The Coming of Dawn

The Coming of Dawn

Library of Congress
Cataloging in Publication Data

ISBN 1-56167-045-6

Manufactured in The United States of America by
Watermark Press
11419 Cronridge Dr., Suite 10
Owings Mills, MD 21117

The Coming of Dawn

Editor's Note

As editor of <u>The Coming of Dawn</u>, I had the wonderful opportunity to review and reflect upon the various poetic selections featured within this anthology. Each piece of artistry depicted within <u>The Coming of Dawn</u>, is crafted with grave originality and design. However, there are a few poems I would like to honor with special recognition.

One of my favorites, "Along the Border," by Pat Gradsky, is an intriguing philosophical piece rationalizing one's concept of now and then. Pat deftly portrays a unique series of events which lead to the ultimate conclusion, "No past and no future... Unless I think it."

In, "Garden of Stone," Aaron Boles uses chilling, clear cut lines in expressing the disheartening companion of patriotism fostered during war.

Brandi Reissenweber presents us with a very picturesque piece full of depth in both color and imagery. Brandi utilizes some wonderful connotations such as, "Red leaves of anger/ Purple leaves of law/ And dead, crackling leaves of guilt..."

Another outstanding poem is, "Ducks," by Abigail Shuler, paints a shadowy scene, bringing to light the mists overshadowing our environment.

Unfortunately, I don't have the time or space to critique each and every one of the prominent poems appearing within this anthology. Yet, as <u>The Coming of Dawn</u> illustrates, all of the poems featured are worthy of merit. The poets artistically presented a variety of subjects and styles, each contributing to the quality of this publication. May all of the artists within this anthology be renowned for their talents and efforts in creative writing.

I sincerely hope that you enjoy reading <u>The Coming of Dawn</u>.

Cynthia A. Stevens

Acknowledgements

The publication <u>The Coming of Dawn</u> is a culmination of the efforts of many individuals. Judges, editors, assistant editors, graphic artists, layout artists and office administrators have all brought their respective talents to bear on this project. The editors are grateful for the contribution of these fine people:

Jeffrey Bryan, Julie Buchness, Lisa Della, Chrystal Eldridge, Ardie L. Freeman, Hope Freeman, Diane Mills, Eric Mueck, John J. Purcell III, and Margaret Zirn.

Grand Prize Winner

Pat Gradsky

Second Prize Winners

Aaron Boles

Irene Brosco

Dana Loewy

Meeka Muse

Edward Pater

Brandi Reissenweber

Abigail Shuler

Shirley Simpson

Reba M. Snyder-Hamman

Laura Whalen

Third Prize Winners

Nik Anderson

Aaron A. Arthers

J. F. Bolinger

Adetokunbo Knowles Borishade

Burl Bredon

Bruce Briscoe

Renee Caggiano

Jean Coggiano

Shaun Collins

Yvon J. Cormier Jr.

Irene Cupido

Madeleine Dale

Matt Damsker

David Rocco DelNegro

Virginia Hunt Donnelly

R. Drullinsky

Perry England

Heidi L. Everett

Francis L. Graham

Madeline Guilli

Jill W. Haley

Martha Sue Shelby Hart

Thomas G. Henderson

Betty Adams Holt

G. Scott Hughes

T. A. Jackson

Mary Jennings

Michael S. Kelly

Dominic Anton Kessler

John King

John Kirkhoff

Lucille Kroner

Dorothy Husar Krosky

Orin P. Lewis

Maura Maher

Gregg Marcellus

Ramona Ann McConnell

Kimberly Miller

Paxton Baylor Mobley

Diane E. Mooney

Nom Nebinger

Carole Ann Parsons

Karen Payne

Piney Woods Pete

J.A. Raymond

Steven Reinhart

Jonathan Russell

Tara Raye Russo

Randall Lee Saxon

Naim Siddiqui

Sara Nadiv Soffer

Walter D. Sweet

Dorothy K. Thomas

Francine Madeleine Tyler

Laszlo Varga

Rosario Villaruel

Richard J. Vogt

Clara Whitney

Sonia Wolff

Congratulations also to all semi-finalists.

Grand Prize Winner

Along the Border
I took the chewing gum out of my mouth
and threw it on the ceiling.
Let it stay there
next to the cobweb and ancient adobe;
like your memory, outside of me now.
No past and no future unless I think it.
Hmmm.
A fly is in the room with me now,
humming as he dances
in the stillness of the air all around my head.
Congenial organism!
Clearly gifted and skilled.
Responding to my friendly mood
he circles, dancing closer.
Enjoying each other and the moment…
Until the fly landed atop the red-checkered oilcloth
next to my jelly donut and coffee.
I thought him filthy and rude and so I killed him.
Outside of me now.
No past and no future… Unless I think it.
            —*Pat Gradsky*

Trust and Love

Love is something very special and can be so beautiful.
A beautiful love that comes from within a true heart.
When the love you feel is strong and getting stronger everyday.
When it comes to love, there has to be a bond of trust.
Without the trust, each couple weaves,
If there is love but no trust a couple cannot become one.

    —Deanna Hodge

Light Through A Door

Light through a door you allow me to see
a bit of what my life could possibly be.

But the door does not yield, nor does it let me in,
but only gives me a glimpse of what is within.

Through the cracked door lies what is left of my life,
all of the suffering, the pain, the loss and the strife.

The light is taunting, daring me to live,
making me give all that I have to give.

And until the door opens, and there's nothing to see,
then I can still hope that there's a future for me.

    —Tobbin A. Bruss

Whispers

Walk delicately through this enchanted forest if you come to seek
a brief but timeless union stolen moments from eternity.
Knowing the difference between what I am
and what I want to be you are continuity

Mystery whispers many promises fate decides which to keep
every thing you say or do falls some where in between
I am drawn to you as you are to my dreams
Yet as you get closer the further they recede

Dark rider into the midnight sun.
Wherever you go you won't go alone.
Burning memories mark the distance ghosts travel to forget
the sparks that lure you forward turn to flames that haunt your past

Living lights between horizons hold the shadows in their place
where reason wanders inward no compass points the way
Look they dance together the laughter and the tears
blink the passage alters the message disappears

Walk delicately across my heart if you come to explore
the circle of innocence around the hidden fire

    —Madeleine Dale

Howard's Song

Raising her face, she pierces the clouds with her gaze,
a challenge of youth and innocence quivers in a crow scream.
Days-old slush loves the mud, French-kissing her shoes.
  Slippy-sliding on sodden earthmounds, she dances on
spiderlegs.
The sun's jealousy of her soul warms her skin, a delicious
burning, ever-so-slightly uncomfortable in her clothes.
Arms like leather wings spread wide, palms open, as she
sings the old songs of trickle-fountain melodies.
Notes that shatter on pebbles smell like moist grass and butterflies.
But their sharpness punishes her for horrible sins never committed.
But Nature never judges her children. Or loves them.
Mother, Daughter, Sister, Lover (?)
distracts us from all purpose and concern.
But still she shouts stupidly, her insults flying in the
wind.

    —Carolyn Garner

Ranch Scene On Maui And Lonesome Paniole

Spring's wide estate runs
  a cliff's edge to the sea,
Welcomes dawn with
  outstretched arms and
Dew-kissed fields of
  bright carnation flowers —
All day long,
Down gently sloping
  mist-shrouded Haleakala,
Jacaranda in clouds of
  lavender cast purple shadows,
Along a dusty country road —
Suddenly, at some ancient
  weathered lava wall corral,
Half-hidden by stalwart cactus,
We pause enchanted to
Listen to a lonesome Paniole sing,
  a tender heart-warm mele,
As his full day's work is done.

    —June Allegra Elliott

"The Cowboy"

White capped mountains, drifted and wild,
A cowboy rides along the hollow,
Leaving tracks upon the powdered surface.
He's checking his hopes and dreams,
From a city of steel and smog to a desolate
  ranch in the Alaskan hills.

The bearded man smiles upon his land,
As his animals swarm around him.
They are not afraid of the gun to which he
  carries,
Because he is a gentle man,
With love and kindness in his heart.
Only does the barrel click to take away the
  suffering or for the game of that season.

The black hat and long coat,
Are all that can be seen on the horizon.
Then over one hill, a single line of smoke is
  formed,
He's made his way home,
  As he does every night.

    —Brandi Christine Voll

Untitled

A little girl danced down the warm sands of
  A creamy beach littered with shells.
A giggle escaped at the water's tickling and
  She gathered a pearly pink shell
    Glossy from the waves' caress.

At a glimpse, a blemish was espied.
Abandoned by the waves, a distorted fish lay.
  As she crept to acquire a better look,
    A dark shadow kicked and
  A corpse shattered as it pierced the air.

The shadow's snicker broke the silence and
Hit by a wave of discomfort was the tiny girl,
  A dull ache deep in her heart: Sadness.
A tear kissed her cheek as she stood motionless.
The pink shell escaped her hand's grasp and
    Dropped to the sand below.

    —Heejung Kim

Heart of Stone

Your heart is made of stone, a priceless gem alone.
A diamond's fire radiates through the portholes of your skull.
Your eyes and mouth spill the energy that some will fear, but I
am not afraid for this priceless gem I'll pay.
For who am I my strengths and fears, you'll find it in my tears
So be my friend not just my love and we'll relive our years
because your heart is made of love, like a peaceful morning
dove. No hate or bad desires. Just to hold me not to shove.
My love for you has grown. You are with me when I'm alone.
Your my energy and my destiny.
Your my priceless heart of stone.

—*John L. Santana*

Janet

Tell me not of shields and bones 'neath Trojan sands,
A dream forever ago.
Nor of bodies bloodless—Time-washed by Normandy's surf—
The black and white of ancient nightmares.

For the saddest soldier of them all
Lies part-buried adjacent my dock,
Its blue helmeted head and painted smile
Popping up from the sand, a child's reach away
From the yellow plastic pail.

And the broken toy shovel that knew the once warm grasp
Of the busy tan first (digging and planting the carved sentry),
Stares like the barbed bayonet ripped from my soul.

"Happy memories heal," advised the fool,
Who never heard the lullabies against which I shut my ears,
Those she hummed over tadpole trenches and coffee can castles,
Squatting frog-like in the foam, pink toes probing wet sand.

Instead, let dirges blow through the aspens;
Let lake lapping lift the last soldier into numbing depths,
And wash away her footprints.

—*David McGrath*

"Blake"

Who are you?
A dreamer who makes her dreams come true,
Or a traveler who has seen the world;
A friend who listens and watches,
Or a rockhound who collects rocks.
Once a teacher,
But, always a friend.
Seeing far away places,
And native sights;
From China with her wall,
And the yellow river;
To the Amazon River,
With her jungle and nature's delight.
A child with stars in her eyes,
Or a thinker wondering-
What's next for you.
You may be small in size,
But, large inside where it counts;
Light on your feet,
And high in spirit.

—*Elsa L. Chase*

Father

"F" is for the figure head of families
"A" is for his abundant gift to love
"T" is for his talent to provide and guide us
"H" is for his hearty sense from above
"E" is for his eagerness to please us
"R" is for his rarity to repair
Put them all together they spell Father
Who, together with Mother, make a Heavenly Pair.

—*Jewell G. Murray*

Memories Before You Went Away

I will never forget the day we spoke.
A feeling of instant closeness I saw.
Trust earned so very fast and never broke
The friendship we have is for a good cause
Like brother and sister so true at heart
The love that we have shared for each other,
A guarantee that we won't ever part
We were always meant to be together
Everyday thanking the Lord for this love
And for the way you always treated me.
Memories we've shared in my head above
Best friends forever we will always be.
I only wish you weren't far away.
Being close together is a great place.
Being there for every time of the day.
Being there for me to constantly face.

—*Danielle Littell*

Laughter

Laughter, is indeed a wonderful thing
A feeling of joy that lets merriment ring;
A hearty expression of both frolic and fun
A luxury that can be shared by everyone.

It may range from a smile, to a giggle or roar
A tonic for the young, the old, rich or poor;
For the boundless happiness that it can bring
Yes, laughter is indeed a wonderful thing.

Tho' things seem wrong and our spirits are down
There's never a cause for a perpetual frown;
Be cheerful with all, get back in the swing
For laughter, is indeed a wonderful thing.

It chases sadness, worry, fear and gloom
Transmits light and sunshine into a darkened room;
The sweetest music known and for all to sing
Yes, laughter is indeed a wonderful thing.

Should I but lose the will to laugh and grin
May the Good Lord beckon to come unto Him;
Where joy will flow from an eternal spring
For laughter, is indeed a wonderful thing.

—*Charles J. Kirchem Jr.*

What You Don't See

A smile upon my face,
  A frown runs through my soul.
A laugh within my voice,
  A cry hidden without a trace.
A shine in my eye,
  A tear within my heart.
A bright light upon my spirit,
  A burning darkness that will never part.
The things I feel, they feel so wrong
  For these feelings come on so strong.
Where to go for I am lost,
  I don't know where I am to be.
These feelings have blinded me,
  I can no longer see.
I am alone far from everything
  awaiting what the darkness can bring.
These are the things you don't see...

—*Heather D. Myers*

My Terrible Lunch

In my bag I wish there'd be
A giant chocolate bar for me.
But in that bag I'd probably find
Something of a different kind.

There's probably something really gross,
Like pickled beets and moldy toast.
And then I'd find that my drink
Had suddenly began to stink.

And when I look inside to see
What my drink might really be.
I'd find something I thought the least,
A can of dried up bacon grease.

My sandwich now is dripping down
In something mushy, gushy brown.
And for dessert, I just don't know
It's a lumpy glump that's starting to glow.

I just don't know what my mom has done,
But I don't think it's very fun.
I never ever had the hunch,
That I'd get such a terrible lunch!

—*Andrew McFaddin*

"The Wall Around Me"

I got involved and bared my soul
A glimpse for all to see
The soft spots in a cold heart
From a hole in the wall around me
Feelings and emotions I keep to myself
Storing them all inside of me
Like dancing close to the flames of friendship
But never letting it touch me
Like a feather blowing in the wind
I lightly touch others lives
And blow away on the breeze again
Leaving behind no lovers, but few close friends
That is the way of my life
And that is the way it has always been
No matter what the situation
I will always find my self running
Hiding away in a shell from others
Only getting involved physically
And protecting my emotions from harm
From behind the wall around me....

—*Kendrell Thomas*

Reminiscence

There is a time of reminiscence, of what was long ago;
A happy sort of thinking back, wherein our thoughts do flow.
We send our minds to wander, and kind of float, you see;
A sort of dream vacation, that sets our ego free.

This thing we own, (It's called a soul,) Is with us all the time.
It soars and weaves such fantasies, that are to us sublime.
And fun it is to roam the past, (In mind it still is there.)
Filed in our memories, for us to tell and share.

The magic of that time gone by, is easy to relive.
It's something that belongs to us, and we are free to give.
So please don't make light of it, those times I want to share.
The fact that I will take you back, means I really care.

Please! Take a moment! Go with me, back to long ago,
Or someday you'll wish you had, but then you cannot go!
Take the time! It's mine to give! I hope you'll share with me!
A faraway nostalgic gift; My yesterday's memory.

—*Clarence M. Owens*

"Turning The Page"

(A poem about picture books.)

Where do they go when you turn the page
A land across the sea?
Where ever they go no one else knows
Not even you or me!?

Where do they go when you close the book,
Sometimes I peek to find out
Do they go "KERPLAT!" or do they "SPLAT"
Or turn plain inside-out!?

Where do they go when you turn the page,
It seems so funny to me
That when you open the book again
They are there for all to see!

—*Bryan P. Smith*

America, The Beautiful!

America, the beautiful and land of the prodigal.
    A Land of the Free and place of distinctive signs,
        Need diapers for my baby!

Why do they live like that in America? says the boy

    Willing to work for food.

I see that sign so say:

    The Ambitious. The Common Man. The Construction man.
The Country folk. The Rich and famous. Even the Politicians.

But, why do they live like that in America, a place of
    the Beautiful?

Everything seems to change, except one thing: All see the
    signs: The Homeless. The Vietnam Vet.
    The Divorced. The Unemployed.

The Unanimous and the distinct of America. America the
    beautiful and a place of honor and distinction.

    A place where freedom rings.
    A place where abound the bold and brave.
    A place of dignity and worth.

But, why do they live like that in America, a land of the
    Beautiful?

—*Charlie A. Guerrero*

The Magic of Love

A wonderful gift that can give you
a life as a blessing from heaven above.
It can comfort and bless.
It can bring happiness.
It's the wonderful magic of love —
Like a star in the night —
it can keep your faith bright —
Like the sun it can warm your hearts too.
It's a gift you can give everyday that you live —
when given it comes back to you —
When love lights the way —
there's joy in the day
all troubles are lighter to bare.
Love is gentle and kind
through love you will find
and answer to your every prayer.
May it never depart from your two loving hearts.
May you treasure this gift from above.
You will find if you do
your dreams will come true
in the wonderful Magic of Love!

—*Sandra Stanley*

Only A Fool Would Play In A Sea Of Glass

...thrust into life of no one's accord,
  A lifeless baby sits on the bench.
It was covered in blood,
A six-inch umbilical chord still attached to its belly.
its eyes were closed and unopened,
They would never see.
Its face was frozen in a grin,
Or was it a smirk.
It looked happy or maybe not.
  It's so hard to read life into a dead baby's face.
  Was it a boy or a girl?
  I couldn't tell.

    —Jonathan H. Shim

Goodbye

    A lazy April afternoon
A light breeze whispered through the air
  The heavens allowed for a perfect day
    But something wasn't quite there

    Many friends' hands were joined
  As flowers bathed in sunshine's light
  The familiar scent of fresh cut grass
    But something wasn't quite right

      Poems were read
      Tears were shed
  As a bluebird serenaded from above
    It was a lazy April afternoon
    They buried the one I love

    —Kim A. Krolak

Self Portrait

She came skipping through my yard today,
A little girl with a bright "hello"
Blowing seed from a dandelion,
Pig-tailed and pinafored as long ago.

With long blonde hair and tear-wet eyes,
I saw her again as from a dream.
She was sobbing, shaking, crying aloud,
Painful, poignant, sweet sixteen.

Then with high-piled tresses and stylish mode,
She engaged me once more with her winning smile.
"I'm in such a hurry again today, Mom.
How I'd just love to stay and visit awhile.

Today she slowly climbed the stair,
"Oh why are my legs so tired?" she said.
I looked at the girl turned old in the mirror,
Laughed at myself and went to bed.

    —Betty Neff Dickens

Valentine Man And Lady

There once were two lovers,
a Little Valentine Man, and Lady.
Who danced to Valentine music,
their love was so great,
they could hardly wait.
They sent Valentine wishes,
before it's too late,
for a very special Valentines date.

Hearts and flowers, to cheer them by the hour,
little magic arrows, flying through their windows,
Sending love notes; and sweet candies, that taste so dandy.

All these Valentines are great,
but I couldn't wait to wish you the very best,
a special Valentine Man from a special Valentine Lady.

    —Sharon L. Drinovsky

Material People

I have listened to it said, by all who are wed
a long litany of things I have given,
There is gold and fine silk, and homes that we built
and great sacrifices I have made for thee,
Long hours and gifts, of red race cars and ships
your dinners, your golf clubs, the flowers,
All the things of our world, even an ebony pearl
yet your heart is still troubled with me,
What else may I find, for the love of my life,
why does your mind seek to alienate me,
You might have given me more, of your love and your soul
and replaced all the gifts with a we...

    —Donald W. Holmes

"The Clairton Sr. Center"

We work at the Clairton Sr. Center which is certainly
a lot of fun
With lots of special people from the start till day is done.
There's always something going on, you should come and see.
Try today or tomorrow be sure you have the whole day free.
The men play cards and shoot some pool, those women at Bingo
are really cool.
We have Arts and Crafts, Ceramics and such, Exercise, Flower
arranging, Pokeno, Boy you can learn so much.
Just come in, to see us we're a heck of a bunch
we'll sit down and chat and then serve you lunch.
Don't forget our parties, they are "oh so much fun"
With gifts galore, maybe you'll win one.
Take little trips, go see a show and shopping,
Come on come see us, we'll keep you hopping.

    —Alberta Cornish

"An Ode To A Surgeon"

I have been given the greatest gift
A love for my fellow man
Skilled hands to touch the people
And help them all I can

Wisdom to know what I'm doing
A calmness in my voice
If I'm presented a life or death
I pray that I make the right choice

I must keep my nerves steady
No matter how dim it looks
Because all the pain and misery
You can't find in medical books

All I can do is my very best
With every muscle and the sweat of my brow
And when I finish an operation, I say
It's all in God's hands now

    —Carl F. Stratton

A Fawn

A fawn that looked out of the branches
A man digging along the road in the trenches
She peered out cautiously from her grassy lay
She looked at the man as if she wanted say
Why disturbs my peace only for your feast
Please go away because you are disturbing my day
The man seem to care at the sight of the lair
What am I doing here breaking up the fawn's care

The fawn's eyes were lit as the man gave her, her gift
The peace of the forest

    —Alex Pek

Twilight

When dusk and shadow mix their paint
To form the twilight haze, that feint
Existing twixt the day and dark,
The rushing world lies down to mark
The time of day so quietly.
My mind awakes from reverie
To realize this hour of day
Is God's own gift to mortal clay.
'Tis quiet then, so quiet that
The shadows can be heard to pat
The darkness nearer to the land
As imperceptibly as sand
Is sifted by the sea, that I
Scarce comprehend the change in dye.
The twilight sailed to seek the sun
The blue-black bark of Night has come.

—*Arthur Patterson*

Suddenly

One day the air is exceedingly chill.
A medley of colors creeps up the hill.
Quiet reigns— song bird voices now are still.
They have slipped away with no farewell frill.
The heavy jawed squirrels scurry to fill
Their caches with nuts. The sun on the sill
Is brassy gold. Down by the little rill
Orange robed pumpkins their cycle fulfill.
A south bound snow goose drops a painful quill
Plucked from his wing with a merciless bill.
Ribbon corn streamers, victims of frost kill,
Rustle and flutter at every wind's will.
Busy farmers hasten their fields to till,
Hopeful of yet another spring. The mill
Of the gods has ground on and on until
Fall again brings its particular thrill.
Unspoken praises for the consummate skill
Of the Master Gardener from our hearts spill.

—*Dorothy N. Denison*

Love

An Ideal Love Relationship includes...
A "meeting of minds",
A sharing of common ideals and goals,
A mutual philosophy on life.
Togetherness without smothering the other.
Some common interests and some diversified.
Able to give the other breathing space.
Full and complete trust.
To feel as secure when apart as well as when together;
To communicate without words.
To respect the other's privacy and not invade upon it —
  physically or mentally.
All four aspects balanced-spiritual, mental, emotional, physical.
To be willing to overlook the other's shortcomings and yet try
  improve upon your own.
To be best friends.

True Love reaches out and encompasses the world.
  It should make life richer, fuller, more satisfying,
And bring happiness not only to each other, but to all
  Whose lives touch yours.

—*Joanna Heitmann*

The Marquee Read

A father
A mother
Born by an act
brothers suddenly uncles-mothers, on cue, baking
why - a ring or a bed?
joining in the light/joined in the dark it's white-is it pure?
is this child of sex or two sexes the mind ponders,
fearful yet ever slightly entertained, glancing at the program acts
can so profoundly change
the course of two bodies
now will non-fictional actors
choose a crib or a basket
murder - the plot, the prop a bed
during climax they
know not the resolution
...curtain call...
a single blood spot
Critics gave bad revues.

—*Jeffrey M. Clemmons*

Hello There, Erma

At the nursing home, on the sixth floor, the east side
A population of special people there reside...

Authors and doctors, professors and cooks
Boys handsomely groomed, charming girls with good looks
Lawyers and firemen, on occasion a baker
All of them made a bit aged by their maker.

They were all children once with bells on white shoes
They all threw temper tantrums during their terrible twos
They all went to school and shared secrets with a best friend
They also all thought that youth would never end.

Those of us who bother to visit and pass by
Barely mutter "Good Morning" without blinking an eye
But do we ever take out a minute to think
That between youth and old age there is a strong link?

Even though Erma sitting there isn't aware of a thing
In her heart there are cherished memories and lullabies that sing.
Stories of good times, of merry moments and laughing smiles
An accomplished lifetime, of love topping piles.

So next time you feed her, barely pretending to care...
Remember that someday, you may sit in that wheelchair.

—*Blimie Frank*

Sonatina Mortem

Above my grave your name became a song.
A pristine, shimmering echo,
Appurtenances in our life, nuances
- I always wanted - had no chance to show.

You never came to leave your gossamer,
In vain, the roses formed a row,
Petals cover to here the path
And winter time the snow.

Rankling was always my part, the ornament was yours,
There is no substance here, no heirloom at the shores
Of dark alluvium, though weightless, concave and hollow.

Timeless is the time, a glimmer here below
    Is eternally long,
All I remember only that astir my gravestone
    Your name became a song.

—*Laszlo Varga*

Some Things Don't Change

The robins are back from their trip to the south,
A promise that springtime is near.
Their wings must be tired from flying so far -
But their chirping and singing is clear.
The wild-geese are honking as northward they go
In their usual formation of V,
Some struggle behind, but valiantly try-
There's a lesson for you and for me.
Though seasons are changing and time passes by,
God's still in control of it all -
The vastness of space or the tiniest place,
He's still within reach of our call.
The world's full of violence, hatred and strife,
But there's beauty and love if we look.
God gave us direction to follow each day.
By sending His Son and His Book.
And just as the flowers come back in full bloom
Through Christ we shall live and be raised.
He's promised new life and salvation to all-
Accept Him, and give Him your praise.

  —Lois Esterline

Friends Asleep

Alone He stood at the judgment hall,
A scene to make angels weep!
Betrayed by friends, abandoned by all,
While good men were fast asleep!

Where are the friends of the Nazarene?
Can they his love forget?
Sinners he pardoned, lepers made clean...
It's early, they're sleeping yet!

Today, as of old, sin's hosts advance,
They're marching 'ere break of dawn,
While heedlessly, as if in a trance,
The friends of the Lord sleep on!

Oh Savior, awake and inspire us!
We long thy harvest to reap,
The victory will come Thou desirest
When good men awake from their sleep.

  —Hugh P. Jeter

The Park

I see you as an image You're just a black and white
A shadow cast from the sun

I'm just an image, a face without any expression, a voice
without any words I saw you in the park, do you remember me?

I was the child on the bench, when you looked at me, I felt
like black writing on white walls, a lot of words with no
meaning you just kept walking

You passed me yesterday, I was the homeless, I saw anger in
your eyes You couldn't look into my eyes, I felt that you
wished I didn't exist I will see you tomorrow, I will be the
elderly I will not have much sparkle in my eyes, I will not
have security I will not have hope, for I'm on borrowed time,
I wonder if you will see me there, waiting for you? Will you
look into my eyes? As you passed by I felt something, it
clutched at my heart As night fell the more pain I felt,
for I've been alone for a long time I wished you could have
said "Hello", I have something to share with you, it's
a sad story, my story, but now it's too late
Tomorrow I will not be on this bench, someone new is taking my
place I'm sorry but you are the chosen one

  —Lessa Potter

Untitled

When her father drinks, he stinks of cigar and rum.
A shagged face or stubble splashed strongly with musk.
Running roughly, twirling clumsily through the garden in the
darkness
Underneath the pale, blunt moon.

Shiny green bottles clenched deep into his fingers.
A voice soft and blunt echoing off the marigolds and vidalas.
Then tap tap
To the window pane, startling her mother in a heap upon the
couch. Tap tap.

Then up again, swarming, prancing childishly like a danger.
His head bobbing, feet stumbling until there he falls, deep into
the waterlilies.
A laugh, and a groan, and a silence to the house.

As the moon glares angrily from the sky above, her father's arms
and legs are spread boldly smoldering the earth.
Like Jesus he lays, his head still, his arms outstretched.
The wind blows harshly... leaves bounce like snakes hard against
the window pane.
He leaves them for sleep as a whisper of relief flickers
throughout the house.
Like a match the lights are out. His daughter can sleep knowing
that the body of her protector
Lies harmlessly in the garden.

  —Justine M. O'Connor

Ships That Pass In The Night

On a vast and beautiful ocean floats a ship.
A ship of once majestic beauty, but now, tarnished.
Its billowy white sails are slashed, and its
wooden planks are rotted. Her scars engraved are
from many battles and storms which she encountered.

Her beloved Captain, who built her with pride,
was thrown overboard in her first major battle.

Since then there has been no one at the helm.
She drifts astray in the naked sea with no direction,
no port to call home.

As I look upon this ship I want to help her.
So with my love I replace the rotten planks and
sew her torn sails.

But I do not stand at her helm.

She will continue to drift, waiting for a
captain to finally lower her anchor.

But until that day,
When she needs wind,
I will blow through her sails.

  —Charles A. Macko

A Beautiful Flower?

Behold a seed, getting food from Heaven's rain
A small seed, distinctive, yet it is still plain
Rain reaches the seed and something begins to take place
The seed grows, not rushing, but at a steady pace
Piercing the ground, no longer in darkness but light
Steadily climbing upward and not to the left or right
With upswept petals it praises the one true power
God, transforming the seed into a beautiful flower
If you are willing, God can do the same for you
If you be in Christ, you will not be old but new
When you confess from your heart Romans ten: nine, ten
You will be set free from the very bondage of sin
God gives us all a free choice to make
Accept or reject him, which will you take?

  —Lisa R. Smith

Batter, Batter...

As the batter stepped up to the plate,
  A silence hushed over the crowd.
For this moment was critical to history,
  And an out simply was not allowed.

It was the thirteenth inning.
  The score was ten to nine.
This swing could either even it up,
  Or, for the Statesmen, draw the line.

A perfect pitch greeted his bat,
  As they met and broke the silence.
The ball was practically uncatchable,
  And third baseman lost his balance.

Runner on third, next up to bat.
  He swung and missed, "Strike one!"
He tried again. "Strike Two!" was the call.
  The opposing team thought they had won.

One last try with all his might,
  It most definitely was a hit.
Both runners made it back to home,
  As the ball rolled off the catcher's mit.
    —*Kristi Posey*

An Old Timer

Another day was ending, silence had set in
A silver haired old-timer was reminiscin'
Sittin' by a window, lookin' down the road
A long life behind him, he was getting old

He'd lost track of his birthdays, he was 94
He had a house and dog, he had nothing more
He'd outlived a family and a friend or two
He relived his past with nothing else to do

In his childhood a convenience was unknown
There was no electricity and no telephone
Families rode in wagons, no one had a car
Planes were unheard of, none came from afar

He got his education in a one-room school
He had tried to observe the golden rule
He'd back a friend through thick and thin
A few escapades he recalled with a grin

He had many memories he'd like to share
With a few friends, who might still care
He turned on a radio, as it began to play
Thoughts of his past began to drift away
    —*Christine Reece*

"True Love"

Love comes in so many ways,
  A smile, a touch, a song.
Two hearts together beating as one
  hopefully lasting a whole life long.
Two happy lovers blessed
    from above
As close as two flowers in a
    garden of love.
When two special people can share
    moments sublime
Be together, forever, till the end
    of time
Let the heavenly bells from
    above ring
For love is truly a beautiful and wondrous
    thing.
    —*Gina McWeeney*

Reflections On A Sunday Morn

Some of the things in life that matter most to me?
A smiling face, a warm embrace, a stroll along the sea,
Babies cooing, hoot owls who-ing, a spirit that is free.

Mothers who care, people who share, the song of the sparrow at dawn,
The colors of autumn, go-getters who got 'em, the smell of a
    newly-mown lawn,
Bread when it's baking, love when it's making, a heart with all
    sadness gone.

A starry night, a soaring kite, the rustle of trees in the wind,
Violets that bloom, peacocks that plume, the voice of a dearly
    loved friend,
A walk in the rain, the beaches of Maine, a love without any end.
    —*Jacqueline Ann Barton*

Which Laws To Defend

'Twas a fun filled day. The sun shined so bright.
A soft, gentle breeze set flower seeds in flight.
  The butterflies flitted from petal to petal,
While my sweet love and I alone lay to mettle.
  It seemed so innocent to kiss and to pet,
But response seized control and "Sweet Love" did beget.

  The winds began to blow and fears began to rise.
"Sweet Love" hadn't matured enough. Such love was unwise.
  A fetus was growing she couldn't afford.
Her parents for shelter and fear would abort.
  A life now was ended and others were bruised,
For God's own authority by man had been used.

  You say "Thou shalt not kill" and "A woman has rights"
Where is the line dawn? How do we set our sights?
  If we follow the "Good Book" from beginning to end
Our creator will show us which laws to defend.
    —*Eulaila M. Greene*

Walking In The Wind

I am walking in the wind,
a terrible wind;
I am thinking a lot,
an unbelievable lot.

Wind blowing hard with sand and dust;
I, walking slowly with an enjoyable heart.

Time flying fast
I, experiencing lot.

When will the wind stop?
I like the walking in the wind.
My face dirty;
My mind fresh.
    —*Elinor Y. Hui*

Beyond Doors

Beyond Doors lies imagination...
A room filled with evil dreams and rage.
But when the rage is fought back
And the dreams are blown away;
The wonderful things you've dreamed before
Soon come back again.
Beyond Doors now newly lives,
The way it should before.
Through my window,
I see the night...
And Beyond Doors.
    —*Katie Johnson*

Reward

I look into the black deep night
A thousand lights gather before me
And as they dance to the music of nature
I feel movement within life so still

Softness overwhelms my aching soul
As calm becomes my heart
I then glance once more to the stars
And find myself beyond them
Into the side of which nothing is known

My heart becomes quickness now
And a tenseness grows in my throat
I behold a sight overlooked by ancient ones
My homecoming, my rest, my life...
All before me - touching me

Such gentleness and such strength
A quietness that fills my ears sweetly
Yes, you I have finally found
Are my grand reward
I only say what there now is...
I love you.

   —Melody I. Lepore

Rare

When I saw your smile so fine.
A thrilling chill went down my spine.
What I felt I did not know.
For you said you had to go.
I saw you once again that night.
With your gleaming eyes so bright.
What I felt was Love for you.
I wished you'd felt the same way too.
Looking up in your eyes.
You've almost got me hypnotized.
But now that it's all over,
I feel it was as rare as a four leaf clover.

   —Kelli L. Avery

"To My Great Granddaughter" (Yet Unborn)

Samantha Sue, this is written for you.
a tiny fragile baby girl,
only twenty two weeks of growth so far.

So many prayers being sent up to God-
asking Him to spare your life,
hoping and praying that you won't be born just yet.

The doctor's say that you would be too small to survive.
if you are born before your time-
you will weigh less than one pound.

So please, please dear child,
stay right where you are-
there you will be safe and sound.

As your young mother, Stephanie Lynn-
lies there in the hospital day after day,
she talks to you, and pray's in her own way.

She is fighting so hard to keep you,
you are her precious little one.

Although she has many problems- she thinks only of you,
If God should spare your life, you will be our miracle baby,
Samantha Sue.

   —Louise Chapman

When They're Gone

I see a sock in the living room, I slowly look around,
A toy lies not much further, and a shoe I finally found.

I see the prints on the walls, I look at them and see,
The little signs of my children, left behind for me.

I glance into the kitchen, a mess is on the floor,
I sigh and feel it's hopeless, to pick up just once more.

A coat lies on a chair, some gloves not far away,
I wonder if they realize, how hard I work each day.

Their bedrooms are a mess, games and toys are every where,
I begin to clean it up, stopping to wipe a tear.

Then all at once it hit me, the day will surely arrive,
When my house will be clean, after their childhood is survived.

Then what excuse will I have, if my home is a mess?
The children will be gone, and then comes the true test.

I know that I will miss it, the mess they leave for me,
I know that I will shed the tears, the pain so vividly.

The hardest part of parenting, is when their on their own,
Stopping by to see me, and then leaving me all alone.

They will realize someday, how it hurts to let go,
I love them more than life itself, more than they'll ever know.

   —Lynette C. Allgood

Birthday Wish

"You say it's your birthday"
A very happy day to you
On this rising Scorpio moon

A better gift than a rug
It'll light your heart like a lightning bug
Think of this as your B-day hug

A personal poem from your honey
More memorable than any money
A birthday wish never bought or sold
Worth ten times its weight in silver and gold

Red roses I know you do desire
How well they light your passionate fire
This little wish may lift you higher
Super love is all that I require
When I see you at last

I yearn to raise a toast
So yet again, I would boast
My love to you with a kith
Today October twenty-sixth

   —Edward Vaks

Life

Life is not what I dream it to be,
a white picket fence and a house with a key.

Things went wrong and things went bad,
somehow life turned really sad.

I try not to worry, I try not to fret,
but the dreams I had, I cannot forget.

I try to hold on and not let go,
for it causes pain, grief and woe.

No one can predict how life will be,
but I have these dreams for you and me.

Life will come, and life will go;
this I learned and already know.

"Please hold on" this I'm told,
but life is short and I'm getting old.

   —Constance Fechhelm

"The State Of The Earth Today"

It was but a few short years ago, no one even thought
about it, how could we know?

Now people discuss the thinning of the Ozone, and tumors that
are possibly caused by your Cellular car phone.

Murdering innocent animals God placed on this planet as
couriers
just to make money for greedy furriers.

Raping the rainforests of their trees, and watching Somalians
begging on their knees.
People complain about Clinton letting the military be taken
over by individuals who are gay, but are they willing to
sacrifice and pay?

Fetuses in the womb can not speak out, do their mothers know
what that's about?

The L. A. P. D. gets away with beating Rodney King, and they
have the audacity to say it's not a racist thing?

We use the Earth's resources at an alarming rate, then aren't
we to blame for sealing our own fate?

—*Kimberly D. Sandlin*

You Said, "She Was Too Young"

You said, "she was too young to hear about or talk
    about, sex or even handle a condom.
See it, touch it, of know what it is used for.

You said, "she was too young to be interested in boys."
After all, she's not even "active" yet.

You said, "she was too young to know about
    safe sex, or sex of any kind, no young man dare!
Would touch a daughter of mine!"

You told me, "not to worry-everything would be okay;
    if we let our daughter grow up ignorant this way"...

Honey - you were wrong! Our child is gone!
Too young! to learn safe sex, A.I.D.S or condoms?

Look at our daughter! You see, she was not
    too young to die!

You said, "she was too young." - Now in the
    morgue she lie!

You didn't know the answers then; no reasons, why?
Honey - "Our child did not have to die"...
    Ignorance kills
        —*Darlene Walker*

Eulogy To A Widow

As the sun sprays its crimson
Across the broad horizon
    And quietly lays itself to rest
I must leave you, my darling,
To join the flight of the starling
    Plummeting toward the west

But lay your mind to ease
I'll be in every breeze
    That tussles your chestnut hair
Don't think for a minute
That you'll not feel me in it
    For, my veiled queen, I will be there

Although it seems my course is run
It's really only just begun
    To take me through another time and space
And I hope the tales they've told of me
And the memories that you hold of me
    Will ease some of the sorrow that you face

    —*Scott Blackstone*

Untitled

On a clear summers night I can see straight through the heavens
above not hate nor fear will scare me up there for all I can
feel is your love most people are afraid of the unknown but up
there-there is no need to cry. But on a night not as clear as
the one before me and the shooting stars have gone by the beautiful
heavens disappear and the valleys of hell arise then all of your
love just disappears and hatred fills your insides besides all
the hate that fills you up the worrying starts to begin your on
the outside of your world and you see no one's really been there
for you and your life goes by in a whirl and you realize you
were left out of all their fun and you begin to cry you know your
cry wont give you what you have lost before they say use your
strength to deal with it but you know you have no more then a
beautiful fairy rises right from out of the blue says your life has
been a bore and always will be too you shouldn't frown or look
down on everything you do be slow for life is more than today
or yesterday in fact but love, adventure, sorrow, pain, it
happened just like that. In a flash, your hell just vanishes away
and the beautiful heavens appear and you decide to take life
just one day at a time and not to frown or ever look down on a
single moment in time.

—*Jennifer Bouck*

"Timely Remorse"

Garrulous maids purge in their place of haven.
Acclamations of nifty parables often irritate the truth.
The emaciated banters alleviate the stained reality
    that tears deeply into life's daily preconceptions.
Prejudices that have contrasting meaning make all of life's
    uncertainty very clear.
Ultimatums and bleak consequences give some meaning to
the word priority.

Rooms of powdered matter, dehydrated rafters of infested
    timber, brooms and dustpans of ruddish-brown rust.
As she awakens and slips into her stale-stained apron,
    she unwillingly arises to her aged lack of concern that
    has attached her to this daily misery.
With years of flogging and self-pity, she finally starts
    to regret her refusal of heavy burden.
Now that the mind is monitored, the soul is barely visible
    under the balls and chains of indexation.
        —*Katie Hess*

"Shadowscapes"

The yearning - a snagging in my soul stirs like leaves scraping
across the sidewalk on a chill autumn evening. I yearn, I
yearn — oh God, for what? For that which can never again be;
for that which is forever lost to me.

The pining, the absolute longing from within, retraces
footsteps into years from which I am relentlessly barred.
The faces, the places — oh, why do I grieve?
Because of lost life; because of unremitting spiritual strife.

The wishing, a raging need pounding on time's portal gnaws
at the void between that which was and that which is.
I hurt, I hurt — oh God, where? Within each time-frozen scene,
against which the sighs of my heart lean.

The memories, footfalls of thought cascading down the corridors
of my years, shimmer in the light of my mind.
The dreams, the schemes — oh how much I ache!
From the depth of my soul; to return home again whole.

—*Margaret A. Schrader*

Day Dreams On A Tree Top, High

Dancing shadows of fluttering leaves
Across the skylight, swept by breeze
From the grand old oak, so strong and tall,
Looking down on the boy so frail and small.

Beckoned the tree from 'way up high:
"Come climb on me—up to the sky.
many are the dreams you'll have with me
As you sail your boats out to sea.

"Build your tree house on my bough.
Oh, come! Come with me now!
Ere destiny deems your fate afar.
Oh, wish you now! on a falling star!"
　　　—Eva McLelland

Farewell To Night

You are the luminous star in the night sky
　　after day gives way to tender night.
The sway you hold over ocean waves,
　　a magic held over from ancient days.

The moon she smiles and begins to die
　　as gentle winds give gentle sighs.
This haven of shadows in silence will say
　　"These mysteries hold true in light of day."

Before she bids her final farewell
　　she kisses the sea that receives her well.
My love cleansed trenched in sorrows
　　that wrenched my heart and feared the 'morrow.

I keep to my heart and mind
　　a love immortal kept safe from time.
Oh tender dove, take me above
　　I yearn for your supple embrace.
　　　—C. Nicholas Morales

Russian Tea

We sat there in the twilight, leaning
Against the universe concentrating on the
Air that fed our bodies dying in the sun
That burned our skins pink fingers of sunset touched
his face and narrowed his eyes the isolation of flesh
Enclosed my searching.

I lack the courage to speak the words
That haunt me to feel their thought become
Questions on my lips, solid against my teeth, bitter
On my tongue I swallow them gently feel them warm
In my belly the Russian tea my mother used to make
Felt like this theses are my choices staked
To the ground at my feet

We are all so little more than voices in the dark
I hate the remarks I spit in self-defense the thoughts
I think as I build this very careful fence piling stones
Against the flood of memory living a life in deliberate
Past tense corralled and herded
Branded with shame loving a man I only know by name.
　　　—Cara Cannon

The Landmark

It's a home for the young and old as well.
A place to rest by those who travel.
A sturdy structure with a strong foundation.
Beauty in it's frame and crafted skin.
It's stood through weather and lasted time.
A landmark to many just passing by.
The landmark they knew stands no more.
They cut the tree down, to widen the road.
　　　—Jesse A. Guthrie

Reflections On A Lily Pad

Beneath this pad there is a bass,
Aggressive, and lurking and hungry.

The plastic worm is weedless,
Long and purple; bass perfect.

The cast is good, the slithery worm
Plops softly on the pad. The lunker moves.

The worm slides quietly closer still.
And then the line discovers the notch.

A Vee-shaped notch half-camouflaged,
In a sneaky pad which snags the line.

And like a pit bull, the pad holds
The weedless worm like grim death.

The lunker alarmed, swims quickly away,
And I am fishless another day.
　　　—Dewey Santmier

Our Heaven

Come with me to the meadow where the grass is green and the
　　air is clean,
There we will find no sadness, anger or pain.
This is the place where the sun will warm our backs and
　　our hearts,
The birds will sing their songs to us and we will feel
　　their love.
We can lay in the grasses and watch the white clouds float
　　slowly across the sky,
The warm breezes will make the green leaves sparkle like
　　emeralds as they flutter.
Small things scamper through the grasses where there is no
　　danger,
Little rabbits scamper across in the meadow happily while
　　the squirrels jump from limb to limb chattering.
We can watch the mighty eagle glide gracefully across the sky,
Song birds will sing their melody to us.
We will know only peace and happiness...
　　For this will be our heaven.
　　　—Joseph D. Ceriani Sr.

I Avow Tomorrow She'll Smile

She night-nested restless in my bent olive arm,
Akin to an owl-nesting hooting from a dark country barn;
For in slumber she moaned from Life's approaching harm.
　　—But I avow tomorrow she'll smile.

Bemused behind her forest of eyelashes clasped,
Like a nymph lost from Artemis my child sadly splashed;
For in the loch of her life she felt her soul taxed.
　　—But I avow tomorrow she'll smile.

For none bear her beauty nor fair aspect free,
Than she whose clean voice seems sung from Life's tree;
As my bright dreaming daughter whose love beams on me.
　　—Thus I avow tomorrow she'll smile.
　　　—Benjamin de Souza-Perez

Judging Me?

Who are you to judge me, when you don't even know my name?
All you see is the outside of the person you put to shame.
You put me at the back of the bus, when the front was rightfully mine.
I was the one that was treated like trash, while you were called a shrine.
You made me drink from a separate water fountain when I didn't understand.
I was the one that followed directions and always jumped at the command.
I was told that I was out of place, when I spoke up for my rights.
The cell that I was put in, I prayed in many of nights.
When I finally got out of jail, nothing more was said.
The only thing that was different, was the knot that was on my head.
　　　—Carol McKay

12

The Evil Inside

It's quite outside, the leaves are all settled, the birds
all asleep. It's nature at it's best, there's no time to weep.
We are only human, pride and true, whatever we do, we do it
to you. Whether it's annihilation of the atmosphere or
journey to the stratosphere. We are always here, night and
day just thinking up schemes whether good or bad to be done
somewhere or to someone.
    The energy in our minds flows by and by, just as one day
we start to die and fade away. We sleep forever in time
where life had no meaning, just where dreams subside in the
back of reality or so it may seem at the time.

   —*David Saah Jr.*

The Pain

Looking out of my window
All I could see is the pain in this world
But if I succumb to the fear
That something will go wrong for me
How will I ever grow
Then I closed my eyes
Something appeared in the distance
Making me feel a glimmer of hope
That the pain will soon diminish
It was smiling and waving me to come
Relieving all of my fears
As I moved forward and held out my hand
The vision seemed to fade
Like a dream that was never there
I woke up and it came to me
It was time to believe in myself
And that's what made the pain disappear

   —*Tammy Duclos*

Shattered Chapel

God - This shattered chapel is all that I have -
all I see - all that is left of this probing disease.
    Why are you breaking me down?
Help me see - I've only stopped here to bleed
in a place I've almost figured out.

    My fragile faith is all I have left -
all I feel - that's why I've tried to be healed.
    Why can't you just give to me -
something real? - good nor raw, I got no end of the deal.
You nor me, this isn't what we wanted it to be.

    My last ignorance has left me alone -
as I kneel - as I call out for you to reveal.
    I do not mean to betray.
All I need - is a chance...in this failing fantasy
and the will to rid my shameful ways.

God - This shattered chapel is all that I have -
all I see - when will you grant my serenity?
    I can not die here in doubt.
Help me see - I am not asking for prosperity,
but I'm tired of treading the clouds!

   —*Buddy Stevens*

Spider, Spider

Spider, spider on my walls,
All you do is crawl and crawl.
You make your webs for food and shelter
And eat on prey to make you healthier.
You appear at times when least expected.
You give me bites which become infected.
At times you move as fast as lightning
And give appearances that are extremely frightening.
Oh spider, spider please stay still,
For now it's time for me to kill.

   —*Lester P. Claravall*

"A Lady Fair"

She stood like a thoroughbred
All poised and reserved
A picture of elegance
And spoke not a word

A great big smile enlightened the face
And the crystal clear eyes of blue
A happy heart pounded beneath the lace
Her emotions showed right through

The ring on her finger glittered like gold
And the smell of cologne filled the air
A serious occasion this moment she stole
The appearance of a lady fair

A large picture hat covered the curls
Dainty gloves stretched up the arms
Around the neck was a strand of pearls
Of this lady so full of charm

In front of a mirror that hung on the wall
She admired herself at her best
For a lady of three there was no time to stall
She had borrowed her mother's new dress

   —*Frank Larabee*

What If — ?

What if for just one day — No! — one hour —
   all the laws of math and science and language
   ya know, the postulates, the theories, the rules,
   the threads that hold together
      THE UNIVERSE snap—
            ped! Yeah. What if?
   And then I expostucircumperambufactured
    my own order of things
      in my hour
        my turn
        my crack
      at running the snow
        and pulling out the stops;
        to slur one subject into another
        to grammatically split the new tron
        to scientifically split the infinitive.
   And the first thing I would do,
I would stand on the chalkboard and prove in two columns
exactly why chocolate tastes better than vanilla!
                              Q.E.D., man.

   —*Kevin J. McFadden*

Crazy Solitaire

I started out playing solitaire with a wrecked deck, and
along came a stranger with quite a dialect. He ask to deal
away, so I said ok. Playing solitaire this way I don't like
much, I could see by his careful touch, he was letting me
win, and he wore a smug grin. So I got out a marked deck to
run, to get even and have a little fun. Sloppily I dealt
them a too, after three or four games across, dealing so he
would win the plays, he knew they were well meant lays, so he
ask, "May I deal and see what we get?" Well I traded back
for the wrecked deck and once more he tried to help me
score. None of the games were being won; in fact, hardly
even begun. Then he found cards on the floor. By his face I
knew what was in store. "I think I've been had," he said
rather sad, and I replied, "Someone most certainly had."
Into my face the smoke he blew, I turned my head as the
laughter grew. "Put yourself out of the game," was my next
retort. "And if it's solitaire with you I'd better not
play!" Was his snort.

   —*Dona M. Nogle*

Time

Time..
always tick, tick, ticking away.
There's never enough time to do all you must do.
There's never enough time to say all you must say.
Give me some time to do with as I please.
Give me some time to spread my wings and sail
upon that warm summer night's breeze.
Give me some time to perch upon the highest mountain summit
and gaze upon the world.
Give me some time to say a heartfelt prayer.
Give me some time to die.

> *—Jalees Muzikir*

Forever

I,
  am haunted,
    by the small ghosts of our love.

They,
  remind me,
    that to you, I once said the word forever.

Forever,
  is a word,
    best left to earth, and wind, and sky.

> *—Richard Bender*

The Angel

She was an angel
An angel from heaven
Nothing could surpass her beauty
He could not look into her eyes

How do I talk to an angel
Far in the sky she shines so bright
How do I talk to an angel
For she is untouchable

How do I speak those words
How do I touch that angel far above
Tell me how do I talk to an angel
For she cannot feel my love

When I look into her eyes
I see the stars shining bright
I wish I knew what to say to that angel
For 'tis her that gives me feelings of love

When the stars shine bright I see the light
How can I live without her
How do the words go when an angel is near
Tell me how do I love that angel

> *—Autumn Newbern*

Dear Misty

What a picture of beauty were,
An aristocrat from the very start-
Glossy black, big green eyes, white whiskers.
  and four white feet,
By a Calendar Cat, you couldn't be beat.

We miss your answering "meow"
Your knock at the door,
Your calling us every morning at 7:30 sharp,
And seeing you curled up every evening in
  the chair.

When you went out that beautiful day
We never thought it would be goodbye.
What happened to you along the way?
Only God knows, but for you we still
  how and pray.

> *—Fara L. Reitman*

An Ode To A Leprechaun

O' I wish I could go to Ireland
an island surrounded by sea,
O' I wish I could kiss the Blarney Stone,
and have good luck come to me.

All over Killarney I would look,
a leprechaun I would try to find,
and if I found him reading a book,
I'd take him home and he'd be mine

O' if I couldn't find him there,
I'd search all over one of those spooky castles,
but what if a screaming banshee with long hair-
O' just give me a shamrock for all my hassle.

I found the leprechaun on Emerald Isle,
as green as it could be,
sitting there looking at me with a smile,
so after all that I picked him up
and took him home with me.

> *—Cory Herrmann*

White As Snow

Drifting downward with a calmness ...
  an overpowering silence ...
  it holds me with a gracious power.

Each flake different, yet it's paintings
  all alike. This creation of a peace
  and deep within a patience ...
  calms my troubled soul.

The grey and drab earth painted white ...
  ghastly decorated by the changing
  of earth's differences.

Lord, if I could stand long enough
  and let it touch me deep enough ...
  then I, too, could be a decoration
  and a part and the holder of
  some beauty.

> *—John Muhs*

Old Fort Laramie

The dust of marching feet, impatiently stamping hooves,
And a by-gone era, lay inconceivably upon the ground.
Echoes of commands, bartering wives with crying babes, and
Ribald barroom laughter, long since drifted to the hills.
A herd of buffalo, sounding through the now hollow structures,
Grazed off into the uncharted grasslands of extinction.
A desk, still cluttered with the important events of the day,
Now passed into decades.
Blanket-cloaked Indians, trading skins and dreams.
The lusty laugh of the redman, silenced by time.
Firearms, hanging on the walls and housed in the gun racks,
Holding secret tales of battles, some won - some lost.
Signing treaties, full of empty words and sincere hopes,
Pledging life and honor, upon soon to be forgotten promises.
Forsaken prison cells, cry out in the eerie silence,
Speaking of the agonies, hidden on the prairie breeze.
The breathless glimpse into the past,
Of a life we shall never know.

> *—Debbe Mese*

Angels In Heaven

Only God knew what our future had in store.
By certain peoples indifference that life was no more.
Did they not know that one of us could be.
A doctor, lawyer, maybe the one who sets this would free?

> *—Ginny Jackson*

Mother Hale

She struggled for food, medicine
and a place to put our children
   Comfortably to bed!
She gave love, laughter and hope
to children that poverty, ignorance
and neglect had left for dead!

She hugged and comforted the shivering
screams that plagued our abandoned and
   sick children lives!
She gave and nurtured without hesitation,
the needed and missing intimacy of love
   our children were deprived!

A Secular Saint we will forever Hail
Thanking God for the woman He crowned
   Mother Hale!!!

   —*Faiz Shabazz*

Corrosion

The battle ax of fate is swift
And a warrior swing is true
And we can't always turn the tides
even if we knew
that time alone deteriorates
and metal can't withstand
corrosion, as the hour glass
slowly looses sand.

And I almost believed
that words were really real,
stronger than the hands of time
more powerful than steel.
I should have known that words aren't iron
And that they can't withstand
corrosion, as the hour glass
slowly looses sand.

   —*Mark Gaspard*

Dearest Grandma Dearest Grandpa

Today as we celebrate yesterday's past
and all of the love that holds true,
from granddaughter's hearts we wish to express
Happy Anniversary from us to you.

Grandparents are a special gift,
one that we will always treasure
from the time that we were little bits,
always and forever.

Love is a mystery, a power, a wonder
to give from ourselves and share with another.
God gives us love every hour each day,
love isn't love 'till you give it away.

So just look around you and you will see,
all the love two people can mean.
Part of you is within each of us,
Fifty Years it means so much.

   —*Kerry L. Dittman*

America's Beauty

America's beauty is shining brightly tonight.
Americas's beauty is in every heart.
America's beauty is untouched by evil spirits.
Sometimes America's beauty turns ugly,
but for all times America's beauty will
survive in all our hearts.
Because to some America's beauty is
irreplaceable, and to all priceless.

   —*Karyn R. Lorenzana*

Beyond the Everlasting Dream

Seemingly I went aboating in a dreamland I went afloating;
and as I drifted free awhile I floated upon a deserted isle
and there forth was no single soul to pay the ransom for my toll;
but I had no indignation, woefully I sat in desperation;
and the water waved with white crystal curls, I noticed
the coral reef of pearls. It sat so seemingly calm, as I sat
do dreaming along, in my boat near the pearl coral reef;
and down, down fell a leaf; so seemingly it floated down, so
seemingly it could not tread, and drifted down as if it said;
"wake-up"; but I could not make myself nor leave this place,
this place of nature in the human race; and as the leaves began
to change, as my face to rearrange and a wrinkles appeared
upon my cheek thereon, there above me flew hereon; he circled
thirty-one times then lost his flight and fell to the ground;
and as the toll I did not pay, instantly my hair turned gray;
and as the night began to fall, I heard a holy spirit call;
"wake-up"; but I did not wake, nor did I stir; for I was
trapped in an aging blur; I looked up and saw one star in
the sky, and as the star fell from the sky so high, it seemed to
   whisper,
"Time to die."

   —*Jennifer Robinson*

Heart Language

   If you are backward and shy
     And can't speak aloud
   Afraid to be heart praising Him
     In the midst of a crowd.

   Just look up to Heaven
     For Jesus is near.
   Just speak in heart language
His ear is not heavy that He cannot hear.

   He will answer heart language
     And bless you, my friend.
   When your heart is humbled,
     The answer He'll send.

   So raise your hand in silence.
     You've nothing to hide.
   For God looks on the heart
     And not on the outside.

   —*Goldie Duncan*

Mykine

Olive leaves patter through unguarded chambers
and, caught by an unexpected gusts, ascend
like smoke toward the gleaming sun and halo of blue sky.

   Who turns to hear the bleating lambs
   and sees how the fair Iphigenia sobbed
   carried through Lion's gate,
     down the rocky path to the sea:
     an offering to the sleeping winds?

   See, who shades her eyes
   to keep her precious child in view,
   and how does her purple garment trail upon
     the patterned floor as she crosses back and forth
     wailing injunctive curses against unjustness?

   —*Deirdre Feehan*

Walking

We walk through the night.
And our faces shining in the moon light.
Still walking by the crack of dawn.
Getting sleepy we both yawn.
So through the night and all day.
We will always be walking our time away.

   —*Loretta Kunzer*

Peace

PEACE will come when people live in friendship, side by side...
and cherish understanding, more than hatred, greed and pride.

Peace will come when people see all people as the same...
and no one has to live in fear of ignorance or shame.

Peace will come when people who are needy can reach out...
for shelter, food or love, and no one has to do without.

Peace will come when people learn to listen and to care...
about the rights and dignity of people everywhere.

Peace will come when love and trust and kindness know rebirth
and on that day all people will rejoice in peace on Earth!

    —*Karen Saelzer*

Poetic Justice

Step into the lawyer's world my friend, land of fees-courts
And crackling hens, judges and clerks and power trustees,
Giving it all away under bankruptcy.
Forget your years of sweat and strain, building a company
Trying to stay sane, they sue and sue and sue again,
Just give a reason out comes the pen. They have no fear
These lawyer breeds, they'll rape and ravish to fill
There needs, ethics are gone, and we'll never see,
Jefferson or Lincoln for a nominal fee. O land of plenty
Home of the brave, how did we become the lawyer's slave.
Will the breath of each morning bring another suit?
From a legal firm looking for loot and the people ask what
wrong today, look at the system, it's the lawyer's way. They
make the laws to suit their needs, justice is easy-just
plant the seeds. Oh Webster—Jefferson—Thomas Paine, where
are you now? Your work was in vain, they've taken your words,
your deeds and your dreams and tore them apart, with their
selfish schemes...so step into the lawyer's world my friend,
Land of fees and courts and crackling hens, let's hope
Someday we all rise up, to kill the system that has run amuck.

    —*Hugh O'Donnell*

Escape

Black velvet enfolds me in a dark soft embrace deeper, deeper
and deeper I sink until no trace, of my buoyant, energetic bouncy self
is found. Heaviness accompanied by an almost stifling warmth —
no sound. A feeling almost of panic pervades my very soul,
Escape is imperative now — I flee to the vast expanse of the
restless sea. At the sea, I walk into the cool rippling water-
slow— slow— slow, to the very depths, fathoms below. Such
blessed relief, such delicious coolness, I'm in a whirl!! I
revel in the beauty of this strange new world, soon this, too,
weighs heavily on my shoulders, like a burden to bear. I
struggle to rise to the surface to breath the pure refreshing
air. Dreams can be exciting, interesting and realistic, my
friend. But we are glad when some of them end.

    —*Gladyes E. White*

Rebirth

Morning brings a day that's new
And frees me from dark fears I left behind.
Nightmare games played by a troubled mind
Become transparent in dawn's lightened view.

Sun's warm breath will make me whole
And turn to nothing yesterday's dark wake
That held me prisoner on witch's stake.
Now, I shall grasp sun rays to heal my soul.

For God has given me another chance to see
New beginnings cancel what I've tried to hide:
A worn-out script of life I need not hold.
So, to the dawn I open heart's door wide
And I shall soar on bird-swift wings that set me free.

    —*Delma M. Rodgers*

Forever

I will love you till the day I die,
And even beyond that.
I will think of you always,
Till summers come to an end.
I will keep your memory locked up in my mind,
Like a murder behind steel bars.
I will cherish the time we had together,
Till winters come no more.
The bad and the good,
The happy and the sad,
The memories of you I will never forget.
I will love you more than life itself,
Forever and more to come.
I will tell you thank you for all you've given me.
I will pray to God to watch over you,
To love you as much as I.
To care for you in his cloud-filled world,
And treat you like a king.
I will love you till the day I die,
And even beyond that.

    —*Elizabeth A. King*

I've Lost My Way

I've lost my way, lost in the dark
The darkness of broken hearts
The hearts that have been trampled
I've lost my way through the darkness of broken hearts
But only if I stay in the darkness,
I also can see the light of beautiful hearts.

If I start now, I should make my way
through the darkness by morn
If I make it through the darkness,
I'll reach the light

The light of you, Mom.
The light of you

    —*Heidi Fields*

Serenity

The apple tree bent to the warmth of spring
And felt the sap stir in it's ancient veins,
It's crooked branches, like old tired arms,
Had known the fresh caress of many rains
And many burning suns, had burdened been
With heavy children, red and crisp and sweet,
Tossing them gently into autumn's lap,
That all the hungry sons of man might eat.
Now— weary, it stood and bore no more,
Yet shading still the ancient cottage door.

The old grandma sat rocking in her chair
And felt the spring sun on her wrinkled cheek,
How long the years had seemed when she was young-
And now a year was but another week.
Once she had felt the eager zest of life,
The pain of love, the mystery of birth,
She reared her handsome maids and stalwart sons
To honest labor in the fruitful earth.
Now she was old, and could but knit and nap—
Yet great grandchildren clustered warmly round her lap.

    —*Eleanor Aho*

"Life Time Of Love"

My youth and growing up years were nothing but dark and stormy and filled with dread. Every spare minute was spent on improving myself with working and struggling and trying to get ahead. I gave all of myself to my marriage, being a friend and wife and lover and, of course, an all around the clock housekeeper and good mother. For a long time I really didn't exist to myself any more. I became lost in my family, loving all, teaching them to help and to love each other. As time passed it seemed the world and outside influences soon would creep in and tear apart the family I took so long to create. With the help of "God" my family was safe and most of the influences were stopped, at least all of the ones I had grown to hate. My family is now on its own and I'm starting to find myself and to create things I had buried a life time ago, when I was not alone. But I worry still about my children's families that are now being brought up in this world where the influences only threatened my own. I continue to pray that "God" will guide my grand and great grandchildren.

—*Gloria Margaret (Clinedinst) Wode*

Temptation

I could walk into your arms right now
　And find no greater pleasure
Than to taste the sweetness of your lips.
　A sweetness long to treasure
I'd know why dawn is kissed by sun
　And earth kept sweet with dew...
I'd know why every stars' a wish
　And why two love birds coo...
The very silence of the night, when
　It's struggle with day has won..
And the rosy blushing glow of day.
　when her lover, night, has gone..
All this, and so much more I'd know,
　My very hearts' sensation..
It might be wrong, but very sweet
　To yield to such temptation.

—*Iris Rogert*

Of Pussywillows, Paperdolls, And Poetry

Rain is pouring down — the day is dark and drear,
And from my cozy corner, memories come fast and clear,
Of pussywillows, paperdolls, and poetry.

For oft, in rainy days of old, my dearest aunt and me,
Would be enthroned on pillows high, a readin' poetry.
Or perhaps we'd stage a fashion show, No queen was half so grand, As our paperdolls, parading across that old night stand.

Pussywillows we gathered by the score,
Spring rains had set them free once more.
And colored chalk 'twas all we used,
To make our pussywillows rainbow hued.

Of all my childhood memories, it's these I hold most dear;
The countless hours Aunt Ruthie spent with me,
In search of spring's first pussywillow, the paperdoll we dressed, And enraptured by all the verse she read.

It matters not how drear the day nor that the rain won't stop,
Still pussywillows poke their fuzzy noses out,
And memories seep in with every drop,
Until it almost seems, Aunt Ruthie's here with me,
A playing paperdolls and reading poetry!

—*Claire L. Workman*

Knit Two, Purl Two

I used to walk a jet black dog Manhattan Beach
and gaze at golden hues caused by the setting sun.
I used to sail the ocean green among white blocks of ice,
the resting place of playful seals having a lot of fun.

I used to fly o'er clouds of snow
to Eiffel's tower of silver steel
to gaze at wondrous works of art
which I could almost live and feel.

I used to climb brown pyramids built
who knows how many years ago;
I didn't hear the beggars shout;
I heard Kings speak in voices low.

I used to watch the changing guards
and hear their drums and fife;
they marched with pomp in red and gold-
a pageant of a royal life.

Relieving memories and dreams
I often sit and knit
or try to write a perfect poem
with vivid words that fit.

—*Eleanor Bardeen*

To All the One's Who Knew Me When

To all who say they knew me when
And had a part to play back then
Tell me where they all are now
As at last I stand to take my bow

Are they kidding themselves or you
Were they the one's who helped me threw
Or did I do it on my own
All the while they should've known

They never wanted to know me
Just took the crumbs I dropped for free
The women that might have been the mate
Who never made it to our first date

Someone I helped or at least tried
A beautiful thing who's insides had died
Or maybe one I couldn't reach
She'd listen now and let me teach

Oh well these are a part of my past
Not the first and not the last
I do remember them you know
But I only live for tomorrow so go

—*Ian M. Wallace*

For the Love of a Country

A sky full of planes both friend and foe, a war full of blood and hate. With soldiers fighting on the ground below, awaiting their final fate. With hearts on edge and bated breath, they await a final attack. Only a split second between life and death, by bombs or guns or flak. A nation to fight for, a country to defend, a desperate cry for peace. Does this fighting have no end? Will the killing ever cease? As the thought of fear fills our minds, the bombs are moving in. A safe place soon we hope to find, before the killing begins. A soldier boy at the age of 18, Lord, I'm not ready to die. Blood and horror is all I've seen, what kind of life have I? I know nothing of life, only of war, it's much to hard to believe. Things will never be the way they were before, my life I will never retrieve. One by one they fall to the ground, never to stand again. How many will live to be homeward bound? These boys forced to be men. As the blast of bullets fills our ears, and flying fortresses fill the sky. We try very hard to hold back tears, as brave young men begin to die. I'll fight to win this victory, I will not suffer defeat. This will go down in history, to make my cause complete.

—*Jean Ramirez*

Every Thought Is A Dream

I'd like to touch what my heart dreams of
And have a winter picnic on the livingroom rug
Because dreams remind me of all the things I've missed
Like a lovely smile and a tender kiss
On a bright sunny day that's covered with a clear blue sky
I like when a lady takes care of herself
Then I know she's worth her pride
The sparkle in her eyes reflects her charm
The moisture of her skin is soft and warm
I'm thankful for winter, spring, summer and fall
Because God's been good to me
And blessed me through it all
Dreams are also for those who sleep
A smile and your health are two things you should always keep
But at least I've had one dream come true
I was blessed to meet someone as lovely as you
And nothing hurts worst than a heart in pain
And to lose a friend who won't explain
So don't step on the one that cares for you
Because hugs and good for your health too

    —Bobby Lawson

The Visit

I sit before my mother in the nursing home,
And hold her fragile hands in mine so she won't be alone.
They're stiffened with arthritis now and covered with dark
spots; her wedding band she no longer wears; it's always
slipping off. As I gaze into her eyes, which are still so
bright and clear, I thank the Lord who gave to me a mother who
is so dear. Some days her mind, it wanders, and she's in a
different time; she speaks of friends of long ago; how life was
oh so fine. She talks of dolls and skipping rope and playing
on the beach, baking pies, clouds so high, a class she used to
teach. I gaze at the hands I hold, wrinkled
and so weak remembering they were once used to brush tears
off my cheeks. They did the wash, cooked the meals, and
mended my favorite jeans, buttoned my coat, smoothed my hair,
and a thousand other things. Mother, your hands are still and
you are feeble now, unable to work or play; but with God's
grace and all you taught, I'm at your side to stay. And when
the Lord calls you home to be with Him above, be assured I'll
ne'r forget your wondrous care and love.

    —Nelson P. Provost

Names

Too many Vangs
And how do you say Xiong?
At least it is short
   and fits in the space in my roll book.
But what will I do with
   Bouaphanh Sonethanouphet?
I was so proud I could say Rodriguez and Juarez
   and before that Sarkisian and Choolijian.
But now a mother's shy voice repeats again
"It's too hard for you, Teacha?"

    —Dorothy J. Buller

Two Ships

Like two ships becalmed near each other for months
and finally rubbing sides,
we found each other.
Slowly, cautiously, we tested the waters.
And when I trusted me
and you trusted you
we began to trust each other.
And love took over
And we didn't fight it.

    —Erin Hithersay

A Better Time!

A mute moment of glory, sped the sun on its way
And I gazed at the starfilled skies.
"You never answered my prayers, dear Lord.
They were wrenched from my silent cries!"
Your GRACE be the wings beneath my soul
A trust that carries me further on.
I hear in my heart, your whispered voice,
"Not thy will, but mine be done."
I'll follow you then through the open door,
Through a silent but not deaf sky.
"It will be a BETTER time, you know,"
Was my Saviors gentle reply!"

    —Borghild Wilson

World?

The snow falls once more; Tragic winds blowing
and i realize that the tender trees shall die
Memories linger on, they shan't be dormant
but they are turning into stone
As the future closes her eyes; She squints at the sun
yet she cant tell her placement in the clear blue sky
Now drizzle is laughing again; Rain begins to pelt
and i realize that the flowers shall drown
Choking presently, they shan't be saved
and the clouds are not weeping
The sun begins to glare; Luminescently against negative space
my heart is buzzing with all its sorrows and broken dreams
Leaves begin their spin cycle; Faces change shades
and i realize her strong voice shall wither away
Until no one can hear it.

    —Kelly Vile

Natures Beauty

As I walk along the lowlands
And I see the splendor there
The flowers standing row on row
There is beauty everywhere

The streams are running down the hill
As the mountain comes in view
The air is so refreshing
It is like the morning dew

The lakes are lying in their place
The deer are standing by
The sun is peeking through the clouds
To brighten up the sky

The fish are jumping in the streams
The birds are singing too
The wind is whispering through the trees
It seems to beckon you

And I just stand in wonder
I wish you were here too
So both of us could enjoy
This awesome mountain view

    —Jim Overton

The Sea

I like to sit by the sea,
and look in the water to see.
The fish swim by as they seem to say hi
and the seaweed sways in the sea.
I like to watch the sea gulls
as they soar just like eagles
they dip into the water and pull out a fish,
I'd like a carefree life like this.
That is why I like the sea
because it is a carefree place to be.

    —Brandy Peterson

A Journey

At ten, my most treasured gifts were books, joys found!!!
And I vowed someday I'd own, First Editions—Leather Bound-
Charles Dicken's "Christmas Carol," or Lytton's "Last Days of Pomeii,"
Poets- Wordsworth, Watts, Burns, and my mind entwined with
Thomas Gray.
A Journey with the printed word!

Then I was there! In Lord Lytton's Knebworth House, his books to view,
In Bedford I saw copies of Bunyan's "Pilgrim's Progress,"old
and new,
Stratford upon Avon, is William Shakespeare's, "spirit owned"
And best of all, Charles Dicken's First Editions, in his London home.
A Journey with the eye!

And now I read—"Splendors of the Ancient World",
My mind remembers, some already seen,
I set my sights on viewing all the rest,
And with the book, curl up to read and dream!
And plan a Journey in my mind!

—*Marge McAfee*

Retreat

The bells were a musical background:
And I walked the hallowed slope: The spirit of the fathers
present left no space or time to mope.

To cope with all the worldly things
Is beyond the human control:
I heard, I prayed, I knelt
And asked for whom the bells toll?

The answer is such a simple one
Of heart and mind, of soul:
Divine sparks in the human breast
Respond to the spirit of which the bells toll.

—*Julia Bell*

"The Way....."

Not everything goes always wrong
and it seems only that bad times are long
the good way to live
is with love to...give.
    Love is great we reason why?
    and years are passing us fast by
    seasons bring us sunshine now and then rain
    and happiness will always win in fight with...pain.
No fearful times will ever last
the bad times will always past
and with each passing of a beautiful day
each hour will lead us in the future in a ....BETTER WAY!

—*Frank Zdzislaw Glinski*

"Somewhere In Time"

I have loved you, your arms have held me,
And I've known love to last through
All eternity, "Somewhere In Time" in my
fond memories, your smile has set
my heart my soul a glow.

I have loved you somewhere so long ago
You face comes back to me, and
Suddenly I know our love will
Last, we'll be together through
All the years, our hearts will beat as one.

I loved you then as I love you now.
Your part of all my dreams, my
Hopes my whole life through
My darling, hold me and never
Let me go, please stay with me.
Stay with me.

—*Hilda Bennett (Breaux)*

Heaven's Streets

Thank you Father take my hand
And lead me to the promised land
Beyond all sin a holy place
I want to see you face to face
My work is done so take me home
It's heaven's streets I am bound to roam

—*George Joji Kobayashi*

Pique On Parnassus

When Music went on holiday
And leased retreat to Rap and Roll,
Despairing Muse was moved to say:
"My Zeus, their noise convulses soul."
"But not for long, Terpsichore,"
Consoling Father flatly said:
"Consider Herod's fantasy,
Sharp price he paid for homey bed.
"Had not Salome learned to prance
On tether to a heady whore
Then executed pristine dance
Flawed house might rule forevermore.
"So, Daughter, let them screech away,
Add footnotes to raw history,
Till Music comes back home to stay
And mates again with Mystery."

—*Judith Pike Boos*

Holy Bible

When you're tired and lonely
    And life has no meaning for you
Just take your Holy Bible
    For from cover to cover it's true

In it you will find wisdom
    It will help you know wrong from right
And you will find peace
    Through the dark and silent night

Sometimes you may have said
    God is unjust
But how can you
    When his Son died for us

So take your Holy bible
    And hold it close to your breast
Then through the dark and silent night
    You'll find peace and rest.

—*Bonnie Hendrickson*

Cadee And Boner

Cadee my lady, yet my little girl, I love her so. She dances
    and prances and jumps to and fro. She wags her tail as
friendly dogs do telling me many times a day I love you too.

We go for long walks twice a day and meet children along the
    way. Boner my black lab goes along too and before the
    children they each try to out do.

The children love this and call them by name while the two
before them exhibit their games. These same children yell
from passing cars, with glee, hello Boner hello Cadee, yet
    neglect to speak to me.

Studies indicate that a child's close association with a pet,
    bird or animal, provides enhancements for the a child's
advancement. So parents take heed and provide that need.

—*Charles W. Morton*

The Golden Rock

The Golden Rock, St. Eustatius, mote of a Caribbean island
and linchpin of triangular trade to the Colonies from Holland,
was a rescuer of our infant nation from the British tyrant.

Sephardim, the horror of ancestors' Inquisition
still in mind and lovers of freedom,
rejoiced in this island sanctuary.

These Dutch congregants of "Honen Daliem,"
"He who shows mercy to the poor,"
gave their hearts to the American cause.

Clever Jewish traders
loaded fleet blockage runners to the gunwales
and greased the flow to Washington's legions.

Alas, the Golden Rock is lost in history!
But British commander, Rodney, called it a "nest of vipers,"
nourishing the American rebellion.

Rodney pillaged the Golden Rock,
banished the Jews and declared:
"This rock has done mortal harm to England."

Recently, Virgin Islands commissioner, Paiewonsky, exulted:
"St. Eustatius and the Dutch Jews changed U.S. history."

   —Charles Bernstein

My Song Of Praise: Amazing Grace

I used to glory in my strength,
 And loved to hike and run,
But then a cruel stroke of fate,
 Said, "With these you are done."
Then, home again, without delay.
 My dear Mary passed away.

Alone, grieving, disabled, what to do?
 But God said with an answer clear:
"Don't worry, my son, just follow me,
And live with my grace from day to year."

 I sold my house, moved to a home.
Made good friends, received good care.
Then met another Mary, younger was she.
 I needed her, she needed me.
 Then God intervened, made us one,
And a new life for us had begun.

"Don't worry my son, just follow me,
 And live in grace for all to see."

   —Lloyd A. Staebler

One Perfect Gift

A star shone down that holy night
And on a stable shed it's light.
Baby Jesus in a manger lay,
On that first wondrous Christmas Day.
With Joseph and Mary at his feet.
And Angel's voices soft and sweet.
There were no trees with tinsel there
No stockings hanging anywhere.
But there was love, a gentle glow
To warm that stable long ago.
So when the holidays are through
And work and worry come to you.
When all the wreaths and trees are dried
And all the toys are cast aside,
Just think of the Babe so set apart
And peace will come to fill your heart.
That loving glow will still be there
To last throughout another year
Give yourself that gift of peace and love
Sent down by Him who reigns above.

   —Dorothy L. Kodesh

Dreams

I stand on a lowly hill,
 And my spirit rises higher still;
  Like a bird with skyborn wings,
   Reaching, reaching, as my heart sings.

I stand on the rugged mountain,
 And I feel within my heart a certain
  Free spirit lifted by the wind,
   And the eagle and I seem somehow kin.

I stand in the meadow green,
 And the wind across the grassy scene
  Brushes my cheek and cools my brow;
   Nothing could be more wonderful than now.

I stand near the river as it runs to the sea,
 And I wish it would carry me
  To far away places of which I dream,
   To take me away from the daily routine.

But standing or gazing or reaching a star
 Comes only when one extends so far...
  That fingers touch the rainbow sky,
   And dreams are grasped 'ere they pass us by.

   —Donna T. Walker

Top Of The Mornin'

The top of the mornin' to you
And of course, to all of your clan
I bring you fondest greetin's
From dear old Ireland

Sure an' 'tis a pleasure to greet you this mornin'
In the traditional Irish way
And I send along me blessin's
On this great Saint Patrick's Day

So wear your shamrock proudly
And no matter where you be
When you take your "celebration nip"
Of course drink one for me

For when the clan is all together
And the fun is about to start
You can thank the Lord you're Irish
From the bottom of your heart

For there'll always be an Ireland
You can bet your life on that
And we owe it all to one swell guy
A saint—we all call Pat

   —John M. McWilliams

"A Glimpse Of A Moment"

The windmills turn on the green countryside
And out in the ocean the porpoises hide
While the seas turning over
And the tips of waves are white
I feel inside a wonderful fright

My mind starts to wonder away from my soul
As the trees and the sky confess to their roll
That they play in this life of confusion and dreams
No one is perfect
At least that's how it seems

Everything seems strange like I've been here before
The world keeps on turning like a king turns a scroll
The birds in the sky are now swooping at flowers
As time passes on
The minutes and hours.

   —Erin Nicole Johnson

Our Twins

Our twins are a wondrous joy, with there big brown eyes
and rosie cheeks, there more fun than any toy that squeaks.

The laughter in there eyes, the smiles across there faces.
God has given us such good graces.

Never a moment that goes by, they run up to you just to say Hi.
With every breath they breath, there's never any sadness or
anytime to grieve.

God gave us these precious, babies, knowing what pressures they
would hold. He had that faith in us, we'd keep them from the
cold.

We watch each step and movement, they eagerly make each day.
There bright and full of sunshine no matter what you say.

We thank God for these ladies. They've brightened up our
lives.
No one could ever know the joys, of having twins for babies.

—*Dena Compton*

Larry's English Garden

I walked through an English garden
    and saw colors that were not able to be reproduced.
I took time when I didn't think I had time
    to do something more important
        than what I thought was important.
I took time to appreciate the natural beauty
    of one man's toils.
This man's garden is not a hobby, but a lifestyle.
A lifestyle more vivid and inspirational than
    the academics that whirled in my mind
        and beckoned my attention.
The knowledge of the earth's gifts were nurtured
    in his garden, his genuine manner,
        and the dirt in his fingernails.
I stood there envying his peace
    and oneness with his garden..
I stood there with a restless mind, a worried disposition
    and clean, acrylic fingernails.
I walked away with a desire to create my own garden,
    even if it just be within the windows of my mind.

—*Margie Irwin-Mostyn*

The Face Of A Young Child

To behold a young child's face so sweet and pure,
And see them so excited for sure,
Of an event of their day, they had spent,
Their faces, all aglow about where they'd went.

Some older people sometimes say,
As they carried on a conversation that day,
"Children should be seen, not heard."
But the children want to talk, not having disappeared

What they really ought to say is just to sit
And wait a moment, then tell me all about it
Then tell them you know it's very important to share
This event of their day and that you care.

As a child is put to bed and sleeping at night
Have you ever watched a more beautiful sight
They are smiling so sweetly
Their faces bright completely.

God has blessed us with children, it's true
So let's take time to listen to them too,
What would this world be without them so pure
To brighten our days with their smiling faces for sure

—*Betty Joan Comer*

Spring Inchoate

I watched mnemonic dust from whirlwind drift
And slowly greet the yellowed page of time
Where restless ghosts of yesterday lift
Aphonicly staging lively pantomime;
Enacting sparks that flare but blink of an eye
When blithesome bubbles burst and fade away
As winds of Armageddon waft goodbye
And spring, inchoate, halts in disarray.

I brushed the dust from weathered book I hold
And saw a radiant flash from summer's trance
That walked the aisle of living hope—consoled
Where whispering tissued gown awaited dance

And bonding flowers, tied with ribbon of hope,
Lie spiritless next to official envelope.

—*E. June Mathews*

Eternal Love

The love that we share is a very rare
and special love that can never be equaled.
Whenever I'm around you, I feel all the hurt
from my troubles begin to heal. You've made
me strong and I'm happy to belong to you.
I promise to remain faithful to you.
My love for you has never been anything but true.
Words could not describe my feelings for you.
My heart soars with undying love and devotion
Whenever I'm with you. When we're together
nothing else seems to matter but being with you.
All of my problems seem to fade away
when you tell me everything will be okay.
Nothing or no one could ever come between us.
If you ever need anyone to lean on,
I'll always be there for you. Our love will
last forever and we will never be apart.
You will eternally and always be forever in my heart.

—*Jennifer Booth*

Bernie The Skull

Bernie the skull is sly as a fox
And spends all his time enclosed in a box
He's witty and clever and tells jokes galore
And keeps you in stitches 'til your sides are sore.

On Acri Creature Feature as we know
Bernie the Skull's the star of the show
When all the joking and fooling is through
Enchanting Bernie has a big smile for you.

He doesn't walk or rattle around
For his body's encased in the ground
So he hopes on a dark Friday night
That you'll be kept in a terrible fright.

So be sure to tune in
With your best girl or beau
To that witty old Bernie
On the late acri show.

—*Kenneth L. Mann*

Alone

There once was a man with no name,
And no one knew from whence he came,
His complexion was fair and his stature tall,
And within his soul lay a silenced wall,
His eyes were complex with features so deep,
His voice was soft with emotions that seemed to sleep,
His actions so silent and yet so sincere,
That no one even noticed he was here.

—*Kathrine M. Moore*

Hourglass

Grandfather had an hourglass that sat beside his chair,
  and stories full of wonder he would tell when I was there.
He'd turn the hourglass over and before the sand was spent,
  through portals into magic worlds my brother and I went.

Those boyhood, sunlit days so fresh in that time long ago,
  forgotten with time's passage as the boy began to grow,
Come rushing back like summer wind as once again I find
  the house, the chair, the hourglass I thought I left behind.

The hourglass sits lonely now with dust upon its case,
  but echoes of Grandfather's tales disturb this quiet place.
I know in time like everything his memory will pass,
  and yet today I think of him and see the hourglass.

What power has that hourglass, what object serves one grain
  that rushes ever faster through and soon is still again?
He lives, he laughs and loves and dies, and in the end does man
  run through a course like sand to fulfill some elusive plan?

    —*Frank Hess*

The Flight

I closed my eyes to pray,
And talk with the Lord today.
Especially on my heart,
Was the thought of your new start.

In my mind's eye I saw a young bird fly,
And soar into the sky.
I asked the Lord to be,
With you and your family.

It's true the nest is warm and safe,
A haven from all that we must face.
But if we never spread our wings,
We shall miss such wonderful things.

The Lord has given us each a vision,
And you are just beginning your mission.
To serve our country, yes 'tis true,
But your duty to God is first for you.

The field for you He's opened wide.
To share with others is where you're tied.
The Lord will do great things through you,
Just depend on Him, He'll see you through.

    —*Brenda L. Bracken*

How Could I Not Be Among You?

Think of me in Spring when violets push through dampened sod,
And tender shoots show forth new evidence of God.
On summer nights when fields are softly trod,
Recall the feel of dew-wet grass on feet unshod.
Think of me when rain pelts upturned faces in the morn
When all the world seems pink and newly born.

But mostly think of me in Fall
When Autumn lets her beauty out in all
Her gold from vaults unseen
And glory leaps the void between;
Who says we die when all this comes anew
Whether I am gone or sitting close to you.

Then think of me again when snow falls softly down
To give you rest and peace and surcease from your frown.
Let sorrow cease, wipe all lines clear———
Remember me with joy—not with a tear.

    —*Helen M. Sheldon*

Remember When...

Remember when you told me that you did it out of love;
and that it was nothing to worry about or be ashamed of.
But when the first hit across my face struck, I felt
my strength had just run out of luck.
It hurt so bad I didn't know what to do, but then I
realized that it was nothing but a little bruise.
But now that I'm ten and the memories are starting to fade,
I'm still scared to see you since three years ago May.
Yet on and on you still drank and drank with that beer in
one hand, and now a table full of crank.
I tried to talk to you about what could happen, but you
wouldn't listen until it was the end.
So here I am looking at a stone sticking out of the earth;
describing everything starting from your name on down to
the year of your birth.
I realize now that I've done nothing to be ashamed of;
I will just always remember you telling me you did it
out of love.

    —*Jennifer Points*

About Forgiveness

It's not often that you find a love,
and that's why I'm glad I found you.

And it is comforting to know that we
can come together and agree.

Agree that we have friendship,
agree that we have love.

I believe that for some reason or another (destiny),
that our hearts are beginning to knit together.

And, maybe your hurt is my hurt,
your pain is my pain,
your care is my care,
and your love ... is my love.

I just felt that I wanted to...
I just felt that I needed to.
I just felt that I should reaffirm my love, and say...
"I'm sorry ... Forgive me!"

    —*Marvin E. Armstrong*

Two Dads

Two dads were part of her life
And the cause of years of pain and strife.
Her biological father was an incestuous beast,
Her offered father to be was a perverted mind rapist.

One young girl so loving and kind,
But tragically caught up in needs that bind,
Physically, mentally, emotionally exploited,
A victim of fun and games, shamely treated.

Her biological father was guilt ridden with shame,
But to his dying day, would not admit blame.
The promised father also denied any guilt
And hides in paranoic behind a court petition he built.

With all her faith and trust in men that really mattered,
Her God given right to marriage and motherhood was now
shattered. Thoughtlessness and cruelty they sought their
pleasure, her life was ruined beyond possible measure.

The wages of sin are death says the Lord,
The higher court ruling, judgment will afford
Justified punishment to end the story,
But neither father was man enough to say "I'm sorry!"

    —*Phyllis R. Gunstone*

Banish Your Hate

The Earth is round, full of hate,
And the corners of it determine our fate.
Our imagination soars above the clouds,
Yet our voices cry more quiet than loud.
Some live today and give love to whom asks;
Yet most reject love and still live in past.
We are selfish, care only for our own lives,
Shan't we be righteous and throw down the sharp knives?
Why kill the innocent if you are no more guilty?
Cleanse your conscience and avoid the filthy.
Hark! People of Earth banish your hate,
For hate is not one to determine our fate.
Love is patient, love is kind;
Love each other and none shall walk blind.
Love God and His Glory for all it is worth,
For soon, my friends, no human shall walk the Earth.
We are in this together, all for one,
So let us fight evil, before evil is done.

　　　　—*James Main*

Shadows Speak

Though the warming sun embrace my back
...and the dancing winds blow through my hair
...and the tiny shape of newborn leaves exact
...the nostalgic smell of the new spring is rare

I've shared my life with lonely dark shadows
...for not a breath of life was here nor there
...in sunlight or moonlight in wide open meadows
...my shadow remained, I've no despair

Soon the darkened clouds took away the sun
...and the cold north winds chilled the empty air
...the beauty of spring suddenly became none
...for my shadow was gone and no one was there

One beautiful but rare bright crisp spring morning
...a thought came to me as I embellished the breeze
..."I was only hurting myself by always in mourning
...and not a shadow on earth was hurting me

Whether the cold north winds begin to blow
...or the still spring air protects the new leaves
...my shadow and I will no longer feel low
...for I will share God's gift, and that is me

　　　　—*Ginny Webster*

Impatiently Waiting

Through the busy, stressful, work-filled day,
And the lonely, restless night;
Your image is captured between my thoughts,
Causing a glorious endless sight.

And as I try to draw your attention near,
To this feeling that makes me whole;
My words come out like a mumbling drunk,
Because you intoxicate my soul.

From that day forth, the time is short,
Since I initially saw your face;
I was hypnotized by your glowing eyes,
And longed for your embrace.

But your thoughts, fears and inner-self,
I've yet to comprehend;
Am I, to you, a passer-by,
Or a growing special friend.

So until that day, when your mind is made,
And your course is set out straight;
I'll be at the end of the narrow path,
As I sit and impatiently wait.

　　　　—*Kelly John Racine*

Dream On

In the heart of every man
　　And the solitude he shares
　　Gives way to what he can amend
　　and Dream on, Dream on, to his care.

In the nights that are so long
　　with his thoughts that are serene
　　the gift of light will bring a song
　　and Dream on, Dream on, all who have seen.

In the harbor of ones being
　　It is there he learns to meditate
　　So he can share in one esteem
　　and Dream on, Dream on, do not hesitate.

In the daily chores each day
　　He goes about to plan and celebrate
　　the joy that bring with no delay
　　and Dream on, Dream on, and circulate.

In the beautiful dreams he has
　　And mountains of opportunity he gathers
　　In the silent and solitude of ones Lair
　　And Dream on, Dream on, do not falter.

　　　　—*Florence R. Duquette*

The Bell Sends Forth a Sound that Is Pure Feeling

The bell sends forth a sound that is pure feeling
And the sound resounds in my heart, peals of forgiveness
And balm

Mercy
Is utterly generous
It cares not how long the heart has remain encamped
In the dark, fetid quarters of its enclosure
Nor why. It has no time for stories, it lives
In the now, breathes of the openness of the moment
And finds it good

The bell calls for you

Will you let the peace sweep in like a spring wind?
Will you let the jonquils caress your soul
Showing it something of the goldenness that has always been?

I cannot speak of the secrets so thoughtfully
Held there for you, or of the flow of the river
That unites night with the first rising of the sun

I can only beckon
Will you come?

　　　　—*Deborah Anne Grandinetti*

"The Ocean's Gift"

When life casts its gray shadows on me
and the tests seem too much to take.
When my heart has been broken once again,
and my dreams have faded into nothingness
The white sands of the beach is where I go.
Running past sand castles and the hidden
treasures the sands may hold
Running past lovers basking in the warmth
of the eternal sun,
I reach for the cool embrace of the ocean's waves.
Far away we go from the shores of mankind,
together we dance to the ebb and flow of the tide of life
and together we stand unafraid.
In the silence of the distance the ocean's
strength speaks to me, enveloping
my soul with the gift of peace it came to find.

　　　　—*Marie Jimenez*

Remember

When things don't go as we think they should
And the world seems to hold more bad than good
When time takes its toll on our body and face
    Remember — A smile is our saving grace

    When prices are high and wages are low
And the spirit is willing but the body is slow
    When music is noise and books are smut
    Remember — A laugh gets us out of a rut

When loved ones have gone and left us behind
  And we desperately long for peace of mind
      When all we do is fret and fuss
Remember — There's someone worse off than us

  When it's easier to sit than it is to stand
  And we don't feel like lending a helping hand
When we think we've forgotten how good life can be
Remember — To care — It's fun and it's free!
       —*Dixie B. Pierce*

First Day Of Retirement

Now has retirement come at long last
And through the work loads no more will I pass
The joys of garage sales I'm now free to shop
When working for money there's no time to stop
On to the dime store where wonders await.
Just go to the handy was always my fate
On to my bedroom I go with great fear
Two years of junk mail has settled in there
Throw it away no way can I do
I must know the news be they ancient or new
On to my parlor I go with a dash
The grime is so settled it's turned into hash
When working for money there's no time to clean
Under the rug makes the dirt go unseen
It's funny how joyous the plain world can seem
When dead lines and schedules are all that you've seen
I can sleep past the sunrise and eat when I please
What a total adventure to just rake the leaves
Old age is upon me and creak though I may
for my aching and paining there's always Ben-Gay
       —*Joyce Willink*

To A Good Friend

It started as a friendship.
And turned into something more.
The love I feel for you I never felt before.
You make me feel so happy,
Whenever I am down.
By telling me your stupid stories and acting like a goofball.

I can't believe you tell me all the things you do.
But I'm glad I can trust you,
and you can trust me to.
Know matter what may happen
I will never let you down.
So whatever you do wrong
I'll always be there next to you,
to let you know your the greatest
friend I ever knew, so I love you.
       —*Charlean Damon*

Elegance

Elegance is beauty,
Beauty is elegance,
but elegance is deeper than beauty,
it's dignified, tasteful, confident, and arrogant
       —*Heather A. House*

The Eternal Dance

Imagine the world we live in one big dance
And we, the dancers of creation

The dance unifies our souls,
And our different rhythms finally blend
To create one glorious song

We become one with the creator and the created
We become the tap of today
We become the turn of tomorrow
We keep dancing...Tap, and dancing...
Turn, and dancing....
Until all that remains is the eternal dance
       —*Cyd Glover*

My Mother's Hands

When I consider where they've been,
And what they've done and undone,
What they've touched, or pushed away,
And what they've lost and won,

The brows they've soothed, the cheeks caressed,
The tears they've wiped away,
The dirt they've washed, the clothes they've ironed,
The mundane things of everyday;

Each wrinkle, every knobby joint,
Each aging spot and broken nail
Becomes a badge of honor,
Bespeaking without fail

Of love for all her kith and kin,
A sign she understands;
How beautiful they are to me ——
My Mother's tender hands.
       —*Donna B. Jones*

Silent Streams Of Death

  Oh where do we go when we die,
and why does everyone always cry?
  We float down a silent stream of death,
where the air's so still you can see your breath.

  We just float down that silent stream,
no breathing, no jumping, nor a scream.
  We float where the water is peaceful and calm,
and the cool raindrops tickle your palm,

  The feisty wind blows so happy and fair,
and the rapid water plays with your hair.
  We float and float till the stream meets the sea,
I wonder if anyone's as happy as me?

  When the sea spreads and breaks into streams,
that's the time when we drift to your dreams.

  When we float down
   the silent streams,

  The silent streams
   of death!!
      —*Kristi Crowe*

Full

My friend, I would make you my love.
But you won't let me breach your walls.
You keep your heart locked up safe and untouched.
What a price you pay, to hold so tightly to your isolation.
Let it go - and I will fill the void with such warmth and joy
You cry out in delight — "I am full up and running over
With sunshine, white doves, and ice cream!"
       —*Kitty Windle*

The Deepest Of Love

The deepest of love is deeper than the ocean,
And wider than the widest sea.
Love is like that ocean flowing out of me.
Love is for that special someone
That brightens up your days.
Love will also come to chase away the
darkness and the gray.
Love is not to take for granted
It will not make you pure in heart.
It is something beautiful; it is something
like spark.
It is better to have been loved than to never
have loved at all.
It is better to have chanced than to have never
chanced at all.
So, find that special someone, and tell then how
you feel.
Then they will know your love's for real!

—*Kara Smith*

It Should Take At Least A Week

It's the sort of thing that makes skin splotchy
    and will add white streaks to your hair
An experience that teaches not to delve too deep;
    until you reach the bottom.

That when looking up, the colors change
    and you feel wet fresh droplets on your skin.

The sort of task best done
    with fibers gathered together—two inches wide

Larger than a toothbrush,
    smaller than a solution.

It's the sort of thing where standing on a chair
    gives you a panoramic view

You have the power to change the complexion of the world.

Humanus Idius is always goal-oriented,
    as though the most pleasing thing in life would be to
    strive for death.
And so, in trying to learn process,

I painted the entire bathroom with a two-inch brush.

It could have taken forever.

It should always take at least a week.

—*Debra Romine*

A Mother's Thoughts

I looked at her, asleep in her crib,
And wondered what I ever did
To be worthy of her trust and care,
She who was so sweet and fair.

Her eyes as bright as heaven above
Shone bright at me with a baby's love.
Her hair so curly and cheek so fair,
She brought me joy beyond compare.

I survey again those blessed years,
Remembering the joy as well as the tears
Her first tooth, first step, first day at school
When I tried to teach her the golden rule.

Now she is a woman grown
With lovely, children of her own.
Even so, to me she will always be
As dear as she was when only three.

—*Helen M. Cheaqui*

"Listen To Your Heart"

When you're alone and empty but the tears inside are full,
And you don't know what to do; listen to your heart,
It'll help pull you through.
Sometimes things can get confusing
and it seems you can't think,
listen to your heart it won't let you sink.
When it seems the world is on your
shoulder and there's nowhere to turn,
listen you heart, it won't let your burn.
If 're ever in despair, listen to your heart,
at least it'll always be there.
You will forget about the bad past,
and to find a beautiful future that'll forever last.
Living in the present is a good start, meanwhile,
be strong listen to you heart.

—*Curtins E. Evans*

The One In The Mirror

When you grasp what you reach for love, money or health,
And your struggle for self finally pays,
Come to this mirror and look at yourself,
To see what that one has to say.

For no one else... friends, parents or wife,
Whose judgement upon you... you must fear,
Because the one whose verdict counts most in your life,
Is the one staring back in the mirror.

Look at the eyes... are they clouded or vacant?
Or do they glisten and sparkle with wonder and hope?
For to see what life has given or taken,
Those windows are cleansed with tears... not soap.

Look at your brow... is it furrowed and lined?
Is your face not a road-map of the years?
So come see the verdict and question sometime,
The one staring back in the mirror

—*James P. Little*

The Nurse

Gentle little lady dressed all in white, you must be an
angel sent by God from the sky to fulfill his command, of
brotherhood and love, while he is guiding you, from heaven
up above. Where there is pain you try to console. Where
there is hate, you speak about love, where there is despair,
you try to bring hope, where there is tragedy you know how
to cope. You know that Goddess Death is lurking in the
dark, you hope she won't come near, you tremble from fright,
but when you feel the cold of the feared lady's wing, that
slowly, without pity, approaches with a sarcastic grin, you
fight with all your might, courageous lady all clad in
white. Sometimes the gray sad darkness, turns into a
shining light, a little baby is born, a new and precious
life, The rising sun's first ray kisses you and the new
born, everything seems so beautiful, like a rose without
thorns. You see then the ugly scorned goddess, scurry with
hate into the darkness alone, full of joy your heart
repeats, "We won little nurse, over death we won".

—*Emilia Salvo*

Funny Patterns Of Life

Funny patterns of life creep over me,
As I sit and brood with my thoughts.
My thoughts are lively and then dull by chance
I know what is happening, I know without doubt.
I know that the Funny Pattern of life
Has given me you, and you me, as I sit and
Brood with my thoughts.

—*Edith Scheuer MacDonald*

Losing A Loved One!

We were selfish and couldn't let go,
Angels came to take his soul!
Like a beast that took to flight,
it came and steered him toward the light.

We didn't want him to die in vain:
So, we kept him from the pain!
He counted on us throughout his days,
But! All we did was hope and pray.

God had come to ease our pain:
We not knowing felt of shame!
We knoweth the Lord had made his spot:
When He lifted him; it felt so right.

So now you see what we have done,
we asked the Lord to lift him home.
We only gave him back to Thee,
Sadly missed by you and me.

But! In our hearts he'll always be;
He's part of you, he's part of me.
As we live the rest of our lives,
Closer to God: We shall be.

—*Debbie Bargy*

He Rides Tall

Now that the cattle drive is all done
    Another trail has come to an end
He rides tall into the setting sun
    Time to see what lies around the bend

Another trail has come to an end
    He is not the cowboy he use to be
Time to see what lies around the bend
    There's not much that's new for him to see

He is not the cowboy he use to be
    He knows the end of his own life nears
There's not much that's new for him to see
    He sure has seen a lot over the years

He knows the end of his own life nears
    Now that the cattle drive is all done
He sure has seen a lot over the years
    He rides tall, into the setting sun

—*Glenn G. Luscher*

A Torch For Humanity

The spark first found in ancient Athenian lore,
    arced an ocean to a fertile, receiving shore.
That spark soon fanned into a magnificent torch —
    flaming and flourishing for all to see, but sadly,
    for many, to die for it heroically.

That spark! That flame! That torch! —still arcing
    to other shores—with enemies deploring it and monarchs
    destroying it. Yet, it still lives on!
In troubled times, it goes underground—even as peat-fires
    smolder long, and burning ever stronger, remain undetected,
    only to arise again as a flaming torch expressing this right
    of humanity!
        Long live liberty!
            Long live equality!
                and may fraternity forever be!!!

—*Lauretta E. Pelton*

Ominous Love

She crossed me with a twitch;
are her ideals that of a witch?
Her face doth drip of molten gold;
Why then her smile so cold?

From her walk no clatter;
however, round-about-her whisperous chatter.
Only her hair falleth into the rain;
yet, her touch chilleth my vein.

Her love in summer doth make a rainbow;
yet, from her kiss, I feel falling snow.
Her laughter maketh me like joy;
No matter, I feel only her toy.

Then her sweet song at night, my delight;
Why then this midnight I feel such fright"
Suddenly, I hear her call;
how with my wisdom did I fall?

Only then she revealed;
my fate had been sealed.
For her name was Mc Beth;
but I was to meet father me death.

—*Jeremy Cooper*

My Private Rage

The words that fill this virgin page
    are merely words, my private rage.
Like all weak mortals I too destroy;
    this blank white page becomes my toy.
And just as mankind takes at will
    I take this page with words to fill.
This space, before I took control,
    was clean and pure, untouched and whole.
The ink-laid words, cold and dark,
    prove some strange need to leave a mark.
And just as mankind has taken space
    to glorify his own dull race,
So does this fool deface this page
    with mortal words ... my private rage.

—*J. Lawrence Keith*

20 Lines Of Verse

The loins of March
are mountains to climb
by night with sightless eyes.
Dispossessed of home and country,
the blind thrive along the impassive mask
of wired holes containing nothing.
No one is there or here to guard or tend,
only this winter night in March
— the month of the vernal equinox
with its sound of dust remains.

Like a flower flowering,
the moon blossoms at its best
in hopes of finding paradise regained
"to earn salvation for the sons of men."
The steps of silent children reach
the mountain top region of strength
where the end vanished to turn
around again and again.
Belief in men and countries like
the worship of gods, still remain!

—*Maria de la Luz Valenzuela*

26

What I Am Thankful For...

I'm thankful for all the things
around me, but most of all what I
am thankful for is my parents for
all the good things that they did to me
for all happy times that we spend
together but most of all for unforgettable
love that they brought to me.
I'm thankful to my parents for guiding me
where is right and telling me
not to look at the side but
stand still proud and not to cry.
I am proud of them and they are
proud of me and that's why we're a family.

—*Irina Pogrebetskaya*

I've Seen The Whole World Come To Me

When it started, my face and all the faces
around me were the same color.
We weren't poor and we weren't rich.
We were old and young and in between
And moved around one another with
great comfort and great strain
And with a great deal of in between.

In time I noticed others that were
different, here and there.
I would see their colors vary
And their numbers grow,
All around me now.

I ask each color what they think
has happened?
And each reply, "I've seen the
whole world come to me."

—*George Roath*

Change

Landscapes change as seasons turn
around to fall with rustic leaves
and blossoms gone
turns to winter with a soft eyed fawn
beaming inward at a snow dripped pine,
Candied apples as red and sweet as hearts
which give warmth to the cold light
resting bravely within another fight
crying to be seen from a desolate street,
A child becoming hungry
searches for growth of spirit
he will love himself
as the ice melts
showing compassion and lavish heights,
With thanks to the caring
a letter of illuminating strength
comes beneath a soaring soul
to turn once again to reassurance

—*Heather Karnis*

The Winter Storm

Cancelled is the early bird's flight,
As snow is in sight.
The animals run with fright,
As it is to continue through the night,
It is not wise to fly a kite,
Or electricity might bite,
Although said to be light,
To me, it is dark and dreary tonight.

—*Kristin Hale*

Too Young

"They tried to tell us we're too young" is known
as a cliche.
It matters not how it's described, it means
"do things our way".
If we spend our whole life doing all the things they
want us to, we'll never know how it should be, the fun,
the joy, the misery, our life would be a sham.
And then when 'ere our day shall come, we'll build our
own dreams one by one, and as the days turn into years,
our love, our work, our play, our tears.
We'll build them strong they'll grow like trees,
they'll soon become our memories.
Then one day many years from now, when our own young
are growing tall, we'll tell them how it should be done
and they won't understand at all.

—*Florence A. Cox*

In My Eyes

In my eyes I see the world,
as a cruel place to survive.
the hate, dishonesty, and cruelty,
seem to combine in one fine piece of art.
An art that can quickly,
transform hate to the human race.
In my eyes I believe the world is unfair.
Even though every person is created equal,
the races remain unequal.
In my eyes I want the world,
to be a safe place to live in.
All the races need to come together,
because in my eyes everyone will
be able to pledge allegiance to,
the flag of United States of America.

—*Latosha Berry*

The Size Of The World

The world stands only about as tall
As a little boy's arm can toss a ball
And wide as the distance from home to school.....
A little boy's feet are a measuring tool.

The world is deep and a boy can tell
How deep when he shouts down as empty well.
The world is big as the span of the sky
And a boy can measure it with his eye.

But a man, when he measures the world, will find
It is deep as his heart and wide as his mind
And tall as his soul... Yes a man can see
The world is as big as he lets it be.

—*Dorys Roach*

Prairie Spring

There's nothing quite so pleasant
As a meadow lark's first song,
Or the gaudy ring-necked pheasant
Strutting merrily along
When the prairie starts to green-up in the spring.
Or the wild geese, high and crying
On their night-time northern flight
When the fresh south wind is sighing
And the moon is shining bright.
And the scent of wild plum blossoms want to cling.
Then the air is fresh and bracing
With the smell of fresh-turned earth,
And it sets one's blood a-racing
With the thrill of spring's re-birth.
Oh, the joys that prairie springtimes always bring!

—*Emily Steinkogler*

Statue of True Dignity Stand Proud

I remember the way I saw you.
As a statue, you stood.
As a person, we remember you.

A statue of metal, a soul that survives.
We bring you life again through word and deed.
If once all steel was all melted,
If once all persons were the same,
We'd join together in a solution.

If we link together, we'd no longer
have room to fight.
Our minds would be linked with hope
of love and friendship.

We need a world image.
If we all stood on one ground at the same time,
the sun would then shine on all people as one.
Soon, we'd reflect each other with the
same goals, the same dreams.

—*Vanessa M. Ballard*

Untitled

Love is like a rose.
As beautiful as a rose is,
At times it can hurt.

Why is love such a deadly weapon?
Love should be kind,
Not to mess with your mind.
The thorns on a rose are sharp and brutal,
As love is sometimes suicidal.
The mindless games,
They pluck at our heart.
And at times, tear us apart.

Be careful to the ones you love.
And be as gentle,
As a careless dove.

—*Jason Daskal*

The Rose

The scent;
   as beautiful as an autumn sky.
The colors;
   like jewels glistening in the sunlight.
The petals;
   like feathers on angels' wings.
The stem;
   like a person standing tall and free.
The thorns;
   that hurt you like a broken heart.
The rose;
   the symbol of love everlasting.

—*Katie Patterson*

My Lee

I felt motionless and still,
As I climbed the hill.
Your singing in my heart, I bore
Long after it was heard no more.
At your grave-my tears I did not hide,
For you my dearest Lee, had died.

I will always keep you in my heart
Our love keeps us from being apart.
One day we shall meet again,
Only God knows just when.
The Lord has gone to prepare a place, were told
My Lee, we shall walk the streets of gold.
Farewell, My Lee, Farewell

—*Dot Miles Karnes*

Broken Hearts

Son said to his Mother
as far as I'm concerned you're dead.
After so many years
those were the only words that were said.

Daughter said to her Father
I'm getting married in May.
I just thought I'd let you know
you won't be giving me away.

Mom and Dad are getting a divorce
because all they do is fight.
Grand-Ma is broken and alone
with only her memories to comfort her at night.

Tears are falling everywhere
there even falling from Heaven
He can't believe that we misused
all the Love He so graciously has given.

—*Connie Erickson Mertz*

Thought

The pressure of this world is great
As for living day by day
The mean'des things that people do
The awful words they say
You would think there were no God at all
That gives us breath each day
That gives us all the strength we need
Yet, we at times - hesitate to say
Thank you Lord,
For all the good blessings you have given me
Thank you Lord,
For all the bad happenings in my life
For it was your will and your will must be done
You made us Lord. "Yes," you know us too!.
So Lord, Please help us?
Please! help us right now
Put your armor of protection around us
for the pressure of this world is great
Save us Lord? Save us now__
Before.... It's to late.

—*Catherine Butler*

The Visitor

A knock made louder by sounds of wind,
As I bade my unknown visitors in
doors swung open, in shadows forlorn,
I knew somehow my demise had been born.
"Hello, Death," said I, come right on in,
I can't say, "Welcome" with smile or grin.
Your visit expected, but with very little joy,
I've put you off for years with efforts coy.
That never a visit you would me pay,
But this is the "moment of truth" as poets say.
I'm not quite ready death to go as yet,
My Peace with God and man has not been met.
Begging your pardon what's that you say?
It's not me this trip, not me to-day!
With jubilant heart I dashed outdoors in flight
As the chimes rang out it was just midnight.
I wanted to laugh, to sing my mouth all numb,
Cried inside, "No, no I'm dead for tomorrow had come.

—*Dolores Szemple*

Each Time I Jump

Each time I jump, I fly higher and higher.
As I reach towards the heavens, and bright blue sky,
I reach towards you. To see your smile, and laughing eyes,
                    just one last time.

Each time I jump, my leg muscles pumping, I fly higher still.
I soar above tree-tops, and glide between misty clouds,
    only thinking of you.
But, what goes up, must come down. And each time I jump,
I must plummet back to the cold, gray Earth,
Into that loomy pit, one more time.

Two lost souls drifting, me, a prisoner of my own body.
Words of hate, words of pain. No one hears my desperate cries.
Each time I jump, they laugh harder.
But they are ignorant, and don't know true beauty.
Those very few that try to understand, shall never know,
                    but, neither shall I.

But still, each time I jump, I soar higher and higher.
On the one hope that our souls may touch again.

— *Kim Richards*

As I Sit Here

What is that glorious scent
As I sit here quietly today
It is the smell of fresh flowers blooming
Which the easterly wind gently blows my way.

What is that lovely music
As I st here quietly today
It is the softly sung wind chimes
Which the gentle breeze whirls into play.

What is that sweet sound
As I sit here quietly today
It is a family of birds perched in a tree
To each other, they have a lot to say.

What is that I see
As I sit here quietly today
It is the withered hillside with green sprouts anew
Sunshine and rain washed the bareness away.

What is that I feel
As I sit here quietly today
It is the gift of life from God
Which he blesses all of us with each day.

— *Megan Hagen*

Boulevard of Broken Dreams

The boulevard is dark.
As I walk along, it is raining.
I think of all the things that might have been.
The people, the places.
The dreams, the memories, come rushing back
Like the rushing of this rain falling from the night sky.
Now, scattered neon lights appear along the boulevard
From various joints that have remained open
To this early morning hour.
The bars and diners along this boulevard
Stand as a refuge for people engulfed with sadness and the blues.
As I pass by a particular bar,
The lonely wale of a saxophone reaches my ears.
It beckons me to enter.
To drown my desperate thoughts with a spirited beverage.
I decline.
I continue to walk, to remember.
Remember the things that might have been.
As I walk down this boulevard.
This boulevard of broken dreams...

— *Kevin Lee Gutierrez*

Middle-Aged Revelation

I have lived my life
As if rehearsing for the main event.
But now, the impact of reality has jarred my bland intent....

I see the one existence granted me
To grieve.....or to achieve!

Perhaps I will not find my "fountain;"
Would it soothe me to believe?

While everybody cogitates
In search of guidelines, goals and God;

The most choose paths well-worn and smooth
And shun the rocky routes untrod;

Yet every avenue provides
A varied view
With promise, too,
Of splendor, just ahead;

But there........
a common chasm;
Then, you're dead.

— *James O. Berkland*

The Hunter

Hunting is the sport of special men whose love for hunting is
as inborn thing, inherited through many generations down
through the ages from prehistoric man who hunted for survival
of his clan. A hunter loves the forests and the hills, the
deserts and the mountains where, afoot or horseback he may
find a trail to follow elk or bear or mountain lion tracking
with his hounds. A hunter loves the challenge of the stalks -
whether the animal is smarter than the man. All animals are
beautiful to him and, he seeks the older ones to grace his
trophy room or make the 'book'. A hunter understands the
constant need for habitat and food enough for all. He knows
that winter often takes its toll when snow is deep and food is
scarce, that some will starve and some will die of cold. The
same in summer drought when streams are low and water holes dry
up, the weak ones die. The hunter then is conservationist- by
hunting older lion, buck, or ram. He leaves the young to carry
species on. That coming generations might enjoy this oldest
sport of man and prove their skill at shooting clean and true
with bow or gun, learning the lessons those before them knew.
They find that hunting is much more than fun.

— *Beryl J. Barney*

The Blank Pages

Life is just a book of blank pages.
As life goes on, the pages fill up.
When you look back on these pages,
they have all kinds of meanings.

The pages of the past can't be changed.
However, the pages of the future have not been written.
Fill these pages with however you want your life to go.

Whatever goal you set can be reached.
It only takes one step at a time.
With each step we fill the empty pages.
When the goal you set is obtained, the page is full.

It's time to set your goals and set them one at a time.
If you fail at that goal, find a new way to reach it.
Just remember the book is empty with all possibilities to reach
whatever you desire.

'Life is an open book.'

— *Daryl Nelson*

A Measure To My Neighbor

Heritage is nebulous, out of reach
As moving thought is spirit of a dream;
Solution-prophecy is spanned by speech
Without the promise of a neighbor theme,
Yet looks not for wrong or evil, yet grieves
At finding sin; the one who ever knows
A measure to his neighbor then believes
The conscience-cry that friend's denial chose
Is questioned knowledge, heritage kept in a vault
Of thoughtful ignorance, as reasoned fear;
Courage is a dread that said its prayers, fault
Is whimsied fancy, witchery's career.

Observe, remark your neighbor with mind-eyes,
Sometimes good hearts show a generous size!

—*Jan McGrew*

"The Sea"

White laced fringes of tides rushing in,
As sea oats whistle in tune with the wind
While solitude flights of seabirds above,
Watch watery diamonds on the ocean I love
And gentle waves break on shell-strewn sands,
As the ocean returns treasures to shell-filled hands
And a small child runs through water so blue,
While mother and father walk along too
For the beauty of the ocean, I do know,
Is Gods creation and natures show
And as long as I can remember,
I've loved the sea
And if I didn't know better,
I'd think it loved me
And as the ocean moon reflects
Upon another night by the shore,
At home I am, by the sea evermore

—*Duane T. Willis*

"The Arm Of His Love"

As sure as the wind whistles through grassy plains,
As sure as the sea rolls in the depths of a rushing wave,
As sure as a drop of dew presses against the soft petaled rose,
The arm of His love is outstretched to comfort all His weary
heartsick souls.

Life can't be weighed by the day to day debts we pay,
Nor can it be compared to the vague misconceptions of time;
If we can see truth even when deceit beckons along an
  intriguing path,
Life can only be measured by our Lord's blessings, so vast.

Experience is the great master which shows us the way,
Patience is required to help us each day.
Open your eyes for it's plainly in view;
The arm of His love is extended to you.

—*Janice Struble*

Roses

It isn't always roses we see in the way,
As we travel together in life.

It can be the thorn's as they prick and burn,
It can be the sorrow we share.

But whatever life will bring, be it pleasure or pain.
It is so much easier to bear when we
each hold the hand's of our Lord so dear,
Who hears every prayer and sees every tear.

So Roll Back the Dark Clouds, let the silver shine through.
For 50 more years together is what I wish for you.

—*Mattie H. Gype*

"Moment Of Grace"

Floral tracings give birth within my heart,
As the first blooms of Spring.
Spirit blowing as the wind,
Touching the gentle petals, softly,
With the whisper of healing love.

Bringing forth new blossoms,
Opening to the warmth of the sun,
Shining upon the graceful flowerets,
Gently encouraging new growth,
Silent utterance of hope renewing.

Enkindling love,
Calling forth a new wisdom-
From my soul's depth,
Budding awakenings to the precious moment,
The stillness espousing this gift of new life.

—*Janice L. Eberley*

Beginning and End

They put warmth but with different results
As the underneath heat blazed my underside
While the topside warmth was like a gentle caress.
My feet were the same without their protection
And the creases on my head felt nothing at all.
With the aid of the mysterious seven,
Our ages were the same, although Bernie
Gave it no thought, smelling rather than thinking.
As my feet inched along, with the water above,
Sisyphus was pushing his rock
And I awaited its fall and my termination,
Hoping that this last search would not end in nothing.
As I blended with the warmth of the ground,
The faithful dog stood over my face
And licked it with his warm and slippery tongue.
The impulse of the moment had joined with
The end of the life and the hope of the vision.
Both knew not the next moment, but in that instance
They had arrived at their definition of
Eternity, each not knowing what was to come.

—*Frank A. Langer*

I'll Come To You

Listen closely to the rustling leaves
as their tethers give way to the breeze
It is there that I'll come to you

Watch as a cloud caresses a mountain top
It is there that I'll watch over you

Smell the newness of an evergreen bough
It is there you can reach out and touch me

Feel the breath of a southern breeze on your face
It is there I am speaking to you

Touch the front of an approaching storm
It is there I will play with you

Listen to the dance of a mountain stream
It is there I will be at peace with you

Look at the grains as they bend in the wind
It is there you will see me

Sit quietly in retrospect
It is there I will share with you

Be there for me in thought and I will come to you
Miss me not, for I'll be with you

—*Lucky Rimpila*

Why I Love Christmas

At Christmas: The darkest streets are so much brighter.
  As this "Festive time" of year,
  Strangers "seem" a little nearer,
  And old friends "seem" more dear.

At Christmas: People "seem" much more forgiving.
  More loving and compassionate,
  Race and Creed make less difference,
  With the birth of Christ to celebrate.

At Christmas: It's hunting out my Grandmas cookie recipe
  And somehow more than ever she is so close to me,
  Teaching me all others to" forget and to forgive,"
  And to be real happy "no regrets with which live."

This is why that I love Christmas I myself couldn't realize
Until I picked up my pen, and started to "itemize."

  —*Lois M. Kohl*

"The Story Of The Firs"

I hear the murmur of the wind
As through the trees I roamed,
Bringing back memories of long ago
When first their stands were sown.
Each tiny trees was planted
By my husband young and strong-
And I was at his side as we carried them along.
They were nurtured carefully with tender, loving care
And now through years of standing
They whisper things we've shared.
They bring back sounds of laughing children
As among the trees they played -
Four lovely daughters grown and gone
Into loving homes where they now stay.
So many things they tell me
Of happenings through the years -
Of loving, happy memories and many, many tears.
Through winter snows and summer storms they've stood there
  side by side-
As we have done my love and I since I was first your bride.

  —*Marie E. Gingrich*

Death

Death flies in on wings of fear,
As time goes by and death draws near;
Fear recedes and joy abounds,
My Lord, and My Savior I have found!
The peaceful serenity of knowing He'll be there,
In that afterlife somewhere;
To comfort and console me too,
Amid my family and friends anew!
The confidence that I have in Him,
Will never shatter, or grow dim;
Faith renewed is strong and well,
I picture Heaven—Devil take Hell!
As I bid farewell to all of you,
Family and friends all true-blue;
I'm thankful for my time here on earth,
Time to share with you, and time for my rebirth;
Fear has left me now and so He comes,
To live with Him, to take me Home!

  —*Isabel A. Kent*

Prelude To Winter

The morning sun
Casts a frosty
Shadow on my yard,
It's October, and
This is winter's
Calling card.

  —*George Druyor*

Seeding —— Thoughts

Our deeds are examples of us,
  As trying to be kind;
  Like loving our - Divine:
Goodness, oh me - Goodness! - Is - Us!

Mis-treatments or Mis-understanding or Lusts;
  Living Death, not to be - Love in Kind,
  And not loving our - Divine.
Deeds are seeds; We do know, our Good deeds- are just.

I, We, They — plant seeds with ideals, with People, with
  Nature. Planting my Seeds, planting my Deeds — And —
  And waiting for the Harvest to Come In!
Them, Us, Me - Sweats out brows; Plow; Sow and Wait for it to
  mature.

Ladies and Men; - Looks at our fields of Harvest of Seeds
And in Deeds; - Reaping our Deeds or our Weeds;
Constructive Deeds or Destructive Weeds.
Nature and Life Beings - Humans - Our Deeds from Seeds for
Needs;
  Indeed; Indeed!
  IN !!! — Deeds!

  —*Howard Wendell Raleigh*

A Tree Fell In The Forest

A tree fell in the forest today,
as we sat in the woods holding you.
I always thought it would be so rare
and an honor to watch a tree as it fell to meet the earth.
And so it was. The splitting and snapping sounds broke our
quiet reverie, as it plummeted to the ground.
We just sat silently watching, not speaking a word.
Watching as the leaves from other trees fell from their
encounter with the Matriarch of the forest.
Watching and waiting until all was quiet again.
The sunshine felt so warm and comforting as we sat there
thinking about what we had just witnessed.
To ease our pain we knew that You had given us a sign.
Everything has its cycle of life and death.
The grand old tree had seen many years and now that life had
been played out. Its time to fall had come.
You, Grand Little Lady, have seen many years too,
and we must let you move on in your cycle.
We spent a wonderful day today with you in our arms.
So Rare, So Exquisite, So Precious.

  —*Maria Slover*

Awful Memory

I'm grateful when my memory is poor,
As when I think too long, in vain
Of starving folk, of wars, and pain.
It's bad enough to read the news
Then watch T.V. and hear review;
The haunting, wretched, anguished poor,
I close my eyes but there they are
The homeless, living on the streets
Where drugs, crime, and gangs compete,
Racial tension, Ku Klux Klan
Greed and cruelty since time began.
Now, add infants raised by babes,
Increasing suicides and Aids!

I've been asked if I feel guilt for the comfort
Around me built..I try each day, here where I live
To do my best, to help, and give. It's plain
To see we've cause to cheer
That our ancestors landed here - and
Good people do out number bad
Keeping our world from going mad!

  —*Lois Smith Triplitt*

"Nothing Is Sadder Than A Wasted Smile"

O' nothing is sadder than a wasted smile.
As when you walk down the street, you go the extra mile for
someone you see and give them a smile.

To hopefully brighten and cheer their day, but they look at you
coldly and not a word do they say. Or worse, they try and
pretend to give you a smile their hearts' not in.

And what happens to your poor smile? It flees to a graveyard
where lost hopes and dreams come.
    It shrivels and dries
        crumples and dies
But soon is reborn, so there's no cause to mourn, and comes back
as a big yellow rose.

O' nothing is sadder than a wasted smile, except for the one
it's wasted on. For someday they shall pluck that rose and be,
pricked by its thorn. Then their soul shall bleed, and they'll
    Shrivel and dry
        crumple and die
And come back as a big hairy spider!
        —*Thaisa Rantanen*

Eternity

I see you sleeping peacefully
As you lie in front of me
Though it will be a long time
Before I see your eyes again
Your twinkle will remain a light
Brightly shining in my heart, for Eternity.

You have meant so much to me
Guiding me through life with
Tender caring loving hands
Now you're watching over me
Guarding me from harm as we
Each wait patiently for togetherness in Eternity.

Tears are shed while sympathies expressed
Above the hum, I can hear your voice,
Reminding me of happy times
Whispering gently in my ear,
"Everything will be all right
Live happily as I wait for you to join me for eternity."

I love you.
        —*Susan L. Roubian*

To Be A Poet

An intuitive poet and idealistic writer, this is truly what I
aspire to be. Creating and documenting a beautiful artform,
for all of the world to hopefully enjoy and vividly see.
Bringing forth feelings from deep within the heart and soul
and me. Expressing emotions taken from life's rich experiences
of all humanity. A dreamer of profound verse and professor of
descriptive rhyme. A composer of complex lyrics remaining
suspended, and frozen in the pages of unending time. A
philosopher of uncertainty, I search to identify within myself
to find my ultimate purpose and underlying meaning, to be
observed and contemplated by all mankind. A collector of
words, sometimes unknowing, abstract and obscure. A
contributor of visions unencumbered and revealing, yet so
simple and pure. A director of conflicting ideas, feeling
apprehensive and definitely insecure. Channeling personal
inspirations and realizations, in the infinite hope my simple
poetry can endure. A poet and a writer, this is where I
purpose my life to go. Treading in dangerous waters, my true
talent I will never actually know. Captured in the profession
of my dreams to continue fueling my imagination to steadily flow.
With my pen in hand and my thoughts on paper, my poetry to
intellectually and professionally grow.
        —*Marilyn Ashe*

Butterfly

Tonight I danced with a butterfly
At first it was a tease to watch her flutter by
Then I realized she was so gentle and free
She fluttered and flirted with such glee
She moved about with such beauty and pride
Oh how I wanted her by my side
I wanted to capture her for my own
Then I realized I could be closer if I left her alone
All of a sudden her wing rested upon my knee
Then she assured the world she was with me
This was all very much to my surprise
Because this was said with her eyes
Now I dance with this butterfly in my mind
And my life is better because of a lady so kind
        —*Edward T. Jones*

The Climb

From the cardboard box of yesterdays comes yet another memory,
at last a fond one that can be played again and again and not
lose it's specialness to repetition.
Looking down on the valley of the glaciers, from a place
where only the eagle could nest, a smile, that hides the terror
in your stomach of the fall into oblivion.
Shades of green mingle with blues and grays amongst the
shadows, and the trees, once giant, are dwarfed by your
exhilaration. Oh, what faith you had in your companions and
their skill; oh what faith you gained in the One who created
these wonders around you.
Oh, what faith you had in yourself to defeat the odds you created
in
your own mind.
Muscles taut, eyes aglow, fingers shoved in the cracks of
granite that is older than any other, you rest before beginning
again, before renewing your assault on your fears and this
place, called Yosemite.
        —*Christopher Black*

"The Mind Of Sorrow"

He broke down helplessly,
At the thought of judgement day.
The drearisome thoughts run closely,
From under a disturbed mind betrayed.

As he sits there sorely,
He thinks of the hour to come.
As the night falls over to hell's boundary,
The threatening of evil is still to come.

As the howling hounds drool,
For the passing of prey unaware.
As the avenge of the saner one,
Comes eternally from below.

As the judgement hour is yet to come,
He sees not the sorrow and pain.
As he sits there in troublesome madness,
He thinks of the world gone sane.

As the coffins shake below,
For the skeleton of uncanny misery be bothered.
He sits in the darkness for the time to come,
For he has no mind for an altar bestowed.
        —*Billy Simmons*

Untitled

    Cold, still dawn
        deep in the wet mist
    A male bird sat in the brush
Crying, a song of a lonely heart
        mourning dawn
        —*Sandra A. Avendano*

The Wind

The wind has many moods, of this I'm sure,
At times, a gentle lamb, or prowling wolf;
Whatever wind may send, we must endure,
The lamb-like breeze, or the fierce wolf, howling.

At times, a gentle lamb, or wolf howling,
its moods range from the gentle to the fierce;
With smile on face, or evil grin, scowling,
No favors here, wind every heart can pierce.

Its moods range from the gentle to the fierce,
And yet, I love the wind, both glad and wild;
The mystery of wind's ways, no one can pierce,
Blustering madness, or a calm, pure child.

I climb upon the wind, and sail the sky,
To heaven's blue = Infinity is nigh!
    —*Goergiana Lieder Lahr*

Untitled

Her alarm clock reads 1:38 a.m. on a school night as she
awakens from a dream, or perhaps the nightmare of reality. It
is a reality in which she feels that her efforts at hard work
have no rewards and school is becoming ever more and more
meaningless. More and more problems seem to flood around her,
never seeming to cease. It is confusing her so much that she
sleeps like a baby, for a few hours each night, only to awaken
to a hunger, a hunger for solutions and answers. After digging
deep inside herself and finding her courage, pride, and
confidence in the future to hold onto, she continues to lie in
bed, awake, watching the alarm clock ticking the minutes away.
She soon realizes that maybe time will solve the problems, and
she starts to drift slowly back to sleep. Her belief in
something so small compared to the world itself pushes her
onward each day, one step at a time: a belief in herself. She
realizes just as the final hand of sleep is laid upon her that
she can succeed and will succeed, if not on the outside where
everyone can see, then inside where only she can.
    —*Lisa M. Goewert*

"Many Years, And Long Long Ago!"

"So many years since then, and long long ago—A beautiful
baby boy was born on this very earth, in a humble stable, on a
starry night out in the evenings bitter cold! And through the
many stages of earthly life, this little baby boy did start
to grow!" "In him, shown all imaginable beauty of life's true
riches of "kindness" and "love"! A gift truly born of heaven,
passed onto all children, a gift from Father God living way
on high far up in "his glorious heavens above!" It was God's
ultimate gift to our earth, to show of "His" bountiful and
undying love!" "Christmas today means many different things in
oh-so many ways, lest "we" not forget it's true meaning, let
us keep silent, take time to reflect, give thanks, and to
pray!" "So commercial is Christmas now it does truly seem,
filled with mankind's many selfish thoughts and selfcentered
dreams! "I" want this, and "I" want that, "give me" this, or
"give me" that! Hurry and scurry, rushing to and fro-what is
the best present to buy Aunt Flo?" "Peacefully, and
thoughtfully, let "your heart" reflect on that special night of
so long long ago! The true meaning of Christmas Day, lay in
that humble manger of straw, out in that evenings bitter cold!
God's gift for mankind many centuries ago!
    —*Cynthia Nazworthy*

Mother

The marble is cold
Even in the summer time
When I touch her name.
    —*Harley Michael Brown*

Thoughts Within Nature

The breeze moved gently through the trees.
barely enough to rustle the leaves,
within minutes, its chilling the knees,
and sooner or later, I'll want to sneeze.

Out here in the woods,
you can't deny it,
if you want to see wildlife,
you have to be quiet.

All the birds, they were singing,
a woodpecker was tappin',
the turkeys were struttin',
but the deer, they were nappin';

Overhead it was gray,
not a touch of blue,
and all of this time,
I was thinking of you.
    —*Eugene J. Pegher*

"You"

HAPPY is the reason for life.
    Be Happy, and resolve not to wonder
about "could have been's"
And not to make any moment
    More than it was
    or ever will be.

LIFE is the reason for life.
    Worry not today for the future;
    Dwell not on the past.
    Live for today, and forge ahead.

LOVE is the reason for life.
Should you be fortunate
and stumble upon LOVE in this lifetime,
Take hold of it.
Study it not too closely;
But read the label:
"DO NOT LET GO.
    LOVE THE BEST THAT YOU CAN."

LOVE is the reason for life.
YOU are the reason for mine.
    —*Kristina J. Gohlke*

Mama...Mommy...Mother...Mom

It might be and usually is the second word you learn. It could
be mommy, mother, mama and even mom as the years go by.
Mothers are usually the first that we tell our troubles and
problems too, No-o-o wonder they like hair color! With the
help of hair color they can look as if they have youth, spring,
color and life. Mothers have sons that are first boys that
turn into men...soldiers. They leave mom, home and their
families to protect, if not fight for freedom, rights, beliefs,
justice and their country. But now girls...daughters,
sisters, mothers... soldiers. They will fight to protect
their moms, dads, sisters, brothers, friends and families.
Even the country they live and believe in. For their freedom,
justice and rights for all. Yes...being a Mother is a handful.
It does drive a person mad, angry, short-tempered and loving...
loving... I love my Mother, Mommy, Mom... I'm also a Mother,
a parent, too. It can be and is a stress, a great
responsibility... But I LOVE IT.
    —*Kathy Anderson*

Sunset In A Raindrop

Tonight's sunset was spectacular
  Because I took time
To view the unpriced gem that was mine
  (It could be thine.)

The rain had ceased
The sky had cleared
The sun set behind the Lindon limb.

A spew of blue thine eyes behold
A shimmering light, a gleaming emerald
A diamond amongst the leaves so bold.

With compass set, and my eyes fixed
I hurried to fetch the diamond set.

Approaching; the brilliance began to fade
To my surprise it is a raindrop in the glade.

A raindrop transforming the suns rays
Into jewels of amber, blue and jade.

Precious gems for us to view
But seen only by a few.

Rainbows have pots of gold
Sunsets have raindrops with gems untold.

—*Luella Ganahl*

"Two Young Fishermen"

We loved to fish on Squash Lake.
Because the bass would always bite.
Much better in the morning,
Than any time near night.
My brother Ben would row the boat,
And I would cast toward shore.
I would cast and cast towards logs and pads,
Until my arm was sore.
We stopped the boat to head for home.
We turned the boat around.
We looked into our burlap bag,
To see how many bass we'd found.
We counted nine, that were quite small,
But one big one weighed 4 pound.
When mother saw the fish we'd caught,
Her face lit with delight.
She said you both are great today,
That's Your dinner for tonight.

—*Charles Mikal*

Little Katie Beers

Little Katie Beers ten years old.
  Been thru hell we've been told.
  Locked in a dungeon, couldn't get out.
 Chained and mistreated by a dirty old lout.
Hadn't been for her brother she wouldn't of been found.
 The dirty old man held her captive under ground.
  Thank God they found her just in time.
  The dirty lout must pay for his crime.
 With a child some people you don't trust.
  All you mothers this is a lesson to us.
 Screen the person before you leave your child.
Then you can come back with an untroubled heart and smile.

—*Georgia Rose Collins*

Special Newborn

Upon a cloud so light and free
 I found an angel just for me
  So gentle and so wee
   And I could see—
She was an angel just like me.

—*Sandy Tauer*

Fall's Last Call

Falls last call for sex and food
Before she set's her wintery mood
—*LeRoy J. Karns*

"A New World Out There"

I saw a new world yesterday,
Before, everything was blurred and gray -
But light came back from a skillful hand.
The blues and pinks and violets too.
Made flowers live, they looked brand new -
The greens of grass and leaves of trees
Filled your heart with thoughts to please -
It's what I've missed for, oh! so long.
Filled my life with love and song
The truth you see, is what was done
He removed the cataract so it didn't block the view -
For to see again God's world,
of beauty and light come thru.

—*Florence D. Hanson*

Unbroken

A playful slap that gets harder with time.
Before I know it, your touch is a crime.
A kick to my leg, a slap to my face.
Now I find myself in my mother's place.
The man she loved beat her black and blue.
Am I destined to make her mistakes, too?

You fiercely deliver a well placed kick.
Figures swim before me; I'm going down quick.
When I finally wake up, I can feel my pulse racing.
I pick up my head, and look at the man I am facing.

You are a disgrace to your kind—much less than a man.
I don't need you now; I don't give a damn.

I need someone who will treat me with care.
Someone to love me and always be there.

You can never give; you can only take.
I won't play a game where my life is at stake.

So get out of my life; I won't take any more.
For I am woman, hear me roar.

—*Amy Winters*

Alzheimer's Mind

Let me go, let me go
Before it's too late for myself
Inside, outside to the right side of the box

Wait a minute, wait a minute
Oh my dear cats and ducks
I need some ice water and my newspaper too

Don't push, don't push
The baby is falling
Is wet, is wet
My stomach is aching

I'm afraid, I'm afraid
Am I suppose to do something?
I can't breath, I can't breath
Did I hear someone's cooking?

Hi! Hello! How are you? My dear friend Little Shorty
Can I have a cup of coffee,
Or do something that makes me sleepy

I want to go home, I want to go home, to my own dear home
Come to me and bring me home
I need to go where I belong.....

—*Bernard L. Songco*

August Baby

The small seed rests quietly within, knowing not when life
begins. Two people in love, who share a goal, will through
this love, give seed a soul. No feeling, yet, but well aware,
knowing that a heart beats there. Suddenly, a movement's
caught, a never-ending pleasure brought; The seed, once
dormant, lies no more, growing, changing, in this core. Weeks
have passed, a month, then two, anticipation all anew. An
overwhelming love has grown, for this being not yet shown.
More, and more my feelings soar to places never seen before.
Many months of trial, and thought, many months my mind had
sought, to look beyond first joy felt tears, to what's held
forth in later years. The time has come, my heart's abound,
closer to this love I've found. My love, my life, the time has
passed, and here you are with me, at last. This tiny soul, so
sweet, so warm, finally rests within my arms. A sadness forms,
and slowly comes, as our souls cease to link as one. Though
our bodies part, you'll still be mine; sharing our love for all time.

—*Lori Hilton*

Magic

Magic happens when your back is turned away from what you truly
believe in and glance at the impossible, the denied,
the dreamed of, the hungered for.
Magic is the soft unrelenting kiss of the lover
begging to never stop never to surface for air.
Air is nothing to the kiss of the lover
Life is nothing, death is nothing.
Only the kiss that holds Beauty itself
in the movement of the lips
the sigh from the Soul
the ache from the begging heart.

Magic is the longing hidden in the folds of the hand,
touching the skin of the lover
feeling the fierceness of desire
igniting the blue fire of intense passion.

Magic is the healer
that seals the open wound
that comes from diving too
deeply into waters that call to them
and dare them to risk all.

—*Barbara Russo*

Beneath the Silver Moon

In the distant glade, sweet sounding music played, at Night
Beneath moon, the sounds of eluish tune. Inside the fairy ring

a distant voice did sing of something from old, a tale of heroes bold.
The wind played a harp, Nearby sank a lark

Melodies reached my ears. Not for many a year had they been heard,
Yet here they were. I stood beneath the sky wondering how and

why these beautiful things were no longer seen but by a few. I wished
I knew the secrets they say, when from faraway

The distant mists parted and little shadow figures darted. They
swirled and danced and didn't even glance at the mere mortal. Only

laughed a chartle. As quick as they came they were away
Leaving me to wait until the day's break.

When back to home I finally did go. Thinking of thing eery, my
hearts more weary. I long to hear their fair voices clear. Night

after night, I stand beneath the sky, hoping to catch a sliver
of tune, beneath the silver
moon.

—*Jody Carlson*

Floribunda

A plot of earth lies near my front doorway
Beneath a coverlet of snow and chill.
I feel the silent strength of winter's will
That ravaged blossoms of last summer's day.
Now comes the time when thoughts are turned to May.
When Spring's sweet breath brings forth the daffodil,
Her tender breast drops flowers soon to fill
This bit of earth. Now Summer's had her say.
Kneeling upon the ground with trowel in hand,
I find the roots of last year's plants still there
Where busy earthworms work. I stand
And smile. I know my garden shows the care
Of sun, of rain, of months that come and go.
All work their magic here where flowers grow.

—*Clara Whitney*

Renaissance

It is the dead of winter and we wait
Beside a window with the drifts piled deep
For one small shaft of warming sun by garden gate,
Or for the rock to move where grasses sleep.

Spring rolls the stone aside, where rivulets
Move hills and lower heights to lengthen days;
And every hour is our Renaissance
To speak of hope, to offer up our praise.

It seems there was an Earth that we forgot,
Still living in accustomed sense and space;
Not dead, but bursting through, alive and taut
With every stem and leaf afire, in place.

All that we ever need is patience, faith
In the brief nap our maples seem to take —
Spring hovers in a snowdrift like a wraith,
Bidding the leaflet and the bud to break.

—*Clair H. Chamberlain*

Death At Cemetery Ridge

There lies the body,
between the rocks at the top of Cemetery Ridge.
The charge was so triumphant,
all those men running across the field.
When they reached the top,
that was when this soldier was shot.

There lies the body,
between the rocks at the top of Cemetery Ridge,
His clothes are torn, his head is slit,
underneath him is a puddle of blood.
On his face is a look of hope,
his gun still lays in his hand.

There lies the body,
between the rocks at the top of Cemetery Ridge.
He fought when the rebel cause was a roaring fire,
now its no more than a flicker, very faint.
There is a lesson to remember,
he entered the army a private, he left a saint.

—*Edward R. Griffin*

"Caution To The Fly"

The spider unliked by most —
Is to me an intriguing host —
With arms welcoming wide —
He'll invite you to come inside —
A tasty, tempting treat to he —
If you stop for a cup of tea!

—*Rosemary Irish*

Look To The Hills

I look to the hills and the mountains
beyond, as if they were placed by a
magic wand. Though I find no
magic in the cool crisp air, just
the voice of God that whisper's there.
   The beauty and peace in the valley
I see, and the rocks and rill's they
call to me. For in this place all
fear must flee, and the grace of the
Lord is all see.
   Now I look to the hills for my
help and grace, till I dwell with
the Lord and see his face.
   I have found in these hill's a blessed
place.

—*Elizabeth Morrison*

Observations

Tractor in a field, plowing, plowing,
Big wheel just turning, turning,
Black crows, cawing, cawing,
White clouds, churning, churning.

Tractor in a field, plowing, plowing,
Big wheel just turning, turning,
White birds, flying, flying,
Red clouds, churning, churning.

Tractor in a field, plowing, plowing,
Big wheels stopped their turning,
Birds, birds, stopped their flying,
Clouds, clouds, stopped their churning.

—*Wyvonne Huebsch Robertson*

January 20, 1993

We have a brand new President
Bill Clinton in his name,
A Rhodes Scholar from Arkansas
Let's wait and see "his game".

Then at his side he'll have his spouse
A real go-getter wife,
But if she sits in on meetings
She could cause Bill some strife.

What's new in the White House this time
Are Chelsea dear, and SOCKS,
We'll hear about their every move
And when they go for walks.

Poor dear - she'll find it difficult
An average kid to be,
Being thrust into the limelight
In Washington, D.C.

Bill will go down in history books
A young man with humor,
We can sit back, relax and watch
Our first "BABY BOOMER".

—*Mae Rommes Christoph*

My World

My world is
just like a book;
I like my new world,
but its just a book.
My world is so colorful
and bright, but I don't
know why it doesn't
have a sight!

—*Abejide Jegede*

Untitled

Spring is here, oh what a sight
Birds are chirping with pure delight
Flowers are coming out of their beds
All you can see is their little green heads.

   Summer is here, the flowers in bloom
   Many a color and taking up room
   Green grass growing, blowing in the wind
   Children running and playing and they sing.

Fall is here now, all oranges and brown
Mother nature has touched it with all her renown
The leaves are falling off from the trees
As the children run in them up to their knees.

   Winter again now, look at it snow
   All of a sudden the wind starts to blow
   We're inside our house all snugly and warm
   Just waiting around for the next big storm.

—*Betty Werner*

Nighttime Dreams

Dark and mysterious, starry night,
Birds of darkness take their flight.
This is where all hatred lives,
Where every little bad thing is.
Finally when the sun breaks through,
The darkness transforms into a shimmering blue.
All hatred and bad is silently lost
At a slight and painful cost.
Yet the heavenly earth still goes 'round,
As I slip dreamily to the ground.
I dream about a horrible, endless pain
And then I see the darkness once again.

—*Brooke Fredrickson*

Mistakes Of Motherhood

The regrets and guilts of motherhood bring grief and heavy
blame, they are weapons that will rob a soul and cause us
to walk with shame. If I were given the chance to undo the
mistakes I made as a mother, there's no-way I'd take the offer
tho I love each son and daughter. I haven't come this far in
life ever yearning for the past, for I remember what it was
like always striving without rest! Human enough to make
mistakes but to undo them I'm not so smart, I've made them and
God will use them to gain an entry into their heart. But to
go back and try again I'd repeat the mistakes again somehow,
cause with babies and toddlers at my feet I
daily prayed to be where I am now.
The mistakes I made in motherhood will help my
children to be strong while they walk with God in life they'll
overcome what I did wrong!

—*Dorothy Logsdon*

The Tiniest Soul

What might they say, the ones that
were tossed
away because they're in the way.
Give me a chance I just might enhance
your
world.
But no, you say, I'm just a tissue
anyway.
Just wait to see I'll have a heart, I have
a soul.
For it wasn't long ago that you were
like me;
But she let you be and look at what
you've
become.

—*Karen Zimmer-Karl*

Wounded

There is no sign of a struggle,
Blood is not to be found.
So this makes you wonder,
Where is this wound so profound?

It is buried deep within her mind.
Somewhere behind those mournful eyes.
You will never know her pain,
Because she is a master of disguise.

She has felt this pain before,
It is nothing new to her.
Never did she think that it would appear again,
But once again it did occur.

Those three words were said.
And she did believe.
That nothing would hurt her.
That he would not deceive.

But once again she failed to see
The lies he did conceal.
So now she is faced with it again,
And must force herself to heal.

—*Kytryna E. Miterko*

The Country Boy

He struts in
Blue jean jacket and flannel shirt
Ready to take on problems
Or calm the hectic world created in his absence

Gentle is his nature
Kind his heart
A spirit—wild and free
Carried on the wings of childhood dreams

A country boy
Blue grass music, soft summer nights
Filled with the knowledge
Of one seeing the hope of tomorrow
Remembering the tears of days gone by

A poet
His words revealing
The depth to which his soul can travel

A friend
Reaching out—Listening—Understanding
Caring for those whose lives he touches
Gently taking them home

—*Janet Luczak*

The Astronaut

A thousand giants, burn midnight oil,
  blue lined paper, with sweat and toil:
Aching muscles, mid racking brains;
  the pregnant still rests on the plain.
Dauntless courage, pressed in the mould;
  high adventure, test for the bold.
Tension mounting, count down is low;
  six, five, four, three, two, one, zero.
Hope is riding, that vapor train,
  man strives to, break his earth bound chain.
A nation waits, now charged with fear;
  they hear his voice, alls well out here.
An infant step, made into space;
  beginning of, the star man's race.
A womb from space, floats slowly down;
  upheld by science silken gown.
Marines retrieve, what giants begot.
  To us is born the astronaut.

—*James D. Barnes*

I Look At Him

I look at him. The frail body lying in the coffin. The same body that used to have so much energy, he wouldn't sit still for an instant. His hands lie clasping a rose. The same hands that were strong in times of anger and gentle in times of love. I look at him. Close my eyes and try to remember every detail of his face. I can't remember... I quickly open my eyes to absorb his face and etch it into my brain forever. I look at him. He is so peaceful as if in a deep slumber. Yet I know from this sleep he will never wake. Never again will I see his eyes looking deep into my heart and more than once saving me. I look at him, a lonely tear runs down my cheek. Lonely... like me. But I know this will not be the only one. As I knew they would, the tears start to come. One tear for every memory of him I have. Will they ever stop? No, I don't think so. They may stop flowing from my eyes but they will never stop in my heart. For this is one time his eyes can not save me, and they never will again. I look at him and can do nothing but remember for there is future and no present. All that is for certain is the past, and only in the past was there life in the man I look at.

—*Penny Reed*

Choo-Choo Train

While tossing, turning, sighing and yearning for that elusive boon called sleep. Late one night lying awake in bed, I saw these happy little thoughts "pop into my head." I directed and collected them into a tiny, little place, where they would help to keep a great big, happy smile on my face. They danced around in my brain, until they became this happy refrain, in rhythm to the clickety-clack from the wheels on the track of that not too far-away train. "We are happy, little thoughts. We have a job to do. To make you smile so you won't be blue. Here's a few smiles to try on awhile; my, they look so nice on you." Mile after mile of this clickety-clack, I smile as those thoughts come echoing back. But, sometimes at night I feel so silly, lying awake in bed, humming that willy-nilly ditty. It "pop" right into my head. I yawn as the train heads for its nearby station, for I, too have reached my destination. I am no longer awake, I'm fast asleep, on that not-too-faraway, happy-little-thoughts Choo-choo Train. All Aboard! All Aboard! You are welcome to climb on board this not-too-faraway-happy-little-thoughts Choo-choo Train. All aboard!!!!!!

—*Catherine T. Nichols*

Today's True Love

Fast happiness like the fast buck, too good to be true?
Brandished, flashing eyes and joyful flushing cheeks.
Old authors knew such crystal clear romance.
Was it true then, but not today?
Peer deep into the pink and blue bubbling gush.
Brush away the perfumed surface foam.
Who's truly there? Hallo. Tell me.
But make it sweet nonsense.
Olde, faithful, spirited love.
I pray.

—*Gregory John Sheffield*

Anthem For Singing

O Beautiful for Spacious Skies
        Scuttles
The unsingable Star Spangled Banner
        And
    Soul sweeping serenity
        Replaces
    War-salving-PEACE

—*Alice H. Senter*

Her Eyes Of Silver Glimmer By The Moon

Her eyes of silver glimmer by the moon
Brighter then anything upon Night's veil
I hope they will descend upon me soon
And that my goddess I want to declare
My love for her will never change it's ways
They say a truthful heart is always rare
Yet, my love will last until the end of days
Oh how I hope she will listen to me
With those ears that frame that pretty face
And understand just how our love will be
For it will live beyond the human race
Oh please, my love, look to me here within
For only then can endless love begin.

—*Chris Hatch*

Winter Time

Winters are so beautiful.
Brightly colored hats and mittens.
Rosie cheeked children with their
outstretched hands catch snowflakes
large and white.
They inhale the frosty air,
Their breath ascends in cotton puffs.

The bite of winter chill
Sleigh rides - tinkle of silvery bells,
The sleigh glides over the fluffy snow.
The trees are shimmering in the moonlight.
Snow glistens like a thousand little candles.
The perfect painting by the hand of God.

—*Bishop Noa Home Poetry Club*

Forgotten Statue

There's a forgotten brown statue, cold and lonely,
Broken hand raised to heaven, the other
At his chest, planted slantedly between
Two modern, storied buildings, but at their rear.

The public seldom glimpses Him, only a few
Employees perhaps. He must wonder what sin
He had committed to be as forgotten as this.
And yet, though forgotten, some of the help pray to him.

Sometimes, just being there for someone
Can be all that is needed. Just to listen
And quietly talk, perhaps to soothe the hurt
No one else cares to comfort; not many listen today.

So, thank you, forgotten brown statue
Of no name, for being there to understand
When no one else could. May you reign
Supreme to all those who come to need you!

—*Bob Forest*

Nana

Wherever I smell
bubbling spaghetti sauce
it is mid-August in Cleveland
and I am sitting on the back porch
swinging in great-grandma's porch swing,
hugging my blankey, and
listening to her sing Mama
until the Italian sausage was stuffed.

But this is not my story
My story is her sleeping in a nursing home
daily losing a bit of the world
until her spaghetti was completely gone.

—*Kristy King*

A Willow That Weeps Soundlessly

I am not a strong bamboo tree, not a palm tree swaying,
but a willow that weeps soundlessly.
It has a mystery that you cannot find.
That only lurks within its own kind.
It looks around in where it stands.
Around it, beautiful, lovely trees are swaying in rhythm,
while way in the back stands a lonely willow weeping.
It wonders with confusion,
Why am I this way?
Always weeping, while the others are gay.
It dreams of becoming like the others
but it knows, that it is different among the rest.
Filled with hope within itself, it knows that it is a
significance to life.

—*Kristell Corpuz*

My Search

I've searched and searched and searched again;
But always it seems, I've searched in vain.
For the things I've wanted and dreamed,
A life's long and weary stream.

Oh if I had a chance to change,
Some things in life, I'd surely try;
To do not some things; I did in life,
And things I failed to give and exchange.

To give more love where love was due;
To give to someone a sheltering arm;
And to give safety, from life's raging storm.
To keep them out of all life's harm.

So I searched, and searched, down through time;
For the things that could have been mine;
That I have missed, because I was blind,
And would not see. What has always been mine.

—*Iva Mae Swinford*

Mother Is In Heaven

Mother died not long ago,
But as she died God's love she did show.

She now lives in heaven on high,
Praying that we will join her in the by N by.

Her prayers were always as we all know,
Someday to heaven we all would go.

The songs that she sang,
Through heaven rang,

Songs of praise,
To the heavens did raise.

She now is in heaven around God's throne,
And we will join her and it won't be long.

Are you ready should the trumpet sound?
Will you be ready to leave the ground?

Mother's prayer was for the world to know,
Christ as Saviour before they go.

Mother's not dead, she still lives on,
In our hearts and around God's throne.

—*Francis Hunt*

What Is Wind?

Is it the past, blowing through the
night, flowing through time?

Does it have meaning
Or is it just there?

—*Kristin Pearce*

Day And Night

Day and night two different things by sight,
  but both created by God's Might.
So who is to say, but He whether or not,
  as you see, if these things are different in deed.
For I am white, but you may be black,
  are we not two different things by sight,
  but were we not both created by God's Might?
So put down your weapons my friends,
  and let us rejoice, in your differences of sight,
For you see, we are all brothers, by God's Might.

  —*Johnny Shannon Dennis*

Blind Man's Bus Stop

By the bible this child was told to learn,
But during the darkness of the night
My heart was forced to burn,
I looked to a room with a candle for simplicity,
While my soul seemed to drift away
From the monster we call society;
Each morning I would wake with fear
To the crying shouts of others,
I then realized it's not the fire that kills
It's the smoke that smothers;
Even to this day I try to bring forth an answer
For one's existence and purpose here,
Maybe in the end while everyone is at rest
The wind will blow and it will all be clear?

  —*Kris Edward Bartley*

Tethered Eagle

The pride of an eagle is in his heart,
But he knows that their souls are far apart.

For the eagle soars above the plain,
But on the reservation he must remain.

His people were warriors strong and brave,
Until the white man came and made him his slave.

His culture was stripped and taken away,
Very little remains to this very day.

The land he was given is unwilling to yield,
The corn that was planted lies dead in the field.

The hand that once held a bow now holds a bottle,
The bar stool now has replaced the saddle.

The elders are unseen and unheard,
And his history is seldom written in word.

On wings of eagles his spirit soars,
Above the fences with iron doors.

To open plains where buffalo still roam,
To open spaces he had once called home.

  —*Janet Hunnicutt*

I Am

I am one who believes in freedom for all,
but I am not free myself, being confined
in a world of prejudice and hatred.

I am a person with great enthusiasm and
a unique character.

I am one who cannot withstand unhappiness
and who loves all people. My love cannot
run out, but your actions can restrain my
love for you.

You are the source of the feelings I
experience, and you are the companion
of my love, like the water is to the rose.

  —*Bronwyn Nichole Blackwell*

Waiting For A Dream

I lay in my bed waiting for a dream,
But I could not sleep because they came.
They dazzled me with their light,
A million flashes in the night.
They filled the yard, the trees, the air
With a constant blinking everywhere. ·
They were candles lit with flame
Then blown out and lit again.
It was fireflies that lit up the gloom,
Their light seemed to fill the tiny room.
They were shining messages to one another,
To each and every distant brother.
When I looked out at the glimmering sky,
I felt smaller than a firefly.

  —*Emily Levinson*

In Search Of...

Oh sisters, my sweet sisters, how I wish that you were true,
but if I cannot believe in me, how can I believe in you.

I've stretched my hand across my life, and with that hand did
send. My love, my trust, my very soul, but could not call you friend.

What does it take to find this dream? What demon taunts my
heart?, that when I give my all to one, what makes that dream so dark?

I cannot wish the worst for those, who wish the worst for me.
My heart though hurt and empty now, still love is what it sees.

How I wish this void were filled in me, with just one loving
soul. So I could find this peace on earth, before I grow too old.

My days are slipping by me now, my heart is going too. I
cannot give you worldly gifts, but I give my love to you.

  —*Pat Pinder Helsel*

Chalk

I am a little piece of chalk,
But it's a shame 'cause I can't walk or talk.

Maybe if I could sing,
I would become a king!
But my voice would be just like a spring!
No, I'm glad I can't sing.

I wish I was a piece of hair,
But all I would seem to do is stare.
I would also have lots of pairs.
I'm glad I'm not a piece of hair.

I'm glad I'm just a piece of chalk,
Even if I can't walk or talk,
Yes, it's best to be a piece of ...
  chalk!!!

  —*Christy Lengel*

Compass Of The Heart

When someone says they care and you believe them
But love is just a mask that they have on
You want to believe the lie they tell is honest
When deep inside you know that it is wrong

If love is always true and always loyal
And to follow your heart, they say, is always best
What happens when you're lead in the wrong direction
And your soul, your mind, and heart are at unrest

Should you try to fool yourself, ignore the obvious
Close your eyes and live without the light
Or do you face the truth and know, though sadly,
That what you did was really what was right

  —*Colleen M. Kelly*

Turning Tides

As the ocean is calm, so is the night
But my mind is confused and full of fright
The darkness around me, in such a lonely place
I feel as though I am lost out into space
Why do you hurt me? And make me lose faith?
I can no longer control my emotions, I'm bound by your wrath
The tide now turns wild and out of control
As the last wave hits, it's taking my soul
If heaven awaits, then that's where I must go
For the stars call my name with an easy tow
Why must life be, so precious but cruel?
Who am I to be? And why must you play me for a fool?
I'm not blinded by love, it's just how I feel
So I don't want it, if you can't make it real
I'm getting sleepy now, I'm afraid I won't wake
So you have my heart, be careful it breaks!

    —Lori-Jean Ferrante

Eternal Ruse

I thought perhaps...
but, no.
A naive Imagination,
confusing the Emotion into it's now familiar error.
Once again teasing the Crimson into it's pulsating flow.
Washing from it's hollow niche,
the ancient Pain of Life;
forever there, yet only a mere echo of itself;
...waiting...
until the Imagination once again turns fool.

    —Gary W. Carter

The Heart Of Hurt

  I talk to them, I laugh with them,
But, now I can't be with them.
  I think of them, I dream of them,
But, now I can't see them.
  I love them with all my heart and more,
But the people took me away,
  From the ones I love more.
I'm not here to talk about the truth,
  To be told what's wrong.
I don't want to know anyway,
  All I'm here is to tell you,
That my friends mean the world to me.

    —Sarah Terry

Love Sheets

You are gone,
But the scent of you lingers
  between the cool pink sheets.
Looking at you as you fall asleep,
Remembering the touch of our toes and our feet.
Oh, how good it felt
  between the cool pink sheets.

You are gone,
And I am left alone
  between the cool pink sheets
which now cling to my body like a vise.

    —June MacArthur

Freedom Flight

Fly away free bird,
High into the sky,
Spread your wings
And soar the vast
Unknown.

    —A. L. Rush

Just Passing Bye

God sometimes I don't even want to try
But then I look up and see the clouds going by
Every thing feels like it is passing me by
I could have let out a scream or a cry
But then God said stop and ask yourself why
Like an eagle soaring through the bright blue sky
That's why life's so hard God wants to see if we even try
To see if we all really even can get by
When God looks down upon the earth it makes him cry
Mainly because of all the children that have to die
The people have to stop living in a lie
Give your soul to God before your own life passes you bye.

    —Joseph Blystone

He's Gone

He's gone like the sun
But there is no dawn
with the gun he said goodbye forever
The moon will always shine
leaving little little light over everyone
The wind blows
Is it him humming? Or yelling?
She made him mad-so he is gone
Can he see her?
See her crying over him?
Is he crying with her?
Or is he laughing at her?
Is he in heaven?
It no longer matters.
He will never come back
She thinks he will-but he won't-ever
He is the hidden sun.
The rock you can't ever seem to find.
He is gone.
Forever.

    —Jenifer Free

Our Troops

It wasn't our fight to fight
  but they were there anyway
Our men and woman soldiers
  defending a helpless country far away

Many left their loved ones
  feeling lonely and scared along the way
Praying for a small miracle
  that might make it go away

Was fighting for our country
  anything they thought it would be
Or was it something you would read about
  not anything you'd actually see

I'll never know what it was like over there
  or even imagine in anyway
But I know the memories will carry on in the future
  and become a lesson every day

I commend the ones who didn't come home
  they'll be in our thoughts each night and day
And we will never forget our dessert storm troops
  who stood for the U.S. of A.

    —Christa Wills

"October Leaf"

October leaf,
Nature's bright confetti,
Falling.
On the streets of autumn!

    —La Retha Adams

"A Country Woman"

Here lies the mother of our hearts,
But through God's will, we had to part.

No one can know the hardships she had,
But to listen to her, they weren't that bad.

A woman who worked and gave her all,
Never dreaming that someday she would fall.

She was never too sick to pray for another,
Always treated everyone as sister and brother.

This basket of country she requested of us,
We thought as first - "Why all the fuss?"

She's picked her share of cotton and peas,
Never having the niceties of coffees and teas.

Over the hills and dales she would roam,
From town to town looking for a home.

A woman who never learned to read or write,
Knowing that God would never let Her out of His sight.

We will never know why He made Her suffer,
Unless it was just His way making Her tougher.

On this day God came and She was told,
"Come on home daughter and walk the streets of gold."
    —*Carolyn Wright*

Dancing

Your lips are not mine to kiss
But to those of the stranger next door
Your eyes are not mine to cherish
But free to wander
The arms which hold me tight tonight
Are not my protection
Those silent words that I hear
Are captured by the night
I am free to believe you love me
Whether it true or false
I am free to follow your eyes
And kiss your lips, if only for a second
I am free to believe in your protection
Even though tomorrow
You will be with someone else.
    —*Doralice Handal*

Atrophy

Used yesterday for your lever, how clever.
But today is too heavy
You're sitting on it, you're screaming at it
And Friday won't help
It can't hear you yet.
It's coming, it's coming but its arms are tied up,
And yours are but clay
There will be no embrace
Your eyes far away, there will be no face.
Rendez-vous, dormez vous
You slept through it, they came for you.
They murdered you when you were not there
They missed you
They offered you the wine you spilt last year
But you licked it up off the ancient floor
Your tongue tied up with splinters,
You said Friday would bring you more.
The days are hungry
You are consumed, leaving me
Atrophy
    —*Jennifer Reilly*

Why Am I A Hero

They call me a hero and I think that's great.
But what about the past what about their fate.
They did their job as well as I.
But I'm a hero and the dead from the past just lie.
I am not a hero unless the past could be rearranged.
They deserve the glory for their life was forever changed.
They were stripped of there honor and they knew no fame.
To them I give my glory so they may never walk in shame.
    —*Bob A. Lowe*

Gods Of The Child Or Children Of God

We are called the children of God
But would a mother kill her children?
Without perceptible reason, tens of thousands
        perish each day.
Mortal man cannot understand Gods plan.
Maybe we are just God's toys.
He finds it amusing to kill one and give good
        fortune to another.

As a child would plunge his toy car off the table;
God plunges innocent men into the pit of death.
And yet, around every corner a sinner's heart lurks;
Waiting to strip a good soul of its body and
        the body of its possessions.

        Why does God do this?
Is he laughing or weeping as we suffer in this
        miserable existence?
Is God like the child, confused and unknowing;
Who, in the end goes on impulses rather than logic.
    —*Chris Kusy*

The Fragile Gift

The cool summer breeze gently danced through my room,
by the accompaniment of the crickets compassionate love song.

Subdued whispers fell from the trees,
telling me the secrets of the night.

As the night air glided across my body,
it stopped to enclose the rose my lover had sent me.

Our love was the beautiful blossom,
while my soul was the tormented thorns.

The petals began to fall,
while the question on my lips cried out to the moon.

How could such sculpted beauty be so effortlessly blown apart,
and brittle to my touch?
    —*Amy Neff*

You Are My Sunshine

The bright shining sun, you are like in every way;
By the brightness, happiness and joy which you have brought to me...
By the warmth you share with me...
By the beauty and stature you show with pride...
By the generous gentleness you give...
By the memories you give to hold in my heart.
The bright shining sun, you are like in every way,
for you like it, are the only one.
    —*Cynthia M. Becker*

Creativity

The awesome moment
An echo of God's heartbeat
Shimmers through my brush
    —*Cathrin Gallien*

Farewell

May you walk along the path of the moon shadow
By the shore of the white fish
May your feet bathe in the coolness of rain-soaked lands
May you tread lightly on the mountain
Leaving the gentle impression
Of your being.

May you obtain from life
As much as you give
Pleased with your efforts for the well being of a people
Echoing into all of nature... all people.

As the sun descends below the horizon
May the peace and harmony of nature
Find its way into your soul
Safely resting in the secrecy of your inner being.

As the daily-ness of life goes on
May the winds of your spirit breathe
Wholeness into a searching people —
Not afraid to wonder
Not afraid to challenge
Not afraid to be.

—*Elizabeth Smith Senger*

The Alarum

These were the days when fire trucks were drawn
    by two white horses with muscle and brawn.
They would dance and neigh and prance about
    When the alarms they did hear and men were enroute.
The men slid down the shiny brass pole
    And assumed their position in the fire-fighter's role.
The horses were led from out of their stable
    To the front of the engine to do what they were able.
The harness was dropped from the ceiling above;
    The girth strap was buckled as smooth as a glove.
The engineer was stoking the boiler with wood in big lumps
    To get up steam that drove all the pumps.
It seemed like only seconds when all work was done
    As the red fire engine started its dashing run
And headed up street with the clatter of hoofs
    Puffing black smoke as high as the roofs.

—*Charles V. Lundstedt*

Do You Have Any "YABUTS" In Your Life?

A "YABUT" is spelled this way: "Yeah, but..." when our Lord you try to resist,
Saying "YABUT" to our Lord is our human way, but trust me, He will persist.
How many times have you said "YABUT" to our Lord just during this past week?
Has it come out your mouth much too quick, even though Him you earnestly seek?

What did the Lord want of you that made you think you weren't ready?
Did you feel unprepared, unworthy, what gave you a feeling of being unsteady?
A "YABUT" easily can become your first reaction to what He sends your way,
What a shame to ignore our Lords calling and wasting another glorious day.

Consider the consequences of "YABUTS" in your life, not giving Him your will,
Bite your tongue when your Lord calls you again...instead, stand very still.
Answer the Lord with your honesty, and HE will provide whatever you may need,
Then that "YABUT" may not come out at all, and with Him you will closer be.

When He next beckons, resist that "YABUT," take a step forward in His name,
Believe me, your spirit will rejoice, and you will never again be the same.
Telling the Lord you will follow His lead, the "YABUTS" will come much less,
You will know He is working in your life, you will never again need to guess.

"YABUT LORD, I don't feel ready...YABUT LORD, why me?"...ring any bells?
Whatever your reasons for "YABUTS" in your life, the Lord you need to tell.
Replace that "YABUT" with "Yes, my LORD, I hear your call, what can I do?"
When you need Him to listen, would you want to hear a "YABUT" back to you?

—*Jill Hoffman*

Happy Birthday, Son

Happy Birthday Son, cherished one,
    My love for you runs deep.
AS A baby you were so sweet,
The times with you made me complete.
    You were a happy child,
Smiling laughing, mine alone for awhile.

As time went by and you grew,
My life became more confused,
    I wish I could turn back time,
Mistakes I made with you, are forever
    on my mind,
I did the best I could, I tried.
    When you think of me, be kind.
Life isn't always as we wish it to be,
Being a parent is like the stormy sea,
But the sun comes out and things quiet down.
    Just a hush, not a sound.
We reflect on times past and we've found,
    Our love and memories keep us bound.

—*Betty L. Moon*

New Dawn

    Anew dawn to ageing eyes,
New solutions to ageless problems.
Sleeping mountains of energy that
have passed to another dimension.

    Something never pass, and can
hurt even more.

    Others sleep until the hurt
turns into a shy smile, from a
faint trail of time, never to return.

    Each patch of roaming clouds
encourages new thoughts, for ideas to
try to better ones self, or bring
whimsical passions that will bring
smiles for others to return without
knowing why.

    Encourage a smile from within,
to cheer up the saddest soul.

—*Brenda J. Miller*

Succeeded Oak

An oaken nut lay brown and shiny
Nestled in some leafy mould.
And lying there, he seemed too tiny
that one should hear his story told.
True his life was unimposing
And unheroic was his fall
from a limb where he sat dozing
Till jostled loose by a sudden squall.
Seemingly, his journey ended.
So suddenly brought down to earth.
Actually it's just suspended,
Awaiting now a second birth.
For this passive little acorn
The very best is yet to be.
In due time, he will awaken
As a living, breathing tree!

—*Bert Hamill*

Well Again

You took me by surprise
by your role playing and sexy eyes.
And, I must say, you had me hypnotized.
Control over my mind was your aim
and I take full blame for letting you play that game.

Self-mastery is an arduous task
for we often wear the mask
we think others expect of us.
How long does it take
before we recognize this fatal mistake?

Death of self for a possible maybe
to satisfy your ego at the expense
of mine is a price
I am not willing to pay
for friends and relatives to throw rice some day.

I let you go consciously.
But you remained in my subconscious
till finally one day my body
erupted in lesions and irritation,
symbolizing the end of you and my recovery and celebration.

  —Elaine F. Schettino

What Spring And Easter Mean To Me

Beneath the snow and frozen ground
Natures beauty lays imprisoned
They didn't die-they awake and cry
Jesus Christ is risen

Flowers grow-still waters flow
Trees grow leaves for shade
All nature sings-Hosannas ring
At what our God has made

So lets join nature in songs of praise
He who was crucified is raised
He bore our sins-we are forgiven
Hallelujah-Christ is risen

  —Eve Luck

"Forever Immortal You Are, Dad"

If I had a wish, that wish would be to have you by my side for all eternity.
The flaming circle has passed us many times, and in that brief moment
 you've shown me ofttimes
That life is too short and that I should know to be kind to those
 people I have loved so.
For one day, they will go away to a place where they will stay, forever.
That span of time we have spent together has been, what, one, two,
 three,...sixteen altogether?
I remember you as the protector of his sheep,
I knew you were watching me as I lay fast asleep.
I would hear your footsteps outside the door and then your great
 shadow sprawled out on the floor
And when you tucked me in your face was a blur, I knew, as I played
 possum that you were immortal.
But I've found out that immortal you're not, you're just as mortal as
 me, I forgot.
For on that dreadful day in October, on the day I'll always remember,
 Mother told me of your illness.
Then in the air there was a stillness.
Shock has slapped me in the face, and then I wanted to embrace you.
But, all I could do was sit and cry, and mutter to myself why? why? why!!
Of all the people that I see, why was He taking you from me?
Although this "thing" is just starting, I fear one day, soon, we will be parting.
Until then, I hope to see you clearly, and try to find out who you really are.
Time may be running out for you and I, and as that flaming oracle speeds on by.
I will live each day as though it's my last, concentrating on today — not on the past.
And when you leave me, I won't be sad because "Forever Immortal You Are, Dad."

  —Liane M. Nishioka

Alzheimer's

Sweet Memory
The Printing Press of Life
You punch out our pages
Of joys and pains and strife
Then
The ink runs dry
The Press moves on
But leaves the pages
Blank

  —Christine M. Anderson

"Red Wrapped Rose"

My baby's wrapped in red today -
Must know this takes my breath away
Like rubies held against the sun -
Like the barrel of an emptied gun
I love it when she looks my way
My baby's wrapped in red today.

Heartbeats doin' double time -
Rose in red just looks so fine -
Like poppies on an open field -
Like apples that the orchards yield -
I love to see this colour bright -
Rose in red looks outta sight -
Must know this takes my breath away -
My baby's wrapped in red today.

  —Frank T. Torpila

My Tracks

The thoughts I think
Have been thought before,
By wiser men
On a different shore.

But the tracks I make
Are mine alone,
And belong only to me
As I journey on.

To that destined place
We all must go,
Whether it's up above
Or down below.

Some swear they know
While angels dare,
It's not mine to know
I've not been there.

Then why should I say:
Follow my track;
It might lead you on-
Or turn you back!

  —James V. York

Love Never Dies

Love is eternal
Love endures in time
LOVE NEVER DIES
Love is a shining light
Love burns deep within ones soul
LOVE NEVER DIES
Love is special
Love is true
Love is a gift I give to you
LOVE NEVER DIES
For our love I must die
Therefore I must say goodbye. . .
Always remember our love
WILL NEVER DIE!
I LOVE YOU!!!

  —Angela Lynea King

Two Breaths Ago

Two breaths ago
filled with such fright
the meaningless war chose that night.
To my surprise a second,
but yet, again, ended by death,
not by war, but by self.
Near third wind,
recognition proclaims me
wiser and prepared for three,
for the third, I will find
what was lost, one, two breaths ago.

  —Christopher S. Bergey

"Childhood Bliss"

Cherub cheeks
Smiles of delight
London's Bridge is falling
down so
Ring around the rosy
Golden sunshine falls
On baby soft
skin
Tender toes prance
On plush grass
FREEDOM
Of all responsibility

—*Angela D. Webster*

In The Course Of Time

In the course of time
we first met in passing
In the course of time
we became associates.

In the course of time
you became my friend
In the course of time
we part in love.

You stand for strength
You are proud as a woman
Your beauty is timeless
You will never be forgotten.

And so these words
I leave with you
That in the course of time
We will be together again.

—*Jeanine A. Hinton*

Return Of A Season

The sun is high
The air is dry
White houses line the street

The seasons change
They bring us rain
The wind, it blows so sweet

The whippoorwill sings
Good tidings to spring
That she and summer will meet
The fireflies light
so incredibly bright
Sheds light beneath my feet

The morning is new
and covered with dew
and an earthly smell of peat

An animal is born
In midst of a storm
and nursed it's mother's teat
These are the things that summer brings.
Abreast her sizzling heat.

—*Elizabeth Yarbrough*

I'll Never Let Go

Well it's been weeks
since we last touched
during that time
my life hasn't been much

I haven't forgotten you
although it may seem
But my heart hasn't changed
and that's hard to believe

Through all of the heartache
you've put me through
It seems like I still
owe something to you

Even though you're the one
that keeps me up in the night
Who's made my eyes full of tears
and my life full of lies

You are the one I tried hardest to win
And you are the one that I've got to forget!

—*Elizabeth Skloss*

Dying

What can you tell a
13 year old about dying?
They're still too young to
understand life.
But who is to say at
what age, do you learn of
life's little problems.
Losing a friend, the hurt
runs deep.
The days go by with a
void.
You will always remember
your friends name and what
he or she looks like.
Treasure the time you knew
this friend.
And always remember they
are in Gods loving hands.

—*Barbara Griffith*

"A Rose"

A rose is God's creation
a blessing from above
a glimpse of pure perfection
a token of His love -
a message straight from Heaven
To people everywhere -
If God gives us roses here
How fair it must be there.

—*Elizabeth Benner Swineford*

The Early Morning

A prime time of the day,
A peaceful time to meditate,
A special time to pray.

So serene the early dawn,
Birds warbling their cheerful songs,
While the dew is still on the lawn.

So pure and crisp the morning air,
An artist palette everywhere,
For mother nature and all to share.

—*Betty Kopatich*

Reality

The teardrops fall.
A child screams
Out into the night.
An elderly man is robbed of his money,
then his life,
And a young girl is raped.
Rivers of blood and tears
Flow all over the Earth.
Peace is obsolete,
Just a dream and a memory.
No one cares,
And no one asks why.
Time passes so quickly,
And the wars rage on
In the hearts and souls of mankind.
Welcome to reality!

—*Brandie Litchfield*

The Mountains

The mountain air;
a cool fresh breeze.
To smell the flowers;
a refreshing sneeze.

A mountain stream;
the beautiful trees.
And all the wildlife;
that you may see.

A mother deer;
with her offspring.
And all the birds;
that you hear sing.

To see a mountain;
stretch the sky.
To see the beauty;
so very high.

The many mysteries;
that never unfold.
The many beauties;
a mountain holds.

—*Crystal Benfield*

Encroachment

The autumn leaves are burning yet,
A crisp gold brown array.
The pumpkin shell is turning; let
The frost fall where it may.

The corn has lost its stately green,
The kernel has its dent,
The melon vines are black, obscene;
Their days already spent.

The hay that's in the o'erstuffed barn,
Like feather pillows fluffed for night;
Like kids intent on fireside yarn,
Awaits its consummating plight.

The cattle low a soft lament
And munch the stunted blade,
Wading icy creeks, intent;
Like visitors o'erstayed

The geese are winging fond farewell
'Til spring shall show her face,
For winter, like a villanelle,
Is creeping in her place.

—*Elmer A. Williams*

"Lightning Star"

What is a Lightning Star?
A falling star
With the speed of light?
Or a little creature,
That shines so bright.

It will show you the way
When you are lost.
It will give you help
Without any loss.
It will be your friend
When a friend is in need.

A lightning star will always be,
Glad to do for you, anything.
So look up at night, look up far,
And you will see your lightning star.

—*Brenda I. Jensen*

"The Future"

A distant life
A far off place,
Yet unknown to me
Is where the cravenness of my mind
Will flourish with creativity.
In this mosaic
I will see my fate
And my destiny.

—*Danielle Parisi*

Life And Dreams

When I grew up I looked into,
A future world without poverty.
That's progress I thought,
But later I saw it was,
Just an illusion.

I saw the wide eyed child,
Its empty staring gaze,
No dreams of future days,
A swollen bowel and meatless
limbs and no illusions.

I asked the wise man: Speak to me,
About illusions and said he,
You are not what you are,
But what your dreams are,
And dreams are just illusions.

Why should I worry then,
Whether life is good or bad,
For life is bad to him who has no,
Future dreams and good when dreams,
Are just elusive dreams.

—*Finnvald Hedin*

Stephen's Promise

Smiles can never hope to be
a substitute for peace
To love a child and nurture him;
to see his strength increase.
Far too many times,
it seems we wrongly represent
Our little ones; our gifts from God
of whom are heaven-sent.
So here and now, I do decree
with calculated bother-
Please let me Lord,
if in your will become a loving father.

—*Christopher Adam Cantner*

Summer Dream

You are my summer dream
A golden illusion
That dances upon
The twilight of my years

The moonlight in your hair
Transforms the magic
of the night
Into the weakness
of my soul

The warm wind blows gently
Upon the softness
of your skin

And your eyes reveal
The pure innocence
Lost to the
hands of time....

.... Yes,
You are my summer dream
A golden illusion
of a love
That might have been—

—*James Rocknowski*

Marriage Love Notes

Marriage is a drama
A play which cast two stars
Both with equal roles to learn
Both with equal parts.

Marriage is a give and take
A let us meet half-way
It's not about just what I want
Nor just about what you say.

Marriage is a union
There is no more "Me" or "My"
"I no longer stand alone
It is now "Us," "We" and "Our."

Marriage is just like Love Notes
Together or far apart
Its melody lingers sweet and long
It's a song sung from the heart.

—*Ella Lemon-Forbes*

"Dear Mother"

Love is like the wind
A small gust will change your life
And if I still do not have yours
For it I shall always strive

I cherish it as a gift
That was given to me from above
To be able to be your creation
And deliver you all my love

To you I can only say
Our love will always be
For you are the seed of a Rose
The most delicate part; you see

I hope that you understand
How much I really care
And how much I appreciate
All the wonderful things you share

So have a beautiful day
And forget of what's behind
An eternity awaits ahead of you
And my love you'll always find

—*David Mathias*

Good Or Bad

When good is good and bad is bad
A sort of balance can be had.
Should good decide to go astray,
And bad retain its evil way;
The world would be a dreary place
Unfit to hold the human race.

Prohibit habits that abound,
For something better can be found.
This then can turn the tide to good,
Where right from wrong is understood.
With moral values on the mend,
Good could prevail unto the end.

—*Bob Krajnak*

Ars Poetica

My pen has struck parchment
A thousand times to scribble
Original, genuine irresolution
Each stroke is raucous in
Hope's that someone will hear!
My poetry is my sculpture regard
Each stroke, it speaks for me.

—*Carolyn W. Crumby*

Years

I feel like I've cried
a thousand years
And heard a million lie
Saw hundreds of unhappy faces
Along this road of endless miles
Seeking those who can hold
heart-felt smiles
Knowing they have been through
difficult trials
Seeing their pain was a strain
And they were those of compliance
Longing to hear the sound
of real happiness and harmonious
music from hearts filled with love
and arms of gentle affection
That display tenderness of love
A true complexion
Seeing those of innocent
and honest perfection

—*Carol A. Contine*

Untitled

Oh look, the flowers are talking,
About you and I, I think
I wonder what they're saying?
For they're really turning pink.

I think they think I love you
You know I guess they're right
And they look so embarrassed
Because your holding me so tight.

I think they think we're silly
Because they're giggling so
I think we'd better get along
It's really time to go.

Can you imagine flowers
Blushing like they do
I guess it's just because they think
I love you, and I do.

—*Constance Ann Hammersley*

Yesterday

Many suns have shone there,
above the cloudless skies;
and much sand has shifted,
spoken whispers, uttered sighs.

Many hearts were broken
because of foolish pride;
old romances, torn like paper,
little tidbits, left aside.

—*Joyce LaVerne Lloyd*

Recipe For Peace

Little competition,
Acceptance of what's done,
Recognition apprehended,
Joys of will shall come.
Games in love and marriage,
Silently resolve,
What is said is lived as truth out loud.

Fears of troublesome nature,
Are confronted and worked through,
Compatibility, cooperation, trust,
Become our strength; anew ....
   a pinch of heart's affection
   a tablespoon of time
   the kind of pride from within
   formulation of mind
   all mixed up together
   at every human's pace
   creates a completed feast
   nurtured by all race.

—*Century*

Don't Act Old

Don't act old
   Act young

Be on the move
   But don't run

Get in the act
   And do your part

People will know
You have a strong heart

   We are only old
When we are weak and feeble

And need the help
From other people

You will be glad
When you can say

Thank you Lord
For this wonderful day
   —*Joseph Gleinn*

With All My Heart

The heart controls the blood of life -
   all the way from head to toe,
   With every other body part
      dependent on its flow.

The same may be said of emotions -
   as I now express to you,
To say I love you "with all my heart"
means I would give my "life" for you.

—*Carol Frederick*

Remember That Night"

The waves crashing
against the shore,
   Each time giving off
a gentle roar.

   The wind as silent as
can be,
   The skies as clear as
I can see.

   I saw you standing,
looking out,
   Oh how I wondered what
your thinking about.

   As I look into your eyes.
   The sparkle beautiful
as the great blue sky.

   As the moon rise above,
Our eyes meet and
   We fall in love.
      —*Debbie Greene*

Racial Hate

   A man is crying in the night
      All alone, scared in fright
   He has a bruised and bloodied face
This was done to him because of race
      Why is there all this hate?
That spreads across from state to state
      Will it ever stop someday?
   God please help, that's all I pray
      —*Dustin Smith*

Fill Me With You

Like glasses I get empty
All humans sometimes do
I thirst not for water
Instead fill me with you

Quench this burning thirst
By sharing your love with mine
I will not take it all at once
Only a little at the time
Let love between us flow
As rivers into the sea
And intermingle sweetly
To satisfy you and me
   —*Bernice Newsome*

Mom's Room

A room full of Avon
All spic and span
Everything in its place
To make room for her clan.
With plates and photos
Ivory carvings and flowers
She's made a new home
Since leaving golden towers.
Nuts and candy in bowls
An open door with a coat
Plenty of fresh coffee
If you believe the note.
For news and letters,
And love and debate
A visit with Nana
Is always first rate.
   —*Carl Crosman*

The Candle

Endless hours of secret passion.
   Alone in the world they created.
Two souls searching, reaching for
the warmth that only love can bring.
   Lies melt away secrets
   not told in the inner circle.
      Happiness vanishes,
      flame burns endlessly,
      destroying their world.
Love once started in the soft,
   flickering candlelight,
   ends unrecognizable.
The candle devoured by the flame.
   —*Ellen Chateauneuf*

Freedom Of Life

To be happy,
Also means to be alive,
With plenty of sunshine,
Within your life.

Look at the sky,
To the birds up high,
Look at how pretty they are,
And how swiftly they fly.

Wouldn't it be great,
To be in their place,
To be able to fly,
And also to race?

Race across the sky,
So swift and fast,
To have that feeling of freedom,
That would always last.
   —*Billy Walpole*

Childhood Memories

Childhood memories
Always bring joy.
Two close friends,
A young girl and a boy.

Childhood memories
Always bring sadness
Of a day a boy had to journey
And the start of a terrible miss.

Childhood memories
Always bring a smile
Of days where two children played
Within the reach of a mile.

Childhood memories
Always bring a frown.
A boy and a girl torn apart
By many, many towns.

Childhood memories
Both good and bad,
Lie in the heart of a girl
Who wants to be with her childhood friend
she once had.

   —*Andrea Bellemore*

Metamorphosis

I felt like a grain of sand
  amidst all the others, lost
  in the crowd.

Then I floated into your arms
  and you held me and
  showered me with kindness.

And when I emerged from the
  ocean of your love,
  I found
    I was a
      pearl.
      —*Dawn Goodnature*

Dust and Feathers

The falcon paces
among Easter Island expressions
waiting to become
deathmasks.

Spiked talons
dig stone faces
making them cry tears
of dust and sand.

Their last days are cloaked
in indigo
and cushioned by pine.

One feather drifts down.

The cliffs crumble.
    —*Holly Kuehlwein*

Untitled

I look at you
And
All I see
Is a reflection of myself
Caught
In your stare

I touch you
And
All I feel
Is myself wound around you
Caught
In your arms

We kiss
And
It's all I can do to resist
But, I'm
Caught
    —*Diana Olive Kennedy*

"Tomorrows Pleasure"

Beyond the hardships of today,
And all the pains along the way.

Stand the pleasures of tomorrows
To help you deal with all the sorrows.

So as the sun sets on this night,
And you think of taking flight.

Remember always the sun will shine,
To help you pass the days of time.
    —*Christina D. Crudgington*

A Robin's Promise

Today I saw a robin
  And although it's very cold
He had a little message
  A promise for me to hold

Now all through the winter
  The Juncos I have fed
And the bright red cardinals
  With the crest upon it's head

The tiny black-capped chickadees
  And the little tufted titmouse
Have been frequent visitors
  Just outside my house

I have enjoyed these little friends
  But the winter was cold and long
So I was glad to see a Robin
  Now I'll wait to hear his song

For the message that he brought me
  Has made me feel so gay
He said "Spring is just around the corner
  Warmer days are on their way."
    —*Geraldine L. Haley*

Untitled

If I came to you
  and asked you to hold my hand,
    would you reject me?
      would you understand?

If I asked you
  to hold me close in your arms,
    would you push me away?
      would you do me harm?

If I was alone
  and I asked you to stay,
    would you remain with me?
      or would you run away?

Please....
  don't answer,
I'm too afraid to know
  the truth.
    —*Jon Rodriguez*

Touch A Child

To touch a little child today
  and change his life a bit,
To give him something new to hold,
  perhaps a goal to hit.

To touch a little child today
  and try to stretch his mind
To seek and wonder every day,
  to probe and not be blind.

To touch a little child today,
  it isn't hard to do,
He's looking for someone to say,
  "I see, I care for you."

So put aside some time each day,
  To ask the one to whom you pray,

For courage, patience and vision to reach,
To touch one child by the way you teach.
    —*Dean S. Pickens*

A Day Has Gone

A day has gone
And come
I still remain.
Speechless night
My friend—
Surrounds me
With its darkened cloak
In the silence of the hour
I hear the earth's heart beat
I am refreshed
As a baby
In its mother's womb—
Contentment.
    —*A. Charles Dana*

Stay In School

When I was much younger
And going to school
I just didn't care
Yes, I was a fool
Life was one big party
And school was such a bore
Fun was all I wanted
All the time, more, more, and more
But, as I grew older
With my career in a coma
All potential employers told me
You have no high school diploma
Things are not always that easy
But it's never too late
To fix things done wrong
So stay in school and control your own fate
    —*Edward Plazek*

A Christmas Message

My thoughts are with the Christ child
and His lowly stable birth -
We've read the Bible stories
And know them for their worth!

We're told about the Wise Men,
Who saw the magic star -
And came to see this baby
With love gifts from afar!

The three men bowed and worshipped
This infant in the manger,
And presented their precious gifts
To this little baby stranger!

He is "Jesus" — the Messiah,
Named "Emmanuel" as He lay,
Who was sent as our Salvation
To take our sins away!

The message for this Christmas
Is: — "to celebrate His birth
By spreading of great tidings
To everyone on Earth"!
    —*Helen Arlynne Lord*

The Fisherman

Oars slicing water
Foggy with the morning mist,
River and man blend.
    —*Rosemary Parsons Torrez*

Gods Tapestry

He wove a tapestry of Love.
And hung it out in space.
He used vibrant colors of every hue,
"Twas such a lovely place.

He gave it then, to mankind,
To live and flourish in,
And they, in turn corrupted it,
With fighting, greed and sin.

If we don't right the wrongs we've done,
And mighty quick, I think,
All life upon Gods tapestry,
Will surely be extinct!

—*Carol J. Coyer*

"Old Glory"

I was once a sailor
And I fought for the flag
To me it was a symbol
Not just a colored rag.

It stood for rights and freedom
My country's joy and pride
So many thousands fought for it
And many thousands died.

Those folks who want to burn it
Should go visit a grave
Of some departed service man
Who died so young and brave.

He gave his life so you'd be free
A privilege most don't earn
He died for just the very thing
That you so freely burn.

So please don't desecrate the flag
Or we fought and died in vain
Remember how we suffered
And how many died in pain.

—*Fred Wood*

The Dream

At dawn, I begin to see the sun,
and I look down
realizing what I have done.
The darkness of the land
had kept me from seeing
the blood upon my hand.
My trusted friend
now lies there still;
with no longer any will.
And as she lay there,
her eyes still bright,
with her skin a creamy white,
I know I want to cry.
She is gone now.
An important part of me is dead.
But as I look upon her head,
I notice something queer.
It is not her, my friend, I see,
For it completely resembles me.

—*Erin Tobin*

Equilibrium

Never more...
Never less...
Starvation's world in excess.

—*Ryan Schmidt*

My Daddy

My Daddy died this morning
And I'm feeling very sad.
He wasn't the greatest father,
But he was all I had.

He wasn't afraid of dying,
He was more than ready to fly,
He said he was very tired,
He said he was ready to die.

He was a quiet, private man,
He hated any fuss.
He folded his hands and went to sleep,
He just did not wake up.

My Daddy died this morning
And I'm feeling very sad.
He wasn't the greatest father,
But he was all I had.

—*Helen Arlene Engelsman*

The Reader

My name isn't Corrina,
And I'm not from Pari,
But I come from that Kingdom
That all of us see...

I'm not much to look at,
But then look! Wha'd ja see?!
A twinkle, a sparkle,
Deep within me...

You have seen something
That many agree
Is the glimmer of wisdom
That all of us seek...

Yes, I may see some things
That you cannot see...
Unconfined... Not from 'this world'...
Inspirationally...

I'll look to the sky,
Then look around thee,
And see what is coming
Naturally...

—*Cynthia Freitag*

You

Tonight I am crying
And inside I feel like dying.
Because you are gone.
Just like the morning dawn.
Your warm embrace
The smiles on your face.
But really what I miss
Is your tender kiss.
I don't know what I would do
Just to spend another moment with you.
I love you more than you know
Or what words would ever show.
If you were here with me
I would want you to be.
In my arms for the very last time
So I can keep you pictured in my mind.

—*Holly Davidson*

The Music Is Over

The music has ended,
And just like you, has gone.
Like the moon fades away,
Bringing the morning dawn.
A newness, a beginning,
Always comes from the old.
Sometimes it's even more special
And more precious than gold.
You are the old part,
Gone away now to stay.
But here I have your baby,
Which will never go away.
Its bits like the music
That seem to linger here,
And a gentle peaceful feeling
That washes away my fear.
For the good or the bad,
I don't really know.
Just looking back on memories,
I wish you wouldn't of had to go.

—*Cheryl L. Herpich*

My Brother

If you could come and sit with me,
and look across the room,
there sits a man who used to be,
a young good looking man was he.
He went to war and came back sick,
as sick as he could be.
Half of his brain is dead and gone,
and there are days that he just sits,
and do not know who he is.
He knows his name and where he lives,
but there are days,
not even this!

—*Amparo J. Fernandez*

My Friend

I have a friend, that is so true
and loves me without measure.
It is so great to look in his face
Because he gives me so much pleasure

His face is the first thing
I see in the morning
The last thing I see at night.
All the things I do during the day
I do with him in mind.
Quickly I do the chores
Preparing for his return.
The clock strikes four
He appears in the door.
My heart skips beats,
Oh what a treat!
My husband, my friend.

—*Hazel F. Crane*

Kindred

Often I think from whence I came
and of those who gave me name.
To the Beech and Oak I trace my kin,
and find the veins below my skin
are as the seasons of a tree.
Like the leaves, then, I must be.
Clinical tests show it red,
but green is the imbued.
A tinge of orange, a touch of brown,
my roots are deep in Kentucky ground.

—*Camila Haney*

Untitled

Thoughts and things
  and memories
All together they appear to be
  the making of me.
And when I reminisce
  of good times long ago
I ask myself
  Am I now forgetting
To act upon the experience
  of having been there before.
To pave my way to better things.
To more pleasures of the soul
  with more contemplation?
  with more self-exploration?
  I wonder!

—*Catherine A. Fuleky*

A Moment For Prayer

I got up early one morning
and rushed right into the day;
I had so much to accomplish,
that I didn't have time to pray.

Problems just tumbled about me,
and heavier came each task.
"Why doesn't God help me?" I wondered.
He answered; "You didn't ask.

I wanted to see joy and beauty,
But the day toiled on, gray and bleak;
I wondered why God didn't show me,
He said "But you didn't seek."

I tried to come in to God's presence;
I used all my keys at the lock.
God gently and lovely chided,
"My child you didn't knock."

I woke up early this morning,
and paused before entering the day;
I had so much to accomplish,
That I had to take time to pray.

—*Carlyle R. Bryant, Ph.D.*

My Window

I look out my window
and say a short prayer.
I imagine a scene
and I find myself there.
The sky is so tranquil
it's colors so blue.
In this scene all my wildest
of wishes come true.
These moments in life
can't be taken away.
Although many will try
in your heart they must stay.
Hold fast to your dreams
and they'll stay by your side.
They may even provide you
a refuge to hide.
Look out your own window.
What things do you see?
The dreams you hold onto
will set your soul free!

—*Judith M. Hamilton*

Open Your Eyes

Open your eyes.
And see the baby's cries.
Open your eyes.
And see the man's lies.
Open your eyes.
And say your good-byes.
Open your eyes.
And see how the bird fly's.
Open your eyes.
And see the blue skies.
Open your eyes.
Before time dies.
Open your eyes.
Keep your mouth tight.
Open your eyes.
And maybe, you will see the light.

—*Jerold L. Magnuson*

"The Night"

I love to watch the moon at night,
and see the stars that shine so bright,
I can feel the breeze across my face,
as I walk along at a certain pace,
But soon the stars will disappear,
The sky will soon begin to clear,
everything will soon be bright,
and we'll no longer face the night.

—*Cindy Loureiro*

On Losing A Mate

When Two have been One so long
and shared the joy and pain
We grieve and wonder how can we
be only one again.
No one can say, no words can heal
the wound cruel death has rent
We wonder how such things can be
And still be Heaven sent.
But we think of the promises
Of Jesus Christ our Lord.
We cling to the strength He gives us
when we believe His word.
For we are promised by Our Lord
In the Hereafter we'll happier be
when ones we've loved and by death lost
Again in Heaven we'll see!

—*Jewel Woodard Simon*

Lost Love

He gave me a single red rose,
Although he didn't propose
  The day was special
I'll never forget the day
  I loved him in everyway
too bad he couldn't stay,

The next red rose was very special,
  It just wasn't the same
what a shame
  I kept each rose,
and held them near to my heart,
  even though we were apart.

—*Amanda French*

The Rose

God's perfect example of life.

Being both soft to the eye
  and sharp to the touch
It's beauty is shrouded with pain

A splendor exists
  and danger is always there

Love and hate.

Control of the life is found
  in realizing they must exist
  and good can come from both.

The Rose
  It's petals comfort the
    warmth of the heart and
  It's thorns protect the
    scars of the soul

A release of the soul
  brings peace to the heart and mind
    and life goes on.

—*John D. Puenner*

Turkey Cobbler

I saw a big turkey gobbler
And started thinking of turkey cobbler
I chased him to a cave
And thought I saw him wave
I just knew he was trapped
And would very soon be zapped
I'd have that turkey for dinner
He would really be a winner
I went right into the cave
And was feeling very very brave
When I flashed on the light
I saw a very strange sight
It wasn't a turkey at all
A dinosaur stood against the wall
I turned white as a ghost
And planned on eating milk toast
Or I might be the gobbler
A big dinosaurs thanksgiving cobbler.

—*George H. Hutson*

Desperado

We covered ninety mile today,
And still it ain't enough
Them bandits are not far away,
By gar, they sure are tough!

My trusty pistol by my side,
But no relief in sight.
It looks like we will have to ride
Until the morning light.

My pony swims the Rio Grande,
But then he comes up lame.
He tumbles down upon the sand
I yell, "Keep up the game!"

His breath is coming hard and fast,
He turns his weary head.
"I'm tuckered out," says Dad at last,
"Besides, it's time for bed."

—*Brett Palm*

My Fear

Have you a fear of mirrors
And the image you might see?
Sometimes it is a stranger
Looking back at me.
Then...It's all too familiar
And I do not like what I see.
For I am fearful and depressed
That I am less
Than what I want to be.

—*Edgeleth Martin*

Life Goes On

When the fearsome North Wind blows,
And the lily no more it grows,
And when life all around you allows,
And long forgotten is the rose,
    Remember life goes on.
The sun it blazeth warm and bright,
The moon it shineth in the night,
When the air is cold with fright,
    Remember life goes on.

Only in the darkness lies,
A spark of light, a warm surprise,
Deep in the shadows does it cry
"Come find me," cries it, by and by,
    Remember life goes on.
A candle blazes tirelessly,
Its light burns brightly which you can see,
It shines untouched by the roaring sea,
    Remember life goes on.

—*Carrie Kiessling*

Untitled

Cap comes off, once again,
    and the scent is released
    to my 'ole factory.
This fresh smell has not been daily,
    and that is "OK," but not for some.
Bright blue, bright blue is what I see,
    but with some quick moves,
    a streaked top of white.
It says "Effective 24 Hour protection,"
    and that is great,
    but who smells me when I'm sleeping.

—*Christopher X. Dougherty*

Shepherd Of The Hills

The hills are full of wonders
And the trees all say Hello
As we, wonder down the pathway
    to the waters edge below.
Know one can make these
wonders
Only God has made them real
For we are all his sheep and
he is the shepherd of the Hills.

—*Iva Siler*

The Death of Young Love

As he stood and watched,
As a single tear rolled down his check,
He pulled his class ring off her finger,
And held it close to him,
He watched her casket lower.
This is all because,
She didn't say "nope" to dope.

—*Courtney French*

Untitled

You are a rose
And when you leave
I will die,
But when you come
I will cry,
For I know
I cannot keep you
Here with me
For Eternity!

—*Heather Borovitz*

A Baby's Cry

I'm crying for you Mommy
    and you too dad.
"I never wanted to die," I said.
They're ripping and tearing my
    body apart.
I told you I never wanted to depart.
I never saw you mommy or
    you either dad.
"I know I would have loved you," I said.
I wouldn't have cried much.
I would have been good.
But you never gave me a chance
    like you should.
So bye mommy and daddy.
I love you, I forgive you.
Even tho it's very sad.

—*Jana Russell*

Equal Under The Moon

For every pair of lips that kisses
Another is being kissed good-bye.
For every mouth that savors
Millions swallowing scraps.
For every mouth that gorges
Thousands dying of famine.
For every dog that dog eats dog
Unequal dogs are eaten.
For every foot treading red carpet
Millions treading the gutter.
For the many traveling for pleasure
The myriads fleeing for their lives.
For every arm waving a banner
Another throwing a bomb.
For every hero put up for a medal
Another put under a memorial.
For every dollar spent on charity
Billions more on enormity.
All are equal under the moon
But unequal under the sun.

—*Jonathan Russell*

Love Song

Your head upon my pillow
As we shut out the dawn
Left a place for my head
    To settle on.

And your body curled nicely
Like a schizophrenic smile
With many a gulf and valley
For mine to fit all the while.

And your smile fixed above me
Came and went...like Christmas time,
A New Year's kiss in the memory,
Or a summer's taste of lime.

—*Jack Pettey*

Fall Gift

November's brightest colors
Are visitors to the sycamore,
Splashed with red and yellow
Upon surviving green.
It's poison ivy showing off these hues,
Endeavoring at this late hour to make
A worthy contribution.
Sycamore leaves turn brown
And fall like scorched love-notes
To the ground. Frost-dabbed ivy
Spirals upward, flashing color,
Cloaked in gaudy new identity.
Autumn celebrants from distances
Are fooled, believing some new star
Outshines dogwood, gum and poplar.
Closer looks reveal the brown and hairy
Vines that wrap and cling
Like boas on host limbs,
Seeking substances to make
Fresh itches come next spring.

—*Gerald L. Cooper*

Fading Monument

Beside a wide-open
Arizona highway
sits a Navajo woman
with a loom and a shiny
shuttle in her brown hand —
fading monument.

Patterns, designs
by word-of-mouth —
through Indian generations.

Red cinder dust
quietly settles on
carefully pulled-back
black hair.

Purple and crimson
velvet cloak —
draped.

Silver, turquoise, jingle
against her buxom breast.

Unfolds her forbearer's
treasured secrets.

—*Diana Yu*

As A Mother

I need a hug, too.
As a mother I need a hug
    from my little one
I need to know they love me, too
In the morning when I'm awake
And you knock at my door, I say
Come in sometimes I ask what
you need or want. You say, I
just want to hug you.
    That makes my day.

—*Elizabeth Ingram*

Rage

Witness the furor of the sea,
As it beats relentlessly,
Upon its rock - strewn shore.
Fighting its never-ending war.
Much as we humans when —
We pit ourselves against all men.

—*Bill Ernstberger*

Treelogy

I heard a tree scream
As a trembling limb
Rent itself earthward
The raw wound at the mercy of the wind.

Came a gentle breeze
Caressed the torn and tortured rift
Soothed the quivering branches
Till all lay still,

Save the faint throbbing
Of the heartwood.

—*Irene Brosco*

The Father And Son

Under a star
As bright as the sun,
On a cold winter night,
She bore a son.

She heard the angels
Singing on high,
She saw the shepherds
Kneel for prayer.

And then again as
Joseph's hand clasped hers,
On this cold night,
They think of that birth.

He came from heaven,
And when he returned,
He became her father,
And also her son.

—*Hazel Sawey Duncan*

Our Pastor

He and God walk hand in hand,
As he travels o'er the land.
He guides us, so we will not stray,
He speaks with God, so some say.
He mends our minds, he saves our souls,
He tells us there is only one goal.
He tells us there is only one master,
The man I speak of, is our Pastor.
Through others do this work to.
For us there is only you.

—*Charles Wurtz*

The One Who Holds The Key

I think about it often...,
....as I lie upon my bed.
How two hearts came to be one,
and the path of tears we've shed.
The many things we've been through,
....the many things we say.
I've loved you for so long now,
And love you more each day.

And though we've come so far now,
our hearts remaining one.
We see life all so different,
from when our hearts were young.
Our lives have changed around us,
...and in so many ways.
And you, my love have entered in,
...and there will always stay.

—*Enzo Leo*

I Saw a Stranger

I saw a stranger, the other day,
As I was going on my way.
I wondered, just who was he,
Of what did he, remind me?

I was puzzled on what to do.
Was this thing, a de-ja-vu?
Why by him was I impressed,
By some memory still unexpressed.

Did we meet in some past life,
Was I the husband or his wife?
Was he a part of my family,
Or just a part of my memory?

Can you say I am to blame,
If I dare not ask his name.
Oh Woeful! Woeful memory!
What did that stranger mean to me.

—*Ervin H. Chase*

Alone

Darkness covers,
as if a shroud.
    No cause,
    No reason.

    Vision turns,
a world of grey.
    No form,
    No clarity.

Emotions dulled,
void of passion.
    No love,
    No hate.

Mind is numb,
without order.
    No spark,
    No thought.

    Future dim,
Oppressive.
    No hope.

—*Erik Alexander Prince*

Listen To The Wind

The wind is very mystic,
As it rustles through the trees,
Bringing a sense of freedom,
To us, as we breathe.

As it blows through the window panes,
Listen to it sing.
There's nothing there to see,
An untouchable thing.

At times it brings a chill.
At times its just a breeze,
Passing by us quickly,
Like the waves from the sea.

The wind is in every season.
Spring, summer, winter, fall.
Feeling the unexpected,
Is the beauty of it all.

—*Carla D. Clontz*

Kitty Cat

Kitty cats are sweet
As sugarcane.
Each one is special.
Their fur is soft
As a mother's touch.
I like the way their eyes sparkle
Like the stars in a dark sky.
I like the sound of their purr
Like a hum to a soft song.
Meow!

—*Amber Pennington*

Dress Rehearsal

Their fingers poised for flight;
As the conductor calls for attention:
One eye on the music;
One on the conductor.
The baton falls,
And the first movement begins!

How skillfully the conductor
Blends the strings with the brass,
And the woodwinds.
The Cymbals crash—and
The music resounds
Throughout the theatre!

How flawlessly the musicians perform;
Each one concentrating on their own
    contribution,
Yet mindful of the sound of the whole
    symphony.
What a blessing for we poor mortals
    to share.

—*Jan Hanna*

New Beginnings

It's raining,
As the tears roll down my face.
The memories taunt my heart,
As new grass grows.

—*M. Catherine Rice*

The Colors Of Your Crystal Heart

I saw you shining as a glassy crystal
as you sparkled in the light
the way your smile lit up the room
the darkness became so bright

The souls that surround you each day
are ignited by your fire
you lift the people who are down
and you take the happy ones higher

The colors of your crystal heart
are radiant and so bold
you touch the hurting aching ones
and their hearts you always hold

When sitting in the sunlight
your spectrum of colors are seen
and as I look at you
my face just has to beam

—*Connie Medford*

Beauty

Beauty is the springtime
Beauty is the dawn
Beauty is the early bird
With his morning song

Beauty is the newborn foal
By his mothers side
Looking at the sun so high
His mothers eyes with pride

Beauty is the springtime
Beauty is much more
Beauty is the love of God
Which opens up The Door

—*Donna Susan Friedman*

Oh Daddy!

I cried only for a while
    because I knew I had to let go.
You never wanted to hurt me
    my mother told me so.

She explained these things to me.
    How daddies don't always stay.
But I was the only Baby
    At least that's what you'd say.

This family stole you from me
    taking the first man I'll ever love.
Leaving me with prayers
    to be answered from above.

Will you ever love me
    the way you did before?
Or will I be frightened
    that you'll leave me once more.

—*Denise Villarreal*

Signs Of Spring

The change of the season is near
Because the warm days appear.
        We also can see
        A scene that is free
For twelve signs of spring are here!

        Snowdrop.....Narcissus
              Crocus
        Hyacinth.....Daffodil
        Tulip........Pansy
              Iris
        Violet.......Lupine
        Azalea.......Banksia
              Enjoy!

—*Hazel Sawyer*

Thanh

Thanh was my cousin.
Boy, was he dear,
Every time I think of him -
It makes me go to tears.

Thanh was a good person and ....
.... God took him too fast.
I didn't believe it -
I didn't believe when the
car crashed.

I love him so much
Why did he have to go?
Now he's gone forever.
I miss and love him so.

—*Elizabeth Luong*

An Illusion Cast

As we grow and age in spirit
Becoming the man we want to be
    An illusion is cast to the world
    Showing all, that we are free

Invisible shackles are born unknown
Ignored as each link is firmly set
Many are blessed and won't restrain
Others will bind as the future's met

    Each tie we make in our life
Changes our freedom just so much
Not always in wisdom nor by choice
    But ever adding a binding touch

    Our freedom has boundary
    Controlled by other hands
    As gentle as they may be
They are as solid as steel bands

But we cast an illusion to the world
    To show that we are wholly free
    Then we age and grow in spirit
Becoming what our bonds allow us to be

—*Dee Washburn*

"Abused"

All alone -
Being beaten
Until black and blue.
Someday it's gonna go too far.
Everyone will feel guilty for
not seeking help.
Don't let it happen anymore!
Be a friend. Get help!

—*Carrie Hemsath*

Untitled

    Some part of you
      belongs to me;
      a part of me,
        you own.
A special bond that's true,
        yet free,
        is ours
    and ours alone.

    Though loves and years
      may pass between
      our meetings,
      there remains
    that part of each
    that for the other
        smiles
and comes to life again.

—*Edie Patrick*

Basketball

Rolling
Bouncing
Dribbling
Out of bounds
In bounds
Up... Down...
Center... Forward
Two points, three points
Slow ... fast
Slam dunk!

—*Earl Ogburn*

Hell Bent

In a journey of the mind
Between the rust colored bone
Laid out mangled
with bones split and bare
Like you would never see
In a land so darkened
To hell you think
To hell
The sky so black and dark
In a place you see nothing of
Between the acid filled seas
That you can only imagine
In a place so hated by many things
For it is not in hell but in your mind;

—*Jennifer McAlpin*

Tiger

I am a tiger
Big and vicious
I am always being very malicious
I enjoy sunshine
I am a tiger
Sweet and warm
I like to cuddle
And stay warm
I am a tiger
protective
of my den for
it is my own.

—*Angelic Gomez*

Justice

Justice for all,
Black, White, Brown, Red,
Short, fat, thin or tall

Why so much hate,
Violence and shame?
Can't we all be friends?
Can't we let each other be?
Soon it'll be too much to take.

We all are one color,
Alike in so many ways,
We are all human. And to me
That's the way the world should be.

—*Angie Kanthak*

Winter Doldrums

The dreary days of winter
    blight fragile hopes of spring.
The cold rainfall in winter
    drown happy summer dreams
      in sadness and
      despair of brighter days.
Let us burn a cheery candle
    and watch its friendly glow;
    Listen to fav'rite lilting tunes,
      fond songs of long ago.
Let us delight
    in simple pleasures,
    and be in touch
      with those we treasure
        to dispel the heavy gloom.
The sun will surely reappear
    to bring its warmth and light
    to a weary, troubled, aching soul
And give comfort in our plight.
"But when," I cry, "Oh when?"

—*Harriet O. Rauch*

Blind

Blind to the ways of human nature
  Blind to thought of the mind
Blind to everything but the stars
  Waiting for them in the morning
  Staring at them in the night
The only way to communicate to him
    Is through the stars
  The autistic mind of a child
Blind to everything but the stars
        —*Christy Thrush*

March

March is a month of many moods,
Blizzards and winds and a sky
    that broods.
Then out comes the sun so warm and
    bright
Once again the world is warm and
    right.
The season of lent - to pray and
    repent.
Then comes St. Patrick's day — lets
    jig away.
Birds on the wing start to sing -
    it's spring it's spring
Majestic trees start to bud —
Now please be careful - watch
    that mud.
Hip, hip hooray — 'tis a
    lovely March day.
        —*Grace H. Auman*

The Summer Breeze

The summer breeze
blows through the trees
and I can hear it calling!

It whispers here, it whispers there.
It whispers to everyone, everywhere,
and I can hear it calling!

Everywhere it follows me
and I am never lonely, for
it keeps me company!

The summer breeze
gives me ease
and caresses my every thought!

'Tis the summer breeze
that blows through my hair
it floats upon its fresh debonair!

Alas when the summer breeze is
gone, I shall shrivel up and freeze!

The summer breeze can change
and be mighty, it can be
destructive and cruel!

'Tis when the sun is out
I can hear it calling!
It is gentle and fresh, lovely and new,
for the summer breeze blows through the
trees...
and I can hear it calling!
        —*Jamie Lynn Webster*

Aware

Green is the sea
Blue is the air
I am me
I am aware

The birds fly free
The fish don't care
I am me
I am aware

The day dawns free
The night is bare
I am me
I am aware

I try to be free
People stare
I am me
I am aware

Set me free
If you dare
Is this me
Am I aware
        —*Diane D. Wells*

Secrets

They are hidden in a dark well
Buried deep within me.
Not visible to my outer shell
Dark ugliness only I see.

Their excruciatingly sharp sting
An ulcer of the mind.
All the hurt and pain which they bring
I am trapped in a bind.

These are the cruel, bitter realities
I will never show anyone.
I fear the rejection of he who sees
My secrets...known by none.

Please do not to anyone tell
Of the dark ugliness inside my well.
        —*Cara Jackson*

I Whispered Those Words

I whispered those words
But he soothed me
With his loving words
He never left my side
He made me feel like a God
    For awhile
    But then
    I guess he heard or saw he's action
He changed so fast
He was never the same
Sweet and sensitive guy I knew
That every girl would love

    Was he or I ?
        —*Genevieve Robertson*

A Haiku Of Two

    An empty kayak
resting in the stream land it
    and set off again
        —*Michelle Villa*

Swore It Was Forever

Swept me away
But now I'm lost in the dark
Set me on fire
And now I'm left with a spark
Alone you left me beyond the haze
And now I'm lost within a maze.

Too far apart to bridge the distance
  But something keeps us hanging on
Pretending not to know the difference
  Of denying what we had is gone.

Every moment we're together
  It's just breaking me down
I know we "swore it was forever"
But it hurts too much to stay around.
        —*Jennifer McClinton*

Laugh

Its hard for me to remember
But what you did
is imbedded in my mind forever
Why did you do it
You didn't seem troubled
In spite of my problems
You always made me laugh
You would get me on my feet again
How I wish you were here now
For my problems have piled up
And I can't laugh them away
I guess you never knew
How important you were
To me you were everything
If you had told me I could of helped
But now its to late
Cause Honey,
I just can't laugh that gun away.
        —*Darcie Bye*

The Wrench That Climbed A Tree

My little toe was damaged
By a wrench that came from a tree.
The toe was on my left foot,
And was very painful to me.
It took thirty stitches
From the hands of a surgeon fine
To repair the damage that was done
On that small phalanx of mine.
I was putting up an antenna
So I could talk on my radio
When this wrench came hurtling down
To deal that blow to my toe.
It was a mystery to all and sundry
What type wrench in a tree could be.
I said to them, "It's really no
mystery.
It's clear enough for one to see,
Only a monkey wrench climbs a tree."
        —*Charles H. Thornton*

February

February, month of love and hate,
But hate was the main rate.
For my friend her date was late,
She got mad, he got glad
Cause he likes it when she's mad.
But when they broke up
He woke up!!!!
        —*Candace D. Kittinger*

Country Nights

Cool country nights,
by the warm firelight.

Warms me up so,
and set my heart aglow.

This country living,
how I love it so.

There is nothing quite like it,
it fits me just right,
and fills me up with such delight.

Country picnics, Barbecues, fun in
the sun,
the fresh air, room to roam.

This ...the country,
is what I call home.

—Joyce E. Reilly

"My Granddaughter"

A special little girl,
    came to see me —
She was made in heaven,
    As sure as can be...

Her smile was contagious,
    For all to see -
I could feel her energy,
    Flow within me...

When she touched my hand,
    My heart did melt -
It was as though,
    She knew how I felt...

The sweet words,
    That she said to me -
My dear "Tata,"
    I love thee...

I shall never forget,
    That beautiful phrase -
Her words, will be with me,
    For the rest of my days...

—Bill Johnson

Transfiguration

In a cave.
Candles linger,
Aimless shadows.
Souls and burdens
Smokey stares.
Most return.
Inside a circle,
The Wizard.
Colors surround
As the rite goes on.
Dreams designed
Mirrors eyes.
Past erased
Institution
The End.
The Same.
Broken straw.
Last call
while looking at an answer.

—David Sleppy

The Important Side

We always stress the way we dress,
We fuss about our hair,
We flick some frosting on our face
If we're going anywhere.

When the outside's sleek and polished
We feel a sense of pride,
But unlined garments turned about
Will have a seamy side.

I'll always do the best I can
To keep my outside shining,
But, Lord, I want no seamy side -
Please help me with my lining!!

—Jeane Nylander

Ducks

Dirty woolen mists
cling to a placid, fluid mirror,
two sets of eyes trace
ducks' ends slicing
through the grease on the surface.
One hand clasping the other's.
The charcoal mists,
pure in those eyes;
The swarm of ducks,
a dance of swans.
Two sets of eyes
metamorphosing the
arctic, adulterated beauty
back to the paradise it was.
And now is to them.
Their eyes cutting through the present,
as the ducks cut through the dirty water,
Seeing the pleasure of the past
And the shame of the future.

—Abigail Shuler

Cold As Ice

Here I stand like a stone,
Cold and tired and all alone,
Watching the silent falling snow,
Wondering where it all will go.

Will it melt and run away,
Or stay and stay for days and days,
Will it freeze and turn to ice,
Or leave as quickly as the light.

As here I stand all alone,
No place at all to call my home,
Not a person within my sight,
Just me the snow and the night.

As I walk along the street,
Not a person do I meet,
I guess they're all in bed asleep,
Not giving a thought to snow or me.

—Etta Jane Fifer

The Beauty I See

I love the beauty of the snow
    covered trees.
The feel of the crisp winter breeze
    The springtime, crocus, tulips
    and daffodils, and rain.
And colorful wild flower over the hills
    I love the sun, the moon and stars
    And the fresh air we breath.
I love watching little children
    playing happily.
My wonderful family you gave to me
    Thank you God for all of these
You made them all.

—Ida Szostak

No Answer

Lost in a barren wilderness
Coveting an unending torrent
False images rotting your
    perception
A wilderness of pain
Out here there is no
    sanctuary
Only the screams
    of the fallen seraphs.

—Christopher Lee Saenz

Unseasonal Season

March, first day of spring past
Crocus and daffodil
should peek from earthen bed,
Snow covered ground instead.

Trees bow with white wet weight
Above the deer;
It's head erect, snuffling the air
Poised, alert, ready to run
A dainty hoof paws away the snow
To find a morsel just below.

The squirrel, only yesterday
busily carrying leaves to line a nest,
Peeks from its hollow oak
Then turns back to rest.

Winter's last blast
raged through the night
leaving the quiet woods
Glistening White!

—Emma L. Carnaghi

Creativity

The awesome moment
An echo of God's heartbeat
Shimmers through my brush

—Cathrin Gallien

So...Can You?

Can you close the sky?
Cut water in half?
Make an end to the bottom of the sea?
Can you control the weather,
Or stop nature from reproducing itself?
Can you grab, see or taste air?
Can you fly like a bird,
Or say to the future, "Stop?"
Can you stop your bowels from moving?
Or say to the grass,
"Turn another color?"
Can you say to the sun, moon and stars,
"Don't come out today?"
Can you say, "Time, come to an end?"
Can you know what a person is truly
Thinking from day to day?
Can you stop yourself from dying:

Can you?

So...can you?
—*Gail Trait Williams*

Untitled

Catherine
Dakini
Dances In Sky
Coming and going without obstruction
In vast space

Totally empty
She who dances
Gives without hesitation

Encompassing all
Those who know her
Dip pleasure without limit

Like the sea
She accepts everything
Taking you home
—*Frank J. Howard*

A Short Life...?

Here I run through the valley of
darkness, upon a watery cave that
leads to no-where, even home. I shot
from my sub-temperate hiding place
to meet my destiny. Screams of
painful joy burst as I begin my
journey towards the un-fertile land.
Probing inner life as it appears cold
and bloody in a harsh and acidic
environment. But there over yonder
breaks, the gross conquest of my
mission. Approaching the unsurpassable
red-zone I leech my way in, to find
life as a garden of eden that breeds
new life.
—*Francis Michael Xavier Olay*

The Future

As the tears roll down
From my eyes
I know I will have
To say goodbye
And give up all the dreams I had
And hope some good
Will come of this bad.
—*Erin J. Brewer*

Song Of A Hawk

The hawk flies
delicately, strongly
up and down, both
forward and backwards,
as I sit here,
on the low, high ground
watching with lust, abounding!
Oh what power this
bird contains, and
will never know from
start to finish.
How I wish for that
natural act.
Lift me up sweet hawk.
And carry me, shuddering
from this chill, into
the brave new dawn
of calming knowledge
with no basis of
comparison needed.
—*Ben Hammonds*

Memories

All is lost and gone
Disappeared with the rain.
But those odd, sweet memories
Seem to still remain.

True love and friends
All are hard to find.
All are lost and gone
But forever in my mind.

Generations lost and gone
As minds go to waste.
Children fearing awful things
We should not have to face.

All are lost and gone
But forever in my heart.
Me and my sweet memories
Never will part.

Memories are forever
They always will remain.
Staying ever so close
Never leaving with the rain.
—*Brandi L. Manning*

January Peace

Amidst my
    disciplined working-woman
        holiday caring-for-others
self?

I'm missing STILLNESS:

come, January snow
come swirl without sound
    and cover my ground
        and center me
            softly
                gently
                    down.
—*Jane Telfair Stowe*

Someone's Treasure

Bidding was high as the auctioneer
Displayed a box of intricate design.
"Going, going, gone!" He called -
The small velvet box was mine.

Inside no jewels or money,
Only a photo of a baby girl -
A faint smile, two tiny teeth,
Hair in dark brown curls.

A tiny brooch adorns the neck
Of her dainty, lace trimmed dress.
She was someone's pride and joy,
A baby girl - so picturesque.

No name, no date on the photo -
A sentimental, untold tale,
Someone's treasure of long ago
I bought at an antique sale.
—*Bernice M. Bottoms*

"Bewildered"

Am I a poem?
Do I stand on solid ground,
Quicksand or loam?
What about meter?
As for structure, I must confess,
I know even less,
Am I for real, am I alive?
Can I pay the rent, work and strive?
As for the poetic word
Will it touch, feel or see?
Am I to be censored
Or happily set free?
Would heartbeat and emotion
Create verses neat
Perhaps thoughtful, fluent or magnetic
Hopefully proving,
I'm neither genius nor fanatic
But a puzzlement quite gigantic!
—*Frederick M. Spuhler*

Of Five Men

Five men standing round,
each to his own life is bound.
One a liar, one a thief,
One who brought his wife to grief.
One a gambler, totally hooked,
the last a good man, overlooked.
—*Brian F. Allan*

My Dad And I

My Dad and I might be apart
But we are always in each
    others heart
When we are together we stop
    for some bait
Go on a picnic and fish by
    the lake
We are alike we both do say
Our eyes, our hair and even
    our ways
We say good-bye, but that's okay
because now there's a
reason to look forward to
our next sharing days.
—*Christopher G. Kulp*

There Is Only NOW

Do not dwell
too long on the WHY.
There is only NOW
for each of us.

Important to the NOW is how we respond.

Taste ACCEPTANCE. It is an herb that,
mixed with TRUTH,
MUST be digested. Once done,
know your strengths......
they are antidotes
to hate within
that comes from pain.

Defeat exists ONLY if
we mutely accept the blows.

—*Cathy Wright*

"Abortion"

She was in the operating room...
Doctors and all,
Waiting to kill,
Before the world even saw.
Her screams echoed,
Through endless halls,
Taking the life of a baby,
She never even saw .
He'll never see,
God's bright and shinning light.
He'll never see,
A star sparkle in the night.
He'll never dream,
A dream worth dreaming.
He'll never understand,
Life's precious meaning.
He'll never get to live,
A life living.

—*Andrea R. Smelley*

Blast!

A blast goes fast, but
does not last, like a cast,
that's from an arm or a leg.
With some firecrackers inside
the cast, with one fuse lit, the
firecracker would then fizzle
out slowly, until it hits the bottom
of the fuse, With the rest of the
firecrackers that light up, the first
firecrackers would then go ka-boom,
While the rest of the fireworks are
ready to go off, they'd go ka-boom,
ka-boom one after the other. There are
cast would then explode wide open, with
shimmering pieces of the cast flying
apart. While the rest of the firecrackers
go off, they would show those beautiful
bursting colors, that shoot up in the sky
on the fourth of July.

—*Dale Hendrickson*

Freedom

Freedom is gone
Freedom is Non-Existence
Freedom is Dead
Freedom is Controlled
Freedom is Censored
Freedom is Money
Freedom is Power
Freedom is what freedom isn't!!!

—*Geoffrey L. Smith*

Good Shepherd

Good Shepherd, stay close to me;
Don't let me stray far from Thee.
Teach me to lie tranquilly;
In meadows green.
Flow Thee Still waters nearby,
Reflecting Rainbows, on high.
Make Thee my home 'til I die;
This peaceful scene.
Tho' dark shadows creep around me;
Sleep me like a dove.
Fear me not life's perils 'round me;
Guard Thee me, with love.
Grow me old, weary and slow;
Lead thee me gently, and Lo!
The whole wide world's sure to know;
'Tis Thee I love.

—*John Boyd Finch*

Winter

The snow falls like stars
dripping from the sky,
As they dip into the cold
but unfrozen lake,
The last of the birds
chirp silently
As death creeps across the land
The thick white snow
shimmers in the falling
light of the day,
the last of the sun's
rays slowly melts into the
frozen ground.

—*Donna Kirk*

Lone Wolf

Without destination he runs alone
Driven by an unknown hunger.
Instincts pulsate in silence,
constantly seeking a purpose.
Absence of insight
unrecognized need
cause oblivion to companions.
Inside himself further he flees
to the only refuge he knows.
Reality equals survival
as he blindly hunts for tomorrow.
Solitude ensures security
when desires begin to haunt.
A quickening pace,
the illusion of freedom.
Without destination
he runs.

—*Cameon Lynne*

Images

Images in my mind,
Distorted figures of reality
destroy my heart with time.
Images of hate, war and death.
What's happening to me?
I used to be a quiet young man,
but, now my youth is gone.
I'm forced to accept the reality
that I must mature or else,
those images in my mind
will be my reality.

—*Carlos Colon*

My Companion

Jesus is my companion
Through the hours of every day
He leads and guides my every step
As I go along life's way

I don't always do His bidding
But He's there for me the same
If I ask for His forgiveness
And call upon His name

Yes, Jesus is my companion
He's with me day and night
Because He's been so good to me,
I want to do what's right

—*Mary E. Long*

Gold Star Mother

The fire burned
Drums talked
They spoke
Of brave young men.
Osage warriors danced.
But not her son.

Her son lay
On some Pacific Island
Far from Oklahoma
And the dance.

He had been brave,
The medals he had won
Said so,
Japan had lost,
This was the Osage victory dance.
She danced for him.

The gold star on the blanket
That she wore
Gleamed in the fire in the night.

—*Don McIsaac*

Put a Smile On Your Face

The sun always rises
Each day without fail
Every day the sun arrives
Not unlike the mail
The sun will never stop trying
Through rain or sleet or hail
So on this one thought,
The sun is like the mail
Maybe people could learn
From the habits of the sun
Not to let a cloudy day
Stop you from having fun
For another day is on its way
Another chance to have some fun
So put a smile on your face
And you'll be like the sun.

—*Daniel J. Anderson*

Poetic Life

Life is like a poem
Each in its own way.
Some being very different
Others complimenting what they say.

As in rhyming lines,
Life has its own verse,
Some have good meanings
While others have worse.

We go through life's day
On our own dramatic stage.
Without rehearsals of unknown lines,
Written on each moments' page.
As through the point of a pen
Lines of poetic life tend to flow.
So does each person's daily verse,
Tell of the path each one should go.

All poems have rhyme or reason
Each with a certain message.
So life is like a poem,
All stating its own passage.

—*J. Roy Burgess, Jr.*

Parting

And when the hour of parting will come,
Each will go his way.
Then clever shall we be,
Each his mistake will see.

Great will be our words -
Phrases of "Freedom and Tomorrow"
That are higher than love and dreams
And painful, heartfelt sorrow.

And we both will fool
Each other and ourselves,

In our heart will glow a pain
Born of tears repressed.
Poor, Oh, very poor we'll remain
Each one for himself

—*Jeannette Pangborn*

Requiem

The glow of wealth and fame
Embrace but few
Fame is only fleeting
While memories of loyalty
Withstand the warp of time

When you depart this earth
A ballot count on judgement day
Need only say
You passed this way
And took your turn on watch

—*D. V. Wedeman*

Untitled

There can be no faith
for such as we
Unless faith has cause
which we can "see"
Yet not the faith
of a mighty tree
As it buries its roots
To an eternity of darkness
From which it gains
life and the beauty of being.

—*Henry Idzkowsky*

Wanting To Know You

There are many people, I know up above,
Especially two little ones whom
I really love!

I lay on the grass at night and
look up high,
Searching for your faces in the
Darkened sky!

I often wonder, my darlings, why
you had to go,
Always coming up with the same
answer,
"I'll never know!"

There's not a day that goes by
That your not thought about, my
lips form a smile
But, then I begin to pout!

Your with our heavenly father and
one day soon,
I will be with you, my children
next to the stars and moon!!!

—*Cathy L. Thornton*

Memory Lane

I love to walk down memory lane
Especially when I'm blue,
I think of all the pleasant things
I used to do with you.

The evenings when we'd sit and talk
Beside the fireside bright,
Its glow was cheery in the dark
'Twould brighten up the night.

At other times we'd take a walk
Out in the fields of green,
Where flowers bloomed profusely
Along a sparkling stream.

We'd sit and watch the shapely clouds
A sailing cross the sky,
Nary a care would bother us
As the afternoon flew by.

But that was then, and this is now,
Where do I go from here?
From cherished thoughts of memory lane
The thoughts I hold so dear.

—*June F. Lemos*

The Quintessential Muse

Poetry - demon of the spirit;
Exquisite mistress of thought and art;
Thou daughter of all graces;
Interpreter of the heart.

In times of trial, whirlwind, tempest;
Enjoin to even keel
Rivers of refreshing
With linguistic zeal.

Food to empty spirits;
Ode to every start;
Add to each new sorrow
The happy counterpart.

Be thou always our expression;
Be thou our joyous song to sing;
Be thou ever our obsession;
Be thou our eternal spring.

—*Irene Cupido*

The Hole

I saw the eyes of a man
fall into a hole,
falling down, down,
into the dark.

He reached out for me,
but I did not care.
He just fell,
and I saw him cry.

I know what he feels,
falling into an abyss.
The loneliness sets in
and you pray to die.

You need to call for help,
but you're so scared
You can't speak.

Still I see his eyes
as he reaches for anything
to stop his fall.

Still I don't help him.
I have my own problems.

—*Jason Prodinsky*

"Sounds"

I love to hear the gentle rain
Falling down upon my roof
And when it softly taps
Upon my window pane
A newborn babies cry
The beckoning sound of a distant train
Happy sounds of children at play
On a warm, bright summers day
The ringing bells of Christmas time
People rushing to and fro
Grandfather clocks when they chime
Fog horns when they blow

A puppy's first bark - a meadow lark
Boots crunching in the snow
The sweet-sad songs of turtle doves
The north wind when it blows

Yet - Sometimes - The one that is the
most welcome to me - You see -
Is the joyful bark of my little dog Blaze -
Lovingly-Waiting-At the door for me!

—*B. J. Phoenix*

Untitled

Shadow of the night
Falling silently
echoes of the past
calling you to me

Haunting memories
Veiled in misty glow
Phantom melodies
Playing soft and low

In this world - a dream
Life is here and gone
But somewhere in the afterglow
love lives on and on
Dreams of long ago
Meet in rendezvous
Shadow of the night
Calling me to you

—*Bobbi Tusa*

Reflections Of A Cowboy

I once was a cowboy
Far, far out West
I was the real McCoy
In fact one of the best

I'd sing songs at night
And always get into a fight
I'd sock 'em with my right
And knock 'em out of sight

Now I'm old and gray
And haven't much to say
But to think of memories past
Which with me will be to the last.

—*Joseph L. Wegrzyn*

Three Dimensional

By the way of three dimensional
   far from a myth
when living in a world traditional
   from the Dept, Height, and Width.
A planet alone we learn to bless
   for producing newborn birth
upon a time without success
   when predicting planet earth,
Living in a world of prediction
   as Astrology search far beyond
separating the facts from fiction
   before the light of dawn,
The time is night, the world is merry
on December the Twenty Fifth
with precious words for us to carry
   to the Dept, Height, and Width.

—*Ed Lewis*

Kingdom Of The Blind

Mothers without daughters,
   fathers without sons,
   dehydrated water,
   anti-aircraft guns,
   the day of coalitions,
   the politics of ammunition,
the gone but not forgotten art
   of carpet bombing runs.

   Anti-missiles,
   warheads full of death.
   Baby in a gas mask
   trying to catch his breath.
   This is not a simulation.
   This is not a drill.
They intend to keep on killing
'til there's no one left to kill.
   Massing on the border,
   communication lines,
   following the orders
of the Kingdom of the Blind.

—*Harold F. Shannon*

Insight

To live and to learn
From each moment in life
Be sure no to spurn
What seems to be strife.
Each issue is a lesson
From which to glean
What the next session
Of self-study may mean.

—*Edie Stephenson*

Walking In The Rain

I was walking in the rain,
feeling sad and so forlorn,
and was splashing through the puddles
on this rainy summer morn.

I heard the thunder roar,
up in the sky so high;
it was shaking all the earth,
and there was lightening in the sky.

I watched the people hurry,
as I walked along the street;
and I tried to catch the rain drops,
as they splashed down on my feet.

I had my red umbrella
held above my head so high;
it was dripping pretty raindrops
that were falling from the sky.

They looked like pretty crystals,
as they glittered and splashed around;
but as I held my hand to catch them,
they just splashed down to the ground.

—*Doris Schill Huber*

Living In Oblivion

We go circles, we do.
Filled with rhetoric,
Laughing at our cleverness
Until tears fill our eyes,
Purging our sight.
Still, we can not see ourselves.

We watch the stars shimmering
In the mid-day's sun.
As the children dance
The young and young at heart
Watch one another uneasily.
The latter knowing,
The former in blissful ignorance.

We are simple-minded imbeciles
Who see our own words of stupidity
As quick-witted humor.
Those robes of purple
They rest heavy on our shoulders.
We carry them with ease-
In all of our immaculacy.

—*Jerry E. Courtney II*

A Birthday Greeting

We, walked in meadows green
   Filled with trees and flowers
We always made the scene
   Enjoyed such precious hours

We gave each other gifts
   That were especially chosen
To give our spirits a lift
   Also faith to grow in

Happy Birthday, friend
   Although we're miles apart
I love you till the end
   I'll always keep you in my heart
My dear, dear friend

—*Elsa Allison*

A Child's Kiss

Merrily we hopped into a trolley car.
For a free ride to Georgetown.
The driver ding-donged here and there,
How good to leave behind awhile
The many current cares.

Winding back to Foggy Bottom,
We slowly made our exit;
A Jamaican mother and child
Still sitting, caught my glance:
While we exchanged amenities.
Her little boy of two gazed at me
With the sweetest love on earth.
He drew his face towards mine,
And puckered his pretty lips
Into a fragrant budding rose,
I stooped and kissed this angel rare!

He only knew one thing—LOVE!
It was like a cascade
Gushing down from FADELESS HILLS,
To pour its limpid waters
Upon a troubled, turbid world.

—*Adele Haddad*

Eulogy

Speak softly of me with kindness,
For I was a wounded bird,
Who fell too swiftly
When leaving the nest,
And my sweet songs were never heard.

Do not profane my memory
With sorrowed tears for self,
Neither place my ashes on
Some soon forgotten shelf.
But scatter them instead upon
A gentle Ocean's swell,
Where they may ride a Dolphins back
To the place where mermaids dwell.
And on a future Summer's Day,
When sweet scents fill the air,
Breathe deeply of the fragrance —
And know that I am there.

—*Betty Adams Holt*

Friends

Happiness is here to stay
For Sadness has gone away.
It feels good to not be blue
When you find friends are true.

They will help when they can
A friend can be your biggest fan.
Always ready to dry your tears
Help to stop your biggest fears.

Always ready to lend a hand
When you've had all you can stand
Talking to someone is real good
After they have done all they could.

To make your troubles a lot lighter
Making friendship a lot tighter,
Smiles of love show on your face
Friends make a difference at your place.

Select a person you want to know
Sow the seed and watch it grow,
Blossom into a real good friend
Who will be true until the end.

—*Eva Cook*

Spring

The earth prepares
for the advent of Spring
as the snow
lying in coves and ridges
silently dissipates.

A blade of grass
and a swelling bud
extend themselves
in welcome.

The ground warms
in encouragement.

Birds return,
performing in recital
a serenade of exuberance.

The harmony of creation
is resurrected
in anticipation
of rebirth.

—Doris Baillargeon

"Having A Good Day"

I'm repenting my dear Lord,
For the sins that I did commit,
I beseech thee of thy Grace,
So again, a smile will be on my face.

Not abiding by your laws,
Has given me reason to pause,-
To stop, think and pray,
For a better life and day.

When the sun shall rise in the morn,
To the East I will face,
"Dear Lord, make this my day,
One to cherish, not one to erase."

Starting my day making peace,
Love will follow with ease,
"Love thy neighbor as thy self,"
Will guide me through this day,

When sundown doth come to me,
For my soul, I do not have to plea,
I cometh to this shore to pray,
My soul, for you to keep another day.

—Harold L. Sargent

Untitled

I want to thank the Lord
For what he's done for me
He has blessed me so many ways
I can walk and talk and see

He let's me greet the sunrise
As he starts each day a new
It's golden rays sparkle on the grass
Like diamonds in the dew

But most of all I thank him
That he loved me enough to die for me
To put his back to that old cross
That I might be made free

And someday when my life is over
My spirit will take its flight
To yonder world with great delight
And there I'll meet him face to face
And praise Him forever, for His saving
grace

—Effie Doles

The Perfect Gift

How do I find the right gift
for you?
One that will say how I feel
and appreciate all you do.

Candy will be eaten,
Clothes wear out too soon.
Tapes will lose their
excitement and become an
old tune.

Books and magazines only
get read once or twice.
Knick knacks and things to
collect dust aren't really
that nice.

I could give you dishes, glasses,
or another coffee mug.
But the most perfect gift is
God's love and a great big hug!

—Ann Moody

Mother To Son

As pure as the color of a bud,
Forever family, forever blood.
This love runs deep into my soul,
Loving you is all I know
To watch you grow into a man,
To be there when you need a hand.
Just like the song that we sing,
It's our love that we need.
Forever yours, forever mine,
I'll love you 'til the end of time.

—Judy A. White

"A Child's Metamorphosis"

Watch them bud, grow, and bloom,
    from full to empty rooms,
from child to adult,
    from ragged to svelte.
From unruly to sophisticated,
    from needing to leaving,
Dreaming and growing,
    Loving and glowing,
Learning and failing,
    Laughing and wailing,
From diapers to dresses,
    From PJ's to jeans,
A child is an image of oneself,
    For they are part of Life's Schemes.

—Dorothea Colangelo

Shaq Magic

Out of college comes a star,
From half-court he shoots so far.
From the floor and above the rim,
That's his team it must be him.
One slam dunk comes in your face,
Michael J. he has taken your place.
Number 1, there is no doubt,
There he dribbles in and out.
Although he is both young and new,
That's his jersey number thirty-two.
There he soars above the rest,
Mr. Shaq O'Neal.... You're the best.

—Heidi Johnson

The Seasons Of My Life

In early spring, when flowers awake
from their Winter's rest,
My soul seems to say, "Get up, get going
and try to do your best."

In Summer, when the days are hot
and nights are long and sweet,
I sit under the cool shades of a tree
to escape the unbearable heat.

In Autumn, as the leaves are changing
from their green to red and gold,
I want to make the most of my life
before I grow too weary and old.

In Winter, snow just seems to cover
everything in sight,
All the earth is peaceful and calm—
my heart is filled with delight!

—Dori Kregar

The Baby's Face

(Dedicated to Alyssa Margaret)

The baby's face
Full of innocence
Trustworthy as could be
Never afraid of anything
What it hears or what it sees.
The baby's face
Full of laughter, happiness, and joy
Content as could be with nothing but a
favorite toy.
The baby's face
Holds the secrets of the future
Behind the rosy cheeked facade.
The baby's face, you see, was an
encouragement sent by God!

—Cassandra D. Hirsh

A Memory

Each day as I
glance at your
favorite chair,
I see a book
entitled "Ships"
that you've been
reading while
sitting there.
Your glasses
are off-
They've been laid
in your lap,
You've decided
to take a long
peaceful nap.

—Jean Bruning

Night

Shiny streets, after rain dark.
Greedy buck toothed poets
Consume midnight vibrations,
Nukular beatniks, fed thru straws,
Filled with breath, they rage and roar.
Neon lights spit snarled sparks
    at madmen playing after dark,
Daring not to dream of corrupt paradise
    or paper empires
But roll in mirth and muse
    as sunset dies

—Guy Henley

Sunset At Lake Wallanpaupeck

The red sun
Glistens off the
Icy lake, I
Felt pure and
Holy. The red
Sun glistens off
The icy lake
I felt happiness
In my soul
The red sun glistens
Off that beautiful
Lake, I felt
Reborn not torn
And joy not
Scorn. The
Red sun glistens
On that lake,
I felt the
World stopped
And so did hate.

—*Gary Chiaramonte*

A Nation Blessed

God bless America's first sunrise
God bless America's clear blue skies,
God bless America's pioneers bold
God bless America's hearts of gold.

God bless America's plants and trees
God bless America's birds and bees,
God bless America's social mix
God bless America's will to fix.

God bless America's rivers wide
God bless America's subtle pride,
God bless America's Indians brave
God bless America's freedom crave.

God bless America's Bill of Rights
God bless America's awesome might,
God bless America's strong who seek
God bless America's poor and weak.

God bless America's bountiful seas
God bless America's Industries,
God bless America's right to be
God bless America's You... and Me.

—*Ben Lang*

Perhaps

Perhaps that is why I watch the sky,
God watches me with starry eyes.
When heavens clear and the day is new,
I look into His eyes blue.
His Holy Face I behold
among clouds glinted in peaks of gold.
So simple finding peace of mind,
just look up into His eyes so kind.
Sometimes He opens the universe
that I may wonder and converse
Alone with Him under the stars,
a night that totally is ours;
He lets me pass thru barriers,
by telling me it is truth that matters,
and all takes to know Him.

—*Carolyn Grace Wilkey*

God, The Enabler

Why should God enable me - - -
Grain of sand that I am?
Creator of all land and sea,
Is He not the great "I Am"?

Maker of all that grows on earth
Or lives in the depth of the sea.
Why should such a marvelous God
Take note of one like me?

He called the heavens into being - - -
The sun, the moon, the stars;
And, even so, takes time to know
The people of earth with their scars.

He heals our wounds and broken hearts
And gives us strength to cope.
He does it through His love and grace
And His Son, our beloved hope!

His Holy Spirit dwells within
The true believer's heart.
He teaches, comforts and promises
He never will depart.

—*Frances Taylor Smith*

Winter Loneliness

Cold is the breath of the northwind,
　Grey are the winter skies.
Icebound the hills and the valleys
　Defying the sun to rise.

Cold is the breath of the northwind,
　Laughing in icy glee,
Breaking the lonely silence
Like a ghost from the Arctic sea.

　Frozen, and vast, and silent,
　Drift after drift of snow,
Loneliness sobs through the music
In the North wind's song of woe.

Oh God, will it soon be springtime
With love and life and flowers,
To chase away the loneliness
That dwelt in the winter hours?

—*Beulah Lidahl*

Decision

Dilemma of dichotomy
　gropes my common sense
　ropes
　pulls strings untangled
　in my known self.

Walks wires for balance
Jumps fires to dance

My practical fantasy of need —
　fulfilled in my
　intangible theater

Costumes of birth —
　feelings of worth

My gold adorned wig frames
　my face
My forearms cradled by
　diamond studded bands

I sit on the stage —
　cross-legged,
melted with lace, lame, and lavender

Mid-night blue the curtain opens.

—*Beth Anderson*

The Truth

Glaring reality -
hard to face,
Children as adults -
Innocence erased.

Friendships falsified,
family untrue -
Strangers as blankness,
Sky of faded blue.

Why is there no value
to what we hold so near?
It is because it has no worth
But still we believe it's dear.

Hearts become as stone would be -
hardened, cold, and rough,
and alone we stand, and wonder why...
It is we that made life tough.

Still the edge is jagged
and the truth is hard to swallow,
So try to find the truth and then
Just follow, follow, follow.

—*Grace Young*

Meditation On A Violin

A beauteous Violin
Has a human soul and
Expresses love, sorrow, elation —
As I draw my bow
Across the strings
It sings in glorious sublimation.

Of beloved memories
And rich days past —
Sweet hands entangled in the snare.
It cries for loved ones who lie still
In slumber—biding no return —
The music lives—the sweetness, bare.

My violin wakes the sounds
That yield my dreams
With brighter realms to come—
From autumn leaves
to grass turned green,
I play.. I live.. I hum.

—*Doris Patz*

"Goodbye... For Now"

It's the hardest word that anyone
　has ever had to say
It echoes through my heart each
　and every passing day
So many things I should have said
　things I should have done
But my time ran out too quickly
　for your time to pass had come
You will never be forgotten, memories
　shall linger on
I'll never be able to convince myself
　that you are really gone
Weep no more, my mournful heart,
　for this I have to say
Goodbye is not forever,
　we shall meet again someday.

—*Chandra Ernsberger*

"World Of Poetry"

The World of Poetry
Has now closed its doors,
But many good thoughts remain,
Even though, heavy rain pours.

To Sears, we went out shopping,
And Arlene bought me nice clothes
Which really helped my ego
From my head top to my toes.

Arlene and I attended
The "Las Vegas Conference,"
While this was my first plane ride,
And my! What a difference?

For my poem "Still Learning,"
I spoke at the room twelve base,
And received a nice trophy,
Now, it's right in my show case.

Several poems were printed
In a few different books,
Which makes me feel honored
For the neat published looks.

—*Eleanor M. Dirksen*

Kids On The Corner

Kids on the corner
Hats on tight what a
pretty sight.
Boys be walken
Girls be talken
Talken "bout" them boys
When the sun goes down
Every one goes in.
And the nextday it's just the same
Kids on the corner
Hats on tight what a pretty sight.

—*Brandi Winstead*

The House You Call Home

May the house you call home
  Have sturdy walls
And windows that face the sun.

With doors that swing wide
  And a welcome inside
To greet you when day is done.

May the echo of laughter
  Resound from each rafter
And peace and contentment dwell there.

May the house you call home
  Be a haven of rest
Secure 'neath a roof of prayer.

—*Arden Wetzler*

Good-Bye My Love

How can I say good-bye
how can I let you go?
The plans so big, so high,
and wonderful memories of years ago.
My life is crushed, my hopes are gone -
how can I face the life so, so alone??
Good-bye my sweetheart,
good-bye my love,
sleep the deep sleep,
sleep my little dove.

—*Ingrid Chalone*

Dairy of a Week

Christopher had his first concert.
He played a drum duet.
Cynthia dislocated her thumb, and
had to have it surgically set.
JoAnne washed the dog, and
boy, did she get wet.
Sean lost his bag and his books,
is he in trouble? You bet!
Aaron is having fun reading. He
goes through all he can get.
Matthew is such a little sweetheart,
but sometimes he really gets het.
Joshua continually rolls fuzz. But
it doesn't go up his nose yet.
Doug is fighting his inmates. They
still think that he is all wet.
Cindy is singing and writing and cooking
and sewing as much as she is let.

—*Cindy Stever*

The Unknown Hero

Gifted with knowledge
He rushes to a scene
Sirens in the background
He helps someone in need

Time is of the essence
He doesn't take a pause
He quickly sets to work
Before a life is lost

Quiet as a mouse
His will is strong as steel
He takes someone that breaths no more
And helps to make them feel

When his day is done
And he's finished saving lives
He's another type of hero
In his children's eyes

—*Bonnie Seiser*

My Vision

When I keep my eyes on Jesus,
He uses me each day
'Tho one step at a time
We walk along the way.

When I look around at others
The burdens pile so high,
And what the Lord asks me to do,
I answer, "By, and by."

When I see the things that I have done
Then I begin to fall;
For that's when pride gets in my way,
And I don't hear Him call.

Oh, Master, keep my eyes on Thee,
And use me day by day;
That I might give some burdened soul
New hope along life's way.

—*Cora Dreher*

Clyde's Catch

Running around the house
I tripped upon a cat
The screech that followed
Was anything but hollow
When I found in his mouth a rat!

—*Dana L. Lang*

"Listen, Then Help"

Don't turn your back on children
Hear what they have to say.
Ignoring it won't help it
Or make it go away.
It's so hard to believe
That those they trust and love
Could abuse such little children.
I just pray the Lord above
Will help them to survive this
Get over the hurt and pain
Not keep it deep within them
Thinking they're the ones to blame.
When guilty ones walk freely
The innocent children pay.
And the hurt they have inside them
Stays with them, night and day.

—*Dolores Jean Rapp*

Untitled

Their slender fingers reach
heaven bound,
  And one can see the peaceful
rest they have found
  They are fragile frames
left from days gone by
  They have lost their refuge
but they shall not die.
  I look out my window
and I see,
  The truth of the winter
trees.

—*Hope Cheree' Howell*

Rainy

Spend a rainy night with me
  Hold me through the storm
When the thunder rumbles
  Keep me safe and warm
Lets watch a raindrop trickle
  down the window pane
Lets then pick a new one
  and do it all again
When the showers over
  hold me through the night
Whisper to me gently till
  the storm is gone from sight

—*Floyd McCarty*

Solitude

I once knew
How to share love
But now I
Only know solitude.

You left sometime ago
But time only helped
My love to grow.

And I guess you've
Started anew
I only wish that
I could forget
"Our" days too.

Instead all that I
Can do
Is say that
I never stopped
Loving you.

—*Brenna Richardson*

Can You Hear Me?

Can you hear me
I am alive
Feeling the vibes
Sniffing the air, my body is bare
But yesterday I heard a dove
I can't deny, yes! I can fly
Measly amounts of residue
Stain the carpets, times are new
We seem to be
Like an old rotting tree
No places are left for children like me
We standup they shutup
They shutout our feelings
Will they ever realize
Proportionilize down to size
Our senses are mental
Were kind, were gentle
We are one to be.....
Raging in the sea

—*Jennifer McCarter*

Untitled

Great day to be alive!
I am inspired to dream.
The wind lifts me up to the sky
    higher.
    higher.
  I close my eyes —
  feel warm all over.
  My body burns —
I catch on fire from the sun.
  I dive into the water
    deeper.
    deeper.
  O, the soothing coolness.
  I am out of breath!
So glad to be alive today,
  pleasant, pleasant day.

—*Bonnie Westmoreland*

Untitled

I loved you so much
I cannot lie
But now she's got you
And I wish I could die

I thought it was over
Between the two of you
But I was so very wrong
I feel like a fool

I should have told you
But I knew in my heart
You still loved her
Loved her from the start
Now the dream is over
It burst into flame
But I'll always love you
Nothing has changed

—*Jacquelyn Driggers*

Spring

I hope spring never goes.
I like the grass between my toes.
I like the wind in my face.
I hope spring doesn't leave this place.

—*Daniel Crum*

You Are There

The sun came up you were there,
I could feel your spirit
in the air, and all day long
you held my hand, you told
me of the promise land.

At the dark of night I lay asleep
I ask my Lord my soul to keep, your
spirit comes down at the break
of day. I can feel your presence
not far away.

And at night when I pray I
know you are not far away I
sleep in the palm of your hand
come morning my God will
help me stand.

—*Freida Lucas*

"The Night"

My loneliness surrounds me,
  I dare not think or dream.
I lift my teary eyes upward,
  But dark clouds are all I see.

The night shadows dance around me,
  Their evil eyes are filled with glee.
I feel as tho I'm being smothered,
  As tho another day I will not see.

I feel numb with pain and sorrow,
  I have no emotions left to fight.
How can I face a new tomorrow,
  When I can't even face tonight.

—*Dixie Lansberry*

Smoke Tickled The Air

"Just how do you do it, Fred?"
"I don't worry about nothin';"
That's what he said to her.
(My Aunt asked the question.)

  He puffed his cigar,
  just the stub end of it,
  a toothpick to hold it,
  as he sat in his chair.

"Yes, but how do you do that?"

"They ain't nothin' to it;
Ta do it, ya' do it!"

He kissed the tip, again;
Smoke Tickled The Air.

—*Douglas M. Bauer*

A Mountain And Its Beauty

Sitting next to a fountain,
I remember a far off mountain.
Tall and slender,
Beautiful and tender.
Tree's and animals dwindle with care.
Mending in and out everywhere.
Leaves starting to fall.
Children playing
with their feet in the sand
Oh, how grand.

—*Danielle Chavez*

I

So alive, so bright,
i feed
On your radiance.
i, a malevolent shadow,
Watch you,
Stealing flashes of your
Light,
With my dark eyes.
My hunger compels me
To wrap my black cloak
Around you,
To capture
Your brilliance
And make it my own.
But to take you,
For myself, would,
Extinguish
That which i covet.
i return to the shadows
And starve.

—*Christopher Weiss*

Searching My Heart

As I search my heart
  I find nothing
  But despair.

When he walked away
The pain he left me
Made my heart throb
  So painfully.

Longing and yearning
  for what?
I have not yet found.

  But now I know
  There's something there
  Hidden so deep
  That it may take
  Such a long, long time
  Before I find it anywhere.

The pain is fading so very slow
And the love I've been searching for
  is finally coming
Inch by inch towards my hearts's desire.

—*Greta Yang*

Faith And Love

I remember the day,
  I first saw you;
I wanted to date you,
  but what could I do?
So I left it up,
  to someone who cares;
He is my father,
  my Savior upstairs.
And that one day,
  we were at the phone;
I knew shyness was out,
  or you'd be gone.
And ever since
  from that day on;
You stole my heart,
  and it has shown,
I know we said,
  we would take it slow;
But as time goes on,
  My love for you grows.

—*Donna Alexander*

The Darkness Between

I watched a woman die today;
I held her hand so tight.
Pale and restless, as she lay;
It was not a pleasant sight.
She did not know I called her name
While in the dark of night,
The two of us, wanting the same
To feel the soul, take flight.

I think she knew that I was there;
Just standing by her side
Waiting while we tarried here;
In darkness, deep and wide.
Rest now, oh little weary one!
They soon can say, you died,
Life here on earth is almost done;
Death has taken you in its stride!

—*Charlotte A. Folk*

Anemic Freedom

Dwarfed in a shell
I hobble through the motions of ghettolife
Where you have spit me out
Like a broken tooth

You - the garroter of all my hopes and
dreams
and I have bled
in your schools, your parks, your
darkened hallways
and your jails

—*Catherine Anderson*

Baraka Qabalah Kahuna

A new way of thinking about me
I love the, "I" in me, even in my dreams
I pray before I sleep, eat, or play
I gaze at the moon and stars
I am the reader of signs and poetry
I live to die and be initiated again
I take deep breaths, count to ten
And wait to meet the God of Abraham
Abracadabra om lomylomy amen

—*Grave Yard Moss*

Invocare

Walking down a darkened road
I see a faint yet steady glow.
It beckons me to follow it
Just where, I don't yet know.
The deaths of friends and family
Had encompassed me in grief,
But a few steps closer to the light
I begin to feel relief.
I step a little closer,
Doubts and fears start to decay.
Hate and prejudice are shattered
When a stranger smiles my way.
Black and white and red together
Walk the street in peace.
I shake my head and stretch as if
To wake myself from sleep.
I reach the source of light and what
A power is invoked
Standing 'neath the sun of love
Bathed in rays of hope!

—*Darleen Cobbs*

Colors

Black is the color
I see inside
The color I create
With the things I hide
Red is the color
Of my rage
My hearts pain
When I'm betrayed
Blue is the color
I feel inside
The color of those sad songs
Every time I've cried
Green is the color
Of my wildest desires
The men I love
That light my fire
Purple is the color
Where I love to hide
The color of dreams
Where I choose to die.

—*Angela Marie Gamble*

Secret Kisses

Secret kisses are all I've ever known
I send him kisses when I'm all alone.
He doesn't know just how I feel,
Or that my love is real.
He's the right guy for me,
But this is something he does not see.
Every night I hope and pray.
That he'll return my kisses one day.

—*Jill Jones*

Goodbye

I hear the sound of music,
I think the thought of pain.
For nothing else could matter,
When I was weeping in the rain.

On that dark and stormy night,
Memories mingled in my head.
For when it came to talking,
There was nothing to be said.

I miss the conversations,
And the comforting abode.
For then I couldn't imagine,
There being an "End of the Road."

Time will go by slowly,
But I never will forget you.
I hope that you will find someone,
To share your thoughts and talk to.

—*Elizabeth Webster*

Untitled

I do not "wish I were sixteen again".
I wish I could trade one yesterday...
　　　back when...
　　　for two tomorrows.

What days would I choose?
The wisest would not know.

Falling in love...
The birth of a child...
Anyway, I would lose.
The day I was closest to you, Lord..
If only I knew... I would choose.

—*Betty Bishop Sovinski*

Time and You and Me

Oh where has the time gone?
I wish I knew.
I'd bring it all back.
And spend it with you
We had good times
And we had some tears
As we went through
All those years.
It seems like yesterday
Our children were small
But oh how time
Has changed us all
A lot of good friends
Have gone away
And we will too
Some secret day
Oh where has the time gone?
I wish I knew,
I'd bring it all back
And spend it with you.

—*Della Kromer*

If I Were An Angel

If I were an angel
I'd give the world a fright.
I'd shower it with sparkles,
Oh so shinny bright.
I'd send it down a ribbon,
For all to hold on tight.
For each and every person,
For them to see the light.
Around the world this ribbon,
Would everyone unite.
For peace upon this earth
Would be a very lovely sight.

—*Carmen Bozzone Michels*

If I Knew You And You Knew Me

If I knew you and you knew me,
If both of us could clearly see,
And with an inner sight divine,
The meaning of your heart and mine,
I'm sure that we could differ less,
And clasp our hands in friendliness
Our thoughts would pleasantly agree,
If I knew you and you knew me.

If I knew you and you knew me
As one knows their own self,
We could look each other in the
Face and see there in, a true'r grace.

Life has so many woe's,
So many thorns for every rose.
The "why" of things our hearts
Would see,
If I knew you and you knew me.

—*Diana Lynn Rice*

Autumn

Man too is like a leaf
In that he may be caught up
In the joys and sorrows of his seasons
The winds of his life
And vary his soul with a bright myriad
Of colors and hues
Only to be tread upon and crushed
By the indignant footfalls
Of society

—*Erich Doser*

"Journey's End"

At the end of my journey
   I'll see Him and say,
"Oh, Lord God
   what a wonderful day".

To be so alive
   and see you face to face.
And bask in your
   precious amazing grace.

For the sound of this grace
   you've given to me,
Is sweet music to souls
   that have been set free.

Free from the burdens
   that weighed us down.
Now clothed with a fine
   white linen gown.

Ready to praise you
   for an eternity.
Because on Calvary
   you died for me.

   —*Carol Kamaile*

For You

She's a fire
I'm burning
All feelings
   aflame
   blazing
    desire
   Reeling
   Insane
   Falling
   about her
I whisper
   her name
She's afire
I'm Burning
   a fire
   aflame.

   —*Fred Wasnak*

Starting Over

For the first time in my life,
I'm starting over.
I don't know what I'm doing
Or where I'm going.
I'm lost,
Confused.

So many ideas flying around in my head,
But can I remember them all?
All the times.
Each time.
This time.
What now?
Where to go?
What to do?
When to do it?

I suppose it doesn't matter.
I feel like going splat.

   —*Clyde E. Willey*

Just Ask

There is someone I like
I don't know who,
But if you ask,
I'll say it's you!

   —*Erin Harris*

Changes

Do we walk passages of darkness,
In faith of finding the light .
Do we sit and wait,
For time that's slipping away.
Do we hold on to doubt,
And never revive the trust.
Do we save the hope,
To find it being shared.
Do we sleep in peace,
So the soul can rest.
Do we seek the clean heart,
Then dare to tell the story.
Do we announce the strength,
By continuing to watch the weak.
Do we want to change it all,
But never face the challenge?

   —*Caroline -Louise Shaaber*

To Come And Die For Me

You can see the sadness
in His silent eyes
As His bloodstained face
turns to the skies

Then a steady rain
begins to fall
It is finished, it is done
As He dies for all

Jesus, oh Jesus,
You completed Gods great plan
As the pain raced thru Your body
the nails thru Your hands

Love, such love
but oh, how can it be
You would leave the splendor of Heaven
to come and die for me

The quiet tomb was empty
where they had laid Him dead
For Jesus Christ had risen
just as He had said

   —*Hope M. DeLarme*

Untitled

I wake from you
In late afternoon sun
And watch
The shadow of birds
On my paper shade
I hold my heart
Against trespass
And wonder
How long you slept
With your first love

   —*Jazz Morgan*

Life

Life what makes it so interesting
is it like loves deadly sting.
As beautiful as a ladies dress
or God's hands ready to bless
As wonderful as a spring morning air
or a ladies skin so fair
As a rowdy as a man that doesn't shave
or a child who miss behaves
As painful as a murder's stab
or a mother mad extremely mad
It's all these things all wrapped in one
that makes life so much fun

   —*JaNeice Jones*

Sultry

Drawn forward by attraction,
in march of nervous treading,
to see the silklike vision.
Her sultry, wind blown hair
was thick to the palming touch.
Smooth—the joy of wondrous strands;
a mark of clearest beauty.
Sweet flowing, purple jelly
was the image of her dress.
Sweeter still, were her silent lips
awaiting a moist response.
Glazed eyes from a sharp sun
meet the shadow of his silhouette;
with freshness alive to vibrant tears,
her weep is gathered in his soul.

   —*James Wesley Duren*

Patience

When I'm cozy
   in my bed
with my pillow
neath my head
and I close
my sleepy eyes
and I tell myself
such silly lies.
How I can stand
to live without you,

   and there are
Better things to do

Then wait and wait
'til such time that
you might tell me
you are mine.

   —*Jessica Marks*

Kaleidoscope

Some of the beauty I have seen
In sixty-five years or more,
Is the thrust of a bird's wing
As he climbs the skies to soar.

At home on a summer's eve,
A departing sun shafts bold.
He strikes across the window-pane
Shattering my room with gold.

When thoughts of spring have left me,
The soft, pink peonies bloom -
I rush to toil on bended knee
Before this altar of June.

The unfolding of a flower
I saw one moment in time.
Five spurred red petals unfurled
And became the columbine.

A cache of beauty I have caught,
Hidden deep within the brain!
In winter's subduing sleep,
I shall see it all again!

   —*Francine Madeleine Tyler*

Pain And Desire Mingle As One -

In the heights of heaven -
In the depths of hell -

It isn't always easy to tell -

I see my soul reflected in your eyes -

Bound to you with such fragile ties -

So difficult to build -
So easy to destroy -

Even so: Knowing you has
Been a joy -
　　　—D. Bowen

The Visitor

Tiptoeing into my room
　　in the quiet of the night,
She bears the gentle prodding
　　of a distant memory.
I am grateful for the gift she brings;
The mood is light, - 'til longings
　　for days gone by,
Down the bird of joy in flight!

She greets me at the seaside
　　while I gaze from the shore;
And whispers not; but
　　sighs, with silent eloquence.

Then, "Spread the canvas wide,"
　　I say, "and paint the colors
Boldly! For life is life
　　and breath is strength!"

My visitor obliges, as
　　echoes of the past return
And both sorrows and delights
　　give wings to my tomorrows.
　　—Carol Barron-Karajohn

The Scar

The wound He healed had festered long,
Inflicted deep, by sin and wrong,
For years it pained, so deep inside,
That hope of healing all but died.

But Jesus saw and felt the pain,
He gave His hope and love again;
In time He healed the wound within,
The healing hurt, but He can win.

The wound has closed, but now it made
A scar that never more will fade.
So permanent, that ugly scar,
My life forever it will mar.

I turn my eyes to Jesus pure,
I see His scars, He suffered more!
They symbolize a victory won,
The power of Jesus, God's own Son.
　　—Evelyn E. King

Love

Love is good.
　　It runs and leaps,
and lots of secrets it keeps.
　　People can love.
　　People can hate but,
　　people who love really
　　rate.
　　—Andrew Tan

My Secret Garden

I have a secret garden that's deep
inside of me.
I go there when I'm troubled and let
my mind go free.
Its where I rest and meditate,
and weed out all my cares—
I just lean back and close my eyes,
and no one knows I'm there.
I'm glad I have my secret place
where no one else can go,
Its where I heal all my wounds,
and this is where I grow.
　　—Dorothy A. Leavers

"I Remember Spin The Bottle"

A boy from the past has come
　　into my life
No longer a boy, but a man
　　fine with strife.
The man, like the boy still
　　likes to play
Hurt by his loved one's
　　every day.
I care for this man
What does he want?
A companion, a friend, a lover
　　or knot?
A casual encounter, soon
　　for got.
Perhaps a bridge from the past
Releasing him from his exile.
　　—Holly C. Ward

Saunter down the lane by light
Into that splendid noble night.
Linger among the bows of trees.
Pause to feel the pleasant breeze.
Smell the fragrance of the grass;
Pick a flower as you pass.
Sing a lilting, charming tune
As you gaze up to the moon.
Climb a tree, sit on a limb,
And look out o'er the city.
Paint a picture with your mind,
And make it very pretty.
　　—Angela Clodfelter

The Mist

The mist came softly creeping
Into the city late one night;
Surrounding each and every thing
Till none was left in sight.

It's damp and swirling motion
Engulfed each lamp and tree;
Each building was an outline
That one could barely see.

It danced around each moving thing
Consuming in its quest;
Creating shadows here and there;
Not stopping once to rest.

Now as the dawn approaches
And we see the days first light;
So quiet as it first appeared
The mist creeps out of sight.
　　—Bobbie Dickinson

The Future

Is it fair to try to see
　　into the future?
Will God forgive
　　if I but take a look?
But the strength He gives is for
　　our daily burdens.
Dealt out as though a mother
　　to her child.
A hand held out
　　to help the blind that stumble,
to help the weak and weary
　　on their way.
So let contentment be
　　my dish at present.
Let me enjoy the days
　　as each one comes.
Looking to the future
　　as a blessing,
That I may meet my trials
　　one by one.
　　—Juanita Fuss

To Love And Be Loved

To love and be loved
　　is a beautiful theme,
If your lover is real
　　and not just a dream
Sweet is the kiss in true
　　love's esteem, but

Deep is the sorrow when
　　reality meets dream
To laugh and be gay is a sign
　　of love's bliss. But
To laugh then to cry at
　　the loss of that kiss
Is a pain that is classed
　　as a pain of its' own
For little can change love's seed
　　once it is sown.
　　—Helen Rude

Why Do People Make Fun Of Me?

Why do people make fun of me?
Is it the way I look.
The way I see.
Or the way I hold a book.

It makes me very sad.
When people are bad.
And decide to make fun.
Of people who can't run.

Sometimes I wish.
That I was a beautiful fish.
So that I can swim away.
From people who act that way.

Now I don't care.
When people stare.
Because I know that I am smart.
And God's precious work of art.
　　—Bunny Martin

Rumor

Rumor
  is like
  a week old bag of garbage...
  while waiting at curbside
  for impending burial...
  is torn into and carried
  about the community...
  by ravenous canines.

Oh - the stench
Oh - the irretrievable collection
Oh - such needless waste!

    —*Judy Terry*

Joy

Joy
is my enemy

Sorrow
my only friend

Happiness
is only a dream

Pain and suffering
my constant companion

Peace
deludes me

Misery
stays by my side like a faithful dog

Love
avoids me

Loneliness
embraces me

This melancholy wind
keeps dispersing the accumulated leaves of
my joy;

Come kind soul; gather my scattered
leaves, heap me together

Make me whole

    —*Howard Torrence Allen*

Untitled

Is there a face behind that mask?
Is there a soul-a being-one to
  love-one who loves-one who
  cares-one who is cared for?
Why hide?
Is it lonely behind there-is
  it cold-dark-are you scared?
I would help-but how?
Is the mask irremovable?
Would a heart-a rose-a
kiss-unstick that fearful-
demon-like-unreachable mask?
Tell me how?

    —*Brett Richards*

Untitled

It's hard to smile when
Life's so blue.
And someone you love
Is thru with you.
I know it hurts
But hang in there.
And maybe you'll
meet someone who's fair

    —*Jeff W. Wight*

The Phantom Lover

The lover I have dreamed of,
Is yet to come to me,
I see him in the distance,
Beneath the old oak tree,
I can smell the blossoms,
He holds there in his hands,
And when he turns his head,
He smiles at me,
I know he is from a foreign land.

Alas I hear my Mother call me,
As she climbs the stairs,
I quickly blow a kiss to him,
Before he disappears,
And as I gaze out of the window,
As I climb into my bed,
I tell him in a silent prayer,
That when I'm all grown up,
It is him I'm going to wed.

And when I wake each morning,
There's a RED, RED ROSE ON THE
PILLOW BY MY HEAD.

    —*Eunice Clarke*

Joy

Joy is deep lasting contentment
It colors everything you do
It invades you
With a bright warm glow—
The absence of loneliness
Brings joy!

Ecstacy cannot be sustained
By it's nature
It must be brief.

Friends give joy
All those who share with us
Add to our joy—

Lovers must share joy
To stay lovers
They must share all the parts
So they can unite
And experience ecstacy

    —*Gabrielle Weiss*

A Future Hope

As I walk along the shore,
it is the waves that I adore.
I see the birds that fly so high,
in the clear blue yet cloudy sky.
The sand below is golden brown,
that glistens like a jeweled crown.
The green trees glow from within,
as they sway in the gentle wind.
The snow capped mountains rise so high,
that they seem to touch the cloudy sky.
And as I walk along the shore,
it is this world I do adore.

    —*Julie A. Thies*

Birthday Thoughts

A milestone here, a birthday there,
It makes us still and thinking.
Where are we going, where, oh where?
Will beacon-lights keep blinking?

We came to live, link of a chain,
Forefathers' blood and virtue.
Pass many stations like a train,
One day, we discontinue.

On goes the circle, God's intent,
Your body leaves, your spirit stays.
Part of your soul remains content,
Whenever child and grandchild prays.

The birthdays come, the birthdays go,
Dwindling by years as taught by time.
With happy heart go to and fro,
Take ev'ry day as gift sublime!

    —*Eberhard W. Gress*

Fog

Fog is a mist that covers my heart,
It never lets me love.
It haunts me all during the night,
It fits me like a glove.
It blocks me from the warm sunlight.
It hides me from the moonlit night.
Through it there shall seep no light.
For the fog holds mournful cries.

It leaves no future for to see.
The past it truly hides from me.
It leaves no decisions for to make.
It only leaves chances one must take.
All lonely hearts left here to break.
For the fog holds mournful cries.

    —*Angela Sherwood*

"What Is Love?"

Love is what makes the world go 'round.
It picks you up when you are down.
It makes you happy when you're sad.
Love's the best friend you've ever had.
Love is like a butterfly.
It can bring you down, or make you high.
What is love? Here's a clue.
In just one word, love is "Y-O-U?"

    —*Jessica Stinson*

The Cliff, Alone From Within

It's majestic, to look up at.
  It's fearsome, to look down from.
It's part of the mountain.
  Yet stands alone.
It has its own beauty.
  But is part of the picture.
The daring may climb it
  An eagle may glide from it.
Time sculptured it.
  The elements, enhanced it.
Its rugged features, give it power.
  It's skyline, gives it grace.
The sunrise, brighten its color.
  The sunset, changes it.
It stands alone,
  From within.

    —*Gary L. Spack*

A Case For Lust

True love finds
Its root in lust:

When passion's fruit
Is nipped by frost

And falls desperate
To frozen ground

Love can reach
Farther down

And break its fast
On the very decay

Of those too righteous
To do the same

—Daniel Newberry

Love

Love needs time to spread
It's wealth;
Is not peace a form of
Mental health;
Is not time a special gift,
When given to your Love who
Needs the lift.
Sharing Love in equal parts;
Opens minds, and, touches
hearts.

—G. A. Panttila

...For Him Only

He understands...
   just how I feel.
He feels...
   when I'm gay or depressed.
He senses...
   my every thought, mood, and emotion,
And when things go wrong ...
   He knows best.

He's patient and tolerant...
   when I don't do as I should.
He's warm and tender...
   when I'm lonely.
And I love him deeply...
   for all that he is.
And I live my life...
   for him only.

—Donna Kolojeski

From Esenin

Oh ploughed fields magnificent,
Kolomna's saddened air,
On my heart beneficent
Shines Russia bright and fair.

The versts go by like fleeting birds
Beneath the horses pace.
The brilliant sun in handfuls
Throws showers in my face.

O noble land of sudden floods
And gentle wafts of spring!
Here the schooling I received
The stars of dawn did bring.

And I thought and pondered
On the Bible of the winds.
I herded golden cattle
Which Isaiah helped me tend.

—Edward Jamosky

Sammy Salamander

Sammy Salamander
   Lay snoring on a rock,
And when I woke him for the time,
   He yawned, "I have no clock!"

"Oh, Sammy Salamander,
   Why have you just four toes?"
"Because my friend," he smiled at me,
   "They take me where I goes!!"

"But Sammy Salamander,
   What do you do for fun?"
"A-h-h," said he, "I snap at flies,
   And lie here in the sun."

"But Sammy Salamander,
   Won't you get a burn?"
"Oh no, said he, "Because you see,
   I'll do a big U-turn!"

Then Sammy Salamander,
   Closed his eyelids to the morning.
He didn't see me wave good-bye,
   For, he just lay there snoring.

—Beulah Weeks

Alone

Deserted, stranded...
left all alone,
gazing bitterly upon the emptiness.
A search for the familiar,
a quest for the known.
I still can't see it...
forever alone!
What's lost, can't be found;
what's desolate, remains barren.
Left to wander
in this dwelling place,
forced to accept the bleakness
of each and every
empty...
space!

—Jennifer Sommer

Incessant Wind

Incessant wind,
Lend me your speed
So that I may heed
the calling of the universe.
Being freedom bound
you surround me
only momentarily
before your departure
to never heights.
What is your essence
for I only feel your presence
as you fleeting glide
across me,
touching so softly.
Seemingly you have no end
yet no time to spend
In this solitary place
where I hide my face
   from others.

—Beverly Day

To The Men Who Died At Pearl

The shells and bombs are silent now,
Lest those who sleep awake again.
Tread softly here, and breathe a prayer
That these brave men died not in vain.

Their bodied lye in honor here,
While we who tread the decks above,
Can only offer them our tears,
And to our land undying love.

Pray they rest in confidence,
That we who live will n'er forget.
Pray the spirit of these men,
Deep in our hearts, lingers yet.

—Edgar H. Stevans

My Best Friends

Kids are people too
Let me tell you
I have two daughters
Who fill the house with laughter
Reba is seven, and Gabrielle is two
If I didn't have them; I don't
   know what I'd do.

Reba is normal
Gabrielle is not
She has Downs Syndrome
But Oh, what a tot.

They encourage my work
They encourage my play
Dear God, I couldn't do it
   without them
I thank you, day by day

—June Roberta Patmon

Grey

There is no black and white
Light turns to dark
And darkness to light
As sure as the sun rises and falls

There is no good
There is no evil
There just is

How can I live when
I have no dividing lines
To show me the way

How can I walk the path
When all I see is grey

Never knowing where to turn or why
Never knowing who is really at my side

I want to see through the mud and murk
I want to see through the clouds of the day
But all I see is grey

I am grey

—Claudia E. Price

Wondering

Looking in your eyes
   Makes me wonder what you see.
Listening to you
   Makes me wonder what you say.
Your hugs and kisses
   Make me wonder what you think.
Watching you leave me
   Makes me wonder what I did.

—Beatrice Veronia Rasdon

Blushing Diety

Glide upon the clouds,
Lightly scale their highest peak;
Gaze at hidden light —
Sun's cross-beams gently beckon,
Trek rugged cobblestone path.

Seek your beloved
Who dwells 'midst thistles and thorns.
Ponder Sun's burnt face —
Blushing Deity's embrace!
Accept ye, "Poor Jesus" grace?

Cherish life's challenge
For Love dwells within, without;
God bears human face —
Homeless, hungry, out-casts cry:
"Transform our lives; become Christ!"

Joyfully walk path
Marked by Jesus' blood, sweat, tears,
Follow his footprints.
Descend to your hollowed space
Surrender to LOVE's embrace!

    —Sister Barbara Mary Lanham,
O.S.F.

Inside My Heart

It's not something you can see
Like a bird in flight
More like a smile, not seen
In the dark of night
It's not something you can touch
Like a muscle rippling tight
More like a feeling
In the early morning light
It's not something you can hear
Try hard, though you might
More like two hearts beating
In bed, side by side tonight

But, if my heart were open
And you could look inside
You would see and touch and hear
The love that sometimes hides
But, the love for you my dear
Is for you and you alone
And I hope that you know
It has never been as strong

    —Jackie Klipfel

"The Long And Short Of It All"

When you wonder about things
like I often do,
You can put yourself in a story book
just like Winnie-the-Pooh.
As you know he's just a fairy tale
bear,
He doesn't have wrinkles or long
Curly hair.
He doesn't have to dream to make
wishes come true,
They're already his, he got them
from me and you.
To make a long story short and to
end it all,
Live life to it's fullest, let's all
have a ball.

    —Donna Southers

Final Farewell

I was cleaning out my bookcase
Like I once cleaned out my heart.
I came across your picture
And It caused memories to start.

Memories not feelings
For you my hearts asleep.
The giant first that it once was
Released the hurt so deep.

It's been awhile since then
I'm over you for now.
I had to learn to trust you
For I'd forgotten how.

I'll put your picture back in place
Between the pages of my mind,
And leave you as you once left me
So very far behind!

    —Christy Lynn Stojak

A Gift

A gift from above,
Like three precious pearls,
Was sent to this earth
As three little girls.

The first was so rare,
And such a surprise,
With gold silken hair
And large China-blue eyes.

The second bright gem,
Not like the first-born,
Had sand-brown tresses
And brown eyes so warm!

The third to appear,
To claim a new place,
Had deep pools of love
Glow forth from her face.

They flowered and grew
Beneath God's bright sun.
They loved; and were loved,
By just everyone.

    —H. Louise Frenz

Urban Raindance

Sheets of teal, and indigo
like wings of giant ancient birds
strung on wires to fly dry
the sky grimaces, and barks.

Counted threads hung to gather
the air, the depth of smell.
The freedom of dream nets
made to lie flat on a bed.

Finally then it rains
and the wicks are taken in.
Frames of glass pulled down
outside flower petals fall.

    —Heather Gyles-Lingard

Our Friendship

I've never had a friend
Like you,
To teach me things
I never knew.

To guide me through
My life on track,
And never saying things about me
Behind my back.

Our friendship to me
Has too many words to say,
But all that really counts,
Is that we're here together
Today.

    —Alicia Young

Tuesday

You play golf and the piano
Like you play me on the phone
You schedule me like a tournament
And I am happy to be caddie
Your message smacks of massage parlors
So I offer my weary flesh for a lesson
We plan our dinners like battles
In West Hollywood we go Italian
Squeeze me in between classes
Call me on your cellular phone
Grateful I go home to wait
Your tactile voice crawls to me
While my courage shrinks
Like the ball under your strike
I am the tee you barely touch
Or the keys that tremble Debussy

    —Dana Loewy

Little Red Robin

Little red robin, what you doin'?
Little red robin up so high.
Little red robin, what you doin?
Gonna fly away in the bright blue sky?

Little red robin gonna try your best?
To find another and build your nest?

Little red robin lookin' so lonely.
Little red robin don't fly away,
I love you the way I see.
So won't you stay another day?

Little red robin, try your best,
You need a reason to build your nest.

Little red robin, I wish for you,
To build your nest as soon as you can.
Way up high in the sky so blue,
With wings spread out like a Japanese fan,
Another will find you very soon,
And together you'll fly off to the moon.

Little red robin, you did your best,
I see you've another to share your nest.

    —Ian S. Osborne

"Kayla"

Little tiny fingers
Little tiny toes
Little tiny mouth
Cute button nose.

Angels are tip toeing
In your peaceful dreams
Protecting you from harm
At least that's how it seems.

So little princess of slumber
Sleep, and sleep away
May Jesus' safely keep you
And bring love to each new day.

All to soon the little
Will turn into the big
And all these precious memories
Give us the will to live.

—*Anita Gale Moore*

True American Cry

The American Indian of this land
Lost and wandering alone.
How do we raise our children
If we have no home?
  The white man takes
  And gives us dust.
  They make us promises,
  But we know not to trust.
This land was ours before you came.
You gave no chance for us to share.
All you did was give us shame,
And you never asked if we did care.

—*Evelyn Ramsey*

Alley Cat

He's the king, that alley cat,
Lot's of muscle, little fat.
White boots scamper across
  the floor,
Empty's food bowl, begs
  for more.
Minds his place within
  the house,
Doesn't touch the kittens
  mouse.
Learned his lessons as a
  stray,
Touches only what he may.

—*John McReynolds*

Love

Love is a game
Love is a word
Love isn't always
  the same
Love is like a bird
Love comes and goes
Love feels good from
  head to toe
Love is crazy
Love can be silly
  at times
But we all have been
  or know what
  Love is.

—*Christina Lynn Hiles*

Love

Love is here
Love is gone
Love is true
Love is wrong
Love is great
Love is bad
Love is happy
Love is sad
Love is Love
and Love is
alive.
Love shouldn't
be debated Love
will survive.

—*Jennifer Emerson*

The Test Of Time

Love stands the test of time
Love will survive the climb
Of the mountain of life
And survives the slash of a knife
So go, go your own merry way
You will be back to love another day
I have faith in you
Whatever you do
You will always be mine
You will wear my love like a sign
So where-ever you go
I will love you so
In this powerful climb
Love will stand the... the test of time.

—*Erik Sternberger*

A love poem

Ocean blue no longer
love's depth patiently fed the fish
scaled children.
Fury crashes the rocks
seeking union;
mist reaching out to sky, finding
companion ethereal.
Playful clouds romance the wind
and caress the gulls
with trust.
Heat fills the cirrus with desire
as his friends come to celebrate,
thunderclap ecstacy releases sweet.
Passionate storms cry tears of joy
to rain love on itself
giving back all
the ocean gave.

—*Jeff Johnson*

"Untitled"

A pure aura breezed through
  my lethargic soul...
The sea gulls gossiped a consequential
  bit about you...
How I wanted to find an impeccable
  emerald of purple majesty...
You took my hand and led me
  to the place
Where we first wrote love poems
  in the sand.

—*Dena Narese*

"The Golden Age"

They tell us 'tis the Golden Age,
Many times you've heard it said.
But for some the only thing "Golden"
Is the fact that they're not dead.

For the hair has turned to silver,
The teeth "They're not there,
The joints have frozen over,
There is stiffness everywhere!

But yet when you mull it over,
And all is said and done,
'Tis better to be living it,
Than to have the other one!

But it's still a lovely life and I
Thank God for everyday I have —

—*Betty Hargrove*

Happy Birthday Jesus

Happy Birthday to you Jesus
may you have a Joy filled Day
may all your Children please you
in the things they do and say.

I'd love to give you a birthday gift
Stained glass windows or a new Church
But we know this is impossible
So my mind keeps on the search.

But what would please you Lord?
What can I do for you?
You gave your life for me
That's it! I'll give my life to you.

I'll praise your name every day
and I'll do what you'd have me do
So take my life and use it
It's my birthday gift to you.

—*June Cooksey*

Untitled

To have an unmade bed
Means I have a place to sleep
Dusting, mopping, cleaning,
Means I have a place to keep

The stack of dirty dishes
Means that I've had food to eat
The ringing phone and doorbell
Means I have friends to greet

A pile of dirty laundry
Means I have clothes to wear
Two cups upon the coffee table
Means I have some one to share

To hear the words 'I love you'
Means happier I could not be
To know peace and contentment
Means God is taking care of me

—*Dawn A. Yost*

Family

Sometimes being family
means more than just
smiles and good times.
It means caring for each
other and building brides
of trust. It means not
being afraid to ask and
answer difficult questions.
It means accepting one
another for what they
are. It means pulling
together when things
get rough, knowing that
love will be there forever
no matter what.

—*Ethel Anderson*

En Route

Drops of rain, or are they
Melting ice?
Rays of majestic sun
Warming my window pane.

Seas of clouds, or are they
Passing alps?
Scene of simple purity
Outside my moving plane.

Suddenly, view of tiny isle
Looking like a gem
Before my very eye, though
Faraway from my reach.

Descend I must,
My heart is filled with joy as
I fulfill my dream of seeing this
Land of charm and harmony.

—*Julia H. Low*

Real Living Really

Waking up to a brand new day,
Mixing work with a bit of play,
Putting faith in our God to pray,
That's real living, really.

Giving thanks for the joys in life,
Asking help if sad times are rife,
Feeling sure of true peace, not strife,
That's real living, really.

Loving folks with all kinds of faces,
Opening doors in all kinds of places,
Serving God as we run life's races,
That's real living, really.

—*Frances Tunnell Carter*

My Love For You

Each time I look at you
    my heart goes crazy,
This kind of love is hard
    yet so easy.
You don't know I'm there,
You don't know I care.
I feel visible to everyone
    except you.
Some day you'll have to see,
My love for you
    will always be.

—*Jenne Wilson*

Love Is

Love is what it is,
More than mortals can describe.
It defies description and
Demands attention and
Commands you to call it a vibe.
But, call it what you will,
Love will be love still.
The question asked,
What is love?
Deserves an answer.
And the answer is,
Love is an emotion,
Not some silly notion;
Sent to us from above.

c. — 1989/1993 Alan O. Burrell
Up To Par Publishing Co. BMI
reprinted by permission of
Up To Par Publishing Co. BMI.

—*Alan O. Burrell*

Untitled

My dearest baby
    my angel child
    your skin so soft
    your eyes so mild

My eyes fill with tears
    when I see you there
    in your fathers arms
    in an easy chair

Your birth to us
is a dream come true
        until today
    we didn't know you

We thank you baby
    and we thank God too
for the blessing he gave us
    when he gave us you..

—*Deborah Lynn Quaale*

Untitled

Twelve years we've been together,
    My four-footed companion and I.
    I've watched your muzzle fade
        With the passage of time,
    Your eyes not as clear and bright
            As they once were.
    Those legs which romped around me
    Now stiffly move to match my stride.
        You know me better than anyone,
    Having been there when things were grand
        Remaining when life seemed hopeless.
            You trust me implicitly,
        Always loving and utterly devoted
            Even during those moments
            When I feel most unworthy.
        Why must your time on earth
            Be a fraction of mine?
                When you've gone
            The best part of you
            Will live long in me.

—*Demrie Alonzo*

"Steping Forward In The Sand"

There I stood peering,
My future in my hands.
I took a deep breath,
And stepped forward in the sand.

Unknown feelings filled me,
Until I could barely see.
But with each step I took,
I knew this is what I wanted to be.

The road was very rough,
And the night was ever so long.
But the unknown feelings inside me,
Were finally once gone.

Everything became familiar,
With each day that came along.
No longer were things impossible,
But all my fears were gone,

Here I stand knowing,
My future is in my hands.
I took a deep breath,
And stepped forward in the sand.

—*Christie Jane Whittaker*

Without Love

My body trembles
my heart pounds
blood rushes
to my head,
hands, and
with these hands
I can make you see
that I can kill
I can destroy
like a wild man
like a little boy.

Oh, but...
I can love,
love
like a savage
like a mother.

Oh mother
can you
hear me?
I'm fading
fading
like a whisper.

—*Carl Vreeland*

Midnight Splendor

Across this frozen land,
Never man's hand raised -
This virgin soil,
Life unspoiled,
As from beginning of time.
Wild life abounds,
Man's never found,
This midnight rest.
Full moon rises -
White gleams on nature's breast.
Ice crunches underfoot.
North wind cries,
Lone owl hoots.
There, alone, in silence, waits -
Time suspended. Eternity unending,
The promise - waits.

—*Janet Dunning*

Pain

Icy hand upon the heart.
One emotion that will not part.
Always there, underlying,
even when you are cheerful
you are still fearful
of the pain that is yet to come.
Chilling breeze of the soul,
constant steady always cold.
Frightened, always ever scared
of the pain that lies ahead.
Warm, soothing, stronger than you and I.
You must let it seep way down deep
where the cold winds blow
to ease the pain that we all know.
To lessen the hunger of our souls.
It is something to hold and treasure,
something you just cannot measure,
something to keep forever.
You should know what this is and know it well,
for if you don't your life is and always will be hell.

—*Shannon Roff*

Into The Darkness

In the quiet calm of darkness, lies the root of all emotions.

It is where they hide. It is where they gain strength.

It is where we as people hide!, but when we let our emotions

emerge from darkness, that is where we gain our strength.

—*Shelly Duquette*

A New Beginning

As I sat and watched the sun rise, I thought of many things,
The pain and joy that life can bring and the way God's birds will sing.
Each day's a new beginning and his music fills the air;
I have to look inside myself to see what I can share.
My brother hurt my feelings or a sister hurt my pride;
I have to keep my distance, so my pain I'll easily hide.
The days pass by, now months are gone—what's happening in my life?
I'm filled with rage that boils out, and cuts others like a knife.
Now I'm the one that hurts a friend, and my loved ones feel the pain,
All because I can't forgive, such behavior seems insane!
Jesus said, "Just come to Me and lay that burden down,"
But without the faith to leave it there, it will trail you like a hound.
Now as I watch that little bird, I hear Jesus softly say,
"You mean so much more than one of these, why do you act this way?
Jesus paid the highest price and forgave so much of us,
Not one of His has the right—to argue, feud of fuss.
I feel my spirit healing and I cannot wait to find
That once dear friend I would not forgive and really clear my mind.

—*Rodger Wedan*

The Lost Girl

Running through a field I see
A girl in my dreams
She stops to pick some flowers
Then she suddenly screams
Dear God, creator of our universe.
Cover your ears when I curse
Close your eyes when I sin
I'm special, take me as I Am
I don't need salvation, I deserve heaven for free.
So when I woke up from my dream
I thought to myself that poor lost girl
Good thing she's just a dream

—*Mark Evans*

Somewhere Inbetween Heaven and Hell

The sea whispers as the wind howls.
A bird chirps as a baby cries!
Hope and happiness are troubled by
    fear and fury.
NOTHING is totally virgin.
NOTHING can escape the evil that surrounds
    everyday life.
For, No thing or No one is totally pure.

Even the first breath taken by a new born
    child is full of evil.
Deceit, lies, lust, greed: All evil,
Love, hope, destiny, warmth: All good.
One plus one,
Equals somewhere inbetween Heaven and Hell.
A place without a face or name.
Yet we've all been there and know of it
    quite well.

—*Michelle L. Zweifel*

A Halloween Tale

The pumpkin's face looked somewhat sad.
A bit slumped to one side.
Tears made of wax from his eyes all aglow.
Made his end seem oh so near.
I truly believe that the pumpkin can see,
through those mystical man-made eyes
and I know in my head
the Great Pumpkin's not dead!
That's a falseness, of Great Lies.
And on Halloween night, a year from now
when witches and ghosts abound,
sad tears they will flow
From the eyes all aglow.
I know the Great Pumpkin's around!

—*J. Paul Malczewski*

The Wonders Of God

A grain of sand
    A blade of grass,
The blue, blue sky above—
    All show the power of God's hand,
The wonder of His love.

The perfect crystal of a flake of snow,
    The perfume of a rose,
Cannot be equalled by work of man,
    It's something no man knows.

God has given man the gift
    Of a seeking, working mind;
But the act of creation, the miracle of life—
    These, dear Lord, are Thine!

From life alone comes further life,
    Even science can't change the sign
That only God has had the plan
    For the Beginning unto the End of Time.

—*Phyllis Seifrid*

Afraid To Try

            I cannot say I am alone.
But the true warmth of love, I have never known.
    Many have less, and face greater despair,
        yet I feel like a sock without its pair.
    Why am I different? What was done wrong?
    Am I to be punished for not being strong?
        The risk of love is a gamble to great.
    For it is better not to be known, than to feel
            the deep pain of hate.

—*Shawn Quelch*

The Bay

The moon,
a bright gold piece slipping into a black velvet pocket,
is slowly descending, as if it were stuck in the muck and
mire of a swamp.
The torrent of thrashing giants,
with white peaks slish sloshing over and over,
cascading as if the streamline of whirs would never stop.
Warned you of its rage.
Then as quickly as it started the violent fury of slick mass
was put in a trance.
A slow, peaceful, endless, dark journey of nothingness.
But my friend you may think it is calm,
for you are a fool.
The bay has just warned its enemy that it can defeat and
overcome him.
The defeat of your worthless soul being sucked out of your
body by the lifeless waves.
You may think you are smarter,
but the bay has more knowledge of death than you ever will.

—*Nicole Hanko*

A Little Girl's Wish

So many years ago, Dear Lord,
A cross you had to bear
You had few friends, my mommy said,
Oh, I wish that I had been there!

I'm not very big - just "going on three"
But I'm sure I could understand
I couldn't have helped you to carry the cross,
But I could have taken your hand...!
Chatting together, we'd trudge up the hill
I'd pick flowers along the way
Together we'd laugh and we'd cry at the things
That had happened during the day.

As we reached the top, you would turn and smile,
To make me understand
That your burden was lighter — your heart hummed a song
Because I had taken your hand—!!

—*Liz Briggs*

One Sunday In Bolivia

A small boy shouts, a late rooster crows,
A distant drum beats, a thin flute blows,
and bells break the tension of the crystal blue air.

White man sauntering in your immaculate best black,
What message can the bells be ringing now for you?
Indian treading softly in your very own way,
What do you hear as the bells break the blue?

Come, toll the bells, the clear ancient bells,
We speak of beauty to heal what hate is creating.
Come, call the bells, the deep ancient bells,
We speak of comfort to endure while you are waiting.

Hush, we tell you of the way to perfection;
Listen, ask mercy - you may yet be set free;
Know the heart's conciliation still lies in reflection,
Know poverty still hangs with Christ on the tree.

—*Mary Jennings*

Kindness

No matter how many ways one may
Choose to divide it kindness it seems
Always becomes a full measure when
Love is the principle ingredient "Be Kind"

—*Joseph C Conowal*

A Cat's Meow

A cat's meow
a dog's bow-wow
there is something that is missing
while the cats meow
and the dogs bow-wow
there's a kitten who's spitting and hissing

There's nothing wrong with hissing
a bow-wow, a purr or a hum
but the kitten needs a meow
but where will we get one from

So I took her down by the river
where the pussywillows grow
one sniff, she purred,
then she let out a hearty meow

So if your heart is in it
and you want your kitten's happiness to show
Take her down to the banks of the river
where the pussywillows grow

—*R. K. Hooker*

A Shattered Dream

I had a dream
A dream of flight.
Of flying kicks across the floor
Like an eagle about to soar.
To kick, to punch, and to compete.
I thought to never accept defeat.
To be involved in a physical banter,
A fight or flight encounter.
We are poetry in motion
Doing flying kicks in slow motion.
A dream I had to become the best
Shattered within my hopeful breast.
And dreams gave way to harsh reality,
With needs to fill with materiality.
A reality needing food and sleep and mundane things.
To no longer compete in the fighting ring,
Was a bitter pill to swallow.
But swallow I must this bitter pill
and dream my dream tomorrow.

—*Michelle Dupuy*

Castaway

A chill, dreary day finds me sitting at the door staring out at
a gray, sodden world. My thoughts are my own as I sit here
alone and dream of the love of another... Adrift on the Sea of
Life, am I, pushed by the currents of Time. No anchor to hold
me, no steadying keel, no direction as I roam, I search for an
island to call my own, where my strivings have purpose and
value. As sometimes happens as Life ebbs and flows, I found my
island in Her. The seed of my love, buried deep in my soul,
slowly blossomed and took fragile hold. She cradled that love
in a grip of steel, soft as the fluffiest down, but would not
let it root in Her torn, battered heart, having just emerged
from a storm. I tried to wait, as the painful wounds healed,
for I knew Her love was alive. To a standoff I fought the Winds
of Change, trying to bide my time. Oh, I could not hold out,
the Winds took me away, adrift upon the Sea. With no star to
guide me I may never find the Love I left behind. A chill,
dreary night finds me still as I was, staring out at a gray,
sodden world. My thoughts not my own as I sit here alone and
dream of the love of another...

—*Richard J. Vogt*

A "Hearts" Desire

A heart should be honest
A heart should be true
A heart should be unbroken
And never made blue
A hearts dreams should be fulfilled
With the joy of living
A heart should never be deceived
but filled with happiness, that is freely given
A heart should never be shattered
True Love it should hold
It should be treated with tenderness
And loved as if it were gold
For when a Heart is broken into
To put it back together, is a hard thing to do
So treat it with tenderness, as if it were gold
And a heart will stay young and never grow old.

  —Patricia Wilborn

Questions From An Answer

suicide — a double-edged sword
a killer that fails to cure
as the pain of the dead ceases,
the pain of the living is pure.

it never fails to amaze
for the real reasons are rarely known
and those that are closely tied
are left hanging in the unknown.

a question with no answer,
yet an answer of many questions to some
as anger and pain are mixed together
to leave a searing frustration.

as the strong brush is aside;
the weak submit to the calling.
they claim they never fit in
and can never keep from falling.

suicide is always painless
for those that commit the crime,
but look how it destroys
the lives of those left behind.

  —Sandra Franzen

Bloom

Midnight strikes, the bell has rung.
A lady cries out a song that has been sung
 through and through.

Have you seen the way you grew?
You were loved like a flower from
Bloom to wilt.
Is this she at her bloom?
She was not loved to cherish,
But hoped that she would perish in spring
When she is to bloom.

The song that she sings always brings me tears
 and horrible fears.
But I can't help her now.
She is dead.
Now the rose that was to be loved is gone.
But it will bloom again soon.

  —Steven Payan

Wrong Way

Logic maybe the answer to many questions,
But when its a question from the heart
It is many times wrong.

  —Pete Chow

The Tattered Hat

As I was walking down the street.
A man in a tattered hat I chanced to meet.
He was unshaven, and his clothes were old,
He looked like he had slept out in the cold.

And as I turned aside, about to go,
He looked up at me and said "hello".
With a gentle smile upon his face
"Haven't I seen you before someplace"?

He told me about his lonely life,
And how he missed his lovely wife.
Then he said, "how are things with you"?
"Just fine", I said, and off I flew.

The man in the old clothes and battered brim,
Showed more love and concern about me,
Than I did for him.
God bless the man in the tattered hat.

  —James F. Walker

The Wrong Side Of The Boat

When fishing with his grandson
 a man would always note;
The young man always caught the biggest fish
 on the right side of the boat.

For years the two fishermen
 laughed at the joke they shared;
And then one day his Grandson knew
 how much his Grand-Dad really cared.

It was then that he remembered
 what he'd so often him quote:
"That the biggest fish could not be caught
 on the wrong side of the boat."

It's not the size of the fish we catch
 that makes life all worthwhile;
It is sharing love with others
 and facing problems with a smile.

  —Marjorie W. Lewis

Twice, Twice Blessed

I think that I shall never see
A more loving happy family
Than at the recent births on the 4th of July
That left many of us with a misty eye.
Four little babies - Oh, what joy!
Three little girls and one little boy!
Their mom and dad thought of many names
For their first born son - Douglas James.
The next arrival on the scene
Was the sweet face of Rebecca Jean.
Following close as anyone can
Came the third little darling - Frances Ann.
And last but not least as the saying goes
Was our little charmer - Laura Rose.
Adding their welcomes were Sarah and Connor.
All in all, it was quite an honor.
I thank Thee, Lord, on bended knee
For these newest additions to our family tree.

  —Regina Galanaugh

ENCHANTMENT

The raging storm was still at last,
a pale moon lit the sky,
as I paused there in wonder
I heard the wild geese cry.

Strong and clear, their song rang out,
with rush of mighty wings,
they soared above the sleeping land
to keep their tryst with Spring.

Soft mist gently touched my face,
dark branches breathed a sigh,
then, wild and free and far away
I heard the wild geese cry.

—*Rose Chism*

Rhythmic

A rhythmic pattern passing by
a pattern running through my mind
I see it all at once some how
and then I know that I have found
a magical mystical place inside
a place where I can run and hide
but all I see are those special patterns
and those colors passing by
yellow, orange, red, and green
and the blue right from the sky.

—*Venessa Bibry*

Home Is Where The Heart Is

Home is where the heart is
A place of eternal love and trust
A shelter from the storms of life
With arms open to console and comfort.

Home is the center of family affection
The hub around which activity revolves
The socket of its extended arms
And always the focus of the network.

Home is the constant gathering point
For all the birds who have flown the coop
Disseminated though they all may be
They still come home to roost.

Home is much more than a dwelling
More than walls, a roof, and floor
Home is the core of our existence
Our true being reverts to the home.

Wonderful home, that comfortable niche
Where pieces come together, as in a puzzle
Each one a person, solid and whole
Though not complete until united.

—*Joan Pace Kennedy*

Ode To Martin Mines

Death, you evil sinner take off your
    cloak of sadness.
For the one who has gone, Martin Mines,
    has left us a basket of flowers, to pick from.
Patience, learning, beauty, flowers, understanding
    were some of his traits.
So don't pick sadness, pick a handful of flowers.
So, you see my brother has left me
    Many pleasant moments to pick from,
        from his basket of flowers.

—*Rosette Mines*

The Secret Place

There is a secret place I'd like to see.
A place that many have told me.
    A place where there is no anger and there will
never be hunger.
    This secret place is not faraway,
We could create this secret place today.
    All we have to do, is not to feud.
Try to be kind, and try to find, This secret place.
I know this secret place did once exist,
    and its so deeply missed.
In this secret place,
No one has a strange face. Everyone could get along,
We would all sing the same song.
    There would be no killing or stealing.
Instead we'd all be healing.
    From all the years of shedded tears.
This secret place is still very much alive,
    to find it all we have to do is strive.

—*Sabrina Maritnez*

Employ To Use

In this land there is said to be
A place where all who live are free.
And in this land we can accomplish goals
Enabling all to achieve.
But the facts that deem to be true,
The American dream now works for few.
Rich getting richer, poor getting poorer,
Those barely meeting ends are only getting sorer.

Costs skyrise, wages are poor,
After paying Uncle Sam there is no more.
With what are we supposed to live?
An extra effort did raise the pay,
But now the work only completes the day.

Life is for living that so few can do,
Merely to exist is what we strive
Hoping wages extend to feed.
Bare necessities we do thrive.

—*Ramona Ann McConnell*

Sticks And Stones

A blossom, blooming in the path of a mob,
A porcelain figurine, beautiful and falling to the cold,
    hard floor,
A painting, shriveling before the flame,
A dream, bent and broken by a nightmare.
Sticks and stones may break my bones, but words can never
    hurt me.
A prayer, just out of reach.

—*Shawn Bakken*

Pretty Little Red Bird

I glance out my window. What do I see?
A pretty little red bird looking at me.
He is decked out in scarlet, with a plume on his head.
Another soon joins him, I think they are wed!

The tree is quit barren, winter now is at work .
If I don't quit my gazing, my chores I will shirk.
The leaves have all fallen, no foliage in sight,
Small brilliant red birds are sure a delight!

My neighbor's their host, super lavish they dine.
When their tummies get full, in my trees they unwind.
Dishwashing's no fun, lots I'd rather do.
Yet the task is much lighter when I'm looking at you!

—*Omega Lucas*

Raccoon Roundup

It all began when it was discovered
A raccoon invading the kitchen cupboards,
To say the least it was quite appalling
That this raccoon had come calling,
The coon had entered through a door designed
To accommodate the family felines,
Much thought was given to devise a plan
How to capture Ol' Coon in a garbage can,
The can was placed outside the door
Ol' Coon made an exit and was free no more,
After taking him to a new location
The arrival home brought more frustration,
For Ol' Mama Coon was found there waitin'
But this time there was no hesitatin'
With garbage can positioned, it was fate
That Ol' Mama Coon would soon join her mate,
Back home again was coon number three
But Little Coon was caught speedily
And sent on his way to join Ma and Pa,
A happy ending for one and all.

    —*Marie M. Taylor*

Dark Room!

The candle flame is burning.
A relationship is dying like a burned out flame.
Is it right or is it wrong?
Only God shall know.
Is it me or is it them?
What will come in the end?
We learn from our mistakes.
We better ourselves through our errors,
So what ever will be...
Will be in his hands
Leave it there.
As the dawn dies down,
We now shall light the candle again!

    —*Laura Ferrier*

Roadside Oasis

Traffic wound slowly this morning
a sea of red eyes shined through
thick waves of morning fog.
We slowed and slowed,
and stopped
on the same pavement I drive every morning
and every night.
I glanced to the side—
shocked to see flowers where
before I had seen only road.
Bushes covered with bright yellow spiky flowers hung back
soft lush grass bent in the breeze,
trees covered with needles and leaves reach toward a rainy,
bright blue-gray sky.
Thick white clouds crawled across
the horizon toward the distant
mountains.
The red eyes closed,
traffic began to move again
pavement pulled me away.

    —*Maura Maher*

Rainbow

A smile chasing away the shadows of rain.
A slide of dreams that takes you to your pot of gold.
A river of color that pours in your heart to overflow it
with joy and happiness.
A ribbon of promise to show life's new beginnings.
A waterfall of light to shine on the paths of righteousness.
The finger-paint of God to remind us of his love.

    —*Kelly Knowles*

My Journey

Unknown to me there lies a love
A secret compassion hidden from the world
A yearning to see the dreams of people
To seek the mysteries life creates

To sail on the silvery sea on the ship of hope
To fly to distant shores on the wings of freedom
To walk on lands conquered by many
And to touch the lives of unknown people

I will awaken to a new sunshine each morning
Dawn will bring me new beginnings
I will see the sunset from the four corners of the earth
Evening will bring me through the galaxies of heaven

Carry me to far off places and lift my spirits high
Bring me to the land of eternal happiness
Bring me to the land of dreams
But love, always bring me back home with you
For it is there that my journey begins.

    —*Oralynn Mulvey*

The Laughter Of A Child

As the sound of sweetness fills the air,
  A sense of happiness is everywhere.
It is cute yet beautiful in its own way.
  Bringing love and understanding
    To all whom it may.
Joined by a hug or a smile that cares,
  The laughter of a child
  Will always be there.

    —*Julie A. Lawrence*

Death Unnecessary

Broken glass, covers the pavements
a sight that is not pretty.
Chills move over the corpse
of the dying individual.
The heart that once beat rapidly
is now barely audible.
The once rhythmatic breathing
is now fleeting.
The once powerful mind
is now in a state of unconsciousness.
This once healthy young body now
mangled, twisted, and hopelessly dismembered.
The once attractiveness of this innocent face
is now horridly disfigured.
This once guileless youth now lifeless
meets its maker before its time.
The cause of a few too many
Definitely not the result of a sober mind.

    —*Stephen Davis*

The Tornado

  Oh God, here it comes the whirling terror,
    Destroying the path without any error,
The friction of the wind concocting a locomotive sound,
  As the slender, black funnel touches the ground,
    We pray for it to stop and its only reply,
  Is hurtling our belongings through the dark sky,
    Just as it came it went with a flash,
    Distributing falling debris and trash,
    How dark it got and how the wind did cry,
    Thank God it's over is our rejoicing reply

    —*Vanessa Wade*

The Rover

Avoiding reality.
A situation drenched in brutality.
Why face a world bearing sobriety?
How could this be the way it has to be?

In the face of death- I'm lost.
May God Bless- this unholy cost!

I no longer see definition
Of what it is we call life.
A rude awakening and revelation
to the Ultimate killing knife.

How it is- the dead still dance?
Or is the music eternally over?
Completely overwhelmed with insignificance
Lost in the skies an aimless rover...

My insides ache an empty, undefinable, indescribable
Unwanted, morbidly haunted, torturistic vision- of an end...
Insignificance of love and friends.
The brain, the nerves, their electrical roots,
All that signifies organism life...
Vanishes at a Flash of the killing knife.!

    —Laura Susan Brady

Christmas

Christmas is holly and mistletoe,
A sleigh ride in the falling snow,
Popcorn and presents, cookies and cakes,
Racers, rag dolls, and roller skates,
Apples and antlers, books and bears,
Being with loved ones who really care.

Cats and children, Santa and sleigh,
And you know very soon comes Christmas Day
Turkey and trimmings, family and friends,
A world full of hope, a song without end.

Anthems and angels, shepherds and sheep,
On that starry night their watch did keep,
Wise men who followed a star shinning bright
Jesus was born that holy night.

    —Wanda Rice

I Thought It Was About Death

A man turned and smiled at me,
a smile of a thousand starts that beckoned
   to me as if this were not my home.
That I should move,
I questioned my limbs
as fear paid the toll
and distance grew between us.
His hand became a hatchet as he struck
   the first blow.
With the second blow, he pierced that
   which was once a soft
     beating heart.
Oh, darkness! Wrap me in that sweet
   smile.

    —Shannon Gvara

Spring

Spring is when you hear running water,
And see kids playing on the teeter totter.
Spring is when the deer come out to play,
And birds begin to chirp everyday.
Spring is when the clouds disappear,
And wild animals have no fear.
Spring is when it's time to mow your lawn,
And that's when you know that Winter is gone!

    —Nikki Gause

The Guardian Of The Site

In an old ghost town by the light of the moon,
a solitary owl begins to croon.
his lonely call echoes through the night.

Across the lake one can hear the shutters bang-
where the hyacinths bloomed
   and the hummingbirds once sang,
when the dew was wet
   and the warm sun cast its light.

This beaten, weathered shack now stands alone;
these days no person dares to call it home.
The previous owners have vanished from sight.

A slinky, black cat with eyes of orange
each evening creaks open the rusty door hinge.
This faithful feline is the guardian of the site.

    —Amy Rebecca Cinpoliti

The Volunteer

This poem is written especially for you.
A special person always saying "I Can Do".
As days blend together and years fly by,
You are always faithful, on you we rely
To remember that people's needs are great
And to those you give, yourselves forsake.
For deep within us is a longing to love.
Some keep this love small and restrained,
While others know the blessings gained
In giving of self, talent, time and concern.
These are characteristics that through love you learn,
To do something good for someone each day,
That helps him through life's difficult way.
We all journey from birth to death.
But what do we know at life's last breath?
It's what we've done for others that's measured.
Not all the false illusions we may have treasured.
"Our Thanks" is such an insignificant phrase,
Compared to those received as Heavenly Praise.

    —Marge Zima

The Four Seasons

Summer - Magic moments are made of simple things-
A thought to share - A song to sing
A waltz around the dance floor - A hike through the woods
Those happy times will not leave you if you keep them in your
   memory bank!

Winter - Winter is near -bringing torrential rains.
I seem to have forgotten how to cry -
But the sky remembers and sheds the healing tears that
   experience and sadness have taught me to discipline and dry.
The sky and I have an agreement about pain and I welcome the
   rain.

Fall - Life Has Returned Somehow!
One time it slipped away and the night welded its chain of
   grief -
Causing me to give leave to all who are near and dear to me.
Fall is approaching so let us allow the winds blow away the
   sadness and regrets in our aching hearts -

For Life Has Returned Somehow!

Spring - Spring sometimes rushes in like a roaring tide -
Into a world of grief and pain - Flowers Bloom! Even then.

    —Kay Schlinkman

"The Path"

The beginning- where does it end?
A trampled path - trampled by retraced footsteps,
Footsteps leading to a destination eagerly sought.
It hugged the edge of the buckwheat field
Waving in the wind like a huge flowered blanket.
It meandered down a steep bank and pebbles bounced underfoot.
I reached into the brush for a handful of juicy blackberries.
Sugar sweet juice oozed from the berries
Like an overturned inkwell and dribbled through my fingers.
Ahead, water flowed under a narrow footbridge.
A willow branch laced with twine and hook
Propped against the bridge, gave evidence
Of a stream full of slumbering trout.
The path climbed the crest of the hill and lay against the sky.
Yonder an old maple tree- its branches wide spread
Exposed the ripped bark where the ropes
Holding the old wooden swing were hung.
As the swing moved slowly, silver hair glistened in the
sunlight. The aroma of fresh peeled apples held in her lap
Wafted through the air as the beginning found the end.

—*Norma Smith*

A Box On The Shelf

There is a box stored high on a shelf,
A treasure you take down and look through by yourself.

These are treasures and memories, things of the past.
Wrapped in paper and ribbons holding memories that last.

You take out each item and reminisce as you look.
It's like looking back through your life's scrapbook.

These are pictures made with crayons and snapshots, too.
Things that would mean nothing to others, they are only for
you.

You think over your life going year by year,
Things happened so long ago but seem so near.

What a good life you've had with friends old and new,
Your husband, your children, and grandchildren too.

You smile as you place the box back on the shelf,
Feeling content and proud of your life and of yourself.

—*Rozella Law*

Untitled

On your 50th anniversary celebration,
a Valentine's Day gala,
your most cherished anniversary ever, remember:

This is a golden time for you both,
a time to be cherished,
a time to be loved,
a time for family and friends,
a time to remember forever,
and a time to celebrate the years to come.

A time to remember the 50 years
you've been together,
to think about the family you've had together,
the families they've had, and
the families they will have in the years to come.

Take the time on this golden day to remember
the good, the bad,
and the yet to come in your lives.

May the love you've shared in these past 50 years
last for the rest of your lives,
and go with you through eternity and beyond.

—*Victoria J. Broekhuizen*

My Vision

One day I had a vision
A vision of no homeless people
A vision that everyone was treated equal
A vision of no diseases, or sicknesses.
A vision that the whole world was one
A vision of no war just peace
A vision of no hatred just love.
A vision where no one was judged
Everyone was excepted for who they were.
A vision you could walk down the street
without being worried.
A vision that the world was full of sunshine,
The chirping of birds, the laughter and joy
of people from all over sharing together.
A vision of a world with no dark clouds or rain
A vision of no prejudice
No one was judged by race or color.
It's just too bad all of this has to be a vision.

—*Virginia Smith*

A Peaceful World

We need peace in this world we live in
A world full of mistrust and sin
We need to rely on each other
like a brother to a brother

We need to keep our world clean of guns
so we can appreciate our magnificent sun
We need to appreciate peace
and wars we need to decrease

We need to look all around us
and turn from hate to trust
The world can be beautiful again
if there's no more bloodshed and stain

A world free of war
A world full of peace

—*Lynn Patt*

The Wonderful Rainforest

Would you like to enter a world, a world that is breathtaking!
A world where only the heavenly sounds of nature are welcome.
A world that is exhilarating, yet oh, so beautiful.
A world where trees are huge, so very tall;
Where flowers come in the most brilliant colors ever seen.
A world where miracles can and will come true -
A world that will capture your soul and enchant you -
A world where the passion of nature truly lock together for
all of eternity -
A world where rain drops slide, down the greenest
Leaves and touch the tip of your tongue -
A world that is and will always be.........a rainforest.

—*Reghan M. Chesney*

Waves

Technology spills over nature
as the waves spill over the rocks.
Rubbing, chafing, and wearing them down
until they are smooth, soft, and round,
and fit neatly into the palm of your hand.
The rock sits and waits patiently, peaceful
for the sea to come crashing down upon it.
After years of stealthy waves,
and devastating splashes,
There is nothing left.

—*Rene Almeling*

"Winter: Harbinger of Spring"

(Dedicated to Donna for always being there to care and support me.)

If there was no Winter, there would be no Spring.
A year without Winter, would change most everything.
You see, we need the cold of Winter, the dark, dreary days,
A time when trees are bud-less, the sky shades of grey.
Were it not for Winter, a time to climb within
ourselves and rest for the days ahead,
The "hope" that Spring brings us, would surely be dead.
We need contrast in our lives to appreciate
that which is good,
Could you revel in a field of daffodils not having
seen the frozen earth? I doubt you could.
The "hope" that erupts in Springtime wouldn't be so great,
if not for somber Winter, wherein we wait.
Enveloped in warm clothing, by a fire to tame it's chill,
The solitude invades my soul, and all the earth is still.
Winter is the "harbinger of spring", the messenger
announcing her arrival,
Spring is a time of joy and hope, but it is in
Winter we concentrate on pure survival.

—*Tana Giusti*

"Perhaps"

Perhaps there was another time,
   a yesterday my mind will not recall.
Could there have been another day
   that never was at all?

Perhaps a place in time
   where dreams are made and set aside to think about,
   or could it be that time stands still,
   to leave bewildered minds confused
   and filled with doubt?

Perhaps someday I'll wake to find this life I live,
   I never lived at all.

Perhaps the future holds a place in time
   that's yet to come.

It seems that we can't comprehend
   that time is not our own to judge or plan,
   but play the part the best we can,
   though sometimes, all alone!

—*Mary C. Rose*

To Tammy

You ended your life early
abandoning our family
your selfishness damaging my life forever.

At 16, how could you hurt so?
Teenage turmoil ate away your heart,
as God chose to take you home.

In friendship we were never close
yet nothing could break a sister's bond:
your final words, "I love you," I hear still.

Why you took your life
I will never know, but I feel
you're where you wanted to roam.

—*Michelle Kingery*

Longing

The day is cold and long
The sky dark and grey
How I wish
I could escape
This little country place.

—*Raymond Joy*

My Blessed Angel

One sleepless night I lied awake so troubled;
About the major problems in my life
It seemed as though my fears and woes were
doubled; and then my darkest hour turned into light.
For I opened up my eyes and I saw glory, an angel bent
and touched my shaking hand.
The softness in his whisper eased my worries, he said
"God won't put on you what you can't stand."
At first I thought that I was really dreaming,
Until I saw the love light shining bright, of the
Angel softly smiling down upon me, prepared to
Watch over me all through the night.
I closed my eyes and felt my burdens lifted, then I
prayed and thanked my father from above,
For my blessed angel standing near me,
And always abiding with me in his love.

—*Rebecca Burnside*

Roots Of Life

Standing among birch and pine, a tempered oak,
above them all so he can see.

Forced by wind he does not bow,
his mighty arms not give an inch.

His thoughts are deep as roots of trees,
it is his life and his decree.

Withering forces others demise, he stands tall,
among them all.

He is a fighter and will not quit,
thought slight of frame,
he has the fame,
of Hercules and bow to his name.

Nourishment is from within you see
and it is for that which he is free.

—*Anthony J. Marquis*

Grandmother

This tree so grand, standing out above all the others,
afraid of nothing and no one,
knowing no feat too great.

As time grew on she developed into a tree.
Knowing no boundaries, she set out to bring meaning to her life.
No ordinary member of the group.
She was special.

Her roots nourishing the young and helping them to grow.
Hoping that they would become loving and compassionate like her,
but none could surpass the love and compassion
as she had shared it with the world.

As her branches became brittle,
none of her gained knowledge was lost.
Slowly it had trickled down to new generations of saplings.

She would not die but continue living.
Her seeds would become seedlings and, one day, trees
to pass on what they had learned and been taught by her.

It would be something new, an adventure which she would explore
with that same compassion which was passed
one by one throughout the world!

—*Amanda Lubit*

Loneliness

The sun has settled behind the western sky - its night time
again. Time when the still sound of loneliness creeps in. The
stars in the moonlit sky twinkle and seems to say. Come join
us - be happy and gay. You begin to reminisce over things you
should've done. Days and years that've been long since gone.
The sudden rustle of the wind. Welcomes me too - saying come
and be my friend. The moonlit nights gives that awesome
feeling that all is right with the world. For a while I'm
caught up in an imaginary wind of whirl. In bed the cold
sheets soothe my flesh. I lay awaiting the long needed rest.
Soon I'm warmed by the covers. Waiting to be joined by my
lover. Only to awaken to the reality that it was all just a
dream. Oh Lord, my only refuge, it seems. What shall I do?
How can this be. Can there be no one in this life for me.
Fate has dealt me a cruel blow. Lonely and loveless through
this life I relentlessly must go.

—*Ruth M. Lewis*

December

In December I hear the howl of the wind
Against the house,
Some people have no heat or any warmth.
Some freeze and some die and no one knows.
No one seems to care.
In December the snow falls.
Christmas comes,
They don't have blankets just a run down shack.
And no fancy dinner on Christmas Eve.
And no new clothes or toys for the children,
No laughing.
Just cold winter.
And Christmas is just another hard day for them.

—*Melanie Magathan*

Counterfeit Criminals

Counterfeit criminals folding their arms
    against the soft white linen
    backing, never - ending
    shattered hearts unlike the
    message beyond the river
      of lost souls, revolving,
        moving far away from the streamlined
        garbage disposal,
          holding up their heads dissolving
          into logic and despair,
          filing their taxes sheltered by
            the wind, hymns of
            innocence growling
            between the cracks
not a gun in sight to
    be released in the
    red hot air
children cracking their gum
    coming up softly in the
        sun

—*Meryl Sheppard*

Wet

The tap of rain tapping on tile.
Resurgent, droplet after drop
It gluts dry hollow, guttering
Roof's ridges to fall
In sudden stream absorbed.
And strung about with sweet beads,
I lick tasting

—*Priscilla Hilton*

Worry Costs Dearly

Can you tell me that when you worried, your worry solved or
aided. We waste the Power we posses with thinking that is
jaded. I don't deny that concern is proper in your desire to
ease the pain. Of those you Love who are ill or hurting and
cannot stand the strain. Don't jump in bed beside them and
join them when they cry. It only makes things worse, no matter
what you try. Always remain very positive in matters of this
ilk. Picture how you want them, stay calm and smooth as silk.
Affirm that which you desire and know that it is yours.
Visualize things as they should be and leave to God your chores
He knows fully well the things they need, long before you ask.
Have faith, you can will these things, to ease your present
task. Worry enervates, and lessons your potential. Affirmed
thought and visualization are the things that are essential.
So try to do the things I've stated and put it to the test.
You'll find that worry's useless and that 'His' way is best.

—*Sal Coniqliaro*

The Reply

The grand inquisitor stood majestically on the rock
All glory and power in his act of malignant
    ignorance.
I stood there looking at him
    from across the shore,
    the sound of the sea pounding its
    breast hoping to catch his
    attention.

He will fade in his glory though
Like all, and the sea will continue
    to pound its breasted reefs
    to others who stand there
    like the grand inquisitor -
Ignorant to its message.

Millions will die at their feet,
    and still they, like the grand inquisitor,
    will die in the name of
        God.

—*Shannon Sullivan*

Searching For Friends

All my life I've searched for friends, in travels far and near;
All my life I've looked for those whose purpose was sincere. I
looked for kindness in their eyes, compassion in their heart; a
soul enthroned with godliness—a friendship we would start. And
I would do the best I could to be a friend in turn; We'd share
the good and bad in life, each other's trust to earn. It was
strange how I could recognize the one whose heart was true; The
ones who really meant it when they said, "I care for you." Some
would stay through sunshine hours but when dark shadows came,
They drifted off into the fog, they hardly knew my name. But
true friends always stayed near by, though things were good or
ill; No storm could tear their friendship down, it just grew
stronger still. That day you came-I saw your smile, I heard
your sincere voice; I knew right then that you were one in whom
I could rejoice. You always fill my heart with joy because you
mean so well; The warmth and love I feel toward you my
stammering tongue can't tell.
So take my hand and kiss my cheek, tell me again you care;
"Cause all my life I searched for you, and now I'm glad you're here."

—*Wayne Drayer*

Thoughts On Passing Time

How fleeting are life's cancelled days
All the years that swept so swiftly by
Like a sunset, fleeting, yet always missed.
Still, when I view each rising sun,
New faith and hope are won.

So down the valley of pageants past
We watch the leaves fall from life's tree
And those leaves seem dead to all who pass
Still, from their mold will spring new life
But this, alas... our eyes will never see.

—*Wayne J. Spence*

Alone

Here I am.
Alone.
Watching the rain's blue time.
I'm feeling such a voidless pain.
Only wanting to refrain.
Has everyone gone?
Not a friend alive.
Hell seams to scream alive.
Here I am.
Feeling cold.
Only wishing I had something to hold.
What's wrong tonight.
I want to watch a fight.
No thrill watching the rain spill.
Grey fists of the lonely shatter my iced window.
Alone.
Here I am.
Alone....

—*Paul C. Stanworth*

Old Man In The Park

No one notices the old man in the park,
always sitting from daylight until dark.

Feeding the pigeons with his morsels of bread,
Using the park bench at night for his bed.

He is covered with rags, no soles on his shoes,
Wind battered hair, and his breath smells of booze.

No one knows of his long weary past,
No one cares of how long he will last.

Someday that bench in the park will be gone,
His home in the park he used to live on.

This man will feed the pigeons no more,
His existence in life is not the same as before.

He lived his life, his soul they will take,
He went asleep, never to wake.

—*Lori Ayyub*

Untitled

Darkness sets In I'm not sure where to go.
Am I dead or alive
I don't really know
I feel as if I'm being slowly pulled away.
My conscience tells me that I cannot stay.
Everything is cold
Cold like death
And as my fear goes away
I breathe my last breath

—*Sherry Oswald*

Illusion/Wonderment

What is it that we really see?
Am I you or are you me?
Are we separate souls far apart
Or part of the whole within one heart?
Are we me or are we you
When we do the things we do?
Is what we touch all that is real?
Are emotions a thought that we think we feel?
Where is Heaven? Is there a Hell?
Do we search for answers yet know them well?
Have we known life before and lived upon earth
To return again through a brand new birth?
Are dreams that occur in the darkness of night
The future—to unfold when the time is right?
Is reality yours or is it mine?
Within this realm we know as time?
Perhaps the answers that I think I find
Are part of a game within my mind.

—*Arlene Mary Langellotti*

The Whisper

As I lay by my countryside trail
Amongst the leafy woodland dale
Beside the ferns, the weeds, the cress
I dream of her being and sensual dress
Behold! Dear heart, is she your want?
Maddened by dismay and unjustly daunt
"Yes" is the answer I know to be true
This magnificent love was sure to ensure
"Call out her name," a voice contrived
Resurgence of excitement hath distinctly revived
With dry lips perched, a whisper long feared
Danced out in the air bearing name so revered
"Janet" billowed out like feathers in a gale
As solemnity blossomed in this fine woodland dale in closing my
eyes to relish thy bliss. My cheek entertained a most tenderly
kiss. The most beloved of joys is the reality of life. When
beside your body is laying your wife an enchanting dream, a
golden treasure. The only woman to offer such pleasure as I
lay by my countryside trail. Amongst the leafy woodland dale I
thank Lord God so high up above for my wife, my angel, my love.

—*Stephen Whisper*

Oops!

In the year nineteen eighty-nine
An embarrassing moment was mine.

A cat sweatshirt I was wearing that day
When out at recess we started to play.

One friend thought the outfit was attached—
Probably because it was so well matched!

After I jumped out of the swing,
My friend Amber did a crazy thing.

On hips she placed her hands,
Gave a tug, and pulled down my pants!

There I stood, pants around my knees
While feeling a mighty cool breeze.

Although I was feeling quite bare,
I guess I just stood there.
Embarrassed and angry, I suppose I turned red.
What I'd have liked was to hit Amber in the head!

—*Alison Slattery*

One Hundred Percent

One hundred percent. That is how sure I am.
An inner peace of my commitment to you.

I want to walk side by side with you.
Not in front, not behind.

Be my friend, my lover, my confidant.

Let me hold your hand, caress your cheek,
enlighten your mind, and protect your heart.

Share your life with me. Your hopes, your joys,
your dreams, your sorrows, and your laughter.

Be yourself with me. Come home to me.
But most of all, love me as I love thee!

—*Regina Holton Muller*

This Locket

A heart shaped locket on a chain of gold
An old time trinket I am told
But I treasure it in a special way
And wear it with pride every day.
It hugs my neck like a fond caress
And brings peace to a heart once in distress.

And as it touches me softly like this
It reminds me of a lovers kiss.
Your picture is there, and a lock of hair
In this locket that I wear.
All the tears that I have cried
And all the sighs that I have sighed.
Like my memories are locked inside.
This locket that I wear.

—*Mildred E. Jones*

Little Brown's Chapel

On a hill is the Little Brown's chapel
   And a beautiful valley below
A little creek at the foot of the hill
   To the river gently flows

The little church is dear to me
   So many memories there
Where we attended in our youth
   With the friends we loved and shared

The ones who were with me then
   Have passed on long ago
And sleeping in that church-yard
   Where I often go

I can hear the songs their choirs sang
   And the sermons the minister preached
And the congregation listening
   To the message he would teach

I will always love the chapel
   It seems like home to me
But all have long passed away
   That worshipped there with me.

—*Anna Sparks*

Untitled

Of all the words I say-
There are a few that I hold today.
But the words I mean the most,
Only a few who can propose.
That the words I only knew;
Are the words to say "I love you."

—*Edison Navasca*

Promises

You promised me a rose garden
And all I got were thorns;

You promised me golden rays
And all I got were rainy days;

You promised me the sun and moon
And all you do is sleep 'til noon;

Empty promises and a broken heart
It's time to make a brand new start;

Let me just say this to you:

If I promised you a rose garden
You would get a rose;

If I promised you a golden ray
You would get a sunny day;

If I promised you the moon and sun
You bet your bottom dollar it would get done!

I'm gonna make a change for the better
That's why I've written you this letter;
Goodbye to you and your promise game
I'm leaving you and I feel no shame;

Goodbye Mister Promise man Goodbye.

—*Stephanie Sheppard*

The Years Of Your Life

There is often the fickle fight,
and all is disrupted as some watch the sight.
The classic ton of homework to do come night,
one struggles to finish by dim lamp light.
All the notes and essays you must write,
and all the answers you strive to get right;
Is High School worth all the fright?

But what of the side that is bright?
What of the amorous love bug's bite?
In the end, isn't all that accumulated knowledge alright?
The honors given to the excelling elite,
watching school football games is most definitely a delight,
and, of course, the elation of the Graduation Rite;
Surely these years are far from trite.

Though, at times, school may be nothing but a plight,
the undesirable things are relatively slight,
compared to the knowledge and experience one might
learn for your life and future. So it's quite
well worth the fight.

—*Rebecca Lynn Simonton*

God's Power

God's Word tells us how Great He is
   And all the power belongs to Him
In our beginning He went way beyond
   By creating this earth to live upon.

Unto His Son He shared His power
   And raised Him up to help rule the hour
Before Christ ascended He said to His own
   My power I give you to serve here at home.

Whatever we do in serving Him here
   Must be in His power and not our own
We are just vessels He will speak through
   If we are cleansed and to Him be true.

Our God is the greatest, nothing can compare
   To the strength He'll bestow upon us to share
The work He has chosen for you alone
   No one else can do it like you, His own.

—*Keitha Arnold*

81

"The Falling Star"

We were at the lake one real dark night;
And all the stars were all in sight;
One of them decided to fall;
That's as pretty a sight as I can recall;
We all saw it as plain as day;
And hated to see it when it went away;
It looked like it fell in the water so clear;
Somebody said it wasn't even near;
I don't know where it came from or where it went,
That's not all that God can do he just gave us a hint.

—*Willie R. Byerly*

For The Childrens' Sake

There are knots in my stomach
and an aching fledged raged

and full fledged rage
where there was only concern at the start

children are missing one by one
from a public place going to or coming from
or while outdoors, innocently having fun

what kind of monster could do this kind of thing?
are they sick individuals
or a part of a much larger, market type scheme?

some people turn their heads
pretending not to see
especially when they get their mail
or buy a carton of milk...
and see a child's face
asking ...."have you seen me?"

no one is exempt from this terrible crime
and if we don't find a solution
the next child missing could be yours
or even mine.

—*Lorrie Montes*

Untitled

It's said that plants will become animals
And animals will evolve human qualities
Man will then become divine and harness atoms
By lifting his hand and saying, "It is."

Then factories will grow products as do plants
Their cells self-building and drinking energy from the sun
No animal human will labor for food nor clothing
Nor housing nor ships nor furniture nor flying machines
The human animals will hold out their hands
For animals trees to lick and they in turn
Will pet and cherish the animal trees.

Man will no longer be born and reborn
To suffer the trauma of birth and death
But clothed forever in his spirit body
Having cut his roots from his mother, Earth
His soul freed from sun and rain and soil
Will spend his year-days in astral communion
With the Lord Abundant of all Beginnings
And the Lord Triumphant over all Endings.

—*Mary D. Stegers*

Not To Store On A Barren Shelf

Love is here so very clear,
And as real as life itself,
Love is to care, love is to share,
And not to store on a barren shelf.

Love isn't bought with a foolish thought,
And thrown in a corner to store,
Love is to care and to always be there,
And to have within evermore.

Love is to give and love is to live,
And it makes this world go round,
Love is your time and it won't cost a dime,
And is the greatest thing ever found.

Love is our life the edge on the knife,
That cuts through the dark and gloom,
Love is the light that cuts through the night,
And lightens this big darkened room.

—*Orrin C. Farnsworth*

Business In The Park

Mr. Jingles retired early
And bought himself a vending machine;
He decided to peddle in the park
Where mothers with children convene.

Mr. Jingles depends on a monkey
And a parrot as added attractions;
Kids giggle at their antics
Which serve for welcoming distractions.

The rainbow-colored wagon
Is host to many a treat;
Popcorn and candy highlight the fare-
Ice cream and popsicles that beat the heat.

When all goodies have been parceled out
And pennies part from tiny, sweaty hands,
Mr Jingles unleashes his balloons
That kids imagine whisk them to fairylands.

—*Peggy Tucker*

"Wilfredo"

I saw Wilfredo for years but didn't know him.
And by the time I knew Wilfredo, alas, Wilfredo was gone.

Already I miss Wilfredo; his big nose, his small voice.
I knew he had a 'preference... some guys just make that choice.

Wilfredo was so quiet; he never ever let on.
His disease made him so old... and took him quite young.
Just little him. He never meant any harm.
And by the time I knew Wilfredo, alas, Wilfredo was gone.

His walk grew more painful. Noticeably, I dare say.
His face went from smooth tan to something like rough grey.
He never cried, never sobbed...that wasn't his way.
Wilfredo seemed to make the best of what surely was a bad day.

In my quiet moments, I kind of scheme to see him
again, of course in a dream.
I wonder if Wilfredo would smile during that time.
Wilfredo didn't smile much walking by in his lifetime.

His flesh and bones did suffer,
but now his war is won.
In heaven, Wilfredo won't suffer.
Lord, Wilfredo is gone.

—*Peter C. Logue*

May There Be Peace

Young hearts are filled with hope
And carefree young voices ring
But there is no way of knowing
What the year 1993 will bring.
Even now, not far from our boundary waters
Heavy clouds lower a dark mantle of gloom
Over the many greedy and restless nations
Where those murderous war guns boom!
Their echoes of horrible combat
Reverberate on dear America's shore
Making our cries be one for peace-
America shall go to war no more!
Have we forgotten those heroic lives
Given that we might live in peace:
Forgotten the prayers of dying lips-
That war among men would cease?
Oh, that brotherly love may prevail
As this new year is unfurled;
Through faith in God may there be peace
In 1993 among all nations of the world!

—*Myrta Weatherhead*

God's Treasures

The tides of the ocean come to wash the shores and the lovely
   sea shells
and clean the grains of sand and relics of the deep which tell
stories of great voyages and journeys to far-away lands,
as the swiftly-rolling tides reach out their hands
to gather the treasures of the water's depths and swelling waves
which rush back and forth with strength of will to stave
off uninvited guests who seek the innumerable treasures
of these vast waters which can never be accurately measured.
The foaming, gushing tides pluck and store the sand into a round
   figure,
then, the intricate grains of sand grow into a ball, ever bigger.
As our old friend Time wanders on his endless way, this ball of sand
quietly, unnoticeably steals itself into an unobserved oyster clam.
The tedious labor of the ocean tides rides on for hours and hours
until the ocean stops to think and decides to combine its Godly powers;
for days, months, and years, the clam and sand are whirled and whirled
until the useless grains of sand and the clam are joined to make a lovely
   pearl.

—*Mary Margaret Farnsworth McBride*

Prayer For An Interview

Dear God,

Please guide him safely to his destination. Give him strength
and confidence essential to his appointment. Let his honesty
and sincerity shine through for those who await him. Keep him
loyal to all causes that are right, and faithful in your love.
Let his words flow like poetry to those ears of men who hold
his destiny in their hands. Let his frustration turn to hope.
Let his mind and heart work together in his fight to convince
men of power of his dedication to himself, his family, his
friends and his job. Carry him like the wind through this
anxious time and keep him secure in his position, so that when
it is over he can be assured that he gave all he had and that
with your love, others will have had the benefit to have met
him. — Let it be his turn to win.

—*Wendy Walters*

Inspiration

In a world where love is overruled by hate,
And couples are separated because of fate,
You showed me how I could be happy and free,
And how I could have what was made for me.
You told me what I wanted to hear, no lies,
You sang me sweet songs, all lullabies,
You touched the heart of me, deep inside,
You taught me to smile when I could have cried.
But all this was just the beginning,
You helped me in a game I never thought I'd be winning,
You told me in this world of dreams, it could all be true,
I just had to believe, and I do, but I wouldn't if it weren't
   for you.

—*Melissa M. Cullen*

Ode To An Aging Lover

So what if time has taken youth away
And dashed your dream of earlier, sunny time.
And what if youth has nothing left to say
That used to tempt and thrill you in your prime.
And what if smoothness leaves your eye and cheek
That once ennobled beauty's battle field
And wrinkles in her place comes court to keep;
Despite the best of ointments, will not yield.
Beauty not from outer things is wrought,
Of raven hair, or cooings of the dove,
But is from hidden, inner sources brought,
The heart, the soul, the you I always love;
   And so as time his wing`ed passage flies
   My love for you forever multiplies.

—*John Morley*

"Together Forever"

Do you know I feel for you
And do you know I care
Do you know I still dwell
On the fun times that we share
We laughed and loved on those first few day's
Till the cool nights took its place
And when we parted each other arms
I still kept the memory of your face
You held me in your arms
And squeezed me till you slept
Our touch was something special
It was a dream how we met.
Those nights were cold, our bodies warm
And you were all I could feel
For the love I felt inside my heart
Was truly something real
I need the love that once was true
And the happiness that I held
From the guy that I once knew

—*Natalie Cassar*

Vanishing Light

In the year of the vanishing dream,
A fantasy that hides the tears of desire,
The dark is a place that is filled with seclusion,
The torn, withered rope that once had bonded us,
Is now to separate us; The rain is a sign,;
A momentary reasoning deep within,
The times we shared had to end,
To move onward bound, the road waiting for me again,
I see no sleep, the rope had been a good friend,;
Today it will break, along with the love I forsake,
And memories will lay eternally upon the forever trodden road.

—*Tim R. Payne*

Vermillion

Today I wandered back in time
And for several hours the world was mine
  The man I love was by my side
Though he draws away like the ebbing tide

  The lake so blue with a gentle breeze
  That rustled softly through the trees
Where like sentinels they guard the waves
That crash against the shoreline caves

The picturesque town is of years gone by
  Built when life was rich with style
When home was where the heart belonged
  And all were welcomed with a smile

We trampled paths, well trodden routes
     Appreciating all we saw
  Enjoyment deep within our hearts
With this contentment who needs more

  —*Barbara Decker*

Sonnet VIII

The crystal tears slip gently down my cheek
And form a pool as blue as Neptune's eyes.
From shaking eyes of sorrow do they leak
Like rain from dolphin-gray clouds in the skies.
My face holds tributaries of my pain
That feed the steaming rivers on my skin.
The loss streams through my heart and floods my brain
While silver tears spill sadness off my chin.
But even though the tears flow steadily
Like droplets in a deluge racing through
The stinging, lightning sky to reach the sea,
The countless tears are quite in number few.
For were my tears to fill the ocean's size
They could not match the hurt seen in my eyes.

  —*Kevin White*

To War

As we leave our merry shores
  And go to where there are no more.
Let's look back and view ourselves
  And see if this is the way to war.
I dearest say to all who hear
  I do not wish a way to war.
We can only ask ourselves
  Do we have to go to war.
I wonder as we close upon the shore
  Do we have to go to war.
I pray for America free and others who seek to be
  Must I go to war.
It is not what we think or feel but
  I must! go to war.

  —*James O. Stephens*

The Sea

White crests rolling their bits of starfish, and sand dabs,
and golden braise of seaweed entrapping the shoreline.

A barrier of rock and reef to slow the pounding surf.
Enraged as it is, the waves caressing the cliffs sending
spewing eyelets of water in the warm air and crashing into
the covered walls of barnacles enormous and mighty.

It glows like a diamond pendant. The sea gulls cruise
the air... they find a morsel of fish in its vast city.

The horizon goes on forever. The islands near, yet so far.
Is it beginning here or stopping on this shore for a moment to move on?

Yes, the sea... it will be in strength an eternity, or will
it last moments...???

  —*Sherri Trout*

He Can Be Your Comfort

Jesus can be your comfort
And He can be your guide.
No matter what,
He'll never turn you aside.

He can be your best friend
And on Him you can always depend.
Believe and trust in His word,
and your prayers will always be heard.

Jesus will give you happiness and peace.
His love for you will never cease.

He'll share your burdens and make them lighter.
Give them all to Him and your day
will become much brighter.

He'll help you from day to day
With whatever troubles may come your way.

He'll help you when things go wrong
And it seems there's nothing else to do,
If you'll just look to Jesus, He'll always
see you through.

  —*Tayran Watkins*

The Tears Of A Child

If I could grasp a shedded tear
  and hold it up to the light;
What information could it reveal
  that might help you through this plight?
Would it tell of all the sadness
  that has entered into your heart;
Or whisper of the hidden love
  that you have begged to depart?
Would it show a collage of memories
  that you want to hold so dear;
Or reveal a palette of confusion
  that you must now fear?
It's only a tear, but it's the tear of a child;
  A child in pain, a child filled with sorrow;
A child desperately reaching out
  In search of a safer tomorrow.

  —*Wendy Blunt*

I Care

My life has been given to me as a very precious gift.
And I always want to help those who are down, and give them a lift.
Whether it be in a radiant smile, or a kind word to share.
I love everyone, and I really do care.

I am so grateful that God has made me.
And instilled so much of this wonderful world for my eyes to see.
I care for all people and everyone in pain.
Whether or not I may ever know their precious name.

Sometimes my heart becomes so overjoyed, and I'm very glad.
Of this wonderful, caring life that I've had.
I care most of all because God lives within me.
And this is the only way I'll ever want it to be.

I find it so easy to show my kindness to everyone around.
I care, because I know that God is always looking down.
I am so appreciative for all things on this earth for me to
  share.
That's why it's so simple, for me to love and to care.

  —*Ree Bullock*

To Be With You

I hope you realize just how special you are,
And I hope you know you defeat everyone by far.

You bring happiness to my life, both night and day,
And together, forever, and for always we'll stay.

I never dreamed there'd be someone like you,
Who'd care for and love me the way that you do.

When you're near me, warmth swallows my heart,
And feel safe and secure, as though we'll never part.

I endlessly long to see your wonderful face,
And I dream of drowning in your deep, strong embrace.

I respect and admire, your hopes and your dreams,
And I'm not mad and unhappy, as you think it seems.

I would be foolish, to ever bid you goodbye,
So please comprehend, I'll never leave, cheat, or lie.

I love you, I mean that, so never be blue,
Because all I ever want is to be with you.

—*Misty Rheingans*

I Am

I am tired,
And I need a place to rest my soul,
but I can't seem to find a place
where peace and calmness rest.

I am weak,
And I need a place to rest my thoughts,
but my time keeps spilling away,
and my thoughts keep slipping.

I am alone,
and I need a place to rest my tears,
but my heart keeps breaking,
and my fears are still calling.

I am desperate,
and I need a place where I can
be with one.
but I can't seen to find a place
where I can be happy and free.

I am tired and weak, alone and desperate,
vulnerable to emotions, I am living.

—*Amanda Caesar*

Winter's Children

I watched my children playing, outside in the snow.
And I remembered when, not so long ago.
When we played for hours and braved the wind.
And we always hated to go in.
We'd play so hard you couldn't feel the cold.
We were young and strong and oh so bold.
But now the children that I have
Are the same as me when I was a lad.
But now the cold hurts my fingers,
Not theirs, no how!
And yes they hate to hear Mom say
    "Kids come in now."

    —*Troy W. Gowler*

Death By Firing Squad

Stand straight little man.
Move not a muscle.
We do not want our
Fine executioners to miss
Your flinching heart.

    —*Laurie Boisvert*

Why Is It?

Why is it a soul can stare in wonder
and idolize a beautiful creation,
Such as an explosion of a sunset on
the glistening waters of a crystal ocean bay?

Why is it a soul can wonder of the
creation and beauty of a majestic
snow capped mountain scene on a crisp,
cold winter morning?

Why is it man idolizes the beauty in the
creation of a powerful eagle in its flight of
pride?

Why is it he can see the most terrifying
beast in an awesome wonder of hatred,
and respect his beauty for what it is?

In all the beauty of creation,
why is it man can not idolize God as
creator, for the beauty in all things,-
He alone is the wonder of our existing creations.

    —*C. E. Hull III*

Mike and Jeff

Mike and Jeff are their names
And I'm their uncle Jody.
Easter is a happy and joyous time,
For Mike and Jeff,
It was a time with their uncle Jody.

Easter is a fun time,
For Mike and Jeff,
It was a time of rolling a ball across a table to their uncle
Jody.
And him rolling it back.

Some may say uncle Jody is a cripple.
But to Mike and Jeff
"Uncle Jody just has a neat chair with wheels and we play in
it sometimes."

Mike and Jeff are four and nine
But others are older
And don't understand things.
Like Mike and Jeff.

    —*Joe Hemphill*

Promises

Promise me that you will stay by my side
and in me your deepest thoughts you will confide.
Promise me you will be here through the storm
and I promise to keep you safe and warm.

Promise me that you will always care
and I promise that when you need me I will always be there.
Promise me that your love will be forever true
and I promise for you there's nothing I would not do.

Promise me that you will always believe in me
and I promise to love you unconditionally.
Promise me that your inner beauty will never die
and I promise you will be the only woman that will ever catch
    my eye.

Promise me that your love will remain strong
and I promise that even when I'm right I'll be wrong.
Promise me that you will stay as gentle as a feather
and I promise to love you forever.

    —*Ali Muhammad*

Powdered Dust

You were in the clouds and in the earth
And in the sea, waiting, waiting there
For me, from powdered dust it was that you
Were formed with water added.

Through the air, around the earth, across
The sea, I came searching, searching
Until I found you.

Quickened, engulfed by care's perfume, I held
The earth in these two hands, I held the sea,
I held them close, I held them close to me,
If I could slow the sun, I would have
To stretch those days forever.

I see you in the desert wind and deep
Within the sea, in the morning's mist
I see you waiting, waiting there for me.

—*Max L Johnson*

These Ole Shoes Of Mine

Lord its a mountain you gave me to climb,
And I've had my share of mountains behind.
And each time I climb I depended on faith
To guide me along with each step I take.
But Lord, the path gets so rocky sometimes,
I feel I can't go on in these ole shoes of mine.
Rugged and worn, torn and abused,
I sometimes forget the purpose for which they are used.
Please give me strength to continue on,
Please give me courage for this journey unknown.
And when my shoes no longer hold to my tired and weary feet,
Please help me to remember, shoes are not needed on
Heaven's Holy Streets.

—*Kim Keeton*

Questioning One's Reality

I often speak of mythic things
And maintain reality within myself.
Reality is said to be a true existence
Within the world of man and woman kind.

Yet I speak of things that some would
Not count as a true existence.
But what man can actually speak in
Say this is not reality?

For reality in ones eyes could be his truth.
And yet in another mans eyes it is untrue
Because he cannot see ore perceive of such
An existence in this world of today.

I speak of things seen with eyes beyond this world.
In other words; with the eyes of a dreamer!

Therefore; one must use his own imagination
And be able to maintain his self existence
And know where the line of reality lies and
the point that leads to insanity!

—*Larry Newkirk*

Alone

There once was a man with no name,
And no one knew from whence he came,
His complexion was fair and his stature tall,
And within his soul lay a silenced wall,
His eyes were complex with features so deep,
His voice was soft with emotions that seemed to sleep,
His actions so silent and yet so sincere,
That no one even noticed he was here.

—*Kathrine M. Moore*

Mama's Cleaning Spree

When Mama goes on a cleaning spree there's nothing safe but you
and me. All our clothes and all our toys have found their way
to other boys. When Mama's in her cleaning mood, she'd grab a
broom and I'd be shooed out to the other side of town - I
didn't want to hang around to see my treasures disappear - The
things I'd saved for nearly a year - My baseball bat, all
cracked and splintered - And my baseball glove that the ball
indented - A football that was much too soft - A kite that
wouldn't stay aloft - My favorite sneaks that I outgrew -
Somehow I guess I always knew, they'd find their way to the
city dump, but I just can't help getting a great big lump.
When I came home, 'twas to a room like new - Space in the
closet, an empty drawer or two, just calling out for a new
collection - I cast my eyes in every direction - And I could
see around every bend, the makings of a brand new friend - More
treasures to keep within my room 'til Mama comes in again with
her broom.

—*J. Patricia Holohan*

Untitled

My fingers grasp for some unreal spot
And my eyes wonder solemnly to the past.
I hold on to what I have
But end up only letting go.
The silence of my dreams
And the darkness of my thoughts
Only come together to form something
    that no one would ever understand
I reach in my pockets and grab what is not there
I feel I may never see again
Though my eyes adjust to the light.
I may forever wonder over daring seas
Knowing I will never see his face again.

—*Shelby Failing*

My Everlasting Love

Just being with you makes my days much brighter
        And my heart a little lighter.
        My nights are without a cry,
    Within me this love will never die.
    An intimate love that has just been born.
        A love that will linger on and on.
        A love that will last past eternity.
    A love I want to keep under lock and key.
    Without this love there's no comfort within,
    This warm and loving feeling must never end.
        I love you with all my body and soul,
        This love — I'm going to keep and hold.

—*Rosa L. McQueen*

Because Of Your Love

These heartstrings are tight inside my chest
    and my love seems so lost, so hollow.
Then those tears once again fall
    slowly down my cheeks,
I try to hide the pain on my face
    from your eyes.
But sometimes I cannot
    as the weight of my love pulls these strings tight
I find myself crying,
Because you give your love so freely;
    you believe in me.
Because you want only; for me to be free
    with your love; you have shown me.
To look upon this pain
    that I feel and smile.

—*Mona R. Burk*

Troubled Times

My pen is dry
And my page is blank. The stream is to cry
As the river overflows it's bank.

The sky is rosy and pale blue. Nature is calm.
But I'm not, what should I do?
All my life's decisions are here in my palm.

Trapped in confusion. By family and friends.
The question is only an illusion.
The answer posses only pain with no amends.

So pain, I bear.
And with doubt and confusion still in my mind,
My heart continues to tear. Without much love of any kind.

All I ever wanted was for two worlds to meet and come together,
For all my problems to disappear
But all I got was outside this evil weather,
And within me pain and fear.

You can't have your cake and eat it too,
Because life's full of all kinds of choices.
You're the only one who can choose what you are to do,
All through your life's courses.

—*Tracy J. Emberton*

The Ring

In her mind she thought she failed
And now she lies there, meek and pale.
In her heart she thought it was right
And so she ended a future that was clear and bright

She had finally found the love of her life
And hoped to soon be his wife
But things went wrong and they had a fight
And now she's in a world of white

Now, as he sits there and stares at the ring
He remembers the joy she used to bring
And all the fun and love they shared
He cried as he realized she will no longer be there.

As they lower the lid to her eternal bed
He sees that his only true love is dead.
And as the birds sorrowfully sing
He catches a glimpse of the ring.

His friends gather at her sides
And quickly, his tears, he tries to hide
But down his cheeks they slowly roll
As she disappears into the snow.

—*Kimberly Vidiksis*

Messenger

They found me in stones
and old cheeses
and when they unplugged the telephone
Lo, I was there!
I scurried with rat's feet under fat sofas
I delivered telegrams
I flew.
I carried clouds in my pocket
and laid my fires everywhere.
I am so astounding they paper-backed me.
I played leap-frog.
I bragged, I brooded.
I watched my shape.
I died, I lived.
I am always catching them.

—*Roxanne Lanier*

A Friend?

I flew a kite up in the sky
and on the string lit a fly
I looked at him and him at me
at first I thought he was a bumble bee

I flipped the string and away he flew
disappearing up in the blue
Suddenly I felt something on my leg
this same fly rubbing his legs as if to beg

I swung at him with a loud slap
he flew up and lit on my lap
What do you want? I suddenly asked.
apparently he wanted to sit in the sun to bask.

I know a fly cannot be a pet
a crazy thought, perhaps; and yet
To this day I remember flying my kite up in the sky
and on the string lit this fly

Was this fly friend or foe
I guess I will never know
From this small insect, can we learn a lesson
Everything on earth is sent with a blessing.

—*C. J. Moshell*

Untitled

The battlefield looked grim,
And our chances were quite slim,
To conquer our opposing foe.

With so many lying dead,
While so many people bled,
There were somber voices, solemn thoughts of woe.

However, they pressed on,
And we'll never know who won,
And all around were canons crashing loud.

But no matter who did fall,
'Twas all for one and one for all,
And the flags' still standing, flying, waving proud.

—*Alex Norris*

One Final Goodbye

The uniform that magically transformed you into a man— so tall
and proud— My young cousin. The snapshot accents those
laughing Irish eyes and that friendly, lop-sided cocky smile.

The coffin closed — bits and pieces inside — A 21 - gun
salute that shot spaces into my being — And thirty years of
tears have finally dried. A small-town boy from Little Rhody
— our first casualty. Those letters from hell — full of
pride and full-blown patriotism. Your role as hero secure —
but your assassination, cruel and unfair.
Billy, we hardly knew ye.
As memory blurs, I want to celebrate your life, but no
Orphic music can charm or change the fact of your death.

I rant against violence; my passion silences me.
I force my pen in hand — but write I must,
Not to dwell on your death, but to link myself to it.
But I guess I lied about the tears. There's still one left,
And I can feel it rolling down my face, so very slowly —
Over my cheek, my lips, and my chin, where it stops and,
finally, drops. It splashes onto this paper and lands at the
end of this sentence, exactly on the spot where I was going
to place a period

—*Peggy Desmarais*

Frustration

I struggled planting seeds
And pulling everlasting weeds,
Trying to get my garden going and to thrive.
The aching of my arms
Didn't diminish any charms
As my garden seemed to groan and come alive.

The little shooting sprouts
As the beans and peas popped out
Gave promise of the full crop yet unborn.
I sprayed and fed and nourished
As my garden grew and flourished,
And I dreamed about the sweetness of my corn.

I could see the jars of pickles,
Onions hanging like icicles,
And my larder filled with good things I would sup.
I could taste the ripe tomatoes
Savor all the new potatoes
Then the rabbits came and ate my garden up.

　　　—Virginia Hunt Donnelly

Senior Refusal

Would that we could feel the glow of youth again,
And race again headlong toward the unknown,
To face the world again undaunted
And never have to look back where we've been.
Would that our paths had come together sooner -
A meeting that might well have stirred the stars
And rained down on us all His countless blessings
And borne us off to heavenly joys afar.
But, lo, our golden years are now upon us;
To deny it, dear, we do not dare pretend;
But, please, forever know I do admire you,
And with love, just let me be your Special Friend.

　　　—Virginia B. Dobbins

A Mother's Prayer

Oh John, my son, I sit and gaze upon your room
And remember the times we shared so long ago.
I hear your laugh. I see your easy smile.
I feel so close, yet we're so far apart.

Remember the times and talks we shared together
Though long ago, their message still rings true.
I tried to teach you honor and to show you love.
It's ours to treasure - a gift from up above.

There are all kinds of love - you've experienced a few.
There's love for all mankind and love for the smallest flower.
But my favorite love - one that is always strong and true
Is a mother's love, like my love, my love, is for you.

Oh John, my son, I think of you night and day.
Stay safe and well, my God, oh how I pray.
I wish I knew what tomorrow holds for you.
Only God can tell. Oh God, my trust is in you.

Oh John, my son , I'm filled with love for you.
Take care of yourself. I'm praying for you.
You've outgrown my lap, I know so well it's true,
But never my heart, no, never my heart.

　　　—Anne Grove Taylor

Are You Coming Too?

Where is this place with streets of gold,
And rivers of milk and honey, as it is told.
With pearly gates and high jasper walls,
And you can hear the souls of millions call.
The lights of the city is not of moon or sun
Everyone is invited. Are you going to come?
No hunger or pain and you'll never be blue.
I'm on my way. Are you coming, too?

　　　—Kelli Steele

If I Had Been There

If I had been there, at the birth of Christ
and saw that star on that Holy night
I think I would have done, as the Wisemen bore
and followed that star to that open door.
Then I would have pondered at the sight
of all things that happened, on our Saviors birth night.

But now as I study His holy word
and sing the songs that the angels heard
I can not doubt the word of God
But believe His word, as I onward trod.
Then some time later when this life is done
I shall rise to my home, with His chosen ones.

　　　—Neoma Knight

Reality Or A Dream

As I walked down the long white sanded beach, I look back
and saw the sun setting above were we once made love.

I saw your image appear, I walked toward's you, each step
I took I seem to get closer.

I blinked and you were fading away. I ran to catch you,
But you seem to have disappeared.

I knelt down and ran my fingers through the warm white
sand, I remembered the time when you held my hand and told me
how beautiful you feel when I love every part of your body.

A tear ran down my face, I wondered if it's a dream or
reality. I felt the breeze go through my hair, I took a glance
across the ocean and saw a shadow behind me, as I turned you
grabbed my hand and ran through the ocean water, as the breeze
blew threw our hair.

I then realize this is reality, and we once again lay above
the sunset.

　　　—Michaelina Birrell

True Love

I'll never stop loving you,
No matter what we go through,
The thick the thin the big the small,
You'll always be the one I call,
The one to depend on,
To share my secrets with,
The one who knows love,
Is much more than a kiss,
You're the shoulder I cry on,
The person I trust.
The man I adore,
For much more than lust,
You'll always be with me,
Deep down in my heart,
And as long as you are,
We'll never drift apart,
Our love means so much,
Much more than just a touch,
That's why I love you so,
More than you'll ever know.

　　　—Charlotte Bird

88

A Mother's Day Tribute

Mother, I think of you today
And search for words to try to say
How much your love has meant to me.
No greater human love could be.

Your labor of love on others heaped high,
Like Alpine peaks reach toward the sky.
In eternity's skies your rewards will be.
They could never be paid by sons like me.

A greater poet than I could be,
Said, "Only God can make a tree."
But trees and poems, all so fine,
A mother's love will far outshine.

Someday you'll leave this vale of tears,
For your heavenly mansion, free from all fears.
Then I will come where you have gone,
When my time on earth is over and done.

What a grand reunion when we meet over there;
When glorious rapture with others we share.
Then, I believe I can better tell
How you loved so much and served so well.

—*Raymond C. Barr*

The Sky Looks Down

The sky looks down upon my brow
And sees a furrowed frown of lines
That tell of toil and strife with plough
Through parting soil with wanton whines.

The trees look down upon my face
With rigid wrinkles placed not there
By things that time cannot erase
But rather fleeting wear and care.

The hills look down upon my form
All bent and braced for nothing great
But rain and drought and coming storm
That often spawn both love and hate.

The clouds look down upon my wraith
Once here once there but not in care
Of life that feeds on foodless faith
But something else of empty air.

The sky the trees, the hills the clouds,
Is nothing there to let me stare
Up where to find not shapeless shrouds
But rather truth that's truly there?

—*John L. Drehner, Jr.*

My Dream Girl

You are the one whose singing laughter
and soft loving voice fills my day,
yours is the smile that moves me onward
and chases the dark clouds away.
Your face is all that my lonely heart longs for,
a vision I truly miss -
all the warmth in those brown eyes
I'm remembering - the heaven we shared
when our lips touched
in one sweet tender kiss.
You lead the way with grace and beauty
and touch every life for the good,
effortless giving is your passion -
at work or in Motherhood.
Your love returns when you find my love for you
outliving the stress of time -
ever lost in your brown eyes, I'm remembering
the heaven we share
both in life, and in my dreams of you sublime.

—*Keith Sheridan*

A Missed Daddy

Who will wipe away my tears
And softly settle all my fears?
Who will assure me things are right?
Who will tuck me in at night?
Who will tell me what to do?
When trouble strikes, can I count on you?
Who will walk me down the aisle?
Who can always make me smile?
Though you may not be here in the flesh,
You did not leave upon your death.
For you'll always be here in rain or shine.
Daddy, can I still be your valentine?
Thanks for all the good times. I can't recall any bad.
How come this time of year always makes me sad?
Perhaps I'm reminded of the last time I saw your face,
Touched your hand, or heard you sing "Amazing Grace".
I love you, Daddy. I always will.
Your little girl remembers you still.
You are my hero, my best friend, and most of all I pray,
You will be my guardian angel whose love will always stay.

—*Amber Paige Cordell*

Looking For Heroes

Everyone looks for a road to travel
And sometimes a path away from the road
For his own reason in his mind,
And a path back to the road in time.

Who among us can say
Which road belongs only to him
For who is born on a road with his name,
And who can say he failed if he died without fame?

There's a decision at every stop sign
And we weep not for roads untaken
If the one we took was in truth,
For we are not teachers in our youth.

What is greater than true teachers
Who are stewards and caretakers
And know at child is in their hand,
As they try to mold a woman or a man.

So while you search your road for heroes
You are blessed while upon your path
If you can look not for another
And can consider your father and mother.

—*Arnold D. Rife*

My Grace Is Sufficient

My grace is sufficient for thee
My Savior has promised with love.
So when my heart is burdened
I look with trust to above.

Though problems seem to overwhelm me
And no one seems to care,
I look only to my Savior
For He is always there.

Do not feel so downhearted
My Savior has said to me,
For I will never leave you,
That, my child, you can believe.

My grace is sufficient for thee
So lay your cares at my feet.
I will bear your burdens for you
And all your needs I will meet.

This is a promise He gave
So trust in Jesus above.
His grace is sufficient to sustain us
And carry us with His Love.

—*Doretta Mills*

Wellspring Of Grace

The old windmill stands straight
and strong, ascending from earth
to heaven. Its steepled shape,
a church-like spire,
inviting family prayer.

The circling paddles spin
to winds that sing
within the turning arms.
Working fins hum low-pitched
hymns of country psalming.

The windmill pole bows down,
then up, with stop-and-start-like
rhythms, genuflecting
in mixed-meter time to winds'
uneven breathing.

Like organ pipes that swell
with music for the soul, the windmill
brings from hallowed ground
new songs of water born;
the cup fills, holy and life-giving.

—*Mary Willette Hughes*

"Ginseng"

My husband loves to go out in the wild.
And survey around, mountaineer style.
He takes his lunch, in a pack on his back,
Because he don't know when he'll be back,

He searches the shady and outward places.
You'd think he was lost, in outer spaces,
He looks the hills and dales over.
You'd think he's looking, for a four-leaf clover.

He usually starts looking in the month of September.
Because that's the best time, as he remembers.
Sometimes he even starts to sing.
Because he's looking for the herb Ginseng.

—*Juanita McIntosh*

The Seasons

It has been said that Love has many seasons,
    and that with each season the heart and
    eye knows a new face of Love.
It is spring and the face is young.
    There is the delicacy of peach blossoms
    and the sweetness of lavender; there is a
    trust that is Love.
In the summer of love one can be honest.
    The face has set with the lines earned
    from the passage through spring;
    there is the smell of ripening fruit.

With the coming of fall the taste of Love no
    longer tantalizes the soul
    and the face can look on the sweet bird
    of youth and smile.

How akin to winter is the face of that season,
    mellowed and scarred from the caresses of love

No longer dreaming and not yet ready for death
    a face with a faint smile and fleeting
    remembrance of seasons passed.

—*Art Baker*

Two Dads

Two dads were part of her life
And the cause of years of pain and strife.
Her biological father was an incestuous beast,
Her offered father to be was a perverted mind rapist.

One young girl so loving and kind,
But tragically caught up in needs that bind,
Physically, mentally, emotionally exploited,
A victim of fun and games, shamely treated.

Her biological father was guilt ridden with shame,
But to his dying day, would not admit blame.
The promised father also denied any guilt
And hides in paranoic behind a court petition he built.

With all her faith and trust in men that really mattered,
Her God given right to marriage and motherhood was now
shattered. Thoughtlessness and cruelty they sought their
pleasure, her life was ruined beyond possible measure.

The wages of sin are death says the Lord,
The higher court ruling, judgment will afford
Justified punishment to end the story,
But neither father was man enough to say "I'm sorry!"

—*Phyllis R. Gunstone*

Until We Meet Again

As the lights begin to dim
And the day comes to an end

Fond thoughts of memories, until we meet again

As the candles cool, once lit
And the time that once was spent

As it was shared with you my friend, until we meet again

The music starts to fade
And the vows that we had made

Makes this moment more special, until we meet again

The time to leave draws near
So I let you know I care

For it's something we can think of; When?
Until we meet again

Just one last embrace
That brings us face to face

With desires I can taste, until we meet again

Until we meet again, until we meet again

I'll be thinking of you, until we meet again

Until we meet again, until we met again

Because I think I love you, until we meet again

—*Joe L. Clayton Jr.*

Good Bye

When love is gone and dark has come
And there is no one there to hold you
All you can do is sit and think of all the
    lies he told you.

Oh how you wish his love was true
And that he had meant all of the things
    he said to you.

I know it may hurt, but don't you cry
When your love tells you the sad words
    "good bye"

—*Michelle Hendley*

Bloodcage

The beating heart in the cage, they fed it day by day
And the things they fed it made it strong and black
Once it was young and thin like you with dreams to keep
  it up
But they pulled out the dreams one by one and said
  never go back

They sucked the blood and drove the stakes
Till the crimson dripped its sweetness from their lips
Praying to their laughing Gods who ruled through their
  injections
They buried it in bloody scabs from whips

The sweet red blood couldn't defend itself against
  their evil lies
And so soon they had the red all drained away
They fed it on the things that it had once so much despised
And ran when it grew bigger than the cage.

        —*Amber Dye*

Feelings

When the lights go out,
And there's no one around
All my thoughts go straight to you.
The way you make me feel when you
Touch me,
The way your smile brightens my cold and cloudy days.
This lets me know that you are someone special,
Because no other person can make me feel the way you do.
There are not many men who have this affect on me,
And sometimes I wonder why it had to be you.
I guess it's true that for every one woman
there is a perfect man,
And you just happen to be the one for me.
From this day forward, I'll strive to make you happy.
To do all the little things to show I care
To let nothing come between us.
And to make these feelings last forever and ever.

        —*Sonya L. Bell*

The Simpsons

This is a little poem about the Simpons you see,
and they are a great cartoon for kids on T.V.
There is the Mother of Marge to be,
and Homer is the Father we all see.

They have three fine children by the name of,
Bart and he is eleven years old.
And a daughter of Lisa ten, I am told,
also only two is Maggie, more precious than gold.

One time Marge and Homer went to a buffet dinner,
and Homer ate all the foods, that was there he is slimmer.
But the owner got disgusted, and kicked them out,
and Homer went to the judge, and told him about.

The case went to trial and Homer won,
and back to the restaurant he did come.
And he did eat more of the food again,
doesn't he know that over eating is a sin.

Marge the Mother has beautiful blue hair,
and Homer is bald, nothing to cut there.
They all get along, just as fine as can be,
perhaps in their cartoon next year, a new child we will see.

        —*Sharon Walker*

Along the Border

I took the chewing gum out of my mouth
and threw it on the ceiling.
Let it stay there
next to the cobweb and ancient adobe;
like your memory, outside of me now.
No past and no future unless I think it.
Hmmm.
A fly is in the room with me now,
humming as he dances
in the stillness of the air all around my head.
Congenial organism!
Clearly gifted and skilled.
Responding to my friendly mood
he circles, dancing closer.
Enjoying each other and the moment...
Until the fly landed atop the red-checkered oilcloth
next to my jelly donut and coffee.
I thought him filthy and rude and so I killed him.
Outside of me now.
No past and no future... Unless I think it.

        —*Pat Gradsky*

"Dear Mom"

I drove by your old house today
And through my tears, I groped my way
Through all the rooms so dear to my heart
I wandered, looking for you, but found no part

Of your loving self anywhere there
Dust had covered your old rocking chair;
I got lost in the memories of the good times we had
Of you and the others .... the kids and Dad

Of sweet gentle moments I spent at your knee
The things that you taught us are still part of me
Of honor and truth and God above all
To always be humble and to always stand tall.

So Mom if you can, please let me know
My heart is aching for I still miss you so
I wiped at my eyes and sat in your chair
I was wrong, dear Mom, you are everywhere.

        —*Rubye J. Simonton*

Freedom's Window

I watch at my window when the world is still
    And through the dark and lonely night
      I hear a whippoorwill
For what she cries I have no doubt
    The shadows of the past are gone
      But still creep all about
I look with dread upon this night,
    For sorrows held so very near
      I pray with all my might
And as I watch, the Dawn breaks free
    Like the spectrum of lights
      On a christmas tree
I know in my heart the night feels fear
    Afraid of the Foe,
      Yet I shed a tear
And over time the Night has vanished
    Slowly disappearing into daylight
      Or wherever it was banished

        —*Tricia A. Hobbie*

Moonlight

As I sit in the dark on the edge of the sea
And watch the shimmering waves in the moonlight
I am reminded of shiny scales on a giant fish
Gliding to and fro in aimless waste
My fears, frustrations and feelings of uselessness
   rise to the surface
Oh! pale moon, what is my destiny in the sea of
   life?
Am I to be tossed and crumbled into broken fragments
   of despair as the shells on the shore?
Or shall I rise as you with determination to meet
   the night
And slip into peace at daybreak?

   —*Lauralee Trent Stevenson*

Roots

The branch is still standing
   And waving in the wind,
And the roots beneath the soil
   Are still giving life to the body.

The roots are growing upward
   Leaving its everlasting mark
Reaching for his soul
   An imprint of eternal torment.

The roots are still climbing
   Closer and closer to the branch
Reaching for its staunch solidity
   To remind it, that it is his beginning.

The roots are now beginning to twine around the branch
   How can the branch survive
Does it break for its freedom
   Leaving his soul behind?

Or does it continue to struggle
   Hoping for the death of the roots
And the fallen seed of a new life
   That can belong to it and be with his soul.

   —*C. J. Villani*

"Said My Neighbor The Fish"

I took my swim in the middle of the sea
And who was there to welcome me,
My neighbor the fish, who said to me, of sad looks,
And sad eyes, this waters fine for both you, and I,

Only you humans, have been cruel, all your lives,
To the sea, and especially to me, seeking as you have
To invade my only home from earth, and sea life,
As you destroy us poor fish, whenever you please,

I replied with tears to my human eyes,
And remorse within my heart, for my neighbor the fish,
Terrible tragedy, terrible deed indeed,
But let us swim together from sea, to sea,

And will both protect the sea of purity, with our peace,
And with our love, or cause a stormy sea wave,
And start a great flood, to drown a race of cruelty,
And wicked hearts, yes that's what will do,

As I'll be the one to spread this warning news, from sea,
To every fish, and from every fish, to sea of bliss,
Said my neighbor the fish, who swam with me,
To sea of happiness.

   —*Samuel Cohen*

Peek-A-Boo!

Why are the hands of a clock called hands
And why the face called face?
From it's earliest beginning in foreign lands
I cannot find a trace.

I know it gets it's name from France
The original word, 'cloche'
Thought it still means bell, is there a chance
That long before it's day

An Alfred the great or a Chinese make
In nine hundred ninety A.D.
Saw a lady's hat in an odd bell shape
From the twentieth century? (E&P?)

Then both it's hands flew to it's face
As some men's do today
And ever since they're kept that place
On clocks, the French cloche.

   —*Valerie Boyd Howell*

Untitled

Sometimes I look at the world
and wonder why we're here.
Some have it nice,
while others live in fear.
Theft and murder is a crime.
I sit and wonder,
will they do time?!
There are teenage runaways on the streets.
Some are cold and hungry.
Some are down under six feet.
Mommy's are having abortions.
Killing their own.
Let me have them,
I'll bring them into my home.
Daddy's are figuring the bills,
Wondering how he'll manage to
buy our meals.
Again I wonder why were here.
then I remember God is near.

   —*Laura Siders*

The American Way

So proudly we fly the Red, White, and Blue
and Yellow Ribbons for our American Troops.

Their lives they might give, so that we may have peace,
from the blood shed that came so far in the east.

They showed not a sign of being afraid,
but fought on the lines the American Way.

Some lost their lives and left families behind,
while others came home with wounds from the lines.

Awards were passed out, Purple Hearts on their chests,
while others not lucky — were all laid to rest.

Now peace has come, Our Troops we Thank You,
We owe it to God, and the Red, White, and Blue.

   —*Sherry Shelton*

Untitled

Life is but a mystery,
A road that we must follow.
We walk on flats and up on hills,
And sometimes fall in hollows.
At times the road is full of traffic,
At times the road is clear.
But the most important thing of all,
Are the people who are dear.

   —*Larraine Gardner*

Legacy

Sadly leaving life, even perhaps a lonely wife,
    And, yes, a world of hopeless rife,
Fretted worries, none so an unborn tainted ecstasy
Long ago, youth's pangs and dreams, that painful strife
All for the unattainable throne of a hollow legacy.

If only the physical held its fleeting own
To return almighty for the ever-grasping of men
Then a man's remorseful remains would claim victory,
    Laughingly unknown
Who gets what, this man's cruel voicing "Amen".
    Again and again, say when!

So, we little people live and begrudgingly die
And then we quietly lie in state there,
While dumb dastard faces mimic grief over the cold flesh
    Of a worn-out funeral director's fantasy
Life's best deal, now for all surviving to dare,
"Where in the hell," he pleads, "is my worldly legacy?"

—*Arthur Stafford*

In Memory

First there was you then there came me
and you loved me unconditionally.

From my little pony tails, down to my
patent leather shoes, and you were always
there for me when I was feeling blue.

Then came those teenage years with the
argues, fusses, and fights, but we still
remained to be, tight! tight! tight!

Now we're older with more responsibilities
forced to be role models for our new
families!

No longer is it we now it's only me because
death had no mercy, and stole you 1, 2, 3!

Now I'm forced to think back with you on my mind,
when I was yours and you were mine;
oh how I wish we could borrow more time!

And now that day has come for me to mend my
shattered heart, while keeping in mind that
death can't tear us apart!

—*Tonia L. Gandy*

Will The Blind And Deaf Be Different In Heaven

Will the blind and deaf be different in heaven, will the arch
angel say.
You cannot hear, you cannot see, I have no need of thee.

In faith I believe there will be a smile on our Saviour's face,
When he looks deep in the heart of each one, and his a toning
blood we plea.
You used the gift you had, you did please me.

He will say my child you did not see as others did, you saw
with an understanding heart.
You did not see the things I told you not to see, you are a
special child, you did a Christian part.

And to the deaf will be the same reply, you did not steal, you
did not lie.   Many things you did not hear my child, you did
read and obey my word.

You used your eyes for the needs of others see, as you did to
these you did to me.

I believe all angels around our Heavenly Father will crowd,
the blind will see the deaf hear loud.

When the hallelujah around us ring, our hearts will sing glad
hosannahs to our King.

—*Ollie Simms*

Dying Love

"Oh happy dagger there rusts and let me die"

DEATH
ANGUISH - she said she'd die for you.

She looked down on the pale, lifeless body
resting peacefully in a bed of blood,
this bed suffocating a pile of flesh that once
embodied the soul of a beautiful, young girl.
She looks on not in sorrow, but in relief-she
said she'd die for you.

FOREVER. A word of broken love, once meant everything,
now means nothing. A last word. It was for not
that wound that now bleeds openly that stole her breath,
for it was your breath, your word. Her love could not
hold you, but she said she'd die for you.

Her heart bleeds for you, it will never palpitate
against human flesh again, her chest never to heave in
the heat of passion, her lips, oh! her sweet lips never
to be sweetened by others again for they are cold,
chilled by the loss of your love, I SAID I'D DIE FOR YOU.

—*Amber Harker*

Wondering

Turning the edge of a broken heart; feeling lonely and ripped
apart. Wiping the tears that roll down her face; wondering who
will be the next to take her place. Day after day just
wondering why; people fall in love then say goodbye. Nothing
in the world can heal the pain; when he said he loved her was he
playing a game? All they shared, they laughed and cried; the
troubles they overcame because of how hard they tried. Just
thrown away to never have again, it wasn't suppose to be this
way, it wasn't suppose to end. All these questions but she'll
never get an answer; nothing on her mind except for times they
were together. Wondering what he could be doing right now; it
all slipped away and she just wants to know how. Breaking that
point until it fell to the floor; it was perfect and forever
but not anymore. When everything they said and times that were
spent; the best things in love sometimes hurt in the end. What
does she do in this lost and lonely world? Striving for the
answers just a typical girl. Is it worth all this pain that she
was put through?; can she wish upon a star and find somebody
new? Should she just stay alone and never love again?; will
she ever trust another when they say it will never end?

—*Melissa DeNoia*

Youth

            The days pass as swiftly..
                As a wind whirling by;
                    Youth comes and goes..
                In the blink of an eye.
The mirror reflex a sweet young child;
Content with her Barbies..too young to be wild.
A changing reflection seems by 'marrow's morn;
Now finds a young lady..with heart slightly torn.
Then in a flash, as she's turning around;
That youthful reflection can't seem to be found.
Her heart now so scared..it shows in her face;
She longs to return to that past youthful place.

She glances once more..at that mirror on the wall;
Finding her youth isn't lost after all.
        For there in the mirror...
            She sees at her side...
        Her loving young sons..
                Where her youth...
            Now resides.

—*Rowena Hadley*

Turmoil

Silence is golden, so I was told when just a child. Today things
  are different, there is no such word as mild.
From world situations down to our personal lives—no peace and
  quiet found, we're like bees in a troubled hive.

There is a war in Asia—fighting in the Middle East. Heard nothing
  but squabbles at our Thanksgiving feast.
Suffering-violence-pollution and explosions, with little
  thought given to its final corrosion.

A trip to the moon, truly a great endeavor! Fifty-thousand lives
  lost to autos, aren't we clever?
International helper—the good ole U.S. of A.; while our people
  suffer, our government has gone astray.

The elderly mugged, robbed, beaten and left in the streets; but he's
  an addict—deserves a chance, oh what a pretty speech.
A police-officer is shot, a storekeeper gunned down—capital
  punishment is cruel—unjust, listen to how we sound.

This turmoil and frustration has hurt all society; respect and
  love are gone today, there is no piety.
Divorce is in and marriage out—what's the world come to be, when
  men are women, and women men—there's no propriety.

As the world goes, so goes our families and happy homes; material
  things our first thought—just to stay with neighbor Jones.
No love, no respect—just you for you and me for me, so blind
  that to look into a mirror will not help us see.

But let us wait—what's for our children, the world yet ahead?
  Should we worry—should we fight—or close our eyes instead?
This utter frustration and havoc will surely spoil all our
  childhood dreams forever—turmoil ahead, turmoil.

    —Tom D. Brown

"My Mom"

Moms like you
are far and few.
This I have found
to be very true.

It takes a special woman
to devote her love and life.
To be totally unselfish
to be a mother and wife.

A thankless job
some would say.
A job for which
you earn no pay.

Money doesn't mean so much
you can't buy love or laughter.
You've surely earned your family's love
for now and ever after.

Thank you Mom for being you
so loving and so caring.
And thanks for giving love to me
That I may go on sharing.

    —Patricia Corney

The Journey

When the trail narrows as you near end
And the ultimate enigma lies 'round the bend,
Pick all the flowers along the way
And enjoy the beauty of each precious day.

Look over your shoulder down through the years
Re-savoring the pleasures, ignoring the tears.
Drink in the stars … relax in the sun,
Mayhap your journey has just begun!

    —Marie Heathco

Danger Zone

You've broken the rules, now where do I wait?
Are there any clues? No, you can't negate
The ballot or the bullet, still we rise
The electric chair, and the poor man dies
School books, Magazines, and the New York times
Presidents, Preachers, don't commit no crimes
Politics, toothpaste, no, I'm not lying
Just look at my wings, you'll see me flying
We've been pushed to far, now leave us alone
Relinquish, surrender, give up the throne
Figure it out, any old kind of way
But leave with no doubt, its no game to play
Can you smell the swine, cooking off the bone?
Police man, billy club, look danger zone

    —Ronald Jones

"I Must Not Quit"!

    When days are dark and times seems few there
are things that I must do. Although so short I
must admit, I've got to hold on and I must
not quit! Though down the hills of hurting
sorrow, I look to God for a brighter tomorrow.
I hold my head down just a bit, but I've got
to hold on and I must not quit! Ere the tides
that come and go washed upon us white as snow.
    Yet the evening draws the night in my
heart, I will not cry and if my thoughts they
do not fit? I've got to hold on and I must
not quit! So now the time for woes to depart,
    I keep the love of God in my heart. Although
it's been a hard long climb I know it will be
worth it all in time. And yet all these things
seems so unlit I've got to hold on and I
must not quit!

    —Mary Case

"Mud Dolls"

The moon was full, the air was still,
around the house in that small town,
of Three Springs, Huntingdon County, Pennsylvania.
Evonne and Reba were snuggled in bed
before their sleep comes nigh,
to talk about the things they did that day,
they were thankful their Mud Dolls stuck so
firmly together, with their tiny stone eyes
and their lips made of sticks,
could be held by their grateful hands.
No money to buy a doll at the store,
their Father had died before they were four,
but happy were they, as they curled up in bed,
looking forward to sunrise and the day just ahead,
to play with their Mud Dolls laying next to their bed.

    —Reba M. Snyder-Hamman

Moved By Things Of God

Lord, what beautiful patterns You put in the sky!
And what a privileged person am I!
Each time I take time to think of the "How?"
I fall at Your feet and most humbly bow.

The beauty on this earth You've placed for me
Just hurts me to look at, and yet I want to see
Every hill and valley, forest and glade -
Lord, all of the beautiful things that You've made!

Man-made creations are pale when compared
To the beautiful, bountiful things that You've shared.

    —Myrtle Cox

Where Dreams Go

I build my dreams
as castles of sand,
And gusty shipwreck gale forces
Blow them into the carnation-fragrant air.

The windy gusts cry back to me:
let them be -
Be for thee.

They float through misty tomorrows
As paper kites
whose strings have broken in the March wind.

With passage of time
slow but distinct,
I rebuild my dreams
of dandelion weed.

But Fall enters and up they drift
through rough currents
of icy blasts
to land
and grow
in foreign grass.

—*Linda G. Taylor*

Class Ring

Closed by the door he paused to stand
as he took the class ring off her hand.
All who were watching did not speak
as a silent tear ran down her cheek.

And in her memory her mind ran
of all the times they have laughed in the sun and sand.
But now her eyes are bitter cold
no longer would she have his hand to hold.
They all watched in close as she bent near
and whispered, " I love you." very soft in his ear.

With the ring from her fingers she kissed him good-bye.
Remembering she wore it she begin to cry.
Then the door opened and the wind begin to blow.
As she carried her self out into the snow.

—*Jennifer Doyle*

Out Of The Loop

Saturday. The mailbox flag is raised
as I post a weekend wish for better reception.
Call it "snow" or "ghosts,"
this interference blurs the playoff game
I'm watching, and resists the robot stampings
of the integrated circuit.

So I lose interest in Toronto's one-run lead,
turn to the field just outside,
where fall plays out in yellows
and retreating greens—these ghosts resolve
my view of summer drained through drooping marigolds
and the webbed, whitened mulch.

Suddenly the screen is clear, bat cracks me
to attention and I follow the sharp one-hopper,
smooth-turned double play, three outs.
Between innings now, I marvel how that Bradford pear has grown;
and how, like thievery's clue or clockhand's crawl,
the mailbox flag is down.

—*Matt Damsker*

My Beloved Sea

The sea breeze swept against my face
As I took one last look at my once very clean blue sea
When I was young the sea glistened in the bright
sunlight - but all is gone, no more does it glisten, no
more does it sweep against the hot sand where children
once played.

Come back to me my beloved sea
Come back I say with all my heart
Do what I say for I am lonesome
Come back I beg of you, please come back

On your beautiful sand I built a sand castle and made the
Daily News
This beach is apart of me and many others too
To me you are my friend and always will be

I will always remember you no matter what
You hold a special place in my heart
Night after night, day after day, I came here when I was lonely
I must go now before I start to cry

Good bye my beloved sea good - bye!
—*Kimberly Nestor*

America Mine

Why do I love you, what are you I wonder?
As I watch my TV and hear the great thunder
Of worsened delinquency, more and more crooks.
Enemies bold, bad news, drugs and books
But then one small child is dying for sure,
All America hears, and prays for a cure.
America tries to help the whole world
She stumbles a lot, gets herself in a whirl,
But where else in this great wide world can you go
You can rise to such heights, yet fall so low?
Then pick up the pieces, try again and go on
And America still will stand by her own.
You're beautiful, humanly free and true
Reason enough to stand by you,
And for all of the chances you've given me.
American Mine, I truly love thee.

—*Martha A. Edmunds*

Love

I have loved but once before
As I will feel that love no more
Because love is different unlike sin
But the powers within once again will win
My heart would soar
But then you tore
My heart in two
As I no longer love you
The next time I love it won't be the same
For it was you in whom I blame
Soon your heart will feel the pain
As you will never love one the same
I hope you feel all the shame
But love I will once again

—*Bernice Rivera*

Understanding

A black eye.
A hug
A tear
A smile
A question
An answer
A child
A teacher

—*Sharon DiBiase*

Danniella

She was born on the beam of light from the moon,
as if an Angel was sent by God.
The little angel was as lite as a
feather floating in the wind.
With her chestnut hair blowing as she plays.
She runs thru the spring grass,
stopping to smell the different flowers in bloom.
Trying to catch a gentle butterfly in flight,
and wondering where it went to.
Her smile is so bright and happy,
it could melt the heart of the meanest person.
With eyes of poppy blue,
her looks can hold you transfixed in time.
She was given to us and the world to
bring joy and laughter to everyone.
My Danniella, my little dreamer, Danniella my granddaughter.

—*Terrie M. Burns*

Empty Places

My family does not feel the same.
  As it did year's ago.
To many places empty
  And this makes me feel real low.

I wish just one I could go back
  We'd all be together again.
I'd say something's I wished I'd said.
  When I had the chance back then

But you can't go back and change a thing
  Neither the bad nor the good.
So if there's anything you want to say.
  Take my advice "you should say what you wish"

Don't be afraid "you'll win all your bets"
Then you won't be setting one afternoon.
  Just thinking about regrets.

There is a bright side in this world.
If God has it like I think up there.
We all go to be with them
And get another chance to share.

—*Paulette Evans*

"The Road Of Life Will Take Me"

The road of life will take me
As it goes up and down
In and out
to take me and set me free.
To hear the wind in soaring air
To set the death of Christ to burning flare.
To watch the bird who comes to flight
Through burning flames in the night
To set upon the road of dust
To set my life's journey here I must
But if I watch, I will see
The road of life will take me.
To bring about the peace of life
To bring about the death of Christ
To walk among the road of dust
To say
To play
To pray I must.
But if I watch I will see
The road of life will take me.

—*Jennell Shaw*

The Night Of The Swan

The night of the swan,
As it stre'ches out its wings
And swoons over the trees,
Gliding ever so slightly over the moons' shadow,
Dancing ever so gracefully.

Until suddenly a pair of eyes
Defiantly looking at the innocent white swan comes into view,
He reaches out and grabs the wing of a soon to be lover.

Together they dance and make all the others envious
Skating on the water of a pond wile the lights illuminate all
   that is around them.
Engulfed into a world of their own
One of beauty, peace and love!

A world so strong not even the evilest power could destroy it.
Through the pits and flames of hell,
The flowers of the meadows
To end only as the sun sets over the unknown horizon!

—*Jennifer Waller*

Black Iris

Temporarily refreshed slumped over she gazes
as lyrical movements gush dow the drain
The cold dampness diffused the burning like black clouds
covering the hot and swollen sun from the day before
painfully leaving returning at dawn
The clock strikes and tells her its time and time
again when her spirits darken and the sky grows sullen
with the curtains lowered she
prevents armored thoughts from showing
an audience what goes on behind the scenes of
the flesh of a painting deep sensual petals
shattered torn from its frame in the corner
of their bedroom floor
Her mind stirs and dust settles on skeletons of
romantic interludes past of
his chest adorning tie dyes faded like
mottled pastures of woolen flowers
damaged cut and bleeding
obscured under a snow white veil
left in the dead of winter

—*Tara Raye Russo*

No Name

I feel great sorrow
As my thoughts wander throughout the night
I stare into the darkness
As I hope for a better tomorrow,
I grasp my pillow tight
As a tear rolls down my cheek,
I quickly brush it away
I cannot seem to forget these memories
But I hope to find a away
I try to think of better thoughts
As another sleepless night passes me by
But all my thoughts seem to darken my tomorrows
And I feel want to cry
One day, after all these sleepless nights
I hope to find a way
But until then, I will keep hoping
And longing for that day

—*Michele Harrington*

Together At Last

When we can see the men we judge
  As neither black nor white,
When the sun will rise and rising,
  Kill the choking grip of night.
When walls will not be built again,
  To fence a brother out.
When the meekest cry for mercy
Can drown out the harshest shout.
When we will never have to hide,
  The truth from children's ears,
When frosted hearts can burn again
  and dry these children's tears.
When bombs can never find their way
  To earth to scar her face,
When buttons can't be pushed by men
  to rid her of a race.
When the lies and sins of everyone,
  Can steal into the past,
  Then it is when we can say
WE ARE UNITED AND HAVE FOUND PEACE AT LAST.....
  —*Nikii Davis*

Insight From The Storm

I walked the muddy creek one day
as storm clouds disappeared.
The rain had beaten down the clay
and eroded what was there.

I saw the earth reshaping then
before my very eyes,
As the ending of the streams poured in
And trickled down the sides.

I thought how fierce the lightning struck
and the thunder boomed so loud.
And then the first rays of the sun
pushed past the dark storm clouds

And when the beams did reach the earth
with great reflecting light,
I found the mud had given birth
to a precious jewel delight.

For there washed clean, a diamond lay
sparkling in the sun
That would be lost until this day
had the down pour never come.
  —*Nelda R. Grenier*

"The Arm Of His Love"

As sure as the wind whistles through grassy plains,
As sure as the sea rolls in the depths of a rushing wave,
As sure as a drop of dew presses against the soft petaled rose,
The arm of His love is outstretched to comfort all His weary
heartsick souls.

Life can't be weighed by the day to day debts we pay,
Nor can it be compared to the vague misconceptions of time;
If we can see truth even when deceit beckons along an
  intriguing path,
Life can only be measured by our Lord's blessings, so vast.

Experience is the great master which shows us the way,
Patience is required to help us each day.
Open your eyes for it's plainly in view;
The arm of His love is extended to you.
  —*Janice Struble*

Lifetime Memories

I stood on the deck - while a breeze brushed my cheek.
As the curtains of night slowly closed.
Memories flowed like the swift running creek
Painting beautiful scenes of long-long ago.
A bright summer moon slipped high in the sky
While its light shimmered gracefully below
Rippling sounds of the water as it quickly ran by
Gave sounds of music that I knew long ago.
I listened intently to the tune that it played
A melody quite dear from the past
Lifting my eyes to the heavens I prayed
That my lifetime memories would always last.
  —*Norma Dotson Payne*

The Golden Years

Many the halls in years of old
As truth be told slowly unfold.
They were all the tomorrows lored
And yesterday's bygones stored.

Memories of gold rest in souls
Through smiles, through sweetness, least it shows.
Enduring 'til the end, hearts pound.
Lost loves cannot seem to be found.

To grow old not like dust that blows—
Of strength and courage polished gold.
Thy wood cane, they snarled fingers
Youthful once with grace still lingers.

The apple, peeled and then exposed
Books once read cover to cover, then closed.
Dark clouds rage in heaven's aglow.
They've seen fear of storms bring rainbows.

Listen for every tree must fall.
Walk the wayward road, Angels call.
My mind delights - never forgotten
Golden apples cling unrotten.
  —*Margaret Gaudiosi*

Children's Magical Moments

It is time for children to go to bed...
As visions of dreams will come in their head...

Dreams of sugar lands and cracker jack towns...
Toy soldiers and funny clowns...

Dreams of mermaids and giants so tall...
Merry-go-rounds, and a Big Bouncing Ball...
Dreams of amusement parks and talking cats...
Water slides and walking Base Ball Bats...

Dreams of giant lollipops
and her shy kisses...
In a land where no one misses...

Dreams that only children will keep...
In their minds when they are asleep...

Dreams of fairytales all their own...
places they are not scared to go all alone...

As they wake, in their heads, the dreams will stay...
until time for sleep, when they can play...
  —*Wendy Baguio*

97

Evolution

Image
Association
Concept

Rationalization, memory, comprehension, inspiration.
  Reflection.. now after a greeting from these distant
    players their hands gripped onto mine, many times.

    An impression was bonded in gentle arms, a collectivism

    This journey marched down the halls of aging desires.
      Organized precise it felt right to dare the space,
        when infertile dreams were hungry for so long.

      The wings of their actions were frozen by
        disbelief of a better tomorrow the inception
        moved on.

        Emotion was dressing its creation
        the precision of design, maybe a new
        birth.

        This evolution being rooted before me
        the potential in its worth.

—*Patricia Fritsche*

Shannon

What a day when Shannon became twenty one
At least three people didn't think it much fun
The twenty one year old with the most sparkling eyes
Is number two now with Shannon is view of the guys
The one score and one who was first in sweet spice
Is now only second with Shannon still on the rise
And still another who is twenty plus one
Is so disappointed she may become a nun
For her title of most lovable has passed away
Gone to Shannon where it surely must stay
These three are sad and feel they have lost
They feel that way because Shannon's now boss
The good news for them is they'll be twenty two
But shortly thereafter Shannon will be too
Number one in their year they can only hope to stay
Until the time comes next year for Shannon's birthday
But rather than be sad and cry
They could tell a believable lie
They could carry flags that when flown and unfurled
Would say Shannon is to lovely to be of this world.

—*Tom Gaumer*

My 1930 Spectacular Experience

Just above the Luke paper mill
At the foot of the hill
One fourth of a mile from civilization
Twining left on a narrow, winding dirt road
A spectacular experience was about to unfold
On the right an unbelievable stone cliff formed a wall
Stretching skyward out of sight, expecting stones to fall
Spellbound, I saw for the first time - the wild savage river
In a hurry, untamed it sped like no other
Rushing and gushing over large jetting stones
I felt a chill in my bones.
The only sounds were birds chirping
I hurried on without lurking
Before me was a large grassy area
Noticing picnic tables, stoves for cooking - I could eat a bear
Following a path among tall trees, I could see log cabins there
In the distance, I could hear the thunderous roar of the unique
Savage river.

—*Marguerite L. Arnold*

Deer Hunter

Sleep, sleep, sleep
Awake early; eat quickly; dress warmly.
The air will be cold.
Out before dawn.
Walk to the stand; make the climb.
Tired, tired, tired
Relax, relax, relax
Daylight arrives.
Gun is cocked, but set on safety.
Watch, watch, watch
Wait, wait, wait
Listen, listen, listen
Birds sing, squirrels cavort.
Jet planes pass high in the sky, time passes too...
Then it appears!
Heart pounds, body still, breathing deliberate.
The prize moves on, never within range.
Discouraged, discouraged, discouraged
Make the walk home.
Sleep, sleep, sleep.

—*Mark Angel*

The Walk

If I could walk along the beach, I would want the sun at my
back, and you by my side.

Like the driftwood on the beech you have drifted into my life;
adding beauty and form.

Like the artists' portrait of the ocean and
all it's wonders, my feelings for you are as awesome.
As awesome as the sunsets disappearing over the water.

As the midday sun warms the water,
You my love have warmed my heart.
You have lifted my soul.

Lifted to the heights only known to the great white birds
that scan the sea and disappear into the clouds.

You have rushed into and invaded my every thought.
As the frothy foam rushes to and invades the sandy beaches.

And I thank you my sweet, from the bottom of my soul;
Which is as deep as the waters in the portrait;
For the chance to explore your heart.
As we walk and drift together on the sandy beaches of life.

—*Ann L. Waldon*

Footprints In The Sand

I walk across the sandy shore
Bare feet sinking deep in the soft earth, searching.
For what, I do not know but leaving behind me Footprints.
Showing where I've been
Yet expressing nothing of where they will lead me.
Like footprints on the shore
A life is made richer, deeper, worthwhile
By the special touch from someone you call a Friend.
A friend cannot pass through your life without leaving something—
A footprint on your heart.
You will never be the same again.

Like footprints in the sand
Friendships come, friendships endure, and friendships go.
The waves of time may sweep them away
But will leave everlasting impressions
To share with the next 'sole' you have a chance to meet.

Like footprints in the sand, you left a footprint on my heart.
Impressions, you touching my life in a very special way.
Footprints may wash away with each passing wave on the shore,
But the memories will last a lifetime.
Your footprints will be mine to cherish. Forever.

—*Sandy Hiskey*

Come Walk With Me

I am a small child
  barefoot and hungry
  and yet I must walk
  to get water and firewood
  for my mother to cook our meal.

Come walk with me.
  Is the way long?
  Yes, I know, but walk with me just for a day.

I'm hungry.
  I have no hands but yours to extend to others.
  I have no feet but yours to pound the pavement.

My way is earthen
  but we go the same distance.

On my path
  I pass by huts and banana trees.
On your path
  you will see beautiful homes
  with well-manicured lawns.

Come walk with me... please
  Saturday, May 22, 1993.

  —*Rosemarie Moews Scarbeary*

Balkan Queen

Shadow cast upon my door
barefoot... dancing in my soul.
Pen and journal...clutched in hand
unframed wisdom...bridging lands.

Quest for truth...set her apart
betrayed homeland etched in heart.
Ethnic revenge...horrors past
her shattered nation...an outcast?

East-West destined to collide
on bloody bridge of genocide.
Far East led her to unfold
prodigal son...in search of gold.

Blood lines...archives...reconciled
Prince of Balkans...a bastard child?
Her silence revealed betrayal since
West unthaws exiled Prince.

Horizon vanished in the storm
through fog...we lost her flickering form.
Barefoot...dancing in my soul
...a mere shadow upon my door.

  —*Sonia Wolff*

I Was Late For School On Monday

  I was late for school on Monday
because I thought it was Sunday and I went
to church by accident because I thought it
was the Sunday in lent. I was all dressed in my Sunday
best all ready to go. Until I got there, there wasn't
a single person there I know. I was late for
school on Tuesday because today is dues day.
I had to go and help my parents pay the dues
for all the week. I had to attend a wedding,
I was the best man. I got kissed by the flower
girl and got hurled by a girl named Pearl who is
the toughest girl in the world. I was late
for school on Thursday because today is birds
day my family goes around the neighborhood feeding
birds of every kind. I was late for school on
Friday because today is My Day!

  —*Randee Patillo*

Reflections

The sunlight shone from between the trees,
Basking your face in its warmth and gently
  touching the hair hiding
  your blushing cheeks.

It illuminated the softness of your
  mouth and stirred the darkness
  of your eyes.
Your eyes spoke to me, reflecting
  the love I offered you.

What right did that beam of light
  have to capture those lips?
To feel their warmth and listen to
  them speak.
To swim in the pools of your eyes.

Alas, the sunlight has gone.
Evening tide brings shadows—then
  darkness.
How fickle that ray of light
That once caressed your face.
How empty my life without your love.

  —*Norm Hobbie*

Echo

The blizzard of ninety-three echoing from the past
Bathing everything in white no other hue was cast.
From Florida to New England wrecking havoc all the way
Nothing in human power could hold the tides at bay.
Streets were awash and power lines became a worry
As the blizzard raged, tornados vented their fury.
Strong gusty winds racing at seventy-five miles
Dwarfed people by snowdrifts of gigantesque piles.
This whiteout brought thunder as dangerous lightning flared
Some states came to a standstill when mother nature reared.
Snow normally measured in inches, switching now to feet
Made our winterland become a scene no eyes should meet.
The Blizzard of ninety-three, now a memory of yore
Caused death and destruction like an echo from before.

  —*Violet Hilderbrand Kane*

Prejudiced

People look at me, smile and giggle.
Because I am different they think it gives them
  the right.

But they judge before they see what is inside
  of me.

Everyone thinks I am crazy for just being me.

But I think they are crazy for discriminating me
  before they see me for me.

Time will go by and I may change my ways.
But if don't and stay the same people may still
  smile and giggle, but see if I care.

I will be me for me, and knowing what I know let
  other people act there way.
I hoping they will realize there ways, change let
  people act there way.

But they may without knowing that everyone has a
little wired inside just put there big fat foot
in there mount.

  —*Spring Damron*

Death

Death is something I don't like to see,
Because it is very awful to me!
It's something I know I'll be,
But, I still hope it won't happen to me!

I hear and see about it everywhere,
And I can imagine me being there!
I don't think I can bare,
All the things that are happening
    around here!

I know I'm almost thirteen,
And people say I'm still a young jelly bean!
I know all these things are mean,
But Death is a very awful thing to be seen!

    —*Tiffany Tyler*

Christmas

Christmas is a time to cheer, not to be sad.
Because of an exceptional, astrological event.
One of life mysteries was unfolded
The birth of a Savior.
It was a spiritual birth, a Holy Birth
It was magic that drawn, the wise men to follow a Star.
To pay homage to a Baby Boy.
We should understand it's meaning.
Christ is good, Good is Joy, Joy is music.
Music that makes the angels sing.
As I listen to those Christmas Carols.
Gift of love, the wise men bring.
To glorify that gracious child. Christmas full with love.
That is what it, will always be. Christmas morn, so merry,
so bright. Bright as that Holy Child. Who brought love,
To the shepherds on the hill. To share with all mankind.
I can hear the jingling of the bells,
And peal of laughter from children, with delight.
"Santa, don't forget that fun gift at Christmas ".

    —*Kenneth Bolton*

Loving Your Father

You came to this place called earth
    Because of your Father
You came with love, joy and peace for all
    Because of your Father
You touched the hearts and lives of people
    from thousands of years ago
    and still today and tomorrow
    Because of your Father
You told us to love one another unconditionally
    because of your Father
You died for my sins and the sins of
    every creature on Heaven and earth
    Because of your Father
You knocked you filled me with
    Love, joy, and peace for all
You let me be a part of your glorious family
    Thank you Jesus
For loving Our Heavenly Father

    —*Vickie Voyles*

Lines from the Bard of Balgonie

As I lay dying dying
I heard a sweet bird crying
Oh Donald don't go
We'll miss you so
So I got up and walked
And everybody gawked

    —*Donald Russell Carman*

The Twinkling Stars

Each night when I was a little child-
Before I would go to my bed
I'd look at the twinkling stars in the sky-
And then I would lay down my head

"What magic kept them from falling"?
    thought I-
It must be a powerful thing-
To see them just hanging so high in the sky-
Such beauty and wonder made my heart sing

They'd twinkle like diamonds so pure and
    so bright-
They were like fairy playmates to me-
But when I'd awake in the morning lite
My twinkling stars I couldn't see

I thought someone took them away from
    their place-
And then I'd begin to cry—
But then when darkness-the heavens would grace—
They were there again—then happy was I

    —*Ann McNamara Heintzelman*

Untitled

Some nights I remember what I had been
Before it was over and before it
    Began. The contrast is clear. The forfeit
was full. Had it been worth it? Imagine
    The end. Utter darkness enveloped
The following Pluto days. In love? Yes.
    That much I know. Happy? 'Tis still a guess.
Sometimes- yet too often discontented.

Craving bliss as the soldier yearns the dove
    I languidly lost my 'I' at great cost.
Then I realized the reason for my fire
    Was not the girl, but my own desire.
Tis it still better to have loved and lost
Considering you lost, so as to love?

    —*Tom Kaplan*

Did You Ever

Did you ever get the feeling that there was some-one there behind you but there wasn't?

Did you ever get the feeling that if you turned around real fast you would see him try to hide?

Did you ever have that feeling that the dream you had the night before just came back to haunt you one too many times during the day?

Did you ever get the feeling that you were the only one in the world and there was no one there to help you?

Did you ever feel as if you were lost even though you were at home?

Did you ever have that feeling that some thing was going to go wrong but you just didn't know what?

Did you ever feel so scared that you just hate going to bed at night and you feel the morning just will not come soon enough?

Did you ever feel that you missed out on something but you just have not figured out what it is or was yet?

Did you ever feel so lonely that you just want to die?

    I DO

    —*Wanda M. McIsaac*

"Grandma, What Are You Doing In The Pond?"

I'm so happy on this bright and sunny day.
Being only six years old; I think I'll go out and play.

I've played all morning with my dolls and I just put them away.
I don't see my mom around so I guess it's ok.

It's hard to put my shoes on, but I don't need them anyway.
I am just running down the hill to the pond, like I did
yesterday.

The grass is cool and soft, underneath my feet.
I can smell the water and it smells very sweet.

I don't remember the water ever being quite this cold.
My hands are turning kind of blue, like grandma as she got old.

"Grandma, what are you doing in the pond?", I heard the other
kids say.
I turn and look behind me, but she must have swam away.

"Come on in the water and play with me." I said,
But the other kids brought me a towel and put me in my bed.

I am really kind of glad they did, because I was getting cold;
And I think my mom would like them to, because I am getting
old.

—*Sylvia Noble*

The Geese Are Flying South!

The geese are flying south!
Below, by day, cars race them by,
Then turn, and see
A-Neatly-Typed-Line-Against-The-Sky.

The geese are flying south!
Arrow straight - a brow - lash of eye.
Urging each other on:
"You can do it! Try! Try!

The geese are flying south!
A-swim through clear, thin air,
Looking down on houses, highways,
Snowy mountains blue with cold;
Autumn trees of fire and gold.

The geese are flying south!
Following their map across the sky.
Dropping lash
       by
         lash
To a warmer lie,

Flying! Flying! Flying south!

—*Marie Froome*

Sorrow

In her sadness
below those blue eyes
above the waist
underneath the fake smiles
behind the forced laugh
beyond the hidden tears
within the girl
with the fake blond hair
inside, deep down
is the sorrow that love left,
that hides stubbornly as possible
behind her painted mask.

—*Tiffany Muctari*

Jehovah-Jireh (God Our Provider)

In solitude I sought my Lord, feeling wan and weak in spirit,
Bemoaning all that I am not and works devoid of merit.
   ... and I said ...

My Father, I am destitute of all the gifts that bless,
So many sins and weaknesses I woefully confess.
Great dearth I see in all I do, console me with Thy pity,
No fortress seems encompassed 'round my saddened earthly city.
   ... and God said ...

You lack for nothing in your life, My Word reveals so much,
Rejoice, dear child, each promise lives for your faint heart to
   clutch.
My own receive unbounded love poured out on calvary,
Pardon, comfort, peace and joy, and power for victory.
   ... and I sang ...

Praise God from Whom all blessings flow, my outpoured heart is
   filled
With strength and inspiration, and my striving is Grace-Gild.
I'll ne'er again proclaim a lack, but glory in my Source,
Since Christ my Lord, from rich supply, anoints my charted
   course.   ..... and all the people said .... AMEN!

—*Meralyn Evans Peterson*

Chaos And Hope

I walked along the path of my life,
Beside the river of reality,
So many raised their voices,
Our social system is hurting,
So many asked me to come by,
Raise their spirits and instill hope, joy and love,
Let them know that "God" and I, their friend - love them.
So many hurting from ego-need pain,
Inflicted by one - who only has themselves in mind -
I asked Him, "Why"?, and no answer came,
Only time can heal these hurts,
And alleviate the pain and repression.
Why, I ask, must there be all this loss,
When all, most all, only wish to do their best,
And be left alone in untrammeled peace.

—*Dr. Roger J. Barnaby*

The Tree

At the start of the day that tree's in full bloom —
birds nest in its branches - there's plenty of room
until people pass by and start pulling and tugging
the leaves - they don't even realize they're mugging
the tree.

By the end of the day that tree's in a state
of depletion, it's weakened, a horrible fate —
it seeks restoration and salve for its ache,
without it its bare drooping branches will break
sad tree.

Then fate intervenes and along comes a child
sauntering by and he stops for a while
and leans up against the trunk that's so strong
and finds himself humming and singing a song to
the tree.

The gift of the song that the child did give
restored the tree's spirit and its will to live
so that by daybreak new shoots did appear
that would give birth to blossoms later that year
with love.

—*Michele Mateo Wood*

After Midnight

Standing on the afterdeck watching the stars falling on the
 black horizon,
I am mesmerized by the wake churning up sparkling foam
 as chalky white caps fly over black curling waves.

Tears run down my cheeks. I'm not sure why. Perhaps because
 you said goodnight
and now the vast expanse of stars reinforces my
 insignificance.

In this microcosm that is our small world, I am but an atom,
 too infinitesimal
to be reckoned on the scale of time -
 as ephemeral as the tide.

Yet in my world here and now all that matters in this hour
 after midnight
is your presence. I wait and watch the waves until the
 wasteful flow of watery tears dries on my shining cheeks

as salty drops rest on my lips where an hour ago
 you kissed me.
 —*Nancy O'Malley*

Like You

Don't hate me because my skin is white, brown, yellow, red or
black. Like you I was an embryo who swam in amniotic fluid in
mother's womb, then made a perilous, tiring journey down a
narrow passageway to emerge to life. This bony base, the frame
upon which I am built, is in all ways much like yours. The
organ that lies within my breast beats in measured rhythm, just like
yours. The muscles, tendons, veins and tissues that compose my
body are just like yours. Don't hate me because my eyes are
blue or brown or grey or black. They see the inequities of
this world; how voracious humans fight, lie, steal and kill to
gain fame or power or amass great wealth. Like you, I see
those who are victims of that greed. I see vast need in all
places on this worldly globe for tolerance, peace, friendship,
understanding, hope and love. With those who do not know those
blessings, I feel their wretched, hopeless despair.
When my course is run and life' deeds are done, this shell of clay
that I call me will return to that plane from whence it came and I
will pass forever from this domain. Can I then say I was one
who loved my neighbor as myself. Like you?
 —*Virginia Stevenson*

"Black"

Black, not just a color, but a race.
Black, not just signifying darkness, but a light.
Black, not being dirty, but, in fact, being pure.
Black, three hundred years of oppression in the past,
 maybe a nation in the future.
Black, not as bad as it is made out to be,
 indeed, it's something special.
Black, it's my race, but not my color,
So why do you call me "black"? I'm brown!
 —*Tyeese Lateefa Gaines*

Writer's Block

What do I do with this
blank page staring up at me
so white, so pure -
Do I defile it with this ink?
Inspiration is such a fickle lover,
teasing me with fleeting kisses
of thought but then leaving me,
alone and unfulfilled.
And I am left with this once blank page,
raped of its purity by my incessant rambling.
 —*Jennifer Haddock*

Untitled

"There she sat near the pond,
Blue eyes, rosy cheeks and curly blonde hair.
Can anyone describe the perfection
that is the miracle of life?
I see in each child a promise,
another world,
a poem with a flaming flash of hope.
In detail,
the hand of the Lord's making
is present in these fragile creatures.
It cold only be translated into beauty,
love and tenderness;
to look for other adjectives
would be fruitless
for they can not be found or
expressed
by any poet, dreamer or realist,
for this work of God."
 —*Jorge Gomes Da Silva*

"Raindrops, Dewdrops And Many-Colored Faces"

Raindrops come down in sheets and mist
Blurring even the sharpest sight
We glare eagerly through the drops
For just a glimpse of yellow light

Dewdrops cling so tenaciously
To sidewalks, flowers, and leaves
To shake them off onto the ground
Takes a brisk and a cooling breeze

Many-colored faces in crowds
In countries, cities, large and small
Build a sense of community
No matter what truth may befall

We crane our necks to see raindrops
We bend down low to see the dew
But we look to other places
When we see many-colored faces.
 —*Kellie D. Gore*

Books

Where would we be today without books
books, books, books, books, books
Books here, books there
books everywhere. Who loves books
I do, I do, I do. Where are the books
Here, here, here. What kind of books
All kinds, All kinds
Books here, Books there
Books everywhere. Scary, funny, love stories too
Western's, true stories, dogs, cats and dinosaurs too
Big, tall and small animals of all kinds
Trucks, cars, small and large are also there too.
Books here, books there, books everywhere
There's plants, trees, bushes, and vegetables too
All kinds of things you can learn there too
That's why I love books too.
 —*Velma Bruchmiller*

Second Of Silence

I breathe, but I hear no breathing
 I listen, but I hear no sound.
 I see, but I see nothing.
A mist of white spreads the air.
 It is the second of silence.
 —*Jessica Prince*

Life Like A Rose

You bloom into this world without choice. As you're born and open your petals for the first time, you do not know what will be out to get you or what your life will become ahead of you.

You're not sure if you like being alive and healthy, or if you want to wilt and die. As days go on, your petals reach their peak of full bloom. You become better than what you used to be.

As each day drifts by, a different petal wilts, and then falls to the cold hard ground. All, but one petal is gone, you know you'll die soon, but you really don't care because your life has been dull. A cold day to make you sick, a rainy day to make you depressed. Finally, the last brown wilted petal falls, and your life is over.

—*Sara E. Hopp*

A Sonnet; Ah! Mustang

Great valiant horse with wild unfettered heart
Bow not to man. You're meant to be a part
Of this great land, this desert where you roam.
You're master here, and here should be your home.
You toss your mighty head, your nostrils flare.
You fling your ringing challenge through the air.
A fiery thing of beauty and of strength,
You claim your ground distinctly. Then at length
You vanish. You are gone with such an ease
As smoke upon the rising desert breeze.
Across the high wild desert land you race
With nothing but an eagle keeping pace.
Rush out of sight, you king of all you see.
Far better gone, than live and not be free.

—*Alta Smith*

It's Christmas

I'm bent over in the driveway,
breath billowing against knees,
the basketball sneering up at me
as I mutter time out, time out.

The haloed wreaths hang in disbelief,
green outlines of coaches' mouths
calling out different plays,
screaming for motion in the snow:

they've seen the missed lay-ups,
the bobbled dribbles. They need points.
So I lift the ball above my head,
slam it down like a commandment,

and fake loose a defender at the key.
There, in the cold of the foul line,
I realize my winter-numbed hands
can't grip the game's final shot:

the same fear that I'll fumble
the communion cup on Christmas morning
and lose the taste of salvation,
blood spilling through my calloused fingers.

—*Mark Allen Cunningham*

Freedom

I looked through the fence
at the children playing
thinking of all the freedom they have
while I sit here in captivity.
Are they really free?
I see a friend holding a bird
the bird is not free either
a cage is his life.
Who is really and truly free?

—*Eileen Paul*

Leprosy Of The Soul

Beyond the realms of life, through the lighted tunnel of
    brilliance and amidst the infinite abyss of the crystal
    whirlpool,
Unchained and no longer earthbound souls refresh themselves in
    an eternal youthful bliss.
Looking out with demonic eyes from a shadowless inferno of
    night, tormented spirits let out bloody cries of drifting
    anguish.

    Burning among their hellish fate
    Paying for their evil activities
    Tortured for their stubborn human selfishness
    Slaughtered by vicious sanity for mere amusement
    Devoured by their own relentless fear and horror.

... slowly the flames overpower them
... one... by... one...
and soon is replaced by the embarking darkness.
What good will repentance and the holy sacrament of
    reconciliation do them now?

—*Thanh Tran*

Bitter Sweetness

The bitter sweet thought of thee,
brings joy to me! This I domineer Merrily!!!
The bitter sweet sight of thee,
brings a tickle and a sharp.
Start-stop pattern of my heart.
Thrilling and treacherous all the same!
The bitter sweet touch of thee,
brings a chill to my spine
and makes me think, "How divine."
The bitter sweetness of all of thee!!

—*Nikki Kohler*

The Environment

I visited a park, I thought there would be nature there,
    But all I saw was trash piled everywhere.
I tried to find a forest and tried to find a field,
    But I only found some ashes,
A burnt forest, was never healed.
I went looking for the ocean
And a bit of sand and soil,
But I couldn't find any beaches
clean and free of oil.
I looked up to the sky
    But saw nothing
Only smog and blackened clouds,
And dirty, stuffy air.

Let's all get together and let's all clean up
And give this planet rebirth.
Everyone has a duty to ourselves
To clean our planet Earth.

—*Rachel Otte*

Tides

Carried over the waves
Behind they crashed, destructive
The icy warm swells pawed at my feet
My forehead forced against the shoulder heated by the season
The arms woven around my childish form.

Breezes chilled hairs I wasn't aware I had.
And as the heat enveloped me, my slick legs
    wrapped around him.

His thighs were soaked and the ocean rose.
I warned him of the depth, I, his careful, wary side.
Puddles did not inhibit me, I feared only this massive water.
Back on the burning grains I curled up and slept.

—*Anne Kouri*

103

To P G J

Ticking silently the clock beats with timeless effort
but can the minute catch the hour?

He waits alone afraid and desperately delivers invisible
shades of sorrow that surround the heart.

He can't change the distance, the time between, but his
clock is set three times to the west.

The clocks were wound, their hands have touched, and
their hollow faces mock the flickering candles that
yearn for the brazing northeast wind.

But can the minute catch the hour and can the hands of
times embrace their flickering candles and shelter their
timeless glow?

—*Robert E. Harley*

"God Blessed Me With You"

God blessed me with you; a tiny baby girl born way too soon,
But God kept you in his hands and took care of you.

Even though I couldn't always be there; you were always on my
mind, in my thoughts and in my prayers.

Some days seemed to go on forever, I thought they would never
end till I could see and touch your face and tell you I love
you once again.

The day you came home was a happy one indeed, the best day of
my life it will always be, when I laid you in your own bed in
your own room, it was the best feeling ever known, for after
five long months you were finally home.

It seemed time stood still when you weren't here now I look
back and wonder did time just disappear, as time passes you do
new things for all to see, which always brings great joy to me.

If things aren't going the right way, your sweet smiles and
funny laughs brighten my day, so I always thank God for sending
you my way.

You will always be very special and very loved, for you are a
special gift from God above, now all I need is just your love.

—*LeAnne C. Daffin*

Nature

I can appreciate the beauty of nature around me,
But I can't spend all the moments I'd like to,
Sitting quietly in awe.

I can enjoy the morning sunrise,
But often find myself too busy with routine things,
To catch a glimpse of the setting sun.

I can plant my bulbs of tulips, jonquils, and crocus-
   a few a time.
But wish that I could run like a child in springtime,
To watch every one push up from the warm earth.

I can take pleasure in the warm colors of the leaves of fall,
Much like I can the pleasure of a crackling fire
   in the coldest of winter.
Yet the fall is too short lived, just as the winter is too
   cold for too long.

—*Joan Crooker*

Beauty Of The Blossom

I sit and look in the mirror and all I see is me
But I close my eyes and it's all I wish to be

The vision I see in the darkness is of no sin
And far more beautiful than the world I live in

No pain nor shame consists in the visions of my mind
But they are only memories to never again find

Memories so precious of a blossom of such splendor
The beauty of the bloom I will always remember

Once filled with wisdom beauty elegance and grace
Never a frown but always a smile upon her face

Now she stands alone in wonder as the night due settles
The weight of the water weakens her tiny pedals

She strives to hold on until the coming of the sun
But soon to realize her struggle for hope is done

Her stem is wilting as her pedals start to fall
She knows she must now answer God's call

—*Shelly Holley-James*

Reality

   Wealth and popularity, their O.K.
but I will go to them another day.
   Looks and hair color, what's the
sense? Those things just make people
uneasy and tense.
   Personality and kindness, now there's
something to look for someone with
these qualities will be your friend
more and more.
   Some people don't like other for
the oddest reasons I say, because of
clothes, how much one knows or because
they talk in a different way.
   But I always called that being
prejudice and I still live by that rule.
   I'll be your friend even if
some people don't consider you cool.
   So, if you act O.K. and you have
a great personality.
   You'll be my friend in my
mind and in reality.

—*Mindy Bradford*

In Search Of...

Oh sisters, my sweet sisters, how I wish that you were true,
but if I cannot believe in me, how can I believe in you.

I've stretched my hand across my life, and with that hand did
send. My love, my trust, my very soul, but could not call you
friend.

What does it take to find this dream? What demon taunts my
heart?, that when I give my all to one, what makes that dream
so dark?

I cannot wish the worst for those, who wish the worst for me.
My heart though hurt and empty now, still love is what it sees.

How I wish this void were filled in me, with just one loving
soul. So I could find this peace on earth, before I grow too
old.

My days are slipping by me now, my heart is going too. I
cannot give you worldly gifts, but I give my love to you.

—*Pat Pinder Helsel*

Tender Age

Save the children around the world
But lets not forget our own
Their crying out in despair
Feeling helpless and alone

Four young teens, who took their lives
For them we grieve and pray
They made a pact, to end it all
Friends forever they shall stay

Oh! what a shame this loss of life
At such a tender age
I fear this is just one paragraph
From a painfully growing page

A loving parent, understanding at times
Their problems for you to mend
You must know when to be a family
And when to be a friend.

　　　—Wayne J. Russo

God's Glory

God is near if we but hear and give a mere,
　　but positive response.
When the heart, the mind, the soul replies
　　in faith, in truth, in Him confides...
we gain the glory of His power, the way to life
　　and the love; His dower.

His beacon glows from every bower...
　　it flows to cease each weighty tower.
His word is wisdom for the soul,
　　with peace and joy it makes one whole.
Toil not in vain or e'en disdain...
　　for when He comes we'll live again.

Stay near...
　　He'll hear...
　　　God's glory from afar
　　　　will light your path from every star!

　　　—Jean Beardsley Allen

The Pain Of Fire

Scars are lonely without touch
But recalling what my mother said:
"The Rose and Butterfly are yours,"
forever designed with the Pain of Fire
Such a tender voice and a tender touch
She is gone now, and no one to heal and aching heart,
Ofttimes I have wished to go
Up in a cloud of hazy smoke
And like a genie from above
Look down on these mortal Folks.
I see them struggling for what they know not of
Some seek for station, power, and gold.
When all that really counts is love
So I say, "Scars are lonely
without touch"

　　　—Mildred Russell

Through My Eyes

I'd like to tell you Just how I feel
But, words alone Aren't always real;
So look inside Through my eyes you'll see
Just what you love has meant to me;
For through my heart And, through my soul
It's through my eyes my love will show;
So, hear me now As if words could say
You are my life my night and day;
And if you wonder how far I'll go,
Just look inside, for there you'll know!

　　　—Tammy Combs

A New Day

It's weird how some things can be so kind
But some things like that are hard to find
But that's okay, even if days are a little dark.
You'll soon find something to set of a spark.
A spark to make things a little lighter.
A spark to make things a little brighter.
It might takes some time.
Just think of a little rhyme.
You'll get through it just wait and see.
Just close your eyes and count to three.
Things might seem just as worse as before.
But something will happen, then there's the open door.
Go through it and see what lies ahead for you.
Maybe a new day with fresh morning dew.

　　　—Angie Yarbrough

The Wall

Once I thought that love was inborn,
　　But that was before mine was sundered and torn,
My emotions were once both tender and vicious,
　　I loved but one,
　　I hated but one,
My love was as strong and as wild as a storm,
　　And my hate was but mildly malicious.

Then my love, she left me alone,
　　With nothing at all but a heart made of stone.
I built a wall of broken dreams,
　　I hid my love,
　　I killed my love,
My love, is gone, and as I roam,
　　My hate is all that remains.

Now I hate many, at that I'm appalled,
　　But try as I might I can't break down my wall.
I built it with power and mortar and rock.

　　Once I thought that emotion came from above,
But I have lost my love.

　　　—Zac Showers

Confused

I met a man this past year,
But there was something that I feared.
He seemed to be coming on too strong,
It always felt like something wrong.
I wasn't ready for what he wanted
　　or at least I thought I wasn't.
But as the days grow long
I feel myself growing fond
　　of hearing his voice and knowing his song.
I got confused because I want so much,
I only looked at the outside and such.
What's inside counts and it always has
I was just blinded by the real worlds fad.
So what I feel for him won't sink
I just need more time to think.
He may not always wait for me
Until I finally clear my mind and see,
That what I really want is standing in front of me.

　　　—Tina Davidson

Blue Genes

I am not saying that you're full of beans,
But this is not about Levi's jeans.
No, we refer to those really sad genes
Involved in heredity in human beings.

There is splicing and slicing entailed in this mix,
A complex chemical that gives science a fix
On this unit of chromosomes that's always playing tricks:
A carrier of heredity that gets in its licks.

Better to stick to the blue jeans we wear
Than the blue genes that can mutate without care,
And in so many ways can affect our welfare,
Just like you are bald and I have red hair!

Perhaps these genes don't like what they do,
But it's all that they know, so it's better if you
Let them follow their sequence (for I have no clue),
And perhaps they'll be happy in their DNA glue!

—Ted Brohl

The Gift

God's gift to mankind, makes us think look and wonders
But will never find, the gift of happiness, pleasure, and pain,
One tends to notice the sunshine rather than the rain,
The gift of love, contentment and health, that give something
More meaningful to life than just money and wealth,
How sweet it is to love and the gift, because it is like
A lion that not only runs fast but he run swift,
How do we use the gift and what can we do with it,
Sometimes we forget about how wonderful
The world can be when you use your gifts
To deal with you problems bit by bit,
For the elderly as well as the young, that's the questions,
That make the problems we have are small
Instead of us making them as big as King Kong,
That's renders our hearts into confessions
That is God is our gift to mankind and all nations,
For truly, truly, man and women are his greatest creations,
So the gift or gifts that you have you should
Use them the best way you can,
Because it is meant for only you and God to understand.

—Temmie Lee Hughes

Innocence

A child looks through innocent eyes seeing only beauty in the
butterflies; oblivious to all the worldly charms, knows nothing
of their hurts and harms. A winged creature falls to the
ground, not one flutter, nor a single sound. Along with the
insect, some innocence dies within the soul, the child cries.
This youth, till now, remained untouched. By senseless evil,
as this was such. The child will never be the same,
The innocence gone, a blameless shame.
This untimely misfortune of the butterfly
Changes the image life was meant to imply.
The young one knew only of life and the living,
Didn't know of taking, just of giving.
As the hopes and dreams of the innocent shatter,
Nothing else seems to matter,
Except what she thought, and what she now knows,
The innocence lost, reality grows.
With this reality, comes unwanted maturity,
No longer one of innocence, but one of impurity.
Now aware of all the disgrace on earth,
What is unattainable innocence worth?

—Amy E. Almeida

Altamira

The beast swayed and ran with others
by fires across the wall,
by men like you and I,
hide-clad, mushroom induced, chanting;
and out of a fever rode the beast
pierced by one man with stick smeared
with blood.

The moon rose full,
men without sleep and women without men,
the dogs were kept outside.
What language was spoken between the unspoken
was little,
was as the flames that leapt and subsided
until the heart awoke in a stampede
down a mountain side
through a mind that can conceive
between the smoke and the flame;

Beast and man are one,
in union of forms
like a painting on a cave at Altamira.

—Marc Clarkson

In A Morning It Happened All Of A Sudden

Morning shapes our soul with its shining sun,
By giving us a new chance to catch,
We are too far away from God.
We are too...
Is nature really our enemy?
Really, what happens every morning, so we should be aware?
G-o-d h-e-l-p-s u-s w-a-k-e u-p
...not only our eyes, but also our souls.
Even,
Despite the singing of birds,
Without noises of humans, cars, industry, television and
My words,
It is very unlikely to shape my soul.
For one second, the Universe has lost its orbit,
The sun has resigned, mountains have begun to walk, oceans...
Help!
They had kept staying long enough not to move towards lands.
Where am I? .....far awaaaaaaay from God.
As far as I know,
Morning is not able to shape my soul,u-n-f-o-r-t-u-n-a-t-e-l-y.

—Muzaffer Alacaogullari

Memorial To My Father

When the time had come and you were called to your place
by His side, I felt so lost and insecure, can't count the
times I cried.
It seemed unfair that you were taken from those who loved
you dear, my memories are always sweet, but often bring a tear.
But memories also made me see that you're still here today,
It only takes a look around to see the many ways.
The hands you helped to train so well to carry in the
crops, the sense of caring you instilled, a love that never stops.
The pride of self that one must have to proceed when times
are tough, to stand your ground and carry on even when the
going's tough.
So when I feel a little lost, depressed cause you're not
there, the comfort of our family makes it easier to bear.
For in their lives and loving ways I see so much of you, from
the many years of giving teaching all the things you knew.
So know that there will always be within our hearts so dear,
A very special place reserved to keep you ever near.

—Pat Mesnard

Season In Transition

I feel winters beckon call
  By the falling leaves that rest beneath my knees,
And as I walk over the rusty leaves,
  I know soon the crunch will be of snow,
As if transform by fairy to fool mankind.

The snow will come; the leaves will go
The windy nights will howl a ghostly call
  That tells of barren hills and valleys,
The creeks will freeze with jagged rocks,

And all animals that walk the ground will hide,
  To only leaving the winter birds,
  That open their wings to the frosted sky,

And winter rests its head as a child at night,
  To awake to bright morning light (Spring).
    —*Rome Louis Hughes*

The Rescue

Overwhelmed, oppressed, feeling consumed
By waves of memory, old hurts exhumed.
I'm sinking lower beneath the deluge
Without hope, or peace, no place of refuge.

Depressed, can't move, no self defense,
Awash in apathy, nothing makes sense.
Submerged, arms flailing unable to cope,
Descending in blackness without any hope.

What? What's this? A light up above
Arouses me, I reach feeling such love.
Hands are sent forth, nail scarred and torn,
They grasp and uplift me, I'm quickened, reborn.

His promise excites me, energizes ....breakthrough,
What relief, I'm delivered, exalted, renewed.
The decision is mine, keep holding His hand
Repent and submit...Will He understand?

Bind my will to His will, allow it to be done
Then relax, give Him all, to be called His son
Will I drown in depression, ignore His last call,
Or be uplifted, saved, and have peace after all?
    —*Patricia C. Berkram*

Parents Can Hurt

You remember all good times
By your vacations and games
You have feelings put in place
Thinking your parent's will never hurt you
They get a divorce
And they don't realize how it hurts their children
It breaks our hearts
Taking our father or mother away
By being together all those years
Knowing one has to go
Either mother or father
You spend more time with one
And hardly see the other
The children never revives
The hurt and pain, that we all go through
But I wish parents would realize
That children have hearts too.
    —*Robert B. Minnis*

"Nativity"

One with, two called for sense...
Called to, from birth, home of, life was...
Two yet three to journey, soul moved, drawn back to Beth...
When received, away turned, at every knock...
Sent to hay and straw, to lay, a place of stock...
Oh how Mary, a womb cracks, feel the joy, peace is here...
At rest in the field, the sheep's men are called...
Angels sent forth, to show the light to glory...
Walking, riding drawn, to the child of Beth...
All people pulled, by the heart with that same string...
Away, far by twelve, kings are sought, and sent forth...
Sent to star light, sight so bright, as glory shines.
Kings of three, sent by fate, bring a saving word...
The word with hold, still the greatest gift brought to...
As angels sing, glory to the name, glory in it's highest...
Jesus, son of Mary, the King of kings is born.
    —*A. Mendoza Jr.*

Dustin's Dream

I sat alone one early morn, when he
came to me, he was my first born, he told
me of a dream he'd had, it broke my heart,
it was so sad, He said that he was walking slow,
along the sidewalk, his head hung low,
he did not look where he was going,
just at his feet, his shadow showing.

And with a bump, he came to halt, I'm
sorry Sir, it was my fault, a voice came to him
and said, there's no harm done my precious son,
He raised his head, his eyes grew wide,
for his Daddy stood right by his side,
he said his heart was filled with joy,
when Daddy knelt to hold his boy.

He said he tried not to awake, he
knew this dream was just a fake, then he
looked at me with tear filled eyes, cause
Daddy's never at his side, he ask me, why don't
Dad care, does he even know the color of my hair?..
    —*Tina Sulifridge*

I Pray

  Can you?
Can you hear it?
The love within my gentle voice.
I saw you once, that's all it took,
for my heart had made its choice.

  I tried so hard so desperately
hard to hide my love within, to love you,
I can't though it's what I want so.
But I fear my love is in sin.

  Why?
A question you silently ask,
so silent I can not hear.
The answer is found deep within yourself,
It's absence makes your love unclear.

  Your love, it's there,
this I know true,
for who, I dare not say.
For you'll find me soon.
Heart and soul.
And for this, each evening, I pray.
    —*Samuel W. Ward*

Untitled

Overwhelmed, overwhelmed. I am overwhelmed.
Can't decide, can't decide. No I can't decide.
What to do, what to do. I do not know what to do.
So I sit, so I sit. So I sit a little bit.
Pass the time, pass the time.
Oh how I can pass the time.
And when I awake, and when I awake,
From my stuporous state,
Nothing is resolved, nothing is resolved,
There is nothing that is resolved.
Except that I am late, I am late,
I am so very, very late!

—*Laurie McElhannon*

A Caring Church

Amid tall trees it proudly stands,
cared for and nourished by loving hands.
It's a Bible church - teaching what's true.
presenting God's word for me and you.
Tho some would look and call it small,
to me it is the best of all.
The members care for one another,
loving each other as sister or brother.
Is your heart aching - do you cry?
there are more to pray than just you and I.
Any members pain is big - felt by all,
with worship and prayer it's quickly made small.
You'll never feel alone, lost in the cold,
support of the members is precious as gold.
Open arms and open heart,
sets this little church apart.
Always loving, praying, giving,
it makes life so worth living.
What a joy, a dream come true,
a caring church for me and you.

—*Betty L. Thomas*

Cherokee:

The Cherokee once roamed free; they lived in Georgia, North
Carolina and Tennessee. The tribe thought their future was
set, when Sequoyah developed their alphabet. A people that
were tall and proud, to always remain peaceful they vowed.
Their bountiful land they did not abuse,
but the Federal Government said "too bad you lose".
Soldiers chased them from their homes in the middle of the
night, though it was winter there was no compassion for their
plight. The Cherokee realized their greatest fears,
when the government marched them on the "trail of tears".
On this impossible journey over 4,000 died,
before they reached the distant Oklahoma side.
Now, restricted to the reservation,
the Cherokee promised their own preservation.
For years they worked themselves to the bone,
to buy back the land that had once been their own.
The Cherokee are still a powerful nation, in their own right,
though the years of suffering will forever be part of their sight.

—*Nick Allen*

Incestum

Deep doth lie the soul entrapped
With stifled wings of circumstance.
That from a child, so pure and free
Now driven deep - repressively.

For lost freedoms search at last
The wings unused grow strong - amass.
Snapping bonds of cruel entrap
The flight of freedom, at last.

—*E. Dale Pemberton*

Who's Crying Now?

A bleeding heart with the rising sun
Caught off guard I am born to run.

Seconds, moments, refusing to last
Long for tomorrow yet grasping the past.

Bittersweet memories turning the page
Ambitions that smolder a soul filled with rage!

Days that are bound in black stormy nights
Steel bars imprisoned forsaking all rights.

One lonely need feeds into the fire
Explodes into passion a full blown desire.

Haunting regrets that continue to grow
Are buried and melted like vain April snow.

Words with no voices that shatter a vow
Eyes with no tears and yet who's crying now?

—*Toni A. Bootz*

Arthur Ashe

Apartheid is not playing on your
center clay court, today.
Rackets are over priced.
Teaching of obediency at an
early age gave you the upper hand.
Hitting an ace for tennis
and one for justice was always in your duffle bag.
Under the stress of not belonging wears
out the heart and the immune system.
Racism shall not last forever.
AIDS was created in whose laboratory?
Speaking to young people was another
joy of your life.
Highlights of your life will
help ease yours pain.
Emancipate this Captain with honor.

—*Anniece McCaa*

Mood Of Love

If you have someone that you love,
Cherish him with tender care,
In a blink of a teary eye,
There could be a vacant chair.
Don't take life with a grain of sand,
For all things wondrousness are in God's hands.
If you are out for a quiet walk,
And love happens to enter into the talk,
Lend an ear to what he's saying,
Don't be left in life always paying.
Words not spoken from the heart,
Will not help by drifting apart.
Like clouds in the endless sky
Love could pass you by with a sigh.
Hold out your hand for him to hold
With unbound pleasure you'll enfold.
Take the journey of life you measure
In him you'll find jewels you'll always treasure.

—*Ruth Broome*

Illusion

My hands,
My body,
A figment of my imagination?
I feel and speak,
but still I am only an Illusion.

—*Stephen Lee*

The Family Friend

Loneliness, fear, depression, guilt, emotions so strong in a child.
Hate, vengeance, revenge, even murder, when emotions scream so
wild. No stranger this man, a family friend, a man so liked by
all. The mask he wears is seniority, his deeds against all
laws. An innocent child, so small, so frail, with thought of
friend and treat; Will take his hand and hug his neck, with
visions of good things to eat.

Ice cream he promises to the child, but first a walk he said.
She leaves her mother, talking gaily, he takes her to his shed.
She feels a fear within her heart, for what she does not know.
The man, his hand, a cry, a whimper, his kindness only for show.
The threats he makes will seal her lips, her fear will stay inside.
The shiny quarter in her hand, their secret when he lied.

The nightmares,the shame,the innocence gone
of a little girl only four.
The fear it lasts forever,
But the shame lasts even more.

—*Nancy L. Harrod*

Spring

The sight of a robin digging for a worm,
Children flying multi-colored kites,
Purple crocuses raising their heads above the recently thawed
    ground,
Families visiting a nearby park for a long-awaited picnic,
Nurserymen advertising—"It's time to fertilize your lawn!"
Sometimes an unexpected snow squall,
Windy March days with warm enough weather for just a sweater,
Rainy April and the just-on-the-safe-side feeling for carrying
    an umbrella,
May tulips, blue bottles, and daffodils—welcome signs to any
    gardener,
Easter, Mother's Day, and Memorial Day—reasons to celebrate!
The season of the vernal equinox has arrived!

—*Anne Fahringer*

Bundo's Son Walks Like A Soldier

Stand at attention tall and proud,
Cold eyes of blue like that of a cloud.

Castled face of stone with softened brow,
The little boy is an old man now.

His uniform was laid to rest,
In a Brown old fashion cedarchest.

Gently folded by Irene's hands,
Never again to have seen foreign lands.

Tattered and torn old Army boats,
Worn by a man of Italian roots.

The hat was worn with determination and will,
Now it lies forever still.

Gold medals on his coat still shine,
Just like a rare red vintage wine.

Even though he is old and gray,
He is a little boy in every way.

He is the son of Bundo and Cuddline,
He was born of a king and queen.

Still Bundo's son walks like a soldier
Still Bundo's son walks like a solder.

—*Shirley Ann Ferenczy*

A Prehistoric Time

a fine
collection
a gathering
of acorns, wild garlic and russian olives

we laid our rocks
side by side
and roofed our heads
with pine needles

it was a days work...

no poison ivy this time
the wild garlic
gave me away
everyone knew where I'd been

—*Robin G. Gauthier*

Soaring Like An Eagle

'Tis February '93 - amidst the winter doldrums;
Comes the pain - the Intruder - that sends me smoldering.
At age 59, and now without much time....
This pain, and suffering renders my body immobile!

I know that yesterday is today's memory, and tomorrow is
today's dream. Yet, I embrace the past with remembrance, and
the future with longing. However brief my days may be,
briefer still are the words I have spoken! And should my
voice fade in your ears, and my love vanish from your memory.
Dear loved ones, my life is only a token.
Relinquish not my soul just yet Dear God.
Physical strength, I may lack, however not the power of Will;
I submit to Thee, striking off pride, self-love, self-pity
Father, I will swallow this bitter pill!

I know Thy love is divine, you will make this mystic temple
Thine. And when I am sapped, by this malignant growth, and
weary with strife.... When darkness gathers over me, and I at
last fall. Take this poor dust, thy mercy warms; and mold it
into thy heavenly form.

—*Barbara Money Wolfington*

"Change"

The passing of time, an institution-a relic of change.
Committing oneself to a world of strangers.
Holding hands with only yourself.
Wait for a difference, a revolution. When will it come?

Yearning for an extra hour, a lifetime, an eternity.
Fighting of death, warding off love.
A desire to confess,
feeling sick, disgusted, unworthy.

Hate.
It lingers in of all places, the heart.
Rippling and tearing, searing-wearing my heart on my sleeve,
a smile on my lips.

Crying inside, sobbing, weeping, dying...help.
Fear, fear, fear, I laugh at it...makes me vomit, makes me want
it, My hands wrap around it, squeeze its neck, claw at its eyes
Hug it... make me strong.

A death wish, a love wish... wanting it all.
Hold me, I don't want you to go.
Too short, it's over, it's almost over, you're gone...
I love you....

—*Tricia Theis*

Vampire

My shadow drifts from town to town
Continent to Continent.
My heart is of ice as the dead of winter is.

I once had a savior; he was snatched from me.
My faith?… No More!
I roam the deserted streets of night,
I hope to overcome my new life—my new death.

I hate this new world that suffocates me.

I clearly remember the sun, even though,
Now I can not look upon its growing light—its warmth.

Darkness has become my son, my home, my companion.

I am walking the streets for eternity with mortals.
I am their shadows that take them at sunset.

A plea from my black lost soul:

Take me—End Me…before my shadow crosses
the path of thee.
—*Venessa Castillo*

Listening Sounds

Can we control our future, our destination.
Convincing lies and deceiving trues, as we walk
Daily blind but unaware. Death is common,
Birth is out. T.V. media paints our defenseless minds.
Being up and positive is considered a madman.
Fear is large while peace is ant-like.
Happiness is obtained by few,
Hate is controlled by the rest.
Gossip tears friends,
Lovers and anyone apart,
Yet it is so easy and fun to do.
Right, wrong morals are becoming stranger
And stranger and more distant every second of every day.
Who is to blame,
"We the people are".
Accept or deny it.
Think…Before…You…Act!!!?
—*Michael Forthman*

Treasures

Is there something special on your shelf
Does is possess an appearance of wealth
Or is it something old and worn
That belonged to someone before you were born

I've been to many places before
And wondered what history a certain item bore
Was it given to them by a special friend
Or did they find it at the five and ten

Was it the symbol of a significant date
Maybe it told of the owner's fate
I wondered if it cost very much cash
Or did they forget to put it in the trash

It could be something given as a gift
Or a funny thing bought to give them a lift
I've kept things and heaven knows why
Putting them in shelves and drawers with a sigh

Thinking they might be of later use
Or give laughter to keep away my blues
But deep down within my heart
I know I've enough junk to fill a cart
—*Marge Warner*

The Black Rose

It stands alone loathing the light,
    corruption awaits ready to strike.
        Evil is present which seems evident
            by the pungent odor; it's poison to my eyes.
                With the killing of innocence
                    never escaping its grip.

            Many meanings within a flower
                different colors change the whole character.
            Yellow is the meaning of friendship,
                red portrays the message of love,
            while white is known as the flower of serenity.
            Where does this sinister appearance
fit with all the above?

    How could one flower mean so much?
—*Stephen Spina*

Our Day At The Zoo

My Dad, my Mom, my sister and me went to the zoo to see all we could see
We talked to the monkeys and said hi to the whales
We saw the zoo keeper carry food in big pails
We heard lions scream and tigers run
We had yummy hamburgers on a big fat bun
We saw an alligator's wide mouth and an elephant's trunk
We saw a cage full of skunks and oh how they stunk
My sister saw a pig and I saw a bear
We saw ducks in a pond and water splashed in our hair
A hippo whaled and very near by a flamingo sailed
But above us high we heard a clock song
    The afternoon chimes Ding Dong, Ding Dong
    It was time to go home, but we really didn't want to
    We said goodbye to the animals and the zoo keeper too
    We got in our car and drove all the way home
    We each took a bath in the bubbly bath foam
    We got in our beds with our blankets so new
    And said to each other WASN'T THAT A GREAT DAY AT
THE ZOO.
—*Sarah R. Glick*

My Act

Morning comes, time to paint my face.
Covering up my tears so they leave no trace.
The tears shoved away, trying to hide.
My act begins now as I step outside.
The world only sees the smile I wear,
Instead of a sad lonely girl wanting someone to care.
I feel like a child's smiling faced clown,
But under this mask lies a deep and painful frown.
Struggling through the day, keeping the wall up high,
Longing for the night to come so I can break down and cry.
The night is long but it feels so good to let the tears go,
And on through the night, even as I sleep, the tears still flow
I wake up wishing I could run and hide from this world,
Wishing I could go back to being a little girl.
These things I know won't come true,
So there's only one thing left to do,
I get my make-up and start all over again,
Walk out my door, and once again my act begins.
—*Mariann Bolinder*

Untitled

A glint of moonlight cannot compare with thee,
    but I would rather have the moonlight.
For it radiates your face
    and I see your beauty.
—*Kenneth R. Wolfe*

A Plea For Help

Our world, our earth, our precious land
    Created by Thy loving hand
As mankind's haven and his home
    Beneath the heaven's star-filled dome
Given in trust to us to tend
    That life on earth should never end
See what today we've done, and weep
    Our trusteeship we've failed to keep
We've decimated forests, trees
    Polluted rivers, lakes, and seas
Contaminated once pure air
    Tainted earth's soil without a care
Our greed and lust for power and fame
    Are our besetting sins and shame
Please, great Creator up above
    Help us change avarice for love
Teach us to nurture and preserve
    Thy bounty, which we ill deserve
Open our eyes that we may see
    Our duty to posterity.

    —*Lois A. Bracken*

Messages

The entry is down, dove, beneath clutch of barbed wire,
creep in through crawl space and gather your grain
that still pulses with blood flow;
taste fear in the code of the seeds that you pick;
listen to language of heart-beat
that only earth hears on plain that is frozen
or hot shifting sands that echo with groan:

Then spread out your wings, dove,
open them up to familiar space;
cross lines and frontiers and carry the whisper,
the last secret wish to the forums of power -
only then will your olive be green, dove
and springtime bloom in the branch you carry.

    —*Nancy Horton*

America

Your snow-frosted peaks, lush green mountains,
    crevices and trees,
Your fields for harvest swaying in the gentle
    breeze,
Your fertile, rocky, flat and multi-colored
    land,
Your river banks bountifully layered with sieving
    sand,
America, with all you have shown, be it right
    or wrong,
America, you are my own.
America, you are my home.
America, where have you gone?

    —*Ruth McCarson Bowen*

All Around Us

For it's always happening around us
but we due not see the changes,
For time changes everything from day to day,
its all around us for we all together
make things change, we are all apart
of life, and what we all due each day
will help the world to change,
For what we all together due, will change
the world all around us.

A world of people is a world of hope.

    —*Michael Breheny*

A Morning Star

A morning star, watches from afar...
Crowning the skies, flickering,
Borne to overcome the darkened night.
Extending it's light, it's glimmer of hope.
A morning star, as I long to be-
In the midst of God's grandeur of heaven,
Seeketh out with eyes of flames.
Shining forth brightness
Upon the shadows of the earth.
In God's vast paradise with my very being,
Standing alone, amongst so many.
Angels, martyrs and prophets walketh forth,
Borne in the grasp of the potters hands-
Unknown, silently the illumined star
Fades away as does earth's poverty.

    —*Patricia J. Elliott*

Introspection

I'm captive here, inside this prison,
Dark, solid walls obscure my vision,
A book, forgotten on a shelf,
No one to talk to, but myself;

Filled with ideas, full of dreams,
Almost bursting at the seams,
All the things I might have been,
Frustration building, closing in;

I want to scream, I try to shout,
I raise my voice, no words come out.
So many thoughts I long to share,
But all I do is sit and stare;

Where is the answer? I'll find the key,
To unlock this door and set me free,
I see a flame burning, clear,
Thank God I'm not alone in here!

    —*L. S. Waldo*

Storm

The anger of the storm
dashes waters against the shore.
Thundering, crashing, spraying, splashing.

The anger of the storm
shouts from the very heavens.
Booming, flashing, shrieking, howling.

The anger of the storm
drives all before it.
Bending reeds, breaking trees.

The anger of the storm
paints the sky in billowing grays.
Wind driven clouds pushed along.

The anger of the storm
passes to reveal a new sky.
Bright, cheerful, washed clean.

    —*V. G. Silverman*

Velvet Fingers

You were so dear to give gift of glove,
    Filling each hand and finger with love;
For now, I know , with each gloved hand —
        Loved as I am —
    I can give the passion of compassion
    Or even the glove, if I must,
        To a meeker, needing one!

    —*Jenna V. Ownbey*

Belated Opportunities

Retirement? It is only the work - a -
    day career that has ended.
Stretching to eternity are opportunities
    once passed by.

Aim high - play with words, they
    call it poetry.

Or another aesthetical game, playing
    with color - called ant.
Try the ivory keyboard for
    pleasant sounds.

Playing the knitting needles or crochet
    hook; pondering and preparing food;
Clay - modeling and mood - carving -
    all have their devotees,
Whose active minds and bodies
    cause each day to seem too short.
But - eternity seems farther away!

—*Ruth Ann Hohler*

Life's Road

We learn many lessons as each
    day goes by,
There are songs to sing and a
    few tears to cry.
There are blessings to count,
    happy memories too
And sometimes disappointment
    in things we do.
There are cups that run over and
    years that are lean,
With bright day and dark days
    and long nights between.
But one choice we can make
    as we carry life's load
If we look to the sun, how it
    brightens the road.

—*Ranjeev Sanjay Nobbee*

"The Eternal Game"

Day in - day out, it's all the same
Day in - day out, living in pain.
Day in - day out, nothing will change.
Day in - day out, it's all the same.

Sun comes up - sun goes down.
Teardrops fall - hear them hit the ground.
World keeps spinnin', 'round and 'round.
One life lost, two more found.

Baby's born - baby cries.
Old man tired - old man dies.
See the pain - behind their eyes.
Nothing can help - they've already tried.

Day in - day out it's all the same.
Day in - day out dying in pain.
Day in - day out nothing has changed,
And still we play - The Eternal Game.

—*Rachel Oppel*

Untitled

Though she had not a single problem that seemed important.
Death has always on her mind.
She tried to remember the good times,
Yet there was not a single one she could find.
She thought of committing suicide.
She thought death was her only way out.
Nothing was keeping her from dying,
For she had not one single doubt.
She thought of many ways to die,
Each day at least one more.
There was not one day she did not wonder
What she was put in this world of ours for
She thought that nobody cared what she did,
Yet her family and friends knew that was not true.
They were all extremely worried
About what she might try to do.
Although she killed herself just the other day,
The time that has passed seemed so long.
And so in the end, everyone did care.
For once she would have been happy to know that she was wrong.

—*Stacey Horton*

Truth And Deception

Truth, the absolute endures-
Deception, double-cross, betrays-
Yet judgment, the discerner decrees the verdict in the end pure-
The seeds of judgment are sown with the deed done always-

Wisdom, good judgment is justified of her children-
Knowledge, enlightenment comprehension, perception, known fact-
Understanding, comprehension perceived, knowledge given-
Prudence is the eye that sees truth and deception back to back-

Never hand in hand walk truth and deception as they cannot agree-
Opposite directions they go-
Like two magicians whose paths cross when the shows over, each
his own person must be-
Discretion, said to be the better part of valor, is so-

—*Berta McGlothlin*

Monotony...

Winterstillness gently shrouds
deep ravines and mountain trails.
Where we walked rise misty veils.
Circling Ravens pierce the clouds.

Winterweary birds, like torn
strings of Hematite, enhance
symmetry on the picket fence,
endless, black in grey forlorn..

Busy little Sparrows sing,
hardly touched by any Season,
chirping without rhyme and reason
songs that echo deep within.

—*Maria Forster de J.*

Lost Friends

The picture is worn and very old,
But to me the picture is just like gold.

It reminds me of people who have gone away,
To see the light of a bright new day.

At night to them I say a prayer,
During the day, I wish they were there.

I know I will see them in that special place,
But to get there, it is not a race.

I'll go on each day wanting more,
Because I don't have what I did before.

—*Stephanie Dawson*

The Excellence and Essence of Beauty and the depth of Its All

Oh to know beauty, in its multi and diversified and descriptive depth in character, and to be well hid within it's confines of excellence. To know beauty, is the awareness of it's essence, in great depth and detail. Let us look into it's never ending excellence and see if we are hid within it's definitions. The little child who born handicapped, is well within it's confines. For it is admired by those who have sought and searched for it's endless depth. The hobo who is lying face down in the street, is also hid in unseen beauty. For there are those who extend the hand of great mercy and help. This too shows forth the evidence within. The excellence and the understanding of the depth of beauty is far greater, and goes far beyond the outer person we see. Shall we find beauty in only a glance of the outer dimensions. I should say not. There are those who long to be beautiful as far as their outer silhouette. Yet except they understand the true meaning of beauty and it's depth, it will not be understood at all. A whore can be beautiful, even though she is not found within the spectrum of outer respectability. For her inner beauty is hid behind the mask of demented association.

—*J. D. Bailey*

Best Friend

Many meanings to best friend flow around,
Different words to describe best friend can be found.
I've read many poems in cities and towns,
Looked high and low, up and down.
Searching, I have, no written word I see,
Can possibly describe what I believe.
With awesome wonder I look up to Him,
The Lord knows the beginning and the end.
He spoke a word, there stood a tree,
He spoke again, there stood you for me.
Not any written word can compare or say,
What a best friend He gave me that day.
He knew the path ways our lives would take,
The bond between us, He would make.
How can I describe a best friend with words,
Using all my knowledge of words I've heard?
How can I write what is in my heart,
When only He knew my desire from the start?
Again with awesome wonder I look above,
Thanking the Lord for a BEST FRIEND to love.

—*Sharon E. Bunton*

The Other Woman

Here you lie in dignity with love
Dirt and flowers cover your grave
Dare I pluck a flower to save?

May God forgive us all our sins
I couldn't come to see and hear
I had no right to be so near
I can only dream what might have been.

Here I stand lonely and bereft
For us no more tomorrows
For me it's only sorrow
But our decisions were for the best.

All the tomorrows I will be alone
Your laugh, your smile, your way to tease
My love for you will never cease
Good-bye, good-bye, my precious one.

—*Velma Lipe Brown*

Heartache

Dirty face
Dirty clothes
Scathing through yesterday's garbage
What will I eat?
Spare change?
Always having an open hand, but still being ignored by
your fellow man.
Streets that are safer than some shelters
Where will I sleep?
Soup kitchens
Cardboard box houses

Please help me!
Will work for food
hope

—*Aronda Veal*

Imagine That

Imagine that the world was flat and America was never
discovered; Christopher Columbus would have explored
the Earth and that theory would be uncovered.
History would have changed its course,
And stars and stripes would have no source.
Pilgrims would not have hit Plymouth rock,
And the Mayflower would have never docked.
We would never have a Thanksgiving feast,
Or celebrate a holiday at the least.
The Boston Harbor would be free of tea,
While there would be no American democracy.
American soldiers would not be needed,
For there would be no enemies to be defeated.
There would be no declaration of Independence to be signed
Because there would be no thirteen colonies to find.
World Wars would not have been fought,
And the Louisiana purchase would not have been bought.
Natural resources would be preserved...
And the American Gold Rush wouldn't be observed.
But luckily the world was round, so America was found!

—*Mera Goodman*

The Revealing

As I look upon the enclosing horizon, a light gleams in the
distance. From all sides circling me, it pulsates and buzzes
silent. I wait amidst the corroded landscape as the
brightness of gold pierces my eyes of knowledge.
I will not shun my sight!
I will not shy!
No, not today, for the hour of judgment has come!

Death is the unknown Angel. Death is a friend I know.
Take me to see the sunflower start to sprout and grow.

Damn you Byron! Where are you now with your witty offerings?
You taught me to know that all I am is what goes on around me.
And you Blake! Have I indulged enough?
Have I reached the Palace of Wisdom?
Ah...it's mine. Just me and this wonderful light.

Swallowing me, the force of billions of years cry
and decades of days hold me in weightless hands like a cup.
Entering the flash of existence, the light and I are one.
All my thoughts are now revealing as I float, float slowly into
the calm, trapped in this cold damp, but warm isolation
waiting for a sign of acknowledgment.

—*Troy Amidon*

Futility

We tried by waiting endless hours in that sterile room —
distracting her darling daughters, until it was official; We
tried by extracting several slivers of glass from their hair,
as they told us her words just moments before... A teacher
desperately talked of The Green Gardens of Paradise and His
Wisdom. We tried by tenderly attending to the details of her
camphor, muslin, and musk — while whispering sacred words;
We tried by listening to the loud silence as the throng gathered
to pray — clinging to each other to stifle sobs; A Southern
white, a Northern black, and a West Indian huddled — fingers
interlaced, wet cheeks pressed together. We tried by reciting
from His Book as we rocked her angelic infant through agonizing
days and nights; We tried by being a face that he could trust
in that time of white coats and stethoscopes — pacifying him
with fresh linens, baths, and hugs, when needles and tubes were
terrifying him; A nurse absurdly insisted that he must accept a
bottle. We tried by getting senators and bureaucrats to let
her sister come from across the ocean, to help her small
daughters; We tried by returning her cherub-baby back over the
same waters, to her mother, who craved this tiny vestige of her

—*Ama Folayan Shabazz*

The Child

Who is the child who cries in the night?
Do you know her name?

Can you find the words, can you somehow explain?
Can you take away her hurts or relieve her pain?

Can you hold her in your arms?
Do you know her name?

She cannot tell you, all you need to know.
She's too young to know the words, she cannot explain.

She just sees pictures of distant memories,
And feels their awful pain.

Do you know this child?...Do you know her name?

If you do, then help her...
Hold here close, hold her near.

Help her dry her eyes and wipe away her tears.
Maybe, then in time...you can take away her fears.

'Cause all this child really needs,
Is to feel loved and safe and dear.

—*Beth Estrada*

Barrenness

Battle's over, multitudes dead,
cords of wood stacked under a grey winter's sky.
A mother's worst dread,
funeral pyres lighting the cold, ebony night.

Remembering her lad's laughter
she questions, why the slaughter.
Now he rests in the harsh, frozen ground,
nothing but cannon fodder.

Which war, doesn't matter,
each the same, doomed to be repeated.
Mothers query the senseless splatter
And clutch their memories, to hold back the emptiness.

—*Rhonda S. Tiller*

Dragons In The Spring

Dragons in the spring,
Coiled above us, entwined
The smell of ozone accompanies their coupling
A tribute to dragon kind
A blue arc, a welder's kiss,
The dry clash of scales against scales,
The wild, pagan cries, the raspy breath,
Heavy lidded love
Pennants, banners snap to the wind
Irises open, thinking that Dawn has come.
But the fiery flow'r signals another sort of beginning,
Another sort of end.

—*Scott Maddix*

Changing, It Is At Rest

edge always edge   wind guides refreshing
denominates   one guiding
one over one   over strong river
into one   always dry
tides edge   at edge

wind knows
no changeable winds
denominating one
over one
into one.

—*J. Jordan Hoggard*

Plastic Jesus

I slip my coat on for a walk
A midnight stroll around the block
Stuff my hands into the pockets
Fleshy plugs in cotton sockets

The cloying air like love's embrace
The grimy sidewalk without grace
The dropping trees like fallen foes
The whores who sport a sultry pose

I venture into Churchill Square
With'ring under Winston's stare
And as I stumble through the park
I hear her dying in the dark—

My ears direct me to the sound
I find her fallen on the ground
A stricken girl I kneel to aid
My fingers strike a buried blade

"It's all right," she whispers low,
"Between the crosses, row on row"
And for me the moment seizes—
And cold hands drop a plastic Jesus

—*Earl J. Woods*

Wise Men

Midway along the road
A man without a hand -
A red flower grew from the wrist.
We shed a tear
We would have built a calvary
But something moved us on,
A file of refugees
Handcuffed in twos
And slowly losing speech.

—*Peter Broome*

Cloud's Sphere

There's another realm
beyond this world.
Its white knights
ride along in massive formations.
Their horses' hoofs
never feel ground.
Their shields
let anyone pass
and close again
behind one
in a twinkle of an eye.
No boundaries
hold back
whatever wants to leave.
And no walls
give harbor
for the ones
who want to hide.

—*Anette Nuhse*

Our World

We weren't born racists
but look around you
A world full of hatred
People never look beneath
the surface of the skin
At my mind, my heart
and soul
And the love deep within
What is love to us?
Love is easily said
But not truly meant

—*Kathy Mpatsos*

It

Night After night
in my dreams
it came.

Day after day
It came in reality
until it was with me
all the time.

Hovering, threatening, taking, hurting,
always there in the blackness.

It was always reaching out,
reaching out to reach me,
suffocate me with its needs;
Its wants I didn't understand

Eventually it become my life
and my understanding that this
was how my life is to be

This is my reason for life
This is why I am here;
My purpose has been fulfilled
Has it not?

—*Julie Goodwin*

My Other Half

The friendship we share
A bond so rare
The odds we've faced
We always came out without a trace

My love for you as friends, so true
I'll always remember you
You brighten my day
Your smile is like a sun ray

Valerie to me means
A friend I'll always need
Even though you don't see it Valerie
You are a part of me

—*Natalie Duperreault*

We See A Work...

We see a work
A life, an edifice grown
Shaped by time
By many lives
Standing tall and free
Of some significance
Having weight
And far reaching influence.

If we have had
In our lifetime
Some small part
In its formation
We too are part of its whole
We too having contributed
May with it stand tall and free
And humbly walk
With thankfulness
In its becoming

—*Queenie M. Allen*

Unnamed Poem

A lite bit of light
A lite bit of mist,
A lite bit of love.
And nature can exist.

In one little beam
From natures big star,
Oh how lively a sunbeam is
Even in a jar.

It can dance across the table
Or dance across the room,
It can bring happiness
And never gloom.

—*Shawna Rae Hammond*

Untitled

When I was just a boy of three
A puppy dog was given me
And holding puppy by the hair
On hands and knees climbed the stair
Dragging doggie across the room
Little puppy sensed his doom
Biting at my griping hand
Trying hard to understand
Mommy knowing the doggies fate
Ascended the stairs at a terrific rate
Then shuttering in her frightened soul
Watched as puppy dropped in the hole

—*Harry T. Colman*

After The Show

When I was a little boy
A sheet of oil paper
Was my movie toy:

In a chariot, a Russian king
Pulled by a slave, wearing nothing

A woman diving and diving alone
A bearded man with a slab of stone

A big man with a long sword
A small man on a wreckage board

The silhouettes came to life
Became greater
When I moved the candle
Behind the paper

My only little spectator
Asked when the show was over

Where all those gone?
Blew out the candle, I replied
Where are all those gone?
He asked, again, as if I lied.

—*B. H. Kaseem*

Love

To man and woman
Add love
The sum total is
The humanity.
To hate and distrust
Add love
The resultant is
The hope.
To chaos and crisis
Add love
The outcome is
The peace.
To doubt and despair
Add love
The prize is
The faith.
To fear and destruction
Add love
The gain is
The immortality.

—*Krishan Kant Verma*

Taking Life In Our Stride

A person tries to hide,
    All the hurt they fell inside;
But it all boils down to pride.

And in the meantime,
    A wild snowstorm rages outside.

A person tries to hide,
    All the fear they feel inside;
But that too, boils down to pride.

In the middle of the night-alone,
    to whom does one confide;
From God - our feelings we cannot hide,
And in our faith -
    We can take great pride.

So all in all it always boils down to -
A good many times I nearly cried;
But we have to learn
    to take life in our stride.

—*Winnified A. Cleaves*

Untitled

Is it morning ... is it night ....
Am I suffering from a fright ....
Is there something in the air?...
I've lost my teddy bear!

In the moonlight there's a freak,
And I hear a strange loud creak;
But I wouldn't so much care,
If I could find my teddy bear.

I'm chilled right to the bone,
And I'm left here all alone;
But I wouldn't turn a hair,
If I had my teddy bear.

—Claire Russell

Freedom

As I look out my window,
And across the water.
I see freedom.
The freedom of the sea gulls.
As they fly over top,
And dive down deep.
To have that kind of freedom,
For even just one day.
Is what I wish,
And seek day after day.

—Tina Myra

My Classmates

I am now so sad
    and at the same time sorry
Why they say that I am that bad
    and a big worry

Two of my classmates
    did the same thing
But why are they late
    to tell the same story

All faults are shouldered to me
    I am now repenting why I was afraid
To tell her what I wanted her to be
    and now I feel that I was betrayed

Betrayed is not the right term
    but saying so is like what has done
It feels so hurt...
    so alone.

I want to pour my anger to someone I trust
    but now I think that it is useless
For that someone is whom I now hate
    and that I think that SHE is valueless

—Gloria Carmela D. Manalac

Mirjam

I see sunshine in your smile
And beauty in your walk,
Grace in every movement
And wisdom when you talk.
The touch of God upon your brow,
The patience of a saint
A heart so pure and gentle
Which no outer force can taint.
Your eyes, they captivate me
Like a priceless work of art
And in them, I see true love
Which soothes my aching heart.

—Andrew Salmon

The Illusionist

It encompasses your heart
And captures your soul
It clouds your mind
creating the illusion

I walk in a reality
Made of my dreams
This is my life
And what it will be

But what becomes of them?
Their reality; their dreams
The souls of others
Their very existence

As I wander around
Trying to find what's right and wrong
Reality slips by
Leaving my dreams behind

My soul; and the souls of others
Trapped in a dream
And I the Illusionist
Am caught in the dream of my reality.

—Mark Klatt

Those Vitamins

I've got Halibut oil
and Cod liver oil
and pure olive oil on Tap
I'm filled to the brim with Vitamins
My eardrums whistle and flap
There's Vitamin A and Vitamin B
There's Vitamin D and Vitamin C
With a booster tied in to top it all
that is labelled Vitamin I
So if I turn pale
Or wind up in jail
All a Frenchmen's Jamboree
You can blame it all
My Rise and Fall
On the one marked Vitamin I
which created illusions of Youths Dream
Though I'm long past 73.

—Leslie Bodolai

Through Time And Distance

(Dedicated to Tiram)

Time is an element which passes
And fades into eternity.
Yet it can always be turned back
By your heart as a memory.

And though distance be as far
As the stars in the skies,
It too can be dissolved
If you just closed your eyes.

So if you are lonely,
Or just feeling blue,
Whenever you wish
I am there with you...

Just close your eyes
And think thoughts of me,
Then there by your side
Is where I will be.

—Krista J. Millar

Missing You

Just thinking of you, brings a tear,
And I want to make something clear.
I do not take love as a game,
The way things ended, I was to blame.
I was scared to show you how I feel,
For my love for you is truly real.
As I think of you, I begin to miss,
The sound of your laugh,
The softness of your kiss,
Even the warmth of your smile,
And your touch with tenderness.
If I ever get one last chance,
I'd hold you close like we first danced.

—Tina M. Gamble

My God You Answered Me

When I was out and down
And life came falling apart,
No one cared if I lived, or died;
I was just another dying soul,
But down on my knees I cried to my God,
And he answered me.

When I was weak
And in pain,
And hope was gone
He cheered me up,
And he made me strong
So I could live again.
My god you answered me.

—Derrick Allenger

Epitome On Disease

Mostly, disease to those who harm;
And need no use any arm
Against, but if takes anything,
Even not a time to do that thing;
Disease, if you been unfaithful,
Otherwise when done harmful;
Disease, if you obey wickedness
Or disobey righteousness;
For who do not confess their treatment
Against, it is mostly a punishment;
So prefer a narrow way to follow;
And do no harm to any fellow.

—Solomon S. Raj Talluri

Distant Tides

I long to view the sea again,
And rest upon the tide.
I long to hear the sound of men,
A fishing by my side.

The sea does call me back again,
And waits for me to come.
But I am lost upon the shores,
Where voices are but dumb.

Now it is here where I must sit,
And dream of that far day.
When I shall view the sea again,
And watch the currents play.

—Margot-Anne Barefoot

116

The Storm

The waving waves come crashing down
    And roll across the shore
The wind blows like a hurricane
    And sea gulls screech no more

They hide in clifftop shelters
    Which face the roaring surf
The ocean shows no mercy
    it fights for all it's worth

But when the storm subsides
    And warm air flows in gently
Seagulls come from our their nests
    To sort among the debris

Tiny fishes they may find
    Or a crab or some small thing
Little creatures stand no chance
    Against the sea, they could not win

Little boats sail out again
    Thankful for the calm
No fear of the mighty sea
    They'll come now to no harm.

    —*Sheila Gower*

Gratitude

As I awake each Morn
And start a new day.
I give thanks to the Lord
And go on my way.
My health is good
My mind is clear
My footsteps light
My intentions sincere.
When meeting people
Both young and old
I listen to their thoughts
Their fears their goals.
Life after all is a journey
With many twists and turns
Some are able to overcome
While others become forlorn.
As I retire each night
In my prayers I say
"Thanks Lord, for the Bonus"
Of another Good day.

    —*Thomas J. Thomas*

Grandpa's

Grandpa's are supposed to grow old
and take you fishing in the spring
and hand out hard peppermint candies
so hot they make you wanna sing.
Grandpa's are supposed to tell stories
that start out "when I was small"
there not supposed to go away
or leave our sides at all.
But our Grandpa was called home
and we feel so sad, inside
we sit and talk about Grandpa
and many times, we've cried
our families have a lot
of wonderful memories
that won't fade away or grow dim
cause when we grow up
if we do everything right
We'll grow up just like him.

    —*Shelly Galipeau*

To A Friend

We met.....
And the storm engulfed us.
We could not see each other.
Then our fingers touched,
And the storm lightened.
Our fingers hooked...solid and firm.
The beginning of a friendship.
The storm could not shake this bond.
As our fingers drew our hands closer,
So our friendship grew.
Our link did not break, as most do...
So our friendship grew.
Now.....
The storm is gone.
The friendship emerged.
In my heart
I know
In time
Our hands would have met.

    —*Poet Millar*

Hope

From amidst the mournful sighs,
and whispered cries,
hope appears.

At first it is but a tiny light,
and not so very bright,
but hope is there.

It helps you find the answer
to why you must fight this cancer.
It helps you see
that love of me
is more than enough reason
to fight the body's treason.
And hope remains firm and steadfast.

    —*Catherine Wilson*

Untitled

"I" is such a little word,
And yet, my love
It is all I have
All I have to offer you
So take it now
And keep it true
Until someday
When I return
To claim my self
To ask it back
Then you can say,
That I am yours,

    —*Ayesha Athar*

Untitled

    He roams the sky
Eyes sharp, wings spread wide.

    He keeps watch over
    all the lands
Watching his children roam.

    He roams the sky
    Eyes sad.
He sees their world crumble
    as they give up hope.

The white man has come.

    —*Kimberly Harlow*

Your Child...

When it seems it's only you
    And you yourself alone
Look to her for comfort
    You'll find you should have known
That every time you need someone
    She's waiting by your side
Forgiving and adoring you
    No matter what the tide.
She loves you unconditionally
    Without adult restrain
She understands your feelings...
    She comprehends your pain.
Take this day to make a vow
    You'll love her as she loves you now
And I promise you in years away
    She'll love you as she does today.

    —*Sandy Lee Gravel*

Forthcoming

Approaching was reality
Anticipation -
No longer thought

Extended beyond was faith
To know the security
Of God's own mind

Yet with contempt I met him
Scorning his ideal
Hating his freedom

I saw desire to know his soul
Cries of passion and anger
No longer existed
But in serenity the understanding
Of true friendship

The peace of God within me
Defaced shadows about me
With an embrace
I shared his soul
Jesus.

    —*Thomas Fish*

Beyond Words

Emotion, frustration, and anger
Are words to describe how I feel
When I see what this world is becoming
And I know that it seems all too real

Pain, heartache, and fear
Are words to describe what I see
In the lives and on faces of others
That's not how I want it to be

Put-downs, curses, and lies
Are words to describe what I hear
I cannot believe they have meaning
How senseless they sound to my ear
Hope, relief, and great joy
Are a few of the things found inside
When I sense those sweet waves of peace
That my God will always provide

    —*Lisa Purvis*

Serene Thoughts

In the light of the cross
At the end of the day
I sit with my thoughts
As serene as the light.
I know God is near.
That I need not fear.
The unknown shall be known
And all will be well.
For the Lord, up above
Will take care of His own.
I sit and ponder
On days gone by,
There is so much undone.
I often wonder
What God would have me do;
Then I realize
He asks only
That I do the best I can.

—*Judith Dahl*

Old

Be old doesn't mean
be annihilated already
come to old denote
enrich the alive soul.

If the spirit is young
the mind transmit life
contribute innumerable
valuables to the humanity.

If You feel you rejected
for the young people, it isn't
because you don't value
its fear for to be displaced.

Live Your life intensely
divide your experiences
transcribe of your mind
what tomorrow will be Bible.

—*Guiomar Orjuela*

Seeing Blind People

I think my cane is more than gold,
Because it helps me walk,
I rather wouldn't have it sold,
'Cause that would be a shock.

It takes me over all the land,
Because I don't have eyes
I operate it with my hand,
And o'er the path it flies.

I couldn't walk without my cane
Unless I had some sight
But with my cane and with my brain,
I think I am all right.

So, fear not, blind man, you're all right,
Because you have a cane,
Although you haven't any sight,
I'm sure you've got a brain.

—*Jason J. Entz*

UN

Behind the tall narrow door
Below the steep narrow stairs
There was:
As a child, deep black corners
Cobwebbed and cold.
Flickering candle light
Casting ghostly shadows,
While bombs raged up above.
Our deep dark cellar kept us safe
For those we love.

Behind the tall narrow door
Below the steep narrow stairs
There are:
White walls, bright lights.
Pop music fills the air.
No longer dark and dingy
A place to work and play.
While traffic roars up above.
Our deep dark cellar still keeps us safe
For those we love.

—*Janet M. Jones*

The Pain Of Loving

She lay on the beach in her bikini,
Bitching about her runaway fiance.

But what had that got to do with us?
Us, only sailors on the sea,
And all that bunkum!

The jocular waves
Could not soothe her,
Neither could any of us
Stroke her down,
Being on different waves.

She sprawled in the sand,
Outpouring her inner fears,
Her eyes suffused with tears,
Her voice wobbling
Like the tide of sea.

It was not until now,
As I ruminate on her outpourings,
Our inner feelings synchronized,
Does it bring to memory,
The pain of loving.

—*David K. Chimwaso*

Remembrance

A mass of fiery gases:
blazing orange and scarlet red
outline your shadow.
A feverish feeling besets me.
I remember you.

And yet, your somber presence
sends a sudden gust of wind
Bleak as a wintry ocean blue.
I am left cold and empty,
alone and bereaved of hope.
I still remember you.

—*Gilda Alfiero*

Ode To Motherhood

She dipped her hands.
Both hands into the pot
The pot of strongbuild
Decked with mirror
In the inner and outside.

Committed to the function
Dipping empty-handed and coming out
With a full hand
Sapped of strength
Calling on the will from a look.

Look that reach out
Speaking volumes of plead
Small hands reaching out
Wanting to be held
To be led every small step.

Every move that is made
Reflected on the surface of the pot
A woman of heart. Distributing among her fruits
Bringing on the rain and the sun
Right from the reservoir of her heart.

—*Kemi Ogunniyi*

The Dunce

He says no with his head
But he says yes with his heart
He says yes to what he knows
and loves
He says no to the teacher.

He stands and he is questioned
And all the problems are passed
Sudden laughter seizes him
And he erases all
The words and figures names and dates
Sentences and phrases
And despite the teacher's threats
To the jeers of infant precocity

With chalk of every color
On the blackboard of misfortune
He draws the face of happiness/

—*Glenora Stephens*

Through My Eyes I See An Old Man

This man I see is wrinkled
but his eyes still had a twinkle
when his hand held mine
I knew I'd never find...
anyone as caring as he.

He never acted old
for he was bold, he knew he was old
but in his heart he was young as I
Whenever I cried,
he was always there to confide...
until he died.

This man I talk about was old, bent
and wrinkles, but he was young at heart.
Through my eyes I see an old man
and this man is my Grandpa,
whom I now hold in my heart.

—*Jennifer Pirot*

I May Seem A Little Different

I may seem a little different
But really I am not
I don't go to your school
But I'm still being taught.

You talk a little faster
And walk quicker too
But I just like to take my time
But I'll catch up to you.

Don't treat me any different
As I won't to you
And we'll get along just like fine
As all people do.

When it's all put on paper
And seen in Black and White
We're just human beings
with all the same rights

So don't treat me any different
And I won't to you
And we'll be the best of friends
It's all up to you

—*Irene Sutherland*

Help Save The Dragons

Robbie 'd heard of the bombs
Called nuclear arms,
That welded the nations
With suicide charms.
He'd heard of the men
Who cared about none,
And without even knowing
He was destined as one.

Now, wiz kids are great
And computers are fate;
But please,
Please help save the dragons.

The witches, the knights,
The dragons and elves
Just have to be a part of ourselves;
so please,
Please help save the dragons.

—*Elizabeth Blanchette*

Where Mystery Inspires

Falling,
Drifting,
Going deep,
New inspiration,
Extra foundation.

Great mystery,
Secret smile,
Waiting;
A while,
Longing mind.

Willing eyes,
Wanting heart,
Open arms,
Watching;
In portent.

Loving care,
Intriguing life,
Laughing,
Spooky love,
Great inspiration.

—*Elaine Barr*

Untitled

My hair unbraided
by Becky's gold
turns silver grey
at dusk.
I contemplate
moving lips
colours essences
images from a far time
women of my youth
frozen in their innocence.

As she moves
her arms motion
a circle
across wide skies.
She speaks breathes her soul
upon my soul restoring it.
In the penumbra of the sunset
Becky's gold becomes the sun.

—*Dominic D'urzo*

Guilty

I feel so guilty.
Didn't go to work today
I read a book
enjoyed the scent of nature
spoke to a stranger
paid a bill in cash
I felt so alive
But then I remembered
I had a degree, a dental plan
responsibility
A brass sign marks my door
my hands are manicured
spring water in my coffee
my smoking habit cured
I floss my smile
avoid red meat and never see the sun
but for a moment I almost got away
I feel so guilty
Didn't go to work today

—*G. T. Reader*

On the Street

I always said I would never,
End up on the street
And here I am forever,
Feeling defeat.

I could pick up the phone
And grab my coat
Maybe I wouldn't be alone
Maybe I could find a way out

I see the children's eyes
And it is hell
I hear their cries
But I can't dwell

Cause I'm here
On the street
Full of fear
Feeling the city beat.

I made a mistake
I need a helping hand
This isn't fake
I wish you could understand.

—*Bobbi Roulston*

Moved

Moved
by his touch, his look, his smile
I wish to remain unmoved
I wish to be untempted
I wish to be strong and firm
and yet
I wish to touch, to look, to smile
to move
to tempt
to show that I am strong and firm
and so in his undoing
allow myself to be undone
of my own doing

—*Richard A. Sutton*

Why Life Is Special

Our life is so special,
don't give it up now,
there's a lot of pollution,
that we wont allow

Don't ever give up school,
at least get your degree,
you'll get your education,
just wait and see.

Don't do drugs
you'll miss up your life
at least start off good,
or it wont look nice.

your life is so important,
So special for you and me
you should live a good life
the way you want it to be.

—*Terri-Lynn Penney*

Untitled

You change your identity
for a mission
to deceive
at a high rank
for if something goes wrong
you can fix it with ease
But some things can't be fixed
because they don't tolerate spies
For if you are found out
You'll be tried
And then executed
So you'll do anything
to not be caught
For a person will sacrifice themself
for you
to complete the mission

—*Randy Naugler*

Standing Feet

Feet standing
feet standing on the edge of the street
standing, waiting to cross over

The street looks so wide
Standing feet are in a hurry
to reach the other side

Cars keep coming fast
Standing feet impatient
Cars! Hurry up and stop
before the sun goes down

Cars have finally stopped
Feet standing
now is your chance
the street is clear

Standing feet can no longer cross
Waiting so long
Standing feet have melted
into the ground
and are no longer around
—*Elizabeth Navratil*

EVOCATIONS

O Israel, don't shoot storks
    Flying toward Africa
Because they teach you the Bible
    O f   r e t u r n i n g
From small spirals to the huge
    Mega — Cycle of Milky Ways

O India, don't shoot turtledoves
    Flying to Himalayas
Because they know the letters
    Of A — U — M
Throbbing with cedarwood scents
    In every Maha — Mantra

O Poland, don't shoot comets
    Flying to Super — Chaos
Because they tell Maddonnas
    O f   o u r   c h u r c h e s
To wet outer eyecorners
    For future Mega — Music
        —*Serafin Korczak - Michalewski*

Song Of The Virgin

The hour waits...
    For the innocence of flesh,
Aroused is the first impulse...
    Within the virgins' nest.
    'The cock begins to crow'
    'The bird begins to sing'
The dance of courtship ready...
    On the peak of spring. Soon...
    The air fills with scent,
    When sudden urges fill to bust,
The cock rising up to triumph...
    At this first awkward thrust. Then...
    The mingle of purity,
    So quickly dismissed..
    No more than a blood-stained memory,
    Left upon the wings. And once more...
    'The cock crows'
    Now, to hear 'the bird sing'
As the dance of courtship settles,
    On the peak of spring.
        —*Linda Evans*

Lost

One child forever lost
Forever lost in time
Lost because of hurt and sadness
And the hatred that she's seen
Fantasies shattered
Dreams crushed
One frightened innocent child, alone
Who was forced to grow up
If you had just had the time
To give her love, praise and hope
And if you had stopped to see
What your cruel, sting words and hate
had done to her mind
Now she'll never know what love truly is
For who was this crying child
from hurt, tears and loneliness
That once crying child was me .....
        —*Natane Wilson*

Freedom

Freedom
Freedom
Freedom
Across the world it flies
the cry for freedom and for liberty
It shrieks before my eyes.

A mother's shrunken bosom
a dying baby's sighs
gunfire down a ruined street
it brings tears to my eyes.

Desecration of sweet life
in search of better living
brings flowing blood and gaping wound
to those who seem not willing
to listen to your point of view
'till bayonet's thirst is filling
seems to me a given obvious
Freedom cares not who it's killing.
        —*Morgan Kendell*

Dragons

Dragon's fire blows
    from his mouth
        when he
flies he is faster than
        the wind.

His enormous neck
    points his
    direction.

And his gigantic feet
    are rough
    his toenails are
sharp and dangerous
His green bumpy skin
    covers him.
His cave in the
desert is stupendous
        also Dark

I should always be
    aware of the
        Dragon
        —*Edward Manclark*

Were You

Shadows in the dark I saw,
Gleaming lights outshine;
Were you a lovely maiden fair.
I'd wish that you were mine.

A heart is such a fragile thing
It hurts and shatters fast.
Were you a shining diamond
You'd be mold in glass.

Sometimes 'tis hard to love
The one whose love is sure.
Were you a rich girl in sight
You'd be welcome to my door.

I am a little willow tree
With boughs that break and bend.
Were you the teardrops in my eyes.
Then you would be my friend.
        —*Cardene M. Sobers*

Dying Dreams

A white light
Gleams in my eye,
It brings me closer,
closer, yet, it seems so far away.
It is so tempting to go too,
Yet I know if I did I would not return.

As it pulls me toward it
I feel a strange sensation
of freedom, peace, and tranquility
overwhelming my body,
as if my soul has been lifted.

I am lifted into the air
Thinking it is the end
But as I begin to awake
I realize that I will
never see the other side,
Until it is my time.
        —*Kristina Koll*

Love Is Like A Tree

Love is like a tree,
growing every day,
from one day to another
you don't notice any change.

But when you pass by in winter,
and then in spring again,
you can see a host of blossoms
and leaves that had not been.

As summer passes by,
the blossoms change to fruit,
and all the world feels high,
and everything looks good.

In fall you think the tree will die,
it's losing all its leaves,
and all the world does cry,
like being stripped by a thief.

But when you pass by in winter,
and then in spring again,
you see a host of blossoms,
and leaves that grow again.
        —*Kirsten Menk*

Love

Love is madness
Hard brutal madness.
Love is fire
Hot blazing fire.
Love is an Ogre
A hard relentless Ogre.
Love is a chameleon
A camouflaged dangerous chameleon.

　Hot Fiery Love,
　　I beg you…
Put out your blazing flame:
Because you I want to touch
Because you I desire to feel,
　Hard remorseless love
Please change your stance
Before the fire of my youth
　Is Quenched.

　　　—Susan N. Kiguli

Consolation Of Widows

Consolation of widows: the cat.
He shares the hearth and the warmed bed,
comes and goes as meals dictate
and keeps his comments in his head.

By day he sleeps, by night he hunts
for mouse or rat or cautious queen,
then softly seeks the favoured bed
and uses bloody claws to preen.

He drinks but little. As for food,
he delicately nibbles it.
He loves to chase a little ball
and elegantly dribbles it.

Old age does not arouse his scorn,
but offers him a parking place
where he relaxes and accepts
caresses with indulgent grace.

He keeps his claws as sharp as knives
and best of all, he has nine lives.

　　　—Jean Edmiston

Cowboy In The Band

I met him in a country bar,
he was playing in the band.
He sat down at our table,
we began to play our hand.

We looked into each other's eyes,
we laughed and talked and smiled.
We touched our knees beneath the table
our hearts becoming riled.

I went home with my friends that night,
my heart had stayed behind.
That cowboy playing in the band
weighed heavy on my mind.

Now that cowboy he's all mine,
I knew right from the start,
that special twinkle in his eyes
played right into my heart.

　　　—Audrey Richardson

Commuting Words

hello.
hello?
Dead.

The wires,
lifeless, hang.
hung.
Hanged.

Tied in word
sentence chained
to sentence miles
before and
after miles.

Germany, Japan
　England, Thailand…

North America.　hello
sorry but　　(Sorry but I can't
　　　　　answer the … please
　　　　　leave…
　　　　　Bzzt)
Dead.　　　(…after the beep)
hello?

　　　—Anita Kleinschrot

No Phoenixes Here

Fury raging redly through cold veins
Hot, hotter
I am the sun.

Don't look at me
you'll go blind.

Don't come too close,
don't touch me;
shrivelled to ash.

Hands hanging at my window
clinking bones in the wind.
Blood drips from the fingers
flesh melting in a pool.

Burnt, burnt, all is burnt.
No phoenix here.

Burnt and twisted?
In you go
burnt before long
ninety-nine years to go.
I'm warning you though,
no phoenixes here.

　　　—Rachel Ruhannah

The Non-Importance Of The Aged

I must remember
I am invisible
This silvery crown
Comes with a curse
Worse

The emperor has no clothes
The empress no body.
Already, before death,
Ethereal

How easy to slip
From non-being
Into nothingness

　　　—Maureen MacLeod

My Son

Sometimes, I sit and wonder
how meaningless life would be,
if the heavens hadn't made you
especially for me.

You came with perfect fingers
and ten tiny toes,
upon your precious face
God placed a button nose.

He made your eyes from the skies
and gave to me my sun.
I realize now,
my life has just begun.

Little things,
that mean so much.
Your smiles, your tears
and your loving touch.

I hold you now, and wonder.
How meaningless life would be!
Thank you Lord,
for making him, especially for me.

　　　—Marie Bisson

"Me"

Oh I'm eighteen today you see,
How wonderful! just to be me!
There's so much to see and do,
And surely a special one, who?

Oh, I'm forty today you see,
How wonderful! Just to be me!
I've a beautiful child to enjoy.
And of course, what else but a boy?

Oh, I'm eighty today you see,
How wonderful! Just to be me!
My mate, I have loved and lost.
In life you must pay the cost.

Today I'm still lucky you see,
I have grandsons to hug,
And good friends to bug,
How wonderful! Just to be me!

I have many blessings you see.
It's wonderful! Just to be me!
There's so much to see and do.
I treasure each moment, do you?

　　　—Mildred Doull

True Loving Wife

Darling to day
I heard you half
You were planning to go far away
The day had been bright but it then
turned to night
as I pictured you out of sight
You're the sun the moon and the stars to
me
My Darling that's what you are
So the moon wouldn't shine and
the stars would be dim if you
were to wander so far.
Stay here with me
and soon you will see
together will make a good life
and as time goes on you will
soon realize I would make you
a true loving wife.

　　　—Hazel D. Leaky

Untitled

I know that he is gone
I know that he's not here
But forgetting all thoughts of him
Is what I really fear.
He knew that he was ill
But had it in his mind
That he would get better
But a cure they did not find.
I guess the time has come
That I have to face the fact
The fact that he's gone forever
And that he's never coming back.
All the time I spent with him
Was so special and so fun
He tried his best to beat the illness
But I guess we know who won.
Even though we're not together
We'll never be apart
For he has his own special place
Deep down in my heart.

—*Kelly Fairchild*

Yesteryears

Alone in my window,
I look into space.
The children are playing
No cares in their face.
I look on with envy,
This used to be me
But now all I've left
Is the fond memory.
I dream of the yesteryears,
Time was my own,
I was the child.
Now my children have grown.
I sit and remember
My childish grin
I think on what was
And what might have been.

—*D. W. Avery*

Fading Greatness

While walking down Melville one night,
I saw a boy,
and his dog.
His retriever was old,
one eyed,
toothless,
and one leg was amputated.
Yet,
the boy praised him fully.

They new each other since birth,
and did everything together.
This dog who received constant praise,
from his master,
was looked disgustedly upon,
by people who,
lacked knowledge of
his past.

—*William Azeff*

Can't Give You

Across the world
    I see you.
Wanting to be able
    to love you.
    Being confused
    about my life
    and you.
    You love me but
why can't I love you.
Love is the Death of me.
Love is what you need
    From me,
The only thing I can't
    give you.

—*John A. Carter*

Civilization At Daybreak

Through the eyes of a child
I watch as the world changes
Through the dreams of a world
I watch as hate and wars erupt

Through wars of power and wealth
I may be abused and homeless
Through my homelessness and fear
I may triumph fear with love

Through love and brotherhood
I search for forgiveness
Through forgiveness and acceptance
I search for the meaning of life

Through my life of denial
I pray for peace and understanding
Through peace and hope
I pray for tolerance and self-love

Through self-acceptance and tolerance
I see a world of genesis and wonder
Through the eyes of a child

—*Laura Farquharson-Myers*

Why

Everyday day, and every night
I wonder things way out of sight.
I wonder things real far away
When the world was better than today.
I wonder why the children cry
Why there's pain and people die.
Why I'm always asking why
and why the time seems to
fly right by. I wonder when
I scream real clear why no ones
there to even hear.
People seemed to lost their
touch to trust and care for
each of us. It doesn't seem
to matter why, when no one's
there to hear my cry.

—*Michelle Savage*

A Heart

When I was just a younger lad,
I'd often wonder why,
That God had given me a heart,
That get broken by and by.

But through the years I realize.
It was the most precious gift to give,
For a heart that hasn't been broken once,
Is a heart that hasn't lived.

—*Hal Walters*

Wouldn't I

If I could fly high above me -
If I could shout like the wind
Then I could ask all the people:
Isn't it time, to
dry up the tears now?

If I could move like the ocean -
If I could bend like a tree
Then I could reach all the people
and let them be free -
Give them tomorrow

If I could be like a window -
Then I could open the clouds
And I could show all the people
This is our home,
Once and for all.

If I could ease all the achings
If I could cool all the pain
If I could keep the sun shining...
Wouldn't I do...
Wouldn't I do that too

—*Anna Nasz*

Monster Stickers

I'm one forgotten firecracker,
I'm the key without a lock,
The search for perpetual motion
And a grownup's old toy block.

I'm a penny in a sewer out of reach,
I'm a late arrival at school,
A dream of paralysed escape
And the court jester's fool.

I'm all these things
And what's more
I'm waiting for you
Behind the never-opened door.

—*Tom Scura*

Treasures

Little children are like flowers
In each, the beauty is unique
As they grow, we watch with wonder
From bud to blossom, so to speak.

Flowers thrive in warmth and sunshine
Children grow with love and care
Stop and take a look around you
Both are found most everywhere.

Some are shy, just like the violets
Others bold, more like the rose
As we shape and mold and nurture
All so special, our love grows

Take the time to smell a flower
Love a child along the way
Spare a moment, just the to ponder
How they both, can make your day!

—*Marie Chapman*

Together

Together we've spent so much time
In letting our love shine through.
The tears, the laughter and the pain
Will always remind me of you.

You're the one who changed my life
And gave me so much love.
The pride I feel when you're next to me
Is like a golden dove.

Sleepless nights I'd think of us
And wonder if we'd last,
Only sadness fills my heart
When I think about the past.

We've both made our share of mistakes,
There's no need for more
Up all night and crying make my eyes
So sore.

But I want you to know that I love you
And I never want to see you go,
What would I be without you,
That I hope I never know.

—*Charlotte Yury*

Over News

I love swimming
In poetry
Over bad news at radio.
O black sadness!
I do not like
Dangerous travels
Neither you in this
Air plane breaking out
Into an explosion.
So do I write more and
More.....about love and war.
Sometimes but
I feel tired
Because violence...
Over news,
I smile also!

—*Michele de Laplante*

The Calm

Mountains are flying
In the deep blue sea,
The calm now decaying;

Black-grey stone,
Now a blur;

The engines now roar,
The beast then soars;

Smoke from stacks,
Sky in black;

My retreat of inspiration
Now in desperation;

But it won't last long.
Just wait for the calm,
It will be as strong.

—*Trevor Ward*

Untitled

Children
innocent, happy
grow, play, learn
generation, dependents, people, heirs
trust, love, observe
helpless, frightened
victims
—*Maria Bober*

Nature's Palette

Nature's palette
Is forever changing
And yet it stays the same.
The greens and gold
Of landscapes old,
The trees in forests blazing.
With fire red and quiet brown
Each mixture new is made.
With shade and light
All things look right,
Each rock and plant persuading.
Blue water flows,
Grey-white clouds roll,
Now falls a golden leaf.
The seasons change
The color range
A new hue soon is breaking...

—*Carolyn Bailey*

The Me Generation

The me generation
Is now coming to an end
We realize that what we need
We can't find without a friend
We want exoneration
From the mistakes that we have made
The wisdom of our elders
Makes us realize we've strayed

We don't want a future
Without God's gift of trees
To be trapped in a concrete jungle
Where there isn't any breeze
We need to see our Children
Freed from this despair
We want to leave a legacy
Of hope, health and fresh air

—*Susan J. Wood*

Your Fellow Man

To respect your fellow man
is the way it was meant to be
injustice to others
is slavery for us all

Ignorance and fear
is bred in our young
we're born with our eyes closed
and raised the same

To learn another culture is taboo
unless you're a different colour
then it's forced on you

People bleed and hurt the same
whey does colour matter
for in our makes eyes
we are all born the same

—*David Smith*

Outcry

I went to travel and saw the world,
it's beauty and it's terror,
the sky, the beach, the deep blue sea,
but what I saw was error.
The news box flashed beatings and rape.
the homeless, poor and hungry.
the presence of crime everywhere,
no solitude, no escape.
As we tear out our hearts, our souls,
cause each other pain,
the thought so strong in our minds,
is how we are to gain.
There is no gain from pain and fear,
self-destruction getting near.
We need a vision-clear and true,
a bonding, hand in hand,
if we're to help each other,
join to take a stand.

The peace you'll find within yourselves,
start to see the way,
take your brother by the hand,
start a bright new day.

—*Natalie S. Berger*

Pensive Poet

I ask myself a question
(I've asked it many times!)
Why is it, when I take a pen
My thoughts translate to rhymes?
Is my brain on a turntable
Just like a phonograph?
And, what is this compulsion
To make other people laugh?
Deep down, I know the answer -
I've had to wear a smile
Concealing scars of childhood -
I occupy an isle.
'Tis there I feel the pounding
Of rhythms on my shore.
'Twas ever so and will, I know
Continue, evermore.

—*Gwen Park*

The Face of Love

As we behold the face of Jesus
Leaning against the tree,
With all the pain and grief and sorrow
Endured for you and me, ——
We see a loving tenderness
Shining from his eyes, —
Assuring us that full forgiveness
Within his mercy lies.
Hope, he gives us, in our work.
With faith, our love release
To all our fellow beings,
To unite our world in peace,
With gratitude for countless blessings.
We haste, without delay,
To let our spirits rise in joy
With Christ, on Easter day
Composed with love by Martha

—*Martha Aschenbrenner*

Leave

Run
Leave me here
If I am not wanted
Than go!
Turn your back
Take no mind of all
The rejection
I feel
Goodbye.
I know it is sad
Isn't it?
That my life is
Worthless
To my friends?
To my family?
Go.
Leave.
Now!

—*Nikka Hugo*

Life

Time
　Life's most precious gift,
　　　Love
　Life's best feeling,
　　　Family
Life's most valuable possession.

　Without Time all is lost.
　　Without Love who cares.
Without Family nothing matters.
　　Time, Love, Family.
　The elements of Life

—*Karen Jean Campbell*

Our Friendship

I've never had a friend
Like you,
To teach me things
I never knew.

To guide me through
My life on track,
And never saying things about me
Behind my back.

Our friendship to me
Has too many words to say,
But all that really counts,
Is that we're here together
Today.

—*Alicia Young*

Where Love Is Real

Mystical dreams
Magic kingdom
All is fair
That ends fair
Love is real
Sorrows are forgotten
Dreams come true
In this wide world
Some may die
Most will live
To realize their destiny
And what is to become
This place?
A far, far away place
Where dreams come true
And love is real

—*Dianne Clayton*

Woman!

Love
Love for Woman
What a passion for the human?

What are thou that before thee
I fall false of the man in me?

How I wish in the now
To embrace and cherish thee as mine

But lo! Time in egg.

O' Providence! Tender her
Tender her sweet that as one

We may embrace Love's yoke
When mother time hatches the moment

Tender her sweet
Sweet that when
Mother season tolls

We may sprout
On the silt of chastity
Tenderness undefiled

I love you woman.

—*Mangeni Patrick*

Memory

White line on grey
Marking where he fell
With no warning
Under the weight of the bullet...
Years ago this was
And the line is now gone,
But when I walk by
It jumps out at me still,
Peeling from the pavement,
Wrapping itself around my neck,
Tightening,
Until I turn away.

—*Sara Montgomery*

"Garden Of Eden"

I lay deep as was dead
My hand push as was laid
My mouth shake as was gone
Being that it was all done

My agony stays endless
My heart looks dim and painless
I shift myself
I stood by myself
Sorrow for fear
O, dreams are not sometimes fear

What was in the dark
As we went in the ark
Where it's all open and day light
Would appear!
Would appear!
would appear!

—*Edna dura Ray*

Shock

Your suicide came so quick I did
not have time to blink.

For I am still in shock and I
Just sit and watch the clock.

And listen as it does tick by
Thinking all the time why O why.

For you were life for me and
now my life has ended.

I blame my self for all you
see your death was probably dew to me.
I think of all the times we had
some great, some good and some bad.

Why did you not speak to me
of your worries and your thoughts
I would have listened I do not judge

And now I aim the gun to my head
my grief for you will be at an end.
P. S. I will see you soon my friend.

—*David N. Howarth*

The World We Live In

Running down to forever land,
Not knowing where to turn.
Alone is where you stand,
While the whole world burns.

Slowly drifting away,
Not long to go.
Awaiting another day,
Hurting us so.

Being washed away,
By what we do.
Nothing will stay,
The future is so blue.

While we stand here,
Alone and afraid.
There is lots to fear,
If the world decayed.

So here we stand,
With questions in our head.
But to keep our precious land,
Let's keep it from going dead.

—*Callonie Roy*

Teenage Years

Teenage years are a time of confusion,
Of depression, of rebellion -
Stuck between childhood and adulthood,
Not knowing where we belong.

It's a time of learning,
Of wondering, of seeking -
How to look and how to act,
So we will not be set apart.

It's the time of discovering,
Of exploring, of experiencing -
All the complicated feelings,
Which are part of being human.

It's the time of transformation,
Of growth, of decision,
As to where our future lies -
For the rest of our lives.

—*Marie-Anne Quigley*

A Wedding

We are the captors
of each other's heart
having shared a romantic,
passionate,
surrender.
Bejewelled and resplendent,
we come to rejoice
in the capture,
and embrace
the respect and honour
due such a splendid union.
It shall be our prize
to let grow
and have last
an
eternity.

—*Jean Katchanoski*

A Message

(Dedicated to Ken Wayner)

If you but knew the splendor
Of the long corridor
The peace within transition
All void of dark suspicion
The passing in review of self
Retrieving from the akashic shelf
The sum of all the credits earned
Dispensed love to be discerned
Naught counts for more
On any plain nor shore
Than total tally of given love
To living matter as from above.
View any and all with eyes of love
In to their space, do not shove
Know all will journey to the light
Live - LOVE and all will be right.

—*Carol-Ann Bosley*

Untitled

The broadened joys
of the new found life.
The cries, no longer of sorrow,
are now tears of ecstasy.

Oh the sadness felt
for those who dared not grow;
those who remained behind
in the coldness of mid-stream.

As the great condors,
I too now soar
through my life
exploring the beauty
in the meadows of my mind.

The fullness of every day,
every month, every year,
that is what my soul now seeks.

What joys awaken inside
whilst the sun peeks through
in the east.

—*Lee A. Smith*

My Vision

I vision distant gleaming heights.,
Of things I would attain in life.,
I dream of far off places fair.,
With someone patient waiting there.,
Where joy and peace ever abound.,
Amid the oceans rushing sound.,
And sea gulls gliding in the sky.,
Are heard to call in passing by.,
Where white caps cross the shoals galore.,
To splash against my homeland shore.,

I vision now back in the past.,
For golden memories seem to last.,
Of yesterday's forever gone.,
Where once a silver star it shone.,
A moon lit trail "a winding stream.,
I vision in my twilight dream.,
And glimpse a rainbow in the blue.,
Then all at once I dream of you.

—*William T. Sturgeon*

An Idea

The morbid race,
Of time and space,
Runs over the valley,
To no place.

The time capsule broken,
And nobody has spoken,
It's just the rules,
Of the game of fame.

When the fires out,
Your thoughts are tossed about,
Explaining them,
Is a task and a half.

You can scream all you want,
Because nobody uses their ears,
Exploding dreams,
Erupt!

—*Tracey Gauthier Blair*

"Missing You"

Looking back, reflecting,
On being there with you,
Didn't know, you felt so low,
And now, I feel it too.

Didn't mean to stifle,
To cramp or crease your style,
But, that's me, I couldn't see
Beneath your treasured smile.

Leaving, was not easy,
You're always on my mind,
The tears I cry, may never dry,
Love is, sometimes, unkind.

I guess it's true, of what they say,
That love is often blind,
I wish I knew, a love as true,
To me, as you were mine.

—*Lynda D. Evans*

There's A Boat Comin' In

There's a boat comin' in
On the late evening tide.
"Oh, I think it's my father"
A little boy cried.

They were out in the gale;
Now the sea's calm again.
"Dry your tear, mother dear,
There's a boat comin' in."

When you feel all alone
On the big sea of life,
And your heart is beleaguered
With conflict and strife

Just raise your head high
And stick out your chin:
For nine chances to ten
There's boat comin' in!

—*Agnes Fisher*

Australian Autumn Love Poem

I send waves of love to you
On this sullen autumn day
With salt breeze crystal tang
In air of southern cold.

I dance a song of love for you
With naked feet and chest,
Toes curling in the carpet
Of my haven room.

I shall sleep and dream of love for you,
Curled warm in flowered covers,
Incense slowly wafting through
The curtain-flapping window.

What came before and what comes after
Is not of my concern.
I followed the pathways of my heart
And they have led to you.

—*Ondine Evans*

Song

I will come to you
On wings of song
When you least expect it.
You cannot deny me.
You will be powerless
In the face of my insistence
For my desire is born
Not of greed nor primal need
Because I come from the regions
Where the unsullied is the brave
Where the victor is devoid of all conceit
So when I come to you
In song. At dawn.
You will be mine.

—*Guadalupe S. Sta Ana*

Winter

The north-east wind blew
mercilessly,
and the rain cried
hysterically
on the window pane,
begging to get in,
tremulous of the dark
that loomed heavily
behind her.

...Alone, I comprehended all...

—*Carmel Calleja*

I Love Thee

Art thou in mournful gloom
or be in joyful boon,
I love thee.

Bustle along with the day
or in quiet slumber lay,
I love thee.

Wakes thou in darkness of night
or fall on sleep in the palest light,
I love thee.

When time ripens and cold shadows
of death, embrace in silent sound,
I'd love to walk upon ethereal meadows
for ever to thee bound.

—*Lola De Paola Dunston*

Cranberry Mnemonic

Cranberry picking:
Oval globes of light,
Crimson droplets in a yellow pail.

Lovers kneel on a
Springy turf
Crushing leaves, fruit.
Juices intermingle.

Bruised, tart smell
Berries and kisses
Greet each other
In sour grimaces

Musk of earth and moss
Nimble fingers tickle plants
'Til red lanterns fall.

—*Jennifer Bayly-Atkin,*

Autumn Masterpiece

Hillsides speckled with black cows,
painted trees against grey clouds.

Horses playing in the field,
Autumn winds of cold do yield.

Swarms of leaves fly near the clouds,
and freely fall back to the ground.

Life is drawing to an end,
as sleepy trees in Autumn bend.

Old stone houses near the road,
embrace themselves against the cold.

Snuggled on the rolling hills,
old clapboard houses resting still.

Rushing sounds of swirling trees,
sunlit tree tops in the breeze.

Miles of fencing decorate,
a lonely passage through a gate.

Where calves and lambs are having fun,
playing in the evening sun.

I look above majestic skies,
God is watching with wondrous eyes.

—*Robert O'Connor*

water skirmish

midnight
rains
silver
spears
on
their
nylon
shields

Sends
the
others
running
for
cover

—*Leonard Desroches*

Kingdom Come

The child is falling down
remember the school days
those wonderful days
tripped on acid and ran away

sees red roses and hammers
painted on the wall
walks down royal road
and believes it leads to anywhere

kingdoms come
and kingdoms go

razor blades on fragile wrists
check out if blood is blue
but the red roses keep pulsing on
thorns for some and flowers for others

another kingdomless king
gave away royal line
for a red rose and a bottle of wine

—*Kira White*

The Moon

At night, it runs.
Rides the waves
And walks on water,
Slicing the darkness
As it scurries off to the horizon
To meet with night.
I look into the black cone
Spangled with diamonds,
Intoxicated by a musical silence,
Enclosed by gaping night's cape,
And the light at the bottom
Is a hole in the sky,
An eye at midnight
Watching over me.

—*Kim-Anh Nguyen*

Despair

The elusive future summons
the impotent past
to the precipice of doom.
Soulless and cold
the nebulous depth awaits
its victims
who contemplate
the wraith-like wisps of hope
that spiral heaven-ward,
beckoning.

—*Donna Peterson*

Evolution

Lightning flashed in a newborn sky
Sent the spark to the element brew
It enraged, it engaged, it commanded
— Life — before it withdrew.

Through eons of time, it travelled
And merged with the earth and the sea
It fed, it convulsed, it conceded
As it progressed, it ceased to be.

While the very air was tormented
The chameleon triumphed and failed
It harassed, it neglected, it spawned
In each new world it regaled.

Journeying beyond the possible
Separating and joining in the dance
It learned, it survived, it remembered
Yet somehow, it was all only chance.

Mothering now, and protecting
Loathing its own bareness
It slithered, it roamed, it soared
Ready to create — awareness.

—*Jeannette Chase-Garagan*

Heartbreak

Depression
Sets in
Like the scarlet dusk.

The setting sun,
Vanishes
In the distance

Happy memories-
Echo
Dark walls of doubt.

As a ship
On the tossing sea,
Wavers-

So my heart
Is pulled
And torn apart.

—*Jodie Schmidt*

Grandma Giggles And Old Fred

Grandma giggles had a cat
She named the cat old Fred,
Fred the cat weighed fifty pounds
From staying in his bed,

Grandma Giggles had a plan,
She told Old Fred to go,
Fred refused to leave his bed,
He didn't like the snow;

Grandma Giggles grabbed Old Fred
She threw him out the door,
Fred the cat got very mad,
Back in the house he tore,

Grandma Giggles plan worked well
She did this five days straight
And after working very hard
Old Fred had lost some weight

—*Carrie Borg*

Living With It

Holding on to the past,
shedding many tears,
hoping things will get better,
trying not to relieve your fears

Living with a secret,
Living with the pain,
You've lost everything you had,
There is nothing more to gain

The man was a good friend of yours,
Until he became much more,
he harassed you on the telephone
and banged upon the door

You hope someday it will happen,
he'll get put away,
and instead of looking behind your back,
everything will be okay.

—*Sarah Stew*

Love Hurts

We walk in the moonlight,
side by side,
Glad that we are alone

The waves whisper in our ears,
in an odd sort of tone.

He stops, looks at me
with tears in his eyes.

He says it hurts too much,
to tell me any lies.

He says it isn't working out
That it was never meant to be

I can't believe he's saying this
Why is he doing this to me.

Tears are rolling down my cheeks
I thought we'd last forever

I can't bear to think what would happen,
if we were no longer together.

Right now my thoughts are very blurred
But the only clear thought I have,
Is that love hurts.

—*Angela Beaudry*

Balkan Knees At The Swan Cafe

Around the sumptuous table,
Sits a girl dressed in sable,
Eating ice-cream sundaes,
On the holy churchyard sundays,
And roaming from cafe to cafe,
Escalloped in shimmering silk,
And a tasting of the buffalo's milk,
From Indonesian Cathay.

Red red lips has she,
Like a dozen kneeling salmon,
Whose fins are far but from a knee,
In a Balkan undressed cafe.

Tea cups dance
A merry prance,
Of Olivetti swimsuits,
A laugh of a girl is sitting up,
Off the sofa in her lingerie salutes,
Of red black and blue.

—*Philip Roland Lucas*

Smoothly

Smoothly things will happen;
Smoothly people are a nappin';
Smoothly people will be dancin';
Smoothly will be prancin';

Smoothly people talk;
Smoothly write with chalk;
Smooth is soft when you touch;
and in the car you move the clutch.

Smoothly is when you brake at night;
Smoothly is when you stay in sight;
Smoothly is when you talk on the phone;
Smoothly is when you brake a bone;

Smoothly is when you ride a horse;
Smoothly is when you take a course;
Smooth is when you erase the board;
and in the church you talk to the Lord.

Smoothly is when you fight with your brother;
Smoothly is when you talk to your mother;
Smooth is when you paint you house;
and after you will kill a mouse.

—*Liisa Pesonen*

People

Funny, how people treat each other
Some days they call you down and
other days, just look and frown.
But now, some people just can't see
what others have to be.
Because of all the tear's and fear's,
Who are people suppose to be.
But if people only see
what they want to see,
Hear only the words
they want to hear.
Then those people are very lonely people.
So people don't you see and hear,
just what those people see and fear.
Then people can say
we are who were suppose to be.

—*Connie Derhak*

Spring

Some think the sun makes winter fade,
Some think March winds lead the parade.
Their blustery gales still fan the flame
That lingers in the fairest name - Spring.

Some think that winter has a time
When it should cease - or be inclined
To start to melt its icy chill.
It's on a calendar - mark at will.

But if we watch so carefully
Through the years we might just see
It's winter that gives needed rest
To land and tree, and nature's best.

And when spring yearns to come alive
It sits with winter - side by side.
They do not fight as we suppose,
But mix and blend - crocus and snow.

The merry stream gives ice a ride.
Each has its time; each has its pride.
One says "Hello", one says "Good-bye",
And we can see it if we try.

—*Carole Haney*

New Wine

New Year's wine,
spilling hope the color of blood,
fragrant and rich,
but brief the joy,
that tips cold crystal
to the lips of the holy that abhor
the sacred drink of pagan heroes.
Sacrifice made from human hands,
and fields of sun,
survives blame,
and given for a kingdom made of beasts,
to consummate a love so rare,
drinks sorrow to the dregs,
and finds its happiness there.

—*Julie Rudrick*

Dream Switch?

Am I dreaming of being a debater?
Surrounding by lots of circles,
Like a great announcer,
Announcing a long story.

Or am I dreaming of being a doctor?
Doing on operation with assistants,
Like a puzzle player
Playing a serious maze.

Or am I dreaming of being a designer?
Sitting in front of computers,
Like a cool guider
Guiding a pretty mask.

Does my dream stop, yet?
Maybe they are just controlled by a switch
Needed to be turn off
Or a never-ending story?

—*Carol Lin*

Untitled

Tension,
Taut and silent
Forever prevailing,
Needing and desiring
More, never obtaining
Living in desperation,
Every move
An act of frustration
Lost in a world
Of enchantment
Losing in reality
No reason to live
No reason to die
Appeals to fade away

—*Philip Corkin*

Taken

He speaks aloud
To tell about a thing
That happened across the sea.
His voice makes me melt into nothing
He laughs, I laugh
I'm taken by his voice
Truthfully I'm not good enough
for him.
My thoughts of him and I
are dreams never true.

—*Denice Gail*

Settle With Man

It was on St. James street, man
That I tried out for bar, man
Braman not in thought, man
It happened every time

Inflammation nation-wide, man
Of bowl end inside, man
Strain ends inside pain, man
It happened quite sometimes

O! Doctor shall you say?, man
Be well, get cured today!, man
Will your life God's way!, man
It happened after mine.

Although near reach eighteen, man
Not yet of legal age, man
Nor yet of tender aid, man
   To be a man!

—*Dominique Behroozi*

Sixtieth Birthday

Who could have told
that the world grows lovelier
as we grow old?

Red cliffs at sunrise
burnished by the dawn,
will they still be red
at sunset
with daylight almost gone?

We made the climb at daybreak.
That was long ago.
When we returned
at sundown, yes,
the hills were still aglow.
Rose-red in the setting sun
and the sea was indigo.

Sixty years are not enough.
I need another century
to find my Poinciana tree
and watch the burnt-sienna cliffs
turn first to copper, then to gold.

—*Mil Pettigrew*

The Conqueror

The girls are gone
The bold men are gone
The drums are being beaten
Calling men to battle

Where are the men of war?
They are in the marble quarry
Labouring for survival
Remembering their motherland

Alas! the bold men return
Holding the shield of faith
The sword of the spirit
Armed with the armour of God

They proclaim love and peace
The men of war disarm
They file into the waters
In Jesus' name for remissions of sins.

—*Ebenezer Ayeh*

The Painters Life

The pictures so perfect.
The colours so bright.
The scenes so real.
Real like his life
With a delicate touch
his hand strokes the brush
up and down, across, and all around.
the soft touches are like the
happy moments of his life
But the rough and tough strikes
on the canvas, are the angry
painful moments of his life
running out of the end of the soft
bristle brush. Like the tears falling
from his eyelashes, his life is
all in pictures. Not life or reality.
Something it will always be as
a painter this is his life.

—*Lisa St. Denis*

Roses

Natures most clever creation
the magnificence that is a rose
petals as soft sheeny velvet
most glorious flower that grows

Richness of deep green foliage
rainbow hues both pretty and bold
no sculptor did mould a perfection
as the curve of each petals fold

A rich blazing glory of colour
they give us the greatest delight
they titillate our deepest feelings
our senses of smell and of sight

Paradise is a garden of roses
as the freshness of day has begun
droplets of dew veil their petals
glistening as jewels in the sun

The most delicious of perfumes
fragrance that's heavenly sweet
a work of art that is flawless
It's a God given beauty complete

—*June Fletcher*

A Sharing Friend

Can wisdom ways ever declare,
   The mystic strength of love?
In diverse frames and vigour bear,
   from man or God above;

Some cry for love, some die for love;
   My friend doth truly share,
A mortal frame with inborn love,
   No spoken words to bear.

He'll lick my hands and wag the tail,
   For a pat and caring word.
Biscuits, bones or a dish not stale,
   He'll nibble, no regrets heard.

Habit or duty, it matters not,
   A sentinel gallant and true,
A friend, in games a partner got;
   A guide, for trips, a crew.

He has no hate or wicked look,
   A trust no power could yaw.
At death he'll seek a lonely nook,
   Yet share my pain and go.

—*Oliver Wije-Tillake*

A Prairie Evening

As the sky turns black
   the night wind whispers
the storm starts to attack
   a strangeness stirs:
don't turn back
   it has yet to occur

The first drop splashes
   upon the dry earth
the dust leaps and dashes
   the soil soaks in mirth
as the thunder crashes
   witnessing a birth

Then the sun beams
   while the wind is warm
and the grass gleams
   fresh after the storm
answering farmers' dreams
   as new life is born.

—*Melanie Hill*

Storm At Mayrhofen - Austria.

There's darkness in the valley now
The rain comes lashing down
The morning sun which shone so bright
Has left this little town.

And yet when at its burning peak
One could detect a chill
It shines too bright, it cannot last
Now rivers have their fill.

What of tomorrow? Hope again
The sun will soon be here
And every storm, however black
Brings forth a day so clear.

—*Ray Pearce*

Remembrance Day

Today is the day
The world takes a stand
To remember all the soldiers
Who fought for our land.

With monuments and poppies
We adorn each grave
Of husbands and fathers
Who were ever so brave.

The freedom we enjoy
And often take for granted
Scarred the lives of many
From whom people have been planted.

Our wounded lay in numbers
Unaware of their loss
Lying there waiting patiently
For signs of the Red Cross.

High up in the sky
Freely glides the dove
To remind us every day
Of those we dearly love.

—*Shayler Higgs*

Babies

Babies come into our life
These tiny miracles
To change us forever
And make us better people.

When we first bring them home
They are so tiny and new
We love them so much
But aren't sure just what to do

But soon we see
That it is all so natural
And that having a baby
Is truly wonderful.

To see them grow and learn
And gain their independence
They can soon walk and talk
It is all an amazing experience.

When you sit and wonder what is it all about?
You look into their little faces
And you know they are people this world couldn't do without.

—*Diane Howes*

Silenced Cries

Listen my friend, Do you hear.,
Those cries that tell a tale.,
Of hungriness, of loneliness.,
Of strong hands growing frail?

With caring eyes, we would surely see.,
Their dark eyes stare astray.,
We might even feel their emptiness.,
If we chose to look their way.,

But deafness, it surrounds us.,
Blindness steals our eyes.,
We no longer see the pain they feel.,
Nor hear their silenced cries.

As tomorrow fades to yesterday.,
As one less tear is cried.,
One less dream shall be fulfilled.,
For one more hope has died.

—*Laurie Golocevac*

The Mommy and the Wind

I am the mommy,
To three girls under four.
I laugh with them,
And cry with them.
Get mad at them
And they at me.
Then we make up,
Usually!
We have good days,
And bad days,
But always very busy days!
There's never too much quiet time!
But last night I fed the baby
In the early morning hours.
It was a stormy windy night.
I sat by the window with a quilt,
And let the wind sing to me.
Why? My girls would ask.
Because! I am the mommy!

—*Jackie Miller*

"A Daughter's Insight"

It took a little child's cry
To awaken me in the night
Not just to the things around
But to some new insight.

As I began to console
A thought comes right to mind
Of how you've done this for me
Time after time.

Yet I never realized
The patience that you had
How tenderly you'd hush me
When I was feeling bad.

I never heard you complain
No matter day or night.
Constantly staying with me
Until I was feeling alright.

Now as I wipe my child's eyes
A thought makes my heart glad
I couldn't have been blessed with anything better
Than the love of my Dad.

—*Darlene J. McIntosh*

Broken Heart

I've searched the world
To find true love,
Then you came to me
Like a gift from above.

But you broke my heart,
I couldn't help crying.
The day you left me
I felt like dying.

They say life goes on,
I don't think it's true,
Because I stopped living
The day I lost you.

—*Anna Klassen*

A 30-Second Work of Art

If God Almighty
took six days to finish His work
why wouldn't we create machines
much faster than Him ...

for the men live little
and prove every day
drops of death.

And the one Sunday left
which to rest should be
is taken to calculate
our next evil step.

Inconsiderate, as it may seem,
life is adorably short.
Because, as a poem,
existence is a 30-second work of art.

—*Monica Eboli De Nigris*

Untitled

A chestnut mare,
travelling across,
a scythe moon,
a silver crescent,
canoe moon.
a lone loon,
calling across,
a half moon,
a lost wolf,
howling to,
a nearly complete moon,
finally, falling in love,
with the full moon.

—*Richard Mooney*

Life

I sit and stare at a window,
Trying to think past that same window.
Then I think about life,
Just as I look at a knife.
People think life is a waste,
Even before they take a taste.
To fall to your knees,
When you see the trees.
To see the snow melt,
It looks much like felt.
To feel the leaves,
Rather then look at the leaves.
what a waste,
For not taking a taste.

—*Melissa A Medina*

Inheritance

If you searched long enough you'd find
under a Belleek tea-pot, on a corner
shelf in the kitchen of her heart
a photograph of a great ancestor.
Generations have polished its frame
with bees wax from the honeycombs
of wombs so that it remains unwarped
by either tears or rolling rain-drops,
and if you were to press an ear against
the lavender hill of her pillow you
too might hear the musical red rivers
that run under the crust of her dreams
where one note relates to another
like the face in the photograph to
that of her new-born daughter.

—*Ann McKeever*

Poison

Take a sip,
we'll watch you fall;
Take a sip,
You'll have to crawl,
It's deadly stuff you're playing with,
If you don't think so, take a sniff,
You'll feel numb, you'll feel stiff.
So don't try this stuff.
It's no bluff.
But if you try it and live,
Just remember we can't forgive.

—*Shyanne Suben*

What is Hurt?

Hurt will seem eternal
When time comes to a stop
Eating away like acid
And confusing every thought

Hurt does not really care
Its hunger has no class
It grips a tender heart
And shatters it like glass

Hurt then takes a turn
And bitterness sets in
To twist all your emotions
And again, hurt will win

Hurt will leave you scars
No matter what you do
And pieces of your broken heart
Will build a wall for you.

—*Rachelle Desormeau*

On Freedom

Into a space
where a man once
existed, comes the love
of knowing freedom,
the freedom of yourself.
It is your idea
of what you are
which sets your image
of this freedom
which you can be
or reject, as you wish.
But how many wise men
are there among the fools
and how many children
amongst your men,
can show you the face
that I know so well?

—*M. M. Shadov*

Alone

I'd like to live in my own little world
   where nothing could hurt me
And no one would be hurt by me

I could do anything I wanted
   and no one would be harmed
Except me

But if I was all alone, I would die
   because you can't live
Without love

No one would miss me
   and no one would care
So I could go silently to Death

Death would be loving and caring
   and would accept me for who I am
He wouldn't care about my problems

He would stand there
   with open arms and give me
The love I never had

—*Kelly Giesbrecht*

Waterfall

Amidst the depth of green verdure.
Where shrieking bird protest man's entry.
And streaming fern does not endure
That this be paths of aimless gentry

There rise to the very cloud
In hurtling rainbow hue
As though a breach in that white shroud
Had 'loved this beauty through

A pure cascade of simple rhythm.
In all abandon of the body leaping
While from its lips majestic hymn
Flows bubbling laughter or soft weeping.

—*E. Heatherington*

Love

Love can be a moon-beam
   which we never capture,
or it can be a cloud on
   which we float in rapture.

There is love
   which takes the form of passion,
and love
   which comes and goes with fashion.

There was a time
   when love endured forever,
but these days
   we seem to see it never.

It flares like
   fireworks in the sky,
there for a short time
   only to die. Why?

—*Yolande Porter*

Winds Up

Winds up, snows on the move.
White micro-bits tumbling across
Saw toothed crystals of former selves.

Winds up, trees stretch
Against frozen fibres.
Untouched by the rustle of green.
Mere images of former beings.

Wind up, clouds tear apart
Over lowered skies.
Earth and air push together in
A skeleton embrace.

Winds up, driving frost
Through bone marrow into ones soul
Creating a longing for things
That aren't cold.

—*H. C. Wyness*

Grandchildren

Grandchildren are special and sweet.
With their sunny smile and muddy feet.
They sometime's laugh sometime's cry.
Always asking what and why.
They have vigor spunk and will.
Have many a tumble many a spill.
Always stuffing their little face.
Spilling thing's all over the place.
But what a joy we are to each other
These little tykes and old grandmother

—*Addie Shaw*

Grandfather

I know an old man
Who's kind and gentle
And caring and loving
In everyway

He is my grandfather
Who I love very much
He's a special part of me
That I never will forget

He takes me places
Here and there
So easy to talk to
Because he's a true friend

My mother says
He's such a wonderful listener
He loves to hear your problems
And help out where he can

Now I see how special grandfather is
He brings that extra warmth
In what he does for me
I love grandfather dearly.

—*Michelle Navratil*

The Glories Of Morn

Purple yawns adorn the ragged roads
With a darker purple epicenter
An inner sanctum
Magnificence of creation
Upon despoiled concrete cement
Spilled earth all over

Quiet, calm, unassuming
Not glory-seeking
Yet glorifying

A day or two
She lasts
Moments of glory
That's all
For moments in life

And the angels heralded her
As she trumpeted heavenward
And as the wings clasped
Turned golden eternal glories
For moments - everlasting

—*Sheilla Clement*

Mother

You brought me into this world,
You gave me love and life,
You taught me how to be a man,
You were my father's wife.

You're a woman of many faces,
You do it so right.
You cooked and cleaned and went to work,
You tucked me in at night,

A poem won't do you justice,
Let me show you how I feel,
If not for you dear mother,
My life would not be real,

So gather round little children,
Boys and girls don't delay,
Remember that sweet woman
Not only on Mother's Day.

—*Peter Gannon*

Take Hold

We work, we toil our spirits away
with fingers worn down to bone.
We hustle and bustle our time away,
with happiness scarcely known.

Our candles are flickering out.
And darkness is setting in.
What will your final thoughts be of
when death has the final win?

Will your mind be full of fond memories
to have, to hold, and to cherish?
Will you have the warmth in your heart
to stave off the cold when you perish?

Or will you end in a lonesome state
with no one there by your side?
No one to hear your last whimper.
No one to see that you've cried.

Take hold of your time, and love.
It's all that we have my dear friend.
The time is steadily approaching.
What will you have at the end?

—*Jarrett Alvin Thompson*

The Man Inside the Bottle

He's, lost inside the bottle
With his fantasies and fakes,
Not a single way to remember
all the promises he makes.

He's the man inside that bottle
There's no fear and no regrets,
Problems he thinks are little
Family members he forgets.

We pray to God that someday,
He will realize he'll drown,
Inside that damned old bottle
That just keeps dragging him down.

I hate that cursed whisky,
That has taken my son from me,
He was once sweet and loving,
Now he's just a shell of what he used to be.

Son, please leave that bottle,
This thing that you call home.
I will always love you, son
Signed by a sad and lonely Mom.

—*Joan Gray*

Untitled

Generations behind you
You are remembered
Your fragile image presses
Between pages and pages of frayed edges
Yellow and cracked

You are of the same name
And of the same blood
And yet who are you
To prey on my thoughts
Your past doesn't give you the right
Your past shouldn't give you the right
Should it

But here you are
Blurring my vision with your memories
Though you belong to the past
You hold fast to the present
Just as your pages hold fast to your image

—*Sylvia Chow*

Never Say Good-Bye

They walked into the room,
With satisfaction in their eyes,
With laughter on their faces,
Yet a tear held deep inside.

When they look at each other,
They wonder what each will be,
They wonder what each will do,
But tomorrow they cannot see.

They look back through their memories,
They look back through their years,
They see a lot of laughter,
And recall a silent tear.

It's so very hard to say good-bye,
It's hard for them to let go,
But each has a separate dream,
As they turn down a separate road.

As they leave and go on,
They watch the time go by,
But yet through it all,
They'll never say good-bye.

—*Shannon L. Anderson*

Shining Armour

In the museum,
You stand tall and proud
Behind meticulously polished glass
And cushioned by velvet.
People come to look at you,
Full of awe and admiration:
You have effortlessly withstood age and
time.

Long ago and far away, you witnessed
battles
And rode with conquerors whom we know
nothing about.
You hold many answers, yet stand silent.
Proud, you look down at us and watch us
blunder:
You have seen eras more exciting,
Men more heroic than those of our time.
And yet,
As you stand so seemingly indifferent
Your silence is a call we can never ignore.

—*Danuta Rajska*

"My Request"

I want to meet the infinite power
Don't care what place - don't care what hour;
But, when he looks me in the eye
I'll be so happy I will cry.
He'll lead me o'er his vast domain
I know with him I will remain.
When he seats me at my place
My soul will overflow with grace.
I'll tell him there is just one other
I'd like to meet - that is his mother.
I only want to kiss her hand,
For bringing forth a son so grand.
He had to die upon the cross
For our sins she bore the loss.
I humbly thank you for this favor
You gave to us our dear, sweet savior.

—*Betty Marie Slifko*

Intercessors Hands

God save Canada, Heal our land,
Your grace shield her
with Spirit of love and truth this day!
In thy love and grace!
Lead her to your Holy word,
Ancient of days in Jesus name
Your help we pray
God give Canada faith in Thee!
Speak to our Country and tell her,
Your Grace sets men free
A crown for every soul,
Be born again in Thee!

Ancient of days in Jesus Name,
Our help comes from Thee we pray!
Let our lands be humble,
Put in a clean heart!
Our Prayer to do right,
For sight and Thy Council!
Wisdom we pray!
Holy-spirit Guided!!

—*Lorraine McIsaac*

Back To Primitive

Eagles in the air and flying
Dreamers in the night are dying
Girls in bedrooms raped and crying
Here, alone, I sit denying

Evening lady of the avenue
I wish to sit and talk with you
In hopes to find my fears untrue
For, life's surprises, for me, are few

Sunshine girls on midnight's streets
Down where all the animals meet
To taste of life; so bittersweet
And prolong our journey from the trees

Falling further into the dream
Where life and love are as they seem
To hear their call, again we cry,
Once screamed be eagles in midnight's sky

Eagles in the air are falling
Dreamers in the night keep calling
Girls in bedrooms, now resolving
Here I'll stay, alone, recalling

—*Francis Wayland*

My Love

My love be she far away
Does she still know me today?
As the skies are now so grey
There's nothing left but to pray.

My heart be with you day and night
Sweet princess whose love be so bright,
How I wish now to see your sight
So beautiful than life's light.

The wind be blowing all day long
Perhaps she is listening to my song
Wearing her flowery sarong,
Waiting for me to come along.

—*Mark Migita*

How Much Is A House Worth?

"How much?" "How much is your house worth? The auctioneer
called. "How much?" How much? Do you hear me say?" "Well,
I do not know. I'll have to count and see the rooms it has.
And, do they suit me?" "How much?!" How much?! How much I
again say?" "How many can sleep in their big and little beds?
Does the fireplace heat to warm our hearts on a cold and
wintery day?" "How much?! How much?! is my house worth?"
"Are the walls painted nice and a lot of windows giving light?
Oh yes, is there a cheery hall, a breakfast nook?" How much?
How much is my house worth? "I guess I have considered it all
and the things a house must have. But to say how much it's
worth, I am puzzled. To say what's inside and is it 'alive'?
The house I live in? With little ones and their givins?
And Dad and Mommy, too. Well, when I think of you and you and
you and my own, I then begin to know How much my house is
worth one, two, three, four, five six, seven, eight, nine, ten
million or a billion more." Only God, I think, can really know
how much is our house worth? A house is worth what's inside of
it. Oh, not furniture and stuff — but you and me and others.

  —Madge Stiehl

Christmas Wishes

Less military-industrial thinking.
Calmer people.
Bigger angels.
More talking with trees and animals.
More respect for insects and stones.
And more Santas from the minorities and parades
 of silly Santas from 3rd World and U.S.A . and . . .
 an exchange program of Santas from
all nations, and no nations thanks.
Quick hurricanes of mistletoe, devil in a headlock.

And an oak for President, a redwood for Governor,
 roses for the mayors of cities, thank you.
For Christmas I'd ask the world for enough love
 to give me goosebumps.
Homosapiens sitting in a ring of joy
 their hats on backwards.

  —Clyde Sanborn

They Say She's Gay

The talented song, dance, and comedy girl
came south when she retired.
She had so much fun giving birthday parties
at the restaurant where she was hired.
They say she's gay - They drove her away.
Gentle of heart and always kind,
never guessing what was on his mind,
She went to the doctor one sad time.
He got the sheriff, he got the judge.
Claiming violent behavior, all three did sign.
They say she's gay - They took her away.
How frightened the lovely lady was in the car.
Darkness came as they took her far.
Up the crooked mountain to the hospital at the end of the road.
They say she's gay - They locked her away.
Locked in a cell behind a door,
Such pain the shock treatment she never felt before.
They broke her body, they broke her heart.
Saddest part; the talented dancer could walk no more.
They say she's gay - they did her away.

  —Jane Edwards

Lost Lovers

The rag-tag dreams of mice and men
can be all that keeps us going.
Uncertain dreams for an uncertain world
and it's killing us not knowing.
In light at this a prayer, a plea,
yearning from the depths of me
Please, forgive me, for I know not what I do
All that's certain is my dear love for you

The time that's spent has gone and went
quickly as the changing seasons weather.
Through thick and thin, smoke and gin,
It's lasted we're still together.
My love for your you and your's for me
has stood the test of time.
Why tear down what we have built?
That would only be a crime.

There is something I leave to you
as pure as a white dove.
For eternity I leave to you my dear,
All my love.

  —Darli Bell

Nourish That Love

Love can be beautiful, and often mysterious.
Can make you feel happy, or maybe just serious
But it needs frequent feeding from the one you adore,
Or it will be lost - to be found nevermore.

So if you want someone to love you alway,
Close by her side, you always must stay.
For just as a flower, untended will wither,
Her love can grow cold, unless you're together.

As a fire needs fuel to keep it aglow,
A love must be nourished - ('tis well you should know)
She needs you close by, if things should go wrong,
'Cause the touch of your hand fills her heart with a song.

If you're far away, and problems arise
She'll find someone else her needs to supply,
Then after a time, though it hadn't been planned,
She'll find her joy lies in the touch of his hand.

  —Ethel M. Kuhn

My Humming Birds

Seldom in this world of stress
Can one have moments of pure bliss.
But they do come, in my own garden,
When native Honeysuckle flaunts its scarlet trumpets
And Humming Birds arrive to sip the nectar they so love.
Whirring wings support their tiny bodies
As they drink the liquid nature caringly provides.
I watch those fragile wings working at magical speed
To fulfill their owners' need.
Standing in silent awe-
Mesmerized by the swift and fluid motion
So different from my own pedestrian pace.

  —Edith S. Taylor

Revolutionalities

A decade of rationalities facilitated pluralities,
Fostered inequalities and legalized brutalities.
Racial and ethnic realities were lost in generalities,
As double-faced dualities preached about moralities.
Absent all integrities, they spoke about complexities,
Denying opportunities, based on less abilities.
But tiring of their hypocrisies, couched in stale banalities,
We made them their own analogies with political fatalities.

  —Catherine B. Laws

Somewhere Along The Way

I know that it wasn't supposed to be this way.
Can't blame God or the innocent child.
Maybe the whole world's just gone to Hell
'cause it seems that so many just don't care.

To dream of Western Movies when the bad guys wore black hats,
   The old sheriff and the cowboy hero
   The sound of campfire songs and bring 'em back alive.

Somewhere along the way the romantic days of long ago were
   forgotten and chaos took over.

Unseen enemies on the 6 o'clock news, a generation of
   revolution, and now kids get their philosophy from MTV
   and their heroes mock the leaders.

The sirens on the black and whites scream
   and the men in them are black and blue as another criminal
   goes free.

Somewhere along the way priorities were forgotten
   as another Steel Mill is locked closed
   or a tractor sits silent on a foreclosed farm.

God save the children before they learn about what adults do
   or the foundation gives out from under them.
   —*Joseph Goralczyk*

The Birth

An infant
carefully transformed,
wakens from his somnolent state
and cries and cries.

To hands that gave him life,
and instruments that reached
into the privacy of his being,
there he lies.

His naked body
exposed in all its perfectness,
like a piece of music the struggle begins-
the lows the highs.
   —*Elizabeth Osborn*

Life's Highway

My brown leather satchel
   Carries its look of import'
      At rest on the cushion
         Beside me

Finally acknowledged
   I rise to present my cause:
      The "Estate Tax I.D."
         I am the Executor

Thirty years saw her save this money
   She may have waited in that very chair
      And looked on past
         This very highway

Her eyes—blue as the summer sky
   Emitted a twinkle loaned
      From the stars, beguiling
         Till day was done

Aye, my "official" look is but a sham
   My eyes well up as I reach the door
      For in the mist softly
         I see her depart
   —*Doris M. Bryce*

Your Strength

I could tell it was you from many feet away. You have a way of carrying yourself. It is almost as if you are giving off a warning. "I'm tougher than I look." I know better. I can see the smile in your eyes. The same look that a child has when he has come up with a plan, a devious plan to do mischief. Then there are times when you have another look. I can only describe it as determination. You know what you want. You don't hesitate to follow it. I know this because you followed me until I stopped walking away and faced you head on. The best thing about that was that now we walk together, both carrying ourselves in the same way. We were both strong individually. Now our strength is brought together and is multiplied. When something breaks through you, I will come up in front of you and shield your weak places. You have showed me how to do this, for you have done this for me many times. Each time we separate for a time, I watch you walk away. You have a way of carrying yourself. It is almost as if you are giving off a warning. "I'm tougher than I look." You are, because I am always walking beside you. Multiplying your strength.
   —*Cindy Carte*

Sunshine

The sun shimmers down in gleaming
Casting golden light to reflect life's days

It is like God's love
pushing through fleecy skies
No human could duplicate it, not in a million tries

Even in winter
When frosty snows layer the ground
Sunshine and shadows can always be found

Old Father sun hanging way up in the blue
Sunshine, the essence of a fragrant rose that's new

All of life's downs seem to fade in the rue
Of the first peek of sunshine
When night's round is through
   —*Delene Montgomery Beaty*

Magic Valley

There, where the sun in its zenith reposes,
   Casting visions of gold on the valley below;
As the wind in the trees a lullaby discloses,
   Untold mysteries in the night's afterglow.
Then soft as a gossamer's fragile wings,
   The fragrant mist caresses the hills;
Where, far in the distance, a mocking-bird sings,
   Of peace in the valley where true love spills.
Like a magic curtain which sparkles and glows,
   To capture the wonder of a falling star,
Which, like a diamond, rich favor bestows
   On hearts which beat high, seeking love from afar,
Then softly enfolds this valley in peace,
   Etched with grace and charm, and more love to increase.
   —*Josephine Cordaro*

Tell It To Jesus

If you love Jesus tell Him don't tell me,
For Jesus will know, If it's so, Don't you see,
And if you love Jesus, He'll cause it to show,
Till even the vilest of sinners will know.
For when you love Jesus, it's hard to disguise,
It shows on your face and gleams from your eyes,
In the things that you do, and the things that you say,
Even when life isn't going your way.
   —*Donald King*

Old Bridge

It spans the width of a restless stream,
Catching the gold of the noon sun's beam,
A shelter for many a youthful dream—
Ancient, forlorn, silent treadworn—
Old Bridge.

A sentinel it's stood for many a year,
Quiet observer of handclasp or tear
Shielding the memories that others hold dear,
Haunt of the past, silent, steadfast,
Old Bridge.

Bearing the record of each rhythmic beat
Of merciless wheels, or languorous feet,
Of swift passing steps the echoes repeat.
It's strength now is marred
Weathered and scarred, Old Bridge.

Recalling with pride each service displayed
In memorable moments of sunlight and shade,
A God-given dream inspired him that made
Unprotestingly dutiful, this rustic and beautiful
Old Bridge!

    —Kathleen C. Dempsey

As A Shadow Passed Me By

A shadow passed me by today.. I felt it's coolness first, then
caught it at a glance as it was rushing forth in haste, perhaps
to find it's master of reflected light someplace. And searching
out it sought, and wondering why forgot it seemed to reach
out with a hopeless, helpless hand. And touching out at
everything in blindness like futility that it so deeply
saddened me I turned away. But not before I beckoned it to wait.

It paused against a tree with hollow eyes and looked at me as
if expecting me to be the one it sought.
And I could feel that it's transparent soul was crying out for
me to hold and warm it from the onslaught of the night.
I knew my help would be in vane, that shadows need their own to
claim and dusk would fall to ease it's pain, consuming shadows
once again. And saddened too it turned away.

I had seldom given thought before to shadows.
Or even knew one had a heart and soul.
But know If I could help them find I'd gladly give my life
sometimes, and even walk with two as mine now.
As a shadow passed me by......................

    —Glen C. Sherman

Streams

The gurgling, bubbling sounds of a stream
causes one to pause awhile, and dream of
tinkling bells and rushing winds, elfin faces
peering down from limbs, of fairy bright birch trees,
with leaves of yellow, and amber lights that shine so mellow.

Oh, to live by the side of a stream
with a mountain behind, and all green in between.
With a fire in the hearth, and a friendly face,
what more could one ask for in this beautiful place?
Tis God's true light shining down from above
which fills this spot with all pervasive love.

    —Marion Millwater

White Cloud Shapes

Lying on my back in the grass, I watched as white clouds
Changed into chariots drawn by white horses,
Into dragons, whales, camels, laughing children
Changing almost instantly into white bearded men
Even as we do.
And my idle thoughts reflected on the brevity of life
And of how long years seem only days as we remember,
Our childhood one brief spring, our youth one lost summer
And our mature years passing like the days of fall,
Gone but well-remembered.
And now we are in the short winter of our lives;
What have we done to warrant being born,
To having enjoyed the blessings each day brings?
Have we, like the clouds, been only forms
Which left nothing lasting before we, too, change
And drift away?

    —Margaret Anderson

A Fair And Lovely Face Is He

Lady: What ails thee child? Thy face 'tis an ache to me.
Child: 'Tis me mam, mi lady, sick with fever is she.

    A fair and lovely face is he,
    A face as woe as me.

Lady: And you be not aside her? Bestowing smiles of comfort?
Child: Me mam sleeps for days fain be I if none wert...

    A fair and lovely face is he,
    A face as woe as me.

Lady: If I wert she twould I like to awake by thy face.
    A buss of wellness and not a child's woe in trace.
Child: True, mi lady? Thence I betake to await nigh her bed.
Lady: Say not and thou shall have the profit of what I said.

    A fair and lovely face is he,
    A face as woe as me.

Child: Very well and welcome, mi lady.
    Here, a flower as pretty as you.
Lady: And I welcome you, child, for thy joy given for two.

    A fair and lovely face is he,
    A face for all to see...

    —Laureen Ruiz

Childhood Is . . .

Childhood is constructing masterpieces with Legos.
Childhood is that special magic you feel when you whisper your wish
    list into Santa's ear.
Childhood is roller coaster and ferris wheels, carnivals and circuses.
Childhood is endless hours playing in the sun.
Childhood is well developed imaginations and "invisible" playmates.
Childhood is skinned knees and bruised elbows.
Childhood is innocence and love.
However, sometimes childhood is ... a dingy one-room apartment.
Childhood is no father, only men who occasionally spend the night.
Childhood is gang wars in the streets.
Childhood is cocaine sales in the halls of the apartment building.
Childhood is taking care of brothers and sisters while mother
    works the night shift.
Childhood is no escape from the violence — in the streets, in the
    schools, and sometimes, even at home.
Childhood is going to bed hungry and waking up to no breakfast.
Childhood is poverty and fear.
Childhood becomes adulthood.
Childhood is the future.

    —Nancy Schorr

Sintelle

A fair young babe in stillness lies; asleep, dreaming her childlike dreams. Visions only she and her angel sees. Unknown to all but those two it seems.

Fingers twitching, that secret smile speaking of dreams oh so very sweet. I see you there, soft wholesome child, on your back with wiggling feet.

Thinking of all that you will see; walking, running and the trees you will climb. Whatever and whoever you will grow to be I hope to live and see, given time.

So be a child, as long as you can. But never be afraid to laugh and love. Live life to its fullest; lively and grand. Always give thanks to our God who is above.

Someday when you are older and wiser than me, perhaps this little poem you will see. When you do; maybe you will and remember me, for a little while.

—*Larry Hardy Willis*

Some Americans Had Tried

At the great wall of granite, with names
   chiseled in stone
A sightless war veteran sat bereft and alone.

He had fought for his country in far away Viet Nam
Now he was lost and forsaken, the war
   conceived as a sham.

A hand with three fingers reached out
   toward the wall
On a leg maimed and tangled, he tried
   hard to stand tall.

He wore bright shiny medals he had won at
   great cost
For while fighting for freedom, pride and
   dignity were lost.

He sadly remembered how many traitors had turned
As protesters marched daily, American
   flags had been burned.

His broken body dropped slowly as blinded eyes cried
In his heart he remembered some Americans had tried!

—*Eleanor Sneed*

Easter Memories

In the memory of a child today, Easter will always be,
Chocolate eggs, jelly beans, and decorations on some trees,
Easter baskets, egg hunts, and pretty colored grass,
Memories of having fun-memories that last.
Now Easter memories, for me, are quite a different kind,
Not chocolate bunnies, jelly beans, or eggs for me to find.
But, on good Friday, without fail, when the school bell tolled
the last,
We scampered home, changed our clothes, and got on the road so
fast!
A two mile hike, not many cars, the danger was not there,
Across the bridge and up the road, and we would stop and stare.
Before us now, it seemed for miles, all that we could see,
Were fields of yellow lilies, pretty as could be.
We picked, until we could not hold, another single one,
And back across the bridge we'd go, we all had so much fun.
When Easter comes again this year, I'll bring from memory,
The lovely Easter lily fields-that folks no longer see!

—*Edna B. McCann*

Your Way Or God's

Though you may sin and go astray,
Christ loves and woos you to His way;
Let evil go, give up your sin.
God yearns your life - your all to win.

Sometimes your heart may be most sad,
But God's dear Son sore trials had;
Not for His own sake did He bear
The shameful cross - the crown so rare

The cruel ones who pierced His side
Knew not how blessed to abide
With Christ the Savior in His will —
Though wicked hearts, He loved them still.

God's will for us is always best,
Though hard it be to stand the test;
Our way must go! His will must stand!
Don't walk alone! Hold fast His hand

—*Lola Mae Collings*

Transformations

Peaceful waters flow through my soul
Cleansing my mind, my thoughts, my feelings
A gentle breeze caresses my body
Serenity reigns about me
Nuzzled in the security and the grips of comfort
I rest in the calmness
Aching limbs begin to relax
The mind moves in a glow
A refreshing rain glides over my presence
A renewal of spirit
Tenderness envelopes me
Peace bounds
I am restored in the arms of love
Connected with it
Esteemed by it
Supported in its reverence

—*Kate Masters*

Remember Me

If I must die, don't weep beside
Cold marble stone for me,
Come ride the wind across the lake,
   For that's where I will be.

Share the warmth of red-gold leaves
That blaze and fall too soon.
Or meet me by a waterfall
   Quick-silvered by the moon.

Walk barefoot sands and laugh as waves
Toe-dance along the shore.
Look down. Just lift a curving shell
   To hear my voice once more.

Smile at strangers. Lift a heart.
Mend a broken wing.
Live each hour in the sun,
   And let each hour sing.

Remember me....but not to mourn
   The love so cruelly taken.
   Remember that we lived our dream...
     That I have only wakened.

—*Billie Dove Hughes*

Spring

Daffodils and violets,
Color in the grass,
A symphony of springtime
That all too soon will pass.
The air is fresh and full of dew,
It carries a promise
Of old things made new.
All the world shall now rejoice,
Flowers open,
Songbirds find a voice.
But no good thing can ever last,
Soon spring will fade into the past.
And then all of the earth shall mourn
The death of the glory that's yearly reborn.
But next year the glory shall once more take wing
And renew the bright beauty
That we know as spring.

—Kristen Murphy

Morning Glory

The silent voices of the past
come back to haunt me again and again.
Fleeting memories of a distant time
ever-present in my subconscious mind.
Stronger now; weaker then
the ebb and flow of the interior world
shaping the exterior form of the interior being.
The morning glory evolved from the precarious cocoon
radiant in all its splendor
reflects and perfects the painful journey
of a soul new-born and nourished in the protection of love.

—Elizabeth O'Connor

To Be Lifted

How extraordinary to have a friend thoughtfully
Complement me for a brave action taken
While the world at large decries my intention.

How good to be lifted unexpectedly when knowing
That derision for certain will be the popular
Denouncement...fanned by the winds of the world.

Like the golden sun breaking through stormy
Clouds, or refreshing soft rain-water delightfully
Caressing a parched earth, the complement

Sincerely evoking the best from my soul...
Calling forth an even greater reverence for
That which is sacred, whole. The truth.

But even a finer, richer find in having
The enemy pay the complement. The adversary
Beholding to a change in attitude and

Direction. The unexpected, to be sure.
However, the surprise reflecting the possibility
That the essence of maturity can touch
  All of our lives.

—Louis C. Riesch

War

Sharp swords, piercing arrows
Clashing with the human body
All is dead with their blood so red
No body left to fight
One claims victory
One claims sorrow
When it's over, no one's left
Except the human corpse that are ready to rest.

—Giancarlo Jacobini

Untitled

She stands, observing in awe
Confused, tired and starved
Pondering memories of the past
Horses, grass and dirt, venison,
beads, freedom the good days
Her father is dead, her mother is wounded
Silence among everyone
Scarce firewood, empty guns, arrows and bows
The white men are gone
Tattered hides, bloody trees, ruined families
The beast of foreboding having preyed
Soon enough-men building, women cooking, cleaning and caring
A civilization once more rising from its inevitable grave.
Thinking with its minds, not hearts
She and the rest, starting again
Trying again, living again.

—Hima Tadoori

Royalty

My silly love and I awoke the other morn,
Convention and decorum we laughingly did scorn.
He was dressed in blue jeans and a sweatshirt for the day;
I was still in robe and gown to watch the birds at play
And enjoy my morning coffee and the warming, winter sun,
To share a word, a laugh, a prayer; the day had just begun.

He pushed his elbow out to me and raised his head up high;
I thrust my arm, entwining his and heaved a solemn sigh.
Then slowly we descended, arm-in-arm upon the stair,
And waved to subjects mute below—the piano, couch and chair.
My escort grinned appropriately, but with brow in deepest furrow,
"Don't ever stop, my dear," he said, "thinking about tomorrow."

—Marlene Carol Spalding

A Prayer For Peace

A prayer for peace, for the battle to cease.

But the war has begun.
Countries with soldiers on the run.

Men praying for their Mother Land.
Soldiers waiting with guns in trembling hands.

He waits and waits for word of attack.
A mother's young son, she wants him back.

For safety's sake a trench is dug,
But bombs are blasting, soldier catches the slug.

He dies a hero, loyal and brave.
He died for the country he was trying to save.

Where a Patriot was once loyal
People made of backbone and gristle.
Today's Patriot, however loyal, is not a person, but a missile.

The war is on, the battle has begun.
From dusk to dawn, in light of moon and sun.

A prayer for peace,
For the battle to cease.

Soldiers, quick, come home safe and sound.
Make the next plan of target homeward bound.

—Jenna Shook

Daddy

My daddy's name is Bill, but grandma calls him Billy.
He's lots of fun and sometimes he is very silly.
He shows us how things are done; he is very smart.
He can cook, and he can make the car start.
Mostly he really likes to tease,
but at bed time he gives us a kiss and a big squeeze.

—Colleen Kachlic

Home Of The Brave And Land Of The Free

Lord, things in America are not like they used to be   Our
country is no longer the home of the brave and land of the
free, oh, we hear from every street corner about freedoms and
rights. The devil pushes these seeds of thought with all his
might. As Christians our rights are being violated, and one by
one taken away. The laws of our land are stifling our voices
as they push us back, day by day. Prayer in school, teaching
of your word, family values, sanctity of life—have all been
compromised for a land filled with hatred, confusion, and
strife, yet, because of your gift to all mankind 2000 years ago
on Cavalry's tree America has the opportunity to turn from this
bondage of sin, and be set free. So Lord, give your children
added strength and courage to live for you everyday no matter
how hard and bumpy the road along the way   Allow us to once
again be brave and our voices loud and clear so that all of
America could wake up and hear; your truth, not the truth that
the world proclaims—your truth that would cause America to
fall on her knees in humility and shame! We can then, once
again, join hands and hearts with thee And truthfully declare
as a Christian Nation, that we are "The Home of the Brave
and Land of the Free."

—*Betty P. Brown*

D-day

Red mist
cracks my window.
The horizon drowns in flame,
and smoke floats to the surface.

At the side of the road,
fire feeds
thick clumps of tumbleweed,
fields of grass
nourished by the heat.
Flames, like snake tongues,
strike the trunks of virgin trees.

With the crash
of falling oak, pine,
and cedar that once stood 180 feet tall,
ignorance and fear echo
against a white sky.

Ash coats
my yellow skin
like pollen.

—*Lara Kjeldsen*

A Plea For Help

Our world, our earth, our precious land
   Created by Thy loving hand
As mankind's haven and his home
   Beneath the heaven's star-filled dome
Given in trust to us to tend
   That life on earth should never end
See what today we've done, and weep
   Our trusteeship we've failed to keep
We've decimated forests, trees
   Polluted rivers, lakes, and seas
Contaminated once pure air
   Tainted earth's soil without a care
Our greed and lust for power and fame
   Are our besetting sins and shame
Please, great Creator up above
   Help us change avarice for love
Teach us to nurture and preserve
   Thy bounty, which we ill deserve
Open our eyes that we may see
   Our duty to posterity.

—*Lois A. Bracken*

Pop Music

Diamond star that glitters above,
Creates the lengthening shadow of...
Pop Music.

Glimpsed in top hat/clothed in mist,
The phantom turns illusionist...
Pop Music.

He peers from modern works of art;
Sings the lyrics that arrest the heart...
Pop Music.

A gentleman debonair/so chic;
Whose timely message is exotic...
Pop Music.

Sky scrapers of steel/glass;
Fresh, sensuous concert in the grass...
Pop Music.

Rosebud in the climax of slumber,
Opens to the beat of summer...
Pop Music.
Pop Music.
Pop MUSIC!

—*Evelyn Judy Buehler*

Tenth Frame

Miles away a black sky forms
Creeping in bringing danger
Its size frightens its presence warns
All mortals beware of its anger

Hovering above it haunts
With strong winds blowing fiercely
Pouring rain mockingly taunts
People running for safety

Under a tree the people hiding
Protecting themselves from the storm they try
A spark of electricity a bolt of lightning
A streak of white in the black sky

Startled by the thunder rolling
It's just the angels bowling

—*Diane Murray*

Summer Shadows

Summer is slipping away
Crisp Autumn breezes are chilling the air.
My mind searches for a simpler time
Reminiscent of childhood wonder
And carefree days.
Summers that lasted a lifetime,
And a world yet unexplored.
Each ray of sunshine was as priceless
As an once of gold,
And imagination and enthusiasm
Were the only requirements for
a full day of play.
Now the responsibilities
Of adulthood permeate my life,
And I long for the joys of
Childhood daydreams and the
Innocence of youth.
Where have all the summers gone?

—*Janice Severance*

137

Remember Me

Think of me when the sea winds blow
Cry for me when my loved ones go
Cherish me when you need a friend
But remember me when you're at the end

Think of time that we foolishly wasted
Cry for time that can never be tasted
Cherish the time that we had together
But remember me forever

Think of how we loved one another
Cry for how we avoided all the other
Cherish when we walked along the beaches
But remember me when you come up with empty reaches

Think of how I foolishly hurt you
Cry to know I can never do what you do
Cherish all those last words I said
But remember me and how I lost my head

Think of how you sobbed all day
Cry for how they pulled you away
Cherish how you never saw
But remember me when the sea winds call

—*Dawn L. Frye*

Deaf

There is a girl sitting by the ocean,
Crying tears saltier than the sea.
Talking to her mother earth,
letting the wind set her soul free.

She watched the gray clouds,
it is about to rain.
She used to feel such happiness,
but now there's only pain.

The cat sitting at her side,
tried to comfort her,
He sat calmly,
then began to purr.

But the girl did not know he did that.
She was only full of fear,
The girl was trapped in her own
Soundless world,
the girl could not hear.

—*Leigh Cavanaugh*

Fearlessly my wings of hollowed bones unite with the fleeting
    currents.

I ride the wind; its power gently lifts me to heights never
    ventured. . . . SOARING!

We embrace my friend the wind and I savoring our new-found
    freedom.

As the clouds above me place their moist kisses upon my brow,
    muted earth tones below me blend resembling the complexion
    of a human mother beckoning my return.

Earth her majesty once awesome now shrinks elliptically,
    egg-like.

No longer am I a bird, nor am I human, nor do I require the
    company of mortals.

Instead, I glide through TIME escaping its talons. No longer
    am I held its CAPTIVE. ETERNITY is now MINE and I its
    CAPTOR!

—*Lory Anello*

Nature Within You!

I walked along the fields of
daisies with no shoes upon my feet,
    Never did I feel so warm,
confident, secure, and complete,
    As my hair blew along with the wind,
As so my soul did too,
    I knew deep within myself
that nature was divine and true,
    For nature grows within your
heart and becomes a part of you
    And can ease throughout the
years to come and shows
through the woman in you
    Nature will never turn on you
    Nature is a friend
    Nature is a bond between two
    That will never really end!

—*Lara Lee Conder*

This Is How I Am

Nightly, I gaze out my paint chipped window. I find I see a
dark blankness, both out there and in me.

I search then for dreams of happiness and then I feel like,
a wave stopped in time, never to reach a sandy shore and
leave my mark in the eyes of the wondering observer.

But again I must come back to the spotted pane of glass,
glinting in the moonlight and again I play the role of a
plunked piano key, chipped, grayish yellow and out of tune.

—*Lynn Paprocki*

The Angels Cry

Silent lightning flashes bright.
Dark clouds roll in the sky.
A fearless storm forms tonight.
Tonight is when the Angels cry.

I feel their tears on my skin.
Through my hair, over my eyes.
Blessed tears wash away my sins.
For I am grateful when the Angel cries.

Families are home beginning to pray.
A loved one is slowly dying.
They could not bid her stay.
Joining the family, the Angel is crying.

Washing the sins of the world away.
Tears bless those who have died.
Tomorrow will be a brand new day.
Thank the Heavens the Angels cried.

—*Chris Gannott*

Coo of the Dove

The night was
dark the moon was high.
Not a creature stirred,
beneath the sky.
Little doves cooed their mournful cry.
Passing winds whistled on by.
The gentle night air was enough to keep cool.
While old willow tree gave them a look so cruel,
They flew away
Without a sigh, up into that very dark night.

—*Gretchen Seiwald*

My Mother

My mother was a beautiful rose in the
darkest of night. The prettiest you
ever saw. I asked God to let me
keep her but I had to let her go.
Her smile was like an angel. Her kiss
was worth more to me than gold.
The love she unfolded in her
precious hands told us children
what we wanted to do.
She loved to sing to us children
her songs never grew old.
She would rock the babies in the old
rocking chair and told us stories of so
long ago. We would sit silent and take it
all in the wind blew outside the our cabin
with our mother we were safe to the end
when she puts us to bed at night she would
always whisper a prayer God watch over
my children keep them safe day and night

—Marie Roberts

Dawn

The sun stirs in the sky and I think of you. In this country,
dawn is a prayer, but misguided, I pay homage west-ward. You lie
beyond the wet horizon a gull spirals overhead calling to no one and
the ocean's waves rise and tumble an inward storm.

Our fingers first touched in a country where lovers shed
each other like dread skin. We call it home and may soon meet
there again in the transient dawn of a camera flash. Our lips,
sea salt on them, will circle like butterflies; our hearts weigh
heavy with waters and our hands reach out to one another's
instinctively. But what becomes of those hands, once more clasped
in a fleshy knot? What do they hold the sun has set and the ocean
turned dark?

—Christopher James

My Log Cabin Dream

My log cabin dream, is a fantasy, I've had since my boyhood
days, and sometimes I can imagine it, in a foggy mountain haze.

A chimney made of rugged stone, and a wooden shingle roof,
The cracks are filled with red clay, grass and tiny roots.

The logs are hewn with care, so that each notch fits just right
and mud is placed between the joints, so they all fit airtight.

I can see the logs placed neatly, one on top of the other,
Now they have turned gray with age, a beautiful sight,
like no other.
I can see the fireplace, huge and such a sight,
and I can see the flickering embers, cast shadows, on the
cabin walls at night.

I can see a winding path, that leads to a mountain stream,
I picture wild life along the way, this is truly a country boy's
dream.
I long to go back to a simpler life, that I believe was meant
to be, away from fast living, with all it's greed and misery.
I hope that when my race is finished, and I may enter
Heavens Gate, that somewhere beyond the mansions,
There's a cabin by the crystal lake.

—Jerry D. Ross

Words Of Kindness

There's nothing like words of kindness to brighten someone's day
Just a smile or a big "hello" is all you have to say!
It makes the day seem brighter and takes away the gloom.
Kind words can surely sooth and heal a mental wound!
Should we speak kind words all through our busy day,
Results will be fulfilling and joy will come our way!

—Chris Grimes McCoy

The Strength Left Behind

Once upon a life,
Days were long and boundless.
It was a time of freshness;
Everything was new.

Achievement was precarious,
But fun was never vicarious.
Some were pretty and some were smart,
But most were waiting for a grown-up start.

Your parents were brave;
Your brothers and sisters admired.
Lessons and facts not always stayed with you,
But teachers and books inspired.

And now time is a stream
That reflects back upon me.
It may glisten and it may gleam, but it soon flows away,
Revealing only the memories that will never again be.

Go on; don't waver to seize each day, to seize each moment,
   this very second, before it ripples away.
Put your hand in the water and let it glide the current over;
This is your past and present, your own pool of splendor.

—Jean McClelland

Tenet

I felt a poem swift suddenly stir
deep within my soul.
Its musical line so soft serene
like a great iron bell it tolled.

Bewildered at first, this event so new —
confused I wondered what to do!
Will I announce this movement fresh,
or shall I quietly let it rest?

"Not fair!" a voice vociferous cried,
to stifle me is but a lie.
Sing out your poem to cock and dove
for your soft stir is unwavering love.

Oh cease not softness, please transverse
my soul across the universe to hearts and minds
of myriad throngs,
and back in place — here — along.

—John A Newkirk

Untitled

Amidst the raging battle I see an angry steed
Defiant to the throngs of death-strength is all he needs.

The challenge spurs him onward; nostrils flare in might.
Through smoke and fire, sword and shield he feels his rider's fight.

But look! The mighty stallion stumbled and as he fell
Death gripped the faltering pair and pulled them down to hell.

Silence engulfs the warrior. Stillness enters in.
Nostrils once breathing life give way to death's mad grin.

The noble one lay dying. The battle still raged sore:
Never seeing, never caring for those who'll fight no more.

They lay in deadly silence-the man and faithful friend-
While death looked on victoriously at their fateful end.

But look! Amidst the battle, amidst the fallen ones
I see alive their spirits and death, it seems, has gone.
-he never really won.

—Lesley G. Murphy

Untitled

You, to me, are never just fine
Delicate, elegant... I'm kept on cloud nine
There should've never been questions of trust
Dilemmas, enigmas... not letting us just crumble to dust
A feeling... my heart begins to swell
Elation, relation... without you is hell
Like a fish I pulled you from the sea
Timid and scared, you wanted to be free
But I nursed you into my world
And what came out is my greatest joy unfurled
I cared, and you shared... secrets
With no one else you would have dared
Thank you for bearing, your patience and your caring
With you I'd like to spend forever
Eternity to fulfill every endeavor
To cry and be shy, bashful, confused
Holding each other, molding the two
Into one glowing ember
Of a beautiful fire
... called Love.

—*Brandon Remick*

Friendship

I have lived eighty years and on this truth I am sure I can
depend, that there is nothing more precious in this world than
a long-time, faithful friend. There are some, I know, who
value money, or precious jewels through life, but I would
rather have old friends, good friends, for with them there is
no strife. And the knowledge that good friends reciprocate
makes life worth living. I have found, to reach that goal I
must apply several things, the most important is giving. To
have a friend you must be a friend with tolerance and
understanding; to be a friend you must be patient also,
without being demanding. The Son Of God, known to us as Jesus,
left us this truest of friendship advice; he said, that, laying
your life down for a true friend is the ultimate sacrifice. As
the sands of time trickle through the glass and the days that
are left are numbered, I would rather they were filled with a
host of good friends, than being with fame encumbered. When I
review my life, reminisce, searching for pleasantries
encountered. I find the most enjoyable are with old friends,
good friends, on whom I have counted.

—*Fred Lee Cooper*

The Search

Why did God put me here on this earth?
Did he put me here to love?
Did he put me here to hurt?

I ask myself this so many times,
I ask myself this and I search my puzzled mind.

Love I gave from the depths of my soul,
But hurt, loneliness and sadness seems to be the price of my toll.

I tried to live the life that he gave,
Sometimes not doing right,
Sometimes not knowing how to behave.

Loneliness seems to be the path that he has sent me down,
I don't know why and still I look around.

I give and I give my heart with such ease,
Trying to love trying to please.

The more that I search the less that I find,
Is loneliness and sadness what God had in mind?

Each day I pray and I pray to the heavens above,
Dear God keep all this pain and just give me real love.

—*Dave Baker*

Reminisce

A door high in a tree. Open it. What do you see?
Did it scare you? Are you scared of me? Close the door.
Another door appears-other side. Open it.
Ahhh, yes... Now I see you trembling.
Beware, for I did not scare you child. It was you-your own mind.
What was it you saw there? Who was he? What did he want of you?
What did he do to you? Did you let him do those things to you?
Did you like it? Oh yes, I almost forgot to ask, How is your cat?
Do you still have the plant I gave you?
It doesn't mean much anymore. Me asking, I mean.
Maybe I'd fluff up your pillow for you.
If I was in your bedroom tonight.
Where you sleep alone only sometimes.
I don't think I'm ready to live yet.
The space where you once were is empty.

—*Christopher Lo Giudice*

For Our Own Sake

Have you ever wonder about our world?
Did you ever think about its future?
That might have passed your mind (not just by words)
But that's not enough for a place of nature.

You have to see that it is in danger,
And sooner or later we're going to die.
It's not a matter of a stranger,
It's the truth of our life and it isn't a lie.

Look around yourselves: seas are getting dark,
Animals are vanishing from the crust,
And nobody seems to care, but just lark.
Oh! Please let not our beauty be the past.

Just do something about this pollution,
Don't let it become our own destruction.

—*Eleonora Cervantes*

Remembering Paul

So full of positive energy
directing hopeful expectations with careful aim
at children who haven't yet
"planted their own gardens and decorated their own souls."

A pioneering spirit
gaining satisfaction from the smallest accomplishment,
hopeful it would be a building block for a bigger one.

Recognizing everyone has some special gift
the must be shared if it is to flourish.

Laughing with us at our mistakes, problems, antics
and his and the world's.

Helping children
to battle the evils of poverty,
hatred, misunderstanding,
scorn, abuse.

Loving unconditionally.

—*Deborah Peale*

Suspense To Survive

Defiance and desire breeds the existence of life itself,
Deprived of emotions creates destruction to ones mind and soul
Mysterious affairs of harm and hope, make decisions
to which I must cope.
The future is bright they say,
But to whom does this quote indicate?
Life is what you make of it,
So force yourself to risk and take it.

—*Diana Avanessian*

Ageless Passion

I am inspired
Divine inspiration
Mystic voices
Voices of lust's fleshly appetite
As fresh and new as day lilies bent in summer breezes
Sensual
As easy as eating, drinking, breathing in and out,
In and out
Lust's final plunge
Sensual folds of imperfection made whole
The smell of faint gardenia perfume brings on
Flames of smoldering embers long overdue
Arms, Legs, lips, breasts entwined
Embraced in total surrender
Enflamed youth
Experienced woman
Becomes ageless passion once again.

— *Ellen Hicks*

Loneliness

The mind deteriorates ever so slowly.
Do not think, do not dream, and whatever you do,
Do not imagine dreams of fantasy, joy, and majestic ways.
You may fly, but do not use the Dragons fire, Unicorn's horn,
or the Sorcerers staff.
Be a legend; pretend, you can't be real.
If you could, you would, but you can't so you wither away.
You scream; cry, yes cry for help,
The heroes are deaf, they will not hear, who could hear?
There's nobody there now, everything's quiet, you can't hear
yourself scream.
Everything is slow: time, hearts, tears of fear and anger
It chases, but will not come or move,
It stares hungrily with bloody claws.
Loneliness envelopes you; you cringe, flesh hangs, you burn.
It's black now; listen...there's nothing to hear.
Peace, comfort, life: Don't come back.

— *Ingrid Jacobsen*

Used To Be

What do you see when you look at me?
Do you remember how I used to be?
Do you recall your breathless request
to be kissed by me so you'd feel blessed?
Is our love lost under the weight of years,
of problems, boredom, financial fears?
Is there any chance of getting back,
the former joys that we now lack?
I'll never forget the hours of sharing
our innermost thoughts with love and caring.
We were truly meant to be one, we two.
Whatever happened? Why is it all through?
Do I still love you, or just the memory
of how close we were, of what used to be?

— *Geraldine Ballou Reece*

Love, Forever

When, they say love is forever, they ain't lying.
Do you feel it deep, down in your heart, I do.
I want the LOVE, to FLOW through me, and be like it was.
You and me FOREVER, ALWAYS, TOGETHER.
I want you to hold me in your arms and never let me go...
But just for now, I have to keep my heart on a lease...
Until the day, I know when your LOVE is true, and you will
never leave me...

— *Jennifer Walczak*

Searching Life To The End

How would you define the word "life"?
Does it begin with "Man and Wife"?
Or, does it exist in the conception and birth?
What is the true meaning worth?
There is no specific value put on living it,
Just that each individual opinion is different.
Each answers for how they live,
Whether it's to take or give.

It's been known that life, is what you make!
Is it full of truth, or is it fake?
Life, to the fullest, can be short or long.
Depends on if the person is weak or strong.

Living it is hard, sometimes, as you face each day.
Wondering if the torment and hell, in living, is the price you pay.
Life has, for each, a different way to begin.
Like everything else, it's a mystery as some seek the end.

— *Catherine M. Ayers*

Untitled

This gorgeous blue-eyed boy whose name is David Mark,
does not like to play with dogs, because they always bark.
He has been bitten by one
and now, they certainly are not fun.
This dog bite him on the face
at his father's home and place.
Dad and step-mom did not come to his aid,
no doctor, no cleaning of wound was made.
Just deny and threaten him,
and make it sound like a whim.
They said they had no dog at their place
but David had a ripped lip and face.
How did this happen to our little boy?
Oh, his father said he fell on a toy,
But David told his story, not of a fall,
to two doctors, three nurses, his family and all.
The Board of Health came to check the doctor's report
and there was the nasty dog, fluffy and short.
But, it certainly left David with a lot of doubt and fear,
Much, too much for a four-year old to bear...

— *Emma Lord*

Cat-Of-A-Thousand-Names

Dearest Hobo. Cat-of-a-thousand-names, and homes...
Dog-like and kind; even the tiniest clutching fingers;
no alarm. Calm and patient.
Black cat, black, with no malice of color.
Yellow-green glance like mustard flower.
And smooth, so smooth in motive and feel.

Dearest Hobo. Life could not be lived without you.
Bringing us all together as friends, not just people.

Oh, cat-with-three-owners, (or perhaps three thousand),
All own you. All love you; and you, all; as we should each other,
without strings...attached, or judgements...made.
Trusting us your little gods, for your next meal.

Such great faith have I not found with anyone in all my world.

Oh, that I might trust my Heavenly Father, as you trust me,
and have faith for all the world to see...

Dearest Hobo. Cat-of-a-thousand-names, and homes...
You are my brother, my friend, my teacher...
You make my house a home, my eyes to see, and my world
full of faith.

— *Kimberly Gene Hernandez*

Largess

If and when I get old and lose my mind, don't let me linger on.
Don't let them put me in a Nursing Home where people are
forlorn. I want no one to wash my back, or feed me with a
spoon. I want no pills to kill the pain, or visitors
afternoon. I want to go when anyone can see that living is no
longer part of me, And that will be when my will is gone and
others have to care for me. I want no tubes to keep me living,
I want no respirator to keep me breathing. Just let me go with
dignity and pride, leaving worldly cares behind. I want no one
to be burdened down with me, as they have burdens of their own,
Just let me die, if meant to be, if I have lived, they'll still
have a part of me. So if you see that I am gone, take all that
can be saved, My eyes, heart, kidneys to someone who is
depending on someone to give, In order for a life to live. I
do not know when I will go, it is not in my command, but
someone far greater has control of my life, as I am guided by
His hand. So do not grieve, for I will be in the place He has
prepared for me. All that I ask, is that while I live, I will
always be willing to give.....

—*Dorothy Phillips*

Dream

Through bushes stands a man your
dream has just gotten fun.
His eyes as blue as the moon, and
hair as dark as night.

His face is familiar and now you
remember he is your love from long ago.

    As you thought new was dead now
you're crazy in the head.
    You look at him with a sight
cause his eyes so red and bright. You
get frighten as it brightens. And he
grabs your arm and says.
    Your life is my life and my life
is yours, keep it in your heart, and I'll
be with you forever, through the thunder
and the rain, through the snow and wind.
I'll be with you again
    Everything went silent and your
love was gone. But you remember it was
when He'll be with you again.

—*Brandy Williams*

The Moon

The Moon floats in a silent sky,
Drifting along, resplendent on High.

It reflects the light of a day now done,
Its place in the Heavens is the place of the sun.

That silvery orb keeps watch through the night,
Bringing us comfort, bringing us light.

We watch it as it waxes and wanes,
Sharing our joys, sharing our pains.

The crescent sliver shows us a side
That's mysterious, as if it's trying to hide.

But once again the full Moon beams down,
Sharing its love and its light with the ground.

Why are we fascinated with the Moon up above?
It's the vessel of dreams and the image of love.

—*Laura Robeson*

Thee Bins Of Existing Time/Life

For my life of existence in comparison to bins of earthly
dwellings that rots and reconverts vast surface existence final
contribution unto the fertile containments of plowed earth
where the explicit bins provision balances waste not want not
want not much life any advances cultural food chain.

For my life of existence in comparison to bins of exploration
developments congest over land, sea, air and space traveling
means.

For my life of existence in comparison to any bins top secret
concealments of surpassed power and authority over all
international decisions pending abolishment of oppositions
future life's succession.

For my life of existence in comparison to lost bins of very
mental cause and effect unto any atmospheric or earthly
dwellings of vast existing species mainly man of whom are the
soul creator of these bins potent valued effects.

Pending improper disposal of all bins waste potency error but
causes only flourishment of these bins detrimental aspects once
exposed unto man/vast wild life's environmental safe haven of
which I'm of existence.

—*Crypticion M. Priest*

Thank You God

(To my children on my 55th birthday.)
Each are so special in their own way
I think of them all everyday.
Not a day goes by when I don't recall
of bygone days when they were small.
It takes me back when something takes place
and right then and there I can see their face.
Their smile, their tears, their love and their trust.
And that is when I know I must.
Let them all know how deeply I care.
To know they are loved and each get their share.
These special people are my soul and my heart.
To each of them I give a part.
They're my reason for being, my purpose for living.
I thank you God, you were good in your giving.

—*Eleanor K. Thomas*

The Compass Flower Always Faces East

I watched you grow from little sprouts,
Each day I passed your way.
And in my mind there were no doubts,
You would grow stronger every day.
From dawn until the setting of the sun,
You flourished in the wind and rain.
The fields were tilled, a days work done,
The farmer dreamed what he would gain.
Green leaves appeared, the stocks grew tall,
God, man and nature did their best,
Preparing for the harvest in the fall,
with a gainful product, new in the west.
At last the sunflowers were in the blossom
Fields of golden yellow to behold,
as far as one could see, it was awe-some.
God's promised crop to be harvested and sold.

—*Edith L. Dresser*

A House

What is a house you might say, sure you see hundreds of them each day. You look at them and never give them a thought, you only wonder how many dollars it took to be bought. You look at a house made of wood and stone, not realizing a house is made of flesh and bone. You see, we as people are a house made by God, he took a little piece of clay and a hunk of sod. He breathed life into our body, we were made pretty and not to shoddy. Yes, each of us is a house within we must live, the beauty of this house is judged by what we give. Oh no-money and dollars I don't mean, but importantly how by the world you're seen. We can primp pretty and look so nice, and yet live with a heart of ice. So you see if a house is to glow, we must build it carefully so it will show, worry not if it's brick or stone, remember our house is of flesh and bone build your house and build it strong, put your trust in God and you'll never go wrong. Heed these words I've had to say, because surely I'll never again pass this way.

—*Earl R. Behnsch*

Meadow Wind

Meadow wind blowing fields in spring,
　Each eddies skittish pass,
Caressing, consoling, brushing, cajoling
　The waving sea of grass.

Meadow wind lofting a fluff of seed
　The disappears from sight,
In the brilliant hue of sky so blue
　Drenched with noon day light.

Meadow wind soaring thoughts and dreams
　Remembered with smiles and tears,
On a waft of draft up a sunbeam shaft
　To keep for a thousand years!

Meadow wind sprinkling scattered seed
　As its gentle currents flow,
To flourish, nourish, enhance the earth
　Where dreams and ideas grow.

—*Edith P. Dill*

Reality

I try, try, try...fail.
Each path taken toward writing becomes
a dead end experience. Resentful I fight to
recapture enthusiasm, my established career.
I fail even the familiar. Despair again!
Climatic depression.

Mania comes. I reason differently.
Above the clouds, I plan perfection.
Exhilaration is felt. Thoughts are delirious.
Feelings are expressed easily with determination.
Not yet free of the yoke of ecstacy,
its Siamese twin perplexity is miraculously nullified.

Lightening strikes! Time has passed.
Instantly I am authentic, whole, merry me.
Imaginative. Normal.
I visualize graceful flight,
singular not ordinary, slowly...
to heights unknown
into beloved warm sunshine.

—*Louise Woods*

Life is Like a Highway...

Life is like a highway
Each road breaks off into different directions.
Everyone has their minds set on an individual lane.
And some people are just followers and may get lost
or deserted in the wrong lane.
Existence means life and life means existence
Everybody has an extra ordinary task
to fulfill by being on this earth
Don't sit back on the couch watching T.V.
and carrying yourself like a slob.
Be all you can be. Be your best!
Do what you have to do
Because after this life you don't know
What extent of tasks your
master wants you to do!

—*Teratineka Thomas*

"Soliloquy"

Like drops within the ocean wide
Each soul does in the whole abide.

God rules by love and not by fear
I feel His presence with me here.

Spiritual man, created first,
Shall mortal rule less he be cursed.
But mortal man a will shall have
To rule himself for good or bad.

The clouds of night
In sunshine bright will quickly disappear.
The light of noon disperses gloom
Revealing God is here.

4,000 more years from his birth
Christ shall come again to earth,
To rule in truth and rightness
And all the waiting souls to bless.

—*Francis M. Black*

Nine Lives To Live

I feel God has given me nine lives to live,
Each time I weaken a new one he gives.
Soon the old ones gone with the breeze,
Then I float to new territories and seas.
He blew a new life to me in the wind,
Made me better and washed away my sins.
Now I'm happier everyone sees,
There's a change a big change in me.
So many loose ends and things to do,
But I'll make it he's helping me through.
I feel he's giving me nine lives to live.
For each time I weaken a new one he gives.

—*Christine L McDaniel*

The Star

The star in the sky its been seen twice
each time its been there its mare of gold ice
sparkling, glitter, beautiful gold.
I dare not compete for I am not bold.

I see the sun, it glitters too,
but I know the star is only in you,
You have the talent to be that gold,
bold beautiful star that's now inside me.

—*Danielle J. Reynolds*

My Little Cowboy

My little cowboy, sits on my knee
Eating his popcorn, while watching TV
He knows all the cowboys, of the great golden west
And it's hard to say which one he likes best.

When the story is over, and the popcorn is gone,
He lies there listening, while I sing him a song,
Before I am finished, he is fast asleep
Dreaming of horses, cowboys and sheep.

My little cowboy, asleep in his bed
While visions of horses run through his we head.
He is up before day break, and goes all day long
A whistling and a singing an old western song.

Straps on his gun belt, and rocks to and fro
Pretends he is a star of some great rodeo
Before he is twenty, I know he will say
That all the cowboys, with money are on TV today.

—*Rita Welch*

Now It's Achey, Breakey Time

I sure worked hard to bring up my kids
Eight of my own, and (two ready dids).
Four girls and six boys, can use up your youth
You get aches, and heart aches, sorrow and pain.
Then the kids are all gone, it is quiet again,
The old achey, breakey takes over again.
Your fingers and toes, start aching like sin.
Your knees and your back start aching, and then,
If you have a love life, that's over too.
So— old achey, breakey has moved in on you
There is a solution, I know to be true,
In spite of it all God still loves you.

—*Bessie Beekman*

Problems In A Mind

Visions of death in the back of my mind
Eighteen and under and we're all going to die
Scientist can't help and politicians lie
Brainwashing communism in foreign places
Malnutrition and crying faces
Tears—in my eyes—seek the truth
There's death in that streetside phone booth
It's lurking in the worst of all
The criminals that never fall
The Lords who push the drugs
The ones who use and the streetside thugs
Privacy hiding child molestation
There's something with our nation
End the way it is today
Make those people pay and pay
Am I the only one who cares
Or do people like me come in pairs.

—*Jason Allen James*

"Different"

He speaks, but they don't hear it.
He smiles, but they don't see it.
He extends a hand, but they don't touch it.
He offers an apple, but they don't taste it.
He holds a flower, but they don't smell it.
Then why is it when he's no longer there,
They remember?

—*Gretchen Schwemer*

Untitled

Joy.
Elusive Joy.
What are you? And from where do you come?
The world offers everything. Anything that you can imagine.
Any pleasure—any delicacy—any riches your heart can hold.
Ah! But the quest is for joy and emptiness is what I found.
Where is joy? That sweet, rich perfume—that perfect delight
That fills us with gladness for life—that gives our hearts
Peace and our minds rest?
Then I was brought before a child.
A child so full of grace.
And the answer—love. Only love.
And it—it is a gift. Free to you. Free to all who do truly
Seek real joy.
For it is in believing. Just that simple act.
And joy, unspeakable joy will fill your heart and life.
Joy is in the child who came.
The glory of creation.
And joy—
Jesus is it's name.

—*Christine Snyder Milton*

Why

The haze fills up the valley,
Emptying from the hills,
As it rolls and tumbles along,
I watch as it envelopes me,
I am lost in the clouds as if the world is gone,
It is here that I feel safe,
As I stand alone and search,
Search for the meaning of life,
And shout at the haze "why,"
For I feel I need to know,
Deserve to know
"Why so much dying and worrying?"
"Where did peace go, why did it run away?"
And it seems as if the haze whispers, there is no answer.
"You should try to change it;"
As the haze rolls away,
I sit and ponder the reason for my life,
For I know I am the only one who knows.

—*Carla D. Hartzog*

The Love of My Flag

Now that I and aged. Withered and gray.
Endless observing I have done each day.
What soars my spirit and anoints my soul
Is to see my flag waving on a pole
Occasionally the wind slashes through
Dancing the stars and swaying the red, white and blue.
The larger the flag, the better I feel.
Yet, no matter the size it is still a big deal.
For this flag I would gladly die.
When it is treated unfavorably, my heart does sigh.
If I lose sight of what it actually means,
It would demolish all of my dreams.
We could not bind together and staidly stand
How could we preserve our land?
Old glory is her magnificent name,
To change that would be a shame.
We are to love, honor and obey
Exactly as husband and wife on their wedding day.
The final object I wish to see,
Is old glory flying for me

—*Delores Z. Martin*

Operation Restore Hope

Land, air and sea troops arrived in Somalia today, unloading
equipment and humanitarian needs under a sky of gray.

Two American flags are waving high in space, seeing the stars
and stripes has put a smile on each face.

A tent city is going up pronto and fast, we're sure this
mission of need will last.

Many countries are joining in to this effort of good will and
peace, that all hostilities which prevailed will cease.

When all is accomplished and true life restored, homecoming
reunions with family, deserves thanks to the troops and the
Lord.

  —Beatrice Delorier

Now And Forever

Tempered with timeless energy, I build my life upon a rock.
Erosion slowly punctuates the span of air upon the bank.
Headlong, I romp among the dying tombs to no avail,
For you have wandered from toll to toll,
Ringing bells of greeting to souls unknown and known,
Sparing only energy to rest amid the fragrance
And the beauty of the Universe,
All bursting with the sounds of yesterday and now.
Joy, oh joy, that has no walls
To close upon its grinding sounds of life —
Of death. The death with yesterday's tumultuous tears.
The life of now, forever sounding in our ears.
Oh wondrous God, how can we ever bear to feel Thee near
And know we filled our lives with endless fear!

  —Kitty Welch

A Changing World

The world affords so much of everything
Especially for those who have a lot of energy.
Most people are prone not to limit their hours
In whatever profession of work they might be.

Of course, some have set goals in life
Which truly gives a high score for them.
But, the next person seems ecstatically happy
With just whatever comes naturally for him.

To everyone who aspires to do their best,
Laying plans must begin very early in life.
Essentially, high school on through college
Earns so many opportunities without strife.

With many libraries full of modern lore
Along with the seminars and all that T.V. allures,
Beside specialized courses in every trade,
All of these assets can open wide many doors.

With the numerous changes in the world today,
A trip to the moon may be next in one's life.
Men, the ladies are passing you by, so beware -
The next astronaut could just possibly be your wife!

  —Bethel Nunley Evans

Untitled

 Beauty walks the night alone,
Her grace revealed in moments of laughter,
 Smiling with eyes that hide passion and
Desire known only to the one who holds her heart
 She walks — leaving behind, a world full
Of fairy tales and innocence heard only in the
cry of a child

  —Jason Sexton

Together

To be young and in love is a scary thing,
especially when you see the one's who've gone before;
To have nothing but grief knocking on their door,
from what was once a thing called love;
But a love so true and pure like ours,
can go unknown to such feelings;
However, when were apart it feels as if the heavens
have separated from the sky,
and not a moment goes by that I don't yearn for your loving;

All it takes is a sight, sound, thought, touch, smell,
feeling and everything around fades into the background
and all I can see is you and I together;
But perhaps the worst is when I daydream you're walking
to me with your loving arms open and I reach out to
engage in a sweet embrace, only to open my eyes and
see myself reaching out for something that isn't there;

It is for all these reasons why the time we share
Together, just you and I, is so special and sacred.

  —Sara L. Lange

Peace

She was to be named Peace,
Even before I got her, I knew she was special.
She brought peace into my life,
And taught me lessons in love and time.
Her fluffy fur and soft cotton tail,
Made me love her from the start.
I never thought she would go away,
But I soon learned life is short.
The large dog that had gotten into the yard,
Made Peace into fear.
There was no escape, not in her small wire cage,
Her eyes were filled with terror, when we found her,
Her soft fur and cotton tail no longer shines.
Her floppy ears no longer jump at the sound of my voice,
Her tiny nose no longer wiggles with excitement.
Peace taught me a final lesson in love and time,
Love is everlasting...but time will never be long enough.

  —Catherine Ellison

Tree

Restlessly I float along,
Ever following the winds desire,
I am not my sovereign,
For my destiny is with another.

Flexibly I bend with the wind,
Will this protect me from the storm?
Strong and sturdy as a bulwark,
Will this be my demise?

But my true strength lies below the surface,
The wind's wrath cannot penetrate me,
But too much rain and I become rot,
Too much sun and I do wither.

With pride and arrogance I do stand,
Believing myself to be ever perennial.
Each member alone cannot stand,
But as one we form a bond that endures
 natures fury forever.

  —Jo Blount

145

Teacher/Children

We do the day's work
Ever wondering which of those we are with
Will be touched by our wonder.

Fresh, eager faces,
Not yet knowing, caring
Theirs the unheralded world beyond.

Shudder, do I, the pain of it
Knowing more of the triteness of our actions,
Meaningless thought,
Tragedies of trying not.

Elated to feel the beauty of need,
Of spirit released,
Kindness offered, with smiles
Accepted with love.

In each, the spirit of renewal
Wanting of horizons, yet unseen
Grabbing, grasping, demanding
Reaching for kindred souls
Let the meek...

　　　—*Elizabeth J. Johnson*

Lana

Don't pretend you haven't noticed her.
Every season of the year she's waiting
　　to be invited into your heart.
Never expecting to receive any more
　　than was given.
She's like the warm gentle breeze of summer.
Touching you with a pleasant grace and
　　expecting nothing in return.
You met her years before in the voice
　　of a robin's song
An amiable fawn in the wilderness, naive
　　as the first petals from a newborn rose.
With visions from her sandstone pearls she
　　perceives good in everyone.
Asking no favors, ready to give when asked
　　and concerned about every matter of unimportance.
She touched you with the innocence of a new morning sun.
Brought you to life with visions of reality
And taught you caring and loyalty is a gift worth sharing.

　　　—*Danny Haynes*

My Love

My love is like a pink rose,
every time I see you I bloom,
every time you leave a petal falls,
and my heart bleeds with every fallen petal.
The rose of pink is my love for you, your thoughts,
feelings, and dreams for a relationship.
The rose of yellow is my fear of a relationship.
The rose of red is my passion in the dream of a relationship.
The rose of blue is the color of you and me,
it's the future we hold and the future to behold.
The rose of black is the death of our relationship!
Please, black! Never the black!
I wake in the morning and roll out of bed,
I walk all over the books I've read.
I make it to the door without touching the floor.
I wondered why you swore,
you dropped your supper on the floor.
Skies of amber gray, start to fade away,
nay, nay, don't fade away, please stay for the day.

　　　—*CT Markus*

Missing You

Missing you is something that I do
Everyday when my heart is oh so blue
because I'm so far away from you
Thinking of the good times we have together
keeps me happy even thought I can never seem
to keep from missing you.
The thousands of miles that keep us apart
is what weighs so heavenly upon
my heart
Missing you is the only thing I
will do as long as we're apart.

　　　—*Deborah Rohlf*

Patience Please!!!

I remember the first time I walked into this place,
Everyone had a smile on their face.
I just came to visit; I didn't plan to stay, but every time I
went to the exit, they told me to turn around and go the other way.
I use to go to all the activities, especially exercise; but
now I'm so tired, I don't even have the strength to rise.
I even went down for all my meals; but that's before I got
sick and had to be put on the pills.
I guess I'm getting old and really going down; I just
realized the other day, I tried to talk but couldn't make a sound.
I can't remember how long I've been here - has it been six
months or has it been a year?
I have a large family; I have many friends. But to be honest
with you, I don't even know who's kin.
I guess this place is where I'm supposed to be; I can't go
home, for who would look after me?

　　　—*Donna Stansell*

"Sapient"

The trees were still bare of leaves,
except for those with green needles.
In the distance lay jagged mountains scraping color
out of the sky. The moon striking a blinding glare off the
still calm waters of the lake. A deer staring out across the lake
unaware of how near death is. A wolf with only one thing
running through his mind, blood! The delicious warmth
flowing down his long, dry, scratchy throat was all he
could understand. The scent hits the air and the race is on;
the deer running leaps and bounds, his sole thoughts are of panic;
blind panic; leaving clean crisp prints through the
snow as he moves with the agility of one who knows his time
has come. As he leaps another dead tree his life ends.
A wolf with only one thing running through his mind, blood!
The delicious warmth has finally sated his long dry thirst....

　　　—*James K. Blocker, III*

Los Angeles

energy, chaos, radical and alternative
　experimentation, undulation
　overcapitalization
　obsessive and progressive
wilderness of human folly
where the first rogue
　met the first fool
　making the first rock legend
to pour the wild vigor
　of sound
into the ears
　of the worldwide
it's just culture releasing
　the angels
as she slithers
like the sidewinder
　into the desert
musically...

　　　—*Peter Macaluso*

May I Be the Ray of Sunshine In Your Life

(Dedicated to Roger)

You bring such a ray of sunshine into my otherwise cloudy
existence.
Our relationship is not strained one,
virtually with no strings,
no bartering,
very little commitment.

And yet,
is that what life is all about? To be without a companion,
to be alone?
We are so very many worlds apart and yet,
could that be what brings us so close together?

I hope and pray to a power greater than myself,
that I NEVER lose you,
I never hurt you,
that I'm never the cause of your pain.
I hope I may only bring at least a portion of the serenity
and
"happiness" you've brought into my life.
I pray that I am only responsible for a smile in your eyes
and
not the sadness in your voice.

I thank you for sharing yourself with me.

—*Elise Jacobson*

Restoration

This Planet Earth provides for us
Existing comforts, luxuries, wealth;
The land, some heights then valleys deep,
Some lush, but some in stricken health.

Where all was beautifully serene
A cankerous fissure struck in power;
Today's science cannot eradicate
And deaths in staggering numbers tower.

Yet wisdom discerns the startling cause,
And there's hope if man acts in his might
Governing conduct in righteous accord
To correct the insidious plight.

We can rise like the Phoenix in legend,
Soar high o'er charred ashes and dust;
Renewed from the scourge of destruction,
Rise up free! We can, and we must.

—*Doris C. T. Smith*

For You

I would climb the world's highest mountain
Explore the world's darkest and deepest cave
I would battle the mightiest warrior
Just to prove to you I am brave

I would explore the white sands of Egypt
I would challenge the wildest sea
I would put out the fires of Hell
Just to have you believe in me

I would seek to acquire wisdom and knowledge
And to time, I would add an extra hour
I would switch the sun and the moon
Just to prove to you all of my power

I would reconstruct the earth
Changing it from round to square
I would build a castle of illusions
And quietly wait for you there

—*Delores J. Morrison*

Windows

Stars are the windows of the heavens
Eyes are the windows of the minds
Most of the windows are clear to see through
And mirror their reflections on time.
Windows are made in pretty shapes
Many are made in colors
Some have pictures in stained glass
And tell us stories of saints.
The bay windows catch the scenery
The picture windows show us trees
The dormer windows are for sleeping
So the light's not to bright on a face.
All windows have a good reason
For being the shape they are,
So if it's a bright and glorious day
Not one bit cloudy and gloomy
Open your windows and say a prayer
While the blessed sun shines in.

—*Dorothy Delaney Roberts*

Ode To The California Condor

The Ice Age ending, meadows appeared, mountains were awash with
falls oceans found their shores, as the great sun warmed the
lumbering giant of space Man came into being and looked to the
skies in awe of the flocks of Condors in their humble flights
of grace the heavily bodied birds with ten foot span of wings
that whistled in the wind came to represent God, death, and
fire to Stone Age Man who would draw upon their cave dwelling
walls, where there had been scenes of Condors circling
sabre-toothed tigers, mammoths and mastodon "holhol - one of
the Sky People" later to the Chumash Indian it would be heaven
that rested on its good wings and the solar/lunar eclipse that
it would bring though homely, eyes curious, bare head and neck
bowed to the God that made it free its wings held high, arched
in a prayer the Ages and All Eternity could sing tender parents
who mated for their seventy-five year life reared their young
hidden among the remotest peaks, in caves, near drinking
grounds of shallow depth, midst the sloping California
chaparral that Time had spun where, from the Pleistocene era
the Spruce and Cedar still it found there it listens to the
lingering mirth of the hush of closing day the rosy hue of
sunset on the peaks imbue as it weaves its loom, All Heav'n,
All Earth All Time, All Space as The Condor soars 'til at
15,000 ft. it stays whilst Angels preen its feathers, Gods
assure The Condor of its worth.

—*Sarita Davis*

Untitled

He eased into my life like a gentle breeze
fanning across my face.
Tall, proud warrior; confident, compassionate, kind.

There he stood with twinkling eyes, a look
that turned my legs to liquid fire, my mind
into a blank and set my body a tremble.

A figment of my imagination; a sweet unending dream;
a shadow on my existence.
Elusive, evasive tumble weed rolling across the desert.

Like a new born babe, fresh and curious. Waiting to
explore the world - to run wild on the white sands
of Cancun; to enter quaint cafes in Páris; to walk on
the ancient soils of Africa.

Spirited, intelligent, man of many shades.
His shadow reaches far and wide. I know.
He's cast his shadow upon my heart.

—*Carolyn F. Cole*

Power In A Whisper

I gazed out of a window not really noticing what was near or
far, thoughts wondered and seemed like a mist had covered my
mind. But as seconds, minutes and even seemed like hours had
passed, I would always return to that hopeless feeling inside.
I walked away from the window searching and pondering on the
questions that kept running through my mind. My God is
sufficient, and I know His love, but sometimes feeling,
sufferings and heartaches take my thoughts off of things above.
Many a time I have been there receiving that warmth that is
continuously near. But again and again, and over and over, my
emotions plunge to a deep end. But as I look back at all the
times in need, the voice that hushed the waters and spoke the
moon and the stars into the sky... whispered, in an ever so
soft reply, my child, do not tremble in anguish, do not crumble
in defeat; for the Lord your God calms your fears and throws
away all despair. So that in all of your troubles and trials
your Father always knows your pain even before you cry.

—*Rhonda Patterson*

What Would Jesus Do?

One time I thought if people treat you wrong you ought to
fight. In fact, I questioned what was wrong, and wondered what was right.
And many times I just decided things the best I knew.
Until I found it best to ask, "Well, what would Jesus do.?"

One time I thought it best to settle things in my own way,
And many times I did not even stop to sing or pray.
But now I try to seek what course is better to pursue.
And it is easy when I ask, "Well, what would Jesus do?"

One time I thought that any man should dictate to his wife
And help to shape the destiny that she should reach in life.
But they who seem to get along appear to be so few,
That now I find it best to ask, "Well, what would Jesus do?"

The world would be much better now and so much strife would cease,
And doubtless there would shortly be a universal peace;
I'm sure that people everywhere would be more kind and true,
If men would only ask themselves, "Well, what would Jesus do?"

—*Ephraim David Tyler*

Doodles

Little trees and happy faces,
Fill up all the empty spaces.
So many classes are boring to me,
So instead of taking notes I draw a tree.
I draw a daisy or a dog or a cat,
I draw a stick figure or a cane or a hat.
Doodles fill my paper to the bum,
And then my mind wanders with thoughts of him.
We're sitting on a park bench happy as can be,
My minds opens up with that turn of a key.
We're sitting real close staring at the stars,
Or we're leaping through space somewhere in Mars.
But then suddenly I'm brought down to earth once again,
When the teacher asks me a question and then...
I stare at my doodles and start to turn red,
For this is the one thing in life that I dread.
I say I don't know and she turns to someone else
And then I can return to the dreams in myself,

—*Gale G. Goodfriend*

Prairie Lament

The black hat won today.
Finally,
The code is broken.
Campfires are quenched,
Thirsts, tempered.
Hero is a word the wind dares not whisper.
Across the range drifts the cowboy's dying song.

—*Gregory D. Brown*

Life

Life has a purpose
Find your niche in this diversified and crooked culture
We have too many misfits already
Rise above the limitations and strains
Be all that you can be
Find your passion in life
You hold the power to your future
Make your life worth living
Strive everyday for your goals
Don't let society or its pressure ruin your dreams
No thief, rapist, or racist can take them away
Protect yourself, be aware of the life you're living
So much corruption and greed
Money rules the world
Don't let it rule you
Success is not a monetary measure
Rather, success is internal happiness
Stand tall, rise above it all!

—*Jessica Abrams*

The Old School Houses History

Friend's - Let's keep history alive by.
Fixing up the old school houses
Let's save the old buildings as the
material is better - then you can buy
material for and build new ones
for - so let's keep history alive
by saving the old school houses
and with all the memories alive
from the past and also save the little
old towns history too.

—*Irene M. Larson*

The Storm

A foreboding cloud blocks the afternoon sun
Flames engulf my tired eyes
My lungs gasp for a cool, clean breath
The only breeze carries the stench of death
My body aches for an hour's rest
Fury forces ten steps at best
The oil turns the sand into a burning lake
War had only these things to take
My health, my respect and peace of mind
Since we have won, they've become so blind
Because only they have left the war behind
It still shadows me each day
Pain and fatigue take my breath away

—*Eric D. Kesterso*

A Springtime Sunrise

The darkness of night lifts, and the golden sun rises—
    flaming the sky
with a magnificent splash of rosy sunglow.
    Sunbeams stream between trees
Casting shadows that playfully move over the lawn,
    And the verdant grass, bedewed,
glitters as though covered with precious diamonds.

A spider's intricate silken web glistens as it hangs suspended
    from twig to twig,
swaying in kinetic motion started by its beady eyed
    occupant owner.
A springtime sunrise, a new day's pulse of life begins—
    the same today
as was in the ancient past when it was first awakened.

—*Jean Bausman*

"Angels In Camouflage"

The famine was in, Mogadishu, just before dawn, the helicopters flew. The textbook maneuvers, on amphibious float, like descending angels, "Operation Restore Hope".

The children looked on, they thought a mirage, to boats unloading angels, in brown and green camouflage. The Marines came forth, with guns in their hands. To save the children, in this foreign land.

These angels will stop, this abuse and curtail, these cruelties of mankind, that made them so frail. The babes skeletal bodies, brought tears to trained eyes, death lurking around, where all hope dies.

The camouflage angels, were long overdue, this mission of mercy, all hope was renewed. The planes winged across, the sandy beaches. All Soldiers' hearts, compassion teaches.

The camouflaged angels, showed controlled skill. They won't leave the children, before their act of goodwill. On Somalian land the angels trod, Warlords armies in their jeeps, I know there will be a smile from God, as camouflaged angels feed his sheep.

—*Nellie Lloyd-Jent*

Springtime Revisited

Springtime has revisited us by
florescent flowers breaking
through the scented earth,
Song birds harmonizing their glorious song.
Springtime brings butterflies all
yellow, blue, and green, fluttering
softly past my window screen.
Bumble Bees go buzzing by, searching
their golden nectar, and the little star
flies sparkle up the skies and erases the
blackness of the night to laughter
The sunshine's beams in warm, within
my window sill, fresh soothing wind
embracing my thoughts of moonbeams and
starry nights. Springtime has revisited
us again this year.

—*La Verle Sager*

Spring

Oh yes, it is spring
Flowers are out and the bees sing
Also the fish are all wet
Time to bait a hook, you bet

The flowers are coming out
Many of them, if we look about
Outdoor stuff, cut grass, pull weeds
And a host of other springtime deeds

Birds singing, and frogs croaking
Stand in the rain, gets you wet, no joking
Spring causes one to wash cars
Stay up late to look at stars

Doing many things for no reason
Just because spring is in season
Kite flying, fishing and all the rest
Seems springtime is really the best

—*Benjamin J. Hilderbrand*

Running Free

He is grazing, his flank twitches,
he shakes his head. Then he rears
and takes off. He charges the fence,
sails over like he's flying. His mane and
tail are flowing in the wind. He whistles
shrilly, and stops, running free.

—*Jesseca Goodman*

"Love"

Love is beautiful,
Flowers are too.
The person who could make my heart beat,
Could only be you.

It's just like wishing on a falling star,
Love can take you just as far.
Love can work in many ways,
Fall in love it really pays.

When you feel sweat pouring down your face,
When your heart is beating at a faster pace.
Fall in love if you're really sure,
Love is something I adore.

—*David Scott Simpson, II*

Signs Of Spring

Signs of Spring are wonderful and gay,
Flowers bloom and the sun warms the bay.

Daisies, tulips, and periwinkles smell real nice,
You don't have to worry about winter and ice.

Straight from the gray rain cloud core,
You can hear the thunder roar.

The sound of thunder never gives me fright,
When I hear it I feel pure delight.

—*Daniel McLean*

Dream World

Glimmering shades of pastels and metalics appear
Flowers so spectacular their colors blind you
Water so bubbly and clear is shot up by a spring
Fragrant lilacs and lilies blossom
Clouds so soft are the color of creamy white
S I L E N C E
White doves hover over the clouds
Trees have branches that oddly twist and curve
Mountains are hidden in the mist
Eternal life

—*Kristin Varnum*

Closed Curtain

Black and white
flowing agelessly across the silver screen
suspended now for always
to be heard, felt and seen.
A dimension and a time
now truly of their own
history repeated over and again
in the deep, dramatic tone.

Today's heartache and sorrow,
tomorrow's unjust pain
played before our eyes
on an all to realistic plane.

We expect a happy-ending
as the credits begin to roll
but happiness
can only be found
when there's oneness
and contentment
with the soul.

—*Kendra Leah Melson*

The Poet

Detached thoughts flow into his head,
Flowing through his pencil lead,
The words are refined,
The images combined,
A scowl; a vacant stare,
A discouraged sigh, a tug of his hair,
He mulls it over a bit,
searching for a word to fit,
And then he thinks his head will burst,
With the load of rhyming verse,
Aha! His pencil moves at a hastened speed,
Buried thoughts sprout like a seed,
A series of lines, curves, and dots,
Interlocking, forming thoughts,
It stops. He contemplates,
What to write, his mind debates,
Which word to use, he squints his eyes,
He finds a word that will suffice,
Finally the title comes,
He shuts the book, the poem is done.

—*Jacob Duncan*

Retirement Home

We sit in patient circles — just waiting
for a meal, the mail, something creating
a division from our self-centered selves.
What could stir us?. A bomb? A pack of elves?

And since we wait for things to come to life
as if life were a band with horn and fife..
we've made waiting our main occupation.
Our one statement—quiet desperation.

There is in each of us a belief still..
It could be quickened by a role to fill—
someone to help, a task to do, a view
of life that won't begin and end with you.
Reach out with a hand, a smile, a word.
You will be welcomed and so gladly heard!

—*Helene Rosenberg*

The Crying Man

There's a child on the corner. Selling his dreams
for a quarter to the wealthy. Who doesn't know
his face nor his name, for their rich.

He takes pride in his country living to gain our
self respect. Yet, never achieving nothing
more than shattered hopes. As he tries to become
worthy of our pity.

He's still on the corner. As life around him gets
better, for those who can climb the corporate
ladder. He sleeps with his back against the wall.
Covered with his dreams.

He has nothing left at all, but the tears of a
crying man. That makes him fall.

—*Julia A. Stevenson*

First Love

Her eyes are shining, big and bright
flecks of green sparkle in the light.
Her smile alone sets apart from the rest.
She's constantly happy, a slight fluttering
within her breast. The girl is not sick, nor
crazy indeed, she's simply in love, so pay
her no heed. There is not a cure for this
bittersweet way so just hope that this girl won't
meet heartbreak one day.

—*Erin Billings*

A Rainbow

To see a rainbow, you have to look high,
 For a rainbow is an arc of light.
A light with colors of bright,
 And they spread over the sky.

A staircase of beauty for the old and new,
 The colors will be yellow, green, red and blue.
After the wind has blown a rain away,
 A rainbow may be seen on that day.

You may see it once a year,
 And that can make fun and cheer.
Only you cannot see it everyday,
 But the rainbow will always be here.

The rainbow fades in and out,
 As the colors dance in the clouds all about.
The rainbow with the arc, so bright,
 Will always be part of this world of light.

Something pretty for all people to see,
 A work of art, for you and me.
Look for the rainbow, the people will say,
 A rainbow will be somewhere everyday.

—*Charles E. Hopkins*

Youth And Age

Few things resist the ravages of Time,
For age-old ramparts rock at last to dust,
And many metals moulder from their prime
By crystalline decay and surface rust.
Just as the season, budding in the Spring,
And rip'ning to the warmth of Summer days,
But, fading when the migrant birds take wing,
On Winter's bier its withered beauty lays;
So mellows Youth to Nature's grandest whole,
Maturing there in beauty and in form,
Till erstwhile fading, Age assumes its role
Of wrinkling in the roundness of the corm.
 Youth is a flower, blushing in its pride;
 Age is its remnant, graceful ere it died.

—*Basil W. Wilson*

My Gratitude

As I lay here thanking you Lord,
for all the blessings you have bestowed me.

I reflect on the times I resisted your will.
Not understanding the purpose of it all.

All the times I took control.
I've always needed you to take it back.

And thank you Lord, because you
always do take it back and make it right.

Thank you Lord for the gift of faith.
As everyday, I realize more,
just what a wonderful gift it is.

With out you Lord I'm alone and scared.

But with you Lord I have the strength,
the courage, and the hope to go on.

As you Lord are; my shield
and my protector.

And with you Lord,
I know all things are possible.

—*Linda Eidsness*

In Honor Of My Dead Neighbor

Someday the sky will shine
For all those who believed,
When somebody die
Another star sparkle in the sky
In the middle of the night
Is painful I know, but
This is the way it should be
You didn't know me,
But I feel the pain
The pain of another soul who lost the game
The game of the life
I don't have more time to talk with you
I just hope you find the key
To rest in peace
See ya there (where you are!)

—*Cindy A. Baide*

Crystal Rose

A baby layette made out of snow white, I crochet with love,
For "Crystal Rose" is on her way,
With shiny silver threads reflecting light throughout,
Like the light that's sure to be in her little eyes,
She comes to us from Heaven above,
So perfect, like a gentle cherub angel,
With a beautiful smile, that will warm your heart,
Leaving no soul untouched by her "being."

I can hardly wait to cradle her in my arms,
Rocking her gently while singing sweet lullabies,
And ever so softly, kissing her warm cheek,
While brushing the soft curls from her eyes,
So much love is waiting here for "Crystal Rose,"
Our kindred hearts eternally entwined,
I await my blessed angel with arms open wide,
For she is my granddaughter to be!

—*Deborah Chamberlain*

Life Is For Living

Life is for living, every precious hour.
For doing our best, as God gives us the power.
For serving our church, our community and school
And in all things; practicing The Golden Rule.

Life is exciting, if we live each day
Truly for others, not seeking our way.
Certain of our motives, yet not questioning God's will.
Taking what befalls us, e'en though it be ill.

Never doubting, never wishing for things not meant to be
But gratefully accepting the judgment of the Man of
Galilee.

—*Charlotte Spahn Rice*

A Thankful Heart

Lord, help me to have a thankful heart
For the many gifts of this life.
Thanks for a bird's song, special and free,
For the music of the universe that falls on my ear,
For the rhythm of a heartbeat, the hum of a motor,
For the things that I feel and the things I can hear.
I give thanks for all the little things,
For the sandgrains of life,
For each tiny raindrop of my existence,
For a brush of air, that touches a leaf so gently,
That caresses a child's hair.
Lord, help me to have a thankful heart
In all I do and touch and see,
Keeping the challenge of life ever fresh.
Thanks for the chance to be me.

—*Martina Sonner*

Untitled

The Lord bless me through my times of trouble
For he knows how I feel.
And even though it will only get harder,
I will love him more with each passing day.
I can no longer find the words to say
"I love you" like I used to.
It has all changed.
Life, love and pain. So it goes.
We were young and restless-
What happened to the simple pleasures
That filled our lives with such joy?
Where does it all go?
Why does it have to leave?
We don't understand it, we're not going to change it,
We have to live with it.
No matter how hard it may seem-
God is always there - He's in our dreams and our souls.

—*Karen D. Webber*

I Am the Shoes

I am the shoes of a great young man
for I carried him overseas
I am the shoes from a great hero he won the war for me

I am the shoes that watched him lie in a lonely bunk and cry
I am the shoes that carried that man on that very field to die

I am the shoes who were shipped across to the
American shores
I am the shoes who watched a mother cry for she would
have a son no more

I am the shoes that stand with pride against
a very large wall
I am the shoes that stand here catching each tear that
happens to fall

I am the shoes that was with the man when he dropped
the shells and bombs
I am the shoes that carried that man to a place called Vietnam

—*Jennifer K. Biglin*

Don't Ask Me Not To Cry

Don't ask me not to cry, dear friend,
for, if you do,
Where, then, would you have me turn?
What would you have me do?

Would you ask me to bear this suffering
with no balm of release of it's pain?

'Stead, let my tears flow freely
and just be there as my friend.

Listen and know that just your presence
will help to get me through.

And with time, the pain will heal itself
by sharing it with you.

For, 'tis now but half the load
that my heavy heart must bear,

And soon, again, my heart will smile,
of that you must not fear.

So, please, dear friend, I would
ask again. Sincerely would you try.

Be there for me and listen.
But, don't ask me not to cry.

—*Gail J. Bourgeois*

Wonders

I wonder why people call me a nut,
  for in life, we are all nuts.
I wonder why people do what they do,
  for in life, we are all nuts.
   Some people eat cookies and water,
They are the nut, not I!
   People put gum in water,
for in life, we are all nuts.
And that ends my poem, you may think
   I'm a nut,
For in life, we are all nuts.

　　—Raymone A. Barnes, Jr.

When I Consider.....

When I consider your smile,
For its warmth, I'll walk a million miles,
Your tantalizing eyes
Sets me on a glorious high,
And fills my hearts with a delicious sigh.
I could praise the perfection of your components,
And it'll be a thousand years before my words are spent,
To me you are godsent,
For when I consider the exciting things you do,
Life is so wonderful being with you.

　　—Keith L. Hosannah

Somewhere

Somewhere in the world there has got to be contentment and love
for me.
It's just which way do I go east, north, west or south.
You look around and know it's their but you just can't reach it.
It seems like you have it for awhile and then its gone.
Where does it go and why does it leave then you are left with a
empty feeling.
But God tells you its alright just keep on searching.
Because one of these days you will find it.
And it will never disappear again.
The love you have will be forever and then it will be the way
it was meant to be.

　　—Linda Biggs

The Plight of Unemployment

　　Unemployment brings with it an ugly connotation
　　　For most nationalities of people.
　　It produces a sore and leaves a scar
　　　That never heals.
　　It tears people's hearts to pieces
　　The dragon burns - stinks - disintegrates
　　It even leaves men with a feeling of rejection

　　What does unemployment bring with it?
Alcoholism - Stress - Strain - Family Abuse - Divorce-
Violence
　　Just naming a few (in its worse form)
　　　Unemployment of the 80's
Can you give (us) the America's people some relief?
　　How about some pride and sense of direction?
Better still some reassurance and hope for tomorrow.

　　　Unemployment can you hear my plea
　　Yes, I'm crying for the human race of today
　But most of all... For our future generation.
　　　The adults of tomorrow
　　Let them hear the word employment
Rather than the connotative Sound-Unemployment.

—Bobbie Crudup Qualls

"Precious Lord, Reach Out To Me"

Precious Lord, Precious Lord, reach out to me,
　for the burden of my heart, is oh so heavy,
　I know you're there, and I know you care,
　　"Precious Lord, reach out to me..."
though my path is dark and no light do I see,
with your love and guidance, my heart shall be set free,
　you said, "Ask and ye shall receive",
　　oh, my Lord, how I grieve,
　　"Precious Lord, Reach out to me..."
For in sin I was born, into this world of hell,
　but through your grace, I know I'll prevail.
With your guiding light, I'm assured I'll be alright,
　In everything I do and everything I say,
　Let your ever shining light guide my way,
　And when things get more than I can bear,
　　Let me know that you are there,
　　In times of trials and tribulation,
　　Be my strength and my salvation,
　　"Precious Lord, Precious Lord,
　　　Reach out to me..."

—Billy Crain

Nightfall On The Lake

As the sun sinks slowly out of sight - nature prepares
for the coming night.
Wildflowers bow their heads to rest - while birds chirp -
as they settle in their nests.
Twilight gently slips away - marking the end of another day.
The lake water glistens in the changing light - as a large,
silver moon sheds moonbeams bright!
Fireflies sparkle everywhere - creating magic in the air!
Stars with shining faces - look down from vast heavenly spaces.
Sleep surrenders to the tranquility of the night - sleep,
blissful sleep - before the light!

　　—June A. Bundschuh

To Granma:

I remember seeing you after the accident and searching to
find some semblance of strength, some sign that would remind
me of the woman I once knew...
But there was nothing...Nothing but bandages and monitors and..

And I thought of the able feet that daily faced the elements
to feed and clothe not one but two generations.
I thought of those hands that cooked and cleaned and oiled the
tourists' backs...and I held those hands...
But they were weak, limp, cold and your feet were covered with
plaster and swollen veins and...

And I was losing you. Not only I but your children,
grandchildren and more...the hundreds more you had been mother
to and...

And I thought of life and how hard it had been for you...
You who had never been inside an aircraft, a classroom nor a
restaurant;
You who had never had the simple pleasures you caused us all to
enjoy...Left now to die...On a hard bed in an overcrowded room.
Among strangers...And my heart said "There is no justice" and..

And I wept... and wept... and wept.

　　—Joy Marie Moncrieffe

Tears Of Sorrow

The tears of sorrow drip down from my eyes.
For the one I loved those tears I cry.

I am now on my own,
Suddenly all alone,
Trying to comprehend,
Why no one has a hand to lend.

I loved him dearly,
But that was not nearly,
Enough to keep him here with me.

So now I shall cry,
Cry the tears of sorrow.

—*Emily Shioleno*

My Search For "Happiness Town"

"Happiness Town" is the town I seek;
For the people there are really neat.
They sing, they dance and play all day;
Beneath the sun's bright golden rays.

The flowers bloom the whole year long;
While birds fill the air with cheerful song.
The trees bear fruit that's ripe and sweet;
And the bushes bear berries, so good to eat.

Yes, "Happiness Town" is the town I seek;
I wish to dwell on its' mountain peaks.
Where the people love me for who I am;
And there's only smiles and never frowns.

Where all there strive to be their best;
As they work to achieve their personal quests.
And though the game of life has its ups and downs;
They seem easier to resolve in "Happiness Town".

So which road leads to "Happiness Town"?
Is it the one going up, or the one going down?
I'll keep on traveling until I find;
The "Happiness Town" envisioned within my mind.

—*Lynn Haynes*

Baby

Please don't think of me after I am gone—
for then it is to late to draw back the hand of time
to undo the things you have done.
Yes, I may suffer and you will feel my pain,
but how could you have been so stupid to let
someone love you that did not mean what they said.
Yes, you will shed a tear, probably many more than I;
but I will feel the pain, the refusal, the life go from
my body, and from yours.
If you feel that it is right, that we don't have a chance,
then maybe I shouldn't feel so sad, maybe I should be glad
that you did not bring me into this tormented world
full of hatred and worry.
I will still love you and think about you always,
and I know your heart will always yearn for the warmth
of my touch, my curls or my blue eyes,
but mother we cannot make it on our own.
Goodbye - though we hardly knew each other
I felt your love.
and you felt mine.

—*Naomi Katrina Ball*

Flaming Promise

They've dressed themselves in colors bold and bright and gay
For this, the gala season's last affair
In trembling expectation now they stop to watch and wait
Shivering in autumn's cold and frosty air.

And then, as though reluctantly, like shy young maids
The brilliant leaves begin their glittering dance
The tempo quickens as they swirl and dip and glide
In swift retreat and decorous advance.

They fling themselves about in strange and wild abandonment
Like painted Indian braves around a fire
Then gather close to softly whisper one last time
A final, fleeting effort to conspire

Against old mother nature's wise and far flung, ageless plan
To hold them close upon her ample breast
Then suddenly, in sweet surrender, with contended sighs
They sink to earth, and grateful, peaceful rest.

As with a saddened heart I contemplate the winter long and drear
Swift footsteps hurry homeward through the rain
She enters with her sparkling eyes and lovely, youthful air
And God has spoken: "Spring will come again."

—*Edna Lane*

"A Day To Remember"

Make this a day to remember.
For thoughts of other instead.
Have a smile or compliment.
A kindly died or phrase.
That they are loved and thought of.
As, they walk along this way.
Show them a ray of sunshine.
and, a big friendly smile.
Be a friend that helped them.
Making them forget, today and yesterday as mild
Keep thinking, that life is worthwhile.
For how little we realize about things,
as time passes by on our way.
It's the sunshine and laughter,
That makes for a memory,
and holds for any day, yes -
they say, Love is more precious than gold
  "Need we be told"

—*Georgia A. Holt*

Be My Voice Lord

Lord I pray guide my every act and thought.
For through your loving son I have been taught.
You are ever present in my soul,
Like the whiteness of the dove.
Use me to bring peace and love.
Be my voice Lord, that I may share your love.

Lord let me reach out to those in pain,
if only with a touch.
May they see not me, but you
let your presence shine through.
Like the sun with its glory after the rain.
Be my voice Lord, that I may share your love.

Lord we are all your people,
whether Jewish Indian black or white.
May we see your image in each other,
reflected in your divine light.
May your love restore peace and the end of woes.
For in each culture beauty is found,
like the colors of the rainbow.
Be my voice Lord, that I may share your love.

—*Margaret Ann Seipel*

Turn A Blinking Eye

Revived in such an all glorious day,
forget the sunset hangs in heavens dripping wet.
fall upon weary knees, rest these glooms in budding May,
capture nature's essence in moon's crescent.

Be protected from all turmoil about,
the angry skies fear not the outer shield bore,
in ancient age tidal waves crashed their thundering noise out.
until calmness regained the windswept shore.

To turn a weary eye to nature's destructive ways.
nothing can stop the clamor breaking world's slumber,
perplexes the giant mountains with these darkened days,
yet still feel powerful in one's singular number!

Issue me some secret answer of protection.
Can't fill up with rage and not be able to react.
if not your bounty hangs on planet's discerning deflection.
then can sun's rays melt, what's said to be fact!

—*James Onuska*

I'm a Nobody Here Today

I'm a nobody here today, no faces do I know in this God
Forsaken City. There's people all around and yet I've never been
so alone, Oh what a pity! People here don't care about people,
they're self-centered, selfish, rough, And if you're not one of
their little group, why that's just tough. I'm a nobody here
today, the world is just passing me by. Once I was everything,
the center of attention, not sitting with a sigh. Wondering if
it's this busy city or is it just me? Have I ventured out to
make friends and the better side of people to see? I came to
this big city from a little country town, where everybody knew
everyone, But here you don't even know your neighbors name
although you see them go and come. If you say, "Good morning,
Oh Morning to you today." What's good about today they'll
say?" A greeting like that sure dampens the spirit, that's why
I say I'm a nobody here today. Don't bother them they don't
have time for a simple hello or a smile for me, If they talk I
might learn how narrow minded they think and how they live so
carefree. So I'll go on to work tonight as I'm getting use to
change, with all work and no play, I'll come home in the
morning weary and tired just to remember, I'm a nobody today.

—*Elizabeth D. Seay*

He Has Only Been Lifted

I knocked on her door and to my surprise,
found a broken hearted woman with tear swollen eyes.
As I stepped inside my heart in my hand, she looked up at
me, my very best friend and said "he is dead." "He is
gone," I thought God loved me but I see I was wrong."
As I knelt down beside her the words came to me
"God does love you don't you see" I know this for sure,
because it happened
to me." Our children are loaned to us for only awhile,
they belong to God when we think they are ours." Her
eyes met mine, the tears were all gone, it seems to me
she could have sang a song." Thank you she said, I know
he is not dead; he has only gone home. Yes! She said,
As her dear face I kissed it, my son is not dead,
he has only been lifted!

—*Gloria Chism*

Vernal Blossoms

Blossoms Blooming everywhere
fragrance fills the air.
Red, yellow, purple variegated too,
What beauty, what a hue.

Little birds have returned to cheer
us with their song.
All day long they sit and sing to tell
us Spring has sprung.

Humans skip about once more,
Some to their gardening, some to the seashore,
Some to the seashore, where they
romp and play.

Some more serious hasten to their trade.
Some go fishing, hearts aglow, hopes
refreshed, well-wishing.

—*Elmer Dailey*

Free From Bondage

Free from rusty chains from iron bars.
Free from unsaid words from reluctant promises.

Free from rejection from staring eyes.
Free from emptiness.
Free from the World.
Unlocked doors
Opened the true reality.

Free from pain, from lost hopes.
Free from silence, from locked away emotion.
Free from the cold, from ever changing winds.
Free from prejudice.
Free from hate.

Bitter memories.
Broken hearts.
Shattered Dreams.
Free from mankind, from day to day life.
Free from the voices, from infected minds.
Free from the sicking air. From love,
Free from it all.
Free from bondage.

—*Jason King*

Freedom

Years ago when this nation was young
Freedom was on the mind of every one
They fought a war for freedom's sake
A free great country they did make

Then down the years when slavery ruled
The north and south for freedom dueled
Everyone should be free just like you and me
Be black or white or what'ere we be

Then Reverend Martin Luther King a leader came
Bringing no wealth but a lot of fame
His message to all for freedom bring
And have the nation freedom songs to sing

The fight's not finished push on again
In the sunshine or in the rain
Keep Reverend Martin Luther King's dream going strong
And keep on singing freedom's song

Sometime in the future we all pray
That freedom will be here for all each day
And as the years go right along
So everyone can sing freedom's song

—*Charles Gaylord*

Reality

Soiled gray clouds raced within ashen drab-dreary skies as
    frenzied roaring winds roughly seized and shook trees
    mercilessly.
Endless pelting rain relentlessly washed and churned the earth
    while moisture cold seeped and searched every
crack-n-cranny
    tenaciously.
The call came as a bolt of lightning-no hints-no warnings-
    nothing but sharp sizzling shock!
Cold water of reality come in one fell swoop-to stun-sadden-
    and rock.
Years have tripped and fallen headlong. Spring-like gaits
    wilted-stopped-never more to bend with ease.
No more promise in the air to be snatched and severed like
    dried leaves fell from Autumn branches and then clothed in
    snow sleeves.
A lifetime of pain and suffering ends.
Lifelessly cloistered, the casket descends.

—*Karen Bartlebaugh*

Friends

What are friends?
Friends are people who share their inner feelings with each other,
the feelings they don't even share with their mother.
Friends are always seen together.
There are special friends such as best friends, which I share with you.
Our friendship can't compare with any other, I don't even feel the
same with my brother.
You are the best thing that ever happened to me, which I
wouldn't trade you for a fee.
I ask you, do you feel the same? If not, was this whole thing
a game?
I hope if our friendship was true, maybe it will last until we
die, I hope we never say good-bye.
Tell me you love me and I will do the same.
Friends to me will last forever and ever.
Let's make it happen.

—*Cynthia Darnell*

Earthly Turmoil

As this moment, I recoil
From all this earthly turmoil!
Life in this age of noise and space
Gets harder, day by day, to face.
Upon our door-step comes of late
War, anger, riot, hate.
Everywhere "beat" music blares
As over this island's quiet air,
These raucous off-key beats resound.
What happened to peace and quiet
In this unhappy world of riot?
Reflect, think back, oh, we of declining years
What would we change, what can we say?
To make this world a better place to yearn
For grace and goodness, love and peace!
Turn back to decency, and prayer, and sow
The seeds of love and goodness,
And we'll grow and
Peace will reign once more!

—*Emma Williams*

For Mark

On a routine flight on a whirly-bird, they were coming back
from Champagne. They were near the base and the noise they
heard, was the wind that precedes the rain. It was hard to
control the shaking and the clouds were as black as pitch
there was no chance they were breaking, would they somehow have
to ditch? I'm sure there was a silent prayer from all the men
on that flight, that the God who must be everywhere would keep
them in His sight. Then the Lord in all his wisdom said, "I
must help these men, I guided them to the heavens I'll lead
them down again." Then he bade the winds to lessen, and He
told the clouds to yield. Then he ordered a spotlight
of beautiful sun, to show them the way to the field.
And for those poor souls who think there's no God I'll
have to question why. Not a mortal man who ever lived on
earth could open up the sky. And every man who returned that time
on that almost tragic trip, knew that God had answered each silent
prayer and that God was on that ship.

—*B. Metko*

I Thank You God For Blessing Me..

Your light has shone down on my life in such a special way,
From childhood thru adulthood I should thank you every day.
It was in nineteen fifty-five, when I was just sixteen,
You sent someone to share my life who'd treat me like a queen.
He's been a special blessing, more than anyone can know,
For his deep, true love and caring ways seem every day to grow.
He sheltered me through hard times, more than I could ask,
Nothing seemed too much for him, he'd handle any task.
I can't forget in '65 when we lost all we had,
He was at my side and with him there, it didn't seem so bad.
He quickly said, we must be strong and realize the best,
We have our son, God's greatest gift, so just forget the rest.
Together we can work real hard and build our home again,
Remember that the sun will shine after all the rain.
Yes, he is the perfect husband, besides a dear, true friend,
So please let us share happiness until the very end.
And now Dear Lord, in thanking you, I have but one request,
Shine down on him your brightest light for he deserves the best.

—*Jerry D. Lemoine*

I'll Love You Forever

This poem to you I truly write,
from deep inside with all my might.
Never before have I felt this way,
'til I laid eyes on that special day.

If you remember, the truth I said,
I'LL LOVE YOU FOREVER!
And ever since that day we met,
my promise to you I've always kept.
Under lock and key those words I keep,
my love for you could never be so deep.

I think about you day and night,
those feelings and memories make it feels so right.
I even sometimes cry, then hide the truth,
'cause I am so proud that I am your guy.

Whenever I am with you or I am not there,
I want you to know that I always care.
You must also know, you're my one and only,
without you I am so lonely.
It's you I truly treasure,
I wanna be yours now and forever.

—*Randy Habben*

155

I Listened Too Late

We have everything money can buy
From our parents with goals set too high
Most when I needed their sweet loving touch
they weren't there to listen the price was too much
they were always too busy being society bred
To hear silent pleas how I wish I was dead
but I'll make them listen one way or another
then you'll get my message dearest father and mother
I went to my room I bolted the door
won't soil their bed
So I laid on the floor
My suicide way I will not mention
For it really doesn't matter
I got their attention

—*Judith K. Griffin*

The Draw

What man has not felt its pull
    from some uncanny, inward place?
When pangs of thirst drive us to be full,
    'tis the cool urn of water to which we race.

"Nothing quenches quite like it",
    we say, and are amazed.
But we would stand as bone and grit
    without it, the scene of man unplayed.

Rain has an emotional quality.
    It stirs the best and worst of us.
The farmer who worships the drops on his rye,
    the child, housebound, in a fuss.

I dare say if any a woman or man,
    could stare out across soft, swelling tides
or storm clouds swirling without rhyme or plan,
    without feeling the power they hide.

The draw is strong and unyielding,
    timeless as the sands it moves.
Dead and yet linked to all living,
    water has nothing to prove.

—*Howard E. Franklin Jr.*

The Letter

I got a letter today,
From someone dear to me.
Is she my girlfriend?
No, but she used to be.

She told me "Happy Birthday,"
And that really showed she cares.
The letter brought back memories,
Of the times we used to share.

I was kind of surprised to hear from her,
But I'm really glad she wrote.
Words can't describe the way I felt,
When I opened up the note.

I would really love to talk to her,
Face to face, or on the phone.
And let her know I'll be there for her,
On the nights she feels alone.

Lord, if you can hear me now,
Please grant me just one prayer.
Let that beautiful young lady know,
That I'm her friend and I'll always be there.

—*Brian C. Falls*

"Toys"

Quick let me sweep these toys up
From the floor now they are broken things;
The ribbons will fly no more.
My thoughts are placed in a birch wood box
Long ago bought to pack away puppets clothes;
Fancy is buried with the harlequins
I chose to become skeletons.
Deep in my breast is an attic
Where shadows of toys ar pressed
Like the perfumed gloves of old women
Who caressed but one summer of love.
Quick I will sweep the torment in;
I will not think of this windmill again
Or look upon the eyes of this tattered clown.
I have torn all of my playhouses down;
Perhaps this is the wonder of growing up
To enter the town called surrendering.

—*W. Edwin Ver Becke*

Leaving Home

"Where are you going?" I asked the lad, as he was passing by,
"From your pack, I'd say you are leaving home, why else would
you cry? Why not come sit and rest a spell, your journey may
be long, smell the flowers, watch the birds and listen to their
song. You say your Daddy was lost at sea and Mommy is marrying
another man? Why he is taking your Daddy's place you just
can't understand. You say your Daddy was a super guy when he
went away to fight. And you miss him just like anything,
mostly when you go to bed at night. That's a purty big load
for a lad to pack when he is all alone. But what do you think
your Daddy would say if he saw you leaving home? Why don't I
walk you back home; you see, I have no car, I'll bet your
mother's worried sick, not knowing where you are. Why not give
this man a chance, maybe he will succeed, and prove he too is a
super guy and exactly what you need. Give it a chance for a
year or two, then if you find you just can't stay, come on back
and meet me here, and we both will run away."

—*Irvin Blanchard*

Sweet Spring

Spring is coming slow but sure soon it will be at our front door
Brown tan black and grey, colors soon to fade away.
Trees with hues of green and red will color the country side instead.
Flowers budding peeking through what wonderful sights
we soon will view.

Birds in flight what a sight... please nest in our
trees so we may hear Mother Natures gifts you soon shall bear.
Wonderful insects big and small, armies of ants over the garden walls.

Creeping myrtle solemn but true forever returning
budding blue. In warm sunny windows hyacinths bloom
sweet trumpets of nectar fill every room with natures perfume.

Sweet spring has once again returned to share its beauty!

—*Janet Link*

Living In Irvine

I love Irvine where I've lived a long time
Friendly people around me, I list in this rhyme
The post office, restaurants, Colonial Hotel, doctor,
Church, Citizen Bank, everyone is kind and nice
Even there in the grocery store called Shop Wise.
I cannot tell anything bad about this city
Only that Irvine is so lovely and so pretty.
When I am walking daily upon the street,
I see smiling faces of people I meet.
What do you think as you read my each line?
That living in Irvine is really fine.

—*Blanka M. Atwood*

My Wish

I look up at the gleaming night. I see the dreams of the
future. I look up at the deep blue sky. I wonder how the
children will get by. I look up at the stars shining bright.
To see each country struggling to find that morning light. I
look up at the moon. Longing to hear the night tune of
silence. I look up at the clouds so black. I see the pain
that keeps coming back. I look up at the colors of the dark.
And see where my people have left their mark. How this beauty opens
up: I see the accomplishments we have made. I see the
failures I cannot change. I see the ideas that will never be
heard. I see the goodness that will never form a word. I see
the caring gone but not forgotten. I see the apples that fall
and there is only one rotten. I can't deny I want to close my
eyes. And wish that all these things could pass. And start a
new with love in our hands. What a wish to demand!

—*Detra Roberts*

They Came Home Alone

We sent them to war young boys to be men
Gave them assurances
Took away their freedom
All that they did, they did to survive
The killings, the bombings, the babies that died
It had to be done it couldn't be helped
We pushed them, we shoved them
They gave of themselves
For once in a war all becomes fair
It's either get them or die over there
They came home to be hero's
To find backs that were turned
"Baby killers" we shouted
American flags we did burn
It's been twenty years
Since no one has won
The missing in action
The lost many sons
They carry the scars of bad memories
We have to respect them, we sent them you see

—*Nick Bjergo*

Forever

As I sit here looking out the window
gazing at the stars
I can still smell her perfume, see her face,
hear her voice as she says "I love you
I'll love you forever."

Just then as I look down
a tear runs down my face
as I realize my forever is over.

As I wipe the tear away
another follows and I do the same,
while doing so I look up again wondering
is forever longer somewhere out there
because my forever is over.

—*Keith J. Szalankiewicz*

Music of the Heart

The music in my heart began to play caressing my soul in a
gentle way, the drum softly beating like the rhythm of the sea,
rolling to the sands on a starlit beach. Then to a melody free
as the wind as a calming breeze thru my spirit is sent,
listening for the very reason, it began to play my life's
season, opening all windows and doors, tunes filling my dancing
hearts floor. Allowing my waking eyes to see the wonderful
music you've composed in me.

—*Julie Vruggink*

Gossamer

Halloween, Thanksgiving, and Indian Summer
Geese and their down in old Germany, cobwebs
Dripping sunlit sparkling autumn dew
The gossamer of spring is out of season
Say the best authorities on words
Never mentioning that it is the stuff of art
The costumes of the dancers, the actor's props
Spider lines in a good architect's design
Brushstrokes catching light and whole people
Singers weaving their spells, writers casting nets
Sculptors hew out of stone or shape from clay
Gossamer, sly deathtraps for human insects

—*James Greenwood*

A Heart Near Death (A Sonnet)

Along the winds of change lies a stray heart
Gentle gusts throb through arrent halls of past
The lively red flow pierces like a dart
A pulse from which beats from beginning to last
In the depths lingers pale soul of life gone
With thoughts and memories threaded within
Dismal fates, fleeting, fading, faces showing done
A fad to black bares the end, keep high chin
Passage is easy, readiness never present
The tunnel somber, the light misleading
Muscles over ridden, gloomy slow scent
Termination nearing, the gates greeting
A faint breath saves the grief laddened organ
The winds of change have swayed back once again.

—*Andrew Graham*

Hey It's April

Is it the horses long hairy mane or is it the children playing in the rain?
   Outside is where I wish to be for now they are climbing a big oak tree.
Why would they want to leave me out?
For I am just a kid who wants to play and shout.

—*James Franklin Baldwin*

Born To Run

That ole' road
Gets lonely and cold
When you're missing your family
That you left back home.

You start wondering
If it's worth being on stage
When all the fun gets up
And starts walking away.

But when you hear the crowd start cheering
And see the lights dim low
You'll know it's your calling
Doing the things you once loved so.

I spilled my soul
For the music they heard today
Every drop of energy
Went into every note we played.

When that last note sounds
And the curtain goes down
You start packing up your things
For another dead end road to another dead end town.

—*John E. Badnewz*

Recognizing Spring

Drop. Drop. Here comes the rain
Giant black clouds drifting over the plain
Sprinkling it's translucent drops
Falling from the sky- into puddles it flops
Then all of a sudden, the process all stops.

As the giant black clouds slowly drift away,
It's the sun's turn to come out and play
As it shines over the plains in rays
Finding it's path through fields like a maze
It slowly dries up everything in sight
And everything's dry well before the night
As flowers and tree buds continue to grow
And when it exactly happens- we just don't know.

—*Amy Pitcher*

Untitled

A leaf in a stream flowing past reflection,
glimmering my vain attempts.

Butterflies drifting splashes of color decorating
my otherwise
drab visage.

A thought of you made tangible, floating
up into a
cloudless sky.

Beams of brilliance, spreading forth warmth
against my
chilled skin.

A kiss remembered, holding me captive against
all self-imposed rationality.

Another touch felt in the night, releasing me
from myself again
but your words, spoken in a whisper,
giving meaning to lonely nights.

And our love, springtime splendor
is all that I wish it to be.

—*Frank Grasso*

Just A Little Thing

A smile is just a little thing; from your glance it seems to
    glow. A touch is just a little thing— so easy to bestow.
    A kiss is just a little thing; no one need e're know.

But Darling, from these little things our love began to grow,
And like the mighty oak from a little acorn grow,
Today your love is all the world I know.

Just a little thing, just a little thing—a smile,
A touch, a kiss—was our love to start;
But Darling, from these little things you captured my heart.

Today your love is everything to me,
And life with you is all I dreamed it would be.
Your smiles, your touches, your kisses make me see
That without your love I could never be free.

Just a little thing, just a little thing—a smile,
A touch, a kiss—was our love to start;
But Darling, from these little things, you captured my heart.

—*Nelson Arnold*

Life Being A Bum

A crisp wind rips through the air
gnawing at my insides
The leaves of the naked trees rustle at my feet
Loneliness has come to greet winters commencement.

Trash cans, paper, dirt whirl down the alley
Creating a whirlwind of hopelessness
The streets are desolate and cold
All my memories permeate my very being.

Regret, grief, sorrow, and pain envelop me.
Yester year is distant and so is home.
Why did I make that decision - were they
right and I was wrong?
Burrr - my torn jacket lets the cold
Air cling to my bones
Well this is my life and it's future.
My endless choice
My run-away decision.

—*Jennifer True*

Willie

I'm a friend of the family
Go often to visit
We met very long ago.
Though I'm welcome to stay, I'm soon on my way
Always hurrying to and for.

Some say I'm nought but a loner
See, I like to be on my own.
I'm not the sort goes to parties
And I never would chat on the phone.

But I have my eye on the girl next door
Such a lovely young thing is she
So slim and petite and so very sweet
Don't know what she could see in me.

We developed a friendship
So lovely and rare
For a loner like me it seems odd that I'd care.
But it's not such a mystery or curious that
She's perfect for me… She's a beautiful cat.

—*Carol Osinski*

Faces and Tears

Children of my life, tell me "What can you expect?"
God knows there are places you can hide where no one will detect.
But if you listen He will tell you just what you should do.
"From now until forever, to yourself you must be true."
Never hide your faces. Never hide your tears.
Hold your head up high in places filled with all your fears.
And though it's hard; let your tears not fall in vain,
For every time you drop your head you're adding to the pain.
This world is full of four letter words and some of them are bad.
But, life and hope and love and help are just a few that can be had.
Now, if you're really listening, take these words apart.
Then stand before a mirror and listen to your heart.
Your eyes and nose and ears and lips make up your precious face.
Four letter words are each of these though none will cause disgrace.
Now watch as you cry, "See the Tears?", that four letter word again.
But know you now what He has done for each of us and then.
Remember you look just like Him and He has cried for years.
So, never hide your faces. Never hide your tears.

—*Robert N. Brown, Sr.*

Untitled

God painted me a picture with the trees so frosty white
God painted me a picture—Oh, what a glorious sight!
I'm sure he's trying to tell me how he'd like his world to be
Our hearts and minds at rest—and with a calm serenity.
The setting is so peaceful on this February morn,
And I wonder if it weren't the same on the day that Christ was
born. There comes a stillness in my heart and it seems to make
me say thank God for eyes to see and a heart that wants to pray
For a world so full of fear and hate
We know this makes us second-rate
Make us over—kind and good
And then we'll do the things we should
To have us claim the right to be
Citizens of eternity.

  —*Florence DeWall*

Shining Light

When life hands you the tough times and we feel we are never
going to see the light again,
We feel as if life is being so unfair to us as we face the
darkness so deep,
We feel hurt so deep inside of our hearts and souls,
And sometimes we feel like giving up instead of fighting
our way to the light again,
When we hit the deep dark times of life,
Try to remember we have a friend that shines brighter than
the sun,
And he can see you through any darkness and lead you into
the light of day,
Jesus is our shining light in the darkness of our lives,
And with Jesus on your side you can't lose any battle,
Because as his child he will always help you through any
darkness you face and brings you back into the light that
shines so bright in our lives.

  —*Elizabeth G. Crombie*

What Is Gold?

Gold is the color of the bright summer sun.
Gold is the grass and leaves in mid-fall.
It's a tiger's fur and a lion's heart.
Gold is the color of stars shining at night.
It's the ripe corn in the field.
Gold is the gates to heaven and the wings of angels.
Gold means love and happiness.
It stands for peace and courage.
Gold is the sound of a marching band.
Gold is the feeling of a warm camp fire.
It's the taste of ice cream in the summer.
It's a baby's hug and a mother's kiss.
Gold is the sound of coins jingling in a child's pocket.
It's the feeling of being tucked in at night.
It's the glow of a candle warm and bright.
Gold is the key to a young girl's diary.
It's the thorns on a rose.
Gold is the feeling of being a winner.
Gold is brave and will never fade away.
Gold stands for friendship.

  —*Jennifer Ott*

Death

Death is my dark angel
With wings so bright —
Filled with holy light —
Lifting me
Past transmuting Calvary
The old marble Earth I see
That dream is done for me:
True morning is now.

  —*Jean Candee*

Angels Do Hover

As I watched you today
Golden hair now turned gray.
My thoughts raced back in time
When my Lord said come and dine

You taught me wrong from right
We've laughed and cried together all night
The grandest mother to my ones so little
Being careful of every jot and tittle

My heart cries as you stumble today
As the Lord prepares to take you away
To the place so much better than this-
That wonderful, heavenly bliss

You taught me the beauty of life,
Not to fret over trouble and strife
My pal, my friend my sister you are
The greatest blessing to me by far

I've seen Christ throughout your days
And His will in your ways
As I watch angels do hover
Over my precious Christ like mother

  —*Judy Davis*

A Teacher's Thoughts On Changing Grade Levels

  Kindergarten

Good-bye to runny noses
And boots on the wrong feet.
Good-bye to zipping zippers
'fore they trundle up the street.

Good-bye to broken colors
Scattered on the floor,
Good-bye to hugs and kisses
'fore going out the door.

  Seventh Grade

Hello to combs and brushes
And lipstick by the ton.
Hello to all the chatter
About the game they've won.

Hello to love and romance and cars they wish they had
To buzz about the town at night and worry poor old dad.

Hello to acne problems and teeth so full of wires.
Hello to motorcycles and the squealing of the tires.

If you'd give me a choice, which group would I choose?
I'd work with either, I could not refuse.

  —*Lillian Nordman*

My Friend

Of all the folks that cross life's scene,
Good friends are few and far between.
Tests tell us what a friend can mean.
I need you for a friend.

A Friend is slow to criticize
And yet will freely sympathize.
And though in me some weakness lies,
He still will be my friend.

On Friendship Lane some rain must fall,
Mixed with the sweet will be some gall,
Else, could we try our friendship's call
And prove ourself a friend?

I long that I could always be
As true as friends have been to me.
So while we sail on life's rough sea,
I want you for a friend.

  —*Oran Skaw*

Holiday Princess

Decked out all in her
gown of green
she sparkles with glitter and bows
casting her shadows-
hues of yellow, red and blue
twinkle against my walls

Beautifully crowned and standing tall
her scent fills the room with holiday cheer
While Christmas songs ring in our ears
children all a chatter
awaiting his pitter patter
to bring them toys -
and Mom and Dad the
presence of joy

—*Deborah T. La Croix*

A Prayer For Peace

God grant us wisdom to do the things, we know that we must do.
Grant us trust within our selves, and faith dear Lord in you.
Help us please to understand, that hate for our fellow man.
Will bring us naught but more hate, and our planet will not stand.
Teach us to love each other, take our prejudice and fear away.
Teach us to ask our neighbor, how can I help this day.
We don't need nuclear weapons, to protect us from ourselves.
We need to take forgotten love and care, from off the shelf.
It does not matter our color, or what country we are from.
Each of us are responsible, no matter whence we come.
So please dear Lord I ask you, grant us peace within our heart.
That we might share it with others, then distrust will soon depart.
And maybe like a garden, the seed of peace will start to grow.
Until it covers all the land, and war will reign no more.

—*Lois E. Cook*

The King Jesus Tree

Born of David's roots, Born of Virgin Mother,
Grew in Nazareth's shoots,
To be our elder brother.

Messiah, King, of us all!
Children of our God, keep us close, lest we fall;
Branches from His sod.

Worker, miracle performer!
On the stage of life, eternal life transformer!
Remember our strife.

Crucified as pretender!
With a duet of thieves, for claiming royal tender!
With God, as son, who sees!

Gifted with a heritage,
Of royal dignity, as friends of His lineage!
Enriched through eternity!

Tree of life, producing,
Embrace our heart-full thanks; for each painful prodding,
Choose us! Count us in your ranks.

—*Margaret Ann Kelly, S.C.*

Relationships

Friendship came to call, we responded.
Held a hand out, offered our hearts.
Invested seeds of affinity, nurtured them.
soon blossoms of love emanated.
We touch each other-share as needed
mutually bond our souls in harmony.
Generate impulses upon one another.
Never penniless within our hearts as
we enrich ourselves beyond monetary wealth.

—*Dorothy C. Lobel*

A Friend In Need

Would you cry and shed a tear for her as you share with her the
grief? Would you sigh and hold her close to you, somehow offer
her relief? Would you try to dream a dream for her when she
cannot dream at all? And tell her of your visions, make her
feel ten feet tall? And when she cannot feel a thing, would
you comfort her and hold her? And promise that you'd care for
her, though the days would make her older? And when her pain
is too much to bear, and she just can't hold it all, would you
stand beside her, firm and strong, making sure she doesn't
fall? And when she's feeling sad and lost, in darkness all
alone, be sure to leave a light on so she'll find her way back
home. And when her days look brighter, when she feels confident
to cope, fill those days with her laughter, grant her love and
joy and hope. And when you cry and dream and comfort her, when
you mend her heart anew, remember her forever, for she's the
child inside of you

—*Ruth M. Cardinel*

Understanding

Patrick Henry and John Paul Jones
   had things in common
So I'm told, liberty and truth
   in days of old.

Battles and victories,
   Smoke and fire,
Guns and ramparts
   Throughout all time ceaseless.

Could it be so the endless
   Process brought together
By strife and peace
   End in a merit of understanding.

—*Jois A. Gould*

Untitled

Last night,
hands rippling in dish water
the steam rose about your face in the dank shack

I felt my heart gather like the
bubbles around your wrists
before the water grew cold.

I watched you from beyond the wall
My bottom-heavy emotion sunk in a chair
and my tears reclined
in front of the old black and white.

I felt you shatter softly in the kitchen
your bare toes sinking again
as you wiped away the grime
and offered the plates to the shelves.

Even habit does not prepare me
for your sudden withdrawal
I find myself drowning
as you dry your hands

swirling with the bubbles and the grime
down the hard cool drain.

—*Cindy L. Walker*

"Dear Angel On My Shoulder"

Dear "Angel" on my shoulder, your help will see me through.
I have a lot of faith with you in charge, cause I believe in you.
You are a beautiful "Angel" pin that I wear above my heart.
Each day gets a little easier, and I pray we'll never part.
When life through me a heartache, and changed my days to blue;
the sun began to shine when I caught a glimpse of you.
So..."Angel" on my shoulder please stay a little while, you
make my life seem better, when my frown becomes a smile.

—*Loretta Rine Marschner*

Remember Me

(In loving memory of my son, Paul Fusco

Remember me not with sadness, but with the
happiness I gave others.

Remember me not with tears, but hear my gentle
laughter.

Remember me not with bitterness for the short
time that we had, but with all the special times we
shared that will forever last.

Turn this card and see my eyes look totally in
disbelief, for I have seen God. The total happiness
and peace I feel you too will someday know.
Until that day, remember me, for I shall never
walk this way again.

—*Diane Fusco*

"Mother"

I hope the seed you helped to tend;
Has become a living tree.
And if blessed, through prayer, will
   bare fruit of which you will receive.
Though some may be bitter,
   because of weakness is diseased,
   I hope the sap of kindness
   will be flowing through it's leaves.
That most of its fruits, which it will produce,
   may provide for you it's goodness,
   and it's sweet refreshing juice.
That which I speak of can only come
   from above,
For what God has planted, is nurtured by,
   A mother's care and love.

—*Derek Hendrickson*

"Discern to Know and Grow with God in 93"

What changes in life would you consider "fulfilling"?
Has your time clock been set by God's all-knowing hand?
Or has indecision trapped you in a never-never land?

Jesus has planned for us a day of rest to fellowship,
worship and pray. His words keep reminding us "Abide with me.
I know the way! Trust and obey, fear not. I am your shield,
your heart's desires I know. Gifts of treasure, time,
and talents are already at your door."

Jesus the righteous "Holy One," the "Rock" on which to stand.
His presence will never forsake a "hope" for all mankind,
a "home" prepared for us when we enter that promised land.

So trust the new year with Jesus. Live the abundant life
each new day. God has promised to make us fruitful.
A challenge to trust and obey.

—*Edna Thurrott*

Glass

It is very delicate
   handle with care
It is so very beautiful
   when kept clean.
It breaks easily
   and when it does it hurts.
You can always find it
   but it takes time to find what is right for you
When broke or not kept clean
   It can always be fixed.

The thing called love....

—*Chastity Lapierre*

The Note

Midnight, Tuesday morning,

the candle blows out near the
hastily scribbled note.
Black ink on yellow parchment
and all the things she was afraid to say....
goodbye..I'm sorry...I didn't mean it
In another time maybe...

The screen door slams loud in
sleeping house. He woke
to hear the old rabbit starting in the driveway.

Seven A.M. Tuesday morning in an empty kitchen.
The coffee is cold and so is
the white linoleum floor.
The newspaper is soggy. And the radio only plays
music of poignant associations.

Thousandth time and twelve and
the note still says the same things.

Tiny signs of once human presence.

Lipstick in the bathroom.
Underwear in the laundry.
And scars across his heart that cold coffee makes
feel a little bit better.

—*John L. Micek*

Comment On Cosmic Thought

Now, let's deal with Modern Cosmic Thought.
Have we the Universal Things we ought

That we might make projection
In some specified direction?

Should we take the gnat, first of all?
Oh, there are many things less small.

Ah, the finite atom. We hardly see it.
Damn it to hell! It must be in orbit.

If it is, it's found "its" place,
Perhaps in infinite space.

Search the Cosmos! Relieve our troublesome load
In some manner, shape or form! It's the mode.

—*Glenn Abercrombie*

Shy

Have you ever wished you could just say hi?
Have you ever just wondered if I would reply?
Just one word and I would be happy
Just to know that you tried
Or should I talk to you?
What would you do?
Would you walk away
And laugh at me today
Or would you just say Hi
And reply?
To find an answer is hard
But its up to me
I guess I'll find the strength one day
To stop and stay
Would you turn away?

—*Angela E. Rigaud*

161

Have You Ever?

Have you ever walked away from an outstretched hand?
Have you ever thought yourself better than one from another land?

Have you ever turned your head from a face with a smile?
Have you ever refused when asked to walk that extra mile?

Have you ever turned your head the other way
because you felt they were not as smart?

Have you ever chosen to be apart
because you felt you were better than they?

Have you ever turned from a child in tears
and not taken the time to soothe her fears?

Have you "looked down" on a child for he didn't measure up to
some without considering the home he may come from?

Have you ever thought that when from this world we part
we may be asked, "Did you give from your heart?"

—*Barbara DeLuca*

Untitled

Have you notice the weather?
It seems as though, your winter clothes are all put together.
Sometimes things won't go your way.
Smile and be grateful, for being able to see another day.
My favorite color is navy blue.
There is a message that's true and must go through.
This is not the time to relax or sit back.
We must take our sacks and face the facts.
Time is moving on, and waits for no one.
When your child, is in trouble that's no fun.
To someone who is in school, obey the rules,
stay cool, you won't loose.
Keep the best set of tools.

—*Henrietta Vaughan*

For The Memory Maker

I saw a shadow in the mirror, a fleeting glimpse, somewhat a
haze, darkness descended but still I stood amidst the silence
with intense gaze.

I swayed against the wooden door and felt it's grain like a
playful maze, as quick, I straightened, afraid I would miss a
scene being shown in the mirror's rays.

A carousel turned — so quiet and slow, but without the horses
as most portray, I saw images in picture frames revealed before
me like grade-school plays.

The shadow moved as each memory circled the mirror of bye-gone
days, my emotions surged — I smiled, I cried, reminded of past
forgotten ways.

Showers of laughter and clouds of pain whispered around like a
restless blaze. Mystical illusion, "No I say!" and my tears
spoke out and cleared the haze.

'Twas not a "shadow in the mirror," distorting vision with dusty
grays, simply a "mirror in the shadow," holding my memories day
by day.

—*Carolyn Harris Hensley*

JFK, The Captain Lives No More

He was a gift of God to the people of this land,
He was a gift of God to men everywhere;
He came amidst a gathering storm around the world,
As the captain, he guided the stern and commanded the ship.

We became one of his before he was ours,
We took him to heart like we never did another before;
He portrayed our vision as we did his,
He was noble and he enabled us all.

—*John Rattan*

God's Greatest Gift

Whenever God needs something done,
he always sends a child.
He bestows his love in some form,
on those, like himself, are gentle and mild.

Poetry and Art are wonderful, in many ways,
it is created by God alone.
It's depths, it's powers, it's agonies,
seem to literally tear at flesh and bone.

The pen of the poet, the brush of the artist,
are guided by his hands for creation.
He gives us love and guidance,
and bestows it to our imagination.

Poets and Artists are God's special servants,
he is there to answer us all.
Love of our work, to do, our lives to live,
'tis the greatest gift that God can give.

—*Dorothy C. Blackwood*

"Daddy's Little Girl...Remembers"

No more national anthems on Friday nights,
He can't hear the tune,
He can't understand the words,
The lines are new and confusing,
The door has been opened....or has it?

No more golf games on Saturday mornings,
He can't swing the club anymore,
His iron has divoted too deep,
The tee has been broken once again,
The golf cart drives on....or does it?

No more bowling matches on Sunday afternoons
The score sheet is clear
The alley is too slick
The ten pins are all down and slightly in motion
There's only strikes being made and heard
Or are they all gutter balls?
Daddy's memory is dead....or is it?

—*Jennifer Van Fossen*

The Rebellious Sheep

There was a rebellious sheep, who wandered from the fold,
He didn't like the fences or the things he was told.
"There's a better way," he kept thinking to himself,
As he headed out on his own and ignored everybody else.

The glitter of the world attracted every sensual desire,
And soon there were cravings that set his soul afire.
He desired those things that hurt his body and mind,
And soon the peace he sought, he could no longer find.

His determination is something he had an abundance of,
When others tried to help, he ignored their acts of love.
"I'll make it on my own," he kept saying to himself,
But in reality, a need to be loved grew inside himself.

Jesus is still looking and searching for this lost sheep,
He keeps on looking even though the pits are deep.
He won't give up until he's brought him back home,
For he is one of the lost sheep, he stills calls his own.

He may have turned his back and gone his own way,
But Jesus' love and mercy is still reaching out today.
He'll never give up, on that you can be sure,
For he has a great mission and a heavenly future.

—*John Bullard*

"Ode To A Hummingbird"

Love is like a hummingbird,
He goes from one flower to the next,
Until the flower with the 'best nectar',
The nectar he can not live without, he finds.

The hummingbird knows not when or who,
He will find this 'sweetest' flower,
Except he knows one day,
He will find the nectar of love.

There is many nectars to try,
Some might never find the 'sweetest nectar',
Many believe they find the right one,
But are crushed to find it is not so sweet.

Can there be a nectar for me?
There is nectar for everyone,
No one knows where and when,
Unfortunately, if they don't look,
They will not find the 'sweetest nectar'.

I found the 'sweetest nectar'
But lost it!!!

—*Chris Novak*

The Final Play

The pressure was tough as he stepped up to the line.
He had to make these shots because his team was behind

The arena was lit up with many dazzling lights.
The fans were all cheering all full of delight.

The coaches looked on steadily while the first shot was there.
It has beauty and grace when it had floated through air.

The fans were all relaxed, among all the children and men.
The score was all tied and he would shoot once again.

He took one dribble then eyed his goal.
He followed through and his shot and let the ball roll.

Silence spread through the arena, and no one heard a sound.
The ball hit the rim, and rattled around.

That got the fans up and they screamed and booed.
But that wouldn't not help because the ball fell through.

The fans took a deep breath and started to cheer.
The sound of them was so loud it was very hard to hear.

The teams ran of the court and started to laugh.
For they knew it wasn't over because they had another half.

—*David Nefouse*

A Cat's Eye View

I have this funny cat, "Beat-It" is his name.
He is always in the way because he is so tame.
He sits upon the sill outside my window pane.
From this position, a cat's-eye view to gain.
He watches me with great concern as I my meal prepare.
"What is that human up to now." He continues to stare.
Does he think it is fun to watch what humans do
As though he is the keeper and me in the zoo?
Yes, there is a frame of glass that makes me look shut in.
I'm sure that has crossed his mind as I see his catty grin.
"At last," he smiles, "The role is in reverse.
Maybe humans now will know life could be much worse."

—*Bernice Hudspeth*

Jesus Is the North Star To Me

Jesus is the North Star to me, my friend, my life, my guide,
He is my compass both night and day, Without Him I'd be
   sore-tried;
When I'm confused to Him I go, No other star can guide me so;
When I'm out of touch, He helps me much, He's my health.
Jesus is my radar to me, my watch, my radio, my all;
He is my coach, my friend, co-pilot, Without Him I would fall;
He sends directions every day, He dispels missiles that comes
   my way;
Millions of stars, One only star, He anchors my day.
Jesus is constant forevermore, A faith-rest above the uproar;
I trust Him now, I'll trust Him when, Life's fleeting days
   are over;
Following His beam I know I'm right, He's my range-finder
   both day and night;
He keeps me on course, No matter the storm, He's my sight.

—*George Lynch*

A Little Ditty

Joseph had real sense in his head
He left his coat and fled.
If men today would listen to what I say,
They'd run like Joseph did.
They'd run, run, run, run,
Run like Joseph did.
He fled fast on his feet,
Got away from the heat,
He left his coat and hid.
He got away from Potiphar's wife,
Put in prison. Kept his life.
He ran and ran but stood like a man.
And so today, any man can.
When you're tempted to sin, don't give in.
Remember this little ditty,
And run, run, run,
And you'll be thought to be witty......

—*Winifred G. Hodges*

"He Left Me"

He left me, and the night is so cold.
He left me, now I have no one to hold.
He left me with the sweet dreams of the past.
He left me, and these dreams they end so fast.
I wish that life could have stayed the same,
   Nothing gone, nothing changed.
Now I must live with the memories that
Seem unknown; and in my heart nobody's home.
   I wonder if he knows how I feel.
That my love is strong, the emotion is real...
I guess I'll just have to live in the dark shadows
   Of my emptiness.

—*Jennifer Klimauskas*

Rainbow

Rainbow, rainbow so colorful and bright,
Fades away into the sunlight.

Reds, yellow's, purple's, and blue's,
Full of beautifully painted hues.

The clouds, the rain, and the sun in the sky,
It's becoming clear oh my! oh my!

You may find a pot of gold,
At the end of the rainbow it is told.

—*Darlene Anderson*

The Holy Spirit

God planted a seed in the mother's womb
He nurtured it and brought it to bloom.
The embryo proved to be a blessing
To those who loved our "Maker in Heaven".

He planted a seed in the human heart,
He called it the Holy Spirit.
It serves as a constant guide
To those who will only listen.

The Holy Spirit doesn't intrude
But always there to those in need.
We have to cultivate to keep it growing
By constant adoration and love for Him.

To feel the Holy Spirit,
One has to live by his word.
Sunshine and showers from Heaven
Cultivate the blessings from our Lord!

—*Edna G. Paschal*

The Poet Died

The poet died.
He passed out, breathless, among crumpled half-written pages.
He succumbed while accepting the mindless void of M-TV;
contributing to the facade,
believing a commercial;
he buys the hairspray and looks for chicks.
He suffocated while noting the Wall Street Journal's daily
tabsheets, in a pair of unused, prewashed, Guess jeans.
The poet smothered not seeing life in the garbage littered,
people ridden streets.
He neither talked nor asked about it.
He didn't feel it,
or smell it.
He wouldn't touch it.
The poet: the people's savior;
Made his exit as he slipped in behind the wheel of his car,
instead of walking.

—*Catherine Mary Vance*

Confused Sea Lover

From the hill window into the bay,
He saw the ships go by every day,
The young man had his dreams very clear,
To go to sea without fear.

He went in search during the depression,
He kept it a secret without repression,
Finally his dreams came through with destitution,
To sea the young man went with determination.

He found freedom sailing the seven seas,
He suffered good and bad in the strange ports,
He was like a bird having many love affairs,
His thoughts were of having one life to spare.

Time came when he wanted to maintain a home,
But, at the end his girlfriend with someone else took off,
He kept sailing around the world to healed his wounds,
And found another love that landed in a honeymoon.

He suffer a destitute which he didn't accept,
He was a prisoner of love by force,
He had will power, but talk too much,
And his innocent woman pay for his past and all.

—*Luis E. Cuevas-Cardoza*

The Poet

The poet is forever young,
  He speaks that one immortal tongue
To him the wonder never dies, as
  youth is looking through his eyes.

Pale listener of the heart of things,
  He hears the voices and the wings,
  He hears the skylark overhead—
    The footsteps of the mortal dead.
The poet is forever young.

Strength of the mountains, power of
The seas, if only our minds could
Feel what he sees... The warmth
of the flowers, The softness of
a kiss... All true poets feel like this,
the poet is forever young!

Strange people seem to come and go,
  but there are only some who know,
The feelings that the poet had,
Feelings that were often sad!!
"The poet he is forever young."

—*Lois Celani*

Ryan

God sent a little angel from heaven one day
He stretched out his arms and said, "Grandma, I'm here to stay."
Now, he was on order for a very long time
But the order wasn't filled until God opined.
Since he came, he has brought a lot of love and cheer
And all the family wants to do —— is be near!
I want to thank God for this gift of joy
For, finally, giving us this wonderful baby boy.

As time went by, Ryan grew by leaps and bounds.
He walked in his walker around and around.
From the playroom, to the kitchen, to the living room and den,
he was so busy exploring from end to end
There were so many things to share
And he had to be watched with lots of care.

Now, he is the apple of grandma's eye,
And she is so pleased to see him try.
Every week he learns something new,
and she is happy through and through.
For all who have met him they can't forget
that he is the most precious gift from God, as yet!

—*Germaine M. Henry*

Untitled

Searching for the road, the pathway of his desire.
He travels along the way, making decisions and "friends"
As we say
He comes to a hard obstacle, like other in the past.
Trying to go around, he doesn't make the task.
For he thinks this obstacle, has finally stopped him.
Now he copes with it, he almost accepts it.
Something inside, makes him strive,
To over power this problem which he has in his mind.
Trying and trying, he won't stop again.
He begins to see the light.
He's almost there,....done,...that obstacles taken,
He moves down the path way, of his desire.
Waiting to come upon, other obstacles to devour.
He struggles down the road, trying to find the "easy way"
But finds there isn't!
And keeps on going!!!!

—*Marc Len*

Hurting Words

Pointing in anger, clenching fists in rage
He tries to contain his anger in an internal cage
Pointing his finger like a make believe gun
His bullets are words, piercing his son

"Juvenile delinquent, never really tried
No respect, complete lack of pride
I've tried to show you the error of your ways
But now I see I've wasted all those days!"

The hands are folded, look of pain
The boy's tears are falling like the rain
He bites his lips and fights back the tears
That accompanied his sorrow through all his years.

"Failing in school, doing so bad
You're the father I never had
Never here for me, you never cared
All the memories we never shared."

The smoke clears as his anger subdued
His methods are lethal, his words are crude
The disappointment in his son he can't deny
He doesn't see his son in the corner cry.

    —Grant L. Preston

The Outsider, The Mirror, And The Achiever

There once was a boy. I won't say his name,
he wanted to be like others, just the same.
When he wanted to be like the rest, kind of cool,
he winded up looking stupid, being the fool.
When he walked and pranced, trying to please them
he realized they weren't laughing with him, but at him!
But then he saw the light, his self-image,
the Distorted Mirror—his worst enemy!
He looked in the mirror and he said, "Why?"
"You made me this way," it said, "that's why!"
By doing better in his life, he reshaped the mirror,
and he looked to his surprise, he saw the Achiever!
Then people started to accept him, for himself, his concern,
"Everybody is an individual!" he said, "that's what I
learned!"

    —James Johnson

Once...

Once, I met a bright, shining Knight.
He was as cold and hard as the steel he
    wore for protection.
I challenged him until he removed his armor
    and I discovered his heart was made of flesh.
I knew him then as he knew me and we lived
    together happily until our deaths.

Another time, I met a Prince.

He was as charming as any fairy tale ever told.
He won me with his warmth and smile.
I knew him then but I discovered that
    his heart was made of steel.
He was bitter and cruel and the rest of my
    days were spent in misery and fear.

And then, I met you.

You protect yourself like the Knight.
You charm me and disarm me like the Prince.
So, I will not let you know me until you answer me this:
If I were to pierce your heart with a knife, would you bleed?
Or would you break the blade?

    —dena

A Stranger's Christmas

There once was a poor stranger, all alone,
He was driven away from his very own home.
No friends or family by his side
He really had no where to abide.
Out of the lonely and cold night air
There came another stranger from a far.
Come and stay with me tonight
I will give you rest from your weary flight.
These are the words they say
Were said on that self proclaimed day.
The two than went together to a lowly home
That wouldn't be considered that by some.
A cot with rags were laid for a bed
but with the richest of foods they were fed.
So in a strange land the strangers had the best
Christmas that they could ever wish.

    —Eddie Arnold

"Dr. Martin Luther King Jr."

Dr. King was born on January 15, 1929.
He was one of the best civil rights leader in his time.
He married Corretta Scott in 1953.
Kings non-violent program reached as far as Washington D.C.
In Washington D.C., King gave his "I Have a Dream" speech,
    on August 28, 1963.
He thought all men were created equally free.
In 1964, at the age of thirty five,
Dr. King received the Nobel Peace Prize.
He had four children and a loving wife,
Just because James Earl Ray didn't like him he took his life.
At the age of thirty nine, on April 4, 1968 in Memphis
Tennessee
Dr. Martin Luther King Jr. was no longer to be.
James Earl Ray, a white escaped convict, pleaded guilty in
    March 1969
His convicted sentence was ninety nine.

    —Kemba Sophia Eugene

Jesus

Jesus Christ our Lord and Savior was once a child like me
He was sent down by God His Father a Savior for us you see.

Mary the Mother of Jesus was astonished as could be
To birth the greatest son on earth
To go down in the Bible of history.

At the age of twelve and only a lad
Jesus was missing, his family was sad.

Three days later in the temple he was found
Discussing God's message to the people all around.

He did not die at thirty three
He bore the cross to set us free.
We thank you Lord Jesus for all that you have done
You are the greatest one of all
You are our Father's Son.

    —Evie Kittrell Williams

Nature

Look at the bees, they act so funny
Have you wondered why they produce honey?
Look at the stars, they shine so bright
If they were higher they would be out of sight.
Look at the flowers, how they bloom
Don't they smell like the scent of perfume?
Look at the moon, it shines so high
Look at the sun, it lights up the sky.
Think of the power that was brought forth
We should take care and love our earth.

    —Leslie McGiffen-Newkirk

My Special Friend

Into my life entered a special child,
He was then just a baby, so meek and mild,
Year after year I could see how he grew,
He was truly very special, this I knew.

This child has become my special friend,
I want him to know, my hand I will lend,
If ever needed, whether big or small,
I'll do what I can and give him my all.

Life is full of wonders, life is full of strife,
My special friend has taught me, so much about life.
He has taught me how to love, and how to care,
And all about kindness, and how to share.

God had a special reason, for placing him here,
A special Mom and Dad to be ever so near.
A special friend, he taught how to care,
Linger's in my heart and beyond compare.

The sparkle in his eyes, and his tender smile,
His giving and caring makes you linger awhile.
Lord be with him and take care of him I pray,
For he is my special friend Lord, he is Jay.

        —*Charlotte E. Whitesel*

Tom

Uncle Tom has a new and dignified look.
He wears expensive suits and Florisheim Shoes
And prefers Bach and Battle over the blues;
Drives a Lexus, BMW or Mercedes Benz,
And lives in the suburbs with his wealthy friends.

On Oprah and Donahue he loves to appear
And preach the right-wing conservative line
The right-wing conservatives love to hear:
How lazy blacks are need to find
Self-help as the key to a life so sublime.

Tom doesn't seem to be able to comprehend
What happened when slavery came to an end;
The slaves unprepared to survive in a nation
Reeking with hate and fear and discrimination;
Self-help was the only means of salvation.

Tom doesn't seem to know or understand
Self-help practiced by many a woman and man
Working the worst of jobs for meager pay
And with sweat and suffering paved the way
For the ignorant and self-righteous Toms of today.

        —*Joe Henry Kelly*

Blue Beginning

A.D.'s a mongrel dog. And old - too old.
He wheezes, head against his master's side.
His senses fade; sight dims; smells petrified
In times long gone. Poe's dungeon walls will fold,
Dull red, upon his world, all frozen, cold
And dark. One sense alone he still can slide
Between those walls - the dream of love, to glide
Through space and time, their secret to unfold.

A.D.'s alone now, head on empty sleeve.
His simple love still searches while he dies.
But now he feels a shining through the fog.
Love cleaves to love! This only - death's reprieve
That will not fade. And then the greatest prize -
That dear hand's touch, the glorious words:
            "Good dog!"

        —*John W. Bowling*

Birds

Why do birds go to sleep so early, hiding their
     heads under wings in trees, some burly?
Why don't they bathe in evening dew? sing at night,
     dance for their love, and coo?
Don't they want to see the moon, the stars, the color of Mars?
Have they seen a shooting star fall so near, yet is so very far—
Have they ever met a bat in flight,
     or tried to catch the firefly with its signal light?
Do they know ants and worms at night are crawling?
Do they hear a hunter's footstep falling, and the frogs'
     and katydid's shrill voices calling?
Have they watched a rabbit the farmer's cabbage nibble?
Have they eavesdropped on lovers' quibble?
Do they gaze at man as their superior —
     or do they think him somewhat inferior?
Is man happier for all his knowledge?
How could birds be smart without a college?
Would study make them wiser, or indifferent?
Would birds be birds if they were different?

        —*Marie Pilny*

Sailing Away

Walking through the tunnel of loneliness
Hearing nothing, but the echo of our footsteps
And the echo of the thoughts in my head

Before we entered the tunnel
We had talked about everything
Except my true feelings towards you

In our long Journey, through the tunnel
Silence was our companion

Unconsciously we might have decided
To be left alone, in our world
Or we might have deliberately wanted
To keep that space, to keep that void

At the end of our trip
You may pick up the phone
And call your best friend
That you're coming home…you're taking the train

And I, left behind, raising the sails of my ship
To continue my journey alone
Fighting the waves and the wind
Sailing away…so not to remember you again

        —*Eid Masri*

Satisfaction

Sitting high and dry, alone on a sandy seashore
Hearing the roar of the surf,
I luxuriate in richness of undisturbed peace
As I watch wave after wave
From beginning to end, over and over again.

Each wave rises and forms from the sea,
Peaking and falling downward in glowing curve,
Spreading to reunite with its' source,
Foaming in rainbow-hued bubbles,
Racing to completion on the shore.

Time exists not as I watch to my heart's content
The rising and falling of waves
That perform, unceasingly, sensuous song and dance
As they live brief, passionate moments of beauty
Gloriously displaying, in roaring sound, pulsing color and
     light.

        —*Ester Akersloot*

Love

What love binds can't be easily broken. The place in your heart where only that one person can fill, no matter how hard you try to fill that spot with substitutes and diversions. Once that kind of love has been shared, that gap can never be filled with anything or anyone else. Make no mistake, what is said to disprove what's deep inside only makes for a pretentious situation. Pretense can't take the place of fact, even though we put up a good facade. A look into the eyes, a touch of the hand, breaks through the facade of hidden emotions, and the love that has been suppressed and hidden comes through like the ocean, with waves of expressed love, passion and tenderness, flowing one to another. Even though the moments maybe only from time to time, the love never changes. It only disappears back behind the facade, the wall of protection they use to survive from day to day, until the time comes again when the two can be together as one again, because the love they share at those moments sustains them, day to day, moment to moment, because they know love never fails.

—*Jean Havlen*

Untitled

My teardrop like rose petals...
　Heavily,
　　Softly,
　　Quietly.

Never stopping like the sands of time...
　Slowly,
　　Thickly,
　　　One by one.

Pure like the virgin's life...
　Sweet,
　　Innocent,
　　　Without touch,

Waiting for you forever
　　—*Christina Robinson*

Am I Alone

Hello is anyone out there?
Hello does anyone care?
I have feelings to, you know.
Just let me prove it, let me show.
Please give me a chance.
I'll make you laugh, sing, and dance.
I'll make you feel good when you are down.
I'll make you smile when you frown.
I wish you would keep me.
I'd really like to be.
A boy or a girl, it really doesn't matter.
Just don't make my life shatter.
I want to live, I want to grow.
I'll say I love you, I'll let you know.
Even though you might get upset.
I know that you won't regret.
So here I am and I love you.
Please say you love me to!
　　—*Christie L. Sutcliffe*

Children

They are so very special,
sweet and innocent are
they. The world would be
lost and gone without
them. Always love them
and they will always love
their children. For GOD
LOVES ALL HIS CHILDREN.

　　—*Benita Atkins*

Untitled

The Lord held me up and the devil knocked me down. The Lord helped me back up off the ground. I looked at the devil and asked him why he wanted to start trouble. He said I'm sorry brother. I said you no brother of mine Satan you one of a kind. He wanted me to go with him that when it all got dim. He said let me show you a good time you see. I said keep on going and let me be. I told him I might dress funky and look kind of wild but I am not no devil's child. It put him into a shock the old devil could not even talk. He went straight back to hell when he got there he just about fell. He thought what was it about that De Berry kid he just could not keep the love of Jesus hid. Just let him beat me just once more who know he just might make it into Heaven's doors. Don't let the devil beat on you just tell him to shew.

　　—*Daniel De Berry*

Philosophy

I have a plan—to me it seems right—
Helping others find their delight.
But if there is naught that I can do,
I'll flee to the mountains; take my adieu.

When problems arise—enthusiasm lags
I'm not a quitter to raise a white flag.
I'll get back of the wheel and give a big shove
For I want you to know that you are loved.

Life is much like a song, from experiences I knew:
I have had much joy, yes, and tears, a few.
I've had many falls—they say that's no sin—
But the biggest problem is getting up again.

Again life could be like a crowded state fair;
I looked all around but you weren't there.
I find life exciting, even at day's end,
But I want you to know I have a wonderful Friend!
　　—*Charles L. Durbin*

Erin

Her hands were birds
Her heart of thrush
Painted by the butterbrush
Hues of the afternoon

'neath fire's tress
Eyes of emerald field
Foretold the thoughts her lips concealed
And fell amid the soil

Her inner life
The hoarfrost skinned
Held at bay the bitter wind
Which clings to the hem

I've walked her breadth
Consumed within
Upon my tongue her salty skin
Stirs the shadows of solitude
　　—*Daniel J. Deasy Jr.*

Friends

Neither opal or sapphire
　will make one an Earl,
tho they have their desire
　like diamond and pearl.

　For riches in life,
　the values in friends;
for they are more precious,
　than jewels or gems.
　　—*Charles Cecil Ward*

Untitled

Hair as golden as the twilight's glow
Her mothers traits begin to show.
Grandma's ears, hands like father.
Whose eyes are those? Not to bother.

A mystery lived day to day
A puzzle piece thrown away.
The clues are close, the answers far.
Let go from her roots like a falling star.

Chosen selectively, like a tomato from a vine,
By people she refers to as "parents of mine".
Told "follow your dreams", "Believe in yourself",
The courage they have shown, is no match to wealth.

A chance, given to an abandoned soul
Offered from angels with halos of gold.
Mom and dad have given me
The gift, of my identity.

Given to me, this chance at life
By this man, her husband, and she; his wife.
Some say that blood is thicker than water
But I am the one they call their "daughter".

—*Jill Carr*

A Willow, I

Beneath the calm exterior,
Hidden behind unfurrowed brow,
Stored among catacombs and convolutions,
Lies the place of imagination, fantasy, and memory.
Ideas flowing furiously fast,
Thunderous passages of thought,
Insightful flashes of lightning,
Conveyed through the window of the eye.
The trouble storing mechanism
In league with concealed joyous rapture,
All stored within the human computer,
And all a hair's breadth from outlet.
Living on the edge of insane/sanity,
We walk the narrow line between what is
And what we wish the world to be,
Gazing with wonder as we pass.
We must crawl before we run,
Branches creak and bend before they break,
Neurosis before psychosis before oblivion.
A mind is a terrible thing to waste.

—*Philip A. Eckerle*

Saltwater Taffy

Tides so low I can see through the earth and beyond. Tides so high I cannot breathe. Rocks, crater through the course sand which is so slick that I melt. This breeze, so lively, I can blow as a kite in the sky. My breath tastes the lemon sunlight to the honeydew moon. Just add some salt and the water will chill my toes and tighten my joints. The clouds can freeze the rain, but the water will melt the snow. The shine will fill your lips and the sun will fill your eyes. Your body tastes so sweet. That bright blue sky cannot beat that star lit night. Staggered out so plenty, my jigsaw puzzle of dreams, my nightmares of flight. Nature so plentiful, nature so bright. Evergreen forests and fields barren of life. I cannot hide behind a shadow, so I hide my face within the light. Dust is filling our hour glass, but the sands fill our empty hearts. So many shapes in the clouds, many more faces in the crowd. Even more grains of sand to keep filling our hearts with joy. Open up the window, let in a little sunshine, let out a little sight.

—*Jason C. Roe*

Once Upon A Time

Remember the passenger pigeons flying
High in the once blue sky and
The buffalo taking days to pass by
Remember watching the deer jumping
out of sight, it was a beautiful sight
Know that there all gone and the birds
Sang there last song. We sit in here and
wonder where we went wrong.
The sun still shines bright but, we
will never again see the night.

—*Bob Hayes*

August Phenomenon

As I stood gazing at an August sky
High upon a grassy hill;
The sleeping village down below,
The houses darkened, all was still.
Except the far off barking of a farmer's dog,
The sleepy sound of peepers,
And the throaty chortle of a frog.
The stars shown brightly,
A cool breeze stirred, and faintly,
The sleepy lowing of a herd of cattle
Echoed on the rolling slopes below.
And then in the north
I saw a streaming glow
Of a meteor putting on a night time show.

—*Madeline Davis Hoyle*

That Old Man

That old man was just sitting all alone in his old easy chair. His babies are all grown up now, they don't seem to care. His oldest son walked in and stopped at the door And said, "You need to quit dropping things on the floor". "If you keep doing that, you'll have the filthiest place in the land". "I didn't know I dropped it, son. I guess it slipped out of my hand". "Well, I've got to go to work now". He didn't even say good-bye. That old man, with the back of his hand, wiped a tear from his eye. He saw his other coming. He was drunk on that old beer. He closed his eyes for a minute, hoping to hold back another tear. His son sat down for just a minute. He sat there real still. Then he looked up and said, "you need to make us out a will". "You know it can't be too long now before you surely will die". "And we need to know what's going to happen before you say good-bye". That can't be my boy talk'n, it must be that old beer. That old man, with the back of his hand, wiped away a tear. His son got up, swayed a bit, then staggered across the floor. He was having a hard time finding his way to the door. That old man is just sitting there in that old easy chair. his babies have grown up now.

—*Hollis H. Noble*

Kiitos, Jallu

I remember rocks that steamed and spit
hissing from wooden ladels and melted snow

you beat me with birch
branches thawed in buckets opening
pores fissures on my exposed back
issuing lava streams of sweat meandering
along skin collecting in pools beneath toes
and thighs darkening cedar benches

your mouth rimmed with salt
tasted of vodka and buttered eel
charcoated black

—*Heidi L. Everett*

Silver Shadows

His black glittering eyes of steel
his boyish features
his adult attitude
his rigid body, wound tight in a coil,
    ready to strike back at what has hurt him.

The hand that reaches out to comfort him,
    comes away bloody,
    to reach out again only to be severed

His life not taken, for it would be too kind,
    and kindness is not welcomed in a life so dark

What is the fear of him?
    of his anger?
    of the life he has led?

Or is it the mirror?
                        —*Kelly J. Brigham*

An Angel Named Hoot

    There once was a man who compared to no one.
His friends were countless, his enemies were none.
        Pure in heart, gentle and kind,
        Honest and direct he spoke his mind,
    A devoted father and husband to his wife,
He loved the animals and the simple things in life.
To know him was an honor, his friends held him dear.
His family, his loved ones thought he's always be here.
    But then he took sick here in his own home town
Where proper medical treatment just wasn't around.
So they sent him away, and we hoped he would heal.
    He fought for his life with incredible zeal.
        But the horrible damage was already done,
        And today we miss our beloved one.
We hold close to our hearts the love that he gave us.
    His spirit we believe will always be with us.
    For someone this special is a gift from above,
    And there is no end to our everlasting love.

                        —*Eda LaPolt*

Knute' Knutson

Knute' Knutson is a most interesting new friend.
His stories are enjoyable from beginning to end.
One I never tire of is about his mother-in law.
It involves a locket which is unlike anything I ever saw.
At the age of seven when in 1888 the Cuban Revolution
Was making date,
Her class she attended was asked to write
To soldiers fighting there,
To help them bear the war horrors and show them they care.
So off went the letter with a surprise return gift,
A locket that opened with a moon-watch that went tick-tick.
A cherub with pitchfork fed the moon, all set in jewels.
But Dorothy, his wife, had tiny baby teeth she used as tools
To remove a few sets which are still missing today;
But now Knute' knows why Dorothy wanted it her way.
For the jewels are sparkling in the heavenly crown in her hair,
She retained them for this purpose
To make sure they'd be there.

                        —*Dorothy Vander Lind*

Untitled

The sun shines
The flowers bloom
Springtime smells
Like sweet perfume
                        —*Max Altman*

To Make A Change

                Little, X, El Shabazz
            His trip to Mecca now in the past
        The words that he spoke are still loud and clear
        And for that infamous white man he had no fear
        Violent, militant, a Black Muslim he was named

            But for all those titles he bore no shame
        For his race to be equal would be his pot'o gold
        Not taken from their motherland later to be sold

            To slave and serve for those who are so great
    Caused his race to grow angry, fight back, and to hate
    To blame those of today for what happened in the past
    Is not right nor fare, a change must come and fast
    To understand each other with open hearts and love

            Has always been the message sent from above
    Hand in hand, heart to heart, man and woman we must be
Equality for you, equality for me is the only way to be free.
                        —*Marva L. Mason*

A New Mothers Thoughts

While you sleep
History is being made
There's rioting by people of every color and shade.

While you sleep
Worlds records are being broken
Gun control is always spoken

While you sleep
Nations death tolls climb
Through famine, war, aids and crime

While you sleep
There's talk of global warming
Political elections send people swarming

While you sleep
There's tornados, snow storms, rain and thunder
Enough environmental hazards to put nature under

While you sleep
Your inner peace touches me deep inside
Are you tomorrow's future, tomorrow's pride?
                        —*June H. Schultz*

The Promise

Good always prevails in the end
Hold on to this thought and a guardian angel God will send
For no matter how rough the road we travel when the journey begins
God is always there to forgive our sins
Seek ye not of ways to gain riches and fame
For if you're of pure heart, God will give you a name
Rather seek ye the slow and sure
And the ways and means with much to endure
Look not to the life that will take a harsh toll
For in the end it will show up on your soul
Look to God, allow him to enlighten
For surely my friend, your days he will brighten
Although the road is rough
Put your hand in God's hand, for he is tough
stronger than we, if we allow him to be remember...
He promised to walk with us through eternity
                        —*Diann Fowler*

He, Did It

You'll never know the beauty that the world
holds just for you.
Unless you believe in God, and the things that
He can do.

It seems He took the mountains and sat
with brush in hand,
And began to paint a picture, the most
beautiful in the land.

On every tree He painted leaves of green
and red and gold,
And when orange was mixed with yellow,
It was something to behold.

Only once a year He works like this,
for each of us to see,
Tho the world is full of beauty, only
God can paint a tree.

—*Harriet E. Lewis*

A Blessed Christmas Tree

At first a tiny seedling planted in the ground
Hoping no one will tread on it; stirring at every sound.
Yes, stirring is the proper word, tho no one else can see
It has a heart inside like us, this tiny little tree.

See how it grows so sturdy, stretching up so high,
Each branch a lovely picture, reaching towards the sky.
Hark! What's this, the final day?
..The time has gone so fast!
It must be taken from the ground — if only life could last.
But listen to the voices — singing out with glee,
"Oh, there it is .. look over here, it's such a perfect tree!"

The tree begins to shudder, it knows the time has come,
Like many trees before it, a duty must be done.
For God gave them all His love and care and makes them
  a lovely sight,
So they can stand in Blessed Beauty
  On His most Holy Night.

—*Helen Pichetto*

Breath Of Spring

Good morning world!
How are you today?
Hope you're telling the sun to shine
So the children may come out to play.

The naked trees are robed
With their bright colors of green,
And the beautiful flowers
The most radiant color you have ever seen.

The birds are singing in the trees,
The day is so pleasant, just like an ocean breeze,
And the robins are chirping on the lawn,
Calling loudly for a mate to call his own.
So dear world, let the sun shine today
So the children may come out to play!

—*Jessie L. Taylor*

Untitled

Brothers, sisters, husbands, and wives
together we shared each others lives.
Brothers sisters forever friends.
love like ours shall never end.
Sisters and brothers forever more.
someday in heaven together we'll soar.
Together forever we then will be
the best of friends for eternity.

—*C. Wright*

Aboard Amtrak

The rolling rails meander past village and street
How different the perspective, through the window
  by my seat
The powerful river; its edges frozen still
As swans paddle fretfully against winter's chill.
Commuter conversations whispered ear to ear
Like telephone line messages you can barely hear.
Endless barren trees form images in my mind
Of a day when mother nature had not been so unkind
Snowflakes snag over barbed-wire fences
And into hibernation go all of my senses.
As wind and whistle release their dreary drone,
My eyes walk a path which to me is yet unknown.

—*Deborah Sloane*

Angel Rose

Angel Rose, heaven knows
How I wish I could watch you grow.
Angel Rose how I wish I could touch your golden hair.
Do you know how much I truly do care?
Angel Rose with eyes of blue
I just want to say I love you.
Do you forgive me little one?
For all that I have said and done.
Do you wait for me at heavens gate?
Safe from this cruel world so full of hate.
So many times I wish you could come down to play.
Even if it were only for a day.
I would spend the hours with you so carefully
I would hold you ever so gently.
Angel Rose, heaven knows
I should have never let you go.
Angel Rose, please forgive me
Open your arms and wait for me in eternity.

—*Deborah Lawrence*

"Dream"

Waiting, Waiting, Waiting.
How long must I wait?
It seems like a life time.
Sunset after sunset, sunrise after sunrise.
All I do is wait and she never comes.
Where is She?
Does she even exist?
I hope, I dream and I pray that she does.

Can I live without her?
I have been, I must, I will.
Maybe she'll be there tomorrow or the next day.
Maybe I'll never be with her.
Have I already missed her.
Has she missed me or have we missed each other.

I'm alone as I wait.
Waiting in the light.
Waiting in the dark.
Dreaming she'll be with me.
But that's all she is.
A life long dream that doesn't seem to exist.

—*Brett M. Spedden*

Empty Promises

Beware of Empty Promises,
The shallow songs they sing.
For empty rhymes
In empty times,
An empty lot will bring.

—*Bradley Schwartz*

170

"Sorrow's Spell"

In this saddened state,
How my heart does ache.
For I can feel no love inside,
As if I had just died.
Emptiness fills the air,
With no one to hear my cries of despair.
Given up all hope,
I can no longer cope.
Captured by sorrow's spell,
Happiness I can not tell.
For loneliness is all I know,
And I wish it would all go.
Waiting for you to set me free,
By giving me the love I can not
    currently see.

—*Derek DiGiacmo*

Impressions

How can I show my love for you?
How often I am alone in this tiny bedroom
Cubed and swollen
Trapped by its harsh angles

How many times I have sat beneath some starry night,
The swirling lights dancing for me,
As I lie alone on some crooked mountain

Often I am lost among my towering haystacks,
Like any dull needle

So I'll nap again in this grey field
Dreaming of you
As flocks of dark crows blanket me.

Now I send you this portrait of myself
See how my face melts into the background
Even more imperfect than before

Two saddened eyes Two dry lips
But only one hollow ear
For you have stolen the other,
And traded my straw hat for white bandages.

—*Christopher L. Cussat*

Untitled

One day on the couch my son said to me
    "How old do you think that cap of yours to be?"
I said, "About your age, which is thirteen,
    You should see the sights this cap has seen."

The fuzz tassel on top is no longer there,
    But that's not bad considering the wear
It's seen rain and snow and hail and sleet
    And when wind blew, it lit at my feet.

It's been knocked off by willows when I rode through,
    And messed on by cows when they had to go pooh.
The days tagging calves while having bad luck,
    And their mothers bluffing me back into the truck.

It's been washed and shrunk and stretched to my size,
    And sometimes it falls down over my eyes.
It's still black and blue, but not from the dirt,
    It's just getting old and feels the hurt.

—*John W. Rieber*

Grandfather's Attic

Origins stir in that attic, there in the gloom
Huge trunks piled high, spill forth in colorful disarray;
Hats with trailing plumes,
Tunics, knee breeches, elegant gowns,
Homespun, and well worn leather, all smelling of grease paint.
And what an assemblage of minds!
On pages yellow,
Homer and Aristotle,
Genesis, Jefferson, Poe, Copernicus, Kant.
And in the far corner,
The cradle stands - waiting.

—*Kathryn Spillman*

The Day I Do

There is no one else in this life,
I am able to love.
There is no one else in this world,
That I can trust.
There was you and only you.
Now you are but a whisper, and I am a dove,
Circling above you, your place forever.
Tears flow from me as I fly above you,
But they are meaningless now
As my life from here and forever.
Gone is your promise that you once knew,
Until I can find the courage
To be with you forever again.

—*David M. Park*

Untitled

I am stranded and lost.
I am helpless and hurt.

Will you stop and love me the way I am?
Even if my body is tired and worn?
Even if my fur is unclean?
Will you stop and say hello even if I am lonely and old?

Could I be one of the many who came to comfort you,
Only to be thrown out into the cold night?

I sit alone by the fire,
its warmth and company are all I have left in this world.

Wherever the fire goes I will follow.
The fire of life.

—*Luis C. Fuquen*

I Am Never Alone

Each time I take a walk
I am never alone
Because I have a friend
Who walks beside me
His footprints I can not see
But he is there to guide me

I look at the world around me
And see all the beauty that surrounds me
Between the evergreens and pines
A fresh smell of God's woods-lands
That relaxes me and make feel good inside

I stand and watch a mother deer and her baby fawn
Stop for just a refreshing drink
And in my mind it gave me time to think
God made everything beautiful
He said, "I am with you all ways
And everywhere you go I am your shadow
And in all the beauty that you see
When you look at all the beautiful things around you
It is me."

—*Judy Ann Brown*

171

A Light In The Darkness

Time is short, my breath grows weak.
I am slowly dying of confusion.
Come and save me, pull me out of the cloud.
Hurry, hurry things grow dark.

Wait what is that light I see,
Is it love for me?
No, no it is just a smile from thee,

A smile that means nothing
For you give it to her... and to me.

—*Cheryl Tangeman*

Woman's Reasoning

You look at me, a question in your eyes.
I answer you and you appear surprised.
  Why?
Do you think
That I would lie?
  Not I!
Except, perhaps to spare you pain,
I might lie then. . .
Or some small thing
Like a new hat,
I might not explain
But to lie? Not I!
Lies
If one's not wise
Can boomerang
  I realize.

—*Hazel Ashton Millasich*

A Little Prayer

One night I sat down to talk with the man above
I asked him to send me someone I could truly love.
He sent many people, but they were all the same
never really wanting love, and only playing a head game.
  I got a little worried, I thought he didn't care
So again I sat down with troubles I wanted to share.
He told me to be patient and someday I would find
Someone I could love and someone who'd be kind.
  I dated around for what seemed a year and a week
And I still couldn't find that someone who made me feel
complete. Then one night it happened, you walked into the
room, I hope and I prayed that we would meet soon.
My eyes were affixed upon your beauty and grace
And that beautiful smile that light up the whole place
The time came and we could finally meet, my heart
began to throb, my knees became real weak.
It was then that I knew you would make my life complete.
  "So now when I sit down to talk with the man above
I can't thank Him enough for sending me the one I love!!"

—*Kim Hubbard*

At The Piano

Fingers slide smoothly, jump joyously
Hesitate, then span a dominant diminished chord.
My left hand thunders, thumps out octaves,
Shifts to silver seductive harmonies
That change as sunlight on a stream
While the right spins out a soothing melody.
The fingers get entangled,
Snarled on double sharps
Designed to trap the hapless;
But I don't mind the dissonance,
For in my mind I'm hearing Rubinstein.

—*Erica H. Stux*

"Why Santa Travels At Night"

It was almost Christmas, a beautiful day.
I, being a golfer, decided to play.
I grasp my club, and put a ball on the tee,
Then suddenly, I felt someone watching me.

The ball lifted off, as the club made a swish.
When I looked up, I just could not believe this!
There was ole Santa, He was coming my way.
The ball hit Rudolph, who was pulling the sleigh.

That reindeer was so mad he could hardly see.
He said to Santa, "bring that golfer to me!"
But ole Santa just laughed and quickly said, "no,
Ah, come on Rudolph, and let that golfer go.

We'll fly at midnight, so we can be alone,
When all of those golfers, will surely stay home!"
I sighed with relief, and I left in a run,
My day on the golf course, was really no fun.

I learned a lesson on that Christmas eve day
I think you should listen, and hear what I say.
If you hit a ball and it goes out of sight,
You better be sure, it's not Christmas Eve Night!!

—*Evelyn Busby*

My Mind

I'm big, I'm scary, my eyes grow in the dark.
I bet that's not what you would think
a monster would look alike.
OK, I admit it. I'm special and unordinary. I'm one of a kind.
When I was five I ate my brain.
A few weeks later I lost my mind.
When I threw up my brain, they put it back in my head.
However, I still didn't find my mind.
Could it be in my hat, hiding in my hair, or just stuck between my
  teeth?
Oh...I honestly don't think it will ever be found.
My mommy said that if I lost my mind, I must be going mad.
Yet I'm not mad at anybody, I'm just simply sad.
Could my mind be lost forever? Will it ever come back?
I don't know about you, but I think this is worth another check.
The last time I checked, I checked everywhere.
Under my nails, in my nose, even in the mid air!
I've been looking, and looking, looking all my life.
Yet, I just now realized, that I don't even know
what it looks alike.

—*Dobi Zalewska*

Untitled

Master of my mind,
  I call to you
I ask you for your help,
  for you know that I am blind
Point out to me the things that I must do
I know not where to go
So I must ask for you to help me,
That my heart and mind mind grow
I believe you in the things that you have said
I'm open to you and ready to be lead
Guide me wisely, oh master of my mind
Open up my eyes, for you know that I am blind

—*Dani Dennis*

Mother

Moma, Mother, Mom - no matter which I say
I can always count on her night and day

She's my very best friend
On her I can forever depend

She teaches me what's wrong and what's right
Her smile is always sunshine bright

She always provides for me within reason
Even if sometimes I think she's teasing

She's more beautiful than the prettiest rose
As she does my hair with lovely bows

For all she does for me, I will always love her so
I never, never want to let her go

Now I know why God lets me see
Why He gave my Mom to me

She's more precious than my favorite lucky charm
She's my very best friend - she's my Mom

  —Joy C. Moss

The Trap

They've slammed the door and turned the key;
I can be as mad as I care to be;
I can laugh and shout and cry and rage,
No longer in society's cage
Where it's: 'Work. Be serious.
Don't laugh. Don't cry.
Conform, you bastard,
Until you die.'
The world is mad. In here, I'm free
At last. I'm able to be me.
But wait! They've heard me laugh and shout
And come with drugs to put me out.
They'll use their pills and shots and potions;
Here, too, to stifle my emotions.

  —Betty Joyce Grossberg

Our Unborn Child

As I carry you so deep inside,
I can feel myself swell with pride.
To think your dad and I were filled
with our deepest love,
Now you are being sent to us from our
Savior above.

The days seem long, but the time is near.
We can hardly wait to hold you, Dear.
To see your face and stroke your hand,
The wait is almost more than we can stand.

I know you are so lovely,
Because you are your dad's and mine.
We will always love and protect you,
Until the end of time.

Until the day you decide to come,
We will welcome you with open arms.
We will love you each and every day,
And guide you in the only way —
God's way...

  —Leah Brown

Thinking About You

Looking out across the ocean
I can only imagine you here with me,
I am hoping to see you Real soon
So I can tell you how I truly feel.
Talking on the telephone,
Only limits what I can say.
But seeing you in person,
I would have it no other way.
You make me smile like no one else has
When you tell me you really care.
Walking hand in hand along the shoreline,
Whispering secrets for me to hear.
Hearing you talk and seeing you smile,
Makes me feel so good inside,
Because I know you'll be there with me
Through the good and the bad times.

  —Kemberley Wheatley

Untitled

Where have you gone?
I cannot reach your heart.
Your love eludes my grasp.
I stumble, lost, unleashed from its hold.
Where have you gone
that our minds do not flow
together?
Your soul flies above the treetops.
I cannot reach it.
I am bound to the earth.
Where have you gone,
that your absence leaves me
dying
(slowly)
alone.
Where have you gone
that I cannot touch your heart?

  —Jennifer R. Sidlo

Conception

I stole you from a ferocious father.
I coaxed his seed into my soul
and nurtured it with all the love
of one drowning in an ocean of unconcern.

Cold and damp, the chill wind of nonexistence
burned deep within a broken heart.
I almost lost you in my steamy self-denial,
sinking deep within the whirlpools of forever.

Yet somehow, within my profundity, your spirit
quickened a passion that burned within.
The enormity your existence
would ignite fires of continuity.

We are one outside the existence of others.
Our blood is bound by intricacies of illusions.
I exist within your image,
even as I conceived you within my own.

I sold my soul for a spirit I never owned.
I gave to you my gift of life
and long for you to live it
in a lyric I have never learned.

  —Anita Lee Daniels

My Walk

I was walking down a lonely road, how wide
    I could not tell
  The road so broad, the road so wide,
    It would lead me straight to hell.

And then one night with troubled heart
    upon my knees I knelt
  'Twas there that night upon my head
    A precious hand I felt.

He lifted me from that awful path
    I'd traveled for so long
  And set my feet on solid ground
    and cleansed me of all wrong.

Sometimes I pause to just look back
    at where that I have been
  Then I realize if I look back
    It's just a place of sin.

So I look ahead instead of back
    to the light that shines for me
  The light of love, the light of grace
    of His Majesty.
      —*Dave Wyche*

Departing White Emperor City At Dawn

As the sky grew lighter with the dawniest colors,
I could tell that something was going to happen.
The radiant white clouds started to appear.
I dashed out of the WHITE EMPEROR CITY AT DAWN,
I got there in a day was I tired or what,
I could hear the monkeys chattering on the huge cliff,
There was no end to their bawling.
As the light boat slipped past the 10,000 mountains,
I could tell that everything was alright.

    —*Darshana Shah*

Last Sunday Night

I was sitting in church, one Sunday Night,
I couldn't understand, why my feet were so light.
I pat my foot to every tune as I stared toward the moon.
I sang songs, I never sang before,
and I asked, Lord, can't we sing just one more?
My hands shook, and chills ran down my back.
I wanted to move, but Satan wouldn't cut me any slack.
I was scared and confused too,
when a voice said, My son, do as I tell you to do.
I walked down the isle, knowing everyone would see.
I cried, Lord, give me the strength and place your hands on me.
I prayed for forgiveness and the cleansing of my heart.
And I asked God to show me how my life could have a new start.
As he touched my heart and washed away my sin,
I knew I had a life long Friend.
I fell on my knees and began to pray, these words I heard Him say.
Sing praises unto My name and tell of My love.
Tell of the home I have built in Heaven above.
Go now and tell of your delight,
for I laid my hands on you last Sunday Night.
    —*Jerry D. Allen*

Broken Heart

Love is blind, and only you could see,
How I care for you, but you only hate me,
I see you in the hall, and then
you turn away,
Only if I could be with you night and day.

The day has come for us to part,
Even though you're still in my heart,
I think of you everyday and night
Only wishing you were holding me tight.

    —*Kelly Stallard*

Love Me

I remember talking to so many today.
I cried for I hurt from the pain within.
I have reached out to others, saying:
Love me, just love me.

I had a long talk with my friend.
She gave me a hug then said, "I'm sorry."
Yesterday my father, my best friend, died.
He was buried today, he loved me.

Today I was told to leave, to get out.
I am only sixteen, I have no place to go.
This is my father's home, I said.
"Not any more, go, just go."

I asked my aunt if I could live with her.
She said no in a kind way.
I sit here on my bed wondering what I should do.
When I hear a gentle voice say:
You are my child. I will go with you.
I am the spirit of your father.
I love you.
    —*Shirley Gillum*

The Tree and Me

While standing under a tree one day,
I decided that tree and I are similar in some ways.
From a seed, it sprouted out of the dark, warm ground,
From an egg, I developed inside of my Mom.
The tree grew, and I grew, we both were getting strong,
Branches for it, and I had arms.
The tree had leaves, and I had hair,
To keep us from looking so very, very, bare.
The tree had roots, that are very, very, deep,
I have roots also, "Gee, isn't that neat!
The tree needs food in order to stay alive,
I need food too, in order to survive.
Like the tree, sometimes we are alone,
Until the birds come back, and from college, I go home.
The tree grows old, and so do I,
Eventually, we both must die,
See, how similar we are inside.
The Tree and Me.
    —*Crystal L. Roberts*

My Dream Of Love

When you first smiled at me,
I didn't know what it was.
But it was like a streak of lighting,
and this was because.

It was like it was just you and me,
Above the clouds and skies, together,
With no one in between,
I have felt this way forever.

I know our relationship isn't the best,
But we can try to make it better,
To me this is the biggest quest,
That we can face together.

Will we stay above the stars,
for awhile longer.
And touch the forever bright Mars,
and make our love a little stronger.

Or will we go back to our earth,
When our dream is forever gone.
And not give our love it's chance of birth,
Ending like the sunset meeting the dawn.
    —*Courtney R. Snell*

174

Death of the Cherub-Like Kitten

Outside, the rain is falling into its past.
I do want this black dawn to continue.
In the bedroom,
an area of winding sheets cave in.
The spring day was turned to ashes
angels flew over the city
angry enough to behead the world.
They carried away my words of rage
-their nourishment?
The cherub-like kitten, and myself are one
with angels who fail.
I didn't even want to look at its innocent,
forgotten body, its brave, little fight lost
over life the same life, the whore
who now fornicates with those who abandoned
its gracefulness to death.

—*Gladys Zaldivar*

Dark Women

Being a dark women is what I am I
I don't go by names like sallynorsam
Because I'm a Dark women and that's what I am
My words are always coming out wrong
Sometimes I stand to tall or to strong
There's two sides to me that I can see
One is dark and the other is light
One is morning the other is night
One is wrong one is right
One is Blind one has sight.
Love doesn't come easy for me
I stand as strong as a tree
Because I'm a dark women that's me
My soul stands alone and free.
It's very reveled unlike me.
Because I'm a dark women that's me
Dark, dark, women that's me!!

—*Lauren Pellicci*

Something

Something: Something is carrying me on.
I don't know what it is.
Only time will tell when and where I should go.

Something: Something is telling me I will be safe.
Just something, in my soul makes me believe'
Of where it might take me.

Me is all I have and I will struggle on.
May it be, in the night alone,
Or the day alone I will carry on.

Something is carrying me on.
It is telling me, to be strong;
So, wherever, I may go, my journey will be worth-while.

I've travelled, and travelled, things I've seen;
Some I wish not to remember, others, I will always
Hold, in my memory.

Something: Like the love I have found along
The way. I will hold it close to me, deep, in
My soul I will always with to remember.
Something: it carries me on.
Only time will tell when and where I should go.

—*Eugene R. Zelmer*

Sunsets in the Blue Skies

Sunsets in the blue skies,
beautiful pinks, blues, and purples.
Draining off the edge of the rocky,
flat earth.
The wonderful magnetic force pulling
the sun down to a nightly sleep.
And depositing the space aged moon
In its bright place.
Scattering dreams, and spot lights
along the fading horizon.
Soothing everything to sleep.
Till the hot shining sun rises,
and sets again, and again.
Till the sun itself disappears
Into the darkness over the years.

—*Vickie-Marie F. Richardson*

"The Quest"

(Dedicated to JS)
In quest and dreams in half-light and water written
In pale rose and the glistening ring
Was your scent the censer of our guilty crusade,

You sought my body like a carnal blade
As your touch clove the wound both flesh and soul
Would our limbs weave our own brilliant armor desired,

From your mesh rose its voice its moan beneath my lips
Your mouth your hips your healing tongue
Anointed light upon the dark source of our shared redemption.

—*Will Miller*

The One That Got Away

A coyote hunt late one night,
Left us in an awful plight;
And gave us all one hell-uv-a fright.

We were sitting on a buicks hood
Shootin' at anything we could
And raisin hell like anyone would.

Well then ole trouble took his toll
And down off that fender we did roll.

We scooped up gravel, not to say
That damned ole coyote got away.

—*Maggie Burns*

Candy And Gum

I have a candy in my mouth,
Its flavor is butter rum.
I'm having trouble eating it
Because I'm also chewing gum.

You may wonder how I do this,
It takes a certain knack.
But it makes one thing interesting,
That's my in-between meal snack.

I shift the gum from east to west,
And the candy from west to east.
I really have lots of fun
With this tiny feast.

East is east and west is west.
I hope never the twain shall meet.
Because then I'll have crunchy gum,
And that's no good to eat.

Why do I look so glum?
I caught my candy in my gum!

—*Brian W. Browne*

"Borrowed Angel"

We borrowed are "Special Angel" she was called "Angela."
Because she was our "Angel" - when Angie was 5 years old.
She played with the kids next door - she's get tired.
Come in the house say Mommy I can't play anymore.
She would walk and talk to "Jesus" down to.
Church on this old country road - she'd tell Jesus Mommy.
Called me Angelica - I was her "Special Angel" through.
She was 5 1/2 years-old - her little heart grew tried too.
Doctors said they could fix it but our little Angelica died.
We prayed to God to save her, but are prayers were all denied,
but God had his special reasons for taking her from our side.
God whispered to me that day - I'm going to take "Angie" to
heaven for "Angel's" are hard to find-
Right before she left us this is what she had to say.
Mommy I'm going to heaven with Jesus.
So please don't worry about me - I'll pick Jesus flowers.
Swim in his rive of blue - I'll set on Jesus lap and tell him
How much I really love you. Mommy it's very important for you
to trust in Jesus too. So when in heaven with Jesus we both
will wait on you. Jesus please Jesus let her pick the flowers.

—*Marguerite Facemyre*

Love Forever And Always

My light shines in the sky of little Jesus,
of my mind, in the sky where Jesus and Mary and God is,
and where we are yes in Heaven with Great Grandpa,
and Mama, Hudson and Angie, up in heaven with the
stars and sky - the moon at night will shine in his eyes
Mary up in heaven will live with Jesus and God,
every time I see Mehlinda and I look in her eyes
I will cry with the tear dropping from my eyes,
of my Dad will be happy, and my love with me a baby
with my mom holding me in her belly I am grateful,
Jesus with my love in the heart with one 5 years old
in the sky, Jesus love me yes I know for the Bible
tells me so. Little one to Him belong they are
weak but He is strong yes Jesus loves me the Bible
tells me so.

—*Tawnya Lee Ann Facemyre*

"Tried and Convicted"

Without a jury he stood on his own,
No honorable mentions, no emotion shown.
They tried and convicted a helpless man,
Just trying to get by, the best that he can.
He used a bottle as a means of escape,
His problems were gone, until he did wake.
But because of his actions stones they did throw,
Hurting a man that nobody did know.
A man who is loving, is honest and pure,
But who had a problem no one could cure.
He saw his life crumble and shatter,
But to those who judged it did not matter.
All he wanted was to live his life,
Have a daughter, love his wife.
They tried and convicted his faults and mistakes,
But he's only human and love's what it takes.
Love someone for who they are,
Not for what they've done and they'll go far.
Don't try and convict try to give help,
You never know it might be YOURSELF.

—*Dawn M. Stinson-Colean*

Hunter's Haunt

I have walked with gun across my shoulder
Along an ancient road around hill...
Three crumbling caverns, old and growing older,
With constant-dripping water never still.

I have walked a road grown high with grasses;
It bends around an old abandoned mine.
The wind from off the river slowly passes;
The yellow broomsage marches in a line.

I have watched for rabbits in the thickets,
And heard the bushes dripping in the rain.
A broken fence, with scattered warping pickets,
Surrenders to the creeping weeds again.

I have walked with gun across my shoulder,
And left it there, as luckless hunters will.
And often have I been the one beholder
When yellow broom came marching up the hill.

—*Burl Bredon*

Ships Of Fate

I stood alone upon the pebbled beach
And watched dim ghostly ships shrouded in grey
Steal silently away from harbour, quay,
Ships of fate sailing beyond the reach of time.
I knew a story they could teach,
As I watched them from the lonely shore that day
Merge into night's dark mystery away,
And felt their loss my aching heart impeach.

Even as you and I, with hands entwined,
Before a solemn altar exchanged rings,
And tossed the glorious bouquet to a friend,
Turning our backs on all we left behind,
To sail into an unknown sea, that sings
With hope and love, until the sunset ends.

—*Lucille M. Kroner*

The Gathering

We met there relics of contracts wars
huddled against the winds of indifference
remembering one who left our tattered
ranks.

He was avalanched, as we, on the floods of
paperwork, calculators, machines, data
while the currents of compassion, flowed
past doors never opened.

We strewed flowers of remorse, as we
eye clutched each other at the soon
to be forgotten land, that became
your home.

We withdrew, our steel insulation,
not blocking out thoughts of our
morality.

We will gather again.

—*John Kirkhoff*

Untitled

He's walking up the calm countryside road
Golden-red trees arch up from either side of him
    Creating a barrier
    Blocking his sacred view of the sky
As a stray breeze swirls the leaves at his feet
I watch the hero of my childhood lore
    Hunch his shoulders
    Searching for warmth

Alone

The breeze strengthens
    Red leaves of anger
    Purple leaves of law
    And dead, crackling leaves of guilt
Swirl around his strained figure
And I want to cry out
    Do I cease to exist
    Once the expenses are too great?
But the wind is top loud
And I don't know if I mean it
    —Brandi Reissenweber

Love Game

Life was smooth
Like champagne and peanut butter
until
one rainless afternoon
you looked my way
your foolish wistful attempts
to capture my sheltered essence
faltered and failed
but
time diffused perceptible awareness
and hours days years blended into oneness
life sang a cantata of pure brilliant reality
my existence became yours
oblivious of other worlds
heartwhelmed that surrender of identity
when
love was merely
a pretense
    —Carole Ann Parsons

The Flower

I saw a flower growing, in a crack along the wall.
I stopped to gaze in wonder, at this fragile thing so small.

It dared to raise its tiny head and spread its pretty bloom,
and all it asked of anyone was just a little room.

It grew in silent splendor, unaware of grief and strife.
It never knew the greed and pain, that man creates in life.

While man continues in his quest for all that he can gain.
The flower grows there patiently waiting for the rain.

It asks naught of anyone, yet its beauty freely gives.
and in spite of man's pollution, the tiny blossom lives.

So when we leave this life on Earth, who can say who really
won? Man, in search of greater things? Or the flower in the sun?
    —Francis L. Graham

Untitled

I get around
  and so does my writing
    —John Mazur

A River's Lore

The churning liquid sterling
slowly bubbling-ever brewing;
mumbles secrets of the willow
passing tales of forgotten lore.
Vastness spreading the silver sterling
Never ceasing,
Never learning,
Never knowing of its origin,
always seeking forgotten lore.
The Alder's desperate for the answers,
gathering hope among his branches,
but foaming pearls are all he bores.
The moon's gloating, gleaming-
gently taunting at the shore...
he's the one that knows the answer,
the silent knowledge
of forgotten lore.
The river's muffled curing-
haunts forever more.
    —Jill Carbone

Carriage Ride

The horse mane was trimmed with bows
She might have been stuck up who knows
The coach was black with flowers of yellow
And the coachman was such a nice fellow
As Madame went out the door
She knew the ride was going to be a bore Madame
sighed deeply and she approached the coach unhappily
The ride was bumpy and long
From where she rode she could hear the church bells
Ding - Dong Madame took these trips to flatter her Father
But if it was up to her, she wouldn't bother
She would rather be with her monsieur
Because he is the one she adore
She thought about the night before
When they snuck out through the servant back door
With monsieur was the only time she was happy
But she had to please her poor old pappy
She was happy when the ride had ended
Because her and monsieur had planned a day that was splendid
    —Katrina Henderson

Lady Cocaine

She's white, but not prejudiced
Virgin, but not pure
Friendly, but deadly.

She's warm and exciting.
Although she is easily used,
she is very possessive.

She asks for only one chance
to prove herself worthy,
Then she moves in for the kill.

She has no preferable choice of sex
For her deadly portion
adheres to whomever she seduces.

Men, women, boys and girls
will kill for a sniff of her substance,
and then crave for more.

When she is snorted into the body
she can't be seen, but is always there
destroying her victim, endlessly.

Cocaine is quite a lady. She leaves an indelible impression
on the brain, the mind, the body and soul.
    —Mable Duffie Mitchell

Mother's Day Tristesse

I raised four precious children
I bless them name by name,
No cards, no telephone calls
But I love them just the same.
So...
I'll pin a white carnation on
A notion now thought queer
And at the mother's mass I'll pray
To honor my old dear.
I'll buy me a few flowers
To take to my small room,
And dream that I'm a mother
This family afternoon.

—*Madeline Guilli*

Spring

It's Spring, it's Spring, I know it's Spring,
The Johnquills bravely face the rain
Their cups are filled to overflowing.

I've heard the little peeper frogs,
They've worked their way up through the bogs,
Cheering on the north bound geese to where they are going,

A meadow Lark with golden throat,
Announce each day with happy note
and mother cows by babes are softly lowing,

Oh yes, it's Spring, I know it's Spring
I see it now in everything
There was just no turning back for all the green things growing.

—*Mabel O. Smith*

Struggling Fish

Lost battle.
Struggling fish.
Black waves,
oily streams.
Sounds of hell.
Fins try to move.

Struggling fish.
Stormy purple sea.
No surface above.
Broken corals.
Snaky eels with confusing tails.
Rusting cans of Pepsi cola.

Struggling fish.
Medusa's song from depths,
fear around.
Pain of splitting Mermaids' tails.

In my days
sorrow spills into my mind.
Then I am,
a struggling fish.

—*Sara Nadiv Soffer*

"Rats In The Fast Lane"

I hid myself in a chariot of steel
Which flew on black rolling wings.
I did not see the creamy clouds
As they sipped silvery zephyrs from apricot oaks.
My rumbling steel belched tainted perfume
And masked the crimson sunset from my bloodshot eyes.

—*Walter D. Sweet*

Nursie, Nursie

Nursie, nursie, help me quick!
I ain't sure, but I think I'm sick!
Fix my throat and rub my back—
I sure hope you're not a quack!

My arm - she hurts; I think it' broke.
Why, I might even have a stroke!
Hurry, hurry - wrap me up.
I feel as sick as that ole pup!

My tooth she aches; I can hardly see;
My ears they hurt and - ow! my knee!
Please, oh please, get your pills
And settle for once all my ills.

My belly aches - I ate too much.
My neck I can hardly touch.
I'm just plumb miserable all over.
Hurry, or I'll be under the clover!

I've got flat feet and bow legs too;
I've got knock-knees and pains brand new.
Oh nursie, nursie, to you I tell
All my troubles, so get me well!

—*Walter R. Cecil*

Garden Of Stone

The direction of the eye
 so very quick
The direction of the soul
 so very quick
I don't question
 our existence
I just question
 our needs in life
After all is done
I am still alone
I won't be taken
But I will still go
I walk with my hands bound
I walk with a bloody face
And I walk with a shadow of my flag
Into my garden of stone.

—*Aaron Boles*

What A Tear

A liquid form of soul innocent and pure,
Born to die when emotions stir,
Never looking up to see the face of its maker,
Simply slipping away separating giver from taker,
Quite possibly the most precious thing on earth,
Yet not for sale and owned by everyone since birth,
Frowned upon by many suggesting its parent weak,
Not seeing the mountain of emotion rather a bothersome leak,
With each salty trail we are carried further away,
Closer to the heart where the fountain of youth lay,
To witness ones creation is to be truly blessed,
Savor that moment and be thankful it wasn't missed.

—*Aaron A. Arthers*

On Top Of The Mountain

On top of the mountain close to God,
how free I feel.
 On top of the mountain close to God,
how pure the air, how soft the clouds, how
sweet the angels sound.
 On top of the mountain, I can see farther
than ever before.
 On top of the mountain I am one with God and
one within myself.
 On top of the mountain I am free!

—*Linda A. Attanasio*

Thought Pattern

The tinkling crash of shattered rules
was ever music to my ears,
for I was wisest of the fools
who gaily bathed in falling tears.

Some splendor and some slight renown
were fleeting as a comet's trial.
One freezing glimpse of fortune's frown
condemned me into deep travail
as quakes shake mighty structures down.

Now deadly thoughts of wasted years
peal bleak enough to numb and blind me,
and every forward view appears
to show my future far behind me.

Glory and wealth are slaves to health,
and when a lordling grows infirm
no less than paupers does he squirm
at keeping trysts with wake and worm.

—*Edwin B. Weissinger*

Eudaemonic Net Worth

Although not mentioned in Forbes' latest list,
Or earth's most wealthy men, I curb a sneer
At names included there, whose wealths consist
Of dollar credits, while my blessings near
Desire's apex, above all banking count.
My asset list ... (one more would be excess)
Begins with health: the four-score large and free
Enraptured years I've had of living well surmount
The sum most men can dream of or confess.
What's more, I've found a perfect place to dwell—
Five sylvan acres ... firewood, fruit and vine,
A time-tried pampering spouse, deep, debt-free sleep,
Five loving dogs — all these combine to keep
My wealth accruing past all measurement.
Compared with me, Don Trump's an indigent!

—*Edwin B. Weissinger*

So Hard To Pin Down

Wags' loose tongues—snoopy neighborly minds close in—on sin
Miss Emily said—"Poetry" made her so cold no fire could warm
Her yet a Boston Brahmin claims she slept with Her in-lawed
sister yet a midwest professor says Her secret love was a
Philly clergyman if you compare Miss Emily and Sir Sam to
them—for Romance lives Heloise and Abelard of France shrink to
Lilliputian tiny size— Her older brother Austin and Mabel
rocked Amherst—linked likewise He—Amherst College
Treasurer—she the local Astronomer's wife with
justification—You wonder where the ruckus went wrong that
vulturous biographers flocked Her roadside kill—ate alive Her
song—far few facts fit justly the Memory we readers rely on
and hate dirty scenarios of our American Icon with capital I
Miss Emily Elizabeth Dickinson—pre-eminent poet
worldwide—Yes
Shakespeare the Bard bows—Celebrities only Romance writers
create but writers—they wrote—now someone tells lurid tales
about these Saints—both bards subjected to intense
scrutiny—
the facts wait so hard to pin down—but Miss Emily
said—Poetry
is only real if what she read took off the top of Her
head—an
Editor laughed

—*Bill Arnold*

Garden Of Life

In my dream last night, I saw a garden of breath taking
delight
splashes of color spilled across the land within my sight.
From shoot to blossom, and then to seed went the dance,
as I watched, I realized my dream wasn't by chance.
God's special garden was here for me to view,
at first everything appeared to be beautiful and new.
I heard a voice say "Look this garden grows as a mirror on
life."
Seeing the garden in another way, I saw some grow with ease
and some
with strife.
There were plants with beautiful blossoms and seeds,
some withered as they began to fade, and others were just
weeds.
Watching now the garden continued to change,
something happened which seemed very strange.
Stricken plants were at random ripped from the soil and sand.
Vacant unfilled jagged holes spotted the land.
I couldn't help but wonder what was happening to these
plants?
Gathered at random, torn from the soil, was it just chance?
The voice now spoke again as I heard it say,
These I've selected to join me this day."
"They now live, transformed into perfection forever."
As I awoke and understood all life to revere.

—*C. S. Roberts*

Paradise Or Bust

It's a long road to paradise, too long for most who try. It's
full of evil temptations that promise an easier life. I've
taken an easier road once myself, only to find it isn't an
easier life you find just the one of pain and sorrow you tried
to leave behind. You'll know they are leading you to the wrong
road when they promise you all the glory you've never known,
but if glory is all you seek then you're going to be left
behind. If you decide this isn't for you, you must find your
way back to the road you left in hope of a compromise. It gets
harder to find your way back to this road every time you try.
You will be traveling this road alone most of the time. Most
do not have enough lasting faith you will find. The evil ones
will tempt you saying "Travel our road our company is many."
Just remember my friend when you have come to the end, your
company may be few but GOD is with you!

—*John R. Leos III*

Torn Love

The black dark hole I couldn't see
was not a stranger to me.
I knew the touch, as he opened up
and put the pain right thru me.

My heart shall ache, my eyes will tear
the pain is overwhelming
He's robbed my soul and cut my heart,
and left my body moaning.

Rage has filled me up I fear
It's very lonely deep in here
He's taken someone's love away
The one I thought would always stay.

Her smiling face is in my mind
and death can't enter in here
it keeps me strong to know I'll find
the grandma's love she left behind.

And in the end it's safe to say
not to all, just some
that I will win on judgment day
and love will over come.

—*Debra A. Forsman*

179

Darkness And Light

Tempests roared,
Torrents gushed:
Billowing sea
Towered above
With monstrous gobs
To swallow up
The sodden shores.

Two frazzled fishermen
Tossed up and down
Struggled hard
To keep afloat:
But the surging surf
Sucked them down.

Tranquility.
Rippling wavelets
Sparkled in the morning rays
And fragrant breeze whispered by.
The sharp shrill notes
Of a new-born babe
Echoed from the banks.

—*P. A. Variath*

Reflections

I need not look outside to see
The butterfly on my favorite tree,
For God has through my mirror lent
Reflected rays the sun has sent.

I need not go to outer space
To have experience of His grace,
For every day I start anew
In spite of all the ills I do.

I need not go to foreign lands
To preach the good works of his hands,
For gazing not, my neighbors see
The God I serve manifest in me.

I need not live a hero's life
For everyday I combat strife!
And every night before I sleep
I view the harvest which I reap.

I need not see Him face to face
To prove the facets of His Grace:
For there! 'tis writ on every face -
Differences innumerable - but yet a trace!

—*John S. Tait*

A Walk In The Valley

As I walk thru the valley
I can see the wild rose buds
apple blossoms and clover
Spring is here, Winter gone for a season
Everything around me is clean,
bright and beautiful
I sense the presents of Our Lord
It is plain to see His hand
has touched everywhere
Like the gentle stroke of the artist brush
Like the gentle hands of a gardener
We plant our seeds
He prunes and shapes
We have only to ask to receive
the touch of the Masters Hand.

—*Charlotte Anne Davis*

Life

Life is full of ups and downs
No matter where you go
Just turn the corner and there they are
The troubles you wish wouldn't show.

Wish you could have a miracle
To ease your heavy mind
As each day goes by
They are much harder to find

Just say a little helpful prayer
For all that is on your heart
And soon a great miracle will come
And the troubles will fly apart.

Yes, life is full of struggles
For each and everyone today
So keep a happy smile and pray
And soon you'll smile your struggles a way.

—*Debby Larsen*

Friendship

My gentle friend hold back your tears,
No more crying, No more fears.
Soft little patters of the rain,
Open your heart, Tell me your pain.
You are my friend,
I care for you so I want to be there,
wherever you go.
I know you are hurting,
It's sad but so true,
I just want you to know,
I'll always be here for you.

—*Emily Steinbauer*

Daddy's Girl

Where did you go?
No more mornings
filled with laughter...
animated face, love glow.
My memories thirst for more.

Tiny rays warm the heart
with smiles that never go away.
These are the things
I no longer know.

Dr. Seuss before bed...
We snuggle and squeeze.
Silently, I weep
and wish we were one.

—*Jon K. Mills*

Footsteps In Your Mind

You said you felt so empty,
You were always so alone.
You said you hoped that someone
could fill your heart of stone.

When darkness came to haunt you
and sleep refused your soul,
your heart cried out for someone
but misfortune took its toll.

When footsteps in your mind
were all that you had found,
you searched to find the answers
but you couldn't hear the sound.

—*Heather McKinnon*

Dreams In The Past

Yellow sand on my tongue
Not a drop of rain to spare
The sky of light to lead
Children follow in fear

With courage of the few,
The ones to lead go further
Unbelieving of my past,
I join the other members

Through the endless pain of life,
The days become much longer
With too much guilt and torture,
The sun grabs just another

We create the fun before we wake
Another dream another mistake
Shrieks we made the day we saw,
The past was true; to death with us all.

—*Daniel Taber*

We Wear A Mask

Would that you could look at me
Not lightly, but deep inside
Could you see what lies in there,
The secrets that I hide?

Can you see each time I smile
A teardrop I hide so well
A tortured soul that plays a part
But why, I cannot tell.

To weigh each word I utter
To myself I can't be true
Does everybody wear a mask?
Come near, let me look at you.

Let me see if in your eyes
Some curtain has been hung
So that no other mortal self
Knows the real song you've sung.

—*Doris Fontaine Sargent*

Untitled

Show me the way
    not to fortune and fame
Not how to win laurels
    or praise for my name
But show me the way
    to spread the great story
That thine is the kingdom
    and power and glory.

If we send no ships out
    no ships will, come in
And unless there's a contest
    nobody can win.
For games could be won
    unless they are played
And prayers could be answered
    unless they are prayed.
And no burden is to heavy
    to be lighten by prayer.

—*Daisy Sopigao*

i try, i tried
to find what is real.
i cry, i cried
knowing nothing can be said.
i lie, i lied
frightened by my own disbelief.
i die, i died again.

—*Bob Bari*

Troll Doll Dude

Don't wear a lot of clothes
Not trying to be lewd
But cha' got to understand
I'm a troll doll dude

Sat in the stores
For years ignored
But now we're hot
Basically adored

Once just an oddity
Now we're a commodity

They buy us for luck
Trying to win a buck
Rubbing on our locks
To increase their stocks

So what you gotta' do
For your next endeavor
Is come on get with it
Catch troll doll fervor!

—*Cheryl Ashton*

Nothing

Nothing has no feeling
Nothing has no care
Nothing has me thinking
Thinking I should be there
But where is there?
Nothing has no emotions
Nothing has no words
Nothing has me thinking
Think I've bed
But what is a lie?
Nothing has no form
Nothing has no spirit
Nothing has me thinking
Thinking I should be someone else
But who am I?

—*Jason Gordon*

The Cycle Of Life

Once young
Now old
Once happy
Now sad
Fair haired
Now gray
Once alive
Now dead
Once remembered
Now forgotten

—*Charles W. Wright*

Untitled

Light.
Water.
Wave to wave,
Dancing together.
Diamonds on silk.
I look, I dream,
I see you, I see me.
Dancing together.

—*Jason A. Hedke*

P-E-A-C-E (God's Peace)

'Twas a starry night
Now so long ago
When the PRINCE OF PEACE
Came to Earth below.

'Twas a Priceless gift
That GOD offered MAN
Whether black or white
Red, yellow or tan.

'Twas CHRIST'S LOVE FOR ALL
That HIS LIFE HE GAVE
So ALL of mankind
Could come and be SAVED.

Whey then this fighting
With heartache and pain
When love should be shown
There's so much to gain.

The PEACE that CHRIST brought
Is not far away
Just 'LOVE THY NEIGHBOR'
There's no other way.

—*Charles H. Alles*

What Have We Lost?

They took the Bible out of school
Now we have lost the Golden Rule.
The Ten Commandments can not be found
Have you seen them any where around?

We know when we do wrong
But there is no rule to keep us strong.
Men with guns are everywhere.
Why is it, that they do not care
And murder others unaware?

It seems so easy to learn to hate
Love we need to cultivate.
When you know someone did you wrong
And I know sometimes they do
Then try to follow the Golden Rule.

We used to learn these things in school
But the Ten Commandments can not be
found
Have you seen them any where around?

—*Edna Strahm*

Today

Today is a new beginning, the rising
    of a new sun.
  It is my chance to start fresh,
    and really experience
    the full beauty of life.
  Today is all I can count on
  because yesterday is past history,
  and tomorrow is beyond the horizon.

So, today I will live and share my life,
  And, I will not dwell on yesterday
    or worry about tomorrow.

—*Cynthia Nemec*

A Rose

Bloomed a rose, in all its glory,
Shattered by a rainstorm, then,
There it lay, beneath the rose bush
Back from where it's glory came

—*Havanna Allison*

My Vital Lighthouse

(Inspired by the beauty
of Lisa Ann Andrews)

My vital lighthouse
Enduring the storm
She stands alone
Glowing with grace
Casting her beauty
In a desperate look
I scan the horizon
In search of shores
Guiding to her
Shores of comfort
Shores of shelter
Shores of trust

—*John D. Pitsenberger Jr.*

Love?

Lying under the bright shadows
Of tall pirouetting trees
Vibrating to the rhythm of the wind:
Encompassed, were contagious spirits...

They were clutched in bright embrace
like magnetized souls, love-clad;
it sea engulfing the amorous whales.
I could see.

Their world lost to the world,
two infants in ethereal innocence;
the milky way, their path.
I could feel the vibration of love...

Yet, when the lassitude of the shore,
the chilly current of the rest
caught the strides in my steps
into frozen icicles

Hovering around them everywhere,
Anon, were big strands of discord
Taming the love I had left;
Entrapped in the manacles of its mundanity.

—*Benjamin Kwakye*

Baby Power

Have you ever stopped to wonder maybe
Of the awesome power of a baby
An infant sucking on his thumb
Can make a man out of a bum.

The worlds fury and it's fuss
Makes cynics out of most of us
A tiny bundle six pounds - ten
Can cause us to believe again

The majesty a baby brings
Can make peasants feel like King's
And macho men and rough, tough guys
Are softly crooning lullabies

Dance to the fiddler. Pay the piper.
Wrap your love up in a diaper
Hold him up for all to see
Your child, your joy, you destiny

—*Jack Kelly*

"It Seems Like Only Yesterday"

I'm sitting here just thinking,
of the day's gone by,
And I must confess,
A tear comes to my eye.

It seems like only yesterday,
And yet I know that's wrong,
It was many years ago,
In a past-we lived-long gone!

How sad one fleeting moment,
Etched upon your heart,
never to be forgotten,
Because you had to part.

with nothing left to dwell on,
But a fleeting memory,
of a special place in time,
that keeps haunting me.
All too soon it ended-

and time went swiftly by,
It seems like only yesterday,
When we met-and said "Good-Bye"!

—*Adeline Fleischer*

Sun-Kissed Days Of Youth

Oh, you caught me dreaming,
of the sun-kissed days of youth
of innocent love,
and holding hands to cross the street,
of sand-box days
and firefly nights,
of warm summer breezes
and the first snowflakes of winter
of endless laughter
and secrets never shared,
of breathless running
and watching clouds pass.
Oh, just the memory of it
makes me young again!

—*Misty D. Lawrence*

Rondolay

Life's a green time,
Oft between time;
In
   the
     meantime —
       Rondolay.

Day's a work time,
Oft an irk time;
In
   the
     meantime —
       Rondolay.

Night's a dream time,
Oft a team time;
In
   the
     meantime —
       Rondolay.

Death's a dance time,
Happenstance time;
In
   the
     meantime —
       Rondolay.

—*Andrea Burke*

Untitled

Old thoughts,
old dreams,
long time ago,
not forgotten.
Set aside
for rainy days
and lonely nights
when my spirit
takes flight
reliving the times
I've laughed and cried.
Sweet times,
bittersweet times,
of the past
are still the present
and the future
when I remember.

—*Iris Grossman*

Blanket

He was my warmth
on a single bed in my
rented room. Alone we lay
through the sunburned nights -
him over, surrounding
clothing me till I folded him
at dawn.
Such a protector!
The perfect companion!
Look at the bed now- without him
see how cold and naked I am
and I don't even have shreds.

—*J. A. Dunne*

Untitled

As I lie here
On my bed
I look back on the puzzle
Of my life
I take each moment
Each event
And place them together
Until finally
A picture is formed
No longer are there
Oddly configured pieces
But a beautiful picture
Of a mortality I have experienced
Yet
The picture still
Is incomplete
One last piece is missing
Death
Death is the last piece
Of the puzzle

—*Jeremy M. Nihiser*

The Ivy Plant

There's a little plant of ivy
On my window sill, today.
It speaks of joy and comfort,
Without a word to say.

The world outside my window sill
Is cold, and friends are few
But this little plant of ivy green
Restores my faith anew!

—*Beulah V. McKnight*

To My Friend

To a friend
on sweetest day

The love you give me
will forever stay - in my heart

The comfort I feel
when I'm with you
will never stray

The tenderness of your touch
will always be soft

To my friend
who has never let me down

To my good friend
who makes me smile
and not frown

To my very good friend
who loves me
no matter what I do

To my best friend,
I LOVE YOU.

—*Christy Manley*

Consolation

Summer came and fled away
On wings bound for winter.
Winter sings its melody high
Covering fall in vast whiteness.
Come, sweet spring - your breath I miss!
O summer, where are you?
Seasons unceasingly flow.

Yet visible above
And ever unchanging
Stand the stars, the moon
Unhindered
Against inconstant earth.
O sweet comfort of the skies
Heavenly boundaries wide
Patterns evidently woven
Invariable throughout the years
Remind me of God's steadfast love
And births my consolation.

—*Carol Urman*

Waiting For The Ship That Never Comes

Waiting in the dawn,
on your lonely boat,
in a sea that leads to nowhere,
for the ship that never comes.

Waiting in the light,
on your lonely dock,
in a land you cannot see,
for the ship that never comes.

Waiting in the dusk,
on your lonely beach,
in a bay that's non-existent,
for the ship that never comes.

Waiting in the dark,
on your lonely harbor,
in the fog that never lifts,
for the ship that never comes.

—*Daniel Delorey*

Dark Candle

All alone, quiet in the night
One candle, lit low
Giving the only light
Shadows, Moving with the glow
The only seen sight
Is the flame, burning slow

Silence, surrounds like screams
Darkness, hiding all tomorrow's
Fading, lost childhood dream's
Enclosing, into self sorrow's
Black, stealing light gleams
Night, candle flame borrows

Life is the same, as we know
For one's light, is another's darkness
What may seem, as one's glow
May be conceived, one's black, in harness

—*Gerald F. Hinkle*

My Mind

They split my mind in two.
One, they gave a name,
The other, a room,
And with divine eyes,
They said,
"This is all."

But with my tiniest fingernail
I picked my way through.
And when I saw light
I knew
I could find my name.

—*Darice Evans*

Song Of A Vagrant - On The Highway

What is eternal?
Only the sun
before me,
but I never catch it.

What flies passed?
Not scenery,
but glowing time
more beautiful than flowers and jade.

Truly, we are no more than
travelers
in this world.

My fortunate friend,
you need not roam about
like I do.

The place you are going
you know
where someone who loves you
waits day and night
with a wide open heart
for you.

—*Jim Zhang*

The Berlin Wall

When the wall went up
The tears came down
Many tried to escape
Many were injured
Many were killed
When the wall came down
The tears came again
This time, of happiness.

—*Janel Attig*

Soul Possession

Your eyes
Opaque windows of your soul
Shadowed, tortured images in the dark.

But the drapery, pulled away,
Allows the fairer hues:
Laughter, mischief, fantasy,
Warm companions to the lighter shades
Of my own soul.

The chasm
Cluttered distance of history
Child of pain and age and choice
Hangs the drapery,
Beckoning darkness to come again.
But the darkness cannot have you.
You are mine.

—*Cynthia Wright*

If

If I can give one bit of joy,
   Or comfort to your heart,
If I can ease life's hard pathway,
   Or peace to you impart,
If I can say one kindly word,
   Or give a thought of cheer,
Then life shall be worth living,
   While I'm remaining here,
You little know the joy it gives,
   When trials sore dismay,
You seek my voice and counsel,
   To ease life's hard pathway,
It filled my heart with gladness,
   It filled my heart with joy,
To hear your voice across the waves,
   To know that you, our boy,
Had given us your burden,
   That we might humbly share,
And may you always feel that way,
   It is our ferverant prayer.

—*Edna Rush*

Mind And Heart

I cannot steal away to pray,
Or sing a song to start my day;
Yet from my bedside indisposed
I count my blessings, heaven knows.

I cannot rise to start my day,
But in my heart and mind I pray;
Whatever then, the day might bring,
That in my heart I still can sing,

I yearn to rise as others do,
My body be as good as new;
And from my bed, then walk away,
With each and every brand-new day.

I must accept what e'er will be,
In space of time, now left for me;
And from my bed, in quiet lay,
In mind and heart, I'll steal away.

—*Edmond C. Woods*

Midland Town

The year was nineteen fifty,
Or was it forty-Eight?
I was so young and pretty,
Only eighteen and so free,

But Midland town was harmony;
So quiet, so serene;
Your main street was so special,
For everyone we knew.

Yet, Thursday nights were extra,
The whole town out;
With those pay check in pocket,
We spent, and spent, and spent.
And so back home we rushed,
Our pay check not all gone.
Our doors and windows open
Play canasta and radio on.

Midland Town of Churches,
Beautiful and warm.
Did strangers overcome you?
Were your boundaries overrun?

—*Carmen Adams*

Her Name Was Carol

At the age of thirty-four
Our dear Lord opened the door.
He took her from her suffering and pain,
Never to appear on earth again.

I still cry and I wonder why?
Two years have now gone by
But I loved her so;
She was all aglow,
And it was hard to let her go.

Thru' the years there'll be many tears
Remembering all the happy years;
Her smiling face was such a grace
Her happiness she'd interlace.

With the angels she'll always be
Waiting there for you and me.
That will help to ease the pain
Until I can be with her again.

—*Isobella Burns*

Untitled

If Someday
Our world should end
Along with you
My love I'll send
I'll miss you more
Than you could know
I'll miss you more
So please don't go
In my mind
Are many fears
And in my eyes
Cry many tears
All the time
You were with me
I thought our love
Would always be
Loving, Caring
And special to
Just like all
My love for you

—*Bob Murphy*

Home Sweet Home

A fire is burning in the fireplace.
Outside snow is blowing all around.
And in the oven in the kitchen
The meatloaf is getting brown.

How nice it is being home
Smelling the burning wood
And the aroma of the meatloaf —
My - it sure smells good!

Yes, it's nice being home
During a winter's storm,
Where everything's so cozy
And everything's so warm!

I only wish the birds and squirrels
Eating seeds and bread
Could come in out of that weather
To get warm and be fed!
        —*Dorothy A. Bodfish*

People Love People

People love people in every sort of way.
People love people every single day.
People love people young or old.
People love people weak and bold.
People love people short or tall.
People love people large and small.
People love people good or bad.
People love people happy and sad.
People love people black or white.
People love people dull and bright.
People love people rich or poor.
People love people more and more.
        —*Brandi Edds*

"The Spirit Of The Soul"

A stone skips the water's surface
Pertly kissing - again, again.
The silent musical rhythm
Saturating the spirit of the soul.

Mission ends, rather quickly,
As the stone submerges into depths
That accepts it with an embrace,
And those kissed areas dissipate.

A later time, a different stream
That same lad, now full grown,
With a need of spiritual renewing
Will stoop to select another stone.
        —*C. Crawford Webb*

Untitled

so i see a bullet
piercing the skull
of innocence
A fire; torching
innocence
A flood: smothering
innocence without remorse
a single Rose in a
garden of cacti
I crY
        —*John Casarietti*

Come Little One

Come little one and stay a while.
Place your tiny hands on my forehead
And erase with your gentle fingers,
The worried frown.

Come little one, and
Let me look again at your
Beautiful sky blue eyes,
And feel the joy they bring
To my ailing heart.

Come sweet, dear little one
To my outstretched arms.
Place your beloved head
On my lap, and stay a while.
Make me believe you are going
To stay with me, forever,
That this is not a sad good-bye.
        —*Edith Broad Daniel*

Men Do Scheme

Relationships are a joke
Please excuse me while I choke
Men do scheme and that's no lie
Let's salute to them goodbye
Shoot them, shoot them, one by one
Goodbye forever, watch them run
Liars, liars, that's all they are
They aren't worth it, they're a bore
Women, women, everywhere
They will hurt you so beware!
Are you with me?
Do we all agree?
Independence is tranquility
Men are for dead
And women rule
Lets kick them out of the gosh darn school
They are too dumb to even be
Smarter than women, we all can see
        —*Elizabeth Duvall*

US

A field of stars with stripes appears
Pole top, sending heart-warming thrills.
Flashes brightly, red, white, and blue.
Glorifying green area hills.
Proud emblem of great history,
Signifies work that built success,
Freedom, liberty, despite wars,
In a place called U.S. - that's us.

Hooray! Our flag flies next to God,
Speaks much meaning high in the air.
We honor, cherish, and love it.
Lord, keep us close in our prayer.
Beacon, light of United States,
Keep high to show respect, Oh yes,
Bravery, courage, plus union,
God's people in U.S. - that's us.

Thank you, God. We're grateful to You.
Distinguished country does impress.
It's the greatest, land that there is,
Peace-loving United States - US
        —*Grace Pierce*

Spring's Song

In the spring, flowers bloom,
    popping up as they please,
Then, just in the nick of time,
    the trees regain their leaves.

The grass turns green,
    and daisies grow,
The world takes a more,
    beautiful glow.

Silently, the days warm up,
    for the sun shines it's rays,
Then, everything just comes alive,
    finally, adding beauty to the days.

Gallantly, the birds fly back,
    to greet you with their singing,
To make you happy once again,
    to hear their glorious ringing.

Almost as quick as it came,
    spring sings it's final song,
To take it's place———
    summer comes along!
        —*Danica Yoder*

Chateau

Tall green grass,
    porch swings in peace.
Roaring guitars and barefoot dogs
    dance in the dusk with
    the heavy summer breeze,
    deep with humidity
    and smells of the woods.
Laughter and songs of youth
    slip into the pages of an
    ill-written book -
    to one day be reopened . . .
    . . . questioned.
        —*Holly Bennett*

Orion

Oh mighty hero,
protector in the sky.
Older than Nero,
Above us you fly.

Great hunter from lore,
friend of the Moon.
Mightier than Thor,
yet death was too soon.

Killed by your love.
A trick by the Sun,
and their father above.
She shall love no one.

Immortal forever,
suspended in night.
The moon's endeavor,
to keep you in sight.

You can down any beast,
from a stag to a lion.
With you all could feast
Ode to you Orion.
        —*David Wayne Helba*

Footstep On The Ocean Sound

In times of Peace let music
reach the Bluebird song of
happiness. It waits upon the
shore of a rainbow as sugar
feeds a horse. Let it ride, ride
on an ocean bay looking into the
warmth of Sunset, sun of deep
love which shines forth your light.
A child hope for people of the
world to keep together join in
harmony and drumful laughter
as one. The color of time will
have nothing at lost.
Life and art brings knowledge
and party that our land bring us
back to our walk of footsteps in
the sand. As I look through ocean
blue eyes I see the world coming
together. Singing many new songs of
eternity peace of song.

—*Donna Pistilli*

"The Touch Of War"

little hands, and little hearts,
reaching out into the dark.
running hard,
from shots.
   The touch of war.
massive battles, and massive guns,
killing those who run,
until there are none.
they are just tots.
   The Touch of war.
little smiles, and little desire,
little minds that aspire,
trapped within, the field of fire.
for a touch of love, they ache.
   The Touch Of war.
the bloodless trust,
the possessive lust,
dreams buried in the dust,
with the lives it did take.
   The Touch Of War.

—*Janice A. Wyatt*

The Bible

The Bible is the Word of God.
Read and study it to be wise.
Then when Jesus comes or calls
you'll meet him in the skies.

The Bible is the Word of God.
It's the book for everyone.
It doesn't matter who you are
nor the things that you have done.

The Bible is the Word of God.
It tells us how to live,
shows us how to be happy
and also how to give.

The Bible is the Word of God.
Believing it gives you power.
So read it prayerfully every day
and think about it every hour.

—*Edna Blankenship*

"A Phone Call Away"

You get up in the morning,
Ready for the best.
Even thou your busy.
Your mind just won't rest.
I wonder? What she doing.
Is there so much on her mind.
Give, her a little call.
A word of love or praise.
And, as a reminder tell her.
I think of you each day.
You'll always be in my mind.
   as of yesterday.

—*Georgia Holt*

Take Time

I woke up one bright morning
ready to start the day.
The glow of the sun was hot
Home offered a cool place to stay.

The day grow hot and long
Sickness within me arose
I soon began to tremble with fear
And I could no longer dose.

The thought of leaving my loved ones
Ached and tugged at my heart.
For I did not take time
to cherish the moments from the start.

My heart felt heavy
A hug from my husband and boy's
I would no longer feel
or the loving words I love you.

But I knew I was not alone
God was with me all the way.
So take time to smell the flowers
And share your love everyday.

—*Donna Wetterstrom*

Holding My Lover In a Way

That lets her
really know
I howl from
the place she
has touched
suddenly poems
explode cool
blue September
green stars
thunder through
my mouth
I want
a thousand
nights like
this

—*G. Monroe*

Untitled

The tears we shed are just a reminder
Of how welcomed death could be.
If not for what we'd leave behind
a favorable retreat.
Ebb and flow, rise and fall
heart and soul entwined
Purge and rest, strength and fear
with no recourse save shed a tear

—*Gail Ann Gula*

Favorite Foods

It sticks in your mouth,
Refreshes your belly,
What else could it be,
but peanut butter and jelly!

Anchovies, pepperoni,
Pepper that makes me sneeze,
Mushrooms and olives,
It's pizza with cheese!

Vanilla, chocolate, strawberry,
Cookies and cream,
Chocolate chip cookie dough,
I love ice cream!

—*Erica Lieberman*

Untitled

Creation
remains
   life's bewildering question.
Wise fools relate
   the bang
   the crunch
   even singularity.
But whence
   the stuff of that small pea
      or
   how came
      the vast empty heaven
   waiting to be filled?
Existence.
   How can it be?
Existence.
   How can it not be?

—*C. S. Hartley*

The Art Of Love

The art of love
reverses hate
and treads the path
of soul's own fate.

To become a part
of the cosmic one
we all forgive
when hate is done.

Transcending what
we are mad about
gives us time
to mellow out.

We learn to laugh
and to understand
we only grow
when we share a hand.

—*Carolyn Ashe Stokes*

The Key

Red, White, Blue,
These colors are true.
I love my country,
This I do.

My country is free,
Free to be,
Whatever I wish,
I hold the key.

—*Brandy Sims*

Birth and Death

Dark, wet warm
Round and round floating
Pain, pressed, pushed
Tight, cold, bright
Am I here??
I don't want to be here
They don't want me here
I feel fear!!
Shivering, shaking, screaming
They scream back
Shut up brat!!
No pain - No more pressure
No more struggling
I'm floating back
Back into the darkness
Where I came from.

—*Finny J. Burns*

Forsythia

Molten gold falls in a circle
Round your feet, Lady of Light.
Sun spills a halo, surrounds you.
Golden bells sway in sweet air.
As a small child I sipped honey
From your lithe yellow cups,
Laughed, to run eager fingers
Through your gleaming blonde hair —
So fragrant, luxuriant, shining
Brightly on drab earth there.
Spring needs your golden laughter,
Spilling, thrilling through rain,
Lighting its landscape, oh lovely
Goddess of lively grace.
Spirit of sun, Golden lady,
Leave me not. Let your light laughter
Gleam and glow in the sun.
Leave me not, Golden Lady;
I have loved long, — Loved Long.

—*Doris S. Arnold*

Inner Beauty

"I am so very ugly"
Said she with that crooked smile
But it's not the outward beauty
It's that which lies within

The beauty of her smile shines forth
From out those tender eyes
Showing therein the answer
So many cannot realize

Her sweet and tender nature
So full of happy love
Blesses all she smiles upon
Like the love of God above

That heart that beats within
Holds love and sweet compassion
Helping hands and loyal heart
That God alone could fashion

So look down deep into those eyes
They surely will reveal
Whoever wins her wins a prize
Of love that's warm and real.

—*Edwin P. Spivey*

Autumn

Like leaves falling in autumn
Sailing softly through a breeze
  Is just like my heart
So soft, so light, so free.

Like the sun shining brightly
Through the bare autumn trees
  Is just like my heart
So young, so alive, so free.

Like two people walking down
Autumn chilled streets
  Is like my heart
So in love, so happy, so free.

Like looking in beautiful eyes
So colorful like autumn when they see
  Is like my heart
So caring, so mysterious, so free.

Autumn, the days of color and laughter
When all hearts feel free
  Autumn, when whispers float as freely as
Leaves through the chilled streets.

—*Angie L. Shepard*

Oceans

Oceans are big enough to
see inside
  Able to see all the creatures
that live and die.
  The form of the sunlight
shines like a Golden Nugget,
  The blue watery waves
share the great moment of life.
  Joy and Romance finds its
way of husband and wife,
Across the open sky;
  The open sky and the big ocean
blue share its memories
for the rest of your life.

—*Debbie Martin*

"For My Children"

I used to have some children -
Seems I don't have them anymore,
They all have seemed to scatter
Beyond my outside door.

Those Sunday evening dinners
Now just seem part of the past,
I guess I should have known
That Heaven couldn't last.

The years that they grew up in
Gave me joys beyond compare,
Each tender loving moment
How I wish they were still here.

My very soul - my being here
Was to see them grow each day,
And I'd give them all the guidance
They would need along life's way.

And now that they are grown
I wish for just one day,
Their little arms could hold me tight
And kiss my tears away.

—*Jerry Newmiller Beleny*

Mother's Loss

Her muffled, mournful cries
Seep (ever so persistently)
Through the paper thin walls,
  A cry of help,
  A cry of need,
  A cry of want,
As I sit and feel her pain,
  Wanting to help -
    Needing to be there.
I feel she needs her time ——
      Alone
  To want
  To love
  To miss
  To mourn ——
So I sit in quiet anguish
  And listen to her muffled
    mournful cries —

—*Debra Radish*

The Ant

I don't want to do it.
  Sharpen the blade,
  Dig with my spade.
I don't want to do it.
Take the spherical grass
  And build my house.
I don't want to do it.
Let the winter frost come
And chill my speckled heart.
  I may bruise and die
  In the seasoned cold.
  I won't prepare
For the winter's discontent.

—*George T. Vaughn*

"A Wren"

I saw a little wren today,
  she was singing lustily.
She sat proudly o'er my head
  perched our old cedar tree.
She challenged all "Gods" birdom
  her happiness to defy.
A note of greeting she warbled
  to each one as they flew by.
Whether sparrow or spunky blackbird,
  it mattered none to her.
Not even a dove or flashy cardinal
  could change her tune, "No Sir".
After formalities were over,
  her serenade began in real style.
Feathered friends were not only charmed,
  for I too listened all of the while.
When her performance was ended,
  her audience still somewhat awed.
She lifted her wings and departed,
  a real little trooper, without any reward.

—*Glenis Gilliam*

Kristy

Kristy is my kitty
She's soft and warm and sweet
She stays very close to me
Not far from my feet
If I sit down.
She jumps on my lap
Snuggles close and takes a nap
She is my sole companion
I've had her twelve years now.
She is a very special kitty
Loves no one else but me
And so I have a problem
As you can plainly see
If I should go and not come back
She would wonder why
I don't come care for her
And hold her on my lap,
And so I wonder who,
Will take care of Kristy
When I am no longer here.

—*Esther H. Hubberstey*

Untitled

Moon,
Shining down upon
Solitary rider.
Forgotten leaves
Along side the road
Dance to an unknown melody
The gusting breeze
Plays upon his body with
Sweet, stinging kisses
And the barren, childless trees
Reach to embrace him,
But his heart is not
For those cold, mysterious
Spirits of the wood.
He eludes them this night
And returns,
Blissfully unaware, to the
Realms of Man.

—*Erin Eckhart*

"Dead Of Winter?"

Pristine whiteness —
Silence —
No sign of life we see.
Wait a moment, friend of mine —
A tweaky nose behind that tree!
A rabbit's floppy ears appear —
A ball of fur leaps past!
The little cotton-tail of him
Waves as flag upon a mast!
Lift your eyes to yonder tree —
A twitching tail does there betray
Little Nutcracker on a branch,
Warm in his winter coat of gray!
And there upon the forest floor
Are footprints small and neat
Which I am sure I've seen before
In my back yard
Where bird-friends
Meet!

—*Barbara J. Currie*

Poem Quest

I wish to write a poem
Since I'm bored beyond my mind,
But the words to write on paper
I simply can not find.
I think as hard as a body can,
But the words just will not flow
And deep inside my heavy head
A poem awaits I know.
Perhaps the poem is hiding there
Deep behind my eye
Or perhaps the words just float about
Till they form a poem or die.
No matter how the poem flows
From the corners of my mind
I know if I keep writing words
My poem I shall find.

—*Drema Bowles*

The Cannibal

Big money is
Smooth and sleek and
    Silent.
as a snake.

Big money moves
    Unseen,
behind black glass
in the Fast-lane.

Big Money
Never sleeps
as a shark
    Never sleeps.

Big Money
is INC.
        and
    has no
      name
        in flesh.

—*Douglas Riston*

Thinking Only of You

Dawn falls on the ocean,
    so calm and graceful,
Birds chirp their merry song,
    so soft and beautiful,
Everything is in its place,
    nothing out of place,
Every rain drop,
    falling to my face,
I sit here in the open,
    not doing any harm,
Staring into space,
    thinking of your charm,
Daydreaming all day long,
    nothing else to do,
Just sitting on the beach,
    thinking only of you.

—*Barbara Austin*

Time

The life is best and richly blessed
that has a busy beat within it;
So let each hour bloom like a flower
and live every precious minute,
For when Today has passed away,
no second may we borrow;
Today is gone and with the dawn
we greet a new Tomorrow!

—*Evelyn Kintop*

Untitled

A dream
so distant, faraway
infinitely out of reach
it escapes our grasp
the dream
where the impossible occurs
where lifelong wishes can be
fulfilled in an instant
a mirage
ever eluding our rival
until reality is realized
we are then cruelly snatched
from that wonderful fantasy
where happiness is ever ending
our fairytale wonderland vanishes
until we dream again
to return
to that paradise
which is only
ours to see

—*Gregory Hodges*

Prayer For God's Presence

There are those spots upon God's earth
So filled with beauty, sweet perfume,
Ablaze with color, majesty,
As though God made Himself a room.

In such a place I find with ease
His presence deep within my heart,
Communion sweet and joy complete,
And of His kingdom I'm a part.

But such a bower is most rare.
Most of my days are plainly laid,
And Satan's work is everywhere...
My life a battlefield is made.

Oh, God of beauty, joy and love,
Reach down amidst life's ugliness,
And flood my very heart and soul
With Thy dear self, Thy righteousness.

—*Elizabeth Packer*

Save The Earth

Save the earth
So it won't burn
Reduce birth
Is first concern

The earth's resources
Don't abuse
Use less, reduce
Recycle, reuse

Use less gas
Don't pollute
Take a walk
Travel in a group

Save the forest
For the rain
Plant a tree
To grow more grain

Save the wildlife
Don't overuse
Give nature a chance
To reproduce

—*Anita L. Alexander*

On The Wings Of A Dove

On the wings of a dove
Soaring so high
Across the distant sky
Soaring so high to Heaven above
On the wings of a dove
Telling of PEACE and love
Love for each other
As sister and brother
Someday we will all stand
Together hand in hand
There upon the golden sand
Singing in sweet harmony a new song
Of PEACE forever long
On the wings of a dove
Soaring so high to Heaven above
Where blessed PEACE and love
Will always be found
On ever higher ground
There upon the golden shore - of forever-
more

—*Billie Jeanne James*

Something More

I look around and see so many faces
Some are familiar
But they are just faces
It make me feel so alone
It's not that I need someone to love me
Or to have fun with
But something special
Something that would fulfill me
Someone to understand me
A little something more
I can't describe it
But it's beyond comparison
To any dream I want or have gain
It's just a little something more
I need it
Yet I have no idea how to achieve it
It depresses me for no seeing where and
    what it is
I receive so much pain in search of this
    thing
Why must I go in agony
For this little something more

—*Helen Wong*

Some Are Friends

In these, the days of living time
Some are sprung back, to wake in mind
And caring not to pause for kindness
Lurking within some shrine of blindness
Through memories they're weaved and bent
And in the timeless time,
Some are friends
Need one describe their small majesty
Within the earth, within ones heart?
You can never recapture the essence,
But in time you see the art
And weaved and wound,
With reassurance to mend,
These small jewels of misery,
Yes, some are friends

—*Gracie Odonavon*

Roses

Roses are Red......
    Some Yellow, Pink and White
As you walk through your garden
    What a wonderful sight.
In the early morning hours.....
With the pedals all covered with dew.
    The first rays of sunshine
Cast a beautiful Hue.
No matter what color.....
    The fragrance of a rose
Will linger in your memory
    When the pedals are faded and gone.

—*Frances E. Dorward*

A Friend

A friend is someone you care for.....
Someone you listen to and help out....
    Someone you love
        with all
            your heart....
That is why you are the
    greatest thing
        in the
            whole
                world...

—*Juliet Alvarez*

"Trapped"

        Ding dong
Something has gone terribly wrong!
The child inside me has to get out
I cry and shout but I can't escape
        Is it too late?
        Will I ever escape?
No use to try... I'm stuck inside.
    All bottled up,
    Like a flower starting to wilt
I feel no pain, but a lot of guilt
    I'm trapped though. I haven't
        yet begun to fight.

—*Jennifer A. Heimann*

In Memory Of Nick

    A dog's love has a special glow-a
special kind of light.
    They make us smile when we're
feeling low, and makes things seem all
right.
And though they often leave
this earth long before we do-
we'll keep their love within
our hearts 'till our
    days are through...

—*Bonnie Van Deventer*

nursing home

claw hands twist with mindless anguish
squeaking empty plastic cup
plastic tag on bony wrist reads
name and numbers adding up
cheery heavy nurse from poland
pushes at the highback chair
sees the dribble smells the colon
notes the desperate vacant stare
take oh take these shining glasses
earrings teeth away have done
no more playing god with pills let
body go where mind has gone

—*John King*

The Eternal Song

Black ink
Splotched
On the brown stained paper
Of your memory book,
Grandmother.
The words
Your hands bled
At knotted knuckles
Now feed my mind.
I feel your youth
Calling across the ages;
The eternal song
Of humanity.

—*Janice Lorraine McDavit*

"Spring"

Winter's come, winter's gone,
Spring is coming like dawn,
See the sun rise in the sky,
See the birds begin to fly,
Watch the flowers as they bloom,
Look here comes the month of June,
See the days go flying by,
As the days turn into nigh,
Feel the sunlight in your hair,
Take a chance if you dare,
Enjoy the time while it is here,
For it will soon disappear,
Then you'll have the snow once more,
Then you'll have the shoveling chore,
You will soon begin to hum,
For spring is just waiting to come.

—*Angela D. Orshesky*

My Daughter

Stand, my daughter
Stand in my power
I hold your hand
In your darkest hour

Satan would have you
Sift you like wheat
I am beside you
Stay at my feet

You are special
I have placed you where
The strong winds blow
But remember, I'm there

To sustain and guide you
So never give up
Remember your Savior
Drank HIS bitter cup

I have already won
Your battle, you see
So run with the WIND
Of my SPIRIT, stay FREE

—*Evangelist Jean D. White*

Untitled

The silence of your absence
    sounds like thunder in my ears.
It hurts so much that
    it brings my eyes to tears.
To hold you again
    is one of my fervent wishes;
And, besides,
    the sink is full of dirty dishes.

—*Chester Povolo*

"The Peat Lamb"

Jam-coated, black-sooted lamb
Stands orphaned by famined ewe.
Light-binding, rock-climbing lamb
Mounts christened in nettle dew.

"From muck to luck" shepherds' bleat
Seeks suck for perishing flocks.
Sun-starv'ed, rain-sogged peat
Yields troves cupping nurture works.

Wind-ravaged, craggy jagg'd wall
Cleaves unsifted thistled field.
Hearth-crumbled, thatch-trundled knoll
Founds temple in pasture sealed.

Lamb bleeding, feeding its own,
Hosts harvest of bleatings sown,
'Thrones remnant by light impaled,
Hails daybreak in glory veiled.

—*James Edward McCurry*

Strangers

Uncaring strangers
Stare with scornful eyes.
Pierce my heart,
Strip my soul,
Judge my character.

To them I am trouble,
A waste of time,
Nothing.

They see no value in my existence,
No hope in my future,
A failure I am branded.

They know nothing of my goals,
Laugh at my dreams,
Think that I'm confused.

By them my decisions made,
My life planned,
My dreams shattered,
My name given.

—*Giselle Julien*

Distant Spring

Spring night
Stars behind the woods
Tiny lilac lanterns along the path.

Granted by a dream
The lilac petals I touch
And mix them with the stars

Believing that
The night is mine
You are with me.

But how hard to believe in solitude
When love is possible here
On this lilac path.

Spring is no one's dream
In the age of carnage,
Of exile and the homeless.

You are not here
Distant Spring you are,
The shredded one.

—*Han Misyou*

The Spirit Of The Solar Wind

The "Spirit of the Solar Wind" am I
steering a course through a gale,
blowing forth from that eternal sun
that powers my metallic sail

Outward I travel from worlds below
sailing untroddened paths alone
upon the particle trails I follow
to points and quadrants unknown

Amidst the black of space, I sail
to worlds no man has trod
riding freely before a stellar wind
as if pushed by the hand of God

I seek to explore the outer worlds,
the stars and the universe of old,
searching only for my destiny
in the sights of worlds to behold

There I am free to be myself,
to be as a spirit in the solar wind
and traverse the dimensions of time and space
on a quest that has no end.

—*David A. Rowney*

From Them To Us

Ending never
stream of movement
running blinking
flashes oblivion.
Sounds ambient
undertow dissonance
voices murmuring
times some billions.
Symbol circles
flashing flicker
like so many
dancing fires.
Silent watchers
walk among us
careful not to
let us know them.
For if too close
we will persist
then future never can exist.

—*Gregory P. Asproulis*

A Capital Offense

Lying down with killers,
Suckling at the breast,
Tissue leaking from the seams,
Plunging from my nest.

Honor. Duty. Thank-you.
Cower in the halls,
Bittersweet cyanide-dust,
Kiss my taunting walls.

Leather breathing, shortly dead,
Pulling at my eyes,
Choking on the rotten meat,
Covered now with flies.

Silent piercing echoes,
Nothing left to sell,
Faces blend together,
I was one of twelve.

—*Chantele Denae Giles*

Untitled

Jingle Bell
Suzukis smell
Honda laid an egg
Kawasaki lost its wheel
Banshee lead the way

Jingle bell
Suzukis should smell
Kawasaki ran away
Rocks flew, Honda knew
He better get out of the way

Jingle bell
Suzukis shall smell
Honda fenders flew away
Oh what fun it is to roost
Kawasaki, while laughing all the way

Jingle bell, Suzukis still smell
It happens everyday
The race was done
Banshee won
It will be no other way

—*Jacquelyn Lau*

Dream Poem

The slyly sneaking Eyes of Night
sweep slowly 'cross the darkened room.
Replaced, just now, by morning light
they leave, reluctant, with the moon.

Waking from our warm soft slumber
we see few traces of the their stay.
Hidden shadows of their feasting
in the corners darkly lay.

The eyes of night (that's all they are)
converse with souls of men asleep.
And scatter to the darkling place
When sun and light cause us to wake.

—*Hugh McDonald*

Virginia Summers

Damp nights
swollen with
the smells sweet of
the gardenia and vine rose

Moons leashed to the lions

The chill of red clay under bare feet
and the lone cricket

Never missing
a beat
a beat a beat

—*Dana E. Payne*

December Snow

Crystal is the snow that falls;
The first snow of the year
Brings laughing echoes that remind
Of days when you were here.
Crystal days you gave to me
With friendship through each one,
As diamonds kept for precious trove
On silver thread are strung.
Crystal is the snow that falls
To softly end the year,
And memories of crystal days
Are polished with my tears.

—*Christie Winter*

189

A Day Of Life

Take my hand and lift me up.
Take my arm and show me the way.
This I ask my friend to do,
At the beginning of each new day.

I'm not blind.
I know the world is mine
I see the birds,
I see the flowers.
The bees have been busy
Gathering the honey,
For many hours.

It will only be a few hours.
Across the meadows
The sun will be setting.
The birds will become still,
Darkness will once again fall on the hills.
With this I will have added.
Another day to my life,
And become another day older.

—*Betty I. Newman*

"My Love Is Like A Rose"

More beautiful and intricate
Than a folded rose
Each petal soft and delicate
How it blooms and grows!
Among the many flowers bound
To earths' rich fertile fields
It's grace and color can't be found
In ordinary yields
My love for you is like this thing
Passionate and red
It lives - expands - it takes to wing
From a nourished bed
The rose attracts and seduces
With beauty and sweet scent
It heals, it calms and amuses
With lines so eloquent
But with this beauty comes a price
For the stem is thorned
So do take care is my advice
Count yourself forewarned

—*Gregory C. Mason*

The Oklahoma Wind

Will the gusting never cease?
That blowing, twisting thing,
Which seems only to increase,
Giving everything a fling.

I'll not wear dresses,
For I'm never sure,
Is it my hem or tresses,
I must make secure?

The wind of which I speak,
Blows in every direction,
It slaps at my cheek.
'Tis almost an affliction.

Though the wind must be,
It tests my perseverance,
And I'd sign a decree,
Declaring its disappearance.

—*Carol A. LaCroix*

"A Valentine's Gift"

People may give you flowers
That have many special powers
 They may give you balloons
Everyday in the month of June
 They may send you hearts
Of silk chocolate parts
 They may send you teddy bears
With ribbons in their hair
 But all I have to offer is
Hugs and kisses full of love
 And
You can have them all!

—*Denise Carina Hernandez*

There Is Something In Your Jeans

There is something in your jeans,
that I can't live without.
I try not to think about it,
but, my life won't be fit.
I need what's in your jeans,
there is nothing I can do,
for the something in your jeans,
makes me stick to you like glue.
So, give me what's in your jeans,
please don't make me beg.
I can't get on my knee,
because of my bum leg.
I need it and how,
please don't make this a mess,
for I need the money now,
to go shopping for my dress.

—*Ann DiMeglio*

Old Pup—Old Gran

We run the place,
That is when we're not sleeping.
A half hour trip
Out in the snow and
Into the house he's creeping.

Flat on the floor
Or on his back,
A grin upon his face.
His paws, they quiver,
His tail it wags—
He's dreaming of a race:

A rabbit or coyote,
Perhaps the old brown cow.
Whatever his dream
It's a happy one,
And so is mine by now—

'Cause I'm dreaming of
Grandkids.

—*Hester A. Godwin*

Poets

Behold the upright poet,
the ragged soul of man.
Once honored
mostly in Ireland.
He had a place in the past;
whether good, or bad or last.
Now, once again he comes
to be heard, perhaps to sing,
one hundred in a lexicon castle
once more to speak and wrestle
with wisdom and history
and every kind of mystery.

—*Dorothy D. Warner*

Man

This is the final stand,
 That last day.
 It won't be long
Till man will have to pay

For destroying our earth in an
 Unmanly way.
 Does man realize
 Or does he care
That he is destroying our world
And that it's not really fair

 For the kids of tomorrow?
 What will they have?
 How will they know

What the world looked like
 Not so long ago?

—*Christie Flynn*

Love Sings

There is a spirit in everything,
That makes life sing.
In the trees and flowers:
All the earth is full of love,
Love makes things bloom:
And all life zooms:
Early in the morning blossoms open up.
Their love must come out of the air-
The rain does it's share,
We have had plenty to spare.
Love comes down from the heavens,
And spreads all around.
There is love in children's laughter,
And in every bird that sings.
Let us all capture this love-
And carry it with us, and give everyone a
hug.

—*Carolyn M. Warner*

Shells

There lies the shell
That once cradled my embryo
And gave me life to give life
My shell, I pray
Will rest with more love
Than hers
 Adieu, my Mother
He too, long since gone
They, not side by side now
Alas, he too, I found not dear
But our souls surely touched
Else, why the pain, until again
 Adieu, my Father

—*Bettye Maglaris*

Together Again?

Together again
That's my dream
It'll never happen or so it may seem.
All that we have been through
Doesn't it mean anything to you?
I see you in my sleep
Upon you my love will creep
Drifting further
Further away
Dawn and night passes another day
hours spent, up all night
Why did we have our last night
Well it's over now

—*Brooke Gaylor*

Someday Somewhere

We must hold on to the faith,
  that someday our children,
    will all live in Peace.

Someday Somewhere.

And learn obedience and respect,
  for the people who are,
    sent here to teach.

Someday Somewhere.

And they must all keep in mind,
  that eventually in time,
    things will be better.

Someday Somewhere.
I only pray,
  that we all see that day.

Someday Somewhere.

    —Dolores L. Green-Jackson

"Sister And Brother"

Quarrel, fight, and bicker
That's all they do.
Constantly, at each others throats.

Annoy, pester, and holler
That's all they do.
Constantly getting the other mad.

Sister and brother
Do they really love each other?
Of course they do.

They try so much to hide it all,
But isn't it obvious.
They love each other.

    —Christina Lineberry

Lights Of Tranquility Are Blue

Imagine a room
that's white with four walls.
The ceiling's too short;
the floor is too tall.
(lights of tranquility are blue)

Imagine a bed
with no springs nor a mat.
A frame you sleep on
of hot, silver brass.
There's a bird in the corner,
staring at you;
you're lost in its eyes
of tranquil blue.

You see with your ears,
and your hear with your eyes.
You speak with no voice,
yet it's no surprise.
(lights of tranquility are blue)

    —Crystal Luv Fox

Spring

The dog woods are blooming
The violets are out
Daffodils popping up
Here and about
The brown stems of winter
Are turning to green.
The birds are all singing.
It's beautiful Ozark Spring.

    —Hilda Ferachi

"Me, That's Who I Am"

Me,
That's who I am.
The reason why, I'm me,
Is because you are you
And I am me.

I'm glad to be me.
I've never wanted to be thee.
Just turn the key
And there's me.
I'm as happy as can be,
Just being me.

I'm as busy as a bee.
Traveled from sea to sea.
Learned a lot from A to Z.
Even climbed a tree.
Busy just being me.
Never wished to be, anyone but me.

Me,
That's who I am
And who I'll always be.

    —Carmen J. Smith

Here Where I Am

To many rivers have ran here,
  that's why I'm building the dam!

To many feet have crossed the rivers,
  that's why I am who I am!

To many problems have surfaced,
  mountains are starting to form!

I seems I'm always at the lowest point,
  and always in a storm!

I find myself in valleys,
  with no way to get out!

The rains keep talking to me,
  but what are they talking about?

Someday I wish I'd see the sunrise,
  and get out of this pit!

But until I'm over the mountain,
  in this valley is where I'll sit!

    —Barbara Ringstaff

Night Wind

The light on the path,
The brightness of days,
For the fraction of a second,
Our minds here to stay.
The perfection of a moment,
Not here to last.
For time fleets on ever so fast.
The lighting fast wind upon the leaf.
The hush at days end soft and sweet.
The summer's fleet passing,
On a dark, clouded moon.
A hot sultry day, over too soon.
Like the flash of a comet.
Summer passes, too soon.

    —Elaine Sturm

Journey

I went to the wall to find you,
  the brothers I left behind.
Your names are etched in black stone,
  they're also etched in my mind.
The lessons you taught me were plenty,
  of giving and of life.
The pain of losing you forever,
  cuts through me like a knife.

I mourn your passing, brothers,
  with each new coming night.
That I came back without you,
  somehow just don't seem right.

I try my best at living,
  the way you taught me to.
But the ghosts of my transgressions,
  make this very hard to do.

I went to the Wall to find you,
  the Soul I left behind.
To finally bring you home with me,
  is foremost on my mind.

    —David M. Stemen

The Second Time Around

Grandparents no more,
The children came to stay.
The second time around
Is cause enough to pray.

Pray for energy
Pray for patience
Pray for knowledge
Pray for time.

From grandma to mother,
From treats to rules.
No mid-winter break
We are back in school.
Pray for guidance
Pray for peace
Pray for them.
Pray for me.

The empty nest syndrome a myth,
The house is quiet no more.
It's filled with love and laughter,
Sorrow is present no more.
Pray for the children
Pray for the parents
Pray for the daughter who died
Pray for us all.

    —Emerita Phillips

Beginnings

I believe in the stripes
  The red white and blue
    The pledge and the allegiance
  I also believe in the fight
    The fight from persecution
    and the foundation

It was clear as white and black
  now shades and delusions
    The idea was lost

But preserved by some
  We must return to the Beginning
    —Ethan Worthington

Tomorrows

Nothing is for certain
  The exception being death,
Nothing is forever
  It ends with our last breath.

We all take things for granted
  A foolish thing to do,
Like there will always be tomorrow
  For us to follow through.

Don't always count on tomorrow
  Or be certain it will come,
It never does for many
  Tomorrow might be the one.

Life is so uncertain
  Just live it day by day,
Don't plan on many tomorrows
  They may never come your way.

Death is the one thing certain
  Who knows when it will call,
Tomorrows are wishful thinking
  They may never come at all.

    —Gilbert L. Hilderbrand

"The Beauty of the Four Seasons"

The beauty of the Crocus.
The First Flower of Spring.
the Daffodils and Tulips.
And the Robin's that come to sing.
The trees are full of flowers.
New buds on every tree.
Yes spring has come in beauty.
That we all love to see.
Then comes the beauty of summer.
Vacations we love to share.
Family reunions and picnics.
And Gods beauty is every where.
Then comes the beauty of fall.
Colored leaves on every tree.
God paints a pretty picture.
For everyone to see.
Then the beauty of winter
White snow has covered the ground.
The beauty of Christmas season.
Will soon come around.

    —David L. Knepp

President

Listening to our president
the other night could see he
was going to have to fight to
do what he thinks is right.
When in his campaign did he say
the American people would not
have to pay? I wouldn't have
his job on a silver plate not
even if there were millions of
dollars as the bait. If could
be seen at a glance - many
people don't even want to give
him a chance. People keep
your opinions to yourself
better yet, put them on a shelf.
Folks please take it day by day,
take time out and for our
president pray. He is really
trying for all mankind and a
man like that is very hard to find.

    —Heather Tucker

In Love

A lady lives whose smile conveys,
The fun she is, the tricks she plays;
I wish to see that smile always,
The one who loves her so.

A lady lives whose voice is dear,
Making one wish her ever near,
Sounding as music to my ear,
The one who loves her so.

A lady lives whose eyes control
My eyes, as meeting soul to soul,
Helping me feel not half but whole;
The one who loves her so.

A lady lives whose hand is such,
That holding makes me wonder much,
Why I receive that tender touch,
The one who loves her so.

A lady lives, yes, thankfully
Her love to know is heavenly,
I pledge her mine eternally,
The one who loves her so.

    —Gale H. Younkins

Echoes And Embers

With the passing of time
the heart searches on
for the hopes and dreams
of a love long gone.

Hall of memories
Where once, dreams did come true.
Now seeped in sorrow
for a love it once knew.

In this wilderness of hope
where destiny awaits
love moves on
to meet it's fate.

For out of the ashes of time
the heart does remember
memories of loving
of echoes and embers.

    —Debra P. Coupel

When...

When the sun sets,
  the moon rises.

When night ends,
  day begins.

When a door closes,
  a window opens.

When death strikes
  birth is given.

When a heart breaks
  a tear falls.

When love is true,
  there is always a smile.

    —Bethany L. Canfield

I Am The Clay

The more I try to give my heart away
The more God fills me every day

As I empty my loving cup
He's always there to fill it back up

He who turned water into wine
Has filled my life with his love divine

All that I am, or hope to be
Reflects the love he's given me

He is the potter I am the clay
He mold and shaped me day to day

To be vessel of his love
Filled here on earth by God above

    —Johnny DeWayne Aaron

Good-Bye

I saw him standing in the light
The night before we had a fight.
What it was over I do not know
The tears that I cried did not show.
I cried so hard when he was asleep
In fear that his heart I could not keep.
His heart was so full of love and joy
But I went and used it like a toy.
Now he's saying goodbye to our hearts.
Knowing he'll tear one of them apart,
Our lives are no longer one
I wish our relationship had just begun
So now it's time to say good-bye
And dry these tears that I cry.

    —Danielle Kaiser

Opening

Time stood still
  the night still young
    who were we to judge?
  what we had felt

Gazing time away
  each eye ablaze
    how were we to know?
    what fate had dealt

The time had come
  for move being made
    a moment intense
    of hearts being laid

Time travels strangely
  a second of desire
    as moment goes by
      we stand by the fire

    —David E. Wallace

No Tomorrow

My family is in sorrow
  There will be no tomorrow

They saw my bloody face
  It was a disgrace

I laid there helpless and dead
  A bullet in my head

I wish I would've cried
  But instead I dead.

    —Christine Laramie

We Will Not Despair...

This life is long and dreary,
the path is bleak and bare
Our feet are worn and weary,
but we will not despair...

More heavy is my burden
more desolate my way
But Jesus it is You,
who took the sin of the world away.

The clouds lie thick around us
In the dark and gloomy night
and the winds blow strong above us
but the stars have hid their light,

But blacker was the darkness
upon Calvary's cross that day
and Jesus, it is you, who took the
sins of the world away.

Our hearts are faint with sorrow
heavy and sad to bear
For we dread what comes tomorrow,
but we will not despair.

—*Brenda Larson*

Lace Red Embrace

Lace
The pattern of romance
Flows like a wave in the ocean
Before I place it on the ground
And wait there
Daydreaming
For the rest of my heart
To arrive
Wine and roses
Red
Complete the setting
And blue birds sing a song of love
Just as I awake
To receive a kiss
That goes along with my forever
Embrace

—*Heather Gatheridge*

Inaugural Poet

From rock, a river and a tree
The Queen of Sheba is reborn,
Her sources true and bold and free.

A figure cloaked in majesty,
Her words spring forth as summer morn
From rock, a river and a tree.

Her wealth in words a horn of plenty
Makes gold in contrast seem forlorn,
Her sources true and bold and free.

Ideas are epiphany
Whose origins are grey moss shorn
From rock, a river and a tree.

In noble thoughts, simplicity,
Emeralds and rubies left to scorn,
Her sources true and bold and free.

There is no greater purity
Than simple truth in nature—torn
From rock, a river and a tree,
Her sources true and bold and free.

—*Janet Shoholm*

Untitled

Stones thrown over
The river the water
Answers in circles
Responding
Expanding
For a lost moment
When gentility
Runs away
Acts cast
Done past
The ripples remain
After stones in the river
Unmeant violence
Echoes of innocence
Injuries
Untended
Expanding
Fading

—*George Ferriter*

"One More Gone"

Crash
The sickening smash of
metal,
and a life is over
He was only twenty-five

He was driving-
Hit head on -
DEAD-
another life is
G
O
N
E

No one wanted to let go
but we had to.

He left behind his memory
and it was a great one.

Good bye Uncle John
—*Angela Marie Thiel*

Who's In Charge?

NO TRESPASSING
The sign shouts its command
Through February woods.
A full - tailed squirrel
Scampers past the
Harsh, orange words.
Crows perch nearby...
I wonder if the sign
Thinks it controls the sky?
Just wait, I tell myself:
The winter's old,
And brightening buds
Promise that very soon
The trees will cloak themselves
In forest green.
Then springtime's gentle voice
Will rule the woods.

—*Emily E. Clarke*

Memories Of An Aunt

Her love, her kindness
the spark in her eyes
Her tinkling laugh
the times she made fly

Her strawberry blond hair
that peach colored complexion
Her freckles all over-
On shoulders and nose

Her three sons
with fire red hair
She left them on Earth
when she left here

Her face won't be forgotten
it's stuck in our minds
Our hearts have an empty spot
not soon to be filled

Her soul is God's
she gave it in trust
We loved her, we loved her
oh so much...

—*Heather G. Herdt*

Urban

Wrapped around the twilight,
the streets become moonbeams
blasting holes in the night.
Forging destruction out of rubble
there's pain in the dogs eyes.
The wind never whispers
like the mistress of your mind,
she found her solitude
in the rhetoric of rhyme.
But do not be dismayed,
catch your infinite desire,
commit your bloody crime.
No evidence is presented
in a world short on time.
Graphic scenes of ocean waves
pound your shores,
falling to your knees you ask
"Lord, just what am I living for?"

—*Bruce Budge*

Beauty

Always will it be unknown
The tale no tongue ever tells
That stone alone tells unto stone
When rains refresh the hidden wells
And all the rivers sound as bells

Walk upon the timeless noon
Taste the primal dews that gleam
Glimpse the secret psychic moon
Reflected in a hidden stream
That whispers to the hills of dream

Tale of the woods! vast history
Of fens beneath the twilight skies
The hill enciphered mystery
That tells of she who ever lies
Who waits and waits and never dies.

—*Joseph A. Ionno II*

Untitled

Hold my hand and walk with me
The way we use to do.
As we stroll, lets reminisce
Of the times that we've been thru.
The years we've toiled, the hardships,
The good times and the bad.
The years of raising children
The trials of being mom and dad.
The little spats, the disagreements,
The laughter and the tears.
And the love that's grown stronger
Throughout these many years.
The coming of the grandchildren
Which filled our hearts with pride.
Lets thank God for all our blessings
As we're walking side-by-side.

—*Donna Weber*

This year I weathered
the winter with the maple trees,
brittle and frozen
even under sun-filled skies.

Passionate, subtle change in light
Blood pulsing to the tips
of my fingers
Rabbit shedding old white fur
   skips, nibbling on green
both preserved and growing

Sap rising, pound through
my veins and limbs
filling my trunk with desire.

Oh, tap into me, release me.
Let me flow on a page like ink,
flow and let me share
the Unsharable:
   the mysteries of my core

—*Jill W. Haley*

Generation Gap

Look around and what do you see,
The world is just one big map.
And the kids are taking over,
In the generation gap.
It's no good pretending,
I'm not that kind of sap.
For the old world is ending,
In the generation gap.

Look at that mini skirt,
She knows where she's at.
They've got their own world,
In the generation gap.
This is a new day,
The world is in their lap.
Everything is going their way,
In the generation gap.

—*Bettie Cook*

Love Is a Rose

Every person is like a rose.
They grow so beautiful, as each
day goes.
A beautiful bud grown with such
care.
Warmed by the sun and warmed by
the air.
A rose needs love and tender care.
A beautiful rose for everyone to
share.

—*Deama Hodge*

Observing Mind

How long ago, when life was young,
The world was different then
To my young mind, I always find,
The conflict one in ten
The skin, the eyes, the blue, the brown
The rich, the poor, the smile, the frown
And everywhere progress abounds
What difference now from then?
With age arrives a planet ill and sad
For man with all his knowledge
More people learned from college
I'm old and gray
And I must pray
That God can bring us back
To unlearn the damage
That has been done
And once again
To see the sun.

—*Francine Frances B. Bianco*

There's No Doubt About It

Trees are green, flowers bloom
The world's crowded there's no room.
Faces laugh, faces cry
Different faces say good-bye.
Snoopy belongs to Charlie Brown
Wood stock stays on the ground
Places empty, places full
Different places are in school
I'm too young, you're too old
Let's not wait, let's be bold.
Guys and girls get together
Guys leave girls forever and ever.
People live, people die
Different people, do they cry?
Guys grow up, girls grow out
Flowers and plants they just sprout.
There's no doubt about it
What would we do without it.
Without all these changes in life and you
A person wouldn't know what to do.

—*Jennifer Peters*

If Only Our World Was Peaceful

If only our world was peaceful,
Then everyone will be glad,
No more fighting and difficult problems,
Which to us was very bad.

We would hold hands in victory,
And talk, and laugh, and play,
But what we are most thankful for,
Is the friendship that we made.

But now our world is in danger,
A threat, then a murder, and a fight,
And many people are dying
   because of these problems,
How can we save our world from this
   horrible, pitiful sight?

If only our world was peaceful,
What joy it would bring to us.

—*Bori Kim*

Beauty

If beauty is a as Beauty does
   Then it becomes a worthy cause
It could be a pretty face
   But not without a Heart of Grace

There is Beauty all around
   All it needs is to be found
The sun goes down
   And darkness comes

The stars come out
   In all their glory
'Tis then that Beauty becomes a story

—*Ione L. Wallis*

At 19

Be happy, my heart
There is joy in the world
Life awaits you with open arms
Ready to enfold you in all its wonder.

The birds sing
The rain falls
The flowers grow
And life is beautiful.

Breathe deeply the sweetness of life
Enjoy forever
The fresh new Spring
That comes with each new day.

Open your eyes
To the beauty of the world
Open your heart
To all life's riches.

Stop—
Look—
Listen—
Life awaits!

—*Donna R. Parks*

A Troublesome Bee

Once upon a time,
There was a bee,
He committed a crime,
By stinging me.

He was sent to the ground,
With one hard pound.
There was not a sound,
That could be heard from around.

It seems he was stunned,
And still couldn't fly.
He hadn't had fun,
So he said good-bye.

—*Jennifer Swafford*

Carousel Of Life

Life is a Carousel.
To ride the
elegant painted horses
of water-colored
rainbows
is to ride the
turning, twirling, orbit of time
for as long as
you are permitted.

—*Heather Moore*

There Were Spiders

There was thunder in the jungle
There was murder in the trees
The killer found his answer
When the jailer lost his keys

There was moonlight on the river
There were spiders on the shore
His fingers found the handle
And he slithered out the door

The rats were on the gallows
The hangman snored in bed
The killer staggered down the street
His hands were on his head

There was fire in the mountains
There were spiders in the trees
He reached the edge of town
And he paused there on his knees

They found him in the morning
And they shuddered in distaste
The killer lay in silence
There were spiders on his face

—*David Pickar*

Honoring Secretaries

When Secretaries' Week comes round
There's not a frown in town;
It's a "Hi," "he," or twiddle-de-dee,
Or what can I do for thee?

The men lap it up with glee,
As they bask in such revelry;
But it's all "game" without a name,
Which gives the boss such fame.

So here's to the gals who type,
From the men who often gripe,
We think you're all the greatest,
As we express our latest.

So to all the ladies up front,
Who smile and never grunt,
Who put up with all the gaff,
Welcome to this heckling staff.

—*Driftwood H. Rucker*

Kids!

Kids are a wonder!
They make us ponder
as to why some are funny,
sunny,
sad,
glad,
or bad.
And often we ask why
some are shy,
or cry.
Remember, they're kids!
There are some who are small,
tall,
but whatever the height;
black or white,
red or brown,
all kids frown
and fight.
And you know why?
they're all kids!

—*Elaine Steiniger*

Enslavement

I see the slaves working
They toil to reach their goal
Insignificant foolishness
Calling uniqueness grand
But still struggling for conformity

They sculpt themselves
Chipping away both flaws and gifts
Washing their souls in bleach
Leaving still the shackles
They forced on themselves

I see the slaves breeding
They won't ever die
Only a change in occupation
They still find more recruits
Enslaving each other

—*Jenny Brundage*

Kids Are People Too

Kids are people too.
They're big and small,
short and tall.

They smile, laugh, and cry
And sometimes tell a little white lie.
But kids are people too.

We sometimes forget,
That they aren't grown up yet
And they still have time for fun,
So kids are people too.

Be patient, understanding,
And show that you care.
Because kids are people too.

So when we think of kids,
We think of ourselves and smile.
The terrible two's,
The troubled teenager and,
The aging adult.
We laugh and realize,
Kids are people too.

—*Delaine M.L. Davis*

Awakening

When you think your life is over-
Things become so very clear.
All the things you took for granted-
You see through all the fear.

You take a look around you-
But this time you truly see.
The things that God has given you-
And all of this is free.

Things so beautiful as a sunset-
Maybe flowers or an ocean breeze.
If you stop and look around you-
It will bring you to your knees.

God sets this all before you-
The rest you have to do.
All things with time get better-
I know this to be true.

Your life is never over-
God shows you what's in store.
When things go wrong and times get rough-
God opens a brand new door.

—*Faye Preston*

Fear Not

Lovers high, lovers low
This is one Lover that will never go
Love you Love you
That he will
For his Love for you is very real
It may seem like a dream at first
But you will soon see his love burst
Burst into flames
Touching the sky
His Love for you will never die
So let his love
be the key to your heart
For his love for you
will never part

—*Edgar Mejia*

"A Leaf On The Wind"

I awoke to a voice in a garden
"This is where life comes to grow"
"Which are the weeds, which are
flowers? Please tell me for I
need to know.
The voice so softly whispered
"You are home now my friend
you aren't a weed or a flower
you are but a leaf on the wind."
I told her I felt I was dying
She said "Don't you worry at all.
We are all of us born in
the springtime and pass away
day by day in the fall
We all must go from green
to gold to brown
To float on the breeze
and do as we please
when the wind stops
we all must come down

—*Scott Thomas Lowe*

Trials Of Senior Housing Management

Residents are very old,
This makes them quite bold,
    When things begin to go wrong,
    They don't wait very long,
Before they really do a scold.

There is a brick garbage dump,
Many bags piled like a rump,
    He says she made the mess,
    She says hers is less,
Pick-up man leaves the hump.

Maytag washer for all to use,
Big load knocked it loose,
    She says he made the mess,
    He says his wash is less,
We wonder who's the goose?

They move and make a loss,
Around the doors grow the moss,
    His life with son is unhappy,
    She is sorry for being scrappy,
Too many want to be boss.

—*Charlotte Martin*

This New Love Of Mine

I held her hand and said goodbye to
   this new love of mine.

My heart is bursting with sadness
   and my eyes are full of tears for
   this new love of mine.

My arms are empty for
   they will never hold
   this new love of mine.

For tragedy came to her early
   and now she is gone
   this new love of mine.

Please, God, take care of
   this new love of mine
   For She Is Only Two.

—*Hunter Gayle*

"The Pervading Spirit"

Feelings of inadequacy
threaten to take control
   of a usually certain,
      dominating mind.

Wherein lies such a person of
   higher intellect
Who could imagine that just
   one repulsive thought
could turn one into a mass
   of sobbing submission?

Deep into one's psyche
   Lurks the sentience
that gives full rein to either
   good or evil.

For whichever one prevails
   will be the culmination
   of one's lifetime.

—*Debbie Renfro*

A Mother's Loss

   Love growing beneath my breast
   Throbbing sounds of happiness
   Flutters of life deep inside
   Abounding ecstasy and pride
   Planning, hoping for the future
This tiny soul that I must nurture
   Unique and blessed from above
   Full of talent and God's love
In this world of pain and strife
   You brought joy into my life
My Child, my Teacher, my Best Friend
   Why so soon, must it all end
   Taken away in your prime
Loaned from God, for such a short time
   Loved by all who ever knew you
Lives so changed for the better, too
   My heart aches for you each day
   A pain that never goes away
Somewhere in time and space we'll meet
   But for now, that's bittersweet

—*Carol House*

Some Freedom Thoughts

Is freedom something new
to be enjoyed by a select few?
Freedom should be fair play
and could be enjoyed everyday!

Free as a bird as we've heard
being always aware
of which season or time to share

Freedom allows us choices
tolerate expressions and voices
no limits or control for the young
and very old.

Freedom to learn much about our nation
to persevere with dedication
Freedom to be a self starter
to continue and grow smarter

With courage to be sensible
through conviction and principle
Freedom may not be here to stay
protects it or it could slip away

—*Izola Couther*

Painted Faces

We wear painted faces,
To cover our pain and disgraces,
So that we can fit into places.
With this world we live in,
People feel they have no sin,
Thinking, will always win.
Looking at their own real world,
Just to find the pure white pearl,
Not feeling in the heart,
Never fearing truth being torn apart.
Many do this with no regret,
Just as long as their life is set,
To get, what they can get.
Others though do feel sin,
Thinking they may never win,
Praying to see what is reality,
hoping to be set free.
Yet through us all
One thing is true,
We all wear painted faces.

—*Dean Allen Kircher*

The Pain

To have or have you not
To find and kiss
A tender spot
Of endless shadow of your lips.
To touch or touch you not
To dream of a light
Vanishing thought
And catch I haven't got

Side and side
No words
Just flying above us.
Giving so much each other
In the perfect fuss

Don't go away my silent pain,
There is a chance to change
Maybe it's easy to gain
When you are for yourself strange.

—*Jack Mozdzynski*

He Loves Me

He loves me, and is willing to
   To give me everything

I asked him for his eyes
   He painted me a picture

I asked him for his mind
   He wrote me a poem

I asked him for his ears
   He played me a song

I asked him for his heart
   He gave me love

I asked him for a fortune
   He gave me himself

I asked him for tomorrow
   He gave me his children

—*Heather Lynn Coffman*

Bell

I wish I had your soul
To keep me from growing old.
You can go all day long
And no matter what goes wrong,
You never give up; you never quit,
you always stay after it.

What a loving soul
That keeps my world from being cold.
You make it all worthwhile
When you make me smile.
You make the world a better place
By simply kissing my face.

What a precious soul.
You're more valuable than gold.
I need you,
A friend that's true,
On whom I can depend.
You will always be my friend.

—*Eddie Summer*

Untitled

To feel you just enough
to make it right put a
little music on I want
to give you all the love
so hold me tight I want
to feel you just enough
to make it right your
the only one who can
fulfill my dreams so
much confusion when it
comes to loving you
should I say yes I wish
I knew you better we
maybe different but there's
one thing that stays the
same I know I need you
in away I can't explain I
want to feel you just
enough to make it right.

—*Elizabeth Tarin*

Remember

It's so hard
to say good-bye
to someone you love
when they die.
They are really
still in your heart
even though
you're far apart.
If you still remember
all the fun times you
shared with them,
You know your memories
have nothing that can
compare.
You will never be really
sad
if you remember
all the good times you
had.
No one ever really dies
they just sleep away and
close their eyes.

—*Chanel Floyd*

My Answer

I followed the path
To see where it led.
It led nowhere.

I bought the dream
And paid with my love.
The dream was empty.

I looked for answers
Even within myself.
There were none.

I prayed for faith
So I could survive.
Where is it?

I waited for daybreak
Hoping for warmth.
Alone is cold.

I called out for help
Feeling abandoned.
There you were!

—*Eva J. Jones*

That's What Love Should Be

To trust in one another
To share with one who needs
To never put down a brother
Oh that's what love should be.

To hold on to a memory of someone
You use to know
To hold on to a feeling
And never let it go.

The keepsake of an old dream
Gives hope we sometimes need
The thank you to the giver
Oh that's what love should be.

God-he is the real love.
He's the one who'll never leave.
Through him we live tomorrow,
Oh that's what love should be.

—*George Lendley*

Narcissistic Love

Could I but take you
to the depths of my Being
and there introduce you to me
what joy that would be…
The depth of despair to share
to let you see the glaring pain of
blood and flesh combined
in spirit three,
to love but you
into eternity;
You,
who WILL not
to see…
but thee.

—*D. Jeanne Peterson*

Come With Me

Come with me, as sundown comes,
To watch the glow of the evening sky,
With its vivid colors all ablaze.

Come with me,
And we'll sit by the ocean,
Listening to waves and reminiscing
about years gone by.

Come with me,
And we'll laugh together at the silly
Sea gulls crying the blues.

And as the sun sinks below the sea,
And as the moon and stars appear,
You and I will surely see,
That we are one forever dear.

—*Debi Moeckel*

Darlin'

My number you got
too, my name
slumber I do not
do you play a game?

I'm waiting for your call
away I am just a mile
from my sweetest darlin' of all
please pick up and dial

Maybe I'm rushing you
but it's been so long
I've been so true
and suddenly you're gone

I hear you're getting married
I heard it through someone new
oh, this ache I have carried
so long now for you

Someday again we'll meet
possible, I'll look you in the eye
tell you my life is so sweet
don't you realize I'd lie?

—*Bernadette Eberli*

Commute

Grey/white country
travels in a blur.
Stations reduce
people to the size of
canvas bags
or muted
business envelopes.

I beg
for a quiet place
to read
the names of boxcars
filled with the freight
of responsibilities.

—*Ernest J. Oswald*

Trees

Trees are exotic and biotic
Trees capture you not devour you,

They sing a melody and delight you
They form a symphony to relight you,

The leaves are green don't you believe
For they shall sing to you and me,

The leaves float like a feather
For it is Fall weather.

—*Joshua E. Wann*

"Date With An Angel"

Last night I slept with an angel
Truly one from above
She felt so warm and soft to me
As she gave me her sweet love.

She's very kind and caring
Just like an angel should be.
I'll never really understand
Why this angel was sent to me.

She gives herself unselfishly
She bring joy and happiness too.
Just when I think she's done everything.
She comes up with something new.

I could talk about her forever.
I'm very proud of her that's true.
And I know I never say it much.
But I do love and care for you.

In case you're really wondering
Just who this angel can be.
Her name is Tonya Lynn.
And she means the world to me.

—*Bill Sympson*

Life

Sometimes I sit alone and wonder,
Waiting and listening to the thunder.
Some days I look upon the sky,
Even though they say I'm shy.

Day after day and night after night,
Sitting and wondering upon a star light.
I sit and sit and wonder why,
But when I think it makes me cry.

As the past go's very fast,
It seems it might not really last.
As life may not be the best,
But usually, sometimes a test.

—*Jeannette Hendrix*

I Feel

I feel I am made up
Trying to be what I'm not
And
What others want me to be

I feel I am someone else
All mixed up
And
Turned dnoura

I feel I don't exist
As I was originally supposed to
And
Not fulfilling my original purpose

I feel through the tunnel of life
With a dimly lit future
And
And bright PAST

I feel I am made up
Trying to be what I'm not
And
What others want me to be
　　　　—*Jennifer Feather*

Genuine Love

Lonely today all alone
trying to pass time away
I think of happy days

Oh! what a joy
when we were young
dancing the night away
memories of days gone by
linger today

Love is the answer
given and shared
to life as we live on
happiness is within
ourselves and passed on
　　　　—*Eva R. Sullivan*

Happy Recognition

Sparkling eyes
Twinkle brightly
With excitement.

A radiant smile
Stretches itself
Across a happy face.

The heart
Palpitates
With anxiousness,

Surprised
By the sight
Of a friend.
　　　　—*Allan C. Kaufman*

Progress

Escaping from long cylindrical tubes
to permeate the land
chains of grayish-white smog
filtering out in a cluster
The odor is present, easily detected
the waste product of progress
is not discarded
but remains with us
　　　　—*Joanne Parry*

The Keeping Of The Green

The world cradled in silence
under a snowy cover prone,
on the eve with evergreen, is
Keeping sacred the hearth, the home.

My heart and hearth's romance
leap upwards as if blown,
and around the tree wave and dance
Keeping sacred the hearth, the home.

Do I now discard the Norway, now
when green within my heart is grown?
Rather deck it near my doorway to
Keeping sacred the hearth, the home.
　　　　—*Danae : Ida S. Barton*

Trust

By giving we gain
Understanding.
Proving, with time,
Everything to each other.
Meaning more to us
Than our air and water.

We exhale.
The secrets of our lives
Flow from mouth to ear
As rivers to the sea.
Or silent lips restrain
The turbulent waters of our minds.
Breathing nothing of our own
To the World.

Then the flood rushes forth.
Destroying all we have created.
Nothing left
But Air,
And the chance to rebuild
All that we have destroyed.
　　　　—*Dominic Paris*

Unknown Love

Love is like a stranger,
Unknown but so close.
Is it real, or perhaps a ghost?
An illusion, spirit, hallucination
Be the customer and pick a fragrance.
Towards a distant, dim light,
blurry, not bright.
Through the corridor of loneliness
blindly seeking the door to bliss,
hoping for the light to shine happiness.
The journey is almost complete,
While the road and rocks hurt the feet.
Pursuing the treasure
Striving not to get beat.
And finally once the light
produces sight,
NIGHT...
　　　　—*Jimmy Koffel*

"Life"

The wind blows beneath me,
waiting for my response.
I look but then turn away,
for it is hard to see his face.
Tears of redness fall down my face,
as I see him wilt away.
For death is hard to see,
When it is he it takes away.
　　　　—*Carla J. Brown*

The Taj Mahal

Perfect within, perfect without
Unmarred by war, untarnished by time
White marble beauty, exquisitely wrought

Reflecting gold in sunlight
Absorbing silver of a full moon
A white marble jewel, encircled

In a frame of dark cypress
A tribute of an Emperor's lost love
The Taj Mahal, Peerless beauty!
　　　　—*Francis Mason*

Where The Moguls Grow

Up on a hill
Up where it snows
Up where the skiers are
Where the moguls grow
The skiers ski down
To the bottom of the mountain
Then ride up the lift
Like a water fountain
Then I stop to rest
In the chalet
While more skiers ski down
In fancy, like a ballet
As I swish down the slopes
As free as a bird
All full of hopes
Like you've never heard
And while the snow comes down
On top of our heads
Angels give us snow crowns
And put the moguls to bed
　　　　—*Dana Mohr*

The Splash

When I feel the cool water splash
upon my face
through my head goes a flash
of love and grace.

Your eyes, your hair,
so light, so fair.
Your arms so strong,
We kiss so long.

When I feel the cool water splash,
I wake alone,
In my heart is a deep gash,
a heart that once was stone.
　　　　—*Henrietta Schuller*

Our Father

Think of all the wonderful
ways of your own father,
then think of all the
qualities you admire in others
How smart, how kind, how
understanding, how good,
how sympathetic.
So many ways we admire
and respect others.
You know that the creator
of all these people has
all these qualities in abundance
to be able to create the
traits that we so love in others.
"How great thou aren't"
　　　　—*Clara D. Smith*

Angry Words

Listening to the anger as you spoke
Using words that brought tears
Looking into your sad eyes
A part of me died inside.

The words were tearing us apart
Taking the love we both shared.
Lying down hoping to sleep
With open eyes I lay and weep

The empty feeling leaving be sad
Knowing the love we once cherished
Had withered somehow.

We shared that love
For many years
Yet lost a part of our hearts
Through angry words.

—*Ella Mae Marsee*

Bleed

Feeling so totally exposed,
Vulnerable, and, and so raw.
That, if you would touch me
I would bleed
So profusely
The my heart would
Pump itself dry.
And in moments,
My life would be over.
But in reality, you listened.
Smiled softly to yourself,
Gently took me in your hands,
And set me down, right side up.
So that I may go on
Being open, honest,
Vulnerable, real.
Without bleeding one single drop,
of life.

—*Chip Hawkins*

Desert Storm

Orange blossoms perfume the night,
Wafted in on the cool breeze.
Lightning flashes
Illuminate the stately saguaro,
As coyote howls
Intersperse with rolls of thunder.
The clouds move closer -
The sprinkles turn
To sheets of rain,
Deluging the parched earth
With welcome moisture.
Quickly over,
The wind pushes the clouds away,
And shakes the water from the trees.
The pungent smell of creosote
Refreshes the air,
And crickets begin
Their evening song.

—*Jean Tersey*

Snow Fairy

Snow fairy, snow fairy,
You make the snow cold.
Snow fairy, snow fairy,
You make the snow gold.
Snow fairy, snow fairy,
You make it like ice.
Snow fairy, snow fairy,
You make it so nice.

—*Erin Enderlin Hoyt*

Across The Plains

Look far across the plains
Waiting for someone of the same
Troubles, problems, depression
Hoping that somewhere, some place,
    someone will be there
An answer will appear far
    across the plains
Searing, always searching for one
    small detail to explain
Reasons unknown for now for what
    ever reason
Will soon be solved, just wait
    be patient in the right season
Looking, always looking beyond
    in hast
Slow down, be patient, wait for
    the answer that comes far
    across the plains

—*Catherine L. Jacobs*

Do A Little

Give a little, take a little,
Want a little, buy a little,
You can spend a little,
But a little can cost a lot.
Live a little, die a little,
Take a little, kiss a little,
Hold a very little,
Because a little's all I've got.
Run a little, laugh a little,
Eat a little, sleep a little,
You can even lie a little,
But the truth is what it's not.
Steal a little, swear a little,
Burn a little, break a little,
You can do a little,
But a little can get you caught.
I'm so little, you're so little,
Life's so little, Forever little,
We all do so little,
While our little Earth does rot.

—*Dennis G. Vinal*

Reaching Out

I come to you with a broken heart.
Wanting to mend my love for you.
If I were to go to you with my arms
outstretched reaching for you, what
would you do?
Dare, I dream you would grasp my
hands, pulling me close to you,
letting me hug you?
I come to you with a broken heart.
Wanting to mend my ways with you.
I come to you with my arms and hands
outstretched reaching for you.
I come to you wanting a hug or two.
I swear to you, it will never go
beyond that.
Because I think it best not to.

—*Gretchen Duncan*

Hidden Beach

Redwood lies on black sand,
washed up bones
from a great, primeval creature.

Heavy
with the growth of centuries.

Silent and smooth
among cliff worn rocks,
decaying seaweed
and foam.

Waiting.
For the tide to return.

Waiting
To be lifted,
Swung against rugged faces of boulder.

Waiting
for the ocean
to pick up her sticks
and play her bass drums,
deep and salty
on the dancing shore.

—*Cheli Mennella*

Shadows

Walking in the shadows
Watching sunshine from the dark
Walls deep inside
Keep the sunshine out

Hiding in the darkness
Yet searching for the light
Needing to embrace the sunshine
With each beat of the heart

Warmth, light, wonder
Start filling every space
To leave behind the dark cocoon
With every taken pace

Lightness fills the darkness
Hope and love now fill the soul
New freedom of expression
Allows it to be whole

—*Deborah J. Strickland*

The Storm That Is In Us

Should we or shouldn't we.
We can't decide
What's going through our mind
So many decisions to make
It makes your mind feel like a milkshake
Oh, no! But you know what you can do,
Say a little prayer to God
And do you best
At the positive
Push all the negatives away
And see only the positive
It's like that song
I believe above the storm
The smallest prayer will still be heard,
And relax
It's all in the palm of God's hand
And rest and relax
God will take care of all of it.

—*Andria Faye Meyers*

"Remember When"

Remember when:
We first met
The night we fell in love
Some call it destiny or
Love at first sight
Remember when:
We made love
For the very first time
You were so scared
So I held you in my arms
Remember when:
You were lying in my arms
When I told you
You meant the world to me
The way it made you feel
Remember when:
You said it was over
Words will last a lifetime
But in my heart
The dream will never end!

—*Donnie Alexander*

Childs' Disgrace

Unto the children
We must stand
Stop - The anger
Stop - The hand

Darkness Shadows
Courage battles
Tears of sorrow
Grave tomorrow

Battered children
Come what may?
Hark, the angels
Join to pray

Treasure children
Shield the way
For their innocence
Cannot say

Stripped by violence
Acts of insolence
Human traits
Childs' disgrace

—*Carol A. Johnson*

No Room?

When Mary came to Bethlehem
Weary and longing for rest,
No room was there within the inn
For the expected Guest.
"No room today"; the words sound bare,
No room for Christ to share.

But will our hearts be crowded too,
Hustling and bustling about?
As we our Christmas chores pursue,
Will we leave the Baby out?
The Baby born in a stable bare,
No room for Christ to share?

So let us now prepare our hearts,
The room where He will stay;
For He, His love to us imparts,
To live with us always.
And then our hearts will not be bare,
With room for Christ to share.

—*Evangeline Bushacker*

The Answer

And I asked the moon,
"What am I feeling?"
And the moon said,
"It's written in your heart."

And I asked the stars,
"How will she know?"
And the stars replied,
"Let her read your heart."

And I asked the night,
"How can we grow?"
And the night told me,
"Let her embrace your heart."

And I asked myself,
"Is what I feel love?"

And the answer came
As I looked in your eyes
And saw you smile

And together we turned
The pages in our hearts...

—*Jason W. Otoski*

Heart Attack

I thought I knew you well
What did I really know
All your words of kindness
I feel were only show

All of your meek charm
Displayed for eager eyes
Worn only for adornment
Until you got the prize

A vicious game of hearts
Where no one wins at all
And in the end, the Victor
Takes the greatest fall.

—*Barbara M. Demers*

Spring...

Spring is a time
when all of the snow is
melted. All of the trees, flowers
begin to blossom, bloom all over.
The grass is greener than you
could possibly ever dream
Children laughing, flying their kites
in the park. Some children don't
always like to fly kites. Instead
others simply just like to ride
their bicycles to get some exercise.
For guys spring
is a good time of the year
whenever one of them
spot a young lady he will fall
in love, with her instantly.
Then he will calmly ask her
if she would like to date or go out
with him.

—*Inga Nelson*

To My Wife Janet

When I leave here and go to heaven
When I have passed the test.
They will let me through the gate
And show me to my rest.

I'll have all my tools again,
My wood and nails and glue,
And I can work to my content
While I wait there for you.

I'll leave word there at the gate
So when you show up someday.
And come to be with me again
There will be someone to guide the way

I know if they give you a map
You won't know south from north,
And you will be all over heaven
If they just send you forth.

We drove many, many miles
In every kind of weather.
If they give you a map.
We will never get together.

—*Robert Boysen*

Misery

Some people say I'm cheery,
When in fact its all an act.
What doesn't show is the Misery
that grows inside.
I've seen so many hurt and
most of them are me.
I'm hoping and praying
someone will break these
chains and set me free,
at last.
Because all the things that
are hurting me is mostly
from the past.
But until that day, I know,
still that Misery will grow.

—*Erica L. Liske*

Untitled

Cry to the fallen stars
when you feel lifetime mars
upon your face with intent
of a great demon's repent.

Cry to the rising sun
to hurry and be done,
so the lashings of the whips
won't send loves to their crypts.

Cry to the waning moon;
tell it death shall come soon.
So loud shall ye curse out,
others will whisper their shout.

Cry to the one you love;
send tears on the wings of a dove.
Die from this evil race,
for my arms are your place.

—*Alexander Hay*

Illusions

Growing up is hard to do
When your heart just wants to play
We all cling to the dreams
That come at night
As they fade away

Yesterday's a bird in a cage
That will never fly
Today is a dream you'll wake from
Always asking why
Tomorrow's just a vision in your heart
In dream you may never see
Today will be a memory
Tomorrow is eternity....

—*Brenda Bradley*

"Without You"

When the loving is gone
Where can I turn,
When the needing is gone
How can I learn,
To live without you?....

When you're no longer there
To hold me at night,
How can I bare
Losing love that was right,
And live without you?...

When I'm sleeping at night
And you're in my dreams,
How can I face daylight
When it finally seems,
That I'm without you?....

All the memories bring pain
Oh, where will it end,,,?
How I'm going through life
With a smile pretend,
Now, I'm without you!!

—*Dianna James and Lynda Lance*

Green Mansions

Come into my garden
Where it is quiet and cool.
Come into my garden;
It's so peaceful — as a rule.

Some days it is not peaceful,
Some days it is not quiet,
But the trouble is within me —
I need to set things right.

My prayers are not so many words —
They are only thoughts instead
Of praising God and thanking Him
For all the things I've had.

Come into my garden
Where it is quiet and cool.
Come into my garden —
Let Him and His love rule.

—*Frances Marie Leigh Bryant*

Life

Round and round it goes,
Where we'll stop nobody knows.
You've heard this saying before,
From shore to distant shore.
Too many lives in strife,
To them, what's the point of life?
How do you define success,
Is it your house, or how you dress?
The goal of life isn't money,
It's caring for and loving your honey.
The one who sees you through,
Even when times are blue,
It's also living for the Lord,
Not by the cutthroat sword
And standing up for what's right,
Even when faced by fearsome might.

—*Gary Lee Sergent*

Shadows

I love not the shadows
Which lurk in the night,
With leering and peering
'Round my small arc of light!

I love not the shadows;
My mind is too clear,
With eyes wild with terror
And a heart faint with fear!

I love not the shadows
For the ghastly lurk there,
In the nooks and the crannies
I feel their chill stare!

I love not the shadows;
Speed the glad day to me,
When my soul shall soar upward
And the shadows shall free!

—*Delmer R. Hite*

My Life, My Love

How often I think of you
while sitting all alone
How memories of us come alive
when I hear our favorite song
A million miles away from you
still I wouldn't be afraid
Because I know deep in my heart
You're in my life to stay
Your sweet, tender, loving ways
they're always shown to me
And there is no other person
with whom I'd rather be
You're my life, my love
you make my dreams come true
The most wonderful person in the world
is what I've found in you
So when you're down and lonely
And feel you haven't got a friend
Just remember that I'm here for you
And I'll love you until the end!

—*Christine Donato*

A Sand Castle

Calm and collected were my thoughts
While walking along the waters' shore,
Feeling the sand fill my sandals
'Til I dumped it in a pile!

A pile of sand from my shoes
Was the start of a sand castle,
A send castle with lots of space
To have fun and to enjoy life!

The castle grew like a mountain
As each grain of sand took a spot,
As my hands shaped the sands
Til a home became its' top!

A sand castle near the water
Disappeared into all Destiny,
The tide of nite took its toll
Leaving me without a castle!

—*Doris L. Burleigh*

Remember Miss Muffitt?

Remember Miss Muffitt
who always ate curds and rye?
Which she loved to stuff it
only it made her cry.

She says she's way too fat
and she wants to be skinny,
Who can she call for a chat
because she wants to be like Minnie!

As she began to dial the phone
with big tears in her eyes,
It's when she's all alone
she enjoys eating cakes and pies.

She stands about five feet two
and about as big as she is round,
But she wants to be skinny like you
and this way she can lose every pound.

So losing weight would be ideal
and she will have to change her style,
Losing all that weight she will feel
that being skinny will always bring on a smile.

—*Herbie Rowbottom*

I'll Follow You

I believe in the Lord above
Who created you for me to love
He picked you out of all the rest
Because he knew I'd love you best
I once had a heart and it was true
But how it went from me to you
Take care of it as I have done
For you have two and I have none
If I go to heaven and you're not there
I'll paint your name on a golden stair
I'll give the angels back their wings,
Golden harps and other things
And if I see on Judgement Day
You have gone the other way
To prove to you my love is true
I'd go to hell and burn with you.

—*Debbie D. Abazia*

A Man I Once Knew

I once met a young man
who had a good life plan
to treat all people good
as he knew all people should

To love his sister and brother
despite their skins color
for the young man he knew
and as he grew
he found it was true
there really is no difference
between me and you!

—Dean E. Meyer

Epitaph

Here lies a man like most of us
Who lived his life with little fuss
He never asked what it was about
Just did his best along the route

He looked on life with gentle eyes
Tried hard to make it an easier size
For all who walked, or swam, or flew,
Or gave themselves as flowers do

He asked no pity, said few prayers
Knew good and bad in equal shares
Offered to all along life's road
Peace, and justice, and moral code

He gave the best that he was able
Took only enough to fill his table
For he always knew he was only dust
Loaned to him by the earth in trust

If there's an end as dreamers say
When some will pass and some pay
Then this man now lying here
Will find his roadway free and clear

—Elmer Coffey Sr.

Transformed

Have you sometimes really wondered
Why God chose, for His Son's Birth,
A dark, dirty, smelly stable
'Tho He made and owns the earth?

I often wonder if that stable
Such a ugly, dirty gloomy sight
Was transformed to shining beauty
When our Lord came there that night.

Just as on down through the ages
Where Christ dwells, the gloom departs.
Filthy stables...changed to Temples
When He came into our hearts.

—Mrs. Bert Lafferty

Untitled

Fog and mist surrounds,
Within mysteries hide.
Fleeting glimpses,
barely seen,
stays within the mind,
to play upon the senses.

Elf-like creatures,
magic in their own,
flit to and fro
along the edges of the eye.
hands held out, reaching,
for the magic just out of touch.

—Everree West

Eye To Eye

When you and I no longer see eye to eye,
will we sit quietly,
feel what needs no sanctity.
Diversity fade away in a sea of love?

Just then, we're miles apart.
Can our separate hearts
beat together in the night,
while no one's right?

Though we don't understand each other.
Can we still be friends?
Loving each other, so close united
on different ends.

We can't see eye to eye.
Our lips meet.
We can't see eye to eye.
Our souls embrace.
We can't see eye to eye.
Lying face to face
making love.

—Cookie Sappington

Bright Tomorrow

I covet bright tomorrow,
With dreams I have at night.
I give each day my very best,
And long for morning light.
No matter what my victories are,
on any given day:
Without the hope of each tomorrow,
There's nothing to convey.
Of all the wishes I could make;
There's only just this one.
Give me a good tomorrow,
Like the shining sun!

—Frederick A. Wood

Beyond The Passion

There lies a valley
with edges obscured in mist
beyond the passion

Flat, cold, empty, lonely
and seemingly vast
where the flame flickers slowly
into numbness

  He: does not notice
  She: chooses not to
They: exist

Vague sense, diffused hope
that warm, solid, sunlit hills
may lie ahead in time
If time would only move

Majestic Passion-peaks
however
will remain behind
and the Supposedly Wise say,
time to grow up.

—Claire E. Horn

The Circus Parade

I remember as a child I watched,
With joys and thrills abound,
To the greatest spectacle of all...
The circus was in town!

Along the curbs the people stood,
Excitement filled the air,
Big red balloons and animals
And bareback riders fair.

First came the funny happy clowns
Cavorting on their way,
Then dancing girls with spangles,
With tambourines to play.

I can't forget the horses,
Proud heads and nostrils flaring,
High-stepping and in rhythm
To the calliope's loud blaring.

The popcorn and the peanuts
And cotton candy sweet...
The circus held enchantment
As it marched on down the street.

—Elizabeth McFerren Youtz

Sister

Woman of mystery
with miles of knowledge

The writer of words
The singer of songs
The teller of tales
The worker of miracles

A salty tear
A rainfall drop
A drip of blood

Unite me with your love
make me overflow

An idea in motion
An embryo in a womb
A child in her mother's arms
A daughter on her father's lap
A lover by my side

—Deborah Doran

High Hopes

The high peaked mountains
With rushing trout streams
Can send a man off——
With only his dreams

A chugging old car
A tent—— a reel
Hopes of tomorrow——a large fish
In his creel

A time to think——through
Problems of the day
And it—all comes
Under disguise
Of outdoor play

—Anita Fenner

Touch Of Beauty

The mountains adorned
with the beauty of snow
glistening all around.

The winter has engulfed
in eagerness with a
noiseless sound.

The trees are silenced
with heavens treasures
as redemption embarks.

The earth has received
the beauty of God's
creative and eternal love.

—*Beverly Jenkins*

I Wonder

Sometimes as I sit
With the rain falling softly
On my clothes
And the sun is blocked
And the cool wind blows
I wonder how it could be
How are you?
How is me?
In this maze
A swirly, cloudy haze
I wonder...
And no answer comes to me
Can an answer
There ever be?
I wonder

—*Erik Chapman*

"Broken Wings"

In the valley of darkness
With wings on their sole
They're trying to fly to heaven
But the ground won't let them go

Lifted by the word
Brought down by man
If there's anyway to get to heaven
I bet that they can

Angels of Christmas
With harps and wings
Saviors of salvation
Trying to find their king

Faults are not for finding
And enduring will tell
If I hadn't broke my wings
I'd be flying there as well

Broken wings, broken wings; help me get
to heaven
   "To honor the King"
Broken wings, broken wings; I hear church
bells ringing
   I know what it means

—*Billy Wayne Collins*

Plastic Silence

I actually caught some yesterday
   —wrapped it in cellophane
      and scotch tape.
      I want to keep it
      for a while.
   Where did I find it?
   Oh, I don't know.
I thought I wasn't listening
      to anything
   —but there it was.
So I grabbed it.
Before it could get away
(I think I was over there
   by the rubber whisper.)
Strange thing. this plastic silence.
   Doesn't really do anything
   —it's almost like it's not there
      But I have it here.
      wrapped in cellophane
      and scotch tape.

—*Catherine G. May*

Alone

Surrounded by loving care
   yet feeling all alone
No one, feeling can she share
   still feeling all alone

She felt confusion, anger, hate
continuously feeling all alone
with no one could she relate
   always feeling all alone

All it takes is you
to see her feeling all alone
But you couldn't see it through
   still feeling all alone

All it would have took
as she felt all alone
For you to take a look
forever feeling all alone

Look to what it led
   feeling all alone
      Now she's dead
      all alone

—*Brian Morgan*

Cousins

Me and you.
You and me.
We'll always be
cousins forever.
Always together.
You live there;
I live here.
In our hearts,
We're always near.
Through thick and thin,
This is where I've been.
To your house and mine,
"that's fine".
We'll go explore;
Find something more.
We can do;
Just me and you.

—*Christy Caldwell*

When You're In Love

When you're in love,
you feel like you have it all,
and you're ten feet tall.
When your eyes meet,
your heart jumps a beat,
and you have tears in your eyes
from it all.
There is so many things you
learn from each other,
it would take a lifetime
to tell.
You're my best pal,
who loves me for myself.
You become one,
and know you've won.

—*Angela Haralampopoulos*

School Children

Children are here now and today.
You hear them talk, laugh and play.

Amidst all the headaches and sighs.
You know that their goals are set high.

I know that I will always see.
Inquisitive children filled with glee.

But most important, I know someday.
What I have taught, they take their way.

—*Ercilia Cantu*

Corners

We stand on corners
   You in your grace
      I in mine
   An edge between us
      Drawing the line

   I stand on promise
   And things unseen
   You stand on truth
   That falls between

And while our footsteps
      can be heard
walking between the edge
      across the line

   We stand on corners
   You in your grace
      I in mine

—*Dale G. Noggle*

Dying Pain

The pain grows deeper,
With each passing day.
The hatred, pain and hurt,
Don't seem to go away.
I never got to say goodbye,
But I tried to let it go,
I tried to fight the pain off,
I refused to let my feelings show.
But now I'm telling you I hurt,
And it's not so easy to say goodbye.
So now I admit it hurts a lot,
to see someone so special die.

—*Angel McFarland*

Emily Michelle Hartman

You were born in Alaska.
　You were so very far away,
Now you live at Fort Campbell,
　Hooray! Hooray! Hooray!

In rain, in hail, in sleet or snow,
　In most any kind of weather.
In a few hours, you know,
　We can all be together.

Charming in your lacy dresses,
　With your gorgeous ribbon bows.
You will look like a fairy,
　As you are dancing on your toes.

You're always there to "help" dad,
　"Fix" what ever he commences.
Stephanie will call you her,
　"Little Sister Princess."

Soon you will take on the world,
　Doctor, Nurse, Missionary, you'll see.
Changes by one little girl,
　May of Majestic Splendor be.
　　　—Etta J. Strickland

God's Letter To Teens

I have loved you for so long.
Your heart is heavy and confused.
You feel unloved and rejected.
Why have you rejected me?

I Have loved you for so long.
You feel everyone is against you.
You feel you are not needed.
Why don't you feel you need me?

I have loved you for so long.
You feel beaten and run down.
You want to walk away from it all.
Why won't you walk with me?

I have loved you for so long.
I will always love you.
Can't you see that?
Let me take over your life.

I have loved you for so long.
I can make your life better.
Trust me with your soul.
I love you and want to help.
　　　—Denise Norris

Untitled

Can't you see, can't you see
You're a person just like me
We love to eat, we like to smile
We just want to stay awhile…
But, here they come after me
Tryin' to catch me before I'm due
Can't you see the pain
Can't you see me withering away…
Don't you see my tears
As they carry me down that lane
Can't you feel my heart beat
Before I die of defeat,
Can't you see…you're me.
　　　—Hugh Brunson III

BARRIER

i want to let you in
you're so much more than a friend
but if i let you in
i'll be hurting in the end

maybe i'll let you in
love may possibly grow
if i let you in
my trust you'll probably blow

if i don't let you in
i'll wonder in the end
since i wouldn't let you in
did i lose a friend

i will not let you in
my heart buried deep in snow
i refuse to let you in
i care more than you know

So i let you in
my trust to you i lend
as i let you in
don't hurt me in the end
　　　—Delores Nuernberger

The Doctor

Push away that Doctor's hands,
He fixes nothing,
He can not mend
Your soul, dear child,
And when the organs
That he plays with
Have been famished
And destroyed by Death,
The soul will remain untouched
And all his work shown as useless.
Take care of your soul,
Feed it healthily
And exercise regularly;
You cannot get a transplant.
　　　—Keller

Loneliness (Without You)

I walk alone in the night
Not knowing where or what may come
Visions of darkness no one in sight
Loneliness is near or has it just begun

I search for it knowing I am not wrong
No one to turn to or hear me shout
No where to go I can't go on
As the fire of belongingness burns out

Nothing to do as time passes me by
Just to sit and thing as to what went wrong
Endless sorrow wanting to cry
Emotions are heartbroken cause I do not belong

I close my eyes, everything's clear
Even through the foggiest weather
All I loved and memories disappear
Sonia, why will there be no more together
　　　—Adam Moramarco

Cruel Life

I whispered the sweet lullaby
But still the child died.
I sung a softnote
That only she could hear.
I touched her pale skin
And it was a cold kiss to my flesh.

I whispered a screaming and tortured prayer
That only God could hear.

I whispered a thought into her little heart
And a song into her soul.
Yet the child grew more pale and still….
I uttered the name of herself
She would never hear.
Into her eyes, I dropped a tear
With a wish for her to have no fear.
Under my breath trembled
A wish that my breath was hers…
A wish that for my soul and my life
she could live.

I whispered nothing.
Tears no longer fall.
A soft cry I hear within my mind.
For the sake of sanity
Let it echo on…
　　　—Aleisha Brooks

And This Will Last Forever

He touched her face,
she cried a tear,
He said I do,
She held him near,
He gave a smile
As they walked up the aisle,
A loving marriage,
this will last forever.
She gave a cry,
They both smile
They love her dearly,
A parent's love,
this will last forever.
Home forever,
Lord our Father,
Loving, caring,
It has and will last Forever.
　　　—Reynda Pratt

To My Students

One day a long time ago,
　I chose a path to take.
Walking the path has been slow
　With many choices to make.

I made a plan from my scheme,
　To guide you as my own.
I'd be there to help you dream,
　So you would never walk alone.

I am the keeper of your dreams,
　And the molder of your mind,
I am the shaper of your lives,
　As forceful as any you will find.

My wish for you as you go by,
　Is that you will find a road.
Release your dreams, let them fly!
　May you never in life be slowed.
　　　—Valerie J. Church

Missing You

A clear crystal-like pond surrounded by tall whispering weeping willows;

a family of happy-go-lucky frogs finding, at last, a home—their
dreams come true. Joyous contentment found here? No, I'm afraid not!
There is a yearning for a friend lost; Miss Lillipad and her flowery
white tenant—with touch of pink—helps make a house a home.

Gloriously green, a meadow sits peacefully in the early morning's mist,

while listening to the lighthearted song of a lark as he welcomes the
new day. A lovely picture, or so it seems, but loneliness is known
throughout this lea—where is Dandelion? She fills the emptiness
felt by both with her sweet perfume scent and bright yellow color.

The sky is a beautiful pale blue today, a fantastic setting for the

magnificent big red sun. But as splendid a sight it is for us, they
are not as happy about it as we. You see, they miss the soft fluffiness
of their white featherlike companions and their gentle caress as they
slowly and majestically flow along.

As we have seen with the little whist pond, the meadow, and the sky—

beauty and happiness are sometimes more than they may appear to be.
So if I seem to you a happy sort—that's fine, but let the truth of
my poem be known; until she is here with me and we are one,
I'll be as alone as the frog, the lark, and the sun.

—*Tom D. Brown*

The Locked Door

You can unlock the lock that keeps you away your hopes and your
dreams. You can unlock the lock that keeps you away from
rainbows and sunbeams. And the way you can get that key,
Isn't very hard to see.
You travel through your mind looking to find,
The key to your happiness.
In your mind, search for a memory,
Something that will make you smile.
Search for a song and sing right along,
And enjoy your thoughts for awhile.
Remembering these things, will make you think you flying with
    wings.
Fly right up to that door, and stand proud and sure.
And the lack will unlock,
Leaving you with lots more memories to create.
You'll be happy living in a fantasy,
There are things around you that you've just got to see.
Look around, open up your eyes.
Because around every corner there's waiting a surprise.

—*Stacy Thayer*

November Portends

Bleak is the sun in the shortening days
Drear, the sad, soughing wind,
Autumn leaves fly in a swirling blaze
To usher the long winter in.

White hoar of frost laces the ground
In the early moments of dawn,
Earth is assembled in russets and browns
And the crow of the cock is forlorn.

Down thru' the valley, bone-chilling blasts
Sweep from the crown of the hill,
Forcing us in to the hearthside at last,
Where a gentle warmth lingers still.

—*Sara Hewitt Riola*

The Drip

The
drip came
on a cold
winter's night.
It's in the bathroom
sink. In the night it drips
more than in the day, I think it
does it just to annoy the house -
hold. Every drip seems to say, "Am I
annoying yet?" My mind seems to reply
"Yes, very much so." The drip continues.
The drip stayed for another year then it became
a constant flow of water and it asked "Am I
annoying yet?" But this time, my mind
said "No, you're relaxing!" So it got
mad and left and now I wonder who
it bothers on cold winter nights!

—*Amy Heskett*

Shadow Meets Light The Confrontation...

I took light of all you had said.
Drunken verses of life's fine thread.
Misery dismisses comfort in empty words,
a weak foundation in your edifice of support.
If ignorance is bliss, then you're euphoric.
Unable to distinguish the shadow of truth
or the whisper of a lie.
Daylight only hides the truth,
that's when we keep our shadows behind us.
If you cried a river of all your confessions,
you'd only drown in your own regret.
I used to wear my heart on my sleeve.
Now there's just a tear.
I mended it with all of the hurt,
for that was all I could spare.

—*Steve Belcher*

Should

Passing the hour with wet words.
Dying flesh lying across the table,
I stare into the fervent eyes of desire.
Walking away from the prey which left no nourishment.
Nocturnal birds feeding on my being.
Poisoned kisses sting my soul as I run.
Burgundy drops of pain slip from my wounds
and scream into the thickening air.
Mindless creatures surround me,
sucking my innocence from every pore.
Alone with cells caked beneath my nails,
I sing. No light, no color, no dark, alone,
chewing viciously upon my own rotting brain.
Touch me no more, let go, stop the bleeding!
Rich, rank streams flow from my eyes
and puddle around my feet.
Give no more, take no more. Release

—*Senna Waldo*

East Of The Garden

Enter the pores of a valley
Down where the reflection of still water
Ripples away from a stone of delight
Although calmness has discontinued
Fallen angels remain in a shell of rage
Back and forth against an outer crust of a pond
A tadpole swims in circles with no worries at all
Dusk grows near as does stillness to the water
Until another shocking moment unfolds

—*Russell Fox*

Daydreaming About Sean

Sometimes I dream about holding you, breathing into your
ear and melting all your inhibitions, kissing your lips to
share passion I often feel for you, doing things to your
body it will surely become addicted to.

Sometimes I dream of you feeling exactly how I feel, caring,
Desiring, needing me as much as I need you.

Sometimes I say a prayer thanking God for the chance to know you.

Sometimes I smile because I know its really you who should be
thankful.

—*Alicia Fernandez*

God's Earthly Rainbow

There's many colors, in God's rainbow, and many colors, on
earth here below. God needed many colors, of humans too, He
made a rainbow of colors, me and you.

We're all humans many colors of skin, all God's colors, in a
rainbow, made by him. No matter what color, we are born in,
because God made us, an image of him.

No color is greater, or better to him, He needed each color,
for a rainbow, below. What ever the color, He made us all,
for a beautiful color, in his earthly rainbow.

You, me, the grass and the trees, houses, barns, cattle and
pigs. All different colors, for us to see, all part of the
color, of you and me.

When you see a rainbow, after the storm, look at the color, a
beautiful scene. Then look around, you can see, God needed
many colors. He made you and me.

Look at the flag, red, white and blue, standing for unity, me
and you. Lets all stand together, side by side, as a rainbow
of colors, in God's eyes.

—*Marcie Burkitt*

Heartbeat

Whispered thoughts deep within the trees
Echo back their questions
Silently one pine needle falls
Unheard, unseen.

Angel query beckons me come
Glistened wing bends on high
Answers pour forth before my eyes
No word, no cry.

Fear melts into a pool of love
Pouring from heart of rose
Wrapped in the heart of Jesus
Behold, foretold.

Two hearts beat one resounding joy
Praise, glorify the Lord
Echo back radiant reply
Listen, rejoice!

—*Sally Swart*

Yellow

If I could be just one color, just one color,
I would be yellow.
Ohh... not just any yellow,
A yellow so bright that the sun would be jealous.
A yellow so bright that people wouldn't want to stare.
A yellow so bright, my house wouldn't need lights.
Even at night people would think
I'm a piece of the sun that had fallen off.

—*Nathan Bell*

Everlasting Friendship

Thoughts and words of distant times
echo within us, soft currents of
yesterday's moments, flood our minds
with school time memories.

Tears may fall and disappear
behind a smile of remembered laughter;
of the times that meant so much -
now a rich treasury, forever a part of us.

Our hearts have met, loved a little
and loved deeply, every shared essence of
time is etched within us, binding us in
the united bond of friendship.

Fears mount as tomorrow's uncertainty approaches,
but the knowledge that we have been loved by many,
is enough for us to strive ahead towards the future.

It's time to turn, time to change.
An individual journey now beckons us all.
But faint hearts grow strong,
because though we may be far apart,
our friendship is everlasting.

—*Anne W. Poisson*

Circles

Circles abound me corner to corner
Edge to edge they surround me.
You are born knowing little
You live, learn, grow wise
So your mind may return little.
As today you will not be tomorrow,
For someday tomorrow may never come
Believe in the God who created you
Because your circle will become fully round
You have been born, you have grown with
Knowledge so that you live, learn, grow wise,
You grow old and die knowing the same thing at birth,
NOTHING

—*Monica Kuhlmann*

One Poet

Awakened long before sunrise, once again a poets heart.
Emotions to be defined, a time to make a new start.
Feelings creating a view, coming from depth of soul.
Finding the hidden answer, of the eternal longing to know.
A poet can pass beyond boundaries, of space and time.
Stirring the midst of souls, exalting into the sublime.
Moved by the spirit within, knowledge is now in reach.
The ideal and emotion, with understanding ways to teach.
Many are great writers, in their rite they hold a sword.
With words of passionate understanding, and forevermore.
Going all the distance, while walking this trail of life.
Touching the inner most reality, of what lies inside.
Words traveling into darkness, or revealing blinding light.
Giving meaning to relate too, feeling void of wrong or right.
Explaining the unseen deliverance, of that not held in hand.
Enlightened by the knowledge, with compassion to understand.
Being dreamers of vision, seeing verse flow into rhyme.
Pouring out senses of the soul, reaching then to find.
Inspiration moving as water, rains from Heaven above.
A seed grows with wisdom, giving its fruit in love.

—*Paul Staples*

"Angel Like Face"

As I walked I began the journey of emptiness. You say what is emptiness its alone its lonely. Do you feel it, and you say no so I show you. I bring you down the road of emptiness you slip away and fall into a shadow you watch me from a distance and tears flow down your angel like face. You watch as I fall deeper into my emptiness. The sound of my heartache began to drain out your thoughts I began to fall into the hole of emptiness you begin to fight the sound of my heartache you regain your thoughts and leave your shadow and you begin to run towards the hole trying to save me but I fall faster into the hole of emptiness the emptiness begins to set in but something grabs me I don't feel alone. A voice speaks words of love and hope I open my eyes and see it was an angel like face my friend. She who would be there until the end.

—*Melynda Tyminski*

When You Love Jesus Like I Love Jesus

Jesus, my Saviour and my friend, always true until the very end. When in trouble or in sorrow, and feel there is no hope for the morrow. Then I look to Jesus, and He helps me through each day. By my side I know He will forever stay, if I will continue to pray, and pray. When days are long and dreary, and everyone you love seems far away, only trust in Jesus. He will guide you across life's bay. Wait and see there's no other way, come to Jesus with out delay. Friends may come and friends may go, but there's no friend like Jesus. It is so wonderful and sweet to know, that all our blessings from Him so sweetly flow. He gives us courage and strength each day, He died upon the cross for our sins, that we may live. Now may we all turn to Jesus and never, no never again from Him go astray. When you love Jesus like I love Jesus, all your fears will disappear. He will make your life complete, when you lay your burdens at His feet. Then confess to Jesus that the worldly goods on this earth were your defeat. He will bring peace and joy into your heart, and from this you will never want to depart. When you love Jesus like I love Jesus.

—*Pauline Dougherty*

Untitled

Scream, and feel the drumbeat in your heart and mind pound endlessly on and on. The tribal storm of fury and fear has caught you up in it's song.

Making unfelt love the enemy and your stirring mind it's spear. Keeping the fiery patterns of the dark dance a mystery, not too near.

Blaze the heated symbol across your rock-hard soul. Toss in the sharp, hot spear, it is a shattered image grown cold.

—*Jeryl Welsh*

"A Mothers Love"

The sorrow that I feel,
Escapes thru the tears that fall from my eyes.
Within my eyes, lies the windows to my soul.
Deep inside my soul, dwells the love of my son.
Why Lord must I feel this pain?
If I asked "could this cup pass from my lips"
would it be so?
Or this my own prison, for in which every mother must live?
My body aches for the feel of his warm little hand in mine.
My heart brakes for the reassuring words.
His little mouth speaks.
Oh oh why Lord, must I feel this pain?
Is this so unlike the pain that Mary must have felt?
Oh I beg thee Lord,
Let this cup pass from me!

—*Regina Lacy*

From Darkness To Light

Hatred grabs the world in an iron fist!
Even the biggest and brightest star can't
  loosen that hold!
The black plague of darkness has a hold on
  the world, and on me.
Alone am I, shadows I cast among people
  imprison them.
No one cares or thinks twice about my tears
  and cries for help!
I am like a black widow without legs.
As I sit without hope to live, I think about
  death!
Then hope from a friend came, your smile is
  bright, your so friendly!
You break the iron fists!
The ice melts away with your warmth and charity!
When you talk and understand me, my legs grow back,
  and I am reborn!
Able to go anywhere or do anything!
  Thank You My Friend!

—*Virginia Ann Schmitt*

Friends Stay Friends Forever

Friends stay friends forever
even when times go bad
and everyone is sad
friends stay friends forever

If you do something wrong
stand up and try to be strong
because, friends stay friends forever

If your hurt their feelings
and they shoot up to the ceiling
don't worry, because friends stay friends forever.

—*Trisha Bryan*

Steppingstones

Trouble is something no man can escape.
Everyone has it in some form or shape.
And the wise man accept whatever God sends.
Willing to yield, like a storm tossed tree bends.

For trouble is part and parcel of life
No man can grow without trouble and strife.
The steep hills ahead and high mountain peaks
Afford man at least the peace that he seek.

Blessed are the ones who learn to accept the trouble men
try to escape and reject.
For in acceptance one is given great grace, courage
and faith. And the strength to face,
The daily trouble that comes to us all
So that we may learn to stand "Straight and Tall".
For the grandeur of life is born of defeat.
In overcoming we make life complete.

—*Mazell Parker*

Too Fast

I'm in the fast lane, driving with the feeling of excitement and thrill
everyone is slower. I'm in power, they are at my will.
Faster and faster exhilarated by speed,
I don't care what anybody needs.
But soon I will arrive at the end of my road,
from where there is no return and no hope.
A tunnel is ahead and I can tell,
it is the one straight down to hell.

—*Silvana E. Pellegrini*

Untitled

No one said a word as she slowly walked forward.
Everyone saw the tears
Flowing softly down her face.
She stopped in front of his casket,
And kneeled down beside him.
She reached inside,
Gently running her hand along his face.
Her one true love,
Gone from her forever.
One moment in time,
Engraved on her mind for all eternity.
Never again will she hear his voice,
Or feel his kiss on her lips.
All that is left are memories,
And his class ring.
Slowly she slips it off her finger,
Gently placing it over his heart for all time to come.
She stands and watches them carefully close the lid ready
To carry his casket away from her,
And into the softly falling snow.

—*Theresa Koster*

My World

I took a trip to my world last night,
    everything looked strange.
It was time for a break from this realistic fright,
    I had missed my time alone.
The demons of the real world were left far behind,
    to drown in their own fear.
My place in their world I have yet to find,
    they repent me.
I run screaming to my secret shelter where I know I am safe,
    for maybe awhile.
The things I keep all bottled inside I let out in this cave,
    that I call home.
Darkness quickly cools my angers with her soft hand.
    I slowly relax,
As much as I can dare let myself in this time of demand,
    and total confusion.
This chaotic time of not knowing, well, much of anything
    is more than I can handle.
I can feel the peace of home and the life of Earth in...
    My World.

—*Sarah Granstrom*

The Unexpected

It started out as a beautiful spring day
Everything was alive... birds, grass, trees, and the sun
By noon there were a few clouds dancing in the sky
At two o'clock there was a strange uncertainty in the air
The sky had turned from sunny to an evil darkness
Out of that darkness came torrential rain and pelting hail
Lightning and thunder flashed and roared with incredible
intensity at that moment everything became quiet as if frozen
in time then, in the distance, came a sound that will never
be forgotten it sounded as though an entire herd of stampeding
buffalo was right outside our home.
We knew exactly what was on its way to visit us...
An odds maker with no favorites!!!
To survive we all had to act as one with cunning quickness
We huddled together for what seemed like an eternity...praying
and hoping.
As fast as it arrived it departed, taking with it all monetary
value belongings. But the one thing it could not rob us of was
our love for each other just as the day began it ended - with
everything alive - my family.

—*Shirleen R. Beynon*

Feline Felicity

Tail curled 'round, he sits by the bedroom door
Eyes seemingly boring through
As he diligently waits

Open-eared, he rivets his eyes to the door
Ears face front, eyes gazing up
The door knob turns, the door swings open

A foot! Does he know it?
Solemnly his nose sniffs for the scent
It's her!

Clambering up her leg with his front paws
He stretches his length as far as he can reach
Meow? he inquires

She reaches down toward his elongated form
R-r-r-ow-r? he purrs
Moving his head beneath her touch

Presently he sniffs the air for the bouquet of his morning meal
That partaken of, he seeks a sunny spot to repose
In the land of Nod, his tail curled 'round, he sits by the
bedroom door

—*Lynn Porter*

Untitled

In a world where the lilies bloom lingers a man with an ivory
face. Such the beauty of a fair frost has he which creates
faint smells of innocence that cover his frail bones. The
fullness of his ruby lips shaped in a crooked smile, drip clear
colors onto a blank canvas of still water.

His broken eyes stare out into the wounds of the field as
memories saturate his weak joints, decayed from rhythm.
Bleeding in silence, his mute words call in heartache but deaf
ears do not respond. Across the dewy grass, unclean air he
breathes, a sweet gasp lost over a silent scream echoes though
a hollow tree. The leaves whisper back the confusion.

In a state of ivory and black the web spun over his mind shines
on the pond reflected in an array of running colors. Sunshine
ripples the water creating a portrait dream of him, all too
quickly rushed away by depth.

—*Nichol Boruch*

Old Man Appeared

Old man appeared bookkeeper for
Face, though worn, no labor lines bore.
On wooden kitchen chair he sat,
Giving white wispy hair soft pat.
Frayed denim collar's edge revealed
Black-pitted pores pocking neck-field.
Through giant mug of coffee's smoke
Poured quick one shot Old Overholt.
Then full-scrubbed but silt-peppered hands,
Bent from briarwood-root-like wrists,
Tamped tumbleweedy tobacco tight
Into many-match-blackened pipe.
And gulping once but puffing twice,
He growled, "Hoy! Is my bucket packed?"
And fixed carbide lamp to miner's cap.

—*Paul Abram*

Success

Failure is just success turned upside down.
Failure is just success that always lingers 'round.
Failure is just success that makes you never want to quit.
Failure is just success whirled into a catcher's mitt.
Failure is just success that pushes you on and on,
Grasp failure quickly for success is just beyond.

—*Sharita Robinson*

"I Didn't Know"

I didn't know as He prayed in the garden,
Father, It's not My will but Thine,"
that the sorrow that weighed so upon Him,
was the sorrow that should have been mine.

I didn't know as the soldiers came forward,
and I heard Jesus say "I am He"
that the cross today He must carry,
would be carried to Calvary for me.

As they drove first one nail then the other,
and they hung Him on Calvary's tree,
I didn't know that He loved me so greatly,
He'd be willing to do this for me.

I heard Him say "Child I give all,
I'll suffer the anguish and pain,"
then He spoke every name ever written,
as He prayed "Let it not be in vain."

Then I heard Him say "It is Finished,
It's for you that I've suffered the shame,
My purpose on earth is completed,"
Then He died softly whispering my name.

—*Mary Pittman James*

Angelic Feathers

Every time an act of kindness occurs, an angel blows a
feather into the air. Every child born receives a bag full of
angel feathers. Their angel waits expectantly, ready to reach
in and release their first feather. Our bags never empty as we
grow. They are magical. A kind person can never count the
feathers that have been angelically picked from their bag.

Angels know that kindness travels much the same as a
feather. It falls lightly upon an individual, only to be
passed onto another. The one who originally released the
magical feather is seldom aware of the distance it incurs, or
the amount of people touched by its travels.

Angelic feathers can never be broken, torn, or crushed. An
act of loving kindness is forever imprinted in history. A kind
word, patience, sharing, politeness...these all release
feathers into our world. And when enough feathers fall, it can
change the environment in which we live.

Angels know the power of a single feather, and with a sense
of honor and humility, lightly blow each wisp of softness into
our world.

—*Kaye Sanderson*

Song Of Life

January's babe is new,
February a toddler true.
A struggling adolescent March,
Turns to April's dazed teenage hue.

May with her bloom of sweet youth,
Soon gains insight of June's truth.
July grows in maturity,
But August pauses sultry and uncouth.

September reluctant for the decline,
Gives way for October's flaming design.
November her hoary head emerges,
And to December's elegy we resign.

—*Mary L. Bombino*

Anger

I hadn't thought my behavior, towards you could make you
feel so strong, hate is such a harsh word, used liberally is
wrong. I really don't understand, I truly don't see what I did,
but I guess it must have been something, that you seem to keep
hid. I've heard those words a thousand times, they echo in my
mind, they scream from all directions around me, but a reason
I cannot find. I don't know what I can say, it's evident I
can't change your mind, it's an answer that I search for, but
an excuse I can only find. Was I really so harsh? Did I
really hurt you that much? I'm having a hard time, maybe I
went over just a touch.
Anger is such a strong emotion, but keep yours so well
hidden, from others' lips those words they fell, and I knew
they were not kidding. Why cannot you tell me, directly to my
face, the reason for your hate and anger, I know you could,
but that's obviously not the case. I hadn't thought my
behavior, towards you, could make you feel so strong, hate is
such a harsh word used liberally it is wrong.

—*Shawn Lee Murphy*

Warring Desert Grounds

Walking down the camp,
Feeling agony from the hatred I held,
I closely examined the useless examples
of leaders laying motionless on the desert
grounds. I imagined what might be waiting
for me was so hopeful.
Almost running to the hole of darkness...
Slowly the hunted man
moved toward me with his weapon,
anxiously he wrapped his weaponry
around my neck.
All things went through my mind...
I was to close the door to war
and open the door to peace.
He pushed me into the Black Hole.
Pain ran down my back to my legs.
The excruciating pain made me close my eyes from
hatred and open them to love.

—*Katarzyn Jasiurkowska*

Sir Brown

Entering the dead mans home
Feeling his half spirit
Feeling his sad feet drag upon the brown of the rooms
The coat rack neatly holding four hats which were placed as
I
could see upon his head
Knowing nothing of this man accept "he died of aids"
The state will be here soon to pick up his belongings
I saw his trees outside his window of bare white
A small sanitized ashtray carved puerto rico, of ceramic
I felt half a spirit settling
I felt my eyes crying to see a picture of him
Upon his soiled grey couch, in his brown home
Sir brown may we meet one day
I'll see your room of Brown, if you desire
If you desire I'll show you my views of black
I'll greet you sir Brown
By each passing of your tree
As I close the door in necessity of an outer pull
I greet you sir Brown
And I'll catch up with you soon, some day.

—*Nicole White*

Endless Forever

Being under the stars with you is a wonderful
   feeling I never shall leave behind.
I feel you hold me, I hear your heart beat
   next to mine.
The words you said will never be forgotten,
   I long to hear your voice through out the day.
No matter what it is you say just as long
   as you speak to me.
Just as long as you realize I'm there, and
   if you understand me that's all that matters in my life.
You mean more to me than anyone else,
   than anything.
I miss you more today and even more tomorrow.
The longer we're apart the more my love grows,
   the more I feel, the less I hate,
   the less I am afraid.
I forgive you for everything, I hope you do me.
All I really wanna tell you is I will
   forever love you and need you.
My love will be endless for you, I love you!

   —*Tiffany Drop*

Fighting

A day not spent well, a walk to church in the rain,
Feeling wet drops run down a wetter cheek,
Wrapping my arms round an inner pain.

Conversation without can't make me speak.
Thinking is illness so I only walk,
Feeling wet drops run down a wetter cheek.

Squashing snow as thick and sad as melting chalk,
Hot beneath the hat too warm to wear,
Thinking is illness so I only walk.

Friends, don't think me rude if I only stare
At the nothing I see in the glare of the night,
Hot beneath the hat too warm to wear.

I don't want to be talking, only to fight
Up the lifesmear of mud on the hill
Through the nothing I see in the glare of the night.

I've haven't slipped but I've been caught, so I will
Walk out my days to church in the rain,
Up the lifesmear of mud on the hill,
Wrapping my arms round the inner pain.

   —*R. E. A. Doman*

Memoirs To A Mother

Words were never said that should have been
Feelings never expressed in the way that I meant
And the day came too late that I tried to tell you,
So now I'll carry those lost words with me forever.

You have to know that I did respect you
And all the life lessons you tried to teach me;
But for one foolish reason or another
I thought I knew more than you.

Today a lonely daughter on her own
I painfully realize that I should have listened-
Because when those lessons hit me in the face
I want to crawl into a dark hole and cry.

This probably doesn't matter to you now
But I want to tell you I'm very sorry
For not being there when I should have-
So tomorrow I will visit your grave.

   —*Tracey Wynn*

From This Black Day

I sit and ponder from those lazy days of sun gathered wonder,
Fields enriched of breath taking rays of gold
Piercing spears challenging twilights haze as the day
beckons time, night is asunder,
For the shadow awaits, building in haste
A force to be reckoned as each day is faced.
Mocking dreams of lives once passed,
Break to the birth of this one at last.
INNOCENT is the dawn, a breath of fresh dew
And mushrooms spawned to this earth renewed.
Bleak is the morn.
This early weathered scorn until the later is placed by
flowers adorned.

   —*Sean Woodcock*

The Serenity Of Spring

Spring is here, in the air, in the
fields, everywhere.

Before dawn I hear the warble of the bluebirds blending
together as one, to welcome the morning before the rising
of the sun.

The robin with its red-breast is singing a cheery
roundelay from an apple tree, while a band of birds flit
around, which we recognize as the black-capped chickadee.

The plain little gray titmouse has been ousted everywhere
and is making his home in our birdhouse.

I see the wrens, finches, and warblers of every
hue; olive, red, green, yellow and beautiful shades of blue.

The song of the mourning dove marks a joyous season,
of the sounds of birds claiming a home, courting a mate,
and making life take on a new reason.

Dear Heavenly Father, Let us always keep this earth
like Spring, a place of serenity, peaceful and green,
a place to enjoy, is my constant prayer.
May we never let it be destroyed through greed and
fear and hatred, but may we all be united in Thy care.

   —*Loma Susan Hart*

Marriage

Loving and Sharing,
Fighting and Caring.
Changing from only pleasing me.
Thinking now in terms of "we".
First, to myself I must be true;
Enabling me to be true to you!
In sorrow or joy I'm no longer alone,
with understanding like I've never known.
Whether laughing or crying there is someone to hear,
to hold me, comfort me, and dispel the fear,
Touching in a myriad of ways,
Emotionally, physically, even to play.
A blending both of body and mind,
I'll live in your heart - you'll live in mine.
Let us always hold on by holding hands,
through life's constantly shifting sands!

   —*Scotty Rosenbach*

Together Again

In spite of all your hate
in spite of all your fear
their is something inside you can not hear
it is the love you have had for me
something only we could see
it'll bring us together once again
and heal the fights we alone could not mend

   —*Melanie Wood*

Wayfarers

The din of crickets and a lonesome whippoorwill
Fill the night with mysterious sounds
On this cold September night as soft breezes blow
Withered leaves that float gently to the ground
A bright orange glow slowly rising overhead
Its face mocks a smile from the sky
Silent stars Orion, Mars, the Pleiads
Through the fog try to light up the night
I'm stirred by remembrance of another Autumn eve
We shared not so many moons ago
'Twas more beautiful, warmer then, a starrier night
Or perhaps you made it seem so
But love like the season also passes
Just as briefly it flourishes then dies
Two who once gazed at heaven together
Become like ships that pass in the night

—*Shelby Cockrell*

As I Sit Here

As I sit here thinking, silently weeping where no one will
find me. I can't help but wonder what causes the thunder inside
my head.
As I sit here dreaming, the tears keep streaming, so hard
to hide. I dream of a rainbow and dew, but something is
missing, that thing is you.
As I sit here humming, my heart is bumming, quietly inside
my chest. The pain is so much deeper, deeper than anyone could
have guessed.
As I sit here hiding, constantly fighting with the demons
inside my head. I know I shouldn't, but sometimes I wish I
was simply dead.
As I sit here just sitting, how misty my eyes are getting,
wishing I wasn't so alone. Hoping my fate hadn't already been
shown. Knowing my past had already been blown.
As I sit here crying, my heart slowly dying from all the
lying, I realize, it's only writing.

—*Amanda Givans*

"Independence Day"

Parades, picnics and fun for all,
  Fire Engines, Marcher, And Kids,
Parks filled with games and Baseball,
  Fireworks the last to bid.

We show our true "American Way",
  And fly our Flag day long,
We join our friends in fun and play,
  And sing "America The Beautiful", Our song.

How then could Independence Day be had,
  And without it our "Honor And Glory",
This is not a passing fad,
  But a true and living story.

It's our Past & Present & Future we insure,
  For Nations all to see,
That we have and will forever endure,
  The struggle to be Free.

For America we have fought and won,
  So we could live and till her soil,
Which God Had First Begun,
  And we must always be Loyal.

—*Tom Harrington*

Late Summer

It is strange to hear the locusts cry in the late summer evening
As the sun courses low from high and lingers in its leaving.
I breath in the death of day and reflect for but a moment.
I feel as the creatures do and join their sad lament.

—*Ashton John Fischer Jr*

Charlene Heart Beal

Charlene Heart Beal was a real package deal.
First she was here then she was gone.
Now all I fear is that I waited to long.
To tell her how to let her know.
That it wasn't a trick I really love her so.

And if I could I would let her know.
That she could stay with me and never have to go.
And if she would stay for just another holiday.
Would it be done her way to let herself happily stay.
Could I go to a children's store and look around with fear no more.

And if I could would it be my choice that I would.
I don't know unto this day.
But I can say Charlene I love you.

—*Bernadette Vanslette*

Lovely

Her velvet red dress with the bow in the back
Fit lovely like a vision everything was in tack
She waltzed around on the great dance floor
The big band playing near the open door.
She knew every step to perform with her feet
When the music stopped playing she ran out in the street
There she would tell everyone she would see
To came into the ball and have a dance with me.
You see lovely was a portrait hanging on the stair
A beautiful lady with skin so fair
And when the music started playing she became aware
To join right in and not to just hang there -
She was beauty to the eye as everyone could see
Her dark black hair flowing down evenly
Moving ever so graceful as a dancer should be
They enjoyed the company of their Lovely.

—*Alice M. Bateman*

Someday

The ocean running deeper than it ever did before
Five streams fulfilled and centered
round your golden shore
you walked the road of destiny
And the road led to me
Enter now my circle
and together we'll run free

Take my hand, we'll fly away
To find anther, better day
In your arms I'm safe and sound
Then say it wasn't meant to be
But there's no doubt when you're with me
Together we will change the world
Someday you will see

—*Jennifer Chiang*

Shadow In The Night

I'm a shadow in the night,
For I've been left behind.
My wonder cannot unite,
For I have a lonely mind.
Feelings are held within me
Without any reason to be shown.

I'm the shadow of the night.
Dealing with this right, somehow, someway,
I'll see the day to treasure my guiding light.
Although I'll never be the same,
For myself I will be without and
Forever be unknown.

—*LaCarr Ricks*

211

David

Eventide holds a hunter's moon
Flouroscoping the opalescent earth.
You come to me on a Zephyr
Like opium
To dulcify.
There is no epistle… only an evolution.
Virgin femaleness, you sculpt.
Maleness, tumid.

A weathercock turns slowly.
The night becomes tempestuous - a toxin
Flesh molds into one.
Zenith.
Masculinity erupts. The cologne of male seed
Scalds.
In these Elysian Fields - a falling star,
A metamorphosis.
I am Pallas Athena. And you,
Hyperion.
    —*Mary Jo Belongia*

Dad's Little Farmhands

Two youngsters, a sister and a brother,
Follow their father rather than their mother;
Dad does so many interesting tasks,
"Just pay close attention" is all that he asks.

They have to be careful in the jobs they perform,
Because work on the farm can sometimes bring harm;
"Take care 'round the hogs and the cattle as well;
Make sure not to spook them" they hear Daddy tell.

John Jr. carries water, and Norene carries feed,
They know just how much the animals need;
A trough full of grain and a warm bed of straw,
The livestock are cared for, one and all.

A ride in the tractor always brings thrills,
Or watching the combine as the trailer it fills;
And helping Dad unload that grain at the bin,
Then back to the field to do it again.

Having a farm dad can be a great joy,
And lends encouragement to a young girl and boy;
It teaches them a worthwhile way of life,
So they will want to grow up to be a farmer and a farm wife.
    —*Sharon A. Miller*

Faith

I looked into my soul and I found it marked unclean. How
foolish of me to think that because I love the Lord, I would be
blameless. Even when I held him so dear to me, there was sin
in my heart. I tried to understand the words of God, but even
as I searched, I couldn't find answers. For I knew that Christ
and his love were based on faith but what did this mean? I
asked, could he love me even in my sin? I was saved by grace
through my faith I am told, is this enough? Is this all I have
to? Just believe in his love, in his name? Some say there is
more, live by the law, also the say. Then I asked, Can I live
without stain? Can Satan's mark escape me? I'm not that
strong, I fear, but I have a promise no one can take from me.
I was bought and paid for long ago, So if I stumble or if I
fall; I know the Lord will pick me up. For I am his child and
he is my father. He would not cast me into the pits of fiery
hell, Even if I fall short or somehow fall to temptation, He
will look upon me and have pity, for I am HIS. For no father
shall turn away his own flesh; So it is with my God and
Saviour, He weeps in my sin, but welcome me when I call out his
name.
    —*Paula Boyd*

What A Day

When life first started where were you
For even your life started a new.
As I grew I felt your heart beat so near
I thought to myself, "I have nothing to fear".
For I was warmly and softly tucked away
Because in your body I rested all day.

Then one day a hideous monster did appear
and with its mouth it started to suck and tear.
It ripped my flesh and bones away
Until I was all but sucked away.

Even though I screamed in pain beyond belief
To you it was but a worry that found a relief.
Greed, lust, and fame has taken your heart
That caused you to tear a life apart.
Go a head and work and slave
For in Jesus's arms will I stay.

Then one day before a large throne
You will give an account for that life you thrown away.
No mercy will he give that day, even with your teary eyes
For I will watch the mother that caused me to die, what a day.
    —*Johnny F. Payne*

"Penguin Pride"

Who are these birds strutting formal attire
For everyone else in the world to admire?

Who created this truly magnificent sight,
These strange little creatures wearing just black and white?

Looking like waiters with short legs and no knees
Conversing with others in their best pengui-eze.

I'm sure you know the answer … it's as plain as can be
The designer was the same for both you and for me.

I think that the penguins got the best of the deal
At least, that's the way that most folks would feel.

In life's little races to win, place or show
The penguins will win because they're all dressed to go.
    —*Annabelle Weishan*

"If"

For every bit of happiness we have upon this earth,
For everything that happens good, 'til death from time of birth
There are heartaches, woes and miseries and discontent and
Tears and worry, grief and sorrow, and there's illness, pain and
    fears.

These things are all the aftermath of Eve and Adam's sin,
Had they but done the will of God, how nice all would have been
Instead of toiling day by day for food and clothes to wear
Those things we'd need to get along: forever would be there

We wouldn't age, we'd only grow to reach adult perfection
Our whole lives never marred by pain or sickness or infection.
And when the days allotted us to be on earth would pass
We'd be transported heavenward to be with God at last.

T'was thus I think it might have been if Adam and his mate
Had not offended God that day and closed us Eden's gate
But, though we toil and curse the sin that doomed the human race
Would you or I or anyone have done better in their place
    —*Rita V. Guertin*

212

My Linda

In reluctance to admit what I know is real,
For fear that infatuation is what I feel.

For the ignorance I observe all around,
In eagerness to comprehend what I have found,

In all I behold and cherish there is few,
For thy passion I feel in my heart for you.

Thus I rest my eyes in the night I lose sleep,
My fantasies are within the dreams I keep.

For such utter emotion so obvious inside,
Sometimes those feelings are thus hard to hide.

My admiration for you exceedingly grows,
Beauty and warmth for your intensity bestows.

In haste I wonder and in my thoughts
I imagine there be,
My never-ending devotion an entirety
To be set free.

For what I see in my Linda
　　　—*L. Whiteley*

The Beast

I'll never want for this creature called love again,
For I have seized this cryptic beast,
And tamed it.
I am no longer loves captive for I have conquered it
And now it belongs to me.
I alone control this creature.
Once I thought it to be a mythical beat,
And if it did exist, where could it be found?
Now I know it to be real,
And it exists within me.
　　　—*Melissa Steh*

Why A Poem?

There's a reason to write words that rhyme,
For me it is a release
Of adjectives that clog the mind
And never seem to cease.

The lilting speech that poems exude
Can only brighten lives
Though some let sadnesses protrude
And some can hurt like knives.

Some can make you laugh out loud
At words in the comic vein
And some can leave you in a cloud
With a meaning you can't ascertain.

But if you let these words roll from your senses
With verve and zest and flair
You can cut through any and all pretenses
And completely freshen the air.

Even an amateur just like me
And a senior citizen at home
Can live the life of the wild and free
Through the vicarious words of a poem.
　　　—*Malcolm K. Rivkins*

Untitled

Can you tell me where the lilies grow?
I kissed a rose,
And instantly its petals fell and withered
Into black crisps of paper,
Like the ashes of a momentary fire.
I think I would like something more pure now.

　　　—*J. P. Lawrence*

My Friend

My friend Joseph died today.
For my friend Joseph, what can I say.
For my friend Joseph, I cried today.
For he is a friend I shall truly miss.
I will miss him more than any one will ever know.
I will miss the sound of his quiet gentle voice.
I will miss the certain way he smiled at me.
I will miss the way he always had time to listen.
I will miss the long walks on the lake front.
I will miss the quiet moments together.
I will miss his strong arms and tender touch.
I will miss the joy in his laughter; the smile on his face.
Of all the things I'll miss the most; I'll miss his face.
　　　—*Susan Rucker*

Miracle Of Love

Sweetheart Day is every day
For my love and me,
Our thoughts, our hearts, each hour we live
Are shared in perfect harmony.

So long ago we pledged our love,
Yet it seems like yesterday,
The joy of life, family, and friends,
So many blessings along our way,

The miracle of love that holds us close
This special day I'd like to say
You are my love, my love forever,
My Valentine each day.
　　　—*Virginia B. Brainard*

The Perfect Rose

A more perfect flower never before had I seen.
For my love the flower did beam.
Purest of white touched with sweet blush of love.
Innocent as his eyes like heaven above.
For my love a single perfect rose as
Perfect as my love. You come to me
In the image as if as a
Perfect rose.
　　　—*Becky Spencer*

There Still Is Hope

The world must feel some pain
For not only itself, but us
The world must hold much anger
So make saving the world a must.

If we raise our hands in hope
And all stick together,
With just a little patience
We can make this world much better.

From land fills to forest fires
From oil spills to AIDS
Still there is a difference
In this world that we can make.

If the world could cry tears
Or loudly shout out
I feel the world would say with fear
"What am I coming to, what am I about?"
　　　—*Tiffany Nicholson*

213

Untitled

To ink my verse is dangerous trade
for poem belies the promises made
of being Confidant, and Confessional-Stranger.

Your lyric sins, attuned with mine
are coded chords in every line
and tho' of meaning encodedly bled
if musically noted...
decoded and read.

Soft! Priest's piano?
Danger! Danger!

—*Jon Paulovik Corager*

She'll Live Forever

She's proudly flapping in the wind,
For she's been victorious once again.
I gave all I had because I care,
I'm one of many reasons she's flying there.
Her stripes and stars they shine so bold,
Her beauty is worth more than gold.
She's not an idol to love and adore,
She's merely a symbol of what we stand for.
Her red, white and blue fill me with pride.
For her to live I would have died.
She'll live forever through strife and toll.
She'll live forever in my heart and soul.
She symbolizes the freedom for which we've paid.
She shows the way of life that we have made.
To tear her down, many have tried.
To keep her flying, many have died.
Through it all, she's given up never.
The Star Spangled Banner will live forever.

—*Jason N. Davis*

My Thanksgiving

I thank you, Lord
For the birds that sing.
I thank you Lord, for everything.
I thank you for the stars that shine;
For flowers that bloom:
Blue skies without end,
And a warm, and lasting love.

I thank you for a few fine friends
Who, if measured, would stand quite tall.
I thank you, Lord, for my neighbors—
One and all.
I thank you, Lord, for favors
Large and small.
But I thank you for my family—most of all.

Lord, you were with me
At my life's beginning,
I trust you will be with me
When my life ends,
And for all the blessings in between-
I thank you, Lord, Amen.

—*Anne F. Miller*

Untitled

It was midnight on that old New Hampshire road. The
evening fog was lifting. I saw a tall white steeple on the
church, rising above the lonely street. The clock in the
center offered a time aged, tarnish brass face for everyone to see.

Its long tall thin hands, moved slowly, aching and grooming
as it kept its pace with time. The minute hand crept slowly to
the top, when it reached the top bell, tolled once, across
the sleeping village.

—*Mike McGann*

Good Bye To A Lover

Good bye.
For the thousandth time... good bye.
It gets no easier, only more difficult, each time.
Why? Answers are not to come at this early date even though
the true date was earlier still.
It would seem after so many good byes it would be possible
to answer the whys... but it is not so.
It is not because I love you. Love enters into the whole only
by accident.
It is not because I need you. Need is only a position of mind.
It is not because you give me what I lack in everyday
existence, for existence is only, also, a position of mind.
Living is the utmost, and in order to truly live, life must be
full and promising...
That is the answer.
The good byes hold no promise of any future living...any fullness.
Only the emptiness of bright days turned gray, overcast.
Emptiness, not only of hours, but of minutes...of all time
gone beyond any recall...no promise.

—*Johnnie Riley-White*

Caretaker

My feathered friends feed on what I have laid out for thee
For the time is right, the dawn has come
Fill your stomach, warm your body, gain your strength
Fly away, come again for you bring much joy
Your vibrant colors in the dawn, toward dusk, fill my heart
with ecstasy.
I'm reminded what was created, I must become my caretaker.
For only then will you survive the elements and enlighten my life.

—*Patricia Leonard*

Gratitude

I have searched my mind without success
For the words to express my happiness,
The generous thoughts and deeds of great wealth
You have offered daughter, son and myself.

Thank-you so very much
For our lives you have touched
With a new healthier start in life,
Without daily survival of strife.

Three years have now past
The mountains of pain surpassed,
Children thriving in their talent,
Our lives fulfilling and each person content.

—*Pamela K. Kvestad*

Everyday, "A New Beginning"

Thank you God for this fresh new start,
for this clean slate upon which to write.
For this brand new play and my new part,
for this new race I'll run with all my might.

This day has nothing to do with yesterday,
and tomorrow will have its own beginning.
Remembering not things done - I'll start anew, today
for with the night came the old day's ending.

Thank you Jesus, only you could make it possible,
for me to have this welcomed new chance.
Even though messing up again is quit probable,
God, will forgive me in one prayerful glance.

Yes, thank you for a new day, exciting and full,
of things never done before - not on this day.
Thank you Jesus for erasing my sins in full,
making me a new person in God's eyes - this day!

—*Mary L. Liddell*

Politics

Beck to the call of your leader
for what he repeats deserves being heard again
for the first time,
for the last time.
What should not be repeated should not be said.
Add drama,
mix with four parts deceit
and the importance of forgiveness will become
lost
in the flow of fury:
the flow that's taken all our heros.
Stolen them.
Centuries ago, our lamps were full with genies.
But all the wishes have been wasted on
petty politics,
and there are no more heroes left.

—*Miriam Hall*

Without You

We will try to never part,
for without you there's no love in my heart.
Without you I'd be all alone.
Like an old rock or a cold gravestone.
Without you I'd surely die,
either that or forever just cry.
For in my heart I can see,
that we'll both live happily.
Until the day that we must part,
but you just look in your heart.
Look in your heart and you will see.
My love for you living endlessly.

—*Sondra Viveiros*

Death Or I

Would you rather death or I,
Fore death at least hath pity,
But hell will have no wrath,
Like a man scorned by another.

Like a bomb of anger, I burn thee,
An explosion of all feeling of remorse,
The white fire melting heart of man,
Yet history stays its course.

With the anger of one thousand years, I strike thee
Fore those that ever wronged me will pay this day,
By the hand that holds my sword I will avenge,
Nothing nor no one will dare taste my steel.

I ask again, who dare you choose,
In all I will strike till no one remains,
Till blood flows from the wounds of all men,
And left, I will be laughing over you.

By this blood on my hands, my anger is unleashed,
And your wrongs I will judge,
Would you have me gone and leave way to escape,
No! You will die alone!

—*Jerry Warner*

Existence

As life winds its way through the tunnels of time,.
Dreams hover above you.
Memories linger behind you,
Hopes flash in front of you,
Fears creep up beneath you,
Emotions roll around you,
But friends will always walk
Beside you............

—*Jeannine Hays*

Thank You Lord

Our Father, thank you for this special day.
Forty three years seems so far away
But yet, Oh Lord, they were spent so fast
It is hard to remember all of the past.

There were times when life seemed so dim
And the future was hard to foresee.
Though we were unaware, you were always there,
Watching over we three.

The days of joy have been may too, knowing love,
Friendship and caring.
Touching lives, unbeknowing to us, through her beautiful
Life of sharing.

Being physically less in many ways has been sometimes
So hard to bear.
But the blessing you gave in her beautiful soul
Has abounded in joy and helped so many to care.

Thank you dear father, for your precious gift,
A life we have been privileged to share.
Whatever be your plan may we go hand in hand
And, Oh Lord, may our Beth be there.

—*Mary G. Marler*

True

Truth is found in enemies
    found in lovers
        found in struggles of the mind and body
        found down the easy road in life

Truth is found in pain
    found in laughter
        found in friendships
        found in memories

Look around and there is meaning

Find your truth and you've found peace.

—*Montse Garriga*

The House Of Brotherhood

Stand here ye walls of Brotherhood
Foursquare against the strife
Send clear the message to all men
That this is part of life.

Hold over us the roof of love
Designed by God's great hand
That man may learn to live with man
And peace be in the land.

The door thro' which we reach your care
Is ever opened wide
And yet we shall not enter there
While we're possessed with pride.

With open eyes we do behold
The window of your grace
And so, where Brotherhood is found
'Tis a beacon for the race.

And underneath in strong support
Foundations of faith we lay
We go from here with courage new
To help someone to a better day.

—*Sanford Bender*

A Very Rare And Lovely Rose

Like a budding rose was she:
Freshness, laughter, majesty,
The petals slowly opening wide,
Revealing simple beauty, void of pride.

A flowering rose upon the tree,
Its perfume flows, embracing me;
But not without the nearby thorn,
And not without the dewdrop tear of morn.

An aging rose. Maturity.
Its beauty grows in dignity.
Then in his time, all-knowing God,
In death, sows seeds of wisdom in the sod.
　　　—*Stephen B. Elmer*

A Sonnet

The rosy-fingered Dawn carries the sun,
Frightening away the darkness of night;
Bearing a new child with golden rays spun,
Its yawn breaks the clouds and gives way to light.
Fresh dew on the ground dances with pleasure,
And sparkles like diamonds so brilliantly;
The waking flowers open with treasure,
Petals extend in morning glory.
Innocence fades to sophistication,
Giving way to bright new discoveries;
But, soon Earth sleeps for regeneration,
And waits for Apollo to bud again.
We watch this symphony of life and death;
Sometimes for granted we take its sweet breath.
　　　—*Angela Chancey*

Death Can't Take You Away

Today I caught a memory,
from a very long time ago.
I tried to look back at the face it
portrayed,
but as I looked back the wind
started to blow.

Of only the face that I could not see,
Yet, I could hear the laughter,
What a sweet melody.

If I could only see you again,
just to hold your hand,
and, when I needed someone,
you would be the one to make me
understand.

Oh the beautiful memories that
life use to portray,
but we will be back together again,
I just look at this as a flight delay
　　　—*Michele Naney*

A Matter Of Course

From birth's instant spawns death's inevitability.
From love's first look comes heartbreak.
From the child's mouth comes the damning curse that
From that child's first thought has not deferred.
From lone isolation spawns happiness bliss.
From constant elation dawns misery's spite.
From afternoons end comes the morn of the night.
From an over ripe fruit drips the juice.
From difference the probability that
From the gallows swings difference's neck in a noose.
　　　—*Sean Patrick DeSilva*

The Gift

Seed of man and labor of wife
from eternity torn
thrown by a hand to a cell in the tower
where the terrors of life wait for you to be born:
Go not unarmed.

Take for your heart the love of your mother
who of her essence fed you, an unknown.
Temper your judgements, your failures and pride
in one selfless fire too brilliant to hide.

In the will of your father where his strength meets his faith
take hold in the knowledge: There your courage is sewn
to fight not in fury for anger or blood
but to stand by a brother and turn trouble's flood.

So Adam or Eve you are now of mankind
you are naked and new, start to stretch, to unwind.
Guard your dreams, seek your visions,
make a song of your pain.

May this gift [call it Power],
when your sight becomes hazy,
clear your life like good rain.
　　　—*Jan Read*

"Little One"

The time it comes and goes so fast
From little ones 'til now
For soon you'll be just 1 year old and I just don't know how
I often feel it was yesterday that I gave birth to you
Now time has gone by oh so quick and look how much you grew
You're trying your hardest to take a step
As tears come to my eyes
For soon you'll become independent and start to say goodbye
Goodbye to all the little things that you did as a baby
So do you think that you could please slow down a little maybe?
For then you'll soon go off to school and soon you'll be a lady
But in all the world just always know your always mommy's baby.
　　　—*Karen L. Romano*

Life As A Submariner

The hatch shuts...
　　From the outside world we now depart.
　　A diving alarm sounds, followed by the ships call
　　to the deep.
　　The echo fills the ears with a final departing cry.
　　Then there is nothing left but 160 men asking
　　themselves, "WHY LORD?... WHY?"
　　The void is filled with feelings of torment and despair
　　All mental resistance is absorbed by the metallic
　　hull.
　　The thought of reality is torn from the mind,
　　And no other world is permitted to exist.
　　The ship possess no sense of time.
　　The clocks on the bulkheads are merely gestures of
　　events yet to come.
　　Separation from the life we once knew is now complete,
　　And with no others will this life compete.
　　We are the submariners of the NAVY,
　　A team known as the ELITE!
　　　—*Robert V. Schittone Jr.*

Untitled

　　My shadow is my best friend.
always there with me at night
(the time I feel most peaceful)
During the day I just chase
　　butterflies
　　　—*Mariel R. Beaumont*

Hurt

You creep in when I least expect you to. I've tried to hide
from you, but when I least expect it, you find me.
You seem to find me on the best of days. Days when I'm in good
company and content. You find me on nights when I'm alone.
You have even dared to find me in the arms of a new man. You
have the damndest ways of finding me, don't you. You smile
back at me from old photographs. You tempt me with the smell
of cologne. You reach out and grab me through the words of a
lover. Tell me, old friend, what must I do to be free from
you. Perhaps, I know there is nothing I can do to totally be free
from you. Only time can soften your sometimes powerful blows.
Do you know how much I despise you. I despise you for stealing
the rug from under my feet and watching me fall. Do you also
know, old friend, that I love you, too. I love you because
each time you find me. You make me think twice about what I'm
doing, where I'm going.
But I love you most of all because with each of your
powerful blows, you make me stronger and for that, old friend,
I thank you.

> —*Phyllis Pires*

"Popping Vertebrates"

Young pup - he hit the street
Full of energy he could really go
Never burned up the route with fast feet
Some day he'd be older and slow.

Middle-age came quickly and forcefully
Slightly rounded shoulders and uneven hips
Fast pace kept he, hair dark and coarse
Sudden rocks became boulders - His back had dips.

Always smiling, now even slower afoot
Retirement raced to him like the end of his route
Legs bowed, slanted hips, curved back, thinning hair
Outward features that hid the beauty within!

> —*Ronald J. Becherer*

The Woodsman!

From the earth, arose "The Man"
Full of spirit, ax in hand:
His roots mingled with the soil
A happy heart, he feared no toil!

His home he hewed, from God's own trees
With a mattress soft, from Autumn's leaves:
While his traps held only necessities
And he whetted his courage on adversities!

He was "The King" of this vast domain
Yet, knew "no letters" or owned gold ring:
Still, "The Woodsman" was rich indeed
His earth provided his every need!

He quarreled not with summer's sun
Or tried to channel river's run:
Nor blast the mountain tops away
For foolish coins, termed "honest pay"...

Instead, he honored the virgin land
And meadows green, bowed in command:
His thoughts were free, his back was strong
To earth and God, he did belong!

> —*Ruth McPherson Kilby*

Yellow Carnations

Yellow carnations,
Full of sweet sensations.

Yellow carnations,
Full of risky temptations.

Yellow carnations,
A flower in many different nations.

Yellow carnations,
One of earth's most beautiful creations.

> —*Robert Boehm*

It Is

It is a mystery and
full of trickery.

It is a soft peaceful snow fall
and wonder for all.

It is a horror story full of fear
some times death is near

It is a lazy Summer day
and we watch the creation play.

It is a storm ripping every thing a part
we hope it doesn't rip open our heart.

It is a bubbling brook on its merry way
Where it is going we can't not say.

It is a nightmare where we feel we will never wake
could it all be a fake?

It is unbridled joy
like a child with a toy.

What is the things with so much havoc
yet so peaceful and sublime?

Like, my children, life.

> —*Sue Mayfield*

Jenny Left Her Shadow

Eyes like emeralds in the sun
Fur, a mesh of grey and white
I could have sworn her soft M.E.O.W.
Was dancing with the wind last night.

Yesterday I snuggled up on Jenny's favorite armchair,
And though my lap was empty surely I could feel her
lying there.

Gosh, I miss her dearly, though I know she's gone to
greener meadows. Never will I be alone, she left a gift —
her shadow.

I feel her presence in the room
And know she's playing hide-n-seek,
I'd give the world to feel my Jenny's cold, wet nose
Upon my cheek.

She thinks that I can't see her
So she sneaks around the room at night
For now I'll play along with her,
I'll let her be my guiding light.

One day when I am ready, probably not until tomorrow,
I'll return her precious gift to her, and give her back
her shadow.

> —*Rachel Young*

The Seasons Of Life

Birth - the Alpha, the beginning, the Winter of life.
Future to unfold, still untold, promises of happiness and
inevitable strife...

Youth - as Springtime, carefree, showers and scattered clouds.
Lessons of wisdom to store, and battles to remove the shrouds..

Adulthood - intermediate existence, breezes in warm Summer air.
Love, laughter, one with nature so free and so fair...

Middle Age - contentment, as Autumn's leaves fall and settle.
Life lived to it's fullest, the essence of precious metal...

Old Age - once again Winter snows, yet numerous delight.
Fulfillment, wisdom, alert to the final battle with dignity and
insight...

Death - the Omega, the ending, the nucleus of Winter's molecule
Peace, yet feared and pondered, as life's final duel...

  —Ann Clenard

Granny

Smooth face and white hair
Gentle eyes that really cared
She wore an apron everyday
Granny was special in every way.

She never judged any of us
She loved us for what we were
Granny would take us anytime
We were all special to her.

Old westerns, Perry Mason and fried cornbread
Just to name a few
These things remind me of her
Like so many more do.

Granny is much better now
We know she's over yonder
Days and days will go by
And thoughts of her we'll ponder.

I think of her so often
As I know you do too
I believe she's smiling on us now
Because she loves me and you.

  —Tamera M. Lee

Scalding Shame

Droplets splatter, running fiercely,
gently over her nakedness.
Attempting to pierce the blinding terror
inside her. They fail.

Uncleansed like a bloody newborn
beating water scalds her
offering forgiveness of a sin
that is not hers.
For she should be the one forgiving
not forgiven.

Chiseling away religiously, he is refused
like the water, forbidden understanding.
She has smudged the dingy windows,
guarding the raging within,
Hidden like a bride's innocence under a white veil.

She revolts from his touch as her eyes betray her
Shame and guilt screech their memory
searing through the depths of her tainted soul.
The burning continues though the drops stop.
Its just another day.

  —Kerry McDonough

Homes For The Homeless

No matter where we have ever roamed we are always so happy to
get back home. Because I am so happy to have a modest home it
really makes me so sad to see the homeless and down-and-out.
The homeless rate is growing every day. No place for them to
sleep but in doorways and on grates. Some are so tired of
searching for work and food they fall asleep on the cold
ground. That has happened to our great country? A place that
was so prosperous it welcomed all who came. We have reached
out and helped so many countries; why can't we now take care of
our own? Our shelters are over crowded and there aren't enough
houses to shelter the down-and-out. Jobs are so scarce and
wages so low, how can there ever be a place in our society for
the present poor? My prayer and greatest wish is that all our
homeless children may soon have a home and an education. God
forbid they just be forgotten and continue to be victims of
drug dealers and taken into gangs. Let us all try to do our
part to help the homeless and just not complain. Home is where
the heart is. Just think of all the hearts that are in pain.

  —Mary C. Schooley

Patience

Why are you looking down with your head hung low, problems
getting you down sometimes you just don't know? You say I just
as well, hey what the heck's the use, when all that really is,
just a poor low down excuse,
You say, I'm giving up, yet deep down in your heart you know
it's just the beginning of a brand new start, you want to give
up but that's not the wise thing to do, God didn't give up, he
had a lot of patience with you. If God was like us and he gave
up so soon, we'd all see eternal fire, our lives would be
doomed, praise God he's long-suffering, full of love and his
mercy sustains, because if it wasn't for the Lord, in life we'd
never be able to maintain, you see our problem is that we don't
like to suffer, it almost kills us to take a little pain, yet
when it's all over with we scream hallelujah, because of what
we've gained, patience is the best virtue, at least that's what
I've always been told, patience is the best thing and you
should treasure it as if it was gold. God said wait on him, be
of good courage and he will strengthen thy heart, stay with
the Lord, don't ever think that you should part. The harder
times get, the more you praise God's name.

  —Zandra Long

We Who Still Proudly Serve

As we stand proud and straight in military formation
Glancing neither left nor right
Eyes glowing, hearts racing, looking to the future
We who still proudly serve

As each ROTC cadet snaps to attention and smartly salutes
As we pin the medals, decorations, and ribbons so richly won
With a hearty handshake and words of wisdom
We send them on their way
We who still proudly serve

For us retirement has lost its glitter
Alas, as our restless spirits soar
With misty eyes, greying heads, and noble words
We send our cadets to their destiny
We who still proudly serve

We the retirees of our military forces still augment the
fighting machine
As we pass the awesome torch of liberty to those standing
before us
And give our helping hand to the future soldiers of the land
For we who still proudly serve, SALUTE YOU.................

  —Stanley D. Sagan

James Christopher Conaghan

God created a masterpiece only one of a kind.
He had a mission designed for him already in His mind.
The perfection of God's work was not to be concealed.
So on the morn of September 7th the completion was revealed.
In the hands of loving parents God entrusted to their care
The future of His little one who is beyond compare.
This little boy is unique in very many ways.
For he'll bring love and sunshine to brighten all the days.
Each time you're in his presence or look upon his face
You'll see the hand of God and feel a warm embrace.
The heart will be overflowing at the thoughts of this baby boy.
For he radiates God's love and fills your home with joy.
Through the tender care of the parent direct him to God above.
So he'll know whence he came and was showered with such love.
The grace of God is something you can never measure.
Give thanks and bless the day you received this heavenly
Little treasure.

—*Mildred O'Neill*

Selling The Farm

"I'm Bertie's daughter," I had told him,
"Gone a long time, but born and raised here."
And the auctioneer, with squinted eyes accustomed to appraising
Searched my face for any trace of her.
My first auction and I made myself an outsider by saying so
To people hunched against their pick up trucks
Complaining that they missed the opening day of hunting season.
Their closed faces never telling their surprise -
As if I'd said, "my first wedding," "my first funeral."
My first auction and I took a number
- the rules seemed easy as Monopoly -
To find that hunting season had not been canceled after all,
But was happening here among my mother's pots and skillets,
And they were giving me a sporting chance
To save a fragment of her life.
I polish the copper pot -
Needing the green bile smell of its corrosion.
Needing the angry circles of the polishing.
Needing to feel at last that she is gone.

—*Barbara Armbruster*

Why Did They Leave

(Dedicated in Loving Memory of my
Grandparents, Robert and Rose Marie Jones)

There were two people
Who were very close to me
But now they're gone
Why did they leave?
He said to the first
'Come and go with me'
And so she went
Willingly
And to the second He said
'Let us go my child'
Now they are both
beyond the clouds
Why did they leave?
Why couldn't they stay?
I hope they know
I think of them everyday
Although they're gone
I know there will always be
There love here on earth
Protecting me

—*Nakia Coles*

"Craving"

Storm lines, you leave your imprint
graved into my soul
My eyes burning, desire to know,
existence, yours alone.
Touch me I cry out.
Let me experience the electricity as
I see it surging, radiance beyond any known.
I feel empty when you are far,
I contain no shape nor
reason for my continued breathing patterns.

Storm lines, let me take hold.
I crave your contours,
As no other has ever taken possession.
I am tired and weary
from the repetitious patterns
which consume my being.

I need to claim shape.

Your form is so delicious.
I crave you constantly.
Patterns.

—*Lynn E. Perrin*

Legacy

Snares set, traps sprung
Greed, captured its victims one by one.
First lies told seemed minuscule
Deliberate actions, cunning and cruel.

Selfishness ruled with lust and pride
Exposed by death, impossible to hide.
Deceit, fraud, dishonest deals
A legacy the deceased cannot repeal.

The lid snaps shut, the box let down
Trumpets play that mournful sound.
Departing can't erase damages left behind
Kinship of man; all lives intertwined.

—*Tiaynah Ann Mikol*

Thoughts

Running rampant through the mind,
Groping for answers they cannot find,
Speaking to the innermost part,
Communing with the innocent heart.

"Lord, let my thoughts be fixed on Thee,
The source of true serenity;
That I would be unharmed by all
The thoughts delighting in mankind's fall."

Recalling details from the past,
Determining to forever last,
Affecting both the body and soul,
Striving be in complete control.

"Lord, let my thoughts be fixed on Thee,
Keeper of my destiny;
That they would never dim my view
Of spending eternity with You."

—*Sandy Haney*

Gods Love

I look up and what do I see
But God's hand of love touching me.
I look away just for an instant;
I look back and he seems so distant.

What has made him act this way?
What can I do or say
To make him love me again?

—*Karen Zach*

Sleeping

Footsteps in the back of my mind
    growing louder each day.
     The dust on my boots is becoming annoying.
Stretching my arms to the sky,
    I can see the stars above me.
   I twirl myself around this small fire,
     grasping the joy I feel from the music.
   The song completes itself within my head
    peacefully.
Mother Sun softly lowers herself into the
    cleanliness of Father's Ocean's arms.
   I sit here on the edge of this hill,
     looking out onto Nature's art collection.
   I lay my body down upon this earth,
    knowing myself safe
     from all man's cruelness
   and close my eyes to sleep.

    —Mika Sorak

Dreams Of Reality

Upon a dream of reality, none may come true.
Hardships come to those who do not have wealth,
for why, you think, must it all come down on you.

Awakening from the dream, you wish you had never,
for the dream of hardship and grief, is better than
what you have taken.

Back in your head, your wildest dream, you think
there must be better, there must be better that
what life does seem; you think there is a place where
whether win or lose, there is no gain.

The day dream of pleasure and gain is soon awaken
by the nightmare of reality.
But why is the dream far fetched, you think.
Then you realize the world isn't what was supposed
to be.......
It's all upon a dream of reality.

    —Paul D. Williams

Harmony

Harmony makes the world laugh, and cry, and shout.
Harmony's not just a word, harmony's all about.
Harmony's the earth, revolving in it's place.
Harmony's the universe and all the rest of space.
Harmony's a feeling; deep down internal calm.
Harmony feels so good from my feet up to my arms.
Harmony's a meeting, some jolly holiday greeting.
Harmony's this poem, the way it flows and rhymes.
Harmony's a clock, the simple way it chimes.
Harmony makes me see, it is all over me.
If harmony is all this, then harmony's also a
good-night kiss.

    —Saul Herbert

For Parents

The most precious things I've ever had
Have been my loving mom and dad

Not a day goes by you don't cross my mind
You're both so understanding and kind

You are the reason I live on this earth
You created my life when you gave me birth

So these humble words to you I now give
"I'll cherish you both every moment I live"

    —Nadine Spears Law

The Homecoming

His soft departure through life's gate
Has left our hearts ajar;
God saw him home while it was late
They passed the morning star.

We shall smile who loved him so
Who gave him hate will weep;
But for him soft winds will blow
There at his Saviour's feet.

Past Jordan's banks, through Canaan's fields
Life's secrets are no more;
Gone all earthly mysteries
Through Heaven's open door.

We cannot see the way he came
Nor can we bear the cost;
That debt was paid so long ago
Upon a rugged cross.

Somehow I know he sees us
He shares our sorrows too;
And he'll be there to save a place
For me...and each of you.

    —Michael D. Mantooth

Real Love Heals

Dwelling in a world so sad while loved ones die at our feet
Hating one another with malice surviving life living in defeat
Lying to each others hearts and speaking in slanderous ways
Feeling without walking in their shoes and standing for what
    most dare not say
Living in a world with peace while people keep healthy and whole
Loving as the Creator commanded to you this plea is my goal
Turn this world around so we can survive
With hope in hearts keep love alive
United we stand laying down sin and strife
Holding youth in our hands stopping drugs guns and knives
And I vow if we all do our part
Standing God by our side
With respect self-love and self-pride
All together we'll cry
For the peace found deep in our souls
Embracing Supremeness we will all be made whole
Then we'll walk hand in hand with each other
    to a new world healed with real love.......

    —Melaine E. Patterson

Feeling Inside

Hollow is my body, no feelings in sight.
Hatred comes right to me, envy is my plight.
Feelings have to leave me,
I hope it goes so soon.
I struggle in and out of life,
but, the thoughts come back too.
I see happy moments,
but they are never mine.
These feelings have to go away
which are implanted in my mind.
I have to look inside me,
deep within myself.
It hasn't had it's time to grow
for hatred took its chance
Let me, take a breather.
Let me, just lay back.
Let me, erase the memories
and let the love grow back.

    —Amy L. Good

My Trip Down South

My trip down south to visit my family, but only one thing has haunted my memory. They called me "yellow", though I'm dark and brown, They said I didn't belong there, and spit on me as I walked around. They whistled when I passed down the street, they pushed me down when I could not retreat. I wondered why they did this to me. If I could not be my colour then what could I be? They called me sneaky. What had I done? They shouted "chinky," though I knew I had none. They pushed my face into the dirt, I felt them in me. As I screamed through my hurt. I wash myself to erase the pain. I scrub hard, scratch and wonder if I'm half sane. When I realize I can't, I feel hopeless and cry, I ask the Lord how come and why? Through these eyes is all I could see, only God knows what had happened to me. To this day, I dare not open my mouth, to what happened on my trip down south.

—*Tenzin C. Tsorpon*

Cries Of Silence

Unto us a child was not born. For all the days of my life I have been barren. Then there appeared a glimmer of hope, and a
drop of desperation. Drawing us closer to her beams.

Unto us a child is given. Our dream has become true. Sleepless nights full of frights, and long days filled with delights.

Unto us a child is taken. I hear his soft cries no more in my ears, nor do I feel the sweet wetness of his tears. Dreams that once were gay, now have been swept away.

Unto us a child is taken. I hear his cries no more. Nor do I feel the little heartbeat, that was so close to mine. The dream is slipping away and the nightmare has become real.

Unto us there is a child no more. Days are long and empty, and the nights are endless, while somewhere in the distance, I hear the cries of a child.

Only more dreams to dream. With our hearts still aching, for the only thing, our own bodies will not allow.

—*Trish Smith*

Escape Route

Like the mighty eagle when tangled in the snare
Have we been caught in a trap, And now going no where
Must we all sit and wait, Until the captor appears
Or make the necessary sacrifice, Of what ever it takes

We have defeated a much stronger enemy than this
First we must remove all greed, And racism from our minds
And we must cancel discrimination, In all creed or color
If we escape from this trap, That is destroying us together

Now make fast to your brothers, And offer your hand
For we are all the privileged, In this promised land
All of this old world, is our neighbor, we must agree
All man kind must learn to love each other it is said
If we ever expect to claim, our fathers victory

—*Joe J. Staker*

Goodbyes

Goodbyes are hard to say, the words get in the way.
Goodbyes are hard to write, the pen just stops in flight.
I simply cannot smile, that smile is a frown.
The sparkle in my eyes is a tear trickling down.
The only thing that comes to mind is a big embrace.
The frown disappears and a smile is then replaced.
Memories of the past will forever stay.
Praying that your future is blessed with happiness today and everyday.

—*Theresa Ann Santos*

Better Than A Friend

He opens the doors where two hearts greet.
He allows them time to really meet.
Will they share His name?
Will they say it out loud?
Will they ask Him in?
He's hoping so; He's really proud.

Then at last, the moment comes!
The angels shout, and sing from above,
"He'll always be there.
He's better than a friend.
That's for certain,
And now you're ready to begin."

—*Vickie L. Kaiser*

Secret Ambition

There once was a man with a secret ambition;
He came to this world on a special mission.
To his mother a gift God gave her;
A son to be born in a lowly manger.

The child grew and became a man;
Always holding out his helping hand.
He tried to teach them just to believe;
But all they wanted was to receive.

Even though he had done nothing wrong;
The people just didn't think he belonged.
With hate and anger they nailed him to a cross;
But his death was his enemies loss.

His death lives on even today;
For his mission was to give his life away.
God walked as a man on the face of the earth;
Giving the gift of second birth.

—*Alison Brewer*

Mother

God had many things to do, this, that, and the other,
    He did a grateful service - He created Mother.
Who was suffering in sunny calm, or raging storm?
    'Twas your dear Mother, when you were born.
Who diapered you, and fed you baby gruel?
    And taught you to sit on the stool.
Who watched you, from morn to night?
    Really, you were never out of her sight.
Who taught you that to get along with each other?
    You accept all human beings as your brother.
Who advised you from liquor to abstain?
    And never take the Lord's name in vain.
Who asked you that during all your teenage years?
    To adhere to the ten commandments, you'd have no fears.
Who came to assist at your first baby's birth?
    Her help was appreciated like no one else on earth.
Who influenced you to invest your soul?
    And you joined a church, which was her goal.
When in jeopardy, you know there's no other,
    After beseeching God, you call on Mother.

—*Arbor D. Fields*

The Elusive Fog

A veil-like fog settles upon the earth,
Hiding the surrounding scenes in mystery and intrigue.
Entering the fog, the shadowy shapes and figures
Momentarily take form, make a grand entrance, and leave.

Acting out a suspenseful play on a mist-
Covered stage, they join a panorama
Of sights and sounds along roads that twist
And turn to journey's end, finale of the drama.

—*Marilyn Jane Vedder*

The Man In The Mirror

Is he a "mere" reflection of love or an image of my life?
He does not walk on water, yet when he speaks, I listen...
He does not make me over to his own perfection.
He talks of truth, honesty and reflects on the beauty of love.
We comb through the pages of our life history and brush
through the pain as if we were heroes or heroines.
He shares his dreams, his failures and compromises to vision
in me he knows not well—
We try on each others emotions and find they fit over the
creases of time.
We speak, we touch, we love and the man in the mirror
becomes one within me.
We laugh, and taste the salt of tears and he sees I am but
his image of love's sweet and sour taste.
We reflect on loves past and the stained corners of our
mirroring image of love.
We are but two in the image of God—Seeing each other's smile
reflect on a life incomplete as one.
The man in the mirror's love fits so I will wear it
fittingly..

—*Sharon Moller*

Without Him

He sees my face weeping.
He doesn't care about my feeling of
hurt inside.

I am no one to the world-
a loner, depressed and hurt.

He doesn't even say "sorry"
but instead he treats me with
such disrespect.

"What have I done to you?"
I cry. "I don't deserve this!" I say
as I dry my tears of sorrow.
"Good-bye," I shout, "I will
miss you and always love you."

—*Meredith-Joy Petersheim*

Just Another Nigger

When the creator of all things looks down,
He doesn't see our race, color, or creed
He only sees believers and nonbelievers.
But when mere mortal men look at me they only see one thing...
the color of my skin.
And some white men judge everything by this
Not my personality, nor the way I treat him, not ever what I do well.
None of this means a thing to him
The only things he know is that my ancestors were once owned by his,
And back then it was alright to treat his dog better than he did me
It was alright to call me a coon or a spook or whatever his
heart desired because he was my superior.
I was not his equal. I wasn't even a human being.
Just another piece of property,
And in his mind no matter how many degrees I receive or lives
I have saved I will still be just another nigger!

—*Marisa Y. Lockett*

Friend In My Life

Once a friend comes into my life.
I can't just let them slip away.
I cannot accept that.
Friends are too important
Once I care for a friend, I will always care.
For friends, I will always be there.
Friends in my past are part of my life, part of who I am,
And I don't want them to disappear.

—*Sherry Ann Charran*

A Perfect Life Cut Short

Aaron had the perfect life.
He got good grades, he never fought with his parents.
He had a girlfriend and was popular with the guys.
He was president of the Class of '94, and the athlete of
everyone's dreams.
He liked to help others and never let anyone down.
His outlook was always sunny and he had plans for a fulfilling
future. Aaron thought he was invincible and took everything
for granted. He thought nothing could happen to him...
Until one night, spent with some so-called friends.
They'd gone to the bar and drank till they were sick.
Just as the new day was beginning, Aaron drove his friends
home. But what he didn't know was the he would never make it.
It all happened just two blocks away.
He lost control and drove head-on into a telephone pole.
In those few horrific moments a young man lost his soul
And two parents lost their precious little boy...forever.
At his funeral, three days later, many tears were shed
For the young boy who had the perfect life.

—*Kimberly Haines*

"Little Boy Blue"

Little boy blue can't blow his horn
He lay on highway near a field of corn
No one knew this little boys name
People of Nebraska took him in just the same
This small town had a burial for this little boy
On his grave placed many a toy
His father had thrown him on this lonely highway
They couldn't charge him with murder, that's what they say
It was bitter that day, snow coming down
When on this cold highway a small body was found
They didn't know his name so called him little boy blue
The town of "Chester" knew what they had to do
You might have read this story somewhere in a book
About a father of a boy whose life he took
"God" reached down for this little boy
Gave him Gabriel's horn for his new toy
He has a new father who will hurt him no more
In Heaven with Angels, with them he will soar
Blow your horn for us little boy blue
The people of Nebraska will never forget you

—*Norma Jean Williams*

Payback

Making time with the reaper
He leaps from the edge of the precipice
Into nothing, infinite space and time
A master at his art
He lands atop of the helpless victim
Claws outstretched, the shiny black panther
Shreds his prey
In the span of a moment
The poacher discovers the meaning of retribution
And the panther climbs back up to his perch in the tree
For a nap.

—*Sean Freston*

Friend

As the sadness sinks into my skin
I sometimes wish I could have been
Could have been there when you needed me most
I know that I wasn't the best host.

I know it must have been your time to go.
But I wish it would have gone a little bit slow
I know some day the sadness will end
But I will always remember you until the
end....

—*Nikki Price*

222

A Little Ditty

Joseph had real sense in his head
He left his coat and fled.
If men today would listen to what I say,
They'd run like Joseph did.
They'd run, run, run, run,
Run like Joseph did.
He fled fast on his feet,
Got away from the heat,
He left his coat and hid.
He got away from Potiphar's wife,
Put in prison. Kept his life.
He ran and ran but stood like a man.
And so today, any man can.
When you're tempted to sin, don't give in.
Remember this little ditty,
And run, run, run,
And you'll be thought to be witty......

—*Winifred G. Hodges*

The Stranger

He walks down the street with his hands in his pockets
He looks away from everyone with an ashamed look
His stubby beard and dirty face is wrinkled by his frown
He walks for hours on a long and unused road
The expression on his face is as long as his journey
His clothes torn and shoes worn out, he ventures in the night
He speaks to no one but himself in a mumbled tone
As he moves through the night all is silent
All is silent but the sound of the old man's voice
No one talks to him
No one looks at him
He just moves on

—*Adam Laudicina*

Life

Life is a beautiful thing, which is made from the one above
He made each one of us special, not to kill,
or hurt, but to love.

We take life in the wrong perspective,
We lie and cheat instead of share and give,

We should see life as God meant it to be,
Not the way we live it but through his eyes you see,
We take life as a senseless game,
That's why each one of us lives with shame,

We must change our ways and make our decisions wise,
Because, what's living life filled with pain and lies,

To lead a good life you'd probably say,
Forget it that's a bore,
But you can't think that way, you
have to understand, that life is so much more,
To change how you live you must start
on your own and you must know what to do,
In the end God will decide if you've
proven yourself, by the precious life
He's given to you!

—*Nanette Campos*

Things We Know

White as snow and the clouds passing by.
I see white sparkling off every tree in the sky.
Planes up high birds down low.
Clouds lakes and rivers that flow,
make every thing grow.
Stars at night
make everything bright.
Those are the things we know.

—*Sarah Dale*

A Brother

A brother is a glorious thing.
He make's you laugh, he makes you sing
And when he looks at you awhile,
You always see an innocent smile.
When he get's you mad,
He always tries to make you glad
All he wants is his sister's love.
I thank God up above for making brothers.
When I look into those little eyes,
I see feelings curious yet wise
I truly see he loves me.
Loves me with all his might
I see he loves me day and night.
I love my little brother
With feelings bright and strong.
That's why I cherish his love
As though it was a loving song.

—*Aliya A. Khan*

We're All Good For Something

After God made all that He could
He sat back, took a look, and said, "It was good!"
From the smallest to the greatest
From the oldest to the latest
Everything created was created for good.

Mistakes are man made, men make mistakes
To learn of a better way he should take
Hearing the right voices
Making the right choices
Finding out what good is in goodness sake.

Sometimes we look on the surface above
Without searching deep down inside for true love
Worth it's weight in solid gold
A sight of all sights to behold
Is the treasure in us that is sent from above.

So if you think that your life is worth nothing
Everyone and everything is made out of the one thing
Look inside of yourself you'll see
The greatest treasure ever to be
And remember that we're all good for something.

—*F. Daniel T.*

The Love Of My Life

He looks up at me, with those dreamy eyes,
He seems to be bored, then lets out a sigh,
He looks all around, lays his head on my side,
Snuggles up close, as if trying to hide.

As minutes pass by, I don't hear a peep,
So quietly, I rise, he is fast sound asleep,
When I cross the room, I sit and just stare,
At this precious child, with light golden hair.

A baby just yesterday, and now that has passed,
The years fade by quickly, he's growing so fast.
He's taught me so much I didn't even know,
All the love that I feel continues to grow.

Amazed with the wonder, and all of the joy,
So much I feel, for this little darling boy.
So curious and active, at times there is strife,
He's inspiration for living, he is my whole life.

There's so much to teach him, even more to learn,
To guide and protect him is my only concern.
I hope he'll be happy, and his dreams will come true,
And I hope for success in all he may do.

—*Rachael Turcotte*

Forever Yours

Yes, He's here beside us today
He sees the sins of our world
Momentarily try and you'll feel Him
Knocking on the door to your heart
Occasionally, you open it just a little
Too afraid to let Him completely in
You can see His outstretched arms
And His diamond-piercing eyes upon you
Then He echoes your thoughts out loud
"Are you afraid to open this heavy door?
Afraid to give up the sins of your world?
Only I can give ultimate peacefulness
One that you have never known
And together we'll become as one"
Oh Dear God, take my heart and take my soul
Cleanse my impurities and make my life whole
He lifts your spirit ever so gently
"As far as I see, you've done no wrong
Because you've given yourself freely
Your love is now where it belongs"

—*Sharon Matthews*

The Mockingbird

I can hear the mockingbird singing in the magnolia tree.
He sings a song so sweet and clear
It seems that he is serenading me.
When I see the beautiful full moon shining in the sky,
Then I know that the song is really for a mate
Who is sitting on a nest nearby.
This bird sings and trills so many songs,
Maybe a hundred or more.
It can even imitate and mimic animals too,
Hear the sound of a kitten's mew!
Listen to the imitation of the rooster crow,
What a talent this birds can really show!
The mockingbird likes to perch up high and sing,
When it comes to song, he is truly the bird king.
Sitting on a TV chimney antenna and singing could last the
night long, that melodious tune coming down the chimney is the
Mockingbird's song. This music puts me to sleep at night and
I think of God up above. I thank the Lord who made Heaven and
and Earth, the mockingbird is singing me to sleep and showing
me God's Love.

—*Annelle Stuckey*

No Thinking

Over the wall comes friend
He stands triumphant
Cloaked in memory
Shielded by the evergreen lush
Of childhood dream
Striking down the guard-adulthood
Denying the loss of youth
But the voice rang out
"Call out the dogs!"
Loud as thunder
And ringing like defeat
And the hounds of militarism drag him away
Never to be seen again.

—*Shane Holmes*

Spring Is Near

The snow is melting, spring is near,
Hooray, hooray, give it a cheer!
When spring is here, I'll laugh and giggle,
And my little dog's tail, will wiggle, and wiggle!

—*Anna Marie McIlroy*

Silently Lay

While he lay silently in his bed,
He thinks up songs in his head.

He thinks of two but one soon dies,
And now he stares up at the skies.

As he lays and quietly thinks,
He knows he shouldn't but he drinks.

All of the poison that the snake gives,
Kills his brain, but helps him live.

He's floating now high in the air,
But now it's time to pay the fare.

From drinking all of the dangerous drug,
That came from that deadly mug.

He realizes now its helping him die,
And faces up to the fact that he has lied.

To all of the people that once loved him,
And to himself-when life was dim.

He's gone now from the land of the living,
And it's too late to begin giving

To the people that he once loved.

—*April Lynn Olson*

"What Dad And Mom Meant To Us All"

Dad worked hard all through his life.
He was married to a very faithful wife.

The strength he had to work, the farm, each and every day.
You must learn to eat, rest and take care of yourself he'd say.

When the chips were down he was always there.
It just goes to show our Dad really cared.

He taught us all to have Humor and LOVE.
It's a gift sent to us from the Lord above.

Mom worked hard to care for each and everyone.
It's hard to believe they had two daughters and four sons.

She cooked the meals for all of us.
With all her LOVE without a fuss.

When we were sick she'd hold us tight.
Sometimes it would be all through the night.

We shared our Mom with many other children.
She taught school so they all could learn.

Thank you from all the world and the Baby.
You were both the best for the world to see.

We all LOVE you so much it's hard to let go.
However, we must as each of us truly know.

—*Arnold L. Raether*

Mardi Gras

Night drums,
hearts dance,
harlequin millipedes pop in rhythmic grace;
Sequin constellations flash the midnight air
when eyes of purple glass smile at mirror fire
and sparkling Venus dangles from the moon
like a diamond on a string;
There a shadow falls a moment,
tripped up within the urgent beat,
but passing, unseen hands reach fast,
return it to the Carnival of Life.

—*Patrick Laurence Cronin*

Fall

Speckled leaves of gold and crimson
  Herald in by Autumn winds
Air so crisp, to fill my senses
  Comes at last, the Summer ends.

As the blossoms, fade away
  Into slumber, they do sleep
Resting, now in natures order
  Thru the Winter, cold and deep.

Feathered friends, their songs now silent
  Leave to make their journey far.
Home again, from whence they came from
  Guided by some far off star.

Winter snows, will soon be with us
  Clogging streams that flowed so free
Thru the meadows green as emeralds
  Not till spring, again we'll see.

In the hollows and the burrows
  Dwells the creatures, large and small
Shielded from the cold around them
  In this season, we call fall.

—*Robert M. Stapp*

Stray Bullets

Looking on these dangerous streets at night,
here we are living our lives in fright.

Staring into the barrel of a gun,
we need to do something we can not run.

Taking on this fearful task,
looking for safety, hiding behind a mask.

Tears from a mother who lost child,
a screaming bullet that was so loud.

As they think of their yesteryears,
they are crying out with falling tears.

Birds fly by day, bullets fly by night,
stops this senseless war you fight.

We have to solve this one step at a time,
here stand our lives at the toss of a dime.

There really is no other way,
if we wait any longer we will pay.

—*William John Pallaris*

Silent Shadows

The Great Horned Owl is back.
He's perched atop the old pine tree.
I hang a bit of suet up
Where he might see
And find it tempting to his appetite.
I know... I read, or, maybe, heard
Owls like to hunt
For things alive;
A field mouse scurrying to and fro;
A snake, slithering soundlessly
Thru drying leaves.

In times like these
When wild things find less of their prey,
A bit of suet might help stay the day
When Great Horned Owls
Make no more silent shadows in the sky.

—*Alice O. Wilber*

Untitled

Fuzzy shadows from the blinking lights
hides the filth and the shame of the city nights.
Her words a small place the size of a corner
who sits up at night and secretly mourns her?
Secret fantasies forbidden illusions
become dangerously clear seductive delusions.
High silk stockings stiletto heels
too tight skirt her fate is all sealed.
Come one come all the look to entice
whatever your pleasure all for a price.
Then the streets grow quiet the crowd starts to clear
Making it audible for all who wish to hear.
A soft humming noise a cry in the dark
of a heart broken woman who walks through the park.
She wishes it all to be taken away
she's lost all hope never knew how to pray.

—*Alan Sayarot*

The Mystery Man

He walks the city streets alone
His clothes all tattered and torn
Cardboard fills the holes in his shoes
That the concrete sidewalks have worn

The park bench is his bedroom
His cupboard, the garbage can
His travels have taken him everywhere and nowhere
What is the mystery about this man

Society meets him on the sidewalk
They cross the street just in time
Where they won't have to mingle with him
Or hear his pleas for a dime

As Winter sets in on the city
The Mystery Man with no place to go
His hands and face half frozen
By the hard winds and drifting snow

The weather became too much for him
And the lost meals took their toll
When death came to the Mystery Man
And finally relieved him of the Cold

—*Raymond Buarques Sr.*

Rose To Fame

His wisdom wavered, he fell from grace,
His fans and family grieved.

His enemies are reminded daily of a hero
cut off at the knees.

Each paper ran the story, each station spread
the news, his enemies were ready to light the fuse.

Our loss was great, his punishment severe, for a
sickness called gambling claimed his career.

Great men before him have fallen to their knees,
but how many can lay blame to a disease.

Presidents have taken the fall for much greater crimes,
only to appear on the lecture circuit line. To be labeled
as an expert in foreign affairs, and handsomely paid for
the views they share.

They are not banned from the Smithsonian, to date, only
history will determine their fate.

Doesn't Pete deserve the same and his place in the Hall of Fame?

—*Susan P. Jones*

In My Place

The angels stared in wonder as
His robe dropped to the floor.
His crown of royal jewels was tossed aside.
At His word the servants ceased their praising,
He sped to earth, all heaven cried.

Once God, now man, He walked the dusty roads.
He knew hunger, sorrow, pain and joy...He wore cloths.

They nailed Him to a cruel cross.
My throne of shame upon His head.
The nails were driven through my shoes.
On my jeans He bled.
—*Paul Larsen*

Still Standing

He stood stout and resolute, like a pine,
His roots planted in a small Southern town.
His branches reach out, all hearts to entwine,
Symbol of strength, never to be hewn down.
What of this pine, why was to so great?
It was king of the wood, admired by all.
Standing unmoved, though life's storms would berate,
Bearing nature's torrents, still, proud and tall,
But silent illness had blossomed in the tree.
Splendidly handsome, mere men could not tell.
It suffered it's affliction quietly,
Forest time spent, alone and weak, it fell.
Do not grieve the loss of the evergreen spear,
He's eternally in my memory dear.
—*Tammy Fleck*

"Where The Heart Is"

Home is where the heart is or so the story goes.
Home is where you shared all your joys and woes.
But what if you don't have a home
And no-one really cares
What if you are down and out
And everybody stares
You try to find a reason for being where you are
It's no good just sitting and wishing on a star
When you're down on your luck and your back's to the wall.
Put your troubles behind you and stand up tall
Remember that where there is life, there is hope
Believe in yourself and you'll be able to cope
Then one day you'll find that you're feeling just great
Your health will be good, and life is first rate.
Then you'll know in your heart, that wherever you roam.
You can always go back to the place you call home.
—*A. Christie*

"If I Should Die!"

If I should die,
How would I be remembered, in your minds eye?

Would it be money or material objects, you could see?
That would spring a memory of me!

Or would a smile, laughter, a hug or precious time shared?
Bring to mind memories, that I "Really Cared!"

For if it takes anything less, for you to put the memories
into actions,
My whole life, involved in yours,
has been but an infraction.

You see love is something money can't buy,
And it's my love I want to leave you with,
when I die!
—*Sam Weichel*

HOPE

Hope you've learned to love, for what are we if we can't love.
Hope you gain understanding, knowledge, and wisdom, to make you
a better person. Hope you find the truth and peace every man
is looking for. Hope the path you take is the path of
righteousness. Hope you can see; the beauty of things, the
things that God created. Hope you can imagine, imagine the
world, imagine peace, imagine everlasting life - in your hands.
Hope you can comprehend and discern, between what is right and
what is wrong. Hope you understand the importance, the
importance of life, the purpose, the reason. Hope your reason
is the right reason. Hope you are blessed, blessed with the
opportunity to know God, so your children will receive
likewise. Hope you realize, without faith, your are without
hope. Hope you know that faith is: the substance of things
hoped for; the evidence of things not seen. So why, why hope?
What is Hope? And why do you hope for me so? Because it is
hope, that brings us prosperity, fulfillment, and life! So
it's rightly so that we should hope -For- Every Person Owes
Him.......................their life!
—*Wade Sanchez*

Be Grateful

Walking down a one-way street,
Hoping to find someone to meet.
I will always feel like an outcast,
Because I will always think about the past.
As I walk,
I see poverty stricken people,
Who are stuck in their own world.
Food is like a well, running low.
Adults and children,
Skinny as a stem on a plant.
They have no future,
They can't remember the past,
The present time is running away,
Right before their very own eyes.
All around,
Time is stealing their life away,
Like a thief in the night.
I see myself,
And realize how greatful I am,
To have, what I have.
—*S. Hunter*

True Love

How can I tell you my feelings,
how can I tell you my fears,
if you ignore me when I talk,
and I don't think anyone hears.
You never seems to worry about it,
You never seems to care,
when I need you the most,
you seem to never be there.
We've had our share of making up,
we've yelled, screamed, and cried,
but to tell you the honest truth,
if I lost you I would die.
Even all the broken promises,
The lying, cheating, and sleepless nights,
we've worked through it together,
not anyone else, just you and I.
We've made it through the bad,
let's start working on the new,
because now you're there for me,
and I know you love is true.
—*Renee Whaley*

Tell Me

Tell me, oh my soul,
How many dreams have gone
for myriads of generations,
into earth's memory.

Tell me, Oh my soul,
in the depth of the deepest breath,
how many tears do I need
to avoid the pregnancy of hope,
and to deliver the birth of joy
to my eternal sea of blinding darkness.

Whatever be the answer.
Whatever the outcome might be.
Give me the enlightening word
to share it with my brothers;
to put it among the States as divine linkage,
not to split us but to unite our hearts
with the cement that your sight spreadest on me.
Give me a tear, Oh sweetest sweetness,
to lubricate the wonders of my dreams.

—*Zerolf Z. Oiluj*

Love

Is there really such a thing? I really do wonder
How someone can say - I Love You,
Then disappear from your life,
If that is love then I
Don't ever want to believe
That I am in love again
Oh, what a great feeling
It is for awhile
Then all of a sudden
You find yourself all alone
And they say they are sorry
But they don't love you anymore
And that they have found someone new
You often wonder what you did wrong
Or if you did anything at all
Or if it was all just a lie
For now I really don't care
For I will never say I love another
But I think I will always wonder
Is there really such a thing as Love?

—*Tammy Flynn*

Poverty

Poverty is like a jungle on an alien planet.
Humans lingering there develop strange patterns,
   Foreign to their fellowman.
Special talents are required to avoid the hidden pitfalls;
While covert traps lie at the end of one-way paths,
   Whose poison foliage allow no turning back.

Abysmal cries echo in the void,
As denizens plea desperately for help.
   It comes as wolves in sheep's clothing:
Ten dollars down; only one dollar a week;
Loans made—no credit necessary;
A hundred dollar watch? Sorry, I can't let you have but ten.

—*Vernithia D. Fitzgerald*

Untitled

Faithfulness is fleeting. An endangered species of morality.
Hunted by deceit, skinned of its respect.

So two have been deceived, but only one realizes. The other is
unaware, believing his spouse is true.

As for me, I too was ignorant not knowing of the oath
You gave to another and then flung aside

I know we are not alone - similar occurrences have happened
before. During the course of a war hearts died as well as souls

At least they had the courage to tell their lovers or mates
Even if it turned the soldier into a Dear John.

Instead you lived a lie - telling neither about the other
Betraying your man's trust and using me for cheap pleasure

Thus I hold contempt, as should your husband. Perhaps I should
get to know him so he knows you

Then you'll walk the streets and two betrayed will be free
But you're not - charge thirty pieces of silver

—*Scott Allen Gammon*

The Glass Pane

Walking in the garden on a cool summer day
I admired the different flowers and their fragrances
saw the bees and butterflies go from flower to flower
every one different, yet fitting in to give an exquisite beauty
'cause there's no glass pane between them.

As I watched, suddenly something touched me. I stopped
looking up, I saw, facing me, a figure indescribably beautiful
Our eyes met, she smiled and so did I.
It seemed we had known ourselves before
where there was no glass pane between us.

Slowly we drifted towards each other without uttering a word.
The look in our eyes told what was in our hearts.
Close now, arms reached out for the lovers embrace
No; close we were but yet very far apart,
There was a glass pane between us.

We never expected this strange barrier
Should we break it? The consequences might be eternal
Hoping to melt the glass with our hot lips, in vain we tried to kiss
Homo sapiens sumus, understand and don't be stubborn
You torturing glass pane between us.

—*C. E. Ita*

"I Am"

I am a person who was created by God,
I am an individual nurtured through family.
I am a child who on other's paths has trod,
I am one who cares to leave my own testimony.

I am a citizen of this great country,
I am a follower of those who have led me.
I am a member of every community,
I am a leader to those whose needs I see.

I am always that which you see before you,
I am forever growing and reshaping on my own.
I am the result of all of the things I do,
I am the product of those lives that I've known.

I am the foundations which have been laid before me,
I am continually questioning what came before.
I am one who has delved deep to see,
I am what I am and I cannot ask for more.

—*Sallie McCutchen*

229

"Conversation With A Troubled Youth"

Man! I'm in a mess.
I am experiencing pain, tension and stress;
I am a washout, burn-out, troubled teen.
Don't be angry at me-
I've got low self-esteem.

Man! I'm in a mess.
This low self-esteem, they figured out from a test.
I've been tested and counseled,
Since my expulsion from school.
Don't be angry at me—
I'm just an uneducated fool.

Man! I'm in a mess.
Being uneducated, I thought I would be free from stress
Life is tough, it's getting me down;
Stealing cars is no way of getting around.
Don't be angry at me-
Give me a hand.
Help this troubled teen,
Before I'm a man.

—*Richard R. Inniss*

Reminded

As I sit and watch the children play,
I am reminded of all the yesterdays,
And all of the days to come.

As I sit and hear them laughing,
I am reminded of all my jokes,
And heartbroken tears.

As I sit and watch the sunset,
I am reminded of all the days,
Coming to an end,
And all of my new days and new feelings.

An as I go inside my own little playground,
I am reminded of the loneliness,
That I do now feel.

But as children play,
As they laugh and cry,
As days come and days go,
The pain goes,
And a fresh new feeling comes in.

—*Andrea Michele Walker*

Nature's Love

I am the stars, that sparkle so bright
I am the moonlight that glows at night
I am the sun's rays that brighten the day
I am the flowers that blossom at noonday
  I am the air of life you breathe
  And the energy of life you receive
  Like a golden harp that plays
  My heart opens up for you always
  Real love can never be measured
  Only hope to find real pleasure
  The tree of life is the key
  Maybe one day it will find me

—*T. H. Nettles*

I Don't Mind Being A Senior Citizen

I don't mind being a senior citizen.
I have a comfortable place to live.
I can sit back and enjoy what life has to give.
Big oak trees shade the ground,
Friendly neighbors all around.
So I sit back and reminisce about the things in the past.
I shall enjoy the rest of my golden years as long as they last.

—*Sadie S. Eaton*

One Night

One night when I went to heaven
I asked God, about you.
He wouldn't tell me what you looked like, or how we would meet
But he said I would know what to do.
I said why won't you tell me?
Because I felt so sad at the time.
Then he looked at me and gently graced my hair.
And said my heart would feel you inside.
So then I begged him for a clue, right then he looked
at you and said
You'll do things with her you thought you'd never dare do.
So when I woke up the next morning
I tried to search for you
But yo were still asleep, and asking God the
same things too.

—*Stephanie Morgan*

Wordless Blossom

When my tongue fell out my mouth
I bled a dictionary before it scabbed,
It left a hollow hole, a dry cave.
I gawked and gargled, spit up Agony
As words echoed deep and disappeared,
Bellyflopping into back black waters;
They drowned and washed away beneath unconscious tides.
My throat grew lonely to share a verbal joy,
Desperate fingers flipped and flitted
With longing to release the sounds to
Someone who never knew the Signs and Symbols.
I shut up tight like a safe with treasures...

...As time eroded canyons on my soul,
A Wordless Blossom broke a dam inside me,
Spilling water over heavy craters
Exploding at my tender fingertips.
A blind ineffable rush of Sensation —
Like a tickling wet fury on fertile soil,
Sunflowers grow, like all that grows from
Ground and Sun — is silent, magnificent, powerful.

—*Ruben Claveria*

Moon (Child Bride)

The moon rises as the blade is illuminated by surrounding fire;
I breath in and gag on flames while anticipations burn higher.
To close my eyes and be another is the demand made upon me; to
become one and be His lover - a child-bride loose, free...
Within the chambers of medieval times the chains clasp upon
legs and wrists; freedom only comes when one dies and upon the
last breath; death is the wish.

Follow the blazing blade, to never lose sight or it might find
your flesh weak; and enter on the full-moon retching night when
the underground reaches it's peak. To run is an intellectual
and ignorant mistake to listen and do is the best; follow and
learn, to be blessed with 'snake' maybe one day there shall be
rest. The child-bride knows the moon and abides strong in mind
she follows the gold; never disobey and mustn't ever hide for
her soul has already been Sold!

The full-moon and child-bride are one in the same;
Should you ever cross them; you must kneel in His name...

—*Anne Hazard*

230

I Let My Pen Do My Talking

I can tell you how much I love you,
I can tell you that you're beautiful,
With a piece of paper and a pen.

I can tell you how much I miss you,
I can release feelings that are true,
With a piece of paper and a pen.

But when I feel I need to explain
All the feelings that I hold within,
The tongue gets tied and the mouth goes dry.

And every time I want to begin
To bring feelings out in the open,
The tongue gets tied and the mouth goes dry.

I guess I'll just have to continue
Expressing all my feelings for you
Through my paper, pen and loving touch.

So if instead of speaking I do,
I'm telling you how I feel for you,
Through my paper, pen and loving touch.
　　　—Thomas A. Dile

My Love For My Son "Bob"

I love you, Bob, so much it seems
　　I can't bear ever to let you go,
And that's natural, that's human, warm and dear.

But the true test of my love is not
How fervently I clutched you to my breast -
But how willing I am to release you.
It was not only my job to teach you to walk -
　　But also to walk away.

When the day comes that God's ready for you
I will not urge you "stay, Oh stay with me"
But "go, be free and walk again and be
　　At peace forever.

　　I'll love you forever
　　　Mom
　　—Roni L. Skaggs

The Renegade Minstrel

My treason stands revealed, and as the crime
I clarion annealed, metallic rhyme.
Though I've no leave to persiflate and poke
My gibes, and peeve at blank, iambic folk

Who, surely in their stammer fraught with throes
Of life's sore straits, ought grammar then to prose
Consign; and wield the scepterdom of lit-
'rature from fright, y-clept, or from a fit,

Yet I cannot conform, lest I blaspheme
Diaphanous, when norm must be extreme
Staccato drumming blood space this churn-
ing mold to flood the grace by which I burn.

What pulseless coos of views, these vapid claques!
Frail fry who plug abstruse rose-colored wax
Within their ears - to nonchalance of jowls
That champ at consonants, and gulp on vowels! —

No, I'm spun not of mortarboard, nor hewn
Of cap and gown's reward, but I impugn
Atonic realms where thunderbolts are drowned
In platitudes and plunder of the sound!
　　　—Raymond S. Kauders

Something Unique

Somewhere in the forest, I found something so unique,
I could not help but pluck it, from its hiding place.
I took it home, oh so gently, so as not to efface any of its beauty.
It was placed, high upon my mantlepiece, for all the world to see.
I went to bed; joy in my heart,
with the thought of this treasure high upon my hearth.
But somewhere between the dusk and dawn, that piece of beauty,
it was gone. It was withered. Its uniqueness shattered.
Somewhere in the forest, I found something so unique,
I could not help but leave it, in its hiding place,
so that I can sneak; softly, quietly, to take another peek.
　　—Pamela K. Lanners

Tranquility

Somewhere up out of the dewy mist,
I could picture a feather swaying, dancing to the breeze,
with ever so much ease.

Up out of the dewy mist came the gentle rustling of the
wild flowers, as they bowed respectfully to the sway of
the breeze.

Up out of the dewy mist came the chirping of birds, offering
a melody ever so sweet,
as they danced around the outstretched limbs of the trees
lined up in rows so very neat.

As I focused my eyes I could see tiny squirrels darting
back and forward playing in the under brush, caught up
in the dewy mist.

As I saw butterflies landing on flower pedals, and I could
smell the aroma of honeysuckle as it rose out of the dewy
mist, I was totally encompassed in tranquil peace, calmness
invaded me and held me captive, within the dewy mist.
　　—Vera M. Douglass

At Night

At night when all are sleeping,
I creep into the kitchen and hear her voice weeping.

She looks up to me with hope,
Then in my heart I know she can cope.

With all her troubles, all her fears
A smile shines through, instead of tears.

She comes and plants a kiss on my head,
And tells me I should be in bed.

But something makes me stay,
"It's okay, sleep," she would say.

Slowly up the steps I go,
A smile comes to her face, a glow.

Without a word between us two,
I know she feels the same as I do.
　　　—Rachel Horn

Emotions

How can each time I see you be more memorable than the last?
How can my feelings for you increase each time I see you? And
each time we are together; you are more beautiful to me!
The reason, my dearest, is that my love for you grows each
and every day. Please be my love, and together we will share
our lives together, as man an woman, in true loves embrace.

My emotions burn with my love for you. My emotions are running
rampant with thoughts of you; my dearest! I want to write and
read love poems to you for the rest of my life! I truly am
blessed with a subject like you; how can I not but write my
emotions in love poems to you.
　　　—John S. Urban

"Hiding"

When I was oh so very little,
I do remember hiding,
Hiding from all those nasty men,
During that war,
I was so very little,
But remember so very much.
People being killed,
Because of their color or religion.
Gunshots and bombs everywhere.
I saw so much,
When I was so very strong,
I survived through those times.
I wish to never have to see those times again.
Hiding, hiding because I would be killed
If I were to be found.
Mom and Dad were oh so proud of us all,
For hiding ourselves.
I hope to never see war again!
To hide what I am so proud of,
Myself!

—*Lisa M. Elek*

My Little Buddy

My little buddy, why do I love thee?
I don't know why I don't say good-bye
My mind says leave but my heart pays no heed
I hope I am doing the right thing
for I'm afraid of the sting
I am caring, thoughtful and nice
but you keep thinking twice
I just wish you would take a chance
and give me that special glance
My Satellite and I would take you to the sky
Who else will carry you when hurt
or will beg for forgiveness upon a annoying flirt
We have many things in common
and we don't do too much stomping
I apologize for being jealous
but you are just too full of zealous
So little buddy, please be my little buddy
For I am grasping the last straw
and am going for it all
Life is but a walking shadow without you!

—*Tex Hawkins*

Stormy Dream

Resting in my bed listening to the soft cool rain,
I drift off to sleep where I should feel no pain.
In a dreamy sunset a raging storm comes,
to thunder, lighting, and wind do I succumb,
I stand looking out over a stormy bay,
as crashing waves make the land give way,
the birds and all the creatures make escape their goal,
and the cold, cold rain beats a path to my soul,
I fall down and feel the sand under my knees,
as I pray to the Lord to calm these stormy seas,
the storm rages on, I must get away,
but there's nowhere to go on this stormy bay,
oh! I see a light shining down the sandy shore,
then it's gone like the sudden slamming of a door,
so I wander in the darkness searching for that glow,
maybe someone is there, someone that I may know,
the lightning dances, the thunder cracks,
the restless wind drives cold rain down my back,
I don't think I'll survive this terrible storm,
but then I wake up in bed, all safe and warm.

—*Terrence Colbert and James Harper*

The Feelings Of The Sun, Sand And Surf

As I look into the sky,
I feel as free as a bird flying over the ocean,
While the sun beats down on my face,
I feel as if all of life's problems disappear.
As the wind blows through my hair,
I feel as if harmony has found its place,
When the sand sifts through my toes,
I feel as if all the tension in my body has been released.
As the surf crashes on the beach,
I feel a sense of power beyond belief.
Yes there is escape from this cruel world,
Were there is the sun, sand, and surf.

—*Monica C. Quantz*

A Perspective From The Crease

As the enemy approaches
I feel the tensing of my muscles
my shield is raised high
letting the enemy know this will be no easy fight
my three allies with their long swords drawn are my only help
no matter, they will fight to the death
I shall ignore fear
For I am afraid
my only thoughts are defending my ground
from the evil sphered demon
to yield to it is to yield to death

—*Anthony Cascio*

All Alone

I feel scared and alone in the world
I feel unloved and neglected
outside I look happy
But inside I'm crumbling with sadness
    like the earth under my feet
I feel like the rain
    when the tears fall from my eyes
I feel like the darkness
    engulfing me when I'm in despair,
    keeping me away from all living things
I feel like stabbing myself in my heart
    to put myself out of my misery
I have nobody to talk to
Nobody to trust with my deepest secrets
No one to love
And no one to love me back
I want to die
To be swallowed up into the earth
And never be seen again, except in peoples' hearts

—*Mercy Descallar*

Julian

When you, my child, were inside of me,
I felt as if my body, my womb,
Was a warm embrace wrapped gently
Around you.

Now that you are here,
I can smell your hair and touch your skin
And hear your soft voice.

Now that you are here,
I can hold you gently
Wrapping you in the warm embrace
Of my arms.

—*Nora Trogdon*

Parallel Pathways

With my chin in my hands and my elbows in the grass
I gazed, hypnotized by the ants as they passed.
With my head bent down, I'd view their industry,
In childish wonder I'd be filled with awe as I'd see
Their nodding heads, their racing feet,
Sometimes bumping as they'd meet,
The loads they carried and how each did his bit
For the organization into which they fit.

Now from the high rise building, I look below
And see the traffic in its steady flow,
Sometimes bumping as they go.
From east to west and south to north
They race around and hurry forth.
So I wonder at buses and trucks and moving cars,
Who is going? And where? And why? And how far?
Moving like the ants which piqued my imagination
I'm watching again, still filled with fascination.

—*Myna Gardner*

Black Eyed Susan

My name is Susan my eyes are black
  I grow by the old railroad track;
I live and thrive without much care
  Just sunshine rain and a touch of dare.
Mystery nature is my mother
  Besides God there is no other,
I prefer the wild to city soots
  Gardens disturb my hardy roots.
Not much to look at some may say
  To others I brighten their day.
Don't compare me to a regal rose
  I have more stout than one of those.
So if you should pass by
  I'll show my eyes of black
And continue to grow
  By the old railroad track.

—*Ruby Bostwick*

The Flame Of Eternal Love

When I was a young man many years ago
I had a vision of a young girl who's love
for me would grow on the day we met sixteen
burning candles began burning brilliant
white just sixteen burning candles burning
day and night. In my heart they will keep
burning as an eternal flame without
her love I'll never be the same. Then
there came the day you said goodbye, you
told me you were leaving, but you would
not tell me why, my love for you is a once
in a lifetime thing as my tears flowed like
rain, I could hear them hissing in the flame
sixteen burning candles burning brilliant white
just sixteen candles burning day and night. Many
years have past and though you say it's wrong
the heat from those sixteen candles keeps my
passion burning strong. Through the years
I close my eyes and see the glorious light
of sixteen candles burning day and night.

—*Rosetta H. Linger*

Mother

I know I'm getting old.
I hastily jot down ma's lyric earthy homilies
In both languages,
Strain for a compliment from her.
I overstate the excellence of meals -
Profuse ahs.
Find excuses to touch her frail frame,
Open mouthed on soft cotton pillow.
"I'm duty bound...," I say, in order
to idle more minutes with her.
At night I unwrap the icon, replenish the oil.
I love this broken woman, and want the privacy
to affirm the merit of her life.
She does not know I feel.

—*Nicholas Vourkas*

Heart's Desire

The man who broke my heart is no longer in my life,
I have found a new man that treats me like I'm his wife.
I love him deep in my heart,
What would I ever do if we come apart.
Before he was just a friend,
but now I love him and I don't need to pretend.
He is my heart's desire.
I can feel it inside, it feels like fire.
I know he loves me
I can see it in his eyes
I'm so glad he's not like those other guys.
It was a shock when this feeling came
What was I suppose to do when he felt the same.
He is the one I will always admire.
That's why he is my hearts desire.

—*Allison Stover*

You Only Live Twice

I have heard it said in school.
I have heard it said in the streets.
I have (even) heard it said from the pulpit,
As if that makes it correct.
In my struggle to convince people of
the inaccuracy of this statement I see no finish.
Sometimes I wonder myself (if I am right).
But, I know that I am (because he is).
Just like I couldn't care less (as opposed to could)
and letting a basketball roll
Off of your index and middle finger.
Only different.
I have heard it said in places of higher education.
I have heard it said in places of low income.
I have (even) heard it said in places of religion.
"You only live once!"
Don't believe it may child.
Don't believe them.
Believe him.
You only live twice.

—*Stephen A. Bailey*

I Wish. . .

I wish upon a star each night,
I wish the same thing every night.
I pick the star that shines so bright
and concentrate on the little light.
Each time I wish it's from deep down inside,
always something special that I would never hide.
I wish of heaven and of earth,
I wish for happiness not of hurt.
I wish for signs from the heavens above
never from greed,
always from love.

—*Angela Greenberg*

To M____

When I look into your eyes I see my Forever.
I have kissed your lips; now I don't need food.
I hunger only for the taste of you.
You have encircled me in your arms,
I've felt the pressure of your hands.
Now my body aches with longing for your caress.
I want, I want....but what?
To feel the soft tickle of your breath on my skin,
To hear your husky whispers in my ear,
To feel the length of you against the length of me,
Flesh to flesh!
I want to spend all my energy on you,
And drain you of yours,
Then lie in the hot, sweet exhaustion of your embrace,
Knowing the energy is never really gone, but rebuilding,
So, that we can burn each other in passion,
And laugh softly in the embers.
Then start with little loving kindness towards the next bonfire.
Let me make love to you.
Please.

—*Teresa Cecchetti*

Take Us By The Hand

I haven't a single reason.
I haven't a single clue
As to the reason that the seasons
Talk to me. And do they talk to you?

I haven't the right knowledge
Nor any eloquent speech.
But to you, Thoreau,
I do sincerely beseech.

Use your knowledge and wisdom
To aid this crumbling land.
Use this profound wisdom,
And take each of us by the hand.

Lead us to our home again,
To pleasures we forgot, my friend.
Take us to the country, to freedom I have to see.

—*Jessica L. Wyman*

This Man

I read the story of Footprints
I hear His name everyday sometimes used in vain
I read His book and follow His word
I try to reach out to people who haven't heard
  of this wondrous man
He brought us here and He will take us away
All His believers will meet Him someday
Some hear His call, others never do
If you believe and trust in Him He will be there for you
This man will love you through the thick and thin
Not just every now and then
This man has helped me
This man will help you
This man is right beside you in everything you do
The man I speak so generously about is the man none of us
  can live without
Our Lord Jesus.

—*Jessie L. Gilligan*

A Better World

I look upon the village and my eyes beseech the trash.
I hear the neverending bouts of gunshots, because of hash.
I feel the dead surround me looking for a dream,
a world lost to corruption is all that is seen.
I'm dreaming of a better world, one not sold to hate.
I dream of children unknown to their own fate.
I dream of peaceful interaction of all race, color, and creed
a world that lives for peace and not to deceive.
Dreaming of a better world in which there are no lies
and people are not killed because someone is high.
I'm dreaming of a better world unfortunately I know
that I can only dream, and it may never be so.
So tell the world around you to dream of better lives
for only those intuned with the heart can make those dreams
come alive.

—*Allison E. Long*

My Grandmother

As I lie in bed, not asleep,
I here my grandma up stairs walking around,
I laughed and snickered without letting a peep
cause she was slamming the cabinets for something unfound.

She want's to be cooking or baking a pie,
by the sound of the cabinet doors, I bet she could cry.

Never mind I thought, go back and dream,
the kitchens all hers for the stay,

well it was one more slam, then a scream,
she yells down, where's the dam pan, I want to bake this today.
So I laughed, and that's not being kind,
but grandma is looking for things she can't find.

—*Troy Reilly*

Secret Life

My name is anonymous,
I hide in the shadows of the night.
Pleading to be noticed,
Hungry for the light.
My life is a secret wearing its disguise.
No one meets my sadness no one hears my cries.
I feel like the forsaken one,
Living all alone.
Crawling to desolate corners fearing the unknown.
But there must be others like me.
Afraid to show themselves
Hiding their true feelings
Stashing them on shelves.
We are the chosen ones,
Running in life's race.
Wanting to be winners,
But settling for second place.
Trying to speak up, give us courage, we pray.
Our chance comes and goes,
Well, perhaps another day.

—*Shannon Tudor*

Girls

Girls are girls and boys are boys,
I'd like to say we are not toys,
We deserve respect and freedom too
For we are humans just like you,
some boys are Sexist and mean,
they put down girls, this I've seen
All people are equal no matter what sex or race,
It shouldn't matter your sex or the color of your face.
All people are equal , I'd like this to be clearer
All men were created equal, but all females
were created superior!

—*Sara Konvitz*

The Turning Of Hearts

This is a valentine poem;
I hope that you'll enjoy
It is meant for everyone
All the girls and all the boys

I know there are a lot of lonely people on this day
There are also a lot of them in here
A lot of empty hearts;
But none of you should fear

Without a friend on Valentine
A person would fell so blue
So look around this room
To find your love come true

For this poem I dedicate to you;
To let you open your eyes
To help you conquer the fear of love
So here my love lies.

For Valentines a time of happiness
A time when we can all be together
A time to share our joys
A time to love forever
— *Angie Chau*

We Knew

She touched my hand,
    I kept her heart.
The forest only was singing
    But then the world laughed out loud.
The day had dawned gray in my head.
    My hours had dragged busily on.
Then, in the middle of noon,
    The sun rose in her smile.
Sudden Joy! Sudden fear.
    Standing now on the edge of tomorrow,
Was also the launching pad to the rest of life.
    Lives, however, come... and stop.
And Love,...Flashes and fades.
    A deep breath, an immediate yes,
Praying that the rigor mortis of good sense
    does not set in.
I took her hand again.
    We loved the silence along the path.
— *W. Paxton*

Just Another Hole In This Glass World

Walking down this long dusty road of life
I kicked the fallen leaves
That covered my memories of you
I zipped my jacket
But just couldn't seem to break the chill
You left behind
When I reached the end of this dreary road
of sadness
I found you buried beneath me
I turned and walked down that same
Road with pockets full of memories
That somehow left me short changed.
— *Ronnie Gordon*

Faith

You was the one who stood by me in time of need.
You're the one who told me I could do anything if I put my mind to it.
You told me don't be stupid and mess up your life.
You said to get an education make something of your self.
Don't be stupid and drop out like the rest.
You believed in me and then showed me down the right path when
no one else would.
— *Amanda Gordon*

"Not Letting Go"

When I'm feeling down because of you
I know not letting go is the worst thing to do
For I really do feel as its been said
You can't bring back a love that's already dead

So no matter how bad I ever feel
I'll not hang on to a love that isn't real
But I'll just try to make it the best that I can
And believe at another time someday I'll understand

Yes someday I'll be over this pain
And feel the joy another love again
With so much behind me I'll start anew
And be all the stronger for what I've been through

For love never gives up we know for sure
But just keeps on rolling like old man river
So you don't really lose even when it's gone
For love has a way of keeping on
— *Judy McLallen*

Someone Will Take My Place

As the sun shines on my face
I know someday someone will take my place
As the blue sky turns to gray
I know you'll leave me someday
As the light dims to darkness
I know your protective ways I'll miss
As my tears drip into the stream
I think — is our love what it seems?
As the image of breaking away to
be with you comes to my mind
I wish today was that time
As my love for you grows strong
I wonder if our love is wrong
As you hold me, close so tight
I wonder if it'll be the same tomorrow night
My heart breaks and I
don't know what to do but tell you
I really do love you
But as the sun dims on my face
I know someday someone will take my place.
— *Nicole Drobnack*

The Miracle

As I look at the heavens above,
I know that you're just everywhere,
Or how could you have expressions of love
And not be right here and right there?
You remind us in spring
When the earth comes alive,
And again when the Summer goes by,
And the fall when the foliage tries hard to survive
When the Winter settles down with a sigh.
But whether it's spring with our hopes riding high
Or winter when everything rests,
Our hopes always seem on you to rely,
'Cause we know you'll give it your best.
— *Mary Lou Stuart*

Love

Love is like a rainbow
a promise for all to see,
Love is like a river that flows
so deep and free
Love is like the sand
a paradise just for you and me
Love is like the gleam
in your eyes that only I can see.
— *Melody Davis*

How Can It Be True?

People are saying some things about you.
I know these things can not be true.

They said you were dying
and were very sick.
I hope it's not true,
just a very mean trick.

They said you wouldn't live
much longer than now.
I asked them why;
I asked them how.

Please tell me yourself
this isn't about you.
I'm asking you this
how can it be true?

—*Lucy Davis*

Silent Cry

I'm cold, I'm hungry, I'm all alone;
I live in a box and call it my home.

Many can see me, but does anyone care?
Most only take time to idly stare.

I'm a person with feelings buried deep down inside,
but you don't care if I'm dead or alive.

I hold my sign high in the bitter cold,
"Don't look at them", as a child you are told.

I once was a child who of the future would dream,
my only dream now is of a warm bed it would seem.

So many pretend this problems not true,
it's only by chance this persons not you.

"Lazy bum, get a job", many would say,
but would you hire me in your office today?

You with your riches, your family, your home;
remember me in the cold all alone.

Just keep walking and never look back,
I'm sure you know it's compassion you lack.

I will survive living day by day,
and it is you I will think of tonight as I pray

—*Marci L. Sturgeon*

For Grandpa

There is a darkness within me
'Cause you are not here.
Yet there are memories of when you were near.
You brought a world of happiness and joy
That will never be forgotten.
My love for you will always remain
As you look down upon me.
You are in a place of peace and harmony
And someday I will join you.
You were among the wise and the brave
And you taught me well.
I would just like to say - I will miss you dearly
But until my day comes, you will remain
In a very special place within my heart,
And there you will never leave.
Every day I will remember your smile and spirits
And I will look up to the heavens
And thank the Lord for having you in my life -
And thank him for taking you in his arms,
George Earl Crawford Dec. 14, 1922 - Oct. 31, 1992

—*Ronnelle Seelke*

Lamentation

In the peculiar, the inconsistent, and the contradictions of life;
I live. In spite of the evil that threatens my very existence;
I am. Even when that which I do is clearly not in my best interest;
I err.

Like the moments when I feel free to confront the Almighty,
to demand an answer to the question of my Father's
disappearance.
Where in the world have you taken him? — I ask.
I demand that you tell the earth to give up his body at once;
I plea.

Then suddenly...
Out of the blue, holy boldness gives way to silent weeping.
Weeping turns to wailing, growing louder, and louder each
second.
I sigh, I gasp, I shout: Surely there's more!
O death, where is thy sting?
O grave, where is thy victory?

Then suddenly...
Out of the blue, sorrow gives way to rejoicing.
Rejoicing turns to singing, growing louder and louder each
second.
I surrender to the melody escaping from my inmost being.
Instantly, my lips bring forth the lyrics of a too long
unsung song.
"When we all get to heaven, what a day of rejoicing that will be!—I
    sing.

Yes, in the wonder of the peculiar, the inconsistent, and the
contradictions of life — I believe.

—*Rosetta Robinson*

Forever And Always

Memories of you will stay forever.
I long for the time when we had each other
What happened between us—I don't understand.
You walked away but never turned back
You left me alone in the shadows of earth.
I stood there alone, hoping you'd come back
The tears streamed down, spilling over my face
I called out your name but you were deaf to my voice.
I watched you walk out of my life
Forever and always.
I wanted to run yet I could not move
I stood silently in place.
Shaking with fear
For now I was alone
No one to comfort me or care
Forever and Always.

—*Sandra Di Santo*

Where A Poem Can Be Found

A poem can be found in the most obvious of a place.
Everyone has been there before.
Yet no matter how you try, you cannot get there
By sea, land, nor by air you cannot get,
Where a poem can be found.
Not in the ground or in a tree.
In the clouds above or in a heart full of love.
Do not search for sound,
Where a poem can be found.
Now I will tell you how to get there.
Just think and you are where,
A poem can be found.
And as you can see you don't have to move anywhere,
For the place is always station,
Because the best place to find a poem is your imagination.

—*Armando Zavala*

I'll Wait Forever

On the wall hangs the painting,
I look at, while I'm waiting
Listening silently to our favorite song,
Deep inside I know something is wrong.

Another long hour slowly goes by,
Then I realize a tear in my eye.
I turn away from the painting and look out the door,
And there on your face I saw a look
I'd never seen before.

I stood up and ran out to you,
Then I realize something that couldn't be true.
How could you think I wouldn't assume,
The fragrance on your body wasn't my perfume?

The tears in my eyes showed that I knew,
It was over between me and you.
I bowed my head and went inside,
To myself I silently cried.

I looked up at the wall at the painting,
And continued my life long waiting...

—*Melissa Denny*

Thoughts Not Of Tomorrow

Growing up thinking not of tomorrow
  I looked around and did not see
A comforting face to relieve my sorrow.
There only was an emptiness
  Expressions of love just didn't exist.

O how I longed to be held
  By someone special and close to me.
For every child who knows not love
  will suffer dearly in years to be.

And when this emptiness fills a life
  Bringing darkness instead of light.
The pains of today which bring such sorrow
  Come when thoughts are not of tomorrow.

—*Timothy J. Carter*

A Simple Touch (Is All It Takes)

Every simple touch, every passionate kiss
I meant and mean it all,
But it seems you have only helped me up to only fall.

I've tried to show you, and make you see,
but no matter how hard I try you'll never break free
I wish you could be certain and sure
close out old memories and open new doors
I realize you can't shut these feelings out but,
at least try to burn down old bridges and make new routes.

I've given you a piece of my heart
I'm more than willing to help you out with a new start..
I'm willing to give it a chance and try
for you I would be willing to die.............
You've got to be willing to give it a chance and try too,
I can't do it myself, I also need you..........

—*Tera Flack*

Death

Death comes with its icy fingers
Clutching your very soul,
Watching its prey with silent movements,
Ever watching, waiting to lunge.

Death is the final, lasting institution,
Dreaded and feared by all.
Death is a hunter with no preference;
None can compromise - none can resist.

—*Mary Jo Wilson*

Untitled

I am not a victim, if there are days I feel like one,
I must remember I made myself feel this way . . .
By relinquishing my control to others.

I mustn't find fault with myself on these days.
I must remember I am human and will stumble and even fall...
I must find forgiveness and strength to rescue my "victim".

I am a powerful individual. The only one in control
of my feelings and life. I have the ability to interpret
yesterday... change today... and envision my tomorrow.

I am an honest person who deserves love.
A person who has been blessed with the ability to love.
No conditions attached since all my needs are met by me.
Likewise, change isn't necessary to fill another's needs.

—*Kriss Kenyon Ellis*

"Simple Things"

Let me rejoice in simple things;
I need no wealth to buy:
For needs, not just desires:
The sunlight from my window: With
dawning of a new day, in which I may,
Do some good deed, for someone who needs:
My loving care,
Lord grant this that I may not outgrow affinity:
That for these, with grateful heart may with simple things:
Treasures to hunt:
Who can say there's nothing to do life is boring:
Will never find middle merely snoring in bed:
So many things one can do;
Then life cannot get boring; with paths to walk:
Stories that need telling;
These are the treasures of a simple day:
To soar with wings as of eagles, rejoicing with the simple
things each day.

—*Lillian Hergert Brill*

Death

What will I do when I die?
I often wonder with a sigh.
What do you say?
Where do you play?
When do I sleep?
Will I ever weep?

When will I go?
Does only He know?
Are we to ask this question?
Or should we get each day's full satisfaction?
I have seen many people die.
I ask the question and get the same reply.

I always end up with a sigh,
When I ask what will I do when I die?
But one thing I do know,
Is where I'll go.
It's my Savior's Place!
And I'll finally see His face.

—*Season Smale*

Lullaby Of The Stars

You snuggle in your bed at night
And quickly go to sleep
A thousand stars high in the sky
A silent vigil keep.
They twinkle brightly and seem to say
Sleep little one
While we watch for day.

—*Kathryn E. Mason*

Reflection

Watching my little boy
I perceive a mirror of myself
Reflecting my evolvement and philosophies
Expressing soul deep emotions
Emanating happiness and vitality
Shedding streams of tears
Throwing darts of anger
Stargazing dreamily and unfocused
Pensively drawing from intellect
Singing out to the world with innocence and sweetness
Energizing with crackling, intense inner fire
Innovating from the intuitive
Surviving from the instinctual
All reflecting wisdom learned through evolution,
Remembered by soul.

  —*Lois Ziemann*

The Lesson

 These words that now burn true and hot,
 I pray they'll linger and leave me not.
  For if time passes without expression,
I'll find once more I've learned "the lesson".

 That words are useless, unless they're free,
 to encourage, stir-up, or strengthen thee.
  And so I wait not till the dawn,
 to write my words, my thoughts, my song.

  I caution not to write them down,
  but fly the pen, on lines and crowns.
  And so once more, my soul's at ease.
  I now can greet the night with peace.

  —*Koral Lee Reefman*

Wings

To let you go is the hardest thing that I will ever do.
I pray to God that I've instilled helpful values in you.
I've seen you grow from a little child, to that grown up
Teenager who sometimes was even wild.
I've seen your accomplishments, and helped you day after day.
I would give anything and everything just to have you stay.
But there's that great big world out there that you want to
see, and every time I look at you I see a part of me.
Wings is what I give to you to let you wonder free. To touch
that horizon, and be all that you can be.
If you ever are in trouble, or need that special friend, all
you need to know is I'm right around the bend.
No matter where you are, or where ever you may roam, there's
always that special place waiting for you at home.

  —*Amy Marie Augustowski*

Through The Eyes Of A Child

Through the eyes of a child, I revisited my youth today.
 I remembered the importance of patience, kindness,
 tolerance, and love.

Through the eyes of a child, I was reminded of the
 importance of feeling special and being accepted.

Through the eyes of a child, I learned that big things
 are not so big, and small things are never small
 at all.

Through the eyes of a child, I was reminded that promises
 are things that should never be broken, never ever.

Through the eyes of a child, I met a hero today, and who
 would have thought it to be...the hero, to the child,
 was me.

Through the eyes of a child, for the very first time, all
 over again, I met me.

  —*Lillie B. McIntosh*

Smudge

In your presence ...
I rise to dissolve and disappear,
much like the last wisp of smoke from your pipe
as it curls up and into the air and is gone.

Then the part of me what was,
but is no more, floats broad
across the room where it clings
to the walls and the bookshelves
and the dying plant in the corner.

I am but residue clinging
to that plant behind your chair—
a smudge upon a jaundiced skeleton
that once stood fleshy, strong and sturdy
but was not nourished and now
withers, droops, and dies
...in your presence.

  —*Vicki Hinson-Smith*

His Peace I Give To You

Leaving my body after open-heart surgery
I rolled into Heaven about half past eight
Surprised to see no pearly gate
Magnificent beauty surrounded an unknown land
Beyond all known to the world
Indeed, I'm one lucky girl!
Great speed of passage of white light WITHIN a tunnel
St. Peter did not greet me—but HE,
The Lord Jesus Christ.
Majestic love and beauty of the Lord
Truly Omniscient beyond score
For such to perceive for a sinner like me
Casting away any doubt about what I believed
"Go Back! You have something To Do." as he
 put up his hands
Not wanting to leave
From a blue light came a friend named UNDERSTAND
God gave me peace to take with me
Carrying me through
'Till my dying day, HIS peace I give to you.

  —*Sharon Derrico*

Circle Of People

A circle of people link hands.
I run around them
Trying to become part of this caring warmth,
But there is no door.

Why am I not accepted?
I need to become one of them.

They don't seem to notice my presence
Though they tighten their grips.

Why won't they let me in?
Don't they see?
I'll give them all the love in the world.
I need to be accepted.

Turning away,
I embrace myself
And become my own circle;
My own love.

  —*Kerri Johnson*

The Test

You think life is a test;
 I say it's a quiz.
Sit down and number your soul one to five.
 Answer in no words or less.

Why am I, me?
Is life a contradiction of death?
Can you find your fate?
How is world a word?
Does love have a reason?

Now fold your soul over;
 it's become oversoul.
Grade your answers with all your cents
 and hope for a c, see.
You've tested a quiz.
 —*Peter L. Schneller*

"Your Not The Only One"

When I think I have it bad,
I see a car accident and it makes me sad
When I think it can get no worse,
I see someone driving a hearse
When I think my troubles have increased,
Is when I realize my neighbor is deceased
When I think I'm hanging from a rope,
I realize people are hooked on dope
When I think life is not fair,
I see someone in a wheelchair
If you would just stop in thought,
I'd be thankful for what I've got!
 —*Roxanne Tully*

The Mirror

What do I see when I look in the mirror?
I see me.
I see a person who loves and cares,
I see a person who is free.
A person with a good home, food and love,
A person who gets her love from above.
But yet not everyone is as lucky as me.
Not everyone is free.
Free of pain, and hunger,
Not free like me.
I have a house, and a bed,
And I don't have to dread,
Dread of where I'll sleep at night.
I want to know what will happen to these people.
I want to know if they will be lucky as me,
I want to know if they'll be free.
This is what I see when I look in the mirror.
I see you and me,
And together we can make our world a better place to be.
 —*Megan Lanz*

Contradiction Of A Ghost

Talk to your mother, she always seems to know.
I however am ignorant, don't trust such a fool.
Talk to your father, for he is wise, I am not.
The most you will get from me is a pack of lies.
Ask your best friend, he'll help, he understands
You, I do not. Why are you crying? It can't be
that bad. Yes, even tears can't help you. Would you
like a cup of tea? For, I am wonderful in the kitchen.
Unfortunately, espresso is not what you desire.
I know, forgive me? I must be going now, things will
workout, you soon will see. This I am sure of
because ghosts just know.
 —*Richard Balanaw*

Places

In the still of the night, I hear their voices.
 I see their faces;
Faces of loved ones gone on and old forgotten places.

Places of memories, places of childhood, places I hold so
dear, in my yesteryear.

I see myself as a little girl, surrounded by love and warmth
and I am at peace with the world.

Now, I've come near the end of my time. Life, sometimes, has
been hard. I've traveled many highways and the road has not
always been easy. But I know that soon again, I'll see their
dear faces, and will rest in the love of their sweet embraces.

I'll walk with them and I'll talk with them, all the
disappointments and hardships will be forgotten.

The mistakes of life will be forgive. We will all have peace
as we rejoice in the love of our Father above.
ONCE AGAIN, I'LL FEEL THE LOVE AND WARMTH OF MY
CHILDHOOD.
 —*Rachael McKee Greenwell*

Memories Of You

When at night I go to sleep,
I see your smiling face.
I think of all the times we've shared,
The warmth of your embrace.

If I could stop the time,
I'd make it stop right here.
I'd hold it as a precious stone;
Then you would be so near.

Our love is growing stronger
Each and every day.
It's you and me together-
Only us along the way.

You're the friend I've been searching for
To look out for me and care.
You're the lover I've been dreaming of;
Nevermore shall I despair.

There will be times when I make mistakes-
I apologize right now.
But know that I'll always love you.
That is my solemn vow.
 —*Megan Schott*

Love That Kind Of Love

I should have been a star
I should have had the fame and all of its glory
To have been a new Hollywood story
To have become beloved

I like that Hollywood glitter and glamours
Like those Hollywood manner
Love all the stars and all of the banners
Love that kind of love

I would liked to have walked up that golden ladder
Love dreams in my heart that mattered
Golden coins upon my platter
Love that kind of love

I guess I missed those Hollywood boats
Missed sowing my Hollywood oats
Someone played some very mean jokes
Love that kind of love

Give Hollywood an honorable mention
A golden deed award
Hollywood has given me my reward
Love that kind of love
 —*William E. Miller*

The Devil's Crotch

(A double black diamond run at Breckenridge, CO.)
I skied the hill that only a fool would try,
a man called Dan and me.

We started down, my life passed by I knew this was my
last mistake, the dare I had to take.

I smelled the hot breath of the devil himself
I begin to cry, hell I don't know why
All I knew I was about to die, that's why.

They named it well, this place called hell, as cold as ice,
"only that cold", but twice. The devils Crotch, a mean
mountain stretch, for fools on board called skis. What are
you
doing here? Old bastard Bill? You should be at home in a
rockin' chair and in your hand an ice cold beer. It all
begins at a spot called Vail, where the wealthy come to play.
If I had one wish, at a time like this, I wish I was far
away.

We reached the base, I fell on my face. Ouch, I did it well.
I skied the hill, I did it well and damn near went to hell.

It was better than sex, well almost Tex,
now let's belly up the bar a Jack Daniels I'll have, maybe
a double too, and a hot cup of coffee and pie... We skied
it well the Devils Crotch Daniel, Michelle and I.

　　　—William L. Baltezar

Branching Out

Eighteen years alive and
I stand on the brink of a new life.
Uncertainty has turned to unsight,
Has lead to hopes and dreams.
Wide open prairies wait to replace
The rolling landscape that is home.
Big buildings, big cars, big people
Wait to replace the routine that is England.

Living on the hopes of a dream,
The media shapes my imagination,
But I am glad to be proved wrong,
Content to be unsure, aware that
Uncertainty has not gone but is
Now accompanied by hope.

　　　—Lucy Large

"Fear"

As the wind blew against my face
I still was unable to understand the reason
Why did he have to lie?
Was he afraid to hurt me or did he want to?
I don't understand
I told him I didn't love him but he didn't care
But why am i hear crying?
There should be know reason for tears.
Now I find myself all alone and insecure
What am I afraid of? I don't know
But there's a fear coming through me
That I don't understand
Is it being alone?
Or is it just something uncontrollable
inside me?

　　　—Maddalena Nuzzo

Called To Witness

One anxious night as I tried to pray,
I stopped to hear what Our Lord had to say:

"Pray for all my people and be a witness to my love.
Pray for all creation and be a witness to my power.

Count on me as a shield against doubt and despair.
Trust in me as a light in the darkest night.

No matter what happens, even at the hour of death,
I'm always at your side; with all my angels and saints.

Your unfailing friend, Jesus of Nazareth.
　　　—Tim Chwala

Blue Vases

While walking down a shady Avenue
I stumbled upon, something new
Lovely crafted vases of blue
Reminding me of flowers, when the winters through

Reminding me of warmer days
Of crystal clear mornings, without haze
Of tulips, roses, orchids and maize ,
Of a tree-lined park, where a child plays

Ah, warm days 'n cool nights
A stroll along a lake of reflecting lights
A walk along a park absorbing the sights
Blues, greens, yellows, blacks and whites

Colors of the rainbow, confront my eyes
These warm days under sunny skies
The horse will graze, and the bird flies
Choirs sing and the baby cries
Ah, spring will come when winters through
And these vases crafted in blue
Will hold flowers for her and you
And the scent will remind of the morning dew.

　　　—Keith A. Bell

"Is This Poem A Living?"

Once upon a pompous poem
I thought I found something-damn 'em?

Those silly idiotic question marks
Shaped like quarks?

Alone, alone-they are so very alone
Is a genius in hell just a stepping stone?

Just when I prayed the nightmare was over
Another sadistic one-leaf clover—?

Stares me in the eyeball and says-
Where oh where has your sentence gone?

Life is but a breath in the sky
Why oh why must beauty whither and die?

Death is just a jigsaw puzzle
Can we repair a burning bubble?

Taxes are killing us; so be happy and sing!!!
Is everything just questioning???

We must find God before it's too late
And become the thing that we create?

Chain reaction, oh no, — OUT OF CONTROL!!!!!
—disintegration total—
　　　—Richard E. Walker

I Thought

I thought that I could make it easily on my own.
I thought it wouldn't be tough being all alone.
I thought when you left my heart would be o.k.
I thought I'd find another, until you went away.
I thought I wouldn't cry, or wish that you were near.
I thought I was alright, until I dropped a tear.
I thought the nights would destroy all the memories.
I thought I could forget the way things used to be.
I thought all my fears, in my smile, could hide.
I thought my true feelings would be covered by my pride.
I thought the pain would be nothing, nothing at all.
I thought I'd walk with my head held high, but on it I seem to fall.
I thought the warm embraces had no effect on my pain.
I thought your love was nothing, that it was all the same.
I thought I'd get over it, but I guess I was dreaming.
I thought, I thought, I thought. That's what I get for thinking.

  —Tracy Dugger

Student Lament

A huge tornado lifted up my house into the sky,
I thought, "Oh, no! This is the end! I'm really gonna die!"
The twister vanished suddenly as it had appeared!
I thought, "This is too strange for me; it's getting very weird!"

The house began to plummet and I screamed and screamed and screamed.
A dragon flew and grabbed it, helping me, it seemed.
But then it started eating it; I was in a bind.
I then leaped out the window, scared out of my mind!
I started falling swiftly, heading for the ground.
Everything was quiet, not a single sound.
A sudden wind came at me, blowing me away.
That is why I did not hand my homework in today.

  —Michael A. Kaplan

The Oldest Child

As a baby you were so strong
I tried to teach you right from wrong
Because a father you never had
To your younger brothers you were a dad

At a young age responsibility you did assume
And because of this you became a man too soon
A mothers joy you have always been
Your kind of loving is not often seen

Although right now you are away from home
Your love for your family does not roam
In another city right now you live
In spirit your love you still give

Someday my first born you will return
Where your mothers love forever burns

  —Nilsa Broughton

The Garden

As still as the shrub behind me,
I watched the leaves sway in the breeze.
Sunlight and shadow mottled the ground,
And the weeds whispered to me,
Lulling me like distant voices of children at play.
Closing my eyes I pretended I was in a magical place,
Safe from pain and sadness and death.
Slowly I opened my eyes like sleeping beauty in an enchanted forest,
But all I saw were weeds and bushes...
And I was all alone.

  —Tiffany Brown

"Growing Old"

Where, Oh where has youth gone?, seems it just slipped away,
I used to tend a big garden, but then, that was yesterday.

I could thread a needle in the blink of an eye,
But somehow those days have all slipped by.

My beautiful auburn hair has turned to dingy gray,
Yes, it seems that youth has just slipped away.

This is the time the privilege to take,
To slow down a bit for old age sake.

Yes, now it is dentures, bridges, glasses, a wig,
You're no longer up to "cool it," "chill out" or "I dig."

My young springy step is now a slow pace,
So I'm resigned to just grow older with grace.

  —Amelia Schipper

The Earth In Space

Sages talk about aliens in outer space,
 I want to talk about the human race
And the earth with its technology, pomp and grace,
 But we can't say were really on home base.

Unlike other known aliens we cannot fly
 With such contraptions that look like a pie.
This just happened to be a most scenic domain,
 Where we could see snow, also hail or rain.

We might have been delivered on the planet Mars,
 Or scattered around like a billion stars,
But God had a real purpose for our creation,
 He bade us to beautify the nation.

He wanted us to cultivate and seed the soil,
 Or fly to Arabia...in search of oil —
Go prospecting for silver, gold nuggets and ore,
 And populate the earth forever more.

We always consider we're living on home base,
 But the earth is only hanging by grace.
We are really aliens, or a human race,
 Living on planet earth in outer space.

  —Alberta Williams

"My Dear Friend"

My dear friend, I miss you so,
I wanted to write you, to let you know.

Your in my every thoughts, day and night,
Even though we are miles apart, you are always in sight.

Your being thought of, believe me it's true,
I think of all the good times, and I really miss you.

I think of all the laughter and the fun we have shared,
and a warm feeling comforts me because I know how much you care.

When I close my eyes, the picture is very clear,
your love abounds with me, and you feel so near.

I can see your smile on your glowing face,
I can feel your touch of your warm embrace.

I can feel your warmness surrounding me,
and it makes my heart shiver and filled with glee.

I thank the Lord for our friendship true,
for when I get lonely, I just think of you.

Thank you friend, for your love and tender care,
I know in my heart, you will always be there.

We will bond together, until the very end,
I love you truly, my dear friend.

  —Tina Fina

A Cold Dreary Night

On a cold dreary night
I was lost and I began to pray.
Please help me Lord to find my way.
There was this peace and calm came over me.
I knew the Lord had heard my plea.
Out in the distance I saw a bright light
twinkling like the stars above.
I slowly followed the glittering light
the Lord had sent to light my way.
I began to thank the Lord for each and every day
and to Praise Him for all the things which he had done.
I asked the Lord to please have mercy on me
and forgive me for all of my sins
and to help me never to lose my way again.
Lord I'm so glad you sent me the light
and saved my soul on that cold dreary night.

—*Agnes Johnson*

You've Gone Away

Remember the kind of friends we used to be?
I was there for you, and you for me.
You were my "big brother,"
There was no other
That I could look up to,
Like I could you.

Summer was leaving.
And you were dreaming
Of all the fun you'd have
Working to be a college grad.
The empty feelings I wouldn't know
Until you had to go.

Now looking back,
The past went so fast.
I had no clue
How much my life would change
Without you.

—*Kristi Baker*

Untitled

Though now sixty seven, it was when I was eleven,
I was told by the dear nun to write a poem.

And through the alphabet I would go
rhyming words until I reached the letter "O",

It was fruits and vegetables I had in mind,
until I got to "orange" and no rhyme could I find.

I knew nothing of iambus and meters,
of poetry I had not been a reader.

Through every thesaurus I searched and I sought
to rhyme a word with "orange" but all for naught.

There was "apple- dapple", "carrot - parrot", "fig - big"
"melon - felon" and on it goes,
but the rhyme for "orange", no one knows

Though now I am old, but not yet frail,
like those who search for the Holy Grail
I will spend the rest of my time
searching for a word that "orange" will rhyme

And should it ever come to pass and my detective
work has made me famous, I may go down in history as being
a very persistent shamus.

—*Mildred I. Fitch*

Hopes and Dreams

As the wind blew outside of my window
I watched the trees whisper words of despair
The sky is no longer spectacular
The land that was once plentiful
of hopes and dreams
Is now empty and uncarried through
Yet over the hill
One solitary rose struggles to grow
On unfertile land
One day the sun will rise over that hill
And that solitary rose will blossom
with demanding hopes and dreams
With a great ability to carry them through

—*Sarah Jane Ashbaugh*

One Moment In Time

For just one moment in time.
  I wish that I could hold you.
For just one moment in time.
  I wish that you could be mine.
For just one moment in time.
  I wish that I was more than a friend.
For just one moment in time.
  I wish we could share a special night.
For just one moment in time.
  I wish you could see me through different eyes.
For just one moment in time.
  I wish you would have me.
For just one moment in time.
  I wish you would say, "I Love You."
For just one moment in time.
  I wish this was not just a dream.

—*Lindsay J. Gunneson*

Racism

Prejudiced people are in the world today.
I wish their racist thoughts would just decay.
It's not right, it's not civil, it's just stupid, that's all.
Just think, what they say, "You're not one of us," they call.
Burning crosses is just one immature thing that they do.
I think, though, that we're equal. I just wish they did, too.
"How can we stop these racists?" you say.
"How can we make their thoughts go away?"
It's impossible, it's unthinkable, they don't just disappear.
They're always here, they're always there, they're always very near.
Just ignore them and don't let them convince you to say,
"You don't belong here. You're not one of us. We don't want you
  to stay."

—*Vanessa Pratt*

Without You

As I sit in my chair; lost in thought,
I wonder if life is all for naught.
The best part of my life has been taken away
Nothing's the same; nothing's worth while
Must I live out my time just day by day
With my happiness gone, not wanting to smile
I miss your voice; I miss your touch,
The pain I feel is just too much
Will we find happiness together once more?
Is this what God really has in store?
Will we be together in a different place?
Will we hug again; will I kiss your face?
I have to believe it will be that way
Or I could not live through another day.

—*Mary Vreeland*

Sunset Over the Ocean

As the sun goes down,
I wonder, where it goes next,
The color is so pink,
With a little blue and purple mixed in it.
Sunset over the ocean,
How romantic it can be.
The two lovers walking hand in hand watching,
The sunset over the ocean,
I wait patiently for it to rise again,
So I again can watch,
The sunset over the ocean.

　　—*Rebecca Finch*

I Am

I am small and get scared easily,
I wonder why there is war.
I hear my dog meowing.
I see rain when its not really raining.
I want the whole world to have money and not be poor.
I am small and get scared easily.

I pretend I'm a famous person.
I feel the moon dancing on me.
I touch the birds high in the sky.
I worry about what my life would be like when I'm out of
college. I cry when I think about something happening to my
family. I am small and get scared easily.

I understand why everyone gets sad when people make fun of them
I say they should let girls be President too!
I dream that someday I'll be President of the United States.

I try to get good grades in school.
I hope that everyone lives a long and healthy life
I am small and get soared easily.

　　—*Samantha Burkhardt*

You Found The Key To My Heart

I would kiss the moon, and melt the sun,
I'd grab all the stars, and give you one.
I'll stand in your shadow, I'll fly higher than the sky,
you heard me say I love you, but you thought it was a lie,
you know our love is true I hope we never drift apart,
call the locksmith, you found the key to my heart,
when you sleep at night, I'll dream, I'll stop the thunder
and the rain, there's an opening in my heart that you fall
under, when I see tears fall, I'll take away the pain.
I'll pick up the world for you, and throw it as far as you
wish, I'll breath all the air for you, and hope to end our
lives with a kiss, I'll hold you tight, as our words collide in
the dark, call the locksmith, you found the key to my heart.

　　—*Joseph Dale McCortney*

How Could I Ever Repay You

How could I ever repay you,
I'd love for the whole world to see,
Just how much two special parents,
Have really meant to me.

How could I ever repay you,
I'd love to write it across the sky,
How much I really love you,
More and more as each day goes by.

I guess the only way I could ever repay you,
Because you've done so much for me,
Is pass down the love and understanding,
To my daughter, Anne Marie.

And let her know just how much two special parents
Have really meant to me.

　　—*Rose Ann Bordino*

Mother Love

This simple gift I send to you, in value is so small.
If I was a fairy my magic would fall.
All your days would be sunny, your skies blue and fair.
Plenty of laughter and sunshine, with never any worry or care.
You would be queen and live on a throne, have a castle all of
of your own.
There would be a wee prince and a princess too.
Then you would know how mama felt about you.
Love that will last until you're withered and old.
For God's greatest gift is love and not gold.

　　—*Jean White*

The Gift

These feelings I feel in private are lost -
if not given away - regardless of cost.

Shyness clouds endeavors to touch -
my reaching to one - needing so much.

Confidence wanes - security escapes -
you'll laugh at my lines - I've made a mistake!

I cover sincerity in laughing tones -
to hide my earnest and not let it be known,
that someone here - sees a need -
so I try to amuse - with my little poem.

My timid spirit is deep in these lines -
locked in the prison - shyness confines.
I must offer something - I feel compelled -
to give my feelings and throw doubts to hell.

So know when I approach you - wanting to flee -
your accepting the gift - is your gift to me.

　　—*Ann Baxter*

You Are

If we look deep enough,
If we look past the pain, the confusion of life.
There is elation.

There's a cool, free space in your heart,
There's nothing but you there,
And you are,
　　You just simply are.

Tides of thought lap the shores of gold,
gentle, quiet things drift across the sky,
The peace greets each new day,
And every word means joy.

The sweet sounds of silence caress you here,
touching your mind with a soft, sweet passion,
The reality around you fades with the setting suns,
Fades until it just melts away,
And you are,
　　You just simply are.

　　—*Quentin Bounds*

To My Granddaughter "Ara"

I love you while you're young and small
I'll love you, too, when you're grown and tall
You are one of life's greatest treasures
Needless to say you give me many pleasures
I count my blessings every day
I love you in a special way
Whether you are far or near
Your voice and laughter ring in my ear
I just had to tell you in my own way
How much I love you and miss you this day.

　　—*Sylvia Katz*

Soul Flight

Let's let the night, this night.
Ignite with light. The light
that shines within our souls.

In the world we are in. Our souls
seem to dwindle deep within.
Compassion for others is pushed aside,
For practical purposes of everyday life.

In the night amidst our sleep.
The soul flies free.
We see ourselves in a world that exists
in perfect harmony.

Society teaches me to think of I,
First and last. When we all can agree.
Our souls will fly free, as we think of you and I.
Two tiny parts of a worldwide family.

    —Robert Reichelt

Tonight Show And Forever

Johnny, Johnny, what more could I say
I'll miss you more than Tammy Faye

I've watched your show since I was six
Back then, I knew you were a hit

My parents brought me up right
Watching your show every night

But now I'm twenty-three
And a better show I'll never see

You've had monkeys on your head
And had your feet read
You're a man defined as-gallant and well bred

We'll take Jay with open arms
But you'll always be the king with the charms

In some states your show is on late
Let's just say you brought up the birth rate

Sentiment is not my style
But across the country, you've brought a smile.

    —Mary Koehler

To Share Your Name

I don't know how to slay this; but I think it's time I do
I'll never forget how scared I was; when Chuck left me here with you.
I was just stranger; who you welcomed into your home.
You greeted me with open arms, and treated me like your own.
In you I found a friendship; that would last a long long time
For you are lovely people; who wasn't hard to find.
You're shown me lots of good times; and helped me through the bad.
Your there in times of trouble; and cheer me when I'm sad.
I want you both to realize; how much I love your son.
I will make him happy; and show him lot's of fun.
As time flew by so quickly; I proved chuck was my life
I shall give him all my love; as you except me as Chuck's wife.
I just want to thank you; for your understanding and your care.
I'm glad we now are family; and for all the things we share
I'm proud to be a walker; it makes me feel so glad.
I just want to tell you now; I love you Mom and Dad.

    —Roberta Walker

Sorrowful Afterthoughts

I surrendered to bleak thoughts that occupied my mind
I'm all alone now, just a prisoner of time.
Darkness surrounds me, yet still I can see
The vacant places where I used to be.
Mother is sad, and I hear her cries
As I stand and watch her, tears fill my eyes.
Forgive me, Mother, but it was for the best
I'm different, very strange, and unlike the rest.
I wish I could talk to you, and tell you why
I took my life without saying good-bye.
I never meant to hurt you, you did nothing wrong
I just had so many problems, and didn't belong.
It's all over now, everything is in the past
Your pain will pass with time, for nothing ever lasts.

    —Rebecca Shannon Palk

Look Up

Don't grieve for me-
I'm as happy as can be
For I am with Jesus now
And all the angels are nearby too.

When you look up in the sky at night
You will see me for I am the brightest light
Cause I am the newest one there is
Right up here in this beautiful place

I would not have wanted to live
On your earth so unaware
That there was someone that needed care.
Life on earth can be so cold.

So look up at night and see me
And know that I am much better off than most
And I will be caring and sending you love,
And someday we will meet and that's how life is.
So smile Mommy and Daddy-
Cause I am happy right up here.

    —Ruth Tooley

My Best Friend

She's gone now her life came to an end.
I'm longing to see my very best friend.

She was so young with a long life to live.
She was helpful caring and willing to give.

We joking and laughing on the side of the street.
The wind was singing its songs so sweet.

Around the corner we heard a loud noise
Coming in a distance a truckload of boys.

The truck swerved as it sped down the street.
Coming at me as quick as a beat.

My friend jumped over pushing me aside.
The truck hit her and instantly she died.

I held my friends bloody body as the medics came.
How could this have happened, life would never be the same.

I owed my friend my life but couldn't give.
For she was dead and I had to live.

I didn't get to tell her how I loved her so.
I'll hold her in my heart forever and never let her go.

    —Alison Dobbs

"Just Plain Me"

I'm not Alan A,
I'm not Phil D,
I'm not an 80's man
I'm just plain me

I don't fly like a bird
I don't sting like a bee
I'm not an 80's man
I'm just plain me

I can be sensitive
I can be sweet
but I'm ruff around the edges
and I'm not too neat
I'm not an 80's man
I'm just plain me

I made some mistakes that brought me shame
but I did it my way and I took the blame
I'm not an 80's man
I'm just plain me

I'm not an 80's man
I'm just me.
—*Steve Tsantis*

(Why Do I) Mean Nothing

Why do I get the hint
  I'm not wanted
maybe it is the people surrounding me
  or just the way I am
but in other words I can be especially happy
  why do I talk the way I do
people are always looking at me
  they think I have mental darkness
why do I have such a preoccupation in guys
  they think I'm unusual
so what if I don't interest them
  I'll find some one out there
why do I look the way I do
  I am pleasing to the eye in a way
I am slender and have pretty hair
  but I usually call myself over weight
but am eye?????!!?
  if you find this entertaining
please tell me you like my extraordinary writing
—*Monica J. Groff*

Life

As I look back to think about my past,
I'm reminded of what God has done for me,
I'm finally happy with myself at last,
I've struggled through hard times and now am free.

Too many years I've spent depressed and sad,
Not knowing who to trust or to believe,
But now I've seen that life's not all that bad,
And now I have God's love I'm now relieved.

As I walk down this awesome road of life,
I count my blessings and I kneel to pray,
For I know that life will be full of strife,
But I can handle it needles to say.

It's by doing what God gives us to do,
That we find real love and happiness too!
—*Angela Skierski*

Impressions Of Pop Singers

I'm falling, pick me up
I'm sitting, stand me up
They don't know what they're doing, but it hurts
They ask me for this, ask me for that,
What next, my shirt?

Don't say anything, I'm trying to be quiet
Yelling at me as if I'm on fire
Have I done anything wrong?
Have I done anything right?
Got to please them, got to please them - right on sight

They don't realize, they've shattered me
Into pieces, into pieces thrown
blindfoldedly in the sea

Make me cry, make me try, stand
on one foot, fall on the other
—*Mark Resendes*

How I Wish

As I dreamt of how I wish the world would be
Images of fruitful fields come to mind.
With cotton in the sky and water in the sea
These hopes seem so close to me.

But as I come to where I was before
I see pollution where the birds were to be
A black storm on the ocean shore
Has now taken over and is destroying the earth's core.

I wish we could change our ways today
But it seems as if people do not realize our needs.
If beings on this planet change their views
Hopefully one day the world will be Okay!
—*Lynn Mobley*

Dreams Don't Die

Creativity is in the air.
Imagination is on the wind.
All good dreams never pass.
The pot of gold is around the bend.

Hold fast to life.
Because the rain can drown you out.
Then you can live in solitude
And do without... creating.

Sometimes we use sadness.
As an excuse not to write.
Just sit down and analyze
And let the pen take flight.

Wipe the tears away,
Whether of sadness or joy.
Then capture on your paper
The hearts of a little girl or boy.

Because ... dreams don't die!
—*Richard H. Perkins*

Animals

Animals are for their beauty,
Not for their skins.
They are used once,
And never again.
One is dead.
One is alone.
Pretty soon they will all be gone.
Now I say, they're killing for fun.
They cannot move, they cannot run.
Without being killed by somebody's gun.
—*Colt Collins*

Pippa's Muse

On a dark December afternoon in a little town near Surrey
In a tavern there where people go, when they are in no hurry,
Pippa sits all by herself, like many times before.
While the tavern clock tolls the hours, Pippa's in her muse.

Smoke drifts from her cigarette around a glass of wine.
Alone there, in the corner, where she spends most of her time,
People passing by her sometimes stop and say "hello",
But only faintly stir the still, enclosing Pippa's muse.

Raindrops drizzle slowly from a great, gray, English sky.
That's given her the quiet time that she is dreaming by.
Perhaps, she's lost in hazy thoughts of country in the spring.
No one knows what fills the hours embracing Pippa's muse.

Afternoon is evening now, the day has slipped away.
She knows that soon she'll have to leave, she really cannot stay.
The lively crowds are coming soon and that will end the stillness.
And all the thoughts that nestle deep in the depths of Pippa's muse.

She walks into the misty night, the streets slick from the rain.
She wants to find another place to sit and dream again.
She goes back home and to her room, her refuge from the world,
There to shed the lonely tears that fall from Pippa's muse.

—*Peter C. Lynch*

Faceless Beauty

I've seen your faceless beauty
in anticipations of many times before.
Your emotions will always give me inspiration
to write forever and more.

Last morning, you bewildered me once again;
nothing like I've ever envisioned in the past.
You alluringly becalmed me to a stand still;
a memory that will always last.

I didn't see a face on your misty blanket,
but I could see your eyes were sparkling blue.
Your beauty was so eerie, yet excited me;
You took away my breath with your point of view.

You are so simple-hearted with all of your free honesty.
You are transparent yet evasive; that you cannot deny.
Your emotions are: oceans, land, moon, rain, and sun;
You are simply the earth and also the sky!

—*Mary A. Olczyk*

Reflections Of Vietnam

Pain sharply etched on one man's face,
In appearance of age, youth quickly erased.
Memories mirrored from the past, living echoes resound,
Unforsaken, unforgotten, still graphically found.

A pledge of three decades, intrepidly shared,
Harsh cruelties of mankind forever lay bared.
Heaven's cries filled the earth, death seized its toll,
Freedom's quest bravely sought by each tortured soul.

In honor and defiance, truth gallantly hailed,
As the valiant and proud in justice prevailed.
They seized victory, each man, from his predestined grave.
True sons of courage borne by the price they had paid.

Their legacy written, an epic monumental in time,
Their bell of liberty yet peals for your seed and mine.
Today's undecorated heroes, yesterday's unclaimed pride,
A bitter memorial to the young who have died.

—*Michelle Engmann*

Life

We search for meanings
in between layers of seconds, minutes, and hours.
We search for answers
while we're gazing at that distant star.

We try to understand
and give it some new meaning
when all the while
in our minds we know
it is oh so fleeting.

The journey at first
seemed never ending.
As we go through it though,
it's not the taking, it's the giving.

Try not to take it for granted.
Tend to sew good seeds,
nurture them while their planted.

We must learn from it,
and pass its secrets to the young.
Life is an opportunistic journey,
today your life has just begun.

—*Alfred Boyd Jr.*

Untitled

There must be mad romances
in every man's vision.
Life, there must be more...
the ugly isn't ugly enough,
Bum trips aren't bummy enough,
to struggle more than challenge,
For blood, not for game.

Something else than riches or fame,
Sincerity isn't neither are facts enough.
To memorize more than know,
living most lies, beyond Being.
Taking dark paths, instead of Enlightenment.
Every day the war, the poverty, the disease,
The population, and people pollution.

Life, there must be more... Than blind alleys.

—*Merle K. Lai*

The Boy I Love

The boy I love is not a star
In fact, he doesn't live too far
Its Picayune, you see
But he is always passing me
I see him in town, I see him in the streets
But the most current place I see him is in
my dreams
Without him, soon I will go crazy
If his heart does not stop being lazy
All he has to do is open up to me
And I'll be happy and no longer free
If he were only here to restore my confidence
Am I making any sense?
Sweetheart, the only thing I have to say to you is:
Colby, I love you!

—*Becca Coco*

The Dove

A dove sings for her long lost love beneath the pale blue sky
In flight she searched the countryside waiting for his cry
Each evening she would perch alone upon the branch they'd
shared. Placing yet another feather for the nest they had
prepared. So white and pure she seemed to me, a shy and gentle
bird. And while she sang her song of love, I watched without a
word. In silence, covered by shadows, hidden by the night
She waited for the morning, with the coming of the light. As
dawn approached, there came a rain, with mist upon the land
Why her love did not return, she could not understand. No song
was heard that morning, with her head beneath closed wings
I knew her only comfort, was that which true love brings
My heart did rend within me, at the sight of one so fair
For now she was unable to sing in her despair
With tears, I whistled softly, hoping she would hear
As the clouds that had surrounded began to disappear
And lo, the heavens parted before the earth below,
Sending forth the shining sun upon a rainbow's glow.
A graceful dove descended, through a ray so bright
As a union, oh so splendid, transformed before my sight
For a love thought lost was found again, singing in the light.

—*Mary Ann McIntyre*

Sacramento

The Book of Common Prayer, in printing "Rites",
in older books meant words-as-used. Not actions.
In the New Book, Rite One, Rite Two, indites
those who naively tolerate false factions.
Rite? In the singular? Rise! And resist!

The Blessed Sacrament, Sacramento,
means quite the opposite of Eucharist.
"Do this..." elucidates the way to go—

Jesus, at his Last Supper, said "Do this..."
Those words, resounding like a trumpet call,
send "in remembrance" close to that abyss
whence few ascend. Vertiginous, the wall!

If we are branches, and he is the vine,
why do the grapes when trampled, turn to wine?
Then, sanctified, create that unique sign!

—*Phebe Alden Tisdale*

"Love Again"

I remember the night not to long ago you told me you loved me
in that voice so soft and slow.
You told me I was beautiful and I thought it
to be true for a second I saw another side of you,
but times have changed we've went on with own lives.
These lovers have become strangers and
everyone can see that falling in love again just couldn't be.
You never call, you never write, it's only my heart so
let's not fight.
I thought it was love I guess I was wrong,
so why when
I close my eyes I see us dancing
to our song? My head is saying
forget you, my heart is saying your
the one. I guess my dilemma has
only just begun. For now just let
me say, I'll take my heartache day by day.

—*Melanie Wood*

Help Me Through The Dark

Sometimes I close my eyes at night to sleep and I shudder
in the darkness. I open my eyes to escape this void, just
to find I'm still in the dark. I cry for a light that never
fully appears. A flicker, a spark, and darkness returns.
I fumble in the dark, searching for a way out, but I only move
in circles. I hear laughter, whispers taunting me, mocking
me, and I beg for my sanity. I see a sliver of light, maybe a
crack in a door, but the darkness holds me back. I scream,
"Help me through the dark!" My screams are silent. I sit in
the dark. Do I rush to the light? Do I break open the door?
Or will my way be blocked? Should I yell a little longer in
the hope of extending the crack? I'm alone in the dark. Tell
me what to do. Open the door. Help me through the dark. I
need to be free to love. Did I make the darkness? Can I be
free? I'm so very scared. PLEASE! Help me through the dark!?

—*Matt Roman*

"I'm Here For You"

I see the pain you harbor there,
In the deep recess of your mind.
I see the struggle to hold it in,
You won't release it, you're not that kind.

You fight your battle all alone,
The hurt struggling to be let go.
You've pushed it deep within yourself,
So deep, it really shouldn't show.

I tease, I touch, to draw it out,
So I can share the pain you hold.
A gentle smile plays on your lips,
But your eyes! They're still so cold.

I touch my lips to your face,
And kiss away your fears.
I touch my fingers to your cheeks,
And wipe away the tears.

A tiny smile turns up your lip,
Which you quickly try to disguise.
But this one travels up your face,
And ever so beautifully, warms up your eyes.

—*Linda J. Ballard-Harney*

Morning Night

It was a beautiful morning night,
In the hot cold morning night air.
The grasshopper crickets were chirping,
And the coyote wolves were howling.

The beautiful flower tress,
Were dropping their petal leaves.
The sun moon shone bright,
And the water land glistened and shined.

The early late bird sang its tune song,
On a small cherry peach tree.
The small gray red fox scamper played,
In the tall short grasses and flowers.

The deer fawns ate the sweet grass,
Out in a meadow field.
A little squirrel chipmunk scampered,
Up a cherry oak tree.

It was a beautiful morning night,
In the hot cold morning night air.
The grasshopper crickets were chirping,
And the coyote wolves were howling.

—*Julie Christensen*

Waiting Game

Bent fingers twist damp cotton. The photo
In the silver frame looks unblinkingly
From the dresser into nothing. To go
Where he is. Into that void. To tingly

Surprise or emptiness. But she waits.
They visit. Her daughter. Her sons. And a
Girl who goes to school nearby. And as the dates
Change on the calendar and float away

Her daughter and her sons say, "We love
You. How can you think of leaving. Come on."
So she sits alone and memories of
Laughter keep her company. Now all done

With and more real to her than anything
Happening right here. She knows them to be
Ghosts — floating by and through her. Not touching

Her at all. Feels their chill. A mere presence
In her room. She plays along. A waiting

Game. Fueled by her thoughts. Serving her sentence.
Her husband is free and she is waiting.

　　—*Sylvia Lamb*

Soaring With the Eagle

The eagle soars so high
in the sky, so carefree, never
questioning why,
No feelings of love or hate
searching only for his perfect
mate. He soars from tree to
tree. Not realizing it's wonderful
to be free. Free from all
the war down on the ground
no homeless eagles up here to be
found no poverty no visions
from drugs. No bumps and
bruises from street thugs. No
worries of tomorrow - no dreams
to be shattered. Just the soft
wind and the eagles chatter,
Born to soar born to fly free. An eagle
must be a wonderful thing to be

　　—*Amanda Lane*

When Winter Comes

The light of life dawns
　in the soul of the babe.

The warmth of love
　nurtures the body growth.

The gift of friendships
　mold the character.

The pursuit of knowledge
　tempers the mind.

The union of love
　regenerates the cycle.

The passage of time
　guides one to summer, autumn, and...

The recall of all that has past
　signals when winter comes.

The Frost, the Wind, the Ice, the Snow
　when winter comes man must go.

　　—*William J. Gary*

Summer Pajamas

My Mama washed me
in the tub.
I am so fresh and clean.
The sky's deep blue—the sun has gone,
and shadows now are seen.

My feet are bare.
The grass is green.
I feel so free and light.
The stars have lit and hung themselves
for the coming of the night.

I romp and skip,
I roll about.
I'm in PAJAMAS—See!
It makes me feel like a summer elf,
or maybe a fairy.

　　—*Robin Meier*

The Immigrant's Dream

The immigrant's dream forgotten
In urbanity now rotten,
Where the metallic maggot's steam,
Escapes the corrupted streets unclean.

"Make things better," people shout.
"Yes, change," leaders return with false clout;
For decay continues through their smiles,
Through those fix-it-all guiles,

And the ants that beneath us hide,
"Fools!" fools!" they would chide,
For we are complacent complainers,
The hand of progress's detainers.

We want everything to be right,
But are no sooner out of sight;
Waiting for rewards unjust,
Waiting 'til we wither from the crust,

So heed well the legacy of the ants,
They respect the dead and the chance
To work to adapt
To decay around the world wrapped.

　　—*William Daley*

A New England Villanelle

Eat the bread and drink the wine of wisdom;
Indulge the Self; withdraw to Castle Destiny;
The thing that hath been is the thing that shall be.

Plow evil; reap iniquity;
Behold, O Israel, there once was Sodom;
Eat the bread and drink the wine of wisdom.

The Earth doth point to surety—
Righteous shadows stalk the Sun;
The thing that hath been is the thing that shall be.

The oblique ray doth plunder its fiefdom;
The yield is blizzard, ice; wild Winter's bounty;
Eat the bread and drink the wine of wisdom.

The telescope of Time doth reveal Time's sum—
Enola Gay in flight, the bomb's prophecy;
The thing that hath been is the thing that shall be.

Despise the law; to defeat succumb;
O Israel, heed the scriptural decree;
The thing that hath been is the thing that shall be;
Eat the bread and drink the wine of wisdom.

　　—*Nora M. Walsh*

Untitled

My life was a series of ups and downs.
I would never change the good things only the bad.
For I would never change the memory of my first puppy.
But I would change the memory of it dying.
I would never change the fun with my friends.
But I would change my father's unexpected death.
For I would never change my marriage to Jill Marie.
And I would never change the years we spent.
Seventy to be exact.
But I regret the way I left her
With the words "I love you" never leaving my lips.

I would not change raising a son and a daughter.
But I would change my son dying in a bloody war
And my daughter dying giving birth to my grandson.

My life was a series of ups and downs
I never saw it before.
For when you are alive you can't dwell on mistakes.
But isn't that what death is for?

—*Andrew S. Day*

Angelic Child

Gazing upon your face, looking for the angels
In their place; knowing that they are there.
Of course they are with you everywhere!!!
————Always...

Your eyes are without hate----without lying or deceit.
There's only an angelic expression of innocence
That is so sweet........Always.

Angelic child....angelic child stay awhile
And bless the crippled with your smile.
Angelic child——let the light of your heart
Heal the sick and for the poor be a loaf of bread.

Angelic child ....Be angelic........Always.

—*Waunidi Changamire*

A Prayer For The Shelter

Praise God for little kittens
(all nine lives we want them to live)
For all the staff and volunteers
for the love and support they give
For sleepy little puppies
Adoring dogs and cuddly cats
For every one
of God's little creatures
In all their habitats
We try to make a difference
and though can't save them all
To save just one
means we'll save more to come
and we'll be there to answer their call
A house that is blessed with animals
is a home that is filled with love
But just know
if they're not
adopted by Man
They're for sure claimed by God up above.

—*Nancy Werner*

From a Child, to a Teen, to a Mom, and then a Memaw

When I was young and had no fear,
I washed away many a tear,
Tears of happy. Tears of sad. Tears for mother.
Tears for dad.

Life was pure and very clean,
Then all of a sudden you become a teen.

It seems to me you grow very fast. Then all of sudden you are
in the past. Just always remember friends from your past.
Because life will go on, but your friends always last.

Your children will come. Your children will go.
They can pull at your heart, sometimes very slow. No matter
what they may do, or where they may go. They are my life that
I do know.

Now here comes my grandchildren so healthy and smart.

Another
big string to pull at my heart.

My husband and I have had a great life. "I wish I could share
it", with all of my might. "My will" is my hero the love of
my life. Does anyone wonder, why I'm his wife!

Now I look back I surely can see. I know that God has been
walking with me.

—*Charlene Giesy*

The Big Fight

She's running like a cheetah after a prey.
In her expression seems to say Ahhh!!!
She hides in a corner, with no way out.
She out maneuvers her friend; between the legs.
What a trick, but the next time she's not as lucky any more.
She's in the arms of her friend now; now what will she do?
Will she attack or will she just wait it out?
She goes with a right then a left, but her friend is enjoying it.
Now what will she do?
She goes for the right and the left once more.
Look!! Look!! She's free!
Ya!! Ya!! She Won! She Won!!

—*Angela Mathern*

My Turtle Dove

(Dedicated to my son, Alan (Mitch) and
my daughter and friend, Mayumi — love mom.)

Is it lust or love? Is it hate or is it fate?
And time will not reveal; frustrations, torments dictate.
Is it so, can this be real?
Deep down you scream within your soul
Without much clarity to understand.
I want to help you and try to make you whole.

I hear your cries into the witching hour.
I fear so much, yet feel so helpless; have I lost the power?
What can I say? What can I do? Is this another deja vu?

With your mind that's so oppressed, accompanied with raging
thoughts, You hurt on endlessly.
I would take your torments, pain so gladly
To save you from this misery

With all my hopes and dreams I'll say,
"You need to think and strive, to rise above.
Shed all of hell's temptations
My little turtle dove".
For I'm the one that you call mother
Who gives so freely
Her undying love.

—*Brigitte Wheeler*

Heaven

Heaven means a lot of things to people,
16 Fudge sundae on a bright, sunnyday;
God's paradise some say

I on the other hand think of,
Gods kingdom with streets of gold;
Walking through a beautiful green
meadow;
Talking with my best friend;
But most of all my heaven is when;
I'm in your arms,
Or when I'm next to you.

So please don't leave
For if you did.
you would take away my heaven.

—*Peggy Bentley*

Today

We are asking for change.
1993 is a watershed year.
Never will things be the same.
We are awake.

Awake to the need of frugality
Awake to the challenge of conservation.
Awake to the limits of expansion.

Our world needs us.
The choices are not endless.
The constraints chain us.

The globe has become small...
An orb where starved ones in Somalia
Sit in our souls in USA...
Where oil spilled in Spain
Spoils everyone's environment...
Where sensitivity to small variations
Is essential to survival.

Man, stay awake.

—*Margaret Gaffney*

A Bookworm

A bookworm travels anywhere.
A bookworm doesn't seem to care.
He rides "Black Beauty" by the hour
Or climbs up fair "Rapunzel's" tower.
You'll find him chasing "Mother Goose"
Or "hobnobbing" with Dr. Seuss.
Sometimes he dashes through a book
Or else he inches for each look
But whether fast or whether slow,
It's fun to go where bookworms go.

—*Vivian Mackey*

Magnificent Nature

A butterfly,
A butterfly.
Light as a feather
Floating through the air
Tiny and colorful as a
Painted stamp.

I wonder how
something so delicate,
could live?

—*Michelle Amy Alexander*

A Mother's Prayer

November Tenth, 1972
    A day I'll never forget
A day when our world came
    crashing down
And our lives were all upset.

The words still linger in my ears,
    The lump still in my throat.
Dr. Sigler, with compassion said
    "It's leukemia - but there is hope."

He's just a child, beginning life
    He has so much to give
Please spare my son - take me Lord
    I've had my chance to live.

—*Shirley A. Richardson*

Untitled

It lay beneath the skin,
A demon not a friend.
Whose mysteries hide within the heart,
Not knowing if you're torn apart.
Before,
You hide in shame.
Yet now,
You find fame.
Hoping they'll let you in,
Without a lover
Without a friend.

—*Jennifer Sarrgent*

What You've Become

It all began so long ago,
A dream you thought you'd never know.
That's now become reality,
For what you'll give is a specialty.

You've found a career,
That's rewarding and true
Something that no one can take from you.
You've seen life...
Followed through by death,
And what you've given has been
part of the test.

You've seen a birth,
You've held a hand,
You've learned many things that
are part of a plan.

And now the best is yet to come,
Only because of what you've done

—*Leslie Ashby*

Love

    Love is like a knife.
    A knife that will cut deep if
        you're not careful.

    Love is blind.
    Blind enough to make you believe
        it will last forever.

    Love is sweet.
Sweeter than candy. Addicting!

    Love is strong.
Stronger than chains. Keeping you close.

    Love is dangerous!
    Love is forever!

—*Michele Johnson*

Young Love

A moment, a second,
a fleeing thought.
Things you've never felt,
things you've never seen.

It could be two best friends
or two people who've never met.
No one ever knows
what will happen.

As they say,
love works in mysterious ways.
It can't be planned
and it can't be changed.

Suddenly, it's the right moment,
the right light, the right music.
Then, somehow, in some way,
you know.

—*Teresa Fernandez*

Heart Song

A woman's heart to God's eyes seek
a gentle heart for Him to keep

Revealing sorrows tender laid.
His masters touch to heal the pain

Joined by multitudes from days
of yore, her voice doth
cry to the maids first born

Oh Rose of Sharon and gentle lamb
Mighty conqueror, hope of man

Consider these thy savants tears
And draw me near, draw me near

—*Pamela Moreno*

The Brooklyn Bridge Birthday

The Brooklyn Bridge
A giant harpsichord
Plaything of the wind

Vibrant strings echo
Soft humming Summer Breeze
Bellowing tenor, North Wind

Brooklyn Bridge
Aglow at sunrise
Envelops your body
In a glorious mantel

Light of dawn
Golden and mellow
Looks upon you
As its own.

—*Yvonne Ross*

Gator

Is you ever seen an alligator
a gliding through the swamp.
'ith just his eyes above the water,
and he's ready to take a chomp?

And he sidles up real slow,
and you don't know he's there,
and his teeth are long and sharp,
and he yawns - - like he don't care.

Just remember he has one purpose
in everything he do,
and if you ain't real careful,
that purpose will be you!

—*Jim Bildeback*

"The Greatest Gift"

Many times we cease to show
 a lack of appreciation
For all the blessings we receive
 with love and inspiration.

Pursuing dreams of the future
 occupies much of our time
As we keep pressing forward
 Toward goals we have in mind.

But lets not forget our parents
 As we tread on victory lane
'Twas their hands that led us
 To joy, success, and fame.

May their golden years be happy
 As they walk side by side
And each sacrifice remembered
 by the children, you, and I.

After all that life has given
 The greatest gift I've had
Is the love and guidance
 of my mother, and dad.
　　　　　—Ada Bullock

Longing

I long for a touch
A look
Any little expression
Of your love
Not much, not gifts,
No long soliloquy
Maybe a pat, or a peck
Or a tear dropped unexpectedly
Maybe a sudden smile
Or a wink
Or a leg rubbed surreptitiously
Let me know, day by day
In a routine way
That I'm still special
Unequivocally
Don't wait for that calendar date
To remember me
Hurriedly
Just one word from your eyes
Will suffice, absolutely
　　　　　—Marian W. Maxwell

A Fool's Dream

　Once I cried myself to sleep
　A memory came and so I weep
　I felt my days would be none
my life in darkness, without a sun
　My heart was two instead of one
　All was sorrow, no room for fun
　My body felt as I would die
　In prayer, I asked "Oh God why?"
Eyes which begged, but she went away
　　　　　—James W. Arnold

Jets

Sleek and small,
As fast as them all,
Gray but still with color,
Hot as fire and cold as ice,
Engines roaring,
Metal under tension,
Still capable of flying into the sunset.
　　　　　—Trey McCrea

The Measure Of A Man

A two-fisted bandit,
A mind all his own.
Unbridled justice,
He stands all alone.

A well of pure hatred,
A soul of deep need.
He's been left unaided,
To suffer and bleed.

Hears no vile rumors,
Speaks no evil lies.
Wants no part of friendships,
Attachments, or ties.

Walking in darkness,
Masking his hate.
Laughing at nothing,
For him it's too late.

"A cold-hearted monster,"
He's been called much worse.
He knows their existence
Is their own private curse.
　　　　　—Joseph Mazza

The Choice

She lay upon the bed
a pitiful bundle of suffering
and fear

She should not have done it,
for she had no excuse
for her actions

Perhaps in ages hence it
would not be thought of in
so hideous a light

But the thought offered no
comfort, no ease, only
more torment

For the child that would never be.
　　　　　—Melissa Amateis

Untitled

I once was mommy's little girl
A precious tiny perfect pearl
Whatever mommy went to do
She'd turn to find me with her too
I'd snuggle close to her in bed
And tell her things inside my head
I'd tell her things I'd like to see
And mommy always played with me
But mommy's little girl's gone bye
And mommy sits alone to cry
I try to tell her that I'm near
But mommy doesn't seem to hear
I try to touch her troubled mind
And tell her everything is fine
I'm happy here where I must be
Not earthly bound my soul is free
I wait the day when mom will come
When mommy's earthly job is done
Then I'll be mommy's little girl
Forever precious perfect pearl
　　　　　—Lawrence D. Collins

Praxis - My Heritage And My Pride

I am an African-American Woman.
 A proud African-American Woman.
I know who I am
 And I love me.

No one can tell me what to think.
I am free to think,
 Free to sink…
Into my mind and heart's desire.

 Free to expand…
 My Life is on Fire!!

I am Proud!
I am Woman!
I am African-
 American!
 Free…
 That's me!
　　　　　—Paula Lynette Neal

Spring Posy

Spring capture my heart so dear.
A season to relish upon.
Gaze straight ahead, you can see.
Endless view natures beauty.

Listen closely you can hear
Wind whispering in your ear.
Nature is calling for you
to come closer and seek near.

Traveling through the vast field.
I couldn't help observing
The endless stretch of posy
flower, flower everywhere.

No time, there is too much time.
Grab a handful of posy.
Slowly smell the aroma
the fragrance is enchanting.

Leisurely take in the view.
Its a shame to leave heaven.
However like yesterday
I shall return, the next day.
　　　　　—Timothy Wagner

"True Love"

Deep into his eyes I stare,
A soft breeze blows and moves his hair
Gentle hand upon my face
Hearts intertwined in loves embrace
A mystic fog as in a dream,
A sparkling, clear, little stream
A piercing cry through forests dark,
A day to remember this does mark,
The day he said "I love you dear"
As down his cheek ran a single tear
Upon my finger he placed a ring,
Elated now, my heart did sing,
"Forever darling, you and me,
Just like our names carved in a tree,
I love you now like I did then,
As much now as the day I gave my pin,
Marry me baby, I love you so
God, I hope you don't say no
If you do, I'll be a mess"
But, I said "Yes!"
　　　　　—Melanie Fisher

Streams Of Anger

Anger is like a stream,
a stream running down a mountain.
   It starts as a small trickle,
than builds up as it doubles with
other streams.
   It gets bigger and faster as it
runs down the mountain, and when it
gets too big and too fast for the
mountain to handle,
the mountain lets it go,
rushing into the ocean.

—*Kelly Howard*

Visions of Splendor

We see a sunrise at dawn
   A sunset of gold.
   All things in between
Are sights to behold.

We see blue skies above
   Mountains below,
   Meadows of green
   Rivers that flow.

   We see on a lake
Two snow white swans
We see out in the woodlands
   Two graceful fawns.

We see birds of all colors.
   Perched up in a tree
   All singing together
   A sweet melody.

Now there is no charge
These sights are all free
   Created through love
For you and for me.

—*Verla Perrine*

Dark Encounters

Shadows in the dark
A tall man and a woman

Blinded by the darkness
Who is it?

A closer look
A bit of light

Could it be?
The two I know

Committed to his wife
Committed to her love

I thought,
I was naive

The two are kissing
The lot is empty

Darkness surrounds them
Gone is the light.

—*Nancy Quattrociocchi*

Thoughts Of Life

The ripples of the waves
   Bring tender moments
For this is all we have
   Moments of the tide

—*Zandria Martinez*

A Child's Cry

What relates to a child's cry?
A thunderstorm that's passing by
The pouring rain like rolling tears
The darkening sky like a child's fears
A quiet wind like very soft moans
And just when the child feels all alone,
A beautiful rainbow fills the air
A smile seems to come from nowhere.

—*Kristen Dixon*

Why I Love Elvis

I love Elvis because of memories
   A Virgin's sensual awakening
      The rebel voice of love
         Emotional Explosions
         Passionate Fantasies
         Sweet Soul Music
         Allows Freedom
            To Dance
            And Be
            Me

—*Alice A. Gray*

Butterflies Are Free

"Never catch a butterfly"
A wise man said to me
If you hold him down, he'll die
Cause butterflies are free.

Exploring every fragrant flower
Sailing with the breezes
Living out each happy hour
Doing as he pleases.

And so I leave you with this word
In the hope that you will hear it-
The saddest thing in all the earth
Is the crushing of a spirit.

—*Beth Bailey*

To My Friend Ruth

The morning mist brings visions—of
A world we used to share.
I hear you and I touch you—and
I see you everywhere.
Your whisper in the evening breeze
That warms the late night chill.
Your laughter breaks the silence—and
I walk with you at will.
Your presence in the flutter—of
A Monarch butterfly
Fills all my heart, my soul with song
With thanks for stopping by.

—*Virginia Williams*

"What I Taste Is Fear"

(In memory of Anne Frank)
All I see are dreary sights,
Dead bodies here and there.
All I smell is death and a hint of
   gun powder in the air.
All I hear are screams and shouts,
   pleas for help and mercy.
And all I feel is weakness,
And what I taste is fear.

—*Karen Payne*

"Within The Shadow"

Hiding in the shadows,
afraid to be who I really am
   Try to be myself, but I
don't think I can
   There's a heart behind
this pretty face, a soul deep within
   My life's so incomplete,
where do I begin
   Feelings of rejection,
behind a smile
   Signs of hate, so I'll
just hide for awhile,
   Deep within my shadow,
the shadow that expresses my hurt
   Nobody's ever looked within
the shadows, and within the shadow stands
me

—*Lacy McHone*

In Memoriam

Snow crackling at my weight -
   Air like a note upon a night:
Inside the pews were full.

The Father (donned in white)
   Emoted words as if
It were to me he spoke:

That evil men will break a heart
   And give a letter of divorcement
And cause a spouse to sin.

And all the world had come:
   To join the dear, departed
To whom I once made vows.

I heard myself repeat:
   The words "To Death us part"
Then it was she it parted.

And as the white-clad cleric
   Said "Shine His light upon you"
I tiptoed past the pillar.

Out to the waiting snow, into
   The arms of an acquired shadow.

—*Jens. T Carstensen*

Silent Friend

Standing in elegance
Alert, graceful, cautious, curious
Non-suspicious
A quiet woods walk
Refreshing cool dampness
Ruddiest complexion

A scurry ahead
White tails aflurry
Except for one young buck
Alert, graceful, cautious, curious

We stand in mutual admiration
Stillness reigns, courage gains
He moves majestically, closer
Then up a mound

A glance back to a one antlered friend
More recalcitrant than he

Oh, young buck
I listen to you and hear
What balance does to fear.

—*Patricia Willems*

Alone

I walk through the forest,
all alone,
A lone wolf's cry,
sends shivers to the bone.

You feel its presence,
Yet it isn't there,
Things are watching you,
every where.

I still walk alone;
Yet I am not,
They are waiting for me,
To make a wrong move,
Then they'll pounce,
And strike me down,
But I'll be watching,
All around.

—*Andrea Kjelland*

The Faces Of Old

On days like these,
all cloudy and cold,
I wish to see
the faces of old.

To reminisce
a little while
Of my grandmother's
ever present smile.

Or a boyfriend's grin
and twinkling eyes
Enticing me in
by telling lies.

The graying hair
on my old dog's chin.
His pleading stare
to let him come in.

The faces of old
do comfort me.
Unable to hold,
yet mine to see.

—*Ann Kemling Zweifel*

Never Say Goodbye

I saw you lying there
All cold and alone
Wishing you had a reason
To make you carry on

I think you saw me there
I'm really not for sure
I know you felt my touch
And will remember it forever more

I know your much happier
In your own little world above
I hope to see you again
And return to you all of my love

I know that God has taken
You away from me
But not from my heart and mind
And Papaw, even though
I know your gone
I will never say goodbye

—*Missy D. Smith*

Winter

January snows are deep
All the lakes and rivers sleep.
Frost is on the window pane,
And snowflakes floating down again.

Icicles hanging in a row
Along the roof from melted snow.
Some of my fur and feather friends
Come to my place when snowstorm ends.

Jays in blue and grey attire.
Grosbeaks red as a fire.
Nuthatch up and down they go.
Chickadees fluffed like balls of snow.

They eat berries from the crabapple tree
And sunflower seeds put out by me.
There are carrots for the bunnies too
Cottontails and the snowshoe.

—*Verla Tollefson*

Walking By Faith

No it doesn't matter to me
All the trouble I see,
And though it may surround me
I'm walking by faith.

There may be times,
There may be places
When I can't see my way,
And nothing seems for sure,
But I know if I just
Keep my eyes on Jesus,
He'll bring me through
I know he will.

You know his word
His word lets me know
That I don't walk alone,
If I just call on Jesus in time of trouble,
He'll sit me up, upon a rock,
And keep me from all evil.

—*Udelia Coesens*

The Hourglass

Internal hourglass
Allows our time to pass
Now it's all fun and grand
Until there's no more sand

Once the sand runs out
No time to go and pout
When you sleep at night
you still see fogged black mass
when you're dead on sight
an empty hourglass

Will our beliefs pay...or
Will we just decay
Life after death...or
Given no breath
Given creation...or
Embalmination

The hourglass
Time ticks away
The hourglass
Towards judgement day?

—*Jeff Mores*

"Desert Storm War"

It's war, war in the air,
Almost more than we can bare;
All we can do is to have prayer
For our loved ones over there.
Some will loose a precious one,
Because war has just begun.
Oh God! have mercy on the U.S.A.
Give them strength in our peaceful way.
There's many a tear will fall
As uncle Sam just made a call;
Do Dear Lord give them power
To do their duty at any hour.
The gate for peace will open wide
For God is always by our side.
It is always love and peace and not hate
You can count on him and not hesitate,
In all of it we'll wait for the hour
For Dear God its all in your power.

—*Alma P. Williams*

Untitled

A child
alone and scared
love
an illusion
reared and scarred

An empty vessel
for years and days
a longing soon
but never to wane

Revealed to me was then
the fight I would not lose

Your warmth consoles me
in the darkness of night
such visions
dance
the power of life (is love)

Beyond these dreams so blessedly
fill my soul with love

—*C. G. Place*

About A Candle

I stand tall in darkness path;
Alone I wait the daylight wrath,
I wonder if I'll ever see,
Another candle quite like me?

Then suddenly the sky shines bright,
And on my head it does alight,
And tears fall down my waxen cheek,
I feel so strange and cannot speak.

But I feel great, I do not know,
Just why I feel all aglow,
Somehow I know this feelings right,
And I will make it through the night.

Could this be why I'm here, I ask,
To shed some light in darkness path,
And bring a little cheery glow,
To people I don't even know?

The answer comes at morning call,
As daylight's face beams off the wall,
And I was placed so tenderly,
With short, small candles just like me.

—*Richard L. Meadows*

"What It Is Like To Be Me"

To be me you must feel pain and sorrow.
Always crying never feeling happiness.
It seems like no-one cares.
That is what it is like to be me.
All by myself I carry this pain,
can't anyone help.
This is what it feels like to be me.

—*Alexis Orane*

"What A Teacher Does"

A teacher is:
Always there,
Right by your side
Helping you along.
She'll give up her time
To grade a test,
And do fun projects.
That can make you feel good.
All she asks, is that you
Try your best.
Those are the best things
A teacher can give.

—*Allyson Prater*

Old Glory

There seems to be animosity
Among those on the ground
What are all these freedoms
Are they really sound

I've been around for years you know
On calm and windy days
The courage you've displayed for me
Explains why I am raised

I wish that you would honor me
Rally round me when it's time
Why set me all ablaze
When it should be a crime

Look upon me with desire
And treat me with respect
When I am old and ragged
I'll then die with no regret

—*Millie Woodruff Hetland*

The Angel

She was an angel
An angel from heaven
Nothing could surpass her beauty
He could not look into her eyes

How do I talk to an angel
Far in the sky she shines so bright
How do I talk to an angel
For she is untouchable

How do I speak those words
How do I touch that angel far above
Tell me how do I talk to an angel
For she cannot feel my love

When I look into her eyes
I see the stars shining bright
I wish I knew what to say to that angel
For 'tis her that gives me feelings of love

When the stars shine bright I see the light
How can I live without her
How do the words go when an angel is near
Tell me how do I love that angel

—*Autumn Newbern*

Untitled

man
and
woman.

wolfschmidt
and loose
tongues.

a startled
moment, then...
a long kiss.
hot, sweaty, humid
and sticky
bodies.

straining, seeking
semblance of ?

he leaves,
she is left—
alone.

she doesn't
mind.

or does she ?

30 aug. 1988

—*rachel p. snapp*

Halloween Night

Goblins and goons
    And all sorts of moons.
Owls and howls
    And all sorts of growls.

They fight all night
    with the moon shining bright.
Creatures and screechers
    are the main features
        of Halloween Night.

—*Miggy Mason*

Untitled

Time between Valley Forge
and Apollo Eleven
Is the distant
we have gone

Thus all stars
become the bars
For man's will
to leap

From earth's gorge
to God's heaven
and the impossible
dream......

Like the will of George-
Who forged the fortitude
of Valley Forge

...And whose birthday today
was noted in a small town editorial
and a local dollar sale

—*A.L.A. Viola*

Cats

Cats here cats there
Cats sleep any where
nice cats cute cats
cuddly cats those are
the cats I like.

—*Rachel Mariah Taylor*

The Friend's Way

If you are hungry
and ask me for food
I will teach you to fish.
If you are thirsty
and ask me for water
I will give you a jar
and teach you to collect it.
If you are fearful
and ask me for protection
I will teach you to defend yourself.
When you have tired
of this world
of pleasure and gain;
and seek the way home
to God once again
I will teach you
The Friend's way
that leads beyond birth
death
and pain.

The Friend,

—*Adhyatma Bhagavan Sri
Babajhan Al-Kahlil*

The Lost Chair

I sat upon a tiny chair
And could not see it anywhere.
I looked around
Both up and down,
But the little chair was gone.

I finally decided why
The chair I could not see.
For when I rocked from side to side
My underneath was much to wide.

—*Kathy Taylor*

On Being A Handyman

In order to maintain a home
And give it proper care;
You must have the necessary tools
To handle each repair;

Because things just keep on breaking
And always need attention!
Why this continuously happens
Is beyond my comprehension!

First you identify the problem
And observe the situation.
Then look at your equipment
And survey your information.

In order to be really ready;
I'll pass on an important clue!
You'll need bungee cords, duck tape,
And lots of super glue!

—*Marilyn Schrotenboer*

Untitled

Does the snail lament and wail
    and gnash his teeth?
Does he know that life is brief
    and has he grief?
Does he know he has no tail?
Does he care within his shell?
Has he thoughts of Heav'n and Hell?

—*Ann Rhodes Miller*

The Flowers Bier

You had drunk a draft of eternal water
And had been leaving to eternal life
That the sight of your back
Were just looked very lonesomely.

On the heavy snow
When your lonesome soul was leaved,
In my heart
Had been dying a cells of life.

You had been kissing of alien love
but delivered coyly for me
that a draft of smile
You were looked like lily.

When it is crying the wind
I have seen lastly
that your flowers bier
Stay and leave in my exhausted soul.

—*Mi Hee Yoon*

Mirror

I look in the mirror
    and happen to see
A sad, sad face
    that looks like me.
With tears on her cheeks
    not a smile to be found
Not speaking a word
    there is no sound.
Alone in her place
    she sits and cries
Saying softly to herself
    No more lies.
One day, she whispers,
    My prince will appear
And whisk me away
    Far from here.
And on that day
    her broken heart will be pure
For she will have found
    her true amour.

—*Kim Krause*

Return To Eden

Jesus wore a crown of thorns.
And He went through the fire,
To show us the only way out
Was through the flaming sword.

There would be no good
Without evil,
And no evil without good,
Not in this world.

So choose who you will serve,
Choose one and deny the other.
That's the only way out,
So sayeth the Lord.

Choose the good and deny the evil.
Come with me, my children,
Milk and honey will sooth the burns.

The only way out is in,
And the only way in is out,
Out through the flaming door.

—*Naman Lewis Crowe*

"Thank You"

For skies of blue
and hearts of gold
for the greatest story ever told

For parent's love, all my life
That never wavers, in times of
    strife

For leaves that turn an autumn hue
For rain and snow, as well as dew

For the smile of a baby to cheer my day
And good news from family, far away

For sunshine and flowers, all summer
    through
For all these things, Lord, we thank you

—*Lucy Spence*

"Ebbing Tide"

The sea cracks
and I am awakened from sleep
from dreams I've taken too deep
to drift in the ebbing tide.

The gulls cry
standing on the wreckage of ships.
Invisible to knowledge, they dip
in the waters of the ebbing tide.

We believed
waves could hear
the chaos that they caused
on the unsuspecting sand.

The twig breaks
as we walk unnoticed through leaves
that fell down upon us in dreams
when we were the ebbing tide.

The girl plays
by herself in a corner unknown
waiting till her sister comes home
so they can swim in the ebbing tide.

—*Matthew Sinclair*

Untitled

The room goes dim,
and I hear you again.
    You're very near,
I feel your breath on my ear.
    As you're walking away.
I hear you delay,
    As you pause for a second.
But then something does beckon,
    You away from me,
And I never do see.
    That smiling face,
Is gone without a trace.

—*Karen V. Pruitt*

Untitled

There was a time when I had felt
    all the blows that fate had dealt
I used to cry and weep and rage
    but fate had gently turned the page
I left my future in your hands
    and now we both have many plans
Fate has dealt the blow of love
    now I fly as free as a dove.

—*Becky Ayres*

"Old Times"

I walk down the country lane
and I see the old family homeplace.
Where Grandpa and Grandma raised
twelve kids—poor but with grace.
I can almost see Grandpa walking
behind that plow all day,
Grandma cooking and washing
in that old fashioned way,
and those twelve young-uns
hollering and running at play.
I wish I could go back there
when you always had the time
to be a neighbor, friend to
a stranger along the way.
Time to have fellowship with
the family at the end of the day.

—*Joy Black*

The Breeze

I feel the breeze blow through my hair,
And I see the sky above.
I have the sun shining on my face,
And yet I have no love.

Love takes time a wise one said.
But time, I have not.
I only want someone to love,
Through the good and not.

My heart is filled with love to give,
And I see no one there.
So all I have left to feel,
Is the breeze blowing through my hair.

—*Jo Scott*

To Love Me As I Am

I'm not a little girl
And I wish that I can
Release the hurt inside me
And have someone understand.

You see that I am hungry
For a life of understanding
And somehow you put up with me
When I am demanding.

It's not for me to decide
What is right for me,
What my life is like,
And what the world can see.

The only thing I really want
Is for you to understand
And for you to be able
To love me as I am.

—*Marijane Bachmann*

Poor Man's Blues

Everybody wants what I ain't got
and I'll be the first to tell them
I ain't got a pot;
Poor is poor then there's starvation,
wonderin' where your next
meal's coming from is anticipation;
I'm so far in debt I can't wait to
see what the hell next is going to
happen to me;
I wish I could say I had the money to
pay my dues, but wishing is only another
way of singing the poor man's blues.

—*Robert P. Campbell*

255

Nowhere Moon

The owl eases his wings over the limb
and into the crotch of the old snag
he stills his murdered prey and gnaws
through the fur and blood
until only bone-dust
sifts to the earth below.
The owl falls into sated slumber
morningtime comes over the hayfield
and insects spring into the waiting air.

—*Mary A Ryan*

Innocence Lost

The crime that overshadows all,
And leaves its victim lost,
Is one that happens in the home,
The place we love the most.

It happens at a time in life,
When we're so young and open.
It slowly drains our innocent hearts,
And prevent our minds from coping.

Our life becomes a jumbled mess,
Of feelings we can't determine.
When stress invades our troubled mind,
Living is lost in the struggling.

If only time could right the wrong,
And replace the broken parts,
To give us back our innocence,
And heal our broken hearts.

—*V. Jean Allen*

The Seasons

Snowflakes and freezing storms
And lots more chilly days
Before the last of winter comes
To end its stormy ways.

Spring days surely are welcome
As they bring the nice warm weather
And the sharp thunder and lightning
That, of course, must come together.

Then the red and gold leaves
That hail the approach of fall;
The seasons must come to an end
As each year does, we recall.

So to finish this long story
As it very happily closes;
Remember that we were told,
"To take time to stop and smell the roses."

—*Kathleen O'Brien*

Easy Trail

A turning from the rush,
And racket of the road,
On to the quiet hush,
Of lane near old abode!

Variety of life,
With work and play and rest,
Number of interests rife,
Including travel, guest!

Enthusiasm, zeal,
Alert awake, aware,
True and sincere, quite real,
Honest and on the square!

—*Margaret Crimes*

The Hopeless Dream

The sparrow takes flight;
And oh how it soars;
Through the beautiful sunlight;
Over hills and moors.

If I were that sparrow;
That so gracefully took flight;
I'd be as fast as an arrow;
And as high as a kite.

I would explore many places;
Far and near;
So that I could see the faces;
Of people who are dear.

But it would seem;
To me and to you;
This is nothing but a dream;
That will never come true.

—*Missy Anderson*

Snow

The snow is white
And oh so cold
We are all inside
No one's out to play
The fires's lit
The T.V. is on
Hot cocoa in a cup
The kitty cat
Is oh so quick
Out to her dishes
In the kitchen
Now for some petting
She is in her box
Now for some napping.

—*Judy Rice*

When I Am Gone

(Dedicated to my sons, Thomas F. Dale
and Russell E. Dale — to my parents
Mr. and Mrs. Frederick A. Jobe,
and to others whom I love.)

I'd like to think, when I am gone,
My loved ones will recall,
All the joys which we have shared,
And how much I loved them all.

I hope they will remember,
Bright and shining lovely days,
And laughter, and understanding,
And encouragement, and praise.

I want them to remember me,
And know that I am near,
For love remains forever,
To give a blessing, and to cheer.

Let the days we've spent together,
Like a comfort, soft and warm,
Wrap around them, with my love,
To keep them safe from harm.

And when their tears are wiped away,
And as their lives go on,
I hope they will think about me,
Like a lovely, lilting song.

—*Alice Jobe Dale*

Who?

She looks into the mirror
and sees a stranger's face
her past etched all in black
unwilling to erase.

Footprints in the sand
Imprints on the beach
Belong to someone else
to whom she cannot reach.

She never really knows
just quite where she stands
Where she's ever traveled
Through such foreign lands.
As she leaves the beach
and looks back on the sea
she wonders what she wants
and who she longs to be,

One day she'll discover
the most uncommon wealth
one day she'll discover
the woman within herself.

—*Stacey Murello*

Dream Weaver

Stop by for a visit
And she'll weave you a dream,
From whimsy and make-believe
And from things she has seen.
She'll weave you some magic
For just stopping by,
A smile and a hand wave
And a wink of the eye.
Some dreams told by friends
And some dreams of her own,
How they started out tiny
And how they have grown.
The soft touch of a birds' wing
The smile of a friend,
A wild flower from a meadow
At her loom she will blend.
She weaves threads from star light
And magic moon beams,
Come by for a visit
She's the weaver of dreams

—*Margaret L. Hall*

Look Beyond

There is a rose for every thorn we have,
And sunshine for every rain.
But we must look beyond the clouds,
To find the rainbow again.

The days I do not think of you
Are few and far between!
In the night you're in my prayers,
And often in my dreams!

I pray the Lord will touch you
In a very special way;
Heal, care for, and comfort you
Today and every day!

—*Alice Tohill*

My Beloved

I'd climb the highest mountain,
and swim the deepest sea,
I'd build the biggest castle,
just to have you here with me,
I'd write a play just for you,
that would put Shakespeare to shame,
I'd give my life and all I've got,
to hear you call my name,
all these things I'd do for you,
without a second thought,
'cause now there's nothing in my life,
your memory's all I got,
just give me one more chance to say,
all I never could,
I'll give you all the love I know,
and treat you like I should,
if I could, I'd change it all,
the past would disappear,
but for now, I'll cry for you,
one deep and lonely tear.

—*Kara Wraase*

Larry, Larry

You don't belong go back
And take Jamey along.
Go back home where the aliens rome.
Maybe it's mars
where you'll be behind bars.
Maybe it's saturn
Do you notice the pattern.
Maybe it's the milky way
What do you say?
Which do you choose
to win or to lose?

—*Mary Ann Belew*

Pain

The sound of the rain
And the pounding thunder
Along with this pain
Is putting me under

As I watched a dove
And the rolling sea
I knew I was in love
But was he?

As I tried to understand
And felt my innerself die
I clutched my hand
And began to cry

These tears are like rain
And for him I'd kill
But although all this pain
I love him still.

—*Amy Lynn Vaughn*

Untitled

He's a Queen
But She's no King
And the President just quit
The Clown wears a mask
but so does the Surgeon
the car had only one owner
the Salesman said.
And the Check's in the mail.

—*K. D'Andrea*

Encouragement

When things are dark
    And the road is rough
Let us call on God
    For in Him We can trust.

Pray for guidance and strength
    in all our tasks
For he knows what is needed
    Before we even ask.

So keep on believing and
    turn not away
Our strength and guidance
    Will come in His day

Life may seem long
    Dark nights and drear
But with Him, our Savior,
    We can have great cheer.

—*Patsy R. Francis*

Broken

The sun rises in his smile,
and the stars light his eyes.
He is my friend.
I grow close to his smile,
and his eyes call to me.
I love him.
A shattering noise floods my ears.
I will not regain sanity soon.
He does not love me.
I am broken, not on the surface,
but in my heart and down to my soul.
He will never love me. I must go on.

—*Anissa Mealer*

The Morning After

The sun rose
and there was no trace
but a memory of your face
Tears ran down my eye
as I knew it must be time
to say a last good-bye
My heart split into two
as it knew its job
must of been through

—*Terri Opatrny*

Unicorns

They run and jump in the sun,
and they always have lots of fun;
Their happiness is by the ton;
with hair of colors from every nation;
their golden horns are very sleek,
and they act very meek;
there is no hate
where they live;
for their hearts
will welcome you in,
If you love all mankind;
then you may visit one of mine.

—*Jamie Lightcap*

Friends

Through all of the laughter,
and through all of the tears,
from the very beginning,
through all of these years.

We have become friends,
and friends we will stay.
Free to be ourselves
and let come what may.

To me our friendship
is something to cherish.
Something to valuable
to ever let perish.

We are there for each other,
through life's triumphs and sorrows.
We have shared the yesterdays,
and together we will meet the tomorrows.

Knowing that our friendship
is from heart to heart,
and even though we are not perfect,
our friendship will never part.

—*Sherry Miller*

I Would

I would swim the mighty ocean
and touch the roaring tide,
I would dance on the rolling waves
and on a flying sea gull I would ride.

I would reach out for a star
and watch in glow in my hand,
I would ride on an "Antarctic glacier"
and crawl through the "Sahara" sand.

I would climb the peaks of Switzerland
for one look from your caring eyes,
I would do wonders, if we didn't have
to hear or say anymore goodbyes.

I would caress a wondrous rainbow
the reds, the blues - colors so bright,
I would hold the sun in my arms
if that would bring you here tonight.

—*Melody Harblis*

Forgetting That You're Gone

I woke up this morning
and turned to see your face,
but you have gone and left me.
In your mind my face replaced.

I tried to hold back tears
which sprang into my eyes.
I should drown in my sorrows
so you won't hear my cries.

I can't seem to forget
your eyes which sparkled bright
and mem'ries of us dancing
in the pale moonlight.

I sometimes wonder where you've been
and if I'll carry on
'cause the real pain deep inside
is forgetting that you're gone.

—*Monica Jennings*

Traces

I walked the dunes at Wingaersheek
And watched the tide wash in.
Upon the sand, the fragile tracks
Of where a bird had been.

But changes come and traces go,
Like tracks upon the sand.
The traces of our fleeting steps
At the wind and time's command.

And where do traces go when time
Has closed another door?
And who, but I, will ever know
A bird walked here before?

Must all our footsteps lie beneath
Some fickle shifting sand?
Must time betray the beach and dune
As it betrays the hand?

Must all the fleeting joys of love
Leave no imprint to say
That "Upon this place in time and space
Two lovers had their day"?

—*Joanne Birks*

Wings

I look out my window
and what do I see?
A beautiful mountain,
so lovely to me.

I wish I could fly,
but there's no hope,
or maybe I could swing,
by the end of a rope.

There goes the air plane
up in the sky,
and it's leaving me here,
oh why? oh why?

If I had one wish,
you know what it would be.
It would be the wish for wings,
So I could fly, oh so happily.

—*Tracy Walter*

"People Stay Out Of Jail"

I am writing this for black
And white, who are not in jail
If this message does not get
Across to you, then I have failed

What I want to do is reach
You, so other you can teach
I have been in jail, so
I hope you can use my speech

It is foolish to be in jail
Jail makes you feel weak
When you go into court
That's the worst time to speak

You can get ten years
For a candy bar that you steal
You can get more years
For stealing an automobile

—*James M. Evans*

To She Who Joins the Wind

You are the gentle mist of the pre-dawn,
   and with the gold of day
you join the sun.

At dusk you stretch with the luxuriant
   shadows,
and with the setting sun you race across
   a wind swept sky.

You are the light that has crept
   into my fog and turned what was
dank into fragrant vapor that
   touches my cheek.

The wind blows.
   I breathe and my senses detect the
fragrance of the mist.
   It touches me.
It is you.

—*Karn W. Griffen*

The Skeleton

He rises up with burning eyes
And yet to us its no surprise.
To see him smile his clever smile
And then he sits to think awhile.
Again he rises to greet the night
The look from him is quite a fright.
He takes a step that shakes the world
His eyes a white and glassy pearled.
His laugh trembles throughout the air
He has no skin and grows no hair.
And as his eyes cast an eerie glow
He goes back down, back down below.

—*Jessica Bunker*

Temagami

The Indians dance for the
animal that could kill
them....the wolf.

The wolf lies before the ghost that
frightens him... the fire.

The fire burns unknowing
Of the bringer of much
life that can destroy it....the water.

The water holds the fish that a
superior bird can
destroy....the loon.

The loon is the holder of the
power that we can't
prevail over....the rain.

The rain that we are
worsening in spite of the God's
that the indians believe in.

—*Alex Sellers*

Fall

I see a tree,
As tall as can be,
Reaching up into the sky.

It's branches are long,
It's trunk is strong,
It's leaves are waving goodbye.

The wind is whispering,
To all who are listening,
Fall has finally arrived.

—*Louise Stewart*

My Shoes

My old shoes I walk in
Are battered, don't you see
They hurt my feet, many times,
But they don't fit you,
They fit me.

Don't judge the shoes I walk in
Cause my heart will guide my feet,
To the best road I know to travel
Don't condemn me,
These shoes fit my feet.

I've only walked in my shoes
And I hope you understand
That I haven't walked in your shoes,
So I can't judge my fellow man.

If I could walk in your shoes
And you could walk in mine
They'd be more understanding,
As we pass each other by.

—*Margaret W. Keyton*

Questions

The sights of the world
Are mysterious things.
From how the dolphin swims
To how the bluebird sings.

How do the trees
Stay so tall and towering?
And what makes the lightning
Look so overpowering?

How does the chameleon
Camouflage itself?
And how does a fox
Move around with great stealth?

Why do the leaves
Flutter endlessly down?
And why does the snow
Blanket the ground?

What makes the world
The place that it is?
It must be the gifts
That nature gives.

—*Rachel Weiss*

Into The Past

The walls of the past
Are what I am walking through
My journey is peaceful
Full of memories of you.

I see all the people
Who I saw before
And, for a moment, I wish
I could stay forevermore.

But now it is time I bid them farewell
Finally, at last,
I have said my good-byes
To the beautiful past.

—*Katherine Longosky*

Fragile

Take each day
  as a separate dream
Try not to frown
  make it better than it seems
Take time to love
  each and every one
And once in awhile
  watch the rise of the sun
Take someone's hand
  just to show you care
Open your heart and love
  always be there
Take a different outlook
  don't dwell upon the past
Life is much too fragile
  not to make it last

(In memory of Dana Micone)
　　—*Toni Surian*

A Whisper To The Sky

The wind blew through my hair,
As I stood over there,
Watching the waves crash down
Not even making a sound;
With the water cool on my feet,
I wasn't bothered by the heat.

As a tear rolled down my eye,
I whispered to the sky...
"Why'd my baby die?"
　　—*Michelle L. Cervantes*

Untitled

Time squandered
As if it did not exist
Forgetting about tomorrow
And tomorrow
Unknowingly to subsist
On day dreams
Dreaming of another
She could not resist
Seeing the face
Touching the lips
Desiring to be kissed
　　—*Susan S. McGonegal*

A Kiss Is Fatal

A rose turns black
As it yet dies
Its petals fall like fire on ice
People fall
But only a kiss can be fatal

A heart broken can be life threatening
Life threatening to the heart and soul
Some will die
Some will live
But remember only a kiss can be fatal

Deep and fulfilling
Luscious and craving
Warm or cold
Some poisoning and venomous
But only a kiss can be fatal
A kiss can be fatal
　　—*Melanie L. Easler*

New Girl

As she walks down the hall,
as lonely as can be,
she sees a group of friends,
laughing joyfully.
She wishes she could join them,
but too afraid to try,
if only she were popular,
there'd be no reason why,
she'd have to stand alone, again,
the way she was before,
if only she could be with them,
and laugh forever more.
And so she walks on down the hall,
searching for someone to call,
and so I say from me to you,
I hope you never feel this blue.
　　—*Abby Wirth*

"Master Manipulator"

clouds move swiftly in the darkening sky
  as night falls silently
    silently
      as if it knows
        silence is less painful
see his face in the dark
  handsome angel
    grotesque demon
      charming
        fiendish
master manipulator
  plays cruel mind games
    to test
      "undying" love
ironic twist of fate
  vicious mind games
    killed
      "undying" love
　　—*Tammy Short*

Untitled

I said, "I have shut my heart
As one shuts an open door,
That love may starve therein
And trouble me no more."

But over the tree tops there came
The wet new wind of May,
And with it, a passionate lady
So strong, and warm, and gay.

My room was white with the sun
And love cried out in me,
"I am strong, I will break
  your heart
Unless you set me free"
　　—*L.H.K.*

Mother

I still can hear my Mother
As she prays on bended knee
And told our Heavenly Father
Of the needs for her family.

As she talked to the Lord, Divine
She named us one by one
And she told of her hopes for each
Of the good race we must run.

How many days she prayed
For her children everywhere
And how many ways she showed us
How much she really cared.
Oh Mother, My Dear Mother
I'm so glad you prayed for me
For now within my heart I know
Where I'll spend Eternity.

She is waiting now in Heaven
And still calling out each name
While the Angels stand beside her
And sing their God Refrain.
　　—*Jenny Clark*

Endless Pain

Crying as I write this,
As tears fall down my face,
I wish this pain would end,
And the fighting would erase.

I hate this feeling inside,
It's a pain that I can't explain.
I want "us" to be forever,
With neither of us to complain.

Maybe it is God's plan,
For us to be apart,
But the most part I dread,
Is when the plan will ever start.

I was there to see you grow,
Into a very handsome man.
And now I watch you drift off,
And leave me here to stand.

But wherever you leave me standing,
I won't be there for long,
I'll get back on my feet again,
And rebuild my heart so strong.
　　—*Jana Chiasson*

Life Anew

There is nothing quite so precious
  as the sharing of mutual love.

Determined to cherish and behold
  with divine blessings from above.

In all hopes and dreams sown by
  manifest promise.

To always inspire and support
  through circumstance amiss.

And forever dwell in the house of
  happiness true.

For nothing is greater than the spirit
  of building a life anew.
　　—*Mary Miller*

"Roses Are Red, Violets Are Blue"

Your hair is afire
As the swaying amber grass on the plain
Your heavenly beauty compared
To the warm summer's rain

Thine eyes shine as stars
In the midnight sky up above
Your voice is so gentle
As the calling spring dove

Your skin is so smooth
Rippling as gently as wine
Life would be meaningless
Without your lovely shine

These words I give
To your heart from mine
Know that I love you
Be my only valentine

—*Tim Spencer*

A Spring's Bloom

Spring is near and life blooms,
As the winter freeze is thawing
and sending water to the streams.
The birds feed on the pests of the world.
The green flourishes as the days
get longer and warmer.
The pink blossoms pop open.
The wind rise to bring colorful kites
soaring through the sky.
The fluffs of clouds change color
from a gray to white, because
it is spring time.
Spring time is coming closer
each and every day.

—*Winter J. Phoenix*

People And Ants

I see people
as they see
an anthill.
Some like to
stomp it out
and watch
the ants flee.
Others like to stop
and watch
the ants
build their shelter.
Still others
do not have
the eyes
to see
the anthill
at all.

—*Linda Sievers*

Raindrops Are Never Alone

While I sit on the front stairs
At the end of my summer,
Raindrops decline to drive
Down along straight lines—
Float to their meeting on my skin.
They bind like brothers.
Each fraternity grows
Into a satisfying number
Before the journey down steps
Into puddles.
They lie together.

—*John L. Bowles*

Lover In Your Mind

I take you by the hand
As we lay down by the fire
We make love in the sand
And I give you all you desire
The moon is full and rising high
I feel you tremble and give a sigh
I see you smile with delight
Cause you know that it felt right
  "I'm the lover in your mind
  My love is easy to find
  Lover in your mind
  You want no other kind."
You awaken from your fantasy
Just to face reality
You sit in bed and start to cry
Thinking was my love just a lie
But if you go back to sleep
There'll be no reason to weep
You know I'm not hard to find
For I'm the lover in your mind.

—*Todd Allen Johnson*

Living

Life isn't all roses,
As we live day by day,
For we will encounter,
Some thorns on the way.

Think thoughts that are pure,
And from trouble don't borrow,
For we don't know today,
If we'll have a tomorrow.

Don't always be taking,
But be generous in giving,
Just think of the time,
That we spend in living.

Knowledge and wisdom,
We gain through the years,
Some days full of sunshine,
Some nights full of tears.

Through trials and errors,
Through trust and through doubt,
Our lives are for living,
Day in and day out.

—*Virginia V. Crosby*

Summer Interlude

The evening was soft and warm,
as we paused under the huge tree.
Our talk was whisked away on tendrils of
dust as the wind whipped
about us.

The tree bowed and swept the sky,
and its upper branches were bathed
in ethereal moon light.

We talked and laughed, a common
bond of love enveloped us.
A feeling of new beginning ascended
in a shaft of light,
binding us eternally.

—*Yvonne F. Rose*

Living

As black as night
As white as light
The earth turns from day to night

As rain falls, tears run down your face
Just to share a simple grace

As blue as the mid-day skies
For you're not blue
So you must be gay

As you seek to find,
New dreams,
And new hopes,
At some points you are weak

As you always shall remember
Never let go......
Like a bow, unties

As an example of a knife
Remember
A knife will never be as sharp as life...

—*Lori Smith*

Untitled

Life deceives me
as you do
and I do you
too many
too few
how much
how many
why
life dreams and wonders
and soars through
darkened skies to be seen
I know you
do you
maybe
within the darkness
of my life
which is in you

—*Pamela Sommer*

Wind Crest

Wind crest,
As you meet the bird's nest,

Blow, blow wind,
Carry on my friend.

Love shall see you through,
Nothing shall hurt you.

Never stop to play,
To see me on your way.

Oh, wind crest come to my side,
And please give me a ride.

Over mountains, under rainbows,
Between clouds' rows and rows.

There is a land wide and free,
Come along with me.

Alas, it will take time,
Before I find the rhyme,

With the key,
To paradise and sweet tea.

Till we meet again,
Good bye to all the women and men.

—*Susan D. Martin*

Silent Harmonies

Fragile new melodies gently push
Ashore, one by one, in staggered
Meter, on unseen cue, as a
Score of crystal refrain
Plays up from the surface in
Twinkly unison, in
Tacit harmony, while the
Freshborn orchestra bobs in
Fluid tempo to the
Composer's unhurried wand,
Warmed in the silent cadence of
Spring's first morning.

—*Robert W. Short, Jr.*

Love Flight

We were jet fuel igniting
at high octane ratio
afterburners glowing
red hot and passionate
in the evening shade
we fired machine gun bursts
twin guns blazing
direct hits to the heart
we conquered a world
few would dare to fly
breaking the sound barrier
turbosupercharged into
truth
reality
and make believe
an earth shattering
fourth of july
fireworks show.

—*Lois DeFriece*

Somehow

You've gone away
At last to play
Upon the Streets of Gold.
Where the Son's sweet rays
Shine through the days
And you're ne'er to grow old.
You filled my life
With warmth and love
And ever seemed to care.
I know one day
We'll meet above
And forever will we share.
But, until the day
When next we meet,
I'll say good-bye, for now.
Though, without your love
I'll not be complete.
But I'll make it through...
Somehow.

—*Ava V. Anderson*

Lost Without You

I look out the window
at the fading sunset,
knowing,
you recall the first time we met.

I was just a baby then
when you first held me.
Day after day, you sent
me love in melodious symphonies.

Over the years,
you cared for me just the same,
from times of joy and tears
that is why I call your name.

Grandpa,
the angels came and took you away.
I last saw
you on that grayish day.

Since you've been gone,
I miss you dearly.
I'm absent inside like a pawn
looking for guidance yearly.

—*Jill R. Peterson*

From A Different Perspective

Through the window I gazed,
At the foam on the tide,
The Ocean quite near me,
My cat at my side.

He purred as he watched,
The things that I do,
And I wondered, right then,
What was his point of view?

I wondered what he felt,
As he watched the world die,
From the all acid rain,
And the pollution in the sky.

My mind whirled,
While I sat, deep in thought,
And suddenly felt grateful
For all the things that I've got.

—*Stacey McGinnis*

I Reach For You

By darkness a pale moon rides high.
At this hour, nightfall will take sight
Ending our journey through the night.
Stars will cry and winds shall sigh.

Dancing jubilant parades sway.
Somewhere musical bands shall play.
Champaign popped; placed in array.
Listening, my heart turns away.

Flowers grow and petals will raise
And blossom into soft bouquets.
Falling slowly through sweet spring air-
I shan't care - you are not there.

My hands will silently open-
I reach for you by night's broken.
Leaving me helplessly soken,
Your life be given, God has spoken.

Fire from heaven only God could provide.
Love encircled - now stored in a shrine.
My soul set free - taking high aim.
Heaven's doors are open wide I claim!

—*Peggy Gaudiosi*

Lock 1993

The water has filled the lock.
At twelve, the vessel floats forward
Into the next level.

The gate closes behind it.
Gradually, it too will fill
With days lifting the boat.

Two levels below you left.
I was swept on reluctantly—
Hating to move alone.

It will be this way, I know,
As each passing year leaves behind
Our journey together.

Yet moving through, gate by gate,
My barge will also come to rest.
I will be set ashore

To discover, after all,
You were not left behind, but there,
Traveled another way.

—*Nancy E. Hanel*

Gavel Sovereignty

Goods, assorted by origin and worth,
Await next owners to find new berth.
Service and elegance stake a place;
Historic items find their space.
Professionals and public collect,
Preview quietly and inspect
Wares displayed...offered in masse...
To spark intent of those who pass.
When hawked in gallery sale
Rounds of silent-signals pale,
"Sold," proclaims the gavel's strike.
Price as heard on auction mike
Sloughs each hesitant luckless guy
And champions outbidder's choice buy!

—*A. C. Helfesrieder*

Untitled

A small girl sits along the murky
banks of a swirling fountain
of dreams and fantasies, lost
to the majestic hills of
rock that rise up over the city
casting their shadows upon it.
Clouds sway and dance, shielding
the faces of the towering
masses from the view of
their admirers.
Flowers leap and sing before
the young girl's eyes
enticing her soul to leave the
coldness of reality for
a world that promises everything
while giving nothing.
Her hair turns white and
wrinkles cross her face as
the girl sits and ponders her
decision before she sleeps.

—*Michelle D. Barnhart*

What Is Beauty?

Beauty is a morning sunrise
Beauty is a walk on the beach,
the sunsetting
Beauty the full, the trees in
a wintry snowfall
A field of beautiful flowers.
Beauty seeing the ballet
the smiles on little ones faces
the holidays families gathering
Beauty the friendship we share.

—*Addy Cox*

He Wonders Why

He wonders WHY, I told a LIE!
"Because he wasn't fair."
He wonders WHY, I felt so TIED!
"Turn around and He was there."
He wonders WHY,I can't CONFIDE!
"The trust just wasn't there."
He wonders WHY, the love has DIED!
"And left Him standing there."

—*Nellie Farrens*

Deep Within

Behind the tears are sad eyes
Behind the sad eyes is a mind
Filled with depressing thoughts
Behind the mind
Filled with depressing thoughts
Is a heart
Heavy with sorrow
Behind the heart heavy with sorrow
Is a wounded spirit
But deep within the wounded spirit
Is a joy in knowing
No matter how bad things seem
The love of God
Surpasses all things

—*Sharyl L. Smith*

Beyond

Lets take a ride
Beyond the mind
Beyond all thoughts
And destinies

Clear the mind
From now till birth
Everything that has passed you
Is no longer an effigy in the mind;

It's all primordial
Your once more you
No longer a hostage
In this cruel and demented world.

The name in it's eulogy
In the demented dimensions of time
You look and see
But you cannot help

For you will lose yourself once more.
Your soul now purified
You awaken
Beyond all imagination

—*Jonathan M. Varga*

Question

Brittle as bone
Bitter as the Cold
Commissioned to frailty
Man to bestow
Forever mounted in shame
What price did I pay for such fame?
Bound to live within four walls...
I signed no papers
For this heap of junk
No annual check up
To fix what is wrong...
The mold was broken with me
One of a kind
Shame for all to see
Where do I go from here?
A question I posed to the maker
His reply, "That's the price I paid for such fame."

—*Louis E. Nelson*

Burnout

Stars fell again tonight
blazing a trail for dreams,
on a collision course
with reality.

Unmindful,
I reach out
to touch their glory;
foolish forgetful
of the
    distance
between.

I catch only a handful
of darkness,
as together,
stars and dreams burn out...
somewhere
    out there on the edge
of yesterday.

—*Lyn DeNaeyer*

In The Name Of Jesus

In the name of Jesus
  Bless his name
In the name of Jesus
 I am strong again
In the name of Jesus
  I weep
For joy, cause he'll always keep
  My soul, I pray
  To live his life
  Each and every day
In the name of Jesus

—*S. Lorraine Giles*

A Mother...

A Mother delivers a child on that
Blessed day of birth.
A mother transports life for
Another human here on earth.

A mother understands the distorted
Chatter of a baby learning to talk.
A mother is the parachute for a
Falling child desperately yearning
to walk.

A mother is a role model and a
teacher who institutes the rules.
A mother is the guidance counselor
Who's absent from most of our schools.

A mother will often worry when her
Kids go outside to play.
A mother praying for kids to be
Unharmed when gunshots go astray.

A mother has a love that reaches
The pinnacle of all measures.
A mother has a love that is elite
To all worldly treasure.

—*Anthony Ellis McGee*

Chains

An invisible wall
blocking my way
heavy chains
holding me back
You are just one step away
but I cannot move,
just one small step away
but I have never moved in my life
I long to be free
and to dance in the wind
There is even in reach a key
but I cannot, will not use it
It is safe in this prison
at least I'll never be hurt.
Throw away the key!

—*William P. Seeley Jr.*

Desires

I want to wake up to
blue-skied mornings
to appreciate the
everyday events of life.
I need to smile, knowing full-
heartedly that I'm happy,
and in love with "Mr. Right."
I long to discover the world—
and watch the sun set
a million times...
I wish to adore the change
of season,
and taste the finest wines.
I'd love to hear birds singing
love songs, and wade in crystal-
clear creeks, then sunbathe on
the rich green bank, knowing
that I'm complete...
In peace.

—*Lynn A. Leshinsky*

Bottle Rocket's

Bottle Rockets, flashing lights
Bright stars, lights of the nights
As the smile on your face
Gave your heart away
My mind wonders when we will meet
Again.
Or were you just an illusion
of bright lights and falling stars
Like Mars, my heart
All aglow.
With memories of your face and smile
All of the miles that are between us
Could we ever be more than friends
Like the bright lights that fade away
Into the nights
Bottle Rockets exploding
With the smile on your face
Throwing my heart your way!

—*Kim Krick*

Heartfelt Promise

Wrap those arms around me
   bring me oh so near
When the lonely nights roll in
   wipe away the fear
Love me for all lifetime
   by no means just a day
And if the darkness closes in
   don't keep your love at bay
Keep away the thunder
   that lurks beneath the storm
Guide me to that love of yours
   that holds me safe and warm
Fill me with the wonder
   that love can bring to light
Bring about the fire
   that we've learned to ignite
Keep at hand the promise
   to mend all broken dreams
Melt away the heartache
   that only love redeems.

—*Pola Christoforou*

Diet

Jenny Craig will make you skinny
Bring out your best points
And somehow steer you clear
Of fatal fast food joints.

Weight watchers will furnish a book
Filled with diet recipes to cook-
Count the calories, read the labels
Before you fill your dinner tables,

If you take a Dexatrim each day
Nine pounds of fat will melt away.
'Tis a miracle to behold
The pill is worth its weight in gold!

Common sense will show you
How to eat a little less
Move around more rapidly
Go try on a new dress!

—*Patricia Donahue*

Christ Is Born

May this holy Christmas season
Bring thee blessings, gaiety,
For the Baby in the manger
Was a gift from God to thee.
This dear Baby was the Christ child
Who was sent to give us Life;
He's the Spirit of each Christmas,
So bring out the drum and fife,
And write anthems to His glory —
It the birthday of our King!
Let us celebrate with music
And let Christmas carols ring!
It's a time for joyous giving,
Time to praise the Diety;
It's a time for jubilation —
"Glad Noel!" to thee, from me!

—*J. L. Harris*

Fire

I am witnessing passion
built from fire,
it pours out of your hands.
As the light flickers
for something of a tormented past,
and is doused by liquid pain.
And I wonder why
you must escape
the lucid heat.
As we drink from a well of fear;
the vulnerability begins to overwhelm,
these hands desire living salvation.

—*Ruth Westergren*

For a Sweetheart

I would give you a rose
but a rose goes away
So I'll give you something
that will stay
That something
is my heart
Please don't worry
it will never depart
When your feeling down
just think of me
This heart full of love
will make you happy.

—*Elizabeth Ballstadt*

Look Upward

I recall the day I did espy,
Mounted mightily in the sky
In a framework hinged by
  blue and white,
One of the world's majestic
  sights:

Seated firmly in his chair:
Eyes in an unfocused stare;
Mouth, though closed,
  bespeaking his thoughts,
Reaffirmed by a chin
  determinedly wrought;
Head bowed down in humble
  prayer,
Exposing a heart of deep
  filled care
Was a man by all called Abe,
Who in God's likeness had
  been made.

—*Joseph Rappazini*

My Mother - My Child

Mother; I remember your eyes,
but I do not see your face.

I remember your fears,
but I do not how they feel.

I remember your sorrow,
but I do not know you pain.

I remember your shame,
but I do not know why you hide it.

I remember your jealousy,
but I do not know why you had it.

I remember your anger,
but I do not know why it was there.

I remember your actions,
but I do not hear your words.

I remember your dreams,
but I do not see them.

I remember your spirit,
but I do not feel apart of it.
I remember you as a person, separate from
me
not as a mother, but as a child unable to
run free from me.

—*Anna Birch*

Melissa

Melissa is only just about one
But I understand her fine
She hasn't learned to speak yet
Just telepathy kind

She makes a sound no one can stand
but for a second or two
She keeps it up because she's found
what it's urgency can do

I have been awakened many times
and found to my surprise
The source to my stirring and waking
came from quiet Melissa's eyes

—*Johanna Morris*

You Hurt Me

I know you said it wasn't you,
But it still hurt me.
You said you didn't mean it,
But it still hurt me.

When I talked to you,
You laughed and teased me.
I trusted you to keep a secret,
But you told and hurt me.

When you laughed,
The tears burned in my eyes.
Anger boiled up inside me,
And it hurt me.

How could you not know
it would hurt me?
Did you really think
I wouldn't care?

You once were my friend,
but my heart will never mend.
For what you did to me,
Made me hurt.

—*Amy Worley*

Potential Danger

Great is your potential
But lazy are your ways.
You pick the easy way out.
Can you please make a Turn-about?

You have a super grin
But with that alone
You cannot win.

Your Brain is very potent
Give it the right notion,
And a bit of locomotion.

It will always give you satisfaction,
If you put it into action.
A little commotion is essential,
With it comes a great potential!

Potential Danger is to waste it!
Success can be yours
If you choose to taste it!

—*Ulrike Basile*

Life and Love

Life may end,
But love is forever

Love may ascend,
Life may endeavor.

Love is so strong
Life is so weak

I may be wrong,
But you may seek.

You are seeking for love
You are seeking for life

You have looked above
You have hit the knife.

You have said "goodbye,"
But the love is still there

Your love is so high
And you are aware.

—*Marisa Moker*

Impassioned

These words I say come from my heart
But merely can not speak the part
Nor strike the chord to resonate
True feelings I shall not negate

I think of you, my life, my love
And feel you, as in my blood
Remember, always, I'll be true
For one and only, only you

"So please remember this," I say
"I'll love you till my dying day."
For no one else will be for me
Just you alone, eternally

I ask you to, and hope you do
Believe me please, how I LOVE YOU

—*Ron Cowette*

Adopt A Child

God gave us life; He gave us friends,
But most of all He gave
The chance to guide another's life,
Perhaps, his soul to save.

Upheaval in the Middle East
Have forced the poor to flee;
Like Christ of old the innocent
Seek love from you and me.

Exchange in mind your place with him,
No food, no friends, no home;
In tattered clothes and worn out shoes
Forced o'er the land to roam.

But for God's grace it could be you
Left shiv'ring in the night;
Like Bethl'hem's star light up the sky
And help make this world bright.

Another Mother Teresa be
And lend a helping hand;
Adopt a child to prove that you
Both love and understand.

—*Mary E. Murray*

A Sincere Prayer

Lord, I have no special talent
But my life I gladly give
Use me somewhere in your service
Let me witness where I live

Make me Lord, to be more humble
Show me Lord what is your will
Help me to know when to witness
Teach me sometimes to be still

For its when I stop and listen
That I hear you speak so clear
And in these still quiet moments
Feel your presence ever near

All my strength for daily living
Comes to me here as I pray
Oh dear Lord, let me be worthy
To live for you again today

Help me to bear somebody's burden
To share with someone your great love
To bring the message of salvation
Then meet them in heaven above

—*Lucy Lott*

Swore It Was Forever

Swept me away
But now I'm lost in the dark
Set me on fire
And now I'm left with a spark
Alone you left me beyond the haze
And now I'm lost within a maze.

Too far apart to bridge the distance
But something keeps us hanging on
Pretending not to know the difference
Of denying what we had is gone.

Every moment we're together
It's just breaking me down
I know we "swore it was forever"
But it hurts too much to stay around.

—*Jennifer McClinton*

Lost In the Mind

A sky is blue
But so is the ocean
Caught in the middle
Doing no motion
Everyone's happy just being there
Forever wondering if anyone cares
Going nowhere and
Hurrying there I often wonder
Just how they exist
Kites in the sky
Like balloons in the mist
Moving all over and
Nowhere to be found
Over the ocean
Pulled down to the ground
Quite often they fall and lose all their air
Running in clouds
Soaring through the air
Together we see
Unlike nothing before
Very beautiful birds
With their wings spread about
Xray the beauty
You see on this day
Zipper this in for it can all go away

—*Wesley Arnold*

"The Miracle Of Life"

The miracle of life is so grand
    but some people refuse
        to understand

Black, white, blue, or green
    God made you just like me

        He knows our fate
        He knows our lives
        He controls the lakes
        He controls the time

        He made the woods
        He made the seas
        He made us realize
        That we are we

    We are equal in his eyes
    We know we cannot argue
        With this guy

Not one better than another
It doesn't matter race or color
The miracle of life is so grand
At least I know I understand

—*Robin Dale Ritchey*

Friendship Lane

We may not meet as often
    As we would like, it's true
But there's a place in friendship lane
    Where I meet in thought with you
And always as we meet and chat
    As friendly as can be
Quite magically, the hours take on
    New happiness for me
And it's grand to know that always
    Through cloudy days and fair
Whenever I walk down friendship lane
    I'll find you waiting there

—*Kent Zeller*

'Tis Not For Heaven

'Tis not for heaven or hell men yearn
But that thy deeds will not be spurned
And when thou takest man away
No other mortal one can say

Thy spent thy life with end in mind
And lied and cheated all the time
And gave not what was given him
To help and aid one lesser than

Nor spoke so boldly of another soul
Nor coveted what thy neighbor hold
And yet the slate of life be cleaned
Exemplified and so brightly sheened

For thou were here to glorify
Another spirited one so high
And as thou wonder bout yon star
Tis not important who thine are

Importance lies within thyself
To discover love with thine spirits help
For this thou live and thou body shall die
And forever be immortalized.

— *Marion T. Collins*

"The End"

Many take what they have for granted,
But they all will soon learn that
   someday;
The ones they love and care for,
Must die and go away.

It could be a loved one,
A mother or a friend;
We find it's hard to cope when someone
We know is facing the end.

We wish they could live forever,
Although that long they cannot last;
We mourn and are regretful,
For many things not said in the past.

We wonder why it's like this,
Why life comes to a sudden close;
Why must we give up the ones that we
   love?
No one really knows.

— *Patricia Hopper*

"Judge Not - Lest Ye Be Judged"

It is so easy to judge others-
By the standards we have set;
So easy to condemn another
Whilst our own faults we forget.

Some people we expect to be perfect-
We forget they are human too,
The best way to judge another
Is to step into their shoes.

Put yourself in their place-
Be honest with yourself,
Quite often you may find
There's someway you can help.

Instead of a life being spent
With sorrow, anguish and tears,
A life can find happiness
That will last throughout the years!

— *Pat Joyner*

Serenity Be

Your Sunshine's hidden from me
By a cloud that's grey with gloom
I hope my sunshine finds you
Sitting safely in your room

Your sunshine is important
To those who feel your pain
So please accept this gift of mine
To clear the clouds and rain

A healthy heart is one that loves
And maintains the body's health
A healing prayer I've said for you
To restore to you your wealth

This gift that's given freely
From the heart unto the heart
Will surely help end the pain
And let the healing start

So know I give it freely
My sunshine for your rain
And let my love for you be
A shelter from your pain

— *M. Piper*

Mystery Lady

You see her walk
by so you stop and
stare. The lady on the
corner with the
reddish brown hair.

She's dirty and
scraggly and lives in
a box. You see her
feet and she has no socks.

We've stopped and talked
She's just like us
I don't see why you
Make a fuss:

Whatever happened
to the lady with
the reddish brown hair
I just want her to
know I care.

— *Kim Burmester*

Shipwrecked

Bitter is the wind
by the troubled waters
of this shore.
I'm wrecked,
as I drink
the morning air.
Strangled into a scream
I wake my soul
to pain,
sailing in a sea
of souls
with lesser depth
than mine.
More than one death
I must die
but again
my soul will be free
for it's home,
is the sea...

— *Marily A. Reyes*

Friends

If you're sad or unhappy,
call on a friend.
They'll listen and understand,
your sadness soon will end.

True friends are hard to find,
but when you find one you'll know,
for love and understanding,
They will always show.

So when your so very unhappy
And you think your life is at it's end,
the person who stands beside you,
You know is your true friend.

— *Adrianna Westbrooks*

A Snowflake On My Finger

Snowflakes,
Came down, down, tumbling down.
They made themselves look
Like Mother Nature's gown.

As I stopped running.
Where, oh, where did one land?
On my finger,
On my hand.

As I looked closely,
What I saw.
Told me that this tiny snowflake.
Didn't have any flaw.

— *Samantha Frost*

"A Little Faith"

Just a little faith
Can go a long, long way
Have a little faith
And don't forget to pray
He's waiting up there
To take you by the hand
When no one seems to care
He'll say "I understand"
Just open your heart
Let him come in to stay
Put your faith in him
Don't waste another day
No burden in this life
Will seem heavy to you
When a little faith
Lives in the heart of you.

— *Veronica Van Koppen*

Just Me

Today I am twenty-one!
Can I do the things I've done?
What is the magic of this age,
Is it a kind of growing gauge?
When your twenty one you know,
You must be careful where you go!
Don't do this, don't do that,
Perhaps you should wear a hat.
Forgive me all, that's not me
I'm really just what you see.

— *Mildred Williams*

Free...

No wind, fire, rain, or snow
can stop me as I walk down
this dried out creak.

No one will stop me on my
way to be free.
I will not look behind me
but only in front of me,
for as far as my eyes can see.

I'll leave no marks to
find my way back.
For what lies in front
is my ticket to be free.

Free from agony.
Free from pain.
Free from any religion
Free from any laws.

Now I have reached by eternity,
for at last I am free....

—*Paul Nadler*

O' Gentle Rain

Speak to me, O' Gentle rain,
Caress my face,
with sweet whispers of
thy dewy breath,
springing from effervescent pools.
In thy Alpha dwelling place-
O'Gentle rain,
Show God's grace,
Draw me from this slumber
that carries me
on swift wings of thunder
to my Omega place.
Speak to me, O'Gentle Rain
stay me for awhile,
from the paths -
of ascending soul's-
'til once more I see-
the quickening of your smile.

—*Sarah O. Saey*

Love

Lips
    caressing me softly,
words speaking truth.

Arms
    embrace my body
without fear, motive to love.

You being me no fear
    no shame,
Just love
    and a beautiful future
full of dreams.

Attraction brings us together.
A bond unites us.
Our hearts become one.

No words
    speak our love.
Our hearts
    know the real meaning

—*Marangely Melendez*

Northern Lights

Stars, oh stars of the silvery night
Catch a ray of Northern lights.
Bring them to me from afar.
Red and Blue and purple delights.
They are pretty don't you agree.
Make them shine of Midnight blues.
of sky and sea's dividing you.
I'll be here for Northern lights
So bring me them so big and bright.
Stars oh stars of the night.
bring to me the Northern lights.

—*Theodachia E. Cartwright*

The Laugh

Oh! That intense screaming sound!
Causing a grief so profound!
Oh! It is so loud and shrill!
It makes my heart to stand still!
Dark as an ocean or sea!
Causing my insanity!
Causing my legs to quiver,
and spinal cord to shiver!
Oh! What ill force has caressed?
that cry to so possessed!
Sending once dry eyes to cry,
Wanting to fall down and die!
Failed have all your escapes!
So your eyes again it rapes!
Write this in my epitaph:
"Dead he lies due to The Laugh!"

—*Michael J. Paddock*

"Weeping Willow"

Winds flow through her leaves,
Causing them to be wild curls of hair.
Tears of anger and sorrow flow.
Down in her side is a sharp pain.
The pain makes her frown and weep.
The winds try to comfort her,
But she says she cannot accept pity.
She feels so hurt and alone.
In the far corner of the forest,
She can weep.
All of her friends have gone.
The cruel men of the world,
Left her to stand alone.

—*Shannon Kelly*

Untitled

protonic polka
chaotic travel
your arrival
singular characteristics
that particular moment
in time
particular space
universe
your unique surroundings
peculiar
incalculable
life cannot be but
most precious Priceless Miraculous

pass the word _____

—*K. E. Nesbit*

She'll Never Be The Same

Tall majestic mountains
Clean lakes and streams
That's how she once was
At least that's how it seems

Once a world of beauty
Now don't look so bright
Comparing now to then
As different as black and white

Change was not her choice
This brought on by man
Not caring what he ruined
Just making all he can

We'll never put her back
Clean and pollution free
We can only remember her
The way she used to be

—*Olin Conner*

The Sunbeam

Hello Sunbeam! I see you there;
Clinging playfully to my wall!
You sneaked in through my window-pane
And came to pay a call.

To dance around on golden feet
And toss your streaming hair
Against the wall; behind the door.
I see you hiding there!

I bid you welcome, Golden Spot;
Tiny offspring of the Sun.
So, come on in and stay awhile;
The morning's just begun.

Highlight with lovely, lacy gold
The decor of this room.
Let your dazzling, shimmering brilliance
Chase away the gloom.

Now, why are you dimming, Little Spot?
It's time to leave, you say?
Well, remember where my window is
And call another day.

—*Linda L. Hughes*

San Juan "Islands' Time"

The locals call it, "Island time."
  Clocks don't run down,
    They......slow......up.

Rhythmically pulsing tides
  soft measure halcyon
    days, weeks, months, years.

Time is a quiet
  friend stopping by
    for a cup of coffee.

Life flows,
  a soothing sea breeze
    upon the brow.

"Island time,"
  gentle marriage of the
    soul and island reverie.

—*Ted Fromm*

266

Inward Joy

Reclining in an easy-chair
Close by my window wide
I looked upon a Robin-bird
So busy for his bride.

He gaily jumped from limb to limb
With sticks and cotton string
To build with pride his lovely home
A place fit for a King.

Great expert skill he plastered it with
Mud and pressed it thin
To make it tight from nature's cold
For those who dwell within.

Instructions came from female bird
Perched high on limb above
Her crooning song from throbbing breast
Revealed to him her love.

Two birds in love with future bright
They built with fervent care.
From them I felt an inward joy
That every home should share.

—*Myron H. Sanders*

The Poet

Sitting alone, staring at words
colliding in my mind
Colours abound, no one around
to witness a heart exploding

A clown passes away
no stage paint before him
His tears run down in tides
forever within, out of control
dreaming of the play
The poet's words

Dying embers seek out the
flame of youth
Never caring, never wondering
What is the use
As he sits alone
staring at words

—*Ronald J. O'Rourke Jr.*

Quest For Omnipotence

From the depths of anguish
   Comes an appreciation of joy.
From the clutch of fear,
   Comes an understanding of hope.
From the fires of rejection,
   Comes an awareness of self-esteem.
From the pain of sorrow,
   Comes a comforting of love.
From the wounds of destruction,
   Comes the solace of peace.

Quenching a perpetual thirst,
   From the chalice of life,
      Reveals the soul of man.
Alleluia!
The Image of God.

—*Mary E. Rocco*

4-H Queen

Hello Queen....hello-o-o Queen,
Comes an echo from the homeland
   and the stream,
You have pledged your heart and
   hand to the future of the land,
You will guide our youth in
   all you say and do,
As you follow your dream
   you'll be leading a team,
God Bless You,
   We Love You,
      4-H Queen.

—*Waneeta Lanham*

Glass

Crystallized sand
composed for a view
Crying and cracking
harm did ensure
Splintering spires
a mound on the ground
Gleaming and glistening
a new beauty found.
Alluring danger
shimmers in wait for you.

—*Jim Hanson*

"The Christmas Spirit"

Why can't "The Christmas Spirit"
Continue all year long .....
As hearts are overflowing
With hope, and joy and song?

Why can't the age old saying
Of "Peace, good will to men"
Continue on, undaunted
Throughout the year, and then,

Why can't the population
Of this, our planet Earth,
See good in one another?
Each soul is of great worth.

GOD gave us an example
That is beyond compare;
Meant to be lived and practiced
By mankind, everywhere.

Why can't "The Christmas Spirit"
Continue all year, then?
When each soul does its equal share
Through LOVE, dear hearts, it can!

—*Joyce Hodge Davis*

Summons Of Infinity

I have heard the howl of death,
In an eerie winds song,
It echoes ominously in the hall of my soul.
It chills and calls to the depths of me.
Come to me child of destiny,
Come to know the great unknown,
Come to see eternity.
Never to be, forever to be,
Where so ever we shall be.

—*Christian J. Lefebvre*

A Flow of Emotions

Evil The mind interprets corruption
corruption breeds destruction
destruction instills fear
fear draws chaos
chaos uproots goodness
goodness falls to terror
terror reigns supreme
supreme lust signals the end
the end winters evil...
LOVE
the sight brings intention
from intention grows a meeting
a meeting sees enlightenment
enlightenment glows with feeling
feelings seed closeness
closeness forms excitement
excitement generates happiness
happiness brings eternal flowers
eternal flowers summer knowing
knowing determines LOVE!

—*Lucious Wilson*

Struggle to Struggle

I'm just a good man, doing the best I can,
I'm just a good soul, trying not to let go
I'm just a good man, trying to make a stand,
In this world oh so cold
Struggle to struggle, it never ends
Battle to battle, it's only a trend
Got to go forward, cause I can't go back,
If only someone would give me some slack.
Time to move and nowhere to go
Cold weather coming along with the snow
Things could be better,
And things could be worse
Sometimes I think that I've been cursed
To live on the edge,
And walk a thin line
Taking chances time after time
Waiting for the break that should be mine
I'm just a good man,
Doing the best that I can.

—*Rick Rhythm*

Dreams

This is a poem about myself,
I'm not a giant, I'm not an Elf,

I'm not to short, I'm not to tall,
I'm not to big, I'm not to small.

A very kind person I will agree,
So loving and tender, and smart as can be.

To start with my head, I have brown hair,
Big brown eyes that shine and glare,

With tiny lips and cheeks of rose,
With two dimples and a little nose.

With a body full of pep, with silky skin
and looks I've kept.

With miniature feet and tiny knees,
And beautiful legs as you can see,

I have an imagination that glares with beam,
For all I've told you is a dream.

—*Linda Zablocki*

To You My Love

The silence fills the walls inside my head,
I don't remember the times I've dread.
    The only thing that lasts, stays with me now,
Are thoughts of you and I, somehow.
    So if you think the love we have is gone,
If you think it's time to move on.
    I know it may look easier to say good-bye,
It maybe just as hard to leave behind.
    Remember day and night together,
And talks through the never.
    You were the one that caught my eyes,
I tried to be there for you when those who died.
    So if this is where we stop,
Then let us say good-bye, just don't forget my touch.
    For you I would have died.

—*Jon Amsden*

Mental Hospital

Hearing echoes in the mental hospital
I enter the door leaving my shadow outside
An empty elevator opens, closes
The clock ticking the hours away
Alone in the quiet waiting room, my body waits for my mind
I didn't want to be there long,
But I stayed in the waiting room, waiting and waiting
The morning sun soon turned into a hot blazing fire
Penetrating the window
A hand reaches up and pulls down a shade
A branch's shadow then waves in the window and is gone
Lives come and go and come again in this building
Soon a presence of a masked doctor pushes an empty wheelchair
along the corridor
I was then guided into a room
There I found her huddled on the bed
In the corner of the mental patient's eye, I exist
In the room the sun don't shine
She screams then breaks into sobs
All lights shine on her face

—*Jennifer Tomboc*

Smokey River

High in my tower
I feel like a king
The power of this land, is such a
beautiful thing.
The smell of the damp air, strikes my very soul.
Oh my Smokey River, I truly love you so.
    All the memories I have here, will never ever end.
    Little otters, playing, just wanting to
be my friend.
    But suddenly! out of the brush, a large
moose appears, nostrils wide smelling the air.
    Pushing the brush from here to there,
another moose", does appear.
    He found his mate for this year.
    I watch them leave with a tear.
Goodnight my smokey river as you move downstream.
    I will try to follow you in my dreams.

    —*Goldie Hale*

Untitled

It's a night warm with the summer heat
Looking into the starless sky making wish
Over the mountains and over the trees I fly
Viewing the oceans and torrential sea
Eastern sky brightening an orange hue
Begs achingly that it stays at such wonderful view
Entering into seasons of winter brings me chills
Not knowing whether it's you.....

    —*Maria Lee*

Children Moved Far Away From Grandmother

I'm thinking of you, the ones I hold dear, the ones in my heart
I feel so near.
Never before have I been so at loss, but know in my heart that
your minds must have crossed some of the pain that I feel.

I know your are safe, for in God you do trust, but my own
selfish love says, "Why? Do you must - go so far from us?"

Just a short trip down the road I could trod, grab all the hugs
and kisses and love. Now only dream - in the day, or at night
of the feelings of hugs, kisses and love. The little arms
squeezing and pulling my hair, the little lips telling me,
"Please take me there." The little eyes shining, so big and so
bright and dancing with laughter half of the night.

Oh, how I love you, my children my life, I miss you so badly
and feel so much strife. But——I know someday soon you
will be back in my life, giving me hugs, kisses and love.

God bless you all till we meet once again and I pray for your
happiness that goes deep within. May God in His infinite
wisdom above give you all more than I know you deserve

    —*Dottie Hyden*

Loneliness

In the darkness of the room,
    I feel the loneliness closing in.
    It weaves it's way around the room,
a spider spinning it's web and trapping it's prey.
    Me, the prey of the loneliness, the sadness,
    the utter emptiness, the darkness,
sucking me into the epitome of the black hole,
    the center of all feelings.
        My head spins,
thoughts drowning in the bitter sea of my emotions,
    a mixture, a solution all combined.
I start falling deeper and deeper until...
        The lights come on
    and my life flows back together again,
    the loneliness gone until the next eclipse
        between the darkness of my emotions
            and the light of my life
drags me back to the solitude of my being.

    —*Kristyne Vine*

A Breath

As I turned, you were there and
I fell, right into your stare.
Caught me up and held me fast,
I searched for you in my past,
    And I found you — everywhere

But I know we've never met ... a breath

A step toward me, open mouthed,
Consciousness bridged, without sound.
I see you searching for me,
    Familiarity keen,
And there, too, in you, I am found

Eternity ebbing fresh ... a breath

Time just swayed there,
    Slow and hushed,
    And came over me a flush.
I know not this outer shell,
But you, within, I know well.
    My soul to you in a rush.

Aye, shown here, life knows no death ... a breath
    —*Helen Louise Amptman*

A Beginners' Prayer

The greatest fears I've ever know were burdened in my heart
I felt that I was all alone, my world was torn apart
Each morning I would wake and cry, "How will I pass this day"
I never thought to take the time to seek you out and pray

Through ignorance and self retreat I had nowhere to turn
And then one day I hear your word and knew I had to learn
That happiness is found in you and love that knows no end
For you Lord Jesus teaches me on you I can depend

To guide me through the good and bad, to find some peace and joy
For in your kingdom I am loved and that can't be destroyed

Now each morning when I cry, "How will I pass this day"
I know that you are in me, Lord, you've taught me how to pray
And now the greatest fears I know that burden in my heart
I'm giving them to you, My Lord, through prayer and a brand
new start.

—*Lisa DeRita*

For Today's Teens

The nights are short and the days seem longer.
I get up every morning; I have to be stronger.
To go to school and do what I can,
To one day help my fellowman.
Drugs and sex are wiping us out,
Killing all people without a doubt.
Sex may be fun - it may feel really great,
But couples shouldn't have sex on the first date.
Go to school! It's the key to life.
To have a family and a wife.
Do what I say and you'll be okay.
Don't be like the brothers that are dead today.
Teachers are the roads and we are the cars.
If you don't listen you could end up behind bars.
I am telling you right, not wrong.
I am telling you something to help you along.
Many teens are thinking that twelve years will do,
But we need sixteen to do what we like to.
There is not very much more to say,
If you want to excel in life — this is the way.

—*Robert Lamont Hedrick*

Daddy's Little Girl

Daddy's little girl I seem to be,
I grew up so fast, and that I see.

You tucked me in on cold winter nights,
I was afraid of the dark, you turned off the lights.

You read me stories almost every night,
I said my prayers and you kissed me good night.

To this day, I'm still Daddy's little girl,
I'm spoiled rotten, that's for sure.

But even though we're miles apart,
You're still with me, here in my heart.

I love you more each and every day,
I appreciate the things you do and say.

I'm Daddy's little Girl, I am, I am,
So don't you ever forget, you're a great man.

—*Gabrielle L. Grahn*

My Limitation

The light in my room is dim.
I hardly seem to notice.

The window blinds look like prison bars to me,
As they let in some light and keep some out.

My room is too small,
And my walls are too high.

On my day off I go out and about,
But not very far. I'm afraid I'll get lost.

I ride the subway and look at graffiti.
The words mean nothing, but I like to look at the pictures.

I study the faces of the people I meet.
This tells me who I am.

At night I watch television.
This tells me what to think.

When I go to work, my job is hard.
I don't shuffle papers.

I scrub floors and clean toilets.
I know where I am by the pictures on the doors.

My boss can read me the riot act at any time.
But as for me, I can't read.

—*Beulah Cordell*

Eddy's Addiction

I admit it
I have a problem
I'm a junkie
but I'm not addicted to any drug
you'd find on the street.
You're the drug I'm hooked on
I need a short of your love very often
A fix every day
especially when I'm sad and lonely
I look forward to getting high on you
The urge for a fix is upon me now
but I know I must quit this self abuse.
My supply has run out completely and is no
longer within hands reach.
I'm sick of hustling for another dose.
My body will soon start to reject this craving
when withdrawal kicks in.
So I must bleed you out of my system
entirely.
Then, I will search for a different drug.

—*Edmund Azzolino*

This Man

I read the story of Footprints
I hear His name everyday sometimes used in vain
I read His book and follow His word
I try to reach out to people who haven't heard
   of this wondrous man
He brought us here and He will take us away
All His believers will meet Him someday
Some hear His call, others never do
If you believe and trust in Him He will be there for you
This man will love you through the thick and thin
Not just every now and then
This man has helped me
This man will help you
This man is right beside you in everything you do
The man I speak so generously about is the man none of us
   can live without
Our Lord Jesus.

—*Jessie L. Gilligan*

New Fallen Snow

My sister's up.
I hear, "There's no school today" in the distance.
I go to my window and look out.
Snow, snow all around outside is snow.
There's quietness everywhere.
The dog's not barking, the birds aren't
chirping while eating our dog's food that
we spilled, and the cat isn't meowing for it's meal.
The temperature is so cold that nobody wants to be outside.
Then new fallen snow covers the leaves and sticks
we never raked or picked up, the garden we never
planted, and the pile of sticks and brush we never burned.
In the afternoon when the temperature rises,
there won't be quietness anymore.
The children will come out in their colorful
snowsuits and make snow angels, snowmen, go
sledding and some may even make a snow fort,
maybe the children will pretend to guard a
castle, play house, or maybe have a club in their fort.
Whatever happens, the new fallen snow is responsible.

—*Danielle Tvedten*

The International Child

Child,
   I hear your cry
      From the far corners of the world-
   Your plaintive cry
      To be held secure,
      To be free of doubt,
         fear, anxiety, and the perplexities of life.

Child,
   I hear your laughter
      Ringing down through the ages
   Laughter that rebounds
      Against the walls of time and rings true
      To the future of the universe.

Child,
   You will face the woeful challenges of life—
      The devastation, splinters,
         and shatters of earth.

   In you lies
      The secret of love-, hope-, peace-
      The destiny of mankind.

—*Marlene Bachim*

Longing

As I watched the waves roll in,
   I heard a sigh -
It followed what seemed to be
   a silent cry -
   "Is there some way I can return and flee?
   That I might abide with Mother Sea?
   My time has been so short
      and the world is so wide.
   Is there someone who would
      help and turn me aside?
For this forlorn wave it was
   not to be.
And never again would eyes
   this wave see.
Its hopes were drowned as
   it rolled up to the shore,
And its life did end forevermore.
But do not grieve, do not mourn,
For a thousand others are
   being formed!

—*Joseph Rappazini*

To My One and Only Love

To my one and only love....
I hope you're listening from above.....
With all the strife and stress of
Living here on earth...
I cherish the thoughts of what....
You considered life's worth....
Love, patience, teaching right from wrong...
In every way...
If only the present youth could learn..
Not to go astray....
There could be less concentration on
Sex, hate and violence...
Because we would learn to live with
One another and God's omnipotence.........

—*Carmela Siciliano*

Over Now

We always talked to each other together.
I hoped that we could stay that way forever.
We went through laughs and also cries,
Then say how much we wanted to die.

We got closer and closer each day,
Mostly because of what we would say.
Sometimes I would feel just really tied up,
Get really down and feel all out of luck.

I only wanted room to breathe,
But you would only be mad at me.
It seems that was so long ago;
Memories together just come and go.

In a way you turned my life around,
You picked me up when I was feeling down.
Now at night when I when I go to bed,
I think of all the things we've said.

I think of it as love, but it's over now.
It was told to me without a sound.
I know that nothing lasts forever,
I'm glad we spent that time together.

—*Betsy Brooke Davidson*

Sympathy Extended

My dear friend's long sick husband died,
I hugged her close to me. She cried.

I said the senseless things we say,
"He's suffered enough, best this way."

"Flowers are lovely, aren't they all?
You need someone, give me a call."

I left her then as others came,
Their words and feelings much the same.

She's under control, she's okay.
Women have to be strong today.

Sorrow overwhelms, friends look askance,
She's a wallflower at life's dance.

Loneliness grows, the bills increase,
Phone calls slow, invitations cease.

In ancient times in other lands,
A husband's death brought dark demands.

Widow's body on the pyre,
Cremated live in his fire.

But maybe when we think it through,
It was the kinder thing to do.

—*Florence Whalen*

Esperance

Continue on brave soul
I know not how you function
So very deep inside of me
I cannot fathom your courage
Or how you seem to make it mine

Could it be you know some thing I do not
Do you hide that missing link
That will firmly anchor me to my dreams
And as you despair I fall down further
Yet as I fall I see the bottom so clearly
I know there is a top

—*Betsy R. Norris*

Untitled

A heart commitment is one of gold
I know one that never was sold
Oh yes, there was a price upon it
And I think of Him often when I knit

For He spoke of lambs, of whom I am one
And I have been sheared, since I begun
To remain as He said is my aim
To stay close to Him is better than fame

He's the King of Hearts, the creator of All
Meek as a lamb, teaches how to stand tall
Though I work with yarn, pen, ink, whatever
His words will win you and keep you forever

—*Imogene Mayr*

"Someday, Someway"

O' God I have a Lover I truly miss, one I long to kiss,
I know only God can create such magnificent love that
feels like a heavenly blest,
    At first glance I couldn't wait, O' boy did I want a date,
I was out to prove I could be a good mate, O'God what will be
our fate, please let me have this date, I'm rushing not to be
late, hoping, praying my place no one else will take.
    My mind began to say, got to get this lover someday,
someway, maybe he'll propose take me home to be his wife, give
me the best years of my life, and there I'll stay,
    You should have seen when our eyes first met, I wanted you
to come home with me and be my pet, I was willing to bet, I
would get you yet, it's meant to be, this romance between you
and me, I'm determined to get you over and over again to be my
lover, my friend, so honest so true, someday, someway, I hope,
and I pray...

—*Gloria J. Burnette*

Tomorrow

When times are good and all goes well,
I know you are here.
When the babies are happy and the rent is paid,
I know you are here.
When we make love and stars are shining,
I know you are here.

But, will you still be here, tomorrow?
When life is hard and times are bad,
When I start to fade, the babies are grown,
And the stars have dimmed.
Will you still be here, tomorrow?

Today, I have tamed the drifter in you,
But, will it come back to haunt me, tomorrow?
To fly free and never look back
On memories both great and small.
Will you still be here, tomorrow?

—*Evelyn Broussard*

Curiosity

On a hill that overlooks the Earth,
    I lay in curiosity of how things work.
Questions unanswered and uncertainty remains,
    my mind just wanders and my answers detained.
The most obvious knowledge leads you to believe,
    that answers to your world you can't conceive.
Simplicity itself can hold a meaning so true,
    maybe the sky above isn't really blue.
You learn to live from what they give,
    from the day that you were born.
Passed on through generations until this day,
    the knowledge has been worn.
Change has come and altered your way,
    giving a new sense of freedom for you to obey.
Waiting and wondering what changes are in store,
    your curiosity seeks out for you to explore.
No traces of Earth are left in your mind,
    only to lay back and slowly unwind.

—*Mark E. Byttner*

Tear Drops

A tear drop flows down my cheek,
I lick it, it tastes like a salty substance.
Then I start to think about the sea.
The sea is beautiful, its blue, a wave splashes
against me, I get the salty water in my mouth.
Then I start think about water. I take a shower,
the water comes out like as if they were rain
drops, then I start to think about the rain.
The rain comes out of the clouds and then I think
about a cloud. A cloud is white and fluffy,
it becomes grey, and the sky goes dark and then
I start to think about a thunder storm, "boom"
goes the thunder. The lightening is gold and
it looks like an old tree limb. Then I start
to think about an old tree. The tree is old,
the wind blows, and the tree makes a loud creaky noise.

—*Kristen Noel Vielbaum*

The Aspen Leaves

"You are so lovely, Dear," he said
"I like the gold upon your head.
The shining look on your sweet face,
So full of wonder and of Grace."

"If I glow and shudder with delight,
My secret can't be still 'til night."
She told him, "It's time for joy,
Perhaps a girl or a little boy."

"Do you mean we've made a seed?"
He glowed at her and she agreed.
"Come Springtime," bounced the leaf with glee,
"We'll see our darling Aspen tree."

He curled around her with his arms.
The snow fell gently on their charms
They floated happily to the ground
To nourish their precious little mound.

—*Frieda P. Davis*

Little Gray Cat

Little gray cat tell me where you have been.
Little gray cat tell me where you are from.
Little gray cat tell me where you are going.
Little gray cat tell me what you hear.
Little gray cat tell me what you see.
Little gray cat tell me the truth.
Little gray cat do you love me?
Little gray cat, I love you.

—*Kim Plancarte*

Lack Of

My ears began to ring-a-ling-a-ling.
  I listened to the bell go cling-a-ling-a-ling.
He was up again.

How can I make him understand?
He is most definitely a morning man.

I love the peace and morning calm.
  I love the feel of his warm skin next to mine,
    while our bodies do the sleepy dance until dawn.

How can I make him understand?
He is most definitely a morning man.

My body shouts a big HEAVE-HO.
  I just don't want to let him go.
I only ask for a little more sleep.
  It seems that I can only weep.

How can I make him understand?
How can I make him understand?
How can I make him understand?
He is most definitely my morning man.

—*Valerie Anderson*

Just Like The Wind

At first there was love and then there was none.
I live the days one by one.
I count the seconds, minutes and such
'Til I find the love I need so much.
Looking to the right and then left
My heart was stolen just like a theft.
I saw you standing there looking at me.
There was love in your eyes, I could see.
I thought you liked me, I thought you cared.
I felt that my love could finally be shared.
I turned once, and turned back again.
And you were gone just like the wind.

—*Brandy Sheppard*

Safety Lights In The Night

I am wide awake. I cannot sleep.
I look around the dark of my room perforated by lights.

The red, yellow, green buttons of the alarm system.
We barricade ourselves in while thieves are rampant outside.
Safety.

The soft glow of a night light to prevent stumbles. Safety.

A neighbor's yard light casts a swath of light
On the ceiling. They'll turn it off when they come home.
Safety.

The red light tells me the fire alarm is working.
The smoke detector, too. Safety.

A loud drone and flashing lights of a plane
About to land. Safety.

Ever-changing numerals of the digital clock.
I hear there is radiation from proximity.
I must exchange it for a wind-up alarm. Safety.

The cold, pale beam of the moon.
God's light that man cannot extinguish. Safety.

But, wait. I can shut out all these lights merely by
closing my eyes. And drifting off to sleep. Safety.

—*Janette G. Greabell*

I Love My Grandma

I love my ma
I love my pa
But I really love my grandma!

She's full of love
And like the dove,
Softly flying above.

She loves me whether I'm right or wrong
She likes words in a song
She may live an hour away, but that's not long!

Four grandchildren has she,
All of them love to see
The truth about grandma, that's me!

We can't wait until she walks in door,
She's never a bore.
After her stories we ask for more!

—*Laurie Bodenmiller*

This Earth

Oh, God!
I love this earth,
This orb on which my soul alit
Some years ago
From God knows where.

And though there is the sacred place
Where souls abound in Heaven's face,
That's test of faith.
That's what I know when spirit graced.

But on this plane of twenty-four,
Despite the pain,
In spite of lore—

I choose Life's side
And long for more;
I love this Earth.

—*Christine Webb*

"Dad"

I love you dad, day after day.
I love you dad, now and always.
With each passing moment, I think of you.
I think of the things you did without.
And all of the times you never would pout.
You gave to your children and your loving wife.
You've given me love all through my life.
You've supported me time and again.
You've been my father as well as my friend.
You looked ahead for tomorrow to bring;
all good things to every offspring.
You taught your sons how to survive;
you taught your daughters how to build their hive.
A lot of luxuries we never had, but all
the necessities made me glad.
Glad to be raised by my mom and dad.
You're the best father a girl ever had!

—*Lois Firkins*

Body Language

A man with clean hands,
May not mean an unadulterated sole.
A man with dirty hands,
May not mean a stained sole.
There once was a man with immaculate hands,
But a sole as cold and dark as the moonless night.
I want the man with soiled hands, and a sole as warm and
bright as the shining sun.

—*Kimberly Acquistapace*

Untitled

On God,
I love you so much
Every time I loose you I feel crushed
You make me laugh
You make me cry
You made me say hello
You make me hang and say Goodbye.
Your the best thing that has happened
 to me, since birth
There is no one quite like you on earth
It hurts me to see you lie
Every time you do I cry
Love is in the heart
I hope we never get turn apart.
Believe me, my love to you is tender and true,
I am faithful, but only to you.

—*Desiree Walton*

Mutual Respect

I desired a person someone special and true,
I made up my mind and began to dream about you.

I wanted to hold you close, close to my heart,
 I couldn't even imagine us apart.

I wanted to visit and knew you'd understand,
just how much it means for you to be my fiancee and friend.

I know your time is limited while you establish your career,
 Not hearing your voice forever is all I fear.

You are my connection to a goal,
And without you I'm not whole.

A person who is devoted to show you how much I care,
In your dreams, through life and love, I'll always be there.

—*Chris A. Liscomb*

I Love You

I believe this is the way love was meant to be
I mean you are so dear to me.
If only you could just understand
I love to be with you hand in hand.
When you are by, I can't help but to almost cry.
Even when you're near, I have no fear.
I love you so much
Now only if we could touch.
I want to be with you forever
And never separate from you, never.....
"I LOVE YOU"

—*Erin L. Bradovich*

My First Love

As I walked the other day.
I met a friend along the way.
I told him what a beautiful sight to see.
He said all this was made by me.
I ask how do you make such beautiful land?
He said with just a wave of my hand.
Don't you know I'm always the same.
Ask anything in my name.
Who made the day and the night?
And place the stars in the sky
Just right.
Hello morning hello noon.
Night is coming very soon.
Thou who made the heaven above.
You are always my first love.

—*George Williams*

Silhouette

I'm the dramatic actress on the stage
I model clothes that are all the rage

The prima ballerina who dances for kings and queens
I've been crowned Miss America

I've conducted a symphony

I've waved my wand and did magic tricks
I'm captain of my ship

A scientist, I've won the Nobel Prize
I'm Mata Hari in disguise

I can cut a figure eight on skates
I'm President of the United States

The Prima Donna who sang "La Scala"

A puppet on a string, I can be anything

I've piloted a plane
Been around the world in a balloon

I've reached for the stars and grabbed the moon!

You see...
When I cast my shadow on the wall, we could be...?
My shadow and I we're...

F A N T A S Y
—*Felicia C. Severini*

Simple Love

I think of you all the time
I need you to make my lonely days shine
Would you ever consider being mine, or me being yours?

Just me and you sitting on an empty beach shore,
 with my hand in yours and your hand in mine.
Watching the tide turn in the afternoon sunshine.
And it seems in this world it is only us two.

Though the sun sets the day still seems to be new,
 and we both do whatever we desire
Until our eyes take over we begin to tire,
So we walk to the beach and lay down in the sand,
And slowly and peacefully fall asleep hand in hand.

As a ray of light pierces through the clouds above,
The wind whispers it is only me you'll ever love,
and it'll be just us for the rest of our years
through all the happiness and all the fears,
 and all the laughter and all the tears.

—*Fred W. Voss*

In My Dreams

You look at me then look away
I never get a chance to say
Just the way I feel inside
When you are by my side

I look into your eyes and stare
I see that you don't care
I've said to myself before
"You can't think of him anymore"

I know we'll never be together
Even if I wait forever
I don't think I can wait that long
There's no chance I'm that strong

There is a place where I'll always love you
In that place you'll love me too
That place is
 In My Dreams

—*Kathy Kowalski*

Until We Know

I crooned a little tune one dreary day.
I never knew it was so very fine
Until I heard somebody sing it right,
With each note like a lovely golden chime.

I made a feeble little joke one day.
I never knew it was so very funny
Until I saw smiles and heard the laughter,
And knew others thought that it was punny.

I made a garment for somebody once.
I never knew how lovely it would be
Until I saw the owner wearing it,
How nice she looked, and how she was so pleased.

I wrote a poem once upon a time.
I never knew that it was really good
Until I saw the joy and tears it brought,
How it moved people as a poem should.

We do so very many different deeds,
And know not the effect these acts can bring
Until we see reactions from someone
That say we've done a very worthy thing.

— *Bertha Woods Greenwood*

Back Pages Of Joy

I worked so hard that I wore my fingers to the bone
I never knew the "Diamond Man" even though I never left alone
At eighteen I meant this lovely girl who said her name was Joan
But it was this sin which my age has never been able to atone.

One day when the sun was hot I gave a cry of rage
How can this nasty summer weather cost me my old age
I came down the back alley pretending I was walking on stage
But the man watching me gave me a look to say,
"Is that your wage?"

I know this saga sounds like nonsense as I've written it thus
far it probably will again but that's the way that poets are
Life in this life can be pretty crazy like sometimes a new car
I'm glad that when its over I'll just begin to be a star.

Written in an elegy of exultation was this poor boy's blues
I came into the city like so many fools do
My suitcase of hope was emptied of all but prayers and heavenly
clues it's been so many years ago I've missed how much I grew.

— *Dallas Marshall*

A Sonnet

I know that when you are asleep you dream,
I often wonder if our dreams are shared
Because when I'm asleep I also dream,
And when you're near me, I am often scared.
From the first time we met I've felt something,
A connection existing between us
There, beneath the surface swirling, churning-
Its presence known, nothing could redeem us.
When I look in your eyes I see it shine,
Could it be love from a common past life?
If so, dare I name it and call it mine?
It may not be and cut me like a knife.
   If only confusion would let me go
   And I heard it in your voice, I would know.

— *Benjamin D. Loudermilk*

Tear

Darkness...
I open my eyes
images cloud my vision
but I see nothing clearly

The swelling in my eyes gives way
a tear forms
A moment's thoughts, a soul's conversation
It beheld my emotion, it carried my sorrow
Release
the tear runs from my vision
left in utter astonishment
   no more
loneliness dispenses down the skin

I search
   only to find oblivion
      — *Cathleen Fong*

Recognizing Realization

   I saw you with my eyes,
I passed you by.

   I saw you with my heart,
and I began to cry.

   I judged you from a far, and didn't
realize, how rare and special you really are.

   I tend to judge by the outside
look, but shame on me! Your not a book.
      — *Cynthia J. LaComb*

Lady Life

Once, it was my ambition, but love got in the way
I paved half the road to hell, decided not to stay.
With passion, I pursued it, that which slowly ebbed away.
Seeking madly after it, unawares I became it's prey
Tho' years have passed and pleasures brought.
This I have to say,

That life and love go hand in hand - it's all a game we play

Now, it seems, my children seek, that which I came to know
That game of chance (called romance, mystery sets it a glow)
Sincerely you may seek her, the lady known as life.
Tho' you love her deeply, she will not become your wife
When you need her most,
when all your friends have gone their way
You'll sit alone and realize, the pursuer is the prey
So heed my words and hesitate, when in this tricky game
No matter what the stakes are, what's "fair" is not the same
You've gathered many memories - had fun along the way
Yet all those years whilst you pursued,
You truly were life's prey.

      — *Dolores LaBianco*

Without You Near

Each day is a fight and I hold back the tears.
I guess it's time to face my fears, you're never
coming back it's clear to see and I don't blame
you for hating me. I know I was wrong for
letting go and I do regret it but you'll never
know I still have memories too precious to
let go and they often hurt me, oh how I wish
you could know. Each song that I play reminds
me of you, oh my darling why can't I tell you!
I miss you each day even though it's been years.
Now can you imagine my darling what life is
without you near.

      — *Carole L. Johnson*

Untitled

God is powerful, wondrous, and wise
I pray to see him with my two eyes
If I don't get this chance at glory
I'll still be glad to tell his story
He started it out, everything you see
And will last forever, past you and me
He is all knowing, loving, and kind
The only true God that you'll ever find
He sent us his son to save us from sin
And through his sacrifice we all can win
So if you want to live forever
Believe His Gospel and sin not ever
Spread your love both far and wide
And then from you he'll never hide
Faith, hope, and love these three remain
But love above all is the highest gain
So listen my brothers to this story
And seek after forgiveness, love, and glory
Through his son is the path to above
To the holy realm of the God of love

  —Dirk A. Myers

The Letter

I received the letter, a loving letter,
I read several times, looked at many times.

It took me down the memory lane,
It brought back my golden days.

She played with me when I was young,
She showered her love when I was hurt.

When I was sick she cried with me,
She felt the pain more than me.

Never did she let me go out sight,
Always pointing wrong from right.

Now away from her thousands miles,
Fragrance of her love comes with smiles.

I am in her thoughts and dreams,
She is in my heart and soul.

She prays for me night and day,
O'Lord guide and guard my son everyday,
With courage and strength to be on right,
Let him shine and be a star in the sky.

This is how she ended her letter,
Is she not a wonderful mother.

  —Anil Khanna

Patty

When she was gone, oh how I loved her.
I remembered so many things about her.
Longing, longing to be with her, to hold and to kiss her.
Now she is home and I find fault with her.
So many things about her irrate me, things I did not foresee.
What has happened? For I knew her before she went away.
I knew her well, and when she was gone,
I wanted her back so very much.
Now she has returned to me, and I am acting this way.
I still love her, surely it must be me and not she who is to blame.
There she is, I'll just think as though she's gone.
How very beautiful, Oh how I love her and want her.
Is she thinking like me? Because she does not respond.
I will do a hard thing to do.
I will act as though I've gone away.
Yet really will here stay.
Perhaps she'll realize as I did, how very much she loves me
And wants me when I'm gone;
And when she does, why of course I'll respond.

  —Norman E. Scriven

Disappointment

Across the snow laid fields,
I saw a dream lie still and breathless
'Neath the rising sun.
Weariness and sorrow
Crept into my very being,
Overwhelming sadness blots out the rays
Of sunshine cast upon a faded dream.
At dusk, I felt it die
With agonizing pain,
This dream I held so close.
I saw the sadness in the sunset
And the faintest glimmer of hope
Disappear beyond the hills.

  —Jeanette R. Swenson

The Woods

I walked into the woods today and looked up in a tree.
I saw a little bear cub looking right at me.
I said, "Oh little bear, don't you know the rule?"
He said, "I'd not be sitting here, if I could go to school."

I went on a little further and over at the gate
A white tail deer was standing there, looking for a date.
Soon a pretty little doe came quickly as could be.
She blinked her eyes and said to him, "Come along with me."

I saw a little Chipmunk go scampering around,
Hiding for the winter, all the treats that he had found.
He looked at me as if to say, "I'll be safe and sound
When that pretty white stuff starts covering the ground."

I came across a little stream, just trickling along
I stopped to watch the water and hear its merry song.
I watched the little fishes and saw some tadpoles too.
A big frog on a little pad said, "Hi, how do you do?"

The day was growing late and I really had to go
But I vowed that I'd come back in just a day or so.
Next time you come with me and see just what I mean.
Take time to stop and listen, it's so peaceful and serene.

  —Florence Fuller

Through The Eyes Of Love

Our world today is full of,
I say, everything but love.
Today we think more of silver
 and gold,
Than the love God showed in
 times of old.

Some examples, which I can think of many,
Show the lives of people which
 some compare to a penny.
Shown in our world is much
 racial tension,
But of love - there is no mention.
The people in Somalia are crying
 just for food;
But when it comes to sharing,
 there seems to be no mood.
In Yugoslavia, there is much fighting,
But of peace - there's only writing.

If we look through the eyes of love;
Someone might help us from above!

  —Amanda S. Zuber

Foster Lake

I see a reflection of light;
I see a reflection of green massive spikes-
that are being smoothed by a slight touch of a breeze.

It caresses the mass to flatness, and a feeling of calmness:
wrinkles unaged.

It's a reflection of a heaven
unseen at night, and-
the air that's a gift from the trees.

—*Erin Maureen Mize*

"Waves Of Time"

The evening sky slowly consumes all my thoughts.
I see a sea of belonging sight, a sea of beauty, a sea of
    might.
Only one can see this somber sight,
the waves can crush a perfect night.
The reflection in the waves, gave me a message.
A shameful message of sight, her beautiful face shaded in
    black.
Yet, I've waited too long, I've been too silent.
How can a person love another so much?
This undying pain keeps us apart.
Although, I really love you in my heart, as if I didn't from
    the start.
I stand here watching the nightly stars—alone.
And I wonder where our love has gone.
Perhaps it was only the waves of time.

—*Chris Grafford*

Once Upon A Time

As I close my eyes,
I see a time long past.
A time when things were different,
Better

A time before missiles and atomic bombs.
A time when you took someone's word.
A time when teens didn't carry guns.
A time of trust.

A time when you could let your kids outside and not worry
    about their safety.
A time when there wasn't gangs.
A time when there wasn't rape or incest.
A time of hope

Was there ever such a time?
Will there ever be such a time?
No one knows
All we can do is hope and trust in a better world to come.

—*Erin Slavin*

Violence

When I look out my window, I see stars in the sky,
I see the moon and it's shadow, and the people walk by,
I see rumbles and fights in the streets just below,
I see trees and the grass and I see blood in the snow.

I see one, two, three, a bang and a shot,
Someone just got hit, he's dead on the spot,
People run far away, as the sirens come near,
No one to stand by him, and no one to be sincere.

What did he do and why was he shot,
Was it his fault, I really think not,
He was just being a friend, like you and me,
He was being sincere, as clearly as can be.

The sirens come closer, they take him away,
He's dead in his grave, with nothing to say.

—*Darlene D. Gray*

The Cat

As I kneel to work among my flowers
I see a vision of black movement, something cowers.
What is that underneath the car?
Why its a cat, a black cat, meowing and meowing.

Come here cat.
What do you want?
A kind word? A pet? A scratch?

The cat slowly walks toward me, hesitant and cautious.
He finally reaches toward my hand.
A sniff, then acceptance.

I rub his head, his back and tail.
Purring, he comes forward for more.
Now bold and demanding attention, he is everywhere.
I cannot reach and pull the weeds
He is there, demanding
His needs.

Then he walks away and ignores me.
Evidently he has had enough of the attention he craved.

Oh, cat its you who decides where you go and what you do.
No one ever really owns you.

—*Della Fowler*

What I See

When I look out the window
I see all the things you once loved
the flowers, the birds that soars high
in the bright blue sky on a warm summers day

I miss the way you used to laugh
all the funny things you would do

I remember how I felt
the day the doctors said,
well, you know what they said

And, well, what I came to say
isn't easy, but
I miss you everyday
and I love you.

—*Michelle Lynn Tidwell*

I'm Numb Because I Feel

I seek, but don't find; I am false, yet I'm real;
I see, but I am blind.
I'm numb, but yet I feel.

I'm deaf, but yet I hear; I run, but still I walk;
I'm brave and shake with fear; I speak, yet I don't talk.

I sleep, yet stay awake; I stand, though I sit down;
I give, but still I take; I smile, while yet I frown.

I laugh, and still I cry; I move, but I am still;
I give up, but continue to try.
I'm numb, and still I feel.

I shrink, but yet I grow; I'm crazy, while I am sane;
I stop, but continue to go; I hurt, but feel no pain.

I'm strong, though yet I'm weak; I'm hot, but shiver with cold;
I'm in the valley while on the peak; I'm timid, but yet I'm bold.

I'm wet, while being dry; I get injured as I heal;
I'm grounded, but I can fly.
I'm numb because I feel.

—*Edward F. Dake*

Why Not?

As I caress the smooth silk long dress,
I see my room is a mess,
I see dirty shirts and socks on the floor,
I open my door to see what's in store,
I lay on my pillow and watch the willow.
What a day to go out and play,
But not today for there is no way.
My neighborhood is so bad, how sad.
I want to play, but maybe another day.

—*Kimberly Howse*

"Ode To Yesterday"

Upon the broken visions of the past,
I see remnants of things not meant to last.
Faces of old friends that are burned eternally
    within the far corners of my mind,
Are placed there for a day when my
    life is only death, and it is they with whom I will
    find again.

The days of today are but fleeting moments,
Like the berries of February—gone, yet just here.
When each year, just past the Jolly Season,
    I smell again what I know,
And always I am taken by the mind to that first
    sensual overflow.

Those images of youth fade with the setting
    sun into silhouettes,
And upon my looking, only the warmest I
    re-kindle for those I have met.
Today, as of yesterday, few, if any, shall know
    me in the light,
As I, myself, fade into a silhouette forever into eternal night.

—*David B. Abrams*

When I...

When I look into your eyes.
I see the golden sands of time.
Counting the timeless minutes
that my love grows for your
uncontrollable lust held by the
bonds of your sensuous beauty.

When I feel the softness of your skin.
I feel the unquenchable smoothness
of the ocean's water glistening in
the glamorous moon's rays dancing
down upon the nonmoving silence
of the ocean's breathtaking wetness.

When I dream about a lifetime with you.
I dream only about the everlasting
burning flame of our unending passion
that is forecasted through the test
of time in this ever-so-perfect
dream we share and hold as one.

—*Lance Barnum*

Memories Of You

Memories of your smile,
Memories of your tender touch...
Memories of how I loved you so much.
I'm trying to let go,
I'm trying to move on.
I'm trying to accept the fact that you're gone.
But deep in my heart,
I know I'll never get over you,
Memories of you will never fade away,
In my heart, that's where they'll stay.

—*Blia Thao*

Hiawatha's Brave

Oh mighty brave and spirited horse of mine,
I see you in the grassy fields on a sunlit morn.
Happy and contented where ever you may go,
from the plains of Minnesota, and then to the rocky pastures
of Arkansas, you have been the valiant one,
With fond memories of our younger years riding in
the Kentucky blue grass country.
Putting on one fine show here in the animal kingdom,
then, onward to the high country of Colorado,
where we have rode in the thin mountain air on a brisk fall day.

I just want you to know you have been the courageous one.
The time you became foundered, and the long battle we fought,
but, we got you on your feet again.
Then off to more pleasant rides, we would go.
When summer has come and gone,
I'll still see you "Hia" galloping off in the distance,
and there you will always be, in my memories.
Now, the great warrior you are "Hiawatha's Brave,"
I lay you to rest beneath the blue skies, in the hills of Colorado.
I Bid You A Fond Farewell Old Partner Of Mine...

Your Loving Companion,
Karen...

—*Margie B. Jeffers*

Perceptions Vs. Feelings

On the outside
I seem to be a calm green meadow.
On the inside
I feel like a dry empty brown desert.

On the outside
I seem to be a chittering busy sparrow.
On the inside
I feel like a lonely hawk searching, searching.

On the outside
I seem to be a calm lazy calico cat.
On the inside
I feel like a caged cougar desiring escape.

On the outside
I seem to be a lively mountain creek.
On the inside
I feel like a pond shrinking before a relentless dry spell.

On the outside
I seem to be a plain piece of window glass.
On the inside I feel
Like a mysterious kaleidoscope of music and bright colors.

—*Frances Abbey*

Untitled

When I seen the star fly in the sky
    I seen the twinkle in your eye,
    How It looked I can't explain.
    You asked If I made a wish
I said yes but its only a silhouette.
    I think you got my drift
But then again that star was only a myth.
    You came and gave me a kiss
        Your lips were as soft
        As the sheet I laid upon.
    Then you turned and disappeared
    In the lonely moonlight night.
        Where you for real
    Or were you that star in the sky
    That we looked upon every night.
        This I can not explain
        For when I awoke
    I see that star fly in the sky
    As so the twinkle in your eye.

—*Christina Mosqueda*

In The Darkness

In the darkness
I sense the presence of something with no sound.
While my heart starts to pound,
I reach out but nothing can be found.

In the darkness as I lift my head and open my eyes,
It is a smell ever so lightly.
I sense the familiarity of something.

In the darkness as I search the empty space.
It is my spirit I have found.
For there is truly no sight, sound or smell
That can capture the inner spirit.
For mine is as individual
As each person's darkness is their own.

 —*Frances Dietz*

A Mother's Day Decree

 On this Mother's Day I took a journey down Memory Lane.
I stole away within myself to be alone with you. I caught
up with you, touched you, wrapped you up in love, and I took
you home with me.

 Your presence overwhelmed me. You laughed with me.
You hugged me. You absorbed me in your love. You were
gigantic and enormous, and the ebullience of your love was
undetermined in boundaries, in height, and in depth.

 Many times I had held you in my arms and loved you. My
world seemed to erupt with endless perceptions of your
"magnitude". Indeed, your unspoken love with such grace was
of cherishing quality and worth in my mirrored eyes.

 You mom, were my visions of reality. Therefore, I
send out this decree in search of you today. You are the
lady that I beheld in my moments of solitude. You are the
woman that I have set among the stars in the heavens.

 —*Isabelle Brummer*

The Wind Will Tell

With passions rich in ancient lore,
I sweep across the plain before.
Emblazoned by a righteous hand,
In ageless might I seal the fate
Of those whom destiny awaits.

I come sudden, voiceless, then disappear,
In my path all will fear.
The gallant, meager - all are one;
Swift justice is mine to rend,
When I pass the deed is done.

My furor breaks mast and bow,
Gale force to the rocks they fall.
Yet through my stillness may be heard,
A distant sound on wings unfurled -
The brave and fallen, their honor served.

Ever onward shall I be,
Forever as the hills and seas.
Those who hear me, listen well
To the echoes of my vast embrace,
Tomorrow is what I foretell.

 ` —*Shamus P. O'Meara*

"Winter Love"

 As I walk outside on this beautiful day,
I see the snow in which I soon will play,
 But before I frolic in the crystal white,
I look up into the new dawns light.
 A beautiful sight to gaze upon,
out in the snow on this wintery morn.

 —*Jason Vogt*

Sis

(In memory of Sabrina Ann Hall)

As I sit and think of you,
I think of the good times and wish they weren't through
you was my best friend,
and was always there
Then I found you truly cared.
We are always together,
From beginning to end
You was my sister, and a true friend.
Your in my thoughts when I'm awake
And in my dreams when I'm asleep,
I know your love I'll always keep

 —*Crystal Hall*

Pictures In The Sand

Walking alone on this lonely beach
I think of you and to you I reach
I think of all the good times we've had
But now you're gone it's so very sad

Looking around in our lonely home
Through every room each night I roam
Pictures once hung on these empty walls
But now only memories fill these halls

Pictures in the sand, scenes of you and I
Thinking of how I hurt you, almost makes me cry
Pictures in the sand, scenes of days gone by
I don't know what to do with those pictures in the sand

It's been five years since we said I do
I meant every word that I said to you
My darling if only you could come back to me
For together forever is where we should be

 —*James Walker*

My Best Friend

My school library is my best friend,
I, to far away places she will send.
She reads with me of the present, past and future,
Yes indeed! She is just my favorite teacher.

At recess she enfolds me between her walls
Other students play, plan mischief or talk in the halls.
She helps me to speak correctly, to study and learn well,
She helps with oral reports that in class I must tell.

If you want your grades always to be top notch,
Your physical fitness and etiquette to have not a blotch.
You must also spend time with my best friend too,
I'm poverty or wealth she will see you through.

 —*Kathryn Bacon Mauldin*

The Telephone

Mr. Bell invented a most needed thing
If only it knew when you wanted it to ring
It rings at the very worst of times
Like when you're trying to make some rhymes
Or when you step in the shower and turn the water on
You hear the rings of the telephone
You turn off the water and dry off quick
Pick up the receiver and hear it go click
Or when you go to the table to eat
You fill your plate and take a seat
The phone starts ringing loud and bold
And when you get back your food is all cold
So if you have something important to do
Unplug the phone or you won't get through.

 —*Jan White*

I Told...

I told you not to.
I told you thousands of times.
But, it ended, it ended in a bloody massacre.
Why did you do it?
You had it.
All of it.
You had a good life and lots of friends
who now are in sorrow.
So why did you do it?
Why did you do it so painfully?
I've told you to get help.
But, you wouldn't listen.
You wouldn't listen to me.
You wouldn't listen to your friends.
It's funny you know,
To talk to a dead corpse.
I told you so.

—*Briean Losego*

Keep Going

I keep going from day to day
I try to forget the past,
Life is happening so fast.
Who are my friends, I can't say anymore

People will hurt you
And slander your name
Then think it puts them ahead in this game
If only they could see just how lonely we all are
They'd hug you instead and give you the stars

Love is missing in this broken world
Can we possibly mend it before we end it

Wars, pollution, poverty, greed
The people they fear, that's why they're so weird

So many have crossed to the wrong side of the tracks
Satan's winning and that's a fact

We must ban together and turn it around
Only then will peace reign and happiness be found

—*Jean Marie Reiff*

Myself

I have to live with myself, and so
I want to be fit for myself to know.
I want to be able, as days go by,
Always to look myself straight in the eye
I don't want to stand, with the setting sun,
And hate myself for the things I've done.
I want to go out with my head erect,
I want to deserve all men's respect.
For here in the struggle for fame and self
I want to be able to like myself.
I don't want to look at myself and know
I'm bluster, a bluff and an empty show.
I never can hide myself from me;
I see what others may never see.
I know what others may never know,
I never can fool myself, and so,
Whatever happens, I want to be
Self-respecting and conscience - free.

—*Diane M. Lewis*

Moon Beams

(Dedicated to all the men I have ever loved.)
I want to meet with you,
Where the wind blows across the sandy shore.
Where the mists meets the moonbeams.
I want to meet you at twilight, and have you
hold me, enfold me in your arms.

or I want to meet with you, where the water
washes upon the sand —
where waves rush, and crash, and spray
upon the ledges, and the land.

Or lets meet perhaps, in the path of yellow
sunlight slashed between the pinetrees, when
it appears over the seas horizon, and casts
a glare across the bay.

Or would you, perhaps rather meet with me on a
foggy and drizzly day?

When land and sea and rocks, are dressed, and wrapped,
together in skeins of grey fog? Like I wish to be wrapped
in your arms, when the evening mists meets the moonbeams.

—*Jacqueline Barstow Sorenson*

My Daughter

My womb was opened in fifty one
I wanted a daughter God gave me a son
Again in fifty-three the daughter I longed for wasn't to be
Fifty-six this will be the one
Again God trusted me with a son
Sixty one, I was afraid to hope, but God knew this was the time
To give to me this precious daughter of mine
He knew when in life I would need her most a daughter
A friend are wrapped up in one, that precious day in sixty one
Sixty-five a little brother, you loved him like a little mother
Now truly years later I can see
The path we walked was meant to be
Tragedy, triumph, tears and laughter
A road map from birth to the here-after
I wouldn't trade one moment
Laughter Joy or sorrow
From the time God favored me with you
My daughter

—*Frances Dollie Mooney*

Have Mercy!!

When I was quite young, perhaps twenty-four,
I was often reminded, "You've said that before!'

I'm now getting old, full seventy years;
My "thinker" plays tricks in shifting its gears.

I'm constantly told, when a tale I recite,
"You've told that before!" or "No, that's not right."

I just want to say, "Be patient, Dear Friend,
"You might just already commit the same sin."

I want to blurt out and let them just see
A few things THEY'VE said that tend to bug ME.

So back off, Dear People, and give me a break—
Withhold your compulsion to mend my mistake.

It's awful to me when I can't find my word.
I once was articulate—now, a rambling nerd.

But it "don't" make much "diff" if "I saw" or "I seen"
As long as you listen and "get what I mean".

Ah, well, SUCH IS LIFE; I'll go with the flow.
(But please love me anyway—and please let it show!)

—*Bonnie Brinn Phillips*

Small Miracles

I watched the sky so blue today
I watched the clouds so white roll away

I saw the sunset so fiery red
I saw the sun sink low "to bed".

I looked to the stars so clear, so bright
I looked at the sky so dark as night.

I noticed the sun come up this morn
I noticed another day being born.

All these miracles are done each day
Take time to notice in going your way

For the more you notice and appreciate
The more love happens instead of hate

When hate leaves the world to you and me
Love takes its place abundantly

—*Diane Silvis Lundblad*

My Tree

I planted you when I was young
I watched you grow from a stick to a tree
You were there through my whole life
Many a tear I've shed on you
I told you my troubles and sang to you
Even though you could not respond
I know you were listening to me
Talking and crying, Oh so free
Even on a summer night
All alone just you and I
Then School came And I went away
All alone during the day
But in our hearts the love will stay
You are my best friend
Now I'm old and can't journey where you are
Eighty two years I've come to see you
Now I'm eighty six and waiting to die
But you'll continue to grow

—*Deanna L. Cavins*

Untitled

I wish we had Christmas where Jesus was invited;
I wish we had Christmas where hearts were reunited,
Where love and warmth of days of old
And the Christmas story to all could be told.
No forked tongue workers of Satan's schemes
Who could cause unrest and destroy our dreams.
Our country was founded by the Pilgrims' quest
For religions for all which was best.
Now they say we violated some other rights,
Took prayer from the schools and got guns for their fights.
There's violence in the streets and we wonder why,
It's really so simple, it could make you cry;
We've forgotten to invite Jesus to His own Birthday party
And we're paying the price in commercial lust from devils so hardy,
But we still can win if we see things right,
Lift up heads and sing "Oh Holy Night".

—*Lois Strawderman*

Loneliness

It sounds like a distant voice ... calling
It feels like petting a vicious dog that's
waiting to attack
It tastes like old rotten cheese
It smells like smoke all around
It looks like an old beggar standing alone.
It is called loneliness

—*Christina Rushing*

I Am

I am an unusual thinker and wonderer.
I wonder how the world is going to end.
I hear the sounds of debris floating along the street.
I see mud reaching up to the sun.
I want peace and love to fill our world.
I am an unusual thinker and wonderer.

I pretend that I am the queen and you are the village.
I feel the soft vibrations of rushing water streaming down
    a beautiful waterfall.
I touch the flowing blue gown of Mother Nature.
I worry about not having enough love for nature to fill our hearts.
I cry for the birds and fish, trapped in misery.
I am an unusual thinker and wonderer.

I understand the cries of protesters against pollution and carelessness.
I say that if you do not have a bit of love in your heart, you should
    be banned.
I dream that one day the world will lick itself clean like a cat.
I try to persuade people, with an extra push, to care.
I hope that society, together, will work one extra day to fill the
world with peace.
I am an unusual thinker and wonderer.

—*Cynthia Santogue*

"The Flag of Feelings"

I am the United States flag glamorous and brilliant.
I wonder if bullets will ever stop flowing in the air as I do.
I hear screams of torture among the states.
I see the mourning of loved ones.
I want people to feel the pride of their states.
I am the United States flag glamorous and brilliant.

I pretend that people care, and they want peace.
I feel the evil blowing in the air.
I touch the spirits hoping to be awakened.
I worry the evil may be spread among us.
I cry for the deaths of so many lives.
I am the United States flag glamorous and brilliant.

I understand the hurt that many feel.
I say the words of wisdom only to get returned bewilderment.
I dream the day there is peace.
I try to shout the truth but no one wants to hear.
I hope my crying blows across someday.
I am the United States flag glamorous and brilliant.

—*Melissa Yongue*

Starvation

I am intelligent and caring,
I wonder if the world will ever cease to exist.
I hear people calling my name for help.
I see people dying from starvation.
I won't to help them, but I don't know how,
I am intelligent and caring.

I pretend to not hear them call
I feel a helplessness inside me.
I touch a child's hand who needs me.
I worry if they will live to see their birthday,
I cry to know they won't
I am intelligent and caring.

I understand that I can't help everyone
I say that I have to keep on fighting.
I dream one day that everyone will be happy.
I try to keep on trying.
I hope that one day no one will have to fight for their lives.
I am intelligent and caring.

—*Chase Parkey*

"Will You Be There For Me"

When I am down on my knees and crying
If I am down in the dumps and feel like dying
Will you be there for me?
When life has got me turned around
And I am feeling death bound
Will you be there to pick me up,
To lift me up, to bring me up
Will you be there for me?
Everybody needs someone
If I needed you, would you be that someone
Would you be there for me?
When I am feeling that there is no hope
And don't think that I can cope
Will you be there to care about me,
To worry about me, to be concerned about me
Will you be there for me?
There is only so much that one person can stand
Will you be there to hold my hand?
Will you be there for me?
To care and understand.

—*Lori D. Seabon*

A Warrior Indeed

A World's need is a Warrior's deed
If in all the World there be a need,
that need be, a Warrior indeed.
For in a Warrior his need, is a struggle indeed.
Find a Warrior with a need, and set him to a deed,
and yes, indeed you have satisfied the Warriors need.
The world is in dire need of a Warrior who never falters in his deed.
If there be a thing for a man to be, let it be a Warrior with a need,
and in that, satisfy a world's need for the deed.
His need indeed is a Warrior's deed.
A World's need indeed.

—*C. J. Bodiford*

If only "Yes" Were "Yes!"

If only "yes" were "Yes!" But it isn't (mostly);
If only "no" meant "No!" But it doesn't (sometimes).

Then what's the good of "no" and "yes"?
Why must we always have to guess?

We hear the "yes" but sense a silent "but..."
We hear a "no" but know it covers up "and yet..."

If only "yes" were "YES!" and "no" were "NO!"
Is there no way for us to know?

Just listen to the voice; ignore the word.
And watch the eyes,
And see the hands.
They speak the "yes" and "no" behind "no" and "yes".

From yes to no and no to yes is not so far (sometimes);
Though no to yes and yes to no is very far (mostly).
If only "yes" were "Yes!" and "no" were "No!"

—*Henry R. Huttenbach*

For The Love Of David

For the love of David would I sell my soul
If the Devil had such fine gifts.
For it would be worth it
To lie in the warmth of his arms
And know the beauty of his soul.
Oh that I should find such fortune
I would abandon these trappings
And follow him to the corners of the earth.
Even if for only a moment to stand by him
And know the meaning of ecstasy.

—*Beverly Ann Dexter*

A Way Of Looking At Things

When you look upon a person do you see the face
If so you see the color and race
Try to look further deeper inside
There you will see a heart a spirit that has tried
It doesn't matter what's on the outside
What counts is what's within your respect and pride
No matter if you're red white black or blue
I don't look upon the colors I look upon you
I look up to you with great respect
For I know you are being you I can detect
Your true friends are the one's that can see
You are you and it makes no difference if you don't look like me
I feel you should hold your head up high
Because your soul and spirit should never die
Because someone was careless and made a mistake
Live your life on happily that's all it will take
Some things in life are not always fair
But always remember you'll have loved one's there

—*Jacqueline Sitch*

Just Wishing

Maybe—
    If we would sing together
    Instead of talking indifferent
        Maybe——we could—Harmonize

Maybe——
    If we would shake hands and greet one another
        With warm embraces
        Maybe——we could—Fraternize

Maybe——
    If we would sit and listen
    To one another's
    Ideas and views
        Maybe——we could—Compromise

Until the worm which causes the rot
    Is cleansed from the core of the earth
        And the foul and filth
        is filtered from the air
        Maybe then——
        A world called—Paradise
        Can be——Recognized

—*Elaine Brown*

Stay In School

Right now you may think that it's cool
if you lay out, skip, or quit school.
But in the future society will only
classify you as a fool.
So just stay in school,
And be the coolest of the cool.
The long life ahead requires an education,
so just tough it out, have a little patience.
With drugs, you shouldn't think about or bother
because if you do, in life, you will get no farther.
Now you make think that it's cool,
if you lay out, skip, or quit school.
But in the future, society will only
classify you as a fool.
So just stay in school.

—*Chris Green*

Leaves

The first frost
ignites the fire.
Soon, treetops are blazing out of control.
Flames, caught in the wind, dance
through the air.
Yellow, orange, then scarlet
until the whole world is engulfed.

I stand in the middle
surrounded b the fiery blaze-
paralyzed in awe,
oddly wishing it won't go out.
A loose flame falls upon me.
The glowing ember will shortly die out.
Crack, crackle   as I walk away.

Nature, also the arsonist, extinguishes
the fire.
Surely torching it again next year.

—*Francie Barone Josephsen*

Racism

Racism;
Ignorant, pointless, scary.
It makes no sense. It makes you tense.
Racism;
Black or white -it makes no difference.
We're all brothers and sisters in the end,
Each one of us will be another's friend.
Racism;
Black, white, brown, orange, red, it's all
in the head.
We're all here on this earth, from the day of
our birth.
Racism;
It's so dumb to be beatin' a drum in a
war of race, because of the color of our face.
There is good and bad in every race
So let me close by saying this -
In the end, it makes no difference,
It depends on what kind of a friend you were.

—*Francis Otto*

The Orchestra

They take their seats, review the beats
Ignore their pounding hearts

And their sweaty palms, only applause can calm
As the warm-up starts.

The oboe plays, while the crowd, amazed,
Anticipates the show.

All the instruments fuse,
Which produces a soft, melodious flow.

Then, trumpets blasting, flutes contrasting
And the soothing violins

Ring and pound in harmonious sounds
Causing many a grin.

Crashing cymbals, fingers nimble,
Pulses racing fast

Pitches ranging, quickly changing
With each note and rest.

The feelings strong, are expressed through music
With each passing measure.

The orchestra, alive and vibrant,
Is full of life and pleasure.

—*Emily Haas*

Eternal

I love you
I'll never forget you
and though we may never be together again
I'll always hold you...
In my heart, in each teardrop, your image shatters me
your voice an echo, like a shipwreck
you make me bleed...
Distance shall not erase you
you are forever in my mind, an etching of security
a reminder I once was blind...
so truly it is over, you may never hear these words
I love you, but then I always did
and it was you who wasn't heard,
I hold you closer now than ever
I've realized to late, he who cries the wolves cry
comes to seal his fate...
I love you
I'll never forget you
and though we'll never be together again
I'll always hold you...

—*Kenneth A. Barrick*

"A Poet I Am, Says I, Says I"

A poet I am, says I, says I -
I'll take you a word and twist it around
And fill it with so much glee!
I'll take you a word and rhyme it around until you believe
what is me!

A poet I am, says I, says I -
I'll take all your love - I'll take all your sorrow and rhyme
it around for thee!
I'll dance on your graves and throw you red roses and rhyme
all your troubles away!
For love for thou and love for thee - it's all a part of me!

Oh, you say, you are a poet - a poet, a poet like me?
Oh, no I say - for I am me and you are thee
You can never be a poet like me!

A poet I am, says me, says me -
A poet I am - tra lee!

—*Dorothy M. Center*

A Re-enactor's Brooding

Well, it's said that after a storm comes a lull.
I'm afraid that they're wrong, it's nothing but hell.
The cries of the gone make a sweet Southern breeze,
While the dead voices of friends ring through the trees.
The dead and the dying lay bloated and black
And even in death the flies insist to attack.
The sounds of the wounded are as mean as the breeze:
"Some water, a Bible, just one bullet, Mister, please."
But as with a storm we eventually take wing;
We go, the Yanks go, and then the birds sing.
But unlike a storm that leaves everything fresh,
We've left the place black; man's dark hole of death.
And one hundred years hence they'll come to admire
Where their ancestors fought and died in the mire,
And the people will look, though they will not remember
But it's sacred to us for now and forever.

—*Chris Cotz*

Thank You

Thank you dear God for any talent I may have,
It came to me with great surprise,
When I discovered the things I could do,
Whatever it may be
It is your gift to me.

—*Jeannette Lamoutte*

Me

Look at me, can't you see
I'm an African American, with great respect and human dignity:
Look at me, can't you see my dream is to build a better world
for my fellowmen, not just for you and me.
Look at me, can't you see I have my eyes on the prize, and will
   always think positively.
Look at me, can't you see the freedom gates are open, are you
   ready to accept your responsibilities.

—*Mamie R. Manuel*

Untitled

One moment it's there, the next it's gone
I'm asking myself what on earth's going on.

It hurt me so bad, but I just can't cry.
I want to crawl up in a bundle and die

From love to hate, from passion to lust
Isn't there anyone here I can trust

There's nowhere to run, there's nowhere to hide
I'll just have to keep my emotions inside

No one can listen, no one understands
I feel as if someone has tied up my hands

I'm lost in a world, I've never been in
I'm swimming around in a puddle of sin

Throw me a rope, please help me out
I'm all alone in a state of sheer doubt

No one can hear me, they don't even try
I'm all alone, in this world, here to die

—*Christine Hearne*

White Stuff

I can hardly wait for the snow to go,
I'm so tired of watching the blizzards blow.
It's white in the morning, it's white in the night,
The piles go up 'til they're out of sight.

I shovel the driveway, I shovel out the car,
I shovel out the dog houses, to find out where they are.
I clean it off the stairs, I clean it off the deck,
I clean it off the roof to keep my house from being wrecked.

The kids go out to play, they bring the white stuff in,
I clean it up, then they go out and bring some in again!
For months it's been nothing but cold and white stuff,
It's time for it to go, I mean, enough is enough!

I dream of green grass, spring flowers, and the Sun,
When it finally gets here, I'll have, oh, so much fun!
I can hardly wait for the snow to go,
I'm so tired of watching the white stuff, you know?

—*Diane K. McIlroy*

Love

Could this be love
Could I feel so wonderful inside.
Wanting to be with you each and everyday.
Never wanting to be out of your life.
So.....
Could this be love
Hoping you feel the same
Having my heart pounding for that
   special someone.
How can I know
   If this is really love
Could it be real
Could this be true.
Could it be love.

—*Romina Rojas*

Our World Earth

As I look around me I notice,
I'm standing in fire.
But it's not a hot fire it's a cold fire and
I realize it's the fire of love.
The love for our world, Earth.
While I try to warm the fire with my love
nothing happens so I look around wondering why.

Then something happens.
Suddenly I can see all there is to see,
but all of the other people can't.
They only see themselves.

As the time goes by I'm still trying to warm the fire
but it keeps getting colder and colder.
Then this enormous chill came over me.
It's like I'm standing in the Arctic.
So I look around and the fire is gone.
It turned to ice and fell to the ground,
and our world, Earth, perished with hate and fear.

—*Angela Davis*

I'm Gonna Be Bad

Oh I'm gonna be bad ..... so very bad
I'm tired of this baloney, of being so sad
I'm gonna run along and try to catch the sun
Drink me some wine ..... have me some fun!
I'm gonna chase all the butterflies ..... everywhere
No where's will I get ..... but who the heck cares
I'm gonna jump in the rain puddles ..... splash you
   all up ..... ain't that a shame
You're bound to get angry, call me some bad name.
Hold on to your ice cream cone ..... cause when I'm bad
I'll knock it right out of your hands ..... and that will
   make you so mad
I'm gonna put a bee in your bonnet ..... and a tack
   on your chair
Oh ..... my goodness, does it hurt you there?
I'm gonna reach for the sky and then smack you
Yeah, you better watch out ..... for that's
   what I'm gonna do!

—*Dorothy Husar Krosky*

"25th" Anniversary

With this ring I thee wed, the vows were made quite clear.
In a little country church, "59" was the year.
To love honor and cherish 'till death us do part.
It has to do with matters of the heart.
A girl took a husband a man took a wife,
This union will last for the rest of your life.
There have been ups and downs, good and bad,
Serious and silly, happy and sad.
Sometimes you've felt like throwing in the towel,
But what is the use of quitting now.
Pushing away or pulling together,
Marriage is a kind of like the weather.
Raindrops are your tears, sunbeams are your smiles.
It takes a lot of rain and sun to get you through the miles.
Hold on to each other in a dear and tender way,
Keep your love safe and warm, don't let it go astray.
Spend time with each other like you did back then.
When love was sweet, you remember when.
Rise above all the fears and tears,
You have come a long way in twenty five short years.

—*June Anderson*

Daynot

Gleaming white satin covering a bed,
In a moon-lit room where I lay my head,
The night brings many sounds, some near some far.
Like the chirping of a cricket or a passing car.
The night brings darkness, the absence of light.
It makes the ocean pound the shore with all of its might.
The nights brings out the romantic in all of us,
It puts children to sleep without a big fuss.
The night brings water, the grass covered with dew,
Each and every time it brings morning anew.
The night brings a chance to view the stars,
And planets like Venus, Mercury and Mars
The night brings ghosts, goblins and ghouls,
Some would say to believe this makes us all fools.
Bright-eyed moon staring down from above,
Oh' mysterious night I cannot tell thee
How much I love.

—*Cliff Otte*

Greasy Creek

Fossils, entrapped
in a tomb of sand and dirt,
wait for new life.

A floating oak leaf,
caught in a current of
Rippling water, drifts away.

A wrinkled man in his weathered overalls
sits on the darkened riverbank,
casting his cane pole
to the edge of the diving rock;

He waits, knowing that time is short.
Lighting his corn cob pipe, he listens
hearing only the mechanical monsters
crawl down the molested mountain,
stripping it of its skin.

Backwards people without a care
become naive in their greediness.
Their black wealth tumbles into the water.

A crawdad darts away.
Nature becomes civilized
The cycle begins again.

—*Gregory B. Campbell*

"Bethlehem Star"

We look to the heavens with questions
in a world filled with hunger and grief.
As in the time of Christ's birth;
    we all seek "Peace on Earth"
and pray in humble belief
That today as Christmas approaches
and our loved ones are scattered afar
as they heard on that night
    the angels of light
We find hope in the Bethlehem Star.
We look to the Babe in the manger
as the Giver of life from above,
Though we anxiously pray
    for our dear ones away
We still believe in this
    Season of love.
For the families of those who are serving
we ask for a time of release;
With Good will toward all Men
    for those we seek to defend
the gift of the spirit of Peace!!!

—*Bobbie Russell Broumley*

The Second Dirge

The stormy panoramic picture of a land
In agony ebbs and flows. In stark disbelief
The people's voiceless screams are frozen; and
They are compelled to watch the creeping cortege of their grief
Before sunlight beams stabbing remembrance of death.

Slow turning spokes of caisson catch the sun's brilliance.
A saddened people stand mute along the martyred way—
The nation's ever growing resilience is apparent as the
Staccato rattle of horses hooves
Portends, perhaps, a quickened pulse and purpose.

Riderless black horse with up-turned stirrups speaks
Eloquently. Speaks of loss and lack of concord;
Asking what part they've played in this deed they can ill afford.
Speaks of a nation suddenly thrust into a great void
Questioning its lated concern for unity.

They stand dry-eyed now—remembering and shamed.
The drumbeat roll echoes the rhythm of their hearts
Slowed after the initial shock and horror.
Pained by history's insidious warts
That intrude to remind that hate still infests and kills.

—*Helene L. Anderson*

His Love

If we could just love one another
In all parts of this world,
"How great, He would cheer,"
"Do put malice out with your fear."

His love can change our attitude
And make us all so loving,
That one can sense the multitudes
Of grandeur in our doving!

So, give your all, your very best
And love one another to the top of the crest;
Then give, and give, and give some more
For it will bring you joy that really soars.

Then, greet your neighbors and your friends
Of near and of far away;
Many of you may have to make amends
But always show your love in full sway!

—*Carla Ruth Finke*

My Dear Son Lance

You entered my life like a deer, slipping
    in and out of the woods.
You touched my life, as I stopped to
    look at the deer, they disappeared
    as quietly as they came.
But I feel, blessed, for having your
    presence, and your gentle kind touch,
And gave thanks to, "God", for the joys
    you brought to me - to fill the voids
    in my life.
What a beautiful, beautiful, and
wonderful precious gift of love of life
Of a dear son, who is so dear to my heart
    May, "God," bless you and
Keep you safe from all harms,
    with motherly affection, your "Mom,"

—*Julia Mackay*

There Is A Spirit Awake

There is a spirit awake on earth;
  In days gone by, I hailed it glad,
  But now the Spring does make me sad;
What if the flower, I muse, has birth?—

Spring, you can but grow the new:
  Dead herb and grass, forever lie,
  The loveliest rose but grew to die,
Its days of life—how short and few!

Birth multiplies, keeps stride with death;
  But no twin from loss will spring;
  O, man, what great, what unique thing!
So matchless in loss—so same in breath!

Let great men rise, and meek ones, fall;
  Break the last heart of mortal, lone;
  We haven't from the lost years, won
A likeness, from that absent role!

  —*Faery Harper*

A Very Special Man

A very special man,
In his little girls big blue eyes.
She grows up always thinking she can,
Knowing she's got love that no one else could buy.
He always used to hold her hand, when she would cross the street.
Or put her on his back, when she had tired feet.
He used to tuck her in at night,
And tell her everything's alright.
He used to scare the monsters out,
He was the greatest without a doubt.
He taught her how to ride her bike,
And everyone she should always like.
The love she felt deep down inside,
She knew would always there abide.
She knew that she'd never forget, the memories they shared
And that this special man, would always show he cared.
They laughed together, cried together too.
And she knew that his love always would be true.
Nothing could take away the feelings for her DAD.
She knew she had the best dad that ever could be had.

  —*Jennifer Kernodle*

An Unknown Destiny:

The sunset fell on glistening clouds,
in hues of red and gold.
As silently the jet flew on,
in a sky so blue and cold.

And so does life seem to swiftly pass,
with it's dark, foreboding days—Alas!!
Despair not! For patiently the sun,
Will shine through clouds one by one,
and see how beautiful they become.
Like ships at sea, majestically,
sailing on to an unknown destiny,
like the unchartered lives of you and me.

  —*Bruce K. Jacobson*

Wildfire

  Starshine falling from velvet skies
    Kindled a light in my loves eyes.
    Wildfire flamed as we stood apart
  Wedding the beat of two tender hearts.
    Under the heavens he vowed to me,
  "Our magic enchantment will always be -
    I'll love you, sweet - forever be thine.
    Whisper the words - say you are mine."
  Now kissed by age and crowned with silver
  Our hearts' sweet wildfire glows forever.

  —*Jean T. Lavota*

Eternal Marriage

(Dedicated to Angie England, my married love,
in memory of our marriage in Christ.)

Love, honor, and cherish, in the Christian marriage,
Is an affair of the beating heart.
With the touch of God on the marriage,
even physical death does not us part.

The physical bond is severed,
when one of the married died.
But the knot that binds the soul
is forever, by God, in eternity tied.

The essence of the soul:
memory, intellect, and will;
being joined by God in the ceremony
lives, though the beating heart is still.

The body will be resurrected
when the Angels trumpet the last day.
Then the married body and soul together,
are joined for an eternity's stay.

So, do not grieve, my darling.
Our love, in our souls, is not still.
We will forever be married in God's eternal heaven.
Our glorified bodies and souls joined to fulfill His will.

  —*James D. England*

Opening Night Jitters

Elegantly decked out
  In my low cut black evening gown,
I'm ready to face my audience
  In my first piano concerto.
I peer into the dressing room mirror
  Seeing myself as the crowd will.
A little more lipstick here,
  A little more eyeshadow there.
There is my cue to enter the stage area
  As the conductor gives the nod.

Already I can feel my stomach tightening;
  I edge my hands to the keyboard.
I flex my fingers preparing to play,
  But they don't move - they're frozen!
My stomach is a running board for panic;
  Like barbecue coals I'm burning inside.
Aware of my imminent failure to perform,
  The maestro softly smiles at me.
My dormant fingers instantly react;
  The opening bars run themselves harmoniously!

  —*John Callas*

"Why?"

Why is there so much hatred
  In our wonderful world where all could be free
Why isn't there any answer
  As God never meant this to be.

Why can't nations love one another
  Live and let live as we may
Lay down guns and dangerous weapons
  Stop drugs and killings every day.

People kill for no good reason
Life has no value at all
Where are the values we used to know
We aren't even safe in our malls.

Is there no fear of God anymore
  Instilled when we were small
Or is the fear of God put aside
  And never thought of at all.

  —*Loretta D. Doyle*

The Window

Passing the essence of reality
In prosperous hope and fear
Mainly for the love of those
Who may not want to care

Looking up to star filled skies
Living up to the aspect that lies
Inside Everybody's surrounding eyes
I hear the eyes of a person are a window

a way to see into one's inner soul
But I've pulled down my shades
And I've turned out the light
Because I was scared of being hurt

I closed myself off
Until one day I found
A person looking through my shades
Who broke my window down

They weren't there to hurt me
They were only there to care
But why they chose to love me
I will never know
    —*Jamie Sarras*

The Scourge

(Historic Sonnet)
In Romania now, is a harsh winter and snow storm
The peasants have no heating and no food:
Last fall the payment was not good
After they worked in a "collective" by "norm".

Under the king (in past), they had fine mood,
They didn't starve, their houses were heated.
But now the peasant's clothes are patched
And their fur-lined coasts no longer good.

As if was not enough the poverty,
Ceausescu started now the abolition:
—"Half number village is set to be!"

Gnashing bulldozers urge on the demolition,
But those "bare - hungry" in scourge they see:
Approaching a judgment day for their salvation!

(Baldwin Park, 21 December 1988)
    —*Dumitru V. Bejenaru*

April's Day

Happy hearts were felt that day,
In such a warm and wonderful way.
There first new born had come to stay,
With a love that would often stray
Only to return another day.

Family and friends came by far,
To see what lay at mother's bay.
The hopes and dreams she must make,
For time is short before you wake.

As you lay in the nursery of babe's
And adoring father could only say.
"She's the beauty of the day."
He never knew his heart could feel so gay.
The day that April came there way.
    —*P. Rash*

The Family Reunion

The children were playing and singing.
In the background the horseshoes were clinging.
Picnic baskets were being unpacked,
It was a joyous day, everyone in the act.

The weather was sunny and bright.
The families had their own prayers in mind.
We all sat down, the food was great,
Meat, vegetables, fruit pies and cake.

There were some empty seats that could not be filled.
The spirit of them were with us still.
We were all thankful for the blessings of time,
And hoped God would reunite us each year down the line.
    —*Mable F. Marsh*

The Abbey

I am sleepless
in the glow and shadow
of the lamplight.
My heart at peace,
dreams and breathes
the incense of dedication.
The cloister bells quiver
in the soft early morning breeze.
The courtyard shuts in the deep darkness
of the starlit night.
The Northern Crown crosses the sky
cut by the chapel roof
where an iron cross soars into the blackness.
The chanting of prayers from hooded monks
floats from the hall.
The fading sound of bells eddy by my bed.
Tomorrow into the sunlight
I will walk in the blossoms of the fields
and weep over the yellow crosses
that cover the dead.
    —*Henry P. Pelletier*

And The Still Waters Run

The mighty buffalo solemnly stands,
In the haughty pens of steel.
Where once he roamed prairies grand.

Blazing camp fires kept watch over the bold,
Dotting the undaunted, unrelented horizon.
The coals now long gone cold.

Rippling waters crawled aimlessly,
Down through the hills and valleys.
Now cut up by roads not meant to be.

Tepee willow poles now in store,
Wait for solemn celebrations.
Stirs the valiant heart forever more.

Brave unbroken spirits not stilled,
By white man's interventions.
And forever the still waters run.
    —*Margie Testerman*

Untitled

Why is it the water flows yet appears it still remain?
    It's like feelings flow but emotion still sustains.
    I come across so valiantly, brazen some might say,
but I need fight for what I want don't let that scare you away.
        The trees amongst the water,
            the reflection's still live on.
    A ripple in the water and suddenly their gone.
    Now they reappear again and yet so, time goes on!
    —*Heidi Cron*

My Prayerful Desire

Help me to do the right thing,
In the right way,
For the right reason.
For that I pray most every day,
Every week,
Every season.

You are wise, you are good, you are strong.
I am weak, lacking love, sometimes wrong.
Put in my world today
Some lovely thing,
Beautiful and true,
That will only count
For your great cause,
In all that I do.
As time today passes, may I have a part
Of giving and taking with joy in my heart.

—*Lois Norberg*

A Walk With God

I tried to walk in God's footsteps
In the same direction He goes
But my feet were heavy with worries I kept
And I carried all my woes.

I'd changed directions too many times,
Not listening to those who tried
To keep me going in God's straight line
And keep him by my side.

I shall ask his forgiveness
For which he died.
For all who strayed from his side,
And put my heavy load away
And be Born again, in the Lord today.

—*Charlotte McDaniels*

Love's Memorial

A flower drifts through breath before my face
In time now comes so fresh to save the day
It lands so sweet upon the sullen place
I stoop to touch the petals on the clay
The heat swells up to scorch the gentle floor
Its fragrance fills the air so still and slight
It gives its all for me in summer's door
Reminder of the joy which mourns fall's night
Now echoing the hollowed sounds of dread
To be the knoll that rings the toll so long
Oh past, it swirls from heart to head
Of love's brief stay in Eden fair now gone
As tucked within the purple velvet fold
And silent lies through winter's nights untold.

—*Gregory C Rogahn*

A True Friend

A true friend will help you out,
In time of need without a doubt,
In times of need they'll be there,
And their advice with you they'll share.
From the rest of their friends you won't be set apart,
For they've seen you for good and straight to your heart.

In a true friend there are qualities to see.
You'll know when you find them, for they're no mystery.
There is one thing that is a must,
In true friendship there will be honesty and trust.
When you find a true friend you will know!
Their true-self they will show.

—*Joseph Bentivegna*

What Is Poetry?

Poetry is you, Love is you, everything you do; I find poetry
in you. When I look into your eyes, I hate good-byes;
Poetry is you. You're my dream come true, with you I'm
never blue; Everything you do, I find poetry in you. As the
sun shines in the sky, my love for you will never die. With
you I always want to be; even after eternity. You are my love;
you are my life; I want to be your wife. Your touch is filled
with ease, I hate it when you tease; you always please.
Everything you do; I find poetry in you. The earth goes round,
with you I'm always found. I'm floating on cloud nine;
My feet never touch the ground. I am truly blessed,
with you I'm at my best. All these things I've found in you;
You're my dream come true. Everything you do;
I find poetry in you.

—*Belinda M. Robinson*

The Psychologist

He sits in swivel, ambiguous chair while I sit on the
infamous couch (lying down is for sick people) gently
probing the mind, the emotions, playing the game,
"Bare Your Soul." My answers, like me, are anorexic
I know this game full well: Silence.
Silence, and the other will speak fill in the uncomfortable
void with banquet revelations.
Like calories my words are measured carefully
Bearded, patient, staring, he waits but he will not
get full on my answers
For what the mind gives up the soul suffers
repentant repentant agonizing self-analysis
We are not adversaries, not true friends yet share an
intimate relationship trying to mend the mind the body
conversational surgery recuperating slowly, slowly

—*Karen Swatowy*

"The Crying Out"

Your words have been the hardest blows
Inflicted not by physical hands
Yet as tones of anger to my soul
Not flowers in bloom, I had been worn
As an unwatered rose
Whose petals fall, whose petals float
On tones so bitter away.

The blows have been the sting of shouts
Of not children's joys of arms taking me in
Only in eternal frames of rage pushing me out
Some say it ever stays, yet I will look
Beyond pain now
As I still march from hate to love…
For the rose in heart will never die,
Today is it's spring to bloom fully again.

—*Karla Semczuk*

Hostage

Folded neatly in a box
Is a yellow ribbon
And a broken watch
I know the watch can be repaired
But I know not what the ribbon's for
So I search my soul and ask again
What's the yellow ribbon for?
Is it for the men
The men on earth who follow war for peace,
Who choose to kill for freedom at least?
I ask you, which man has killed another
And felt a freedom from his dead brother?

—*Brenda Nollmeyer*

Front Page / Back Page

HOMETOWN USA: Front Page: "Alan King dies as a result of injuries received in traffic accident... Back Page: Gifts in memory of Alan King may be directed to MADD, Mothers Against Drunk Driving."

What dwells within
a woman, mother
bids her drive,
blurry eyed...
to harm another?

King his name —
'Tho from his birth
a prince of peace
and caring,
for this Earth.

On bicycle he died.
His passion's choice
of carrier. Rather than
pollute the air
she lives...to share.

—*Carol M. Reed*

PRO - FUN - DITTY

Along the coast
Inside the swing
Words don't mean ... a blasted thing

Deeply we look
A word at a time
For inspiration ... something to rhyme

Slant a meaning
Distance a thought
New ideas ... fervently sought

Thoughts that endure
Senseless to guess
Brilliance of words... meant to impress

Continue to ramble
Write something deep
Look for a meaning ... all words are cheap

Wind up the poem
It's now or never
To win a prize ... one must be clever

—*Gloria Opferman*

"The Pain"

Tame and sound and level-headed.
Instead of doing homework, I'd rather be riding.
Fun-loving but full of pain, for I stay home to practice again
For now in my life is a confusing time,
I don't know which one I'll choose between those parents of mine.
Now and then the pain will rest it's rearing head.
Yelling and screaming 'till the anger is dead.

And now and again I can sleep at night;
Never a need to shut off the lights.
Drowning out my parents words,
Reaching for my radio so instead it can be heard.
Everyone ignores that girl; too much spite!
Will someone please tell me what I did to be brought to this
Hell they call life?

—*Tiffiny Andrew*

Time To Face Reality

Thoughts circle my mind
Intense emotions that aren't kind

I am badgered each and everyday
I am reminded in every way
I am useless

Seconds turn into days
Months turns into years

Time slips through my hands
As sand flows through an hourglass

The clock is ticking
Now and to the end

I live a life of shame and tremendous pain
But worry not, time goes by with the tick tock of a clock
Life goes on
—*Barbara Ann Bavlsik*

Requiem

Before broken bones are lost to the grave,
Interred alone within sepulchral cold,
The hard clay is belimed, no movement save
The quick graceful dance of wings painted gold.

From the darkened shroud of silence has grown
A hopeful song from sweet but fleeting rhyme;
A single grain of sand aimlessly blown
Across the incessant desert of time.

But by the tombless crypt I do recant
The sorrow I've shown, the tears I have cried,
And only murmur a requiem chant
For those who survive being killed inside.

I barely breathe — my butterfly has flown,
My soul dry as dust, my heart cold as bone.
—*Justin Shaltz*

Maled

Absorbing all its warmth and light bright serenely spilling
into a white bright hallucination
mellow and unaware of its existence
The fetus spins like a flower on water where each cell is
a petal dividing and floating into microscopic divisions
a whole organism is magically bonded
lured to the blinding beam and destroyed
and left in no comfortable grave it nests with others
not allotted one breath of air eyes eclipsing
A sickly grave embryos melting black and seeping
into an earth and the evil of this contamination
melts into the earth as well
the soil is turned and we must begin again malediction
A lovely white pigeon moves in unusual
grace and in a second its wings liquidly flap
silently soaring circular into a stone well
where all pity it's demise
swiftly floating to a secret
land in divine comfort
—*Jessica Anne Smith*

Gentle Spring

Have you ever seen a lemon drop?
It looks just like the sun so hot.
The baby fawn stumbling along,
Looking to his mother to see if he's wrong.
A child's eyes for the first time
When seeing the Easter Bunny fill with surprise.
These are the signs and things
that blossom into a gentle spring.
—*Jennifer Yon*

"It's Time"

            Sin - has no distinction
Into this world - born within all - It was

        Wrong is wrong -and- Right is right
    Why bring down the world - in YOUR fight
        Because of - 1 or 2 - or a Few

        We as Friends - Sisters - Brothers
    The Color of skin - let it not brings us down
            Before it's to late - in God
                Lets come Together
        It's His ways - We should come to know
                And His ways of Love
                We should Always show

        Different on the outside we maybe
    But the Blood - that's in All - is All the same
        Yes! That life given color Red
        It's - what keeps Us - All - Alive

    Don't - bring down the World - in your fight

    Come - Together Friends - Brothers - Sisters
        Come together once and for All - In God
                    It's Time
            —Dianne Bonty (Sylver)

Forerunner Of Paradise

Joy; clandestine images of serene beauty
Intoxicating in the upward spiral of grace.
Sorrow; for the now perishes, a soulless mobility.
The touch goes unseen, the feeling penetrates.

For the cleansing has begun,
Weep not for uncertainty,
The sacred unknown embraces the tortured soul.
A divine purity goes unnoticed,
In this knowledge we sustain.

Cast feather to the wind, embark on emotion;
A new reality emerges, the journeyman is immersed.
Dark unto light: regrets diminished:
Yet another age.

Joy; existence unfolding in passages of
Surreal current, the traveler is overwhelmed
Forerunner of paradise.
Sorrow; love lost, cease the romantic heart.
Forever knowing,
Forever mourning,
......Forever
            —J. A. Staffieri

How Quickly Flies The Time

The passing of time
is an occurrence that none can halt
We have no control over
How fast or how slowly it will happen
Why do we let this precious time be wasted
as though we can recapture the yesterdays
already beyond our reach
We take for granted God's beauty surrounding us
How many opportunities we let slip through our fingers
the chance to be a friend to one who is lonely
a few words of encouragement to one who struggles
loving arms to hold one who is in pain
to neglect to say to those we love
how much they mean to us
to say "I love you" to someone every day
Why do we not share the joy of life and living
extend a hand in friendship and caring
Let us be thankful for all that is ours
be ever joyful, and be fully aware
of how quickly flies the time
            —Jewell Castro

Great Grandpa

Out in South Dakota on the great prairie
Is a small graveyard I want to see,
Where Great Grandpa is buried beneath the prairie sod.
He froze to death, the living was so hard.

Someday I'll go there and find his resting place,
I will bring some prairie flowers that he loved so.
We will have a nice long visit until I have to go.

We shall talk of things I have to know,
Like how you survived when the temperature was so low
And were you there when the buffaloes died?
Were you there when the Indians cried?

You can tell all about the West,
And why cowboys always wore a leather vest.
How far would the arrows go
When the Indians shot them from their bow.

Your old Kentucky rifle still hangs over our fireplace.
I still think of you laying in that cold place.
When I get old and die, I will come and lay beside you
Then we will be together in the land of the Sioux.
            —Norman Gilbert

To Anyone

The depth of loneliness
Is beyond measuring.
Reach out.

The touch of a hand on the face,
A passing kiss,
A handclasp,
An arm across the shoulder—
Simple; human touches
That soften the journey
Through the lonely days.
Reach out.

Each touch will be remembered, cherished,
And who can know but that a life is saved,
A human being decides to live another day,
Remembering your touch.
Reach out.
            —June Hayward Fifield

The Moon

The clear lustrous moon
In a black velvet sky
Shown upon the snow.

Snow like burnished pearls
With shadows of barren trees
Contrasting.

Stars trying to be seen.
The moon so bright and clear.
Such a cold, still night.

So quiet, so still.
No woodland creatures
Telling their tales.

The clear lustrous moon
Hypnotic
In its solitary glory.
            —Jane S. Langton

Untitled

Pain and suffering, where does it end
is it a message he is trying to send?

Why does this have to be,
the pain and suffering inside of me?

Love and happiness, when will I see
what beauty it will come to be

I may never see happiness again
for the pain and suffering will never end.

—*Dana Boreland*

The Note

Your love,
is it only in the mind's eye,
the product of bodily fluids or
a gift from God.
My heart, my life, is like the night sky
before a storm,
like the grey rolling sea before the tempest.
And yet, I feel alive, alive and wonderful
amid this misery I delight in your eyes,
your voice,
the heat of our bodies.
I will wait for you and I will carry our
grief, our pain, through out all eternity.
This bittersweet emotion will rally my
cause and pacify my heart.
This is only a note,
from me to you, to let you know I love you,
I love you.

—*Karl A. D. Brown*

"Just For Me"

A shimmering light glistening through the shade of a tree -
Is it shining just for me?
A twinkling star over a bright blue sea - Is it there just for me?
The rain cooling off a hot and humid day -
Could it be showering just for me?
A flower bud opening - its colors bright and gay-
Is it growing just for me?
The sun beaming its heat to the meadow and the lea -
Is the warmth just for me?
The good earth with all its mirth and glee
Was it created just for me?
A bird chirping at a distance I cannot see -
Is it singing just for me?
Snow falling to the ground without making a sound
Covering the earth with a white crown -
Could it be these snowflakes are just for me?
Isn't it a wonderful miracle God performed
Doing all this - just for me!

—*Nancy Miller*

Innocent Years

Oh when do we leave our innocent years?
Is it when we are young, when we are old?
When the smiles leave our face and turns to tears?
When our innermost feelings we have sold?
When mom finds the lipstick mark on our mug?
When we touch the hot stove after she says no?
When she asks for a kiss and we act smug?
Our young maturity we yearn to show?
When we talk and talk all night on the phones?
Or is it the time when we deny pain?
When nothing can hurt, even sticks and stones?
When we kiss a boy outside in the rain?
Oh when do we leave our innocent years?
It's when we're lost and all hope disappears.

—*Emily Frydrych*

Rock And Roll

To the many Hippies of today, Rock and Roll
is music—"of a sort",
June 28th in California, — 'twas the earth
that moved with a loud report!
To live through such an experience, no one can describe
what you feel—
It's like the hand of the Devil, and it's eerie, weird, and unreal!
And after the shock is over, with all the destruction in it's wake,
Man stands in awe and wonder,—for only God can make an
earthquake!
To all those non-believers who say Religion is passe,
This terrible ordeal is a message of what God is trying to say;
Like Noah and the Ark in the Bible, immortality
pervades the land,—
Drug addiction, sin, and corruption beyond what the Almighty
can stand: Such depravity and pollution destroys the mind,
body, and soul;— Thus God in his wisdom is warning;—
purification must be ecology's goal!

—*Corinne Nawells*

Friendship

The value of a friendship
Is something yet unmeasured.
It is, like heirlooms old and dear,
Something that should be treasured.

Don't ever take a friend for granted,
For they may come and go.
The friend that yesterday you thought you had
Today may be your foe.

Friends share a common bond of trust
But this is easily shattered.
The things your friends thought trivial
To you may really have mattered.

True friendship is often
Very hard to understand.
Honesty, trust, fate, and faith,
All must go hand in hand.

Everyone needs a friend,
Someone that they can trust.
But in order for you to have a friend,
First be a friend you must.

—*Jennifer Ann Anderson*

Love Is Beyond the Rational

Love is beyond the rational: the mind
Is strong, and yet the heart has far more force.
Despite your firmness, I cannot rescind
One word of love, nor relinquish the source
Of life and creation. Thus, what you were
In times long since past, and what you now are,
And whom you loved, and whom you love, matter
Nothing to me. I am fixed as a star.
I will cast light to the far bounds of my
Firmament, seizing at love, forgotten
By you; and when I finally must die,
Not ever having reached your shining sun,
The darkness all around me will be bright—
Though gleaming cold—with self-created light.

—*Dolores A. Ruzicka*

The Bible And Common Sense

The Bible that has led my life
Is the rock on which I stand -
And in all these years are no doubts
Of the faith that I understand!

My respect for my family taught me
How to honor one and all -
And I really tried to forgive and forget
If one faltered, and took a fall!

But today there are so many wars,
And are based on hate and greed -
The ones in power seem intent to kill
To make less mouths to feed!

The Ten Commandments God gave to us
Seem covered with webs and dirt -
"Love Thy Neighbor" is gasping its last
From the demons of starve and hurt!

Now, even the Bible is questioned,
After all these many years -
And the over-powering know-it-alls
Are filling the people with fears!

—*Jane R. Lee*

A Thing Called Love

Across the room a tender glance.....
   is this a thing called love by chance?

A laughter shared, quiet solitude....
   this thing called love is joy true!

From his hands a gentle touch....
   am I a fool to care this much?

A passionate desire to hold you near....
   why does it hurt, what is this fear?

To say I love you is much too bold....
   his words and touch have now turned cold.

Laughter now is full of tears.....
   quiet solitude is not so dear.

This thing called love is full of pain.....
   that fear I felt was not in vain.

This thing called love is not to be.....
   it's just a state of mind for me.

—*Diane B. Martin*

Enormous, Enormous Wings

Is your life alive?
Is your darkness dark?
Are your arms open enough?
   Open your enormous wings, enormous wings, enormous wings
   Don't forget that freedom without caution dies here
   Open up your enormous wings, enormous wings, enormous wings
   My loved ones

Where are you going?
I am going nowhere

What do I do with my enormous wings?
   It is not about an exile from reality
   It is about going through your world (not our world)
   It is about an opportunity to be alive
   It is about opening up another possibility you and I in our
   minds, so

Open up your enormous, enormous wings!

—*Kirara KIKI Kawauchi*

Ode To Your Rose-Blush Colored Pony-Tail Holder

A gentle color, like on a rabbit's tender ear,
is your plum colored ponytail holder, which I hold so dear.
See how it rests, so quaintly against my curly blond strands,
like a rose colored horizon on wheat colored land.
No flower I know of, no tropical fish can boast,
of this exact color,
except the light hitting the thinnest part of my grape jelly on toast.
It whispers a color too quietly to be heard,
a combination of rosy-purple, plum and white;
ingredients forgotten once they were stirred.
This ponytail holder is a non-conformist,
a color for the tenderest of eyes with the tenderest of hearts.
I'm afraid that my little ponytail holder and I, we cannot part.

—*Kristen Suarez*

Untitled

I remember very well and I will never forget.
It all started late one cold dark wet foggy stormy night.
While walking down a muddy dirty road,
I was sore tired that I could hardly barely make it home.
All of a sudden to my surprise,
I took notice to that gorgeous woman,
struggling and striving very hard to survive.
Snapping into action and without hesitation immediately,
I did my best to rescue her.
I told her that I'm in love with you and I love you
all the way I want you I need and this
I'm asking you to do tell me my love me too.
I think of you every day,
I want you for bride when I walk down the streets
please there by my side. I love you too.

—*Fred Caldwell*

A Mother's Love

A mother's love is a beautiful gift bestowed on a precious few.
It blossoms like a fragrant rose and is exquisite to behold.
It shines in the night like a wishing star
That can make all your dreams come true.
Its warmth and compassion keep the fire going on a cold winter night.
Its freshness is like the morning dew.
A mother's love is a great tapestry;
An ornate design for the world to behold.
A mother's love will guide a child throughout his life:
Through the struggles, heartache, and despair;
Through the happiness, and springs, and summers.
A mother's love is always there;
For a mother's love is a never-ending song,
Providing a candlelight of hope for the world to share.

—*Heidi L. Hartmann*

People Pride

Whatever has happened to People's Pride?
It sure is missing today.
Honor and morals are cast aside
With the things folks do and say.
Many dress like they're off to the beach,
But go to God's house instead.
Some lifestyle, our children, we teach;
Takes greed and power to get ahead.
Man's home is no longer his Castle,
The yard's all littered with trash.
Extra effort — why that's just a hassle,
If we work it's only for plenty of cash.
Time's running out, we must be responsive
For our lives and surroundings, if we're to survive.

—*Geraldean B. Roy*

A Word to the Wise

Wisdom is not quite the same thing as knowledge,
It cannot be taught, like the latter, in college.
Nor can one pursue it, or bring it to hand
With mountains of words that prove useless as sand.

The gold of a Midas, or wealth of a Croesus
Can't purchase a trip to that plane past noesis,
And even pure genius, from earliest age,
Is no guarantee to the title of Sage.

True wisdom it seems, only happens to those
Who can break through the walls that all credos impose,
Then stand unencumbered, alert and aware,
And see 'neath the rubble what really is there.

The wise man gives credence to both dream and fact,
And tries to discern how all things interact,
Whether they're real, or unmeasurable things
That are, and are not,—like a hummingbird's wings.

For truth is an echo of things as they are,
A concept in context, like sound from a star.
The sage finds but one perfect truth ere he dies:
To lay claim to wisdom is not very wise.

—*Jaylocke Neller*

Suicide

When love has broken the human heart
it desires the body to die.
Know your heart will heal,
it's only a matter of time.

If drugs become your inner voice
and beckons you to kill,
beware, you're the victim,
even against your will.

Maybe you're in prison,
the punishment of a crime.
First seek forgiveness,
then serve your time.

Those traveling through a tunnel of pain
at this very hour
hold sacred your gift of life
and pray for a brighter tomorrow.

—*Connie Vainavicz*

The Deserted House

The deserted house stood on a hill.
It features were attractive but it gave a chill.
The rumors that were heard through the years,
made the house quite threatful as though we hear.
A glow of a light that shown during the night,
made you see a maiden in white.
It was told I hear that she carried the light.
Hunting for her true love that disappeared one cold night.
The sounds of her crying was carried in the wind
from the deserted house that stood empty through the years.
The maiden still appears once every year.
Hunting for the true love that one true love that she held so dear.

—*Crystal Spencer*

"Don't Look Back and Throw Stones"

Looking back in Common,
   It happens all the times;
So if you're fond of looking back
   Make sure its good you'll find.
Let there be an open window,
   To every channel of your mind;
Don't let there be a dark horizon
   In every thing you leave behind.
There so much you can accomplish,
   It's all left up to you,
To many minds lay cluttered
   With the things they didn't do.
"You are the one who makes the ripples
   In the gentle flowing stream",
"It's your thoughts that make the difference,
   You are the things you dream".
Don't let your presents falter!,
   Though you may stand alone;
Be the very best you can,
   Don't look back and throw stones.

—*Charles H. Norman*

The Old Quilt

Stored in the attic is an old quilt..
It is faded and worn..
The woman who now affectionately touches it; is old and tired.
The stairs to the attic seemed to get longer.

As she spreads out the quilt, her mind wonders back to days
gone by.
Some days her mind plays tricks on her.
But not today, the trip to the attic had some how made
everything seem better.
Like when she had made the old quilt.

The many different shapes and colors of material told a story
of her life.
Starting with a piece of white silk from her christening gown.
And ending with a pale blue piece of satin from her husband's
coffin.
The old quilt felt like a long lost friend.

—*Joy Butler*

Angry Cries

The world is no fun anymore
It is filled with garbage and lots of war
We as children do what we can
But they as adults don't understand

We see what no one else can see
The hunger and homeless which is called poverty
This is no game
Nor any fun
For this will be our world
To fix up when they are gone

We love our world
And do what we can
To clean up our home
And have a clean place to stand

We care and share
And throw our love everywhere
But soon it will be all gone
And we will grow up and be like you
Isn't that what you wanted all along?

—*Erin Vivero*

"God's Greatest Gift"

Perhaps you'll wonder then exclaim
It must be health and wealth or fame,
What matters wealth without contentment?
Some have their health but deep resentment
And as for fame, what's in a name?
For when we die we're all the same.
You gaze about and look with doubt
The world's not right is what you shout!
Why is she crippled? Why is he blind?
What did they lose? What did they find?
They lost resentment and gained contentment
For in happy souls you'll always find
God's greatest gift is Peace of Mind!

    —Joseph D. Barone

Time

    TIME is such a funny thing,
    It passes by each fall and spring.
    With each new year it comes and goes,
    What lies ahead TIME only knows.

    TIME heals the wounds that we endure,
    Once it ends there is no more.
    TIME turns the day in to night
    And turns what's wrong in to right.

    TIME forgets what's in the past,
    It needs the future for it to last.
    Rain or shine, TIME's always there,
    To help the one's for whom we care.

    TIME is so precious as you'll come to learn.
    It's not to be wasted, but yet not be earned.
    For it is a gift to us all to use as we choose,
    So important to cherish, too important to loose.

So always remember that TIME is your friend
And never forget someday it will end.
But for now just recall that it comes and it goes,
And what lies ahead TIME only knows!

    —John Shaffer

The Cries Of A Child

My life! My world! My dream!
It seems like only yesterday my life was like a child at play
Free! Free of all the hardships and the sins in this God
awful world. Free! free as a bird to fly through the heavens
and soar upon the midnight moons

Yet there was an air of pain, pain, it was a face with no name.
No one wanted to listen to the cries of the dear, dear child.
Her cries were little but not so little to be ignored. Her
cries were only but one of the many in the world.

People listened when the blood was shed of one or the other.
But is the world such a cruel, cruel world that no one cares of
the cries of a child. Little do they know the blood will
never be shed of one or the other, not in the eyes of the dear,
dear child. She will not shed the blood of one or the other, never!

The little cries of the child one day must be heard. Maybe
when she is old enough to express her life dreams in a proper
manner. But never too desperate to shed the blood of one or the
other.

    —JoAnn Humphreys

A Painter's Moods

Yesterday, God's canvas was a blue mass
It showed not a stroke of His mighty brush;
Motionless trees stood like hostile giants,
Birds flitted by without a merry note;
I yearned to express my thoughts for so long
Yet at day's end my canvas was a blank.

Today, I looked up in search of God's moods
His canvas was glowing from early dawn;
The rising sun is sending warmth to earth,
The Great One is splashing hues here and there;
My moods merged with the Great Painter's spirit
And my canvas is a show of sunrise.

Tomorrow, I hope, will be like today,
I will be with myself in earnestness
And fervently sketch the sea and the surf;
Birds will be courting and young buds bursting,
Perfumed breeze will be playing around me
As I paint Hawaii's springtime grandeur.

    —Ed Y. Kish

Life's Voyage

Life is like a mighty ship when it sails out to sea.
It starts at port on its voyage
with everything that it will need.

New material you start your voyage
with a captain and his mate.
And you know in their hands your ship is very safe.

Second voyage out to sea waves keep coming in.
Still your captain and his mate hold your
ship with a stern hand.

Third voyage, with all new crew
the weather is getting bad.
Tidal waves twist you about
as your ship heads toward the land.

Fourth voyage the mighty ship is old and worn with time.
Material things that you picked from life
the old ship no longer requires.

Up ahead the light house beams
sending out a bright light in the storm.
The Captain that waits there for you
will guide your ship safely home.

    —Lavada Robbins

Roses and Daisies

A wave of courage surges in the tranquility
    It's creation crushing the earthly weakness
Arisen in its wake a livelihood of security
    Hidden from sight is meekness

The bold and insightful will rule it strongly
    All will be one; no one without
What once was forever is never done wrongly
    The locked soul screams to get out

Severed are the binding chains of society
    Appearance overshadowed by the beauty inside
Unlock the secrets of prosperity
    Fear shall duck its head and hide

Death received in its prime
    The strength of the masses
Fulfilled; not nearly enough time
    Silently the rose with the daisy passes.

    —Nancy Jesiolowski

Big Black Is Back

I once made a rocket named the Mean Machine,
It took off with a shower of gleam,
It flew to a height, and it gave me a fright,
But it didn't come back that night.

We looked and looked in yard and tree;
We looked and looked, my brother and me;
We looked in a tree and in a yard,
But finding this rocket sure was hard.

The weeks they came, the weeks they went,
But I never knew where that rocket was sent.
I couldn't stop, I simply would not,
That rocket I had to spot.

One day with my brother I was riding
When I saw where that rocket was hiding.
I saw it all bent squeezed in a can,
But I didn't care, I took it and ran!

I raced straight home and into the workshop,
I worked and worked and couldn't stop.
And when I finished my massive attack,
I ran out and announced, "Big Black is back!"

—Dennis Schell

The Joy Of Given

As I walked down the street to work there laid a seed I picked
it up, placed it in a pot and covered it with soil, one day
later it started to bloom into a beautiful flower. As I was
walking down the street I saw a small child standing in front
of a candy store looking through the window. I gave him a
quarter he smiled for I gave him hope. As I sat on the bus an
old woman stood there tired and in pain I gave her my seat.
She smiled and said thank you, her relief was the smile upon my
face. As I walked home on a cold winter day I saw a homeless
person laying under some newspaper. To keep him warm I gave
him my coat. He looked up at me, his eyes was filled with
thank's for I gave him another day. As I laid asleep in my
bed, I remembered an old saying from my mother. The joy of
given is what keeps the heart at ease. Bring a smile to
someone else face will enable you to smile. As I was walking to
work a man dressed in a long black coat came up to me and gave
me a note and the note stated "you gave me a coat to keep me
warm, for that I'm thankful and if you should ever fall by the side
I will be there, I will always be there. One hand reaching out with
an untouchable love, one world builded with the joy of given.

—Charles L. White Sr

Sinner's Guilt Destroys

When darkness falls and all is still,
It waits for me upon the hill.
What is it that I do not see?
For I hear it and fear it as it calls to me.

Death? With its frigid yet unsubtle calmness?
I dare not think it.
My fever grows so weak now,
Chills overcome my body.
No escape, no relief from this selfish,
Unjust creature of darkness with piercing,
Cold metallic eyes.

And so on the last thread of life;
I whimper out at the night with unsure moans,
"Take Me" for living any longer is unbearable.

Satanic? No doubt for I deserve no less than
What destiny and free will have brought about.

—Carolyn Phinny

The Baby Quilt

Before you were born, I made a little quilt for you,
It was mostly pink with just a little bit of blue.
I made so many things, worked on them every day,
And all the while praying you'd be healthy and ok.
Sometimes I really got carried away,
Making cute little dresses, it filled my heart with joy.
What would I have done, if you had been a little boy?
At last the day came for you to be born,
A little bit early, but alright they'd sworn.
I took that little quilt to the hospital with me,
You entered the world, I named you Tina Marie.
I couldn't wait to take you home,
All bundled up in that quilt I had sewn.
But you weren't well, we couldn't foresee.
No one went home, except the little quilt and me.
Years have passed by, those things are stored on a shelf,
And all I have, is the memory, deep inside of myself.

—Betty Sines

An Empty House

I entered an empty house one day,
It was quiet; damp and chill,
And I thought as I wondered from
room to room
With everything so still:
What if my life were as empty as this;
no cheer or comfort to give;
I'd fill it with things from our
Father above
And start all over to live.

And as I pondered o'er what I'd like
to fill up this emptiness with,
I bowed with an uncovered head in the quiet
And asked of my Lord just this:
Lord, fill up my house with things from above
And into each room pour abundance
of love,
Then all through the year 1993
Will come comfort and cheer
from a mortal like me.

—Louis W. Lucas

A Mother's Love

As I slept, a visitor came to see me.
It was the mother I never knew.
She brought a message no one else could deliver.
A story only a mother could whisper.
It was written to a child,
But took a man to understand.
Her story of undying love,
Told of sorrow, pain and tears.
I was too young to understand back then.
Because she left before I was four,
What joy she felt at my birth,
Known only to a mother here on earth.
Watching and waiting as I grew older,
Having to leave before the story was over.
Only now do I begin to understand,
She came to see her child grown into a man.

—David Shantz

294

Winter Wind

Facing the bay window I feel the sun's rays.
It's a cool, snow covered windy day.
I watch the tops of the trees move and sway
Pointed wooden fingers point up and away.

The wind appears to blow in random gusts
At once calm, then soon a swirl of dust.
It blows through the woods and onto the pond
Making snowy swirls and then it is gone.

It moves all about like a giant cool sea,
Wraps around us and shivers our knees.
Like watery oceans, with peak and trough
It comes and goes, then on then off.

Where it starts where it ends, who could ever know.
Is it all the elements that cause highs and lows?
From my window view the trees move back and forth,
For all I know it came from the North.

Now the wind has stopped blowing through the trees
And all that is left is a very soft breeze.
It's the stillness in the woods that catches my eyes.
The wind is all gone now, I realize.

—*Earl W. McKennon*

Political Games

The way they spend money in government;
It's a good thing they own the Denver Mint.
They keep on spending like there's no tomorrow;
Come election day, there'll be real sorrow.
A man named Ross said "Vote for me;
I'll cure it all and vote for free."
Then came a man said, "Take a hint;
I'll save you, my name's Bill Clint."
I swear I'll take the deficit down;
If you'll let me wear that golden crown.
Said on spending we must save;
As our taxes he did crave.
In the end, our time we'll bide;
To see what spending they will hide.
He'll try to them his plan to sell;
I hope and prey he will do well.
The truth be known, he's only one;
taking blame for Congress can't be fun;
Sir, please don't mind the fun I poke;
Mr. President, it's meant as a joke.

—*Becky Grumet*

Immortal

It's odd I can not remember the first time we met.
It's as if she has been with me a lifetime;
Our souls must have known each other forever.

Sometimes I know just what she's thinking.
It's as if her heart connects directly to mine;
I flounder with the energy I feel for her.

Do I acknowledge it, and hope it goes away?
Do I cherish it and grab as much as I can?
Do I just feel it and know she's my lifeline?

Things are changing all around me.
My life is changing; and so responds my body;
The energy I feel for her reminds me of how alive I am.

Yet my body betrays the energy I feel.
Her skin is vital and alive;
I ache to be connected to her.

Maybe I don't want to remember the first time we met.
Maybe then I would know there was a beginning;
There would have to be an end.
I want us to live forever!

—*Faith Wunder*

Life's Journey

Through foaming waves and billowing surf we tread,
Like ships we brave the tides that loom ahead.
No looking back to fearful clouds that rise;
For God, our Captain, rules the stormy skies.
He walks upon the waves 'til night is done,
And daylight brings the joy of rising sun.
So live each day in hope through pain or sorrow,
For each today is yesterday's tomorrow.

—*Catherine Elizabeth Currans, S.P.*

The Education Train

The Education Train is old and strong.
It's been traveling in our school system for oh so long.
Hurry up and jump on, be still and be quiet,
For regurgitation is working all right.
The train rushes by in authoritarian style,
With boxcars full of worksheets you can see for miles.
The conductor yells, "All Aboard, if you can,"
But some students need a kind helping hand.
Educators of the future please stop and take heed.
An educational revolution is what this train needs.
Slow down in the classroom and make room for change.
Responsibility and creativity in the student will reign.
Society must realize childhood is not a race,
It is a journey of learning at the child's own pace.

—*Judy Ann Prothro*

Remember The Day When The Earth Was Green?

The sun is rising slowly in the sky
It's deadly rays beat down on you and I
Cancer eats away at skin
Nothing left
The earth can't mend

Man must eat to survive
We are the only animals left alive

Remember the day when the earth was green
and all we had to do
Was to keep the air clean

But we wouldn't listen to cries from the sea
We didn't care if the sea creatures died

They weren't as important as you and I

—*Gloria Hood*

!!! The Inevitable Question!!!

Everyday we put our mind and body to the test
It's embedded in all of us to do our very best.
We live our whole lives in the shadow of pretense
People condemn us for not having good common sense...

I look in the mirror and tell at a glance
Living with myself has been no romance.
I have few wild oats left to be sown
Come August I'm forty-three and fully grown...

The older I get the more I have to hurry
The more I do and have the more I worry.
I feel pretty lucky but who put me here
I get lots of answers but none that are clear...

I'm told don't take life serious it's only a game
But as my life passes by who am I to blame.
We live our whole lives without ever knowing
Where we came from or where we're going...

I've had plenty of questions since my birth
What was I before and why am I on earth.
One more question because I do care
If we're here then who's out there...???...

—*Bill R. Duke*

Untitled

It's hard to explain how I feel
It's like nothing I've ever felt before
Whenever I'm with you it seems unreal
It's like a dream, but so much more

I want a love that lasts forever
With you I'll be till the end of time
Reassuring we're always together
I want you to tell me that you are mine

I often wonder if you think about me
Or if what you say is true
No matter what may be
I want to say I love you.

—*Andie Darr*

The Desert Rose

It lies upon a dry and barren ground
its petals that were once a ravishing vermillion
now wilt to a fragile black decay.
All the days it gave vitality and a buoyancy spirit
now brings a touch of sadness to your soul.
You feel a wet, lonely tear silently escaping
as you wipe it away
the tenderness of your cheek
reminds you of the silky petals
of the now
    DESERT ROSE.

Wishing you could give it the tear
and bring its blooming smile back
and desiring its sweet smell just one last moment.
Although the beauty of the fragrance
still locked timelessly in your heart.
Never to forget the happiness and sadness it gave to you.

—*S. Balkovetz*

Autumn Haze

When summer turns to autumn with warm days short and few,
    It's then the leaves are turning to shades of brilliant hue.

The emerald grass is tarnished and Jack Frost chills the ground;
    It's when the geese fly southward with a honking sound.

It won't be long till winter when autumn breezes blow;
    Soon nature's leafy carpet will hide beneath the snow.

Then evening shadows lengthen o'er the leaves that fall;
    It's just a pause till winter when autumn comes to call.

The mountain is quite hazy, oh so bleak and bare,
    As autumn winds blow stronger through the frosty air.

In the woods and forest the hardwoods stand so still,
    Stripped of all their beauty on every dale and hill.

It seems as if by magic the fir trees take command;
    The pine, the spruce, and hemlock so tall and stately stand.

Upward lifts their branches of broad and emerald bowers;
    The pride of all the mountain in aging autumn hours.

It's just a pause till winter, these airy autumn days,
    When nature hides its sorrow in the autumn haze.

—*Carroll Buffum Sr.*

My Friend

You've been there for me right from the start,
It's too bad that after this year our ways must part.
I promise I'll always stay in touch,
For I'll miss your friendship so very much.

I'm going to miss your warm and generous smile,
When something was wrong, calling you was worthwhile.
You have an awesome personality,
You have helped me through some harsh realities.

I can't express in words the way you've touched my life,
I wish you the best always for the rest of your life!
You are like a sister to me,
And I know that you always will be.

When I was down, you'd listen to what I had to say,
You tried to help me find the right way.
You'll always be beside me in my heart,
No matter how far our ways do part.

—*Angela Lamb*

Christ

    I gaze up at a shining star and make believe
its what you are
    A bright unfailing beacon in the night drawing
souls into heaven with your glorious light
    Trying to understand your sacrifice which is beyond
comprehension and awestruck by the result that
defies imagination
    Brought about by unselfish love to a world
speeding rightfully toward hell, to defeat a
clever foe who has fought hard and well
    But if He had won the result too terrible to
comprehend for the blessing of this love would surely
have met a tragic end
    Praises be to You oh blessed Son of the Father,
and may You always be, revered like no other

—*Bill Eardley IV*

48 Without A Date

For heaven's sake, I'm 48.
I've been single for 5 years,
and I'd like to have a date.
It's time to shift into some higher gears,
but to start dating, gives me great fears.
So, where do I start to meet a man.
I could sit on a bar stool,
but I'd feel like an old fool.
The best men are all married.
The others, I'm sure, are all dead and buried.
So what am I missing, by not having a man.
Maybe a helper to bring out the garbage can.
Well, as they say, "things will turn out in time".
Things better hurry, I'm about out of my prime.

—*Faye Kars*

The Black Lens

I wear a black lens, it's part of me,
It's so I see one instead of two of thee.
Jacob Lang hit us, my head broke the glass,
My knee hit the dashboard & shattered alas!
The car I was riding in didn't have belts,
So I couldn't stop my body from smashing its 'self.
So please wear your seat belts, it's even the law -
You'll survive to the next day, to live one day more.
I've learned to live one day at a time,
And it isn't that easy & writing in rhyme.

—*Marilyn R. Brandon*

A Reflection

A face familiar to me now
I've seen in other places.
Not masked in features so familiar,
But surely the same.
Strangers, one and all,
Yet invisible bonds unite us;
Our love for one another.
Where ere I go its roots
Have sprung above earth's firmness,
And always with open arms
Awaits the need of one.
A stranger to some, yet ever present.
Whatever acts of goodness we perform,
It's pollen, kindness, goes forth to fertile soil,
Takes root in other hearts
And blossoms forth with radiance
To inspire new souls to higher deeds.
Thus, the face familiar,
It's the love within we recognize
As one we gave away so long ago.

—*Joan M. Ghio*

Fulfillment

Teaching music to little kids has made my life worthwhile,
I've seen them run and march and jump, and watched them laugh
or smile. They've shared innermost secrets, some happy and
some sad, told of newborn pups and cats, or tiffs with Mom and
Dad.

I've watched my students as they've matured, and had
children of their own, and now I'm teaching their offspring,
a fact that makes me groan. I look into their little eyes that
sparkle as they sing, and my mind goes back to bygone days,
fond memories to bring.

I'll soon be moving to the side and finishing the race,
I'll hand the torch to someone else, a bright new shining face,
And the music will go on and on, bringing happiness and cheer,
And the singing deep within my heart will keep my students near.

I'd like to think as I travel on and the years go along,
That someone in his daily work will begin to hum a song,
And as he remembers the lyrics, his memory will-fill
With a music teacher he once had way back in Painesville.

—*Ellen Gilkerson*

Mommie Don't Cry

Mommie, please don't cry
Jesus sings to me a lullaby.
We run through fields of shimmering gold
He tells me stories of days of old.

I run and play now, and climb a tree
Did you know, he even plays with me?
Jesus said I could write to you;
He knows your days are sad and blue.

But, Mommie, there's no pain now; it's gone away.
I'm home again and I really want to stay.
I've seen Daddy pretend to be strong and brave,
But I see tears flow at the foot of my grave.

Daddy, don't you know I'm really not there?
I have a mansion here, high in the air.
Mommie, hold Daddy close and be happy once more,
I'll be waiting to greet you at heavens door.

Together we'll run through fields of gold,
And, you know what, Mommie? We'll never grow old.
Mommie and Daddy, please don't cry;
Jesus sings to me a lullaby.

—*Linda Eyraud*

"What It's Like"

The dishes are melting in the sink,
John's talking,
and my head is beginning to swim—
nostrils narrowing, eyes unable to focus,
and my breath smelling like garlic:
my belly bulging as though I was just
beginning to show, and wearily I think
I'm not even ready for motherhood.
My behind spreads like melting lard each time
I sit down, and I think I must not have
a very good opinion of myself.

—*Jeanne Weiss*

Good-Bye My Friend

Oh, we never will take as I know,
just a ride on the wheel.
And we never know when death will take us.
And we wonder how we'll feel.
So goodbye my friend.
And though I will never see you again,
but the time together through all these years
will take away those tears, it's okay now.
Good-bye my friend.
Life so fragile, love so pure,
we can't go on but we try.
We watch life quickly disappear.
And we never know why.
But I'm okay now, good-bye my friend.
You can go now.
Good-bye my friend. Good-bye.

—*Janet Poore*

Rest In Peace

Warm white water slowly sifts through the Earth's silky sands
Just as my life has sifted through Destiny's indecisive hands
On majestic cliffs that rise high, resisting God's wicked winds
I stand contemplating and despising not resisting my own sins
Sunlight steadily shimmers and reflects off the glassy sea
But I can see no light. Just darkness all around me.
With all the beautiful scenery, somehow I can find
Thoughts of my death darting across my demented mind
I take my leap, for in God I Trust
Ashes to ashes, dust to dust.
And as my mortal body floats steadily to the East
Maybe now my pure spirit will rest in eternal peace.

—*Adrian S. Potter*

Friends

Friends are forever
Just like me and you,
So let's stay together
And help each other through.

Our friendship is true blue,
And it will always last.
We stick together like glue,
And always have in the past.

We've known each other for a long time.
And I really love you a lot.
High and low mountains we have climbed,
And I don't think we've ever fought.

I am your friend, and you are mine;
We belong together and deserve each other.
I love you a lot and hope that you find,
That you'll never leave because you are my mother.

—*Chrissy Ward*

Just For Today Unconditional Love

Just for today I love and accept you just the way you are. Just for today I will do my best to love you always. Just for today my truth is I love you no matter what. Just for today, my friend, I will share with you my heart. Just for today God abides within my soul. Just for today I believe we are one.

The greatest gift we can give to another anytime of year is love. Love is something we can't see or smell or touch. But love is something we can feel, a feeling that changes everything and everyone it touches, a feeling so powerful it removes everything in its path. No hard feeling, anger, resentment, hate, or negativity can survive when it's around.

The only gift if there is one that we can give that is greater than love is UNCONDITIONAL LOVE. Unconditional love, no strings attached, no bargains made, no if you are, if you will, if you can. Just "I Love You" just as you are no matter what.

Just for today I love and accept you unconditionally. Just for today you are my loved one and just for today you are truly my friend.

—Dottie Stockman

One Lonely Tree

One lonely tree grows along the roadside
Just how it got there to no one will it confide

Perhaps someone dug a hole and planted it there
Or may be the wind blow in a seed from who knows where

What good does it do standing there all alone
As to such great height and beauty it has grown,

In its boughs many a bird has built a nest
And many others in flight have stopped to rest,

Those passing by have beheld its beauty
As it offered its shade and protection to fulfill its duty

The summer season ended and its leaves turned all shades of gold
And gently fluttered
    down the ground to enfold

It stands there alone and bare and sleeps for awhile
Suddenly its spring and it must reblossom with a smile

—Helen Irwin

Changes

I close my eyes when I am in thought,
just thinking of you and times we've shared.
I only wish I could cherish those moments forever.

As the clouds part and those bright stars shine through,
I dream of the days we might come together as one,
and share the remainder of our lives in happiness.

Slowly the night sky turns dark blue and an arrangement of red.
As the night fades into the early bits of morning,
we lay in grass and gaze at the beautiful sky light.

The natural beauty takes me away to a place where nothing can
be less than perfect.
The dawn air is filled with a mild breeze,
I picture myself slowly sailing down the bay with you,
on a hot summer day, the sun beaming its warmth upon my shoulders.

These endless thoughts and memories continue to ease in and
out of my mind.
A tear of happiness slowly slips down my cheek, then subsides.
As a smile appears across my face,
The morning air now becomes crisp and the sun begins to rise.

—Teri Yost

My Niece

She laughs and giggles:
Just like she should,
She jumps and wiggles:
Just as she would.

A new born baby
What a dream,
She is so dear to me
Her and I - what a team.

And so I think about the future,
I wonder what she will be -
She has so much to offer in that little body
I guess I'll just wait and see.

A little bundle of joy!
She laughed and pointed my way,
I jumped and screamed oh boy!
I'll never forget that day.

She shows me her toys,
And makes lots of noise:
Her mother is my brother's wife,
I can't wait to watch her grow in life!

—Jessica Robbins

Untitled

Zooming up into the sky
Just my little plane and I
I get a thrill, when looking down
I see the hills and all the towns

The purple mountains spinning by
Look just like giants, I can't tell why
The horizon with the setting sun
Seems to say, Gods will is done

Now comes the greatest thrill of all
For now the plane begins to fall
I feel alarmed! but not at all
For the dear Old earth, has checked my fall

—Eunice H. Francisco Stumpf

Untitled

Went walking down by the creek.
Just stopped, sat down, cooled my feet.
My thoughts floated on down the stream.
Closed my eyes, and remembered my dream.

Hand in hand in the fields green,
oh, how simple it all seemed.
The sky was perfect, just perfect blue,
nothing else mattered, except me and you —

Restless and young, sitting on that fence,
the simple breeze, filling each sense.
Kisses were just gentle fun,
laying in the grass, soaking up the sun —

Opening my eyes, the sun had set,
as did my dream, pain and regret.
Wanting your love, so much to grow,
but like the wind, you had to go.

—Christine Aldrich

"Once Upon"

I returned to a marriage that was no more.
Just to pick up my kids.
Then came barking, at my "used to be" front door.
My old faithful friend,
There he stood.
He didn't recognize me.
Then I spoke.
"Master?" I know he thought,
"Is it really you?" That I see.
It's been a long time since we played.
I told him "sorry I couldn't stay."
He wagged his tail.
Somehow I do believe.
I saw a smile cross that hairy lip.
I wished him well, as my heart began to swell.
My kids came out, as we walked away.
I tried to look back, but I turned.
I couldn't look at my old friend.
I just wanted to remember.
The joy and that "Once upon a time, We used to spend.

—*Lawana Sue Craig*

The Deepest Pain

(Dedicated to my father, Theodore I. Roberts,
killed in Vietnam — May 4, 1970)
A gaping wound in the Earth.
A gaping wound in my heart.
Catharsis.

I run my fingers over the blackness.
The name slips through.
I can not catch it.

Rain—internal, external—shimmers.
Reflects in eyes and on the granite
For the survivors.

Thoughts and visions
Continue to haunt millions
Who come for relief.

Will I always cry
When I walk by?

—*Carolyn J. Roberts*

A Speck of Old-Hat

Standing in drizzle in a silhouette of trees
Kittycorner from an old store and apartments
Two shades of gray and peeled paint
The brick building of the old county hospital in view
Its upper floor a row of windows with little pillars
Cracks in the sidewalks serving as rivulets
To veteran trees plying their well-worn scars
A new residential complex a huge affair
Bordering the old bohemian hispanic sector
Further along the midway leading to the big street
Little girls wearing pretty, soft pastel dresses
Ruffles, lace and satin trims, happy faces
Like all the world's a merry-go-round!
Aromas of burritos, pizza, and oven-fresh goods
Shocking pink, blue-striped, confetti cookies, brown alligators
The big street with bright yellow bus markers, heavy trash cans
On sides kittycorner to serve as polyglot riders munch on the run.
An old ballpark and an entrance to the freeway
A rolling park with memories of the Cinco Mayo fests
Concluding the sweep of view from north to 101 south!

—*Carmen I. Doerner*

Remembering

The first time I saw you I
knew that I had just fallen in love
With your cheerful ways and I saw
that your eyes were looking for love

Then your eyes of wonder, finally met my eyes that night
When I walked up to you and your loving blue eyes
I knew you were the one, because your
loving blues gave me a big surprise

We went together for awhile
And then something happened to our love

Your loving blues I still see today
Even though we have parted away

I can still remember that night we met
How could I ever forget

—*Marie Davis*

I'm Only A Beginner

I'm making a nice red plane, but don't
know the name of it,
after all, I'm only a beginner.

I'm trying to fly that nice red plane, but it
won't fly, I won't know why,
after all, I'm only a beginner.

I just glued a piece of wood on the nice red
plane, it flies now! I don't know why,
after all, I'm only a beginner.

I have to fix a plane motor, I'm not sure how to,
after all, I'm only a beginner.

Hey, I'm tired of being a beginner!
I'm going to do this more often and be a pro!

.... four weeks later......

I'm a pro!!!!!!!!!

Hey, now I'm going to work on car models.
O.K., here goes! Whoops, I made a mistake!
After all, I'm only a beginner.

—*Christopher Abdow*

Learn Not To Burn

If you hear a loud noise in the middle of the night:
KNOW WHAT TO DO!
Stay calm and show no fright.
LEARN NOT TO BURN!

If you hear a loud noise while doing work at school:
KNOW WHAT TO DO!
Walk quietly and be cool.
LEARN NOT TO BURN!

When smoke fills the room and you need to get out:
KNOW WHAT TO DO!
Just crawl and don't shout.
LEARN NOT TO BURN!

If your clothes are on fire and you're running around:
KNOW WHAT TO DO!
Try not to make a sound.
LEARN NOT TO BURN!

Be tough. Be like Miss Toll.
KNOW WHAT TO DO!
Just STOP, DROP, and ROLL.
LEARN NOT TO BURN!

—*Deborah Toll*

Young Folk, Please Listen!

Learn value, earn respect
Know your foundation in every aspect.

Hunger for education, master a trade
Be self-prepared...
So your life won't be delayed.

Love yourself...and your fellowman.
Be understanding...offer a helping hand.

There are choices, so start your quest
Be constructive and productive
It's a guarantee for success.

This is a heartful premonition
Be precise, and work with precision
It's all about you,...so make the right decision.

  —Clara Retha Graham

Untitled

Me thinks me an angry child and fearings are deep within
Knowing not, so daring not to ever allow love in.

Taught me well these life long roles, they've even let me feel.
Though deep within that dungeoned cell she whispers, it isn't real.

Never knew a safe place of a child's trusting soul.
Never could believe in truth, its either borrowed or too cold.

For she is me, as I am her, tired guardians in a blur,
And bankrupt to face a starving soul.

But pity me not my path in life for 'tis mine to venture true
Mine to escape mediocrity and find God in me and you.

Pulled in by many forces whether friendly of foe,
Always beckoned by my nature, a lost but searching soul.

Its true I look forward looking behind and dining with the
pain. To share my empty plate with ghosts, to face what
was insane.

You tend to raise your brow with intent to show your
 disapproval though you've never lived inside my shell with this
 yearning for fears removal.

  —Dawn C. Fisher

Acrostic Winter Poem

Saturday nights my grandfather used to give me sleigh rides
Lazy David lies back to enjoy the ride
Endless rides until midnight
I wish I could go up front,
 and guide the horses through the night
Grandma yells "Look out," as a branch flies by my head
Hard, but fun, we ride the night

Rabbits pass the sleigh really fast
I'd love to pick the rabbits up,
 and feel their soft, snow covered fur
Dozing off to wonderland
Easy to be distracted by bells, that jingle along the way
Sing a song before the night ends,
 morn is on its way

  —Jessica Lee Clark

Compression

 Who must say much in little space,
  Let him say it in poetry.
There, weightless words take on the force
  Of ultimate density.

  —Herbert W. Edwards

Spring Comes

Spring comes early.
Let me dig, play in the dirt,
Sniff the air, fresh, virgin-clean,
See the well-spring of life, tiny green swords
Among shards of frost crystals and
Dead tan tufts of last year's
Summer gone forever.

Give me some soil.
Let me turn it with a spade
To prepare for new life, new seeds,
New plants, new flowers, new trees, new Season.
Let me feel the cool crumbly clod.
See how the worms do wriggle
Making room for life.

Dirt,
 dig, smell,
  turn, feel,
   step, crunch.
Spring. Peace.

  —Gene Peters

The Dream Feather

Old man, as I look into your eyes
Let me see the winter of ages past:
Winters of war under dark and dreary skies
And promises of peace that did not last.

Old man, look into my eyes
See hope and bliss ever dear,
Summer fields under blue skies,
And sparkling rivers mirrored clear.

Old man, look into my mind
Bring about unfurrowed brows.
Let your vision with my youth entwine
Intermingled with love. Now!

  —Dolores Gandia

A Plan

Give me a chance to reach my goal
Let me suffice the desires of soul
Give me knowledge and let me learn
Let my grip on life be fixed and firm
Guide my thoughts to higher plains
Let not my losses surpass my gains
Teach me to be righteous, staunch, and true
Let me smile when successes are few
Plant my feet on solid ground
Let my heart with love abound
Equip me for my works here on earth
Let me remember those things from birth
Help me to make others glad
Let me be happy when they are sad
Prepare me for the life to be
Let me set sail on the open sea.

  —Charles Manly Pack

Lost

Confusion is a trap you see,
 Is everyone confused, or only me?

Smiles and laughter on everyone's face,
 Is it real, or is it feelings misplaced?

Dark and gloomy I feel inside,
 Is this natural, or is it something I should hide?

Life is what you desired it to be,
 Is it real, to want to be happy and free?

  —Kathy Ann Rutledge

You're The One For Me

When I'm around him my heart always pounds
like a speeding bullet that makes no sounds;
he never calls me by my name,
but I love him still the same.
He's like a lost butterfly in the wind;
but he always find's his way back in.
I love him dearly with all my heart,
that's why I would never want to part.
I will stay forever you see and we will live as a family.

    —Crissy Cole

Give The Children A Better Chance

Give the children a better chance
Let them laugh and run to play
Give the children a better chance
Let them learn to sing and dance
Let them dare to dream of a bright tomorrow yet to be
Forever free
From bitter strife and sorrow
Give the children a better chance
Let them laugh and run to play
Give the children a better chance
Let them learn to sing and dance
Let them be
Forever free
Let them be
Forever free forever free

    —Billie Jeanne James

Silent Days

Two chords playing side by side
let them play till you hear no sound
Then listen in the silence I am found
In and out breathe the mystical silent song
Breathing life, breathing hope, sadness
Hold with it till you feel it too
In silence I am found
I'm found in the pause between the ticks of a clock
Two musical notes, or even between rings of a phone
Nancy is found in silence
Listen to the silence, hear what is not there
Understand what I have to say
The candle and the rose sitting side by side
Stare at neither candle or rose
But the space between
Nancy is there and between table and chair
I'm found in silence, loosing life, loosing hope, despair
Please listen to my silence

    —Nancy Lowry

A Mother — A Son

My child may say to me this is my life, my life to live
Let this errant child not forget his life is His but I did give
A part of me is in His life without this gift he would be naught
can he forget has he forgot
The pain of birth still floods my mind
Of years of endless wait, of motherhood, of being kind
Giving when their was nothing to give, yet you say 'tis your
    life to live
Blessed be the mother who has not sat the endless wait
Listening for a footfall at the door, the clocks ticks back 'tis late
    'tis late
when at last this same child is home safe in bed
Say's thank you God, He's safe, He's home I ask no more all has
    been said
now this same child must choose his way, he asks to be alone
he turns his back his voice says let me
be the one, don't you know I'm grown

    —Glynda Fitzgibbon

"Let's Share A Blanket Of Love"

Let's share a blanket, somewhere in the grass at a park,
Let's share a blanket, on the sands of a nearby lake after dark.
Let's sing a song...steal a lyric from a passing lark,
Let's dance along...keep in step with a schnauzer's bark.
Let's put a sparkle in the moon, a twinkle in a star and
    watch the romantic rhyme...
Let's share a blanket of love, one more time.

Let's share a blanket, on a floor, next to an old-worn-out broom.
Let's share a blanket in bed, preferably in my room.
Let's cement our marriage - let's think baby-carriage.
Let's eat a little...chicken, beef, fish or pork.
Let's make a baby...and deliver one for the stork.
Let's share a drink with a twist of lemon or lime.
Let's share a blanket of love, one more time.

    —Andrew J. Hanacek

Label On A Frozen Turkey

Inside this wrap of plastic and foam
    Lies the turkey you'll take home
He'll be stuffed and roasted gold brown
    Then your whole family will all sit down
You'll carve him into slices thin
    Hundreds of teeth all tearing in
Tearing his flesh clean off the bone
    But let me tell you about my home
Me and my brothers will sit around
    Scratching and picking food off the ground
We'll cry long and we'll be sad
    Because, Dear Consumer, you've eaten our Dad.

    —Charles N. Cantella

The Ritual

She methodically exhales her last few breaths of seasonal
life, as she deliberately slips into her annual coma. Her
warm green coat of life has gradually wilted down to a
rust-like covering, as her exterior being drifts into
temporary death. Her thriving and tangled fields of soybeans
have been transformed into giant barren table tops. Her
once-upright and proud stalks of corn now resemble hordes of
dead and dying soldiers on countless battlefields of hope.
The merciless combines that had strategically roamed the
fields and screamed their defiance of the incoming crop now
sit lifeless under the shelter of metal roofs. The chilling
rains pepper down to slowly alter living soil into slick, cold
mud and drive her keepers inside, to drink in the heat of wood
stoves. For the harvest season is over, and Mother Earth lies
dormant as her tillers reflect and thoughtfully anticipate her
awakening.

    —Greg Elam

Look Through Your Pain

So many people turn away from the pain. The hurting are
left alone. Beaten, abused, and used I looked to my God to ask
why. The answer was unclear. I gave up; I tried very hard to
die. I could not! I did not understand why. Then the day
came, I looked away from myself and saw him; A troubled man,
standing alone, and hurting ever so bad.

We have now grown very close. After being asked many times
over what I see in this man that's more like a child? How do I
live with his anger? He's so confused, why do I stay?

My answer now comes very clear. It is because of my pain I
can understand. It is through the pain I have found love.

    —Carla Saylor

Untitled

I think...
Life is a dream, dreamt by God
We live out his fantasies and nightmares
Like actors on a stage performing to an
Audience of one
The director says "cut!"
A child dies
And another is born in its place
But when God finally wakes
  Apocalypse
    The end
I think... life could be an illusion
What is reality? Where is it?
Is it a product of our over active imagination?

I think... The sky is green and the grass is blue
Two and two... Who says it equals four?
Why not three or five?
I think... There are no right answers
Only answers that lead to more questions
      —Chelsie Owello

"Reflections On A Neon Night"

Sun's got the blues - sky's cold and gray,
Life on the street - sign says one way,
Last cigarette - ain't got a light,
Reflections - on a neon night,

Emotions cold - not much to say,
Give them a little - but not today,
Bellies are empty - belts drawn tight,
Reflections - on a neon night,

Senses are numb - pain doesn't pay,
Bitter cold air - no place to stay,
The homeless - we know their plight,
Reflections - on a neon night,

Some really care - most look away,
One more at peace - death came today,
God's vagabond children - go into the light,
Reflections —— on a neon night...
    —Len Iovino

Alive

The Jaws of the mountains seem to swallow you whole,
Life was thrown again and again.
The fuselage soured like a rocket with no wings,
Finally coming to a stop across the cold snow as if it knew
This were its home.

Cries of pain, pain, pain.
Blood shed more than most see in a life time.
Horror raged, raged, raged.
Night was just beginning, would the light survive?
Death, death, death, again, and again.

The days rolled by slowly, like the steep mountains on
Which they passed. Mountains, everywhere.
Survival was hopelessly difficult, yet the people cried...
Nando, Nando,... over and over again.

You seem to pull them through with ease.
God blessed you with strength, courage and wisdom.
You fought the mountains miraculously,
Life, life, life and you won.
    —Marcelle T. George

Living In A Fantasy

When I look at you I often wonder what
life would be like if my fantasy could
come true.
When I hear her soft voice caressing my
mind I wonder is there any way is there
anyway I could ever make her mine.
When I think of her ever so sweet touch
in my heart I know what is right.
I must let this fantasy stay a fantasy
for that is the only way my love will
last through the night.
    —Dylan Souza

Lake Of Dreams

If you look into the lake of dreams, shining like the eternal
Light cast from the stars shining bright.
You will find the image of the everlasting love I have for you.

In the night you look into the sky and see the moon laughing at you,
For only she knows where your love lies for me. Search your heart,
Search your soul. In the deepest depths you will find me there.

Only in the lake of dreams can you see us together, dancing
in the eternal blue depths of the deepest sea.

If you look into the lake of dreams, shining like angel's smiles,
You will see our fates, eternities away, cross

I will always love you and remember you until times and times
Are done, we are forever one. In dreams dancing, singing, laughing
At the moon, because not even she can take our dreams away.
    —Lacy Scarborough

A Gold Ring

In the air is a Victorian Carousel piece,
Light, lovely music that plays to my heart
That transports me to my childhood,
To a day at Coney Island, on a carousel

On a white horse, a charger, a noble steed, in a child's mind.
A warm summer's day in a child's life, salt air, bright sun,
Laughter, hot sand, and music, always music, Waltz music,
Rump bah bah, Rump bah bah, elegant, joyous music,
Music for the child's heart, for a child on a white charger,

With a carefree, athletic reach for a gold ring
Each time around, round and round, rump bah bah,
Laughing and reaching safe and innocent right from his heart
For a Ring of gold.

One outstretched arm, leaning way over the side of the horse,
The rhythm of the music and the leap of the charger, up and down
to the beat of the Waltz music, the beat of the Carousel Music.
Delighting in the music and the reach and the overflowing heart.

Now a wedding day approaches. And the child is a man.
And the Ring is still gold.
    —John R. Scotti Jr.

My Beloved Son

I held him in my arms
looked down upon a face so sweet and fair
and I thanked God for a little bit of heaven
that was delivered there.
I watched him grow to manhood
a boy of which any mother would be proud;
always cheerful and happy, but never loud.
Then one morning God picked a flower
for his bouquet; one that was sweet and fair.
Oh that awful emptiness left here to bear,
trusting God some day we will meet again up there.
    —Nina Hazel Backstein

Ask The Moon

I look at the moon and miss my homeland
Like a silver sickle shines the moon
  -I am homesick
  -You are homesick
  -He is homesick

I lift up my head and look at the new moon.
I drop my head and miss my old home.
The silver sickle hanging-
How homesick I am!

Like a jade plate glows the round moon.
  -At the New Year, I dream of my home.
  -At mid-August, I dream of my home.
  -Each fifteenth of the month, I dream of my home.

How perfect the sky's round moon!
Imperfect the earth's half moon.
How much homesickness the jade moon holds!
    —Hang Ching Yip

Hurts

A son can hurt you
like no one else can,
little hurts when he's little,
big hurts when he's a man.

To show you that I loved you,
at bed time when you were little,
stories were read and songs were sung.
Do I deserve what you're doing to me today,
after giving you my all when you were young?

Did I love too hard and give too much,
now that it's all said and done?
I can't change your feelings toward me
but I want you to know
Regardless, I love you my son.
    —Blanche French

Untitled

Thoughts of a pretty face in black lace clouded my mind
like strong elixirs, drugs and wine.

"Some-Thing" about you gave me a natural high, an intense
rush, that made me seek the sky.

Your smile inspired me to write and your openness I took
for an invite.

The door to your heart, at the moment, closed. It's
doing time for unknown woe's

I never considered you frivolous at heart, but in the
way's of the world I am none too smart.

For a while, I'll wonder why you smiled and why I feel
you played my mind.

Relax I am not insane, just a man in some kinda pain
that's difficult to explain.

But if you only knew, if you could see the view, you'd
know that in my heart I made room for you.
    —Jose Marc Rios

Fire

Bitter rage courses through my veins,
like the fire of the amber dragon's blood that
I seldom drink to give my limbs an extra push
when endured in battle. The flames of hatred
burn deep behind my eye's as I envision my blade
thrusting up between my enemy's ribs puncturing
the heart. But now I am faced by an enemy I
never would have expected. "My Twin!" Now it is
her who I see dying at the end of my unmerciful
blade. It is her who ignited the fires in my blood,
and the flames behind my eyes. As I realize that
it was her who I wished to be and take her place
at my father's side. And all it takes is one blade
easily slipping into flesh. But behind all her power I
saw her weakness, she lacked compassion. The
one thing I have, the one thing I would loose if
I succeeded in killing her. Then knowing who I
really was, the fires died and I walked away the winner.
    —Crystal LeeAnn Brooks

Thank You

I look back to my old people (pause), my great ancestors. I
like to say thank you, because it took courage to go through
what you did. It took courage for you to be bound in chains
like animals. It took courage for you to be beat, just
because you wanted to educate yourself to a higher level.
It took courage for mothers to watch their children sold off
from them. It took courage for fathers to watch their wives
and daughters raped. And I know sometimes in life you wanted
to give up. But you looked to the one and only God and he
restored your strength, your dignity, your pride and your
respect. Without there being a you...there would not have been
a me. Now, I like to say thank you to Dr. Martin Luther King,
Jr., one man who stood and risked his life to improve the way
for the African Americans. He taught against hatred. It is
time again for Americans to rise up as a nation and to
surrender to love, to wipe out these three words:
prejudice, violence and ignorance. Last but not least, I want
to thank my parents for stressing Salvation first and Education
second. My ancestors left me the last step of the ladder to
climb. When I reach my goals in life; I won't forget who I am.
    —Darlene Sutton

Tornado Alley

My home's in Alabama In the Tennessee valley, Right in
line with Tornado Alley. We'd like you to come visit us and
come without any fear, because we have a storm pit that's
dug very near. We laid good block and poured a good floor:
Put a vent in the top and one in the door. The steps ain't
much-don't let that bother you, 'cause if you see a twister,
you'll slip right through. Now take Miss Annie-she's big
and she's stout, but when you hear it thunder, you can't
keep her out. Come bring your wife and children, but keep the
little brats quiet, because we may be in that hole 'til way
past midnight. Lord gave me words to write this poem, so it
might help protect someone from a storm. It used to never
bother me, what happened this valley; but now I set on my
front porch and watch, down Tornado Alley. We now have lights
and water, we're almost up-to-date. Guess that's all that
we can do, until we get our tax rebate.
    —Benton Browning

Today's Care

Hospitals and nursing homes
Lingering illness and long term care
Days, weeks, months, years
Fill the heart with unquestionable fears.

Medicare and co-insurance supplied
Bank accounts closed
Savings depleted
Insurances shriveled and died
CD's like a breath from heaven
All used to pay the bill
No stocks or bonds
Social Security is nil
Pension usurped and applied
Homestead swallowed - out of sight.

Bent, broken, and forever spent
There is nothing left to heir
For Public Aid is TODAY'S CARE.

    —Julia Irene Hardy

Tenebrae

As I sit gazing at the cross, draped with the purple veil, I
listen to the story again, I feel the agony, the pain, and
sorrow that because of me, Christ suffered death upon a tree.
I feel the crown of thorns they placed upon his head. I hear
the angry cries of crucify him, crucify him, how could they
want him dead? I feel the lashing of the whip, the searing
pain of scourge, the shame of their scorn. The weight of his
cross lays heavy on my back, the nails as they are driven
through his flesh, pierce mine. I know the ache he felt of
being forsaken, of being denied by a trusted friend. I wonder
at his compassion, when he asked forgiveness for those who took
his life. I then begin to realize, Tenebrae has opened up my
eyes. How could I know joy on Easter day, unless first I
walked the Calvary way? So, to this thought, I will hold fast,
when this dark, dreadful night is past, as a dead bulb bursts
forth in bloom, Christ will come forth from the tomb. And we
will know of life reborn, on a bright and glorious Easter morn.

    —Lavonne Long

Space

  Infinite blackness beyond all measure.
Lit only by lonely stars in their slow spiral.
  A vacuum filled with dust, rock, and ice.
    Desired by so many.
      Denied to all but a few.
  A dangerous, unforgiving void,
where only the foolish and adventuresome dare to go.
  Harsh and beautiful it invokes a love,
    a passion,
an uncontrollable desire to live in the void,
    the vacuum,
    the blackness.
    My Desire.

    —David M. Allen

Yesterday

"Yesterday I wandered back down
  memory lane;
I met him there — we shared our
  times of joy and pain.
He loved me then — I love him
  still — and though he's gone
  beyond my reach, it want be
  long until — I'll meet him — in
  that other land - where Jesus walks
  and we'll walk hand in hand — with him."

    —Bette B. Taylor

All Mixed Up

How silly it would be if:

Fish had feathers and birds has scales
Little kittens had puppy dog tails
And pups would meow instead of bark
And owls would sleep when it got dark
And bees, well they didn't make honey
And days were all gray and never sunny
How about an elephant with a giraffe like neck
Or a chicken with lips how would it peck?
Oh I could go on and on how about a
snake skin covering a swan?
Or worms that walked on flamingo pink legs and
Cows laid baby calves in big white eggs
Or people had nest in the top of the tree
Oh my, how really silly that would be.

    —Martha Reedy

Life Is Brief

The flowers were so beautiful this year, but they did not last
long. So remindful of life, we are here today and tomorrow we
are gone. Millions of folks observed the sunshine yesterday,
and left this old world with a sigh. Yet I know that my
journey on earth is far along, and tomorrow so will I. Why was
I left here today, while so many were take yesterday that did
believe? Could it be that God has given me another day for
something to achieve? Many may gather gold, silver and food
for tomorrow it does seem. Yet we know that we will carry no
more out of this world than out of a dream. If wealth becomes
your baggage on this road through life's trials. You will be
weighed down like a mule with gold, after many miles. What
dying man would not exchange all his gold for another breath.
Lord help me to use this day as if it is all I have left.
Today I will love the wife of my youth, and the children God
has given me. For tomorrow they will be gone, and so will I,
don't you see. And if God should see fit to give me another
day of life, I'll thank Him for His grace. I will ever ask for
guidance and strive to serve Him in the right place.

    —Carroll Hoefer

The Wind

I sit here in the warm sweet breeze,
Looking down a hill covered with trees.

The sunshine dances on the forest floor and
The wind whispers through the leaves,
The sound is a musical score.

A concert of nature, sweet and pure.
The rustle of oak leaves, the whisper of cedar,
The wind is playing follow the leader.
It rushes through fast, then slow.
Just when you think it has ceased,
Again it begins to blow.
It sings its song so gentle and sweet,
It makes this beautiful day complete.

    —Dianne White

Powered By Greed

America the beautiful
Powered by greed.
Lustful spending; the demon's seed.
Great towers reaching upward, to the sky
All wanting more, a bigger piece of the pie.
  Dig down deep in the earth,
reach in and pull out its soul.
All for power, and the lusting for gold.
Cut down the trees foul the air and the streams
Kill all of God's creatures, for riches and dreams.

    —Arthur K. Barnes II

Yellow Ribbons

Living in a worry free time, taking chances without a care
Looking for adventure, never passing up a dare
Graduation was upon us, then an endless summer of fun
We had no idea of the final test that was to come

Then came the news early on a Sunday morn
A son, brother, and friend from this world had been torn
In a state of shock we went to the service
Wondering if his death had some secret purpose

He touched our lives in so many ways
A lifetime of memories in seventeen years, eleven months and
twenty-eight days
We flew our yellow ribbons in loving memory
Only wishing we had sooner realized our own mortality

Our lives have changed because of his leaving
We now know that each encounter could be our last meeting
The pain of our loss lessens with each passing year
But the memories of laughter and friendship just grow
stronger
    and more dear

            —*Brenda J. Pierce Almquist*

Closing The Door

Slowly I removed my coat from the rack and stood quietly,
Looking — just looking, for one last time.
After twenty years of living in my delegated corner,
Freedom, so often longed for, would very soon be mine.

The steady hum of the typewriter had been silenced.
I will miss you, dear old trusty friend. You were always
waiting, ready to be of service, especially on those hectic days
I thought would never end. Tall metal sentinels coldly standing
at attention, one last glance took in the row of office files,
Erect and proud, unaware they were adorned with dust caps,
I closed an open drawer and couldn't help but smile.

A pencil fell onto the floor and rolled itself beneath my desk.
Then I noticed something that had been on top for many years,
A white mark left by my favorite, but leaky coffee cup.
Strange that such a trivial sight should cause my eyes to tear.

Tomorrow, a new day, another secretary, my name soon to be
forgotten. I had to leave — a farewell lunch was waiting,
then nothing more. I stood for a silent moment and felt the
beckoning call of Freedom, with mixed emotions,
I left my office home and softly closed the door.

            —*Ellen Loyer*

The Silent Tree

In the house I sat confined,
Looking out the window at a tree I once climbed.
I sat there dazed and stared at the tree
And the tree stared back to me!
I sat there and stared at the way it moved
This way and that of and I approved.
I sat there and stared in wonder at the tree,
But it just stood there looking glorious and free.
Free, free, free, how much those words meant to me.
I suddenly felt that I wanted to be alone,
I wanted to get out and away from my home!
I ran outside and stood by the tree's side
Tell me you're free how come and why I cried!
But the tree said nothing, nothing to me,
It just stood there a silent tree.

            —*Iris Fravel*

Let Me Live On The Desert

Let me live on the desert, where the cactus
    Looks to heaven as though in prayer,
Let me walk among the giant saguaros
    That stand as silent sentinels there.

Let me live where mountains rise like smoke
    From the quiet and peaceful desert floor,
Where flowers cover the ground like clouds
    That hang across the tallest mountain door.

Here I'd finally rest, away from crowds
    That buzz like swarms of angry bees,
And I'd dream my dreams while coyotes
    Move like shadows among the Joshua trees.

Here I'd live a life as quiet and mysterious
    As the tallest mountain cloaked in mist,
And I'd momentarily forget the world at war
    And enjoy the desert that I have missed.

        —*Guy V. Ryan*

Prelude To Lost Cove

Smooth ribbons of water
    loop twice downward
    then funnel underneath
    the wave-rocked pool.

Cliff walls push back the sound,
    doubling and redoubling
    the thunder of crashing water
    reverberating my soul.

Two half rainbows carved by the morning sun
    rise in the mist filled air
    above the rock bound pool.

        Imagination must complete the arc.

Forward in space - backward in time,
    The waves of mist
    Billow down Linville River
    to Lost Cove.

        I hear the prelude of tomorrow

            —*Kathy H. Howell*

She Waits For Him There

A memory and a tear, contentment and fear:
Love, and hate, destiny and fate:
When does it end, where does it start?
So close together, yet so far apart:
Knowing the reasons, yet questioning why,
Laughing one minute, and the next she will cry:
So many faces, so little friends,
So many smiles, she always pretends:
A faded picture, sometimes clear,
She pushed him away, he held her near:
Now he's given up, she's holding on,
She becomes weak, he becomes strong:
A hopeless dream, an endless prayer,
He walks away,
She waits for him there...

            —*Leanne Lamb*

Daughter

I behold the precious gift God gave to me and ache with
    love deep and pure.

I hear the hurt in her voice as she tells me her troubles and
    suffer in her pain.

I look upon her angelic face and dread the loss of innocence.

I see the clear vision in her green eyes and scorn the event
    that will cloud it.

I watch the exuberant energy of a child's play and regret when
    that energy might be misspent.

I anticipate the trusting love that someone will see in her
    steady gaze and despise him for the betrayal that might
    forever make her doubt.

I watch her guileless approach to life and long to help her
    circumvent disappointment by imparting the wisdom of my
    years.

Yet, I fear the prematurity of too much knowledge.

I know she must, as did I, grow, unfold, grow some more.

Yet, I long to simplify and orchestrate the experiences that
    will mold this winsome creature into a woman.

   —Kathy Day

Defining Love's Purpose

Love is our refuge - Whatever the strife
Love is the truth - springing to life
With love in our hearts for giving and caring
Then love is renewed because of the sharing
Where-ever one goes this blessing is there
Above and beneath us - its touch everywhere
We can rest quite secure in our innermost thought
Knowing with love, doubt and fear stand for naught
With such facts in mind into consciousness stole
That to love all mankind is the ultimate goal!!

   —Constance M. Johnson

Love Is A Teammate

A teammate is someone with whom you can depend on to endure
life's atrocities as well as share life's whimsical delights.

Someone who supports you in pursuing a dream and trusts you
to shut down the financial drain, if it fails to evolve.

Someone you can go to when you are hurting and feel safe, not
like a victim.

Someone who does not lecture when they can see your own
conscious is beating you with guilt.

Someone who is equally determined to work hard.

Someone with whom you can accept each other's weaknesses and
faults.

Someone who leaves, but never goes away.

Someone with whom you can identify, plan a family, build a
future, and share a history.

A bud of physical attraction, grows into a relationship of
commitment, and blossoms into a vast past of cherished memories

An individual once said, "Love is a frame of mind." I believe
it's a lifestyle.

Not all marriages are made up of teammates, I'm glad ours is.

   —Cindy Niles

Untitled

   Love is the answer.
   Love knows what to do.
The known and the unknown unite, to move
   In perfect balance in the hands of love.
   Love is the answer.
   Love knows what to do.
Love is present.
   Love sees what cannot be seen.
   Love listens and hears.
   Love gives without question.
Love acts.
Love waits.
Love belongs.
Love stays.
   Love is trust.
   Love is song.
   Love is laughter.
   Love is easy.
      —Leslie Steen

Can I Go Back?

Can I go back to someone who...
Loving me so, knows nothing of you?

Can I go on and dream of the past
Only as joy, too perfect to last?

If, when I weep in the dark of the night,
You hold my hand...show me the light

Give me the courage to live and to bear...
Then come what may, I shall not care

And I can go back, but not to stay.
I'm coming to you...somewhere..someday.

   —Edith M. Ennis

Winter Wonderland

The snow that fell last night
Made everything so very white!
It made of my yard a wonderland
As if every change were truly planned.

Snow plastered against every tree
Was, to this beholder, good to see.
It was atop each branch and limb
Even on those that were very thin.

Icicles along the roof hung straight.
They became bigger as it got late.
At the house across the street
The evergreens with snow were quite replete.

Snow covered the last leaves of Fall.
It left every evergreen so tall
Weighted down with beautiful snow.
It was then a strong wind began to blow.

My yard is such a pretty sight
As I look out one window toward the night.
God has shown me the beauty snow can give
And, through it, I can more abundantly live.

   —Lorraine Umbdenstock

Question Of Birds

The birds are gathering up in the sky;
Making beautiful designs as they all fly.
Now a dark cloud, swirling with flare,
And then disappearing like smoke in the air.
All of one mind, they turn and flow;
Flying in formation, sweeping so low.
Again disappearing as directions they turn;
Together they flit, and fly as they learn.
Who is their leader, what keeps them together?
All of one mind, the birds of one feather?
How do they know with so big a group
Which way to go when they make that last loop?
And then take off; I would like to know why
How birds fly their formation up in the sky.

—*June Stalder*

The Whispering Tree

To feel the soft kiss of a breeze.
To give rest to humming bees.
To drink up the new fallen rain.
To feel the warmth of day again.
To give home to birds of song.
To feel proud when looked upon.
To hear the voices of dreamers and lovers.
To keep their secrets, I'll tell no others.
To sway at night when crickets sing.
To shed cool shade to a child's swing.
Oh to be able to give breath to a single cry.
To wish you Hello.
To wish you goodbye.
Oh if only for a single sigh.
But whispers of silence I must hold.
For they are my treasures
Whispers are my gold!

—*John Ritz Powell*

Awakening Of Peace

The sunlight filters through the trees
Making tiny shadows among the leaves
The dew kissed grass sparkles with a shine
That makes the morning seem sublime.

As the birds begin to chirp and sing
My old alarm clock begins to ring
I awake and rise with a hopeful sense
That the world today will be less tense.

As I prepare to go to work
I flip the radio dial on a quirk
They finish playing a sad love song
Then the news reporter tells all that's wrong.

Pollution, floods and acid raid
The world is full of hurt and pain
Our world leaders can't agree
The threat of war now reality.

I hope in the future, we can grow to love
And trust more in the one above
Tis the only way for man to survive
So that generations to come can thrive.

—*Billie McHenry*

In Loving Memory

*(Dedicated to baby boy Tully, Wayla
Marie Tully and Andrew Joseph Joyce.)*

Though I only carried you a little while
You were still a part of me
And I know we'll be together someday
And your little face, I'll one day see.

You will always be in my heart, Little One
And I will always love you so.
But you are happy in Heaven now
Though the reasons why, I do not know.

Although I'll never raise you
Or nurse you at my breast
I know you'll never suffer
And you'll always be at rest.

You're now a flower in God's garden
You're now living among His grace
And I look forward to the day
That I again will see your face.

I know I'll know you, Little One
Of me, you were once a part
Someday I may have another child
But you will live on in my heart.

—*Lisa Coulombe*

Seeing Isn't Believing

For art thou's child's eyes are masked —
masked by a so called lighted dimension.
it went off —
like a switch.
so sudden —
wondrous of why it was.
All that was question,
was now all answered.
For all it was
was a rare "flashlight,"
it strikes, but one in a thousand.
But it strikes.
Even experts are confused.
But the one in a thousand child knows
that it's such a simple thing.

—*Emily Willcox*

Just Where Did The Gods Really Go

Just where did the Gods really go
Maybe "Mercury" would know
And travel to Athens
To proclaim - we still care what happens
To reach the heights of "Mount Olympus"
And search for the goddess of love "Venus"
To spread the word of joy
To "Zeus" not to destroy
The mortals who no longer believe
In greek mythology
To bond a renewal with the Fates
Who determine human destiny
To awaken from a sleep that states
They're as real as real can be
Mighty in words and deeds
The will once again plant their seeds
To all the lands near and far
Touching us no matter where we are
So each of us would really know
Just where did the gods really go

—*Francis A. Targowski*

Our Dog Penny

We were a happy bunch when you came into our life
Me my three kids and my wonderful wife

You ran, you pranced, you jumped with ease
There is no doubt you wanted to please

One time you blundered, you lost your way
The good ranger found you, saving the day

You found a new toy, it really stunk
We forgot to tell you, don't play with a skunk

The kids boarded the bus, and went to school to learn
You waited and worried, would they ever return?

They dressed you in costumes, I'll never forget
You seemed to enjoy it, you never did fret

You loved to chase squirrels with youthful glee
As time made you slower, you just let them be

Penny sit! Penny lay! Penny speak! Penny stay!
You loved to perform in a wonderful way

You slowed to a walk, you could hardly run
You filled us with pleasure you were still fun

You are gone now, the Lord knows what is best
We hope you are enjoying a very peaceful rest

—*Ardie Zimmer*

Missing You

I missed you today, but I don't know why because you never left me...not my spirit, not my soul. I fought with myself to resist calling to hear the words flow from your lips that would reassure me that you were just a touch away.

I missed you today when I was napping in my bed, but I don't know why because it was still warm from when we last made love.

I missed you today since it was your birthday, but I don't know why because you have just become a year wiser for the purpose of teaching me more about love...life...us.

I missed you today, but I don't know why because you never left me...not my spirit, not my soul, not my heart. I'll never expect to miss you because you've promised to always love me and never leave me...

—*E. Taleshea Holland*

The Plight Of The Spotted Owl

The spotted owl sat in a tree and laughed and hooted. "Lucky me! These little men in such a tizzy who run around, (they make me dizzy), trying to learn about my bed and how they can protect my head, supposed they've even worried so and wondered where my droppings go. I'm surprised they've not built houses for us to live in with our spouses, with carpets fine and la vatories and radios to tell us stories. So that we won't get distressed and so we won't be too depressed. Actually it seems absurd, in fact, the silliest thing I've heard. To try so hard to protect a bird. When trouble strikes I think that we could fly off to another tree." The wise old owl then cocked his head and thought just what those "big shots" said. "They just cannot foresee tomorrow the trouble they are soon to borrow: More homeless people everywhere, no jobs for them, no clothes to wear, children with no food to eat, crying homeless on the street, more crime and stealing from the "Riches", from those who should be digging ditches, instead of only on the prowl studying the habits of the owl". But as the old owl poem said, in Mother Goose you may have read, "the wise old owl sat in an oak, the more he saw, the less he spoke.

—*M. Daniels*

"Shadow"

The way he looked... the way he smelled... is now just a memory...
He's in the back of your mind... waiting to be thought of...
He was like a book waiting to be read...
He comes when darkness falls and dances away like a dream...
He has feelings like you and me... but they don't shine through him.
Instead, they come like daydreams waiting to happen...
And fade away in the morning light...
Shadow's can come and go as they please...
If you shine a light on it... it fades away...
If you keep it in the darkness... it stays...
The moment you care for it... it slips away...
Everything's gone... all that is left... is a shadow...

—*Jessie T. Trovato*

call me from hollywood

i'm applying my makeup first thing in the morning
mentally reviewing the acts of the day
i practice my lines and dress for the part
then head out to face what the critics will say
oh, i'm so hopeful that if i'm good they might call me from hollywood
in all situations i don't have the script so i naturally improvise
some take no notice, while others make faces
and there is occasional applause as my prize
i'm so optimistic if i knew the whole story
i'd make it if only they would — call me from hollywood

in my spare time i'm dreaming of four stars and critical acclaim
i'm so relieved today's rehearsal ended
and i made it through the scene just the same
i'm still alive and my knees aren't shaking
so i'm ready if they should — call me from hollywood

i write out acceptance speeches
and my scrapbook is ready — my memoirs in mind
i practice my autograph on magazine photos
i know i'll be their "find"
oh, life is so wonderful just knowing they could
call me from hollywood.

—*JoAnn Mick*

I Stand Alone

I stand alone.
Midst the hue and cry
of sheep who follow blindly,
I stand alone.
You didn't dare to question or to wonder why,
as I have done.
It would have been so easy, so 'sensible' to acquiesce,
to merge into the anonymity of the herd. Following. Cloned.
I could have given up my own integrity
to become a part of the masses,
where criticism wouldn't make a devastatingly direct hit.
But, as some great one once said,
'To thine own self be true...'
I am. I have been.
I find no fault with what I have done.
Actually, I've spoken for many of you,
you of the clone community,
you, who didn't have the courage to speak aloud.
And now, true to myself still - and to you,
I stand alone.

—*Dorothy B. North*

All Moms Nightmare

The days and nights have come and gone.
Mom I'm sixteen years old.
I'm grown. If only you'd listened to
what you'd been told, maybe you'd take another road.
I'll never forget those beautiful eyes looking at
me saying good bye Mom I'm leaving home
Leave me alone, I'm sixteen years old I'm to old for
you to hold, why couldn't you listen from right and
wrong? It's hard for me to grasp what I've been told
through all the moans and groans.
As you lay there so hard and cold
all I can think of is what you'd say,
Mom I'm grown I'm old enough to be on my own.
Now you're with God sitting with him on his throne.

   —*Carolyn Dooley*

Inseparable Pair

As children we played without a care;
Mom used to call us the inseparable pair.

We fussed and we fought, as all siblings do;
Soon friends again, starting anew.

As time passed and we both grew;
Adults with separate lives, look what we've been through.

Our lives have not been easy, there's been thick and thin;
Your friendship is precious, but best of all we're kin.

I feel many emotions, some anger and rage;
As this disease that has touched you at such a young age.

A sickness that has attacked many, both bad and good;
Giving judgement of death, whenever it could.

To others with A.I.D.S., your such an inspiration;
Giving encouragement and hope, in place of desperation.

I love your laugh, your smile and eyes;
In me you have woven unbreakable ties.

No matter how long, God has in store;
I'll cherish every moment, and long for more.

There is one thing that nothing can sever;
I love you dear brother, I'll love you forever.

   —*Lori A. Goldensoph*

From Death to Life

Sunshine at daybreak
Moonlight at night.
Peace is in sight.
It glistens like the edge
of a knife.
It's sharp but mellow.
It's loud but soft.
It will take your spirits to
A new dimension.
Colors will mesh together like
Unseen camouflage.
Inanimate objects will become alive
You can move without touching
the ground.
Your physical boundaries are gone.
You can fly on the wings of
a prayer.
Fly on proud bird, you're free at last...

   —*Lee Butt*

"A Gift From Heaven"

More than I could ever dream of.
More than words could ever tell,
God sent you, such a wonderful gift
from heaven above.
A virtue of God's love.

   Through the years you've been
my friend, my teacher, my sister,
my brother, both Father and Mother.

   Sometimes that old roller coaster of life,
through the ups and downs.
At times wrong seem to be right,
Our heart to heart talks seem
to bring me back into the light.
   One day we'll all be together,
for God has something better,
Until we all go home to heaven.
   I'll thank God for you,
      "My gift from heaven."
         —*Lee Evans*

It's So Hard Not To Cry

It's lonely in these golden years,
Most joys have passed on by,
There's little but a ticking clock,
It's so hard not to cry.

The panic every morning,
Will my legs hold up today?
Will I meet each deadline just in time,
Or pride be peeled away?

Each hard-won simple effort
Seems to ever go awry,
Left dazed and gasping for each breath,
It's so hard not to cry.

Oh, to find another's hand in mine,
To hear another's voice,
To know my day's fulfillment will
Depend upon my choice .

Can I feign another smile or two
A guffaw if hard I try?
Don't know if I'll be able, when
It's so hard not to cry.

   —*Evelyn G. Mortensen*

Our Lade Of Guadalupe

Dear Virgin of the roses,
mother of us all,
gather us 'neath your trellis,
where your love like roses petals fall.

Let the sweet perfume of your blossoms
all of our senses fill,
as you did for Juan Diego,
high on Tepeyak Hill.

When we weep in bitter frustration
let our tears water the sod
that nourishes such royal beauty,
O magnificent Mother of God.

Mary, please lead us to Jesus
and when we feel we can carry no more
prick us gently with the thorns of your roses
to remind us of the crown that He wore.

And when our journey is over
please let our reward be sweet
Mother may we be the roses
that you spread at Jesus' feet.

   —*Irma Delacnoix*

Carousel

Horsey backs of carousels, ups and downs of life,
Motioning from high to low, from somber waves to strife,
Carnival music gaieties sets the mind at ease,
Again up at the peak of life with arms of joy to seize.

Then life's sustaining matters, laughing fools leave unattended
Anxieties slowly building, broken bubbles can't be mended.
Confronted with complexity, afflictions of life's quest,
No longer empty laughter blinding fools to their distress.

Master Understanding, riding with the skill to win,
Horsey at his lowest point he must go up again!

—*Karen M. Mackie*

A Horrible Sight Is A Shadow's Delight

The sly serpentine shadows of the night
Move hauntingly in and out of the light.
They possess no strength and obtain no might;
But when seen; oh, what a horrible sight!

They slowly slyly slide along the ground.
At every turn you take, they can be found.
One is seen; then a yelp and howl of hound.

The shapeless shadow shows its dark being.
The lines and curves help to give it meaning.
If it proceeds to move; I'll be fleeing!

The ghostly graceful gliding in the night
Possesses much more beauty than if in light.
More dark than day, will it produce a sight;
It can make a man turn a ghostly white!

—*Christopher Volosy*

Heart Break

I'm trying to be strong, to not show just how
much this experience is affecting me.
Try not to show how much my heart is hurting,
struggling for breath against the strangle hold it has on the
memories.
I can't believe you're gone.
I never even got the chance to tell you good bye, so long, or
tell you how I feel.
Now I have a mind full of regrets.
Things I should have done, should have said.
I keep remembering the times we had.
The parties, the laughter,
Even the teasing arguments over whose ice-hockey team was
better.
There could have so many more events and conversations
to add to our memories.
There will be no more new memories of you,
only the yesterdays, now, only memories for today.

—*Heather Hart*

Untitled

Why she asked with a sudden cry
must you go with no good-bye
Dressed in black ready to go
why he left her, she did not know
She felt his touch, his kiss, his cry
why he left, no one knew why
The prayers, the tissues, the heat of the day
she felt like a stone, nothing to say
His parents were there, shattered and torn
as they stared at the grave of their very first born
Time passes you up, like an arrow in a bow
take life to it's fullest and just say no.

—*Heather Barish*

"Going Back To Texas"

It was a cool and early morning, when I went out for a ride,
My Appy was a trotting along, I had my six gun on my side;
I don't know what got into my head, but I never turned around,
I just saw those big Ol'Mountains ahead, and lots of open ground.

Now I strayed from kansas city, went on up to the yellow-stone,
Saw a beautiful valley, and decided to make it my ol'Home;
There were beaver in a beaver pond, with the water crystal clear,
And Big ol'Griz-zly bears, and lots of white tailed deer.

Then one night in my valley, I heard an Eagle cheer,
There's a pretty girl in Texas, all lonely and crying tears;
He said to me "Go get that girl," way down in San Antone,
And bring her back here with you son, and make this place your home.

Well I'm going back to Texas, to make everything al-right,
And I'll be seeing you in the morning, and I'll see you in the night;
I'm going back to get that girl, and bring her to my home,
up here where the nights are long, and the cool winds forever blow.

—*Michael S. West*

To My Baby Sister:

November 7th was the day,
my baby sister passed away.

She had little time to look around,
before she was heaven bound.

I still don't know why she had to go,
that little sister of mine.

If only I was there for her,
things would have worked out fine.

When mom came home and said, "She's gone,"
I had no hopes of seeing dawn.

But I said that I'd wait for my baby dear,
And hope that someday she'd be here.

I think I found her in my heart,
now I know we'll never part.

I wish I could have her back with me,
because there is so much she didn't see.

All I have instead of memories, it seems,
is all those times we had in my dreams.

Baby sister is you can see this too,
Please remember: I LOVE YOU!

—*Erica Therrien*

Mom And Dad

Some songs talk about love and beauty, some poems, books, and
movies too,
But none can compare to the love and beauty inside of both of you.

From the minute I get up, until the day is done,
You make me happy and treat me like a special someone.

Whether I'm fine and running about or even stuck in bed,
You stop what you're doing to make sure I'm comfortable, rested
and fed.

Since the day I was born you've taught me good values, what is
wrong and what is night,
That I should never be mean to others, never to start a fight.

You taught me to be grateful for all the good that's come my way,
Never to be selfish, and to enjoy each and every day.

You are always there for me and lead me towards success,
You push me towards the good in life and offer me the best.

Now to you I'll quote a line from a song in case I didn't mention,
"You are the meaning of my life you're my inspiration."

—*Geordana Margolies*

Young and Carefree

When life was new and days so sweet. My feet would skip through
leaves like wings. Through snowy ground and moonlit paths. The
cry of Earth it beckoned me. Fields of clover, ponds so deep.

On grassy hills I'd lie my head. The clouds of white and skies
of blue. They were my teacher, He my God. Never was I closer
than, when He and I would speak of life. Of love and truth and
good and bad of ups and downs and things so sad.

I'm glad I listened in those days, it helped me make it through
my life. In later years, life wants much more. There's Family
work and endless chores. Music, art and love and time goes by.
As jobs, careers all fall in place.

And now as looking back on life. I know He had it all
arranged. The time to listen and to learn. The way to take the good and bad.

Our life reflects on what we are. Examples shown and choices made.

I'm glad I listened when He called. When I was young and so
carefree I've felt each day He guided me. Thank you for those
lessons God. As through this life I bravely trod.

—*Flo Lensky*

...Was Taken Again

-But now with age in its autumn years,
my eyes serve to keep with foot apace
and my heart the same clear rhythm hears
this soul of mine weeps longing tears
that soon will I a new road face;

For this very one upon which traveled long,
seems 'twere only yesterday when all alone
from within so deep came a made-up song
that is now whistled by others without wrong
and I've no right to claim it as my own;

Since they too are as I once also was
standing afront where two roads diverged
choosing this the same only just because,
a search for truth is a heart that greater loves
all the more so am I now urged:

Towards there that road where before me lays
its fallen leaves still with virgin dew
whispering those footprints where sunlight plays,
just beyond the bend of these youthful days -
knowing well it will make all the difference too.

—*Herb Buckland*

A Child's Eye

I watch through my child's eye the things I had long since
lost sight,
Monsters in the closet at night,
Raindrops falling gently, reaching as they touch down,
A smooth rock on the ground
Snow that comes at last,
Only knowing today, no future-no past,
A mother's gentle hand, a father's kind word,
By his own shadow is he quickly allured,
The words that are spoken,
The chimneys when smoking,
The color, the shape of the birds as they fly,
Things forgotten now seen through a child's eye —
As he looks at me to smile so wide — I can only
hope and wonder the treasures he holds inside.

—*Barbara J. Johnson*

Love Is

Love is when you care for another.
Love is you share things with each other.
Love is spending time together.
Love is friendship that lasts forever.
Love is losing or giving one's heart.
Love is not being hurt.
Love is being hugged.
Love is being kissed.
Love is being faithful to another.
Love is being truthful to each other.
Love is what makes the world go around!

—*Jennifer Lynn Koniarski*

Alone!

Although you've gone away from me.
Into the web of deaths dark mystery
In the long still night I think of you.
And all the things we used to do.
In my dreams you're with me still
Warm and close and very real,
You tease and I laugh aloud in glee
And then you laugh along with me.

You take your hand and turn my face
And hold me tight in a warm embrace
And as we stand there, can't you see
I feel you close, still loving me.

Then I awake and you're not here,
Oh! how can I go on my dear?
I cry aloud, "Why did you go?"
I want you here, I need you so!

You can't come back, so I must go,
For how many years I do not know
Through these wasted days and nights so blue.
So wait there dear and I'll come to you!

—*Ada Jones Bergren*

Petoskey Stone

Along the shores of Lake Michigan.
In the water
On the sand
This is where the stone is found.
Once a living organisms.
Now a symbol of our State.
Cold, hard and pitted,
fossilized and completed.
Our State stone,
the Petoskey Stone.

—*Lorraine M. Pond*

Where The Black-Eyed Susans Grow

I love how they sway
in the warm spring breeze.
They look like dancers
all in a line.
In a patch
of the garden bed,
WHERE THE BLACK-EYED SUSANS GROW.

They look like bananas
surrounding kiwi.
When I lie down,
you never see me.
Down where I plant
all of my seedlings...
WHERE THE BLACK-EYED SUSANS GROW.

—*William M. Daussin*

311

Easter Wishes

Easter Lilies,
Cradled in the wind,
Chilled and dampened,
Holiday wishes bring;

From nearing spring,
For folk and nature,
News of a joyous time,
And sad chills' departure.

From songbirds who,
On teeming branches preen,
Tales of fragrant blossoms,
Hiding in the green.

From the sun, whose warm eyes
Look down upon the meadows,
After winter dreams,
Waking all the shadows.

Happy Easter!
Choirs of angel sing,
Echoed by the trees
Dancing with the wind.

—*Barbara Janik*

Untitled

Pretty little socialite
Cries in bed most every night
He's walking through the flower bed
She never passes through his head

The feelings that he harbors here
Grow stronger for her every year
She gives up and walks away
Sick and tired of wanting to stay

The talks they have don't mean a thing
She lacks the strength to even sing
He'd like to think that they're alright
He can't hear her when they fight

If they could see where it went wrong
He'd love to have her tag along
Instead she's running very scared
Dreaming of the times they shared

—*Amber Raggie*

Only An Hour

Eyes of hurt,
Crimes of passion.
Needs of one,
Wants of another.
Both needing something
Neither knowing what.
Only knowing that,
When thrown together
   their fires burn.
Consuming those
   needs and wants.
If only, for an hour.

—*Jennifer L. Hager*

Birth

Breathless with ripping pain
crying with intensity
wishing for the coolness of rain
again comes the pain-in high density
then the sunshine appears in form,
a new mother is born.

—*Tammi Ross*

Dancing Choices

Memories lost and tossed away
cry out with tiny voices,
love can not come out and play
or follow the dancing choices.
With wings of sadness laughter flies
above the silence of the smiles,
razor sharp become the lies
as they nurse on angers files.
There needs to be an answer
to a question asked in pain,
truth has become a shadowed dancer
spinning madly and in vain.

—*Robert Daniel Terry*

"Seasons"

Birds chirping in the morning chill
Daffodils sitting on a windowsill
Lilac buds beginning to sprout
We herald spring in with a shout

Birds singing at the break of dawn
Fresh clean smell of a newly mowed lawn
Bright red roses so soft and sweet
Summer is as welcome as a treat

Birds retreating to a warmer clime
Plentiful harvests to last a long time
Trees in splendor oh so tall
Reds and golds announce the fall

Birds diminished to a few
In the dark green branches of a yew
The christmas star that shines so bright
In the cold clear silence of a winter night

—*Margaret A. Grela*

Autumnal Etude

Wakened dead
Dance hand in hand
With children still born.
Little yellow
Autumn falls
Stuck in matted hair
Adorn.
No
Longer red lips sing
In spiral tone
Parallel
To their steps.
Chants alive
Electric air
Feet in
Sky dance circling.
Wakened dead
Above the eye
Dissipate in
Moonlit wind.

—*J. S. Johnston*

Untitled

Can you see my crying
Do you feel my tears
Deep inside I'm dying
Strangled by my fears

Alone I walk a darkened path
Never forward, always back
Be myself or be no one
But who am I...

The lonely one

—*Shelly A. Gray*

Snowfall

The snow is falling gently,
Dancing down its stairs,
Twirling, leaping, rolling,
Down the steps of air.

There is a sound that they create;
It is a peaceful song.
To hear it, there's no special date;
It last the winter long.

Listen, do you hear it?
It's melody is young.
The earth they choose to sit,
Tired since they've sung.

But even on the ground and trees
They shine and call out cheer;
They cover up the old dead leaves
And welcome a new year.

Creatures of the air are these,
Meek and wild, both;
But rarely are they ever seen,
To us, they are just ghost.

—*Kristine Law*

Sunray

The sun it danced with
dappled hands.
From leaf, to bough,
to the mass below.
It lit the forest with a
soft green glow,
Slid the browns and grays
from sight.
It stayed all day to my
delight.
Until the mountain stole
colours hue.
It stole the light,
the sun from view.
I say good-bye,
please come again,
I will be waiting for you
my friend.

—*Julie Cliett*

Untitled

Gray sky,
Dark night,
Eerie, lazy lullaby.
Song to draw the
   children in.
The time of lies will begin
You will rule for him,
With an iron hand.
Until its his time to
   take command.
Then our world will be
   destroyed.
By all the little girls
   and boys.

—*Karla Hasund*

Gifts

Thank you, Father, for precious gifts-
Dear bejeweled bluebirds,
Memory-filled words,
Timeless ties of love,
Your blessings from above.

—*Patricia Michael*

Prayer

A well
Deep ...
Deep ...
Down

Breathing in and out
The fathomless nothingness
Which is everything

In the deafening silence
Darkness penetrating

Resting in the Mystery
The stillness consumes

Cradled in warmth ...

Pulsating presence ...

Home
—*Patricia Canty*

Acquisition Of A Lesser Law

It's nothing perfect that ye seek,
despondency so pallid, weak
To own a spirit
of reprise, encounter untimely
demise. Devouring moth
doth tear away
what thieves stored
for the coming day
Thy increase spent
for filth and lust,
thy gifts of gold
yield dismal dust.
The price of passion
paid in full,
ye desecrate
the white, clean wool
The gentle plea
ye turn away,
and look with pride
to judgment day.

—*Stewart W. Brewer*

Mom And Dad

Pain, guilt,
Disappointment,
Love so strong I cry:
Heart burns,
Unconditional love, yet boundaries/
prejudices exist
The force of emotions grips
my heart; seems unbearable,
Is this normal?
I won't survive without them-
don't really care if I do,
My foundation; my essence was
built from their values,
Shared accomplishments become
treasured memories
Special secrets, golden warmth
Waves wash away precious time.

—*Kathleen M. Murney*

Question...?

Am I here, Are you there
Do we exist anywhere
What is real, what is not
Is our life ours to plot
Is there a beginning, is there an end
How do we tell enemy from friend
Am I deaf, am I blind
Is life just a trick of the mind
Is it a cycle,is it a phase
Is it just an endless maze
How do we know, how can we tell
Does it all end in hell?

—*Tim Carmichael*

Time Passes By

Do you hear what I hear?
Do you take the time to listen.
Some of us take for granted
What others are missing.
Can you see what's all around
You, for it is a beautiful place.
Some cannot see, for it is
dark upon their face.
Can't you speak, but keep
silent the words you feel
are there.
Share them with your loved ones,
to let them know you care.
Precious are our lives, for
our time grows near.
Give your life to Jesus and
know no fear.

—*Melody Smith*

Love Is...

What is love?
Does it fly,
Like a dove?
Does it feel,
Or only "is"?
This is what I ask myself.

Love is cruel,
Love is kind,
Love is whatever you want it to be.
But, above all,
Love is...
To be cherished.

—*Katy Bishopric*

City Of Dreams

Oh my city of dreams
don't you know how it seems
and when I arrive
I know I will survive
in my city of dreams
now I feel so cold and alone
pretty soon I'll have a home
I don't live in the danger zone
cause all I really need is a home
God bless the world I live in
I don't do anymore sin
if I could love you
Forever baby I know I won't
be that crazy. Oh my city of
dreams don't you know how it seems
and when I arrive in my city of dreams.

—*Robert Berenter*

Untitled

A child so frail
does not know
What his future holds
As he grows older
he may know
He will go threw hardships,
and the maze of life
Just to see what the world is like
As he gets where, he wants to go
He feels compelled
for now he knows
He finds,
Threw sorrow, and pain
his accomplishment are better off made
Now he's a success
With the fear of old age running threw his
chest
And when he dies he will feel secure
Knowing he was the one who got
the job done

—*Kelly Adams*

Distant Friend

Feeling sad I shed a tear, why?
does some lonely spirit cry for me?
Does life's equation have equal
parts of joy and sorrow?
I think not, only what we hold
most dear merits tears.
Distant lonely friend I share
with you this lonely night a
sense of sadness.
We are so close because I shed
a tear for thee.

—*Montana S. Cook*

Untitled

Looking for wealth
Don't teach!
Looking for respect
Don't teach!
Looking for Recognition
Don't teach!
Looking to make a difference in
someone's life
Teach!

—*Mary Stephens*

Why

Why oh why must the children suffer so?
Don't you know what you're doing?
Don't you care? Does it show?
Look at the pure sweet innocence
of a young child.
Then abuse their body,
their mind, and their soul.
Let them trust you, admire you, and
love you so much.
Then hurt them unmercifully
with your words and your touch.
Hey, it's not your fault.
After all, it's all you've known.
God knows you're not to blame.
The children were wrong.
The children are grown now,
with children of their own.
Do they know what they're doing?
Do you care? Does it show?

—*Tamara Stroupe-Hartman*

Progressive Prose

Pursue Pushing aside
doubts, blindly I endure
yet, struggling engulfs me with hope
to win.

I wait, through life I last.
Time we share together
knows not the future-dreads the past.
I love.

Clocks chime steadfastly they
tick away, securely
stealing the inevitable,
our fate.

I fear the path to choose
rises much too sharply
causing cowardly me to change
my choice.

Sleep comes sweet to those whose
heart is free from guilt as
contentedly they lay their head
to rest.

—*Terri J. Sperber*

Clip Clop Go The Little Ponies

Clip, clop go the little ponies
Down through the valley of the sun.
With their black, sleek leader
Leading everyone.

Through the stream and big black forest
They go at lightening speed.
And then they stop at a clearing
With a bubbling spring and all
The fruit trees you could name.

It was fun for them
All the little ponies.
All the little ponies on the run.

—*Jodi McGill*

Untitled

It often comes as the Spring rain,
drop,
by drop,
by drop.
Pieces of the past begin to
collect in my mind,
making pictures as big as puddles.
Muddy puddles,
Muddy memories.
Will the skies never clear
and dry up my thoughts?
Must I always have muddy memories?

—*Mikki Maddox*

Mom

No other Mom is just like mine
God picked her out for me
He placed me in her loving care
He doesn't make mistakes you see

Thank you mom for all your love
Your help and understanding
Thank you God for giving me
A Mom that's quite outstanding

—*Winona G. Hauck*

Homeless

Some people are homeless because of
drug and alcohol addiction,
and some from family confliction,

Some are homeless from loss of jobs
and some from landlord snobs denying
children places to stay that should
not happen anyway,

Homeless is bad to be for children
it seems like eternity,

When it rains those people are hungry,
cold and wet, some are vets; that is
something they will never forget,

Our communities are not safe any more,
we cannot go peacefully to the store;
There are beggars in the street begging
for money to buy something to eat.

—*Ruth V. Parks*

Untitled

Plastic flower lies bleeding,
    Dying in the rain.
Endless cascade of deceit,
    Promises in vain.
My conscience twists the truth
Crawling, reaching in pursuit -
    Of the broken love,
    The flying dove,
    The only face,
    No one can replace
What I lost when I lost you

—*M. Westerback*

Days Of Paradise

Each day I spend in your arms
Each day I look into your eyes
Each day we kiss and make love
Are days of paradise

Each day I hear your voice
Whispering in my ear
Each day you say you love me
Those days of paradise are here

Each day that ends
Each measure of time
Each day that you and I are together
Paradise will always be your's and mine

—*M. Craig*

Untitled

Waves have crashed against the
Earth for an eternity

Endlessly hitting the shorelines
of the world around

Driven by an unseen yet
powerful and mysterious force

Destructive and life threatening
calm and serene

Bringing life to the under sea
world in which it bestows
Forever changing the environment
as time goes on.

—*Thomas Adam Dedering*

Untitled

Rain
Each drop
Different
Yet the same
Maybe different
Colors
Maybe different
Shapes
But yet all the same
Still rain

People
Each one
Different
Yet the same
Maybe different
Colors
Maybe different
Shapes
But yet all the same
Still people

—*Sunny L. Bavaro*

Emotions

Emotions
Each one passing
    Like wind
    Fast quick
Lightning bolts
    In a storm
    A storm
Of emotions
In your mind

—*Maria L. Willett*

The Seasons

A parade of seasons provides a race.
Each one vying for first place.

Here is spring!
It's majestic grandeurs are free.
The reviving of life
The verdant foliage of each tree.

Here is summer!
It's time for work and time for fun.
Continuing growth of crops
Labor and pastimes are never done.

Here is fall!
For blessings special thanks are made.
The harvest of happiness -
An important part of the parade.

Here is winter!
A time of worship and of pleasure
Faith, a feeling of peace,
Qualities in great measure.

The parade does away with strife.
It's a challenge for a greater life.

—*Thelma Williams LeGette*

Love Is Like A River

Love is like a river
Flowing for an eternity
If one is not loved
It's as if the river is dry
So everyone should love
Or the world means nothing

—*Sara Phipps*

A Wacky Animal

The dog
Eats anything
Scratches everywhere
Will knock you over
With its tail
Will bite you
If you're bad
And give you
The worst kiss
You ever had!

—*Tim Higgins*

In Love Adorns

A wreath of flowers
encircles the head
to last for hours -
their fragrance to spread:

The sweetest perfume
To tickle a nose -
seductive and gentle
a soft, deep red rose.

Its a mild reminder
of the beauty within
much kinder
than the ugliness of sin.

But what of this rose
And it's forgotten thorns -
Which in beauty grows
And love adorns?

Which withers
At the hour's end
And brings hither
broken hearts to mend.

—*Nicole M. Guilbault*

War

Today, is a time of bombs,
Every day people die;
Seeing blood and bones on the ground,
While the enemies fly in the sky;
As the sun goes down,
A cannon booms in the night;
Ashes float to the ground,
Hours later, the sky is light;
When too many are killed,
People will stop the fight.

—*Kathy Estep*

"The Bomb Has Been Dropped"

Destruction every where,
Fire and radiation in the air,
Death is all around you,
The bomb has been dropped.

The air eats your lungs,
It melts your skin,
It dissolves your bones,
The bomb has been dropped.

Feel the pain,
Feel the horror,
Feel the nothingness of death,
The bomb has been dropped.

—*Jessie A. Insley*

Treasure Above!

Forty and 8000 was all I had to spend
Every dollar a dollar
And every cent a cent.
First I drove to Dallas
Then to Idaho
I tried at Sears and Roebuck
And Kingston's IBM
I checked for all the imports
The gifts from Singapore!
All fashions in from Paris
The best and even more!
But inner city children
Were starving on the street.
The inner heart was pleading
The mothers' hearts were dead!
How then my heart it melted
The money it was spent,
Relieved from all my burden
My treasure is "above."

—*Paul G. Kaiser*

Big Bertha

Big Bertha lies
    face up in a box
Surrounded by Mums
    Gladiolus and phlox.

Given in lieu
    of respects not shown
Before ever that
    she was gone

Abuse and foul names
    were her lot
And that's about all
    that she ever got

For Bertha was not
    Her name, you see
But a nickname given
    by a beneficiary.

Now derogatory names
    are neither binding or real.
But it seems she forgot
    when signing her will.

—*Alvie Garrett*

Old Ghosts Revisited

Bitter
Falling, salty, down ...
Rapidly.
Overwhelming.
Damnation no escape.
Delirium,
Desire,
Pain...
Not knowing how to stop the game
Wooden,
Void...
Lack of noticeable feeling.
Bleeding,
    Heart broken.

—*Lisa Marie Brady*

Frozen Teardrops

I sat and watched the frozen flakes
Fast falling to the ground,
Like thousands of silent tears
They touched without a sound.

I marveled at the shimmering scene
That floated before my eyes,
Whose tears were these a falling down
From away up in the sky?

I pondered thoughtfully for a while
Then suddenly came to know,
They were God's frozen teardrops
Falling to earth as glistening snow.

—*Teresa Willis*

Sometimes You're Alone

Many times you're alone
Feeling like being home.
No one to hold or feel bold.
You think why am I here no one is near.
You stop and think when you see a wink.
Not knowing who you say boo to you too.
When you wake you think
that was a dream how wem.

—*Sarah Rieland*

The Heart

Filled with love,
Filled with joy,
The heart is something special,
    between one girl and boy.
A heart is hard to steal,
    it takes a lot of time.
But once a heart is broken,
    it takes too long to heal.

—*Salyna Drake*

Scales Balance

Seeing her loved
Floating on a dream
depth in her eyes
But not for me

Rainbows in the sky
another touch of the hand
Birds singing spring
But not for me

Looking this way
Dew on the leaves
a lingering kiss
But not for me

Scales balance
in mournful tragedy
Roses smell sweet
But not for me

Seeing her loved
Floating on a dream
depth in her eyes
But not for me

I wish you were

—*Lorin W. Doolan*

Snow

Little gifts from heaven fall
Fluffy snow, so light a ball.
Which descends upon the land,
And change it to a wonderland.

Little ones come out in bands
Bundled up by caring hands.
With bright eyes and rosy cheek,
They are happy as they streak.

As they chatter with delight
At the magic of the sight.
And the frosty soft white air,
Plays upon their flying hair.

—*Laura Atkins*

Fired Up

The wings of a bird
fly high upon the wind
as do the dreams of a dreamer.

The limbs of a wolf
push hard against their limits
as do the goals of a winner.

The hoofs of a horse
reach the sky after victory
as do the fists of a fighter.

To choose one is to choose all:
To be a winner is to dream of the fight,
To be a dreamer is to fight for the win,
To be a fighter is to win the goal.

—*Lyle Skains*

Give Me A Heart

Give me a heart that pants with Thine,
For a World that's lost in sin.
A concern for souls, Oh make it Mine,
A passion that burns within!

Press to my heart an imprint Clear,
Of the debt of love I owe;
To the lost sheep, to Thee most dear,
Lord help me Thy love to show.

Fill me with holy zeal dear Lord
And let me not count the cost,
Move me to bring thy precious Word,
To the last soul that's lost.

Oh for a heart that will not rest,
knowing souls are lost in sin,
Help me, Oh Lord to give my best,
That one lost soul to win.

Give me a yielded heart I pray
A heart toward thee most Tender;
My all consume, let come what May,
Let me know full surrender.

—*W. J. VanDree*

Love

Love is something I have not seen,
I wish it was not so mean,
But although I've known some pain,
There's something I felt but can't name,
Now I've seen it what a shame,
It feels like a flame,
What do I do about the pain,
It feels like a hurricane!!

—*Jamie Cook*

Care-Actors

There are those who have murdered me
  For in their hearts I'm dead
They have gone as far to dig
  A hole to lay my head.

Do they know I hear them,
  Talking behind my back.
Just because I'm not screaming,
  All the honest facts.

They say I'm the reason,
  They're in such misery.
Because I couldn't be the martyr,
  They wanted me to be.

I hear them keep on saying,
  I've got a splinter in my eye.
I would let them remove it,
  But I see their railroad ties.

No I do not see so perfectly,
  But I see well enough to know
That If we really love someone,
  We have to let them go.

—*Nolan Fitzpatrick*

Mother's Day

I ask my mother how I could pay,
For joy she gave me yesterday
For working hard to guide me right,
For faith to light my darkest night;
For love and kindness through the years
For ways of calming all my fears.
She answered, you can pay me, dear,
And even when I am not here,
Give someone else what I gave you.
A friend, a child, or someone who
Will need your love and care as much
So, give and give with my old touch
If I have brought good things your way
Just pass them on and that's my pay

—*Sally Pipkin*

In A Denver Coffee Shop

  Meina Zimmer sits and waits
    For life's final act
    1987's now
She remembers the Cassacks
    Prussia, Austria
    And Warsaw before the war

Meina Zimmer sits and waits
    For life's final fact
    1987 ain't new

  Communism is no life
  What have the people got
Here I have three rooms to myself

  Meina sits and waits
"Meina knows too much," she said

"The Cassacks were murderers,
  Warsaw was beautiful,"
    Then was 1912

  I don't know his name
I have nothing against him
He does his job, doesn't he

  His name is Reagan, Meina
  She sits and waits

—*Michael N. Wilkins*

To My Bride

I want you as my wife
for my entire life
When all is said and done
You'll still be the one

As we walk together
through calm and stormy weather
Our hands will band together
From now until forever

When we kiss goodnight
And hold each other tight
We will know for sure
Me and you are right

And when I get old
And in my rocking chair
I know you'll be there
because you always care

—*Terry Entzminger*

Waiting For Love

Here I wait, hopefully, not in vain,
For something that has
Been said to be wonderful.
It has been said that
Life without it is almost worthless.
What I am waiting for is
Something I have never truly
Had the sensation of feeling.
I'm not looking for it
Because, when I think
I've found it, it turns out to
Be fake.
So here I wait, hoping that
It will come to me, that
It will find me and
Take me places I've never known.
I'm just here waiting,
Waiting for love.

—*Antonette Marie N. Dorado*

I Cry

I cry,
For the pain I've known,
inside and not showing.

I cry,
For you because it's new,
the feeling of being a worn out shoe.

I cry,
For all the times I've tried,
and all the times I've lied.

I cry,
For all the unfairness,
and the lack of uncaringness.

I cry,
For all the lost love,
and for all the lack of faith in above.

I cry,
For all the people I thought I knew,
and how far apart we grew.

I cry,
For me and you.

—*Marsha Gunnerson*

I Will Be There

For times of hope,
For times of care,
For times of sharing,
I will be there.
For times of bedlam,
When we all are scared.
For times of crying,
I will be there.
For times of triumph,
For times of dare
For times of victory,
I will be there.
For times of defeat,
For times of despair,
For times of agony,
I will be there.

—*Kevin Welch*

"Refreshments Will Be Served"

What is this magic potion
For which poor mortals long
That beckons as the temptress ocean
With powers vast and strong

It calls to all - come here, come ye
Come join the celebration
What is it that they crave to see
Whatever the occasion

They come from far, they come from wide
It lures from glade and glen
They throng and crave to get inside
This nectar casts its spell on men

Aha! We know its magic well
And why the yearning to partake
Do you not hark - it rings a bell
'Tis naught but coffee - yea and cake

—*Pearl Greenberg*

A Woman's Choice

A face of majesty
For young or old
Faces of death
Bodies Cold.
Twinkle of light
Around the eyes
Waited for a new beginning
Saw only a demise.

—*Michael F. Magill*

Hope

When you walk in the
forest the birds sing out
your name, when you swim
In the ocean the waves
Call out your name, when
you hike in mountains the
winds whisper your name, when
you fly over the rain
forest the trees cry out
your name, you, your name
is hope,
you are the hope of the world.

—*Tara Lee Drew*

How Much You Mean To Me

One minute without you seems like
forever. Days have gone by without you
by my side. I never really told you
just how much you mean to me. And
just how much it hurts me to see
you when your down. But when your
around me I am so happy because
I am where I belong right here
in your arms. I wish I could take
this moment and turn it into eternity,
that's how much you mean to me.

—*Jessica Moralez*

Dream

Water, water in the stream,
forever flowing like a dream.

It seems to me that this dream,
should be shared, so it would seem.

In this dream forever blue,
comes life within you.

Limited to a certain extent,
life can be sometimes bent.

In a way, no ones sure,
but life each day can be very pure.

—*Matthew Burcham*

Untitled

Just when you think you've
found someone,
no - one is there.
You search all around you
but your heart remains bare.
Your mind can travel farther
than your eyes can see,
she's just out of reach,
nothings for free.
You feel her presence like a
magical force
You chase it forever
but never get close.
You'll climb mountains
and swim seas,
at the end of your journey
You've been chasing a ghost.

—*Randall Gene McSorley*

A Mother's Tears

The time is too short
    from cradle to grown
That child in my arms
    was there on a loan
Too soon she is eager
    to live out her life
To taste of its joys
    sorrows and strife

My story is told
    by eyes full of tears
The pain of my loss
    the depth of my fears
I pray that her path
    won't pull her down
From the dreams symbolized
    by her veil and her gown

—*Patricia A. Munson*

Pearls

Time rushes away
    from me.
A day can pass
    while I'm still
In the moment.

That's how I live,
    moments...
With gaps in between,
    like a poorly strung
Set of pearls.

—*Julia Winsor*

The Uses Of Passion

Provide a continuance of space
from the crazy wind

Plant the seed
perhaps the possibility
of Russian empresses

Whisper window
a size so slight

Nearly color archangel wings
or ribbons of packages never received

Promise to print
parts of speech
(or were they articles
boiling with no place to hide?)

Splash vermouth
big sirens and little dreams.

—*Mary Garrison*

I Lay There

They all stand above me,
full of sorrow;
I lay there.

They weep and cry;
I lay there.

I've closed my eyes
to fool them all;
they call for me,
but, I lay there.

Now I see I won the game.
They have cried only for
me and still,
I lay there.

But now it grows dark,
and the worms begin to
eat and my cavity shows
no light.
My screams are never heard.
and still, I lay there....

—*Troy Fleming*

"I Dream"

I dream I were a princess.
I dream of nice dresses.
I dream of purple flowers
And the nice breeze.
I dream of nice friends,
Just like me.
I dream of a nice bed,
Just for me.

—*Kellie-Ann Cahill-Epstein*

Dancing Melodies

Pretty are songs
gently drifting in windless
space touching entire bodies
and leaving them dreamy
in flawless worlds
of ultimate lyrics and melodies

pretty are smiling women
with pleasant attitudes
and innocent wits of
fine qualities dangling
on the edge of perfection
leaving most men in awe

pretty are my thoughts
of you as beautiful
dancing melodies that
uplift my desire for you
as friend companion and lover
and moves us even closer to TRUTH

pretty is you your song is pretty
—*Marion A. Moat*

Values

Friendship and honesty
go hand in hand
These values I demand

Freedom is the best gift of all
you can hear the liberty bell call

Caring holds the world, together
It will be with me forever

These values I share with all
And that is why I stand up tall.
—*Tanya L. Stewart*

Life In The Light

The moon hangs like
God's
Lightbulb in a fixture of
Sky
He watches us.
And knows what we are doing
To the world.
The moonbeam is the
Flashlight of a policeman
Interrogating someone he just
Pulled over in the
Darkness.
Suppose when
God
Gets tired
Of watching us,
He may just turn the light
Off?

—*Stephanie J. McCorkle*

Untitled

Going down the river
I can see all of the world
Without the troubles

A minute of time
Watching clouds, feeling a breeze
A lifetime of dreams
—*Jeffrey Jason Hanisch*

What Would I Be Without Jesus

What would I be without Jesus?
God's one and only Son,
What would I be without Jesus?
And life's battle not yet won.

He's the spring of living waters,
He's the joy down in my soul,
He died on the cross to protect me,
His love has made me whole.

He came to save all sinners,
And set the prisoners free,
He made the lame to walk again,
And caused the blind to see.

He's building me a mansion,
Up there in Heaven above,
One day I'll be with Jesus,
In that blessed home of love.
—*Virginia K. Hutto*

"The Passing"

He drifted away in glory,
Going down like a setting sun.
I met his eyes one last time
Before his life was done.

What was it he was thinking
As he quietly slipped away?
Did he know where he was going
And will he find the way?

What was he reaching out for
When he held out his hand?
Did he want to stay with me
Or did he see the Promise Land?

When he crossed over that threshold
That is not yet for me to see,
Did he pass into a Heaven
Where he will wait for me?

It's for me to only imagine
These answers that I need
While I patiently await his call
To come and follow his lead.
—*Sheila Burnham*

Silly Goof

Silly is the way I like to be....
Goofy, Laughing, Ticklelishly,
Playing, Clowning, Joking around.
Spinning and spinning
Until I fall down,
Dancing,
Singing,
Screaming out loud.
Forgetting everything,
Feeling like floating on a cloud.
Laughing, Laughing,
'Til my stomach hurts.
Out on the playground
With my toes in the dirt.
Silly is the way I like to be.
'Cause...
This is another side of me.
—*Marcie D. Rice*

Understanding

Patrick Henry and John Paul Jones
    had things in common
So I'm told, liberty and truth
    in days of old.

Battles and victories,
    Smoke and fire,
Guns and ramparts
    Throughout all time ceaseless.

Could it be so the endless
    Process brought together
By strife and peace
    End in a merit of understanding.
—*Jois A. Gould*

Untitled

    Their faces are wind burned
Hair is blown and streaked of sun
The wranglers they wear are faded
    Their boots are of warring
The stetsons they wear with pride
They often appear tough as old hide
    Some are quiet and shy
    Some are terribly refine
    They love the land
    And love to ride
Out where the sky is clear and blue
The mountains are broad and tall
    The trees are of pine and few
    This is Wyoming
Seen through the eyes of a midwestern girl
    Whose left Hoosier Hysteria fur
    Hats, Boots and Spurs
        To be her dream
    That real western girl
—*Tamberly L. Newton*

"Allen"

If one spent the minute...
Half of it going, not knowing where,
And half coming, for you saw nothing,
You will find no wisdom there.
And if you find it hard
To deal with life
Beneath the eyes of God,
Go ahead...just ask...
A one armed person
How one learns to applaud,
For we are all bound to reality,
And that reality gives back
Little peace of mind,
But a candle losses nothing
By lighting another candle,
Even of a different kind.
So, when you are searching
For where reality is at,
Maybe...just maybe...
The search is just that.
—*Vince Woodwick*

Untitled

When no one cares about me
I go somewhere to see
a beautiful sight
to fly a kite
there is no fee to the happiness key.
—*Jessie Ehlers*

P.M.

The man is laughing as her
hands reach out

And the eyes and the mouth
do not bend

Downward the faces move
to disappear

Into the light and away
while I

Watching, was alone
and inside

It's cold and darkness
has no color.

—*Anne Mackie*

In Search Of; New Avenues

The avenue lined with lilacs
    has been travelled many times
    no longer there yet every walk,
    every step, brings it back to me.
If her solitude and silence could
    bring the strength I require, I would
    walk her many times to build
    a fortress within me.
For her essence could free
    the angry soul and find paradise.
The almighty endowed her
    with perfumery sweet to enlighten
    the breath of every creature.
A hundred miles away her memory
    embraces you to seek out
    a new avenue and the comforting
    powers of its beauty.

—*Valerie J. Wiley McGuire*

Family

    Love throughout the ages,
    Has started in the home,
    Caring, molding, nurturing,
    The teachings never done.

    It comes from Mom and Dad,
    Brother and Sister too,
    Their guidance and examples,
        Make you into you.

    So remember when you go,
    All that they did do,
    It seems upon reflection,
    The learning's never through.

Small things are often overlooked,
    When youth is in full bloom,
    But as the seasons carry on,
    Change can come so soon.

I send these thoughts to comfort,
    Don't worry, fret or cry,
    We all have a family waiting,
    Somewhere beyond the sky.

—*Anthony Otis Burkholder*

I Don't Remember

I don't remember climbing trees.
I don't remember playing games.
I don't remember very much
Except being me!

—*Jeremy Scheff*

Peace And Love

The peace in the world
Has to come from within
Like the snow that is swirled
By the winter winds
It has to come from the heart
Deep within each of us
So now is the time to start
And lots of love is a must
We all have to live together
On this beautiful earth
Life's storms we have to weather
Right from our birth
Through out our entire life
With all our hopes and dreams
When broken, cuts like a knife
And all is lost is seems
But with all of our love
Right from the start
We hear a call from above
Deep within our hearts

—*Judy Obuchowski*

The House You Call Home

May the house you call home
    Have sturdy walls
And windows that face the sun.

With doors that swing wide
    And a welcome inside
To greet you when day is done.

May the echo of laughter
    Resound from each rafter
And peace and contentment dwell there.

May the house you call home
    Be a haven of rest
Secure 'neath a roof of prayer.

—*Arden Wetzler*

The Deaf Mute Cowboy

The deaf mute cowboy
he is also blind
silent cool slouched
the only sound he makes
is the hoofbeats of his horse
with the exactness of a clock
he rounds us up
he corrals us
through the northern gate
into the northern field
we his cattle
seemingly free
follow obediently
not one strays away
not one.

—*Berta Burleigh*

"Isolated Loneliness"

I sit alone in my room,
gazing out the window at the moon.
I feel isolated and alone,
to most people I am unknown,
so I just sit in my room...alone.

—*Katie Haas*

Typing Psalm

He is my teacher, I shall not pass,
He maketh me knuckle down and study.
He leadeth me into the classroom.
He restoreth my memory.
He leadeth me into silence for
my classmate's sake.
Yea, though I continue typing,
I fear my teacher,
For he is above me, and my
fingers surely bother me.
He prepared a test before me,
In the presence of my classmates;
He compelleth me to remember,
My knowledge runneth out.
Surely keys and words shall
follow me all my school days;
for I shall dwell in the
typing class forever.

—*Lena Irene Hurd Sleet*

In Memory Of A Man Who Cared Beyond

He gave more love than he would take
He showed each of whom he cherished
What of each precious moment to make
Strong was he in the acts of love
To swim against the tide
And to reach above

As changes of stream
Ran into new bold waters
And crowded stormy days
His heart and wisdom conquered
Even the highest of sultry waves

Green in his pocket
Was not the ideal of his shore
A green light for welcome
Always shown upon his door

An eye's twinkle said life
To transform and to feel
Pours forth the rain
That spins the spiritual wheel

—*Norbert Markiewicz*

Forgotten

I know one of you
He sits in the cold
He fishes through cans hoping for gold
A tin with food
A sweater with a tear
He looks for anything to help in his
    disappear
He nests in a van
walks through the day
hopes for a miracle to fall his way
God has forgotten
    he thinks in his head
People that love him believe he is dead
He begs on the streets
He holds out his hands
Change is spread from those who can
Hours become days
    days become years
Life is not changed for the
homeless portrayed here.

—*Thais Torres*

The Child

As I sit in the wild
hearing a whimper, a weep,
a cry mellow and mild of a
small child.
Searching, looking, stumbling
in the dark
Wondering which way to
turn or even for the
slightest spark.
Wondering how this infant may feel.
Will it have a life?
Will it have a dream?
Hearing this child it
doesn't seem.
Who could do such a thing?
Someone who doesn't care
about what life can bring
My heart aches to hear the cry.
There it goes fading.
Goodbye! goodbye:

—*Shawna McConnell*

Carole's Passing

An angel whispered one dark night
Heaven's waiting, take your last flight;
Away you went, without a word;
God's open arms, so I've heard.
So safely now you do sleep,
Leaving me here only to weep.
A child that was left behind
With a broken heart,
Her soul robbed blind.
Each day I look
And find no end;
To the unanswered "why?"
I can't pretend.
I await you arrival,
But know it will never be;
Because he left us here,
Your grandson and me.....

—*Meredith J. Kott*

Untitled

I used to go around with a girlie
  Her name was Shirley
   With her so curly
   And teeth so pearly
  Then I had to go out of town
   Which made me frown

Because I knew this guy named Hurley
  Who was very burly
Who wanted to make time with Shirley
  And I knew I would get squirrely
   So I called my boss
   That I was at a loss
   And I may get surly
  Because I may lose Shirley
so the boss said with a frown

   Go back to town
   To see Shirley
  With the hair so curly
  And teeth so pearly.

—*Nicholas Roman*

While Away

While I was away, another claimed
Her, not for wife, exchanging vows
In church as if higher powers ordained
The choice, 'twas nothing so highbrow,
More like a caveman's mate she went
Unwilling victim—or was it in assent?

My mind forgets, refuses, stops
Short like a rusty watch. No hand
Rewinds me, cleans the gears, drops
A hint, for who could know better than
Myself what reckless impulse left
Her courting danger if not death?

The blame is mine. The guilt, if guilt
There was, belongs to her.

—*K. S. Carter*

A Hermit Thrush

I watch from camp a Hermit Thrush
he's shy as he can be.
When he thinks no one's around -
he comes and visits me.

His color brown, a reddish tail -
his breast a spotted gray.
His voice it's melody, just great
flicking tail, gives him away.

He feeds amongst the willow brush
that grow beside the stream.
Where worms and bugs are plentiful
Speckle Trout his friend it seems.

He mates in spring around the camp
in brush not far away.
They build their nest upon the ground
and four blue eggs she lays.

Then he becomes a hermit
as he was before they met.
But every night he sings to her -
as the golden sun sets west.

—*Walter R. Bell*

Tight Rope

The rope stretched taut
High in the sky
On the rope I'm caught
Twixt my future and the past.

I balance there
In the air
And carefully traverse the span
On the rope stretching infinitely.

Should I leap
Or should I keep
  to the path before me.

Step by step
Making my way
Day by day
And sometimes I dare
To dance there
On the rope.

—*Vera M. Mulnix*

A Tribute To My Dad

He was my Knight in shining armor
His faith my shining shield
He gave his love so freely
His patience never failed
His words of wisdom led me
His arms of love he gave me
No matter when, no matter where
Whatever I needed Dad was always there
This man of strength and courage
His heart was full of love
His life he gave to all of us
From morning until dusk
He had the ways of a servant
This gentle Dad of mine
He was my Knight in shining armor
I'll love him through the end of time

The shining armor that he wore
It was the armor of God
And he wore it
RADIANTLY

—*Peggy L. Moore*

Someone Somewhere

Look he's bleeding
hit him again
break his ribs
Yes, he's bleeding
look, his blood is spewing
  from his mouth

I don't see any blood
I don't either
hit him again
pretty soon he might be dead

No, no way
he might be hurt
he might feel pain
But, no
hit him again

—*Susie Sing*

A Penny for Eliot

Heaven help those
hollow men frozen
chickens

sleeping in a closet.

remember me when
you get eaten.

seven pink lips crunch
until daybreak. please

forgive

my god for being only
one. over broken glass
eliot's feet bled like
an ocean.

dreaming of kingdoms
whilst he sang inside
a

refrigerator box
in the park.

—*J. A. Raymond*

Victory

A road of palms;
Hosannas ring.
On a donkey rides
The King of Kings.

An upper room;
The cup; the bread.
Not just a meal,
But souls are fed.

A garden called
Gethsemane;
Our Saviour prays
In agony.

A crown of thorns.
By friends denied.
He is led away
To be crucified.

An empty cross;
An empty cave.
Our Lord has triumphed
O'er the grave!

—*Kathy Martin*

House Of Pain

Where did all the memories go
How did all the feelings die
Please let me know
Why I always cry

Mama never listens
Daddy always shouts
Little brother never learns
Why I gotta get out

This place ain't for me
Mama doesn't know
And Daddy never learns to stop

Why is life so unfair
No one understands
No one really cares

Where did all the memories go
How did all the feelings die
Please let me know
Why I always cry

—*Josie Grindle*

Discovery

Aids testing
How far will we go?
What if we all
Have a nuclear glow?
What if it's true?
What if I have it?
What if it crawls,
And I have to stab it?
What will they say?
Where will I go?
Why couldn't I
Be smart and say "No"?
I don't want to die,
I'm much too young,
I did it all
Just having some fun...
And now, look at me,
I'm really sick,
They say it's because
We didn't protect it.

—*Kelee S. McKean*

Seeing You Again

You'll never ever know,
   How I've missed you so.

It's been far too long,
   since you're been gone.

Where you went to stay,
   was too far away.

Why did you go so far,
   much farther than a star.

What would or should I do,
   I couldn't follow you.

When I'll see you now,
   It's more than a big "Wow."

I've got a hunch,
   you'll know,

I love you a whole bunch,
   and so -

Seeing you again, seeing you again,
   is so — wonderful.

—*Margaret Corral*

How The One You Love

Isn't it strange,
   how the one you love
seems to hurt you the most?
   Isn't it strange,
   how the one you love
seems to apologize the most to you?
   Haven't you seen,
   how the one you love
   is forever in your debt?
   Haven't you seen,
   how the one you love
   is not making it on his own?
   Haven't you seen,
   how the one you love
just wants to be held by you?
   So why don't you,
put aside your grief and feel
   how the one you love
   is now full of relief.

—*Neil D. Rivel*

A Boy - A Girl

A boy - a girl how can we tell?

Wait nine months then we will yell

A boy - a girl who really knows

Wait nine months see how it grows

A boy - a girl
How will we do?

After nine months
our dreams will come true

A child is born.
A boy - a girl

The gift of a child.
The greatest in the world!

—*Sandra Sexton*

Fantasy

If only I could have you,
hug you,
kiss you,
and tell you what I feel.
It would bring me happiness,
to realize what love really means.

If only I could be like a bird,
hold you under my wings,
and show you the world.
It would bring joy,
to know that I can conquer the world.

But now I realize,
this is all a dream,
something I fantasize about.

If only I could open my eyes,
snap out of my dreams,
I would accept life,
for what it really means.

—*Kericee Baugh*

In The Fields

In rice fields
Hungry children
Stunted growing
Coolie hats on
Troubled heads
Weary bones without
Soft beds.
Hold your rice bowl
Raise them high
Do not let the leader
Pass you by.
Raise the standard
Beat the drum
Some day the Peace
You seek will come
Do not whimper do not cry
For the glory day is nigh
No more hunger, no more pain
All is right with the world again.

—*Roberta Sue Gibstein*

Smile

I used to never smile at all
I always wore a frown
And when someone would look at me
I always hung my head down.

Until one day I met this stranger
He said my dearest child
You ought to smile more often
You have a beautiful smile.

I'll always remember that very day
And what that stranger said,
So now when someone looks at me
I always smile, I never hang my head

A smile is such a precious thing
Lots of joy to the world it brings
It gives sunshine to a rainy day
And brightens up the skies of grey

Life is short and so unsure
To waste a moments time
So smile my friend and you will have
A smile as great as mine.

—*Rowena Ray*

Greatest Love

We are together but not forever
I am deprived of many things but
still I go on. Through this world
is becoming more like satan I
feel that I can no longer go on,
Many things occur to many to court
So I have to say goodbye. I know
you may not miss me, but I still
say it. Now I am in a more
pleasant world where nobody can no
longer hurt me. I am safe. Now
both of our worlds can sleep in peace
—*Jere Mills*

"I"

I am independent;
I am intelligent;
I am motivated;
I am extrovert;
I am robust!

I am compassionate;
I am optimistic;
I am seventy-seven inches tall;
I am ambidextrous!

I have a strong willpower;
I get along well with tout le monde;
I love languages;
I love traveling;
I love drama!

I love beach;
I love swimming;
I love beach sports;
I love summer!

I have long term goals;
And finally, I enjoy life!
—*Nicholas C. Kreonides*

The Tree Of Conformity

I am a seed ready to grow
    I am stepped on
One faithful boy waters me
    So I strive to grow

I am a young plant
    I am nibbled on
One faithful sun warms me
    So I strive to grow

I am a blossoming tree
    I am burned
One faithful cloud shades me
    So I strive to grow

I am an old tree
    I am chopped down
One fateful man kills me
    I stop growing

I am a shaped tree
    I am polished
One faithful man sits on me
    I can no longer breathe
—*Amanda Nelson*

Destinations Of Art

I can make life come alive.
I can express feelings, emotions
    and beautiful things.

For I hide not feelings
    and wondrous ideas,
But can tell them in my own
    mischievous ways.

You understand the way I am
Because I show deep feelings;
    feelings of expression;
    feelings of love, beauty.

Though I show love,
    I can show hate;
And though I show courage,
    I can also show fear.

I can show many,
    many things.
For I can make life
    come alive.
—*Michelle L. Hake*

Beetle In A Jar

I am a beetle in a jar,
I can't climb out, I can't go far.
Around I run in endless rings,
While in my breast, my sad heart sings.

Of clovered fields and lofty trees,
Of flowers visited by bees.
The dewy grass; the warm moist ground.
I think of these, as I go around.

I dream some day this jar will break
Or from this nightmare, I shall wake,
And then my heart will shout with glee,
Rejoice with me. I'm free, I'm free.
—*James Snyder*

"Rainy Day"

I quench and satisfy
I cleanse and purify
I love falling and being absorbed

I am in the rivers and seas,
I am the ultimate please..

To growth, I am life,
Everything's my wife

So drink of me
My sons and daughter,
    I am water
—*Terrence R. Boudreau*

A Midnight Dream

The colors of the sky passes
high as me and my Romeo fly on by.
All across the great mighty oceans
just more and more does are hearts
feel POWERFUL emotions.
In stormy corrupt weathers you knew
our LOVE will hold us through.
Oh God, how I love you.
But now I cry and scream, for you
were just a midnight dream.
—*Sienna A. Wallace*

When I'm No Longer Here

When just a little girl
I coveted the lavalieres
Mama said they'd be mine
When she was no longer here

Oft-times I'd ask her
To show me the lovely gems;
"I want them for my own;
I'll take good care of them."

When mama passed from this life,
A little box was found tucked away.
As I gazed at the diamonds and ruby,
I could almost hear her say...

Here are the lavalieres,
The diamond and the ruby,
I kept them both for you;
Please keep them safe and securely."

"Please keep the lavalieres"
My daughters now hear me say;
"The diamond for one; the ruby for the
other
When I have gone away."
—*Mary Blanche Fox*

Peace

One man's eyes to another man's hand,
    I do believe that the two will meet
and become friends as we all,
    learn to become a part of Peace.
—*Nancy D. W. Sheedy*

Arrogance

When I cease to be
I do not wish
The earth to stop turning
Or the earth to stand still -
    (Though I hope someone will care)
But the fog should drift quietly
Over the forest,
And the birds stop their flight
    (Just for a moment)
And a perfect shell
Should wash up from the sea.
—*Shirley Hesalroad Dykman*

All I Want

I don't want a diamond ring,
I don't want you to buy me a car,
I don't want a brown/white pony.
All I want is your love.

All I want is
Your heart close to mine,
Your attention when I'm speaking.
Your arms wrapped real tight around me.

I don't want to run your life.
I don't want pretty red roses.
I don't want a cute puppy,
All I want is
Your body close to mine.

I want your understanding,
I want your arms around me when I'm
confused,
I want your fingers to wipe my tears away,
Your kisses to soothe me when I'm
nervous.
All I want is you and your love.
—*Julie Hamlin*

322

Back Surgery

As doctors wrestled with my flesh,
I experience cardiac arrest.

Another dimension——
I've been set free!
What a discovery—
My soul is me.

Into a tunnel, black as night
Beyond the black, a golden light.

Floating through this strange atmosphere—
Rushing waters tumbling somewhere near—

I'll cross that river
Leave this void so black
When suddenly a voice sings out

"Go back"! "Go back"! "Go Back"!

It was my mother
——Dead——
Ten long years!

The yellow glow faded
The tunnel disappeared.
    —Mary E. Heimbaugh

Love Un-Returned

When I met you -
  I feel hard and deep,
You awakened feelings,
  I thought forever asleep!

You accepted my love-
  With nonchalant care,
And your cool indifference
  Was hard to bear.

I gave you my heart-
  But it was all in vain
I've nothing more to lose-
And nothing at all to gain.

There is no reason to try
Its time that we part
And, perhaps passing time;
Will mend by broken heart.
    —Mary Harris

Untitled

  Whenever we are together
  I feel safe and secure.

  The strength from your hand
holds my secrets and feelings.
You know how I feel about you.

    You know what to say
    when I am depressed.
    Nothing in this world
    would compare to you.

  Every night I thank the Lord
  for bringing you to me.

  You may not always be with me
    when I need you.
  You are always there
  in my mind and in my heart.

  You save me from the hard times.
  Holding me calm in your arms,
  I can feel your heart
  beat against my chest.

It's reassuring to know you are there.
    —Kylene Baney

Alone

So when I cut the T.V. off
  I felt lonely-
No one to share time with-
No one to call the day quits with-

  Just a clean house
  and all work in order.

The cats laid up where they feel like-
  and outside noises
To fill the void-
  or is it to make, the void,
  more noticeable?

Was busy day.
  No time to stop; reflect-
Accomplish - that was the tone.

So when I cut the T.V. off,
  I felt -

  Alone.
    —Steve Shires

"The Sea Gull"

Wing on wind
I fly and I'm free.
I admire my reflection
admiring me.
Pursuing perfection
inseparable we;
laughing like lovers
myself and the sea.
    —Karl Roseman

Untitled

The memory of you, my albatross...
I hasten to add the slender rope
will break if given time.

Then when you're fully dressed
proximity to my desire quenched
and I have moved away,

the image blurs.
Deliberately I close the hunger
for everybody knows the mind is ravenous.
    —Ruth Avitia

I Love You

Night and day, day and night,
  I hope that everything's alright
You and me were meant to be,
  for always and eternity.
Your on my good side on the spot,
  the summer nights they were so hot
You ask me if I mean, what I say,
  or if I'm only out for a play.
I'm telling you now my love,
My heart only belongs to you is true.
  I don't know how to define love
  the word, I can only tell you
  what I've heard.
  Whenever you gone I'm feeling
  blue. I hope you feel the same
  way too.
    —Andrea Maldonado

My Wish

When one wishes upon a star,
I hope their dreams come true.
But when I wish upon that star,
I only dream of you.

For when I see that far off star
I think of you my love.
How you are like that far off star,
The one sent from above.
    —Nicole Pfeifer

Puppy Heaven

There's a puppy heaven
I know there has to be
a place to roam, explore
a final home to be free

There's a puppy heaven
I know there has to be
a place to receive the last reward
for all the loyalty

There's a puppy heaven
I know there has to be
a place to return to God all creatures
that are extensions of His love for me

There's a puppy heaven
I just know there has to be

Farewell, my dear Lady
    —Nancy A. Ditges

Miles Away

You are the one I love and the one
I long to kiss the one I am deprived
of and the one I miss

Fate bought us together and you
quickly stole my heart but although
I love you miles keep us far apart

When we are together it fills me
with such love I feel like it's a
match made from up above

But when I can't be with you my day
seem dark and gray for I know
tomorrow you'll still be far away

If you could look into my eyes it
wouldn't be hard to tell that the day
that we first met for you alone I fell

So I send this poem to you cause
hidden deep inside is a love I have
for you that can not be denied
    —Ralph A. Gorofolo

Two Cardinals

A cold chilly snowy morn as
I looked out the window there,
I saw a red Cardinal sitting on
the branch of a tree;
It looked as though he was perched
looking back through the window at me.

His mate was there next to him with a
brown and rusty coat.
The two Cardinals sat together singing
songs cheerfully.
As the cold white snow of Winter dropped
to the earth peacefully.
    —Una Blanche McKenzie

Weeping Willow

Shedding the tears that blew away,
I lost a love that could not stay.

In Winter and Spring, Summer and Fall,
My children dream of their fall.

Awaken my child for the time is here,
The wind is mild but death is near.

Mother, Mother I will pray,
That in your heart I'll always stay;

So please, oh please remember me,
And In your heart I'll always be.

I now must go, I hear my call;
The wind must blow and I must fall...

—*Martin Wierzba*

Cause

God must have known
I needed a friend
Exactly like you
Honest and sincere

So, if I cause you sorrow or pain
I'd never intended my friend
'Cause your Friendship, you see
Is something special to me

'Cause you're like the rainbow in the sky
That makes a cloudy day bright
Or just like the flower that blooms
Makes everything look pretty soon.

—*Manuel O. Padilla*

Memories

Listen there is silence,
I no longer hear,
the happiness far and near,
I am numb from the hurting,
And the crying too,
For there is nothing,
No one can do,
I have to find a way,
to release these things inside,
but the more I try to release them,
the more they try to hide,
One day I will release them,
but at least until I do,
I will always wonder why,
You never took our memories with you.

—*Vickie Brunei*

Regret You Asked

It is with deep regret, my son,
I tell you the whole thing ain't;
The myth of battles lost or won
Is costly marble and paint.
Crescendos and arpeggios
Majestic arches of sound;
The rosy structure gleams and glows,
All products of the ground.
The million aged whirling spheres
Take up the sweet refrain;
Through corridors of weary years
We drag the load and stain.
Forgive, forget; let hopes chase fears;
What was; what is, is gain.

—*Richard McKeon*

Creature of the Night

In waking to the sun
I realize I miss the moon.

The sun, full of itself
rises quickly and consumes the land.

It's intensity dampens the shadows.
It's brightness eclipses all.

I must prefer the moon
and the world of night it shows.

The shadows, it seems
hide the pain and fright.

Enveloping us in a warm blanket;
sheltering us from life.

But now we have a manufactured sun
whose light intrudes.

It intrudes on
the beauty of the night.

—*Troy A. Haag*

Reproach

I saluted a nobody.
I saw him in a looking glass
He smiled so did I.
He rumpled his forehead
frowning so did I
Everything he did I did.
I said, "Hello, I know you,"
But I was a liar to say so!

Ah this looking glass man!
Liar, fool, dreamer, play actor,
Dusty drinker of dust
He will go with me down
the dark stairway
when nobody else is looking.
When everyone is gone!
He locks his arm in mine.
I may lose all but not him!

—*Margaret W. Ash*

Untitled

Live - Live!
I say to you!
Live your highest high,
and your lowest low
As if there were
no tomorrow!
Be not afraid to laugh
nor afraid to cry.
Don't let the last that
you say
Be a gasp
Before you die.

—*Judy King*

Dawn

Peeking through the shadows
I see a gleaming light,
It seems to split the clouds in half
And chases away the night.

Its rays extend like outstretched arms
And dries up the morning dew,
I wish that I could capture it
And give it all to you.

—*Barbara Mc Guire*

Love Nevermore

In the deadly calm of night,
I see a light warm and bright
"Tis her, tis her," I say
It is but she only turn's away.

Love will kill the pain forevermore
But love I will get nevermore;
The pain inside is growing
Until I feel my heart exploding,
Now the pain I will feel nevermore.

—*Jason Yarbrough*

The Wish

When I look above up high
I see a star in the sky.
I wish of love throughout the world,
because I don't see it around me.
Not just me alone in my room
but flying away in a zoom.
People say I'm mighty unusual
So, who's unusual?
I'm just me.

When I look above my head
I see a man in the stormy sky.
But I know who he is.
It's just my Lord looking on my life.

I always say, "Why me?"
When it should be. "Why us, that have
to live in a world of bigotry?"

—*Jeannine Annette Johnson*

Winter Dream

i catch a sound
i see it crawl on my ear
It moves the stillness around me (and i)
my body grows cold
but my heart becomes warm

i hear the fear of the everyone
and i see the deer ever end
and the dears we become
We start to wish to a never end,

Before

We wished it to end
but it all ends every anything does
now that we don't want it to end
before it begins

—*Aaron Bowman*

Image In My Heart

As I sit here by myself,
I wish that you were here;
sitting right beside me,
to take away the fear.

I close my eyes to see you
and suddenly you're here;
but then I open them again,
and you slowly disappear.

As long as I have my vision,
we will never be apart;
because you are right beside me,
from an image in my heart.

—*R. J. McCray*

Untitled

George has his face on the dollar
He lived through riches and squalor
He never did grin, his teeth were not in
He lacked sex too as no heir did foller.

—*Laura B. Hawes*

Life And Sight

Holding onto the light-
I see it from my height-
And my sight is good-
Do not let blindness in your life-
Do not follow the bad
For temptation is motionless-
When you're notionless-
And wonder where it leads-
And sight from the height-
Lets see the light-
And one day it shall be yours-
For do not fold it-
or hold it too long-
Those good things in life-
And have the light-
Let the blind see-
All the realms
and life's films-
let it be yours forever!

—*Lindley Graves*

Forever The Moon

In the night when I look up,
I see the shining moon.
I gaze at the silver paradox.
as it pierces the dusky darkness.
Like a flower in a meadow.
A note in a melody.
A light in the dark.
Always, the moon is there.
I can wish all my wishes.
tell all my fears.
I can cry for the world.
It's light dries my tears.
I can say anything.
It doesn't even flinch
I can tell all my hopes.
The light is always there.
A beacon on a mountain top.
A dream in an endless sleep.
the glassy surface of a lake.
Always, the moon is there.

—*Shayne Muelling*

Needed: Friend

As I write this poem,
I think about friends

They try to help,
The process never ends.

All of my friends,
They care about me.

But there is so much
That they can't see.

How I'm hurting inside.
How long can I hide?

I wish I could share,
My secrets so deep.

And that a friend,
My secrets would keep.

—*Katie Wright*

Blizzard Of 1993

Where were you in the blizzard of 93?
I thought of you and wished you were me
I gazed out the kitchen window
All I could see was snow aglow
I prayed you were safe at ten
You were on the road again
"The power is out" a voice did shout
"Turn on the radio with the battery"
Your life sure mattered to me
The snow drifts were enormous
I know I'm making quite a fuss
I don't mean to smother
I'm only your loving mother!

—*Pauline Tatiana Guman*

Summer Ecstasy

When I was but a girl of five,
I used to love all things alive,
I used to love to laugh and play
In the meadow, day by day
And in my bare feet I would wade,
In laughing rivers,- in the shade
With slippery pebbles 'neath
my feet
And berries growing sweet
To eat
I'd run along the cow path
Curving,
Through the green wood cool
and luring
Such happiness will be
remembered.
Through many June's
and cold December's
"Happy Birthday, Mother"

—*Rhoda Wilson*

Love

Like seawashed sand,
I was carrying love
in my palm.
Fleeting whiteness -
it slipped away.
Between my fingers,
it left behind
a captive breeze,
a smooth sea-pebble.
I couldn't give you a stone
as a charm or a gift.
So I patched the pebble
into the stone steps
that ran towards the sea.
Let it wear flat
like love
when one treads over it.
In this world
protrusions don't last
too long.

—*Val Avens*

A Day-A Life

I wake, and wonder why
I reach for the sky
Enjoy what I attain
Then rest, then sleep again

—*R. H. Brock*

Kristin

She was a picture on a page, missing,
I was filled with rage

As I read on, for weeks I would wait,
Only too soon I knew of her fate

I knew this girl, not as a person,
but deep in my heart,
of this I am certain

As I looked in her eyes I was filled
with sorrow, because I knew for her,
there would be no tomorrow

She was so young, had so much to give
A special person who should have lived

Now it is over, and soon will be past
I just can't forget her, her time
went so fast
But for me her memory will always last

She's in Gods hands now where he wants
her to be
She will paint for him pictures,
the world will never see

—*Marcelle Elmer*

Ode To The Bedpan

While recovering from surgery
I was terribly annoyed
For the toilet was denied me
And the bedpan was employed.

I tipped back on my shoulders
Soon my legs were stiff and numb.
The odds were all against me
I'd die before 'twould come.

When, at last, I got results
I grew faint with dread
Did I hit the bedpan
Or was it on the bed?

So the laws of gravitation
Have proved, as sure as fate
You cannot stand upon your head
When you evacuate.

There is a future for some genius
To invent some kind of diaper
Or a back adjusting "Thunder Mug"
With an automatic wiper

—*Shirley Hudson Fetterolf*

Color Me Teal

Red, my endless terror —
Fearing the blood of this life,
Spilling the fuel of this body,
The fuel of energy, of tomorrow.
Blue is so chilling so cold
So far off-it's black
Don't let me go-
There's no turning back.
Green is the light saying, go...
Go on-toward the white and silver
And further beyond.
Count not by numbers
Use colors to guide,
For if we had no color,
How easy we could hide.
Don't be your brownside, be bright,
Bright gold,
Live by colors, be bold.

—*Tony Nardi*

The Last Cry

A single tear, rolls down my cheek
I wonder, shall I speak?
Now that its over between you and me
The memories remain of what used to be.
One minute you were here.
The next, you were gone.
I can't help but thinking
If life really goes on.
Now that I'm leaving
I will see no more.
I remember the dreams
But are now never more.

—*Amber Carter*

Why Do I Worry So?

Why does it have to be this way?
I worry about every one,
And I am so lonesome and blue,
And worn out when the day is done.

God watches over his children,
And I pray for Mine each day,
That he will love and watch them,
And guide them along the way.

He watches over the Sparrow,
And on all things on earth,
And he has watched over me,
And he guided me since birth .

I know he watches my children,
So why do I worry so?
I know he loves and guides me,
Until it is My time to go.

—*Willie Johnson Cumming*

Untitled

If I could fly
I would fly to you
and want to be held
close and tight

If I could love
I would love only you
and want to be loved
by only you

If I could die
I would want to die with you
being held in your arms
and the last words I hear
would be you saying
I love you

—*Annette N. Smith*

To Any One Who's Lost A Child

To anyone, who's lost a child,
I write, this note, to you.
I know the pain and sorrow,
That, each day, will put you through.
I also know the sadness;
So many tears I've cried.
My heart goes out-to anyone,
With news their child died.
Some say, with time, the pain will fade;
But I know, it's not true.
It seems like only yesterday;
When I lost, my child too.

—*Deborah Carpenter*

Time Flies And Mosquitoes Bite!

When in my teens, long years ago
I'd write to friends I used to know
and write it all in rhyme.
They used to smile and say to me,
"Why do you waste your time?"
They'd say to me, "Oh Josie, Honey
Use your talent. Make some money."
I laughed it off, like any kid
Packed my dreams and closed the lid.
A busy life filled many years
Sometimes laughter, sometimes tears
Now there's time to fool around
Maybe I've become profound.
Here it is! I wrote this rhyme.
Could it ever earn a dime?

—*Josephine Cerniglia*

"I Think I Would Die"

I think I would die,
if never in life
I could have one joy fulfilled.
To sit on a hillside
overlooking a lake,
and watch all the world stand still.
To feel the wind against my face,
and smell the fresh-scented breeze.
To see a bird on a distant tree
filling his throat with air.
Such simple things make a joy inside,
a peace that lies deep in my soul.
Yes, I think I would die if never I tried,
to live, when I know life is there.

—*Susan Roseburrough*

If You Like Me

If you like me and made of fur,
If you like me and make me purr,
If you like me and don't like her,
If you like me and don't make me burr,
If you like me and don't call me "sir,"
If you like me and you're not dirt,
If you like me and drive a herd,
If you like me and have a bird,
Then I like you,
and I hope you like me, too.

—*Veronica Bacio*

Nightmares

Darkness finds me, once again.
I'm all alone.
It feels like the end.
It walks with me while I sleep.
I can't go back
I'm in too deep!
I feel the chills crawl up my spine.
I realize that it will soon be my time.
My eyes don't see what my heart feels.
Evil overcomes me to where I can't heal.
I know now that this I cannot end,
So I will never ever sleep again!

—*Merissa Ann Progar*

Being Strong

I have Mc Ardies you see.
I'm always hurting, I'm not happy.
When will the hurting end,
When will my muscles mend?
It hurts to walk, it hurts to write
When God, will I be alright?
I have a lot of muscle pain,
Everything lost, nothing gained.
Some say I'm lucky its not worse,
Hey you're not me when it hurts.
When it gets bad I can't even move,
What If I'm alone, then what do I do.
I try to be strong for my husbands sake,
But sometimes I feel like I could break.
It could get worse as I set older,
Please God, give me strength to be bolder.
I'm scared and that's the truth,
Just look at my tears, there's the proof.

—*Sherri Brewer*

Untitled

I think of you, I hurt inside
I'm drowning in my pain

I wonder, what is my life
With nothing left to gain

I wanted you, I needed you
I loved you day and night

I see you in another's arms
I must give up my fight

I cry for you and only you
I fear you'll never know

The feeling strong, they burn inside
I'll never let them go

Forever, I will wait for you
Without the question why

You my love, you, my life
Without you, I must die

—*Tamara J. Rose*

Love

Everybody needs a hand to hold
I'm glad you're holding mine
The way I look at you
I'm showing you a sign
Sometimes the things I say
Just don't come out right
When you and I together
Alone during the night

The way I hold you
It's easy to see
The woman that you are
Means so much to me
With your hands upon my shoulders
And your lips within reach
This thing called love
Has so much to teach

—*Matthew Thebold*

Untitled

Tiny seed planted by the gentle wind
in a fragile place
unknown to all but few.
Slowly,
silently, growing,
a life in making.
The sun is shining.
The rain is falling.
Tiny being loved every day,
peace surrounding.

Place unknown
is found by others.
They pick the flower yet to bloom,
tearing life from fragile ground.
Turmoil, chaos,
are resulting.
The sun is shining,
not as brightly.
Rain no longer falls, gently
from the sky above.

—*Julie A. Hoffman*

The Center Of Our Days

We begin by getting in some kicks
In a fun and healthy way
By doing some aerobics
To get us going for the day.

Making crafts is a lot of fun,
Creating lots of pretty things;
Look at what your hands have done
And all the pleasure that it brings!

We add variety in many ways—
Cards, Bingo, our hand at games
Bringing enjoyment to our days
Staying fit is one of our aims.

In chorus, singing songs of cheer,
Hymns that guide us from above—
Recalling memories of yesteryear
Fills our hearts with joy and love.

Helping others we do our share;
Taking pride in what we do,
Showing the center that we care
Gives us an upbeat feeling too.

—*Lorraine Steiger*

save me

when fear grips you
in her steely claw,
no one can save you
from your endless fall
into the darkness
of unknown terror.
only sheer weakness
to combat my error
of creating life
without the gold band.
mistress, not wife,
possesses the bare hand.
my screams unheard
as the knife gleams -
i have no final words,...
only dreams.

—*wild irish rose*

My Wish For You

Without noise, my life all,
In love, let's go and fall.
World is open, not closed.
Then, we can't stay morose.

Near you for evermore,
I'd always like to stay,
To kiss you everyday.
To love you more and more.

My wish for you, you know…
Let your tears on me flow.
Don't wait your tender face,
Your rare face full of grace.

Do not be shy, but free,
Your own free will with me.
True love is made to give,
Enjoy the time to live.

Under the sky so blue,
There is only one clue:
The one to love pleasures,
Which is lover's treasures.

—*Mark M. McNally*

The Cloud

I paint a cloud
  In my dream;
    The sun colors it
      With a rainbow.
    I gaze at it
      Feeling the attraction
        As my lonely cloud
          Dresses in blue
            Like the sky…
              Vanishing
              Forever
                Into nothingness
                  Like my dream
                  As I awake.

—*Tarcisio J. Bagatin*

True Love

The love that I have for you
In my heart is true.
When I look in your eyes,
I see time gone by
And times to come.
The way you show your love to me
Makes me dream of our love to be
I know people can change
And find someone new to love
And I wish that would not be
Because I want your love for eternity.
Remember I'll always be here for you
No matter what you need
Whenever you hurt
I bleed
As I lie here thinking tonight
I realize………
Our love is my life

—*Amaia Frandsen*

The Woods In Late Winter

We're walking and looking
  in our woods so fair.
We're watching and listening
  to the sounds, aware
Of small animals rustling
  to burrow and lair.
And the birds, oh the birds,
  as they dart through the air
Their colors so brilliant
  with the trees winter-bare.
We prod at the leaves
  that mat everywhere;
We search for the first sign
  of Spring—anywhere!

—*Thomas F. Brown*

My Place

The moonlight plays at waters edge
In silence through the night.
Shaking from the casted stone
Which skipped from left to right.

And music sprang from natures land
To serenade the peace.
And truly here I could relax
And put my soul at ease.

From the crickets steady rhythm
To the bullfrogs mighty roar.
I let myself fly to the stars
And let my spirit soar.

I watch in awe the battle
'Neath the shelter of a tree.
How nature lives and dies
Without a single thought to me.

A place I will remember
And it's here I will return.
A place where teachings at it's best
Come on let's go and learn.

—*Thomas J. Bosso*

April's Day

Happy hearts were felt that day,
In such a warm and wonderful way.
There first new born had come to stay,
With a love that would often stray
Only to return another day.

Family and friends came by far,
To see what lay at mother's bay.
The hopes and dreams she must make,
For time is short before you wake.

As you lay in the nursery of babe's
And adoring father could only say.
"She's the beauty of the day."
He never knew his heart could feel so gay.
The day that April came there way.

—*P. Rash*

The Garden

I walked in my flower garden today
In the lovely month of May
The sky was a pretty blue
an' the flowers were colorful to
It took my breath away
In this lovely day in May

—*Arthur Trezzo*

All Alone

Truth cannot be easily found
In such a world turned upside down.
There is no better place to hide,
Then below the man inside.
Since truth has been lost,
Lives now have little cost.
Since she died
It's over, we tried.
All must remember
The words she rendered;
But the separation of death
Our memories of her are cleft.
O'tis the hatred left.
With her gone its become a test.
To live from day to day
In a world I think is insane.

—*Joey O. Sais, Jr.*

Rain

God cries with me
In tears as they fall
Rain clouds billow
As thunderstorms cloud
Soft drops now falling
Through daylights mist
Softly I cry
From kisses I've missed
Dreams now awakened
Too far to come true
Makes my heart deepen
From thoughts of you
Sprinkles now thicken
From rainbows come true
Water from sky's light
As God cries too

—*Patricia Keefrey*

You Could Have Heard a Pin Drop

You could have heard a pin drop
in that lonely room that night.
The sound of heavy breathing
hear through a dim mist of light.

People filled every corner
of that dimly lighted room.
They sat in sickly silence
as time passed on.

A close friend, a few relatives,
his wife there by his side.
Once in a while a whisper
then a sob she tried to hide.

Now that this life is over and
heaven has opened its door,
the lights up there will shine
brighter than they ever have before.
Don't worry it's ok to carry and to be
sad for he will be missed by all.

—*Liz Swift*

Korsakov

The reason I like Rimsky-Korsakov
Is because I love his piece,
"Flight of The Bumblebee."
I sing along and it sounds realistic.
There's just one problem.
Why is it so short??

—*Nina Hsu*

My Attic

I like to curl up
in the attic of my mind
and review the cobwebbed memories
stored away there for so long.
loves I've had
loves I've lost
their trinkets never kept.
But I have never swept my mind
of what it treasures most.
the glad times-
the sad times-
they all have special meaning.
I do not try to balance them
but let them in my being.

—*Pamela Millay*

Untitled

The old tree stood shivering
In the cold morning air
Its leaves had all fallen
Its branches were bare

A few flakes of snow
Tumbled around
Kissed the bare branches
And fell to the ground

The wind died down
Everything was still
As the pale winter sun
Crept over the hill

There in the light
The old tree stood
An art work of God
A sculpture in wood

—*Jean Card*

Summer Evening

On a fragrant summer evening
  In the fading sunset's glow
Songbirds find their secret places
  We can't follow, where they go.

Wish for me a silver moonbeam
  I can climb to find the Maid
Of the Moon with golden halo
  Coiled from her own moonlit braid.

—*Mary A. Fowler*

To Run Away

If another day I stay
In this dreaming place
  of humanity
I don't think I'll make it
  through this night
Without losing my own
  sanity.

So I run as far as
  I can
To get away from the
  Burden of it all
In this crude society
Yet I haven't gone far
  enough
Cause I could still hear the
  screamings of this chaotic world.

—*Rod Sims Legaspi*

Bystander

There it was.
innocent as a flower.
Never did any harm
Shut out from the world
into a glass cylinder.
So many dreams, ideas,
wishes, goals,
Destroyed.
Sucked into the vacuum of
Horror.
Never to come back to this
day and time.
Why??

—*Kelly Morton*

"Read A Poem"

Read a poem
Inside your home
And you will surely find
Troubles go right out the door
And you'll have peace of mind.

Read a poem
Inside your home
When you have work to do
And you'll locate
A system, great
With inspiration new

Read a poem
Inside your home
When all the work is done
And you'll find treasures God designed
Beneath each setting sun.

—*Pauline L. Green*

Untitled

I am the one that laughs
instead of cries, and smiles
instead of frowns.

You will never know if I am
sad because that feeling and
all the other feelings have
slowly drained away. Just
like I am slowly draining
away from life.

I'm the one that confuses your
mind into believing my happiness
is for real, but you shall never
see the true sadness that lies
beyond my smile, the tears of
pain I go to bed each night with
and the true horror I wake up with
each day.

—*April Wakefield*

First Meeting With Mommy

Her face
Interesting
Arms holding me tightly
A tear dropping down from her eye
New world

Heart beat
Rocked back and forth
Exploring each other
Hand in hand the love is growing
New life

—*Lisa Feldstein*

Touch Me

Hello, is anyone out there?
Can you hear me,
Or does it pain you
To listen to my words?
Help me, the dark is coming.
My veins are poisoned with a disease,
I lie here too weak to escape its grasp.
I am dying.
Not only my body but my soul.
Why won't you come closer to look at me?
Are you too scared to look beyond my sickness?
My lips are salty from my sorrow.
Dry my tears,
Or is your heart too frightened?
It's alright to be scared,
learn from me,
Find the cure for this disease.
Though your lack of understanding
destroys me no end,
It's okay to touch me
I will not harm you.

—Elaine Bridger

Adamedia and Elle

And GOD created Elle
Si douce, si candide, si belle
That to do her justice
The sun remained in solstice.
Naked the beauty wazz
With a little natural fuzz...
- And she was not ashamed
Only to cover sins, garments ought to be made! -

And ADAMedia saw ELLE
- So sweet, so candid, so frail -
That he created jealousy
Cos his entrails tortured him with envy,
To the point that they began to ache
And transformed him into a snake;
Tis how the very first of pang
Metamorphosed into a fang.

It didn't prove to be wisdom
To try to inject some venom
Cos to alter Divine Beauty
Wasn't to be evil duty.

—Maryse Ledru

Mom

As a mother you raise your children the best way you know
You love and protect them as they grow
You guide them with love and happiness,
Tears and fears you teach them respect

And then you reflect
You hope you have taught them all you can
Then you realize they're your biggest fan

As your child, I realized you did this all for me
I am now becoming the best person I can be
As an adult I have the pleasure of being
Your friend as well as your son
But it's not over, it's just begun

And now you have two grandchildren
You're still a mother and still a wife
This is now the time for you the time for your life
A new life, a life for you to do with as best you know
This is the best part for me; to see what
you do, and to watch you grow
So on this day I send all my love
Wishing for you all the powers from above

—Dean Moulton

There Is Only Jesus

There is only Jesus, standing there alone,
Jesus is the only One I see;
There is only Jesus, Jesus all alone
Being ridiculed for you and me.

There is only Jesus, hanging there alone,
Jesus is the only One I see;
There is only Jesus, Jesus all alone,
Being crucified for you and me.

There is only Jesus, sitting on a Throne,
Jesus is the only One I see;
There is only Jesus, Jesus all alone,
Interceding there for you and me.

There is only Jesus, coming from above,
Jesus is the only One I see;
There is only Jesus, Jesus all alone,
Coming for His own, yes, you and me.

—Columbine Thompson

A Sailing Cloud

Today as I looked up, I espied
A cloud sailing across the sky
And a question came gushing through,
Whence did it come, and float whereto?

As a child I was told,
'Tis water droplets that clouds hold;
And, at times gathering together,
They cover the sun, changing the weather;
The rain then falls on the earth,
Soothing its burns, quenching its thirst.

But Oh! the clouds in my sky
Always and always sail by,
Never stopping to gather and shower,
Never blossoming a single flower;
Am I a barren desert sky?
Whence clouds will always fly;
'Tis said trees entrap clouds,
I'll grow trees, tall and proud.

—Atul Singh

Ode To Raindrops

Oh, for the stillness of a summer's night,
A gentle breeze and a bird in flight;
A meadow lark perched on a hill,
Its voice melodious, clear and shrill.
But most - a rain that comfort brings
to every dead and living thing.

A warming rain, a gentle rain,
A soft and soothing quiet rain
Pattering on my window sill.
While the thirsty earth that fallow lay
With beckoning arms once parched and dry
Breathes free once more as the tiny drops
Taint its hue, and then subdue
The abysmal thirst of its inner soul.

—Mike H. Tkachuk

Love

Love is as rich as a diamond
In the morning sunlight
Or it's as poor as a lonely
Mountain stream.
Love can be daz'ling and make
Your eyes shine bright
Or it can leave you with
Nothing more than a dream.

—Allyson Jones

I

You vanish in the mid hour of July,
a lethal letter talking of your sickness.
Far away, a flock of birds
alone chant,
to an unknown soldier, to a garbish man,
to an isolated artist.
Only they honor each all,
Guests of the unpardonable earth.
But, looking back on his early days,
he remembers a number of misfortunes and
injuries. "Who will pay the debts of
my youth?, "he says.
I, old supporter of human lives will rest
in peace, not so the intellectuals whose
names are uttered minute by minute by liar lips.
Now, a voice at this back calls him,
No one answers, nobody is there,
Nothing can be done.
His thoughts were stronger than his needs.

—*Anays Avila Zambrano*

Whispers The Wind

An electric glance.
A meaningful smile.
    "Give it a try." Whispers the wind.

A tender greeting.
A fragile moment.
    "You can do it." Whispers the wind.

A feeling of love.
A future of hope.
    "See, you did it." Whispers the wind.

A broken promise.
A lost fantasy.
    "You did your best." Whispers the wind.

A time of trials.
A feeling of loss.
    "Just keep trying." Whispers the wind...

—*Katie Bambauer*

The Prisoner

I'm locked in my prison by no metal bars,
A sad victim of life, with invisible scars.
The demonic voice fills me with such dread
Please won't you help me; look inside my head?

Mutely I wait and pray you will hasten,
The great doors will open, if you will but listen.
My mind whispers to you, "Come in and find me,'
Won't you enter my prison and help me break free?

But why be so cautious. Ah, you don't feel safe,
Deep down you're afraid of this poor insane waif.
You warily ponder, that I too, was once free,
'Til the voice in my head made a prisoner of me.

Ambivalence takes you, as the prison doors open.
Should you come in and find me, as you have bespoken?
Is the dread that assails you, this terror you feel,
The fear of contagion - getting caught in the wheel?

You enter, you touch me, but a dark abyss yawns,
And I gleefully laugh; you mad fool, it dawns.
Your horror as sanity slips from your grasp,
When I slam the doors, locking us in your past.

—*Dorothy K. Thomas*

The Smile Of A Child

There is a hand reached out to you,
a smile, a look, so trusting and free.
A child that knows that there's someone,
to hold the hand, answer the smile that's
how it should be.

But it seems that more and more children,
don't learn how to trust no more.
They have been abused by family or friend.
So what have they to smile for.

There is no hand that reaches out,
no smile, no look, they don't trust or feel free.
They don't know what to think at all,
is this how it is supposed to be.

Please keep the children smiling,
full of trust about the people they see.
Because they know that they're loved and secure.
They will grow up knowing what love is meant to be.

—*Maaike Borst.*

"Pas De Deux"

Emerging as the theme filters out from inner night,
A song of love fills their steps, to create a bond of light;
Her face, a wreath, touched with snow,
expression pure as white,
beckoned by his kingly stride, that's present in her sights;
Their fingers embrace at the music's queue,
she unfolds her classical limbs,
as a blooming rose feels the kiss of the sun,
she feels the kiss of him;
The clinging threads execute his claim,
and animate swayed emotions,
stretching with a timeless care, and drawing like the oceans;
Merged by the score that rises and falls,
conveyed by the night's caring eyes,
gestures of grace flow under the stars,and reinforce their
ties. The motions ascend and bid him to carry her
down to the last lover's trail,
and with the hush of the notes, and the motion within,
comes a perennial end to the tale.

—*Trina Stelmaschuk*

Untitled

Allow me to describe,
A transformation between,
Two events, one tangible,
And one that cannot be seen.

The latter is an emotion,
Although difficult to detail,
Transforms your body into an ocean,
Of emotion, to surface, and prevail.

For at the surface, it takes on shape
For then it becomes quite clear.
Of the transformation between these events
One emotion, becomes, one tear

So when it's time for this event
To surface, and exit the eye
Don't be afraid, don't let it drown
Let is surface, transform, and cry.

—*Paul Lascelle*

A Better World To Live In

Oh! for a better world to live in
    A world without evil and suffering
    A world without war and death
    A world without famine and plague
    A world without Tornado and Hurricane
    In which all mankind will live in peace.

Oh! for a better world to live in
    A world without strife and fight
    A world without hate and anger
    A world without quarrel and litigation
    A world without struggle and contention
    In which all mankind will live in harmony.

Oh! for a better world to live in
    A world without doubt and unbelief
    A world without skeptics and agnostics
    A world without scoffers and critics
    A world without objectors and sneerers
    In which all mankind will live in faith.
        —*Sampson Eghan*

AIDS

Have you heard about the new scourge?
Acquired Immune Deficiency Syndrome
From East to West, from North to South,
From all nooks and crannies of the world,
In Europe, in America, in Australia, in Africa,
In all the continents of the World,
It rampages; it destroys; it wears down; it annihilates.

With AIDS the body no longer holds.
With AIDS the mind falls apart.
With AIDS the body immunity is gone.
AIDS is a killer disease
AIDS defies all treatment
No vaccine to protect you,
No drug to cure you.

AIDS can be caught through sexual intercourse
AIDS can be contracted through unsterilized needle,
AIDS can be transferred through blood transfusion.

The best antidote against aids;
"MAN, BE FAITHFUL TO YOUR WIFE!
WOMAN, BE FAITHFUL TO YOUR HUSBAND."
        —*Mac Aderele Araromi*

"Old Things"

Remember when old laces were fancy smiles?
all our fondest memories were embraces
our longing for sunsets never ceases,
sunsets gave us breadth for senses.

Remember when old faces were pure glances?
all our fantasies for happiness were dances
our calling for the end of sadness
window panes of treasured nights of solitary madness

Remember when old things called for sentiments?
all our keepsakes were letters, notes and photographs
they were kept hidden in our own soulful chest
boxes of bundled destinies reopened for memories' sake

Remember when old times came our way?
"like death was so stubborn to die"
they were our first moments stolen forever
kept sacred by the wandering mind.
        —*Mary Rose A. Lagunsad*

Sunday Masochist

It left her in a sweaty state of
agitation - permeated with rage,

The 'Believers' - those white, doughy
middle class bodies - a sea of them,

Each one covered in 'acceptable' clothes
- each one pampered, powdered and sprayed

Their minds also - with suffocating

Self-righteousness personified - aglow -
with seemingly great compassion/charity.

At times she'd try to converse -
stumbling with banalities - inwardly
articulate with profanities...

Long afterwards she'd still be smoking
cigarettes and gulping sweet, black
coffee in catharsis mode...

Blunting the horror or truth was just
one thing - more comforting and concrete

She held no golden, honey sweet Jesus
but a God who wept till snot ran

Unchecked by human vanity - whose eyes
were gouged out by the sight and horror

    Poisonous Compromise

Whose flesh ached, rotted and ripped
with the arrows of pseudo-spirituality

Who choked, gagged and vomited on the
anguish of humanness...

And that was reminder enough for awhile
- 'til she'd forget, and would try church again...

    Sunday Masochist.
        —*Mary Nikoletos*

Wish Upon A Star

Down at the log house dancing to the beat,
Along came a fella I could hardly wait to meet.
We were stomping to the music "Fishin' in the Dark",
When he brushed my shoulders and threw off a spark.
Eye to eye contact, we started dancing up a storm.
Quick, quick, slow, slow, we sure were in form.
Two bodies touching, holding one another near
He caressed my hand and whispered in my ear.
The romance was climbing, my battery was all charged,
Someone to drive me down the freeway of love.
It all happened so fast, the next thing I knew
It all came to an end before it even grew.
There was a flash of bright lights and I awoke.
There I lay alone, my heart was so broke.
You see, this was nothing but a dream.
The love I have to offer, my tears washed down the stream.
I'll just hop back into my ice box of a car,
Head down to the log house and "Wish Upon A Star."
        —*Vicky Clark*

To Catherine Lynn Armour

I wish to tell you my beautiful one,
I'll cherish you forever, old or young,
    Poor or rich, my blood burns Armour,
    I love, I yearn, I want, and more.
    My needs fulfill whenever you say,
        "I truly love romance this way."
Your blonde hair, mystic eyes blue,
    Your figure askew, and I love you.
        —*Wayde Kenji Brown*

The Flea

Was there ever, in the days of men,
An allegiance among strangers and friends?
Was there ever, in the history of the earth,
Another dominating race, not yet un-earthed?
Perhaps the dinosaurs ate all the first men,
And after their genocide, returned again!

Was there ever, preceding the universe, so big.
An implosion, like the one they say that we'll meet?
When the universe collapses all of its energies,
Sucked together into one single entity;
Making way for another big bang to prosper.
Allowing moments like deja vu to occur?

And all other majesties of the mind.
Little things, not implanted, that you find.
I'd imagine if we answer all the questions,
We'd begin an evolutionary recession!

Invisible, but an echo system depends on me,
Universe, in a giants bowl, on top of the T.V.?
Or take a tiny atom from the giants, dogs, flea,
And if someone split that atom.....

—*Lee Martin*

A Thunderstorm

A loud rumble as the sky groans
And a flash illuminates the darkness.
The folks on the inside cry their moans
As the rain begins its soft caress.

The clouds that darkened in such a short time
And the wind that began to blow
The force of the wind causes bell to chime
As another flash makes the sky glow

The rain that started as a small sprinkle
Starts falling in a torrent of rage.
Drops hit the window pane, sounds like a tinkle
And the insiders view it as a stage.

But soon the lightening ceases to flash
And the thunder stops its grumbling
The rain slows its steady lash
And the birds begin to sing.

Children come out to play once more
Raindrops, on tree leaves, cling.
The scent of rain we all adore
And that my friends, is spring.

—*Brenda Schubert*

I Want To Be Someone

Have YOU ever ever wondered who YOU would like to be -
   a doctor, lawyer, banker, the President, a dentist, accountant or
   an Indian chief?

Maybe a carpenter, a plumber, a musician, a tailor, a poet or a chef
   or a teacher of the blind, mute, dumb or deaf...

Sometimes I feel like I can never decide
   even after thinking and pondering about it over and over in my mind

So I have come to the conclusion that the only true answer to the
'Who do YOU want to be test?' is to BE SOMEONE AND BE IT AT YOUR BEST!

—*Theresa Minus*

Prize Fighter

Savouring the night.
And already the sweet scent of coronation
   is within contemplation.
This one last leap will make conspicuous renown.

Raw noise will witness challenges
   against himself and his mystery,
as he creates a noble fragment
   of an always appalling history.

But the plan has gone awry.
   His grasp for splendid fame aborts.
Long hands shrink, heavy and hurt,
   Fingers swell, gloved pain congeals,
relief is sought.

The shame of imminent defeat erodes
   just before stars inside his head implode
and darkness descends from heavenly above.
   Again he denies, is denied, love.

Post fight discussion will not record
   that out of ignoble, inappropriate rewards
we have holy fellowship, blessed and noble Lord.

—*Rod Milgate*

For the Children's Sake

There are knots in my stomach
and an aching in my heart

full fledged rage
where there was only concern at the start

children are missing one by one
from a public place going to or coming from,
or while outdoors, innocently having fun

what kind of monster could do this kind of thing?
are they sick individuals
or a part of a much larger, market type scheme?

some people turn their heads
pretending not to see
especially when they get their mail
or buy a cartoon of milk...
and see a child's face
asking... "have you seen me?"

no one is exempt from this terrible crime
and if we don't find a solution
the next child missing could be yours,
or even mine.

—*Lorrie Montes*

A Simple Question

I dug in deep
and came up with my arms full
of severed limbs. He slumped
on the step, broken
by the weight of his question.
"Why is poetry always so esoteric..."

I was stuffing branches into bags,
stomping down thorns and pulpy flowers,
cracking twigs with intent, my hands
stained and slashed.
"The child was crushed," I said, "killed
in a freak accident."

"...or brutal?"
he said.

—*L. R. Young*

Music To The Song Of Our Dreams

My son sleeps to the sound of tractors in the field
And awakes to the singing of the bees.
Birds are the music to the song of the dreams that he sees.

As he slumbers in peacefulness
I take comfort in the warm summer breeze.
I work with the richness of the land
In a dance with the aging maple trees.

And one on one with mother nature
I'm an artist on my own
And I reap the harvest of the
Bounty I have grown.

The warm sun, blue skies
And peacefulness entwine
And I rejoice in the claim
That's yours and mine.

And we sleep to the sound of the creatures of the night
And awake to the laughter of our son.
And our love is the music to the song of the
    dreams we've begun.

    —Laura Hamilton

December

The first snow falls like down upon the hills,
And covers up the earth with that same care
That nature loves to take with all she wills —
And so she dresses now what lately bare
And barren lay, with garments white and fair;
And every spruce and fir tree in the wood
Is hung with ornamental ices, rare
With prismic colours, like a gem that's good.
And ah, where yesterday there plainly stood
For me to mark and smile upon with grief,
The gauntness of an oak, all stark and rude,
Without the saving grace of one last leaf,
Today is lovely with the finest lace
That nature and December snows can trace.

    —James D. Humphreys

My Love

Though you have left me
and have taken away my reason for living,
don't shed any tears for me.
Know in your heart that I have loved you
and will love you until the end of time.

I will forever cherish our special memories.
I look forward to the day,
when we stop acting like enemies.
I remember your loving smile,
those unspoken words that said so much.
If you should ever think of me, please know!
You are forever on my mind.

    —Devo Dyette

Temper Tantrum

I'm out of control
I'm losing my temper
I'm feeling low
I can't see straight
I want to say no
I want to surrender
I want to make it stop
But it's much too late
Oh no it's a temper tantrum

    —Ronnie Gunnels

My Heart's Mother

She lead me into an intoxicated land,
and held my hand, as we walked through a garden.
This garden didn't spawn fruits and vegetables...
but naked people.
She taught me to harvest these people and use them
impractically.
We kicked the stalks and shells, of harvests gone by,
and began...
She showed me that we are democratically oppressed.
    (But we may still fall in love)
We held hands and kissed passionately in small rooms,
so no one would see.
She thieved the essence of my innocence.
    (Or whatever took its place)
She lead me through a forest,
we climbed its looming trees, drank its sparkling water
and rolled love through its velvet moss.
I loved her... I hate her.
I passed her... walking the forest's trail...
(and she was with another).. as I returned to the garden.

    —Brian Carey

Untitled

The sun comes up each morning, and goes down for the night,
and in its place comes shining, the moon and oh how bright.
Each day we feed the future, with all its unknown tales, at
once an awful creature, but time retrieves its ails. Of one
thing we can rest assured, the whole consists of parts. Our
daily toil will bring us fruit and shoot light through our
hearts. And so with every word we learn and phrase to unlock
hearts, we'll find we yearn and live to see our sweat has born
new parts. These parts make up the whole, the whole is then
our goal, and with surprise and full of glee, the mind has now
run free. English we'll have mastered, with all the world to
banter...and that is then the reason, we'll wring out pearls
of patience, and trudge through the confusion, and tame our
tongues with vengeance. The grammar is confounding, but new
hopes are surrounding...wart's ab du Sprache, so ist die
Sache, wir zwingen dich auf die Knie! Motivation

    —Gloria Villalon

Your Name I Do Not Know

Although my hands are withered,
And my walk is rather slow,
I lived an active life not so very long ago,
I see your smile, I feel your touch,
To me they mean so very much.
    But your name I do not know.

If perhaps I utter some unkind word to you.
Just remember in your heart that none of them are true.
You are my nurse, my best friend
You'll see me through to the very end.
    But your name I'd not know.

Late at night when I lie to sleep,
That is when I weep.
I pray that God in all His mercy
Will lay His blanket at my feet
    Because your name, their name, I do not know.

    —Norma McArthur

The City Of War

The human race is at war.
And the people have stopped to love.
Death is around the corner,
Waiting for your fathers, mothers, children.
The bullet shots are common,
For the residents of The City of War.
Dead people on the street is nothing new,
Just another casualty of The City of War.
Families begin to get smaller,
And funerals are an everyday occasion.
People pray over the bodies of loved ones,
While bullets rip through the air.
The tears have almost run out,
For the residents of,
The City of War.

—*Yasam Kaspan*

First Memory

That September morning,
and the shadows of the roadside
mixed with cool,
and the ground echoes when you touch it,
and it's time for school.

That September silence,
and the murmur of the water
in the brook,
and the ripples sway the pennyfish,
as I stop to look.

That September feeling,
and the melting mist made yellow
by the sun,
and the greenly spruce companions stand lone,
for long the days' begun.

—*J. L. Makela*

Ruler Of The Night

Who knows what happens in the sable night
  Any better than the all seeing moon?
To whom is it more day at midnight's noon?
  Who possesses this all-powerful might?
Who sees and hears the events without light?
And keeps himself company with a tune...
  The merry dancer's glory is the lune.
Is it the moon? Is it something so trite?

Surely not, for the moon will pass away!
Just as soon as the Son begins to rise.
The moon will give its scintillant splendor
  To the One who's the ruler of the day,
And unlike the moon, this One never dies.
  His sovereign pow'r never to render.

—*Nathan M. Stricker*

Forever Love

My love to you
Is forever and true
Our love through the years
Has surpassed all the tears
Although we're apart
We're still lovers at heart
Through all this time
Our love has been a crime
But with wishes on a dove
And prayers from above
You'll always be
My forever love

—*Katie Cleveland*

After 50 Years I Have Come Home

Places here, there and everywhere
Are scenes that I once knew
Emotions stir as I recall
The memories that grew.

I'm like a lamb lost in a wood
Being so world weary,
If someone will watch over me
Life won't seem so dreary.

Dreams and doubts clear like misty clouds
Upon the hills of time,
Though man be proud he's thistledown
On winds of every clime.

We come and go, ripples on streams
For all that we may know,
And every time we say goodbye
We die with stricken woe.

For life's a sparkle and a span
Yet still how proud our ways,
While time shuts up in silent graves
The story of our days

—*Beth Morris*

Alone

The damp, misty air of the arena fills my lungs.
As the black skate guards depart my old scuffed skates,
A newly sharpened blade is revealed.
I feel the cool air whip through my hair, and the glassy ice under my skates.
The arena is empty and silent.
Alone.
I am alone.

My heartbeat quickens, as I set up for my first jump.
Then I jump. One, two, three rotations. Then...boom.
The rink echoes as I feel that smooth, glassy ice under my left hip.
As I am sitting on the cold ice, I look around the arena.
Alone.
I am alone.

A train sounds in the distance.
I stand up, brush the snow from my knees, hold my head high,
And try again.

—*Lori Macklem*

Palm-Wine Smile

One Ukwo market eve
At sunset
When the chickens have gone to roost
In an open-air Apa bar
In the third moon
Of the year of Nigeria's census result
That famished men
Outnumbered better life woman
In the market place of this famished land
Brow - beaten
From ekeing-out a lean living
In the world's thirteenth poorest Nation
OCHE, OKO, AMEH and I
Sat on broken bamboo seats
Savouring sour up-wine
Froth with booze
Smiles long-forgotten
Played momentarily on our worn lips
"It is a new day!", we all sang.

—*Ada Ugah*

334

Untitled

An old indian man, maybe a chief or warrior, looks
at the river, the sun, the moon, the mountain and bear
  to him they're dancing in nature's own way.
    To him they all have a reason to play.
    But you, you coward, you crucial beast,
you look at these beauties like they're all a feast.
    With chemicals and hate you fight in Kuwait
    The river, the moon for supper you ate.
    The old man laughs as he holds back a tear
  he knew it would happen, just not this year
and when you die and when you're with God
      I've seen it before,
You won't smoke or drop your can on the floor.
  Just thank him, the indian man that is,
    the one who crawled into your dream
      and helped you see
the river, the sun, the moon, the mountain and bear.

    —Curt Brownlee

Thae

Ever wunder if Thae'r reelee az smart
az Thae'd hav uc beeleve Thae ar?
I don't mean just abowt art
but win Thae tel us wea kan't goe far
beeyond the limits Thae'v set for uc.
Ferst Thae teach uc not tw explore tw much
and tw oebae withowt maeking a fuc
bie kripling uc, thin proeviiding a kruch.
Thae tel uc Santa onlee brings toys
tw'gud littul gerls and boys
and korn bred and switches
tw thoze hw beeleev in witches.
Thae deelae ower lerning tw read
bie maeking letters undeapindubul.
Thae waunt tw reestrikt ower feed
tw what will keep uc malleabul.
Thae put tha fear of 'The Lord' in uc
beakawz that waz what waz put in thim.
We'ar tawt not tw lie and not tw kuc
tw trust thim ower wings tw trim.

    —Donu Karuneenu Share

Julianna

Julianna by night whispers to the moon,
Bathed in Angelic light for dreams that pass too soon.

Bubbles of time woven together with thread of gold,
Chase the ancient rhyme from the generation of old.

Quiet lies come from the stardust elves,
As she cries for those who will not cry for themselves.

Madly alive within her beating breast,
Are the five broken promises that will never rest,

Life, love, truth, anger and lies,
As seen by the lamb with the eternal eyes.

As she suspends her dreams in the stars above,
The night air sends a tremor to the flight of the dove,

Forsaken by the Son of the desert sea,
She sighs knowing she will always be,

Now and forever seeking the light,
Now and forever Julianna by night.

    —Kevin J. Wowchuk

Destitution

I was born with a rich mind but did not mind to be rich.
Because of illiteracy I yielded to exploitation. I knew I was
been exploited but had no choice. Day came, day passed, but for
me nothing changed, time left me empty handed. I was hard
working but when my ability vanished, my boss fired me. I
became a drunkard and my wife fired me. My country is wealthy
but the wealth is a distance from me. I sit hungry from sun
rise to sun set watching with distress the few enjoying the
wealth that I made. I am condemned to poverty by both friends
and enemies. Those who talk to me are those I share the
plight, with. I am deaf and can't hear what is said about me.
I am ever sad. I fought in world war II for reasons known to
my colonial masters. During bombardment little did I knows
that my hearing was leaving me. I am fortunate I did not die,
but sometimes I regret having lived. Whether the rate of
inflation is high or low, whether they is drought or not,
whether the standard of living is high or low, to me
situation remains the same. I don't have food, I am diseased,
live in squalor and have no clothes to cover my bones. I have
faith that heaven will be better than earth.

    —Dama Mosweunyane

Masquerade

Sti'f masks stick to skin
Beneath the winking lights
Above the babble and din
of rustling silk,
Silk high blown, blown wide along the floor
Or standing rigid near the open doors of open verandas
cupped in shrilling laughter;
Arms bare and brown brushed with gold
Caught in mocking gestures;
In the frosty cold
of drinking glass dizzy with feigned delight,
The mask puckers lost in blurring sight.

But I remain silent self-contained
(As them that wear the masks remain)
In an idea formed of one to take the chisel and the knife,
to cut and scrape
To see beneath the downward smile and laughter shallow
The inside is but hollow.

Soft in thought; softly as the night descends upon her flaking speech
of this she likes and that she loathes
(Dependant on which company she keeps).
Oh, who will be the one to say, 'The Emperor has no clothes!'

    —Yael Shapiro

Things Have Changed

I read it in story books and I heard it on the farms
But when Grand-dad told me about those gone by days
Lord I jumped and hollered - hearing what he had to say
Then as I sat and pondered - about those days of slavery
Grand-dad took me on his knees - and with a smile he said
Son - things have changed.

He told me about the cotton fields and old Mazaruni
His Mom, his half white brothers - and years of agony
Then he took his shirt off - and showed his back to me
Lord I'll never forget - the sight it revealed.

The cotton fields are still there - and so is old Mazaruni
But Grand-dad is no longer with me - only memories
Lord how I wish I could forget
The agony his face tried to conceal
As Grand-dad took me on his knees and with a smile he said
Son-things have changed.

    —Harold R. Adams

"The Chief"

He sits alone on a wooden bench
Beside the pool hall door
He feels a thirst that just won't quench
As he speaks of a time before

Once my people rode this land
They were proud, and they were free
Then the white-man came like the drifting sand
And stole our dignity

They gave us whisky, and treaties wrote
Not one that was sincere
They sent the law, with the bright red coat
And made the buffalo disappear

Then they told us to go to a desolate place
They called an Indian Reserve
Now you'll be a part of the human race
And get what you deserve

Then he bowed his head and the silence grew
On that bench by the pool hall door
And in his heart, the old chief knew
That the Indians would dance no more

—*Elmer J. Peterson*

Autumn Leaves

Torn from your mother tree, dancing and dying,
Blown to the mother earth, withered and lying —
For days not numbered, decay and rotting,
Nourishing God's good earth for its reviving.

Delicate buds, to your mother tree, holding,
Waiting for warmth, for the joy of unfolding —
To look on mother earth, thanking your Maker,
Knowing that death's but a wondrous creator.

—*Mary Pickard,*

In Commemoration (Of Patrick Kavanagh)

I sat beside you on your seat today,
Bronze Bard of the common man.
In nearby Grafton Street your verse he bunked
from his bill of fare, A La Carte poems for the shoppers there.

My son sat on your knee today.
He touched your nose and hat, I didn't think you minded
as you stared into your still, dark redemption.
I wanted to touch you but feared you'd startle and leave.

The sculptors hands have shaped
you well but missed upon your greeny shell
one thing...
no clay upon your boots.

—*Gerry Callaghan*

What Makes Me Feel Special

What makes me feel special
Is all the things I do.
The hours of every day
Really are to few.

A special teacher who guides me,
Who shows me how to work and play.
And is always ready to help me
Through out each and everyday.

I know I have a special friend
Who's always there to show
The right and best way
For me to go.

—*Terri Barker*

Dying For Pleasure

Not only in back streets and alleys so dark,
But also in playgrounds you'll find the black heart
Of dealers and pushers who live by the pain
Of addicts who pump deadly drugs through their veins.

Needles are shared, AIDS is a threat,
They no longer care they're caught in the net
Of cocaine and ecstasy heroin and smack,
For some it's too late, there's no turning back.

Cold empty faces, death in their eyes,
Bodies that shake as they wait on supplies.
Hooked on the venom they took just for kicks,
Horribly tortured until their next fix.

Bodies invaded by dope that they shoot,
Into every vein from head down to foot.
Veins all collapsing, lives sadly wasted,
The sweetness of youth is no longer tasted.

Their habit is fed by sex being sold,
Just children in years with bodies so old.
Destroyed by the drugs which keep them enslaved,
Please let them find help and not early graves.

—*Margaret Walker*

What Is The World Coming To?

Sometimes I feel like dying.
But always I end up crying,
People say they need me.

The world is becoming cruel.
Where evil individuals rule.
True peace is what I long for,
Now only found at the great door.

What is the world coming to?
Total destruction maybe it's true,
All I know is that I'm scared,
That somebody the world can't be shared.

My life your free to destroy.
But save the world for others to enjoy.
There are people I love and trust.
But I can't help feeling this painful lust.

I feel like dying.
Instead I'm just crying.

—*Shari Dayment*

"She's Lost"

There's someone I would like to know
but getting close is very slow.
There's a lot of pain she's trying to hide
and over this she's never cried.

When you have been emotionally abused,
it's you yourself you accuse.
Low self-esteem is what she excels
For this is the only thing she does so well!

But there comes a time for everyone
When the pain you've tied comes undone
One day she will realize
To know herself she has to cut the ties!

But for now what can I do but wait,
Support her and pray she does it before it's too late!
It's amazing what childhood cost,
When it causes an adult to be lost!

—*Patti Leitch*

The Rugged Beauty Of Scotland

I have seen some beautiful places,
But nothing quite compares,
To the rugged beauty of Scotland,
And the memories I found there.

The rolling hills of purple heather,
Reaching up to meet the sky,
Seemed to say, "Welcome Friends!,"
As I was passing by.

The winding roads that never end,
The endless fields of rye,
The graceful rivers flowing across the land,
Made it hard to say good-bye.

I have seen some beautiful places,
But nothing quite compares,
To the rugged beauty of Scotland,
And the memories I found there.

—*Jackie Miller*

Yesterday

I know the answers are supposed to be wise
But the world is still young behind this disguise

Not only myself I speak for us all
We still think of spring when it really is fall

The days flash on by ever faster it seems
Each one filled with more of yesterdays dreams

For some on the outside it's wrinkles and grey
But here on the inside it's all yesterday

You can melt any time into this ladder of years
With your dreams of the future or the past and its fears

It's hard to believe that you've walked thru the field
From the first planting 'til it's ready to yield

There's only the comfort as time comes to call
It's the love of past seasons as spring turns to fall

—*Walter H Gale*

My Dad

He walks a little slower now,
But will not use his cane
He is too proud!

He used to seem so tall,
But not so now,
His shoulders bend a bit.

I love his mind and always have,
His memory and his humour and his wit
Time has not changed.

Sometimes I catch him dreaming of days gone by,
of battles fought, and places he has been,
But now, only in his mind can go.

—*Shirley Gauthier*

The Song Of Life

My life is only one note
in the song of life.
Some people cannot hear the song
only their note
A note without a song
is a wasted note.
I listen to the song
and sing my note
For the more joy in life
the more harmony in the song

—*Sarah Jackson*

By Chance

I'm sitting beside my window, looking at the moon.
By chance can it be, that you are looking at it too?
If so, I wish I was the moon looking at the world below
Just to be gazed by you.

I wake up in the morning to see the sunshine.
By chance can it be, that you are awake too?
If so, I'd like to be a ray of the sun
That shines beside your window
And slowly rest upon your hand.

As I walk on the meadow green, look up at the blue sky.
By chance can it be, that you've noticed it too?
If so, I'd love to be a part of the blue sky,
That brightens your day.

I'm sitting on a rock, enjoying the sunset.
By chance can it be, that you're viewing it too?

I am sure this sunset will bring me dreams.
By chance can it be, that you feel the same way too?
If so, I'd slave to be this sunset to sweeten your dreams.

—*Cecilia Ratna David*

One Path

What I need to do before I leave,
Can only last a certain finite time.
Of all life's expanding infinities,
Only a tiny chunk, a narrow line.

That which forces me to this chosen path,
This juggernaut, which slowly draws me near,
So that never by me, the starry skies, will be won,
This lack of knowing, by far, my greatest fear.

So, when I consider that all these wonders are there,
Within my sight, but rudely torn from grasp,
I think this to be an unacceptable fate, but then,
I know that the ability to try is all I ask.

—*Nathan Riddle*

Phoenix Born Queen

The ethereal Queen of rock and roll.
Captives the people grasped in her hold.
An ageless spirit from fairy tale days.
In red satin slippers, with gypsies and knaves.
Dances on high with the stars and the moon.
Sways to the rhythm, a black chiffon haze.
Lost in the music, forget everything.
The beautiful white witch has started to sing.
Lets her feelings reach out so far and wide.
Touches fiery emotions deep down inside.
Your music inspires life, love and dreams.
Can you ever know how much that means?
Magical, mystical Phoenix Born Queen.

—*Kirsty Louise Stevenson*

A Puzzle Piece

A puzzle piece
Is a puzzle too.
It could be a paper crease
Or an elephant's shoe.
Or perhaps a dress.
It could be a face.
Maybe a person
On a hike keeping pace.

More or less, more or less

A puzzle piece is a wonderful mess!

—*Lila Selim*

The Itch That Would Not Be Scratched

If you were who I am, you might expect talk about a certain
characteristic Mozartian;
Or about the tragic Marilyn;
Who in a film won renown
While tenaciously and virtuously she held down
Those fluffy summery skirts
A subterranean draft,
From a passing behemoth underground,
Forced upward against her will.
Rumour has it that what civility
Demands we cover, ne'er was — really!

The itch I could not scratch
Was absolutely mundane,
For I was supine, jaws agape
And filled with hardware and a bit of India fare
With an occasional fist therein
And, all the while,
The numb'ed chin had that itch
One that would not be scratched.

—*Ruth R. Gordon*

A Tormented Mother's Past as Presented by One Child

Your Child was Born innocent and sweet
Coming to you with no great feat

Memories were to be your making
As your child, this is where it becomes shaking

Memories of the past, are haunting
Never to be forgotten, yet wanting

You profess to have been a good mother
Yet you have never proved this to another

Cruel treatment has been denied
Yet my heart has always cried

I remember, yet will not say
You have constantly made me pay

A child is a child until it is grown
What you receive from that child will be shown

Your rewards will be just
As in your making, it is a must

—*Lydia Prentice-Hill*

Untitled

Oh, moon your silver pathway on the dark night sea.
Could I but walk it to the one I wish to see,
Clear as a diamond pathway to me
Cold silver moon on a deep dark sea.
If I could walk that pathway on the sea
All my dreams would come true you'd see.
We'd love and warm that cold dark sea
My love and I with a warm warm love of the sea

—*Ada Reed*

Love

The dark grim animosity
is growing
into
a gnarled twisted
hate
that slowly progresses
into
a hopeless nonsensical
love

—*Sara P. Hausman*

Trinity

We watched when sunrise warmed the Earth
(Crimson lit the sky);
But when the moon made colours fade,
All alone sat I

We watched when summer's sun did warm
(The Autumn breeze drew nigh);
But when some winter winds did blow,
All alone sat I

We watched when stars made heaven bright
(Angels sang on high);
But when some crosses nails did make,
All alone sat I

We watched when peace did rule the world
(Hatred seemed to die);
But love did missiles soon replace,
And all alone sat I

We watched when sunsets scorched the Earth
(Crimson seared the sky);
And when Mankind made colours fade,
All alone sat I

—*Andrea England*

Last Farewell

Angeline, Oh Angeline!
Cry not that I surrender
To eternal grace;
Wondrous delights prevail
To which I must make haste.

Do not mourn this
Fading star;
Your rage will not last,
When reborn, my sacred flame in
Mortality doth pass.

Soon shall I understand
That which we have sought,
Cloaked within a new eternal peace;
Floating through a world as yet unknown,
Where darkened thoughts, my love, forever cease.

Recall the memories
Etched within your mind,
Laughter which we shared and grew so fond;
Awaiting my return my tender love,
My companion through the door which lies beyond.

—*Cynthia Syme*

The Door

A lake in the still of morning, The sun at the break of
dawn. The clouds at the end of twilight, A deer standing
there with her fawn. The smell of the trees in summer,
the sound of a waterfall's roar, the look of a moose as
it's feeding, All this I have seen - and more. The ice as
it freezes in winter, The snow as it falls from the sky.
The sound of ducks going southward, These are things that
a man cannot buy. And still I keep looking for new sights,
that will touch me right to my core, I keep looking ahead
down the pathway, all this I have seen - and more. The
road keeps going before me, the road that never will end.
I will follow it all through my lifetime, I will travel
each byway and bend. And when I come to my ending, When
before me there opens a door - I will say as I make my way
through it - All this I have seen - and more -

—*James Carson*

Letting Life Pass You By

.... He continues to sing. The world is falling at his feet,
destruction emperor of human desire
Hatred dances in the flames left by the heat of war.

.... He continues to sing. Perdition reins within all that is
good for us to not have. Poisoned energy, thoughtless cares,
afraid and unsure of the unknown where.

.... He continues to sing—a melody droned and monotonous,
repetitive—it lacks poetry. One bit of a song oblivious to
tempo, his tune off beat and flat
One song we ridicule in fear while sounds carry over the winds
towards stranger's ear.

A melody immune to us, creating a world of fantasy within the
walls of his sanity, yet beyond the boundaries this sweet song
inside his opinion plays forever in his mind, but we cannot
hear the rest of the tune we so feverishly blocked out. Not
listening hard enough to his innards to hear the melody that
tastes of his love and brings his emotions high, we are immune.

And when we are able to open our hearts unto the peace and
enchanting tune which calls out to the passions of time,
it is then we fear we have missed the sweetest songs of life.

—*Jennifer Guay*

Mother

Mother you've given so much of your life
devoted to children and being a good wife.

You've given your best years without much despair
Unselfishly loved me when I was unfair

You taught me to love since I started growing
defended my wrongs without even knowing.

You taught me of courage as well about prayer
You've never regretted the times you've been there.

My debts you have paid for that you did not owe
I cannot pay back but want you to know.

The good I've become is all part of you
for you're the foundation on which I grew.

In my gift of life there will never be one
whom I will love more than you, Mom....

—*Roberta Schneider*

I'm No Stranger To Suffering

I'm no stranger to suffering
Did my mother no retch and retch
Whilst the pungent onion smell
Whiffed through the kitchen door
Engulfing my whole being

Did I not endure the noxious fumes
Of many a car down the road
Little comfort did the womb provide
But still I survived
And my mother bulged and bulged

Today I look aside
Knowing looks and wicked grins change faces
Like weeds I thrive
With grit I survive
I'm not stranger to suffering.

—*Gloria Kadyamatimba*

You And Me

Among us there lies a special breed
    different then the rest
When we, our mates do find
They to are a special kind -

Though the devil lays the rules and eyes
    us with suspicion
Still we challenge him with our intuition
Together we will stand and fight
    for what we believe is right.

Our love lies deep within our very soul
    and cannot be stole.
And when within you deep I lie
    there comes a shutter not a sigh

As if from the depths of hell
A beast rises on a swell
And as the swell subsides
Gentleness appears in your eyes

    Yes, my dear we do stand apart
        And for these reasons we should never part
    —*Joachim Sparmann*

Digital Romance

What's on the menu today, dear little PC of mine?
Does it feel good when you're booted and finally on line?
Interactive behavior exploits your Megabytes,
Dialogue reveals depths and hidden delights.
One could not wish for a more compatible friend,
Except during a power cut, or at the weekend!
Your resolution and peripherals are quite out of this world.
Your carriage and footprint are a joy to behold.
Are you heavily into fanfold my love,
Or will single sheets do 'til we've both had enough?
My language is Basic, you Remember of course,
It's how we communicate, in fact it's our source.
How can we control the feelings of lust as
Configured and formatted we exploit you clusters?
I open up windows on your intimate screen,
In awed silence you wait for my next drag routine.
The world's a network of hooked-up nations,
And we, a part of telecommunications.
Amid passwords and glitches and Lans and tritons,
Let's escape dear, lose control dear, and wallow in icons!
    —*Ken Harper*

At The River Bend

When the sun always sparkles and the birds sing a song
Down at the river bend that's where I belong
The water is so clear
That at the bottom it seems so near
The little breeze
Will sway the trees
Down at the river bend where my dreams never come to a end.

I had a secret friend
Down at the river bend
We had so much fun building giant sand castles in the sun
Then one summer day he said goodbye and moved away
But the memories will keep us forever friends
Down at the river bends!

But my secret friend returned again,
Somewhere other than the river bend,
He was not the same as he used to be,
And the memories started to fade away from me,
So know I wonder about down at the river bend,
Maybe dreams can come to an end!
    —*Ann Ranson*

To Mom, From Your Daughter

Last night sleep didn't come easy.
Dozing off, waking up, my mind on you.
The pitter-pat of raindrops on my window.
Wondering, like my thoughts of you.

A grey, cold day, appropriate, suites me.
Grasping unto memories of you, as you were.
A sunny warm day wouldn't fit, not today.
My hands are cold, my eyes are tired, and my thoughts are
     with you.

In this day and age, leaving life behind is easier.
Freedom from pain, worry and fear, and uncertainty.
I take relief in knowing God handle things better than we.
He can make our dreams come true, and when there are no more,
     takes us home.

The pain will hit me, the tears will flow,
For what wasn't said or done, for hopes and wishes left behind.
For the piece of my heart shattered, and the lost part of my
     life so cherished, that which gave me life.

    —Kimberly Lilgert

The Old Mans Dreams And Tears

The old man sat in the swing, on his porch
Dreaming of yester years,
Of things he had planned and things he had done
And slowly his eyes filled with tears.

He thought of the woman, his lover, his wife
Who stood by his side, through all their strife,
The hard times, when their life together began
And down his cheeks the bitter tears ran.

He thought about long cold winter nights
And of the gentle summer rains,
Of cattle grazing in pastures green
And beautiful fields of waving grain.

He thought of the lovely daughter, they raised
To that wondrous age of seven,
Then GOD, in HIS infinite wisdom
Took her back home to HEAVEN.

His wife and daughter are together again
Two weeks ago, his helpmate died,
That's why the old man sits alone
And the reason why he cried.

    —A. C. Tillett

"Spring Is Here!"

The ground hogs are out and sniffing around,
Eating the new clover close to the ground.
The trees are budding with yellow-green leaves
And everyone's gardening with rolled up sleeves.
The Red-Wings, Robins and Swallows are here.
Building their nests for another short year.
The ponds are full and pulsating with life
Where frogs and peepers chorus all night.
Bright, happy daffodils and dandelions too,
Dance in the breeze, their hats all askew!
Grass fires burning with a heavenly smell,
Branches and dead leaves bid winter farewell.
Skies overhead are a beautiful blue.
Painting the lake with the same colour too.
Young May is such a glorious time,
When the earth comes alive and the days
are sublime!

    —Muriel E. Dundass

The Beckoning Sea

Close to my heart, is the song of the sea.
E'en o'er the many miles,
It, keeps on...
Calling to me.

Beckoning thru remembrances
Of sea shore, sand dunes, shellfish and gulls,
Sea grasses, brown pelicans,
Ol' fishing boat hulls.

To stroll on the beach
For many a mile
'T would do the heart good
Etch one's face in a smile.

Peace, peace, there
By the water's edge.
Alive, alive, as wind current
Waves sea oats and sedge!

Undulating waters, exuding surf's foam
Entrapped in a rhythm, like my mind...
Here at home.

    —Mary Olan

Snow

Look upon your serenity
fill my desire till dawn
Quietly falling you sedate me
in the glow of evening moon

Mountains welcome your adorning
ice water, freezing cold,
but you're warming

Unforgettable moment
stays with us but for a while
till seasons pass
like a child growing
maturing fruit from the loins of the bearer
Nearer doth summer come and take you far from me

    —Shane Cris Pyers

Searching Soul

High across the heavens I soar
Fleeting grandeur, with silver-tipped wings I dip
To view below the bustling of life;
A mixture of colors
Clashing in fervency to find
Its pattern line of perfection.
Power and stress its obstacles;
Creating fusion in disarray;
A faint thin line glimmers
Majestically weaved throughout the chaos
An illustrious ray in quest for right of way
Fortified by sincerity and purpose
Dauntless in its theme
Little by little it gathered the threads of colors within its beam
Majesty could not be denied the guild
That one day would coat my flight
As the colors would be one
At the journey's end of life.

    —Arlene M. MacKenzie

Spring

Spring flowers grow and the stream flows.
While the May winds blow!
Some birds flutter by, while they sing.
Because it's now warm spring!
A puppy barks when he walks to the park.
The leaves start to bud and there's a lot of mud!

    —Samantha Demers

340

In Libraries

In libraries you search and look
    For audio, video, fiche and book

Learn from sources, learn from tools
    Knowledge, sciences and its brooks.

Information, statistics and the log
    Are filed in one or more catalogue

Books are memories, fiche are treasuries
    Biographies, Dictionaries and Directories

Research is the name, reach is the game
    read, search and accomplish aim

Attain, achieve and also find
    Ideas, inventions and beyond.

Request, ask or demand
    Librarian will always be at hand

Yes! you'll find your track
    In Yearbooks, Encyclopedias and Almanac
        —Suzan Nabih Metry

You Mean Everything In My Destiny

You mean everything in my destiny and then war and ruin
For long, long in that chaos about you every news was lost.
That voice of yours, voice of yours, which was dead,
After many years once more shook me.

I was reading your testament in the night
And then I woke from soul swoon.
To people I hurry, to crowds, to the morning bustle and chores
And then I cannot understand my trial
But I would like to order them - be nice!

Suddenly I impetuously went with them
And I had a feeling that it was the first time for me
When I saw the street covered by snow
So it was easy to feel the deadness and silence about it.

I felt for the people, felt for them, like I were having
all their parts, I was melted like snow heated by Sun
and again like sky I was clouded over.

But hearts already are sturdy, the days which are coming
strict the faces with fastidious despise
That is the last thought.
You mean everything in my destiny!
        —Barbara Potempa

Time

Did you visit to-day with a shut-in
From whom time runs out like a sieve?
Can you pile up your most precious moments
And one of them cheerfully give?

Will you brighten one hour with sunshine
Of his which are mostly all grey
Relating a choice bit of nonsense
Thus changing November to May?

Can you offer your handclasp when needed
And smile into eyes dimmed with pain
Or quietly speak with assurance
To give him fresh courage again?

Can you pray to the Heavenly Father
To ask that all suffering cease
And note on the face of the sufferer
A look of contentment and peace?

Have you thought then, of those needing comfort
Whose heads oft in loneliness bow?
Enough of that Procrastination
The time for that visit is now.!
        —Joan Cecile Lugg

The Waiting

Just around the corner it waits,
Full of anticipation, I'm its bait.
I fell into the stupid trap,
Now I have to pay for all my crap.
I'm walking towards the coming dark,
Behind me are the singing larks,
But it's funny that they sound so sad,
My interpretation is completely mad.
I have self-pity and a dying dread,
that around the corner, it's dressed in red.
If only the time could rewind.
If only the one above didn't mind,
then I'd know my mistake would be fixed.
Everything wouldn't be so mixed,
but I know that just around the corner,
Will be a painful dark red blur.
It'll pull me towards it, not let go,
My blood will never stop the flow.
I'll deserve the approaching blow.
As soon as I get around the corner...
        —Hema Mulrajani

High Above

Amidst the vastness of the endless heavens,
Glows infinitely a dim, romantic twilight.
The soft tiny pearls of its quiescent light
    dance slowly above the fragile beauty
    of the sleeping roses.
Its delicate, dewy, svelte moondrops slither
    across the land like liquid golden silk
    poured from the heavens.
The sparkling silent beauty called moonlight.
        —Sonia Dass Sethi

Death

Death you are the king. The king of no mercy. Wherever you
go, you leave them crying and mourning. You come when you are
not invited and leave them a trail of panic and confusion.
Your visits are accompanied by fear and terror. When you come,
you come like a hungry vulture descending upon a carcass. You

strike randomly and indiscriminately. You don't choose or
select whether the victim is young, old deaf or dump. You even
kill the unborn ones, those who know nothing about you. Death
you don't have mercy or spare where you stroke last year, this
year, last month, this month last week, this week, yesterday or
even today you strike even when they that are mourning - When the fresh
sad memories of their beloved are still in their minds. Death you
are the most known and respected king. You are even feared by
the most respected and feared king of this land. Those with
millions of soldiers don't want to hear your name. Death
you are the commander and the general of yourself. There is not
even a single war which you fight and loose, you are the
conqueror. The mentioning of your name causes panic and
confusion among the living. Death, if you were a human being
the rich people would use their wealth against you.
You, the conqueror of life, no one hasn't been affected by you one
way or another. When are you going to stop taking or visiting
our beloved ones?
        —Shingie Magwera

Insurance

Depths fall under pressure,
Together, finding old treasures of reassurance.
Gaining insurance.
Of ancient ways of seeing,
and believing.
        —Richard Johnston

341

God's Presence

Spring is here, and as we can see,
God's gifts are amongst us on land and on sea.
We see God's flowers, oh what a site,
that God's given powers are with us tonight.
The sunrise of a spring mornin', the smell of God's rain,
only to feel God's presence,
will we be blessed again and again.
We read the bible, and what do we find?
How God made the Earth and also the Sky.
God asked Noah, to build a great Ark,
and to remember his achievement with his whole heart.
The flood was a coming, like our emotions inside,
God asked Noah to gather all the animals that he could find.
So off on a whirlwind and out with a roar,
the Ark set adrift, to find something more.

—*Terry Jackson*

A Suicide

Neptune spreads his silver-white fingers
Hard on sheer black rock-face,
And drags down, down...
A spray of white rose petals scatters in the wind
And is lost.
Sea, wind and moonlight fuse in mesmerizing trance;
Storm clouds roll laboriously over the horizon,
And a lone crusade of waves
Rush at the girl' imagination.
She stands, clothes billowing out to sea,
Encouraged by the persuasive wind from behind
Persistent and forceful.

Visions of her life flit and waft through her mind
Like drugged butterflies;
Beautiful, fragile, sadly crushed.
Tangy salt in her throat as she cries...
Then is gone.
Grasses on the deserted cliff-top wave in unison
And a salutary caress from the shifting waters
Covers her.

—*Miranda Montgomery*

My Poem

As I journey inward, many aspects of my life
Have become clearer with the strife.
I was lonely in our house of three,
Just my mother, brother and me.
Hugs and kisses, were never given,
I never really knew, "What was living?"
No childhood to remember, it seems to be a crime
I grew up an adult, way before my time.
Tears didn't come, with all the pain,
Sometimes I thought I would go insane.
So each and every day, I soothed it all away
The food in youth, and smokes at teens,
With booze and drugs following early it seems.
These escapes helped me to hide the truth,
But one day I realized I needed proof.
I wanted to find the real me, to look inside and really see.
So, you must deal with the past,
Forgive, and then Love yourself.
The day it finally happens, it's like being born again.
The old cast is broken, your heart has become your friend.

—*Sue Lipohar*

People Of The World

People of the world in outer space,
Your relationship is as delicate as lace.
Keep your culture your beliefs and your ways,
For those are the most important things these days.

—*Anna Du Vent*

Haiku On Anglo-Japanese Cultural Interaction

Eager, from the east,
The Chrysanthemums arrived:
Roses have returned.

—*Edward R. Pater*

Just Be

Lord, I want to serve You.
  He answered, "Just be you."
Lord, I want to learn of You.
  He answered, "Just be you."
Lord, I want to give to You.
  He answered, "Just be you."
Lord, I want to sing for You.
  He answered, "Just be you."

I couldn't understand why all those things were wrong.
I want to give so much, myself, I want to belong.

"There's nothing you can do, My child, to earn My love and care
You must trust I love you, while My ways with you I share."

"All I want is the child I saw when you gave you life to Me,
There's no way you can rush ahead, you only have to be."

"So trust in Me and I'll show you, it really isn't far,
For as you trust and lean on Me, you'll realize you are."

—*Debbie Ingoldsby*

Arabin Horse

On his small, tough legs and feet,
he is able to withstand the greatest heat.

Provides a great deal of pleasure,
Is a great friend, and for must people a treasure.

He is about 15 hands in height.
And as most horses is very bright.

All are fast and very sensitive,
But they are quite expensive

His silky coat and flowing mine,
Is as soft as cat's; he is the Arab's fame.

—*Iwona Magdalena Gozdz*

The Reason I Like Rimsky-
Heart Over Mind

The yearning of the human heart
Is different from the mind
The heart wants dignity, love,
The courage to be kind.

The mind can never be
a truly meaningful guide,
Because when we use it for thinking,
It stumbles over pride.

We can overcome our cluttered mind
That thinks with careful thought,
Weighing each fact we think about
Against bigotry that's taught

For if we follow within a path
That our humble heart relates
There is a beautiful soul within
That can do as God dictates.

The soul and heart within us
Can our salvation be
The mind can stifle and restrain
The heart can set us free

—*Wanda L. Young*

342

He Was Too Old...Too Bad

I saw him there that evening,
He was at work, you see.
He asked me what my name was
I fumbling said, "WHO ME?"

The days, they were heaven sent,
And fortunately I saw,
That the days did not come
So quickly...as they went.

So, there I went every day
In a dream, you might say.
And when he did come closer,
I did not pull away.

We talked a lot, day by day.
And when I thought I was bringing him closer,
I soon found out, I was only,
Pushing him away.

To think now, it makes me sad,
But I have now come to see
Although he seemed just right for me,
He was too old...too bad.

—Krystal O'Shaughnessy

'Dina'

Her shadow of motion is stillness,
Her apparel is of the night.
As a tiger, she quantifies all around her,
Freeing conceptual light.
Her visage is pure delight.

Her beauty is as the inception of radiance;
She emanates flaming light.
A constant in pure madness,
I thank the creator for the gift of sight;
Her beauty is pure delight.

Her voice soothes my home,
When she speaks, there can be no pain.
Conversing with her, there is no-one else,
I would for that time again.
Her voice please, once again.

Though this time is brief,
I try with all my might,
To recapture her presence again,
To see that conceptual, emanating light.
Her person is my delight.

—Senarath Wijeyesinghe

Children In The Garden

Here come in the garden,
many big and small children.

They sit, they sleep under the tree shadow,
they dream about seeing a puppet show.

It is the dawn of the human life,
when they run, they chat, they laugh.

They talk with their dolls, they have lot of spirit,
they eat the cake, they are exquisite.

It's you the horse, who drags the cart,
It's me the coachman, who stops and starts.

Life has four stages, childhood, adolescence, adult and old,
purity of childhood inspires the old like gold.

The mouth of children are full of murmurs,
they are rosy and full of fresh air.

—T. G. Hema

Painter's Canoe

Stretched upon the woodpile
Her bottom to the sky
Scrapes and scuffs of summer
Patched by snowy dye.

The lake nearby is glassy with ice and snowy bank
Drifting up the landing where water last they drank.

The canvas snow her cover, her ribs will rest of pain
Waiting for the painter to green her up again

In springtime she'll be mended then turned upon her keel
By the painter now impatient with brushes he would wheel.

The lakes recall her prowess
The streams her cutting ways
Like the painter knows the islands
And the forest by the bays.

For now upon the woodpile
'Neath snowy canvas dream
Of spring and autumn colors
The painter will redeem.

—Garnet Hewitt

Tarnished Dream

My father, what hope you had for me,
Honesty, integrity and all virtues to be.
Promising I was, no doubt,
Now no more than a lout
My father, forgive me for I have sinned
You were my base, my cornerstone,
The fulcrum of all my actions.
Nothing is left for me but to atone,
For disregarding my inherent unction.
My father, forgive me for I have sinned.
Little did I do to fulfill your dreams,
Whatever achieved is tarnished indeed.
My life is falling apart at the seams,
Falling prey to my unholy misdeeds.
My father forgive me for a I have sinned.

—Nalinesh Arun

Lost Love

How you walked into my life
How easily I opened up to you
You swept me off my feet
How you showed me happiness

You showed me what, true love was
Whispering to me, that it was for good
How joyous we were together
Nothing could stand in our way

Girl I did not do no wrong
But it all went wrong
Why did you leave me out there in the cold
With nothing for comfort

All the happy times that we had together
Your smiling face brought me joy
Just seeing the sight of you
Made my insides turn with joy

Now, every move I make,
The memories of you, just won't fade.
I have many, a sleepless night
Life without you, is just not right.

—Aman Ravindra Singh

1993-03-07

The moon is closer now to the earth, than it has been in one hundred years. In Britain people are wondering if the tides will flood up to their ears.

The moon is closer now to the earth, maybe that is the reason why my blood is rushing whoosh through my ears and my emotions are running high.

The moon is closer now to the earth, dogs howl and I want to cry when I see the beauty of la lune up close and count all the stars in the sky.

The moon is closer now to the earth, our cycles are all out of kilter. Insomnia keeps me awake with the skunks till I breathe with the aid of a filter.

The moon is closer now to the earth, aborigines are running scared but I'd love to make love in this light of the moon, when all inhibitions are bared.

The moon is closer now to the earth, than it's been in one hundred years a remarkable wonder made just for me to celebrate my forty-three years.

—*Dinah Lee Waddell*

Infinity

As I sit here through dark and dreary days,
I cannot help but wish I'd changed my ways
and done the things I always said I'd do,
But time grows short, the days are getting few.

Our days are numbered, we are as the snow,
One day we're here, the next no more,
We drift away as if we'd never been
and move somewhere to an unknown scene.

I wonder what it's like, I feel afraid
of the things unknown; have I paid?
Enough to earn the place I hope is mine,
Have I been loving, thoughtful and so kind?

We live on through our children we are told,
This thought will be my peace if I grow old.
I pray to God to grant me this full life
and free me from my worry and my strife.

—*Jeannette Harris*

I Gave You Love!

Love is a precious thing so hard to find.
    I gave you love!
Faithful, honest, true and kind
    I gave you love!

I have never cheated with other guys.
Never had reason to tell you lies.
Never even wanted to.
    I gave you love!

I see more clearly now, years down the line,
Heartache, so real, most of the time, and still.
    I gave you love!

You have used me, abused me, and always
Denied me the right to care.
When I needed you most you were never there. Yet,
    I gave you love

So incredible was the love we once knew,
It's hard to believe that none could be true.
Now I know, if I stay,
I truly will be in your way.
So, I'll go. But please know
    I gave you love!

—*Isobel Smith*

Trust

When I was a girl, I thought I could trust my parents
I grew up and made mistakes
Which made them doubt about me,
Now they don't trust me the same.

Then I started to trust my friend,
She was my best friend so, why wouldn't I trust her?
Later she betrayed me, I never thought she would.
And I lost all my hopes in having someone to trust.

As I kept walking in my life,
I had problems and I had no one to trust.

Then in my walk I found someone,
He was a stranger to me at first but slowly,
He become my friend then my partner,
And now he is the man I love, the man I trust.

I hope he will never turn from me
Even if our love stops,
I pray that he will never betray me like other people did.

—*Pia Quintana Beristain*

I Am Faster Than Lightening

From the time I came on this planet earth
I have succeeded in destroying lives
I am no respecter of persons
The rich, the poor black or white

I have been traveling around the world for years
I don't need a plane, a car, a boat
I have brought heart ache to the human race
And loneliness to the world

Medical science and doctors have tried everything
They are just working in vain
Polio was the number one killer
But I have over powered polio
I am the champion of champions
The only cure for me is a miracle
From God
You want to know who I am
I am aids.

—*Joyce John Baptiste*

Red Slippers

Bright worn outward appearance with rubber soles, I hid them in the far-off corner of her bedroom. She, my grandmother, found them the next day, and struck my tender little bottom. Discipline is carried out as a ritual, and the "Red Slipper" is often used as a part of the performance. A young innocent child's face showed pain and anger when the rubber soles struck that tender skin.

I developed hatred but not enough to heal my pain. One night, I went against her will, and the "Red Slipper" struck again. Tears ran like water pouring down my face like a river running wild, meandering towards the ocean, and I realized I must have done something severe to deserve the "Red Slipper" once again.

My horrifying grandmother's strict rules of discipline carried on, and I realized the punishment I had been receiving would not have occurred if I only listened to her call.

The "Red Slipper" is hidden once again, but this time my grandmother put it away. I suppose I had been well-behaved but lately I have come to despise any object made out of red.

—*Janet Millendez*

A Lesson Learned Late

I listen with ears that do not hear;
I look with eyes that do not see.
I pray to whatever power there be,
To clear these senses and set me free.

I love with a heart that's grown cold;
I quake with fear from being bold.
I cannot bear this growing old
Without someone to have, to hold.

I drifted through life from start to end,
And although its road had many a bend,
There's never been one real, dear friend;
Our fancied troubles we each could mend.

Now as this life does slowly fade,
The Fates I surely can't upbraid;
For it was I alone who sat in shade,
And never one meaningful effort made.

Learn this lesson, learn it well:
Enjoy a bird's song, a flower's smell;
Friendships make, and make them well,
Then in your heart true love can dwell.

—*Jon Christensen*

On the Death of an Eccentric Old Woman

For years she walked these woods.
I often met her,
Fingering the flowers,
And muttering kind scoldings to the trees.
She measured out the seasons
Watching the leaves,
And calling to the birds.
Now she is dead,
Mourned by none save I.

Her paths remain,
Green trails through brown bracken.
Her birds fly overhead
Chittering cheerful song,
While speckled lizards flit across her ways.
Now I walk with none to find.
This kingdom, now more lonely,
Now is only mine -
Until I too am gone.

—*Laurie Sullivan*

Dracula

As I stand alone among the dead a great fear is born within me
I search for a way out all I see is miles of tombstone
Then I hear it the howling of the wolves
I look up to see a full moon then I see it
In the moon's faint light resting upon a mound of fresh earth
A lordly tomb centuries of years old
Slowly it opens
To reveal a creature
With scarlet fresh blood
On its mocking, sensuous lips
I turn to run only to be stopped
By an army of the dead
Slowly closing in upon me
I look towards the creature
A strange force draws me towards it
I walk beneath the moon towards it
As I reach it, it grasps my hand
Then in a sudden whirl of darkness
I find myself in the vaults beneath a desolate castle
It then pronounces a single word "Dracula"
And sinks its sharp ivory fangs into the base of my neck

—*Natalie Bussiere*

The Altar

As I walk up the isle with a bouquet in my hand,
I see my fiance there who can barely stand.
His knees are wobbly, and he is white in the face,
He looks at me nervously, I'm dressed in satin and lace.

I look at him calmly and give him the smile,
That says he is gracious, has class and style.
His knees stop shaking, his face is now pink,
He is so self-conscious of what I think.

My bridesmaids follow with such delight,
And then there is the flower girl so full of fright.
The ring bearer so cute and so charmingly sweet,
Is dressed in his tux so tidy and neat.

We reach the altar and what do I do?
I trip and fall, and off goes my shoe.
It glides through the air and where does it land?
Right in the comfort of my fiance's left hand.

I am doing the splits but up I go,
I have given my guests enough of a show.
My dress is all wrinkled, my veil on the floor,
My pride is hurt, and my ligaments are tore.

—*Billie-Jo (Chiles) Ferguson*

Wondering

In a corner by myself,
I sit alone wondering.
Watching people stealing,
Hitting, yelling, fighting over stupid things.
Why? I ask. Why can't we just be friends?
All of us.
Black, white, red, brown, yellow.
The rich, the poor, the homeless, the hungry.
If everyone would just try,
Life would be much better.
If the rich would give to the poor,
And the white would stop fighting with the black.
And everyone liking people for what's inside,
Not out. I wouldn't be here now,
Alone,
In a corner,
sitting by myself,
wondering,
watching,
Crying.

—*Deanna L. Spinney*

Yesterday

Seems like it was yesterday
I was sitting in the kitchen watching you.
You were baking something, I don't remember what.
I followed you all around.
If I got in your way,
You gave no sign.
Seems like it was yesterday,
I was kneeling beside you in church.
You were teaching me how to pray.
You gave me something to believe in,
In a world where nothing seems fair
Seems like it was just last night,
You tucked me in, and said good-night.
But now I'm wide awake,
And I can't find you anywhere.

—*Krystal Chamaillard*

345

Please Remember!

I would like you to know that when you get hurt,
I will be hurting just as much as you are.

And I hope that you will always remember,
I'm on your side.
For everything that you do

I am here to laugh and also cry with you
But I am always here to love you

I know that there are moments we all try to
do the best we can.
And we try and give it our all.

Those feelings come from our heart and souls.

But from my heart to your heart please remember,
That I will love you forever...
And ever!

—*Leslie Brown*

I Wish

I wish you were still there
I wish you were there for me, waiting for me

I wish you were there, laughing, enjoying life
I wish we were together

I know now it can't be
I know it's late, too late

I have no regrets whatever we've done
I have no regrets whatever your life was

I wish you told me again you love me
I wish I stayed longer in your arms

I wish you were still there.

—*Karine Christelle Ardault*

Black

Black reminds me of the sorrow I keep inside.
If I let it out it will destroy things around me.
I run and hide but it does not care it wants to break free.
It claws at my insides and makes me cry.
I try to think happy thoughts but it comes back to haunt me.
What can I do to ease the pain?
I try to tell people but it comes out all wrong.
My life is a lake and I am drowning.
This is the end I can't live any more.
Help me save me bring me back.
I'm falling further into the black hole of despair.

—*Olivia Ouellette*

To My Wife At Harvard

Enchanted by full-fraught Harvard
Inspired by Fulbright award
You took flight ten thousand miles along
Leaving me alone here to endure amorous pang
Day in and day out your absence I painfully feel
Your charming look, elegant make and sweet talk I miss all
Think of two hundred days and nights of separation
My heart sinks deep into suspended animation
Spacial distances along the longitudes
Carve utter temporal inconveniences
When I dial you to tell "Have a nice sleep, dear"
Sense of global times prompts you to reply "Have a nice day,
dear": Should our brief separation mean cooperation
For you to expand your intellectual horizon
I appeal to my reason to boss over my emotion
And wait for you to come home with greater emancipation.

—*A. Ramesha Rao*

Friends And Me

What a wonderful place it would be,
If it was just the earth and me.
I could laugh and sing and have some fun,
all beneath the sun.
No houses, no walls, no cages, or anything in their places.
Yet I would get quite lonely, for I am very homely.
If I could choose just one friend
I don't know who I would pick;
Still if I searched my heart of hearts, it would come in a
click. Not many people think this way, but still I want to
obey. He picked me up and put me together, with all
the right pieces.
His name is Jesus.
Yet a human voice I would like to hear,
With my very own human ear.
I choose my friends, my teacher, and all my kin
Some animals and yes, even Kim!
So now the world is back with me,
And it's still a wonderful place to be!

—*Eryn Austin*

The Autumn Ball

You're invited to a party which takes place in the fall.
In a great, great, forest it really is a ball.

The theme is "Autumn Splendor", the music, is the breeze.
Which seems always to be gentle,
As it rustles through the leaves.

There is a great excitement among the many trees.
As they don their favorite colours, for all of us to please.

The pine, the spruce, the hemlock,
In shades of green and yellow,
The dogwood and the birch, to make it all so mellow.

The maple and the sumac, in shades of red and gold.
And many other colours, too numerous to be told.

I'll keep my invitation and I'll return next fall.
I wouldn't miss the pleasure to attend, "The Autumn Ball"

—*Jan McCourt*

Lucien

I see you as you sit so peacefully
    in front of the man we all call Jesus.
There is no sadness as I look into your face
    only happiness and a sense of peace.

My heart hurts for those you left behind
    many cloudy days to come they will find.
There will be tears of sorrow
    any lonely days ahead. ·
Special times to face they will surely dread.

To each and every one I would like to say
    you really did not die, you have only gone away.
Take the time you need to heal
    cry the tears that you must.
Knowing always He is there, in that you can trust.

Goodbye for now our friend and neighbor
    your pain is gone, no need to labor.
Know you are loved and missed by all,
    and that we'll meet again
As we each receive our call.

—*Esther M. Ternes*

Ashes

A hand came
In the cover of wisdom,
It was the Hand that holds the key,
To life and to death
Death's door opened and you were taken in
Away from us,
We loved you;
Away from me,
I lived for you
You were my inspiration,
Everything you said,
Everything you did,
Held the spark of love and the fire of life,
The spark has died down now
And the fire is but ashes
Leaving only a memory,
Of the warmth and light it gave.

—*Teri Lynn Kyler*

Brave Son Of America

America, the Savior of Africa. You have obeyed God's
inspiration To wrestle dictators of Africa. Opposition and
sedition are synonymous in Africa.

You wiped the tears of Kenyans. Bush administration sent
Ambassador Smith Hempstone. He came and conquered.

Democracy dawned in Kenya in 1989 December,
The month Smith Hempstone landed on Kenya soil.
A valiant and persistent soldier he has been.

In April 1990 he proclaimed American Congress Order,
No more American aid to dictators',
Americans' tax must nourish democratic institutions only'.

'Proclamation is a dream, a nightmare', President Moi
exclaimed! Bullets of abuse were shot at Smith Hempstone.
'Racialist and drug pusher', he was called by Kenya Government.
'Forward ever backward never', Smith Hempstone replied. 'Aid
squeeze is unbearable', yelled President Moi and succumbed.
Multiparty politics was born in 1991 December.

What a great achievement within 3 years of determined effort!
We, Kenyans owe Americans immeasurable debt of gratitude.

—*J. G. Nderitu*

Untitled

To live life without feeling
Is to never live at all
You have to let the emotion give way
To answer the questions life will call.
Listen to the wind
And feel its full sound
Let the breezes take your heart
To a place no one else has ever found.
Learn to feel the sunlight
For it is joy and it is pain
Let the tides of sensation take you away
And bring you back again.
Do not be afraid to live and love
Or to reach out to a feeling within
Life is to be lived with both joy and pain
Feel, and your life will begin.

—*Jennifer Douglas*

...At Sunset

I watch the sun as it dips out of sight;
It gently welcomes the cool of the night.
The clouds shine red long after sundown;
Floating on air like a giant crown.

The night sets in-the stars begin to dance;
Holding me fast in a steady trance.
I watch the moon, a tiny crescent,
Start its slow, but steady descent.

The city lights pierce the darkening air,
I find myself thinking "they're really not there".
My awakening was rude , so sudden and tragic....
Time brought an end to my evening of magic.

—*Promeet J. Singh*

Beauty

Beauty withers like a flower
It is the grade vineyard created by God
It is like butterflies floating above the flowers
Mass of flowers on a bush, a sight of beauty
What ever portrays the human feature
Is what has gone mad and destructive
Beauty withers like a flower

God the creator of mankind
For under His creation He molded beauty
The land ploughed with creational beauty
Where man doubts himself in excitement
He is like a child crying for this and that
Beauty withers like a flower

If beauty is love, if love is beauty
Beauty is guilt of love, it is smeared with hatred
Man has died, obtained injuries because of love
He divorce, lingers because of beauty
The beauty that withers, that disturbs promises
Tears hatred and killing the picture of beauty
Beauty withers like a flower.

—*Patrick Ramolefhe*

The Butterfly And I

Although it was just a butterfly,
It was more than that to me.
So beautiful, small, and graceful
Its coloring was of golden yellows,
Glorious greens, and unearthly browns.
But why? Why was it more
Than just a butterfly to me?
Suddenly a young boy, no more than ten,
Took his net and caught the butterfly
Now I knew.., It was I entangled in that net
Except, it was not a net anymore,
But a web of different emotions.
Sadness, happiness, anger, even fear.
Irrationally, I ran up to the boy,
"Let it go", I screamed, and he did.
Suddenly I felt care-free, not a worry in the world.
As if my emotions had been untangled,
Thanks to that one little butterfly.
It was then that I knew, there would always be a bond,
Between the butterfly and I.

—*Stacy Strutt*

Solace Of The Night

I'm happy to be out of there.
It was very crowded.
Behind the wheel of my pickup, driving.
I'm past the streetlights, past the asphalt.
My blood is hot, my soul, restless.
Turning off the dirt road and onto a unused trail.
Small trees and branches bending under my grill and
sliding off my windshield.
I stop, turn off the headlights, take a breath of cool
night air and begin walking.
"Where am I going?"
"It doesn't matter."
My eyes are locked on the full moon above, hanging.
I stop. This is the spot.
A tall pine tree on my right a towering poplar on my
favored left. I lay myself down on the damp moss,
grasses and soil.
My eyes see above me a crystal clear conglomerate of
fiery stars which fade to black as my heavy eyelids close.

—*Elton LaClare*

Did You Hear The Wind

Last night did you hear the wind.
Its crying and howling stirred me within.
I laid there and listened a minute or two.
It seemed to say I'm howling for you.
Come out, come out, it seemed to say.
I see you, I'll get you, so don't run away.
Don't batten the hatches or brace up your doors.
Cause I'm out to get you like never before.
I shivered and shook at the sound. My head went spinning
round. I pulled the sheets higher to muffle its cry.
But it was still there. As hard as I tried.
My bed seemed to roll like a ship on the sea.
The wind tugged at the walls to get in at me.
Its eerie sounds encircled my room Then I passed out for an
hour or two. When I came around. The sun shone so bright.
The room was all finished in hospital white.
He told me this morning. A doctor in blue.
We fought all night. But we pulled you through.
All I could answer When I spoken to him.
Was doctor did you hear the wind.

—*Naomi Griffin*

Untitled

Today, I lay before you
   It's my Judgement Day
On the wings of a dove
   I too, will be whisked away

The magical unicorn with my carriage awaits
   Ready to take me to the pearly gates
My spirit family is close
   Ready to show me my host

There is always a beginning but no ending
   Just life revolving, always mending
Ashes to ashes, dust to dust
   To you Lord my soul I entrust

—*Judy Schlichenmayer*

His Eyes

His eyes, how they hold and intrigue,
Iris blue, and seeing deep;
Searching windows of the soul.

Ever reminding of secrets
Yet hidden in their depth:
Esoteric rites of passage.
Sudden blinks, the spell is broken.

—*Laura E. Williams*

Two Lovers Walking Hand In Hand

Two lovers walking hand in hand,
Kissing one another by the sand.
The sun was warm and going down,
As a bag lady feel asleep without a sound.
The wind was hissing very light,
For she knew she was with him tonight.
With his arm around her after a while,
He gave her his jacket with a strong smile.
Telling her she was beautiful with his charm,
She felt happy and safe in his arms.
His hand was gentle on her face,
And love she felt by his slow pace.
The water moving at a slow rate,
Together forever by loving fate,
A dream they dreamt in a magical land,
Two lovers walking hand in hand!!!

—*Luisa Raffa*

Different Eyes

Life is hard, we both agree,
Life is hard, even for me.
But I guess it's easier to take the stain.
If you have somebody else to blame.

Am I so different from you?
I am your brother, can't you love me too?
And the question springs from the young and the wise.
Is the world so different through different eyes?

I may not understand you, I ask you not that of me.
But is it so different, what we do and what we see?
We are all human, black, white, yellow or red,
and we all have something that needs to be said.

Am I so different from you?
I am your brother, can't you love me too?
If we do something about it and stop telling lies.
The world can't be so different through different eyes.

—*Amanda Corbett*

The Bard's Malediction

There are times the SVGA screen stares back
Like a chilled grey corpse in a morgue in a sack
When brain storms and stimuli usually here
Are as flat in the noggin as yesterday's beer

A writer must write every day so they say
Or face never making the damned career pay
Doubts and rejections swirl round in my head
As the bank balance stubbornly hovers at red

Uncomfortingly, the editors hopelessly blind
Unappreciative of genius and brilliance like mine
The expectations of course are the limited few
Who purchase my works to them merci beaucoup

What's wrong with the doctors prescribing the pills
Who claim to know oodles about everyone's ills
Never acknowledging black funk which writers' minds block
It's not just imagined, don't hand us that schlock

Time to shut down computer and printer and screen
Before I go bonkers and getting obscene
Maybe a hot bath, a tumbler of scotch on the rocks
A toast to myself and to hell with the blocks

—*Richard I. Thorman*

The Storm

She walks amongst the shadows,
Like a creature of the night,
To the edge of a cliff.
Alone.
Stands looking out to dark clouds fleeing,
Before the storm.
The pounding of waves against the cliff,
is the rhythm of life,
of a heartbeat.

The sky begins to gray at the dawn,
But no birds call out.
There is silence. She stands tall.
Calm.
Illuminated against the sky,
And for an instant life is perfect,
'Till she leaps into the air,
Hurtles downward as the thunder peals,
Like a death-toll.
   And the pounding of waves against the cliff,
     no longer speak of life.

      —*Laura Coristine*

"To A Troubled Teenager"

Hello friend - this is "God"
Looking down on you
I see your life is in a turmoil
You know not what to do
School is a bore - life is a chore
Adults do not understand you
A double standard exists in the land
Your problems are far too outnumbered
Most time you feel you cannot cope
Everything is going wrong and no one cares
But you have forgotten one thing my friend
I'm here my hand is outstretched
You only have to reach and hold tight
I'll pull you out of the depths of despair
Life will certainly turn around for you
Things will get better parents and friends will respond
So grab my hand and hold on tight
I will not let you fall
Put your trust in me - I care for you
And soon all will be well.

      —*Hester Curtis*

The Night

There is something about the night that makes people...
Makes them something that they are not at all times.
What is it of the night that causes us to live, cry and dream?
Does the night instill the confidence to write a song?...
Or to feel a fear so frightful the only solution is weeping?
Or, to wistfully wish that their reality was not their own?

The night is filled with stars, love, or the unending drive to dance.
Yet it holds the shadow behind a streetlight
And the constant wonder of whether the door is locked.

Have you ever lay in bed and chill at an infant's scream, or
the siren of the police?
And when it disappeared, felt your own relief and warmth?

The night owns it own country serenity and by the same token,
its city bustle.
Both can be so mysterious, cold and unnerving,
But still can be relaxed, joy filled and unerring.
What is it of the night that makes some people inadequate?
But others confident?

      —*Jerald Collens*

Man And Human

I am both man and human
Man in the sense that I have spirit and soul
The reflection of God's image
So idealistic, perfectionist and moralist
Human in the sense that I cannot control
The biological needs of absolute
Human condition that sometimes tends to be animal.

      —*John T. Hingco*

Telephone Calls

disembodied voices asking to be there,
material as the magic box of demand,
so much sound wound so cleverly
between place and place,
transmitting an "Here I am!"
day after day, year upon year,
between space and space,
blank face to blank face.

disembodied voices: "All of me -", they croon;
"Why not take all of me?"
"Soon.." is the answer, "soon..."

disembodied voices slopping around long-
distance, slop-pails of reproach
tilted into the receiver. (worse still,
the barely audible sob in the barely audible whisper,
"I am here, I am here.")

even the answer-phone has its mechanical fate.
serves up a helping of contact on a cold, mechanical plate.

it is hard, sometimes, to sleep.
"Dream now -" says a voice, " - after the bleep."

      —*Olga Maginsky Larrett*

Wonderful You

The sky is blue and everything that I see reminds
   me of you wonderful you.
I close my eyes for a moment and suddenly tear
   come falling from my eyes,
and rolling down upon my face, and darling
   you are the reason why.
Now from my heart come's a little pain,
But I don't mine, it happen all the time
Because I am always thinking of you wonderful you

I walk by the sea every day
And I watch the ships go sailing by.
Wishing that one day, one will being you back to me.

My mind is always drifting back in time
And I guess cant help it,
Because I never loved any one but you,
I was a fool to let you go, Wonderful you

I see your face everywhere a million times every day
And as always, I try to reach out to touch it, but it isn't
there, it's all in my mind. I have no one to blame but myself
for my broken heart for that is all I have left with me.

      —*Derrick Allenger*

Untitled

The miles I've travelled.
The things I've seen
The many things that might have been
The wine the women
The raucous song
The things I've done I know were wrong
The nemesis that within me smoulders
The pity old heads don't grow on young shoulders

      —*C. Hall*

The Waste Land

Film is the cruellest medium, mixing
Memory and desire,
Breeding, imagery out of a dead land
Sublimating, fact out of fiction: and imagination out of both.

An endless cycle of marketing and bottom-line,
Brings knowledge of motion, but not of stillness,
Knowledge of speech, but not of silence,
Knowledge of words, and ignorance of the Word.

Where is that knowledge we have lost to information?
Where that wisdom we have lost to knowledge?
Where that vision we have lost to visuals?
The age of images is upon us
Rendering - all that was private, public
All that was holy, profane; all that was eternal,
A sound-bite.
That follows like a tedious argument to formula, to
The Waste Land.

—*Wayne A. Hunt*

Ode To A Friend

My dog, no, not really and true,
    More like her father the wolf, all silvery blue;

She filled my life with sunshine
    She filled my heart with cheer,
        She was even know to steal
            The odd bottle of beer:

One day, she was happy
    Just playing alone,
        The next, she was sick and I knew
            Her time had come;

I held her all day and far into the night
    For fear she would be gone, before daylight;

In the morning she was still there
    Not making a sound,
        She couldn't eat or drink
            She was just lying around:

She died in my arms later that morn,
    The only sound she made was a WOLF's lonely death song;

My SMOKIE-NAHANNI, is still with me I know,
    I hear her voice calling me, when 'ere' the wind blows.

—*June Rolson*

Mother

    —'Twas only yesterday in the gay and carefree
morning of life—our days were full—our cares were
few—no time for thought—only a mother knew.
    —Yet never a word of hardship and strife—
there was cooking, mending, loving, caring—and luxury
was naught—but the world was good then—
in the morning of life.
    Now today and much too soon we've reached
the mid-day fair—and you in your evening years—
wear a crown of silver and gold.
    Little we knew of silent tears, countless
prayers—a heart so full of care.
    Look swiftly—see the toil worn hands—
my mothers grown old—when I close my eyes
and remember—I can see her—in the twilight there.
    Today will be yesterday tomorrow—but
forever in my heart will be-a silent prayer—
that God in his kingdom above—will tenderly
keep, protect and let you see—before the
darkness falls—my deep devotion, understanding and love.

—*Karen Rundberg*

My Perfect World

There are so many things Lord, that I would like to do;
Most of these are ways to serve You:
Like feeding the hungry, teaching a child,
And taking the homeless in from the wild,
Giving a penny to every outstretched hand,
Wiping out poverty from land to land.
Lord, had I the power to do all this,
The world would live in perfect bliss:
No enemies, no wars, no sadness would there be,
Just peace and love and camaraderie.
But each of us have our trials to face,
And those with faith will carry the pace:
So, I will strive to serve you in every way
And pray that each tomorrow will be a better day.

—*Cindy Ann Too-Chung*

My Oasis Of Love

When life becomes unbearable and
    my dreams begin to fade
Yours eyes become the well of hope and
    your touch cooling the shade
Your voice quenches like the desert spring and
    drowns those saddened faces
And like the cactus I will not die for
    your love is my oasis

—*David B. Wyatt*

Autumn's Artist

My eyes have yet to see,
    An artist, though he be fine,
Paint the leaves of autumn
    The way nature has in mind.

Oh the pride that she doth bestow,
    While she portrays her color so grand,
Her beauty, no other can capture,
    Like the brush in her creator's hand.

—*Jennie Himmelman*

To Those Who Wait

When all was lost and life seemed stale,
My faith in mankind, shaken and frail;
The lights of the city are beacons that show,
Souls that are wondering aimless and slow;

While I walked along on the crest of a dream,
To a far destination, that's never been seen;
The island called Lonely, in the midst of dry land,
Beliefs I had shifting, like winds across sand;

Then hands that mould mountains and stir up the stars,
Parted the clouds and down came light, in glorious shards;
With the joy of a blind man, who now can see,
The rescue line was hope, you threw out to me;

If your heart was a garden, I'd tend it with care,
The seeds bloom with kindness, showers of beauty to share;
Your music is rainbows, that come from the soul,
Sanctuary lyes in your smile, making me whole;

Life's quest and its journey, never will end,
I'm not likely to stray, with you as my friend;
You've given me something that no one else could,
Without money or riches, you are all that is good;

—*Diane E. Mooney*

November 21 1992

A year ago today
My father past away,
His memories will always last
Of all the wonderful things in the past,
Although I will never be able to touch him
Or hear him one more time,
I know he is always with me
In heart and in mind,
If I ever need someone
I know he'll be there,
For he is father
I am daughter
and I know that he cares,
He will always be in my memories
and forever in my heart,
God put us together to love each other
and cherish each other
and I know we will never part.

—Alysia Gabriel

Philosophy of Life

With these words I send to you
My hopes and thoughts to help you through.
Don't be forward don't be shy,
Just be yourself, I'll tell you why.
At yourself you're best of all,
If you pretend you'll surely fall.
Always smile through smooth and rough.
Think positive when the going gets tough.
Do unto others as you'd have done
Or disappointment will surely come.
Everything comes to those who wait
But don't wait forever it could be too late.
Take each day as it comes along,
Try to do what's right not wrong.
Happiness and feelings come from within,
You only get out what you put in.
These few rules are easy to follow,
Live for today and maybe tomorrow
You'll still be there with a glint in your eye,
Content and watching the world go by.

—Alfie Hillyard

This Child

This little child, out in the cold,
No one to hug her, no one to hold.
There in the dark she cries all alone,
Wanting someone, someone to call her own.
She cuddles her doll, her only friend,
The only one on which she can depend.
She talks to her, there in the night,
To convince herself things will be alright.
She closes her eyes to hold back her tears,
She holds on tight to fight back her fears.
She lies awake, the nights are so long,
She can't understand things so wrong.
She falls asleep, dreams of a happy place,
Someone to hold her, a loving face.
But for this child, it is all dream,
Never to happen, it would seem.
They are her dreams, though, never to die.
But for now, alone this child will cry.

—Sharon Graham

Waiting

Sitting in the empty room, not knowing what to do.
No-one to talk to, No-one to listen to.
Sitting in that empty room,
Through a glazed window you look - into darkness.

Sitting in the empty room, at night; the stars are still not out.
You're left there sitting alone, to suffer, weep and mourn.

You hear the rain, but cannot see it,
You feel the ray of warmth, but cannot see the sun.
You're left there sitting alone,
waiting, waiting for a ray of 'hope' not 'sun'.

"Why?" you ask yourself, "Why? Why me?"
"Why?" you say again, "Why in this empty room?"

Counting as the seconds go by, hours, days, years.
You hear the wind and think - it's safer to be in here,
But see outside and think - it's nicer to be out there.

Sitting in the empty room.
Wondering if anyone could possibly be as miserable as me
Wondering if anyone cared.
Waiting, waiting and waiting
O God, answer my saddest question - "Why me, in this empty room?!!!

—Nasreen Hijazi

The Time Machine

The time machine is running down, its oil smoothed gears are
noisy now.
Sometimes it 'weeps', and the whole world feels its gasping sobs.
Those who feel its hurt the most
Are filled with grief at the horrors foreseen.
Riots, wars, race against race, nation against nation,
The atoms split and mushroom, and are windswept ——
Across the ever seething bloody seas to other lands ——
Whose people are silently watching
And waiting for the heat seared hands to clasp and circle the universe,
The time machine is running down —— listen,
It's slower and slower with each anguished sob
With only a few to dry its tears and try to mend its
breaking core. Soon, too soon, its fiery clouds will spread.
The whole world will ignite in a brilliant flash of white hot fire.
The time machine will explode in a mighty roar, then —— Stop.
Man and his world will be no more.

—Irene Guest

Apples Of Gold

Someone who sees with pleasant understanding and one who judges not,
Precious joys that make up life and the cheerful things he ought;
Mellow of chimes with kindles of hope embrace warmth anew,
Bring the light of passive mist and roses drinking dew.

Dancing flanker, whisper wind, through the warm-night air,
Silent music, dripping laughter, gallops the ebony-mare;
Seizing darkness, fields of trickles open up the skies,
Down the breathful path of blissness, tranquil heavens lie.

Full the willow, honeysuckle, flicker cooling eyes,
Sweetest truth and wisdom portrayed, pleasing in its sigh;
Playing pleasure, with the moonlight shimmers golden ice,
Soothing strokes of gentle shivers bathe in paradise.

—Betty Murrin Barry

Nature Speaks Through Love

The cold river flows rushing to the sea
Now I feel your love grow sweetly through the trees
The wind caresses me and you're gone
It's true I cannot feel you although I respond

The birds are so fury in their nest
Showing love their mother holds them close to her breast
Now I'm free from your embrace
I know it's true your love has left a trace

Now the hot day melts into the sun
I tip toe gently not wanting to wake anyone
Again I crawl within my humble abode
It's easy to think of you in your mansion bold

I refuse to sleep, my mind caressed
I know by all your vapors I am possessed
My sleepy eyelids shut, my head deepens
I sleep with the hope your love is still keeping

    —Wilda Cresswell

The Mirror Of The Roots

Four months ago, I started to picture
of a root so winding and trees too small
I held my paintbrush and started to paint
of an old root that stands strong
then I painted a girl sitting on it
how strong is the root that it held fit

Leaves are long but stem too small
great is the tree for it was the smallest
but it was never denied that it was the strongest

Then I stood and watch the finished canvas
of a couple who wants to own it
I stood one more time for my pride
for I was so proud of it
to tell them it wasn't about me
but of my parents whom I'm so please.

    —Mary Divine Grace D. Painaga

Dear Grandma

I see much in the wisdom
  of your kind gentle smile,
    please,
  sit down and talk with me awhile.

There is too much,
  in this world for me to understand,
  my heart is a frightened bird,
    that has no peaceful place to land.

You have seen more than I,
  have lived a richer life
I don't know where to begin,
  because I'm afraid of the evil and the strife.

Oh Grandma, I love you so much,
There is too much to say for a poem,
  but I'll always be grateful for your love,
  and see your beautiful smile as home.

    —Tami Van Dusen

Rage

Watching the moon rise up over the ridge
He notices that it seems to radiate
An aura of hypnotizing power.
He listens to the wolves howling at the moon.
For him and him alone their song soothes the
Soul. Their woeful cries are but lullabies.
Now he too howls at the moon. Rage! Rage!
He let his feelings free, let them find their
Way to fall on the deaf ears of the man on the moon.

    —Suzana Ivanic

Souls United

I am sheltered in darkness
Oh how tranquil, fluid
I blend in here
I'm yielding, yet forever

I am the water and the water is me
My only warmth being the quiescent glimmer of light that you send
You're the light in my deepest depths

Although the day mocks you, your omnipresent
For you have broken the impervious surface and were absorbed

There's peace on earth
When I hold you upon me!

    —Calvin Roy Petrie

Valley In Mourning Thoughts Beside A Woodstove

I'm drawn to a comforting flame right here
On a bright but chilly day,
As I stoke the blaze and lift my thoughts
Past these tragedies—and I pray,
That, what's come to our Valley,
In recent times: the futile drive;
And that fateful crash; plus that mother's loss
Of a bright little girl; and now burnt out dross;
And a young boy gone;
Can soon be healed by the Maker's Balm
And restore us all, in penitent calm
Through the Peace that comes to human aid
And leads us now to a price that's paid
As we seek our God for a missing link
In nurturing youth as it broaches the brink
Of adulthood. And surely think
That the world must offer more than this:—
The tragedies of life, amiss.

    —Sheila Pearce

Soliloquy (Sister Mary)

What have I? An eye, an ear, a voice
One cried in the wilderness; sighed on The Cross.
Have I crossed my bridge of sighs?
Clean the 'fridge, sweep, dust, wash-holy
His feet were washed, meek, lowly.
Kneel, scrub the floor, mary how contrary we are
Trivial, convivial, conniving, thriving, deceiving
Killing, thrilling to senses-perceiving
Perceptive, perpetrating; knowing nothing
Naught, ill, the pill, unproductive
Unselective; reflect, reflect, reject.
Do the shopping, eternally hoping-
Hope breathes eternal. Maternal Mary,
Make me a place to hide by thy side.
I have a small soul to save, salvage, salve.

Seek and ye shall find, knock....
Why is it blocked I hate cleaning drains?
What remains? No guile, perhaps a smile
And a child to chase, race to the
Winning post.....?

    —Kathleen Ross

A Little Bean Sprout

When I see you sprout above,
Oh my heart is filled with love.

What I'd give for another bean,
I'd give up my throne, and stop being queen.

    —Rachel Timmins

The Lonely Bench

The little park, with a lonely bench,
One small tree, not even a fence.
Were we would sit, all day, and half the night,
Talking and laughing, sometimes till daylight.

I miss you terribly, each and everyday,
Sitting on the bench, but nothing to say.
It's lonely here now, by the tiny tree,
Thinking of the things we did, you and me.

Watching the traffic, and the people go by,
Remembering the night, we sat here and cried.
Wish you were here, beside me, on our bench,
In that little park, without any fence.

Some of us have gone away, from home,
And the little park, seems so all alone.
We have made a life, the best we know,
But we still miss you, where ever we go.

The tiny tree is bigger, it has grown,
But it looks so sad, since you went home.
As I sit and watch, while the seasons change,
On the old faded bench, nothing's the same.

—Sharon Dingle

Cry Of A Poet

A cry of a poet, like the screams of a baby new,
Or a siren of a curfew,
A poet cries, for some attention,
Of some recital she has mention,
For she has written, quite a few,
But they were all just for you,
An audience of understanding,
Of what a poet was commanding,
You should know her intentions,
A poets cry to be mention,
And for some of your audience branding,
Would help to decided her standing.

—Mary Jean Smith

The Anniversary

It's not the diamond watches,
Or the golden wedding rings,
The fancy cars, the jewels,
Or the many other things.

It's a little bit of kindness,
When you're feeling kinda down.
The simple cup of coffee
On a pleasant Sunday morn;
Or a kindly gesture, When a child is born.

Someone to share a smile with
and remove the ugly frown.
The things you want the most,
Are the things that cost the least.
To be treated as a person, who is worth listening to,
To share your hopes, your dreams,
and your troubles too.

Love and kindness should
go hand in hand but,
They are the things most lacking
In this troubled land.

—Marjorie Griffin

Sit Among Friends

Oh why can't we sit among friends wherever we maybe,
Please can't they stop the wars for you and me.
Why must it always be the little children of the Lord to die.
It would be a peaceful place if all were children in their hearts.
Please find the peace in your hearts to stop the dying.
The war maybe in someone else's yard but it could jump the fence.

—Shirley Verch

Memories

There's an old, old house set far back from the street
Protected by trees from the snow and sleet
Lonely and haunted standing there
With broken old shingles and windows bare
And once in awhile in the warm summer air
A little old lady with silvery hair
Sits on the gallery, her hands in her lap
Dreaming her dreams as she takes a short nap
What does she think as she rocks to and for
Back through the years to the long ago
Thinking far back when the children were small
Picking the apples, the leaves in the fall
So many memories down through the years
Now she's alone with her troubles and tears
She smiles as she rocks, with patience to wait
To join Dad once more as they open the gate
She knows he'll be there on the warm golden sand
To lean on once more as they walk hand in hand.

—Jessie B. Alguire

The Corners Of The World

Who is hiding in the corners,
Protected from the stings of others?
Who is hoping not to be found,
As they weep their pains away?
Is there ever a new day,
A fresh start for those hidden?
What makes them become a corner-dweller?
What drives them to anonymity?
Is life too painful?
Is it too difficult to show failure?

Protection is the material that creates the walls.
People are too harsh, too callous;
They painfully chip away at the walls.
Corners are a refuge,
They disguise true feelings and internal strife.
The world is taking refuge,
    disguising,
      hiding.

—Bonnie L. Olson

Five Miles From Insanity

I am five miles from insanity, my mind is unravelling,
revealing my northern stars. I'm two miles from insanity, my
mind is opened almost all the way. Soon I will be gone. One
more step now. I dance and try to reach the little stars far
off in the distance. I've jumped now, over the edge of
dimness and into a world of kaliedescoping beauty, my axis is
spinning out of my perimeter. As I jump, my stomach floats to
the sky like an excited ball of fire waiting calmly to explode.
Work my mind all night. Blackness glows out of me, I am deep,
I am black, people get lost within me. I can see past the
perimeter now and into the insane dimension of my stars. My
ocean is rolling inside me, wildly. Jumping towards the full
moon of my eyes. I forget about my worries and pain and dance
away into darkness, my never ending dimension of eternity.

—Laura Whalen

Different Lifesytles

Overhead, a single engined plane goes by
right away, I look up to the sky
Maybe because its presence broke into my tranquility
or what I thought peace to be
But, before too long, the plane with its sound is gone
so, it's no longer something the likes of me needs dwell upon
The smell of woodsmoke reaches my nostrils, and I sigh
for, being out in the bush, to me brings on a natural high
Picture, in your mind, a place so dear to your heart
now, imagine it slowly, ever so slowly being taken a part
Wouldn't that about push you over the brink of insanity?
I can only say, a pretty picture it wouldn't be
Two very different lifestyles not only for I to lead
but, which of these two do I really truly need
One, for sure is out of pure necessity
so, the other must mean the world to me
Anyhow, that's how it is today
I win and lose either way.

—*Sarah Jane King*

Behind Castle Walls

The black knight of delusion
Runs rampant through my brain
And the white knight of compassion
Is dying just the same
For the dragon of deceit
Doesn't care who he flames
While somewhere Unicorns are dancing
To a song without a name
And the jester sits back laughing
At everyone's silly games
The henchman sits there waiting
He doesn't care who's to blame
While the prince of knaves is some place in hiding
Trying to ease his pain
He grieves for his lady fair
And it's driving him insane.

—*JAK*

Controlled Freedom

Like a stranded sailboat lost without a sail,
Sea of disappearing dolphins with only one whale.

Blue-green sea turns a muddy brown,
All species within are sure to drown.

Nothing they can do how they fight back,
They're once colorful world has turned a dark black.

Maybe to beach themselves is they're easy way out,
Resembles the Ethiopians trying to fight the drought.

World's busy fighting in our battlefields of hate,
As the world's delicate mammals face the hands of fate.

Victory for them is to survive another day,
Living in a controlled world they strive to find a way.

Like an eagle soaring through the sky
And dinosaurs before our time,
They all seem to someday disappear
Where's the justice to fit the crime?

To hear these mammals cry makes my heart miss a beat,
Trying to fight the world's cruel ways
And the final sound of defeat.

—*Danna Marie Schaubel*

The Wind Blows Softly

The wind blows softly
Sending ripples across the once smooth lake
That holds many memories of the past
And is waiting for the memories of the future.

The soft sand that surrounds its uneven edges
Waits for the touch of a human foot to tread upon it
And silently it moves as if it were alive
Or as if it were being sifted.

The landscape that surrounds the area -
It is painter's delight
It gives the finishing touches
That bring romance into a moonlight night.

And everything is natural
As if never touched before
And no power can control this everlasting beauty
And no one could ask for more.

In this high state of serenity
A leaf falls off a tree
And then again - there is no complaint
As the wind blows softly.

—*Madhuvanti Mahadeo*

From The Earth...

(Personification of the Earth During War Time)
Shadows of night pass quickly over my self
As the flame that surrounds my self beds down
Silent darkness is a welcome sanctuary
Redeeming souls tortured by the light
In time recollections fade
But still, My self remembers the way my self was
Floods of warmth the color of my core
invade my self
Demanding acceptance and approval from my selves
Russet visage, why do they pound, strike, deface
For no wrong done my self
My self issues a playing field for games of discontentment
My self left bruised and alone
Hopelessness and uselessness of trivial misunderstandings
Those who fall victim vow eternal silence, complete resistance
And I, myself accepts them into my depths
Sheltered from the wrath of misconceptions
They live on
They, My self, myself
And so do they...

—*Tara Betts*

Is This Love?

Sitting here thinking about the times we've been together,
Sharing the happy and upsetting times forever,
Now knowing every day draws you nearer,
A teardrop from acknowledgement of fear,
A fear of one day losing you,
A love so blue but yet so true,
Every time I hear your far away voice,
The sound of your voice shuts down the noise,
A voice inside my head,
Combines with the tears I've shed,
Why do I care so much about you?
Your the one who helped me through,
The good times and the bad,
Life can be upsetting and sad,
Life is like a door you can open and go through it,
Or you can close it and throw the key away.

—*Crystal Collison*

The Conclusion

Our waitress in a bar:
  she didn't look exceptional,
yet she aroused my desire;
  I was infatuated by her.
I so craved her
  I could imagine her taste.

She smiled at me and roused
  her lips to speak,

  (I could feel her need for me,
   it was obvious.
   I longed to feel the sensation of her words
   coursing through my spine.
   This would make my night complete.)

she said:
  "It's getting late
   I would love it if
   you would, please...
   clear your tab."
              --Allan Boss

Untitled

Another sleepless night of tossing and turning
she lay trembling under her covers
knowing that the monster might come tonight
her fists are clenched around the blanket
and her eyes are squeezed shut so that she won't see him
if and when he comes. She listens carefully
and then she hears the footsteps coming
slowly the door opens, she beginning to shiver now
wanting to scream, but it won't come out
The monster grabs her hair and face, her arms and legs stiffen
and she feels the hot sweaty body weight on her, then
the piercing pain inside her stomach
she's not sure what causes it she only knows it hurts
after a few moments the monster leaves exhausted.
She cries and wonders "Why me?" I'm only five years old.
We must find a way to end this "horrible monster" child abuse!
              —D. J. Petrella

My Very Dear Friend

A happy face, an encouraging smile
She left without a good-bye over many a mile
She went peacefully, no hurt no pain
To have her gone life won't be the same.

She never got to fulfil her goal
So weak was her body, so happy her soul
If someone wanted comfort, that's what she would give
Her dream never came true — the dream to live.

She would make you laugh, she would make you cry
So calm even knowing she was about to die
She tried to comfort others when they were down
Often acting as though she were a clown.

So many feelings she could not place
She hid them all with a happy face
If ever you needed a hand, her hand she would lend
And now she's gone forever ... my very dear friend.
              —Cynthia Hann

Comment

With my close friends they think I am the tops,
I correct my reaction to the praise with unsettling stops,
To prevent my problem which needs improvement,
The joyful moments for my friends should be so dominant,
A comment to make for beautiful friendships
  should be caring and understanding,
I want to be the tops for my friends with partaking.
              —Catherine E. Pawloski

She

She woke up this morning to start a new day.
She smiled and stretched and up she got
to shake the sleep away.
Soon the family demands crowded in her mind-
then they were gone to live their day
and she was left-behind.

Alone at last her thoughts crowd in
her deep sorrow is back.
For what she thought would fill her world,
has only brought her lack.

Each day she decides will be different,
her sorrow she can't ignore.
Is this what they meant, when they said-
you should give 'till you can't give no-more.

She dreams of flight into the night
where she might set it free,
this endless beating of the butterfly wing's
that she tries so hard not to see.
              —Charmaine Horsburgh

Untitled

She took my breath and my heart's beat
She wrote and sorted and stamped, so neat
With Oh! what wondrous patient look
She relieved me of my library book.

I often relive that brief encounter
As I stared and loved 'cross the library counter.
She with her manner so prim and proper
As I paid my fine with a hand-warmed copper.

And yet, I thought, as she stamped my card
I wonder does she read the bard.
Would she care to listen, and hear
My rendition of old Shakespeare?

But to ask might seem to be too intelligent.
To a library girl he might be irrelevant.
Nothing ventured, nothing gained
So I asked and she refrained.

So now my heart is lost and broken
Like my useless library token
For what are books without her looks
And what's Shakespeare without her near?
              —Paul Wilson

Why You?

I remember when I had you in my arms,
It was just the other day,
On our one year anniversary,
I finally said I love you.
Even though I knew it from the beginning,
I was afraid of what you might say.
I remember whispering into your ear,
And you gently kissed me.
Then said I'll always love you till the end.
I was the happiest person in the world,
Until today, now I am full of tears and guilt.
Why did I ask you to come over?
It's all my fault, if I hadn't asked you
To come over last night, then I would
Be talking to you right now.
Instead that drunk driver came out of no where,
And threw you over the cliff.
He just got a scratch, that's so unfair.
I miss you, I want you back, but I won't ever see you again
'Cause I asked you to come over here.
              —Beth Nelson

Untitled

How beautiful the ivory light of the moon
shines deeply onto the mountain stream.
The outline of the shiny silver reminds me
of something I saw in a dream.

Marvelous angels aglow with bright white
with wings descending from their hinds.
One walked towards me holding out her
great arms and said,: "Come now, and hold on to my hands."
I reached out to hold the hands of the angel
knowing I would not be here much longer.

She guided me towards the silver mountain stream,
getting closer, closer, stronger, stronger.
I was able to walk on top of the water.
Each step I took I rose more and more.

When I reached the top I knew it was the end
because someone reached out when they opened my door.

I slowly woke up to the end of my dream and
when I opened my eyes I saw a marvelous sight!

Someone came in, held on to my hands and
pulled me towards a bright ivory light.
  —*Diana Czarkowski*

Universal Reversal

We men fought and foiled our enemies
Simply to feed our families
We worked sweated toted our wares
Survival being our only cares

We took our beatings from the bosses
Then brought home pay after losses
We drank smoked and "joked" awhile
Till we got home to reconcile

Our wives would all be a glare
Enquiring "How did we fare"
Of course we answered straight and true
"God 'Twas hard. We're black and blue"

We've worked, we've fought and won our battles
Now we're turning over goods and chattels
We've borne the brunt without perks
Due to some undeserving jerk's

Gays and lesbians have been re-arranged
But real men have not changed
So now women, after all this fuss
I hope you will kindly remember us.
  —*R. E. Sibthorpe Sr.*

Untitled

She walks the night with beasts
Sits before their laid out feasts
Through the darkness she stalks her prey
To stay alive stay out of her way
When darkness falls all is her domain
What evil lurks in hidden shame?
She rules with evil and hateful grace.
With pent up anger at the human race.
They took from her what she could not give
And when all was done left her to live
To think of the past brings back pain
Her tear drops fall like showers of rain
And then the sun comes up from the east
To slay the evil and kill the beast.
  —*Katharina Dueck*

Winter

Silky snow across the land
Skating children hand in hand
Rosy cheeks and twinkling toes
Snowmen with a cherry nose.

Stained glass windows all aglow
Overhanging mistletoes
Houses filled with Christmas cheer
Singing bells for all to hear.

Winter soon will pass us by
Summer will be next in line
Then, back to school we must go
Until, again, returns the snow.
  —*Giovanna Marrelli*

One For Another

Why Worry? The world is wide, pastures are green,
Sky is vast, and sea is deep.

Why fear? When countries prosper,
Science gets better, and technology stronger.

Why care? Forests are burnt, another species is dead,
And another cloud has cried, its acids tears.

Industries' expanding, sea is rising, coastlines are
disappearing, waters are poisoning, does it matter?

Indeed! The sea is not so deep, the pastures not so green,
That it can swallow all the filth, and hide all our deeds.

The earth is only a gift from God to thee.
It is there to bear for you and me.
It gave us food, and gave us shelter, it gave us beauty and
lustre. It gave us air so pure, it gave us life so dear.
It did the best it could, to give us all it should.

So why don't we give it a little thought,
Before our last chance is lost,
Why not hold hands together, learn a little to share and care,
Why not to do the best we can,
To save the only home we have.
  —*Vineeta Nand*

Home Sweet Home

Mountains loom under cloudless skies,
slight winds utter to the restless trees,
of feelings: serene, peace, joy.
Senses of bitterness and sorrow,
dawn a facade of tears.
A place I once called Home Sweet Home,
a place I'll call home no more.
To leave this place, to never return,
and enter a world unknown,
A residence I'll call it for eternity.
  —*Tammy Evans*

The Knew Life

The innocent child
Lies gazing up at its parents' faces
Gurgling sounds that are incomprehensible to the adult ear
Emerge from the baby's throat.
The meaning look —
The questioning gaze —
What is the child thinking?
Wondering?
Asking?
— Can you idiots afford Harvard?
  —*Chantale Sarrasin*

To Bloom

It dawns on me this awe filled revelation
So late in life to fathom meditation.
To delve beneath dark shadows deep
And such a harvest there to reap.

It dwells in silent isolation
The fruit of patient meditation.
Still, beautiful, unique in fashion
A flower of brilliant hue and passion.

The smiling Grace is welcoming,
The warm embrace encompassing.
Knowledge of the past appear
A flash of recognition here.

The seeker and the found unite
A glorious love of life takes flight.
The garden grows in sweet delight;
Dim shadows now, the gloom of night!

For in the darkness of the night
You caused a blinding cleansing light
That set the struggling flower free
And slowly I am finding me.

—*Veronica Raynan*

"Imagine"

A dusty road lies ahead
So we care, as our minds wonder
Like we are not there at all
Your mind travels to places unknown

The road we travel grows bare and narrow
So we hurry to the end
Then hope on another less bare but safe road.
And let your mind takes you on more, ventures

As we continued to imagine
Time comes, time goes
Our past, our present and our future
Your mind works over time, looking for a better place

Another day has come and another day has gone
We imagined it away too
And when it gets the best of you
You get the best of it.

—*Gail R. King*

Unfair Fate

A broken neon sign flickers above their heads.
Stacks of old newspapers or cardboard boxes
Are their beds.
They huddle under blankets, sheltered,
From the rain.
Wishing someone, something,
Could take away the pain.

A fire burns in an old garbage can
In the background you can hear the muffled
Cough of a dying man.
Their hands and feet are frozen to the tips.
They have no hot meals to hold to their lips.

A small girl cries, and thinks of her mother,
And grasps the hand of her only brother.
Hatred fills their minds, what did they ever do?
No one seems to care. Or do you?
These are the homeless, their signs are unseen
They pray for a miracle, how could life be so mean?

—*Jennifer Miller*

On This Night — Earthshake

Sun rubbed some gold on the hills
stark against the dark purple sky, face like a fist against
the earth, teeth clenched in tight wooden trees and fences

As the sun slides a
lazy smile beyond
the long loins of the valley and

Turns in her slumber A rolling of
bulk the town sleeps in
her embrace her hecatomb Pachydermatous they
dream in her soiled flesh

Liquorice twisting in her purse melting
in her molten eyes Snaps and bursts her
snake skin face her swollen dreams its dambust guts

Opens her mouth and yawns and
the world collapses sucked in to her restless
flesh Cities bore her porous hide her primeval psyche
her belly ripples swells but hungers.

—*Ioluc Matthews*

The Drifter

On a cold and windy autumn evening while driving down a city
street, I came upon a man hobbling on a set of crutches, he
struggled as he crossed in front of me while I sat in the
comfort of my car.
he had a rugged look to his face as if it had been over exposed
to many weather conditions.
His hands were large and strong looking but revealed a
condition of arthritis as though his fingers were branches of a tree limb.
He was wearing a badly warn parka and with an enormous backpack
hanging from his shoulders that may have held all of his possessions.

He continued on showing no indication of complaint or
discomfort and then he paused for just a fragment of a moment
and looked towards me while the headlights of my car lit his
face as if he was auditioning for a better part in life, and
then, a slight smile appeared on his face and he winked
just before turning away as if in his own way saying "it's
Ok".

—*John Coon*

I Watched The Raindrops Dance

As thunder rolled and lightning lit my way through darkened
    streets -
I stomped my feet in rhythm with the raindrops that fell,
    Harder....and Harder.

I hated the rain.
It ruined my day with its unexpectedness.

I raised my head for a moment to make sure my path was clear -
I saw a beggar. He looked up at me and smiled.

"I love the rain," he said. "It washes me free of this dirt
I must sit on; and the dust that is kicked in my face.
It bathes my tired hands, and soothes my aching feet."

"It cleanses this world of its filth;
and breathes new life into the seeds of our futures."

I looked up and let the rain wash my face free of its frown.
I opened my hands out of the fists they were in —
I took off my shoes.

I skipped home in rhythm with the raindrops that danced,
    Happier....and Happier.

—*Melissa Faye Maduro*

357

Little Tree Upon The Hilltop

Little tree upon the hilltop, with your branches bending low,
Summers' gone and autumns' coming, soon you will be covered in
snow, after you have slept all winter, you will wake up in the
spring, when the sun is shining brightly, as the birds begin to
sing. Little tree upon the hilltop, how you tremble in the
breeze, bow your head to all who's passing, how I notice all of
these. Little tree upon the hilltop, when I've wandered far
from you. There'll be a spot where I am welcome in the shade
that's made by you. When the strong winds rock the maple, and
the tall pines murmur low, I feel lonely, someone's calling, I
cannot stand it I must go. They recall to me my boyhood, with
my playmates resting there when we wandered in the wildwood we
were happy true and fair. Now the breeze is getting stronger.
From your branches fall a leaf, time has passed us; oh so
quickly, we knew no sorrow, pain nor grief. I stand gazing in
the silence, I seem to hear my playmates call, 'though I know
there's no one calling. Little tree you answer all. So little
tree upon the hilltop you're most beautiful of them all with your coat
of many colours; see them flutter as they fall. Time is flying
I am sighing;as teardrops gather in my eye, the time has come.
I must be going little tree I'll say good-bye.

—*Hazen Sturgeon*

Untitled

Our teenager is some sort of terrific David
teachers can't control her
the neighbors are calling us every second day
and she steps beyond the law
with divine Kohlberg ration
at times she can be truly malignant

Her words are brilliant
slaying stones
it's too bad they're draped with her youth
just as her lips with garish two dollar lipsticks
on her way to school

The other night we watched one of Welles' old flicks
she turned and said
  we are the most dangerous product of evolution
  we have become alien to this earth
  we are food forethought

She can be positively horrid
I wish we had never taught her to read

—*Scott Fiddes*

Cries of Protest

Oh, my sweet Lord, please,
tell me where your sorrows have gone
tell me where the scarfs scaped
when the acid winds of Chernobyl
darkened the skies, lungs and shadows?

Still there are plenty of sunshines
that are waiting to raise up
and thousands of solitary moonlights
that want to bright and dance.

Therefore, let us stop the machines guns!
Let us stop the smokes of our cars!
Sea gulls and trees are expecting
a single answer from our hearts!
(Also the quiet shells of the sand...)

Oh, my sweet Lord, please, I beseech you:
show me the right way to save Mother Earth
or just draw us the magic road
in order to find you at the end...!

(It will not be necessary a bloody strike
because nothing is so far from our hands...)

—*Manuel Saavedra Duran*

The Beauty Of Light

The darkened sky rumbles warningly,
Telling all to run and hide,
Wind and snow blow mercilessly around,
Whispering death to the homeless.

Snow piles high in alleys and streets,
Homeless huddle around a small fire,
Hoping to fight off the cold,
Says one, "Do not worry little thing, we have done it before."

The storm dies off, withering away,
Dawn spilling all over the winter diamonds,
Making the storm a dream,
Lightness scares off the darkness,
Uncovering a field of pearls.

The little one brushes the snow off,
Catching sight of the winter jewels,
Dazed by the wonder and brightness,
Thanking God for the beauty of light.

—*Tiffany M. Siek*

In A Life Time

So many things happen, in a person's life time
That thou never forget.
The time they met
That first romantic night they spent together
And that first kiss.

In a person's life time there's so much to remember
and will never forget.
Like that time he put that ring on your finger
That day we said, "I Do"
That was forever.

To wake-up in each others arms
To hear the baby crying in the next room
To lay back and remember the time
We met, your romantic night together
and that kiss.

Those are the things, I'll never forget.
Those are the miracles of life.

—*Kimberly J. Marion*

Mashinanna

My name is Mashinanna, ancient sign of peace,
The aim of my life, one that shall never cease.
Bringing unruly hearts to know this sign,
And its meaning real, true and sublime.
I am a daughter of the seven fold light,
Crossing the bridge way from darkness of nights.
A real double rainbow over my head,
Brothers of written word use my right hand,
Brothers with wisdom of Solomon I do stand.
Tempting, testing, lifting every step I make,
As the long journey into the unknown I take.
Through mystical haze, my hand I did give,
To work through me to prove that they live.
Invisible brothers of righteous men made perfect,
I ask my mission you give due depth of respect.
To any who, with sincere thirst to drink,
The essence of my message for which I stood abrink.
A welcome, to my humble presence I make,
To view the beauty through them I did take.

—*Barbara Franklin*

"Guilty"

From a very early age I was made to feel guilty. Sitting on
the Chara at the magical age of seven. Pleading my innocence
age ten and being convicted without trial and the injustice of
not knowing of what, cruel lies and more guilt heaped upon my
young head aged twelve. What was this family I loved so much,
just deceit and lies, deceit and lies. Joy at seventeen
marriage at eighteen but guilty of feeling free. Freedom,
freedom no more lies or deceit. A new life away from cruel
relatives and feelings of guilt, and then fate that devil rears
its ugly head. A husband who buys toys and expensive games to
pass away his time. What do I do play the dutiful wife or go
my own way. I cannot walk away I have a son who is life itself
to me, and so it begins again guilt, guilt, guilt. Doing my own
thing made to feel guilty. Years and years of it, I cannot get
away from it. Guilty if I'm happy, guilty if I'm sad, guilty
if I'm there, guilty if I'm not. Guilty for loving too much,
guilty for not loving enough, guilty for leaving, guilty for
staying, guilty for longing, guilty for yearning, guilty for
being but not guilty of dying.

—*Pamela E. Betteridge*

Repose

Marmalade sat on the shanty-roofed porch,
The cold wood underneath,
Looking left, then looking right.
All he sees is snow - white snow, melting under the warm, hazy
   sky.
His orange fur, standing on end from the cold,
His paws, tail, and feet neatly tucked under, to keep them warm
The silence is disturbed by a westbound freight-train,
clicking along the old line, speeding like a cheetah.
Suddenly, it's quiet again.
Marmalade turns his head again, whiskers and all,
to the left, then to the right.
Bored, he scampers away.
What is marmalade?

—*John C. Murney*

To A Mosquito

I was sleeping very soundly, when there was a gentle hum:
The "Dive Bomber" lit on target, but I didn't hear him come.

He didn't use his tail lights, nor drop his landing gear;
He nosed in on the airstrip, which was me, I fear.

The pierce of his propeller, was like the poking of a pin;
He wasn't very gentle, as he eased his motor in.

The earth tremor was terrific, as I let out a yell,
I bombed that poor mosquito, and then I scratched like hell.

His fuselage was broken, his fuel was splattered round;
It was a total write off, so the agents found.

Now you dopey pilots, I am posting up this sign;
Find another airport, if you wish to wine and dine.

—*Maurine Becotte*

Friendship

Friendship is like a rainbow,
It shall come and it shall go,
The colours represent its many stages,
From joyous to sad through all the ages,
Though the rainbow may fade it will always reappear,
So if something falls apart why should you shed a tear,
For if the person is truly your friend,
Even through fights that bond should never bend,
Yes friendships have their highs and lows,
But same with all else including rainbows.

—*Monica Marton*

T.V. Communion

They huddle around their idol in passive adoration,
The electric oracle of radiant magic power.
Manifesting marvels, it enchants their indolent souls
As in languorous trance they slouch, or in vacuous ecstasy,
Programmed for belief, their responses preordained.
Their marble eyes are gazing at photogenic visions,
And at times they are illumined by official revelations,
Or they hearken to the sermons of unctuous hierophants
Who preach instant faith in miracles they're selling.
Weird is the languid orgy of the soulless metal body,
The blue electric blood, the fluorescent transfiguration,
The transient surrogate life, the ephemeral paradise,
The fleeting bliss they borrow to fill their inner void.

—*T. A. Jackson*

Flying Over Kilimanjaro

I behold the eternal Kilimanjaro again today,
The highest mountain peak in all Africa;
We rushed to look through the window,
Of the aircraft flying us towards Dar.

Two travellers clicked and flashed their cameras,
To register the splendor of the sight;
Three just crouched and watched without cameras,
Speechless as they flew past the Kilimanjaro.

Yet some stood and stared and talked,
Not loudly but in hushed measured undertones;
Four pointed at this, others at that,
As they saluted the mightiness of Kilimanjaro.

It rose proudly above the morning cloud,
Its snow capped summit swathed in majesty;
Somewhere there must be a supernatural force.
No human artisan could have crafted Kilimanjaro.

—*Adelola Adeloye*

No More

Aren't you tired of all the pain,
The hurt that goes along,
When the one you thought you cared for,
Totally ignores you?

After many years of searching,
You thought you'd found
The one, who would be always there with you,
To share your every joy.

No looks, no words, no smiles:
They all have disappeared;
And left behind a sharp, sharp pain,
And many tearful days.

It's as if you never used to know,
You never came across;
You never used to talk before,
You never used to smile.

One bitter look - one broken heart,
I guess that's how it will be.
Just hope it all ends quickly,
So that life can start again.

—*Jennifer Grant*

Empty Promises

Beware of Empty Promises,
The shallow songs they sing.
For empty rhymes
In empty times,
An empty lot will bring.

—*Bradley Schwartz*

A Penny for Your Thoughts

The mirror in the back of my mind reveals
the last remembrance of unspoken feelings I
share deep in the myths of my heart.
The pages turn, like the pile of leaves I used
to kick over once when I was a small child
walking down the street in the haze of an
unforgotten dream.
The thought I share with you both present
and future are unspoken crystal tears that will
always shine through the days of humanity.
I have collected pieces of mirror that once have
been broken in my life, but can't find the time
to mend them together.
Time, time is so relevant and uncared about,
but time I spent is time I lost.
As the tears of rain braced past my view as I
stop to think!

—*Anamaria Gonzalez Haupt*

Souls Pass In The Night

They sit in the cold.
The lonely, starving children
Of an alienated world,
An enclosed hell.
Buried alive in their own corpses.
The suffering, the pain, is a part of
Their life.
They know no other.
Do we see them? Do we care?
We close our eyes, but our hearts bleed
As their sores fester.
They die in the night, as we sleep peacefully.
Their torment is echoed in the sorrowful, moaning wind.
But as the sun rises,
We do not notice
Their
Quiet
Passing.

—*Lorie Ann Silverson*

"That's Life"

Once gainfully employed now wiped away
The minor recession is here to stay.

Evaluation time - the 40's you know
My direction has changed but which way to go.
Jobs are few and thousands apply.
Will my name be noticed or carelessly flipped by

Advise is plentiful if only they knew
Have they tried lately, it would silence a few

A family to support which way to turn
Start my own business or back to school to learn

No need to worry your path is set they say
So Lord I'm ready please show me the way.

—*Grace M. Snider*

Gems of Caring

What priceless gems of caring can a man in love collect,
The while that he is with or lingers nears,
Someone whom stone-cold reason would advise him to reject,
But anu asked-for magic has made dear.

Then every little happening is a jewel for this store
- a treasure house close-guarded in the brain -
Like other precious stones, they will exist for evermore,
Though used to deck his thoughts, time and again.

Lips brushed against a temple as he holds her fondly tight,
A stroke of silk-smooth cheek in soft caress,
The entwined clasp of fingers, what a diamond of delight!
A ruby smile to temper his distress.

Just being close together, to listen to her voice,
To press a loving kiss upon her hand,
He gathers up his gemstones, poor fool he has no choice,
Tight-snared by deep emotions all unplanned.

He looks into her eyes - which are the brightest gems of all -
And feels his very being tear apart,
To see, so very deeply in those mirrors of her soul,
A reflection of the yearning in his heart.

—*Raymond Mitchell*

Untitled

The Madonna of Ludzmierz
the Woman from Tatra Hinglands
the Gratification of our hearts
the Gate Permanently Open
Reph.: where She is - we are where we are - she is
    in the Tatra Hinglands in Washington's land
she is our Queen Mainstay - Rescue
our Mountain Path to the Peaks our Luminous Ray
the Mother of constant Returns and the Link of Unity
Life - Truth - Love
and a smile of Freedom
in her Great Goodness
she chose the Lord
a Pole - a Servant of humanity
to her Gratitude and Glory
Reph.: where She is - we are
    where we are - She is
in the Tatra Hinglands
in Washington's land

—*Franciszek Lojas-Kosla*

Focus

Focus on the positive - stop and take the time
The world lies in ruin at your feet you have no hope the future's bleak
For it's easier to run away yet it takes strength and courage just to stay
Take time to focus on your life a quiet time at end of day
Reflect upon your gifts and goals you just may be surprised
Perhaps you've touched someone's heart you know not what
around each corner lies
Be thankful for each trial for it usually ends in triumph!
And we are usually called to grow with life's ups and downs
and little bumps
So before you fall down into deep despair plant a garden
breath fresh air
While others 'round you pout and flounce smile! your alive
and that's what counts!
For beauty lies within us reach out and lend a hand
For the joy is in the giving take the time to be a friend!

—*Doreen Gwilt*

Autumn

In this world of darkness
There is still beauty to be found
In the red gold leaves of autumn
As they fall gently to the ground

The roses all have gone to bed
But one who lingers on
Must go before the winters snow
Find you unprotected here alone

The blue bird soon to leave us here
Has sung her last sweet song
As she wings her way across the skies
To join the merry throng

The flowers too have done their best
To spread beauty far and wide
But now it's time to say goodbye
As they sleep together side by side

The winters snow so soft and white
Will come quietly drifting down
To warmly cover all sleeping things
Till spring once more abounds.
 —*Genie Core*

Their Love

Their love is all so strong
There love will last forever long.
She waited all her life
And now all she wishes is to be his wife.
They said from the first
They would love each other through the
best and the worst.
Now here they stand
United together as woman and man.
It may be to others only a dream,
But to her, real it does seem.
For to her when she sees him at night
She knows her choice was right.
For he is kind and never cruel,
A man is he, not a fool.
Now here it comes to the end
Will her choice be a man, or a friend?
Her decision is made and she's not afraid.
For now she has found out
What marriage is all about.
 —*Wanda Slauenwhite*

Untitled

Life was dark a deep night black
there was something missing something I lack

It was not cloths money nor praise
but someone to turn to throughout my days

When he met beauty that was fine
but when I met you. You blew my mind

I leaped with joy in my little heart
I swore we would not turn, ignore nor part

But here I am and there you are
we are not close and yet nor far

For your in my heart my memories my dreams
you know I do miss you by all means

So when you read this I shall think of you
oh by the way I love you.
 —*Shelly Picard*

"Dark Secrets"

We all have our secrets, in the back of our mind,
They distort our vision, and our senses we cannot find,
They can consume our thoughts, and make us insane,
They turn our happy times into pain.

They make us so restless, that we can't sleep,
These dark secrets, in our minds we must keep,
We confuse our brains, till we can't cope,
To get rid of these secrets, there seems no hope.

There's no one on earth, to whom we can confide,
All these dark secrets, in our heads, we must hide,
Because, if we told them, someone, we loved, would get hurt,
If they knew about our secrets, they would think, we were dirt.

People never forgive you, for what you tell about,
But friends listen to me, for I found a way out,
If you have secrets, that's as black as the grave,
You can tell it to the Lord, your soul he will save.

For all your sins and secrets, to him you must atone.
But he will keep it scared, so you won't carry it alone,
He will tell it to no one, he will hold it in trust,
He will help you carry it to the grave,
And then turn it to dust.
 —*Marla B. Coburn*

Remembrance Day

Remember those soldiers who fought and died in the war,
They fought for our freedom but sadly, they are no more.

Their screams are silent, almost faded away,
but we still remember them on remembrance day.

Flander's fields are where cross' stand,
Row and row, hand in hand, poppies bloom
Around the graves, they are the symbols of war,
bloodshed and rage.

Remember those soldiers one and all,
who fought and died to save us all.

So wear a red poppie on remembrance day.
So the memories of those heroic soldiers will never fade away.
 —*Dwayne Oake*

Leaving Home

Going westbound on a train
Things will never be the same
Can't get blamed for the trouble at home
Heading in the world all alone
Finally got to the city
Suits look and say, "What a pity."
Such a young kid should be home in bed
If not a survivor, he'll wind up dead
Don't worry I came equipped
With a jack-knife on my hip
Thinking I'm so smart
At 15 years it's only a start
Hotels, for dollars a night
Pimps and whores, a sure fight
That's right life on the city street
Standing on your own two feet
Walking passed department store windows
Seeing a reflection of someone, you don't know
Now nineteen, oh what I've seen
No doubt time to straighten out
 —*John Bierman*

361

Shaktisthal

The boy extracts self-pity
through the tainted sinners eyes
from mirrors of constructed truth
on which he so relies.

Like the moth who flutters by the sill
to engulf himself in light,
this boy in need of suffering
gives chase to something right.

From scholars joy and life's sweet breath,
he seeks to touch on this;
to learn of beauty's solemn wine
by senses abstract kiss.

From this crimson fruit upon the wine,
the nature of his love defined
vague creature freed and harnessed up
with aged frolic soul declined.

With beauty found and love embraced,
he can assail the task at hand;
to enshroud himself in naive ideal
and live to free the exiled man
—*Charles Demian*

Friends

A friend should always be there
Through thick and thin
Caring and sharing
All of life's trials
Friends should stick together
You should always be there
Friendship is a partnership
Everything has two sides
It takes two to make a friendship
It takes two to conquer the world
All we need are hopes and dreams
All we need are friends
Everyone needs a friend
Whether they are black, white, yellow, or red
Whether they are Irish, Indian, English, or French
Race, color, and religion do not matter
All that matters is what's inside
That's what makes the difference
Because friends see below the surface
Friends can make a difference.
—*Lisa Paddock*

A Passion

The world around us is a long road ahead;
Through twists and turns and curves instead
Love is what I said before,
But some may stay and some ignore.
My answer is waiting for you to come along
I will prepare you with a song.
Don't be scared and stay away
Because I will be waiting for you day after day.
When the sunset ends and turns to mist,
My love will linger and stay on list.
If the world would end by only a song,
I'd sing it for you all day long.
For passion is strong and hate is rare,
The time I spend thinking of you
Is a sign not saying beware.
So think of me like I think of you
And maybe someday,
We can be a pair of two.
—*Lindsay D. Palamaruk*

Aftermath of the Storm

It came suddenly, pelting upon our village like bullets,
thunder rolled, and lightening cracked the sky lighting up the
County like an olympic stadium. The rain fell in torrents all
evening, enveloping the mountain in a thick white sheet,
making it impossible to see anything for miles around.
Oh how we'd prayed for the rain during the long, hot endless
summer, and now, on our hot tin roof village houses it played a
joyous, melodious symphony, warming our hearts, while our bodies
cried and tingled with indescribable excitement. Eyes
glistened and hearts rang out, as we told stories of old
fishermen...stories of sad hearts and merry hearts."
Every child, woman, man boy and girl felt the magic, and in the
circle of their individual homes, clung to the moment and
wished that time would stand still and capture a portrait no
great artist had ever painted.
In the wee hours of the morning, the rain stopped...I crept
outside, running into the woods inhaling every fresh, new and
exciting scent, my naked brown feet left prints wherever I
passed, and the birds sang like never before. The rising sun
sparkled on a dewdrop, creating a kaleidoscope of colours...
Oh how perfectly white washed my native land looked!...Maybe I
was dreaming! Then I walked along the beach, and saw the
gather of debris and fossils, things that were left after only
one thing "The aftermath of the storm."
—*Bernis Brigitte La Mothe*

Our Precious Son

It's late at night and all is calm
Time for reflection, need be until dawn.
Before you arrived we were living a lie,
Not alone but still lonely, not knowing just why.

We'd accepted our fate, without children we'd be;
Though we loved one another, was not enough, don't you see.
We pampered our pets, took up hobbies galore;
What we really required was a child to adore.

We must have been blessed, for how many can say
They believe they were chosen in some divine way
To raise as their own, such a beautiful boy
Who gives us such pleasure, such wonderful joy.

Now we'll never be wealthy, have rich jewels or car,
Or take lavish vacations away and afar.
But our rewards are many, though by far the best one
Is our pride when we tell folks, "That's our precious son."
—*Brenda I. J. Burgess*

Untitled

I'm right to be in a place of green,
to be a deciduous in between-
two trees that die in the summer's heat
and place bouquets at my feet,
    And know...

That my amour has engulfed me so,
away from all the rain and snow
with the heartbeat of the forest strong
my death will be both faithful and long
for I'll live within the raven's song.
    And keep...

A place for me
When the seasons change
my demise is certain...cremate my remains.
—*Louise Lees*

Country of Contrast

From subtropical forests
 to desert wastelands
From vast open spaces
 to imposing mountain ranges
From deep ravines
 to sunny golden beaches
From pulsating city nightlife
 to restful silence off the beaten track
Such is the breathtaking scenery
 of a country embraced by
a variety of contrasting people
Beautiful South Africa.

—*Glenda Lourens*

Lasting Love

To meet my dream girl, and be your best friend.
To fall in love and that friendship not end.
To misunderstand, yet make up so fast
Is proof that our love definitely will last.
To get up quickly after I fell,
To worry myself silly when your not feeling well.
I want to help you feel better, and strong
So I try to do it through a poem or a song.
However you need me that's how I'll be
Because sweetheart you're the greatest thing
 that's happened to me.

—*Dale DeBodt*

And The Darkness...

And the darkness is mine
to hold and breathe,
which never sleeps and dreams
of unholy lands and styptic things,
of rotting heads mounted upon
great stakes in a field of blood-soaked wheat...

And you realize that all you have
learned and seen is a lie
but the lie is somehow the truth
because it was only a lie
in your own ignorance and youth,
and you scream and you wail
and the bleeding skeletal heads distort
and moan as you run...
and the inky paste and the stiff wheat
stains your skin and clothes
and you run, thrashing,
filled with the moans which echo your own
as you reach to that unknown place
It is life eternal...

—*Piera Incitti*

A Gypsy's Prayer

Oh, please God, help me find a home
Somewhere, someplace, I can call my own
I'm tired of all this moving around
There must be somewhere You want me bound
I can't handle being so confused
So please, God, show me what to do
I know You have other things on Your mind
And You don't need me taking up Your time
All I want is for You to help me out
and if it takes some time, Lord, I'm not going to pout
Well, I must be going now, it's time for moving on
But from my mind, Lord, You will never be gone
So please, God, help me find a place
And stop me from moving at this deadly pace

—*Maureen Van Den Bussche*

Married To A Miner

Being married to a miner, I know how it feels at night,
to lay awake and wonder, if my husband is alright.
He's working nightshift this week, I hope the phone won't ring,
and break the silent darkness, that the nighttime hours bring.
I knew the day I married him, a mining man I had, and we'd
be forever joined together, through the good times and the bad.
He'll always be a miner, for it's the only life he knows, and
I'll always be that miners wife, as daily my love grows.
Danger constantly surrounds him, has he drills the rocky
ground, so I pray each night that he'll stay safe, and soon be
homeward bound.
I've seen him suffer silently, when a fellow miner died, the
hurt and sadness in his eyes, was something he could not hide.
He knows the risks involved, bravely facing them each day, but
does he ever wonder - 'is the price too high to pay?'
But I'm married to a miner, so I push it from my thought, and
try to be always grateful, for the precious time we've got.
So tonight again I offer thanks, when I feel his warm embrace,
knowing that when he's lying next to me, he's in his rightful place.

—*Sheila O. Hillier*

Friendship

Friendship means a lot these days,
To many people in many ways.
The world is full of trouble and strife,
We try to be happy all our life,
Work and toil from dawn to night,
Amongst our neighbors, do not fight,
Bury the hatchet, shake their hands,
Make everyone smile throughout the lands,
Peace, not war, is what we need,
Love and friendship we must breed.
Help each other every way,
Your reward will come some day,
It may be a smile or two,
When you need it, they will help you.

—*Elsie Peer*

One For One

I wish for peace every day
To the people of Hartley Bay

You need to bond, you need a friend
We'll be together 'til the end

Smiles happiness, I wish to see
Not the glare of an enemy

With hugs and kisses, you've got class
Forgive and forget, for the rage will pass

So reunite and work as one
From this life we can no longer run

United we stand, divided we fall
Our motto, I recall

—*Angela M. Bolton*

"Sight"

Close your eyes and reach out your hand,
Towards me without stammer,
Now grasp my hand with all thy might,
What do you feel?

You feel my chapped old hand trembling,
But no more,
You know nothing of me.

Now close your eyes and open thine ears,
To the sound of my soothing voice;
The words pounding through your soul,
Emanating love and joy,
Fulfilling your every desire.

But then you open your eyes,
To see your new found friend,
And all you can see is race...
No more do you hear the soothing voice,
Nor feel the nervous gesture,
Of the one you imagined friend.

—*Jason Found*

"True love"

True love can thrive anywhere. True love knows no hindrances.
True love crosses every bridge. True love climbs any
mountain. True love crosses any river.

It knows no impediments. It knows no but's. It knows no
conditions. It knows no borders. It knows no discrimination.

Love that says I will always love. Love that says I will
always forgive. Love that says I will always try. Love that
says I will always smile. Love that says I will always stand.

Once started there is no going back. Once begun there is no
finishing. Once accelerated there is no stopping. Once
switched on there is no switching off. Once provoked there is
no recovation.

No mistake is too much to be forgiven. No problem is too big
to be resolved. No person is too ugly to be loved. No disease
is too great to be healed. No wrong is too dirty to be
condoned.
True Love

—*A C N Nchunga*

Our Far Away Land

We gaze into the sunset not a worry in our minds
Unable to name our emotions due to so many kinds
I tell him secrets I know he'll believe
For if I turn my back I know he won't deceive
I love the way he holds me in his arms at night
In total darkness not counting the moonlight
That shines in his face and makes his eyes glisten
Looking in his eyes and hearing his voice, I listen
As he talks breathlessly in my ears
Telling me his desires and his fears
We may search alone but together we will find
The gift of love, peace, and happiness
The gift will spare us nothing less
I see him in my dreams, I see him in my mind
Words to express my feelings I wish I could find
I want to tell him the feelings I have in my heart
To tell him the loneliness I feel when we're apart
I think he'd make an effort to listen and understand
And take me away to a far away land

—*JoAnne Bartniski*

Illusion

Toys of the attic in my mind
   unwind
Spread like thyme gone wild
Skateboard memories quantum leap
Light years collide and crash.
Was my life a dream?
The contents of a dusty book
   forgotten?
A broken doll?
Or was it a bug in a jar transfixed
   so crystal clear
It shattered glass?

—*Charlotte Morris*

Talking About Drugs

Drugs are very serious substances,
Used by people for treatment and diagnosis,
But some guys you know they are kind,
They take bad ones until they're blind.

Some guys use drugs to play cool,
But they end up even lower than the worst mule,
Come on guys, don't be fools,
Say no to drugs and go to your schools.

Now this is about those guys who smoke cigarettes;
Smoking around the place, like a real menace,
But the world is getting more health conscious,
You smokers; your breath smells atrocious!

All you drunkards, who use alcohol,
Calling off the girls, through your spit and drawl.
You're a social outcast and you don't realize,
Cause it's too late, the stuff has got to hold on you.

There are some people, who don't realize,
That taking drugs is not all that wise.
You know the right and the good from the wrong,
So make your choice and you had better be strong.

—*Brent Craig*

Broken Hearts

Roses, roses, perfume fills the Hall
Vines clinging to the wall
will give their harvest early Fall
Raccoons will share it all
   as broken hearts with falling petals vie.

The fire in the hearth seems doomed to die
because men will fancy fly
and sometimes test the rule of do or die
to leave their dreams in tatters lie
   as broken hearts with falling petals vie.

The home is still, the grief is strong
whilst loved ones wait
to glimpse the destined fate
of a past that once was great
   as broken hearts with falling petals vie.

Men who want to stand up Tall
will all the harder stall
to stilt the truth to save the gall
And rather leaved a treasured perfumed Hall
   than hear the sound of broken hearts with falling petals vie.

—*Di du Toit*

Africa, 500 Years Ago

Africa, 500 years ago
Was a dramatic time and pure
People of old lived in peace and in unity
With no differences among them
Full of hope and understanding.

Africa, 500 years ago
Was a dramatic period
People of old lived in strong culture
Through tradition and spiritual belief
That their Gods provide and protect
Full of strength and magic

All along the people surrounded with superstition
That the great spirits of their ancestors guide them
Through famine and calamity
With strong feeling of contact to the dead
That unity comes only perfectly with the unseen
companion,

Africa, 500 years ago.

—Joseph E. Appiah Sr

The Cloud and the Sun

A dark cloud in the sky
Was floating quietly
While the sun, so shy
Tried to smile brightly

The cloud hid the sun in a flight
Besides the efforts it made
The sun could still send its light
And prove that it would not yet fade

It calmly warmed the air
And caused a soft breeze to blow
Some people might say, "it's not fair"
But the breeze forced the dark cloud to go.

Life is almost like that
Difficulties rise everywhere
But we have the strength to react
And calmly to say, "we can bear"

Violence can't lead anywhere
Except to the loss and despair
But love and the adequate care
Can do like the sun: warm the air.

—Rosa Maria Barboza

Pre-Schooler

Young in years with cherubic face,
What do you do for the human race?
Do you work the land, the traps or the sea
To make the world better for you and for me?
Do you teach us valor, or courage, or grit,
Rush off to fight wars for the fun of it?
Perhaps bags of money is what you've got
And you pit it against Old Poverty's rot?

Respected, revered, my dear old Treasure,
I'll answer you in the self-same measure.
I can't work the land, the traps, or the sea
To make the world better for you and for me.
You have lots of valor and courage and grit;
And I won't fight wars for the fun of it.
Bags of money of course I've not got,
Still, p'rhaps I've something for Poverty's rot.
Young in years with cherubic face,
I can grow in Hope, and Love, and Grace.

—Don Hinton

Stranger

I feel as if I don't belong. Hidden wishes to be other then
what I am; a connection to something I only feel at unexpected
moments, and could never explain. Yet...this is as much a part
of my essence as is a flame to a lit candle. Uncertain.
Always the sensation that my strangeness marks me, in some

obscure, subconscious manner, as a person of another place:
accepted, yes, but never family's member. I feel I know
something. Something that is life's necessity. I am frantic
to impart my ephemeral, all-embracing knowledge. The world
will know me, then, and will say, "This is why she always stood
aloof, outside our thinking."

I boil and explode to expound...What? What is it I know
With a certainty and serenity so deep it's melded in my bones?
When it comes to it, I cannot say. How to describe a feeling:
How to explain what haunts me like a silver mist I can see, but
cannot grasp? It is a good thing, this which separates me. I
feel that it is. In fact, in moments I feel far superior to my
fellows, for my inner whispers mark me so. And then, I am
struck. Superior? They, or I? Even in the words, themselves,
"They " stands among friends.

—Wendy L. McNeil

The Blind Man

Blind from birth he could not see
What is taken for granted by you and me.

The golden sun and the drenching rain
Beating against the window pane

But he loved life and to his ear
Came the sound of music loud and clear

Happy was he when he felt our hand
Clutching his, like a band.

Sightless he knew he had to be
But his gift of touch made others see.

How lucky they were to see the sky
So they stopped to talk on walking by.

Such happiness shone from their face
as he heard their footsteps and their pace.

Blind he was for evermore
But he knew he could knock on any door.

This man, so steadfast in his prime
Received our love and all our time.

Sightless he was for all to see
But that gift of touch meant much to me.

—Madeline Van Horrik

Master Quest

What a lost soul am I
Where can the Master be
Searching the world how can I find thee
Some I asked had vacant eyes
Seeing that all hope was lost
Others had delightful joy
But behind the smile it was all a lie
I found many claiming to be His
Refusing to look beyond their blind ways
Finally I found what I so longed for
It was not in people or strict up bringing
There it laid in front of my eyes
My craving soul read the wondrous words
The quest is over to find thee
Holy Bible you have set me free

—Virginia Sofronuik Kehler

The Splendour Of Natural Beauty

Take one look around and you will see,
What splendour there is in natural beauty.
This picture of reality is a perfect work of art,
You will know, if you look at it from your heart.

See the sun rises to bring a new morning;
Its magical rays strikes the forests and the birds begin to sing,
The lovely buttercups awake and give such sweet-smelling scent
in the air;
The light morning drizzle on the grass casts a freshness everywhere.

The magnificent hills and mountains stretch across the land;
And the wandering rivers and streams carry their deposits of sand
Through the tributaries into the vast sea.
Oh! what splendor there is in natural beauty.

As the evening approaches the faithful sun descends in the west
And from the distant meadow the cattle come home to rest.
The night birds and insects begin to make a distant call.
Just look with profundity and you will see the great splendor
of it all.

—*Emily Husain*

The Ocean

Forever, I will glorify thy name;
What would the earth be, without thy fame.
On top of thy ridges,
I feel elated;
The comfort you bring to my tears,
as much as the soothing to my fears,
is like an aura of light,
after crossing a dark tunnel.
And always, will thy midnight sun,
enlighten my last long run.
Above thee, the reflection of the sunshine rays,
make thy sand grains,
look like a collection of precious jewelry.
Here and everywhere.
will the ocean be big and fair.

—*Nathalie Maillard*

Looking At The Moon

Up in the sky you shine so bright,
When darkness comes you give us light.
As the world rotates you keep in touch
With all earth's creatures, there is so much
For you to see,

Young lovers stroll beneath your glow,
As hand in hand their love does grow.
For days to come - they make their plans,
So vast an area your view spans
From sea to sea.

The dark side of people you also witness,
The environmental issues bring such stresses,
The bombing, killing and so much starvation.
As you look down on the devastation
From war and greed.

Men with curiosity went into space,
So they could land upon your face
And look down on this world below.
A resolve to protect it, in their hearts did grow
With haste and speed.

—*Kathleen Miller*

Born To Die

'Twas a grey morn
When she was born to a young couple
A joy to the home and a hope for the future
Wrapped in innocence she feebly cried and writhed in pain
A frail child of dust
Couldn't suck her mother's tits
Her tongue sore
Her diarrhoea endless

Solemnly the doctor finally pronounced "I have no aid"
To aid the skeleton life soul
Tie the dreaded aids
That has sapped her innocent soul!

She was gone in the misty morn
Never lived to say good-bye
Never lived to see the rising sun
For she was born only to die
Her parents glancing sideways
At once knew that they too had began the lonely journey
As the world tormentally wallows in a circle of death
The trumpet full blown proclaiming the end of the world.

—*Christine Ombaka*

Orpheus

Orpheus, you sing of love but gather hatred,
When you tell us of our sorry state.
The truth can often seem like terrible blows,
But still, I cannot turn away from the majesty in your songs.
The longing trembles in your voice,
Bittersweet, like ale or muscatel,
We'll drink of that sad wine until the very end.
Your songs, that touch the soul, shall be the path,
Nine muses, they will take us to Elysian fields,
There your lyre still floats upon the air,
There Eurydice waits upon those Thracian notes of love
and Calais wanders restless,
In the shadow of a long white robe.

—*Tom Emmens*

Autumn Drive Through The Woodlands

A drive through the woodlands, enchanting to see
Where nature commands every creature should be
As free as the air and as tall as a tree
    In this great land or ours

Look down at huge marshes, with their shades of brown
Water streaking through cattails, and green blades around
Easter palms they resemble when spread on the ground
    In this great land of ours

Rustling gold and red leaves in wind so strong
Like an orchestra playing the September Song
A woodpecker's staccato beats steadily along
    In this great land of ours

Like dying embers, shades of orange at Earth's feet
As darkness surrounds the after-glow in retreat
Wild game head to water, for their time to eat
    In this great land of ours

Watch a thousand eyes blinking as downward they stare
Feel the power that guides them, since time they are there
Pray tomorrow you awaken to smell tree-scented air
    In this great land of ours

—*Norm Abraham*

Food

Here in Canada we have plenty of food,
Which tastes so super good.
Hundreds differently shaped meats,
Oval bulby bushy beets.
The ever ugly starchy potatoes,
Big bright red juicy tomatoes.
There's plenty little round radishes,
Most humans differently hate doing dishes,
Cats and Indians crave fishes.
Green jungles of squash,
Whip up a delicious hamburger maush.
Baking new things will make you think,
Please keep my kitchen from stink.
Chinese unbelievably adore rice,
Arrange the table splendidly nice.
Our bodies demand plenty of milk.
Peaches feel smooth like silk.
The digestive track requires large leafy greens,
So, so many high vitamins in beans,
Hope third world countries can find the means.

—*Lawrence Kasprick*

Our Master

The Lord is our master for us He set the rules.
Which we all should follow in and out of office, home or school
Never should we neglect or throw these rules aside
For in this world not one of us, from God our life can hide.

He loves every one of us since the day that we were born
Yet to so many of us He still remains unknown.
We were all made equal no matter what color of skin
Yet this world is so full of hate and of racism.

'Cause all of these men made rules that are being allowed today
Are the downfall of our children, whom are quickly lead astray
Everything that was wrong before is now assumed as right
Which leads man to murder, steal, abortion and even fight.

Every child that's born has a father and mother
But have lost the love and respect they had for one another
Life's now become nothing but freedom, money and sex
Yet everybody lives in fear of what's going to happen next.

How can any one of us find love and peace today
When we forget there is a God and find no time to pray.
Let us turn away from sin and all that shameful hate
And ask the Lord to help us, restore back our love and faith.

—*Annie Martens*

The Mystery Of Love

Who can explain love,
For surely there are many ways;
Is love the voice of our beloved when they speak,
Starry eyes that shine brighter than gold?
Is love the fragrance of roses in bloom,
Their unveiling, a beauteous sight to behold?

Who can explain love,
For surely the task would be great;
Is love hearing the voice of unspoken words,
With a smile from eyes that are gleaming?
Is love a bountiful gift from the heart,
And by sharing it, we resolve its true meaning?

—*Evelyn Brown*

Best Friends

Best friends are people
Who share their secrets
They won't tell another
They'll always keep it

They'll stay close together
And defend for one another
Treat each other like a sister or brother

There'll be good times, bad times,
But they're always together,
Best of friends forever and ever.

—*Treska Sweeting*

Untitled

I didn't expect I could live this long,
Why am I accorded the privilege?
Age hasn't made me wiser - I'm no sage -
Among the blunderers do I belong!

So many are the things that I've done wrong,
How can I ever undo the damage?
Fear, sloth and pride - they hold me in bondage.
And the lure of self-interest remains strong!

But I'm blessed with loving kinfolk and friends
Who freely accept me the way I am.
They have faith in me - no qualm, no pretence -
About my failures they don't give a damn!

They've stood by me through many a rough day,
I owe them a debt I can never pay!

—*C. H. Chia*

Content To Love

Many times felt more than little confused
Why I still care if I'd only been used
Taking my stand to make a decision
Saying no will soon end repetition

I'd like you to try, as hard as it seems
Believe when I say, he's out of my dreams
Actions now, no result of a rebound
All - long since passed, he just kept coming round

As time wears on, feeling less of the pain
I begin to hear myself call your name
I'm asking your help to leave past behind
Even happy memories don't feel kind

To me there is nothing that you can't do
My heart's changing every time I'm with you
Fear of caring slowly begins to drift
In its place, love, as you accept my gift

Time makes me feel like we fit - hand in glove
Feelings of contentment, growing is love

—*Patricia D. McCourt*

Nippon Shines

With Ginza's towers as backdrop behind me, I gaze
With wonder at the little gay lacquer bowls and
Food arranged in beautiful symmetry. At the door,

Uniform bows and salutations remind me of
These people's love for order and collective
Mentality. What's more, I recall polite and

Friendly faces, rows of neatly trimmed and covered
Autumn trees: dressed in spiral ropes and ready
For winter's cold, and the scores of lovely cherry
Flowers that bloom in spring.

—*Rosario Villaruel*

367

Enigmas

When I asked as a child for the answer
Why the stars made me want to cry.
Where eternity ended or where it began,
Were we really all part of some prearranged plan,
Or do we really matter we dust motes called man.
I was told "You will know by and by.
You will know by and by when you're older
The answers to all of these things,
Why each leaf's a poem in gold, green or red,
But you're just a child and you should be in bed
So go to sleep now dear "That's all that they said
And I dreamed of the butterflies wings.
And no one could answer my questions,
Now I find that the older I grow
The riddles from childhood increase by the score.
And I batter my fists against knowledge's door,
And I am no wiser than I was before,
All I know is - that I'll never know.

—Shirley Simpson

The Dying Rose

Sometimes I feel trapped inside a dying rose
    with petals so hard as cast iron
However brittle and frail to me I see.....
    to none I display this character.

A proud rose is what my life has been
    a free soul, alone beauty silently swaying
With beauty sustained, and thorns to prick.....
    a combination of love and hatred.

For man is black and unfair with torn leaves
    and I will not give, for my own sanity
So here I will grow beneath turmoil skies.....

Even though I may be cut, and on a table stand though every day
shortens, one by one. So proud I will stand...

A when at last the water runs dry and slowly my petals begin to
die ... I will become withered and cold with decay. Nobody
will ever take my sweet fragrance away.....

For though I may feel that I'm trapped within a dying rose...
    I remember my pledges of past life untold.
And will continue to cherish the red balm and green....

Because I'll know once I saw life the way I perceived it to be.

—Daphne Lapenna

A Mother's Love

I sit here and remember you,
with the strength and courage you had
the fight for your life
God what a battle you had.
With dignity and pride you asked, if you taught
us any values in life, I hugged you and told you,
you had. I asked if you were afraid to die, your
answer was no, we had to accept it, but I couldn't let go
You said I had to and be brave. I held you in my arms
and you asked me to stay. Mother and daughter we are.

And now she lies here, beneath the fallen snow,
I feel her presence of before. There is no pain only sadness.
With a heavy heart, teardrops fall, to cleanse the soul of
guilt, of wishing her to go. You fought and lost and now we
mourn or weep. Now God and angels have you in their keep.

—Lauralynn Hankins

Northern Soul

I search for my soul at times in this vast northland.
With the wind it seems to leave me during cold winter nights.
I wander alone and lonely, empty with a hungry heart.
I yearn for the warmth that comes from within.

The north at times makes me restless, it makes me think.
Countless memories haunt and trill me as every season sets a mood.

There is no place like home, a gentle summer breeze reminds me.
How soon I forget when fall appears with colors so bright and
the north wind trailing, not far, gut briskly behind.

Winters bite is close now, and spring seems like a faded memory
of being a child.
I remember the growing and the changes over time.
At last summer will arrive again.
It makes me happy and content, just the thought.
I feel that I have found myself
Yes, I have found, once again, my northern soul.

—Russell Teed

True Love Never Fails!

You look so sad with your blue eyes why! darling what is
wrong? You can tell me, my love, you know I care about you,
let me share your good thoughts. Give me your hand, and sit beside
me amongst the beautiful flowers here on top of the hill.
O'look! A pond! a family of duck's, proudly holding their
head's high, calling the pond their home. The sun is warm
and touches our skin, it feels so good, and your beautiful
blonde hair is blowing in the wind, how nice you look!
I know why you are sad, it is because I have to go, it will
not be too long, and I will be back with you, and our little
son. In the meantime we can write and share all nice things,
and about all our problems, what this world brings.
That we can share together, and solve them for the
better, because true love never fails. This world is full of
problems and other things, but if we have love, we can master
them. We must look around us, and see! How we can help others
also in need. So darling give me a kiss and a hug, and look at
the flowers. They remind me of people, because they are
different kinds and struggle just like people, against the
wind, but ours are problems what this world brings. But that
makes it worth while, to be strong and keep our faith. Because true
love never fails we will carry on.

—E. R. Verhees

Ode To Canada

Canada, I love you; you are my native land.
You're beautiful from sea to shining sea,
And no matter where I wander
From your skies of thunder
You're the greatest nation ever to me.

I've made every port of call from Vancouver to St. John's;
Sat in the igloos of the north;
Spoken to all peoples within your tender embrace;
Magnificent, oh Canada my heart.

I've seen the sunset dying in crimson above your hills,
The golden fields spreading out below;
Watched the gray goose flying high
And heard the wild loons' call
From the doorstep of my Canadian home.

I have roamed your quiet woodlands;
Scaled your granite crags
Feeling dizzy and drunken with the scene;
I have heard the north wind roaring
And felt the blizzards blast;
Magnifique, oh Canada my home.

—Frederick Laing

What Is the Question?

the West is the best
Yes is the best

unless you follow Trudeau
then vote No

my roommate did not care to vote
a rain soaked Canada flag did not fly

was my father voting yes
to Canada or economy
Senate reform
Native autonomy

A friend called from San Francisco
he would not be voting
he did not care about political jargon
he lived under the Constitution of Uncle Sam
the land of life, liberty and inequality
Pot is an herb
Bush is a dope
maybe we would be a little better off if he inhaled

the west is the best
yes no veils the mess
—*Michael D. Hill*

I Adore You

You can feel the weather change.

When scudding clouds leave the sun to shine,
Warmth begins to penetrate winter garb
For the first time in months ...
And I know that you are mine.

The earth retains its moisture from the recent rain
Yet welcomes us with a cushion of fresh green grass
On which to lie our heads.
The sun blankets us with its warmth,
Shining gladly on our bed.

I look into your eyes
And there see all your love conveys.
Passion, pleasure, and soothe tranquility -
Love in every guise
To see us through another day.

I arch my back to heaven
And dream of summer days gone past,
Panting, shaking
With the pleasure of our love
As you complete your sweet repast.

I can feel the seasons change.

Once again we venture forth outdoors,
As the love I have to give you changes too.
The intensity of my feelings
Now rivals the elements themselves.
Put simply, I adore you.
—*David Keogh*

Untitled

If I were a poet, I may
write a poem and title it
"My Last Will and Testament

To the young, I leave dreams of the future
To lovers, I leave shady lanes and moonlit night
   To families, I leave togetherness
To the old and infirm, I leave faith
To the forlorn, I leave hope

And to all the world, I remind you
of salvation thru the Lord Jesus Christ
—*Ronald David Neufeld*

Forthcoming Event

A tadpole with undeveloped limbs
you curl within my womb.
Can you feel the caress
as I press my fingers to the swelling shape
that seems to be part of some other me
- an unexpected self - Earth Mother
revelling in the joy of this creation.

Rocking your body
in the cradle of my hips
I am at one with you
in the intimacy of our sharing.
Unreasoned caring for
I still know nothing yet of who you are
or what you may become.

No harm shall touch
whilst I can shield you
little one. Calm
are my waters for this precious time
when I am yours to learn to love
and you are mine.
—*Heather Chandler*

Mother Kristine

Now take a look and tell me what
You really think you see.
Am I the child you used to know,
Or what I've come to be?

You've watched me grow from then 'till now
And saw how I have changed.
Sometimes you wish that I were still
A tiny child again.

You know the shadow of my past,
The child you used to see.
And even though I've grown tall
A loving daughter I'll always be.
—*Donna Clayson*

Beseeching All Poets

Dip your quills in the stream of my tears, oh poets!
You tell of us; I can write no more.
Maurice said it was time to part,
And thinking of him reopens the sore.

Our caresses have long faded
From my skin as well as his,
Though my mouth does softly linger
To the warmth of a long kiss.

I gave all, he gave little;
And after so short a healing time,
I'm still too weary - oh poets!
To turn my pain into rhyme.

Write about my bleeding heart,
Pierced by cruelty's knife,
So that Maurice, repenting,
Might yet bring it back to life.
—*Laura Chalar*

369

A Distant Friend

My heart was pounding when I met you
You were sitting on the grass and me staring at you
I know you like me as much as I do
But you couldn't do it my friend
To tell me the truth and what you really intend
Until you said goodbye
But I promise to see you again sometime
We didn't know each other's abode
And didn't think of each other for a long time untold
I prayed that you still know me
Though we didn't care much like it used to be
One day the good news came
I was allowed to go to your place
Sorry when I felt irascible to see you
'Cause I was afraid you might have someone new
But God was kind that we still longed for each other
And planted new feelings right there in the center
Sad to say it's my time to leave
Just by seeing you gave me great relief
I'll relish and treasure the time we spent
Even though it was short, it made a crescent
A melancholic incident to be apart
I miss you dear with all my heart!

—*Farah Lisa A. Lazatin*

Friends

When you are born on this earth,
You're born happy and full of mirth.

Not one hateful thought comes to mind,
Until someone's hate turns you blind.

Because someone is not the same,
doesn't make them animals and fair game.

They live and breath like you and me,
so why can't we just let them be?

If your truly do believe in God,
then become friends instead of not.

This world would be a better place,
if all we ever did to one another is give
a happy face!

—*Debbie L. Mawusi*

The Hungry Hearth

Oh, Hearth of cold wet icy dampness Don't let my heart be one of same,
The trapped wind invites me beckoning with tinkling silver refrain.
You seducee and delude one by one who are entranced by mauve marble pit,
With mysterious overtones, moaning grey darkness, yearning to be lit.
Yes! I should run to wilderness abducting kindling of pine and oak tree,
Or should you desire cherry, maple, birch? Whichsoever would quench thee?
"Anything" you murmur or was that a withheld smoldering tortured scream,
"Anything that burns brightly with fervor," chesire smile, "As you deem."
I turn, a cool gust rustles, swirls and billows under my calico skirt,
Coincidence, doubtful a conscientious move, a rogue, a knave, a flirt!
Perhaps that was to prod me on merrily for your desirous aim,
All important, a quivering crackling canary, marmalade, and azure flame.
My youthful allure oh hungry hearth I think is quite deceiving,
I've trodden too many a disparaging path with slammed door, "I'm leaving."
"I will not haven of glorious trees to Hearth or any likeness feed,
For hollow cold enshrouding emptiness has ravenous constant need.
Hungry Hearth I leave you as you are insidious, debunk with frosty cold,
Me, I seek my rapture in towering Greenery abundant, adoring branches enfold!"

—*Adriana Hinder*

The Words

The darkness slid away
on that very special day
The one on which you said
I love you
So strong
my heart began to pound
Then you held me
indeed a special day
I have had no feeling
none of this sort before
Weeks have gone by
Seemingly getting stronger
is the love I have for you
Hoping it will never end
for the simple reason
Losing you would be
my greatest loss
My first love
I'll love you forever
till death tears us apart

—*Thomas C. McGuire*

You Were the Harvest

The harvest time.
I,
    the sweat of summer.
She,
    a sylvan breast
I watch her through the undergrowth.
She bit a branch,
    and impressed her teeth.

It's hot
    I thought
The hours of the day were sinking
    her shadow danced
    on the warm earth.

I sang to her:
    "...black hair,
    eyes blond
    like luck."

I'm coming! -she said
    disappearing into my belly.

—*R. Drullinsky*

"The Lie"

Alone in my tower
In the dark lonely hour
Alone in my tower of night

Desolate was the dark
Then there came the spark
Then there came an hour of light

But only an hour!
Then retreat to my tower
Retreat to my tower of night

Oh, I'll come at one day
But how long I can not say-
How long I'll continue to fight.

—*Mike Daskal*

Autumn Masterpiece

Hillsides speckled with black cows,
painted trees against grey clouds.

Horses playing in the field,
Autumn winds of cold do yield.

Swarms of leaves fly near the clouds,
and freely fall back to the ground.

Life is drawing to an end,
as sleepy trees in Autumn bend.

Old stone houses near the road,
embrace themselves against the cold.

Snuggled on the rolling hills,
old clapboard houses resting still.

Rushing sounds of swirling trees,
sunlit tree tops in the breeze.

Miles of fencing decorate,
a lonely passage through a gate.

Where calves and lambs are having fun,
playing in the evening sun.

I look above majestic skies,
God is watching with wondrous eyes.

—*Robert O'Connor*

Wisdom's Song

Oh, precious God! Through my mothers' hope you gave me life
Lovely life from the very first cell of my conception
To what will eventually, God willing lead to my old age;
From my very beginning to my final earthly end
I will sing a wondrous song, the song we all need sing
The sweetest song of gratitude

Gratitude for others' lives - those good and generous souls
Who live kind, unselfish and faithfilled lives
Gratitude for sun and wind and beauteous stars
For animals, their loyal love and natures' sweetness

When the time comes I will move joyously through
The birth canal - throbbing, rejoicing, grasping, pulsing
With lifes' desire, a life too wonderful for words
I will cry aloud when I reach the outside air
A cry of hope and faith and love to God in my soul!
Ah! magnificent soul carry me in grace and goodness always;
In this world let us all love, hope and sing!
Stop the horror of abortions now and always!

    —Jane Thompson

The Coming of the Storm

The thunder of the waves casts visions against the rocks.
The sound soothes the mind of everyday trials and the wonder of
   its nature enters our minds.
The sun cast rainbow lights over the rocks and forms a rainbow
   over the sky.
And then time passes and the sun falls behind the clouds and
   the water now has a grey cast to it.
Every so often the sun re-appears and forms silver glimmers on
   the rocks.
Soon the cast of grey turns to a near blackness and chills go
   down your spine.
The trickles of water on your face now become water droplets
   and the storm has started.
A mist rises over the water line and the visibility becomes a
   cast of white smog.
Upon an alcove, a bird seeks shelter from the elements.
The wind whistles through the trees and the serenity is now
   lost for the day.
People depart to escape to safety!

    —Adele Mary Kraft

Windy's Christmas Gift from Heaven

This was my first Christmas in Heaven and oh what a beautiful
day, for Jesus has helped me send something special on its
way. I sent you gift from heaven, especially from me just
hear my love, as it whispers through the trees. I have
sprinkled moon dust on your face, to dry up the tears so you
can only remember all the joy we shared each year. So listen
in your heart and whenever you hear a bell ring, know that it's
me in Heaven, with the words that I can finally sing. For
today as I watched and waited, Jesus finally came. It was then
that he told me, that it was you who gave me my name. Now I
can finally understand how my life came to be. But I feel a
sadness in my heart for I know how much you must miss me. So
I just want to tell you Mom, you don't need to cry. For I'm
safe with Jesus, beneath his watchful eye. So whenever you
need to know that I am with you there, just go outside into
the breeze and feel my fingers run through your hair. Because
you know I loved Christmas when I was with you there. So let
me tell you now that Christmas in Heaven is beyond compare.
For Jesus told me how he was born on this most holy day. As
we strolled among the Saints stood along the way.

    —Diana Irish

Nine

Take me back
Back to the days of Peaches and Scooter
Take me back
Back to the days of the boy and the girl
Take me back
No!
I was never good enough
I was your embarrassment
I would never be anything
Why?
They had no blood
I was what was yours
I let you decide
Why was I all lies?
Why did you let me die?

    —Tim Barr

For Levie

You're full of unanswered questions
Questions that don't make sense,
You ask yourself over and over
But only end up all tense.
You feel that you're to blame,
You can't help how you feel,
But he knew it was going to happen,
It would've ended just the same.
You're full of unanswered questions
You don't know what to do.
I just want you to know
That I'm here forever for you

    —Clarissa Layugan

Tears

When you turned your back,
you thought I didn't care.
You refused my love,
you thought I didn't care.

You wondered about the tears,
the tears that should've wet my cheeks,
and stained my shirt.
You wondered about my unshed tears.

If you look into my eyes,
deep into my soul,
you will see my heart,
and the unshed tears in my heart.

    —Carrie Snyder

You Are My Everything

You are my everything.
My friend when I need to talk.
My lover when I need to be held.
You somehow seem
to make my days a little lighter,
and my nights a little brighter.
You are the one that took the time
to teach me how to love.
You are the one that took the time
to see the real me.
You held my hand, and comforted my
heart
when I thought all hope was lost.
You are my everything,
and there's one thing you should know
You are my light
in the darkness of the night,
and I love you.

    —Mysha J. Hodges

Cooking Tips

A favorite part of being home
is having the chance to make
Cookies, candies, pies and such,
just being able to bake.

I sit and look through recipe books,
what I choose just doesn't matter.
You see, I never see an end result,
I always eat the batter.

I sample creaming, mixing, beating,
while enjoying every bite.
The ingredients are what make it good,
to make it turn out right.

There are cooks who have great knowl-
edge,
but I have figured out the trick
Is not the time and temperature,
it's stop testing before you are sick.

I figure God must like a lady
with a little extra hip
or He surely would not give us
the delightful chocolate chip.

—*Tracee Ford*

Vision

The blind man
is her father.
She guides him
across the street.
In eight years
he has never
seen the blueness of her eyes,
the radiance of her smile,
but he has felt
the thick ringlets of curls
around her tiny face;
people tell him
they are red curls,
but that means nothing.

He pulls them out
till they bounce back
in the same form
like magic
like nothing he's ever dreamed
before.

—*Pamela L. Laskin*

A Loving Way Always Your Surprise

What you are
is important
as one of God's
    stars.

Who you are
will lead you
    far.

Where you walk
you can always
    talk to God
sand or sod.

—*Lola Hansell*

One

One who is
is many things, not

one, alone, but
more, because, like life

and world, and universe, and all, the
whole of him is bigger

than the many faces are, alone,
though they tell who he is, this
one.

—*Patrick M. Kaufer*

Facing The World

Cold
Is the stare
As the world peers into my soul
Its magnificent immensity
And complexity
Barren, yet full.
What is my life?
What happens to the small and
Insignificant?
Will it become lost?
What is my purpose?
Great or small among humanity?
What if great?
People are small against
The face of time.
Where is warmth
And sustenance?
What is important
In such a trivial thing
As life?
Friends.

—*Anthony David Keller*

Has Christmas Come To Your House

Has Christmas come to your house
Is the tree there all aglow
With trinkets from the bygone years
And some lights to make it show

Is there a wreath hung on your door
A circle filled with love
In memory of the dear christchild
Sent from heaven up above

Have you filled a great big basket
With things to give with care
And delivered it to that other house
Because you really want to share

Has Christmas come to your house
Are the children there with you
They give us joy from another world
And bless the whole year through

With all the memories in your heart
I hope the bad are few
For all the times we've been apart
I'd hope to be with you

—*Velma Futrell*

Life

Life is like a speeding car
It can pass you by bed it won't
go far
Life can be a real drag
When all you do is whine and nag
But life can have its good side you know
Like when you win the megabadse
you can spend all that dough
So don't give up your life just yet
It will be better-I bet.

—*Lee Waller*

Life

Life is like a comet
it comes and then if goes
where we go when we die,
no one really knows,
We've heard many rumors.
We've heard many lies.
But I don't really want to know.
I'd win the surprise.

—*Anne McDonald*

Untitled

Love is an image,
It drifts and sometimes fades.
You cannot always see it,
But it will always be inside you.

Love is a dancer,
Moving to the rhythm inside.
Sometimes you miss a step,
But the music is ever forgiving.

Love is a kaleidoscope,
Colors twisting and turning.
Continually changing,
Yet always the same.

—*Mara Weston*

Emotions

I cried the day we said good-bye,
It hurt so hard I thought I'd die.
I knew the pain would go away,
If only you were here to stay.

I think of all the happy ways,
In which we spent our youthful days.
From late nights till early dawn,
My love for you goes on and on.

Then suddenly the pain is gone,
I feel "Emotions" running strong.
A stranger walks into the room,
And once again loves in bloom.

Its funny how "Emotions" can be,
If only we, as humans, could see.
It changes lives from afar,
But, that's the way "Emotions" are.

—*Linda Pleiman*

Untitled

The mountains call,
The trees listen,
The sky holds on,
The water answers.

—*Nicael Leistikow*

Only Friends

We started out as friends
It slowly turned to more
I thought it was a good thing
but now I'm not sure.

Even though I want to
the words I just can't say
I hate you would be so easy
if only I could feel that way.

But the truth of it all
is that you mean a lot to me
and that maybe even someday
it could be how it used to be.

Your friendship meant a lot to me
much more than you'll ever know
I act like I don't really care
I try not to let it show.

If this is what you want
I hope life makes you happy
but do me one last favor
and promise you won't forget me.

—*Rhonda Rearick*

Pressure

It storms inside my head;
It wants out,
But I can't let it out.

I try to forget it,
But it builds up even more.

It builds up inside my head.
Now I must let it out,
But I don't know how.

Sometimes I let it out to hurt someone;
My mother,
My father,
My sister,
My best friend.
Sometimes I let it out to hurt myself.
Pressure.

—*Melissa Alwine*

Untitled

It was a new environment,
It was a new place,
Everything was new
The teachers, the people, everything.
Then I met you.
You were weird and did everything.
You knew what to say and do to put
a smile on my face and I thank you.
Now you've gone,
It's been so lonely.
I never knew how much
I trusted and cared for you.
This is for you, just to
say I'm glad that I got to know you.

—*Yvonne Dauterman*

Close

Distance
touched you first,
more directly.
This was necessary
for the presence of your hand.

—*Cindi Laukes*

God's Love

God's joyous love is so dear,
it will even draw a tear.
God has plenty of love
just taste it, and you will
flutter like a dove.
God's love is so strong,
so take it, and pass it along.
God even loves you, no matter
what you've done.
His love is powerful,
it will give the wicked a stun.
You can't say His love is weak,
if you don't believe me,
just take a peak.
God's love is so true,
one day it will Hit you, out of the blue.
Go ahead, test it, I dare you to see,
It will overflow sweetly and abundantly.
In God's love there is laughter, and peace,
and you will find God's love will never
decrease.

—*Richie Watford*

For A Beloved One

If I could paint Love,
It would feature the radiance of your smile,
Your blindness to my faults,
And accent your zest for life.
My painting would be
In brilliant rainbow colors,
Reflecting the many facets
Of your personality.
It would sketch in kindness—
Thoughtfulness—
Spiritual beauty.
There would be splashes of compassion,
Areas of understanding
And strokes depicting
An uncompromising concern
That embraces
All of God's creation.

—*Naidene Stroud Trexler*

"Maybe"

Maybe isn't yes or no,
It's a word that's in between.
Only the person using it,
Really knows what it means.

Many parents say it,
It's an easy word to use.
"Maybe", we'll see", next time",
It's a phrase that can not lose.

If you come up with a choice,
Of yes or no to say.
Just use the word maybe,
It works the live long day.

And when the day is over,
If you still can not decide.
Just tell them "we'll see", maybe,"
Ask your dad, he's just outside

—*Vickie J. Oates*

Untitled

Run from sanity,
   It's knocking on your door.
Curse the darkness,
   and hope for nothing more.

Whisper in the night
   To drown the crazy siren screams
Blow out the candle,
   and focus on your dreams.

In your mind there is a clown.
   with a tear strained face.
Why is he so sad,
   In such a joyous place?

Is it just an act,
   The tear stained clown?
Awaken with a shiver,
   and notice, the sun is just going down.

—*Michell Ansley*

Mother Nature

This is Mother Nature's harmony.
It's not a negro spiritual,
though it could be sung to God.
It might simply be a celebration
of the dawning of a new day.
A glorious dance in which all her
children are choreographers.
A first-run play in which:
the clouds;
the sky;
the trees;
the dew;
are actors.
Oscar winning performances
without a thought,
Performed every morning.

—*Kevin Mills*

The Past

The past will always haunt you
Its power makes you weak and frail
Thoughts of it will never escape you
For it covers your emotions with a veil.

All you need is a moment's respite
But the chance will never arise
For the past is a powerful enemy
Despite the fact that it dwells inside.

Take the chance to expel it
Drive it away from your thoughts
Get it out in the open
For your future is in its grasp.

—*Kevin Fury*

On A Snowy Friday Afternoon

When freak winter weather
   deposited diminutive dunes
      snow softly illumined boulders
         ordinarily sedate ocher stones

            I
broke N through
feeble S protest
   wane P light
            I
            RATION...stoneware addressed

—*Eardie A. Curry*

The Wind

The wind is such a mystery
Its such a source of power
It can be just a soft and gentle breeze
To kiss the violet flower
Or it can command the very biggest tree
To shake and bend so low
It can gently move them in a waltz
That sways them to and fro
You will never ever see the wind
But you can see its wrath
If it becomes real angry
And your caught up in its path
The mighty wind no one can control
Except for God on high
Only he can speak and even the winds obey
From his throne up in the sky.

—*Linda Rakes Keene*

Untitled

Your eyes fill with fire
Its the fire of life
Your mind tears through
Locked doors of nostalgia
Making you live your whole life again
Then suddenly there is a
Gust of unearthly mental wind
Which blows out your heavenly fire
And leaves you with nothing
But dirty gray smoke which rolls
From the burning embers of your soul
The smoke fills your eyes
And blinds you of life
It leaves you with the eternal sight
Of packed earth around your soulless body
Now you must lie there for eternity
And wonder if this is really better than life

—*Paul Moore*

For Jud

The moon is full and high...
It's time to say goodbye!
I'm sorry I don't know to lie
And say to you happy new year!
Because tonight, my ever dear,
Before my last
And your new year,
I'll be the past.
The moon is full and high...
Goodbye my dear!
You have my last goodbye!

—*Petre Carje*

Untitled

A single red rose
on a grey stoned path.
One candied heart
for a pretty little girl.
A stray puppy
wandering streets of nowhere.
Fire in the eyes
of a new mother in love.
One purple orchid
in a field that was once filled.
Lustrous on the faces
of a young couple feeling new desires.
All this painted
in one single picture.

—*Linda M. Smith*

My Best Friend — Theo

She's my very best friend
I've know her for years
We share joy and laughter
Also sorrow and tears

She's always around
If I need her today
She'd be here in a minute
And come to stay

As dreams we have shared
And fond memories too
We sit and talk
Or be quiet and blue

We can smile and laugh
Or if I'm sad
She holds my hand
And helps me be glad

Our family and friends
Have all moved away
But our love for each other
Is here to stay

—*Vera Wille*

Untitled

Through my eyes....
    I've seen our love grow
Through my thoughts....
    I picture our happiness
Through my emotions....
    I show you how I feel
Through my arms....
    I hold you close to my heart
Through my kiss....
    My passion goes free
Through my heart....
    My love burns for only you
Through my life....
    I'll be committed totally to us
Through my touch....
    I'll never let you go
And through my love....
    I'll cherish you forever

—*Antonio Alfaro Jr.*

Winter Drama

Squeaking squawking speckled Starlings
joined by rude rambunctious Sparrows.
Warming up on the barn's sunny side,
cheering up the mid-winter morning.
Taking over feeder and suet
hung on bending cedar branch.
Daring to land in view of the—Tom,
himself sunning on the old well cover
perhaps dreaming of feathered lunch.
Flicking ears adjusting to sounds,
tail tip beating, eyes pretend closed.

Quizzical, quibbling, quarrelsome
flock of Starlings and Sparrows
watched by lounging yellow—Cat.

—*Anna H. Bohling*

Pearl Harbor Haiku

The **Arizona**
Its broken stern in the air
Juries the atom.

—*Lillian Baker*

There's A Panda In My Room

There's a panda in my room.
It will be there, I assume.
It's black and white
and does not bite.
It eats bamboo and also my shoe.
It always answers my telephone,
so I give it an ice cream cone.
I think it's happy in my room.
It will stay there, I assume.

—*Kellen Alexander*

Someday

It seems as though he'll never know,
just how much I really care.
Why can't I tell him that when he's gone,
I always wish that he was there.
I try to find the words to say
I think about him everyday.
Every time I look into his eyes,
I want to tell him so much;
That all I want is for him to
feel the same way and tell him
how I care for him so much.
Someday I'll finally tell him.
Someday I'll find a way.
And maybe then I'll find out
that he also felt the same way.
Someday.

—*Molly Lumsdon*

Early Morning Beauty

Did you ever see a meadow
Just when the sun began to shine
See tiny bits of lace hung out
Like clothes upon the line?

Each weed in that big meadow
Became a clothes line it is true
And fairies hung their wash out
For passers-by to view.

Each tiny piece of lace
Became priceless too
When studded with sparkling diamonds
Etched in by the dew.

The sun shining so bright
The gentle wind that blew
Made a rainbow of color
Just for me and you.

The woven web of a spider
Studded with tiny drops of dew
Created this beautiful sight.
That early rises might view.

—*Mary Elizabeth Chapman*

A Troubled Child's Prayer

"I lay me down to sleep," please Lord
keep my parents from fighting.

"If I should die before I wake," will
my parents get a divorce, I hope not.

"The Lord my soul to keep", please
God let everything be okay.

—*Jon Bixler*

My Own Coon

My own cat, full-grown now;
keeps me safe.

He's got light-green eyes,
Silver and white fur
with a long fluffy tail.

My main coon kitty,
Saved my life!
He's very precious to me.

Knowing he loves me so much,
Makes the life I lead easier.

His tail is like a raccoons.
His eyes sparkle.
He's even a great hunter.

My coon is nice, good, company.
He's someone I can talk to and lean on.
Sometimes he leans on me.

My coon is a grandfather now;
Being a father wasn't enough.

No other will ever replace mine.
Mine's a miracle!

—*Marrianne Gossett*

Remembering

I wonder where in play
Lady Strider romps today.
Does she twitch her freckled nose
sniffing, searching as she goes
for some memory of me?

Does she on clumsy puppy feet
Fall around in fields sweet
with fragrant flowers and locust trees
chasing butterflies and bees
only she can see?

Does she cock her curly ears
and grow homesick as she hears
me stepping on her squeaky mouse
calling through a lonely house.
"Strider, do you miss me

AS MUCH AS I MISS YOU?"

—*Mary Overfield*

Life

When you see a bird fly high in the sky,
    Land at your feet
    Take off again,
Can you see we all are free?
    Warm then cold now warm again,
    Blossom's Flower's Bird's and Bee's
    Green leaves on the tree.
In the world of Nature
        No negative's,
The season's change and life goes on,
Why do we Humans make the
        Seasons long?
Fly high lovely bird.
Bloom on pretty flowers.
As in the day's of Yore,
Why do we wish for more?
Nature will survive the
        Human race.
If we do not use our mind's
    To state God's grace.

—*Jean Hawks*

"Pineapple Delight"

From clearing banks of Beauty's spoiled
Lasting homes of golden knowing
From spots along this River's bridges
I alone do wait for glimpses
smiling singing hardly breathing
whispers form to make up reasons

For why I cannot be myself
And utter what I know the best
You decide, then tell me so
Since I no longer have the key
That gives the waters time to be
You've always stood the Dam to me
And ways to set the rivers free

Do not pour your words on me
The Gooding world that I shall see
Rains on me

—*S M Thomas*

The Boys Of Summer

Running through the fields
Laughing under trees
Sunshine reaching down
Hair blowing in the breeze

Faces all aglow
Smiling cheek to cheek
Exploring all around
Wading barefoot in a creek

The boys in sunshine play
with all the friends they meet
Fun times all around
Till old man winter takes his seat.

—*Laura Weisser*

The First Time (12-21-92 1:22 a.m.)

A fragile rose of red
Lays neatly on your bed
Between the satin and lace
It symbolizes your grace

Now that your innocence is gone
The white sheets no longer belong
The blood red rose
Is laying where you posed

It's been an hour or so
Since you let your man go
Slowly you start to cry
Still wondering why

Your innocence was picked
Much like the rose he flicked
Upon your bed
Your sheets are stained red

—*Finney McCloud*

Salvation Fish

Swim swiftly, little mandarin flame!
Sear fiery vermillion seas with haste,
Eluding cravings of ravenous vermin
Soiled, unworthy; let them waste.

Flicker, flash your gossamer fin!
Leap free of oceanic purgatory faced,
Allowing dregs to sink as stone
No idle prey for praying taste.

—*Semi Aboud*

Mistake

Break my heart and make me frown

You said I could trust you, then you
let me down

I don't know why I fell for it like a
fool

You're just like everyone else, you
Don't care that you're cruel

It was just a game that you were
Playing with my heart

I let you in, and you tore it apart

I don't want to play your game
anymore

There's too much pain and I must
Fix the sore

So think in the future about
The promises you make

And try not to make another mistake.

—*Jenn Luhr and Michele Smith*

Let Me Be Your Eyes

Touch my hand as we walk
Let me lead you through life's
Winding road of pain and sorrow,
Of happiness and love.

Each step is a journey
A beginning and an end,
Make each step count
For again will never be.

Live to the fullest each day
Sing songs of love for others to hear,
Sing songs of love
For others to feel.

Whisper words of inspiration
To those in despair,
Send prayers to the heavens
To ease those in pain.

Look toward the sky above
Beyond the clouds the sun shines,
Enjoy life, smell the flowers
Touch my hand.

—*Sergio N. Domondon*

Blessed Communion

With this bread and with this wine,
Let our souls with yours entwine.
And as we leave filled with your grace,
To make this world a better place
To live, to love, to work, to pray,
To thank You for each blessed day.

So now dear Savior take my hand,
Pour out Your blessings on this land.
Let your radiance shine through me,
So others too, will come to Thee.
Our souls together now will soar,
And all shall love You evermore.

How wonderful to know I'm thine,
But breathtaking to know you're mine.
One day we will meet face to face,
In Your heaven that Holy Place.
When in your arms to hear you say,
By My side you'll always stay. Amen

—*Theodore H. Runyon*

Nostalgia

Discarded treasures of the past
lie buried in the crowded room
and memories of long cherished times
surround me with nostalgic gloom.

Beneath obscuring shrouds of dust
lie toys of children long since grown
and keepsakes from my younger years
remind me that I'm now alone.

Mementos gathered through the years
lie scattered in the disarray
and like the stories of their past
have faded from the years' decay.

Discovered in a cobweb cloak,
an album of old photographs
has been the keeper through the years
of timeless smiles and silent laughs.

A pressed corsage disintegrates
among my special souvenirs
as I recall the times we shared
with bittersweet, nostalgic tears.

—*Xylia E. Paredes*

Reflections

In the still place of my inner self
Lies a silver pool of tears
So smooth, a hard and glassy pond
Unrippled by my fears.

The sunlight, while once safe and warm
Now casts a dangerous glare
And the pool remains unmelted
Keeping you locked up in there.

No pain, not hurt from caring
Or the honesty of your eyes
Can reach inside this mirrored place
Where my soul no longer cries.

My dreams live on the distant shore
Of this frozen lake of tears
And when the lovelight reaches in
A dazzling rainbow appears.

I cannot look into that prism
Where healing and love bring pain
And memory brings your touch of sadness
Along with the melting rain.

—*Kathy Fiedler*

Straws

Twenty years and
  life's a bitch,
The small things
  become huge.

Have a care
  or you may
Find our
  unity unglued.

Camels breaking
  backs are not
Just platitudes
  to me.

But encompass
  saddest truths
That there could
  ever be.

—*Barbara J. Vuocolo*

Jimmie's Eyes

The light that shines within your eyes,
Lights up my life and tells no lies.
I try to read what it all means,
It seems to reflect all your dreams.

I see such love shining bright,
Its brightness lights up the night.
Your love gives off a special glow,
Its bright enough to melt the snow.

I hope that light will never dim,
It fills my heart to the brim.
I feel so special in your eyes,
I hope our love never dies.

Your eyes express how you feel,
They make your love very real.
I hope my eyes tell you the same,
I am not playing any game.

I've searched so long just for you,
Please don't ever make me blue.
Our love I pray will grow strong,
And will last our whole life long.

—*Phyllis "Armi" Snider*

Envy

I too would shriek
like a barn owl ,
buzz like a locust,
on the high-wise,
in the nutty shade.
Tail like a boa
flicking, dancing,
I'd swear at the curs —
"shit-nose"…"bone-tail" —,
angle for the chase
and last-second
leaps at the trunk.
I'd sprint for my mate
on flimsy branches.
Sky-crazed,
I'd tangle my nest
in the tallest oak
where hawks land,
fantastic wings
clobbering the air.

—*Marcel G. Gauthier*

Jason

My love for you is wild,
Like an unruly child.
Like wildfire on the plain,
Or dancing in the rain.
A freedom I've never known
Is what to me you've shown;
You taught me how to fly,
And how to say goodbye.
Our love will always be,
Though you're not here with me.
For the love of a common friend,
Our love was destined to end.
Such a very noble choice…
Oh how I miss your voice,
And being held by you
As the chill wind blew.
And our sorrow had no reward.
The three are together no more.

—*Autumn Wright*

Thoughts For Peace

Let   Thoughts for Peace
        Like flocks of geese
        Overwhelm the sky.

Be   Sure to know
        On earth below
        The best of leaders fly.

One   Course they chart
        In seasons part
        Returning up on high.

Peace, Peace! Peace, Peace!
        From flocks of geese
        Resounding is their cry!

—*Ruth Goloff*

Empty

An empty life
   Like hollow hallways
   Echoes silently

Time passes by
   Like a vacuum
   In a black hole

—*Pauline Anderson Slovak*

One More Time

I sit here amazed, of how I feel
Like I'm going through a maze.
The pain of it is so unreal;
It's hard to explain how I feel.
As I walk down this rugged hill,
I pray for the Lord to heal,
My broken heart.
Where did this all start?
Did I deserve every part?
Lord, please help him to see;
Just how much he means to me.
My wish is for us to stay together,
As one forever.
But Lord if it was never meant to be,
Just one more time before I die;
Lord …… let me tell him,
Just what he means to me.

—*Amy Cooper*

Night Visitors

Oh, all my fears come out at night.
Like wayward ghosts in lonely flight
With carping cries, reciting lists
Of prizes lost, of chances missed,
Of costs too great and gains too slight.
Oh, all my fears come out at night.
And all my doubts appear at night
Like rodents hidden from the light,
They creep about inside my head
Till any hope for sleep has fled.
If I were small, I'd ask for light
To cope with phantoms of the night.
My father would, when I was small,
Leave night lights burning in the hall.
He understood my childish dread
Of ghosts and goblins round my bed.
But now I'm grown much too tall
To leave lights burning in the hall.
My father has been dead for years,
It's up to me to quell my fears.

—*John A. Jordan*

Russian Roulette

Give and get
Live and let
Russian Roulette
Gamble and bet
   ...your life away.

Live and let
Death and dying
Fly and flying
Cries and crying
   ...in remorse.

Shot in the hall
Spots on the wall
Blots on it all
You lost it all
   ...'twas such a waste.

Neither now or never
Life isn't forever
Shot and severed
This game so clever
   ...laughter in the distance.

   —*Johnny Thomas*

A Prayer

Dear God, please quiet all turbulent
   lives I pray
That we may love all people, all
   creeds, everywhere today.
There is so much hatred, prejudice
   and slight
Cluttering up and obstructing your
   highway of right
People trampling one another in
   the mad rush of the throng
Each thinking his right - all
   others are wrong
Show us that this highway is
   wide
There all feet may trod
Once we be still - and listen,
   and know. Thou art God.

   —*Minnie M. Allison*

The Gun

It's a metallic demon
Long, slim and hollow
Hungry for red
It spits, but doesn't swallow
The evil idol of hell
An illicit in society
It's the unforgiven symbol
of death and insanity.

The dark hole
Of the demonic figure
Awaits the message
Of a so called trigger
The perspective of the hole
Determines fatalities
Victims and witnesses
Unfortunate realities
Ellipses make you a witness,
Circles- a victim,
Hope you'll never see,
Or feel- what's in them.

   —*Roberto Vargas*

If You're Watching Over Me

(Dedicated to Steven Stern, I love you)
Look into my eyes, my friend
And tell me what you see —
A tear that's shed when you were lost
A heart that's found empty

Listen to my heart, my friend
And tell me what you hear
A hollow hole without a beat
A rhythm lost without you here

Reach out and touch my hand, my friend
And tell me what you feel —
An ice cold grasp without your warmth
A feeling only you could heal

Steven, I'm lost without your love
Just your soul can set me free -
All you must do is follow this
And please don't forget me.

So if you're watching over me
Look, listen and feel
The pain you've left inside of me
A pain only you could heal.

   —*Risa Tanania*

My Prayer

Father,
Look on me - This day I pray,
Please grant me - That I may,
Bring joy I hope, to those in despair —
   Help Dear Lord, to help - repair -
Pain and anguish of this life,
Help me Lord, to touch a life.
   Grant me your love,
      When I'm blue
   Give me strength to see me through
   And then Dear Lord
   When day is through
   Think of me - When
   I think of you.

   —*Amantha Starr Dunning*

Depression:

Utterly and completely alone
Lost in nothingness
It hurts so bad
This void inside me
Go away
Take flight
Set me free
So strong is my depression
I can touch it
Taste it
Such a burden
It weight me down
The pain so immense
That it bleeds
The pain of heartbreak
Lost of friendship
My loneliness is eternal
My grief infinite:

   —*Sharline Barstowe*

A Good Nite's Sleep

As I, prepare for a good night's sleep,
Like one walking in cotton feed,
Where my mind is fertile,
That makes one's nite complete.

   —*Vernon Ross*

Untitled

Have I got it, have I
lost it.
Can I keep it, what's the
   cost of it
Shall thou fall upon a stone
will there be Light to guide me home
   constantly Dark, is this my life
Consistently sharp is this your
   knife

   —*Sandra Kelley*

Everything

There are many ways to describe
Love...

If Love is to give then
there is nothing in this world
good enough for you.

If Love is friends, then
it's you I confide in.

If Love is time, then forever
would be too short for us.

If Love is kindness, my hands
are yours.

If Love is family, then let
our name be one and never end.

Love is for those who seek
and believe that true
happiness can be found in
innerself and beyond.

   —*Kevin Nolder*

Love

Love is tender, kind and sweet
Love is great and can't be beat
Roses, cards and good luck kisses
All the things that used to be wishes
Hours spent on the telephone
And detestation when no one's home
Once true love is found inside
You'll always want it by your side
Once there's love you won't regret
All the ones you've never met
Through the many, many days
The feelings-they won't ever fade
The feelings of love can't be mistaken
They're like a dream ne'er to waken
On the face and in the heart
The feelings you thought would never start
Now they're here and going strong
The feelings you know just can't be wrong

   —*Patricia J. Truesdale*

Remember Me

Remember me when the gentle sun rises
Remember me when the first wind blows
Remember me when the first beautiful
   grass grows across the prairie
Remember me when the canary sings its
   last song
Remember me when all hope is lost forever
Please my friends remember me when the
last angel rises to heaven in harmony.

   —*Christine Seese*

Untitled

What is love?
Love is just a word
Just a word!
Love is much more than a word
Sorry!
I mean it's just an idea
Just an idea!
Love is much, much more than an idea
Well I mean love can't be seen
Can't be seen!
Obviously you have never seen love
Nope
Me neither!

—*J. Robins*

Love

Love is confusing.
Love is true.
But how do you
Know its Love?
Is Love wanting
To spend your whole
Life with him,
To spend time with him,
To kiss him, to hold him
In your arms?
What is Love?
Melting when he talks to you
And crying when he doesn't.
Wanting him, hoping
He wants you.
Can some one tell me
What Love Is?
Is there even an
Explanation?

—*Melissa M. Manes*

Tiger Eyes

Long red hair and tiger eyes
Love, just over the hill
I'm not there now, nor yesterday
Tiger eyes, be still.

Wait for me, my tiger eyes
Be faithful, stay, be true
I'm coming soon, my tiger eyes
And I'll be back for you.

Tiger eyes are roving eyes
Tiger eyes are bold
Tiger eyes are never true
You have them, so I'm told.

Wait for me my tiger eyes
Be faithful, stay, be true
I'm trying hard, my tiger eyes
To hurry back to you.

Long red hair and tiger eyes
Love, just over the hill
Now someone else's tiger eyes
And now my heart is still

—*Katey Schlank*

Mountains

The mountains stand tall,
majestically above all.
Looming blue and white
in clouds high above the world.
Mountains are peace for people.

—*Kristin Parchem*

Departure

The year had passed
Love was there and gone.
He had thought they were enemies
But was very wrong.

They found each other once more
Only to find love again.
Singing had brought them closer
A friend had given help too.

The love never departed from the two.
Knowing it would last forever
They touched before departure.

—*Tiffiny Ingram*

My Light And My Darkness

You are my light
Loving and dear
He was my darkness
I was filled with fear
You are my light
Warm and bright
He was my darkness
Cold like the night
You are my light
You hold and love me
He was my darkness
Always standing above me
You are my light
Full of trust
He was my darkness
Consumed with lust
You are my light
Our love goes on
He was my darkness
The evil I've known

—*Tammy S. Liles*

A Poem Just For Girls

Kissing is a hobby
Loving is a game.
Boys get the pleasure
Girls get the pain
He tells you he loves you
You may think it's true
But when your tummy swells
He says the hell with you
60 minutes of pleasure
9 months of pain
2 days in the hospital
And a baby with no name
Your father is a bastard
Your mother is a whore
You wouldn't be here today
If the dam rubber hadn't
TORN!

—*Jennifer Gates*

If It Weren't For You...

If it weren't for you,
  my life would have no light.
If it weren't for you,
  I'd stay in at night.
If it weren't for you,
  the night would never end.
If it weren't for you,
  I might be dead.

—*Allison Pratte*

Second December

There is a song that bleeds
Lying face down on the concrete
Sucking into its body the murky water
That gathers there.

Oh, to speak of the Old Republic
is to break a back,
smother a worm,
feed soup to strangers.

Bring the fireflies
to burn the city while its vermin
remain unable to escape.

—*Sigmund*

Sunday Afternoon

The big blue chair and I
Make a pocket
Only a small person
Can crawl into.

She folds herself
Neatly into it
One leg akimbo

Filling me in on Fantasia
Her whispers
Tickle the side of my face

I don't remember being this small
Yet I can feel the warmth
Of my Grandmother's
Large love for me.

If I can't be in a pocket
I know how to make one.

—*Janet Mahan*

Take Care

Hearing those words you say
makes you seem so far away.
So I pray
from day to day,
that you'll be safe
and no troubles will come your way.
Happiness you seek you will find.
Just keep in mind
the family you left behind.
I can't bare
not having your care.
You say I'm strong
But you've always been my strength.
Leading me,
while I follow in your tracks.
Which now I lack.
Please come back!

—*Laura M. Watts*

Dragons Fight

Dragons fight
Pierces the night
Spears through
Pain which
Tries to win
The game
The blood is splattered
The dragons are battered
The fight is done
The old of course has one

—*Michelle McClintock*

Our God: King

Upon the new earth God knew dearth
man was not yet out of His mind
solely He breathed one into earth
Adam reflects the Lord's own kind.

The need for a real companion
from God's Adam woman we find
living with their oblivion
together created a bind.

They were given a tree of life
knowledge unto them became real
meddlesome Satan gave them strife
patrimony loss they would feel.

The flood came all was lost but hope
salvation was in the shadow
of Emanuel on the cross
and later beyond human glow.

Again departure we can save
our victory is with a ring
loyal followers we are brave
one-by-one we choose Our God:a King.

—*Pierre LeBlanc*

The Real Me

The earth revolves around
many things, and I know that
I am missing,
    An eagle has the sky to sore
through, all I have to sore
through is an empty room.
    I need some space like a
field where I can run free, and
feel the night wind or a cool day
breeze.
    Right now I can't find me,
but will continue to seek.
    The sadness and madness
holds me into deep.
    Hoping that someday it'll
set me free, so I can find
The Real Me.

—*Sandy Lee Olivo*

Remembering

Hello, Kiddo! Mud in yer eye.
Ma's old apron, apple pie.
Grandpa's beard, his big mustache
Fireplace clutter, piles of ash.

Bicycle wheels, fuzz-faced boys
Kids a sleepin' in fogs of joys.
Velvet muffs, high buttoned shoes
Time's been flyin', none to lose.

Horse a chewin' clumps of hay.
Me, a sleepin' cares away.
Evening comes for happy women,
Blueholes full of catfish swimmin'.

Catfish's fryin', day's a dyin'
Me in clover just a lyin'.
Scarecrow waves, "Hello" to me,
I'm awake and filled with glee.

Childhood's gone, but I remember
Smokin' hams in mid-November.
Golden peaches canned in jars,
picked by mommy from the stars.

—*Velma Scafe*

Circles

Tomorrow the day brought
me to that place I've
been before a bridge to
no where leading to
this day that is no
more so where can today
bring me if tomorrow
has passed away and
will I ever forget
the pain felt by yesterday

—*Lisa M. Broe*

Prisoner

A shell on a white sheet
metal as your captor
You cannot move but stare
with glossy eyes of blue
like my own
The black pit in my stomach
opens, swallows my cries
as you are held prisoner
of your own body
which is not yours anymore
but theirs
with needles and tubes
you are trapped inside
yourself
And I cannot free you
I'm sorry
but I love you.

—*Julie Forseth*

The Black And White Of It

Billy, Billy, where are you
    Momma knows you are near
    Come closer back in view
    So Momma will not fear

    Here Momma, here I am
    I was not far away
I was visiting my friend Sam
Though I know I should not stray

    Sam lives just a little way
    Its really not far at all
And I'll come back when you say
    I can hear you when you call

Oh, but Billy, Sam is black you know
    His family is not like us
You may not think it matters though
    But I know it will cause a fuss

    Oh, but Momma, can't you see
    The fun Sam and I enjoy
    And how Sam's black family
Lets him play with your white boy

—*William R. Bastin*

Dreams

A dream is a wish you make in your sleep.
Ready or not you only remember a peep.
Sometimes you dream of a wedding cake.
Before you can eat it you wake.
You might think these dreams are weird.
Just like seeing a man with a purple beard.
But may be when you meet the right man.
You might have a dream you understand.

—*Barbara Preston*

David

Uncles, aunts, and cousins,
More numerous than I can count.
I have at least six grandmothers,
And a grand father I'm learning about.

And yet with all these relatives
Not to mention a sister or three
I felt very lonely and lost in the crowd
Like no one ever noticed me.

Then my mother announced,
(In the midst of my gloom)
That another baby was due.
That baby turned out,
To be the buddy I needed.
And I found that he needed me, too.

He needs me to read him his stories,
When he's tired and ready for bed.
And I seem to be his main comfort,
When his bittersweet tears are shed.

—*Terri Lynn Deluca*

Mother At Her Sewing Machine

I was a pig tailed girl of three
Mother said "come sit by me"
She with her long skirt and blouse
Sat by the threadle machine
She had a smile on her face
Was happy at what she was doing.
She sewed and sewed same more
Sewed for a family of sewer
Made dresses for the nieces
Even out of left new pieces
She seemed to be next to Heaven
When by that machine she sat
Almost without a glance
She sewed boys pants
Now mother is at hers earned rest
She waver after best
Now she's up there with God
Helping take care of the angel
Auditing their all about
Sewing where threadle machine.

—*Alba Moravec*

Got To Keep Moving

Got to keep movin'
    Movin' along
Got to keep moving'
And singin' a song
A song to the moments
That fleet in the wind
    Got to recover
    From original sin.
Got to keep moving'
    Moving' along
Got to keep moving'
And singin' a song.
But what do I sing now?
    The words melt away.
What do I sing now?
    In this new day.
Got to keep Moving'
    Movin' along
Got to keep movin'
And singin' a song.

—*Tom Penaskovic*

For My Brother, Elijah Brown

After a year of life
my baby brother died from
a blood disease.

Loving is what I did
not show him.

Sadness is what I felt
because of not showing my
brother I loved him.

Unfairness is what I think
he's thinking of me right now.

But uncontrollable was
his death.

Forgiveness is what
I hope he gives me.

—*Kawana Wilson*

A Naval Officer's Lament

My mother stays in Boston.
My daughter's at her school,
Way back in New Hampshire
Where the nights are always cool.

My son's still at Annapolis,
My wife is in Hong Kong,
My furniture is in Texas,
And here I am at Guam.

I voted last in 'Frisco,
Was born up north in Maine.
Pay club dues in Manila
And in Washington the same.

Own property in Florida,
Joined a lodge in snowy Nome
And I'll be dam if I can name
A place to call my home.

—*Wm. W. Galt*

hope

still the dawn has not illuminated
my eyes in the open sepulcher
that cold refuge
given to me by the angel of darkness

still not a docile quarry
of the archers with envenomed crossbow
nor of the artifice of their words
sketching a world abandoned by Gods

still it is not the portal of pain
that opens and pulls me in
vanquished by turbid waters
of despair where i cannot see myself

still they have not found our songs
nor decoded the sharp edged lyrics
where everything is seeing us flying
or looking at us full from inside

still i know you are there
loving me in the umbra of the moon
willing to save me from my own madness

still it is not the foretold end

—*Pablo Perez*

Willard

Although my steps are faltering
My eyesight growing dim
My mind's not what it used to be,
I stumble now and then.
Sometimes I don't hear what you say,
Or think I've heard, but naught
So if you have to say it o'er,
Don't think that I'm a clot.
I'm lonesome for the good old days,
The friends I knew back when
Someone to take hold of my hand
And share our thought's within.
Some of you think I'm funny,
And strange in many ways,
But someday you'll be in my shoes
And long for friends and play.
Now when I come and sit beside
My new found friends, I pray
"Don't turn your back and snub me"
Cause your turn will come someday.

—*Rebecca Fleet*

One Year

It was winter when
my heart first knew
that wonderful things
would happen with you.

It was spring when
love's first bloom
rose up from nothing
and chased all gloom.

It was summer when
we joined together
and thought our love
would last forever.

It was autumn when
things began to fade-
quarrels started,
apologies unmade.

It was winter when
my heart finally knew
your love was gone,
that I'd lost you.

—*Jennie Hutchins*

Forever Tree

I stand as a tree—
my leaves
flutter free—

One by one
I see
them blowing from me—

Barren in the
chill—
no leaves for
a quilt—

Shielded from the wind
I stand—
for those whom had held
my hand—

fertilize my
roots—
out from which
I shoot—forever.

—*Jill Schlumpberger*

Promises Accepted

While walking down the path of life
My Lord is always there.
All I need is to reach out to Him
For I know that He does care.

He helps me in my sorrows,
He helps me through all woes,
He heals me from my sickness,
He helps me fight all foes.

He gives me happiness and joy
When daily chores are complete.
He gives satisfaction and blessings
As I witness to people I meet.

As I walk closer to Him daily
May His word be in my heart,
And I promise to give Him my best
And from Him I will never part.

When my days on earth are ended
And I cross the great divide
I will feel safe and secure
With Christ Jesus at my side.

—*Verna L. Welsh*

An Ode to Marriage

To my love,
My lovely dove,
Who I may covet,
May I always love it.

May I love you for,
Your mistakes and more,
For your patience and sharing,
For your kindness and caring.

Until death do us part,
A work of art,
May we forever hold our peace,
And it never cease.

—*Penny Rose*

Poem To My People

My country,
My nation,
My home.

Let us come together as one,
every father, mother, daughter, and son.
To play in the fields of life,
to swim in the pools of glory.
Set aside your differences,
and past wrongs.
Come dance in the streets,
while singing joyful songs.
We are all part of each other,
therefore, we mustn't fight one another.
Let us rejoice,
using our loudest voice.
It is time to come and go
in peace and love.

My country,
My nation,
My home.

—*Sarah Parmley*

Bedtime Prayer

Come beside my bed tonight
my poor sick mind is all but bright
the scent of madness comes to me
but only sinners I can see
the ruthless mind of yours alone
can turn my eyes into stone
the sight of me comes to an end
for only hate must I send
careless secrets in my soul
my heart is gone, what you stole
as I lay in a trance
my memory is still in its dance
wake me up, for I might die
the things I say are all, but lie
can you break my trust in you?
The birds in the sky all but knew.
Carry me away from this fantasy
this must be what they call ecstasy.

—Melanie Berry

As Raindrops Fall

As raindrops fall my heart does too
My sunshine's gone, It's there with you
As I look out the window near
Through lonely dreams I sadly peer
My thoughts drift out into the rain
Lo, the face that brings me pain
Not a pain from something wrong
But something right that now is gone
This barrier-dark, ominous
That holds our love away from us
This space that holds my heart from you
Malicious friend, I can't get through
As raindrops fall they separate
And for your love a patient wait
As raindrops fall I think of you
And as they break my heart does too

—Kevin Bradley Kline

New Day

As my sun sets slowly in the eve
My tomorrow is almost today
Today is surely yesterday
And a new dawn is on the way

The days add up to months gone by
My months total up to years
Years fly by and become decades
And growing old is my fears

Because you've been here to share my life
Has bought joy to many years
Whenever my sun is not so bright
You cast out my shadows and fears

So when the shine has gone from my sun
And darkness is my only light
I'll know tomorrow is today
And in peace I'll die tonight

—Judy J. Turner

You

There was a storm and sand,
my hands were full of pebbles.
There was you and a child.
You made a kite out of
some strings and plastic bags.
There was also a woman
who saw you-
close-up and further away.

—Micheline Morgan

Frosted

    Always stay inside
    Never say good-bye;
  As the cold silver of winter
    Paints over the
      Colors
Mixed and meticulously applied
        by
    the other seasons.
  This new silver seems
    Rather gray to me
    since it's all gray
      when...
  You always stay inside,
  Feelings forever hide in
  fields of lifeless gray
    on a heart of
    burned out black.

—Mark Smith

Horizon

All alone walking on the beach,
no one can see me,
I'm out of reach.
It's been a long time
since I've had a good friend,
whistling to myself
as I walk into the horizon.
The edge of the horizon
is like the edge of the world,
stepping over the side
into the roaring tide.
Strange new faces,
fresh new tears,
I left my world
because nobody cared.
I still watch the horizon,
but from the other side,
next time they'll know
just why I cried.

—Shanea Taylor

My Secret

Inside me there is something
    no one knows about
      like a secret
  This secret tells me I
  will never grew older
  never laugh with friends
never be who I should if I
    ever reveal its name
      outside me
      I am blooming
    inside I am dry
If only I could understand
  the reason for my crying
If only I could stop this fear
    of dreaming that I'm
        Dying!

—Summer Marian

Childhood Love

He said he loved me
Never would lose me
Instead he shoved me
Only to accuse me.
He said I'd lied
I wish I'd tried
But, instead I hid
The fact, that I was only a kid!

—Melissa Quesenberry

Creation

No one knows the year,
no one knows the date.
Why it happened, I can't say,
but I think it was fate.

The world began to shudder,
the world began to quake.
All the dry, barren land
soon began to break.

And the mountains, standing proud,
peaks began to blow.
And the heaven's pale blue sky
soon began to glow.

The world was set
amidst a fire.
While the sea
formed a choir.

With all the fury
and the scorn,
amongst a blaze
the earth was born.

—Nathan Mendes

I Saw You Today

Your little body all alone
No one to care
Once happy in a home
Maybe good, maybe bad

No one to look for you
No one to care
A happy little animal
Never more to run and play

Do they miss you
Do they care
All alone on the street
Silent forever more.

I care
I saw you today.

—Thais V. Merrick

The Praying Tree

The tortuous path
no sad, no word
diminishing out of sight
The virginal tree
no air, no voice
standing on the hill
She put her hands together
and gazing a white cloud
and saying without sound
Oh, my friend in the remote country
You give me a dream
Let me dream my dream
You fill my heart, my world
Now the drift cloud
bring my words to you
bring my world to you
The small tree
so happy, so still
praying on the hill
praying in the depth of her soul

—Yi Cheng

Voices Kill (No Suicide)

Voices kill I do it for a thrill
No suicide they won't
make me die.

All the children in New York City
They all shall die
All the mothers of the children
They all will cry
I foresee a nuclear attack
When I get to Russia I'll
Pay America back
I'll live forever I'll live
As one with my woman and a
Horse and a gun
Some say I'm the driver
And you're the slave
But I know I'm a sinner
And now I'll be BRAVE
Some say I'm so crazy
I've lost my mind
But I'm really evil
And I'll lead you blind

—*Robert Berenter*

The Way We Face

Not east nor west,
Not north nor south,
We face not direction.

The light it pulls,
It pulls this way, that,
Yet we face not direction.

Which way, they ask,
Which way? Do they not know?
We face not direction.

—*Becky Phelps*

Do You Hear It Too?

I sit here thinking of you,
not really knowing what to do.
I call your name out,
I hear it.
Do you hear it too?
They say I talk about you often,
but its hard to get my mind off
you.
I hear you tell someone I love
her.
Do I hear it? Yes, I love you too?

—*Tonya L. Mantz*

My Love For Him

I love him with all
my heart. I knew right
then we would never part.
He holds me tight each and
every night. My love for
him I can no fight. His
eyes are blue like that of
the sky. I fall so madly
in love I could almost die.
His hair is like rays of sun,
which is always so neatly
and perfectly done. Yes, he
is a gift from the God above.
For he is the one I will
always love.

—*Shanna Bingham*

Celebration

Birth of mornings, crystal sun.
Night surrenders as days begun.
Spring reigns while winter succumbs.
During coronation of the equinox.

—*Paul Arnold*

A Wild Dream

I smelled the flowers bloom in May,
Not so, 'twas just freshly mown hay:
I turned my head the other way in
Time to see the light of day.

Moonbeams still danced on the wall
And I began to stumble and fall:
The barn door swung wide leaving me
No place to hide.

A tractor rested in one corner
Somber as any mourner: I turned on
The ignition switch and backed into
A muddy ditch.

Throwing the gear into reverse only
Made it worse: With too much speed
I mowed down a whole row of newly
Planted seed.

Next I headed for the barn before
Causing any further harm: When I
Awoke I was chewing my pillow feeling
Like a weeping willow!

—*Melvin Manwarring*

Spring Days

I was fast asleep
   Now I'm awake!!
Sunset to sunrise,
Brings a new, sunfilled day.
Sunfilled days — with spring
         Smells
      songs, and
         skies
   Skies filled with
   Billowy clouds,
   Colorful kites, and
   Hot air balloons
Spring, can I come out and
   Play with you —
         Today?

—*Margaret Griffin*

Two Hearts

S ilent dark shadows
O blivious of a Pale Horse,
M ust dodge scorching rays
A nd winds of swirling sand.
L ive on, wide-eyed children,
I n spite of it all;
A wait the still rains...

A n army will come
M arching over the waters,
E agar to chase ill spirits;
R elieving Grim Reaper's hold.
I t may take time you do not have.
C an you keep the vigilance
A s still, the rains don't come?

—*Vernice Ankerstjerne*

The Spring Of The Fall

Leaves curl and fall
Obeying the call.
So do we all.

Leaves, snug, repose
And, snug, decompose.
So do we all.

Leaves, ever loyal
To life, become soil.
So do we all.

Soil, through history,
Shows us a mystery.
So do we all.

The secret is out:
From rot comes the sprout,
Reversing the fall.

The start of belief
Is the curl of the leaf,
The spring of the fall.

—*Ralph E. Grimes*

From Your Dreams

From your dreams, I see the night,
   oceans, tides, an endless flight,
   waves abound on shores moonlight,
a love I've found with endless sight.

The soothing feel of an ocean breeze,
   I see the shore with swaying trees,
   and on the beach upon the sand,
   I see us walking hand in hand.

From your dreams, I see the love,
   as I look down from up above,
   you look up as if to see,
   feeling, knowing, it is me.

The sky is black, the stars are out,
   the wind is cold, without a doubt,
you have no clothes, but yet your warm,
   the moonlight dances on your form.

—*Paul F. Guyer*

"Spirit Of `76"

Thine eyes have seen the glory
Of a battle fought and won,
We have lifted sword and missile
And all too soon our gun,
We have died for our father
And would die for our son,
To keep peace in this nation,
For each and every one
There were words that day invented,
That lifted spirits high,
And we knew that very moment
The Lord was smiling on us
And we knew that word glory
Implanted in a million men's
Hearts was something no gun
Or missile could tear apart.
Yes, we knew the words,
Glory, glory, hallelujah!
Would echo through the years,
And represent victory's voices,
Along with victory's tears.

—*Marie Lee*

Untitled

What can be the meaning
Of a misty winters morn
When not a bird is singing
And the gray world seems forlorn?

Who can find a purpose
In the gray and weeping sky
Or the brown and somber fields
Where the sleeping flowers lie?

My soul seems curled in sleep
As the sleeping world outside
And there my nestled verse will keep
'Til by springs warmth revived.

When winters murky mist retreats
And spring revives the bloom
My soul will sing with verses sweet
And pierce the fleeing gloom.

—*Scott Thornton*

A Mother's Love

There's nothing like the love
of a mother for her child.
It's there before each one is born,
it comes from deep inside.

She loves each child completely.
Her love grows from day to day.
Each one of them is special
and unique in their own way.

Her heart is filled with memories
of each one when they were small,
of sparkling eyes and dimpled grins
and fingerprints on walls.

She remembers how she rocked them
as she soothed and calmed their fears,
the lullabies she sang them
and the times she wiped their tears.

And though each one is grown and gone,
to her they're always near.
She holds them close, within her heart,
and will throughout the years.

—*Joan Ray Brown*

"Clouds That Drift"

The Intertwining
Of a thought
In the mirror's clouded view...
Reflections of a childhood.
I once knew.
In the mirror's view
The fog of memory lifts.
And becomes a clouded sky
With raindrop tears to cry...
Landing, rippling
In a pool's reflection.
A different shade of blue
A place in time
I once knew.
But clouds that drift
Upon a sky
Reflect a brighter
Point of view - a golden hue
From childhood's view.

—*Stephen W. Young*

Young Butterfly

Enchanting the moment
of an opening dream

Come innocent beauty
now gracefully seen

So cheerful a welcome
when in passing you fly

With wings ever gently
caressing the sky

Wander so freely
across nature with ease
To land ever softly
on whatever you please

Then sudden wings flutter
with a last wave good-bye

To a place that's more suited
for a young butterfly.

—*Wayne Benefiel*

Enlightenment

If love be the weight
of enlightenment,
Then let me be crushed
by tons of light.

If hate or vile Emotion
be remnants of the Heart,
Then bring to me a lantern
to drive away the dark.

—*Ronald E. Cross*

The "The Black Magic Rose"

Is gathered from the hills
of lavish thoughts
Near the streams of positivism,
High above the golden valleys of love,
And each picked for a very, very,
Very Special Person!
May your life be highlighted
And your dreams come true.
It's magic is a good notion
Just For You!

—*Luther Stanton*

Little Speck

Little speck
of many more

What is your
unfeigned chore?

When you move
I cannot see
your flitting back.

Perhaps it's something
intricate
that I lack.

But now and then
When flying by
I feel you perching
on my eye,

Which causes me to
weep, lament.

Are you the end of
some great statement?

—*Robert V. Cunningham*

Once Depressed

Mold grew in the darkness
of my mind
Cold, dark and wretched
green and grey and blind
And suddenly out of the blue
and darkened corners that I
did not know were there;
Beautiful flowers grew and entwined
With light dancing on their vines,
And wrapped their coiling stems
Around the moldy mess.

And made it beautiful.

—*Roberta Mate*

Winter's Ire

Swirling mounds
of raging snow,
from building blocks
of flakes they grow.

While cow'ring trees
and limbs alike,
bemoan the blast
of nature's might.

The crueling winds
that chill the hide
and render white,
our world outside,

Wreath pillowed crowns
of purging sky,
with crystal glaze
of winter's cry.

—*Roy G Hill*

The Child Within

Children are God's way
of reminding us
of how he planned it.
The eyes of a child
are full of trust...
their lips speak the truth...
their hearts are filled with love.
All of this until
we teach them
to be adults.
How wise we would be
if we allowed them
to teach us....
to be children.

—*Marj Winters*

Memories

When we're apart
I'm so alone
It hurts my heart
and burns my soul
So I keep thinking of things gone past
To make our memories last and last
For without them, I'd not survive
My life would be worthless
and not a day un-cried
So stay with me now
and always be by my side
At least until the end of time!
I love you

—*Paula Gaio*

Gay Michael's First Wife

Gay is like a breath
of spring
So lovely
Shining face
Glistening eyes
Lovely teeth and auburn hair
She looks great in those
Beat up jeans
The bubbly talk
Like rare wine
and smile
She rambles on and on
What subject does she take
Their all wrapped up in one
There just isn't
Anyone else like her
All the soap operas
There ever were
All the movies and books I've read
She makes life an adventure and fun

—*Maria Restaino Kowalchyk*

Untitled

It's like a commitment
Of the heart
Sometimes in the middle
It gets torn apart
It's hard to say forever
Without a doubt
But then you get swept away
And that's what love's about

—*Martha McAdams*

Sun-Kissed Days Of Youth

Oh, you caught me dreaming,
of the sun-kissed days of youth
of innocent love,
and holding hands to cross the street,
of sand-box days
and firefly nights,
of warm summer breezes
and the first snowflakes of winter
of endless laughter
and secrets never shared,
of breathless running
and watching clouds pass.
Oh, just the memory of it
makes me young again!

—*Misty D. Lawrence*

My Love

I sit and listen to the sound,
  of the waters upon the rocks.
I sit and dream of my love.
  My heart beats,
In rhythm to our song.
  His words,
Still fresh in my mind,
  we've shared so much,
Now it is gone.
  I must learn to let go of the past,
And love some one new,
  But on the sand each day
I will always sit,
  and dream of my love.

—*Jennifer Ware*

Behind The Walls

Behind the walls are sounds
of wind,
And songs within the mind.

Behind the walls are mice
and rats,
That chew away on an old
man's mat.

Behind the walls are
little places for little men
to play,
"But that's ok," says the old,
man,"It's only for one day."

Behind the walls you'll
find someday,
Little things going their
own way.

—*Tonya Odom*

Sleepless Moments Daydreaming

I spend the daylight hours, daydreaming
  of you and how I might spend some
  of my daytime with you.

I daydream of all that we might do
Daydreaming of the moment that I can
  only see you standing there in front
  of me and all my daydreams then
  come true.....

—*Armstead Swann Jr.*

"Saint Agnes Highway"

Planting daffodils at the base
of your Mahogany marble door
always clearing the stray blades
of grass that grew between the cracks
A bright blue Cathedral ceiling
held in the beauty of the
sponge painted Ivory clouds
that seemed to touch the
tops of the rounded stones
and it brightens the garden
where you chose to relax
to soak up the suns rays
I remember when I was the only one
who ever visited bringing you a touch
of love along with a smile and a tear
I just couldn't shake the vision of the
cool soft satin like velvety moss
that lined your coffin......

—*Tina Marie Brierley*

Devoted Molly Mutt

My devoted Molly Mutt.
She got up from a warm bed
To lay at my feet.

I think God gave her to me
As He knew I would be lonesome
After everyone died.

Poor Molly, she didn't have a home.
From place to place, she had to roam.

I am grateful for her presents.
Though I have to watch it,
That she doesn't trip me up
Laying with her head on my feet.

—*Margaret Ethelyn Hunter*

Only A Prayer Away

Many times when I am troubled,
Often times when I'm depressed,
  I try to look to Jesus,
as I am being put to the test...
  An answer there is waiting,
  I only have to ask...
  And patience beyond measure-
will be my greatest task!
  Just wait upon the Lord,
I've so often heard it said,
But I found myself miserable,
facing fear, doubt and dread...
Don't be like that, my child,
his voice would softly say...
I'm coming to your rescue...
  I'm only a prayer away.

—*Marion P. Phillips*

"My Tree"

  My tree
Oh, how I admire you so
You stand so tall and firm
You look so very proud
  My tree
Oh, how I wish to be like you
Nothing can move you
Nothing can break you

  Then one day while visiting
  My tree
  I saw the worst thing
  They tore it down
  They chopped down
  My tree
That was once so tall and firm
  Once so very proud
  Once nothing could move it
Once nothing could break it...

Except, of course, the monster of
  Man

—*Valerie Soto*

The Wonderful World

The beautiful world goes by,
Oh my! Oh my! Oh my!
So beautiful as it goes.
With guys with ties, and girls with bows.
A wonderful life for sure!
Across the wonderful shore,
Over the wonderful mountains,
Through the wonderful plains.
Oh my! Oh my! Oh my!

—*Mike Hoffman*

Peace

Peace, Peace, Peace,
Oh why can't there be
peace?
Why are there weapons?
Why are there killings?
This world is falling apart,
because no one uses their
heart.
We could all work together,
and love one another.
Peace, Peace, Peace.
Oh why can't there be peace.

—*Sharon Robertson*

Untitled

It passes me by
on a sailing wind
Who knows when
it will come by again
But down it swoops
and takes my love
Shatters my dreams
and shoots them above
Slams them down into
hurt and pain
Cold, dreary and stormy rain
The sun comes out
But not too soon
It will be long
before a sunny
afternoon.

—*Uhura Jones*

Quiet Morn

The street is quiet
on a Sunday morn
as I look from my window,
just after the dawn

Birds are just beginning
to sing a song
high up in the trees
I would sing along

The sun is now peeping
over yonder hill
and touching the flowers
on my window sill.

Now a car goes by,
and I am forlorn
For it has ended
Ended my quiet morn.

—*Louis F. Valente*

Happy Spring

"In the morn barefoot moms
On green lawns kissing flowers,
Dads in garages
Whistling for hours.

Concerts, puccini
Great sounds to hear,
How good is life
This time of year.

Bluebirds and Robbins
Blossoms and berries,
Raincoats in yellow
Make us feel merry.

Moonlight and lawnchairs
And rust on our rake,
Drag out the charcoal
And lets grill a steak.

Bring on the wieners
The matches, that's right,
Break out the cognac
The song and the night!"

—*Mary M. Baldwin*

Untitled

The yellow porch light shined down
on her chestnut curls
messed by her trembling hands.
She puffed on her Camel,
the butt starting to burn,
and wiped a tear away.
More followed as she sat
at the picnic table in the yard
and read to me—Five pages
of pent up emotions and confusion
poured as freely as her tears.
"Only the people I trust
and care about may read this..."
But I couldn't read it.
My eyes were overflowing, too.
She turned to a typewriter
when her world was closing in,
while so many others have turned to death.
She's looking for answers, alone.
Does she realize that a lot of us are, too?

—*Amy Foreman*

Evanescence

Like a gull's feather
On the drifts of sand
I have made my mark,
But your barefoot heel
On the edge of dunes
Leaves a deeper dent.
The feather breaks,
Soon will be afloat,
In little pieces,
Upon some daring wave,
It no longer cares
Or remembers the drifts
Of sand where there is no mark.

—*Wilma Stafford*

Untitled

Would you like to play
On the playground of my life
Do not be afraid for
There is no pain to be met here
The swings so long forgotten
carry us to our childhood
The days of yesterday
Prepared us for tomorrow
The smell of the clear blue sky
Filled our hearts with purity
The power of the sun
Compelled us to seek safety
The world was united
Peace was the word for the day
Looking through the eyes of a child
I yearn to return to
A day where there were no worries
Secured in a paradise
Locked out of life that contains our body
But can never trap our mind

—*Randy Antin*

Untitled

Darkness is a glue
Nothing changes in the nighttime.
The void barks
Not the dog wondering inside of it.
A brotherhood of lost loneliness
Everyone is friend.

—*John Nicholas Jones*

Sight

My thresh spirit blossoms at night,
On wind travel, to who;
Cheek pressed its pillow, closed orbits.
Absconding the essence of letters
Abound from their envelopes.

Quiet face in peace sheeting,
A presence unknown.
Unreturnables.
Taffy flesh figures, muted colours
Spend my sight, vis-a-vis.

Disclosed viscosity, your smooth digits
Touch disregarded malevolent manitou.
In morning, crackling all reaches with
Hot fingers, sun liquids have you.
Eyes gone at moments of time passing cup.

—*JayAnne Jaederland*

Apex Discovery

The opening of a flower unique was
once something I knew
As it withered and died, my hopes,
my dreams vanished as closed
eyes that had always been
When I opened them, the flower
was there, and I knew my hopes,
and dreams had never died

—*Amber Krapsicher*

One Flag, One Country

One flag to unfurl,
One nation to behold,
One flag, one country,
Never separatism.

May by the strength of her might
Under the stars and stripes
Red, blue, and white,
Perfect sanctuarism.

In this great land of ours
Or wherever she towers,
A beacon amidst other powers,
Great magnetism.

And may her people be
Filled with humility,
Waving a banner free,
Devoted patriotism.

—*Louise Dent Smith*

Dyeworks

A poppy petal,
puffed away by a south breeze,
falls on my notebook.

The petal extract
slowly blots out the blank
and runs over the page.

The tinted piece gives off
a spellbinding incense and
intoxicate me.

Eventually,
the tint soaks into your soul—
especially dried ones.

—*Keiichi Ito*

Our Love

A love
One so inviting
So powerful
This feeling
I am left to fight

The instant I sense
Your presence
I smile

A love
Such as ours
I have discovered
Cannot be stopped

We belong
Belong together
Our hearts entwined
Such as our bodies
In a lovers' embrace

Forever,
Our love
—*Rosemary Warrington*

The Two

Two sat beside a fire.
One was truthful,
The other a liar.
The liar saw the fire dim,
Then the truthful said to him.
"We need a log for this fire."
"I don't have one," said the liar.
But behind him the liar hid
The log that finally did him in.
The truthful one does live today.
But the liar has passed away.

—*Rachel Webb*

"Lovers"

Tonight lets roam as if we
only knew of one thing.
Love is in our hearts lets
not let it die.
For which losing you is one
loss I cannot sustain.
Be here for me and I'll be
there for you.
So walk me home and kiss
me until the sunrise.
We won't tell a soul for
only our hearts will know.

—*Sabrina Richmond*

"I'll Always Remember You"

Our walk along the beach,
Our love that was so true,
The first date we ever had
I'll always remember you.

The first time you kissed me,
You thought it was a joke,
But what you didn't know,
It was my heart that you broke.

I'll never forget the times we had,
I hope you'll remember too,
You may not remember me,
But I'll always remember you.

—*Sarah Soule*

Without You

Without you there's no laughter
Only lonely cries of pain.
No sun to shine upon me
Just days of pouring rain.
The nights are cold and empty
I feel so all alone
I long to hear your voice
As I sit and stare at the phone.
The time goes by so slow
The tears always fall so fast.
Inside my heart is dying
I wonder how long it will last.
I want you here with me
To wipe away my tears
To hold me in your arms
And take away my fears.
I try to hide my feelings
I say my love has died.
But I'm still sad and lonely
Without you by my side.

—*Belinda Tapley*

Inspiration

You inspired me
Opened the door
So I could see
Now emotions can soar
High above the rest
There is no end
Only the best
All shattered can mend
Kingdom to stars
Leaving behind memories
Breaking away the bars
So give me your keys
I will unlock your door
Provide you with a new view
One with so much more
Many shades and tints of every hue
From purple to yellow
Everything is beautiful
Believe me - I know
Nothing will ever be dull
I will show you the way
To a wonderful day!

—*Kari Hovet*

Blue

Blue is an ocean,
Or a lake,
Just like someone,
Who is late for a date.
Bluejays, blueberries,
And the sky are blue.
Just like ice,
That would make you feel nice.
You feel cool when you get
Out of the pool.
Blue is known,
To be depressing, sad,
And for feeling down,
But listen to some blues music,
And you'll feel,
Like saying
"Wow"

—*Melissa Moreland*

Life's Questions

Can you hear the birds that sing,
Or do you hear not anything?
Do you see the flowers so gay,
As they dance in fields today?
Can you taste the salt of tears,
That shower forth from unknown fears?
Can you smell the new moan hay,
As you walk the fields this day?
Do you feel the kiss of love,
That showers down from God, above?
Do you touch man, one and all,
And beckon to a higher call?
These are the questions we must ask,
As we fulfill our lifelong task.
Each life is precious, that is true,
And holds a promise for me and you;
Help one another to find the way,
To make our world better every day.

—*Maxine Christian-Jaouhari*

Love

Love can be good or bad
or even make you mad.
I've never figured out
exactly what love is all about,
sometimes it even makes me
shout most of the time it makes
pout.
When things are so bad it's
worse then anything we've all had
I would even go running
to my dad with all the
problems I've had that's pretty bad!
Love can make you very
upset and makes you totally regret
the things I've said and done
makes me feel like I lost 'cuz
I have not won.
I remember all the fun
but now what's said is already done.

—*Kim Blair*

Anticipation

Our little boy will be so fine;
Or, he may be a girl,
With a laughing eyes and dancing curls.
Our little girl will be so great;
Or she may be a boy
A freckle face, our pride and joy.
Dear Lord, "thank you for your goodness,
To our family; An heir to cherish
Through eternity"

—*Bertha Snyder*

Untitled

As the dying embers
of another day
drift into the auburn sky,
Within a coat of heavy leather
I sit and ponder why.
To the beat of wind blown feathers
the fine dances in my eyes
and with the chill of soft resign
I speak my last good-bye.

—*Robin Harvey*

The Memories Are Always There

Whenever I see your face
Or hear your voice
I realize I'll always care

Someone has to bear
The plans we had
And the dreams we shared

Dream come and go
And feelings sometimes change
But the memories stay there
And there's no one to blame

The world is hard
And the road is rough
After a while your heart gets tough

Sometimes when I sit awhile
My mind goes far away
To a place that's warmly enchanted
And where the people really care

And then I wake and remember
The memories are always there
　　　　　—Linda Hise

A True Friend

Sometimes I'm lonely,
　Others I'm blue.
I never am joyful,
　I never feel new.

Sometimes I'm silly,
　Others I'm rude.
I just can't be satisfied,
　With the things that I do.

I sing a sweet tune,
　Or dance under the moon.
Yet I never am happy,
　Being me. I need you.

You help me to cope,
　You see my life through.
You cheer up my day,
　When I'm down and blue.

In times of trial, or times of doubt,
　You've stood right there to help me out.
Dearly loved friend, I wish you knew,
　How much I truly care for you.
　　　　—Kathlyn Grace Coulter

"Near The Place We Call Home"

Near the place we call home,
Our loving memories will ever roam,
There, I'm never alone,
Near the place we call home.

Where a loving smile will greet me,
Under that weeping willow tree
Where a loving friend will meet me
There my home will always be.

When the road you walk is dreary
And the way always seems weary
And the places desolate you roam
You'll find there is no place like home.
　　　　—Albert J. St. Cyr Jr.

My Garden

Through my window clear and bright
Out in the garden full of light
The trees are swaying in the breeze
Pretty flowers and green green leaves.

The birds are in their bath
Splashing and singing
Sweet notes are ringing
To me, all joy bringing!

Above the tall trees in the sky
Heaven is truly, very near by
Our thoughts so profoundly deep
Into the future, dare we peep?

The flowers so gay and so sweet
To me, such a very great treat
Nature is all at it's best
And we are very much blessed.
　　　　　—Aline Nunes

Dreams

I often gaze through the meadows
over the hills, through the rivers
throughout the creeks, across the
mountains over their peeks, until…
I see the great ocean, and over
it I soar thinking of loved ones
left at shore, but still my thoughts
ponder with ease, as I move on through
the chilling breeze. I have things
on my mind, people one person
to be exact, his face pale white
his hair coal black, I can see
him clearly now across my
mind, to London I'll go just
to find his name very simple
it may be a bliss, but I'll never
forget him, his name reveals as
　Robert Smith.
　　　　—Sara Scacco

Untitled

Life in the hourglass,
　passing time by the grain.
Destiny gives the order,
　to live it all in vain.
So desolate is the mind,
　ever lonely is the heart.
Selfish is the flesh,
　they all are soon to part.
Smothered by the earth,
　sand becomes the breath.
Anger fills the soul,
　for fear of certain death.
Freedom is now a mission,
　It's the only thing that matters.
Love is now a reflection,
　as the mirrored window shatters.
　　　　—R. Bohnke

Untitled

With Jesus picture
　on the wall
Are two churches
　with steeple tall
Together shared—
　happiness and tears
For many, many years
　with fond memories
　　　　—Lila Siewert

"The Road"

In a world for two
People always find
A way to become one
In a very special
World called love

Have we found that
Road that leads to
Love or is it a
Diversion that leads
To an end

As we walk down that road
We become closer
And the road becomes shorter

At one point
The road divides
And we must choose

I know we chose right
Because we are in that
World for
I Love You
　　　　—Shawna Marie Shaw

Winter Afternoon In The City

A chill light rain,
　people, puddles, and passing vehicles
engage the outer senses;
but the inner senses
　flit and linger over other things —
　pleasant thoughts, prickly thoughts,
　tearful thoughts;
memories are an old man's "Walkman."
　　　　—Arthur R. Dornheim

The Closet Of Memories

Where do we store our memories?

In the closet of days gone by
perhaps we have a hang up
that brings a tear drop to our eye.

Is the closet of memories somewhere
off the hall?
With the memories of a lost love
that never returned a call.

The contents of the closet will last
forever more.
There's the memory of a loved one
that never returned from war.

In the closet of memories my love for
you remains,
Although you are no longer with me dear
I've adapted to the change,

In the closet of memories not every
garment sad.
We have some glad rags hanging there
So life is not all bad.
　　　　—Alexander G. Galbraith

Jazz Music

Bass plucking
Piano playing
Drums beating
That's Jazz

Feet thumping
Fingers snapping
Heads bobbing
That's Jazz

Drinks flowing
People smoking
Everyone listening
That's Jazz

New Orleans rhythm
Memphis blues
Harlem nights
That's Jazz

—*Mark L. Taff*

Will you?

Will you set my words to music?
Play the tune on your guitar?
I have thoughts that need repeating,
And I'll listen for a star.
Set my words to music singing...
Set my thoughts to rhythm ringing...
To your body my arms clinging...
Silver chords from earth to star!
I have words that need repeating;
Play them well on your guitar...
For my heart its last is beating,
But I'll listen from a star.

—*Sal O'Brien*

Sweet Little Girl

Sweet little girl sound asleep
Played ball and went for a swim.
So now you hear not even a peep,
Sweet dreams little miss.

Sweet little girl can swing a bat
And send a ball sailing in the air,
Eyes shaded with the tilt of her hat.
Good show little miss.

Sweet little girl swims like a fish,
Going side to side in the pool.
To go in the deep end is her wish.
Keep practicing little miss.

—*Margaret Schanz*

O, Shadow Of Fear

O, shadow of fear,
Please go away
For the flower that blossoms,
Forbids you to stay.
The sun that shines brightly,
Will help her grow strong
With nourishing food, drink, and love,
To help her along.

So shadow fear,
There is no place for thee,
For only love in her heart,
Shows the flower she's free.

—*Angela Eathorne*

The Bible

Pick up your Bible
Read it every day
Don't let it collect dust
It'll help you find the way.

Keep your mind on
Our God above
You may want to read it
You will learn to love.

When you start reading
You'll hate to put it down
Continue to read
You'll win every round.

It's like a magnet
Drawing you to it
It's like a candle
After it is lit.

Love and accept
The three in one
You will be happy
When your work is done.

—*Juanita Wearren Jordon*

Poetry Is...

Poetry is color,
Red and blue and green.
It's a sure work of art,
Something often seen.

For some people it's work,
For others it is play
But sometimes it's hard,
To think of what to say.

Poetry is funny,
Everybody giggles
Poems come alive,
It may start to wiggle.

Poetry is words,
Forming a song.
Verse after verse,
Some short, others long.

Poetry always ends,
Like this one.
You may not like it,
But its got to be done.

—*Melissa Klein*

Songs Of The People

Sam Sosi
remembers the
soaring joy
when he first
saw her
at the
gathering
of clans.
At ninety two
he sits
facing East
in Sears flannel shirt
and Levis
gazing at
the Sacred Mesa
his mind
clinging
tenaciously
to the pieces
of his past.

—*Marian M. Davis*

Time

The tick-tock of a clock
   reminds us of the TIME...
TIME that slips away too soon....
   to waste it is a crime!

TIME is a priceless gift from GOD...
   more precious than silver or gold;
Today is all we have to spend
   on something that we cannot hold!

Today is the day to use TIME
   for we cannot stash it away...
Cannot put it in our pocket...
   nor save it for a 'rainy' day.

So wisely live every moment...
   for tomorrow may never come...
When TIME runs out and we must face
   our CREATOR for all we've done.

Grow in the Faith and trust in GOD;
   let us choose 'right' over 'wrong'...
And make a difference in this world
   so to GOD'S family we'll belong!

—*Marie Ostrander*

Untitled

Just the right amount of cream,
   right amount of sugar
One sip, perfection.

Turn on diner stool to converse
   with old man in wool cap
Waitress comes by, means well, pours.

Start over again

Just the right amount of cream,
   right amount of sugar ....

—*Shari A. Young*

The Lyric Dawn

The night did shimmer
   ripple by
Hushed quiet music
   wafting high

Through treetop leaves of
   greenish hue
Praise, ancient as time
   softly new

Mingling with sweet tunes
   of the air
To glide in strains of
   rapture there

Furtive rose beams blush
   midnight sky
New day reborn with
   peaceful sigh

As the darkness hides
   a weary face
The dawn enfolds with
   wondrous grace.

—*Lesa Tessensohn*

The Wooden Dancing Man

Rain falls like BBs,
rippling the puddle,
wound after wound after
wound, and
a piece of pinestraw
lies on the surface,
the way a stick man would
or the wooden dancing man my
father bounced on his
knee when I was
small, the one
that died in childhood.
Bits of waste at the edge
taint, and
everywhere I look there is
rapid fire.
I am careful;
I step over and around
the sacred graves.

—*Kerra Virginia Riley*

He Left The Party

I sit in here
Room walls white
I'm tired and
The air is tight
No longer can I run
No more can I play
A drunk driver came
And took that away
I'm sure someone offered
To drive him home
He probably told them
To leave him alone
So, he left this party
On a road not wide
He had his fill and
Took this ride
They say for days he'll need a cane
But I'm the one who suffered the pain
Here's the key to stay alive
Don't go out and drink and drive!!

—*Monica D. Schwartz*

Beyond Touch

Waves crashing at my feet,
Salty air filling my body.
Walking away, far away,
    a little closer each time.
Floating up, up into a world
    beyond touch.
Away from all the evil,
and all the anger of this stupid
    make-believe land,
Light, bright lights stinging my eyes.
    Coming closer;
The angel's hands outstretched
Walking towards me,
My hands fitting into hers, walking away
    far away
to a land beyond touch.

—*Stephanie Maxey*

Seven Cousins

Seven cousins all so long ago
Sang of Christmas, so sweet and low.
All grouped together in a rocking chair
Their sweet young voices filled the air.
Those seven cousins where are they now?
Each gone their separate ways I vow.
But, still in spirit their song is heard
As clear in sound as a cheerful bird.
Three of the cousins sang very well.
Their voices clear and true as a bell.
The other three of the cousins sang too
Their young voices so proud and true.
The very youngest of the seven
Sang as sweet as any angel in heaven.
Those seven cousins so long ago
Who sang of Christmas so sweet and low.

—*Theresa Mangiantine*

The Storm

Drifting darkly through the Heavens,
Scowling, sulking, swinging low,
Always angry, never smiling,
Dropping water down below.

See him dashing, darting, daring,
Swept before the winds of might,
Surely, swiftly, surging forward,
Now the day turns into night.

Rumbling, rumbling, rising, rising,
Roars the restless wind before,
Hear him laughing-sounds like thunder
And the rains begin to pour.

Pushing, pressing, passing onward,
Reeling, rocking roaring by,
Now it's quite, the storm is over,
Now the sun is in the sky.

—*Melvin Echols*

Children

Loud, yet in command,
Screaming, yet sleep.
Children, no matter
What they do, we love them.
If there were no children,
There would be no future.
Save the world for our
Children's future!
They may be scoundrels,
They may misbehave,
They don't always listen,
But we still love them.
They may hurt us emotionally,
But they love us.
Because if it weren't for us,
They wouldn't be here,
And eventually the world
Would die.

—*Sarah McIlvanie*

"Spring"

Gazing out of the picture window.
Season changes begin to show.
When the snow starts to melt and go.
Soon little streams will overflow.
Trees and bushes begin to bud.
While the dirt roads turn to mud.
Bright sun rays streaming down.
Warms the plants in the ground.
With the spraying of April showers.
Will bring an array of May flowers.
The chirping sounds as the Robin sing.
All of this is called spring.

—*Marilyn Dragon*

Beauty's Eyes

Beauty's eyes are ghostly,
Seductive, still and haunting.
Ugliness can never taint them,
And Evil finds them daunting.

Beauty's eyes are infinite,
Mysterious and true.
Within them span the worlds of dreams,
Deep as ocean blue.

Beauty's eyes are mischievous,
Playful as a child.
Peaceful as a sunlit lake,
Ringed by heather wild.

Beauty's eyes are quick as wind,
Seeking out the true.
I quest not for Beauty's eyes,
For they are found in you.

—*Sergio Valencia*

Addiction

Drugs can make you high,
Sending you to the sky,
Where you feel you could fly,

But when you hit the ground,
And reality comes back to hound,
You know the drug must be found,

And when you haven't a dime,
Then you must turn to crime,
And go steal what is mine,

Again you are high,
Your up in the sky,
Feeling like you could fly,

And then you hit the ground,
And reality comes back to hound,
And the cycle goes round and round,

You go to a clinic to try to be saved,
On this road temptation must be braved,
Following a path where others have already
caved.

—*Kristina Tenney*

The Meaning Of Orange

Orange is the fruit of
Raging waters rasping
Against sullen rocks with
Notches in them. It starts a
Glaring love of freedom and
Eternal life forever.

—*Lara Slimmer*

Lessons In Submission

Spanish steel will strike you down,
sever your limbs,
spill your blood,
But slice your heart—
there is no 1st degree worse
than the blind slash in the night,
the quick penetration,
The ravished lamb screams,
bleeding innocence over the linen,
silence and guilt.

—*Sarah Eyerly*

The Artists

We are all sculptors;
Shaping our thoughts, our feelings.
Conforming our minds to function
As we desire.

We are all painters;
Combining different ideas
As one would colors
To express just the right mood.

We are all dancers;
Showing emotion with
Gestures and expressions:
Happiness, fear, love…

We are all musicians;
Composing our notes to fit
A certain rhythmical pattern,
In synchronization with life.

We are all artists;
Confused at times,
But with the needed effort
Will make ourselves a masterpiece.

—*Jacqueline A. Steedly*

Love And Friendship

Lord, All I want is a gift to give
She helped me cry, and learn to live
She let you use her gentle hand
Surrender to your healing plan
She let my life be one with hers
A blessing there to lift the curse

Beyond the panic
Beneath the fear
I yearn to always
Have her near.
Show me how to
Give this love,
And gentle push
When I needa shove.

A rainbow bridge to cross the pain
And happy tears that fall like rain.
An angels' song to lift my heart
A love that can't be torn apart.
The gift of how to be her friend
A love that doesn't have to end.

—*Michael Allan Forry*

Fist of Flowers

(To Jesse W. Paine 1974-1993)
She is beautiful, like poetry
She will give me a child
And she will smile with labor pains
She will whisper its name in my ear

I love her

She has made me a son
That was all she really could
My child lies in her arms
He listens with newborn ears
As her blood and breath stops flowing
He cries the tears of a failed song
And although she is so beautiful,
Like poetry
I am not a poet,
And I cannot keep her full of life now.
She is drained away like a dried flower
So sadly tragic, so poetically beautiful.

—*Kate M. Gibson*

The Color Of Her Shadow

Paradise in hell, well done?
She just lies in there
Finding more and more despair
Depression sinking deeper and deeper
And I pray and care
Death do you dare?

Why torture
Show her special grace
And study in her face
What given in the future.
Sensitive, sweet and spoiled
Always to spoil her more
Have my lectures worked?
Or will she, them, overlook!

And as I pray and care
Dignity fades further from her door step.
Love will suffice and conquer the world.
My life for her life
Happy memories taken in stride.

—*Maureen K. Jones*

Radio Tina

Young Tina loved to listen to the radio
   She listened to it day and night
         Without sleep.
   One day in school antenna grew
         Out of her head.
   Tina Rina thought she was dead.
         But she wasn't.
   And, by the time she got home
She knew something must have been
wrong.
Because she was a radio singing a song.

—*Kristin Carothers*

Earned Rest

So active, most summer days-
   running, writhing, gurgling-
sweet liquid gushing forth,
   bringing life to withering limbs.
Now, winters comes
   and there in calm repose,
gracefully coiled and silent,
   lies the garden hose.

—*Thelma Hull*

Shimmering

When I see Venus,
shimmering
white,
under the sliver of a waning moon
I remember the dark,
cool nights,
walking out of the golden pyramids
in Iowa,
looking up,
and seeing myself in the vastness.

—*Michelle Demers*

Weather

Spring to the raindrops
Shine to the summer
Fall with the leaves
Snow with the winter
   They start to tap
as they fall on your lap
   Tap tap tap tap
Suns a shinin' on your window
It's nice, hot and sunny you know.
There they go blow blow blow
around your yard acackaling hard.
   Little white flakes is all it
takes for a cool day in a white
blanket pool.

—*Michelle Munroe*

Fluffy

We heard a puppy crying somewhere,
Between our trashcans she was there.
Queeny had four puppies of her own.
How cruel it was to be left alone.

Queeny was kind and took her in,
The puppies treated her as their kin.
For years she felt she was outside,
Until the day came, when Queeny died.

She grew big, the others stayed small,
So Fluffy took care of them all.
She was so gentle and so kind.
No better friend could anyone find.

She grew within our family,
Then she was so happy, and so free.
We loved her, with all our heart,
Of all us she became a part.

At eleven she passed away.
No more we'll hear her bark and play.
In our hearts she will always be.
We miss you so much, sweet Fluffy.

—*Ervin H. Chase*

Untitled

On a starry, breezy, beautiful night
An old man decided to fly his kite
He crept out of the door without a sound
Once he was outside he looked around
Until he found a place just right
It was there he launched his kite into flight
This old man's kite reached an incredible height
Until in the sky it was but a speck of white
Oh what a sight
A sight to excite
A kite on this starry, breezy, beautiful night

—*Carrie E. Meier*

Tennis Is A Racket

People who watch tennis games have swivel necks that turns to see
.air the through lightning like streaks it as going is ball the Where
Speeding like a bullet it returns to where it used to be.
.affair mad this watch to turn heads all and back batted it's There
Tennis was a quiet game for ladies and for gentlemen.
.metamorphosis a been there's; years passing with changed has This
When the game was played for fun there was no thought of money then.
.avarice with stars super to changed has this shows History
Rows of people in the stands can watch the game and see up close.
.display on tantrums their put brackets highest the in Players
Chosen for their tennis skills they are instead quite bellicose.
.dismay with on look people; rackets their pound and curse will They
Turning heads do more than watch a tennis ball fade to a blur.
?anyhow game old the to happened what ask patrons Scowling
Earnestly they shake their heads in sad dismay, and you concur.
!now moving is your's as just is heads their move people the How

—John G. Sprung

You Had Everything Right But The Date Mr. Orwell

The fat-cats selfishly breathe the air.
Yes, these educated Philistines
Assume it will continuously be there.
They ponder problems of more import,
As the rate of their receding hair.

"Receding rain forests" in response they bellow.
"Are those trouble-makers at it again?"
"Find an ozone-layer for those demented fellows,
And tell them we will save them a tree."

They rape the planet like there is no tomorrow,
And for them there probably is not.
Their legacy consists of tax write-offs,
And the planet a parking-lot.

"Why save a whale or bird", they ponder,
Will they ever really know?
There is nothing as permanent as extinction,
But to them their stocks will always flow.

—Robert Chinery Barkas, Sr.

Africa Dreaming

Although rife with struggle and hardship
And torn asunder with dissention and strife;
   Let the trees whisper her name.
   Africa, O Africa — I dream of home.

Even when need renders her breasts dry
And carves sinewy details along her strong body;
   Let the winds waft her fragrance.
   Africa, O Africa — I dream of home.

In spite of rivulets of brine that run
Along her gleaming blackness;
   Let the sun testify of her beauty.
   Africa, O Africa — I dream of home.

Though lost to touch for generations past
And with face shrouded in compelling mystery;
   Let the rivers pronounce the names of her children.
   Africa, O Africa — I dream of home.

Despite being soiled for ages by the feet of strangers
Still she rises from desolation clothed in riches.
   Let the world bow to her mastery and her majesty.
   Africa! Africa — O Africa!

—Adetokunbo Knowles Borishade

Exposed

How scary my life it could be,
If the traits I could hide, they would see.
Do I stand? Do I run?
Does my life lose it's fun?
Or do I learn that it's just part of me!

Of course I don't wish to expose,
Or stand naked from head to my toes.
Have my hurt, have my pain
wrapped in sheer cellophane,
If I could hide it in layers of clothes!

Some things about me make me blush.
And others they give me a rush.
Show the highs, show the dumps,
Expose my goosebumps.
It's best that I keep me hush! hush!

Do I run from all who can see?
Keep their eyes far away as can be.
Is it right? Is it true?
Not their eyes, but their view.
Is the person I run from - just me?

—Ron de Jaray

Memories Of Grandpa

I sit here looking
at the chain you gave to me.
My how it brings back,
Many a fond memory

Memories of the ice-cream parlor
Memories of the fair.
Oh and I'll never forget,
Memories of the time we shared.

Although I knew you shortly
Not long enough to blink an eye.
When I think of you sometimes,
I still break down and cry.

You gave me many things,
toys, candy, and play things.
But who ever thought most precious,
would be the sweet memories

—Kristy Meyer

The Gift Of Love

One day while sitting on the beach,
A conch I grasped within my reach.
A withered note it did contain,
I knew not of the wealth I'd gain.

It said, "Love is like the deep blue ocean:
Nurture it with great devotion.
Hold it close, but let it flower,
Or drown helpless in its power."

Who sent this message from far away
That in my Heart will always stay?
I knew it came from up above —
The author was the God of Love.

I placed the note back in the shell,
The gift of love in me does dwell.
I cast it back into the sea;
No longer a mystery to me.

And this my prayer for all of you —
That one day you will find it too:
This conch I grasped within my reach
One day while sitting on the beach.

—Jacqueline Mills Shornak

The Vulnerable Brute

I thought he was omnipotent
Most powerful of all
But at a brief and weary time
I saw the monster fall

He made himself up big and strong
A humbling sight to see
But he himself was humbled
To one more powerful than he

Though no harm came upon him
The decision came to one
And I sat there in confusion
When I saw the monster run

When he returned, he just laughed
In the dark his teeth did gleam
But I could not feel his fear
Until I heard the monster scream

Then a calm swept o'er the room
None there more relieved than I
And in the darkness of that room
I could hear the monster cry

—*Rachael Murray*

Snowflakes

They fall down, down, down, into
the white blanket of warmth. It
is it's protector it's guardian
from wind people.

As the snowflakes dance in the
air a hush falls over nature.
They all share the laughter of
children passing through their
performance. All dancers are
unique and eccentric.

When the blanket fades and the
sun comes out visions of just
simple flurries pass through the
heads of adults. But the beauty
of snowflakes lie in the hands of
children. For they'll never
forget snowflakes are performers
in disguise.

—*Lindsay Anvik*

Intention

Our words lash out
With no emotion or feeling,
You had just cut
A heart that was healing.

Your heart was in motion.
Your mind didn't agree,
Sometimes hurt is what talks
It projects without speaking.

If our concept of people
Was judged on how we felt,
This world would be problem-free
Cause we understood their guilt.

Some words aren't intended
For their warm hearts to hear,
Yet they tune to their listening
And rejection is what they fear.

So next time you're angry,
Back up words with thought;
Cause your intentions have been taken
But an apology is what was sought.

—*Aerie Shauger*

No Pain

Tonight as I lay in my bed
I found a pillow to rest my head.

Just when I thought I was going to sleep
A huge stabbing pain went through my feet.

I sat up in bed and grabbed my feet
And the pain went away with deceit.

Oh well, I thought; as I wondered why
I have such a pain in my eye.

I grabbed my eye with my hand
and then the pain went to my brain.

I told myself, "Now that can't be"
And then the pain went to my knee.

I said to myself, "now this pain has really got my goat"
And then the pain went to my throat.

And then I thought; I might as well give in
And then the pain went to my chin.

And so, I decided to rest my mouth
And then, the pain left my body, and left my house.

Now, I don't hurt anymore, I can go to sleep.
Good Night!

—*Jeanette Jones*

My Biggest Fear

My biggest fear in life is to loose you.
You're the one I cry for in the still of the night.
I see your eyes when you look back into your past.
I see the loneliness that will shine forever more.
But, how am I to let you go to a place that's unknown?
How am I to set you free, when now your a part of me?
This fear grows stronger and is slowly killing me.
But, hell we both know this ain't where you want to be.
So go and be free -
But, please take my heart and think of me.

—*Stacey M. Payne*

While You Were Away

This morning I awoke
to a beautiful day
but you weren't here
you were away
gone on another
business trip
but I'll describe to you
three wines I sipped
the birds orchestrated
a song of Spring
but you weren't here
to hear them sing
the sun was bright
and made the air warm
but you were on your way
to a military dorm
the breeze was nice
and blew in to say
that soon you'll return
to share, with me, this day.

—*Sonya Roland Hainstock*

Life

Life is grand,
Life is great;
Life is what you make it.
You have to live it.
You cannot fake it;
You can bend or you can break it.
This big world is not a cake,
But can you meet this mighty fate?
Life is not happy date,
You can't go in by the garden gate!
God gives us backbone and strong will,
But does this give us power still?
No !!! - There is a challenge we must
meet,
A fire within that can be beat!
Young and old,
Smart or dumb;
We all still scream give me more,
Give me some;
Of this thing called - Life.

—*Jessie F. Varner*

392

"The Window"

As I look through the window of my life, I feel an emptiness
inside myself.
I notice the cracks in the glass - each representing a
shattered dream, a broken promise, or a moment that passed me by.

As I examine the window further, I realize that the pane is no
longer gold; but instead silver - resembling all the broken
friendships, lost loves, and distant relationships.

I notice a beam of sunshine peering through the window.
For a moment, I feel all the laughter, joys, and triumphs.
But, as the sun fades, darkness comes once again and so do the
memories of the tears, the heart-felt pain, and the disappointments.

As I open the window, the gentle breeze comes to a halt and all
time stands still.
Leaving me to wonder how the bruises heal; but the wounds scar.

As my cuts bleeds once more from my haunting past, I again
close the window to heart forever.

—*Tanisha Hamel Randall*

"Hands"

These hands held my life and cherished it,
Fed me, clothed me, wiped my tears.
Gave instruction thru the years,
Served the dinners, washed the dishes,
Always submitting to my wishes.
Baked favorite cookies, bread, and pies,
And under blue adoring skies,
Cut the grass and planted flowers.
These hands saying little and giving much,
With just a single touch, can brighten up my day.
They've said hello, and waved goodbye.
And not much to the human eye,
They're now wrinkled, broken, and worn,
These are the hands I love so much,
Serving God with every touch,
The beautiful hand of my Mother

—*Jeannette L. Ciliberto*

Nature's Saying

I pushed my feet deep into the sand,
As the wind swept waves to shore,
Another sunset displayed beauty so grand,
As breathtaking as any before.

The gulls were screeching as a pelican dove,
And the sandpipers' bills prodded for a meal,
White caps formed on wave tips that drove
Water shoreward for my feet to feel.

The clouds turned many colors as a sailboat passed by,
Little coquinas reburied with each receding wave.
As a magnificent painting took shape in the sky,
I knew in that moment, only my mind could save.

I felt close to nature as only one can
When her gifts, we take time to enjoy.
There was no shame being here as a man,
And acting like a little boy.

As I glanced down the beach, it was obvious to me,
Many people allow life's burdens to steal away,
Opportunities to relax so they can clearly see,
Nature's saying, take time to enjoy each day.

—*Hugh W. Ruckdeschel*

Have You Ever Been Thankful

Have you ever been thankful for being a human
Instead of a Doberman pinscher or hound?
For instead of the warmth of a cozy, soft bed,
You would sleep in a box or on ice-covered ground.
Instead of a strawberry punch and a steak,
Your master would feed you with dog food and scraps.
Your pail would be filthy with water and dirt,
And life would be mangy with boredom and naps.

Have you ever been thankful for being a human
Instead of a pig or voracious old hog?
For instead of a plate of delicious spaghetti,
Your trough would be filthy and worse than a bog.
On a miserable morning your master would kill you,
And scald and dehair you for succulent meat.
Your master would bleed you by slashing your throat,
And your flesh would be butchered for humans to eat.

Have you ever been thankful for being a human,
For having a life-span of eighty or more?
And with knowledge of science and change of your habits
Your life can be longer than ever before.
If the doctrine of reincarnation is true,
Let us pray that your soul will be human forever
For it's sad to be anything other than man,
To be mastered by humans so cruel and clever.

—*Alfred Leon Wallace*

"The Pain"

Tame and sound and level-headed.
Instead of doing homework, I'd rather be riding.
Fun-loving but full of pain, for I stay home to practice
again
For now in my life is a confusing time,
I don't know which one I'll choose between those parents of
mine.
Now and then the pain will rest it's rearing head.
Yelling and screaming 'till the anger is dead.

And now and again I can sleep at night;
Never a need to shut off the lights.
Drowning out my parents words,
Reaching for my radio so instead it can be heard.
Everyone ignores that girl; too much spite!
Will someone please tell me what I did to be brought to this
Hell they call life?

—*Tiffiny Andrew*

The Winds Of Change

I feel a great wind blow by. It brings a tear of joy
into my eye. Why it is the wind of change it has come
at last to blow away hate and rage to pass.
Secure your self prepare to change as it blows softly
across the plains.
Forget not your hurt and sorrow. Endure the wind
of changes through a new tomorrow.

—*John White*

Community

All around me all I see,
is a very disturbed community.
We must unite together, hand in hand.
Boldly and take a stand.
We must stand tall and proud,
Because that is what existing is all about.
Fighting crime pain and sorrow,
so that there will be a better tomorrow.

—*Sara Wilson*

Jesus Asks

Do you trust me in everyway?,
Is all our Lord would ask today.
Have some faith and watch for me,
and every dream you have will be!
Go safely now, with faith on high.
Because I love you, I'm always nigh.
You say you believe and trust in me,
then just receive, what I have for thee.
I wish you more than your hearts desire.
It pleases me so when you inquire,
in prayers I feel your heart on fire.
Stay strong in faith, with eyes on me,
and before too long you will foresee,
all the promises I have for thee.
For in my heart there's treasure more,
of things for you I've kept in store.
The Lord will bless you beyond compare,
stay true to me I'm always there!

　　—Sonia Pinder

Wolf Haven

　　　A wilderness without wolves...
　is like a tropical island without palm trees,
　a spring time without butterflies and flowers,
a beautiful woman without a warm and tender heart.

　Something vital and important is missing!
The wolves' destruction is a symbolic example of
　　Man's destruction of Mother Earth.
　Perhaps, if we can save the wolves...
　　we can save ourselves, as well?!

　　—Stephen F. McCormick

The Bitter End

The bitter end for the old,
Is not dying.
It is abandonment,
That is where the pain is lying.

It is when they are forgotten,
Tossed into an old folk's home,
Kept in storage,
While their children roam.

Or left on the side of the road,
Because they are not a puppy anymore,
No longer needed,
Because they are not as cute as they were in the store.

But they have wisdom,
The young are just too self righteous to use it.
So they just ridicule,
And care not a bit.

The bitter end for the old,
Is becoming a burden,
And the plain lack of respect,
Practiced by their children.

　　—Tommy Taylor

Shadow Walker

I see you walking in the wake of my shadow
used to the darkness that you have come to accept
like a small child looking for its own way
choosing what I have chosen before-doing what I have done
feeling only a bit of warmth from the sun
then to plummet back to your cold dark world
never really realizing what I had done
seeing eyes of someone I once knew
the rest is just a shadow
of a small child who never found its way

　　—Sara Bone

Wondering Writer

Sometimes I wonder, am I really a writer?
Is that what I was meant to be?
People pull me in so many directions,
I wonder if it's a possibility.
My mother thinks it's a hobby.
My dad thinks so too.
I don't know how to tell them
that that's not true.
If only I were stronger
and really knew how I felt.
Then all their words of criticism
wouldn't make me melt.
They say I might not be good enough
and might not survive.
In a career based on opinion
that might be suicide.
Am I really a writer?
I wish I knew.

　　—Morayo

"The Revelation Of A Rose"

The last rose of summer,
Is the sweetest of them all,
Before it is kissed by the frost
And welcomed by the fall.
There's nothing so perfect,
As the delicate rose,
Nor as sweet and beautiful when
Touched to the nose.
God surely loves beauty,
Because he created the rose.

Anything as sweet and lovely was
Surely grown by God.
To grow from an ugly thorny bush,
Nourished with God's love, care and earthly sod.
This is a revelation to us,
That we, too, as ugly and sinful as we are,
With God's love, care, and forgiveness,
We can also emerge as the rose from a scraggly, thorny bush,
A person reborn with beauty within and once again shared with
love and in fellowship with God.

　　—Shirley M. Pounders

True Love

True love is a sickness. It is a pit which
is very deep and dark. A pit in which many people
fall in, but once you fall in it is tremendously
hard to pull your way out. True love is a blindness,
a blindness which blinds millions. True love is
forgiveness, but what is forgiveness? Is it a mirror
of our souls? Or are our souls mirrors of our love?
True love is saying "I love you." True love is a
relationship in which two people share, but what is a
relationship? Is it one passionate night? Or is it
years of passion and love? Passion, what is it? Is it
what we base our love on? Or do we base our love on our
friendship, our faithfulness, our truthfulness, and our
forgiveness? The pit in which we fall in is our blindness,
our sickness, and it is our passion. Together we can pull
each other out of this deep pit and we can overcome our
blindness. We can fall in love with our eyes open and our
hearts listening to our souls. True love is you and me!
True love is what I meant when I said ... "I love you"

　　—Rachel Leanne Bishop

Love Remembered

Alzheimer's such a sad disease,
it breaks your heart to see
the one you love with all your heart
as "lost" as he can be.

He's forgotten how to dress himself,
or bathe, or comb his hair.
He can't remember what to do,
or when, or why, or where

He used to know so much about
so many different things.
Folks came to him to find out how
to make, or fix, or clean.

He worked so hard, yet loved to play.
The children loved him so!
He fixed their toys. He played their games,
and helped their knowledge grow.

The damaged mind forgets so much,
memories are lost, that's true,
but each day he remembers yet
to tell me, "I love you".
　　　—*Ruth Hickman Clay*

Love

　Love can be good and love can be bad,
It can be forever or just a Fad.
　You cannot love just overnight,
You must make sure your feelings are right.
　Love can mean something or love can mean nothing.
It can tear you apart or pull you together,
　make you feel like there's nothing better.
Love grows inside stronger each day,
　makes you feel like there's no other way,
It makes you see things differently than before,
　You begin to fantasize more and more.
If the feelings you have are different and new,
　that could be because you've found someone true,
Your knight in shining armor and a whole lot more.
　In simple terms you've found your amour!
　　　—*Tina Marie McGrory*

What Is Love?

A love can be long and oh so lasting.
It can be short, romantic and gay.
It can be brief as an early spring,
Or as cold as a long winters day.
It can struggle like the crest of a wave
That spells itself on the beach it nears.
Or get lost, like a child in a mountain cave,
Who cries for help, but no one hears.
It can continue on from day to day,
And grow stronger from year to year.
Or, like a budding rose in May,
Wilt and die then disappear.
　　　—*Robert R. Speno*

Life's Seasons

In the beginning the spring of my life
Time meant very little
As day turned to night

Then in the Summer everything changed
I noticed the sunshine even enjoyed the rain

Then came the Fall, I look back and find
All that I have is what's left of my mind

Then comes my Winter with a heart full of pain
And everything different except for my name.
　　　—*Emogene McGraw*

O' Faithful Guide

Faith cannot fill empty hands;
It can only guide thy hands.

Noah's hands built an Ark;
Although there wasn't a cloud in the sky.
People mocked him daily;
But when the rains kept falling,
They no longer questioned why.

Faith cannot fill a mouth;
It can only guide thy tongue.

Miraculously, the Red Sea divided;
And the people of Israel crossed its path.
From up above came their guide;
Nevertheless, they spoke forth their aftermath.

Life always has two paths:
Either go your own way,
Or have faith in the ways of God.
　　　—*Wayne G. Perry Jr.*

What Is Love?

Love is true, something from the heart,
It can't be given to just anyone

Love can't be held with bars or chains, or kept in a box

Love is shone by the way you act,
holding him when he awakes from a bad dream,
surprising him with gifts from the heart,
keeping in touch while you're apart

Love is something that never dies,
It brings you through the quarrels and fights

Love forgives for the broken glass,
Love never accuses or remembers the wrongs of the past

It keeps you warm in the middle of the night,
Holding close and tight

Love is special, love is true,
So remember this before you say "I love you"!
　　　—*Michelle Templeton*

The Tree In Pain

I'm chilled, chilled by the ice that hang
　It covers and freeze my limbs
It will soon fall as the south winds sang
　Yet glitter in lights bright and dim

I am stripped of my clothes, lying below
　My branches are nacked and bare
I was robbed by dryness and wind that blow
　But no one seem to really care

Tomorrow that ice will sparkle under the sun
　Like diamonds under the light of the moon
They will be trotted upon while hunters have fun
　That chilly ice will melt away soon

'Tis coming another season, it will be spring
　I'll stretch my branches upward toward the sun
Then I shall hear the birds and robins sang
　then I shall rid of this pain
　　　—*Joyce Lee Johnson*

The Debut

Peace, an alien so rare on stage
reading script from an empty page
unwritten leaves except one place
(Approaching hell is the human race)
　　　—*Riley T. Evans*

395

Precious Time

Time does not stand still for me,
It does not stand still for you.
It rushes by like an angry wind,
Changing things anew.

It races towards the future,
Like a bullet through the air.
And no one, despite how hard they try,
Can stop it from getting there.

Every soul must keep with time
Though it may seem to go too fast.
For the future's waiting, and if we don't hurry,
The present will be the past.

So live your life right here and now,
Don't wait another day.
For if you keep living in the past
You'll waste your life away.

Time is to be treasured.
It is a rare and precious thing.
Use it to live, and love, and laugh,
And happiness it will bring.

    —Laura Souliere

"The Quiet Enemy"

It has no brain.
It has no mind.
It comes and sneaks upon you one person at a time.
We all need to be aware of this dangerous thing.
Because Aids is an enemy, not your friend.
It's not prone to pink, blue, black, or
white people because it doesn't care about color.
It could even be lurking within your sister or brother.
Aids doesn't just sit there, within you it does not soak.
It hits you all of a sudden, Aids is no joke!

    —Tara Marshall

Straight From My Heart

If my heart had eyes it would cry.
It hurts to know,
You are gone and you might never come back.
Like a thief in the night you came and you left.
It hurts when,
I feel the missing so much.
I tremble sometimes thinking I saw you.
It hurts seeing,
The things you left me with.
My days are filled with disharmony.
It hurts wondering,
Where you are or if you are?
Now you are just a memory that lurks in my heart.
It haunts me,
The tragedy that has happened.
I'll always remember the love we shared.
I'll always want you back,
To stay with me forever.
What I feel for you is indeed,
Straight from my heart...

    —Joanne Guppy

Life

Life is filled with mystery, exciting to explore.
It has challenges to conquer as well as trials to endure.
We're but a speck of humanity in an ever changing world
with power to discover and conquests yet unfurled.
Living is more than existence, it's more than what we think.
It's growing in an awaking zeal that sees beyond the brink.
Life's seasons speak of Gods own plan through changing scenes of life.
That bring quiet self-renewal overshadowing human strife.

    —Ruth Thunberg

The Child

The child's eyes went blank - her smile once was so bright yet it is nevermore. Her cheerful laugh made everyone smile yet it is only an echo in the wind. Her strength to fight has long been gone. Her courage has vanished from her mind - her heart and her soul. Her crisp clear voice is now harsh and hoarse - she is afraid of her own words and voice, so she speaks no more. Her mother holds her hand but barely touches her daughter. She sings so soft, sweet and low to ease her child's pain. Foolish people drew her away. She looks at everything yet she looks at nothing. Foolish people set her fate. Counting the hours, counting the days the child sinks deeper within. She knows what happened - she knows what is going to be. All her hopes and dreams were lost after one foolish mistake by some foolish people. No begging for a beautiful dress just for the prom. No tears of joy - No wedding bells to chime this day. No more parties - no more fun. Everything crushed by one foolish act. This child has no more pain no more fear. By a foolish mistake which became a fatal one, the child got a scary, and deadly disease; she died of AIDS.

    —Amanda Cowan

Once Moments...Now Memories

A carved image of that time we spent together seems to go away
    It just seems like yesterday we were strangers
        living in another world.

We had no idea that our forces were going to join to make one special bond
    For I knew when we met had something
        which could never be taken away.

Time went by too fast, moments were turning into memories

every second
    I wish we had more time to share that magical glow
        embodied within my heart I call friendship.

Many things have changed because I met you, you taught me to believe
    in myself and my ways.

One thing that's hard in our relationship is the distance..but that
doesn't matter.

    At times, I wish I could look at you or tell you
        how I feel when I need it the most.

I stare at your picture, hoping that you can hear me, but it's not the same
    I look back to those few days and thousands of memories
        and laugh...they were the best times yet in my young life.

I found someone in my life that I can call a true friend which is you,
    Our friendship is so special to me that it will
        last for an...ETERNITY...

    —Michael Lee Clanin

The Journey

T'was a cold dark night and the wind blew strong
    It seemed it had snowed, and blown drifts for so long
I had put off my journey, till now could no more
    Cause I knew if I did what would then be in store
So I started with boots to my kneecaps laced tight
    All bundled up well to head into the night
The wind bit like a snake as it whipped cross my face
    Of the path that was there, there was now not a trace
So with shovel in hand, destination my goal
    I must shovel yet faster to ward off the cold
It seemed like forever, this journey would end
    But there's comfort at last just ahead round the bend
When I reached out, the door had a welcoming touch
    Cause by now my discomfort was really too much
I could now tend to duty and turned around butt,
    To my horror the old out house lid had froze shut!

    —William R. Morris

Mask

Confusion, it wonders in everyone's mind.
It makes us weak and starving for answers,
Yet questions always seem to be unanswered.

Mysterious, the word thought of when looking
In a mirror.
A temporary mask covers the face of many.
It hides the truth and happiness,
And reveals the pain and sorrow.
It discovers the unrevealed.
Darkness then appears within yourself,
Struggling constantly behyond reason.

The mask can be pealed away, but only by faith.
Faith in oneself.
Having the strength to achieve and accomplish
Anything desired, can take the mask off.

The mask will only return when we are weak and
Starving for answers, and this is when we need
to be the strongest.

So believe in yourself, give yourself a chance,
Prove you are the best and give the mask a rest!
—*Laura Shurtz*

Gold

Gold is first place.
It makes you feel successful, gold.
Gold is the best.
It makes you feel better than anyone else, gold
Gold is winning.
It makes you feel part of a team, gold.
Gold is team spirit.
When you worked together and tried your very best, gold.
Gold is disappointing.
Because you didn't win, gold.
Gold is unfairness.
Because we deserved it and they got it, gold.
Gold is ANGER!!!
When you worked together and tried your very hardest
    but didn't win...
        gold.
    —*Leminh Phan*

It Rained All Night

It rained all night while we had slept,
    it rained and rained and rained.
        The splashing drops
        had glossed the walks
        again, again, again.
A baby's slumber and mother's breast
were left, untouched, by strain
        Although outside
        the water screamed,
        yet screamed it did
            in vain.
        For not a snore
        and not a dream
        were slashed by
            noisy pain.
    'Cause when she cries
        He shuts our eyes
        and leaves her soul
            to drain.
—*Omer Pearlman*

Missing You

As I lay and watch the rain from the sky,
It reminds me of the many tears I cry,
Each day when I think of you.

Missing you more each day.
Oh what a terrible pain it's true.

God bless "Ma Bell"
For without her
Where would we be?
Waiting and hoping each day to find,
A letter from you to me.

Crying each day is not the way it should be.
Please don't ever forget —
    me.
        —*Marla M. Walker*

Hope

It comes and goes, just as the sun rose
It rises in the East and sets in the West.

It stays in the heart, just as a body part
It pumps our spirits up and filters despair—
Into a sweet Kool-Aid up.

It resembles an unreliable friend,
Fluctuates as conditions change
It leaves us at a lonely coast
Just when we need it the most.

It comes and goes, so have no remorse
Just hold on to it because it's HOPE.
        —*Ashlesha Sharma*

Tho I Wish Upon A Star

Tho I wish upon a star
    It seems thy never get that far.
I might as well put them in rhyme
    For posterity at some later time
Then they can wonder - how many fools like me
    Were set adrift on an endless sea
Wishing for things that can never be?
    Maybe someday in the "Great Beyond"
I'll get my wish and we will be
    Together through eternity.
Until then I'll just stumble along
    And wonder what my mission here was to be
And if I'll accomplish what, God, meant for me?
        —*Maxine M. Sperry*

Empty Train

Looking back at what was
almost (and shuddering)
I can hear sometimes
the swiftly decaying whistle
of a long, slow moving freight train,
its old red, rust-freckled wheels
hammering
into the empty spaces between
the rail-ends
of a curving track mindlessly
determining the train to a course not its own
and this,
the abrasive sound of destiny,
the friction of steel on steel,
travels to the place where I am
listening, across a dry, grass field,
between yellow blades that riot in the wind.
        —*Jay W. Driskell*

We Have To Learn.

We have to learn to get along.
It starts when we are small.
"Why is Masana's skin different from mine?"
"I see little difference at all.
And anyway-underneath that skin our hearts all beat the same."

We have to learn to get along.
The questions continue us we grow.
"Why does he act so superior-as if there's nothing he doesn't
know?" "I'm not sure. I do know that some people only seem to
be able to make themselves 'bigger' by trying to make others
'smaller'. But anyway-inside our heads our brains all work the same."

We have to learn to get along.
I suppose questions never end.
We need to learn to look beyond, to accept, to care, to bend.
Because anyway-inside these beings our very souls are all the same.

—*Marleen Strebler*

The Book

There is a book that I hold dear,
It tells of love, joy and peace,
O' what would I do without this book.

If you read within its pages,
You will find the love of Jesus,
And the joy of living, and the peace of God.

You too can find a better way of life,
It will make you strong in spirit,
Rich in love and mercy, a joy for life and the
Mercy of God.

And when it comes your time to die. You
will have peace to die by. So if you feel
Lost and lonely then take your tear stained eyes to the Bible,
and leave all your sorrows with the master of the Book.

—*Annie Spears*

The Sadness

I knew what it was, I was afraid to let it show.
It was creeping up slowly, I felt my body moan.
It had started at my feet, making them tingle.
It climbed up to my knees, making them buckle.
Going on up into my stomach, I felt my stomach lurch,
as if not wanting it to go further.

But it still kept on going, on up to my heart.
Wanting my heart to break, to try to tear apart.

It went to my brain, making my brain pound.
Fighting to keep control, the weakened brain
gave command for the eyes to rain.

The sadness had won, I was defeated.
It will show somehow, someway.
For the sadness is too powerful,
you cannot keep it away.

—*Neria Jester*

Poison

A poison swallowed in haste.
Repercussions shroud souls unspoken.
Feelings scream in foreign tongues.
Bleed and bleed and bleed
on gravel and stone.
Heartbreak and pain.
Pleading but never said.

.............I'm sorry.

—*Thomas A. Davidson*

I Found A Leaf Or A Pen

I found a leaf in the sand just the other day,
It was green and brown and just a little gray.

I picked it up and took it to my teacher,
She looked at it and acted like a preacher.

She threw it to the ground.
It landed on without a sound.

"What did you do that for?" I said.
"I don't want it, so give it to Ned.

I picked it up once again,
But dropped it 'cause I found myself a pen.

"Hey, my pen !"
Yelled Big Ken

I found myself in a controversy.
Between a pen and a leaf don't you see?

So I dropped the pen,
Into a lion's den.

And I dropped the leaf,
Like a chunk of beef.

It was all done,
And no more fun.

—*Matt Silver*

The Story

"It all happened", she said.
"It was my life and I don't want to lose it.
I was young once.
I played with my sister.
My mother cared for me.
My husband courted me.
My children were born and grew.
I was strong and courageous.
Nothing kept me from hoping,
Nothing made me give up my dreams,
  Now the dark frightens me.
  The pain is a sorry companion.
  I feel that I must defend myself
  and I feel defenseless.
  Please help me remember this
    life that I have been a
    part of.
  Please make the pictures stay clear.
  It happened, it is my story.
    It is my life."

—*Nancy Hayman*

Clarence

If I could open a window to my heart
It would show you my burning love that
Resides there for you
You could see that I love you
I want to be with you always
Every time you go out the door
My heart has a pain that stays until you return
Never before has anyone touched me
Reached out and grabbed me the way that you do
Your love could never be replaced
Thoughts of your body against mine
Leaves me feeling intoxicated
I feel so alive and a part of you
Knowing that you love me
Gives me the courage and the will
To give my all to you and life
You've added hope and meaning to my world
I could never begin to thank you for
All that you have given to me

—*Julie Holz*

Missy And Her Bill

Bill and Melissa have set their wedding day in December
It will be beautiful, it will be remembered.

Look!
In her beautiful gown of white, accompanied by her dad,
  Melissa is coming down the aisle
Where Bill will be waiting for her, he is all smiles.

Bill and Melissa have bought a house,
  someday soon they will have something
  running around the yard, a fence I mean, of course, I do.

In a couple of years if the Lord tarries,
  there may be a little girl in curls,
Who will have all our heads in a whirl.

Or it might be a handsome little lad,
To follow in the footsteps of his dad.

Bill and Melissa if God gives you one of these little bundles so neat
You will know that, that is his way of making your homecomplete.

   —Ruth E. Bettenhausen

Never Be the Same

Love once fought hard for went away,
It would always leave never stay.
Long ago he was my one and only,
But when he left me he left me lonely
Occasionally I see him and we will embrace
I know he still loves me it shows on his face
He admits he still care's to this very day
I only wish I could find away to stay together and never part
Just to love and be loved from heart to heart.
I think of him when I lay at night
His smile so sweet his eyes so bright,
I wake up crying, yelling his name
I've lost him forever I'll never be the same

   —Ginny Foster

Yesterdays Sorrows

My heart cries for your sorrows-
It would paint pink... all your tomorrows
Take the worries away from your eyes-
Dry the tears! Whenever my darling cries.
  Life is cruel my dear!
  But, there shouldn't be any fear
  Because the Lord loves us so.
  He takes away your worries-
  Protecting you... wherever you go.
There will be another bright tomorrow!
The wind will blow away all yesterdays sorrows.
All the heaviness in your heart:
Will fall away... fall apart!
On this lovely-lovely earth.

   —Aino Kohaloo Kabe

Teachers

The story's been told time and time again
Just another poor soul, never wanting to grow old
And now he's trapped with no way out
Him and his distorted mind filled with fear and doubt
  So friend, heed my warming
Life's too short to live your days with no mornings
  Love is the only way
  To accept each and every day
  Live for the children
  And teach them a better way.

   —Phil Gutchess

The Caged Bird

The icicle is suspended above,
  It's life hanging by a thread.
For upon it's fall the life would vanish.
  The fabulous beauty? Dead!
And if the hot sun, in the cloud filled sky,
  Should decide to reappear:
A slow death the icicle must endure.
  Even that, the bravest fear!
But if someone were to take it inside,
  The beauty would start to fade.
And soon only plain water will remain.
  Behold! The captor repaid.
Is it not possible to view, from afar, the beauty?
No, you must possess it, even if it means caging me!

   —Rae Hanson

The Message Of Springtime.

Springtime brings a great message to all,
It's neither summer, winter nor fall,
Look closely and you'll surely find
A robin, a bluejay or a bird of some kind,
Flying by to tell us, a new time is here
And a chance to start over and hopefully share,
Our laughter, our blessings and also our time
With others in need to hear the bells chime.
Springtime brings breath,— it's a way of reviving
The flowers, the grass and every human being.
It's God's own form of communication,
Our time is ripe for transformation.
So live and let live should be our motto,
Aiming to reach life's highest plateau.

   —Joan P. Seales

Life

Life is like a test
It's not easy, no it's not easy being young
Not easy being a young christian
Not easy being a young christian who's black
For we always talk about other people, as christians,
And think nothing of it
But I challenge all my friends,
Girl or boy, man or woman—now to pass the test
For through all our tears, trials and tribulations
There's always a teacher—his name is Jesus
Jesus not only will pass you with flying colors
But he'll give you extra credit at the gates of heaven
For whether you make an "A" or an "F"
Always remember God will tutor your life for you
Yes my sisters and brothers
Life is a test—a test for human love!

   —Maurice Robinson

Anticipation

  Everyone's awaiting spring,
    It's time for a change;
  I'd like to shed this heavy coat,
    Cut some flowers to arrange.

  This winter hasn't been too bad,
    Like some years in the past;
  But let those flowers pop their heads out,
    They're in for one more blast!

  The days are getting warmer now,
  The sun shines bright and steady;
    You can tell Old Man Winter,
    "That's enough, already!"

   —L. S. Waldo

The Desert Rose

It lies upon a dry and barren ground
its petals that were once a ravishing vermillion
now wilt to a fragile black decay.
All the days it gave vitality and a buoyancy spirit
now brings a touch of sadness to your soul.
You feel a wet, lonely tear silently escaping
as you wipe it away
the tenderness of your cheek
reminds you of the silky petals
of the now
   DESERT ROSE.

Wishing you could give it the tear
and bring its blooming smile back
and desiring its sweet smell just one last moment.
Although the beauty of the fragrance
still locked timelessly in your heart.
Never to forget the happiness and sadness it gave to you.

   —*S. Balkovetz*

Love Is Godly

Love is but a tool, God permits us to use,
Its purpose in life, to kindle virtues,

Each love through the years, we may have known,
Without our knowing, a seed was sown,

Let us look back, through the pages of time,
When first love of mother prompts us to mind,

As brother came along, we lost our singularity,
But found instead, more love, t'was that of charity;

Through adolescence we feel the wanting of a soul,
Unknown to us, it later reveals, a search for love,
   to make us whole.

And too, we know that through this growing age,
Many loves come forth, each in our book of life,
   leaves an indelible page.

And then it is through marriage, we begin to distinguish,
Love is a sacred thing, we cannot extinguish.

And so, you see, even though love give us pleasures
   of mind and of body,
That's not the purpose for which t'was meant,
It's a gift from above, and truly, is godly.

   —*Shirley E. Dragoone*

Democracy

Democracy is something more than just a word
It's something grounded in the heart of a man.
Something that cannot be taken by the sword
Man's right to the freedom of the land.

It's greater than the cannon roar
And its flag shall ever wave.
As it has and does and will forever more
This land shall be the homeland of the brave.

A gift bestowed upon all mankind
That he might worship God as he sees fit.
That he might have freedom of his mind
And his offerings wholly unto God submit.

It gave to him freedom of speech
And satisfies the longing of his heart.
It gives him the right to study or to teach
And gives him the right to stop or to start.

We may think that it has had its day
It may be dim and sometimes seem to wane.
If that be true take heart, rejoice, be gay
For like a flower it shall rise again.

   —*John Henry Davis*

Worry Wins

I can feel the chill,
It's the wind of worry.
It blows through my mind
And it freezes my thoughts.
I try to forget the possible future,
It makes me sick, but builds character.
I learned from my mistakes, but it's sometimes too late,
As my car takes control, I meet my fate.

   —*Michael D. Lutz*

The Auction

The auctioneer was loud and bold,
"I've here," he said, "things new and old,
Now what am I bid for these things of worth,
Food and shelter, a plot of earth?"

"Gems that sparkle, power and fame,
They're here to take, for you to claim.
We offer knowledge, advanced degrees,
Ladders to climb, the social type, if you please."

A clamor arose throughout the hall,
And bids were made by one and all.
Some gave everything—a life of work,
For a moment of power or a plot of earth.

"But wait," said the auctioneer, "Before you go out,
I've one last item; please forbear your doubt.
'Tis a friend, with honesty and goodness for girth,
Now what am I bid? Please tell me the worth?"

A silence fell on the auction hall,
And none dared speak, though one and all,
Searched their psyches for a price to expend,
But none could tell the worth of a friend.

   —*Marguerite Shurte*

This Land

This land they say is not our home and yet this is where
I've lived, learned and grow.

This nation they say is not yours alone.
We've come here to make us a new home.

When the white man came to this strange land.
We offered peace and a helping hand.

Freedom for our children is what they would say.
When the children from both worlds were taken away.
Thru murder and death they took away the land of
our children to grow up and play

This land they say is not yours alone
we've taken it to make us a new home.

   —*Linda G. Placker*

The Storm

   Her crystal Blue Eyes
   Jolt me from my morning slumber.
Their Energy sparkling a forgotten emotion
   that pierces the void
  of numbness that shelters my heart.
   Slowly, the storm passes
     leaving me
      Alone
     in safety.

   —*Mark Dixon*

Colorblind

Can we make this world a better place
Judge people for them and not their race

Can we learn to love instead of hate
Yes! We can start now it's never too late

We can learn to love for the person inside
We all can learn to be colorblind

I see others judge people upon their skin
When will this stop can you tell me when

I can tell you we can start today
We can learn to judge in a different way
   —Karen McNamara

Mailbox Blues

Looked in my mailbox, what did I see
Just a little vacant space waiting for me.
I got the mailbox blues
I got the mailbox blues
I'm telling everybody I'm a-getting the mailbox blues.

I'm telling that postman mail's a must
All he ever puts in my box is dust.
I got the mailbox blues
I got the mailbox blues
I'm telling everybody I'm a-getting the mailbox blues.

Something in my mailbox, thought it was from you.
Just a little notice saying "Box rent due".
I got the mailbox blues
I got the mailbox blues
I'm telling everybody I'm a-getting the mailbox blues.

I wrote me a letter, asked Montgomery Ward
Send me please a letter or a package or a card.
I got the mailbox blues
I got the mailbox blues
I'm telling everybody I'm a-getting the mailbox blues.
   —Alvis M. Coleman

One Of God's Gift To Humanity

 As you are driving up Lopez Cyn Rd.,
just above the foothill freeway
you will see the open gate to our retreat.
When you enter the Ground's, your eyes
will marvel when you see our oak trees,
that have withstood time and weather
living in timeless splendor,
for all the world to see
we all are heavenly blessed, living
in this time-span, where we can
still enjoy peace and tranquility
in places like Forester's Haven.
   —Milo M. McFarland

Amanda

 Polka dots and purple bows
Put the paintbrush to your toes.
Take a step and turn your back
A femme - fatal, they'll never attack.

Flip your hair to the right.
Sing and dance and kiss all night.
Make them think you've really got it
Even if not, baby, flaunt it.
   —Jacqueline Hayes

Walking In Le Havre

Come walk the walk on the boardwalk
 Just down by Old Tydings Park.
You will enjoy the walk on the boardwalk
 At dawn, while it's a bit dark.

There's a chill in the air in Tydings Park,
 It all but makes one shiver.
The sleeping birds, squirrels, and ducks
 And the stillness of the river.

As we pass the museum by the boardwalk,
 Not a sound that we can hear.
We keep on walking the broadwalk
 Because we are almost there.

I like this walk on the boardwalk,
 We meet not a single foe.
It's fun to keep walking the boardwalk
 And it is healthy too, you know.

We have come to the end of the boardwalk,
 The lighthouse is there to see.
Oh, what a Heavenly adventure,
 Just God and you and me.
   —Mabel E. Hart

Survival

The world is in a mess-we all know it,
Just how can we straighten it out?
People are such creatures of habit-
Of that there is no doubt.
If only there were more love of people
And understanding of problems at hand,
Instead of the greed and discontentment
That seems to possess our land.
Some struggle thru life more than others
The elderly, the ill, the hungry, the poor,
While the wealthy and prosperous among us
Always seem to want and get-more.
Is there no end to our struggle
As we try to survive each new day?
Will the world ever be more peaceful?
Let's all pray that God will show us the way.
   —Alice M. Goldman

Thanks Mom!!

How do you let someone know
 just what they mean to you?
When they're the one that's taught you life,
 and showed you what to do.
Always there with love in their hearts,
 and discipline in their hands.
Each lesson taught more painfully to them,
 than we will understand.
Someone who's always there for us,
 when we are right or wrong—
Someone who's guided through the years,
 helping us to be strong.
The one that shows life can go on
 through pain and trials each day.
The one that's taught with truth and love,
 "you can always find away".
See, there's no other love more true and kind,
 than that which a Mother gives.
So here's to MOM with thanks and love.
 She is part of us each day that we live.
   —Barbara D. Osborn

Only

I could've sworn I saw your face
Last night in the dark
But I didn't see you with my eyes
I saw you with my heart

You came to me and held my hand
You said that it's alright
You wiped all of the tears away
You brought my heart to light

Then you gently told me
That you would not return
I wept bitter tears and begged you to stay
You simply said "You'll learn"

I held your hand tightly
So you couldn't go
So you couldn't leave me alone
But you just disappeared
And I sadly looked down to see
The hand that I held was my own
        —*Angela A Reis*

Acrostic Winter Poem

Saturday nights my grandfather used to give me sleigh rides
Lazy David lies back to enjoy the ride
Endless rides until midnight
I wish I could go up front,
    and guide the horses through the night
Grandma yells "Look out," as a branch flies by my head
Hard, but fun, we ride the night

Rabbits pass the sleigh really fast
I'd love to pick the rabbits up,
    and feel their soft, snow covered fur
Dozing off to wonderland
Easy to be distracted by bells, that jingle along the way
Sing a song before the night ends,
    morn is on its way
        —*Jessica Lee Clark*

Are You Afraid?

When you fear your dreams, you
let go of them.
You are afraid of others, you lie
You fear yourself, but still convince
yourself you are just like the others.
You are afraid of death, and you see
your life crumble.
You fear life, you kill it.
You fear hate, it will crush you.
You are afraid that love will forget
about you again.
Are you afraid?
Are you like me?
        —*Tuuli Saarela*

Untitled

Those unseen people
say that time heals sorrow.

Perhaps.

But sorrow heals,
washing separation's pain
as gold from sand,
leaving
clean, close communion.
        —*Linnea Nyman*

Open A Book

Open up a book my child
Let it take you to
Lands you've never been before
Mystical and true.

Let the pages talk to you
Let the pictures show
Let it tell of all its wisdom
And guide you as you grow

Open up a book my child
I'm sure that you'll agree
It will be your closest friend
Until eternity
        —*Regina Phillips*

The Birthday Ribbon

I lay dormant on a roll until smooth hands pick me out,
    Let me tell you what my plight is really all about.
My color pink, baby soft, my size is long and thin,
    Around the pretty package is where I will begin.

The scissors cut about two yards -
    And around me they gently wrap with ease,
Careful not to juggle, squash or even squeeze.
They tie me in the center in a double knot,
    To make the gift more special worthy of what they got.

The scissors run vertical down my length -
    To curl my straightness out,
Much prettier is the package now that goes without a doubt.
    Another strip cut and curled lays gently by my side,
I really wonder why the gift they fuss and try to hide.
    Another strip then four or five curled and in its place,
My purpose now is to bring smiles to the little child's face.
        —*Sharon McGuinn*

Thank God For Today

"This is the day which the Lord has made;
Let us rejoice and be glad in it."
It matters not if the sky is gray
Or that rain may fall any minute.

God never said, "Rejoice and be glad
Whenever you hear the birds singing;
Or when flowers bloom along your way,
And bells in your heart are ringing."

Let's be mindful He made all our days,
And though some may be filled with sorrow;
What counts is how well we live today,
For we may not have a tomorrow!

Then let me help somebody today
Who may be carrying a heavy cross;
Because it's in giving we receive,
And a gift of love is never lost.

"This is the day which the Lord has made;
Let us rejoice and be glad in it;"
Forgetting mistakes of yesterday;
Knowing His grace is all-sufficient.
        —*Miriam D. Phifer*

Joy

Joy is better than everything,
Just like spending Christmas with everyone.

Joy is like a sunny day in spring,
With hopping and laughing all around.

Joy is love, joy is peace, joy is friends,
That's all we need.
        —*Toni Meagher*

402

Contentment

Life is so uncertain from today until tomorrow,
Lets live life to the fullest and no trouble barrow,
Live peacefully with all our neighbors,
Support and help him with his labors.

As we travel along our busy separate way,
Let us try to make it better each and everyday.
Try to make each day a little brighter.
When you share a load its lighter

Sometimes helping or just listening is the key.
That brings peace and contentment to you and to me.

—*Alice Rogers*

Life Is As It Is

Life can be fun, it can keep you on the run!
Life can be bad and it can be sad.
When things go bad we get mad.
We do not know that life is a thing
That no one, can give on earth but God.
Everybody want it so they should be glad.
Life is as it is.
When you live your life,
There is not other life that you could have had.
Life is a beautiful thing to have so less
don't go around, looking and feeling so sad.

—*Ricky Teagle*

Slow Down My Child

Slow down my child you're trying to grow up too fast,
Life is too precious, you must make it last.
I know there are so many things that you want to do,
Just slow down my child and see each day through.
Many say you act so much older than your age,
Always pretending to be older, using life as your stage.
In your dreams you already have your entire future planned,
Full of life's finest treasures and all that is grand.
Each day I'm amazed at how fast you grow,
It's not always sweet growing older this you must know.
You act so much older than what you truly are,
So full of ambition, I know you'll go far.
Just slow down my child, and act you're own special age,
Think of life as your story, book, you must fulfill every page.
Each day I see you growing faster than the speed of light.
Yesterday you were my little girl, now a young lady overnight.
So please slow down my child, learn to take each day in stride,
Remember all you've learned and lived and let God be your guide.

—*Robert Wisniewski*

Patterns

We gather into us the silken strands of
   life of generations gone.
To meld with our peculiar traits and weave
   a whole new pattern
Passing this along.

And though we vision not the whole
   Assured we all can be.
Life's quilt of colored fashions
   Needed you and me.

—*Mary Ann Studer*

The Real Me

I never knew just what bothered me
Life was fine as far as I could see
There were times when my emotions
   were out of control
But I never really knew what hurt
   So deep in my soul

I had emotional seizures and I never
   Knew why
At times it was so embarrassing
   I would just sit and cry

I lived a good life but something was wrong
Little did I know that I felt like this
   since the day my innocence was gone

He took it away and he changed my life
It was as if he stabbed me with a knife

Now I know and I'm fighting back
I will now start my life and that's a fact
And I ask you all to hear my plea
Let me Stand as a Person and finally
   Be The REAL ME

— *Nancy A. Waters*

Devastation

So many things you said echo in my head, I'm halfway through
life where others took a stand, and I wonder if I'm sane
because, I haven't got a plan Yes, I've ran from the past and
I've lived with the pain, and I've watched the days go by in a
world that's not the same. So take me for the moment, quick
-
before the change of time, I want to stay but I'm so dazed,
locked up within my mind. I tell myself this ain't life, it's
not the way it ought to be... but the fear grows and the
anguish shows, in the world surrounding me, and I'm standing
here facing lifelines that I'm tracing, wondering where they're
gonna lead, because I can't stop the fighting and it's so
frightening to me. Yes, I've ran in the past and I've lived
with pain, now I watch the lives go by in a world that's not
the same. Now the world is in a frantic state, a massive fate
and I'm just trying to survive, as I wander through these man
made dreams where nightmares come alive. I tell myself this
ain't life, it's not the way it's got to be... but the loss
grows and the hatred shows in the world surrounding me.

—*Virginia Jensen*

Walk With Me

Sit with me, before going again
Life will not stop as you rest
Talk to me to ease your pain
Feel better as the time pass
I've been there you see
Come walk with me

Over there stands a big tree
Provides you shade in the heat of the day
The grass bows down to me
The soil, the rocks are here to stay
Both together, as you can see
So come walk with me

The flowers smile as the wind blow
Little children laugh with glee
Big one, little ones, all colored like a rainbow
Beg for love and to be free
I can not grant this alone
Too many in need, too many is gone
It's not too late to walk with me

—*Bernice Petty*

Silence Is Not Golden

Silence is white,
  Like a wisp of smoke here and there -
  a frozen lake or pond
  with an occasional fishing shack
    huddled against the wind and storm.

Silence is awesome,
  as the snow whirls and drifts -
  as the pines sway in the wind,
  as one child calls to another
    across the white expanse -
  and then silence -

Silence is peace -
  It is a winter scene in New England
  far from the hustle and bustle of the space age -
  not in miles but in feelings -
It is a closeness to God.

    —Robert J. Covert

"You Are As These"

Like sunshine after drizzling rain,
Like soothing balm to aching pain,
Like roses found in the desert,
Like the relief from deepest hurt,
Like the brightest stars shining above,
You are as these, my only love.

Like light of day destroying night,
Like courage over dread of fright,
Like spring replacing winter's grip,
Like home again after a trip,
Like music, poetry and art,
You are as these, my dear sweetheart.

Like shelter from the raging storm,
Like heat after cold, glowing warm,
Like water after thirstiness,
Like news restoring happiness,
Like faith in everlasting life,
You are as these; my darling wife.

    —Robert B. Herriot

Song For The Dishwasher

So plump, and so, so round,
like the grinning Cheshire cat
that swallowed whole a canary yellow balloon,
howling like a flat-butt baboon at the moon,
happy from large morsels of fat
cookies and frosted cakes. The sound
of laughter mocking Sea-hags
and the sensible thoughts in normality
ricochets smiles off of steel walls
(like the raindrops he sprays on the bathroom stalls).
His eyes blink quick smirks at formality
as he abandons greasy pans and rags
to massage the backs of both waitress and cook
with groping hands and dishpan-eyes
that stick his world on them like jelly
which can no longer be hid (just like his belly);
for there's no need for him to disguise
his feelings that we sometimes overlook.

    —Shawn P. Regan

Faith In Love

My feelings for him I often must hide
like the tears that fall at night or my slightly
    bruised pride
I wonder if he'll ever let himself see
what I have to offer him, what love should
    really be
Yes I understand he's tied up with another
But I know that we should be with each other

My heart and the stars, they say we belong
life everlasting-our love just as strong

As our hearts are bonded together for life
our feeling too strong to be severed with a knife
Dreaming of our love as each day passes by
I'll faithfully leave my trust in the sky

For now I'll be patient and hope he'll let
    fate win
before time covers up what could've been.

    —Rebecca DeGannes

Sterile

My mind crusts over
like the wound
on the back of a cat,
caught by the exposed springs
of a bed.
Lonely,
he reaches under
the locked door
with a paw,
hoping there is something there
that will touch back.
The world is sterile.
Cleanly, faces rush past
with eyes set
like stones in a ring,
unwavering.
There is nothing
reaching back
from the other side
of the door.

    —Mitchell Gang

Robin Red Bird

Little Indian papoose girl
Little English White Baby
  Half and half,
Hair of golden red
Eyes of almond shape and marbles brown.
Skin silk soft and olive milk cream.
Nose turned up with button dirt dobber holes
Little mouth that opens wide with smile
from side to side
Curved little lips in the middle, where
Laughter rolls out and a little giggle,
Pink little tongue that drools clear drops of
honey.
Little Robin Red Bird with
A perfect Hampton Head,
Robin Winona-Eyes like almonds
And marbles of brown.

    —Norma A. Hampton

Do Green Vegetables Have Feelings?

Far away, long ago, deep inside
lived a boy, or a cabbage, but it died
a head of lettuce, a mind of guilt, heart of pain
an unknowing farmer, an adulterous father, excuses lame

Whip the child and chop the vegetable from the vine
wash it clean, sanctuary inside the mind
for a time, a safe haven, refrigerated crisper
see the reapers, fear the argument, hear him whisper

"It's not my fault. I grew best I could, just a poor harvest.
No... I'm a bad kid, really didn't do my best."
cry for sleep, tuck him in, little zucchini
scared to death, gone insane, feelings? vegetables haven't any

—*Michael Williams*

Monkey On the Shelf

Bug-eyed, big ears, sitting on the shelf,
Lonely, boring, sitting by itself.
Big teeth, brown skin, flashing red eyes,
Horrid smile,
That's what I see at my size.
Happy, cheerful, and gay,
But when I see it,
Trouble's on its way!
Head bobbing, cymbals clapping,
Always makes me feel
It's laughing.
Gave to me as
A gift from gramp,
Ever since I had it I felt like...
A champ.

—*Samuel Thompson*

My Flag

My Flag, with colors of red, white and blue,
Long may it wave for me and for you,
Each of the stars are for each state,
Which are now fifty, but were then forty-eight.

The stripes are for each old colony,
Of each is a memory for you and for me.
The first flag flown was a long time back—
Let not our patriotism ever be slack.

May it always be honored wherever we go,—
And never be tossed around to and fro,
Or put in a corner, all covered with dust,
But fly it in honor of "In God we Trust".

My flag, dear flag, may it long always wave
For the land of the free, and the home of the brave.
Thanks to the dear soldiers who gave their own life,
That we may have Peace and be free from all strife.

—*Victoria Sandberg Peterson*

New Beginning

Through a small crevice of her guarded wall
Peeks out a shy but eager young lady,
Her eyes see wonders and terrors through all.
While hopes and dreams for the future are still shady
Slowly the loosened chains fall from the father figure.
For this child did once plead but now hesitates
Building strength and courage is all she can rigger,
To make her place in the world to which she relates,
Support and comfort installed within her wall
Allows this soul to push steadily into the stream,
Having no intentions to slip or fall,
She reaches out achieving a special life lived dream
Deep down inside every persons heart
Lives this young lady that needs a little push to start.

—*Darcie Coulson*

Families

Are
Forever
"Families
Are Forever"
And were always
meant to be; Not just
for a span of time, But for
ETERNITY. Fathers and Mothers
with Children, With Grandpas' and
Grandmas' to see; Together, they form
a UNIT, It is called, "The Family Tree."
The GOD who dwells among them, Is closer than
a brother; And He blesses them in HARMONY, With
LOVE for one another. They often dream of REUNIONS...
And the times they've shared together; Even FAR AWAY,
Across The Miles
"Families
Are
Forever."

—*Billie R. Russell*

China Doll

Hey there, China Doll! Can you hear us as we call?
Look around and you will see the world was watching on T.V.
Your beauty and your youthful grace,
Your hopes and dreams shown on your face.
You have to know that we were there—
We have had our Tiananmen Square.
We saw your Lady, proud and tall,
Reaching for freedom for you all.
Smashed and gone, but in her place
A sacred spot for you to face
The future, as you know you will
Although it be a poison pill.
Doll of China, dry your tears,
Teach them how to face their fears.
Tell them how they have to try
Although your comrade had to die.
Our hearts are breaking in your plight.
We pray that things will turn out right.
Scale Heaven's Gate—on to the wall-
We'll greet you there — brave China Doll!

—*Pat Dozier*

Good-bye '89

1989, is gone. Yes, this is true.
Look at the disaster it took us
    all through Hurricane Hugo in September.
Earthquake in November. Oh, don't forget
    the snow that made our Christmas white,
What about my neighbor whose house
    caught on fire New Year's Eve night.
1989, you brought us some pain,
hopefully in 1990 our strength will be regained.
To me it won't hurt to say good-bye '89,
    I'll always remember you for putting so
many lives on the line.
    You tore down the Berlin Wall, oh, that
was great you taught us how to work together
    and not hate. Farewell '89 your time is up.
Here are the 90's we hope it will bring
    us good luck.

—*J. Thaddeus Chapman*

Untitled

The world is full of hungry people,
    look at them all hungry and feeble.
Help them to establish their human rights.

Don't buy them guns to put up a fight,
    cutting down trees, for cash a solution?
Won't solve problems just increase pollution
Who's in control of this place, our home
Look at that you buy, and what gets thrown
    —*Mark S. Smith*

Her Soft Gentle Way

When I look into her eyes I see her soft and gentle way.
Looking at her I can see her age.
I know in my heart she's not going to stay,
Not for too many days. When she hugs me
I feel her warm and caring way.
When I look into my grandmother's eye,
I can see the love that's filled in her heart.
Her soft gentle voice is always soothing to here.
Knowing in my heart that maybe a day soon,
She will no longer be near.
So, my heart breaks, and I shed a tear.
I also know that God has a beautiful set of wings just for
her.
Wishing she would stay but God is calling her.
    —*April Elaine Bailey*

We Have Not Learned At All

It sits there untouched, but threatened,
    Looking at us with mournful eyes,
For the ones on the other side have
    learned to be happy,
While we have not learned at all.

The thorns crawl up our side of the brick,
    Breaking into roses at the top,
But the flowers are facing the ones
    on the other side,
For they have learned to be forgiving,
    While we have not learned at all.

    The door of rotted wood,
    In the midst of the gloomy brick,
Will open for the ones that have learned,
And lead them to a world of peacefulness,
    While it remains shut,
For those who have not learned at all.

    We have not learned at all.
    —*Kendra Leyda*

The Wind

I sit here in the warm sweet breeze,
Looking down a hill covered with trees.

The sunshine dances on the forest floor and
The wind whispers through the leaves,
The sound is a musical score.

A concert of nature, sweet and pure.
The rustle of oak leaves, the whisper of cedar,
The wind is playing follow the leader.
It rushes through fast, then slow.
Just when you think it has ceased,
Again it begins to blow.
It sings its song so gentle and sweet,
It makes this beautiful day complete.
    —*Dianne White*

White Flag

I scan the film clips on the six o'clock news
Looking for a glimpse of your face, head, or even
    the back of your hand.
I pray you're there, alive,
Captured by camera in the gulf or Somalia.
What conflicts have you faced since that Army-Navy
    same when only my mouth and your ear
    made it on T.V. from the stands?
It was some time ago
Before I spoke and you heard way too much.
No war could come close to our clashing minds.
No love could survive.
We stockpiled our feelings while cadets hailed the goal post.
I pleaded, but your staunch heart saw no white flag.
I pray that some small kindness can balance
    on your points of honor-for your sake.
I pray that some small solace can be found-for my sake.
I pray every night at six o'clock-for our sake
Because I do not know if you are alive,
    and I do not know if I am alive.

    —*Loretta Viscount*

Suicide

He stood on the high burning coal
    looking into the deep, deadly pool of maroon,
listening to the voices,
    the voices of his destiny—
Something and Nothing talking to him—
Something telling him to stay;
Nothing telling him to go away—far, far away!
Wanting to listen to Something,
    but responding to Nothing,
    looking into the deadly pool of fire and
    blood swirling beneath him,
        hypnotized by the maroon swirls,
wanting to be there...

...aching to be there! Dropping to his knees then

    plunging into the fire and blood,
feeling the beautiful sensation
wanting more pain!
Floating away from the Words of Hell.
    floating toward his destiny—
    the sensational pain of Hell!
    —*Alecia Blaire Clark*

The Victory

Her opponent was time
Losing to him
Was considered a crime
She chased and outraced him
Her lead had erased him
She was fast
But he was stronger
Each time she leaped
His strides grew longer
While her legs became lame
He mastered her game
Time ran ahead
She could no longer win
She felt her head begin to spin
Hopelessly defeated she stopped to relax
Time stopped
And fell dead in his tracks
    —*Aliza Stevens*

Love

Love is the thing that grows in the heart.
Love is the thing that is there from the start.
Love is the thing you get from just being there
Love blooms around us everywhere.

   —Leslie Woodring

Borders

Brown, yellow, black, white — courtships, marriages, families
Love, hate, toleration, prejudice. Hope?

Manmade / natural disasters, violence, war
Deaths, injuries, tears
Volunteers, law, arbitrators.

Mosques, synagogues, temples, churches — isolation,
   misunderstandings
Prayer, indulgence, togetherness, brotherhood.

Droughts, starvation, fleshless frames, pestilence
Sympathy, benefit concerts, donations, airlifts, medical personnel.

Have-nots — homeless, ill-housed, ragged, shoeless, hungry,
   crippled, sick
Resignation, despair, desperation, supplication.

Haves — extending: empathy, medical / technical know-
   how, necessities, material possessions, education.

Black, Brown, White, Yellow —
Resilience, unity, love, bonding. Hope!

   —Tillie Atkins

Love is....

Love is a patient, love is blind.
Love is hate, love is kind.
Love is strength against the wind, love is a shoulder
that you can lend.
Love is the sweet kiss, that we would not miss.

Love is gentleness that soothes and brings out our passion.
Love is the fire that holds our burning desire.

Love is maturity that holds our security.
Love is anger that we hold deep inside.
Love is the person that unravels our pride.
Love is our tenderness, caring and happiness brought together
to build a bridge of a life together.
Love is fate, that won't build hate.

Love is familiar, love is something that we share.
Love is knowing one another, and showing we care.

Love is worth the wait to be together forever in love.

   —Kealia Gray

Love

Love is finding someone to care.
Love is having something to share.
Love is a blanket full of pain,
where you feel you have nothing to gain.
Love is trying hard to find,
the person you dream about in your mind.
Love is learning to find someone new,
after you lost who you thought loved you.
Love is a feeling deep inside,
where you bubble with joy you just can't hide.
Love is a link between the two,
that makes them happy instead of blue.
Love is lonely, when only one's in love,
that makes you ask the God above,
"Why oh why do we fall in love."

   —Melissia Jo Bryant

"Love"

Love is something that you can't get over
Love is something that never dies
Love is something that you can't get over
until it makes you want to cry.

Love is something that you can't see
Love is something that means everything to me.
Love is something that the whole world is built upon.
Love is something that always goes on.

Love is something that is pure
Love is something that is not always sure
Love is something that is always a pleasure
Love is something that you can always treasure

   —Michelle Romero

My Love For You

My love for you is like a golden twine of
love that cannot break with a thousand swords,
or a thousand knives, but what's a twine without
another. Its hard losing something you
never really had, My real love for you will never
break, My real love for you use to bloom like
a flower in spring. But all things must come
to an end and winter is near but like flowers
it will never die but just fall in a deep sleep.

   —Sheldine Murrell

"Nature's Creations"

Love the wilderness so fresh and pure,
   Love the beauty
   Of that I'm sure,
   Love the animals
   For their precious ways,
But don't love the hunters for they shorten their days.

Love the flowers for their waves through the airs,
   Love the petals
   For they come in sweet pairs,
   Love the trees
   For their brilliant fresh smell,
But don't love the woodsmen for the trees they do fell.

Love the crickets for their faint chirping sounds,
   Love the canines
   Which include the bloodhounds,
   Love the birds
   For their snapping a twig,
But don't love the teens for their boom boxes big.

Love the wonders of nature no matter where they are found.
   Love all of God's creatures in air or on ground.

   —Jeanine Menczywor

City

   The night was black, shadows at every corner
lurked luminously over steel towers of glassy reflection,
   light rays bounced gleefully off the eroding, shineless
metal, cold, for no heat came from the heart of these
   monstrosities that dot the horizon, for everyone to
see through their smog covered windows, no sunsets to be
   observed by the "nature lover".
Black clouds of pollution-filled smoke crowd the black
   night air, suffocating small birds that loom
cautiously nearby hoping to find a descent meal before
   a hidden sun gives light to the prey for it to scurry
away, smelly fumes fill the air, people turn away praying
   to breathe country air in their city town.

   —Tamara Krause

Daddy

Daddy was a hard man he worked all of his life, he had three
loving children and one understanding wife. He always took for
granted, that everything would be alright. Then he awoke one
morning, with a totally different life. He had lost his job,
and times were gettin' hard, momma thought we'd never make it,
but we made it this far. Daddy started drinkin', drinkin'
every night, along came the worries, of his children and his
wife. Along with the drinkin', came an anger with a hurt, not
so much the hittin', but so much the words. He always made us
fill bad, he tried to make us cry, he never said, he was sorry,
cause alcohol was his pride. He never knew exactly, of what
he'd said or done, goin' home was a nightmare, going home, was
no fun. Daddy still drinks, and now he's all alone, Daddy has
no where, that he can call his home!

—*Tammy Keaton Miller*

Mamma

All the cows are in the barn lot.
Mamma is there whether cold or hot.
She's a faithful farmer along side my Dad.
A faithful Mamma, I've always had.

She's up before sunrise and working hard.
In the deck of life, she's quite a card.
She gives her all and asks for none,
But she's ready for bed when the day is done.

There's more on her shoulders than I could bear,
And Mamma's the one who's always there.
No matter the trouble, no matter the pain,
Mamma is the one who can see the thru the rain.

She's always been my shoulder and dried my tears.
She did her very best throughout all the years.
No better Mamma has their ever been
And most of all, she's my best friend.

—*LouAnn Russell Stargel*

Things That Always Stay The Same

Years pass by in swift succession
  Man's inventions still progress
    'til they dominate our living
      Bringing on a world of stress.

But we have some peaceful blessings
  Stressful living cannot claim:
    Things that give us mental comfort
    Things that always stay the same

Joys that always come at Christmas,
  Friends who help through troubled days,
    Faith in God's eternal promise,
      Joy that we are free to pray.

Man's inventions may reap chaos
  The inventors may reap fame
    But we will reap both strength and comfort
      From things that always stay the same.

—*Sarah E. Johnson*

The Encounter

Timing was bad, so sad. Program - reprogram
love like hot candied yams, sticky sweet
with feelings hard to beat. Moving through scenes
mostly unseen wondering what does it mean?
Time approaches, we mosey down to get something
to eat, as time calls we travel our separate
ways till we meet again in our own minds.

—*Richard Alvin Snow Jr*

Serenity

A field of death stretches beyond human sight.
Massive markers are the only remains of character.
The silky landscape welcomes my curiosity.
Finality disguised by nature's beauty.
What traitor desires immortality?

—*Jenny Hughes*

The Indian Maiden

I am an Indian maiden, standing high, upon a hill,
Marveling at the beauty, of the world so quiet and still.
It makes me feel so regal, almost like a queen, to be here,
At this place, so peaceful and serene!
  There are no other voices, only natures sound.
I came here to be alone, with no one else around! I came to
Seek the solitude, I know this place would give. I'm here to
find an answer, to how we all should live!

  There is a wondrous beauty, to see the world from here,
To let the peace surround me and not feel any fear!
I know there is a reason, for everything that I see!
I know that there is an answer, why all the world should be!

  I am an Indian Maiden, standing high, upon a hill.
I seek to find the answers, to everything that is real!
I came to seek the truth, of why I am me!
I came to give thanks, for letting me be!

—*Tressie O'Kelley*

Finding My Love

Destiny is a future of which we do not know my soul
mate comes from my heart and who I've been searching for
  all my life.

To endure life alone is not impossible, but to find the
  one you search for and grow old with, this is what I seek.

I often think that in the end when my soul mate and I are
  together at last, only then I
will feel and know the true meaning
  of love in all its wonderment and beauty.

  The years are going quicker
now and the seasons pass with a
  hurling speed and I'm tired of
counting all my grey hairs. But the only
  thing I still believe that it's
better to wait then to go with
  anyone else other then a soul mate

—*Suzanne Ashraf*

"The Brain Child"

The brain child, a well known entity of extremes
May struggle in the darkest abyss of despair,
Or reap fame and fortune in the golden harvest of their dreams.

Marconi and Edison gave us firsts', in energy and light
To ease the drudgery of daily toil.
Bright lights for tired and eager eyes, better to see
Some, by cruel fate, succumb at birth,
While others, just wilt away as juveniles,
Into total obscurity.

Who but mortal man, where ingenuity applies,
Can do so much, for so many, where so much misery lies,
Who, but the one whose only son, the Christ Child,
Gave all that we might live
And promises to come again, and still forgive..

—*William Bernard Raines*

A Child's Wish

Why doesn't dad go to Sunday School?
Maybe he doesn't know he's my hero,
Heroes are tops but they can be fooled,
His neglect bothers me so.

If he would come once or twice,
And hear me read and sing and pray,
I think he'd say "That's Nice,
I believe I'll go another day".

We learn about God and His love.
He was a Hero, when He gave His Son,
Sent Him all the way from Heaven above,
And the battle over sin He won.

He said to the disciples who followed
"Let the children come to me forbid them not"
Sunday School, is an institution that's hallowed,
And all brave men should cast their lot.

—*Mary Biggs*

Need

the walls felt as if they were trying to shut me in, trapping
me for life. I need you here with me, but you are nowhere to
be found. The need for you increased, as I was pacing the
floor out the window I saw the old stoplight swaying back and
forth in the wind. It is the only noise you could hear on this
very cold, lonely night. The intense need for you made my
lungs ache with desire, taking short jagged breaths in, and
slow breaths out. Wanting to hear your voice made my head
spin, dialing the number, it rang, but I knew no one was home.
Wanting to see you so much until I couldn't think, my heartbeat
quickened with the thought of you gone, so now I am sitting on
the floor listening to the squeaking of the old stoplight in
the cold, lonely night, needing you more and more.

—*Nicole Mason*

Me

Me is the one I know the best
Me is the one so different from the rest
Walking around with the expression of glad
When all in all, I'm really sad
Looking at the future, thinking of the past
Wondering if it was up to Me, would I last

Me is the one that I don't like that much
Even though others think I have a gentle touch
The touch that makes them feel good about themselves
While most of the time, I feel like a single book on big
shelves. I try to explain my feelings, but end up frustrated
Then I start to feel as if I've faded

Faded from existence among the human race
Feeling so alone and so out of place
No man in his right mind will give Me his love
Which leaves me to predict I'll always be as free as a dove
I'm to the point now where I don't like myself
If you feel this way, please get some help

—*Rochelle Maple*

My Rescue

If my days seem to assail me and all things eventually fail
me... Let me not be petulant, only patient. If temptation
causes a diversion for me; help me to commend thee, in
actions and in words. Help me to not deplore you, but always
adore you. If novelties or fatuous things creep into my
thoughts; forgive me God and always know that you are in my
heart.

—*Natalie Ranton*

His Cry For Help

We were on the dance floor having fun,
    Me, my brother, and even my grandmother son,
I don't remember who all was there,
    and when the music started it gave me a scare,

The lights went out and I heard someone scream,
    I don't know who was the one screaming,
The music went off.
    and I heard an unusual cough,

I was so scared I didn't know what to do,
    or where to go,
I started to cry when I saw my brother lying on the floor,
    when I found out he was dead I cried even more,

I found out that the man who killed my brother,
    had killed himself and even his mother,
I will never forget all the crying that day,
    nor will I ever forget my one and only brother.

—*Kristy Zumr*

Lost World

It is January 23rd, 1993, I am setting and typing a poem about
me. My thoughts today are deeply in pray,
Hoping to see more easier day,
I am searching for an answer to relieve my pain,
But a search in this world could destroy your brain,
(Tomorrow) is a word that never ends,
Only a new day really begins,
If life lasted only eighteen years,
No hurry, no worry, no long lasting tears.
This world is so full of brain scrambling tests,
Not a moment to spare or a bit of rest.
But (tomorrow) is also a word that brings hope every day,
As my heart gets weaker I knee down and pray,
For tomorrow to be a more easier day,
Now I lay me down to rest,
For tomorrow to be the very best,
——(Amen)——
—*Terry Waits*

"Shadow"

The way he looked... the way he smelled... is now just a memory...
He's in the back of your mind... waiting to be thought of...
He was like a book waiting to be read...
He comes when darkness falls and dances away like a dream...
He has feelings like you and me... but they don't shine through him.
Instead, they come like daydreams waiting to happen...
And fade away in the morning light...
Shadow's can come and go as they please...
If you shine a light on it... it fades away...
If you keep it in the darkness... it stays...
The moment you care for it... it slips away...
Everything's gone... all that is left... is a shadow...

—*Jessie T. Trovato*

Memories Carved In Two Hearts

The lovely days, how they were spent;
Now only memories for us who went.
The sunlight above the heart of the tree;
that held the lovely words, you plus me,
Shall always remain there with shelter beyond,
The love and joy we used to live upon.
Now life has separated two hearts from then;
I just wish you had lived to see it begin...

—*Shaye Lucas*

"The Bloody Battle Site"

Dead bodies all over the battle site,
Men fighting with all their might.

Streams of blood running everywhere,
Not a trench to spare.

Men being eaten away by vultures,
People cleaning up using mulchers.

Men getting trench foot,
With burns that look like soot.

Medical attention needed everywhere,
Not enough people to give care.

People having to be brave,
Visiting relatives in their graves.

Seeing men falling one by one,
Wondering when this nightmare will be done.

Every soldier saying "Please God let
me live through this nightmare,"

—*Tonya Hall*

Untitled

As we walk beside the park I think of what
might have been and of all the things that are.

I listen to your voice and smile with inner joy
knowing that this moment is all I need.

I see the faces passing in the crowd and wonder
if they can see the serenity that is me.

I touch your hand and sense the beating of your
heart as it joins mine in harmony.

And I know that what I feel is a love
born of destiny and painful memories.

If there be a heaven then it is here each day that
I gaze upon your face and touch you with my eyes.

And the memories of the past fade away and the pain
is replaced with joy and I know that love is real.

—*Karen W. Sherlock*

What Can I Eat?

Milk acid causes ulcers, and beer causes gas, so, I put
Milk, and egg in my beer, and call it —An
Ulcered...Bloody Mary!!!
I avoid, aspirin, and coke, and vitamin
Poisoning???!....And my calories +and- = Diarrhea!
And ....empty....apple extract!

Since my dog eats orange slices, orange crush people
are fewer .....Acid-deals
From stomach-flu, anyway!!!

Dogs, and cats; howl back! —— as people
Bark back at each other, like Roman parlors, and
Spas of Ben Hur—times!!....

—*R. C. Miller*

Mirror Eyes

Your mirror eyes
reflecting my own.
Not mimicking,
but understanding.
I do not need words
to tell me how you feel.
Your mirror eyes tell me
how I am feeling too.

—*Victoria Watson*

The Dream

On the shores of our beaches we
mingle briefly with absolutes
see sights - hear sounds that
will keep us from insanity
in the face of being alive.

There, briefly, was a pattern and purpose;
there was a glimpse of continuity;
there was the DREAM
the Great and Private DREAM
which rhyme and ritual were created
to be keepsakes of.

If our beaches were to be polluted
the damage would be incalculable.
What was secret would become commonplace;
What was holy desanctified.

And a species
kept from lunacy
by it's DREAM journey
would be left unhealed.

—*Stephan Wassel*

Recipe For The Greatest Mother

Take a cup of kisses, give it a caring shove
Mix in three teaspoons of affection and 1,000 pounds of love.
Blend ten cups of happiness, sprinkle some caring hearts
Add lots and lots of joy!

Whip up some loving care, grate it so it's fat,
Add some understanding hugs and give it a friendly pat
Take out all the arguments by squeezing really tight,
Scoop in the loving relationship and take out all the fights.

Add a lot of sweetening, remember to spoon in some pride,
Mix in all the fairness for the Mom who's always on our side
Press out all the problems, smooth till it's all smothered
Simmer some compassion, and you'll have the greatest Mother!

—*Laura Leigh Latham*

Different Eyes

"Please sweetheart, don't play in the sand,"
Mom says to me as she takes my hand.
And even though I'm only three
It's very plain for me to see...
We see the world thru different eyes.

"I'll do what I want! It is my hair!"
My mom is so stubborn. She doesn't care.
At sixteen the future looks so grand.
My mom is worried. She can't understand....
We see the world thru different eyes.

"Oh now mom, don't be sad.
You know I love you and dad."
I'm nineteen. My day is here.
The man that I love is standing near....
We see the world thru different eyes.

"Please sweetheart, don't play in the sand,"
I say to her as I take her hand.
It's been twenty years since I was three
And getting very hard for me to see.....
Did we see the world thru different eyes?

—*Jaydine Good*

A Child's Eye

I watch through my child's eye the things I had long since
lost sight,
Monsters in the closet at night,
Raindrops falling gently, reaching as they touch down,
A smooth rock on the ground
Snow that comes at last,
Only knowing today, no future-no past,
A mother's gentle hand, a father's kind word,
By his own shadow is he quickly allured,
The words that are spoken,
The chimneys when smoking,
The color, the shape of the birds as they fly,
Things forgotten now seen through a child's eye —
As he looks at me to smile so wide — I can only
hope and wonder the treasures he holds inside.

—*Barbara J. Johnson*

Grandfather's Farm

Fences unmended, barns fallen
Monuments to a time since gone

Autumn harvest is in
Stubbled fields snowladen
Sepulchers for Winter: renewing season

Silos—unbricked and void of grain
Huddle as stock standing in chill and rain
Both breath and earth, misting strains
of lost warmth—remain

Aging into the hills
Faded to grey, squeaking if yet working, mills
Stammer to answer the wind's whisper and whistle

For now no more does summer breeze sing
Replaced by forthright beat of hawk and eagle wing

Beacons once where was life, still life teeming

—*Timothy Mitchell*

Intaglio

Years rushed by faster than expected.
More sunsets, more moons, fewer stars
In eyes overflowing with living.
Then, an immense void.
Earth assumed a dullness that was unbearable.

As quickly as spring lightning
You appeared in my universe.
Fresh, alive like young roses.
Your breath, warm and sweet
Appeared and etched your spirit into mine.

But where now?
Contemptible loneliness abounds.
Strange, unlikely beings loving and entwined.
You incised my stone heart and soul
And gave me profound reason to be.

Intractable to supple.
Thoughtless to caring.
But still an imperfect engraving
In need of completion.
I anticipate the artist's return.

—*N. Patricia Yarborough*

Island Paradise

Here is the Island Paradise.
Most are happy, everything nice.
The Hula dancers are swaying-
as the guitars are playing-
under the palm trees, so very cool.
You want to dip in a pool.
This place so ancient, things of the past.
Visions of bygones left so fast.
Listen to the ocean waves rise and fall.
With the roar, makes the Island seem small.
This is a paradise, out of the blue.
a dream come true.
The natives are bringing in a canoe.
They paint it blue for it is new.
The girls wear garlands around their neck
They've come from the ship, and been on deck.
This grass house is dark inside.
Our island home where we abide.
Farewell to thee, remember me
It is an exotic place to be.

—*Mary E. Watkins*

Nora

Who was Nora? She was my best friend. She was my wife.
Mother of our three children. She was my counter part.
Nora was everything to me and I to her.

We did everything together.
Nora always went fishing, together.
She was a good bowler, not for me, for herself!
Nora could play Poker with the best of them.

Nora and I could hold our own in Bridge.
If you think we did everything together, we did!
She was a Damn good driver, never had an accident.
Her children, husband and family was her whole life.

Nora got sicker and sicker and I think she knew the end was
near. She loved life and she fought as long as she could.
Nora didn't want to leave me after 37 years!
She didn't want to leave her children and grandchildren.

Nora asked me if I would marry after she died.
I told her I'm not a man meant to be alone!
But, after having a perfect wife, what could I find?
After 3 long and lonely years I haven't found one half as good.
I guess I am Damned for having had perfection!

—*Alvin E. Grimmig*

Signal Lights Of Life

One thing you can count on, as the light turns to green,
Mother urges, go my child, there's a world to be seen.

Her love is the ultimate, in this race you have begun.
For her praises, as you go, makes it well worth the run.

Your bruises are healed, with the touch of her lips,
And you keep on running, as she gives you tips.

As the race continues, the light has turned amber,
She's still saying, press on, though you've slowed to a canter.

Mother knows you're a winner, she taught you well,
And the'cup' you receive, the story does tell.

It's now filled with trophies, won through life, as you sped.
Ease up on the throttle, because the light's turning red.

—*Wanda Hendon*

Mothers -A Wonderful Creation

(Dedicated to my late Mother and my Grans.)
Mothers are there no matter what you may face
They are problem solvers no matter how bad.
And does it with charm and grace
She's the **best** friend I **ever** had.

They are always there to protect
They're like a lioness in her lair.
And for them we should **always** have great respect
For they certainly can be trusted to give the greatest care.

We should **never** forget to express our love
Yes, they're due a **daily** celebration.
And be **grateful** to the stars that shine above
For such a **wonderful** creation.

One should **not** cause her so much pain and strife
Because a **Mother's Love** will be with you all your life.

—*Barbara S. Atkins*

Indian Brave

He was running from the law,
moving with grace and speed,
his long hair blowing in the wind.

Could he outfox the men in blue?

When I saw him a chill of excitement
ran through my being.

What he is considered now is nothing
comparable to what he might have been.

My mind drifts back to an earlier
time when he would have been
considered quite a man.

Maybe he would have be an Indian Chief,

I can see his long hair blowing in the breeze
as he rides his pony on some adventure.

I can see him commanding the respect of his many tribesman.
But alas, my mind ventures back to the present.
And, on he goes fleeting around the corner,
down the darkened street.
Once again he has eluded his predator.
But, has he really?

—*Yvonne G. Engel Davis*

A Heart In Hiding

Her heart hold's pain, deep in her soul. She loves him so
much, she doesn't want to let go.
A dream that was dreamt, so long ago, heated by passion,
frozen in snow.
A rose that bloomed in the warm summer sun, but in the fall
wind, it becomes undone.
A flame that can't shine for him to see, she hides
in the cowardly side of me.
Afraid of showing pain, she hides behind my smile,
while I act like a fool, all of the while.
The many tears she's cried have come from my eyes,
her loving you is the me I despise.

—*Misty Hammond*

"Mother"

Her hair was silver, her eyes were blue.
Nowhere in this world was a heart so true.
The stars are not as bright now,
The sun's a little duller.
For I had to say goodbye to my
dear sweet mother.

—*Wm. R. Schwartz*

Go Gently Into That Good Night

I want to go gently into that good night.
My age would burn and glow at the close of day;
Sing and cheer at the dying of the light.

Each of us know there is delight
And we will all travel this way.
I want to go gently into that good night.

To many persons, the end is in sight;
Christ's words can guide them over the way.
Sing and cheer at the dying of the light.

We know of persons who sing of light
And have learned of hope on their way.
I want to go gently into that good night.

Brave ones, near death, see with tender sight
A bright path beyond every hope.
Sing and cheer at the dying of the light.

And you, my dear friend, there in that sad fight,
In victory can hope and dream and pray.
I want to go gently into that good night.
Sing and cheer at the dying of the light.

—*Ava L. Benn*

Blue Eyes

My blue eyes cry for you,
My blue eyes love you,
My blue eyes speak of undying love,
They say you are the one,
Blue eyes cry in the rain,
Dance in the sun,
And float with happiness when you are near,
My beautiful blue eyes love you,
And I love you, too!

—*Melodee Goodermote*

"Still Loving You"

"Today you said you're gonna leave me." Tears rolled down
my cheek. Even though we had our ups and downs and I'm very
sorry for that, you promised you wouldn't ever leave me. The
love I feel for you deep in my heart, I know it will never
leave. I love you so much, I just hope we can work this out,
Before its over with us!

—*Kym Knight*

Mom

From morning rise to kiss goodnight
    my children frequently recite
The single word that sets things right:
    Oh Mom! Hey Mom!

"He touched me, Mom." "She called me fool."
    "The cat has fallen in the pool!"
"Look what I did today in school!"
    Oh Mom! Hey, Mom!

It tires me so, day in and out,
    to hear each child repeatedly shout
The unthought word that leaves the mouth:
    Oh Mom! Hey Mom!

How could I chose this occupation
    from which there is no silent vacation
And no relief from the incantation:
    Oh Mom! Hey, Mom!

Yet time will come too soon for me,
    the kids will grow and away they'll flee.
Then I'll miss their every plea.
    Oh Mom! Hey Mom!

—*Patricia L. Sullivan*

Something Dark

Shadows form a folding motion
  my dark passions passing notion
I sing a silent tune of death's disaster
Of frowning laughter— of tragic tears that fall too soon

And no one seems to care
I reflect black windows
Glazed darkness seethes in silence
And the glow of my image fades into fallen realms
  of forgotten fear

Something dark dares damnation
  with a wicked wrinkle of new temptation
And the fear finds faces that cower while death's daughter
  seduces the man in the tallest tower
And no one ever leaves there
I sing this silent tune hoping the darkness
  might be leaving soon

But when the window breaks the light never shows
The master of disaster knows the fear of failure grows
  then falls - like passion
And after all it's just a passing notion
  —*Paul Alexander Raineri*

Am I the One?

Overwhelmed by a sudden spate of curiosity
My eye caught by a wandering
cluster of dandelion seeds.
Like a gypsy caravan touching down
but gone again without direction.
White and delicate, yet seemingly
impervious to the summer breeze.
My focus now drawn like a magnet,
drifting to unknown territories.
Deeply distraught but filled with
excitement, I free myself of control,
riding passenger to a mesmerizing power.
Wave after wave floods through me as
this vision floats closer and closer.
Anxiety stricken I extend myself towards it.
Will it descend and lite by my side?
Is it time? Am I the one?
  —*KAS*

My Window

I stood by my window -
My eyes were traveling far and near,
This must be the last snow of the year.

The snowflakes were softly coming down,
Soon a white blanket will cover the ground.

The crocus were peeking through the earth,
As the season has signaled time for rebirth.

A formation of geese were flying high,
Streaking northward through the sky.

A rabbit was scampering across the field,
To the approaching dogs it cannot yield.

A cardinal was fluttering in the breeze,
As the wind rustled through the trees.

The robin was singing his usual song,
Knowing spring will return before long.

The Master had painted a beautiful view,
For me to enjoy as I stood and looked through.
  —*Verna Gallimore*

My Special Holiday

When first I looked upon the dark little curl,
My first thoughts were 'It's a girl.'
And then I held that bundle of joy,
And found to my surprise it was a boy.
Then I thanked God again,
And named this baby Johnny Lynn.
Many years have passed and this child is far away,
But each year I'm reminded of this event on St. Patrick's day.
  —*Ollie Mayes*

"Shadows"

You know I'm all alone,
My friend's, they are not around
Everybody's gone to the garden, the garden
of happiness.

The garden is like beautiful brighten trees as green as the
greenest grass, the flowers are bright red as red as your heart
I can't see anyone, but they can see me.
It's so dark, all I can hear is the voices that are left, of
the friends I use to know.
Our friendship was like a rose that kept on blooming. Now!
it's like shadows which I can't touch.
Shadows of what was like a clock that kept on ticking
Now! it's like death.
When my fears subside and shadows still remains there's no
one around to blame or talk to, I feel waste like garbage that
was just thrown away. So why see the darkness we still can
find away cause nothin' lasts forever.
  —*Veronica Nieters*

Sweden

Sweden is a distant land across the deep blue sea
My grandparents were born and raised there
Till the distant call and wandering feet
Found their way to a sailing ship
That took them far away
They wed one April day in a new land
That we call the U.S.A.
Here they built a home
As years passed and they were truly blessed
With 5 sons and 1 daughter to carry on their name
In their twilight years they looked back to see
What their life had turned out to be
We have had a good life you and I
Just look what our children has given us
Years of joy and sweet contentment
This life you have given to me
  —*Albertina C. Serpa*

Touch My Body, But Not My Mind

Laughter broke from my lips.
My hair slid from my face.
Pure knowledge of guarded thoughts,
And I know I won't let you near me.
If you break through, then I'll feel you,
And I can't let you near my mind.
But you can touch my body,
For there is no purity there to find.
Oh, I want so badly for you to touch me,
If this is what you do
My heart will have one gentle sigh.
My mind won't fold and die
If you can penetrate into my thoughts
What fascinating you will confront.
What secrets you will find
What madness you will have to consider.
My body's here for the taking,
But leave alone my mind.
  —*Nancy E. Hinrichs*

The Achievement

I woke up in the morning
My head spinning 'round
Just wanted to let you know
Where-ever you go I'll always be around.

It matters not how many curves lie within our road
No problem will escape unsolved
Love conquers all;
Or so I've been told.

Do not falter; dare not to fear
Our love will always endure
Soon again the day will come
When I can hold you near.

Never again will we part
For I love you with all my heart.
We will achieve within me and you
A life-long love shared by few.

—*Tammy Lavoie*

A Roaring Fire

As I sit by a roaring fire
My heart is filled with desire
The weather is wet and cold
I sit in this rocking chair feeling alone and old
I wish the girl I love was sitting in my lap
I would hold her tight as she rested her head on my neck to
take a nap I would softly touch her face and kiss her cheek
Loneliness leaves me sad, cold, and weak
I want a girl who will love me in every way
Like Juliet loved Romeo in Shakespeare's play
I look deep into the flames
I know I will lose but I still want to play love's game
But a roaring fire can't warm a broken heart
Only love and passion can warm that body part
The fire disappears as ashes are made
And the dream of that girl in your lap begins to fade
As the cold hits you again you miss that girl in your fantasy
As you lay down to sleep you wonder if it can become reality

—*Jon Harrison*

Memory Of You

I love you, darling, I love you, dear.
My heart is lost, I live in fear
Of loving you again some year.

So long ago we laughed together
Found happiness and made life better.
Still lingers on the memory
The joy your love has brought to me.

I love you, darling, I love you, dear
All through the weeks and months and years.
But, all has changed and you're not near.
I love you, darling, I want you here.

—*Verna Wooten Bryant*

First Light

When I first see the light of day
    My nightly fears just fade away
I stand in awe of the rising sun
    Which makes the day for everyone
It brings hope to me and all my friends
    And this is how our day begins
    We work - we play and all agree
    For us this day was meant to be
    As daylight now begins to fade
    We all enjoy the progress made
With time we've spent from light to dark
    We close our day with thankful heart

—*J. Warren McDaniel*

My Son

I love you, my son. I love you so much.
    My heart longed to be with you.
I often wondered where you were
    and what you were going through.

Only the Lord and I know what I've
    experienced after leaving you.
He knew my heart and my desires,
    He made my dream come true.

We've finally come together after years
    of hope and prayer.
You must have felt I didn't love you,
    You must have thought I didn't care.

When I heard you call me Mom for the very
    first time my heart was filled with joy.
For I wasn't there to hear those words
    When you were just a boy.

The Lord has kept His watchful eye on you
    He knew this day would come.
Such happiness you've brought me.
    God bless you, I love you, MY SON.

—*Linda Young*

December Of 1992

A crisp December night brought you into
    My life and I don't know it happened
I remember you and a crowd around us, yet
    You and I weren't there together.
Your eyes were piercing and I was afraid
    to make any direct contact.
Each time I'd glance over, they'd capture me
    And I'd have no where to hide.
Then I hear your voice on the other end of
    My phone and I cannot believe it's true.
We began feeling more than a friendship forming.
Then the day came when you told me you loved
    me, my heart fell, my eyes filled
And the glitter of the gold shined brighter
    than I've ever seen before.
My tears almost fell as it looked into your eyes,
    then you brought a smile to my face and the
    emotions flowed from my heart.
"Alan Lee, I love you, from today until the
    last tomorrow I live to see!"

—*Tiffany M. Drop*

Always Near

    So much like the ocean that's how
my life is, I spend all my moments
wondering of the years, the years that
have passed and the ones that are near.
    Just as the tides go in and out my
fears fall about, fears of being alone
and scared for I know my year is ahead.
    Just as the sea gulls that fly overhead
my dreams will live on even when I'm dead.
    Just as the sea shells wash upon the
shore, so many people will stop and adore,
so it is what they will say,
how we adored her even on this day.
    Just like the water so pure that's how
I want to be remembered that's for sure.
    Remember me only with love and cheer,
don't be sad I'll always be near, let
me wash upon this shore for I want to
be here forever more.

—*Nikki Duffie*

Mystic Love

The moon-
My mystic friend.
Luna my girl-
You shine eternity.
You reflect your man's rays-
Support the sun as a woman should.
You never grow old- never dim-
You age well, beautiful still.
You control romance-
You create love.
Yet, evil lurks under your dark powers.
Maniacs roam- rapers rape- murderers kill-
Yet, you still smile and look on.
Is that an evil smirk on your brow-
Or is it a pure enjoyment of life itself?

—*Vanessa Reinhart*

Perspective

"You're young," said the calendar on the wall;
My own heart answered, "I'm not young at all.
I've seen so much of this world and its life;
I've suffered so much of its pain and its strife.
I'm weary and tired; there's nothing to see
In all this world that would interest me.
You say I'm sixteen and so young — but then
You're wrong— "I shall never be young again."

Tempest fugit

"You're old," said the calendar on the wall;
But my own heart said, "I'm not old at all,
There're many things I have never seen,
A million places where I've never been;
There're countless numbers of joys yet to know
Life and adventure the world can still show,
You say that I'm fifty, and life is cold?
Oh, but you're wrong — I shall never grow old!"

—*Pearl Borchard*

Stop, Listen, Pray!

You spoke Your word, Your call I heard.
My path was paved with sin I questioned,
if not now Lord, when?
You answered with the same words again.
I've had to run a difficult race; You pleaded my case.
You promised me a better place, if I'd humble
myself, and look upon Your face.
I meditated on Your word, You spoke to my heart.
I understood things better then.
Lord, when you took me in, as Your word proclaims
my new life did begin. You set me on a course,
kept me at a steady pace to stay,
You revealed to me a brighter day.
The one thing You asked in return,
is that I submit to Your way.
I'm so glad! I took the time to, Stop! Listen! and Pray!
My trials were many; times were hard;
it's all over now. I Thank You Lord.

—*Barbara Thomas-Brown*

Body And Soul

For what I am Human, my thoughts pure,
My destiny rough rugged with a sense of calmness.
What I feel becomes unstable at times,
Not all seems clear, but here I am strong,
Weakened at times, happy and sad.
From day to day I continue to move forward.
Time is of importance.

—*Allan Carson*

Why I Always Have A Good Night Sleep

Every night I think of you as my head rests upon
my pillow waiting for sleep to overcome me.

I see your face and hear your voice and can't
help but smile when you laugh that stupid
laugh so much.

I see the way your hair flips over your forehead,
not caring which way it goes, so free, just like yourself.

I see you drawing or reading as you so often do alone,
putting great concentration in the color of the
sky or a line of poetry.

With these thoughts, I finally fall asleep and it's
always with a smile.

—*Melissa Slavick*

Victorious King

I dreamed that I awoke on Easter Morning
My precious Savior did I behold
Descending form heaven surrounded by Angels
Swathed in white with a crown of gold

I looked around in utter amazement
At the crowds gathering form near and far
And my gaze was drawn toward a voice from heaven
To a gigantic twinkling silver star

"Behold my son the risen Savior
Who from the cross has set you free
He has broken the chains of sin that bound you
And conquered death eternally"

The angels blew their golden trumpets
They spread their wings and began to sing
"Hallelujah, Hallelujah, he has come for the faithful
Praise the Lord, Our Victorious King

I awoke reluctantly from my dream
Peace and Joy now filled my heart
And I looked toward heaven and cried aloud
"Oh my God, How Great Thou Art!"

—*Jean Chinchillo*

My Beloved

My beloved who is the whole of my being,
My soul belongs to God alone
But my heart, my life and my love belongs to you.
My Lord gives me the breath to live,
But you are the one who makes me want to keep on breathing.
The world would be empty without you here for me.
Death alone is all that can take you from me,
And precious memories would keep me living on if you were gone.
I pray that God will grant us perfect peace and happiness that
no one but He alone can give.
My love is strong and no demon in hell can take it away.
My love is you, my hope is through God,
And my happiness is being with you until I can make Heaven
my final home.

—*Sharon Bridges*

Another Day

Each thought races off, before I have time to
place them in my memory. Temporary subsided. Life
stays the same. Reaching, dreaming yet still reality.
Ties to cut, but dreams too far to grasp, soon in the
past. Life is here, dreams are there. Bringing forth
hope, happiness, life, and death. Is there yet more.
Only in my thoughts racing off to yet another day.

—*Shelley Miller*

Consorting

In the darkness past midnight
    my soul longs
        for the rush of coolness
            that waves the grass and
                stirs the dust over the prairie.

The mind window plays me
    the sing of snakes,
        the slice of heat thunder,
            the sweat smell of horse.

My soul remembers and
    wastes for the past;

It rams my heart
    with each tick of Time.

Its unhappiness drains my energy, my
    resolution.

Yet, I am afraid it will leave me.
    I would break brittle
        as a scorpion carcass in the sand.

My soul remembers
    and stays.

—Mary Jane Madden

More Than Just A Girl

She is my blanket of protection,
my sunshine on my darkest of days,
her loving arms acting as warm rays.
She makes everything sweet,
faster my heart beats.
I have so much to gain from her-
So much to lose when she is gone.
She means so much to me.
I feel her love.
I feel the need for her love.
My life rises to a higher
plane of being when she is there
Everything about her makes my emotions twirl.
She is all this, but...just a girl.

—Seth Pociask

Growth

The tranquil autumn sky grows stormy
Mysterious wisps disengage the brilliant sun
It denies the landscape its vibrant expression
Thunderous deliberation sways the magnificent silhouette
Its limbs outstretched in an inquiring disbelief
Turned upward to its Creator as the sky unleashes its fury
The raging storm beats upon the mighty being,
Only to be absorbed for its greater strength
Questions encompass this gift to the heart
An outpouring of feverish awareness consumes its mind.

—Jeffery L. Clark

What Is Happening To Us?

'What's happened to society?' asked one man of his
neighbor, after a long discussion about one man's mother
and another man's dog, both of which are now dead. "It
seems to me that each must better the other's tragedies to
make his life more pitiable and sad. Sympathy from our
peers is the reward of a constant contest of depression."
"How depressed are you?" asked the neighbor of this
man, "Does it surprise you that sympathy rhymes with
apathy? Does this make you understand indifference of
another kind?"

—Marie Polley

It Cannot Be Told

Life is but a dark hallway
Never able to be lit
Unable to determine what happens next
Many times you just want to quit

You just can't appreciate that the future
Must remain dark and mysterious
Because the sensation of curiosity
Dwells in all of us

We all ask the question
What will the future hold
But we'll never find the answer
For it cannot be told

—Tabatha Gerdon

Virgin Sleep

Many ships have crested the surface of my sea.
Never before has one dove into the depths of me.
The wind of romance brought you here.
The waves of passion drew you near.
Up and down your ship did roar.
In and out like never before.
All at once you dove in deep,
And woke me from my virgin sleep.

—Robert C. Wilbanks

Ships That Never Come In

Most all of our lives we dream... and wish... for things that
    never can be.
If only... oh how many times we've all been heard to say.
    I'm waiting for my ship to come in, I know it's on it's way.
I've been waiting for it forever so long, it's how I make it
    through each day.
I know that I am not alone in my waiting don't you see? There
    really are a lot of us waiting out each day.
A waste of time? I don't know. Who am I to say?
    So here's to dreams... and wishes... and hopes... and
ships that never come in.

—Sylvia Hendrix

Missing You

Never thought that you would be gone.
Never knew I wouldn't have you for very long.
Now I'm always thinking about you,
Knowing now, there is nothing I can do.

Never thought it would hurt this bad.
Never knew a person could be this sad.
Now I think of what we could have done.
Knowing now, that we could've had lots of fun.

Never thought everything would be so out of place.
Never knew how much I'd miss your smiling face.
Now I wish I would have made the most of every day,
Knowing now that it's too late because you've passed away.

—Tori Lambert

Sharky's Education

Sharky's was only a small candy store
Next to the Astor Theatre
And I passed through it with the impatience of youth

But the memories of an old man
Who really wasn't there just for the money
Stay with me longer then the movies I've seen

An old man's time is his own......
I wish I'd known that then

—Paul Carr

416

Early Morn

Jack Frost has painted my window again sometime during the night
As I look out it's easy to be a child again
To wish that I could paint designs so beautiful and bright
Beyond that glass the snow now falls so silent and so white
It lands just so on bush and tree
Oh what a wondrous sight!
As early daylight fills the sky I almost feel I could
Take down the sleigh and don my hood and venture out to play
My mind let's me trudge up the hill my dog not far behind
And when once there I take the sleigh and down the hill I slide
The cold air reddens up my cheeks I feel I'm all aglow
For just a little while I can appreciate the snow

—*Shirley Whitbeck*

Parenting

When parents expect their child's birth
Nine months of both bitter and sweet
They behold that great moment of mirth
After they count hands, fingers, toes and feet

Their first year should be the beginning
Of knowing when you are playing and not
Be consistent and firm, not yelling
Remember you are both teaching the tot

The years before school are the pattern
of the responsibility and obedience you start
As they grow and flourish, not cause concern
And these traits are from your heart

Those who teach religion, respect and trust
Will soon see dependable young ladies and men
And when God looks down on you, as he must
He'll say you've done a good job up till then

The position of parent never retires
Because the children need help from time to time
Give advise and listen to their desires
But your older years should be sublime.

—*Nadine Sloan Southern*

Without You

If there was no sun to warm your face,
No breeze to give you its cool embrace,
No stars to twinkle in darkest night,
No moon embracing in loving light,
No grass to tickle between your toes,
No bright flowers to arouse your nose,
No trees to sway in the strongest wind,
Life would be hopeless but would not end.
But without you and your soft, sweet touch,
That warms my heart and I love so much,
An eternity of endless loss,
It would be too long a bridge to cross.
Death would be sweeter to let it end,
Than pain and despair at every bend.
So let me love you and hold you tight,
And hold and love me with all your might.

—*Rebekah Anne Sanchez*

The Coyote

He runs real fast like a streak of light
prowls and hunts at the edge of night
He runs a vast and lonesome land
Through the sagebrush and the sand
Though he still keeps running by the fear of man.

—*Tom Dieke*

Vampire Nihilist

I am a Vampire Nihilist;
  No memories of my own
  Thus I must dip my shriveled
tongue in yours... and yours
      and more
So as - to loose my own
    - to be as my own
    - to feel your night through my pores
I have yet to fill my yearning, so -
Quickly! Grab at another's life...
For I am empty, and soon I will cut my own throat.

—*Mike Flynn*

Return To Silence

...When I am ready to die,
No miracles there will be
  Miracles are for the living,
  ... Only shattered illusions
  Illusions are for the striving,
No more resisting reality....
  Reality thicker than the walls of Ilium.
  ...Dreams that captured man's fancy
Will go with me into the ground
  Slowly as a blessing
Or pounding as a Sledge.
  ...The things I wanted to Change
  Ideas that would create
Values that would lift
  A brighter, Better, Safer world
Now will bring futility, anger...
  ...And hope turned to ashes
    will be your Burden,
  vague, nameless shame, your Guilt.
But, in the ground, I will be silent.

—*Thomas A. Flowers*

Alone

Alone in love, alone in silence, alone in life
No one to here your worries and sorrows
No one but a heart beat pulsing in the mist of the air
No fears, no hopes, no dying, just you no one else

Alone in silence
No little boy or girls prayer to be heard
No sounds of joy or happiness

Alone from the environment
Alone from loved ones from the one who really cares
But really who is that person looking back at you
Through the broken glass sweet and innocent on the outside
But inside, burning full of rage

Nobody to hear your scream, to hold you when you wake up
From a cold wet, deep sleep

Alone, last being on the face of the earth
No Adam or Eve or even a simple apple tree
No one around in the deep black hole you call earth

—*Nichole Gillespie*

Our Love

Our days are Long,
Our Nights are short.
Our love is like a game of Sports.
Waiting for the ball to land in our Court.

  I say a silent prayer of hope,
That the Good Lord will always give us
His patient and kind support!!!

—*Michelle Wylie*

Retirement

It's nice to wake up — with thoughts only hazy
   No problems at all — a day to be lazy
Don't care if the weather — brings sun, rain or snow
   You're staying inside — with no place to go
Enjoy eggs and bacon — good coffee to drink
Ignore all those dishes — now piled in the sink
No TV of interest — no book to be read
Yawning could mean — a return to your bed
Boredom's set in — depression's felt, too
   So many long hours — nothing to do
Isn't there someone — with whom you could share
Your time and your knowledge — show them you care
By helping each other — simply to cope
Fill both of your lives — with a new sense of hope!
   —Alice E. Coggeshall

My Changing World

As I gaze out my window,
No sun, no one moving, but LO!
Into my world so dim
I see in the maple tree, a squirrel so trim.

Bushy tail up and sounding quite an alarm,
Something sinister meaning to do him harm
Is coming across the lawn, I see,
And Squire Squirrel has good reason to be free.

For in my attic, we have found
Deep in the insulation, in a squirrel pound,
Four baby squirrels and Mom,
Their scampers sounding like mini bombs!

So, Papa Squirrel sets up a fuss!
Not a hair or whisker does the sinister one muss!
"There's Beebee," he chatters, "It's the Cat!"
She wants in the house! and THAT'S THAT!

The danger is gone and I see,
With a smile on my face, and with glee,
Squire Squirrel again happy at work.
"Come in, Beebee." And I open the door with a jerk!
   —Nell Aaron

Listen

Be proud of who you are my child.
No, you don't have long straight, silky hair.
Your hair is thick and tightly curled.
Better known as nappy!
Honey, we come in all shades of brown.
There's vanilla, taupe, chocolate, and hershey.

Mommie, mommie I know this color;
As she points to and rubs her arm with gentle strokes.
"It's beautiful brown."
That's right baby it is.
And you're beautiful brown.
   —Stephanie A. Rogers-Moore

Emptiness

I had a dream last night that I died,
Nobody cared, nobody cried.
My soul walked along a path of dirt and stone,
My skin melted away revealing the bone.
I came to a man dressed all in black,
He told me to turn around and go back.
Go back to what? There was nothing there,
Just an evil world that was all but fair.
So I stayed in the dark and empty place,
Vanishing from the earth without a trace.
   —Jennifer Terry

Love Is Purple

Whispering around on soft
Noiseless paws, like those of a
Cat, she watches with knowing
Eyes.
The outstretched arms, always
Accepting and forgiving,
Warm those who are cold. Her
Tickling fingers replace frowns with
Smiles, and her soft lips
Caress the ill.
The perfume of wild flowers and narcissus
Flows behind her as she
Enters our lives and minds.
Winter rain drops fall to the
Earth and land on our tongues as we
Think of her.
Rich, flowing juices of delicious foods
Run through hungry children,
And we are reminded of her.
   —Sarah Wahrenbrock

What You Mean To Me

No words can explain,
Nor can any words describe,
The friendship that I feel for you,
Comes from deep down inside.

Like a gift sent from our Father above,
Like the sweet pureness of a spotless white dove,
Just to know we have a Godly love,
Is what you mean to me.

For you were my answered prayer
   when I cried to God for a friend,
And I pray a Abba Father
   that this friendship will never end.

So I give this special gift back
   to the One who first set it free,
So that Jesus Christ be glorified
   by both you and by me.
   —Patricia J. De Hoyos

Love Suspended Forever

Here we are,
Not close, but not far,
Stepping, one, two, three,
The two of us, you and me.

Where are we going you ask,
Where we're going is worth the task,
People look high and far,
To try and find out who they really are.

The waves crashing on the sandy shore,
We run up and down to see more,
The sand sliding in between our feet,
While the water and salt also meet.

The earth is silent and free,
Think only happy thoughts, one is family,
Leaves changing colors, making no sound,
While snow falls to the ground.

Sun sets in the west,
Never giving up is always best,
Everyone must have an endeavor,
Ours is love suspended forever.
   —Rachel S. R. Goldfine

Untitled

Why do I set myself up for all this anguish?

Why do I give my love to one who will
   not except it, return it?

Why do I try to be loved by one
   who will not herself know of love?

Why must I have this bittersweet
   love? Is love so damned important?

Does love feed the soul?
Does love set the heart free to fly
   upon wings?

Why does the answer evade me?
Is love to be lost, wasted on a heart
   of stone?
Will I cry insane tears of sorrow?

I with all my sins, desires, lusts and
   lies, do I not deserve love?

To love and be loved, I myself,
Do I honestly know, want or need love?

   —William Kelley

Progress?

Back in 1593 this land was a brand new destiny
Not much was known about it, but people wanted to see
Not knowing whose it was or whose it would finally be
But, they weren't happy where they were and wanted to flee

When 1693 went by, people came from Europe by the score
They were sick of being robbed through taxes and took no more
Where they came from people were getting the short end
Freedom restricted and taxed 'til they had nothing to spend

1793 rolled around and the U.S. already stood her ground
After becoming a free nation, great peace of mind was found
No more paying high taxes and being bossed around
Land of the free, home of the brave-let the guns sound

When 1893 got here the U.S. was strong, so never you fear
A man was judged by what he could do and that's damn clear
It didn't take a lot of money, just a strong will and back
Some sense to go along and there's nothing you'd lack

Now it's 1993, all over again people would like to flee
Justice is short, taxes is high-I don't see anything free
A working man can't get ahead, he'll barely keep his family fed
It's progress someone said? Is it him or I-that's being misled

   —Terry L. Ashlock

Being A Man

A Man is not measured by the height he grows
Not the muscles or brawn or the seeds he sows
He measured by kindness and love and things that he does
That people don't see but the Lord alone does

He'll reap what he sows be it good or bad
He'll learn as he grows, often things that make him sad
He'll wish he had extended his hand to a friend
or helped someone in trouble along life's way
Maybe just being quiet when he really had a lot to say

Being a man, be he short or tall
Extending his friendship and love to one and all
Being a man means many different things
Sometimes if only its a smile that he brings.

   —Mable B. Belcher

Time

Without her, the world has stopped spinning.
Nothing moves; we are separate.
All has ceased
Without her, nothing flows.
Sadness, melancholy fill the stagnant air I breathe.
Time does not exist without her; no time passes,
   yet tune us all there is.
With her, all is one breath
The days are nothing but a kiss, a peck;
Nothing but a smile, one caress it seems.
Time comes in on the wind then goes,
   Staying only to brush her hair on my face.
With her, time does not exist.
One movement is all; one warmth of touch,
Then gone.
   —Kurt Moellering

"Friend"

Happy memories of our first meeting,
November '87, with tentative greeting.
Hoping each would find good rapport,
Praying that neither would go out the door.

Ready to join lives and our living,
You, always unassuming and giving.
Your quiet needs daily perplexed me...
I confess, freely, sometimes you vexed me.

Blunders, I made them, but not from my heart.
Practice was needed to play proper part.
I saw your errors with perfect 20/20.
Blind to my flaws, you gave love a-plenty.

Sharing our journey for lifetime's race,
Happily basking in friendship's place,
Without further ado - without solitary barrier -
Curtis, I love you, my smooth Fox Terrier!

   —Aldena M. Moise

"Missive To Xanthippias"

And now that all has died,
Now Aphrodite's love in its dying throes;
A wife hovering neighborly at a cruel distance
kills me yet with her honeyed kindness
subtly mixed with horned myrrh and bitter aloes.

Xanthippias,
   She never loved me truly... this I truly know.
   She is dead to me now, a love that never could live,
     and hence I must go. Am I so sick to clasp
   that which was never alive - coiled sting of death,
   suck at the hemlock root, my bitter heart, and never
     to revive?

Xanthippias,
   Would that I had plucked
   from your masculine wings the apple of wisdom,
   a marital oath, once so solemn, traduced and pierced by
     Eris' stings...
   while Pallas Athena led me weeping to the sacrosanct purity
     of love
   and you eternally trusting, my Xanthippias,
   whom I have loved like my own soul.

   —R. E. Weinstein

Autumn Leaves

Leaves, once green,
now ripened to glowing shades
of gold and brown and red
flutter like bashful maidens
as they listen to the wind
seducing them, with promises of freedom -
Infatuated, they whirl and twirl
they spin in the arms of this fickle lover -
break free from the nurturing bonds that hold them
until abandoned, they fall to the ground,
a sodden blanket to warm the feet
of the Mother tree who bore them.

—*Roberta Hawkins*

Child of the Universe

Child of the universe you are — a point in time and space.
Now you are "through a glass darkly," but "then you shall see
face to face,"
Understand the ordered disorder, the chaotic will discipline space.
The "big bang," basic helium and hydrogen
Stars are born, super novas, stars die.
And you, carbon cycle, made of star stuff —
For answers so deeply you pry.
If you want to know clearly your forbears —
Look homeward, Angel — the sky.
The energy that causes this universe in space gently curved
everywhere.
Einstein's intergalactic equation, E-MC Square.
and this energy, the power of nature kind.
The bond that is holding you fast,
Ontogeny recapitulates phylogeny
Links all to the prehistoric past.
What is good, what is man in the universal plan?
To learn about the universe are you really free —
Or does the universe seek to know itself through THEE.

—*Marylynn Markowitz*

Growing Old In 1993

It used to be that growing old was just a natural thing, but
now you have to watch your weight and your step must have a
swing. You can't invite your special friends to taste a fresh
baked treat, they take a look and have to say it's the calories
we can't eat. When you take out a nice pork roast, they can't
eat that at all, there just might be a little fat to give
cholesterol. Then there is the chocolate cake with frosting
thick and white, A lemon pie and custard too they cannot take a
bite. I'd like to sit down to a meal like it was years ago,
with second helping piled up high and not a soul said "No".
Everyone enjoyed the meal it really was a treat, not to think
of diets but just sit down and eat. Another thing you
shouldn't have is hair that's turning gray, I like to think I
earned each one as I went along life's way. On wrinkles,
graying hair and fat much money's spent each day, to keep the
face and figure young but it just don't work that way. When
you get up from off the chair and all your bones complain, no
amount of wrinkle cream will help to ease the pain. So I think
that growing old no matter what they say, should be fun and
food with all your friends, they too are getting gray.

—*Vivian Rice*

A Man Without Age

A man without age is free from worry
Told of time; no reason to hurry
He keeps to himself the burden to carry
One without an epoch; becomes a surrey
To transport the depressed to the merry
A being divinely perfect and able to parry
Is by purpose omnipotent to answer your query

—*Nathaniel D. Grant*

Ode To Politicians

You'll promise us anything to get elected;
Now you're the ones we've selected!

Read my lips, "No new taxes";
Four more years, you'll get the axes.

We should be willing to do without;
So you have money to travel about.

What can we do to better our lot?
Thought so long, I forgot.

Maybe someday it'll be better;
Don't count on it to the letter.

Payday comes and payday goes;
Doesn't cure the money woes.

Everything I own is in hock;
Hope I stay well, can't afford the Doc.

You send our children to foreign lands;
They lose their lives, feet or hands.

What'll I do, Oh woe is me;
Well, you say that I am free.

—*Margaret A. Stith*

Good Witch

Every summer I vow I'm going to cut it down.
Nuisance red berries dropping to ground
staining feet, shoes and inside carpet.
For the firewood stack I swear I'll mark it.

Then I remember late Februaries
when the yard 'n' garden
and trees are bleak.
It is this fine plant's
tiny yellow clusters
that first muster courage to peek
and initiate the inevitable crescendo
for winter begone.

You may stay on,
my good Witch Hazel,
stay on.

—*Michael R. Hardesty*

I Saw the Eagle Cry

Waves of white topped blue, slam against the miniature rocks
of a solemn beach.
Humans lay in the sun, like basking Sealions.
Adventurous souls brave the fast moving ridge of the waters
surface.
Sounds of man made boxes assault the air with Furious Beats!
Black Swill takes to the water, and gains a toe hold!
Vessel leaks oil from five miles out.
Like an evil entity, it chokes all that venture in it's blind path.
I see the head of a Water Foul, fighting not for flight, but for life!
As it struggled against it's Great Captor, I glanced skyward,
and saw the king bank on a breeze. As he flew by, watching
it's, inedible quarry die.
My eye's strained to see, what my mind told me could not be,
For Noble him, humbled by, uncaring, self righteous, Man.
Could but turn, fly for the sun, and as he left, I swore
I saw the Eagle Cry!

—*Alex R. Hayes*

The Tree

I am the tree!
Of all sizes and a lot of colors.
With the wind's blow I compose beautiful melodies!
I shelter wooing hearts and conceive fantasies...
But, like you, I have my fears, you know.
I am the tree!
I need not to introduce myself,
because I represent the nature and I am everywhere.
I adorn and I feed all continents!
But... there is always someone to cut me down.
I am the tree!
I, too, have been created by God!
I am alive! I miss being loved.
I adorn your days and dancing, I soften your sweat away.
Then, why do not they hear my moanings?!
I am the tree!
Please, do not make me bleed with your saws!
One day, when you are not able to see me anymore,
and there, in the Holy Field you have gone to dwell,
certainly I will sway your eternal sleep.

—*Ruth Vianna*

My Best Friend

I've just realized, that, you're my best friend
of all the friends, that, I've had; you're the one.
I know, that, I can count on until the end.

When no one else has time for me.
You're always there to make me laugh.
Everyday, that, I spend with you is trouble free.

After those hard days at work
and all those embarrassing moments
You're the only one, that, doesn't make me feel
like a jerk.

Even when my wife seems unsensitive.
I know you'll be there to cheer me up.
because, I know you'll never say anything derogative

Thanks for being such a good friend to me.
Your sense of humor, your reliability have
proved, that, there is no better friend than
your T.V.

—*Ronald H. Mason*

Untitled

Whether a doctor or a priest, we all started out as a piece
of clay or an empty piece of canvas.
Our days of youth and schooling have molded us into whatever
we are today.
Daily experiences and our attitudes towards them are what make
us individuals.
No matter what our skin color, religion or nationality we have
the power to mold ourselves into whatever we wish.
For it is not our social success which makes us great, but our
personal satisfaction.
Some of us grow into beautiful pieces of art while others
remain as mediocre decorations.
The beauty of each of us is not our appearance but our mind
and how powerful it is.
Our knowledge is what makes us a beautiful sculpture.
We are able to make our minds as attractive as we desire.
Although our physical appearance is with us the rest of our
lives, it has no significance.
Our appearance is permanent but we have the ability to mold
our minds into whatever we desire.

—*Bannon Dencler*

To A Robin

If you would like a quiet moment
of enjoyment to know,
you need a birdbath you can watch,
as various birds do come and go.

The high point of this vigil kept,
is to see a robin come your way.
When he takes a bath, it's serious
business for him, for the day.

He'll dip and splash, and I mean Splash!
The water flies all around, and then
He'll preen his wings and feathers, and
then do the whole bit all over again.

So what if I do have to fill
His bathtub all over again, too.
To watch his joyous fling gives me
a lot of pleasure, and could also do for you.

—*Natalie V. Fletcher*

Eternal Peace

Innocence experienced the coming
  Of eternal night

In blissful serenity, Innocence awaited
  That final flight

Innocence was guided by moonbeams
  Of glimmering, magical lights

Innocence was lifted up
  To the angels so bright

Innocence said promise me
  You will tell them why
I was chosen to soar
  Through a different sky

A promise was made
  For the precious innocent one

The caring were told about good deeds
  "Innocence's have all been done

Innocence brought and taught
  So much about love

That all the innocent ones were granted
  Eternal peace in heaven above"

—*Siubhan Dewar*

Mind-Country

History is the recording
of man's culture and times.
A warning reminder
of his follies and crimes.
A remembrance of a generative energy
and zest
A creative mind-country
where man's at his best.
A mind-country so vast
every soul's welcome there
Whether lover, or poet,
or statesman who care.
To all who contribute
their large or small share.
The gates are wide open
to all who will dare.

—*Susan F. Selby*

The Gift Of Love

I remember a picture I saw once ago
of my grandmother when she was a girl.
"Grandma was pretty," I said to Granddad.
"No, she was beautiful", his eyes shining he said.
The love in his eyes was so easy to see
As deeply today, as when she was seventeen.
Through good days and bad days, for fifty years
Through the birth of their children through laughter and tears
they've loved each other with a love that is true
a love that has blossomed since they both said, "I do".
It was the hand of God that brought them together.
Before time began he made one for the other.
True love is the most precious gift of the heart.
When placed there by God, it can't be torn apart.
As God made our souls forever to be
May your love last a lifetime — and through eternity.

  —Monica Crump

Untitled

  Jealous are we of the keen eyes we see,
    of the confusion and worry
      that they will bury;

      the love, the kind
    that they won't leave behind;

      the curve of the smile
    that will be only for a while;

      a heart broken look,
    a girl's heart that has been took;

    children's laughter and play
      that has been taken away;

        drugs on the street
        that we can't beat;

  friends and loved ones killed day after day,
    we want time to stop but there's no delay;

      our lives vanished into thin air,
but it really seems to me that no one gives a care.

  —Ajanet D. McClain

Affirmation

The tree seems ageless and strong as it withstands the lashes
of the mid-winter storm. The branches make brittle sounds of
cracking as the storm rages and howls. It's been long since
the tree felt the embrace of the sun, it's roots froze as if
time had stopped. Alone it seems, unable to move with grace
its arms and hands and dance to the sun. Perhaps, it fears God
has abandoned him, left him alone to battle the raging storm.
It wishes to reach out as in spring but it feels its energy
immobilized, froze, locked within its soul. He feels himself
ugly, all stripped naked, exposed, as he ponders his destiny,
not feeling the worth of life. Now time has passed beyond the
cold wintery nights, and the sun shines steadfast. Just as
reassuredly as the sun that penetrates the haze of the woods
with hues of amber and misty white. Nothing is outside the
sun's vision, for he is the light. Slowly the light begins to
reach the heart of the tree and it heard the soft sounds of
words. "You are a part of the family of trees and at your feet
lie the flowers of spring. Look around you, for even as I have
given to you, so have I to all that surrounds you. Relax your
arms and trunk, the storm is over, and I will embrace you.

  —Sandra Branson

In Loving Memory

In the loving memory,
Of the one who stole my heart,
But as soon as you came you left,
You stayed just long enough to do your part,

When the Lord took you away,
He took a part of me,
I've done all that I can,
To be what you want me to be,

The future is for you,
And I'll strive to make you proud,
Even though you're so far away,
I can see you in the clouds,

Just stay right by my side,
And never leave me again,
Don't make me have to wonder,
Where you are and where you've been,

Watch over me Mrs. Gootee,
Dry the tears when I cry,
Just promise to stand by me,
But please, never say good-bye?

  —Tammy Stivers

My Dreams

Along life's dark and gloomy pathway, amid the adversities
of the world but, apart from the world, through toils and
tribulations I strive, I strive for success

Before me my dreams are my inspirations, behind me, beside me,
beneath me, my failures are many, inside of me the fire burns
day and night as I struggle, struggle to fulfill that burning
that yearning desire within

Until I reach that place inside excepting no failures along the
the way, from dawn to dusk I press, I press on toward that
burning that yearning desire within

With God above me below me, before me, behind me, beside me,
and within me, my trials, my struggles, my adversities,
though they are many I will achieve, I will excel, I will
accomplish my dreams in spite of.

  —Virginia Edwards

Understanding Love

Love, what is love? I've asked myself this question thousands of times.
But for someone to stick with another no matter what the situation is,
To care of someone so deeply and to have such an intense pain
Within because the one you love is so extremely close,
Yet so far to take hold of is a true act of love.
A quality not everyone can grasp, a quality I tend to admire in one,
A quality so many people lack, a quality which is so unique
It only blooms in special people one in a blue moon.
For a person, as emotionless to everyone as yourself
To open your heart to only one lucky person is something that
So many people wish for and it is so rare to find.
In all of the acts I've seen in my life I believe that you are
not an act but reality.
I just wish life was not just one big "Tug-of-war"
However, I do want to thank you for sharing and unlocking your
heart with me.

  —Jennifer Harrar

Inside

I'm having these nightmares and they're getting worse,
Oh God help me I think I'm cursed
The devil came to me and he said,
Sell your soul or your family is dead
It's you or your family what will you choose,
Shut up and leave me both ways I loose
Ok your family I guess you said,
When you awake tomorrow they'll all be dead
Wait don't take my family tonight,
If you let me choose you can take me if you like
No son! A figure appears,
It's not the devil it's just your fears
The devil can't hurt you as you know,
He can only trick you to sell your soul
The next day I woke up to see,
My dead family in front of me
I looked to the devil and said I don't understand,
He pointed down and I saw the dagger in my hand
As I looked away I felt a tear,
Cause the devil and I were one in the mirror
        —*Donato Rigg*

Love Of My Life

Oh, love of my life,
Oh, wonderful guy,
I love you so much,
I hope you know why!

You fill my life with smiling faces,
You make me happy,
And treat me gracious.
I love you for this!

I'll never, no never, love a man
As much as I love you!
I hope I never have to love anyone else
From now till the end. This my love, is true!

Oh, love of my life,
Oh, wondrous man,
Love me now,
As tender as you can!

Never, no never,
Leave me alone,
I'll love you forever,
On my own!
        —*Rebecca Turner*

Faded Youth

As I sit here alone in the dusk of eve, bended down on one old knee,
I see behind me all the years of youth, of joys and sadness
And of glorious truth. I think of the loves I used to have;
Numerous they were and this heart made glad.
Now I am wrinkled and gray and can hardly see
As I sit bended down on this old knee.
But my heart is young and restless and hot
With the love I once had but never forgot.
True love is precious and true love is rare;
Worth all its burdens and all its cares.

But the day is over - the sun has set;
The end of my days I have surely met.
So not long shall I sit here in the dusk of eve,
Bended down on this old knee, thinking of life and its treasure
chest. This old self is weary and wearing out; worn by time
and the face of age. Up I'll rise from this long lived life
full of tears and of strife. I'll pluck a rose from the bush
next to me; its life, too, gone out; finished with Earth as I,
Oh Earth, am finished with thee, bended down on this old knee.
        —*Melba Lee Atkins*

Facts Of Life

The joy, the pain, the loss, the gain,
    On my heart it leaves a stain.

Happiness, fault, and jealousy,
    These are elements of you and me.

Certain things will bring me fears,
    Inspiration, emotions feelings and tears.

I laugh, I cry, I weep a while,
    The power of depression can halt a smile.

Love grows distant and hearts will break,
    The thought creates a giant ache.

Live with this fact, it's part of life,
    But don't give up, conquer strife!
        —*Angela Bayliss*

Untitled

You drift through my window
    On radiant beams of sunlight
And gently warm the inner depths of my soul
    Banishing the cold emptiness of night.

I rise then-to greet the morning
    Which seems most glorious, fresh and new
And I feel not the slightest sadness
    For though alone, I am not without you.

Your warmth, your love, your tenderness
    Permeate my world and gently fill
My hungry soul with more than words can express
    And though we are apart, I feel you still.
        —*Mary Eileen Dressell*

In An Empty Room

Your memory haunts me
On the flashing glint of a searing blade
in the shadows of a drowsy night.

The eyes of dark when time
    stood still
        silently screaming to see the next framed piece
move faster than words could pass
between minds and mouths together

        alone

Carelessly cut, cursed, like a scar,
Remaining forever
unwanted.
        —*Melissa Jaten*

If We Wish

Have you ever heard of, "Hungry Hollow,"
    Or seen those living in a Similar Wallow?
So many seem to thrive — others always follow
    To this place called, "Hungry Hollow."

    Sometimes known as, "White Trash,"
        By those who are so Brash
    Loftily thinking the Phrase a Smash
    While knowing not — caring less of backlash
        By such Balderdash.

History is alive with, "Hungry Hollows," blight
    And shows a future not to bright
We can, "If we wish", correct the plight
    Of, "Hungry Hollows," and make things right.
        —*Wendell E. Hauenstein*

The Introvert

What is she fit for? but solitude,
One day perchance she'll have a friend,
But the greater part of her future days
Will be spent in utter seclusion.
We cannot complain
We've got to understand her.
But we cannot perceive what is solitude
and how far it extends.
And so she struggles on through life,
Through every sorrow and difficulty.
For to her a crowd is not company,
Faces are just a gallery of pictures,
And there is no love.
What other possible comfort could she
have, but solitude?
None, none that could make her happy
in her unhappy state.
A desolate woman, fighting within herself,
Crying for peace, and yearning for happiness,
Yet only finding self-destruction.

—*Jennis M. Paul*

Wanted

Wanted; one goodhearted man, to fulfill all my dreams.
One who can be trustworthy to be part of my team.
Must be a tall, handsome gentleman, that is sweet.
He should be willing to give hugs and kisses along with lots of
    treats.
I also require a lot of attention.
A devoted man that would share his love and affection.
In return this man will receive a woman that will do her best
    to make him the happiest man ever.
If you qualify you can be my valentine for the rest of eternity.
My last requirements is that you have the name Donald Dettman.

—*Rose Mary Hunter*

The Poet

Only the poet can see day and night.
Only he can see fear and danger.
His words are powerful, strong, and useful.
Only he knows the meaning of life and death.
Why is it only he? Why is he the only to know?
Because he watches. He listens. He tells.
He is the guardian of nature, the world.
He controls the way we feel about things.
He could see a rock as a group or race,
Bonding together, to form a mass that can—
Never be broken. His life is paper and pencil.
Nothing more but his mind. His imagination.
He has no worries. No dangers. He is the poet.

—*Nicole Kendall*

Untitled

Exchange with me what's inside.
Open up your heart.
Close your eyes.
Allow your mind to become completely free.
Search your heart and soul.
Am I there?
Can you see?

Grey clouds lurk amidst the sky.
As the options enter in and out of your mind.
Fear overpowers you - what you have longed for.
If there were some way to be certain -
    that the keys within your grasp
Could somehow permit your entrance.
I have but one question -
Would you take a chance on unlocking the door?

—*Lori Turbyfill*

Jessica

We returned a little body to earth today,
Only the shell that housed her soul.

Her spirit lingered on awhile,
Not wanting to leave that day.
But her soul yearned for her Father,
With Angels waiting to guide her way.

She wanted to tell each loved one,
There was nothing to fear.
She tried to talk to Mommie, but Mommie couldn't hear.
She tried to talk to Daddy, but Daddy wasn't near.

She spoke to me, finally getting thru.
"Hi Gamma, it's pretty here, everything just like new.
There's lots of children to play with.
Picked you some flowers and a Daisy too.

Now Gamma don't worry about me,
I have to go.
One day you will see me again,
And Gamma you will know."

—*Verna D. Collett*

Loves Uncertainty

The darkness of the room is comforting,
Only the silence is broken by the heartbeat
which seems incredibly loud.
Pounding, pointing out thoughts and memories
of a days past, filled with joy and then sorrow-
So beautiful it was, and then as if the mighty
powers of fate commanded,
It was suddenly ripped away-left to melt in the
rain-echoing back like the heartbeat-
the heartbeat that the ear upon it pounded for its own.

In the darkness sleep is waiting, but the sleep must wait.
The heartbeat is much too intense, the memories
have too much meaning.
The heartbeat pounding out a cadence reminiscent of
leaders fallen before, just as it did today.
The night is long and empty-sleep would be a grateful release.
But then, what now of tomorrow? Will the emptiness still be there?
The heartbeat still pounding for what was-or is-
or never to be—.

—*Sandra Bishop*

Our Lonely World

I scream into an empty room
    only to hear the silence,
A tear trickles down my cheek
    As I recall all the violence.

Once innocent and pure,
    full of colors so bright,
But colors soon fade,
    leaving us with a world as dark as night.

The homeless kids sleeping on streets,
    and drugs that control the mind.
Look at the mess we've got ourselves in,
    I hope someday the old world we will find.

What happened to children's laughter,
    and the smell of roses so sweet,
The roses, like our dreams, are broken,
    and our children, by parents, are beat.

We must fight back at all cost,
    if we're ever to see happiness again.
To not even try and only give up
    would be our most tragic sin.

—*Beth Anne Butler*

Them And Us

You and I could maybe visit him and her
  Or, they could come and visit you and me.
I think that they and we would certainly get along,
  Especially him and me.

But, I don't see how you and me
  Could quietly stand by
While you and her just talked about
  The faults of he and I

We could explain to her and him
  How the two of we both feel,
And then let them brief you and I
  On how him and her think. Still -

Would be nice if we and they
  could positively agree
That he and she (or him and her?)
  Concur with you and I. (me?)
    —*John E. Hemmert*

Deep Blue

  The sun rises over the horizon, on a burst of yellow and
orange and red and blue.
  Blue forever running beautiful; light strikes your eyes with
a sparkling enigma.
  When I gaze into your eyes, I see blue sparks, blue that
never runs, blue sparks of life.
  Not of just any life, life being so precious, it is my life.
  The blue runs so deep, deeper than the soul, deep as my love.
  So modest, as you hide from the light, but your beauty
cannot be masked.
  Your eyes are so gentle, but the beauty springs forth at me.
  Love surrounds us like bees surrounding the queen, love
protecting us.
  My love runs deep as the blue sea, as broad as the sky, as
dark and mysterious as the universe.
  So reach deep within my heart and mind, and let me know you
will be there for me, for all of time
  Reach deep within your heart and mind, I will be there for
you, for all of time.
    —*Roland L. Hernandez*

To My Son

As I look at the sunset behind the horizon, I wonder, how many
other horizons it is setting behind, and to amaze so many
wondering young eyes. As dusk falls on this lonely town, a
church bell rings calling the people to commune, and a man
on the corner, with a guitar, plays a sad, sad tune. In the
graveyard, many in black are gathered around, their loved one,
who is now being lowered into the ground. A man in a uniform
gets out of a car, a man proud of his country and what he has
done, and now cries, as his family comes running to greet him,
so happy that he is home. And me, I sit in this open field,
with my senses observing every little thing, from seeing the
deer come out to feed, to hearing the whippoorwills sing. And
as a wind blows across this open field, creating these waves
of gold, my Grandfather told me this story once, when I was
only 6 years old.
    —*Tremayne Harer*

"There"

There is pain in the mind of the plan of the future
There is freedom in the corner of the room of the unknown
There is trust in the hand of the lord of the lonely
There is humiliation in the way of the glory of the hatred
There is sorrow in the eyes of the weapons of the masses
There is truth in the crevice of the soul of the man
There is where I am
There is where I am
    —*Robert Schnoor*

Chimay

Up top and straight ahead, chipped rock.
Others step to it, creviced and clayish
At the mouth. Lizards mate, away from there.

Shady, the sun leaves in the sky
Alone, its own wintry orbit
And scorches a way through seasons
To make other sides visible.

Cut.
A blood-red run interrupts
One clear ripple, you wading in
With directions of wind across water.

Eternities from here, in windows
Scaled corpses laid in ice
Preserve stares, iridescence, the scent
Of burning feathers on the riverbank,
And memories of the way this path bends in two

Hiding when suns go down.
    —*Shari*

As One

Though my skin is not of the same shade,
Our blood runs true like that of our ancestors.
Together we soar with the eagle.
Our spirits are as free as the wind.
As one, we run with the doe,
And swim the stream like the fish.
In the mountains, trees whisper,
Telling of our people and their past.
Today, we need to stand as one
Fighting together to keep alive all that
they believed in,
And taking pride once more in what it means
to be Indian.
    —*Lisa Forrester*

Home

Can there exist a better place than this,
Our house hidden far back in these trees?
With walls so tender as a remembered kiss,
So wonderful are the memories of these.
Is there a home on the face of the earth;
A residence shared with nature alone.
With gardens risen carefully by gentle hand;
With the powers of unity so known.
Surely there are those believing in better;
More special than the touch of our ways.
But there lies no shame in the minds of these debtors;
For they're struggled long, tiring days.
Is it true there are spaces more precious than these,
With streams spilling into clearer rivers;
Holding within its grasp in eternal seize
The true beauty of being a giver.
There simply cannot be a place more special than ours;
Where the land and the men become unified.
With our plush green lawns blooming in spectacular flower,
And the most important aspect is having tried
    —*Sheila Marie Springer*

Day By Day

There's things to remember as we grow older
There's things to remember to strengthen the soul
In the midst of the darkness there is always the light
The moon in the midnight the sun in the mornings
So beautiful and bright
There's things to remember as we grow older
God made it this way to strengthen the soul
    —*Ruth N. Mims*

Eternal Journey

Before mortal birth, as here on this earth;
our journey we did pursue.
    Intelligences there, in that place somewhere;
when life was thought to be new.

    Then in spirit form, as child in Gods arm,
that first estate to live;
    In wisdom to grow, His grace was to know,
allegiance we each did give.

    Decision we made, His laws we obeyed,
to salvation plan agreed;
    That agency to use, the evil refuse,
our souls would thus to be freed.

    We to earth, through this mortal birth, so came;
probation to fulfill;
    That journey we took, heavens comforts forsook,
to exercise our own will.

    In mortal sojourn, our destiny earn,
by what we shall here to do;
    In heavenly place, those steps retrace,
eternal journey pursue.

                        —Rodney Perkins

...In The End

All of us make mistakes that we regret;
Our minds filled with illusions trying to create the perfect
Life that can only be found in some fairy tale.
"Easy Street";
Only to find out the meaning of life is what we forget.

Sure, I too would love it if life were peaches and creme;
But that would take out the fun and there would be no challenge
Ask yourself this:
"Who likes everything easy - Without a challenge?"
Not I!
It would be like a hypothetical, illusion-filled dream.

We have to take our lives day by day with our honor to defend;
Taking the bumps and bruises, the ups and downs that life
Has determined for us.
To open our eyes and cope with the reality that does not only
Exist in a dream world or in a fantasy novel,
And to take on hardships we normally ignore.
Only to find out that somehow, someway it'll all work out...
IN THE END.

                        —Kevin A. Zubeck

Our World Turns Round And Round

Cold and icy, warm with sun,
Our world turns round and round.
I swim through the ocean of crashing waves...
Then my feet touch the sandy ground.
Still our world turns round and round.
I trudge through the snow covered tundra,
The wind whiplashing my face,
I have long to go, I am far from home,
But I try to keep a steady pace.
Still our world turns round and round.

                        —Rachel Billos

Ode To The I.R.S.

I was sittin' at home with my feet propped up
Out in my drive came this pick-up truck.
Then came the bangin' on my front door.
I don't ever have company any more.
As sweet as I could I said "Who is it please"?
We're the I.R.S. puttin' on the squeeze.
We'll sell your house, pictures and car
We don't give a damn who you are.
We did it to Red and Willie too
Now we're fixin' to do it to you.
All these years of work gone in a flash
Cause someone was to lazy to earn his own cash.
Let me tell you something, hear what I say.
Count your own money and do it every day.
I've got a surprise for you revenue men.
I made it once, I'll make it again.
With this little ditty I'm goin' for the gold.
That's all there is my tale has been told.

                        —LoNetta White

Sculpture By The Inner Child

Sculpted family—frozen time, fleshed in stone,
Outlined by the hand's clear, artistic trace
Of childhood perceptions we saved in bone.
A mapped memory of a foreign place
That shows hurt, shame, and fear standing unnamed
Behind Mama and Daddy. All blocked, made untrue
By the viewer who comes with feelings lamed
To examine this portrait carved in rue.
Strong, dark, dreadful stroked connect in the heart.
Child artist's intent achieve—past broken
Into—the adult can accept his part
When anger and grief, at last, are spoken.
Becoming real, in commune, we can bring
Our child out to write hymns of self to sing.

                        —Marie Kochick

"Ode To Friendship"

Friendship is a thing to treasure
Over the years it gives a lot of pleasure
It may be simple like a walk in the park
Or perhaps bringing sunshine, when things look dark.

Through your illness friends are there
All your life they show they care.
Good friends are always there to help you.
They also encourage you in all that you do.

They are there with you if you have to cry
Always accepting you and not asking why.
Give your friends the time of day.
Listen patiently to what they have to say.

Friends will come and friends will go.
Each one is someone special you know.
Times may come when you don't agree
But all will turn out fine because you're friends you see.

If tragedy should befall a friend
Be there with them to the end.
Don't take advantage of a friend please
Or you may find that friendship will cease.

                        —LaVerne Bauldry

Fly My Child

Fly my child, fly higher than birds dare to soar!
  Overcome the obstacles I surely cannot predict.
Learn from my mistakes, my pains, my tears.
  Conquer the errors you must encounter.
Hold tight to ethics that will heighten your flight.
  Walk proudly! Step surely!
Dance by the music that is righteous and wise!
  Not that which is prerecorded for you.
Know where you're going
  and the road
    that will take you there.
  Fly my child! Fly higher and farther than any one dare!

—Shirley Howell

The Summer House

The summer house sits high on a hill
Overlooking a stretch of smooth white sand.
There two small children search and find
Small bits and pieces of contraband.

The waves are slapping the rocks offshore
Creating a cover of sea-green foam.
An old man goes by with his dog on a leash,
Keeping him close, lest he should roam.

Sea gulls overhead rising and falling
On air currents with graceful ease,
Now and then gliding down to pluck
An unknowing fish from the sea.

Far in the distance is a small white dot.
Could it be pirates? Of course not, you say.
It's just a boat with several large sails
Riding the wind on a glorious day.

The surf, the sand, the sun and breeze
All combine to make a true dream,
For those who come to share quiet times
At the summer house by the sea.

—Nancy J. Kidd

The Refuge Within

The world is full of pain,
Pain's instruments are always within reach,
But refuge is always within reach too.
With each beating,
Pain emerges.
With each shouting match,
Pain arises.
With each slap,
Pain erupts.
Cruelty is reality,
Pain is reality,
But dreams are a refuge.
Within I escape,
I escape pain.
Within I find a world,
A world of peace, love and kindness.
Security and safety are discovered within me.
Dreaming becomes my refuge's building bricks.

—Juanita Jones

Heavenly Meditation

Wild are the animals that roam this earthly surface.
They combine with the universe, the bright and soft
expressions, to rule the world with heavenly meditation.
With unique coordination and mad determination, they
travel with the wind and are known to pretend, but the
natural essence which is truly beheld is expressed by God,
His gift to this world.

—Tanya Dodd

Commute

In my mind's eye...I see
Paths unfolding right before me
A myriad of cars in lineal procession
Moving onward in a continuous course
Through a confusing network of passages
Impediments thrown in periodically to hinder the flow
Unforeseen obstructions to block the circulation
Numerous faceless beings in cars rushing together
Craving for harmony in the parade
Making that daily journey through the course
An objective to reach that destination of employment
Tomorrow...unfolds another week of commute.

—Suzanne Notario

The Rose

The beauty of the rose lies deep within,
Patiently waiting for life to begin.
It must be nurtured, and given care,
Then it can find its way anywhere.

And with the warmth of the sun,
It knows its life has begun
Its journey to find the way
And reaches for the sky, it begins today.

And in the spring when life is new,
A bud will form just for you.
If you gently care for it, I suppose,
Soon you will see the beauty of a blooming rose.

Roses touch the hearts of some,
But some touch only the heart of one.
And in that moment you see and feel,
And know that life is very real.

—Allis Joyce

August

August, a time for reflection and redemption
  paying for emotions that were unexposed

Everything matters, whether small or large
  regardless of timing and circumstance

  Life's many faces remind us that
    human existence is significant

Fate, destiny, and luck control and guide
  the reality that we encounter and endure

  It's a game of inches applies to
    every facet of personal intervention

  August reminds us of a story about
    thirteen little birds on your doorstep

  Singing songs of freedom, but
    what does freedom create?

  Happiness? Sorrow? Joy? Anger?
    Maybe, but not necessarily

Therefore our struggle must continue through
the hazards of uncertainty that clutter our path

Because the cliches of freedom, perseverance,
and success will become the reality that we seek

—Vincent Taliano

My Head On A Stake

A stiff piece of wood intrudes my skull,
Penetrating the chant that is my brain,
Shadows dancing over my cold flesh,
Dark red rain falls where my feet once stood.

As my flesh begins to darken, and my blood begins to harden,
The cockroaches of humanity begin to sing
A hymn of sorrow, thinking of unattended lesbian desires.

Then the sky begins to darken, and the mourners,
close to orgasm, begin to harden,
And they all rip off their shrouds of black,
Fulfilling erotic daydreams, they hit the sack.

And my head, still on a stick, opens its eyes, begins to weep
It knows my body is gone, never to have pleasure again.

Insects buzzing, bizzing, chirping,
Smell rotting flesh, free for the taking.
The worms come together for an Orgy!
To be held in the shell where my brains once stood.

—*Michael Ray Wallace II*

City Life

    Big cities; have lights and sounds,
People happy, sleeping, talking, and full.
Big people and small people in the city.
Do you have any pity?
People begging with all their might.
Do you have a dollar?
People dancing, drinking, having fun.
Not a lot of harm was done.
Dogs barking, children laughing, and
cars screeching.
Too many people and things in the
city.

—*Trish Rhynes*

Alive

From the artist's hands spread emotion throughout
    People's limbs, making them feel alive.
From the musician's instrument pours something relative
    to life.
From the comedian's witty lines contagious laughter
    is ignited.
From the painstricken homeless emanates a tragedy
    Not to repeat, but to fear.
From the old bookkeeper's deepest wrinkles remembrances
    of old loved ones come, making them feel alive.
From the poet's viewpoint of life, tired and abused,
    Come the underlying reasons,
    Making people question
        Feeling alive.
—*Michelle L. Martin*

Peppermint Peppermint

Peppermint peppermint, tasty and yummy.
Peppermint peppermint, there good for your tummy.

You can eat them for breakfast
You can eat them for lunch
But whatever you do don't eat them with punch.

Peppermint peppermint, I really love you.
But you must understand I can't really hug you.

Peppermint peppermint, I can eat you, I can lick you.
Peppermint peppermint, But I dare not kick you.

—*Amy Gundersdorff*

Reverence For Life: Tribute To Albert Schweitzer

One of the gifted 'giants' of our time —
Physician, theologian, musician,
Philosopher, humanitarian,
Medical missionary and writer —
He subscribed to "a reverence for life",
And belief that man's God-given talents
Should serve to humanize this great, good Earth.
The memorable scene of a kitten
Walking across his desk as he sat writing,
Portrayed his respect for all living things,
In exchange for a comfortable life,
He chose to live in primitive quarters
In French Equatorial Africa,
Struggling to build medical facilities
For deprived natives in the wilderness.
To the query, "Why are we in this world?",
He would, unquestionably, have replied:
"Man should have a worthwhile mission in life;
Mine was to faithfully serve my brethren,
Ease their pain, and strive to enrich their lives".

—*M. E. Steiner*

Helen

The ebbing away of timeless hours, the forgotten
places, the loosing of belongings, and finally the
loosing of one's self. With this illness there appears
to be two deaths, one of mind, one of body. In the
beginning we tried to compensate...how simple to
believe she was just a bit forgetful, slow or confused.
She lost her grip on life as she witnessed the death
of her confident, her lover, her best friend. They
stood great time together, this woman and her
husband. Sadly we watched as this whistling, gentle,
fun loving lover of life retreated into unknown
world all her own. She didn't understand, she didn't
know us. She was oblivious to our world, the very
one she helped create. She was the fabric of our
lives. Now, left with only poignant recollections of her
all too short life, we feel quite alone. Our one true
connection with the world has been severed.

—*Barbara K. Rice*

A Prayer For Amanda

What a special little girl who's come into my life. And what a
pleasant personality full of sugar and spice. Though she does
have her moments and is not a pleasant gal. She is today and
always will be my special little pal. And that sweet

irresistible love that she seems to spread all over. Oh, the
many things in my heart I have yet to show her. That special
twinkle in her eyes that always makes me smile. I promise to
guide her through life's every mile. And when my years have

passed and I have grown old, she'll be just bursting into life
so beautiful and bold. Oh, sweet Amanda you're such a
beautiful person and have so many gifts to give. Hold onto
that talent and your values for as long as you shall live. And
whenever life gets you down and things just don't seem right,

just look my way and I'll be there to give you my advice. And
when my time comes to depart this life of frustration and
confusion, I'll be happy just in knowing that you are real and
not an illusion. And you'll carry on without me with your
strong courage and hope. And with the many disappointments in
life I know you'll be able to cope. May God always bless you
and keep you very close to his heart. AMEN
—*Tammy L. Blankenship*

Who Am I

Who am I? Though I be me.
Please show me, dear God, that I might see.
Who am I, as in this life I stand.
So as of this world, I may better understand.

This flesh and bones, that compose my body,
Does not even start to be.
These billions of cells and nerve fibers
Are still only a part of me.

If I were dead and only my body left.
Still yet it would not be me.
For we are two, my body and me
I'm so much a part of it, as it is a part of me.

Then who am I, though I exist, in the confines of
  this skeletal being.
As I go through life, and it carries out my every desire
  and need.
Who am I? This I think I will never get to know.
For who I am is a secret, that only God will know.

—*Lou Dishman*

"Living For Jesus"

Living for Jesus, Oh what peace
pleasures abound me never cease,
trying to please him in all my cares,
Seeking assurance that he is very near.

Drying my tears pressing along,
Thanking him for a heart of love songs
Discipline my life in strict obedience
Knowing his sweet holy spirit is here to stay

Knelling in prayer and finding him there.
Casting upon him all my troubles and cares.
Praying with strangers that come to my door,
pointing them to the heavenly shore,

Witnessing for him in the streets,
Talking with people I happen to meet
Seeking last souls that's gone astray
pointing them to the heavenly way.

—*Kathleen Buchanan*

Baby Fingers

Little fingers in the air
  pointing, patting everywhere
In his ear, mouth and eyes
  can't control, and so he cries.

He feels of everything he sees
  pulls and takes things off the shelf
Hasn't learned to say please
  selfish wants all for himself.

As he learns and can control
  he'll learn to count his fingers and toes
He'll learn just what they are for
  tying shoes and opening doors
Writing, painting when he's five
  creating things before his eyes.

—*Mary Turner*

Weather

The wind blows, the rain falls.
The tornado hits, mother nature strikes.
Trees falling, sea rising.
God tries his best, mother nature keeps on going.
God wins, mother nature gives up.
Finally the storm stops, the sun comes out.
O' what a beautiful day, lets go out to play.

—*James Henson*

Two Waves

Two ocean waves of blue. Top by crowns of heavenly white foam.
Poised and cocked like a scorpions tail before striking.
Strong, powerful, fragile and vulnerable.
Dominate, in control, racing mindlessly forward.
Rushing in far to quickly.

A short, intense existence.
Determined to experience all they can.
Speed their addiction. Propelled by natures breath.
Reaching,
Surpassing natures summit of narcissism.

Suddenly, violently they crash. Crumbling, disassociate from
the past.
Desperately attempting to reach further and further inland.
Wringing out all that is within themselves.
Reaching and retreating. Reaching and retreating.
Frantic and futile.

Exhausted and spent they recoil.
Resting, recuperating and refueling.
Regenerating themselves for the return to the vicious cycle.
Once again to delve furiously into their world.

—*Michael Byrne*

The Idea Of A Lifetime!

The sands of time slowly
  polishes away.
Our painful thoughts of yesterday.
  As the grind-stone easily eats the knife.
We all loose our lust for life.

  The city will always have its lights.
And all the days will have there nights
But the singers won't always have their voices
  And the conformists won't
  always make the choices.

There might always be a God above,
  But no matter what lovers like us
  will always love.

—*William T. Hawkins*

Gift Of Our Father

  Hark now what this roaring thunder
  pounding through my head and chest?
  Help me now I'm going under,
  my love for you won't let me rest.

I see your face, though in a frame,
  (the water's come 'tween us again)
my heart goes reeling, calls your name,
how can such joy come through the pain?

For though we're 'part, cast shore to ocean,
  heart and soul we're bound in love,
  I, even here, feel your devotion,
  gift of Our Father up above.

  So when the tear runs down my face
  it speaks of pain, but sheer delight,
our love transcends all time and place
  while dreams of you and I unite.

These words of script are vain essay,
  no verse can ever hope express
  the ecstacy you send my way
  when I but glimpse your loveliness!

—*Andrew C. Buckland*

First Born

Dainty little baby hands, tiny baby feet,
Precious little rosebud lips, chubby chin so sweet.
Button-nose, two lovely ears, two sleepy, sleepy eyes,
Little angel all my own, to treasure and to prize!

You're such a tiny little thing, so sweet and so dear
I've waited such "an eternity" time, finally you're here!
I feel tightness around my heart, throat feels tighter too,
Somehow it seems incredible that I also belong to you!

I hold you gently in my arms, caress your soft, smooth skin,
I feel an overwhelming love "spring up" from deep within.
And so I hold you closer still, such joy I never knew,
Now I hold within my arms, my "dream of dreams" come true!

　　　—*J.M. Rusti Keith*

The Rain Begins

Waking to the morning light, I feel it's going to rain,
Pressing hard against the wind, I watch the birches strain.
Clouds so gray and ominous, chasing across the sky,
Twisting and turning silently, they quickly hurry by.
Lightning flashes, thunder rolls above a misty vail,
I see the massive shapes that form within the vapor trail.
Dragons, hats and castles and boats with flowing sails,
And trains go speeding through the dark, on shiny silver rails.
One by one each in turn, the drops come falling down.
Then slip away in unison, without the slightest sound.
Then ever so rapidly the rush becomes a roar,
As harder and harder, the rain begins to pour.

　　　—*Jeanne Arnold Liska*

Looking

I looked out the window, and what did I see?
Pretty birds looking for food, in the deep snow,
Because they are very hungry
The wind is blowing the snow wall around,
And the snow is getting deeper
Covering up there food more on the ground.

As I keep looking out the window,
the snow is coming down so fast,
And the snow keeps on blowing and drifting
Oh! The pretty birds are flying away
For cover and protection, as they knew they wouldn't last.
And it's very bitterly cold, windy and
snowy, for them to stay.

I looked out the window again, and what did I see?
The pretty birds came back
Looking for there food in the deep snow
As I know they are still very hungry
Pretty brave little birds, finally got
Some food on the ground, And I am still looking out the
window again, and that's a fact!

　　　—*Priscilla J. Galek*

The Wrath Of Dusk

As the day sun begins to fade,
Purple haze fills the room,
Darkness threatens and shadows loom,
Memories creep in the mind and thought
　　takes over,
A time gone by wanders in the heart,
A cry of pain is heard as the wrath
　　of dusk drives itself deep into the soul,
The body settles into unconsciousness
　　as it awaits the rise of the sun.

　　　—*Kimberly Fitzpatrick*

Seeds

Seeds that in a garden sow
Producing sprouts
We watch them grow
Depending on the type of seed
Could be a flower, vegetable or weed
Flowers unfold with petals so bright
Reaching to the sky for their sunlight
Soft falling rain bathes them ever so clean
Making them a glorious sight to be seen
Words are seeds we plant inside
Of every person we may greet
Some give laughter, some give dread
It all depends on the way they're said
Master gardener of all above
Till our soil with your love

　　　—*Sophie Maly*

Untitled

　　The brazen and brown arms of day,
　　pull my limp and uncaring body from
　　the soft and spellbinding lips of night.

　　Night understands my tears
　　Day dries up my oceans of loss,
　　　They both care for me.

　　Day knows of my secrets
　　Night hides all the unspoken truths,
　　　They both protect me.

　　Night listens of troubles
　　Day consoles the dark spots of my soul,
　　　They both sympathize with me.

　　Day hardens the cast around my true self
　Night cloaks the daggers of hurt from the curious,
　　　They both hide me.

　　　—*Nicole A. Hermann*

Society

The people of the time begin to realize the horror and anguish
　　　　　　　put forth.
All of them begin to visualize what they have become, what they
　　　　　　　are worth.
Entrapped in a world created by those of the same kind they
　　　　　　　attempt to make change.
Yet they do not succeed because many still believe and act in
　　　　　　　the old ways.
Therefore nothing has been altered and some wonder why their
　　　　　　　lives have not been rearranged.
And the time continues and passes by with life still the same
　　　　　　　everyday.

　　　—*Karin Coger*

Dare To Read

Go ahead, take a trip through life,
Read a Book;
Romance, adventure, and new places,
Just have a look.
Peek into the future,
Look back, into the past;
Let your mind wander,
Read slow, make it last.

Learn new ideas, remember the old;
Books and words can be tables of gold.
So learn to read! It's the right step ahead;
Seek it! Find it! Let your mind be fed!

　　　—*Pamela Stewart*

430

Listen To The Wind

Listen to the wind, hear what it does say
Read the stars, and you know where your destiny lay
Listen to the river, as the water does flow
It is telling me, my life is aglow.

Life is not always as it seems
'Til I hear the birds chirp and sing
Then I know, I can always have my dreams.

Listen to the wind as it gently blows
Just like two hearts that already seems to know
Love is like the wind, it can be harsh and cold
And at times very bold, or it can be gently and true
When you really know it's clue.

Listen to the wind, when it talks to you
When our lives we make each other blue
Listen to the wind, as we start each day anew
Then in your heart, you will know, I will always love you.

—*Nicole M. Aldrich*

The Mockingbird

Have you ever listened to a mockingbird sing?
　Really listened?
What mechanism to produce such thrilling
　notes of melody!

Need we ask what Infinite power
Put together that magnificent reel
　Of pure melody, intrigue, and song?

This tape of God unwinds
And plays and plays.

—*Velma O. Owen*

Untitled

Yes, there it stands; a prey to nature's knife
Rejected - lost forever from all that is today.
It's now an ancient relic - so they say
That house which proudly bore the fruits of life.
But once before it's current age of strife
When sun had shined on paint all fresh and gay
And windows mirrored hope from every ray
Its hearth was haven to a man and wife.
Abandoned now, a grave above the ground
With timeless tales of love forever sealed -
Its shattered glass upon a dreary mound
Lies with the fading paint that time has peeled.
Not wind nor rain will ever cease their sound
'Til all existing things are forced to yield.

—*Salli Bright*

Walking With The Wind

Some times as I walk through the city at night, I
remember back to when I was a boy living in the country.
I was born and raised in the mountains and that is where
my heart will always be, walking with the wind, and only me.
Looking at snow capped mountains year round, with a cool
breeze and fresh air, pine trees as big as the eye could see,
I think that was the only time I was truly happy. There
was never a hurry or a rush of people moving frantically
about, but always a happy smiling face to ask "how ya doing"
and really mean it. Everyone had the time to listen because
there were no strangers to these people.
Sometimes as I walk through the city at night, I look up to
see those billions of stars I used to see, only to be saddened
by the lights, sounds and screams of the city.

—*Sean D. Russ*

Our Friendship

In that period when you feel shut out remember our friendship
Remember how it lasts through the deepest, darkest moments.
How our friendship would last even though we were and still
are totally different. But we've shared so many feelings,
we've shared so many thoughts, we've shared so many laughs
that it tore me apart to think that we will drift apart. But
I will remember you until the day I die. You were there for me
when I needed you and you encouraged me but most of all you
made me feel important when it seemed like the world had tossed
me out. I told most if not all of my secrets to you and I
cried on your shoulder and laughed at our jokes. And I thank
you all for the memories and I list you not because I could not
fit all of your names on one piece of paper. And I remind you
again that you're my friends and what we have together, our
friendship will last forever, even if we drift apart.

—*Stacey Hughesman*

Remember

Whenever life is getting you down,
Remember I'm here. I'm always around
When nothing seems to be going your way.
Remember I'm here, only a phone call away.
Whenever you feel you're losing your mind.
Remember I'm here, I'm not hard to find
When everything seems to give you a scare.
Remember I'm here
Remember I care.

—*Jacqueline Ann Irvin*

"A Story Retold"

A picture, A color, A story retold
Remember the good times
Now you are old
Think of the bad times you tried to forget
Remember Mike, a guy you once met

Everything that happened
Seemed like a dream
Remember cheering for your football team

The music you listened to
The groups have all faded
Now the good stuff is all outdated

It's a picture, a color, a story retold
A faded life made out of gold

Tears form, the stars shine bright
Your life will be gone by the end of the night
The sky is dark, the moon is out
Your whole life is all you think about

It's a picture, a color, a story retold
The time has come
You are no longer old

—*Marcia A. Gauthier*

Prayer For Truckdriver

Oh Lord I am on the road with a heavy load
Please help me make it day and night
Keep me safe in good and bad weather
So I can keep it all together.
Give me the strength to deal with others
So I can think of them as my sisters and brothers
Now I can go collect my pay after my load
is delivered today.
I thank you Lord for your guidance in every way.

—*James W. Krull*

"And Then To Start Over Again"

The depth and darkness in his eyes,
reminds you of the darkest skies.
Reminds you of a secret passion,
staring at you in a fearless fashion.
A kind that finds your deepest sense,
and you can feel your body tense.
Then he seeks into your eyes,
sending your heartbeat into a dive.
Never have you felt such fear,
a single glance reveals a tear.
A tear of sadness or of joy?
A tear of pain from an inner boy.
One who cries for someone into oblivion,
and also the help that you are giving him.
Hold him close and never release,
hoping the moment will never cease.
Painful cries and angry shouts,
that's what heartbreak is all about.
Giving up and giving in,
and then to start all over again.

—Melodie Mathieson

"No More Deceptions"

How come it always seems, never to be able to
Remove these iron bars?
That we keep putting across our hearts.
Always feeling torn,
Our love has already been worn.
It was so full of glitter.
Then you made me turn so bitter
I've searched every season,
Trying to find a reason

Even though we've gone our separate way
I think about you every lonely day.
I wished I could forget the past.
Even though you said it would last.
All the deceptions.
And unwanted questions.
It was over so fast
We both knew it wouldn't last.

—Martha Jordan

Devoted 2 You

Are love, it is in your eyes wisdom always on your lips
respect in every touch.
When you speak the tones are so sweet the birds envy you.
Your hair is long and beautiful
a knight in this world of trolls
You are what every man only wishes he could be
You are not a fantasy or myth, you're real my love
Your name is the name of kings wisdom of centuries you possess
Who are you, your name is love, but I'll call you George.
My knight in shining armour love

—Terry Sunderland

Public School Death!

I escape from all fears.
Run out through a window or maybe a door.
Smoke comes you cough.
Escape from death.
Five feet from the door you drop.
Someone pulls you out and puts a sheet
over you. Now your family grieves for your
Lost life and then they put you in the ground.
Goodbye, you feel like saying to your family.
Goodbye pets. Goodbye everyone.

—Stephanie Harrold

"What's The Use?"

Can you figure out why...
responding to a cry for help often causes you to cry; or,
trying to find a problem's solution brings on a sigh ... a
sigh of frustration; should we "do-gooders" relent to the woes
of the world; and say: "What's the use? Why's the flag
unfurled?" Perhaps we should ... let things take their
course; but then, what satisfaction is there in remorse?

The newspaper beckons us to read the bad news; the newscaster's
style seems somewhat subdued; is it too much to ask that some
feeling be shown when hunger and death abound; perhaps it would
spoil the delivery or allow true character to be found.

"Oh, Say Can You See?" ... the beginning of truth; when you
walk down the street and you sense people's ruth ...lessness!
We could reach out and touch, in a sensitive way; but why get
involved; no one hears what we say!

Has life just become one challenging charade? May ...be. We
must look beneath surfaces we ourselves have made; so our
feelings and emotions long hidden may rise; and our true sense
of spirit will lift to the sky.

—Mickey Campbell

Stepping Stones

The clutching razored talonings of grief
Retracted and eased back their choking grip,
As gentler, warm-fleshed, outstretched hands and arms
Reached through the trance-like unreality
Of loss, re-opening small channelings
To verbal interchange.

Soft bandages of empathy, concern
And low-voiced muted words unrolled and wrapped
Themselves around the victim's raw-nerved wound
That healing might begin and "normalcy" return
On close-laid stepping stones invitingly
Untrodden, new and strange.

The very first uncertain, hesitant
And trembling step, though painful, lent a strand
Of courage for the next succeeding ones,
As like a healing limb, the healing mind
Grew stronger through maneuvering — to reach
And then surpass its former use and range.

—Mauricia Price

Retirement Age

Maturity has its rewards, though often hard to find;
Retreat in peaceful silence, search the channels of your mind.

From generations past, fond memories retrieve;
The hoarded pleasures in your heart, your thoughts again receive.

Don't prod your aching body, let it rest and meditate;
Contentedly relax and smile, recall and concentrate.

The picnics and the sing-a-longs, you enjoyed them most of all;
The children's funny antics, you laugh as you recall.

Participating in the sports, you gave stiff competition;
You joined in all the merriment, without false inhibition.

Now you deserve the honor, you've reached commencement stage;
Accept award in graciousness, enjoy retirement age.

Your life's lovely tapestry, woven in your mind;
Day-dream and reminisce, cherished beauty there you'll find.

—Ruth M. Kattau

The Lake

The lake mirror's the moon's full glow
revealing a serenity I long to know.
Beckoned here by a still, small voice
I came not by chance but by choice.
A pink, pale sky announces day's dawn
And very soon now I must be gone.

As light begins to steal the night
I pledge to return when the time is right.
Hoping the next time that I can stay
and no other voice will call me away.
Before I leave this much I know
amid these woods in sunshine or snow
Lies a faithful friend true and serene
the likes of which I have never seen.

You gave much more than I gave thee
You gave me peace and a lasting memory.
Farewell my friend until another time
When I'll return to claim what's mine.
A way of life apart from the rest
enjoying God's grandest and very best.

—*Ronald Bailey*

Solitude

Clear echoes of mortar shell
Ring ominously on shattered ears

Deaf to human suffering
Blinded to graveyard tears

War's devastation surrounds us
Wrapping its cloak of terror

In a choke hold indifference
To suffering scattered thereabouts

How brutal are the thoughts of man -
Whose solution lies in weaponry -

Lo, these many centuries
Controversy wears the mantle of war -

When will we end this heretical dissonance
Replacing it with rationality's tune -

Time is running out, mother earth -
To repair your battle - scarred face

Each second of conflict portends
A threat to the human race

—*Stanley S. Reyburn*

We Used To Touch

More than with our hands, we used to touch. Our
Hearts and minds and eyes were bound with steel. Back
Then, our souls were welded; much of life's sweet
Bounty flowed to us. We never felt the
Prick of ripping thorns; our love was armor. We
Did not know what anguish we would feel.

Oftentimes my face was soft with laughter;
Months and years escaped a hint of pain. I
never knew that death could strike 'til after
Lifeblood ceased to flow within my veins. My
Face, my face no longer soft; disaster had
Loomed with heavy gloom, and brought the rain.

Now, however far the sunbeams venture,
Or how sweet the perfume of the Spring, my
Eyes will always doubt, and look with censure
At the promises that lovers sing. My
Heart won't stand another deadly wrenching ... I'll
Never trust my all to love again.

—*Elvera J. Holroyd*

A Bed Of Roses

Hey! As we walk thru this life, we are walking thru a bed of
roses. And oh-o-o! The lovely fragrance, of those precious
roses to our noses! But hey! They're not always blossoming in
their fullness - opening up at all times their full beauty our
eyes to bless. But there's leaves, and bugs, and thorns which

also them adorn. One stem had none, another forty two, while
another had one hundred three thorns. For every bush has many
more thorns which prick, hurt and even scratch by far than
there are blossoms within a rose garden path. So unless you
walk in care as you pass by there and heed the dangers lurking

there with care, you can be hurt as well as blessed! So you
must heed the signs as along life's pathway we tread while
being aware of the times. Enjoy the beautiful vision therein
as the roses in various colors flair for roses stand for love,

and love says in sweet fragrance for you I care! So enjoy and
receive the lovely fragrance and beauty of each flower, knowing
that one must walk in care and appreciation while there. Being
thoroughly aware of the rose bed and of every detailed part is
a very necessary knowledge deep down in our own heart, for as

we walk in life, we too must have the knowledge for total
success, we too must heed and walk in the fullness of our
Saviour to be blessed!

—*Virginia Todd*

Dave

He's a person who seems
    rough and tough.
And at times he is.
But when you spend sometimes
    and get to know him
    you'll find that deep inside
    he is really sweet and kind.
Dave is a person who can talk a lot,
    when he's in a good mood.
But when he's mad
    and he's not always glad,
    he'll hit the wall and not talk at all
He'll always be rough and he'll always be tough.
He'll always be sweet and kind
And hopefully Dave will always
    be a friend of mine.

—*Stephanie Crisman*

Free

I'd like to be a horse that's free
    Running long in the night with no fear, no fright.
The moon is lighting our way,
    The herd seems to frolic and play.

I run to the lake crystal clear,
    I see myself standing here.
It reminds me of the winter days
    That were filled with nothing but snow and haze.
With eyes of steel and a heart of gold,
    I shudder at the memory and push out the cold.

The wind is at my back, the morning will awake
    Soon the sweet breathe of dawn will herald another day break.
The field is quiet, cold, and still the only thing swaying
    is the daffodil.
    I dream of what I'm not, a horse that's free
But when I wake I must walk, not trot.

—*Robin Laskey*

Poets And Poetry

The kingly bard of ancient days, a poet of high esteem,
  Sang of his golden age and the many deeds of tribal fame.
The poet of today also speaks of victorious deeds supreme,
  Thoughts of love, life, joy and sorrow, and even blame.

Poets write tales of sad affairs, but also the melody of chimes
  Sometimes in the narrative, lyric, and even the humorous.
Poets agonize over words, and search for simple rhymes,
  For the poetic tale is always salient and marvelous.

Poetry is a way to recite a brief story never before heard.
  Imagination and a sense of beauty helps the tale along.
Poetry is a pleasing piece of fiction set to a rhythmic word,
  A three or four foot iambic helps create the scale of song.

Every word makes the song, lovers and even the fairy-king,
  Sound forth in lyrical language to tell a tale agog.
Poetry is a delightful way of saying things, even challenging,
  Or as some have said, Poetry is itself a thing of God.

One word more should be said, a poet must forever write.
  He hopes his favorite verses will give people pleasure.
Poets love to hear other poets and with ardent delight,
  And as long as man lives, poetry will remain a treasure.

—*Omer E Williams*

Autumn Has Arrived

The sweetness of Autumn all about us,
School days beginning with a polished flurry,
  Mums flaunting their bronze and golden glory,
  Leaves once verdant now drifting down.
Time to sit to dream of Summer's treasured fun,
While a languid haze shrouds the morning sun.
Skies of brightest blue and shorter days,
Lengthening shadows and flaming sunsets,
  Make us hasten now to collect
Odds and ends of fleeting Summer's fruits and seeds,
  Adding to our hoard for Winter's needs
    Ceasing Summer's active rush,
      We await Winter's solemn hush.
The sweetness of Autumn all about us
Holds the promise of another Spring.

—*Alta R. Johnstone*

Thanks Be To God

Thanks be to God for this land of ours. From sea to shining
sea. For mountains high and prairies wide. The rivers running
free.

Thanks be to God, for skies of blue. For the drifting clouds,
and the rainbows hue. For the glory of the setting sun, The
moon and stars, when night has come.

Thanks be to God, for those calloused hands. Which held the
plows, that plowed this land. For men of courage, and
integrity. In preserving this land's liberty.

And thanks be to God, for the right to vote- To help when 'ere
we can. Tho choose good laws, to live by. To protect the rights
of man.

Thanks be to God, for children's laughter- For the touch of your
loved one's hand. We have so much to be thankful for. In this
great and glorious land.

Thanksgiving day is every day. Every week, every month, every
year. God bless this land of America. The land we hold so dear.

—*Sandy Cron*

Descended From The Sea

I have eyes the color of the
sea on a stormy night, raging
and full anger yet, beautiful
and full of wisdom.

Like the sea I am angry for
all the hate and war in our world and as
waves of wisdom roll across the
shore, and tides of beauty wash up I
grow stronger, descended from the
sea me.

—*Amber Yankulov*

Timely Emotion

As the moments pass and each sequential
second brings forth a new tomorrow,
the thoughts and feelings of this
unstoppable future attract every feeling
of love and loneliness one heart can summon.
Although not only the future, but also
the past and the present fill my heart
with emotion. Frightening thoughts of
what may lay ahead compelled by joy and
troublesome moments which lay behind.
I can only hope that the love and joy
will fallow me when I am gone,
but I believe it shall, for it is
ever so strong.

—*James A. Wheat*

Crying Pain

Sit at your window.
See the rain.
Cry on your pillow
Feel the pain.

No one loves you,
No one cares.
No one hears you,
No one dares.

The blood is on your hands,
Resentment in your heart.
They take away what you love the most.
The pain is on your part.

They dangle your world in front of your face,
Then hide it from your eyes.
They think you'll forget all about it.
Out of sight, out of mind.

—*Sandy Kozina*

Bird Feeders In Winter

Slate Juncos are so very nice
Running around like little mice,
Down on the ground under the feeders
Picking up crumbs dropped by the eaters.

Blue jays run the small birds away from feeders
But then come downeys, red bellies, and flickers.
The harris sparrows are bullies too,
They even quarrel with their own crew.

The male Cardinal, a splash of red against the snow,
They come no matter how hard it blows.
Black caps and tufted titmice are my favorite sight
They take one seed and go, back and forth till night.

—*Russell L. Kelch*

Spring

Of the beauties of the seasons, nothing can compare with Spring
See the robins and the Sparrows, gleefully we hear them sing

From the swamp the Frogs are chirpin', in the air warm breezes blow
On the trees the buds are poppin', then green grass begins to grow

Now the snow and ice have melted, see the creeks a flowing high
See the Geese and Crows and Eagles, flying northward in the sky

Soon the flowers start a blooming. Soon the bees are buzzing round.
Then crickets start a creakin'. Spring has sprung with special sound.

Everyone has Springtime fever, kids a skipping school and such
They've been cooped up all the winter, you can't keep them
inside much

Such a pleasing, pleasant feeling, as the sunbeams warm the earth
Makes it seem a new creation, as the ground give forth new birth

All the seasons have their favor, all exceed in some great thing
There is one that tops the others, it's the season we call Spring

—*Roy Newland*

Merula

The fire in your eyes
Shows me the deepest, darkest part of your soul
The part you hide from all others
Where the real you lives with the real me
And your Raven locks tell me of your flight
While I sleep you lurk in the shadows
Waiting for me to give you life
But I'm scared of the sacrifice
Yet spellbound by your beauty
Then once more I look deep into your ruthless eyes
And in a second I am seduced once more
Your psychotic charm intrigues me
The alluring amulet of your being
Beckons me nearer
Enthralling me to rapture
As your lust for the crimson goblet
Thrills me, Chills me
Till I am brimming with terror
At the sight of your ivory skin, framed by your ebony hair
Until ultimately I am irreversibly inebriated by you.

—*Joni Diane Giallonardo*

Unconditional Love

Papaw was a wonderful man who always had patience and was kind
Patience is a virtue and rare when dealing with a child
Never harsh, but firm and someone to laugh with

Love that was unconditionally given
Never expected but always received
Unrestricted and complete
That is the Love that Papaw gave.

God is the same way with his children
Excepting our faults and loving us
Even when we hurt Him-this is what Love really is

Love that is unconditionally given
Never expected but always received
Unrestricted and complete
This is the Love that God gives.

I hope that because God Loves me that I can Love others
I want the Love of God to glow through me
I want to be able to forgive without a second thought

Love I hope I unconditionally give
Unrestricted and complete
I hope to show the Love God gives me.

—*Jennifer Repp*

Judged Too Quickly

Some folks proceed through life with tunnel vision.
Seeing in others only what is there
not bothering to look beyond
as they just do not seem to care.

Some refuse to see the good in others
they judge too quickly and they condemn
not realizing that the others may
think the same thoughts of them.

Never be too quick to judge others
on how they may seem to appear.
Open your mind warm your own heart
and your own vision shall become clear.

First impressions can be lasting ones,
seldom are we given a second chance
so always be the best you can be
as if you lived in a manse.

—*Peggy Sue Bernards*

Headstone Of Technology

Monday, February 8, 1993.
Seldom do the raindrops fall.

Earth bleached by the beaming rays of the sun
Deep cracks cut through
Giant pores of wind burnt skin.

Seldom do the raindrops fall.

Sharp, dusty, shrub rounds pierce the surface,
Clinging to the only moisture found in the air
Lonesome blades of gasp.

Seldom do the raindrops fall.

Once a forest,
  Once a field,
    Once a farm,
No more.

Seldom do the raindrops fall.

For the marks of human nature lay deeply
embedded in this stone.
Left beaten, raped, and forever now,
hardened and alone.

—*Phyllis C. Franco*

Tying The Knot

She is beautiful, she'll fit my needs.
She is perfect for my dirty deeds.
I stroke her strands, yet she doesn't feel.
Soon, without knowing, she'll make me squeal.
I position her after a while.
"God," I think, "she is so versatile.
She has the power to kill me dead.
She can save my life, perhaps, instead."
Slowly I enter into her hole.
I see she's stealing away my soul.
As I move and thrust I feel her tense.
The thoughts of pain and bliss are immense.
I lose all my breath as we unite.
Her strong hold on me is deathly tight.
Soon it's over and I do not move.
I told them I had something to prove.
I wasn't making love to my wife,
With rope and a tree, I took my life.

—*Scott Sanders*

Untitled

Out on the corner everyday
Sellin' the dope to get my pay
Dropped out of school at the age of 14
Told my parents to drop dead
And they asked what do you mean?
As you can tell they were high and drunk
On cloud 9 cuz of a single blunt
So they didn't care what I did or said
I don't even think they know I'm dead
Yeah I've gone to a better place
And I'm really glad to be out of that
   disgrace
Now I see that I was a fool
I should have said no to drugs and
stayed in school.

—*Angela Malarkey*

Moments

The moonlight drifts through the golden curls of his hair
sending a dreamy glow about him. A soft breeze comes to
dance with the highlighted leaves while the winding stream
races past carrying with it the soil of all life. The
stars glimmering in the warm, ebony night symbolize peace
and romance, and birds sing of sweet surrender. The touch
of his hand takes me to a place I have never known.
Children dance full of joy and life. An elder couple walks
hand in hand stealing a kiss as if they were teenagers, no
food is lacking in the world and no clothes worn. This is
a place of unbelievable love. This majestical night, my
beloved, is because of the bond we share.

—*Amy Clark*

Glorious Day

There once was a man
Sent from above
His name was dear Jesus
With a heart full of love
He walked on the earth
Just spreading God's word
There was so many that never observed
For upon on a cross his blood was shed
They pierced his side with steel instead
Then on the third day the rock rolled away
Jesus had risen! O glorious day
He promised his return in a fiery way
So kneel down to Jesus he'll save you today
Now the devil will deceive you in many ways
But never lose faith child there comes a great day
For Jesus is returning! Just as he said
It's life or death child your choice to be made
For Jesus is coming one glorious day!

—*Timmy Keen*

Public School Death!

I escape from all fears.
Run out through a window or maybe a door.
Smoke comes you cough.
Escape from death.
Five feet from the door you drop.
Someone pulls you out and puts a sheet
over you. Now your family grieves for your
Lost life and then they put you in the ground.
Goodbye, you feel like saying to your family.
Goodbye pets. Goodbye everyone.

—*Stephanie Harrold*

A Day In Paradise

There is a glare over the horizon, just as the silvery mist
Settles on the morning dew. My eyes follow the dark rough
Bark of a tree up into the blue sky until it meets a thick
Green blanket of leaves. The sound of the birds' harmonious
Song floods my ears and makes me feel as if I were singing
Along with them. As the wind blows the tall golden stalks
Of grass, it sounds as if the stalks were whispering to each
Other. An aroma of honeysuckles fills my nose as the breeze
Refreshes me. As I stroll down the path, I look to the right
And see the amber leaves drift slowly downward until they
Settle on the rippling water of a pond. Along the path is a
Beautiful light brown buck and his family feeding happily on
The green carpet of grass. As I casually stroll back down the
Path, I gaze wearily at the horizon. As the dark red ball of
Fire sinks into the water, I know that darkness will soon fill
The sky, and the day will come to end...in paradise.

—*Paul Mayer*

A Promise

Children of love see only light,
Shadows and darkness never in sight.
Beauty and color are endless pleasures.
Children of love bestow their treasures.
Heartless souls are those who would abuse,
Hopelessly frustrating, trying to confuse
These innocent souls, children of love,
Glorious gifts from the heavens above.
It is our duty, given maturity,
To protect these children and give them security.
Children of love, children of light,
We promise you guidance, love and insight.

—*Linda Caray Rude*

A Silent World

Her cries in the darkness of the night drown her dreams.
She cannot even hear her own tears fall.

Her pillow catches each hopeful wish as a leaf
blows by her window, soundlessly.

Silence envelops her every movement, every thought,
no one hears her scream for freedom in her trapped
shell of deafness.

Listening to the silence, she lets her heart absorb
all the sounds she can't share.

Each word slips through her precious hands.
No stranger understands her peaceful language.

She feels like a daisy in a field of yellow roses.
Although she is together with them, she has never
felt more apart.

A cricket plays a ballad on a hot summer night,
and the ocean whispers a story to the sand.
She cannot hear the familiar sounds that assure a
childhood memory. She revolves around a silent world.
Forever kept from the beauty of a reassuring voice,
or the echo from her own words.

—*Renee Caggiano*

My Mother

She's made of a sweet smelling rose
that blossoms its love to all she meets.
This special rose is
watered by God.
The warmth of the sunshine brings her joy.
Her sweet smelling perfume is as sweet as she is.
There is no other sweeter rose
than my mother.

—*Jean Bosman*

Mommy's Junk

This is a verse for my mother
She is not at all like another
Most mothers like cookin' and sewin' and such
But my Mom loves going to garage sales so much
Her house is a museum for second hand stuff
I've told her often that she has enough
The closets and drawers are full of used trash
I hate to think of all that wasted cash
Books, jewelry and stuff animals, too
Christmas trees, doilies and pairs of old shoes
Buttons, coasters and pictures ev'rywhere
This house is a jungle of junk I'll declare
She'll buy all of these items no matter the cost
Don't ever come visiting or you will get lost
I really must say she is sweet
Even though this house isn't neat
I can't find a place to sit down
If you don't believe me just take a look around
Every time the leaves I get ready for the junk to pour in
I still love my MOMMY and I think she is "TOPS"
But I sometimes wonder is the trash line will ever STOP!!

—*Susan E. Horton*

"What A Special Lady"

Her character was good, she had a good name,
She treated everyone equal and loved the same.
She was a Godly lady and taught us to do good,
She hoped and prayed that every one would.

She always had a lending hand,
Saying, by this, I'll help if I can.
No matter what color, race or creed,
This lady would help anyone who was in need.

This lady had faith, and she believed,
If you believed in God, you would receive.
She said, do good for evil, not wrong for wrong,
A home in heaven you will have, and it won't be long.

This special lady I've been talking about,
In my heart I love her, there's no doubt,
She is no other,
Than my sweet mother.

—*Anna Belle Cox*

A Lilac Flower

The stars are shimmering down tonight:
Shimmering down on you and me
And down on the little lilac tree.
I'm hoping that one will fall
Or, better yet, let them all
Come streaming down in a radiant shower
So I can choose seven to pin in your hair
And linger forever to adore them there.
But all I can give is a lilac flower:
Just my love and a lilac flower.

The star are glittering down to night:
Glittering down on you and me
And down on the little lilac tree.
These heavenly gems of light
Are leaning so near tonight
I'll pick some and with a mystical power
I'll fashion a veil for you of star lit lace
And with its star light I'll frame your precious face.
But all I can give is a lilac flower:
Just my love and a lilac flower

—*Mabelle Wiard Willmarth*

Untitled

When the noises stopped crashing around in her head
She found she could open her eyes
So ashamed of the horrible life she led
Untouchable, her world was all lies

How she got there she could not recall
Nothing since then had been too clear
She reacted badly if ever at all
Her sole motivation was fear

She moved as though she had no past
So confused, where could she start?
A life she knew would never last
For he had taken with him, her heart

—*Alexandra Pipitone*

Freedom

As he unlocks the chains with which he is bound,
he looks one last time at his friends all around.
He opens the door to see if it's clear,
without a sound for anyone to hear.

One last look at the cotton fields afar
which made him prisoner and gave many a scar,
one last look before he flees,
"At last," he says, "I'll be free!"

With his dark skin he is hidden against the night;
he is hopeful for freedom, yet full of fright.
He hides by day and runs by night;
he is scared, yet he continues his fight.

One dark summer night the sight of lamps appear,
and the bark of hunting dogs echo in his ear.
He knows he must run quick, or soon he will be dead,
for if the hunters catch him, they will hang him by the head.

Now cornered in the forest the hail of bullets start,
as the white men come upon him, he is hit in the heart.
He looks up at the white man as he feels his chest go numb,
and whispers to the murderer, "Now I have freedom. . ."

—*Bethany Hahn*

Hands

The Light of the Lord shone through his hands and
Left a delicate stain of love on
Everything he touched.
The gnarled knuckles pounded nails truly,
Bringing out beauty in the uneven symmetry of
Raw wood.
The Light drew warmth from fresh, dark earth
Squeezed through his fingers and
Rearranged in random rows.
The uncertainty of the future of a brand new
Leaf, turned over in the tender fingertips,
Grew into confidence.
The pages of a treasured tome, singed around the edges by the
Embers of time, were reverently turned
Without so much as a fingerprint
Left to signal the intrusion.
The love of a woman was gently kneaded,
Protected by a feathery cover of care and
Allowed to rise in the glow of independence.
They were the hands of a husband lifted up...

—*Deborah Donley*

Fear Of The Dark

There it stood with a black angry hood hovering over your
shoulder. "You turned in fright," there it was standing
in the shadowed light!"
You've taken a second glance and began to dance for it was
your shadow you glimpsed!
"You sigh in relief" and shake your head that you could of
scared yourself with such a lie!
You slowly turn and wave good-bye, and again you sigh!
Whew! I thought I was going to die!

—*Becky A. Becker*

The World's Most Valuable Resource

Speak softly to a child;
show your love and tender care,
Teach a child truth and goodness
and that beauty is everywhere.

Encourage positive, creative thinking,
help it grow and flourish strong,
Teach a child that to harm anyone
is very, very wrong.

Help a child know that nations
struggle for joy and peace,
Through methods of due process
That must never, ever cease.

Share the golden rule with all the children,
Who walk this earthly sod,
And know that every child is the handiwork of God.

—*Marie Therese Emery*

The Holy Brave Earth

The mandarin red sizzling sun hid itself once again,
Shutting down, in an ever ordered fashion with exactness,
Soooooo opposite from the white mans' chaotic mind,
Unordered, stubborn, these days tuned into universal evil!

When will so-called earthman learn what is real?
Inside adobe walls with manmade pillars, secrets are
contained.
The "anasazis" knew the sacred realities, of life, love,
Of balance and centering, of the "great spirits" truths!

The sacred lands still resound with life—if one
Will but listen with their hearts. Spirit guides roam
The lands, and their words echo through the canyons
Rimmed with wild red berries, and mossy green grasses.

Matates rhythmically tapped out the crushing of sacred corn,
The hunters ask permission of the deer to skin him,
But now silent screams from mother earth's parched lips
Show another side, the coyote howls for waterdrops,
Once more the givers of life have changed mother earth's
face!

—*Linda A. Sandknop*

The Escape

Although it still is only seven days
Since I first crossed the threshold of the cave
And emerged once more into the light,
I feel as though eons dragged by
While I was imprisoned there.
My soul lay, in shackles bound,
My mind huddled, fearful, bat-like
And shrinking from the light of day.
Until, with choking throat and bursting lungs,
Out of the fetid darkness I could explode,
Soar and glide into evening's golden glow
And exultantly inhale the free and fragrant air.

—*Mary M. Ince*

Remembering When

I was walking in the park today.
Sit for a while, and watch the children play.
Memories came back, to a time in my younger day.
In spite of myself, I had to say.
I wish I could really be a child again.
So happy, free, young, and innocent then.
And as I sit there, my mind wander again.
To a birthday, a party and now I can't remember just when.
Was it six or was it seven.
All I really know is that it was sheer heaven.
And so as I sit and watch the children play.
I decided, today would again be a special day.
So I got up, and went to play.

—*Aaron Watson*

Untitled

I'm sitting alone,
sitting, wondering if I'm going to come out of my sleep.
I'm sitting alone,
sitting and watching,
I'm sitting and wondering if I should stand, and if I
do who will catch me when I fall.

—*Tess Wickenhagen*

I Sit Beside Myself

I sit by a river of thoughts that roam my mind. There is a
slight storm in my brain, for my river is filled with flowers
of love, fires of hate, winds of change, and hearts
of loneliness, that create a waterfall of pain that aches in my soul.

I sit beside a rock that is in the path of my dreams. No
sleep can I get. I even have nightmares while I'm awake. In
my nightmares my dreams are corrupt, my life is destroyed, and
my soul aches more than before.

I sit beside my friend, my imagination. Big and brave it
is. It sits in the storm beside the sleep I cannot get. It is
thinking of the future that will never be. Of diamonds and
pearls that are set before a table given to a queen, of peace,
not a hint of war in the centuries to come, of happiness and glee
throughout history.

I sit beside myself, knowing that may never be.

—*Shauna M. Poete*

A Love Way To Equality

We are slowly climbing the protracted ladder to equality.
Slowly but sure, step by step,
another past due equity is bestowed.

> ...the end of slavery
> ...the end of segregation
> ...the right to vote

A haunting whisper and grey portraits of black struggles tear
at our consciousness. "It will get worse before it gets better"
(Hopefully the worst has past).

Nearing the top of this acclivity - the turn of the tide -
looking back, there is a feeling of achievement.

The funk of slavery is not in naked view and the revolting
bout of segregation is mere blur.

Yet, I look forward and surmounting racial degradation is still
quite a distance.

But I do see a dim light ahead. Lit by our white brothers and
sisters as well as our black brothers and sisters.
Lit by those who have opened their eyes to love.

And with this love, we will optimistically rise on to a bigger
and much brighter light ... and finally EQUALITY.

—*Latoya Green*

438

Great Struggle

I stand liberated in the midst of emptiness.
Slowly filling with revengeful anger
That's much closer to completeness,
Than the mind that's in danger.

Dignity and self respect were taken
Before I knew they were mine.
My life had been forsaken
And used by one so unkind.

I mourn my loss with some reservation,
For this mourning has nothing to gain.
The unwelcome thoughts of my deprivation
Threaten the mind with intimidating shame.

The days of abuse continue to teach.
Like the cookie jar on a shelf
I keep it just out of the reach.
For neither dare I, trust myself.

—*T. Wayne McLeod*

"The Lonely Teardrop"

The lonely teardrop running down your face.
Slowly magnifying everything in its way.
It falls so slowly, yet so gracefully, just like the
 first raindrops of a storm.
That one perfect teardrop running down your face.
So innocent yet meaning so much.
When it rains I watch and carefully listen to find that
 one raindrop that reminds me of you.
Yet, while I watch a lonely teardrop runs down my face
 remembering everything about you
Those lonely teardrops wondering where the other is,
 just like I'm doing now.
Wishing and hoping you'll come back, but you never do
So my lonely teardrop falls one more time hoping to be
 reacquainted with your one teardrop
And so the rain slowly comes to a stop, the lonely teardrop
comes to the edge of my cheek dropping off,
 hoping to become part of your teardrop.

—*Shannon-Elizabeth Kelly*

Purple

Purple is a woman who is exotic and desired,
 smelling of sweet fragrances that waft from her soul.
She floats in the sky at early dawn,
 flourishing it with beauty.
She blooms in the ripe, wild orchids,
 that are plush with silky petals.
Lustrous and majestic,
 she enchants her surroundings and fills it with magical life.
Shedding her bliss and peace to others,
 there is no need to worry,
 for her spirit lingers everywhere...

—*Nicole Jacobs*

Best Friends

You always know how to make me
smile and for that I'd walk a mile.
You always know just what to say and
for that I'd be there any day.
You always have a good time when we're
together and for that I'll never bother.
You always have a positive style and
for that I'll always be here when you dial
And what separates you from the rest is
your the best at whatever you do and
I love you.

—*Jessica Wills*

I Alone

I long for your protective embrace. I settle for your sweet
smile of amusement at my childish ways. If only you could see,
the passionate woman within. I wish for your love. I am
granted your friendship which, I must confess, I question. I
am afraid that, when you look at me, you miss what you are
"seeing" I fear that you do not see me, but merely my
appearance. I knew of my love for you at first glance. Only
I, not you and I. Only I, I alone.

—*Rebecca Douglas*

Rainbows

Rainbows smeared into the ground,
 smiles turning into constant frowns.
Everyone asks for a reason why,
 and all I am able to do is cry.
I reach for security in life,
 but this constant battle is full of strife.
The sky above is full of clouds and rain,
 giving the impression that it is in pain.
Salvation is far from near,
 there is always a feeling of overriding fear.
The tears begin to sting me,
 and it is becoming hard to see
 the blood-red sunset that sets the mood.
The truth not only hurts, but is sometimes rude.
One day the gold will be found,
 from that rainbow that fell to the ground.

—*Tiffany Polishan*

Jonathan

Jonathan sits by the window with his cherubic face
Smiling a chesire smile as the other children
Play games on the dusty green carpet.
He leaps down from the windowsill
To stampede over the carefully balanced
Pattern of wooden blocks
Leaving a frenzied mass of crying eyes
Who overlook their masterpiece
Now scattered in a jumbled pile on the floor.
Jonathan rushes frantically into the hall
And throws his pudgy baby arms
Around my leg, so I can drag him
Step by step across the floor.
He slowly releases his death-grip on my pant leg
To skitter away and pull Kate's cookie
On his way back to the windowsill seat
Where he sits and smiles a cheshire smile
And waits for the next stampede.

—*April J. Robinson*

Old Man Winter

With weary dread I face the day.
 Snow oh snow
 Please go away.

Unbented fury, the winds will blow.
 Winter old man winter,
 Won't you just go.

For spring like air I long to smell, enough of you.
 Enough of your Hell"

 Green grasses,
 Fields of flowers
Summer days, idle hours.
Dreams of running barefoot through a summers field.
 But peaceful slumbers, the only place they'll yield.
So dream must I, or face the days I dread.
 For Old Man Winter, keeps raising his dreary head.

—*Lynn Robins*

My Travelling Buddha, Or The Cats Out Of The Bag Now

My travelling buddha is a Batik that goes everywhere,
so I can ride the rapids down the nectar river of purity.
Does Buddha know public hairs don't print or that I drink behind
everyones' back?
That I really want to be Ms Harley Davidson 1993?
So I can fell the undulating pulsating motor on the nape of my
neck. Of course, he knows, Buddha knows - all and what is-is.
So he sits everywhere - in the hall, on the wall on the
bookshelf, on the T.V. in the car, my desk, at the sink, in my
hat on the surface of the cloth in my mind and in my heart,
Knowing what's best, pulling me closer to the truth.

—*Sarah Jane Boyd*

Untitled

The world is collapsing;
so I turned on the television,
just to see what was going down.
It told me the rainforest was dying,
so were the wildlife and spotted owl.
They had to leave without their homes,
their homes given to us...taken by us.
The Lord gave the world to Adam;
yet I believe He gave, thinking Adam would give,
not take.

Commercial Break.

Then it told me the ozone layer was wearing thin,
but not to use my aerosol, airfreshener, or hairspray.
I feel we all are going to die;
but no need to fret. I hope.
But have a good day!

The world is still collapsing;
but we have learned to live with it.

—*Morgen Sizer Rose*

Life Goes On

Winter comes, and the birds go,
Soft snow falls,and flowers fade.
Why must one beauty die for another to live?

Snow melts and disappears,
Trees turn green, flowers burst
forth with brilliant colors of spring.

Quickly the days become hot,
Quietly burning all the green beauty
to a warm golden brown.

Gently the winds whisper, and autumn arrives,
The golden colors softly fall and cover the ground.
Slowly the days start to freeze and...

Winter comes, and the birds go,
Soft snow falls, and flowers fade...
Life goes on.

—*Tania Taylor*

Friend

To start the day, I need to be
Rested, relaxed, to talk to thee.
Time to be thankful, time for prayers
To start the day and know you're there.
Refreshed to live the day for you
And know that you will carry me through.
The joys, the fun, the sorrows, the tears,
The peace, the love, the doubt, the fears.
For comfort, assurance and love you give
Always forever as long as I live.

—*Melvelene Dean*

The Silent Giant

To God's creatures big and small,
Some misfortune does befall,
As the "Giant" begins to crawl,
The "Silent Giant" of urban sprawl.

Harsh is the trampling of forrest and farm!
No woodland creature to sound the alarm!
Deer by day, eagle by night.
To avoid any harm, have taken to flight!

Tranquil and sturdy the country house.
A yard for garden, grass and flowers.
Now replaced by duplex-dwellings.
Condos and multi-highrise towers.

Carried along on invisible feet,
The banner of "Progress" advances.
With metamorphic stride the footfalls repeat,
I wonder just who this 'progress' enhances?

Gone is the blue-bird! When again will it sing?
Gone is the duck pond that rippled with spring!
No longer with trout does the summer stream bristle!
What will tomorrow bring?

—*Richard Bialy*

A Poem A Song

Some say love is like a flower, how they bloom in the spring,
Some say love is like a river, how it flow to the sea
Some say love is like a picture, how it hang upon the wall..

I say love is the Father, for He gave His only Son
I say love is the Son "Jesus" for He died for us all.

Some say love is like the trees, how they grow so tall and strong,
Some say love is like the moon, how it shines threw the night
Some sat love is like the winter, so cold and blue...

I say love is like the sun, shine so bright and so warm,
I say love is like a mother, so kind and so dear
I say love is love for it come from above... the love of God.

—*Barbara J. Woodley*

People

You meet people off and on.
Some you meet are very strong.
Others may be weak in heart,
Some may even be very smart.

There is a lot a different people on this earth,
But God paid what all was worth.
He gave His Son for everyone,
Now all we need is to just learn.

We may know but others my not.
Are we just going to stop!
All the different people need the same,
Just to know his loving name.

How Jesus died even for them.
That they may be with him.
What is it that we need.
Just someone to go and plant the seed.

—*Melissa Colquette*

Dare To Be Different

Dare to be different,
Unusual, and not commonplace.
Laughter may follow you.
Scorn may annoy you.
But dare to be different,
And someday others will copy your ways.

—*Jerrel Thomas*

Thoughts On Children

Tomorrow they're our future...today they offer life
Someday our daughter's becoming a wife
Young and carefree protected from daily harm
Hearts ringing and singing in silent alarm
Our sons' electricity offering life's eccentricity
Life offering life to overcome our electrical perversity
Someday our sons' beckon our dream
Perplexities of life into the main stream
Aunty's and Uncle's a bit melancholy
Grandma's and Grandpa's a bit of folly
The crying... the laughter of our happiness
The tender moment of yesterday's tenderness
Tomorrow they are our future
The best of our country's stature
Yesterday's spectacles becoming tomorrow's reality
The reality of our diversity
In the circle of life we are the ultimate gift
Yesterday, Today and Tomorrow, the outer edges of the circle
    we can not lift.
    —*Robert G. English*

Happy Birthday Honey

I wanted to buy you a wonderful gift
Something expensive, to give you a lift,
Something real great that cost lots of money.
I'd do almost anything for you, My Honey.

I thought to myself, now what does he need?
Maybe a golf cart, like Mr. Sam Snead.
(If I got one of those, and he went all the way,
I'd end up a golf widow most every day).

A helicopter from Montgomery Wards?
(I'd fight him first, at point of swords),
I know he wants one, cause that's what he said.
(He needs it like a hole in his head).

Or maybe a boat that could sail on the ocean?
(But where he might sail to I haven't a notion).
He might find a place he liked better than this,
And then I'd be missing his hugs and his kiss.

Now, none of these things I could really afford.
(With anything less he would surely be bored).
So it just seems to me there is nothing to do
But to hug him and kiss him and say "I love you."

    —*Ora Wayman*

A Broken Heart And Empty Chair

This old house sometimes don't feel like home
Something is always lost when a loved one
passes on

Precious memories of a love once shared
Flows through your mind while you pretend
Your loved one is sitting there

In the stillness you feel loneliness
And despair is this how the story
Ends with a broken heart and empty chair

It seems at any moment you'll hear a
Voice, your loved one is home but the
Emptiness you feel reminds you
You are alone

You know someday your life must end
But you have faith God will re-unite
You with your loved one, again

And all your friends and loved ones
Who care you'll leave behind
A broken heart and empty chair

    —*Stanley Jonston*

My Son

Time moves swiftly and though you live each day,
Sometime in haste, in love, yes, even in hate,
Yet you live as you feel it, and in your own way,
With the strength and courage to accept your own fate.

So, to perform the duties assigned to you,
Without regard for personal consequences,
Is the test of bravery and dedication to
Your country, home and moral senses.

For a great man never cringes or backs away
From the responsibility and obligation of each day.
Remember, son, in the measure that a man is brave,
Also, in that measure is a man great.

There is nothing more strengthening than a prayer.
There is nothing more rewarding than a job well done.
I shall think of you always, and I will be there,
Whenever the going gets rough and you need me, my son.
    —*Virginia L. Dewar*

Ours Forever

Desire, for good grades, a beautiful girl, maybe, maybe not.
    Sometimes even I take for granted all that I've got.
        A nice car, showy clothes, the perfect look,
            What does all this mean?
    Sometimes what you own and desire is something not seen.
        All we have is our dignity and emotions,
    I sometimes feel lost in emotion and full of commotion.
        Anyway, I don't want to fall too deep,
            Short and sweet.
    What we truly own is what we forever keep.
    —*Yong Shim*

Married With Children

I'm not always right, but I try to be fair
Sometimes I get angry, but always I care
I know I'm not perfect, but I know what it takes,
to say that I'm sorry, when I've made a mistake
I love all my children, with them I've been blessed
My love for their mother, is more now not less
They know I can't give them, all the things they desire
Still their love never flickers, it burns like a fire
I know they'll be with me, for the rest of my life
God answered my prayers, with my kids, and my wife
    —*Wade Pritchett*

A Heart's Illusion

We do not live in a perfect land,
Sometimes it can be quite dreary and bland.
But beyond the moons and planets and stars,
Lies a world that is by far
A world of fantasies, hopes, and dreams
Where everything does not quite seem
So complicated and so very confusing
There is no war and there is no losing.
In this place there is always peace;
The friendliness shall never cease.
And then, way up in the sky,
The geese and birds fly way up high.
All the animals roam round free
Seeing all that there is to see.
I know you say this wonderful place;
Of it there is no slight trace.
But to me this world is very real
And I will forever feel
That if we try and try and try,
We'll find this paradise by and by.
    —*Kara Soos*

An Age To Hope

Each day is a struggle to survive,
Sometimes only in tears do we seem alive.

We hurry and run to and fro,
Sometimes wondering which way to go.

A tender light inside of us breaks forth,
Suddenly knowing who is chartering our course.

Our Creator has always been around,
Sickened within (New Hope unseen) we almost fall down.

By Love we are picked up, Thank God just an injured knee,
With supreme patience and Love all can learn to 'just be.'

Throwing off false human reality must be the Start,
The invisible Kingdom of God is ripe for Love's Heart.

Always knocking on our conscience, this inner door,
Every Hope of Love's faith to open this door to new lore.

The door once opened no more room for ignorance of mind,
His Universal Mind established to connect all mankind.

"Heart-to-heart" the One Principle brought to light,
The new mental age is here, darkness unveiled, and made bright.

  —Susan Bette Hebert

Sometimes

Sometimes a heart must break before we find its gold,
Sometimes we wake too late and find love has grown cold,
The hand we fail to clasp may want to dry our tears,
To calm our fears, sometimes, sometimes.
Sometimes we have a second chance to right the wrong,
Sometimes we hear the silent music of love's song,
We turn away from pride and look into love's eyes,
Ah, we are wise, sometimes, sometimes.

  —Alice C. Walker

Health, Harvest, Hope

Full half the settlers died first winter,
 sore test of faith.
Yet did they minister unto one another,
 full seal of charity.
And wrote Pilgrim Father Bradford, winter two
 drawn near, "They begane now to gather in
 ye small harvest . . . being all well recovered
 in health & strenght, and had all things
 in good plenty . . . ther was great store of
 wild Turkies, of which they took many . . .
 besides . . . Indean corne. . . ."
Their hope became our creed,
 their health became our hope,
 and we their harvest now.
So say we then with them, "And thus they found
 ye Lord to be with them in all their ways. . . ."

  —William K. Bottorff

Oh! Moon

Oh! Moon, Oh! Moon.
Shining bright and clear.
Image! what you see as you drift along.
Revolving in the air like a spinning wheel.
Flashing your light merely as you Rome.

Traveling North, South, East and West.
Spreading your light, while children at play.
Then your eyes disappear like a
shadow and fades away.

  —Susan R. Bridges

"A Hearts Winter"

Someone lost...Someone found,
Souls passage cost...to be unbound.
New snow falls gently on rocky, hard, frozen ground,
The old is claimed, taken quietly from view,
We wait, watching with different eyes...anew.
As within longest winter, grows...
Seeds of silent hope only the heart still can know.
That once again the grace of spring shall call,
Prayers of peace and union are spoken,
And what once was hidden will be known by all.
No one lost...No one bound,
Truth undenied will turn us around.
Sun and smiles and children's laughter bringing,
Songs of joy within singing.

  —Steve Davis

"Christmas"

It's Christmas time as again with the Jingle Bells Rings of sounds of Joy and love. The Holy winds is blowing the snow flakes around. It's Christmas time again of many, many, many presents in the world. The Horses are driving in the mountain trail woods along the snowy road with the sleigh. As the snow flakes fall in the world. The sleigh with the Horses, people, and present drive toward, the sacred snowy castle. As the Drawbridge open into the Holy Icy Castle. They put the presents under the nine foot Christmas tree. Along side of the fire place on Christmas Eve and go to midnight mass and wait for Santa Claus in the morning on Christmas Day for the children in the world. It's Christmas time again with the Jingle Bells rings of sounds of hope, faith, joy, and love on this Holy Day.

  —Paul Dunn Jr.

Portrait Of An Unbroken Spirit

Gently, gracefully poised and ready for battle,
Sparkling child of the Universe,
The night has already made its mark.
The wound has begun to shape you brittle.
Fear and scrutiny have all to soon devoured the wide-eyed innocence.
Reticence and ridicule now your guarded guides.
The dance of angels, turned the stance of demons,
Clasped firmly in the cobwebs of your mind.

Speak to me, oh lovelorn one, of secrets
That bind the very essence of your soul;
And scream the silent sound of fallen tear drops.
Allow the living passion to unfold.

There's safety here beneath the weeping willows.
There are bridges back to trust for broken starts.
There's hope and joy and life and love eternal.
With outstretched hands....
I offer you my heart.

  —Pat Ellin Lakin

Our Special One

To most parents he seems like just a son,
to us he is called our special one.
To the day we saw him lying there,
looking at us, and with all that red hair.
Such a special one to us,
the very first time we could touch.
The day we brought him home with us,
has been filled with precious love.

  —Lorri Gum

Sunday In October

'Twas Sunday, the blustery twilight of October,
Spring had sprung and Summer had gone, and the
Fall was nearly over. I took a stroll in the park this day,
With a friend so close and dear. Although we're so close
I must truly say, I've only known him for less than one year.
The crisp brown leaves fell from the trees, and whimsically
pranced about our feet. I laughed out loud as they soared
in the breeze, as my friend smiled a smile so sweet.
Walking the same trails, sighing the same sighs
As I had with my father in Octobers past,
The passersby saw the likeness in our eyes,
And in our faces as we laughed.
My life has been one of Thunder and Storm,
And now the turbulence has finally ended,
My pride does soar and my heart glows warm
With this person whom I've befriended.
As the winds blew cold and darkness did creep,
I gathered my friend in my arms,
And I took my dear son back home to sleep,
Away from the cold wind and all harm.

—*William McCollum*

White Candle

White Candle,
Standing tall,
burnt by it many times.
Watch the flame for it might go out.
Watch the wax rolling down for it might collide.
White candle,
Standing tall, how do you keep your flame?
You're so sturdy in her hands you don't play cards
White candle,
Gave me light in the deep dark whole,
now and then I see you and happiness is told.
White candle,
Give me strength this very day,
for instead of happiness you gave me love in a very,
deep way.

—*Stacey Renee*

Untitled

In a glimpse of time undefinable, where progression
    stands still as its enemies pass never to
    return

Where only one eye is touched by the glimmer of sun
    reflecting off a brief splash of river water
    refusing ever to repeat itself

Peering into a hologram of mosquitoes unwittingly
    dancing in their cloud of insect matter as a
    passing breeze would go unnoticed but for the
    cold it leaves behind on the sweat covered
    parts of my brow and upper lip

And I can pull nobody, planted no matter how close in
    my grasp or range of sight or sound, into my
    memories

Memories trapped like bodies in the ashes of
    unrecorded eruptions in unrecalled places
    melted, mixed, and churned, only to be blown
    out in another form at another time to trap a
    different body with a different memory

—*Michael S. Kelly*

The Warmth Of The Blizzard Of '93

How I watched everyone hustle about, gathering all emergency
staples 'till the store ran out. I guess everyone thought it
was just a scare, as I waited in the checkout line, my arms
full, as everyone else there.

When I reached home, I felt secured and looked to the snow
filled sky above; "Dear Lord", I prayed, "please protect all
those that I love". I wondered where all the little creatures
would go, with the prediction of hurricane winds and three feet
of snow! I guess, God has His way of protecting his little
animals and us, so with faith in my heart, I shoveled the first
six inches of snow and did not fuss.

Then as I sat by the fireside with a cup of tea, the telephone
rang, "Hi, Hello there, Sweetie"! Oh, such joy filled my heart
such warmth ran through me! It was my love from England, far
across the sea.

As we exchanged news from each shore; his voice, his words
warmed me up, plus more! No longer shall we be divided by
distant shores, for Spring shall not only bring sweet blossoms,
sunshine and laughter, it will bring my English Love, to hold,
now and everafter.

—*Mary Anne DeLongchamps*

The Little Ones

Look at the little ones with tears in their eyes
Staring at their Mama and asking her why
There's no food on the table no heat in there home
They were told it would get better but now it's all gone

Look at the little ones they can't read or write
They grow up in the streets and learn how to fight
Some go for a bottle, a pipe or a gun
Then look at us and say, "See what you've done."

If we only did it different and taken out time
If only we could see but no we are blind
If only we could go back to another place in time
If only there were a solution that we could find

Look at the little ones with no shoes on there feet
Standing on the corner begging in the street
Yes look at the little ones they are our own
See what we've taught them, see how they've grown

—*R. A. Nappi*

Marriage

Look at us laughing, smiling at each other
Staring into each other's eyes
Wine glasses half full, or are they half empty
Did you smile ???
Talking about old friends and new ones
My friends now, your friends then
Agreeing instead of arguing
Compromising on what to eat
Looking good for each other
Hugging like we mean it, this time around
And then I reach down to retrieve my napkin
Our eyes meet and we kiss
Nothing fancy, just a soft short sweet sensuous kiss
Looking at us now, who'd have ever thought
We're no longer married

—*Meeka Muse*

Exiting Sweet Hell

She walked slowly down the mountain side,
Staring into space.
Not aware of the world around her,
Yet knowing of the fate she held within.
Her feet began to slide in the sand;
Every breath became a struggle in the hot, dry, air.
With every step she grew closer to the future.
She sat on the desert floor and began to cry.
The tears ran gently down her face,
Yet she was not afraid.
Her hands shook as she cradled her weapon.
She lifted it to her head,
Set it gently at her temple,
Then whispered, "Goodbye sweet hell."
She pulled the trigger.
The shot then echoed throughout the night.

—*Krista Mangano*

Amaryllis

A beautiful lady haughty and proud,
Stems that flow softly through
The sky like a cloud;
Very stubborn and difficult to grow;
Yet when in bloom you should
See her glow,
No morning dew touches the pollen inside;
For in the night her head she will hide;
Not many friends, for many despise,
She is too arrogant in their eyes;
Perhaps it's the way she holds
Her head so high;
As if to say "Just walk on bye!"

—*Amy Martin*

Mystery Creature

In a silver pasture on a moonlit night
steps a regal creature spun from light.
As it lifts a hoof of gold
its outline shows up clear and bold.
When it buries its nose in the fragrant grass
upon its head a beam is cast.
As it goes to the river for a drink
it sees you there and seems to think.
Then, as softly as a cat
it steals back to its habitat.
But you saw it anyway
when a beam had gone astray.
It was a silver horn
Belonging to a unicorn.

—*Melanie Wilson*

Untitled

Tie this arm off, friend.
Stick this bruised vein again.
Suck the red life, enough to fuel
One more dreary day.
Both lives tired, grey.
My lifeblood thins, goes twice the distance,
But there is no Chanukkah miracle here.
And I feel old and you feel old.
The life, diluted to two half-lives
Would be better balanced as yin-yang.
But tie this arm off, brother, sister
For I do not wish to deny you
Even the most weary existence
And I can live without
Red, furious life
For one more dreary day

—*Adam Seehaver*

Overwhelmed

In the deepest dark,
stillness and quiet embrace me.

Feeling somewhat haunted and alone,
my mind sensed a superior power,
a greater existence somewhere
beyond the darkness of the night.

You are not in control of life,
however,
there is control, what will be is-and

I'm driven to the earth on my knees,
Salty tears sting my eyes,
stain my face,
I gaze towards the heavens
and realize a blanket of humbleness enfolding me.

—*Sheryl L. Hammond*

The Love We Choose

My eyes were closed but I still heard the sea, my ears were
Stopped up but I still saw the trees

My mouth was closed but my voice came out, my arms were folded
But you still took my heart

In all my life I saw up ahead of me, so why in the world has
This come to be

I never saw the warning signs, your love made me truly blind

You won me over with your ways, your smile brightened all my
Days

I saw everything in black and white, but nothing prepared me
For last night

When you held me and kissed my lips, from head to toe to finger Tips

I still never really realized, but it was always in your eyes

Last night was heaven, my love it's true, no one can move me
The way you do

Once it's done you never lose, unless you're unwise in the
Partner you choose

But you chose me and I really must say, "Darling I wouldn't
Have it any other way"

—*Valen Buels*

The Star Traveler

The Nebula, in form of stallion 'd-head;
Strides, with coat, all in gloss —, of ebonied-sheen!

'Crost, the vast, of cosmic-sea;
'Midst, the velvet, of deepest-space!
Framed, 'gainst, the cluster of star-field;
Bathed, in the network/of its afterglow!

The stellar-Object, encompassed, 'bout;
With, luminous - backdrop, — in, crimson'd-flow!

Stands, in silhouette,—and, beckons-now;
The Star-Traveler!

Its beauty - as of, a star, — bless'd;
Adazzle, in faceted - brilliance!

Affixed, in scene, — as, towards-unto;
A many, Splendored-Dream!

—*Milton C. Watson*

A Child's Lament

All alone you trod life's road —
Struggling, fighting to survive;
Both father and mother to your children,
Striving to keep your family alive,
To keep your children together.
You gave so much of yourself:
Your strength, your courage, your caring.
Each of us KNEW we shared a special love,
But the words were never spoken.
There wasn't time.

I needed to hear "I love you"
To let my heart be free
To soar above the highest clouds,
To face reality.

Today my cry was answered —
You heard my silent plea.
Today my heart is singing,
Today my heart is free!
Today I am sixty years old.
Today you told me you loved me.

   —*Ruth E. Moomaw*

A Strand Of Pearls

Oysters make pearls when something irritates by covering with a
substance it manufactures within its own body.

I'll make a strand of shining pearls upon my soul to wear, I'll
make each one a precious gem a pearl of beauty rare.

The trials that come upon my way I'll count - not loss - but
gain and cover them with love till I no longer feel the pain.

Each victory will be a pearl that I have dearly won and only
God and I will know how each pearl was begun.

I'll count it joy whatever test the foe against me hurls and
when I stand before my God I'll wear a strand of pearls!

   —*Myrna L. Franks*

The Other Side

My mind has set the blaze , full of thoughts of death and
suicide. There is no return for the man that has lost his way.
Have I lost my way or gone astray. The answer lies just beyond
the other side, but for me the other side is place of death
from suicide. The depths of Hell are here for me and now I
wonder how I got this way. Just beyond the other side the
answer lies, shall I wait or shall I die. The man that has
lost his way has no return, so have I lost my way or gone
astray, the answer lies just beyond the other side...
Hear these words I have to say, for I speak them in a sober
way. Life has lost its way and death has found the only way.
Fear not of what I say for death will come in a grander way.
Cry not for I have found my way, death will be welcomed in the
best way...

   —*James Emmert*

"Memories"

Carefree thoughts of bygone times drift slowly through my mind,
Sunfilled days and starry nights I soon would leave behind.
Emptiness came creeping in as silent as the night,
Fading shadows quickly pass so silently from sight.
Staring at the lifeless from where once a light did glow,
Crying out in anguished pain please help me to let go.
Sitting and remembering the time I first saw you,
Sunshine filled my empty heart and life was born anew.
Seasons pass and time moves on we laugh-we cry-we are...
Searching for tomorrow's dreams-alas, they seem so far.

   —*Alice E. Overly*

The Freedom Land

I walk down this street alone,
 Sun glaring in my eyes.
  I can't see,
  And suddenly I am
  Being pushed and pulled
  In every direction
By too many people to count.
 I am no longer alone,
  No longer free.
There are voices in my head
Screaming for me to conform
And little hands pushing me to follow.
  I refuse.
 They use harsher methods,
 Brainwashing me into nothingness.
What happened to my thoughts and actions?
 They have been buried and now
  I am a zombie,
Walking through this wonderful place we call
   Home.
   —*Katrina Smith*

Untitled

Tiny, cottage cabin with a woodsy, autumn floor
Sun-streaked, cloth drapes near a thick, splintered door

Cozy, stuffy loft- feathered blanket cover
Faded egg carton mattress, represents a simplistic,
comfort lover

Low- flamed wick casted on soft, shadowed walls
A sleepy, drowsy essence drifted thru the halls

Only the loft window, looked- in perfectly clear
To see the little girl hiding, within her own fear

Her small, sheltered world, could never try and survive
By venturing thru the forest and coming back alive

For sure the animals would devour, her ignorance and naivete
Engulf her with their norms and turn her into a tree

Yet in time she'll become part of the forest, and her old self
will be left behind, some say now she's grown, yet to others
she's lost in time

Precious sweet world a child loves to cater
We all must say goodbye... sooner or later

   —*Jean Coggiano*

Tiscornia Beach

It will never again be the way it was that day;
Sunlight sparkled radiantly in a dazzling array;
The great lake's waves cascaded toward the shore;
From eon to eon: an unrelenting encore.
Just one day out of quadrillions we observed:
Sea gulls fresh fish on the beach were served.
We saw gulls dive; we watched them soar and glide;
We felt at peace: as if on God's side.

We purged our souls and cast our failings to hell;
Our spirits then clean as quartz, bubbled like a well;
While temperatures and sun dropped slowly in the sky,
The most luxuriant colors were presented to the eye.
Though intruding mosquitoes finally threatened our serenity,
The indwelling calm transcended infinity.
When the jewel that I love slipped silently toward home....
Precious memories and moments live longest in a poem.

   —*J. F. Bolinger*

My Thoughts Of You

Everything I see—every sound I hear—reminds me of you!
SUNSHINE—The way I feel when I'm with you—so alive!
RAIN—The tears that flow when I'm missing you.
THUNDER—The pounding of my heart at the very thought
and sight of you.
LIGHTNING—The sparks that fly when you touch me.
STARS—The galaxy I have in you.
MOON—Alone in the heavens as I am when you're not with me.
FLUFFY WHITE CLOUDS—The softness of your touch.
WIND—Your breath upon my skin.
DARK CLOUDS—The fear of never seeing you again.
All together a love so very precious—
A love that should have been kindled long ago,
But how was I to know—
That we would meet again, and I would feel as
young as I did back then?

—*Pauline Wilcoxson*

Superstar

Like a whore in the dark
Swallowing something unborn —
I — Too — Am a superstar —
I dress the ritual and the poverty of your beliefs —
(Discarnate - cold - Perishable things) —
Knowing that everything is sacred —
Not just what you tell me is —

This thirty second baptism
Moves me promiscuously through the halo —
With no sense of repentance —
(So close to the grave) —

On my knees - I hopelessly clutch the paraments of my altar —
And facing the guttered walls of eternity —
Know I need to follow no laws
When I can think for myself —

I am reality —
Committing acts of ecstacy in the streets —
Assassinating an old priest's fairytale —
As any superstar would —

—*Richard J. Di Via*

Home Sweet Ghetto

Oh for the feel and smell of the ghetto, it's a hot, steamy,
sweaty, summer night. Enter the ghetto and it enters you -
it envelopes your very soul. Dark, dank, musty, wicked, hazy
air presses in, seeming to encourage one to draw closer. Will
you survive - only to come back again.

Asphalt streets filled with wet, half-naked kids, with
hopeless, terror-filled eyes, bathing at a hydrant. Downstreet
the bugs shootin' crap with their welfare money, mommie
hustlin' for dinner and dope, she say - ain't no hope.
Sidewalk strewn with blown trash, beside a drunken neighbor, no
hope round here, save those innocent tads.

Two blocks away the b-ball courts are empty, the young head
be watchin' the home-boys sellin' crack. They Superman in
these boys' eyes, they makin' out this hood, man. Five or
six, maybe seven, sharp, shocking, night-cracking, skin
piercing shots later - yeah they made it blood. Sometime,
most time, it like that . Cold-blooded. They capped the bros!
Damn - ain't no way out this. Someone made it, only to come
back again, and again, and again..

—*Raymond J. Harmer*

The Nighttime Visitor

The night is still; the clock strikes one,
Swiftly she glides in.
Her face is old and white as milk,
Her hands as black as sin.

She neither looks to right or left,
But makes her way instead,
To a small bare room where an old man lies
Asleep in a cold, hard bed.

The clock ticks twice; her work is done,
She quietly leaves the cell.
No one has seen, no one has heard,
No one was there to tell.

Five more the lady must visit tonight;
Five more; her task is done.
Two while asleep, two on the roads
The other alone with a son.

The gloom has passed; the day dawns clear
The lady is gone with the light.
But the ones she touched, what of those six?
Their lives are gone with the night.

—*Mark Douglas Eubank*

Reality

True essence of life, a matter of perspective
Take alcohol or drugs to make life effective
Stop reality when things don't go your way
Decide it's not worth it, to live just one more day

A fairy tale world, so far from the truth
Escape life, juggle death all within your youth
Fantasies are real not just imagination
Life's more than a trip, an occasional hallucination

Existing on purely a natural high
The true essence of life will never slip by

—*Amy Amerman*

Ground Yourself And Know Your Mission

Think of others and your own misfortune will diminish
Take each step and follow through if you intend to finish
Detach yourself from earthly wealth, it anchors you to grief
Invest in self, respect your health, and stick with your
belief
Do not dwell on ancient past or hang up in the future
Live for now and it will last, the present time will nurture
Show compassion and the lasting feeling will sustain
Friends will always be a natural healing to your pain
Keep your attitude sincere and your thoughts pure and clear
Know your strength when called upon will always persevere
Do not hesitate to share the wisdom you have learned
Give away and multiply the knowledge you have earned
Set your goals and do not be afraid to reach the sky
Know the Soul will be your guide and teach you to aim high
Ground yourself and know your mission, do not deviate
Use the power that you have, envision and create
Meditate and find your center, enter it at will
Know your fate will come to be, even standing still
Rejoice in life and know your birth was destined to begin
You chose the time, date and sign, it all came from within

—*Sharynn Rose Schibig*

One Conclusion

Many thoughts running wild tangents
   tiny bits of emotional flax
the electric state of the souls life force
   filling
      filling every level of mind
Coming together in one final conclusion

—*Robert L Stagg*

Challenges

There's many of challenges that we
   take every day.
Some of them challenges we can't
   seem to beat.
It doesn't mean were to weak,
Its a challenge we can't meet,
Challenges in life there to big and strong,
Only a prayer could help us linger on,
The prayer doesn't mean were big and strong.
Our father knows when to linger us on
His our challenger that challenges us all,
We could all pray that's not wrong,
Our father wants to know how strong
   our prayers really are.

   —Tammie Meaike

The Rainforest

The flames roar with insensitivity
taking away all life
Not much will be left for me
The cat that tears her to pieces
leaving shreds of hopelessness
Bringing down all life to the hell we'll see tomorrow
Killing the cure that just might be the key
to a future
No future of this is no future of us
A dead, dry desert a symbol of all
the hate we put into it
The rain that will pour until no tomorrow
a symbol of God's sadness
He cries because he see's no tomorrow for us
Just an empty place of hate
"I wish there had been something I could have done"
-they always say
All this sacrifice for a road

   —Misty Costa

The Sunrise

Slowly it covers up the land
Taking its time
For it knows that no one can harm it
It moves silently
Like a mouse pushing its way through the underbrush
Bright colors
Covering everything that stands above the ground
Its beauty
Showered upon the world creating a perfect cast of the earth
It knows only love and care
Bringing joy to the world
The colors of hope
The cast of a beginning
The sunrise.

   —Rebecca Wilkinson

Untitled

Thoughts of anguish realize;
that hatred not shows in all our eyes;
mask by many a painted disguise;
on faces hidden so well with their lies.
Here the wind blows, the storm arises;
those with no shelter, are those with disguises.
Eyes of hatred tinged with red;
conjuring wicked thoughts in their heads;
leaving upon others horrors of dead.
Still the wind blows, the storm arises;
those with no shelter, are those with disguises.

   —Becky Monohon

The Cathedral Of Trees

As I close my eyes in memory I see
Tall stately pines standing guard over me
And a cool sparkling mountain stream
That's warmed by the sunlight's beams
As the soft light filters down through the trees
I hear music created by a gentle breeze
With the birds and crickets singing in harmony
And the tumbling of the water adding to the melody
The music seemed to lift my wounded soul to
   heights unseen
Where God healed it, then returned it pure and clean
Now as a wave of confusion sweeps over me
I long to go back to that place of serenity
To hear the soothing melody of the breeze
And feel God's cleansing power in the
   Cathedral of trees.

   —Yvonne Baxter

When Time Began

Is this the way it was when time began?
Tall trees standing in stately splendor
peace and quiet in early morn
bird songs rising in heavenly chorus
paeans of praise at New Day's dawn.
Is this the way it was when time began?
Beautiful sounds of the ocean's roar
sea gulls drifting above the waves
before man covered the earth with graves
of men who died in another war,
Is this the way it was when time began?
Beauty of desert and mountain and stream
the hope and promise of everyman's dream.
Is this the way it was when time began?

   —Sarah Daniel Vaughan

Build Me A Man

Build me a man of bold stature and might,
Tall with a heart, and of mind clear and bright!
Character shines from his face and his frame,
One who builds bridges, yet loves just the same.

Build me a man who speaks kind words and true,
Never to think of himself before you...
Handsome of body, yet loving his Lord
More than his life on this earth is adored.

Staunchly he stands at the side of the truth.
Gracious he grows to a man from a youth.
Justice and Mercy shall serve as his guides.
Kings will respect him and stay by his side.

Build me a man who will shine like a star,
Never afraid to dream dreams from afar!
These will come true because God is his source,
Goodness his fruit, with God's Spirit his force.

   —Winnifred Coe Verbica

Our Timeless Love

A ripple of gentle thoughts are the sweeping sensations
that paramount my longing for your touch.
You are my inspiration and joy which flows within me
continuously as the tides of great oceans.
My wanting to exist is your existence.
My wanting to touch is your touch.
My wanting to smile is your smile.
And so my lovely, my love for you reaches to the farthest
star in a universe of stars.
You are my love and I your lover.

   —Richard Capalbo

An Adopted Daughters Prayer

Does she love me
tell me true
please Dear Lord
what to do

Tell me about her
does she look like me
oh, sometimes how I wish I could see
for myself what life with her could be

Dear Jesus
does she ever think of me
are there other children, brothers and sisters
do they know about me

Dear God
could it be
that she has forgotten about me
Please Bless her and her family
Amen

　　　—Teresa Hackett

Oh Gossamer Sheaves

Oh gossamer sheaves tongued-tied in the breeze,
Tell me what you think?
So fragile you could sink,
Yet so strong of fabric,
You could withstand Winter's cold havoc.
You have a heart of gold, yet feet of clay.
Getting stuck in life's quicksand so easily.
Behold there is hope for you!
Behind the curtain you see only dimly.
Above I see your brilliancy, and promises to keep.
Promises to yourself first.
Promises to others secondly.
Promises that bring you to the cross-roads betwixt.
Opposer of rigidity, are you willing to surrender?
Embrace self-discipline vigorously,
To breadth the goals you explore.
If, this is true happiness,
Go for it,
If it is not,
Reject it.

　　　—Susanna Corning

"Little Boy Blue"

Hey, Little Boy Blue come blow come blow your horn....
　　Tell the world that the Christ Child has been born.
Hey, Little Drummer Boy, don't shy away....
　　Come sit by Baby Jesus's crib, this Holy Day.
Hey, Little Shepherd Boy, all weary and worn...
　　Won't you see the Boy Jesus, who was just born?
Hey, Little Maid Girl, all dressed with care....
　　Won't you come and help up to share?
This Holy Child of God Our King.....
　　Won't you lead us as we pray and sing?
Hey, Little Children everywhere...
　　Won't you grow up and then won't you care?
For the Christ who is now gone above....
　　Who shines down on us with his sweet love.

　　　—Joy Black

Little Star

God has a new little star tonight,
To give us infinite beautiful light;
To guide us on our earthly way, until the
　　breaking of the day;
So when you look at the heavens above, know
　　he shines bright, with our God of Love;

　　　—Virginia Lisenby Thompson

Where Have The Values Gone?

Solemn expression,
tending to business as if it were pleasure.
Sneering grin,
while wiping away natural beauty.
Industries growing,
Polluting the air with bitterness.
Destroying conscientiousness.
Slowly, steadily, hardening many hearts.
Awaiting fortune,
hoping to make the "American Dream" a reality.

　　　—Trisha Renee Lund

Words Of Perfections

More than once I've heard it said, "That the pen is mightier
than the sword." It must be true, because for me I'm as happy
as can be when I'm reading or writing a little bit of poetry.
Just as there are many a beautiful and unique kinds of birds,
there's also a lot of magnificent sounding words. Sometimes in
my dreams at night many lovely words comes flying into my head
But, incidentally it makes me very sad to say, "Most of them have
taking a fancy flight by the early dawn of daylight, with
some exceptions of course, and I say that without any remorse."
I call them my WORDS OF PERFECTIONS. and they are
REPENTANCE;
REDEMPTION; SALVATION; RESURRECTION; SAVIOUR; and
LORD.
These are just a few of the sacred words my mind wants to store.
Could it be, because I know in my own heart that God and His
son JESUS CHRIST is FOREVERMORE! Now who could ever forget
about all
of Jesus's agony in the Garden of Gethsemane! Not counting His
slow, and very painful death on the cross at Calvary. And with
the shedding of His precious blood he paid in full for all of our
salvations. It seems that the choice is left up to all of us, to
accept and believe, because mankind has a God whom would never
deceive. I can't help it, if I get a sweet smile on my face, when
I think about how I was saved through His painful, loving grace.
And as sure as all of the Sea Gulls love to fly by the vast seas;
I will continue to love God and His son Jesus, for all time and
eternity no matter what befalls me and my future destiny!

　　　—Nina Maphis

Other Paths

There may be other paths, other ways
Than those tradition has decreed.
Paths wild and windy through lands of promise,
Where Desire leads the way, while duty falls far behind.
And the collective conscience no longer bars the road
For him who would stray from mankind's patterned way.

There may be other paths, other ways
Than those convention has decreed.
But those paths are dark and uncertain.
And he who would swerve from the herd's common rut
Must forego the animal warmth
Of the wandering, channeled mass
For the stinging cold, the echoing loneliness,
The formless fear of untraveled, uncharted realms.
Must trade present peace
For phantoms on the horizon.

There are other paths, other ways
Than our elders have decreed,
But those lanes so lonely
Are for heroes only.

　　　—Norm E. Hamlin

God's beautiful Creation!

Having the opportunity, to contemplate
Thanking God, as I meditate
For all the beauty, He has made!
One cannot help but marvel, to see
A speck of sand, right by the sea
Where bare feet, roam and delight with glee
We gaze at the moon, the beautiful stars
Makes us aware, how small we are!
We see the sun, so big and bright, without it
We would have no light
Then there are Mountains, trees, rivers, waterfalls
When God, made nature, he thought of all
He made man with heart and a soul
He loves us so much we don't have to
Be told!
How blessed are we, that we can see,
Gods beautiful creations, for you and me.

— *Dr. Mary Elizabeth Groeger*

A Mother's Pride

On this special day of yours, just had to let you know
That as your mother I am proud, and had to let it show

You've been a joy and always will be everything to me
Through your life I've come to see that dreams are meant to be

You saw the things you wanted and reached for them each day
Nothing was too hard for you, you knew there was a way

A beauty you have come to be, a lovely one so rare
But truly on the inside you shine beyond compare

For in your heart lies such a love of life and creatures all
And through your life I've come to see the dreams I can recall

Of having a dear daughter whose caring, loving, true
And God did richly bless me with a child sweet as you

— *Phyllis Rubadeau*

Why Do I Love You...

I love you because of your caring attitude
that can be heard anytime,
All I have to do is pick up the phone and call...

I love you because of your warm smile and sweet voice.
Whenever I'm having a bad day
All I have to do is either see you or hear your voice
And that usually brings a smile to my face...

I love you because you always know
what to say and when to say it...

I love you because whenever you are around
People or friends that you act yourself
And don't put up a front and show off...

I love you because you make me feel good inside...

I love you because when we're apart
Your absence makes my heart ache
And I feel that this is love
Because I've never felt like that before...

Most of all I LOVE YOU because you're you!

— *Tianna J. Wilson*

A Teenager's Lament

All at once it happened...so fast.
That cancerous disease that took him a past.
He was so loving, so sweet, so kind,
His memory will never leave my mind.

How could such a horrible thing happen
To such a wonderful man?
Tell me Lord, how could it be,
For I can still see his sparkling face
Shining at me.

I still can't believe this happened.
My soul is oh so numb.
I put on a smile; is it real
Or is it there to hide the pain?
But he is oh so joyous for he did gain.

I hope he knows how much I truly love him.
How I would give anything in this entire world
To hug him again and see the lights shine...not dim.
So I could just have my chance to say good-bye,
I wish I could have; but then the time had come
For his body to die.

— *Lori M. Haase*

A World's Nightmare

I dreamed that summer never came
That cold rains and winter winds never ceased.
The trees, once slightly green turned drab again
Tulips, daffodils, and crocuses, once sprouted
wilted, and were dead,
Then the hope within my breast for warmth and summer's sun
died, when the robin taking wing
flew south again.

Oh cold, bleak, rainy days
who visits you upon us here?
Can this then be our punishment for waging war
exploring atoms, yet not for peaceful means?
The H bomb, voyages in outer space,
Science answered all we thought; yet now we know
for the warmth of spring and summer's beauty
there must be God.

— *Barbara L. Brown*

Little Girl

A little girl is an angel's kiss
That comes with the breaking of dawn;
She's the twinkle of dew on fresh spring grass
On a carpet of emerald lawn.

She's the sprite who skips from the tree,
Or peeps from behind a flower,
And spreads her magic over the face
Of your blossoming garden bower.

The musical sound as she lightly skips
And dances with friends at play;
Or giggles with joy at the some wonder of God,
Brings loveliness to your day.

Be thankful to God for such as she,
She's only a child for awhile,
But in your heart she always will be
And remembering will make you smile.

— *Marjorie Seiber*

"Did You Ever Need?"

Did you ever need love so bad-
that even the thought of it made you sad?
Did you ever need someone to touch-
Who would touch back just half as much?
Did you ever need to be kissed-
and to know when you're away-you are missed?
Did you ever need a smile-
and to know for you-someone would walk a mile?
Did you ever need someone to caress-
and know with you-someone is obsessed?
Did you ever need to know someone would
follow you to the end of the earth-
for good, and for bad, and for all it was worth?
Did you ever need to hear 'I Love You'-
and know deep down inside, these words were true?
Did you - ever need?

    —Sally (Gustman) Lyngen

My Prayer for the World

My prayer for the world, Oh Lord, is this;
That fettered mankind shall be free to lift its eyes and
worship Thee;
To feel the sun upon its brow, to hear the lark and guide the plow;
To read a book and walk about, to hunt for birds and fish for trout;
To see and ad and get a job, to help composes a circus mob;
To get a ticket from a cop to be reminded red means "STOP."
To join a club and say a speech, to listen to a negro preach;
To run for sheriff or for clerk, to tip a friendly soda jerk;
To use machinery in a mill, to try a case or pass a bill;
To bake a cake or make a bed, to kiss the tops of babies heads.
To live a life of simple peace and then in dignity—decease.
It may be prayed a better way but this, dear Lord, is what I pray.

    —Ozella Burns

We Met In A Dream

We met in a dream, of what was to be
that hot summer night, when you came to me
through the mist of my mind, in a lovers sleep
you stole from me, the heart you would keep

You bade me come unto you, discover visions that you knew
you bade me leave my mortal shell, to fly the night with you
we floated through the cool night air, ever warming by our
sighs we tasted pleasures few have dared,
lost the wanting from our eyes

As the night grew on, our bodies intertwined
the heat of our love, left glowing embers behind
I had found a love that I knew I would miss
on the taste of your lips, from your soul quenching kiss

But alas my love, the night draws nigh
And away from your arms must soon go I
for when the dawn breaks, and the dew falls anew
then the sadness shall come, of me without you

Then I'll go through the day
though an eternity t'will seem
and wait for you, my love in the night, for we met in a dream.

    —R. Wheeler

Sleeping in God

Sleeping in God, waking in light,
Under his wing, kept from all harm,
Blessing and praising, He rules in white.
Now at His throne, seated with Him,
Glory resplendent, the Omnipotent reigneth.
All glory to Him, given in power,
Darkness no more, Sight of all might,
Sleeping in God, waking in light

    —Alexander Douglas MacPhail

The Essence Of Leather And Hide

A tree is born from within a cavity
that housed a sense of five
A light is on but no one's home
in the cranium of desire
The kitchen table once full of truth
now sprouts alfalfa grass
And a crack or two reveal a new
brick-wall of red and brown
A butterfly with peacock's eyes
investigates the hollow mass
While the sky hears not Rembran't laughter
to scorn the shadow cast
Of a once gracious ring-nose player
who followed the rules and guide
Now reduced to the decaying reality of life
and the essence of leather and hide—

    —Paxton Baylor Mobley

Autumn Love

I thought that on my wedding night, as stars shone bright above
That I had reached the untold height and depth and breath of love.
But oh young friends it wasn't so, as life was soon to prove,
For on that night so long ago, I'd just begun to love.
So many years have come and gone that we are man and wife,
And with each passing year is born new joy and love in life.
I know now that young love can be as ashes in the dust,
Unless like acorn into tree it grows with faith and trust.
The love that filled my young heart then was but a tiny part
Of what would lie around life's bend to fill my aging heart.
he's not so tall and straight today and I am not so fair.
The years have turned his brown to gray and dulled my yellow hair;
But oh young friends, our love is tall and fair, not old and gray.
The acorn grew, now it is Fall. An oak tree stands today!

    —Rosemary D. Ludeau

Dreams Of You

Looking into your eyes I see an innocence
That I wish was me, I feel so tense
Next to your fragile frame, wanting to protect you from
  everything
But wanting you to play the game; I want to hear you sing
In your eyes, so eager to learn; learn about life and love
See more everywhere you turn, seeing more below and more above
Let your heart take you, to places you want to see
And give you the strength to be who you want to be
Trust your bright eyes, to show you the way
To show you the lies, to show you the new day
When you look up at me, I feel so proud
Waiting to see who you'll be,
You'll never be just one of the crowd
And when your heroes fade away, I'll always be by your side
Anytime; Night or day, we never have anything to hide
When you smile your eyes shine, with that vulnerable innocence
I'm so happy you're mine, now I don't feel so tense
I know you'll be alright, with the love we share
You eyes will always shine bright, our love is so rare
And our love is so strong, that no one would dare
Stand between for long; we'll always be a pair.

    —Keith Gabbert

"Helpless"

Helpless is the young and the old
They could be hot, or they could be cold
Seems no one cares, they just sit and stare
The old stare into death, and the young stare into their future
While they sit there crying, no one cares to lend a hand.
So reach out and calm their mortal cries
They are real just like you and I
But help them, they count on us.

    —Misty Miller

Pondering Thoughts

What is there in my life today
That keeps me contented and free?
It's a person who has never stood in my way,
Or kept me from being me.

In our world of the here and now,
Everything has been changed around.
The very words we used before,
Have such a different sound.

Once I would say "she is always gay",
meaning my friend wasn't different than I,
But it would show she was happy that day.
So for the changing in meanings I sigh.

What keeps me going, some want to know,
Well, I'll tell you it this way.
It's been my husband who's kept me aglow,
Even on our worst down day.

The beautiful children he and I have
Of course our nine grandchildren too,
Take heart my friends for what you gave,
You'll receive many skies of blue.

    —*Moyra B. O'Neill*

Polarity

I simply say
that life is evolving good.
Would you have me tear the seed apart in winter's blow
to show you how we spin in air,
disgrace, despair, discovery then, deliverance?
Too much to bear unless it's simply stated.
Until a spring of consciousness, a summer of belief
are forged within an autumn of awareness,
the mind and heart cannot
forgive disgrace, forget despair, discover faith,
deliver up the self to non-illusion,
deliver up the self to boundless joy.
The round smooth shells of seeds
are simple words.
They will be solved in time,
and understood.
I simply say
that life is evolving good.

    —*Yvonne Youst*

Soul Food

Our souls need special nourishment
That meat and bread cannot give.
God has given us four basic soul foods,
To guide us in the way we should live.

The "Twenty-third Psalm" gives the way,
All of us should always think.
It contains essential nutrients to sustain us.
In times of trouble, we will not sink.

The "Lord's Prayer" empowers us -
To freely talk to Him.
Without this daily bread,
The chance of happiness is very slim.

The "Ten Commandments" guides us -
Leads us, and shows us the way.
As we feast on its contents,
We are able to make it through each day.

If we trust Him, and obey Him,
And in His word believe -
The "Beatitudes" reveals the rewards,
That all of us will receive.

    —*Adella D. O'Neal*

Divorce

There is no act more tragic, than a cold divorce decree.
  That separates a man and wife, and parts a family.
    Some people never seem to care, or ever stop to ponder
     About those solemn words! Let, no man put asunder.
    How can they ignore Gods Law, and go on their selfish ways
     Unmindful, of those sacred vows taken just yesterday.
    They! Must have loved each other once,
     With hopes and dreams to treasure
     The after math, of painful divorce
     Is far too much to measure.

    —*Suntina L. Orr*

Baby Harp Seal

You laid down on the carpet of snow
that spreads out with no ending
Your powerless body
rolled to the left and to the right

Steps came from a distance,
steps from the angel of death with his black rope
You tried to run away
but your movement slowed by the freezing air
You tried to scream for help
but your voice disappeared, swallowed by the wind
That steps came closer... closer... and closer
you knew that the time will come very soon
You closed your eyes when finally the steps stopped
and pearls of tears fell from your innocence eyes

The angel of death peeled you alive...
Your red blood left on the white snow
becomes an internal witness of cruelty
of man.

    —*Sally W. Tirtadihardja*

Choice And Chance

  "It is written in the cards." They say.
  That the key to life is in the games we play.
To show love with diamonds to the hearts you've found.
To find with spades the clubs buried in the ground.
To fight with pen, lance, bow, battle-axe, and sword,
The pain, and strife brought on by the unholy horde.
     That mercy, and love
    Are in the flowers the women bear.
     That punishment, and war
    Are in the weapons the men wear.
     That answers to questions
    Come from below as well as above.
     That all around are the symbols
    Of death, riches, weapons, and love.
    That with the queens we all may dance,
And face life's kings through choice, and chance.

    —*Victor T. Greene*

My Little Blue Flower Forget-Me-Not

There grows a little flower behind my shed.
That use to grow in my flower bed.
The wind must have blown it to that spot.
I like the little flower a lot.
So I put it in a flower pot.

I set it on the window sill, in a sunny spot.
So I can look at something real, because I day-dream a lot.
My little blue flower forget me not!

    —*Ruth Culver*

Let's Keep On Learning

And now it has been sixty years, it seems so long ago,
That we received diplomas - what more did we need to know?

We had studied hard and made it to that graduation day,
Thinking all those gifts and wishes would just never go away.

But as days grew into weeks and months, and months grew into
    seasons,
We wondered about many things, and mostly looked for reasons.

Why did we need to find a job? Why did we need to strive?
Could someone else provide for us, so we could still survive?

We've been through good and not-good days, we finally did find
    out,
We didn't know quite everything or what life was all about.

There's always need for learning, no matter what our age,
We may not always find it upon the written page.

We learn from those about us who might quite different be,
They may have even come one day from far across the sea.

Their language and their customs may be hard to understand,
But trying to will help us keep our minds at our command.

One thing we didn't realize in 1932,
Our world would countless changes have by 1992.

        —*Viola M. Valentine*

Home

  The cold crisp air gently sways the trees
    that will tell a story of springtime.
The fields of brown, once scattered with seed,
    stretch to the edges of the evergreens.
  A lone bird flies across the expanse of sky
    in shades of blue and grey.
    And as I sigh, I remember this place,
this place where my heart is and always will be
        It is my home.

        —*Kimberly A. Wobbleton*

All I Know

No one knows me better than me of course.
That's a reality that is very clear.

I realize from the very start
Almost from the minute I begin to walk my life
I goes further and further
As I progress thru the years.

I know who I am and what I want;
I know where I stand.
It's that simple.

Nevertheless, maybe I'm just too proud of myself.
Perhaps, not too humble...
And that makes a fool of me.

Frankly, I don't even know hereafter,
What is there beyond beyond.
I don't even know the numbers of my hair
Even though I'll try to begin to count it this time.
All I know, I have been young
And now I'm old.

        —*Melchor M. Manjares*

"Lost Love"

Remember me;
    that's all I ask
      Before you turn away.
Remember me;
    And all the things, we used to do and say
  You gave me hope, and made me feel
      That love could "flame anew"
But all we shared, was broken dreams
      That never did come true.

Remember me;
    That's all I ask
      and I'll remember you...
        —*Marlond P. Balcer*

"A True Love"

Faithful is a love,
That's based on true.
No feelings can say
The way I feel about you.

You make have the strangest desires,
For they feel my heart with tears of fire.
God's love is what we both share,
His love is soft as an easy care.

It's the love he's put in us,
His decision is always a must.
If he meant for us to be together,
Then his will is for us to be never,
Whether near or far or whatever,
If it's God, It's us forever.

Yes, my love,
Your love is like my Lord's Dove,
It's yours and I possess it.
And your love in my heart is a perfect fit.
As long as God's in the mist,
In my heart your love will exist.

        —*Belinda Sellers*

Matthew

Lay out your truths that has been shown and give all love
that's within, so once you and I can come together as one
for as one you. Can understand and love me just as much as
all the love and understanding. That I can take, lend not a
tear from your beautiful eves for that only shows love with
sadness; yet don't give a heart that has been closed for that
only shows ones misbelief built up yourself to hear all the
Joyest words of the only women to love you.

        —*Tiffany L. Kirksey*

Beyond the Bars

Beyond the bars I can see
The beauty of a house, pound and tree
Dark clouds are rolling across the sky
But don't give up and start to cry
Misery is a state that can not help
Take it from your mind and put in on a shelf
The sky is crying and looks so gray
For the simple reason were so far away
Look past the gray and into my heart
The love we have will never fall apart
Your heart is strong but your mind is your defeat
It breaks our bond and makes you weep
Open your heart and tether your mind
My love for you is true until the end of time.

        —*James Maynard*

A Love Not Meant To Be

Falling in love was supposed to be
The best thing to happen to me
The months we were together felt so right
But all that was shattered one awful night
The night they came and told me my love was dead.

I cried and cried till I could cry no more
I ask and ask the Almighty what for
I went to bed and dreamed about
The love of my life standing big and stout
He was telling me not to be sad
Because the place he was at wasn't at all bad
When I awoke that morning I shed not a tear
For the death of one I had held so dear
I knew he was happy in that heavenly place
I could tell by the angelic smile on his face.

—*Sharon Kaye Wells*

Flying High

The sky is high
The birds can fly
And so can I...

The birds fly high
And the sun shines bright
And the water flows in the river under the sky
And so can I.....

—*Meagan F. Dugan*

Winter

The sun is out of sight,
The birds have left last night.
The wintry winds do blow,
And then down comes the snow.
I like summer, spring, and fall,
But I like winter best of all.
And then comes Christmas with its joy,
To every little girl and boy.
The holly and the mistletoe,
The bells ring out let's have some snow.
And then the Holiday Season's done,
And so has ended all the fun.
But here's a greeting from me to you,
Merry Christmas the whole year through.

—*Nina L. Ervin*

My Beagle Hound's Field Of Trails

My little dog runs swiftly through
    the calm chill night,
As she lets out her call to the woodland
    it just doesn't seem right.
The rabbit she's been chasing through
The golden stands of wheat,
plays its trick like when two
    people meet.
She unravels the trick,
    and understands it quick.
She lets out a cry,
    he doesn't know why.
She runs him down,
On that long trail that belongs to my
    little beagle hound.

—*Rebecca Schopmeyer*

Our Capsule

While we are entangled in each other
The Capsule surrounds us
Embracing us till suffocation
Constricting time
We are all occasional presence

Some sit motionless in one spot
Letting the walls tumble upon them -smashing what is
They fog their view and blur their sight

Let us away the Capsule boundaries
Inhale a renewing breath of life
We will laugh and taunt the Capsule - and jade all sorrow

When the door- rapping fright comes
We shall be flung forth
The Capsule still encasing mortals
Imprisonment a memory

We embrace not in graves
We will forge through the endless outward
Infinite togetherness
Two bodies engaged with time
Two souls married to eternity

—*Sheila McCallum DeBlonk*

The New Covenant: The Age Of Clinton

I had a vision of the ship of state.
The captain ruled by love, not by hate.
The waves were rough, but the course was sure.
The goal was justice, not hate or fear.
No longer words to separate us and them,
but all joined in a conscience filled union of women and men,
My captain stands waiting with outstretched hand to turn
the swords of hate into ploughshares, to restore our land.

Let the flowers bloom again.
Let peace fill all the earth.
Let an era of justice come to all women and men.
Let the land know its full worth.

Let the bells ring,
and the anthems swell,
their message to mankind bring,
That all is well.

Let our goal be human good,
An era of conscience among all women and men,
joined in a common sister and brotherhood.
Let the flowers bloom again.

—*L. E. Ward*

Youth And Old Age

Hand in hand, they walked together out across the desert sand,
The childlike woman, and the silvered man, with a look of
admiration shining in the sweet child like gaze, caused the
man to stride with pride out into the desert haze.

What was their destination, only they and God could know,
this was hot sand all around them. The distant mountains
clothed in snow, still they traveled on together, talking
and holding hands, this childlike woman and the silvered man.

I drew a little close, so I could hear what they had to say,
As they trudged along life's pathway in the desert on that hot
summers day. Life is surely never easy, sometimes it's dark
and rough the way but with God here to help us, we can be free
from the hardships we find along the way.

—*Roma V. Ball*

The Flight Of A Soul

The church of God is a church of nonsense.
The church of Satan is a church of lies.
Choose yourself, the soul inside of you.
From this does truth derive.
Jump inside, jump outside of yourself and kiss
your severed soul.
As your soul and freedom entwine,
And your soul and earth untie.
Awake now from your sombering sleep and
watch the gods and devils weep, as truth
Upon them slowly creeps and painful tears
Slide down their cheeks.
You realize now you've only you.
Your body, heart, and soul are true.
The soul that through God's shadow flew.
The soul the devil never knew.
The soul now rises above the pain.
As it listens to its only shame.

    —Rachel Kerr

In light Of Desperation

I reach into my soul, in light of desperation,
The conflict still grows, a quiet separation.

As the building blocks grow, between one another,
How can I honestly love myself when love is shown,
By the way I treat my brother.

In search of a safe haven, to exist with no real existence,
How far must I go, or can I go the distance.

There'll be wars and rumors of war, so I am told, and there is
no bargain are these just lies, should I believe,
Or pass this off as senseless jargon.

To live as one, to exult, in perpetual transformation,
All people unite, in concrete affirmation.

I reach into my soul, in light desperation,
But to live as such, is certain annihilation.

    —Michael F. James

Dragonfly

Shrouded in the fog and mist,
The crew team practices diligently on the water.
From my perch on a nearby hill,
They more resemble dragonflies on a wet causeway of ribbon.
One scull stands out from the rest.
It is the one sitting idly on the bank.
Waiting for someone to maneuver it onto the ribbon,
To slice it's long oars through the sheet of glass.
Day after day, through good and inclement weather.
That one scull sits idly on the bank.
Its shiny lacquer tells of a life suspended from water.
It is not an old shell, an experienced eye could tell.
And yet, I've never seen that certain dragonfly skimming the glass.
I wonder why.

    —Kristina Murray

Circles

    A gray spray of rain causes her ashy-blond hair
to fall in ringlets over her shoulders,
while the damp earth swallows water in rusty puddles.

    The mourners quietly, gently —
step around the shiny mirrors,
and engulf her tiny frame in their embrace.

    Their cheeks stained with tears,
and coats slicked with rain, they
stand in a circle.
Doing the only thing they know to do.

    —Amy Fletcher

How Can I Forget

How can I forget
the day we met
How can I forget all the days we spent together
Memories that can and will last forever
How can I forget the love that I feel for you
Honest and forever true
But the most that I can't forget is the day you left me
You left me in pain and agony
But what most hurt me was when I saw you with
that other girl
You knew you destroyed my whole world
and you broke my heart, but most of all you tore my
life apart
How can I forget the tears I've shed
How can I forget the words that were said
I shall live in silence and keep my memories
Silence is the word to my heart and my head
But I can't forget that our love was never meant to be
And that my heart is scarred for all.
Eternity.

    —Mercedes Camacho

Like A Rose

A bud is...
    the delicate beginnings of a friendship.
As it grows...
    it becomes beautiful and grows stronger.
Within its folds...
    unforgettable memories of happiness are hidden.
The sweet smell...
    is the care and love shared.
Dew upon its petals...
    the tears of happiness and sadness.
Beautiful bright colors...
    bring hopeful dreams warming the heart.
Sharply made thorns...
    to be protected from unbearable hurt.
Its beauty brings...
    complicated feelings to a deeper love.
Leaves of green...
    a sea of deep conflicting emotions.
At full blossom...
    love is shared to its fullest.

    —Raisa Vaow

The Night Before Christmas

'Twas the night before Christmas and all through the house,
The family had gathered and were quiet as a mouse.
They had come to see grandpa and grandma too,
To eat all the turkey, the cakes and the stew.

The tree was loaded with tinsel and toys,
To grant all the wishes of the girls and the boys.
The grown-ups were waiting with faces aglow.
Though they were as anxious, they dared not show.

Grandpa was seated with his Bible in hand,
That the true meaning of Christmas we might understand.
He read a story from God's Holy Word;
The sweetest message that ever was heard.

Of shepherds and wisemen, of angels and a star,
Of a man and a woman who had traveled afar.
When they came into town, no room was available;
Only clean straw in the Innkeeper's stable.

They welcomed this place, for Mary to give birth
To the greatest man who ever lived on earth.
He was Jesus of Nazareth, sent down from above.
Praise God for His Son, the true meaning of love.

    —Pearl C. Wyatt

Catching The Perfect Fish

Casting out her line into a vast sea of fish,
the fisher-woman knew exactly what she wanted.
Her bait... Innocence, Intrigue, and a well hidden
vigor which was yet to be discovered
in a sugar-coated mystery soon to be uncovered...

The overconfident fish took the bait
never having been so intrigued... Inhibited
by blind emotion, the fish submitted himself
to the excited fisher-woman who reeled in
this sugar-coated mystery only to find indecision.
For this sugar-coated mystery was not all she had envisioned.

The fish dangled helplessly at the mercy
of fisher-women's line. Now, out of his
element and into hers, he could no longer
survive this game of hers.

A wounded fish can no longer swim,
for this same fish, who only comes
once in a lifetime, would not be back again.
But as they say, to justify their ways:
"There are plenty of fish in the Sea"

—*Michael Chrabascz*

Childhood

The innocent laughter that once was shared;
the fun times when no one cared,
the outrageous things that once were dared.
When daddy's love was all that mattered,
mama's cooking and bowls of batter.
Little toys that wind up,
drinking from a sip-it cup.
childhood
Summers spent with friends and foe,
playing in sandboxes with kids you know.
Changing clothes twice a day,
doing things the simple way.
When reading books was mama's job,
and little teeth had problems with corn on the cob.
Little handprints on the wall,
little feet pattering down the hall.
childhood
No responsibility, no rules,
blow up pools.
childhood, the perfect lifestyle.

—*Annette Compeau*

A Child Of War

I look upward at a bleeding crimson sun;
The glaring white light of day grows faint
And fades along with my waning strength.
I hunger for today's sustenance as I
Press through the daylight's torments.

The loud raucous music of gunfire and bombshells
Bombard the air,
And the foul stench of withering, rotting flesh
Stings and sears my nostrils;
Rapier like pains cascading through my brain
Enervate my body sapping its life energies,
And I am swaying on the edges of life and death —
Each at times taking the other's form.

I speak in an ancient tongue born of the first
Stage of existence—inner spirit voices.
Piteous wailings bemoaning my cruel bitter plight
Soar toward the heavens—the cradle of my beginning.
For me,
Where is the sweet savor of the gift of life?

—*Vivian Jordan*

"The Candle"

The wick is you and I intertwined,
the glow is love.
It stays steady and still.
It holds the same shape and size.
Our love warms the base of life,
releasing the hurt and sorrow.
Letting it slowly drip into the pool of
confusion.
It knows not where to go,
But the competitor finds control
the wind if hate blows steadily against the flame,
slowly killing the love!!

WE THEN BECOME COLD ——

As we wait for the match of happiness,
to make us glow once again...
I realize...
Love lit us up...
Hate put us out,
    Causing the pool of confusion to harden,
    and the base of life to be shortened.

—*Loretta Holec*

"Through The Years"

I found you mother after years of searching
the hard times have passed;
and the future is just beginning.

After years of wondering where you were I knew in my
heart the day would come; when we would be together for the
first time and our hearts would become one.

When I see your smile I realize the years that have passed;
for now that we have found each-other the moments will
always last.

The regrets of giving me up it was all you could do;
for you wanted me to have a loving family and God
did that for you.

My life's so beautiful now like a rainbow in the sky;
we have so many years to catch up on ever since that
moment you said good-bye.

We have the future together for this is true;
just remember that I will always love you.

—*Michelle L. Posma*

Spring In The Verbiage

I walked through my garden.
The heavenly hyperbole, the dangling participle,
The purple prose, the hardy cliche,
All were budding and about to bloom.

I parsed the rambling sentences, watered the pathetic
fallacies,
Split infinitives to later transplant,
Conjugated some transitive verbs for my lunch,
And plucked a tiny shibboleth nestling midst the
parentheses.

The hyphenated syllables warbled sweetly in the metaphor.
Spring had come!
Time to compost winter's clotted ambiguities,
Coordinate the fresh conjunctions of May.

—*Jane C. Flowerree*

The Old Pine Tree

The old pine tree out back stands tall and proud
The home of many creatures, chirping loud
It's hard to believe it once was a weed
The pines are so full of life and green
As a small child I went there all the time
In a way I kinda felt like it was mine.
When my day was sort of sad or dreary
A source of protection, it didn't fail to be
Everyday I'd just run out and sit there
I'd sit and think into space I might stare.
When I look at the tree through the window
I think of what I knew then and now know.
I don't run out to my tree anymore
I talk to friends that's what friends are for.
And as I've grown older, I can now see
That friends are a good thing to have and to be

—*Kristin O'Callahan*

My Little Angel — Christina Nicole

Sometimes I see her looking at me, with a smile upon her face.
The innocence of a babe untouched, full of elegance and grace.

An angel, so beautiful, with hair of sunshine gold.
And eyes so blue, they illuminate my very soul.

I see her reaching out to me and never do our hands meet.
I long to hold her in my arms and tickle her tiny feet.

I see her in a field of flowers, her hair blowing in a gentle breeze.
I want to have her close to me, and pray to God upon my knees.

Please take care of my little angel, for I'll never hold her close.
Please let her know how much she's missed, and that Mommy
   loves her most.

I'll always have this image of her in the depths of my mind,
And some day I hope I'll see her again, and peace we both shall find.

—*Tracy Lynn Schiro Vokac*

Lotus-Love In Angel-Cities

'Come, my un-domestic flower.'
The kind without the usual, looked-at look -
Can I trust this disinterest in dower;
This rarity of sultry, lunar night?
Will such nocturnal budding brook
Mornings antiseptic, skeptic' light?

Evenings everywhere are warm and dimly lit,
Mystic, ethereal earth of the art;
Where a pale face rises from the crowd to hit
Ones gawking surface; and stand apart
From dancing, shadowed waves: the other fools.
How she shines; like Buddha's bloom from darkened pools!

'So come, my foreign femme-fatale. I can't resist you; not at all!'

Her perfume's a potent dopamine.
Her lipid stare disarms; and trembling, sets the scene
In this floating-garden of coined delights.

To assure escape from other circling fins:
'Let's share moon-set on the dune (and endorphins),
Far from discoasis. '....On this night-of-nights!

—*Steven L. Reinhart*

Nature Domesticated

The parakeet out of its cage flying around the room,
The kitty scratching its post with head held high, purring,
The terrier sleeping curled on its rug in front of the fire,
The hamster running in its wheel and getting nowhere,
All these are my friends:
They make me feel good.

—*Richard Tuerk*

The Lonely Lamb

When a lamb walks alone, no mother to care,
the lamb is no longer in sight of its mother.
The lamb walks alone on the braces of the moon,
while the moon shines on its' tail. The wolf
of the forest can see the blazing light of the
lambs tail. He goes for a jump and grabs the
lamb, and what is left of it; the fur, the bones,
and a little blood to sprinkle over the waters,
for the lamb who never had a mother.

—*Katie Lucier*

Spring Is Here

As I look upon the world outside,
The light blue sky slowly turns hue, then black.

I hear the soft pitter-patter of the rain.
This moment in time will never be the same.

I am in a trance; then fast asleep.
Being put there by it's hypnotic beat.

Awakened by the warmth of my room,
To shadows chasing each other on the floor.

Light is blinding as I step outside.
Beautiful songs hit me one at a time.

Daffodils bloom above new green grass.
New life has come as I realize spring at last.

—*Melissa Smith*

Spirit of the Light

Darkness, unfortunately has come
The Light, she is gone
She brought us joy and happiness
As all Light brings warmth and comfort
She was special to all of us
But, the Light has faded

Darkness, has diminished the warmth
With this brings a feeling of sadness
As all Darkness does
But Darkness passes, as does the Light

She will be seen again
Only in our hearts and minds
The Light will again bring us warmth
As her everlasting spirit
Will forever be with us
Darkness, cannot take her spirit
Her Light will be here, again

We must remember the Light, not the Darkness
Light, will keep her true spirit, alive within us
Remember, she will always be with us, The Light, she is gone

—*S. Reynolds*

The Storm

Once upon a stormy night, alone and scared, I shuddered,
The lights were down all over town; the candles gently fluttered.
The strong winds screamed a morbid cry like Gaelic banshees
mourned,
As rains extremed, the lightning and the thunder-blasts forewarned.
Briars struck my window with such fervent, shackling, ardor,
Attaching, scratching, snatching at my nerves to make me
martyred.
The moon was teemed, and so it seemed the sky had one vast eye,
To cast a foiled glare down on our world that's gone awry.

—*Traci Nikole Billingsley*

Ode To My Mother

When I think of Mother and home
The likes of which I thought I'd never roam,
And as time goes by, year after year,
Memories of mother become more dear.

And when I think that in her nest was eleven
Plenty of everything and of love there was even
More than enough for each and everyone,
As we grew in stature and wisdom at home
Whatever our goal in life might be
"You can have it if you want", said she
"But work you must and in God put your trust"
And that is the secret don't you see?
To instill success in the hearts of you and me
What a blessing to have had a mother like her!
No one can take her place, that's for sure.
Mother love has always stood the test
But I'm sure my mother was the best.

And with my descendants I can only pray. That they will
remember me some day In reverence, as I do mine today In having
instilled love and trust in my own way.

—*Rena B. Strong*

Move Towards The Light

Coming out of my room, I drag myself across the warm carpet of
the living room floor to open the wooden door. As I step out
into the bright sunlight, I inhale the energy of the morning
sun. The sky glows with its beautiful rays as if God were
opening out his arms spreading his love. The spirituality that
I share with the Lord is something that I cherish above and
beyond reality. But why do I turn back to the darkness and the
dysfunction that is present in my homelife? I see the grung of
a scrabbing punk just outside my window hoping to seek
rehabilitation. He is now released from behind those silver
bars and our good Lord watches him closely, yet from afar. As
I sit in my room early in the morning, I read about the
discombobulated bodies that stem from the darkside. I pray for
this crooked, miffed, and blasted world of today in hopes that
it will change and display the wonders of light from the heavens
above. We will all one day die; but, hopefully we will live in
the eternal lights of heaven and not the torturing flames of hell.

—*Lisa D. Cisneros*

What Gifts Bring Ye

Hark! Can you hear the shepherds say,
"The Lord of Heaven Is born today?"
The words are the same but ever new.
Christ Jesus came for me, for you.

Listen! As the shepherds extol his birth;
Tell how God was brought from heaven to earth,
Was wrapped in swaddling clothes, placed in a stall.
This Jesus who came and died for all.

Harken! To the words He has to say
On this most happy, holy day.
As you buy your gifts and trim your tree,
Can you not spare some time for me?

Think! What gifts bring ye to this God's son
In thanks to Him for all He's done?
To keep Christmas real to make it true,
The best of all gifts would just be you.

—*Ruth S. Wilson*

"Reality"

This land pours the fears from within-
The lost soul of our destiny.
With uncovered eyes we trudge the hill,
What? over the heap that our restraints
And responsibilities are.
To be able to express an era or an ora?
Can any-one hear the teachings of the forgotten ones?
Open the senses to all that is real,
And the light will shine
So, you bold adventures,
Express your lost meanings
And follow the dream;
Because to believe
Makes all of your wild
visions: Reality.
　　　　　—*Norman Rice Jr*

The Love Of The Birds

The love of the birds
The love of the bees
The love of the windy day breeze
Love is like a flower
Growing as tall as the highest tower
Love is when you mark your initials among the kissing tree
Love comes from the heart and a special friend holds the key
Love doesn't come from what you see
From the beauty inside is what it'll be
Love is when you share a secret
And deep down you'll know sure to keep it
Love is when you stand side by side
Helping each other during the times you cried
Love will stay as long as you know
The special bond will grow
The love of the oceans
The love of the lands
The love of people reaching hands.

—*Angela Darby*

Aftermath Inaugural '93

　　　This land that stretches from sea,
the merging of the states borders like infinity. The people,
　so diverse, have their hopes. We are one people, so why
are we divided? Everyone speaks of his or her own passion,
　Where else could you do this, but in the land of the free.
　　We owe this land which supports our styles.
　　　We took it and molded and melted it down.
　　It's a sad land which waits for resurgence.
　　　She sent her young men to do battle,
　don't we owe her a little something of our self?
　　　We have torn and spit on her flag,
　Then why do we hasten to stay within her borders.
　　　Freedom has to be lived, not explained.
This is your land, your country, don't you want to stay?
　May the hope of patriotism stir in your breast today.
　　Go out and fill the cracks, build the mountains
　Go and shine her stars, say the pledge of allegiance.
This land that stretched from sea to sea for you and me.
　Hate and animosity for each other must be laid to rest,
　　Take King and Kennedy's call and make it last.
　　　　　—*Anna L. Holobach*

I'm So Glad

I am so glad the world is so nice,
The snow is white, the snow is bright.
The leaves are green, the leaves are seen,
The flowers are pretty, they smell like spice,
I am so glad the world is so nice.

—*Mary E. McIlroy*

My Fat Poem

Oh! tired and weary, sick and sore, I took a look at me in
the mirror once more. What did I see? A fat jolly person
that couldn't be me. That's not me I'm not as fat, as fat,
can be. I like to think that I am thin, but the mirror says
the diet must began. I'll put it off day after day, hoping
the fat will just melt away.

To make myself the calories count is hard for me to bare.
I measure my food, and weight it, to make sure I get my fair
share. My tummy cries the whole day thru, oh! why are you
treating me so? Give me some pie, give me some cake, quit
making me have a belly ache. I want some coke, I want some
candy, I want everything that's handy. I tell my tummy the
whole day thru that this will not do. The fat is on, it must
go, we are on a diet don't you know.

I get so tired of all the diets, and weighing of the food.
I wonder why God didn't let me be thin. Oh wouldn't that be
grand, if the diet I didn't have to plan, and the weight
would go and I would be thin.

    —Patricia A. Patterson

Young Night

The stars were shining like diamonds in the dust,
The moon was bright with majesty in all its lust,
The wind was warm and the sky was clear,
I looked at the shimmering water as shapes and shadows danced
on it and whispered in my ear.

The night was young,
It had just begun,
It was such a longtime till my eyes meet with the brisk warm
summer sun,
I danced with the trees and let the wind run through my hair,
The night was so lovely I couldn't help but stare,
The grass laughed and flickered in the moonlight with a flare.

The night was so amazing that nothing could compare,
All the night birds gave an orchestra of songs,
All of the creatures and me just danced and sang along,
As I laughed with the wilderness friends,
I thought to my self, I hope this young night never ends.

    —Amy Testerman

Rock Of Peace

    Remember the feeling of immortality
      the mountains so very high?
        God's country before me,
      this beauty no one can buy—
        there he sat.

    Down in the valley, and up the trail
      flow streams of sunlight and dew,
      glimmering wheat fields a swaying
        atop of the mountain view—
        there he sat.

Tenderness glistened in each tiny wrinkle
      features were so defined,
the silence comforting was ere' so sweet
      the scent was "peace" of mind—
        there he sat.

    He remains etched in my heart
      like the heavens above,
      unforgettably immortal
        infinite love—
        The Rock of Peace.

I love you both—God and my Dad.

    —Arleta M. Sage

My Question

So many questions, never any answers
The music is playing but I don't see the dancers,
I wonder if you love me or am I a game?
The person in the movie doesn't have a name
Am I just something to fell your extra time?
I can read the poems but the words never rhyme.
Do you care for me? Or am I just a fling.
I hear a beautiful song but no one wants to sing.
The dancers and actors, poem and song
all have a place where they belong
There's only one place I'd truly love to be.
That's wrapped in your arms with you loving me.

    —Jamie Hunerjager

Me and My Car

When I was young and strong I liked to fight,
The new car I had was a beautiful sight;
The girls would watch for that new car to come,
When I got in sight they would some on the run;
As the years went by I don't fight no more,
Springs sticking thru the car seat make my rear end sore;
The good times we had in that car were more than a few,
The engine now sneezes and coughs like its got the flue;
That car liked rough roads the best,
that's when I got a pane in my chest;
If the ear went dead I would get out and walk,
I am sure glad that Car can't talk;
when the battery run down on it wouldn't start,
sometimes I wished I had a horse and a cart;
I fell out of bed trying to open that car door,
My dream ended when my head hit the floor;
My head is bold now down to the tip of my ears,
I out lived the life of that car over sixty years;
I crippled out in the yard with my hat on my head,
To see that old car rustin' away out by the shed.

    —Raymond Walker

Life

One minute you are here,
The next you are not.
We live in fear,
In hopes to never be forgot.
God gave us life,
We cherish it so,
for the heaven above will be our next home.
We make and lose friends day after day,
never forget to follow His way.
When getting depressed and giving up hope,
just remember one thing,
life is not a joke.

    —Rebecca Klees

Choice

      I think of my older days
        the ones yet to come
          as if I own them
      yet life is never owned.

    I think of walking with a cane

      I think of dying
        of simple causes
not some 20th century disease but from old age and a good life

      I think of my older days
      will they be more pleasant then now?
      will love have eluded me always

      I think of my older days

    —Sunshine L. Brown

Mother

I will always love you for,
the pain at birth, the time your worth.
For the meals that, I turned my nose up at.
For the clothes, washed and mended,
For the spankings not intended.

I will always love you for,
The time we shared, because you cared.
For the love in your heart when we're apart.
For the letters you write,
When you can't sleep at night.

I will always love you for,
The teenage troubled years,
When you would ease the fears,
For that special day, my dad gave me away.,
For the days you were there for me,
For it's you I came to be,
The woman I am now,
For that you deserve a bow.
    —*Mary Jane Stone*

The Palm Strewn Path

Our precious Master rode through,
The palm strewn streets of Jerusalem,
Seated on a borrowed, lowly donkey,
Jesus rode at the break of day.
A curious, noisy clamoring crowd,
Of hopeful people quickly gathered,
Shouting Hosanna to the King,
As they followed Him along the way.

Their great expectations were for,
A mighty, triumphant earthly King,
But Jesus was just a gentle, all-knowing man,
Whose time of ruling had not come yet,
Who knew their cheers, and praises,
Were destined to be short-lived,
And the mighty sound of their voices,
Would fade away, before the sun would set!
    —*June Rose Smith*

"Unspoken Love"

Twilight once again approaches near,
the passions that have slept begin to appear.

The soft lines that contour your face,
begin to form.

Desires to embrace the gentleness of your essence,
to quell the storm.

Slowly as darkness returns to dawn,
your image remains though you are gone.

A vision to hold,
a memory to retain.

A love I never told,
which is still the same.

As the years pass,
I place destiny to blame.

"Forever to Exist "
A love with endless flame.
    —*Michael A. Kotlinski*

At the Taj Mahal

Serenity and peace —
The peace that passeth understanding —
To outward eye surround the ethereal tomb;
And on a moonlit night
One can see tears transformed into marble domes,
And elegies engraved
In arabesques of resplendent hues.

But no one hears the mute sepulchral sounds,
Nor sees the resurrected royal pair
Aghast at the massive profanation
By multitudinous crowds
Who come to see the temple, not the gods,
With prying eyes, unfeeling hearts, ill-mannered tongues.
    —*Naim Siddiqui*

Darkness

The day fades, breaking into dusk,
The peaceful time as the sun falls below the mountains,
Night-creatures come alive, and day-creatures hide,
As darkness ensues, reaching it's tentacles down on the earth,
    creeping.

The wind howls—beckoning forth fear borne years ago,
Fear that can never be abated; that will exist forever.
The darkness awakens, this is it's favorite time
To pry into secure places, making them doubt their security.

The nights when we're together,
The evil of darkness doesn't seem so near,
The other side of the window, that's the place to fear.
Where loneliness awaits, to claim another victim

And oh! Those nights when you are away,
The loneliness threatens to overwhelm.
I reach out to touch you, saying your name,
When only emptiness embraces, and shadows answer.

Darkness smiles, as it has again proved;
Anyone and everyone is subject to it's desires. It's power
grows and therefore, darkness shall never be defeated
    —*Michelle Cloutier*

Seventh Sense

Silent soliloquy, the slow burn of hell.
the phone never rings,the door has no bell.

    Of the people come and gone,
    so few matter in the long run.

    People walk by, faces unseen,
    until one in the crowd asks,
        "Where have you been?"

    Where do you know them,
    your memory can't find,
    the time or the place,
        the reason or rhyme.

    Deja'vu, seventh sense,
    a walk beyond the mortal fence.
    A love once lost, but now found.
    A stroll along forgotten grounds.

    Where do you know them,
    your memory can't find.
    But what does it matter?

    No reason to rhyme.
    —*Sandra Crivello*

Oh My Son!

My quiver lies empty and my tomahawk broken in two.
The prairie is on fire,
our village lies in ruins.
I've seen the fire of hatred that burns in
your eyes,
but I hope that you can still see what
hatred has done to our lives.
We watched the wagons coming, and the buffalo
disappear,
We fought the white mans bullets with our arrows
and our spears.
But oh my son.....If only the words that were
spoken would have held some truth,
we'd still be together, three......
instead of riding two.

　　　—Paul Roberts

To Vera May On Our 57th

People have asked me
The problem they see
How you make differing people agree.
You don't but you try,
And you sometimes ask why;
But the Lord has a plan
For His family of man
And He surely expects us to be
A part of His world family.
So how did we live with the joy and the pain?
For the love of each other each day
And I'll tell you frankly — we pray!
And I'd do it all over again!

　　　—Darrel C Maxson

Eureka - They Found It....

By the sea, the ominous sea
the profanity of pollution
depresses one's soul and spirit
brown foamy pungent water
so filthy none dare go near it....

Skyline filled with stacks and smoke
the breath of monstrous mills
chewing up the scalped and naked landscape
leaving naught a single ancient tree
for future generations to see...

Mountains standing barren against the cold
their forest blankets being stripped and sold
trucked by smoking road hogs across the land
loaded on ships that sail with speed
bound for ports so calloused with greed....

Long ago, before the mills reigned supreme
when the trees were tall and unafraid
ocean pure and pristine, clean were streams
for the redman then ruled and dreamed
nurtured harmonious life, now gone forever....

　　　—T. M. Morris

Wants

The greed has taken over us- the whities on the shore
They take whatever pleases them and then they ask for more.
Where nothing ever is enough we take what isn't there
The children cannot comprehend- presumed their unaware.
I fright with ease this dream of night, this monster in the
make; Never to give for seconds live- the culture grown to
take. Asleep we lay pray we'll arise and see our evil deeds
I hope it so yet still I know-
　　We've made our wants our needs

　　　—Tracy Haus

Vision

I sit in an apartment, filled with empty space.
The room is black with the nights invading darkness.

I can hear the whistle of the wind,
blowing through the autumn trees.
Beyond, I can picture the sound the freeway makes.
Passing cars, humming along at a brisk pace.
The glow of headlights giving their identity away.

Above I can feel the moon; although, it gives off no heat,
I feel its radiated glow fall upon my face.

You shake your head in disbelief,
"How can you see these things?"
You're blind, you mean to say. Nauseated, I reply,
I see with my mind not with my eyes.
Maybe you should close your eyes sometime.

　　　—Wade L. Epperson

Fate Of The Fallen Tree

A fallen tree- tipped away from Mother Earths life giving body.
The roots entwined; veins, drawing life from the Mother, are
　　still reaching and absorbing the gifts she offers.
It is sad, for you are not yet naked as is a withered old tree
　　that has grown tired, and has withdrawn from the Mother's
　　tender bosom.
You do not know that you are dying.
I see you before me, covered with finery, an emerald veil about
　　your head.
The wind stirs and the edges of your veil gently sway in a
　　flirtatious dance.
Soon, very soon, the faltering sun and chill of night will
　　force your kind to adorn their heads with crowns of crimson
　　and gold,
But not you;
By then you will be gone from Mother Earth and her tender
care-Always remembered by me as a slender young maiden, in an
emerald vail flirting with the wind.

　　　—Suzy Kaminski

Winter Remains

A heart that knows:
The season of winter
And of pain that turns to numbness
The freezing from the outside in
In a cold and distant indication
Of a pale and failing light
The days of brief respite
From the reign of darkness
And black, cold-hearted nights
And the suffering of winds
And the cold that creeps
Through cracks and spaces left breathing
Letting cold weather in
And the cruelest of winds
That tear through a soul
In frigid weather again
And a heart frozen
Remembers the pain before numbness came
Before darkness reigned
Now only cruel winter remains

　　　—Ron Zillmer

The Sentinel

In a foreign, distant Land,
The sentinel stands alone.
A terrible heat reflects from the sand.
Yet he is chilled to the bone

Only his thoughts of another time, another place,
Keeps him from loosing his sanity.
A slight smile caresses his face,
But this too, disappears so very quickly.

Soon the sun will burst upon the horizon
Instantly hot, to burn man and sand
A tear stains his cheek and blurs his vision.
His body quivers and sweat touches his hand.

Over head, the planes begin their daily drone,
Sending the enemy scurrying to their shelters.
Shattering his thoughts and dreams of home,
Yet his vigilance never falters.

—*Robert E. Martin Jr.*

Tian'anmen Square

The forgotten sound of night pierces the ears.
The silence of something that has been cleared away, but is
certain to return hangs on the surface like a thick fog.
The fire of rain scatters the locals and the tourists.
Only a few isolated guards remain to enforce their nocturnal
domination.

A forbidden darkness buries the unhealed wounds of years past.
An invisible blanket that hides the truth,
Pulled over the eyes of the Chinese people.
A blanket woven with apathy and denial that they cannot see,
Or do not want to see.

Darkness gaping with the emptiness of lost hope envelops the
vast square. A darkness so intense, so full of emotions that
it is difficult to breath. An internal sensation of lonely
peacefulness passes through the body as you float through what
must be a dream. The new fallen rain exposes a smell that
lingers with traces not of weather, but of human souls.
Rising from the pavement, rising into the sky,
These spirits find a new home glimmering in the stars of night.
A light for every soul that once sheltered the flame of freedom

—*Andrea Wenzel*

A Country Walk

While walking down a country lane,
The sky opened up and poured the rain.
A little bird flying in the air,
Left a deposit in my hair.
A car driving by, tooted his horn,
The driver laughed in scorn.
Trying to rest on a tree stump.
I fell off and bruised my rump.
Squirrels chattering in the trees,
And I could smell that country breeze.
Lying down on the ground to rest
A snake slithered across my chest.
Arriving at a quaint country store,
Literally falling through the door
"Point me to the nearest phone," I said.
They stared like I was soft in the head,
No phone, or taxies, could be found,
But, good ole, Clem would take me to town.
Country walks for some might be fine
But, give me the busy malls anytime.

—*Pat Frey*

Dissolution

A steady, pitiful pulse beat down on the window pane.
The sky was a black shroud covering the Earth.
A steady procession trudged down the muddy lane.
This all seemed such a mockery of birth.

Life was a perfect crystal sphere,
Now completely shattered.
Happiness, sadness, frustration, fear;
It seems it never really mattered.

It is the end,
It is the beginning,
This reality we cannot bend,
The spiral never ending.

The wind wails, the sky cries,
The body dead, the soul has passed.
A new dimension, the spirit flies,
We can't go back, the die is cast!

—*Trigg Bowlin*

Heaven

Last night I dreamed of Heaven.
The sky was fantastically blue.
The buildings of gold towering above me sent
   chills up my spine.
As I walked along a silver street I met God.
He asked if I thought I deserved to be there.
Of course I told him I was unworthy.
Then he smiled and said:
"My child, I know how hard life is.
But even while you are a child of the world,
you are still my creation,
beautiful and flawless in my eyes.
My love for you is unconditional.
I will not make you carry your burdens alone.
Just put your faith in me and go in peace,
knowing that I am always here."

—*Angie Hanners*

The Wind Blows

Soft is the night breeze
The smell of a light fragrance is in the air
The way it caresses a face
A gentle scent of ginger floating on the zephyr
Strands of a child's hair flying free from the mane
Everything is so calm for only a moment
Then I watch the leaves begin to dance swaying softly
The blades of the grass seem somewhat confused
Moving this way and that, not knowing which way to go
In a rhythm all their own
In a moment's notice the rhythm is broken it's still now
In a second, the swaying begins again the lights are shining
The shadows play with one another
As lovers, acting out some romantic love scene
They seem to be in need frantic to find a connection
The sun is beginning to rise breaking over the clouds
The lovers sleep now the breeze has faded
Leaving only an impression in my mind
Of the whisper from the wind

—*Windy Wilson*

The Rose

Your love is like a rose for all to see
The smell so sweet with hope to never die
With stems unbroken reaching up to the sky for me
A color so true it keeps me from wanting to lie.

To see the rose lying there all alone
Makes me think of you more than before
I smell the scent so sweet all through my bones
And slowly wish to be so near you more.

The petals softly brush against my hand
The feel as soft as velvet brings you near
I wish that you were here to take a stand
So I could love you more without a tear.

My love for you has grown throughout the years,
Much like the rose which grows without much fear.

—*Nicole Atkins*

When Homeless Is Your Name

The bitter-sweet cold burns briskly against my face,
The snow, it piles up, leaving me no escape.
The wind keeps on blowing, has it any pity?
Or is it like the rich, uncaring of the homeless in this city?
The people continue walking, not slowing for a glance,
To see someone who really knows he does not stand a chance.
"Please come and save me, Lord." I pray this every night,
And soon, I know, he'll come again and sweep me out of sight.
Still I lay here, quietly in my box,
Though I may not have much, I am thankful for my shoes and socks.
Oh, this land of liberty, how sad she really must be,
To know her people starve to death from sea to shining sea.
Young or old, boy or girl, homelessness is still the same.
So don't be shocked when you wake up and "homeless" is your
name.

—*Sonya Owens*

A Fissure In Life

You better believe it!
The sooner you know it,
The quicker your out of it.

No matter how you got there,
It's a prison - don't stay there,
Look up! Look out! God's there!

Don't say, "Let it be - let it be."
Don't think, "It had to be - had to be."
Don't listen, "It's meant to be - meant to be."

God knows your in it
Be patient while in it
Time brings you out of it.

Love and grief are truer while there
Laughter and insight for being there
Living in peace when your out of there.

Reach upward and outward - let it be.
God can touch you as He did me - let it be.
He is waiting for you - Oh, please, let it be!

—*Marian Koerner-Anderson*

What It Would Be Like To Be A Snowflake

I am a snowflake up above. I am above the ground and ready to
tumble slowly then I start to fall.
As I am falling I hear the joyful laughs of little ones. I
smell the fragrance of the Pine and the mist of the bitter wind
blowing upon me as I suddenly land upon the big meadow soon to
be filled with snow. I have been let free to begin my life
once again but to spend it on the ground waiting to be found.
I am now a part of the world, that is until I melt.

—*Melissa D. Snyder*

Love

It is the vision by which the blind can see.
The sound by which the deaf may hear, and
the voice by which the mute may speak.
It creates life by the power of God and it
exists after death. It is the foundation of
faith and the congregation of joy. It is
freely given so that all may share in its
wealth, and it does not discriminate so that
all races may shine in its glory. It is
a power by which all human and animal kind
are connected with the almighty

—*Ronnie Weaver*

The Man In The Moon

Next to the laundry mat
the street whittles away its days by rubbing against
the balding heads of car tires
and rubber bottomed shoes kicking stones'
rubble loosed in pot holes and weary gutters.
The fantastically fat man who lives in the apartment
above washing machines watches
as the street guides jelly bean colored cars,
stops them and goes them,
even at night when the colors look the same
and the cars seem as empty as the moon.

He grows larger, as the days grow longer
and lean upon one another on their elbows,
bending and scraping as
the world turns over itself and curves
over the streets, and the man drinks water
from the faucet without a cup
and sings to himself about angels.

—*Marci Whiteman*

Night Watch

Tonight, as on many nights, while my family sleeps, I patrol
the streets of our town.

And tonight, as on many nights, I wonder why I spend the
night out here instead of with them.

Then, I think of them safely asleep at home and I realize
why I am out here.

It is because of my love for them, so that they can sleep
safely while I am here watching over them.

—*William O. Rainey Jr.*

Light Fades Into Night

Another earthly day has ended
The sun has set in western sky
The light of day has slowly faded
As moments of this day fleet by

The birds have found their resting places
Midst leaves and branches of the trees
To wait the dawn with all its graces
Their brood with open mouths to feed

We too must lay our cares aside
And rest within His sheltering arms
The God who holds us near His side
Till day break keeps us from all harm

The stars keep vigil through the night
As guardian angels o'er us bend
As all God's creatures see new light
We pray to God new strength us lend

—*G. George Ens*

Untitled

As the pounding waves come and go,
The sun will shine, the moon will glow;
Time will pass, trees will grow,
My heart is caged, love is foe;

As a warrior stands watch all
   alone on a hill,
Waiting on the light to make him
   feel stronger;
Every eternal second hoping for still
The fight is long, but the night is longer;

I have been wounded by love
   somewhere along the way,
Joining an alliance with time to
   heal my pain;
Planning my return by building a
   bounty for the dues I'll pay,
Praying for a treaty of love, so I
   can have peace over fear once slain.

      —Art Hufnagel Jr

Destiny Of Death

The wind blows my hair about my face.
The thunder roars like an angry lion and
the lightning lights up the pitch black
       night sky.
The leafless tree branches look as if
they are motioning for me to follow them
and follow I do as the rain begins beating
      down upon me.

Now, as I stand at the cliff's edge I can
    hear the raging ocean below.
Suddenly the sound becomes louder as it rushes up at
      me.
Fighting against the current if foolish for
   I cannot, but at last I am washed
     upon some rocks.

As my blood turns the white surf red
   I look up into the sky
and smile, for with a rib in my lung and
a stick in my heart I die the death
    which I was born to die.

    —Angelia Ross

God, The Father

Our God, both father and mother lives forever.
The ties of the flesh eventually sever.
Fleeting are our years on this earth
But life begins forever in re-birth.

Birthed in JESUS, the Holy one
Brothers and sisters of God's only Son,
Living a life over troubled waters
As adopted sons and daughters.

God the Father forever so gentle, so kind,
Our home of rest... a settled heart and mind.
If we would daily choose to believe
All of His unending riches to receive.

God the Father is not one who is changing—
Always the same.. in beauty exchanging—
Sorrow and grief are fleeing.
His truth brings joy and gladness to our being!

    —Phyllis M. Mezzera

Underlying Belief

As arid twilight tints the sky, left mournful joy behind.
The time arrives to praise the night within its tainted mind.
Bewildered beasts to charm the soul, from up and coming grief,
Sent blackness lifted through the boundaries of untamed belief.
Throughout uplifted illfulness, beyond the descent wake,
Forms iridescent livelihood among the men he'll take.
Beyond the crescent waking moon above the deathened sky,
Forms trifle, mirrored images among sinners left to die.
Portrayed in vivid evidence, masked with doubtful steel.
Torments with playful ignorance foretook in blind appeal.
For senseless mindful games are played, to torturous mounts
upheave. To bring upon a faithless tread to those who don't
believed.

The morals are not wrote clearly, nor are they hard to
understand. But the words are not wrote merely just to
criticize the land. Simplicity is the basis for complex, yet
trifle things, and to minimize your intelligence for the
ignorance it brings. It may not fit together. It may not be
described. But all the work that's done to live, deserves the
chance to die.

    —Leslie Willis

Little League Excitement

It's spring time and it's finally here,
The time we've waited for all year.
It's time to hear the umpire say,
"Batter up" it's opening day.
You can feel the excitement in the air,
The ball caps perched on player's hair.
The bleachers are full, the parents can't wait,
Hey look, "that's my boy", he's number eight.
Little League baseball is the name of this game,
Once you experience it, you're never the same.
The major leagues can't begin to compare,
With the joy and happiness these players share.
So come on out to the ball park, I'm sure you'll agree,
A Little League game is the only place to be.

    —Rolanda Barton

"Pierced Hearts"

My heart bleeds,
The tip of his wicked tongue has pierced it.
Blood trickles down like rain on a window,
He leaps at the chance to drink it.
For I am wounded and weak against him.
I fight back all the wickedness I can muster,
Yet, he is too powerful.
I call for the mighty of all who walk the earth.
Yet, no one appears.
I am challenged and with fear in me,
I can overcome any beast that crosses my path.
For my heart will mend itself,
Until the future day where it is pierced once more.

    —Nancy Desmond

A Winter Day

The sun had sunk beyond the trees,
   The trees bowed down to welcome the breeze
The frail limbs curtsy, their trunk to squeeze,
   The dew in helplessness will freeze.
The leaves will fall, the earth will seize,
   The blossoms are gone, no honey for bees.
The circling wind twirls, the geese to tease,
   The cracked hulls curl with absented peas.
The toad will sleep on bended knees,
   The summer is past, the winter to please.

    —Roy J. Harris

Village Farmer

Under scorching sun ray when wind rises high
The village gets deserted and well gets dry
The dry leaf, tree top, half bent boughs
Search for the passerby for few drops more.

Sweat runs profusely when heat gets high
The far off farmer still tills on the land
Dry sand blows up, covers his limb
He never pays attention, tills indeed.

With half-bent force on, he pushes his plough
His weak body drags on with slow paced cows
His throat gets dry quickly, the little pond far
His thought for a stopping place but to finish up the land.

His skin looks like ash color, his eyes get red
His little turban, little hope to wipe sweaty head
His feet get sore quickly, blisters many more
He tears up the rag turban to heal up the sore.

When sun touches horizon, time for him to come
He lifts up the little plough, waits for none
His face gradually glares up, his glance goes far
His joy makes him home-bound to touch his little star.

—*Prativa Mohanty*

And Now I Understand...

With a proof, you appear and vibrate the growth of me
The vision of your soul grips my mind so tightly
And it might be a realization or an expectation unfulfilled
That kills other's passions
But still I can remain silent
And you respond to calm the stormy waters in my dreams
When you entered my space and time anxiety died
Contentment was born unto me
Six pounds nine ounces
With ten fingers and ten toes
Shy and bold
With laughter drowning dripping tears
Blowing breath into me for the lost loves of a thousand years
All inhibitions faded into yesterday
And now I understand what it means to say.....
   I Love You
      —*Niki Rene' Webb*

Great Grandfather

I remember you.
The visits I dreaded.
I am sorry I didn't enjoy them.
Never had the chance to really know you.
I was too little to understand.
I missed out on all the wonderful stories you told mom.
Now you are gone forever.
But I still remember you.
Wrinkled and frail.
Feeling as if though I touched you
You would fall to dust.
I regret what I missed.
But I am glad I still remember you.

   —*Sarah Woodhouse*

Robert And Me

When I'm down, without any hope
With no chance of reason,
little time to cope.
I have a light that shines inside.
It heats up my wisdom and dust off my pride
The light tells me why we're free,
because Robert Kennedy was once a
seaman like me.

   —*Patrick S. O'Shaughnessy*

Breaking Through A Reality Of Dreams

Rainbows caress the hillsides
The warm silky feel of her skin resounds from the
sunlight
Dancing clouds fill a mind with rapture
Questioning movements explode in the air

Has she left an unfinished dream in his heart
Wallowing for the sake of self-pity
The ocean mists drift in, taking out the memories of the
past.

She has gone!
Lifting with ease like an invisible wind
Torrent as ocean waters heave on cliffs
Pain envies a once happy soul
A troubled tension shadows his brow
Reality shows the null void she has brought
In leaving,
He fights truth like it was his last temptation, he its prey
Crying out with the screams of a gull
This dream state must not bind reality!

Awaken,
She breathes besides him...

—*Michael Hooper*

A Fighter's Strife

My heart burns of fire, my mind burns of fear
the warrior inside me grows stronger year by year;
my heart beats thunderously, my mind thinks fiercely
the volcano inside me erupts almost instantly;

Just like a tiger, I hunt down my prey
ready to attack, not a sign of delay;
I pounce on my victim and denounce his reign
letting him know who the hunter is, and who, is the game;

I come out of the fury with a devastating deliver
leaving my opponent, standing there to shiver;
The signs of first blood give me a sudden chill
like a shark in red water, I move in for the kill;

With a relentless attack, and an undermining terror
I drop my enemy into a state of despair;
I take pride in the victory, and pray that I'll never fail
for come the next battle, I shall also prevail.

   —*Nick Cortesi*

"Mirror On The Water"

As the blue waves roll into shore
The white sea gulls fly so high
The sun is brilliantly bright as always
While we're dreaming of days gone by.

We stroll the sand hand in hand
Enjoying the thoughts of yesterday
Knowing that our time is not long
But our love is really strong to stay.

The waves come in, they hit the shore
Bringing us thoughts of Love once more.
The shore is very long so they say,
It stretches for miles along the way.

The sun was so bright that day
It shone like a mirror on the water that way
Reflecting back lovely thoughts of you alone
Time may soon be gone, dear,
But your memory will always linger on.

   —*Merrilyn Fitzsimmons*

Moonlight

When I see you standing there,
The wind blowing through your hair,
Your eyes sparkling bright,
In the warm summer moonlight.

When I hold you standing there,
With the touch of your skin ever so fair,
I'll hold you ever so tight
In the warm summer moonlight.

When I kiss you standing there,
I'll caress you with such care,
I'll embrace you - because it's right,
In the warm summer moonlight.

When I see you standing there,
I'll be here for you because I care
The gentleness of your touch puts me in flight,
In the warm summer moonlight.

—*Marvin Putman*

The Coupon Cliptomaniac

Heaven help the supermarket junkie
The wretched coupon cliptomaniac
Driven on by her addiction
She has only one conviction
She must try to get the monkey off her back.

Her husband tries to read the daily paper
His wife is driving him to misery.
With relaxation on his mind
He is soon appalled to find
Empty spaces where the coupons used to be.

She's become a victim of her habit
And everyday she has to have a fix.
She's a maiden with a craven
And her shopping cart is laden
With the discount coupon items she has picked.

Fearing that she's going to loose her marbles,
She's decided to consult the family Doc.
He said "your sanity's intact
You're not loosing it, - in fact,
I'd say you're just about as crazy as a fox."

—*Maureen E. Johnson*

My View Of The Vietnam Memorial

They stand there in silence with tears in their eyes
Their reflection is vivid of their friends that have died
The wall that they stare at is forever and deep
With their comrades in arms & the families that weep

For a sacrifice given let no one dismay
They would do it again God made them that way
Don't cry for your comrades their battles are won
but weep for old glory that waves in the sun

Be forever vigil a watch must be kept
So that freedoms not lost for those that have wept
Tell those we elected the right way to go
For God and his power knows what seeds to sow

Whether the fruit of our planting will be
Bitter or sweet it is all up to thee
So join in the cause with all you can give
For all that have died so that freedom may live

—*Terrall Hanson*

If Eyes...

If eyes... fading eyes find ecstacy in love,
then I will be the flower who whispers thy name
in the fragrance of time.

If words had no meanings, and
dreams were the same without any reason,
then I will be that cup of wine that was sweetened
by thy presence.

If all the oceans be wine and all the deserts garden.
If fishes are to be drowned in water,
and tears were to be laughters
then I will be the idol that drinks wine from your cup.

If my eyes were stones carved into thy image.
If memories were thy shadows,
and you suddenly became a flower,
then I will be the last vision seen by those fading eyes.

—*Shahzain Husain*

The Affects Of Her Essence

Before day break it is oh so dark and lonely and cold and
then over the eastern horizon she rise! She is bright, ever
so bright, shining brilliant light that ushers in the dawn.

With the dawn it is a new day. A day like no previous day
and it is filled with new hopes and new dreams and new
aspirations and new ideas and new directions and with love
like never before imagined. A day with new horizons brought
to me by this warm yet hot radiating beautiful beaming
mystical star. She inspires my soul morning, noon
day, and afternoon.

I become sad as she fades deeper and deeper into the western
distance forcing darkness in where she once shone so
magnificently. As the darkness thickens I am already
becoming glad because I know she will rise again for me.
Rises again to give me another day like no other.

My sugar loaf, my betroth, my wife, this is the effect of
your essence on each day of my life.

—*Willie Stocker*

Quiet Praise

If only you could see yourself through my eyes,
Then you'd know perhaps, you'd realize
Just how beautiful you are to me.

If only you could feel my heart beat or my passion rise
Whenever I touch you or you touch me.
Perhaps you'd realize.

I cannot say with words and ever make you understand
The many things that make me love you so.
Words, no matter how they're put, seem slight,
And can't describe the love my heart can know.

Poems from this poet's pen are all in vain,
Ways of saying to no one, the things I wish to say to you.
So I live each day and love each hour,
See you smile each chance I find,
And think about you when you're gone,
Leaving my trail of poems behind.

—*Steven D. Brandlein*

As Years Pass

As darkness falls upon me. I think of the times I've shared
with you though they get fogged as the years passed. And the
memories are no longer. You will always hold a special place
in my heart forever, that I promise.

—*Melissa Dann*

First Line

The sea is calm tonight,
There is a slight breeze.
As the sun sets in the Western sky,
The sky becomes filled with color.
The stars begin to appear one by one,
The moon grows brighter by the coming of night.

The sun is now completely gone,
The stars fill the sky like little diamonds.
There are too many to count.
All the color has disappeared, the sky is a deep blue.
The cool breeze blows gently.
The sea is calm tonight!

—*Kimberly M. Johns*

Reflections

When I look into my mirror
There is a stranger that I see.
Who is that old gray haired woman
Staring back at me?

How dare she, with her wrinkles,
Invade my precious space!
Where is my long black hair
And my eager, shining face?

Seems it was only yesterday
That I sat daydreaming the hours away
Wondering if my young man
Would ever ask daddy for my hand.

For just a moment I can see
That care-free young girl looking back at me
But in a flash and twinkle of her eye,
She is gone and I breathe a sigh.

How fast the years have gone by.
Suddenly, I realize why
That white haired woman stares back at me.
My youth has been replaced and I am she.

—*Julia Guenther*

The Noise We Made

There isn't any starlight,
There isn't any moonlight, it's just black tonight,
Like the screen when a camera does a "fade",
And I wonder...whatever happened to all the noise we once made?

Whatever happened to all the noise we made?
The Passion we displayed?
Was the laughter a charade?
I always thought more than this could be saved,
Considering all the noise we made.

For future investments in new starts,
For future investments in our hearts,
For future stories when we're apart,
We should remember nothing was betrayed,
It's just a piece of us that got away in all the noise we made.

It seems it takes too long,
To find out where our hearts belong,
But don't wait...don't be afraid,
Can't you hear it? ... It's almost like the noise we once made.

--*Stephen Meyer*

The Door

The door opens.
    There lies an infinite road.
    Stretching nowhere.
    Going no place special.
    Going where sands of yesterday once were.
    Where musk-scented flowers sway in the breeze.
    Where cherubs weep for famished mortals.
    Where icicles dangle from the hearts of men.
    Going.
    Abandoning.
    Leaving.
    Leaving all the shadows of slumber.
    All the fears.
    All the dead.
    All the spiritually correct.
    Choking no more on the stench that once kept me amongst
        the living...
Behind the door.

—*Jennifer L. Rogers*

My Lady Love

As I awoke, and peered out my window this day
There was much in my heart for which I have to say,
I looked at the snow covered ground
and still remembered the Love we both found
The purity of the newly fallen snow
is like our Love for each, as we both know!
It has been a difficult time for just us two,
to attempt to get our love back, and start anew!
And to put the feeling, back into our lives,
as we only know, which is worth all our strives!
No matter who, or what they may say,
This is a Love, for which they can't take away.
So, as we look back to the day's that have past,
The Love I have for you, and you for I, must last,
Cause as I stand at our spot and watch the bird's
soaring far above,
I think of my one and only "My Lady Love"

—*Richard T. Risco*

Only One

When someone you love is taken away
There's a hurt in your heart day after day

What did I do!! You scream in a fit,
You try very hard to understand it.

Was it something I did that was so bad?
Is that the reason God was so mad?

Your told it gets better and time will heel,
Yet still inside you know how it feels.

As time goes by its true what they say,
The hurt get less day after day.

Still in your thoughts now that you've grown,
All the hurt comes back when you're alone.

To take their place there is no other,
For there can be only one mother.

—*Mary Moore*

"Love"

They say, love makes the world go 'round.
They say, it's better to have LOVED once, than not to have
    LOVED at all!
They say, love your neighbor as you would LOVE yourself.
They say .....

Too bad so much energy is put into the words of LOVE,
and not enough into the acts of LOVE!

—*Lori Lampron*

Smiley Faces

I love to look upon smiley faces,
They bring such a joy that only love embraces
  From black to white to yellow to brown,
To all the little children that hunger and frown
  Hang on to some hope and dream on a star,
That a fairy will come, but she won't take you far
  To a joyous place of no sorrow or pain,
You can run, you can skip, you can play in the rain
  For it is destined, for dreams to come true,
Just believe and I feel it will happen to you
  And when its all done and your dreams become real,
Look back where you came from and see how you feel
  Then bow on your knees and thank God for his graces
For special children like you and your sweet smiley faces.
        —*Tina Christine Burkett*

Census

They counted us all up
They call it taking census
Nursing homes and condos
And behind our prison fences

When they got to some
It cut them to the bone
When they had to answer
Sir, I have no home

There is a lot of us
And our planet is in trouble
With every new sunrise
The population seems to double

A people so self-centered
Weakens our defenses
Could it be St Peter
Will conduct our next U.S. Census
        —*Mary Frances Powell*

Vivisection

The hallway with those white lights a scent of pain and death
they carry. My friends are locked up and one is strapped down.
The pain he feels I know is great and tears come to my eyes as
he succumbs to deaths dark wings.

  I dream of an open window where the moon comes in and the
good fairy takes us away from this sin. The morning brings no
sunshine only an eclipse of death. My once proud and mighty
heart now clouded with worry and doubt. The pain will be great
beyond imagining and no void can fill its, space. I can only
pray to the father of heaven for the ounce of courage he once
gave me and a chance to rest inside his gates. Some people say
I have no soul or place in heaven. Then why with no soul should
I be put through hell?
        —*Jess Melendrez*

All In Unison

Ghandi, M.L.K., and Malcolm X
They didn't just fight to save their necks,
They believed everyone should be equal,
every face, no matter what sex, no matter what race.
From the slaves to the riots and the Rodney King jury.
There has always been something and it is fury.

For decades and decades many people have tried.
Some have succeeded but a lot have died,
The barrier is part broken but not enough
So try not to forget all this stuff,
All the races should make amends,
And not be enemies, only friends.
        —*Richard Ridge*

The Eye's

Two eyes are watching you!
They have no colour
They don't want to be racist.
They are clear and sparkle.
These eyes love you and everyone
These eyes love watching and protecting your every move.
These eyes hold no hatred.
These eyes care full of wisdom
Your future will get brighter
Your bodily movements so gracious.
But when will this happen?
But why don't you feel these things now?
But surely you are living?
But is this all true?
Yes, the two eyes belong to you!
        —*Natalie Attrill*

"Trust"

Trust is a being extinct, I think,
They hunted it down and hounded,
Until it found it could resist them no more.

They tortured and harassed and betrayed it,
Dismayed it,
They played it like some sick game,
Now it's not the same.

This thing trust no longer exists,
Nothing but a shadow of what once was,
And will never again be.

Soon it will be no more than a memory,
You'll see,
And they'll wish they had never destroyed it.
        —*Stephen Louis Boyd*

Abortion

I don't understand the world we live in today.
They made abortion legal, which is wrong in every way.
They are aborting babies in a mother's womb at 6 months old.
That's a full grown baby, God only knows.

I'm telling you this because it's so.
We have one, fully developed from his head to his toes.
People wake up, you're destroying a human life.
When you do you are going against Christ.

It makes God sad to see this day after day.
But He picks up the pieces and remolds his little clay.
There are so many couples who would love them in their life.
Please put them up for adoption, that's only right.

So please people, help by taking a stand.
To save our babies, our futures throughout the land.
Let's prove to the government, there's many Christians left.
Let's save our babies, because they can't save themselves.

I support the right for life, my opinion I've spoken.
Abortion is wrong, one of the ten commandments is broken.
Mothers, don't let the doctors fool you and lead you astray.
That's a human life inside you, they are killing everyday.
        —*Wanda Gray*

"I See Your Eyes"

I see your eyes
they make me cry
you are so beautiful, I love you so
without you I die

I see your eyes
they show so much of you
your compassion, tenderness
and how your love is true

I see your eyes
when your in pain
come to me, I'll comfort you
when you feel your in the never-ending rain

I see your eyes
when your happy and joyful
they express your true emotions so much
you are so kind, loving and thoughtful

I see your eyes
as they well up with tears
as you walk down the aisle
to join me through the years

—*Troy S. Schade*

Untitled

At times I feel I am a puppet to the words.
They march forth from my soul in their authoritarian garb,
The mighty soldiers tugging my strings,
Seducing my mind with images
In the middle of the night
Until I am scrawling phrases on tiny scraps
By the dim light of the moon.

Yet, other times, the strings are umbilical cords
Binding me to the truest expressions
Of my reality.
The words, my treasured creations
Though separate, as much a part of myself
As the hand that wrote them,
If not more so.

—*Ottavia Piergiovanni*

Love Is God

God said, "Set me as a seal upon thine heart, as a seal upon
thine arms, "for he is love, strong as death, jealousy is as
cruel as the grave, so gimmy love, for its as a dove, not a curve.

Search the world over, joy, gaiety nor happiness you'll not
find, 'til this love you take of, and be consumed by its coals,
for they are the coals of a consuming fire, take it on, and
this you can cheerfully judge, then serve, for it comes from above.
Time will tell you see, cause many waters cannot quench it,
laps of time, nor can floods drown it, for it comes with a
surge, that comes from the Lord, 'tis without end, and fits just
like a glove, tis satisfying to the nerves.

Ain't' Love great? Ain't' it wonderful? Tis grace you see, its
salvation unto ones soul, and cannot be purged, tis Love; Tis
Love'm which is all, it is the essence of life, for the essence
of Love is God, for God is Love, that's what love is can't you
see, can't you know that Love is God? Love is God, it is He
then, that I shall serve, tis this love for all my neighbors
in this world, especially the old, tis all RESERVED.

—*Roy Lee Burns, Sr.*

One More Night

It can't be true,
Things can't be over between me and you.
We've worked so hard to get it right,
Let's just give it one more night.
One more night to discover,
All the things we need to uncover.
One more night to decide,
Weather we've got anything to hide.
I want you to hold me tight.
I want to feel your kiss so light.
Just one more night so we will know.
Just one more night to let the love flow.
I just know we could make everything right,
If we just give it one more night!

—*Melanie Barry*

Someday!

There's going to come a day of reckoning for a lot of the
things we allow. Like talking Christ out of Christmas and out
of our schools as well. Someday this nation will crumble like
Rome, and those of old for we are sewing seeds in rubble, seeds
that will surely grow. Rebellion and riots are commonplace in
most every part of our land. The children are doing their own
thing and no one is raising a hand. God began our life with
freedom with his own perfect plan. But man with his will, is
working hard still, to see what he can command. Someday the
heavens will open and the Master will show his face, then
those here on earth will know what He meant when He said, "I
will repay." Their knees will bow without question and homage
to him they will pay, they may have denied Him while here on
this earth, but they will not deny Him that day! We are given
a life, such a short time to do what we must while we're here.
Why spend it all fighting against Jesus when he is the reason
we're here? If He hadn't come down from heaven and lived and
died for our sin, what hopeless and helpless people we'd be,
better if we'd never been. So take down the signs if you want
to... Don't mention Jesus ever again.

—*Barbara S. Brewer*

What Can I Do For Jesus

At the beginning of each new day,
Think "What can I do for Jesus?"
"What can I do for my Lord today?"
"What can I do for Jesus?"

When you help someone whose way is
hard, you are doing if for the Lord;
and God will bless your as a reward,
if you do things for Jesus.

As you go through each passing day,
think "What can I do for Jesus?"
Watch for the chances that come
your way; think "What can I do for Jesus?"

When you give someone a friendly smile,
you make your own life seem
more worthwhile; and God will welcome
you as his child, if you do things for Jesus.

—*Wanda Pennebaker*

Born In The U.S.A.

In fifty eight, when I was born,
Thirteen years past the great world war;
Some years went by, young camelot fell,
We thought the nation had gone to hell;
A young King had dared to dream,
He died to soon, so it seemed.
To Vietnam in such a hurry,
Then came home to no ones Glory;
They tied us up, put blindfold's on,
They toppled Jimmy from his throne;
An American Challenger raced to the sky,
A shattering thunder, five Angels died;
A little man, showed his neighbors scorn,
We went an fought him in a desert storm;
There was a people with need, because of people with greed,
Our young soldiers were sent to feed;
From Arkansas a star came forth,
Bringing promises of America's rebirth;
From my birth, to my last day,
I will live with pride in the U.S.A.

    —Roger Horton

Untitled

I have become one of the infected ones,
This common and rare disease has struck me
and soon it will tear me apart.
It has infested on my rich blood
As it has many of those before me,
For it has practiced on others.
It strikes anytime
and will not abandon until complete,
Passion or obsession,
It is quite happy with either
yet never satisfied with neither,
And when the disease is gone,
I will be happy it departed,
But oh, I will relish for it again
No matter how much pain love brings my way.

    —Sam Graham

To Wait

To insanity which I am close,
This human mind suffers so.
Cursed to wait from long ago,
By forbearers own petty souls.
Concerned for none but their own,
Scarring an innocent child for life.
To believe the cure can come from the edge of a knife.
Through his neck, wrist, or eye,
But this child fearful to die,
Will wait and suffer,
For years to come.
And accept no death,
But a natural one.

    —Jerome A. Smesny Jr.

The Sands of Time

The Sands of Time and Mother Earth
The great gifts of life and birth
The mere existences of this interactive planet
Is a firm, reliable rock, like granite.
The clockworks of the universe, of space
Are rhythmic and full of grace
Mother Earth and Father Time
Sent this huge clock to chime
To renew the harmony
Between human kind, you and me
To restore the truth and trust
That was lost in greed and lust.

    —Trina Bullard

"What Is A Tomorrow"

The day you are born, you are marked to die,
This is the pattern of human life, as the years go by.
Childhood is a fantasy, where everything's bright and gay,
And tomorrow is a time, that comes most every day.
The teenager finds out life is not to keep, only God gave it to borrow,
Then starts living reckless and fast, cramming every thing in their tomorrow.
One day the fun is over, and they've grown into a man,
Selective service now calls them, and they're ready for Uncle Sam. Off they go to Vietnam where there is a war of horror,
Hoping and praying, that they'll live to see another tomorrow.
And then comes Old Age, Social Security, and State Medicare,
And with this kind of income, this old world looks barren and bare they should not be shut out, because they're ill, or that they're growing old, but instead of neglect, should be living, and happy, in a palace made of gold. They don't feel needed anymore, so their old days end in sorrow, feeling lost, scared, and lonely, for to them, there is no more tomorrow.

    —Molly Magee

A Farewell To Winter

Shall I compare thee to a cold winter's night?
Thou art more distant and ungiving
Windchill doth bring more comfort and delight
And winter's trees seem to be more living.
Too hot the eyes of Satan shine
And often his desires burn thy soul from within
And in his midst all darkness combine
By thy will to be a temple for vile sin.
But thy eternal winter shall not reign
Nor for thy wretchedness myself I blame
Nor be victimized by my temptress's pain
Even though thou has crucified me with shame.
So long as I shall live and am free
So long alone in darkness thee shall be.

    —Angela D. Strange

Untitled

I call to thee...
Thou who halt thrived and survive in astral health, come!
I summon thee, my consorts, my allies, let us harvest...
Let us spend the coin of cosmic wealth...
Come before the net of nerves, my mind,
I call thee my guiding image...
And within the depths of my truest knowing,
the center, my soul, I call thy guiding whisper.
Speak, speak out the yield of yester years.
Speak your perceptions of the present.
Come aid me to divine our forming future.
Teach the truths you have learned,
since the burst of creation...
Say that we may cross the aeons,
into the unfoldings of eternity.
Speak! Aid me to form Eden anew.
Upon our wounded world. Come guide this lone speaker,
seeker to rituals of divine power.
Power for salvation.. the salvation of all.
I call to thee... my ally.

    —Amy Roberts

Here I Sit Waiting

For what I'm not really sure
Thought I'd have a call from at least one friend
But no-way
Looking back over my life
I wonder why some romance came my way
Yet, I'm left alone today

This must be what life is all about
Just waiting for time to run out
Life isn't fun anymore when you're alone
All I can do is look out a window or a door
I can't go anywhere anymore

Was that my phone or a doorbell ringing
Could it be an angel singing
No
It was just my ears ringing

Why do I sit here waiting for what or for who
Could it be all those dreams that never came true
Or am I sitting here
Waiting for God
  Just like you
    —Sandy Jo Roemer

Thoughts

Thoughts come from deep inside,
Thoughts are something you shouldn't hide.
Occasionally you speak them out loud.
Sitting around with the crowd.
Someone ask "what did you say?"
You return with "all nothing just thinking - "out loud."
Do we hide behind those words.
Cause our thoughts are not to be heard.
Or do we just shun away,
For no one would believe our thought, today!
    —Patricia Robinson

Death, My Friend

Doth gather fully, as the Sage of time,
through every sprig and lowly bending bough,
the sounds of life emitting nature's quake.
A season captured for the earthbound thou,
Uncaring whether smooth or furrowed brow.
It's only death, my friend.

An ever moving, changing sky doth show
a vision clearly seen, a blackened sky turn blue;
Blown by a flow of wandering wind a circle make,
a land, a sea, a sky shown constant, ever true.
Regret. Return a bolder, brighter hue;
The way of death, my friend.

So shake the soul from comfort's sanctuary held,
a union chartered by that realm so high.
Life's limb hath gathered fruit, now to refrain.
A changing will, life's breath grown still, no breath to sigh.
Earth's claim remains. Another death to die.
It's only death, my friend.
    —Margaret J. Baker

Do You Hear It?

It is more than lyrics put to melodies
Through incredible talent and time it becomes Art -
A type of expression for the musician...
    An escape for the listener...
It becomes a peace between cultures -
It allows you to listen...
    to think...
      and to feel..
This is Music.
    —Sharon Myers

Window Of The Past

I'm lying here, feeling so lost so empty inside, looking out
through the cold window of the past I see a small three year
old boy, looking up at me with love in his eyes when I think
of all the times the little hugs and kisses he gave me "all
the joy" I see all this looking out the window of the past
This is my youngest and only son who had just started college
at 23 then there it is the window of the Past calling me: Come
look here's your son at four his dark shining hair, eyes all
aglow with a boyish grin why did my handsome strong son die,
Why? It was a cancer of the lymph nodes something, that with
treatment, would be gone but chicken pox came along and now my
son is just a memory a beautiful song all I see is this window
to the Past beckoning to me all my hopes and dreams for my
beloved child whose life had just begun but out from (this
Window of the Past) it keeps saying - from sickness, pain and
untold agony your 23 year old son is safe at last, he sends his
love, "mom don't cry", my soul has survived and someday we'll
meet again and not through this cold Window of the Past.
    —Sandra Stevens Casalinuovo

A Circle Of Love

Round is the world, a circle of love
tighten with ribbons to keep inside
all the spirit, all the strength,
all the grace, all the talent.
Round is the moon, shining so bright
to light my road, to light my life.
Round is the magic crystal ball
where my destiny and fortune are wrapped.
Round are the pearls that form my necklace
hanging so gentle around my neck.
Round is the wedding ring, a circle of love,
to keep the heart warm forever on hearth.
    —Salua Janett Torfan

Love

Love is quicksilver, just when you think you have grasped it
tightly in your hand, it slips thru your fingers.

Love is wind, you know it's there and can feel its touch,
but don't try to grasp it because it's not there.

Love can grip your heart with laughter, happiness, sorrow
and pain.

Love can leave you floating on a cloud or leave a scar that
will never heal.

Love is so hard to find and yet, be lost easily.
Sometimes without a reason, love eludes us and slips away
and we never know why.
Love can't be explained or reasoned, while you have love.
savor it and never take it for granted for tomorrow it may
slip thru your fingers.
    —Patricia Jean Pinz

The Law Of Balance

Let not your tears drop like falling stars
to crease your cheeks in vain,
for the cause of it was wrought of anger
and jealousy, to inflict pain.
That shall harm only the giver.
So waste not those tears on such as those.
For their time too shall come,
At an unbeknownst and untimely day or hour.
For Universal Law shall mete
Out its justice in full.
    —Amanda Bartz

Bleeding Heart

10... Angel of death, I see, without care for tiny yellow feet
tiptoeing on broken glass of elders' folly.
9... God of valor, I see, avenging eyes melted by the glaring
red, westerly sunrise.
8... Guinea pigs, I hear, squealing in a fenceless cage,
seeking escape of experimental incision.
7... Eagles cry, I hear, pronouncing its battered pride across
a world rotating reluctantly on a hated axis.
6... Must I sponge the tears of a million helpless screams?
Feel the pain of burning flesh, falling in a forest fire of fury?
Retard myself to animalistic, Social Darwinistic Nazism and
complete the full circle?
Am I the American Fuhrer trapped in a decisionless cockpit
pulling the trigger to a personal holocaust?
2... A true man wouldn't...
1... but I did. Bombs away!

—*Jeff Powers*

Bestfriend

To a bestfriend who has never lied.
To a bestfriend that makes me feel good inside.
To a bestfriend that will always be there,
I want you to know I am here to share.
The wonderful memories that we can still see,
Like a clear ocean, with a little summer breeze.
We laughed, we cried, we even fought
But not being friends, we never thought.
We have many more years to party hard,
Before we can charge our stuff to a credit card.
Our friendship will never end,
And I'm here for you with a shoulder to lend.

—*Melissa Stein*

The Painter

I, me, see, what can I say,
to be like the color or shade of gray,
That's not me, oh no it is not,
there are many lessons to be taught.

Oh, no I might, oh, yes I may
I won't use this shade of gray,
Do you think I should, if I could,
be myself, yes everyday or should not say.

Can I do without my favorite colors today,
pink, purple, orange and red,
Without my pastels, I will dread,
I hope, I hope, I can find them.

Oh, I found them, yes I found them,
and now I can be myself again,
Because it's not what you do,
if it's not you.

—*Sarah Marie Reyes*

To Be Free

To see the world as I did when I young.
To believe in all I did when I was a kid.

To have the hopes and dreams of a child again.
To be able to believe in something (anything).

With all your heart and soul.
As only a child can believe.

But best of all to love totally and with out
reservation.

As only a child can Love.

—*Marcus P. Padilla*

"My Best Friend"

You're just the kind of friend I need
to brighten up my day,
And when I'm sad and feeling down
you know just what to say.

There's been a lot of times that I
have needed a helping hand,
And you're always there to help me
letting me know you understand.

And then there's times when I need someone
to tell my troubles to,
You sit and listen while I talk
as a friend will always do.

A friendship is a special thing
it flourishes like a rose,
And because it is so beautiful
it grows, and grows, and grows.

It doesn't happen overnight
It takes special love and care,
To make a friendship that will last
That we will always share.

—*Pamela Atkinson*

The Loss of Mozart's Pet Songbird

(A starling in prime of his brief time,
to drain death's bitter pain," Mozart)

Dear reader, please, with me, shed a tear,
For my saintly little songbird, I prized so dear.
That he is now, eternally, so high,
Singing and winging, in his heavenly sky.
Yet, so sorrowful I remain, that death,
Has taken from me, his melodious breath.
As my own music, from my heart,
Is so suddenly, and sadly, shorn apart.
My faithful little songbird, so lively and bright,
Has left me grieved, in his final flight.
My musical little angel's earthly days are done,
He who once made my life, first begun.
Now, my days are over, for happiness and cheer,
No longer his wondrously spirited songs, to hear.
My musical universe of love, is gone,
Without my little bird, of enraptured song.
Dear reader, please, with me, consider my deep extremity,
For any future song, sonata, or symphony - from me!

—*Richard A. Senser*

The Spiritual Threads Of Time

Elevated from a time of betrayal...
To enter a moment of total abortion
And to finally see, without
The blind coral tiers of rain...
As an amethyst glow begins to cover your mind
There no longer is any pain.
And in your hand, your fears subside...
Like crumbled pieces washed away by the tide.

The spiritual threads of time return to the body,
And the mind fills up with darkened grays...
And the escaping is gone until the end of our days.

The escaping of the spirit, to find some peace...
To clearly see, the part of life we now know,
And to see it with ease.

As you quietly slip from a dream, grasp what
Can, for sweet as it may be...far as it may go
The mind ties the spiritual threads of time
From past you present,
Where in lies our future.

—*Terri King*

The Sea

What a wide, beautiful area
            to explore
    From ocean to shore,

    What a welcome release
for gulls, egrets and herons
        to escape once more
            from land to shore
        to explore the sea.

        Mankind
        often in a bind
Inland, on a weekly basis
        discover the oasis
    of the shore and seas,

    Mainly, to benefit from
            the ease
        of the rolling tides
            of the seas.

                —*Joy E. Stone*

"A Little More Time"

A little more time, I need a little more time Lord,
To finish my tasks here on earth;
To nurture the sick and help clothe the poor,
Lord, I need a little more time.

We all have our problems-whether big ones or small,
And your love needs to come shining thru;
So let me help dry a tear and cast out a fear;
Please, a little more time Lord for me.

Each day your love grows and in people it shows,
If only they'd let it come in-
We all need each other-no matter the color;
Lord, we all need a little more time.

Our hearts have been seeded and understanding is needed,
To make each one flourish and grow;
But what good is growing, if love is not showing?
Lord, please give us a little more time.

                —*V. June Wilkins*

To Make It To The Dawn

To make it to the dawn we must make it through the night
To get to where were going we must put up a fight.

The world we are living in may not be the best
So we must live for the good times and grow from the rest.

We may not have our future laid out into our hands
But we have the heart to share our dreams with those who
understand.

To make it to the dawn we must make it through the night
Cause living in the real world not all things are black and white.

                —*Tiffany Wolf*

My Friend

Sleepy little towns sing happy, merry tunes,
The willow trees dance in dark and dreary dunes.

My friend and I stand watching the past go flying by,
Just one glimpse of hope goes speeding by my eye.

I wonder could it happen, could that hope just once shine through,
But then I realize for me dreams do not come true.

My friend and I go walking home and as we reach my door,
My friend just looks and stares at me and then she is no more.

                —*Jane E. Murray*

Thankful For What I Do Not Have

I am thankful I do not have
to go hungry every night.
I can sit down for my meals
and enjoy every bite.
Thirst is another thing I do not have
and lack of I do not have to fear.
I also do not have to feel His presence
to know He is near.
I am thankful I do not have to be cold,
For I have warm blankets on my bed
I do not have to sleep on a park bench
with no pillow under my head.
I am thankful I do not have bad health
I am as healthy as I can be.
For you see I am very fortunate I can walk and talk and see
Another thing I do not have that I am thankful for
I did not have to hang on a cross in pain
Because Jesus loved me He took my place
Now eternity I have to gain.
As I come to a close do not get me wrong
I am thankful for what I have as well
But the most important thing I do not have,
That is to spend eternity in Hell!

                —*Veronica Wood*

Show Me The Way

    "Show me the way," we say,
        to God, to our parents,
        to the ones we obey.
        "Show me the way,
        I want to do it right,
    give me a sign, let me see the light."

        It's hard sometimes
            to find the way,
    in these hard times we live in today,
    we need some help, we need a friend,
there has to be someone to show us the end.

    So why is it, still to this day,
        so hard to find the way?
    Are we really trying, and if we are,
    there must be someway we can go far.
        But here we are left alone,
    and no one's there to answer the phone.

So it seems all we can say, is Please,
        "Show me the way."

                —*Thomas Cottrill*

Love Is Relative

Most young men dream of owning classy cars
To impress peers, female and male as well,
But nothing so impersonal will quell
That agitation caused by moon and stars.

Though men can now fly up to planet Mars,
No one has yet been found who can dispel
Ideas that basic sense of touch or smell
Cause deep emotions; sometimes lifetime scars.

How sad a situation it must be
When finally a young love is revealed,
A love unique, never like another,
He's totally enslaved...no longer free.
She crushes him with feeling she's concealed,
"Sorry but I love you like a brother."

                —*Mary Ann Bandemer*

472

Song To My Child

I know now what it's like
  to live among the angels
For God has sent one down to me.

I know what it must be like
  in heaven
For any one can see
The stars fell down and I found them
Shining bright as ever deep down in your eyes.

The sun rose,
  smiled at its reflection
Found in your sunny smile.

Now there is no doubt
All things here and above
Know, my darling,
That it's you I love.

I know all that's left
  to do now
Is pray to be worthy of you.
    —*F. Barbara Guidone*

Memory

Scarcely a minute I look out the window. Before I've come back
to look inside having grasped nothing of all I've passed or
touched at one point.
    The sky is larger and more beautiful then ever and at the
last minute. The land turn going by. The footsteps over my
head of all that's in motion some one comes to a stop. Let the
world go on as it will and anything in it.
    The dancing lights and the speeding shadow. There more
space looking straight ahead inside a cage a living animal
leaped with an identical gesture of a beast with arms.
    A women laughed. Through back her head and someone took the
one of us for the other. All three of us were strangers and
formed already as one a world of hope.
    —*Kathleen Howard*

The Buccaneer

I stole the gay shades of a rainbow
  To prove to my love that I cared,
And clipped the bright skeins from a moonbeam
  To drape in her shining hair,

Took the lilting notes of a wood thrush,
  To give her a voice of love:
All mixed with the song of the rivers
  And the cry of the mourning dove.

Then I caught the wild grace of a wood fawn
  And the poise of a swallow in air;
Grabbed a handful of stardust to sprinkle her eyes,
  Made the wild rose her red lips to share.

Yea, I raided star-jewels from the heavens,
  Buccaneered all the Great Milky Way;
Clipped the sparkling tail from a comet
  And carted them all away.

Robber-mad, I plundered life's treasures
  For only my love to adore,
But then, when I placed them all at her feet,
  My love, was all—she asked for!
    —*Roy Ritchie*

Rhythm

'Twas when the cotton grew and greened and broke open white
to punctuate the leafy forest with puffy snow balls,
that school bells rang.

The Fall clock pendulumed between days of chalk dust and
Chaucer and twilights of flinging arms stuffing tubes
before darkness called.

Darkness beckoned us with promising voice to supper
and kerosene lamps winked our way to Morpheus' welcoming arms,
our math in unopened binders.

This daily rhythm snatched a Saturday syncopation of day long
urgency before the Sunday gatherings with Jesus in the mornings
and cousins after noon.

When the empty stalks were sliced
to renourish the black loam which mothered us all,
we gentled into winter, constant in blackboards, corduroy and
chase till spring called us da capo
to the first bars of the familiar symphony of the years.
    —*L. Wayne Bryan*

Yellow Ribbon

Tie a yellow ribbon on the old oak tree
To remember all the boys that did not go free.
Pray every night that God will see,
That he will bring them home to their family.

So much suffering is so wrong,
Let all pray together and bring them home.
Tie a yellow ribbon on an old oak tree
And pray that god will see, and bring them
Home by easter to their family.

So tie a yellow ribbon on the old oak trees
To see our boys and girls will all be free!
    —*Marie T. Sweeney*

Grey Ships

Grey Ships stand at anchor awaiting the morning dawn,
  to slip from Lindon Harbor before the coming storm.
  They have stood in silent grandeur for years untold,
  ready to sail that westward course as endings unfold.
  The voyage will be long through perilous dark seas,
always searching westward for forgotten paths and breezes.
  No other ships, no other sailors may follow this dawn,
Grey ships will sail from Lindon Harbor hopeful but forlorn.
Aboard their proud grey wooden decks a host soon will stand,
after great tribulation they would finally leave this land.
  Just before the break of dawn the wind begins to blow,
  casting off their silver lines the time had come to go.
  Silently the high grey bows cut through the harbor calm,
  passing into the boiling mists beyond the worldly storm.
  Those aboard took one last look at the land left behind,
sensing their good works would fade like colors do in time.
  Than all at once they were gone no land could be seen,
those on the shore could only see the fading starlite gleam.
    —*Anthony T. Panico*

Past Lives

Past lives flash within my mind of who I was in another time,

I dreamt I was a lady once, in flowing gown and peek-ed hat,
with chiffon veils all floating down - I did not know my name.

And then I was a pilgrim man with shiny buckles on my shoes,
standing by the sea break wall, waiting for news - I knew not what.

I come back to my conscious self and realize my life today,
then wonder what my life will be in times to come - I cannot say.

I pull from deep within my mind more lives I lived in another time.
    —*Jennifer A. Ebeck*

For You My Dear

The things you loved I have not put away
To smoulder in the darkness year by year;
The songs you sang, the books you read each day
Are all about me, intimate and dear.

I do not keep your chair apart,
Lonely and empty, desolate to view;
But if one comes a weary, sick at heart,
I seat him there and comfort him for you.

I do not go apart in grief and weep,
For I have known your tenderness and care;
Such memories and joys, we may keep.
And so I pray for those whose lives are bare.

I may not daily go and scatter flowers
Where you are sleeping 'neath the sun and dew
But if one lies in pain through lonely hours,
I send the flowers there, dear heart, for you.

Life claims our best; you would not have me waste
A single day in selfish, idle woe.
I fancy that I heard you bid me haste
Lest I should sadly falter as I go.

    —*Allen F. Brandon*

Listening With The Heart

Words can oft be spoken with little thought or care,
To someone who is suffering and deep down in despair;
We cannot hear the heart beat if the words are loud and strong,

Or hear the gentle music lost in the noisy throng.
There are times life may overwhelm us-our trials seem
too great to bear;
It's then we need a listening friend-someone with whom to share,
Someone who is ready by thought, word, or deed;
To reach out a helping hand in our time of need.
The heartaches may be heavy and the burdens too,
But a friend who listens from the heart can help us
make it through.

    —*Wanda Benson*

Mama And The Blanket

The blanket, soft and warm,
To soothe but a lonely dame.
It's cotton weaves like gold,
And Mama just the same.

Her smile was soothing and bright,
Her hair like silver and gold,
And one more trait in common,
They both were very old.

Mama loved that blanket,
Stitched it all herself,
But when Mama died,
We placed it on a shelf.

But the memory
of it on Mama's lap
Made us put it back there,
for Mama's final nap.

    —*Natalie Wolc*

Innocence Lost

Without a cause, her Integrity was taken away.
Without indication, her Song was left without its Melody.
Without a definition, a Void occurs.
Without light, a Soul survives in darkness.
With Innocence Lost, her Smile has vanished.
Without direction, Confusion abides.
With Innocence Lost, Life's Fullness is Denied.

    —*Karan Hubbard*

Somalia Christmas

Duty called the young marine
to spend Christmas in Somalia.
Distributing food among its
starving people.

Leaving behind the holiday
gala of home.
Trimming the tree and festive
family gatherings.

Regardless, never did he feel
such an intense Christmas spirit.
For, the gifts he received were heartfelt.
Warm smiles, handshakes, and gratitude.

Never will he forget his
Somalia Christmas.
For the words peace and goodwill
had a renewed meaning.

    —*Pat Bordner*

Dreamscape Seashore

I wander into midnight dreams...
to the turn...and turn...and turn around -
that shields me from my ceiling skies—
and scatters my mind on my ceiling tiles—

All to the whirling cadence that
drowns the sounds which waver timeless—
transcending the years beyond—

While my feelings here, long alone—
but for the whine of electrons pounding
the facile images of faraway eyes—
to sellout emotion behind hideaway blinds...

I stumble through these cackling echoes and ephemeral
strolls in cloudy gardens that might yet run away with me—

Oh take me down to the ocean, please!
Take me knee deep in the rapture—

Where I can bury my feet beneath hourglass sand—
in fast retreat through tidal hands—

That wrought the pale echoes—

Which dance across the flickering sea
and wink aloud to the flicker in me.

    —*Anthony D. Estes*

Dare To Dream

I would follow endless winding rivers
to the very edge of eternity itself
if I were certain that I could find a
sacred kingdom where peace and love would
comfort all those who desperately seek them.
I would travel across bitter cold terrain
to find the warm flickering flame of hope
and return it to the peoples of the earth
in this time when all struggle to hold onto
their fleeting faith.
But where does this kingdom lie where the
trinity of faith hope and love flourish
and the gift of life is purer than the blue
sky behind the falling rain?
I know that it truly exists,
and I also know that as a people we can find our
way there if we refuse to let loose of our faith
and put the broken pieces of our own shattered
individual hopes together as one whole hope
and dare to dream.

    —*Paul Jones*

Denied

Children gunned down in the street,
to this day the reason unclear.
The hate filled race wants everyone different,
to quietly disappear.

They take our youth in states of depression,
and twist their minds into puerile slabs of clay.
Before they mature through their ancestors morals,
they have already been taught to make others pay.

Where will this oppressive dream state land us,
on the door step of heaven or hell?
Consumption of materials have selfishly blinded us,
for one more possession, our freedom we'd sell.

Suffering since the day you are born,
your dreams die from self-mutilation,
Pray to God your born without difference,
your punishment-eternal degradation.

It has gone to far to stop this madness,
with one political stroke of the pen.
No one cares to waste their energy,
on the underprivileged who wallow in sin.

—*Sheila Tharp*

Rude Awakening

How rude it was of Mother Earth to quake,
To toss my house, and rattle me awake.
She shook and nearly threw me out of bed;
She could have knocked me right out on my head!

Oh, what a way to open eyes from sleep!
I was so scared I couldn't make a peep!
It's not the nicest mode to greet the day.
I wish that I could simply move away!

But if I moved, what new calamity
Or terrible disaster would there be
To frighten me, and knock me out of bed?
I think I'll just stay here and quake instead!

—*Mary Eleanore James*

Grandma's Rocker

As I sit in Grandma's rocker my mind drifts back in time
To when I was a little girl of eight or maybe nine
I close my eyes and see her in a long old fashioned dress
With silver hair and wrinkled skin from age and toil and stress
She told me many stories about when my Dad was a boy
And as she talked I'd watch her eyes light up with pride and joy
She told how my Dad helped her after Grandpa went to heaven
He had to be a man now even tho he'd just turned seven
She washed and ironed for others at her small log cabin home
To feed and clothe the seven kids she was raising all alone
There was never any bitterness, no malice, hate or scorn
Instead her home was filled with love and respect from those she'd borne
As I sit in Grandma's rocker recalling life from way back then
Sometimes the memories make me wish I was a little girl again

—*Sammie Tidwell*

The Little Silicon Chip

Little silicon chip, did you know
You blasted the world wide open?
I picture you, delicate as an iridescent
Fish scale, long hidden in a crystal cave.
Patient, knowing the secret you held,
Would send such a shock wave flowing
There would be no end to it.
Nothing would be the same again.

—*Rosamond Ellis Scott*

Wind

It is everywhere, all around.
To where could it be bound?
It searches here and then there,
The fluffy clouds to bear.
But has it found what it's looking for?
Or is there much more?

I can tell that it grieves
When it moans among the eaves,
And sighs throughout the leaves.
But when it heaves,
And tosses leaves into the air
I know it's not just sad up there.

—*Kate Dowling*

Lost Love

Wait! Wait ! Oh wait my dear! I call
to you, but all is silent, all is clear
nothing is left but a sample of
my falling tear. What will I do, without
you. I continued to say, but you
are gone, left, went on your way.
My hopes my dreams, have fallen
far. I wait for you like the morning
star. I loved you once, but it was
not true, darling you have turn
my heart in two. Dear! Oh dear! Why
did you flee, please, please! Dear come
back to me.

—*Sarah Jean Vexter*

Then, Now And Forever

Tomorrow is an elusive time you dream of.
Today can be a depressing experience you wish would end.
Yesterday is a fond memory of good times and good friends.
Put them all together and it adds up to a lifetime.
Will you spend it doing or dreaming?
Will you look back in fifty years and know
You've done your best to make the years count?
The present can hurt you if you let it.
The future can delight you if you want it.
As the years go by and the seasons change
Live your life to it's fullest and
Remember me - then, now and forever!

—*Tamy W. Wight*

Today Is The Day…

Today is the day I came to say, Bye.
Today is the day I am going to die.
So much to live for; as I step out the door,
You'll never see me anymore.
So much in life to do it all,
In years from now we'll think it was dull.
As I walk out the door,
I fell,
I fell into hell.
The devil greeted me, with a shake of a hand,
I wondered into an unknown land.
All around me was my friends,
I guess my life had to end.
As I started to rise, I felt my soul let go.
I was scared to death,
Nothing was left,
All of a sudden,
God came down from heaven.
And took me back up with him,
To him I had no sin.

—*Tina Bozzi*

The Gift Of Life

A man and a woman linked by the soul
Together have created their ultimate goal
The woman of course bears this new life
A miraculous feat, the hero, my wife
A man must watch as she copes with the pain
All along reassuring her all there is to gain
The pain she has experienced she never had before
For that very special moment they both will adore
I love her so much for bearing the gift of life
We are partners forever, me and my wife
When I think of the pain she had to go through
A tear comes to my eye, if only she knew
This miracle is something I can never repay
I will spend eternity cherishing this day
You performed the art that nature conceals
In my eyes you're an angel, I truly do feel
For a moment my tongue seems to be tied
If I say I was not nervous, I would have lied
You've given me the greatest gift of life
You are my darling, my precious, my very dear wife.

—*Troy K. Holman*

Night Trains

My grandpa, who I would have to say is pretty old,
Told me of how, when he was a boy in a world small,
All of his dreams rose from what he learned there in that town.
Down the hill to the creek he'd wander, and then he'd fish,
And wish, and dream about small boy things, and then go back.
The track ran just past there, past his life, curving slow around.
Sound from the chugging trains would split the night country air.
There, in bed, he'd feel the house moan to roaring thunder,
And wonder on the click-click, click-click of pounding rails,
And wails of the whistle as it split night from the dawn.
On it went, 'round the curve, then fading to dreams.
It seems to me there was magic in the huffing
And puffing and roaring and rhythm of those old trains.
The gains we've made since then might be good, I would suppose;
But those gains brought with them a price to pay, a high cost.
Lost are the night train sounds of Grandpa's country boyhood.
Could I wish, I'd choose to lie and hear night trains pass through...
WOOOO! Wooooo! Wooooo!

—*Richard Larson*

Hope Is Gone

Hope is gone and out of sight. The thought of you appearing tonight.
I'll go on with others than you, although the whole time you know I feel blue.
I walk alone pacing the sand, when you walk by holding her hand.
After you're gone and out of sight, I fall to the ground and cry to the night.
The hours suddenly fade away, It's time again to face a new day.
I slowly get up and decide to move on, I've finally realized your love is now gone.

—*Jessica M. Sharp*

Never Ending Love

The love I felt for you, hasn't faded one tiny bit,
your the one lover my heart can not forget.
I know because I've tried so hard to make my mind
move on, but is just will not expect the fact that
you are really gone.
And even though it's hard to do, I've realized it's
true for the rest of all my day's I'll be forever
loving you.

—*Roxanna Gale*

Flowers Of The Field

The "flowers of the field" God made
Too many in number to calculate
So different in color, size and shape
They dazzle the mind to contemplate.
Flowers do not sew, nor do they spin
Yet more admiration they win
Than the glorious robes of Kings.
Their colors invite blissful contemplation
And raise the mind to adoration
Of Him from whom all beauty flows.
If the flowers He made are so breathtaking,
What must be He who did the making?

—*John D. Sauter*

Nemesis Of My Nightmares

She wasn't like anyone I knew.
Totally different.
Evidently true.
Practically infallible.
Her eyes were like diamonds;
And her they were beyond incredible.
Never have I seen someone so mysteriously beautiful.
Inner essence of beauty was
Equal to outer beauty, soft and incomprehensibly wonderful.

When could I meet her
And talk for hours on end while
Gazing at the stars?
Nemesis of my nightmares she would be, allowing me to
Endlessly dream of utopia and
Realize that I could truly love her.

—*Tim LaFave Jr.*

Dream Of Fantasy

I often dream of sailing down a stream.
Touch the stars and the ray of moonbeams.
I see fair maidens with gold of sunstreams
In their hair. They watch the unicorns,
In the mist as they lie in their lairs.
Majestic castles way beyond the hills.
Seem to beckon me upon will.
The wizard with his crystal ball, see the
Colors do their magic, when the wizard
Gives them his call.
Just close your eyes and dream of sailing down
That stream. Touch the stars and see the beautiful
Moonbeams. These are the quiet times of my dreams.
That fulfill my heart, and make me sad when I must
Depart. This time of happiness is as the hourglass,
Never to fade away. Will remain my own private fantasy.

—*Patricia Swankier*

Robins!!!

Robins! — in my yard today!
They've come at last, I hope they'll stay.
They'll pick and choose which tree they'll use,
Which yard they think will feed them best
And then perhaps will build their nest.

I hope my yard has just that tree,
That perfect crotch and promised greenery.
I hope my tree's leaves may proudly wear
That nest of Robins in its hair.

Each warming dawn now has the sounds
Of Robins starting to claim their grounds.
Their happy chirps and warning calls
Are freeing me from winter's pall.
Robins!!! in my yard today!

—*Virginia H. Hurley*

Can You Hear The Snow Fall?

Candy Sue is the name of my good friend, a friendship that
truly God did send. Why is candy sue so unique? She is deaf
and cannot speak. Candy can only "see" what makes a sound or
sometimes feels vibrations from above or from the ground.
Candy in her curiosity asked me about sounds one day. What
prompted it was voices I heard far away. I heard the voices of
her father and a friend coming down the hall. She asked me how
I knew when she couldn't see them at all. What things can I
hear she continued to ask. Trying to tell her was such a task. The
tapping of a fingernail on a desk, can I hear that? I shake my
head yes, please stop that! The clinking of keys on a key
ring, does that make a sound? She keeps wondering. Then she
asked the question that touched my heart so deep. The question
that made me want to weep. It was in the winter time when she
asked, "Can you hear the snow fall?" I looked at her and
responded quietly, "No, candy, I cannot, not at all."

—*Patricia S. Van Den Berg*

The Hawk

Today I saw a small hawk, so strong and so bold,
  try to land on a branch and take a firm hold.

The branch started to tremble, it was only a twig;
  the hawk couldn't hold on, for he was too big.

For some strange reason, I thought of our love,
  as I watched that hawk flying above.

We had shaky times, but we always pulled through.
  We were determined to make it, me and you.

That hawk was persistent; he kept trying to land.
  And I thought of those hard times, when you'd hold my hand.

When you'd hold me and tell me that we always would be;
  I believed in you, and you in me.

The hawk tried it again, he landed so light.
  The branch wiggled and wobbled, but he held on tight.

As he perched on that limb, up there above,
  I was reminded again of the strength of our love.

When you believe in something, and want it to be;
  You can make it happen - like you and me.

—*Susan Callahan*

The Diary of Levi & Louisa Cornell

In a log cabin, near Sugar Creek
two newlyweds, a diary keep.

First they write of their wedding day
and list the gifts that came their way.

Then each day they note the weather
and then the chores they did together.

Little they realized, way back then,
a hundred years later it would be read by kin.

We wonder how they survived the trials
of pioneer living, all by themselves.

The birth of their children with no doctor near.
No greater love than to hold her child dear.

Wind and storms and rising water from the creek
Grandpa gathered his brood, refuge to seek.

Hoeing, planting, reaping, saving,
Loving, playing, teaching, praying...

It's all in their diary. We read of their faith
in each other, but also in God for strength.

What lessons this diary has taught us, all of us.
To work lovingly together and in God put our trust.

—*Reatha Fivecoats Femyer*

Love Of A Thousand Miles

A thousand miles apart,
Two young hearts connect as one,
Love is all they have to hold on to,
They wonder if it is enough,
Too young to be together,
Too old to be alone,
Kisses at midnight in their thoughts;

She sees his face as plain as the first sight,
She dreams of him day and night,
She sleeps on the satin sheets he once used,
She feels his arms embracing her,
She runs to him in the shadows,
Then realizes he's not there;

He looks in the baby's eyes,
He sees his love's beauty in the child,
He looks at the sun,
He remembers she is his sunshine,
In the darkness she is the starlight,
He close his eyes to feel her touch,
In his memory she is here;

—*Patricia McIntryre*

Milestones

A child, I oft tripped over them,
Unaware that these were, (in the jargon of the 60's)
happenings,
And sometimes I did pick them up
And momentarily looked
But gave them short shrift,
As I tossed them negligently over my shoulder;
  Seldom did I deem them worthwhile.
  I left most of them disintegrating into shifting sand.
  I have come to look for, search for them,
  Possessing the patina of time and age.
  They gleam in the distance, luring me on.
  I take my time to reach them,
  (They will not disappoint),
  Savoring each step toward them.
  Now I cannot negligently toss them over my shoulder.
  Like a rare jewel they must be fondled,
  Treasured and stored in my memory.
  Reluctantly, I lay them down, and
  Perforce, turn toward another milestone in the offing.

—*Hester B. Eyler*

In The Light Of The New Day

I know sometimes you can't control the sorrow that you feel, I
understand the feeling, it's painful and so real. You may have
often wondered why it must be this way You're looking forward
only to the ending of the day. Don't tell me I don't
understand, I've been there in your place. I've felt those
burning tears of frustration running down my face. I know it's
hard to tolerate, but please try to understand. We'll get
through it together, side by side and hand in hand. You and I
together in the light of the new day we'll find a way to climb
the wall that's standing in our way. And you know as well as I
do that these obstacles we fear will pass as quickly as our
evening sunsets everyday of the year. With the setting of the
sun, my friend, and the darkness of the night, there's the loss
of that one obstacle as we have won the fight. And with the
morning sun comes peace of mind because we know, the obstacles
we conquer help our hearts and minds to grow. As our good Lord
brings you happiness, and as our lives go on, you may not
always feel fulfilled, you may not be so strong. Remember I'll
be there for you, and together we will see, we'll find the
strength we need in the bond of our unity.

—*Nancy Nashed*

Red Rituals

I arrive home to a paradise
Unfitting to my sadness.
There in my mother's eyes—
I see my clear, rippled tears.

We, sixty, gather as one amidst the
Ghost-like incense and heeding chinese chants,
Taoist tradition is so foreign, I think to myself,
Not at all like Christianity.

There are no words to speak,
I fiercely clench my sister's perspiring hand,
Blood rushes to my stubborn fist.
Onerous rituals continue, undaunted by our prevalent misery.

Her face is unfamiliarly peaceful.
She endows me with her pain.
Now, I cry burdens,
Popo is free.

　　　　—*Jona M. Goong*

Clouds

　　In the true blue sky,
　　Up above the world so high,
　　Enclosed in a place unknown,
You are seated on the highest throne.
　　　　Some are silver,
　　　　Some are nine,
　　　　But all deliver
　　　A feeling of divine.
　　Once upon you will wander,
　Getting down you will not ponder.
　The wind becomes your friend,
And your journey need not have an end.
　Your throne will take you higher
　　　If you have the desire.
There are no limits of speed nor height,
　Nor will obstacles stand in your way.
Float until you can't float any longer,
　　Fly until your goal is defined,
Fly until you have left the world behind.

　　　　—*Lisa Izzo*

The Country Boy

As I stare out a window
Up so high above a paved world
I think, how tragic that men have so lost themselves
in the modern scramble for a life
that consisteth in the abundance
of the things one possesseth
that these imitations of a better world
fall on ears utterly deafened!

I cry, the world travaileth in pain
reality, hard reality of this artificial age
have caged the walls of my heart.
In time, I will go home,
and fly with the birds,
play in the cool grass,
pray in the open air.
For you see,
there the intruders of loveliness
are not tantalizing jests of an ironical fate.

　　　　—*Timothy D. Lang*

"Kinship"

Here I lay
upon my mother's soft breast
Akin to a baby bird
who lays asleep deep in it's nest.

Though we're as different
as the sea and the sky
Someday we'll see our reflections
within each other's eye.

I shall see in it's feathered beauty
the work of God's creative hands
While it, in turn, shall see it's Creator's image
in God's imperfect man.

　　　　—*J. Hilton Kinsey*

Battle Hymn Of Aging

We reach the age of 65, our golden years are here. They tell us that the age begins a happy new career, For now our Uncle Sam becomes our permanent cashier. As we go marching on. Our social security from Baltimore is sent. We buy a little bit of food and maybe pay the rent. And after that we're stony broke and left without a cent. But we go bravely on. And as for medicare will someone tell us how? There's always doctor bills they sadly disallow. And dental costs as well we know they wholly disallow, But we go bravely on. We don't know how we make it as we live from day to day. With income fixed and prices up there's always more to pay. So minding our arthritis let's keep on our knees and pray. That we go bravely on. Now first of all let's thank the Lord that we are still alive. The dreams we have may still come true when we are 95. So please, dear Lord, give us the strength our troubles to survive. As we go bravely on.

　　　　—*Socorro F. Oboab*

Once In A Lifetime

Once in a lifetime!
　Usually, not even then,
There comes a brother, full grown.
　You wonder—where has he been?

Once in a lifetime!
　Responsibility—despair.
Betrayed, abandoned, Broken.
　Life preserved! Grief. Memories dear!

Once in a lifetime!
　Uniquely. Out of the blue.
A brother appears! My own!
　God gives people. God gave you.

Once in a lifetime!
　(In the heart of a mother.)
Always wished for, never known.
　God alone gives a brother!

Praise the Lord!
He's given us each other!

　　　　—*Ollie Kraska*

New Found Love

This is so new to me; these are things I've never done.
Yet everything I do with you seems to be so much fun.
I don't know how I lived before I ever met you.
The love I feel inside feels so simple yet so true.
I always want to be with you, to never be alone.
I want to love you always and have you for my own.
I never knew I could love as deeply as I do.
I never knew until I loved you.

　　　　—*Amber Allen*

Poets Joy

I seek words from the heart to describe my passion for poetic verse.

Often the words come not to mind but seem to intertwine.

Frustration is a poets lot when what our mind and spirit
think can't be placed in rhyme, but sinks and falls on deaf
ears not to speak in silence the inner words locked in some
firm embrace one knows not where.

Verse the joyful sound of the soul tears at the poets inner
most being when locked away.

But joy abounds when the flood gate is released to spell
bound even the poets thoughts.
Words come from he knows not where to fall on unknown ears.

—*Marvin Cool*

No Longer A Passenger

Moving slowly as if backwards the stately white shimmering
vessel approaches the worn out rotted pier.
It is here to collect the spirits of the departed.

The salty sea water mixed with tears pounds the sides of the vessel.
A mist of sorrow is lifted as you see them.
Faces that live in the family album smile at you.
Children cling to their parents while grandparents tightly
squeeze their namesakes.
It is here families are reunited.

You look up to see a warm face with arms extended eager to
help you as you step aboard, suddenly you pause,
something stops you, the echo of a familiar voice grabs hold
pulls tight and you turn away the weight of the ship shifts
as you step off and return to the pier no longer a passenger.

You watch the vessel back away, powered by grief turning
it cuts through the fog, it's course already set for an
eternity far beyond our reach.

—*Lorraine M. Stirpe*

Untitled

The walls of my silence
vibrated from the weeping winds
that sought refuge in my tears.
The ancient wailings of my ancestors
did little to awaken the Sleeping Prince.

"A sacrifice will bring our somber
warrior to his senses", cried the frenzied mob of shadows.

The whisper of the cackling hen
froze beneath the cave
where the fragile heart hid.
So with diligence and
Godspeed, the ceremonial
fires were ignited and the lamb
was placed in the rapacious maw of the beast.

So foolish were the hopes of the
vaporous mob that when
Death required another,
the sounds of shattering hearts
left the Laughing Man tone deaf.

And the Sleeping Prince went back to his Dreams
—*Raymond Charles Brookter*

Kaleidoscope

All nature since time began
Viewed through life's Kaleidoscope
The passage of things ancient
Long since removed from the scene of action
Hidden in the crevices of the far horizon
Beclouded by shadows that never knew the sun
In darkness that no light can penetrate
Begging for a relief that embraces
In love and sympathy the anguish
Of souls whose pain is searing
Where resides the power that can release
The chains that bind, and bring the solace
That all mankind is seeking
To rid this planet forever
Of all its miseries and into the sunshine stare
Into a brightness never before experienced
Never before known.

—*Lois J. Clarke*

Sometimes

Sometimes we don't know what we had,
Until we loose it;
Sometimes we don't know what we really want,
Until we get what we thought we desired;
Sometimes we think we know the way,
Until we find ourselves lost;
Sometimes we think we're in control of a situation,
Until we find ourselves caught in a trap;
Sometimes we think someone really loves us,
Until times get rough;
Sometimes we think we know what's best,
Until God shows us what He has for us!
—*Matthew K. Olson*

Sunday Masochist

It left her in a sweaty state of
agitation - permeated with rage,
The 'Believers' - those white, doughy
middle class bodies - a sea of them,
Each one covered in 'acceptable' clothes
- each one pampered, powdered and sprayed
Their minds also - with suffocating
Self-righteousness personified - aglow -
with seemingly great compassion/charity.
At times she'd try to converse -
stumbling with banalities - inwardly
articulate with profanities...
Long afterwards she'd still be smoking
cigarettes and gulping sweet, black
coffee in catharsis mode...
Blunting the horror or truth was just
one thing - more comforting and concrete
She held no golden, honey sweet Jesus
but a God who wept till snot ran
Unchecked by human vanity - whose eyes
were gouged out by the sight and horror
Poisonous Compromise
Whose flesh ached, rotted and ripped
with the arrows of pseudo-spirituality
Who choked, gagged and vomited on the
anguish of humanness...
And that was reminder enough for awhile
- til she'd forget, and would try church again...
Sunday Masochist.
—*Mary Nikoletos*

Leaf Eternal

I watched you come, I watched you grow,
I watched you change, I watched you go.
Spring burst forth your lime-green glow,
Summer fed you, full birth to show.
But, autumn slipped in and now I know
The color you share now golden, the shade of life's
Ending flow.
Leaf eternal, life aglow! God's fulfillment a positive desire.
Blazing with life, living...dying...dedicated, surviving life's
Strife.
Pass away now to await new life!
Leaf eternal, sadly, life sends you on your way.
Go then, to dark sleep within nature's welcomed breast.
You will return, again, after winter's long needed rest.
Bringing forth, God's promise once again.
God's eternal promise safely kept deep within.
All will anxiously wait and watch for your glorious return!
Knowing with melancholy, you will repeat an eternal need.
No need for dismay! The promise repeats over again,
God's promises shall ever and ever eternally grow.

—*Carolyn Burchfield*

Street Gangs

Sacrificial victims lie, among bare bones so white
Stripped of meat and tender thighs, beneath the earth,
innocence lies.

How can men be callous and cold; cowardly are the murderer's souls.
Afraid of love and life, they take, life from the youthful and the old.

Men should grow from youthful boys, laugh and kiss and breathe fresh airs.
But for the use of ungodly toys, lost forever, who really cares?

It'll never happen to me, we say. Our ignorance keeps us safe.
Lost one moment, no time to pray, or ask to see just one more day.

Please give life a chance, I say.
Love has power, hate has none.
Men should come around one day, and we'll all be one in God.

Until that day I'll always grieve, for trusting ones deceived.
Starlit skies see through man's wrath, and hold lost angels in their light.

—*Anne S. Gettler*

The Old Quilt

The old quilt rested on her bed, each patch so soft and worn.
The colors had faded long ago and a corner had been torn.

Gramma bent down slowly, and touched a patch of gold.
"I remember Mama quilting this. I wasn't very old".

"My brother wore a handsome shirt from this patch of blue and brown.
This yellow one was a summer dress. It was a hand-me-down."

"That red one was a cotton dress with lace along the sleeve.
I remember proudly wearing it to church on Christmas Eve."

Gramma seemed to drift among the memories on that bed,
and I stood nearby listening, and treasured what she said.

She recalled so many memories, some happy and some sad,
of friends and fun and family, and loves that she had had.

That day with Gramma has come and gone, now the quilt rests on my bed.
And I lovingly remember all the things that she had said.

So many little pieces, each a fragment from the past,
sewn lovingly together to help the memories last.

Now my children hear the stories, and I tell them what she said,
for one day this precious quilt of hers may rest upon their bed.

—*Patricia G. Sushil*

Wisdom's End

In the storm that covers
all our fateless futures, a man struggles,
a beaten warrior, so tired and so cold,
at the end of all the answers,
at the end of all the roads.
Empty cities, devastation
is the desperate prize we've won...

All, the wind embraces with its mortal chill
while playing with the bony shadow
as it whispers secret songs to the corners of the world.
The mind flows like restless spirits; the deep, dark whirlpool
swallows all and in its arms it carries him
to the edges of the world...

Unearthly castle, secret hideaway...
heaven to all lost, tired desperate souls;
timeless jewel of this and other
self-destructive, faithless worlds, where no law is king nor
rule divine and dreams are just a whisper in time,
the hidden path to your pearly gates, I beg to show...

...to the long lost fortress at Wisdom's End...

—*David Rodriguez*

Eagle Talk

The wind whispers under my wings
sending me soaring effortlessly
Above the red cliffs and valleys
of Canyon de Chelley
Past White House Ruin I glide
Then up on high I circle
searching, reaching, stretching
responding to subtle air messages

Brother Sun beats heartlessly down
baking the Earth and my feathers
Diminishing the life source called river
from a roaring force to a quiet trickle
Still the Navajo corn struggles valiantly
barely winning the fight to live

Spider Woman teaches her people to weave
with wisdom as woof and belonging as warp
A beautiful harmonious pattern to see
from high up above as I ride the wind

—*Little White Bird*

Fire

Once fire, water and
air, elect to combine
and join as one
all will be peaceful.
A violent man has no place
in a peaceful world, and
when a cat and a black dog
named Bobo decide to forget their differences
and put down, their teeth and
claws and join the sea
and sky, day and night,
and the eye's and the mind's
eyes in one great
ball with black and white.
There will be peace or pieces
of man's mind
will be left
To run free in the fields of grey.

—*Kenneth Massey*

The First Kiss Of Nectar

A Still Silent Moment Hangs in the Air.
Transparent thoughts and Delicate laughs
Float in the Candle-lit Room.

A Hummingbird, Green and Shining,
Greets a Bouquet of Flowers
In the Garden - Hovering.

He meets the depth of her Dark Brown Eyes.
Silence. Their hearts
Beating in the Silence.

The Flower waits, A pause
in the morning Breeze
filled with Nectar - Sweet.

Absorbed in one another's Gaze,
A Deep Breath is drawn...
They draw closer
To the lips of their desire.

And the Gentle Hummingbird
Hangs in the Air...
How Sweet! How Sweet!
Is the first sip of Nectar!

—*Coby J. Lyons*

I Believe

I believe in God the Father, ruler of all he surveys;
I believe in one bright heaven, pure and mystic in its haze;
I believe in life eternal, living day to glorious day;
I believe in wondrous miracles, each one special in its way;
I believe in loving families, sharing each new ray of joy;
I believe in peace and harmony, holding hands each girl and boy;
I believe in precious moments, holding close to their embrace;
I believe in one great nation, filled with one kind, the human race;
I believe in sharing wisdom, for those wise can teach the world;
I believe in a free America, let the melting pot be stirred;
I believe in love all knowing, kind and gentle, honest and true;
I believe in helping others, for someday you'll need help too;
So let us stop all the fighting, for the God we're all the same;
Enjoy the life he's given and embrace his holy name!

—*Traci Lynn Welborn*

Suicide

The pain is inescapable, I can no longer survive.
The nightmares and memories engulf me like the tide.
There must be some cause for the pain I bear.
What is the reason? Or do I even care?

My body goes on but a soul doesn't seem to exist.
Yet, there is a memory, a damaged child engulfed in mist.
But that child hurts and she has truly tried.
It seems the only way out is suicide.

The pain is so great I can handle no more.
I've endured such tragedy, I've been hurt to the core.
I can't cry out, no one cares to hear.
At every moment I make sure death is near.

I want to die, but there's no one to stop me.
I would try to survive, but there's too high a fee.
Can I possibly blame this imprisoning cage,
For all my pain, anger, suffering and rage?

The sound of my thoughts is driving me mad.
There's been so much trauma. My soul is so sad.
I cannot stop the rising tide.
This time it's rescue or suicide.

—*Karen Lee Fowler*

Step Dad

Life is difficult at times I've found
To raise a family that is lovingly bound

But I was lucky when I as a mother was left alone
With four little angels and a dog needing a bone

For I found a man who was full of good wit
And you know my dear Jimmy that you were it

No where in the world if we traveled far and wide
Could we have found a heart so truly wonderful inside

Though my sons will be bigger than you someday
So you say
That's why you're nice
But I really don't believe all that sugar and spice

Because when I for my children did pick a Step Dad
I found a world for us all
Through you
I thought I'd never of had

—*Linda Conroy*

A Conversation Piece

Brooks and bridges cross the path
of her enlightenment.
Hands shake as voices rise and cups
overflow
with some potion called Happiness
in the crowded space
that leaves the Two of them too near
to touching
too near the speaking, too near to acknowledging
the less than precious tension strung
between the faces that connect their glances
which, by the way, are short and stealing
emotion of the eyes
says a lot, don't you think
that before the event closes these Two
will want to, or have to
Bridge the Brook, made of Stones,
and chock full of Beavers,
that runs swift and cold
between them.

—*Kara E. Hansell*

At Death's Door

Many people feel lost in the world
They feel as if they are falling snowflakes
being mixed in crowds
being smothered and suffocated
being frightened and uneasy
These people want so very much to melt away
They pray each day, not for their survival,
but for their death
A feeling of well-being is what they lack,
depression and sickness is what they
have too much of
The rest of the world ignores these people
They just don't care what happens
Soon, because of their disgraceful actions,
the rest of the world will fall into darkness
We will all begin to immerse in misery
We will all become a
part of the disintegrating
universe at death's door!

—*Karen K. C. Yoshida*

Jakarta

Cloves are kind because of their mysticism. The essence of
their Southeast Asia aura. The visions one gets when smoking
a clove. They make me see Jewish mosques and temples of
Sala Bim. Aromas of sandlewood and curry permeate the air like
a cloud of sunshine.
　　The earth is crisp and sandy brown to the white man's touch.
　　The water has a blue transparent shine that glimmers
Like the sheen of a moon Goddest after a shower of heaven's
Light — dripping slowly down the curve of her back,
　　into infinity.
And her other real waves of hair untangle slowly to the
open spread of humanity; - creations' child will be born
to a universe of chaos, then fall into the pit of nothingness.
　　the moon, she shines on me, - I know. Sweet is the summer
air she brings with open arms; the fresh sensual smell of
night blooming jasmine and scents of the falling twilight.
　　Just a glimpse of the future come to past.

　　　—Yvon J. Cormier Jr.

Flight

In Heaven's stark white purity
Through golden mists of angel-song,
God breathes to life a small new soul.
An angel as security
(lest this small being journey wrong)
Is pledged as guide to Heaven's goal.

The earthward flight is swift and dark,
　　all memory of
Heaven erased, except dim longing for God's love.
Two silver threads, the angel's mark, within the
newborn heart are placed to be the guiding reins
　　thereof.

Hope gleams, one silver rein to guide the heart
from all despair, and Faith shines strong, a
　　constant light.
Eternal love a soul must gain. Yet even with an
angel's care, free will may cause a bitter fight!

This is the test flight of a soul: it circles in
the sky of time, half-blind, flies over earthly sod.
An angel cannot quite control the path a soul must
somehow climb in flying back through time to God.

　　　—Virginia Dyer O'Dowd

Guilty

Another morning I awake from the dreams
The same horrible visions keep coming it seems

I don't know if my conscience is telling me so
But I feel guilt for the accident that occurred weeks ago

I could have saved him, the blame is on me!
He shouldn't have suffered, he was only near three!

I'll tell you my story, it has to be heard
So my heart be less painful, my sleeping less stirred

It began on the beach, on that unforgettable day
I was watching my son, Kurt innocently at play. Amy I yelled
seeing someone I knew. Why I hadn't seen her since back in grade 2

I forgot about Kurt, he was like a shut door, so of course I
didn't notice him run to the shore. He didn't know better it was
my fault I say! The last time I saw him the tide carried him away

If only I stopped him, if only I knew. Now there was only one
thing left to do. I look outside at the ground seeming so far
away. I stand on my windowsill and without delay.
I jump to the air like Kurt to the wave; knowing I'll rest in
peace buried next to his grave.

　　　—Nicole Davenport

This Life's Only Lover

　　There's still your pictures, records, and a brush with your
hair, yet it's you I still miss and about whom I care.
　　There's the memory of laughter and of the times we've had,
still, I wish there were more of them good or bad.
　　Still even with this hurt and all of the pain even if I
could there's nothin' I'd change.
　　It was you that brought meaning and purpose to life, and
though I loved you when young, I loved you more as my wife.
　　Our love burned like a candle from both ends, and maybe that
is why this heart never mends.
　　I've loved you always and then you become my bride, I loved
you from our wedding until the day you died.
　　Although some may find love in the arms of another, for me
there was you, "This Life's Only Lover".

　　　—Terry Tinsley

"The Girl at the Y"

She works with Jennie and Jennie says
the people there don't want her
they try to get her fired or
hurt her into quitting
but she hangs on
with her large head and misshapen body
and a lisp that conceals the intelligence
behind her eyes
men make crude remarks and women turn aside
as if she isn't there
and she cries softly into her pillow
in the middle of the night
in her room at the Y.

　　She stops in to say hello
　　and I cry softly behind my smile
　　Because she is a mirror, cracked
　　and I want to turn aside
　　lest she see the reflection
　　in my eyes.

　　　—Nom Nebinger

On My Wings

Take away the sadness from your eyes.
　　If I found your tears I'd gave them back to you.
　　　Love stills your pain.
　　　I watched you walking.
As the moons eyes slowly open to the night.
Rain drops dance around your feet.
Make you sing an' smile.

Take away the sadness from your eyes.
Hold your hand move away from it all.
　　We could kiss down by the sea.
Walk an' speak of the things we've done.
　　Your shyness an' beauty.

Are fragile.
Kindness can never be injured.

Take away the sadness from your eyes.
I'd hold out my palms for you to lay it down.
Then like a bird I'd fly up to the stars.
With your sadness on my wings.

　　　—Tony Kavanagh

"I know How Much You Love Me"

I know how much you love me,
  for I see it in your face.
When you put your arms around me,
  and we share a sweet embrace.
I can hear it in your gentle voice
  and know you understand.
I can feel it in your tender touch,
  each time you take my hand.

I know how much you love me.
  for I see it in your eyes.
The look that reassures me.
  more then you may realize.
I can sense your real concern for me.
  In everything you say and do.
And no other man could ever love a woman,
  Any more then I love you.

— *Jeffrey A. Saum*

It's All Right

A small wasted body here...disjointed words
With a mind that spends most of its time somewhere else.

Eyes like the windows of an old empty house..
  Webs and shadows, dusty memories,
Seen through the shiny purple glaze of aged glass.
  Eyes with smiles in the corners.

Between bites, as I lied to her about how hot it was,
  spooned the mush into her now lineless face
  and smoothed her soft brown hair,
the words I heard were "It's all right if I die"...
  spoken to the wall...or the wind...
    or to a memory.

And then, for a moment the eyes were sharp.
  She held my wrist..looked into my eyes..
and the second time, from deep inside her somewhere,
from the Mother to her child... "It's all right if I die"...
  And took another bite of pineapple.

And that night she did...
And she told me...
It's all right... And it is.

— *Martha Sue Shelby Hart*

Autumn

Hot days of Summer
are eclipsed in Autumn hues of forest rainbow
Dancing in the sultry air,
Rivers flow much quieter
As the earth prepares to sleep under silvery blanket
Waiting to cascade everywhere.
All the earth is busy
With last minute things to do before Winter comes
Trumpeting upon the scene.
Migrating birds are leaving
As animals fill their storehouses with food
For when times are lean.
Silences are deafening
Across the fallowed fields where crops once grew
To harvest fullness.
All the earth is ready
To celebrate the grand season's blessings
In its colorful dress.
Day and night bring changes in climax enjoyed
In autumn of wonders fair.

— *Merle C. Hansen*

Ye Did It Not To Me

Why are God's children homeless and hungry;
  When the body of Christ is so rich?!
  Why are his children crying out
    for someone to show compassion?
  But they are being denied,
    When Jesus teaches —
    that the children of God;
      are suppose to be,
    compassionate and kind!
I'm hearing that God cares
  about saving souls;
    And this is true,
      He does!
But the Jesus that we've learned of,
and have so deeply grown to love —
  meets also the physical needs,
  of His precious chosen ones!
    Jesus looks out for,
    and He has extreme pity;
      on the poor!

— *Rene Humbert*

"Leaving You, Daily"

How long and lonely are my hours
  sitting alone, staring into space —
I cannot seem to abide by reality
  As my mind ever concentrates on your precious face.
For almost two years I've fared alone
  Since my inadequate strength wrought loss of you —
Loss of your presence, around-the clock, haunts my life
  However I fare, whatever I do.
If I could walk into the room wherein you abide,
  Any hour of night or day since we're apart, —
Concern for your benefit of comfort and ease
  Will ever be the prayer of my caring heart.
In our brief "togetherness," two "fleeting" hours each day —
  I leave wearing a mask as I walk away.
At each moment of leaving, agony sieges my heart —
  Most times I blindly walk a blurred path to depart.
From every "leave-taking" I count the hours—
  Until arrives the time "seeing you" flowers.
Often I've wondered if your own loving heart shares —
  With a mute agony, of your own, speechless despair.

— *Piney Woods Pete*

A Grandmother's Thoughts

I want to come to my Autumn years, with the silver in my hair,
And always have the Children stop, just to visit by my chair,

I'd like to reach October, free from blemish or mortal taint,
As splendid as the maple trees which artists love to paint,

I'd like to come to Autumn, with my life's work fully done,
And stand a little like a tree, that's gleaming in the sun,

I'd like to think that I at last, have come by care and tears,
And still as lovely to be around, as I was throughout my years,

And when I've came to November, then full contented I shall be,
If those with whom I've walked in life, still have love for me,

Nor shall I dread the winter's frost, when brain and body tire,
If I have made my time in life, some memories all can admire.

(Written by an old man, "In memory of his wife.")
— *Orin P. Lewis*

The Dyerville Giant

Awake!
Sunlight bleeds through a ceiling's break.
Hundreds, years thousands, of struggling souls.
Aware of some, a thousand years old.
Time affords thee, of thoughts which to dwell.
Yet pay thee no witness to young bodies' swell.
An old Mother's hair, pokes a young shadow's eye,
Obliging ye upward, to touch a warm sky.
  And now stands a Giant, what a sight to behold,
Yet none as defiant, none quite so bold.
Kings of the Giants, his defiance so righteous,
Summons Thor's presence to bestow on him violence.
The thunder-god wields myth's hammer down,
In battle the King, reveals his crown.
The battle unfolds, a King's crown explodes,
Our hero goes down, his feet are exposed...
  So farewell to thee, Grandfather no more,
May ye rest in peace, on Dyerville's floor.
All that remains is to bid you adieu,
A toast to the future, a forest renewed.

—Bruce Briscoe

The Grace Of Self-Denial

Land and Sea
Mountains on High
Clouds of Glory
People do deny.

Candles glow, children cry
Where are the people
Who really care.
But still deny.

The rain comes, the rain goes
The Son of God appears with a rainbow of colors,
He is the One that does not deny!

We the people that should set our priorities,
Stand back and ask God
To show our children the faithfulness
The Grace, the Love, and Glory,
The blessings of self-denial.

God comes and never goes away,
So come all ye children,
Let us pray,
For I love you all!

—Mildred Hall

The-Old-One

He sits there, without stirring.
This man without a name.
He wonders what, he is doing there?
On whom to put the blame?
His body is old and feeble.
His eyes reflect despair.
He is looking forward, to his death now.
For there is no one left, to care.
There are people, passing around him.
Like life's, ever shifting sands.
Yet no one, is passing close enough.
To reach his pleading hands.
We spend millions, for bombs and missiles.
Even space stations, in the air.
Still we pass by our elderly sick and homeless.
Without the slightest care.
We have here, in our Great Country.
A generous, and bountiful land.
It takes very little effort.
To reach out, to that outstretched hand.

— 1989 —

—Ralph Southworth

Only the Shadow Knows

In the shadow, I can glimpse an ugly woman.
Always lurking; always following; always there.
I am immune to her impulse
Devastated by her desires
Annoyed by her anger.
She is racked with rage
I, repulsed by it
She is loud and lewd
I become embarrassed
She screams sarcasm
I shut down.
Deathly afraid she will emerge, from the shadow
I watch and push her back,
As only I know how.
If she comes into the light, there will be no more control
I keep her hidden
Thinking this keeps me together and whole.
I know this woman, full of passionate anger
For her ugly face bares great resemblance to mine
She is the element of myself, living in my dark shadow.

—Sarah Strock

Hard Lesson Learned

You gave me a vision, of what I was to be.
You showed me the world, what I was to see.
You promised me love, said you'd always be there,
To lend me a hand, to show me you cared.
We'd walk through the day, never rushing our steps.
We cherished our time, for the time was well spent.
Then suddenly one day, you weren't there by my side.
I rushed through the days, by myself, all alone.
I cherished our memories, although to anger has grown.
Then one day I thought of you, and sighed a bitter sigh.
The long awaited sadness pierced my heart, then I cried.
I cried for all the empty dreams, that people have these days.
I cried because I had a dream, and then it slipped away,
To endure through out eternity, the present, the future, the past.
And although I wouldn't have changed it, in my heart I know it's true,
A lesson learned the hard way, is the price of loving you!

—Dee Lindsay

A Fleeting Moment

As a child, I can look at my father, and remember
The days of gladness, and some days of sorrow.
And now in this life, for he and I there is no tomorrow
The time has come, and now is past.
For life on this earth does not last.
The love, the joy, the caring he gave.
The teaching, the laughter, the path he paved.
Was sometimes rocky, and hard to discern.
What does a man do, who has come here to learn
About life, and pleasure, and God's untold treasures?
He may spend a lifetime, and come to the end of the line
And look back and ask? Where went my time?
A fleeting moment was given to me.
To look at life, to God, and to see.
The magic of love, of giving, and of sharing.
Of knowing that someone is really caring.
The mistake he made was not in knowing.
That to each of us he was showing
This journey on earth is one with gladness, and sorrow.
Give to life your best today. You will have a better tomorrow.

—Laura E. Jackson

Jewel or Stone

How are the children preserved?
As tiny jewels in an expanse of larger ones?
Or as jagged stone in the midst of desolate rubble?
It is for each passing of judgement by many unfit to judge,
that this decision is made.

Children may be hidden within any true form
as jewel or stone or a cemented portion of each.
With the most burned branding or blessed touch.
Not forever simple to witness from their exterior
only discovered in a vision of their soul.

The astute are graced with the kind heart
to embrace either child with love.
The hard are emblazoned with the notion
of forming stone from jewel.

—*Wendy Perron*

Heavens Unrest

I dream a lot
and in the day I always try to keep
notes on the dreams and visions
that I dreamt of in my sleep.

There's usually a message
that is meant for all to see,
and last night I had such a dream
that really bothers me.

So, in rhyme,
I'll attempt to write the sadness shown to me;
this view I had of heaven
where all souls should be set free.

I saw row upon row of tombstones without any signs.
there were jars and baggies
with fetuses of all different kinds. Then - I saw God,
with an aborted fetus on his knee,
and his distress was apparent as far as I could see.

Tears were flowing down his cheeks
as I heard him sadly say, while cuddling the "baby,"
"I didn't plan it this way!"

—*Paula Bridget Haury*

Sarajevo

Early morning
a police officer locks his flat and heads for work
like any other day
His tattered uniform
soiled and grey,
but creased and pinned neatly at the knee
Slumped on crutches lifted from a corpse
he views the city below, and sighs before his descent
The narrow streets, cold and damp, strewn with concrete
from buildings mercilessly bombed
Muted voices hide behind the walls of homes that survive
but no longer live
By midday he approaches a soccer field
now a graveyard of 1500 stones
An army flatbed, tracks freshly laid in the snow,
idles at the end of the field
He counts as twenty more fill the gravesite
"cleansed" of this horror
Buried under sod tossed hastily, between rounds of gunfire,
the dead are envied by the living
The crutched man looks to the cold sun
of the Sarajevo hills
His hollowed eyes can no longer cry
and he whispers dryly,
"am I...in Hell?"

—*Gregg Marcellus*

Stranger In My Mirror

An image that appeared in my mirror
Was one that looked so unfamiliar
A reflection that wanted to mimic
And it seemed to have no limit

I closed my eyes to lose this character
And found myself on a psychological rollercoaster
Bewildered from this bizarre episode
When I opened my eyes I expected to be consoled

Relieved to view an identical image
The experience unveiled a transitional vision
I understand now how this could be
My mirror exposed myself to me

—*Mary Woods*

Poetic Prisms

It's hard to break the rhymes and rhythms
Of words that form poetic prisms
Catching light from mental corners
Bouncing off emotion's borders
Memory's wavelengths separating
Form the spectrum I'm creating...

Crystal images in words
Silent voice of mind is heard
By all who choose to focus eyes
On my reflections cast in dye!

—*Trish Iwanski*

Centenarian

He had a face of old leather
and tired blue eyes,
dulled as if swept by the dust of time
into forgotten pockets of least resistance.
His nose retreated
from the advance of years,
small signpost on the face of age.
Cheekbones of prominence
sloped downward
and in,
opening on to sunken pools
where dimpled youth had slowly settled.
Lips as thin as November ice
parted from the left
to reveal stubs of teeth
leaning like yesterday's guardrails
to prevent errant morsels from slipping over the edge.
Hair the color of new-fallen snow in afternoon light
swept down across his brow,
defying the ravage of years, boldly proclaiming,
"I am!".

—*Randall Lee Saxon*

The Watchman

What is the measure of a man or woman,
When all is said and done, now do they stand?
Heads held high eyes reflecting to heaven,
Ready to receive the promised blessings?
Or heads downcast trying to hide, wondering why.
I believe in the tallyman.
I believe that a man or woman can change
in the midst of life, in the midst of grief,
In the midst of death.
This light, this phoenix, that has shone so brightly,
its mere existence is sure to guide someone else's way,
So they too can stand tall on their day.
Sometimes purpose shrouded lays undiscovered,
For many years until uncovered,
by the watchman who waits, to improve his or her own fate.

—*Mark Armstrong*

Health For All Year Two Thousand

As the century draws to a close, many aspects of world health
are in decline.
Rendering health for all by the year two thousand an empty outcry.
Diseases once vanished from the scene are back in form.
Cholera being one of them.
Cholera is stirring awe
And threatening humanity out of existence -
As if pushed by a sinister urge to repeat history.
A contagion suppressed today is tomorrow succeeded by another.
One more contagious than the afore.
Contagious diseases, diseases sexually transmitted, cancers and
all, diseases in the form of the rampaging knights, they all
dash out of this damned century scrambling for conquest in
the limelight of the century tomorrow -
Dressed in abattoirical costumes in nature,
Demanding recognition, and challenging the world medics and
health organizations.
Health for all by the year two thousand is a failure.
Aids remains unmoved.
No cure yet is found.

—*Sitidziwa Ndoya*

Cave

(An alternate route to the subconsciousness.)
My lips and lids are useless.
Hands feel out every fold and nook.
Blacker than a trillion midnights.
And it's wet and smooth.
This neon cave awaits me to fall;
Deeper, its call.

I go. Trapped - ceaseless visions and specters collide in my mind.
I live on orange-colored fudge;
and rats with miscellaneous munchkins in bondage gear
look for the golden earring in my skull.

I drop back into it.
Smelling the mildew and dank fungus grow.
No fresh breeze around.
The gauze on my fingertips deadens my sense of pain.

Her pink berries smell so moist.
My tongue is dry & I can't see them.
Only my nose knows this time, for sure.
And the pleasantries seem so far away;
Lingering in the anteroom's door.
How do I get out.

—*G. Scott Hughes*

At Days End

Is anybody happier because you passed his way?
Does anyone remember that you spoke to him today?
The day is almost over, and our waking hours are few.
Is there anyone to utter now, a kindly word of you?
Can you say tonight, in parting with the day
that's slipping fast, that you helped a single brother
of the many that you passed.
Is a single heart rejoicing over what you said?
Does the man whose hopes were fading, now with
courage look ahead?
Did you waste the day, or lose it?
Was it well or sorely spent?
Did you leave a trail of kindness, or a scar of discontent?
As you close your eyes in slumber, do you think God will
say, "You have earned one more tomorrow,
for the work you did today?"

—*Michelle L. Toney*

Xenophobia

Insects, Insects big and small,
Hairy and crawly, I hate them all.
Should they continue their family line,
I shall hate them throughout all time.

Caterpillars, spiders, and ants all are,
Representatives of insect's par.
If the world they overtake,
I will be leaving in their big wake.

And if they think they have some class,
I would like to submit them to the looking glass,
And show them their existence so pale,
Way down low on the evolutionary scale.

A microscope has let me see,
Their fearsome features with relativity.
And if they should grow to mammoth size,
I hope I don't see them with mine own eyes.

With this word
I bid thee farewell,
But when I see an insect,
I'll be running pell-mell.

—*Nik Anderson*

Let Your Feelings Show, Please

Woke up Sunday morning, feeling out of tune
Wrapped my eyes around you and love came in the room.
I'm gonna let my feelings show
My love will grow and grow
Laughing into midnight, letting you be my guide
We approach the morning, feeling good inside
Paying dues and changes, living day to day
Love is necessary, to help you find the way
Try not to hide
What you feel deep inside
If you care, you must dare to be free as the air
Fairy tales and stories that we fail to see
We will tell the story of our reality
Tingle in your heartbeat
Softness on the clouds
When softer words are spoken
Action speaks out loud
Time is the healer, our love and our fire
Bringing feelings closer, is all that I desire
If you care, you must dare.

—*Kathy Reed*

Skin Deep

This tall siren turns,
Sequinned,
Reflective as a champagne flute.
Her bare throat has a memorable use.
The purpose of that fine-grained skin —
To announce the advent of bruises or beads,
(Black blushes, pearls from sand)
Glimpses, through symbols, of impassioned nights.

Her instinctive life now manifests as flesh
Clad in pebbles that show purchasing power—
They wink like bidders. Other eyes click as, quickly,
Numbers are added and the value dawns. Ah!
So much!
For such pained instants, at nature's expense,
Here is beauty, whose effect on sense is pivotal,
Like the first star.

—*Jane Gardner*

Garden Of Life

In my dream last night, I saw a garden of breath taking delight
splashes of color spilled across the land within my sight.
From shoot to blossom, and then to seed went the dance,
as I watched, I realized my dream wasn't by chance.
God's special garden was here for me to view,
at first everything appeared to be beautiful and new.
I heard a voice say "Look this garden grows as a mirror on life."
Seeing the garden in another way, I saw some grow with ease and
some
with strife.
There were plants with beautiful blossoms and seeds,
some withered as they began to fade, and others were just weeds.
Watching now the garden continued to change,
something happened which seemed very strange.
Stricken plants were at random ripped from the soil and sand.
Vacant unfilled jagged holes spotted the land.
I couldn't help but wonder what was happening to these plants?
Gathered at random, torn from the soil, was it just chance?
The voice now spoke again as I heard it say,
These I've selected to join me this day."
"They now live, transformed into perfection forever."
As I awoke and understood all life to revere.

—*C. S. Roberts*

Oil to Burn

'Tis midnight, and all is well…
the walls are quiet, but…
my mind is racing, running like hell
there must be something to put out this fire…
until I find it, I'll sit—
pen in hand, waiting, wanting to inspire…

The oil is burning, so they say
I'll sit and write
until a new day…
Tis midnight, and all is well…

I'll write of living,
loving and learning,
for all these things, there is a yearning…

Take time to read what I write,
and I'll stay up past midnight…
The race has begun, it's second gear
another page, I feel, is very near…

Tis midnight, and all is well…

—*Kathryn Palmer-Bryan*

Ode to an Unknown Sweetheart

Recognizing your almost forgotten beauty, twenty years later -
Like the first time, captured again by those intense, awkward
    feelings.
Seemingly unchanged - as if time had stood still…just for a moment -
A moment in timeless remembrance of innocent teenage love.
Of feelings, long forgotten…but suddenly, bodily remembered -
As if a time capsule had just been opened.
The same "heart in my throat" feeling,
Still, and perhaps always, the indescribable yearning.
For what? After all these years, I can never fully know.
Partly, for even the tiniest recognition of my being.
Now, as then, wanting somehow to express my silently pounding affection.
You will always be that which was not and can never be.
That endless search for the perfect love…
Are not life's roads taken with such dim awareness of their ultimate
destination?
Seeking answers to unknowable questions -
That lead, in the end, back to the face in the mirror -
And finally surrendering to the puzzling experience of one's heart,
In all its pain, joy, sorrow, and eternal hope.
While the mind relinquishes so grudgingly the questions,
And still wonders…if the answer was indeed… you?

—*S. John McDonald*

Passing Wonder

Passing time and myself
along turbulent thoughts
Waiting for a gust, bell or guard dog
to go off, awaken or quell

Emotions mixed by some
long forgotten recipe
Rapid quietness contorts itself
all shapes need boundaries

Perplexed, perhaps a philosophical plumber
could fit pieces which don't matter
It is uncertainty and solitude which collide
producing some vague notion of aimlessness

The metaphors themselves
dilute, deprive feelings
Occasional vision, perpetual void
hover and taunt simultaneously

Reaching armlessly yet grasping
so much nothing, it weighs heavy
On my mind in mere moments
wonder and loathing overlap

—*Patrick Fombert*

"Watching The Rain"

I sit here, staring out the window.
Watching the rain fall.
I sit here, remembering as the rain comes down.
Our moments shared together in love.
I sit here, with tears rolling down my face.
Making my own gentle slow rain.
And remembering: the way we talked,
The way we laughed, the way we cared,
The way we loved.
I sit here, staring out the window.
Watching the rain fall.
I sit here, remembering you, our love,
And us being together.
I sit here, remembering as I stare out the window.
At the falling rain.
Wondering, are you remembering too?

—*Mary-Michelle McCorkle*

Untitled

You look at me so differently
Say I really changed so much from
who I used to be?
We're both too wise for alibis
We talk, but there's so much we
don't say
I guess I've gotten used to it this way
But… In the past, you promised
me the moon
And when I fell, you couldn't tell,
It happened all too soon
But… In my world, we were foolish then
Make it happen again
Even though I'm reaching out
It feels as though nothing's coming in
And you know that this is how
it's never been.
But… In my heart, you took me
by surprise.
I know you heard my every word
Just by looking in my eyes
But we were crazy then
Make me crazy once again.

—*Kathy Reed*

The Sea

Ah my vast and glorious sea
You lie with arms outstretched to me
And gather me with all your charm
One doesn't think of how you harm

Yet your power far exceeds your beauty
Why the world is always at duty.
For always in history since time was observed
It's been the freedom of seas we have tried to preserve

But not only here does your power lie
Not if you view it from a seaman's eye
For a seaman who has been embraced in your arms
Knows that your power transcends your charms.

Know this too, my beautiful, outrageous, tempestuous sea,
This insignificant writer, will always, always be addicted to thee.

—*Leanora Casey O'Donnell*

Beauty

Beauty comes from within'
so deep only God knows where.
Beauty could be in the little children,
laughing and playing or praying
it can even be in one simple rose,
it could be in someone just saying hello
or it could be in a simple caterpillar showing its
beautiful colors that God gave to them.
Beauty can be anywhere; in you and in me.
It comes from the heart, maybe even deeper
than that; in the soul; your own self. So
bring out the beauty in you; show it to
someone by just loving or even just do a little caring.
Beauty comes from the soul and heart;
where you can always find God; willing to help you
with your problems, even questions or some answers.
So next time you look up to Him, thank Him for the
beauty that He gave to us.

—*Michelle Tanigawa*

Pain

So much pain, what do you do?
Just hide it deep down inside of you.
There's that hole in your heart where you keep it hidden,
Where everyone, but you is forbidden.
Everywhere you turn you can find pain,
It's enough to drive someone insane.
Pain comes in all shapes and forms,
It comes weather it sunshines or storms.
That certain pain caused by someone you love,
Does it mean something, is it a sign from above?
You want the pain to go away,
But it won't no matter what you do or say.
Pain is a part of life,
Some try to end it with a gun or a knife.
Others are afraid of death,
The true fear is with the ones that are left.
From the pain I want to be free,
Dear God, please release me.

—*Amy J. Enevoldsen*

Crying

And he cries
For the first time he cries uninhibited
Hoping the tears remain
For they are so real
Lost is the desire to hide behind a tissue
Is there something in his eyes?
Yes
Saltened drops
As he lay on his back
These drops freely gush forth
Drops roll everywhere
And are not wiped away
For the first time they are not wiped away
But left alone to plunge over
His cheeks, chin, and temples
For the first time
In his entire life
He is genuinely sad
And his heart warms at the thought

—*M. K. Vaske*

Life

I know not anything,
but that life is not for me.
My existence is without joy and lacking harmony,
and my death is not marked by crying but by joyful screams of
glee.

My mind races through the tunnels of time,
not knowing how to stop.
For when I can finally stop,
and my life has run its course,
Then I will cease to be and not to be remembered but discarded
as debris.

My life searches for a meaning,
and a reason for my being.
My heart yearns for love and care,
but instead all it knows is hate and despair.

My soul is searching, searching, searching,
for the cup of forgetfulness and to keep drinking, drinking,
drinking,
hoping to forget the hurt and anger,
and knowing whether to live or die in sublime humility.

—*Johnny J. Gom*

Someone

Someone has gone
We all cried.
Someone has gone
That someone died.
Someone has left me
I'll always regret it.
Someone has left me
I'll never forget it.
Someone has died
It will never be the same.
Someone has died
No one is to blame.

Someone is in heaven peacefully singing.
Someone is in heaven and bells are ringing.
Someone is clear across the sea.
The someone is still within me.
Someone has died, but is still everywhere.
Someone died but is still in my prayer.

(Age 10)

—*Kelsy Lonergan*

For You

In singing my songs of sorrow
and unhappiness
I am hushed by the presence
of someone so free
Like the wind
        Like the dove
        Like the ripples
That come and go on the
Surface of the sea.
Sorrow, Unhappiness
Overshadowed
Till they disappear
into the rays
of the sun
And fun freedom fun
        To create
        To be
    To love the sea
Is there for me to hold
For me, For me
        —*Theresa Hamilton*

Untitled

I think about you every day in class
visions of you just could not pass

I gave you my heart and you threw it away
you told me lies each and every day

My heart is breaking, but you don't care
the words you said, I couldn't bear

I thought our love was all so true
but all it did was leave me blue

I struggle each day as my life goes on
I never thought you'd really be gone

I'd wake up each night with a horrible dream
you wish I was dead, you were so near

I was hurt so much from the stab in back
I was crying and screaming but all you did was laugh

You haunt me as I lay on my bed
visions of murder danced in my head

You came into my home with a loaded gun
I tried to yell, but you said it was just for fun.
        —*Keltia Petroskey*

"Ode To A Portrait"

Portraits exude many things.
Voices soft, course, passive, and vain.
Eyes smiling, starring, piercing and pain
revealing love, mystic, fear, cheer and fame,
expressions of care, rapture and disdain.

Portraits say many words.
How, where, when, devise and weep.
If only they could recollect and speak.
What secrets they might divulge or seek.
Some secrets untold remain theirs to keep.

Portraits of old and new,
Reveal imagination superstition, fanaticism,
Tales in paint of today and yester years.
Geniuses of power and astonishing vitality,
Expressions of strength, devotion and fears.

        —*Nadine T. Willis*

Snow Days

When it snows the world stops
Waiting eagerly
For more and more white stuff to cover the earth

Creating ever more a wonderland of sparkling beauty
Especially under a full moon
Diamonds in the snow

Snow days make us joyful and childlike again
Phone calls are those from friends and family
because all the jobs are stopped

Suspended
With baited breath
And the hope of getting a break

In this busy world
To stop and reflect
Amend and create

To be ourselves

Snow days
        —*Raney Rogers*

Life Is Like A Flower

Life is like a flower, just a seed in the beginning
waiting to grow. Then it begins to grow and grow
until it sprouts. Then its just a little stem with a
button waiting to grow. Then it grows and grows until it
can't grow anymore. Then it gets old and useless all its
happiness and delight of being young is gone.
Then the petals begin to fall until it is a flower no more.
Soon it will die and all that will be left is its
remembrance of its growth, it's childhood, the memories
and where it stood, and what it used to be,
but most of all it will never forget all the happiness
it brought to others and how it made them laugh,
and how it brought a smile to them when they needed
cheering up.

        —*Karina Lopez*

Some Day

I will catch a moonbeam and swing across the heavens.

    I will hopscotch across our Solar System and
        walk on the Milky Way.

I will enjoy the delights of other galaxies and
        count the constellations, in each.

    I will wink at the stars and smile with the moon.

I will sit on a ring of Saturn and sprinkle
        shooting stars through space.

    I will catch the tail of a comet and ride
        around the sun.

I will paint Black Holes with all the colors of
        the Northern Lights and roll them down the
        streets of gold.

I will ride the Gulf Stream to the top of a cloud
        and sit forever at the feet of God.

        —*Nina Whittlesey*

Untitled

A child of careless innate innocence
Wanders nature's wonders without a thought;
Turning the stones of winding streams and creeks
Never knowing the names of creatures sought;
The purest of pleasure in plain nature
Lasts but the life of living in childhood;
Romping the grass without nomenclature
Mindless yet truly by time understood;
Then comes the clear call to perpetuate
As mindless pleasures fade into fancy;
Callous commands come romping through the gate
That once was the portal of purity:
Innocence may be blessed and beautiful
Though unblessed it can never be dutiful.

—*Nelson L. Jones*

"Soulmates"

The lake lies still, waiting..soft breezes, with southerly warmth,
Touch us, caress us, as summer breaths its dying breath.
Storm clouds pause, in North and West.
As thunderheads peak over their horizons...waiting.

We embrace, the lake and I, our surface calm...
Our souls as one, our hearts...unrest...waiting.
A loon swims by, without it's mate, calling,
Plaintive, lonely, haunting....

The breezes cease, the grasses still, the calm deceptive.
Soon the wind will shift and dominate...the sea deepens,
As night approaches, the sky gives off it's last glorious light
My posture, still and waiting....

Darkness descends, as fall comes on winter winds.
The sea trembles...it's surface blending with the night.
Only sounds and air now tell of the changing season.
Waves build, winds howl, our spirits blend..in life...

No longer waiting.

—*Sally A. Mellon*

Sweet Memory

Kept high on a shelf all tucked away,
was a special tin saved for Christmas Day.
Filled with the sweet things Mother had made,
while the little children around her played.
Each child had a favorite and waited in line,
to taste the goodness at samplin' time.
Sugar cookies packed that they might keep,
so not to disturb gingerbread boys fast asleep.
Popcorn balls, carmelled just right,
wrapped in waxed-paper nice and tight.
Soft white fondant, chocolates dark and sweet,
brown sugar pan-fudge filled with hickory meats.
The tin was filled and tied with a ribbon of red,
and all were twice reminded before going to bed...
That sweet dreams are made of special things,
like red ribbon and tins and rememberings.
So when Christmas comes, make a memory to share,
with a special tin packed with love and care.
Have a "Merry Christmas" right from the start,
and recall a moment of the past that you hold in your heart.

—*Lois W. Suhr*

Untitled

To fall in love with you
was such an easy game.
And now you're telling me
that you feel the same.
To fall in love with you
I must have been so right.
Because I feel it when you hold me
each and every night.
To see your smiling face
to feel you hold my hand
Or the way you sit and listen,
to your favorite band.
The songs as they'd come on
the way you'd sit and sing
Or how about the day
you handed me my ring.
Just a gratitude of love
to show the way you feel
I just hope you realize
my love for you is real.

—*Angela Templeman*

Easter Morning Sonnet

Mary gripped the disciple's arm as John
watched the oaken cross sway in the fierce wind.
He listened to cruel jests of the Romans.
The Arimathean, his tomb to lend
to the Virgin's Son, neared the bloody rood.
John observed the soldiers rattle the dice;
His savior's body nailed to the coarse wood.
Women brought the scent of burial spice.
Tears filled the eyes of the Virgin as they
laid her son in white internment linens.
Bloomed garden flowers strewed the rocky way
to the somber humid crypt entombment.
The burden of the mighty cross alights;
glance Eastward, behold glimmers of sunlight.

—*William T. Hitz*

"Life's Angles"

A gray dawn is breaking over the sea.

Morning mist rolls over the mysterious
waves that dance and sparkle in the break of a new day.

Seafoam laps on the virgin sand
giving a gentle sigh of relief.

A perfumed wind blows in
from the doors of heaven.

A spray of mist hits me in the face as I sit and watch
the morning break along the beach.

Soon this morning to remember will be gone, it
will fade into my heart, soul and mind.

It will become a part of me.

I hope to remember this morning in years to come
when my life seems to have turned astray.

To remember.

Life is a simple thing to enjoy, and when you look at it
from any other angle, no matter how hard it is, it will
always look better than it was before.
But for now, dawn is breaking along the beach and I shall
sit and watch it until it is no more.

—*Lauren Ann Caminiti*

How're Ya'll?

Down here we all speak with a southern drawl.
We address each other with a "How're Ya'll?"
I isn't good grammar, but the warmth is there.
We meet no strangers. All are neighbors here.
We like to fish and we don't mind
Whether one bothers to get on our line
For while we sit on an old creek bank,
It gives us time to stop and think.
The good Lord didn't mean for us to push too hard.
We'd grow callous and mean and old and tired.
He said, "Love thy neighbor" and we live that way
So if by chance we should meet you today,
Join in, don't cringe when you hear us call,
"Howdy Neighbor! How're Ya'll?"

—*Audrey Madeline Markos*

"Imagine That"

There was no pain to feel a gain
We all had a place and enough room for our own space
There were no fears so we would not cry any more tears
"Imagine that"
There was no confusion
And everything was an illusion
The fast lane made sane
And everything was tame for the sake of fame
There were no disease, oh please.
We had dreams without screams.
"Imagine That"
No guilt or shame placed on our name.
The struggle of life could someday be explained.
The unknown would be full blown.
We would not judge or hold a grudge.

—*Lynn Yonko*

Untitled

It was just a year ago,
We all had to let you go.

We take a step each passing day,
With God the one guiding the way.

We miss your smiling face and sparkling eyes,
Many times these things make us sad and make us cry.

But in this long and rough past year,
We've retained memories of you, so dear.

We have a comfort as we battle each day,
We know God had it his way.

We know as we look up to the clouds of white,
God is holding you close and holding you tight.

When the time comes for us all to meet at the golden gate,
We'll realize this while was much worth the wait.

We'll all turn and smile at one another,
Realizing we have eternity to spend with each other!

—*Summer Dietz*

Day Dreams

Look into my heart and tell me what you see
Visions of my loneliness, day dreams of you and me
To walk along in silence with your hand held in mine
Finally to see our paths have crossed, slowly intertwined
We sit and talk for hours and sometimes not at all
I'll always be here to catch you if you ever lose hope and fall
I'll keep you in my heart to shelter you from the pain
Holding you close inside myself where there you will always remain

—*M. R. Cain*

Untitled

In the frantic search for peace of mind,
we cautiously probe the boundaries of the
imagination. Looking for that daring escape,
often tipping but never toppling those
delicate scales of thought. Commonly during
this self examination we learn of the
existence of an alter ego we perceive to
be more fascinating than our normal selves.
However, for as much as we know this being
will relieve our anxiety and conquer all we
never release "ID". Often improvising for its
strength, usually adapting to the situation,
and seldomly overcoming the dilemma. Thus
suppressing the dominate force and concluding
the search in vain.

—*Avery Hines*

When You And I Were Young, Mary

When my sister and I were little kids
   We did all sorts of things
We made doll clothes from flowers and leaves
   And fashioned pretty clover rings

We had necklaces and bracelets
   Made from wild red clover
Roses trimmed our play house
   There were rich mud pies all over

When we washed the dishes and dropped a knife
   That was a romantic sign
It meant a boy was sure to call
   Would it be her beau or mine?
But if we happened to drop a spoon
   That meant a girl would call
Mama said it meant carelessness
   She wasn't romantic at all.

—*Jean L. Sexton*

Basic Ingredients

Thank you for being with me in the confines of our cauldron where
we each ask why. Why I am anything that adds to the spice
always alludes me. And the paradox remains that I find my
insecure grip on the end of the ladle.

I stir and need your ingredients to ensure a pleasant texture.
Only through being lost—and through you—do I find it more
palatable with purpose and comfort when there is more of you
and less of I.

Because you are so important to the direction of my quest,
I implore of you to become aware of how insignificant we remain;
but how important we are while lost when we hold the lantern for
another.
You—you are one or you are all I am able to touch. I am
nothing without you, but together we are twice as good as we
think we are and often half as good as we want others to
believe; but the Almighty Ten will always help.

—*H. Bus Bondurant*

Goodnight

You went back to the Earth through surreal sceneries.
   You, my sweet brother with the fog and
     you my sweet sister, with the snow.
   The Earth decided to cushion everything
     with fog and with snow.
She wanted you back through the surreal sceneries,
   to rock you in your last sleep,
     with fog and with snow.

—*Palma D'Alessandra-Marchesi*

"I Didn't See The Children"

My wife and I had done real good this year,
we had bought the family Christmas, paid for free and clear.

We were in such a hurry to make it all right,
we overlooked a most important sight.

On Christmas morning it came clear,
I didn't see the children to whom Christmas is so dear.

I didn't see the children that a doll would be their cheer;
I didn't see the children, to me it wasn't clear.

I didn't see the children that a coat was their need,
I didn't see the children the joy a bike would bring.

I didn't see the children who didn't have a home;
I didn't see the children who walk the streets alone.

I didn't see the children for food they grieve;
I didn't see the children who had special needs.

For our family, we had done good,
but I didn't see the children and didn't do what I should.

I hope not a child did without, cause in a hurry I couldn't see
I made a promise this year to answer their needs.

I hope the Lord will forgive me,
'cause the children I did not see.

    —Kevin D. Perrine

A Last Prayer

Oh dear God, forgive us for what
we have done.
We've made war on your star and
nobody really won.
What once you created fresh, alive and new.
Man has DESTROYED with his wars and
wonders what will he do.
In six days time you made all things.
Now after two thousand years of war,
There's nothing.
Soon man will be gone, just like the
Dinosaurs, the cave man, and the past.
The once again there will be peace
on this star.
God help the next breed to make it last.
I know from the beginning man against man.
Death and suffering was not Gods plane.
May God have mercy on us all.
When this war is over that we hear the final call.

    —Jennie D. Jones

Third Day's Morning On A Trek Out Of Pokhara

Out of Ghandruk en route to Biranthante
we hike down the steep slate steps
to the rushing glacier melted river that
roars along with a chorus of crickets.
The path grows narrow,
cobbled, run with water and leach filled weeds.
Waist high
fly pairs of plump yellow butterflies
with black rims, and blue-winged dragonflies.
Now these, one or two electric-green
grasshoppers, and huge and tiny
tiger striped moths give chase
across the riced and flowered meadow.

    —Marilyn Wilkey Merritt

Our House

Welcome to our house, we're very glad you came.
We love to have friends over and we love to entertain.
In the kitchen you may find some coffee or some tea.
Just make yourselves at home, that's how we like it to be.
And as you leave this day we hope you've seen the one
The Saviour of the World, God's one and only Son.
For God so loved the World that He made the perfect way
to reunite ourselves with Him when we leave this life one day.
God sent His only son Jesus to die for you
and me so we could live with joy in this life and eternally.

    —Patti Redman

On Our Journey

On our journey
We saw the truth, the light
Our destination we said, our fulfillment, our fight

And it's just over there, surely we draw near...
We could both tell the closeness
From our rising fear

Our fear that we would actually get there
And be complete at last

To find the reasons for going
had gone - had passed

Well fear not my love
Our road doesn't go there at all
Whenever one of us is up
The other, is soon to fall

And standing both we must
Were there any hope of reaching
The space to be aware
Of the lesson life's been teaching

That life's one and only true call
Is the sharing of our love and ourselves, with all

    —Todd Marshall

What We Believe

We have no explanation for death.
We search and look
but there are no answers.

We want to trust.
We want to believe.
But with no one to answer us
sometimes its hard to conceive.

It will always hurt
the pain will never go away
It will never be easy
but we must go on and continue to pray.

We have to believe
that there is a better place
and someday we will meet up again
within God's good grace.

So, when someone you care about
life comes to an end,
just look into your heart and believe
we will be with them, another time, another place, again.

    —Paulette S. Anderson

To Thee, Wind

Oh mighty wind, invisible god,
We see what the power of your touch hath wrought-
Danger, destruction here now abound,
Limbs, leaves in disarray line the ground.

You're funny, you're fickle
In a strange sort of way-
Summer breezes, gale forces,
You bring each, come what may.

You elude our sight still,
But your touch vainly confirms
You are here in control,
Oh mighty wind, we forever extol!

　　　—*Nancy S. Hudson*

Sensory Memories

It seems it was in dreams so long ago
we strolled in streams of light. But who could know
how swift the breath of day could play against
the remnants of what was? And though I'd sensed
that rain was in the air, I'd no despair;
for I'd be strong as long as you'd be there!
Yes, I remember sunlight and the way
it filled your hair; and how a ray
would gently kiss and glisten. How your lips
invited, so excited that it grips
me even now; how I recall the taste
of honey! Yes, it's funny how we waste
what most we treasure, for the pleasure blinds
us both; much as the moth whose spiral climbs
up to the fire, ever higher, to
it's destiny, it's quest remaining true.

　　　—*Scott Lewis*

You Will Always Be In My Heart

　The best times I ever had were with you
　We talked, we laughed, and we even sang too
　You told me things that meant so much to me
You said such sweet words I never thought could be
　But then came the tragedy which tore us apart
　You had died and left a whole in my heart
　I never thought this would happen to you
　I didn't want to believe it but it was true
　I thought we would always be together
　I didn't think I would lose you forever
　But I now know we will never really part
　Because you will always be in my heart

　　　—*Jessie Sarauer*

Untitled

Today I danced with an old friend of mine
We walked to place we used to know.
The time passed quickly and that was all right
with me, the distance between us was felt.

We finally reached our destination, after many stops.
Here we parted ways,
the ghost held inside for so long was put to rest
and we, two separate lives move on.

The ghost I had danced with for many a day,
is put to rest,
not forgotten, but peace between us is made.

Into our separate sunsets we fade.
Living from what's been learned,
forward to what has not.
So, here again, I'll say good-bye and forever in my
sanctuary, you, I'll love.

　　　—*Sarah Tucker*

Lessons Throughout Our History

He and I opened a book that we've shared from the start;
We were writing our history, words that came from the heart.
We filled every page with friendship so dear;
The friendship grew stronger by the day and by the year.
One day we saw something that we hadn't seen before;
There was much more between us than our minds had in store.
We consummated our interests knowing everything would change;
And then we separated by distance, nothing would be the same.
The book still existed after all we'd been through;
but our friendship had suffered much more than we knew.
If we could tear out the last few pages, our friendship would again
be strong;
but once history is written we can only learn from our wrong.
The book held things together for us with binding and glue;
but to stay friends forever, our intimacy had to be through.
There were a few more pages left to write on;
we wanted to fill them with happiness before the pages were gone.
Love became part of the friendship we shared
Everything we had was precious and nothing made us scared.
We suffered the strains of distance and time;
But our friendship survived all the mountains we climbed.

　　　—*Theresa Lynn Hardesty*

A Family Reunion

Like the rainbow after rain; like the clear sky after bad
weather, there's something wonderful about getting a family
together. A reunion of caring, loving ones must find a way to
often meet and create an exceptional, special day. The
memories shall be engraved in each mind and heart as it is so
sweet to hug and kiss as we meet; hug and kiss as we part.
Let there be a full time of laughter, games, food and fun,
Storing joys to be implanted by everyone. Parents and children
could choose to swim, boatride or ski, catch upon on family
news, tell jokes, play games, watch T.V. Hilarious at
midnight, "Where do I sleep?" is the call, though beds,
mattresses, couches, pallets are wall to wall. A brunch
breakfast of sausage, eggs, muffins at every will, followed at
dinner with casseroles, salads, or steaks on the grill.
Until another reunion our cups overflow with joy and love
That cements us in harmony such as taught by the Lord above.
Compassion for each other we shall always keep anew. From
hearts having been touched by voices, "I love you." So like
the rainbow after rain; like the clear sky after bad weather,
there's something wonderful about getting a family together.

　　　—*Vera Lee Hall*

In Search Of A Queen

　　Come my beloved enchantress
weave your incantation onto my battered remains.
　　Purge the incertitude of your passion
　　and replenish my soul with resolution.

Destiny has propelled my inner-being to search
　　　for your alluring touch.
　　Bewitch me with your voluptuous desires
　　compel me to remain spellbound.

　　　Vigor will cast a ring of love
　　Devotion will seal our hearts to one.
The sword has been removed from my heart of stone
　　　now you are Queen.

　　　—*Artemio Murillo*

We Are "Woman"

We are "Woman", We are survivors
We're as strong, as strong can be.
We are "Woman", We are invincible
We've been around, since Adam and Eve.

Big or small, We are survivors
We've survived, All famines and wars.
We out lived, the little do-do
And all the great big, dinosaurs.

We love our men, We protect our children
If you doubt this, just study our worth.
We protected them close, thru out the ice age
And cuddled them during, the flood of the earth.

We have survived, as God intended
If we did not, this world would fail.
We bear the burden, of reproduction
For us All, both male and female.

We are "Woman", We are not different
We are just, what we should be.
We were created, by the Master Maker
God All Mighty, for eternity.

    —Sallie L. Desmond

With All My Heart

You and I together
We're going to last forever
With the love we've both shown
We share laughter and tears
We share dreams and fears
But most of all we share the memories
By all the love you've shown for me
I know we were meant to be
My love for you is just as strong
There's no way we can go wrong
We know each other inside and out
We'll survive good and bad without any doubt
Knowing that we'll never part
I'll love you with all my heart

    —Shanna McCartney

A Little Girl Likes To Dream

Many delightful hours in dream world
Were mine as an imaginative little girl.
Now as I think back and reminisce,
I recall the dreams of that little miss.

As I walked down a winding road,
I watched with interest, a playful toad;
And wandered in the meadows green
Where beautiful flowers could be seen.

The pleasing fragrance was everywhere;
Overhead, birds could be seen in the air.
I watched the spectrum in sunlight beam;
Oh! What a wonderful place to dream!

A young man would enter my life,
In love and gentleness take me as wife.
I planned my home, as it would be;
The mail-order catalog was a help to me.

My dreams as a little girl are reality now;
On that truth, I will take a vow.
You see, dreams do come true;
That is a promise from me to you.

    —Martha Herbert Jones

Golden Years

Once in awhile you stop to ponder,
What about this world you wander?
You eat, you sleep, you work toward goals,
Each year flies by and takes it's toll!

The children that you loved and bore
Are grown themselves, and what's more,
They think their parents' life is spent;
You ask yourself just where it went.

What happened to the golden days
Filled with work and a golden haze?
Your mirror tells you truth, you know,
The silver hairs begin to show.

And yet you're young inside, I'll tell,
Just inside that body shell.
Youth's there all right, just slightly hidden
Beneath white hairs that grew unbidden!

Don't let them count you out, I know
You'll be around for years to show
Your children and their children too
What Pa and Grandma can still do!

12-11-75
    —Sandra Spruiell

A Cry For Help

Somewhere a prisoner of conscience is counting on you
What are you going to do?
In the night horror begins, dragged from homes
Taken who knows where
Yet you are remembered with love and prayer
Languishing in prison, where human minds are bound
Hearts broken, encased in chains, somewhere outside of main
torture continues.
Hear the cries, feel the pain
Brothers and sisters, not suffering in vain
Issue for human rights for all
Is beckoning the call
These actions, criminal before bar of human rights
and high court of Heaven
We are out brothers keeper holds still
Golden rule still holds true
So do for others what you'd have them do for you.
If this strikes a chord in your soul then make it your goal to:
Support human rights and dignity with your prayers and cash.
Prisoners of conscience and loved one you are not forgotten.

    —Richard Weaver

If Your Hair Is In A Knot

What do you do if you can't find your shoe?
What do you do if you have nothing new?
What do you do if your hair is in a knot?
Do you use remover for a spot?
Do you play connect the dot?
Or just leave it to rot?
You do none that is above,
You write a letter to Seventeen and mail it by dove.
They work on the problem in their limousine,
and print the answer in their next magazine.
If your hair is in a knot, what do you do?
Seventeen simply replied, just comb it right through!
So what do you do if you can't find your shoe?
Or if there is nothing new?
But if your hair is in a knot, you know what to do!

    —Lucy D. E. Coburn

494

No Prayer In Our Schools-Who Will Answer???

When someone is sick or near death,
What do you do or say?
It matters not your religion,
You get down on your knees and pray.

And if things in your life,
Aren't going just right,
YOU probably say a little prayer,
Before you go to bed at night.

But the world has grown away from GOD,
Become wicked and vain,
And now has taken prayer from our schools,
Oh GOD!!! — What a shame.

The very One you call on
In your dire time of need,
You've taken away from you children,
To make their schools religiously free.

But one day you'll have to answer,
At the Great White Throne in the air,
Why you denied your children the right,
To start their school day with a prayer.

—*Tommy Moose*

What I Would See from Space

Look at the world from space.
What do you think you see?
I would have to look real close to see.
I see cities and people that crowd them.
I see people sleeping in the street.
I see people starving and digging for food.
I see vandals and thieves.
I see children, adults, and animals looking for
love, care, and some friends.
Get to work and find a solution to our problems.
Help stop the fighting, ailing, and vandalizing.
What our world needs most of all is PEACE!
Help find peace, before it's too late to do
anything.
Save our world! Please!

—*Nicole Suter*

Let Us Be Together: The Man

She's talking again.
What do you want from me?
I cannot be what you want me to be.
You talk, I listen, yet you want more.
More than I can offer.
Leave me in peace, I like silence.
Silence you break when you enter the room.
She's angry.
Why can't we survive without words?
Let us not talk trivial.
Let us explore our souls in joint solitude.
Let us sit in silence together.
Let us be together.

—*Julie Gregory*

"X'mas In Our House"

X'mas in our "house" is best of all.
We have a X'mas tree
stately and tall.
Stockings are hung by the chimney with care.
They are filled with presents that say we care.
Jolly old St. Nick comes with his pack
He leaves us some presents, then he starts back.
We sing some songs and go upstairs
We thank the Lord and say our prayers...

—*Katherine Ham*

The Soul Needs A Resting Place

He's all grown up. Gone through life, seen and lived
What most people would never begin to dream of.

Never had much need for a church with preachers
Telling him how he aught to live. All religion
seemed the same. Pushing this, pushing that
confessing your sins, you'll be forgiven before you
turn around to leave.

Now the time has come for his soul to rest. It's
fighting to leave the trappings of the body. He is
not at peace, so therefore he fights with every
fiber, filled with frustration, anger and fear. He
can't let go, he doesn't know how.

When the world is asleep his soul tries to leap from
within. He refused, so for now. His soul will find
no rest or peace!

—*L. Susan Johnson*

Children Learn

Children learn what they see,
What we do to them, is what they will be.
Children who hurt themselves or others,
Were probably beaten by their father or mother.
Children who cry or shy away,
Didn't have any love in a simple way.
Children who leave their homes,
Are ones who were left alone.
Children who kill, had someone say it's a thrill!
Children should have the love,
a gentle touch, parents who care,
someone to be there on a dare.
Children should be happy all
The time, but not for a penny or dime.

—*Sandra Pickett*

Why

What are dreams? What are we?
What were we meant to be?
Dreams are fantasy, we are real.
We're meant to be whatever we feel.

Why are we here? Where are we at?
Why when it rains do we wear a hat?
We're here to succeed on this place called Earth,
We keep our heads dry, like taught at birth.

What is that ball that shines from above?
What is the meaning of the word, Love?
The ball is the sun, that's one of a kind,
To answer the other there's only one place to find.

To find love, look deep in your heart.
It will keep us together, never part.

—*Vernon White*

"The Gifts Of Love"

There comes a moment in everyone's life
When happiness dwells in heart, soul, and mind,
When friendship and joy transform out of strife,
And all give honor to love of each kind.
Love starts as a twinkle in someone's eye
And grants a sense to which all can revive.
It grows from the trust the world will supply
In order to keep its power alive.
Love is a feeling between two who care;
A thought designed to convey what we feel
So that all can partake and all can share.
Its meaning bonds an unbreakable seal.
Love bestows kindness for the world to bear;
Love is a feeling between two who care.

—*Mary Pat Frey*

What Would It Be Like?

What would it be like if there wasn't any violence?
What would it be like if there was no drugs?
What would it be like if everyone had jobs
   and there was no one out of work?
What would it be like if there was no fighting
   and everyone got along?
What would it be like if there was no stealing?
What would it be like if my sister and
   brother listened to me when I babysat?
What would it be like if parents were never grouchy?
What would it be like if everyone was
   happy and no one had problems?
What would it be like ?
   But the world isn't like that and sometimes
you need to hide from the world and
dream of what it would be like not
to have these problems in the world

      —*Letitia Coulter*

If Ever

If ever we should meet again
What would we say to each other
Dearest one I would tell you of
The dreams I've kept undercover

The loneliness of each passing day
From morning till evening
Thoughts I carry in my head
Of the countless ways of scheming

We never should have said goodbye
For this I alone am to blame
Thinking it was best for you then
Why oh why do I sigh in vain

If ever we should meet again
Be it near or some distant plain
Please soothe a heart that is broken
'Tis then it will be whole again

      —*Marie Jane Franciose*

"Good Idea"

I got a bad grade in my Math class!
What'll I do?
I forgot to mow the backyard grass!
What'll I do?

I forgot to go to the grocery store!
What'll I do?
I tracked mud across the kitchen floor!
What'll I do?

On the way to school, my homework tore!
What'll I do?
I forgot to do my weekend chores!
What'll I do?

I broke the window with a baseball!
What'll I do?
I tripped and fell and put a dent in the wall!
What'll I do?

Maybe I'll blame it on somebody other,
Maybe I'll blame it on my big brother!
THAT'S what I'll do!

      —*Arran Klosterman*

My Father's Angels

My Father's Angels are always there,
   When accompanied by a child's prayer,
As he listens to their cry and plea
   To have protection aid for thee.

For the future is held in the palm of His Hand
   He alone can turn the tide and shifting sand
And make those things which seem all wrong
   Misfortunes, incidents that come along.

By helping the hearts of His following few
   To get prospective and clear the view
When things are dim and people aren't compliant
   And the way seems far, rugged, and defiant.

Our father is closer than you think
   A hair's breath away to tap and link
You to His resources of His Love and Care,
   Where you'll find an angel awaiting you there.
For it had travelled on the wings of prayer
   As you have entertained angels unaware!

      —*Sarah Elizabeth Stanley*

A Love Lost

I can remember a time,
   when first our eyes met in quiet desperation,
   and all the pain of injustice were washed away.
I can remember a time,
   when two arms reached out to me,
   smothering the remnants left of past sorrows.
I can remember a time,
   when the warmest of hands caressed my heart,
   and released all the emotions I had buried there.
I can remember a time,
   upon hearing the words spoken of true love,
   restored the faith of the little girl in me.
Now, I have so much love to give,
   I don't know what to do with it,
But, I can remember a time.

      —*Lillian Nardone*

Surreal

Strange dreams fill my head
When I got to sleep

When I get up in the morning
I don't know if I'll ever go back to sleep

This morning it took me a couple of hours
To try to sort it out
Something's gonna happen
That I have to figure out

Am I going crazy
Or am I just a little insane
If I ask someone to help me
They probably wouldn't know what to say
Oh.....strange dreams just go away

Is it a quarter after
or is it a quarter 'til
minutes seem like hours when you think you're meant

The sun is going down
Shadows elude the night
Afraid to go to sleep
I dream things that just aren't right

      —*Steve Vitek*

The Forever Lasting Bed

I remember that day so long ago
When I looked at your coffin
Not knowing where to go.
As they lowered you into the ground,
I couldn't help but to frown.
Tears fell down my cheeks, and
My knees felt terribly weak.
I held my head as I cried.
All I wanted to do was die.
Memories rolled through my mind
Of the times we shared and
Times we cared.
My heart kept saying, "She can't be dead,"
But my brain said, "She's in that forever lasting bed!"

—*Kelly Edgar*

Blinddate

It was near midnight
When I made my exodus
You kissed me good-bye
saying I was going foul.

I didn't even get your name
Hillrich, Bradsby, or was it Adirondack?
You came from mixed blood
A fine black and white beauty.

Look up in the sky.
It's a moon shot.
Is that Coogan sitting on his bluff,
nodding his head?

Announcer sings his hymn.
Look at me. Hardly a mark.
Yet, I cracked him,
tar oozing out of his wound.

He gave his life for me.
A moment in the sun.
Now we sit together
cuddling in Cooperstown.

—*Matthew G. Lesniewski*

Life Is a Book

Life is a book.
When it is opened, the adventure begins.
When it is read, life is enacted.
When it is skimmed, life is hurried lazily by.
The pages are days, read swiftly and then under strain forgotten.
The chapters are years of long life.
The index is a personal biography, a diary for reference.
The table of contents is an overview, setting ideals for the future.
Headings represent holidays, and
Paragraphs are special occasions.
Pictures are a tale in themselves, a life of color and variety.
And text is daily living, life taken moment by moment, pieced
    together by sentences, words, and
Letters, which are hours, sometimes slow and sometimes hasty
    and strenuous.
And then the life is done, and a new life is begun.
For when the book is closed, death has come.
And a birth is soon to be lifted and opened and undertaken.
A renewal of fond memories now lost in cogitation.

—*Shane R. Pitkin*

Time Will Tell

I feel I don't know you,
When I've known you all my life.
When you left I kept thinking you'd be back,
But then I realized it was true;
    you'll never be back.
I always see people that remind
    me of you.
And think, "Could it be possible
    that you're still here?"
Everyone says that time will heal
    all wounds
But they've never hurt this bad.
I think of the future,
    the future without you.
My kids won't be able to meet
    the incredible person I once knew.
They'll just see pictures of a man
    they will never really know.

Will the hurt ever stop?
.....Only time will tell.

—*Nike S. Ruiz*

"The Dream"

When I dream, I dream of a day,
    when man will walk with peace.
All of the suffering,
    will be no more,
    and war will be at cease.
The man-made poisons,
    that inhabit our earth
    will be gone without an invitation back.
And for each person,
    not color of skin,
    it is prejudice they will lack.
So when we dream,
    we should dream of a day,
    when the world is a safe place to live.
No one would worry about receiving anymore;
    everyone would love to give.

—*Nicholas Hopkins*

A Little Something

Sometimes in this old world,
When nothing seems to go right.
The path of life seems cluttered,
The clear path out of sight.

Have you ever felt you couldn't make it,
And yet, somehow you knew you would.
Have you ever felt like running away,
And against all odds you stood.

As long as you have love for another,
The rest will fall in place.
If you stand together in the struggle of life,
There's nothing you can't face.

So next time when life seems so hard,
It makes you feel so blue.
Look to the one you call your love,
And say, "Baby, I love you".

—*Ricky Dummitt*

The Mother Deer

The mother deer lay still that night
When the hunters come to prey.
She listened on the whole night through
Lest they might come her way.
The long awaited dawn then came; her heart was now at rest.
She turned and watched, her young in peaceful sleep,
And her heart beat proudly in her breast.
She rubbed her soft felt-like tongue
Across her youngsters heads then arose to find some food
And left them in their beds.
They lay for a while in peaceful sleep;
Then one roused up and look around
The little fawn began to cry; its voice denoted tragic fear
It turned just one way then the other,
But its mother could not hear.
For down the road its mother fought;
She died to save her little ones, and only their safety
sought.
Now this mother's love would put some humans to shame
For animals have the gentlest hearts,
Even the wild and untamed.

    —*Virginia Byron*

Observation and Examination of the Self (Part 1)

My shadow is my only friend
when the moon is full
when the man is there

Like spit on the sidewalk I am
ignored, stared at and disgraced

I am distressed. Oh yes!

I am more than mortal
with a tiny head

I am estranged, I confide in me.
I am different, but only I can see.

With my eccentric reach
Sometimes I grab, but I never hold.

I give all I possibly can afford to give,
that's why I'm broke,
broke in more ways than one, even two, even three.

I am relied on, never relied for.

But I'm still me and change I won't.
Not for man.....

    —*Scot M. Leith*

"All Alone"

When the sun goes down, the nightmare begins
When the shade is drawn, it dances on my shin
It laughs in the darkness of my weary world
It screams in the blackness of my dreary cold
It takes away my covers and whispers in my ear
It watches me over and wants me to care
It strips me of my pride and chuckles at my nakedness
It turns to the side and shows me its emptiness
I know of nowhere to go, nowhere to spill my sorrows
For it makes me feel low, and shows me no tomorrows
And it can dig into my bones to show me the despair
Reminding me I'm alone with too much pain to bare
So, where will I turn, or will I just fade away
Because it makes my soul churn, and won't leave 'til the day
At last I know my fate, at last I give up hope
For this constant circling date is far too much to cope
And when the light breaks through to brighten me- safe warmth
I'll be long overdue, in the cold and dreary hearth.

    —*Udaya Amtey*

Million Miles Away

Looking at the night sky,
When the stars,
Are bright,
Feeling millions of miles away.
Seconds are eternity,
Forever the night,
It does not matter,
That I am millions of miles away.
I am forever young in the heavenly night,
Flying off into the heavenly world,
To another world,
Not knowing what to feel
I know I will be forever young
In the heavenly world.

    —*John North*

I Shall Wear Daisies

I shall wear daisies,
  when the sun, the moon, and the stars shines bright.

I shall wear daisies,
  when your heart, your soul, your very being says
  "This is mine!"

I shall wear daisies,
  when you feel flutters, your body trembles,
  while sharing that very special moment.

I shall wear daisies,
  in my hair, 'round my neck, a corsage perhaps!
  I will lay one on your pillow as it answers to his name.

I shall wear daisies.
  when the moon, the earth, the heavens come together,
  such as a field of daisies in bloom
  takes your breath away!

Yes! For that one shining moment in your life,
  I shall wear daisies for you,
  on this, your wedding day!

    —*Shirley J. Bench*

My Master

I met Him in the garden
When the sun was going down,
I knew it was my Jesus
On his head he wore a crown.
His cloak was white,
His sandals were tattered and worn
His hands I could see the scars of the nails he had borne.
His eyes were kind
His face a radiant glow,
A gently smile as he whispered so soft and low -
Come unto me - be not afraid,
He beckoned with out-stretch arms,
My peace I give you, my love so tender and warm.
I knelt at his feet, on my head he placed his hand,
Thank you Lord for your blessings
Sometimes I don't understand -
But this I know that I accept, not just a part
But all the blessings that you give to me
To live in my heart.

    —*Pauline G. Thompson*

The Eve Of Emigrant's Leaving

When in the autumn are empty the trees,
When storm is shaking the whole garden,
When on the ground the fallen leaves
Lie, when the wind is howling
In chimneys, when light will never be seen
In the windows, there's no evening, it seems.

    —*Alice Medveder V*

Black Roses

Tis a bleak and rainy day
When the weary girl lay down
Curls upon her pillow
Red roses in her hands
The young girl closed her tired eyes
And drew her one last breath
Roses upon her breast
A smile upon her lips
She took the hand that leadeth her
To everlasting bliss
Thou to her death comes as a friend
To help her cross the threshold
To guide her towards the light
Though her roses are withered black
Family, friends and others shall
smile through their tears
For will evermore her laughter
Ring true in the hearts of
those who love her.

—*Nicole Coats*

Dreams Of The Sea

Sometimes you can scent the salt-sea air
When the wind blows cold
From the storm-torn coast.
And you stand in the wind with your hair blown free
While the grey clouds roll
And the wild waves foam.
Then the thin mist clears, and a ghostly ship
From a time long past
Fights the howling rain.
But you open your eyes and the dark ship flies,
And you stand in the sun
On the grassy plains.
Though still, in your dreams, when the salt-scent calls,
And the sad sky cries,
And the seabird flies,
Then you're back on the cliffs in the stinging fog
When the grey clouds roll
And the wind blows cold.

—*Melissa Halstead*

A Tear For The Storm

Why when thoughts of you penetrate my mind's eye, do I cry?
When whirled winds blow, finding foe, not friend, but why?

You...who resembles Walter Matthau, an olive skinned birch,
cherry mouth protruding,
pushed by a flabby chin, that looks like Cupid's bottom, rising
up within a vexed smile,
while all the while frowning.

A storm has broken on the horizon, a prisoner in the wretched
winds am I, a gentle leaf.

Oh, pitiful storm, leaving me barren, like the contents of your
heart...revealing nothing...
Nothing , but destruction in the profile of a cursed
awakening
and a tear for the storm.

—*Victoria Anne Burkhart-Navarro*

Expressions

When you write me, smile
When you fall, yell
When you feel happy, laugh
When you feel sad, frown
When you have won, jump for joy
When you have lost, congratulate the winner
When you are excited, be crazy
When you hurt inside, tell someone
If no one will listen, tell me because
I can be trusted and I will listen

—*Melissa Breedlove*

Don't You Judge Me!

Hay! What give you the right to judge me? Don't you know,
when you judge me; you will never be free. Stop throwing
stones at me; while all your sins just flee. The laws of this
world apply to you too; so bare in mind that which you wish for
me, returns to you. Help me not to fall into the lies, and
deceptions of the evil one. Father, help me to stop looking
at what my brothers done; instead keep my eyes on your for-
giving Son. Everyone, will one day give account, and meet
the judge, on judgement day; therefore we all need to say, "If
I just look into my mirror today; I know that I too, have sinned
in someway." Now, Jesus wants to forgive you and set you all
free; yet first you must forgive me. Then go straight to your
heavenly Father, the ultimate judge of us all; he will vindi-
cate you when you call. You see, life is a ongoing game
of love, and forgiveness; we need to stop judging one
another's weaknesses. Let's look beyond their faults, and see
their needs; for God is watching and taking the final score,
don't be surprise if you can't get through heavens door. I
forgive you, now you forgive me, we'll call it a cease. Now
finally we can all have PEACE!

—*Ramona G. Knight-Womack*

The Wind And The Willow

The wind in the willow reminds me of you
When you sighed in the night like a sweet country tune
For the wind sings the willow a sweet lover's song
That leaves the tree swaying long after it's gone
...just like your sigh still lingers on

How can you capture the wind when it plays
It dances, it teases, it breezes away
I never believed in your need to be free
I thought you contended to love only me
...but how can the wind love only one tree

In all of the seasons this willow is torn
The wind shows no mercy when he takes her by storm
And just when I think I've left you far behind
Your memory will tear at the peace in my mind
...yes, you and the wind are two of a kind

So I'm sitting here under this old willow tree
Playing, replaying old love's melody
And the willow, she hangs down her head in pity
And weeps ever gently with me
...oh, I'm like this old willow tree

—*Ramona Q. Blackledge*

A Miracle

Nine months you were totally a part of me.
What you were I could not see.
Then delivery day finally came.
A daughter, to whom you were given a name.
The cord was cut and rent apart,
Yet the same blood flows through each heart.
I go my way, she goes her way,
Yet that special love is there to stay.

—*Aina H. Olson*

Death

Death is something we will never overcome
When your time comes there is nowhere to run
Standing still afraid to move forward
Thinking every breath you take is your last
You must fight to live
Everything has a purpose
Meaning good or bad
Who's to say you will wake to see another day
Time is precious and it's all we have
Take pride in what you do
Make each breath you take mean a little more
Who's to say you may not take one more.

　　—*Travis J. Horstman*

To My Son

Life away from you isn't a battle I ever thought I had to win.
When you're without me and I think of you, where do I begin.
Flowers that I see are only visions wilted.
Tree's dark, no beauty to shed.
Little sleep comes when you're away
I miss the house a mess, the toys on the floor,
　　your unmade bed.
Feelings run deep, thicker than my skin,
More than a mortal soul can bear pain within.
The clock sounds...was I awake or asleep.
Fantasy, reality - all an illusion, no time do I keep.

Life away from you isn't a battle I ever thought I had to win.
When you're without me and I think of you, where do I begin.
Thinking of words unspoken, feelings too heavy to lift.
When you appear, I see your smile,
　　glaring baby blue eyes.
It makes my heart start pumping.
Your life is my gift.
This poem is yours my son. Yours to keep.
Like my love - wear it well and plant it deep.

　　—*Paul E. King*

"Indispensable? I Think Not!"

If ever you feel on top of the world,
Whenever your ego's in bloom.
If ever you feel that you must be
The best qualified in the room
Sometime when you feel that your leaving
Might leave an unfilled hole.
Pull yourself up by the bootstraps
And this thought may comfort your soul.

Take a bucket and fill it with water
Stick your hand in - up to the wrist.
Pull it out! And the hole that's remaining
Could measure how much you'll be missed.

You can splash all you want when you enter,
You can stir up the water, galore.
But, soon, you'll find that in no time at all,
It looks quite the same as before.

The moral to this little poem
Is to do just the best that you can.
Remember, nowhere in all this wide world,
Is the indispensable man!

　　—*W. David Golden*

City Vs Country

I live in a metropolis...beneath polluted skies...
Where crime abounds relentlessly...and screaming sirens
cry...and oh! The crowded freeways...the potholes...
bumps and jars...fast moving eighteen-wheelers...
and the endless rush of cars...there is no doubt...
I need a change...to cure these city ills...so
I'll count on the county...the rivers...rocks
and rills...where I can do the simple things...
as in the days of yore...and my mind again
can linger...on the things I most adore...
I'll climb high on a mountain...where eagles build
their nests...meander through the pine trees...then
pause awhile to rest...I'll thrill again to music...
from the wind up in the hills...while listening
to the melancholy sounds of whippoorwills...
I'll also savor fragrance from the honeysuckle
vine...then store all natures beauty...in the recess
of my mind...the country's near Utopia...and one
thing's sure I know...if there should be no
heaven...the country's where I'll go

　　—*Hazel H. Wells*

Where Have All The Hours Gone

Where have all the hours gone that fled so fast away?
Where have all the roses gone that bloomed just yesterday?
Gone with all the dreams I dreamed in those halcyon days.

Where have all the young girls gone who used to dance and sing?
Where have all the daisies gone that blossomed every spring?
Gone with all those blithe spirits that only youth can bring.

Where have all the young men gone who used to be my friends?
Where have all the summers gone we thought would never end?
Gone to find more quiet time that passing age portends.

Where have all the children gone the little ones at play?
Where has all their laughter gone that sounded through the day?
Gone and now just memories for us to store away.

　　—*Paul Ebaugh*

Return To Destruction

When it declined only they can say.
where it stopped it stays today.
Under rough seas, frozen...as if to pause.
"I wonder who was there,
　　who was spared,
　　　what the cause?"
Items of hope and love forever untouched, left to rot
not ever to return, but not buried from thought.
From a universe hardly begun,
all can see, nobody won
leaving behind a mental camera of undeveloped memory
now realizing survival was the only key
Move on, move on, from my return to destruction.

　　—*Paul Kenneth Diamantine*

Pretty Little Dixie

A wiggly, waggly, feathery tail
Which thumps a welcome without fail,
Two curly, folded, furry ears,
And throaty growls for what she hears
That's Dixie Lee, our precious dog.

Her naughtiness we can't dispute
But when she's naughty, she's so cute,
Sweet Dixie, apple of our eye,
To daily life a constant tie.
Her puppy personality
Gives pleasure to reality.

　　—*Wilma Stock*

Our Old Farm House

I remember the three-room farm house
Where my sisters and I were born.
The rooms were large and plain,
The carpet was tattered and worn.

The kitchen with its oil lamps burning,
The aroma of fresh-baked bread,
The kettles on a wood-burning stove,
Sleeping on a soft feather bed.

Mom frying chicken and baking corn-bread,
Mending clothes and darning socks,
Canning fruits and vegetables
And sewing pretty frocks.

These memories of the three-room farm house,
Where I was born and raised, you see,
Are cherished and dear to my heart,
As I want them always to be.

—*Kathleen Boehm*

The World Of My Dreams

Oh, how beautiful that world of my dreams
   Where people relate with no need for schemes
And the outcome desired is always achieved
   With every persons's word always believed

Where lies and deceit are a thing of the past
   And only truth has the power to last
Where love and kindness are as common as caring
   And people are concerned with how others are faring

Where hostility and aggression are meaningless terms
   And the most violent creatures on earth are worms
Where medical science has conquered all germs
   And man has no problem with controlling his sperms

Then I awake with a sudden start
   And reflect on my dreams with a taste oh so tart
Cause what I see is not what I dream
   And those beautiful thoughts aren't what they seem

Oh how different that world of real life
   Besieged with misery and cluttered with strife
So I'll close my eyes for a little while
   And dream a dream that will make me smile

—*Maurice Levy*

Anticipations

Waking from a dark distant land of unknown
Where the conscience knows of no friend or foe,
The heart is troubled with uncertainly and disdain,
As the mind seeks a more complacent, comforting plane.

Penetrating the thick heavy early morning air
Where the feet wander deep in the midst of a foreign land,
The heart awaits anticipations which are to unfold,
As the soul finds comfort in revelations it is to behold.

Halting at a vibrant green forest clearing
Where birds are fluttering and nature is singing,
The heart stops beating for a moment maybe two,
As the eyes behold a sun drenched sky of blue.

Peering up from beneath leaf laden branches above
Where the vision of serenity takes its mighty form,
The heart is consumed with joy as well as fright,
As the body stands before this manifestation of site.

It is here from a distance that she can see him. The man whose
presence so far away awoke her. The man whose being led her
along this pathway. Her heart is filled with unbounbful love
and peace, as his arms surround her without notions of cease.

—*Polly E. White*

Loneliness

I am sitting here in this little room
   Where they locked me in and left.
There is nothing but loneliness and sadness
   In these walls that I stare at.

I can tell something is wrong in here.
This room is full of lonely and sad memories.
A lot of sorrow has passed through these walls,
   Left behind for some unlucky soul to conquer.

These little rooms that I talk about,
The ones that create sad and lonely memories,
   There are dozens of these little rooms
      And each one has its own occupant.

They destroy the mind and soul
   With all the loneliness they have in them.
Loneliness is a destroyer. Yes, that it is.
Loneliness is being locked in this little room.
   Loneliness is forever and forever.

—*Wayne Woltering*

Reflection

Throughout the deep corners of my mind
Where within myself I begin to bind
I have found the reason why
There are no friends or foes in which to hide
From inside there are no answers to the cry
I can only find questions with which to try.

Throughout the deep corners of my soul
I can see the brightest sun and deepest hole
As poised above the truth I lay
And beneath the lie I try to stay
Deep within I can see that it's only I
That shall take me up that high.

Throughout the deep corners of my heart
I feel the rage and love torn apart
The beating almost driving me insane
As the reason behind all my pain
Is all at once a revelation
Though a quick glimpse at my reflection.

—*Mary Galindo*

Grandma's Always Been There

Grandma's always been there for us
Whether a broken heart to mend, or a helping hand to lend

She taught us to make our favorite pies
And could always see through our childhood lies

We could even talk to her about our favorite guys
She could tell when it was love just by the look in our eyes

And when love made us cry, she'd say with a sigh
"There's more fish in the sea, just let them fly"

Grandma's always been there for us
Whether to kiss a skinned knee or yell "Hey you, get out of
   that tree"

She taught us to work for everything, cause nothing comes free
There's been times when she wanted to say no, but would just
   agree

Grandma's always been there for us through good and bad
She has a way of making us glad

She always makes life seem as easy as flying like a dove
You'll always be the grandma that we cherish and love

—*Tami Merkel*

501

Faces

The faces that I see, are all a mystery to me.
Whether black or white, green or blue,
By your face I will not judge you.

Through prejudice and ignorance,
The people have put up a resistance,
Against anything that is different or new,
By your face I will not judge you.

A face is something used to express ourselves,
Not to label people as a group,
Or to turn our world into a zoo,
By your face I will not judge you,

Not by color, race or religion,
But by your personality,
Will I judge you.

—*Sheila Seshadri*

Happiness

To breathe very slowly the smell of fresh dahlias
which always bring me back a sense of nostalgia
and help to enliven fond childhood memories
of my own native land I so dearly cherish.

To listen to the sound rather melancholic
of old immortal songs, all my favorites
which do transcend my soul to the ultimate state
where sadness and joy can be defined the same.

To watch a tired sun hardly lighting the sea
where the sailboats and the ships drift away silently
as I wonder, if by magic, they could have carried me
to some far-away place only dreamed of by me.

But my true happiness is somewhat primordial
hoping that when I join the promised paradise
I will be remembered by my fellow mortals
For having loved life fully until I died.

—*Maudlin Lamothe*

The Little Old Woman

It was a dark dreary night. There was candlelight shimmering
which you could see from outside the little cottage.

Inside the little cottage there was a little old woman
struggling into her night clothes.
Then she knelt by her bedside as she folded her hands.
And she began to speak softly, "Dear God, thank you for letting
me survive another day, but I know my time is coming soon.
And I don't know if I can accept it! And I'm scared to die."

As the little old lady finished up thanking God for everything,
she slowly climbed into her bed. As she lay there trying to
catch her breath.

Then she slowly pulled her blankets over her body. As she
laid there and closed her eyes.
The little old woman slowly drifted into a deep sleep.
While she was sleeping she started to think again about how
much longer she had left. As tears slowly rolled down
her soft, wrinkled skin.

Morning approached; the bright, orange sun slowly rose
over the horizon. The sun shined brightly the day of her
funeral. But I never knew I would end this way!

—*Moira Ackert*

Untitled

Walk down the street at night
While it's raining sometime.
Look if you are under
the street lamps.
Notice how the rain forms
patterns that lull you into
profound dreams?
They change so fast you blink
and they are gone- left without a trace.
But look, there's another one, and again
and again and again and again.
People passing by may think
you strange because
the rain will put you in a solemn mood
and you are holy for a while
and they are not, then it is
gone and the rain quits and
and you get drawn right back
into this...

—*Adam Robertson*

A Teardrop

A teardrop is so gentle
While running down your cheek,
Tears are not only made,
For the young and the meek.

The teardrop can not only be gentle,
But powerful,
Powerful to someone who loves you.

When you are all alone,
And you remember something from the past,
Tears relieve the pain fast.

When you have a fight,
And nothing is going right,
You know you will feel better,
After you shed them together,....
In each others arms.

—*Allison Kearn*

Night Of The Fleet

I felt the blackish reach of the beast
While the sea was still breaking violently
He held me as he steamed into the fleet
He drowned the black man and screamed silently
Light flashed from his eyes and onto his marble feet.

I'm scared with the coiled, hurdling muscles of his thighs
As I glance at the bloodless corpse
With my greenish shivering eyes.

With the beast octopus dogfish face
He turns to me in disgrace and dreaded to confess
I tried to leave this place
But I'm powerless compared to him.

He blinks his heavy lids
From the whirlpools of faces upon his body
With his earthshaker tentacles
He throws me to the ground.

I feel the empty winds they're twirling all around me
As the beast moves around me
I can feel his breath
He disappears suddenly the sea gulls tremble at my death.

—*Tammy Lloyd*

The Intruder

In the quiet at break of day,
    While under quilts I warmly lay;
I hear the pitter pat of feet,
    As they intrude upon my sleep.

Over me there comes a creeping,
    Something to disturb my sleeping;
'Neath my covers it slinks and slides,
    It's little body there to hide.

It wiggles in and snuggles close,
    It's breath as warm as fresh made toast;
I dare not open up my eyes,
    For fear of shock and shear surprise.

I've no idea what this might be,
    But out of curiosity,
I cannot wait, I have to sneak,
    An eyelid open, and take a peak.

And there a glowing face I see,
    Softly smiling up at me;
My heart leaps, and I am glad,
    When that face whispers, "Morning Dad"!

—*M. S. Davis Jr.*

A Winter Day

Snowflakes fluttering to the ground,
Whirling, twirling all around,
It's cozy and warm inside to stay
On such a gray and snowy day.

Two little birds sat in a tree,
House finch singing happily.
Where do they go when the snow comes down
And covers all the roofs in town?

Children going out to play
How they like this wintry day!
Warmly dressed from head to toe.
Their little faces all a glow.

Sliding on sleds down the hill
Oh, what fun! What a thrill!
Skaters on a pond nearby
Skating so fast they seem to fly.

Soon the snow will melt so fast
When warm days come, it will not last.

—*Vivian L. Holloway*

Untitled

Lightly the snow flutters to the ground. No sound it makes
whisking through the air. Too much snow befalls a branch and
it collapses. A nearby bird takes to the skies in search of a
safe haven. The silence is broken by neighboring children
attempting to make Frosty live again in their backyard. They
start with a small ball and roll it until it is bigger than
they are. The snow begins to fall harder and the young ones,
heeding their parents, leave to go inside. Silence returns to
the scene once more. Inch upon inch it continues to fall,
turning a dull landscape into a winter wonderland. Fields
beyond fields given blankets of snow to keep them warm through
out the winter. Hours pass and the sun slips into its night
hideaway. Inside a roaring fire illuminates the darkness and a
cup of hot chocolate warms the hands as well as the stomach.
All too soon it is time to sleep and dream. From the bed, a
window shows the streetlamp lighting the way for the snow to
land. The covers are cold at first but quickly yield to the
body's warmth. The pillow is a welcome sight as thoughts of
tomorrow's snow enter the head. Falling asleep, the night has
begun.

—*Matthew J. Zellers*

Music Box

Music box play a song of peace and harmony,
Whisper chimes that may rhyme
All done so charmingly.
Hopes and fears of treasured years I recognize the tune,
Songbirds that sing along with spring
When flowers are in bloom.
Nature's beauty of tender care created from above,
Charming trees and endless seas
Through wings of a gentle dove.
Mysterious sky of cotton clouds and stars that only shine,
White velvet grace dancing through lace
Inside this world of mine.

—*Robin Lynn Will*

Beautiful Cardinals

How beautiful the bright red cardinal this glorious sunny day,
Who comes to bring me cheer as I meditate and pray.
He's sent from heaven above as I complete my daily chores,
To bring remembrances and love from Dad, whom I miss and
    adore.
And as I do each and every day, I lay my plans and do my deeds,
I always find the time and a way to care for God's wildlife and
    their needs.
Though funds are slim and meager God always comes through for me,
Because he knows I'm so eager to show him how good I really can be.
And each night at dusk when the cardinals bid me goodnight,
They know as well as I do that again tomorrow all will be alright.
Oh beautiful cardinals, I love you today.
Oh beautiful cardinals, please keep coming my way.

—*Mary Ann Woischke*

A True Woman

A women of courage one of the finest sort
Who faced the world; leadership was her sport.
She was an example to the community
Brightness she portrayed, love and unity.
The one man she swore to love, abandoned
Her, and came back. Ten times he returned,
Ten times she forgave. But it was not in vain, for
In return she was blessed with ten fair
Treasures that no one can acquire. She had
Ten beautiful offsprings, nine fine ladies, true fairies of
    Leningrad;
One unique, handsome young man that was full of chivalry
Strange at the time. All this fine children were
Brought up well and single handedly. For she was more
Than a mother to them, but a father and a true friend.

She had beautiful brown curly hair, her nose was elegant, her
eyes honey color and fair. Her mouth had lips that were soft
and red. She dressed in a simple but elegant way, in stature
she was of a moderate length, with wonderful agility and strength.

—*Alma G. Cisneros*

Colors Of Britain

Nine black-eyed swans were tinted orange
while the ivory queen strolled by in lacy dress
plaiting a white-petaled chain,
frowning upon deep brown stalks with tails.
Her skirt brushed and grasped some purple-scented heather
as she stooped and gathered tiny green spikes to add to her wreath.
Tiny buttercups and tall thistles began a frenzied dance
as she, the queen, turned to walk along the incomplete wall,
herself as fragmented.

—*Shirley F. Jackson*

Untitled

What cruel, remorseless reprobate is fate?
    Who from beneath my watchful eye did steal
A love so dear none better can abate,
    Through ceaseless time and earthly pleasure heal.

And what distant, paltry deed is this?
    To one so young and innocent deny
A life adorned with tenderness and bliss;
    The fortitude of life it self defy

Yet, though the hand of time and fate divide
    They make my own years melt away e'er fast
And draw me near'er reunion at your side
    That moment when I too, shall breathe my last

For when mortal existence meets its end,
    Then once again we shall embrace, my friend!
        —Thomas Pirozzi

My Friend, Myrtle

I found a friend some time ago
Who in my life has been a glow,
Of truth and love along the way
Giving of self, from day to day.
Times have, our strength and love proven
Our lives together have been woven.
Together we've laughed and cried
And our friendship often tried.
Tho distance separates us at times
But ever present in heart and mind.
True friendship gives and forgives
Love for each other lives and lives.
This truly is what I've found in you
And may this friendship always be true,
Until our days on earth are done
And in Heaven a new life begun.

        —Lora Dunaway

Divine Stubbornness Of The Peace

It will be granted to all
who of course ask of it.
It will always be available.
The love of Christ
will fill your empty soul.
You will never
be able to outrun it or hide from it.
It will not be deceived.
It will turn up
time and time again
like a bad penny.
It will embrace you in its arms
and take you away from all you do not care to see.
It will take you above
all the chaos of the world.
If you just realize it will
always be there for the taking.
It will never fail
to follow you wherever you go.
That's the divine stubbornness of the peace.
        —Tracee S. Fuller

The Unknown

As I look upon whom I follow,
Whom I follow looks upon me.
I try to pretend that nothing will happen.
But yet I know something that is not known,
Will be placed upon the shoulders of whom
looks upon everyone,
Which are the shoulders of God.....
        —Vanessa C. Nelson

Carlos

It all began with red roses.
Who would've thought those red roses would be
The start of the most magical friendship!

You introduced me to a world I've never known...
    Playing poker, smoking cigars with five Marines,
    The BBQ chicken that nearly set your BBQ on fire,
    Countless movies we critiqued,
    Numerous experimental cooking.

Seeing you in the morning is like seeing a sunrise.
You give me the comfort of a child in her mother's arms,
    The security of infinite peace.
You give me that comforting feeling as if I've known you forever.
All the treasures in the world wouldn't be enough to
    Trade the times we spent together. But,
All the laughs we had would be enough to cure
    All illnesses in the world.

The sheer joy of seeing you,
    Being with you,
        Is enough to keep me contented forever!
        —Moon Choi

Love

I found a person full of love
Whom I'm always thinking of.
Before these feelings were even known,
I always thought I'd be alone.
But now since these feelings are very clear,
I never cry a single tear.

I always tell him the way I feel,
And the affection never goes downhill.
Sometimes our love is like a red, red rose,
Other times its peaceful like the wind that blows.

Love can be soft like the heavens above,
It can also be made into what you dream of.
Love seems like a glowing candle light,
Always burning with passion throughout the night.
        —Alicia Hudnall

Why Can't I Reach The Moon?

A small, discouraged boy said aloud,
    "Why can't I reach the moon?
        The response came-
    "Be patient, it will be soon."

The young man, still discouraged,
    "Why can't I touch the stars?"
        The response came -
    "Be patient, for they are not far."

The grown man, now full of frustration,
    "Why can't I hold the warmth of the sun?"
        The strong voice replied -
    "Please be patient, we are not done."

        The small girl asked
        "Did he have it all?"
        The calm voice replied -
"I have held the moon and touched the stars.
The warmth of the sun is still with me. Some day
    you may also have it all."
        —Melody Stubblefield

People Are Starving

People are starving
Why can't someone help them
They don't have anywhere to live
They don't want to see what the next day will bring

People are starving
Yet there is enough money in this world to buy jewelry, cars,
clothing, boats and mansions
We have money for weapons and bombs and tanks
We have money and prizes to give away on game shows

People are starving
If I were president the first thing I would do is help the
homeless
They are human beings
If you were human you would help too.

—*Beth Scalone*

Humanity

Why can't we put the human back in humanity
Why can't we see what God meant us to be
Why can't we see the right from wrong
Why do we sing the same sad song

Why do we view strangers with hate
Why can't we just learn and wait
Why do we use race and creed for the fault
Why don't we just learn to forgive and cope

Why does fear and hatred rule our live
Why can't we learn from the wise
Why do we view everyone with fear and lies
Why can't we see the love in their eyes

Why do we use violence as our tool
What happened to the "Golden Rule"

Where is the love, where is the forgiving
Just what is our reason for living?

—*Marianne A. DeCamp*

Our World

Look at all the beauty in the world limited to what you can see
Why is God's creation suddenly been taken away from me?
People dying in the streets, freezing, starving,
Whose expectations do these meet?
If I could heal the world of pain, make peace throughout this land,
Everyone would get along
Come with me, just take my hand.
It really is a short ride if we could all just have a little pride,
Be proud for what we have
This would be a happier place with more than one smiling face.

I wish I could heal the world of pain cause there is so much
that we would gain.

—*Melissa Rudolph*

On the Street

Help the people 'cause they don't know,
Why it is the world treats them so.
For they don't have a roof over head,
No feather pillows on a big warm bed.
They go to sleep hungry each and every day,
All there is to eat is what we throw away.
When they get help it's never enough.
To get off the street is very tough.
All that they own they wear on their back.
No walls to hang pictures or even a tack.
They walk the street all day threw,
With no money to buy anything new.
Think how it would be to live on the street,
Together this problem I hope we can beat.

—*Rhonda Lee Allee*

Untitled

I am sitting here wondering.
Why my heart is thundering and thundering.

Could it be because I can not see?
Yes! It is my eyes for they are dying
and my soul is crying.

Because there are so many things I want to do.
Now! While I can still see.
Time yet to see and spend with you.

Can you understand?
Will you hold my hand?
for life is short and upon my sight
I have little command.

Friend I have spoken the truth,
I need not lie,
Take me now before I die.

—*James Williams*

"My Wonders"

I have only one question,
Why'd she have to go so soon?
Sure I think that's an easy question,
Our world is completely messed up.
She'll like your world better,
but why'd you have to take her?
Your world has speak - free air,
Ours has 1,002 tons of pollution.
Yours has healthy lungs, packed with fresh air,
Ours has garbage lungs, packed with pollution
Sure the odds are against us,
but why'd you have to take her?
I was just beginning to like and respect,
that truly beautiful lady.
I'll always wonder somewhere in my mind,
why did you take Sue Teegarden away from me?

—*Theresa Stinson*

For The Love Of A Child

Look into the eyes of a child. Feel the love and emotions go
wild. Gaze into those deep and curious pools. Within them
lie future rebuilder's tools. Each child is tomorrows shining
star. But not the one in the alley face down on the tar.
The light extinguished, life taken away. No explanation for
the body that lay. Think! Think of the injustice done. What
was this baby's crime to be hidden from the sun.
What was there for this child's mother to fear?
As she robbed a life did she even shed a tear?
When will this most horrendous of crimes end? Why does mankind
turn their heads, walk by and pretend that this is not of their
concern and cannot be prevented? Stop! See! Let your
outrage be vented! Reach out and touch a life unwanted. Don't
allow your heart to remain blunted. There is a child craving a
look, a smile. Give some happiness if just for awhile. Let
every baby nurture and grow. Let every child feel the wind
blow. Give a piece of yourself to the meek and the mild.
If for no reason, but for the love of a child.

—*Paul Lebkuecher*

The Wolf

He stands all alone in the cold night,
While his shadow never moves in the bright moonlight.
He howls a tune down through the land,
And the echo is heard by every man.
As the noise fades into the night,
No birds, no sounds, nor nothing in sight,
Only the voice of snow falling down,
As the wolf just stands there looking around.

—*Ann Havard*

I'm Here, Too

Does a road get very lonesome when few people pass it's way?
Will the path that I must follow lead me to a brighter day?
Will the knowledge that I'm seeking bring me a better life ahead?
Will the world not judge appearances, but look within my heart instead?
Will my "strengths" be enough to carry my "not-so-strong" abilities?
Will opportunities knock on my door as I try so hard to please?
Is it so important that my hands or feet be quick as they can be?
'Cause I want to be the best I can - and the best I am... is me!!

  —*Patty Nickless Hinman*

Winning At Life

Life is a game we all must play
winning and loosing each and every day.
Sometimes it gets tough and you think there's no way out,
till someone reaches and helps you, then away goes your doubt.
Some people play to win and some play to loose
Deciding which is right for you, only you can choose.
Some people quit before the game is over,
some like it so much they wish it continued forever.
It's a shame that it doesn't
that's a fact we can not change
But we can make the best of the time
for wasting it's a shame.
Like everything else, life comes to an end
Some people's lives by others - then away they descend.
That's a reason to live all you can,
not by the rolling of the dice
So at least you can say you were winning, at the game of life.

  —*Renee Polletta*

Courage

"Courage!" she spoke
   with a gentle firmness
  flowing from her years
    of accumulated wisdom,
 addressing my moment
    of angry confusion and pain —
     and even denial of what
   the test result had shown.
At first the word
  sounded hollow —
   like a cold rejection of my inner struggle,
    as though I had manufactured the conflict
     to gain her sympathy.
Later, I would come to cherish
  her simple word of encouragement —
   even as I learned to accept,
    and eventually, adjust my lifestyle
    in response to the test results.
 These adjustments would, indeed, require
    an extra measure of courage!

  —*Tricia J. Culverhouse*

You Are My Heartbeat

Like the rising sun touching the dew covered rose
Whole world sparkling by the ray it throws
You keep me alive plus going strong
As your my heart beat all day long

When things go wrong and I'd like to quit
Sad song singing, in me there's left know wit
I don't give up I keep going on
As your my heartbeat all day long

We're together for life's roller coaster ride
As together we go side by side
Things will work out how can they go wrong
As your my heartbeat all day long

  —*Robert Detweiler*

April

Winter, dramatic and beautiful,
With all of its ice and snow
Is gone, and spring has returned to us
With her very special glow.
The miracle of April has come once again
On time, and without a cue;
A miracle that is always the same,
And yet it is ever new.
Trees that were etched with charcoal
Are now brushed with pastel with pastel pink.
Gentle rain falls in new leaves and blossoms
To give them a welcome drink.
Colorful crocuses open;
Tulip and lilac buds swell;
Hyacinths, purple, pink, and white
With scent so sweet to smell!
Wild geese fly in a v-shaped wedge;
Robins sing in the trees;
Damp earth pushes the tender young grass;
Pussywillows nod in the breeze.

  —*Arlean Moser*

The World We Live In

The world we live in is very hard to see,
With all the smog that's all over this country.
We have so many kinds of pollution
That we breathe all the time,
And in this world theirs all sorts of crime,
From beatings and killings and other such crimes.
I can't stand most,
I'm not trying to boast.
People are dying and committing all sorts,
Unfair treatment of immigrants and ports.
People being arrested of unfair crimes which
Is happening a lot of the time.
We need to start to clean up this world
We live in because there's only one world
And so many of us.

  —*Rebecca Kramer*

Untitled

Once a peaceful family, calm as can be,
with apples and oranges sitting calmly by the tree.

But as everybody knows a death tore it in three,
The children suffered but no one noticed
because they were busy with three themselves.

We the children saw may things, like lying and crying.
We sometimes cried too but within ourselves so nobody could see.
We the children were torn apart from grandpa, aunts, uncles,
and cousins too.
We did not like it but we could do nothing.
But when Christmas came all was jolly.
We were confused and unknowing that one person kept the family
together and that was our grandma Jo Ann.
We love her, I love her, all loves her.

Thank you Grandma for what you did, you kept our family together
and not apart from all.

Grandma please remember I'll always love you.

  —*Amber Tedesco*

The National Library of Poetry - The Coming of Dawn

On Apples — On Life

GAZING by fireside, as snow is caressing,
With blankets of white, its tender blessing,
Over all manmade and God given creation,
Trapping by white barriers - gloating satisfaction.

GAZING and dreaming of friend apple tree,
Bare branches hold snow, but soon will be
Warmed by showers and sun so bright,
Bringing soft pink blossoms, to our delight.

GAZING with thoughts drifting of the old rope swing.
Bees pollinating. Robins chirping "`tis spring!"
Pink petals floating gently to tender grass of green
Being replaced by green apples and leaves - minute, but seen.

GAZING - anticipating the hot summer days
Under branches covered with leaves filtering rays.
Hammock or chair, the swing now replacing.
Limbs laden with tempting fruit need bracing.

GAZING - glimpsing the yellow-red harvest of fall.
Both leaves and fruit must answer the call.
Aromas of sauce, cobbler, jams and pies have arose.
Stagger
or
Swagger
back to fireside as a cold winter wind blows?

—V. Irene Dean

Beautiful As A Rose

Beauty was my mother so majestic as a rose,
With elegant reflection in grandeur pose.

Gentle as the breeze, soft as the dew,
Glorious in depth by things she knew.

Like grand perfection of shimmering wine,
Delightfully sweet, this Mother of mine.

So poised and true and piously pure,
Straight from the heart, characteristically sure.

Each petal in place bursting forth aglow,
In refined beauty, as a prize to show.

With dignity and grace of true color serene,
Beautiful as a rose, was my mother queen.

—Nellie L. Evans

On The Golden Pond

I see golden light in the pond,
    with fishes below.
I see a boat wooden and meandering,
    where the currents flow.
The oar I see is half hidden by the water,
    the well used strength of the oar rests in peace,
    leaving behind what matters.
There is no human hand to hold it,
    it's challenges are all done.
The peaceful tides learned, keep it company,
    no room for fears that are gone.
The human desires and rules are not needed,
    because the peacefulness of God is heeded.
So the peacefulness of God gently guides the boat,
    to it's resting place, where nothing is wrong
    and nothing is rote.

The light beyond it's golden dream, is a place to belong in,
    it's meandering stream.

—Alena M. Roberts

A Freedom Carol

Sing softly, sing softly, glad tidings proclaim
    With glad Alleluias sing praise to His Name!
The little Lord Jesus came down to the Earth
    The lame to make walk, the blind to make see.
To make all men brothers, like you! - like me:
    Saying, "Peace on the Earth, to all men of goodwill".
To wars on the Earth saying "Peace, be still."

"Sing softly, sing softly, glad tidings proclaim
    With glad Alleluias sing praise to His Name!
The little Lord Jesus came down from the sky-
    The lame to make walk, -the blind to make see,
    To make all Mankind free."!
    —A. Lois Butler

Family Trees

Rooted in the south, many years ago;
With God's loving grace we continue to grow.
Our branches sprout and multiply,
Determining the beauty we display with pride.

Our roots are strong and intertwined,
Bringing forth a robust and noble line.
We share the juice of life, you see;
I am of you; you are of me.

Our tree is not apple, peach or pear;
Their seed won't produce the fruit we bear.
The arbor of life for you and me,
Is appropriately called our family tree.

This tree traces our ancestry;
Its branches compile our history.
We celebrate, while holding dear,
The link to life that brought us here.

So, never forget from whence you come.
And to those who ask where you come from,
Stand tall, for it is an honor to be
A Redwood in the forest of family trees.

—Sharron L. Solomon

Who Couldn't Love The World In May?

Who couldn't love the world in May
With green and gold replacing gray?
When bird-song fills each sunlit hour
While roses bloom on every bower,
And hearts are young and light and gay
As frisking children at their play—
Oh, wouldn't we love this world too much
If every month could be May or such?
Still, ours as much in August's heat,
Or bleak old December's frozen sleet
When rain in torrents gushes down
And all that is seen is seared and brown.
Hearts filled too with the selfsame gloom
Filling the world outside the room—
Then will be the time to remember May:
Days that tripped lightly on tiptoes gay,
Sunshine so golden and warm and bright
The mere thought banishes winter's night...
Wouldn't we love this world too much
If every month could be May or such?

—Audrey Brown Craft

507

A Love Without Meaning

He was the greatest; the greatest guy on earth. Every moment
with him was like a new love's birth. But then something
happened our "perfect love" shattered. Then all our precious
moments together had scattered. For ours was a love without
meaning, with no love; caring; or a shoulder for leaning, after
that all my feelings of happiness were drained. Now all I feel
is that between us there is an unbreakable chain. My days are
depressing and my nights are grim. For ours was a love without
meaning, with no love; caring; or a shoulder for leaning. Here
I am today so sad and lonely. With no one to love; except for
me "the one and only", he doesn't understand I loved him more
than life itself, because he doesn't love me; only himself, for
ours was a love without meaning, with no love; caring; or a
shoulder for leaning, even though I know we don't have a change
I think about him by and by or some nights I think about him
and start to cry. I know I'll always love him so I'll have to
let him go, and my life and heart will heal; but very slow.
For ours was a love without meaning, with no love; caring; or a
shoulder for leaning.

—*Jennifer Meyers*

I Call Him Dad

He sat on his bed
With his hand pressed
Hard on his face
In his beat-up suit
With sweat that turned cold,
And I knew there wouldn't
Be a new one
Because of a stain
On the inside
That would never go away.

I could see that
His eyes squeezed water,
That tasted like salt,
In a place where a real bell rings once a week,
And that he went to his mother's new house,
To build a dirt roof
Next to his father's bed.

—*Joseph Huelskamp*

With Liberty - Now Justice

In this time that all's fine
with humans emerging from the blind.
Science understanding our God,
Man depressing His flock.
We go forward to educate, but not to emancipate!
We teach only what's right, only to give man more fright.
Different paths, Different Faiths, Different Beings,
Different
    Grace.
We who have walked the edge, were only there to stand for
    this countries Pledge.
To stay and to say, that this bastion of Human Rights
    won't allow the gay.
We love, we care, we achieve, we scare
We are the new niggers of fear
All who have come before us also were labelled without care.
Someday, Someway our lives will become one
Individuality is a way.
Were not on the prey
So let us play, the American way.

—*Michael G. Creek*

A Cowboy's Dream

A cowboys's life is hard, they say,
With long hot days and very little pay,
The gathering and sorting for dusty cattle drives.
He knows not to look up cause there's no sign of rain
    in the sky.

The sun and the heat are constantly there,
And the choking dust he knows he must bare.
The smoldering heat that chafes his hide,
After each gritty day he turns in with a sigh.

He's always so careful not to start a stampede,
Not to spook the cattle, his only heed.
He and his companions sit around the campfire
Wondering if he'll ever be the one that gets to hire.

Owning his own ranch, his constant dream,
With lush green grass beside a cold stream.
He wakes that morning right before dawn
And remembers that those years are all long gone.

—*Angela Neal*

Meditation

If you haven't viewed the ocean
With majestic waves on high,
Or sea gulls skimming on the surf
Then zooming to the sky.
Come with me to surf and sun; and pick the cockle shells.
Hear the distant clanging of the ghostly light house bells.

the hot melee, searing, glow of the setting sun,
Will meld two people together and our thought's become one.
Oh joy! ecstatic joy! Gods artistry in view
With silent observed by this melancholy two.

Another time of redundant, mystical charm,
The sea unfolds to reclaim the rapture of ruminating past.
We are refreshed and tranquil in God's glory,
Of the sea's elegant art and fragmented whispered story.
Oh yes, we'll come again to this most precious place
and watch the voluminous waves roll by.
Ah! feeling placid and refreshed,
our thoughts rise to the sky.

—*Barbara S. Thompson*

"If You Only Knew"

If you only knew how much I cared for you would you stay
with me another night, cause I never felt like this before
    You're the first that could make me feel brand new
    And no one else could make me smile the way you do
    So stay a while and hold me in your arms and tell me you'll
never leave
    Tell me a joke, tell me a story, but most of all tell me
not to worry
    Cause you'll stay that one more night, and as we hold each
other tight, I hear you whisper in my ear that you care and
everything's going to be alright, but those last few words
that you said to me was close your eyes and sleep tight cause
I'll always love you and then you said good night.

—*Janet Hamlett*

Untitled

I lie in my room at night holding my pillow tight,
With memories of you filling my head.

It was then I wondered why you said goodbye!

As tears filled my eyes, I couldn't hide the cries,
Wondering why we couldn't give our love another try!

—*Wendy Pryce*

Untitled

A house stands alone out in the middle of no where
With nature and the clean air lingering all around it
I am wandering endlessly taking in everything surrounding me
Waterfalls in background; water crashing against the rocks
Birds chirping and flying; squirrels in trees
House above; furniture made from forest
People walking in and out
Time to leave here
Don't want to
Please stay
Fallingwater
House built into the mountain side
The furniture made of the forest
The dark and dreary hallways
Bright and colorful rooms
Waterfall underneath it
Nature unharmed
Fallingwater

—*Katherine L. Silvius*

The Lie

Why do they do the things they do?
    With no rhyme or any reason.

Is it fear they feel? That we might steal;
    the corporate ball in mid-season?

Give us a chance, that's all we ask,
    to show all that we can do.

They'll be surprised, that in GOD'S eyes,
    no difference between me and you.

It's a crying shame, that some point blame,
    at people of different color...

Don't they know, when will they grow,
    to live with one another.

Will it ever be, will they ever see,
    how ignorant it is to hate.

Some will never know, what the BIBLE shows,
    doomed eternal is their fate.

Will they hear these words, become perturbed,
    because it may have some meaning...

Doesn't matter though, you reap what you sow,
AND WE WILL ALL STAND FOR THE FINAL SCREENING.
    —*Michael Gerald Williams*

Hope

The future calls to us as hope,
With possibilities that are wild and free,
Like a butterfly called into being from a chrysalis,
We break free and fly.

Our openness is part of hope,
We see small openings for new efforts,
And give birth to new efforts from small openings,
Our world is changed through us.

We become instruments of new values,
Transforming our small slice of history,
Step by step, through insight and creativity,
Hope opens the world to what it might be.

    —*James Jacobson*

Moving

Moving can be as in dance
With rhythm
With feelings - good feelings
Moving can be as in changing locations
With good feelings and bad
When I am in the in-between
Half of my belongings in one place where I'm going
Half of my belongings in the other place where I'm leaving
The silence of both places is hollow sounding
And empty like me
With the nothing feelings that make me feel so much pain
Will I ever be home?
Where is home?
I want to find that warm place that is in me
And I can move to there.
    —*N. King*

Sing a Sad Song of Love Intertwined

    Sing a sad song of love intertwined
with silver songs of carillon.
    A boy and girl hopelessly in love
as they look from above.
    To watch the fallen angels fly.
    Sing a sad song of love intertwined
    Sing the song with your eyes.
    Sing a sad song of love intertwined
and I will pledge with mine
    Sing a sad song of love intertwined
we fly like the birds
    And sing the sad song of love intertwined
    Sing a sad song of love intertwined
with silver swans of carillon.
    —*Sonja Marie Henegar*

To Bettye

Our lives are a funeral march
With slow and, toward the end, reluctant
Steps from habitat to Home.

Living is not much more
Than picking here a leaf and there a flower
Or, at best, planting a tree in uncertain loam
To grovel, dwarfed among its kin, or tower
In autumnal gown waiting among the Philistines
For its David to bring it down.

As I wave goodbye to you, my forever Dear,
I wave to leaf and flower,
To my enduring tower
Through the passion of a tear.
    —*Randall W. Hoffmann*

"It Ain't My Fault"

Paralyze me with your race, power me
with you fear. Whose the majority? We power
our race with the revenge of our fore-fathers.
Pre-judged by my skin color and you become
the enslaver, I the enslaved. You turn the ta-
bles, tables built around centuries of prejudice
and hate! You are owed by me...what I never
took! There is a void and in this void, a room
full, full of us all. Yet you're alone, I'm alone,
we're all utterly alone. Alone in a kaleidoscope
of togetherness, in a world of non-existence. A
sea of waves, a forest of rage and, hopefully,
one day, a prairie of peace. But today, today is
a life of connivance, a pretended ignorance of
what lies ahead. Whose the majority?
    —*Antonia Pepaj*

Tint Hint

The steel blue eyes are turning pale,
   With specs they can still see.
The teeth have long since gone their way,
   So it's denture time for me.

The once lean frame has gone to fat,
   Taut muscles have toned down.
The skin which once was clear and "tan,"
   Has age spots now, they're "brown."

Oh, I don't grieve 'bout gettin' old,
   Why should it get me down?
My heart's washed as "white" as snow,
   I know I'm heav'nward bound.

I've not much "green" to leave my heirs
   But there's hope in this "gray" head,
That when I've passed beyond the "blue,"
   My poems will be "read."

    —Mel Brookshire

Murder Near The Children

The gang gunman had just completed his task,
with the bus stop broken glass surrounding the victim.
Nearby children squealed with delight and fun,
unaware of the danger around them.

The teachers cringed in anger and fright,
hustling to bring the fun loving children inside.
The rest of that extraordinary March afternoon
death hung heavy over that day-care corner.

    —Peter J. Gillen

From Above

The fields are rustling today
with the rich fulfillment of summer.
The gossamer webs fall silently on the bushes
and the hay is stacked in the barns.
God is above! Autumn is here!

Soon the seasonal colors will be
loosened from the trees
And the apples will roll and roll
over this splendid land.
God is above! Autumn is here!

The heavens share the sun and moon
with the abundant harvest.
Ah yes, we can proudly proclaim
God is above! Autumn is here!

    —Sallie Cooney Girard

Ode To My Right Hand

You caress my body with it's sensuous curves
with voluptuous sighs and strident pantings you
stroke my manhood

You unfold the secrecy of my inner sanctum
with tight pinchings you draw would-be milk from my teats

Ah! my right hand
You have loved me for decades.

You have loved me,
and I thee,
far longer and better than
ary a man or ary or woman,
save Christ,
who first taught me,
by gentle promptings,
your fond embrace.

    —Thomas J. Kuna-Jacob

"Land Sakes Of Life My Child"

When you come to me my child
With your problems all told
How much I feel like a hypocrite
As I am growing old.

Land sakes of life my child so innocent and sweet
It certainly not easy when you ask why
There are all these problems to solve and meet
They seem to reach up to the sky

If I always act before I think
Or if I take drugs, smoke, cheat or lie
Or I'm bossy, selfish, rude or take strong drink
Or don't work but just try to get by

The list goes completely wild
Lord you put a real burden on my shoulders
So land sakes of life my child
No wonder I'm growing so much older.

    —Alice M. Faulk

Like Us

A star is like us. It gives all it can give, and slowly
Withers away, like us. It is born then it dies, like us.
Sometimes it is beautiful, sometimes it is not just like us.
If you see a star close up it's ugly and if you look at it
From a distance it gives you a wonderful feeling.
So maybe a star isn't like us they probably never have wars
Or murders. They probably are all in peace. So stars are
Not so much like us. I sometimes wish we were like them
But they are so lonely up there that it changes my mind.
So maybe they are just like us.

    —Mary Rosanne Summers

Rewards

When I practice telling the truth, I develop honesty
within myself.

When I obey and respect my parents, I learn to
respect myself and others.

When I am kind to others, kindness comes to me.

When I learn to do/say the right things, I care
about myself and others.

When I love God, family, myself, and others, I am
beginning to understand life.

When I work towards practicing and understanding
morals, I am growing towards a good life, character,
freedom and peace.

    —Marva Boatman

Key Chain

Unchain your mind. Unchain your mind;
within your mind exists the key.
Free your mind from the chains of dependence and doubt;
within your mind exists the strength that shouts.
Free your mind from the chains of procrastination;
within your mind exists sweet and divine inspiration.
Free your mind from blind, ivory tower academics;
within your mind exists the key to fulfilling subsistence.
Free your mind from the chains of passion;
within your mind exists love in the purest fashion.
Unchain your mind.
Change your mind. Free your mind.
Within your mind exists the key,
to be all that you aspire to be.

    —Melvin T. Ingram

510

Shadow Of You

You walk and it follows,
Without it you may feel hollow.
It is always near in the sunlight,
Yet it disappears in the dark hours of twilight.
Just like a friend that won't dare flee,
Flip on a bright light and I promise you'll see.
The glorious figure awaits you,
Open your eyes wide and stare.
The precise piece of imagery that
forms your personal glare.
Your own individual portrait,
that you may or may not admire.
Surprisingly it shows in the flickering flame of a fire.
A murky and gloomy figurine awaits you,
you can't shake its hand.
It happens to be sweet and simple,
not very hard to understand.
Something unexpected lies in store,
A lovely silhouette of you.

  —*Marie VanAssendelft*

"He Can't Stop Crying"

Do you see the patience of His endurance
Without Jesus you'll have no after-life insurance.
Beware of imitations, the old ways are a lie.
To the world and yourself, for him die.
To some his spirit is a loss of breath,
For others it will determine a judgment for their death.
Just listen and hear it, that voice isn't just in your head,
It's from the Holy Spirit.
All living things are of his beloved creation,
You shouldn't deprive yourself from his Holy Nation.
The eternal Father is waiting for you to make a choice,
Will you contribute to damnation or choose the light to
Rejoice?
Soon satan will have you as a target within his range,
Better make a big change.
Can't you at least try,
Jesus paid the price and
Satan was not the one who made the buy
God's tears continue to run, your time has come,
He knows your dying, He can't stop crying.

  —*Rosa Sanchez*

Sleepless Nights

I'm lying here in my own bed
wondering if you're experiencing
the same difficulties I'm having without you
I picture you in my mind
The way the lights reflect your beauty and your smile
From the first time I saw you
No one person has ever affected me the way you do
When I'm with you I never want to let you go
We are in two different countries
And the distance is what's keeping us apart
Someday we will be together
And maybe, just maybe
That will end my sleepless nights.

  —*James E. Herron Jr.*

Once More The Night

Rambling through the hours of night.
Wondering why so long 'til the light.
Tossing and turning, endless it seems.
Taken away into countless dreams.
Trying to endure the restlessness within.
Seems there is no end.
Daylight is here—and a new day begins.
Now another sleepless night ends.

  —*Shirley Hutcherson*

Death

I sit crying in the dark lonely and confused.
Wondering, will he ever come back?
Or why he even left.
I don't know why God had to take him.
He was apart of me, I needed him.
I felt like a dead rose losing its petals one by one.
It's like I died along with him.
Coming back into reality I realized that the clock was
Still ticking, and the world was still revolving without him.
And I needed to face the fact he was dead, and I wasn't.
It was time for me to come out of the dark
And back into the light.

  —*Amber Jeffries*

"Jumping In"

They caught one another's eye, two people meet, thinking the
world beneath their feet. Hearts in a zoom, as love surely
blooms. Wedding gown and tux, hoping for a life deluxe.
Pools of joy in their eyes, not comprehending mothers cry.
Leaving in that long black car, never suspecting, they won't
get far. Believing in happy ever after, as they hear the echoes
of laughter. Now the love turns from hot to cold, there isn't
anything left to hold. In creeps the temptations of life, cold
as steel and sharp as a knife. Dreams left shattered, as
hearts and trust are scattered. The attorney's handle the
rest, attempting to divide up this little nest. Before
commitment, you have choices, so be very careful and listen to
all those little voices. Till death do us part, is a very long
time, it can either rain or shine. Right or wrong, there is no
one to blame, you made the choice, just the same. Even if you
haven't a penny, the rewards of Marriage can be many. Work
hard together, through the ups and the downs, "Love", learn the
meaning, you might like the sounds. And pray every night
before bed, that God give you strength and a clear head.

  —*Rhonda McCarthy*

Recognition

It seems to me that recognition is what makes the
world go around.
A vital part of life, from birth to an epitaph in
the ground.
Recognition is like a precious metal that you can
give to young, or old.
To some not worth a nickel, and to others more
precious than gold.
Think of it as a medicine that only you can give.
Be careful not to make an addict, and give it
as a reason to live.
If you don't believe in recognition, and the miracles
it can do,
just try some on your friends, and children, and a
little bit on you.
For who would want to climb the highest mountain,
or build a mansion on the hill.
Without some recognition, our world would just
stand still.

  —*Robert L. Beavers*

The Assemblage

Life is:
 Youth, new eyes on the world.
 Learning, remember not only good is taught.
 Hurt, the broken heart is forever scarred.
 Life is an accomplishment.
 Love, strongest of bonds.
 Youth, the retraced beginning.
 Realized, the final breath.
  Life is an assemblage....

  —*Aaron Kloberdanz*

Prejudice

A disease
Worse than my frightened eyes care to see
It eats at the heart
It poisons the mind
It lingers … in everyone.

We see color
We sneer at those who are different
We see religion
We see race
We see sexuality … differences

Beaten
Beaten for something they cannot control
Kicked out
Ridiculed
Knocked down … killed

Fear of those who are different
Minorities
Gays
Jews … but still people.
—*Renee S. Heroux*

Opened By Innocence

Black hands reach out to the little white child.
Wrapped in sheets,
        hobbled and wounded,
            the men respond to the presence of the child.
Faces light up with smiles,
        hands reach out,
            bodies bend nearer,
            voices beckon,
                see me—
                    touch me—
                        acknowledge me.
The innocence of the child reaches something deep within.
She is a reminder perhaps of another,
        a child at home,
            a child unborn,
                a child lost to
war.
The presence of the child breaks down barriers of suspicion
and fear.
We laugh and reach out to touch her.
Through the child we touch each other.
We smile and eyes meet eyes,
Opened by innocence.
—*Sharon Nelson Arendshorst*

Moments Of Dawn

I awoke from sweet slumber,
    Yawn, stretch, my eyes flutter open.
A grey shaft of light begins
    To pierce the darkness.
Outside my window gentle breezes,
    Bring waves softly lapping on the shore.

Somewhere, a dog barks, from afar comes an answer.
In the distance, a cock crows, and a chorus begins.
The chirping of birds, join in the melody.
A soft orange light, begins its spreading ray.

Nearby, a car motor comes to life,
    Workers begin their daily pilgrimage.
On the river a boat's horn,
    Splits the air with its passing.
Audible voices can now be heard,
    On the waterfront.

The sun peeps up, over the horizon,
The smell of coffee permeates the air.
A great cacophony of sounds emerge,
The world is awake—it is morning.
—*Ruth Stancil Parrish*

Geraldoaholics

It's six fifteen in Timbuctu,
Yet eyes entranced by plastic thought still reach to sip
Geraldo's wine.
The King of Compromise, that hollow fellow,
Takes grasp of Satan's lips.
Our morals melt and ethics sink.
It's six sixteen in Timbuctu, and you,
deep in a boiling cracker jack of drink,
still view the box of hell that's glued to you.
You guzzle, mesmerized and hypnotized,
from goblets plated thin with silver fake on bullshit cups,
now drunk and google-eyed.
On your sofa, vegetated, long past intoxicated,
you're never fully sated.
During Happy Hour, your devour each bubble and shot glass
of sensationalized, commercialized propaganda booze.
It's six eighteen in Timbuctu
and all the clones of apathetic trash switch the station,
drunk in degradation.
Geraldoaholics slaughter our nation.
—*Mischa Jakupcak*

Untitled

I went to the store to look for a card, I looked through them all and I looked real hard. I tried to find one with the right words to say, but none of the words were the words from Ray. A pen and some paper is all that I bought, then I left the store with those and a thought. I went to my room and pulled out a chair, then I opened the window to get some fresh air. I sat in the chair wondering just how to start, but the words were so easy because they came from my heart. So I write these words for you to read, knowing my family loves me is all that I need. This is a thank you to you mom and dad, a thanks which makes me very glad. Glad to say that I'm your son and this thank you has just begun. My life has been full of so much love, for that I thank the good lord above. But most of all, I want to say…thanks mom and dad for leading the way. You have given me so much advice, some that I may have just denied, but never ever losing my sense of pride. Pride that you've given to set my bearing, the support, the sharing, the loving, the caring. These are small samples of what you have done, that deserves the highest praise and thanks from your son. For all the thanks that you should get, there is something you both will never forget. You are loved and respected, not only by me, but are both loved so much by the whole family! When I stop to think of all you've done, it makes me proud just to be your son. One of these days I will have the same, to be a father like you dad and have a wife like you mom, to carry on the family name. A name that carries with it some many friends, the name I am proud to say is LAVERENZ. A name for so many is hard to say, and for some the spelling could take all day. I am always willing to help them on their problems with my name, a name I will always stand behind and take pride in just the same.
—*Raymond E. Laverenz*

A Vision Within

I envision greatness,
Yet, I have many obstacles to overcome,
Some greater than others, and many sacrifices
In between, my life is filled with puzzles,
Where not all the pieces fit,
A combination that is not completely solved,
Seeking for answers I discover new parts,
Things I was not aware of,
But not really surprised
Content with achievement,
Success is sure to follow,
Still, something is missing
Leaving me somewhat hollow,
Fulfillment is fantastic,
And love may not always be the answer,
But, happiness holds the key,
To opening the doors to all,
Your endeavors.

—*Vieanna D. Huertas*

My Uncle Cuco

My Uncle Cuco had a one track mind.
Yet, through it all, he was one of a kind.
He left us so young, without saying a word,
His emotions and thoughts were left unheard.
He left the world without saying good-bye,
He brought his family and friends lots of tears in their eyes.
He brought us laughter, to each and one of us,
We will always remember him, for he has gone without us.
We love him so much, what love cannot buy.
We mean what we say, because emotions are not lies.
We will treasure his memory, deep in our hearts
Forever and always, till death do us part.
We will meet him in heaven, in eternity.
"Please God," I say, "let this be."

—*Monica Jackson*

Thank You

You came into my life, I knew you not.
Yet we were drawn together by a common bond.
We shared our stories, hopes and dreams.
We cared a lot it seemed.
You walked beside me when things were good, as I always knew
you would.
You walked beneath me when things got tough, you made it seem
not so rough.
You walked in front of me to help me along.
Together, nothing could go wrong.
You walked behind me to bring up the rear and kicked me a
little to get me in gear.
You gave me your strength when I had none and told me often
life had just begun.
To you, my friend I owe a lot.
Your kindness and caring will never be forgot
When we part your friendship will be always cherished and
carried with me.

—*Kristy Jahner*

Faith Unknown

Like a river by the sea, my faith for
You is unknown. I read the writings
or so I say. I pray and pray every day
for someone to come and save me. When
I cry my Lord's face smiles down on me.
He knows I'm hurt, He knows I'm sad, He
I've been treated bad. Even though I
may not say how sorry I am, for all the
sins I feel He'll always understand.

—*Angela Black*

Climbing

Many unspoiled paths to seek,
You and I -
Untold visions of sought-out places to unfold,
You and I -
Let us lift our hands toward the light of dreams
To catch those distilled precious and tantalizing
Drops from the cup of heaven;
We shall saunter through the woods and fields,
Climb a craggy mountain,
Sometimes to rest beside a pure pool
Under the boughs of whispering pines;
Cross the scorched sands of desert,
Until we stand naked
In the cold waters
That break against timeless fog-floating bastions;
Like guests at the brief feast of the earth,
Stand poised to absorb the gifts
That vibrate beneath our feet,
And in wonder
Lie under the silent stars at night.

—*Thomas W. Chandler Jr*

My Guardian Angel

You came into my life on a special day.
You answered my questions and showed me the way

You showed me the one true meaning of love
We fit together as a hand fits it's glove.

God knew that I needed a special friend.
You are my guardian angel the one He did send.

You really do make my life seem complete.
With you by my side there is never defeat.

I know that you love me.
I know that you care.
Please stand by my side,
And always be there.

—*Patricia Hood*

This One's For You

This one's for you and all the things
you do, it's even for the things you've
put me through. You've been my lover
and my best friend, I wonder will this
thing we have, ever find an end.
You were my strength, when I was
weak, you were even my eyes when
I did not see. You taught me I
was a survivor, when I wanted to
go under. The strength you showed
me it's made me grow much stronger.
You told me there was nothing, that
I couldn't do, because I had a mind,
and you were so true. So this one's
for you and all the things you do.
I'll never find another to love like you.

—*Phyllis Annette Robinson Rodgers*

Destiny

Which is the right road, left or right?
        You pick the right one,
            you worry all night.
    Around the curve and on the way,
things work out and you have a great day.
The sun is bright and everything is fine,
        knowing that your love is mine.
        Happy days are here again,
    I've got the right road, Amen.

—*Theresa M. Burgess*

513

Harpstrings

If once in all your errant years of flight
you found someone whose greeting-song rang true
and made no dissonance; and if for two
that song were gold as day, and cast no blight
upon the sun, nor woke the beasts of night,
would you impose the caustic bonds of youth
and then demand veracity of truth
to test against an alien world, your might?

Let them be brief, my love, those bonds of words,
prison bars of sound against the heart.
Speak if you must, but let it be with song
to free the soul. Observe the flight of birds
flung like the Blind boy's shaft, a dart
of joy! With music may our time belong.

    —*Thomas M. Beck*

Untitled

You're an island in the sea of despair. Your arms a fortress,
you hold me close, I find safety there. Your lips and oasis
in a deserts burning sand. Inside an ember becomes a flame
at the touch of your hand.

You're a port when the storms are at sea. I harbor there,
lower my sails and find security.
And when life's storms have ceased to roll and winds no longer
blow. You're yet by me, you take my hand,
Oh, how I love you so.

A life alone without you near I can't imagine this. No gentle
touch, no soothing voice, nor any soft warm kiss. Without
you now my world would be an empty page in life. Too many
battles, empty emotions, bitterness and strife.

I'm glad you're here to be my true and very special friend.
I'll love you dearly, stand by you always, until our journeys
end. The love we share may not be perfect, but somehow we
know, Someday we'll share a life together. Dear, I love you so.

    —*Susan K. Hanifan*

Untitled

I wake my friend, I wake My eyes stun you and my voice shakes
you. I wake and look for you. Look at you You think I am an
enormous plant, a carnivorous plant And I come to eat you off
the surface of your life. And I am, And I will You shake at
the thought that I am free to walk as my own shape To move my
feet free from the pot they have been buried in, They are free
I walk and as I walk you think I am knives and revolvers You
think I am war and murder, And I am Friend, I am. You think I
make judgement on your small dark life And I do my Friend, I
do. You sit and you sit, You hear movements The carpet, the
wall tack, the sheet, and you blink your eyes, You hear me, and
I am here my Friend, I am here. I glow like a comet rising in
the sky, I am painted blue and orange. I jump the way fire
jumps, I am explosions and steel. I am buttons and silver, I
am books and thread, I am tongues and laughter, I am song.
Electricity is the way I touch, Night is the way bend my legs.
And my Hair, my Hair revolves the Sun. I knock at your door
and I am leather and lace, gems and silver. I dance, I laugh
and you think I have come to kiss your face, You think you
won't hear me, you think you won't touch me,

    —*Sambrina Gordon*

I Love You

I love you so much, but you don't love me
you like the other girls, and that I can see
I tried to tell you how I felt and that
I'd always be there
But you turned away and said you didn't care
You hurt me more than you'll ever know
Or more than I'll ever let show
I tried to get close but you turned away
Then acted liked you didn't know me the next day
I'm not sure about anything or why I feel the way I do.

I just wish you felt the same way too.
But I do know something right from the start
and that is, you never opened a door into your heart.

    —*Tina Kolsun*

Listen Or Lose

Darkness, quiet, solitary rooms of nothing
You listen keenly, hear the songs they sing
The music's the steady beat of ones heart
Rhythmic breathing, Concentration broken with a start
With your insides out - N - outsides in
You face yourself - N - try to grin
With pain dispelled, troubles gone
Heartaches healed with natures song
Rape, Robbery, Murder, world a mess
Dog eat dog, would you have guessed
Worship's out, Drugs are in galore
This would of Hell, You asked for
By standing by, Out of your mind
You lose yourself - N - become blind
But you best get with it, Wake up fast!
This planet you're on will not last
Check all the angles, search deep in your soul
For when the world dies, You'll be in the toll
Choose, the darkness, quiet of our solitary room
Or a burnt out cinder of Nothing, DOOM

    —*Sandie Margerum*

The Sorrow Of Despair

    Life is, but a game, to win is to be popular. To lose
you must be different. For I am different, but do not
care. The guys pass me by. I do not weep. The blackness
of my life is too deep. It swirls around, my thoughts
go spinning my soul rages through me when no one's
about. The love, tragedy, hate and sorrow it can not be
stopped. The pen touches the paper. I begin to write.
To be different is the way for yourself, you can not
hide. Your pride can not be demolished if you believe.
You are all that counts not what people think of you.
So express yourself, for you may be tested, do not be
discouraged, one day they may look up to you. So do not
change to fit your friends. Take it from me, be yourself.

    —*Melody J. White*

"If's"

If "if's" were ever to be
your life would be shared by me.
These times found in fantasy
would be warmed in ecstasy.
But, here I stand
afraid to touch you by voice or hand,
not knowing if you would understand.
the fear of knowledge of desire,
moments unfulfilled as time transpires.
I stand watching you walk by
and think of moments that were and are denied.

    —*Roland Rose*

Winter Nest

Atop the highest limbs.
You perched the foremost of the flock,
Securely fixed twixt vees and sprouts -
A spacious nursery -
A haven hid through spring and summer foliage,
A squawking site your neighbors peckered at,
Then flew to other trees to do the same.

Yet swayed your modest eyrie
Through rearing season, 'til end,
Then left, vacated totally -
Driven forth not by squabbles or squawks,
But fruition of self's destiny.

Abandoned, starkly grey and lone,
A blot amid the topmost limbs
Intact, you last through storm and snows
Empty, waiting.
Who knows if your cycle shall repeat itself -
A gentle monument to life.

    —*L. K. Murphy*

"Say A Little Prayer"

 I prayed to God to send me someone real.
You should know that you're my inspiration,
You gave me something I could really feel.
   All I wanted was your full attention.

See the changes I have been going through?
 You should know I will love you forever,
Just because I still want to be with you.
   Can you see should still be together?

Was it all that hard for you to cherish?
I'll soon find that you don't want what I do,
   When I imagine I get what I wish.
Oh, this was the real love I never knew.

Even though it's much better we forsake,
 I'm now having an eternal heartache.

    —*Roberta Michelle Perkins*

"The Hearts A Funny Thing"

   You come to me in silence, cloaked by the night
you stay with me always to the morning light

   You never stay for very long
to someone else your heart belongs

   so I take every moment I can steal with you
knowing that when the night leaves, you must too

   Why do I go on this way
knowing that you'll never stay

   the hearts a funny thing you see
it dreams of things that can never be

   You fill my head with hopes and dreams
then your gone once more, or so it seems

   returning to the life you live each day
never knowing if you'll come back this way

   several days go by, and nights too
still I sit and wait for you

   Why do I go on this way
knowing that you'll never stay

   the hearts a funny thing you see
it dreams of things that can never be

    —*Terry Smith*

Untitled

I bide high the moon
You summon low the grave
Light of moon gives you sight of dead
And grave will serve after moon to be my home
   Only moon and grave exist after belief

Behold in the garden a rose not planted
Next comes a weed with reason
Bewildered is the gardener with no seed
Where is the scope on things not planted
   Cycles ending each season

But mightier a world with will to begin
Now light the dark and unchecked goes fear
More a titan a God when twisting a man
Man then spites the question to breed an answer
   Realize only man pays heed to God

    —*James Palazzolo*

As Good As Gold

You were my coach when I was eight years old.
You taught me everything about the game.
You told me I would be as good as gold.

I remember how you taught us to be bold,
And if we failed we should not be ashamed.
You were my coach when I was eight years old.

Our skills were something that could not be sold,
To get us to Regionals was your aim.
You told me I would be as good as gold.

When you left, the team started to unfold,
From then on nothing was ever the same.
You were my coach when I was eight years old.

Cancer was what you had, so I was told.
I wanted to believe they had the wrong name.
You told me I would be as good as gold.

When you died I needed someone to hold.
I now know nothing would ever be the same.
You were my coach when I was eight years old,
You told me I would be as good a gold.

    —*Nicole Durand*

Kaleidoscope

What a wonderful invention you are
   You thing of yellows and reds and blues.
Your bright and changing colors
   Pattern themselves into countless shapes and hues.

How fascinating to hold you in hand
   And gently turn you round and round.
I see hexagons of mostly brown and orange—
   A twist, and lavender stars I've found.

Your creator must have laughed with delight
   When he brought you forth to show the world
That colored chips of glass together in symmetry
   Can entrance us like bejeweled cloths unfurled.

I think life is a kaleidoscope, too.
   It's an ever changing assembly of shades.
There are vivid moments of gladness
   And sometimes the happiness fades.

So, here's to you, my pretty rainbow toy.
   Your power to bring forth a smile
Is a tribute to an ingenious, cheerful someone
   Whose handiwork lives on to charm and beguile.

    —*Alice B. Yeager*

To My Daughter

All the hugs and kisses I used to get
You turned thirteen, that was the end of it
You were such a pretty little thing
Just to watch you made my heart sing
I watched you grow into those teenage years
Like any father, hiding my fears
I wanted nothing but a good life for you
I never wanted to see you blue
I tried so hard to teach you the right things
Wanting you to be ready for what life brings
Sometimes things don't appear as they are
They seem close, but they're really far
You'll never know the pain that I feel
Knowing that maybe this will never heal
You've got your own life to live
I'm sorry I didn't teach you to forgive
Life is but a one shot deal
When it's over, that's for real
I hope someday you'll love your Dad
Maybe then life for you will no longer be sad

— *Thomas Mallett*

Kastel Stari

Little Kastel Stari by the blue Adriatic sea,
You will never know how much you mean to me.

I remember the wonderful smell from the bakery
Each day as they sold their bread,
And the market place with fish, fruits and
vegetables from which Kastel Stari's people are fed.

Each morning the ladies share gossip and turkish
coffee to start their day,
And somehow they never seem to run out of
things to say.

The children, neighbors, cousins and friends,
Shared their stories while giving me memories no end.

Little Kastel Stari with your sunshine galore,
I can still picture in my mind your beautiful
tree lined shore.

I love your wonderful old Saint John's church,
And your new church with the steeple,
But the most precious thing you have to share
Is your happy, carefree people.

— *Patricia Vrtlar*

Friends

You were my friend in my time of constant sorrow
You would lend any peace that I could borrow
You were there
And if I ever felt alone or scared
For all the people in the world I knew
At least one cared.

You'll be my friend, and though soon I must be going
I will spend some gentle moments knowing
Friends are rare
And when everything's been said and done
For all the people in the world I'll know
That I've got one.

You are my friend, joined to me within my heart
Till the end as you have been from the start
We can share
And if you ever need help beyond prayers
For all the people in the world you'll know
At least one cares.

— *Jude Grant*

Hungry And Homeless

With all the progress that's been made
You'd think that no member of the human race
Would have to survive without enough to eat
Or shudder from the cold of living in the street.

Yet no matter where one might roam
They can always find those hungry and without homes.
Such victims of life should not be blamed
And for their misfortunes they shouldn't feel shame.

What a horrid frightening life they must lead
Wondering if tomorrow there will even be air to breathe,
Never sure of what they can or should do
In order their lives and spirits to improve.

Across the globe many are those
Who offer them food, shelter and clothes.
Sadly, though, there is never, ever enough
To permanently lift the hungry and homeless up.

The only way for humanity to succeed
In sheltering the homeless and the hungry feed
Is if every single human being
Slows down their taking and speeds up their giving.

— *Tammy Rose Walter*

"I See You Redman"

I see you Redman; moccasins caressing earth, whisper soft,
Your heart beating free as the golden eagle aloft,
brother to the wolf, the sun and the sky,
Mother Nature and you as one, never to die
but live on in the rain and the wind and oft

Reborn in new flesh or wild flower,
or growing within the giant Sequoyah to tower
above all, walking with the Great Spirit,
  I see you Redman.

July suns melt grieving mountains' tears
for your war cry and chant, the years
swallowing sounds of rivers and freedom and the buffalo.
Perhaps one day the whole world will know,
when topside your magnificent piebald, you appear,
  but already, I see you Redman.

— *Annie Golightly*

The Pull

Warm pull, the pull of the tides
Your pull
The need to be with you

Silent pull
The need to be alone
At the long time inland place
A radial pull, spreading from here
Meets the shores in all different directions

Sometimes I need the sound and feel
Of your rocking and turning
Even your breaking is beautiful, for all its grind
With its pass it always leaves us
Floating, swaying in rhythm
Curling up, then gently bubbling over
Small rumbles of laughter, growing, we share together
Before we both draw in again
Until the next time we feel the pull

Sometimes I need to be at the inland place
No sounds do my feet make when they are standing,
Silently planted and deeply rooted in this ground

— *Susan Ross*

My Knight

When first we met you challenged me like a Knight on a quest.
Your softness in manner but strength in deeds captivating me
Casting a spell of love, desire and need over my heart and mind.
Searing my soul with your eyes of Blue desire.

Later you serenaded me with your body
How heavenly you played the music of lovers.
Covering my nakedness with your long beautiful mane.
Creating a quiet heaven for us in our bed of candle light and
     incense.

On my love I waited for you night after night hoping for a
     place in your heart—
Hoping—for your soft and tender touch
Bliss such as ours is surely a gift.

The Knight has won his quest.
My love is eternal my devotion unquestionable
My soul is yours and I bow in humble reverence to my Lord and
     Master.
          —*Terry Sunderland*

To A Spring Shower

Sweet Spring!
Your warm, moist winds whisper through the trees
And dance playfully across the new green grass,
As sunflowers sway, keeping time to your music.

Clouds flow in on a damp breeze,
Covering a blue sky with soft muted gray.
Your melody builds as small droplets
Fall like tears upon the virgin ground.
Again, and again, the droplets fall,
Until the mass sounds like a chorus of laughter.

Lightning rushes in setting the sky aglow
Thunder rumbles with a boom,
Making all in its presence quiver.
The trees and their leaves now swish and sway,
Bow and bend like a bow on the strings of a violin.
The instruments of nature builds in sound, and in power!
Ah, the symphony of a spring shower!
          —*Tara Ratliff*

Whispers

He only has eyes for you, when you're looking.
You're lost in those coffee-comfortable depths, so you trust.
But when he holds you tight in his possessive arms,
his eyes are mine.
Do you know that he watches me like a hawk appraising prey?
That his feet search for mine under our dinner table?
That he strokes my hair with a furtive hand
while he fondles yours boldly?
Surely you know his brief visits aren't only for you.

Sister, your lover is safe with me.
I've never touched his silky curls,
never returned his footly caress,
hardly met the powerful stare.
But it's so hard.
I want to drown in those rich, deep eyes
and feel his warmth next to mine.
Keep him close and forgive me,
for one day,
Temptation will whisper "Do it" too loudly in my ear,
and I will.
          —*Suni M. Edson*

Crossroads

I've travelled roads, some good some bad, all alone
You've also travelled these roads on your own

Then we met at a crossroad and had choices to make
We stopped and looked around at which road to take

We could have stopped for a while then pass on by
But this choice we did not take, neither you nor I

I may have glimpsed at one road and you at another
But we each knew there was something more that we must discover

We didn't pass by but each decided on one direction
It was here that we made our true connection

We decided to take one road and walk down it together
Once we met, we knew that we couldn't walk alone forever

We saw more down this one road in which we decided
we saw love, the kind which our eyes had never seen, and to this we
     confided

We confessed our love and passion to each other
And knew in our hearts we could never love another.

There will be many more decisions and choices to make
But now we can decide together which ones to take

There will be many different roads we must travel along our way
I have faith that we'll face them together, forever, day by day
          —*Valerieanne Milosh*

The Dilemma Of The Big 4-0!

Well ole boy, it's finally here
You've hit the big 4-0

The time has come to say some things
That you've just got to know.

You may feel on top of things, and be bubbly in the mornings,
But we're sincere when we tell you, we're giving you a warning!

You'll find that you'll have aches and pains you never had
before. And to wiggle out of bed sometimes - is even quiet a
chore.

Your joints will swell, your feet will too - you'll have some
trouble walking and when your gums start to recede - you'll
have some trouble talking.

Your eyes begin to fail you, you can't see very far
You become disoriented, and wonder where you are.

Your hair begins to gray, and then begins to thin
You come to the conclusion, that there's just no way to win.

It begins to be an effort, for everything you do
You'll check you mirror often, to make sure it's even you.

There is no end to all this fun, once it has begun
For exactly one more year from now, you'll be 41!
          —*Monica L. Gribble*

Courtney Marie

Dear sweet child from God above
     you're a symbol of their love
An innocent child so sweet and pure
     who could ever ask for more

Dave and Shelly's pride and joy
     whether you'd been a girl or boy
But a beautiful girl was born that New Year's Day
     and not one of us could stay away

For we all had to come and see
     the miracle that came to be
And I will never, ever doubt
     that this is what life's all about
          —*Kathryn M. Csuy*

Tristan's Lay, Off Cornwall

It is done,
Yseulte;
We have drunk together
From Brangane's cup.

The mind, perhaps,
Was ill-prepared;
But not the heart,
Whose ancient wisdom
Long foresaw
This confluence of destinies,
This sealing of a fated pact
Which binds us now till death.

But death will come too soon,
Yseulte,
So let us ride the sea's dark shoreward surge
In one last fierce embrace,
One night-long song of love
Whose echo neither dawn nor Cornwall's coast
Nor Cornwall's King nor all of time
Will still.

—*Niles Bond*

Sleeping With The Stars

The stars watch me
when I am sleeping.
They protect me from
the jaws of darkness.
They light my dreams
with sad and demented songs
and feed me stale bread.
Come dance in the stars with me.
Lay your head on my pillow and dance.

—*Kathy Marie Kelly*

Ode To Greed

Greed, your sting is significant!
You start out innocently enough as individual endeavor—
You end up as grief to many.

Capitalism is your spawning ground, but somehow you lost touch with humanity.
Get ahead! Get ahead! Get ahead! Is drilled into you from the beginning.
The glamour is there, you just have to seize it.

Values? What are they? They just interfere.
What really matters is collecting George Washington's face printed on some green paper.
You started out with just a few — enthusiasm gleaming from your face, sweat the indicator of your labors.
But along the way productive work became your dinosaur; investment is the way to your god, Greed.
Is the enthusiasm still there? Do you want more? Or are you weary, Greed?
Set your goals — reach your goals, day-after-day.
Dad, would you please play a game with me?
I can't. I'm busy. Greed's got a hold of me.
More! More! More! I've got to have more! For me and for my kids.

Profits, I don't have enough profit.
What can greed buy to increase profits?
Why housing and real estate — greed flourishes there.
Hypertension — I've got to buy some medicine to control my hypertension.
Why couldn't you just buy a pill for health and fitness?
But the competition's fierce. Doesn't greed ever let up?

The market crashed and my company took a beating.
I'm suffering from AIDS (Advanced Insufficient Dollars Syndrome) and
    my friends are shunning me.
I need a transfusion — make that gold or green plasma.

I'm addicted, I didn't believe it could happen to me, but I'm addicted (to greed).
Greed, why didn't you warn me as to what I'd become?
People are suspicious about me. I just wanted to get ahead, but they're still suspicious.
I'll help them now — they'll see how decent a guy I am.
But what's left for them or me? I've ruined all that was worth living for — with greed's help!

—*Jim Player*

Friends

Friends are hard to come by,
    and are very hard to choose.
A real friend never dies,
    this friend you will never lose.
Friends are like diamonds,
    very precious and rare.
The closer you get to know one,
    the more there is to share.
A friend who has a comforting smile,
    has cheered my way for many miles.
Good friends are often found 'tis true,
    that's why God sends friends like you.

—*Byram L. Williams*

Dreams

I want to live a life to see
what I'm really like. I dream
of loved ones and ones I love. I
wonder if there's anything
to see in my life. To have a
life and to take one of
another. Maybe one dream is
to come true or if it will, what
will it be? It's a dream and
a life that makes it come true.
To me, it will last for eternity, a
dream, that will one day come true.

—*Misty White*

An Empty Soul

An empty soul
What does it know
A life of hurt and pain.
An empty soul
Where can it go
When the loss is no more to gain.
An empty soul
How can it grow
When the water is very scarce.
An empty soul
Low and behold
The burdens it must bare
An empty soul
All alone
There's nowhere to run and hide
An empty soul
In the cold
Still must have its pride.

—*Roberta R. Thomas*

Trail Of Tears

Why can't they see,
What they are doing to me,
Why don't they know,
Why must we go,
If our land we should give,
Where should we live,
If we all die,
Who will cry,
Why all this pain,
Why can't we remain,
Our home is here,
But we leave in fear,
If you make us go,
We want you to know,
As we cry,
And as we die,
Our hearts will stay,
At our home far away..

—*Katrina Stephens*

Untitled

What is God?
What is God-but an illusion?
A dream perhaps -
Something created in the mind?
What is God?
My hand, my soul, my conscience?
God is everywhere, God is nowhere.
And what of me?
What of Nature? - the elements?
No.
They've been there.
They've always been there.
Yet God is without me right now.
He merely is a word, a memory,
Something long forgotten -
Here in Hell.

—*William De Guzman*

Untitled

At night,
When all are asleep.
The cold wind howls.
And the house it creaks.
No one is there,
But I'm not alone.
I look to the wall.
And discover my friend.
There in the darkness
Sits the one I adore;
Raggedy doll
With the button eyes.
Comfort it comes,
And to my surprise,
Her smile never fails
Nor the twinkle in her eyes.

—*Nancy D. Roberts*

Untitled

Once upon a midnight clear
When every thing was dark,
There came a bird to our house
Whose name was Johny Stork.

He left a little bundle
That turned out to be a baby.
When I asked if I could name him Tony
He said, "I think so maybe."

Now this little baby bundle
Was as ugly as could be,
But everyone who saw him
They said he looks like me.

Now this is what I'm mad about
And you would be mad too
If they said an ugly baby
Was the very picture of you.

So I think I'll buy an airplane
And on it I'll embark
Until I find that aunry bird
Whose name is Johny Stork.

—*James B. Puckett*

To My Wife Janet

When I leave here and go to heaven
When I have passed the test.
They will let me through the gate
And show me to my rest.

I'll have all my tools again,
My wood and nails and glue,
And I can work to my content
While I wait there for you.

I'll leave word there at the gate
So when you show up someday.
And come to be with me again
There will be someone to guide the way

I know if they give you a map
You won't know south from north,
And you will be all over heaven
If they just send you forth.

We drove many, many miles
In every kind of weather.
If they give you a map.
We will never get together.

—*Robert Boysen*

Friendly Shadow

In my darkest night,
When I think that I'm alone.
I'll always have a friend,
In the deep crevice of stones.

A light is shining dimly
On my back, a ray appears.
I turn around and see my friend,
So startled with fear.

Who is this friend of mine,
That stay so close to me?
My shadow in the dark still night,
To rest and comfort me.

He'll never be a passer-by,
He'll only be at my side.
Imitating my every move
Right there, so sheer and shy.

—*Megan Herber*

"Where Did Billy Go?"

Why do they call it a search "party",
When I'm not having any fun,
Where did little Billy go?
Is he hiding or playing in the sun?

He's done this sort of thing,
So many times before,
Always saying he's "sorry",
Promising not to do it anymore,

But, here we go again!

Armed with our trusty flashlights,
As day draws to a close,
Hope we can find little Billy,
So I can punch him in the nose!

For he's ruined my 7th Birthday,
Leaving no time for play,
"Oh Billy, where are you?"
"Come out, come out today!"

—*Anthony Herpich*

Time

Time passes so quickly
When one's life is alone,
Narrowed by everyday's expectancies,
And long lasting hurt from inside.

Remembering youth, the easy ways,
Doing nothing, not having to care,
Running through open fields
Playing ball, or just lying there.

Climbing tall pines
That sway with the wind,
Their great boughs hold me safe,
Nothing could hurt me.

Lying on sweet smelling hay,
The loft in quiet and warm,
Rain gently falls upon the tin roof,
Slowly, I drift asleep.

—*Norene J. Harns*

Black Death

What are we to do,
When skies instead of blue,
Turn black with rage.

How are we to deal,
With facts like death so real,
When we ourselves don't know.

When songs of death are sung.
And heads not high but hung,
Are seen all over streets.

When feelings have been mixed,
About things that can't be fixed,
And you cannot run away.

As we bow our heads in sorrow,
Hoping for tomorrow,
We see another death.

In the distance children weep.
Trying to wake their Mother's sleep
Don't they know she's already dead.

What are we to do,
When skies instead of blue, turn black with hate.

—*Pallavi Sonia Rao*

When The Birds Flutter

When the birds flutter,
When the birds sing,
When the birds sing about
happiness they can bring,
Then you will see a land,
a far where troubles are gone,
The world awakes,
A breath it takes,
As the morning fresh dew
rises to a clear white sky,
The trees start to sway,
As the birds say,
Alas its morning,
When the birds flutter,
When the birds sing!

—*Jennifer Butler*

Oh Captain, My Captain

You're the anchor in my life
When the seas get rough
And I feel battered by the storm
your my port of safety.
My warmth in the dampness.
The brightest star that guides my way.

It's been sometimes choppy
but you are the calm after the storm.
The deep quiet in the
stillness of the dark.

—*Wanda McQueen*

White

White is the color of elegant birds
White is the pale skin of ugly nerds.
White to me is sweet and nice.
White to me is yummy rice.
White is dice with black dots.
White is not a yucky spot
That is what white is to me.

—*Sara Nore Davis*

Untitled

Our love is like coal to fire
When together we burn as one
When apart we are nothing.
Your voice so soft, so gentle
Gives security to my soul
And brings hope for the future
Your touch so delicate
Just as a porcelain doll
And the hand that crafted it.
Your heart is understanding
For all the times I faulted
You forgave me and still stayed.

—*John Mesmer*

Mother

She's the one who really cares,
When we fall in traps and snares.
She's the one who pick's us up,
She gives us tea in our cup.
She's just the loveliest dove,
I call her "Mother", the one I love.

—*Raina Leon*

"Joys"

A springtime treat
When we meet,
 a flower in full bloom!

A summer boon,
A watched cocoon
 Sprouts wings and flies!

Many gifts of fall,
But most of all,
 the greens to bright gold!

A winters delight,
when we sight
 a bird on the wing!

—*Michael Begley*

True Friend

It's hard to lose a true friend,
When you have to say goodbye.
But sometimes they'll make you
Happy, as days go by.

They'll make you laugh.
They'll make you cry.
They're honest with you,
And they never lie.

Being a friend is hard to do,
But I know it's not easy for you.
You make my fears disappear,
You make my dreams very clear.

You're the friend I've never had,
Because you never make me sad.
I hope our friendship will never end,
Because you are my true friend.

—*Keri Eidson*

Time

In the days of my youth;
When you'd let me run loose;
I'd skate with great speed,
For that was my need,
I really could fly, in days gone by.

I could dance until dawn;
Without so much as a yawn;
I cared little about sin,
Because you were my friend.

When the sun would go down,
I'd be wearing a frown,
just who would think,
that you'd shorten the link.

I shed many tears,
when I think of those years,
Without a doubt,
the sand has run out.

—*Sharrye R. Cooper*

Aquarius

Aquarius,
When your moon touches mine,
When you throw yourself into orbit,
I feel so beautiful inside,
Aquarius,
Your star shines down on me,
And let me see the light,
Aquarius,
Your sun warms my heart,
And your romance plays a song
 in my mind,
Aquarius,
Your love will stay with me forever!

—*Samantha Weiner*

Me

So... here I am.
Where am I?
I don't know.
Lost behind two jealous hazel eyes
Or swimming
In my tender lake of tears.
Or maybe
I just don't exist.
Or maybe
I just don't want to.
After all,
Who I am today
Isn't the astute voice
I spoke for yesterday
Or the tranquil soul
I will cry for tomorrow.
If tomorrow ever comes,
That is
And if it doesn't,
Will I know?

—*Kellie Conley*

Time

 Time.
What can I say about time.
I really don't have the time.
Maybe some other time.
 Time.

—*Rami S. Hanash*

Search For Expression

How deep my thoughts;
Where are those words I cannot find
To say the things that
Weigh so heavy on my mind.
I search and search -
And then become distressed,
I cannot find the words,
For thoughts I must express.
The beauty's there —
The love, the joy, the pain,
But still my search
For words is all in vain.
Oh what pictures!
Oh what beauty we could share!
My heart cries out,
For words that are not there.

—*Mary Etta Richards*

Without You

When the loving is gone
Where can I turn,
When the needing is gone
How can I learn,
To live without you?...
When you're no longer there
To hold me at night,
How can I bare
Losing love that was right,
And live without you?...
When I'm sleeping at night
And you're in my dreams,
How can I face daylight
When it finally seems,
That I'm without you?...
All the memories bring pain
Oh, where will it end...?
How I'm going through life
With a smile pretend,
Now, I'm without you!!

—*Dianna James and Lynda Lance*

The Quest

I sought God in lofty cathedrals
Where I would kneel to pray,
And though I sensed a spirit there,
God seemed so far away.

I thought perhaps in mountain crest
Where air was fresh and bright,
I'd glimpse the majesty of God,
But saw no heavenly light.

I went again to oceans blue,
Where waves break white with foam,
I marveled at the seas of life,
But still felt quite alone.

I stooped to lift another up
From depths of black despair,
As I reached out in love to heal,
I found God standing there.

—*Lucille Oliver*

Love To Share

I walk in the fields of flowers
Where my love has found its way
perfumed-sun-warmed showers
A rainbow wants to play

I try to give my love like toys
From a bottomless bag of joys
It is too precious, for one to keep
A happiness to make one weep

To the winds-to the sky
Increase my love, make it multiply
Take the pollen of my flower
To every lonely tower

—*Sean O'Rooney*

The Trip

I have tasted the cool
Where the dye in fashion
Was autumns dress
I heard the cry of babies
Born in Spring
When bulbs were rising.
There was I a fool in love
As was the cause of Summer
But it was mine.
And now the frosted pane
That hides the hill
Where bulbs are sleeping
And missing the cry
Of babies born in Spring.
Perhaps another Spring
The pond in spawning.
But once for me.

—*Leslie Gordon Lindley*

In The Shadows Of The Morning

In the shadows of the morning,
where the frost and dew still lay,
the spirits of the future,
and the past and present stay.
They're waiting for tomorrow,
and some for yesterday,
yet some are on a journey,
through the treacherous world, today.
Their mission is to live,
but some can only die.
Yet some are only thought
of as the teardrop in your eye.
In the shadows of the morning,
where the frost and dew still lay,
the spirits of the future,
and the past and present stay.

—*S. J. Weir*

Gina Marie

There have been times in my life
When I've felt all hope was lost
And yet you stood by me
No matter what the cost

You gave me your shoulder
When I needed to cry
And when times were tough
You were by my side

Few people are as lucky
To find a friend so true
So don't ever forget
I'll always love you

—*Kurt Griemsmann*

Escape

Escape to a far off land.
Where the sand looks like a
twelve day tan.
The sun is so bright some is
left for twilight and the
ocean looks like an electric
blue strobe light.
The natives come out to
meet you and greet you
with coconuts and pineapple.
You stay for a week or two
and you start to get used to
everyone serving you.
When you're ready to leave
you try not to greave over
the escape that you once
wanted to retrieve.

—*Marlene Bleau*

Imagine That...

Imagine that you're in a land,
where they play a great big band.
Imagine that you're in a place,
where everyone has a silly face!
Imagine that you're in a state,
where you never have to hesitate.
Imagine that you're in Greece,
where there's always world peace.
Imagine you're in a place called love,
where angels sing up above,
and the sky's the limit,
where you have every single minute.
Where you can stay,
and say the things you want to say.
Come and see,
just you and me.

—*Melissa Ginczycki*

The Closet

Inside there's a dark closet
Where very few have a key
What you find may be sad
And it may be a mystery
Many things are disorganized
Confusion is the only light
A maze of pain and pleasure
No one can ever discover the secret
Of what the closet might hold
A puzzle with missing pieces
Warm but yet very cold
The door has many scars
From where hurt has made its way
In loneliness is the only cry for help
Happiness a true sin
So if you ever come to the closet
Keep in mind if it seems so cold
That packed away are years of sadness
From so many days ago...

—*Kim Sellers*

My Dearest One

Remember my dearest,
wherever you are;
you'll always be the nearest,
even though now you are far.

I could search this whole earth,
for someone like you;
but never in a million years,
could I find one like you.

I miss you morning, evening,
especially when I'm blue;
it's then I get the meaning,
of love that's really true.

Your letters are a part of me,
hope mine mean much to you;
to my heart you have the only key,
which I'm saving just for you.

When you'll be here beside me,
our hearts will beat as one;
God keep you safe for me dear,
until your work is done.

—*Mary A. Devanko*

The Sickness

Love is like a sickness,
Which is very sure to spread.
Although it seems to last forever,
Its really all just in your head.
If a love is true, it never stops,
Until the day you die.
Your bond will grow and prosper,
And strengthen by-and-by.
When a love is blind,
And all but true,
Its like a gust of wind.
It starts to blow, and then it stops,
And that love can't be replaced again.

—*Allison C. Senette*

Reality Or Fantasy

Reality or fantasy-
Which of the two are for me?
Reality or fantasy-
Why can't one alone be for me?

There's a large gap between the two.
A middle word is not a rule.
I have defined both during school.
As an adult, I am a fool.

Is trusting God reality?
Is having faith sheer fantasy?
Are thefts and rapes reality?
Or just results of fantasy?

Which one of these should I believe?
Which one will help me to achieve?
Does reality sole conceive?
Does fantasy only deceive?

Please tell me quick the word to choose.
To keep dreams in this world of fools.
Fantasy can not pay my dues.
Reality gives me the blues.

—*Pamela G. Coleman*

Dirt Daubers

Some people are like the mud daubers
    Which spread their mud with glee,
But after all what they do
    Genuinely is for their family.

Other people are like the black sheep
    Of the mud dauber family.
They spread their dirt with laughter
    And do not seem to care
    How much harm they cause,
As they gleefully proceed
    Pretending to believe
    In the hereafter.

We cannot keep the dirt daubers
    Who are so difficult to suit,
From spreading their dirt here,
    There, and everywhere.
We can, however, do the best we can,
    Never letting the dirt daubers
    Get the upper hand.

—*L. M. Wallace*

Childhood Memories

Childhood mem'ries have a magic,
Which wondrously is wrought,
When dreaming weaves a pattern
Upon the loom of thought,
The scent of Lilac blooms in may
The nightingale's sweet roundelay
The baseball game upon the green
Is pictured in the summer scene.
September fields all ripe with grain
The rainbow's glory after rain,
The peal of bells at Christmastide
Across the snow clad countryside.
But best of all at twilight glow
When mother settles down to sew
Then father reads to children three
A tale of knights and chivalry.
    The spell is deftly woven
    And oh what joy it brings
    For when the pattern is complete
    My glad heart homeward wings.

—*E. M. Lowery*

Relics Of A Distant Past

Odd missionaries
Who keep ascetic ministries
As interstices between seasons
Securing Wisdom to her children
From the solstice to the equinox:

    Evergreens

Consummate seamstresses
Who with their needles
Stitch the seams of seasons
Twice, Fastening their secrets
To mysteries of Eleusis:

    Evergreens

The seneschals
Of sacred groves and holy spaces
Who steward oaths of hopefulness
Long rooted in our souls
Whose lonely words are poems
Composed of longing and of sorrows:

    Evergreen.

—*P. Marguerite Forcier*

Math

I saw a ghost
Who was eating some toast,

I gave him a fraction
And he had a reaction,

I gave him addition
And he went on a mission,

When he came back
He stepped on a tack,

So I gave him multiplication
And he went on vacation,

Then I tried division
And he lost all his vision,

Maybe some subtraction
will put him back in action.

—*Melissa Ricca*

Life Of The Same

Puppy-
Why do you do
As you do?
Chewing on ground up bones.
Hiding from sounds unknown?
Barking at the independent
Nine lives?
"Because," wagged his tail
"Someday,
"I hope to be a dog."

—*Abner G. Nissen*

Stairway To Heaven

Every tear shed for me
Will lead me to a higher step
On the stairway to heaven.

My suffering has ended
And my mind is at ease
God has taken me in his arms
To forever hold me in peace
On the stairway to heaven.

Memories will be kept in the heart,
And joy will come within
Like life in death we too
Must choose a path,
And my path is the
Stairway to heaven.

—*Jody J. Korf*

Storms

Rain trashing the shingles
Wind howling its' name
In solitude I shiver
Trying to push back the pain.

Neath blankets of sorrow
Trying to ride out the storm
No warmth is provided
Your love I do mourn.

Bolts of lightning crack the heavens
Tears of rain pelt the earth
From life's storms rise the challenge
Plant the seeds of rebirth.

—*Sharon Akahoshi*

'Tis Spring!

Sounds of rain splashing oe'r my
Window, droplets watering down my
View of a somber sky,
    And why!

Fresh smells of earth-of growth
Green, with beads of life clinging
To each laden bow,
    And now!

The cycle eternal renews its
Vow-of rebirth, kindled by the
Gifts that nature brings,
    Tis spring!

—*William T. Crowl*

"Labors' Of Love"

A pen is the tool of the
window of my soul,
guess I'll correspond with
letters 'til my eyes grow old;

Letter-writing appears to be
a lost art,
I think that it is ashamed,
more people don't write
from the heart.

My pen is used as a labor
of love,
a God - given
talent from
the Lord above.

—*Mary C. Kelly*

Blizzard

Snowing
Windy
Hard snow blowing against my face
Blinding me
Scary.

Dressed in warm clothes
But still freezing
Shuffling along
So I won't fall
Sun is hiding.

No school
No fun
No playing outside
No friends.

—*Alicia Lawrence*

Long Walk Home

She walks briskly,
With an air of tailored suits
And college education,
Brief case swinging to and fro
Like cars that go whizzing by.
Now on a side street,
Sweat beads on her midnight flesh,
Tiny drops of diamond dust give
    shine to
Coffee-black and silky skin.
She wipes her forehead with a hanky,
As two young boys, white and lanky,
Peddle past in rags and ignorance;
Call to her, "Nigger!"

—*Antara Satchidanand*

Dreams Of Love

Staring at the stars,
With all the beauty from the glaring sky,
As a shooting star falls,
So does a teardrop from my eyes.

Twinkles of light,
Stare endlessly to no end,
Thinking, dreaming, wondering what's in
store,
To heaven our love will extend.

Holding each other tightly,
On a cold winter's night,
With the flames of the merciless fire,
Shining on our faces bright.

Laying on a deserted island,
With a beautiful sunset in the west,
Peace, love, fulfillment, and joy,
As our tired eyes want to rest.

Dreams of happiness,
Where nothing is ever wrong,
It's only us making love,
The creation of our most intimate song.

—*William Scott Hinson*

"The Birth Of Day"

It is up at night,
With all times might.
As it grows,
With its shining light.

It likes to show,
What all it knows,
Before it goes at dawn.
Now it is setting low.

With it's shadow on the lawn.
Now it is totally gone.
With a new flame,
At the crack of dawn.

It has it's own fame
The day has came
And it will never be the same.
And it will never be the same.

—*Amy Noell Furnish*

When Grandma Rocked the Baby

When Grandma rocked the baby
with flawless tender love
the light of wonder in her eyes
out-shone the stars above!
Her felt-clad feet set the beat
for the rocker's patient song.
The fireside's glow flickered low
as her soft voice hummed along.
She crooned a tune sweet and low
a nursery rhyme from long ago.
In whispered tones a lullaby
for little ones of years gone by.
At last, bright eyes are sleepy
lulled by motion and sound
for Grandma's rocker is magic
but only when Grandma's around!

—*Mary Grimes*

My Son

My son was born not long ago
With his big brown eyes that glow
He has his Mother's chin
and his Father's nose

Then one day My Son was sick
I watched as the doctor passed by quick

Then that day the doctor said
you know your son should be dead
I didn't know if I heard him right
So I turned to my husband and
asked if that was right

As he replied! I saw fear in his eyes
As I sat in the chair and cried

I prayed to God out of despair
Hoping he would hear by prayer

Now I know what My Son means to me
As God did listen to thee
My Son is home where he should be
I thank God on my hands and knees

—*Kathleen Keglovich*

Old Gray Winter

Old gray winter you come again
with icy frost and sleety rain

You chase away the autumn leaves
and leave us bare so we can freeze

There is one thing we all know
that only you can bring the snow
This is one thing in your favor
even though we have to labor

We know that you belong in season
but just the same there is no reason

For you to blow your winds around
and shake the plants right off the ground

We shut our windows good and tight
to make sure you stay right outside

You know you are not welcomed here
because you spread such mighty fear

And when it's time for you to go
we start to reap to dig and sow

And when you sense that spring is here
finally, you bow and disappear.

—*Elizabeth Detsis*

The Mountain

I love the mountain oh so high,
With its great tranquility.
I love the way the clouds float by,
And sink into the sea.

The mountain with its snow white peak,
A purple hue against the sky.
The top which men try to seek,
But cannot tell you why.

—*Sharon L. Sanders*

Tranquility

The hills are ablaze
With leaves of red, gold, and green-
I must honestly admit-
The most beautiful sight I've ever seen.

Nature has to show off
The brilliance of God's plan
Such glorious colors could ne'er
Be achieved by a mortal man.

The feeling derived from such a scene
Fills one's heart with peace
The leaves will fall, the snow will come,
But the tranquility will never cease.

—*Barbara Gould*

Threads Of Time

So little time to spend
with lessor thoughts to share.
Executed in robot style trends
stilted love, tenderness to bare.

This life, our loves depleted
the days like blinking eyes.
Quick flashes, memories receipted
for a time when our soul cries.

Yet tenacious threads which bind
past events, loves and friends
Overpower and seduce our minds
healing, helping us to mend.

—*Stacy Augustin*

Food For Thought

A dinner is nice
with meat and rice
and vegies on the side
and a piece of bread
and milk instead
of a glass of sumpin'
it died
but foods all dead
the feller said
so what's the use a "Freetin"
Just shove in the fork
they're beef and pork
and 'commence t' do the eatin'.

—*R. Arlin Genzoli*

Untitled

My face was a mask
Of indifference and pride
It did not shadow
The way I felt inside

My face was a mask
My soul felt the pain
The face you can coach
The heart you can't train

My face was a mask
Nothing could break
Until I met you
Now it's a smile I can't shake

My face was a mask
Now there is you
I'll love you forever
And you'll love me too....

—*Susan Valkar*

My Muses

When the muses leave and I am left
With only my paper and pen,
I can do nothing - just wait and hope
   They'll deem to appear again.

The paper stares blankly;
And my pen refuses to move -
As if for me to write the words,
   Then my muses must approve.

I'd like to think I'm special,
Chosen by scribes of long ago,
Who left this world, perhaps,
   Before their stories were told.

Their words and mine now combine
Our hopes and dreams and fears,
Our passions and joys put in words
   For others to read and hear.

To gratify my muses, to make them smile
At each word I have penned -
I try very hard to make them proud,
   So they'll return to me again...
      —Linda Brooks Goins

Black's And White's

Black's and White's are awfully tight
with their own color's.
Because we took a flight
back to slavery nights.
Let's forget the past
work on the future.
Make peace, with all races.
Let's take a bite out of history
and put in the new generations
Nation of Unity.
      —Venus Stone

Thought Of You

This night I traveled far and fast
With thoughts of you I knew would last
Our last good bye it seemed so clear
You said the words I love to hear

And traveling in this winter night
Where colors change in mystic light
My eyes are blurred with thoughts of you
The dreams and plans I pray come true

Then lights flash on before my eyes
I'm here again to only drive
To wonder how this came to be
To hope you dream of loving me

And miles pass in endless mass
With thoughts of you that always last
The dreams of love and reckless nights
of tender times when all is right

Then shake my head to clear the mist
How can I drive and feel your kiss
For coming home I hope to see
Within your eyes, please still love me
      —Kevin Larsen

Untitled

There once was a kangaroo
Who lived in the city zoo
   He heard an ouch
   Come from his pouch
He knew who it was, too.
      —Aron Michael Higgins

A Touch Of Autumn's Beauty

A lovely blue bird
   With wings widely spread
Flew gently around
   In the sky overhead

While golden wheat stalks
   Swayed in the soft breeze
As if to a tune
   That God gave to please.

A fleck of bright blue
   On canvas of gold,
A pleasure to watch
   A sight to behold.

His own rocking chair
   Was one stalk of wheat.
His meal for that time,
   Nearby grains so sweet.

With fluttering wings
   He soared from his chair.
Now blue upon blue,
   He graces the air.
      —Mary Ann Melson

Poet's Song

The world is filled with poets,
   With words they sing their songs,
Their words are sweet or bitter,
Their writings short or long.
No matter how its written
   Whether good or even fair,
Their words do pull the heartstrings
   Sometimes to render or tear.
But often making one smile
   or ponder along the way.
The world is filled with poets
   With words they sing their songs.
      —Tammy Cherni

Susie

Pretty little country girl.
With your head of chestnut curl,
In your satin, yellow dress;
I gaze upon your loveliness.

Little girl in nature rest.
Lean upon warm sunshine breath.
In a field of emerald green,
All is quiet, peace serene.

Little girl, I do recall,
Black-eyed susans straight and tall,
In a lovely meadow scene,
Blend with scents upon the breeze.

Pretty little country girl,
In a field of daisies twirl.
In this lovely rural scene,
Summer's kiss of love and peace.
      —Lil Toomey

Bedtime

To close my eyes
   without a sound.
A moment of peace
   yet to be found.
The screaming the yelling.
   Oh the noise.
The fighting the pulling
   the tugging of toys.
The tension is mounting
   the stress is real.
Patients are needed
   for me to deal.
Waiting for bed time
   with plenty to do.
I have a daughter, she two.
      —Shiela Grunwaldt

The Comptroller's Credo

Collecting the green is never obscene
Without it business fails
Successful business men, it seems,
Must be as hard as nails

The timid fellow holds his tongue
Concerning accounts receivable
For him to prosper, I profess,
Is truly unbelievable.

Business growth is slow at best
When needed funds are lacking
And bankers shun most any one
Without collateral backing.

So heed these words of good advice
Collect the money due you
If you do not, beware, my friend,
Your creditors will sue you.
      —Robert G. Mogg

Pondering

Did you ever stop and
wonder on a dark and
dreary day?
Just what is up above
those clouds so far away,
Is there sunshine up
above so the angels can
come out to play, or
are there just more
clouds forming to rob
us of another sunny
day.
      —Ruth McCann

Spring

Spring's the most
   wonderful time of
The year, because...
   Mother earth starts
Over anew; she brings
   out the beauty of
Trees great and small...
   flowers and shrubs...
And that's not all...
   the streams they all
Whisper a tune, cause
   they know, there's
A duty mother nature...
   soon will unfold.
      —Mary Louise Myers

Rainbows

Without them the world
would have
No hope no faith no dreams

We chase them as a child
Searching for the
Pot of Gold
The Wee Leprechaun

We chase them as a teenager
Trying to ease the pain
To stay a child
Forever hopeful

We chase them as an adult
Trying to find our elusive dreams
Looking for our lost childhood
Always knowing it's one step ahead

Rainbows
One of life's enigma's
We never stop chasing them
Rainbows, elusive rainbows

—*Sharon Holman*

Nam

He bowed himself over the bread
wrinkles redoubled
by the hand at his head.
A frown deep
spoke of no peace
in eyes dark
since some ancient war.
Sausage and bread
or cheese instead
was the feast
to be eaten again.
The scowl gave way
to curse or to pray
and once more he picked up the bread.

—*Morris Gillett*

Yesterday I Went On Horse Back

Yesterday was a summer day,
Yesterday it was warm
I saddled up my big black horse,
Hoping it wouldn't storm.

I rode into the deep dark woods
and tumbled on a rock.
Then I heard a screeching sound,
Kind of like a hawk.

I quickly ran as fast as I could,
With my horse coming behind.
Finally, I found my way out,
Which I thought I'd never find.

—*Tamara Webster*

Visage

Perhaps today, a martyr
Yesterday's forgotten;
Sometimes new,
Always hidden.
Love meeting truth
When it ends
Or sees that it never began;
If we ever meet, welcome
And goodbye,
forever.

—*Allan S. Kane*

Daddy

Daddy died years ago,
Yet he breathes and eats.
He sits alone, cries a lot,
And sleeps upright in his seat.

He says he can sleep standing up.
He learned to in the war,
On German boxcars as they swayed
And jerked and stalled and jarred.

Packed in so tight he couldn't move,
He prayed he wouldn't fall
Into the smothering feces
Where he couldn't breathe at all.

I'm not so sure that prayers helped.
I think that's where he died—
In that Nazi boxcar,
He smothered deep inside.

—*Lynette A. Riggs*

Leo's Life

Leo's life is full of strife;
Yet, he has a daughter and a wife.
His war is over;
His battle has been won.
His life is spent,
Not on two legs, but one.

No matter the circumstance
Nor the tradition;
Leo comes out on top
With all his ambition.

He mops, he cooks, and reads his books.
He answers the phone, and
is ready and prone;
To give advice or just be nice.
That's Leo we've said;
This poem you've read.

—*Rose Metros*

Earth Angel

Earth angel,
You appeared in my dreams.
When I woke,
There you stood,
With eagles' wings.
Glowing like the moon,
You're sure to visit me again soon.
You gave me a kiss,
And I realized,
That you're my earth angel.
You're here to stay,
So I have to say,
I love you,
Earth angel.

—*Jennifer Lynn Stewart*

"True Love"

You've made me laugh,
You've made me cry,
You've made me wonder why.
I've loved you so and always will,
until the day I die.

—*Andrea Basdeo*

"Oh Little One"

Oh little one, a joy to be,
You are, for now, a fantasy
That grows within your mother's womb,
A life to be, a rose to bloom.

Oh little one you'll be my pride
When in the park you climb a slide
And romp and play and ride the swing
While swaying by, a tune you'll sing.

Oh little one, my precious hope,
I long to watch you skip a rope,
To kiss you when you skin your knee,
To gaze in awe at things you see.

Oh little one, my innocence,
A life ahead of fond events,
Like seeing creatures at the zoo-
Intriguing places all anew.

Oh little one, my heart, my soul,
Success for you is my true goal
And as you grow and day is done
I dream of you, oh little one.

—*Fennell*

"I Am"

I AM.
You are. I will and you came to be.
I sent HIM that you may see,
That I AM indeed.

What more can I do
That I've not already done?
I gave you MARY MY daughter
And JESUS MY SON.

You have THEIR LIVES as example
That you may be like ME.
Depart not from THEIR counsel
For you'll be sorry.

So repent of your sins
And return to ME,
So that where I AM
You may be.

—*Anonymous*

Our Son

You have red hair and freckles.
You are joy and laughter.
You have strength and truth.
You are Dad's little helper.
You are Mom's best friend.
You are proud and you are brave.
You are love that never ends.
You are tears that seem to fade.
You are sunshine when it rains.
You are our gift from God
A child, our child.
You are to be cherished and praised.
You are special in every way.
We will love you till our dying day.
Our Son, Our one and only.

—*Rebecca Lynn McAlister*

To My Wife And Sweet Heart

You are my whole heart,
You are my very soul,
You are everything in my life.
You are so very sweet,
You are so kind and gentle,
You make me proud being my wife.
You know life can be rough,
You know life can be tough,
You know this can happen any time.
You know I'll always love you,
You know I'll always cherish you,
You will always be my valentine

—*A. Sahler*

My Lord

You are here,
You are there,
Oh, my Lord,
You're everywhere.

You watch by day,
You watch by night,
You're even there by candlelight.

You're with us all
In wrong or right.
You know us high,
You know us low,
You know us, Lord
No matter where we go.

—*Jere S. Sloan*

The Crossing

With words that were so fair
You did build upon the air
    A bridge of promise
In a voice that rang so true
I most absolutely knew
    You'd be there
A friend
Until the very, very end
    By your promise

But then, with words to break and bend
You did blow betraying winds
    Upon our bridge of promise;
Now, where one was bridged of two
Dangle lonely halves of me and you
    In silence
Halfway crossing empty air
Reaching only what is there
    A broken promise

—*Todi S. Carnes*

End Of Time

You don't care what people say,
You don't care what people do.
You defend me when I can't
defend myself.
You accept me for who and what I am.
You will never leave me,
for you love me and I love you.
I can trust you with my thoughts
and my fears.
I pray we'll be together 'til the
end of time.

—*Rachel Fulp*

My Friend

  My friend,
You exceed the realm of beauty
Your dark eyes pierce the night
Like a bolt of lightning
That lights a warm summer night
Your smile lightens my heart
Every time my eyes come upon you
The warm glow and vibrations that
Come from your pleasant self
Make me feel like I am reborn again
This is what my friend, Yourself
Means to me

—*Larry D. Smith*

Not Your Fault

When a friend dies in an accident
You feel lonely and sad,
but when a friend
Kills themself,
You don't know
How to feel!
You may feel
Like it is your fault,
You should've been
There for them,
Or
You should've talked
Them out of it!
All you can do
Now is mourn the loss,
Then get on with your life!

—*Jennifer Sommers*

The Taken Child

How could someone take
    you from your family and friends
This horrifying thought
    in my mind never ends
I see your face, I hear
    your voice
You haven't even lived
    to be given a choice
My life is so empty and
    filled with such pain
What could this person
    possibly have to gain
I need you here,
    to be by my side
Where did they take you —
    where did they hide
If I could only touch you
    and see your face
You belong back home,
    this is your place

—*Jamison*

One Up

It's clear to see
you're not the one
But after all
you had your fun
yea...you said you thought about it
But you know—I know
It's just as I suspected
you was short from the get-go.

—*Linda Frazier*

Deep Inside

  Hush, Hush my darling
  You need not say a word
Whatever's in your heart to say
  My ears already heard;

  Listen not my sweet one
  You shouldn't use your ears
I'll tell you through my heart
  So no one else can hear;

  Speak not to others
  To tell me how you feel
Your actions just around me
Tells me your love's for real;

  Look not my loved one
  You do not need your eyes
Everything you need to see
  Is hidden deep inside;

  Leave not my dear one
  We mustn't ever part
I couldn't live without you
The shock would break my heart.

—*Aaron M. Turner II*

You Mean the World to Me

You've been there since day one for me.
You never left me out,
You always cared so much for me.
You never caused me to shout.
You never left me in the cold,
Nor the snow or rain.
You always kept me warm inside,
And somehow you kept me sane.
You helped me through the bad times,
And through the good times too.
You always acted responsibly,
And never caused harm to me or you.
You've been there from the beginning,
And to the end that's where you'll be.
Because as I've said before,
You mean the world to me.

—*Katie Powell*

Wind

Oh blustering mad winds.
You untamed tempest.
Reckless gale, rudest of all —
Who'll repair the oak
After you've been by?

Oh blustering mad winds
What savage behavior
You dampen my dignity
As flying down the lane I chase
A fleeing, darting cap.

Oh devastating mad winds!
Clattering the shutters and
Blasting in through windows cracks
Who's bringing you to court
For unruly violation?

—*Magdaleni Kaiser*

526

Only A Dream

It was all so beautiful,
  you were holding me tight.
Sitting by the fire,
  on a cold winter's night.
You told me how much you loved me,
  and I told you the same.
While our love seemed to burn,
  like an eternal flame.
Nothing could come between us,
  we were like one.
And when I looked into your eyes,
  they were bright like the sun.
But reality hit me,
  so bluntly you see.
For this beautiful night,
  was only a dream.
But I can only hope,
  for this scene to come true.
Because the one I truly love,
will always be you.

—*Jennifer Adams*

"Only to Wander Away"

I found you on a sunny day
  you were so cute and fat
Only to wander away
  my wayward, solitary cat.

I took you home to stay
  there you sat on a mat
You wanted your own way
  my wayward, solitary cat.

Then came the day
  when you ran away
You left before I could give you a pat
  my wayward, solitary cat.

—*Pamela Batey*

Mother

My mother was the nicest lady
You would ever want to meet,
She carried candy in her purse
To give little ones a treat.

I learned from her example
To be nice to everyone,
Her cheerful smile lit up the day,
It was constant like the sun.

Her blue eyes twinkled as she laughed
While telling me funny things
That happened many years ago
As she pushed me in my swing.

She was so very happy on my wedding day
As we stood in the receiving line,
She was most proud of me
Because she knew this was, indeed, my day
to shine!

She is no longer with me, but when I'm
feeling down,
I think of what she would say to me,
"Be patient when it's raining,
There's a sunny day coming around."

—*Phyllis Parks*

Missing You

I'll never forget
Your smiling face
And my favorite thing
Was your warm embrace

Your sparkling eyes caught my attention
Your kindness caught my heart
Then something happened
And my dream fell apart

Wanted so badly
For you to be mine
But all you could say
Was, "It's not the right time."

Then all at once
You were out of sight and mind
And believe we when I say
You're the hardest person to find

One day I'll find you
And I will hang on tight
And just wait for you to tell me
Everything will be alright

—*Keith Allen*

Grandma's Advice

Remember, my child,
You're special, unique
You're one-of-a-kind
None can compete.

Always give your all
And accept nothing less
For you are special,
You deserve the best.

The love you give to others
Is returned ten-fold,
Family and friends
Are your silver and gold.

I pray God's blessing
And love you will know,
That he'll keep you safe
When from this world I must go.

Always remember,
My dear little one,
Your grandmother's love
Is an eternal sun.

—*Pam Von Hagel*

"Neither When, Where, Nor How"

I'm sure, dear reader, that
you will quickly agree,

That into the misty future
we would all like to see...

And know the circumstances
of our demise,

But, alas, our imagination
shall have to suffice!

—*John Bruce Wolford*

Promise Me

Today you are beautiful
You've been here so long
Keeping me cool
Keeping me company

Soon your color will change
And then fall they will
To the ground
And you will stand bare

Then soon the ground
Will be covered
And all will be cold
And some will freeze

For so long you will
Look of death
I cannot see the life in you
If it is still there

When the time comes
So I can be sure
Please promise me
You will come back again.

—*Stephanie White*

In My Corner

Once again, thank you, Lord;
You've really helped me out.
With you in my corner,
Why should I have doubt?
When I ask for help,
You always come through.
Unfortunately,
I get tangled up,
In all I have to do.
And forget I need not be,
Struggling, and all alone,
Or losing sight of when,
Your light has shown.
Thank you, Lord,
For being patient,
As you stand by me;
And for getting me to focus,
When I simply can't see.

—*Tammy E. Seaman*

Sweet Tooth

I think I'll bake
myself a cake

while, I'm waiting I
will eat this pie,
I just went to buy.

I may have a chocolate chip
cookie instead, that could
widen my hips.

Or maybe these M and M's
than take a run
around the gym.

Oops! I can not seem
to be able to have
any after all.

Why you ask?

Because, my sweet tooth
just fell off.

—*Rebeka Vasquez*

Drizzly Outside

It's night time and it's drizzly outside,
The fog is descending upon the foliage,
Moistened leaves amass on the sidewalk,
They even out beneath my shoes.

The air has a soggy woody balm,
The rainfall drips slowly from the limbs,
It settles on a blade of grass and
  burbles before melting away.

The dripping of the rain is very
  pronounced as it flows forcefully down
    the water spout,
Its range blends with other sounds of the
  night and coins a somber piece of music.

—*Duane P. Shaw*

Untitled

Beyond your thoughts and through to your soul
The forces of love have taken their toll
  With no words of warning nor writing on the wall
  Just the innocent and the honest destined to fall
Confusion runs rampant in a heart not content
Hearing what's said and wondering what's meant
  You'll tend to lose faith in the word we call love
  Thinking it's punishment sent from above
Love thrives mysteriously in so many ways
Its complex dimensions trap you in a daze
  From moments of hope to hours of doubt
  You now pray to God that it all works out
To believe in yourself is the only way past
The pleasures and pains that make a love last.

—*Dave Johnston*

Untitled

Some morning in Winter I wake up to see
The frost on the weeds and bushes and our big tree
The frost is on everything all around
From the top of the trees to the snowy ground
Everything is white to the edge of the town
Even the trees with their few leaves of brown
I look out to see a fairyland before me
It glistens like diamonds and sparkles like jewels
The don't know how it's made, they say, as a rule
I hate to see it disappear so soon
But the sun frightens it away towards the noon

—*Cheryl R. Hamilton*

God Gave Me A Present

God gave me a present, It didn't cost a dime
The gift is free to all, you can except it anytime
It's not a gift to put under a tree
It's not a gift that you can see
It's a gift that live's in your heart
When you receive it, that's the time to make a new start
Time to throw away the old and put on the new
Time to learn the true meaning of Christmas, too.
Christmas is a special time of year
It makes joy and love to all seem very clear
When you know Christ, you'll know the true meaning
Of Christmas past and the shining star gleaming
So when you celebrate His birth
The one who died for us when He agreed to come to earth
He took away our sins, and gave us the gift of life
So think about all I've said on this Christmas morn
The very day our dear Savior was born
I wrote this from my heart the place He lives in me
If you haven't excepted Him as your personal Savior
Try it and see how happy you'll be

—*Darlene Patterson*

The Dawn Of Conscience

Woulds't that I only heard better
the gifts of God,
that through the Angels do pass to me true.
Could I only bear better
the truth that they tell,
and not find what they say to be new.
For to hear their whispers
I must listen real hard
and abhor my own thoughts to the core;
lest I lose in that quagmired wilderness,
the light that I there once saw.

For as children we know but have forgotten
what once were our souls' desires.
Lost in meaningless emptiness,
we've become false destined sires
of pain turned to pleasure
and pleasure to pain:
a forfeit of reason and love.
For what we have lost in that wilderness,
is the lamplight that comes from above.

—*Mark J. Stumacher*

Elegance

The flickering flames in a fire place.
The golden glow of the sunlight rays.
The contour of a lovely face.
The glistening diamond look of a frosted
snow flaked window pane.
A rainbow in the sky.
The moon in it's silvery splendor as it follows
Your every move guiding and protecting the world
through the night always a guardian angle in flight.
The russet orange and yellow hues of the trees framed
against the blue sky, a peek of light seeping through,
a whisk of wind blowing the falling leaves to the
ground whirling, dancing around like the sounds of children
at play the beauty of laughter.
A love that has endured through the years triumphant
through fears and tears.
Thanks be to the master builder.
We have these memories.

—*Ida Newborne*

The Test Of Motherhood

A ceremonial birth does not induce
the graduation of motherhood.
For, misconception of conception
can lead a woman astray
until the official birth-day.
Then it is the true test for a mother
to do her best. Pacifying ones past
plans by putting them aside and
sacrificing for the future so he will
be able to provide. Responsibilities
become a must everyday from dawn to dusk.
Remember a baby is not a doll so be sure
you're ready or don't have one at all.
A diploma for motherhood must be earned
by tests of life and love and
honored by both mother and child
making it all worthwhile.

—*Gayle Carter*

Technical Death

The sky is gray, the trees are brown
The grass is dead and so is the town
There is total silence, the night is deathly still
There's nothing left to roam, nothing left to kill
No more birds soaring in the sky
No pretty flowers to catch the viewing eye
Technology is definitely the main fault
Bringing our world to a very abrupt halt
"Nuclear energy is the way to go!"
This is untrue, cause little did they know
Nuclear energy would deliver the final blow
There was nothing to do with all the waste
It didn't stop them, they even quickened the pace
that was the age of nuclear death
Taking our earth, taking our breath
Technology is gained at any cost
It's too late, we've already lost

—*Joshua A. Hill*

Segno Silence

From the rising of the sun to the going down
The hours are multitudinously long.
But in each human heart there can continue the song —
That's the only way a person can spend
The years that move on-and on to the end.
There are still steep slopes to fondly face
When so many you've loved have left this place.
The silhouette of things that used to be
Keep beckoning on and you can see,
There are many problems needing to be solved
So there's a purpose and reason to get involved.
Think of all the children and youth to keep on course
The Power who strengthens will grant the force
To the self who follows with a strong will,
And that one can continually climb over the hill.
From the rising of the sun to the going down.
The hush of all the years that have past
Comes to keep company with us until the last.

—*Hazel Martin*

Suspension

Right before the rain is worst,
The humidity building.
I stand at the sink
Sweat trickling between my breasts,
Down my stomach.
Skin so tender
It feels like ants.

The storm at sunset is a tempest.
From the house wide-eyed
Watching the wind-tossed trees,
Heart racing with every rush,
Senses heighten.

The trembling shadow of the chiawarra—
Elongated horns and arched neck
Silhouetted against the lone yellow light—
Speaks of the animal night.

The human side seeks shelter,
Pulling horizons inward to a light,
A warmth, the very present moment,
Echoing, outside, the ancient muezzin call to prayer.

—*Linda Voss*

Endless Rain

Grey skies fill with black clouds.
The kids watch Saturday cartoons, as the adults shake their heads
Over the weather forecast.
A chill wind screams outside the door, echoing their feelings about the
Predicted three days of constant rain.

The first fat droplets of water fall.
Soon the rain is coming down in sheets and people start warning others to
Move their cars up to the high areas.
The rain is endless and soon the water has reached our second step.
The creek has started to flood the park.

The merciless rain pours on and on.
It is Sunday evening and we light candles since the electricity is out.
My family and I are trapped inside.
The water has engulfed the seven steps to our porch; it is too cold to wade
The icy liquid that has us surrounded.
The endless drone of rain finally ends.
It is nine p.m. and I prepare for bed, knowing I have school tomorrow if
The water is low enough in the morning.
As I sleep, the weather is calm, the skies are clear, the
stars shine.
I awake and find the ground clear if soggy.

—*Brenda Jumper*

Mother Nature's Decorations

Summers here, the flowers have bloomed
The lawns and gardens are well groomed,
And with Mother Nature as their guest
The world dresses in their best.

Fall is now very very near,
Mother Nature is making it clear,
She's turning the leaves red, yellow and brown,
Then she'll toss them to the ground.

Winter now is on its way
As the weather gets colder day by day,
The leafless trees on the mountain crest
Resembles lace on Mother Nature's breast.

Spring is just around the corner,
The days seem to be getting warmer,
The birds and butterflies are being seen
And everything is turning green.

Summer has flowers
Fall has colors
Winter is white
Spring is green and bright.

—*Ethel A. Fath*

We Need A Little Pain

Contentment is too comfortable for a writer.
The lazy days slide by with no ennui.
I see him lie beside me in the night;
No fights. Our words weave the fabric of our lives:
soft as silk, warm as wool. Sweet words.
We never switch to that cutting pitch that
spirals higher with each thrust.
We trust our hearts and know the care is there
to keep the loving safe. But
contentment is too comfortable for a writer
Sometimes it takes a dream
to squeeze out sleeping memories and spur
a little anxiety. A dream
to pique a long-forgotten flash of pain.
Contentment is too comfortable for a writer.

—*Carol Wilson*

529

A Light In The Night

No matter how dark or windy or drear,
   The light in your window is a token of cheer,

I look for that light, and when its not there,
   The night seems so dark, I almost despair.

So thanks for your light, that token of cheer,
   Which sends out the message that friends are near,

And may my light be a token to you,
   "I thank the good Lord for neighbors like you,"
         —*Ethel M. Meade*

Nannie

The Nannie I knew is gone, I fear.
The lights no longer shine,
And 'tho her body is still here
Meaningless words and blank gazes sign
The collapse of all she used to be.
The hands that sowed, and sewed, and tied the bows
Now fidget and pluck at what only she can see.
Her children, and theirs, she no longer knows.
And even her mate of, oh, so many years
Cannot pull her back into a world that's real.
That's all for the best, it appears,
For she's left no dignity, now. I feel
The cruelest blow of all would be
To know her personal needs others take care of.
She would never have withstood the indignity
Even 'tho those needs were met with love.
'Tho age must come and with it the disease
That leaves its victims mentally bereft,
I seek for Nannie a kind release.
There are some things much worse than death.
         —*Daniel D. Oesch*

My Daughter

I am only one of your early lovers.
The love in your heart goes as far as eternity,
You can walk on the clouds
You're the Venus of my heart. A goddess of beauty
You're a Princess, Knights risking there lives to serve your love.
You're the one they look up to.
You're a beautiful rose an Iris a
Morning glory that awakes every morning to a happy new self.
Your eyes could put any one in a trance.
I am glad you are mine.
         —*Brittney Barnett*

The Face Of Woman

In the dark, dismal, fetid cave
The man child lay on animal skins
His tiny fists fumbling blindly
Hungry mouth seeking suckling.

In the place of the Pharaohs
The infant regent on vermeil throne
Slept amid golden and sapphire scarab
A cobra scepter guarding his head.

Laughing as the wind tickled his face
The papoose swung from the birch bough,
In a meager manager on a bed of straw
The hope of mankind was cradled.

Crouched in the dark cave was a watcher,
In the palace walked a silken robed queen
The squaw picked blueberries, Mary smiled,
Woman is the life force of the world.
         —*Marie Gilligan Mahan*

Dream I Alcohol: Killer

The cards were revealed, but abrupted quick,
The man flushed with anger, now a lunatic,
The warpath was set, blood rushed in his eyes,
Now no other force or man could defy,
The decision must kill his heart and mind,
Both are disrupted in such a short time,
The sickness, forever, all in sorrow,
Rage for now, sorries are for tomorrow.
The killer in his bloodstream, leaving all dead,
Mentally not physically, Dependency is left in his head,
What was once weaker, is now more powerful and rough,
Leaving the road ahead even more tough,
The killer has given pain and rage,
When will he break out of this dependent cage
         —*Sean Ruffing*

The Lost Moment

One little moment born to be,
The master of a destiny.
Lived only once, without having done,
The miracle for which it was begun.

The little child at play could not see,
That this moment might hold his destiny.
The youth let it slip idly by,
The lover could not see for tear dimmed eye.

So onward it winged into outer space
Unheeded in times, unprecedented in race.

The aged man reached out with zest,
For here at last was the end of his quest.
But this moment held little in store,
For death, stood waiting at his door.
         —*Brenda M. Fenners*

God Gave Us All Things

God gave us these things, when he passed by;
The mating dance of the butterfly.
A tiny baby's laughter, too;
And a rose bud, kissed with dew.
A lily refreshed; by the rain;
As it beats down on our window pane.
A bee gathering nectar, for his queen;
As we marvel at what we've seen.
A beautiful song from a bird;
As we marvel at what we've heard.
God gave us, the warm gentle breeze.
He also gave us, giant oak trees.
He gave us angels, with gossamer wings.
To enhance our lives, God gave us all things.
         —*Carol Armstrong Holt*

Life

The summer breeze came in the open door without an invitation
   The new accompanist was welcomed by the ceiling fan
      Gleefully, both swayed to the same rhythm.

I watched as the five origami, intricately folded
   Moved as graceful dancers on the tiny thread
      A thread almost invisible to the human eye - so fragile.

And, so does our life balance on a delicate thread.

Then I said a silent prayer, asking forgiveness
   For the young woman who had given the origami to me
      Who took her life last fall.

The delicate thread and the origami sometimes dance to
   different rhythms.
         —*Jean Twentier Robinson*

"I Am Very Thirsty"

Mommy feed me, my eyes firmly fixed to
the mirror displaying myself
the face a sickly chalky white
the eyes a bloody red
Which cast sinister red glows
Along the midnight walls, I want it all
I would like to be fed
No it can't be, it's more difficult to see
My ruby red lips, open just ajar
the awaiting flesh not so far
Oh she's late and the night awaits
My mouth lifted open
the childish yellow teeth
grew into sharp teeth blades
the mirror image soon fades
Now on my own, bloody thirst through my mind
I must seek and find... flesh
No please help me it can't be
I shall not bite, however I suppose that's just not right
for I am now a creature of the night
  —*Michelle Legris*

The Creation Of The Earth

You see the light and the darkness falls. I open my eyes as
the moon rises. My life is under the stars. I rise every
night with the moon. The wind blows softy as I move. I pick
up where I left off knowing that my creation is not yet
finished. My paint brush is there waiting for me. I open with
a stroke of green to color it. Then a soft blue for the
oceans. My creation it is done. The mountains are perfect,
and the skies are clear. I sculpt it into the universe knowing
that it is mine. No one else can touch this beautiful thing.
I have made good in all directions. I take a few moments to
ponder on this perfect picture. I sit back in my chair to
think and wonder, "what shall I call this thing I have
created?" I hear a voice behind me say, "earth I understand
now why it is called earth. Earth means beautiful.
  —*Diane Pan Konie*

Through the Eyes of the Aged

I laid my book down on my lap and looked out the window;
the new signs of spring had made it's grand entrance in glorious splendor.
The memories of the gay festivities of days so long ago past;
with close family and friends gathered together in my mind at long last.
I let out a deep sigh as tears came to my eyes;
as family gatherings at holiday is no longer alive.
The loneliness had snuck into my life like a lingering shadow;
with no control over such designated existence in life's final fallow.
To have outlived family, friends and other acquaintances to fates;
was a secret fear I had hoped I would never have to face.
With no family left to carry on the family tradition, heritage and name;
to be chosen as sole survivor of extinction in a family line so maimed.
These keen eyes of mine have seen many joys and sorrows of years past;
not only my own but of family, friends and a world made of fragile glass.
To have given so much of myself in later years to those in need of wisdom and praise;
to prove I was not a weary old woman with no mind or heart left as they say.
A nurse's aide handed me a card and replied: "This came for you, Mrs. Sand."
I smiled and replied my thanks as I open the card with unsteady hands.
  —*Cynthia A. Hallenbeck*

"The Pilgrimage"

My pilgrim's progress has one goal, I've faith it's not in vain,
As life on earth, to live is Christ, my hope to die is gain.
So to arrive at the Holy City, not on my own accord,
As to be absent from this body, to be present with the Lord.
The Holy Spirit's with me, the promise of this age,
When the journey's over, I'll lie down, and end my pilgrimage.
  —*Gordon Sironen*

America's At Risk

According to President Bush
The New World Order's good for us.

Such talk's been heard before, we fear...
In hist'ry, when did it appear?

There's nothing new under the sun.
The Bible points to Babylon.

'Twas imported! - from dark ages,
By modern, rich, mattoid sages.

What they are selling, labelled new,
Is old world's feudal nobles' brew.....

With such order would come trouble,
Like another Tower of Babel.

If truth's no guide for Mister Bush,
His deception's clearly treas'nous.

Although some people will be fooled,
America's at risk to lose.

New World serfdom awaits for all
If we would buy that old snake oil.

We, The People, cherish freedom
And we say, "Away, deception."
  —*John Nevin Shaffer*

The Night City

Neon glare springs from fading day;
The Night City lives.
Born again alleys hide awakened
street children performing survival
as the weary thief hopes for discovery,
stealing through the dark.
Shadows, fear chased, leaping curbs,
flicker against lamp-lighted streets,
turning to reflections on the opaque
storefront.
A silent moment cries out, its echoes dying
in the sudden, awkward stillness,
Unheard by dawns false sanctuary.
  —*George A. Jette*

Unnoticed Love

Someone is there - I hear him in
the night, he is the only one I
love-my guiding light
My love for him is strong, burning
deep inside my heart—the way he feels
about me, we will always be apart
I hear his voice every where, I call
to him but he does not care
My heart is broken, the two parts die-
I look to him to ask him why
The sky is bright, a crimson red my
love turns to anger inside my head
I grab my knife-I see him there
I take my life -he doesn't care
My life is over-with one small mistake
My deep love he can never take
  —*Melissa Jaylene Smith*

The Meaning Of

To be is not to be forgotten, To be alive to
to be heard, to desire all can lead to nothing.

  The meaning of can be heard in the
soft sound of the single breeze.
  —*Christina Parra*

A New Day Dawns

I have a peaceful feeling as the day begins to dawn.
The night is ending and I know the shadows will be gone.
I hear the sounds of early morn as the night begins to fold.
Light streaks across the sky and turns each cloud to pure gold.

While the dew still sparkles on each unfolding bloom,
The butterfly emerges from the bonds of it's cocoon.
As the birds sing out their praises in an early morning song,
I feel the presence of my Lord as I pray and walk along.

As the day breaks bright and clear,
I must believe that my God is very near.
For I see His Hand in each and every wondrous thing,
My heart overflows with the joy this day will bring.
If only praises to my heavenly Father I will sing.

If some sorrow should come my way.
I know my God will Hold me close and ease the pain away.
I need never fear the storms that in my path may lay,
Only trust my Savior as He leads me through each day.

—*Ann Koberg*

"In The Night"

The night is so dark, peaceful, and true,
The night was made for me and you.

Near a lake with your someone special by your side,
  Holding you tightly and watching the stars up in the sky.

He holds you with his warm embrace,
  And you gaze up into his loving face.

Could this be real or make believe,
  Only you would know can't you see?

—*Derenda Gentry*

What Is the Sound of Poetry

The steady beat of a tom tom,
the nightly song of a loving Mom;

Or maybe rain drops hitting the window,
with a pitter patter both fast and slow;

How about a cat crying with fright,
perched on a fence in the middle of the night;

Soft sounds, loud sounds,
from small babies or large hounds;

And even the leaves on my pear tree,
rustle and whisper like poetry;

Poetry is all the sounds you hear,
and all the thoughts that you hold dear.

—*Frances Bucaro Mc Climent*

To Vera May On Our 57th

People have asked me
The problem they see
How you make differing people agree.
You don't but you try,
And you sometimes ask why;
But the Lord has a plan
For His family of man
And He surely expects us to be
A part of His world family.
So how did we live with the joy and the pain?
For the love of each other each day
And I'll tell you frankly — we pray!
And I'd do it all over again!

—*Darrel C Maxson*

Asked The Word: Beauty

Asked the word, what is beauty;
the only seed, I could breed,
within my soul, a flourishing tree in autumn's wind,
the beholder's eye, the harvester of sights' seed;

The seed buried beneath,
in the mind's arena of optional beauty,
grows with every hour, within the eyes where beauty lies,
through the gardens, my seeded rose flower, come with me;

Peering through with the thought of beauty,
within the emerald genial embrace,
seen with different aspects, and through a different window,
like everyone's taste, and everyone's face;

Within ones' eyes, every hideous or radiant appearance,
appears as an Aphrodite or a Medusa,
within someone's eyes, whether blinded or wise,
within the core of love, where beauty lies, lies desires' utopia;

Within the sea of eyes, in the web of beauty, I'm writhing
blue, drowning within through and through; if there is beauty,
my wanting one, their seams are sewn up and down within you.

—*Crispin Demers*

Mirror Of Life

Like a bird on swift flight
  The past year has flown by
  Leaving memories, sad or bright
  As seen in the mirror of life.

May this year be highly blessed
  With significant events
  As we strive to do our best
  In serving our Community.

Awakening at dawn to the cock's crowing
  We rise to the daily challenges-
  To those in need, our hands extending
  And with caring hearts, remembering -
  Solving problems, to achieve our goals
  To enjoy a life of harmony.

May the future be bright as the sun
  Illuminating our universe
  By fulfilling our cherished dreams
  Of hope, good-will and lasting peace
  As reflected in the mirror of life.

—*Fumi Migimoto*

Our Final Journey

Will you walk with us our Saviour?
Will you take us by the hand?
Will you lead us down the pathway?
That leads to the promise land.

When that morning breaks so clearly,
And our toils on earth are through;
Guide our souls within thy kingdom,
With your love forever true.

See us past the vale of shadow,
Hear us when we call your name;
Help us on beyond the river,
As our souls are seared with pain.

Guide us down the path to glory,
Safe from earthly sins and shame;
As O, Lord this is thy power
Hallowed be your precious name.

—*Patricia Mackie*

Land Without Tears

God saw the hills were getting steep
The path was hard to trod.
He whispered "Come to Me and rest
There'll be no tears with God."

He gave us a loving mother
Who always calmed our fears.
But then He called her home to rest
To the land without tears.

With heavy hearts and tear-filled eyes
We watched as life grew dim.
In pain, she whispered, "Which way, Lord?"
There would be no tears with Him.

She's sleeping now on the hillside
But still we know she hears,
The many times we call her name
To the land without tears.

Friends may think we have forgotten
But ever through the years,
Our empty hearts wait to greet her
In the land without tears.

—*Levada A. Parchey*

Death, Near, Far And Beyond

People die, I don't know why.
    The people you love go up above.
The people you hate, it was there fate.
    The people you care for, the people you know no more.
Death is a part of life,
    for kids, mothers, and wife.
It's for everyone, not just one.
    It's not something to wish, because you will be missed.
Suicide is the answer you say,
    but it's not the way.
People die I say, everyday-day after day.
    People will die, you and I.
There is a hope, no need to mope.
    Love, caring,
        children sharing,
        that's the hope.
People die, I don't know why.

—*Chrystral Jirak*

Sonnet On A Photograph

In trying to describe a memory,
The photographs around me seem more true;
Than subtle shades of synapses grey hue
Can ever recreate less faithfully.
Yet, some details are difficult to see,
Without a tensely concentrated view
That bursts the frame. Exploding thoughts renew
Each color, blending fast in harmony.
A narrow road that winds up the steep slope
Like Christmas garland; The violent cliffs loom
Above an ice-blue sea whose currents doom
In time the shore. Its cyclic fingers grope
The ancient rock, as now erodes my hope:
To copy truth within this silent room.

—*Margaret Alkinc*

My Teacher

My teacher is happy
When she gives something with value to one of us.
I can see it in her eyes.
I can hear it in her voice.
She says she loves teaching.
But I think she loves me.

—*Bente Pedersen*

My Valley Is Gone

My beautiful valley near my home
    the place where I liked to roam
I watched rabbits, squirrels, chipmunks, and deer
    they roamed in my valley with no fear.

Men and machines took my valley away
    they filled my valley with dirt one day
Now I have a new place where I like to roam
    and the animals have a new green carpeted home.

Isn't God wonderful, isn't he great
    this didn't all happen just by fate
God, man, and machines took my valley away
    my valley is gone, but my life goes on each new day.

—*Garlinda Mathews*

Birth Of Life

The light of a new day, it is dawning
    The promise of beauty, a peaceful morning

The arriving of light, over-coming the night
    It pictures the power, that gives us sight

All is anew, yesterday is gone
    Never again to see, its memory alone

As pages of life, are turned each day
    Memories in making, before us they lay

What is life - some may ask
    What's our reasoning, what is the task

There are answers, but we must look
    Our Fathers diary - our hand book

Its filled with stores, ancestor history
    Its full of wisdom, tells our destiny

It tells of peace, but also of strife
    Instructions to follow, all about life

Where are we going, we can see
    Just ask our Creator - while upon our knee

Our end journey, leaving this site
    To life eternal - our Fathers delight

—*Helen Miles*

Old Fashioned Thanksgiving

The corn stocks are stacked in steeples so high -
The pumpkins been made into sweet-seasoned pie!

The 'tators are cooking and so is the corn -
We've been preparing since way early morn.

The turkey is roasting to a golden brown -
The leaves in the orchard have all fallen down!

The children are out in the fresh autumn snow
And playing about as to church they all go!

Dear Mother is busy - now kneading the bread -
And out in the workshed is hard toiling Dad.

The tables are set now - Dad begins the Grace -
"Thank God for Thanksgiving in our humble place."

—*Zelma Moorman-Hunt*

A Visit From Santa Claus

I was lying in bed Christmas Eve night,
When all the sudden I saw a bright light.

It was Rudolph; the gang and Santa, too,
I was so astonished that my face turned blue!

I rushed downstairs and there he was,
So Jolly and Happy my dear friend SANTA CLAUS.

—*Sarah Ruth Wright*

Reflections

The window pane, with sunlight glare, brings warmth into the room.
The radiant face that can be seen, as a bride walks to her groom.
Our image brings reality, (as others see us) through a mirror that doesn't lie.
Unlike — the shadow that walks with us, it's deceiving to the eye.
The clear, calm water reflects the scene, of mountains, trees and sky.
And the darkness brings the moon-lit night, shining, from on high.
An echo resounding words that are said, from a mountain high above.

The peace of mind reflects in those, who have faith, contentment and love.
How we sit and think of by-gone days, remembering a most happy time.
Ideals we had, that we made come true and some that are still in our mind.

When consideration is shown by those you love, you seldom do feel blue.
The reflection you see, from someone's eyes, when-their-in-love with you.

—*Dolores V. Hager Keller*

Deaths Other Kingdom

In deaths other kingdom,
the road that leads beyond
becomes the beaten path
where those without feet,
tread upon the wind.
Just as a shadow leans on a wall,
a soul floats between
the known, and the unknown
tightly weaving it's essence
into what is
and what is not.
Both are the same,
they achieve this
by taking turns becoming each other
until they can no longer tell the difference.

—*Alan Braun*

Lachesis

Lachesis determines the length of the thread of life
the sands of time whip about the tailor as he sews
some grains lodge in his eyes
hurtful years, invoking tears
that can't wash memory away
still he blinks and thinks up lies
or through the swimming vision tries
to gaze back to a better day
but like Lord Tennyson looking back along the run
he feels the pain reflection brings
"Sorrow's crown of sorrows in remembering happier things"
still he sews never knowing when
the thread and he must go
and of these haphazard stitches in rows
he finds himself less than omniscient
will the garment formed keep him warm
will it be sufficient to hold back the chill
of Eternity's winter and when he is done
the needle passes to the son
but the question goes unanswered

—*David E. Hicks*

Heartfelt

The pain in a child's heart is carried deep,
The scars cannot be healed, only comforted.
The tears that fill a child's eyes
Should be wiped away with love.
Some children suffer
With no one to wipe away their tears.
To hold a child's hand,
Touch a child's heart,
Is such a wonderful happening
It cannot be replaced by imitation.

—*Andrea Rauch*

Life

Life is grand,
Life is great;
Life is what you make it.
You have to live it.
You cannot fake it;
You can bend or you can break it.
This big world is not a cake,
But can you meet this mighty fate?
Life is not happy date,
You can't go in by the garden gate!
God gives us backbone and strong will,
But does this give us power still?
No !!! - There is a challenge we must meet,
A fire within that can be beat!
Young and old,
Smart or dumb;
We all still scream give me more,
Give me some;
Of this thing called - Life.

—*Jessie F. Varner*

Light Fades Into Night

Another earthly day has ended
The sun has set in western sky
The light of day has slowly faded
As moments of this day fleet by

The birds have found their resting places
Midst leaves and branches of the trees
To wait the dawn with all its graces
Their brood with open mouths to feed

We too must lay our cares aside
And rest within His sheltering arms
The God who holds us near His side
Till day break keeps us from all harm

The stars keep vigil through the night
As guardian angels o'er us bend
As all God's creatures see new light
We pray to God new strength us lend

—*G. George Ens*

A Day At The Beach

The sand is soft, the waves are strong.
The sun is hot, the day is long.

A day at the beach is so much fun.
I love the shells, the sand, and the sun.

A little crab comes crawling by.
He carries his shell. I wonder why.

I built a castle in the sand.
I thought it looked so very grand.

The tide will come later today,
and wash my beautiful castle away.

It's time to leave the beach once more,
and the sand, the sun, and the seashore.

—*Julie Susanne Riley*

The Living Church

The beautiful Church of the Living God. Like a light-house by
the sea. Is beckoning to the troubled world. "I will help
you! Come unto me." The world is o'erflowed with confusion
and strife. With souls in the deepest grief. But the 'Light'
from the Church of the Living God. Beckons - - "Here you will
find relief." As you join the Saints in sincere prayer.
You'll find sweet peace for your soul. Leaving your cares at
the Master's feet. You'll know you've been truly made whole;

just read God's Word and obey His will. He'll reveal Himself
to you. You're a part of the glorious Body of Christ - Set
apart from the world - and true. A member, yes, of the Church
of God. Not a Church that's ruled by man. But guided -
instead - by the Spirit of God. Whose plan is "The Perfect
Plan." In the beautiful church of God, you'll find God's
heaven is now your goal. Confusion and strife are left behind.
Peace and joy daily flood your soul.

 —*Dorsie G. Davis*

Beautiful Lips

Beautiful lips so red and full and oh! so ripe.
The smile they help create, let me know my heart is right.
So soft and tender, most luscious and full;
Most beautiful the sight I see, will never be dull.
Ones life with you, would forever be full.

To have the most adorable lips press upon mine;
The spark in my heart would never decline.
These are the most beautiful and succulent lips to possess;
Beautiful they are to give ones heart, forever life.
Forever to be etched, in ones mind so great.

To touch your soft and tender lips upon mine,
I know my heart will have no greater find.
Soft and tender they may be, my heart will forever shine.
From the smile they help create, there will be no greater find.
The spark within my heart, will forever shine.

Within the moisture that lies upon your lips, so sweet,
Would make the biggest, strongest man bow at your feet.
Just to receive the smallest taste, would make a man so great,
Would be to you, his heart and life's greatest fate.
To make your heart, his hearts life's mate.

 —*David L. Paugh*

Spring

When the snow starts to melt, letting the grass grow.
The snow that melts runs into the rivers and streams.
Flowers and trees begin to grow.
Ponds come alive with fish and ducks.

Animals come out from their winter sleep,
Birds come back from the south to sing.
You wake-up to the sounds of a new generation of animals.

As the sun stays in the sky longer.
The nights are shorter then of that of before.
The days are getting warmer.
Where yellow, pink, and green remind me of spring.

If all above is true then it is truly spring.

 —*Christie Conrad*

"An Early Sunrise"

When the first new light fills the sky,
When all the morning doves like to fly,
The lazy flowers slowly open their petals,
And the champion inch worms earn lots of medals.
As the sun gets warmer and cheerfully brighter,
The earth opens up and becomes much lighter.
The dew on the grass quietly melts away,
As a twinkle of joy starts a beautiful new day.

 —*Hilarie Lloyd*

Soundless

I hear this sound in the back of my mind
the sound of hate that kills all time
I cannot vanquish this sound I hear
It lives with me, I live in fear
A saddened sound that brakes all hearts
An empty noise that fills all parts
These words of pain that never end
With no voice, but always begin
A tear for what these sounds have done
They made me see, they made me run
To forget what I said, and all the pain
The loneliness begins, it's all the same
I'm running from...my minds thoughts
Thinking back it will not stop
I'm turning to you for some help
It's the only...other way out
Stretching my hand I reach for sounds
There's none in sight, there's none around
I've been running from this love I feel
The love of a family, this love is real
I've been missing what has always been there
The thought that someone actually cares

 —*Jason Nakonsky*

Scenes of Winter

The trees are barren, the grass is brown
The squirrels are searching for food
The evergreens are now more beautiful,
As snowflakes set the mood
The cool brisk wind bites the tip of my nose
I'll be glad when spring arrives
And puts life back in the rose
The earths silent moments are now taking place
The stars shine so brightly in the great outer space
Life is as a vapor that quickly passes by
Enjoy the things of nature as you wonder
"How the hummingbird can fly"

 —*Judith S. Cook*

Alone

A cold, dark room
The steady trickle of a faucet
drip drop (drip drop) drip
A coyote howls in the distance —
The moon shines, and makes a patch of light
 upon the floor
And here I sit, against the wall
Shivering from the cold
Listening to the faint drip
And the lone coyote
Staring into the mesmerizing moonlight
 Alone, Again

 —*Amanda Sue Whittington*

Snow

The silence of the snow envelops me.
The stillness of the landscape beguiles me.
  Nothing stirs
  Nothing sounds.
All is silent.
All is snow.
Selena rides slowly above the white.
Etching shadows darkly in reflected light.
  Nothing moves
  Nothing whispers
All is silence.
All is snow.

 —*Eileen Foulks*

Untitled

The dawning day awakens like a symphony
    The subtle flutes are trilling in the light
A cacophony of birds sing obligato
    As the sun shows signs of conquering the night.

Morning glories fold their petals outward
    To view the spectacle before their eyes
Colors are reflected in the dewdrops,
    As shades of pink and yellow paint the skies.

Sunbeams straight from heaven pierce the forest
    Making shadows dance throughout the trees.
Rustling leaves join in the sunrise chorus
    Swaying in the gentle, morning breeze.

The world is now awakened, bathed in splendor.
    The symphony composed, beyond compare,
While music fills the soul in all its grandeur.
    Condolences to those so unaware.

    —Jody A. Aldrich

A Cold Morning

    The alarm goes off and it's six a.m.
     The sun is shining but very dim
The weather report said it's cold outside
And the feeling I had I just could not hide

I jump from the bed and to the bathroom I go
    There's no time to waste and this I know
     Nature is calling and I can't wait
And there's an appointment to be made at eight

    I lowered my PJ's and took a seat
And what happened next made me jump to my feet
My body was warm and the commode seat was cold
    And that gave me shivers from head to toe

    Then I realized that the house was cold
     So I guess I'm not quite that bold
To sit on the commode in a house with no heat
    Now and forever I'll always check the seat

    —Joseph T. Edwards Jr.

Little Girl

Little girl do not cry.
The sun will still shine when he is gone.
He will always be remembered in your heart.

Little girl do not be shy.
A new day begins at the break of dawn.
You will find another, now is the time to start.

Little girl do not fret.
Someone will always be there for him.
He will never be alone.

Little girl do go to sleep.
Dream of the joys of yesterday.
Still unknown, but he loves you.

Little girl, the memory of him is yours to keep.
Do not ask him to stay.
Let him go, you'll find another that will be true.

    —Bernadette Lake-Willcutt

Untitled

When I am all alone I think of you.
When I walk alone I think you are with me.
I call out your name, I hear no answer.
I look for you, but I do not see you.
I wonder if you are playing games, but I know not.

    —Katie Musgrove

Beyond The Sky

    A beauty beyond endurance;
The sun's glorious, magnificent diffidence
spills its somber coloring o'er the sky.
    Pink and orange,
    a blue of diamond brilliance
    and of coming twilight.
The departure of the day signals
    the same going of my soul-
too far away, down, and low
    beyond the beauty-
    beyond the flow of
the sweetest scented rose-
where no one else dare go.

    —Kirsten Houssell

Spring Break Fever

"Bonaparte, prone Europe's master..."
The teacher's voice pounds on - we do not listen.
All those yester-years coursed faster
Than these dull days now lagging at winter's end.
Who heeds Plato when Sappho sings?
Sings, and we desert our alphabetic rows
To follow her whenever Spring's
Blandishments destroy the fetters of our minds.

Then, farther south our fancies go,
Searching for love and life 'neath smoldering skies.
We seek, dream, but we do not know!
In those youth flocks, strewing sand and splashing sea,
We hope and risk and dare to chance
New love and laughter under a metaled sun,
And a festive ritual dance
To beating, blatant rhythmic sounds which reflect
The desires of our hearts set free
In future fields, picking the flowers of tomorrow.

    Now, fever, sand and sea are gone
    But the sage's voice still pounds on!
    —Kenneth A. Byrns

Beauty Rose (In memory of my grandmother)

It's twilight in the rose garden,
the thorns do fall away.
The petals only part old grandeur,
no longer in their day.
The garden wilts, the garden mourns
its own passing time.
It fears the chilling frost that comes,
the frost called Old Man Time.
The rose had beauty, the rose had scent;
cherished by love and God's assent.
But the garden clouds over and the sweet petals close,
Undaunted frost cometh to pluck Beauty Rose.

    —Joanne Altman

Day's End

Day is ending and the night begins,
The time for souls and living things
To rest and dream, or watch the stars,
For dogs to yap and clocks to tick,
And in the fire, dying embers flick.
Dear God, again I faltered from your way,
I did not try, and this you won't deny,
To curb my rapier tongue or make a friend,
Nor did I always seek your face
In everything, or pan the dross,
To find the golden grain.

    —Anita G. Dugger

False Security

She is the rose - delicate yet strong -
The thorns protect her from all the wrong.

Lovely to smile upon, painful to hold -
Fragrance mystifies and entices the soul.

Cultivate with love, the rose will thrive -
Try to possess it, surely it will die.

If cut at the root where life begins -
The petals will drop, life's juices will end.

Dewdrops are tears waiting to fall -
The thorns stand guard, challenging all.

Long after death, the thorns remain strong
No longer can they protect her, for the rose-
   She is gone.

She was the rose, delicate yet strong.
The thorns betrayed her -
Now she - is - gone -
   —*Lynn Grant-Berger*

An Old House

Out front where Louis played,
The Tiger pads the creaking boards
pouring holy water on the evening.
Ringing Saints in iron frames
count bread, and fish
the hungry crowd.

Rain drums Ory's Tin Roof
Beating out Melancholy Blues to the
Johns listening at the long mahogany.
The frails hustle bitter tea and
hint of four poster hospitality
up the back veranda stairs.

Bechet's band, playing Dear Old Southland,
sweats down the afternoon street,
Takes five, to get down some bets, and
spends the late afternoon on hot mattresses.
They burn a roach with the strippers
as the beds are made.
   —*Dan Morrison*

"Time"

Time is a verb, a noun, an adjective, a magazine
The time of birth is recorded, the year, the month, the day,
Now we have to work so much time
To receive some pay.

Time is a factor always moving forward
In all kinds of business and industry,
Time is bought and sold for great sums
In radio and T.V.

In travel, time schedules are prepared
For each aeroplane and each train,
For an automobile to operate smoothly
Depends a lot on the timing chain.

"Oh, I haven't the time for that task"
Is an excuse some people exercise,
But the time is always there
That they fail to efficiently utilize.

For the time of our lives we enjoy
It is God we wish, "To Thank,"
If you wish your time to accelerate
Borrow some money at the bank.
   —*Don Hensleigh*

"Remember"

Remember the way he made me smile
The times that we have shared
The way he held me in his arms,
Remember that he once cared.

Remember he was my world
How much he was meant to be
Now he has found another girl but,
Remember deep inside he'll always be with only me.

Remember how much fun we've had together
The laughter that will never fade
The times we've cried to each other,
Remember our future that we once made.

Remember I only want the best for him
If he is happy now, I will try to be too
She might be better for him than me but,
Remember, I'll always love you!!!

Remember the memories we would've held
Our life we would've shared together
Counting the sleepless days and nights but,
Remember now he is gone forever.
   —*Jaime Dunadee*

Leaves

Winters here again once more, reaching out for things to clasp
the tree's do shudder within it's grasp
while upon their limbs, the leaves prepare
for the long journey, each year, they dare
they change their colors, to form a coat
to keep them warm while they do float
upon the currents, of air they ride
to reach the place, where they shall hide
beneath the nice white, soft, new snow
till spring does make the waters flow
the old shall pass, the new shall rise
from the shells of old, where seeds now lie
to furrow themselves beneath the soil, so alive
to await the rain, so they'll survive
to reach up, from the ground, free of things now a shroud
to try in vain to reach the clouds
   —*Gerald N. Bridgewater*

April

"It's winter still,"' we moan, huddling in coats and scarves.
   The trees know better.
Their waking arms reach for the sky,
Their buds burst joyfully into green.
   For them it's Spring!

"It's winter still," we moan, watching snowflakes fall.
   The flowers shout, "No!"
Their shoots push confidently toward the sun,
Snowdrops, crocuses, daffodils proclaim rebirth.
   For them it's Spring!

"It's winter still," we moan, keeping the thermostat high.
   "O ye of little faith,"
The birds sing out their message of new life,
So lustily, you'd think their tiny throats would burst.
   For them it's Spring!

"It's winter still," we moan, but suddenly winter clothes hang
   heavy. And hearts are lighter.
We laugh as bold, gaudy dandelions usurp our lawns,
And green thumbs itch to prune and plant.
   For Us it's Spring
   —*Gwenda Fenessy*

Image

She grows up with an image to fulfill, as the rest of us. She's
the type when you meet her she's almost perfect. The blond
hair, long legs, smart, and great smile. Daddy's little girl.
Growing up she realize's life isn't full of all the
beautiful pictures daddy painted for her. Seeing homeless,
diseased, drugged out people on the verge of death. At the
age of 14 we think we know how our lives are going to turn out.
But do any of us really know how our lives are going to turn out?
They tell her drugs are bad through most of her childhood.
But as she reaches adolescence she's tired of being the
perfect, daddy's little girl, and the image that was placed
on her shoulders at birth. She wanted to be wild, try new and
exciting things that her parents didn't even want to her
thinking about. She was like a soul of death walking on the
edge of destruction, not caring who or what she destroyed in the
process. The only one who could understand her was messed
up in her own emotions. They wondered how something this
good could ruin you so bad. She finally got tired of all
the hatred, the sorrow in her life, and the world. The
pressure, the work, the constant act that she wonderful, while
really dying inside. She wonders, "Why don't I just end it
all right now?" With one last sallow, she finally fits the
teenage image.

—*Jamie Isom*

To Mother On Mothers Day 1976

Thank you for everything you've ever done - to help us along the
way.

For every hug and every kiss and for smoothing our sorrows and
troubles away.

You were never too busy to help us, never too involved to say.
No matter what happens "I've be here and I love you anyway"

For every wonderful meal "I thank you". There never was a
better cook. Lord knows you fed us well and kept us clean.

I thank the Lord you've with us and in whatever way I can I
hope I can make this Mother Day, the best God and I can plan!

—*Kathleen H. Brockwell*

A Year With No Hope

The crackling of the leaves in fall,
The way the sun shines when it's very cold.
Brown, orange, red and yellow,
I look up and see this walking fellow.
The man looks over to catch my eye,
I quickly turn then I wonder why.
Is it the way he looks that I turn away?
Is it fear that's leaving me nothing to say?
His clothes were torn, ragged and dirty,
He looked somewhat familiar to me.
I took a deep breath and approached this man,
He told me he knew and that his name was Sam.
We went to school and graduated together,
We went to parties and laughed with one another.
We were friends that had lost touch with each other,
And now I found him here in the gutter.
I felt so bad for him it ached inside,
He had been laid off of work and that's why.
He's been on the streets for a year with no hope,
No place to live so I took him home.

—*Jackie Fowler*

"Deadly Silence"

What is happening to earth they say?
 The weather is going crazy and everything
is washing away.
 It's so hot you can barely get your breath.
 There's storm's every where and causing so
many deaths.
 The ozone they say is being destroyed.
 If this keeps up can we survive much more?
 There's famine and disease spreading through-out
the land.
 The survival of mankind is growing quickly
at hand.
 We all wonder what has brought this destruction
to past.
 That earth is dying and being filled with trash.
 So all earth mourns and pangs of death
are heard.
 As we all drop our head in silence and
never say a word.

—*Mary V. Pauley*

They Call Him God

The long reeds lined the murky water like a barrier,
The wind blew warnings to those who would disturb
their master's sleep.
On his island, the mighty willow stood sentinel
as the weaker trees reached to the heavens to grab
the life giving light.
The wind blew messages through the reeds, telling those
who could hear, to be silent.
The waters of his river became still as he passed,
Animals shrank from sight, birds became silent, the wind
stopped talking, and the willows cried.
Only he had such power to cause this.
He was inferior to none, and superior to all.

—*Keith D. Koene*

Full Moon Rising

A candle is lit by a spark in the night
The wind howls by cold as the mirror reflects the light
The image appears from out of the gloom
The fear begins but is broke by doom
The candle blows out as slivers fly by
And the image is no more but a wink of the eye

The wind comes back to howl through an opened door
The moon shines bright on a bare wooden floor
A wolf howls in the forest in the moonlit night
Only to disappear with dawns early light

The door is now closed and the wind only flows
The slivers now show only eyes that glow gold

—*Karen Denise Bowers*

Heaven And Us

There once were days when life was dead.
The world was standing still.
At night I would toss, and turn in bed.
My life was not fulfilled.
And long I thought my days would be, a woeful empty pit.
But since you've come, much ecstacy has made my
pieces fit.

No other girl could take your place.
My heart has told me so.
And let's continue face to face.
To heavens gates we go.

—*Dennis Pohl Sr.*

Iowa

The snow keeps right on snowing
The wind keeps right on blowing
It's wet and mud, and water everwhere
Isn't this a crazy thing
Snowing when we know it's Spring
And everyone is cold but you and me.

The temperature just goes on down
No bright spring colors can be found
There's snow around my favorite apple tree
The birds have stopped their singing now
The only noise is the snowplow
And everyone is cold but you and me.

We live in the middle west
This season is our very best
Mother Nature has the last laugh now
Yesterday was simply great
The temperature was 88
So we'll just keep our home state anyhow.

—*Jean Jesse*

A Call To Love

Poets write about lovers the greats of them all.
    The wise pray for wisdom, love answers the call.
Loves bonding is holy no words can express.
    It's faithful and hopeful, loves gift is the best.
Love has no color, love has no race.
    can speak every language and goes every place.
    It's love that nourishes the soul.
    Its love that keeps you in control.
    To hear the human cry that's there.
    'Tis love that's needed everywhere.
The language of love is the romance of the soul.
    It gives you new life and makes you feel whole.
Puts a song in your heart, with a spring in your step.
    Refreshes the mind with a surge of new pep.
More precious than diamonds or silver and gold.
    It reaches the needy, the young and the old.
The greatest gift that's meant to be, which goes into eternity.
    To love one another, that meets Gods' command.
With a peace that will follow can heal all the land.

—*Jennie M. Wiggin*

Easter Greetings

The cold dead of Winter is in the past
The world again stirs to life at last,
Buds burst forth, to blossom soon -
And song-birds send forth a cheerful tune.

I bid you tidings of Easter cheer
Health, and happiness throughout the year,
Yes! The little song-birds on the wing -
They hail so joyful the arrival of spring.

—*Clifford F. Harp*

Mother

My memories of you, will always be, so often I think of
the worries I put you through. Your twinkling eye's melted
the angry word's our straight from the heart talk's were
sincere. For ever and always you will be, always loved an
remembered by me. Letter's together will spell a word, I
need no other, than you my mother. If I could turn back
the time, I'd still be the same, wanting your love, was like
playing a game. You blamed your self an that's not so, there's
no way to change what was to be, no way to change, what
you mean to me.

—*Judith Monds*

The Shell of Pride

I have lived so long from within a hollow tree. Looking out at
the world, such a view I can see. Only daring to be touched,
afraid of what I'd find, My actions were so coarse, like a toy
I'd let them wind. It seemed the thing to do, prying open
others' lives. To show them theirselves, let the bees from
their hives. I felt so safe inside the fortress I had made,
But upon my childish ways the sun began to fade. The wind
began to blow and the rain came falling down. It wasn't very
long before I lay upon the ground. Who would help me up, did
anyone see me fall? Will this nightmare ever end, will anyone
hear my call? To stay here would be foolish, another house I'd
surly find. I was sure it wouldn't be that hard, but found
myself entwined. I struggled to get free, but it had been so
many years. The time at last had come, I must address my
fears... I could feel from far outside someone looking in.
And thought of such a view, how it might have looked from Him.
Myself I'd never seen as my heart began to swell, I turned and
took a look and saw two eyes deep in a well. There was no
mighty fortress gleaming in the light, Or a tree so tall and
strong filled with hope and might. I'd lived like this for
years, I thought and wondered why? When suddenly the ground
shook and I could see the sky. A grip upon my hand pulled me
to my feet. I couldn't see his face, I was sure we'd meet.
I touched the wind around me, this I'd never felt. With the
warmth of the sunshine the ice began to melt.
What glory had I seen, what is this strange new place?
A taste of salt it seems, water taken from my face.
My life had passed before me, my selfishness was gone.
Me tears of pain and sorrow had closed my foolish song.
No more will I just look, at others' joy and sigh,
I have my own desires and I will place them high.
As I stand here by myself I'm part of all around me.
A piece of the Lord's glory, my heart I finally see...

—*John Starrett*

Happy Golden Years

Oh, the days of dancing and prancing are over
Their echoes now, are found in the hills
Now, we resort to fine memories
And loaded down with varieties of pills.

Now, take 2 in the morning
And take 2 at noon
And if the pain returns
Take 2 but not too soon.

The colors of pills are bright yellow
And some even purple and green
How do they know to treat ailments
They haven't heard and been seen?

So, this, then, are the golden years
But, the gold goes in pockets unseen
There is the doctor, the dentist, the therapist
They come in all sizes and big pockets too
So now as we watch all go down the drain
We wonder, would we do it all over again!

—*Emanuel Rosenkrantz*

Looking Glass

Looking glass so honest, how painful you can be
When searching you in desperation for the reality of me.

I looked at you a long time and turned to walk away
When I caught a side long glance a glimpse of yesterday.

I smiled in recognition at the image you projected
For deep within were childhood dreams, pampered and
protected.

—*Carol Hogan*

A World Of Hope

Did the World turn before destruction?

The trees were green. The seas were blue.
Their edges tinged of yellow and brown.

We play, we sing. Do we really care?
The soul is scared and deep with tension.

Sand disappears. Forests fall.
Brightness becomes dim.

I see a light. Bright, Brilliant.
Are the trees green again?
The World begins to turn.
I'm home again

—*Floyd B. Malone Jr.*

To Princess

Will there be pets present on the Great Judgment Day?
Their life span ended and they wandered away —
Surely to a place in the realms above
To warm themselves in the light of His eternal love.
My precious Princess' faithful devotion
Cannot roll off like the waves in the ocean.

Father God, love her - still lead her anew
In Your World Above with its Eternal view.
Keep her safe in the shade of the pastures green
'Til the mists roll away and she's part of the Heavenly scene.

—*Frances M. McCue*

"Allegiance"

In our D.C. home kitchen are the "Congress Cooks". Who cook
their own recipes, menus, and books. They are fond of their
own bank and their "Gourmet Awards". From those unidentified
"GOURMET LANDLORDS." Who gave OUR "representatives"
those cords?

And who raised their salary, pension and term?

It was "we the people" because we were infirm!

We've been hibernating far too long! And that, in a

Democracy,
is very wrong! We have the precious right to be free. But
also the duty to oversee! We need that old Yankee recipe!

Volumes 1776, '87, '91 as our guide. We recall lost memories
and revive our pride. We give rebirth to our obligation. To
our beautiful "Freedom Nation."

With renewed "Allegiance" in our volume 1993. For justice,
peace, and harmony. For our "home of the brave and land of the
free." Let's remodel our kitchen in Washington D.C.!

—*Georgia Kiml Pilous*

A Floweret

A floweret I picked swinging on a vine
Then held its beauty in my hand
Life did open a petal at a time
As if upon demand

How could one forget this feeling of love
To see the birth of a Floweret,
As in flight of many doves
Or a band of clarinets.

Stop touch the flower where ever may be
One will find beauty so great
All these things are free
And never, never too late.

—*Georgia E. Hacker*

Life's Passing Parade

O! How they march these men in grey and blue
Their stride was slow but the path is true
Then came the doughboys marching to the band
Their steps are quick and with rifle in hand
Row after row soldiers returning from France
The yanks are home after kicking the Kaiser in the pants
My gosh look at that, here they come more and more
The uniforms are different, but I've seen these before
Hey there goes Bob and there goes Joe
But my God they were killed in the war years ago
What is this parade I'm watching go by?
Why do they seem to be coming from the sky?
What's this, some one is grabbing me by the hand
Let go, let go, I don't want to leave this land
How long have I been watching this parade go by?
No, No, it's not my turn to join the ranks
But here I am and all I can say is "no thanks?"

—*Arthur F. Wilhelmy Sr.*

For The Service-Men Who Restored Hope In Somalia

Deep within I can feel Somalia's saying THANK YOU, for making
them smile. And for every little things you've done, to help
them live a while. Thanks for your time and for all the
the concern, that comes so naturally.
The giving of food as if Somalia, were part of your very own
family. You risked your lives, left loved ones behind, the
mission to restore hope.
By giving children food to eat, and just trying to help them
cope. You traveled many miles you had a very difficult,
strenuous job to do.
Sworn to, "Be the best you can", praying God will see you
through. I know that it must be hard, seeing little children
starve to death.
No clothes, no shoes, no hope, and in the very poorest of
health. You have brought Somalia hope for tomorrow, which
is a mighty good thing. To fill a child's heart with hope,
and the happiness it will bring.
Please continue working together with Care, Feed the
Children,
and the U. N. And hopefully we won't have a situation, like
this ever again.......

—*Evelyn Fuller Scott*

Sylvia Ruth Williams (nee Howard)

For nine months you carried me inside of you
Then in painful labor, feet first, I entered this earth
But as you held me in your arms you knew
It was worth all the pain to give me birth.

You watched me grow day by day
Teaching me right from wrong
Working hard, often without pay
So my life would be better, and long.

You couldn't give me much in material things
Yet you gave me the greatest gift of all
Your love, greater than a million diamond rings
Could never be considered small.

If I was offered my choice of a mother
It would always be you I'd choose
I would never want any other
With you I could never lose.

I love you mother so very much
It's hard to find words to convey
How I always loved your gentle touch
That brushed all my tears away.

—*Ethel June Williams Knox*

The Long Tightrope

Life is like a tightrope, getting thinner and thinner each day.
Then something tells you it won't be getting easier along the way.

For giving up is an easy thing to do.
But the tough part is going all the way through.

You start out in first grade, which wasn't hard at all.
You speed right through elementary, but after that you're
afraid you might fall.

Now you're on your tippy toes, on a thin piece of thread.
"It's impossible, there's no use," is what you said.

You want to turn for help, but find no one around.
So you turn to a crowd, but realize it's nothing but trouble
you have found.

It's up to only one person, now you see.
For life isn't as easy as one, two, three.

Life is what you make of it, that you must realize,
and remember, in their own special way everyone is wise!

—*Katie Rzadkowolska*

Why Me?

You kiss me with passion and tell me you care
    Then without warning you yank on my hair
You say not to fight and no one gets hurt
    You push me to the ground and I taste the thick dirt
I feel your cold hands brush my soft skin
    Your face looks of evil, your lips crack a grin
Without hesitation you rip off my dress
    Your hands, they explore, as your lips to mine press
Numb from the fear, I feel physically ill
    You undress yourself and I wish I could kill
My body becomes weak as I feel you inside me
    You say I enjoy this, it's in my eyes you can see
Finished you smile and tell me not to cry
    You lightly kiss my cheek, with love you say goodbye
I lie there motionless, without a single scream
    Jerking, I awake, it was all horrible dream
But my mirror tells another tale, as I scream to heavenly grace
    My reflection shows a different girl, with tears and
    a dirt smeared face

—*Jennifer Noel*

Untitled

If love be true,
    then you be you.
And I on gossamer wings will fly -
    to comfort, inspire and free your soul,
    my being ever nigh.
I will not weep at your departing,
    for it heralds your returning -
And distance creates our yearning.
    When at last there comes the quickening -
    our beings sense the mingling,
of, fingertips, lips and gazes -
    we navigate the mazes, that time
away doth cause, and for an instant,
    there is pause.
Then a look of adoration - I am reflected in your eyes.
    Oh come to me my darling, for your presence
bids me haste - to tarry would to waste,
    this moment of jubilation and
        fulfilled
            anticipation.

—*Margaret A. Stuart*

Angel's

Angel's are forever, and never are they blue.
There always near, but never far away from you.

Angel's are Gods spirit for guidance and
Protection of his people. Some angel's
were people that we knew but, some were
strangers from far or near.

When someone dies, they don't always
become an Angel. Most of them are suspended
in a world, to wait until God comes for them.

Most people that die, go before their time.
They don't even get a chance to live a full
life of their own. All of that's taken from them
and there isn't anything that can be done

That is what happened to my sister.
It also happen's to a lot of other people.
People say that life is unfair but, life
isn't what's unfair.

Death is what's so unfair. It claims the bodies of
people who deserve the right to life.
Death will always rule over life.

—*Johnny Odom*

Towards The End

The garden flowers are still blooming
There are green leafs on the willow trees,
But can you see the snow on the hills
The freezing winter is almost here.

How can you prepare for the winter
When pain and misery will enter,
When you know no more spring is coming
To warm up your soul and cold body?

No one can help you, and you hate
To face the suffering and pain
Which will surround you like a rain,
What can one do, it is too late!

It is too late to change your life
To love more and ignore the might,
But you can try to fly some kite,
Laugh and be happy for a while.

—*George Z. Libertiny*

What Is A Prayer?

(In memory of my foster sister Janie Kern)
There are many kinds of prayers
A prayer may be a simple little thank you
A child's prayer or a message from the heart

A call for help in time of need
Or for aid in making a decision
A prayer may also be a conversation
When you are alone and need to talk to a friend

Whatever the kind or reason for a prayer
God is always there to listen and understand
But most of all to answer!

—*Lorrie K. Bowers*

541

There Are Times

There are times when I am quiet and you talk
There are times when I am talkative and you listen
There are times when I am sad and you are compassionate
There are times when I am child like and you are gentle
There are times when I am loving and you are loving
There are times when I am independent and you are dependent
There are times when I need someone and you are there
There are times when I am lonely and you are comforting
There are times I need understanding and you understand
There are times your faith, wisdom, love, and understanding,
Are the only things that give me the strength to go on.
You are the Only One I need when there are times

—*Frances C. Hehn*

Peace On Earth

Ever since God made two people
there has been a fight.
Each blaming the other
When nothing went right.
Jump back honey, I smell a spat,
Get out of the way of our dog and cat.

Can a snake hypnotize a bunny?
In more than a psychological war,
everybody fighting near and far,
hold your guns on shore, jump back honey.

An eye for an eye, tooth for tooth,
the bird of the sky sweeps down.
WE have more planes and teeth, honey that's the gospel truth.

They surrender to the great speckled bird,
and the pilots guided to flight by the Great I Am,
Three cheers of the red, white and blue
yellow flying ribbons and support of uncle Sam.
If world peace comes and I pray it will
Send our boys home give the united nations the bill.

—*Clara Ingram Sandridge*

"Disease"

Amongst all the cemeteries of the world,
there is a deep, shadowy grave.

Encompassed by a gagging mist,
and lit only by the naked moon.

An endless pit growing,
spreading disastrously every hour.

Buried in the gloom are hearts bleeding with
sorrow, and emotions croaking with betrayal.

A song of misery is what they cry,
a chorus singing on their deathbed for eternity.

They cry about their murderer,
a disease so terrible it rots yours soul.

A disease...called love gone bad.

—*Ryan Fleming*

Farmer

I am a farmer,
Watch me plant my golden, yellow, white
and red dreams.
My harvest shall be,
Magic...
And music...
With some glass clear tears,
To last a million, billion, trillion years.

—*Denis Allen Trehey*

Lake

Gathering mist - a premonition
there is a full moon tonight, and stars
through the clearing can be seen

Illumination, chill of the air
not far, the lake
with me, sanctuary

The moon beckons action,
and with it questioning, common disbelief.
dispel reservations, actions shatter the facade
the spotlight, the stars: under a blanket of nature
feeling at last natural, and at once complete

Actions however clumsy
words painfully spoken:
attempts to define elusive cognitions;
a point not clear but mutually understood

The night is still with me,
forever occupying my mind
supporting my spirit, your existence
the best of a world, us
home at last...

—*James V. Hillegas*

People

We are all the same.
There is no difference.
We are sisters and brothers.
We are one,
All the same.
We all live,
We all die.
But most of all we have feelings.
Everyone cries;
Everyone lies;
But why don't people see,
That everyone is the same inside.
It doesn't matter what's on the outside,
What counts is on the inside.
For those who see past the hate,
Will see more into themselves!

—*Lisa M. Rimpf*

Where To Reflect

In today's busy world, with the push and the pull
There never seems time to review,
All the beautiful thoughts that come whisping around
And vanish before I pursue.
But, I found a place to dream a dream
Tho' my dreams may never come true.
And I found a place to think a thought
and follow it all the way through.
Where the mighty ocean meets the sand
And the gulls fly into the blue,
Where crested waves roll to etch
Their prints for a moment or two,
Where peace and quiet reign supreme
Where the vast sky covers you,
I found a place so full of space
Whole thoughts abound anew.

—*Marie Matson*

"The Contradiction"

Once in a great while.
There passes before thee,
A contradiction.

The black comes forward
With boldness and reform.
It is rigid and encompasses its heir
With shivering standards.
It is cold...It is unable to show feeling.

Amidst the solid black structure,
Is white.
It floats and comforts,
Releasing a gentle love,
And a tremendous value within the soul.

Entwined, the two transform,
They shallowly adhere to the inability to unify.
They simply are,
The contradiction.

—*Brooke Loucks*

Ivy Lea

Once upon a sunny day,
There walked a girl named Morgan Faye,
Hair so golden lips so red,
She stumbled on a flower bed,
Beside the flowers was a translucent pool,
And oh the water felt so cool,
Gathering up her skirt she waded ankle deep,
And watched silver coy swim near her feet,
Before her lay an ivy lea,
In the center there grew a great tree,
It rose far above the rest,
As if to greet its lovely guest,
The tree invited Morgan to dance and play,
Beneath it's canopy for the rest of the day,
When night fell,
It broke the spell,
And Morgan was alone,
It caused her such great sadness she went home,
Yet she knew of all the places she could be,
She'd rather go to ivy lea.

—*Etanna Sack*

God Chose To Loan You An Angel

I knelt beside my daughter's grave—but found
There were no more tears left to shed—only emptiness remained
I wanted so desperately to forget, but I remembered well,
The winsome smile of my sweet, little Gabrielle,
With her soft, bouncing curls of yellow gold
And sparkling, sky blue eyes.

I remembered the horror I felt that day, when I
Looked up and saw a drunken driver had jumped the curb
And was swerving across our front lawn
To strike down the innocent little child playing there.
There was such panic as I rode beside her in the ambulance
And shock and disbelief when the doctor came to say
"I am so sorry but your little Gabrielle is gone."

I became aware that Grandma was beside me,
Come to comfort me and share my grief.
"My child," she said, "There will come a day when you'll
realize your little Gabrielle was needed up in heaven,
And when your hurt and pain subside you'll be so thankful
That God chose to loan you an angel—
Even if it was only for a little while."

—*Mrs. Kenneth L. Slaughter*

All My Tomorrows

All my tomorrows are in God's hands.
There's nothing for me to fear.
Hard times may come, disappointments abound,
But the Holy Spirit and victory are near.
The Father looks down from His Heavenly throne;
Nothing escapes His watchful eye.
For He loves us so much, He had a plan;
His Son, our Mediator, on high.

Jesus can give us Eternal Life;
Paid for by His shed blood on the cross.
Now accept that sacrifice, so supreme;
For Life, rather than loss.

Your soul is worth much more
Than all the wealth on the Earth.
You'll not regret the day
You receive a brand New Birth.

The Son of God is coming again;
A promise He made before He went away.
Could be any day, "look up"
It could even be Today.

—*Eileen M. Just*

I Am, You Are

Gaze into my eyes
There's so much love
I'm the blue sky that hovers above
The fire that warms you in winter
You are the flowers that bloom in spring
You are my summer sun
You are autumn's golden gown.

I am a mighty oak so firmly rooted in your love
You are the rain which nurtures my growth
I am your shelter when the storm rolls in
You are the water which quenches my thirst for life
You are my food for thought
I am the wind which parts your hair
I am the evening star which guides you home...

—*David G. Harrison*

A Friend

A friend is there when you need a lift,
They are there, even when away you drift.
They are there when you feel like you want to die.
They are there, to hold your hand, when you need to cry.
They know when you have a need to talk,
Or stay quietly by your side when you'd rather walk.
A friend always knows when you're feeling depressed,
They reach out and touch with a loving caress.
They are always there when the going gets rough,
To prove that your need for love is always enough.
They are there for you through thick and thin,
Maybe they leave but return again and again.
They are there when you're scared, when you drift afar,
They don't ask where, when or why, they just are.
They are always willing your pain to share,
Like me, they show others they really care.
For riches will not buy this kind of friend,
This kind is always there and will be to the very end.

—*Leuna Perry Ferguson*

Remembrances

Impressions we accumulate are treasures of the mind,
they bring to us again the happy days we left behind.
They open wide our memory gates and bid us come within;
and oft they bring us back to where and
what we might have been.
The saddened woman wrinkled, aged and bent with many a care
thinks often of the carefree girl with flowers in her hair.
The old man with a cane who walks the square each day at three
smiles sadly as he sees a little urchin climb a tree,
or yell so lustily while playing tag or hide-and-seek,
or take off his shoes and stockings to go wading in the creek.
These treasures we can never bring ourselves to leave behind.
Although we may be old and worn they're always in our mind.
The outer shell may tarnish and grow dull 'tis very true,
but the inmost part is just as bright as when it was quite new.

—*Elizabeth Trouve' Callison*

Queen

Unadorned, she sleeps amidst the garbage of the street;
they call her Queen, those that do attend her—
the rats and birds of the alleyways.
Her blanket is a garbage bag, her undergown of colored rags
peeks through, and a belt of hemp encircles her waist.
For a crown, the birds brought bits of string and foil
to nest in her tattered hair; the rats gave her a scepter,
fashioned from a piece of broken iron pipe.
The Queen would walk her fief scavenging bits of food;
hoarded morsels she shared nightly with her subjects as they
gathered in the great hall of the Alley, decorated with
tapestries of soot and graffiti.
When the feasting had ended, the Queen would retire; throughout
the night, her subjects kept watch o'er her safety, lest
intruders venture too close and threaten the Domain.
If perchance an intruder threatened, the birds, encircling his
head, would peck at his eyes, then the rats would scurry
forth to gnaw at his feet. As the sun descends upon her
chamber, the Queen smiles; so rich is her kingdom, so loyal
are her subjects.

—*Marilyn A. Leahy*

Getting Old

No one wants to grow old today,
  They emphasize staying young.
When wrinkles begin to appear on your face,
  The ageing has just begun.
Your hair may turn gray or bald just a bit
  Your walk start to falter you're not quite as fit.
Teeth may become false eyeglasses a must
  We must try to look young
Stay in fashion or bust.
  So what can we do.
To accomplish all this?
  A facelift for some
Brings happiness and bliss.
  Color your hair,
It cannot be gray.
  Join a gym, be healthy,
Keep extra pounds away.
  Whatever path you choose we are told.
If you just live long enough
  You're bound to get old.

—*Ethel Hiller*

Brother Let Us Pray

Two men walked in the darkness,
  They fumbled, they stumbled, grew lame.
Each man complained to the other,
  And each thought the other to blame.
The way grew rougher and steeper;
  They longed for a light on the way,
Then one man said to the other,
  "Brother, let us pray."

It doesn't matter who spoke first,
  His color, his caste or his creed.
What matters is one of them did speak,
  And the other man heard and took heed.
Profound the truth, yet so simple,
  For when they two could agree
To look for light from Jesus
  They found they both could see.

—*Irene O. Gulledge*

Romp

When is it to be listened to and when is it to be heard. When
they grab your wrists, bruised, lace your blood with chains
that have attached themselves to the ground, taunting you with
dreams you can see through the cracks of the skyscraper fences.
One more day, one more closer to the cold, black ground.

From your fingertips escapes the desire through the cracks and
you can no longer see it, the wall so blinding, and you are so
close to the ground and so hollow as you realize you've
forgotten it anyway.

And you are so close to the cold, black ground that you no
longer have fingertips or wrists and your blood is slowly
sipped, once spent on that dark, dark day.

I mean to tell you I was wound so tight, his eyes so pure, deep
as infinity itself and he stared with an inexhaustible stare,
but I had to break it, broken as my soul into tiny bits,
emptied like turning you upside down to let the pocket change
fall to the ground, but that's all it is, pocket change
scattered helplessly on the cold, black ground.

—*Carmen Dempsey*

Down Memory Lane

Life is filled with many things
they happen to beggars as well as kings.
Each has fond memories he holds dear
perhaps, to bring a loved one near.

Life could end in complete despair
if we had no one our dreams to share
and, youth must have that kind of friend
who always helps his woes to mend.

Then, when you reach your golden age
and, your life turns over another page
you can rejoice and feel much bolder
because he walked with you shoulder to shoulder.

—*Ellen Biggerstaff*

The Wind

The wind is a soft white swirl.
Though you may not always be able to see it,
The wind is still there.
It sways in the high tops of trees.
Hides in the bottoms of the oceans.
Floats through school windows to its desk and chair.
Then it winds back up to heaven where it there dies down
And rests for the night till the next windy day.

—*Kristin Gigliotti*

Fledgling

Robert Fulghum has a theory that whatever people know.
They learned in kindergarten, a long, long time ago!

   Examining this further, he has also theorized.
   That the reason we are sent to school is to come out
   civilized!

Though his proposal makes some sense, I can't fully agree!
At least, in my experience, it meant much more to me!

   It marked the day that I had grown enough to spread my wings!
   To leave the safety of my home, and try many new things!

My journey back through memory reminds me, too, of tears —
The vastness of the place new rules, aroused so many fears!

   Important to this reverie, my teacher! Giant — Tall!
   Incredibly, as I grew up, in turn, she grew more small!

Until this time, I'd always felt firmly attached to ground!
Another separating force—the school bus came around!

   It swallowed all the little folk, leaving the moms behind,
   And journeyed far away from home, fear swelling in my mind!
As time went on, a wondrous thing began to come to pass,
The roots so anchored in the home transplanted to the class!

   I didn't need to sever roots while testing my new wings!
   Experience has taught me this - each journey, firmness brings!
      —*Joyce A. Poirier*

Then There Was One

There once were two creatures, one big and one small.
   They lived well together, no problem at all.
Until the rain stopped and the land went dry,
   the small one couldn't reach the food that was high.

The tall one was hungry and it didn't care,
   as long as it could eat the food that was there.
The small one cried out before it died,
   "I thought you loved me. I guess you lied."

The rain returned, the tall one ate.
   It missed the small friend, but it is too late!
Animals or people, I'll let you choose.
   Either way, the small ones lose.
      —*Linda S. Ripley*

The Sands

Tears trickle down my face, I am in much disgrace.
They represent a love gone bad, they represent a world
gone mad. I live on my broken dreams, my life is like a
flowing stream, always moving, constant motion,
pouring out into the ocean. All my fears I try to hide,
this pain that I must disguise is taken with the tide.
I'm just another grain of sand, lost along this ocean band.
A bird is flying over head, it represents the love I send.
Each grain of sand under my feet, the waves thrashing on the
beach, further and further they try to reach.
The shells left behind in the sand, like the ones that stayed
when I was sad. The crystal cool water splashing on my thighs,
like the memories coming back from my early life.
Soon the waters will be calm, my purpose here will be done.
Nothing will remain, except a sea of grains.
      —*Casey Hickman*

A Tribute To My Friend

We were like sisters, you and me
They said Siamese twins is what we should be
together all day, together all night
never apart, never did fight.

Then one evening, during the fall
8 o'clock came and you never did call
It soon became late, "Traffic" I said
While horrible pictures flashed through my head.

And then the phone rang, a tale of bad news
A tragedy happened, my friend I did lose
A drunk driver, a wild man, a nut or a loon
What ever he's called, her time was too soon!

He was real drunk, he hit them head on
He totaled their car, now she is gone
He walked away with a mangled fender
They rolled her away, in a bag, on a stretcher

Am I selfish? I often wonder
To want my friend here, and him 6 feet under
      —*Becky Tita*

Ground Hog Time

When all the old men get together
They say us ground hogs can predict the weather
And all say the ole women say it's true
That we ground hogs come out on February two

Dean Sturgill knows and probably a few others
The mating urge awakes us and we dig from our burrows
If the skies be black or if the skies be blue
We ground hogs are out all February through

You see ground hogs must frolic in the February hay
If our young are to be born in the green fields of May
Romeos and Juliets we could very well be
But weather forecasters we're not, you see

If this untruth you have believed for 66 years
We hope the truth will bring you laughter instead of tears
Still on February second we would like to say
We and Dean wish you a happy, happy ground hog day
      —*Dean Sturgill*

Troubles

Troubles are something we all have
they seem to follow us every where.
I have learned to deal with it in
such a way that now I don't care.
The more you try to avoid these
troubles that seem to follow you.
When they come to you on these days
it seems the entire world turns blue.
Some people call these days, days
of depression or maybe loneliness.
What ever they turn out to be to you,
you will be one or the other I guess.
So let it be, troubles will come
on this there is no doubt what so ever.
If you can beat these days on your own
you can assume you are very clever.
      —*Dudley Woodward*

Where Do The Tears Go?

Where do the tears go when they don't fall?
  They well in your eyes, then disappear.
So where do they go? Where do they disappear?
  They fall to your heart with a tightening pain,
    filling it up a little at a time.
Absorbed into your soul are those tears,
  gripping your heart with pure pain.
Each time you prevent your tears from falling
  is another time you cheat your heart of love.
    Love for yourself!
So where do the tears go when they do fall?
  They whisper away with the wind and the pain,
    releasing your heart once again.
To show yourself love,
  you must cry now and then,
    washing away at least some of the pain.
  —Kimberly Pennington

Requiem (For the Living)

And why should they have Eden-like surroundings?
They who cannot see or feel
They who cannot talk or hear
They who cannot take a breath
Why the flowers that they cannot smell?

The lawns are carefully manicured and groomed
The trees provide more than ample shade
For what? For whom?

They cannot see the beauty, feel the shade
Nothing in them moves, nothing in them lives
They sleep without dreams, undisturbed
The wonder of the earth does nothing for them

Is it for us, the living, that we do what we do?
Is if for us, the parks, the flowers, the trees?
Is it for us, the living, the wonder of the earth?

The dead cannot see or feel
They cannot talk or hear
They cannot take a breath

For what and for whom are graveyards for?
  —David Lessard

The Women Who Won't

The modern day women won't take no talk,
They'll knock you down, and over you they'll walk.
Very few women are left in the kitchen,
The ones who are there, are still bitchin',
Women have filled many a man's shoes,
They smoke, they curse, and even drink booze.
They speak their minds, and walk like men,
She don't kiss no ass, but she'll kick yours in the end.
They're not old fashioned, not today's young girl,
You'll give her some money, and she'll rock your world.

  —David Usery

"Wind"

The wind is clear invisible to the eye,
The wind is alive whirling, whispering, waving
I wonder how we know it's there,
I've heard people say the wind can talk
Quietly, secretly, silently, and now
I know that is true, for in the night
Sometimes I hear the mournful cry,
Of the wind...
  —Laural Schweiger

Celebrating 40

Not many marriages left to say
They've made the 40 years today.

Perhaps they may just give it up
Or maybe they never had the love.

The years of love and sacrifice
Have given you rich memories of your life.

Together you watched your dreams come true,
Richly deserved by both of you.

Keeping a marriage takes hard work,
Determination and a feeling of self worth.

It takes a very unselfish love.
All of which you both sure have.

So stand up and be proud today,
For many never see the way.

Of giving and caring the joys and tears
That brought you two to 40 years.
  —Teresa L. Wells

Portrait Of A Painter's Death

He liked to paint—not masterpieces, chalk pastels—but useful things
Like weathered garden charis, window trim, and backyard swings.
He liked his painting clothes; stained hands and face
Were part of that painter's portrait. It was a case
Of one man working against time's erosion
Of everyday possessions. Some days he'd take a notion
To repaint all the flaking trims of windows here and there,
His ever-present stogie in his mouth, his right arm
brushing in the air.
And that's what killed him. The day he died
He'd planned to finish all the backdoor trim—
A bright, cool, sparkling time in fall when pride
Could be taken in a man's work; but for him
It was his last. He sat and rested from the job beside a
gutter spout,
Set down his lit cigar; and then its spark, and his, went out.
  —Jean Costen Carr

It Is Faith

Now faith is the substances of thing hoped for the evidence of
things not seen. Through faith we understand that the world
was framed by the word of the only King.

It is faith, It is faith, It is faith that I'm standing on.
It is faith, It is faith, It is faith that will lead me home.
It was faith that made the lame man walk, and caused the blind
man to see. Faith made the dumb man talk, and faith has got
a hold of me.

It is faith, It is faith, It is faith that I'm standing on.
It is faith, It is faith, It is faith that will lead me home.

Now it is faith that keeps us standing upon a very high
mountain top. Faith will let us know when to go, and let
us know when to stop.

It is faith, It is faith, It is faith that I'm standing on.
It is faith, It is faith, It is faith that will lead me home.
  —Donna Buzzell

Lost Child

The walls of time grow thick between us
There is still time to reach through the cracks
And pull ourselves to one another
But if you wait too long the walls will be
Too thick for our fingertips to reach
And we will be lost to one another forever
For death is the thickest wall of all
  —Dike E. Deitchler

Always And Forever

As I walked along the sea,
Thinking of him,
Watching the waves come crashing down,
And the form that slowly disappeared,
I saw my dream disappear with it.
The dream of a perfect romance,
My first love and my first kiss or so it seemed.
And as I sat there all alone,
I remember him
And our perfect romance.
And I remember him saying:
"When you dream, dream of me always and forever:"
The waves disappeared, but I knew
That my perfect romance would always be there,
Always and Forever.

—*Dawn Lee*

The Romantic Fantasy

While I sit in the warm summer sun
Thinking of things that will never be.
A picture of you slowly drifts into mind
I think of you and I together
Walking hand in hand down a sandy beach at sunset
The waves are slowly washing over our feet
All of a sudden you drift away
Just as you had drifted in
I awake to a gentle breeze and a memory of the romantic fantasy
With hopes that you will see the same fantasy as me

—*Holly Wollin*

Cancer Of Mind And Soul

Death approaches me soon, for I have cancer.
This cancer has strained my mind and body for the lust and love
of life.
Why me, Oh God, and I pray for my soul.
Many of my relatives and friends have died this way, there
bodies ravaged with pain.

I think of this and it reminds me of what lies ahead of me,
But my love and belief of God will ease my pain and I will die
in piece.

How thankful I am to know that heaven awaits me, to be with
loved ones that were lost.
For those that I leave behind, I leave my love to them in
remembrance of me.

There belief and prayers for cancer cures that will soon come.
will be blessed and well deserved.
For you who follow my path, the way to glory and God is prayer
and belief in him.

—*David E. Conrad*

This My Land

This is my country proud and free.
This is my country my liberty.
My faith in God.
My willingness to give.
Makes it a better place for us to live
Those men who have fought and died
With loyalty and pride
So why do we take it all in stride.
Stand up and be a proud American
Remember those who died for this our land
Learn the way and help our fellowman
This is my country proud and free
Let's keep it that way
Our land of liberty

—*Deborah Foutch*

"A Country Boys Dream"

Since I was a young boy. I have always had
this dream. That someday I would stand on
stage and pick my guitar and sing. I want the guys
in the band, who are called the Chances R to play
the music loud before a country music loving crowd.

This country boys' dream is to sing a country
song. For the love of country music lies deep
within my soul. Mama always told me, son, be
proud of who you are, and don't you let nothing
stand between you and your country boy's dream.

Now you know there ain't nothing like giggin
with the boys in the band. To get to play in some
honkey tonk every now and then to play that
favorite country song in my cowboy hat and jeans
is only just the start of this country boys' dream

I have to follow this dream that I have. No
matter where that it may lead. For if I don't take
the leap, then how am I going to take the fall.
I have to know that at least I tried to make
this country boys' dream come alive.

—*Brenda Birchfield*

The Children Are Gone

The children are gone, and all that I am left with————
Is this house which is no longer a home. So much freedom I've
never known. Now I'm free to go where I want to go and do what
I want to. But now it seems—there's nowhere to go, and
nothing to do. Because-wherever I go and whatever I do————
There is a part of me that is always blue. The children are
gone——But the Love and Responsibility lingers on. The
feeling of motherhood is strong—— And it hurts down in the
marrow of my bone. I can't sleep at night————Because I
wonder if they're all right. I want to hold my baby tight,
Everything is wrong and nothing ain't right. God please help
me make it through the night!!!!!! And if I make it through
the night——Then I must get up and face the day. And as I
live through each and every day, I must continue to pay.
Because I took the wrong way. Lord, I must be a sight, my life
of pain is at it's height. Before it was too late. Why didn't
I ever——see the light?????

—*Peggy J. Collis*

Addiction

It is so hard to resist you
This I know for I have tried many times before.
You have this unbelievable power over me
And danger is what I pay with.

I can do without you though
I have proved it many times
But I ask myself why I have to prove it over and again.

Do you still have control over me or I over you?
Can you be controlled or must you always take over?

Well, you cannot have me for I am all mine.
You cannot have my life again
Because no more will I walk down that bitter road.

I do not want anymore pain.
I do not want anymore hurt for anyone.

As I sit here and write
I ask God of any religion
Or if a greater power simply exist
To give me strength
For I do not want to lose anymore.

—*Marie Felix*

547

My Prayer

Lord, make me poor in spirit,
This is the prayer I pray.
I want to be your servant
And live for you each day.
Teach me to mourn Lord
For my sins and the sins of others;
To be meek
So that I might serve You and my sisters and brothers.
I want to tell others who need to hear
Their hunger can be satisfied and He is near.
I long to be merciful as You would have me be
So the mercy of God, I can clearly see.
I pray to be pure in heart my whole life through,
To walk in righteousness and be more like You;
To be a peacemaker beginning now, -
Lord, help me today, show me how.
When treated unjustly I need to be strong;
I want to rejoice when things go wrong.
This is my prayer as I live through each day.
I know God will answer and show me the way.

—*Helen B. Hanson*

Mystery

There is mystery in never having seen one's own face
This mirror reflects the inner self
The heart beat is a love song
A soul satisfied with its own goodness
Simply being, is a joy

Likewise, the mirror may portray a life of pain
Depict thwarted intellect,
Destroyed self esteem, and distorted emotions
These victimize the perception
The face is a caricature

After encountering various passages
The facility to discern changes
With time, comes new insight and deeper dimensions of thought
Beautiful and ugly become relative
And alas, the realization that beauty is only an idea

—*Mavis McKenzie*

Reminiscing

Grandpa George has a twinkle in his eyes
Tho' his hair is as white as the snow.
He's a lot of fun just to sit and listen to,
And there's so much he seems to know.

"I remember the time—", he so often starts;
His imagination runs high and wild.
"And there I was, surround—", he expounds!
What thrills in the mind of a child!

And like all other normal old-timers,
He relives those days he once knew;
Like a key to a chest of great treasures,
His stories let the past come through.

He jokes and he laughs ever freely,
A pleasure to all loafers near by,
But wait! What is that dark shadow
Lying deep behind the twinkle in his eye?

Could it be he's laughing through sorrow
Over a loved one who has gone by the way?
Still he laughs as daily he mingles,
Spreading pleasures along on his way.

—*Joe B. Herron*

Strange Dream

You wake up wondering why dreams seems so real,
Those strange scenes they sometimes reveal,
Watching a woman at the end of a cottonfield row,
In anguished pain break the handle of a garden hoe,
Not wanting to look at her, but I knew I must,
As she watched the billowing trail of the wagons dust
A few days ago it happened at the market clock,
Watched her children being sold at the auction block,
No one could know this woman heartaches and fears,
But you could feel the pain unmasked by tears,
All the memories that are left for her to keep
Just shadows in dreamless sleep,
This dejected woman devastated and forlorn
Mourning loved children she wished were never born,
Mothers loved and mothers tears are all that's left for the
coming years, callous man has torn her world apart,
Leaving an earthly shell with its breaking heart,
Not able to stand this life shattering blow,
She falls asleep forever
Across the broken garden hoe......

—*George F. Brown*

Be Encouraged

At times it seems that nothing is going right, God. It's as
though my trust is growing weaker and weaker each day, and soon
my whole purpose will wither and die. I feel so useless, so
unnoticed! Sometimes, I think that no one would even notice if
I were gone. So, I cry out to You with all my heart. "O Lord,
please strengthen me, fill me with joy and let love shine
through me!" As I finish praying to the only one who can help
me, I lift my hands toward heaven. Lord, what a wonderful
feeling to have You reach down, lift me up, and hold me close
to You. In Your presence I feel a great peace and warmth.
Then I realize that even if the whole world was out to destroy
me that you would be with me. To strengthen me, love me, and
give me courage to endure. My desire is to be in your arms
forever and to be in sight of your caring eyes.

—*Kerry Luckow*

It's In The Stars

I know that I care for you
Though you don't care for me,
But, darling, I can't live without you,
See me bending in my knee.

It's in the stars that you and I can never be,
So for just a little while, we can pretend.
It's in the stars, together we shouldn't be,
So for now, you will be my friend.

A friend can be so special,
That he becomes my love,
And now it can be very crucial,
Will I ever be his love?

It's in the stars that you and I can never be,
So for just a little while, we can pretend.
It's in the stars, together we shouldn't be,
So for now, you will be my friend.

—*Lynn E. Henk*

Paper

Glaring white blindness
Threatening edges lined with precision
Foreboding corners that keep you ensnared

Paper should be more seductive
Enticing your secrets
Your essence absorbed
Into each of its cells

Instead of the standard
8 1/2 x 11
Manipulated carcass
Of a dead tree
—*Chrys Egan*

Nine Long Months

  First one then two, before I even know
Three then four, before I start to show
  There's no mistaking at, five and six
Starting to get big and feel the kicks
  Getting uncomfortable, at seven and eight
Starting to hope, that I'm not late
  Then comes nine, the worst of all
The labor and delivery, I still recall
  The unbearable pain, I promised never again
I thought that labor, would never end
  Then delivery, with pain so real
Finally the doctor said, "It's a girl!"
  He set you in my arms, you looked like a doll
It was that moment I knew, you was worth it all.

—*Linda L. Gray*

Prospective

Baby, this that is felt that comes from with-in you;
Through physical and Psychological Views,
Always at Peace, No matter what others seem to do;
This Tranquility, Still keeps shinning through.
Love to feel your loving and tender touch,
If torn apart, My heart would crush!
Enjoying your Perspectives, That are good,
No matter what the situation, You've always understood.
Time has given you a special kind of "PROSPECTIVE."
Not to anyone, Have you been in anyway Disrespective.
Obtaining the Ultimate Essence of In-sight,
Heart and Soul of you, Shines through like a light.
Since you've came, A projection of strong desire,
A feeling of Security, and Love has been transpired!
Receiving your knowledge, Puts joy in my heart,
Just by being yourself. Don't ever want to part.
Having such a good attitude on Social Objectives;
So glad to have you near, with your Over-all "PROSPECTIVE".

—*Carr O. Root*

Untitled

The shade lifted momentarily,
through the ice spattered window
mountains stretch strongly and delicately
upwards as we bounce through their blanket
of clouds. Rolling green and growing
cities hold tight to these ice age
remnants. A small pool of melt still stands,
reflecting upward shards of new sun shimmer
in the sunlight. Up here it's still a beautiful
gift from God. The shade closes. The aerial
portrait now just a memory, breathtaking, but
the real beauty shares the memory and sits by my side.

—*Keith Soffner*

Thoughts

The peacefulness of the night air with the wind whispering
  Through the pines, sings a song that soothes the soul.
'Tis great to be alive enjoying God's late show. The heavens
  Above and the breeze below makes you never want to go from
This mountain meadow to the valley below. The night air is
  So fresh and clean, the stars so clear and bright. As
You gaze in awe at the vastness of the universe, you realize
  What a small part you play. You become aware of the
Complexity of the soul. How you came to be, what will become
  Of humanity? Is it the kindness that you show or the deeds
That you do, that will cause people to remember you. It is so
  Quiet and peaceful here that you forget your fears, you
Forget your tears as you bring back the years of your youth.
  Oh how long ago they seem. When times get lean we like to
Look back to when it was fun, when we were young, when troubles
  We had none. All these thoughts and so much more,
Wait for you when you venture into the great outdoor.

—*Charles Robert Fransham*

Special Mothers

Mothers are so special
  Through the years of our lives.
They're there when we're young,
  And also when we're wives.

They teach us the good things,
  How to avoid the bad,
And never to regret
  The things we never had.

We never really miss them,
  As through our lives we go,
But when they go to Heaven,
  We really miss them so.

Oh, Mom, how I miss you!
  You seem so far away.
Thank God, just not as far
  As you will be some day.

So, while I have the chance,
  I'll say, "I love you so,"
Because, I won't be able
  To say it when you go.
—*Janis Happy*

"Kindred Spirits"

I face heaven for wings to sue
Thy tender kiss through global dawn.
Muse glides higher and fealty swan
Beams rays of sunrise upon you.
Quondam words of thine accrue,
Furled Christmas morn and gift withdrawn,
Spent laureled crown and hilltop lawn,
African plains and skies clear blue.

Yonder glowed moon in gay entire
Calms curves of sighs to sleep,
Where Angels whisper and conspire,
And midst constellations speak...

  'Nary Soul could be nigher
  Than thy breath upon my cheek.'
—*Elizabeth Dawn Bender*

Resurrection

The tiny seeds sleep in the warm brown earth
'Til the call of the gentle spring rain
Awakes them from slumber to a new birth
To grow tall and lovely again.
So shall it be when in dreamless sleep
I lie in the heart of God's earth.
I shall hear silver notes of a great trumpet sound
And shall rise again to new birth
For death cannot hold, 'tis only a dream,
Of silence and calm through the years.
Til the great, glad day of Jesus' return.
What a promise to still all my fears!

—*Iva Campbell*

Reflections

We raised our children as best we could,
To be honest and loving - as all children should.
We taught them their lessons to help them get smart,
We taught them to love from within the heart.
We gave them the courage to stand out alone;
"Be not a pebble - but be a stone."
We gave them their wings and helped them to fly,
Encouraging them to aim for the sky.
Our hopes for our children are the best we could give,
And will go on forever - for as long as we live.
These are our memories of days by gone,
Our standards of life to be carried on.
Though futures do change, the basics remain,
For future generations to have and maintain.
We pray that our children's children will share,
In the goodness of life and loving care.
We've had our share of good and bad,
Our ups, our downs, our happy, our sad.
Our family is close - as close as can be,
For this is our Family History.

—*Donna Crabtree*

Life's Steps

The early ones are timid and meek,
To be—the only goal they seek.

Soon, they're quick and light and free,
Surging with their youthful energy.

Then they crest the apex of their tenure,
Here perhaps, their purpose to inure.

But down the curve they surely must go,
And finally become bent, and low to slow.

Oft times, they have born a heavy load,
And cares have pressed them to the road.

Yet all will finish their own race,
And all will come to the same place.

Into eternity to be cast——
Now is it the first—or the last?

Some glance to the past, some will pray,
What was held back—or tossed away?

The crossing to forever——all must pass,
The bridge——is yesterday's looking glass.

—*Janice Collins*

Daddies Little Girl Grows Up Too Fast

Today is my only daughter's marriage and all I have is memories to cherish.

As memories begin to form, I see my little darling just being born.

As I walk her down the aisle, I felt the father's love flowing for my grown child.

Report cards, scraped knees, bedtime stories and trips to the zoo help bring loving memories into view.

Her first date, school activities and keys to the car, I then knew this day of reckoning would not be far.

As I hold back the tears from my eyes, I know I must release a father's ties.

She has grown to a beautiful woman with a mind of her own, and is starting on a trip of life I have known.

—*Gary Lynn Grice*

"I Am Retired"

The older I get, the more I'm inspired
To do all the things that I have desired.
But very close budgeting is now required,
For money is short since I have retired.

I won't do today, and feel no sorrow,
What can be put off until tomorrow.
Times goes by so quickly for one who's aspired
So long for the joy of being retired.

I sleep in in the morning, stay up late at night.
There aren't any business rules for me to fight.
Though housework and paperwork are not admired,
There's no rush to do them - I am retired.

I talk with my friends, and sit with the kids,
Play with the dogs, do what volunteer work bids.
I'm reading the books that I have acquired.
Happiness indeed is being retired.

I watch some TV or am on the go.
As an at leisure person, I'm now a pro.
No matter what I do, I can't be fired,
For I'm now my own boss - I am retired!

—*Jeanette L. Lascelles*

"A Dream"

I have a dream, as if I may
To dream alone, on a windy day
as I dream, I often pray
Oh Lord, who's so far away
help me please, as I pray this say
apart my bondage, as I abide your faith.

Oh Lord may I say this today, as I
often pray, to you who's so far away, to
abide your holy faith.

Oh Lord as I pray, may I be to you and
all the rest, faithful, loyal, and honest, nevertheless,
be divine, and keeping in mind, your faith, I've
searched to find, is a blessing to me, and mankind.

—*Martha McCree*

Winners Are Losers

Everyone wants to be number one
to finish the race, and be the first one done
well, somebody always has to be last that's how it is, was,
and will be in the future, present, and past
Have you ever thought losers are the best?
they let the others win, and take all their jests.
Never stopping, but keeping going,
all the while thinking and knowing,
that in the end no one they'll face
nobody will know that they finished the race.
That is why losers, the trophy should get
for they are the ones who never quit.

—*Jennifer I. Solem*

Legacy Of Love

A divine love was sent our way,
To guide the disciples of Christ.
We love God first, mightily or pay.
Our neighbors as our self we suffice.

Love of heart we find, trust and sincerity.
It can be felt together or apart.
Love one another is a Godly law of clarity.
An everlasting love he had at the start.

A deceptive love is always around.
Guard against subtle destructive lures.
Good conscious and peaceful hearts are found.
Let brotherly love continue for sure.

A spirit was given also to guide.
One spirit bears witness with another.
When two loves are tested and tried.
By this you know your true brother.

—*Elwanda C. Partin*

A Spring Day

A spring day, what a day! The ground seems
  to have nothing but flowers.

Which is such a beautiful scene. It could
  possibly be stared at for several hours.

Each side of the driveway was outlined with
  at least fifty or more roses.

Which was pleasant smell for my little
  puppies' noses.

My puppies are very sweet; maybe one a
  little more petite than another;

or maybe one is a little more neat
  than another.

They each have a little black nose,
  and each have a beautiful soft
white fur coat. They play with
  one another, like they would rather
have no other brother.
It's completely different in my case.
  I, myself and my brother would
rather not know one another.

—*Eric Black*

America Is Calling

America is calling, the young, the brave, the free
To join its strong assembly lines and work for liberty!
The workers in the factories are loyal to their vow,
The struggle for democracy unites the nation now.

The challenge has been answered, with brain and brawn and skill.
The people do not hesitate, but work with iron will.
The farmers plow the fertile fields and harvest bumper crops
To overcome the shortages and feed the folks in shops.

The miners tear the earth apart and dig for iron coal.
No effort is too burdensome till we achiever our goal.
Our victory must break the chains of hate and poverty,
And bring a lasting brotherhood— the true democracy!

—*David Boyd*

The Pain Of Letting Go

God could see that he was tired, his body ached with pain.
To leave him here on earth there was nothing more to gain.
He had lived a good life, his regrets were but a few.
From Norwegian-Swiss decent, was this man that we knew.
We'll remember those strong hands, that stuccoed houses and built hay
mows. They drove the trucks and tractors and reined his horse
to check the cows. He declared his earthly race was over, he
had made a long hard run. He was now leaving "it" with The Father
and His Son. With his hands clasped in prayer, asking for
forgiveness and relief. He told his family members "It's ok"
don't be filled with grief. The Lord was ready now, reaching
out to take those hands. Burdens and cares of this world
lifted, leading him to a peaceful land. The last several days
and weeks have been hard that is true. But with the faith that
we all shared we've all made it through. Thanks Dad for all
those moments in life we shared. All the things that you
taught us showed that you cared. We will meet you afar in
a life that is new. Where there's no pain or sorrow and the
skies are always blue. With tears of sorrow and the pain of
letting go. We will hold tight to fond memories of this man
that we loved so.

—*Linda Harpster*

Mother Earth

The Earth deserves another try,
To let this horrible century pass by.
To let the pollution float away,
The ozone to recover;
And the atmosphere reconstruct nicely.

The pollution is the hazardous chemical,
That pollutes the air we breathe;
It's killing us all and all things.

The ozone has a hole from the pollution
Not protecting us from the sun's rays;
The whole population is going to fade away.

Without the ozone,
The atmosphere has no chance;
To reconstruct and enhance.
Do you feel the same?

—*Bonnie Burns*

Time Flies

The old years fly by as if they had wings
Time grows short as the pendulum swings
Man has to hurry and stay on the run
Not enough time to get everything done
The road is not rough, but goes steeply downhill
The old buggy tips, one by one we will all spill
Seems a darn shame to go, and leave all this behind
But that's the way of the world, to make room for mankind.

—*A Remle Ramble*

Untitled

I spread my wings and soar like a dove,
To look at the earth from high above.
I see the water as crystal blue, the grass as dark green,
It forms into the most picturesque scene.
The earth looks at rest, when seen from afar,
Like a place of happiness, below twinkling stars.
Everything is calm, like in the dead of night,
When everything is still, relaxing, and quiet.
The land full of peace is nice but not true,
Our world is crumbling because of me and you.
We are ruining the world created by our Lord above,
We are teaching our children to feel hatred instead of love.
World hunger and poverty, aids, and the homeless,
Environmental disasters, we've created a mess.
The land was once beautiful, until powered by greed,
Thinking only of ourselves, instead of the earth's needs.
The environment is going to hell in a hand bag, do we care?
No and we will never give a damn until it's there.
As for me, I stay a dove, and remain flying high,
Because the earth seems better off, when seen from the sky.

—Chuck Booth

Sensing Addiction

Easy fortunes! Riches to win!
To look away, the gambler's sin.
Excited hearts come quick with speed!
Feel trembling hands, the gambler's greed.

Run! Don't walk! Come push and shove!
For a taste of fame, the gambler's love.
Invest in chance! What's to lose?
The smell of green, the gamblers choose.

Now the money's gone, it's time to leave,
But listen close and you can hear them grieve.
For beneath their breath they reveal a dream,
To start again, the gambler's need.

—Chad Brian Rohman

My Dad

Farmers do the best they can,
to make it through the year at hand.
A jack of all trades; they have to be,
to keep their ship a float, you see.
They challenge mother natures wrath
through floods and droughts they trudge their path.
They take the good and bad in stride,
and to the family, instills pride.
My father was this kind of man,
if in need, he lent a hand. Our families
loss is heavens gain
And we all know that in the end
we'll see that wonderful man again.

—Mark A. Kurtz

To Have Had

To have had a Mother's touch.
To have felt a Father's guiding hand.
To have experienced your first love.
Marriage and all of your dreams come true.
The miracle of a first newborn.
Your child's recognition of you.
Friends near and far that helped you grow and expand.
Faith, knowing that there is a higher being watching over you.
Sunsets and sunrisings that bring new tomorrows.
Yesterday's that have allowed us to reflect and continue
on in our Quest for life.
If you have had these things you have had it all.

—Barbara A. Johnson

"The Forgotten Ones"

Sing me back home with the songs my mother used to sing
to me when I was so young an free, please don't let me die in
a forgiven land without once more feeling the soft touch of my
mothers hand upon my face, for I fought without question as
gallant as could be.

Captured an no longer free after all these years my tired
face is etched in unforgotten pain, an untold fear,
continually moist with tears, even after all these years.

I want only to be remembered, reunited with my family so
that they may wipe away the memories as though tears that
trickle down each cheek, my body is now shackled an weak but
my mind carries me through each day, so that I may endure to
once again be set free.

My tour is more than complete, for I fear we are The
Forgotten Ones, left upon forgiven soil forgotten and alone
always thinking of a place so dear to our heart, called home.

Please remember us now in our hour of need, please do
what you can so that we may hear once again the tender song
a mother sings to her young son, even though the war we
fought was not won, please remember us The Forgotten
Ones.....

—Shawn Busch

Untitled

The beast within has no desire
   to melt his heart and set his soul on fire
The fire blazes beyond control
   but yet he'll never let it go
For passion leads all those who know
   to a place which was foretold
It's a Fiery place of doom
   where the sinners are to loom
The demon there has no heart
   he was that way right from the start
He's cold and cruel and wicked to
   but what's the matter to me or you
We are one of the chosen few
   we lead the crowd and cast the rules
We'll watch them dive into the pools,
   which were filled by the blood of fools
We'll obey his wishes and demands
   it will give us time to make our plans
Cause one day soon we'll give the commands
   we'll be the masters of the darken lands.

—Brenda Tiedt

Can You Give Without Loving?

Can you give without loving a small helping hand
To some little youngster in some faraway land?
A child who is homeless and hungry and poor,
Can you turn his pleas away from your door?

Can you give without loving a little old man
Who is tired and crippled and done all he can
To live a right life in the world he was born?
Can you turn him away unkempt and unshorn?

Can you give without loving to friends close and dear
In time of their sorrow, a word of good cheer?
A word of uplifting for deeds they have done?
Can you do these things in the name of the Son?

Can you give without loving as God did His Son
Who died on the cross with a victory won?
You can give with loving and I know you will find,
So many more blessings among this mankind.

—Eileen M. Taylor

Human Rights

To think for oneself with impunity
To read without censorship
To speak up and protest
To write without fear

    Human rights

To breath fresh air without pollution
To touch the grass, sand and water free of contaminates
To enjoy the companionship of a variety of people
To work at something you love

    Human rights

Some people are punished...
For thinking for themselves
For speaking about corruption
For writing about atrocities
For reading "what some call" subversive materials
For protesting against institutional crimes perpetrated on the
    common man

Our survival demands the preservation of.......

    Human rights!
    —*Diana Henry*

Extending Hands

You have given me so much, I'm glad you are my friend,
To say some day I'll repay is not a thought to send,
I felt your hand extended, given from the heart,
You gave and gave, and gave some more without the need to return,
You gave me your attention, listening quietly to my inner thoughts,
You passed no judgements over my utterings of fear and self doubt,
Your hand was simply given with tender loving care,
So I could find my inner peace without shame nor guilt to bear.

My friends, neighbors, and relatives, and people I didn't know,
Were so kind and loving to me when my spirit was so low,
They touched my mind, touched my heart, and touched my flesh too
You dear friend reached down inside of me, deeper than all
the rest - and touched my soul!
Yes, I hope I can be there to extend my hand too,
When you are struggling... struggling with your inner you,
That's what friends are for, I know you understand,
For I've learned to love from you by gently extending my hand.

    —*Alan Jubenville*

To Know You Care

It is nice to know you care.
To share all our happiness together.
To know my dreams have finally come true.
To know you are in my arms every night.

It is grand to know you think of me.
And the smiles you bring to me are
Filled with more then the
Heavens above.

It is nice to know I will never be alone,
And that we will walk hand in hand down
the road of happiness and sorrow as the days
pass on. But, there will always be
the love that we share no matter
where we go.
That is why I love you so.

    —*Jamie Melton*

Waking Up

It took 30 years to finally see the light,
To stop chasing ungodly delights.
I have an enormous list of sins,
That my merciful Lord has forgiven.

Fornication, lust, covetousness, I will no longer participate,
Love, charity, and hope I will illustrate.
I have experienced death, sorrow, and guilt,
These characteristics are component of my humble heart you've built.

Dedication, devotion, forgiveness, and affection,
Will percolate my soul, without discretion.
"Glory To The King", is my motto,
I'll take my chances with you, and not the Lotto.

I'm listening Lord, waiting for you to speak,
A room in your kingdom, I shall seek.
I'm praying, asking, and knocking,
Anticipating the day, I hear you speaking!
    —*Kathleen M. Harvey*

"Someone Special"

To someone special
To someone dear
To someone I love everyday of the year
To someone who cares, listens and understands
To someone who holds my hand
Someone who walks beside me
Who's there when I need you the most
You'll do anything I ask and not boast
You're a lover and a friend
And no matter what I'll love you until the end
You listened and cared
You bear with me in times of hard
Love is something dear
In which you share with someone you care
And I really do with you
Thanks for being here for me
And I'll always be there for you.

    —*Belinda Michelle Huggins*

Unlike A Bird

I would not want to be a bird,
to take flight when things aren't right.

But like that bird I can sing,
sing of things I've learned, so many things.

I can spread my winds in flight,
soaring up with wings of life.
Things I've seen and things I've learned,
can become like the wind,
and lift me up to soar again.
    —*Della Koster*

Which Way?

Here we go again playing the singles game not even bothering
to ask for each others name. Putting up a real good show
when we ourselves don't even know which way to go.
Do we go this way? Do we go that way? Questions we seem to
ask ourselves each and every day. So we keep going down the
road trying to loosen our load. The load to us seems lighter.
We are now a survivor no longer a fighter as we age it's like
turning a history page. We all live and we all die, sometimes
we wonder why we even try. We all try because we hope to live
and learn, and anything along our path is just one more bridge to burn.
    —*Karen Bishop*

Family Request

Son: I would reach to the end of earth
To test your worth.
I am more than your dad; I am also a friend
But I need the son I had for never in my life
Have I encountered such strife
For you are hooked, son.
I am the one who loves you
For you have no family or home
But this one will do.
If you could stop the roam
That burns deep in your feet;
If you could leave the crowd
You have formed to defeat
Yourself right out loud;
You could come home again;
Be a part of this tiny group;
Maybe wash out the stain of that strange troupe.
I love you son;
But a son? I have none
Until you are done.

—*Gene J. De Lain*

Lost Love

I've lost my love, oh where can he be; did he wander off, down
to the sea? I've lost my love, oh where can he be; is he down
in the meadow under a tree? My love, I fear you've gone away
and I know not where to look, I've roamed the hillside all the
day; are you perhaps hiding down by the brook? My heart is
grieving and I am scared. A storm is brewing-dark clouds are
rolling in. Where are you, where are you - can you hear my cry?
The winds are gusting - no stars are in the sky. The clouds
have burst-the winds are blowing with hurricane force. The
trees are straining as they sway trying to hold on till the
storm goes away. Where are you my love - can you hear my
prayer. Be safe for I'm waiting for you over there. Slowly,
slowly the storm has past. Maybe I can find my love at last.
The moon and stars have been born anew and the world seems
to present a new view. Lo, over the hill my love does stand.
I look and call out - come take my hand. Have you heard my
love what's in my heart. I love thee forever-till death do us part.

—*Johanna Weinstein*

They Ran A Great Race

It was a serious business
To those who came to make the run.
They wanted to get the good land
On which to build new homes.
And so they lined up on horses, and in wagons by the score.
Some even rode in buggies,
They'd never done this thing before.
So when the gun went off to start them,
They took off at a killing pace.
For every man and woman it was a stampeding race.
There was no time for slowness, if they were to get the best.
  No Matter how tired the horses, there was no time to rest.
  So they raced on for miles and miles
  To see what they would find.
  They needed grass and water,
And a place to raise food of all kinds.
Some wanted lots of timber, some wanted prairie land,
Others didn't care much which, just beauty on every hand.
Just a place they could call home, and raise their families,
And never have to roam, but live their lives so happily.

—*Marcia R. Morris*

"Two Hours Till Daybreak"

We can hear the war hoops and tom toms
  toms beating from over distant hill.

Two more hours till daybreak, then they
  will come riding in for the kill.

The women and children are hiding in
  fear, and our ammunition is
  dangerously low.

I just pray our scout made it through
  the enemy lines to let the cavalry know.

Two more hours till daybreak, then all
  hell will break loose, but we will give
  them a damn good fight.

Without reinforcements, I doubt if we
  can last another day and night.

But wait, I believe I hear in the distance,
  a bugle loud and clear.

No doubt now, our scout made it
  through, and the cavalry is very near.

Two more hours, till daybreak, and we
  are going to win this fight.

—*Floyd A. Simon*

God's Touch

Sea mist billows above the waves,
  towards the rocks they do rage.
Tumbling, rumbling, on they roll,
  magnificent beauty in God's control.
Relentless pounding of the shore,
  the waves roll on o'er and o'er.
Upon the rocks the waves do pound,
  transforming edges smooth and round.
The pounding force makes shifting sand,
  what once was rock sifts through your hands.
Like the rocks, jagged and rough,
  God will round you with his touch.

—*Kathy Ladd*

In Silence We Fly

In silence we fly, leaving heaven behind us,
Towards the stars with Zephyrs by our side.
Sour tongues leading us nowhere, because
Everywhere has been taken by Father Time's bride.

The moon dances slowly, to escape its true duty
Of joining and reuniting two futures into one.
Blind of commitment, everlasting beauty,
Surrender your beams to the almighty sun.

By day the imperialists laugh as they steal
The roots of a heart and seeds of a flower.
A dolphin's eyes water at its wasteful last meal,
As Mother Nature's tears bring acid rain showers.

In silence we fly to escape splintered love,
Soaring with prophecies, powerful in word.
From the echoes of sunsets to the wounds up above,
A familiar heart breaking can hardly be heard.

—*James P. Linse*

Dead Ends

  Danger Ahead! the sign read.
Total disregard kept motion in my feet.
  Suddenly, I came to the end of the street.
Surveying the scenery, I saw nowhere begin.
  Once again, I've hit a dead end.

—*Donna Handoe*

554

"Trapped In Love"

Flowing with a strong wind;
Trapped in a corner, I'm pinned.

I want to follow my heart;
But my mind wants a new start.

I feel my face break into pieces.
My feelings of lonesome drastically increases.

Our minds suddenly collide.
My arms struggle to open wide.

Holding you is like a golden sunset.
My dreams could come true if you would let.

But since you are on your way,
Trapped in my bed of tears I lay.

—*Gina M. Weatherlow*

Rejected Reflections

My mirror is an out and out liar,
Tries to tell me I'm getting old.
That can't be my reflection,
You're as young as you feel, I'm told.

Those aren't wrinkles that line my face,
Which proves a mirror can fail.
What actually now is happening-
I am just seeing more detail.

What looks like a sag at each side of my mouth
And that extra chin? Let it pass.
It just has to be a distortion,
A flaw in that old looking glass.

There is still a reasonable spring in my step.
I can swing to a Glenn Miller song.
My appetite's good, blood pressure just right,
Cholesterol is low, nothing wrong.

So, I'm saying my mirror is a liar.
And I seldom do anything rash,
But I swear if it still tries to make me feel old,
The damn thing goes out with the trash.

—*Bill Foster*

He Gave Me Poetry

He works in mysterious ways, His wonders to perform.
Trouble was in my days, I got in the way of harm.
I'm paralyzed since "71."
Now stuck in my bed, "What a bummer," I said.
"I can't get out and run around."
But the Lord doesn't want me to be tied down.

God works all things together for good.
For those who are called according to His word.
So he gave me a mouth with which to shout.
and He tells me things to talk about.
He is faithful ever more.
If He closes a window, He opens a door.

And so in 1989,
He began putting words in this mouth of mind
In the form of rhyme.
To praise Him some, or to comfort someone.
Or maybe bring a grin when humor is thin.
And maybe share some love from our Father above.

—*Juanita Powell*

I've Always Loved Eyes Of Blue

Blue as the skies, his eyes of blue
    True are the eyes of clear blue hue
My first love, my husband — Paul Newman — true,
    Each has eyes of clearest blue
Not green, not hazel, but purest blue
    Straight to the soul, they mirror through

I've always loved eyes of blue

Dark as the night, her eyes of brown
    A moonless night — so large — so round —
With longest lashes, sweeping down.
    This first grandchild, who smiles at me,
As I hold her, oh so tenderly
    With eyes so dark, do they really see?
They laughingly shine, as they dance in time,
    to the music they make in my heart.

Now I love eyes of brown.
    —*Barbara Hedden Hertz*

"Come Along"

We all have dreams and wish that they come true
True as dreams could be
We plan and try to make them the best things that could be
But yet dreams have their own way of thinking

Come along and we can sing songs
That's made for just you and me love
Come and share my golden dreams
We can build our own world around us
And share all of our dreams together

How can I show you just what I mean
There must be a way? Where do dreams began?
And how can you show them to others?
To let them know what you really mean

Come along and we can sing songs
That's made for just you and me love
Come and share my golden dreams we can build our own
World around us and share all of our dreams together

Oh; how I love to feel your charms
Your lips so soft and warm
And the thought's of just being close to you
    —*Grico Samon*

Say No To Drugs

There's people that are getting rich
Trying to get anyone on a fix.
You never know if they are bugged,
The best you can do is Say No To Drugs.

If you see someone in your home town
That you haven't been seeing around.
From them, you never take no slugs,
The best you can do is Say No To Drugs.

This has caused too many deaths,
The victims saying with their last breath,
I want you to please watch out for mugs.
The best you can do is Say No To Drugs.

People just don't care who they may hurt,
As they spread all their kind of dirt.
If they get to you just let your shoulders shrug,
The best you can do is Say No To Drugs.

When you get old and look back in time,
Be thankful you didn't spend a dime
On all that crack and other drugs,
Thank your God, you said No To Drugs.

—*Eva Nell Sheppard Davis*

The Garden

As playful thoughts fumble around in my head.
Trying to remember how it use to be.
 Those thoughts are all but forgotten.
Carefully I pull together the way we were.

 I get lost in a maze of rose bushes.
Many the flowers few the tears.
 As I trip over the old fountain;
Memories come over me that seemed lost for so long.

 Caring for people who are gone forever.
Memories linger, linger.
 My heart is wilting away just like the flowers.
My soul sinking as in quicksand.

 My heart a tremble in the wind.
My soul crumpled as a piece of paper.
 Around, around it's the same old thing.
Wishing, doubting, wishing back those memories.

 Carefully putting the pieces together.
As in a puzzle.
 If you make a mistake it could cost you a memory.
If you get it right it could cost you your heart.

—*Jenny Christianson*

"Our World"

Spinning, spinning suspended in time.
Trying to save your world and mine.

We can save our world if we really try.
Otherwise we may have to say good-bye.

Our world is crumbling, falling apart.
If only everyone would play their part.

We could protect where we live.
If only everyone would learn to give.

It doesn't take much, just a piece here or there.
Soon maybe people would learn to care.

—*Erica A. Brezinski*

Remembering the "Good" Days,

Times and Years of the Elderly

Remembering the days "grandma"
 tuck us in and kept us warmth from the cold.
Remembering the days grandma"
 worked hard all day and night to keep food for the poor"
Remembering the days grandma"
 rocked and cuddle, when sick in bed with the flu cold.
Remembering the "Both"
 who nicely took everyone to church
on Sundays to keep in good work with the
Lord, was their goal!
And, thanking them when those days we had to be scold!
And remembering all the goodtimes,
 when we were young, now that we're gotten old!
Thanks to grandma and grandpa for those
good days, which were began! Amen! Peace

—*Brinda E. White*

Beauty Of Spring

The dogwood with chasuble of pink and white
Tulips with panorama of color so bright,
Narcissus and other bulbs, in symphony of flight,
The lush emerald lawn with each new dawn
Herald the bird with song brighten the day all along.
The busy bees seek their way among blossoms all day,
Tasting delicacies of cascading azaleas in formal attire,
Squirrels frolic on stone benches to enjoy their desire
To eat from cones beneath magnolia and pine tree
While all Nature, creatures, and man is happy and free.
The doves with their young near-by to care for and love,
Gentle warm rains, sunshine, dew (diamonds from above)
Herald the love pair to sit, preen each other with loving care.
Children, young lovers, the aged or infirm Spring's Beauty
share. Humming birds return to the nectar feeding place,
Monarch and other butterflies all Nature face
With wisdom and mystery of Nature's intricate place,
To herald the wondrous New Spring, all to enjoy, a new song
sing in Spring's concert of spinet, harp and lute sounds,
As joy, peace, beauty and serenity of soul abounds.

—*Perry W. England*

Hush, The Dinosaur Is Sleeping!

Hush, little clouds, the dinosaur is sleeping!
 Tumble playfully over each other
 guided by the wind
Hush! Do not waken him.

Hush, little flowers, the dinosaur is sleeping!
 Grow cheerily among each other
 guided by the sun
Hush! Do not waken him.

Hush, little grasses, the dinosaur is sleeping!
 Sway gently among each other
 guided by the wind
Hush! Do not waken him.

Hush, little sunbeams, the dinosaur is sleeping!
 Dance happily with each other
 guided by life's energy
Hush! Do not waken him.

—*Eva Hibma*

"The Mark of Life"

What am I looking for?

A house full of rooms?- every door exciting;
Two couples running naked on a beach, foolishly in love.
A ballerina in a clear global sphere,
Two red headed boys playing with fire trucks,
an 'ole cowboy movie, or two colored
people dancing very slow on a huge lawn in broad daylight.
A room for me, a brush of reality, and sharing an adventure?

What am I looking for?

A hand full of sand, with patches of moist seaweed,
the feel of a young one's wet hands,
A warm stream in an open forest;
Lots of trees and glittery rocks, each one holding a glimpse of
a life that is unreal?

What am I looking for?

A way to a lost friend of mine;
Something,... something huge to patch up this hole in my heart.
A rose of every color, blooming with freedom in every such way,
A reason to leave this world with such remembrance, a mark of
my own? All in all, who I really am.

—*Corinna Dominguez*

Gypsy Violin

In the cold chill of the solitary park
two forms just passed and vanished in the dark.
Where the pond reflects, a mirror deep,
black silhouette of a willow tree
a gypsy sit alone; he bobs and sways
to the long sobs of his violin at play.
Appearing only a shadow draped in a luminous moonlit glow,
his hair on the lofty boughs of the air in streams flow.
His eyes were alight and wild with despair,
vaguely taking notice of his onlookers' stares.

Low in the air of the city streets
the echoing song of his violin weeps:

And with long, lustful sobs, the violin throbs
    to the gypsy's despondence at play.
And all the restless shore tides heaving upon the ocean side
    swell with a passionate dismay.
Yet few know the cost of the gypsy's lost
    love who is now gone away.
For wherever she goes she hears the woes
    of her gypsy's violin wild at play.

—*Kimberly Miller*

Untitled

One night,
    Two lovers walked along the coast of the world,
    the oceans lapped contentedly at their sandy feet,
    he turned to her, moon-framed and star-filled, to entreat,
    "Will you be the sea to my ocean-bed,
    making sure my hungry beaches fed?
    Can I cradle your vast expanses,
    hearing only your siren's romances?"
She merely laughs, and casts her glance across the sea,
    "I would die for you, would you lie for me?
    when the winter comes will you cover me,
    and when the summer reigns, will you release me?"
She merely laughs, and casts her glance across the sea.

—*Eric Hansen*

The Path

In an old shabby inn on the outskirts of town,
Two men were boarding and the mill was shut down.
"Let us go for a walk," I heard one man say.
"You go on ahead. I'll come later today."
One walked by the brook by the old broken tree;
The most hideous thing you ever did see.
The pathway was stony and far much too long
And nettles might sting you as you passed along.
By the brook it was muddy — on his shoes it got grime.
He thought it was purely a waste of his time.

The other set forth with no definite goal.
His only objective — a rest for his soul.
He heard a bird sing in an old rustic tree;
A sweeter song was never to be.
He searched in the weeds to see what could be found,
And there were sweet flowers all over the ground!
He saw a green frog on a big lily pad,
Watched it splash in the pool and his heart was made glad.
He returned from his walk with his heart light and gay,
And felt he had spent a profitable day.

The story is ended and now you may laugh.
They each had followed the selfsame path.
And I ask, as I journey on life's pathway,
Which of these men do I portray?

—*Oran K. Skaw*

Milestones

A child, I oft tripped over them,
Unaware that these were, (in the jargon of the 60's)
happenings,
And sometimes I did pick them up
And momentarily looked
But gave them short shrift,
As I tossed them negligently over my shoulder;
    Seldom did I deem them worthwhile.
    I left most of them disintegrating into shifting sand.
    I have come to look for, search for them,
    Possessing the patina of time and age.
They gleam in the distance, luring me on.
I take my time to reach them,
(They will not disappoint),
Savoring each step toward them.
Now I cannot negligently toss them over my shoulder.
Like a rare jewel they must be fondled,
Treasured and stored in my memory.
Reluctantly, I lay them down, and
Perforce, turn toward another milestone in the offing.

—*Hester B. Eyler*

Jenne's Goodbye

Though the years give way to
    uncertainty
Nothing shall strangle the will
There's a part of me, a part of you
Though sometimes it's very hard to see
It's never far from me
    alive to eternity

I can hear the steady shallowness of your
    sleepy breath
While your muscles, gently quiver and twitch
    into their relaxed state
I will think of you now as I thought of you then
My heart will brighten and gently will a tear
    slide along my silkened cheek

So I'll let my disappointment pass
Let the laughter fill my glass
And not let the past
Remind me of what may be....

—*Mark Armijo*

Theirs Not To Reason Why

Theirs not to reason why, theirs but to do or die, the
stories
unfold an epic of old, nobody counted news vendors shouted,
guns volleyed and thundered, everyone wondered, horses dashed
by, to late to retreat pressure was great, someone had
blundered orders obeyed into the fray banners held high, rode
the six hundred— Theirs not to reason why.

Today heros zeros in the blazing skies, while on the ground
Armies are numbered, gas masks and protective gear the whole
Idea someone had plundered. Marching in hundred armies soon
departed bombers to fly, orders okayed hostilities started;
Theirs not to reason why.

Before all this started for peace we cried nobody answered
Nothing arrived, the deadline had passed still hoped for the
best alas all hope departed, just broken hearted could do
nothing less but we surely tried, all bombs away into the
fray
troops multiplied— Theirs not to reason why.

—*Kathleen Kay Lewis*

"Let's Make Space"

Little white heads, sad eyes, tired or happy,
unsure steps; shaky, pained bodies
that at the slightest blow of a breeze
can bend.

Your mission completed, your goals
having been reached. Yet you are very tired!
Let's not be selfish. Let's leave our
space!

To find a more beautiful space,
another space that will be eternal.
Let's leave our space here
Let's be generous; lets do it now!
We shall rise to another space, more beautiful!

Our earthly space is transitory;
A visa, given by "God," and
by "God" it shall be cancelled!
Let's give up our space, for
another visa extended by "God."
            —*Carmen M. Ramirez*

Orinda

At sunset in my village, the sky catches fire, and burns
    until it melts into the river.
Then, all is gold, and black.
Fishermen and their families simply appear, without sound,
    Casting out their nets like giant webs
    upon the silken water.
They move as if in a dream, their bodies bronze silhouettes
    against the molten sky.
Diamonds of light flash from their fingertips
    with every turn of net, every surge of wave.
I am transfixed by their beauty.
I drown in their completeness,
    and, in all the world,
    this moment is enough!
            —*Wolfheart*

Untitled

Outlaws of the heart,
Utilizing the only light.
Red flows through the cracks.

Dawn of silence,
Eels electrifying the space of our souls.
Altering our course
Through the final
Hour.

Hatred is kind
And blood flows from the
Serpent's mouth.

Coming to realize,
Open for the kill, she reaches her
Moment, and shoots the arrow
Erupting my soul.
            —*David Schmitz*

Day Dreams

Look into my heart and tell me what you see
Visions of my loneliness, day dreams of you and me
To walk along in silence with your hand held in mine
Finally to see our paths have crossed, slowly intertwined
We sit and talk for hours and sometimes not at all
I'll always be here to catch you if you ever lose hope and fall
I'll keep you in my heart to shelter you from the pain
Holding you close inside myself where there you will always remain
            —*M. R. Cain*

"`An Expression Of Me"

I gaze in a wondrous state of euphoria,
upon the splendorous, rapturous beauty
of creation.

Filled with the feeling of awe and
amazement, trying to conceive the total idea
of what has flourished.

Overwhelmed with sentiment of the infinite
wisdom of the "divine" force, I zealously
search the heavens.

Passionately reaching out, I silently
express my gratitude for having been
enriched with this enigma.
            —*Jean M. Lutz*

Wound Unhealed

The word as sharp as a shard of glass
Used as a weapon of destruction, it cuts deep within
When resistance to trespass is naive and immature

The wound as bottomless as the weapon will allow
The weapon as damaging as the users intent
Now inside, where it causes it's worst mutilation

Morals torn and twisted
Love slashed with conditions
Leaving disorder and misery
The weapon is painfully withdrawn

Skin slowly closes over the void
All evidence remaining trapped within
Scar tissue forms
The weapon shelved, wound unhealed
            —*Edward Mello*

Unfair

Shattered piece of a ceramic doll
used to remind us all
of failed attempts at racial peace
writing on heads place for lease
murdered for selfishness
punished for selflessness
put behind bars for having wrong feelings
running free for illegal drug dealings
held back by an unknown force
too powerful for a single man to endorse
with the murder weapon in his hand
still claiming he didn't kill the man
morals of strings not bars
ten men die over fuel for cars
black print on white paper
pleads insanity the reason he raped her
made a mistake he gives her a ring
then he leaves doesn't say a thing
it seems this world doesn't care
I guess life just isn't fair.
            —*Karen Carney*

While You're Not Here

Each day I think about you and wonder how you are
Wanting to reach out and hold you, but the distance is too far.
I'm here missing you, and you're there missing me
I want to have our lives back, the way that they should be.
I want to feel you near me at the closing of each day
I want to erase this emptiness I feel when you're away.
For you to return and dry my tears is only one thing that I yearn.
And so I say a prayer each night and request a safe return.
            —*Diane Gallagher*

Third Shift

Puddles beam yellow on the oily tarmac; the sodium
vapor glow struggles in dense wet blackness.
It is cooler now, after the cloudburst, though
stale tobacco and sweaty polyester
still sour the air. Too late for baseball,

he stretches the coat hanger on
the battered old radio, and reels in
pure pedal steel. A soft slow wail
washes the shack like firelight. Lunch:

three liverwurst sandwiches and fruit sloshed
with black sludge left at the bottom of the
first pot of the night. At least it is hot.
Feet on the counter, paper spread
to the scores. It will be some time before

trucks rumble in. Four hours, two nights,
ten months, twenty-eight years
till retirement. The greasy dollar
in his pocket will buy a chance
for two million on the way
home in the morning.

—*James B. White*

Verticals

I catch my breath at your
vertical climb on surfaces
offering no perch for wrens
where masterful of the life you risk
you rise with the zest of light within
to enter a universe out of the reach
of belly crawling moles and worms.

And when you belay on
the slant sun's light
with storm in a cauldron
of far clouds brewing night
your eyes still tell of an eagle's world
that you cannot share with a troglodyte.

—*Henry Noyes*

Voices in the Night

When I was half asleep or maybe half awake, I heard strange
voices calling me is this my imagination, maybe just a dream
or could someone, something be calling me but nobody's home they
left hours ago I'm starting to fear, fear the unknown for what
could these voices be trying to say with their deep screaming
sorrows of suffering and pain then I see, see on the wall
shadows, faces I hear the voices once more now the shadows move
from the wall to the floor into darkness I can no longer see
them any more but I can hear light creeks from the wood floors
things gently stepping as if not to make noise I pray this is
only a dream that soon I will wake but what if it isn't I pray,
(please don't let me die) the moaning is getting louder my
heart more faint I swear I hear the sound of heavy breathing by
a hundred people or more, "suddenly!!", I hear loud piercing
screams then I hear the last beat, beat of my heart my eyes
close I die my soul quickly parts. Restless souls have caused yet
another death now off to collect another life, if they too can be
scared to death.

—*Shawn Norling*

Forever And A Day

I just sit here by the phone,
waiting and waiting all alone.
No one to talk to, no one to hold
you might as well tell me, "I told you so."
You said that I would never forget,
but all I do now is regret.
We had laughter, fun, and joy.
Now I know that you are no ordinary boy.
You took my heart and tore it in two.
You made me cry, but I still love you.
Now your with her and not me.
I just wish that people would leave me be.
They ask me if I'm O.K..
They ask me if I want to cry.
All I can say is, "I gave it my best try,"
You don't love me, so that's what you say,
but I'll wait for you forever and a day!

—*Brenda Styber*

Indecision

Trying to catch a bus. The driver sees me-standing,
waiting. Closing the door, he pulls away. I chase him.
Frantically I race down the street, just behind the bus.
But not close enough to catch. Days run into weeks - then
months. Pleadingly I beg him to stop, to wait.
I chase him harder and harder - And harder.
Stopping, finally he opens his door.
I don't approach, I don't get on.
I wait, I wait for the door to close.
Staying open, the driver reaches to coax me in.
He assures me it is warm inside.
He tells me I'll be comfortable - And protected.
He says I can ride the bus forever.
I step on. I jump off.
I look at the bus, I look at the driver.
Another bus approaches. Trying to catch
that bus, the driver sees me - Standing, waiting.

—*Kim Marie Grabowski*

Untitled

When the earth was golden I was there
Waiting for my timely share
Things look brightest with the sun in the sky
and I wonder loudly who am I
Waiting- waiting for things to be right
The sky will darken soon it is night
Do I wonder about what shouldn't be
Or ponder too much about me?
Is there an answer that I will know
Will good times come and bad times go
Do all my questions get answered in time
Or must I keep pretending that all is fine?
Soon the days will end for sure-
And then I will ponder and question no more.

—*Hazel Pfrommer*

Untitled

When I am lonely, you are there.
When I am abused, dear Lord, you care.
When I am sad, to my heart you give cheer.
When I am afraid, you say "My child do not fear".
When I am happy, in my heart you put a song.
When I want to be alone, your love tags along.
When I am tempted, you give me strength.
When I think I can go no further,
You take me great lengths.
When I ask "My Lord, what for you can I do in return?"
You answer "Love my father,
and for his word your heart to yearn.

—*Crystal McAdoo*

line drawn in the sand

Like the night before Christmas
war eve excitement
has the world eager with anticipation.
At long last, a tangible terror awaits us.
Nothing so subtle as holes in the ozone
or incomprehensible debts of the nation.
For war's graphic horrors
We know how to weep.

The night before deadlined withdrawal from Kuwait...
Nationwide, U.S. religions hold vigils,
"World peace" prayer vigils,
to temper the hate.

An orthodox ministry opened its doors.
In came some Moslems, a Buddhist, some Jews.
In came a Peace Prize recipient from Ireland.
In came a sampling of Christendom fractions.
In came the chill of the night before bedlam.

—*Christina Larson*

"A Rating Between One And Ten"

My rating as a mother when the children were all so small
    was in the high numbers, as far as I can recall
They were loved and cared for and also disciplined when
    they disobeyed or were bad
They were the most wonderful family a mother ever had
Now they are grown and sometimes need to be advised
I want to help, but not interfere too much into their lives
I still get upset when they say or do things that I don't agree
And I'm sure they also get aggravated a good many times with me
I pray to "God" to help me overlook and to forgive
The small things that come up in this life that we're trying to live
And to let my family know I loved them from the start
And that love still and always will fill every corner of my heart

—*Gloria Margaret (Clinedinst) Wode*

Moonwatchers

Cold white light of late night heaven
washes over the two moon watchers.
Silver fingers through hair,
over skin,
smoothing away anxieties.
Late night lovers, so distant by day,
pour out their hearts in the moonlight.
Where have the nights of moonwatching
Gone?
Except, with the full moon,
Away.

—*Jennifer Wade*

Hungry For Hearts

Somaliland's stumbling skeletons
Watch guns on wheels rattling
Away to dusty street corners
To wait for transport of food.

Peacekeepers of all brands swagger
Before the cameras and pick a skeleton,
Grin sweetly on the shriveled skull
To signal to charity that mission is done.

Hearts don't march up to miseryland
Nor in unison cry out nevermore!
But cling to TV and journal's gore
Dismissing the faraway darkness
In favor of their own fairyland.

—*Dominic Anton Kessler*

From A Teacher

I like to be in the know with you; it gives me a reason to
Watch. Yes, I am a watcher, a drinker, not a beggar; a
Soldier, not a lover.

The seeds of a pumpkin: I can show you how to count them. And
When we get the answer, who can say that I know the answer
Better?

There's fear in that, I know. But just don't say who knows the
Answer better while we're counting, because I like to be in the
Know with you, when I'm watching.

—*John Leighton*

A Beautiful Unicorn

A beautiful unicorn pausing on a mountain top,
watching the rain fall to the rocks.

Unicorns may be fantasy but,
there's one animal I'd love to see

Close your eyes a dream to be
a beautiful Unicorn galloping.

So if you see a horse flying through the sky,
It just might be a Unicorn, well alive.

—*Jamie Keeton*

Forcing Through The Mist

Wheel slowly churning,
Water splashing, steam bellowing, on we push
Through the mist of the majestic river.
Heat the coals and we will slowly move.
Splashing, sputtering, spinning,
Confined to the path of the camouflaged banks,
The vessel trudges through the murky solid
Onward moving with the constant current.
Turning, spinning, making its mark,
Forcing further to its final destination,
This solemn soldier pushes on to gain
Victory over the turbulent waters.

—*Dina Kinnune*

My Get Away Path

   My get away path seems so clear to me, its located on the
waters of life, easy to come by but not easy to follow.
   The beginning and middle of my path is of great challenge,
if you don't fight it you'll find yourself pushed back to the
very beginning of poverty and war by the waves of suffering and
ignorance.
   But at the end you'll find yourself floating with the
currents that are as silent as a newborn sleeping....
   Soon my path leading out of the world of problems, will sink
into the silent destructive earth soon to come again the next day!

—*Chloe Spencer*

Untitled

If one could go back to 1779,
To the tragedy at the old Opera House in London Town.
Martha Ray was a victim of murder at the time
Her death caused an old hack to pen these lines,
Of the man who took her life,
    "A clergyman, O wicked one
    In Convent Garden shot her
    No time to cry upon her God
    It's hoped He's not forgotten her".
How would one phrase those lines today
Of the woman who died
Cause to her suitor she said nay.

—*Elfrida Walker*

The World

The world is a great place in which
  we all must try to live
The world is where the love we
  have we must give

The world can be only what we ourselves
  can make of it. When the going
Mighty rough, we must remember not to quit.
  The world can only be as strong as the
people are that is in it

The world we need everyone's that's in it
  we can help heal the wrong if we
Put our hearts, souls, minds, hands, legs
  back, and everything else and mean it

The world yes your place and mines
  lets end misery and strife and replace it
With joy, smiles and the laughter of a child

We can do, not with a pill or any drugs
  We can do it by extending our helping
hands and work up to an everlasting hug
  The world joy begins with each of us
    —Barbara K. Bynum

Bury Me With Dylan Thomas

Bury me with Dylan Thomas
We are blood, he and I
For we both soar through the mists of minds
Bury me with him when I die
Bury me with Dylan Thomas
Inside the earth of Wales
We'll protect the land together with wise words
And strengthen minds that are frail
And may Dylan and I be trodden upon
By the feet of those in trust
And may one of them follow in our steps
And be buried next to us
If I should wake with Dylan Thomas
Above my bed of dirt
In eternal peace would I then be,
To dwell in sacred earth
Bury me with Dylan Thomas
When to this life I say goodbye
Then over the land of Wales we'll rein
And write our poems in the sky.
    —Gracie Odonavon

Untitled

This place we live is called our home,
We call it earth, our place to roam.
I hate it here because of all the wrong,
It makes each day seem so long.
With all the racism and all the fights,
And all the power given to all the whites.
Even though it may seem that way,
Were killing our selves off everyday
It's not the Mexicans, whites or blacks,
It's all our hate, and the love we lack.
If we could just put color aside
Scared people wouldn't run and hide.
There's more and more killing on the streets,
And more and more kids are being beat.
Were starting to make killing a hobby,
That along with rape and robberies.
What if we gave loving a try,
Maybe we'd stop living this lie.
    —Dory McCollum

My Daddy

We didn't do much together, you and I.
We didn't even agree much either.
Right from the start, I knew you were
bigger, and stronger than me.
You almost seemed like God standing there.
When I looked in your eyes, I never saw love in them.
I knew you didn't love me.
Yet, I learned to respect you, obey you.
Out of fear and knowing what you'd do to me,
if I didn't.
We'd hide our feelings, and lived in our own little worlds.
A family full of lies and secrets
My dad and I.
I grew up and moved away,
We'd talk, lots of empty words.
Then you got sick, and died on me.
And I can't say I love you, or I miss you anymore.
So please tell me I can come, and be with you again.
    —Jeannie McClister

Crazy For You

Since we've met it's been real sweet
we discovered new worlds and it was kind of neat

We broke up suddenly, things were said and done
We were known as two and no longer as one

We're now back together and we're making it great
We're going out steady and didn't need to just date

I'm so happy things are working out fine
You say "I love you" and it's not just a line

Things are so simple like the sky above
but this time I realize I'm lost in love

We're back on track there's nothing left to say or do
except one thing, I'm crazy for you!
    —Kimberly Bordo

Dear America

I thank you for the freedom you give me every day.
We elect a new president to help you run your way.
So we can take away the bad and put in the good,
so everyone in America can do what they should.
We try to clean up in each and every way,
so you can have a very, very Happy Birthday.
Some countries don't give as much freedom as you do,
So when you help us, we love helping you.
You may think that this is the end of the poem I'm sending you,
But it's not.
God created a special everyone like me and like you too,
Happy Birthday.
    —Chris Bilecki

The Wind

Oh how beautiful the wind
To set the ships unpinned,
I feel the air cool and moist
That sets the sails a hoist.

Oh how I love thee gentle wind
Thrown upon my hair,
As I watch the water go by
And see the birds fly by.

Oh how these memories past
I find that I'm too old to last,
And find my legs can't take me to the sea
But can still smell the cool summer breeze.
    —Katina Rice

To Our Graduates

In your spring of life and season,
We gather here to celebrate
For the very special reason:
You very soon will graduate!

Graciously we share your pride
That this plateau marks for you.
With hopes and joys we scarce can hide,
We wish your goals and dreams come true.

Our selfish rue we must suppress
At thoughts the larger world will share
In all your dreams, your sure success,
Your promises beyond compare,

Too bright's your promise to restrain;
Too strong's your urge to gain and grow.
The world's in want and need and pain.
So swiftly, surely you must go.

So spread your wings and fleetly fly
Above and beyond the present earth.
Boldly soar toward sun and sky,
And live your live for all its worth!

—*James F. Rasmussen*

Winterfest, Winterfest, 1992

Winterfest, Winterfest, of 1991 is overdue.
We had some beautiful days in February, too.
The temperature was as high as 80 degrees and you could see some green covering the trees.
Let it snow, let it snow, It's so peaceful and quiet in the valley below.
God knows we need this snow to kill some bugs and also we need this snow to help the soil and make things grow.

Don't fret it out! Pine or shout! Yes this kind of weather is turned inside out!
Now, I'm watching all kinds of beautiful snowflakes by my large bay window. My bay window is a Heaven today. Let it snow!

Yes, I'll miss the St. Patrick's, Dixie Land Stomper tonight.
I won't won't sweat it, though. Enjoy the wintertime (over fest). Snow! Such picturesque beauty only our omnipotent God can paint.

—*Donna Belle Rowe*

Come Home, Come Home

Our world moves fast.
We have to follow it or get left behind.
It doesn't matter if you come in last.
Do your best and let others see your work.
Things happen that we have no control over.
God rules our lives and this world.
Keep him in your heart.
Ask him to guide you safely through this world.
Use the wonderful talents that he gave you.
Let his light shine in this fast world.
He will be there for you when you need him.
He is a good listener.
He is patient with those lost in the world,
He loved us enough to let his son die for our sins.
He can help if you will let him in.
Don't let others dissuade you from finding your home.
Look at the world and see where you fit in.
God's hands are open and ready for you to come in.
He will protect you from the evil of this world.
He is waiting for you, his lost child.
Come home where you are always loved

—*David Wayne Counts*

Untitled

We know how you felt,
We know how you feel
But, was your love, for him ever really real?
You loved him less than he loved you.
You never really liked him, but,
His love was true.
It'll never be how it was before,
And look what you did,
His heart is now tore.
To you he was so sweet, so nice.
Next time you dump someone,
You better think twice.
You were together, never to part,
That's what he said straight from the heart.
Together forever, that's what we thought.
Together forever, well, maybe not.

—*Claire Lewis*

Love Steps Unknown!

Love steps unknown in this fantastic place this world
we live in; as we press forward in unity
Intimacy and passions. The magnificence of its
many flavors to excite pleasurably. It'
excellence sent forth from the Gods;
We feel what we think, I keep thinking I'm
still with you and you're not here; I'll
always remember your loving, lovely compassion;
You were to stay with me to stimulate my
heart and soul to think in tranquility;
But now you're only in a song to be played
over and over again and again; As I listen
eagerly in quietness like always; And when
Love steps unknown into a stranger's door;
When a visit is better than nothing, when
a sensation is Love, I'll accept this new phase
in my Life I'll open my heart with Love.
Like always; Love!

—*Margurite Scott*

How Could I Not Love You!

How could I not love you, when Love circled around us,
we moved along in amusement; Raised our glasses
with delicate champagne bubbles; We touched very
softly, interlaced, warm and ready without
hesitation; When Romantic Love is on floating Words,
Its the most fabulous surge - promising much, much,
more; To peek into stain glass windows with wall
to wall poems to read; How could I not Love yours
as soft silk music surrounds us, reaching
gracefully at full length, loving at the very best, to
Linger and pamper ourselves to the good life,
Knowing in my heart, she charm, the enchantment,
is now, this day, this moment is only on loon.
But my love for you will be for much longer
time like always Love.

—*Margurite Scott*

Red

Have you ever really looked at Red?
What's the first thing that pops into your head?
A valentine surrounded with white lace,
covered with hearts and a cupids face,
Or juicy red strawberries piled high in a basket.
Or the red satin lining in a vampires casket.
Santa Claus in bright red duds
or lively red petals on rose buds.
A red cape waved at a roary eyed bull.
Well, I see a red sportscar with its gas tank full.

—*Joann Raymond*

An Ocean Of Experience

As the sea of life roars,
We open those doors
In which we bring the future
Together with the past.

As the ocean wind blows,
We have our highs and our lows
But only through experience
Can we find our flaws.

As the tide rises and falls,
We hear faint calls
Of new reason from somewhere
That helps break down tremendous barriers and walls.

As the shore becomes dry with sand,
We hold in our hand
The key to our future
Which allows us to open those locked doors.

As we come to rest,
There is only one way best
To show the young how to be wise;
That is through our own eyes.

—*Jeremy Paul*

Three Cheers For Nettie

Three cheers for the most talented cook
We recognize her at once, as we take a look
When the postmaster delivers the magazine for farm wives
We find a cozy corner and have the time of our lives
We look for Nettie's page her best recipes, then plan
Which one to try on our favorite man-
For the way to a man's heart is, you know how
So why delay the experiment, but do it right now.
It's a challenge to try recipes other cooks have won
In whatever contest it was they had fun
For them to be chosen the "best in their class"
Tempts me to produce that when tested will pass
For it to be judged best, if I carefully measure
Thus experience the joy that gave them such pleasure
We also enjoy your creative and interesting hints
On homemaking, family living or maybe its mints
So we patiently look forward to each monthly issue
For what's new, and the best of everything we wish you.

—*Esther G. Fahning*

War

War.
We send our children off to battle.
They fight...
With honor...courage...dignity...
Their struggle is "justified"...
They give their very existence for
"Our cause".
Does the pain hurt them any less?
Do their wounds not bleed?
Are their cuts not as deep?
Babies...
Who only recently left their mother's arms.
At home...
We are filled with pride. Then... Death
Unmarked graves. Lifeless bodies. But...
They died "in the service of their country"...
And "for a noble cause"...
Yet,...
They are gone just the same...
War.

—*C. Leigh Myers*

Fifty Years

Its hard to believe these fifty years.
We shared have gone so fast,
But there's nothing we can do
To change what we've done in the past.

I look at our beautiful son and daughters.
Who God has blessed us with
It makes me feel so thankful
To share our lives with.

We are growing old together
Many memories we left behind
There's many times we blundered
While going through this life

I love you dear with all my heart
We have shared so much together
Through this old troublesome world
We always stuck together

Our memories are slowly slipping
I know we are changing too.
If we keep our faith in Jesus
I know he will see us through.

—*Dora Gibson*

Just Like Candles

Just like candles
We stand
Illuminating in tiny flickers,
Fluctuations that
Burn
Us
Down
And
Wear
Us
Out
Eventually.
The consolation is
That someone somewhere used us to see by
While we lasted.

—*Lou Ann Sears*

A Tribute To Our Mother

As we look back and realize where God has brought us from
We stop and thank him graciously for all that he has done

He placed each of us in your life and gave us one another
And even when we caused you strife you stayed right there
Dear Mother.

You could have said "I quit, I'm done!"
You could have said "I'm through."
You could have walked away and left,
Feeling there was nothing else to do.

But Mother, Oh Mother you stayed and prayed
with God right by your side.
Giving your will and way to him,
allowing him to be your guide.

—*Carzadean Y. Baker*

Mom Says So

Long ago, back in the fifties,
We thought we all looked pretty nifty,
With bobby sox and saddle shoes,
We listened to Elvis singing the blues.

Our poodle skirts swayed side to side,
And our puppy-love feelings we did not hide.
We sang along with each new tune,
One of which was the big, "Blue Moon".

The local D.J. spun the Top Ten,
We did the stroll to the slow beat of Big Ben.
We popped the phlobees in our glass of Pepsi,
Ate fries and burgers with Ann and Betsy.

We made our way home where Mom was baking,
To beg for a party with our hearts all aching.
She gave us a "no". We gave a big sigh.
The reason was, "Mom says so", that's why!

We're now in the nineties. It's my turn to bake,
My teenager's driving, for heaven's sake.
And when it comes to asking, with that same big sigh,
It's no, cause "Mom says so", and that is still why!

    —Judith Roach

Loving Prayers

As we sit beside a loved one who is ill,
We understand their future, is really "God's will."
Knowing surgery is needed, yet dreading the outcome,
We cry out to the Lord, "thy will be done."

We pray to our Lord for comfort and peace.
We know His love for all, will never cease.
Sweet is the trust we do have for thee,
As prayers go forth while on bended knee.

For those who are troubled, sacred oil is needed
By priesthood-holding Elders - their prayers are heeded.
We place names of the sick on Temple prayer rolls
And these become beacons to God, from our souls.

Dear family and friends add their thoughts to ours
And relying on angels and Heav'nly Father's powers
Full of the Holy Spirit, we rejoice in our hearts
To give thanks for the knowledge, His gospel imparts.

    —Elsie J. Staska

We Had Such A Wonderful Time Today

We had such a wonderful time today,
We went to the park and I watched you play.
You found a new friend with who you could laugh,
And later we discovered an old moss covered path.

Now you've taken your bath and brushed your hair,
Your nightgown is on and you have your bear
But before you close your eyes for the night,
Let's go outside while there's still some light.

Sit on my lap and listen to the leaves
Whispering to each other in the evening breeze.
I wonder what tales they have to tell,
Or if they're just nervous a storm might swell.

The first fireflies flit across the yard,
Each flash of light like a beckoning star.
A cricket comes out singing his song,
Then others join in to urge him along.

I hear you say "I love you" as I kiss your cheek,
And when I look again, you're fast asleep.
The rays of the sun have all slid away,
We had such a wonderful time today.

    —Carolyn Crandall

Beauty And Hair Fads

When we entered this lovely world
  We were blessed with locks so fine.
Some were curly, others were straight, but
  A thing of beauty, whatever the kind.

As a child those flowing locks can
  Add charm to a happy face,
And through those teenage years
  Its beauty we hope not to erase.

As the years have passed by
  The styles seem to rule the day.
The snarling and fluffing and teasing
  Has tossed hair's beauty astray.

The long locks, the men's pony-tails,
  And kinky, unruly hair half covering the face,
With long skinny bangs distorting one's view,
  On both men and women, look- a disgrace.

So why not shorten the bangs
  And let the facial features show through,
Brush out the teasing, put a wave in the kinks.
  And enjoy natural beauty, anew.

    —Irene Coughlin

A World In Conflict

A world in conflict, searching and longing for peace.
  Weary of wars, violence, and crime,
from these they want release.
  Conflicts rage, brings fear of the world's destruction.
Men will destroy themselves, if there is no arms reduction.
  Is life so cruel that conflicts, becomes our only fate?
Through violence and wars, we promote the bitterness of hate.
  Hate bears its bitter fruit, when vengeance becomes an outcry.
The sorrows of a wounded heart, is pain we cannot deny.
  Is there hope for a world, enduring suffering and pain?
Will peace be restored in the future, to be mankind's greatest gain?
  When men can reason together, and put all differences
aside. Let them establish a brotherhood, where peace and
and love will abide.

    —Elvin E. Storey

Glimpses Of Reality

Fire compelling, bright as day,
  Weaves enchantingly in thy sight,
Holding at bay the shifting gray
  Mists that playfully mimic night.

Arise, throw off blind entrancement,
  Free thy mind to see the bold truth;
Fiend fire sends bright enchantment
  That keeps thee bent in its tight booth.

Leave the flame and follow the lure
  Into those mists, and thee will see
Many mysteries fay and pure,
  And Glimpses of Reality.

Human Souls dwell there, dancing free,
  Knowing not what is yet to be;
And living governments they'll see -
  Aging biologically.

Truth and goodness and piety,
  And youth for all eternity,
Await the brave whose Souls seek free
  These Glimpses of Reality.

    —Donald Gilbert Carpenter

Welcome Home

Welcome home King descendants,
Welcome home.

Welcome home to Barlow Bend your birthplace,
Welcome home.

Welcome home children to the site of your childhood memories,
Welcome home.

Welcome home to the joys and sorrows shared by sisters and
brothers,
Welcome home.

Welcome home to Papa's and Mama's resting place,
Welcome home.

Welcome home King family,
Welcome home, welcome home.

—*Linda Diane King*

Wendy

Wendy, you're the lady in my heart as
Well as in all my thoughts, who I so
Greatly admire and truly desire.

You're the lady who is so rare and
Way beyond compare from anyone
Else I've ever known, for you're
One of a kind that is so hard to find.

Wendy, you're the lady who looks so
Fine all the time, and who I wish
Was truly mine to love, cherish,
Comfort, and adore, both night and
Day in every sweet, caring, and loving way.

You're the lady that will always
And forever have a warm and
Loving home in my heart.
Wendy, beautiful I just want you
To know that sweet heart, wherever
You may be or go, whatever you may do,
  I'll Always Love You."

—*Frederick Harold Arnold*

A Perfect Excuse

"We often hurt the ones we love." -so goes a mournful song.
Well, I'm an expert at that stuff. I wonder what is wrong.
"Tell me the truth", a friend will ask, "How do you like my hat?"
And I rise nobly to the task: "It makes your face look fat!"
And on and on I tell the truth that no one wants to hear.
I've done it since my early youth , and always will, I fear.
It doesn't help my cause a bit. I never get repaid.
Sometimes I think I ought to quit to call a spade - a spade.
What makes me act so ornery? Why do I play that game?
The answer finally dawns on me: my parents are to blame!
They chose the time when egg met sperm, and so - my date of birth.
After the proper nine-month-term, I found myself on earth.
That, which sends Zodiac on the march by its eternal rule,
Put Sagittarius in charge of me - its earthling tool.
The archer with the honest soul - he guides what I will say.
To tell the truth must be my goal, to speak out, come what may.
To sum it up: I wasn't there to lay my corner stone.
My parents were the guilty pair. They chose the date alone.
I cannot fight the stars above, and so I'm doomed, you see,
To sometimes hurt the ones I love - this "Sagittarian" me.

—*Hildegard Geller*

No Bugle Boy

No Bugle Boy played taps that night the FITZ
went down, but markers on the maps
Show where the men did drown.

Rough and heavy seas in sight, whipped by winds
of 60 knots, gave many a man a fright-
Un-cured by double shots.

Now on the muddy bottom, her hull broken in
pieces, is where Davy Jones gott'em-
Down where all life ceases.

Down by the bow the FITZ went, down into the
deep she plunged, so her use - full life
Is spent- her future expunged.

17 Miles north of white - fish
Point, and 88 fathoms deep,
The ship has become a fetish
For those who worry and weep.

No Bugle Boy played taps
That night the FITZ went down;
No more will those brave chaps
Visit their own home town.

—*Frank Ahern*

The Death Of A Dove

A wounded dove, alone and lost
went wandering through the night,
trying to find the snow covered path
of which it had lost sight.
Traveling far and for many a day
with neither food nor rest,
its weak, bedraggled wings gave way;
it never reached its quest.

The snow falls steady, and deeper still
the path is covered by the shroud.
The snow falls steady, as is man's will
death from a dark and mushroomed cloud.

And how will this dove understand,
how can it hope to see
the great nobility of man
and pay him eulogy?
Because somewhere its remnants lie
buried in the dust;
because of man it had to die
and man's most evil lust.

—*Linda M. Dettmann*

God's Gems

The most beautiful gems I have ever seen
Were brought about by the sun's bright gleam,
For the trees all sparkled in colors bright
Upon ice-laden branches, a rare delight.
Such glory to view on a cold wintry morning
No gem on earth could bring such a warming
To the heart, as the colors changed with each breeze
At the tip of each branch of the silvery trees.
Nothing on earth could ever compare
To the wondrous beauty that God had put there.
I deemed myself blessed, being able to see
The glory God wrought upon each sparkling tree.

—*Eugenia R. Mulligan*

A Family Thru Adoption

It's been a year, it's time to cheer,
we're living a Dream come true.

It's hard to remember, the past without her,
a bundle of joy at age two.

All of our fear,
turned into tears,
the day she came home to stay.

The long long wait, time we used to hate
now passes faster each day.

The simple pleasures, become instant treasures,
each day an adventure brand new.

There are times that we felt, like we wanted to melt,
when she hugs us and says, "I love you."

Nothing can compare, precious moments we share,
the feeling it's like no other.

The oyster has its pearl,
we have our little girl,
but there's still plenty of love for another.

—*William S. Campbell*

The Other Side

I found little things that got no mention
were often the culprits of stress and tension.

There was no second glance from the men I would meet
It took much longer to cross a street.
My memory lapsed and I couldn't hurry.
I was "Oh so tired" and my vision was blurry.

I preferred resting over having fun
and felt like I must weigh a ton.
The music I liked was soft and sweet.
My tummy said "Watch what you eat."

Yesterdays and tomorrows were the same as today.
I didn't dare enter a crowded freeway.
My bones ached, my feet were sore.
I said to myself "How much more?"

Then I heeded advice of those who had retired.
I found a quieter life on the other side.
My name was not listed for perpetuity
but it was on the list for Social Security."

—*Fannie M. Lacey*

Won't Be Pushed Around...

I tell you, I thought we were meant to be. Me knowing that
we're young, but that couldn't stop me, and nothing else
would... I thought you were the one, it was meant to be, until
the end. Though the end came pretty fast. Don't you agree...
Now I must go on with my life! I have to face the world. Be a
strong woman, not for you but myself. Have to put all the
negative things away! I have to admit, I am still captivated
by your love and affection that you brought towards me. Me
being gullible by each word you speak. Yet I must move on...
move on to be strong, stand out for my rights and achieve my
goals. Must put all the past away. Even though it may be
hard, I know I'll make it. I've come this far and there's no
stopping me NOW.... No one can stand in my way, a young strong
intelligent, determined lady like me can't and won't be pushed
around, not by a man or anyone else. There's no stopping me
now!!! I've come too far in this world to be stopped and I
won't, not by a man or anyone else!!!

—*Jamila H. Thomas*

Of Leaves And Love

Leaves, green leaves
What a sight to behold
Leaves that brighten nature
Leaves that echo back the past.

Leaves - so green and tender
Fresh and untouched by human hands
But then, slowly they wither, die, and fall
And gently blown by the wind.

Leaves - were just like my love
So green and tender when it first bloomed
So full of dreams, promises, and sweetness
Which later cooled off and died.

Leaves - they form a part of my life
They impart joy now that I'm alone
They cause the pain which I suffer
And because of them, my heart bleeds.

Leaves, green leaves
They would continue falling, I know
Continuously, they would hurt me
And continuously, too, they would torture my heart.

—*Maria Teresa C. Lazo*

When You Look Around You

When you look around you.
What do you see?
Poor souls, pitiful people,
Who need to get on bended knee.

What's happening to this world of ours?
Where to the trouble lay?
Instead of people getting better,
They're falling by the way.

We need more love in this world.
We need it so very bad.
When you look at the world and it's situations,
It's really very sad.

You don't expect a perfect world.
This would be asking too much,
But people will have to learn to live,
With a little more love, and a lot of trust.

When you look around you.
What do you see?
A world that need to get better,
Or never need to be.....

—*Bonnie Jean Taylor*

The Honey Grove

The unseen and unbelieved
What in life to be conceived

Don't he know he's not wanted
That spiritual life that is haunted

All darkness and sadness...
How could he break the chains of madness

No more mornings no more light
Just the blackness of the sight

Then he looks at the cold-blood

No hate, but the silence of love

As he whispers in the dark...
Descansar mi unico ecanta

—*Kimberlee Davis-Minniefield*

The Blind Man

Blind from birth he could not see
What is taken for granted by you and me.

The golden sun and the drenching rain
Beating against the window pane

But he loved life and to his ear
Came the sound of music loud and clear

Happy was he when he felt our hand
Clutching his, like a band.

Sightless he knew he had to be
But his gift of touch made others see.

How lucky they were to see the sky
So they stopped to talk on walking by.

Such happiness shone from their face
as he heard their footsteps and their pace.

Blind he was for evermore
But he knew he could knock on any door.

This man, so steadfast in his prime
Received our love and all our time.

Sightless he was for all to see
But that gift of touch meant much to me.

—*Madeline Van Horrik*

Searching For Some Sort Of Peace

The people of the world are dying at extraordinary rate.
What is this disease that is killing us all,
(mentally and physically)?
Could it be AIDS, hate, money, drugs, power, cancer
Or no communication between people, what?
We are born into such a crazy world
And are forced to pick from right and wrong.
How will we know the difference
When our parents don't know the difference?
How can we help others when we can't help ourselves?
How can we help ourselves when we don't have help from others?
I don't know the answer to these questions.
All I know is that I need God
And so does the rest of the world.
So God please save us all from destructions?

—*Esther Rosenberg*

Two Shades Of Blue

Two shades of blue, blue heaven and a blue day.
What more can a lonely person say?
My beautiful blue eyes in a head, hard as nails.
My ship just came in her ship's ready to sail.

Two shades of blue, one for you, one for me.
I have followed those blue eyes over the world
Each time I think I have her at arms length
She gives me a whirl.

Time and tide waits for no man, my life is
fast slipping away.
I could follow her, rest of my life.
No good for me, she will never be my wife.

I will sail on blue yonder
Let her wonder what happened to me;
When she hears the loud thunder
Maybe those blue eyes will think of me.

—*Hazel Huffman*

Words of Encouragement

Loud! Bossy! Vulgar! I'll-mannered in every way! This is
what they say. I know this to be untrue. For you are me and
I am you. You are my sister, my beautiful black sister.
Violent! Abusive! Ignorant! Ill-mannered in every way! This
is what they say. For you are me and I am you. You are my
brother, my beautiful black brother. We have suffered so much
from the destructive hands of others. From the rapings of our
sisters, to the lynchings of our brothers. Stolen from the
land from whence we came. Brought to a land who in-bred in us
guilt and shame. They have stripped us of an identity once so
proud. And now today this is something they greatly disavow.
They have taught us and have firmly believed that Black is bad
and white is good. I ask, why is it then the "good" insist on
wearing those damned white hoods. Ourselves they have taught
us to hate. Have we believed them? Angry towards her, your
sister, to your brother, to him we need not be angry towards
each other. I love you my sister! I love you my brother!
African kings and queens of Shabazz, Zulu and Ashanti strong,
intelligent, beautiful black people are we!

—*Carla Lynette Forster*

My Shadow Is Mine

My shadow is mine, it comes where I go.
Whatever I do, it always keeps low.
When I go for a walk, it stays by my side.
My shadow is with me, stride after stride.
Sometimes I jump high in the air.
My shadow jumps too, it always knows where.
When I go out, to play with my friends.
My shadow plays too, until the day ends.
My friends bring their shadows, they all play together.
They have the most fun when it's nice sunny weather.
If clouds come by, they come from the west.
It's time for my shadow to take a short rest.
My shadow is mine, and mine all alone.
Whether I'm little, or big and full grown.
At night when I go to my bed to sleep,
I know shadow's sleeping, I don't hear a peep.
My shadow is smart, it knows what to do.
Aren't you glad your shadow's with you?
No one can take my shadow from me.
You have your own, just look down and see!

—*Laura D. Hale*

Retirement

Life's full of strife
When a husband and wife
    Are suddenly together all day,
His retirement's great
But not for his mate
    "Cause she won't conform to his way.
He's not very cool
If he thinks her a fool
    Who can be molded and taught to obey -
She's ready to scream
Since he once was a dream
    But now, he's turning her hair to gray.
She tries to compromise,
But he thinks he's too wise,
    And schemes to make her pay.
He has no one to boss
But that's strictly his loss
    She'll do as she pleases, Ole'!

—*Harriet M. Rosenman*

Life's Extras

Always be aware of the heavenly beauty of the night,
When all things are transfigured by the full moon's light.
Enjoy the wild mocking bird's warbling song of release,
Which can surely bring the joys of beauty and peace.

Sunlight, air, water and food are needed to survive.
Moonlight and starlight are extras to enjoys when alive.
The stars in the sky above twinkle and brightly shine,
And are everlasting proof God's love is forever thine.

One of life's extras is a fresh, lovely flower,
To be appreciated the same as an April sun and shower.
Music and perfumes are extras for us to always enjoy.
While the necessities of life we must ever employ.

When with deep grief, take a walk in the wood,
The birds, the fragrance, the wind will do good.
Music will often remove one's deep and keen sorrow,
If from troubles one does not always stress borrow.

For strength that is permanent, one on faith must lean,
With that, hope, trust and things unseen we may glean.
We can always enjoys the extras from high above,
And know that they are from God's mercy and love.

—*Ida Mae Lehman*

When Comes The End

(Hopeful Thoughts of a Combat Soldier)
When comes the end - when these shadows lift,
When the roar dies out, with the bomb's haze-drift,
When the "light" breaks through, when it's peace we hear,
When brave-scared men can forget their fear—
'Tis then my joyous way I'll wend

Back home to you; when comes the end.
When comes the end of this bloodiest toil?
When will be reclaimed all the tyrant's spoil?
Not one can say we can only fight,
And deal out evil for the sake of right
Till we steadily forward force our trend

And our's is the victory, when comes the end.
When comes the end, may I be there,
To fling my helmet into peaceful air.
May I laugh and shout with many a friend

That we cheated death - till comes the end.
When comes the end, then I'll return
To the things I love, to you who yearn.
'Though we long were parted that time we'll mend.
We'll begin anew when comes the end.

—*David S. Bowen*

Sonnet 1

"Tis love I'm told that must as pillars stand
When doubting wind doth levy weak'ning blow,
To crack and raze the strength of sweat-stuck sand,
To slay and bring the monument full low.
This love I'm told must soar as mighty wings
Amidst the breezeless heights and restless sky,
To dodge the arrowed darts and flighty stings
That glory in the fall of winged cries.
'Tis love I'm told that as the lonesome oak
Resides atop the weather beaten knoll
In rigid pride, all anger to provoke,
Inspiring jealous wrath from mightier souls.
Nay, I say love's the sapling sprig that bends
And with life's pressure humbly doth contend.

—*David E. Manley*

Untitled

Oh what wicked battles go on in the mind.
When everything around you is peaceful.
Wisps of daydreams flutter before your eyes.
Wishes and fantasies fight back haunting memories.
Smiles come and go, only less often than they used to.
Thoughts without feelings become hopes without souls.
Sparks are gone, fleeting moments now too rare to remember.
Dazed into a nowhere stupor beyond imagination.
Creativity is dead in the disdain of reality.
Knowing anything would be better, but not knowing how to get
there, or even how to start.
Dreading tomorrow's sunrise and yet greeting it gracefully
in the morning's new light.

—*Kelly McGrew*

The Holidays

The everyday doldrums of life disappear
When first we feel the holidays near.

The hustle and bustle and careful preparation
Of food and drink for friends and relation

Soon turn to silence and quiet reflection
of those who had come from every direction.

We laughed, we loved, and cried some to
for all too soon, we knew - we knew.

We stood at the door - with tears in our eyes
Expressing our love while bidding good-byes.

—*Constance Jo Kluding*

Days Of The Past

Just sitting here, thinking of a day gone by,
When happiness seems not to lack,
Where humor always covered up the bad,
And seriousness made no match.

Those days are gone,
Replaced by bitter cold stares,
Harsh words spoken,
Friendship broken.

Try to retrieve those days,
Cannot reach that far back,
To where the days were fine,
You have left it all behind.

Grown up, grown old, grown cold,
Memories slipping away,
Some warm summer day,
You find yourself fading away.

Lights go out, silence all around,
Nobody's home, left all alone,
You'll find yourself just sitting there,
Trying to remember those days gone by.

—*Brenda Kloss*

Led By His Hand

I love to walk alone in the dark of night
When stars deck the sky with diamonds of light
And a small silver of moon hangs low and dim
It's then I almost see God; I talk with Him
I thank Him for the blessings of the past day
I thank Him for leading me on in His way
That I should walk to be worthy of His grace
And I'm sure if He could; He'd reveal His face
But it is enough to feel His presence nigh
And know He reigns from heaven on high
I put my life completely in His command
Secure in the thought I am led by His hand

—*Lillian L. Schrader*

568

"Love Is"

Love is Christ's love for all mankind,
when He gave His life all of us,
That we may have forgiveness of our sins
and His promise for eternal life.

Love is friendship, like a flower,
it buds, blooms, and groves.
Like the beauty of nature itself.

Love is kindness, patience, understanding,
sharing giving, helpfulness to others,
always willing to lend a helping hand.

Love is like a beacon in the sky,
showing forth its light, like a gem,
with its sparkle and radiance.

Love is overpowering, towering high above,
like a mountain, with its continued strength,
as of a mighty shield.

Love is a splendid thing,
no matter what form it may be.
It's like a circle, never ending.

—*Helen McHale*

"Blessings"

We all were blessed; by God.
When he gave us a partner called "woman".
But we undervalue those blessings.
And some of us even forget about that "woman"
Woman that is our mother.

But mother today — mother tomorrow.
Mother when we were children;
Mother when we are grown-ups.
Suffered mothers — mother suffering now.
But nobody knows it.
Because she's always happy and smiling.
To care for her children.
Though they all forgot her.

—*Luis Munoz Guevara*

Trust Me

Oh how can I ask one as lovely as you to trust me,
When I am not even sure that I can trust myself;
For when I look into those lustrous pools:
Of splendor and beauty that are your eyes,
I see the flames of passion burning bright;
Oh how they enchant me I just want to take you in my arms:
And never let you go,
But we our friends and that can not be;
Oh Lord when we are close I can not trust me!
I have tasted the sweetness of your kiss,
But once an only for a second;
But that second seamed like a life time to me!
How can I ask one with kisses as sweet as sugar,
To trust me when I long to kiss you forever;
And fill the warmth of your love ever close to me:
But we our friends and that can not be,
Oh Lord when you are close I can not trust me.

—*Charles S. Lepore Jr.*

Retirement Enthusiasm

I never thought that I would see the day,
when I could vacate desk, files and computer
and slightly drift away
To a permanent change which we all look forward to
When one reaches the age of course,
there is not much more to do.
But look to the time when we are fancy and free
to do whatever one desires; that wonderful
wish comes from me.
The greatest thought appearing in the mind
Is covering everything you wanted to do,
but couldn't find the time.
I dare you to compare how great retirement can be!
Traveling, relaxing, and volunteering for services
that seniors delight to see.

—*Lois P. Marks*

Long Ago

There was once a time
When I felt the soft breeze on my face,
rejoiced in its warmth -
the gentle glow that keeps souls warm and content.

There was once a time
When beauty was so intoxicating;
I was overwhelmed by its mere thought.

That was long ago...
I feel cold now.
The shaking hands you see are mine;
They shiver from the cold and cannot be warmed.
My eyes, too fragile to look upon,
Shy away from what they see.
How can I be so lost?

—*Jacqueline Allard*

"Lovin' You"

In the past there have been times
When I have started something new,

But never have I been happier than when
I started lovin you!

If I had to quit everything in my life
and there was only one thing I could do,

I would put everything down around me
and keep on lovin' you.

I have seen gold shining so bright
And when I touched it, I knew,

That if you could give me all this shining gold-
It still wouldn't equal lovin' you.

When I think of all the experiences
This man has been through.
There's none better,
Than simply "Lovin' You!"

—*Carole Velde*

The Wine's On The Counter

I'm in the chair.
We're both alone in our own rooms
separated by air.
I've danced and I've sung
and done all that I dare.
Only when I knocked things off the wall
did you even seem to care.
At times like this it's hard to explain
why I should even be here.

—*Cynda L. Nelson*

Your Eyes: Sea Of Tranquility

Your eyes are the sea of tranquility.
　　When I look into them I can see indefinitely.
They are very much a Revelation to me.
　　Exposing much more than reality.

Your eyes have the effect of a hypnotic trance.
　　I'm completely mesmerized in an immoveable stance.
When they focus on me all my cells dance.
　　My eyes forever want to glance and glance.

Your eyes have a calming effect on me.
　　They are very stimulating like a hot cup of tea.
They are as beautiful as a sunset to me.
　　Your eyes are forever captivating me.

Your eyes are truly a sight to behold.
　　My yearning for your arms to enfold me has become bold.
In other words they sparkle and shine like glass, silver and
　　gold. When my eyes meet yours, the pupils say SOLD.

　　　—Charlotte W. Cue

The Stronger Sex

I thought I could answer the problems of all mankind.
　　When I thought I understood life's riddles.
　　　When I thought I knew the female mind.
　　　I discovered I knew very little.

　　When I thought we were the stronger sex.
　　　And there was no task on earth,
　　　　that was to complex.
　　　Yet we could never give birth.

　　　I could never take the pain.
　　　Nor could I take the stress.
　　For the strongest sex I must explain.
　　Wears not the paints but the dress.

The female is not just an object of beauty.
　　Or an object of lust.
　　All men have a sacred duty.
　　Show them love honor and trust.

　　I will try to understand,
　　the ways of the opposite gender.
I'll be a gentleman when ever I can.
　　And lovingly treat them tender.

　　—Frederick Alonzo Reuling

Remaining Sham

An old tree stood in the middle of the lake,
When the motor boats passed it shivered in their wake.
"It's the one remaining sham",
Said the man who built the dam.
"We tried to pull it up with a crane
And the bulldozer tried to knock it down in vain."

Man's city needed a new water supply
So he flooded a valley in the hills nearby.
The animals fled and refuge was scarce.
A weasel choose a limb the lake didn't swallow.
The opossum hid in the old trees hollow.
The old tree had a purpose to fulfill,
And it was strong enough to defy man's will.

It's only a hollow shell today,
But it still stands, as if to say:
"Don't take away all open land,
Wild life is valuable too: please understand!
The balance of nature is tried and true."

　　—Dorothy Scrutchin

To My Husband

Oh what a lonesome summer this has been
When I walk through the garden alone

The grass and the trees are the same and the birds keep
calling your name but I don't hear your whistling their reply

In the car as I'm riding, I keep seeing you beside me
Commenting on the views that we pass

I keep your cap on the seat beside me
It seems to help guide me along

I feel like I'm moving around with 100# weight in my chest
How long does a heart have to keep dragging this load,
Before it can have some rest

I just can't adjust to this being alone,
The hours that drag are just endless

I'm so glad we enjoyed the little things that we did together
Even a little ride before dark always added a spark
To the quiet evenings before us

There is a reason they say to keep pushing along
As yet I still haven't found it

It's a lonesome old path we have to bear
When we've lost someone who used to care

　　　—Edith M. Mellon

Best Friend

She is the closest person to me.
　　When I'm with her,
I feel so free.
　　It is easy to talk to her,
And also to cry.
　　Everything about me, she knows.
Oh I would never try to lie.
　　Nothing is ever to secret not to tell.
'Cuz even if I kept it inside,
　　It would be ever so hard to hide.
I never want this friendship to end.
　　Because, she is my best friend.

　　　—Kristina Speck

The True Story Of Gordon Jackson

Back in the days when texas was young,
When men packed six-guns and horses thieves were hung,
Gordon Jackson rode north singing one day,
Waving to friends aa he went on his way.
He was headed for Kansas on a big cattle drive-
never to return to Texas alive!
The cattle were sold and the men left for home,
But all of them parted, and each went alone.
The rest were united with families and friends,
But Gordon Jackson's life story in this way ends.
His wife was forever to wait in vain,
For she was never to see him again!
Did he drown in a river, was he killed by a fall,
Was he shot by a stranger in an Abilene brawl?
Through all the long years, this mystery remains
Of a man who drove cattle across the Great Plains!

　　　—Miss Bettie Geren

"Yesteryear"

Oh, to have lived in yesteryear
When skies were bright and streams were clear
When man could live by the work of his own hand
At peace with God, in love with the land.

Oh, to have lived in days of old
When nature's wealth meant more than gold,
When we understood from time of birth
The need, the duty to care for earth.

Oh, to have lived in days long past
When human ties were made to last,
When trust and fidelity were better known
In friendship, love, marriage, home.

Oh, to have lived in the long ago
When one's immortal soul could grow
In understanding, caring, faith,
When life moved at a slower pace.
—*Germaine Davis Williams*

Friendship

You ask what your friendship means to me
    When the heart has a lonely hour,
It's a kin to the silver rain that falls
    On the petals of a flower.
Or the tinted hues of a bright rainbow
    As it spans from hill to hill,
The twilight hour when I first hear
    The call of the whippoorwill.
It's the sigh of the South wind through the pines
    The blue-green depths of the sea,
All of these and so much more your
    friendship means to me.
A meadow in the morning mist
    The mountains tipped with blue,
The star that pales in the western sky
    With the promise old, yet new-
That these things shall not pass away
    Nor will the moon beams end,
Each star-bright night, each sunlit day
    Will bring you near, my friend.
—*Hope Kreiger*

Cats

Cats are soft, furry and sweet
when they've just came in with muddy feet.

Cats are busy little things,
when they've been outside, they'll bring in a birdie wing.

Cats like to see the Whisker Lickens label.
And they like even better to walk on the table.

Cats like to play with strings,
jump in windows, and knock over things.

Cats like to hide in boxes and drawers.
And do their business on the floor.

Cats like to go up and down stairs.
They like to get the newspaper and tear, tear, tear.

Cats are sweet and lovable pets.
They're just the nicest things you've ever met.
—*Linda Thornburg*

My Heavenly Visitor

The calling of God in my Christian life
Was a Bible miracle - you must agree
I had never seen God's good Book
When Jesus came to visit me.
I do believe in Christian miracles
As strange as they may seem to be.
With God, all things are possible
For Jesus came to visit me.
I will help you Sayeth the Good Lord,
Come with me - the way of truth.
I have made a promise to the Almighty
To share God's Gift with all of you.
—*Leopold C. Martinez*

Has Been

We know that it is a special time of the year
When those arrive who carry wood, leather and sphere
Showing up on green fields both far and wide
To bat, field, throw, run and slide
Arms release balls like so many darts
Legs glide between bases after very quick starts
Hands pick up rockets that are hit their way
Moving in a blur no orbs go astray
Bats make contact with effortless swings
These guys are blessed by those with wings
I marvel at their speed and grace
And realize time flies by like a race
Decades ago I could play this game
Performing well enough to put them to shame
Those older then thought now as I do
Just once more couldn't I be like you
For my book of life has reached a back page
You see for me it is called old age
—*Eric Gluck*

Hope For Tomorrow

Sometimes, Dear Lord, I lose hope for tomorrow
When today seems to be full of sadness and sorrow.
Please teach me, O Lord, to then call on you
When it seems like the sun will never shine through.

As in nature, with storms, comes also the showers
That water, nourish, and strengthen the flowers.
So I know with the sadness comes a strength that you give
Which helps me to grow, to mature, and to live.

But when times of trouble do come my way
Teach me, O Lord, to just kneel and pray.
I must not lose hope, for tomorrow I'll find
I've become stronger in body, in soul, and in mind.
—*Eddy Logan*

Untitled

I'm sitting here thinking about you
Wondering if your thinking about me
I sit in the darkness missing you
I sit alone wanting to hold you
I sit sadly thinking of us
I also sit happily thinking of us
I daydream of our futures together
Wondering if you are or soon will be thinking the same
Then realize that I really do love you
—*Ann-Marie Cilwa*

Magic Johnson

Many of us watched him play pro-basketball for 12 years...
When we heard he was retiring, there were many tears; He was
the unique superstar from Michigan State... His consistently
outstanding performances were always first-rate.

Suddenly, a nation was shocked to learn that a supposed
three-day bout with the flu concerning Magic — one of the
all-time greats — was just simply untrue.

He held a nationwide press conference telling the world he
tested positive for the HIV stunning people virtually
everywhere as they asked: "Can it happen to me?"

He is now in a bigger arena, And his opposition — a much more
formidable foe — His fight against AIDS will require much more
than his eternal smile and glow.

As fans, we will never forget him, he always put on quite a
show; A man who has shown his courage, And when faced with a
challenge, Never said "No."

Here's his chance to improve the world as he did in his sport,
And even if he leaves us too soon, his life will not be for
naught.

— *Howard S. Bealick*

Toward the Unsetting Sun

And in that strange moment
when we view the aristocracy,
their smooth mouths and pointed noses.
Even after revolutions from 1789 to 1917
we all sense an instant of inferiority,
that innate desire to be commanded
like the pitied person once bonded to the fields.
Their graceful motion and infallible speech
intensifies the bred beauty
which swims forever in their blood.
I could never question their integrity
which flows so generously in their gestures.
So white, untainted are the thoughts
behind pampered skin and child like translucent eyes.

Marx, our guidance, when will it happen?
Our rise toward the unsetting sun,
The revolutions are over, and
has anything changed or will we always be their subjects?
Subject to the opinions and cravings of the aristocracy.

— *David J. DePippo*

Daddy

I'll never forget my sweet dad
When we were sick at night
It was he, who turned on the light
He'd lead us in a happy way
And we knew "Every things gonna be OK!"

He'd read our Bible late at night
He tried his best to teach us right
He taught us one thing money can't buy.
A happy relationship with Jesus on high
I'm looking forward to that Day so nigh
Where well never say goodbye

So friends hold your heads up high
These troubles will soon pass by
We'll all be in the arms of Jesus
In that sweet By and By
No pain nor sorrow in this earth
Can compensate our precious Saviors birth

— *Kathleen Goodin Carr*

Precious Daughter of Mine

I treasure that April Day, you're first moments of time,
When you were born, precious daughter of mine.
As a babe, I forever carried you,
Time went on and you grew and grew.
Then you were always under my feet,
Time went on never missing a beat.
Next you started getting in my hair,
Time went on, it just wasn't fair.
Now you're off and on your own,
Without you around, I feel so alone.
So as the clock beats on in time,
Together we'll grow, precious daughter of mine.

— *Andrea Wisniewski*

Ah... Memories

You don't think much about memories
When your heart is young and gay
For your life is far too busy
With the schedule of the day.

But in golden years, how precious and dear
Are the memories that come to mind
Recalling times and days gone by
And of dreams long left behind.

Some fill your soul with peace and love
So vivid, real and clear.
Some put a smile upon your lips
Yet fill your eyes with tears.

And as you grow old, I'm sure you'll find
The sad ones are but few,
For God in His infinite mercy
Has hidden them from you.

You can't live yesterday over.
Take care what you do and say—
For the memories of your tomorrow
Are the ones you are making today.

— *Elizabeth Stewart*

Through The Eyes Of Children

It all seems so grand
When you're just a child
The world is a giant playground
Spinning loving dreams all the while.

Suddenly you've grown full bloom
Romping through the house
Climbing monkey bars
And dreaming dreams to reach the stars.

All you hear is true
Questioning everything and nothing
High is up
And deep is blue.

Far away from all life's harm
Wouldn't it be wonderful to remain
Embraced in this charm
Caught up in a child's song of sweet refrain.

— *Francina B. Sorey*

A Special Seal

One seal stands surrounded by other seals,
    yet she is different.
She is white and the others are brown.
This seal is not shy or lonely though.
    She's just happy to be alive
      and to be a seal.
    Seals are like people,
    only sometimes even smarter.

— *Jessica Honor Carleton*

Where Dreamers Go

There is a place where dreamers go
Where all the colors of the rainbow glow
They call this peace, it is not
It's the heart that lives without caring
It's the heart that we've forgot
The soul that no longer can bear it
There is a place where dreamers go
In a room of flowers that only wither away
They feel there's no tomorrow, they have no today,
and to them there was never yesterday
It is a peaceful place where dreamers go
The sky never darkens, the sun always glows
There are no burdens, no sorrows
In this place there's always tomorrow
There's always a hand out to welcome you in
And your dreams will never be shattered again
Everyone there is the best of friends you know
For my friend you see
It's the most wonderful place to be
In this place where dreamers go
　　　　　—Debbie Meadours

Growing Up

Looking around I wonder
Where all the time goes.
Yesterday I was starting kindergarten,
Wow, how one grows.
You spend half your life wondering
What you'll be like when you grow old.
The rest of your life you spend wishing
How to go back to being young and bold,
Looking in the mirror,
Watching yourself change.
Hoping the days go slower,
Wishing the future didn't seem so strange.
It seems so crazy
How the days fly on by.
I remember being a little girl gazing into the sky.
Now I sit here wondering
What I did with all the time.
Thinking about my future,
Will I shine?

　　　　—Deborah Stone

MNPY, 1986, Mir (Year Of Peace, USSR)

I met you in Kalinen,
Where are you today, Lana?
Where is your peace?
Is it the peace of God that passes all understanding?
Will you find peace as someone finds this balloon?

The world, as these words, has
Too many questions,
Too few answers,
And too little Peace.

　　　　—Lorine A. Gleue

Despair

Despair, why have you come to visit?
You were not invited into my mind.
You have no place with me.
Go away from me now.
If you don't leave I will be forced to cry.
I am trying not to think about you.
I want to sleep but you will not allow me too.
You bother me with your constant whisper.
Lose yourself before I lose my mind.
Flee from me. Now I'm free

　　　　—Clinton D. Hobdy Jr

December Scene

I plod
Where deer have lightly trod.

How neat
The petitpoint of sparrows' feet;
The watery bower
Where watercress spreads its snowy flower;
The shape,
Bravely erect, of Oregon grape.

I look
And wonder at the maternal murmur of the brook.
And see
Branches of light reflected festively.

I plod
Where deer have lightly trod.
　　　　—Charlotte R. Grawn

Equality

Equality…to be made equal
Where did it begin.. with man
Was it with the woman's vote
Could it have been the color of our skin
Perhaps…equal rights
Lets try the labor laws
Along with equal pay
Maybe it is the right to speak
The right to worship
With freedom of choice
The right to be who we are
Does it really exist
…Can it be…
Yea…for you see…it all began
When the son of God came
Willingly to walk and represent man…kind
Is man…kind willing to see
And recognize truth
With freedom and equality
　　　—Pauline J. Richards

Bad Times

As the October cold starts to come
Where do the street people go?
Do they hover in dumpsters, and doorways
Or do they sleep in the snow.

Not every one has a job.
It's not as easy, as you think
We are cold and hungry to.
And yes we'd like a job to do.

Did you ever eat from a garbage can?
And be glad you found it there
Did you ever go so long, without a bath
Or, watch, others at you stare

If there was working, like they say
I'd be working, yes for pay
I'd have a warm bed to sleep in
I'm just like you, I need a friend.

They sent our jobs, off to countries so far.
And they hired, a robot or two
And Mr. Manufacturer, just please do tell me
Does other countries, and robot's buy a car.

　　　　—Marvel Feltman

The Sea of Margo

All day I'm in this sea, wave after wave,
Where do they start where do they end,
I see them coming at a distance
Cresting and sounding - they are bluish green.

The sea of Margo it is called
Where few venture and shortly are beyond recall.
Set sail - go forward with the evening tide,
Set your ship on course and let
The stars be your guide.

Way out there, there is a new landfall,
Reached only by the prevailing winds
And storms and test of time.
The sea of Margo it is called,
Where few venture and a good sailor
Often rows, paddles and swims to
reach and touch the gentle image in
his mind.

—*Henry Cota*

Halt Disaster

Where are the birds, where are the trees
Where is the rain, where is the breeze?
Winds always blow hard, dust in my face
Even the snow misses this place.

When I was young, hedges grew tall
Birds had their nests, food there for all
Did you cut the hedge, did you cut the trees
Did rabbits and squirrels follow the bees?

Think before acting, don't ravage the earth
Conserve and replenish for all you are worth
Listen to others and strive to replace
All of the damage by our human race.

Halt the erosion, there still is a way
Plant trees and save wildlife, help us today
Plan for the future, I hope there's still time
Let's make it a beauty, your land and mine.

—*Juanita O. Gilbert*

I Know This Place...

I know this place which we have not yet seen
where light streams, ripples and enfolds
where past and future lose their shape and find it
again in crystal harmonies of thought.

I know this place where we have not yet been
where stillness plays a music of its own
where time and distance come apart and meld again
in the vast forests of the forever of the mind.

I know this place which we have not yet reached
where all enigmas are unraveled and explained
where plan and chance collide and yet embrace again
in a continuum of calm and peace.

I know this place which we will find still
where there's no pain, no anger and no tears
where we are never left to feel alone or estranged
for every soul we have ever touched and every being we have
ever known is here...embracing us with joy and tenderness...
Life touching Life. Meeting here in this place meant for all
of us..for we are all alike...and we are to each other
Children of the same gentle and ever loving God.

—*Cleo Laszlo*

A Writer's Dream

I searched my life through to find my true person,
Where my ability may lie at the beginning was quit uncertain.

I tried so many areas of all types of work,
From a factory worker to even a shipping clark.

As time went by I lived as many others,
Only to find myself looking for me within my personal cover.

I found myself suddenly with pen,
That's when my true self really began.

The words flowed from my mind like a rushing brook.
As out of control all my true self pored out into a book.

Unsure to submit, and in great fear of rejection,
To be told your work is good enough, is
a writer's dream that can never be perfected.

—*Marie Irwing*

Imagining

Have you ever been to a magical place,
Where they don't discriminate on your color or race,
Where the sky is the color of aquamarine,
And unicorns tread on the patches of green.
Where dragons and children lay down side by side,
They stay sleeping soundly with nothing to hide.
Where strawberries grow when the summer days are long,
And hummingbirds' wings beat a melodious song.
Where butterflies arch their wings and take flight,
And a star shines brightly in the twilight.
Where a firefly's goldness illuminates the sky,
And moon-kissed water catches the eye.
But then you realize the image is leaving,
And to you your mind has been quite deceiving,
For nothing this beautiful could ever be real,
This place is something you can't touch or feel.
We know in reality this place can't exist,
It stays in your mind an unreachable wish,
Have you ever been to a magical place,
It vanishes into the night ... without leaving a trace.

—*Angela Rosenthal*

Don't Wake Me Now

Now that you have found your way into my heart;
Where will we go from here my dear?
Now, when the power of our love makes mountains tremble
     and seas part;
When will Cupid's dull arrows signal that romance end is near?

Now when I cry, my tears are tears of joy;
And my greatest worry is that our lips shall not soon caress;
Now, the bed with satin sheets is another wonderful toy;
Instead of just a piece of furniture to slumber upon and rest.

Now, when rest is upon my mind, I undress and rest with you;
You—that magnificent animal that God created just for me!
Then joyous songs we sing to sleep and to meet the rising
     sun to;
Oh, with love to light the way, life is as simple as can be!

If this is a dream—my love—it's dream that I have never
dreamt before; And if asleep I am, then I wish to
sleep for days, years and even more!
Because I want more of this stuff that makes me giggly called
love; And many, many more nights singing joyously to the
stars and moon above!

—*George E. Pope III*

Reflections...

Reflections...
  Whether good or bad
Are what we portray
  In this life that we have.
A reflection...
  I pray that I am
Of His beauty and love
  Reaching out to family and friend.

Do we reflect a mirrored image of Him?
  Are we in His likeness or an antonym?
Are we a mirage, an illusion to see?
  Or do we reflect His divinity.
Can others look in and Him do they see
  A reproduction, a copy, this Jesus in me!

Formed in His image.
  Yes! In His likeness I am.
Working and loving and abiding in Him.
  Letting my light shine before all of man
That others might see
  This reflection of Him.

    —Donna Horn

I Wonder

I wonder
Whether he knew
Death was waiting outside his door
As we kissed him goodnight
And said, "We'll see you in the morning, love."

I wonder
Had he had strength to speak
Would he have whispered, "Stay.
Death is just outside my door."

So many times we'd held him tight,
Our arms around him close;
Though Death we knew awaited him,
We wouldn't let him go.

I wonder
Had we stayed the night,
Whether one more time
We could have pushed Death back,
Death, waiting just outside his door.

Sad and lonely, I wonder.
I wonder.

    —Bernice Musick

Duel In The Sunshine State

For months they dueled
Whether knowingly or not their zeal never cooled
Until the fatal shot.

Their duel need not have
Pitted one against the other.
There should have been no feelings personal
Only love as for a brother.

Though their beliefs were different
Their actions should not have been significant
America is a country with divergent views
Less emotion would have provided less news.

The gunman disliked the law
Permitting the doctor's action
He felt compelled to correct the flaw
His emotions must have satisfaction.

The victim had won a duel with polio and realized his ambition
Overcoming adversity, he had become a physician.
But this duel he would not win, what a shame
The murderer toted a "38"; the only gun Dr. Gunn had was his name.

    —Harold Newman

My Homeland

Why comes this black cloud that I see
Which casts a shadow on my horizons?
A spiritual barrier that impedes movement
Swiftly envelopes the yearnings within my mind.
My thoughts reminisce to a forgotten time
When only the daybreak limited contemplation.
It seems inconceivable as to why it must be
That dreams provide no longer any comfort.
Alas, the illusions of a hopeful youth
Have no bearing on omnipotent fate.
Eyes that view the dominant summit of life
Seldom believe in the distance required.
How maniacal does existence appear
When imagination and reality do not intersect.
I find it amusing when those who are younger
Relate to me that I failed my own hopes.
No one is capable of neglecting dreams
Unless circumstance provides a more stable mind-set.
A ghost of an aspiration emerges in my head
And my homeland is again under my control.

    —Douglas Farmer

Love

You look into my eyes and say Love is emotion
Which causes you to value and crave my body;
You press my lips and swear that Love is not shoddy,
But when you speak of possession I question devotion.
You milk my breast and declare Love is an ocean;
That you are not magna, but summa cum laude;
That I must not think of you as being cloddy,
Yet I see you are merely drunk with lotion.
I look and say Love itself cannot be defined;
Caring and sharing, yes; a product of thought, no!
I behold you and say freedom Love guarantees.
I look and say Love itself is for all mankind;
Caring and sharing, yes; a product of thought, whoa!
I behold you and say Love itself frees! frees! frees!

    —Letty M. Shaw

The Many Thoughts Of The Teenage Mind

There's your own personal love life
Which he doesn't even know exists
So you drag up the courage to talk to him
And see him the very next day
But you forget your lines
And run away.

Then there's the problem with the ECO system
Which no one seems to get
So the earth keeps melting away
Day by day, by day.

We need to educate people more today
To help our children and save what we may
Learn all you can about the facts of life
And TEACH IT! TEACH IT! Left and right.

If we clear the minds of teenagers today
We can educate them for the fight of tomorrow
And if we know what is needed to know
Teach young and old, to and fro
And we'll be ready for the biggest fight
The one you and I call teenage life.

    —Josephine Leone

Legacy

Part of me is in this land
Which nurtures me and earns my love
Part of me is everywhere
Across the seas and at land's end
In everyone whom I have touched
And every song I've sung
In every poem I have loved
In all the faces I have met
And lovely paths I've walked
The rough roads and hills I've climbed
To my dear children I give it all
May their paths be smooth and mountains high
So they may know the glorious climb
And find it great as did I
        —*Carol C. Larson*

Which Way Now?

All the gates are open now
which one I choose to go through is now my decision.

Various options can be found at each gate
I will look at them, evaluate them and decide what I really
    want.

Then I will run like hell through that gate
Time is wasted by looking back
Because the circle is empty now and the memories are in my
    heart.

So I will use my knowledge and God given wisdom and run
    run like hell and hope the wind will dry my tears.

        —*Martin J. O'Malley*

A Mouse in the House

There's a mouse in the house - what shall I do?
while I sleep - He comes out to chew

He chews the wall beside my bed
He runs across the floor 'neath my head
Then darts to the kitchen - to eat my bread

I'll buy a cat to catch that mouse
who dares to live in my house

But a cat will meow, as all cats do
And wake my dog, and he'll bark too
Oh quiet little mouse, I'll just keep you.
        —*Dennis L. Dotts, Sr.*

Why?

Why do children die.
While other children cry?
Why do people get illnesses without cures
That leave them less than pure?
Why do we have wars that people fight?
To me that doesn't seem too bright.
Why do people get addicted to things?
Or join gangs?
Why do some people not have homes
While others practically live in domes?

Why do people play with guns?
Don't they know that's rather dumb?
Why do women get raped?
After all, wasn't it supposed to be a date?
Why do people steal?
Why don't they get real?
Why do people kill themselves?
Life can't possibly be a living hell.
Why doesn't any of the answers to these

        —*Heather Maurice*

She Sits There

She sits there quiet in another world,
while she screams in her mind;
Wishing to be like the others,
but herself she must first find;
If only she would be able to think
about her future,
but remaining there will always be
her haunted past;
And there will be problems in the present,
for this is the time that for awhile
will last;
Wishing she would have thought
about what she was doing in the
years before,
maybe people now would have looked
at her with joy;
Things will never change between her
and this place called Earth,
for she will just sit, and sit, and sit...

        —*Christine Luebke*

Unanswered Prayers

Wondering, wandering,
Whispering unanswered prayers.
Thinking, Pondering,
Dreaming unrealized dreams.
Within,Without,
I am alone inside myself.
My hopes have been shattered,
My dreams have been lost,
My prayers have gone unheard.
I have nothing, except my love.
I have no one, except Magdalena, whom I love,
But I cannot tell her this.
She is the only purpose my life has,
My only reason to live.
Her perfection is unmatched,
Her beauty knows no equal,
She is the incarnation of purity,
But she does not know I exist,
And she never will.
        —*Marshall Fletcher*

Beach

Waves undulating toward the beach,
white tongues lifted to lick the ice-cone tree
and lap the glazed and frosted shore

Grey clouds overhead fade to the horizon blue
The sun tiring of Hide-and-Seek will also fade,
as will the sparkle of the ice encrusted tree-limbs

Still beauty remains as pipe-organ ice-tubes reach
up from the roots toward the limbs as if to see,
and perhaps to hear also the waves and the wind, and more

Two bundled against the cold, linking arms as lovers do
Seeing nature's beauty, they stand as if bade
by nature to listen to her, and memories that won't dim

Of other walks and distant shores, moments that teach...
Souls open each to the other — it had to be,
for only then could love grow and each the other adore

Gazing into each other's eyes, pain fades, they love anew
A bond beautiful and too strong to die is made,
while nature shares her secrets by Lake Ontario's frozen rim
        —*George F. Bergman, Jr.*

A Teenager In Trouble?

Where is that cute little boy
who, as a baby, brought me so much joy?
I would like to find him if I can.
I believe he is hiding in the body of a man!

Too big to be spanked when bad,
My son does some things to make me mad!
He tries to stay on the right track
But his young inexperienced mind is easy to ransack!

Girls seem his problem to be.
They cloud his brain, and he can't listen to me!
I believe he wants to leave her,
But she confuses him and renders his mind a blur!

One good thing about the problems of youth,
Usually one recovers like after a sore tooth!
I have faith in the way he was raised,
And am sure he will soon again be praised!

    —*Elsie M. Beard*

"Hidden"

The majestic mountainside and immaculate plains, are like she
who holds everything inside and covers up her pains.

If you really got to know her you'd know there is more to her
than meets the eye. When on the outside she was smiling on the
inside another part of her soul gradually begins to die.

When a monarch butterfly gracefully soars overhead, she no
longer gazes at it wondrously-she wishes it were dead. In may
when the spring flowers beautifully bloom, her heart and mind
is still cold and buried below the snow while she silently
cries in her bedroom.

The sorrowful day will eventually come when she will give up
and take no more, soon she will take her life into her own
young hands all the while wondering what she's been living for.

    —*Charity Tumblin*

Truly An Angel

    You truly are an angel
      Who in my eyes I see
   Your friendship that is measured
   By all those little treasures
    You have given me.

Always being there when I needed you
  When I was feeling sad and blue.

For sharing laughter, tears and smiles
  That reach out for many miles.

I really am so lucky to have a friend like you
    For you truly are an angel,
     I will never forget you.

    —*Deb Prunty*

The Children's Hour Reply

This is your blue eyed banditti, who long ago scaled your wall,
who knew that a moustache as you were, must have been a match
for us all.
But you allowed yourself to be taken, by those of us yet so
small, the locks and the chains that had bound you, were of
kisses and hugs, that was all.
Do you think oh moustache of mine, now that I have grown, my
love is not equal to that of the young girl you had known?
Yes, now my life is busy, spare moments I have few.
Life brings change, as we all know,
but nothing could change my love for you..........

    —*Cathy Messina*

Heroes

I saw homecoming victorious soldiers,
Who saved fatherland from oppressors,
One falling behind, both legs amputee,
Pair of crutches tied to his armpits.

With his hands he used deadly machine guns,
Missiles and rockets while shedding his blood.
Victory medals adorning his chest,
Unselfishly served to save his country.

But now has no hands to salute his flag,
Neither to caress his beloved child.
Has no legs to put his foot on the land
So valiantly fought to free his homeland.

    —*Ferdinand Kaimakamian*

To My Daughter Nancy

I knew a little girl
Who was my pride and joy.
She was a little devil
Should she have been a boy?

But she was for sure all female
From her head right to her toes.
She loved to dress up prettily
With buttons and with bows.

Her brother named her "Cooky"
I can't remember why.
It might have been because
She had a twinkle in her eye.

He was her slave when she was born
No one else dared to touch.
The mother was quite amused
That he loved her quite so much.

The years have passed and we're still close
But for a job she moved away.
I miss her smile, humor, love and hugs
I really miss her more each day.

    —*June M. Genagon*

Peace For All The Children

Hold hands with all the children
Who wish to live in peace,
Throughout the world in any circumstance
Hope and love can be released;
Pray bombs become ghosts of the past,
Cease letting poverty and fear reign
And allowing war to steal life from youth,
Some deny children are in pain
Anguished faces cry out the truth.

Shower little ones with love and qualities they can return,
As priorities in life change, there's so much we need to learn;
Educate our youth of consequences when violence is in control,
Blessings are the world's children. Daily we are challenged
to care. Peace for all God's children is our goal.

Turn tragedy to hopefulness for children every where;
The time has arrived when our offspring should live in safety
Some of the world's riches share, young people become our
leaders. Treasure gifts they offer to the world,
Be grateful for children each day.
Remember they're precious like pearls.

    —*Charlotte O'Donnell*

577

'Vets' Our Hospital & Home

May the "nurses" of this hospital and home
"Who" work with the sick, to make healthy the flesh and the
bone:
Always be at our side", for many of us have cried:
  Nurse
And have been relieved of our pains
And through time have tried to gain,
The confidence of our doctors
  And our nurses
Who stayed at our side thru the good and the bad,
And saved many relatives from being "sad"
For "we all" that are still here "can give a good cheer"
  For our nurses...

—Charles Heeting

Reflections On A Favorite Writing Utensil

An emaciated mustard yellow man
Whose body resembles
A firing post
After the execution
Stands tall in his charcoal boots
That get shorter
As this poem progresses.
Atop his shiny silver head
Deformed from the nervousness
Of one too many calculus tests
Rests a tattered pink beret
That won't survive nearly as long
As he will.

—Jennifer Dahler

Untitled

She follows me with shadows
Whose hazy forms run from the light.
She watches me with unseen eyes
Whose vision can pierce even the darkest night.
She speaks to me with doubt
Whose words echo endlessly within my mind.
She touches me with pain
Whose fingers reach my deepest nerves.
She controls me with fear
Over which I have no control.
She left me long ago,
But the power she held over me has not.
This love, a domineering master,
And its obedient slave.

—Douglas J. Struckmeyer

Alone

As I stand alone in the corner wondering,
Why did this happen?
I can't believe she's gone. I am alone,
hoping she'll come back and say, "I am
home baby girl, everything will be
all right. But, I know this won't happen,
So, I wish my mom knows that I
love her and will never forget what
she did for me. Raised me without
a father , and loved me like no one
loved me before, for 14 years I loved
her and for 14 more, I'll love her as
she loved me, now I have to live
alone without my mom. No one
to call me "Kitten or Baby Girl" I also
have no one to call my mom and
for as long as I can remember she'll
always love me and I will always
love her.

—Molly Brinich

Foolish Boy

Screams of indecision pound my ears
Why does this situation arise from the void?
Decisiveness must be prompt and swift
Do not play the part of weak-minded
Unable to live for one's self
Resist acts of false love
Wings of a temptress reach to strangle
The search for a fallen angel endures
She exists in this desolate land
Hidden behind some rock or tree
To remain from eyesight until a revelation

Judgment day shall be upon us
For some it will be the end
But for others, an awakening
And I have been asleep too long

—David MacLaren

I Don't Understand Why

I don't understand why some things do the things they do.
Why dogs bark and cats meow, I wish I knew the answer now.
How does a plant grow from a seed, and then wither away
  in the wind?

Yes, how does Mother Nature know and plant the things
  we need?
What makes me laugh and what makes me cry,
What makes me end the day with a big, reluctant sigh?
Why is the day full of light, while darkness fills the
  endless night?
I try to think with all my might, but my reasoning never
  comes out just right.
What makes some people do right and others do wrong?
What makes a friend stick through thick and thin?
I don't know a lot of answers, but.....
God does and he'll take care of me till the end.

—Jennifer Andress

Christmas Magic

  Santa was broke and didn't know what to do;
  Why, he couldn't even buy Rudolph new shoes,
  So he said, "Come here my Dear Little Elves,
We've got a problem and have to help ourselves;
    One of the elves began to cry;
    Santa said, "No, no, we'll get by,"
He said," my helpers what can you do?"
    One said, Oh, I know how to glue,
    So he repaired Rudolph's shoes.
  Santa said, "we'll have to make do,"
    So they began to sew and to glue;
    And when they had finished,
  There were gifts for their friends.
Not fancy or new but made with their hands.
Cause friends like you are the best in the land.
I wrote the poem you see because I am Elf Number 3.
    Merry Christmas

—Faye McBee Henderson

Silent Good-bye

  The last kiss is the one I'll always miss.
  Your words echo in my ears your picture burns my
    face with tears.
  Our silent good-bye still makes me cry.
That last glance still sends me into a trance of our
    summer romance.
    That last touch meant so much!
Now everyday I look in the mirror I want to tell
    you I love you dear!
I always thought we'd be O.K. but I guess the odds
    were in our way!

—Marjorie M. Harrigan

"Where Is Virtue?"

I wonder as I ponder the wild blue yonder,
Why I squander my thoughts and dreams.
Can it be that my memory span is too short,
That it can't take the load and must abort?
I ask myself why this must be in this land of liberty?
In this land of chance and change, where is virtue?
Virtue is here and must be sought
By all with careful thought.
Virtue must be protected at all costs,
By every person in this nation.
And in each succeeding generation.

—Elbert R. Moses Jr.

Say A Prayer

Look, see, there's trouble, trouble, its everywhere!
Why, oh why, doesn't somebody say a prayer?
They moan and groan, they pull their hair.
But no one, not one, will say a prayer.
They sit and they cry, cause the sky's not fair.
Why don't they stop, and say a prayer?
They say God's too busy, to hear them or care.
So they've given up hope, and don't even try to say a prayer.
But wait! Wait a minute! It's surely a must that it
    start somewhere!
So, maybe it's 'I' who should say a prayer.
    Thank You God!

—Charlotte Kleiber

Ask

The locust asked the butterfly,
why she was so sweet,
she answered that is just because
I kiss each flower I meet.
The Robin asked the apple, where she got her blush
from swaying with the gentle wind,
and getting in no rush.
The little fish asked the river,
just how far it would go.
For sure I'll go to the ocean,
but from there, well, I don't know.
The little frog asked the lily pad,
to set with her today, the evening brought a big storm,
and washed them both away.
The little tree asked the big tree,
if he really knew his age, the big tree said, I used to.
But now I've lost a page.
The rock cliff said to the waterfall,
go merrily on your way, and maybe in a raindrop,
you will return someday.

—Lily May Yarbrough

Freedom

Once upon a special night, you looked at me.
Your eyes sparkled like emeralds in the dark.
I could see your love, like a new eagle
ready to take flight.
young and fragile, but growing strong and
powerful into the night.
I was so entranced by your beauty and grace,
that I had to question, if I was in the right place.
But I caught myself and realized, this is
where I want to be, dreaming, sweet dreams,
of you and me.

—Debra L. Murphy

God Cares

Have you ever felt like nobody cared?
Why should you ever feel this way;
Have you ever felt like you were all alone?
Living in a real dark place. It seems you
Only have God to talk to. He will never
turn you away. He will always be there,
every time you kneel to pray.

Sometimes the road can get very rough,
And the hill so hard to climb, but
God said it would all be over one day,
And "Peace would Be Thine."
God knows the many times you have called
Upon Him, and the many tears you have shed
He even knows the many times you have wished
That you were dead. So whenever you feel like
no one cares; and that you would never be
missed; always look to God, cause
God still does exist. He will care for you
every night and day, all you have to do is just
kneel and pray cause God cares.

—Dorothy Frashier

A Lady's Journey

I walked upon the stones and asked,
will you be my guide?
They answered, of course my lady,
with each and every stride.
I sat beneath the shady trees and asked,
will you be my tent?
They answered, of course my lady,
please rest and feel content.
I gazed up at the moon and asked,
will you be my lamp?
It answered, of course my lady,
offering silvery beams to light up my camp.
I felt the softness of the grass and asked,
will you be my bed?
It answered, of course my lady,
gently rest you weary head.
I looked upon the earth and asked,
will you be my friend?
It answered, of course my lady,
we shall be companions 'til the end.

—Danielle Martell

Freddie

Oh, how precious those strong young hands
Willing and able to prove the man.
Hazel eyes so filled with love
My gentle giant from God above.

God made him special - it's plain to see
He lent him for a time to me.
I am so proud and grateful too
Though it broke my heart to say, "adieu."

I give him back, Lord, with heartfelt pride
I thank you for a son so fine.
Fred was just too good to stay
Though it broke my heart when he went away.

If Fred could speak, I know he'd say
Take heed my friends as you fish each day.
Be ever careful and let not greed
Make the daily quota your ships exceed.

Let not my death be all in vain
Once lost your life, you can ne'er regain.
Think of your loved ones with their endless pain
Live on to see the sunset - again and again.

—Dolores Fischer

My Silent Stalker

The untrusting moonlight shines its jagged glow all through my
window tonight. I lay but I do not sleep, for fear creeps
through me like the moonlight seeps through my window. I
squeeze shut my eyes, suppress the feelings, the fear of not
knowing, not understanding, somehow it will all come back to me
in my adult life. It might be a dream, or maybe a memory.
I'll run, I'll scream, filled with fright, all because of the
unforgetful night. The fear runs through me like the
untrusting moonlight seeps through my window. It did not
protect me on that night, or any night, like no one in my
house. All lay sleeping, except my silent stalker and I. I
close my blinds as tight as I can, but the jagged moonlight
still seeps in, like the man in the night, who filled this
child with fright. He took away all my rights of pure
innocence only a child knows. He removed the inner safety and
security a child feels within their home and as judge
unknowingly sentenced me for life. So now as the knowing
sunlight shines through my window, it cuts through my room,
like a knife through my soul. I cannot trust this light, I
fear it know my shame, and reveals my pain.
Please tell me what did this man gain, as he moves on like
everything
is the same. Only I am left with my pain, and fright. But the fright
I felt that night, is my punishment for a crime, I was too
innocent to stop, but my sentence... is my life.

—*Marsha Haneline*

Seasons

Winter
Winter comes and snow falls down we sit by the fire and pass
hot chocolate all around the baby sucks on its pacifier while
we all enjoy the warmth of the fire.

Spring
Soon it warms up and flowers bloom animals mate, and springtime
smells fill the room people fly kites, it rains through the
night springtime is such a beautiful sight.

Summer
Summer is a time when we're out of school the days are hot, we
swim in the pool we run, jump, yell, and play we love summer
but it always goes away.

Fall
We're back in school, learning is fun we're anxious for another
year to come the leaves fall down and the people have piles of
leaves all around when the trees are bare and its cold at night
we know it's time for HALLOWEEN fright After this season is

over the year comes to an end the new years beginning and
winter comes again fall has been fun same as the rest I liked
last year and I think I'll like this one the best just hope.

—*Bradley Austin*

Walking With Me

I walked along a darkened path
With a sad and lonely boy
A child so filled with torment
and a heart that knew no joy
We walked awhile, just holding hands
and I could feel his fear
He seemed empty and lost in feelings
for the crossroads would soon be near
The fork in the road is where we stopped
and bid a warm farewell
An uncertain feeling came over him
and the tears began to swell
I walked alone a little while
and rest beneath a tree
I wept once I had realized
That little boy was me

—*Timothy C. Walraven*

Spring

Spring has arrived hooray, hooray
Winter has left a brand new day

Off with the coats, hats and mittens
Grab your rods and let's go fishing

The sweet smell of Spring is all through the air
No one stays inside, they wouldn't dare

The grass is green, the sky is blue
Mom and Dad are in such a good mood

Buzz, buzz, buzz what is that sound
Oh no, it's a bee flying around

The fresh cut grass is soft as a bunny
It tickles my toes and feels rather funny

Speaking of bunnies, Easter is near
So, what will your Easter bonnet look like this year

Baseball and tennis are fun to play
If the Spring showers don't get in the way

I'd pick you some flowers but that makes them die
They are much more beautiful when they're alive

In the evening we sit on our front porch swing
While we reminisce over our favorite things

—*Jamie Curtis*

"Somebody Misses You"

Somebody misses you so each day
Wishes you were not so far away.
Somebody loves you more than you know
Just can't keep from telling you so.
Somebody likes those eyes of blue,
Because they mean that you are true.
Somebody likes your lips for a kiss
They always bring such perfect bliss
Somebody likes the touch of your hand
Which has a meaning that you understand.
Somebody loves you and hopes that you see
Just what you mean to a girl like me.

—*Hilda Stephenson Woodall*

Sin's Of Yesterday

One heart so enormous
With a mind and strength all its own
To see beyond all in depths of another soul
To see eyes full of tears never shed
Raging anger so enormous to erupt instead
Emotions so wild flaring like a mind mad
Yet to see beyond all a tormented soul
Hearing beyond all rage a cry for help

Within another tender gentle full of need
To turn to twist to roar with rage
Erupting from depths all eyes are blind
Dark secrets of evil horrors buried in time
Blocked out a mind so small now grown

Eyes blinded to condemn a love like this
Love to endure all to take one back years gone
To remember all hell when it began
To get it out to let it out tears now flow
Destroying the rage of all time forever
A bond of love remains never felt before
A soul once lost now saved

—*Linda (Ryan) Martin*

Sweet Dreams

As I lay there on my bed,
with a soft pillow beneath my head.
The sun went down and the moon began to shine,
I had this dream that you were mine.
That every time I wished on a falling star,
I had this great feeling that you weren't far.
I knew that I would see you soon,
So every night I stared at the moon
I felt so close to you that I couldn't move.
When this dream began to fade,
I knew that there was a mistake that I had made
So there on my bed I just laid.

—*Karrie Schrader*

David

He was a wild eyed boy
With clear seeking eyes
That yearned for life
And all he could try

A charmer, a dreamer, a traveling soul.
From a very young age
He had taken a hold of the reigns...
Of a very rough life.

He struggled for self
When he thought it best.
And believed in himself.
When doubt filled the rest.
When no one was willing to try
He wasn't afraid...to fly.

He traveled alone thru his trouble and strife
And grew to be stronger
And love life — as dreamers and gentlemen do.

And now he is noble, a treasure to hold.
A man who will never be bought or sold.
Whose visions are perfectly clear.

His heart he will share.
With the one he holds dear.
For today, he will start a new life
With his lover, his lady, his wife.

—*Sherryl Watkins*

The Victor

Smooth, well-heeled churchmen stole my wealth
  With crafty contract, acts of stealth.
    I asked my pastor to please share
  With proven Saints my need for prayer.
Quoth he:
    'Christ came not to make you whole,
    'His mission was to save your soul.'

They smeared my name, they stole my purse,
Left me with kicks and foul-breathed curse
    Bleeding, shamed and all alone.
  Weak Saints hailed me in mocking tone.
Hailed they:
    'Saved is what you claimed to be —
    'That you were lying's plain to see!'

With broken heart and tear-stained face
  Crept I up to the Throne of Grace.
  'Lord!' cried I. 'Hear my plea!'
'Grant peace of mind and victory!' Whispered He:
    'You're hurting much too much to see
      'That I AM the victory,'

—*Keith Kirby*

With Tears In Her Eyes

Even though she knows that she is now dying
With every breath she will never stop trying
  To find the one eternal love with no lies
So she'll search on with tears in her eyes
  She has past up love because they betrayed her with lies
So she searches on helplessly with tears in her eyes
  She's thirty eight and now knows she's dying
And still she looks for that one love who's not lying
  She has seen countless numbers who betray with their lies
So she searches on helplessly with tears in her eyes
  Because her heart was broken by all of the lies
So she searches on with tears in her eyes
  She has searched for love but they were all lying
But until she dies she will never stop trying
  To find that one special love without any lies
So she searches on with tears in her eyes

—*Darleen M. Haggard*

Son

My Son has passed away. I think about it day by day
With gentleness, love, kindness and praise
And that I really cared those very days.

Each day I think of him.
And do the best I can.
For he has left a son.
In which he had loved.
And wants to carry on.

For him I miss, and also I pray
That some sweet day we will meet again.
In the heaven's some passing day.

The path ahead is rough.
And painful is the way.
I feel his release of pain.
And I must live for today.

Still in my heart and mind my love for him will stay
At peace with myself and peace with thee.
Released from all his pain and fear.
He is set free this very day.

—*Crystal Lynn Ransome*

Angles And Nature

Just straight lines and multitudes of squares
with grace of roundness succumbing to the angle,
that all encompassing vastness of the heavens rising
to the beyond, stretching, struggling, to expand
from the womb within.

Now, she is helpless in her nature of serenity, capable of
reproduction of her infinite forms, being able to
be totality in her oneness.

She is grasping her fertile soul, weeping in hunger,
that mankind has done her an injustice.

Where is my green, golden grass, streaked with iron
furnishing the nourishment of my creative forces?

Suffering in turmoil, restless from so little growth,
ceasing to root my seeds, to grow in curves, to smile
to the blueness above, rising to feel the drift of air
fluttering through my blades, touching, feeling warmth from
the golden force pouring into the granules of my soil,
holding the moisture upon my nature, losing, losing to the
form of angles.

Tell me, when will mankind touch me with a gentler hand?

—*Judy Kay Scott*

A Homeless Portrait

I watch the world in my mirror,
With great pity and sadness.
The hope, the fear, the tragedy,
While the worry free watch on with gladness.
I look upon my future,
While waiting to use my key.
It's now old and rusty with neglect,
There are no doors to be unlocked.
I walk upon my territory,
A simple box, with tattered newspaper.
I'm happy with my life as a reject.
I have no hope, no fear, no tragedy,
I have memories and dreams,
That keeps me happy it seems.

—*Dawn Peters*

Alone

Alone after many wonderful years
With heartaches and yes a few tears
And yet as I mourn one I loved so long
I know others the same path have trod
   and been strong.

God in heaven gives strength to all, but oh
at times I feel so small
Like perhaps he has forgotten me, among
so many he needs to see

I have been blessed with a family who care
And in their own way my sorrow share.
But each generation has it own away to make
And one lonely soul cannot their time to take

Life does go on and sorrow comes in different ways
to all. And we are never ready for that call
He is gone, don't moan, You are not alone.

—*Evelyn H. Stewart*

"Treasures"

As a little girl looks out the back door
With her doll in her hand,
She thinks a bright leaf is a treasure
When that girl grows a bit she thinks
a small cup from a wonderful old lady is a treasure.
When the girl turns ten a bright purple big-girls-bike
is a rare and wondrous treasure.
When that very same child turns 12 and is on
the threshold of Junior High, a picture of a
special boy is a terrific treasure.
Now, as I look back, the same child with all the
treasures, I realize that the things weren't the
treasures, it was the people who gave them.

—*Sabrina Sherman*

Alone? No

Sitting alone in my old rocking chair
With my memories and silvery hair
No longer in the house-a pair,
Reminds me of the old grey mare.

Can't play ball anymore,
Can't dance a jig anymore,
Can't play golf and yell fore!
Can't go to the show, too poor.

My children seldom come
Not many call on the phone,
I'm usually here all alone.
But my Jesus is with me till kingdom come.

—*Helen E. Miller*

God Made That Tree

God made that tree for me
   With it's bright colors glistening.
He lovingly touched each leaf
   And they seemed to be listening.
As he stroked gently with his brush
   Red, yellow and orange nestled among the green
There was no need to rush
   To paint this MASTER SCENE.

Each twig was bowing to his will
   Creating with His love for me.
His works make my heart to thrill,
   In His beauty my eyes to see.
My Lord, my saviour!!! shows his love
   To the smallest and to the largest
With His glorious beauty from above
   Yes, my Lord is quite an artist.

—*Manervia Herrington*

A Veteran's Thoughts on Memorial Day

This is the day that we honor the dead
With muffled drums and a measured tread.
For many and many a soldier brave
Lies somewhere in a lonely grave.
Let us keep "Old Glory" flying high
We who were there but did not die.
For shells care not who the victim is;
They were meant to take our life or his.
Of the living, we honor in greater part
The ones who returned with a "Purple Heart."
If you should ask of the fighting men,
"If it were to do over?" We would do it again.
It is well to remember come Veteran's Day,
For freedom, there is a price to pay.

—*Oran Skaw*

Gravity

Ya' know I didn't figure ta' get this old,
With my back all crooked and my legs bent and bowed;

You can sure tell things are startin' to go,
When you show up to a brandin' and grab a' holt of a calf that
   shoulda' been there three months ago;

Or ya' step into a stirrup on a cold frosty morn'
And the colt takes a few steps, snorts, humps his back and ya'
   go ta' grabbin' for the horn;

Now I've got more sags than a prolapse, more wrinkles than a prune,
and from the looks of the swellin' hangin in front of me,
   I figure I'm due about June;

I'm really not that old — I'm only 43,
And talkin' to some folks, they'd really like to be as young as me;

Now, I've heard it called agin' gracefully,
but somehow that don't seem to fit,
   'cause there really ain't nothin' graceful about me;

So, I reckon I'll ponder my fate,
at some later date;

But, for now, it's plain to see,
It's just a simple case of givin' in ta' gravity!

—*Leigh Gamble*

Blessings To The New Era

Dark, Godless era faded - gone -
With nineteen hundred ninety one -
God - Spirit's Love reigns on the Throne
For heavenly father and His son.

God's Loving Spirit is the Might,
Which gives Creation, Love and Light:
He dwells in us by day and night -
Our Still, Small Voice knows the Delight -

You cannot grasp it, like a bill,
It comes like Zephyr from the hill!
And when you Understand His Will:
His Loving Light makes worries nil . . .

God! Bless Humanity's New Era!
God! Bless World's Future, Light and Love! . . .
—*Lydia Venta Dobrovolsky*

The Shooter of the Evil Seed

When you started out - it was all in fun
With no intention of hurting anyone
But speed leads to greed and selfish needs
Love takes a backseat when you plant the evil seed

Everything you treasure is blown away
No clear thinking anymore
Satan held the needle
And you walked right through the door

People listen to me-open your eyes and see
Pain out weighs pleasure by so much you can't believe
When you find yourself alone wondering "what went wrong"
Take a good look inside yourself, because you've known all along

It's a one-way road once you get on
And there's no way to go back home
You've gone much too far along
Now you're dead and gone!...
—*Bill Bacoccini*

Lonely Dove

On the glistening lake sits a lonely dove,
With no one around to fulfill her love.
The reflection in the water so blurred and distilled,
The nest on the bank still hoping to build.

The others have all left to hatch a new life,
For her only breezes and all her strife.
She hears the squeaky chirps of voices oh so new,
For her, only her own chirps after morning dew.

The nights are getting longer,
The days are getting colder,
For her another year will come,
As she is getting older.
—*Becky Leuddeke*

Ellis Meal Site

I'm writing about the Meal Site group,
We're all over sixty, but we don't give a hoot;
We eat, exercised and play cards too,
Come join us, this invitation is for you;
We're a jolly bunch you'll soon find out;
If you come and eat, when you're round about;
We laugh a lot, and love the old,
Just stop by when your cold;
Everyone will greet you, and make you a friend,
That's the Meal Site group and this is the end.
—*Marie Bennett*

Falling In Love

The way the rain paves the walk and street
with slick leaves levels the steadiest of foot
as if they were legless. No amount
of evolution preserves our uprightness
in catastrophes of nature's making
—and she never lets us down easy.

When weather and the trees grease the way
in waterlogged scarlet and wet yellow,
there's no choice of goal but impact;
and caution's as frivolous as the lack of it.
Yet nothing stops this pedestrian traffic
of bodies in mutual attraction.

It's not for me. I keep myself grounded,
stuck at the window to watch the slapstick,
a little sick at the way it keeps happening
even in dry spells, as if the world lay
in a permanent state of canceled friction,
and every season were gravity's.
—*Dana Rapisardi*

Make Me A Tunnel

I looked at the pond of stagnant water
with the debris lying all around;
and thought what a shame it was useless
it's purpose for existence can not be found.

If only it's banks were opened
so it's waters could freely flow;
and if all the debris was cleared away
then the beauty of it's life would show.

And the same is true of the blessings
God gives to me each day;
I'm to look for those in the shadows
and give these blessings away.

For if I'm selfish and keep them to myself
stagnation will begin to grow;
clutter will collect around my heart
and my light will fail to show.

For the purpose of my existence
is to share with others as I grow;
so I ask you Lord, to make me a tunnel
through which your blessings can flow.
—*Christine Stanley*

Waiting

My love for you is unbound.
With the torturous winds of time,
I travel the earth seeking you,
Needing you,
Waiting.

All I've done is love you.
Never having ever known you,
Nor loved another more than you
But still I must stop,
As I'm told,
I'm
Waiting.

Waiting for you,
For you to love,
Love me.
—*Greg Drumm*

The Fall

The leaves that drop steadily from standing, stolid trees,
With the warm October sun and the cool night breeze,
Has one feeling that the end has come
To a beautiful summer whose work is done.

Each dropping leaf like a memory gone by;
Each gust of wind, a reminder that I,
Like the leaves, will remain but awhile;
First a bud, then a leaf, then a faded smile.

May I, like the tree that stands gaunt and bare,
Shorn of beauty that once was there,
Leave a faith to those on Mother Earth,
That with trumpets of spring, there'll be a rebirth.

—*Gilbert D. McKlveen*

"Come See The Night"

Dance in the light of our pitiful day.
With thy own eyes you won't find the way.
Into the fire of our setting sun.
Another day gone the battle rages on.

The good things of our day have now passed by.
Now our pain follows us 'til the day we die.

Come see the night! Walk out of the light!
Into the shadows we'll play!
As our enemies stalk their prey!

On thru life in storms of light.
Nation against nation as we fight.
We gasp and choke on the air we breathe.
Screams come from children buried beneath.

Take a step forward and drop into your hole.
So save our future and pray for our souls.

Come see the night! Walk out of the light!
Into our graves we'll lay!
Now there are no shadows in which to play!

Now we live in the destruction of man!
So reach out people and shake the devil's hand!

—*Eric W. Smotherman*

For Evermore

   Please do not go despairingly into that ever-ever land,
with tight lips, bowed head, unseeing eyes,
nor with flagging steps-unwillingly.
   Go with your old flamboyancy, so uniquely yours:
a toss of your leonine head, a wave of your hand,
a confident smile on your lips.
   There will be new wonders to perceive-there:
the 'other worldly' hues of flowers, delicate, vividly colored,
perfuming the air with spicy and pleasant unidentifiable fragrances.
Some flowers as soft to the touch as milkweed floss,
others, opening full as you pass by.
   There will be beckoning paths,
stunning beauties anew at every turn-
at your feet, 'round about, and above you.
   Go with joy!
Greet each new experience with the wonder and delight
it elicits from an Earthling.
   Go boldly! Our most extravagant dreams are too small-there.
   Go with finality! Could one possibly wish to return?
   Go for all time - for evermore.

—*Helen J. Mayton*

Nursery People

Little people in their beds
With tiny hands and tiny heads.
They're snuggled down inside their covers,
Sleeping 'till time to see their mothers.
These tiny people all snug and warm
Are now innocent and free from harm.
They yawn and move their tiny hands
They're each one marked with small name bands.
Each sleeps all wrapped in flannel bunnies,
Or pastel stripes, these little Honeys.
These little people with chubby cheeks,
Will be quiet and sleepy for several weeks.
They will sleep and eat all through the days,
And slowly grow in many ways.
To parents and families they are a prize,
As they wiggle about and open their eyes.
These little people snug in beds,
With tiny hands and tiny heads
Are those who keep the world alive,
And make the race of man survive.

—*Dorothy J. Moase*

My Father

When I was young,
With vanished pride;
My wings were little and couldn't fly.

His wind blew softly under my wings,
He set me afloat with vitalized strength
and infinite pride.

Days went by and years fled.
A day, lovely and softly;
My father died.

Distorted and pale in hollow ground,
He sleeps now;
The spiritual place where he lies.

There I weep.
In my self this soul exist;
A part of me recreates the scenes and
sentiments held close to my heart.
Of the day, I spread my wings to fly.

—*Billie Joe Taylor Sampson*

Lakota Warrior

A Lakota shade silently dances,
With warrior's bow in the evening sky,
With tattered ghost shirt that enhances
A sublime spirit that shall never die.
Wagon Box, Wounded Knee, and Greasy Grass,
Heralded now in your history stone,
All conjure visions of deaths in masse,
And chant a sorrowful prairie moan.
Search out your wounded soul with gourd in hand,
Tightly grasp the sacred eagle feather,
As Mother Earth rebirths from crimson sand,
A proud people rise and stand together;
   Mystic man, do a humble heart adorn,
   For a good warriors made—as well as born.

—*Alan H. Azure*

Hands Paint, Blood Dolls

... Doubt (low)
With wreckage (wreckage)
Hands across my lap, lap

... Doubt
With wreckage
Hands across my truce

Can't you see the writing on my hand?....
Can't you see the chiding of my youth?...
Can't you see the fist against my sands?...
Can't you see the shunning of my truth?
... Doubt
With wreckage
Hands across my lap

... Doubt
With wreckage
Hands across.. truth!

—*Jennifer Spears*

The Eagle With The Broken Wing

My heart is an eagle which soars through the blue sky
with you by my side. With the love and friendship you bring
to my heart, I fly with a smile peacefully in the sky.   As I
see your smile, my heart grows larger as the seed of a rose
grows with beauty and my wings expand with happiness. I can
fly forever. Days go by and you are gone. Without the love
and friendship you bring, my heart and soul are filled with
emptiness inside. I fly with a broken wing, and the clouds
are dark and gloomy, but the thought and spirit of you will
keep me flying forever.

—*Francisco Alberto Olivas*

Unknown Of Me

The curtains of my eyes cover the shadows of dark.
Within the pain of my soul crushes the unseen light
that punctures outside my world.
The escape of my burden lingers to a path
that searches the mind of my spirit.
As I see objects dominating the closeness
that intertwines my being.
I let loose and scarcely begin to run.
Further in my journey to the end of life.
Fadingly there is death
which has a beginning to my place of life,
"Heaven".

—*Christina M. Lay*

Without You

Without the sun, no plants would grow
   Without the rain, there would be no lakes
Without the honey, a bee would not buzz
   Without you, I would be alone.

Without ink, pens would not talk
   Without the scent, a rose would be just another plant
Without a melody, a song would be just noise
   Without you, I would live alone

Without love, the world would not exist
   I am like the world, without your love
   I would not exist.
Like the plants and the lakes need the sun and
   The rain, I need you.
Without you, I would perish from the Earth.

—*Harold Dalious*

A Ghost Of Love Past

Sometimes I wonder where she might be
Wonder still if she remembers me
Many years ago as I recall
There was a time when we had it all
The years have all slipped away so fast
That she's become a ghost of love past.

I can still see her as she was then
And can't help but think what might have been
'Twas no one's fault we drifted apart
But somehow she stayed within my heart
And her memory will always last
If only as a ghost of love past.

Good times past are remembered the most
Visions often appear like a ghost
Sometimes from dreams we hate to awake
And lose good thoughts fantasy can make
My good thoughts will remain steadfast
Remembering a ghost of love past.

—*Harold L. Russell*

"Wondering?"

Sitting here all by myself,
Wondering where you are,
wondering if your thinking of me,
On the highways near or far.

Some say the road is hard on love,
But yet, absence makes the heart grow fonder
Which one do you think of,
when your mind stars to wonder?

The road is long, and your mind is drifting
What do your think of when the sun is lifting?
As the sun is setting and the sky is blue,
when you wonder what to think,
Think of how much I miss you.

—*Cindy L. Morris*

"Creative Expression"

Colors of beauty, textures that flow;
Words of strength, thoughts to bestow;
A vision so vivid, a sensation conveyed;
A feeling recognized, a creation is made.
The hands of a sculptor, the stroke of a brush;
The gift of a poet, that makes us hush;
A heavy rhythm, a man's distress;
He dances to his pain and brings us unrest.
It's a fluid musician with passion and ability,
Who plays the notes that gives us tranquility,
Like a beautiful painting that's hung on the wall;
It's nothing to own it, it's nothing at all.
To look upon it with appreciation, to admire it is part;
But it is everything to experience a work of art!

—*Christy White*

Loving You

I love you dear, so very much
Your sweet embrace, I long to touch
You make my life so serene
I know its real, and not a dream
Every moment of the day
In my heart you'll always stay
Cause the happiness, that we possess.
You put it there,
With your tenderness
All earthly cares, just fade away
When your near me, every day.

—*Josephine Warych*

Casualties

A sadness envelopes me that cannot be shaken.
Words, paraded mockingly about me, jest in the light of
  foreboding uncertainty.

Or is it me?

Are mine but the only eyes that see?

Is mine the only heart burdened; ladened with the illegality
  of these trespasses?

Does mine need be the only voice exacting equity?

Crippling notions are these; my soul grows lame by consequence.
Stabbing at inner, cerebral peace; raping my consciousness,
  until only the acerbic taste of actualities remain.

And so you wonder; the soundness of your constitution in
  jeopardy.
What you once were is forgotten, what you will become, unknown.

Perilous is this existence we call humanity.
Nothing remains rudimentary, and only the in-humane survive.

—*D. E. Irons*

Extension Of Man And Me

I understand: I see you as an extension of man and me. Is your
world the same as mine? It must be.

We reason, think, feel and talk - my world has extended with
your thoughts.

You are my friend, brother, sister; you may be someone's mother
or father, child. Yet, you are my world and an extension of
man and me.

They tell me you did this or that, how good or bad you are,
said you said this or that. I really do share your part from
my heart; "Oh my," you are just an extension of man and me.

When we go through life, walking mountains or valleys which it
may be, look to see if you're not an extension of man and me.

When we grow pale or older, depart from our world, is it not
true that you will yet be an extension of man and me?

Extension! Extension! of man and me.

—*Hilderd Fields Gunn*

"Peace"

How wonderful it would be if the whole
  world were at peace,
How wonderful it would be if tyranny
  would cease.
Why can't human beings get together as friends,
Iron out their differences and make amends.
Money then that is spent for fighter planes,
Would be spent instead for the poor, the
  homeless, easing their pains!
We hope the Lord our prayers would hear,
We hope that Peace can be achieved without fear,
We hope that John and Robert Kennedy, and Luther
  King too,
Didn't die in vain, cause they believed men could
  stand together again,
Holding hands across the seas!
  Oh Lord, please hear our pleas.
We want so much for the world to be at peace
No more wars, let's be able to
  open our doors,
Without any fears, and without any tears!
  Just Peace!

—*Frances Ritchkin*

Abortion

Dear Mommy, how are you? Me not good because I
would be 16! But they call it abortion! How
would it feel to hold me Mommy? But I'm not
there for you! I'm still as little as ever.
Small enough I don't have to hide I'm doing a
good deed Mommy I am helping you, but you didn't
help me. I'm still a little seed no one ever
knew me. So that means I'm nothing. It's
already done no one cares? It's not fair!
Mommy why did you act like you didn't care. I
could have many friends. But I'm gone. unlike
me I hope you don't abort my brothers and
sisters. I thought you cared until that stuff
aborted me! We could have had fun. It was loud
and clear that we are family. But we will never
meet. Mommy I have to go now! I'm sorry it had
to be this way! Today is another day!
P.S. Why. Love you! Love, Baby

—*Carissa Carter*

Think

Had I have lived when Jesus walked this earth,
  Would I have followed him?
Or would I have been with the angry crowd
  That persecuted him?

  Would I have laughed and urged them on
    As they nailed him to the cross?
  Or would I have bowed my head in shame
    Knowing what the world had lost.

Could I have driven the nails in his hands,
  Or maybe have pierced his side?
What would you have done had you been there
  The day that Jesus died?

Thank God we were spared that choice to make
  As we worship him today.
And thank you, Jesus, for dying there
  To wash our sins away.

—*Margaret L. Sanders*

Postage Due

If Jesus sent you a letter from Him to you,
would you be ready to pay the postage due?
And if He began by saying, "My Dear Child",
would you accept it with a frown or a smile?

And a little further on you read,
"I'm the one true God, I'm not dead.
I took care of you all the while
for you are my child.

I picked you up when you fell.
I even told you about Heaven and Hell.
I tried to show you every way that I could.
But you chose not to do good.

I even told you "Whom soever will, let them come'.
I kept all my promises but you still doubted me some.
So this is my final letter, it comes directly to you.
But, it comes with postage due."

—*Hellen Brown*

Teacher

Teacher, is there something
wrong with me?
Could you let me know about it
so I can see?
Help me to find the way up,
To what you know
A mature mind and healthy
body should be.
For I have been down for so long,
and I'm tired!
I've been kicked around, picked
on, nicked by
Nothing but low grades, and no
satisfaction.
This is bad, real bad, but what
can I do?
Is there a book I can get or follow
some common rule?
I want to improve my grades,
but how do I start? I'm not afraid!

—*Elaine Pauline Laster*

Thoughts Of Yesterday, Tomorrow And Today

The love we once had held dreams of that we hoped for.
That we hoped for was just memories to be made.
The memories made, when remembered, were to be shared.
Somewhere along the way we must have made
A wrong turn or maybe a wrong decision.
It must be that we are to learn from our past,
The things we are to teach others,
Hoping to guard them from our mistakes.
Now, with each new day dawning, the memories
We once had are remembered fondly with smiles and tears.
Maybe a small part of our heart still aches for that
Which we have no longer, yet our heart has grown enough
To hold the memories to be made in the future.
Greet each new day with a smile on your lips
And a song in your heart, for we know not
What awaits with each step we take, each turn we make.
Seek only the best in everyone you meet,
Offer the best you have to give,
And we all shall be truly blessed.

—*Anna Palmgren*

Daddy, I Miss You

A year has gone by since you were taken away from me.
Yet, it's no easier to bear; I still feel the pain and agony.
I long to gently touch you and softly kiss your face.
I want to hug you and hold you in a warm and loving embrace.
I wish that I could see you before my very eyes.
This won't ever be possible, I tearfully realize.
I look on the porch but you're not there, like you used to be.
I see your empty chair and I picture you there, talking to me.
When I look and see you standing in the garage.
I begin to cry because I know it's just a mirage.
The memories are painful, this is so true.
But mostly, they're the happy times that I spent, dad, with
you. I won't ever forget all the good that you've done. A
better father and granddad, there can never be one. I find
comfort in knowing that you're in heaven now because the pain
you felt on earth, Jesus won't allow. He will take care of you
and keep you safe, far from heartbreak and sorrow. From now on
you'll only have peace and comfort in each and every tomorrow.
So rest, my sweet dad, for you are at peace. The hurt and pain
you knew, now it all will cease.

—*Linda Downey*

"The Spinning Wheel Of Progress."

The wheel of progress is in motion,
Yet, there's a new poster child upon the wall.
The school playgrounds are barren,
Not a soul to be found at all.
Hiding from a blood red sun,
Afraid to play out in the rain,
The air unfit to breathe,
Dying 'Amber waves of grain'.
Slowly slipping under
This 'One nation under God',
Prayer refused in schools,
Teachers forced to spare the rod.
Deserts filled with water,
Rain forests parched and dry,
Mother nature's in an uproar,
With a hole punched through her sky.

—*Christopher J. Claire*

Poets Court, Jester, Gesture?

So write a poem was said to me
You always said it came so easily
So rhyme your words
Like rhyme or time
Or dime or wine
Oh my, oh well.
If I could only spell
But wait! said I
If only I could tell
Of the beauty and humor that poets see.
I'll buy it every time or is it rhyme?
See - I'm doing it again
So please take some time and write a poem
Unload your mind and go into overtime, or is in overrhyme.

—*D. B. Bolinger*

Betrayed

When you feel betrayed
you are a little scared,
And a little afraid.

You don't know what is going on
And you think...
That there will never, be a new dawn.

You feel like,
You can't put anymore trust
In anyone again

For fear that, that one,
Won't think that you're a must.
And that they will treat you,
Like you are nothing more than dust.

When you feel betrayed,
You sometimes don't know how. And sometimes,
You don't know in what way.

"It'll get better," People say
They don't know when,
But, you hope it'll be someday.
Soon someday

—*Jenny Stokes*

Overdoing It?

(Remarks to oneself.)
Why, oh why, are not you satisfied?
With more, will you then be gratified?
Fine beauty, by faint flaws, is enhanced;
Perfection is a merciless cause.
So pause, reflect and oh, be entranced.

—*Carl A. Loy*

Garden Friends

Petite guava, with jelly pears
　You are not worried
With what you wear.
　As the little gypsy flower
Wading in her pool of dew.
　And the plump mother tomato,
With her tiny group of two
　Or the chubby plum which dances
Through the air, as the summer breeze goes by.
　This is the garden of fruits and veggies,
They all are kindred folk of time.
　Some old, some new, a sapling or an oak.
They all live in harmony, as God has forever spoke.

　　—*Crystal M. Seyller*

To Lucile

We were the youngest of friends.
You arrived in August, I in November.
The happy years of dolls and mud pies,
the age of innocence and trust. The
age of freedom from cares of today
or tomorrow.

New friends were added with the
coming of schooldays. The larger
circle of girls and boys enjoying
picnics and parties. Eventually dating
and dancing. Romance dawned and
and wedding bells sounded.

Now we are eighty. The two little
girls of August and November are old
friends with memories to share as
only best friends can.

　　—*Frances Nowlan Love*

A Gift To All Who Knew Him

On this day of January 15th.....
You came into the world and departed this day.....
You touched each one of us in a special way.....
You taught love and kindness and for that you will always
　　remind us.....
If patience is a virtue.....
Then you are virtuous indeed.....
Because the world has never met a man as tolerant indeed.....
You lent a hand to all, especially to those in need.....
You will always be remembered for all your unselfish deeds.....
Now the fight is over, the pain that you endured.....
We will meet you in heaven, you can rest assured.....
So to all of us who had the pleasure of knowing you
We would like to jointly say.....
We will forever love you each and every day.....
Your spirit lives on within us, for that you can be sure.....
The qualities you taught us will be valued forever more.....
The hearts you touched were many, I'm sure all agree....
From earth you've departed, but your spirit will forever be....

Love, your son Duane, your family, and all who truly knew you.
Goodbye Bob, We Love You.

　　—*Duane Byrne*

Goodbye

When the earth is cold at night the thought of
you glows like light. Your beautiful eyes, nice
looking butt which I shall never see again. For
night is coming again and you I shall never see,
so I'll have to say goodbye to you but never
to the memory.

　　—*Angela Bruzzese*

The Eternal Love of My Mother

The eternal love of my mother is something you can't describe
You cannot see the love and it cannot be prescribed
The love that comes from my mother's heart
is something I take with pride
Appreciation is the key to a mother's heart you see
Wherever my mother may be I always keep her inside of me
Whatever the time and wherever the place
My mother's always ahead of the race
to comfort me with her comforting face
Whenever I'm in trouble my mother's there on the double
Whenever I'm in pain my mother's there again
My mother's a special person in every which way
I'll love her always from day to day

　　—*Angela Kulesza*

The Game

It was a game, they used to play,
You could enjoy on a summer's day.
Now it's sport; a game—no way.
The play is gone, it's all for pay.

Wake up America!!! Let's draw the lines,
You're turning games into dollar signs.

When a game becomes a sport,
The general public comes up short.
Paying too much, not seeing enough,
As what was play becomes so rough.
The child in us can't understand
Why play requires such greedy hands.

　　—*Daryl E. Smith*

My Little Brother (Tony)

My little brother,
You have grown up to be a handsome man and a wonderful person.
I think that in time, people will know how special you are,
With a little less angry and a lot more patience
You will learn that others do care.
You're not only my brother, you're also my friend.
I see a lot of good things in you
And it just will take time for others to see it.
You're there when I need a smile and you're there
When know one else is (especially our family) there for me.
Little brother, you accepted me for who I am and what I am.
You don't put me down for being a little different.
Even though you're far away now,
You still seem to put a smile on my face.
Little brother, I will be here for you, no matter what,
Because we're not just brother and sister,
we're best of friends.

　　—*Davina Zeitz*

To Big John

I woke with you each morning.
You helped some tears go away,
You filled so many lives with joy,
And now here you lay.

So many people loved you
So many people knew you cared.
You helped so much,
Many smiles we shared.

This is to you Big John,
We love you so very much,
You'll be in our hearts forever,
Just look at all the people you've touched.

　　—*Judy Ann Buchanan*

Qualities Of A Good Person

With kindness and childlike modesty,
 You have healed my heart.
Qualities such as these,
 Have given me hope.

With compassion and genuine concern,
 You have cured my despair.
Qualities such as these,
 Have allowed me to see and speak the truth.

With good nature and gentle laughter,
 You have dried my tears.
Qualities such as these,
 Have allowed me to feel joy again.

With sincerity and honesty,
 You have one my trust.
Qualities such as these,
 Have given me a reason to believe again.

With unselfishness and complete giving,
 You have won my love.
These qualities, above all, have allowed
 Me to once again live.

—*Deborah Humphrey*

Youth's Dialogue With The Self

O gabbling Youth! The golden age of opportunities! Where are
you leading your blue-eyed boys, the future citizens?
What good future holds in store for those chosen communities?
My heart bleeds to see those disillusioned denizens toiling
tedious to trudge on a trivial temporal existence; Their urging
minds groping in the enveloping damnation searching in vain
for succor and spiritual sustenance to guide their way
through the path to soul's salvation; Their dreams nipped in
the bud by perverse presumptions And an excessive effervescence
of unwise assumptions. Who is this that tunes the string of a
frail heart And tries to sing a swan song to their
afflictions? Not I a derelict or a demagogue with a partisan
heat; Nor I a slave with servile modes and sold affections;
But a fair, fervent, and fiery spirit of alignment Standing a
silent spectator to the sad predicament. Enough of this
fiesta, we tarried too long in confinement; Come my brethren,
let us seek light and life's enlightenment; Let us unite our
hands and hearts and sing in sweet unison: "Long live our
nation, the fountainhead of many a noble notion."

—*Katherine Shelley*

But I Miss You Daddy

 Why Daddy why did you have to go
 You must have known how I loved you so

 I can't tell you now for it's too late
 You've met your Maker at the Golden Gate

You went the way you wanted in the still of the night
 With no one there to help you fight

 Your wife and children all gathered around
The day we laid your body in the hard cold ground

 How proud you must have been to see
 All of us together as you wanted us to be

There was hugging and talking, laughter and tears
 We hadn't all been together in many a years

Gentle snow fell that morning then the sun did shine
 That was God's way of saying "Now he's mine"

 I know you're with God in heaven above
 But I miss you Daddy and send you my love

—*Kathleen Owens Keller*

Oh Ye Of Little Faith

Oh ye of little faith, sighed the disciple here one day, that
you only had the faith of the mustard seed, he prayed. But the
crowd just scoffed at his words as if they did not hear.
Comparing us with a mustard seed, they'd said and continued to
mock and jeer. We know that He is dead, they cried, for we saw
the light grow dim, we saw him close his dark, sad eyes, we
heard a sigh from him. And now you tell us that his life is
not yet done; and you talk in parables and believe such things,
yet you seem to be the only one. Had you listened to His
teaching even of this tiny seed, said the disciple to the
doubting crowd, you'd know just what I mean. Just to show the
smallest sign of faithfulness, yes even this small, to blossom
forth and grow within, then His truths would fill you all. His
love is like this mustard seed when planted in fertile earth,
for then it would grow, to do His work, and you'd know His true
worth. So do not mock this tiny seed, but learn from what it
teaches. That it, like you, without his love, can't know how
far He reaches. Have faith, for He forgives us; so did He die
for all our sins. And He has not forsaken us; this knowledge
we must hold within. Only faith will bind us together.

—*Faye Henley*

Feeling Alone

Alone is the feeling you get when
 you speak out and nobody speaks back.
Alone is the feeling you get when
 you arrive and no one says hi.
Alone is the feeling you get when
 you only get noticed when you have something they want.
Alone is the feeling you get when
 you tried to make a friend and she's not willing.
Alone is the feeling you get when
 your friends are only around when you're successful.
Alone is the feeling you get when
 your best friend forgets about you to become popular.
Alone is the feeling you get when
 you try to confide in someone and they don't care.
Alone is the feeling you get when
 your friends get invited, but you don't.
Alone is the feeling you get when
 you are me.

—*Erica Garner*

Eternal Train

When you feel good inside
You want to sing and shout
To let others have a ride
And see, what it's all about.

Christ can bring you to this place
Put your trust in Him now
All yours past He'll erase
If on your knees you'll pray and bow,

Ask Him now into your heart,
It's so simple - you will see
A brand new day - a fresh new start
A joy inside will come to be.

No matter where you are in life
He'll always be there to guide you through
In good or bad - worries or strife
I promise, He'll be there for you.

He saved me too from my sins you know
He'll save you too if you want Him to -
You can choose what seeds you'll sow -
The path you choose is now up to you.

—*Jodie Griffis*

Please Let Me Have My Tomorrows!

You had a lot of tomorrows, why can't I?
You went to school in peace, I go with police patrolling the
    school instead of the traffic.
You went to the stores for a piece of candy, I go and hope that
    I won't be snatched.
You could go to the playgrounds anytime, I can't cause the
    dealers and pushers are always there.
Please can't I have my tomorrows?
You could sit on the steps when it was too hot to sleep, I
    can't sit out too long cause a shoot out is sure to come.
You could go to the park or take a short-cut through the woods,
    I can't cause I'll either see a murder or be murdered.
Please let me have my tomorrows!
Can I make plans for my tomorrows or are you going to take
    them? Please let me have my tomorrows, you had yours.

      —*Inez L. Fulton*

My Daughter Is Very Special To Me

Your not so little anymore
Your all grown up and pretty as can be
Im so glad that you are a part of me
And it will always be that way
Why? Because your my Special Daughter
And, without you here by my side, I wouldn't know what to do.
I'm not sure what else to say
Your always here for me
When I'm in need
I would absolutely be lost in tears
If I ever lost you
Your Love will always be locked up in my heart
You make me so happy, just being here with me
I want you to be happy always
You know why, Daughter?
Because you're very special to me
Always will be
I will always carry your Love in my heart
Because you are that special someone
And that someone is my very own daughter.

      —*Christine M. Shellito*

Bag Lady

Bent, old, cold, weary.
Your broken belongings cart holds you up.
Sick, alone, forgotten.
Garbage is your sustenance.

Victim, target, prey.
Trash are your treasures.
Wet in the spring. Hot in the summer.
Cold in the winter. Dark in the night.

Your lessers laugh, but
you cry no more - what's the use?
When were you happy last?
None know you. None want you.
None see you. None care.
Your's is a fate none deserve.

Who stole your home? Who stole your money?
Who stole your family? Who stole your life?

Where are your children?
Are they bag people too?
Or are they dead?

      —*Henry J. Meyer*

Indictment

Through the laughter of my childhood,
your careless insults cut away the line
of confidence and self-worth,
severing it with sharp, blunt strokes.
You crushed my imagination and happiness,
condemning them as childish pretending and
silliness. You taunted, you twisted, and
you maligned, knowing that I would not answer
for your due respect. And now that I might
look back and see some goodness in you and
learn to like or maybe even love you,
you die.

      —*Jennifer Harrison*

Wait For Me Spring!

  Wait for me spring!
Your days pass much too quickly!
Winging their way across the inviting lawn;
    With budded boughs,pink clouds of apple blossoms.
      Blue eggs and fledgling birds -
        Then you are gone!

  Wait for me Spring!
We braved the snow together.
Waiting for balmy breezes to outride
    The frigid steeds
      Of Winter's stormy weather.
      Now you are free -
        But I am kept inside!

  Wait for me Spring!
I need to touch and hold you;
To thrust my fingers in your warm, moist sod.
    To free from weeds.
      To strengthen growing tendrils;
        And joining hands with you.
          Reach up toward God!

      —*Florence Beans*

Forever Yours

You comfort me with warmth and love,
Your eyes caress me from above,
You make the tears all disappear,
Such caring and happiness is always near.

Never leave me; for in the end,
We will prove to them all; who will make amends,
Our future is planned; our love is ready,
To take that step like so many.

Your eyes twinkle with delight,
Our life together will be so bright,
Our times alone make it worthwhile,
I love your laughter; not to mention your smile.

You've changed my outlook on life,
I hope someday to be your loving wife,
To share our secrets through the years,
Our innermost thoughts and deepest fears.

Our memories are old but yet so new,
Although, my love for you is a little blue,
In hopes that you will come back soon,
To the one you left behind; the one who loves you.

      —*Lisa Marie De Luca*

Happy Valentine's Day Anniversary

How much do I love you? Where do I start first?
Your heart, mind, body and soul quenches my thirst.

Your eyes and your smile brighten my every day.
You have that loving ability to take the pain away.

When we met, the aura around us was as bright as the sun.
Our hearts led us down a path to our lives as one.

I have been so fulfilled since you entered my life,
and love has grown stronger when I became your wife.

You work so hard to make sure we have what we need,
And baby, you have what it takes in life to succeed.

Today, I wish you Happy Anniversary, my love,
For all your dreams will come true from the heavens above.

—*Debra J. Fleishman*

The Sea

Once you have the feel of the sea
Your home away seems dull and drear,
No calm and blue sea on sunny day,
No angry and grey sea on stormy day.

I miss you, you are so faraway,
I miss you at night, the movements of waves,
No sea gulls calling and flying to race,
No sea air washing my eager face.

I love the sea and I always will,
Just waiting for chance to go back still,
I know and feel you calling me there,
I hear your voice and understand.

Before I leave this earthly life
With all its joys and all its strife,
I shall go back to sea and shore
And I shall stay and leave no more.

—*Hedy Wolf Formanek*

A Christmas Prayer

God, grant to us humility and wisdom so that we may see
   Your image in each one we know.

Grant that we may understand and take our brother by the hand
   So that our soul, within, may grow.

Grant us courage to be strong to face the truth when we are wrong
   Yet, tolerant be of imperfection.

Grant that faith with us abide with knowledge so that we may guide
   Our lives in your direction.

Grant that the infant Savior's birth will teach men how to live on earth
   So someday they may wear a crown.

Grant forgiveness to the weak so that the King whom all do seek
   Will, in the hearts of men, be found.

Grant that on this Christmas Day as we kneel down to pray
   The fire of faith will burn within.

Grant it will within us stay, every hour of every day
   So He will dwell with us. Amen.

—*Marie F. Endicott*

Someday

Someday I will make it to eleven.
Who knows, when I die
I'll meet God when I go to heaven.
Someday I will become a nurse
And help people who have been on an evil curse,
Someday God will come down to me
And tell me what a great job I have done.

—*Mariana Mena*

Mother's Meditation

It was a gleeful day, my Little Scout;
Your laughter seemed to turn the tears aside,
And now you are completely given out;
Your daylight by sweet sleep has been defied.
Sir Dream entreats: forth comes a golden smile,
A sparkler bright to cuddle and to kiss.
The days and years are such a little while
For treasure storing up of infant bliss;
I'll print these down in recollection's book,
Enrichment for the days of growing old;
I'll open back its pages dear and look
O'er truest pleasure God gave me to hold.
The mother of a man-and with that thought
My lowest duties will become as naught.

—*Betha Williams*

Your Mom's An Angel

Up in the star filled heavens where God's true glory lies
Your Mom is with the angel's singing loved filled lullabies.
Her love is always with us and her eyes keep watch below,
To smile upon her children's world to watch her love seeds grow.

I've seen her eyes of laughter melt suddenly to tears,
When she'd sit and watch a movie that held a mothers fears.
She filled our lives and hungry hearts with everlasting love,
And gave her all in every way even now with God above.
I can remember how at christmas time she kept you both in
sight, I can almost touch her secret joy in your laughter
of delight. I can see the peace that filled her eyes and I
gather it with greed, for I know the love your mother felt
as she filled your every need.

She enjoyed just being a mother and she changed so much in
life, to make her self with pleasure into a mother and a wife.
Now God called Ann from our world and she walked through
heavens door but her love is always with us for she's an angel
ever more.

—*Bob Sams*

Lost

Huddled in your Shell - My friend
Your own personal little Hell - My friend
Perhaps it's just as well - Pretend
   That nothing really matters

Walking around
   With your head hangin' down
Can't find the Solution
   These rules choke you like pollution
Listen closely
   You might hear the sound of Love's evolution

Trapped in a Prison - of Doubt
Another tricky decision - You shout
   I can't do it!
   You blew it - last time

But you've done your time

Atonement achieved
No longer deceived - by yourself
Proudly you bear the scars of your Strife
Welcome my friend, back to Life

—*David M. Hoskins*

To Holly

When you were little I could hold you in one hand,
Your short, bouncing legs couldn't keep up with me when I ran,
but you tried!
Your downy puppy fur was always messed up, always soft.

When you were older we went jogging together
Or climbed into an old rowboat and when we'd reach the center
we'd both jump into the cool pond water.
Or I'd saddle the horse and you'd trot happily along
and race enthusiastically when we galloped.
Or in winter when the pond froze we skated together and played
in the snow.
You were My Best Friend, really, always fun!

Now when it snows you curl up in your soft, downy blanket
because your cold bones hurt.
Now we go for slow, short, after dinner walks-
but no more jogging, or horse racing, or swimming.
We don't have fun anymore and it doesn't matter.
Every time I leave I hope you'll still be there
at Thanksgiving, at Christmas, because I now know that one day,
soon, you won't.

—*Allison Holloway Frazee*

Mom

The depth of tender love, held in every touch.
You're the reason why I've learned to care so much.

The dew upon the grass, warmed by the sons embrace.
Always kept the sunshine glowing in your face.

Even in the rain, my cloak was always dry.
Your arms outstretched above me, whenever I would cry.

My journey has been rocky, and many times I fell.
But a smile in your heart, assured me I was well.

The times I felt no meaning, you brought me to my feet.
Without that love there for me, I may have lost my seat.

Although I have grown slowly, my strength is like a rock.
And when the beast has withered, you'll be waiting at the dock.

I looked into the days, your countenance had fallen.
And wonder why the Father had written such a calling.

But the wisdom I have seen, and every page I've written.
Cannot pour out fresh milk, to a hungry little kitten.

Today I want to thank you, for the breath of life I share
And for a perfect christmas, and this caring heart I wear.

—*John Starrett*

Waste Of Life

You have no sense of humor
you're way beyond stupidity
you're relentless as they come below mentality
you're a no good filthy bum useless you are
Stupid and dumb you never take a bath
   you never brush your teeth
Your appearance is hideous far beyond belief
You're a lying cheating thief
and you fill everyone
   who surrounds you
with misery and grief
you have an acne covered face
having no moral values
you're covered in disgrace
you're an idiotic schmuck
and could care less to even give a _ _ _ _
your smell sickens me to the point
I obtain a dry heave
From this my body starts to weave

—*Brandon Watkins*

Mental Archeology

Come on, dig a little deeper, you don't have far to go;
You've almost reached the center, the treasure—my soul.

Don't talk about the weather, don't talk about my hair;
Small talk is much too easy, and is getting us nowhere.

Let's unearth some relics, some memories of the past;
Let's dust off those aspirations, shelved by the real world much too
    fast;
Better grab your shovel, the best is always last!

Let's excavate, let's contemplate our buried feelings of fear and love;
I mean let's really communicate for it's getting late,
But forgive me, I don't mean to shove.

Are you frightened? Yes, I'm scared,
But we're just scratching the surface;
We have so much to share.

Have you found it yet?
That treasured artifact?
It's not easily seen.
But the more you dig, the more you uncover;
Buried bits and pieces, fitting together, — forming the real me!

—*Deborah L. Benko*

Loving Jesus

You've got to love Jesus more than father or mother.
You've got to love Jesus more than sister or brother.
You've got to love Him more than your child, husband or wife.
You've got to love Him more than your own life.
He said, "You must take up your cross and follow me.
Regardless of the cost, follow to Calvary.
Deny yourself of everything,
That would keep you from seeing Jesus as King."
Just now, search, count the cost.
See if the seasoning of your life is lost.
Do you let Him rule and reign?
In your heart is He really King?
Do you love Him, love Him supreme?
His praises daily do you sing?
Love Jesus today, Give Him your heart.
Right now, today, your journey to heaven start.

—*Beatrice Haas*

"Dad, Dad"

Dad, Dad, I'm so glad I found out more about the life
you've had. I'm glad you and God gave me that chance.
To know much more about you, more than just a glance.
Thank you for that chance.

I am your daughter and I'm sitting here by the water. I wish I
could be with you even more, I'd give more than just a dime.
But with every little thought, you are with me all the time.
And that's just fine.

You and Mom taught us to appreciate everything so well,
That for the man who had everything I brought you a shell.
Because I know there's been time when I put you through hell.
But, I'm never going to give up and say, "Oh, well."

So as you middle daughter sits here by the beach.
Her parents whom have taught her so well, are never out of reach

I know, now why, you taught us so good and I'm gonna try
With my kids, like I should.
For family is family and ours is so good.
If I had three wishes, I honestly don't know what I would say,
Because with parents like you two, ALL is Okay.

Maybe I'll just save them for a rainy day.

—*Marie Jon Pretzer*

Untitled

Your smile penetrates my soul. Your touch warms my being.
Your suggestions help me grow. What would I be without your
friendship? Because of you, my friend, I am something.

Without you , I am but dust. Thank you, for all you do. I
love you, my friend.

Where will I be and who will I know one year from now? I know
where I've been. Seen too much. It changed my life. I weep;

but the tears are not of sorrow. I cry; not for myself but for
the sweet people who give, but are not given to. Who work, but
that are not treated of any value only used and abused by the
man who made me see too much and know too much.
How life turns and twists. It's path is often filled with
stones and rocks. If we would just turn and look to the side
We would see the field of flowers.

 —Faye Hutchinson-Brooke

Delusion Of Love

It may seem that I'm going crazy
My friends think that I've gone insane,
I no longer have time for right thinking
'Cause I only have you on my brain!
How can I focus on tasks at hand
Or pay mind to the things I must do
When every cell of my love hungry mind
Is filled with desire for you?
If people laugh when I forget
And lose things I never can find,
I just overlook and forgive them
'Cause I only have you on my mind.
I guess that I've totally lost it -
I'm completely wrapped up in your spell
And although I'm mindless and foolish
I've never, ever felt quite this well!

 —Little Turtle

March

 It is March.
My garden lies asleep beneath the snow,
 Cozy and warm,
Waiting for the gentle touch of April
 To spring to life again.
The daffodils, brave souls, are peeking above
 the snow,
They seem to shiver in the cold.
 But yet they tell us
 That spring will surely come
When April lifts her warm hand
 and bids the garden come alive
With bird songs, blue skies, and warm sun
 To cheer our hearts
 and help us forget
The snows of the winters of our lives.

 —Jean Seestadt

Eyes Of Love

When you look at me know that you see love.
The eyes are the windows of the soul,
to look in mine will show my love
for you, like a river - flows.

This love fills my heart, occupies
my thoughts, you inspire fantasies,
so much to say, no words need to be spoken.

Look in my eyes, my love, they speak of
fire and passion, of love.

 —Elaine E. Boyd

An Oak Tree In The Winter

The oak tree, as I walk along the cold track
My great attention does really attract.
A wistful eye, a rueful experience
Now peers amidst bleak and awful silence,
As dreadful winter comes to make things drab,
With no fluttering leaves to grab.
No more the once gorgeous oaken powers,
With sturdy stem and blooming flowers;
With death like juxta posed wings it weeps,
Or, like crazed mankind it weeps.
Come Oh Winter! brag not in fatigue
There is no more room for intrigue.
Mankind did you for years endure
When Sir Spring comes all things to ensure;
Weep no more spring is weeks away
When patience will assume its sway.
Bravo! big sturdy oak tree,
I will count for you, one two and three.

 —Joseph M. Njoku

I Love You My Dear

I love you my dear.
My heart could not wait.
I could not put my heart on hold.
I did not have to be told.
For my heart knew I was for you.
For you are wonderful and bold.
Although it's been years, I still love you my dear.
Now our eyes are dimmer and our hair is grey.
But your touch is still soft, gentle and warm.
When I am weak, you are strong.
But together our life will go on, our heart is as one.
It's never to be undone in this world or the world beyond.
My love grows deeper as the days go by.
For without you I would be so sad.
But our hearts together we will always have.
I love you my dear.
Art

 —Margaret C. Martin

Peace With God

I searched for peace
 My heart desired to know,
Thoughts of money and pleasure
 Filled my mind aglow.

Riches would surely bring peace
 And pleasure would be rest,
But the more I worked for riches
 Pleasures of this world called for the best.

Searching for peace in this life
 Cannot be found in material gain,
God alone can supply our needs
 His blessings we may attain.

When we repent of our sins
 And ask Him to forgive,
Our Heavenly Father comes in our hearts
 And shows us how to live.

My desire to live for Jesus
 The giver of peace and love,
Gave me a life of assurance
 In God the Father from above.

 —Carlene Fry

Suddenly

Suddenly life!
My heart is beating, my blood racing
My vital organs forming, my little body
    Growing, changing

I can make a fist, I can hear your voice
    Softly speaking
I'm warm and ohhh so comfortable
I praise the Lord because I am
    Tearfully and wonderfully made

I feel funny, did you take something?
    I see a light, I feel cold
I see a long, hollow tube
    It's coming toward me, Mommy

It's pulling me, it's sharp, it hurts!
    It hurts so much
Please Mommy, make it stop!

My arms, my legs, my body
    I'm being torn into pieces
        Mommy, why???
            Suddenly, death.
    —*Debby Nelson*

In The Stillness…

In the stillness…of this moment…my child,
    My heart leans its thoughts to you.
Oh, how great my heart's love is—
    To try to show you, it's so hard to do.

I know you're grown and an adult now
    So I have set you free
To make your own decisions,
    Of how your life should be.

But in the Stillness…at this moment,
    Before this moment fades away,
I want you to know you are loved by me
    And in my heart — this love is sealed to stay!

Love forever, Mother
    —*Jeanette Pinkham*

"Time Does Sweetly Fly"

(Dedicated to my daughter Dawn.)
My how time seems to slip away. Faster and faster every day.
It seems only yesterday, I watched you, at play, with all your
little friends In grammar school.

Then as swiftly, you seemed to grow into a sweet young lady,
with a boy who called on you, each night. Taking you here and
there, hearts filled with delight, and too swiftly it seems,
I sat in a church, and watched you, walk down the Isle, with
that same boy.

As pretty as a picture, and as happy, as could be. Starting
a new life, which you know would turn out right.

And now again, I must say, time has slipped so fast away. For
here you are a mother to-be, making a Daddy, of your husband,
and a Grandmom out of me.

Yes time, does sweetly fly.
    —*Margaret A. Brewster*

Thought's

A persons thought's are like numbers on a combination lock.
Without their right combination they are nothing.
But with the right sequence it open's up and one's thought's
comes forth to form one's ideal's which can shape the course of
one's destiny.

    —*James G. Jones*

Diary Of A Sailor

"Drifting" drifting endlessly upon the sea,
my imagination is only a reflection in the ocean of me
luring this sailor to explore for treasure in underwater
caves,
while mother earth absents spawns myths of mystical mermaids.

Fresh are my thoughts of those tropical Edens,
brown as gingerbread are the island girls
that tantalize their seamen, treating him as he were king,
for this sailor has traversed the four corners of the world,
but the beauty they possess is like nothing I've ever seen.

In the comfort of my quarters
I'll scribble the memory of this voyage in my diary,
along with other journeys that have taken me to exotic
places,
indeed life on the seven seas have been kind to this limey,
so have all the ports of call, and as for the crew, I shall
always remember their faces.

Beyond the soft blue horizon
a lighthouse awaits to guide this vessel pass the coral
rocks,
no longer dose the compass point towards the house of the
rising sun, ahead in the distance lie familiar faces to
welcome
us as we dock.
    —*Kevin Fisher*

Tomorrow

"Mommy, when can we go to the zoo
My little girl asked me out of the blue
"Oh, maybe tomorrow," was my vacant reply
Then she frowned with that all-knowing sigh.

"The last time you said that was a long time ago
And we still haven't gone. Why, Mom? I'd like to know"
I felt pangs of guilt and a twinge of sorrow
When she asked further, "Mom, when is tomorrow?"

I was thoroughly amazed and about had a fit
When my child observed with astonishing wit
"Tomorrow never comes," I heard her say
"For when tomorrow is here, we call it today!"

Well, that little comment caught me up short
For I knew full well I'd had my moment in court
So I donned my biggest smile as I most surely knew
That today was the day we'd be off to the zoo!
    —*Gloria Hizer*

You Might Find

In the absence of God you might find I am your maker
    My love my heart
Until that time when all is mine
    In the absence of God
What becomes of what you are and who you'll be
    And, as always, what becomes of we
In the absence of God how will we know if we've found
    What we've been looking for
And how will we know to revel in the find
    As in the making of love
In the absence of God we stand before the mirror
    and question what we see
Who we are
What we know
And what we choose
    In the absence of God love becomes a rouse
Who we are and what we choose
    In the absence of God
I long for you.
    —*Elisabeth R. Reagan*

A Dog Named Star Shine My Master Called Me Bugs

The Lord called me home today, but you can bet I will shine for
my master up in animal heaven. And I will always remember all
our happy times romping together. You, see, I was her first
best buddy. Then came a fluffy gray cat who's name was Annie
to live with us. She was O.K. as far as cats go, but then she
went away, don't know where! Maybe I'll see her again one
day... Now, I liked that horse named Dandy, and that he was, a
dandy of a fellow. You should see us all run like the wind,
with my master upon his back to places you wouldn't believe,
and come home all tuckered out. Then one day my master came
home with this scrawny little four legged doggie, didn't care
much for him at first, but he got to be my friend called C.J.
Now he liked to play and jump and chew up things. I couldn't
go for all of that, because you know I was getting on in years
and set in my ways. But to hear my masters voice say, "Come
along 'Bugs', let's go riding now," was another story. Away we
would all run for that old pick-up truck, and off we would go
in a cloud of dust. Then came this sunny spring day, April 15,
1989. I got laid low, don't know why I had to go. So with no
time to say good-bye, I'll see my loyal and faithful companion in
the big starry sky.

—*Margie B. Jeffers*

Into My Dream

I'm sitting in my room dreaming away,
my mind is running far away

In a meadow of roses and little dressed mice
eating chocolate sweetened rice!

In that same little town ladies spinning their wool
and little men swimming in the pool!

All the children playing games,
all the houses kept warm in flames of love...

The sky kept white, with the light of each day.
Oh my I have just woken up and it's the month of May.

—*Lupe Atencio*

Do You Think Of Me?

When I awake, your all I can see,
My mind, seems to wonder;
And I think, do you think about me?
I picture us, kissing, through the cold,
dark night; so beautiful are your kisses.
When you kiss me good night.
You have so much warmth, I'm beginning to see,
But all I keep thinking, is are you thinking about me?
Your heart, is so warm, when your holding me tight;
I try, not to cry, because it feels so right,
I'm so happy with you, and I miss you so much.
All I can think about is your tender touch,
But still I keep thinking in the back of my head,
Do you think of me when you lie awake in bed?

—*Irene B. Ingram*

Untitled

Somewhere she waits to make you win,
your soul in her firm black hands.
Sometimes she listens to your long lasting cry,
your tears in the darkening sands.
Something makes her see the child,
that she holds inside her heart.
And somewhere she will realize,
how she tore that child apart.
Your smile will now find a place,
in her softening white eyes.
With her false comforting words,
showing through her falling lies.

—*Kiri Laabs*

"Heart Of Flames"

My flaming heart cannot be quenched.
My one passion has come around again.
It all happened with a mere hello and ended up with a
broken heart.
desire within can never be fixed for this heart is cold
It has no warmth which can show no feeling.
What shall I do to quench the pain?
Shall I seek for another heart or mend my broken one.
One does not caress you if they have no feeling.
Yet the heart might lie in a pit of evil.
No one knows what a heart will say or do next.
Don't ever let a heart roam for a broken heart.
It is territory not to be entered ever again,
or it shall shatter into a million and one.

—*Christine Reich*

Stop, Listen, Pray!

You spoke Your word, Your call I heard.
My path was paved with sin I questioned,
if not now Lord, when?
You answered with the same words again.
I've had to run a difficult race; You pleaded my case.
You promised me a better place, if I'd humble
myself, and look upon Your face.
I meditated on Your word, You spoke to my heart.
I understood things better then.
Lord, when you took me in, as Your word proclaims
my new life did begin. You set me on a course,
kept me at a steady pace to stay,
You revealed to me a brighter day.
The one thing You asked in return,
is that I submit to Your way.
I'm so glad! I took the time to, Stop! Listen!
and Pray!
My trials were many; times were hard;
it's all over now. I Thank You Lord.

—*Barbara Thomas-Brown*

Hey Wovoka!

Let's Ghost Dance. Bring back your old ways.
My people have had their chance and their ain't too much praise

Poisoned water, poisoned fish; glass and steel pierce the sky;
Poisoned air, poisoned lungs; no one bothers to ask why? —

Hey Wovoka! Let's Ghost Dance.
Sweep us back into the sea.
Bring the stab of your mystic lance
and avenge the children of Wounded Knee —

Poisoned days, poisoned nights; my God! We broke the sky;
Poisoned child, poisoned man; rally 'round the liar's cry —

Hey Wovoka! Just you never mind.
You don't need a Ghost Dance.
Denying our past, we run blind,
teetering on the killing cliff.

—*Mark L. Chance*

Your Sweetness As Perfume

Your sweetness comes as from perfume.
My senses reel when you enter a room.
Your smile is that of flowers in full bloom.

Your delicate air is as a Summer breeze.
Your moods are mine to please.
Your hair tangles as tatters in the trees.

Your touch is as a feather blown.
Your kisses are as seeds sown.
Your love is as ivy overgrown.

—*J. Pierritz*

Chad

You're my sun that rises in the morning,
  my stars that light up the midnight sky.
You're my trees that blow in the spring,
  my snow that falls in the winter.
You're my link in the chain of love,
  my strong side when I'm weak
You're my tears of joy when I'm happy,
  my tears of pain when I'm in need
You're my voice when I can't talk,
  my raindrops when it's cloudy,
You're my eyes when I can't see things
  my hands when I can't feel.
You're my wings to fly high with,
  my cliff to jump off.
You're my feelings when I'm numb,
  my life I'm dead.
You're everything to me,
    I Love You More Than Anything!

  —*Mandi Stockton*

"Playing Games"

As I sit here, lonely and blue.
My thoughts all gather when I think of you.
The things you did for me gather in my mind
and must to think, you seemed so kind.

I guess we were just playing a game.
I was the loser 'cause you got all the fame.
I know I was messing in the game of life.
I wasn't cheating, but I got stabbed with a knife.

I was the one who ended up being hurt.
All because of nothing, I was thrown in the dirt.
Just now, I realized the truth, you see.
In the game we played, you never loved me.

  —*Carrie A. Campbell*

Sharing

Without you to share
  My thoughts and feelings with,
They would have no meaning-
  No hope;
They would be aimlessly tossed about.
But with you-
They are given meaning,
  And the promise of growing further-
The promise of spreading
  And touching another.

  —*Barbara A. Swartz*

March Minds

March winds briskly blow across the fields,
My thoughts are of this summer's yields.
What could be around the corner but spring,
At which time to are wits we cling.
We'll be hastily busy with tasks at hand,
From morning into the night we till the land.
When rest does come we give praise to the Lord,
Happy that we have room and board.
Only for a moment my thoughts turn cold,
As tales of hail and floods and droughts are told.
Then my soul at peace a smile shall be worn,
For I pursue a career for which I was born.

  —*Eugene J. Scherley*

I Feel

With this love I feel inside,
my thoughts, my hopes,
Were never denied.
God be with me while I cry,
I can't believe, what I'm feeling inside.
        I feel -
I found a dream, that has awaken at last.
        Chris -
My feelings, my actions, words were never asked.
        I feel -
Myself snuggled to my pillows,
holding them tight.
Thoughts of you, praying your alright.
Whispers of you lingering in my mind.
        I feel -
If life takes us separate ways,
with this love I feel inside,
remember it was time for you and I
Love will always remain, A- L- I- V- E !

  —*Florence L. Hemple*

On A Wall About To Be Brought Down

Though I may be a hard stone wall,
My time has come. I, too, must fall.
Thus all things go. Both short and tall,
We all succumb to Fate's cruel call.
No one can hide. No one's too small
To escape the heavy hammer's haul.
Behold my demise. Don't boast at all
That others hold you in highest thrall.
As you go through life, your eye on the ball,
Remember all things are ephemeral.

  —*David Salsburg*

Death Of The Mistress

Crystal ball she holds in her hand
mysteries sought across this land,
Dropping to the silk sheets black as the night
shattered crystal then takes flight,
Misty cat eyes gleaming in shadows
as the fog begins to rise and grow,
Fur so black moves so sleek
rounding the corner gains a peak,
Senses alert sharp to all
for I swear I heard the crystal ball fall,
Through the silky sheets I slip
My whiskers tickling my upper lip,
I come upon the end of the bed
the mistress lying still and dead,
Out her palm silently fell
the crystal ball with a story to tell.

  —*Marsha Myers*

Audience

I have always believed that a person
need not speak loudly to be heard, they
must only have something pertinent to
say. But in the unlikely event that you
still go unnoticed, I strongly encourage
you to rely upon the silent power of the
written word. It has never been ignored
by the intelligent mind.

  —*Jennifer Allen*

596

Reaching The New Abode

Racial slander, hurt and shame
Never treating anyone exactly the same.

Learn to love, learn to be kind
All prejudice is in your mind.

Rid your heart of anger rid your life of wrong
Truly as you talk the bond will become strong.

Never have you spoken anything nice
Now you can't stop, the kindness melts the ice.

Coldness held its hand tight around your heart
Now everyone is together and no one's apart.

Your life continues down that same road
Travel until you've reached a new abode.

Never have you felt this high on life
Making right choices and ending the strife.

As time continues equality will too
Eventually we'll be equal—me and you.

No colors to see no pain to bear
The prejudice will be gone and only love will be there!
—*Michelle Cramer*

Book It

The game was going extremely awful for the Chicago Bulls that
night. Arch rivals, the Trailblazers, sure put up a fight.
Portland was up by 13 with just five minutes left to play,
They were playing for the championship of the N.B.A.

The crowd sensed the feel for heat, no one budged to leave
their seat. For if only Jordan could touch the ball, the Bulls
would surely take it all. But Jordan tired and so did Pippen,
At that sight the crowd did stiffen.
Off the bench jumped Paxson and did what no one could ever do,
And with his sharp-shooting, he cut the lead down to two.

With a minute left to go Jordan took his stand,
For his team was to be the greatest in Basketball Land.
As the clock ticked down in the Bulls old hall,
In the huddle Jordan shouted, "Throw me the ball!"
His eyes were fixed, his stare was steady, he pumped and faked,
oh, he was ready! Ten seconds left, it's now or never,
The shot to silence the Blazers forever.
Oh, somewhere out in T.V. land, graceful birds are tweeting
like a band. Some men's hearts are filled with glee,
and children are romping playfully, mighty Air
Jordan swished the game winning three!!!
—*Christopher Dallaglio*

Weather Or Not!

If we'd just get some rain, you'd not hear me complain.
  No, honest, I really wouldn't.
But we get lots of snow, and the wind starts to blow,
  and I KNOW it really shouldn't.
If the sun would just shine, then we'd be feeling fine.
  But not in Montana. It couldn't.

Then June will break through, July and August, too,
  and we start to complain of the drought.
"It's too dry, rain's a must! I am choking on this dust!
Everything's going dry. Look about!
Crops will probably fail. Oh, great. Look, now it's hail!"
  It's enough to make a sane person shout!

But soon harvest is through. Farmers' psyches 'black and blue.'
  We all settle down for quiet relaxation.
Our minds float off to snow. Skiing, sledding -on the go-,
  and all other forms of winter recreation.
We think of storms and drifts, and of Winter's chilling gifts
  and complain, — a Montanan's favorite occupation!
—*Fred Wenger*

The Last Time Married

One, two, three and four, maybe now there will be
no more. It is a shame it takes so long to find the one
with whom you belong. To go through all the pain, hurt
and sorrow, to find that one who will be there tomorrow.
To find that special one, who will stand there beside you
in all that you do, they will love you and help to guide
you too. The same place in life you both have to be,
maybe somehow that is the key. To have loved, suffered
and lost all you've held dear, gives you some doubts
and a whole lot of fear. To try again and again
takes a whole lot of guts, some even say, "Man
you've gotta be nuts." I say, to those of you
who want to hear and are sincere. "It takes a
whole lot of care and understanding to pull a
marriage through the tough times and through
the years. If you wish hard enough and love
long enough, anything is possible, the last time.
—*Betty Mae Eaton*

Tear Stain

I cry.
No-one knows why.
But when I cry,
I let the tears stain my face.
Oh the pain, of a death,
a darkness of the light shining in my eyes.
She smiles as she walks by, she is beautiful.
I talk to my bird, people think I'm weird,
why is that?
Because I don't use a tissue or my sleeve
to wipe away those tears.
I just let them stain my face.
When I die people will cry and then wipe
their tears away.
I'll get up from my bed in the coffin and
tell them,

   "leave them there",

then I'll go back to death.
—*Emily Tennant Gadd*

Orchid's Twilight

Instant love, it's just a game
No one's a winner, everyone's insane
Was it the smile that captured his attention
Or was it the excitement in his eyes that captured hers
It is the excitement that keeps them together
Or is it a race to see who lasts longer
Destiny brought them together
Fear keeps them apart
Their lips are wrapped tightly around each other
But where is their heart
Soon the game becomes reality
And they're both in too deep
The mind is no longer at play
It is now the heart that has the final say
Tonight the sunsets as they hold each other close
Tomorrow the sun will rise and they'll go
  their separate ways
Only to remember when they were in love
Only to forget those wonderful days.
—*Angham A. Ibrahim*

No Place Like Home

No place like home, no place like Jesus
No place like home, no place like God
In our home, is here with Jesus,
No place like home, no place like God.
Don't go so far, and stay with Jesus
He is everything for you, for me
He's King of Kings, He's the Father
He's Holy Doctor if you believe,
He touch your pain and heart and body,
He make you strong, to stay in wind
He gives His power and His mercy
He gives His grace because he's King.
You can't find a place better than Jesus
No place like home, no place like Him.

—*Maggie Doroscan*

Do You Believe?

If you believe that this world exists, then beliefs would have
no value. Without values there would be no morals. Without
morals we wouldn't have a world to live. So why believe in
something that already exists? If you believe there is no
world, the world would have to believe in you, except the world
would have to believe in you just because you exist. So the
only way to get the world to stop believing in you is to die,
because to the world, you would no longer exist, then the world
believes you go to heaven or hell.
How can the world believe you go to a place that may or may not
exist if they no longer believe in you?
So if anyone is reading this and agrees with me, they believe
in not believing. If anyone disagrees, then they do not
believe in not believing. Because in order to not believe in
not believing you would have to not believe - and in order to
believe in not believing you would have to believe. So how can
this world get anywhere if we keep believing. All it does is
cause confusion!

—*Christian Lees*

Let Freedom Ring

The greatest treasure in the world today, is not gold or silver
nor fine array, but, freedom with her beckoning light whose
beams can pierce the blackest night. Now, let us make her our
most treasured thing, and from that song of old, "let freedom
ring." So, let us spend all that we have not counting the cost
cost, for without this singing bit of freedom all is lost.
It's certain that hours seem darkest just before the dawn,
then let us embrace this freedom when elusive peace seems gone.
For freedom is the light that fills our world when skies
are not so blue, and keeps our spirits soaring until bright
rays shine through. Although, we may tread a rough and rugged
road where briars and thorns sharply sting, may we never lose this
song of the soul that lets true freedom ring. Beyond life's
teeming rapids, well beyond the chaos of the falls, lies a pool
of calm cool where freedom answers crisis calls. Shining like
bright rainbows on the meadow, and moonlight on the shores,
she flies her wingless flight to the Earth's most troubled
doors. Life is like a giant silent sailing ship, ever seeking
freedom's harbor to end this endless trip. She, alone, can
cause our world to sing, as only God's real peace can ride on
freedom's wing.

—*Emeline Pennock Morris*

Thru Grandmother's Eyes

The king sat, crown on head
Soaking his feet before retiring to bed.
The violet lay bare,
Grandma had gently removed its petals to expose him there.
The children were delighted for hours
By her lore of the birds, the bees and the flower.

—*Doris Brubaker Walter*

Untitled

I wish that rhyme and legend-haunted prose did move me less,
Nor wake a hunger sans fulfillment in this life;
Why stories, touched with ancient finger's dust
Should breed in me unrecognized lust
For mysteries, believable by them who told,
Of passions quenched, of sparkling wines, and dancing jewels,
and gold. These fantasies they speak of knowingly,
as real to men, I tell myself were more delusionary then.

It's destiny, though; one marked as I, and touched with fay,
To have a common heritage with such as they.

—*Luise Ankers*

The Anger I Feel

I have an anger.
Not a name called anger,
or getting in trouble anger.
Not a bad grade anger,
or a lost game anger.
But an anger that there are
drugs.
An anger that there are homeless.
An anger that there is violence
in this world.
An anger that babies are being
abandoned by their mothers.
An anger that people have enough
nerve to abuse others.
An anger that children kill other children.
That is the anger I feel.

—*Jennifer Finley*

Untitled

I am not a poet
Not as they are known.

I am a woman with a lot of feelings
And a choice vocabulary.

I am not a poet, not as they are known to you.
But open your arms and envelope me,
Let my tears fall on your shoulders,
Let my laughter fill your ears,
Let the rhythm of my heart enter yours,
And you will hear my poems.

I am not a poet
As they are known to you.

But, Oh, my soul sings beautiful verses.

—*Derita Renee Ratcliffe*

To Lora

One day I met a little girl of nine,
Not knowing she would become a stepdaughter of mine;
Her eyes were blue and her hair was long,
And she usually brought a stuffed animal along;
Now before me a young lady I see,
Where did the time go, it's hard to believe;
That she's grown up now and ready to discover,
On the road of life, all its treasures and wonders;
You have everything needed to make the trip,
Sunny personality, good looks, talent and a sharp wit;
But, if for some reason you need some cheer,
You're lucky to have four parent's near;
Who will be there to offer their love and support,
Just in case your boat gets stalled in a port;
So I wish you the best as you follow your dreams
through each year,
And if clouds slow you down, don't despair,
sunbeams will soon appear.

—*Judy Donnalley*

Yellow

I am the color yellow:
Not cast with illness—pallid and jaundiced,
    Or with a cowardly streak.
But mine is every other yellow
Even that of a lemon: sour, tight, and bright.
And as a daffodil nodding in a sleek snow drift—
    A balmy blast of color amid a winter's peak.
And as a pat of butter melting
    Bubbling, rich, warm, even freckled with brown—
    Hot and delicious with sin.
Mine is the yellow of a bee's bottom:
    Full of itself, busy, and completely pollen kissed.
It is a cosmic spectrum of golds all right,
    As in my cat's chameleon eyes—ocher orbs that are
    Solid saffron suns by day, manic moons by night.
Chin out and jutted, my yellow is a laugh and never a frown.
It's a contradiction,
    An exaggeration, an exclamation point highlighted!
And when my yellow ventures to speak,
    It is not a squeak but a shriek!

        —*Cynthia Belechak-Becraft*

"While Were Apart"

I want you to, know that your constantly on my mind
Not just for the moment, but all the time
We were meant to be, so stay here with me

As each day goes by remember my love
Our prayers have been answered from above
We get closer and closer to holding each other
Sharing, loving, what we do best to one another

Don't think for one moment that your not here to stay
For I wouldn't ever let you get away
You know what our love is, a once in a lifetime
Knowing, feeling, loving, and having that balance
Almost impossible to find

We may be apart physically, but not for long
We know within our hearts, here is where you belong
So my love, counting down the days for us to be as one
Then everyone will know that we too have won

        —*Carole Ann Anderson*

The World That I See

The World that I see, is a beautiful world,
not marred with sin or wrong,
but the world God intended it to be.
A world where all of us are free
A world where there's no pain or sorrow,
This is the world of God's tomorrow.
The world that I see is a peaceful place,
where there will be no more war,
and the nations will never lift up swords.
It will be peace forever more.
The world that I see, will have no night,
for the Lord God shall be that eternal light.
A clear crystal river, will proceed from God's throne,
where everyone will be happy and we will never walk alone.
This is God's tomorrow
This is the world that I see.

        —*Bette Mitchell*

Friends?

You were living in hell, you said.
Not sure of past, present, or future.
You looked behind at a ruined life.
You looked ahead at the hatred that is human nature.

Your phone rang.
You hoped it was a friend.
You picked it up,
And your hopes were dashed again.

You watched the lights out your window.
You listened at the sound of feet.
But the feet passed on by,
And the lights went on up the street.

So there you lie.
Now no one can reach you.
Look at all the people here,
They all cared about you.

You said you lacked just one thing,
    A friend.
But look how many there are
    After your end.

        —*Jennifer Buskirk*

Washed Away With The Tide

How could you do this, how could you leave me out in the cold,
Not telling me if you still want my heart to hold?

Please tell me if you lied, don't hide your true feelings inside,
Because as soon as the flowers died it seemed as if
Your feelings floated away with the tide.

I thought that what we had would last so long...
For the feelings I had for you were oh so strong.

As I sit and hear the telephone ring,
I'm wishing I hear your voice ready to tell me everything,
But then I realize it's just not you,
For you haven't called to tell me if your feelings are still true.

And now I see the water coming back, telling me it's your heart
    that I lack.

I realize that you drifted away in that wave
And now all I have is your memory to save.

Maybe you'll find your way back someday, but I don't know
If I'll accept what you have to say.

        —*Lisa Marie Squiccerini*

Waiting To Bloom Again

Weary.
Not tired...
Not old...
    but weary.
Not tired needing sleep,
But weary in heart and spirit
Like the mighty oak hewn down before its time.
Not by one blow,
But by many little wounds
Until at last, it lies sleeping...
    waiting to bloom again.

        —*Colleen Sullivan-Rusch*

My Identity

Staring emptily into my reflection,
nothing can I gain through introspection.
All I can see is a face without features
and a unique and mysterious creature.

From the depths within
a timid faint voice cries out, "Who am I?"
While life slowly passes me by.
I ask, "Where are you?" "Underneath?" "In the midst?"
As a wondering traveler lost on his way.
You change like the weather every other day.

No matter how hard I try,
this mountain won't go into the sea.
All I want is to duly be me.
It frustrates me so - I just want to cry.
So helplessly, I feel like a mime
only expressing myself in rhyme.

Why didn't you teach me, O sages from my birth?
To talk and to love all in the same verse?
Now I sit lost in time
and trapped in rhyme.

    —*Kyle Kaniper*

Saved

He stood atop Golgotha's hill
Now naked stripped, quiet and still.
Heaven he looked to God he prayed.
The soldiers' hands were never stayed.

They grasped his arms, body pained rack
And threw him down onto his back.
Probed the hands the nails to strike,
And through his feet they struck the spike.

Thus there he hung upon the tree
For all the world he would soon free.
"Father, forgive them", Jesus cried,
"They know not what they do." And sighed.

Though many would accept the gift,
Some are there who'd widen the rift.
To his right, "Lord", a thief did say,
"Remember me on kingdom day."

"I say, you shall verily be
Today in paradise with me."
The thief now had a life anew
By son of God who's word is true.

    —*Edward J. Sleger Jr.*

A Time Of Waiting

In a time of waiting, I grieve for You,
O' Child of the Earth.
The word of love has been sent to you,
But You continue to embrace Aberration.
David sang of Life,
You refused his songs.
Solomon wrote of Wisdom,
You welcomed Foolishness.
Jesus looked upon your cities and wept,
You built walls so not to see his tears.
Socrates told of the Beauty of the Way,
You offered him hemlock.
Budda gave the Precepts in the Deer Park,
You choose Misery and its Absurdities.
Muhammad preached of the Five Pillars
You let Shaitin add a sixth.
Dr. King revealed a Dream,
You narrated a Nightmare.
O' child of the earth,
In a time of waiting, I grieve for you.

    —*Forrest Crawford*

Mother

M-is for Mother the greatest friend you will ever have.
O-is for Over the Years you took care of us.
T-is for the Trouble time that was hard to bear.
H-is for the hard time we all help put there.
E-is for Every time you told us that you cared.
R-is for the Room I have in my heart for you.

    —*Christine R. Holloway*

The Maiden Of Spring

Gatherer of spring; maiden of innocence - now mindful of me
O' spring gatherer; why mindful of me?
I have touched your wind - so fragrant and soft...
   I have tasted your spring when it passed inside of me.
Sweet young maiden, why touch me now?... Why make me feel
   the blooming spring of yours in me?
Was softness of the wind is the innocence in me?
Was the maiden in spring, then the fall was me?
Now, I know, how to pass again; to no more.
I must fly to summer, then to fall, for no more spring for me.
It is to morn again...to fall again...to spring to
   the maiden of spring in me!

    —*Karl A. Owen*

Tall And Slender

O, how great is my love for thee,
O, tall, sweet and slender,
it is mightier than the ocean waves,
in my soul it is louder than the thunder.

Thy damsel-like face covered in thy locks,
is like a pearl peeking through black velvet,
it ignites the blaze of affection within me,
it's like an unquenchable forest fire in my heart.

As thy ruby lips sing mellifluous lauds,
unto the sole and eternally great Lord,
the cherubim and seraphim applaud and rejoice,
for their hearts are merry and their spirit is glad.

Thy breasts are like perfectly curved hills,
on the shores of a celestial dreamland,
tender, fragile and smoother than the fine silk,
specially purchased in a far away land.

Thy pleasantly lean waist is the masterpiece,
perfectly hand-carved by the grand designer.
As I gaze diligently on it, I admire at the
marvels of the creator and his grandeur.

Thy prodigious and exquisite gait has been bestowed
unto thee as a gift, by the infinite one.
Embraced by the fragile shake, thy tender walk causeth
the birds to whistle and flowers to smile in the garden.

    —*John Y. Bhatti*

Perspectives

Fix this to a narrowing point of view.
Observe a mountain of glory, with size unearthed,
Beauty at rest, majestic, unheralded,
One of many, a labyrinth between peaks of crystalline snow.
Reverse this view and harrow the thought
For a mountain is nothing a mind can't conceive
And these tags are just ties that our minds did perceive.
A mountain owns no glory, beauty, or majesty on its own
To the seed it is earth, to the goat it is home
To the clouds it is a barrier, to the woodsman, his yard
To the visitor- YES...MAJESTIC.
But this frame paints a picture each mind needn't share
For perspectives are different-Understand and Beware!

    —*Perry Piazza, Jr.*

Untitled

Creepy, crooked, rusty trees. Near the horrible shrieking of a lady that's in pain agony. Rippled, coky, dripping with oogy grub. The slushy mushy, breath taking, bubbling mud, spurts on trespasser's legs. An owl camouflages with a thick, spiny tree trunk. The branches of the trees have no leaves on them. Dead falling trees, crumble, crack, jerk to the ground. Suspensefully, some chosen one starts choking, shaking wildly, nails spiking through its neck. Bent gates turn round and round, dizzily, someone watches and on the sides of the choppy gate, there are crooked wrecks cracks and slices. Chopped to pieces, the green, slimy bush, brutally bends in whipping notions. Its actions are too fierce to get near. Soaking wet trees, sit there longingly while they get stiff, chunky and thick. In the minds of the trespasser, creative ideas of horror go spinning, twirling and swirling into their minds. Rusty shrieks echo wildly and tingle the dry, musty skins of animals running as fast as a horse on a death run. In the distance, someone can see and smell the rotting symptoms of dusty, moldy, thick, ugly cheese...

—Danielle Ezra

A Pearl Of Absence

Between the heated couple, at hearts
of any swirling interlocked soup,
each thought, balm or irritant
addresses a wound and dissolves
between daffy yammering and desolation
unreflected, clenched, primeval and exhausted

As if having never been. Welded
to the heel of every dilemma, rasping
against every utterance, a hopeless bead
at the surface of every kiss
buoys slightest whispers
or ballasts abhorrence and delight.

For what is not returned may never have been.
And from the beginning, everything clings
to inconclusive memories of self
reaching through destruction
as if in hopes of grasping echoes,
or as if to begin to listen, or to love.

—Don Socha

Alanya's Turquoise Shore

The ages dared not dim the glare
Of brilliant, crowded diamond points.
Alanya's turquoise jewels set free
Possessed the soul of every rock
And reef; consumed the land, the sea.
That coast of blue-green seaside space
Was Antony's expensive gift
To Cleopatra on the day
They pledged their vows as man and wife.
Among the centuries since that time
Mankind has praised the turquoise tide.
They laughed and bathed and bled and died
In waters channeled from its store.
While earthquakes ravaged mountain sides
And men unleashed their endless wars
The thundering violence of time
Created ruins far and wide;
A stone necropolis at peace-
While deathless waves caress the floor
Of old Alanya's turquoise shore.

—Margaret Nienstedt

A Message To My Family

If I must leave without a chance to say goodbye:
Of course you'll miss me and you'll cry —
But do take time thank the Lord on High,
That you didn't have to sit and watch me slowly die.

Please feel no guilt for things undone or said:
Remember only joys we shared instead.
Rest assured the Hand of God has lead
Me to be with loved ones gone ahead.

But if to slip out quietly is not God's plan
I'll try to be as patient as I can.
Don't feel too badly—rather understand
That life and death are in His hands.

Though love of life can be extreme—
No matter how humane it seems,
Don't keep me living? by machine—
Life's race is not run by human scheme.

So when I'm finally laid to rest,
Grant to me this last request:
Be-grudge not my going, we've all been so blest
Accept God's decision, He knows what is best..

—Emily McCall

Juveniles

We read in the papers and hear on the air,
of killings, stealing and crimes everywhere.
So many children are encouraged to roam,
by too many parents who refuse to stay home.
Kids watch movies and read books,
then they start to idol the gangsters and crooks.

Soon they get alcoholic beverages served in a bar,
by the time there a teen they've stolen a car.
You can take the kids off the streets,
but you can't take the streets out of the kids.

—Frances Hermanns

Communion Of Hearts

Thy beauty came on wings of song and kissed the strings
of sorrow's harp,
Evoking treasures hidden deep within the ocean of my heart;
Full many a sleepless nights were spent upon
The shores of studiousness,-
Full many a rose have bloomed and expired,
Leaving their soul's essence upon the soft, fragrant,
Colossal bosom of the wind.

Where art Thou now, sweet Child of Sol?
Hast Thou withdrawn Thy Christly loveliness?
If so, life hath no purpose here; and I must seek a kinder sphere.

O God of my Heart! What shall I do? Am I indeed the Prince of fools?
If suffering is the vital Loom of Life, and Thou art Source of
Pristine Peace, Truth, Wisdom and Light,
For Whom the Sword of Justice shines?
Where is the Promised Dawn of Thine? O Mind Infinite!
Answer Thou my humble plea.
Am I not Thought, Breath, Hands and Consciousness of Thee?

—Eric N. Hylton

Life!

Is life a real thing?
People live in and out the day not stopping
a second to wonder what life really is,
or why certain thing's happen in life.
Every day we hear about bad thing's, good thing's,
but still we never stop to think
about the word life and what it really is.

—Buffy Elliott

Amarillo - The Friendly City Of Texas-

My Adopted State

Amarillo - the friendly city
Of Texas - my adopted state
From the mayor to the
Garbage collector -
From the chief of police
To the tax collector
Even the kids say "H!"

—*Harold Drake*

The Stillness Of The Night

Imbedded in the stillness of the night is the awareness
of the fact that soon; a ray of hope will embark in the
quietness of the early morning sunset.

The evening nightfall is in an indicator of the upcoming
celebration. The stillness of the night appears to be so
peaceful; yet so imaginative.

A light shining as if it has passed through a prism,
distinctly isolating and illuminating many variations of colors
The stillness of the night so deafen that a vociferous sound
drowns out the sound proof of a lesser sound.

Everything is so still and silently digested. It's
scrutinizing, challenging for the night to speak out;
depicting its true meaning.

Many sounds are interpreted, truly distinguished;
definitely recognizable. Some the victims of an
erratic feeling; a fear indistinguishable.

Yet, we are mentally prepared for the stillness
of the night. It slowly escapes into day-break;
causing one to relish the comfort and the security
of the morning sunrise..

—*Lloyd P. Wallace*

Arkansas Calling

I hear your call amidst the winds blowing across the rivers
of time. You prickle my being, disturbing the peace of
another land I have learned to love.

You're calling me home, my beloved land of pine trees and
lakes, of apple blossoms and honeysuckle, of sunflower
seeds and mockingbirds.

The land of cotton and pecan pies, of Piggly Wiggly hamlets,
of mining towns and caverns of diamonds.
I hear your call.

The battle rages on within me to blot out the paths of
memories strewn with thorns and blackberry bushes, of
watermelon rinds, smoke houses, potato kilns and
Arkansas blues.
I hear your call.

—*Hazel Wright*

Finally We Have Freedom

Forever we will be black, and together.
Right, if we go, we will be trapped. To the left, we will be
trapped. I guess we should go forward.
Ever lasting we shall be.
Everything was built on our sweat.
Dungeon - our lives have been like being in a dungeon.
Others thought they had it bad, but not like us.
Mothers have us and that is why we are the joy of the world.

—*Darrin D. Tucker*

One Plus Equals Peace

It takes more than wishing for peace in our time.
"Oh, give us a leader." The people all ask,
So quick to appoint someone else to the job
That belongs to the fellow we see in our glass.

That mirror may show that we know we are weak
And fearful of all that the task could entail
But, also, we see that the job must be done-
For the sake of our future, we dare not fail.

The truth is, each person must work with the others
To make this world better at last,
And multiplied strength can achieve what is wished
By the fellow we see in our glass

We have plotted our course on the eagles great might
The strength of our country no one can deny-
Great deeds in the future are part of our plan
To gain more than wishing or someone's faint cry

Yes, the dove has a place in this future of ours,
For man dreams of peace for all mankind at last-
Which only can happen if peace will be sought
By the fellow we see in our glass

—*Erlzie Burris Cook*

Inside

I'm having these nightmares and they're getting worse,
Oh God help me I think I'm cursed
The devil came to me and he said,
Sell your soul or your family is dead
It's you or your family what will you choose,
Shut up and leave me both ways I loose
Ok your family I guess you said,
When you awake tomorrow they'll all be dead
Wait don't take my family tonight,
If you let me choose you can take me if you like
No son! A figure appears,
It's not the devil it's just your fears
The devil can't hurt you as you know,
He can only trick you to sell your soul
The next day I woke up to see,
My dead family in front of me
I looked to the devil and said I don't understand,
He pointed down and I saw the dagger in my hand
As I looked away I felt a tear,
Cause the devil and I were one in the mirror

—*Donato Rigg*

Dreams

As I sit on the porch on a warm sunny day,
Oh! how I dream away,
I dream of being a movie star all prettied up or
I dream that I'm a pilot trying to control a plane,
I dream of being kissed by a handsome prince like in the
fairytales,
Oh, how I dreamed,
As I grew older I found that some dreams never come true,
Now I've learned to face reality and not dreams,
Even though dreams are there night and day I know
they're not true, their just pictures in the mind's eye,
And that's all they'll be unless you do something about it.

—*Jayme Grass*

602

Cold Hearted

Where can I turn, when you turn away
Oh, please tell me, where will I stay
When your heart turned cold
An awful story was told
The words you said
Went straight to my head
By staying with you what could I gain
Because all you caused me was great pain
The words you said, I didn't want to hear
But you made your point very clear
You never loved me
This I could see
I felt like a slave
Because of the bruises you gave
You made me feel useless
Because my life was a mess
Now this time you'll listen to me
Because I will break free.

—*Twyla Barnhill*

Teacher

Oh teacher why do you come to school?
Oh teacher why do you come to school?
Oh teacher why do you come to school?

Do you come to school to teach me how to count?
Do you come to school to teach me how to read?
Do you come to school to teach me how to plant?

No No No No No
Your hate will not let you teach me how to count.
No No No No No
Your hate will not let you teach me how to read.
No No No No No
Your hate will not let you teach me how to plant.
Your hate will let you teach me hate itself.
But my God will teach me how to love you.

—*Fannie Ann Young*

From A Trees Point of View

Rain is trickling down,
Oh, the burn of acid rain,
You are killing me,
Can you not feel the tree's pain?
You build your noisy highways,
You couldn't care less,
Our lives could end.
Never to return,
All you would know,
Was no more to burn.
Soon you would realize,
No more trees, no more air.
No more air, no more life.
Then you would care.
Please, I don't know how much we can stand.
I feel life slipping out of me.
Life going out, across the land.
Life is slipping out of me.
Oh, but what is the loss,
Of one little tree?

—*Crystal Blodgett*

Song of Joy for Peace

I'm glad I'm going to see this world when Jesus is its King!
Oh, what a drastic change there's going to be to all in everything! Every man will own his home; his wife will stay to her place. She'll keep the house and watch the kids with no thought of home-life disgrace! Every child will have a home;

he'll have love and lots to eat! No bloated stomachs will we see; no sleeping in the street. No young adults will be on drugs; no running off from home, our King will be right there for us to see; no more will we roam. And we'll have peace not war, and joy supreme instead of worldly fun! And every man will show great pride in the work he has done. No more

cussing, smoking, drinking and the bad results they bring! No more stealing, lying, cheating; there'll be change in everything. The King will walk among us then; you'll see no bullet-proof vest. He will love us and we'll share His blessed rest! The desert will bloom as a garden; the lamb lie down by

the bear. We will all be one in our Savior; no racial war - who'll care? No more cripples, hospitals or prisons; no Christmas or Easter will be. King Jesus will be all sufficient, you'll see and at His name, we'll bow every knee!

—*Bonnie Lee Montgomery East*

Autumn Hues

Let me walk the lane of painted trees,
On a crispy autumn day.
Just to see the gold and flaming hues,
Painted on in the Master's way.

The sumac red and the maples' gold,
And the oak trees' russet brown.
The nuts and leaves falling softly down,
For a carpet on the ground.

The woods are at their best today,
Dressed up in autumn splendor.
While the Master's paint brush adds the touch,
To the trees both tall and tender.

—*Blanche McGougan*

Dear Grandma

Flowers, flowers everywhere,
On a stand and in the air.
Grandma, Grandma now is dead,
But always kissed me on my head.
Dear Grandma I loved to see your face,
But now I know you are in a better place.
So Grandma, Grandma rest your head,
But you will always be the best Grandma
a kid could have.

—*Andrew Berry*

A Winter Holiday

When children go out to play,
On a warm and sunny day,
They forget their pinching feet,
And soon slide down on their seat.
They'll skip and run to keep themselves warm
Out of the snow and storm.
They'll go sliding all afternoon
And when they go they say, "We'll see you soon."
They'll dream of skating and frolic and play.
But when they wake, it's another school day.
All through the day they sit at their desks
Hearing the teacher; giving them tests.

—*Bettina Kaiser*

Mother's Love

In this world love's beauty constantly is expressed
On canvas, in symphonies, in a thousand words or less
Beleaguered by poverty, war and death
Man continues to see love as his greatest quest.

Love is limitless, there's an infinite supply
I was taught this long ago, so fortunate am I
For my quest began in the heart of another
Love's eternal hope, I learned from my mother.

—*Jan Stuckey*

Lest You Forget

We are the boys who sleep where tropic breezes blow
  On far away atolls and desolate sandy beaches.
We are the boys beneath the crosses row on row
  That stand by thousands in the vast and lonely reaches
    On blue Pacific's shore!
We are the boys who now from weary battles rest
  In peace for ever more,
So gently cradled on the ocean's coral breast.

We are the boys who lie on narrow beds of white;
We are the ill and lame, so gruesome to the sight!
We are the lonely dead who never more shall know
The joys of home - the summer's sun, the winter's snow.

We are the boys who smile and ask in wordless pain,
"Keep memory always bright, lest you forget again!
  You have tomorrow's world within your waiting hands,
When flags of lasting peace should wave in freedom's air.
  Our plea: Remember boys who died in foreign lands,
That hate and greed and senseless wars have sent them there!"

—*Beulah M. Porter*

The American Flag

A symbol of men who fought and died
On foreign soil - to keep freedom alive
I fly it proudly for all to see
And remember how lucky we are to be free!

Silhouetted against a sky of blue
It's saying "to thine own self be true"
And then in splendor and all it's glory
It symbolizes the American Story!

The most beautiful sight in all the world
Our red, white and blue flag unfurled
Waving boldly and proudly in the breeze
A symbol of freedom - honor it please!

—*Irene T. Bluhm*

Someday

Someday you'll write your unknown name
On history's ancient pages
And it shall stand in honored fame
Among all the saints and sages.

The eager heart must try to find
The best there is in life to do.
Leave cares and troubles far behind
And make all your cherished dreams come true.

But if old age overtakes your way
Before your greatest goal is won,
You still can meet the Lord someday
And hear Him say to you, "Well done."

—*Helen Foy*

Incomparable Love

She felt pain, she felt happiness
On the day I came to be
From the beginning to now
True love she's given me.

My mother is the person
that I am speaking of
Her love is incomparable, very unique,
beautiful as a dove.

I wasn't a great boy,
I'm not a great man,
Regardless of the situation,
she always understands.

My joy, my sorrow, my enthusiasm for tomorrow,
Patience and guidance I received,
Never a time was I deceived,
Sometime a tear, always the moral.

I love my mother from the bottom of my heart,
Nothing in the world can keep us apart,
I thank God for blessing me with a mother so true,
I write this poem, Mom, simply because I love you.

—*Charles J. Douglass*

Tribute To A Nurse

If the night becomes quiet, things
on the floor become slow, take time
to remember you're God's angel you know.
If you've given someone comfort, eased someone's pain,
take time to remember God is moving through you again.
If your kindly word has just meant a lot,
remember that God speaking through you may be all they've got.
And if during the night that word becomes the last sound they
hear, find comfort in knowing now God is most near.
And though angels may grow tired and
think they can take no more, they know that God
moving in them will show them through the next door.
An angel or nurse, whatever you be, if you
comfort God's children, he'll comfort thee.
Because love wasn't put in your heart to stay,
love isn't love 'til you give it away,
And - nurses do that both night and day.

—*Don Wood*

Sharing

We sit together, my dear gray friend and I,
On this old tree trunk, thoughtfully felled
For tired bodies needing rest.
Your sharpest canine hearing responds
To the slightest cold night sound.
Your keen nose scenting smells
Visiting from the pine woods.
You sit, intensely alert,
Your nearby warmth warming me.

Silence, silence - time passes in deep contented peace.

Then you turn your head,
The question clear in your eyes,
Communicating, one species to another.
We rise as one
And step off into the moonlit darkness
Continuing the delayed pleasure -
Our mid night walk.

—*Donna M. Tasker*

Vacation

Often times I feel poetic and I write verse and rhyme, So I was on vacation, having a wonderful time. I saw the great Smokey Mountains, their beauty I beheld The grandeur and the majesty of their scenes words hardly can tell.

I went through the National Park, and an area called Cave's Cove, I saw scenes of primitive living and God's creation as we slowly drove. In a Cherokee Indian village, people made all sorts of things Canoes, baskets arrowheads belts beads and several kinds of rings.

Shopping centers on top of one another, literally, stacked, For things to purchase, a shopper nothing lacked.
When one thought they had a bargain, out came the old Master Card, There went the money for which one labored so hard.

To tell every detail, would take too much time and space, Everyone, perhaps, would not enjoy such a hectic pace, Certainly one would not get bored unless they allowed themselves to be,
Because there is so much to do, and so much of God's beauty to see.

—*Lloyd L. Pope*

Untitled

I am but one
One but all of many
I have been chosen
One of few chosen of many
Leadeth me oh mighty of mighty
Showeth me the purest of purest
Giveth me the power of good over evil
For only thou has the power to give
Guard me from that which wishes to destroy me
Bend me as a willow
Mold me as in your eye sight
Reach out thine hand and bless me
I kneel before thee and kiss thy feet
If it be your wish
Thy heart and soul see only you
Cleanse this temple so as I may cleanse others
Let me not help in this time
But this time through eternity
In thy sons most precious name.
          Amen
—*Eddie Meador*

Love Games

It's a game we play everyday
One I think you're unaware of.
We pretend as though we don't care but then, our actions contradict our words!

We were friends there was something there, unspoken but visible to everyone.
Then it was gone-vanished as if it never really existed.

In my heart I knew it could never be the same-maybe to you and The rest of the world it is.

But to me it's different-different in the way that something so wonderful could cause so much pain and yet once resolved show no visible signs of what occurred!!

To everyone it's over-but to me it's ever present and every time we speak a piece of me dies-so I wait-I wait for my heart to heal the way yours has and wonder why it ended so sadly!!

—*Donna-Marie Zucconi*

Let Freedom Ring

From the north church belfry,
"One if by land, Two if by sea"
Signaled the ride of Paul Revere.

At Lexington our FLAG unfurled
As Minute men fired the shot heard 'round the world.

Three hundred and fifty Sons of Liberty,
In Boston Harbor dumped the TEA.

In 1776 the Declaration of Independence, wrought.
In between and betwixt, Many more battles have been fought.

Our FLAG still flying at the siege of Ft McHenry,
Inspiring, in this manner, The Star Spangled Banner
Once again brought harmony.

Somewhere along the way our citizens lost their fervor,
Where is OUR devotion, spirit and ardor?
"Breathes there a man, with soul so dead,
Who to himself hath never said,"
This is OUR land, So, lift your hearts, Salute your FLAG!
Show your LOYALTY,
"Your FLAG is Passing By!"

—*LouAnn Kelley-Fenicle*

"Quit Smoking"

I read and hear and learn a lot,
One is, good health is a luxury that
can't always be bought.
Many people have reason, now to know,
That cigarette smoking is a no - no,

"Nothing will hit me" - so many say,
But, how sad, that's not true - no way,
That little white roll-called a cigarette,
Using them, is a dangerous habit, you will regret.

You smoke a few, then the harm has begun,
You don't realize, what you've done,
You can't do without out them, though some try,
So, to the habit, say good-bye!

Why do such habits, take a hold?
Even though they've bad for you, you've been told -
Before you know it, you are hooked on the thing,
Come on now, don't be a ding-a-ling!

All you smokers, time you get smart, stop smoking!
Stop smoking! Oh! why did you start,
Don't light up another one, no matter what —
And don't use the excuse — I try — but!

—*Louise Kalpakjian*

A Tribute To My Father

We shared a very special love, my father and me
One of joy and gladness, displayed for the world to see.
Whenever I needed a helping hand, to Father I would turn,
And there he was without fuss, providing whatever I yearned.
The Sitter for my children, He picked them up from school,
Then off to McDonald's for "love" and "sweets,"
Was always his Golden Rule.

How do you honor someone who has always been
A teacher, wise counselor, loving family man,
Really a true, blue friend!
We laughed together, cried together—
And yes, we sometimes fussed; but never did we hold my grudges,
Nothing could separate us.
For when you love and respect one another,
Your hearts shall always be
United, forgiving, caring for each other;
Love is always the key.

I'll always remember your humor and wit, I'll never forget your smile, I'll love you forever...I'll miss you so much, I thank God for being your child.

—*DeArtriss Richardson*

The World

I'm going to build me a ladder;
One that reaches the sky.
And I'll have to climb that ladder,
Because I don't have the wings to fly.

Then I'll look down on this wicked world
With all its crime and sin,
And think of those Pearly Gates up yonder
And wonder who will get in.

Purse snatching is common and so is fraud.
They say the dope is shipped in from abroad.
Murder and rape go on everywhere.
It won't even slow down with the help of Prayer.

We live in a world that gets worse every day,
Besides there's always those taxes to pay.
It seems that since the last big war,
This world has become another Sodom and Gomorrah.

—*Louis H. Grimm*

What I Think Of Racism

To me racism is a dirty word
One that we do not need in our world

With some it is color they spite
To me we all look alike

Who cares if from some other country they came
They are all people just the same

We all belong to the human race
No matter the color of the face

All this great world we share
To be a racist is not fair

Black, Hispanic, Oriental, Asian
I do not care what is their nation

All have a father and a mother
Some a sister or a brother

What have they done to us
For us to make such an awful fuss

For what I can see
They have done nothing to you or me.

—*Amy Hudson*

Footsteps Ahead

A few steps forward, a few steps back, will only keep you on one track. But if you put one foot forward and never look back you'll leave that undefeating track. It's what you see ahead that holds your future in it's path. Now with your eyes focusing forward, and never astray is the only way to complete your day. If you have to look back it only means what is left behind should only stay within your mind. You've done all there was to do, so leave it at that. What lies ahead is much greater than what is dead. So forget the past, only keeping what has been meant to last, and has brought you to this day. And now your on your way to the place you deserved because you've learned your lessons well... You've done what you knew best. And with that you've left the rest who could never quite complete the test. It's them who look ahead only wishing they were there, and where they could buy the fare to get them there. So you see what they don't have is the power in which to grab that tells themselves it's up to them to get ahead. Now step by step and saying I can is what it takes to be a man. For it's only men who can stay, but yes it's done day by day without ever being led astray. Now there's many out there who can only wish they were where you are today, so take heed to them, for they will only try to take you back to that oh so ugly undefeating track.

—*Maria May*

Untitled

The longing. The heavy crush upon
    One's breast.
To know.
To know the emptiness
Will never again be satisfied.

Sigh, sigh, the sorrow to not know the high.
Silence.
Heart racing.
Breath short.
The eyes, oh, the eyes.
The muted cry as the magnetic force can
    No longer be suppressed.
To know the meaning of
    Depressed.

Numbness.
The cloying smell of death.
Forgive me my silent mourning.
The novelty forever lost.
I'm drowning from,
The Longing.

—*Courtney Spore Major*

Flight

I fly with the wind like the eagle,
On wings of gossamer, soaring,
Never weary nor weak nor burdened,
Freedom on freedom builds, roaring.

Below lies all I've forgotten,
The Sun in her palace reigns high.
My flight, like the wind that inspired it,
Undestined, in movement survives.

No rest, never ceasing, the dream not attained,
Too high is the palace of gold.
Yet to fly not all, descending to grief,
Marks the day the young heart has grown old.

—*Lorey Sutherland*

One Last Chance

A brightened day turns into drear;
One's happiness replaced by fear.
And what you thought might someday be
Is now the vision that you see.

A loved one's world has reached the end;
You look for comfort in a friend.
It's hard to know just what to do,
For emptiness is what consumes you.

Even though it's all a part of life,
The heart is stabbed with an emotional knife.
If only you could ease the pain
For the body cannot bear the strain.

And though you long for one last chance
To have more than a final glance.
His spirit lives within your soul
When the final bell begins to toll.

And as the days turn into weeks,
The answers you no longer seek.
Bad memories start to fade away,
The good ones left behind to stay.

—Harriet Gilbert

Sunset

The years have gone so swiftly by,
Only so few we remember, I wonder why!

How many are there left for us to see?
How lonely will we be?

When we are busy with life's problems, so many,
We never think of the remaining years, if any.

Now that the time is past,
Who do we wish to take care of us at last?

Strangers to bathe us, I pray not,
Please Lord give us a better lot.

May someone we love have the last say,
How we are to spend our day.

Maybe we will be of failing mind,
Please, Oh Lord, let them be kind.

May it be the last of our years,
Be not covered by a strangers tears.

Let it be, Oh Lord, instead,
A loved one standing by our bed.

Holding our hand up to their breast,
As we pass through the sunset, to go to rest.

—John M. Burns

Depression

Sometimes she feels so lonely, and wishes she could die.
Or fade into the distance, where she could sit and cry.
Failure feels just like a knife, that cuts so deep inside.
And leaves the wounded open, nowhere to run and hide.
Sadness echoes through the empty spaces contained within.
And every harsh word spoken pricks her heart just like a pin.
Her body is so tired, her mind is so run-down.
Her heart can find no answers, she smiles with a frown.
The only thing she clings to, is someone she can't see.
But knows that He can help her, through Him she can be free.
He can fill the empty space with joy, and peace, and care.
Just because she remembers, that someone's always there.
Even if she feels she's lost everything she'd once won...
She gives it all to Jesus, and He helps her to go on.

—Christine Hanna

June Bride

We traveled on the cusp toward marriage
Or away — as the solstice passed and the year declined.

A year we'd dreamt would not expire
Die like Julian days and weeks
of an ancient order reversed by fiat.
A time strained, worn out with use
and out of step with grander schemes of things.

Equals, if you like postulate the match of souls!
But after tiles are lined and laid
Sunk in their plaster bed like casts of teeth —
Then, observe the final pattern, and
Augur what fate their bond reveals.

Roaring onward toward our wedding
Rattling in the back of a pickup truck like fools
In the fragrant darkness, laughing
Aloud, but silently to myself
Considering time gone by, fading
Like the buzz of wine, and time ahead:
Parabolic, repetitive, unforgiving.

—Douglas Wolford

Not Such A Tragedy

Have you the same love that you before
or has he departed from your life?

The latter.
Our hearts shall never meet again
in the fashion they did before.

I regret to hear of such a tragedy.

It is not such a tragedy,
for I have found a new love.
One more grand than ever before.
Not the sweetest of chocolate.
the richest of gold, or
the clearest of diamonds
could be more
than the love that me and thee hold.

Our love is so grand,
that it shall not depart this world
'till we both are resting in peace,
'till our souls shall meet in heaven...

....and love until all eternity.

—Margaret Tumbleson

Silent Moon

The shadows had never been so defined,
  or my visions so clear.
  And though my path was free and straight,
  I cried for my lost Hope.

I watched as the dragon rose up
  singing to me songs of power and light.
  "Be a knight of truth and power."
  "Wash away your rigors like dust on so many books."

I heard the sage as his song descended.
  And thus ended my age of dreams,
  When heralds announced the passage of darkness.
  When the silent moon cried for the world.

—D. LaPier

607

A Lost Love

I sit alone and I weep,
Over a man who my love for has grown so deep,
He is now forever gone,
And I will cry over him until it is dawn.
Without him around my love for him has grown stronger,
And my days get longer and longer.
I wish that he would come back to me
But my love for him, he does not see.
Instead of running away, he should be with me, to stay.
Until he decides to return, I know that tomorrow,
My heart will still be filled with sorrow.

—*Marie Beckwith*

Them And Us

You and I could maybe visit him and her
    Or, they could come and visit you and me.
I think that they and we would certainly get along,
    Especially him and me.

But, I don't see how you and me
    Could quietly stand by
While you and her just talked about
    The faults of he and I

We could explain to her and him
    How the two of we both feel,
And then let them brief you and I
    On how him and her think. Still -

Would be nice if we and they
    could positively agree
That he and she (or him and her?)
    Concur with you and I. (me?)

—*John E. Hemmert*

Four Score And Ten

The years go by, "She doesn't change!" so many people say.
Or we may hear "It seems that she looks better every day."

There is no doubt that what is said is nothing but the truth.
She must have sought and long since found her own Fountain of
Youth.

The count of years, four score and ten, as once a poet said;
A formidable span for some, to her there's more ahead.

She rises with each sun with hope and prayer to guide her day.
The tests of life are overcome - they don't get in her way.

She's seldom idle, keeping busy, head and heart and hands.
The giving of herself to all, to family and friends.

And so she's satisfied and thankful when day comes to end.
She sees tomorrow as a chance to do it all again.

—*C. Fred Ward*

Raindrops

As the rain drops fell from the thundering sky.
It washes away the dirt, and smog that we leave as the days pass by.

Too bad it can't wash away the crime, and the hate.
Clean up the people, and the environment state to state.

Too bad it can't wash away problems that are on peoples' minds.
Wash away the violence, and purify mankind.

Too bad it can't wash away diseases, and sicknesses that lie within.
So people are healed, and for them a new life they can begin.

Too bad it can't wash away the litter in the streets.
Shelter the homeless, and provide the hungry with something to eat.

—*Jim Mossbruger*

Racism Stands Still

Racism, a disease that diminishes
our being, manipulating the mind
to states of malice, rage, and insanity.

It's covertness enables the contagiousness
to lie dormant, entrapping victims
of all ages, and colors with its mastery.

Conceivably, racism is not an evil
that belies us at birth.
But a malignancy that manifests
through teachings of bigotry,and bias.

Surmountable, is the prevalence of
racism that circles our globe.
In mass fixation, multiplying, and
thriving unrelenting through the
ignorance of mankind.

Racism, notoriously remains the most
poisonous venom of our times.
Unlikely a foreseeable cure, tragically
it is a costly yearning of the soul.

—*Ima Lawson*

The Tree

Like the leaves on a tree changing colors,
Our feelings change for each other.
Like the bright yellow and red colors,
Our love brightens more and more every day.
The leaves eventually fall of the tree.
Our relationship comes to a halt.
The next year, the cycle repeats itself.

—*Bethenie Ruth Ennis*

Coming From The Sky

Tears of joy and laughter...clicking cameras...OO'S and Ah's.
Our little girl is here...Flown to us on silver wings with
roaring motors adding to the celebration.
Our new little one is here.

Four little girls, one boy, added to five family's joy.
Ours is a beauty (the best of all the rest?) so, we think of
our Holly Ann. She brought us joy without the pain.
Delivered to us on Wings and Prayers...
Truly a gift from God... the same as our others.

As she descended from the sky...what a tumult we were in.
We did not look for features.
We did not check for flaws.
This little Bundle was given to us,
And we were told......."She's Yours!"

So as adoptive parents, we felt the joy of giving.
This little 'babe' is living, entrusted to our care.
We wish that you could have been there
To share our tears of joy.

—*Elaine Meli*

Roses Rain

As the song of the rose, plays by the light,
suddenly, but slowly it becomes night.
Not one sound is heard through out the country side,
not even in the oceans tide.

As they walk along the beach,
the water runs beyond their reach.
They start to slip through the sand,
and everyone wondering if they will ever understand?

—*Heather Craig*

Senior Citizen

The wait was long, the years were many,
Our tears and joys were there aplenty.

The tasks we faced were never mild,
We did our best and then we smiled.

We now sit back and enjoy our treasures,
And in every day we find great pleasures.

To our youth we now must listen,
For we've become a 'Senior Citizen'.

Many thanks we give each day,
And know that God will lead our way.

When it's time to bid farewell,
We'll go in peace for we did well.

—*Connie Archer*

Save Our Lost World

America we are destroying
our world day after day.
Killing each other along the way.
Taking life which we can't give.
Please dear world let our
children live.

For God so love the world
that he gave his only Son
So why should we undo the
good that God has done?

So stop killing our boys and girls.
for they are the ones that make up this world.
Please don't put guns in their hands.
for they will go back to school and
shoot their fellowman.

Put the Bible back in their hands.
and more wisdom and knowledge in their head.
Then perhaps our children will not end up dead.
It's up to us to save our world,
and keep our Beautiful Boys and Girls.

—*Lyric Coats*

The Happy Life

The days of before beckon more and more.
Our younger days return in many ways.
AS WE GROW OLDER.
Thoughts of the past come thick and fast.
We have the knack to remember back.
AS WE GROW OLDER.
The memories soften as we think often,
Of the friends indeed we shall always need.
AS WE GROW OLDER.
With mellow reverie of youthful dreams
And plans that nearly came about.
We laugh with glee of our life so grand.
Our hearts give a shout of joy.
AS WE GROW OLDER.

—*Dwaine R. Anderson*

"Home In The Valley"

There's a quaint little home in the valley
Nestled there beneath the trees,
It breathes a home to treasure
Alive on a sweet summer breeze;
The lush green meadow that surrounds her
Gives a feeling of trust and true love,
It's a gift from heaven above
On the wings of a sweet turtledove.

—*George Barden*

We Are

For all that we were, and are, and will become,
Our youth will be emblazoned, ennobled.
As we grow to be who, and what, and why,
Our lives will be challenged, defined.

Our roads will be straight, or tumultuous,
The avenues travelled; curved, yet rewarding.
And, as we aspire, grow, and endure,
We relinquish our youth to a wiser, softer maturity.

We brandish and hold youthful dreams, never daunted.
But, in letting go of youth, we become who we are.
And, we are beautiful in our now, in our us,
We are exquisite in youthful dreams, grown wise.

And, we have fulfilled youths' destiny for today,
The glory of tomorrow is yet to come, to know.
But, we will know it, experience it, grow with it.
For, the future is yours, mine - ours.

—*Jenny Patterson*

Ode To The I.R.S.

I was sittin' at home with my feet propped up
Out in my drive came this pick-up truck.
Then came the bangin' on my front door.
I don't ever have company any more.
As sweet as I could I said "Who is it please"?
We're the I.R.S. puttin' on the squeeze.
We'll sell your house, pictures and car
We don't give a damn who you are.
We did it to Red and Willie too
Now we're fixin' to do it to you.
All these years of work gone in a flash
Cause someone was to lazy to earn his own cash.
Let me tell you something, hear what I say.
Count your own money and do it every day.
I've got a surprise for you revenue men.
I made it once, I'll make it again.
With this little ditty I'm goin' for the gold.
That's all there is my tale has been told.

—*LoNetta White*

Under Five Over Fifty

The best things in life happen when you are under five and
over fifty. A rolly-polly, a butterfly, a funny noise or a
funny nose are oh so nifty. Music is heard all the way down
to our toes, and the people we meet are friends, not foes.

A forest is an adventure, even a few trees in a park; stars are
little diamonds with happy names which make you forget the
dark. A big bowl of ice cream is the perfect medicine for
whatever's wrong; and funny stories always brings out the very
best songs.

Reading a book out loud is a ticket to another place and time.
And hugs always keep the cold and sadness out of mind.
Birds, dogs and cats are friends all the way,
Under five and over fifty would sure be a great place to stay!

—*Charles R. Moncrief, Jr.*

Untitled

I bear not scars from wars that I have fought in
Nor do I flinch a troubled soul to hide,
Of all the knowledge fields that I have sought in
There clings no ugly torment to my side.
I walk alone with many friends around me
The button just fell off the shirt I wear,
Of all the evils searching, none have found me
Yet when were that a lighter cross to bear?

—*Dane N. Stark*

The Storm

There was a storm arising in my heart
Over the love that was lost, as we grew apart.

I thought special love was to last forever,
No matter what the weather.

As the clouds rolled in and the winds increased,
It was then that your love began to cease.

But deep in my heart I tried to understand,
I know you were not ready to take command.

I wanted a husband, but you did not want a wife
But now I have learned and can move on with my life.

The storm is almost over, it has calmed down
I will remain your friend, when you decide to come around.

—Angela Pollard

"Ode To Friendship"

Friendship is a thing to treasure
Over the years it gives a lot of pleasure
It may be simple like a walk in the park
Or perhaps bringing sunshine, when things look dark.

Through your illness friends are there
All your life they show they care.
Good friends are always there to help you.
They also encourage you in all that you do.

They are there with you if you have to cry
Always accepting you and not asking why.
Give your friends the time of day.
Listen patiently to what they have to say.

Friends will come and friends will go.
Each one is someone special you know.
Times may come when you don't agree
But all will turn out fine because you're friends you see.

If tragedy should befall a friend
Be there with them to the end.
Don't take advantage of a friend please
Or you may find that friendship will cease.

—LaVerne Bauldry

To Someone

Quietly her image waltzes through my mind,
Painfully I remember my past mistakes, chances lost.
Yet I still await a sign, an indication of her feelings.
What are her feelings?

Her beautiful name, her glowing face, her enslaving smile,
pull me from the depths of depression onto the threshold of
    a universe I want so much to be a part of.
Yet at this threshold, I still feel so lost, so without.

This tightrope I walk between friends and lovers is not
    one to which I am accustomed.
The anguish this balancing causes is unbearable.
Help me, tell me how you feel before I tell you my feelings.

You see, I am afraid I may hurt you if I told you.
To hurt you would be to drive a dagger through my heart.
But maybe this time will be unlike the past,
Maybe we were meant to be.

—Douglas Crothers

The Fawn Hunter

Little brown skin girl in dress of white
Passed me, smile flashing in the night:
Haughty breasts held high, dark eyes asmolder,
Coltish legs poised for flight.

My allies, man's barest arsenal of charms:
Experience, deceit, cunning and guile with myself I did arm.
As the fawn fears no harm from above,
She whom I desired observed me without alarm.

Pursuit was swift, the prey nobly slain
In a manner most civilized, sophisticated and humane.
Her tears were shed, how shall I say;
In a way designed to ensure me everlasting pain?

The precious prize secured, and proudly enshrined
In the darkest recesses of my trophy room mind.
My solemn vows of abstinence and caution were again made
With honest intent and constance meant to bind.

Ah, then a little brown skin girl in dress of white
Passed me, smile flashing in the night:
Haughty breasts held high, dark eyes asmolder,
Coltish legs poised for flight.........

—James Winsby

Once 'On A Time

Often at twilight I'm sitting and dreaming of days that are
past. Dreaming of days of my childhood. That are gone but
forever shall last. As thoughts come stealing around me of
lands far over the sea. Of kings and queens and fairy
princess. Airy castles and gingerbread trees. Ancient harps
and their mystic chimes. They all come from the region of
"Once `on a Time."

Then visions of people and places come out of the dim misty
past. Unfolding the long hidden story of love that forever
will last. Of trouble, of triumph, of sorrow. O joy that at
present is mine. They rob all the days trials. These fancies
of "Once `on a Time."

I glean from the stillness of twilight. That the burdens now
crowding my way will vanish from memory forever. In the realms
that are fairer than day. And I see a glimpse of their glory
catch a strain of their heavenly rhyme. When the shadows of
evening bring visions. From the mystical "Once `on a Time."

—Georgianna Moen

A Living, Giving Service

White is the ground with new-fallen snow
Peaceful my kitchen, I happiness know.
Love is my banner wherever I go,
God's kindness to others, we, too, must show.

Helping all others who are in need,
Witness for Jesus, sowing the seed.
Of his gospel story, glorious indeed,
To souls who do hunger on His word to feed.

Living for Jesus, His mercy we plead,
And strength to go onward, is all that we need.
So trusting in Jesus, we carry the seed,
Fighting God's battle, we're blest indeed.

—June E. Briner

Wooden Walls

Wooden walls, a fortress wide a treasured queen to surround.
Perched at attention, ears pointed high. Silent keeper within
the cities gate stalked and clawed unwarranted prey. Sudden
puff unlatched the hinge with clever hands. Freedom beckons...
A call of the wild. In freedom she leaves, in freedom she dies

Black hulking figure rushes out into the night. Ears bent
backwards against rushing wind, visions of opossums and other
tender things. Muzzle salivates upon the idea of possibility.
Nature her possession invites with observation. Thumping paws that
lunge her forward transports an emission of husky
breath. Steel ghosts ahead in view fly by.

Blacktop thoroughfare with angry streaks of white. Waits
patiently while nostrils flare low to the ground. Offers a
passageway to fields unknown, but carries the riders of metal
formed evil. That collide and snuff the oxygen from heaving
chest. Labored breath for no longer than a few moments...
She is callously flung into the rugged ditch. Freedom breeds
a cruel death bed.

— *Laurie Thomas*

"The Rose"

A rose is as delicate as a child,
Perfect and ideal in the eyes of many.
Their eyes of innocence look out upon the world,
As dreams and secret desires look for fulfillment.
The rose blooms and matures, as does the child and her
dreams. Not yet realizing the cruel cards fate can deal.
Soon the petals of the rose fall endlessly into oblivion,
The child's innocence rudely stripped away.
She comes to realize that life is not what it seems,
It is disguised to hide the horrors beneath.
The rose begins to die, gasping for breath and salvation,
Looking for security, the child gasps also,
Yet, none is to be found and she stands alone.
She confronts life with vigor and courage,
Only to turn back with bitterness and frustration.
The desires and dreams slip away into the unknown,
Out of their fingers, out of her grasp.
Should she give them up for an unknown existence,
Or should she continue to seek them,
As the rose does for eternal life?

— *Charity A. Marr*

Walk With Me

In the eve of ages past, I walked the road leading nowhere.
Placed myself amid the ruins in desperate hope you'd find me there.
Pleading for the darkness to set me free as I reached out for you,
to touch the somber part of me; unshield the shade of misty blue.
Out cast the shadows that hinder me; allow me into the light.
Perch amid your highest goals to blast despair into the night.
Fade the temper that holds afar the passion we two need,
and in our hearts a warnings dare can't foretell the heed.
If in years, days go by without a severed soul to steal.
The darkness fades into sight and you see a treasures real.
Walk the road alone with me and find the door no where leads.
Enchant the ruins to retract the sore, feel the troth and no
heart bleeds.

— *Linda C. Wright*

Rainbows

Rainbows are joy in the midst of tears
Rainbows are hope for the coming years,
Rainbows are peace as the moments fly,
Rainbows are power as the days go by.
Rainbows are challenge when life seems hard.
Rainbows are comfort when you are tired.
Rainbows are light when you world is dark.
Rainbows release you to make your mark.

— *Grace M. Weaver*

Cape Cod Cemetery

Headstones stand in an irregular line
placed only by the passage of time
some tilted some broken some flat on the ground
I stopped for a moment couldn't hear a sound

My journey that evening had barely begun
when I was suddenly drawn to a particular one
I scraped away some of the dirt and the grime
revealing an anchor and some dirt filled lines

Under the name it said Pirate, hung by the head, age 23
I stood for a moment and thought about he
who in some other life with my name could have been me
it's why I was drawn here and what I was meant to see

I'll return in the daylight scrub away all of the grime
trim the branches so at night the headstone will shine
I'll often bring flowers so he'll know someone cares
I wish that he knew its the same name that he shares

— *Herbert Thompson*

Love Grows

Love is a seed
Planted in the fertile field of tenderness
Nurtured with understanding
Until it bursts open from the warmth beneath
Shoots up into the brightness of new life
Confidently reaching upward
    always upward
Until its strengthened stalk
Becomes a firmly rooted trunk
From which caring branches reach outward
    always outward

Then in spring's embrace
Smiling buds appear
Then fruit

That's how love grows
And blooms and bears.

— *Janet A. Murillo*

Helen's Poem

Sweetheart, if I should go away, across the "Great Divide",
Please know I treasure every day I've had you by my side.
And if I've ever hurt you, dear, by any word or deed,
To have your complete forgiveness is the only thing I need!

Though you won't see me any more, we won't be far apart,
I'll find a space, a hiding place, down deep within you heart,
And in that snug and cozy spot, I'll go around with you.
I'll laugh when you are happy! I'll cry when you are blue!

And should some problem worry you, something that needs a man,
I'll be close by and I will try to help you all I can.
And if events should make you weep, please, darling, have no fears,
I'll come to you when you're asleep and kiss away your tears!

And when it comes your time to go across the "Great Divide",
I shall be waiting, as you know, upon the other side!

— *Petrus G. Pearson*

Erik's Journey

I walk in silent desperation
Searching for answers that aren't there
My heart is as heavy as the boughs of trees
Laden with falling snow about to snap
The tender branches to fall barren to the earth
I wish that I could lay my head down
In a soft pillow of new fallen snow
To sleep for all eternity in peace.

— *Cindi Casteel*

611

Predictions

Dear Mr Weatherman,
Please lend your ear,
For here's something you should hear.
For today, you predicted 85 to 90 degrees
Now your many strong believers are about to freeze.

For tonight, you warned, "expect strong thunder showers."
But all was calm, only I shook fearfully for hours.

For the weekend, you promised, "no rain in sight."
Great! So we made plans for both day and night.
But then came the shock!
The lightning flashed, the thunder roared,
And the rain came, seemingly, never to stop.

Now Mr. Weatherman,
Its not your fault, we must all agree,
It's anyone's guess what the weather will be.

—*Camille C. Steverson*

My Dear Children

My dear children,
Please listen
To the words I say.
Have fun in all your play.
And cherish the moments,
Along with your assignments.
You will then always grow,
Knowledgeable of all the things to know.
Be kind and loving,
Considerate and caring.
And you will be as lovely,
As you were meant to be.
The world's DEAR CHILDREN.

—*Jo Ann Burger*

Who Am I

Who am I? Though I be me.
Please show me, dear God, that I might see.
Who am I, as in this life I stand.
So as of this world, I may better understand.

This flesh and bones, that compose my body,
Does not even start to be.
These billions of cells and nerve fibers
Are still only a part of me.

If I were dead and only my body left.
Still yet it would not be me.
For we are two, my body and me
I'm so much a part of it, as it is a part of me.

Then who am I, though I exist, in the confines of
    this skeletal being.
As I go through life, and it carries out my every desire
    and need.
Who am I? This I think I will never get to know.
For who I am is a secret, that only God will know.

—*Lou Dishman*

Cynical Laughing

They all look like little puppets.
Puppets pursuing vague unexplained pathways.
Puppets making laughing music,
Making laughter —
What a cynical thought.

Joy happens, but is it genuine?
Or is it too cynical?
One would only know through
The thoughts of the Musician
The genuineness of the Music's Joy.

—*Laura Hinkle*

'A Farewell'

The coffee is hot and it taste good, drank from a white
Pottery cup, as I sit here in our cozy paneled kitchen.
And I know I should be busy out and about, packing everything up
'Cause time is running out for me and this home.
I will miss this old place,
although it was a choice that we made.
    It was always a race
to keep everything going at my kind of pace!

    Around the round table, where we all were pretty able to find
laughter, happiness, love, anger and tears.

    Yes, it happened all through the years,
And my heart swells with pride, when I think of my family
Bless their hides! And of the love and joy that I feel.

    After twenty-five years (25) there's a shifting of years and
old father time had his way. And now I bid goodbye with a
finalized sigh, a tear and a smile.

—*Dorma Lee Johnson*

Be Strong

A broken life, torn up with a dull knife
Poverty surrounding everyone, yet I see
    nothing done
Hungry faces, lonely places
Living in dark alley streets, listening to
    each others heart beats
Wishing for the very best, after failing
    the great test
Lucky are the one's strong at mind,
Weak are the ones that stay behind
Listen to the old and wise, they end
    up giving good advice
Don't let no one slow you down, slow
    are the ones who get a frown
Always try to stay ahead, so you'll
be proud before you're dead....

—*Angelina Medina*

Elizabeth's Joy

Praise the Lord! God has finally answered my long awaited
prayer. All the years of frustration, doubt and terror,
Are now turned to joy, it's bitter sting remembered no more.
For this new life within the womb has comforted a mothers heart
of war. It's precious body is being formed by the Divine.
A heart is encased within it's tiny frame, in a wink of an eye.
It's personality and destiny are set on course by His hand of
grace. Shame is taken away only to let full bloomed patience
take it's place. In a moments time, I wipe away the countless
tears, as I run my hand across my swollen belly, I no longer
remember the disgrace of the barren with its fears.
No greater ecstasy can a man and woman attain then the rapture
of joy at the birth of their own. A tiny blossom to be bathed
in dedication, instruction and discipline, to whom my timeless
devotion is sewn. The scales of love have to form an even
balance. Blessed is this child..... It's destination....
Your lips have announced.

—*Brenda Bland*

The Falling Star

Moonlights shined bright on us,
Walking in an enchanted woods,
Her eyes glittering like stars,
Wind blowing soft and cool,
There, a falling star in the sky,
As the sun rises I noticed,
She had gone to another world,
Like the falling stars in the sky.

—*That (Ted) Ly*

Little Jewels

There are diamonds all around us
Precious gems of every kind
Underestimation of their value
Is an almost heinous crime

Neglected and abused
And tools for selfish gains
Shuffled around like cheap little pawns
Amassed with nicks and stains

Making dull their brilliant shine
Darkening their radiant glow
Reducing to nothing their beauty and strength
As if you didn't know

The children are your jewels
Needing tender loving care
They're only allowed to come through you
And God's lessons you must share

The children are so genuine
Polish and value them
Refine each of their better points
For every child is a precious gem

—*Maretta Arnold-Franklin*

First Born

Dainty little baby hands, tiny baby feet,
Precious little rosebud lips, chubby chin so sweet.
Button-nose, two lovely ears, two sleepy, sleepy eyes,
Little angel all my own, to treasure and to prize!

You're such a tiny little thing, so sweet and so dear
I've waited such "an eternity" time, finally you're here!
I feel tightness around my heart, throat feels tighter too,
Somehow it seems incredible that I also belong to you!

I hold you gently in my arms, caress your soft, smooth skin,
I feel an overwhelming love "spring up" from deep within.
And so I hold you closer still, such joy I never knew,
Now I hold within my arms, my "dream of dreams" come true!

—*J.M. Rusti Keith*

My Heart

Promise me you will not harm it, once given.
Promise me you will not break it, once taken.
It is a precious commodity that can't be bought.
It is very fragile and can be yours with a single thought.
It weakens with every word and every kiss,
It remembers certain words that my mind has missed.
It beats faster with every touch of your hand,
It is stubborn, which my mind can't reprimand.
It is easily won and can be deeply touched.
It does not know lies, deception and such.
Take it carefully, nurture it, let it grow,
Innocence, naivety, romance is all it knows.

Better to cut off my arm than to let it bleed,
But you will find that affection is all it needs.
Let it blossom in your love.
Let it soar with yours high above.
But please remember one thing,
Which could be a brutal sting,
Promise me you will not harm it, once given.
Promise me you will not break it, once taken.

—*Charisma Norabhanlobh*

Love

In the mourning of love passions arise strong and clear.
Pure and innocent as a dove, the mind soars without fear.
Free of even time's powerful chains it flies wild and reckless.
Unaware of the coming rains blindly it stumbles into distress.
At midday, love, swells with Herculean passions,
But is clouded by the restraints of aggression.
Dove, water stained, laden with possessions,
bucks against winds of jealousy, and rationalization.
Love in the evening, rare and cherished
Embers of passion burn fiercely, quietly.
The dove rests, cooing lightly
enjoying what has passed

—*Robert E. Bradbury*

Bits and Pieces

I went through my attic the other day;
Pushed aside the cobwebs, dusted around,
Let in a little light, the better to see;
And tucked into boxes and pigeon holes
I found the fragments that helped shape
The fabric of my life.
The singing and the crying,
The birthing and the dying...
I touched them so gently, and placed them back.
Here I found a chuckle, over there was hurt and pain;
Yet I would not change one thing...
Those hurts and pains gave me strength,
And helped to make me what I am today.
There were my triumphs and disappointments,
The dreams that died aborning,
The "kibbles and bits" of my life,
And put them all back where I got them from...
From the attic of my mind.

—*Helen Cecil Pierce*

My Golden Locket

My golden locket, my golden locket
put away in a lead like a treasure of long ago.

My golden locket my golden locket
sits in the box holding precious
memories of my past.

It holds the story of my life
it holds the secrets of my life.

Today I opened my golden locket to
revive the memories of my past
The surge of happiness became sadness.

The smiles inside my golden locket
made me crazed with madness
As tears roll down my face I realize
that I am sad and I also realize the
happiness that my golden locket keeps
of all the memories and all the secrets
that I once had.

My golden locket my golden locket
how I love the memories it holds inside.

—*Luciano Santini*

Stars

When I look upon the stars
Thinking of God in heaven,
I wish upon the first star
For harmony among men.
Strive always toward the stars,
Help others who are down
And then, God will place stars
In your heavenly crown.

—*Nita Sue Gentry*

613

Treasured Love

Each day if find buried treasures within your heart of gold.
Quiet labors of love blend our days into years.........
Years of sharing endearing times, sad times, simple times,
Knowing we have each other to hold.

Reverently I look forward to each day that is to come...
Thanking God for sending you to heal my heart.
Never forget, dear one, you're more precious than the breath
That gives me life...........
For life can fade, but never shall my devotion and passion for
You die.

Your tenderness broke down all my defenses I had structured —
Your loving embrace will forever drape my heart.
No morning light can brighten a day like you've brightened my
Life........
No setting sun can darken my love, nor separation, nor time.

Each day I declare my desire for you anew......
With each day passing, each day to come, my heart billows with
Tender love...........
Love for you, my darling, love for you!!!!!!

—*Kay Brown*

Monuments Of Nature

Stately, and tall, in the forest they stand;
Reaching high, and stretching wide,
They are the mammoths, of our land,
Our monuments, of nature.
For many centuries, they have stood;
Sheltering, many life forms
Silently, standing in the wood,
And weathering, many strong storms.
Highways, run through the base, of some,
A view, that is quite picturesque;
But, now it seems destiny, has come,
To these redwoods, so statuesque.
And our turn, is here, to show we care;
To preserve, these mighty giants,
So that parents and children, everywhere,
Can enjoy, our monuments, of nature.

—*Lorraine Cordileone Burian*

Change Of The Seasons

Of flowers bloom, and meadows green,
Rebirth has swept the land.
Where I soon realize, that now is the time,
For spring has come once again.

To a scorching heat,
My thirst runs deep,
A drop of water I ask for.
That as the child inside, learns the way why,
For summer has now been delivered.

That of a maturing nature,
Rest is the factor,
Which soon all come to endure.
And as we are leaves, spawned from the trees,
For fall has fallen upon us.

So winter arrives, with its blanket of white,
Sweeping the land from side to side,
That of unkindly winds, to the flaming hearts keep,
All life soon comes to silence.
For please don't cry, but close your eyes,
To awaken again in a new year's time.

—*Dimitros Pliagos*

"Goodbye"

Loneliness will be the death of me,
Releasing my soul and setting me free,
Missing the happiness I once had,
Now I sit here lonely and sad,
Thinking I should give love one more try,
When I truly just want to say "Goodbye,"
The end of love creates so much pain,
It's enough to make a man go insane,
   I truly just want to say "Goodbye"
Please Lord let another touch my soul,
Before I decide to just let go,
With my final choice I could end up in hell,
But with the love of God you never can tell,
I'll end this poem before I die,
And I'll say to you,
Never tell your love "Goodbye"

—*Scott Eric Sienkiewicz*

"What Might Patrick's Church Have Been"

Early Patrick! Early Christian church of Patrick, might have
remained to be, had not Lombardi family conquered Far south in
Italy and founded, they-Lombardi family!-all that glorious
setting for themselves; and called it, they, the Papacy. Right
here on Earth, a Holy Father?-more than merely imagined? And
some facts rearranged, so as to make all seem more related to
the newly rich, Lombardi family-and, with some chronological
changes, The actual birth and time of Jesus, would not again be
truly traceable. And, with the lengthy and complete diaries of
the near-invincible Julius Caesar, carefully hidden away by
ambitious Lombardi people A full forty years of time, so
enigmatically could be brought forward!- With mainly
speculation, thereafter, rather than facts to rest upon. If
Early Christian church of Patrick truly had survived and
Eventually had not been incorporated into the political-minded
Power structure of a new-founded Papacy of 590 A.D., what Might
christian Patrick's Church have been? - for, much earlier He -
the former slave of Druids!-had died on March 17th, in 493 A.D.

—*Canadia Collins*

"In Remembrance Of Me"

"Do this," he said, "in remembrance of me;
Remember my pain and death on the tree.
And remember my life, my words and my love,
My mercy and grace which bled from above."

"Eat and drink," he said unto them,
And with his disciples he sang a hymn
Of praise and thanks to Jehovah the Great,
As he prepared himself for the path he must take.

Jesus, the Lord, the only Son,
God's chosen King, the anointed One,
Upon the cross endured the rage
And defeated the evil prince of this age.

The body of Christ they placed in a cave,
To serve the Lord as a cold, dark grave.
Death tried in vain to keep in the Light,
But he broke free in his righteous might.

At the right hand of God forever to reign,
A reminder to souls never to feign.
He still says to those whom he sets free,
"Eat and drink in remembrance of me."

—*James M. Wells*

Shattered Dreams

I was admitted into this world, by two people you see, who were
responsible for conceiving, but incapable of loving me.
I didn't come into this world as a grown-up, I came as an
infant needing love and support.
It seems as though I tampered with somebody's dream, I was born
to parents who were abusive and demean.
It started long before I could walk, the physical, mental, and
emotional abuse, sadly though, I couldn't even talk.
I couldn't see the sun for the raging storm, my dreams seemed
shattered long before I was born. Was the nativity and
responsibility too much to share, then why wasn't I given up
for adoption for others to care. Neglect represses me, but
abuse hurts more, the scars will heal, but my heart will remain
sore. I speak the truth, straight from the heart, I hope that
therapy can mend my broken parts. To decimate my nurturing,
makes me cry, my shattered dreams will follow me until the day
that I die. I'm surmounted by shattered dreams, and horrid
screams, but through it all, I have a life to live, reposing
my dreams, because I have love to give.

—*Brenda R. Bender*

The Joy Of Aging

Slowly the mystery unfolds
Revealing the tragic untold
From beginning to end sum a circle of friends
Bound by music-so haunting,
Emotion-so taunting-
And passion, engripping of men.

As the clock winding down
Releases the smiles, and the frown,
And the tears——
Do the years pass us by
While we try to possess yesteryears?

Shall I learn to be free?
Shall I seek reverie?
Shall the daylight become my best friend?
Or shall I succumb to gravity's plumb
And grown old
As The Great One Intends?

—*Kenna Morris Grushoff*

"Don't Be Afraid!"

Don't be afraid to wander, along the
    Road of life;
With its strange occurrences, and
    unexpected strife!

For, each day seems somewhat different,
    than the day that went before;
And there's no way to foresee the things
    that Fate may have in store!

But, if you live just one day at a time,
    and take it all in stride;
The Night can bring only pleasant dreams,
with happy memories locked inside!

Then, as Dawn appears you can wake refreshed,
    and go along your way;
Light of Heart and energized, for the Events
    of another Day!

Living is just a Unique Adventure, and a
    Challenge at its Best;
For all to see and conquer, then, at
    Life's End be Blest!

—*Leah C. Anderson*

In Our Paradise

Waterfalls rumbling in the distance
Robins and Jays singing in the oaks
And the whispering of Breezes.
Are the sounds of our Paradise.

The never ending earth of Blue and Green
Stars and Moons- Both day and night
And golden, warm sun above us.
Are the sights of our paradise.

Rose's and Wildflower's pastel scents,
fresh air from the peak of mountains
is the aroma of our Paradise.

Come with me to our Paradise.
A wondrous place for only us.
It's a place of dreams and truths;
It's a place for you and me, Us!

—*Gina Smith*

Little Old Lady

Little old lady with holes in her shoes,
Rocking away and reading the News.
Children out back fly high on a swing.
Their laughter to her a beautiful ring.
Announcement of two who have taken their vow,
The tiniest tear starts glimmering now.

Little old lady keeps rocking away,
Recalling her vows from yesterday.
Graduates listed and honor roll too,
Beginning their lives and starting anew.
College comes next and they will date,
Then she recalls of meeting her mate.

Little old lady still rocking her chair,
Sun turning to gold her pure white hair.
Ending the day, forgetting her sorrow.
"Obits" she'll leave until the morrow.

—*Jane E. Manderfield*

To Be Free, At Last

I am standing on the old wooden pier, watching the mighty waves,
roll in and crash against the rotting columns, my dark,
windblown hair absorbs the smell of sea foam, as it whips right
and left in the wind. I watch as the smaller waves and ripples
are thrown back after impinging on the columns and hastily
scattering, not strong enough to overcome the formidable
obstacle. Cries of gulls which once shattered the silence are
now being carried away in the wind. So awesome is their power,
bolting against the breath of the Earth, diving down, deep
towards the churning water, just barely skimming the surface.
They fight with all their might to regain their position high
above the belly of the unforgiving sea. My lifeless eyes focus
on the clashing waves below; they are so strong, unlike the
smaller waves separating into all directions, scattering amongst
the sea, like dried leaves in an autumn breeze. Without
hesitation, I step off the pier, surrendering my soul to the
sea. The seemingly relentless storm has finally come to an end.
A sea gull skims silently over the calming water, like a
dragonfly darting over the glass-like surface of a pond. At
last, I can feel the waves...how mighty they are...how strong.

—*Gina Dorazio*

Time

Time goes by - by to where?
Rolled in a scroll, only God can bear.

Though out of sight - to mortal man:
It's in plain view, where God stands.

He views it all - from end to end;
From last to first, and back again.

Time that's gone - is gone to where?
On this scroll, into God's care.

So brethren rest - for time gone by;
Is not far away, but really nigh.

On the other side - of God's Scroll:
We're in His hands, how ... ever rolled.

So past is near - and future close;
Time not a problem, the Lord Of Host.

Your family gone? Gone to where?
Into God's hands; forever near.

—*Frank H. Jackson*

The Storm And Dear Old Pine

The sky was pitch black—it was only noon
Rumbling—in the distance gave a warning sign
As the lightning flashes, told of its coming soon
This storm!!—may knock down- the dear old pine.

The wind— sang a haunting whistling song,
Trees danced to and fro and down to the ground:
The wild storm is coming— it won't be long
With its rumbling, clapping, whistling sound.

Now overhead— torrential rains came down,
Mother earth shook— with a clap of thunder
The lightning lit up, everything in town—
Dear old pine was struck— but did not go under!!

Suddenly— the sky was a beautiful blue
The sun shone down with a smiling face
It was as though, the Lord knew
Dear old pine though struck— stood firm in its place!!

—*Esther Mazza*

Dreams

In the darkness of your dreams,
Safe from the world—the cruel world,
Your mind open to endless possibilities.
Some never wake again,
Most do, not remembering,
Not remembering what their mind had been opened up to.
Eyes closed, breathing at a slow, peaceful beat,
Like music, like dancing,
1...2...3...4...and on into the night.
Sleep, what a beautiful, peaceful time until...
Falling, falling, falling,
Wake up quick, you're about to hit the ground.
Oh, sweet Jesus, lend me a hand,
Make your hand the ground, it will soften the landing.
You toss over in your bed,
Your subconscious mind with the only knowledge,
Awaking abruptly, forgetting what had woken you,
You drift back off into your deep, silent sleep,
Never to think of the darkness of your last dream,
But to only create a new one.

—*Erica Gose*

Mary Crocus The Star Of Jesus

She Little dwarf crocus
Said Hi to winter
She had bloomed too soon
In the year of the man in the moon
She died of pneumonia before spring
One spruce kept crying it was so sad
Mary Crocus was buried
next to a pine cone
"Never bloom early" was
on her epitaph
One wood of the forest
Lamented and wailed
Because Jesus had
Chosen her as a sample
She too had died a Christ - like
death of crucifixion of her stem like petals
We wonder why what God has in mind
With little like Mary and His son
Mary Crocus one star of Jesus and the man at Dark Cavalry

—*Laura Lambe Burrell*

The Skin Horse

Climb on my back little boy,
said the horse.
He looked up at the handsome white horse with the wondrous
wings.
Climb on my back little boy,
said the horse.
Could it be that the Wishing-Hair wish had come true?
Climb on my back little boy,
said the horse.
Beloved skin horse! At last,
You are here!
Climb on my back little boy,
said the horse.
At once he realized his pain was gone and
he was strong again.
Climb on my back little boy,
said the horse.
So upon the horse's back he climbed and away they flew.
The skin horse and the little boy too.

—*Donna Ross*

The Sailing

Tossed and torn she lists
Sails split, she no longer catches wind
She rolls in waves thirty feet deep
Green walled water frothing, hissing, foaming,
The sounds angry seas make

Orders given to save her
Old salts washed from the deck never again seen
Only cries of help scream from the sea
Their dying breath be salt water indeed
Sinking to the bottom to sleep for the centuries

Sailors have passed this way on kinder days
How calm, how peaceful, they say
This resting place
This watery grave

—*Duane B. Smithem, Jr.*

You're All Man

I came into the bedroom to put away some socks. The sight that I
saw gave me quite a little shock. There you lay in your
innocence, asleep, and never knowing that I watched in proud
astonishment, the dirt you missed, now showing.

You came in from work, showered, ate, and went to bed. You
couldn't stand for me to find you dirty or your clothes a mess.
You looked like such a little boy, I wanted to hold you tight,
But I slipped quietly from the room and gently dimmed the light,
You work so hard in the coal mines, underground you like it
there, you say, but there are times that I cry hour 'round until
I know you're safe.

You treat me like a woman. I'm not like most men's wives, the
men say things that hurt them. You always treat me right. You
act as though you're proud of me, even when they're near
their disrespect you said, shouldn't be: You said, "Love's the cure."

You've never even thought to strike at me, you told me so
yourself. The most of them, they hit their wives: They've lost
hope with nothing left. You fix the car, you pay the bills, you
fix the roof when it leaks. This man, so far, you don't seem
real, but baby, you're all I need.

—*Margaret Buell Colvin*

The Fragile Edge

We lay our ravage dead in the earth,
Scatter crosses, white sentinels to keep the watch.
Quickly we turn away forgetting the horror of the day.

We do not remember
Cold bitter shores, shredded skies, racing bombs to hell
And back, pain, insanity.
We do not remember eternity waits.
We gently lay our heroes to rest,
Soft smiling faces beneath the mask.

The world heals her scars,
Trees give birth to green leaves,
Birds return to build their nest.
We gently lay our heroes to rest.

Like winds smashing waves against the rocks,
Madness unleashed, shatters the crystal edge of sanity.

No heroes lie at rest.
No crosses somewhere in earth.
No earth,
Only ashes in the wind.

—*Edith Stanton-Ingram*

Infinite Thoughts

Through the walls of thought I trod;
Searching for the window of harmony
With curtain's of peace and friendship,
And a comfortable breeze blowing in love and happiness.

I feel someone reaching in,
Reaching to grasp my thoughts and dreams away.
Doing that, would be leaving me with
Complete darkness within myself
And my inanimate shadow would be my best friend.

Dreams are hard to comprehend and leave us with much disarray;
An engraved thought is eternal
And seems to leave me with an intriguing extent if suspense;
even when death visits "sheol".
The thought roams, roams like a stranger to death;
To find another beholder to beheld its meaningful sight.

Though I've found some happiness within my thoughts.
I'm still searching for the full extent of extensive
Love and happiness throughout my revealing mind of thoughts;
For the mind is the poetry of life.

—*Donny McWilliams*

Her

As she walks through the black night, searching,
searching helplessly to find the one she loved long ago,
her naked feet tingle from the scratches
caused by the branches down below.
Her hair a dark black, black as a black stallion,
galloping as the sun goes down.
she struggles a painless struggle
and the trees stare in the deadly silence
except for one nightingale.
Desperately she walks through the forest.
When the pines scrape against her face,
she feels a coldness inside.
And now I think about
that cold, dark night and
the girl that is there no more.
She once came out at night,
searching for the one she loved.
I get a tingle down my spine
and a thrill of excitement,
but now she is...gone.

—*Destiny Lee*

Grandfather Garner

When I cull cerebral crevices of fallible memory,
searching inner limits submerged in surmises,
it is difficult to remember Grandfather Garner.
There are fleeting glimpses which glide like ghosts,
but stay not long enough to fix their time or image;
so there are only single frames of broken film
to piece together a fractured record far from epic,
but recall he did exist, like some nameless portrait
stored in attic corners of my childhood gallery,
a face floating lined and puffed with pink grey age,
a voice warping dimmed and cracked in scrambled years.

I never asked my mother if he wore a moustache,
though my recollection is both yes and no.
It does not matter since he fades from memory
and cancels all but that last time in Baltimore,
when I was six, and he lay in Chambers Funeral Home.
With hushed and solemn family on folding chairs
in grieving groups, I crept alone on tip-toe to the bier
for one brief glance which labeled death's first face,
of orange lips and powdered cheeks, but not the man.

—*Charl Van Horn*

Serpent Song

Looking for the serpent song
Searching without a map
To help me on a journey that's long
Endlessly my soulless feet on the concrete slap
Oh sweet serpent song I long to be you
Keeping me living in such sweet misery
Alive amid only the special few
Lead me to the endless ride
Fly me into the bottomless sky
Jesus don't let me slide
Why do I keep this up why
I wanna get into the serpent song
Hear it's endless melodies in my head
Expanding in my mind all day long
Until finally it's silent and I am dead
Whereupon in a burst of ecstasy I become the serpent song
In my broken mind
Home at last where I belong
Because upon me it finally shined

—*Elisabeth Dasenbrook*

Allison

Dark -
secluded isle of stars;
entered through this everescent gate in your imagination.
You created protruding errors
to help you fight to keep going in this simply-faceted
world icon:
Dormouse to the great and only fear-
feared all alone in this intolerable chamber of
pity-free souls;
stirring around your face, they dance like
wild orchids wet with excitement.

—*Jeff Hickman*

The Coyote

I'm such whom nobody can bear.
Seems not enough to chase me down on earth
I'm often double watched from the air.
I'm looking nearly like a dog
My predicament — I'm not a dog.
I cannot follow owner singing sweet —
On empty stomach looking neat.
Some days I had a longing for a porridge bowl,
Secure corner somewhere to lie down —
This naked hunger takes out all that's mild,
I howl, I grab, I'm cunning wild...
My cubs were waiting for me eagerly —
They disappeared recently...
Give me a moment of a worthy life
If only sweetened poison bait —
And slay me tenderly.

—*Alma Mikelsons*

Ode To March

Blow, blustery winds of March
Send gray billowing clouds across the skies
Then surprise us with sunsets
Living murals before our eyes.

But you can't keep the crocus hid
Under your snows with drifts deep
They awaken in a warming earth
By a restlessness from their sleep.

You can't hide the daffodil,
Who catch a wandering sun ray.
They come to give us promises,
Of a warmer, quieter day.

Gentle April soon will come
To wash the air and melt snows
No longer will you blush our cheeks
And send chills to our toes

—*Hazel Maskel*

Shattered Dreams

Today my life was shattered,
Shattered into many pieces.
Each piece broke slowly,
Eventually, my life was gone.

The first piece broke when I met you,
For I knew we would eventually part.
The more I began to love you,
The more the pieces broke.
The day I learned you were leaving,
Is the day I felt my last piece break away.

Slowly the pieces will go back together,
To make my new life whole.
But with all the times we shared together,
I will always remember and love you!

—*Jami Vodvarka*

Country Kitchen: A Childhood Memory

The black iron range crackles with burning wood,
Sending small whiffs of fragrant smoke
Assail on heated air. I sniff, and smells
Of baking bread, molasses cookies, and
Cinnamon buns tickle my nose.
On this cold winter day, I am toasting
My toes upon the oven door.

Mother's rocking chair, padded with calico snuggles
Teddy and Florabelle my unruly "pretend" children.
There on the "no touch" shelf behind the chair stand
Photographs of old be-whiskered men and sober women,
Looking at the world outside through windows dressed
In white, starched, ruffled curtains.

The braided rug, gleaned from discarded garments,
Is now my hopscotch game board as it fills the room,
Making a frame for the round oak dining table.
I land on Mother's old black Sunday dress,
And quickly hop to Grandma's woolen skirt.
"Step on Uncle Jack, break your mother's back!"

—*Lucille J. Oosterhous*

Sights Unseen

On a sad and mournful morning, one cold January day,
seven roared to the loving hands of God, in tears, history

In the name of Man's greatest steps they rose, a gleaming
white chariot of fire, with ease of heart, calm of soul.

Five brave men and two daring women put there lives into
man's reach for the stars, and joined those unsung heroes of
   lifted flight, riding its crest onto destiny, forfeiting
   too their souls.

From the smallest death in an idea, to the sudden grief of
   that morn, men and women will always dream into the heavens
   for other neighbors, in the faint lights of dawn.

As we morn our brave knights who rode its crest of thunder
   do not lose sight behind their deaths, do not call this
   "blunder"

For Earth is our cradle, civilization of the universe,
   and as its little child we must try to leave,
   mother's warm breast.

And as we reach beyond the confines of this safe cradle
   into its vast universe, heed its child,

For its first steps that need taken or not with its fall.

—*David Lee Hale*

Summer Morning

Peaceful solitude of a new day's birth
Shadows being cast across the earth;
Before humanity is up and about
Mother Nature has her clout.

The innocence spanning upon the land
It is all, in God's perfect plan;
All's well with creatures, large and small
Man isn't causing their untimely fall.

Grass is glistening with needed dew
Unharmed for now, footprints are few;
Trees standing tall and oh, so proud
From their branches birds singing aloud.

Just take some time in early morn
Be glad for another day born;
Listen to the quiet, observe the beauty
Be thankful for our gift, its our duty.

—*Kay T. Story*

Plagued With 'Hard Times'

Roll-up your shirt sleeves and get going!
Shake-off your sorrows once in awhile!
When the going gets tough start your adrenalin a'flowing!
Put your best in every inch of every mile!

'Hard times' make easy ways to make a 'quitter'!
Lady luck turns secret corners and can hide!
No matter where—pure gold will always glitter!
And so will you, if you don't lose your pride!

Shake-off the constant frown and do some smiling!
Take a little time for Love; cast-off your fear!
Pretty soon your 'blessing' will start a 'piling
If you'll fill good days with ways that'll make a good year!

There were other times too, that were hard; so were some people
Who lived, but lacked the courage to tote their load!
Look out beyond your lot and see the 'steeple';
God will help you trod your long, rough road!

With whatever tools you've got, go out and labor!
Work hard through working-hours; show no remorse!
And before you know it you'll discard that 'saber'
And be thankful for the 'guts' that stayed the course!

—*Andrew Thomas Frederick*

Look Up, Often

Look up, see the fluffy clouds of many
    shapes, drifting lazily by.
They make you feel so happy, taking away,
    your urge to cry.
After a sudden rain, look up, you may see,
    a rainbow!
If you're having a sad day, look up or you'll
    never know.
There is so much beauty, out doors,
    that God has created.
Hardly a day, can pass, that I don't go out,
    look up, feel so elated!

—*Ann M. Hollibush*

She's Deserving, So Deserving

God knows, I can taste her kind forgiveness.
She forces my hidden desires to secretly apologize.
Bestow upon this heart of mine,
A dreamer's love.

Her's is a soft, sweet voice I've come
To understand and recognize.
Hunger and recognition stir my writing hand
With a harvest of words, so to capture the pleasures,
I have to struggle to fight, yet I yield.

As I move and begin to trespass across hope and reason
toward her unsuspecting life field.
Oh, God, if only she could see the deserving truth that
has been born under every rising sun.

Shall there be, yet another innocence of caring lost,
Along with a song from life's happiness,
That won't be shared or sung?

Let his the truth be unveiled,
And never broken for
She's the deserving one.

—*Dave M. Blunt*

Untitled

Darkness, implicit silence, shattered by the touch of a hand.
She gasped startled.
As he took her down into the green grass of the meadow,
The sweet smell of poppies brought a tear to her eye.
She felt cold wetness upon her back from the dew of night,
Yet heat rose from their entangled bodies
The gusting wind moaned through the trees, deleafing limbs,
Leaving them vulnerable and bare, to the full moonlight -
As it danced across the river,
While the waves went up and down
Rushing toward the opening into the sea,
A sea of rising emotions.
Feelings rising them so high that they were stars in the sky.
Bright spheres of blazing fire
Ready to burst at any moment.
Then gentle rains came,
Leaving the warm night cool and longing,
For more endless nights of summer.

—*Gypsi Bible*

Lady Liberty

Upon her head she wears a crown, her eyes look out to sea.
She is the mighty symbol of the land for liberty.
    Her left hand holds a Book of Rule
    Pressed against her gown.
    Her right hand lifts a mighty torch
    To light the world around
She stood and watched her children leave
    To fight in distant wars
crying tears in silence to see them never more.

The lady has been ailing, because she's getting old,
One hundred years of salty wind, and better, bitter cold.
    We her children want forsake her
    We'll mend her good as new
    She'll stand in all her splendor
    For all the world to view
And at her feet are broken shackles; she stands on sail that's
    free. The fairest lady of them all, is lady liberty.

—*Chaplain James C. Summerlin*

Untitled

I spied a maid upon the shore,
she leapt and danced upon the sands,
my heart did bleed, she danced the more,
she beckoned me with soft-white hands.
I stumbled 'cross the sleeping beach
to glimpse this beauty closer still,
I sought her arm, with mine, to reach;
athwart the dunes she led my will.
The moon shone in her flaxen hair,
I followed still, forlorn and slow
I'd dreamt of ladies not so fair,
and until now should never know...

(Written in iambic tetrameter with an alternating rhyme scheme.)
    —*Trevor Treller*

VIP - 18 - 110

Thank you friends for asking me
to share a part of John,
fans say my poems are special
and many awards have I often won.
But fate has made me humble
so I am forced to turn you down,
knowing well I'll miss a big one
as well as new poetry friends in town
    —*John Hartzell*

The Stranger

I saw a face of wonder, wanting of happiness and laughter.
She looked at me a while, but when I spoke she did not answer.
I longed to hear her voice, my soul began to cry.
Upon looking up I noticed she too had tears in her eyes.
Why couldn't she respond, why couldn't she be free?
Then I noticed her imprisonment. She was imprisoned there by me.
I wanted to set her free. I went looking for the gate.
I started to feel so desperate and I knew she couldn't wait.
But I could find no gate, no door, no fence, no lock.
There was no entrance to her, no door on which to knock.
I thought I heard her voice, I though I heard her call.
I walked to where I'd seen her and found a mirror on the wall.
How could this have happened? How could all this be?
To not have realized sooner...
that I was looking in at me.

—*Denise E. daCosta*

More Precious Than Jewels

She held me.
She nursed me.
She bathed me.
She kissed me.
She cuddled me.
She kissed my hurts.

As I grew up, she guided me down the right path.
She soothed me through my so-called tragedies.
She eased my fears.
She was patient with me through my teens.
She set me free.

Now, that I am older, she is still beside me.
She cries with me through my woes.
She is happy with me for my joys.
She calms my fears.
Most of all, she still comforts me.
You see, she is my mom.
God gave me a love more precious than any jewels.
He gave me my mom — I love you mom...!!!

—*Barbara A. Yageric*

Into Sunshine

All alone in a corner, forgotten by the world,
She sits and quietly stares out her window, into sunshine.
No one stops to visit, or even just to say hello.
She can't remember the last smile she saw.
No flowers on her sill, or children on her floor,
Her memory is fading; her eyes and ears fail her.
She once was adored by many, so happy and lively.
But now she avoids mirrors and people's eyes.

She scares me, in a way, not because of who she is,
But because, in my future, I see myself as her.
Sitting alone in a corner, forgotten by the world,
Quietly staring out my window, into sunshine.

—*Dori McDaniel*

He Loved Her Anyway

Her name was Henny.
She didn't even have a penny.
But he loved her anyway.
She was skinny.
And though her family was many,
He loved her anyway.

She had a dog
That was no bigger than a frog,
But he cared for it like it was his own.
All she had was an old rusted bike.
But she knew that she was loved by Mike.

—*Holly Burton*

Granny's Songs

She was both old and frail, with mind gone wandering.
She spent the coin of worthless days in squandering
The treasures of her long-forgotten golden times.
Her life was filled with riddles, but no games or rhymes. .

But, let her sit at the piano and the notes
Of ancient melodies would leap across the moats
Of reason. She could play with majesty and power;
Or, delicate her touch, I'd listen by the hour
To her fairy tunes, her fingers swift and sure.
She was a gifted artist whose clear portraiture
Could paint the world in magic scenes with those sweet songs.

And so, in memory, that part of her belongs
To me. Through labyrinthine passages those notes
Escaped to bring me messages, sweet antidotes.
We could not share our thoughts except in songs she played;
But that's enough. I'm grateful for that serenade.

—*Verna Macbeth*

Untitled

He stands by her side, his face looking straight
She touches his hand because she understands
He looks at her face, he feels the love all too well
Her hair, a blond flame in the breeze.

He touches her face, feels the smoothness
She see's that it's hard for him to say something
A tear well's up in his eye but falls from hers
He brushes it away with his finger

She smiles to reassure him she'll always be there
To hold him and love him, to know she cares
He kisses her forehead and starts to leave
She holds him for what seems an eternity

Now he is gone and she is alone
Her heart beats a rhythm by itself
She lays down beside him and whispers
Whispered words he longed to say
"I love you" as she placed flowers on his grave

—*Jackie Chrapczynski*

The Listener

Just like "The Thinker" she is probably alone.
She's just waiting and hoping to hear a certain tone.
It's a very small sound that she wants to hear.
It comes from people who need a patient ear.

An ear that will listen to what they have to say.
One that can listen without forcing its way.
She doesn't always have answers, but may have some clues.
At times in her life, she has walked in your shoes.

There is no guarantee that your troubles will end.
One thing is for sure, she would like to be a friend.
Just someone to be there, when you may need to talk.
Someone who won't tell you to just take a walk.

There is no need to worry about what you may say.
A friend doesn't repeat or want things just her way.
If she starts being nasty or tries to be boss.
There is nothing to gain and it's really her loss.

The door is always open and there's always a chair.
An ear is waiting with a friendship to share.
The one thing I've learned, when all is said and done.
If you really want a friend, you learn to be one.

—*Geraldine Gleich*

Phoebe shivers out seven.

"The Countessa?"
"She's the One,"
I said,
"I do too."
"Her Dacian Trinity drove it's point forth!"
"I hung nailed to the door,"
"Left to flap, to and fro, to and fro."

"Her sweet smile gnawed"
"My five-finger"
"Drummed,"
"Bloom! Blume! Bloom!"
"I adore you," she whispered.

"Six! Sex! Six!"
"Seventh Heaven."

"I abhor you," she whispered.

"Insinuate!"
"Nine, neie, nine."
"She's a ten, dead!"

Snake-eyes rattles out eleven.

—*Carlos Prieto Jr.*

A Loving Poem for My Elisha

Oh, Elisha I love you so much. Your hair is like the sun
shining on my face. Your nose is as sharp as a whistle, and
your eyes are a beautiful green just like mine. Your face is
intricately put together with such awesome beauty, that I could
look at it forever. Your lips are a light pink and they look
so divine, that when you would talk with them, they would move
like dewdrops, dripping from a rosebuds pink, sweet sensational
smelling flower petal. Your hair on your arms are full of
lightness, and when you would put them close to mine I would
feel a love like no other kind. Your ten fingers are put
together so well, and when you would use your thumb and other
two fingers to write with, I would have liked kissing them
slowly one by one. Your thighs are soft looking and firm to
the touch. Your knees are shaped like no other woman that I've
ever seen with my own eyes up close before. I've only seen
your shoes and not your bare feet yet, but I am sure they are
beautiful enough to be met, with lavishing kisses from my
mouth-watering tongue, kissing on each and every part of them.

And now as I gaze one last time into Elisha's beautiful green
eyes, I will be reminiscent of what has come and what has
already gone by, and although we have never met our lips with
a kiss, I will always keep her in my heart, with loving
thoughts of how beautiful she was and still is by far.

—*Dale Merwitz*

God's Plan

I never thought I would live to see forty-nine. But God
showed me he had a better plan.
For you see, I didn't know God loved me as no one could.
He lead me down the road so true to show me I could
love Him, too.
He said, "Follow me. I will give you everlasting life. All
you do is just believe."
He said, "Lean on me. I am all you will need. I am always
true you will see."
And we went down the path toward the plan, hand in hand.
And He showed me love was the plan to see me through
Until he comes back to save me, too...
I will live to see fifty-two.

—*Linda Brown*

"Caretaker Of The Clocks"

Many clocks, not one or two, their faces shown in stately view,
Side by side upon a shelf, timed in rhythm — to charm an elf.
They soothed to comfort in the night
Unveiling each new day in dawn of light.
Like old friends tried and true share sad and happy times
with you.

One quaint old timepiece it's silence wears
A saddened face as if no one cares;
Once proudly stood in aging grace,
Now a mantle shows a vacant space,
Silence urging to unlock the heartbeat of this lonely clock.

Dad's patient hands made to repair
Turned the key of time once more to share,
Of days gone by and times we know
Revealing summers warm and winter's snow.
Spring time breezes and harvest gold
In rhapsody these stories told.
Time goes on remains not still,
Time renders life in God's on will.

From far and near of folks that talk,
Know the caretaker of the grand old clock.

—*Leah Jean Vixo*

Witness

There he stood in all his glory, his beautiful bride by his
side, the sun high in the sky warmed his eyes, and played with
her hair and there they stood all of his loved ones witnesses
to this, two people becoming one
There she stands and listens as he recites the lyrics
to the only music she'll ever care to hear

There they stand looking into each others eyes then gently
they kiss, there they all stand on this day feeling no pain,
no sorrow, why should they on a day such as this
And here I stand a witness to this two people becoming one
listening as he recites the lyrics to the only music
I'd ever cared to hear

Here I stand feeling only pain, only sorrow
A witness to this, the end of my dream
Here I stand in all my sorrow, my beautiful dream by my side
The sun high in the sky warmed my tears
And played with my heart
Yes here I stand no witnesses to my emptiness
Here I stand alone, alone.....

—*Emily Gonzalez*

Shucking

Dragging your baggage by cords of desire, still,
sighing to be understood
Exchanging excuses of meager release for
another veiled sacrifice
On an altar of ego doubt's shadow delivers an
uncertain comfort with price
to knife another oyster washed in fever of tabasco
being newly dead, or simply new unwise.

Adding a new pearl to strands of your wishes, each
beautiful rosary clutch
Sincerely requesting cultivation's conformance of
sand covering scar
Claiming unrealization, attempt rearranging things that
should be as they are
to ignoring the purest passions that don't find acceptance,
Will is unwilling, freedom gets another bar

—*Cynthia Gunter*

1944 - 1981

When I was a girl-child of Hollywood stars,
Sinatra songs, Kennedy wit...
I believed.

When I was a child-woman of infant's smiles,
husband's hands, home's womb security...
I believed.

When I was a liberated divorcee of frenetic gaiety,
financial woes, men's apartments...
I believed.

I believed in God, Country, Motherhood, Love,
Money, Doctors, Love, Presidents, Education, Love...
I truly believed.

Now I believe in God, Motherhood, all the
essential socio-cultural beliefs...
But mostly,
I believe in me.

—*Marlene Barkow-Weiss*

"Michigan's My Reason"

I looked out my window and what did I see
Six inches of snow awaiting to greet me
It's March twenty-second, the storm missed the ides
This beautiful white blanket has covered the outsides

A Michigan White Wonderland is inviting to me
The hill down the road is abiding you see
If I don't sled today I may not be able tomorrow
Thus leaving my sled and me a little sorrow

The sled skis are waxed awaiting the trip
I'll pack up some cups for hot chocolate to sip
Maybe my friends from Jordan will come
The thrills that we'll get we can't get from rum

We'll bundle up warmly all taking a turn
For fun in Michigan's Whiteland we'll all really learn
The soup on my stove will soon be all made
We'll all have a bowl after sledding in today's shade

To let any day pass without some fun and joy
Is a major mistake made by any girl or boy
We're lucky living here where we have four kinds of season
Even with no house - Michigan's my reason

—*James A. Gossett*

The Poconos

Today, I saw the beauty of the mountains reaching onward to the
sky, dressed in vivid colors, with Delaware Water Gap close by.
One could not imagine the sight before my eyes; it was
absolutely awesome as the rain fell from the skies.

The smell of cedar was in the air as the land was cleared to
make room for roads and housing, along the river bank.
Tourists were everywhere with cameras in their hand,
Capturing scenes of elegance of God's almighty land.

The roads were narrow and winding, a canal was laid beside
where mules, at one time, pulled barges, driven by men with
pride. Oh, there's no place like New England with its
boundless mountain land, bathed in all its beauty by the
Master's powerful hand.

—*Karen Nowak Foley*

Nighttime Wonders

Each night as I sit in quiet thought beneath the starry
sky, I feel God's love reaching out and my heart responds
with peaceful sighs.

He has made such beauty our eyes to behold, forming the
whole of creation in just six days we are told.

The clouds pass by at rapid pace hurried by the breeze,
separating at intervals making little ripples on heavens seas.

The moon in all it's splendor hangs against a sheet of
blue, showing forth it's hills and rills in glorious brilliant hue.

Soft breezes touch upon my face like gentle loving
fingers, and even as it passes by the wonder of it lingers.

Thank you God for such beauty it is truly an awesome
sight, and thank you that in quiet peace I can turn and
say "goodnight".

—*Dorothy Irene Eddy*

The leaf fell
    slowly and majestically
        from the tall tree.
As it fell, it twisted and turned
    ever so slowly
        as if in slow motion,
But gravity pulled it steadily downward.

Occasionally it reflected light from the sun,
    as it floated downward on a summer's day.
At night it was invisible
    and its presence was only known
        because it blocked the visibility of stars
            as it flickered downward.

On windy days its path was altered
    and its destination changed
        from a sidewalk,
            to a park,
                to a river.
No one could be sure
    where and when the leaf would land.

—*Kevin Angulski*

Loneliness

Blue was the sky
Slowly fading to black.
    The old woman fed the birds
As one landed on her back.
    Her heart filled with love,
As she stared at two lovers,
    Watching the stars above.
She had too, been young and free,
    The name beauty fit her to a tee.

Now was her time to cry,
To see her lonely life flash by.
    The bird and the beach were to her a friend,
Because she all to well knew that happiness,
    Must end.
While the lovers, sea shells, they tried to find,
    Their hands like two roses intertwined.
The old lady wept,
    As the sky and her tears faded, she slept.

—*Alicia Irvin*

Two Became One

Two limbs of flesh, a cane of wood
Slowly, methodically walk the field.
Foot high, higher to clear the ground
Breathe deep the richness of life.

Never say no, just pray and go
We smile as my love returns.
To others I say break not his will
His will keeps us alive.

Body weakened, courage to die
Bright casket pictures strewn on the bed.
Think tonight, tomorrow choose oak
Our eyes meet, we smile, we pray.

Calm, peaceful, depart with a smile
Hands touch eternity and God.
The angels dance and the saints sing
In celebration. We smile. We die.

Gently I lift his lifeless form
Down the hall, out the door one last time.
A farewell kiss, his presence remains
We walk up the stairs and I die.

    —*Diane M. Childree*

Rituals I Have

It is bedtime. Again I trust my body to the safe white sheets,
snap shut the purses of my eyes, and imagine someone's death:
a parent or both, possibly a brother, sometimes it's my dog.
Could be from fire, disease, a charging Mack truck or
hard freeze and leaking gas fumes. Someone I care for is taken
political prisoner in Haiti and never seen again. Or shot
on the street by the boy who took me to my first Homecoming.
I might be there to see the accident; I could read it in the
paper, or a family member (not dying that night)
might tell me to my face. I trick myself into revealing
what I'd wanted to say before it was too late,
before it is. I hunch in the corner of half-dreams,
eavesdropping on my private grief. Always the same voice says:
Don't leave me, don't leave me, let me go.

    —*Lilace A. Mellin*

A Cold Winter Night

Outside I went on a cold winter night.
Snow coming down like no end in sight.

Visibility was poor and roads were slick.
Snowing so hard, it was very thick.

Night driving in snow was hard by far.
God tonight would bring a new star.

I arrived at work safe and sound,
To see nurses scurrying around.

A couple came on that blustery night,
And a baby boy was born, oh! What a sight.

The snow whirled as the wind blew.
Busy inside was the Maternity Crew.

God was busy throwing snow around,
While inside you hear a baby sound.

The temperature was zero or below.
Happy and content Mom and Dad did glow.

Winter is shedding a heavy winter storm.
Nestled and safe a new life is born.

God not only gave cold winter night,
He sent a baby, a most wonderful sight.....

    —*Marcia Randolph*

To All Patients With Cancer

Life is so precious - in the palms of our hand
snuffed out so quickly like the shifting sand
We try to live - the best that we could?
Didn't I live the best that I could?
We do everything we know that we should?
Didn't I do the things that I should?
Why me I asked with grave concern?
What is it that somehow I needed to learn?
I said to myself, "How can this be fair?
Seeing myself, as I was losing my hair
Suddenly I was losing the will to live
Hadn't I given most all I could give?
To turn back the time I'd give all I own
I watch my family, who must now go on alone
but now "God" calls and to Him I must answer
He's calling me home, healing my 'bout with cancer.

    —*Laura L. Manning*

So As The Many Ways Of Love For You

My love for you is like a daisy;

Compare the many petal's of a daisy,
   so as the many ways of love for you.
Every petal is the same yet each unique,
   so as the many ways of love for you.

A single petal may fall short of the others.
   Yet still hold so much beauty,
   so as the many ways of love for you.

Half of the petals may curve toward the sun
   although one is equal to the other,
   so as the many ways of love for you.

To combine everyone's beauty forms one sweet flower,
   so as the many ways of love for you.
That complete daisy causes an inner warmth,
   so as the many ways of love for you.

My love for you is like a daisy....

    —*Kimberly Honaker*

Country, Sweet Country

Country, sweet country; there! a solace, I can find, Oh! so divine.
There! my love for nature and animals can intertwine.
Country, sweet country, as sweet as the misty dew on the
morning glory vine.
There! I find quiet rest and sweet peace, while basking
in the warm, cozy sunshine.

I leave my "homey", country home to go to the office in the
city for pay.
I return to my "paradise" at the close of a tiring day.
I, then, am in perfect peace with man and God.
Money cannot buy my "little piece of the precious sod."

    —*Lila Cannon Daugherty*

Poem of the Aged

What do you do when your old?
Some just sit around to be told?

Can we only be in the grey,
Just as if, we've had too much hay?

What shall we compensate, remaining time.
Can our God be so kind:

Again will we see the colors, blue, white, and red,
Are the things we're to see, only from our beds?

Will this planet be able to hold,
Both, the very young, and very old

    —*Bernadine Cusamino*

The Mallards

Two male ducks gliding by
So elegant in their rich attire
Dark green satin for their fine heads
Majestically they glide the ebb.

Chocolate feathers adorn their backs,
Snow white accents peeking through.
Scouting diligently for their food,
Preparing the way for Mother's brood.

Thirteen tiny balls of fluff,
Mother duck can get quite tough,
When babies wander inquisitively,
Floating thither and yond; so much to see.

Quack! Quack! the female speaks,
The scattered puffballs rejoin the group.
Elegantly she leads the small formation,
One almost hears the orchestration.

Back through the canal she begins to steer.
The baby ducklings have no fear
As Majestically we see so clear
The two male ducks bringing up the rear!

—*Doris E. Lamdin*

So Far Away

So long,
So far away
Is Africa
Our native land

Forced from our home and all its pleasures,
Africa coast we left on ships to America
Captured and chained by slave traders
Taken from our families

So long,
So far away
Is Africa
Our native land

Bought to America
A strange land and sold for a profit
Belonging to another person called master
Places in the fields
Sometimes in the master's home
Cleaning, cooking and taking care of his children

So long, so far away
Is African our native land

—*Evan B. Farrior*

Recycled Teenager

What I see in my future is "I hope" a long and healthy life.
So I can keep on dancing and cope with air pollution after
sixty-five. I also see a monorail through all of U S A so we
can breath and beat the smog and high insurance rate. I see a
free "will of choice" if I get ever sick. So I can tell to
live; or stop my heart to tick. I also want my kids to pick
their own amount of tots. Only what they can afford instead of
lots and lots. Who has the right to say what I do with my
life. Who says I have to inhale smoke I utterly despise. The
future will be a perfect place in 1992. Give us one year to
unite with one outstanding man. To be our leader, we never saw
before. Let 's count our blessings much, and many more. Have
faith, we're all children from one God. Avoid the negative,
try to laugh a lot. They call us "Senior Citizen," I'd rather.
be called "Recycled Teenager" for that matter. The future I
see and will order. is one of peace on earth, border to border.

—*Kay Riet*

The Tide

As the tide is going back to the sea,
so I follow the motion.

The new found land, now uncovered,
displays new adventure, treasures
and remembrances of day's familiar.
This new land is sought with strength.

the sun warms your face,
dries the mist and grows a smile.

The days tend to be shallow,
Some crisp breezes waft through my soul
Alerting my senses I turn.

There are many faces, many treasures.
the sun warms your face,
dries the mist and grows a smile.

—*Robert John Crosser, Jr.*

The Old House

Old house sitting on the hill,
So lonely and bare and still.
No voices now fill your hall,
Nor laugh, nor whisper, nor call.
There's no patter of little feet,
Nor baby talk low and sweet.
Your hearth holds no crackling fire.
There are no dreams nor desire.
Proud you were with head held high
When loved ones stood warmly by;
Bereft of love you may fall.
Does not love sustain us all?
Oh that I could see them still
Whom you sheltered on that hill.

—*Fred C. Stanley*

Twilight Years

So many races that I'd like to run,
So many things not finished though begun,
So many worldly things in which I might partake
It makes my weary body grieve and ache
To think how many things in life have passed me by
And knowing soon must come my time to die,
So twilight years move slowly, I beg you
I have unfinished tasks that I must do.

There are so many recipes that hide
Within my cookbook lying there untried.
There are so many pictures in my mind
But time to paint them I don't seem to find.
There are so many books that I've not read,
So many things to say that I've not said.
So many full, full hours, it seems that's why
The time speeds on until it's time to die.
So twilight years, move slowly, I beg you,
I have unfinished joys awaiting, too!

—*Margaret Ann Halvorsen*

'Lesley'

You were as a majestic raven
Soaring in the night
You were as an immaculate spirit
Prancing in the light
Your soul shines pure + clean
Brighter than the moon glows
Things I don't have the guts to think of
Come pouring out your spout like rainbows
I thank you for answering me
The burning question
 What's on top of the mountain

—*John Maggs*

A Bird Named Recession

There once was A man
So proud and true
That he knew exactly what to do

Then came the bird
That he wished he never knew
For the birds name was recession
Full of depression through and through

Recession flew high and wide
Causing the economic recovery to hide
And the middle class cried

Indecision was his companion
Mental tic tac toe was his plight
But was he right
This is what he thought of night after night
But recession still flew at morning light

—*Joseph P. Contento*

Fawn

My favorite cow, her name is Fawn
So tall in black and white
Tied in her stall from dust to dawn
This holstein is quite a sight!

Eating her silage, hay, and grain
Waiting anxiously for her turn
To the milking parlor to relieve the strain
Back to the barn she will return.

Milk, milk, milk
Into the tank it goes
It's cool and fresh and smooth as silk
Drink to take away your woes.

She's an excellent at ninety-five
For a long time we hope she survives!

—*Adam Elsass*

War

All are the same as before,
    so totally sad, that's for sure.
We all sit and wait in despair,
    for untold stories from over there.
Helpless as we all feel,
    our tears and worry of the whole ordeal.

God to help them with his strength.
    God to carry them with his faith.

To be strong for all is what we can do,
    listen, cry and be there to help them too.

Just knowing that we are here,
    can make them feel they are near.
We can give them our support,
    to help carry them on to each new port.

Taking a short time each day,
    to think of them so far away.

How we hate to hear the news,
    but can't seem to break loose.
As we watch with tears in our eyes,
    so important to all our lives.

—*Linda O'Hallaran*

A Dream Come True

Once in a dream his face appeared, a smile
so warm almost an embrace
When I awoke I couldn't dismiss the
Thoughts of him though I knew he said
goodbye without a trace.
The desire to say hello once more became
stronger and stronger in my heart
I knew there must be a reason for this
but I was lost at where to start
Through search and prayer I found
him again and heard his beautiful voice
His words were warm and caring too, they
made my heart rejoice.
Now I know why this dream came to me,
it came to mend my heart.
To let it know that true love never
dies and never is in vain.
Years cannot change the love we lose
it can be found again.

—*Barbara Sturcken*

Peace On Earth

This is our world, in which we live.
So why is it so difficult for some to give?
To think about others, not only yourself,
To share in the happiness, and in the wealth.
There are so many people, who are truly in need.
And too many people, with a quality called greed.
We must help the homeless, before time runs out.
We must be able to feed, every hungry mouth.
Poverty stricken people, deserve to be free,
From disease, and all other, types of misery.
No more lives being shattered, by the use of drugs.
Instead, let's all turn, to more love and hugs.
No more abuse, and no more neglect,
No more crimes, such as forcible sex.
Let's all clean our environment
More and more everyday.
Let's all work together,
For a better way.

—*Ellen Gouskos*

Martin Luther Kings Plan

There stood Martin Luther King
Soaring on an eagles wing
I have a dream, he said
and those powerful words
have led to an acceptance
which was long over due
for the black community
this is so true.
Slavery and segregation
is where it began, peace and justice
was Martin Luther Kings plan.
An assassins bullet shortened
his life and took him from
his children and wife.
We must work together to make peace anew.
So Martin Luther Kings dreams will come true.

—*Jodie Thibault*

625

Easter Travelers

High on the Judean slopes
soft breezes whir through
the juniper trees.
Deep in the valleys
lilies wave their innocence.
Not wasted riches, but all
unseen by travelers two.

As they round the bend
pink oleanders dot
the stony courtyards,
wafting their invitation.
Suddenly, a stranger alongside
inquires the despairing souls.
Like a laser, He shares the Holy Scroll.

As the afternoon sun pales the sky
lamps glow in the tiny abode.
Abiding in fellowship light,
we behold His nail scarred hands.
Now we understand
our Risen Lord - Rose of Sharon.

  —*Dorthalene S. Hutchings*

Stages Of Life

Touching the candle briefly, the flame sprang to life giving a
soft, warm glow. It's brightness slowly increased until soft
shadows danced, seemingly happy; about the room, various new
shapes forming and uniting with others until a single, warm
glow reappeared; firm and unwavering, yet still soft as before.

Then the breeze began to rise with infinite gentleness, though
in reality not yet even a breeze, but a warm summer zephyr
that went seemingly unnoticed by the flame until the intensity
increased and the flame wavered back and forth, slowly
diminishing and darkening, then springing ever so briefly back
to life, only to die anew; leaving the room in an apparent
darkened state. Though but a moment in time, the darkness
seemed to continue into aeons as minute sparks, barely visible,
yet not discerned by the darkness, slowly reunited and joined
together, unfettered, and not disturbed by the now abated
breeze. And the light began anew, as before, to shine in the
darkness, And the darkness did never comprehend it.

  —*Francis Lee Mc Carthy*

Black Faces

Black people, the most beautiful and stunning, I've yet to see.
Some are Princely ... Noble ... Stately ... Beau Monde but
all are sacred .... Mahogany faces, the darkest I've ever seen
... with an abiding strength there that speaks of times passed
.... Faces, unblemished and unpenetrated, with an inner soul.
Old faces, scooting along but bent by life's infinite hand.
Faces, frowned in stone, by this America land .... And still
other faces, blurred and slurred, by bigots and radicals.
Almost white faces ... of gentility .... Almost black faces
... subliminal .... Faces, almost sincere and victorious,
expecting life to throw a breath of hope ... yet, determined
to hold on, to linger in spite of life's diversities.
Invisible faces, smashed, crushed and smeared by unfulfilled
dreams. Faces, looking up toward heaven, pondering the reason
for their existence .... Then, they trust their words, in
unison, into inaudible sounds of internal confusion. Faces,
wondering and reasoning the idea of the black man's creation,
and searching for their places in this cosmic flow of creation.

  —*Elliot Dugar*

"Love Takes Time"

Not all love begins at first sight.
Some take a little time;
Some take a lot of time.
Becoming friends is important
when you love the person;
You need to get along
and confide in one another.
Trust is, also, a needed asset.
Some people trust easily;
some people need convincing.
If that trust is broken,
it is not easily rebuilt.
You have to work on relationships;
they don't get better without some work.
Patience is very valuable.
You can't lose it very often
Without seeing some harmful effects.
Love takes time to grow and become strong.

  —*Corinne Dallmann Denloss*

What Does The Flag Mean To You?

Some call me old glory, some the red, white and blue,
Some the grand old flag, what do I mean to you.

I've been in all the wars, just to mention a few!
The civil war, world war I, world war II, Korea, Vietnam,
And the Gulf War, too. What do I mean to you?

Some stand at attention and salute me as I pass by,
And on other occasions they look to the sky,
To see me waving proudly. For the past and future I fly.

Thousands have shed their blood for me and thousands have died.
But all those who have done so did it with pride.

So I say to you America - the patriotic majority,
Not the ungrateful few-keep me flying high, for I'm the red,

white and blue. Don't let them burn me or cut me to shreds,
Or use me for a door mat; Don't let me fall.
Don't let them desecrate me, yes those ungrateful
Few, the ones that don't love the red, white and blue.
For I represent freedom, liberty and justice for all;
And I shall wave proudly as you stand tall.

Yes, I'm old glory, I'm your grande old flag. I'm your red,
white and blue, and I know I mean more than desecration to you.

  —*James C. Lyons*

A Guiding Light

A guiding light is what I need,
Someone to help me sort out my needs,
Someone to help me sort out my life,
To put all my problems out of sight.

Problems I hope to see no more,
Just as if I've shut a door,
A door in my head that can never be opened,
That way my guiding light will win.

But once in a while memory creeps back,
And it's nice to know my guiding light is there,
To help put things back.

So you can see what kind of friend my guiding
light can be,
So take my advice and find someone who cares,
And they'll stay behind you
For the rest of your years.

  —*Kristal Gail Osment*

"I Want to Meet Someone"

Lord - I want to meet someone,
Someone who's loyal and true,
Someone full of love and fun,
Lord - someone more like you.

I want to meet someone,
Someone respectful of what I say,
Someone with ol' time character,
Who'd when I'm right feel the same way.

Lord I want to meet someone,
Whose christian and righteous too,
Someone who both knows and does what he says,
Well Lord - where's someone more
Like you?

Lord - I want to be someone,
Someone sweet and pure and true,
Someone of whom others can say,
Lord - she's so very much. Like You!

—*Elsie McMahan*

A Friend

A friend is someone who really cares,
Someone you can talk to who is always there.
A friend is someone who won't stab you in the back,
Someone that won't tell lies only facts.
A friend is someone who likes just me,
Not trying to change or tell how I should be.
A friend is someone who won't discriminate,
Or someone who will never intimidate.
A friend is someone who wouldn't fear,
And never being afraid to show me a tear.
A friend is someone I can always talk to,
A person who believes in everything I do.
A friend is someone who is there forever and more,
Who will help to heal my heart when it is sore.
A friend is someone for me who will fend.
    Tell me can you be that friend!!!

—*Richard Graham*

A Tearful Good Bye

Her love for him was so very much,
something no one else could touch.
His love for her was just the same,
she was someone he could trust.

But then about a month ago, she changed, so very much.

And now, looking down upon her face, her family cries,
because she died, they miss her so very much.

He realized now that he loved her more than he thought
and he wonders what would have happened if
he had made her stop.
Her drinking and driving caused her death,
I hope you can see, that: Drinking and driving will not
set you free.

—*Christy Hendricks*

Beginnings

The sun arose to signal past
    The ending of the night at last
To spread the warmth and lift the dew
    To mist to start a day anew
Such majesty in silence rise
    And heralded by lighted skies
Who else but God could bring to be
    This brand new day-This brand new day

—*Rod Morris*

If Only You Would Have Known Me

"Mr. Drunk Driver," I need to talk to you today, there's been
something that was left unsaid since that day you took my
breath away. As I only met you for a moment you didn't give
me time to speak, so I hope that now you'll listen though my
voice is still and weak. You see, I don't mean to be
judgmental as I didn't know your friend Jack Daniel's the way
you do, but if only you would have know me you would have liked
me, too. I had so much more to offer than he could have ever
given you, why'd you have him with you——look what he made you
do! There's a favor I must ask of you as I sacrificed my young
life for you, please stay away from my friends and family,
don't meet them on the center line, too. Don't take someone
else's child away, get rid of your old friend, Jack, don't make
someone else's mom and dad wish they had their loved one back.
We were young and we deserved a chance to fulfill our childhood
dreams, for you and Jack to take our breath away so senseless
and so mean. I always thought that death would be lonely but
you didn't send me here alone, you and Jack met three more of
my friends on that fatal dusty road.

—*Linda Boldt*

"Souls In Love"

    Something in me changed since the day you died.
    Something warm and dear—now holds an emptiness inside.
        That emptiness is like a deep, dark hole
    That aches in the darkness of the depths of my soul.
        All those days when I felt I couldn't go on
    The love of our child gave me the courage to be strong.
    All our loving memories shall be treasured until
                the end of time.
        And, it's those same loving memories that
                will help me bide mine.
    Although we'll never again know a love like ours-
Our souls will share eternity when those heavenly bells
chime.

—*Kathy Churchill-Sulak*

Pa'paw Wolfe

Sometimes I feel lonely, sometimes I feel afraid.
Sometimes I feel secure, sometimes I feel safe.
But most of the time I know that you're there,
Because I can feel you when you are near.
You may be close, you may be far,
And I still love you wherever you are.
Wherever you are, wherever you may be,
I still remember the way you shined with glee.
I keep wishing and wishing on that same bright star,
That you are happy wherever you are.
I love you so, so very much,
The way you felt, the way you touched.
I want you to know that I miss you,
And without a doubt I still love you!

—*Angela Dickey*

"It Is Spring"

There's a song in the air,
Soft, smooth sailing!
And a gentle breeze, gives a sense of ease
As the oars splash forth unfailing!

The trees just ahead
Have a comforting spread
With leaves of silver and gold,
Shadows are seen with light in between
And there is a beautiful bird!

Its song that is heard
Strikes a note full and free
    It's spring!

—*Irene C. Pemberton*

"I Am"

At times I do wonder. Just who am I?
Sometimes I have it together - sometimes I cry,
Sometimes I'm happy - sometimes I feel
I'm going insane,
Sometimes things are serious - sometimes
It all feels like a game,
It's all about you - it's all about me,
It's about life, a university,
I am, I am,

At times things are hot - at times they're cold,
It could be young - it could be old,
It could be shaky - it could be sound,
It could be answers - or none to be found,
It's all about you - it's all about me,
It's about life, a university,
I am, I am,
Oh my Lord - I am amen...

—*Frank Commedo*

The Day Our Child Is Born

See him move inside of you, it must feel really weird.
Sometimes I think about it, and I feel a little scared.
Soon we will be Mom and Dad, our names we will be called,
By the child that grows inside of you, and soon he will be born.
It's really lovely to discover what a joy in life can be.
As we wait in expectation for the gift from God to see.
Now we share in love and laughter as we watch him kick and move.
And to think of that creation that has grown inside your womb.
As we're waiting, being patient, as the time and hour is near,
when this child wins a smile from his Mom and Dad who care.
As we spend our time and keep in mind our responsibility.
That we're needed, and to be there when our child has a need.
Give a bottle, change a diaper, give a bath, but not too hot.
Rock him gently, when he's cranky, cause his tummy is upset.
So till then we'll have to wait until that time and hour.
We'll wait and watch and pray the Lord will keep us in His power.
Time will pass and we will have as a new day has dawn,
a chance to see this joy of life, the day our child is born.

—*Daniel J. Beaulieu*

The Guitar

The guitar you gave me lies beside a chest in the attic
sometimes the wind glides across the strings
and I can hear music again listen

I followed your lead as brother and sister harmonized with
notes, chords, hearts beat strong, rackets extended out to slam
ball against wall laughing competitors
you told me you'd always win

The lyric changes
discordant notes wail awhile now
your image alters
withered body and mind, hollow as the guitar frame
I played "Amazing Grace" for you but felt no mercy from Him
then listen
nothing the music stopped just like you

Sometimes I hear your voice
in the wind gliding across the strings asking me to play for
you again coaxing me to hear music
but for today the guitar you gave me lies beside a chest in the attic
while a heart within beats broken rhythms

—*Betsy Goetz*

Faces

We see all kinds of faces,
Sometimes we see...
Sad faces,
Glad faces,
And sometimes we even see mad faces.

We see all kinds of faces,
Sometimes we see...
Happy faces,
Smiley faces,
And sometimes we even see mean, nasty faces.

We see all kinds of faces,
Sometimes we see...
Surprised faces,
Scared faces,
Hungry faces,
And sometimes we even see crying faces.

Sometimes we the saddest faces...
Dead faces...
The hardest for most of us to look at,
or to face!

—*Robert Swearingen*

Life

Life is purely amazing,
Sometimes you feel like balling it up
and throwing it away.
Sometimes you can cherish it
even cradle it like a newborn baby.

Life is sometimes put out of your mind
and everything around you have disappeared,
your locked up inside yourself
motionless, speechless, thoughtless,
without sight.
You're in total darkness.
You lose self control and become spellbound
as if in space.

Sometimes it is a flickering light
that shines in your mind abundantly
and is only conscious of your needs,
hopes, and dreams.

—*Lori Watts*

The Clown

With a single tear he bares the
souls of the children.
Their ear-to-ear smile
stretched and embedded in their cheeks
reflect in his sepulchral grin.

His eyes are prophetic of the
lies they'll hear,
the pain they'll abide.

His brows crouched at their
elders leading the ignorantly
to the shallowness of this
unattainable rainbow
which ends
in a glittering crock.

—*Christine Darling*

The Art of Noise, Moments in Love,

Over and Over I hear the
sound of the music - no sense, it
will make no time, it will
take a song for love, one moment one memory
Love all for a four lettered word
love what a powerful word, it is
love, so powerful, that it can
turn a dead heart and make it sing,
And a put out candle is lit again,
For she is beautiful, she is a true
work of art, with her I will never part
She is a virgin, untouched and unharmed, so
gentle and fragile like a cloud in the sky
or the ocean, love to be or not to be
She is the peacemaker for me
You will love her, she will love you
Love is everything forever too.

—*Bleu Roberts*

Do You Hear The Bomb's?

Quiet my child, do you hear?
Sounds of missiles heading here.
Awake from your slumber one last time'
let me hug you, young heart of mine.

One last glance at your eyes of blue,
in Heaven, we'll meet, me and you.
Laugh one more time, my sweet dear,
for after tonight we won't be here.

Let me hold you close to my heart,
when we die our spirits won't part.
Let me sing one last Lullaby,
close your eyes, please don't cry.

Here they come, they're getting near,
in my arms, you need not fear.
In thirty more seconds we'll both be dead,
close your eyes now, rest your head......

—*Holly Guldenshuh-Krol*

Beautiful In His Time

The words of Emerson, so revered.
Spoken in truth, we should adhere.
"Never miss a chance to appreciate beauty -
For beauty is the handwriting of God" -
To look for such; 'tis a privilege, not a duty -
while on this earthly walk, we trod.

Before us is a visual feast,
Picture dawn-breaking in the east -
Sunset masterpieces, slowly erased,
By twilight, with the Evening star in place -
Our Creator's handiwork, freely given -
Bestowed as gifts, for all the living -

However we choose to view His gifts -
The choice is yours and mine -
To consider, all that is good and fine.
Let us receive and celebrate with joy -
Knowing, He hath made everything,
Beautiful in His time.

—*Frances Moss Taylor*

From Pink

Eraser dust with love to you, Tristesse.
Sprawling, the airport buzzes on the right.
Tailpipes puff smoke rings, you shake your tresses.

A tattered sketch, worn through in places, I'm
a sharp-angled stick figure, bleeding white
eraser dust with love to you, Tristesse.

Tomorrow I scatter from your kisses.
You warn me eons run through this red light.
Tailpipes puff smoke rings, you shake you tresses.

The page is pure for you, at last out West,
across mountains: avalanches of slight
eraser dust with love to you, Tristesse.

The light turns green, the traffic crawls still less.
Will you think of being with me some night?
Tailpipes puff smoke rings, you shake your tresses.

Not that I blame you, Tristesse, I confess.
My heart is cluttered, full of faces, tight
eraser dust with love to you, Tristesse.
Tailpipes puff smoke rings, you shake your tresses.

—*Greg Thorson*

The Seasons

Seasons come and seasons go, each with a gift on us to bestow.
Spring gives us blooming trees, returning birds, beautiful
flowers, warm breezes and refreshing showers. Summer present
us longer days, time for picnics, cook-out. A time for lots
of fun. We work we play, we are ready to go. Summer, oh
summer we love you so! Autumn, colors our world, a sight to
behold. With leaves of yellow, purple and gold. Nature
decides it is time to rest. Relax my children, of forest land
or sea. Enjoy the beauty I have given to you. Winter oh winter
hear my plea. What is the gift you have for me. The flowers
have faded the cold winds blow. Frost sparkles like diamonds
on bare limbs of trees. Beautiful snowflakes fall softly.
Thanks, winter for your gifts to me.

—*Beatrice F. Thacker*

Seasons

The seasons of life have swiftly passed. Youthful
springtime filled with wonder, laughter and love is but a memory.

The fruitful summer days, of promises fulfilled and rich
harvests all too soon were gone.

I walk serenely now among the falling leaves and soft blue
haze of autumn.

Lord when I must go, let me leave in the glow of Indian
summer while I still feel life and beauty around me.

Let me not linger through a cold sterile winter, but fall
asleep unknowing 'til some distant spring when I rise again
with the daffodils.

—*Erma Holden*

To The Sun

When your eyes meet mine, the clocks will stop and so will time.
The feeling will be, that I am yours and you are mine.
The eruption will flow with speed and contempt,
to burn and melt our silent walls.
For it is there that we will feel
emotions...
true and shining as they are.
We must pass in time and spirit, this impassable ordeal.
To realize the love we have; and overcome these things we feel.

—*Freddy R. Geib*

Adjustment

She sat there in the familiar shabby chair now
squeezed into a corner of the small,
neat-as-a-pin room.
She gazed around, seeing only the chest of drawers
that was "hers" and the few
pictures that were remnants
from the old place.

She looked at me a slight smile on her lips and
lifting her chin, said:
    "Oh, I'll adjust."
    ("Of course you will-you'll
      be comfortable here")

At that she looked away from me
and stared out the window,
thinking, no doubt, of the many
adjustments she had made
during her ninety two years.

—*Betty Trezona*

Birds In Flight

Distant mountain, standing guard,
Standing guard in the night. Spider's web,
covered with dew, field so covered, shimmer
frosty and cold, it's magical to behold. Hidden
birds in fields of green, Imperial Valley is
to be seen. Stars like diamonds, diamonds
like ice, that's winter's night. Summer's day,
the dust devils play, the fields, are scorched,
by burning sun. The roads do melt, nothing
can be done, tell summer's night.
Moonlight shining, people running, past
the mountain, that stands guard, people
running in the night, like birds in flight.
Coyote hid, waiting, waiting, will they,
soon, be in sight? Distant mountain
standing guard, standing guard this night.

—*Brenda G. Childers*

"Rain"

Bursts of fury burning the roof.
Steely eyes,
Speculating my every move.
A cloud of dampness lurking.
Tantalizing shadows incarnating my body.
A demon's eye shining darkness,
piercing my heart.
Deadly claws, gripping,
tearing at my chest.
I sit as a soldier
pressed to the surface,
fear of every breath
    movement
        sound.
Silent but deafening.
Outside but inside.
Foreboding clouds envelope my body.
Limp, unconscious.
I enter into my soul
paralyzed, until dawn.

—*Courtney Rosenthal*

Woman With A Knife

Brandings today, you will find,
still show male domination.
Women, when they're allowed to help,
mostly tally and do calf vaccinations.

More and more women at brandings
are lending their help all around,
from roping and dragging critters in,
to wrestling calves to the ground.

But none of the jobs these women do
cause the men such strife,
as when she's cutting bull calves,
and her hand is wielding a knife.

The men on the ground fall silent,
nervous, and wanting to run.
They flinch as the woman nears them
and heave a huge sigh when she's done.

"I don't mind a woman cutting calves,
they do a fine job and such....."
explained one old cowboy earnestly,
"They just shouldn't enjoy it so much!"

—*Gina M. Stevens*

The Storm

There comes a time when the wind
    stops blowing and laughter fades away.
The rain and clouds shut out
    the sun, and want for a new day.
Feelings of anger shatter your heart,
you feel like escape, let your soul be free.
A new idea fills your head,
    you're as calm as you will ever be.
The rain falls as fast as the
    tears start to trickle down your face.
You're like a god, you're in control,
    like a runner you've set your own pace.
Now the rain is pouring down, the clock
    in your head stops, you breathe your
    final breath.
The lightening strikes, the thunder
    pounds, another soul has found
        out about death.

—*Danielle Mroz*

Violence

The streets are crying loud and long
streaming blood through shattered song
there is no justice to be found amidst the tragedy.

Gone are the days of joyful hope where children played and
elders joked and streets were filled with merriment;
when life was more than pay the rent.

There used to be the common specter, rich or poor or in between
life had a purpose far beyond the gathering of the green.

Neighbors shared all that they owned
strangers welcomed into homes and no one need to be alone
unless they so desired.

Now we never ever stop to help those on our way.
We simply go around their pain or pass some another way.

It is no wonder that the streets are crying out with fright
and taking up the violence in the middle of the night.

We must step back into the past and salvage what was best.
We must take up our brothers load
and let the child rest.

There is no stranger in the town, there is no enemy -
more frightening than the violence that lives inside of me.

—*Donna Davis*

Sisters and Brothers Think

The Devotion coming from an innocent black woman with the
strength to raise a child alone and the virtue of envy, for not
having the support coming from a black man.

The illusion of the african man being an endanger species,
hounded by the economic structure, appropriate to the world and
the psyche, attributed to the myth pertaining to white supremacy.

The power connected to an illegal substance, that makes people
abandon the true focus of living a long prosperous life,
eluding to anything to catch that cloud, get that high or fix.

  —*James Keith Wright*

When There Is No End In Sight

When there is no end in sight... the rivers still flow, the
sun continues to shine and the world never stops revolving.
When there is no end in sight... life goes on. When there is
no end in sight... we must find the light in what appears to be
infinite darkness. When there is no end in sight... we have to
carry on. Just take a look at those who have preceded you...
Mothers, grandmothers, aunts and friends... I mention women
because they have been my special inspiration... it seems that
they persevere when no one else can... they make it because
they know they can. I look at my mother, Flora... she moved
and spoke with such graciousness... on the exterior there was
beauty and signs of fragility... on the inside durability
reigned. When there is no end in sight... I look at Mama.
When there is no end in sight... I remember her struggle.
When there is no end in sight... I now know there is no
infinite darkness. When there is no end in sight... there is
a beautiful gateway which opens into a world full of options.
As Mama always said... children, the world is your oyster.

  —*Sammie L. Orr*

Among God's Gifts

Among God's wondrous gifts...
Sun, sky and sea.

Most precious of them all,
His undying love for you and me.

His love for you and me is so great;
He sent His only beloved son Jesus for our sins to
  compensate.

God created mankind to glorify His name,
And be of service to one another.

  —*Martha Soldorfen*

Strange Silence

The intrinsic beauty of love exists in a state of grace —
  surrounded by shadows and lines.
Contrasts of light and dark
  spin in images of love and fear.
   Spinning and intertwining.
Light and dark clinging together, struggling for survival —
  they must exist for each other, against each other.
Wrapped in a visual explosion
  that reflects an insane world.

A thought that tears at the mind, at the heart —
  How one person's feelings for another can
   vanish so quickly —
    without warning.
And the pain it causes the forgotten person —
  an intense eternal ache, deep within the soul —
   and beyond.

But I keep searching.
I reach into that strange silence of existence and I hope...
I hope for the sound of love.

  —*Grechen Lynne Wingerter*

Sunrise

I sit, perched precariously on the edge of night
surrounded by yawning darkness...I wait, I wonder...
dreaming...strangely being drawn into NOW...

The watery womb of Terra will soon give birth to crimson
light of morning... nightingale's song joins in the harmony
of the stars in early morning sky.

Who am I? What am I? How am I? Why am I.. in this moment
of NOW?
(...and the journey into radical nothingness begins)
Child of Terra Sancta...incomplete, yearning, unfulfilled,
restless Dreamer, vulnerable Lover, Sojourner...
longing for wholeness...

Ever being born...ever dying...the ecstacy of choosing
is mine!

  —*Kathleen Kutz*

Lost Thoughts

Lying awake staring at the ceiling
Surrounded with only darkness revealing

Seeing nothing, hearing not a single sound
Feeling nothing, but my heart beat become a pound

Thinking of all the things that bring me fear
Like being lonely, with no one to talk to, nor no one near

Lost in thoughts that stir so deep within
Searching for answers, but not knowing where to begin

Closing my eyes wishing only to sleep
As the tears fall upon my face as I weep

  —*Denise M. Cox*

To a Child Who Isn't Starving

You will wake up tomorrow morning,
Sweet little child of mine.
I know you will see the new day dawning
Because you are safe all the time.

But, in a country far away,
Children are dying every day.
Mothers are weeping, fathers are too,
There isn't a thing that they can do.

The sun is hot, the earth is dry,
They can't buy the food which money can buy.
We have enough grain to build into mountains
And milk which can easily flow into fountains.

That we have so much seems so unfair.
I suppose those poor people must think we don't care.
Perhaps, someone in power will see some sense
And give them the food at our expense.

So, darling child, you can help as you grow.
You can make sure the future will bring
Help and hope to all the people you know,
In the world, who don't own anything.

  —*Barbara Kindon*

631

Drink Me With Your Eyes

Drink me with your eyes...
Take me by surprise...
Our yearning voluminized...

Bring me to your heart—
Let me feel it's beat—
Never let me go, I need you to know—

Bring me to your soul—
I want to live inside—
We, no longer need to hide—

Drink me with your eyes...
Taste the passion inside...
Never let me go, I need you to know—
Silent beauty your face fascinates me—

Thirst for me... cry for me...
Smile for me... belong to me...
  Feel me... breathe me...
    Embrace me...
My Divine and Enchanted Love,
We burn together, we're chained together—
  Unveil my innocent world...

  —*Marie Agozzino*

My Cloak

And I will stand on my own feet.
Tall and straight with the pride
of centuries as my cloak.

See its train, it be stretch'n back
  for centuries.
This cloak is not complete yet and
  probably never will be.

For I will pass it on to those behind
  with this,
"You must add to it, you are part of the
  fabric.
Your life holds it together.
DON'T LET NOTHING, NOTHING SOIL IT,
For you see, this cloak is your history."

  —*John-Douglas McMillan*

The Humming-Bird's Wing

My heart heavy with sorrow, I stood on the hill
Tears were coursing down my cheeks;
Then beside me I heard a sound and turn to see
A humming-bird, sweet nectar it did seek.

But beyond it was a vision
Faint and very pale;
Then my mother's voice spoke to me
She told a heart felt tale.

Oh don't weep for me and daddy
Be glad, for can't you see;
For even in your sorrow
Things are so right for him and me.

There is no more sickness and worries
Just sunshine, flowers and peace;
So my little girl, smile and be happy
Then your pain will ease.

Weep no more—weep no more
Her voice came so soft and seem to sing;
Then with a soft flutter the shadow vanished
On the humming-birds wing.

  —*Gloria Davis*

The Gates Of Hell

I was in The Gates Of Hell, the things we saw we could not
tell. I was hungry and was cold, my body looked so frail and
and old. My parents died without a doubt, so they could not
have helped me out. Somehow I was always afraid the Nazis
tortured me so, they gave me beatings after beatings and one
blow after blow. I tried to live from day to day and managed
to survive, I think I have done very well and now I am alive.
They made me walk they made me scream, they made me torture
with each dream. They made me work they made me sick, they
made my mind just like a brick. They made me crawl out in the
snow, they said walk fast if not we'll blow. They made me
work they made me weak, they made my future turn to bleak.
I have a number on my arm, the Nazis laughed and sneered
with charm. I have survived and am now well, I have survived
the Gates of Hell.

  —*Elaine H. Shanker*

A Mother's Pride

On this special day of yours, just had to let you know
That as your mother I am proud, and had to let it show

You've been a joy and always will be everything to me
Through your life I've come to see that dreams are meant to be

You saw the things you wanted and reached for them each day
Nothing was too hard for you, you knew there was a way

A beauty you have come to be, a lovely one so rare
But truly on the inside you shine beyond compare

For in your heart lies such a love of life and creatures all
And through your life I've come to see the dreams I can recall

Of having a dear daughter whose caring, loving, true
And God did richly bless me with a child sweet as you

  —*Phyllis Rubadeau*

Life's Blessings

Let's count some blessings we all hold
That can't be bought and can't be sold
The many beauties of the earth.
The greatest gift the one of birth,
The spring so fresh, the waking tree,
These all give joy to you and me,
The rose bud opening through the day,
And peace when kneeling down to pray
The wonders of the heavenly skies,
The sadness when a loved one dies,
But God will wipe away all tears,
Still the heart and calm the fears,
We can't begin to understand
The many wonders of this land
All the mysteries of the sea
We just accept that it will be
And so it is with daily life
Sometimes the peace and then the strife,
But even so we all should say
We thank Thee Lord for this thy day.

  —*Trudy Woodford*

632

"Cherished Memories"

Aunt Bertha's house is a cherished place, a childhood memory
that can't be erased. I drove past it the other day; it's not
the same you see, it's tattered and worn, doesn't have the look
of care, it's not the way it used to be. It's blue now, was
gray then, Lilies of the valley were planted along the walkway,
welcoming people in. The grass was trimmed, airy curtains at
the windows beckoned within. Rocking chairs lined the porch
when I was a child of five, and all the rooms would come alive.
Alive with prayer, laughter and song; oh for those days how I
long. Poems were read each night, after we climbed into bed
and cuddled up tight. When dawn would break, and I would wake,
I'd lie there just for comfort's sake. While the hand wound
clock would gently tick, I'd lie there until someone hollered,
"Get up quick!" Off I'd go to the kitchen to see Aunt Bertha
preparing breakfast for me. The table was set with a white
linen cloth; a small shaded lamp sat on top. It's glow was
warm, a comfort to me; those were memories meant to be. We
would gather together to start our day, then I would go out
happily to play. My favorite place to spend time, was under
the grape-arbor vine. It had a swing made of rope and wood;
I'd swing as high as I possibly could. My toes would touch
the leaves above; the aroma of grapes I truly loved. When I
would tire of swinging high, I would play in the back shed,
by and by. What fun I had in that old shed, sometimes I would
play until it was time for bed. Forty four years have passed since
then, each forming cherished memories of way back when.

—*Margaret Kurtzman*

The Moment

I celebrate the prism of paradox
  That embraces the flow streaming swiftly beyond
   The wonderment of our contrary thoughts

  Scattered clouds caress consciousness
  That abounds with miracles laying otherwise unknown

Spirit, feelings, future fanaticism, fragments of the past
When fears of realization touch deep the heart of love

  A reality too real, A dream too lurid
  Unleashing the pure heart where the humble strength lies

  Love in dreaming, Reality screaming
  The scarlet fire flourishes in the night

  Embellished beyond senses, Abolished pretenses
  Concluding whence the coming of the dawn

And again, deep in the eyes of love everlasting
  Emotion is masking the fear lying for all to see, touch, be
  In the garden where only time can free

  And the greatness of life flies majestically

   Life is the moment
    —*Ben Tanler*

My Promise

I made a promise to you the day you were born.
That I would not be like another, the chain would be broken.
I promised you there would be no violence.
Not like another.
I promised you my love would be pure.
Not like another.
I promised you I would safely tuck you into bed.
Not like another.
I promised you I would not be your fears.
Not like another.
I promised you I would be there to protect you.
Not like another.
I have kept my promise to you, now the link is gone, the chain
has been broken.
There won't be another.

  —*Bonnie L. Swanson*

Fond Memories

Of all the scenes from my childhood days,
  That I can remember best;
Is an old oak tree on Ozark hill,
  That stood taller than the rest.

Grandpa would lean on its mighty trunk,
  And I against his knee.
We would close our eyes and drowse and dream,
  And he would talk to me.

He told me tales of days gone by,
  His grandpa told to him;
Beneath that very old oak tree,
  When it was young and slim.

He told me where the places were,
  The Cherokee lived in the hills;
Where the panthers and bears hid out,
  And the hillbillies had their stills.

Now Grandpa lays on another hill,
  In the shadows of an old oak tree.
Those same old tales are wondrous still,
  And live fondly in my memory.

  —*Ione McCabe*

Untitled

Dear Mother, I am not the child I once was, nor am I the adult
That I like to think I am. I am just somewhere in between.
I do know the time has come, and I need to go. But I need
you to let me go too. I may not make it in this world, but
I want the chance to try. I know I came from you, but I did
not become you; nor you, me. We both have our own ideas and
opinions; we need to respect that. Maybe that is why we have
said things to each other that neither one of us meant to say.
Both forgiving, but neither forgetting. I think by my going
we will both grow to understand the other. I hope you do not
think I am leaving out of anger. I am leaving because I care
about you and finally I care about me.

  —*Charlotte Davis*

The Lighthouse

The lighthouse has a guiding light
  That helps all ships pass in the night...
But did you know? When the light grows dim...
  The lighthouse get its strength from "him"...
God guides us through a stormy night,
  And steer us without fear...
But the lighthouse stands alone out there,
  For many a many year ...
So thank you God, for the lighthouse,
  That makes our travel safe...
And thank you God, for your tender touch,
  We hold with such loving grace...

  —*Kay Tee Thomas*

The Thanksgiving Dance

Following the turkey feast
We watched our daughters dance.
We smiled, the two of us,
As our cherished girls performed.
And though it was not our music,
And though it was not our dance,
Still the graceful turning bodies
Evoked such wistful memories
That when our daughters left us
We moved together, wordless,
To distant clocks heard faintly
Counting down our time.

  —*Phyllis G. Roumm*

I Cried

I cry out to you, please hear me.
The cry swallowed by the sea of my torment.

Bouncing back and forth against the tide.
I cry out but my cries are muffled by the
sounds of the gulls.

I struggle to catch my breath, to save my
troubled life. I reach as I cry once more
before the water covers my head.

I cry out as the waves over take me and my
mind swarms with what's to be of me.
You did not hear me as I drowned.
You heard nothing. Not a sound.

—*Glenda DePollo*

Invisible Kingdom

There's an invisible kingdom
That many do not see
But now and then there are glimpses of eternity.

Problems and circumstances are
the "secret passage ways."
The road is dark and foggy. Faith is the light,
And perseverance burns the fog away.

We are being trained for Heaven,
Where there are no barriers.
For we will have won the victory over the devil.

Daily, God provides the passage ways.
Don't look at what "seems to be".
Persevere through fear and emotions.
They are only "road blocks.
Lean heavily on His Word alone.
Don't pay attention to the time passing. Keep on believing!

Each insight or answered prayer, are glimpses of Eternity
In THE INVISIBLE KINGDOM
—*Lorrie Smith*

I'm Thankful

Dear Lord: I'm thankful everyday for the things I have to do,
that not only keep me busy, but maybe healthier, too. I'm
thankful that I'm needed to sweep the floor and dust, or bake
a batch of cookies or lend an ear in trust. I'm thankful when
the sun shines bright but we also need the rain, and when it
comes to wet the land, I'm thankful yet again. I'm thankful
for the many years that "Red" and I have spent together. The
glad, the sad, the caring times, through every kind of weather.
I'm thankful for the home we have, that we're not "out on the
street." I'm thankful for our garden, the flowers, and the
food we eat. I'm thankful for our family, as we share their
ups and downs. The grandchildren - what a blessing sometimes
we laugh, sometimes we frown. I'm thankful for the friends we
have and the good times that we share. The music and the
stories and the memories, here and there. I'm thankful for
each day on earth and hope that I may be the kind of person
that I should. I'm thankful, Lord, to Thee.

—*Mae V. Emerson*

Peace

On the midst of stress and
turmoil and the thundering of war
Let us work and pray
for wisdom and a greater
Brotherhood,
For God is waiting, waiting
to give Peace, the gift of
His love.

—*Pearl Ahlf*

A Rose

They say there are no tears in heaven,
That things on earth are erased away,
But I hope my Savior somehow tells him.
I threw a rose in the grass that day.

I threw a rose because I loved him
No one else here needs to know
But I hope my savior gently tells him,
I threw a rose upon the snow.

I threw a rose when it was raining,
Another when the sun was bright.
If it would ease this pain of hurting,
I'd throw one in the dead of night.

Someday when my days are ending-
And my eyes are growing dim -
I'll pick a rose with the dew still on it,
Take it along to give to him.

I threw a rose because I loved him,
For memories of his love so kind -
And someday when our fingers touches,
A dozen roses will be mine.

—*Carrie L. McThenia*

One Rainy Night

The rain poured from the heaven's above,
That was the night we first saw that beautiful white dove;
We sat by the fireplace and cuddled close together,
Trying to keep warm despite the cold and stormy weather;
We said we could never be torn apart,
And you told me I could never be replaced in your heart;
The dove had come here to stay,
Even though you and I went our separate ways;
Hoping someday we would again meet,
And we soon did in the summer's nightly heat;
Soon after that night the dove flew away,
As if to tell us this time we were here to stay.

—*Kimberly Diane Eldridge*

To My Children

What do I do to be instated on that pedestal of motherhood
that's so overrated?
The cards, and calls that never come make me feel so glum
not to be loved by my own son.
Daughter, one day you will know the labor for it may not
be in your favor due to your behavior
Love and forgiveness are the only waiver I pray for the day
you see the way, and call to say, it's okay, Mommy.
You are no star, but you can be who you are. Your just fine,
You have committed no crime. I will see you sometime.
I love you, and need you. You were a part from the start.
This is from my heart.

—*Debra Cooke*

Those Black Poets

When I was a small child they said: "Respect you elders." And
that's what I learned to do. When I was a little older they
said: "Be sweet to the younger children." And that's what I
learned to do. When I was at the playground they said:
"Play nicely with the other children."
And that's what I learned to do.

Those Black poets said they didn't mean everybody. Those Black
poets said they respect, be sweet and play nice with others
like me. But that's not the way I learned it. Oh, they
sometimes whispered among themselves about the coloreds, the
Negroes, the Blacks, but they didn't whisper it to me, so I
didn't hear it. But those Black poets did, loud and clear.
They lived their live behind the wall of those hushed words.
The whispered voices will die away someday, but those Black
poets will remind us of how it was.

My child will learn to respect her elders, she'll learn to be
sweet to the younger ones, and she'll learn to play nicely with
the other children. She'll learn that means everybody, because
that is how I'll teach it and those Black poets won't write about me.

—*Elizabeth B. Dyer*

Where Have All The People Gone

An old house stands, all alone and falling in.
The barn still stands, out there for all to see.
But—where have all the people gone?
That once ran this field in play, and milked old Bessie out
in that barn.
And filled that house in early morn.
The smell of biscuits in an old wood stove still fill this room.
But—where have all the people gone?
One by one they went away,
left mom and dad to care for the place.
But they got old and died you see.
But, why? Do you walk away? From all the love you shared.
Why—leave it to decay?
For once this was your home.
There's no reason to be ashamed, of what was once your home.
The house and barn can't speak for themselves,
So I'll take their place, and ask,
Where have all the people gone?

—*Jean C. Booker*

Distance Me from a Long Journey

She empty her clothes from the closet.
The bathroom was warm, from the heat coming out of the vent.
I turn around shivering to light the fire place.
Cuddling up by the fire place.
Hawaii dreams come sizzling in the midair.
I found my face turning red.
I'm all choked up with words.
If someone would enter the room, they would scare me
half to death.
Distancing myself from that long overdue journey.
Crumbling up every peace of my inner gut feeling.
Going home were I can smell the green grass and see,
The flowers bloom.
I would give anything for that long journey.

—*Cheryl Smith*

"What Have We Done To Our Country?"

What have we done to our country?
The beautiful home of the free.
What have we done to our country?
The beautiful place it used to be.

The terrible sounds that we hear.
Most people won't shed a tear.
The sounds of innocent people dying.
And abused children crying.
It's hard to believe it can happen here.

People shooting up drugs.
Poor peoples' houses infested with bugs.
People everywhere losing their jobs,
The homeless shelters trying to help the people in mobs.

The environment is destroyed by people, polluting.
Peoples' possessions are destroyed by other people, looting.
Most people say, "it won't happen to me,
I live in the land of the free."
It seems to me that our country is the scariest place to be.

—*Jessica Kornstein*

Dad's Stories

I remember quite well,
    the bedtime stories my dad would tell.
They became so real;
    oh, what excitement I would feel!
We'd go anywhere, my dad, my brother and I;
    from the depths of the sea, to the planets in the sky.
I didn't much like going to the moon;
    they'd leave me saying, there wasn't room.
I would lie there crying in my bed,
    wishing my big brother stayed instead.
It was more than a story to me;
    the creatures out there I could see.
I didn't want to be there alone;
    so, finally they'd come and take me home.
I was exhausted from our trip;
    into a deep sleep I would slip.
Now my children anxiously await,
    each new adventure they will take
Thank you dad, and grandpa too,
    for giving us a part of you.

—*Judy Demers*

Untitled

The silence,
The blessed silence has wrapped
    its comforting arms around me.
And though I know it won't last
I sigh contentedly as I sink into
    the soft, downy blackness
For now I can rest
Without the screams
Free from the blood and the tears
I don't have to run anymore
I'm safe here
For now
But I know I'll have to start over again
How soon, I won't know
But for now it's the silence
The silence that comforts
Kisses,
Doesn't sting.
The silence that I retreat into now
And hide in a dreamless sleep.

—*Jacquelyn Jaye Floyd*

My Angel Unaware

There have been times when I have sought
  The blessing of a friend ...
Someone with whom to bare my soul ...
  My broken heart to mend.

Sometimes the circumstance has called
  For words of counsel true.
My ears have ached for special words.
  God sent those words by you!

Again, my need for loving eyes,
  Which twinkle with God's Grace,
Has been supplied so wonderfully
  When we've met face to face.

When I have needed tender arms,
  To circle me in love,
Your presence has been comforting ...
  A blessing from above.

Praise God for His Amazing Grace ...
  For special friendship rare !
In you, He has provided me
  An Angel unaware!!!

    —Everett Reconnu

A Father And His Son

A father and his son were on a walk one fine day.
The boy looked at his father and asked, "Dad why is
nature so beautiful yet it changes so?"
"Why your mother of course." And he continued thusly.
  The stars try to outs shine her eyes
  But a glance from her surpasses them by and by.
  Then comes a fresh spring day
  But your mother's beauty...well what else can I say
  Then comes summer with harsh yearning.
  Then tries to steal attention by scorching and burning
  When the sun realizes your mother has it all
  Nature tries again with fall.
It's no comparison to your mother, may I be so bold.
  Then comes winter with all it's cold.
  It covers the world with snow to see if we's miss it.
  But its nothing compared to your mamma's kisses.
And like putting on an old grin
  It starts all over again.
"Now son." asked the father. "Do you understand?"
"Yes dad. You're a very lucky.

    —Curtis Baker

Faith

The wind said, "Speak, and they will listen."
  The brave said, "I will".
The rain said, "Ask, and you will be answered."
  The brave said, "I will."
The earth said, "Trust, and you will not be betrayed."
  The brave said, "I will."

One hundred years later the brave returned.
"You told me to speak,
  No one listened."
"You told me to ask,
  No one answered."
"You told me to trust,
  I was betrayed."
"No my lands are gone, and my people are few.
  What do I do now?"

    —Daniel Ferranti

Arrant Bullet

Unmasked, cold, blank,
the bullet killed the gold painter,
shielding thieves taking millions
to mock his hurt, his toil, his worth.

Eighty dollars left to drown in blood
as thieves went free to multiply,
bullet safe, insensate, to hurt, to steal.

Unique foreboding's siren shrill
of outrage failed to force arrest.

The Germs run free
  Strewing
the Van Gogh curse.

    —Dorothy Randle Clinton

The Clouds Know How I Feel

I stare out the window at the rain
The clouds must know how I feel.
They cry for me, hiding the tears that fall.
Every second feels like an hour, as I sit alone,
For your not here and I can think only of you.
I watch the clock, it moves so slow,
The hours go slowly 'til I next see you.
For time has no mercy.
My mind drifts back to the first few days,
The happiest days of my life,
But these thoughts don't bring joy
As I drown in this misery.
I pick up the pieces of my shattered heart.
Knowing only you can put it together.
Time may heal these wounds and this pain,
But time is cruel to me.
You can end the pain I feel, if only you will listen.
I stare out the window at the rain.
The clouds know how I feel.

    —Jennifer Phelps

An Old Man's Lament

My life's greatest tragedy,
  The cruelest stroke of fate;
I was born too early,
  She was born too late.

Through this life our steps were sadly out of tune,
Though our paths crossed,
  I crossed in the morning, she crossed in the afternoon.

Though I love her dearly,
  There's this one last heartbreaking twist;
Though I think the world of her,
  She doesn't know I exist.

    —Charles C. Young, Jr.

After The Storm

All is quiet, after the storm.
The air is still, it's very warm.
The trees are bare, not naked though.
The leaves are gently falling slow.
The sky is dark, without a sound.
Piles of leaves lay upon the ground.
The ground is damp, from all the rain,
that trickled down my window pane.
There are no cars passing by,
my house right now, I wonder why...
The storm is over, the clouds have passed
The rain and thunder are gone, at last.

    —Erin A. O'Donnell

Down... To Sleep

Please don't blame me;
The dark I seek is not a simple end of day.
The thoughts I speak are To The Lord I Pray...
Now I lay me

Down...to sleep;
No more to watch each night crawl past my bed,
And taste the fright, and choke upon the dread;
My soul to keep...

A black so high,
It covers moons that once gave hope of dawn.
I know the starlight, too, will soon be gone...
If I should die.

Before I wake,
I count each beat my heart sends to my ears,
And lie in heat that only feeds my fears...
My soul to take.

I've watched the sun.
I've seen the edge of light where shadows bend.
I know tonight the darkness will not end...
As light and dark are one.

 —David A Conary

Me

Confusion controls my life.
The dark overcast
 that drains the energy from my body.
Hurt,
 that makes my heart cry out for help.
Happiness,
 the thing I just can't seem to find.
Emptiness,
 knowing there is tomorrow.
Anger,
 that turns the sheepish lion into a furious beast.
Love,
 the thing I desperately seek.
Life...
 the thing I wish I could end.

 —Jessica Paulik

The Day That Elvis Died

Where were you on the fateful day?
The day whose memory won't go away.
What could one say when given the word?
The King was gone - no sound was heard.
The day that Elvis died.

Didn't the grief then spread like raging fire?
The cries, the moans - would they never expire.
Then the thought prevailed - Wasn't this untrue?
Leaving is a thing the King would never do.
The day that Elvis died.

Didn't it start on that day we now remember?
And can't let it go lest August be September.
Wasn't there something that wouldn't lie still?
A void in life that only the King could fill.
The day that Elvis died.

So, isn't there a belief now held most high?
Perhaps by you but for certain by I.
It is to savor along with our rallying cry.
Let the King put an end to this dreadful lie.
That fateful day our Elvis did Not die!

 —Campbell L. Smith

A Farmer's Life

In the life of a farmer's eyes,
The days are different by and by.
For one can be rainy, the other one sunny,
The work must go on even though there's no money.
The days can be long, the work's never done,
Hoping tomorrows will only bring sun.
The smell of the air, fresh cut ground,
Can only be appreciated, when a farmer's around.
To plant that first seed, watch it grow,
Brings a little hope in his heart very slow.
For you see, the things that can ruin his crops
Can destroy his life and everything stops.

 —Debra Weatherly

Dream On My Friend, Dream On

Dream on my friend, dream on
The days of yesteryear are gone
Yea tho the sun still rises as I wake
Mid skies of blue does shadows make
The moon above the mount doth rise
The stars yet wink with twinkling eyes
Be still and not a whisper make
The night doth turn to morning dawn
Still the days of yesteryear are gone
Dream on my friend, dream on

The days of carefree times have past
Only memories now linger in our grasp
The days when strolls with friends we'd take
Mattered naught that rain would damp our face
The crackling leaves beneath our feet
The hint of fall, the smell so sweet
The snowflakes fluttering down with grace
Like angel wings of pure white lace
Oh precious memories of times bygone
Dream on my friend, dream on

 —Elizabeth Ann Evans

This Ol' Drought

Been ponderin' this ol' drought
The dry stream; used to be trout.

Grass is short, dries in a heartbeat
Turns to dust, right under your feet.

Ever'where ya look it's dry as sand
Dusty n' gritty, it's not kind to man.

Should it rain, it comes down in sheets
Washin' out gullies n' brings up the creeks.

The ground soaks it up with a great thirst
After a short time, it's dry, like a first.

After seven years of this dry stuff
Been nothin' but wet, can't get enough.

Snow, Hail n' Blizzards packed up high
Ol' Man Winters' back, we all heave a sigh.

Seein' a crick tricklin', ain't seen in so long
It's music to the ears, It's the best song.

 —Jeanny Robbins

Blizzard Of '93

White rain, white rain in the air
Shining, sparkling everywhere
Swirling, twirling all around
Gliding, landing on the ground
  Shovels throw it
  Winds blow it
  Snowplows scoop it
  Children roll it
  Sun shines through it
    Spring
    —*Sharon Perigo*

Once

Coat of wool
Shoes of leather
Home of beauty
Summer weather
Feast of fancy
The theatre
Car of class
Dog of setter
Sail of Waves
Field of heather
Homeless now
But....days....were ....better.
    —*J. M. Bennett Hammerberg*

Saint Joseph

It would be a hard job
Should he do it?
A "Mother to be" kind and lovely
Should he do it?

He had a dream
An angel serene
Put his fears to rest
Mary was "Blessed"

The Divine Child to raise
God be praised
He would do it!
    —*Patricia Scaro*

Charcoal

My head moves from
  side to side.
I'm restrained and
in pain.
I cannot move
It's not from the paralyzing fear,
  because this was
Unnatural.
My upper body
Is covered in black.
I feel sick. I add to it.
It didn't work.
My plan was
  imperfect
Like my life.
Another day
    another try.
I'll try
Try to make it all better.
But first I must be untied.
    —*Anita Furtner*

Yesterday

I entered a room
Silence met me at the door
I stood quietly
Listening for a sound of remembrance
There was none
In this space of time
A room wept
    —*Marian Lackey*

Peace

Peace is not a ghost,
since it has not been
and hence, has not died.

It is abstract, and yet,
when it is, it is known,
and cherished, as it is.

In this sense it is
intangible substance,
nearly really real real.

Is there a fount of pure,
unadulterated, paradise peace
that flows down like snow melt?

Can it quench a thirsty land
like cold water running over
a dry mouth and down a hot neck?

Or is it a rainbow place —
a pot of gold that some grasp
and finally lose to leprechauns?

Peace is, and is not,
all at once, together, forever.
    —*Mike Phillips*

Love Gone By

How long has it been
  Since our eyes have met
  Our hearts have touched
  Our souls have wept?

When's the last time
  Our hands have touched
  Caressed your skin
  Felt your lust?

Has so many years gone by
  Since you can remember,
  The sparks that fly
  When our lips brushed.

Those electric shocks that send shivers
  Threw your body,
  As your hands gently
  Cupped my cheeks.

How does it feel today?
  Do the shivers turn
  To tremors or just fade away?
    —*Teresa Ellis*

The Moon

People think it's just something
  to brighten the night.
What is the moon?

Is it something real?
Is it something special?
  Or,
    Does it just reflect light?
    —*Karalie Vest*

Pierce The Sky

There's a red, red tail hawk
Sittin' on top a power pole
Lord of the sky of the fields
For miles and miles and rows and rows
Now he don't move he just watch
Can see a lot from a power pole
He don't even move when he fly
Man He just glide
All you see is a shadow fallin'
and somethin' pierce the sky -

Now when hawk he takes off
circles wide above the land
for miles and miles - unbroken wilds
Except for the track of human hands
Now he don't work why should he
Knows his role, is right on top
Now he don't even work when he fly
Man he just glide
All you see is a shadow fallin
and somethin pierce the sky
    —*Marc Tilson*

All In You

It's all in you,
  skies of bright and dreams
Come true.
  Sweet and gentle understanding,
A love through the days true and
  withstanding.
A deep caring heart and tender
  kisses,
A rainbow of my most dreamt
  wishes.
Soft and kind comforting eyes,
  It's all in you where
My happiness lies.
  And no one comes
Close in comparison to you,
  Baby you're my skies
Of bright and dreams come
  true.
    —*Tina Bennett*

Am I Not A Man!

Was I not a bonded man
slaving in the desolate fields
for hundreds of years, only left to
dance in the shadows of my tears

I Am a Man!

Was I not the man
Who chased freedom so long
left never to finish!

Am I not a denied Man
beaten with a bat of ignorance,
a tree of Racism, still holding my
head high!

Am I Not a man!

Was I not the one
who built a nation out of
Blood, Sweat, a myriad of Tears,
unable to enjoy the Fruits!

Am I Not A Man!
    —*Mario A. Martin*

Tiny Little Guy

Tiny little guy, all brand new.
Sleeping nights are very few.
You cry until your pants are dry.
You sleep when the sun is in the sky.
You smile just once in a while.
As your laundry has turned into a pile.
And I run around to get things done.
While you swing and suck your thumb.
As you try to reach out to play
You have that look on your face.
You know it will happen today!
Tiny little guy, precious as can be.
You could only belong to me.

—*Sandra Newman*

On the Passing of a Day

Dawn comes early on this valley
Sleepy banners raised on high
Life flickers briefly then subsides
Lone wolf takes up the cry

Icy dreams raised from snow
Melting in the mind
Ignites the heart in desert heat
In footsteps of the blind

Weary mountain stands alone
Gods perched upon a shoulder
Cries bloody rivers to the sea
And mourns the day is older

Roses in the braids of maidens
Mysterious flowers of the soul
Engulfs the senses in its petals
Night steps to gain its rule

As sight bows down to sound
Sun rests its weary head
Black ocean holds that wicked night
And breathes that golden red

—*Timothy William Grebiner*

Death

Leave quietly
Slip away into the night
Cause no pain nor sorrow
and forget your sins
For tonight you leave the
mortal world.
let your eyes see no pain,
Suffering or war
Fear not my child
destiny has been planned and
your future awaits in the
heavens above.

—*Rose Spitz*

Untitled

You're so special, I want you
so bad. And I think of all the
good times and bad times we had. I
remember when we hugged and you
kissed me goodnight, but I didn't
think you cared when I held you
so tight. I love you even more
as seconds go bye. So always
remember your the apple of my eye.

—*Patricia Garcia*

Grandma's Blue Dot

Her eyes sail
small and frail
the sense dim
caught between mind and body
reality thought no longer but by myth
fuzzy, drippings of the past
made worse by loss of memory
tales spoken once in unison
now cloud over in lonely stutters
has there been no season?
no season of which the words were
formed
not so far off
but no emotion triggered
lifeless form draped in blue
what is it dear that has
quieted you?

—*Rob Heller*

Silence

Air turns cold
Snow comes down
On country roads
And in the town
Silence comes.

Like curtain drawn
Noise to shield
Stillness comes
To yonder field
Silence comes.

The rabbit sits
Ears erect
No sound
Can it detect
Silence comes.

Light fades
Darkness falls
No movement seen
No bird calls
Silence comes.

—*Bernadine C. Dostal*

The Rose In The Garden

I look upon the garden
So full of beauty
And I see all the flowers
That caress my eyes

I reach down to touch
A single long stemmed red rose
The softness that I feel
Is like the breeze today

I gently touch the petals
As if they were like crystal
Keeping aloft the beauty today
Of the garden of my life

I can feel a strange life
That comes from the rose
And I know that this is beauty
From my garden, to the world.

—*Rian D. Botts*

Education

And Plato laughed
So hard he cried
And then he died (in my arms)
Singing in ancient Greek.
I couldn't sing along
I didn't know the song
Or even the words.

—*Wayne S. Valentin*

Yesterday's Gift

It was a gift, the giving free
So have no great concern
There's never a necessity
To give back in return.

They call me fool to bare my heart
However fragile made
Yet selfish are the "games" they start
-Coquettish Masquerade!

With love, the seed can only grow
This unrequited way.
I couldn't hide my candle's glow
And thought it best to say.

For when you looked into my eyes
I knew that you would see
The glow shine through the heart that tries
To show the friend in me.

We've nightmares called reality.
My hope is that you'll find I gave to your
Eternity a happy rest from time.

… it was a gift, the giving free.

—*Rosann York*

Eternal Love

What happened to the love we shared
so many years ago?
Does passion slip as one grows old,
or has the spark just lost it's glow?

You used to bring me flowers
from a road side flower stand;
Carnations are my favorite, and
roses with the long stems.

I would press the petals in a book,
the fragrance lingers still,
from memories that used to be
before we both went "Over the hill."

Now that we are growing old,
those things don't mean as much.
Just holding hand, a hug now and then,
seems to be enough.

It tells us both, that deep inside,
our love is burning bright.
That Eternal Flame will never die,
it's just the spark won't light.

—*Marjorie L. Squier*

White Magic

On the first day of winter,
the elegant white swan
slices through paper-thin ice
on the Palace pond,
and disappears
in the snow flurries.

—*Sherwin P. Helms*

The House With A Heart

There is a house
So steady and strong,
As I would pass by
I could almost hear a song.

Many a lonely night
When all else seemed dark
The lights on the house
Uplifted my heart.

Time passed and
I was invited in.
Whatever it was or is
I felt a healing begin.

Out of love
This house came to be,
With a spirit
To last an eternity.

People have come,
People have gone,
And the love in the house
Shall always pass on.

—*Peggy Crilly R.S.M.*

Dear Son

With joy, I write this letter today,
So the whole world can hear me say,
That, I love you so,
Much more than you'll ever know,

When a small child,
On my knee,
I endeavored to protect you,
From all hurt that could be,

However, you realized,
As you grew older,
The world you once knew,
Began to grow colder,

I tried so hard,
To shield you from harm
While warning you about,
Superficial charm,

"Always be wise and cautious" I'd say,
And think for yourself, each and everyday,

Knowing your mom, will always be near,
Forever to listen, to your greatest fear.

—*Lynn Edelman*

A Mother's Supplicate

Awaken my child
  so we may embrace

I dreamt all night
  of your splendid
    face.

My little baby
  oh did you sleep
    well?

How I wish you could talk,
  if only you
    could tell!!!!!

—*Salima McGregor*

I Want to Live In a World of My Own

I want to live in a world of my own.
So what if people said that I am
strange. I want to live in a world of
my own. If I live in your world
would you promise me peace, love,
happiness, togetherness and justice
for all or would you turn your head
as though you should be ashamed. If
you can promise me all this then
I will live in your world. If not
I want to live in a world of my own,
because I can control my own world,
but can you control your world if
so bring back the peace, love, happiness,
togetherness and justice for all in your
world. Until you do I want to live in a
world of my own. Yes, I might seem strange,
but I want to live in a world of my own.
Where there is peace, love, happiness,
togetherness and justice in my world.

—*MaryAnn Freeman*

A Red Shirt For Me

Enfamil, undershirts and socks
Soap powder and foil
Pampers and Crisco oil,
Paper towels and instant tea and
a red shirt for me.
A shopping list found on the
fitting room floor.

That's why we love our Moms-
A Mother's love is so precious and dear,
A little bit of God shows through
in everything they do.
That is perfect love you see, and
last of all she writes-
  And a red shirt for me.

—*Patricia A. Allbright*

"The Most Precious Gift"

God made so much beauty to abound.
Some is breath taking and we astound.
It's God's way of saying, "I love you!"
Do we really know what to do?
God made flowers to freshen the air.
He made birds to fly up there.
He made mountains and valleys below.
He made fountains and plants to grow.
He made animals and fish of the sea.
After all this, he made you and me.
You want to know the reason for living?
It is to be like God in our giving.
Man has made so much stuff.
We never seem to have enough.
The most precious gift I can give today,
Is to walk in God's love and show you the way.

—*Al Thomas*

The Grill

  A one-legged dragon
Stands behind my house.
  In winter he sleeps.
    When summer comes—
      Roaring breath
    Flaming, Smoking
      Children hear
  Their mother scream
'Hot dogs are ready!'

—*M. Megan Conaway*

Talk To Me

Tell me before it happens
Sometime I may not hear
Tell me about drugs also
When ever I am near

I may be traveling the wrong road
The end I do not know
Tell me before it happens
If you have been there before

The Devil knows our weakness
Evil things we will do for wealth
Tell me before it happens
His wages for me is death

Don't wait until I land in jail
And then feel sorry for me
Tell me before it happens
And your conscience will be free

You will not live here forever
This flesh will die one day
I am telling you before it happen
That Jesus Christ is The Only Way.

—*Richard Walton Sr.*

Invisible

Maybe I'm invisible?
Sometimes it seems that way.
People talk around me,
or right through me every day.

Although I stand close by
my words they do not hear,
and most of the thoughts that I express
seem to fall upon deaf ears.

Feelings, although often stated,
are not taken into account,
and I'm left with a great emptiness...
and a feeling of "no worth".

For people, even me, have substance...
so unlike a wall,
that just stands there, and says....
(Nothing at all).

—*Mary A. Ryk*

Earth

People, they think I'll last forever.
Soon I'll be as barren as the dessert.
They throw their garbage upon me
They dump their wastes
Into my bodies of water
They turn my silent surface
To a deafening.
When they make me furious
I'll shake 'em up or
Spew forth crimson fluids,
Wake up people,
I will not last forever.

—*Elizabeth Graham*

A Friend

A friend for life is what we are
We laugh, we smile and look at stars
A sudden glance, our hearts beat fast
This feeling deep, won't be the last
But looking up upon the stars
A friend for life is what we are.

—*Ulrica Peterson*

I Love You!

I love you more than the
Sound of the oceans waves.

I love you more than the
Sunbeams shining on my face.

I love you more than the
Smell of a fresh rose.

I love you more than the look
on a mothers face when her baby takes
its first step.

I love you more than a cup
Of hot chocolate on a cold day

I love you more than the
taste of ice cream on a hot day.

I love you more than the
City lights at night.

I love you more than the
Sight of fresh snow

I love you more than words
can say, without you my life would
surely fade away.

—*Kerry Toomey*

Untitled

A reflection on the wall
Stands and stares at me
Chills my heart
And swallows my tongue
An image in my head
Endlessly tortures me
Holds my breath
And suffocates my love
A sound in my ear
Like the last breath of dying man
Haunts my will
And deafens my soul
A vision of you
Like the brightest star
Warms the world
But steals my sight
My memories of you
Like poison on my lips
So so sweet
But twice as deadly

—*Steven S. Churning*

Father

A man of honor,
Strength and love.
A powerful hand
As gentle as a dove.

A person to reach out to
In trouble and pain
Someone to help you
Over and over again.

The love of a father
Is one of the greatest assets of all
For he will always be there for you
When you stumble and fall.

Through the thick and thin
The good times and bad.
A shoulder to lean on,
To support you when you're sad.
Thanks for everything you've done
I LOVE YOU DAD !!

—*William M. Potts*

Midnight Flight

Lightening storms in skies below me
Starlit peace in skies above me

Caught between
No place to go but on
On, with life's decisions.
Free to choose
To choose? But storm or peace?
Or lifeless life between.

Simple ways of Peace and Quiet
or on to fill one's inner calling!
The happiness of nothingness
or that of things achieved - well done
The loneliness of one who keeps on going
or peace and quiet of the caged in mind.

Go on mind and carry me
Through stormlit darkness - to see beyond
Those things unanswered, unfinished,
unsolved
To live and do, achieve and live
Be happy once again!

Lightening storms in skies below me
Starlit peace in skies above me
Free to choose —
Happiness again!

—*Ursula Eckert-Peterson*

For My Granddaughter Karina

I've neither seen nor held you -
Still, I know you're beautiful.
A fresh canvas on which to
    splash your colors
    and dance your life.
May we love you well
and touch you often,
so you will early learn who you are -
    A beloved child of God.

—*Judy Carlson*

Still

Still on my heart,
Still on my mind,
Still in my thoughts,
all the time.

Still the love of my life,
Still you and me,
Still you're my everything,
I could ever want you to be.

Still in my dreams,
Still thinking of you,
Still making love,
In room number 102.

Still my laughter,
Still my friend,
Still my song,
again and again.

Still filling my day,
Still filling my night,
Still fulfilling me,
It was love at first sight.

—*Sharon E. Sherry*

Giant Of The Earth

Volcano sleeps,
Still, silent,
Year after year.
Suddenly, arising from his bed
Deep in the depths of the earth,
Thundering a mighty roar
He warms all those in his path,
Who flee in terror at his command.
Lava, a fiery liquid, flows;
Flows from his frothing mouth.

Raging inferno;
Curling, thick black smoke,
Poisoning the air,
A mighty, majestic King,
Laughing at his subjects
Fleeing, as lava runs and destroys.
Villages evacuated,
Somber, bleak, desolate,
A scorched, cindered black mass.

—*Moensie Rossier*

Moment In March

Burden-sated I trudged through
Streets, still splattered with snow.
Suddenly an acrobatic squirrel
Scampered across a slatted fence
And in surged Spring, all at once:

A redwing missiled across the sky
Lemon sunshine softly warmed
Budding blades of green
Winged wisps of hyacinth fragrance
Made wonder rampant and in a trice
One heart soared to meet the redwing's!

—*Samuel G Gilburt*

For Land's Sake

Glass, paper, plastic waste
Styrofoam cups and plates
Is there no place
To deposit this case?

The land is filled
There is no place
To make another hill
Of this awful waste.

They tried to tell us all
To recycle the glass and paper
But we were all to tall
To bend to the caper.

Cardboard, paper and bags everywhere
And not a tree in sight
How could I be so unaware
The fate in the night.

If I had only used
The recycle bin
I would not have abused
The land I live in.

—*Linda Miles Landon*

Looking Up

Daylight breaks and space pale gray
Ushers in a brand new day.
Comes morning, after calm, cool, quiet
Lead by silver stars.

—*Ruth Barbara Morgan*

On Never Having Seen The Mona Lisa

We are like distant friends
Such regard I hold for Leonardo
High as the price of visitation
Makes me an immovable pilgrim.

Wouldn't the wait, the lines,
The momentary meeting
Separated by a velvet rope
Diminish all the years of admiration?

Majestic, even in half tone
My old art book open in my lap
I will enjoy you as a rumor;
And I will seem to smile.

—*John T. Eld*

Ice Lace

An airy cobweb,
   suspended
   in a corner
of a white arch,
   gossam'ry,
a 'glitter with ice.

      Or

an airy cobweb,
   suspended
   in a corner
of a white arch
   —breathtaking—
a 'glitter with ice.

—*Agnes Louise Paulus*

Icicles

Long beautiful icicles
Suspended
Shining
Sparkling
Silvered ice, tapering to
stiletto points. They're now
melting
dripping
disappearing.
Your beauty was here
for such a short time.

—*S. June Desmond*

What Else Is There...that Matters

Fighting through these years
Swallowing my tears
I've melted into silence
Hiding my own violence
Scarred myself inside
Ignoring any pride
What else is there...that matters.

Biting through my words
Rejecting what I've heard
I've haggled with respect
Forgetting I reflect
Played myself a fool
Breaking every rule
What else is there...that matters.

I've wallowed in my anger
Satisfied with danger
Plagued myself with lies
And now I close my eyes
What else is there...that matters.

—*The Coz*

Dedicated To The Indian

See the pounding of horse feet
Swaying with the motion of every beat,
Across a carpet of wheat
We are soon to meet.
With hearts a pounding
Our voices sounding,
To our fate
Against white men filled with hate.

To roam the land no more
As we once did before,
For freedom is no longer ours
But our spirit saved by higher powers.
Some of our heritage we did save
To our children we then gave,
For we will not hide
Our Native American Pride.

—*Angelia Reasor*

The Victor Endowed

Though rough the path that wound ahead,
Sweat rolling down my brow.
I'll not turn back, although I dread,
Within me the victor endowed.

Behind my tears escape a smile,
That rings within It's all worthwhile.
I'll embrace the challenge every mile,
Within me the victor endowed.

I'll keep my eyes upon the goal,
Though snares attempt to crush my soul.
Onward toward the mark I'm told,
Within me the victor endowed.

Closer I get, my target insight,
Strength from God, but not my might.
Rejoice, Rejoice I've won the fight,
Within me the victor endowed.

—*Kimberly A. Tidwell*

A Little Child Lives Here

A yard of snow, untouched, unmarred
Swept by the winter wind,
Except for a set of footprints small,
A little child lives here.

A yard of grass, so tall, so straight,
Swept by the summer wind,
Expect for a toy, a shoe, a towel,
A little child lives here.

Our own heart, untouched, unmarred,
Swept by our soul within,
Expect for troubles, worries, and hopes,
A little child lives here.

—*E. M. Coffey*

True Love

Take it slow
Take your time
Your still young
Love is blind
Talk it out
Make your move
Work things out
See it through
Love is priceless
True love few
Once you find it
Keep it true

—*Kristina M. Johnson*

Untitled

Wheels turn in synchronous motion
Taking him any place he chooses
A rough method of travel
But one he semi-understands
A road hums to the tune of passing
And air breathes in displaced noise
He seeks out new points to refer to
Inside his head
As he compiles memories
Fuses, half real moments
To build upon
A basic rhythm beats on
Becoming more complex and beautiful
Accompanied by dancing moments
He takes a moment to try and understand
Vast cosmos
Whirling and dancing in another fabulous
scheme
Yet still linked somehow
He shakes his head in wonder
And drives on.

—*Sam Dutka*

The Tally

Dead kids without names
tallied on the evening news.
Dead kids without names
victims of drug abuse.
Dead kids without names
gunned down while in school.
Dead kids without names
starved by greedy politicians.
Dead kids without names
laid to rest inside the unknown
   soldier's tomb.
Dead kids without names
tested positive for H.I.V.
Dead kids without names
tallied on the evening news.
Too many dead kids
without names!

—*Kenneth L. Powell*

Applauser

Look international farther fetch
Than cruise orderly dream
Shellely, Keats and Byron stretch
Unexplained eclectic team.

Tell how dew reveal no source
At certain time surrender page
Would adhere together force
Include ink soul clever wage.

Assemble mosaic word lover
Poet artisan, display truth
Where 'tis noble to discover
Each heart owns eternal youth.

Poet sincere love fragmental
Assume replace lest concern
Be it passion sentimental
Or flowers at last petal fern.

Let wisdom appear master verse
And publish poem reader pause
Pure assimilation starts rehearse
Then bow calmly when applause.

—*Orien Todd*

Dear Mother

Life was but a fleeting moment
   Tears of love drifted past
   Loving arms warm and tender
   Blanket of gold never last.

   Petals of love was broken
Dreams and hope shattered that day
Beautiful rainbow never as bright
     Since you went away.

   Roses bloomed along your way
Beautiful memories you gave to all
   Sunshine came with your smile
    Your love I still recall.

   Precious moments linger still
Dear mother keep peace of mind
Cherished love you left behind
   I wish we had more time.
—*Uledene C. Bean and Mary C. Brammer*

Untitled

Lady, I have wept one-thousand
tears to claim you as my own

Lived and died only to lay within your
bosom once more

Once more.

Do you wish my back to turn against
Your rejecting heart?

I wish I may.
I am among the heart struck
And fear to face a maddened world
Your virtuous guidance

Sorrowful may it be.

Be mine my lady,
Drink thine lips and recognize my
Existence of never ending loyalty

I am yours to vanquish in a whim.

Or yours to enchant dreams.
Dreams of ashes.
    —*R. Grijalva*

The Embrace

The embrace is stronger
than any kiss could ever be.

A feeling of belonging
and sincerity that heals doubtfulness.

The embrace has nowhere
to hide it's feelings of love.

A feeling so strong —
it holds me forever, it seems.

The embrace of your strength
takes me away from all of this.

A feeling forever lasting
in my memory of one embrace.
    —*Robb Johnson*

Ecstasy

I inhaled the perfume of ecstasy
That awoke my nostrils of desire
My deepest intrinsic passion flay
My innermost being to aspire
To grasp and thrust into that well
From which came that scintillating smell
Captivating me as it cast its spell

My every fibre stood at array
Tingling my emotions to display
Caresses of tenderness and say
Love me and take me today

Might the Creator Affirm to His Created
I Gave the Sweet Spirit of My Will
Your very being to Infill
Let your freedom of embrace
Bring you to my Face
    —*Richard D. Cagg*

"A Chain Of Memories"

There's a Golden Chain of Memories
   that binds two hearts together,
A chain so strong it holds you fast
   through fair or stormy weather.

It's links are forged of love and trust
   of happy memories shared,
Of times it meant so much to know
   that some one special cared.

The years can never break that chain
   but only add new lengths,
As joys, sorrows, hopes and plans
   combine to give it strength.
    —*Bea Morgan*

Love:

Love is like a candle,
That brighten up the heart
Love is like a beautiful dream.
That bring happiness from the start

To live without love,
is like living in a tomb.
It also remind us,
Our love has not been shone.

Some folks say they
don't wear their heart
on their sleeve.
But deep inside they really care.

A friendly smile, a little hug,
Can let you know love is there.
Love, is something we shouldn't hide.
It's wonderful, and so inspired.

So why not love one another,
As God meant it to be, with love
in your heart, you will always feel free,
to count your blessing and trust in thee.
    —*Myrtle Roth*

Rain

   Rain, feels like
Teardrops on my face.

   It sounds like a
Tumbling waterfall.

   It is caused by angels
Crying in the clouds.
    —*Misty Vesterby*

All These You Are

You are the dream that walked;
That held my hand and talked.
You are the voice that stilled-
Deepest longings; unfulfilled.
You are the fire that came-
Into my heart with sudden flame.

You are near to me; the moments spun-
Into a lovely dream; against the sun.
Your hand in mine; we ran through rain-
To capture magic in a misty lane.
Your lips on mine, and time stood still;
To mold my heart; forever to your will.

You are my sun by day;
A star at night; to lead the way.
Music, laughter, heart aglow-
A love too deep; to sweet to go.
All these you are; will ever be-
The dearest one on earth to me.
    —*Myrtle Toman*

Electronic Limbo

I see emotions on the screen
That I have never felt before.
Love, laughter
Lost somewhere
When I left childhood.
Mesmerized by figures
Flashing before my eyes
They share with each other
Feelings;
If I had I could not hide.
Instead, I sit here as a shadow
Of what I could be.
Empty, shallow;
Lost somewhere;
Between realities.
Life pulls me.
Afraid, I push back
Into an electronic limbo
Of dreams and truths
That smash a soul to bits.
    —*Rachel M. David*

Now I Know

It seemed like it was yesterday
That I said that I would change.
Like all my other promises they
all went in vain.
But I know this time it's different
Because words won't come into play.
    —*Kirk Layne*

Reunion

One short week

Did anyone think
that in one short week
so many people
could do so many things
shed so many tears
and laugh so many laughs
go back to old times
while looking ahead
one short week
can be a long time
if in each heart
each moment is kept.
    —*Lori Hilton*

Who's Behind The Voice

There's a voice
that I've heard
  once before
that silently whispered
  sweet nothings
    in my ear.
I don't know who's
  behind that voice
but he's very sweet
    and dear.
I'd like to get together
  with whoever's
  behind that voice
and maybe there will be
something we can share.

—*Tammy Schwien*

A Hope For Justice

This month we remember
  That long hot summer,
When justice didn't roll down
  Like a mighty river
It was when help
  Seemed so far away.
It was an enduring struggle
  Day by Day.
Our question was
  Where can we go from here?
Injustice anywhere is a threat
  To justice is everywhere.
Can for one day,
  Can we all get along?
Together hand in hand
  Singing a freedom song?
Can we not be judged by our skin
  But by our character?
From that we can probably
  Get along together.

—*Margaret Haule*

Release

They released me in a way
that made me feel like I
wasn't apart

I was gone into my life
to seek adventure and
who I am

To feel my inspiration
my belongings to seek
another person in
myself.

They released me and
also something else .....

—*Amy Aiello*

Beauty

Beauty lies in the stars,
The canopy of night.
Peace lies in the tall green trees
Reaching toward the heavens.
Beauty lies in the lovely flowers
That grow along the way.
Beauty lies in the rushing river
And the roaring of the sea.
Beauty lies in the hand of God
As he wipes our tears away...

—*Lucile D. Morin*

Where Is The Innocence?

It is through children
  that we learn to speak,
A light of truth
  for all to seek.
When lies are told
  and truths are lost,
It is our children
  who must pay the cost.

From children to adults
  they grow,
Telling lies,
  no truths they know.
With products of our
  violent ways,
How do we regain their
  innocent days?

When lies are lost
  and truths are told,
Reality will set in
  to take its true hold.

—*Jamie Cooper*

Time Slipped Away

Time slipped away with those things
  that we were,
Leaving me just with the memory
  of warm, gentle hands,
  their touch on my face, and
Pictures of you in my mind.

White daises and gold,
  tender kisses that told
Of sharing in ways to us special;
  though now far away,
  forever you'll stay, in the
Pictures of you in my mind.

—*Wayne E. Suns*

Knowledge

Young people you think you know it all?
That's strange, because you don't,
And it gets even stranger,
Because you won't.
Not you, not me, not he or she.
There's just too much to know;
But if you want to be in the running,
If you want to be in the show,
You have to pay attention,
That will start to flow.
Knowledge is yours to have,
No hesitation
Get all you can,
It prevents frustration.
Participation is a must.
It will give you a rush.
Listen to positive motivation.
Have some great expectations.
Knowledge is not a lie.
Young people it is a natural high.

—*Lydia I. Henry*

Censured

Music is an imagination of the ears.
The noise will conquer your hearing,
and the rhythm will overwhelm your senses.

—*Tina Langeraap*

My Friend

Beautiful young person.
That's what I wish
She would always be.
I remember sitting still
When I was told
My grandma was ill.
She gave me anything
that I wanted,
She told me I was a person
that could accomplish
anything I wanted.
I miss her dearly,
though it feels like,
she's near me.
I remember her personality.
My mom says, she was a
resemblance, of me.

—*Teresa Perez*

Miracles

A gesture, a smile, a wave Hello
  That's what surface shows
But hidden beneath the broken heart
  A different picture arose
The hurt, the anger, the guilt...
  And thought of what to do
Now searching for a miracle
  To wash away the blues
As daybreak nears each passing day
  A hope the phone will ring
And at the other end you hear
  The tiny voice now sings
For Miracles can happen
At least that's what I'm told
And I'll believe in Miracles
  Forever young and old

—*Stacie Franks*

Soldier

The cries of the wounded
The clash of steel on steel
The neighing of the horses
These sounds assault my ears
As I stand in the midst of the battle

Then she comes
Stumbling from the mist
The agony so obvious on her face
And she collapses before me

So I kneel
And cradle her head in my arms
But she is wounded so badly
The hurt, all that pain

I want to help
But what can I do?
I have no bandages
No medicine
I am but a soldier
Holding a dying friend

—*Peter Brimble*

Masks

Masks rise and masks fall.
The courage to let them fall
is greater than the fear to
keep them up.

—*Tim Joachim*

"High Pursuit"

With prudent step on icy walk
the climbers proceed forward,
In caution they refrain from talk
lest rockwall displace toward...

Fine route selected may result
in quested jubilation,
But Mother Nature could default
and steal from their salvation...

Nirvana, so it seems to them
exists on mountain summit,
When eagles and no other men
have touched their wings upon it...

To most a mountain's just a view
and trespass idle chatter,
But life itself for select few
depends on lofty matter.

—*Thomas Petrillo*

Prayer Is....

Prayer is the heartbeat of the soul,
The cry of conscience to be whole,
The throbbing of the aching heart,
The longing as the teardrops start,
The feel of pain at guilt of sin
Or loss of all that might have been.

Prayer is to contact heaven's throne
To touch the great Eternal One!
To feel his love, till all of pain
Sinks to oblivion again;
To linger there in sweet release,
His presence bringing perfect peace.

Prayer is the sweet perfume of praise!
The Holy Spirit's inner blaze!
The listening to His loving voice,
the humble yielding to his choice.
Transcending all—in sweet acclaim
The whisper of the Saviour's Name!

—*Ruth Rose Flickinger*

The Perfect Picture

I am the twilight, the dusk, the night
The dying flower that knows its hour
I am the knight upon your tower

You are the stem, my choice, my gem
The flowing stream that bears my dreams
You are the hem that holds my seams

We are the mixture, the flawless fixture
The soothing love, that reigns above
The perfect picture, my ladylove

—*T. J. Houlihan*

Untitled

Dawn
The early wake of the day
The early morning
The early dawn
The early light
Dawn
The early mist
The early singing of the birds
The early frost upon the ground
The early sunrise
Dawn

—*Lisa Layne*

Inspiration

You are my inspiration
The flame glowing in my heart
Love rushes in to save the burning soul
Keep me from burning so
But the flame catches on
It helps me to think
To understand love at different angles
It is shown through many sunsets
At dawn, at noon, and at midnight
I see inspiration
I feel your presence near
And I know I must go on

—*Josie Ochoa*

Wings Of A Breeze

On the wings of a breeze,
the future
    Left behind, the past
    not yet forgotten
A two sided mirror
of decision
    Painful
    A blade that pierces
        the delicate skin
        of life
Welcome the soft touch
of what is yet to come
    Gently harness,
    lightbeams of memories
On the wings,
of a future breeze.

—*Samantha Jean Doty*

Sea Gulls

See
The gulls
Diving - for
A silver streak
Flashing in the sun.
A life now sacrificed—
Sustenance———for another.
Its raucous cry a grace of thanks
As it soars and dives again — again
And never satisfied———until its end!

—*Oral Widmayer Bower*

Taking In Slow Moments

I hear the clomp, and clomp of it,
The horse, that ghosts once fed,
As passing through the covered bridge,
Aged planks protect my head.

I hear the idle chatter,
Of children counting eggs,
And view the mercantile with,
Its stores, in wooden kegs.

I hear the women fussing,
Over gingham cloth, and lace,
And feel, the freckled wonder,
On an eight year old boy's face.

I am again, in Lancaster,
Backstepping my pace.
The structured walk, is slower here,
Stretching time, in space.

—*Robert F. Vitalos*

An Empty Gym

A half an hour ago -
    the las person left
    the lights were dimmed
    the doors were locked
And here I stand
    all alone in reverie
    within these walls
    where games were played
How this silence screams-
    the vaulting ceiling echoes
    the empty bleacher sounds
    of cheering, hissing, booing
I stand alone by yet I hear
    "Rah, rah, rah"
    "Hey, are you blind?" "Traveling."
Clues remain
    gum wrappers, dixie cups,
    napkins, streamers, banners
Loud silence speaks once again
    band playing, pep club yelling
As I reflect on this empty gym.

—*Alice Braunersreuther*

"Forgive Me, My Son"

You were a vision of love the
the little boy of my dreams
you were a part of me
and I love you dearly
the day you got sick
I didn't want to believe
the little boy I love so much
would ever leave
I looked into those big, green eyes
and told you I'd make it better
I never stopped believing
and I prayed with all of my might
that my sweet little child would make it
through that very cold and dark night
I held you in my arms
I held you very tight
I saw that freckled nose
and had to ask God why?
please forgive me my son
I never wanted for you to die.

—*Jennifer Kuenzer*

Entangled Existence

My eyes, penetrating through
The nebulous darkness,
See the falsity of
Time.
Encompassed in the
Entanglement of existence
Time is nugatory.
Impinging on the mind
It strengthens;
Revolving around the present,
Following me, to surround
My future
Only to leave me without.

—*Lisa Rossario*

Wings

At our peril we perceive only
The adversity of love;
All golden ringlets in the sun,
Ignoring the tarnished bronze of ocean.

Icarus Redux:
Why could you not have seen
Beyond the ecstasy, the turbulence below,
The warmth that melted your waxen wings
And the cold that stilled the heart?

—*Walter M. Bastian*

Is This Love?

Is she the one
The one I've been looking for
Gods chosen mate
To live with forever
Will she bring glorious memories
To carry with my soul through eternity
Is she the happiness
My heart desires
Will I be able to live life
In only her arms
Or will the temptations of life
Lead us apart
Am I ready
Just for you
Or am I still
Wanting to give
To those that don't matter
Is she the one
The one that I shall
Destroy.

—*Shane Maxwell*

A Mothers Love

It starts out with little things
the ones that mean so much.
Watching your children grow up.
With that special loving touch.
A mother teaches first steps
And wipes away the tears.
Chase's away the boogie man
And all their children's fears.
It always seems so special
What a mother can do.
But it doesn't surprise me
When the love comes from you.
I love you, Mom.
Happy Mothers day.

—*Kimberly E. Hippensteel*

On Being Forty

The first course has ended,
The plates have been cleared.
But don't be offended,
There's cause to be cheered.

The first course was hasty,
You must have observed.
The first plate's for tasting,
It's only hors d'oeuvre.

Now comes the real feast,
With time for repast.
Now wanting's decreased,
The best saved for last.

—*Warren W. McCurdy*

I Was A Tree

Asleep in the moist Earth
The origin of my birth
Struggling to get out
Sent forth a tiny sprout

Stretching in the Sun
My life had just begun
Hungry and craving thirst
My roots began to burst

As it was meant to be
I became a lustrous tree
But without warning I was cut down
My branches hit the ground

I silently cried within
As they cut away each limb
It wasn't very long
I heard the sawmills song

I felt the carpenter's hand
Inside walls I was nailed to stand
The children will never see
The tree I used to be

—*Virginia A. Westfall*

I'm Starting to Know Peace

I'm starting to know peace
The pain has begun to cease
Alone in the dark night
I no longer feel fright
I'm starting to know peace
It has been quite a feat
Can't stop the powers that be
The power is not in me
I'm starting to know peace
One day at a time
Each moment I can find
A reason to go on living
A way to go on giving
I'm starting to know peace
Strength I get from above
Giving me real, true love
The one and only great God above
I'm starting to know peace

—*Mickie Barnes*

Togetherness

Uncle SAM
The piper man,
Plays a tune,
"Save Us from Ruin."
Shed no tears,
These Clinton years,
We must band,
And give a hand.
Balance budget,
Bit by bit.
Deficit,
Abolish it.
Meet health need,
Diminish greed.
Cost control,
Aim for the goal.
There's a way,
Trust U.S.A.

—*Margaret Gleason*

Nature Is

The Hawk so hungry,
the plain so bare;
Keen eyes search,
for mouse or hare;
Spots a rabbit,
the rabbit unaware;
Nature is kind and good.

A swift small shadow,
falls out of the sky;
The look of terror,
in the rabbits eye.

Sharp talons strike;
the rabbit will die.
Nature is cruel and bad.

Is Nature cruel and bad?
or really kind and good?

Beyond the cruel, beyond the kind,
There is one thought that comes to mind,

Nature is All, and All is One.

—*Paul Zeman*

A Southern Spring

I do not mourn
The quick-brown
October night
When passions cool
To winter's dream,
For soon southern winds
Will come to green
A naked woods
Of dark decay
And live again
A Southern Spring.

—*Ron Greene*

The Wind, The Sea And The Sun

The wind blows the grass,
the sea waters the ground and
the sun dries it out.
As my hair dries from the sun and
the wind.
The sea shown on me.
I float upon the sea, the wind
Blew me far, and the sun shown
my way.
The men and women,
boys and girls,
gay and straight, they all know
something different about,
the wind, sea and sun.
I run, with the wind near the
sea while the sun guides my
way.

—*Melissa Genua*

Untitled

I once had a slim waist of thirty two
The expansion of it I sorely rue
It is now a bulging thirty eight
The result of too much food I ate
I exercise and do sit ups everyday
Unfortunately so far I can't make it pay
On my stomach there is too much meat
Despite that fact I still love to eat
My wife has let out my shorts and slacks
I hope my waistline has reached its max.

—*Wendell Atkin*

646

"Experience Is Knowledge"

Who knows where -
    The silent tree falls
        If it is not of our forest

Who knows of what means
    Does the caged bird
        Take flight and soar.

Who knows why lights-
    Are in the sky
        To steer the ships in the galaxies

Or why man is man
    And air is needed
        To breathe life.

Or, by which standards
    Should we stand by
        In the face of our dignity

Only, by living
    Can the answers
        Show themselves to us.
            —*Sharon Ryan*

Sandbox

Emotions slide down
The sliding board of time
Into the sandbox of experience
Where they get skinned up a bit.
Oh, they heal
On the trip around to the ladder
And up again,
But they are never quite the same
For the next trip down.
            —*Mack Magaha*

Hopes of a Wonderful Place

The tainted water
The smog in the air
    how I wish
I was not there

I dream of safe water
I dream of clean air
I hope I soon
will be there

A time when the earth is safe
Oh my, what a wonderful place!
            —*Rebecca McHenry*

Lovers

We dance,
the Spring rain
tearing our sight;

we sway in
lover's
young romance.

We dance
like Druid's
in magiclands,

loving life
in free
romance.

We dance,
our bodies one
in our
romance.
            —*Sean Morris Taylor*

African Princess

Naked as the day born,
The sun burns in her walnut tan,
As she walks,
Slowly,
With easy, gliding motions.
Thick, woolen hair protects her head,
From the sun.
She raises up her voice in song,
In a tongue only she knows,
And she runs free,
Like the tigers and elephants,
That surround her.
She has the exact swift, silent movement,
As a jaguar,
And her eyes are watchful.
The power she holds within herself builds villages,
But with the tender love,
Just as a lion softly licks her cubs,
She wets her thick lips,
And poises for the tender kiss of love.
            —*Linda Wells*

New Day Dawns

A new morning arrives
    the sun shines bright
It brings new light....
A new beginning
Begins!

The end of new hope
    that was shallow
Washed in tears of pain...

But, a new day dawns
    and, the sun shines on.
Dreams begin and end.
New beginnings begin again.

Yes, the sun shines bright
    I see new light
On this dream
    that never was...
It only lived in me.
            —*Sherrie Koy*

"When the Raindrops End"

After the raindrops end
the sun will shine for you my friend

All the colors of the rainbow
will dance all around you...

Spinning, spinning ever so freely.
Colors flowing to and
fro, dancing from your own window

You may think of me, when
the raindrops end, for time
and tides have made us friends.
            —*Tinamarie Gaidus*

Photographs and Mirrors

His old, wrinkled hand clutched
the delicate, brown photograph,
and a tear ran down his cheek.

The gold framed, antique
mirror watched from the wall,
and caught it as it fell.

And both caused reflections.
            —*Shaun Collins*

Little Blind Baby

Little blind baby, you'll never know
The sun's first blush nor after glow—

You'll hear the robin's cherry call;
You'll know he's there but that is all.

You'll miss his rosy plummed breast,
The azure eggs within the nest.

The rose's fragrance on the air
Will let you know she must be fair

But lovely petals velvet hue
In darkness will be lost to you.

So tiny and so innocent
Of waywardness or days misspent—

What fate exacts this costly toll
And clouds the windows of your soul?
            —*A. Louise Dorman*

'Explanation Of A Motive'

Seduction of the innocent,
The sweetest corruption,
Can you call it something so base?
If it's sexual beauty,
The love of control,
The loss of your being
In feeling.
If it's nothing but soul...
And all of the flesh
If the thought makes you weak,
And the act makes you fly?
If it is hedonistic?
So be it.
If it makes you all that you are,
Takes you where you've never been,
Becomes everything you've lived for,
Then it's purity...
Angels with tarnished holds
Instead of mortals with tarnished dreams.
            —*Elizabeth Lippert*

My Man Of Music

We were young and hopeful.
The symphony we shared.
You played the rhapsodies;
I listened enchanted
To the notes we loved.

Where are you now playing
The music of the stars?
I knew you loved me then,
And still recall the bars
Of the notes we loved.

My own man of music,
Cherish the memories—
Those days of serenades
And love to the tender,
So soft notes we loved.

Someday, somewhere, somehow
Will I see you again?
Will you come to me here
And play the score and more
Of the notes we loved.
            —*Anne Katherine Hansen*

The Thunder Of Man

Light, smoke and noise
The thunder of man.
Shrapnel that rips,
And scars the land;
Children cower, death near at hand.
Deep in darkness, overwhelmed with fear,
The lonely child who sheds no tear.
Children bleeding, torn asunder,
'Neath the reign of smoke and thunder.
To all who remain,
On this cratered orb of dirt;
Who stops the pain?
Who ends the hurt?
Let's bring our children
Up into the light,
Out of the terror and darkness of night.
The time is now, to take a stand,
To heal the scars upon the land,
And free us all ....
From the thunder of man.

—*Paul D. McCreary*

Christmas Symbols

We know the Christmas symbols,
The trees and wreaths and lights,
Of Santa and the Reindeer
On their famous evening flights.

But Christmas marks the birthday
Of one who never knew,
These symbols we have treasured
As through the years they grew.

It seems we need old Santa
To remind us all once more
Of the blessing in just giving
And the good life holds in store.

—*Leone Lee Coates*

The Woodland

How pleasant is the woodland
The trees no more are bare.
Their swaying tops are bowing
As to greet your presence there.

When far away you see them
Upon a mountain high,
How like a dark cloud rolling
Upon a faded sky.

They too, are in the valley.
Looking down we see
Their tops, a rugged smoothness.
They stir my memory.

They hold a charm upon me.
A thing I cannot tell,
Is hidden in their beauty,
As they nestle in the dell.

When I look upon their beauty,
So pleasant, soft and free,
They make me look forever,
Through eyes that raptures see.

—*Tom Holland*

Ocean Of Love

Like the roar of the ocean,
The waves standing so tall.
She fell in love,
With the best man of all.

Like the depth of the ocean,
So pure and deep.
This feeling of love,
When we first did meet.

Like the voice of the ocean,
So loud and clear.
He expresses his emotions,
While holding her near.

He took her in the walls of his heart.
Together they live and never to part.

Life and love go hand and hand.
Just like the ocean and the beautiful sand.

—*Patricia A. Van Horn*

Words

I felt the wound so very deep
The weapon was deadly silent
The memory I will always keep
Its meaning was so violent

Piercing my soul as an arrow
As it glided through the air
In my mind, it made a furrow
Wrenching my heart, so bare

No, it was not fired like a gun
Nor was it thrust, as a dagger
None the less the deed was done
With a force that made me stagger

So be very careful what you say
Because once you have been heard
The hurt is always there to stay
Tho the weapon was only a "word"

—*Larry Patton*

I Wish

I wish I had
the wings of birds
the arms of strength
the poet's words.

I wish I had
the mind so wise
the answers all
the eagles eyes.

I wish I had
the fame and wealth
the perfect body
in perfect health.

But most of all
what I wish to see
is not my love for you
but yours for me.

—*Richard Dominguez*

We All Must Trust

The teacher has his students,
The wino has his wine,
The cook has food for cooking,
The cop has lots of crime,

The big wig has his little wigs,
The butcher has his meat,
The sailor has his sails to mend,
The walker has his feet,

The banker has his bank,
The fisherman his boat,
The loggers have their logs to cut,
Reporters have a quote,

The owners have their worries,
The workers have their woes,
The cabbies have their cabs to drive,
The tailors have their clothes,

The preachers have their sermons,
The Catholics have their Pope,
We all must trust in God above,
To bring us love and hope,

—*J.P. Horgan*

What Is Happening?

The beauties of the country side
The wonders of the city
Often make you stop and take time
to look at the world with pity
As the highlights shine through
As the flowers bloom
As the birds sing their happy tunes
It often makes you wonder,
What is happening?
Is the world falling a part?
Are we falling apart?
What is really happening?

—*Kim Whitehead*

"Love"

We may not always say-
   The words within our mind,
But deep within the heart,
   The love shows through in time,

We may not always do things right,
   Forget a high, high grade.
But what seeps through the heart,
   Is, one hundred percent homemade.

One thing we all have in common,
   As we close our eyes to die.
We find a true and loving heart,
   That never had to lie.

He told us of faith, hope and love,
   The gifts as old as time.
Of these, love is the greatest,
   This is why I'm sending mine

—*James E. Maurer*

The Nature Of Things

Do you sometimes wonder what makes
thunder battling in the sky?
Smogs, Frogs, and tiny worms and
whirling leaves that fly?
Tears that fall a mother's call
I surely know of this,
So turn around you wonderful sun
and give me a great big kiss.

—*Marie A. Della Sorte*

Best Friends

It's strange that I have never seen,
The wrinkles on your face.
All I see is your loving smile,
And the beauty of your grace.

I see the love within your heart,
The magic of your charm.
The kind and generous person,
That is so true and warm.

I see a person who truly loves,
Her family, home, and friends.
She is aware of things around,
And keeps with the latest trends.

Our covering is just a piece of skin
To protect the God-ly-ness within.
How truly blessed I have been,
To have you as my closest friend.

—Zella Mulder

To My Family

The time flies by
    The years pass too -
I've never expressed
    How much I love you!

Three sons and three daughters -
    We've had trials and sorrow,
    With smiles and laughter
    Nor today and tomorrow.

So now after "eighty" -
    I wonder each day
If you know I appreciate
    Each one along life's way!

I have many grandchildren
    And GREAT grandones too
I love each and everyone -
    Remember! I do!

Just once in a while
    I've said "I love you!"
But I never could say
    What Deep Love! Now adieu!

—Audrey M. Henning

The Summer Of The Gulls

Gulls?
Their beauty
Reflects God.

Order of feathers,
Except when flustered
Lay smooth and quiet.

Walking with wind
From south
Disturbs gray
And brown.

A pause;
An alert eye
And bread nourishes.

Beauty,
Serenity,
Peace,
Waiting.

His perfection
Is mirrored
In them today.

—Ruth F. Gilman

Mother

Her body and blood, she gave to her Son
Then He gave Himself to me,
That's why I thought of mother;
This morning on bended knee.

I'll never forget that union,
When victory o're sin was won,
That powerful, prayerful union,
Of that glorious Mother and Son.

I knew where you'd be this morning,
Where you prayed, 'ere I was born,
That's why you're a wonderful mother;
And I thank Him for you this morn.

You've been such a faithful mother,
In seeing His will was done,
That's why I asked Him this morning,
To help me remain a good son.

I've offered my holy communion,
For you a Spiritual Bouquet, I pledge you my honor,
Dear Mother, To my faith I will always be true,
And I'll thank Almighty God daily, for giving me — to you.

—Vincent Bard

Believe In Yourself

    There is no black,
There is no white,
    Please come together,
We must not fight.

    We all are one,
We've got a mission,
    The deed will be done,
When we stop the racism.

    We dwell on the past,
"But were we there?"
    To criticize each other,
It's just not fair.

    We all are family,
'Til death do us part,
    So face reality,
And follow your heart.

    To the kids of the future,
We still have time,
    To stop the racism,
To stop the crime.

—Tricia L. Worrell

Dreams

We have them when we're young,
They may nestle in our heart
For many a year,
But they will become a reality,
As sure as two plus two, is four.

We have them late in life
And cuddle them close.
Realizing time is shorter
And so very precious
And so very real.

Dreams and love
Go hand in hand.
Both are needed to develop,
The talents, God gave us
To live to the fullest.

—Ruth S. Hill

S.O.S

Electric eyes dancing
They used to shine so bright
You could see when she was glancing
the red, the blue, the white
An American girl
She lives in a dream
But at night you can hear
this young girl scream
And she survives
That's her life
Carries around a switch-blade knife
She's a refugee of pain
Frustration builds inside her brain
I am my own worst enemy
Who lives a life of misery
I cannot speak
These words that I confess
And so I am sending out
This silent S.O.S.

—Sheila R. Hooley

Nebulous

Sitting, watching your life go by
thinking of what should be or
should've been
Nothing...
love in relapsing stages
posing before a goddess
singling out two people
by fate
Roaming the earth
power by hate
building, blind fury
weeks pass by
love is gone
forever - no more

—Millicent W. Uskert

Just You And I

When I sit
    Thinking of you
I feel so blue
    Why do I
feel this way
    I ask myself
everyday
    You're in my thoughts
when I cry
    you make me
feel this way
    I can't stand us
being apart
    I say this with love
and all my heart
    Together we'll be
Just You And I
    always in my thoughts
'til the day I die!

—Tracey McCormack

"Our First Thanksgiving"

Our Pilgrim virtue is upon on us
    this Thanksgiving Day.
Raise the flag of freedom to worship
    and to pray.
Rejoice in fruits abundance that only
    God can convey,
Through these greatest riches our land
    is here to stay.

—Peggy G. Hoffmann

Grandpa Jack

I sit here in the dark
thinking of you with a
glimpse of light shining
from the window unto my face.
The door open and the wind
Blowing my hair back.
Slowly I reach up to get some
of the hair out of my face
and you appear. I get up
and reach for you but I
soon notice you are not
really there. I imagined
being in the room with you
in your arms hugging.
I lay backdown with a tear rolling
you are no longer with us but you
will always be remembered and
loved forever.

—*Yvette Allen*

Blind Faith

I do not understand
This fate that I've been given,

Nor understand the path
That I'm so blindly driven.

All I know is my faith
Is the beacon from which I see

It is my faith in Jesus
That guides me endlessly.

Although I may weary
And in disgust say, "I quit!"

But for all my sins He died for
What more could I forfeit?

So when my life engulfs me
And I've no where left to hide,

Jesus always finds me
Through Him only am I sanctified.

—*Kim E. Whitney*

"A Leaf On The Wind"

I awoke to a voice in a garden
"This is where life comes to grow"
"Which are the weeds, which are
flowers? Please tell me for I
need to know.
The voice so softly whispered
"You are home now my friend
you aren't a weed or a flower
you are but a leaf on the wind."
I told her I felt I was dying
She said "Don't you worry at all.
We are all of us born in
the springtime and pass away
day by day in the fall
We all must go from green
to gold to brown
To float on the breeze
and do as we please
when the wind stops
we all must come down

—*Scott Thomas Lowe*

A Grieving Heart

It happened, without knowledge
This love we now know
It brought only heartache
A long time ago.

For this passes slowly
When your heart is grieving
How could we have known
The happiness we were leaving.

Friendship blossomed to love
That we could not claim
For although we loved deeply,
I had another's name.

We didn't know that fateful day
When we kissed, we held sorrow
For our love once untarnished
Must wait for tomorrow.

In his arms, he held heaven
My once happy life, shame
For I could not hurt the one
Who had given his name.

—*Verna Strause*

Tao

Tao, thou art the way
thou art the light
that guides me night and day
through all my life

Tao, thou art the meaning
and the source
that lights up gleaming
stars so filled with force

Tao, the seen and unseen
move in you
as rhythm to the seasons
ever new

Tao, the glory, wonder,
shining presence
that rips maya asunder
leaving essence

Tao, thou art the act
of life and death
Tao, thou art the act
of cosmic breath.

—*Leslee A. Ellenson*

Frames

You always looked at me
Through your glasses
Before you took them off.
And looked away,
At anything,
Before you put them on.

But when your contacts came
You wore dark glasses—
Sunglasses so dark
I saw myself,
And you didn't look at me
Then.

And now I look for you.
I, who have no frames
To take on and off—
To make artificial
Edges.
And I can't find you.

—*Laura Steinert*

"Your Lover, Your Friend"

Lucky me to have your love
Though we were miles apart,
Our love will feel the gap
Just don't forget...

You're my man,
That warms my heart...
You're that enduring sea,
That cleanse my sight...

Now, I could say,
Let time be the test,
If this love we have
Will reveal the best...

But one thing I would like to say,
You're not the kind of man,
So easy to forget
Just don't forget that...

I could be your lover, your friend
Who'll always here to care
For my love is sweet and tender
To heed till forever...

—*Liv Louise T. Infante*

Jeff

Tears for you
though you are gone
this empty feeling you left-
deep within my soul
how could you be so selfish
how could I be so blind
to not see through your words
to the heart you have left behind
I'll try to be understanding
though I've not understood a thing
how you took your life
and left me here to cry
tears of pain and sorrow
above this subtle joy
that maybe where you are now
you may find the love you died for.

—*Serafina Boxley*

"The Great Griffin"

One two! One two!
Through and through
Aye 'tis the fire breathing Dragon
Oh, Alas the Great Griffin
I shall bring him in tis certain

Such vast fire, breath of fire
Shall I turn back I shan't
As ye whip your tail rave and rant
I have my drawn weapon higher, higher

Oh ye Great Griffin yonder the cave
Ye can overlook into the sea
Swish swash swish swash go we

One two! One two!
Through and through
Aye tis the fire breathing Dragon
Oh, alas the Great Griffin
I shall bring him in tis certain

—*Teri Berta*

Today's Value

She rushes around
Through the bustle
Hectic rush and roar
Of rats
Scurry
In their tall concrete and glass cages

Feet pound
Never in rhythm

Door slams
Another day
Gone

I asked
"Ever watch a sunset?"

"No."

We watched a sunset today
—*Richard H. Tessitore*

I Found a Way...

I found a way,
Through the night.
By waking up,
And seeing the light.

My dreams are over,
My thoughts renewed.
I'll surpass the day,
By being hopeful and shrewd.

New beginnings,
Are the best kind.
The future is at hand,
But what will we find.

Resolutions,
Start the day.
In the final hour,
We'll find a way.
—*Matt Spencer*

Never Lonely Is The Wind

Over the prairie as it ripples
Through the folds of meadow grass
Coming forth in morning splendor
Giving word that night is past.

Carrying with it gentle whispering
As the leaves must part as friends,
And the Frosty snows of winter
Lay their windrows end to end.

Just as springtime meets the summer
Dancing partners of the clouds
As they change the worldly mantle
Waving heaven's brightest shrouds.

Sailing shipmates of the schooners
As they sailed from shore to shore
Opening up the distant boundaries
Of the Worlds that lay before

And we sit in awe and wonder
As we listen to the trees
At this wind that God has mated
To the earth and sky and seas.
—*Robert G. Barth*

Love Is Sweet

Love is so special
thy once one person told
Love is so special
Know one really knows
As once a person said
Love is here now
So don't let it end
The person said you don't know
What love is until it's dead
Some people say that you
Don't know that love is until
You experience it, but
Love thy not in the mind or sole
but thy in the heart
As you say the word love
means so little
but as you show the word love
means so much more
—*Benton J. Monk Sr.*

Life

Life is precious and has its
time,
Do what you can as I must with
mine.
Don't let anyone stand in your
way,
It's your life don't waste it
away.
Life is something to be accepted and
treasured,
It's full of joy and many many
pleasures.
Life is precious and has its
time,
Do what you can as I must with
mine.
—*Rebecca O'Neill*

A First

Sharing times together
Times just you and me
Walking alone into the sunset
Fires among the beach
Not knowing what lies ahead
Or what will come of us
Is there a future that's destine
Or will we smother out
Well, summer's come and gone
A new ground we must roam
It's changed our lives forever
No more past to be found
Holding hands through hard times
Letting our love shine through all
Still looking back in the past
Brings lots of hope and hurt
Nothing will change how I feel
No matter what anyone says
It's a rough road ahead
Together we'll try our best.
—*Rebecca McCormick*

The World's End

The world is coming to an end,
to bad we're not united.
We think our home country is best
that we should kill all the rest.

The world is coming to an end,
but can you say "a world".
Separate worlds is more like it.
We are not peaceful nations.

The world is coming to an end,
with no help from the leaders,
and there's no denying that.

The world is coming to an end,
pollution, discrimination, war,
drugs, this list might never end,
and that is why the world will end.
—*Nancy Lisa LoPreto*

Someone

Someone to talk with
To calm all my fears.
Someone to hold me -
To wipe away the tears.

Someone to be there
When I need a friend.
Someone to reach out
Just to lend a hand.

Someone to love me
When I feel so alone.
Someone to break through
My surrounding wall of stone.

Someone to care
As if nothing else matters.
Someone to let the sun shine
While the rain still patters.

Someone, he is.
So special to me
Someone is one man: Who else could it be?

My Father.
—*T. Sanfratello*

Reverend Martin Luther King Jr.

To help somebody,
To feed all who are hungry,
To clothe the naked,
This is all our Great God's Plan,
And mine, an African man...

In Stockholm they gave
Me a prestigious Award,..
The Nobel Peace Prize...
In Memphis my award was
The lone assassin's lead gift...

Do not speak of my
Education, my degrees,
Material possessions..
I died a Baptist preacher,
Reaching out for Freedom's hand...

Now you make this world
A paradise for mankind...
This means you must pray...
This means you must focus on
The Black Madonna and Child.
—*Martin J. O'Malley Jr.*

Child Abuse

I'm hiding in a corner trying
to find away out.
But all I can do is pout.
The yelling and screaming comes
Stomping in the room, trying to
find me so he can hit me with
a broom.
Soon he starts to yell I feel
like I'm in hell.
I have to come out but all
I can do is shout.
Then he let's out all his
anger and throws me on the bed.
Sometimes I wish he would
get it over with, or why can't
I just be dead.

　　　　—Naomi Toporovsky

Yesterday

Yesterday I wish I could go back
To fix the wrong I've done
I loved her
and didn't mean what I did
The pain I've caused
drew people to hate me
glancing down at her,
her beauty was revealed
Her eyes were
a clear blue sea
Her face was
as smooth as a baby's skin
Walking from the casket
I wished I could go back
To fix the wrong I've done

　　　　—Jason Proffitt

Christmas Is.....

Christmas is, the time of year,
To give the gifted of good cheer.
To show the one, you hold so dear,
The love you feel, when they are near.
Christmas is, a time to pray,
For those who feel, so blue and gray.
To show the way, for those astray,
That Jesus is, the only way.
Christmas is, a time to morn.
Those you miss, who've gone before.
To know inside, when life is done,
You'll join them there, in days to come.

　　　　—Pamela Clem

How Love Blooms

Love starts like a bud of a flower,
Then it blooms, into a beautiful rose.
Love can start at day break or
At the break of sundown.
Just like a rose, anyone can smell
The fresh sweet aroma of love.
Love is about trusting, listening,
And sharing feelings with each other
Like deepest and darkest secrets.
But unlike a rose the love
Will never wilt or die....
　If its the love with that
　　Special Someone!

　　　　—Miranda Paulus

"Yearnings"

I yearn for my woman,
To have and to hold.
　I yearn for her touch,
No matter how bold.
　I yearn for her caress,
The curve of her hips.
　I yearn for the loving.
In her warm tender lips.
　I yearn for her kisses,
Her soft special hugs.
　I yearn for her whispers,
Her playful little slugs.
　I yearn for her thoughts.
And all of her caring.
　I yearn for the children,
Of our's she's bearing.
　I yearn for her sweetness,
A long loving life.
　I yearn for that one,
Who is my wife.

　　　　—William A. Thomas

OLD

To grow older is to know less,
To know more and say less is older.
How old is old?
Old is years accumulated.
Years that speak in colors.
Gray streaks and brown spots.
The heart doesn't know age.
Age tells tales.
Tales are times remembered.
Slightly colored.
To remember when times were different.
Is different old?

　　　　—Madeline Barrale

"Sisters"

Sisters are special people
to laugh with and to cry
Sisters are special people
who are always by your side.
Sisters are special people
to share your feelings with
Sisters are special people
one of God's many gifts.
Sisters are special people
who always know how you feel
Sisters are special people
that no one can ever steal.
Sisters are special people
a very unique creation
Sisters are special people
and there's no closer relation.

　　　　—Valerie Raufer

Untitled

Hope is the answer -
　　to life
　　to dreams.
Without hope we are empty -
　　without life
　　without dreams.
From where does hope come -
　　from life
　　from dreams.
Hope is a circle.

　　　　—Sara J. Brown

True Immortality Ode to the Eternal

We must go where our saviour slept
To reach our true immortality.
Back to the soil which gives us life.
Where the sun and the rain always wept.
We will rise from Earth as the rose
As it blossoms after the morning rain
To be with him as the Morning Glory
Out upon the new life's glorious plain.
Then, we will embellish our new birth
When he has raised us from the Earth.
To be with Him in Glory forever more.
Let us praise such a mighty God
Who lifts us from this Earth
As a beautiful flower, in Eden, restored.

　　　　—Richard Lee Cox

Just For You

I would walk a thousand miles just
to see your face,

I would search the world over without
leaving a trace,

I would climb the highest mountain
just to hold your hand,

I would even swim the ocean blue
or cross the Rio Grand,
If only I could hold you close;
our bodies become one,

And the bond we share will get stronger;
it will never be undone,

So you see, my love, there is nothing
I wouldn't do for you,

You will always be my one and only;
my heart it shall stay true.

　　　　—Sue Alexander

We Ever Yearn

At times we have the need,
　to seek, and somehow find
the peace and sweet content
　which soothes the troubled mind.

Some call it; "getting back to nature,"
　replacing siren and wail,
the roar of heavy traffic,
　with sounds on a muted scale.

Soft as gentle music,
　we hear the sound of stream,
the whisper of the wind,
　and rhythm reigns supreme.

We find a reverence in our heart,
　for the beauty of the space,
that which we have journeyed to,
　a peaceful resting-place.

Reluctantly we leave,
　and vow we shall return,
to find once more the soothing peace,
　for which we ever yearn.

　　　　—Luke N. Baxter

To Emily

What can I say Emily,
To tell you what you mean to me?
Your ready smile, extended arms,
Your joyous words, your special charms.

When I hear you call my name,
No other voice is quite the same.
Oh Gramma-her! Oh, Gramma-her!
No other voice could be more dear.

Your touch so special, all your own,
As tiny fingers start of roam,
Lightly touching as you trace,
Lines of age across my face.

Baby fingers lightly move,
Cooing softly, you can smooth,
Away the worries of the day,
By your happy baby play.

What other child could be more dear,
That one who calls me Gramma-her!

—*Nancy L. Goode*

Price To Pay

The wig dropped down
    To the dirty old ground
As the hatchet was buried deep,
More dead than alive
    She struggled to survive
And managed to keep her feet.
She whirled around
    For the crack of a sound
Was screaming towards her head.
With one swift smack
    The steel struck her back
and indeed this gal was dead.
What a price to pay
    for a real short stay
on this old planet earth.
Why, some would say
    on a far off bay
She would return in a brand new birth.

—*Timothy C. Carnes*

The Poet

The poet caresses hearts
To uplift souls,
Writing feeling charts
For easy rhythm flows.

Measured line and meter
Making pattern whole,
Lyrics that endure
Is every poet's goal.

Phrasing without a symphony
Keeping natural tone,
Following cadence carefully
The poet sings alone.

And the final stanzas
Accomplish the art,
Creating poetic arias
With written music parts

Like candles and arrows
True sighting marks,
Poets as heroes
When - lighting minds and hearts.

—*Stanley W. Schmidt*

My Best Friend

Mother, you were always there
To wash my face, to comb my hair.
You brought me up to be polite,
You kept me safe throughout the night.
Into my teens I grew so dumb,
I didn't heed your rule of thumb.
I caused you such a lot of grief,
I knew best was my belief.
I had to learn the hardest way
So here is what I'd like to say:
I didn't mean to be so bad,
I didn't mean to make you sad.
I have to put these things to rest
Because you really were the best.
You never turned your back on me,
So let me say quite gratefully
I'm glad things worked out in the end,
I love you Mom, you're my best friend.

—*Jean Nickerson*

Untitled

        Parental duties
    too numerous to name,
    once you have kids
    you're never the same.

One minute they're darling
    so lovable and sweet,
    before you know it
your insanity is complete.

They'll fight all day long
    bite, kick and scratch,
it's like Frazier and Ali's
    famous boxing match.

You love and protect them
and guide them with care,
    all you get in return
    is lots of gray hair.

    Don't get me wrong
    they're truly a gift,
just look into their eyes
and feel your heart lift.

—*Luanne Richardson*

Secrets To Tell

Little girl, all alone
Too young, to know what to do.

Wrinkled shirt;
Shorts to the knees.

A secret kept well
When there's no one to tell.

If you heard the screaming,
If you felt the pain,
Don't ask what happened,
Thoughts gone insane.

Nothing can change
What's in the past.
And whose to blame,
The memory of her acts?

Little girl, burning inside
Too much to say, about yesterday.

Innocent body;
Fallen to a sin.

A secret to tell
That's hidden all too well.

—*Kiffany L. Hoover*

Winter Recipe

Take a ton of cake mix
toss it on the ground
on the roof spread fluffy icing
hang glossy popsicles down.
Spread topping on the fences
sift sugar on the walks
dredge flour on the trees
stack cotton candy on the posts.
Tell the breeze to stir
ask the sun to bake
cool it in the night air
then everyone partake.

—*Berniece C. Smith*

The Wharf

See the wind
Touch a waterfowl

Smell the sea
Through its shells

Hear in the shrill
Of stream whistles;
Sounds of my love

Watch fish bones
Floating— the remains
Of souls long gone

—*Soon Chul Lee*

Untitled

I'm here at home
Trying to write a poem.
It has to rhyme.
Want to know the time?
It's 8:22.
I have a lot to do -
Physics, Trigonometry, and English too.
And this poem I'm writing is over due.
It's now 8:29.
Seven minutes passed away.
I couldn't think of anything to say.
Writing this poem is pretty tough.
Have I written enough?

—*Steven Yacco*

"Negative, To Positive"

Turn a negative, to positive.
Turn your frown, upside down.
Turn a negative, to positive,
and your LIFE will turn around.

You can always find some GOOD,
out of everything, that's bad.
You'll just have to TRAIN your mind,
to be HAPPY! Never sad!

You'll CONTROL your life, and destiny,
with this SIMPLE little plan:
Never say, "I CAN'T DO IT!"
Turn it around! Say, "YES! I CAN!"

That's a lesson someone taught me,
and you know? It's really TRUE!
You can change your life and fortune.
Frame of MIND,... is up to YOU!

Turn a negative, to positive.
That's all you have to do.
Find the GOOD, in every bad,
and the "BEST".....will come to you.

—*Pauline Di Benedetto*

653

Multi-Cultural Poem

J - Japanese, Jewish
U - Urkranians
S - Scottish, Spanish
T - Turkish
I - Italian, Irish, Indochinese
C - Chinese, Cuban
E - English

F - French, Finnish
O - Oklahoma, Indians
R - Russians, Romanians

A - Afro - Americans
L - Lithuanians
L - Luxem Borgdians

—*Theresa*

Gray Cat...

Gray cat
Ugly cat
Meowing at me with your
Ugly cat meow
At my open bedroom window,
You come and bother me
I'd let you in, but
I don't know where you've been
Little cat
Standing against my open window mesh
With your little green
Cat eyes that glow translucent
In the light
Striped cat
Long cat tail
Go away
Run away

—*April Ivy*

Shadows Of Shame

Today shadows of shame;
    uncovered.
    Fall has began,
leaves hit the ground.
They crumble and feel pain.

Today shadows of shame;
    mystified.
    The Body Naked;
the tree no longer whole;
    Just branches,
scratching the soul.

    Shadows of shame
        you see,
    No one knows them,
    except the trees.

—*Michelle Stelter Lee*

Untitled

Your hyena laugh rose up
Strong through the cocktail party.
Have another sip of your gin and tonic.
Close your eyes,
All around you the people talking
(You must listen closely)
They sound like a pack of excited dogs
At the kennel.
One dog is going home
The rest are loudly protesting
Their imprisonment.

—*Stephen C. Zimmerly*

My Grand-daughter

I have a lovely grand-daughter
Unique in every way.
She's the only one remembers me
on every special day.

She comes up here to be with me.
She helps me do my work.
She showers me with love to be
The queen for all to see.

It's not because I'm prejudice
It really is just so.
She's one, we can be proud of.
That's true ... because I know.

—*Addie Johnson*

A Shattered Life

    A precious little child wakes
up, alone, in the dark.
    She has no family to call
her own, her life is left
without a spark.
    The clothes she wears
are tearing, while mine are
trimmed with lace.
    And I walk by her
staring, as a tear sheds
from her face.

—*Michelle McInnis*

Untitled

A kiss.....
Upon my lips
While in early morning slumber
Brushed so gently
    yet so real,
Even the essence of your hair
    filled the air.
Half awake,
Reaching up, thou dreaming still,
I saw your tanned and freckled face
    smiling,
        above me.
Could it be some spatial sign
    that you do
        truly
        love me?

—*Viviane Cochrane*

Civil? Unrest

All the angry young men trying
to take back the night - breaking,
looting, yelling at their plight of
poverty with no hope, no jobs, no
future thinking they have the right
(in the name of Rodney King) as the
sons of slaves, as the brothers of
Malcolm X to take, take, take without
looking back those VCRs, those TV
sets that have given them hope for a
moment that the nation couldn't ignore
their broken dreams splayed across TV
screens as people watched in fear as
L.A. burned down in flames.

—*Robin Ikemi*

Politics

Cyclones of rhetoric!
Volcanoes of bombast!
Downpours of claptrap!
Rivers of rodomontade!

Veiled truths.
Half-lies.
Insinuating accusations.
Innuendo.

Where lies honor?
Where truth?
Where integrity?
Where lies hope?

Not in apathy.
Not in indifference.
Not in passiveness.
Not in complacency

Political corruption,
Allowed to flourish
In the sterile garden
Of empty voting booths!

—*Susan S. Hume*

Untitled

His smile is like the sunrise,
Warm and welcoming
His words like love,
Kind and gentle
He swore his love to me always
But soon I learned I was deceived
His smile and words became thorns
Piercing my heart
All the memories and love washed away
Leaving my heart an unfeeling wasteland
He left an impression on my mind,
in my heart, and in my soul
Leaving me alone and helpless
Searching
Forever searching
For the love to fill this void in my life
The only love,
His love.

—*Becky Spencer*

Acquiesce

Your cloak no longer
warms my bones,
I loose the ties
and step out free.
I stare at the
macabre dance
of withered limbs
paying homage to
an unforgiving moon.
The night wind
blows chill and hard.
I am alone
and shiver in my nakedness.
I feel the beady eye
of time trace peaks and valleys
upon my cheek.
Then slowly I turn
and join the wind,
the limbs,
and the unforgiving moon.

—*Barbara Shreder*

Cycle

A young boy
Was born into this world today.
What is his purpose?
This I cannot say.

A young boy
Took his first steps today.
Will he learn to run?
This I cannot say.

A young man
Finished college today.
Does he have a future?
This I cannot say.

An old man
Was taken from this world today.
What was his purpose?
This I cannot say.

A young boy
Was born into this world today.
What is his purpose?
This I cannot say.

—*Michael Jay Magee*

T.L.

The man I always longed for
Was difficult to find.
I searched for him high and low
And found him drunk on wine.

He looked at me through
blurry eyes and tearfully he said,
"I hate for you to see me, darling
I wish that I were dead."

The mattress that he lay upon
Was matted down and gray.
I reached for rags and covered him,
And then he passed away.

I kissed his dirty, whiskered face,
And held his wrinkled hand.
He was the one that I loved most,
My Father was the man.

—*Tereasa Bellew*

Old? Me?

I used to think that growing old
Was just a change of year.
I didn't know your teeth came out
Or that you couldn't hear.

The steps are so much higher
The cars all go so fast
I can't see like I used to
And I love a little nap.

My middle seems much bigger
And my bottom sits a lot,
I think about some exercise
But it's too cold - or hot!

Does being senile come with age?
I'm sure I couldn't say
I can't find the book that tells!
I'll search another day.

—*Peggy Starnes*

Summer Loves

I loved you my love, I think
was stronger. You don't understand
the hate, or the reason I don't love you
any longer.

I thought you understood my
feelings, I really thought you cared.
All the times we talked, the things
you said, the trust we shared.

You will always be in my
dreams somehow this I know.

But your spirit in my heart,
buried under snow.

—*Korrie Henderson*

Like Unto Thee

No more of this uncertainty -
We claim Thy Mercies now.
We've worked and waited -
Fought and prayed
For miracles from Thou;
Our sins died in an ocean....
The echoes took the wind...
Light angels freed our innocence -
And carried it to Him.

—*Myrtle Trott*

Time

How much do we have?
We don't know—
At times it seems
To move very slow,

Sometimes it flies—
as the winter snows—
And we have cause to wonder
Where it goes?

There are moments we find
When our hearts are full
Of thanks for the time
to be dutiful

But pleasures are many
and laughter sublime
When we give to others
The gift of our Time!

—*Anne Mary Bass*

Grandpa's Birthday

It was Grandpa's birthday party.
We gathered to celebrate.
Before unwrapping presents,
We sat down to cut the cake.
Cousin Pam put the candles on,
"Make a wish, Gramps!" we cried.
He thought for a moment,
He huffed and puffed.
And then,
Grandma died.

—*Michelle Fulmer*

Friends

Friends are special people
We meet along the way
Some cross our paths just briefly,
While others come to stay.

Each one adds their brush strokes
To the canvas of our heart
And leaves a lasting touch of love
That sets them so apart.

And as the years roll on, it seems
The colors melt and flow
Till somewhere in our life's mid-stream
The picture starts to glow.

Then we become aware, a new
of God's own plan for us
And know that all the time, it's true
His hand has held the brush!

—*Ruth W. Fields*

"Skin"

When raising a child
     we must begin
Discuss no validity
     to color of Skin
Whatever the color
Whatever the shade
The image of Man
     created not made
Each one has it's own
     style or a way
Let's try not to judge
     and start a new day
And hopeful together
     a Life of peace
But only if the race
     wars cease
For all who are equal
     not outside but in
Cause it never matters
     the color of Skin.

—*Susan Donovan*

Popularity

     What is this need
We so desperately want to be?

     Once, just once we'd
     Like to find the key

To joining in the "right"
     crowd, the "fun" crowd

     This is not the way
     To make your peers
          Proud

You automatically become
     A target of evil hate

Then you begin to wonder
     If it's all that great

     What is this need
We so desperately want to be?

     Once, just once we'd
     Like to find the key...

     To popularity...

—*Monica Buenrustro*

River Drifters

You are darker than the rain.
Harder than the wind
Black river bottom
I've returned again.
Where does your heart lie.
Alongside, hazy in my head.
Or lost swirling dead inside.
Why all these currents of change
Your answers go drifting by
You are unfair placing love songs
In my heart, to carry them away
Before a melody to sing by
Yet in this is the answer.
A circle, a rippled ringlet.
A continuance of your knowledge.
And presence in the cycle.
Which falls and rises over again.
You are an entirety so basic.
Without form yet a formation.

  —Jeff Kemme

Just Yet

Where are you?
I wonder, if by chance,
We ever watch the same sunset,
Or wish on the same
Falling star.
Sometimes,
In the middle of the day,
I'll feel like crying
And I wonder
If maybe it's you
That's sad,
If maybe we are connected
By something not seen.
Are we meant to be?
When I see you,
Will my heart jump,
Or my spirit soar,
Or have we already met?
And maybe,
I don't like you, Just Yet!

  —Tracey Smith

Fade Away

The minutes pass water through my hands
The days fade in and out like the rolling waves of the sea
Time intertwines with the solitude of distant lonely lands
Like the soul inside my mind that leaves my heart to bleed
I'm hiding in my dwelling place at last
Afraid to face the dying dream of life
Yet afraid to turn and step into the past
And be faced with yet another wall to blast
I cannot run nor can I turn away
I cannot rest or find the strength to play
My one desire is to just fade away
As if I was a dark and dreary day.

  —Lori Meier

Thoughts

As I sit and watch the candles turn into a
pile of melted wax, thoughts run through my head.
Thoughts about things we can do, things we can be,
remember keep your dreams in your heart and hold
them there successfully.

  —Johanna Andrews

The Flower of Endless Love

When I think of you, I think of all your love and beauty to behold.
Stop and take a moment to look at the Roses.
They remind me so much of you

With all their ardent beauty so early in the morning, as the rising sun rays
shine upon the buds and the tiny dew drops that gently fade away from the warmth,
so could I make your tears vanish, from the warmth of my touch.

As the bud begins to open, to release the wonderful fragrance of love
and invites us into the heart of it, to partake of the love it offers...
So do I invite you into my heart to accept all my love.

The petals, so velvet to the touch, are so tender and should be handled with care...
so would I handle you with the tenderness of care and love.

As the dusk of eve falls upon them, they begin to gently close
as if to say, hold me through the night... As I would hold you
in my arms until the beautiful sun rays dawn another day.
 The Flower of Endless Love.

  —Garnett L. Hays

Tumbleweed

  I'm like a tumble weed —
which seems to have no beauty...
  Only nature recognizes my purpose —
for the beauty exists within me!
  I'm like a tumbleweed in the desert —
Thousands are all about me...
  yet I'm still alone!
like the tumbleweed —
  I tumble to worlds end; hoping to be free,
The winds not blowing
  I stopped for awhile...
I finally found the answer —
  It all begins with me!

  —O'Dean M. Grant

Through Someone Else's Eyes

This morning, I saw eyes so intense, love so deep, a
relationship so rare being shared by a mother and her
daughter displaying a bond of trust and a heart filled
with so much love.

As I watched, I couldn't help but notice the warmth of
tenderness that radiated between the two binding souls.
Their facial expression was non-verbal yet their
expression manifested;

    a passion of caring,
    a passion of belonging,
   a passion of understanding,
    and a passion of loyalty.

As I continued to watch a mother embrace her daughter
with her eyes, I could see the harmony that lay between
them as they communicated their affection and respect
for one another. Their bonding seemed so pure and
peaceful that I dare not interrupt their world.

As I looked through their eyes, I now understand the
meaning of motherly love, it's the nurturing spirit that
exists between the two binding souls that makes them
inseparable.

  —Naomi Johnson

Dawn and I

List'ning to the dawn creeping up on me;
Watching closely 'cross the mirror-like lake;
At daybreak there's a dim tranquility,
As all, even the sun, begin to wake.

The golden-red sun hesitantly peeks,
Over the water and over the hills;
In the cool quiet the early morn speaks;
And everything around instantly stills.

With new vigor the sun begins to rise;
It glides over the high peaks of the land;
It quickly lights up the lazy blue skies;
And the bluish-gray lakeshore becomes tanned.

The awakening earth seems faintly to blush,
As morning comes in a glorious hush.
        —*Jessica Gerrior*

Old Pictures

High on a shelf for a long, long time,
    Some of them cracked or curled.
They hardly seemed worth the climb,
    What value could they have in my world?

Sorting began, old times and old places
    Brought surprising feelings of pleasure.
Memories awakened by long gone faces
    Made every old picture my treasure.
        —*Jane C. Ellis*

Tell Me Oh Lord

What will I be?
Tell me, oh Lord
Will I soar in the air
Or stay on the ground?
Will I rise to great heights
Or be naive and simple
Be barren or fruitful,
Tell me, oh Lord
What is my purpose?
Will I just lie here
Rolling, rusting and nervous.
        —*Deloris L. Ross*

Canis Eyes

Feelin' confident on a fine spring day
    gonna get my fill.
Sky's a-blue, sun shinin' thru the
    trees where I look out.
Prey's all gone so I come to roam the
    prairies, pastures, and farms.
Hunger drives me to a savage beast
    I ask God for one more feast.
Bitch and beau are afraid of me so
    that they hide behind the barn.
Old man peaks out, I hear him shout
    with such incense, "You dirty sinister bastard!"
Had killer, rippin-shreddin times here before
    but the thrill was never so intense.
So here I go and rip open the belly of the old man's bore:
    Smith & Wesson on sight
        lose game without fight
            ...should've waited 'till night.
        —*David Rocco DelNegro*

Arthritis

They say you've got arthritis,
Because you ache in every joint —
You keep on taking medicine,
but what the hell's hells the point —
Your joints they keep on aching,
As you hobble here and there —
Each year it's a little harder,
To go up and down the stairs —
The Doctor, he keeps on talking,
About putting a new knee in —
He says, "We pop the old joint out,
and put in one of tin' —
I kind of think he might be right,
And though I'm not enthusiastic —
I just might let him do the job,
If the new joint is made of plastic.
        —*Walt Rhule*

Thousands of trees
Holding centuries of life
Waiting
to take their next breath
that will last for eternity.
        —*Michelle Ortwein*

Ten years old they bend and fight,
The Russians come with all their might,
With courage none but theirs to give,
They wield a gun and try to live,
The trollies turned over out in the street,
And bodies lying at their feet.
With freedom blooming ere two days hence,
They fight and fight the great Iron Fence,
What kind are these who would destroy,
The freedom of a little boy,
With blood and guts and Man against Might,
A merciless and dreadful Freedom fight,
The battle rages in its domain,
While ten thousand ride the freedom train,
Why this so young a life to give,
That of a boy for men to live,
With courage true from God above,
They fight and die for Freedom's Love.
        —*Billy Walker*

"Jeannie and Tim
forever to be!"
are the words carved deep
in a hickory tree.

And through many good times
about three to four years,
they've been together
through laughter and tears.

Now those words
are tattered and worn
but a grim reminder
of a love forlorn.

Maybe it wasn't
meant to be,
just a fanciful dream
spelled out on a tree.
        —*Linda Fogarty*

BIOGRAPHIES

ABERECROMBIE, GLENN
[b.] June 4, 1926; [p.] John and Lucy Aberecrombie (Norman, Arkansas); [m.] Divorced; [ed.] Milgore High School, Milgore Junior College, North Texas State Teacher's College; [occ.] Retired Hot Metal Printer; [memb.] ACLU, ADA, AARP, DAV-LIFE Member; [oth. writ.] Scant writings in college newspapers, some writings in veteran's publications; [pers.] Motto: "In Odds We Trust", financially and socially.

ABRAM, PAUL
[b.] January 3, 1930, Windber, Pennsylvania; [p.] Paul E. and Beatrice Abram (both deceased); [m.] Cynthia, October 23, 1992; [ch.] Rebecca Campbell, Laura Stauffer; [ed.] University of Pittsburgh; [occ.] Retired; [oth. writ.] Newspaper news stories, features and editorials during 35 year career. [a.] Johnstown, PA.

ABRAMS, DAVID BARUCH
[pen.] David Abrams, Dave Abrams; [b.] July 6, 1972, Sumter, South Carolina; [p.] Samuel and Adelle Abrams; [ed.] Sophomore at the Citadel: The Military College of South Carolina-Biology, pre-med major; [occ.] Student; [memb.] AOPA, Race Relations Committee, Presidential Advisory Committee SCLEDA; [hon.] President's List, Dean's List, Sophomore Class President; [oth. writ.] High school literary magazine; [pers.] Poetry is the mirrored thought of a poet, and upon their writing, they share with the world, a part of themselves. [a.] Sumter, SC 29150.

ACQUISTAPACE, KIMBERLY
[b.] October 22, 1971, Mt. Shasta, California; [p.] Eugene and Julie Acquistapace; [ed.] WEED High, Siskiyous Junior College, AA-Humboldt University; [a.] Eureka, CA 95501.

AGOZZINO, MARIE
[b.] Raritan, New Jersey; [p.] Joseph and Graziella; [ed.] Bridgewater-Raritan High School West, The Art Institute of Fort Lauderdale; [occ.] Specialty and Theatrical Clothing/Accessory Designer; [hon.] Honor Roll, Fashion Merit Honor, additional Art, Dance, and Music awards; [oth. writ.] Poems/songs appeared in local literature publications; [pers.] Life is a dream, a mystical and magical moonlight...The Divine Love...A path to fulfillment, a secret that allures you, an enchanted melody that captures your soul, and leads your heart to dance...Close your eyes, open your mind, escape the chains of disbelief. Take the hand of the child within you, and let the adventure begin...[a.] Fort Lauderdale, FL.

AHERN, FRANK L. Jr.
[b.] June 20, 1922, Somerville, Massachusetts; [p.] Deceased; [m.] Deceased; [ed.] BS in ME, Cornell, June 1944, and LLB George Washington University, IN; [occ.] February 1953, Retired; [memb.] Lapsed; [oth. writ.] I have an unpublished Ms. about the sinking of "The SITZ", which my poem is about; [pers.] None, really I simply take care of myself in order to stay healthy, and I keep myself pretty busy too. [a.] Covington, KY.

AHO, ELEANOR K.
[b.] July 19, 1920, Kalamazoo, Michigan; [p.] Joseph and Margaret Martin; [m.] Deceased, July; [ch.] Gary, Kathleen, Glenn and James; [ed.] Kalamazoo Central High School, Southwestern Michigan College of Nursing, Gogebic Community College; [occ.] Retired Nurse; [memb.] Range Art Association, Pewabic Pens; [hon.] Only art awards. Best of show, numerous first prizes ribbons, etc.; [oth. writ.] Numerous poems and short stories; [pers.] I have been inspired by my mother who was an author and poet. I feel that this recognition is a memorial to her. [a.] Ironwood, MI 49938.

AIELLO, AMY
[b.] July 29, 1979, Attleboro, Massachusetts; [p.] Anthony and Barbara Aiello; [ed.] 7th grade, Qualters Middle School; [occ.] Student; [hon.] Veteran's Day Essay, Expo Project on Poetry, Together We Can essay; [oth. writ.] Poetry and editorials; [pers.] I enjoy writing because it enables me to express who I am, my thoughts, feelings, and also observations. I was influenced by my Nana Ryan and also many of my teachers. [a.] Mansfield, MA 02048.

ALBANESE, JILL
[b.] September 11, 1972, El Paso, Texas; [p.] Bernie and Valerie Albanese; [ed.] Don Lugo High School; [occ.] File Clerk, United Title, Phoenix, AZ; [hon.] Honorable Mention, Poetry Contest 1992; [oth. writ.] Several poems that I'm trying to get published. [pers.] My poems all have personal interests, and my influence has been my mother. [a.] Phoenix, AZ 85051.

ALDRICH, CHRISTINE R.
[pen.] Chris; [b.] May 23, 1967, Columbus, Nebraska; [p.] Steve and Jeanne Haney; [ch.] Aaron and Adam Davidson; [ed.] Columbus High, Platle College; [occ.] Certified Welder, Behlen MFG Columbus, NE; [memb.] ATA, NRA; [hon.] German Weld Certification, Government Weld Certification, State of Nebraska Weld Certification; [oth. writ.] Several poems published in high school yearbook, poems pending acceptance to Hallmark, Inc., [pers.] Most poems I write are reflections of love, that has entered my life, and made me see, reality through eyes of others. [a.] Rising City, NE 68658.

ALEXANDER, KELLEN
[[b.] February 27, 1985, Strongsville, Ohio; [p.] Donald and Rae Alexander; [ch.] Brothers-Andrew (11), Colby (2), sister-Aubrey (5); [ed.] Strongsville Co-Op Pre-School Dexter Drake Elementary; [oth. writ.] There's A Mouse In My House, The Seasons, My Cat Is Missing, My Baby Brother; [pers.] I love animals and enjoy writing about them.

ALFARO, ANTONIO, JR.
[b.] September 21, 1972, McAllen, Texas; [p.] Antonio and Aida Alfaro, Sr.; [ed.] McAllen Memorial High School, University of Texas at Austin; [occ.] Student; [oth. writ.] Numerous collection of poems not yet published; [pers.] Poetry in its simplest form can create warmth in one's heart.

ALFIERO, GILDA
[b.] October 24, 1970, Montreal, Quebec; [p.] Anselmo and Cesina Alfiero; [ed.] Trafalgar School for Girls, Mariahopolis College, McGill University; [occ.] Student (BA in Psychology); [memb.] The Migraine Foundation, Amnesty International, McGill Literacy Council; [hon.] Samnium '93 Summer School in Italy (scholarship); [oth. writ.] Several journal entries to be published in a volume by "L'Universita'del Molise" in Campobasso, Italy; [pers.] Inspired by the personal experiences, I contemplate the existential nature and the psychological condition of the individual. [a.] Montreal North, Quebec, H1H 5E3 Canada.

ALGUIRE, JESSIE
[b.] October 9, 1918, Montreal, Quebec; [p.] Naomi and Henry Wood; [m.] Arthur, 1938; [ch.] 4 daughters; [ed.] Montreal High; [occ.] Retired-Senior Widow; [oth. writ.] Have been writing poetry since I was a young child. It is a source of pleasure and enjoyment to me. [a.] I use my talents to help people who need enjoyment and a little understanding in their lives-this is my enjoyment. [a.] LaSalle Providence of Quebec, Canada H8P 2J4.

ALKINC, MARGARET
[b.] May 15, 1952, Hackensack, New Jersey, [p.] Theodore L. and Katherine S. Van Winkle, June 28, 1991; [ed.] BA English Literature-Montclair State University; [occ.] Computer Sales; [memb.] Human Race; [hon.] Semi-finalist in your 1993 North American Open Poetry Contest; [oth. writ.] Many poems and several short stories, all unpublished; [pers.] To turn the pages of my lie with humor, hope, and honor. [a.] Rutherford, NJ 07070.

ALLBRIGHT, PATRICIA A.
[b.] January 31, 1938, Scottsville, Kentucky; [p.] James B. and Audrey Gibson; [m.] Robert K., September 14, 1985; [ch.] Gregory Lee Warren, James Marshall Warren; [ed.] 1 year Nurses' Training, Good Samaritan Hospital School of Nursing, Course in Human Services, Anchorage Community College, Anchorage, AK; [occ.] Long Distance Telephone Operator-Retired. Part-time Q.M.A.; [memb.] Order of Eastern Star, Extension Homemakers Club, Garden Club; [oth. writ.] Essay-"A Calling to Care", placed first at Medco of French Lick, sent to ISBH. Writings consist mostly of essays, poems, and personal diary; [pers.] Life is sacred, protect it, care for it and enjoy it. Life is beautiful when you are true to yourself. Everyday is a blessing when you listen to that still small voice from within; you know what is right, so do it, find a place that makes you happy and go there. When you pass through the fire, remember, it will pass, go from strength to strength, things always have a way of working themselves out. A Life is no mystery all of the answers are in the precious book of God and it is so beautifully written. [a.] Shoals, IN 47581.

ALLEE, RHONDA LEE
[b.] April 12, 1973, Oriville, California; [p.] Carol Mitchell and Ronald Lee Allee; [m.] William Landon, September 1989; [ch.] Jessica Elizabeth, Justin James; [occ.] Homemaker; [oth. writ.] Collection of poetry and unpublished children's books; [pers.] Enjoy touching people's lives and hearts with my writings. [a.] Olathe, CO 81401.

ALLEN, JEAN BEARDSLEY
[pen.] Jean Allen - Jean Swengel; [b.] September 25, 1923, Paintsville, Kentucky; [p.] Dr. and Mrs. D.H. Swengel; [m.] William T., July 5, 1984 (formerly widowed); [ch.] Paula Beardsley Steele, Scott, Douglas, and Richard Beardsley; [ed.] BS and Masters, Michigan State University- majors (Human Ecology, Speech and English); [occ.] Retired teacher, Family Focus East Lansing, MI; [memb.] D.A.R. National Defense Church, Fine Arts and Opera Guild of Sarasota, Republican Women's Club, S.D.A. Church Membership, Symphony Guild of Sarasota, Christian

Women; [hon.] Omicron Nu National Human Ecology honorary, Dean's List Mrs. Homemaker for 3 counties in MI; [oth. writ.] Threads of Time, published by Destiny Image, 1993, by Jean Swengel, Mystery of the Messiah, copyright 1989 used in the prison ministry of Florida in 17 prisons, by Jean Allen. Many editorials and various contest entries and few awards; [pers.] My work primarily reflects the Lord's love and caring with emphasis on the Bible as the source of the truth and the need to live spiritually with Him to realize fulfillment of peace, hope and joy in life. [a.] Sarasota, FL 34236.

ALLEN, NICK
[b.] February 9, 1979, Harbor City, CA; [p.] Keith and Judy Allen; [ed.] 8th grade; [occ.] Student; [hon.] Honor Roll 1991, Principal's Award of Excellence, poetry contest winner, Los Angeles Public Library Contest; [oth. writ.] Limericks in the Limelite, "My Hero Geronimo"; [pers.] No matter where you go or who you become part of it all. [a.] San Pedro, CA 90731.

ALLEN, V. JEAN
[b.] August 26, 1947, Hattiesburg, Mississippi; [m.] W. Mac, December 4, 1990; [ch.] Lisa Annette Camp and Teri Marshea Henderson; [ed.] High School; [occ.] Debt Management Representative; [[oth. writ.] All The Silent Children, published in "Mississippi Voices"; [pers.] It is my desire to use my writing to expose and eradicate the horrendous crime of "Child Sexual Abuse". [a.] Hattiesburg, MS 39402.

ALLEN, YVETTE
[b.] June 13, 1979, Litchfield, Illinois; [p.] Mr. and Mrs. Don Allen; [ed.] 8th grade, Litchfield Middle School; [pers.] First published poem-it was written for my Grandfather Jack Holman-who died March 26, 1992.

ALLGOOD, LYNEETE C.
[pen.] L.A. Thunder; [b.] September 21, 1963, Dearborn, Michigan; [p.] Fred and Josephine Allgood; [m.] Divorced; [ch.] Jessica Lynne and Kevin Michael Shoda; [ed.] English major/Delta College, Telecommunication minor 6 years of college; [occ.] Certified Paralegal a writer/full-time mom; [memb.] Writer's Digest; [hon.] I have received many awards for my poetry over the years. Valedictorian of my law class. [oth. writ.] Far and Away, Truest Love, Drugs for a Life, My Twin, Forever Love; [pers.] I believe writing comes straight from the heart. If one wants to write just listen and words will flow. [a.] Inkster, MI 48141.

ALLISON, ELSA G.
[a.] Salt Lake City, UT 84104-2165.

ALM, DONNA M.
[b.] July 26, 1962; [p.] John L. and Kathleen A. Knight; [m.] Glen A., May 31, 1986; [ch.] Karli Rae and Katelyn Dixie Alm; [ed.] Noble Central School and Lethbridge Community College and Olds Agricultural College; [occ.] Animal Health Technician and Rancher; [memb.] Alberta Cowboy Poetry Association; [pers.] I began to write a year ago and it has been a wonderful outlet. I write from my heart and I hope that those who read my work can feel some of what I've felt. [a.] Claresholm, AB T0L 0T0.

ALVAREZ, JULIET
[b.] January 6, 1980, New York; [p.] Luisa and Roberto Alvarez; [ed.] I.S. 73 Junior High School; [occ.] Write poems, draw; [hon.] Reading, Honor Roll; [pers.] The poems I write are about the way I feel (romantic, love, friendship, etc. poem). [a.] Elmhurst, NY 11373.

ANDERSON, AVA
[b.] September 24, 1961, Paopsa Springs, Colorado; [p.] Carl Anderson and Dee Daniels; [m.] Just exes; [ch.] Nichole Antonia Dowdy and Carina Allene Bowland; [ed.] Currently attending an Electronics Technical College; [occ.] Secretary/Bookkeeper; [oth. writ.] Occasional letters to editors, one rejected article; [pers.] Writing is a comfort to me. I write when feeling becomes too much. I hope others will gain comfort from my poems too, someday. [a.] Wichita, KS 67202.

ANDERSON, AVIS D.
[[pen.] A. Denise; [b.] December 27, 1953, New Orleans, Louisiana; [p.] Richard E. , Sr. and Elva A. Smith; [ch.] Albert L., Letitia O., and Juane T. Blake; [ed.] Ganesha High, (Pomona, CA), Sawyer Business College, (Pomona, CA), San Diego City College Dist. (San Diego, CA); [occ.] Operations Control Coordinator, Teledyne Ryan Aeronautical (San Diego, CA); [memb.] National Authors Registry (Troy, ,MI); [hon.] Honorable Mention in the Spring 1993 Iliad Literary Awards Program; [oth. writ.] Published in 1993, Celebrations, Chapter Two and Memories, August 1993 edition; [pers.] I enjoy writing and seeing my creativity of feelings and expressions being published and knowing that it touches other people in special ways. [a.] San Diego, CA 92116.

ANDERSON, BETH
[pen.] Allison Archer; [b.] June 28, 1969, Baltimore, Maryland; [p.] Beverly Bukovsky, Michael and Deborak Anderson; [ed.] MD Institute College of Art, Towson State University; [occ.] Artist; [pers.] I convey the expression of my experience - images, music, words, the finest things of life. [a.] Baltimore, MD 21057.

ANDERSON, CAROL
[b.] September 9, 1944, Oak Park, Illinois; [p.] Dorothy Jean Allison and Arnold Topp; [m.] James, February 22, 1991; [ch.] Tammie, Latanya, Robert Sr., Anthony, Sr.; [ed.] Hirsch High, Southeast Junior College, Laney College; [occ.] Proof Operator; [oth. writ.] Several other poems; [pers.] I write from my heart and some experiences I've had, I also write about my dreams. [a.] San Rafael, CA 94901.

ANDERSON, CATHERINE
[pen.] Catherine Anderson; [b.] April 30, 1950, New York City; [p.] John Battles and Jane Anderson; [m.] Deceased; [ch.] Natasha, Sashene, Joshua and Tashara; [ed.] Julia Richmond High (NYC) and Rockland College; [occ.] Writer; [memb.] P.E.T.A., Bureau of American Indian Affairs, Friends of Society (Quakers); [hon.] Phi Sigma Omocron, Dean's List; [oth. writ.] Article on Martin Luther King, Junior in local newspaper, poem accepted by L'Apache Magazine published in the West; [pers.] I write quite a bit about civil rights, as well as the plight of the Native Americans today in this century. [a.] Bemus Point, New York 14712.

ANDERSON, CHRISTINE MCCOMBIE
[b.] May 2, 1911, "Holly Farm" near El Campo near Belvedere, Marin County, CA; [p.] Alexander Barnett McCombie, Louise M. Heebner (Hubner); [m.] Harvey S. Anderson, April 23, 1948; [ch.] Karen Louise Jurasin, Dan Michael Anderson; [ed.] Calaveras Union High, University of CA, Berkeley, A.B. 1937; [occ.] Social Worker, Highland Hospital (County), Red Cross, World War II; [memb.] California Alumni Association, discontinued others due to age; [oth. writ.] Interested in Learning art and craft of poetry not publishing; [pers.] Like Mona Van Duyn I think satisfaction is found in "loving each other with commitment". "Commitment" is the key to fulfillment. I WISH I COULD "create art this is rooted in love". So much "love" now is based on utility, use. When utility goes, love goes. [a.] Walnut Creek, CA 94595.

ANDERSON, ETHEL
[b.] October 1, 1976, Belleville, Illinois; [p.] Karen McCarver and Carl Anderson; [ed.] Sparta High School; [occ.] Student; [hon.] Honor Roll; [oth. writ.] Just in grade school papers; [a.] Tilden, IL 62292.

ANDERSON, LORENA JUNE MOORE
[pen.] June Anderson; [b.] June 7, 1943, Massey, Maryland; [p.] Elwood and Minnie Sipple Moore; [m.] John Edward, October 21, 1960; [ch.] 1 daughter and 2 sons; [ed.] High school graduate, Early Childhood Development, Certificate EMS Training; [memb.] Local fire department, ladies auxiliary; [oth. writ.] Collection of poems over 32 year period, some published in local paper; [pers.] I find that putting my feelings down on paper helps me deal with the stressfulness of life. I try to keep a positive attitude. [a.] Millington, MD 21651.

ANDERSON, MARGARET
[b.] November 15, 1913, Matthews, Indiana; [p.] Elma Belle Benefiel and Alvin C. Swinnup; [m.] Porter, October 23, 1934; [ed.] Graduated from Bloomfield High (IN), 1 year Indiana Central Business College; [occ.] General Office Bookkeeping-Telemarketing; [memb.] Phi Chi Epsilon, Member of Presbyterian Church; [hon.] Exempted two semesters of English-attended writing class instead; [oth. writ.] Musings by Margaret - collection of poems and other writings; [pers.] I love people and enjoy communicating with them-especially my family. I am no polly anna, but an optimist.

ANDERSON, NIK
[b.] September 2, 1978, Portland, Oregon; [p.] Lloyd and Paula Anderson; [ed.] Freshman Sequim High School; [occ.] Student; [hon.] School Honors Society; [a.] Sequim, Washington 98382.

ANDERSON, SHARON LEE
[pen.] Shannon Lee Anderson; [b.] November 19, 1972, Kindersly, Saskatchawan, Canada; [p.] Arthur and Sharron Anderson; [ed.] Grade 12 diploma from Chaplin School (Chaplin, Sask, Canada); [hon.] Numerous first and second place awards for Remembrance Day poems. Second place award in a Dental Poetry Contest; [oth. writ.] Published in school yearbook, published in "TEEN" magazine, published in local paper; [pers.] I give great thanks to my family, my companion, Chad Campbell and Avery special friend, Lisa Erixon, for standing by me and always believing. "You will never get anywhere standing still". [a.] Chaplin, Sask. CAN. S0H 0V0.

ANDRESS, JENNIFER MICHELLE
[b.] December 28, 1979, Birmingham, Alabama; [p.] Deborah and David Andress; [ed.] Currently enrolled at Andalusia Middle School; [occ.] Student; [memb.] Student Council Board of Directors, School newspaper, Andalusisa Middle School Math Team, Honor Society, Bethany Baptist Church; [hon.] All A Honor Roll; [oth. writ.] Several poems and/or writings published in school newspaper and local literary magazine; [pers.] I enjoy expressing my ideas in writing and in art. [a.] Andalusia, AL 36420.

ANELLO, LORY
[b.] February 18, 1949, Newark, New Jersey; [p.] Henry and Emily Waldron (both deceased); [ch.] Lea, and Joseph Anello, Jr.; [ed.] South Plainfield High attending Union County College working towards an Associate Degree in Occupational Therapy; [occ.] Medical Clerk; [hon.] President's High Honors List; [oth. writ.] Literary work has been published in the SHEAF, Union County College's literary arts magazine which has placed first in a contest-critique sponsored by the American Scholastic Press Association; [pers.] My writing reflects my love for the earth and all its creatures with a fervent belief in freedom. [a.] Union, NJ 07083.

ANGEL, MARK
[b.] October 13, 1959, Sullivan, Indiana; [p.] Dennis and Erma Lynn Angel; [ed.] Hutsonville High (Hutsonville, IL), Lincoln Trail College (Robinson, IL); [occ.] Grain farmer; [memb.] Student Against Drunk Driving, Christian Church (West Union, IL); [hon.] Phi Theta Kappa, Dean's List; [a.] West York, IL 62478.

ANTIN, RANDY
[b.] July 2, 1974, Los Angeles; [p.] Michael and Evelyne Antin; [ed.] University of Michigan; [pers.] The answer to every question lies hidden within all of us. [a.] Los Angeles, CA 90049.

APPIATH, SR., JOSEPH EKOW
[pen.] Big Joe; [b.] May 14, 1952, Elmina; [p.] Mr. John Kwame and Comfort Appiah; [ch.] Three; [ed.] G.C.E. Level; [memb.] Methodist Coir, Methodist Youth Fellowship, Upper Drama Group; [hon.] Best Writer for the Year 1992; [oth. writ.] Poems into the newspapers, Church Forum, Methodist Corner and all student booklet; [pers.] Poem turns the deaf ears into active view, with actions and creativity. It is always true that poetry brings the hearer in the center of reasoning. [a.] West Upper Region, WA.

ARANI, SAROTINI
[pen.] Katherine Shelley; [b.] February 16, 1948, Allur, India; [p.] Venkata Raghava Arani Reddy and Lalithamma Arani; [ch.] Padmaja Sattu, Vindhya Sattu; [ed.] MA-West Texas State University, Teacher Certification -U.T. Permian Basin; [occ.] Not yet employed; [memb.] Sigma Tau Delta; [hon.] Financial Aid Merit Scholarship Holder; [oth. writ.] "Quest" published by West Texas State University English Department Magazine "The Legacy" and several other poems yet to be published; [pers.] I am a staunch believer in the Wordsworrthian motto---Poetry is "Spontaneous overflow of powerful feelings." Shakespeare and the romantic poets greatly influence me and my poems. [a.] Odessa, TX 79762.

ARNOLD, CLYDE NELSON
[b.] March 29, 1944, Trenton, Tennessee; [p.] Clyde Franklin Arnold and Emily Elizabeth Arnold Flowers; [m.] Divorced; [ch.] Keitrah S. Arnold Snider (8) and Kirk S. Arnold; [ed.] Fulton High School, BS-University of Alabama/Birmingham, JD-Cumberland Law School, Sanford University; [oth. writ.] Many unpublished poems; [pers.] Poetry, to me is a snapshot of some aspect of life, taken by the heart and processed by the mind. [a.] Knoxville, TN 37938.

ARNOLD, DORIS SANFORD
[pen.] Doris Sanford Arnold; [b.] June 6, 1915, Irvington-on-Hudson, New York; [p.] Morris and Caroline Sanford; [m.] Raymond, September 15, 1945; [ch.] Diane Arnold Huebmer; [ed.] BA-Mount Holyoke College, MA-Cornell University; [occ.] Retired English Teacher (H.S. and Jr. College); [memb.] Delta Karda Gamma, AAUW, Local Offices (Elmira, NY) State Board, NJ; [hon.] Delta Gamma Honorary, several awards for poetry; [oth. writ.] Magazine articles on practical grammar, also folk stories, included in numerous anthologies, author of book, Poems of Praise and Protest, printing 1992 and 1993. [a.] Winston-Salem, NC 17903.

ARNOLD, FRED
[pen.] Pee-Wee Arnold; [b.] March 23, 1957, St. Clair, Michigan; [p.] Wellington Willard "Duke" and Rachel Olene Arnold; [ed.] Jefferson Adult Learning Center, St. Clair County Community College; [occ.] Poetry and Songwriter; [memb.] National Library of Poetry; [hon.] Several awards from World of Poetry and Jefferson Adult Learning Center for achievements accomplished, and poetry contests that I have won. Also, won a trophy for most creative thinker from a contest; [oth. writ.] First book called "Music From the Heart" (poems and song lyrics) copyright 1990, 2nd book called "My Love Poems to Wendy G. Bowman" (poems and songlyrics) soon to be copyrighted 1993; [pers.] Wendy, I love you so much for you're the lady I want to be mine till the end of time you and me that's the way I feel it should always be. [a.] Port Huron, MI 48060.

ARNOLD, KEITHA M.
[b.] January 11, 1918, Montcalm Co, near Edmore, Michigan; [p.] Jennie (Culver) and Venus Loman Arnold; [ed.] Stanton High, Montcalm County Normal, Central Teacher's College, Mount Pleasant, MI 2 years; [occ.] Country Public grade school -6 yrs, County Schools Bible Teacher and Release Time Bible Teacher; [memb.] RBM Ministries, Inc., AARP, Stanton Baptist Church; [pers.] Just began writing poems last year "92" for my secret pal each month and enjoyed it, so am continuing writing. [a.] Newaygo, MI 49337-0032.

ARNOLD, MARGUERITE L.
[pen.] Marguerite L. Arnold; [b.] April 13, 1911, Elkins, West Virginia; [p.] Robert I. and Bertha E. Smith Morrison; [m.] Robert C. Jr., April 11, 1931; [ch.] Two boys; [ed.] High School and Nursing Training at Sibley Hospital, Washington, DC; [occ.] Housewife; [memb.] Piedmont, W.VA, Presbyterian Church, Piedmont W. VA. Women's Club, Treasurer of Republican Women Club; [oth. writ.] When a S.S. teacher I wrote a religious pageant for our class. The poem that I submitted is my first poem; [pers.] I am inspired by the beauty of nature around us. I have painted flowers and seascapes or amateur. [a.]

Westernport, MD 21562.

ARTEMIO, MURILLO
[b.] July 1, 1971, Chicago, Illinois; [p.] Nicanor and Norma Murillo; [ed.] Wigley South, Lewis University; [occ.] Student; [memb.] United States Marine Corps; [pers.] Dedicated to the one who stole my heart and found my soul. Sandra Tse. [a.] Chicago, IL 60623.

ASHBAUGH, SARAH JANE
[b.] November 17, 1980, St. Louis, Missouri; [p.] Deborah and James Ashbaugh; [ed.] Presently attending Tri-Central Junior High; [occ.] Full-time student; [hon.] Young Author's Award from my school; [oth. writ.] Young Author's Award for a story entitled 'No Where To Run'; [pers.] I love writing and one day hope to become a writer. [a.] Tipton, IN 46072.

ASHLOCK, TERRY L.
[b.] July 4, 1957, Chanute, Kansas; [p.] True and Ionez Ashlock; [m.] Cindy, March 17, 1990; [ch.] Jessica, Luke & Teria Ashlock and Nick Angelo; [ed.] High School grad and Trade school; [occ.] Pipe Fitter and Welder; [memb.] Local Union #397 Bartlesville, OK; [oth. writ.] Dozens of poems and song lyrics; [pers.] My writings are based on my own personal beliefs and experiences from my own life. [a.] Eureka, KS 67045.

ASHRAF, SUZANNE
[pen.] Suzanne Ashraf; [b.] November 23, 1956, Buffalo, New York; [p.] Sidney and Shirlie Warren; [m.] Jack, November 5, 1986; [ch.] Amber (16) and Hailey (6); [ed.] Kenmore West High School, Erie Community College, Associate Degree in Food Management, BOCES Nursing 1, Have SPN-licensed private duty aide; [occ.] Food Management; [memb.] SPCA, Buffalo Zoo, Mansonic (Triangle Gamma); [hon.] SPCA-for finding the most lost animals, school have received merit awards in English; [oth. writ.] at least 95 other poems; [pers.] When writing down how I feel or think and the possibility others will read it to, I feel like a rainbow after the thunderstorm. [a.] Buffalo, NY 14223.

ASPROULIS, GREG
[pen.] Gregory Paul; [b.] December 1, 1969, Rochester, New York; [p.] Andrew Asproulis and Joanne Donaldson; [ed.] Victor High School, Travels; [occ.] Musician, currently with band stillmotion; [hon.] Victor Film Society first place film, NYSATA certificate of achievement in the visual arts; [oth. writ.] Poems published in Youth Conglomerate Magazine; [pers.] I wish to bring out the imagination in people as well as cutting through to what's truly real. [a.] Palmyra, NY 14522.

ATENCIO, LUPE
[b.] February 13, 1980, Sante Fe, New Mexico; [p.] Silviano and Margie Atencio; [ed.] Tierra Amarilla Mid High, 7th grade 3.9 average; [hon.] 4-H awards, Spelling Bee, Oral Interpretation, National Honor Roll, Singing and writing; [oth. writ.] Spring the Brazos Mountains, Squaw, Colorado Bay, Boat Ride in the Bermuda Triangle. I've written these poems on things I've seen and seen and experienced; [pers.] I try writing about the beauty of nature, and about fantasies that occur in the mind. [a.] Amarilla, NM 87575.

ATKIN, WENDELL
[b.] November 12, 1914, Ohio; [m.] Madalyn, November 4, 1983 (2nd marriage each have 3 sons-widowed 1 year; [occ.] Tool and Die Maker (retired); [memb.] Baptist Church Literary Volunteers of America; [pers.] Retired over 13 years, play golf, cards, and the organ. Also teach reading for Literary Volunteers of America. [a.] Venice, FL

ATTIG, JANEL
[b.] October 10, 1979, Albert Lea, Minnesota; [p.] Howard and Imogene Attig; [occ.] 7th grade student, babysitter; [memb.] 5 years of 4-H and 3 years of Odyssey of the Mind (OM); [hon.] 1 purple ribbon in 4-H and 2 OM state competition ribbons and 1 OM Ranatra Fusca Creativity award. [a.] Glenville, MN 56036.

ATTRILL, NATALIE
[b.] September 2, 1973, Barking, England; [ed.] Davenant Foundation School, Loughton College (both England); [hon.] I sing and have done so at the Royal Albert Hall in England. This and poetry are my two favorite pastimes. [a.] Arlington, VA 22207.

AUGUSTOWSKI, AMY MARIE
[pen.] Kennedy; [b.] February 1, 1979, Baltimore, Maryland; [p.] James K. and Kathleen M. Augustowski; [ch.] Sister-Amber Lynn; [ed.] George T. Cromwell Elementary School Bookpark/Lindale Junior, Senior High, Peabody - Annapolis Maryland Hall of Music; [occ.] Student; [hon.] Honor Roll, 1992 Gold Music Award and 1993 Gold Music Award; [pers.] I like to write how I feel about things that I see. [a.] Glen Burnie, MD 21061.

AUMAN, GRACE H.
[pen.] Grace H. Auman; [b.] December 29, 1923, Boyertown, Pennsylvania; [p.] Laura Mest and Edgar H. Heyat; [m.] Gordon R., March 21, 1946; [ed.] High School, Business School and various night schools; [occ.] Executive Secretary-Office Management; [memb.] St. John's Lutheran Church, Boyertown, PA; [hon.] I designed the Christmas card for 1992 for Leader Home which is sent to business firms, hospitals, doctors, families, and friend to many states; [oth. writ.] Personal poems written for friends etc., also designed Christmas card '92 for Leader sent to most states; [pers.] My great love is the outdoors followed by pets, people, and trying to live a good clean life. [a.] Pottstown, PA 19464.

AUSTIN, BARBARA
[b.] May 24, 1979, Cadillac, Michigan; [p.] Lew and April Austin; [ed.] currently a ninth grade student at Cadillac High School; [pers.] Never forget that you have something to give. And by giving only then will you feel whole. [a.] Cadillac, MI 49601.

AVANESSIAN, DIANA
[b.] June 3, 1975, Armenia; [p.] Raymond and Mary Avanessian; [ed.] Crescenta Valley High School - Senior; [occ.] Studying to be Registered Nurse; [memb.] 1991-1992 Volunteer at Verdigo Hills Hospital in La Cresenta, CA; [hon.] 1985-Poem (4th grade) "April showers bring May flowers" published in Glendale News Press; [oth. writ.] Personal writings none have been published, besides April Shower Brings May Flowers in 1985 (4th grade); [pers.] To my dearest family: I love you and thank you for your support. Without your love and understanding I

would be lost. Thank you. [a.] Glendale, CA 91208.

AVITA, RUTH
[b.] May 14, 1946, Madellin, Columbia S.A.; [p.] Dwight H. and Isabell A. Macduff; [m.] Chang Sheng Gu, July 19, 1989; [ch.] Chavela and Terrence Carr; [ed.] St. Mary's, Indiana University, University of Massachusetts; Yale Divinity School' [occ.] Mental Health Counselor; [memb.] Member of Unitarian-Universalist Church; [hon.] Dean's List (U of MA; [oth. writ.] Several poems published in IN.U. School magazine; [pers.] "Do random acts of kindness and senseless acts of beauty"-Anon. [a.] Sotu Dennis, MA 02660.

AVENDANO, SANDRA ALICIA
[b.] January 15, 1977, Orange, California; [p.] Ralph and Linda Avendano; [ed.] Currently in 10th grade, a homeschooled high schooler, attending intermediate classes in cake decorating; [occ.] Student'Cake Decorator; [memb.] 4-H Club, Harvest Christian Fellowship; [hon.] Honor Roll Student; [pers.] My goal is to strive to stay within the plans that Jesus Christ would have for my life. To be a young woman with high moral standards, in my writings and in all aspects of life. [a.] Perris, CA.

AYERS, CATHERINE M.
[b.] January 11, 1951, Campbell County; [p.] Raymond Jefferson and Mary Louise McConville Winnagle, Sr.; [m.] James Gregory, February 25, 1992; [ch.] Charlie Houston Roowser, Jr. (21) and Shannon Nicole Rowsey (17); [ed.] Graduated Brookville High School (1970); [occ.] Casepacker for C.B. Fleet Co., Inc. Pharmaceutical; [memb.] Women of the Moose #1335, International Society of Poets, B&W Rod & Gun Club; [hon.] Golden Poet 1990 and 1991, Award of Merit 1991 Certificate, Honorable Mention Certificate 1993; [oth. writ.] over 200 poems; [pers.] Someday, with God as my guide, my poems may help others through a life which I've seen and still continue to seek. [a.] Appomattox, VA 24522.

AYRES, REBECCA
[pen.] KAET, K.T.; [b.] February 22, 1978; [p.] Thomas W. and Linda S. Ayres; [ed.] high school student (currently); [occ.] High School Student Freshman; [pers.] My writings come only from my personal feelings. It's just the way I express my true self. [a.] Sycamore, PA 15364.

AZZOLINO, EDMUND
[pen.] Edmund Azzolino; [b.] August 3, 1965, Glenridge, New Jersey; [p.] Geraldine and Edmund Azzolino; [ed.] Currently pursuing a degree in creative writing went to Clifton High School; [occ.] Video, Theatre, aspiring writer, student; [memb.] Studio Players Community Theatre Group in Montclair, NJ; [pers.] I strive to be the best writer I can be, but most of all I hope the person who reads my work thinks that I am the best writer there is. [a.] Clifton, NJ 07015-9998.

BABAJHAN, ADHYATMA BHAGAVAN SRI, AL-KHALIL THE FRIEND
[pen.] Bhagavan Friend; [b.] March 29, 1943, Des Moines, Iowa; [p.] Maynard and Marian Douglas; [ch.] John Lee Douglas Jr.; [ed.] BA Psychology, Master's Behavioral Science from California State University, Dominguez Hills, Marriage Family Child

Counselor (MFCC); [occ.] Maitreya Kalki Mahavatara Satguru; [hon.] Founding President of Psi Chi Honor Society in Psychology at California State University; [oth. writ.] The Holy Book of Destiny, Destiny, The Friend's Call to Satya Yuga, My Purpose and Mission, The Movement for Individual Freedom, Parables & Poetry, Adhyatma Prashad, The Friend's Gathering for Meditation; [pers.] It is my absolute Conviction that Freedom is best for all people. It is my absolute certainty that Freedom is the highest Natural State of all People. When True Freedom dawns within a person, a group, a people, a nation, it brings with it a real and abiding Ethic that needs no external enforcement, but which is lived out willingly and energetically by the Free Will and Self-Determinism of those within whom it arises. I know with Absolute Certainty born of my own Self-Realization, that Spiritual Freedom is the Mother and Father of all other Real Freedom. My Adhyatma-Yoga-Dharma is both True Spiritual Freedom and The Way to it. This is my work, my life and my gift to humanity. I welcome all sincere people who hunger after Freedom to come and share it with me. It is my Purpose to create an ever growing Circle of Free People working in a Free Religion for a Free World living in the fullness of Universal God's Pure Divine Truth. [a.] Lomita, CA 90717.

BACHIM, MARLENE M.
[b.] July 14, 1939, Browns Valley, Minnesota; [p.] Luverne C. and Lillian T. Morse; [m.] Anthony C., September 24, 1966; [ch.] Dale Edward and Jodi Lynn Bachim; [ed.] Siren High, University of Wisconsin-River Falls, University of Wisconsin-Madison, Oshkosh, Whitewater; [occ.] Elementary Teacher, Morgan Elementary School-Beloit, MI; [memb.] Delta Kappa Gamma, Independent Order of Foresters, Precious Moments, Educational Organizations; [hon.] Robinson School Teacher of the Year, Beloit Rotary Club Teacher of the Month, Beloit P.T.A. Educator of the Year, National P.T.A. Phoebe Apperson Hearst Outstanding Educator nominee, NDEA Scholarship for Adv. Study in Geography; [oth. writ.] Poems for personal friends; [pers.] I have a healthy respect for what makes each person unique and worthwhile. As a teacher I try to help children see themselves reflected in a positive image and show them how to reach out to love, understand, and accept all individuals. [a.] Beloit, WI 53511.

BAGATIN, TARCISIO
[pen.] Tarcisio Bagatin; [b.] April 5, 1928, Thiene (Vicenza) Italy; [p.] Francesco and Elisa Bagatin; [ed.] College and 4 years of Theology, one year at the Pontifical College for Migration, Rome, Italy; [occ.] Pastor of the Italian Church of "Holy Rosary" in Washington, DC; [memb.] The Missionaries of Saint Charles B. (Scalabrinian Fathers) for the care of Migrants; [hon.] Awarded 2nd prize in a poetry contest in Italy by the Ministry of Education (out of 300 competing poets); [oth. writ.] "Sonnets and Poems", in Italian and "Moments of Life", English and Italian. Contributed with two poems to the anthology: "Italo-American Poets" (Fordham University, NY), other publication in magazine and newspapers; [pers.] Reflecting on people and nature, on the changing pace of struggle and beauty, of pain and joy, I would like to capture the mystery of it all and be able to send a message of hope and love as the gift of life comes anew every day. [a.] Washington, DC 20001.

BAGUIO, WENDY JO
[b.] November 17, 1971, Jackson, Mississippi; [p.] Clara Wiker and Jim Wiker, Jr. (step-father); [m.] Joseph F., March 13, 1992; [ed.] High School; [occ.] U.S. Military (Army) for three years; [hon.] 1 ARCOM/1 AAM/ 1 Good Conduct Medal/ AIT Ribbon/Numerous Achievement Certificates from the military; [oth. writ.] A finished manuscript of "Poems From Within the Heart". Waiting to be published after I find a publisher to whom I want; [pers.] If I can touch one person's heart with my work then I know I have passed the test. [a.] APO, AE 09111.

BAILEY, APRIL ELAINE
[b.] April 7, 1970, Paterson, California; [p.] Sarah Vorwork and Bill Bailey; [ed.] Gaileo High School and some college; [memb.] Lafayette Health Club; [hon.] Class President; [oth. writ.] Several poems, kept to myself also poems in school papers; [pers.] My poems come from the feeling of my heart. I no longer wish to keep my poems to myself. I wish share them with others, in hopes to touch other peoples hearts. [a.] Pleasant Hill, CA 94523.

BAILEY, BETH
[b.] May 14, 1958, Munich, Germany; [p.] Jack and Bobbie Bailey; [ed.] Tift County High, Abraham Baldwin Agricultural College, Georgia College; [occ.] Manager, Jack Bailey's Home Entertainment Center; [a.] Douglas, GA 31533.

BAILEY, JACQUON D.
[b.] August 29, 1956, Memphis TN; [p.] Arcelious and Dortha Bailey; [m.] Mary Jane Bailey, August 31, 1991; [ed.] 2 yrs. college, Written Communication Skills, Oral Communications, Effective Speaking; [occ.] Bocing Co.; [oth. writ.] 73 Framed creative writings; [pers.] To extend an arm to those who are down and out, to help those who have been crushed and trampled by the perilous woes in life.; [a.] Kent, WA.

BAILEY, MICHELLE
[pen.] Amber Ina Carter; [b.] January 15, 1980, Lufkin, Texas; [p.] Rex and Myra Bailey; [ed.] 7th grade; [occ.] Student; [memb.] 4-H; [hon.] Young Author's Award, Farm Bureau Art Award; [oth. writ.] Various books and poems; [pers.] You should live life in your own point of views and you should not fail to reach your goals. [a.] Groveton, Texas 45845.

BAILEY, STEPHEN A.
[b.] January 5, 1970, Port Hope, Ontario, Canada; [p.] Dr. John C. and Rosalyn P. Bailey; [ed.] Fort Worth Christian High School, Arilene Christian University; [occ.] Singer, Songwriter, Actor; [memb.] Society for Theatrical Artists' Guidance and Enhancement; [hon.] Who's Who Among Students in America's Universities and Colleges; [oth. writ.] Hundreds of songs and essays; [pers.] My writing comes from personal experiences. I am inspired by life's struggles and it's joy; by God's creation and his gift to man of creativity. [a.] Bedford, TX 76021.

BAKER, CARZADEAN Y.
[pen.] Josie; [b.] January 24, 1962, Savannah, Georgia; [p.] Lucille E. Tanksley and Joseph A. Baker, Senior; [ch.] Jolene Jeanette Baker; [ed.] Alfred E. Beach High, Savannah Vocational-Technical School presently at Armstrong State College; [occ.] Paraprofessional, Charles Ellis Montessori Academy; [memb.]

Savannah Community Choir, LORD's Ensemble, PZBC Adult Choir; [oth. writ.] "A Pastor's Wife", "In Answer to God's Ca;;", "Dear Leroy"; [pers.] My writings are reflections of real-life situations which I or people around me have experienced. [a.] Savannah, GA 31404.

BAKER, LILLIAN L.
[pen.] Lillian Baker/Liliane L. Baker; [b.] December 12, 1921, New York; [p.] Deceased; [m.] Roscoe Albert; [ch.] Wanda Georgia and George Riley Baker; [pers.] Love makes us survivors of sorrow and sacrifice. Achieve goals that benefit yourself, family, and country. Love of a FREE life deserves dedication and sacrifice. [a.] Gardena, CA 90249.

BALANOW, RICHARD ANTHONY
[b.] April 7, 1973, West Chester, Pennsylvania; [p.] Lois C. and Anthony Balanow; [ed.] Coatesville Senior High School, The Art Institute of Philadelphia; [occ.] Manager for a Print Company; [pers.] By the time they're perfected the toothbrush, my teeth will have all fallen out! [a.] Honeybrook, PA 19349.

BALDWIN, MARY MARGARET
[b.] December 30, 1939, E. Detroit, Michigan; [p.] Tony and Tina Lumia; [m.] June 1959; [ch.] John O. Jr., Pamela, and Shelly; [ed.] Bachelor Fine Arts-Eastern Michigan University; [occ.] Dilettante - former Sales Rep., Executive Secretary; [memb.] Alhambra Metaphysical Institute; [hon.] High School Champion Spelling Bee, Local Art Contest; [oth. writ.] Poems, short stories, nothing submitted as yet; [pers.] Beauty oft times follows tragedy. I have been mainly influenced by the love of the late Chauncey and many life experiences. [a.] Westland, MI 48185.

BALLARD, VANESSA MARIE
[b.] January 23, 1979, Houston, Texas; [p.] Dr. Kenneth G. and Eliana Ballard; [ch.] brothers-Chester and Andrew Ballard; [ed.] Presently finishing 7th grade at Gregory Lincoln Middle School; [occ.] Student; [memb.] National Junior Honor Society; [hon.] First place, 1991 from YMCA in Creative Writing and National Honor Society; [oth. writ.] My Reflection (poem)-published in the 1991 edition of Antilogy of Poetry by Young Americans. I an continuing writing stories and poems as my hobby; [pers.] I try to reflect every thought that I have about my work, so that other people see life through a view that I learn to feel by heart. [a.] Houston, TX 77017.

BALTEZAR, WILLIAM (BILL)
[pen.] Silver Fox Baltezar, The Silver Fox; [b.] May 8, 1924, Butte, Montana; [p.] Austrian father-Louis B and French mother-Mary B.; [m.] Dorothea, June 19, 1949; [ch.] Mark and Michele; [ed.] Butte High School, WWII (18 mos.) and Korea (18 mos.); [occ.] Dental Prosthetic Technician, Watercolor since 1939; [memb.] Washington School of Art, President Silinas Art Club - Ski Club, Flyfishing, Inc. Big Game Hunter of Montana; [hon.] Won Art Scholarship, Washington School of Art May 1944, Toastmasters International, Art of Monterey County Historical Society, Oscar, Theatre, Dale Carnegie-Little Theatre - Watercolorist; [pers.] One in a family of 12 children. I've lived my life to the limit --wine, women, song. I have on my tombstone (it's waiting). "This is the only stone he left unturned." [a.] Salima, CA 93901.

BARDEN, GEORGE
[pen.] Cleo; [b.] May 15, 1897, Yorkshire, England; [p.] Sam Barden and Alice Abbott; [m.] Violet Grace, July 1921; [ch.] George Philip, John Samuel; [ed.] College, 3 years Engineer course for ASC degree in the RAF World War I; [occ.] Structural Designer; [memb.] Associated Member Structural Engineers England; [hon.] Bronze medal gymnastics, Honorary mention for light verse, poetry in motion silver medal, 5 KM walk, senior olympics, 5 bronze medal in play (As You Like It), I walk 5 miles each day, I'm an artist; [oth. writ.] "My Life Story", poems; [pers.] I am the last in the true Barden line. Ii have been an engineer, food producer, horticulturalist carpenter, bricklayer, glazier boiler fitter, and most other trades. [a.] San Bernardino, CA 92404.

BARDO, VINCENT C.
[pen.] Vince Bardo; [b.] April 2, 1925, Fredonia, New York; [p.] Samuel and Carrie (Barone) Bardo; [m.] Phyllis Ann (Meehl), March 28, 1951; [ch.] Lynn Christine Bardo (Ross), twins-Michael Kevin and Christine Ann Bardo; [ed.] 11th year of High School (went into Military services); [occ.] Electrician; [memb.] Clarence Senior Center; [hon.] Honorable Discharge after serving during WWII and Korean War; [oth. writ.] "The World Will Long Remember" (in honor of my history teacher, Mrs. Whitney), "An Undying Sonnet of Our Brave Dead" (in honor of the soldiers that gave all), "Camp Picket I'm Leaving You" (after basic training); [pers.] Born to serve God and country. [a.] Clarence, NY 14031.

BARI, ROBERT
[pen.] Bob Bari; [oth. writ.] Poetry, prose, lyrics. [a.] Santa Fe, NM 87505.

BARNES, MICKIE
[pen.] Mickie Barnes; [b.] June 19, 1954, Oakridge, Oregon; [p.] Leo and Viola Heyen; [m.] James W., March 20, 1993; [ch.] Joshua Lee and Alma Reva; [ed.] Pleasant Hill High, Lane Community College; [occ.] Laborer in chicken plant (Creswell, OR); [memb.] Springfield Church of Christ; [oth. writ.] None published only personal writings; [pers.] My writing is inspired by God's healing power in my life. [a.] Creswell, OR 97426.

BARNES, RAYMONE A.
[b.] December 6, 1978, Philadelphia, Pennsylvania; [p.] Audrey J. Frisby; [ed.] High School; [memb.] Alterboy; [hon.] An award from the President of the U.S., principal awards, a citation and other awards; [oth. writ.] This is the first thing I have written; [pers.] If you try you can do anything. If you don't it's impossible.

BARTON, DANAE: IDA S.
[pen.] Danae, Suzy, Susanna; [b.] June 10, 1920; [b.] Zelienople, Pennsylvania; [p.] Mr. and Mrs. Gabriel Sayti; [m.] James C., December 5, 1943; [ch.] Jacqueline Diane and Timothy Dana Barton; [ed.] Zelienople High, Beaver County Community College, Geneva College; [occ.] Homemaker; [memb.] PA Poetry Society, Word Alive Church, Ellwood City Art Club; [hon.] 14 awards of merit, 2nd place in state contest, 2nd place in local contest, golden poet award, dubbed "Danae" (Golden Princess) for placing 6th internationally; [oth. writ.] Newspaper articles and stories; [pers.] It is my hope that my poetry can enable the reader to see life as beauty in its fulfillment. [a.]

Beaver Fall, PA 15010.

BARDWELL-BROWN, CHARLOTTE M.
[pen.] Charlie; [b.] April 25, 1968, Pascagoula, Mississippi; [p.] Mrs. Joe N. Smith (Doris) and Mr. Charles W. Bardwell; [p.] Ens. Alexander S. Brown, April 3, 1993; [ch.] Alex S. Brown, Jr. (9 years); [ed.] Moss Point High School, Georgia State University, United Business Institute; [occ.] Writer, Computer Operator, Homemaker; [memb.] Alpha Psi Omega, Navy Marine Corps Society, and Mu Alpha Theta; [hon.] The National Library of Poetry, Who's Who, Distinguished Americans; [oth. writ.] Night Life Magazine an advice column entitled, "Dear Charlie". Fun Spot Magazine poems and articles; [pers.] I love writing, any type of writing I would like to eventually write my own nobel and look of poetry. I'm inspired by Maya Angelou. [a.] Moss Point, MS 39563.

BAREFOOT, MARGOT-ANNE
[b.] March 13, 1965, Toronto, Ontario, Canada; [p.] Dorothy and Norman Barefoot; [ed.] Branksome Hall School, The University of Toronto (BA), The University of Western Australia (PhD, candidate); [occ.] Student, aquatic instructor, lifeguard, community liaison officer (Paraburdoo, Western Australia); [memb.] Red Cross and Royal Lifesaving Societies (Canada and Australia), The Anthropology Society of Western Australia; [hon.] Ontario Scholar, community service (City of Etobicoke); [oth. writ.] Dreaming Tales: Aboriginal Myths and Stories from the Kimberley Region of Western Australia. (This volume of traditional myths and stories is ideal for young adults wishing to learn more about indigenous cultures; [pers.] It is my dream to further the understanding of indigenous cultures, particularly those of Australian Aboriginal people, through the medium of prose and poetry. [a.] Paraburdoo, Western Australia 6754.

BARGY, DEBBIE
[b.] June 24, 1963, Columbus, Ohio; [p.] Robert M. and Sandra K. Pullins; [m.] Paul M., July 19, 1979; [ch.] Louann, Sandra, Valerie, and Paula Bargy; [ed.] Westland High School; [occ.] Receptionist; [oth. writ.] Dedicated to the memory of my loving father, Robert M. Pullins, who died unexpectedly 11/29/92; [pers.] I believe there is no greater power than the love of your family. [a.] Thornville, OH.

BARNEY, BERYL J.
[b.] January 3, 1917, Collingsworth County, Texas; [p.] Horace H. and Billie Ann Jones; [m.] Ollie O., December 31, 1953; [ch.] Peter Clyde, Damon Lee, Deanna Sue and Sherry Gene; [ed.] Wichita High School (1934) and some college (1960's); [occ.] Homemaker; [memb.] Ladies Auxiliary to the VFW-DAV Commanders Club; [hon.] 1988 Golden Poet Award (World of Poetry); 1989 Poet of Merit Certificate and Honorable Mention Certificate (American Poetry Association; 1990 Silver Poet Certificate (World of Poetry); Honorary Charter Membership Certificate 1993 (International Society of Poets); [oth. writ.] Poems in high school paper, 1933-34; short stories in Rio Rico Arizonan and Rio Rico Sun, 1986-88.; [pers.] All of my writing is based on personal relationships with family and friends, and about things around me and existing in my world. My husband is a Big Game Hunter and Arizona Lion Guide hence my poem, "The Hunter", and the one about the hunting dog. [a.] Rio Rico, AZ 85648.

BARNHART, MICHELLE
[b.] August 7, 1974, Mora, Minnesota; [p.] Rodney and Rita Barnhart; [ed.] Mora Public Schools, Cambridge Community College (1 year), Sophomore at College of St. Benedict; [occ.] Student; [memb.] National Honor Society, High School Drama Club, German Club, Quill & Scroll; [hon.] Who's Who Among American High School Students (2 years); [oth. writ.] Poems published in High School Writer, several articles for high school newspaper; [pers.] Everyone has a dream, but only the bravest dare to maker theirs come true. [a.] Mora, MN 55051.

BARNUM, LANCE
[b.] May 28, 1973, Sandusky, Ohio; [p.] William L. Barnum and Linda K. Edington; [ed.] Margaretta High School, EHOVE Career Center, John and Wales University; [occ.] Student; [memb.] American Legion, DECA - an Association of Marketing Students; [hon.] DECA-Student of the Year, State Placement in Pepsi Learn and Earn Project; [pers.] My writing comes from the events that happen throughout my life with a little added imagination. [a.] Sanducky, OH 44870.

BARR, RAYMOND CURTIS
[b.] December 19, 1913, Fayette County, Illinois; [p.] James and Amanda Barr; [m.] Ethel Marie (Stockey), December 21, 1934; [ch.] Raymond Curtis, Jr., James Edward, Anita Laverne, John Leonard; [ed.] Mahomet (Il.) High, Olivet Nazarene University; [occ.] Ordained Minister Pastoral Ministry-Church Nazarene; [memb.] Retired Elder-Church of the Nazarene, OnO Alumni Association, AARP-NARFE; [hon.] Dean's List, Cum Laude graduate, THB Degree, Olivet Nazarene University, Ordination; [oth. writ.] Currently writing family biography entitled "Down on the Farm", dealing with parents and siblings over a period of sixty years (not yet published); [pers.] I perceive my purpose on writing or living is to promote optimism and to elevate spiritual values among mankind. [a.] Bourbonnais, IL 60914.

BARR, TIM
[b.] December 8, 1959, Grinnell, Iowa; [p.] Karen and Max Cumming; [m.] Pat, June 25, 1985; [ch.] Matt Barr; [ed.] Graduated Shenandoah High School, Kirkwood Community College-operation of water treatment plants; [occ.] Water works operator. [a.] Shenandoah, IA 51601.

BARRY, MELANIE A.
[b.] August 25, 1976, Camp Hill, Pennsylvania; [p.] Richard A. Jr., and Deborah S. Barry; [ed.] Presently a sophomore at Northern High School in Dillsburg, PA; [oth. writ.] I have no other writings that have been published at this time; [pers.] I write poetry to express my inner feelings, thoughts and emotions. [a.] Wellsville, PA 17365.

BARSTOWE, SHARLINE N.
[[pen.] Sharline Barstowe; [b.] November 27, 1970, Jamaica; [p.] Elaine Robinson and Sidney Campbell; [m.] (boyfriend) Kingsley A. Pryle; [ch.] Khiry A. Pryle; [ed.] Devonshire Academy Bermuda; [occ.] Mother and student; [hon.] BSSC Certificate and diploma; [oth. writ.] Love Is, Waiting, Reality, Black Man, and many more; [pers.] Always believe in God and yourself, totally and completely. Fam-sis- Sharon Gibbons Demitrius and Kiven, Luzan. [a.] Jack-

sonville, NC 28540.

BARTLEY, KRIS EDWARD
[b.] May 8, 1972; [p.] James W. and Michelle D. Bartley; [pers.] Erosional thinking is the mind's way of reminding us that we are still alive and we haven't become what society wants us to be. [a.] Fall River, MA 02720.

BARTON, ROLANDA
[b.] April 26, 1955, Gilmer, Texas; [p.] Geneva and Wayne Thompson; [m.] Larry Barton, July 7, 1973; [ch.] Amanda Gayl and Joshua Aaron; [ed.] Harmony High School; [occ.] Pre-School Teacher; [oth. writ.] Poems written honoring High School graduate published in local church bulletins; [pers.] Poetry writing is a way for me to relax and express myself. [a.] Big Sandy, TX 75755.

BARTZ, AMANDA
[pen.] Amanda Bartz; [b.] February 22, 1908, Milwaukee, Wisconsin; [p.] Marthja and Vincent Poplaszewski; [m.] Rudolph C., October 19, 1974; [ch.] Marie Kowalski, Ellen Bolton and (stepchildren) Randolph Bartz and Jeanne Broder; [ed.] Elementary; [occ.] Homemaker, Retired; [memb.] Oak Creek Lionetts, American Legion Post 434 Salvation Army; [hon.] Editors Choice award, The National Library of Poetry; [oth. writ.] Poem-Title "Listen to the Rain"; [pers.] My desire is to set the individual to thinking of this vast universe and its wonders. Also, of nature and its never ending changes and yet at the same time its constancy in some respects of areas. It is as never ending wonderment and study.

BASDEO, ANDREA
[b.] January 9,k 1970, Guyana, South America; [p.] Cecil and Cecilia Basdeo; [ed.] Franklyn Delano Roosevelt High School, New York City Technical College; [hon.] Dean's List; [pers.] I believe that each of us is driven by the desire to love and be loved. Without love we're incomplete. [a.] Jamaica Queens, NY 11418.

BASILE, ULRIKE
[pen.] Ulrike Basile; [b.] Plainfield, New Jersey; [p.] Hannelore and Wilhelm Neumann; [m.] Steven Basile, July 10, 1979; [n.ch.] Kiona, Kino, Valentino Christopher, and Christina; [ed.] Arizona State University, Institute of Children's Literature; [occ.] Writer/Housewife; [hon.] Track and Field, English Award, Writing for Children and Teenager Award; [oth. writ.] A Doll Named Kissy, I Want To Steal A Little Kiss, Jesus Will Show You The Way; [pers.] I try to instill a moral lesson in my writings. We learn from observation and an open mind. The Young, the older and wise, a-like, can teach us much. If we only open our minds and hearts to everyone. [a.] Bloomsdale, MO 63627.

BASTIAN, WALTER M.
[b.] Washington, DC; [ed.] BA American University (SUMMA), M.A. Yale University; [occ.] Retired Foreign Service Officer; [memb.] American Foreign Service Association, DACOR, OMICRON Delta Kappa, Alpha Sigma Phi. [a.] Chevy Chase, MD 20815.

BASTIN, WILLIAM R.
[b.] July 30, 1925, Shelby County, Indiana; [p.] Samuel M. and Ella E. Bastin; [m.] Marilyn Y.

(Theobald), June 9, 1946; [ch.] Jeffrey Richard (8/20/48), Steven William (5/11/51); [ed.] Manilla High, Manilla, IN, Wooster College (Wooster, OH), University N. Carolina-Chapel Hill, Indiana University (Bloomington, IN); [occ.] Development of Natural Ground Water Resources for Industrial and Commercial Use; [memb.] (Formerly) National Water Well Association Junior Chamber Commerce-Engineer Club, (currently) First Baptist Church; [pers.] Listen not to those who speak out against the newly elected. Lift up prayers for our chosen ones so they may serve us well in their time. [a.] Shelbyville, IN 46176.

BAUER, DOUGLAS M.
[pen.] Doug Bauer, August 12, 1942; [b.] Herkimer, New York; [p.] Maynard Frederick and Ruth Spraker Bauer; [ed.] BS-Hobart College (1965); [occ.] Telephone Professional; [oth. writ.] Local only, but well received; [pers.] My philosophy, if I have one, is self evident in my writing. Other than that, I have only the standard writer's curse of having to do what I do in order to stay sane. [a.] Kalamazoo, MI 49001.

BAUGH, KERICEE NICOLE
[b.] May 31, 1979, Kingston, Jamaica, West Indies; [p.] Anna and Paul Baugh; [hon.] Basketball and Volleyball certificates. Certificates for being an outstanding students; [oth. writ.] Several poems which have been published in my school newspaper; [pers.] In my writings, I try to write my true feelings. I try write the things I experience as a teenager. I was influence to write poems by favorite teacher in Middle School, and by other romantic poets. [a.] Houston, TX 77099.

BAXTER, ANN C.
[a.] Brandon, MS 39042.

BAXTER, YVONNE
[pen.] Yvonne Baxter; [b.] May 4, 1929, Stephenville, Texas; [p.] Henry and Laura White; [m.] Dean Baxter, December 1, 1946; [ch.] 4 sons, 11 grandchildren, 2 great-grandchildren; [ed.] 11 years formal, 64 years school of hard knocks; [occ.] Housewife and mother; [memb.] Church of Christ, Volunteer of America; [oth. writ.] Christmas Story published in The Durango Herald December 1992, other poetry and stories unpublished; [pers.] My writings are from personal experiences and my strong belief in God, Family, and Country. [a.] Durango, CO 81301.

BAYLY-ATKIN, JENNIFER
[b.] January 14, 1971, Toronto, Ontario; [p.] John and Cristine Bayly; [m.] James Atkin, August 22, 1992; [ed.] Sir John Franklin Territorial High School (Yellowknife), University of Calgary (4th year of BA English); [occ.] Student; [memb.] Amnesty International; [hon.] Out of Province Entrance Scholarship (UofC), Entrance Scholarship (NWT Department of Education), English 30 Departmental medal; [oth. writ.] Short story published in Amnesty International Publication for members - one article in The Yellowknifer (newspaper) and L'Aquilon (N.W.T.'s French Language newspaper); [pers.] The poetry I write that is most real to me is always about the North. Its haunting beauty will be part of me forever. [a.] Yellowknife, N.W.T. X1A 2R2.

BEANS, FLORENCE
[b.] July 17, 1980, Linwood, Michigan; [p.] William S. and Maude Brumley Amstutz; [m.] Lloyd P.,

December 19, 1936 (Deceased); [ch.] Donald Beans and Margaret Burritt; [ed.] Bay City High and County Normal Central Michigan University BA from Eastern Michigan University; [occ.] Elementary teacher for 26 years, Retired from Keicher school, Michigan Center 1971; [memb.] M.E.A., M.A.R.S.P., Alumni E.M.U., Jackson Bethel Baptist Church; [hon.] National Honor Society, Bay City Central High 1925; [oth. writ.] Poems Exodus published in Moody Monthly, 1961 (May) 40 page paperback, A Cup of Life published November 1985; [pers.] My poetry through the years has been a journal of everyday life; also a tribute to our Father above, and the friends He has placed along my way. [a.] Jackson, MI 49201.

BEARD, ELSIE MAY
[b.] July 23, 1943, Battle Creek, Michigan; [p.] Loren H. Vogt and Bertha V. Vogt-Sissen; [m.] Phillip M., October 3, 1965; [ch.] Scott Eric and Mark Frederick Beard; [ed.] Belleville High, Olivet College, Michigan State University and Western Michigan University; [occ.] Substitute teacher Pennfield schools, Battle Creek, MI; [memb.] Alpha Lambda Epsilon, Baseline Methodist; [oth. writ.] I have written several other poems in the past; [pers.] I resigned my permanent teaching position to raise our two sons because I believe that it more important. It is this love of my family which influenced my writing of poetry. [a.] Battle Creek, MI 49017.

BEAUMONT, MARIEL
[pen.] Rahcel Beau; [b.] May 26, 1917, Norwick, New York; [p.] Richard and Karen Beaumont; [ed.] Sophomore at Oxford Academy Central schools; [memb.] French Club, Drama Club, Field Hockey; [pers.] Success is accomplished by discovering your true self. Being everything and all you want to be, and to have God in your heart to guide you. [a.] Oxford, NY 13830.

BECKER, CARL F.
[pen.] Carl F. Becker; [b.] March 31, 1908, Kampsville, Illinois; [p.] Geo W. and Ida L. Curtis Becker; [m.] Widowed, 1928; [ch.] 3 all grown and married; [ed.] High School; [occ.] Formerly Building Contractor; [hon.] I have many awards both poetry and songs; [oth. writ.] Songwriter with over 200 songs, all my poems are songs; [a.] Escondido, CA 92027.

BECKWITH, MARIE
[b.] June 3, 1972, Pittsfield, Massachusetts; [p.] Lorraine and Albert Dean (step-father); [ed.] Graduated from Wahconah High School; [occ.] Curtain maker and a ranch hand; [hon.] Physical Education award; [oth. writ.] I have numerous amounts of poems that I have in a notebook, no one has seen them yet; [pers.] I try to be imaginative and creative with my poems. I like to express my feelings in a poem and to make non living things come to life. [a.] Becket, MA 01223.

BEEKMAN, BESSIE PAULINE
[b.] July 15, 1907, Hartford City, Indiana; [p.] Alexander and Orpha Craig (Marion, IN); [m.] Guy C. Boucher (1st marriage), 1925; [ch.] Hazel, Arthur, Joann, Jerry, Floyd, Robert, Donald, Juanita Sue Boucher; [ed.] Elementary; [memb.] The Church of Jesus Christ of Latter Day Saints, Mormon for 32 years, taught Sunday school; [hon.] Golden and Silver Poet awards, Sisterhood Day award for story,

Award of Merit for poem "You Think I'm Getting Old"; [oth. writ.] I'm one of His Sheep, Perfection, I Thank Thee Lord, Hillbilly Hilda, Spring, Acky Breaky, Time and many others. I write for a small magazine; [pers.] Started poetry at 7 years, like poems that tell a story. Favorite poet was James Whitcomb Riley. I write poems to my friends and children. [a.] Marion, IN 46953.

BEHNSCH, EARL R.
[pen.] Earl R. Behnsch; [b.] August 4, 1924, San Antonio, Texas; [m.] Julia (Doolie), January 1, 1946; [ch.] Patsy Sue, Doris Marie, Michael R., Vivian Kay, and Lillian Faye; [ed.] High School and some college; [occ.] Retired Supervisor,, S.W. Bell Telephone Company (40 years); [memb.] Telephone Pioneers of America, Masonic Lodge and Knights Templer-32; [oth. writ.] Old Tree, Cold Hot Day , Farewell to Maw and many more; [pers.] All my writings are from my heart and from things I have seen or witnessed. [a.] Rockspring, TX 78880.

BEHROOZI, DOMINIQUE
[b.] June 23, 1970, Lachine, Montreal, Quebec; [p.] Gwen and Cyrus Behroozi; [ed.] High School diploma and graduate,, electrical technician; [occ.] Electrical Technical and working on cables, industrial motor control specialist; [memb.] CAA Association (Caradium Motor League Association); [pers.] I love life, people and different nationalities. I am single, and looking forward to continue my education and practices as an electrical technician; [a.] Montreal, Quebec, Canada H4U 2G2.

BELCHER, MABLE B.
[b.] April 23, 1925, Richmond, Virginia; [p.] Walter L. and Elizabeth Ann Barfoot; [m.] Robert F., Sr., May 22, 1943; [ch.] Robert F., Jr., Danny E., and Diane B. Marion; [ed.] High School-GED at age 42; [occ.] Housewife-Retired office worker-Bookkeeper; [memb.] St. John Newmann Catholic Church; [oth. writ.] Poems-1-published at Richmond Public Library for History of Old Neighborhood "Oregon Hill" concerning party reunion of many years; [pers.] I write from feelings of the heart. [a.] Powhatan, VA 23139.

BELCHER, STEVEN L.
[b.] March 4, 1971, Port Jervis, New York; [p.] James and Rose Belcher; [ed.] Port Jervis High School; [occ.] Employed by Trail Blazers a non-profit organization; [oth. writ.] Currently working on novel and book of poetry; [pers.] WE spend most of our time celebrating flesh and ignoring the emotions that binds it. I'd like to change that, however I can. [a.] Montague, New Jersey 07827.

BELECHAK-BECRAFT, CYNTHIA
[a.] Ellicott City, MD 21043.

BELEW, MARY ANN
[b.] June 16, 1976, Lawrenceburg, Tennessee; [p.] Alice Belew and the late Vance Hull; [ed.] I am a sophomore at Summertown High School, will graduate in May 1995; [occ.] Full-time student; [memb.] Future Homemakers of America (FHA); [pers.] I was inspired by my friends to write this poem. [a.] Summertown, TN 38483.

BELL, DAWN
[b.] July 6, 1964, Charlotte, Michigan; [ch.] Chris-

tina and Dustin; [pers.] I wish to dedicate this poem to Christina and Dustin Bell. Mom will always love you forever please don't ever forget this.

BELLEMORE, ANDREA
[b.] June 19, 1978, Denton, Texas; [p.] Claudia Barry and Philip J. Bellemore; [ed.] Christoval Junior High, Central High School; [occ.] Student, part-time Veterinary Technician; [memb.] Varsity Orchestra; [hon.] Presidential Academic Award, Top 10%, UIL Writing Medal; [oth. writ.] Fifty other poems written, Uil Ready Writing, Children's Book (not yet published); [pers.] I never realized my potential as a poet until an unfamiliar cousin lost his ability to write. I proceeded on with his beloved hobby. I owe this all to him. Thanks, Mark. [a.] San Angelo, TX 76904.

BELONGIA, MARYJO
[b.] April 9, 1965, South Milwaukee, Wisconsin; [p.] Joseph and Mary Beth Klatt of Green Valley, AZ; [m.] David, February 14, 1987; [ch.] Lauden and Peter; [ed.] South Milwaukee Senior High School, University of Wisconsin-Milwaukee (Criminal Justice); [occ.] Housewife and part-time Medical Records Technician (West Bend Clinic); [pers.] "Eventide hold's a hunter;s moon..." was written for my husband, David, on his 26th birthday. May we always be a "one". [a.] West Bend, WI 53095.

BENDER, BRENDA ROBIN
[b.] July 25, 1954, Augusta, Georgia; [m.] Victor; [ch.] Chuncey and Brandon; [ed.] B.S. and MS in Elementary Education-Ft. Valley State College; [occ.] Teacher-Watterson Elementary School (Louisville, KY); [memb.] National Alliance of Black School Educators (Wash. DC), St. Paul Missionary Baptist Church; [hon.] The Apple Award; [oth. writ.] Several poems; [pers.] I enjoy the pulchritudiousness of each day, and strive to touch someone with an inspirational thought. [a.] Louisville, KY 40250.

BENDER, SANFORD
[pen.] S. Eldon; [b.] April 15, 1936, Grantsville, Maryland; [p.] Harvey and C. and Elva (Yoder) Bender; [m.] Miriam C. (Tice) Bender, August 23, 1959; [ch.] Marlin, Sonya, Twila, Sandra, Donna, Myron; [ed.] High School GED Certificate; [occ.] Minister; [oth. writ.] Several plays given in local church setting and poems printed in church papers; [pers.] My utmost desire is to exalt the glorified Christ. To me 11th century BC has some of the most beautiful Hebrew verse ever written. [a.] Bittinger, MD 21522.

BENEFIEL, WAYNE L.
[b.] June 19, 1956, Des Moines, Iowa; [p.] Merle and Eloise Benefiel; [m.] Kim D., February 14, 1991; [ch.] Matthew and Danielle McVicker; [ed.] Des Moines Technical High School; [occ.] United States Post Office; [oth. writ.] Cupid's Sorrow, In Falling Snow, First Love, At Her Side, Moments of Spring. [a.] Des Moines, IA 50315.

BENFIELD, CRYSTAL
[b.] June 18, 1967, Burke County; [p.] Grover and Sue Pritchard; [m.] Justin W., June 30, 1984; [ch.] Sheena Lynn and Tiara Dawn Benfield; [ed.] Freedom High School, Western Piedmont Community College; [occ.] Health Care Technician; [memb.] State Employee's Association of North Carolina; [oth. writ.] A Child published in "Quest of a Dream"

in 1993, Pacific Rim Publications, several poems published in local newspapers; [pers.] I write poetry to reflect my life, or the lives of others around me. I have been greatly influenced by my friends and family. [a.] Morganton, NC 28655.

BENN, AVA L.
[pen.] Ava Russell Benn; [b.] January 15, 1914, Lawrence County, Ohio; [p.] P.G. and Nettie Russell; [m.] David H., June 5, 1943; [ch.] "adoptees" Lee Soon and Young Newsome; [ed.] Aid High, Ohio State (BS), Miami University (Masters); [occ.] Business Education Teacher, Ohio Missionary, Brainerd Indian School, SD; [memb.] Stonecroft Ministries FBC Coordinator, United Methodist, Church Women United; [hon.] Pi Omega Pi (Honorary Fraternity), Rio Grande College Scholarship; [oth. writ.] News articles for local newspapers, report to Ohio Business Teacher, poem published in the Ironton Tribune; [pers.] My purpose in writing is to benefit others, to bring honor to God and Christ "in whom are hid all the treasures of wisdom and knowledge". [a.] Oxford, OH 45056.

BENNETT, MARIE
[b.] November 23, 1913, Eureka, Kansas; [p.] Emory and Flora Blake; [m.] Widow; [ch.] Janet Weber, Peggy, Velman, Raymond Neal; [ed.] High School; [occ.] Housewife; [memb.] UNA Chapter O.ES, (Hosington, KS), First Christian Church, Meal site, AARP, Ellis; [oth. writ.] Poems for programs as within 6 years, District Aide, a;; una chapter 119 Hosington.

BENSON, WANDA
[pen.] Wanda Severson Benson; [b.] February 26, 1915, Hampden, North Dakota; [p.] Oscar and Edverda (Aardal) Severson; [m.] Carl Eilertson, 1942-46) and Hamar Benson 1951 (deceased); [ch.] Donald, Karleen, Douglas, Bjorn, David, and Beth; [ed.] Valley City Teacher's College 1937, Augsburg College BA degree 1940-Reading Specialist 1974; [occ.] High School English Teacher, Elementary and Title I Retired; [memb.] Family of Grace Lutheran, Women of the ELCA, AARP-Senior Citizens; [hon.] H.S. Valedictorian, College Honor Student, Oil Painting 2nd prize, County Fair; [oth. writ.] Several articles in the Plainswomen University, Grand Folks, ND; [pers.] I strive to express the love of family, friends, and the inspiration of God's beautiful creation in my poems and writings. [a.] Auburn, WA 98002-4815.

BENTLEY, PEGGY
[b.] March 24, 1976, Alexander County Hospital; [p.] Willie and Virginia Bentley; [ed.] Rising senior at Alexander Central High School; [occ.] Student; [memb.] Former member of Future Horsemakers of America, French Club; [hon.] Outstanding Writing Award; [pers.] I think poetry is the art of all literature. Everyone can write a poem, but you have to look deep down in your heart to get the .(point) [a.] Taylorsville, NC 28681.

BERGREN, ADA
[pen.] Ada Catherine Jones Bergren; [b.] June 12, 1915, Tarkia, Missouri; [p.] William Jones and Lille Weable Jones; [m.] Everett Ramsey and Clifford Bergren; [ch.] Junior and James Ramsey; [ed.] High School Equivalency Certificate; [occ.] Farm wife and mother; [memb.] Methodist Church Rebeckah Lodge, Eagles Lodge; [hon.] Second in spelling contest in

Missouri; [oth. writ.] I have written several poems but never had any published before; [pers.] I have a very sensitive nature and am deeply touched by peoples problems and try to help whenever I can. [a.] Red Oak, IA 51566.

BERRY, ANDREW S.
[pen.] Andy; [b.] June 26, 1981, Jackson, Michigan; [p.] David and Jody Berry; [ed.] Andrew is in the 5th grade at McDevitt Elementary School in Vandercook; [memb.] Andrew is a member of the 5th grade band and also the Mileage Club; [hon.] Andrew has been on the all A&B Honor Roll since the First Grade. [a.] Jackson, MI 49203.

BERRY, MELANIE ANN
[pen.] Melanie; [b.] April 6, 1976, Dallas, Texas; [p.] Laura Berry and Bill Day; [ed.] Richardson High School; [hon.] 1st Place New Mexico State Speech Tournament, Albuquerque Junior Symphony Orchestra; [oth. writ.] "The Place", "All Alone", "You", and "Earth Beast"; [pers.] To the love of my life-may you finally find happiness in this cruel and strange world through me. [a.] Dallas, TX 75218.

BERTA, TERI
[pen.] Morgan Cobey; [b.] May 7, 1955, Dallas, Texas; [p.] Michael and Mildred Porter; [m.] David G., June 29, 1984; [ch.] Tracie, Amy, Joshua; [ed.] Graduated in 1973 North Dallas High, attended North Lake Junior College; [oth. writ.] Poems, currently writing a book about Great Great Grandmother; [pers.] I have always said that one is no more or less intelligent that the one he is communicating with because each has to understand what the other is trying to say. [a.] Irving, TX 75060.

BERKLAND, JAMES O.
[pen.] J.O.B.; [b.] July 31, 1930, Glendale, California; [p.] Gertrude M. (Thompson) and Joseph O. Berkland; [m.] Janice Lark (Keirstead), December 19, 1966; [ch.] Krista Lynn (1/20/69), Jay Olin (10/3/74); [ed.] AA-Santa Rosa Junior College, AB-U.C. Berkeley, MS-San Jose State University, PhD (Candidate) UC Davis; [occ.] Geologist; [memb.] Fellow, Geol. Soc. America Association, Engin. Geologists, Sevmological Soc. of America, AAAS, Sierra Club; [hon.] Fellow Lions Club Intern. Foundation Lion of the Year, King of Club Lions, San Jose Distinguished Member Award, Santa Clara County Engineers and Architects Association, Who's Who in the World, Who's Who in the West, Who's Who in California, Who's Who in Frontier Science and Technology; [oth. writ.] Fifty plus scientific papers in Geology. Editor of "Syzygy-An Earthquake Newsletter", editor of "Loose Leaves", Annual Poetry, publ. Santa Rosa Junior College (1951); [pers.] Truth, like beauty, is in the eye of the beholder. It is not achieved by majority vote, but is subject to change with some new data or some new insight. At best a scientific truth is a progress report. [a.] San Jose, CA 95127.

BERKRAM, PATRICIA
[b.] December 27, 1937, Jersey City, New Jersey; [p.] Thomas and Florence Clarke (deceased); [m.] Elmer M., October 24, 1974; [ch.] 4 children, 2 step-children, 13 grandchildren; [ed.] AA Nursing, BA Bible and Theology- now a student at (postgraduate) Assembly of God Theological Seminary; [occ.] Retired Registered Nurse; [hon.] President's List 4.0 2 years, Dean's List, All American Scholar and Na-

tional Dean's List 3 years; [oth. writ.] Many poems published by the National Library of Poetry, and in school magazines and papers. Also many published essays and short stories; [pers.] The Lord of Creation is my inspiration. His spirit endues me with any talents I might have. [a.] Cut Bank, MT 59427.

BHATTI, JOHN Y.
[b.] November 22, 1960, Peshawar, Pakistan; [p.] Yousaf and Sharifan Bhatti; [ed.] BA in English University of Peshawar, Pakistan; [occ.] Currently working for an Insurance company; [memb.] United Pentecostal Church; [oth. writ.] Several poems written, some of them are: To My Special One, Cupid's Cry, Little Caleb, and The Hope of Glory; [pers.] Success is a friend of those who never accept failures as defeat, but rather fresh opportunities to achieve more glorious victories. [a.] Los Angeles, CA 90041.

BIANCO, FRANCINE B.
[pen.] Young Senior; [b.] Scranton, Pennsylvania; [ch.] Angela and James Bonavoglia; [ed.] High school graduate, evening classes at Business Tech H.S., Advertising Diploma ICS 1990, University of Scranton 1982-1985 part-time, studied toward a bachelor's degree-left to begin an art career, recently became certified into the 'Babes' program for the Lackawanna County Commission on Drug and Alcohol Abuse. Through puppetry I communicate with children at schools to draw from them various problems - if they exist, took acting lessons in the summer of 1990; [occ.] Wrote short stories for communication studies at college, hold a fictional manuscript (sent it to a few publishers) it is dormant, at present; [hon.] Received an award as a retired volunteer for Reading to the Blind, on the radio, once a week, hold an award from the clerk of Judicial Records certification for my Celebrity Portrait Exhibit at our Court House; [oth. writ.] Participated in the musical "Mame", dancing and singing, produced by a local theatre group names "Standing Room Only". This was a few years ago. I was a choreographer for several months-teaching tap, dancing to teen-agers, (my very first love was tap dancing). Some of my poems were published by the Scranton Weekly newspaper; [pers.] My very existence along as I can recall-was utilized with every consciousable God-given talent and taken as far as my capabilities and strength would allow. [a.] Scranton, PA 18510.

BIBLE, GYPSI LEIGH
[b.] February 16, 1976, Crossville, Tennessee; [p.] Seth and Charlotte Bible; [ed.] Senior High School 1993-94; [memb.] Play flute in my Symphonic Bound in High School and in the Cumberland Orchestra at Sewanee, TN; [hon.] Received honors in English and been placed in Advanced Placement English classes. In high school Symphonic Band received Musician of the Year, Best Bandsman; [oth. writ.] Several other poems in my personal collection. [a.] Sewanee, GA 30174.

BIERMAN, JOHN A.
[pen.] A.J. Bierman; [b.] June 5, 1961, Winnipeg, Manitoba; [m.] Jody, June 9, 1986; [ch.] Dylan (6) and Jeese (2 1/2) Bierman; [ed.] Grade 11 - East Kildonon Secondary School; [occ.] Restaurant Consultant; [hon.] Volunteer Award, Boy and Girls Club, Kelowna BC; [oth. writ.] Yes, none have been published; [pers.] I would like to see my poem in songs. To send message to young people that "the grass isn't

greener on the other side". [a.] Kamloop, BC.

BIGGS, MARY
[b.] Faith Hope; [b.] January 18, 1908, Peridido, Alabama; [p.] William Thomas and Clara Evelyn Smith; [m.] John Henry (deceased), February 27, 1931; [ch.] Leon (deceased), Charles, Benny, Derwood, and Ann; [ed.] High School Bay Minette, AL, BS degree Troy State College (Troy, AL), graduate work-South Alabama (Mobile, AL) [occ.] Children's Institute of Literature, Homemaker, Mother, Teacher; [memb.] Church, AEA, ARTA, AARP, Cancer Easter Seal Society, Hospital Auxiliary, UMW, others; [hon.] Those that came through motherhood and teaching school; [oth. writ.] Community news reporter, 55 years for "The Baldwin Times". Historian and corresponding secretary for Church; [pers.] Even at 85 years, I still live alone and take care of my home. When friends ask if I live by myself, I say no, the Lord lives with me . He's the center of my life. [a.] Atmore, AL 36502.

BINGHAM, TENEE'
[pen.] Nay-Nay; [b.] October 31, 1980, Indianapolis, Indiana; [p.] Helen and Brian Bingham; [oth. writ.] "As I Look Out of the Window", "MoonLight", "The Old Woman Who Loved Apple Pie"; [pers.] I put all my faith and trust in God, and I am thankful for all he's done. [a.] Indianapolis, IN 46205.

BIRCHFIELD, BRENDA
[pen.] Sue Birchfield; [b.] November 21, 1947, Hazard, Kentucky; [p.] Everett and Nettie Brewer; [m.] Ray, December 19, 1964; [ch.] Michael Ray and Tamara Dawn Birchfield; [ed.] Sophia High School; [occ.] Homemaker; [oth. writ.] I have written several other poems. None of them have ever been published. I give the poems as gifts. [pers.] I enjoy writing these poems, I always write poems for family and friends. To let them know just how I feel about them. I always write them from my heart. [a.] Woodbridge, VA 22191.

BISHOPRIC, KATY
[pen.] Katherine Chloe Bishopric; [b.] August 1, 1981, New York, New York; [p.] Susan and Bob Bishopric; [ed.] 6th grade student, Carver International Middle School, studying French; [memb.] Future Educator of America, French Club, National Honor Society; [hon.] Honor Roll, Gifted Program, French certificates; [oth. writ.] 1st place-Haiku in Dade County Youth Fair-2 years in a row; [pers.] International Exchange student-2 summers in France. "Poetry allows me to express my inner feelings in the utmost way". [a.] Coral Gables, FL 33134.

BIXLER, JONATHON THOMAS
[b.] September 11, 1971, Fort Wayne, Indiana; [p.] Dolly Fluke and Phillip Bixler, Sr.; [m.] Linda Louise, September 7, 1990; [ch.] Christina Renee; [ed.] BS-Civil Engineering, BS Engineering Administration; [occ.] Student; [memb.] American Society of Civil Engineering; [pers.] I have been greatly influenced by Frost, Poe, Hemingway, and King. I try to put in perspective today with my writings. [a.] Fort Wayne, IN 46809.

BLAHUT, SUSAN E.
[pen.] Susan Hoff, Susan Horton; [b.] January 5, 1964, Eustis, Florida; [p.] Del and Molly Horton; [m.] Phillip, Sr., November 2, 1983; [ch.] P.J.,

Mollie, Ashley, Owen, Selena; [ed.] Mt. Dora High graduated, Lake Sumter College studied Psychology two years; [occ.] Homemaker, crafter, poet; [memb.] Navy Wife Club; [hon.] Gifted program in Junior and High School; [oth. writ.] Some published in Navy News; [pers.] Poetry is my diary. My heart. Life opens subjects from comedy to tragedy. My soul. To love, laugh, lose. God to guide the pen. [a.] Virginia Beach, VA 23456.

BLAIR, TRACEY
[b.] June 3, 1967, Welland, Ontario; [p.] Gloria Gauthier; [m.] David Edward, February 12, 1993; [ed.] Welland High, Three Rivers High School (Quebec); [occ.] Upgrading to become chartered accountant; [hon.] Mature student award 1990 graduation; [oth. writ.] I have a thousand writings, but made never tried for publication till your contest; [pers.] My writing is my personal release on life. It's every thought I ever had. It's my way of fighting for my life. [a.] Victoria, B.C., Canada U8T 4E2.

BLANCHETTE, ELIZABETH
[b.] September 12, 1954, Alliston, Ontario, Canada; [p.] James Blanchette and Barbara Love; [m.] Divorced; [ch.] Jennifer Julie-Anne, Kimberly Anne Marie, Earl Wayne, Tony (grandson); [ed.] St. Clair College-Applied Arts grad; [occ.] Homemaker and Professional Cook; [memb.] Cerebral Palsy Association, Alzheimer's Society; [oth. writ.] Several poems and stories published in local papers. Also published a newspaper for children via government grant. Have written a children's book-have not yet sought publication; [pers.] I particularly enjoy writing for, and on behalf of, children. After all, children are the builders of the future. [a.] Airdrie Alta T4A 1Y4.

BLAND, BRENDA
[b.] October 14, 1958; [b.] Springfield, Massachusetts; [p.] Theresa and Edward Kuryn, Jr; [m.] Clifford R.; [ch.] Jason Eric and Logan Ray; [ed.] Springfield High, Jeff Tech College; [occ.] Nurse (LPN), Carroll Health Care Center; [memb.] Assembly of God Church; [hon.] Honor Roll; [oth. writ.] Many poems unpublished; [pers.] Throughout my life, writing poems seemed to be good therapy for me. A release of emotions that were trapped inside. Once released-inspiration-gave birth to a poem. That's when I found comfort...and I pray your comforted too! [a.] Carrollton, OH 44615.

BLUHM, IRENE T.
[b.] April 6, 1933, Aurora, Illinois; [p.] William G. "Bill" and Irene Dissell Stephenson Koward; [m.] Lawrence W. (Larry) Bluhm, December 27, 1952; [ch.] Cynthia Bluhm Meyer and son-in-law Roger Meyer, three grand children - Brant, Dustin and Chase Meyer; [ed.] Graduated from Emmanuel Lutheran, grade school and East Aurora High School - Class of 1950; [occ.] Homemaker; [memb.] Zion Luth. Church, Naperville, IL, Zion Lutheran Church Choir and Ladies AID and Ladies Mission Society; [hon.] National Honor Society (High School), The National Library of Poetry's, Editor's Choice Award for my poem "A Vision"; [oth. writ.] "My Sweet Child", published by Watermark Press in "Another Place in Time", "A Vision" published in "Where Dreams Begin", National Library of Poetry, "Grandma's Love", published in "Distinguished Poets of America" National Library of Poetry; [pers.] I dedicate this poem to my husband, Larry - who is also

my best friend and mate of 40 years. He loves the American flag and what it stands for. He served his country in the U.S. Air Force - and is Korean War Veteran. [a.] Aurora, IL 60505.

BLYSTONE, JOSEPH A., JR.
[pen.] J.J.; [b.] August 11, 1956, Latrobe, Pennsylvania [p.] Joseph A. and Miriam R. Blystone; [m.] Divorced; [ed.] Greater Latrobe School District, Eastern Westmoreland Vo-tech; [occ.] Machine Operator; [oth. writ.] Poetry; [pers.] Try to live each day like it is your last. [a.] Hostetter, PA.

BOATMAN, MARVA
[b.] November 10, 1955, Madison, Florida; [p.] Rosa Lee Boatman; [ed.] BS (Special Ed./Mental Retardation), FL. State University, MA (Ed. & Human Development/Serious Emotionally-Disturbed Adolescent, George Washington University; [occ.] Teacher, Author; [memb.] CEC, National Council of Negro Women, Washington Teachers Union Volunteer; [hon.] Cafritz Fellow, 1985; [oth. writ.] "A Children's Book of Morals", "Reality"; [pers.] Its through the continuous development of faith in that we triumphantly meet the constant challenges of life. [a.] Washington, DC 20010.

BODIFORD, CLIFFORD J.
[b.] December 28, 1957, Freeport, Texas; [p.] Warren and Marilyn Bodiford; [m.] Sherrie, November 23, 1985; [ch.] Jennifer Kay; [ed.] Brazoswood High, Gallaudet University, Southwest Institute College for the Deaf; [occ.] USPS Mail Handler; [memb.] Texas Association for the Deaf; [hon.] Who's Who; [pers.] The one great aim, why even death stands still and waits an hour for such a will. [a.] Fort Worth, TX 76103.

BOISVERT, LAURIE
[b.] February 12, 1974, Regina, Saskatchewan; [p.] Leo and Helene Boisvert; [ed.] Currently attending University of Regina; [occ.] University student, working towards a Bachelor of Fine Arts; [oth. writ.] Several poems and short stories have been published in local and provincial anthologies; [pers.] I don't want my poetry to dictate thought, but rather encourage it. [a.] Regina, Sask S4X 4B5 Canada.

BOLDT, LINDA
[b.] September 24, 1948, Batavia, New York; [m.] Dennis, July 2, 1992; [ch.] Rammy Lynn Fearby and Dawn Marie Ames (Medina, NY); [ed.] Medina High School; [occ.] Medical Assistant; [oth. writ.] I just write for pleasure. [a.] Batavia, NY 14020.

BOND, NILES WOODBRIDGE
[pen.] Niles Bond; [b.] February 25, 1916; [b.] Newton, Massachusetts; [m.] Pamela; [ch.] 2 daughters; [ed., memb., and hon.] U.N.C. 1937, A.M. Fletcher School Law and Diplomacy, Medford, MA, 1938. U.S. foreign service officer, 1939-68; vice consul Havana, Cuba, 1939-40, Yokohama, Japan 1940-41, 3d sec vice consul Madrid, Spain 1942-45; ed sec 1945-46; advisor to U.S. delegation to 4th session Econ. and Social Council, 1947; 2d sec, vice consul Bern, Switzerland, 1947, 1st sec. and consul, 1947; asst. chief div. N.E. Asian affairs Dept. State 1947-49; officer in charge Korean affairs, 1949-50; adviser to U.S. delegation to 4th session UN Gen Assembly, 1949; 1st sec Office of U.S. Political Advisor to Supreme Comdr. Allied Powers, Tokyo,

Japan, 1950; acting chmn. Allied Council for Japan, 1952; counselor of embassy , vis lectr. Bologna Center, Johns Hopkins U, 1957-58, research fellow Ctr. for International Affairs, Harvard, 1958-59; minister-counselor embassy Rio de Janiero, Brazil, 1959-63; coordinator interdeptl. seminar Dept. State, 1963; minister, consul gen. Sao Paulo, Brazil, 1964-68; sec. bd. trustees Corcoran Gallery Art, Washington, 1973-86; pres. bd. dirs. Brazilian-Am. Cultural Inst., 1976-86; mem. ct. study system DC Bar, 1979-81, exec. dir. fee arbitration bd., 1981-87; exec. dir. Project Orbis, 1972; adviser Sao Paulo Bienal, 1969; dir. internat. exhbns. com. Am. Fedn. Art, 1976-77; [occ.] Retired diplomat and cultural institute executive; [oth. writ.] 3 books of poetry: <u>Dreams From A Wintry Night</u> (1993), <u>Elegos</u> (1967), <u>Arcanum</u> (1965); [pers.] In the Old World tradition of the Poet-Diplomat, Niles Bond began to write poetry early in his thirty-year diplomatic career. Although many of the poems in this book were written far from his native shores, while serving in such areas of the world as Western Europe, Northeast Asia, and South America. they reveal few geographical coordinates. His poetic terrain is rather the inner landscape of the human condition, which he explores in an intensely personal way. Mr. Bond was born and raised in and around Boston and now lives with his wife, also a writer, in Old Lyme, Connecticut. His two previous books of poetry were published to critical acclaim in Brazil in 1965 and 1967. [a.] Old Lyme, CT 06371.

BONE, SARA
[pen.] Sara to; [b.] October 20, 1976, National City, California; [p.] June and Clyde Bone; [ed.] Helix High; [occ.] Student; [memb.] Key Club; [hon.] 1993 Outstanding Keycluber; [oth. writ.] Staff writer for Highland Fling, several poems published in high school Lit. mag.; [pers.] I write what I think, I think what I write, my poetry is a reflection of myself. A thousand reflections, one person. [a.] Lemon Grove, CA 91945.

BOOTH, CHARLES (CHUCK)
[b.] March 20, 1976, Minden, Louisiana; [p.] Kenneth Ray and Jean Ann (Quires) Booth; [ed.] High School in May 94; [occ.] Satellite Repair and Installation; [memb.] United States Karate Foundation, American Judeau Association; [oth. writ.] Sweet Dreams, The End, and others; [pers.] The Beauty is in the hands of those who have learned to appreciate it in every aspect of every way. Appreciate the beauty of the gifts God has given you and use it wisely with Grace. [a.] Homer, LA 71040.

BORCHARD, PEARL G.
[[b.] June 27, 1920, Saginaw, Michigan; [p.] Alfred and Gertrude Burnett; [m.] Roy G. Borchard, September 12, 1942; [ch.] Sharon and Gary Borchard; [ed.] High School; [occ.] Housewife; [hon.] Poet Laureate of Saginaw High School, 1939; [oth. writ.] 25th School Anniversary poem, 50th Anniversary Poem, Holiday Poems for a Monthly Senior Citizen Paper in Erie, PA; [pers.] This poem was written as a senior high school. It was inspired by looking at my 75 years grandmother who I lived with. [a.] Erie, PA 16502.

BORDO, KIMBERLY
[b.] June 14, 1974, Scranton, Pennsylvania; [p.] Jack Bordo and Dianne Bordo Mikolaczyk; [ed.] Mid Valley High School, East Stroudsburg University;

[hon.] Who's Who Among American High School Students (3 years) 90-93; [pers.] I enjoy writing poems to express my true feelings on a specific situation. [a.] Scranton, PA 18504.

BORELAND, DANA
[b.] June 11, 1976, Allegheny Valley Hospital, Natrona Heights; [p.] Ellen Szarewicz and David Molnar; [ed.] Fox Chapel High School, Middle Road School, Dorseyville Junior High; [pers.] I take poetry very seriously, I think that is one very good talent that is wonderful to have. [a.] Bridgeville, PA 15017.

BORISHADE, ADETOKUMPO KNOWLES
[b.] April 3, 1939, Cleveland, Ohio; [p.] James and Julia Knowles; [m.] Divorced; [ch.] Mario L. Borishade Andrews; [ed.] PhD Temple University 1993, MA-Ohio State University 1982, BA Wilberforce University 1980; [occ.] Professor of African Studies; [memb.] African Studies Association, Pan African Studies Association, National Council for Black Studies, Liberian Studies Association, African Heritage Studies Association; [hon.] Alpha Kappa Mu, National Dean's List; [oth. writ.] Articles published in: Western Journal of Black Studies, Journal of Black Studies, Proceedings-6th and 7th Pan African Conference, Proceedings 5th Annual Conference, Association for the Study of Classical African Civilizations, and more; [pers.] My writing sets forth my rootedness in and love for the spiritual, philosophical, cultural, and aesthetic modalities and expressions of all things African. Africa is the source of my creativity, my vision, and my reason for existence. [a.] Jacksonville, FL 32206.

BOSLEY, CAROL-ANN J.
[b.] November 24, 1946, Canada; [p.] Eileen Prevost and Arthur Bosley; [ch.] Heather and Brian Hirst; [pers.] Conduct your life in such a manner that you can always like and respect who you see in your mirror. DEDICATION - "The Journey" was composed in honour of Kenneth E. Wayner, my piano teacher and friend. Ken was a dedicated family man, a mixture of strength and gentleness, a man who epitomized the word "gentleman". Your dream of "wanting to be remembered of making a difference" is in fact a reality Ken. On behalf of all of us fortunate enough to have you touch our lives "thank you Ken for being God's blessing". [a.] Ottawa, Canada.

BOSSO, THOMAS J.
[b.] September 11, 1949, Compton, California; [p.] Joseph and Theresa Bosso; [m.] Karen Jean, April 25, 1992; [ch.] Kirk, Jeff, Mark, James; [ed.] Dominguez High School, U.S. Air Force, North American School of Conservation; [occ.] International Society of Poets; [hon.] Award of Merit, Golden Poet Award 1991 from World of Poetry; [oth. writ.] Numerous unpublished songs and poems. Two poems published in a "View From the Edge". One poem published, "Great Poems of Our Time"; [pers.] If just one poem can change one persons life for the better, then it was worth writing. [a.] Lakewood, CA 90713.

BOUCH, JENNIFER
[b.] December 6, 1980; [p.] Sandee and Joe Bouch; [ed.] 6th grade Mohonasen Middle School; [occ.] Student; [hon.] Honor Roll; [pers.] Interests: reading, writing, horseback riding, music, bike riding and being with my friends. [a.] Schenectady, NY 12306.

BOUDREAU, TERRENCE
[b.] November 7, 1947, Rockford, Illinois; [p.] Wilfred and Adeline Boudreau; [m.] Carol, 1990; [ch.] Noah, Hannah, Cole, Denton, Dalton; [ed.] College; [occ.] Consultant; [memb.] National Rehabilitation Association (NRA); [oth. writ.] Poems, short stories and children's stories; [pers.] What is...is. [a.] Laytonville, CA 95454.

BOUNDS, QUENTIN
[b.] September 15, 1927, Chambersburg, Pennsylvania; [p.] Clarence E. and Marie Bounds; [ed.] Currently enrolled in Chambersburg Area High School's class of 1996; [hon.] Johns Hopkins CTY State and Regional SAT Talent Search, District gifted seminar class; [oth. writ.] I am currently putting together a small collection of poetry and essays that I hope to have published within the next four years; [pers.] A dream is what I have here. In time, it may fade, but for now, let me dream. This is all that anyone really needs. [a.] Newburg, PA 17240.

BOURGEOIS, GAIL
[b.] May 9, 1938, Saugus, Massachusetts; [p.] Louis E. Winchell and Mary Winchell Taatjes; [m.] Paul, December 16, 1966; [ch.] William, Leonard, Michele, Marshall, Carol and Paul; [ed.] Malden Evening School; [occ.] Poetess/illustrator, freelance journalist, photographer; [memb.] Cliftondale Congregational Church, Mission Committee Co-chair, Shipper Coordinator, Heifer Project International Northeast Region; [oth. writ.] "And Gail Writes" (self published), an anthology of verse, poems and illustrations. "Freddy Learns About Love", a children's story emphasizing the principle of love; [pers.] Gratefully acknowledge the source of your talents, love and nurture your family and friendships and know that in life, pain is inevitable but misery is an option. [a.] Saugus, MA 01906-4279.

BOWEN, DEBRA
[b.] January 18, 1970, Maryland; [ch.] Travis Edward Miller; [occ.] G.E.D. Southeastern Business College; [occ.] Mother/student; [pers.] Life isn't always easy. It requires perseverance. I persevered. [a.] Portsmouth, OH 45662.

BOWLIN, TRIGG
[b.] October 24, 1977, Lubbock, Texas; [p.] Susan Millsap and Randy Bowlin; [ed.] Lubbock High School, Sophomore, LEAP Honors; [occ.] Student; [hon.] Nationals Power Tumbling Competition 1991 and 1992. [a.] Lubbock, TX 79416.

BOWMAN, AARON W.
[pen.] Aaron bowman, bow; [b.] June 3, 1975, Bloomsburg, Pennsylvania; [p.] Glen and Betty Bowman; [ed.] Central Columbia High, Indiana University of Pennsylvania; Music Education-major; [oth. writ.] This is my first published work; [pers.] I try to put personal experiences into a poem, yet still keep the poem meaningful to everyone. Mostly influenced by E.E.Cummings, Robert Frost and other modern poets. [a.] Bloomsburg, PA 17815.

BOWERS, KAREN
[b.] March 26, 1968; [m.] Roger, March 4, 1989; [pers.] I dedicate this to my husband, whose love gave me courage, I will love you till the end of my days. [a.] Stillwater, OK 74075.

BOWERS, LORRIE K.
[b.] March 11, 1964, Latrobe, Pennsylvania; [p.] James R. and Evelyn G. Bowers; [ed.] Richland High, Cambria-Rowe Business College; [occ.] Bookkeeping and tax service in my home; [memb.] Westmont Baptist Church; [oth. writ.] A short story published in a local paper. Currently enrolled in a writing course from the Institute of Children's Literature. I hope to become an author of children's books; [pers.] I am physically challenged-walk with two wooden canes-but I don't let that stop me from doing things. I just have to do some things differently. If people remember to look to the Lord first, surviving the mountains and valleys of life won't be impossible. [a.] Johnstown, PA 15904.

BOWLES, DREMA K.
[b.] January 25, 1967, Rockledge, Florida; [p.] Larry and Margaret Pennington; [m.] Richard Wayne; [ed.] Princeton Senior High, Concord College; [occ.] Administrative Assistant; [hon.] Employee of the Year; [oth. writ.] I have a portfolio of over 100 poems, however, I have never attempted to have them published; [pers.] Trust in the Lord with all thine heart, lean not unto thine own understanding. In all thy ways acknowledge him and he shall direct thy paths. Prov. 3:5,6. [a.] Princeton, WV 24740.

BOYD, DAVID P.
[b.] March 24, 1906, Chicago, Illinois; [p.] James J. Boyd and Adele Elizabeth Boyd (nee Adele Elizabeth Wandas); [ed.] Bachelor of Science in Journalism, The Medill School of Journalism, Northwestern University, 1929, Master of Science in Journalism, The Medill School of Journalism, Northwestern University, 1932; [occ.] Former editor of C.R.D.A. News, the Chicago Retail Druggists' Association, Chicago, 1939 to 1943, Army Air Corps., February 1943 to September 1945, reporter for the La Grange (Illinois) Citizen, 1947 to 1952, worked for Illinois Bureau of Employment Security from 1965 yo 1974, The Illinois State Employment Service, reporter for the Blue Island (Illinois) Sun Standard, 1929 to 1930, reporter for the Chicago City News Bureau, 1930 to 1931; [memb.] Church of the Atonement (Episcopal) Chicago, member of International Society for General Semantics, member of Sigma Delta Chi Professional Journalist Fraternity since 1929; [oth. writ.] Author of "How to Discover Your Better Self", Vantage Press, 1959, author of "Stories Behind the News", short stories, Vantage Press, 1965, author of "Thoreau, the Rebel Idealist", Americana Magazine, 1937; [a.] 5619 N. Kimball, Chicago, IL 60659.

BOYD, ELAINE E.
[a.] Baltimore, MD 21207.

BOYD, PAULA JO
[[pen.] Paula Jo Boyd; [b.] August 22, 1942, Kennett, Montana; [p.] Betty Jo Brown and Paul Roy Earl; [m.] Divorced; [ch.] Two daughters, oldest was murdered in 1975 when she was 14; [ed.] 12th grade; [occ.] Disabled; [memb.] Baptist Church; [hon.] Merit for poem, Time Gone By, also honorable mentions; [oth. writ.] I have lots of poems, I have not done anything with them; [a.] Arnold, MO 63010.

BOYD, STEPHEN
[pen.] Nick Sane; [b.] October 7, 1972, Los Angeles, California; [p.] Louis Boyd and Carolyn Lee; [ed.] Brentwood School, California State University; [oth. writ.] Numerous other poems, unpublished. Also a few unfinished screenplays; [pers.] One shouldn't depend on others in life. Fear nothing and have no regrets. [a.] Los Angeles, CA 90062.

BOYKIN, ROBYN INEZ
[pen.] Bobbi; [b.] July 27, 1980, Atlantic City, New Jersey; [p.] Felix and Lydia H. Centeno, Junior; [ed.] Arthus Rann Middle School; [occ.] 7th grade student; [hon.] Merit Roll-three times over; [oth. writ.] A poem published in the Atlantic City Press; [pers.] The contents of my poetry are based on events that have occurred throughout my years. [a.] Pleasantville, NJ 08232.

BRACKEN, BRENDA L.
[b.] February 28, 1955, Washington, North Carolina; [p.] William F. and Lilly Inez Godley; [m.] Divorced; [ch.] B. Craig, S. Michael and K. Renae Bracken; [ed.] Laurel Valley High School, Coastal GA Center for Continuing Education; [occ.] Legal Assistant-Bouhan, Williams and Levy, Savannah, GA; [memb.] VP-Savannah Association of Legal Secretaries; [oth. writ.] In the process of compiling a work entitled "Poems from the Heart of A Single Parent"; [pers.] My poetry is from the heart and spirit. [a.] Ellabell, GA 31308.

BRADLEY, BRENDA
[b.] June 26, 1961, Ancourage, Alaska; [p.] Rayburn and Arlene Beck; [m.] Lawrence C., January 27, 1991; [ch.] Jasmine Arlene; [ed.] Bitburg American High School, Bitburg Germany; [memb.] Human Race; [oth. writ.] The Dream Is Real, 1993; [pers.] Love people, use things. [a.] Ft.Walton Beach, FL 32547.

BRADOVICH, ERIN
[pen.] Erin Siegel; [b.] March 27, 1979, Pittsburgh, Pennsylvania; [p.] Rose Rossi and Michael Bradovich; [ed.] Aliquippa, PA Middle School; [occ.] Volunteer at Aliquippa Hospital; [hon.] Academic Excellence awards, Academic Achievements; [pers.] My writings are of my heart and of my feelings. Hopefully one day my writings will inspire younger and older minds. [a.] Aliquippa, PA 15001.

BRADY, LISAMARIE
[pen.] L. W. BRADY; [b.] June 26, 1970, Jersey City, New Jersey; [p.] Cecelia A. and Frank J. Brady; [ed.] St. Aloysius Grammar School and High School, Junior College, Jersey City State College; [occ.] Full-time student, part-time theater employee; [memb.] Society of the Creative Anachronism; [hon.] Award for working on my high school newspaper; [oth. writ.] "Wait For Me", "Candle Waltz" both printed in Quill books; [pers.] I'll suffer anything for my art because my art is my life. It is an extension of me. [a.] Sayreville, NJ 08872.

BRANDON, ALLEN F.
[pen.] Allen; [b.] April 20, 1909, Clay County, Arkansas; [p.] Elijah J. and Dannie Brandon; [m.] Mary Valeria Moore, December 23, 1928; [ch.] I have nine children, all are living except one; [ed.] 8th grade plus one Ark. State Teachers College course 1927, have State Teacher's license; [occ.] Writer, gardener, retired Inspector, F.T. & R. Company; [memb.] American Legion, Lion's Club, United Methodist Church; [hon.] Chaplain, American Legion Post No. 15 Calico Rock, Ar., Golden Lion No.

223 Arkansas; [oth. writ.] Books published Fragments of Thought, 1977, Odyssey to Somewhere, 1987, both are copyrighted, the last one has the poem I sent in; [pers.] What is poetry? Poetry is thought, sometimes philosophy, sometimes argument, but always emotion. I love to write, poetry has love, sorrow, passion, religion, heroism and life. [a.] Calico Rock, AZ 72519.

BRANSON, SANDRA JEAN

[b.] May 15, 1943, Dexter, Iowa; [p.] Max and Myrtle Branson; [ed.] Graduated area XI Community College Associate of Art Degree; [hon.] Dean's List Twice; [pers.] Have always felt a keen interest in observations and involvement in much of life's processes. [a.] Cedar Rapids, IA 52405.

BREAUX, HILDA BENNETT

[pen.] Hilda Bennett; [b.] July 21, 1930, Elk City, Oklahoma; [p.] Grace Vera Hogan and James Blaine Cook; [m.] Divorced; [ch.] Carla Burr, Mark Burr, and Clayton Bennett, Pamela Bennett; [ed.] Lucy Flower High School (Chicago, IL), St. Louis College of Music (Clayton, MO); [occ.] Retired singer, pianist for 20 years in Washington DC; [hon.] 1947 Jr. Miss America Contest, winner in talent, toured England and North Wales, singing sang for Cherokee Tribal meeting in Taliguah, OK; [oth. writ.] Book of 100 poems unpublished. In progress of writing my life story, lyrics entitled, "If This Is Not A Dream". Copywritten for Each Maninoff's Rhapsody on theme of Paganino; [pers.] "Somewhere In Time" was written to be sung with music from movie by the same name written by John Berry. My favorite poetry is romantic and spiritual. [a.] Vienna, VA 22182.

BREHENY, MICHAEL

[b.] November 6, 1954, South Carolina; [p.] Mr. J. and A.M. Breheny; [ed.] Yorktown High School, Nova College, Georgetown University (Washington, DC); [pers.] It means a great deal to me to share a poem with are readers and to ask are readers to read are poems to people of all nations that we may all share these poems. [a.] North Arlington, VA 22205.

BREWER, STEWART

[pen.] Stewart Brewer; [b.] March 29, 1971, Price, Utah; [p.] Ashton Philip Brewer and Janet Sue Offutt; [ed.] Vintah High School, Brigham Young University, Utah State University; [occ.] Student majoring in History/English; [hon.] Eagle Scout-concert master for Utah Community Schools Orchestra; [oth. writ.] Various short stories-several poems dealing with a variety of topics and styles-general research on various topics; [pers.] Through personal, intense prayer, we yield all we are and hope to become to that being. That God, that gave us life, He who loves us more than life itself. [a.] Vernal, UT 84078.

BRIDGER, ELAINE

[pen.] Elaine Rae; [b.] April 6, 1975, Surrey, B.C., Canada; [p.] Raymond and Sheila Bridger; [ed.] Attending grade 12; [hon.] Royal Conservatory Music grade 6 level. Canada Cord (Guides); [oth. writ.] "Friends" published Oct. 7, 1992, Vancouver Sun. As well, two years published in school yearbook. "Autumn", "Friends", "Lost Chance"; [pers.] My words are thoughts and sounds of truth. I say what others sometimes are unable to say loud enough that people may hear them. [a.] Surrey, B.C. Canada .

BRIDGES, SHARON

[pen.] Sharon Bridges; [b.] March 1, 1945, Trion, Georgia; [p.] Mildred and Bill Croft; [m.] Doyle, July 6, 1987; [ch.] Angie, Steve, Paul, Bryant, Kelly and Danny Dodd; [ed.] Chattooga High; [occ.] Home Health Care; [hon.] Several awards on my poetry; [oth. writ.] I have also written over 50 songs, my favorite are gospel; [pers.] My very favorite thing is singing my own songs. The gospel songs. [a.] Summerville, GA 20747.

BRIDGES, SUSAN R.

[pen.] Sue; [b.] October 13, Raleigh, North Carolina; [p.] Dewey and Margaret McKnight; [m.] December 20, 1958; [ch.] Michael Lemuel, Darryl Wayne; [ed.] Ligon High, Saint Augustine's College, North Carolina Central University; [occ.] Librarian; [memb.] Zeta Phi Beta Sorority, Saint Augustine's Alumni Association; [hon.] Dean's List, Service Awards, Wake Medical Hospital, Partner's Award; [oth. writ.] Several poems written ready to be sent to a publisher; [pers.] I select my titles with care relating to poetry. They are realistic, original, creative, deals with mankind and nature. I have always loved poetry as a child. [a.] Raleigh, NC 27610.

BRIGGS, LIZ

[pen.] Formerly Liz Dearborn; [b.] November 19, 1918, Erie, Pennsylvania; [p.] Sam Ingro and Isabell (Henderson) Ingro; [m.] Joseph, September 28, 1982; [ch.] (by former marriage) Diane Lewis Sam Ehret, Larry Dearborn, Barb Evans; [ed.] Millcreek High School; [occ.] Shop worker-Retired; [memb.] Erie Humane Society-American Association of Retired People (AARP); [oth. writ.] Several poems published in Erie Daily Times; [pers.] Many of my poems were written during the long, lonely days of World War II and many memorials to family, mostly. [a.] Erie, PA 16506.

BRIGHAM, KELLY J.

[b.] May 7, 1966, Burlington, Vermont; [p.] James and Sandra Farrington; [ed.] Degree of Associate in Science; [occ.] Administrative Assistant; [hon.] Who's Who in American High School Students 1982-83 and 1983-84; [oth. writ.] Poems and short stories from the soul; [pers.] My writings reflect my healing journey. If I feel an emotion, I write about it. [a.] Burlington, VT 05401.

BRILL, LILLIAN HERGERT

[pen.] Lillian Hergert Brill; [b.] September 16, 1914, Sellwood area of Portland, Oregon; [p.] Mr. and Mrs. Solomon Hergert; [m.] Edward C. Brill died tragically January 12, 1972; [m.] April 14, 1934; [ch.] Beverly (January 16, 1937, Dorothy Patricia (May 4, 1940; [ed.] 8th grade graduate 1928, family was financially poor to allow me to attend higher education; [occ.] Retired paralyzed senior citizen 78 years of age; [memb.] American Heritage of Germans from Russia, Salvation Army Rose Center; [hon.] Painting contests and written true stories-to Reader's Digest magazine of short stories; [oth. writ.] 3 true short stories to Reader's Digest: 1) It's Only Skin, 2) There Is No Government Justice Only Opportunity; and 3) Audibly Heard from Jesus the Christ; [per.] Any talent I possess I owe to my Creator, God. He has programmed faith into each of our beginning given us hope to keep going and a bit of love for beauty. I live and move through God's spirit. [a.] Portland, OR 97266.

BRISCOE, BRUCE

[pen.] B.B. San; [b.] December 1, 1957, Glendale, California; [p.] John H. and Pelan C. Briscoe; [m.] Lisa Marie Chavez; [ch.] Joshua Lawrence, Angela Monique, Joseph Jared; [ed.] St. Victor's, Bancroft Junior High, Walt Whitman High, Shasta College, L.A.C.C. College of the Redwoods; [occ.] Self-employed woodsman, jack-of-all-trades; [memb.] National Geographic Society, Agnes Johnson Booster Club, Site Council; [hon.] From California Department of Forestry for tree planting and fire fighting, Agnes Johnson School for Volunteer time; [oth. writ.] "Requiem for the Dew", published in Where Dreams Begin; [pers.] All of life's questions are answered in nature's daily routine. [a.] Weolt, CA 95571.

BROOKS, ALEISHA

[pen.] Elaine Silverbrooke; [b.] August 5, 1975, Arlington, Massachusetts; [p.] Robert and Tonya Brooks; [m.] (Best friends in the whole world) Karla Ek, Lori Chin, Mae-Keng Louie, Jess Zamora; [ed.] John Marshall High, youth for Understanding Student Foreign Exchange in Germany, applying to Emerson College; [occ.] Writer; [memb.] National Forensics League, National Rifleman's Club; [hon.] Mock Trail, Speech, Journalism, Poetry, Drama, Acting and Directing, Swim Team Championship; [oth. writ.] Poetry: Wishes (A Prayer); Cruel Life, A Gentle Heart, and others, two novels, unpublished, children's stories, unpublished; [pers.] Everything has a right to live and die as it chooses. We shouldn't have to wake up to a gray world and see gunmen at the foot of our beds. [a.] Los Angeles, CA 90039.

BROSCO, IRENE

[b.] August 8, 1918, Kansas City, Missouri; [p.] Anna and Julius Koontz (violin maker); [m.] Al Mardo, August 9, 1937; [ch.] Allen Mardo, Robert Anthony, Richard Vincent; [ed.] Westport High, Kelly-Mack School of Dance and Drama; [occ.] Entertainer, pianist, dancer and singer; [memb.] Musicians Local 47, Alumni "Tower Adorables" Chorus line (Inglewood, CA); [hon.] Toastmistress winner, Toastmasters Humorous Speech Contest, winner-Gong Show, Winner-Live Like a Millionaire; [oth. writ.] Comedy material for husband's act. Skits and educational material for Toastmistress Club, poem in 3rd grade newsletter; [pers.] I hope people will become more aware of the necessity for ecological balance in our life sphere. [a.] Los Angeles, CA 90043.

BROUGHTON, NILSA A.

[b.] December 19, 1941, Puerto Rico; [p.] Agustin and Anasta Sia Aviles; [m.] Widow; [ch.] Kofi A., Quinn A., Kahlil O. Washington; [ed.] Empire State College, Cadwalder Behavioral Center; [occ.] Substance Abuse Counselor; [memb.] Catholic Church; [hon.] Award of Merit from World of Poetry, Certificates in: Alcohol the Chemical, Alcohol and Drug Counseling, Codependency, The Abused Child Syndrome, Relapse and Prevention and Wellness, Chemical Dependency in the Family, Alcohol/Drug Counseling the process, Basic Alcohol the Chemical; [oth. writ.] Two poems published by Infuse local magazine in Houston, TX; [pers.] I write about what affects me in life. The goodness as well as the injustices of man. What influences my writing are the changes I would like to see take place in the world. [a.] Yonkers, NY 10701.

BROUMLEY, BOBBIE D.
[pen.] Bobbie Russell Broumley; [b.] July 17, 1929, Alvarado, Texas; [p.] Roy and Anna Russell; [m.] Oliver, June 25, 1946 (deceased Dec. 6, 1989); [ch.] Lester, Richard Broumley and Janis Broumley-Woodworth; [ed.] Alvarado High School, Durham Business College; [occ.] Retired-Administrative Assistant to State Senators-Arizona State Senate; [memb.] Baptist Church, Freedoms Foundation at Valley Forge, Right to Life, republican Party, International Poets Society; [hon.] 3 poems, Congressional Record, Finalist, World of Poetry (for Post Laureate) 1992, "In Thee We Trust" (book, 1970), have presented poetry in California, Texas, Pennsylvania, Washington DC, etc., George Washington Honor Medals, Freedoms Foundation at Valley Forge-Letters of Commendation for Poetry, Sandra Day O'Connor, (U.S. Supreme Court), Senator Barry Goldwater, Honorable Bob Stump, many published newspapers, several magazines, etc.; [oth. writ.] Have written and presented hundreds of poems, school organizations, churches, state functions, etc., "Precious Feet" poem has distribution of more than 2 million at present time, poems published in numerous pages and publications; [pers.] I think the ability to write poetry us a god-given talent and I've attempted in everything I write to bring honor to God and to hopefully help my fellow man by inspiring his faith and helping him smile- [a.] Oceanside, CA 92056.

BROUSSARD, EVELYN
[pen.] Eve; [oth. writ.] "Collections" by Eve and "Sayings" by Eve; [pers.] "The Earth is in its glory, when all who dwell on it live in peace", "To wake anew and feel life once more, is a miracle in and of itself". Sayings by Eve copyright 1991; [a.] San Diego, CA 92162.

BROWN, BARBARA L., DH
[b.] February 25, 1921, Waltham, Massachusetts; [p.] Hazel (Decker) and Lawrence Lombard; [ch.] Dr. Beverly Foster, PhD, RN and Susan Rogers; [ed.] Eastman School of Dental Hygiene, Syracuse University (Continuing Education); [occ.] Retired-Dental hygienist and Bridal Consultant; [oth. writ.] Published poem, local newspaper articles, commentary, local bridal fashion shows; [pers.] Here in Upstate New York winters are Christmas card beautiful, yet very long; by March we yearn for the warmth and green of spring-hence-this poem. [a.] Syracuse, NY 13206.

BROWN, BETTY RUTH
[pen.] Betty Pickens Brown; [b.] May 18, 1941, Pontotoc, Mississippi; [p.] W.L. and Claudia Carpenter Pickens; [m.] Gerald Wayne, November 14, 1959; [ch.] Sandra Ruth Brown Smith; [ed.] Toccopola High School; [occ.] Physically Disabled; [memb.] International Society of Poets, Shiloh Baptist Church; [hon.] Won National in Recreation in 4-H Club in senior year of high school; [oth. writ.] Poems published in local newspaper, in A Collection of Poems by Louisiana, New Mexico, Mississippi, and Minnesota Society of Poets; [pers.] God has blessed me in so many ways, not with "wordly material things", but with Spiritual blessings. He shares His Love daily with me through the studying of His Word, the song of a bird, the smell of a flower, the laughter of my grandchildren, and the love and support of a God-fearing spouse. My prayer is that my writings will help others to see God's love, strength and power in every line. [a.] Thaxton, MS 38871.

BROWN, ELAINE R.
[pen.] Elaine Brown; [b.] December 18, 1930, New York City; [p.] Mae Dominick and Richard Brown; [ch.] Four sons; [ed.] High School graduate, Nurses Aid School; [occ.] Seamstress, Nurses Aid, Songwriter, Lyricist; [oth. writ.] Staff writer for recording and publishing company; [pers.] Most of my writings are about my feelings, thoughts, and experience. My aim is to move people to good vibrations, and to be entertained. [a.] Fayetteville, NC 28304

BROWN, GREGORY
[b.] September 19, 1960, Clay County, Georgia; [m.] Anita Bowden Brown; [ch.] Bruce, Zachary; [ed.] BS in Education-Troy State University (Dothan, AZ); [occ.] Teacher/Program Director; [memb.] Abbeville United Methodist Church; [oth. writ.] "RenFro Churchyard": A Chancel Drama-published by Meriweather Publishing Ltd.; [per.] I enjoy the challenge of telling a story in as few words as possible.

BROWN, HARLEY MICHAEL
[b.] March 6, 1951, Princeton, Missouri; [ed.] Cerritos College (Norwalk, CA), North Arkansas Community College, University of Arkansas at Fayetteville; [oth. writ.] Voices section of the Arkansas-Democrat Gazette, poem in "Wind in the Night Sky" a National Library of Poetry anthology. [a.] Mountain Home, AK 72653.

BROWN, JUDY
[b.] December 7, 1944, Ohio; [ed.] John McBrown; [ed.] 12th Phoenix Union High School; [occ.] Reaching out to others in our community, those who are old and lonely; [hon.] 3 honor awards and 2 awards for golden poet (1990-91); [oth. writ.] I Am Never Zalone, Santa's Coming Home, Daddy's Special Little Angel; Sunshine Rainbows and Roses; [pers.] In my heart I give thanks to God, for giving me the gift of being a poet and to share my poetry all across our great land, the United States of America. [a.] Engadine, MI 49827.

BROWN, KARL A.D.
[b.] May 2, 1969, Jamaica; [p.] Revella Christie and Vinroy Brown; [occ.] Sailor U.S. Navy; [oth. writ.] Several short stories published in the Jamaican Daily Gleaner; [pers.] Life is a mystery. It is our external task to understand it. [a.] New York, NY 09564.

BROWN, KAY
[pen.] Kay Stephens; [b.] October 10, 1948, Wingo, Kentucky; [p.] John and Mary Stephens (Water Valley, KY); [m.] Gary D., June 11, 1964; [ch.] DeWayne, Melissa and Michael Brown; [ed.] Western Kentucky Tech (Mayfield, KY); [occ.] Clinical Secretary, Western Kentucky Mental Health and Mental Retardation Board, Inc.; [memb.] Little Bethel Baptist Church; [hon.] On Board for West Kentucky Allied Services (Mayfield); [pers.] Writing is a release for any emotion one has, and the freedom to express any idea, thought, or emotion is one of the greatest liberties mankind holds. [a.] Mayfield, KY 42066.

BROWN, LEAH
[b.] February 26, 1947, Eufaula, Alabama; [p.] Willie Lee Britt and Belgia Augustus Smith; [m.] Gary Don, May 7, 1967; [ch.] Tamra Lanise, Gary Don, Jr.; [ed.] Alabama Christian High School (Montgomery, AL), Troy State University (Troy, AL); [occ.] Instructional Assistant - 2nd grade, Ridgecrest Elementary School(Phenix City, AL); [memb.] Artist Guild (Columbus, GA); [hon.] President, PTA, Central High School (Phenix, City, AL); [oth. writ.] I have written many personalize poems for individuals in the Southeast and abroad; [pers.] I use my God given talent to express in poetry, the feelings other people have, but cannot express themselves on paper. [a.] Phoenix City, AL 36867.

BROWN, THOMAS D.
[b.] April 16, 1945, Jersey City, New Jersey; [p.] Firman T. and Mary (Brombacher) Brown, Jr.; [ch.] Thomas D. II (6/17/80) and Richard M. (6/9/81); [ed.] BA in Sociology and Applied Science Relations 5/90 Eastern Connecticut State University-Willimantic, CT; [occ.] Director of Security Emhart Class Corporation; [oth. writ.] As seen in "The Great Poems of Our Time" pgs 194-5; [pers.] Be dissatisfied enough to improve, but satisfied enough to be happy (Carrol E. Word, Jr.); [a.] Hampden, MA 01036-9731.

BROWN, VELMA LIPE
[b.] November 26, 1915, Carbondale, Illinois; [p.] Thomas and Hazel Lipe; [m.] Frank E., August 6, 1941 (deceased 7 1/2 years); [ch.] 4 legally adopted from 4 different biological mothers at infancy plus 3 grandchildren; [ed.] 3 years college plus music education; [occ.] retired realtor, babysit my darling granddaughter 5 days a week; [memb.] AARP, NARFE, OES, NFSPS, Poetry Society of TX, Honorary Charter Member International Society of Poets, Baptist Church, Rebecahs; [hon.] World of Poetry Golden Award 1989, Silver Poet 1990, Golden Poet 1991, Award of Merit Certificate: 2 in 1990 and 1 in 1991, Honorable Mention from Quill books; [oth. writ.] Have had several poems in the local: Huntsville Item paper, poems in additional anthologies; [pers.] Adhere to the Christian teachings stay in control and endure what life has to offer but work to stay with the current flow. Love one another with kindness and compassion. [a.] Huntsville, TX 77342.

BROWNLEE, CURT
[b.] July 31, 1976, Regina, Saskqehana; [p.] Earl and Brenda Brownlee; [ed.] Athol Murray College of North Dame (grade 11); [occ.] Student; [oth. writ.] Different note book poems; [pers.] I see poetry as "different" level of communication. My poetry is written to make people think of things beyond oral intelligence. [a.] Drumheller, AB T0J 0Y3.

BROWN-THOMAS, BARBARA
[pen.] D'Henri Lang Ceril; [b.] February 20, 1955, Opelousas, Louisiana; [p.] Curley and Mary L. Thomas; [m.] Charles, May 29, 1976; [ed.] Leonville High (Leonville, LA); [occ.] Telephone Secretary - Lewis Electrical Company; [memb.] Holy Ghost Catholic Church, African American Cultural Awareness Committee, Block Unity and Spiritual Togetherness (BUSI); [oth. writ.] Articles for the local newspaper, poem for KNEK Radio Station, essay contest winner for a local boutique; [pers.] I aim to convey personal life experiences, unspoken emotions, and sympathy in my writings. My inspiration has been becoming aware of the God that lives within, and getting in touch with my inner self. [a.] Opelousas, LA 70570.

BRUNDAGE, JENNY L.
[b.] April 2, 1977, Phoenix, Arizona; [p.] David and Lynn Brundage; [ed.] Centennial High School; [occ.] Student; [memb.] International Thespian Society; [hon.] Lettered in theatre; [oth. writ.] Previously unpublished; [pers.] If you don't question what you believe, then do you really believe it? [a.] Peoria, AZ 85381.

BRUNER, VICKIE
[b.] February 13, 1976, Statesboro, Georgia; [p.] James and Brenda Bruner; [ed.] Reidsville High School Junior; [memb.] FHA; [hon.] Who's Who; [oth. writ.] Never Say Good-bye, You and Me, Love, But First, Boys, Nature, Atlanta Braves; [pers.] In my poems I am able to express my inner feelings. [a.] Bellville, GA 30414.

BRUNSON, HUGH S. III
[b.] January 1, 1974, Darlington, South Carolina; [p.] Mr. and Mrs. Swint Brunson, Jr.; [ed.] Graduate of St. John's High School, Sterling College Grass roots year; [occ.] Student; [hon.] Eagle Scout, Order of the Arrow, Brotherhood. [a.] Darlington, SC 29532.

BRYANT, CARRLYLE R. DR.
[pen.] Carlye R. Bryant; [b.] January 8, 1917, Ft. Inn, South Carolina; [p.] Carl and Lona Bryant; [m.] Bee Bryant, October 23, 1940; [ch.] Linda, Randolph, Jeanne, Dianne and Donna, 17 grandchildren, 6 great grandchildren; [ed.] Greenville High School, BA and BS, Furman University, MA Duke University, Psychology, PhD University of South Carolina, Educational Psychology; [occ.] Retired former school teacher - Math and Psychology, Berea School, from Navy as Commander; [memb.] American Heart Association, Tau Kappa Alpha, Lions Club, U.S. Power Squadron, Past Adv. of Distributor, retired from Navy as Commander; [hon.] Dean's List-Duke University, Furman University Magna Cum Laude, Doctoral Dissertation published by U.S.C.; [oth. writ.] Sold several science fiction stories to Astounding Science Fiction, others to Asimou's Science Fiction, poems published in World of Poetry books; [pers.] I am happy to write of "Love", and good things of life. [a.] Greenville, SC 29605.

BRYANT, FRANCES MARIE LEIGH
[pen.] Frances Leigh Bryant; [b.] September 6, 1921, Hazelhurst, Mississippi; [p.] Enos Wilder and Emily Wilkes Leigh; [m.] Giles Wheeler, November 5, 1943; [ch.] Ann Whittemore, Giles Wheeler, and Thomas Leigh; [ed.] BS Med-University of Southern Mississippi (Hattiesburg, MS); [occ.] Teacher; [hon.] Kappa Delta Pi; [pers.] I want to have made this a better world. [a.] New Orleans, LA 70124-3320.

BRYANT, VERNA J. WOUTEN
[b.] January 26, 1950, Baton Rouge, Louisiana; [p.] James Vernon and Sarah Lillian Lewis Wooten (Linder); [m.] Mark Edwin, August 12, 1971; [ch.] Vernon Jason and Janna In Hye Bryant; [ed.] Natchez Adams High School, Capiah-Lincoln Junior College, University of Southern Mississippi, College of Cosmetology; [occ.] Bookkeeper and Receptionist; [memb.] William Dunbar Chapter, Daughters of the American Revolution, First Baptist Church; [hon.] Capiah Lincoln Junior College-Special Recognition Award for being on the N-Sights Staff; [oth. writ.] Several articles published in the local newspaper. The essay Our Great Loss about my father and many

poems; [pers.] My hope is that my love for God and humanity will show through my poetry. [a.] Natchez, MS 39120.

BUCHANAN, JUDY ANN
[b.] November 22, 1974, Jasper, Georgia; [ed.] 1993 graduate of North Jackson High School in Stevenson, AL. Recently was accepted to Northeast State Community College; [occ.] Full-time student; [memb.] Beta Club, Mu Alpha Theta, Spanish Club, Who's Who Among American High School Students, B Port Church of Christ; [hon.] Academic Scholarship U.S.A.A. award in Mathematics and Leadership and Service. Voted as outstanding senior, all american scholar, U.S.A.A. Award also in Science; [oth. writ.] "What I Want for Christmas" published in the book Awakening to a Dream; [pers.] Poetry helps me rid myself of grief, anger and helps me express my happiness. I have written poetry since I was thirteen. [a.] Bridgeport, AL 35740.

BUCKLAND, ANDREW C.
[pen.] ACB; [b.] September 9, 1957, Miami, Florida; [p.] Eldwin and Rose Buckland; [m.] Patricia J. (Cleary), March 6, 1982; [ch.] Matthew (10), Rebecca (8), Jason (6); [ed.] High school graduate (1976) Miami Sr. High, Electronic/Closed Circuit Television/Broadcast Television Technician (US Navy); [occ.] U.S. Navy electrician; [memb.] American Red Cross, Shelton Park Elm, PTA; [oth. writ.] Approximately 100 love poems and others inspired by many months at sea, none of them published as yet; [pers.] God has blessed me with a beautiful wife and children who are my inspiration and support.

BUCKLAND, HERB
[pers.] This poem is dedicated to Arthur Larson without whose late afternoon memorized recital of Robert Frost's poem, "The Road Not Taken", while walking in Murray Park, in Murray, Utah, and whose intuitive appreciation of Life's subtleties had inspired its birth, ...without reservation. A special heartfelt gratitude is extended to Professor Lee Bartlett at the University of New Mexico from whose own original poems, heard at a standing-room-only recital, encourages one to know the muse of poetry as a kindred spirit to our heart and soul. [a.] Salt Lake City, UT 84123.

BUDGE, BRUCE
[b.] November 5, 1960, Schenectady, New York; [p.] Harold and Phyllis Budge; [m.] Jessica Dolan, May 21, 1988; [ed.] Scotia-Glenville High, Potsdam College; [memb.] Concerned Women for American, Shelby American Automobile Club (SAAC). [a.] New Paltz, NY 12561.

BUEHLER, EVELYN JUDY
[b.] March 18, Chicago, Illinois; [p.] Marzell (deceased) and Ida Mae (Rubbia) Regulus; [m.] Henry, August 23, 1985; [ch.] Ashley Leonard, Evelyn Judy (Jade); [ed.] Dunbar High, The Loop College, John Robert Powers School of Acting; [occ.] Poet, Songwriter; [memb.] International Society of Poets (Associate member); [hon.] 34 honorable mention awards, 2 special mentions, 7 golden poet awards from World of Poetry; [oth. writ.] The Days of "Billie Jean" in "Poems That Will Live Forever", 1992 by World of Poetry Press; the short story "Enchanted" soon to be published by Drury's Publishing. An anthology entitled, "Envoy Collection"; [pers.] Believe in yourself. a [.] Chicago, IL 60621.

BUELS, VALENCIA
[pen.] Valen; [b.] January 31, 1971, Chicago, Illinois; [p.] George and Patricia Buels; [ed.] Honor graduate from high school and some college; [occ.] Data Entry Processor; [pers.] I feel that if you write wrongs in your writings and let it come from your heart you will never go wrong. [a.] Aurora, CO 80013.

BUFFUM, CARROLL SR.
[pen.] Buff-the Simple Man; [b.] July 28, 1936, Arlington, Vermont; [p.] Cecil and Christie Buffum; [m.] Nancy, March 23, 1957; [ch.] Carroll Buffum, Jr.; [ed.] 10 years; [occ.] Retired from G.E.; [memb.] League of Vermont Writers, Buffum Family Association, N.R.A., Middletown Springs Alumni and International Society of Poets; [hon.] Silver Tray, G.E. plaque, first prize ribbon for Driftwood Sculpture and my book of poems and the International Poet of merit award; [oth. writ.] Numerous poems and news articles published in local newspapers and Grit magazine, poetry in one local book and six nationally, my book of poems in print working on second book (Good Old County poems); [pers.] I strive to write about nature, the good old days, togetherness, Vermont poetry. I have been greatly influenced by the Raven by Edgar A. Poe, The Old Swimming Hole by James W. Riley; [a.] No. Clarendon, VT 05759.

BULLARD, TRINA
[pen.] Evol Reed; [b.] August 8, 1980, Tyler, Texas; [p.] Faye and Harold Bullard; [ed.] Eighth grade, gifted and talented program; [memb.] Cheerleader, student council; [hon.] Duke University T.I.P. State Essay Competition, various scholastic awards; [oth. writ.] Assorted poems short stories, and essays; [pers.] Never stop settings goals and striving to reach them. I pray that by writing from my heart, I can influence future generations. [a.] Van, TX 75790.

BULLOCK, REE
[b.] September 23, 1936, Phenix City, Alabama; [p.] Mr. and Mrs. Minzok L. Chadwick; [m.] Wilbert Rex (deceased 1988), December 24, 1955; [ch.] Hiram Jeffrey Bullock, Sr.; [ed.] Central High School, attended UAB in Birmingham, AL, graduated from Roper Hospital in South Carolina; [occ.] Private Duty Nurse; [memb.] Member of First Baptist Church; [hon.] Has won 7 Golden Poet awards worldwide and also 8 Honorable Mentions awards worldwide; [oth. writ.] Published in Who's Who in Poetry worldwide and also published in many books worldwide published in newspapers in the Bahamas and in Mississippi; [pers.] I strive daily to see the good and inner beauty in all of God's creations. This to me makes life so simplified and understanding. a[.] Pensca Cola, FL 32503.

BUNTON, SHARON E.
[b.] July 21, 1940, Toppeninsh, Washington; [p.] Mr. and Mrs. Clarke Rhode; [ch.] Seven daughters, Darla, Laura, Tamara, Kimara, Carrie, Gina and Patricia; [ed.] Graduated high school 1958, Granger High School; [occ.] Writer (unpublished) Office Worker; [memb.] Four Square Church, Forest Grove, OR; [oth. writ.] I have written 15 poems and several short stories, all have not been published. I love to write and hope to have my poem made into a book called God's Recipes; [pers.] I have had the joy of ministering to friends and family with the poems and short stories I have written. I believe that it is the way

I have been able to help my neighbor. [a.] Forest Grove, OR 97116.

BURCHAM, MATTHEW
[pen.] Dan; [b.] April 8, 1977, South Charleston, West Virginia; [p.] Phillip and Bora Burcham; [ed.] High School; [occ.] Student; [memb.] The National Arbor Day Foundation, Blue Hill Meteorological Observatory; [hon.] Honor Society; [a.] Sissonville, WV 25320.

BURCHFIELD, CAROLYN
[b.] June 27, 1937, Richmond, Virginia; [p.] Deceased; [m.] James, January 14, 1959; [ch.] Rebecca Kaye, David James and Sherrie Beth; [ed.] Hermitage High School, Pan American Business College, Malone College, BS (Canton, OH), Akron University (Akron, OH); [occ.] Kindergarten Teacher Louisville Elementary; [a.] Louisville, OH 44641.

BURGER, JO ANN
[pen.] Jo Ann Thomas; [b.] March 12, 1958, Hazleton, Pennsylvania; [p.] David L. and Joan M. Thomas; [m.] Leonard J., October 25, 1980; [ch.] Jolene, Leonard John, and Timothy John; [ed.] West Hazleton High, Luzerne County Community College, and Lock Haven University; [occ.] Elementary substitute teacher; [memb.] Girl and Boy Scouts of America, Drums PTA, United Church of Christ Activities Program; [oth. writ.] Stories and poems with children in classroom settings; [pers.] If my writings will influence readers to appreciate all the wonderful things nature and life has to offer, my dreams and goals will be accomplished. Mark Twain's writings inspired me to write about everyday life. [a.] Drums, PA 18222.

BURGESS, BRENDA I.J.
[b.] February 26, 1956, Edmonton, Alberta, Canada; [p.] Susan S. Dunlop (deceased) and Adam E. Zotzman; [m.] Richard, February 16, 1990; [ch.] Trace Jared (December 13, 1992); [ed.] Lakeland College, Northern Alberta Institute of Technology/ Red Deer Regional Hospital Centre; [occ.] Journeyman Insulator/Medical Radiation Technologist; [memb.] International Association of Heat and Frost Insulators and Asbestos Workers Local 110/ C.A.M.R.T./a.A.M.R.T.; [hon.] Lloydminster Jaycettes Independent Learner Award/Lakeland College Grade 12 Diploma "With Distinction"; [oth. writ.] Numerous poems written for family and friends, usually of a humorous nature; [pers.] Heartfelt thanks to my husband Richard who encourages all of my artistic endeavors and Sherry, who gave us the inspiration for my poem, our son Trace, for whom it is dedicated. [a.] Alberta, Canada T8A 0C6.

BURK, MONA R.
[pen.] Mahoney; [b.] January 27, 1963, Portland, Oregon; [m.] Richard A. Smith; [ch.] Jenny (10) and Zachary (8); [occ.] Housewife; [oth. writ.] A variety of unpublished poetry; [pers.] Thru my poetry I hope to touch that emotion that is - common to everyone that is so hard to express. [a.] Seaside, CA 93955.

BURKE, ANDREA
[b.] September 8, 1923, San Francisco, California; [p.] Charles and Emma Burke; [ed.] BA and MA San Francisco State University; [occ.] Artist (painting in oil, acrylic and water color), retired high school English Teacher; [memb.] Marines Memorial Asso-

ciation; [pers.] Music, art, and literature have formed the core of my life-either creating or teaching. Rhythm and design are the essence, the elixir of the soul. [a.] Napa, CA 94558.

BURKETT, TINA
[b.] December 27, 1967, Little Rock, Arkansas; [p.] Stanley and Jeannie Ledbetter; [m.] Byran, October 13, 1990; [ch.] Kursty Nicole and Christopher Wayne; [ed.] Capital City Christian Academy; [memb.] Siloam Baptist Church; [pers.] In my poetry, I like to focus on important issues in our world today. I also enjoy taking people to beautiful and mystic places of the imagination. [a.] DeKalb, TX 75559.

BURKHARDT, SAMANTHA
[b.] March 29, 1982, Red Bank, New Jersey; [p.] Lois and Paul Burkhardt; [ed.] Currently a 5th grade student at St. Lawrence O'Tolle School (Brewster, NY); [pers.] One sister, Aimee, age 14, loves animals, plays soccer and tennis, skiing. [a.] Carmel, NY 10512.

BURKHART-NAVARRO, VICTORIA ANNE
[pen.] VyKy; [b.] July 26, 1957, Chico, Georgia; [p.] Ernest and Sally Burkhart, (grandparents) Mr. and Mrs. Earllock and Mr. and Mrs. Leonard Burkhart; [m.] Manuel Cris Navarro, February 14, 1986; [ed.] San Jose State (California), BA Fine Arts, California University-Sacramento Post Graduate; [occ.] Artist and Art Instructor (Art) Homeschooling for Christian Children; [memb.] Sunset Christian Church Art Galley Coordinator; hon.] Honors, Dean's List, Cupertino Women's Club Scholarship and a Peter Amig. Memorial Scholarship Senior Art Award, CSF (California Scholarship Federation); [oth. writ.] Many journals of individuals writings, short stories and poems, private - unpublished works; [pers.] I reflect upon life's experience for my creative expression. [a.] Rocklin, CA 95677.

BURKHOLDER, ANTHONY OTIS
[b.] November 16, 1970, Union, South Carolina; [p.] Eddie Ray and Emily Irene Burkholder; [m.] Jana McMillan, July 27, 1991; [ed.] Broome High School, University of South Carolina at Spartanburg, Keesler Technical School, U.S.A.F.; [occ.] Computer Systems Operator; [memb.] Eastside Baptist Church; [hon.] Beta Club, Honor Graduate (high school), honor graduate (Keesler Tech, USAF); [oth. writ.] Poem published in college collection, "Maggies Drawers"; [pers.] In all that you do keep family, friends, and 600 in your actions. [a.] Honolulu, HI 96810.

BURKITT, MARCELLA
[pen.] Marcie; [b.] June 24, 1935, Gallia County, Ohio; [p.] Mr. and Mrs. E.T. Miller; [m.] Delmar L., November 1, 1955; [ch.] Rick, April, Dawn and Brian; [ed.] 8th grade; [occ.] Housewife; [memb.] Villais Chapel Church, United Methodist Women's Club; [oth. writ.] I have several poems at home, only my family and church members have copies; [pers.] This world is big enough for all people, let's try to love one another and to live by God's plan. [a.] Wilmington, OH 45177.

BURNS, BONNIE
[pen.] Bonnie Burns; [b.] June 29, 1973, Charlotte, North Carolina; [p.] Paul and Linda Burns, Sr.; [ed.] Still studying; [occ.] Unpublished writer; [memb.] Double-day Book Club; [pers.] My prospect of the

poems I write, are to give people the joys of reading them. [a.] Charlotte, NC 28206.

BURNS, OZELLA
[b.] 1952, Hays, Mississippi; [p.] W.W. and Mary Jane Burns; [ed.] High School Business College; [occ.] Secretary; [memb.] Forest Baptist Church; [hon.] Valedictorian Harpersville, A.H.S. 1921, Interstate Medal 1921. [a.] Forest, MI.

BURNS, TERNIE M.
[b.] July 29, 1949, Oklahoma City, Oklahoma; [p.] Juanita Miller and Jack Todd; [ch.] Robert Shannon Stow and Melissa Lynn Medford and 2 grandchildren-David Keith Warren Buckingham and Daniella Marie Mefford; [ed.] Sam Rayborn High, Central Texas College; [occ.] Retired Nurse/Office Administration currently handicapped; [oth. writ.] 'Why I hate Vietnam' published in Catholic Digest; [pers.] If you have the good Lord and good friends, you can always accomplish your goal no matter what the circumstances. [a.] Harker Heights, TX.

BURLEIGH, DORIS L.
[b.] August 14, 1927, Robertsdale, Alabama; [p.] James and Mary Lloyd; [m.] Norman, June 8, 1945 (deceased); [ch.] 4 daughters and one son; [ed.] Junior High with self educated; [occ.] Homemaker, Nurses' Aide, waitress and writer; [memb.] Florida State Poetry, Admiral Fitness Center and Manna Food Bank; [hon.] 5 Golden Poet awards, Poet of Merit Awards and "Who's Who in Poetry" 90-91; [oth. writ.] Peace Sets That Go Worldwide with Many Replies from Heads of Nations; [pers.] I strive and work for peace over the world-what could be more important? [a.] Pensacola, FL 32506.

BURLEY, JANET
[b.] January 20, 1966, Scarborough, Ontario; [p.] C.K. and Genevieve Burley; [m.] Divorced; [ch.] Joshua James; [ed.] Bluevale Collegiate, Open Door, Universal Career Institute; [occ.] Hostess and full-time Psychology and Social Work student; [hon.] Math honors award; [oth. writ.] I have a collection of poems called, "Love Songs from the Heart Written in Ink". Not yet published; [pers.] My poems are inspired by friends and personal feelings and reflections on life. [a.] Haliburton, Ontario, Canada K0M 1S0.

BURNETTE, GLORIA J.
[pen.] Glo, Glory; [b.] January 27, 1943, Ruthersfordton, North Carolina; [p.] Kenneth and Addie Louise Miller Burnett; [m.] Divorced; [ch.] Tawanda Michelle, Randall Bernard, Deborah Denise; [ed.] Carver High School (Spindale, NC); [occ.] Real Estate; [hon.] Honorable Mentions for poetry from World of Poetry, 1993 Poem of the Year; [oth. writ.] Several poems, a short story published in books of poetry to be put in Library of Congress, Libraries in the USA; [pers.] My love of poetry springs up in my heart because of my love for God, my fellowman. I hope and pray it will promote love, peace, harmony throughout the world. [a.] Washington, DC.

BURNHAM, SHEILA
[pen.] Sandia Burns; [b.] November 14, 1956, Lubbock, Texas; [m.] Billy, April 5, 1981; [ch.] Shelly and Ciji; [oth. writ.] Poetry, short fiction and currently working on my first novel; [pers.] I use poetry as an outlet for the romantic side of my imagination.

My fiction, however, reflects my intense interest in the darker side of human nature. [a.] Ft. Walton Beach, FL 32548.

BURNS, FINNY J.
[b.] July 31, 1940, Oil City, Pennsylvania; [p.] Mary F. and Joseph F. Finnegan; [ch.] Larry V. Burns and David W. Seope; [ed.] CSULB (BS-Psychology), LBCC (AA-Business Management and AS-Quality Control), Nick Harris Detective Academy; [occ.] QC Manager-soon to be private investigator; [memb.] American Association Cereal Chemists, World of Poetry-International Society of Poets; [hon.] 3 Golden Poems awards, graduation with honors all 3 degrees, 4 Honorable Mentions, other merit awards; [oth. writ.] World of Poetry Anthology-World Famous Gold and Silver poems-Poems That Will Live Forever-Great Poems For Our Time, Who's Who in Poetry Vol. IV, Hour of Awakening magazine; [pers.] It's exciting to grow old when your chasing the youth in the next life to come. [a.] Long Beach, CA 90805.

BURNS, JOHN M. JR.
[b.] December 25, 1923, Cockeysville, Maryland; [p.] John M. and Minnie L. Burns, Sr.; [m.] Jacqueline Fitch, May 24, 1968; [ch.] John M. III and Cynthia; [ed.] Towson High School 1940, University of Maryland; [occ.] Voc. Ed. Inst. Dundalk Sen., Martin Co. Sen., Catoctin Sen., Florida Inst. Tech.; [memb.] Moose Lodge, American Legion, V.F.W.; [pers.] I would like to include the feelings of life's experience in my writing. a[.] Lake Placid, FL 33852.

BURNS, ROY LEE SR.
[pen.] Tate; [b.] December 25, 1933, Wilkes County, Georgia; [p.] Robert and Annie Belle Tolbert Burns; [m.] Addie Lou Danner, May 2, 1953; [ch.] Roy Jr., Willie E., Nedra A., David L., Daniel L., Anita M. Evonne and Lynn M.; [ed.] 16 years; [occ.] Social Service (Senior Citizens Center Director); [memb.] 32 Degree Mason, National Council of Aging, Coalition on Aging, Ministerial Association of Wilkes County; [hon.] Senior Center Achievement award-State of Georgia, Bronze star w/clasp, Vietnam's Cross of Galentry; [oth. writ.] "It's Not Just A Meal", "The Beauty of Old", "The Measure of a Man", "Memories", "What It Is", "Straight", "All Bout You", "Whole Loaf", and "God Our Source"; [pers.] The voice of the Lord calls unto us as a people, my prayer is that the man of wisdom shall out there will here and we as a people will once again do as we say or our money "Trust in God" and not in money-seems that's what we do today. [a.] Washington, GA 30673.

BURNSIDE, REBECCA
[pen.] Becky Burnside; [b.] August 27, 1957, Baltimore, Maryland; [p.] Stanley and Luellen O'Dell; [m.] Rodney, January 6, 1977; [ch.] Ryan; [memb.] Order of Eastern Star; [pers.] I dedicate this poem to my Heavenly Father, I could not have written it without his inspiration. All glory must go to him. [a.] Rock Cave, WV 26234.

BUSHACKER, EVANGELINE
[b.] May 3, 1920, Austin, Texas; [p.] Peter and Elisabeth Lydia Schneider; [m.] Eugene H., May 28, 1949; [ch.] Timothy David Bushacker and Elizabeth Ann Rackley; [ed.] Graduate of Stephen F. Austin High School; [occ.] Homemaker; [memb.] Grace Lutheran Church (Elgin, TX); [oth. writ.] Poems published in The Austin Statesman in the Sixties - in

the Poetry Corner; [pers.] My favorite Bible verse: My sheep hear my voice, and I know them, and they follow me: And I give unto them eternal life; and they shall never perish, neither shall any man pluck them out of my hand. (Jo. 10:27,28). [a.] Austin, TX 78757.

BUSCH, STANLEY
[b.] March 22, 1952, Castle Pollard, Ireland; [p.] Robert and Pat Busch; [ed.] Alta Loma High, Citrus College; [occ.] Hair Stylist; [hon.] California Veteran; [oth. writ.] This is the first ever published most others are of romantic nature; [pers.] Hopeless romantic that likes to express on paper what people think but can never say, so it seems. [a.] Cucamonga, CA 91730.

BUTLER, A. LOIS DR.
[b.] May 25, 1912, Stockdale, Texas; [p.] Susan Passmore Butler; [ed.] BMus-Violin and, Piano (S.W. Georgetown, TX 1932)-MMus. Composition, The Benjamin T. Rome School fo Music-The Catholic University of America (Washington, DC 1972); MMus Violin, first woman candidate, Peabody Institute of the Johns Hopkins University (Baltimore, MD 1940); Authorization in Schillinger System of Musical Composition, Berklee College of Music (Boston, MA 1949); Paralegal Study, 1982; C. Brenier & G.T. Jones, composition E. Meyers, electronic music; further studies, Violin and Composition, University of Wisconsin, Madison, summer 1934, Legal study, University of Texas, Austin, summer 1935, Violin, Juilliard School of Music, New York, summers 1936, 1937, 1938, Violin study with R. Burgin, Boston University School of Music, 1947; String instrument Workshops of Dr. George Bornoff, Boston University School of Music 1966-70; [occ.] Musician - Genealogist; [memb.] American Music Center and Albun Berr Society; [hon.] Winner in Texas Music, Texas Composer's Guild; [oth. writ.] Musical Compositions-Instrumental and Vocal; [pers.] If at first you don't succeed-don't cry-try again! [a.] Dallas, TX 75232.

BYRNE, DUANE
[b.] August 6, 1961, Norristown, Pennsylvania; [p.] Christel Schenrer and John D. Byrne (deceased); [ed.] AA in General Education, BS in Business Management and Human Resources; [occ.] Actor: Film and TV; [memb.] Screen Actors Guild, American Federation of Radio and Television Artists; [hon.] Circle of Winnows, Bronze Life Achievement, Honor Society, Several athletic related and sales related awards; [oth. writ.] Several poems that reflect my emotional and spiritual journey and growth through life; [pers.] This poem was inspired by my step father who died. I read it at his eulogy at his funeral. His death has inspired me to live each life to the fullest as life has no guarantees. [a.] West Hollywood, CA 90069.

BYRNE, MICHAEL J.
[b.] June 18, 1964, Monessen, Pennsylvania; [p.] Linda L. Wolford and John G. Eloshway; [m.] Rose Ann Greco; [ed.] Monessen ER High School, Community College of Allegheny County; [occ.] Freelance Writer; [memb.] International Society of Poets; [oth. writ.] Several poems for after Image Magazine, several as yet unpublished short stories for children; [pers.] I write with the spirit of my grandfather and the little boy he gave heart, spirit and soul to even though

he passed on 20 years ago. He lives in my writing and my memory. [a.] Pittsburgh, PA 15218.

BYRNS, KENNETH ANTRIM
[b.] February 18, 1912, Dickinson, North Dakota; [p.] Walter and Dorothy Meier Byrns; [m.] Virginia, December 29, 1973; [ch.] Lara, Kendra, Sadhaka, Faik, Fadil, Thomas, James, Maria; [ed.] Longmont Colorado High, University of North Colorado (BA), San Diego State, George Washington, U. M.A., Northwestern University, Canadian National Defense College; [occ.] Retired Foreign Service Officer, Consul General, Lt. Col. USAF (Ret.); [memb.] Diplomatic and Consular Officers Retired, Military Order of the World Wars, ROA, Cure of Ars Catholic Church, Air Force Association; [hon.] Commendation, US Department of Commerce for Work in International Trade; [oth. writ.] Articles for the Foreign Service Journal; [pers.] Have lived 19 years abroad and travelled in many countries. Overseas experiences reflected in my writings. [a.] Leawood, KS 66206.

BYTTNER, MARK ELLIOTT
[pen.] Marcus Havenly; [b.] December 27, 1965, Mercy Hospital, Buffalo, New York; [p.] John and Margaret Byttner and Mary (grandmother); [m.] Joyce C. Duggar (girlfriend); [ed.] West Seneca East Central Schools; [occ.] Silk Screen Operator; [memb.] Bally Matrix Health and Fitness; [oth. writ.] (unpublished) Poems-Always Watching, Sanctuary, Simmering Society; [pers.] We are the key to the universe, ready to unlock it. I am greatly influenced by the Rising of Atlantis and Albert Einstein. [a.] Amherst, NY 14228.

CAESAR, AMANDA
[b.] October 23, 1976, Fairfax, Virginia; [p.] George E. and Susan Vinsinger Caesar; [ed.] Acalanes High School, 11th grade; [occ.] Student; [oth. writ.] A poem published in the school literary magazine, The Akalite, 1993; [pers.] All my thoughts and fears collaborate into beautiful songs of poetry. [a.] Walnut Creek, CA 94596.

CAHILL-EPSTEIN, KELLIE ANN
[b.] October 24, 1985, Mt. Kisco, New York; [p.] Wayne J. and Kathleen M. Cahill-Epstein; [ch.] (cat) Sammy; [hon.] Voted by peers to play Princess part in "Prince of Doom" play, 1993: School Chess Club 1993, member-Girl Scouts of Westchester/Putnum since 1990; [pers.] I don't think people should do drugs because they are bad for your body. I like to write, especially poems. [a.] White Plains, NY 10605.

CALDWELL, FRED L.
[b.] June 16, 1938, Birmingham, Alabama; [p.] Deceased; [ch.] One daughter; [ed.] High school, military school; [occ.] Social Security recipient; [hon.] U.S. Army Reserves, 1957; [oth. writ.] Over thirty-six years back I've written music songs, but none of them has ever been publicized; [pers.] I have music to go with my poem also. [a.] Akron, OH 44307.

CALLAGHAN, GERRY
[b.] October 16, 1953, Belfast; [p.] Maureen and Frank Callaghan; [m.] Sally Callaghan, April, 1975; [ch.] Adam Callaghan; [ed.] St. Mary's Grammar, Belfast, Newtownards College; [occ.] Student; [memb.] Linenhall Library, Belfast, Queen's University English Society, Belfast; [hon.] A beautiful fam-

ily!; [oth. writ.] Some 'wee poems' published in anthologies and newspapers; [pers.] Patrick Kavanaugh would have a good chuckle at being the subject for the poem in this book! I only hope he didn't mind the intrusion. [a.] Belfast BT11 9NL, Northern Ireland.

CALLAHAN, SUSAN
[b.] June 12, 1946, Rochester, New York; [ch.] Pam, Peggy; [ed.] Wayne Central; [occ.] Secretary, Penske Truck Leasing, Rochester, N.Y.; [pers.] I believe human feelings and emotions are mirrored in nature and often reflect on that as I write. [a.] Williamson, NY 14589.

CALLAS, JOHN
[b.] Milltown, New Jersey; [p.] Michael and Ellen; [ch.] Erin; [ed.] New Brunswick Senior High, Seton Hall University, Rutgers University; [occ.] Self-employed accountant; [memb.] Writers Roundtable, Keyboard Club, Music Appreciation Club; [hon.] Bowling trophies, golf trophy; [oth. writ.] Currently writing 2 novels, written 50 poems for eventual publication; [pers.] My poems range in scope from happiness to sadness, from individuals to nature. My fictional novels relate to mystery and double identity. [a.] Camarillo, CA 93012.

CAMINITI, LAUREN
[b.] June 3, 1977, Brooklyn, New York; [p.] Thomas and Dianna Caminiti; [ed.] St. Edmund High School; [memb.] Member and head editor of Saint Edmunds news staff; [pers.] "Life, That the powerful play goes on, and I can contribute a verse..." [a.] Brooklyn NY 11229.

CAMP, JOE III
[a.] McLeod, MT 59052.

CAMPBELL, CARRIE ANN
[b.] July 31, 1980, Glascow, Kentucky; [p.] LouAnn and Gary Stargel, brother, Glynn Parker; [ed.] Shepherd Grade School, 8th grade; [memb.] Gifted and Talented Students of Adair County, Cheerleading Team-captain, basketball; [hon.] Perfect attendance, 8 years of school K-7, numerous athletic trophies; [oth. writ.] Poems for friends and relatives; [pers.] In my writings, I express myself from the heart, in hopes that I will benefit others, encourage hope and peace and inform others of the "real world". [a.] Russell Springs, KY 46242.

CAMPBELL, GREGORY B.
[b.] August 17, 1968, Roanoke, Virginia; [p.] Raleigh and Rae Campbell, brother Joe Campbell; [ed.] Northside High, Virginia Tech, B.A. in Liberal Arts and Sciences; [occ.] Insurance agent, Northwestern Mutual Life; [pers.] I find a lot of the tone and themes of my work are related to how people live and where they were brought up. Greasy Creek, for example, is a small town in the mountains of Kentucky where my father spent his childhood. [a.] Roanoke, VA 24019.

CAMPOS, NANETTE FRANCIS
[pen.] Nena Fields; [b.] August 12, 1978, Chicago, Illinois; [p.] Ricardo A. and Isabel Campos; [ed.] Sacred Heart Grammar, Bishop Noll and Griffith Senior High; [occ.] Student; [memb.] Eastside Girls Athletic Association (softball); [hon.] Two Stevens' Music Scholarship Awards; [oth. writ.] None published yet!

CANFIELD, BETHANY L.
[b.] July 20, 1970, Rochester, New Hampshire; [p.] Roger and Mary Ann Hartford; [m.] G. Andrew Canfield, January 20, 1990; [ch.] Thomas Andrew, Elizabeth Lee; [ed.] Kingswood Regional High School; [memb.] National Rifle Association. [a.] Montpelier Station, VA 22957.

CANO, MARY ARLENE
[pen.] Mari Mast; [b.] January 27, 1931, Sac; [p.] Elmer W. Mast and Evelyn M. Freeman; [m.] Charles Amaro, April 27, 1946; [ch.] Charlene, Brenda, Freda, Christopher and Tracie Cano; [ed.] One semester high school (dropped out), two semesters college; [occ.] Housewife, inventor, writer of poetry and short stories; [oth. writ.] She has wrote about 12 more poems, that I can send to if so requested she had her heart set to be there - and so proud that she was nominated and be recognized for her merits. My wife Mary Arlene Cano passed away on June 2, 1993. [a.] Fallon, NV 89406.

CANTNER, CHRISTOPHER ADAM
[b.] December 17, 1971, Ft. Eustis, Virginia; [ch.] Someday they will know the depths of a father's love; [ed.] There can never be a greater, wiser education than that of my grandfather's and my very existence; [occ.] Museum curator and Public Relations, Mauch Chunk, PA; [memb.] Association of Hopeless Romantics, Bring unto a quest to perpetuate Love; [hon.] I consider life both an honor and an award; [pers.] It truly does make much more than combat gear to make a man. I shall forever remain on the threshold of a dream, in the midst of a song. Thank you so much Mother, you are everything this world should be. [a.] Hazleton, PA 18201.

CAPALBO, RICHARD
[b.] August 19, 1936, New York City; [p.] Rose and James Capalbo; [m.] Anastasia Capalbo, April 25, 1969; [ch.] Martine Capalbo, Matthew Capalbo; [ed.] A. B. Davis H. S., Westchester Community College, University of Florida; [occ.] Self-employed automotive dealership; [memb.] Modern Auto Advisory Board, N.T.R.D.A. associate member, Church of St. John and St. Mary; [hon.] Outstanding community service with city of Gainesville, FL, Dean's list, National Auto Advisory Award; [oth. writ.] 1. mostly poetry on love and nature, 2. short stories about children and animals, 3. also life's struggles; [pers.] I write in order to release my internal and external feelings and the vision which grants me the strength to live. [a.] Chappaqua, NY 10514.

CAREY, BRIAN
[b.] September 2, 1974, Framingham, Massachusetts; [p.] Glenn and Bernadette Carey; [ed.] Park View Education Center; [oth. writ.] No other published writings; [pers.] Live for the day, yet plan for the future, and as the future approaches the fruit of the day becomes more plentiful. [a.] Nova Scotia, Canada BOR 1GO.

CAREY, MEREDITH KATHLEEN
[b.] February 5, 1984, Sarasota, Florida; [p.] Vicki Herbruck; [ed.] Home schooling; [occ.] Student; [memb.] Brownies, 3rd grade, church choir; [hon.] "My Grandmother" won a prize in the Young Authors Project, Raleigh-Wake (N.C.) Council International Reading Association 1993; [pers.] I owe all that I am and all that I'm going to be to God and His goodness.

[a.] Akron OH.

CARJE, PETRE
[pen.] Tica; [b.] August 28, 1947, Bucharest, Romania; [p.] Florica - Iosif; [m.] Denise Carje, December 1982; [ch.] Bogdan - George; [ed.] Economic Academy, Bucharest; [memb.] Pro-Monarhia for Romania; [hon.] Golan University Plaza, Bucharest; [oth. writ.] Several poems in Romania; [a.] Teaneck, NY

CARLETON, JESSICA HONOR
[b.] January 1, 1983, Evanston, Illinois; [p.] Gail Sikevitz and Robert Carleton; [ed.] Willowbrook School, Glenview Illinois, 4th grade; [memb.] BJBE choir; [hon.] 1st place for 4th grade, Pioneer press "Scary Story" contest, 1992 Illinois PTA Certificate of Recognition "Just Imagine" poem, Recipient 24th Annual Illinois Poet Laureate Award; [oth. writ.] "Nightfall" published in Anthology of Poetry by Young Americans, several poems in Worlds of Wisdom and Wonder, Creative Writing Magazine; [pers.] Writing is a gift from God given to people who he knows will use it to bring out love and goodness on the hearts of all people. [a.] Glenville, IL 60025.

CARMAN, DONALD R.
[b.] April 13, 1914, Regina, Saskatchewan; [p.] Russell and Muriel Pigott Carman; [m.] Kathleen Murray Cameron (deceased), April 13, 1940; [ch.] Christopher and Suzanne; [ed.] Grade 8 and 1 year in TB sanitarium which was crucial to my self-education; [occ.] Retired as president of Carman Educational Associates Limited; [oth. writ.] The Bard of Balgonie Travels By Train and Recalls His Past (unpublished); [pers.] "I do not know which witch is which or what is what or what is not." W. B. Yeats, John Donne and Gerard Manley Hopkins are among my favorite poets. [a.] Woodbridge, Ont. Canada L4L 2L3.

CARNAGHI, EMMA L.
[pen.] Auntie Em; [b.] January 11, 1929, Springerton, Illinois; [p.] William and Dora Holder; [m.] Frank Carnaghi (deceased); [ch.] son and 2 grandchildren; [ed.] High school, junior college; [occ.] retired; [memb.] Church; [oth. writ.] Company newsletters, local newspapers, poems, prose. [a.] Dixon, IL 61021.

CAROTHERS, KRISTIN
[b.] November 26, Chicago, Illinois; [p.] Willis and Jacqueline Carothers; [ed.] 5th grade student at Mark Sheridan Elementary School, Chicago Illinois; [memb.] St. Marks United Methodist Church; [hon.] Honor Roll student; [pers.] Do unto others as you would want them to do unto you.

CARPENTER, DEBORAH LYN
[b.] April 25, 1955, Ravenna, Ohio; [p.] William Cheatwood and Shirley Ward; [m.] David; [ch.] Rhiannon Marie (deceased Feb. 1982); [occ.] Licensed Optician; [oth. writ.] "To Anyone Who's Lost A Child", published in "Where Dreams Begin" in March 1993, since my childhood I have always seemed to be able to write poetry, mostly about love, life, and loss; [pers.] This poem was inspired by the loss if Johnny Carson's son, and everything I write is always in memory of my daughter, "Rhiannon". [a.] Phoenix, AZ.

CARR, JAMES S.
[pen.] Jimmie; [b.] January 6, 1933, Indianapolis, Indiana; [p.] James Ruben Carr and Charlene Humphrey; [m.] Wilma Curtis Carr (divorced), January 10, 1953; [ed.] P.S. 26, Crispus Attucks High, IUPUI, Krannert, Ivy Tech Vocational College; [occ.] Retired U.S. Army (SSG) [memb.] Elks Lodge #104 IBPOE/W, Trinity Lodge #18 F & AM; [hon.] Associates degree Architectural Drafting; [oth. writ.] In Selected Works of Our World's Best Poets by John Campbell, "I Can't Understand Why", "The Rise", "Lonesomeness", "Where Did I Meet You"; [pers.] I try to write about life memories and happiness and continually hope for more of the same, wealth included of course. [a.] Indianapolis, IN 46208.

CARR, JEAN COSTEN
[pen.] Jean Costen Carr; [b.] July 4, 1924, St. Louis, Missouri; [p.] James B. and Carolyn T. Costen; [ch.] Carolyn Kehlor Carr, James Costen Carr, Marjorie Carr Anderson; [ed.] Graduate of the John Burroughs School, St. Louis, study at Smith College, Stephens College, the University of Missouri; [occ.] Retired secretary; [memb.] Formerly St. Louis Poetry Center, St. Louis Junior League, Smith College Club of St. Louis, Columbia Chapter of the Missouri Writers Guild, University Club; [oth. writ.] Poems in the Columbia Daily Tribune, 17 years, published a small booklet, The Missouri Poet, in the early 70's with my own poems in this occasionally, religious poems in Episcopal magazines, Living Church, The Torch; [pers.] My sole purpose is t write everyday poems for "everyday people", for the man in the street, glimpses into universal experiences--with beauty and rhyme. I believe a poem should have structure and cadence, with rhyme. [a.] Columbia, MO 65203.

CARR, PAUL
[b.] April 13, 1947, Atlantic City, New Jersey; [p.] Albert H. and Mildred Carr; [m.] Deborah A. Carr, July 9, 1985; [ch.] Paul W. Carr, Christopher Carr; [ed.] High school; [occ.] Business administrator; [oth. writ.] "Love Knows No Reason". [pers.] Jai Gurv Dev; [a.] Absecon, NJ 08201.

CARSON, JAMES R.
[b.] May 25, 1942, Halifax, Nova Scotia; [p.] Rex and Flora Carson; [m.] Carol E., September 1965; [ch.] Three; [ed.] High school, Technical school as a draftsman, 2 years, University of Alberta FAC of Science; [occ.] Truck driver; [oth. writ.] None published; [pers.] ILLIGITIMUS NON CARBORUNDUM. [A.] SASK, Canada S7J 3V3.

CARTER, FRANCES "FRAN" TUNNELL
[b.] May 21, 1922, Springville, Mississippi; [p.] David Atmond and Mary Annie McCutcheon Tunnell; [m.] Dr. John T. Carter, March 16, 1946; [ch.] Wayne Carter, Nell Carter Branum; [ed.] Ed.D, University of Illinois, M.S., University of Tennessee, B.S. University of Southern MS; [occ.] Retired, professor, editor, now National Exec Director, Kappa Delta Epsilon; [memb.] National League of American Penwomen (VP), AL Writers Conclave (Pres), AL Poetry Society (Pres), B'ham Women's Chamber of Commerce (Pres), Civil Air Patrol (Southeast, Public Affairs Officer); [hon.] Who's Who in America, Who's Who of American Women, Who's Who in American Education, Dictionary of International Biography, Birmingham Woman of the Year 1977, Birmingham Volunteer of the Year 1980; [oth. writ.]

4 books: Sammy in the Country, Tween-Age Ambassador, Ching Fu and Jim, Sharing Times Seven, also published: 35 poems, 55 articles, 11 curriculum units (4 programs in each unit); [pers.] I believe all kinds of writing, whether prose or poetry, are important. I want to help in my small way to inform, entertain, share love, and help evangelize the word through religious and secular writing. [a.] Birmingham, AL 35243.

CARTER, GAYLE M.
[b.] October 23, 1963, Salem, Massachusetts; [p.] Ellen L. Hochter and Stephen E. Wilkinson; [m.] Michael J. Carter, September 13, 1992; [ch.] Sonya Marie Wheeler; [ed.] Essex Agricultural Institute, North Shore Community College; [occ.] Housewife, student; [oth. writ.] "Protected Violator", "The Person Within", "The Choice, "Joy", and several others; [pers.] I encourage all-to express thyself on paper, to discover the talent that you may have within. [a.] Peabody, MA 01960.

CARTER, TIMOTHY J.
[b.] December 25, 1954, Washington, D.C.; [p.] Robert W. Carter and Janet M. O'Brien; [ed.] BS Sociology-Frostburg State University; [occ.] Enjoy writing poetry; [hon.] Human Relations award, Dale Carnegie; [oth. writ.] None published; [per.] My poems reflect on specific humanistic problems. However, most are religious in nature that offer prayer and hope. [a.] Cumberland, MD 21502.

CARTWRIGHT, THEOACHIA ELAINE
[b.] March 20, 1962, Springville, New York; [p.] Donald and Audrey Dick; [m.] Michael David Cartwright, March 20, 1984; [hon.] Received high honors of one of my poems in Jr. high about 18 years ago; [oth. writ.] I have been writing poems for about 20 years. The love for poems that I have has grown through the years. I will keep on writing as long as someone will want to read them; [pers.] Living in Washington has really reflected my poem writing. Being married to a wonderful, kind, and loving husband also. I like to spread my love through words of a poem. [a.] Mt. Vernon, WA.

CASALINUOVO, SANDRA E.
[pen.] Sandra Stevens Casalinuovo; [b.] December 28, 1940, New Haven Connecticut; [p.] Ruth and Harold Stevens; [m.] Domenick Vito Casalinuovo; [ch.] Domenica, Lisa Rose, and my only son Domenick Vito Jr; [ed.] Audrey Cohen College for Human Resources; [occ.] Arts and crafts, writing, social work; [memb.] St. Mary's Church, American Red Cross; [hon.] Catholic Brotherhood countrywide art contest some years ago, I won 3rd and one or two poetry contests; [oth. writ.] I've written many poems, one song "Loving You". I've written a book of poems but until now I have not wanted to get them published, but since my son died, I want to share them; [pers.] When I write and I'm stressed, writing somehow relaxes me. I get lost in my own thoughts and the beauty and true meaning I get out of writing. [a.] New York City, NY 10002.

CASTELL, CINDI
[b.] August 15, 1957, Washington, D.C.; [p.] Leo J.. and Lillian V. McConnell; [ch.] William E., [ed.] Elizabeth Seton High School, maryland School of Hair Design; [occ.] Cosmetologist; [pers.] I'm a romantic at heart. I believe if you have love you have

everything. Almost all of my poems come from being in love with Erik Davis. He swims through my blood and tears to catch me when I jump. He's my friend, lover, teacher, and knight in shining armor. [a.] Bladensburg, MD 20710.

CASTILLO, VENESSA A.
[b.] October 21, 1975, San Antonio, Texas; [p.] Cheryl A. and Joe A. Castillo; [ed.] Junior at John Marshall High School, San Antonio, Texas; [occ.] Full time student; [memb.] Spanish Honors Society, English Honors Society; [hon.] English Scholars award; [oth. writ.] Several poems written, but not published; [pers.] In my writing I strive to show the more shocking and mysterious side of reality. The reality that we, most of the time, overlook may be the reality that we need to see most.; [a.] San Antonio, TX 78240.

CASTLE, RACHEL
[pen.] Rachel Ruhannah; [b.] January 6, 1975, Adelaide, SA Australia; [m.] Graeme Evans; [ed.] Penleigh and Essendon Grammar School, Monash University; [hon.] School colours; [oth. writ.] Poems published in school yearbook; [pers.] I aim to present human emotions in a universal context. [a.] Sydney, Australia.

CASTRO, MARIA E. GALINDO
[pen.] Mary Galindo; [b.] September 16, 1967, Los Angeles, California; [p.] Gilbert Jr. and Bertha Rosa C. de Galindo; [ed.] Bach. degree in Communications, specialized in Mass Media; [oth. writ.] Articles published in several newspapers in Eagle Pass and Monterrey, Mexico. Other poems and songs. [pers.] I truly believe that any effort made with sincerity can produce change. Art carries with it a tremendous power to do right. [a.] Eagle Pass, TX 78853.

CENTER, DOROTHY M.
[b.] December 18, 1929, Reading Massachusetts; [p.] Mary and George M. Harrow; [m.] Widow; [ch.] Mary, William, Kathleen, Garry, Christopher; [ed.] Boston Conservatory of Music, private study of piano and violin for concert performance; [occ.] Domestic and international travel consultant for A.A.A.; [memb.] U.S. China Peoples Friendship Association; [hon.] Poetry awards (national competitions) 1991, 1992; [oth. writ.] Travel writer for AAA Today magazine and poem on China published in U.S. China Review and other poems published in AAA magazines and books of poetry; [pers.] My work has taken me around the world in many directions-if we could all join hands forever what difference color, race, or creed? Peace! [a.] Albany, NY 12203.

CERNIGLIA, JOSEPHINE
[b.] August 3, 1922, Brooklyn, New York; [p.] Antonio Fiore and Severina Terranova Fiore; [m.] Stephen Cerniglia, June 17, 1945; [ch.] Joanna, Alice May, Vincent Joseph; [ed.] High school, LaSalle Institute Evening School for Secretaries; [occ.] School clerk; [memb.] Orchid Society, P.B.C., Lake Worth Art League, New Dimensions P.B.C.C. FL; [oth. writ.] Editor for various newsletters in school and homeowners associations; [pers.] He hesitates is last. [a.] Lake Worth, FL 33463.

CERVANTES, ELEANORA
[pen.] Elio; [b.] October 25, 1974, Mexico City; [p.] Jose and Susana Cervantes; [ed.] Lompoc High

School, Allan Hancock College; [occ.] Student; [memb.] Expression Latina (mural group project); [hon.] Principal List, 4 years, Brave of the Month, February, Athletic awards, soccer, and volleyball; [oth. writ.] Several poems unpublished; [pers.] Life for me is full of poetry and music, we just have to open our hearts to see it and hear it. [a.] Lompoc, CA 93436.

CHALAR, LAURA
[b.] July 26, 1976, Montevideo, Uruguay; [ed.] Elbio Fernandez High School, Montevideo, Uruguay; [occ.] Student; [oth. writ.] 1st prize, 1988 National Writing Contest, 1st prize, 1991 Elbio Fernandez High School Poetry Contest; [pers.] I write about the love that I feel, and the sorrow, pain and happiness that it causes. I think poetry is, in itself, a demonstration of love. Because I'm young I have to work hard to be acknowledged. But it's worth fighting! [a.] Montevideo, Uruguay.

CHALONE, INGRID
[b.] November 2, 1926, Czechoslovakia; [p.] Otakar and Marie Ptacek; [m.] Melvin L. Chalone, September 6, 1947; [ed.] Business school, Czechoslavia; [occ.] Retired; [pers.] Poetry and music can do wonders for the soul. [a.] Aberdeen, MD 21001.

CHAMAILLARD, KRYSTAL
[b.] September 28, 1975, Ottawa Ontario, Canada; [p.] Lenora (nee Kelly) and Paul Chamaillard; [ed.] Currently studying music, hoping for a career in music; [occ.] Student; [memb.] Various choirs including the Royal Conservatory choir. Also I participate in plays (acting); [oth. writ.] None of my other writings have been published, but I write about 3 or 4 poems a month; [pers.] I'd like to dedicate this poem to my grandmother Hazel Kelly, who passed away in 1991, but will never be forgotten. [a.] Quebec, Canada JOX 3J0.

CHANCEY, ANGELA
[b.] September 15, 1974, Arcadia, Florida; [p.] Karen and James Chaney; [ed.] DeSoto County High School class of 1992, sophomore at the University of Florida; [hon.] Valedictorian, class of 1992; [pers.] The Lord, God is my Creator and maker of the universe. He and only He is responsible for all things about which we write. Look about you and see Him in the beauty of His magnificent creation. (Colossians 1:16).; [a.] Gainesville, FL.

CHANGAMIRE, WAUNIDI
(African rose, the Sun and a body of water); [b.] February 29, 1948, Virginia; [ch.] Mariama, Diallo, Chioke; [ed.] Educated in Yukon, West Virginia and Columbus Ohio; [occ.] Registered Nurse, entrepreneur; [memb.] Loveland Church; [oth. writ.] Wrote, directed , and produced a play, "Shackles To Shackles", February, 1993; [pers.] Always known as a dreamer. Loves water and being in the sun. Loves reading and writing, Chuck Singleton, her spiritual inspirator, also inspires her writing.

CHAPMAN, JESSE THADDEUS
[pen.] J. Thaddeus Chapman; [b.] October 20th, Charleston, South Carolina; [p.] Cathaleen Legare and Jesse Fludd Chapman (deceased); [occ.] Housekeeping, Medical University Hospital; [memb.] Islanders ROTC Alumni, Bethel AME Church Young People Department; [hon.] Certificate of merits in

poetry 3-31-91, Certificate of merit in poetry 12-12-90 Silver Poet 1990 and Golden Poet 1988; [oth. writ.] "We Are Brothers", published in John Campbell Selected Poets; [pers.] To be able to lift someone's spirits through my writing. [a.] Johns Island, SC 29455.

CHASE, ELSA L.
[b.] April 2, 1949, Camden, New Jersey; [p.] Marcella and Ervin Chase; [ed.] High school diploma; [occ.]] Machine operator, was also a draftsman, sales, and cashier; [oth. writ.] "Jim", "Mother", "Sam", "Blake", "My Friend Jim", "The Death of a Friend"; [pers.] Everything has a light that shines from within that grabs a hold on your heart that is known as "The Dance of Lights". [a.] Camden, NJ 08105.

CHEAQUI, HELEN M.
[b.] April 21 1914, Castleton, Kansas; [p.] Newell Earl and Jessie Marie Fountain; [m.] William M. Cheaqui, May 21, 1954; [ch.] Jack L. Crozzer, Elizabeth Joan Curth; [ed.] High school, Moline, Kansas; [occ.] Was secretary in our own business, The Chikay Co.; [memb.] The United Methodist Church; [oth. writ.] Numerous poems on different subjects, mostly religious, books of poems and for several years drew the pictures and wrote the poems for Christmas cards, and had them printed; [pers.] I try to show my personal and religious feelings through my poetry. [a.] Findlay, OH 45840.

CHESTER-COATS, LYRIC
[pen.] Lossie; [b.] August 26, Smith County; [p.] Arthur and Mabel Warren Muckleroy; [m.] Ira Chester (deceased), June 9, 1934 and Robert Coats (deceased), July 23, 1977; [ch.] 14 Chester; [ed.] High school; [occ.] Retired; [memb.] American Legion, Lily of the Valley Hearion of Jericho; [hon.] Nurse certificate, Mother of the Year, North Star Baptist Church; [pers.] Work as a foster mother for M.H.R. 12 years, kept foster children, 15 in my home, sing in choir, was president of the Star Light Band President of the Mission Society. [a.] Tyler, TX 75702.

CHIANG, JENNIFER
[b.] November 16, Houston, Texas; [p.] Sue and John Chiang; [ed.] Colony Bend Elementary; [memb.] Science Club, Chess Club, Math Club, Rainforest Rescue campaign, Houston Museum of Natural Science, Odyssey of the Mind; [hon.] Basketball, Science Fair 1st place, Math Fair 2nd place, perfect attendance since kindergarten,Geography Bee 4th place, Fine Arts Festival 1st place, Honor Roll, Gifted and Talented class; [oth. writ.] Book incomplete The Other Life of Carissa Thompson; [pers.] I write and draw how I feel like it so no one can say if I am right or wrong. [a.] Sugarland, TX 77479.

CHIASSON, JANALYN
[b.] August 10, 1975, New Orleans, Louisiana; [p.] Bonnie and Earnie Chiasson; [ed.] High school graduate; [occ.] College student; [memb.] SADD (Students Against Drunk Driving), Right to Life (Anti-abortion organization); [hon.] Class Beauty, 1993, Senior Maid, 1993, Immaculata High School. Outstanding Student in Adult Responsibilities (Department award), 7th place in UNO Rally (Management and Resources). [a.] Marrero, LA 70072.

CHILDREE, DIANE M.
[pen.] Dionysia; [b.] September 29, 1943, Rugby,

North Dakota; [p.] Magdalena (Holzer and Philip Lesmeister; [m.] Raymond Children (deceased), March 17, 1976; [ch.] Chris Don Schiefelbein; [ed.] Fargo High, Northern Montana College, Stephen Ministry; [occ.] Former secretary and bookkeeper, office manager; [memb.] St. Jude's Parish Council, Worship Commission, Stephen Minister; [hon.] Honor Roll; [oth, writ.] Short story personal experiences with a humorous twist. Some of my articles have been published in our college and daily newspaper; [pers.] To truly love others you must first learn to love yourself. [a.] Harve, MT 59502-2204.

CHILES, BILLIE-JO
[b.] MaY 11, 1974, Nelson B.C. Canada; [p.] Gordon Chiles and Linda Wiebe; [m.] Brad Ferguson, July 3, 1993; [ed.] W.R. Myer's High, Lethbridge Collegiate Institute; [occ.] Public relations administrator, Taber literacy project; [hon.] Honor Roll at high school w.R. Myers, and LCI in Lethbridge; [oth. writ.] Several other poems that have not yet been sent to be published, a few short stories written when I was very young; [pers.] You shall love only from thy heart. Not from thy mouth and not from thy head. If it is not from thy heart it shall be left unsaid. My family and finance greatly inspire me to be the best I can be. [a.] Taber A.B. Canada TOK 2G0.

CHIMWASO, DAVID K.
[b.] December 29, 1958, Kalabo, Zambia; The late Palata Mulemba and the late Theresa B. Mulemba; [m.] Esther M. Chimwaso, May 3, 1987; [ch.] Kubangu, Inonge; [ed.] Liumba Primary School, Kalabo Secondary School, University of Zambia; [occ.] Quantity surveyor, Ministry of Works, Transport and Comms., Botswana; [memb.] Surveyors Institute of Zambia, Gaborone Toastmasters Club; [hon.] Surveyors Institute of Zambia Prize for Academic Excellence, University of Zambia, 1985; [oth. writ.] Volume of unpublished poems; [pers.] I love poetry. To me, it is one of the best ways of narrating a story or expressing one's feelings with a lasting impression. [a.] Gaborone, Botswana;

CHINCHILLO, JEAN BELL
[pen.] Jeanie Bell; [b.] April 9, 1917, Boston, Massachusetts; [p.[] Roy Bell and Sarah London; [m.] Tory (deceased 3-9-93), June 25, 1939; [ch.] Janet Siemasko and Joyce Griffin; [ed.] Boston University, Malden Business School; [occ.] Retired secretary, presently writer; [memb.] International Society of Poets 1993-94; [hon.] Golden Poet 1991,Per Eddie Lou Cole Poetry editor; [oth. writ.] Book The Caterpillar and Other Poems for Children, published 5-9-88; [pers.] "The Lord is my Shepherd".

CHOI, MOON
[b.] December 19, 1961, Seoul, Korea; [p.] Sook and Charlie Choi; [ed.] University of California, Riverside, B,A. History, M.A. Education; [occ.] Elementary school teacher; [oth. writ.] First poem ever to be published; [pers.] I was inspired to write this poe when i fell in love 3 years ago. [a.] Irvine, CA 92715.

CHOW, PETE
[b.] March 21, 1975, Hong Kong; [p.] Kwok L. and Yuk Woon Chow; [ed.] High school grad going to the University of Illinois at Chicago (U.I.C.); [oth. writ.] "Troubles" in Quest of a Dream; [pers.] Special thanks to Kimberley Betty Stevenson. I will always love you. [a.] Chicago, IL 60645.

CHRABASCZ, MICHAEL
[b.] November 25, 1972, Hartford, Connecticut; [p.] Richard and Eileen Chrabascz; [ed.] Currently attending Salve Regina University in Newport R.I.,sophomore; [occ.] Student, English major; [pers.] For me, writing is just as much a simple unwinding of the mind as it is an attempt to formulate the perfect illumination of confused passions. [a.] Somers, CT 06071.

CHRAPCZYNSKI, JACKIE E.
[pen.] Jackson; [b.] May 22, 1973, Amherst Ohio; [p.] Mary M. Migra; [ed.] Bowling Green State University, English major; [hon.] Two poems published in literary magazine in which I got a letter for in high school; [pers.] I want to make a personal effect on all who read my poems. I want the same emotions out of people that I wrote the poem with. [a.] South Amherst, OH 44001.

CHRISTENSEN, LINDA LOU
[b.] December 19, 1951, DeKalb, Illinois; [ch.] Amanda, age 21, Abigail, age 12; [occ.] College bookstore administrative assistant; [hon.] Awarded 2nd place for prose, DeKalb High School literary magazine, New Pennies, The poem published here, I when my daughter, Amanda, was awarded 1st prize for prose in the same publication twenty years later; [pers.] I believe our futures can only be successful and fulfilling after close examination of the past. I strive to teach my daughters our genealogy, tradition, creativity. My great-grandmother, Mathilda Hendrickson, wrote her life story, the original manuscript a most valued treasure of our family, though never published. [a.] DeKalb, IL 60115.

CHRISTIAN-JAOUHARI, MAXINE
[pen.] Maxine Christian, Maxine Christian-Jaouhari; [b.] September, 19 1947, Washington , D.C.; [p.] Harry John and Marjorie Breuer Christian; [m.] Driss Jaouhari, December 29, 1990; [ed.] Surattsville High, University of Maryland, Catholic University, District of Columbia Technical Center; [occ.] Library technician, Library of Congress, Washington, D.C.; [memb.] Library of Congress Professional Association, Library of Congress Recreation Association, LC Choral Society; [hon.] Golden Poet award for 1991 and 1992; [oth. writ.] Two poems published in Selected Works of the World's Best Poets, and two poems published in "LCPA Journal"; [pers.] In my poetry, I try to show the beauty in the world and my faith in an eternal life. My conversion to the Muslim faith has opened my eyes to the love and kindness in others. [a.] Alexandria, VA 22303.

CHRISTIE, ADA
[b.] December 23, 1934, Scotland; [oth. writ.] Poetry for persona enjoyment. [a.] Ewa Beach, HI 96706.

CHURCH, VALERIE J.
[b.] October 14, 1954, Wynnewood, Oklahoma; [p.] Riley and Jimmie Church; [ed.] McAlester High School, BS/ED and M.Ed East Central University (Ada, OK); [occ.] Special Education Coordinator, Lower Yukon School District; [memb.] Council for Exceptional Children, Alaska Association of Special Education Administrators; [oth. writ.] Poems published in University Anthologies; [pers.] We all have the power to shape a mind, to mold the future, every child is entitled to receive that guidance. [a.] Mtn. Village, AK 99632.

CILIBERTO, JEANETTE L.(CAIN)
[pen.] "Joy"; [b.] May 2, 1936, Atlantic City, New Jersey; [p.] Stanley and Helen Addams Cain; [m] Divorced; [ch.] Dianna, Rocky, David, Mary; [ed.] High school; [occ.] Telephone operator; [memb.] AARP, Pioneers of New Jersey, Girl Scouts; [hon.] Most wonderful award are 4 giving, productive, adult children with "Love"; [oth. writ.] Preparing for a book someday. This was the 2nd poem I've ever written. My first poem was a graduation gift for my daughter; [pers.] I strive to reflect the joy and love I see in ordinary things and God's precious gifts we take for granted! [a.] Parkertown, NJ.

CISNEROS, ALMA G.
[b.] October 30, 1975, Atotonilco el Alto Jal, Mexico; [p.] Alma E. and Mario A. Cisneros; [ed.] George Washington High School; [occ.] Student; [memb.] East Side Historical Society yearbook staff, Student Council, Academic Decathlon, Access 2000 (Science and Math program); [hon.] Hobby Ambassador, Honor Roll, Science Fair, Best Actress in school, Art major; [oth. writ.] Several writings and reports on the school yearbook; [pers.] This poem was inspired on the life of my mother. My mother is the greatest person on earth. She is a mother, father, and friend to her 10 children. [a.] Chicago, IL 60617.

CLAIRE, CHRISTOHER J.
[pen.] Chippy Munk, Skippy Munk; [b.] July 11, 1963, Poughkeepsie, New York; [p.] the late Walter W. Claire II and Priscilla (Claire) Lutke; [ed.] Marlborough High, Newbury Junior College; [occ.] Manufacturing technician, Foods Division, Genetrak Systems Corp, Framingham Mass; [memb.] The Loyal Order of Moose Lodge #1129; [oth. writ.] Cartoons, childrens' short stories, and several poems. None of which are published. [pers.] "To further explore the wonders of life and understand remember that the more we discover, the larger the role mystery plays." [a.] Marlborough, MA 01752.

CLARAVALL, LESTER
[b.] August 2, 1967, Warren, Pennsylvania; [p.] Dr. Leonardo and Gloria Claravall; [ed.] Midwest City High School, Bachelor of Business Administration, University of Oklahoma, Master of Human Relations, University of Oklahoma; [memb.] OU President's Leadership Class, president, OU Student Business Association, president, Mu Kappa Tau Marketing Society; [hon.] AASA Outstanding Senior Student, Who's Who Among Students in American Universities and Colleges, National Dean's List, Banner carrier, head of processional march of the graduates of the OU College of Business Administration; [oth. writ.] Several poems published in the Midwest City High School Anthology, several poems published in the Penn Register, the Dillard's Penn Square Newsletter; [pers.] I enjoy writing about special experiences, humorous incidents, or creative thoughts in general. Over the years, writing has allowed me to reach out and grow. [a.] Midwest City, OK 73110.

CLARK, JESSICA LEE
[pen.] Jess Clark; [b.] October 3, 1981, Middlebury, Vermont; [p.] Kenneth William Clark and Melanie Louise Pratt; [ed.] Student at Shoreham Elementary School; [pers.] This poem reflects on what my life has been like in the past and how important my family is to me. [a.] Salisbury, VT 05769.

CLARK, KIMBERLY PENNINGTON
[pen.] Kim Clark; [b.] May 2, 1961, Fort Campbell, Kentucky; [p.] Robert and Laura Johnston; [m.] R. Kent Clark, January 6, 1994; [ch.] Shalimar Emily, Chanel Renee, Ariane Rachealle; [ed.] Loveland High; [occ.] Housewife and mom; [oth. writ.] I have written over 90 poems and as yet have not published any until "Where Do the Tears Go?"; [pers.] My poetry comes direct from my heart and true life experiences. [a.] Wheatridge, CO 80033.

CLARK, LYDIA
[pen.] Lydia Prentice-Hill; [b.] April 22, 1953, New Westminster B.C. Canada; [p.] Lydia Cowan and Thomas Prentice; [m.] Anthony E. Clark, June 19. 1992; [ch.] Cathleen Phyllis, Christine Selena, Brandon Anthony, grandchild Marcus Brian; [ed.] Rossland Sr. Secondary, Rossland B.C. Canada; [occ.] Homemaker, previous employ, Bank of Nova Scotia; [oth. writ.] Done to date for personal enjoyment; [pers.] My writing is my way of expression, none shall live such a full life as the children. [a.] Williams Lake, British Columbia, Canada U2G 4M8.

CLARK, VICKY
[b.] Vancouver, B.C. Canada; [ch.] Tina, Troy, and Stacy; [pers.] To all my friends down at the log house, it's been fun. Life's a Dance, alright. I thank God for the three most precious gifts in my life, my children, Tina, Troy, and Stacy. I love you kids more than words can ever express. To David, Anni, and Jen, I would like to dedicate my poem in loving memory of Joshlyn. We all miss her. She is our "Star". [a.] Mackenzie, B.C. Canada V0J 2C0.

CLARKE, LOIS JOHNSON
[b.] March 3, 1914, Winston Salem, North Carolina; [p.] Archie P. and Annie Pace Johnson; [m.] Deceased, May 1, 1942; [ch.] Marshall A. Clarke; [ed.] Palmer Memorial Junior College, Sedalia, North Carolina; [occ.] Retired; [memb.] International Grapho-Analysis Society, Chicago; [hon.] Salvation Army, Sherman Corps; [oth. writ.] "Excerpts From the Journals of Annie Pace", Vantage, third book, Poetry, this spring; [pers.] Songwriter, published (lyrics and melody). [a.] Washington DC 20010.

CLAY, RUTH HICKMAN
[pen.] Ruth H. Clay; [b.] May 30, 1921, Hudson, North Carolina; [p.] Jacob Ivey and Ila Downs Hickman; [m.] James Marvin Clay, June 15, 1941; [ch.] Cynthia Jeanne, Carolyn Marvina, Marcus Everette; [ed.] Hudson High, Appalachian U; [occ.] Retired, taught Real Estate courses and Math at Catawba Valley Community College; [memb.] First United Methodist Church (Hickory, North Carolina), North Carolina Education Association, Board of Realtors (Hickory North Carolina), Senior Women's Club of Hickory; [hon.] Graduated Magna Cum Laude, Dean's List, Who's Who in American Colleges and Universities; [oth. writ.] Poem published in CVC college paper, many poems published in our monthly (Epworth Notes) paper here at The Methodist Home of Charlotte. I write short stories, none published so far; [pers.] I write about happenings in my life, and how I feel about them. I believe in the Goodness of God and mankind. [a.] Charlotte, NC 28215.

CLAYTON. DIANNE
[b.] November 7, 1967, Toronto, Canada; [p.] Margaret and Floyd Miller; [ed.] Durham College, Haliburton Highlands Secondary School, Archie Stouffer Elementary School; [occ.] Registered Nurse; [memb.] P.R.A.N.C.E. (Pegasus Riding Association Nurturing Challenged Equestrians); [hon.] Art scholarship; [oth. writ.] Several poems I hope to publish in the near future; [pers.] I kept most of my life all bottled up in me until about five years ago. Then, I wrote it all down. Now, life seems so much easier. [a.] Port Elgin Ontario, Canada N0H 2C4.

CLEMENT, SHEILLA
[b.] June 17, 1967, Singapore; [p.] M. A. and Rosemary Clement; [ed.] Bachelor of Arts, National University of Singapore; [occ.] Administrative assistant, faculty of Arts and Social Sciences, National University of Singapore; [pers.] Poetry is that voice of my inner eye. For me, this world of poetry is one of magic, truth, and beauty. [a.] Rajah Court, Singapore 1232.

CLEMMONS, JEFF
[pen.] Kendolph Clair; [b.] March 20 1973, Mobile, Alabama; [p.] Archie M. Clemmons and Joan L. Schairer; [ed.] ABA Reinhardt College, Etowah High School; [occ.] McCamish Broadcasting Center, RCTV (Reinhardt College), McDonalds; [memb.] Phi Beta Lambda, Phi Theta Kappa, Boy Scouts of America, Reinhardt College Captain (PR rep); [hon.] All-American Scholar, National Dean's List, PTK, 1st place Georgia Regional PTK Poetry/Lit Competition, Eagle Scout, Student of the Month , Rotary International; [oth. writ.] Poems published in college's literary magazine; [pers.] Never judge a book by its cover, and always read between the lines. [a.] Woodstock, GA 30188.

CLENARD, ANN
[b.] October 6, 1944, Chicago, Illinois; [p.] Elsie and Byron Buker; [m.] Gary Clenard, August 7, 1964; [ch.] Kimberly; [ed.] Glendale Community College, Glendale, California; [occ.] Secretary/bookkeeper; [memb.] National Wildlife Federation, Humane Society of U.S., American Heart Association; [oth. writ.] Although I have been writing poetry for years, I have not pursued anything professionally until now; [pers.] I hope to project a positive image in my writing, delving into fascinating truths and amazing connections in this life, both physically as well as spiritually. [a.] Glendale, CA 91202.

CLONTZ, CARLA
[b.] January 24, 1968, Canton, North Carolina; [p.] Foard and Betty Parsons; [ed.] Bandys High School 1986 graduate; [occ.] Secretary - Catawba Memorial Hospital; [oth. writ.] Poet on the school newspaper my junior year, wrote the welcome for Junior Senior Prom. Also have written many poems on love, life, and Christianity; [pers.] Any person who has the ability to dream also has the ability to write it down. [a.] Conover, NC 28613.

COATS, NICOLE
[b.] January 20, 1979, Coldwater, Michigan; [p.] Michael and Cyndra Patch; [ed.] 8th grade, Legg Middle School, Coldwater High; [hon.] Attended writer -in-residence for 2 years, honor award in English; [oth. writ.] "Someone Cares" (poem); [pers.] Anyone can be a writer, but with imagination you can

be a poet. Favorite poet Jack Krietzer. [a.] Coldwater, MI 49036.

COBURN, LUCY DANIELLE EOWYN
[pen.] Eowyn Coburn; [b.] August 16, 1980, Coos Bay, Oregon; [p.] Barbara and Thomas Coburn; [ed.] 8th grade, I plan on going through college to become a lawyer; [occ.] Student, North Bend Jr. High; [memb.] Houser Community Church; [pers.] "Life is like a horse, hold on tight or get bucked off". [a.] North Bend, OR 97459.

COCKRELL, SHELBY
[b.] April 12, 1944, Akron, Ohio; [p.] Geraldine Reckla; [ch.] Michelle Renee, Jennifer Mae, Jerome Swaggerty, grandson; [ed.] Buchtel High, Malone College of Ohio, North Tech Education Center, Florida; [occ.] Dialysis Tech, Realtor Assoc; [memb.] American Cancer Society, American Heart Association; [oth. writ.] Green High School yearbook, Akron Beacon Journal; [pers.] I am in awe of the early noble emperors and have a heartfelt admiration for their exalted grand verse. Deep in my soul I have such envy and aspire to humbly emulate their art. I seek to lift a spirit, give strength, renew peace, and open doors of one's mind wit the universal language that speaks to every need. [a.] Akron, OH.

COCO, BECCA
[pen.] Shelby Brooks; [b.] September 18, 1976, Ocean Springs, Mississippi; [p.] Brenda and Stephen Coco; [ed.] 11th grade Pearl River Central; [occ.] Student; [memb.] Honor Society, Honors English, Beta Club; [hon.] Honor Society, Honors English, Honor Roll; [oth. writ.] Poems and short stories, but none have been published as of yet; [pers.] I strive to reflect the importance of love in the heart of mankind. I have been strongly influenced by my vivid imagination, my intense emotions, and music. [a.] Carriere, MS 39426.

COESENS, UDELIA
[b.] April 26, 1958, Buckholts, Texas; [p.] Mr. Bartolo and Nickolasa Montalbo; [m.] Michael Coesens; [ch.] Matthew Allen, Trina Reene, Stacy Marie; [ed.] Rogers High School; [occ.] Housewife. [a.] Rogers, TX.

COGGIANO, JEAN
[b.] July 14, 1970, San Jose, California; [p.] Michael Coggiano and Janice McPeek; [ed.] Saratoga High School, West Valley College, Cal State Hayward; [occ.] Full time student; [memb.] Alpha Gamma Sigma Honor Roll Club, Psychology Club, @ Hayward, Psi Chi National Honor Society in Psychology; [hon.] Dean's List, 3 years, achievement awards in choir class; [pers.] I admire my father who has inspired me to release my soul through poetry. [a.] Saratoga, CA 95070.

COHEN, SAMUEL
[pen.] Sam; [b.] April 21, 1938, Lower Eastside, New York City; [p.] Sadie and Ezra Cohen; [ed.] Public School 205, High School 227; [occ.] Foreman and truck checker at Bradley Imports, Newark, New Jersey; [hon.] Golden Award from the World of Poetry; [oth. writ.] Poem published with National Arts Society. Wrote to President Bush, based on a patriot poem "Give Us Our Flag", President Bush wrote back and thanked me for it. 8/69.; [pers.] That all things in life is an art, from the graceful flight of

a bird, to the unstill ocean waves, to the way one looks about life and the beauty of it. But the greatest art of all is love, for love is the highest art form of all, known for its own purity. [a.] Brooklyn, NY 11220.

COLE, SHACHRISTA L.
[pen.] Crissy Cole; [b.] February 16, 1981, Oklahoma City, Oklahoma; [p.] Thurman and LaVerne Cole (grandparents-guardians); [ed.] 7th grade home school ShaChrista Academy; [occ.] Babysitter, yard worker; [memb.] Karate; [hon.] Acting, activeness, and art; [pers.] I am greatly influenced by Shakespeare's writings especially, "Romeo and Juliet". [a.] Blanchard, OK 73010.

COLEMAN, PAMELA G,
[pen.] Pam; [b.] January 15, 1954, Chicago Illinois; [p.] Charles A. and Gwendolyn E. Simmons-Coleman; [ed.] B.S., University of Illinois; [occ.] Industry specialist SBA/US Federal Government; [memb.] Trinity United Methodist Church of Christ, Chicago, Illinois; [pers.] Talent is nothing but a gift from God. Therefore, I honor, praise, and glorify God for the gift He gives me. [a.] Chicago, IL.

COLES, NAKIE RENEE
[b.] October 22, 1975, Detroit, Michigan; [p.] Deborah Elaine Coles; [ed.] Freshman year in college; [occ.] Student, Washtenaw Community College, Ann Arbor, Michigan; [hon.] High school Honor Roll; [pers.] My poem is dedicated to the memory of my loving grandparents, Robert and Rose Marie Jones. The love showering down from heaven to earth can heal all wounds. [a.] Detroit, MI 48238.

COLLENS, JERALD
[b.] March 6, 1960, Hamilton, Ontario, Canada; [p.] Verna and Carl Collens; [m.] Kimberly Collens; [ch.] Barry Morris, Jacklyn Louise; [ed.] South Lincoln High School; [occ.] Credit manager. [a.] Williams Lake, B.C. Canada.

COLLETT, VERNA D. (GOLDWATER)
[b.] September 23, 1937, Lubbock, texas; [p.] Alfred and Sadie V. Jewett Goldwater; [m.] Lloyd M. Collett; [ch.] Mary, Dale, Michael, Tina, Myra; [ed.] Battle Ground High School; [occ.] Realtor; [memb.] Yachats Presbyterian Church; [oth. writ.] Writings in local paper; [pers.] In order to write from the soul one must be in tune with their ever present spiritual guide. The spiritual awareness of Emerson, Longfellow, Whitman and Sara Jewett have influenced my writing. [a.] Tidewater, OR 97390.

COLLINGS, LOLA MAE
[pen.] Lola Collings; [b.] May 16, 1915, Dunn, Texas; [p.] Bertha (Head) and S. James Littlepage; [m.] James F., August 22, 1942; [ch.] Vonita Sue (Collings) Clary; [ed.] BS degree, Howard Payne University, graduate work Hardin-Simmons University; [occ.] School teacher, housewife; [memb.] RSVP, Gideon International Aux., DAV Aux., Baptist Church, National Poetry Library; [hon.] Valedictorian of Snyder Tex. High School, 2 Golden Poet awards, 1 Silver award, member-choir awards, superior honor in solo contest - in Ms. San Angelo Pageant 1991; [oth. writ.] Poem book - Keys of Strength; [pers.] Do the best you can with what you have! [a.] San Angelo, TX 76903.

COLLINS, BILLY WAYNE
[pen.] Bwayne; [b.] September 27, 1949, Forrest City, Arkansas; [p.] Basil and Gertrude Collins; [m.] Sarah Collins, June 4, 1977; [ch.] Karen Renea, Jessica Kay, and Chad Wayne; [ed.] Hollywood Junior High, Humes High, Memphis State University; [oth. writ.] "Trapped", Recovery Times, January 1991; [pers.] To create a oneness in the earth in and through the word lest we forget "In the beginning..." [a.] Memphis, TN 38127.

COLLINS, COLT MAKAI
[pen.] Cody; [b.] June 4, 1982, Newton, Mississippi; [p.] William Donald and Mary Skinner Collins; [ed.] 4th grade at Newton Elementary School's Gifted class; [memb.] Calvary Baptist Church; hon.] Two brothers Donny and Jay, Love Jesus and live for him, a student on the dean's list, won awards in math, spelling, science and would like to dedicate this poem to my grandmother, Bobbie E. Skinner. She died January 2, 1991. I love her very much; [oth. writ.] One of my favorite poems is the Rainforest. I wrote it; [pers.] I love to write poems, I love to write about animals and people in my family. Writing is the best thing I love to do. [a.] Newton, MS 39345.

COLLINS, GEORGIA ROSE MCLANE
[b.] January 20, 1920, Grand Rapids, Michigan; [p.] George and Virginia Mclane [m.] Divorced; [ch.] Five; [ed.] Grade and high school in Dayton Ohio; [occ.] Retired from Board of Education; [memb.] National Library of Poetry, International Black Writers, American Poetry Society; [hon.] Library of Congress, World of Poetry; [oth. writ.] All poems; [pers.] My talent belongs to God. And I am doing this to help mankind to show them the beauty of love and goodness of God. Through poems we can do that. [a.] Chicago, IL.

COLLINS, LAWRENCE D.
[pen.] L.D. Collins; [b.] June 6, 1951, Chicago, Illinois; [p.] Florence Evans and Clyde Collins; [m.] Jo-Ellen (Adams), May 25, 1972; [ch.] Lawrence II, Marcus A., Jason A., Athena L., and Dawn D.; [ed.] Crescenta Valley High School, Glendale Community College, Lincoln Land Community College; [occ.] Federal Correctional Officer; [memb.] Local #1145 AFGE; [hon.] Employee of the Year '88, numerous awards. [a.] The Rock, GA 30285.

COLLINS, SHAWN
[pen.] Robert Sundance; [b.] March 15, 1973, Honolulu, Hawaii; [p.] Donna and Kirt Collins; [ed.] Topeka High School, Washburn University; [occ.] Student; [memb.] Greenpeace, The Planetary Society; [oth. writ.] Several poems published in University Magazine, articles for the Washburn Review; [pers.] There are three kinds of people. Those who make things happen, those who watch things happen, and those who wonder what happened. I plan to make things happen, as soon as I find out what happened. [a.] Topeka, KS 66611-1978.

COLVIN, MARGARET BUELL
[pen.] Margaret Colvin; [b.] March 3, 1949, Tremont, Kentucky; [p.] Rufus and Bertha Buell; [m.] Otis Lee Colvin, November 2, 1991; [ch.] Mary K. Crumpston, Lynn Neal and Douglas Neal III; [ed.] Senior-Eastern Kentucky University (Richmond, KY) also attended Southeast Community College (Cumberland, KY); [occ.] Cashier-K-Mart; [memb.] World of Poetry

Club, used to be and was in Kentucky Poetry Society; [hon.] Golden Poet award (1991) award of merit - honorable mention 1990 - spring on cloverlick Poetry Contest 1991 (1st place) [oth. writ.] "Scotia Mines", "Occultant Confusion", "You're All Man", "The Mountains", "Short Reindeers", "Under the Cover", "Over You"; [pers.] With God-where's there's a will, there's a way. [a.] Loyall, KY 40854.

COMBS, TAMMY
[b.] June 27, 1964, Kendallville, Indiana; [p.] Luther and Emma May; [m.] Jeffrey E. Combs, November 11, 1988; [ch.] Crystal Jean, Kaylee Marie, Karen Renee; [ed.] Dekalb High; [occ.] Housewife; [memb.] Four Corners Baptist Church; [pers.] I write poems in view of what I feel or what I see in the emotions of others. I've been writing poems sine the age of 10. [a.] Hudson, IN 46747.

CONAWAY, MARGARET MEGAN
[pen.] M. Megan Conaway; [b.] September 10, 1979, Chillicothe, Ohio; [p.] Robert and Gina Conaway; [ed.] Chillicothe High School, 9th grade; [occ.] Student; [hon.] Presidential Academic Fitness Award; [oth. writ.] "An Elder and a Baby", "A Dandelion and a Rose"; [pers.] Make tomorrow a better day than the one before. [a.[Chillicothe, OH 45601.

CONIGLIARO, SAL
[b.] October 14, 1923, Newark, New Jersey; [p.] Sal and Anna, deceased; [m.] Nancy, April 27, 1946; [ch.] Nannette Fenton, Michael and Bob Conigliaro, Jamie Ann Williams; [ed.] Two years college; [occ.] Retired; [memb.] The Theological Science Society, Inc; [hon.] WWII Bronze Star (2); [oth. writ.] Other poems; [pers.] There is no limitation to your mind except that to which you acknowledge. [a.] Tampa, FL 33625.

CONLEY, KELLIE
[b.] July 26, 1974, Princeton, New Jersey; [p.] Richard and Ruth Ann Conley; [ed.] Princeton High School, University of Delaware, Trenton State College; [hon.] University of Delaware Dean's List; [pers.] Don't compromise yourself, you are all you've got. [a.] Princeton, NJ 08540.

CONOWAL, JOSEPH C.
[pen.] Skeet; [b.] March 16, 1937, Philadelphia, Pennsylvania; [p.] Joseph W. Lola Conowal; [m.] Linda Tinsley Conowal, January 9, 1982; [ch.] Joey, Helen, Christopher, Mary, Michael, Wesley; [ed.] Graduated South Catholic and the college of hard knocks; [occ.] Artist, designer, builder, real estate, land, art , securities; [memb.] All-Governors Development Council, Booster and Community Development Award, former chairman of the advisory board to the Commissioner; [hon.] Served on many board and committees, lived in three states politically. Active in each, chaired one of our two parties; [oth. writ.] Short similar sayings along with short wildlife stories and some as seen through the eyes of the streets were published in local papers; [pers.] I have been greatly influenced by my beginning on the streets. Working from these roots, I have come to believe that we must respect all life in whatever form given it. A must if human dignity is to prevail. [a.] Gulf Breeze, FL 32561.

CONROY, LINDA
[m.] James (Jimmy) Conroy; [ch.] Combined: three daughters, three sons; [ed.] Sacred Heart Convent, Philadelphia, Rowan College, New Jersey; [hon.] College President's List, Deans's List, BA degree, Magna cum laude; [oth. writ.] To family members. Never submitted for publication; [pers.] I gave this poem to my husband twenty years ago on Father's Day. It is still true. [a.] Linwood, NJ 08221.

COOK, BETTIE
[b.] August 6, 2927, Toronto, Ontario, Canada; [p.] Bill and Elizabeth McGowan; [m.] George Cook, July 29, 1971; [ch.] John, Jimmy, Josephine, Richard, Jenny, Jeffery, Jerry; [ed.] High school with business school; [occ.] Booking agent (music) Bluenote Records; [memb.] Red Cross, Republican Ladies, British American Club; [hon.] Writes for a hobby 3 Award of Merit certificates, Golden Poet trophy; [oth. writ.] "Broken Heart", "Love's Memories", "There's A Sadness in My Heart", "My Dreams Are Always of You", "Rainbow Around My Heart"; [pers.] It's never too late to start something new. Today is the first day of your new life. [a.] Mississauga, Ont, Canada L5V 1R2.

COOK, JUDITH SPIGGLE
[pen.] Judy Cook; [b.] July 21, 1941, Edinburg, Virginia; [p.] Samuel L. and Fleta Bowers Spiggle; [m.] Larry C. Cook, April 18, 1960; [ch.] Larry Jr., Lanita, Shannon, Ruth, Carla, Carl; [ed.] Edinburg High School (last graduating class of EHS 1959); [occ.] School bus driver, homemaker; [oth. writ.] Several poems written and used as eulogies for close family members and friends; [pers.] I can only express my true feelings by putting them in writing. I need to be inspired and my prayer is that others will also receive inspiration from my writings. [a.] Woodstock, VA 22664.

COOK, MONTANA S.
[b.] August 22, 1926, Butte, Montana; [p.] Thomas and Florence Champion; [m.] Douglas A. Cook, September 13, 1952; [ch.] Thomas H., Linda J., Janet G.; [ed.] Pershing High, Detroit, Detroit Business Institute; [occ.] Secretary; [memb.] Pen & Palette Club, Roscommon, Michigan; [pers.] The beauty of all things along our path. [a.] Roscommon, MI 48653.

COON, JOHN
[b.] November 10, 1961, Brockville, Ontario, Canada; [ch.] Ryan Donald; [occ.] Retail investigator; [pers.] Inside everyone there is a moment of silence when we realize how beautiful we really are, why don't we show it. [a.] Kingston, Ontario, Canada K7M 6E7.

COOPER, JEREMY
[pen.] Jeremy Cooper; [b.] March 22, 1975, Buffalo, New York; [p.] James L. and Carol Cooper; [ed.] First Baptist Christian High School; [occ.] Student; [memb.] I.C.S.; [hon.] Student Body Leadership award; [oth. writ.] "Tales of Life"; [pers.] I strive to put into words what I know and feel: their past and the present. If people could truly miss both, God is the linking solution for all. [a.] Niagara Falls, NY 14305.

CORAGER, JON PAULOVIC
[pen.] d'Jon Corager, Paul Corager; [b.] November 22, 1944, Biloxi, Mississippi; [p.] L. Townsend and M. Corager; [m.] Ba'Lee (Myrtle), December 3, 1969; [ch.] Alan; [ed.] B.A., M.S., M.A.Ed,

Sandmutopia University; [occ.] Creativity consultant, advertising, technical writer; [memb.] Timberfell Society, St. Louis Chemists, Pi Delta Epsilon; [hon.] Semi-finalist, Manifest Reader and Drummer writing competitions; [oth. writ.] Autobiography of a Sadist, Creativity in the S/M Arts, Pantomime-A Mystery; [pers.[Haiku: There are dark shadows even in full moonlight, which writing enlightens. [a.] Montgomery AL 36109.

CORDELL, BEAULAH
[b.] Madison County, Arkansas; [m.] Jack Cordell; [ch.] Dennis Cordell, Kevin Cordell; [ed.] University of Arkansas-Fay. B.S.E. 1987, M.S.E. in progress; [occ.] Reading teacher in developmental studies at North West Arkansas Community College, Rogers, Arkansas; [memb.] Ozark Literacy: as a tutor of basic reading, English as a second language, and former member of board of directors; [hon.] Gamma Beta Phi, Who's Who in American Education. Hall of Fame Teaching Excellence at NWACC 1993; [oth. writ.] This is the first time that I have submitted any of my work for publication; [pers.] Being able to communicate with the written word is a precious gift. As a reading teacher and tutor of adults, I wanted to describe in my poem the life of the illiterate adult. So many of life's pleasures open up to us as we read. For my students, I want to pry the door open as far as it will go. [a.] Springdale, AK 72764

CORE, GENIE W.
[pen.] Genie; [b.] December 31, 1929, Edmonton Alberta Canada; [p.] Frank and Mary Brown; [m.] Melvin Core;, April 29, 1975; [ch.] Howard Peter, Marie Lorene, Cheryl Ann, Marilyn Eve; [ed.] Scona High, McTavish College; [occ.] Manufacturer for wedding gowns; [hon.] Poet of the Year 1988; [oth. writ.] I have compiled a book of poems, which I would like to publish someday; [pers.] I believe that poetry comes from deep inside someone not learned from a book and should be shared with others. [a.] Bluffton, Alberta, Canada.

CORMIER, YVON J. JR
[pen.] Yvon J. Cormier Jr.; [b.] August 18, 1970, Middletown, Connecticut; [p.] Yvon Sr. and Shirley A, Cormier; [ed.] A.S. from Middlesex Community College; [occ.] Assistant to the director of Middletown Commission on the Arts; [memb.] Editor in chief of the "Free Word Exchange" student literary magazine at MXCC; [hon.] Note of recognition for helping build the "Human Equality" park at MXCC; [oth. writ.] "Child's Play", A Loss of Innocence", and "Noise Pollution of the Times"; [pers.] The experiences that I remember are many and of greater meaning to me now than when I experienced them then. [a.] Middletown, CT 06457.

CORNING, SUSAN
[pen.] Susanna Corning; [b.] July 25, 1943, Salem, Massachusetts; [m.] Neil Corning, September 20, 1964; [ch.] Kenneth, Patrick,Daniel Corning; [ed] Associate in Science degree, North Shore Community College, June 1993; [occ.] Relief staff, Gr. Home for the retarded; [memb.] Phi Theta Kappa, Peabody Historical Society, Association of Retarded Citizens; [hon.] Vice-president of Phi Theta Kappa, Dean's List, Regent's Scholarship, G.T.E. Award, Trustee's Scholarship Award; [oth. writ.] Christmas story, short poems for "Pennant Magazine" (school paper); [pers.] Persistence and determination are omnipotent.

Would like to touch just one person with my writing. [a.] Peabody, MA 01960.

CORPUZ, KRISTELL
[pen.] Kris Hyper; [b.] May 18, 1978, Wailuku, Hawaii; [p.] Jovencio and Cristina Corpuz; [ed.] Saint Anthony, Waihe'e Elementary School, IAO Intermediate School and Baldwin High School; [hon.] Principal's List; [pers.] If you know what you want in life, just do it. A lot of people have failed in life but that is only a beginning. [a.] Wailuku, HI 96793.

CORTESI, NICHOLAS
[b.] January 31, 1973, Cicero, Illinois; [p.] Robert and Kathleen Cortesi; [ed.] Marist High School, Lewis University; [memb.] Lewis University Honor Society; [hon.] Dean's List, Golden Gloves Boxing Champion, Lewis University honor student; [oth. writ.] Other poems, some published in school literary magazine. Editorials published in the Chicago Sun Times; [pers.] Self-evaluation is the key to the door that opens to success. I would like to thank my mother, Kathy and my father, the late Robert for their guidance and love throughout the years. [a.] Lemont, IL 60439.

COTTRILL, THOMAS
[b.] November 15, 1977, Vienna, Austria; [p.] Charles and Betty Cottrill; [ed.] Currently enrolled as a sophomore at Culpeper County High School; [occ.] Student; [memb.] American Cancer Society, school newspaper staff, Drama Club; [hon.] American Academy of Poetry winner, Writing Achievement Award (short story), 3rd place; [oth. writ.] Many other unpublished poems and short stories; [pers.] My writings reflect my mod and feelings when I write. I hope to become a better writer through time and experience. [a.] Rixeyville, VA 22737.

COUGHLIN, IRENE A.
[b.] April 11, 1911, Pierrepont, New York; [p.] Nelson M. and Lula M. Caswell; [m.] George W.L. Coughlin (deceased), March 8, 1930; [ch.] George Donald, Rogene Joann, Naomi Irene; [ed.] High school, Madame Hudson Method of Beauty Culture; [occ.] Hairdresser 1929-1941, secretary 4H Ext, 1947-55, law secretary. 1957-72; [memb.] St. Law. Co Extension, Order of Eastern Star (Gr. Rep. to Conn. 1962-1965); United Methodist Church, AARP; [hon.] poem, "The 4-H Spirit" in National 4-H news during WWII. (George D. serving in the US Navy at the time.); [oth. writ.] Mostly things about friends and family at baby showers, weddings and retirement parties. "Thank you" notes, etc; [pers.] Enclosed is a sample sent just across the hall (from 7C to 7D). Her brother is married to my sister and we Irene P. and Irene C. [a.] Canton NY 13617.

COLUMBE, LISA
[pen.] L.M. Coulombe; [b.] July 24, 1965, Franklin, New Hampshire; [p.] Marlene and Floyd Sargent; [m.] William, June 20, 1992; [ed.] Graduate from Franklin High School, 1983; [occ.] Concord Group Insurance, Co.; [oth. writ.] I have no published writings except a poem entitled, "Just Say No", that will be in the "American Poetry Round-Up"; [pers.] I like to write and hope someday to be a writer. I believe my poems can be an inspiration to people. They are from the heart. [a.] Concord, NH 03301.
COUPEL, DEBRA P.

[b.] June 29, 1956, White Castle, Louisiana; [p.] Dennis and Marie P. Pitre; [m.] Walter, Jr., April 9, 1976; [ch.] Melissa Ann and Chad Joseph. [a.] White Castle, LA 70788.

COUTY, JOE
[pen.] C; [b.] March 27, 1976, Chicago, Illinois; [p.] Faith and Greg Couty; [ed.] Waukegan High School; [occ.] Construction; [oth. writ.] I have written many poems in the past, but this is one of the few I have shared; [pers.] I hope everyone gets something from my poem. It means a lot and relates my feelings as all my poems. [a.] Waukegan, IL 60085.

COVERT, ROBERT J.
[b.] July 22, 1921, Montour Falls, New York; [m.] Barbara (deceased); [ch.] Robert Jr., Margaret, Kevin, Katherine; [ed.] Prep school, some college; [occ.] Retired; [memb.] St. Pauls Episcopal Church, Schuyler County Retired Senior Volunteer Program, Chemans Valley Multiple Sclerosis Assn; [hon.] Voted Life Member Purchasing Management Association of Maine; [oth. writ.] Some poetry and prose for my own personal pleasure; [pers.] Do the best that you can at what you are doing but what is next. [a.] Montour Falls, NY 14865.

COX, ANNA BELLE
[b.] March 21, 1941, West Jefferson, North Carolina; [p.] Rowie and Pliner Woodie; [m.] Walter Cox, May 9, 1959; [ch.] Arna Denise, Dwayne Kenneth; [ed.] Beaver Creek High; [occ.] United Chemi-Con plant worker, housewife; [memb.] Round Knob Church budge committee, music director; [oth. writ.] Several poems published in local newspaper, songs written and sung in churches; [pers.] As beautiful or sad thoughts come to mind, I like to put them in words to share with others. I love poetry. I thank God for the gift. [a.] Fleetwood NC 28626.

COX, CLARA W.
[pen.] Clara Whitney; [b.] July 8, 1909, Cleveland, Ohio; [p.] Frank P. and Maude E. Whitney; [m.] Howard E. Richards, 1937, Thomas K. Cox, 2960; [ch.] Mary Giffen, Charlotte C, Neal, Nancy Neiswander; [ed.] Shaw High School, Oberlin College B.A., CWR University, Library School B.L.S.; [occ.] Retired librarian; [memb.] First Presbyterian Church of E. Cleve., Heritage Foundation, Ohio Library Council; [oth. writ.] Book notes for E. Cleve. newspaper, poetry for high school paper, poetry for St. Nicholas League; [pers.] To my father, my mentor, I owe my love of books and the great English poets. It was he who showed me how to use words to express the beauty and magic of this world. [a.] Willoughby, OH 44094.

COX, DENISE M.
[b.] September 26, 1955, Tacoma, Washington; [p.] Col. Albert and Rose Davy; [m.] Robert Cox, July 6, 1974; [ch.] Aleesha Marie, Ashlee Renea; [ed.] Derby High School; [occ.] Secretary, bookkeeper; [pers.] Through my writing I try to express emotions that stir deep within us all. And as the words come together to create a verse, a thought, a feeling, from this a poem is formed. [a.] Derby, KS 67037.

COX, RICHARD LEE
[pen.] Richard Lee; [b.] November 8, 1933, Wagoner County, Oklahoma; [p.] Etta Cox; [ch.] Richard Lee Jr., Sharon Faye, Donna May; [ed.] Sequoya High,

Tahelquah Oklahoma, Northeastern State University, Tulsa University, Oklahoma; [occ.] Salesman; [oth. writ.] Number of other poems written., One is published in National (Helicon) by Nile High Poetry Society of Denver, Colorado; [pers.] I strive to reflect the spiritual senses of our deeper thought. I was influenced by the earlier romantic poets, such as Byron, Shelley, and Keats, Wordsworth. [a.] Tulsa OK 74110.

CRAFT, AUDREY BROWN
[b.] February 28, 1930, Troy, Alabama; [p.] Thomas Kirby Brown and Mamie Hudson Brown Campbell; [m.] Vernon Thomas Craft (deceased), January 4, 1949; [ch.] Barbara Jane Craft Chance; [ed.] Shellhorn Grammar School, Troy High School, and business course; [occ.] Corporate legal secretary; [memb.] Troy Church of Christ, Florida State Poetry Society, Alabama State Poetry Society, Pike County Creative Writers charter member, Floribunda Garden Club; [hon.] Numerous awards and prizes from Florida State Poetry Society and Alabama State Poetry Society; [oth. writ.] Co-author of four books published in local papers The Alabama Sunday Magazine and The American Legion Magazine, 2 books: Pots and Poems, Pots, Prose and Poems (co-authored); [pers.] All I have seen teaches me to trust the Creator for all I have not seen. I have been influenced by friends who were/ are poets/writers of all countries. [a.] Troy, AL 36081.

CRAIGT, MICHAEL D.
[pen.] Michael Craigt-Hulick; [b.] March 19, 1965, Clinton Township, Pennsylvania; [p.] Rosemary and Thomas; [m.] Terry Lee, September 2, 1992; [ch.] Cayenne, Fred, Damien, Belle; [ed.] Wilde Lake High, 2 semesters University of Kentucky; [occ.] Retired U.S. Army specialist; [memb.] U.S. Army Reserves; [hon.] Air Assault Badge, Army Achievement Medal, Driver Badge, Good Conduct Medal, Overseas Service Ribbon; [oth. writ.] "Ethel's Dreamworld, "The Years Before, "Acceptance",etc; [pers.] My life will be but a whisper. My words will last forever. [a.] Jacksonville, FL.

CRAIN, JAMES ELLIS SR.
[pen.] Billy Crain; [b.] April 25, 1949, San Diego, California; [p.] Johan and Cleo Kearse; [m.] Diane Crain, July 3, 1993; [ch.] James Jr., Robert, Orlando, David, Daniel, Deandrea; [ed.] Samuel B. Morse, San Diego, California; [occ.] Truck and van driver; [hon.] It's an honor to worship and praise the Lord. My award is eternal and everlasting life; [oth. writ.] I believe in miracles, children of Atlanta, Reaganomics, Show is shady, election 80, master of my soul; [pers.] Before you give someone a piece of your mind, make sure you have enough left to do what you have to do! [a.] San Diego, CA 92113.

CREEK, MICHAEL G.
[b.] February 14, 1944, Kalamazoo, Michigan; [p.] Gorman and Lorraine Obert Creek; [m.] Ebert Bell; [ed.] St. Augustine High School; [occ.] Tool and die maker, James River Corp; [hon.] Volunteer service for the United Way; [pers.] To have a vision of Faith and the wisdom of Hope. [a.] Delton, MI 49046.

CRESSWELL, WILDA
[b.] November 5, 1955, Markdale, Ontario; [p.] Mae Wilson; [m.] Divorced; [ch.] Norman Cresswell; [ed.] Grade 12 and Lougheed Business College;

[pers.] Thank you for letting me know for sure that I have real talent. [a.] Markdale, Ont N0C 1H0.

CRILLY, PEGGY
[b.] March 20, 1926, Elizabeth, New Jersey; [p.] John J. and Helen Crilly; [ed.] Mount Saint Mary Academy, N. Plainfield, New Jersey, Georgian Court College, B.S., Lakewood New Jersey, Seton Hall University, M.A.; [occ.] Former teacher, now substance abuse counselor; [memb.] Clown College, Sisters of Mercy, N. Plainfield, New Jersey; [hon.] Dean's List, certified clown; [oth. writ.] Several unpublished, few articles for high school paper; [pers.] I live one day at a time, respecting my wholeness and enjoy my humor and creativity. Helping others to nurture their gifts is my gift to others. [a.] Avon by the Sea, NJ 07717.

CRISMAN, STEPHANIE
[b.] September 22, 1979, Woodstock, Virginia; [p.] Steve and Debbie Crisman; [ed.] Woodstock Middle School, Central High School; [hon.] Academic awards; [pers.] Always follow your instincts. If you write something, take your time: paper is patient! [a.] Edinburg, VA 22824.

CRIVELLO, SANDRA K.
[pen.] Sandra Kaye; [b.] April 26, 1960, Seattle Washington; [p.] Wilson Arnold Bender, and Beatrice Carol Koch; [ed.] ICS Newport/Pacific High School, Scottsdale Community College; [occ.] Software marketing entrepreneur; [memb.] Arizona Software Association, National Geographic Society; [hon.] Founding member Ashton-Tate Corp, 3rd place Scenic Photography by Galen Ravell, Who's Who of the West; [oth. writ.] Current novel work includes "The Crystal Cathedrals", and a book of poetry called Color Me Simple, also have published articles for Arizona Software Association; [pers.] Individuality- it's the point where reality ends and immortality begins... [a.] Scotsdale, AZ 85259.

CRONIN, PATRICK LAWRENCE
[b.] September 30, 1948, South Weymouth, Massachusetts; [p.] Michael f. and J. Margaret Cronin; [m.] Brenda J. Cronin;, August 29, 1970' [ch.] Jennifer Noel, Patrick Kevin; [ed.] Whitman-Hanson Regional High School, St. Michael's, B.A. English, M.Ed; [occ.] Teacher, curriculum coordinator for English Dept, East Bridgewater High School, East Bridgewater, Massachusetts; [memb.] National Council Teachers of English, State leader for program to recognize excellence in student literary magazines (NCTE), Massachusetts Council Teachers of English; [hon.] Horace Mann Teacher, PCEA Honors Award winner; [oth. writ.] Poetry in The Poetic Knight and Feelings magazines, poetry and story in Spitball, articles in Athletic Journal and Scholastic Coach, local newspaper; [pers.] "...I rhyme to see myself, to set the darkness echoing." Seamus Heaney, Death of a Naturalist. [a.] Whitman, MA 02382.

CROOKER, JOAN A.
[b.] July 20, 1940, Nashua, New Hampshire; [p.] Philip and Helen LeFavor; [m.] Ronald Crooker, June 9, 1962; [ch.] Christopher Ronald, John Joseph; [ed.] Nashua High School, University of Virginia, (Bach Sci,Ed), Lynchburg College, (Master of Ed); [occ.] Reading specialist, Fairfax County Public Schools, Virginia, Camelot Elementary; [memb.] NEA, FEA, National Head Injury Foundation, Kappa

Delta Pi; [hon.] Kappa Delta Pi, nominated Teacher of the Year, 1986, Fairfax County Schools, Nashua High School Teacher's Union scholarship; [pers.] I remind my young students-anything you think, you can say. Anything you say, you can write. Writing keeps your thoughts in memory. Enjoy your memories, the beauty around you. Don't be afraid to write about them! I never thought I could write a poem-but I wrote this one! [a.] Oakton, VA 22124.

CROSS, R. E.
[b.] November 10, 1956, Benton, Arkansas; [p.] A. W. and Dorothy Cross; [m.] Cindy Cross. December 18, 1976; [ed.] B.S. Engineering Physic, University of Arkansas, M.S. Engineering Management, Florida Institute of Technology; [occ.] Engineer; [oth. writ.] Revival of the Heart (unpublished), Heartsongs (unpublished); [pers.] I believe in the diversity of the human race. We are all part of this larger family and should celebrate it, not despise it. [a.] Orlando, FL 32833.

CROWE, KRISTI
[b.] January 30, 1978, Great Falls, Montana; [p.] Linda and Charles T. Crowe; [ed.] Sophomore, Cleveland High School, Seattle, Washington; [pers.] Smiling is easier than frowning.

CRUMNY, CAROLYN W.
[b.] March 20, 1968, New Orleans, Louisiana; [p.] Roger and Bonnie Martin; [m.] the loving Thomas R. Crumby, April 20, 1991; [ch.] Timothy R. Crumby, Christopher Aaron Crumby; [occ.] Mother, poet writer, homemaker; [oth. writ.] "Restless Father", a dynamic poem published by Sparrowgrass Poetry Forum; [pers.] There is a novel of thoughts in each of us. My thoughts flow from my pen. Sometimes the expressions make no sense at all and sometimes my philosophy is profound. The pen is the key to my subconscious mind. I thank my mother for her love of literature she shared with as a child. [a.] Slidell, LA.

CSUY, KATHRYN M.
[b.] March 24, 1959, Bellevue, Pennsylvania; [p.] John and Velma Jean Csuy; [ed.] Freedom Area High School, Community College of Beaver County; [memb.] Beaver valley Writer's Guild, Big Brothers/ Big Sisters of Beaver County; [hon.] President's List, Dean's List, Trustees's Award; [pers.] I write from personal experience and for the love of others within my heart. This poem was inspired by the birth of my girlfriend, Shelly's baby, Courtney Marie. [a.] New Brighton, PA 15066.

CUE, CHARLOTTE WILLIAMS
[b.] December 2, 1941, Gainesville, Florida; [p.] Thomas and Rubye I. Williams; [m.] Henry Cue Jr, August 26, 1967; [ed.] Lincoln High School, Edward Waters College, B.S. degree, University of Florida, MED degree; [occ.] Elementary school teacher, Brentwood Elementary; [memb.] Delta Sigma Theta sorority, Kappa Delta Pi Honor Society, Duval Teachers United, NEA; [hon.] Duval County Teacher of the Year finalist, 1985, biography in the Personalities of the South, the World's Who's Who of Women, created Project SEEK; [oth. writ.] I have written poems and articles for special occasions; [pers.] My writings reflect the love I have for the family and friends. They are "feeling" poems. [a.] Jacksonville, FL 32209.

CUEVAS-CARDOZA, LUIS EDGAR
[b.] November 9, 1927, Cabo Rojo, Puerto Rico; [p.] Luis A. and Rosalina Cardoza Cuevas; [m.] Margarita Cuevas; [ch.] Janice, Raul, Dennis; [ed.] P.S. 51, Gompers High School, Bronx, New York; Law's School of Engineering, U.S, Merchant Marine School; [occ.] Retired merchant marine, body and paint shop owner, driver, Youth Movement Inc Advocate Schools; [memb.] Founder, Inland Empire Puerto Rican Association, Club Social Puerto Riqueno, San Juan Festival Event, Masons Society; [hon.] Best new poet, 1988; [oth. writ.] A few poems in Spanish, article in the San Bernardino newspaper, poems published by The American Poetry Assn, The Watermark Press, World of Poetry Press, The National Library of Poetry, and The Amherts Society, also novels; [pers.] Now that I'm retired from everything else, I always keep busy writing novels and more poetry. Writing is my beat. [a.] Riv., CA 92503.

CULLEN, MELISSA M.
[b.] April 14, 1978, Sumter, South Carolina; [p.] Kevin and Kim Cullen; [ed.] Caesar Rodney High School; [occ.] Student; [memb.] Zoroastrian, student literary magazine; [oth. writ.] Poems published in zoroastrian; [pers.] I try to write poetry on experiences I know others can relate to. [a.] Dover, DE 19901.

CULVER, RUTH
[pen.] Ruth Culver; [b.] February 26, 1939, Kaiserslautern, West Germany; [p.] Martha Jensen and Richard Nusshag; [m.] Edward T. Culver, Jr, November 28, 1958; [ch.] Barbara C. Bewley, Edwina A. Richards; [ed.] Educated in W. Germany; [occ.] Housewife; [pers.] Special thanks to my daughter Barbara for being my inspiration. [a.] Mays Landing, NJ 08330.

CULVERHOUSE, TRICIA J.
[b.] October 15, 1946, Birmingham, Alabama; [p.] Carl and Margaret Culverhouse; [ed.] B.A. English and Writing, University of Redlands, M.A. Religious Education, School of Technology, Claremont; [occ.] Church secretary, freelance author, curriculum developer; [memb.] Impact Presbyterian Church, California Association of Persons with Handicaps, Peacemaking Committee of Presbytery of Riverside, Developmental Disabilities Area Board #12, past member; [oth. writ.] Devotions, curriculum, and articles related to disabilities, concerns, and peacemaking issues. I am currently working on an autobiography; [pers.] Despite my physical disabilities, I have always sought to live a productive life which involves reaching out and giving something back to the world around me. [a.] Redlands, CA 92373.

CUNNINGHAM, MARK ALLEN
[b.] May 13, 1971, Chattanooga, Tennessee; [p.] Jerry and Anna Cunningham; [ed.] The McCallie School, University of North Carolina at Chapel Hill; [occ.] Student; [memb.] Co-editor of Cellar Door; [hon.] Argonaut Poetry Award, Stone Scholar, National Merit finalist, Cum Laude, All-City Shortstop; [oth. writ.] Poems published in the Argonaut, and Cellar Door Bi-Weekly, article for The Tornado, short story also published in Argonaut; [pers.] I'm trying to write the kind of poetry which is inherently paradoxical; I want both baseball players and poets to enjoy the poem. That's almost impossible. [a.] Chapel Hill, NC 27514.

CURTIS, HESTER
[pen.] Hester; [b.] January 2, 1925, Windsor, Ontario; [p.] Mr. and Mrs. A. E. Carter; [m.] Rowland Curtis, October 14, 1944; [ch.] Nancy, Allen, Gary; [ed.] Patterson High, W. D. Lowe Vocational; [occ.] Homemaker; [memb.] AWC Anglican Church; [oth. writ.] Article for London Free Press, and The Windsor Star; [pers.] I write for my family, stories and poems that i wish they can read when I am no longer with them. I also wrote a biography of my childhood until I had my children. My grandchildren find my book on my childhood hard to believe because the different lifestyle compared to theirs is hard for them to comprehend. But I feel they must realize the difference and if I don't write it down, how will they know what grandmother's childhood was like, and it certainly was different than their childhood. [a.] Windsor, Ontario, Canada N85 3W2.

CUSIMONO, BERNADINE
[pen.] Connie capone; [b.][March 10, 1947, Birmingham, Alabama; [p.] Paschal and Frances Louise Cusimono; [m.] Barry Lee Ringewold, December 22, 1990; [ch.] Claude Lucky, Jason Lindsey, Philip Laurence; [ed.] Stephen F Austin High, North Harris College, Criminal Justice degree; [occ.] Private investigator, reconstruct accidents; [memb.] Daughters of American Revolution, Liberty chapter, Texas Children Hospital volunteer, Court Appointed Special Advocate for severely abused children; [hon.] Mrs. Congeniality, 1993, Texas, Child Advocate Award of case competition, Texas Children Hospital Award for service and time dedication, Honor guest at the Academy Awards 1993; [oth. writ.] Three novels written but unpublished. "A Taste of Time", "Go Buy Yourself a Heart", "The Prince of Rios", "Spirit of Celebration", "Freckle Face"; [pers.] In all my stories or poems there are two words or statements I follow as a guide-always be kind and courageous-I can only write what I feel and experience. [a.] Cleveland, TX 77327.

CUTTER, OLGA
[pen.] Sonia Wolff; [b.] November 8, 1939; [b.] Montenegro, Yugoslavia; [p.] Ilija and Milica Sjeklocha; [m.] June 17, 1962; [ch.] Stan (29), Buck (26) and Miki (23); [ed.] BA major Education, minor-Russian, law school- 3 three 1988-1991; [occ.] International Trade Broker-Pres. American Business Congress; [memb.] Senatorial Inner Circle, National Association of Female Executives, Russian and American Alliance of Women Serbian Unity Congress; [hon.] William Taft Law School Scholarship, 2000 American Notable Women 1993, Centurion -Cemetery 21 Club, Million dollar Club - Century 21; [oth. writ.] Poetry in Serbo-Croatian contribution editor - "Serb World", "The Road to Siberia"published in newspaper in Far East Russia, "The Balkan Queen" - 3 act play; [pers.] Where we planted seeds of hope in barren deserts, the new generation in converting dreams into realities. [a.] Oceanside, CA 92056.

DA COSTA, DENISE ELIAS
[b.] May 15, 1972, Springfield, Massachusetts; [p.] Mario da Costa and Beatrice and Leroy Williams; [ed.] Commercial Art major with a minor in Spanish from Elms College, Chicopee, MA (BA 1994); [memb.] Art Association, VFW, Ladies Auxiliary of 6189, Springfield Library and Museums, Funai Nerds; [hon.] National Dean's List Student, Who's Who Among College Students; [oth. writ.] Various other writings that have had not been published; [pers.] I believe we should open our minds to the world and other people. Respect others but mostly respect yourself, your ideas, your beliefs and opinions. [a.] Chicopee, MA 01020.

DA SILVA, GEORGE R. GOMES
[pen.] Rob; [b.] Madeira Island; [p.] Martha Douget Fiche and Abeilard Gomes Da Silva; [m.] Maria Isabel Gomes Da Silva (deceased), September 4, 1951; [ch.] Roberta Maria and Elisabeth; [ed.] High School; [occ.] Retired Port Authority Administration, in Portugal, Europe; [memb.] Various clubs in Europe; [oth. writ.] A compilation of 500 poems, several articles for monthly newspaper in Lisbon, Portugal; [pers.] Poems are an expression of my inner thoughts. [a.] Gaithersburg, MD 20882.

DAHL, JUDITH
[b.] September 2, 1912, Kulm, North Dakota; [p.] Emil and Victoria Lundstrom; [m.] Harold Englebert (Bert) (deceased), November 21, 1936; [ch.] Millicent, LeRoy, Rosette; [ed.] Part grade ten; [occ.] Wife and mother, grandmother and great grandmother; [memb.] United Church; [oth. writ.] Poems-published in newspapers in Canada and USA; [pers.] I think on the goodness of man in this troubled world and the words come. [a.] Edmonton, Alberta, Canada T6H 5J2.

DAILEY, ELMER L.
[b.] April 19, 1911, Riversburg, Pennsylvania; [p.] Mr. and Mrs. George W. Dailey; [m.] Ruth C. (Faulkner), December 24, 1934; [ch.] Two sons and two daughters; [ed.] Limited-earned G.E.D. after age 65-Sauk Valley College (Sterling, IL); [occ.] Last 25 years minister of the Gospel-pastor, evangelist; [memb.] Nazarene Church; [hon.] Served WWII honorably discharged served in South Pacific; [oth. writ.] The Domicile" Booklet, short articles, verse, published - gratis; [pers.] My philosophy is Jesus Christ, wisdom, learning. [a.] Milton, FL 32571.

DALEY, WILLIAM
[b.] December 21, 1970, Milford, Connecticut; [p.] Gerald and Mary Daley; [ed.] J.A. Foran High, Housatonic Community College, University of Maine; [occ.] Student; [hon.] Writing awards: Horizon's Service award/Bridgeport Post award (Housatonic Community College), nominee for Arthur B. Hill Scholarship (University of Maine); [oth. writ.] Newspaper work and some short stories; [pers.] Within my writing, I endeavor to resuscitate the good heart in what I feel is an ailing society today. Old films, especially the work of Frank Capra, remain important influences on my style. [a.] Milford, CT 06460.

DAMSKER, MATT
[b.] March 14, 1951, Philadelphia, Pennsylvania; [p.] Sidney H. and Mildred H. Damsker; [m.] Lori Haber, May 6, 1979; [ch.] Jesse Michael, Ashley Jane; [ed.] Central High School, Temple University (Phila., PA); [occ.] Managing Editor, Rodale Press, Inc.; Journalist and critic; [oth. writ.] "Rock Voices" (1980, St. Martin's Press, NY), poems and articles in literary journals, Rolling Stone magazine; [pers.] Poetry is the purest and most rewarding expression of our human complexities and our struggle with time. I most admire Wallace Stevens, James Marshall and Philip Larkin. [a.] Newtown, PA 18940.

DARBY, ANGELA RENEE'
[pen.] Angela Darby; [b.] February 17, 1979, Ohio, Columbus at Grant Hospital; [p.] Mike Darby and Beverly Wolfe; [ed.] Middle School in the 7th grade, A and student; [occ.] Student in Middle School; [memb.] Softball, cheerleading, volleyball, ski club, track; [hon.] Merit and Honor Roll; [oth. writ.] I won before in this some contest, but I never sent anything back in; [pers.] in life, everything that you do, do it your best and do it with pride. [a.] Blacklick, OH 43004.

DASKAL, JOSEPH M.
[pen.] Mike Daskal; [b.] July 3, 1975, New York; [p.] David and Sara Daskal-immigrants from Hungary; [ed.] Ner Isreal High School; [pers.] I believe poetry is the cryptic cries of the mind. Poetry must be written for oneself with no intention of publication. I have been greatly influenced by early 19th century poets such as Edgar A. Poe. [a.] Brooklyn, NY 11230.

DAUGHERTY, LILA CANNON
[pen.] Lila Cannon Daughtery; [b.] April 23, 1936, Pitt County, Ayden, North Carolina; [p.] Robert Andrew (Bob) and Callie M. Cannon; [m.] Shelton Bryan, February 3, 1963; [ed.] High School, 12 grade; [occ.] May 1, 1991 retired from Lenoir Co., Department of Social Services (35 years); [memb.] NCRGEA, NCSSA; [oth. writ.] "Mama's Accident", published Summer 1993 in the "Treasured Poems of America", "Feelings of a Handicapped Person", published in a local newspaper and to be published in the Fall 1993 (August) "Treasured Poems of America"; [pers.] I love nature and family. I grew up on a farm; 14 children in the family, giving me a varied background. I have always loved poetry. In everything I do "verses are always on my mind". I love people and animals, I still live on a farm. [a.] Dover, NC 28526.

DAUSSIN, WILLIAM M.
[b.] November 28, 1980, Abita Springs, Louisiana; [p.] David and Carolyn Daussin; [ed.] Entering 7th grade in the Fall of 1993; [occ.] Student; [memb.] Boy Scouts of America; [oth. writ.] Several and poems as yet unpublished; [pers.] My inspiration comes from everyday things. [a.] Mandeville, LA 70448.

DAVENPORT, NICOLE
[b.] May 15, 1980, Salt Lake City; [p.] Ronald and Carrie Davenport; [ed.] Currently attending West Jordan Middle School. [a.] Salt Lake City, UT.

DAVID, CECILIA RATNA
[b.] May 7, 1975, Pure, India; [p.] Cecil Richard and Mary Beetika David; [ed.] Freshman, College; [occ.] Student; [memb.] Seventh day Adventist Church; [pers.] Nature thrills me. It's creator Jesus Christ helps me pen my emotions. [a.] Nicosia Cyprus.

DAVIS, ANGELA L.
[b.] March 19, 1980, Little Rock, Arkansas; [p.] Becky Channell and Lee Davis.

DAVIS, CHARLOTTE ANNE
[b.] March 2, 1951, Belleville, Ontario; [p.] Bert and Mary Burgess; [m.] Divorced; [ch.] Michael John, Thomas James; [ed.] Quinte Secondary Loyalist College; [occ.] Customer Service Clerk, Ontario Hydro; [memb.] O.A.C.E.T.T. (Ontario Association of Certified Engineering Technicians and Technologists), O.E.L. (Ontario Electrical League); [pers.] To enjoy all people no matter their race, colour or creed and Philippians 4:8. [a.] Peterborough, Ontario K9J3W9 Canada.

DAVIS, DELAINE
[pen.] Elizabeth Margaret Sterling; [b.] December 21, 1968, Lafayette, Indiana; [p.] Lewis and Alta Davis; [ed.] Zionsville High School, Manchester College; [occ.] Personal Fitness Trainer; [hon.] Many athletic awards throughout my high school and college career; [oth. writ.] This is my first writing; [pers.] My writing shows what I see in Society today. [a.] Zionsville, IN 46077.

DAVIS, JOHN H.
[b.] January 23, 1908, Woodland, Pennsylvania; [p.] Ephraim and Katie Davis; [m.] Irene Z., February 23, 1943; [ch.] John C. (deceased), Mary Kay, Elainel, Carol Ann; [ed.] HS Associate Degree in Electronics; [occ.] Retired; [hon.] War Department Ability as Commissioned Officer; [pers.] The strength of a nation lies in the character of the people not in the ability to wage war. [a.] Clearfield, PA 16830.

DAVIS, JOYCE
[b.] July 8, 1929, Eagle River, Wisconsin; [p.] Bertie Albin and Millicent Irene Hodge; [m.] William Paul Jack Davis, June 11, 1949; [ch.] Robert James Davis, Linda Sue Davis Schaller; [ed.] Graduate of Woodland High School and Anderson School of Scientific Massage and Physical Therapy; [occ.] CA State Certified Home Health Aide; [memb.] Charter Member of The International Society of Poets; [hon.] A number of awards of merit from World of Poetry and two Golden Poet trophies; [oth. writ.] "To Those Who Seek", an autobiography with poems dating from 1947-1981. Many of my poetic writings have been received with music as well as words; [pers.] I pray that my words of poetry and the music that has been entrusted to my care will aid in helping to lift spirits and bring peace to the world. [a.] Knights Landing, CA 95645.

DAVIS, JUDY A.
[pen.] Judy A. Davis; [b.] June 3, 1943, Laurel, Mississippi; [p.] David Pascal and Janie Sumrall; [m.] Max H., April 18, 1962; [ch.] Mark, Tammy, Macon; [ed.] Degree in Nursing; [occ.] Registered Nurse; [memb.] Miss Nurses Association; [hon.] Scholarship in Music, Achievement Award; [oth. writ.] 10 Gospel songs, one copyrighted. I am presently working on a novel; [pers.] I believe we are created for a purpose in life and to celebrate the beauty that God has given us.

DAVIS, LUCY
[b.] October 21, 1979; [p.] Elizabeth Davis; [ed.] Mt. Olive Middle School; [hon.] None as of yet, but I hope to have many in the future; [oth. writ.] I have several other poems that I'm planning on submitting in the near future; [pers.] I often write about problems or controversial subjects that touch my heart. My greatest influence has been my Mom. Who also puts feelings into poetry. [a.] Budd Lake, NJ 07828.

DAVIS, STEVE
[pen.] Steve Davis; [b.] April 30, 1953, Chattanooga, Tennessee; [p.] James and Adrianne Davis; [m.] Cathy, June 5, 1979; [ch.] Tammy Lynn Aykroyd; [ed.] Englewood Senior High, Florida Junior College, Concord School of Career Science, Life; [occ.] Respiratory Care Practitioner; [oth. writ.] Various poems, lyrics and attempts to express the inexpressible; [pers.] My writings come from a place of balance within that is not so easily seen or experienced in my outer world. [a.] Lander, WY 82520.

DAWSON, STEPHANIE
[b.] May 17, 1979, Akron, Ohio; [p.] Jeffrey and Mary; [ed.] Copley-Fairlawn Middle School; [memb.] President of Copley-Fairlawn Builder's Club; [hon.] All A's Roll. [a.] Fairlawn, OH 44333.

DAY, ANDREWS
[[b.] January 14, 1974, Lowell, Massachusetts; [p.] David S. and Carol Ann Day; [ed.] Westford Academy; [occ.] Student; [pers.] No one should underestimate the power of words. Write and let your emotions flow. [a.] Westford, MA 01886.

DeCAMP, MARIANNE A.
[pen.] Marianne A. DeCamp; [b.] January 25, 1939, Clearwater, Nebraska; [p.] Blanche and Hewitt DeCamp; [m.] Divorced; [ch.], Chris and Angelita DeCamp; [ed.] One year of college; [occ.] Disabled; [oth. writ.] An Ode to A Love Lost, Emercance, In Your Arms; [pers.] Without poetry, I would feel unfulfilled! The thoughts keep coming to me until I release them. [a.] La Mirada, CA 90635.

DeGANNES, REBECCA L.
[b.] November 26, 1975, Key West, Florida; [p.] Deborah Landrian and Carlos DeGannes; [ed.] Homestead Senior High; [memb.] Thespian Troupe 1710, Homestead Auxiliary Corp., Class of '93 Club, Student Council Executive Board; [hon.] Who's Who of American High School Students 1990-91, 1991-92 Class Presidency, 1992-93 Class Presidency, 1990-91 Leadership Award, Paul Bell Award; [pers.] Eyes in love are blind to imperfection. [a.] Homestead, FL 33033.

De GUZMAN, WILLIAM
[b.] August 16, 1970, David City, Philippines; [p.] Loreto T. and Eleanor P. de Guzman; [ed.] Oak Ridge High School, first year electrical engineering, Pellissippi State Technical Community College; [occ.] U.S. Navy; [memb.] Philippine American Association of East TN; [hon.] First runner up Spelling Bee 1983 Cedar Hill School, (Oak Ridge, TN), high school graduate with honors Biology award. [a.] Oak Ridge, TN 37830.

De HOYOS, PATRICIA JANE
[pen.] Pat De Hoyos; [b.] January 19, 1972. Beaumont, Texas; [p.] Alejandro C. and Elvia G. De Hoyos; [ed.] South San Antonio High School, San Antonio College; [occ.] Full-time student and electronic publisher; [hon.] Dean's list and being a child of the King of Kings; [oth. writ.] The Man in My Life, Friend or Foe, Destined, Don't Capture My Heart, It's Casual; [pers.] I give all honor and glory to my Lord, Jesus Christ, who has been with me through both the good and bad times. He has blessed me with a wonderful family and with good friends. And for giving me a best friend when I needed one the most. I love you, Lord! [a.] San Antonio, TX 78211.

De LAPLANTE, MICHELE
[b.] October 3, 1944, Montreal, Canada; [p.] Jean and Fernande L. de Laplante; [m.] Louis Marie Kimpton, October 3, 1981; [ed.] Letters and Geology; [occ.] Editor; [hon.] Golden Poet 1992, (World of Poetry), some prizes in French poetry; [oth. writ.] Some French fantastic novels. Positive thinking book, poetry. [a.] Berthierville, Canada J0K 1A0.

DeLUCA, BARBARA
[b.] April 15, 1941, Alden Station, Nanticoke, Pennsylvania; [p.] Mary and Nicholas Veronick; [m.] David J., January 2, 1960; [ch.] David, Kevin and Brian DeLuca; [ed.] Newport High School (Class of '59), Luzerne County Community College, Graduated 1981; [occ.] Secretary to school principal Crestwood School District; [memb.] UCC Church (Dorrane, PA), Church choir and several church committees; [hon.] Dean's List, Luzerne County Community College; [pers.] I strive to bring out the good in people through my writing. [a.] Wapwallopen, PA 18660.

DeLUCA, LISA MARIE
[pen.] Sasha; [b.] March 7, 1975, Canton, Ohio; [p.] David and Mary Jane DeLuca; [ed.] High School diploma; [occ.] Cashier at Fishers Foods; [memb.] The Edge; [oth. writ.] Numerous poems and a few short stories; [pers.] Numerous authors and poets have influenced my poetic writings. Through writing, I achieve inner peace and happiness. [a.] Canton, OH 44709.

DeNAEYER, LYN
[b.] July 16, 1939, Alliance, Nebraska; [p.] Joe and Wilma Spencer; [ch.] Barbara, Bill, Russ, Martin; [ed.] BA Mental Health, Sinte Gleska University; [occ.] Cattle Rancher, free lance writer, counselor; [memb.] NE Cattlewomen, St. John's Episcopal Church, Old West Committee, Western Folklife Conservatory; [hon.] First place, 1991 and 1993 for personal column, NE Press Association, 2nd place 1992; [oth. writ.] Newspaper columnist, and correspondent, published poetry in anthologies, and Dry Crik Review, perform and write Cowboy Poetry; [pers.] Stewardship of the land is the only reason to be in ranching; one always cares gently for that which is loved greatly, but there's no reason not to have a good time in the process. [a.] Seneca, NE 69161.

DePIPFO, DAVID J.
[b.] October 1, 1993, Omaha, Nebraska; [p.] Penelope P. Chriss and Dr. Paul David DePippo; [ed.] Barry Goldwater High, undergraduate at University at Arizona; [occ.] Student, Wordsmith; [oth. writ.] Many unpublished poems and songs; [pers.] Through history's eyes we can reflect all, blood, better, victory, defeat, lust and love. This knowledge will perpetuate the process, which is mankind. a[.] Phoenix, AZ 88027.

DeRITA, LISA
[b.] April 8, 1961, Detroit, Michigan; [p.] Vincent and Carol Derita; [ch.] Daniel Vincent; [ed.] Sterling Heights High; [occ.] Gas Accounting Clerk; [oth. writ.] Unread poems and co-writer on songs for my brother's band; [pers.] Many emotions and feelings inspire me to write, but my biggest inspiration is Jesus Christ. Through God, all things are possible. [a.] Antioch, CA 94509.

DeSILVA, SEAN PATRICK
[b.] June 7, 1972, Brooklyn, New York; [occ.] Student; [oth. writ.] Many poems and some essays none of which are presently published. [a.] Valley Stream, NY 11580.

DEAN, V. IRENE
[b.] March 20, 1926, Warwick Twp.-Chester Co., Pennsylvania; [p.] Harry George and Eva Mildred Murray Spohn; [m.] Clinton Wilson Dean, Sr., October 8, 1944; [ch.] Clint Jr., Tom, John, Joyce and ten grandchildren; [ed.] Graduated Norco High School as a Secretary; [occ.] Now wife, mother, grandmother, all commitments involved; [memb.] Christ United Methodist Church-Republican Party, Pottstown Area Seniors' Center, Mahanatawny Chapter of National Society Daughters of the American Revolution; [hon.] Presently Conservation Chairman Mahanatawny Chapter DAR. [a.] Douglassville, PA 19518.

DELLASORTE, MARIE
[b.] August 28, 1937, Yonkers, New York; [p.] Angela and Frank Torre; [m.] William, December 1, 1957; [ch.] Linda, Louise, Angela, Paula and Billy; [ed.] Yonkers High School; [occ.] Teacher Assistant for MonteSouri Pre School Children; [memb.] American Cancer Society; [oth. writ.] Articles published Gannett Westchester Newspaper, poem sent to President Bill Clinton and many others sent to cheer children who are disabled; [pers.] My children and grandchildren inspire my writing. I strive to reflect, and send a message when writing my poems. To put a smile on someone's face and love in someone's heart. [a.] Yonkers, NY 10701.

DELNEGRO, DAVID ROCCO
[b.] October 2, 1963, Somers Point, New Jersey; [p.] Carl V. and Caroline DelNegro; [ed.] Florida Keys Community College; [occ.] Paratrooper and Prizefighter; [memb.] 82nd Airborne Division Association, American Boxing Federation; [hon.] Nominated to Who's Who Among Students in American Junior Colleges, President's List, Army Achievement Metal; [oth. writ.] Yes; [pers.] With no intent to offend, I strive for reality with humor. I have been greatly influenced by the early romantic cave-dwellers. [a.] Princeton, FL 33032.

DELOREY, DANIEL F. III
[pen.] Delirious; [b.] October 23, 1968, Merced, California; [p.] Daniel Jr., and Rebecca S. Delorey; [ed.] 1987 Laramie High grad.; [occ.] U.S. Ar,y Infantry Fort Ord, CA; [hon.] Three Army Achievements Medals; [oth. writ.] A couple of poems published here and there; [pers.] My mind is on a quest within me, and my soul, my mind shall free. I am motivated by inspiration and reality. [a.] Laramie, WY 82070.

DEMERS, JUDY
[b.] May 28, 1953, Glendale, California; [p.] Wallace and Rena Graham; [m.] Joe, January 10, 1981; [ch.] Jennifer and Julie; [ed.] San Jose State University; [occ.] Elementary Physical Education Teacher; [hon.] Olympic Trial Finalist 91972) in Track and Field; [oth. writ.] Accepted works in production include poems in magazines and a storybook coloring book; [pers.] I like to write poems and stories that have a moral to them. I often write to encourage and strengthen. [a.] San Jose, CA 95158.

DENNIS, JOHHNY SHANNON
[b.] May 12, 1975; [p.] Johnnie M. and Michael e. Dennis; [ed.] Cloudland High School; [memb.] Beta Club, Spanish Club, Who's Who of High School Students, Annual Staff; [hon.] Honor Roll, Top 15% of Class; [oth. writ.] O' blue Sky, O' Father, Mother; [pers.] Special thanks to my family, especially my Mother, a poet in her own right, who inspires me day after day. [a.] Elizabethton, TN 37644.

DENNY, MELISSA
[b.] August 2, 1977, Colorado Springs, Colorado; [p.] Michael R. and Debra L. Denny; [ed.] Joplin High; [occ.] Student; [hon.] Modeling, Fitness Award; [oth. writ.] Numerous short stories, working on novel. [a.] Joplin, MO 64804.

DESCALLER, MERCY
[b.] December 6, 1979; [p.] Michael and Olympia Descaller; [ed.] Dan Mini Elementary School, Solano Junior High School; [hon.] Presidential Academic Fitness Award. [a.] Vallejo, CA 94589.

DESMARAIS, PEGGY
[pen.] Peggy Desmarais; [b.] September 8, 1939, Providence, Rhode Island; [p.] Hugh T. and Helen D. Grimes; [m.] Ronald D., February 4, 1988; [ed.] Cranston High, Johnson and Wales Junior College of Business; [occ.] Housewife and Legal Secretary; [memb.] Providence County Legal Secretaries Association, Charter Member; [oth. writ.] A collection of short stories, as yet unpublished; [pers.] My poetry is my personal gift to myself, it is my mode of self-expression and have been writing since early childhood. [a.] Pawtucket, RI 02861.

DESMOND, NANCY V.
[b.] February 8. 1971, Lowell, Massachusetts; [p.] Richard and Virginia Desmond; [ed.] Shawsheen Valley Technical High School, Plymouth State College; [occ.] Student; [hon.] Dean's List, My art has been shown in The Drerup Gallery (Plymouth, NH); [oth. writ.] I have written many other poems none of which have been published as of yet; [pers.] My poems reflect my inner most feelings. I have been greatly influenced by Robert Frost. [a.] Tewksbury, MA 01876.

DESMOND, SALLIE L.
[pen.] Sallie L. Desmond; [b.] June 16, 1928, Celina, Texas; [p.] C.B. and Sallie Taylor; [m.] W.R. Desmond, Jr., May 28, 1948; [memb.] Fort Graham Baptist Church (Whitney, TX); [oth. writ.] Other poems - Have You Met My Jesus?, Our Husband's Hands, Our Muddy Mirrors, Voice by the Sea and many others; [pers.] My poems and writings comes from my heart, so when you read them, you are looking deep inside of me. May you only see love there. [a.] Whitney, TX 76692.

DESORMEAUX, RACHELLE
[pen.] Rachel Desmond; [b.] July 16, 1943, Plantagenet, Ontario; [p.] Eugene and Alda Desormeaux; [ch.] Sandra, Peggy, Tammy and Thomas; [ed.] Grade 12, Adult Education, P.P.H.S. (Shawville, Quebec); [occ.] Homemaker for 25 years; [oth. writ.] I am in the process of writing a book of short stories (fiction) stories on the unexplained; [pers.] A dream come true! I am very pleased to have been chosen and proud to have my poem published.

[a.] Shawville, Quebec Canada.

DESROCHES, LEONARD
[b.] Penetanguishene, Ontario; [occ.] Writer, Drywaller, Resource Person for Workshops on Non-Violence; [oth. writ.] Book-in-progress on the Practice and Spirituality of Non-Violence; [pers.] Poetry for me is distilled observation-of beauty, truth, events, yearnings. [a.] Toronto, Ontario M4M 2H5.

DEWAR, VIRGINIA L.
[pen.] Virginia L. Dewar; [b.] November 25, 1917, Spokane, Washington; [p.] Erwin and Meta VornKahl; [m.] Robert J. Dewar, Jr., December 13, 1941; [ch.] John R. and Dennis R. Dewar; [ed.] High School and Business College; [occ.] Secretary, Bookkeeper and Administrative Assistant; [memb.] Vice President of AARP Plantation Chapter #3173, Secretary of the Broward County Retired Educators, and Treasurer of Sorority Chapter; [hon.] Received certificates of Recognition for Outstanding Service to the community, for Recognition of Dedicated Service from AARP, and Commissioned as a Kentucky Colonel; [oth. writ.] None that I have saved; [pers.] I was born during World War I and married during World War II, so the Vietnam War came at a very difficult time-both my sons were of draft age. Dennis was drafted and to him I poured out my heart in this poem. The made it home safe. [a.] Plantation, FL 33317.

Di BENEDETTO, PAULINE
[b.] Boston, Massachusetts (raised in Brooklyn, New York); [p.] Pauline Cassara and Michael DiBenedetto; [m.] Divorced; [ch.] Four children; [ed.] High school; [occ.] Bank teller and Insurance agent; [memb.] The First Church of Religious Science of Rhode Island; [hon.] Honorable mention , Golden poet award, and Poet of Merit awards; [oth. writ.] I've written two books of poetry. "The Magic of Love", and "Seasons in My Life". I've drawn my own illustrations and am looking for a publisher; [pers.] I am first cousin to Tony Bennett, and although I have never met him, I would love to get to know him personally and share my gift of poetry with him. [a.] No. Attleboro, MA 02760.

DiBIASE, SHARON
[b.] July 9, 1951, Coshocton, Ohio; [p.] Wilma and Leo White; [m.] Warren, July 31, 1976; [ch.] Lori DiBiase; [ed.] Coshocton High, Ohio University, Youngstown State, Kent State, (BS in Education), University of Steubenville, Dayton University (MS in Education); [occ.] Teacher-certified Eng. 7-12, Elementary 1-8, Specialist K-12, Supervision; [memb.] Vice President-Board of Directors-Tri-State Cerebral Palsy Unit, Board of Directors-East Liverpool Education Association, Secretary Columbiana County International Reading Association, Beta Beta-Alpha Delta Kappa Chapter, Ohio Women's Cacus, NEA, OEA, Business and Professional Women's Organization; [pers.] My writings reflect personal thoughts and observations concerning the realities of one's existence. [a.] Chester, WV 26034.

DIAMANTINE, PAUL KENNETH
[b.] February 14, 1971, Hayward, California; [p.] Valerie and George and Christine Diamantine; [ed.] San Leandro High, San Jose State; [occ.] Advertising Student (SJSU); [memb.] Alumni of Pi Kappa Alpha; [hon.] Semi-finalist in 1993 North American Open Poetry Contest; [oth. writ.] First ever poetic contest;

[pers.] Live to laugh, laugh to live. Only the strong survive . I'm interested in collaborating with talented musicians. [a.] Fremont, CA 94555.

DICKENS, BETTY NEFF
[pen.] Betty Neff Dickens; [b.] June 30, 1911,, Pittsburgh; [p.] Richard and May Thomas Neff; [m.] Gordon J., January 1, 1943; [ed.] BA-University of Pittsburgh in English, English Studies, Allegheny College (Meadville, PA); [occ.] Writer of Verse, Articles; [memb.] Pen Woman since 1940, Alpha Delta Pi Sorority, Pittsburgh Poetry Society, Founder of Vero Pen Women; [hon.] 1980 First place in Poetry for Federated Women's Clubs of FL., Golden Poet Award, World of Poetry June 1992; [oth. writ.] Feature writer Pgh Press, Miami Herald, Indian River Life Magazine. Book of poems "Voice on the Southwind", 1980 by University Press, Miami, FL; [pers.] My poetry is about a sense of times, where we are in universal time! Human and animal life struggling for rhythmic adjustment to seasons, tides, day and night. [a.] Vero Beach, FL 32966.

DICKINSON, BOBBIE
[pen.] Bobbie Dickinson; [b.] November 23, 1931, Girard, Kansas; [p.] Willard and Lois Swart; [m.] Samuel, April 8, 1990; [ch.] Dennis James and Michael Allan Gallinetti; [ed.] Girard High; [occ.] Homemaker, Receptionist; [memb.] Christian church (Girard, KS); [hon.] Girls State, Honor Roll, Homecoming Queen, Employment Service Award, Employee of the Month; [oth. writ.] Several poems published in local newsletters; [pers.] I love to express myself through my poetry. It is very satisfying for me. [a.] San Ramon, CA 94583.

DILE, THOMAS A.
[b.] February 15, 1956, Coshocton, Ohio; [p.] James E. and Shirley Dile; [m.] Barbara S., June 26, 1993; [ed.] River View High School; [occ.] U.S. Army; [memb.] Veterans of Foreign Wars, National Rifle Association; [oth. writ.] Over 250 other unpublished poems; [pers.] Most of my poems are based on personal experiences and feelings over the past twenty-two years. [a.] Conesville, OH 43811.

DINGLE, SHARON M.
[b.] November 30, 1945, Yarmouth, Nova Scotia; [p.] Archie and Doris Mitchell; [m.] William E., December 12, 1964; [ch.] Christopher Lee and Diana Lyon; [ed.] Hants East Rural High; [memb.] United Church of Canada, Canadian Sport Horse, Past member Maritime Arabian Horse Association; [hon.] Have worked on Heart and Cancer Associations, also have been active with Boy Scouts, minor ball, and an elder with United Church for several years. Spent a few years working on the Canadian Pony Club, and other Horse Committees; [oth. writ.] Have written many poems, never had one published, but maybe someday, will have my own book of poetry; [pers.] I usually write when I feel down or grieving, it is a way of letting out my feelings, and somehow it only enlightens my mind. Have a great love of nature, trees and horses are my greatest loves in life. [a.] Hants County, Nova Scotia B0N 2H0.

DIXON, KRISTON J.
[b.] December 17, 1982, Atlanta, Georgia; [p.] Carolyn Sessoms Dixon; [ed.] Currently in 4th grade at E.C. West Elementary School in Fairburn, GA; [occ.] Student; [memb.] Girl Scouts, member of

Children's Choir at Bethel United Methodist Church; [hon.] Won Fulton County Young Writer's award at age six for a short story, "Prince of the Woods". In the Talented and Gifted program in Fulton County; [oth. writ.] "Princess of the Woods" several other unpublished short stories and poems; [pers.] I would one day like to earn a living as a writer. I like to sing and play the piano also, I recently wrote my first piece of music. [a.] Atlanta, GA.

DIXON, MARK
[b.] December 9, 1970, Rochester, New York; [p.] Judith and John Dixson; [ch.] brothers-Derek and Patrick; [ed.] Victor High School, Morrisville College and Potsdame College. [a.] Macedon, NY 14502.

DODD, TANYA (HOUNSHELL)
[pen.] Sissy; [b.] April 9, 1960, Baltimore, Maryland; [p.] Barbara L. Gray and Duconze Hounshell; [ch.] Dwight D. Dodd, Jr (9); [ed.] Walbrook Senior High, Community College of Baltimore, Medix School-Towson, MD; [occ.] Medical Office Manager; [memb.] American Society of Phlebotomy Sciences; [hon.] English Honor Society, Walbrook High School Alumnnia; [oth. writ.] Several poems written for local church and other social organizations; [pers.] My goals are to express nationally words of Art to make the reader think deeply and open their minds to new expressions of word Art. [a.] Baltimore, MD 21216.

DOLES, EFFIE
[b.] July 1, 1936, Corinth, Mississippi; [p.] Columbus Criner Counts and Vearl Counts; [m.] Billy Gene, July 25, 1951; [ch.] Stephen Marcus Doles; [ed.] 12th grade; [occ.] Seamstress in a garment factory; [pers.] I wrote my first poem at the age of eleven, I love gospel music and occasionally sing solos at church. [a.] Corinth, MS 38834.

DOMONDON, SERGIO N.
[b.] June 10, 1934, Philippines; [p.] Mr. and Mrs. John B. Domondon; [m.] Rose, June 18, 1960; [ch.] Maria Christina, Laura Domondon Lee, Liana Marie; [ed.] BS-Zoology at University of the Philippines, MS-System Management-University of South California (USC), MPA-Golden Gate University, San Francisco, CA; [occ.] Management Analyst for the Commander-in-Chief, U.S. Pacific Fleet (Pearl Harbor, HI); [oth. writ.] A collection of Haiku Poems - (currently unpublished); [pers.] "Touch others in a special way to make them more caring...For in caring, there is love!" [a.] Pearl City, HI 96782.

DONOVAN, SUSAN
[b.] November 14, 1961, Brooklyn, New York; [p.] Fay and Tony Ruggiero - three brothers and two sisters; [m.] James, April 16, 1982; [ch.] Janine (9) "My Beauty - My Life"; [ed.] Tilden High School, Wilfred Academy Beauty School-licensed hairdresser - student in creative writing course - presently learning American Sign Language; [occ.] Owner-retailing business - woman's accessories; [memb.] American Cancer Society "The living Bank "-sign donor. Registry for Interpreters of the Deaf (RID) member; [hon.] Received letter from President Bush after "Gulf War" - a thank you for poem I'd written about the USA called "Taken for Granted". I am very proud of this; [oth. writ.] Have in my possession over 100 poems I've written, am looking forward to having my book published soon; [pers.] I write about life and what is going on in our world today. I am touched by

so many things others can't see or feel. [a.] West Sayville, NY 11796.

DOOLEY, CAROLYN LOTT

[pen.] Judy Lane; [b.] May 20, 1953, Russellville, Alabama; [p.] Carl Dester Lott (deceased) and Lois Virginia Watson Lott; [m.] Phillip Dale Dooley, Sr., September 19, 1969; [ch.] Phillip Jr., Karen, Carmen and Rodney; [ed.] Parchment Adulted K.V.C.C. College; [occ.] Medical Transcriptionist; [oth.] Four-class Honor Roll for entire adulted classes attended; [oth. writ.] (none published) Reflections From My Imagination and Fatal Obsession stories and a few poems; [pers.] Adult Education gives people a second chance to reach their goals. Creative writing courses brings out your hidden assets. [a.] Kalamazoo, MI 49004.

DORNHEIM, ARTHUR R.

[b.] March 12, 1921, New York, New York; [p.] Gustar A. and Lillian R. Dornheim; [m.] Charleen Egan, July 5, 1952; [ch.] Michael Arthur and Daniel Egan; [ed.] Yale BA 1942, Columbia MA 1948; [occ.] Retired Foreign Service Officer; [memb.] DACOR (Diplomatic and Consular Officers Retired), American Foreign Service Association. [a.] Bethesda, MD 20814.

DOUGHERTY, PAULINE

[b.] February 16, 1912, Carrollton, Kentucky; [p.] Mr. and Mrs. Harry Supplee; [m.] Fred, June 18, 1932; [ch.] Polly June, Jimmy Lotty, and Geneva Ruthetta; [ed.] Carroll County High School; [occ.] Housewife; [memb.] Bedford United Methodist Church, United Methodist Women, Loyal Service Class; [pers.] The love of the Lord in my heart has inspired me in my writing. [a.] Bedford, KY 40006.

DOYLE, JENNIFER ANN

[pen.] Jen; [b.] April 13, 1977, Santa Rosa, California; [p.] Linda Doyle; [ed.] Ninth grade; [occ.] Student; [hon.] 4-H; [oth. writ.] Poetry and short stories; [pers.] I live in Kodiak, Alaska with my mom. We live in a wonderful place with eagles, deers, whales, foxes, etc. [a.] Chiniak, AK 99615.

DOZIER, FRANCES K.

[pen.] Pat Dozier; [b.] August 16, 1921, Newport, New Hampshire; [p.] William and Elizabeth McGranahan Kennedy; [m.] James Walton, February 26, 1946; [ch.] Twin daughters - 43 years living in Atlanta; [ed.] High School - 2 years College (UNH); [occ.] Worked 44 years - New Eng. Tel. & Tel., Insurance Agent, 19 years Accountant; [memb.] Macon County PTA, Friends of Library Sumter Players, Writers Group, Music Club, Concert Series; [hon.] Original Peanut Brigader for President J. Carter, former Mayor of Montezuma (First Female); [oth. writ.] Poems - Prose; [pers.] Music and poetry are the extra fulfillments for extraordinary pleasure they explain life. [a.] Montezuma, GA 31063.

DRAKE, HAROLD

[pen.] Bard of Kennebec; [b.] January 29, 1906, Wilkes-Barre, Pennsylvania; [p.] Elwood R. Drake; [m.] Catherine White; [ed.] Graduate of Girard College (Philadelphia, PA); [occ.] Old bookkeepers never die and they just lose their balance. [memb.] Life Member Maine Society of Poetry - Life member Veterans of Foreign; [hon.] Wars post 9223 Arlington, CA; [oth. writ.] Too many to attempt to enumerate as I have written poems from Maine to California

"Twilight Love" day first; [pers.] Poem was publisher in the first edition and second printing of Maine poets and their poems. In Richmond, VA I volunteered as a "Volunteer Officer candidate and when WWII ended I was on the island of I.E. Shima where Ernie Pyle was killed, I saw grave between a PFC and a Private - now I understand he is on the Island of Oalia near Schofield Barracks. Also, I liked to the command post when Lt. General Buckner was killed or Okinawa, I was promoted to Captain by General Thomas and awarded a Bronze star for bravery under fire. At Gerard College Colonel Robert M. Brvakfield took the officers of the Band and Battalion (I was a Lieutenant) to West Point for a day trip.

DRAKE, SALYNA

[b.] February 18, 1978, Los Alomitos, California; [p.] Sharon Ries and Harold Drake; [ed.] Diamond Bar High School; [occ.] 9th grade student; [hon.] President's Academic Achievement Award, 1992; [oth. writ.] Many poems not yet published. My poems deal with real life feelings and situations; [pers.] It takes effort to be successful. [a.] Diamond Bar, CA 91765.

DREHER, CORA

[b.] May 13, 1917, Grace City, North Dakota; [p.] Laura and George Stedman; [m.] Raymond, November 26, 1938 (deceased); [ch.] One son, Merle Allen, his wife Jackie and children-Sheila, Kay, Jill, Justin; [ed.] High School; [occ.] Housewife; [memb.] St. Paul's United Methodist Church Hospital Auxiliary, Christian Women's Club; [hon.] I won best actress award in play about 1939-40; [oth. writ.] Have none except my book of poetry, lyrics with a lift. [a.] Jamestown, ND 58401.

DREHNER, JOHN L., JR.

[b.] May 8, 1938, Coronoda, California; [p.] John J. Drehner and Louise Drehner Bartole; [ed.] Coronoda High School, California Western University, Chaffey Junior College, San Diego State College; [occ.] Retired U.S. Postal Service Employee; [memb.] United States Tennis Association, National Cat Protection Society, International Save the Pun Foundation; [hon.] Dean's List; [pers.] Man is the only animal that blushes- or needs to (Mark Twain). Despite my agreement with this statement, I have a romantic temperament, albeit colored with tinctures of pessimism. [a.] San Diego, CA 92104.

DRISKELL, JAY W.

[b.] January 31, 1973, Chicago, Illinois; [p.] Jay and Flora Lynn; [ed.] Four years high school, one year undergrad; [occ.] I sell paint and hardware; [memb.] National Honor Society, Phi Beta Kappa; [hon.] Full scholarship to University of Illinois (Voluntarily returned); [oth. writ.] 161 poems, unpublished; [pers.] A writer is someone for whom writing is more difficult than it is for other people - Thomas Mann. [a.] Chicago, IL 60622.

DRUMM, GREG

[b.] August 19, 1978, Sharon, Connecticut; [p.] Timothy Drumm and Pam Powers; [ed.] Sharon Center School, Oliver Wolcott Regional Vocational Technical School; [pers.] There is no peace...Only Annihilation. [a.] Sharon, CT 06069.

DUGGER, ANITA

[pen.] 85 years old; [b.] February 14, 1908, Adele, Iowa; [p.] Evona Robinson and Milo Freeland Salmon; [m.] Died 1981-Claud Dugger, 1927; [ch.] Don-65, Mildred-62, Dolores-54, Lyle-killed-1983, Carl-46; [ed.] High School; [occ.] Home Maker, Dairy Farmer-farmed in Oregon, ND, Washington; [memb.] Fed. Woman's Club, 4-H Leader, Writers Clubs, Grange, Autobon; [hon.] Income now, Social Security $512.00 that's all. Own my little home in the country. Am in good health after four-way-by-pass, 1989. another, 1991. Keep 9 chickens and have a garden. It would embarrass my four living children and 19 grandchildren and 6 great grand kids if I got published; [oth. writ.] Farm Magazine, articles, correspondence with Eleanor Roosevelt, still have her letter. William O. Douglas, State Governors, hosted people from Japan, exchange student from Japan, South America and Peru. I write lots of letters to editors and they get published.

DUKE, BILL R.

[pen.] John Luke; [b.] August 11, 1950, Anniston, Alabama; [p.] Marshall B. and Ethel V. Duke; [m.] Linda K., March 17, 1979; [ed.] Saks High, Troy State University, presently working on Masters in Computer Science; [occ.] Computer Scientist; [hon.] Cum laude; [oth. writ.] Collection of many poems...none published; [pers.] I strive to write my world of reality. My best poems come from what I'm seen or experienced... [a.] Valparaiso, FL 32580.

DUMMITT, RICKY

[b.] October 3, 1968, Portsmouth, Ohio; [b.] Grover Dummitt and Margene Witten; [m.] Lisa, July 15, 1988; [ch.] Samantha (3), Dillon (5); [ed.] High School; [occ.] Construction worker; [memb.] Veterans of Foreign Wars, Defenders of Wild Life; [hon.] George Washington Metal of Honor presented by Freedoms Foundation at Valley Forge; [oth. writ.] Several other poems one of which was published in a local newspaper; [pers.] My poetry has been inspired mainly by being away from loved one during Operation Desert Storm. [a.] Garrison, KY 41141.

DUNAWAY, LORA

[pen.] Topsy; [b.] September 17, 1912, Wesson, Mississippi; [p.] Jessie T. and Lillie Mitchel Granberry; [m.] W. Leon Dunaway (deceased), February 25, 1932; [ch.] Jerry Walter, Jessie Mitchell (deceased); [ed.] 12th grade-McComb High School; [occ.] Retired from Retail Business; [memb.] Veterans of Foreign Wars, Locust Saint Baptist Church; [hon.] Golden Poet 1991 (World of Poetry) New York city, four wards of merit certificates - trophy; [occ.] Special church occasions in bulletin; [pers.] I write for pleasure and about friends and loved ones. My writings reflect my feelings for those people and things I write about. The loved poetry since early school years. [a.] McComb, MS 39648.

DUNDASS, MURIEL E.

[pen.] Muriel E. Dundass; [b.] June 14, 1921, St. Andrews East, Quebec, Canada; [p.] Edith A. Neve and Conrad Say; [m.] Dr. Charles Howard Dundass, June 5, 1943; [ch.] Judith Dale, Bruce C.H., Barbara M.E.; [ed.] High School, Secretarial Course, Art Courses; [occ.] Artist (landscapes, flowers in acrylics, oils and watercolors); [memb.] Women's Art Groups; [oth. writ.] I've written a lot of poems and have never tried to have them published, this is my first time; [pers.] I write poetry to impart all things beautiful close to my heart life <u>can be</u> beautiful. [a.] Magos, Quebec, Canada.

DUNLOP, LOIS JEAN
[pen.] Lois Jean Celani; [b.] April 18, 1956, North Kingstown, RI; [p.] Rocco Celani (father) and Jean McKinley (mother); [ch.] Michael James, Mark Anthony and Barry Alan; [occ.] Homemaker and aspiring singer/songwriter; [memb.] Member of VFW Ladies; [hon.] To be recognized in this book as a true artist.; [oth. writ.] Two songs entitled, "Hundreds and Thousands of Men," and "When He Goes Back On the Road," - copyright Library of Congress 1988; plus other poems and lyrics; [pers.] I am honored to share my poem to all who may enjoy it! Poems are beautiful songs with or without melodies.; [a.] Danvers, MA.

DUNNING, JANET
[b.] September 11, 1954; [p.] Ernestine and James A. Dunning; [ch.] Derrick L. Rodgers and Amantha S. Dunning; [ed.] Twin Rivers High School, Three Rivers Community College; [occ.] Homemakers, Farmer, Registered Nurse; [memb.] Oglesville General Baptist Church; [hon.] Dean's List, Twin Rivers High School, Honors list Three Rivers College; [oth. writ.] Several poems, written for my own pleasure; [pers.] From our own dreams, each of us create our own reality. [a.] Poplar Bluff, MO 63901.

DUNSTON, LOLA DE PAOLA
[b.] December 11, 1922, Rome, Italy; [m.] Dr. Th. J. Dunson, October 24, 1953 [ch.] 2; [ed.] Diploma in Medical Technology, art school in Rome and London, Heatherly School of Art; [occ.] Artist, writer and composer; [memb.] The Academy of S. Nicola of Greece, Club Artistico Rome of the Association Des Beaux Arts Cannes, the Society of Graphic Artists London also member of the Greater London Art Association and the South Eastern Federation of Art Societies, Accademie International de Lutece Paris; [hon.] The World Who's Who of Women 1980, International Directory of Who's Who of Intellectuals Cambridge England 1978-1981, International Register of Profiles 1983, International Book of Honour, American Biogr. Inst. 1987, The Dictionary of SA Painters and Sculptors 1988 and The National Library of Poetry U.S.A.; [oth. writ.] 1973 Far Faraway (poetry), 1975, Young Pretoria (Historical), 1977, Yonder (poetry), 1980, Echoes (poetry) and 1993, Events Have Tears (historical novel); [a.] Voelklip, South Africa.

DUQUETTE, SHELLY ANNE
[b.] February 1, 1966, Stockton, California; [p.] Sue Hellwig and Jerry Person; [m.] Edwund, November 7, 1992; [ed.] Bret Harte High School; [occ.] Office Manager - Floor Coverings; [oth. writ.] Poem-Gathered Thoughts, books-All My Tomorrows; [pers.] I want people to feel my words and to provoke thought when they have finished reading. [a.] Avery, CA 95224.

D'URZO, DOMINIC
[b.] April 18, 1948; [p.] Jerry and Antonietta; [m.] Millie; [ch.] Michael and Jerry; [ed.] MA in Psychology; [occ.] Certified Psychotherapist Marriage and Family Therapist, Teacher; [memb.] International Association Behavioral Medicine and Psychotherapy; [oth. writ.] Speaker at numerous conferences, articles

in newspapers, radio and television appearances. [a.] Thornhill, Ontario, Canada L4J 7J3.

DYER, ELIZABETH
[b.] November 25, 1952, Nashville, Tennessee; [ed.] Belmont University; [occ.] Trainer-Human Resource Development and Dressage Training for Horse and Rides; [memb.] Junior League of Long Island; [hon.] Williams-Murray Writing Award; [oth. writ.] Articles, poems, cartoons found in <u>Shorelines</u> (LI, NY); [pers.] Hoping to promote equality and diversity for peaceful coexistence in a world that belongs to all. [a.] Franklin, TN 37064.

EASLER, MELANIE
[b.] September 16, 1978, Jackson, Michigan; [p.] Brenda and Steven Easler; [ed.] Linden Middle School, 8th grade; [occ.] Student; [memb.] 4-H Horsemanship; [hon.] Michigan State Board of Education for Science, M.E.A.P., Soccer player of the year, two basketball awards 7th grade and 8th grade; [pers.] I'm very busy all of the time through athletics and school but I always find time to write. [a.] Fenton, MI 48430.

EAST, BONNIE LEE
[pen.] Bonnie East; [m.] March 4, 1926, Briggsville, Arkansas; [p.] Grady Bruce and Ocie Wihunt Montgomery; [m.] Edwin L. (deceased), December 4, 1944; [ch.] Bruce W. East Winn Williams, Kathy Travis, and Paul East; [ed.] Hot Springs High School, one semester in Bible College, medical training; [occ.] Retired medical transcriptionist III - 18 years; [memb.] Medical Secretary Association, Arkansas Rehabilitation Services, AARP; [hon.] None except to be married 45 years to one man, have four children, and seven grandchildren, all Christians. <u>Real</u> Christians. I play the piano in my Church; [oth. writ.] Many poems and letters to my friends, and my family thought all were special; all for my own joy or to bless others. One other poem in local newspaper; [pers.] I am blessed with warm and loving Christian parents and family. Only my sister and I are living to pass on our heritage to others. [a.] Hot Springs, AR.

EATON, SADIE S.
[b.] July 12, 1914, Sheridan, Texas; [p.] Madison and Laura Selph; [m.] Tom Eaton, February 22, 1936; [ed.] 6th grade; [occ.] Retired. [a.] Columbus, TX 78934.

EBERLEY, JANICE L.
[pen.] Janice Hebert Eberley; [b.] June 9, 1942, Grand Forks, North Dakota; [p.] Louis and Ruby Hebert; [m.] Ronald N., May 10, 1992; [ch.] Frank Edward, Timothy Alan, and Donald Louis Whitney; [ed.] Gonzaga University (Spokane); Eastern Washington University (Spokane), St. Leo High School (Tacoma); [occ.] Chaplain, Providence Medical Center (Seattle, WA); [memb.] National Association of Catholic Chaplains, Greater Seattle Chaplains Association, Westside Hospice Chaplains, St. Bernadette Catholic Church, Third Order of St. Francis, Secular; [oth. writ.] Other religious poetry, newsletter articles and spiritual meditation; [pers.] My writings attempt to express my deep inward spiritual journey. Much of my writings are a form of prayer and meditation. They attempt to find God and the profound meaning of life. [a.] Seattle, WA 98126.

ECHOLS, MONROE MELVIN
[pen.] Monroe Melvin Echols; [b.] April 9, 1920,

Dallas, Texas; [p.] Monroe M. and Alta Susan Echols; [m.] Dorie Mae, July 18, 1942; [ch.] Melvin and Stephen M. Echols; [ed.] BBA - SMU - Dallas; [occ.] Retired; [memb.] Mason-32nd Mason Degree Mason, President - Lions Club, President Rods Club; [hon.] Captain - Military Int. WWII; [oth. writ.] Ballad of Ft. Phantom Hill, thirty plus poems; [pers.] Live and let live. [a.] Dallas, TX 75229.

EDDS, BRANDI
[b.] October 14, 1983, Louisville, Kentucky; [p.] Penny and John Morrison, Sr. (stepfather) and William Edds, Jr. (father); [ed.] Multi-age classroom; [occ.] Hobbies-Dance, writing, and study of animals; [memb.] Kid's Club, Foxfire Classroom; [hon.] Advanced Placement Writing class, Foxfire Showcase, Presenter for Foxfire Educators, Collaborative made quilt displayed in front hall of school; [oth. writ.] Rewrote Snow White and performed in it (collaborative experience), writes for school newsletter. A book being published "Cross-stitching Generations Together", class-student made books; [pers.] Special thanks to my 2nd and 3rd grade teacher, Mona Jones, for encouraging me to write. [a.] Louisville, KY 40216.

EDMISTON, JEAN
[pen.] Helen Robertson; [b.] August 9, 1913, Southport, Lancashire, England; [p.] Dorothy and John Edmiston; [ed.] Liverpool College Hayton, University College of London; [occ.] University Assistant, now retired for many years; [memb.] Fellow of the Linnean Society of London; [oth. writ.] The Twilight Zone (poems), four detective novels under Helen Robertson (pseudonym), two- The Crystal Gazers and Swan Song published also in America. One novel under my own name, several scientific papers; [pers.] I think I am a humanist, interested in the chemistry of plant colors. [a.] Bishop Stortford, Herts. CM23 3SH England.

EDMUNDS, MARTHA A.
[pen.] Martha A. Edmunds; [b.] March 23, 1911, Boston, Massachusetts; [p.] Lillian and Albert Thorley; [m.] Melville C. Walker (deceased), October 19, 1935; [ch.] Lee Harmon and Bruce Harrison Walker; [ed.] High School, Lasell College; [occ.] Legal Assistant and Medical Secretary and Executive Secretary; [memb.] American Legion Auxiliary, Federated Church of Hyannis R.S.V.P. So. Dennis, MA; [hon.] Poetry 1975, 1988, 1992; [oth. writ.] Editor of In House Newsletters for: Dennis Housing Authority, Station WOMR - Provincetown, MA; [pers.] Life is a constant amazing challenge. [a.] So, Dennis, MA 02660.

EDWARDS, JOSEPH T., JR.
[b.] October 18, 1921,, Petersburg, Virginia; [p.] Joseph T. and Laura Butler Edwards, Sr.; [m.] Divorced; [ch.] Sheryl, Linda Kennon; [ed.] Petersburg High; [occ.] Retired; [memb.] Monumental Baptist; [pers.] I have written many poems mostly containing thoughts of love, happiness and a peace loving world. [a.] Richmond, VA 23237-3214.

EDWARDS, VIRGINIA
[pen.] Kawana Walker; [b.] December 12, 1950, Yazoo City, Mississippi; [p.] John and Jessie Walker; [ch.] George Walker, Andrea, Angela, Alex McNeil; [ed.] N.D. Taylor High School, Alcorn State University and Jackson State University; [occ.] Math Teacher,

Scammon Elementary School (Chicago, IL); [memb.] First Baptist Church; [pers.] First and far most, a strong belief in God, confidence in yourself. Last but not least, patience and perspectance. [a.] Chicago, IL 60644.

EIDSNESS, LINDA
[b.] May 6, 1948, Portland, Oregon; [p.] Juanita Mitchell; [m.] Norman, August 28, 1994; [ch.] Paula Bradley, Shelly Anderson, Troy Eidsness; [ed.] Grant High, College of Beauty, Evertt Community College (since '85, AAM '87, I still go every other term; [occ.] Hair Stylist/Photographer; [memb.] AA; [hon.] Photos printed in Photographers Forum '87, '88, '91, and '92; Monroe Fair 7 Blue Ribbons, Who's Who in Photo '91-'92; The Fire Boys Evertt, WA 100 years, '66-'86 Grant High's 20 year Reunion, '88 Vibrations from Evertt Community College; [oth. writ.] My first time I have ever shared my writing I have dyslexia and I didn't think anyone would accept me; [pers.] Happiness comes from doing the right thing. [a.] Evertt, WA 98201.

ELDRIDGE, KIMBERLY DIANE
[b.] February 5, 1977, Big Stone Gap, Virginia; [p.] Bob and Karen Eldridge; [ed.] Powell Valley High School; [pers.] I try to write of the beauty of life and what I am feeling at that very moment. [a.] Big Stone Gap, VA 24219.

ELLIOTT, BUFFY LEANN
[b.] April 16, 1982, Boone, North Carolina; [p.] Tammy and Gary Elliott; [ed.] Elementary School so far; [memb.] Softball and basketball also play piano; [hon.] 60 yard dash since kindergarten. I reflect attendance 5th grade Certificate of Award for Outstanding Citizen for 6 years at West Jefferson School, Terrific Kids Award 2 years, Beaver Creek basketball Camp '91 - Attitude trophy; [oth. writ.] I wrote the poem in 5th grade 10 years old. I have red hair, bluish green, eyes, and glasses. I like sports a lot; [pers.] I won't to thank my Grandma Beatrice Spencer for everything. I want to thank you my good friend Eric Houck, also my parents. [a.] West Jefferson, NC 28694.

ELLIS, JANE C.
[b.] January 28, 1926, Milwaukee, Wisconsin; [p.] Valeska and Bernard Parys; [m.] Donald A., June 25, 1949; [ch.] Steven, Joan, Barbara, James Richard, John, Patricia; [ed.] North Division High School-courses at Mt. Mary College and Waukesha County Technical College; [occ.] (Retired) Assistant to the President, Medical College of Wisconsin; [memb.] Wisconsin Regional Writers Association, Friends of the Medical College of Wisconsin; [oth. writ.] Several Opinions in major local newspaper, article in Death Studies, 10:297-300, 196; [pers.] I believe a long life is a priceless gift, experience is the best teacher, and the fruit of life experiences should be shared from a positive perspective. [a.] New Berlin, WI 53151.

ELLIS, TERESA
[b.] August 29, 1964, Allegan, Michigan; [p.] Richard and Donna Miller; [m.] Jeff Ellis, August 31, 1985; [ed.] Hopkins High, DeVry Institute of Technology (Dallas, TX); [occ.] Factory/Hobby Farmer as one pursue my writing career; [hon.] Dean's List; [oth. writ.] Currently writing a romance/mystery novel; [pers.] My writing is inspired by the heart. The good and the bad in human relationships. [a.] Irma, WI

ELSASS, ADAM T.
[pen.] Adam T. Elsass; [b.] September 5, 1979, Defiance, Ohio; [p.] Marvin and Judy Elsass; [ed.] Just completing 7th grade this year at Wapakoneta Middle School; [occ.] Student and helping my dad farm; [memb.] Happy Herdsman, 4-H Club - Optimist Soccer Team, Member of St. Marks Lutheran Church, Clay Twp.; [pers.] Written for a poetry assignment in 6th grade English class. "Fawn" is one of our cows on our dairy farm. [a.] Wapakoneta, OH 45895.

EMERSON, MAE V.
[b.] October 13, 1920, Greenfield, Massachusetts; [p.] Louis N. and Margaret Sears; [m.] Paul R., February 14, 1946; [ch.] Margaret L., Gary D., Robert C. Emerson; [ed.] Springfield Technical High School; [occ.] Retired Cook-manager at Cummington School Cafeteria; [memb.] Village Church Cummington; [oth. writ.] A few poems or rhymes on various subjects; [pers.] To put into poetry form everyday thoughts, feelings, or happenings; [a.] Cummington, MA 01026.

EMMENS, TOM
[b.] January 6, 1951, Salisbury, England; [p.] Alan George and Patricia Hooder; [ch.] Patricia Laura, Marsha Paige; [occ.] Musician; [pers.] The poets soul is in us all. [a.] Sherwood Park, Alberta Canada T8C 1H9.

EMMERT, JAMES
[b.] March 6, 1974, New London, Connecticut; [p.] Mildred and James L. Emmert; [ed.] San Marcos Academy, Sophomore at North Georgia College; [occ.] Full-time student and in the Army ROTC program; [pers.] My writing is influenced by my dreams. We sleep in the safety of darkness colored only with a rainbow of dreams. They are by far more real than reality and are the purest most innocent honesty. [a.] Kingwood, TX 77345.

ENDICOTT, MARIE F.
[b.] August 10, 1916, St. Louis, Missouri; [p.] Harry F. and Flora K. (Asmussen) Williams; [m.] Ralph A., June 19, 1937; [ch.] Elaine S. (Endicott) Heine and Francine M. Endicott Armstrong; [ed.] Oak Hill School - graduated 1/1930, Cleveland High School-graduated 6/1933; [occ.] 35 years Executive Secretary to Lawyers, Engineers & Company Presidents;, Executive Secretary (Legal, Medical, Technical), Former Volunteer Girl Scout Leader & Red Cross First Aid Instructor; [memb.] AARP Crestwood Chapter #2913-St. Louis, MO, Sodality of the Immaculate Conception; [hon.] 17 year Member of Girl Scouts, past Pres. Sodality of the Immaculate Conception Sodality; [oth. writ.] Over the years I have written poems primarily for Christmas, Thanksgiving, Weddings, Anniversaries, Graduations and my Marriage poem was published in "Bridges Magazine"; [pers.] Most of my poems were inspired by faith in God and the positive aspects of human relationships. [a.] St. Louis, MO 63123.

ENEVOLDSEN, AMY
[b.] December 25, 1976, Iowa; [p.] Robert and Terri Enevoldsen; [ed.] Sophomore at Humble High School 1992-93; [occ.] Student; [memb.] 4H (Shooting Division), National Honor Society, Girl Scouts, Future Problem Solving; [hon.] NRA Awards, various academic awards, Girl Scouts Silver award; [oth. writ.]

none published; [pers.] I feel that the best kind of writer is one who can put themselves in other people's shoes, and write realistically from that point of view. [a.] Humble, TX 77396.

ENGLAND, ANDREA M.
[b.] March 13, 1971, Halifax, Nova Scotia, Canada; [p.] Herman and Shirley England; [ed.] Guysborough Municipal High School, Universite de Moncton, St. Francis Xavier University; [occ.] Student; [memb.] St. Francis Xavier University, English Society, Canadian Crossroads International; [oth. writ.] I have never sought to publish any of my work up until now, however. I keep a journal and am presently working on my first novel; [pers.] I think that an artist must strive to accurately reflect her society; to do so, she must know both here and there, now and then, you and I. She is, ideally, a master of perspectives. [a.] Sand Point, Nova Scotia Canada B0E 2G0.

ENGLAND, PERRY W.
[pen.] Pierre Michelle; [b.] October 23, 1920, Davis Park Road, Gastonia, North Carolina; [p.] Broadus Henry and Bertie Wilma McAllister England; [m.] Beatrice Froneberger (deceased), December 20, 1945; [ch.] Michael Francis; [ed.] Victory Elementary (Gastonia), Lowell High School (now Holbrook), Newberry College (SC), High Point University (NC-BS), Duke University; [occ.] Naval Intelligence, Psychologist Old U.S. HEW, Athletic Dir. and Latin tutor, Private School, Civil Engineer (Assoc. Degree),, Educator Private School; [memb.] Executive Board RCLC, Charter and U.S. Naval Institute Honorary Life Member Rep. Pres. Task Force, P4F Life Member Post 23, NC American Legion, Gastonia Little Theatre, Gastonia Fine Arts, Gastonia Concert Association, Poetry Academy, St. Michael's Catholic Church, Ronald Reagan Presidential Foundation, Rep. National Hall of Honor by Presidential Commission, Thaleans Lit. Society, Drama Club, Charter Member Honorary Society, Gamma Sigma, YMCA, Newberry Players, Honorary National Rep. Senatorial Commission; [hon.] '92 Certificate of Recognition for Outstanding Service (Bronze name plaque), Rep. Presidential Task Force Wall of Honor, Signature and name on documents (National Rep. Presidential Center Archives), and Ronald Reagan Library (Permanent President pass for admission), special award, Pentagon Educational Center, Poetry Silver Award, 4 time Golden Poet, Chosen for special award trophies 5 times, Honorary Charter member T.S > P.; [oth. writ.] Published writings for newspapers, mags at 9 years), Responses, age 16, dramas and lyrics for music for drama high school and college, short plays for drama club presentations age 14 published by NY Times, Reader's Digest, Newsweek, AMA, NCE, TIME, Gastonia Gazette, Charlotte Observer News. Wrote, directed and presented play A Christmas Story to fullhouse N.O. Book of Short Story, Ms's, Ms's, edited final drafts for publications, 1 musical drama, three short plays, collection of short mysteries, novelettes for a book, two book length murder mysteries, short story collections book length collection poetry, (all lost before publishers saw them), novel: Road of No Return..; [pers.] I've never composed only written (when idea or topic persisted) till completed - whether poetry, philosophy, moral, other, often when something submitted, no revision, but as written. Early poetry often no title, no try to give appropriate

title. Now, title is the protagonist prior to sitting and writing nonstop till completed. I have always and do write from the hyper sheer pleasure to me and that I trust others have and do share my poetry (est. 25)) reflects kaleidoscopic view of life, all aspects; sonnets, odes, mystical, beauty and love. nature, sea, places and locals, dialects. Search for wisdom, knowledge, truth (taught by my parents in love of Arts, writing, music and nature). [a.] Gastonia, NC 28054.

ENGLAND, RACHAEL
[b.] June 7, 1973, Ann Arbor, Michigan; [p.] Barry England and Nancy Wood; [ed.] Graduate Pioneer High School; [pers.] Poetry is directed by a craving for chocolate. [a.] Ann Arbor, MI.

ENGLISH, ROBERT G.
[b.] August 12, 1945, Portland, Oregon; [p.] Mr. and Mrs. Samuel English; [ed.] Ignacio High (CO), two years Adams State College (Alamosa, CO); [occ.] Poet, author, photography; [memb.] World of Poetry, International Society of Poets; [hon.] Merit certificate, Simply A Mouser-Ebbtioe Rivers Crossing-Thoughts on Children-Golden Poet 1991 and 1992, Outstanding Achievement in Poetry by International Society of Poets; [oth. writ.] Books only yours-Susanna My Rose, Poetical Jest my Gestful World; [pers.] I wish my work to reflect a more visual world so a reaper may experience a travel to a new and wonderful place. [a.] Albuquerque, NM 87107.

ENGMANN, MICHELLE
[b.] February 12, 1949, Winslow, Arizona; [p.] Benjamin and Wilma Mileham; [m.] Gary W., December 11, 1971; [ch.] Nicholas Aaron, Antionette Patrice; [ed.] In process of obtaining masters degree for teacher education; [hon.] Article regarding Freedom published in August 19, 1963, Congressional Record, graduated high school in Top 10% of a class of 165 students; [oth. writ.] Several poems published in various anthologies; varied articles and poems printed in local publications; [pers.] This writing is dedicated to my husband, a vietnam veteran. Forever memorialized on the pages of my heart through his love, commitment and ever present character of heroism. [a.] Alpharetta, GA 30202.

ENNIS, BETHENIE
[b.] September 14, 1973; [p.] Julian and Grace Watkins Ennis; [ed.] Homewood High School.

ERVIN, NINA L.
[b.] March 11, 1937, Columbus, Ohio; [p.] Noah and Henrietta Karswer; [m.] David L., April 28, 1956; [ch.] Terry L. Seacrist, Cindy L. Ervin and Polly L. Thacker; [ed.] Hamilton Township High School; [hon.] Three grandchildren, one great grandchild (Brandy, Kelly, Ryand, Grant); [oth. writ.] A Children's Story, local neighborhood newspaper; [pers.] Always leave a place better for your being there. [a.] Grove City, OH 43123.

ERNSTBERGER, WILLIAM J. JR.
[pen.] Erik Dayton Sarke; [b.] May 25, 1940, Baltimore, Maryland; [p.] Jean Lee and William J. Ernstberger, Sr.; [m.] Joyce M., March 6, 1982; [ch.] Tim, Susan, Mark; [ed.] High School; [occ.] Secretary; [oth. writ.] One prose, two other short poems; [pers.] Jesus is Lord. [a.] Owings Mills, MD 21117.

ESTERLINE, LOIS
[b.] July 17, 1924; [m.] Harold, July 4, 1942; [ch.] Five; [occ.] Happy Homemaker; [oth. writ.] Mostly poetry-some-published in local newspaper. Write mostly as hobby or special request for special occasions; [pers.] I have always enjoyed the writings of Ben Boroughs and Helen Steiner Rice whose poetry had a message or hopeful outlook and I find what I write is similar in content, with glory to God for His blessings in my life. [a.] Millerstown, PA 17062.

ESTES, ANTHONY D.
[b.] January 28, 1969, Raleigh, North Carolina; [ed.] Needham B. Broughton High School (BA), University of North Carolina at Chapel Hill; [occ.] Computer Consultant; [memb.] North Carolina Poetry Society; [hon.] First prize Marie Barringer Rogers Young Poets Competition of the North Carolina Poetry; [oth. writ.] Essay: "One Last Beer for Old Times" in Pfeiffer College Review of Literature (1993); [pers.] I plan to teach high school after attending graduate school in Creative Writing or English. I also plan to coach football "I will teach frivolity and coach champions". [a.] Chapel Hill, NC 27514.

EUBANK, MARK D.
[b.] April 15, 1953, Somerset, Kentucky; [p.] Richard Z. and Eva C. Eubank; [m.] Gina D., December 23, 1971; [ch.] Nathan R. Eubank; [ed.] Eubank High, University of Kentucky (Somerset Community College); [occ.] Insurance Agent, Businessman (Small Business Owner); [memb.] NALU, Oak Grove Church of Christ, Eubank PTA; [hon.] National Honor Society, Dean's List; [oth. writ.] Several poems and short stories -unpublished; [pers.] God puts within us the seeds of great accomplishment, but we must water and cultivate them. [a.] Eubank, KY 42567.

EUGENE, KEMBA
[b.] April 24, 1982, Trinidad; [p.] Althea Ingrid and Ralph Earl Eugene; [ed.] P.S. 269 Elementary School; [occ.] Student; [oth. writ.] Short stories; [pers.] I love to write poetry. My goal in life to become a famous poet. I was encouraged to write poetry being my Aunt Allison, and by my favorite teacher Ms. Brown and Mrs. Mendonca. [a.] Brooklyn, NY 11226.

EVANS, DARICE RUE
[b.] November 19, 1968, Santa Maria, California; [p.] Inese and Reuben Evans; [ed.] San Diego State University. [a.] La Mesa, CA 91941.

EVANS, MARK
[b.] November 17, 1976, Valparaiso, Indiana; [p.] Richard and Cheryl Evans; [ed.] Jefferson County High School; [occ.] Student, 11th grade; [memb.] Environmental Club; [hon.] Wrestling Team Varsity Letter for past two years, President's Physical Fitness Award 1993; [oth. writ.] This is my first poem written - no other publications; [pers.]
After this poem was thought about and written, I was encouraged to write my feelings and thoughts in poetry form. I only hope I can touch other people's lives through my poetry. [a.] Dandridge, TN 37725.

EYRAUD, LINDA
[pen.] Linda Eyraud; [b.] July 22, 1940, Los Angeles, California; [p.] Spiritual Father, Bob Brackett and Spiritual mother Lorean Harbor; [m.] Robert, June 15, 1975; [ch.] Guy, Stephen, Scott, Shelly, Laura; [ed.] Dewey High School (Long Beach, CA); [occ.]

Homemaker; [memb.] Ryderwood Community Church; [oth. writ.] Other poems published in local papers; [pers.] God healing my life from child abuse, I try to reflect the very heart of His love toward man through Christ Jesus. [a.] Ryderwood, WA 98581.

EZRA, DANIELLE ROTHMAN
[b.] January 31, 1983, Los Angeles, California; [p.] Deborah Rothman and Eric Ezra; [ed.] Seeds University Elementary School; [occ.] I have my own business that sells food and has other facilities; [memb.] D.E.L.T.A. Animal Rescue, St. Judes Hospital, Animal Shelter, National Geographic; [hon.] National Geographic, Perfect Homework, best daughter and most beautiful and talented; [pers.] I'm ten years old and I'm so so happy to be having mu poem published. I love acting, sports, singing, dancing, swimming, math, art, discourse and writing. I am a talented excited person at U.E.S. I hope you enjoy my poem. [a.] Los Angeles, CA 90049.

FAIRCHILD, KELLY
[b.] January 18, 1979, North York General Hospital; [p.] Sharon Margaret and John Peter Fairchild; [ed.] Grade 8; [hon.] "Tom Gally" award for Soccer (Sportsmanship); [oth. writ.] Racism, Love, The Earth. Suicide, Drinking and Driving, Friends; [pers.] I write about my feelings and important things that really need to be noticed. [a.] Scarborough, Ontario, Canada M1T 2L9.

FALLS, BRIAN C.
[pen.] Brian C. Falls; [b.] March 4, 1976, Shelby, North Carolina; [p.] Herbert and Linda Falls; [ed.] Senior Blackburg High School; [occ.] Student/Video Clerk; [memb.] Buffalo Fire Department Explorers (Blackburg Junior Police), Future Teacher's, Teens Inspired. [a.] Blackburg, SC 29702.

FARMER, DOUGLAS
[b.] October 1, 1974, Ogdensburg, New York; [p.] Daniel and Gail Farmer; [ed.] Haverhill High, Merrimack College; [occ.] Student; [memb.] Merrimack Newspaper and Yearbook; [hon.] 5th in Mass. Voice of Democracy Contest, National Honor Society, Dean's List; [oth. writ.] Various articles in college newspaper and yearbook; [pers.] The world would be a much better place if everyone dropped the veil of insensitivity. [a.] Haverhill, MA 01835.

FARQUHARSON-MYERS, LAURA
[b.] Toronto, Ontario, Canada; [p.] John R. and Barbara (Armstrong) Farquharson; [m.] Alan J.; [occ.] Personal Computer Systems Analyst; [memb.] Leo's Hope, Caring Canadian Crafters for Charity, Junior Achievement; [oth. writ.] A letter to my father; [pers.] Praise the Lord for your many blessings by giving a helping hand to your brother/sister. Only through personal commitment can benevolent heights be achieved. [a.] Toronto, Ontario, Canada M4M 2M9.

FEEHAN, DEIRDRE
[b.] May 28, 1953, Hollywood, California; [p.] Joseph and Kathryn Beal Feenhan; [ed.] BA Immaculate Heart College; [occ.] Technical Writer; [memb.] Henry James Society; [hon.] BA Cum Laude; [oth. writ.] Biographies, Soreta Barbara Architecture, 1975. [a.] Tarzana, CA 91356.

FELIX, MARIE
[b.] November 30, 1968, Manila, Philippines; [p.] Jessie and Eleanor Felix; [pers.] An open mind is a very powerful tool and a person who possess' it has only infinite to limit her. [a.] Arleta, CA 91331.

FELTMAN, MARVEL L.
[pen.] Margo Lane; [b.] March 21, 1924, Onsted, Michigan; [p.] Ida L. Smith and Irving Ross Preston (poet); [m.] C.W. Feltman, March 23, 1968; [ch.] Laura, Doug, Priscilla (by former marriage); [ed.] Ninth grade and still going to school; [occ.] Owned an Adult Foster Care Home for 30 years; [memb.] Baptist Church; [hon.] Not many I did take up art and I love to paint barns; [oth. writ.] I have written a book about foster care, some day hope to get it published; [pers.] I am very hard worker and I enjoy music, painting, I like to make quilts, last year I made seven quilts for my family. I love to sew and I'll admit I can't type very good. [a.] Adrian, MI.

FENNELL, JONATHAN E.
[b.] June 24, 1948, Kittanning, Pennsylvania; [p.] Donald M. (deceased) and Rella F. Fennel; [ch.] Eric G.; [ed.] Indiana Area Senior High School, BS-Indiana University of Pennsylvania and MBA Southern Illinois University; [occ.] Supervisor of Systems Development Delmarva Power, Wilmington, DE; [hon.] Gamma Rho Tau, Beta Gamma Sigma. [a.] Newark, DE 19711.

FENNERS, BRENDA M.
[pen.] Ben; [b.] February 4, 1947, Paterson, New Jersey; [p.] William and Lorretia Jost (left me with grandparents) - adopted by Charlene and Alfred Fenners (aunt and uncle); [m.] DNA Divorced 6/2/79, June 2, 1968; [ch.] Daughter - Heather Mary 15 years old and is a pianist; [ed.] HS - Top half, 5 years college - BA in Interior Design and Theater Arts Minor Sociology; [occ.] Interior Designer and Interior Design Teacher and Theater Set Designer and Makeup Artist; [memb.] Metropolitan Museum of Art Interior Design Society Professional American Lithographers for short time; [hon.] Humane Award, 4 years won - cosmetic awards, Dermablend - for TV actors and actresses covering severe superficial problems show - Midtown and Howard Weise Gallery NYC Paintings swimming - trophies and archery-Atlantic Champ 66-69 School Honor Society; [oth. writ.] Short story - The House that Wanted Me, fiction a TV Story, The Lost Moment; [pers.] Never, forget your heritage learn from your mistakes, make goals work to achieve them and never let go of your dreams look for the good in others and you'll be rewarded. Don;t be greedy for anything you can't take it with you. [a.] Franklin Lakes, NJ 07417.

FERENCZY, SHIRLEY ANN
[pen.] Simply Samantha; [b.] January 30, 1941, Youngstown, Ohio; [p.] John and Mary Schneider; [m.] The Late Steve, June 2, 1962; [ch.] Steven J., Shawn J., and Anastacia J.; [ed.] South High School; [occ.] Day Care Teacher; [memb.] Christian Education Committee, Personnel Committee, Choir, Board Elder, Youngstown Academy of Ballet; [hon.] Voice of Democracy Speech Contest, Optimists Speech and Essay Contests; [oth. writ.] Several original poems: Sander's Hill, Gray Lady Down, Anastacia Still, Simply Samantha, Fonder's Stance; [pers.] Now that I am 52 and a widow, I am just now starting to live again through my poetry of years gone by. [a.]

Vienna, OH 44473.

FERGUSON, LEUNA PERRY
[b.] May 25, 1920, Manatee County, Florida; [p.] Clyde and Thelma Ogle Perry; [m.] Deceased; [ch.] Anita Lane Hutchison, Richard K. Lane; [ed.] Manatee County High School graduate 1938, Several short courses at Florida State Business College; [occ.] Insurance Agent Owner Fabric Store - Sales - Singer, Co.; [memb.] Library Club-Moose Club - Jr. Nomane Club - English Club; [oth. writ.] Unpublished have written short stories, never entered writing - read by family only - except Church Bulletins; [pers.] I have always written but for my own self and family - last 73 felt like others should share my feelings, for that is my poetry my feelings into words. [a.] Lk. Panadoffkee, FL 33538.

FETTEROLF, SHIRLEY H.
[b.] December 27, 1926, Johnstown, Pennsylvania; [p.] Jerome K. and Violet Hurl Hudson; [m.] Frank K., May 12, 1946; [ch.] Sharon Fetterolf Vak, Donald H. Fetterolf; [ed.] Graduate-Johnstown High School, Nurses Training West Penn Hospital, Pittsburgh, PA; [occ.] Homemaker; [memb.] Past President Memorial Hospital Junior Auxiliary; [hon.] Made Honorary Junior Member of Pennsylvania Academy of Science May 26, 1944 by the American Association for the Advancement of Science for Exceptional Ability and interest in science; [oth. writ.] Numerous poems. [a.] Johnstown, PA 15905-3329.

FIELDLER, KATHY L.
[b.] May 14, 1957, Allentown, Pennsylvania; [p.] Charles W. and Mary Lou Lutter; [m.] James J., December 15, 1979; [ch.] Kristen Leah and Meredith Kay (twins), Gregory Steven, and Andrew James; [ed.] North Penn High School, Lansdale, PA, Bloomsburg University (BS in Elementary), Kutztown University (MLS Library Science); [occ.] Middle School Librarian, Northwestern Lehigh School District; [memb.] Phi Delta Kappa, Church Council President Zion Lehigh Lutheran Congregation, Alburtis, PA; [hon.] Graduated with highest honors (summa cum laude) from both universities; [oth. writ.] All unpublished, currently at work on a novel for Young Adults; [pers.] I use my writing as a springboard for personal emotional growth, with each new piece I discover something I didn't know was there! [a.] Alburtis, PA 18011.

FIELDS, ARBOR D.
[b.] January 15, 1897, Sadievile, Kentucky; [p.] Bonnie and Escue Fields; [m.] Lena E., September 6, 1986; [ed.] BA and MA in Education both from O.S.U., four years in Army, was in WWI - 43 wounds; [occ.] Retired - taught both boys and girls for 15 years, Dayton Ohio High School; [memb.] D.A.V, Vet. of Foreign Wars, State Teachers Retirement, Military Order, Purple Heart, American Legion, Social Security; [hon.] Golden Poet Award, World of Poetry 1989 Sacramento, CA, I am totally disabled veteran of WWI. Have "Teacher of Merit" certificate hanging on walls. Have 43 wounds from combat in Battles of Soissons and Chateau Thievery, France. I'm 96 years of age. [oth. writ.] My book of poems published - "Reminiscence of An Old Combat Soldier of World War One, Carlton, Press, NY; [pers.] When I became 16 my mean stepfather took me out of school day after Thanksgiving in 7th grade. Had no high

school. Did not know what a H.S. looked like inside. However, I have BS and MA from OSU. [a.] Dayton, OH 45415.

FIELDS, HEIDI
[b.] April 7, 1979, Walla Walla, Washington; [p.] Tony and Nancy Fields; [occ.] Student; [memb.] National Wildlife Fund-First Assembly of God Church-Orchestra; [hon.] Honor Student; [oth. writ.] Best Friends and many other poems; [pers.] I enjoy reading and writing poetry. [a.] Spokane, WA 99207.

FIELDS, RUTH W.
[b.] August 29, 1921, Weogufka, Alabama; [p.] Rufus and Vida Ward; [m.] William Preston Fields (died 3/61), July 3, 1946; [ed.] Grad. Sylacauga High-AL, Pensacola Junior College - Art, all courses including pottery; [occ.] Retired/Employment Specialist, Florida State Employment Service (now known as Job Service of Florida); [memb.] Member Liberty Church, Northeast, a charismatic, full gospel church; [hon.] Best of Show award for a large Watercolor shown in Ft. Walaton Beach show - same show watercolor took first place - only time I've ever entered a judged show. Art is just a hobby; [oth. writ.] None ever sent any place often have poems come in to my mind. I jot them down sometimes put a tune to them; [pers.] I enjoy meeting new people and I treasure my friends - some I've kept in touch with since grade school - my 'Church family" is also special and I love sharing Jesus and his love with everyone when I can. [a.] Pensacola, FL 32534-0421.

FINCH, JOHN B.
[pen.] John Boyd Finch; [b.] April 2, 1907, Wilson, North Carolina; [p.] Benjamin Perry and Annis Elizabeth Finch; [m.] Anne Vivian, April 1, 1928; [ch.] John B. Finch, Jr. married Marie Spano and 2 grandsons Vincent and Stephen; [ed.] Southport High School (Southport, NC); [occ.] Retired 1971 after 31 years service E.A. Dupont; [memb.] World of Poetry, International Society of Poets; [hon.] Golden Poets award 1988-1989-1900-1992 with World of Poetry, and many awards of merit. Published in Who's Who in World of Poetry; [oth. writ.] 30 some gospel songs. Composed and arranged Anthem for 101 Anniversary celebration; [pers.] I had no idea that I would ever be called a poet. My sister in Southport, NC deserves all the credit - she believed in me. God bless Eunice Huntley. [a.] Penns Grove, NJ 08069.

FINCK, THERESA M.
[pen.] Theresa B. Toennemann; [b.] November 30, 1943, McAlester, Oklahoma; [p.] Mr. and Mrs. John Finck; [ed.] BM and MM - Tulsa University; [occ.] Teacher; [memb.] NEA, PEA, TCTA, MENC; [hon.] First runner up teacher of the year 1992, NEA Grant 1993 (only 7 teachers nationwide), 3rd place - Shakespeare Festival - 1991, 1st place Earthday '90-'92; [oth. writ.] Creating with words, May issue '93, Clouds are breaking - Library of Poetry -September '93, Two plays submitted to Little Theatre in Tulsa; [pers.] Recently, I became very interested in environmental and multi-culture issues. This is reflected in my writings. [a.] Tulsa, OK 74105.

FINA, TINA
[pen.] Tina Fina; [b.] February 17, 1961, Houston, Texas; [p.] Bill and Racine Watson; [ch.] Kristina and Amanda; [ed.] Mineral Wells High School,

Weatherforo College, LVN Nursing School, Jones Real Estate School, Insurance Agent School; [occ.] Insurance Agent, Poetry; [memb.] International Society of Poetry; [hon.] 1st poem published - Oh Dear Lord, 2nd poem published, My Dear Friend; [oth. writ.] Troubled Heart, Innocent Man, Lost of a Great Friendship, One of A Kind, My True Blessing, Longing, A Bad Affair, Return My Love, Without You My Darling, Bobby, Shall We Dance Dare to Care; [pers.] I strive to relate poetry with true life experiences and always include God in my poems. My inspirations are my daughters Kristina and Amanda and God. [a.] Mineral Wells, TX 76068-1127.

FIRKINS, LOIS ANN
[pen.] Lois A. Firkins; [b.] August 28, 1951, New Albany, Indiana; [p.] George and Juanita Dunn; [m.] Robert E.; [ch.] Jason, Valerie, Darrell and Wayne; [ed.] GED; [occ.] Domestic Engineer, painter, writer, and mother; [hon.] Several poems accepted for publication; [oth. writ.] Poetry - Believe, Feelings, Positive Mental Attitude; [pers.] I am inspired by family, friends, and Jesus. [a.] Jeffersonville, IN.

FISCHER, ASHTON JOHN JR.
[b.] November 24, 1952, New Orleans, Louisiana; [ed.] Tulane University, B.A. major in English; [hon.] Dean's List. [a.] New Orleans, LA 70118.

FISHER, AGNES
[pen.] On Sculpture-Senga; [b.] March 2, 1909, Dundee, Scotland; [p.] John and Agnes McJannet; [m.] Leonard, December 18, 1935; [ch.] Lenora Agnes, Robert John, Elizabeth Anne, Gordon Duncan; [ed.] Davidson High (Davidson Sask.), North Island College (B.C., Canada); [occ.] Retired; [memb.] Community Arts Council, North Island Clay Club; [hon.] First for sculpture in juried show at Madrona College, Nanimo, BC. First for painting at juried show at Prince Rupert, BC; [oth. writ.] Many poems in local papers, articles about the rain forest; [pers.] I live in the rain forest by the sea and I care very much about our environment. The sea and the big trees have inspired me. [a.] British Columbia, Canada V9W 2B9.

FISHER, DELORES
[b.] June 3, 1930, Philadelphia, Pennsylvania; [p.] Morris and Ann Wallace; [m.] Neal F., April 18, 1953; [ch.] Karen, Susan, Neal, Brian, William, David, Danial, Frederick; [ed.] West Philadelphia Catholic Girls High - St. Francis Hospital School of Nursing (Wilmington, DE); [occ.] Registered Nurse - retired; [hon.] Compassionate Friends, Knight of Columbus; [oth. writ.] Many other poems published in local newspapers, Women in White Mayisene Newsletter Editor Compassionate Friends, three years - Reader's Digest; [pers.] My poems are about life, its tragedies and its joys and the closeness of God in our lives. I strive to offer a lesson in all that I compose. [a.] N. Cape May, NJ 08204.

FITCH, MILDRED L.
[b.] October 25, 1925, Two Rivers, Wisconsin; [p.] Tom and Dorothy (Boutin) Hetue; [m.] John G. (deceased), March 11, 1943; [ch.] Tom, Gene (deceased), and Randall; [ed.] High School grad, Two Rivers Washington High; [occ.] Homemaker; [memb.] VFW Auxiliary; [pers.] I have endured many vicissitude of life as best I could. Coping with personal losses and hardships, I believe has made me a stronger

person. [a.] Two Rivers, WI 54241.

FITZGERALD, VERNITHIA D.
[b.] Kansas City, Missouri; [p.] Irene Ethel and Joseph Thomas Branche; [ch.] Sheri Long, Kenton Moore, Mark Moore, Cynthia Willis, Carol Terrell, Jackie Bell (deceased); [ed.] Lincoln High, Kansas City, MO, Omaha University, Omaha, NE; [occ.] Retired; [memb.] Bethel A.M.E. Daughters of Allen, Cherokee Temple #223, Daughters of Elks; [hon.] U.S. Federal Employee Service Outstanding Awards; [oth. writ.] Children's short stories--unpublished; [pers.] God Is. [a.] Omaha, NE 68111.

FITZGIBBON, GLYNDA ANN
[pen.] G.A. Fitzgibbon; [b.] December 26, 1932, Medford, Oregon; [p.] James Arthur and Ruth Goddard; [m.] Walter, September 2, 1965; [ch.] James, Patrick, Karen, Michael, Ray; [ed.] Franklin High School, Seattle College Courses, and Veterinarian Assistant Bellingham Washington; [occ.] Dog Breeder of Chinese Sharpei, House of Chan Choi Kennels; [memb.] Chinese Sharpei Club of America, American Kennel Club, Mount Baker Kennel Club of Bellingham Washington; [hon.] Commendations for Search and Rescue of Chinese Sharpei; [oth. writ.] Numerous articles on various dog subjects, books including "On A Dogs Level" fiction research papers on dog health problems, all published in dog magazines; [pers.] Life lets us follow till we are reader to be leaders. My poetry is emotional, from my life's changes, I write when I feel a need to express these feelings. [a.] Camano Island, WA 98292.

FITZPATRICK, KIMBERLY DAWN
[b.] October 9, 1972, Sapulpa, Oklahoma; [p.] Larry and Angela Fitzpatrick; [ed.] Sapulpa High, Eastern Oklahoma State College, Southeastern Oklahoma State University; [occ.] Full-time student; [hon.] Tau Beta Sigma, Dean's List; [oth. writ.] Extensive private collection, none published; [pers.] My writing comes from life. My emotions are my greatest work. I was heavily influenced by Emily Dickinson. [a.] Sapulpa, OK 74066.

FITZPATRICK, ROBA NOLAN
[b.] March 13, 1951, Paintsville, Kentucky; [p.] Carl and Kathleen Fitzpatrick; [ch.] Terra Noelle and Nolan David; [ed.] Fairview High and Wright State University; [occ.] Psychiatric Attendant; [oth. writ.] Poem published in "The Raven" a local literary magazine; [pers.] Working on a compilation of poems and song lyrics. I have been influenced by Bob Dylans writings and songs. [a.] Richmond, IN 47375-0122.

FLECK, TAMILLA LYNN
[pen.] Tammy Fleck; [b.] June 9, 1966, Niceville, Florida; [p.] George and Elma Fleck; [ed.] Niceville High School, Okaloosa Walton Community College, University of West Florida; [occ.] Teacher of Emotionally Handicapped Students, Bob Sikes Elementary, Crestview, FL; [memb.] Church of Jesus Christ of Latter-Day Saints, Okaloosa County Education Association; [hon.] Who's Who in High School 1984, The National Dean's List 1987-1988, Outstanding College Students of America, 1989; [pers.] I thank my Heavenly Father for countless blessings and thank my parents and family for helping me accomplish my goals in life. [a.] Valparaiso, FL 32580.

FLEET, REBECCA J.
[pen.] Rebecca J. Carlock; [b.] December 29, 1928, Jackson Hole, Wyoming; [p.] Earl Simpson and Effie Wilson Simpson (1st white child born in Jackson Hole); [m.] Loren J., December 24, 1989; [ch.] Barbara Klye-Seal Rock, OR., Beverly Miller-Cove, OR, Julie Carlock-Portland, OR; [ed.] Graduate High School-New Meadows, ID, 1 year college, La Grande, OR-805C; [occ.] Retired USFS - now farmer, Rancher's wife; [memb.] LDS Church Eastern OR Singles Club (Secretary), Mt. Emily Good Sams. (V. President), VFW, American Legion Eagles, NARFE; [hon.] The biggest honor is being married to the kindest, most considerate man in the Grande Ronde Valley. Who married me in spite of the disfiguration and traumatic experience of breast cancer in 1987; [oth. writ.] First Spouse: Fred Carlock died July 28, 1977 - cancer; [pers.] I'm a people and animal lover. My hobbies are painting, sewing, flowers. I used to write poetry for special occasions. The one I entered in your contest was inspired by a new member joining our Single's Club in 1991 - a very lonely man, new in the community. [a.] Cove, OR 97824.

FLETCHER, JUNE
[b.] June 9, 1937, Stoke-on-Trent, England; [p.] George and Florence Goodwin; [m.] Brian, December 14, 1957; [ch.] Jacqueline Ann, Christopher Damien; [ed.] Secondary School; [occ.] Housewife, artist, and writer; [oth. writ.] Over 100 poems several of which are on display indefinitely in local library. Have been highly praised. Several children's stories condensed autobiography; [pers.] I like to think that God has guided my hand in every aspect of my work especially regarding several poems which are written in defense of animals. [a.] Werrington Stoke-on-Trent Staffs ST9 0El. UK.

FLETCHER, NATALIE V.
[b.] June 5, 1907, Boston, Massachusetts; [p.] Louise Spidell and Harry B. Nickerson; [m.] Twice Widowed; [ch.] 3 children, 13 grandchildren, 6 great grandchildren; [ed.] H.S. one course B.U.; [occ.] Ret. Town Clerk and Treasurer, Wellfleet Ret. Personnel secretary, Nat. Park Service, Dept. of the Interior; [memb.] Doane Family Association, Nickerson Family Association, Mayflower Society, Boston (Doane Natioinal Org. also Nickerson); [hon.] Honor Award for Superior Service, Dept. of Interior, Grand Marshall - 4th of July Parade, 1992 Wellfleet; [oth. writ.] Short stories and poetry published in local newspapers; [pers.] Live by my mother's creed: "It's better to wear out than rust out." I like somebody else's (?) saying: "It's good to be on the right track, but you'll get run over if you just sit there." [a.] Wellfleet, MA 02667.

FLOREZ T., JULIO C.
[pen.] Oilvy Zerolf Zellet; [b.] June 14, 1955, Valencia, Venezuela; [p.] Robert Florez and Rosalba Tellez; [m.] Anatilde Castiblanco, December 19, 1981; [ch.] Juliana C. and Laura C. Florez; [ed.] Camilo Torres High School, La Salle University (Colombia), Silva Mind Control (Colombia); [occ.] Financial Advisor, Mutual of New York; [memb.] Hispanic-American Association of Artist and Writers (Poetry Vice Pres.). Eclipse Lodge #259/Patriotic Order of the "Sword of the Bunker Hill"; [hon.] Cellular One's Executive of the Month, Hoffman-La Roche's Champion of Sales (Colombia, 1986); [oth. writ.] Several poems (over 500) and short histories published in Spanish lan-

guage. Also writings related to Philosophy/Psychology and Economics; [pers.] I have been influenced by the classic poets from the early Roman Empire as well as the Greeks, but mostly my deepest inspiration has a name: Life (I'm a life lover). [a.] East Rutherford, NJ 07073-1325.

FLOWERS, THOMAS A.
[pen.] The Old Honker; [b.] February 9, 1923, Hoopers Island, Maryland; [p.] Thomas H. and Edna Hall Flowers; [m.] Frances Leonard, November 30, 1947; [ch.] Ann, Jane, and Dean; [ed.] BS Salisbury State University, MA Temple University; [occ.] Retired, Supervisor and Director of Education Dorchester County; [memb.] Vestryman, Christ Church Director Dorchester, Democratic Club President, Dorchester Retired Teachers Association; [hon.] Outstanding Community Service, Joycees; Bronze Star World War II, by U.S. Army; Outstanding Commitment to Children by U.S. Dept. of Health, Education and Welfare; [oth. writ.] Dorchester County, A History for Young People, Eastern Shore Folklore, Weekly Columnist The Times, Daily Commentary Radio WCFM; [pers.] I am totally involved in living and loving people. The earth is a great gift of God that I hope I can pass on to my children and grandchildren. [a.] Cambridge, MD 21613.

FLOYD, CHANEL Y.
[pen.] Rudy; [b.] October 6, 1980, Philadelphia, Pennsylvania; [p.] Evelyn and Theodore Floyd; [ed.] Strawberry Mansion Middle/Junior High School; [memb.] The National Junior Honor Society (Dr. M.L.K. Junior Chapter); [hon.] The National Junior Honor Society/Academics Achievement/Honor Roll; [oth. writ.] Philadelphia Drama Guild, Zora Neale Hurston Storytelling Competition. I wrote "A Ghost Story"; [pers.] If you have faith, nothing shall be impossible. [a.] Philadelphia, PA 19132.

FLYNN, MIKE
[pen.] Felix Meilhym, Ratboy; [b.] July 27, 1976, Huron, South Dakota; [p.] Chuck and Janet Flynn; [ed.] Student at Craig High School; [occ.] Free-lance Social Activist, writer and artist; [memb.] Church of the SubGenius, Reporter for School Newspaper; [oth. writ.] Philosophical stories, poetry and art printed in local mini-magazines commonly called zines; [pers.] The Now is here, it's not waiting to stay for anyone, not even today. Do not hesitate to enthrall yourself in the Now, as laziness is the slayer of great minds. [a.] Jonesville, WI 53545.

FLYNN, TAMMY
[b.] May 8, 1962, Saint Johnsbury, Vermont; [p.] Marion and John Spring; [ch.] Michael Adam Flynn; [ed.] Woodsville High (Woodsville, NH); [occ.] Cashier-Grand Union; [oth. writ.] Published in local newspaper a poem dedicated to my son; [pers.] I have always loved to read. I have been writing for years and have finally decided to try to publish some of them for others to share in. [a.] Wilder, VT 05088.

FOLEY, KAREN LEE
[pen.] Karen Nowak Foley; [b.] April 7, 1938, McLouth, Kansas; [p.] Vendelin Ludwig and Charlotte Matilda Nowak (both deceased), living stepmother Veda Nowak; [m.] William Joseph, Jr., May 25, 1962; [ch.] Charles Michael Bradley, Kathi Leigh Martin, Lisa Kay Williams; [ed.] Belle Plaine Rural High School (Belle Plaine, KS); [occ.] Executive

Secretary to Vice President - Data Center Services, American Airlines; [memb.] American Legion Auxiliary, Vera Christian Church, A.A.R.P., Appaloosa Horse Club, Sooner Appaloosa Horse Club, American Quarter Horse Association; [oth. writ.] Numerous poems written of actual experiences. One poem published in Kansas paper, have not pursued any other publishers; [pers.] Write about true experiences in my life and about actual friends, family and events. [a.] Talala, OK 74080.

FOLK, CHARLOTTE A.
[pen.] Cawfolk; [b.] April 15, 1931, Frostburg, Maryland; [p.] Victor C. and Pansy L. Garlitz Wilson; [m.] Harry W., Jr., November 20, 1948; [ch.] Eugene Lee-Debra Ann-Michelle Lynn-Duane Webster; [ed.] 11 years high school; [occ.] Housewife/mother; [memb.] Church of the Nazarene; [oth. writ.] Poem published while being a volunteer in Hospice unit in hospital in Cumberland, MD; [pers.] I have tried to live my life in such a way as to improve, through experiences and make my life and others a better way to live. [a.] Frostburg, MD 21532.

FORSMAN, DEBRA
[b.] July 7, 1958, Everett, Washington; [m.] Larry, July 7, 1980; [ch.] Benjamin Michael; [ed.] Everett High School, Hiroshima Joqakuin; [occ.] Housewife; [hon.] Marion Award; [oth. writ.] Display poems I've written on wood decorated with artistic burnings, and given away as gifts; [pers.] I believe that words and thoughts are gifts given to us and kept in our hearts, for the sole purpose of knowing, we all share the same emotions in relating our experiences. [a.] Lake Stevens, WA 98258.

FOSTER, BILL
[b.] July 19, 1918, Spencerville, Ohio; [p.] Wilbur Jacob and Bessie Alice (Strohl) Foster; [m.] Dorothy E., December 25, 1949; [ch.] Todd William and Ted Lowell; [ed.] Spencerville High, Art Academy, Cincinnati and Central Academy of Commercial Art-Cincinnati; [occ.] Retired florist; [memb.] United Church of Christ, Child Welfare Officer and Buckeye Boys State Chairman of American Legion Post 191 and 99th, Infantry Division Association; [oth. writ.] Numerous articles poems and cartoons for local newspaper; [pers.] My writing has always been on the lighter side hoping to brighten someone's day. People like Mark Twain and Will Rogers have helped me to develop the philosophy of "when up the creek make humor be your paddle." [a.] Spencerville, OH 45887-1283.

FOSTER, CARLA L.
[b.] December 28, 1972, Newport News, Virginia; [p.] Deborah A. Neal; [ed.] James Madison University; [memb.] Black Student Alliance, Students for Minority Research, LAE - Criminal Justice Association; [hon.] Dean's List; [oth. writ.] My first poem; [pers.] Complete success is a hard thing to achieve - the road is long, but my determination and great will to surpass all obstacles that lie in the way makes the journey a little less rocky. [a.] Hampton, VA 23661.

FOWLER, JACKIE
[pen.] April Stone; [b.] July 29, 1970, Redondo Beach, California; [p.] Bob and Joyce Fowler; [m.] Single; [ed.] Parkway South Senior High, El Camino Community College; [occ.] Branch Manager, Trade Air, Inc.; [memb.] National Association for Female

Executives; [oth. writ.] Several poems but this is the first one published; [pers.] I feel that you can express more in a ten line poem than you can in a five hundred page book. [a.] Torrance, CA 90501.

FOX, CRYSTAL LUV
[b.] March 18, 1972, Keywest, Florida; [p.] Danny J. and Helen Fox; [ed.] Currently a senior at Our Lady of the Lake University (seeking BA in CIS); [memb.] DPMA officer, Sigma Zeta; [hon.] DPMA outstanding member 1992-93 participant in San Marcos programming contest and in DPMA Spring '93 Conference; [pers.] Most of what I write is influenced by the people closet to me and things I cannot change. "Lights" was written for my younger brother, William, who taught me to appreciate words individually. [a.] San Antonio, TX 78207.

FOX, MARY BLANCHE
[pen.] Blance Fox; [b.] September 8, 1932, Livingston, Tennessee; [p.] Ruth Mai and Richard Duke; [m.] J.W. Fox, Jr., June 5, 1954; [ch.] Traci Lynn Fox and Kimberly Ann Fox Sisty; [ed.] Livingston Academy High School; [occ.] Clerk/typist-Marshall County Department of Human Resources, Boaz, AL; [oth. writ.] Poems published in hometown newspaper, retirements, birthdays, sympathy cards, Bosses Day, T-ball Team, T-ball coaches graduation, poems honoring police chiefs, (for friends and family upon request); [pers.] I put my thoughts and mind completely into a situation. My writing reflects my true feelings about my subject. I have to have a complete awareness and appreciation (if only momentarily) for my subject. [a.] Boaz, AL 35957.

FRANCES, DEE
[pen.] Dee Frances; [b.] August 10, 1950, St. Louis, Missouri; [p.] John and Della; [m.] Harry, May 2, 1975; [ch.] Charles, Renee, Jeannette, Micah, Matthew; [ed.] High School; [occ.] Writer; [memb.] International Society of Poets; [hon.] World of Poetry I.S.P.; [oth. writ.] Profile of Abuse, Poems and Growth from me to me, Reflections of a Time, Positive Thinking Easier Than You Think; [pers.] In December of 1990, I began to discover what makes the real me tick. Writing. I believe part of my purpose is to put a positive thought back into a world filled with negativity. I believe we all can, if only we want to. [a.] St. Louis, MO.

FRANCIS, PATSY R.
[b.] April 11, 1929, Vigo County, Terre Haute, Indiana; [p.] Homer P. and Elsie A. (Pugh) Bowman; [m.] James, February 25, 1950; [ch.] Karen Denise, Kevin Douglas, Kathryn Diane, Amy Renee and Krista D' Lee; [ed.] Glenn High School; [occ.] Clerk-Bookkeeper; [memb.] Indiana BPW, Women's Community Service, First Christian Church; [pers.] To serve God and fellowman in furthering peace and understanding among all persons. [a.] Linton, IN 47441.

FRANKLIN, BARBARA
[pen.] Mashinanna; [b.] July 4, 1935, Toronto, Ontario; [ed.] Self taught, tutored. George Brown College, Sheridan College, Atlin Center for the Arts, Evangelical Seminary; [occ.] Artist, Fantasy Illusion Artist; [memb.] Mississauga Arts Counsel, Brampton Arts Counsel, National Chaplains Association; [hon.] Chaplain; [oth. writ.] The Eagle Flies, Angels Sing, Mashinanna, Welcome to my World; [pers.] I am an

artist who writes stories and poetry about what I paint. Being religious mystical and fantasy. I write and paint for the new age, spacemen and all. [a.] Mississauga Ontario Canada L4T 2C8.

FRANKLIN, HOWARD E., JR.
[b.] September 23, 1957, Birmingham, Alabama; [p.] Howard E. and Juanita J. Franklin, Sr.; [m.] Starnell G., January 6, 1980; [ch.] Howard E. III and Katherine L. Franklin; [ed.] Mortimer Jordan High School, University of Oklahoma; [occ.] Physician Assistant, U.S. Army, Vilseck, Germany; [memb.] American Association of Physician Assistants, Society of European Physician Assistants; [hon.] Gulf War Veteran; [pers.] My inspiration comes from a love of nature and family. [a.] Unit #28009, APO AE 09112.

FRANKS, MYRNA L.
[b.] October 10, 1919, Tacoma, Washington; [p.] Mr. and Mrs. L.M. Baxter; [m.] Rev. Lawrence J., April 2, 1938; [ch.] Sandra Thompson, Larry E. Franks, Rebecca Riggle; [ed.] High School, Stadium High (Tacoma, WA) 1937 graduate; [occ.] Minister; [memb.] Peoples Church, Assembly of God Ministers; [oth. writ.] I have two small books of gospel poetry published by ourselves. I quoted my poetry all over the U.S. in our meetings; [pers.] My husband and I were part of a T.V. team known as "The Gospel Westernaires" in Seattle, WA for five years. We also travelled as evangelists and pastored churches.

FRANKS, STACIE
[b.] March 14, 1968, oakland, California; [p.] Clayton and Nancy Rapoza; [ch.] Michael Lee, Amanda Lynn, Corey Daniel; [ed.] Tokay High School; [occ.] Homemaker; [pers.] I structure my poetry from feelings and realities of everyday life. I am greatly influenced by emotions. [a.] Elk Grove, CA 95624.

FRAVEL, IRIS R.
[pen.] Crissy I.; [b.] February 23, 1959, Goshen, New York; [p.] Ethel Oakes and Roy Fravel; [ed.] Ninth; [occ.] Construction; [hon.] A+; [oth. writ.] None printed, personal; [pers.] I got very discouraged and forgot about writing any other interesting poems. [a.] Rooseneltown, NY 13683.

FREEMAN, MARYANN
[pen.] Little Mary; [b.] August 7, 1950, Brooklyn, New York; [p.] Albertha and Henry Fields; [m.] Danny, September 2, 1972; [ch.] Daniel, Jermaine, Yolanda, Tanya, Danny, Jarrel, and granddaughter Iasia; [ed.] Academic received diploma, degree studies in Business Management, Crown Business Institute, Barbizon School of Modeling; [occ.] Poet, inventor, songwriter, author; [memb.] Robert Tilton Ministries, Marilyn Hickey Ministries, Feed the Children, The American Biographical; [hon.] Golden Poet of 1991, 1992, International Biographical chosen as a world intellectual of 1992-1993 "Honor". International Society of Poets "honor" for Outstanding Achievement in Poetry in 1993; [oth. writ.] Manuscript accepted by Vantage Press Inc., to publish my book title Modern Day Poetry, a collection of my poems written by me; [pers.] Keep your mind open and never stop learning, because as long as you live, you can always learn. [a.] Brooklyn, NY 11206.

FREITAG, CYNTHIA G.
[pen.] C. Gail Fridae; [b.] July 4, 1960, Tacoma, Washington; [p.] Della J. and Vernon W. Ham; [ch.]

Jesse A. Noller (age 13); [ed.] H.S. Diploma with 1 1/2 years of Community College majoring in Psychology and Music; [occ.] Disabled food service worker/ poet; [hon.] Who's Who Among American High School Students 1977-78; Golden Poet years 1988-92 from the "World of Poetry" organization; [oth. writ.] Numerous poems, articles for Vashon Island, WA newspaper 1975-76; [pers.] Some people may not readily understand what I have to say, but when they do I make sense. Think about it…[a.] St. Maries, ID 83861-1960.

FRENZ, H. LOUISE
[b.] May 26, 1923; [p.] Hattie M. and Thomas H. Power (both deceased); [m.] William F. (deceased), September 26, 1943; [ch.] Lynne - two grandchildren, Heather and William; [ed.] East High School (Rochester, NY); [occ.] Secretary, Secretary/Receptionist and Executive Secretary, now devote time to daughter's Riding School/Breeding Farm-teaching children to ride and show breeding Paint/Pinto horses; [memb.] Many horse-related organizations, many years was active in Walworth Chamber of Commerce and still maintain membership; [hon.] Received many awards for our horses. [a.] Walworth, NY 14568.

FREY, MARY PAT
[b.] February 5, 1971, St. Mary's, Pennsylvania; [p.] Mark and Ruth Sporner Frey; [ed.] Elk County Christian High, University of Pittsburgh Bradford; [occ.] Student; [memb.] St. mary's Catholic Church; [hon.] Who's Who, National Honor Society, Society of Distinguished Students; Dean's Scholar. [a.] St. Mary's, PA 15857.

FROMM, TED J.
[b.] May 31, 1935, Portland, Oregon; [p.] Ted and Pearl Fromm; [m.] Joanne, March 14, 1955; [ch.] Jeanne, Susan, Carolyn, Glen; [ed.] BA MAED Western Washington State University (Bellingham, WA); [occ.] Educator-WA State Public Schools; [memb.] WEAIR, NEAIR, Presbyterian Church; [hon.] Valedictorian; [oth. writ.] Poems in local newspapers, public school curriculum; [pers.] I seek truth and understanding in my writing and in life. I strive to balance the conscious and the unconscious. I quest for my unique path and attempt to flow along it asking for God's grace and guidance. [a.] Olympia, WA 98516.

FROST, SAMANTHA JO
[b.] July 17, 1983, Iowa City, IA; [p.] Fred and Leslie Gunderson Frost; [ed.] Fifth grader at Wapsie Valley Elementary (Fairbank, IA); [memb.] Immaculate Conception Church, TAG (Talented and Gifted); [oth. writ.] Other poems but none published; [pers.] I feel our earth needs our care and people should recycle. [a.] Fairbank, IA 50629.

FULLER, FLORENCE L.
[b.] August 17, 1938, Dansville, New York; [p.] William G. Paulman (Lillie); [m.] Donald E., September 7, 1955; [ch.] Six children, ten grandchildren and raised 67 foster children; [ed.] High School; [occ.] Study Hall Supervisor - 12 years at Homell High School; [memb.] Free Methodist Church, Youth Teacher; [oth. writ.] Numerous poetry, some published in local literary magazines. Most for my own pleasure and release of my emotions; [pers.] I like to reflect on small things that can bring so much good and yet are overlooked so much. [a.] Hornell, NY

FULMER, MICHELLE
[b.] April 11, 1958, Akron, Ohio; [p.] Gene and Betty Wallace; [ch.] Simon Laurence, Schuyler Gene, Spencer Louis; [ed.] University of Missouri-Columbia; [occ.] Public Relations Coordinator for animal shelter; [oth. writ.] Several juvenile books, collections of humorous poetry for children; [pers.] I love to write poetry that is humorous, philosophical, and that entertains children and adults on two levels. [a.] Tallmadge, OH 44278.

FUQUEN, LUIS C.
[b.] November 9, 1964, Bogota, Columbia; [p.] Maria and Marco J. Fuquen; [ed.] Union Hill, university College-Rutgers, the Art Institute of Fort Lauderdale; [occ.] Student; [pers.] I live life to live it not waste it.

FURNISH, AMY NOELL
[pen.] Noell; [b.] April 19, 1978, Auburn, Indiana; [p.] James E. and Mildred Ann Furnish; [ed.] Ninth grade; [hon.] I got an award for a program call Mathothon for get over $100.00; [pers.] I hope my poem can make people happy. I am going to hopefully get more poems published in the future. [a.] Hamilton, IN 46742.

FUSS, JUANITA WHITE
[pen.] Juanito White, Juanita Whire Fuss, J.W. Fuss; [b.] January 31, 1923, Lewistown, Montana; [p.] Mr. and Mrs. Homer L. Norton (both deceased); [m.] Walter, February 22, 1986; [ch.] Judith Andrews, Pat Calland, Jean Andrews, David White, James White, Jamie Hafley and Barbara Nelson (step daughter); [ed.] Missoula High, one year at University of Montana, Teacher's Aide Training Voc-Tech; [occ.] Retired Nursery School Teacher; [memb.] Retired Senior Volunteer Services, MIS (Montana Institute of the Arts; Literacy Volunteers of America (LVA) Salvation Army at the present time I am taking a writing course from the "Institute of Children's Literature", but I haven't written any poetry since I started the course; [oth. writ.] None; [per.] Most of my poems will either teach a moral, express my religious beliefs or be something to make people happy. [a.] West Missoula, MT 59801.

GABBERT, KEITH
[b.] August 10, 1964, San Francisco, California; [p.] Charles L. and Bonita Kay Gabbert; [m.] Jane, November 2, 1991; [ch.] Kaylyn Chelsea; [pers.] I just try to write from the heart. "Bright Eyes" is dedicated to my daughter, born July 17, 1972. [a.] Seattle, WA 98155.

GAIDUS, TINAMARIE
[pen.] Tinamarie Escape; [b.] July 29, 1959, Jersey City, New Jersey; [p.] Thomas J. and Marie Novembre; [m.] Ronald, April 20, 1985; [ch.] Tiana Marie (7), Tiffany Jade (3); [ed.] Ridgefield Memorial High School, Brookdale College; [occ.] Household Executive; [memb.] Holy Family School and Church; [hon.] Citizenship Award for Truth, Honor and Integrity; [oth. writ.] Several other original poems and writings and original oil paintings; [pers.] I see the world around me as ABC's -1,2,3's and colors, lots of colors. [a.] Union Beach, NJ 07735.

GAIO, PAULA JOETTE
[b.] September 18, 1953, Bowie County, Texarkanna, Texas; [p.] Paul Joseph and Matilda Louise Hall-

Gaio; [ch.] Carl Eugene Jr., and Toni Marie Johnson; [ed.] Martinsville High; [occ.] Vocational Skills Training Specialist; [hon.] Throughout my school years my teachers always displayed my drawings and poetry on the bulletin boards of the schools for everyone to enjoy; [oth. writ.] My only honors or awards have been obtained through ribbons and whatnot at my grade school and high school; [pers.] I have been influenced mostly by my mother's brother Roger Hall and her sister Judith Hall as they both have extraordinary drawing and writing abilities. [a.] Greencastle, IN 46135.

GALATI, STEPHEN R.
[b.] October 26, 1971, Brooklyn, New York; [p.] Richard and Marilyn Galati; [ed.] Xaverian High School, Pratt Institute; [occ.] Electrical Engineer; [memb.] Institute of Electrical and Electronic Engineers; [hon.] ITau Beta Pi Honor Society, Pratt Circle Award; [oth. writ.] The Voyage, a poem published in the Prattler; [pers.] To Janet for her love and support. [a.] Brooklyn, NY 11228.

GALBRAITH, ALEXANDER G.
[pen.] Alexander G. Galbraith; [b.] April 16, 1922, Belfast, North Ireland; [m.] Betty, November 16, 1957; [ch.] Cathy, Bill, Carol, and Bruce (all married) Empty Nest; [ed.] Four years Englewood High (Chicago, IL), one year Studio School of Art; [occ.] Retired security officer Chicago Tribune; [memb.] AARP, Disabled American Veterans, Eastern Will Company Senior Citizens; [hon.] Waiting for $1000.00 grand prize from the National Library of Poetry; [oth. writ.] Freedom of Expression, Geese, Grandson, Divorce Poems, Partition-Irish poem; [pers.] Life is so uncertain so eat your dessert first. [a.] University Pk, IL 60466.

GALE, ROXANNA
[b.] July 17, 1960, Fresno, California; [p.] Ed and Maxine Gale; [m.] William O. Smith; [ch.] Randy Doyle, Roger Wayne, Brittany Nicole; [ed.] Central Union High, Fresno City College; [occ.] Housewife; [pers.] This one is for you, Pretty man, in my life a short time. But within my heart forever you'll be. [a.] Fresno, CA 93722.

GALE, WALTER HENRY ENOLIN
[pen.] Buddy Gale; [b.] October 7, 1928, Minnehek, Alberta, Canada; [p.] Sidney and Lillian gale (deceased); [m.] Marilyn J., September 5, 1953; [ch.] Two boys, three girls, and three grandchildren; [ed.] Grade 8 and the school of life; [occ.] H.D. Mechanic and Welder, Teamster, cowboy, truck driver, equipment operator; [memb.] 52 years working, 80 of outdoors; [oth. writ.] Two short stories published in a magazine in Sudbury Ontario. 1986 a few short stories and about 40 poems, all poems written in about 10 mountains; [pers.] I have suppressed urges to write for years all of a sudden. Poetry seems through is a short space. Its like a lake. When the shallow thoughts are used up you just get deeper and deeper. [a.] Alberta Canada T8A 0V8.

GALLAGHER, DIANE
[b.] August 31, 1965, Scranton; [p.] Paul and Florence McCauley; [m.] George, May 18, 1990; [ed.] Scranton Central High School; [occ.] Financial Examiner, Prudential Defined Contribution Services; [oth. writ.] Personal collection of unpublished poems; [pers.] This particular poem was written to my husband while he was serving in Saudi Arabia during Operation Desert Storm. [a.] Scranton, PA 18504.

GALT, CAPT. W.W.
(PAY DIRECTOR, USN-RET)
[pen.] Submission by grandson-Capt. R.G. Zimmermann, USN (Ret.); [b.] Capt. Galt died in 1934; [occ.] Naval officer; [memb.] Grand Mason of Virginia; [hon.] Special medal for heroism given by the U.S. Congress in connection with the Battle of Manila Bay, 1898; [oth. writ.] "Battle of Manila Bay" 64 pages published in 1900. [a.] Norfolk, VA.

GAMBLE, TINA M.
[b.] May 22, 1974, Rosthern, Sask., Canada; [p.] Gilbert and May Gamble; [ed.] Stobart High; [pers.] In my writing, I write what I believe and from the heart. The inspiration to write comes from the people in my life. [a.] Duck Lake, Sask. Can.

GAMMON, SCOTT A.[b.] July 6, 1973, Hollywood, Florida; [p.] Rom and Peggy Gammon; [ed.] Fernandina Beach High School, University of Tennessee, University of North Florida; [occ.] Student, Security Officer, Ritz-Carlyton Amelia Island; [memb.] Springhill Baptist Church, Republican Party of Florida; [hon.] Dean's list, National Honor Society, Voice of Democracy; [oth. writ.] Various poems in high school literary magazine; [pers.] A liberal may be defined approximately as a man who, if he could, by waving his hand in a dark room, stop the mouths of all the deceivers of mankind forever, would not wave his hand - G.K. Chesterton; [a.] Fernandina Beach, FL 32034.

GANAHL, LUELLA L.
[b.] June 5, 1936, Bucyrus, Montana; [m.] Richard J., Jr., May 8, 1973; [ch.] Cynthia Louise, Gregory Clinton, Leo Alexander (four grandchildren-Clinton, Austin, Emily, Becky); [ed.] Associate Degree in Arts Meramec Community College; [memb.] Hobby-Depression class; [hon.] Note-Poetry Book Review in Ferguson Focus Newspaper; [oth. writ.] Dancing Blossoms Memories in Poem and Verse published 1990; [pers.] The fringe reality with hope, and walk my talk. Born with innocence in a world of knowledge, growing in a world of change. [a.]n Ferguson, Missouri.

GAND, MITCHELL
[b.] May 21, 1971, Philadelphia, Pennsylvania; [p.] Iris And Malvin Gang; [ed.] Bachelor of Arts Degree from Fairleigh Dickenson University, Teaneck, NJ; [occ.] Sales Associate, Record Town (Wayne, NJ); [hon.] Honors and Dean's List; [oth. writ.] Commentary in the WEA Guide, Poems and Criticism published in The Spectator, The Hub, ,and Columbus Columns; [pers.] My work is a reflection of the decline and fall of society under the weight of its own divisiveness and false morality. Wilde and Brecht are my main influences. [a.] Clifton, NJ 07012.

GANNOTT, CHRIS
[b.] July 27, 1976, Marshall, Minnesota; [p.] Barbara Gannot; [ed.] Marshall Senior High School; [occ.] Student; [pers.] All my poems are about experiences and feelings I have had. [a.] Marshall, MN 56258.

GARCIA, PATRICIA
[b.] October 20, 1979, Monterey Park, California; [p.] Lucille Olsen and Richard Garcia, Sr.; [ed.] Eighth grade; [occ.] student; [pers.] I dedicate this poem to my loving boyfriend, Matthew Almanza, I love you! [a.] Brentwood, CA 94513.

GARDNER, LARRAINE
[pen.] Larraine Gardner; [b.] July 9, 1927, North Vancouver, British Columbia; [p.] Brian and Lorna Gardner; [ed.] Peter Skene Ogden Senior Secondary, British Columbia Institute of Technology; [occ.] Overseas Traffic Manager; [pers.] Live Life to the Fullest, as you don't know what tomorrow will bring. This poem was written in memory of Donna and Keith Gardner. [a.] Burnaby, BC V5H 4B8 Canada.

GARNER, ERICA
[b.] March 23, 1979, McAlester, Oklahoma; [ed.] Puterbaugh middle School, now attending Parker Mid-High of McAlester (9th grade); [memb.] Bison Cheerleading Squad, McAlester High School Marching band; [hon.] All-American Scholar Award, United States Achievement Academy Award; [pers.] I am only 14 years old and this is my first publication. It has encouraged me to write even more. I really like to write about things that almost everyone can relate to. [a.] McAlester, OK 74501.

GARRETT, ALVIE
[b.] Pickett County, Tennessee; [p.] Samuel C. and Eunice Heard; [m.] Walter K.; [ch.] Sam, Ron, Cindy, Tony, Mrs. Joan Mauck; [occ.] Homemaker; [memb.] Anderson Poetry Corner, Columbus Avenue Church of Christ; [pers.] From an early age my parents taught me to love the written word for which I have always been grateful. And my children have been a source of encouragement to my writings, but husband was #1. [a.] Anderson, IN 46016.

GARY, WILLIAM J.
[pen.] W.J. Gary; [b.] 1938, Albany, New York; [m.] Charlene Bissell; [ch.] John, Kathy, and Tracey; [ed.] SUNY Cortland, Russell Sage, Institute of Applied Science, Hume Business Management; [occ.] Sales/ Marketing Lee Co., VFC Senior Investigator, BCI, NYS Police - Ret. Private Detective, Criminal and Civil Forensic Investigation Expert-Ret.; [pers.] Happiness is the stalking of truth through the eyes of the great philosophers. It is a blessing that they recorded their thoughts and observations, all should take time to bathe in their product. [a.] Queensbury, NY 12804.

GATES, JENNIFER
[b.] March 22, 1978, Largo, Florida; [p.] Almedia and David C. Gates; [ed.] 9th grade; [pers.] Teenagers should protect themselves from the unknown. [a.] Largo, FL 34644.

GAUTHIER, MARCIA (TAYLOR)
[b.] January 17, 1972, Marshfield, Wisconsin; [p.] Richard and Priscilla Taylor; [m.] Daniel, September 2, 1991; [ed.] Shelton High School, Olympic College (Shelton, WA); [occ.] Homemaker; [oth. writ.] I've written up to 100 poems; [pers.] The poems I write are either on personal experiences or thoughts and ideas of life in general. I've been writing from age 12 to present. [a.] Shelton, WA 98584.

GAVALAS, MARY BEARRY
[b.] February 9, 1921, Limerick, Ireland; [p.] Patrick and Elizabeth Dawson Beary; [m.] Emmanuel, July 9, 1944; [ch.] Alexander, Elizabeth, Mary and Lorraine;

[ed.] National School of Ireland, Bon Secure Nursing School, Royal Air Force in England - WWII - Voice Instruction under Julie Art, Wilfred Academy; [occ.] Nurse, Singer, Cosmetologist, Housewife, Waiter; [hon.] Being accepted by the National Library of Poetry; [oth. writ.] Poems for schools and churches, business writings and promotional material for the fine arts; [pers.] I am interested in the finer things in life - art, music, literature and poetry. I have a natural impulse to learn, so I philosophize in order to avoid ignorance. I am always in pursuit of knowledge, because knowledge is free science. [a.] Malverne, NY 11565.

GEIB, FREDDY R.
[b.] August 28, 1960, Hershey, Pennsylvania; [p.] Frederick D. and Barbara Hirs Geib; [m.] Cathy (Longenecker), October 29, 1988; [ch.] Chyna Marie, Chelsey Rae; [ed.] GED; [pers.] Learn how to read and write but find something else to keep you up all night. [a.] Palmyra, PA 17078.

GENTRY, DERENDA
[pen.] Derenda Gentry; [b.] December 17, 1977, Leesburg, Florida; [p.] Huland and Carol Gentry; [ed.] Sophomore at Leesburg High School; [occ.] Student; [memb.] Latin Club, Beta Club, Kathryn Knight School of Dance; [hon.] Leesburg CofC Essay Contest, Placement at Latin Dist. and State; [pers.] My desire is to touch the heart of people with my poetry. This poem was written for Kenny. I love you. [a.] Okahumpka, FL 34762.

GENUA, MELISSA
[b.] August 2, 1980, Greenwich, Connecticut; [p.] Robert and Susan Genua; [ed.] 7th, New Newtown Middle School Middle Gate Elementary. [a.] Newtown, CT 06470.

GERRIOR, JESSICA
[b.] April 4, 1977, Dorchester, Massachussetts; [p.] Leo and Judy Gerrior; [ed.] Franklin High School; [memb.] Track, field hockey, St. Paul Youth Group; [hon.] Honor Roll, Coach's Award; [oth. writ.] Various poems; [pers.] To me, poetry is something you feel, and it's inside all of us. It's one of the most powerful forms of personal expression. [a.] Franklin, NH 03235.

GETTLER, ANNE S.
[pen.] Annie; [b.] March 19, 1962, Washington, D.C.; [p.] Deceased; [m.] Jeffery A., January 26, 1989; [ed.] 2 year degree in Business, 10 years piano lessons; [occ.] Student; [memb.] The Humane Society of the United States; [hon.] Dean's List, Honor Roll; [oth. writ.] "To the Sea" published in the Lyric Magazine, 1981 Newspapers, Newsletters; [pers.] We should not base our success on what we own, but how we get along with others. That's more valuable. [a.] Spencer, IA 51301.

GIALLONARDO, JONI DIANE
[b.] January 20, 1976, Greensburg, Pennsylvania; [p.] Kathleen M. Wells and Nicholas J. Giallonardo; [ed.] Hempfield High School; [occ.] Student; [memb.] Various school organizations; [hon.] Northumberland County Commissioners Resolution for Community Service, Milton, PA Lions Club Student Excellence Award; [oth. writ.] Various articles in school-related student publications; [pers.] Go out and look at the stars with someone close to you. Because without

dreams and friendship the human race ceases to exist. [a.] Greensburg, PA 15601.

GIBBS, LEE ANN
[b.] September 14, 1970, Seoul, Korea; [p.] Kap Y Spanton-Stern and Donald Leroy Stanton; [ch.] Morgan Jan Gibbs; [ed.] UW-Rock, Blackhawk Tech, Evansville High; [occ.] Full-time student; [hon.] Special Recognitions of Students, Director's Honor List; [oth. writ.] Several poems written on my spare time; [pers.] A person who tries always succeed, a person who doubts their potential sets himself up for failure. [a.] Evansville, WI 53536.

GIBSON, KATE M.
[pen.] Jesse O'Neal; [b.] December 25, 1977, Tahlequah, Oklahoma; [p.] Vance Gibson and Cynthia Gould (guardian - Angela K. Bliss); [ed.] Enrolled at Tahlequah High School in the 10th grade; [occ.] Work as a care-taker for an elderly woman with Alzheimer's; [hon.] National Junior Honor Society, National English Merit award; [oth.writ.] I have an unpublished collection of my own poetry called Contents; [pers.] I live by Tom Robbins' quote, "There is no such thing as a word human being. Its just that some take more understanding than others." [a.] Tahlequah, OK 74464.

GIESY, CHARLENE
[b.] March 1, 1938, Pittsburg, Pennsylvania; [p.] Catherine and Eugene Shuttera; [m.] William; [ch.] William, Thomas, Kimberlee, Sherry, Traci, Carlene; [occ.] Mother and Housewife; [oth. writ.] Small poems for my children and grandchildren; [pers.] Living my life for my six children and my 14 grandchildren and my husband, Will. My friends and family makes my life beautiful for me to write poems.

GILBURT, SAMUEL G.
[b.] September 13, 1910, Brooklyn, New York; [p.] Harry and Anna; [m.] Lillian (Lehds), March 14, 1937; [ch.] Naomi, Judith; [ed.] BS City College of New York 1933, MA Columbia University 1935, 40 credits toward R.of Ed. NYU; [occ.] Retired secondary school principal, Asst. professor Long Island University; [memb.] New York City Association English Teachers, National Association Teachers English (mem. radio and television com.), N.Y.C. Association Assistant Principals (pres. 1956), N.E.A. (memb. audio-visual com.), N.Y.C. Joint Commission Teachers Organization (exec. com. 1954), Brooklyn Teachers Association (legislative rep. 1957), N.Y.C. Principals Association, Junior High School Principal Association, Poetry Society Am., National Council Teachers English (mem. poetry appreciation com.), N.Y.C. Association Junior High School Principals (exec. com.), Council Supervisors Association (chmn. dist. 26), Phi Kappa Delta; [oth. writ.] Author articles editorials, journals, also poems, including I Am Brooklyn (read to U.S. Lio. of Reps., printed in U.S. Congl. Record); [pers.] Diploma with degree of C.P.T. (Certified Poetry Therapist" can aid psychiatrists in this area. Gare "Volunteer" course - Poetry Therapy in Palm Beach Junior College for nine years. [a.] W. Palm Beach, FL 33417.

GILLAN, PETER J.
[b.] February 17, 1940, St. Paul, Minnesota; [ch.] Andrew Peter, Monica Therese, Laura Drew; [ed.] M.A. Metropolitan State University (St. Paul, MN), BSB - University of Minnesota; [occ.] Consultant,

Adjunct College Professor; [oth. writ.] Children's Stories, poems, master's thesis; [pers.] My poems reflect how I look at life around me. I am considered a realist. [a.] Minneapolis, MN 55412-1933.

GILLIGAN, JESSIE
[[b.] April 16, 1978, Alton, Illinois; [p.] Phil and Val Gilligan; [ed.] Attending high school; [oth. writ.] Poems printed in Church newsletters; [pers.] Your life is only as good as you make it cut to be so start living today for you do not know what tomorrow will bring. [a.] Morreno, LA 70072-4901.

GIVANS, AMANDA
[b.] August 24, 1993, Beech Grove, Indiana; [p.] Carolyn and Charles Givans; [ed.] Center Grove High School; [occ.] Student; [hon.] High School Art Award, Bowling Awards; [oth. writ.] Nothing published; [pers.] I've always been interested in the strange and unusual; I've even been accused of being them myself, sometimes I wonder if that's true, but I doubt it. [a.] Greenwood, IN 46142.

GLASSMAN, HAN
[pen.] Han Misyou; [b.] December 4, 1930, Kunsan, Chullabukdo, South Korea; [p.] Jin Wo You (father) and Jung Hi Cho (mother); [m.] Fred, November 1964; [ch.] Diana and Grace Glassman; [ed.] B.A. in Korean Literature, MA in English at the Sukmyong Women's University, Seoul Korea; [occ.] Korean-Japanese Instructor at the Language Lab, NYC; [oth. writ.] Three poems (1990-1992) published in Smoke Signal, called now Nomad's Choir, Flushing, NY and two others (1992-1993) in The New Press, Flushing, NY; [pers.] Through lyrical symbolism I try to retrieve my early countryside life, vanished in a war. Perhaps lyrical power helps in our age of spiritual crisis... [a.] New York, NY.

GLEASON, MARGARET F.
[b.] Windsor Locks, Connecticut; [ch.] Gregory Gleason of Hebron, CT and Gary Gleason of Chicago, IL; [ed.] Enfield High School graduate, University of CT (BA), University of Buffalo School of Social Work - MSW; [occ.] New retired, was active in teaching and school and hospital social work; [memb.] AARP, Board of Directors and First Vice President AARP Englewood, FL Chapter, St. Raphael's Church; [hon.] Served as President of AARP Englewood Fl Chapter, won awards in oil paintings; [oth. writ.] AARP Newsletters, occasional newspaper articles and Quails Call News Bulletin; [pers.] God helps those who help themselves, so never give up but use every resource possible to achieve your goal. [a.] Englewood, FL 34223.

GLEICH, GERALDINE
[b.] July 30, 1933, Westbury, Long Island, New York; [p.] Samuel J. and Florence Quinan; [m.] Frank J., April 13, 1958; [ch.] Warren Frank, James Rudolf and Kathy Ann; [ed.] Westbury High School; [occ.] Domestic Engineer; [oth. writ.] Several poems published by World of Poetry; [pers.] My poems reflect the way I feel about things. They are written from my heart. [a.] Levittown, NY 11756.

GLEINN, JOSEPH
[b.] July 1908, Tarenium, Pennsylvania; [p.] Gertrude and Gabriel; [m.] Blanche, January 27, 1935; [ch.] Three; [occ.] Retired; [oth. writ.] First poem that I ever wrote. Do not act old, now I have more. [a.]

Nairona Heights, PA.

GLICK, SARAH
[b.] September 3, 1982, Baltimore, Maryland; [p.] Diane and Lewis Glick (sister-Lindsey); [ed.] Fifth grade attends William Paca Old Post Road Elementary; [memb.] Harford Dance Theatre member since 1989; [hon.] Honor Roll student, Maryland Council on Physical Fitness Award; [pers.] I enjoy dancing and playing the piano and I like to write short stories and poems. [a.] Belcamp, MD 21017.

GLINSKI, FRANK ZOLRISLAW
[b.] October 17, 1928, Wyrzysk, Poland; [p.] Stanislaw K. and Maria A. Glinski; [m.] Eugenia Pilc-Glinski, September 2, 1950; [ch.] Lech Walter Glinski and Evon Eve Weber; [ed.] Polish-PTE-Warsaw Ind. Ec., German-Middle School, English-Rutgers University-Newark General Business and Computer Science; [occ.] Supervisory Manuf. - retired; [memb.] Our Lady of Lordess-W. Orange parish, The West Nine Country Club-Plainfield, NJ, Moose Legion North Jersey #2; [hon.] Silver pin for work in textile industry-Poland, XV-pin for cultural work in Lower Silesia, Gold pin-mountaineering-PTTK-Poland, Gliders Pilot Pin-Poland, Award for Excellence Pin-Simmons Co-Piscataway-USA; [oth. writ.] Several cultural articles in local and national press - Poland, History of Textile Industry in Lower Silesia - 3V-Poland, 15 years biography-Wroclaw-Poland, Memoir-SGH-Warsaw-Poland; [pers.] In my English-Polish-German writing, I reflect on positive side of humane mind in all variations of life - I have been greatly influenced by European romantic poets. [a.] West Orange, NJ 07052.

GLUCK, ERIC
[b.] January 12, 1938, Yonkers, New York; [p.] Harlan W. and Helen E. Gluck; [m.] Evelyn V., August 6, 1965; [ch.] Lisa Marie Gluck; [ed.] Halsted High Ithaca College, City College of New York; [occ.] Teacher of Health and Physical Education, Robert F. Wagner Junior High, New York, NY (retired) and Professional Baseball Scout, Baltimore Orioles (retired); [memb.] United Federation of Teachers, Former member New York Professional Baseball, Hot Stove League, Inc., NASCS (Age 50 and over seniors softball world series); [hon.] Dean's List, Ithaca College. I have been the subject of articles in the Gannett Westchester Newspapers, Herald News (NJ), NY Times (Westchester Edition), Middletown NY Record, and Patent Trader (NY). Also I've been interviewed on cable tv in NY and NJ and on radio in NY. I was also the subject of an article in the Cape Cod Oracle; [oth. writ.] Years ago, I had an original joke published in Playboy. It was an "unabashed dictionary" joke. I've never attempted to write anything for publication besides that joke and the poem I wrote and submitted to this contest. [pers.] I've had the chance to live my lifetime dreams-that is to coach and to work in professional baseball as a scout. I believe everyone should pursue his or her dream and should continue to persevere without giving up or getting discouraged regardless of the set backs or time it takes. I have my parents and my wife to thank for my success. I'd like to encourage young people in particular - each of you can succeed! [a.] Wellfleet, MA 02667.

GLOVER, CYD
[b.] January 30, 1976, Los Angeles, California; [p.] Elaine Glover Willis; [ed.] Attend St. Bernard's High School; [occ.] Student-Junior; [memb.] Professional Dancers Society (PDS); [hon.] Negro Women Association for Achievements in Academics and the Arts; [oth. writ.] If Only I Could Be, Be Strong, Death - to name a few. None of these have been published; [pers.] Professional dancer since the age of seven. I've been featured in several shows, and one Broadway show, Black and Blue. My love for dance inspired my poem, The Eternal Dance.

GOINS, LINDA BROOKS
[b.] February 1, 1949, San Saba, Texas; [p.] Dewey C. and Melba Jones Brooks; [ch.] Jennifer Kathleen and Charles Michael; [ed.] A.A. Tarrant County Junior College; B.B.A. Dallas Baptist University; [occ.] Writer/editor, Tarrant County Junior College, Ft. Worth, TX; [memb.] National Association for Female Executives, Texas State Teacher's Association, Professional and Businesswomen of Fort Worth, Board of Directors/Trustees for Texas A&M University System, Ciunty Extension Service and Miss Texas Scholarship Pageant, member of (hometown) Azle Rotary Club, Chamber of Commerce, Historical Society; [hon.] Named to Who's Who Among Texas Women, 1986 and Personalities of the South, Outstanding Community Volunteer 1970; [oth. writ.] Weekly column, NEIGHBORS, in Azle News, numerous poems/essays published in college publications, bi-monthly features in college newsletter/tabloids; [pers.] The growth of a writer does not rest in what he or she can do already. It rests in what he or she cannot do yet. I am growing. [a.] Azle, TX 76020.

GOMEZ, JOHNNY J.
[b.] July 23, 1977, Guatemala City, Guatemala; [p.] Pedro and Maria L. Gomez; [ed.] Bridgeham Middle School, Classical High School; [occ.] Student; [memb.] Brown University Medac Program, NC Heritage Panel, Classical High School; [hon.] Second time winner Roberto Clemente award. Organizer of Classical High School's first International Fair; [oth. writ.] Several other poems, on War, Peace, and other topics. Poems in both Spanish and English; [pers.] I try to put into words what I am feelings, and what others may also be feeling. I am devoted for equality and justice for minorities. [a.] Providence, RI 02907.

GONZALES, ANAMARIA
[pen.] Anamaria Gonzalez; [b.] September 23, 1962, New York City, New York; [p.] Cathy Gonzalez; [ch.] Ceili Helen Katherin Sheppard; [ed.] Red Bank Regional High School; [pers.] I would like to reflect my thoughts into the Hearts of Peoples reality. I hope to inspire other writers and I would also like to thank the people in my life that inspire me. [a.] The Netherlands.

GONZALES, SONYA
[pen.] Sonya "Roland2" Hainstock; [b.] May 21, 1972, Ann Arbor, Michigan; [p.] Gaynor and Grover Hainstock; [m.] Michael P., July 1, 1992; [ch.] Anthony, Jenifer, and Alexandra; [ed.] Poway High School, Home of the Titans; [occ.] Homemaker; [memb.] The American Poetry Society (T.A.P.S.) and Trinity Baptist Church; [hon.] Editor's Choice award from National Library; [pers.] Others see in us what we do not see, yet they do not see in us what we see in ourselves. [a.] Poway, CA 92064.

GONZALEZ, EMILY
[b.] January 24, 1969, Yonkers, New York; [p.] Judith and Anthony Gonzalez; [ch.] Christopher, Robert, Heaven Gonzales and David Knight; [ed.] High School Equivalency Diploma; [occ.] Single mother soon to be college student; [oth.. writ.] Several unpublished poems; [pers.] My children inspire me to aspire. My loves inspire me to feel and my feelings inspire me to write. [a.] Bronx, NY 10475.

GOODMAN, JESSECA LYNNE
[b.] August 17, 1978, Columbia, Missouri; [p.] Stephan David and Cheryl Lynn Goodman; [memb.] 4-H, FHA; [hon.] Artist of the Year, 1993-Best Supporting Actress 1993; [a.] Chilhowee, MI 64733.

GOODWIN, JULIE
[pen.] Julie Goodwin; [b.] December 30, 1970, Hay River, NWT (Northwest Territories); [p.] Jim and Betty Goodwin; [ed.] Father Mecredi High School, Keyano College; [occ.] Child Care Worker; [hon.] High School Poetry Award; [oth. writ.] Several personal poems; [pers.] Because of my interest in children I have written several poems about them and am striving towards writing a children's book based on my experiences and knowledge. [a.] North Vancouver BC V7M 1S4 Canada.

GORDON, AMANDA JO
[pen.] Amanda Jo Gordon; [b.] April 4, 1977, East Chicago, Illinois; [p.] William R. Ashley and Paula Gordon; [pers.] An a special thanks to my father (William Ashley) for encouraging me to pursue my writing career. [a.] Gary, IN 46406.

GORDON, SAMBRINEA S.
[b.] November 18, 1940, Lawrence, Massachusetts; [p.] Samuel A. Gordon; [ed.] University of Colorado; [occ.] Soldier of Fortune; [memb.] Children International National Aids Project; [oth. writ.] Arizona Press Women, First Place, Fiction, Arizona State University. Poem used in HIV-Aids Education Through Performance Project Creative Writing Workshop - poetry/plays; [pers.] When the Human Voice Screams: Someone needs to be taking notes. [a.] Phoenix, AZ 85072.

GOULD, JOIS A.
[pen. Jois A. Gould; [b.] December 16, 1929, Newark/Elizabeth; [p.] Charles R. and Ann H. Walker; [m.] John C. Lyons, July 4, 1978; [ed.] High School, college 2 years and 4 years other; [occ.] Poetry-Artist World Peace and Government; [memb.] From school years - World of Poetry and yours; [hon.] Over 150 awards - silver and homer honor and numerous others; [oth. writ.] Classics, children's books-Penshre Thee and Old Glory, The Gamut; [pers.] From Tiny Child - loving it day and night endeavor and all kind of poets, writers, artists and the like before me. [a.] Orange, NJ.

GRADSKY, PAT
[b.] September 26, 1941, Los Angeles, California; [p.] Joel and Iva L. Wright; [ch.] David Joe, Sherrye Lynne, John Matthew; [ed.] Polytechnic High, Texas Christian University BFA, U.T.A., N.T.S.U.; [occ.] Self-employed artist; [memb.] Texas Sculpture Association, United We Stand America Women in Broadcasting; [hon.] World of Poetry award 1991, The

National Library of Poetry award 1993, Radio Public Service Program award 1982; [oth. writ.] Articles, poems, cartoons, short fiction published in a local news magazine; World of Poetry award for poem "Fear Deforms"; [pers.] To transcend the world and others need to conform me into their expectations of me; And, to stay true to my own personal vision for my life according to His purpose - and a good pair of sneakers to keep moving. [a.] Fort Worth, TX.

GRAFFORD, CHRIS
[b.] August 7, 1975, Granite City, Illinois; [p.] David and Debbie Grafford; [ed.] Marquette High; [oth. writ.] Several poems in the school paper; [pers.] I enjoy writing poems relating to my age group "teenagers". I have been influenced by late girlfriends and also the greatest power "nature". [a.] Alton, IL.

GRAHAM, ANDREW
[pen.] Xavier; [b.] November 1, 1975, San Jose, California; [p.] Robert and Catherine Graham; [ed.] John Muir Middle School, Bellarmine College Prep.

GRAHAM, CLARA RETHA
[pen.] C. Retha Grahm; [b.] April 20, 1961, Greensboro, North Carolina; [p.] Mr. Willie Hue and Mrs. Mae Catherine Graham, Clara E. McNeill (grandmother); [ed.] Scotland High School, Winston-Salem State University; [occ.] Teacher Assistant; [hon.] Certificate of Merit (WSSU), Miss Physical Education, Super Volunteer Award Special Olympics Volunteer; [oth. writ.] Several poems written for future publication; [pers.] Poems of rhyme, poems of rhythm, poems from my heart to you are given. [a.] Winston-Salem, NC 27103.

GRAHN, GABRIELLE LOUISE
[b.] July 4, 1972, Elgin, Illinois; [p.] Carole Grahn-Hayes and Gerald Grahn; [ed.] Graduate of Batavia High School 1990; [occ.] Retail Sales; [oth. writ.] "GoodBye" published in "All My Tomorrows" Vol. II, Quill Books. [a.] Batavia, IL 60510.

GRANDINETTI, DEBORAH ANNE
[b.] March 7, 1960, Brooklyn, New York; [p.] Frank and Mary Ann Grandinetti; [ed.] BS, Boston University; [occ.] Proprietor of 'Birthin' Books: A Literary Midwife Service for innovators who want to inspire; [memb.] Human race, self-realization fellowship; [hon.] Boston University Faculty/Alumni Award for Top Print Journalism Graduate; [oth. writ.] Co-author of: Postive Living and Health: The Complete Grade to Brain/Body Healing and Mental Empowerment (Kodale 1990) and four other Kendale books, also published in Boston Globe, San Jose Mercury News, India Times. [a.] Sonoma, CA 95476.

GRANDT-BERGER, LYNN
[b.] October 21, 1950, Columbus, Georgia; [p.] Edward and Enza Grant; [m.] Divorced; [ch.] Thomas Grant Berger, Matthew Edward Berger; [ed.] BS 1973-Vanderbilt University, M.Ed. 1983 Columbus College; [occ.] English Teacher, Cross Creek High School, Pompano Beach, FL; [memb.] Kappa Delta Pi, Broward Teachers Union; [hon.] Teacher of the Year 1991, Who's Who in America, Who's Who in the South, Who's Who of Emerging Leaders in America, Who's Who in American Education, Who's Who in the World, Who's Who of American Women; [pers.] I write to purge my soul and to understand myself. [a.] Coral Springs, FL 33071.

GRANDSTON, SARAH JAKE
[b.] February 5, 1978, Arlington, Washington; [p.] Jack and Lynn Granston; [ed.] Arlington High School; [occ.] Student and Tree Farm worker; [memb.] Human Race; [pers.] Everybody has their own inner demons (fears). My writing is about mine and how I live with them. You must deal with them before you can live in peace. [a.] Arlington, WA 98223.

GRASS, JAYME
[pen.] Jayne Grass; [b.] April 1, 1979, Metaline Falls, Washington; [p.] Dean and Kathy Grass; [ed.] Selkirk High School.

GRAVEL, SANDY
[pen.] Sandy; [b.] April 22, 1970, Hinton, Alberta; [p.] Carly and Danny Gravel; [m.] Joseph Macroux, July 24, 1993; [ch.] Jaime Lee Brianne; [ed.] Grade 12 graduate 1988 (Airdrie, Alberta, Canada); [occ.] Administrative Assistant; [hon.] High School Drama Award; [oth. writ.] Several other poems, mostly reflective of life experiences and personal views and outlooks on life; [pers.] If you can reach deeply enough inside yourself to really see who you are-understanding others and life as we know it comes naturally. [a.] Calgary, Alberta, Canada T2B 2T2.

GRAVES, LINDLEY D.
[pen.] C.D. Graves; [b.] August 18, 1860, Waterloo, Iowa; [p.] Mr. and Mrs. Edson Graves; [ed.] Campbell Sport High School 1979 grad; [occ.] Dishwasher, St. Joseph Convent; [oth. writ.] None-The-Less, released to 100 different radio stations in the United States; [pers.] I think we're here to have and help each other. I think life is a honor. [a.] Campbellsport, WI 53010.

GRAWN, CHARLOTTE R.
[b.] June 18, 1908, Duluth, Minnesota; [p.] Dr. Fred Augustus and Vera Ramkin Grawn; [ed.] BS Spearfish State University, S.D., one year graduate study in medical care at University of OSLO, Norway; [occ.] Nurse (Retired), Physical Therapist (Retired); [memb.] Spearfish S.D. Senior Citizens, Spearfish State College Alumnae; [hon.] $900 Scholarship, St. Mary's School of Nursing, 1932 (Salutatorian), one year study of medical care, OSLO, Norway; [oth. writ.] One poem published in Christian Century (magazine) - "Cup of Antioch"; [pers.] I have no religion except the contemplation of nature. Of course I try to lead a good life. [a.] Spearfish, SD.

GRAY, ALICE (RAIMO)
[pen.] Alice Ann; [b.] May 7, Massachusetts; [p.] Frank and Helen Raimo; [m.] Robert A., April 1968; [ch.] Robert R. and Andrea A.; [ed.] New England College; [occ.] Nurse, Mother/wife, Secretary, writer; [memb.] L.P.N., Seacoast Women's Network; [oth. writ.] Article published in local newspaper, articles published in company newsletter; [pers.] I search for truth, honesty, and the rights of all, especially children and women to express their feelings. [a.] Hampton, NH 03842.

GRAY, DARLENE DEE
[pen.] Taz or Dee; [b.] September 2, 1978, Fall River; [p.] Ted and Susan Souza; [ed.] Durfee High School (Sophomore); [occ.] Babysit; [memb.] YMCA; [hon.] Honor Roll 7-9th grades, Science Fair 5th place, Race 6th grade; [oth. writ.] I have written other poems,

horror poems. I wrote many and I write many more; [pers.] I am influenced by all great poems. I write what I feel and what I have experienced. [a.] Fall River, MA 02721.

GRAY, JOAN M.
[b.] January 5, 1933, St. Catherine's Ontario, Canada; [p.] Leo M. and Blanche M. Book; [m.] Robert, May 10, 1980; [ch.] Linda, Eleanor, Donna, Danny, Patricia, David, four-step children, 24 grand children, and one great grandchild; [ed.] DeWitt Carter Public School, working toward high school diploma; [occ.] Retired computer operator and now housewife; [hon.] Graduated public school with honors; [oth. writ.] Articles and poems published in local newspapers; [pers.] My poems are written about things that have happened in my life or to people I love, or friends I know. Basically, I write about everyday happenings. [a.] Port Colborne, Ont. Canada L3K 2M5.

GRAY, SHELLY A.
[pen.] Shelly A. Gray; [b.] January 11, 1968, Clovis, California; [p.] Ronald D. and Margaret A. Gray; [ed.] Graduate of Poway High School; [occ.] Data Entry Clerk; [oth. writ.] Many as of yet unpublished poems; [pers.] Like most all poetry, mine reflects how I feel or how I felt at the time of writing. I enjoy writing and like the possibility that it will take me somewhere. [a.] Mukilteo, WA 98275.

GRAY, WANDA CAROL
[b.] September 7, 1957, Ackerman, Mississippi; [p.] Coy and Lois Mann; [m.] Sam Wayne, September 18, 1976; [ch.] Michael Wayne, Carlton Lee, Charles Samuel; [ed.] Weir High School, Holmes Junior College; [occ.] Housewife, mother; [memb.] Mississippi State University Alumni, First Baptist Church, Eupora; [hon.] Elected most likely to succeed, and most athletic in high school, basketball scholarship at Holmes Junior College (Goodman, MS; [oth. writ.] Poem published in Reflections in College; [pers.] My poetry is greatly influenced by my family and friends, and with God's help the words come easily. [a.] Eupora, MS 39744.

GREABELL, JANETTE G.
[b.] October 18, 1916, Maplewood, New Jersey; [p.] Walter M. and Mary F. Gray (both from Scotland); [m.] Robert H. Sr., November 20, 1942; [ch.] Robert H., Jr., Richard Scott; [ed.] Maplewood Junior High, Drake Business College, Syracuse University writing courses, West Point art classes; [occ.] Freelance artist, art teacher, East Syracuse-Minoa Adult Education Program; [memb.] First United Church of E. Syracuse, ESTMIM Organ Society, CSEA, 25th Division Ladies Aux., Choir, Fellowship Choral Group, The Organ Orchestra; [hon.] Various Art awards, "Gracious Living" Church award; [oth. writ.] Children's stories-one accepted for anthology; [pers.] Inspired by Maya Angelou's inaugural poem "On The Pulse of Morning" to tell-it-like-it-is. [a.] East Syracuse, NY 13057-9445.

GREBINER, TIMOTHY WILLIAM
[b.] October 23, 1969, Pittsburgh, Pennsylvania; [ed.] Bachelor's Degree St. Vincent College; [hon.] Appeared as guest poet with Muse for Moderns; [oth. writ.] Many other poems and songs, but only a handful that have ever been tossed into the light; [pers.] Play Hard. Live Fast. Love Once, Die Young. [a.] Pittsburgh, PA 15201.

GREEN, CHRISTOPHER DANIEL
[b.] October 9, 1977, Geneva, Alabama; [p.] Jack and Tonja Green; [ed.] Ninth grade Geneva High; [occ.] Student; [memb.] Symphonic Band, Varsity Football; [hon.] Eigth grade perfect attendance, 91/92, Junior Varsity-Best Lineman, third place in Lip Synch Contest 1993, third place in S.E. AL Nintendo Challenge 1987; [oth. writ.] I've written a complete book of poems, short stories, and songs which has not been published and only a <u>few</u> members of my family (1 or 2) and a couple of friends have read. I would love to have them published; [pers.] Most of my writings are about things that go on around me and have to do with my views on society today. Jim Morrison, the lead singer of the Doors has been my major influence. I wrote my first poem after seeing the movie The Doors. Prince has also influenced some of my writings. [a.] Geneva, AL 36340.

GREEN, LATOYA
[b.] January 16, 1975, St. Petersburg, Florida; [p.] Tommy and Laura Green; [m.] Brother-Tommy Green, Jr.; [ed.] Silver Valley High School, Yermo, CA; [occ.] Student-12 year; [pers.] Through the teachings of Malcolm X and Martin Luther King, Jr., we can all learn to love one another, and strive for equality. [a.] Barstow, CA 92311.

GREENBERG, ANGELA
[pen.] Angela, Angie, A.J.G; [b.] January 26, 1976; [p.] Kathy and March Greenberg; [ed.] Currently a Junior at Mountlake Terrace High School, graduating in June of 1994; [memb.] Jobs for Edmonds Graduates; [hon.] Natural Helper, State Finalist in Miss American Co-ed Pageant; [pers.] Poetry is a beautiful wonderful work of art which enables me to express my feelings and emotions freely. Dedicated to Timothy Charles Thompson. [a.] Mountlake Terrace, WA 98043.

GREENBERG, PEARL
[pen.] Grandma (5 grandchildren); [b.] August 13, 1921, Yazoo City, Mississippi; [p.] Louis and Rose Rosen; [m.] Morris Greenberg (deceased), November 30, 1941; [ch.] Joseph, Michael and Eddie Greenberg; [ed.] High School, some adult education courses in Brooklyn College; [occ.] I sell expensive shoes to rich ladies; [memb.] Tennis Club, Bowling League, Singles Club; [hon.] Nothing recently, your letter was an honor; [oth. writ.] I am editor or our Condominium Newspaper - it's a labor of love; [pers.] You've got to be grateful for whatever there is to be grateful for. (My mother's quote.) [a.] Tamarac, FL 33321.

GREENE, VICTOR T.
[b.] March 6, 1960, Columbus, ARB, Mississippi; [p.] Christopher L. and Marion A. Greene Sr.; [ed.] High School graduate Landrum High School; [occ.] Unemployed machine operator; [oth. writ.] Poems published in Great Poems of Our Time, On the Threshold of a Dream, and World's Largest Poem for Peace; [pers.] My hope is that my writing may inspire or touch at least one person in a way that would be beautiful to everyone. [a.] Landrum, SC 29356.

GREENWELL, RACHAEL MCKEE
[pen.] Rachael McKee Greenwell; [b.] December 16, 1919, Somerville, Morgan County, Alabama; [p.] Gilbert and Bertha Prince McKee; [m.] Harold R., December 29, 1942; [ch.] Gilbert Richard, Margaret

Edith, and Susan Marie; [ed.] High school diploma - Morgan County High School; [occ.] Housewife; [memb.] University Baptist Church JUBILEE Singers, Senior Choir, MADD, American Heart Association; [oth. writ.] Letters to the Editor, Huntsville, AL. [a.] Huntsville, AL 35806.

GRENIER, NELDA R.
[pen.] Nelda Ramey; [b.] April 13, 1956, Glasgow, Kentucky; [p.] Harry and Susie Ramey; [ch.] Michael D. and Daniel B. Vaughn; [oth. writ.] Too numerous to name all unpublished; [pers.] We trade time for wisdom, peace for power, and love for only a promise of a greater one. God bless our ignorance. [a.] Bowling Green, KY 42101.

GRICE, GARY LYNN
[pen.] Gary Lynn Grice; [b.] March 13, 1947, Albion, Michigan; [p.] Herbert S. and Vivian M. Grice; [m.] Mary F., August 5, 1972; [ch.] Jennifer Lynn Grice; [ed.] Albion High School, Kellogg Community College, Western Michigan University, Michigan State University; [occ.] Hearing Aid Specialist, Beltone Hearing, Kalamazoo, MI; [memb.] M.B.G.H., V.V.A. chap. 313, N.A.F.C., N.A.H.C., C.B.A., World Bowhunters Club, N.R.A., Calhoun County Republican Club; [hon.] 1989 National C.B.A. Champion, Eagle Scout, Dean's List, one hundred plus salesmanship awards from various insurance companies; [oth. writ.] Several poems published in local newspapers, articles for State Auto Magazine, and A.F.L.A.C. Bell Ringer; [pers.] I draw my inspiration from nature and the foibles of mankind, with liberal use of humor, so that I won't cry. [a.] Marshall, MI 49068.

GRIFFEN, KARN W.
[b.] October 9, 1935, Newark, New Jersey; [m.] Suzanne; [ch.] Mary, Karn, Chris, Will; [ed.] AB in Princeton University, MBA Rutgers University, DMin. Fuller Theological Seminary; [occ.] Pastor Lakewood Christ Presbyterian Church; [memb.] Los Ranchos Presbytery, Presbyterian Church (USA), USGA; [oth. writ.] Other published poems, "The Church as a Therapeutic Community", <u>Theological Foundation for Ministry</u>, T&T Clark, Eerdmans, 1979, Misc. Book Reviews in Memphis, Commerical Appeal. [a.] Lakewood, CA 90712.

GRIFFIN, JUDITH K.
[pen.] Judy; [b.] September 22, 1945, Des Moines, Iowa; [p.] James and LaVina Glenn; [m.] James A., July 15, 1960; [ch.] Seven; [occ.] Housewife and mother; [oth. writ.] World of Poetry, Nashville Poetry; [pers.] Take the time to listen to your children. Every mood swing is a message they're sending. a[.] Ankent, IA 50021.

GRIFFIN, MARGARET A.
[b.] May 11, 1945, Endicott, New York; [p.] Jean and John L. Griffin; [ed.] College Misericordia BS, SUNY at Cortland MS, CAS University of Vermont; [occ.] School Administrator; [memb.] Phi Delta Kappa, International Reading Association, NCTM, Society of Children's Book Writers and Publishers; [hon.] Recognized as an Outstanding Teacher of Reading, NYS, Recognized as an Outstanding Educator in Vermont, Helen B. Murphy Award-NERA, Sylvia D. Brown Award, MA Reading Association; [oth. writ.] Book-Recipes for Turning Kids On, A Mixture of Learning Centers, Articles-Principal Magazine, A School Where Children Teach Children, NRA Jour-

nal-Irish Setters, Big Books and Mother Goose, An Age Old Tradition Still Thriving; [pers.] As an elementary principal I feel it is important to continually demonstrate my skills as a writer. This poem (and many other pieces) was brainstormed and written by me as the students looked on. [a.] Perry, NY 14530.

GRIFFIN, MARJORIE
[b.] April 13, 1923, Manchester, England; [p.] William Bert Giles and Levinia Stephens [m.] Charles Frederick, February 7, 1948; [ch.] Three girls, two boys (one girl deceased); [ed.] Grade 12 diploma, secretarial course, one class in Medical terminology; [occ.] Retired; [memb.] St. George's African Church; [oth. writ.] Several poems and two or three stories; [pers.] Do unto others as you would have them do unto you. I write poetry when something or some happening inspires me, I try to reflect the thoughts behind the picture before me. [a.] Prince Albert, Sask. Canada S6V 7M4.

GRIFFIN, NAOMI
[b.] February 19, 1930, Wayne County, Michigan; [p.] William Andrew Dickson and Lillian Olive Fink; [m.] Orville Eugene, August 2, 1952; [ch.] Kenneth Gordon and Cindy Lynn Griffin; [ed.] Grade 8 Dickson's Corner's School, Ingersoll Ontario, Canada; [occ.] Housewife; [hon.] Merit awards for poems and lyric writing; [oth. writ.] Patria Formosa, I said Down, Giants Bigfoots and Kings, Johnny Red Bird, some on records; [pers.] I enjoy writing song lyrics and poems, and other writer's poems, but don't care for one's too deep. [a.] Ingersoll, Ont. Canada N5C 3G7.

GRIFFIS, JODIE P.
[b.] September 1, 1963, Billings, Montana; [p.] Frank and Joyce Goddard (whom I thank for helping make so many things in my life possible); [m.] Dennis C., January 12, 1989; [ch.] Tiffany JoAnne, Samantha Joy; [ed.] Ashland High School, Western Baptist College (Salem, OR); [occ.] Customer Sales Representative-Budget Rent-a-Car, Mom and housewife; [pers.] Poetry is always a good thing to read or write for inspiration and reflection for all occasions. (Thanks Mom and Dad). [a.] Reno, NV 89512.

GRIFFITH, BARBARA
[b.] November 22, 1955, Bethesda, maryland; [p.] Robert and Mary Byers; [m.] Robert, July 27, 1974; [ch.] Bob, Jr., Theresa, Jennifer; [occ.] Noon-Time Supervisor - Alvin Dunn Elementary; [pers.] I write for my children and children everywhere. [a.] San Marcas, CA.

GRIJALVA, RICK
[b.] April 5, 1970, San Jose; [p.] Ezekiel and Isela Grijalva; [ed.] Mount Pleasant High School, San Jose City College, Evergreen Valley College; [occ.] Production Operator; [oth. writ.] Personal- Journals of Reality; [pers.] Ah, Children of innocence lost, brush your tear-torn eyes and allow the quill to weep. [a.] San Jose, CA 95148.

GRIMES, RALPH E.
[pers.] I believe that a poem should <u>communicate</u>, at a level approaching (or even surpassing) actual experience, something valuable (and apparently understandable) which has not been noticed before (or at least quite in that way). It should approach one in a friendly manner, but reveal (as in any good friend-

ship) more and more secrets with each subsequent encounter. A poem should be, and it should be for all who read it. This is my fervent and deeply held poetic creed. [a.] Los Angeles, CA 90027.

GRIMMIG, ALVIN E. SR.
[pen.] Alvin E. Grimmig, Sr.; [b.] March 2, 1927, Memphis, Tennessee; [p.] Fred A. and Mary Virginia Grimmig, Sr.; [m.] 1-Nora Margaret, June 9, 1949 and 2-June 15, 1991; [ch.] Alvin E. Jr., Margaret Frey, Lynda Rogers - 6 grandchildren; [ed.] Miami Beach High, 1945 8 years at different schools; [occ.] Ret. U.S. Post Office; [memb.] AARP, Knights of Columbus, American Legion; [hon.] Presbyterian Church 19, City of Fort Lauderdale, FL; [oth. writ.] 15 other poems and 3 songs; [pers.] Write what is in your heart, always write the truth. [a.] Ft. Lauderdale, FL 33311-4824.

GROEGER, MARY ELIZABETH DR.
[pen.] Dr. Mary Elizabeth Groeger; [b.] Lone Pine, California; [p.] Hilary Frank and Josephine Oliver Morales; [m.] Earl B., April 27, 1947; [ch.] Steve and daughter-in-law Karin, Ryan and Jeffrey (grandsons); [ed.] U.C.L.A., Loma Linda University, Acupuncture, Research College, Sierra Memorial Hospital; [occ.] Dr. of Acupuncture, Dr. of Chinese Herbology; [memb.] Acupuncture Research Institute, Center for Chinese Med., International College of American Med. Society; [hon.] Doctorate of Acupuncture (1/1982), Doctorate of Traditional Chinese Medicine (9.25.82), three proclamations, from city of Pico Rivera, CA, First American nurse to be Dr. of Acupuncture in CA started in 1969. Chinese Cancer Surgeons, were my professors; [oth. writ.] "The Profile" city hall newsletter, Knights of Columbus (Pico Rivera), newspaper Highlander, local paper some hospitals and churches; [pers.] Thankful to God, for the good I see, people, places things. My writings comfort people lifts their spirits regardless of circumstances. [a.] Pico Rivera, CA 90660.

GUERRERO, CHARLIE A.
[pen.] Chubby; [b.] January 2, 1954, Morenci, Arizona; [p.] Isabel and Charles M. Guerrero; [ed.] Eastern Arizona Junior College/Grand Canyon College-Phoenix, Arizona/Golden Gate Theological Seminary-Mill Valley, OK., Southwestern College-Education, to become a teacher; [occ.] BA Degree, Interpreter for American Express, Phoenix, AZ (5 years); [memb.] DECA Club-E.A.C. Junior College, Letterman's Club-G.C.C. College; [oth. writ.] First writing in Poetry, 1993; [pers.] In writing my first poem, I have been extremely inspired from the less fortunate in the City of Phoenix, and have been touched by their hurts and desires. [a.] Phoenix, AZ 85008.

GUILBAULT, NICOLE M.
[b.] April 6, 1971, Newport, Rhode Island; [p.] Oscar R. and Marguerite D. Guilbault; [ed.] Our Lady of the Angels Academy, Bolton High School, University of Connecticut - 1993; [occ.] Student; [memb.] Volunteer teacher, English as A Second Language; [pers.] How we live our days is, in reality how we live our lives. [a.] West Willington, CT.

GULLEDGE, IRENE
[b.] June 28, 1913; [occ.] Retired piano and organ teacher; [memb.] Loxley United Methodist Church; [oth. writ.] Poems published in two other anthologies.

Songs and responses which have been sung in my church and other local churches; [pers.] Only the giver of life can teach us how to live life. His word is a lamp unto our feet and a light unto our pathway. [a.] Loxley, AL 36551.

GUM, LORRI
[b.] May 15, 1961, Fairfield, Washington; [p.] Glen Meredith and Betty Hanson; [m.] Tom, October 17, 1981; [ch.] Robert Gum; [occ.] Housewife; [memb.] Zinland Northwest, Zoological Society; [hon.] Editor's Choice Award for Outstanding Achievement in Poetry; [oth. writ.] To My Love, published in, Wind in the Night Sky. It was among the best 3 % of all entries; [pers.] I wrote this poem for my son. I try to devote all my time and love to my Husband and my son. And I try to be the best person that I can be. [a.] Worley, ID 83876.

GUMAN, PAULINE TATIANA
[pen.] Tatiana; [b.] February 15, 1934, Jermyn, Pennsylvania; [p.] Michael and Anna Chup Mizok; [m.] Joseph Jr., April 8, 1953; [ch.] Joseph III, Paul G. Guman and Judy Guman McCabe; [ed.] Jermyn High School-class of '52; [occ.] Homemaker, garment worker; [memb.] AARP-Mid Valley Sr. Activity Center, Over Fifty Club of Jessup, PA, WIBC; [hon.] Four grandsons (Brandon and Justin Guman, James and Jonathan McCabe); [oth. writ.] Lost Treasure, "All This and a Meal Too!"-published in local paper "Active Senior"; [pers.] It's a wonderful feeling to be able to express your thoughts in writing. The writer and the reader can both bring out their emotions of laughter or tears. Sometimes you are a poet and don't know it! [a.] Olyphant, PA 18447.

GUNNEK, RONALD W., JR.
[pen.] Ronnie; [b.] March 30, 1966, Houston, Texas; [p.] Ronald W. and Josephine E. Gunnels; [m.] Cherry S., July 13, 1992; [ch.] Amber, Lacey, Cody, and Aaron; [ed.] High School; [occ.] Metal Refinisher. [a.] New Caney, TX 77357.

GUNSTONE, PHYLLIS R.
[b.] June 27, 1915, Heffley Lake, BC Canada; [p.] Calvin L. and Mary E. Dow (deceased); [m.] R. Dale (deceased), April 6, 1935; [ch.] 2 boys-Donald and Richard, 2 girls-Bonnie L. (Foster) Sharon Overstone; [ed.] High School/graduate college course in Accounting Oil Painting classes; [occ.] Accountant (retired); [hon.] Service Award-19 years dedicated service to Morningside, Inc. Training Center for Disabled; [oth. writ.] One poem - to be published - Western Poetry Associate, articles for Church papers; [pers.] Live life in appreciation of the masterful creation of our universe and strive daily to abide by the Ten Commmandments accept Jesus as my Savior and pray for world peace and the time all people live in brotherly love, in harmony with God. [a.] Olympic, WA 98512-9401.

GUPPY, JOANNE
[b.] March 29, 1975; [p.] Wilfred and Julie Guppy; [ed.] Currently attending college at Albany; [occ.] Student; [hon.] Junior High School and High School Poetry Contest, currently on Dean's List; [oth. writ.] No other published writings; [pers.] My poem written in the book is dedicated to my loving father who is a missing person.

GUTCHESS, PHILLIP
[pen.] P.E.G.; [b.] June 19, 1962, Jackson, Michigan; [p.] Fred L. and Patricia A. Gutchess; [ch.] Aaron Michael Gutchess; [ed.] Vandercook High School; [oth. writ.] Personal journal; [pers.] Only through conquering your fears, can you cast the chains that bind your growth as a human being! [a.] Jackson, MI 49201.

GUTIERREZ, KEVIN LEE
[b.] April 13, 1974, Panama Canal Zone; [p.] Rudy and Linda Gutierrez; [pers.] Be true to your heart, pursue your dreams, and live life to the fullest. [a.] Snyder, TX 79549.

GWILT, DONNA DOREEN
[b.] January 27, 1951, Chatham Ontario, Canada; [p.] Dorothy and Cecil Tunks; [m.] John Morris, October 18, 1969; [ch.] Renee and David (grandson-Marty Randal); [ed.] Graduate Arts and Sciences grade twelve; [occ.] Chief Administrative Assistant - Canada Employment; [memb.] Co-leader Resurrection Church Music Ministry; [hon.] Merit award from Director General Employment and Immigration; [oth. writ.] Composed a cassette of ten original inspirational gospel songs - tape called Go Forth Boldly was released in may 1990 (self-management); [pers.] Even if you think your goal is unobtainable - Never give up your dreams! I may never find a record producer but I'll continue to sing and write songs and poetry. [a.] Fort St. John BC V1J4M6 Canada.

HAAS, BEATRICE
[pen.] Bea Haas; [b.] April 21, 1926, Konawa, Oklahoma; [p.] Earl J. and Lee Oxley Quinn; [m.] George Earl, October 27, 1945; [ch.] Harold George Haas and Connie Lee Haas Kay; [ed.] Graduated 1944 from Shawnee High School (Shawnee, OK); [occ.] Housewife and Sunday School Teacher; [memb.] Konawa Free Will Baptist Church at Konawa, OK; [oth. writ.] Several poems published in Shawnee, OK "The Shawnee News Star paper; [pers.] My inspiration comes from my family, sermons that I hear and what God gives to me. [a.] Konawa, OK 74849.

HAAS, KATE
[b.] July 12, 1980, Philadelphia, Pennsylvania; [p.] Richard and Linda Haas; [ed.] 7th grade student at Redeemer Lutheran School; [hon.] Honorable mention in school writing contest; [oth. writ.] Several poems and short stories printed in my school newspaper; [pers.] My career goal is to become a poet or a writer. [a.] Philadelphia, PA 19135.

HAASE, LORI
[b.] October 8, 1976, New Orleans, Louisiana; [p.] Julie Haase; [ed.] Sophomore in High School; [occ.] Student. [a.] Covington, LA 70433.

HADDAD, ADELE
[b.] November 18, 1928, Portage, Pennsylvania; [p.] Edward Haddad and Jamele Nasrallah; [ed.] Portage High School, Georgetown University (DC), Pennsylvania Academy of the Fine Arts, Corcoran Art School, Grenoble University (France); [occ.] Retired; [memb.] Study of Religion throughout the year attendance every Monday; [hon.] Austrian Ambassador exhibited my painting of Salzburg in the State Department exhibit. Congressman Gude awarded me first prize, UPO Director awarded me a certificate of appreciation for services in Senior Citizen weekend

feeding program and many other awards; [oth. writ.] Six poems published in an anthology, an article in Senior Deacon, and a poem in the Georgetowner newspaper; [pers.] My one ambition is to serve all ethnicities and see all universalized in harmony as a society of peace and war thoughts FOREVER ERASED FROM THE EARTH. [a.] College Park, MD 20740.

HAFFNER, MATTHEW
[pen.] Matt; [b.] March 18, 1978, Hutchinson, Kansas; [p.] Bobby and Donna Haffner; [ed.] Ninth grade at Spencer High School, Fairview Elementary; [occ.] Youth Sports Instructor; [memb.] Youth Bowling Association, YMCA Membership; [hon.] Varsity letter for Photography; [oth. writ.] One poem published in the Daily Reporter in Spencer; [pers.] You can do anything in the world. All you need is your mind, a pencil and a piece of paper. [a.] Spencer, IA 51301.

HAGAN, RICHARD C.
[pen.] Richard C. Hagan, Maj. Gen. USAF (Ret.); [b.] January 31, 1911, Griggsville, Illinois; [p.] Warren L. and Mabel R. Brunner Hagan; [m.] Lois R. Holder Hagan, June 19, 1940; [ch.] Richard D. Hagan, PhD., SEIll Community College Official, Ann Lynn Hagan Kief; [ed.] Urbana High, AB with honors Univ. of Illinois, LLB-JD Law School, LLM, Columbia Law School, Un., Fellow, Asst. Prof. Law, Mercer University, (Macon, GA), Comb. & Gen. Staff School, U.S. Army; [occ.] Retired U.S. Foreign Service Officer and Diplomat, Retired Attorney, Retired Reserve Military Attorney (First Reservist with rank of major gen. VFW Am. Legion, various Masonic Bodies in U.S. and in Scotland, Boy Scouts of America, Annandale United Methodist Church (Annandale, VA); [hon.] Phi Beta Kappa, Bronze Tablet 1933, AB with Honors, President Senior Class-Law School, Univ. of Ill. 1935-36, Military Decorations-Legion of Merit, USAF, Pre-Pearl Harbor Medal, President, D.C. Reserve Officers Association; [oth. writ.] Some 600 poems, largely of the personal, life revealing, historical, and humorous type. Oral Interview History Yale, type, USAF Archives, JAG School, Air University, Montgomery, AL; [pers.] I find that writing in the poetic format brings understanding of clarity of concepts, philosophies, life itself, and especially reactions to the people, individually and groups. Praise and recognitions can be to the often genuine accorded kindnesses and generosities of otherwise unknown and ordinary folks. [a.] Cape Girardeau, MO 63701.

HAGGARD, DARLEEN MARIE
[b.] December 19, 1954, Redding, California; [p.] Chester E. and Darlene J. Randall and Desmond R. and Myrtle Keaton; [ch.] Thomasina M. Baker Houk (18) and Daniel E. Baker (16); [ed.] I completed tenth grade before getting married then seven years later I took my CA GED and passed; [occ.] Disabled - domestic engineer and factory seamstress; [pers.] Don't let your life slip away and mean nothing. Each person you meet is to learn from or to teach something to. Touch each persons life in a loving way, so you will be remembered by all you touch lovingly. [a.] Smithville, TN 37166-1814.

HAINES, KIMBERLY JEAN
[b.] March 13, 1979, Pella, Iowa; [p.] David Bruce and Malinda Jean Shafman; [ed.] Southeast Polk Junior High School; [memb.] Altoona Christian Church; [hon.] Honor Roll, School Citizenship Award, Presidential Academic Fitness Award; [pers.] I write poems telling of my own experiences, but try to let others relate to them also. I believe that anyone can do anything if they really try. [a.] Runnells, IA 50237.

HAINS, LORRAINE
[b.] August 9, 1925, Sherbrooke, Quebec; [p.] Edouard Hains and Gabrielle Marcoux; [ed.] College - boarding 14 years in nine different convents; [occ.] Retired; [memb.] U.Q.A.M. University of Quebec, in Montreal; [hon.] Finalist "Les Poetes de la Monteregie" - Le Conquerant, Summer 1991; [oth. writ.] Fifty French and English poems and some prose (unpublished); [pers.] Writing enables me to glorify Nature, it also helps me to better communicate with Humans. Loving Medieval Poetry, I feel I would have been more at ease having been born in the 19th century... [a.] Longueuil, Que. J4J 3E9.

HALE, LAURA D.
[b.] August 4, 1957, Queens, New York; [p.] Barbara and Frank Piazza; [m.] John G., July 19, 1980; [ch.] John Willis and Christopher James Hale; [ed.] BSE Physical Education, Cortland State; [occ.] Movement Education Instructor; [pers.] My intentions are to recreate childhood experiences in an entertaining poetic style. My inspiration, therefore this dedication, come from my children, John Willis and Christopher. [a.] Frewsburg, NY 14738.

HALEY, GERALDINE
[b.] July 23, 1925, Wilmington, Delaware; [p.] Thomas and Frances Loughrey (both deceased); [m.] Lawrence (deceased), October 23, 1948; [ch.] Gregory, Sharon, Michael, also four grandchildren; [ed.] High School, P.S. du Pont, some evening classes through the years; [occ.] Retired; [memb.] Fox Point Association, Sellers Senior Center, St. Helena's Church, AARP; [oth. writ.] I have written other poems just for my one enjoyment and family and friends. None published; [pers.] There are many overlooked pleasures in life. I focus on these in both poems and oil paintings. This gives me great pleasure. [a.] Wilmington, DE 19809.

HALEY, JILL WHITCHER
[pen.] J.W. Haley; [b.] May 27, 1972, Woodsville, New Hampshire; [p.] David and Judy Whitcher; [m.] Elmer, Jr., August 29, 1992; [ed.] Oxford High School, Plymouth State College; [hon.] President's List; [pers.] I have the conviction that the attempt to explain the Wordless is what causes human beings to write. [a.] Warren, NH 03279.

HALL, MILDRED ELIZABETH
[b.] July 3, 1953, Marion, Ohio; [p.] Mr. and Mrs. George Earhart; [m.] Lester A. Hall, January 14, 1973; [ch.] Amber Marie and Mark Anthony Ray Hall; [ed.] Graduate from North Union High School (1972); [occ.] Housewife; [memb.] Essex United Methodist Church; [oth. writ.] Yes, I have at least 12 other poems that have been written but not published, The Grace of Self Denial, is my first to be published; [pers.] My first poem I wrote was on a spiritual walk. This is called The Emmaus Walk. I never written a poem in my life until then. This walk was one year of age, Aug. 6, 1972. [a.] Richwood, OH 43344.

HALLENBECK, CYNTHIA A.
[b.] April 12, 1953, Jamestown, New York; [p.] Frank Ellis and Mabel John; [m.] Married 22 years; [ch.] One son; [ed.] Frewsburg Central School; [memb.] Carroll Rod and Gun Club (currently serving 4th year as secretary); [pers.] I hope to touch many hearts through my writings. [a.] Frewsburg, NY 14738.

HALPERN, LINDA CARAY
[b.] December 27, 1947, Oakland, California; [p.] Philip and Melba Rude; [m.] Maurice, April 4, 1993; [ch.] Jeffrey Duane Barker; [ed.] Paramount Senior High, UCLA, ICS, U.S. Army Women's Army Corp.; [occ.] Artist, Interior Designer and Author; [memb.] The Art of Living Center, California Scholarship Federation, Past Honored Queen, International Order of Job's Daughters; ;[hon.] CSF Highest Honors, Bank of America Achievement Award; [oth. writ.] Poem published in "Helican" anthology by the Mile High Poetry Society; [pers.] Create your reality and enjoy the brilliance. [a.] Flagstaff, AZ.

HALVORSEN, MARGARET
[pen.] Margaret Halvorsen; [b.] October 31, 1924, Lake City, Iowa; [p.] Kate Smith and Henry Buttrick; [m.] Evorn; [ed.] Lake City High School, Drake University (Des Moines, IA) graduated 1959; [occ.] Fifty years in the teaching profession (classroom teacher); [memb.] Iowa State Teacher's Association, National Education Association, National Toastmistress; [hon.] Champion of National Hollerin' Contest 1986 Jackport, NV; [oth. writ.] Threshin' Time (poem), Christmas poem every year since 1952; [pers.] I love to write. I write something every day. I started teaching in a rural school at age 18. College degree was earned on Saturdays, evening and summers. [a.] Lake City, IA 51449.

HAMILTON, JUDITH M.
[pen.] Judith Ness Hamilton; [b.] November 18, 1962, Chanalis, Washington; [p.] Frank and Dolores Ness; [m.] Timothy; [ch.] William Michael, Tangella Marie, and Amanda Jean; [ed.] Jeffersonville High School, Florida Junior College; [occ.] Scheduling Coordinator; [oth. writ.] Several poems have been in the paper; [pers.] I try to always be optimistic and look for the best in people. a[.] Jeffersonville, IN 47130.

HAMLETT, JANET
[b.] March 7, 1977, Berrien Springs, Michigan; [p.] Cristena and Woodrow Hamlett; [ch.] Anthony Dewayne; [pers.] I like to share my poetry with others. When I write a poem it comes from the heart. I would like to say to all the people who's out there, if you got a talent don't be scared to show it or do it. [a.] Hartford, MI 49057.

HAMMOND, SHAWNA RAE
[b.] June 10, 1976, Peace River, Alberta, Canada; [p.] Arthur William Hammond and E. Dale Pemberton; [ed.] Grade ten student; [memb.] Appaloosa Horse Club of Canada; [pers.] This poem was written at eleven years old. Love music and play percussion. [a.] Manning, Alta. Canada T0H 2M0.

HAMMONDS, BEN S.
[b.] May 31, 1968, Naples, Texas; [p.] Henry and Mina Hammonds; [m.] Stephanie, October 20, 1989; [ch.] Molly May; [ed.] High School grad, James Bowie School, Simms TX; [occ.] Day and Zimmerman,

Inc., Lone Star Ammo, Maintenance Department; [memb.] National Rifle Association, Hands Across America 1986; [hon.] Most likely to succeed and top 10 of graduating class 1986; [oth. writ.] Have written many poems and pieces of prose, all non published. All having to do with life and its teachings, the symbolisms of said teachings; [pers.] I have always been an outsider and a loner even among close friends. I tend to favor Jack Kerovan and the Beats in their philosophies, I find life a painful pleasure with hard fought lessons to be learned. Everyone should keep living and learning. write down what you know and what you think 'less you forget. Mankind may find solace in something you take for granted! Everyone should own a '55 Mercury, find the symbolism there! Beware of your excesses for excessiveness will be your undoing. [a.] Simms, TX 75574.

HANASH, RAMI S.
[b.] October 18, 1961, Buffalo, New York; [ed.] State University of New York at Buffalo; [occ.] Author/scholar; [oth. writ.] Several works published in national journal; [pers.] I write not for profit or gain, but only for the world to consider, the infinite pleasures conveyed, by the written word. [a.] San Diego, CA 92122.

HANDOE, DONNA J.
[b.] February 4, 1970, Meridan, Connecticut; [p.] Walter C. Jr. and Bonnie Deckert; [m.] Frank C. II, July 1, 1991; [ed.] Maine Central Institute, Austin Peny State University (currently a sophomore; [occ.] Full-time student at APSU, part-time clerk; [hon.] Dean's List at APSU, graduated high school #3 in class, National Honor Society, National Dean's List Book, Honor Student; [pers.] Never stifle your emotions. You should express them in a constructive form. I do so through my poetry. [a.] Clarksville, TN 37040.

HANEY, SANDRA LEE DANLEY
[pen.] Sandy Haney; [b.] October 26, 1962, Portland, Oregon; [m.] Marty, July 26, 1981; [ch.] Steven John and Sharon Rose; [ed.] Christian High and Julian High near San Diego, CA; BS in Education from University of Mary Hardin-Baylor, TX; [occ.] Remedial Reading Teacher, Rockdale Elementary, Rockdale, TX; [oth. writ.] Several poems published in local newspapers; [pers.] My writing is a reflection of my faith in God, and of my passion for His handiwork. [a.] Rockdale, TX 76567.

HANIFAN, SUSAN
[b.] April 4, 1956, Toledo, Ohio; [p.] Virgil and Karis Hanifan widowed, remarried (Karis Borger); [m.] Divorced; [ch.] Katie (11) and Meggie (7); [ed.] BS Agriculture, Ohio State University, continuing education to obtain masters in Occupational Therapy; [occ.] Student and self employed painter and wall paperer, landscape design; [memb.] Zion Lutheran Church, Waterville Play Shop; [pers.] Life is what you make it. "Bloom where you are planted". [a.] Waterville, OH 43566.

HANISCH, JEFF
[b.] December 13, 1971, Sioux Falls; [p.] Walter and Belinda Dejong Hanisch; [ed.] West Central High School; [occ.] Mechanic; [memb.] St. Anns Catholic Church; [hon.] State Finalist for Junior Poetry Contest; [oth. writ.] Many other poems in my collection at home.

HAPPY, JANIS
[b.] November 12, 1947, Eminence, Montana; [p.] Arthur Verne and Dana Elizabeth (Bales) Orchard; [ch.] Tammy Orchard, Candra McGee, Grant Cochran, Delfina Happy; [ed.] Eminence R-1 Elementary and High, Western Business College (Portland, OR); [occ.] Secretary, but at present, Creel Clerk (MO Conservation Department); [oth. writ.] Poetry over past eight years, none published presently working on western novel; [pers.] Most of my poems have been inspired by God, family, or nature. I thank my wonderful mother for her inspiration for this poem. [a.] Birch Tree, MO 65438.

HARDESTY, THERESA LYNN
[pen.] Tressa; [b.] September 20, 1972, Honolulu, Hawaii; [p.] Kathleen Millicent George and Edmond Lee Hardesty; [ed.] Iroquois High (Pennsylvania), beginning nursing school at St. Vincent School of Nursing in 1994; [occ.] Nanny (childcare) for four boys - Tampa, FL; [oth. writ.] I've written many poems but never actually decided to publish them; [pers.] I dedicate this poem to Darren. I am a hopeless romantic and I hope to reach the hearts that are locked inside of every individual. I was inspired at an early age by a young love. [a.] Tampa, FL 33647.

HAREL, EVELYN J.
[pen.] Evelyn J. Harel; [b.] June 26, 1925, Chippewa Falls, Wisconsin; [p.] Ralph and Alilda Kampf; [m.] Died March 5, 1981; [ch.] Ron, Ken, Louis Jr., Louise, Dan, Lorraine, Renae, Barbara, Dave, and Theresa; [ed.] Chippewa Falls High 1944; [oth. writ.] Phantoms of Indian Summer in "Wind in the Night Sky"; [pers.] I believe nature is the greatest of poetry. [a.] Chippewa Falls, WI.

HARLOW, KIMBERLY
[b.] September 16, 1976, Ladysmith, B.C.; [p.] Brenda and Gary Harlow; [ed.] Grade 11 in 1993 - finished; [occ.] Student; [hon.] "B" Honor Roll; [pers.] I enjoy all life's beauty and live by that. This shows in my writing. [a.] Langley B.C. (V3A 3H6) Canada.

HARMER, RAYMOND
[pen.] Raymond J. Harmer; [b.] May 8, 1953, Philadelphia, Pennsylvania; [m.] Cecelia, September 5, 1984; [ch.] Ray, Christine, Stacie, Tracie, Rick, Joe, Brian, and Michael; [ed.] Currently attending Pennsylvania College of Technology at Williamsport, PA; [occ.] Nursing student; [memb.] Cherry Flats Baptist Church; [hon.] Scholarship award in English Literature, Dean's List; [oth. writ.] Several poems and short stories I have not yet submitted for publication; [pers.] I admire the way Robert Frost describes his feelings and thoughts in his writings. God has blessed me with deep feelings and thoughts. I have had many experiences in life, from which most can relate to. I do my best to share them in writing. [a.] Mansfield, PA 16933.

HARNS, NORENE J.
[pen.] NH; [b.] October 23, 1954, Cherry Valley, Ohio; [p.] Donn Jd. and Norma I. Wagner; [ch.] Jennifer Norene Hunkus, Robert Francis Westgate, Jr.; [ed.] Eleventh grade Grand Valley High School, Orwell, OH; [occ.] Warehouse Laborer; [oth. writ.] Just Going - The Restless Ones - The Hollow - Let Me Go (Let Me Be Me) - Alone - The Ocean Song - Moods of Summer - My Friend - and many others; [pers.] I

write to express my inner feelings of people, places, nature, etc... I was greatly inspired by Rod McKuen at age 14. Soft music inspires me, the same with nature. [a.] Pineville, MO 64856.

HARPSTERM LINDA L.
[pen.] Country Dreamer; [b.] August 22, 1946, Belle Fourche, South Dakota; [p.] Ole J. and Lois W. Johnson; [m.] Gary, August, 8, 1965 (deceased 6/2/68) Don Harpster, November 1, 1984; [ch.] Cindy, Diana, Christy, Charlie; [ed.] Rural Elementary, Carter County High Schoo;, two years medical record correspondence course A.R.T.; [occ.] Homemaker, Office Supervisor-Medical Records at Memorial Healthcare Association (Ekalaka, MT); [memb.] Little Missouri Lutheran Church, State and National Medical Record Association; [hon.] National Honor Society; [oth. writ.] Poems for relatives and friends some published in local newspapers; [pers.] Family and friends are the love of my life. I wish to portray my positive feelings of life in general and the good times of the years gone by for family to enjoy in the years to come. [a.] Ekalaka, MT 59324.

HARRAR, JENNIFER LEE
[b.] May 4, 1974, Doyelstown, Pennsylvania; [p.] Earl R. and Helen J.; [ed.] Palisades High School, Penn State University; [occ.] Student and nursing assistant; [oth. writ.] Other personal poems no other previous publishings; [pers.] Nature is only the beginning of my inspiration and my heart is the blossom. [a.] Pipersville, PA 18947.

HARRIS, ERIN M.
[b.] April 27, 1984, Columbus, Ohio; [p.] William J. and Jaren M. Harris; [ch.] brother-Ryan S. harris; [ed.] Granville Elementary; [occ.] Substitute newspaper carrier; [memb.] 4-H member, Pilgrims Lutheran Church; [pers.] Would like to work at a zoo or with animals when she finishes college. [a.] Granville, OH 43023.

HARRIS, JEANETTE
[pen.] Neddy Harris; [b.] July 17, 1937, Wainwright, AB, Canada; [p.] Bert and Belva Whitehead; [m.] Patrick, February 19, 1955; [ch.] Donald, laurie, Ken, Suelle, Michelle; [occ.] Customer Service Representative - Power Company; [memb.] Sedgewick United Church, Foot Hills Bluegrass Society; [hon.] Nominated for award - Outstanding Community Service; [oth. writ.] Several poems; [pers.] Poetry is influenced by environmental concerns. My love of music makes my life very happy.

HARRISON, JON SHELBY
[pen.] Jon Harrison; [b.] September 14, 1971, Lubbock, Texas; [p.] Terry and Vicki Harrison; [ed.] Coronado High School, Lubbock Christian University; [hon.] Honor graduate Coronado 1990; [pers.] I strive to write what I feel in my heart and that other people feel. I hope in some way my poems help them. [a.] Lubbock, TX 79413.

HARROLD, NANCY L.
[pen.] Nancy L. Johnson; [b.] March 2, 1957, Louisville, Kentucky; [p.] Ralph Johnson, Barbara and J.W. Watson; [m.] Divorced; [ch.] James Christopher, Misty Dawn, Larry Dean, Robert Brentwood; [ed.] Mt. Washington, G.E.D.; [occ.] Homemaker and writer hope to be; [pers.] The degrading experiences we feel are ours alone, can only be washed clean

with the knowledge that we are many. [a.] Mt. Washington, KY 40047.

HARROLD, STEPHANIE
[b.] November 9, 1979, Shreveport, LA; [p.] Frank and Susan Harrold; [ed.] I'm going into 8th grade Adam's Junior High; [occ.] Student; [memb.] Chorus Club, my brother's Tribe of Poets; [hon.] An S.A.T. award for showing up all days; [oth. writ.] Bitter Sweet Love, Release Me, Love, All Eternity. I have more poems some of them are really good; [pers.] I wanna thank my brother James for inspiring me to write poetry. I watched him write then I started. I also want to thank my parents. I was also inspired by Edgar Allan Poe's work. [a.] Tampa, FL.

HART, LOMA SUSAN
[b.] June 22, 1921, Pemberton, WV; [p.] William David and Vessa P. Jones; [m.] Paul G., April 27, 1943; [ch.] Paula Susan Baldwin and Richard Paul Hart; [ed.] Woodrow Wilson High, Mrs. Keys Business College (Norfolk, VA), numerous banking courses, graduate of West Virginia Banking School; [occ.] Retired Banker; [memb.] national Association of Bank Women, Sunday School Teacher, Calloway Heights Baptist Church, Beckley Art Group (amateur artist); [oth. writ.] Several poems, some published in local newspaper. Five Golden Poetry awards from World of Poetry, and several silver poetry awards; [pers.] I try to reflect the goodness of mankind and the greatness of God in my writing. I have been greatly influenced by Helen Steiner Rice, and other religious poets and writers. [a.] Cool Ridge, W.VA. 25825.

HART, MABEL E.
[p.] Charles and Emma Hall; [m.] William Hart (deceased), December 5, 1942; [ch.] Dean B. Hart (U.S. Army Ret.); [occ.] Retired Teacher; [pers.] I enjoy reading the ideas that come to mind. I like to think of others who will read my thoughts and smile. [a.] Havre de Grace, MD 21078.

HART, MARTHA SHELBY
[b.] June 23, 1941, Oklahoma City, OK; [p.] DeWitt and Addie Mae Shelby; [m.] Leslie Dean; [ch.] Shelby Thom and Casey Kittrell; [ed.] University of Oklahoma, South Oklahoma City Community College, Capitol Hill High School; [occ.] Commercial/ Graphic Artist Oklahoma Education Association; [memb.] SEE (State Education Editors), Arts Council, Oklahoma City Community College; [oth. writ.] Many several published; [pers.] "It's Alright" written one week after the death of my mother from Alzheimer's Disease. It eased my grief. I tend to write what I feel. [a.] Oklahoma City, OK 73109.

HARTZELL, JOHN
[b.] January 23, 1945, Hardtner, KS; [p.] Mr. and Mrs. Kenneth Hartzell; [ed.] BA Sociology and AA Nursing; [occ.] Service Tech; [memb.] VFW, American Legion, Kiwanis International; [hon.] Published poems in ten books to date, and I bought them all. (Ha, Ha); [oth. writ.] Several newspapers; [pers.] A modest poet of the common people". [a.] Winfield, KS 67156-1808.

HARTZOG, CARLA DAWN
[b.] October 19, 1977, Jefferson, NC; [p.] J. Edward and Parmalee Hartzog; [ed.] Fleetwood Elementary, Beaver Creek High School; [occ.] Student; [memb.] Future Business Leaders of America, Future Teach-

ers Association, Concert Band and Marching Band; [oth. writ.] "What Spring Is To Me" published in Dimensions/World of Words; [pers.] Trust in the Lord and all your dreams will come true. [a.] Fleetwood, NC 28626.

HARVEY, ROBIN
[pen.] Mary Edwards (occasionally); [b.] November 21, 1961, Kansas City, MO; [p.] Joe and Nina Harvey; [ed.] University of Kansas, Johnson County Community College; [occ.] Photographer, commercial and fine art; [hon.] I have won several awards for my commercial and fine art photography; [oth. writ.] No other works published as yet; [pers.] My prose is a venue for me to release the inner turmoil that we all struggle with throughout our lives. [a.] Kansas City, MO 64117.

HASUND, KARLA
[b.] April 2, 1975, Seattle, WA; [p.] Douglas and Karen Hasund; [occ.] Currently a student at A.C.F.C. high school; [pers.] I express my thoughts and opinions in the poems I write. All of the poems I write are influenced by the people around me, current events, and world problems in general. [a.] Everett, WA 98204.

HAULE, MARGARET
[b.] February 27, 1980, Dar Es Salaam, Tanzania; [p.] John and Elizabeth Haule; [ed.] Harvard Avenue School, Armstrong Junior High; [occ.] Volunteer help for poor and elderly/community service worker; [memb.] Young Astronauts Club, Student Council, Peak Program; [hon.] National English Merit Award, D.A.R.E. Award, Honor Roll, Miss Teen of America Scholarship and Recognition program, American Heart Associate "Jump for Heart", Super Kids Award; [pers.] I hope my writings will encourage children especially from low income families that there can be peace in a painful situation. [a.] Mississippi State, MS 39762.

HAUS, TRACY L.
[pen.] Tracy Patton Haus; [b.] October 20, 1968, Wichita Falls, TX; [p.] Donald L. Patton and Donna Hanks; [m.] Gary J., June 17, 1989; [ch.] Sterie Lynn, Joslyn Lee, Jordan Taylor; [pers.] I have been writing short stories and poetry since I was a small child and though my credits are few, I hope I have and will continue to express my point of view through my works. [a.] Kent, WA 98032.

HAUSMAN, SARA
[pen.] Selene Jacobson; [b.] September 11, 1978, Berkeley, CA; [p.] Diana Petitti and Ken Hausman; [ed.] Going to high school; [occ.] Student; [oth. writ.] Crozel, Flowers in the Cross (unfinished); [pers.] This poem is a love, and no matter how dark it is, it is still a love poem. [a.] Piedmont, CA 94611.

HAWES, LAURA B.
[b.] May 30, 1913, Marion, MA; [p.] John L. and Anna Baker; [m.] Henry A., September 23, 1931 [ch.] Henry A. Jr., [ed.] Graduate Fairhaven High School; [occ.] Quality Control Ocean Spray now retired; [memb.] Lifemember Wareham Historical Society, Life member Tobey Hospital Guild, 50 year member Wareham Unit 220 American Legion Auxiliary.

HAYES, ALEX R.
[pen.] A.R. Hayes; [b.] September 12, 1959, Detroit, MI; [p.] Garland and Nora Hayes; [ed.] North Western High, Central Michigan University; [occ.] Hotel and Resort Manager, Petoskey, MI; [hon.] 1991 Golden Poet from World of Poetry in California; [oth. writ.] Poems published in local newspapers; [pers.] If I can make the reader See, Hear, Smell and taste what I did. Yet still question my motives and meaning. I wrote a good poem! [a.] Detroit, MI 48215.

HAYES, ROBERT LEE
[b.] June 29, 1964; [m.] Sue; [ch.] Jesse Lee and Joseph Montieth; [pers.] The people of the earth need to join together and stop the destruction of the rain forest and wasteful use of the earth's materials and if my writings could make people just sit and think what could happen or what already happened. That would be one step further to the reparation of the planet Earth. [a.] Holland, MI 49424.

HAYMAN, NANCY
[b.] October 5, 1941, Picayune, MS; [p.] Clarence and Lois Davis; [m.] George T., February 9, 1963; [ch.] Frances, Truett, Erin; [ed.] Picayune High, William Carey College; [occ.] Kindergarten Teacher Prentiss Christian School; [memb.] Whitesand Baptist Church, Jeff Davis Hospital Auxiliary, Private School Association; [hon.] Crosby Memorial Scholarship, Who's Who in American Colleges and Universities; [pers.] God has given us a great opportunity for good through the written word. I would like to honor him with all I write. [a.] Prentiss, MS 39474.

HAYS, GARNETT L.
[pen.] Chris Hays; [b.] February 27, 1939, Bowling Green, KY; [p.] William T. (deceased) and Mary E. Hays; [m.] Wife - Patricia A. (Gresh) Hays, June 18, 1993; [ch.] Donna Jean, Keith Allan, Robin Lynette; [ed.] Warren High School, Bowling Green, KY; [occ] Hillsborough County Schools, Law Enforcement; [hon.] Awards and Honors U.S. Air Force; [oth. writ.] Several other poems, none published; [pers.] I feel that poetry is a way of bringing out our true feelings and living complete in this world that God gave us.; [a.] Valrico, FL.

HEBERT, SUSAN B.
[pen.] Sue Mimi Hebert and Susan B. Quick; [b.] October 5, 1949, Worcester, MA; [p.] Ralph and Betty Quick; [m.] Alvin C., June 23, 1979; [ch.] Christina M. Farias; [ed.] some college; [occ.] State Civil Service, 20 years currently as a Data Compiler; [memb.] The International Society of Poets; [hon.] Poets awards 1989, 1990 and 1991 through the World of Poetry; [oth. writ.] "Who Will Answer?" in "Great Poems of the Western World", Vol. II by The World of Poetry 1990. "Flight of the Soul" poet collection "All My Tomorrows" by Quill Books 1993. Completed work of essays and vignettes, ready to publish; [pers.] There remains a humanity destiny awaiting to overcome manmade fear. This destiny can energize soul growth of civilization in all walks of life. John Denver's musical words of love and hope have greatly influenced my own personal growth of awareness. [a.] Lacey, WA 98503-0459.

HEIMANN, JENNIFER A.
[pen.] Jen, Jennifer Ann; [b.] March 25, 1980, WI; [p.] Nancy and Richard Heimann; [ed.] Nelson Middle School grade 6; [occ.] Student; [memb.] Girl Scouts,

band (clarinet), volunteer at Darlington Public Library; [hon.] Silver Award in Girl Scouts; [oth. writ.] Several poems, short stories, drawings. [a.] Darlington, WI 53530.

HEITMAN, LESTEE JOANNA
[pen.] Joanna Heitman; [b.] July 24, 1936, White Plains, NY; [p.] Mary Attisani and Michael DeCarlo; [m.] Karl, October 7, 1956; [ch.] Karl (Chuck), Kurt, Cheryll Heitman-White; [ed.] Doctorate in Divinity from the Church of the Holy Spirit (Vienna, VA); [occ.] Pastor of the Call to Prayer Ministry (Glendale, CA); [oth. writ.] Numerous poems and articles in various publications and newspapers. Currently working on a book entitled, "Reflections On the Gospel of John"; [pers.] Communication is so important. It is the responsibility of each of us to use words, either written or spoken, to encourage others to live up to their full potential, as well as to comfort others in times of need. This is my desire in serving others. [a.] Glendale, CA 91202.

HELLER, MELISSA
[b.] January 10, 1965, Gettysburg, PA; [ch.] Steven Guy Heller (11/20/86); [ed.] 1983 graduate of Biglerville High School; [occ.] Real Estate Clerk, Legal Secretary. [a.] Arendtsville, PA.

HELMS, SHERWIN P.
[b.] November 9, 1917, Boston, MA; [m.] Mary Claire Rhodes, September 6, 1942; [ch.] James Rhodes Helms; [ed.] AB Northeastern University, MS (Journalism) Northwestern University, Thunderbird Graduate School of International Management Air War Colllege; [occ.] Military Service World War II and Korea,, Lt. Col., USAF (Ret.), International Advertising, Foreign Service Officer (USIA) (Cuba, Mexico, Vietnam, Washington), Director, National Historic Site (Jamestown, VA Historic Preservation); [memb.] Sigma Delta Chi (Honorary Journalism Fraternity), Rotary International; [oth. writ.] Air Force publications, USIA Magazines, brochures, pamphlets, advertising copy writing, two poetry chapbooks; [pers.] I strive to write understandable poetry--not puzzles, poems that are crisp, sharp, ironic and fun to read. [a.] Williamsburg, VA 23185.

HELSEL, PATRICIA E.
[pen.] Pat Helsel; [b.] October 24, 1941, Miami, FL; [p.] Howard G. and Dora Pinder; [m.] Divorced; [ch.] Robert E. and Ashley E. Helsel; [ed.] Columbus High School, La France Beauty School; [occ.] Cosmetologist and Home attendant (in-home care); [oth. writ.] Unpublished collection of original poems; [pers.] I long to find the words, that will always paint a picture, as they are read, of sadness, of joy, and finally, of hope. [a.] Okeechobee, FL 34972.

HEMA
[b.] January 1, 1964, Bangalore (Karnataka); [p.] T. Gopala Krishna and T. Savirti Devi; [ed.] Central School, Delhi Cantt., Kalindi College, Bhartiya Vidya Bhawan (French Language, diploma course); [occ.] Free-lance writer; [hon.] Second prize in paper reading competition, first prize in quiz competition; [oth. writ.] Written various poems on philosophical, historical, political issues and on nature and life; [pers.] " It seems that evil is powerful, but goodness moves slowly, gradually and steadily, taking actions in time and wins at last". [a.] Mayur Vihar, Phase II, Delhi.

HEMMERT, JOHN EDWARD
[pen.] John E. Hemmert; [b.] January 8, 1933, Pine Bluff, AR; [p.] John E. Hemmert and Lucy Parker Hemmert Raley; [m.] Bernice Stanberry, October 15, 1966; [ch.] Stepson-Keith Stanberry; [ed.] Pine Bluff High, University, Golden (B.S.) State of California (Master); [occ.] Retired Air Force Major, Retired Aviation Federal Manager and Chief States of OK and AR; [a.] Monument, CO 80132.

HEMPHILL, JOE
[b.] October 25, 1943, Joplin, MO; [p.] Joe and Annette Hemphill; [ed.] Santa Barbara High School, Cypress College, Long Beach State University; [occ.] Consultant for the handicapped and writer; [memb.] United Cerebral Palsy of L.A. County and Dayle McIntosh Center; [oth. writ.] Articles published in local and national newspapers; [pers.] Often the disabled or the one needing help can end up being the one giving help. [a.] Anaheim, CA 92804.

HEMPLE, FLORENCE L.
[pen.] Flossy Hemple; [b.] December 10, 1966, Salem, NJ; [p.] Louise and William Dilks; [ed.] Salem High (New Jersey) and Salem Vo-Tech transfer to Woodbridge Senior High DE and Sussex Vo. Tech (autobody); [memb.] Farmington Vol. Firefighter Station 47 (Farmington, DE); [oth. writ.] A poem published for Woodbridge Senior High "My Study Prayer" for Woodbridge Senior High School "Senior Paper"; [pers.] I feel "God" gives everyone a special talent, but you strive to do everything, you will find what you are really great at. I love to write poetry, poems, songs, and sing. In me I found just follow your heart, cry with your pain, think of all your sorrows, and just write your precious memories. [a.] Harrington, DE 19952.

HENDERSON, DENA MARIA
[pen.] dena; [b.] September 28, 1963, Syracuse, NY; [p.] Jerry and Gina Henderson; [ed.] Graduate of StephenvilleHigh in Stephenville, TX; graduate of Central City Business Institute in Syracuse, NY; [occ.] Branch coordinator for ICS/Executone Telecom, Inc. - a telecommunications company; [pers.] My writing is geared toward life, death, and reincarnation. I try to make people stop and think about a variety of ideas.; [a.] Baldwinsville, NY.

HENDERSON, FAYE
[pen.] Faye McBee Henderson; [b.] June 4, 1949, Gaffney, SC; [p.] R.M and Ellawey T. McBee; [m.] Marshall Henderson, January 20, 1968; [ch.] Mike Henderson (1969); [ed.] Graduated from Gaffney Senior High School 1967; [occ.] Cashier-McDonald's Drive Thru; [hon.] Christmas Magic printed in Poet's Corner of Gaffner Ledger, Hometown paper December 1992; [oth. writ.] Written several poems, not published yet; [pers.] Everyone has poems inside them. I find poems come from the heart and through experiences of life and living. [a.] Gaffney, SC.

HENDLEY, MICHELLE
[b.] December 21, 1976, Piggott, AR; [p.] Jean Russell and Kenneth Hendley; [ed.] Attend Twin Rivers High School; [memb.] FBLA; [pers.] If you believe in yourself you ca do anything. [a.] Qulin, MO

HENDON, WANDA
[b.] March 28, 1928, OK; [m.] Jesse, September 1, 1945; [ch.] Carol, Franklin, Betty; [ed.] Graduated

Porterville High; [occ.] Stockroom Supervisor; [memb.] Southern Baptist Church, ISP; [hon.] Several from World of Poetry, Honorable mention, silver and gold; [oth. writ.] Poetry in the Baptist Association over the years; [pers.] To show love for mankind, beauty of nature, and our part in it all. I am influenced most by my family, whom I love dearly. [a.] Porterville, CA 93257.

HENDRICKS, CHRISTY
[pen.] Christy Hendricks; [b.] January 13, 1993, Harris Hospital: Newport, AR; [p.] Donna Vanwinkle and Chris Hendricks; [ed.] Bradford Junior High School; [memb.] Junior Beta; [oth. writ.] This was my first, I have no others; [pers.] I wrote this to prove a point. I want to make the world a better place (even though I'm only 13). [a.] Bradford, AR 72020.

HENDRICKSON, BONNIE G.
[pen.] Bonnie G. parker; [b.] January 26, 1932, Mt. Vernon, OH, Knoc County; [p.] C.C. and Kalhine Griggs; [m.] Paul E., October 4, 1974; [ch.] Stephen D. Randall, Emma J. Ko. Micheial D. Mason, Patrick Parker, John Parker; [ed.] 7th grade; [occ.] Nurse's aide, short order cook, babysitter; [memb.] TOPS, AARP, AA, Seventh Advents Church; [hon.] Able to be me and be accepted as me; [oth. writ.] Mother in Distress, Humble, I Thank You; [pers.] Work on own, since age 12 year God has blessed me all my life truly by everyone I have met, never met, stranger, smiles are catching. [a.] Newark, OH 43055.

HENK, LYNN E.
[b.] March 25, 1945, Evanston, IL; [p.] Walter H. and Anne L. Seidel; [m.] Charles W., March 14, 1970; [ed.] Evanston Township High School, Evanston Business College; [occ.] Retired after 26 years of working at Rotary International (Evanston, IL); [memb.] Business and Professional Women's Club of Evanston; [hon.] Paul Harris Fellows from the Rotary Foundation of Rotary International; [oth. writ.] Poem "Love In America", printed in "U.S., In Clover '76". poem "A Holy Wish" printed in "Our 20th Century's Greatest Poems". [a.] Cicero, IL 60650-1710.

HENLEY, FAYE
[b.] October 7, 1945, Cowan, TX; [p.] William and Margie French Barnes; [m.] Paul E., October 11, 1963; [ch.] Lisa and Michael Henley; [ed.] Franklin County High School; [occ.] Production Manager The Herald Chronicle (Newspaper); [oth. writ.] Numerous articles and features for newspaper where I work, poems and short stories published in other magazines; [pers.] Although most of my published and printed work is of poems and feature articles, my greatest interest is in romantic fiction and my personal journals. [a.] Winchester, TN 37398.

HENLEY, GUY
[pen.] Guy P. Henley; [b.] April 6, 1971, Hot Springs, NM; [p.] Grace Theresa and Edward Henley; [ed.] Artesia High School (Artesia, NM); [occ.] Landscaper; [pers.] I want my writing to move and burn the untamed heart. [a.] Ruidoso, NM

HENNING, AUDREY M.
[b.] August 24, 1910, Calamus, IN; [p.] Cornelius and Ida Hayes Petersen; [m.] Milton, December 23, 1930 at home (deceased 1962); [ch.] Janelle Ramsey, Douglas Henning, Dennis Henning, Craig Henning, Brenda Aiken and Denice Birdwell; [ed.] Grad of

Calamus High and attended Cedarfalls Extension College - took a few courses at Marycrest (Davenport, IA); [occ.] Rural school teacher six years, substitute teacher and file clerk; [memb.] Lifetime member Our Saviors Lutheran Church and Choir, Clinton County Historical Society, American Legion Auxiliary over sixty years (DeWitt, IA), Women's Bowling Association (over 50 yrs) and WAPSI Oaks Country Club since 1971; [oth. writ.] Many poems for birthdays, 80 etc., some church bulletins. For 80th celebration of mine I wrote and children read; [pers.] Always liked to write and do oil paintings. My mother sisters and daughter entered contests - 25 words or less - limericks etc. won prizes. Have 18 living grandchildren and 3 deceased and 14 great grand.

HENRAJANI, RATTAN
[pen.] John Rattan; [b.] May 10, 1941, Karachi, India; [p.] Hasomal and Saraswati, deceased; [m.] Bina, January 7, 1969; [ch.] Navin, Kishore, Priya; [ed.] Jaihind College, Bombay, Georgia Tech, B.S. and Bradley University, M.S.; [occ.] Export - Import business; [memb.] Masonic Lodge, Port Washington Rotary Club; [pers.] My life's goal is to produce creative thought, not just to struggle for existence and mere survival. [a.] Great Neck, NY 11021.

HENRY, DIANA
[pen.] Diana Henry; [b.] September 2, 1943, Cincinnati, Ohio; [p.] Leslie and Anna Edwards; [m.] Joseph K., June 17, 1973; [ed.] Courter Tech. High Practical Nursing Program, University of Cincinnati, Lincoln University, University of Iowa; [occ.] Fifth/ sixth grade combination class teacher, Longfellow Elementary School (Iowa City); [memb.] Phi Delta Kappa, International reading Association, NEA, Iowa Council of Teachers of Mathematics; [hon.] Project Excellence Grant, 1991 and 1992 awarded monies by the Iowa City School District to implement 1) multiculture support group, and 2) conflict management program for students; [oth. writ.] One poems and two short stories all unpublished; [pers.] To be a catalyst that promotes creativity, humanity and proactive involvement in issues that students can do something about. [a.] Iowa City, IA 52240.

HENRY, GERMAINE M.
[b.] July 4, 1926, Michigan City, Indiana; [p.] George and Mary Wagner Grott; [m.] Divorced; [ch.] Thomas M., Charles J. Henry and Susan Henry Kramer; [occ.] Retired; [memb.] AARP, AARP-Vote, First Congressional District Team Members for the State of Indiana; [oth. writ.] I have written 35 poems about my grandson, Ryan, who is 2 1/2 years old. Each poem pertains to a different experience in his life; [pers.] This poem is the first poem I have ever written. I have never written about any other subject. I have never been able to write poetry before. [a.] Michigan City, IN 46360.

HENRY, LYDIA I.
[pen.] Lydia I. Henry; [b.] July 27, 1955, chicago, Illinois; [p.] Catherine and Alvin Dickey; [m.] Divorced; [ch.] Anthony Henry (21), Leon Henry (19), Stacia Bland (5); [ed.] DuSable High School; [occ.] Teacher's Assistant at Gresham Elementary (Chicago, IL); [memb.] Gresham P.T.A., Chicago Teacher's Union; [hon.] Being chosen by the N.L.P. as a semi-finalist and the publishing of my poem "Knowledge"; [oth. writ.] A number of other poems published in school newspapers and recited in various

school programs, and assemblies; [pers.] I'd like to thank all who encouraged me to continue my writing endeavors. I dedicate this poem to my daughter, "STACIA" and to all the children at GRESHAM Elementary school. [a.] Chicago, IL 60649.

HENSON, JAMES
[pen.] Rabbit; [b.] October 3, 1983, Camp Lejeune, North Carolina; [p.] Lt. Col. Frank and Kathy Henson; [ed.] Stone Street Elementary; [occ.] Student; [memb.] Jacksonville Cardinals, Wabelo Pack 490; [hon.] All Star Soccer and Basketball player; [oth. writ.] Various poems, short stories, and news articles; [pers.] People should never give up no matter how bad things appear. [a.] Camp Lejeune, NC 28542.

HERBER, MEGAN
[b.] March 2, 1976, Reading, Pennsylvania; [p.] Robert and Jean Herber; [ed.] Attending Grand Junction High School - Senior '94; [occ.] Waitress; [memb.] National Honor Society, Cheerleader, Student Con., Chorale, Women's Jazz, Black Illusions; [hon.] English merit award, Who's Who, Outstanding Sophomore for Good Times Show Choir, Unsung Hero, Girls Softball, won several beauty pageants and talent contests, Honor Roll; [oth. writ.] I Believe, Thoughts, To Be or Not to Be. [a.] Clifton, CO 81520-1413.

HERBERT, SAUL
[b.] November 8, 1980, Glenwood Springs, Colorado; [p.] Gary and Rita Herbert; [ed.] Carbondale Elementary and Middle Schools, presently homeschooling; [memb.] (P.E.A.K.) Program for Educationally Advanced Kids; [hon.] '87-'89 CES Excellence in Music Award, Whiz Kid Apple Computer Achievement Award 1988, 1990 Certificate of Excellence Mitts Apple Award, 1990 Certificate of Creative Achievement from Aspen Art Museum, 1990 Markerdrawing exhibited at the 11th Annual Valley Kids Exhibition, 1990 received a Art Scholarship to Anderson Ranch Snowmass, Co., 1991 my design was chosen for the logo at Carbondale Elementary School, 1991 Presidential Academic Fitness Award 1991, I was Wilber in Charlotte's Web musical, 1992 Principal's Award; [pers.] Even a stopped clock is right twice a day. [a.] Carbondale, CO 81623.

HEROLD, SANDRA M.
[pen.] Sammie Marquerum; [b.] May 12, 1948, Philadelphia, Pennsylvania; [p.] Robert and Mildred Marqerum; [ch.] James, Steven, David, Chasey, and Desiree; [ed.] Bonsalem High School 10th grade; [occ.] Grader Birch Tree Hardwood Flooring; [oth. writ.] For personal use a book of poems and a few songs not published; [pers.] A pair of rose colored glasses for everyone, it is would truly help them see things in a better light. Our world could use all the help it can get. [a.] Birch Tree, MO 65438.

HERNANDEZ, KIMBERLY G.
[b.] December 13, 1955, Santa Rosa, California; [p.] Eugene S. and Carmelita K. Canevari; [m.] Thomas R., August 4, 1979; [ch.] Gabriel T. and Sterling T. Hernandez; [ed.] Bachelor of Music 1979 San Francisco State University, Magna cum Laude; [occ.] Home maker and ordained minister along with husband; [memb.] A.F.C.M. (Association of Faith Churches and Ministers); [oth. writ.] Several short stories and poems - unpublished; [pers.] In my

writings, I desire to draw all people into a personal encounter with their creator, savior, and friend, Jesus Christ; his father, Almighty God; and the Holy Spirit who binds us together in love. [a.] Castro Valley, CA 94546.

HERRIOT, ROBERT B.
[b.] December 7, 1919, Adams, Wisconsin; [p.] Robert M. and Ruth C. Herriot nee Brown; [m.] Gwendolyn E. nee Steffen, June 20, 1942; [ch.] Robert Sr., David, Richard, Pamela, Patrick, Floyd, Dawny Deidre, Holly, Mary, Heidi, Heather and Neal; [ed.] High School; [occ.] Retired; [memb.] Life Member of V.F.W., American Legion and Disabled American Veterans; [hon.] Military - Bronze star, Purple Heart - French Croix de Goerre - Belgium Cross of War - Netherlands - Orange Lanyard - United States - Presidential Unit Citation with Oak Leaf cluster - Combat Infantry Badge - European Theatre of Operations - Ribbon with Bronze Arrowhead and 4 bronze battle stars; [oth. writ.] April Snows and many other poems; [pers.] Live your life to the fullest. [a.] Friendship, WI 53934.

HERPICH, ANTHONY
[b.] August 28, 1984; [p.] Scott and Cheryl Herpich; [ed.] Currently in third grade at Garden Grove Elementary School; [occ.] Student; [oth. writ.] "I Had a Dream", "Me and My Friend Tyler"; [pers.] Writing is fun if you give it a try. [a.] Simi Valley, CA 93063.

HERTZ, BARBARA ANN
[pen.] Barbara Hedden Hertz; [b.] May 20, 1937, Dover, New Jersey; [p.] Betty Sue Gilbert Hedden (deceased) and William Chessman Hedden Sr.; [m.] John Frederick, USAF Ret., September 3, 1955; [ch.] John Jr., Joni Sue, Martin Ray and Mark Erik; [ed.] Amon Carter Riverside High School (Fort Worth, TX class of '55, studied under well known artists, coast to coast; [occ.] Professional Artist since 1969; [memb.] Oklahoma Art Guild, Pastel Society of Oklahoma, Central Art Association, Norman Art League; [hon.] Major awards in California, Massachusetts, Louisiana, and Oklahoma. Featured on television. Recent work, "My Heroes, Have Always Been Cowboys" Pastel used on cover of International H.S. Finals Rodeo program, Shawnee, OK, July 1993; [oth. writ.] None only yearly Christmas letters; [pers.] I have deeply emotional feelings that often surface in my art, or in this case, poetry. "Do unto others as you would have them do unto you" (and Right On, Rush Limbaugh!). [a.] Tecumseh, OK 74873.

HESS, KATIE ELIZABETH
[pen.] Anne Liberty; [b.] March 25, 1978, San Diego, California; [p.] Art Hess and Jana Hess; [ed.] Christian High School (Sophomore); [occ.] Student; [hon.] Honors Society at CHS Honors English - one year; [oth. writ.] Includes several unpublished and undiscovered works. This is the first time I've submitted any work; [pers.] If I am understood I take great reverence. Those who take my words into their own context of application are praised. [a.] La Mesa, CA

HEWITT, GARNET
[ed.] Art Student's League (NY, NY 1964), Hunter College (NY, NY 1963), New School of Social Sciences (NY, NY 1964); [oth. writ.] "Canada Council Children's Literature Prize 1981", "Amelia Francis and Howard-Gibbon Medal, 1981 - Children's Li-

brarians", Frankfurt 1982: "Europscap Translations - Netherlands & Scandanavia", "Ytek and the Arctic Orchid", Vanguard Press, NY, NY 1981; Douglas & McIntyre, Canada. [a.] Richmond DC V7E 3Z7.

HICKS, DAVID
[b.] June 23, 1953, Billings, Montana; [p.] Glen and Happy Hicks; [ch.] Glen, Christopher Whitney; [ed.] Statesboro High School, Bullock County Correctional Institute; [occ.] US Navy; [pers.] Poetry is like sex- it can inspire deep and wonderful feelings or it can simply be a stain on the sheet you've worked on. [a.] Summerville, SC.

HIGGINS, ARON MICHAEL
[[b.] August 13, 1981, Seattle, Washington; [p.] Robert Paul and Judith Ann Moffat Higgins; [ed.] At this writing I am a 5th grade student at Assumption School (Seattle); [occ.] Student; [memb.] Boy Scouts of America. [a.] Seattle, WA 98105.

HIGGS, SHAYLER
[b.] October 13, 1980, North Battleford, Sask.; [p.] Richard and Marlene Higgs; [ed.] Grade 7; [occ.] Student; [hon.] First prize winner in Royal Canadian Legion Contest Honor Roll - $100 Scholarship; [oth. writ.] Mother's Day poem. [a.] North Battleford, Sask. S9A 1C9.

HILES, CHRISTINA LYNN
[pen.] Tina Lynn Hiles; [b.] December 19, 1975, Lincoln, Nebraska; [p.] Ed and Diana Dinan; [m.] Boyfriend-Jonathan Conover; [ch.] Zachary Alvin Hiles; [ed.] Kindergarten to tenth grade (working on GED now); [occ.] Meadow Gold Dairy - clean with uncle; [oth. writ.] Forever And A Day, True Love, Moms. [a.] Lincoln, NE 68505.

HILL, JOSHUA A.
[pen.] Josh; [b.] October 5, 1972, Frankfort, Indiana; [p.] Becky Frantz and Mike Hill; [m.] Jennifer; [ed.] Frankfort Senior High currently studying electronics; [occ.] Student; [oth. writ.] Many personal poems; [pers.] Life is what you make it. [a.] Frankfort, IN 46041.

HILL, MELANIE
[b.] May 18, 1975, Regina, Saskatchewan, Canada; [p.] Vivian and Della Hill; [ed.] Imperial High School, 1993; [pers.] My poetry tends to reflect the beauty of the environment and how sacred it is. I have been influenced by great poets such as Percy Bysshe Shelley and Robert Frost. [a.] Imperial Sask, Canada S0G 2J0.

HILL, MICHAEL D.
[[pen.] Miguel Kind; [b.] Ottawa, Ontario, Canada; [ed.] BA Queen's University, Kingston, Ontario, Canada. [a.] Ottawa, Ontario, Canada.

HILL, ROY G.
[b.] February 6, 1941, Rochester, New York; [p.] Harrison and Bertha Hill; [m.] Helen C., September 1, 1962; [ch.] Wayne, Mark and Kristen; [ed.] Byron-Bergen High School, Roberts Wesleyan College; [occ.] General Manager, Village of Spencerport, NY; [memb.] First Presbyterian Church, Municipal Electric Utilities Association; [hon.] D.B.H. Dalrymple Community Service Award; [oth. writ.] Several poems published in church newsletters. [a.] Bergen, NY 14416.

HILLEGAS, JAMES V.
[b.] August 13, 1972, Arlington, Virginia; [p.] Debby Farmer, Ed Farmer and Barry Barry Hillegas; [ed.] Toledo High School; [occ.] Vagabonding Philosopher and Musician; [memb.] Paratheo-Ana Metamystik Hood of Eris Esoteric; [pers.] True loving friendships and a never ending quest for LIFE - the essential comments to create words of joy and a reality too ecstatic for words...[a.] Siletz, OR 97380.

HIMMELMAN, JENNIE O.
[b.] January 22, 1949, Jordan Falls, Novia Scotia; [p.] Lew and Thelma Williams; [m.] James, December 30, 1966; [ch.] Beverly Stuart; [occ.] Bookkeeper; [oth. writ.] Poems for special occasions; [pers.] I love reading and writing poetry. In this poem "Autumn's Artist". I am trying to express the awesome beauty that surrounds the south shore of Nova Scotia in our autumn season. [a.] Nova Scotia Canada B0T 1S0.

HINDER, ADRIANA
[b.] 30 something, Neptune, New Jersey; [p.] Rudolph and Trudy Seemann; [m.] Andreas, January 17, 1992; [ed.] Howell High School, NY Academy of Dramatic Arts, Weiss Barron Commercial School; [occ.] Flight Attendant training, seven years then model and actress; [memb.] Screen Actors Guild; [hon.] Shield and Key award, National Honor Society, many Golden awards for poetry; [oth. writ.] "Your Kiss" best poets of the 90's Library of Congress, Most Distinguished Poets of America written lyrics to songs plus children's stories; I write about experiences that are true to my life and enjoy telling a story with imagery and enlightenment. I wish for mankind to believe in God with truth and love for fellow man for a complete world. [a.] Zurich, Switzerland.

HINES, AVERY I.
[b.] October 26, 1962, Norfolk, Virginia; [p.] Aray J. and Roy Lee Hines, Sr.; [m.] Belinda F.; [ch.] Avery Hines II; [ed.] Norview High School, Norfolk State University; [oth. writ.] Several other poems and thoughts unpublished; [pers.] I believe that even in a world that has become so harmful the mind still can create the ultimate pleasure. [a.] Citrus Heights, CA 95621.

HINMAN, PATRICIA ANN
[pen.] Patty Nickless Hinman; [b.] February 5, 1947, Worcester, Massachusetts; [p.] Jesse and Marion Nickless; [m.] Robert, April 22, 1972; [ch.] Kenneth Scott, David Joseph; [ed.] Charlton High School, attended Worcester State College; [occ.] ESE Paraprofessional at Bright Horizons School (for mentally handicapped students); [memb.] Chronic PTO and PTA Mom, Visually Impaired Children, Group-various committees dealing locally with problems of handicapped youngsters; [hon.] Twice Paraprofessional of the Year, Twice Paraprofessional of the Month, Very Special Arts (Broward County) Music Award, Holiday Verse and Ideas award-Avon; [oth. writ.] Slogan winner in Skating Rink Contest, SACS School "Rap", Say No to Drugs "Rap", Very Special Arts Speech to introduce this concept to Broward County, FLA. Many "intro" speeches for B.H.S. musical/productions and numerous personal poems and rhymes for friends for all occasions; [pers.] I love humor and usually strive to see the "brighter" side of things - I also have respect and compassion for

handicapped children and try to see the positive aspects of these brave youngsters. [a.] North Lauderdale, FL 33068.

HINSON, WILLIAM SCOTT
[b.] June 26, 1970, Brenton, Alabama; [p.] Pete and Meme Hinson; [occ.] U.S. Army; [hon.] Persian Gulf War Veteran (Shield and Storm); [pers.] I dedicate this poem to my girlfriend, Brandy, I love you. [a.] Gulf Shores, AL 36542.

HINTON, JEANINE A.
[b.] May 8, 1970, Elizabeth City, North Carolina; [p.] Stanley Leon and Shirley Delois Davis Hinton; [ed.] Northeastern High School, College of the Albermarle, Elizabeth City State University; [occ.] Secretary. [a.] Elizabeth City, NC 27909-5505.

HIPPENSTEEL, KIMBERLEY E.
[b.] July 28, 1964, Bath Maine; [p.] Donald Asdell (deceased), Robert and Wanita Ireland; [ed.] Lance Cruese High School; [occ.] Factory Worker (Lyons Industries, Inc.); [pers.] All my poems have very personal meaning to them, which I think is very important in writing. [a.] Michigan.

HITHERSAY, ERIN
[b.] October 22, 1975, Plantation, Florida; [p.] Darcy and Steven Hithersay; [ed.] Cypress Lake High, University of Central Florida; [occ.] Student; [memb.] Quill and Scroll, Reflections, Panther Prints, Shadowplay, Panther 4 News, National Honor Society, Spanish Honor Society; [hon.] Voted Most Talented, Cypress Elite, Citizenship Award, Delegate to Leadership Conference, President Spanish Honor Society, First Place State Vocal Award; [oth. writ.] Several poems and interview published in Literary Magazine Reflections. Editorials and articles published in Panther Prints Newspaper; [pers.] "I BELIEVE IN THE RIGHT TO QUESTION." [a.] Fort Myers, FL 33912.

HITZ, WILLIAM T.
[b.] July 6, 1955, Odessa, Texas; [p.] Betty S. and Thomas A. Hitz, Jr.; [m.] Ellen A.,, June 20, 1986; [ch.] David A. and Rebecca K. Jones (stepchildren); [ed.] North Georgia College, Woodrow Wilson College of Law, Gwinnett Hall Baptist College; [occ.] Real Estate Title Examiner (Gwinnett County, GA); [memb.] First Moravian Church of Georgia; [hon.] Eagle Scout, God and Country Award (BSA); [pers.] I thank God for all He has done. [a.] Lawrenceville, GA 30245.

HIZER, GLORIA E.
[b.] July 30, 1936, Dafter, Michigan; [p.] Vilho and Elma Huhtala; [m.] Eugene R., February 7, 1990; [ch.] Donald W., Michael J., and Kathy Quigley and Teri A. Marchetti; [ed.] Superior High; [occ.] Retired - was office manager of local utility company business office; [oth. writ.] Couple poems published in local newspapers. I have a portfolio of over 200 poems and some short articles on personal issues. All my poetry began after August 12, 1991; [pers.] I am a strong believer in the brotherhood of man and writings reflect my study of man and his problems, sometimes in a serious vein, other times in humor. [a.] Kincheloe, MI 49788.

HOBDY, CLINTON DEET, JR.
[b.] January 1, 1964, Lubbock, Texas; [p.] Ruby Lee and Clinton Deet, Sr. (deceased); [m.] Doris Ann, July 1, 1989; [ch.] Amanda Shar Deet Hobdy (9/7/88); [ed.] Estacado High, Texas Tech University, East Texas State, Community College of Air Force; [occ.] Computer Systems Consultant and Software Integration Specialist, Poker Dealer; [memb.] African Dealer Association of South Mississippi; [oth. writ.] The Mall, Uncle Bob. [a.] Biloxi, MS 39532.

HODGE, DEANNA RENE'E
[pen.] Deanna Hodge; [b.] February 15, 1961, Fresno, California; [p.] Bill and Judy Townsend; [m.] Divorced; [ch.] Amber Rene'e (7) and Amanda Ann Hodge (5); [ed.] Graduated high school; [oth. writ.] I started writing poems in 1980. The poems that I do write are about life, friendship, love, also I wrote about my two daughters, which is about (My Gifts From God); [pers.] All the poems that I have written comes from the heart. Also, how life can really be worth living. I really enjoy writing, this is the first contest I've entered. [a.] East McKinley.

HODGES, GREGORY
[b.] December 13, 1965, Los Angeles, California; [ed.] James Monroe and St. Albans L.A. Valley College and West Texas A&M; [memb.] Dead Poet Society, N.O.R.M.L.; [oth. writ.] "A Nation Says Its Sorry" published in last years Anthology "A View From the Edge"; [pers.] My greatest influence has been being truly in love and the chaos that accompanies it. My influences are Jack Kerovac and Jim Morrison. [a.] Amarillo, TX 79109.

HOEFER, CARROLL
[pen.] Carroll Hoefer; [b.] Hutchinson, Kansas; [p.] Alma and Hap Hoefer; [m.] Rose, August 20, 1955; [ch.] Steve, Tim, Ruth; [ed.] High School; [occ.] Dillon's Warehouse; [memb.] Westside Baptist Church; [hon.] Church Bus Captain of the Year 1985; [oth. writ.] Colorful Colorado, Poem of Labor; [pers.] I try to magnify God and His Son in all my poems.

HOFFMAN, JILL A.
[b.] May 6, 1943, Yakima, Washington; [p.] Henry and Lucille Lind; [ed.] BA in Education, Minor in Music and Home Economics; [occ.] Education Technician, employed at Navy Cadena, NSB Bangor, Silverdale, WA; [memb.] I am an active member of the body of Christ serving our Lord and Savior by striving to become more like our father in words and actions; [oth. writ.] Extensive collection of Christian inspirational poems, composed numerous songs with lyrics, creating an inspirational video. All honor, glory and praise is lovingly given to my father, son and holy spirit; [pers.] All that I am and ever will be is given by my eternal father in his grace and love. He is my inspiration and strength, without him I am nothing. To him I give all honor, glory, and praise. [a.] Bremerton, VA 98310.

HOFFMAN, MICHAEL GREGORY
[pen.] Mike Hoffman; [b.] June 7, 1982, Warren, Ohio; [p.] Pamela and Bruce Hoffman; [ed.] 5th grade at Champion Central Elementary School; [occ.] Student; [memb.] HEPP (Highly Educated Potential Program), 5th grade Champion Central Elementary School Band, Champion Youth Soccer League; [hon.] Recognition of Outstanding Academic Achievement of the Presidential Academic Fitness Awards Program, Recognition for Outstanding Performance in the Spring 1993 Elementary Knowledge Master Open, Received Certificates of Achievement for High Standards of Excellence in 5th grade HEPP and 5th grade Honor Roll for all year; [pers.] I strive to inform others in my writing that there is only one beautiful world and we should try to preserve it. [a.] Warren, OH 44481.

HOFFMAN, PEGGY G.
[pen.] Peggy G. Hoffman; [b.] August 8, 1924, Muskegon, Michigan; [p.] Tom and Bernice Anderson; [m.] William D., August 7, 1975; [ch.] Jan, Daniel and Susan; [ed.] Muskegon High School and Glendale College; [occ.] Homemaker; [memb.] Church of the Lighted Window, Council of the British Society; [hon.] Golden Poet of 1991, by World of Poetry; [oth. writ.] Several short stories published by the Glendale Community College; [pers.] I try to achieve a reader's delight. [a.] La Crescenta, CA 91214.

HOLEC, LORETTA
[pen.] Loretta Holec; [b.] December 9, 1974, Barron County, Wisconsin; [p.] James and Laura Holec; [ed.] Cameron Junior and Senior High School; [occ.] I.C. Express (Cameron Convenience Store) and L&L Painters; [oth. writ.] Dog Spelled Backwards is God - Dream Come True - The Crying Rose - I Wish I Was - The Real World - My Feelings - Love Hurts - I Long for a Place to Belong - Child of the Wind - I Love You - A Stare of Silence - The Candle; [pers.] Take in all of life's "Little" pleasures, they may not seem important but if you Look Deep enough, They Have A "Large" - Meaning. [a.] Cameron, WI 54822.

HOLLAND, E. TaLESHEA
[pen.] TaLeshea E. Holland; [b.] January 17, 1971, Washington D.C.; [p.] Solomon and Bettye Holland (Atlanta, GA); [ed.] Frederick Douglass High School, Clark Atlanta University, Spring '93 graduate (Mass Communication); [occ.] Data Entry Clerk, Dept. of Army. Aspired to work in local publishing company in various roles; [memb.] Delta Sigma Theta Sorority., Inc., National Association of Black Journalists; [hon.] National Dean's List, CAU-TV Appreciation award, Spanish Honor Society, MVP award - High School Newspaper; [oth. writ.] Collection of poems and essays: "Emotional Preludes", short stories and monologues; [pers.] Anything in life worth having requires both mental and physical sacrifices in order to be the extraordinary individual you always knew you could be. [a.] Atlanta, GA 30331.

HOLLAND, THOMAS MAX, SR.
[pen.] Tom Holland; [b.] January 21, 1911, Camanche, Oklahoma; [p.] James Allen and Arizona Satterfield Holland; [m.] Theresa Marie Fisher, August 16, 1937; [ch.] Thomas Max, Jr. and John Allen Holland; [ed.] BSA (April 1961) university of Arkansas 1938; [occ.] Soil Conservationist - Agri. Teacher, Agri. Scientist - Sheet Metal Mechanic; [memb.] Alpha Gamma Rho Fraternity, Alpha Zeta, Arkansas Alumni Association, Masonic Lodge, Scottish Rite and Alta hi-Twelve Club Charter Member; [hon.] Alpha Zeta, An Honorary Agri. Frat., Pershing Riflemen - Honorary Highest Score - 1938 Civil Service Exam for Jr. Agronomists U.S.D.A., Soil Conser. Service, State of Arkansas - Highest G.P.A. Freshman; [oth. writ.] Poems - Adela-Trees-October Nights-Twilight-The Robin Red-Breast-At Wintertide-The Woodland- To Jerri, My Pal-Autumn-Something Sure-A Prayer-To A Hyacinth-We Stand Alike-The Night If I Had A Boy-March Wind-Friendship-Little Flower By the Wayside; [pers.] As a sub-teacher, I especially love children and work toward better wholesome nurturing and care in their development - I look to better educational experience for their unique and individual thinking. [a.] Reedley, CA 93654.

HOLLIBUSH, ANN M.
[b.] February 10, 1934, Woodmen, Wisconsin; [p.] Pauls and Maryann O'Brien; [m.] Andrew, April 11, 1953; [ch.] Cynthia A., Mary T., Anna Mae, Beverly J., Patricia A., Joan E., Edward A., and Andrew James; [ed.] Senior High School (Evansville, WI); [occ.] Homemaker, Retail sales demonstrator; [memb.] Our Lady Queen of Peace Church, SeGoe Center Poets; [hon.] Golden Poet, A Vote For Pansy; [oth. writ.] To each of my eight children, Beholden to the Evergreen, Ode to Songbirds, My Beloved Finches, How A Figurine Cheers; [pers.] I have written to each of my eight children about choices in life, interest in ecology also about flowers, birds, in general about how much beauty can be found in the world outdoors. [a.] Madison, WI 53705.

HOLLOWAY, VIVIAN L.
[b.] June 4, 1912, Boonville, Montana; [p.] Henry W. and Lucy A. Holloway; [ed.] BS in Education, Warrensburg State University; [occ.] Retired Teacher; [memb.] AARP, Main Street Baptist Church, Retired Teacher's Association; [oth. writ.] Several poems that have not been published. Poem My Garden published by National Library of Poetry; [pers.] My material for my poems comes from observation of the world around me. [a.] California, MO 65018.

HOLMAN, SHARON M.
[pen.] Sharon M. Holman; [b.] September 28, 1943, Ellensburg, Washington; [p.] Wallace M. and Violet McCullough Huppert; [ch.] Dennis Wayne, Craig Henry, Sheri Marie; [ed.] Ellensburg Senior High, Northwestern University (Evanston, IL) Seattle University; [occ.] VP/Manager Continental Escrow Company (Seattle, WA); [memb.] American Escrow Association, Escrow Association of Washington, National Notart Association, National Association of Female Executives; [hon.] WA State Escrow Achievement of the years 1989/90, Director State of Washington AEA, President EAW 93/94; [oth. writ.] Trade Journals, AEA, EAW, and Gr. Seattle Escrow Association Technical Journals; [pers.] Poetry is a wonderful avenue for the release of my creative side. [a.] Everett, WA 98208.

HOLMES, DONALD W.
[b.] January 3, 1953, Bloomington, Indiana; [m.] Divorced; [ch.] Custodial parent of Ammanda and Wayne Holmes; [ed.] Post High School Technical Degree; [occ.] Computer, Medical, Photographic Equipment Sales and Service; [memb.] None oriented around writing or poetry; [oth. writ.] This was my first ever submission - I am currently compiling a book of poetry and essays, will begin sending MSS to publishers in June 1993; [pers.] I write primarily about everyday people and their relationships, my observations, moral and ethical beliefs and the power of writing to help heal the mind and heart. [a.] Bloomington, IN 47407.

HOLMES, SHANE
b.] November 27, 1972, Rushville, Indiana; [p.] Joe and Cindy Holmes; [ed.] Plainwell High School, life, extensive chemical testing, a touch of pain, a few Don Won books, too much Brady Bunch; [occ.] I get paid by the Air Force, but I get the feeling that my real job is wondering what my job is, and then being told I was wrong; [memb.] T.C.J.T.B.I.A.C. (The Club Just To Be In A Club - president, chairmen of the board, the board, the secretary, all other members); [hon.] This is the only time my poetry has been read by anybody other than my dog, but I don't think he knows what he's reading; [oth. writ.] Incidentally, I did write a book, "Visible Thought Balloons", but it happen to be in a leather bag someone wanted, and alas, I've never seen it again, but am currently trying to put it back together; [pers.] As you have read, I am not much for being serious when asked something. All I can say is this - life is a lot tougher than the instruction manual lets on, I think I am going to sue. [a.] Plainwell, MI 49080.

HOLT, CAROL ARMSTRONG
[b.] January 17, 1930, Knoxville, Tennessee; [p.] Robert and Helen Seiber Armstrong; [m.] Fester, April 17, 1944; [ch.] James Gary, Timothy Jackson, Julia Ellen, Richard Alan, Shannon Delaine; [ed.] Lenoir City High, Athens Area Voc. School; [occ.] Licensed Practical Nurse, Baptist Assisted Living Center; [memb.] Northside Church of God; [pers.] I strive to prove that to have faith in God, and through perseverance one can be a conqueror of dreams. [a.] Lenoir City, TN 37771.

HOLT, GEORGIA A.
[pen.] Georgia A. Holt; [b.] December 30, 1906, Doylestown, Ohio; [p.] Alvin Wesley Smith and Nellie Alena; [m.] Robert L. (deceased), December 18, 1926; [ch.] Norman Eugene Holt; [ed.] High School and home decorating of New Homes also office work of Real Estate and model airplanes shop overseas; [memb.] Methodist Church; [hon.] Built and flew a model airplane in contest, came in second in Ohio Modeling Contest for beauty in workmanship and flying. Built planes and care of most things in modeling and ran shop. Was the first mother and son to fly in contest and won prize for beauty and flying; [oth. writ.] Quite a few poems and many religious ones; [pers.] Received many compliments on poems and would like any help you could give me. This library of poems sounds so interesting. I care about writing poems very much. [a.] Cuyahoga Falls, OH 44223.

HOLTON-MULLER, REGINA
[pen.] Regina Holton-Muller; [b.] September 8, 1958, Ramondville, Texas; [p.] Rex L. and Jeanne L. Tomlinson; [m.] Paul A., October 26, 1991; [ed.] Slaton High, South Plains College; [occ.] Registered Nurse-Operating Room, The Surgery Center of the Woodlands; [memb.] Association of Operating Room Nurses, Texas Nurses Association, American Nurses Association; [hon.] 93-94, Who's Who in American Nursing, South Plains College Outstanding Achievement in Maternal Child Nursing, Certified Nurse of the Operating Room; [oth. writ.] Numerous poems written for private and public events; [pers.] My poetry is an extension of my innermost thoughts and ideas. Most of my poetry is based on emotional events in my everyday life. [a.] The Woodlands, TX 77380.

HOOD, PATRICIA
[pen.] Patty Hood; [b.] March 13, 1953, St. John's Hospital; [p.] Pauline and Raymond Dailey; [ch.] Pacia and Pamela Hood; [ed.] Graduated from Anderson High School and Apex Academy of Hair Design; [occ.] Housekeeper, Beautician; [hon.] Poetry awards from World of Poetry; [oth. writ.] Poems. [a.] Anderson, IN 46016.

HOOKER, RUSS
[pen.] R.K. or Rusty Hooker; [b.] May 11, 1952, San Diego, California; [p.] Ralph B. and Viola A.; [ed.] High School GED, Kelsey Jenny Business College; occ.] Author/Illustrator; [hon.] Volunteer Certificates of Merit from both Lemoncrest School in Lakeside, CA and Lakeside School Board; [oth. writ.] Poem: "Human Under the Bed" which was lauded by former-first lady Barbara Bush, a 15 (so far) story series for children, "Tales of Dunsworth P. Dragon"; [pers.] Goal is to inspire children to read and write and to help instill in them the difference between right and wrong through a virtually kind character who would use violence only as a last resort. [a.] San Diego, CA 92109.

HOOLEY, SHEILA R.
[pen.] Sheila R. Hooley; [b.] September 26, 1970, Goshen, Indiana; [p.] Marti and Randy Hooley; [m.] Teresa, Marcia, and Mike Hooley; [ed.] Northridge High, Elkhardt Career Center; [occ.] Self-employed; [pers.] I will continue writing poems for my own sense of freedom. It's my way of letting things go. "Peace". [a.] Goshen, IN.

HOOPER, MICHAEL
[b.] November 10, 1976, San Jose, California; [p.] Frank and Carolyn Hooper; [ed.] In attendance at Bellarmine College Preparatory; [occ.] Full-time student; [hon.] Saratoga Optimists Club, Citizenship Award, Dean's List, Honor Society; [pers.] Most aspirations seem all too impossible for the people of the world, but I know that if those same people would open their minds and souls, they would understand just how possible their dreams really are. [a.] San Jose, CA 95118.

HOPKINS, CHARLES E.
[b.] January 20, 1936, Paragould, Arkansas; [p.] Edgar and Mary Ellen Hopkins; [ed.] AS and BS Degree-The University of the State of New York, AA Degree-Thomas A. Edison State College; [occ.] 33 years - City Light and Water-Water Maintenance Supervisor, 8 years CL&W; [memb.] American Water Works Association, Arkansas Water Works and Pollution Control Association, Arkansas Sheriffs Association; [oth. writ.] Great poems of our times, selected works of our worlds best poets and Who's Who in Poetry; [pers.] In my writings, I try to write about nature and peace for all the people all over the world. a[.] Paragould, AK 72451.

HOPPER, PATRICIA
[b.] April 7, 1978, Suwon, South Korea; [p.] James and Sun Hopper; [ed.] Kadena Middle and Kadena High School; Katena Air Base (Okinawa, Japan); [occ.] Student; [memb.] National Junior Honor Society; [hon.] Presidential Academic Fitness Award years 1990 and 1992; [oth. writ.] Various poems on various subjects, never published; [pers.] I have been influenced by my feelings on various subjects and happenings in my life. [a.] Okinawa, Japan.

HORN, CLAIRE E.
[pen.] Claire E. Horn; [b.] May 10, 1953, Charlotte, North Carolina; [p.] Carl and Virginia Horn; [m.] Bruce Bodaken, November 16, 1984; [ch.] Conor Michael and Ian Horn Bodaken; [ed.] Salem Academy, Winston-Salem, NC, University of South Carolina and California State University-Long Beach; [occ.] Perpetual Student and mother; [memb.] NOW (National Organization for Women), Sierra Club, Greenpeace; [oth. writ.] Poems and short stories-unpublished; [pers.] I believe that women's lives are replete with creative energy too often stifled by the demands and expectations of those around them. Giving a meaningful voice to that energy would go far towards healing the ills of our modern world. [a.] Los Alamitos, CA 90720.

HORN, DONNA L.
[b.] January 25, 1944, Fennville, Michigan; [p.] Fred and Madeline Beagle; [m.] Arlee, July 7, 1962; [ch.] Mark Owen, Bret Darrell, and James Wesley; [ed.] Fennville Public, Holland Community Education; [occ.] Pastor's Wife, Factory Worker, and part-time secretary; [memb.] Harvestime Fellowship Church; [oth. writ.] I write articles for our church newsletter and special occasions; [pers.] I strive to relate the goodness of God to everyday situations. [a.] Fennville, MI 49408.

HORSBURGH, CHARMAINE
[b.] December 7, 1953, Durban, South Africa; [p.] Bill and Patricia Fleming; [m.] David, July 3, 1973; [ch.] Jay Horsburgh; [ed.] Mitchell High School; [occ.] manager; [oth. writ.] Currently working on a book, with the theme "The Use of Will as an Agent for Change"; [pers.] Empower yourself, feel your connection to the whole, there are no boundaries except that thought has created. [a.] South Africa.

HORSTMAN, TRAVIS J.
[b.] April 7, 1973 (death January 19, 1993), Lima, Ohio; [p.] John and Shirley Horstman (sister - Tiffany); [ed.] High school; [occ.] Laborer. [a.] Contential, OH 45831.

HORTON, NANCY
[b.] Izmir, Turkey; [p.] George and Catherine Horton; [ed.] BA Sweet Briar College, graduate studies, Harvard; [occ.] Wrote for English language paper in Athens and National Press Club, DACOR, Federal publication poets; [hon.] Read at Folger Shakespeare Library, included in best college poetry, on program local radio "The Poem and the Poet". Former president Federal Poet; [oth. writ.] Published in "Foreign Service Journal" Federal Poet, other magazines. [a.] Washington, DC 20016.

HOSANNAH, KEITH L.
[b.] October 9, 1962, Georgetown, Guyana; [p.] Ruby Simpson and Carl Hosannah, Sr.; [m.] Freley Stang, February 24, 1985; [ch.] Kierra Lee and Prescott Andrew; [ed.] Senior - SIV Vocational Education and Curriculum Development and Associate degree - Health sciences; [occ.] Aeromedical Technician - USAF; [memb.] Phi Kappa Phi Honor Society; [hon.] Dean's List, Honor's award, Who's Who Among American High School Students 1981-82; [oth. writ.] "Life", "A Puzzle", "Cars", "Air Force", "Time"; [pers.] I enjoy writing poetry because it allows you to express yourself in any form - from the sublime to the ridiculous. It transforms plain English

into a thing of wonder and power. [a.] APO AE 09464.

HOULIHAN, TERENCE J.
[pen.] T.J. Houlihan; [b.] February 7, 1970, New York, New York; [p.] Edward D. Sr., and Joan P. Houlihan; [ed.] Iona Preparatory School BA in Philosophy and BA in Theology (Manhattan College, NY, NY); [occ.] Student, waiter, lecturer, writer; [memb.] International Society of Poets; [memb.] Manhattan College Grant, Guest Speaker in High Schools; [oth. writ.] Small poetry in Malcontent; [pers.] I enjoy life today, because today is all we have. Man must search for truth in his creator, not himself. Poetry touches the soul, not the heart. [a.] Bronxville, NY 10708.

HOWARD, FRANK J.
[b.] March 14, 1948, Brooklyn, New York; [p.] Frank J. and Jeanette C. Howard; [m.] Gretchen A., November 28, 1970; [ch.] Meghan Claire, Tracy Skye; [ed.] St. Louis Park High School (Minneapolis), A.B. Dartmouth College; [occ.] Insurance salesman; [hon.] National Merit Scholar; [oth. writ.] Forty two pages of unpublished poetry. My first novel is two thirds written. I have been writing for only one year; [pers.] I have been a practicing Buddhist for twenty-two years. The teachings of this ancient faith strongly influence my writing. [a.] Rochester, NY 14610.

HOWARD, KATHLEEN
[pen.] Kathy, Kathryn, Kathleen; [b.] August 25, 1968, Muthean, Massachusetts; [p.] Judith and Peter Broderick and Diane and John Howard; [m.] Ken, May 6, 1990; [ch.] Miranda Rose; [ed.] Northeast Voc. High School; [occ.] Friendly's Waitress and Mom; [hon.] Vica from North East Voc.; [oth. writ.] A View From Long Ago, A Peacefulness Inside Trust, and There, A Child In Us, Friendships, The Smile of A Youth, The Rose of Life, Oh Father Of Mine; [pers.] I always liked Edgar Allan Poe, Emily Dickinson, Robert Frost, and many others. [a.] Malden, MA 02148.

HOWARD, KELLY
[b.] December 30, 1979, Rochester, Michigan; [p.] Judith L. and Kim L. Howard (deceased); [ed.] Barnard Elementary, Baker Middle School - Troy, MI; [occ.] Student; [hon.] young Author's Award - 1st grade, Student of the Month - 7th grade, Honor Student 7th grade, First Division Medal 1993 - M.S.B.O.A., Mich. Education Assessment Placement Certificate; [oth. writ.] "All About Me" published at Oakland University - Rochester, MI, Young Peoples Library 1986 (age 6). [a.] Troy, MI 48083.

HOWELL, HOPE CHEREE'
[b.] February 28, 1975, Adairsville, California; [p.] Vickie and David Howell; [ed.] Adairsville High School; [memb.] S.A.D.D., Tri-Hi-Y; Drama Club, Marching, Concert, and Symphonic Band; [hon.] Band Directors' Award, Most Improved 10th Grade Band Student ('90-'91), Most Outstanding Woodwind ('92-'93), $500 George C. Hooks Scholarship; [oth. writ.] Collection of numerous unpublished poems; [pers.] Dreams shape my life, surge my soul, and lend plot to my poetry. God is the inspiration for my poems. [a.] Adairsville, GA 30103.

HOWLETT, DENISE GAIL
[pen.] Denise Gail; [b.] January 31, 1977, Newfoundland St. John's; [p.] Joanne and Roger Howlett; [ed.] Grade 9 still attending; [hon.] Peer Helping; [oth. writ.] Poems published in school newspaper; [pers.] I write my poems to express my feelings. I feel others could agree with my feelings. [a.] Amherst, NS

HUBBARD, KARAN
[pen.] Cookie; [b.] July 8, 1963, St. Louis, Missouri; [p.] Dorothy Hubbard; [ed.] High School graduate-presently enrolled in Nursing School; [oth. writ.] Unpublished-"You Are", "My Brother, My Friend", "Innermost", "Empty", "Thank You", and "The Beginning"; [pers.] Of all the knowledge I have obtained through books, and in my daily living,s the most important, and the most valuable item I have obtained is understanding. [a.] St. Louis, MO 63115.

HUBBARD, KIMBERLY
[b.] February 17, 1969, Port Huron, Michigan; [p.] Floyd and Jennie Hubbard (brothers - Eric and Kipp); [ed.] Associate in Science; [occ.] Radiologic Technologist; [pers.] Dedicated to K.A.S. "831". [a.] Detroit, MI.

HUDSON, AMY
[b.] August 23, 1975, Warrensburg, Missouri; [p.] Joe and Mary Anne Hudson; [ed.] Bosworth R-V High School; [hon.] Presidential Academic Fitness Award, George Washington Carver Award, and U.S. Marine Corps Academic Excellence Award; [pers.] Live each day to its fullest, for you never know what tomorrow will bring. [a.] Bosworth, MO 64623.

HUGHES, G. SCOTT
[pen.] Richard Encrevasse; [b.] May 20, 1966, Long Beach, California; [p.] Bill and Lynda Hughes; [m.] Not yet, still searching; [ch.] Zero, Honest; [ed.] Long Beach Poly , G.W.C., H.B. CA. The School of Hard Knocks, Long Beach Community College; [occ.] Bartender; [pers.] I write from things I have experienced. Influences: Keroac, Simic, Anger, Baudelaire, Phil Anselmo, David Lynch, Bukoswski, my family. I am always searching for new subjects. [a.] Long Beach, CA 90804.

HUGHES, LINDA L.
[b.] October 27, 1938, Oolitic, Indiana; [p.] Mahlon V. and Delmer Strunk Meadows; [m.] Bobby D., April 22, 1959; [ch.] Bobbi D. Hughes and Karen Hughes Baker; [ed.] Marshall Township High School; [occ.] Central Supply Manager, AMI Brownsville Medical Center; [memb.] American & TX Scoieites for Healthcare, Central Service Personnel, Living Waters Tabernacle Church; [oth. writ.] Two other poems published; [pers.] I am utterly fascinated by the beauty of the created world. I see the hand of God wherever I look. Nature has a voice all its own.

HUGHES, ROME LOUIS
[b.] November 8, 1948, Cincinnati, Ohio; [p.] Theodore and Marjorie Hughes; [ed.] Graduate of University of Cincinnati, BA History, Scholar of Lifetime Academician; [occ.] Accountant; [memb.] Kiwanis; [hon.] Son of American Revolution award citizen; [oth. writ.] Various. [a.] Cincinnati, OH

HUGHES, TEMMIE LEE
[pen.] Tem; [b.] August 20, 1963; [p.] Bobbie Gean and Claudie Hughes, Jr.; [ed.] Arkansas High and

Henderson State University; [occ.] Writing poems to ease the pain the hearts of mankind; [memb.] Part of Michael O'Howell Health Club, the Member of Boldware Temple and St. James Baptist Church; [hon.] Weightlifter of the 1000lb Club, Club member of the 400lb Club; [oth. writ.] Jessie Ray Hughes brother of Temie Lee Hughes; [pers.] Man's known knowings of each and every part of life was made by the wisdom and grace of God in which we all are a part of his godly image. [a.] Texarkana, AK 75502.

HUI, ELINOR Y.
[pen.] Yan Chang; [b.] July 16, 1961, Shanghai, China; [m.] Howard H., August 19, 1988; [ed.] Beijing Foreign Languages Institute; [occ.] International student; [pers.] I have been greatly influenced by Chinese and western poets. I want to express subtle feelings of mankind and I want to make readers think after reading my poems. [a.] St. Charles, IL 60174.

HUME, SUSAN SHOEMAKER
[b.] November 25, 1944, Memphis, Tennessee; [p.] William Millard and Alice Shoemaker; [m.] Robert A., Jr., October 25, 1981; [ed.] University of Mississippi, Bachelor Elementary Education and MED in Reading; [occ.] Restaurant owner and caterer; [memb.] Merchants Walk Business Association, National Audubon Society, National Wildlife Federation, National Arbor Day Foundation; [oth. writ.] Poem-Nature's Jewel published The Florida Poet, 1988; [pers.] Nature is the inspiration for most of my poetry. [a.] Niceville, FL 32578.

HUMPHREYS, JAMES D.
[b.] March 6, 1993, Windsor, Ontario; [p.] William and Laura Humphreys; [ed.] High school, BA (Toronto) greater part of studies on MA in French, (McGill, B.E.D./Dalhousie); [occ.] Retired high school teacher; [memb.] St. Alban's Anglican Parish Choir, Local Mensa Club; [hon.] Only a trophy for knowing by heart my catechism that of the book of common prayer (1549); [oth. writ.] My mother's brief biography in her church burial form - also mine, ready for the day! [a.] Dartmouth, Nova Scotia, Canada B2W 4L9.

HUNT, FRANCIS MARIE
[b.] March 22, 1949, Delhi, Louisiana; [p.] James W. and Geneva B. Dickey; [m.] Rev. Roger D., August 30, 1969; [ed.] Spencer Business College 1984, (Baton Rouge, LA), Baker High School (Baker, LA); [occ.] Secretary; [pers.] Jesus is the answer to all life's problems. He was tested and tempted just as we are, yet without sin. When we have a personal relationship with Christ our test and trials are easier to bear. [a.] Poplar, MT 59255.

HUNTER, CRYSTAL
[pen.] Ophelia; [b.] January 26, 1975, Ardmore, Oklahoma; [p.] Steve and Mary Russell; [ed.] Ardmore High School, Oklahoma State University, Freshman 1993; [memb.] Arts and Humanities Writer Guild, Word Weavers (local storytellers group); [hon.] Anthology award, National Journalism Conference; [oth. writ.] "Eyes Shut Rather Tightly", "Mining for Gold", - High School, Anthology - "82", "Starved Skinny", "Surviving"; [pers.] The lady that wears a glass on top of her head is starved skinny and ready to write another children's crusade. This is not a phonic book I am talking about, it is a truly amazing tale about a gypsy soul that finds a soft spot in the road. Poetry sits

beside me. [a.] Ardmore, OK 73401.

HUNTER, ROSEMARY
[b.] June 14, 1956, Columbus, Ohio; [p.] Walter and Margie Hunter; [ed.] Columbus North High School, three years college at Ohio State University; [occ.] Previous supervisor at Riverside Methodist Hospital; [memb.] Arthritis Foundation Heritage Homemaker Club of Somerset; [hon.] Crisco award for Home Economics; [oth. writ.] Several poems written for personal enjoyment and to share with family and friends; [pers.] Many times events or individuals touch my heart. I find much pleasure in putting these special thoughts into my poetry. [a.] Mt. Perny, OH 43760.

HUNTER, SUGAR
[b.] October 22, 1977, Olongapo City, Republic of the Philippines; [p.] George and Sherry Delk; [ed.] 9th grade attending Kings Mills High School in Cincinnati, OH; [occ.] Part-time cashier; [memb.] Member of the Kings Mills Band, American Heart Association; [hon.] Several Spelling Bee Finalists, Honor Roll, Several Reading Awards, Awesome Award for Exceptional Achievement in the Writing Competency, Field Day Accomplishments, Merit Roll, Civic Achievement Award; [oth. writ.] Short stories and poems; [pers.] I was an orphan at birth, my parents adopted me while they were in the military. My writings are centered on what my life could have been like had I not been adopted and had remained in the Philippines. [a.] Loveland, OH 45140.

HUNT, WAYNE AUSTIN
[b.] Mindemoya, Manitoulin Island (Ontario, Canada); [p.] Austin and Anita Hunt; [ed.] BA (Hon) Laurentian M.Sc. (Econ.) London School of Economics, PhD. University of Toronto; [occ.] Associate Professor, Political Science; [memb.] Mudge Bay Floating Club - Rear Admiral; [hon.] Visiting Fellow, Centre for International Studies, LSE., London England; [oth. writ.] In addition to academic manuscripts, Wayne Hunt has published poetry in a volume by Ian Walton (ed.) Guardian of the State; [pers.] Poetry is politics. Poetry in its very essence works from a potent and subtle political philosophy - potent in the symbols it evokes, subtle in the way these symbols play across our conscious and sub-conscious beings. Poetry takes the rhythm of the stars and makes it flesh, giving it feeling, form. Poetry, being both cerebral and reflective, is the head of the arts, because the heart of art will always be musical, His spirit, divine. Poets are the unacknowledged legislators of a newer, better world - that will only exist in the future. [a.] Kagawong, Manitoulin Island, Ontario Canada P0P 1J0.

HUSAIN, SHAHZAIN
[pen.] S. Khan Bhopali; [b.] February 15, 1974, India; [p.] Ahsan and Saleema F. Husain; [ed.] Moorpark High, Moorpark College; [occ.] Student and part-time Employee at the Bombay Co.; [hon.] Dean's List; [pers.] All poetry is a divine revelation, experience being unnecessary. [a.] Moorpark, CA 93021.

HUTCHINS, JENNIE A.
[b.] February 16, 1950, Darby, Pennsylvania; [p.] Edward F. and Edith M. Blair; [m.] Daniel S., June 25, 1983; [ch.] Nathalie Louise, Daniel Huntington, and Paul Edward Anderson; [occ.] Child Care Provider. [a.] Clifton Heights, PA 19018.

HUTCHINSON-BROOKE, FAYE
[b.] August 22, 1952; [p.] Patricia Ann and Alfred Anthony Laschiazza; [ch.] Joy Ann (16), Jonathon Andrew (14), Joel Aaron (12); [pers.] I wrote the poem one evening while writing a letter. The letter was to my boss who became my best friend, Oscar Sanchez. [a.] Lake Elsinore, CA 92530.

HUTTO, VIRGINIA KING
[b.] January 12, 1924, Lexington County Swansea, South Carolina; [p.] Guymon W. and Edna S.C. (Ott) King; [m.] O'Neal, December 24, 1952; [ch.] Steven W. Hutto and Marget J. Echevarria; [ed.] Wagener Centralized High School (Wagener, SC); [occ.] Homemaker, Babysitter, writer, gardener, wife and mother; [memb.] Christian of Mt. Hermon Baptist Church, Sunday School Teacher Choir; [hon.] Merit award of Honorable Mention 1987, 1987, 1989 Golden Poet award 1989, 1990; [oth. writ.] Weekly newspaper column (Meet Me in Church on Sunday), poems "He'll Be Your Loving Saviour Too", "Jesus Saviour", "When He Comes Again", "I Love You So", "Who Is This Man Called Jesus", and more; [pers.] I'm really blessed to have Jesus as my Lord and Saviour. He's everything to me. And I have a wonderful and loving husband, who encourages me to do all I can. [a.] Salley, SC 29137.

HYLTON, ERIC NATHANIEL
[b.] July 31, 1935, Kingston, Jamaica, West Indies; [p.] Deceased; [m.] Susan Lee, June 16, 1974; [ch.] Aton Zam-Ramanno, Colombe Thazra-Rose, Ras Makarhu, Leo-Rose; [ed.] Self taught current student of Philosophy, Rose Croix University; [occ.] Photography, Artist, printer; [memb.] Rosicrucian Order, A.M.O.R.C., Traditional Martinist Order; [hon.] "Roll of Honors" for humanitarian service; [oth. writ.] Poems published in anthologies; [pers.] Dedication to the recognition of beauty in all expressions of life, the realization that each day is a virgin page to scribe my experience. [a.] Augusta, ME 04330.

IDZKOWSKY, HENRY
[b.] March 19, 1908, Pittsburgh, Pennsylvania; [p.] Harry and Mary E. Idzkowsky; [m.] Velva Seyler, August 30, 1937; [ch.] Betty Hazlett and Gretchen M. Lugar; [ed.] B.S.M.S, PhD, The University of Pittsburgh; [occ.] Professor Emeritus of Biological Sciences; [memb.] Pennsylvania Academy of Science, Sigma X; [hon.] Silver Beaver, Boy Scouts of America, Phi Sigma Honorary, Biological (National) Sigma X, National Honorary Science Society Beta Beta Beta, National Honorary Undergraduate Biological (Honorary Member), Outstanding Educators of America; [oth. writ.] Manuscript in Progress-Biosensitivity-Concepts of an Aged Biologist; [pers.] Having taught forty six years at both the small college and university levels, I learned much about the intellectual honesty and faith of young people. [a.] Johnstown, PA 15905.

INGOLDSBY, DEBBIE
[b.] March 17, 1953, Lethbridge, Alberta, Canada; [p.] Joe and Eva Ingoldsby; [ed.] Currently student at World for Christ Institute of Christian Studies in Lethbridge; [occ.] Secretary for First Congregational Church and World for Christ Institute; [memb.] First Congregational Church; [pers.] I hope my poems show my love for Jesus, my Lord and our Father in Heaven's love for his children. My poems connect me also to my Dad who passed away in 1960. [a.] Lethbridge, Alberta, Canada T1H 0R7.

INGRAM, ELIZABETH
[pen.] Frances; [b.] November 1, 1957, Montgomery Co.; [p.] Odessa Robinson; [m.] Arthur, August 2, 1975; [ch.] Elizabeth, Rhonda, Tara, Nancy, Arthur Jr., William, Kelly, Shaun, 'James'; [ed.] Brotonville, Candor Middle School, East Montgomery High; [occ.] Homemaker; [memb.] Mineral Spring Improvement Council; [oth. writ.] I have other poems but have not had them published; [pers.] Poem seem to be flowing in my mind and the only way to catch them is on paper. I tend to continue to write poetry. [a.] Ellerbe, NC 28338.

INGRAM, IRENE B.
[b.] September 28, 1964, Kearny, New Jersey; [p.] Richard H. and Irene A. Ingram; [ed.] North Arlington High, Montclair State College; [pers.] Poetry has always been a big part of my life. My heart is filled with deep emotions, and those emotions are unfolded in my poetry and inspired by loved ones, that I have loved and lost. [a.] North Arlington, NJ 07031.

INGRAM, MELVIN T.
[b.] October 12, 1958, Milledgeville, Georgia; [p.] Willie R. Sr. and Julia Butts Ingram; [ed.] Baldwin High, Savannah State College, pursuing MBA at Averett College, Quantico, VA & D.D.S. and Meharry Medical College (Nashville, TN); [occ.] United States Marine Corps Combat Engineer Officer; [hon.] Who's Who, Dean's List, NROTC Commendations, Navy achievement medals, unit commendations and various other military awards; [pers.] Any realistic dream, no matter how remote it may seem, is possible. Dream on realistically! Exposure to Black American literature, during my high school years, opened up a whole new world for me and taught me the joy of reading, learning, and sharing ideas. [a.] Milledgeville, GA 31061.

INGRAM, MICHAL TIFFANY
[pen.] Tiffany Ingram; [b.] November 16, 1979, Minneapolis, Minnesota; [p.] Sherol Ingram and Michael Stewart; [ed.] Marcy Open School (Minneapolis, MN); [occ.] Student, writer; [hon.] 1993 IBM Minnesota Twins Student Pennant Race Recipient, Scholar award Mpls. Public schools 1987; [pers.] I have been greatly influenced by my family and teachers, Heidi Bergin and Kathy Scoggin. Love sees no colors. [a.] Minneapolis, MN 55414.

INNISS, RICHARD RANDOLPH
[b.] September 14, 1955, Barbados, West Indies; [p.] Mr. and Mrs. Deighton Inniss; [m.] Elaine, September 5, 1970; [ch.] Anthony and Natalie Inniss (Anthony Peter and Natalie Suzanne); [ed.] Diploma in Nursing Manor Hospital, Epsom, Surrey, UK; BA in Psychology for Nurses; St. Leo College, St. Leo, FL;; [occ.] Nursing Supervisor-MHC, Inc.; [hon.] Dean's List, Most Progressive Nurse of the Year; [oth. writ.] Several poems published in MHC, Inc.'s monthly newsletter; [pers.] I have been greatly influenced by the Psalms of David and the English poets. [a.] Tampa, FL 33618.

IONNO, JOSEPH II
[pen.] Nyborg Batfish, Esquire; [b.] June 26, 1955, Bridgeport, Connecticut; [p.] Joseph and Julie Ionno; [ed.] Dropped out of college (University of Georgia) at age 17, but became self-educated since that time; [occ.] Professional musician (keyboardist with the Dr. Hook Band); [hon.] Qualified for National Merit

Scholarship; [oth. writ.] Anthologized in "Poetry from Hartford", political and satirical articles published in Gwinnet Daily News, Thens Banner Herald, Flagpole, Athens Observer, Classic City Live, The Red and Black, was managing editor of the Athens Bad Press; [pers.] The emergent properties of nature manifest themselves through the matrix of human consciousness. [a.] Athens, GA 30605.

IOVINO, LEN
[b.] September 7, 1950, Chicago, Illinois; [m.] Cathy, May 5, 1973; [ch.] Dominic and Vince; [ed.] Morton Junior College, St. Ignatius High School, Defense Language Institute of Monterey, CA; [occ.] Printer; [pers.] Writing is escapism in its purest form. I can soar above the turmoil of everyday life and lose myself in a world of harmony and understanding. [a.] Berwyn, IL 60402.

IRISH, ROSEMARY
[b.] April 8, 1962, Manchester, New Hampshire; [p.] Paul F. and Margaret T. (O'Leary) Murphy Sr.; [m.] Shawn W., September 29, 1989; [ed.] Memorial High; [occ.] Navy wife; [memb.] League of American Wheelmen; [hon.] Certificate of Appreciation-presented by W.R. Large Caption U.S.N.; [oth. writ.] This is first piece published; [pers.] Always help the next guy-your pay back will be ten-fold. [a.] Aiea, Hawaii 96701-3623.

IRWIN, HELEN
[b.] May 8, 1920, South Dakota; [p.] Bertina and Alfred Olfstad; [m.] February 23, 1954-Divorced; [ch.] Hugh, Matthew Hallie, William and Eva; [ed.] High School-Business; [occ.] Retired; [memb.] Methodist Church; [hon.] Art. of Honor on Poem, High School Queen, Honor Student, Parent of the Year, Parent of the Year Morning Side College; [oth. writ.] Fathers Big Choir, The Mysterious Wind. [a.] Pierson, IA 51048.

IRWIN-MOSTYN, MARGIE
[pen.] Maggie Ryan; [b.] January 16, 1947, Joliet, Illinois; [p.] Bob and Edith Irwin; [m.] John P., September 28, 1968; [ch.] Mollie and John Ryan Mostyn; [ed.] BA Education - Lewis University; [occ.] Math Educator, Prov. Catholic High School, Illinois Math and Science Academy; [memb.] St. Dennis Church, IMSA Fellow, ICTM, NCTM, and MAA; [hon.] Impact II Grant NASA, Newmast Recipient, Who's Who Among American Teachers; [oth. writ.] Geometry and Life, Dear God Prayers for Teenagers, My Son Left for College, Chosen One, A Teacher; [pers.] Never give up, someday, someone will listen to what you write, if you keep trying. [a.] Lockport, IL 60441-3641.

ISLAM, JAMIE
[b.] December 2, 1977, Fountain Valley, California; [p.] Howard and Glennda Islam; [ed.] Norco High School; [occ.] Student; [hon.] Fathers Day Contest, Several writing awards; [oth. writ.] Several papers on history essays; [pers.] I be what I want to be. I don't take things too serious. I'm greatly influenced by my dear cousin, Sarah Scott, my light. [a.] Mira Loma, CA 91752.

JABBAR, NAJAH
[b.] December 10, 1967, Chicago, Illinois; [occ.] Clerk and Student at Sante Fe College; [pers.] My brother once said to me, "The sky is the limit"...When

I only saw the top of my nose, then I looked out and say my first star. [a.] G'ville, FL 32606.

JACKSON, TERRY LYNN
[pen.] Terri L. Jackson; [b.] December 5, 1963, Bow Island, Alberta; [p.] Steve and Doreen Juhas; [m.] Denis, November 6, 1985; [ed.] Tilley High, Community College Southern Alberta Institute of Technology professional cooking course; [occ.] Housewife; [memb.] Scandia Lutheran Church; [hon.] Editor's Choice Award for a poem; [oth. writ.] Several poems for friends and support groups; [pers.] I release my feelings and thoughts by writing poetry. My family and friends especially my wonderful neighbors have been my biggest influence for writing. [a.] Scandia, Alberta Canada T0J 2Z0.

JACKSON, DR. TOGWELL A.
[pen.] Tog Jackson, T.A. Jackson; [b.] November 1, 1939, New York, New York; [p.] William Ralph and Dr. Eleanor Alexander Jackson; [m.] Dr. Chung-Ja C., June 17, 1967; [ch.] Bertrand and Alexander; [ed.] BA MSc and PhD in Geology (from Columbia University, University of Wisconsin, and University of Missouri, respectively); [occ.] Research scientist in the field of biogeochemistry. Working on environmental problems of lakes and rivers; [hon.] Graduated cum laude from high school, freshman humanities prize in college, A.P. Green fellowship in clay mineralogy in graduate school, award for graduate term paper in geology, membership in Sigma Xi, National Science Foundation (N.S.F.) postdoctoral fellowship at Woods Hole Oceanographic Institution, elected to Rawson Academy of Aquatic Sciences (in Canada); [oth. writ.] Several other poems (unpublished), both serious and humorous, many scientific publications, I have also done a fair amount of art work; [pers.] I have many interests embracing a wide range of cultural as well as scientific subjects. I am a professional scientist, but my principal second calling is art. I believe strongly in preservation of the natural world and traditional cultures and ecological balance between man and his natural environment. I have been profoundly influenced by Buddhism. My English heritage is also very important to me. [a.] Burlington, Ontario L7T 3W6, Canada.

JACOBSEN, INGRID
[pen.] Ingrid Jacobsen; [b.] November 2, 1976, Flagstaff, Arizona; [p.] Dorothy A. and Leonard T. Jacobsen; [ed.] Flagstaff High School; [hon.] First place in sculpting and first place in painting; [oth. writ.] Many poems and short stories not published. [a.] Flagstaff, AZ 86004.

JAHNER, KRISTY
[pen.] Montana; [b.] November 25, 1963, Great Falls, Montana; [p.] Shirley Casey and Darrel Kelso; [m.] Divorced and engaged to Mike Hanley; [ch.] Brittney, Brantan, Braxton, and Brooke Jahner; [ed.] Clearfield High School, Allen Hancock College; [occ.] Professional Waitress (Jordan Chateau; [oth. writ.] Several unpublished; [pers.] Life is short, don't waste it on hate or intolerance. Live only one day at a time because tomorrow never comes and yesterday is a memory. [a.] Merced, CA 95340.

JAMES, MARY PITTMAN
[b.] March 8, 1937, Wiggins, Mississippi; [p.] Dunaway and Hilda Pittman; [m.] Billy Y., June 24, 1960; [ch.] Glenn N. Bradem, Michael Gary James,

and Staci Lyn James; [ed.] Orange Grove High (Gulfport, MS); [occ.] Operator, South Central Bell Telephone Company; [memb.] Petal Harvey Baptist Church, Sunday School Teacher, Telephone Pioneers; [hon.] Ribbons won for poetry with Pioneers; [oth. writ.] Poems published Baptist Record, song recorded with Rainbow Records (Hollywood, CA); [pers.] My hope is that these words may inspire many to know the One who gives them, a loving heavenly Father. [a.] Petal, MS 39465.

JAMISON, NANCE
[b.] January 16, 1948, San Diego County, California; [p.] Don and Virginia Jamison; [ch.] Sunee Nicole Ibarra; [ed.] High School, Beauty School, Interior Design; [occ.] Design Crafts, Shirts, Decorate homes/shops; [oth. writ.] I have over 100 poems I've written. Expressions for cards, personal diaries of life's ups and downs; [pers.] My dream is to have all my poems published in my own book and cards to be printed for sale in stores. [a.] Concord, CA 94521.

JASIURKOWSKI, KATARZYNA MALINA
[pen.] Kasia; [b.] September 19, 1973, Krakow, Poland; [p.] Stanley and Sofia Jasiurkowski; [ed.] Our Lady of Lourdes Academy, Naval Academy Preparatory School, United States Naval Academy; [occ.] Student-Midshipmen; [memb.] American Heart Association, St.Richard Church Choir and Lecturer; [hon.] Dean's List, Silver Knight Nominee, Winner of ROTC Scholarship, numerous awards in field of Science, recipient of U.S. Coast Guard Academy appointment and U.S. Naval Academy appointment, 1991 Miss Florida American Coed Pageant; [oth. writ.] Several poems published in Literary Magazine, local newspaper; [pers.] I write to express what I feel about the people. [a.] Miami, FL 33177.

JEFFERS, MARGIE B.
[pen.] Margie; [b.] February 6, 1924, Greenville, South Carolina; [p.] Warren and Mae Beck; [m.] D.L., May 3, 1946; [ch.] Kenneth, Jennifer, and Karen; [ed.] High School - Brescia College, Lea Business College; [occ.] Retailing; [memb.] Baptist Church, National Poetry, Lea College-Women's College Society; [oth. writ.] Hiawatha's Brave; [pers.] Poetry, an outlet for sentiments and memories. [a.] Shalimar, FL 32579.

JEGEDGE, ABEJIDE
[pen.] Tinu; [b.] May 31, 1983, Newark, New Jersey; [p.] Oyeniyi and Felicia Jegede (brother-Oyekunle and sister-Aderonke); [ed.] St. Bridget's Day Care, St. Columba's School; [occ.] Student; [hon.] First Place 1992 Science Fair, Extra Effort Award 1992-93, , 1992 Merit Award, 1991 Creativity Award.

JENNINGS, MARY
[b.] September 10, 1922, Chicago, Illinois; [p.] Payne and Mildred Jennings; [ed.] BA and MA; [occ.] Retired; [memb.] Various humane and scholastic societies; [hon.] Honorarium Social Science Research Council (Washington, DC), Smith-Mundt Grants for Lectureships, University San Francisco Xavier, Sucre, Bolivia and University Francisco Morazan, Teguugalpa, Honduras; [oth. writ.] Interview with Mexican entrants to the U.S., an investigation supported by the Social Science Research Council published in Civilizations by the International Institute of Differing Civilizations in Belgium; [pers.] May the reader pray for Reconciliation. [a.] La Jolla, CA

JESSE, JEAN
[b.] June 17, 1926, Boone, Iowa; [p.] Claude and Estella Shafel Wiley; [m.] Marvin Crouch (1947, deceased 1966) and Roland Jesse (1967); [ch.] Two daughters-Ricki Crouch Webb and Jane Crouch Hagge, one son-Maruin Gene Crouch, died 1993, two step-daughters-Janis Jesse Anderson and Pamela Jesse Munson and one stepson-Roland Lavern Jesse, Jr.; [ed.] Boone High School, Western Union Telegraph School; [occ.] Bookkeeper retired, have small craft business "Counting Cousins"; [memb.] First Methodist Church, Boone County Historical Society, Boone County Genealogical Society; [oth. writ.] I have written many poems and short articles for my own enjoyment. Nothing published other than high school yearbook; [pers.] I try to write about those everyday things everyone can relate to. [a.] Pilot Mound, IA 50223.

JETTE, GEORGE
[b.] December 29, 1961, Pawtucket, Rhode Island; [pers.] Reading a diversity of cultural and philosophical literature helps us gain a health objectivity of the world around us and also helps to stem the subjectivity that creates ignorance and pressure. [a.] Pawtucket, RI 02860.

JIRAK, CRYSTAL
[b.] January 31, 1978, Elko, Nevada; [p.] Jeanie and Ronald Jirak; [ed.] Moapa Valle High School; [occ.] Student; [oth. writ.] Southern Nevada Writing Project Anthology; [pers.] Wrote this poem for Grandma that has passed away. My Mom and my teacher, Mrs. Bev Bradley have both inspired me to write. [a.] Overton, NV 89040.

JOHNBAPTISTE, JOYCE
[b.] September 21, 1957, Dominica; [p.] Ethel Zamore; [ed.] High school graduate; [occ.] Yachting Industry. [a.] Tortola, British Virgin.

JOHNSON, DORMA
[pen.] Lee-Dallas; [b.] August 23, 1924, Beckham County; [p.] W.P. and Lucinda Dallas; [m.] Lonnie, (deceased 1987), April 22, 1946; [ch.] Danny, Kim, Peggy, Diane; [ed.] High school diploma, Dale Carnegie course, Bible Course; [occ.] Homemaker, owner, operator of cattle small ranch; [memb.] United Methodist Church, E.S.A. Sorority, Educational Director 1993, U.M. Women's Circle; [hon.] Past president Treasurer-E.S.A. Sorority, Past president of American Legion Auxiliary; [oth. writ.] Poems not published; [pers.] I enjoy life, like to read, walk, dance, play bridge, eat with my friends, play with grandchildren, worship at church, and visit my children. [a.] Elk City, OK.

JOHNSON, ELIZABETH J.
[b.] March 12, 1928, Grand Rapids, Michigan; [p.] Xenia and John Matijek; [m.] Robert Walter, July 1, 1950; [ch.] Kimberly Fern and Thoren Holt; [ed.] BA, MA - Wayne State University, University of Detroit; [occ.] Retired Art Teacher (Public School-Towson, MD); [pers.] The finest years of my existence have been as a teacher of art, and of the artistry of words. [a.] Towson, MD 21286.

JOHNSON, ERIN NICOLE
[pen.] Erin Nicole Johnson; [b.] July 2, 1962, Oakland, California; [p.] John P. and Colleen B. Smith; [m.] Mark Thomas, January 11, 1992; [ed.] San Lorenzo High, Chabot Junior College, California State University Hay (CSUH); [occ.] Sales-design; [memb.] Oakland Youth Chorus-Alumni, Prometheus Symphony, Kennsington Symphony Alumni; [hon.] Music scholarship/viola; [oth. writ.] Several-emphasis on lyrical; [pers.] I write what I think I know and what I know I feel. [a.] Monterey County, CA 93907.

JOHNSON, FLORENCE W.
[pen.] Flossie; [b.] June 8, 1964, Morristown; [p.] Lewis K. Winstead and Agnes Winstead Johnson; [m.] Larry W.; [ed.] Flat Gap Elementary, Hancock High School; [occ.] Homemaker; [memb.] TRSA Recording of Nashville, TN; [hon.] "Honorable Mention" three times, "Golden Poet award" from World of Poetry S. Cal; [oth. writ.] Many, many poems, short stories; [pers.] I love writing my happiness come in thinking it will comfort someone or make someone smile. This world needs comfort more smiles, and love.

JOHNSON, HEIDI
[b.] January 7, 1981, Santa Barbara, California; [p.] Steve and Becky Johnson; [ed.] Canalino and Aliso Elementary, Carpinteria Middle School; [occ.] Babysitting part-time after school; [memb.] Santa Barbara Polo and Racquet Club; [hon.] Spelling Bee contestant, Environmentalist at school; [oth. writ.] Personal cards to family and friends; [pers.] Thanks to my grandma for introducing me to poetry. I love her with all my heart. [a.] Carpinteria, CA 93013.

JOHNSON, JEFFREY MICHAEL
[pen.] Jeffrey Michael Johnson; [b.] March 26, 1969; [m.] Still looking; [ed.] Clemson University; [occ.] Freelance Writer; [oth. writ.] Op-ed published in the Washington Times, numerous articles for TV, etc.; [pers.] With so many rules and moves and fears dictating how people are supposed to be, writing is a place where I can go and experience unbridled emotion. I yearn for a world where we can be ourselves, speak our minds, and command respect for who we are. [a.] Boulder, CO 80302.

JOHNSON, KRISTINA M.
[b.] may 13, 1973, Eureka, California; [p.] Linda Swaim and Albert Mendes; [m.] David L., November 28, 1992; [ch.] Kyle David Johnson; [ed.] Fortuna High, College of the Redwoods-majoring in Forestry; [occ.] Waitress, Night Supervisor, Hungry Hutch Restaurant (Fortuna, CA); [hon.] College Honor Roll; [pers.] Life is too short to pass love by. Take a chance. The risk may be well worth it, for only time will tell. [a.] Eureka, CA 95501.

L. SUSAN JOHNSON
[pen.] Susan Johnson; [b.] may 5, 1955, Ashland, Wisconsin; [p.] Nathaniel and Lottie Hunt; [m.] William A., December 31, 1973; [ch.] Rachel, Benita, Jeremy, James Russell Johnson; [ed.] Bloomington High, partial Harper Community Junior College; [occ.] Wife and mother; [pers.] Look to the light ahead of you. Not to the darkness behind you. And one day that wonderful light will surround you. [a.] Hutchinson, KS 67501.

JOHNSON, MAUREEN ESTELLE
[b.] September 19, 1933, Chakrata, India; [p.] Alfred and Estell Guerin; [m.] Leroy Frederick, December 11, 1954; [ch.] Mark, Stephen, Michael, Deborah, and Kelly Johnson; [ed.] Elementary English School (Kempston Bedfordshire England); [occ.] Caregiver for Elderly; [memb.] Faith United Methodist Church, Akron; [oth. writ.] Assorted poems-some comedic others in a serious vein some blank verse; [pers.] During times when life's events threaten to pull me in a downward spiral, my writing has proved to be therapeutic for me and entertaining to others. [a.] Akron, OH.

JOHNSON, MAX LAVERNE
[b.] February 4, 1929, New Sharon, Iowa; [p.] Leonard and Ellen Johnson; [m.] Darlene C., June 11, 1988; [ch.] Barbara, Carol, Virginia, Maynard, Douglas; [ed.] University of Dayton, Black Hawk College; [occ.] Retired Computer Specialist, Artist; [pers.] I try to express personal experience. [a.] Newton, IA 50208.

JOHNSON, NAOMI
[pers.] Expression of art is the freedom to explore your imagination inwardly so that you can display it outwardly in song, acting and creative writing for all to enjoy. [a.] Cincinnati, OH 45212.

JOHNSON, ROBB
[b.] April 9, 1969, Carthage, New York; [p.] Lawrence and Judy Johnson; [ed.] Carthage Central High, Regents diploma class of 1988; [occ.] Still Photographic Specialist, U.S. Army (Fort Irwin, CA); [pers.] The embrace was written for Mich'l Klersy and the goodness that is found within. [a.] Fort Irwin, CA 92310.

JOHNSON, SARAH E.
[pen.] Sarah E. Johnson; [b.] November 24, 1901, Connelsville, Pennsylvania; [p.] Mary G. Dilts and Willard H. Johnson; [m.] Horace H., January 18, 1923; [ch.] Robert David Johnson and Mary Nina Underwood; [ed.] BA in Music from Carnegie Institute of Technology, Pittsburgh, PA; [occ.] Teacher; [memb.] Parent Teachers Association, Mt. Lebanon U.P. Church, National Association of Parliamentarians, Mt. Lebanon Women's Club; [hon.] Mortar Board in Carnegie Institute of Technology, Graduated 2nd in class Connelsville High School, Who's Who of American Women, Vice President of National Congress of Parents and Teachers; [oth. writ.] 35 years of original Christmas poetry, compilation of Parliamentary Procedure Book for PTA, "Leaves from A President's Notebook" for PTA; [pers.] Most of my writing as born in some thought in the Holy Bible applied to everyday life. [a.] Pittsburgh, PA 15228.

JOHNSTON, DAVE
[b.] June 1, 1969, Atlanta, Georgia; [p.] Debbie and Paul Johnston; [m.] Fiance - Therese Maffetone; [ed.] High school- part-time college student - Emergency Medical training; [occ.] Bio Med. Tech; [oth. writ.] Misc. songs and poems; [pers.] Racism is ignorance. [a.] Croton Falls, NY 10519.

JOHNSTON, ERIN E.
[b.] January 11, 1971, Kitchener, Ontario; [p.] Bruce and Karen Johnston; [ed.] Waterloo Collegiate Institute, Kitchener Collegiate Institute, Ryerson Polytechnical University (Toronto); [oth. writ.] Over 150 unpublished poetry, several short stories; [pers.] You must believe in yourself before others will believe in you. [a.] Waterloo, Ontario, Canada N2L 1K3.

JOHNSTON, STANLEY G.
[b.] September 1, 1953, Hillsdale, Michigan; [p.] Fred and Joan; [m.] Jacalyn J., August 29, 1970; [ch.] Paul, Amy and Leah; [ed.] Camden Frontier High School, Jackson Community College; [memb.] Cambria Baptist Church, Broadcast Music Inc. (BMI), Gospel Music Association (GMA); [pers.] My heart's desire is to bring enjoyment to others through my writing. [a.] Hillsdale, MI 49242.

JOHNSTONE, ALTA RUTH
[pen.] Tall Friend; [b.] August 15, 1914, Lincoln County, KS; [p.] Robert Theodore and Mary Esther Gabelman; [ch.] Frances Shaff Miller, Robert Eugene and James Clinton Shaff; [ed.] AA degree from Compton Comm. College, CA; [occ.] School secretary, retired; [memb.] National Assoc. of Educational Secretaries, American Baptist Church, Smithsonian Associates, Friends of the Library, Mended Hearts; [hon.] Professional Standards Certificate, NAES Honorary and Continuing Service Award, PTA, Participant at Freedoms Foundation, Valley Forge, PA; [oth. writ.] Fine Arts Society, Indiana Greater National Society of Published Poets, Great Poets of the Western World, Center for Today's Woman, Cerritos College Sounds of Praise, Church Women United; [pers.] Keep on keeping on.; [a.] Bellflower, CA

JONES, ALLYSON
[pen.] Allyson Jones; [b.] January 31, 1978, Detroit, Michigan; [p.] Jeff and Diana Jones; [ed.] Ninth grade; [occ.] Student; [memb.] Student Council, Honor Roll, Tennis Team, Volleyball, Flag Core; [hon.] Poems and stories recognized in Honors English classes, and asked to attend the Fitzgerald Academically Skilled and Talented summer program for six years; [oth. writ.] Extensive collection of poems and creative writings; [pers.] I've always believed that someone can achieve personal gratification from expression of feelings through writing them down especially in the form of poems or short stories. Writing creatively triggers new feelings, better, healthier ones that can improve the sense of individuality that is needed and desired by everyone. Poetry has its place in everybody's life. [a.] Warren, MI 48091.

JONES, DONNA B.
[b.] May 6, 1911, Philadelphia, Pennsylvania; [p.] Dr. Roy G. and Donna H. Barrick; [m.] Victor H., October 8, 1934; [ed.] Iowa City High School, University of Iowa (BA); [occ.] Dental Office Manager (retired); [memb.] G.V. Community Church, Worship Community, P.E.O., G.V. Assistance Service; [hon.] Certificate of Honor from World of Poetry; [oth. writ.] About 50 poems, several book reviews. [a.] Greenvalley, AZ 85614.

JONES, EDWARD T.
[b.] March 23, 1945, Pleasantville, New Jersey; [p.] Vincent and Martha Jones; [m.] Carol M.; [ch.] Lisa, Larry, Ed Jr., Joe, Tyrone, and Ron - grandchildren Orion and Angela; [occ.] Retired police sergeant (Egg Harbor Township); [memb.] Life Member of New Jersey P.B.A. Mainland Local 77; [oth. writ.] Several romantic poems to my wife, Carol, and about other refreshing bits of life; [pers.] I used poetry as an escape from the harsh reality of police work. [a.] McKee City, NJ 08232.

JONES, JEANETTE P.
[pen.] Attorney Jones; [b.] February 18, 1939, Caroline County; [p.] Robert H. and the late Pearl Parker; [m.] Deceased, February 20, 1960; [ch.] Nadine, Sylvester and John - grandchildren: Tunisia Chavonte, Kenneth and Stentyan; [ed.] Union High School, Guinea School (Elementary), Margo's Beauty School, Nurses Aide Training from Woodmont, Nursing Home (Frederick, VA); [occ.] Certified Nurses Aide, Homemaker; [memb.] Maccadonia Baptist Church, American Heart Association; [hon.] An award from World of Poetry and an invitation to attend a poetry convention in California in 1992; [oth. writ.] A poem published in the poetic voices of America summer of 1992. Titled: "Where is Justice for Children and I won an award of merit for a poem titled I am not a little tree, from World of Poetry; [pers.] I try my mind at several poems a night. I have writing and its always daybreak before I realize it. My poems represents life, love, and happiness also sadness and injustice. [a.] Woodford, VA 22580.

JONES, JENNIE
[b.] March 20, 1961, Panama City, Florida; [p.] Cora B. and George J. Switzer; [m.] Jerry A., September 7, 1991; [ch.] Amanda Lynn and Harrison James; [ed.] Part-time student working full-time; [occ.] Housekeeper; [hon.] Having my poem published in your book; [oth. writ.] If Momma Could Write Me From Heaven, Tears in My Eyes, Space, The Death of a Star and Man, The Dream, Heaven's Gates; [pers.] Having someone enjoy my feelings, and maybe understanding how they come from the heart makes me very happy. [a.] Auburndale, FL 33823.

JONES, MARTHA HERBERT
[b.] Brownsville, Tennessee; [p.] Samuel Allen and Ida Herbert; [m.] Dewey, February 8, 1958; [ch.] Dewey Alan and Lorie Beth; [ed.] Haywood High, a course in children literature at the Institute of Children's Literature at West Redding, CT; [occ.] A bookkeeper at the Brownsville Bank for 10 years, now a homemaker; [memb.] Holly Grove Baptist Church and Director of Women's Missionary Union; [hon.] Won numerous awards in arts and crafts for needlepoint, quilting and canning; [oth. writ.] Write a weekly news article in local newspaper. I have written an autobiography entitled, "The Guiding Hand". Poem published in "World of Treasure of Great Poems"; [pers.] My writings reflect personal experiences and my Christian faith and philosophy. [a.] Brownsville, TN 38012.

JORDAN, JOHN A.
[b.] July 15, 1928, Toronto, Canada; [p.] John N. and Ora E. Jordan; [m.] Patricia H., June 24, 1980; [ch.] (step daughter by previous marriage, first wife deceased) Barbara Jordan Conner; [ed.] Associate of Arts, Brevard Community College (Florida), Higher School Certificate, Manchester Grammar School (Manchester, England); [occ.] Retired USAF Senior Master Sergeant; [memb.] NCO Association, American Automobile Association, American Association of Retired Persons; [hon.] First place, short play, 1988, Space Coast Writers Conference. Runner-up 1987, 1990, Space Coast Playwrights Workshop; [oth. writ.] One Act Plays: "The Audition", "My Friend Adolf", "Moving Day", "Welcome Back Elvis". Essays: "A Figure of Authority", "A Taste of War". Unpublished novel: "I Say It's Spinach"; [pers.] Retired after 25 years service with USAF

where I worked primarily as a publicist for USAF Recruiting Service and as a broadcaster with Armed Forces Radio & TV Service. [a.] Cocoa, FL 32926.

JORDAN, MARTHA
[b.] February 24, 1959, Gastonia, North Carolina; [p.] Joel and Betty Jordan; [ch.] April Nicole and David Lance; [occ.] Self-employed; [pers.] My poems reflect thing's that have affected my life or people's lives that I have known. I hope that every one that reads my poems enjoy them as much as I have writing them. [a.] Locust Grove, GA 30248.

JORDAN, VIVIAN
[b.] September 29, 1948, Vienna, Georgia; [p.] Claudia Lewis Roper and Minor Jordan, Jr.; [ed.] BS Secondary Education; [occ.] Teacher/Dayton Public schools; [memb.] Delta Sigma Theta Sorority, National Parks and Conservation Association; [pers.] In my writing I hope to provide the reader with a means of exploring a variety of emotions and experiences. [a.] Dayton, OH 45406.

JOSEPHSEN, FRANCES REGINA
[pen.] Francie Josephen; [b.] April 29, 1967, Stratford, New Jersey; [p.] Carmen A. and Trudy Barone; [m.] Fred J., June 16, 1990; [ed.] BA Communications, Glassboro State College. Presently an M.A. candidate Rowan College of NJ; [occ.] Elementary Teacher, Chelsea Junior High School (Atlantic City, NJ); [memb.] National Education Association, New Jersey Education Association. [a.] Northfield, NJ 08225.

JOY, PHILLIP R.
[pen.] Raymond Joy; [b.] May 2, 1978, Halifax, Nova Scotia, Canada; [p.] Diane and Ken Joy; [ed.] Hants North Rural High; [occ.] Full-time student; [oth. writ.] A few unpublished poems; [pers.] Very concerned about the environment especially wildlife. [a.] Maitland, NS Canada B0N 1T0.

JULIEN, GISELLE
[b.] June 15, 1975, Port-of-Spain, Trinidad, West Indies; [p.] Neville and Gemma Julien; [ed.] Roselle Catholic High School, Trenton State College (Biology major); [memb.] Nature Conservancy, Greenpeace, American Museum of Natural History; [pers.] I write about what I see, what I love, and what I feel. [a.] Hillside, NJ 07205.

KACHLIC, COLLEEN M.
[b.] June 16, 1982, Tyler, Texas; [p.] Bill and Donna Kachlic; [ed.] Fifth grade-Velma Penney Intermediate School (Lindale, TX); [occ.] Student; [memb.] Little Eagles, 4-H Club member of a ballet dance company; [hon.] "A" Honor Roll, 5th place winner in Math Pentathalon; [pers.] I hope that the world is a more beautiful and peaceful place for the next generation. [a.] Lindale, TX 75771.

KADYAMATIMBA, GLORIA
[pen.] ZII Gwinyai; [b.] September 26, 1959, Chesutu, Zimbabwe; [p.] Wilson and Rose Mbofana; [m.] Simon Richard; [ch.] Tanyaradzwa Lazarus; [ed.] Usher Girl's Secondary School, Tegwani High School, University of Zimbabwe, University of Pittsburgh (USA); [occ.] Senior Assistant Librarian, National University of Science and Technology; [memb.] Zimbabwe Library Association, Zimbabwe Women Writers Union; [oth. writ.] This is my first publication; [pers.] I wish society could be more tolerant of

those that are different. [a.] Bulawayo, Zimbabwe.

KAIMAKAMIAN, FERDINAND
[b.] January 16, 1916, Cilician, Armenia; [p.] Haroutune and Haiganoush Maimakamian; [ed.] American College of Central Turkey; [occ.] Radiation Therapy and Radiographic Technologist-Licensed; [memb.] American Legion Chaplin (New York, Post #18 Vet. WW2), Knights of Vartan Brotherhood P.C.; [hon.] John F. Kennedy Award for Libraries (1972), Knights of Vartan Outstanding Achievement 1988; [oth. writ.] First Rhythmic Translation Opera Cavalleria Rusticana into Armenian 1954, Pagan Eras of Church Music 1965, numerous articles on Middle Eastern Music and History, etc.; [pers.] From realities of life's inspiration to constructive ideals applied... [a.] Corona, NY 11368.

KALK, PATRICK
[b.] January 31, 1961, Thunder Bay, Ontario, Canada; [m.] Carmen, June 29, 1991; [ed.] Martin Collegiate, University of Regina; [occ.] Business Systems Analyst.

KALPAKJIAN, LOUISE
[b.] August 28, 1908, Boston, Massachusetts; [p.] Helen and Benjamen Boyajian; [m.] George, May 28, 1939; [ch.] Alan; [ed.] High School but has tutoring, as I was in and out of hospitals; [memb.] Rebekah Lodge, The Women's Division of Odd Fellows and Congregational Church (Milford, MA); [hon.] Rebekah's and a citation from this hospital for creativity; [oth. writ.] I have several poems I have written. I always write poems for friends birthdays new homes, new babies, etc.; [pers.] I am a patient here, going on 9 years, I've had 73 operations, on my leg, which was finally amputated. I last lived in Milford, MA.

KAMAILE, CAROL
[b.] December 9, 1940, Los Angeles, California; [p.] Robert and Harriet Dowling; [ch.] Clifford K. Ahmow, Jr., Cristin M. Ahmow; [ed.] Hamilton High; [occ.] Receptionist, teacher and student of the Word of God; [oth. writ.] Kamaile's Favorites Hawaiian Quilting Instruction Booklet, article and poem for company newspaper, miscellaneous poems and gospel songs; [pers.] In all that I am and do, I try to bring honor and glory to my Lord and Saviour Jesus Christ. He inspired me to write by his holy spirit. Amen! [a.] Honolulu, HI 96826.

KANE, ALLAN S.
[b.] August 1, 1965, Philadelphia, Pennsylvania; [m.] Michelle; [ch.] Lynn Marie, Amber Rose; [ed.] Penn Charter, Stockton State College, St. Joseph's University; [occ.] Police Officer, Galloway Township, NJ; [pers.] The greatest joys, the worst tragedies - all a tribute to the depth of the human experience. [a.] Smithville, NJ 08201.

KANTHAK, ANGELENA DAWN
[pen.] Angie; [b.] December 27, 1981, Tarboro, North Carolina; [p.] Rosa Lee and Ronald Kanthak; [ed.] Fifth grade at present at J.C. Braswell Elementary [occ.] Student; [memb.] Triad Enrichment Program; [hon.] A/B Honor Roll for three years straight; [oth. writ.] Third place winner in county wide creative writing contest (a playscript). [a.] Rocky Mount, NC

KARNIS, HEATHER
[b.] May 19, 1972, Hollywood, Florida; [p.] Edward and Diane Karnis and brother Steven Karnis; [ed.] Stonewall Jackson Senior High School, Wright State University; [occ.] Student; [memb.] Wright State University, Emerald Jazz Dance Team; [hon.] Dean's List; [pers.] The things that are most beautiful are the most simple. [a.] Dayton, OH 45431.

KASPRICK, LAWRENCE
[pen.] Eddie Big Kaz; [b.] July 25, 1953, Winnipeg, Manitoba; [p.] Irene and Len (stepfather) Soloshy (Tugunga, CA); [m.] Barb Kerr, common law marriage; [ch.] Laura; [ed.] Grade 10 plus college course and Math upgrading (Neepawa, Manitoba and Kamloops; [occ.] Restaurant worker; [memb.] Columbia House and CD and video club; [oth writ.] Just poems in poetry contests; [pers.] I love music, sports, and poetry. I like to give reading pleasure to people who love poems. [a.] Kamloops, BC Canada.

KAVANAGH, TONY
[b.] July 18, 1959, Dublin, Ireland; [p.] Mary and Thomas; [ch.] Jack (5); [ed.] Left school at 14, learned how to read and write in Mt. Joy Pinson; [occ.] Writer playwright/poet; [memb.] Screenwriter's Guild of America; [hon.] Top 100 Irish American Award, 1992, 1993, Best Stage Scene, 1992 Best Stage Monologue Smith and Klaus publishers from play Down The Mats; [oth. writ.] One original screenplay Johnny Jump Up, five stage plays, Summerhill Parade, The Drum, Down the Flats, Broken Under and Angel; [pers.] Love She Naver Leaves - sadly we walk away from her tears. [a.] Waterside Plaza, NY 10010.

KAWAUCHI, KIRARA
[pen.] Kirara KiKi Kawauchi; [b.] December 19, 1971, Japan; [p.] Takashi and Yoshiko Kawauchi; [ed.] Maryland Institute, College of Art (Senior in Fall '93), Walt Whitman High School graduate 1990; [occ.] Art student; [memb.] WWF, Smithsonian Institution; [hon.] Sculpture award in 1992, scholarship in art in 1993; [oth. writ.] Poem "Magician" is in American Collegiate Poets: Fall Concours 1992. International Publications, Los Angeles, CA 90044; [pers.] This is a very interesting era we live in, too much information, too many styles, and you get confused. What is life? Why are we here? Who are we? I still look for the answers. [a.] Baltimore, MD 21217.

KEARN, ALLISON
[pen.] Ali; [b.] October 9, 1972; [p.] Mr. and Mrs. John Kearn; [ed.] High school, J.S. Fine; [occ.] Child Day Care - Teacher's Aid Magic Years Child Care and Learning Center; [oth. writ.] I have written a whole lot of other poetry not published, and a story. I am also working on a children's book; [pers.] I am greatly influenced by my childhood cancer-leukemia, and my trips to the hospital in Bethesda, Maryland and the support I was given. [a.] Nanticoke, PA 18634.

KEENE, LINDA RAKES
[b.] April 23, 1946, Dickinson County - Clintwood, Virginia; [p.] Alex and Verna Rakes; [m.] Reggie G., November 21, 1969; [ch.] Wesley Marvin, Cheryl Allison, and Ashley Elizabeth; [ed.] Clintwood High School; [occ.] Housewife, Receptionist; [oth. writ.] Hundreds of literary poems and short stories; [pers.] Much of my writings reflects on personal experi-

ences, however, I love fictional writing and poems of faith. Poetry has been a strong influence since childhood. [a.] Spartanburg, SC 29301.

KEEN, TIMOTHY
[pen.] Timothy Keen; [b.] December 23, 1963, Decatur County, Tennessee; [p.] Charles and Larue Keen; [m.] Cathy Spain, November 30, 1982; [ch.] Ashley (10), Courtnie (9) and Whitnie (7); [ed.] Decatur Riverside High; [occ.] Deputy Sheriff; [memb.] Hopwell Baptist Church (Parsons, TX); [oth. writ.] Oh What A Friend - and Through His Eyes, non-published; [pers.] If in this life you don't want to accomplish anything-do accomplish one thing! Make peace with God. [a.] Wildersville, TX.

KELLER, ANTHONY
[b.] October 7, 1974; [p.] David and Brenda Keller; [ed.] Plainview High School; [memb.] Beta Club, Mu Alpha Theta; [hon.] Mr. Beta, Top 10 percent of Senior class; Presidential Academic Fitness Award, Academic Scholarship to Northeast Alabama State Community College; [pers.] I am inspired by the realities of life and the exploration of my feelings and self. a[.] Rainsville, AL 35986.

KELLER, KELLI MARIE
[b.] July 23, 1975, Evergreen Park, Illinois; [p.] Donald and Bonnie Keller; [ed.] Graduate of 1993, accepted at Harvard; [occ.] Student; [memb.] Student Council President, National Honor Society, Latin Honor Society, Mu Alpha Theta, Animal Activist; [hon.] Valedictorian of Class, Illinois State Scholar, Hugh O'Brien Youth Award, Homecoming Queen Candidate; [oth. writ.] Several poems have been published in school literary magazine and ion Kenyon College's magazine; [pers.] I believe in the rights of all living creatures. I shall always work hard to provide that right! [a.] Chicago, IL 60652.

KELLEY, LOUANNA E. (FENICLE)
[pen.] LouAnn Kelley; [b.] October 17, 1920, Denver, Colorado; [p.] John E. and Violet M. (Griffin) Richards; [m.] Glen R., January 23, 1984; [ch.] Bill and John Kelley, Joan Fenicle (step-daughter); [ed.] Idaho Springs, Colorado High School, Red Rock College (Golden, CO), Dental School Emily Griffin School (Denver, CO); [occ.] 20 years Freelance Journalist and Historian. Society Editor for Mountain Messenger News (Idaho Springs, CO); [memb.] 1980 Colorado Press, 1993, Jefferson County Historical Society, Colorado Historical Society (Denver, CO), Social Ethic Club (I.S., CO), St. James Methodist Church (Central City, CO); [hon.] Listed in: Who's Who in The West, 22nd edition; [oth. writ.] Articles too numerous to list. Most are historical. "Take Your Pick and Strike It Rich" (book). Articles and song and regular contributor Magazine: Today and Tomorrow (historical publication); [pers.] "Read the label before swallowing the Bottle!" (an old Cornish saying). [a.] Golden, CO 80403.

KELLEY, MARY E.
[b.] November 28, 1931, Tulsa, Oklahoma; [p.] John Patrick and Florence Quinlan Kelley; [ed.] H.S. Holy Family School, BA-Catholic University of Puerto Rico, M.R.E. St. Paul's University - Ottawa Ontario, Canada; [occ.] Director of The Turning Point: A Resource Center for Creative Change; [memb.] Montgomery Ministerial Union, Missionary Cenacle Apostolate; [hon.] cum laude (both undergraduate

and graduate degrees); [oth. writ.] Reflective Place Mats; [pers.] My motto, "Timeless Time knows rhythm and beat".

KELLEY, WILLIAM L. JR.
[b.] February 21, 1959; [m.] Divorced 13 years; [ch.] Dustin L. Kelley (13) and Jason D. Kelley (11); [ed.] High school grad self taught the really useful things; [occ.] Had several jobs, right now I'm working in an auto parts yard; [hon.] Being a father; [oth. writ.] All unpublished; [pers.] I wouldn't want my boys to grow up a boring world, one without individualities. Make a bigot mad, smile and hug someone. [a.] Lake Station, IN 46405.

KELLY, MICHAEL SEAN
[b.] August 13, 1968, Seattle, Washington; [p.] Patrick and Lillian Kelly. [a.] Kent, WA.

KELLY, SHANNON DOYLENE
[b.] August 25, 1978, Harlan, Kentucky; [p.] Doyle and Geneva Kelly; [ed.] Attending Evarts High School; [occ.] Sophomore student; [memb.] FBLA, Beta Club, Gifted and Talented; [hon.] First in Spring on Cloverfork poem contest; Governor's Cup, Biology awards, Science Olympiad Competition; [oth. writ.] Why Mother won first place in Spring Cloverfork, submitted several poems to different competitions. Poems published in school newspaper; [pers.] I try to reflect the reality of life in my writing. My writing is inspired by things that are happening around us everyday. [a.] Closplint, KY 40927.

KELLY, SHANNON-ELIZABETH
[b.] November 23, 1976, Elk County, Pennsylvania; [p.] Cecilia and James Kelly; [occ.] Student in high school will graduate in 1994; [memb.] SADD, Mock Trial; [pers.] I wrote The Lonely Teardrop when I was 14 years old. [a.] Clearfield, PA 16830.

KENDELL, MORGAN R.
[pen.] Brylyant Sporatic; [b.] August 18, 1951, Oshawa, Ontraio, Canada; [p.] Deceased; [m.] Yes, thank you, August 2, 1972; [ch.] Two sons, I give up easily; [ed.] Very little (grade 9); [occ.] Sign-maker, dreamer; [hon.] Having Colleen as my wife; [oth. writ.] Love letters ('68-'71) plus some recipes; [pers.] I encourage people to be more serious and not suffer lightly the fools of the world. [a.] Coquitlam, BC, Canada.

KENT, ISABEL
[b.] August 1, 1933, Benson, Minneapolis; [p.] Henry and Gladys Hughes; [m.] Stanley, June 11, 1955; [ch.] Steven, Coleen, Tim, Kevin, Shannon and Shawn (twins); [ed.] High School - 2 years of college; [occ.] Housewife, retired; [memb.] For World of Poetry (1989-93), St. Lawrence Church Catholic Guild, International Society of Poets (1993); [hon.] 1989-1990-1991-1992 Golden Poet Award, "Who's Who in Poetry" 1990-1992; [oth. writ.] "Brian-Eulogy to A Grandson", "Friendship", "A Mother's Confirmation Prayer", "An Anniversary Poem", "What Is An Alcoholic", "Love", "What Is A Grand-daughter" all published; [pers.] My poetry is my heart and soul, reflected by my beliefs and concepts imprinted on paper. [a.] Perham, MN 56573.

KERNODLE, JENNIFER
[b.] June 27, 1977, Harrison, Arkansas; [p.] David and Wanda Kernodle; [ed.] I will be starting my junior year of high school in August '93; [occ.] Student; [memb.] Track, Volleyball, Medical Mission Team to Nicaragua in 1992; [hon.] Honor award in English been on A/B honor roll for three years, lettered four years in track; [oth. writ.] I have written several poems but none have been published yet; [pers.] Even though I am only 15 years old, my parents have always taught me to put Christ first in my life, and always to see the good in everyone. This is dedicated to my loving Dad. [a.] Harrison, AR 72601.

KERR, RACHEL
[b.] June 2, 1977, Morenci, Michigan; [p.] Allen and Faye Kerr; [ed.] Hilltop High School; [occ.] Student; [oth. writ.] Collection of several unpublished poems; [pers.] Society influences us far too much. It tells us how to think, feel, and live our lives. I think we should believe in ourselves and not what society tells us to believe. [a.] Alvordton, OH 43501.

KETCHAM, ANNIE MARGARET
[pen.] Annie Margaret Ketcham; [b.] March 23, 1934, Little Rock, Arkansas; [p.] Annie L. and Willie C. Michael; [m.] Carl Clinton, 1941; [ch.] Six; [ed.] College-Business; [occ.] Poet and housewife; [memb.] The National Library of Poetry; [hon.] Merit award (2), Golden Poets 10 (1992); [oth. writ.] Book printed by World of Poetry; [pers.] I have a great many more poems. [a.] Winchester, IN 47394.

KEYTON, MARGARET W.
[pen.] Margaret W. Keyton; [b.] Kite, Georgia; [p.] Velma S. and Sam Ashley Williams; [m.] William T., March 21, 1942; [ch.] Ann K. Scarboro and Robert Lyn Keyton; [ed.] Graduated high school business course, Swainsboro Tech. Medical Terminology, Continuing Education, Georgia Southern College; [occ.] National Certified Health Unit Clerk; [memb.] Georgia Society of Published Poets, Member National Certified Health Unit Clerks, Nashville Songwriters Association International; [oth. writ.] Many poems and songs. Had two songs recorded in Nashville, TN. Dedicated a book of poems "Poems From The Heart"; [pers.] A poem written from the heart, will reach the heart of all people.

KHAN, ALIYA A.
[b.] November 11, 1978, Danville, Illinois; [p.] Dr. Abdul Hadi and Rose Lynne Khan; [ed.] High School student; [oth. writ.] Carious other poetry and stories - non published; [pers.] You can put your heart into anything, but only your soul into poetry. [a.] Olney, IL 62450.

KHANNA, ANIL KUMAR
[b.] June 30, 1953, Shahjahanpur, India; [p.] Baij Nath and Malti Devi Khanna; [ed.] MSC (Maths), Allahabad University, India, ALCCS, IETE New Delhi, India; [occ.] Software Engineer, (Student of MSE (CSEG) at UOA); [memb.] IEEE, INC, Usa; [hon.] CMC Ltd. (India), Person of the Year award and Special Recognition Award; [oth. writ.] This is my first poem; [pers.] I strive to reflect the passion and emotions of mankind in its relationship with environment, fellow beings and family members. I have been influenced by poets like Mirza Galib and Khalil Gibran. [a.] Jankiduram, Lucknow 226020 India.

KIGULI, SUSAN NALUAWA
[b.] June 24, 1969, Luwero; [p.] George and Joyce Kiguli; [ed.] Gayaza High School, Makerere University; [occ.] Teacher; [memb.] Uganda Society, Uganda Association of University Women; [hon.] Uganda Association of University Women, Academic Excellence Award; [oth. writ.] Poems and short stories; [pers.] My pen is the flower of my heart. [a.] Kampala.

KILBY, RUTH MCPHERSON
[b.] April 29, 1923, Cannon County, Tennessee; [p.] Abandoned at birth, lived 4 years in Tennessee State Orphanage; [m.] Dewey L, Jr., October 26, 1940; [ch.] 2 daughters; [ed.] Hume Fogg-U.S.C. (CA); [occ.] Retired school teacher; [memb.] The Universe; [hon.] State Charter from Tennessee to publish authors of Tennessee. Executive publisher - Ruth McPherson Kilby, Art Director - Dewey L. Kilby, Jr.; [oth. writ.] Historical novel - Parade of Courage, 3000 poems - authors of Tennessee Magazine; [pers.] I arouse from the earth to touch stars. [a.] Murfreesboro, TN 37133-8104.

KIM, HEEJUNG
[b.] April 21, 1979, Seoul, Korea; [p.] Jeong-Soo and Hyerye Kim; [ed.] William H. Ray Elementary School, Kenwood Academy; [occ.] Student; [memb.] City Youth Symphony, Chicago Children's Choir, Academic Olympics, Chicago Academic Games League; [hon.] Third place at Academic Games League Nationals, Excellent at District Six Science Fair, Honor Roll, Latin Olympics, City Art Fair. [a.] Chicago, IL 60615.

KINDEL, JOSEPH
[b.] September 23, 1914, Cincinnati, Ohio; [p.] George Margaret; [ed.] BS in Education; [occ.] Teacher; [memb.] Society of Mary for 57 years; [pers.] I try to make other people happy by writing a poem especially on special occasions.

KING, ANGELA
[b.] November 20, 1972, Fontana, California; [p.] Linda Spratt; [ed.] Thomas Stone High, Charles County Community College; [hon.] Who's Who Among American High School Students, Award of Merit plaque, Pompon Superior Blue Ribbons, Letter, Officer Star; [oth. writ.] Several poems, children stories; [pers.] In my writing I strive to reflect the beauty of friendship and love. Thanks to my mother Linda, my sisters Mia and April, and my best friends Jen and Cynthia. I am able to share my gift with others. I love you all. [a.] Waldorf, MD 20602.

KING, DONALD
[b.] March 23, 1928; [p.] Dan and Dorothy Monroe-King; [m.] Bonnie Runner, May 29, 1982; [ed.] I went to school for about 30 minutes. All I know was given to me by God; [occ.] Me and Bonnie Run - the King Museum; [memb.] Because of the poems and art work all 50 states and 46 foreign countries have come to see what God can do; [oth. writ.] I have over 800 poems and songs, that come to me when I have magazine headaches. I'm a woodcarver, also do Gourd art. [pers.] Like said, God gave me all of this. I was born without legs and hands don't look human and both of them are different. Nobody ever showed me how to do anything. [a.] Vevay, IN 47043.

KING, JOHN
[b.] February 14, 1948, London, England; [m.] Mary Jane; [ch.] Emmeline, Gawan; [ed.] University of Bristol, England; University of Manchester, En-

gland; Marist College, New York; [memb.] Poetry Society of America; [hon.] Bard of the Cornish Gorseth for Proficiency in the Cornish Language; Winner of the Mordon-Caradar Bowl; Winner of the Celtavision song contest, 1984 (Ireland); [oth. writ.] Several plays, stage and radio; fiction and non-fiction, including work on Poetic Technique, History of the Ancient Celts and British Mythology, Cornish Language TV and Radio Broadcaster; [pers.] I am interested in collaborative workshops and/or publication (New England area). [a.] Cornwall, CT 06753.

KING, LINDA DIANE
[b.] April 23, 1951, Chicago, Illinois; [p.] Cornelius and Beatrice King; [ch.] Kendra Nicole Clayter; [ed.] Emil C. Hirsh High, University of Illinois at Chicago, University of Illinois at Urbana; [occ.] Librarian; [memb.] American Library Association, Black Cercus of the American Library Association; [oth. writ.] Bibliographic Study Library Guides, "Know Your Heritage" Study Guide; [pers.] As a researcher and informationist specialist both in my work and personal relations I strive to offer my skills to help others. [a.] Chicago, IL 60649.

KING, ROXIE GAIL
[b.] December 17, 1974, St. Anthony; [p.] Lester and Zoe King; [ch.] Sisters-Kathleen, Linda, Deanna and brothers-Glen and Ted; [ed.] Canon Richards High this fall attending, Sir Wildred Grenfell College; [occ.] Student, future police officer; [hon.] Athletic awards; [oth. writ.] Have written a number of children stories, but nothing published, and enjoyed by the children in the family; [pers.] "If my mind can conceive it, and my heart can believe it, I know that I can achieve it." Quoted the Reverend Jesse Jackson. [a.] Flower's Cove, NF1D Canada (Nameless Cove).

KING, SARAH JANE
[b.] November 10, 1961, Trout Lake, Ontario; [p.] Betsy King (and father deceased); [ch.] One daughter: Annie Elizabeth Courtney King; [ed.] Grade 10, 1979-Queen Elizabeth District High School, Sioux Lookout, Ontario; [occ.] Being a mother to my 3 year old; [oth. writ.] I've been toying with poetry for around 15 years but, never felt that this "hobby" would ever really anywhere so, for me - this is a mirabile; [pers.] Just being alive and to feel free to write down my inner most thoughts and feelings is enough for me. [a.] Red Lake, Ontario P0V-2M0.

KING, TERRI LYNN
[pen.] Terri King; [b.] November 24, 1959, Batavia, New York; [p.] Patricia A. and Lawrence Conway (biological deceased), William King; [ch.] John, Stephen, Daniel and Holly; [ed.] Graduate, 2 years Beauty College "Continental" Beauty School; [occ.] Salesperson, mother, hair designer, crafts; [memb.] MTB Wellness-exercise, St. Mary's Church; [hon.] In hair design, culture; [oth. writ.] "Guardian Angel" published in Sparrowgrass Poetry Forum Winter "93", and "Sweetdream" in the Spring of "93", the "river Edge" will appear in the Winter "94" Anthology of Sparrowgrass; [pers.] Realizing that life is but a dream to be lived out, to touch other lives. Inspirations include, Real Loves, Real Pain,, Reality. The 1800 poetry and dongs by Stevie Nicks, mostly to mention God. [a.] Batavia, NY 14020.

KINSEY, JAMES H.
[pen.] J. Hilton Kinsey "Watchman"; [b.] May 18, 1940, Los Angeles, California; [p.] Al and Betty Kinsey; [m.] Nancy, December 17, 1966; [ch.] Jim, Al, Kelly, Heather, Tonia, Keilani, Justus, Floyd and Kevin; [ed.] Richard Mont. High School (Rockville, MD); [occ.] Founder and president of "Lifeguide Christian Ministries" since 1985; [hon.] First place award in a Montana Wide contest - Fall 1992 for poem called "Of Distant Thunder"; [oth. writ.] Several poems published in local newspaper etc., plus in the process of finishing up my first collection of over one hundred poems to be published in 1994 entitled, "poems of prophecy, poems of praise, poems for Garth's Final Days"; [pers.] God has opened my eyes and my heart that I might be as a voice crying in the wilderness. As a watchman that is called to his final watch. To warn all who will listen that the day of Christ's return now downs on mankind horizon. [a.] Florence, MT 59833.

KIRBY, KEITH
[b.] December 4, 1924, Battle Creek, Michigan; [p.] Paul F. and Ruth M. Kirby; [m.] September 15, 1961; [ch.] Sally Walker and Susan Kirby; [ed.] Battle Creek High, Western Michigan, University of Oklahoma; [occ.] Retired Accountant, Teacher; [memb.] First Baptist, Coldwater, MI, American Legion; [hon.] Prizes of recognition for short stories; [oth. writ.] Short stories for newspapers and industrial publications; articles for Industrial Publications; poems for several anthologies; [pers.] We reap what we sow, subject to intervention by the Supreme Being who presses us into His mold for his purposes. [a.] Topeka, KS 66604.

KIRCHER, DEAN A.
[pen.] DAK; [b.] June 17, 1963, Lansdale, Pennsylvania; [p.] Mary and Melvin Dean Kircher; [ed.] Frankford High School, Northeast Community College; [occ.] Writer; [memb.] Church of Jesus Christ, American Lung Society, Bally's Health and Fitness Corporation, American Rose Society; [hon.] Track and field, drama; [oth. writ.] Several poems published in newspapers, and a song being recorded Skeletons in the Closet; [pers.] I strive to reflect the inner feelings of emotion within my writing. I am influenced by Mystic, Spiritual living and those poesy. [a.] Smithville, TN 78957.

KIRKSEY, TIFFANY
[pen.] Sugas; [b.] February 7, 1971, Bradenton, Florida; [p.] Mae Richardson and Amos Kirksey; [ed.] High School; [occ.] Cashier; [memb.] Tenth Street Church of God; [hon.] Perfect Attendance, Award in Handwriting Honor Roll; [oth. writ.] Several poems written but none published; [pers.] Maya Angelo inspired me alot. My best friend Latisha Kirbsey, Mae Richardson, Dana Brown, Ames Kirbsey, Liz Richardson and Matthew McKinney. [a.] St. Pete, FL 33705.

KITTINGER, CANDACE DESIREE
[pen.] CDK; [b.] September 16, 1980, Huntington, West Virginia; [p.] Ed and Mary Kittinger; [m.] (brother) Parrish Kittinger (7); [ed.] West Chapmanville grade school - Chapmanville Middle School; [memb.] The Eagles Nest Club, Jump Rope for Heart, Junior Member of National Geographic Society, Bates Memorial Presbyterian Chorus; [hon.] Social Studies Award, Reading award, Honor student, Golden Apple

award, several as a page for W.VA House of Delegates, Students of Week, Wheels for Life St. Jude's Hospital; [oth. writ.] Yes, two others but haven't published. [a.] Chapmanville, W.VA 25508.

KJELLAND, ANDREA
[pen.] Andrea Kjelland; [b.] March 3, 1980, Valley City, North Dakota; [p.] Mike and Jan Kjelland; [ed.] Washington Elementary School and Valley City High School; [occ.] Work at my Dad's pet store and I work with my horses; [memb.] American Quarter Horse Association (AQHA) and I am also in 4-H; [pers.] I hope that some of my poems that will be published (in future) will inspire other people. [a.] Valley, ND 58072.

KLASSEN, ANNA
[b.] February 26, 1977, Tilsonburg, Ontario; [p.] Bernhard and Maria Klassen; [ed.] Currently attending East Elgin Secondary School; [oth. writ.] A story entitled, "Patient Love", and I have recently started another story; [pers.] The most important people in my life are my friends and family, and of course my writing. [a.] Ontario, Canada N0J 12O.

KLIMAUSKAS, JENNIFER
[b.] December 19, 1970, Haverhill, Massachusetts; [p.] Teresa Klimauskas; [ed.] Haverhill High School, Northern Essex Community College. [a.] Haverhill, MA 01830.

KLINE, KEVIN BRADLEY
[b.] January 27, 1970, Elkhart, Indiana; [p.] Steven Kline and Jean Inbody; [ed.] Arthur Campbell High; [occ.] Port-secondary student; [pers.] I am interested in the realization of tragedy and dolor as necessary to the appreciation of a beautiful existence. [a.] Bristol, IN 46507.

KLIPFEL, JACKIE
[b.] August 11, 1957; [p.] George Davis Jr., Esther and Vernon Kimbley; [m.] Andrew, April 15, 1978; [ch.] Kristin, Rachel, Andreana; [ed.] Montgomery County RII; [occ.] Housewife. [a.] Wentzville, MO 63385.

KLOSS, BRENDA
[b.] December 19, 1972, Petoskey, Michigan; [p.] James and Harriet Kloss; [ed.] Harbor Springs High; [occ.] Currently employed at Boyne Highlands; [hon.] High school Art and Spanish Competition awards; [oth. writ.] A poem about Ryan White was published in a local newspaper; [pers.] I think, poetry can be expressed, one way, as the tortured songs of our souls. [a.] Harbor Springs, MI 49740.

KLOSTERMAN, ARRAN
[b.] January 31, 1980, Twin Falls, Indiana; [p.] Alan and Cheryl Klosterman; [ch.] siblings-Kara 917), Erik (14), Brandan (8); [ed.] Currently attending 7th grade at West Minico Junior High; [occ.] Student; [memb.] Boy Scouts of America; [hon.] Honor Roll at school; [oth. writ.] I write a lot for fun; [pers.] This is my first published work. I love to write poetry. I would like to receive and answer letters from other poets or poetry readers. [a.] Paul, ID 83347.

KLUDING, CONSTANCE J.
[b.] June 10, 1938, Columbus, OH; [p.] Donald Edward Bateson and Grace (Sunny) Minerva Lewis; [m.] Glenn A., October 11, 1958; [ch.] Scott David

Kluding; [ed.] One year college via night courses; [occ.] Supervisor over Collection Dept. in a law firm; [memb.] Erie County Democratic Women, American Legion Auxiliary , (past - Heartbeat, Pro Life Group, Toastmasters Speech (Public) Group; [hon.] High school - a few awards for honorable mention for scholarship tests in English. Numerous awards for superior work performance during my 30 years as a federal employee, but no honors or awards of any real significance; [oth. writ.] Although I have some poems, I have never tried to publicize; [pers.] My poems are "usually" written based on a personal heartfelt experience - i.e., "The Holiday" was written after all my family left after Thanksgiving and I reflected on that. [a.] Sandusky, OH 44870.

KNAPP, JILL
[b.] Calgary, Alberta; [p.] Daniel and Patricia Knapp; [ed.] Student of Simon Fraser School; [occ.] Student. [a.] Calgary, Alberta T2M 4L4.

KNAPP, DAVID LEE
[pen.] Dave Knepp; [b.] October 3, 1938, Mineral Springs, PA; [p.] Frederick and Dorothy Knepp; [m.] Shirley Ann, October 20, 1961; [ch.] Gary Lee, [ed.] 11th grade Clearfield High School; [occ.] Maintenance Ground Keeper Berg Electronics; [memb.] Glad Tidings Assembly of God Church Lic. part-time Radio Announcer for WPHB A.M. Gospel Station; [hon.] I have received volunteer of the year award a mountain laurel nursing center in Clearwater, PA; [oth. writ.] Songs, I wrote little lights are shining, I Won't belong till will begin home, God's little white country church, One These Day's The Trumpet Will Sound Gospel songs I use in my band; [pers.] I can play string instruments guitar Mandoline Tener Banjo and violin my band. "The Country Gospel Strings", we do not are playing music in seniors citizen center and nursing homes. [a.] Clearfield, PA 16830.

KNIGHT, NEOMA L.
[pen.] Neoma L. Knight; [b.] November 22, 1922, Howard, KS; [p.] Loran and Pearl Bell Shipman; [m.] Gen. M. Knight, September 10, 1948; [ed.] 10th grade; [occ.] Housewife and writing, poems, songs; [memb.] In By Trailes Writers, USAF Air Defense in 1945; [hon.] Plaque of Two Fathers; [oth. writ.] Short Stories; [pers.] I play a guitar and sing, used to play for square dances. [a.] Weiser, ID 83672.

KOCHICK, MARIE
[b.] November 22, 1942, Pensacola, FL; [p.] Charles and Ruth Blanchard (usn Retired); [m.] Clifford, November 21, 1973; [ch.] Charles, Teresa, Patricia, Julia and Lisa; [ed.] Graduated Napa High in Napa, CA 1960, two semesters at Oklahoma Univ.; [occ.] Bookkeeping for Wintco, Inc. (Shawnee, OK); [memb.] Society of Friends (Oklahoma City) and Friends of Library (Tecumseh, OK); [oth. writ.] A few of my poems of "Recovery" or spiritual nature have been in the friends' newsletter and a support group's newsletter; [pers.] Turning fifty has opened my heart to participation in life rather than only thinking about doing so. [a.] Tecumseh, OK 74873.

KOEHLER, MARY KAY
[b.] August 21, 1968, Evergreen Park, IL; [p.] Clarence Koehler and Sheila Seeber; [ed.] Marian College, Fond du Lac, WI (2 years), Marquette High School, Michigan City, IN; [occ.] First of America

Bank, Northwest W. Teller Supervisor, Hacienda-Bartender Michigan City, IN; [oth. writ.] This is my first published poem and if all goes well, won't be the last; [pers.] The main objective in my writings is to make people laugh. The people who have given me the most influence are Johnny Carson and Steve Martin, for their quick wit, sarcastic overtones (when appropriate) and most of all their class that they use in all of those characteristics. I hope that I can achieve that talent in my work. [a.] Michigan City, IN 46360.

KOENE, KEITH
[[b.] December 7, 1972, Sheboygan, WI; [p.] Gerri Quisenberry and David Koene; [ed.] Graduated in 1991 from Sheboygan Falls High; [occ.] Full-time student at LTC. Part-time employee at Bemis Manufacturing; [oth. writ.] The hunter/the hunted; [pers.] I believe that my writing is a way of releasing my aggression without harming anyone. This world's got enough violence in it. [a.] Sheboygan, WI 53081.

KOERNER-ANDERSON, MARIAN
[b.] March 27, 1933, St. Louis, Missouri; [p.] William C. and Mary Kestly Koerner; [m.] Cecil D. Anderson (former), February 7, 1953; [ch.] Katherine Elizabeth, David Roy, Carole Eileen, Jacqueline Marie; [ed.] John Burroughs High, AS Glendale Community Col.; [occ.] Micrographics clerk, Glendale Community Col.; [memb.] First Baptist Church of La Crescenta; [oth. writ.] Poems and essays, storiettes; [pers.] All talent is God-given. It is how we use it that reflects glory to him and moving responses in the hearts of others. [a.] La Crescenta, CA 91214.

KOHLER, NIKKI
[pen.] Colette, St. James; [b.] November 15, 1978, Ottumwa, IA; [p.] Kenn and Linda Koehler; [ed.] Prairie Junior High; [hon.] Young Writer's Conference; [oth. writ.] Other poems (Changes, Love, Liquid, Dreams, etc.) short stories (Void, The Other Side, etc.) some published; [pers.] Live, love, learn, peace! Great thanks to my parents for my unique talent and creativity, and their praise and encouragement. I'll love them forever! [a.] Cedar Rapids, IA 52404.

KOLSON, TINA
[b.] Woodbury, NJ; [p.] Martin Kolson and Ruth Vanlieu; [ed.] Clayton High School; [hon.] This is my first; [oth. writ.] Just many more poems - none ever published; [pers.] I express my feelings and my thoughts in my poetry. It is easier to let people know how I feel. [a.] Clayton, NJ 08312.

KORNSTEIN, JESSICA
[b.] May 11, 1979, Baltimore, MD; [p.] Harvey and Janice Kornstein; [ed.] Friendship Elementary School, Southern Middle School, just entered Susquehannock High School; [occ.] Student at Susquehannock High School, Glen Rock, PA; [memb.] York Junior Symphony Orchestra, Temple Beth Isreal, Southern Middle School Orchestra; [hon.] Honor Roll, Editor of Middle School Newspaper, "The Arrowhead"; [oth. writ.] Several articles and poems published in local and school newspapers; [pers.] I have been influenced a lot by my family who encouraged my writing and helped me learn to believe in myself. [a.] Spring Cove, PA 17362.

KOSTER, THERESA
[b.] August 2, 1975, Washington, D.C.; [p.] David and Marilyn Koster; [ed.] Oxon Hill Science and Technology Center; [memb.] Civil Air Patrol, Future Teachers of Maryland; [hon.] Gen. Billy Mitchell Award, Amelia Earhart Award, Honor Roll, Science Technology Student of the Year Semifinalist; [pers.] My work reflects the happy and sad times a teenager encounters. Life is my greatest influence. [a.] Ft. Washington, MD 2074..

KOTLINSKI, MICHAEL A.
[b.] November 2, 1953, Chicago, IL; [p.] Gene B. and Lottie V. (Koziol) Kotlinski; [ed.] Glenbrook North High School, partial - Lake County College "Construction Course"; [occ.] Mailman-U.S. Postal Service (Northbrook, IL); [oth. writ.] For relative and friends. "The Spirit Star" in the National Library of Poetry ("A Break in the Clouds"); [pers.] Wishing one day to attain the wisdom of thought to understand the wonder of existence and it's infinity. [a.] Gurnee, IL 60031.

KOURI, ANNE
[b.] April 15, 1977, Charlotte, NC; [p.] Katherine Sant'Ambrogio and Moses L. Kouri; [ed.] Attending Germantown Academy, a high school, in Ft. Washington, PA; [occ.] Student; [memb.] Community Service Organization at Germantown Academy, at same location, Debate Club and Peer Counseling; [oth. writ.] "That All-American", short story published in a small, local monthly literary magazine; [pers.] Practice Random Acts of Kindness, Respect the Rights and Choices of Others. [a.] Doylestown, PA 18901.

KOWALCHYK, MARIA RESTAINO
[b.] October 1, 1925, Marsiconuouo, Italy; [p.] Louisa DeGregorio and Raffaele Restaino; [m.] Stanishaw, April 28, 1951, Diane Louise Abdoo; [ed.] Two schools in Italy Grammer, Junior High and High School Night School; [occ.] Housewife, poet, writer, journalist, community leader; [memb.] Many charitable organizations, honorary member of the police department; [hon.] Character personality, Honesty, Industry, Loyalty, Traits, Good manners citizens award, badge for my community work; [oth. writ.] Poems published 1993 by World of Poetry, plaque one as world's best poets, Who's Who in Poetry award merit 1990, golden poet for 1991; [pers.] I was always willing to learn, Carter, Ledyard and Milburn 2 Wall Street started many careers for me. [a.] Brooklyn, NY 11204.

KOWALSKI, KATHY
[pen.] K. Susan; [b.] July 15, 1979, Detroit, MI; [p.] Robert and Janet Kowalski; [ed.] Malow Junior High; [occ.] Student; [pers.] Always believe in dreams coming true, and never stop dreaming. [a.] Shelby, Twp., MI 48316.

KOY, SHERRIE W.
[b.] Trenton, GA; [p.] Mrs. C.R. Young (Houston, TX) and Mr. H.M. Wooten (Trenton, GA); [m.] Milton P.; [ch.] Rodney Paul and Dean Randel; [ed.] Channelview High School--Stevens Finishing School & Academy. Attended: Houston Baptist Univ. and Univ. of Houston; [occ.] Housewife/Mother, Actress/singer/songwriter; [memb.] Houston Associa-

tion for Film and Television (HAFT), Network of Lyricists & Songwriters, Inc., Inspiration Writers Association; [oth. writ.] Songs on my album entitled "Upside/Downside", poems and short articles and stories for various newspapers and magazines through the years; [pers.] To me poetry is the art of language...it's visual and emotional...Poetry is beautiful thoughts and feelings before it becomes a song. It's music for the soul. [a.] Houston, TX 77024.

KRAUSE, KIM D.
[b.] May 8, 1968, Pittsburgh, Pennsylvania; [p.] Drs. Helen & Marvin Krause; [ed.] North Allegheny High School, Clarion University of Pennsylvania, (BS in Psychology), graduate student at Slippery Rock, University of PA; [occ.] Caseworker Children and Youth Services at Allegheny County, Pittsburgh, PA; [memb.] Pennsylvania Association of Children & Youth Workers; [hon.] Outstanding College Students of America; [pers.] My life is based on protecting and helping children and preserving the family. I live and learn day by day and feel that education is the key to success. [a.] Wexford, PA 15090.

KREIGER, HOPE
[b.] April 24, 1920, Cumberland, Maryland; [p.] Father deceased, Irene Kreiger (mom); [ed.] Grade school and high school medical training for medical secretary; [memb.] Fort Ashby, Trinity United Methodist Church, The American Bible Society; [oth. writ.] Some other poems, but mostly lyrics and melodies for gospel music and country music - the "Down Home" music. Guitar and piano my friends; [pers.] I've love poetry from childhood and receive much pleasure and inspiration in reading good poems, moral books. I long for talent that would aid and uplift others. [a.] Fort Ashby, WV 26719.

KROLAK, KIM A.
[b.] March 5. 1970, Schenectady, NY; [p.] Raymond and Jean Krolak; [ed.] Colonie Central High School and Maria College; [memb.] People for the Ethical Treatment of Animals; [hon.] Dean's List; [pers.] Special remembrance to the free spirit who lives on through my words. [a.] Schenectady, NY 12304.

KRULL, JAMES
[[pen.] Jamull; [b.] July 12, 1944, St. Louis; [p.] Joe and Theresa Krull; [ed.] 10th grade; [occ.] Custodian; [memb.] St. Louis Zoo, World Bird Sanctuary, National Wildlife; [hon.] Golden Poet 1991 and 1992, National Bird Feeding Soc.; [oth. writ.] Mother, Father, Giant of the Sea, Giant of the Land, Man Loves Woman, and James all poems; [pers.] To be or not to be is the question, and the answer is, to be.

KUENZER, JENNIFER
[b.] July 7, 1974, Manistee, MI; [p.] Marilyn and Russell Kuenzer; [ed.] Manistee High School, West Shore Community College; [memb.] National Honor Society; [hon.] National Honor Society, Journalism. [a.] Manistee, MI 49660.

KUNA, THOMAS J.
[pen.] Thomas J. Kuna-Jacobs, Jacob, Toussaint L'Aperture; [b.] January 9, 1948, Ingolstadt, Bavaria, Germany; [p.] Dr. Aladar A. and Magdalene Kuna; [ed.] Christian Brothers High School, Georgetown Univ., Johns Hopkins Univ., Quincy Univ., John Wood Community Col., Univ. of Colorado-Boulder; [occ.] Educator, Writer, Translator,

Interpreter, World Market Consultant, Publisher, Chairman, T.L.C.D. Dev. Co. (60% Employee Owned); [memb.] Black Awareness Association, NAACP, Assoc. for World Peace, Legion of Mary, Environmental Defense Fund, Natural Resources Defense Council, Sierra Club, Amnesty International; [hon.] Dean's Citation for outstanding contributions to the School of Foreign Service, Smithsonian Grant to Develop Anthropology Curriculum for 8th graders, Appreciation Plaque for Years of Dedicated Service, Black Awareness Association and NAACP (Quincy Chapter), Dean's List, Who's Who in American Colleges and Universities (1969, 1970); [oth. writ.] "Peace Process in the Holy Land", "On New Economic Citizenship, also called, On Free-Enterprise Socialism, "The Present Moment in World History", "On New Econimce Partnership, Free Enterprise Socialism and the Rise and Fall of the Cold War", "Trees in the Wind I: Collected Poems and Paintings"; [pers.] Sionce the age of 5, I have dedicated my life to finding the proper strategy and tactics for a Just and Lasting World Peace. I have found it theoretically in a Universal synthesis of Marx, Einstein, Darwin and the World Religions and assiduously strive for its practical realization. [a.] Quincy, IL 62306-1214.

KUNZER, LORETTA J.
[b.] September 20, 1956, Queens, New York; [p.] Catherine and Roy Preston; [ch.] Michael James, Derrick Lee, and Christopher Alan; [ed.] Penns Grove High; [occ.] Slot attendant - Trump Taj Majhal (Atlantic, NJ); [memb.] Unite Women's Group for SIDS and Stillborn Babies; [pers.] I write from feelings of people and things that affect my life. It it were not for them, I would not have written. This is for my son, Derrick. [a.] Absecon, NJ 08201.

KURTZMAN, MARGARET ANNE
[pen.] Margarey Kurtzman; [b.] February 15, 1944, Shelby, OH; [p.] Robert and Betty Meier; [m.] Louis, November 16, 1963; [ch.] Robert Louis, Brian Keith, and Stephen Christopher; [ed.] Crestline High School; [occ.] Wife, mother, homemaker, grandmother, friend, and volunteer (all a full-time job); [memb.] St. Joseph Church (Crestline), Crestline Lions Club, Crestline Patio Gardners Club, Crestline Historical Society Board Member; [hon.] Crestline High School 1961 Homecoming Queen. Crestline Lions Club President 1993, Patio Gardners Society 1993, 1992 District 13 B Lions second place speech for courtesy winner. Award from Lions Club for dedication to the club and community, 1992, Crestline Harvest Festival Grand Marshals, 1992 , Designer of Lions District 13 B for 1992-93; [oth. writ.] Two poems published in local news papers. Poetry written for family and friends; [pers.] Persons who influence our lives in positive ways are a blessing from God, Great Aunt Bertha was one of those blessings. She touched my heart with her in my soul and etched memories in my soul with hours of poetry we'd read at bedtime. I miss her. [a.] Crestline, OH

KYLER, TERI
[b.] May 18, 1976, Drayton Valley, Alberta, Canada; [p.] Brian and Louise Kyler; [ed.] Currently attending Frank Maddock High School; [occ.] Student; [oth. writ.] This is one of many that I have submitted but the first to be published; [pers.] "Ashes" was written for a friend who died tragically in a car trash in 1991.

When you have a dream, follow it, at the end is your pot of gold. [a.] Drayton Valley, Alberta, Canada

LACY, MARY REGINA
[pen.] Regina Lacy; [b.] July 22, 1963, Concord, CA; [ch.] Jessica M. DelPrato and Elijah Penn McGuire; [ed.] High school graduate currently attending Heald Institute of Technology; [oth. writ.] Several other poems and short stories not yet released, which I am hoping to put in my own book some day; [pers.] Thru the ink that flows from my pen, I am able to express my love for life, freedom and most importantly my children. I thank God for them all. [a.] Pleasant Hill, CA 94523.

LADD, KATHRYN
[pen.] Kathy Ladd; [b.] March 21, 1943, Portland, OR; [p.] Edmond L. and Esther A. Hults; [m.] Donald L., September 3, 1960; [ch.] Dawn Marie, Owen Neil and Serge Edmond; [ed.] 9th grade; [occ.] Retail clerk, 20 years with the same company; [memb.] Scio Baptist Church; [oth. writ.] Several, none published; [pers.] The magnificent beauty that God has created all around us and his undying love for us are what I love write about and share with others. I thank God for this gift. [a.] Scio, OR 97374.

LAFAVE, TIM P., JR.
[pen.] Berlin Morgan, Sol; [b.] July 19, 1974, Delta County, MI; [p.] Kathryn and Marlowe Greening; [ed.] Little Chute Elementary, WI, Fremont Elem., WI, Weyauwega-Fremont Schl. Dist. (Middle and High Schl.), Weyauwega, WI, Illinois Institute of Technology (ITT) (presently); occ.] Full-time undergrad. Physics student; [hon.] Second place ($100) in ITT's Lewis Liberal Arts College's Humanities Depart. Writ. Contest for the Mollie Cohen Essay Award for an essay (which my senior class English teacher despised) titled Space Station Freedom; 2nd place ($100) for the Lewis Poetry Award for a poem titled "I Hate Words";Dean's list (Fall '92); Who's Who Among American High School Students (two years); Pres. Academic Fitness Award (84 and 88); two Pres. Fitness Awards during the "Reagan Administration"; Academic Excellence Award (Jan. 1992); [oth. writ.] A complete manuscript for a sci-fi novel, Sol Survivor (unpublished). Poems entitled "Heart Condition: Terminal" and "Til The End of Time" published in In A Different Light (1992) and Wind In The Night Sky (1993-Editor's Choice Award) by the National Library of Poetry. I also have had a two-page poem printed in the Weyauwega Chronicle (now known simply as The Chronicle) titled Class of '92. My poetry class at ITT published a small compilation of collaborative works simply titled bloo containing a few of my original works (300 copies). I have completed my second personal compilation of poetry of roughly 50 selected poems which I distribute to a good number of close friends and relatives and has been offered to anyone interested in purchasing it. I plan to publish an updated edition on my own twice yearly; [pers.] I have never been more appreciative of anyone as I am of my present girlfriend Heidi Marie Christofferson without whom there would be no more poetry worth writing. (Though we are 500 miles apart!) I realize that this particular poem is about another girl who presently is a friend of mine still in high school as the first letters of each line of the poem dictate. Within the last two years, I have been extensively depressed and used poetry as an emotional outlet. Now, however, most of my work is

dedicated almost entirely to Heidi as well as becoming much more experimental in nature, for whatever "experimental" means. As before, presently, and well into the future my goal is to "Aid in humankind's understanding of the universe and itself free from militaristic endeavor." [a.] Chicago, IL 60616.

LAING, R. FREDERICK
[pen.] Billy Joe, December 3, 1949; [p.] Port Anson, G.B., Nfld; [p.] Joseph E. and W. Alice Laing; [m.] Dorothy C., October 6, 1972; [ch.] Betty D.B., Ronald J.M.M., Joey L.W., Timothy J.D., Natalie J.A.; [ed.] Memorial University, NFld., Third grade teaching high school certificate; [occ.] Construction Contractor; [oth. writ.] Several poems published in local newspapers, and The Nfld. Herald; [pers.] As a writer, I consider life to be extremely precious, and all life to be worth living and all things living to be given a chance to live, to love and to die peacefully. [a.] South Brook, Green Bay, Nfld. Canada.

LAKE-WILLCUTT, BERNADETTE
[pen.] Bernie; [b.] June 8, 1978, Seoul, Korea; [ed.] Hampshire Regional High School; [pers.] Sometimes things are not meant to happen, but most of the time they are. And when they are, your heart will lead the way. [a.] Haydenville, MA.

LAKIN, PAT ELLIN
[pen.] Sarah Bales; [b.] February 5, 1943, Charleston, Illinois; [p.] Birth mother-Edna V. Dickens, Adoptive parents-S.J. and Sara Mandel Lakin; [ch.] Rochelle Eans Messer and Samantha Evans Arreola; [ed.] Riverdale County School, Syracuse University, UCLA Extension Art and Design; [occ] Vocation-Artist, Writer, Healer and Teacher; [pers.] The transformation of fear into love is at the core of all my work. Personal and planetary healing is my goal. [a.] Ojai, CA 93024.

LA MOTHE, BERNIS BRIGITTE
[b.] April 26, 1971, Dominica (Commonwealth); [p.] Paulina Wallace; [ed.] Convent High, University of St. Martin; [occ.] Cashier at a Cosmetic Centre and part-time tutor; [memb.] St. Maarten Red Cross and Powerline Ministry T.V. Drama Club; [hon.] 1987 Winner of World Poetry Day Contest held in Monsterrat; recent runner-up in St. Maarten Valentine Verse Contest; [oth. writ.] For school assignments; lots of personal writing which I never gave for publication; [pers.] Writing has always been my greatest inspiration; if nations could come together through poetry, I would play a big role.; [a.] Philipsbugh, St. Maarten.

LANE, AMANDA
[pen.] Sally Wright; [b.] June 21, 1980, Spangler, Pennsylvania; [p.] Connie (Prida) and Dane Lane; [ed.] Central Cambridge Clemtery School, Central Cambria Middle School; [occ.] Student; [pers.] I believe that you can do anything if you put your mind to it. [a.] Colver, PA 15927.

LANE, EDNA C.
[b.] August 23, 1911, Loogootee, Indiana; [p.] Joseph H. and Theresa I. Fields; [m.] Jesse A., April 27, 1930; [ch.] Donald J., Nancy J., Elizabeth A., John R.; [ed.] Memorial High school (Evansville, IN); [occ.] Homemaker; [oth. writ.] I have written a number of poems but this is the first one I have submitted for publication; [pers.] I choose to devote

my life to my husband and our four children, instilling in our children faith and have of God and each other. That was my "career", if you will. I love to read and to write poetry, I have 10 grandchildren, 10 great grandchildren who give me much joy. [a.] Springville, IN.

LANG, TIMOTHY D.
[pen.] Timothy D. lang; [b.] November 14, 1963, Boston, Massachusetts; [m.] Laronda, May 24, 1985; [ed.] Criswell College (Dallas, TX); [occ.] Farrier; [oth. writ.] Life with the Old Man (short stories), poems; [pers.] Every one needs their hand held some time --. [a.] Marlow, N.H. 03456.

LANGELLOTTI, ARLENE MARY
[pen.] Arlene Mary Langellotti; [b.] July 12, 1937, Poughkeepsie, New York; [p.] Arthur and Mabel Baird Galuppo; [m.] Thomas N.; [ch.] Mary Elizabeth; [ed.] Poughkeepsie High School, Vassar Brothers School of Nursing; [occ.] Nursing-Therapeutic Touch (private practitioner) - Professional psychic and astrological counselor - teacher/lecturer; [memb.] President-Uranian Transits Astrological Association; [oth. writ.] Other poems, articles for teaching class and inspired articles; [pers.] Striving to be my best spiritual self and live in harmony with all living things. Desire to assist other to do the same. I enjoy teaching others personal awareness and healing. [a.] Poughkeepsie, NY 12603.

LANNERS, PAMELA K.
[b.] March 25, 1956, Clearbrook, Minnesota; [p.] Chester and Betty Rud; [m.] Alan, March 22, 1975; [ch.] Christopher, Lynette, Kirsten, and Jenica; [ed.] Clearbrook Public School, Remidji Area Vocational School; [occ.] Chef; [memb.] Christ the King Lutheran Church, Council member, Choir; [oth. writ.] Something Special published in 1990; [pers.] Nature is our most precious resource, and it is our job to preserve it. To do that means to leave it to be as much as possible. [a.] Orangevale, CA 95662.

LAPOLT, EDA
[b.] March 11, 1956, Monticello, New York; [p.] Norman and Mary Pittaluga; [m.] Howard, September 4, 1982; [ed.] Monticello High, Orange County Community College; [occ.] Secretary; [pers.] 'An Angel Named Hoot' is my first publication. It is dedicated to my father, Norman "Hoot" Pittaluga - In memory of a very special man and wonderful father. [a.] Monticello, NY 12701.

LARABEE, FRANK J.
[b.] March 19, 1920, Portsmouth, Virginia; [p.] Emma and Frank Larabee; [m.] Catherine, April 15, 1945; [ed.] High school graduate; [occ.] Retired; [memb.] American Legion, Veteran of Foreign Wars, Elks; [oth. writ.] A poem published in local paper, "Close Your Eyes and Remember"; [pers.] My poems are written to read to express the way I feel. to help others to take heed and appreciate the things that are real. [a.] North Arlington, NJ 07031.

LARGE, LUCY
[b.]] February 18, 1974, Somerset, Ukraine; [p.] Roger and Maggie Large; [ed.] Completed my 'A' level exams in England (West Somerset Community School) in June '92; [occ.] Student (currently working is U.S. as child minder); [oth. writ.] This is the first piece to be published; [pers.] I've always enjoyed

writing and have been particularly influenced by American literature. I hope, in the future, to have the opportunity to study it at college. [a.] Sherwood Forest, MD 21405.

LARSON, BRENDA
[b.] August 10, 1956, Phoenix, Arizona; [p.] Gus and Marcella Gustafson; [m.] Carl; [ch.] Jesse, James, Joseph; [oth. writ.] To those bound in prisons: Serving Our Lord Jesus Christ, To God Be the Glory; [pers.] I strive to reflect the goodness of the Lord Jesus - Christ in my writing to all mankind! I have been greatly influenced by the Bible. [a.] Sacramento, CA.

LARSON, CHRISTINA ELINOR
[pen.] Chris Larson; [b.] March 26, 1953, Camden, New Jersey; [p.] Rosemary and Herman Baker; [m.] Robert A., June 1, 1982; [ch.] Adam, Mary, David, Rob (plus over 100 foster children); [ed.] O.W.C.C., AS in Paramedics, University of West Florida BA in Psychology, and University of West Florida BA in Religious Studies; [occ.] Foster mom, "Patriots for Peace" organizer, Administrator Larson Sculpture Studio; [memb.] Sorority Honor Societies, PFP, NAACP, Common Cause, Anti Defam. League, Nature Conserv., Greenpeace, Echota Cherokee Tribe; [hon.] Adopted by Cherokee Chief Ponaycatawa Moitee, UWF "Outstanding Student of the Year", and "Academic Excellence" awards 1991, 4.0 Summa cum Laude; [oth. writ.] Mideast Crisis research hand carried to UN Sec. general by Nobel Peace laureate, articles in Unte Reader, Rural S. Voice for Peace, Bishop's Commission for Soc. Justice News, Just Peace, profiled St. Pete Times March 23, 1992 front page; [pers.] Peacemaking is no longer an ideal, peacemaking is a basic survival skill. [a.] Shalimar, FL 32579-5092.

LARSON, IRENE MARY
[pen.] Irene Mary Larson; [b.] September 19, 1921, Lynd, Minnesota; [p.] Andrew and Mary Larson; [ed.] High School; [occ.] Retired farmer and disabled M.S. patient; [hon.] Golden Poet 1990, 1991, An Educated Fool-Education World of Poetry founded by John Campbell, 1975.

LARSON, RICHARD G.
[b.] February 23, 1932, La Crosse, Wisconsin; [ch.] Kurt, Hans, and Renya Lawson; [ed.] PhD Curriculum studies, Northwestern University; [occ.] Professor Emeritus and Children's Poet; [hon.] Standard Oil Award for teaching Excellence, The University of Wisconsin-Milwaukee; [oth. writ.] 70 publications on education, "Why is a Wild Pig Called A Boar?". Poems for kids growing up and adults growing down (a collection); [pers.] Have read own poetry to 38,000 students in 8 states. Active in doing poetry writing workshops for schools. [a.] Wind Lake, WI 53185.

LASCELLES, JEANETTE L.
[b.] September 24, 1925, Battle Creek, Michigan; [p.] Harold J. and A. Blanche Parmelee; [m.] Divorced; [ed.] High School, Augubright Business College, various courses through the years; [occ.] Retired Executive Secretary; [memb.] Life member of Beta Sigma Phi; [hon.] Beta Sigma Phi, Order of the Rose, Silver Circle Award; [oth. writ.] I have written all types of poems and have presented entire programs in rhyme. I have ghostwritten poems for other's personal use; [pers.] I enjoy writing poems for 50th wedding anniversaries. My sister, Doris Bailey, also

writes poetry. [a.] Camarillo, CA 93010.

LATHAM, LAURA LEIGH

[b.] May 31, 1977, Weslaco, Texas; [p.] Connie and Doug Latham; [ed.] 9th grade; [occ.] Student; [memb.] School Dance Team, Foundation Youth Choir; [hon.] Trophy for "Most Talented" in pageant for singing; [oth. writ.] Other poetry; [pers.] I wrote this for my Mom because this is how I feel about her and I want her to know I love her. [a.] Columbiana, AL 35051.

LATUSICK, CAMEON LYN

[pen.] Cameon Lynne; [b.] August 18, 1959, Iowa City, Iowa; [p.] Lynnford and Karen Edwards; [ch.] Shawn and Chelsea; [ed.] Southeastern Community College, University of Northern Iowa; [occ.] Currently a student majoring in communication with a minor in writing; [pers.] Poetry had been a passion of mine since adolescence, increasing continually. It is my hope that any who read my poems find some degree of pleasure and enlightenment in them. [a.] Cedar Falls, IA 50613.

LAVOTA, JEAN T.

[b.] January 31, 1924, Ashland, Wisconsin; [p.] James and Mabel Temby (now deceased); [m.] John R. Sr., February 18, 1943; [ch.] Nelle E., Debra J., John R., Jr., and Jeffre, Lavota; [ed.] Elementary, High School, and Business College; [occ.] Retired at present, was Accountant for many years; [memb.] St. Paul Catholic Church, Ashland Square Ayoers; [hon.] Graduated honor student (from Ashland High), several awards for entertaining at Nursing homes; [oth. writ.] A collection of poems written over 50 years; [pers.] I enjoy addressing life and everyday living through poetic comment. The poets I enjoy reading are too numerous to mention here. [a.] Ashland, WI 54806.

LAWSON, IMA

[b.] May 9, 1937, Denison, Texas; [p.] Mary and Joseph Lawson; [ed.] Jordan High School, Los Angeles City College (Los Angeles, CA); [occ.] Security Services; [hon.] The World of Poetry, San Francisco, CA; [pers.] The ultimate goal in writing to reveal my sensitiveness, and love for mankind in a world where values are no longer a priority. [a.] Winston-Salem, NC 27101.

LAWRENCE-KOEPP, MISTY D.

[pen.] Misty Lawrence; [b.] April 25, 1969, Aurora, Illinois; [p.] Sandi (Herki) and Larry D. Lawrence; [m.] William J., November 28, 1987; [ch.] Devin Michael and Cody Marshall; [ed.] West Aurora High School; [occ.] Interviewer, Milward Brown, Marketing Research Inc.; [pers.] I try to put a bit of my soul and a lot of love into everything I write. [a.] Belvidere, IL 61008.

LAY, CHRISTINA M.

[b.] January 27, 1993; [p.] James and Barbara Aman; [ed.] College; [occ.] Student; [pers.] Poetry is a way to look beyond my imagination. [a.] Ontario, NY 14519.

LAYNE, LISA M.

[pen.] Lisa Marie or Lea; [b.] October 20, 1978, Arkansas; [p.] Ray G. and Deborah G. Layne; [ed.] G.J.H.S.; [occ.] Student; [memb.] School choir, Girl Scouts, and Pen Pals of the World; [oth. writ.] Working on a book, maybe some day it will be published; [pers.] I am influenced by a special person, my mother Deborah G. Layne. [a.] Russellville, AR 72801.

LAZATIN, FARAH LISA A.

[pen.] Lala A. Lazatin; [b.] November 7. 1975, Manila, Philippines; [p.] Meden A. Arellano; [ed.] High school graduate incoming freshman; [occ.] Student; [memb.] Hangad (choir), Killer Whales Swimming Team, Philippines; [pers.] My poems are based on my feelings - usually about romance. [a.] Heroes Hills, Q.C. 1104 Philippines.

LEAHY, MARILYN A.

[b.] March 22, 1955, Monaco, France; [p.] Albert and Bettina Harvey; [ed.] Virginia Commonwealth University, Medical College of Virginia, University of Richmond; [occ.] Adult Education Teacher, Instructional Designer; [hon.] AAET Achievement Award, Outstanding College Student of America, AAET President's Award; [oth. writ.] AAET Classroom Video Series, Medical Journal Case Reports, Cookbook, Freelance Poetry and short story; [pers.] Writing is the art of Magic, the writer magician creates an illusion to capture an audience ready to be owned. To my mother and Anne Duke, the master magicians. [a.] Richmond, VA 23231.

LEE, MARIE

[pen.] Marie Lee; [b.] November 28, 1931, Rockvale, Colorado; [p.] Mr. and Mrs. Tony Davis (deceased); [ch.] Mark Durant; [ed.] High School, Semester College, many hours of training in management on the job; [occ.] Supervisor - V.A.R.O. Retired 1990; [memb.] NARFE, AARP, Women on the Move, Federal Business Association Minority, Business Opportunity Commission; [hon.] Outstanding awards, superior performances, many merit achievement awards; [oth. writ.] Poem-U.S.A.D. and published. Computer programs - U.S. Army being used today in many agencies; [pers.] Strive to achieve productive results. Was inspired to write. [a.] Houston, TX 77072.

LEE, STEPHEN

[pen.] Die Jung; [b.] March 6, 1967, Othello, Washington; [p.] Stan and Anita Lee; [ed.] Centerville High School-Dayton, Ohio and University of Manitoba-Winnipeg, Manitoba, Canada; [occ.] Administrator; [oth. writ.] Several poems published in school's newspaper; [pers.] My writings are influenced from the mind and soul of the individual. [a.] Toronto, Ontario, Canada.

LEE, TAMERA

[pen.] Tammy Lee; [b.] April 14, 1964, Foley, Alabama; [p.] Joe and Claudine Morris, Sr.; [m.] Martin, August 13, 1983; [ch.] Matthew Gary Lee; [ed.] Albany High School (Albany, GA), Albany Junior College, Institute of Children's Literature; [occ.] Homemaker; [memb.] The Nature Conservancy, The National Arbor Day Foundation; [hon.] Who's Who Among American High School Students; [pers.] My wish is that all who read my writings will feel the emotions that inspired me. "...and the greatest of these is love." 1 Corinthians 13:13. [a.] Birmingham, AL 35242.

LEFEBURE, CHRISTIAN

[pen.] Chris Lefebure; [b.] January 4, 1962, Springfield, Massachusetts; [p.] Monique Langlois and Rene Lefebure; [ed.] Community College of the Air Force, Rodger L. Putnam Vocational Technical High; [occ.] United States Air Force; [memb.] U.S. Parachutist, Society for Creative Anachronists, NCOA (Non Commissioned Officers Association); [hon.] A.F. Commendation medal, Two A.F. Achievement medals and Humanitarian Service medal; [pers.] Bi treun, Tha dorus an tuir fargailte, Theid a'ghaoth troimhe. Gaelic. [a.] Springfield, MA

LEHMAN, IDA M.

[pen.] Beckie; [b.] January 9, 1910, Hagerstown, Maryland; [p.] Elmer and Verna Beckley; [m.] Harold Funk, November 22, 1962; [ed.] High school, two years of college; [occ.] Secretary (now retired); [memb.] Hagerstown Business and Professional Club, Ago Organ Guild, Daughters of American Revolution; [oth. writ.] Have written short stories which were published; [pers.] I try to stress the help of God in my writings. [a.] Hagerstown, MD 21740.

LEIGHTON, JOHN

[a.] Waterville, ME 04901.

LEITCH, PATTI ANN

[b.] September 8, 1973, Guelph, Ontario; [p.] Ronald Samuel and Margaret Alice Leigh; [m.] Dale Albert Wyville, June 4, 1993; [ed.] Erin District High School; [occ.] Bookkeeper, Leitch Fuels Limited; [oth. writ.] Personal poems never published; [pers.] I believe that poetry is an expression of your innerself, thoughts and feelings that you can only express to paper. Your free from disapproval from others, you can just let your feelings flow and learn who you rally are. [a.] Erin, Ontario, Canada N0B 1T0.

LEITH, SCOT M.

[b.] September 8, 1968, Texas; [p.] Peter Gordon and Dimitra Katherine; [m.] Nikole Alicia, December 22, 1989; [ch.] Chandi Alicia and Scottie Matthew; [ed.] Chandler High School, MESA Community College, Northern Arizona University; [occ.] Sales Support - Computer Company, Singer/Songwriter; [memb.] NAV Gospel Choir, Advertising Club (NAV); [oth. writ.] Numerous poems and song lyrics included: Mother the Woman (poem), Decline of Brotherhood (poem), The Waiting (poem), Rites of Passage (song), and Circus of Ones Soul (song); [pers.] What is Expression? To me acting out inner sensation. Discovering answers to unasked questions. "Never disloyal your soul, that what makes you, you!". [a.] Mesa, AZ 85202.

LEON, RAINA J.

[pen.] Anastasia E. Lore; [b.] April 7, 1981, Drexel Hill, Pennsylvania; [p.] Norma D. Thomas-Leon and Edwardo Leon; [ed.] St. Clement-Irenaeus Elementary School; [memb.] Junior Dance Company - L7L Dance Production, Band Clarnet - St. Clement - Irenaeus; [hon.] Honor roll, Award of Excellence (school), dance award - first place star power competition; [pers.] I strive to put my heart and soul into everything I do. My influence is my mother who is a published free verse poet. [a.] Philadelphia, PA 19153.

LEONARD, PATRICIA

[pen.] Pat Leonard; [b.] January 16, 1939, Syracuse, New York; [p.] Andrew DeMaio, and Nicholas and Mary Cassola; [m.] Joseph, December 3, 1958; [ch.] Joseph and Mark; [ed.] North High School; [occ.]

Administrative Assistant (Food Broker Business); [memb.] Women of the Moose - Syracuse Clowns; [oth. writ.] Children's short stories - short poems; [pers.] I am greatly influenced by my awareness of my environment and choices of mankind and knowing in the end we all answer to God. [a.] Syracuse, NY 13209.

LEOS III, JOHN R.
[pen.] Jonathan Tudy Leos III; [b.] December 11, 1964, Los Angeles, California; [p.] John Leos and Patricia Ortiz; [ch.] Arlene Leos; [ed.] Garfield High; [occ.] Bookkeeper; [pers.] The Father has placed me on this earth to do what good I can and to make the world a better place for those who follow! [a.] Los Angeles, CA 90022.

LEMOINE, JERRY D.
[b.] October 20, 1938, New Orleans, Louisiana; [p.] Joseph Bonis Sr. and Lucille Ripoll Devenport; [m.] Robert Joseph, April 27, 1957; [ch.] Robert J. Jr., and grandson Bradley J. Lemoine; [ed.] Nicholls High; [occ.] Office Manager; [hon.] Ridgefield Chapter, National Honor Society; [pers.] I enjoy writing in the shadows of the moss draped oaks which provide a tranquil setting in the small country town of Lacombe. [a.] Lacombe, LA 70445.

LEMOS, JUNE F.
[b.] June 6, 1922, Boston, Massachusetts; [p.] Roy L. and Bernice G. Whiddon; [m.] George M., November 10, 1941; [ch.] George, Sandra, Anne and Elena; [ed.] Provincetown, MA High School; [occ.] Housewife and mother; [oth. writ.] Have written many poems over the decades as relaxation and a way of expressing my inner thoughts and feelings at different moments in life; [pers.] My poems are usually a reflection of things I see and enjoy in nature or happy or sad occasions in our family life. Have always enjoyed reading poetry from school years onward. [a.] So. Orleans, MA 02662.

LENSKY, FLORENCE E.
[pen.] Flo Lensky; [b.] May 18, 1918, Detroit, Michigan; [p.] Frances Leibinger and Abraham Masker; [m.] Walter Lensky (deceased), June 15, 1946; [ch.] Mary Lou Rowe, Sal Conway, Daniel Lensky, Paul Lensky, George Lensky, Darlette Blizinski; [ed.] High School, 1 year college, Dale Carnegie, course-Italian class; [occ.] Retired Homemaker, singer professional; [memb.] Lover of mankind. St. Barnabas Church, minister of Praise, Capuchin Guild; [hon.] I say humbly I try to forget whatever good I may have done for my family, friends and fellow human beings; [oth. writ.] Several poems published in St. Barnabas news, poems to all my children and grandchildren and friends; [pers.] I hope when I leave this beautiful world, it will be a better place, because of something I have done. [a.] Eastpointe, MI 48021.

LEPORE JR., CHARLES S.
[pen.] Charles S. Lepore Jr.; [b.] August 5, 1952, Coatesville; [p.] Charles S. Sr., and Mary E. Lepore; [m.] Divorced; [ch.] Matthew and Zachariah; [ed.] Octomara High School; [occ.] Steel worker; [oth. writ.] A Blessing being published in A Break in the Clouds, Two a Day at the North Pole being published by Carlton Press, Inc.; [pers.] Keep trying don't give up. [a.] Atglen, PA 19310.

LESSARD, DAVID
[pen.] David Lessard; [b.] November 14, 1941, Gardner, Massachusetts; [p.] Noah and Gladys Lessard; [m.] Linda Darnell, October 4, 1987; [ch.] Bethany, Shannon, Devin, Darren, Wes, Linda, Lillian, and Danica; [ed.] Washington High, Glendale Community College, VT Community College, Biosystem Institute; [occ.] Respiratory Care Practioner; [memb.] AM. Association for Respiratory Care, AZ, and Society for Respiratory Carel; [hon.] RRT (Registered Respiratory Therapist), CPFT (Certified Pulmonary Function Technician); [oth. writ.] Several poems published in Poetic Wiles of America, articles in Advance Magazine (a Respiratory Care publication); [pers.] I was influenced by Edna St. Vincent Millay, Emily Dickson, Robert Frost Robert W. Service and Ayn Rand; [a.] Payson, AZ 85541.

LEVINSON, EMILY CLAIRE
[b.] August 18, 1976, Carbondale, Illinois; [p.] Marc Levinson and Debra Casleton; [ed.] Anna-Jonesboro Community High School; [occ.] Student; [memb.] President of Future Business Leaders of America at H.S., Forensics Team, Mu Alpha Theta, VP of Catholic Youth Organization; [hon.] National Honor Society, SIV-C English Award, Who's Who in American High School Students, US National Mathematics Award; [pers.] I write in order to record my observations and emotions. I hope my writing will enrich, as well as entertain, those who read it. [a.] Anna, IL 62906.

LEVY, MAURICE
[b.] August 15, 1933, Chicago, Illinois; [p.] Eugene and Jean Levy; [m.] Lois Rissman, September 11, 1955; [ch.] Arden Levy, MD; Andrea Levy, MD; and James Levy; [ed.]]] BS and EdM, University of Illinois; EdD, University of Georgia; [occ.] Associate Dean and Professor at the Medical College of Georgia; [memb.] Phi Delta Kappa Professional Society, Association of American Medical Colleges, American Heart Association; [hon.] Phi Kappa Phi Honor Society; Kappa Delta Pi Honor Fraternity; Gold certificate for Outstanding Scientific Exhibit in area of Learning Values at American Academy of Pediatrics; American Academy of Family Physicians Award for Outstanding Scientific Exhibit at American Medical Association Conference; Outstanding Faculty Award for General Programs Faculty, Medical College of GA; Gold Award for AHA for outstanding service in advancing heart program and stimulating public support in fight against disease of heart and circulation; Honorary membership in American Academy of Physician Assistants; [oth. writ.] 2 books, 50+ professional articles, 10 audiovisual programs, 2 poems; [pers.] My poetry is totally different from my professional publications. In my poetry, I try to reflect the world as I see it. [a.] Augusta, GA 30909.

LEWIS, MARJORIE WINCHELL
[[pen.] Marjorie W. Lewis; [b.] September 29, 1913, Philadelphia, Pennsylvania; [p.] Elsie Stearly and Samuel Dickson Winchell; [m.] Don E., May 23, 1942; [ch.] Dickson Winchell Lewis and (grandchildren) Christopher, Jeffrey and Paige; [ed.] Upper Darby High School (1930), Palmer Business College (1932); [occ.] Legal and Executive Secretarial positions and journalism; [memb.] Past President of a Philadelphia Professional Writer's Club, ARC and various community and political activities; [hon.] Salutatorian of my class at Palmer, ARC awards for

Red Cross instructor, etc.; [oth. writ.] All facets of newspaper writing with the former Upper Darby News and part-time with the Philadelphia Bulletin, and other local papers; [pers.] From academics to secretary, later my son's birth, I combined motherhood and journalism at home, culminating in my love of poetry. My husband of 51 years is my greatest inspiration in hanging on to my dream - as one door closes another opens! [a.] Havertown, PA 19083-1117.

LEWIS, RUTH MARIE
[b.] July 8, 1947, Crawford, North Carolina; [p.] Hattie Burton and Zion Hall Berry; [m.] Stanford Lee, July 12, 1984; [ch.] Larry D. and Thomas E. Richardson, Keesha D. Lewis; [ed.] Currituck Union High, College of the Albemarle - A.A.S. degree, Elizabeth City State University - B.S. degree; [occ.] Secretary/Elizabeth City State University; [memb.] N.C. State Employees Association; [hon.] Alpha Kappa Muy Honor Society, Dean's List; [oth. writ.] Have done several poems - one entitled "My Mother" won a contest years ago; [pers.] I inspire to make a difference in someone's life and to make a contribution to society. [a.] Elizabeth City, NC 27909.

LIDAHL, BEULAH
[b.] August 12, 1911, Esmond, North Dakota; [p.] Ted and Mary Ann Nelson; [m.] Arnold, June 29, 1935; [ch.] Dr. Larry Lidahl and Dr. Tom Lidahl; [ed.] High School; [occ.] Retired; [memb.] Plentywood Lutheran Church; [pers.] "Winter Loneliness" and several other poems were written in 1932 and not discovered until my son found them in the attic in 1990. [a.] Plentywood, MT 59254.

LIDDELL, MARY L. MCCLOUD (WOODS)
[b.] March 14, 1931, Daytona Beach, Florida; [p.] Fannie Ruth Jarris Counts and Frank McCloud, Jr.; [m.] Edward, May 28, 1988; [ch.] Anthony and Andrew Liddell; [ed.] BS in Elementary Education from Bethune-Cookman College in 1962, MA in Education with emphasis in reading in 1974, Specialist in Education in 1976; [occ.] Teacher; [memb.] New Way Fellowship Baptist Church, Sigma Gamma Rho Sorority; [hon.] Several outstanding Woman of the Year awards; [oth. writ.] I wrote for a Miami Weekly under the Bi-Name "Out of the Woods" for four years. Before that and since I've written many plays, poems and stories that I use in my work as a teacher in the Dade County School System; [pers.] I truly believe that any child can do well if he wants to badly enough. For the "want to" will take of the how. As for me, I can do anything through Him who gives me the strength. [a.] Miami, FL 33169-5213.

LILGERT, KIMBERLLY
[b.] June 12, 1960, Wiarton, Ontario, Canada; [p.] Roger and the late Shirley Ebel; [m.] Ron, May 10, 1986; [ch.] Jason Arthur, Sarah Elizabeth; [ed.] Wiarton Public, Wiarton High School, Grand Prairie Beauty College; [occ.] Hairstylist turned Housewife/mother; [oth. writ.] I have had a couple of articles published in local newspapers; [pers.] My man died of lung cancer, me by my side, 2 months after I wrote this poem. In times of trouble and pain, writing is my escape. Words writing is my escape. Words on paper do wonders. The words often flow, and questions get answered, emotions unleased, and no fear, or inhibitions. [a.] St. Albert, Alta, Canada T8N 1Y6.

LIN, CAROL
[pen.] Y.Y./K.K.; [b.] May 4, 1975, Taiwan, R.O.C.; [p.] Jenny and Johnson Lin; [ed.] Burnaby North Secondary School (completing grade 12); [occ.] Student; [memb.] School's Library Club (monitor) and School's Horseback Riding Club; [pers.] A English as Second Language student. Most of my ideas are from my own feelings and thoughts. [a.] Burnaby B.C. V5C 2S8 Canada.

LINGER, ROSETTA H.
[pen.] Rosetta Linger; [b.] April 2, 1959, Buckhannon, West Virginia; [p.] Dessie L. and Wesley J. Tenney; [m.] Gary N. Linger, June 2, 1975; [ch.] Wendy Dawn, Stormy Allen, Sammie Neil and Misty Rose; [ed.] Buckhannon Upshur High School; [occ.] Mother, Housewife, Disabled; [pers.] True happiness makes the heart weep with joy. [a.] Buckhannon, WV 26201.

LINK, JANET
[b.] November 2, 1955, Clifton, New Jersey; [p.] Henrietta and Vincent Mullen; [m.] Gary; [p.] Justin Gary and Diana Patrice; [ed.] Clifton High; [occ.] Homemaker; [pers.] My gardens are my sanctuary where my thoughts turn into poetry. [a.] Vernon, NJ 07462.

LINSE, JAMES P.
[[pen.] James Patrick Linse; [b.] February 16, 1970, Hammond, Indiana; [p.] Jim and Kathy Linse; [ed.] George Mason University; [oth. writ.] Too few and too far apart to ever mention; [pers.] Words are puzzles in my mind designed to connect and clarify my past and future yet to come. [a.] Fairfax, VA 22031.

LIPPERTG, KORI E.
[b.] June 2, 1974, Bountiful Utah; [p.] James I. and Peggy I. Lippert; [ed.] Cross Roads High (graduated 1991) in college; [occ.] Student; [memb.] Nothing current; [hon.] Salutatorian, 1991 Texas UIL Feature Writing Gold Medal, Girl Scout Silver Award. [a.] Austin, TX 78745-0433.

LISCOMB, CHRIS A.
[pen.] Chris A. Liscomb; [b.] April 24, 1970, Bethesda, Maryland; [p.] Eugenia and Jesse R. Liscomb, Jr. and Jeanene Liscomb (sister); [ed.] BA Organizational Communications, California State University, Stanislaus; [occ.] Songwriter/entrepreneur; [memb.] SCA (Speech Communications Associations), ASCAP (American Society of Composers, Authors nd Publishers); [hon.] Top Student Communication Studies at CSUS, National Science Foundation "Excellence" Scholarship; [oth. writ.] A majority of my poems are being converted into songs; [pers.] "To strive for excellence in all you do, so that no fault will be found in your character." Ptah Hotep. [a.] Los Angeles, CA 90019.

LITTLE, JAMES P.
[b.] September 15, 1948, Torrance, California; [ch.] James Jr. and Jason; [ed.] San Gabriel High (CA); Delgado Community College (LA), W.D.S.-Novel Writing Workshop; [occ.] Retired Offshore Oilfield, Deep Sea Diver/Writer; [memb.] Broadcast Music, Inc.; [hon.] 1992 Honorable Mention by Hutton Publications for Short-Short-Short Story: "The Simple Box"; [oth. writ.] Published music, B.M.T., newspaper articles, poetry, have novel-in-progress and

authored a stage play "The Dream"; [pers.] Writing for me is simply an attempt to interpret the refracted and changing perceptions beyond my life's prism through which I gaze. [a.] Covington, LA 70434.

LLOYD, HILARIE C.
[b.] June 28, 1993, Hornell, New York; [p.] Gary C. and Mary Jane Lloyd; [occ.] Student at Alfred Almond Central School - 7th grade 12 years old; [memb.] Alfred Ballet Academy, Chorus,- Piano, Odyssey of the Mind Team Member; [hon.] Regional Winner Team - Odyssey of the Mind, High Honors Academic Achievement, Outstanding Evaluation - Piano- N.Y.S. School Music Association Spring '93; [oth. writ.] "Vacation Trips" Literary Festival winner also many earth poems and dramatic plays; [pers.] There's a place in your heart where the sun always shines. FIND IT! [a.] Andover, NY 14806.

LOCKETT, MARISA Y.
[pen.] Risa; [b.] December 24, 1976, Chanute, Kansas; [p.] Henry and Marie Lockett; [ed.] Sophomore at Shawnee Mission Northwest High School; [oth. writ.] Black Girl, The Universal Love Question, The Secret, My Tree, and The Gentleman; [pers.] This poem expresses the rage and hopelessness I fell after hearing the not guilty verdict of the police officers who beat Rodney. And my hope is that this poem will give people the desire to change so someday we all can truly be free and live in racial harmony. [a.] Lenexa, KS 66215.

LOEWY, DANA
[b.] July 15, 1960, Decin/Czechoslovakia; [p.] George J. and Danuska Loewy; [ed.] Bonn University (Germany), UCLA, University of Southern California; [occ.] PhD Student in English, graduate assistant, lecturer, translator; [memb.] Modern Language Association, American Translators Association, American Literary Translators Association; [hon.] 1992 American Translators Association's Student Translation Award, 1991 Graduate Student Recognition Award, Phi Beta Delta International Scholars; [oth. writ.] Several poems published in German Anthologies, poetry and short fiction are on hold pending my completed dissertation; [pers.] The best poetry emerges from pain. [a.] Los Angeles, CA 90089-0453.

LOGAN, EDDY
[b.] October 2, 1963, South Pittsburgh, Tennessee; [p.] Edsil and Sandra Logan; [m.] Lori, August 8, 1987; [ed.] Ringgold High, Shorter College, Southern Baptist Theological Seminary; [occ.] Southern Baptist Minister; [pers.] It is in the unselfish giving of one person to another that we find true meaning in life. [a.] Louisville, KY 40280.

LO GIUDICE, CHRISTOPHER
[pen.] The Judge; [b.] June 18, 1965, Poughkeepsie, New York; [p.] Judith Mar Schmitz and Santo Anthony Lo Giudice; [occ.] Animal Care Specialist; [oth. writ.] Although I have written dozens of poems, this is the first one to be published; [pers.] Very special thanks goes to my friend Karl Wayne Jensen. If not for him, this poem might not exist today. When I shine, those who love me also shine. [a.] Poughkeepsie, NY 12603.

LOGUE, PETER C.
[b.] June 29, 1958, Chicago, Illinois; [p.] Arthur and Lena Logue; [ed.] Proviso East High, Triton College;

[occ.] Actor; [memb.] AGVA/AFTRA; [oth. writ.] Many, many scripts, poems and jokes; [pers.] My friend died after Christmas and I didn't find out until much later. This poem helped to ease my sadness. [a.] Maywood, IL 60153.

LOJAS, FRANCISZEK
[pen.] Kosla; [b.] October 30, 1946, Poronin, Poland; [p.] Franciszek and Ludwina Lojas; [m.] Lapa Kazimiera, July 11, 1971; [ch.] Darivsz and Franciszek; [ed.] Seven years Grammar school in Poland; [occ.] Wood Sculpture; [memb.] Polish Highlanders, Polish Poets Association; [hon.] 10 diplomas, 23 competition contest of poetry in Poland; [oth. writ.] Three short books of poems, various papers in Poland, poems published in several anthologies, Polish paper (Tatra Eagle) NJ, and Dziennikzwiakowy in Chicago. [a.] 34-520 Poronin - Poland.

LONG, ALLISON
[b.] June 10, 1975, Hammond, Indiana; [p.] Patricia and Gary Long; [ed.] Caldwell Elementary, Scott Middle School, Morton Senior High School; [occ.] Student; [memb.] Drama Club; [hon.] Third place ribbon at U.S. Indiana Bell Superbowl, Drama Letter; [oth. writ.] "Hidden Desires" to be published in Poetic Voices of American; [pers.] To write from your heart and soul. I write what moves me to learn, and saddens me to grow. [a.] Hammond, IN 46323.

LONG, MARY
[b.] March 3, 1912, Salesville, Ohio; [p.] Henry and Della Linn Kehl; [m.] Samuel (deceased), November 24, 1937; [ch.] Linda Johnson, Francis Long, Loretta Wilson; [ed.] Quaker City High School; [occ.] Various jobs - Seamstress Restaurant Manager, School Custodian; [memb.] Q.C. United Methodist Church, United Methodist Women Senior Citizens Group; [oth. writ.] Other poems pertaining to family birthdays, anniversaries, etc. [pers.] I would like to bring the message of the love of God and our love for each other in my poems Helen Steiner Rice has been a big influence to me. [a.] Quaker City, OH 43773.

LONG, ZANDRA
[pen.] Lisa White; [b.] February 19, 1961, Brunswick, Georgia; [p.] Priscilla and Earl White; [m.] Charles, December 25, 1991; [ch.] Toshema Ramkissoon Kussum White, Karama Long; [ed.] Glynn Academy High, Meadows Skill Center; [occ.] EDA, Data Entry Operator; [memb.] Kingsley Terrace Church of Christ; [hon.] Church awards; [oth. writ.] Several poems, songs, short stories; [pers.] I'm out tot win souls to Christ. [a.] Indianapolis, IN 46218.

LONGOSKY, KATHERINE A.
[b.] August 9, 1984, Durham, North Carolina; [p.] Carl J. and Susan L. Longosky; [ed.] Currently third grade at Derrick City Elementary School (Derick, PA); [occ.] Student; [memb.] Girl Scouts U.S.A., St. Francisco of Assisi Church, Recycling Club (at school); [hon.] Honor Roll, Book-It- Reading award; [oth. writ.] Poems, short stories; [pers.] I wrote my first poem in kindergarten and that opened the door to my enjoyment of writing. My second grade teacher, Mrs. Joan Mansour, has encouraged me and I dedicate this poem to her. [a.] Bradford, PA 16701.

LOPEZ, KARINA JACQUELINE
[b.] October 30, 1976, El Salvador; [p.] Lilian Arana Chavez and Francisco Omar Lopez; [ed.] High School,

11th grade; [occ.] Student; [oth. writ.] I have written many other poems, but they remain in my diary, locked up; [pers.] I love poetry, and expressing my sentiments through poetry. I believe everyone is equal, we are the only ones who can make a difference. [.] Los Angeles, CA 90006.

LORD, EMMA BUCHMANN
[b.] March 24, 1924, Jersey City, New Jersey; [p.] Emil and Delia Scott Bachmann; [ch.] John Apgar (deceased), Joan Apgar Hunter and Jean Lord; [ed.] Snyder High; [occ.] Retired; [memb.] Deborah Hospital, Joyce Kilmer Chapter; [hon.] I have always worked with children. Choir mother, Brownie leader, selling war stamps in school, very active in school during my children's school years; [oth. writ.] Several poems published in local newspapers and periodicals; [pers.] My poems are on subject of child abuse. All are true and heartbreaking about my beloved grandson, David Mark French. [a.] South Amboy, NJ 08879.

LOUCKS, BROOKE
[pen.] Elizabeth South; [b.] August 13, 1974, Decatur, Alabama; [p.] Mrs. Nancy C. Lesslie and Mr. John K. Loucks; [ed.] Batavia Senior High School, University of Dayton; [occ.] Full-time student, Swim instructor, Lifeguard; [memb.] American Red Cross, YMCA, HOBY, ATOP, D.A.R.E.; [memb.] Treasurer of Hugh O' Brian Youth Foundation, N.Y.W. Alumni Association; [oth. writ.] Several poems in Stained Glass publication, a collection of unpublished writings; [pers.] Going to college for your years often does not give you the knowledge of watching the ways of a child for just an hour. E.S./B.L. [a.] Batavia, NY 14020.

LOUDERMILK, BENJAMIN D.
[pen.] Benji Loudermilk; [b.] December 10, 1962, Bloomington, Indiana; [p.] Harry D. Loudermilk and Sharleen A. Snapp; [ed.] Bloomington North, Indiana University, BA 1991; [occ.] Residential Supervisor in group home setting; [memb.] Actively involved with local theatre production companies (Bloomington Playwright's, Monroe County Civic Theatre); [hon.] Who's Who Among American High School Students (1980); [oth. writ.] I have written poetry and song lyrics for about seven years, mainly for personal pleasure - previously unpublished; [pers.] Through a love of the theatre and years of active involvement, my greatest influence grew from the classics (esp. Shakespeare). I also admire many modern authors. [a.] Bloomington, IN 47404-1828.

LOVE, FRANCES NOWLAN
[pen.] Frances Nowlan Love; [b.] November 23, 1911, Greensboro, North Carolina; [p.] Meta Budd Grundman and James Francis Nowlan; [m.] Verner R. (deceased), August 30, 1930; [ch.] Verner Richardson, Love Jr., Susan Love Droste and James F. Love; [ed.] University of North Carolina, major-Business, minor-Music(voice and piano); [occ.] N.C. Department of Mental Health - Area Coordinator (5 counties-now retired); [memb.] United Daughters Conferancy, S.C. Genealogical Society - Charleston Chapter Historical Society, American Association Retired Persons; [oth. writ.] Completed 25 years writing of Love and Nowlan Family no w published and distributed - Book "Just For You", thoughts of my early life for grandchildren (now published) Bi-monthly Column for Summerville Journal Adene.;

[pers.] It is never too late to widen your horizons. [a.] Summerville, SC 29485.

LOY, CARL
[b.] July 31, 1927, Ft. Loramie, Ohio; [p.] Albert H. and Margaret Viola (Mills) Loy; [ed.] Ft. Loramie Public Schools, Ohio State University; [occ.] Retired Aero-Space Design Engineer, NASA; [memb.] Society of Automotive Engineers, American Institute of Aeronautics and Astronautics, Auburn-Cord-Duesenberg Museum; [pers.] A causal, inept, mystified, but captivated student of Emily Dickinson's Poetry. [a.] Huntsville, AL 35810.

LUCAS, FRIEDA
[b.] August 7, 1935, Leitchfield, Kentucky; [p.] Albert and Rosa Miller Conder; [m.] Kermit; [ch.] 14 pound white cat; [ed.] Eight years grade school at Leitchfield, KY; [occ.] Housewife, homemaker see ATT paper; [memb.] BMI in Nashville, TN; [hon.] Have a song called A Man in a Robe published on Keith Bradfords Heart of Gospel Tape, I have did many Bible course have a Bible Lay Certificate also Bible History; [oth. writ.] I have 4 songs playing on local radio here, about 2 notebooks full of songs and poems; [pers.] I get songs or poems from looking and enjoying God's creation of the beautiful world. The trees the flowers, hills, valleys and people. [a.] Big Clifty, KY 42712.

LUCAS, OMEGA
[b.] January 13, 1927, Senath, Montana; [p.] Ed (Bud) and Clarsa Jordan Anderson; [m.] William Nix, July 25, 1945; [ch.] Judy Carol and John (Hink); [ed.] Elementary (Bucoda MO) and high school (Senath, MO); [occ.] Retired; [memb.] Coles Ferry Senior Citizens, South Side Baptist Church; [hon.] Volunteer for Retired Seniors, Volunteer for Mid Cumberland, Meals on Wheels, Volunteer for S.C. Coles Ferry Pike; [oth. writ.] Several poems published in "Dunklin County Press". Also in "Lebanon Democrat" (Lebanon, TN); [pers.] When people like my "Little Poems", I'm very happy. I hope that 99% of the population can relate to what I say.

LUCAS, SHAWNEE SHAYE
[b.] November 3, 1978, Nacodgoches Medical Memorial Hospital; [p.] Ronnie and Donnita Lucas; [ed.] Rusk High School; [hon.] Honor Roll at school, awards for beauty pageants and softball awards; [pers.] I believe there is one rule in life, "Love and let Love". [a.] Rusk, TX 75785.

LUCKOW, KERRY
[b.] December 16, 1972, North Kansas City, Missouri; [p.] Kerry and Carol Luckow; [ed.] Crescent Lake Christian Academy, Maple Woods Community College; [pers.] I believe in God the Father-maker of heaven and earth, and in Jesus Christ his only son and I will hold steadfast to this creed. [a.] Liberty, MI 64068.

LUCIER, KATIE
[b.] September 21, 1982, Sanford, Maine; [p.] Paul and Cindy Lucier; [a.] E. Lebanon, ME 04027.

LUDEAU, ROSEMARY D.
[b.] April 15, 1929, Touro Hospital, New Orleans, Louisiana; [p.] Ralph Daniel and Caroline Nolting Dwyer; [m.] John Lawrence, Jr., August 13, 1949; [ch.] Seven and seven grandchildren; [ed.] Three

years college- Loyola University (New Orleans) and U.S.L. in Lafayette, LA; [occ.] Retired editor and publisher, American Heartbeat and V.P. Gazette currently feature writer and columnist for Gazette; [memb.] Formerly Louisiana Presswoman and NFPW; [hon.] Thanks Badge, Gold Medal that is highest honor in adult girl scouting, Girl Scout Hidden Heroine Award 1976, Farm Bureau Freedom Award 1976, Ville Platte Woman of the Year 1962-nomination for same again in 1971, 1975, 1976 included in 1980 edition of "Who's Who Among American Women" received many state and national writing awards for feature, column, editorial and others; [oth. writ.] Feature stories, columns, personal, and cooking, editorials, news stories and others for Ville-Platte Gazette and The American Heartbeat both of which I edited at different times; [pers.] although there was a number of writing awards over the years, this is a first for poetry and since poetry has always been dear to my heart, this really touches me deeply. Thank you. [a.] Ville Platte, LA 70506.

LUMSDON, MOLLY
[b.] September 26, 1974, Brazil, Indiana; [p.] Jim Lumsdon and Sandy Liddil Bayes; [ed.] Northview High School; [memb.] First Christian Church; [oth. writ.] Article published in school paper; [pers.] I have been influenced greatly by my grandmother (Bea Liddil) and my friends who have supported and encouraged me with what I do. "Romans 8:28". [a.] Brazil, IN 47834.

LUNA, SUSAN
[pen.] Susan Luna; [b.] September 26, 1943, Albany, California; [a.] Salinas, CA 92912.

LUNDSTEDT, CHARLES V.
[b.] January 20, 1914, Detroit, Michigan; [p.] Paul V. Lundstedt and Emma Lelia McDill; [m.] Dorothy Marie Bowen, October 6, 1944; [ch.] Christine Marie Howard, Eric C. Lundstedt, Janis Marie Keahin; [ed.] University of Detroit (1931-1939), EE/postgrad Maine '39-'40 Wayne State Music, '69-'70 George Washington Grad, Engineering, '81-'82 Pima Community College AA degree w/honors, National Judicial College, class '83, Taught Meterology and Celestial Navigation '60-'66; [occ.] Engineer (Electronic, Radio, Space) 1936-1979, County Justice of Peace 1983-89; [memb.] Institute of Radio Engineers, Amateur Radio Call WA2UCY, Arizona Constable J.P. Association, National Judges Association; [hon.] Order of DeMolay Chevalier, Phi Mu Alpha Sinfonia (music), Elder in Presbyterian Church, Space Communicator (NASA), American Legion Commendation, Dept. Army Morse Code 25 wpm, Who's Who in Arizona 1987; [oth. writ.] Numerous operation manuals, "Top Dog" (set of poems) unpublished, "Looking Toward Eighty" autobiography unpublished; [pers.] I have a legacy that only I can write to pass on to generations to come. [a.] Green Valley, AZ 85614-3927.

LUTZ, JEAN MARIE
[pen.] Jean Lutz; [b.] July 25, 1958, Utica, New York; [p.] John J. and Helen T. Zajac; [ed.] Hazelton High School and Hazelton Area Voc-Tech. School; [occ.] Intermediate Solderer for Lucas Aul. and a self-employed massage therapist; [memb.] American Heart Association, White Haven Ambulance, Foster Parent Association; [hon.] 1976 winner of the Abraham Guassberg Memorial award; [pers.] Much of my

writing has been greatly influenced from the teachings and beliefs I've learned from my church, "The Fraternity of Light". [a.] White Haven, PA 18661.

LYONS, JAMES C.
[b.] July 20, 1940, Catlettsburg, Kentucky; [p.] Ruth A., and Donald R. Lyons; [m.] Barbara A., July 20, 1972; [ch.] (step) William James, Debra Joe, Judith Kathleen; [ed.] Thomas R. Brown High; [occ.] Retired USAF and Civil Service; [memb.] Air Force Sergeants Association, American Legion; [hon.] Navy Unit Commendation Ribbon, Air Force Commendation Medal; [pers.] I strive to express my most inner feelings in my poetry. [a.] Warner Robins, GA.

M, ANNA
[b.] September 19, 1888, Meade County, Kentucky; [p.] James and Belle Sneider Toops; [m.] John Andrew Sparks (deceased), March 2, 1913; [ch.] Mrs. Wm. (Pauline) Crist, Mrs. Jack (Audrey) Montgomery, Mrs. Gilbert (Charlotte) Nelson (dec.) and Mrs. Fred (Patricia) Larimer; [memb.] Church of Christ; [oth. writ.] Published a book of poems called "Grandma's Poems" for the family; [pers.] Poems written on reflections of friends, relatives and memories over 104 years. [a.] Mattoon, Il 61938.

Mac ARTHUR, JUNE
[pen.] Joon Mac Arthur; [b.] August 12, 1934, Oklahoma City, Oklahoma; [p.] Jewel and Edgar Mac Arthur; [m.] December 22, 1962; [ch.] Christopher and Cameron; [ed.] Graduate student, Legal Administrator; [occ.] Legal Assistant; [memb.] Amnesty International, Wildlife Association; [hon.] National Speech contest, 1956 and District winner in 1960; [oth. writ.] Currently writing a story of my life in journal form; [pers.] I attempt to spread some joy, some sadness, some mystery in my writings. [a.] La Crescenta, CA 91214.

MacDONALD, EDITH SCHEUER
[b.] October 29, 1919, Mishicot, Wisconsin; [p.] Earl and Lillian Scheuer; [m.] Robert A. MacDonald, November 10, 1942; [ch.] Daniel A. MacDonald, Attorney; [ed.] Bachelor of Science; [occ.] Retired; [memb.] Civil War Round Table, Faith Evangelical Free Church, Manitowoc Genealogy Society, Silver Lake College Round Table; [oth. writ.] Several poems published in newspaper; [pers.] I strive to search the inner soul of man and am deeply interested in people.

Mac INTOSH, DARLENE J.
[b.] December 23, 1959, Roseway Hospital, Shelburne Co.; [p.] Mr. and Mrs. Lewis Williams; [m.] Delma S. MacIntosh, Jr, September 8, 1979; [ch.] Joseph S. and Jennifer L. MacIntosh; [ed.] Lockeport Regional High; [occ.] Mother, housewife plus owner of Lamt-Stand Bible Bookstore; [oth. writ.] I have written many poems for family and friends, plus I have written songs for people for weddings, birthdays, anniversaries, etc.; [pers.] This poem is just one of many inspired by God. It is for Thanksgiving on the love of my day. I always thought it was my mother who spend most of her time caring for us when we were ill, but after one night of staying up with my daughter with an earache, I remember my dad doing things to help me get rid of mine, he never left my side. How bless I am for both my mom and dad. [a.] Lockeport, N.S. B0T 1LO.

MacKAY, JULIA
[pen.] Missy-Kay, Gram-Kay; [b.] May 29, 1908, Rocklin Lake, New York; [p.] Susan Ann and Joseph Horvath; [m.] Chadwick C. MacKay, March 12, 1945; [ch.] 1 son, I am widow for 25 years; [ed.] High school, 2 years Junior College, graduate, nurse graduate, millinery design; [occ.] Retired, L.V.N. Nurse, have many hobbies and crafts; [memb.] Senior's activities, church activities, ladies group, widow's group; [hon.] Senior's Handicapped Certificate of Appreciation for Citizen Awareness, good samaritan, helping hand, helping everyday, my poetry started at age 14, I'm never still, always doing something, I walk 5 miles a day; [oth. writ.] Many writings in news, my personal self, favorite poet Edgar Allan Poe, made up poems about people's birthdays and parties; [pers.] Love to help and donate monies and clothing, giving help where needed. [a.] Stockton, CA 95207-5854.

MACKEY, VIVIAN (nee RING)
[b.] March 30, 1906, Bowdle, South Dakota; [p.] Simon Chester Ashley Ring, Lydia Laurentia Lindholm; [m.] Warren Barrett Mackey, August 13, 1932; [ch.] Marzieh Ruth, Joseph Brooks, M.D.; [ed.] PHS, Plankington, S.D., University Washington, Seattle, WA 1930, graduate WK-U. Hawaii, Honolulu and Seattle University; [occ.] Retired teacher 28 years; [memb.] Delta Zeta Sorority (UW) St. John Vianny Catholic Church, Seattle Genealogical Society; [oth. writ.] Poems in " Child Life", "Jack and Jill", (anthology "Best of J & J First Ten Years", 4 poems in " Children's Lit for Dramatization by Geraldine Siks (Harper Row). [a.] Vashon, WA 98070.

MACKLEM, LORI
[b.] June 9, 1976, Winnipeg, Manitoba; [p.] Eva and Dennis Macklem; [ed.] Completed grade 11 (RVS), returning for grade 12, 1993-94; [occ.] Student at Roseau Valley School, Dominion City, Mb; [memb.] Canadian Figure Skating Association, Canadian Red Cross, Royal Lifesaving Society of Canada; [oth. writ.] Several unpublished poems and short stories; [pers.] My writings reflect my feelings and experiences. "Follow your dreams of today into tomorrow". [a.] Manitoba, R0A 0L0 Canada.

MACPHAIL, ALEXANDER D.
[b.] November 2, 1974, Harrisonburg, Virginia; [p.] Ralph and Alice MacPhail; [ed.] Eastern Mennonite High School; [memb.] Grace Covenant Church; [pers.] Jesus of Nazareth is Lord. [a.] Bridgewater, VA.

MADDEN, MARY JANE
[b.] November 11, 1942, Detroit, Michigan; [p.] Willard G. and Lena J. Angel Mullins; [m.] William B. Madden, deceased; [ed.] Berea Foundation, Eastern Kentucky University, Indiana University; [occ.] Communications/media Arts Teacher, duPont Manual High School, Louisville, Kentucky; [memb.] National Teachers of English, National Education Association, Kentucky Education Association, National Wildlife Association, The Nature Conservancy; [hon.] Dean's List, Who's Who In American Colleges and Universities, teacher in a National School of Excellence, Master Teacher Award; [oth. writ.] Feature articles published in The Courier Journal and The Louisville Entertainer; [pers.] Poetry has no nationality it speaks to the inner self. [a.] New Albany, IN.

MAGEE, MOLLY
[pen.] Molly Magee; [b.] March 20, 1909, Baltimore, Maryland; [m.] Widow, September 10, 1927; [ch.] 5 living; [ed.] Junior high; [occ.] Retired; [memb.] A.A.R.P., social clubs, Colts Corral, Minnie Mouse Club and Hill Top Social; [oth.writ.] " The Way It Used To B", " Home Is Where The Heart Is", " Don't Take Too Much For Granted", " Me and The Model T"; [pers.] I write many things for friends and family, anything else that inspires me. I just love doing it. [a.] Linthicum, MD 21090.

MAGWERA, SHINGIRAI
[pen.] Shingie Magwera; [b.] March 30, 1969, Chinhoy, Zimbabwe; [p.] Kayton Sydney and Mirayi Magwera; [m.] Still single; [ed.] Golcomere CPS Masvinao, Vhembe High School, Beit-Bridae; [occ.] Managing director for Inter City Taxis; [memb.] Lion club of Beit-Bridae; oth. writ.] A novel titled My Life, published by Mambo Press; [pers.] Though its natural it is very difficult to apprehend and the knowledge that it will reach anyone of us makes it too agonizing and horrorful. [a.] Zimbabwe, Africa.

MAIN, JAMES D.
[pen.] Eddie B. Merchant; [b.] March 16, 1977, Sacramento, California; [p.] Donald and Susan Main; [ed.] Del Oro High School; [occ.] Student, Del Oro; [memb.] Church Leadership Team, CSF; [hon.] VFW Male Outstanding Student of Class, Honor Society, Cum Laude, numerous sports awards, top student in both Science and English; [oth. writ.] Many poems, numerous genres of stories and essays; [pers.] The diamond cannot be polished without friction, nor man perfected without trials, to live is good but to be alive is better. [a.] Rocklin, CA 95677.

MAKELA, JOYCE
[pen.] J.L. Makela; [b.] August 3, 1943, Amherst, Nova Scotia, Canada; [p.] Lorraine and Frank Landels; [m.] Matti Makela, October 10, 1964; [ch.] James Burnett; [ed.] Toronto Teachers' College, Mount Allison University, St. Mary's University, Simon Fraser University; [occ.] Teacher, St. Charles Elementary, Amherst, Nova Scotia; [memb.] Art Teachers' Association, Scottish Cultural Society; [oth. writ.] Letters in education, children's stories; [pers.] One cannot write poetry without the pen of music and the ink of philosophy. [a.] Nova Scotia, Canada B0L 1B0.

MALDONADO, ANDREA
[pen.] Andrea Maldonado; [b.] November 21, 1978, Stockton; [p.] Linda and Eldon Allen; [m.] Single; [ed.] Passed 8th grade, starting high school in September; [occ.] Student; [memb.] I am a member of the Lodi Boys and Girls Club; [hon.] My 8th grade diploma; [oth. writ.] Working on other poems; [pers.] My feelings about poems are that you can express your feelings honesty within poems. [a.] Lodi, CA 95240.

MALLETT, THOMAS
[pen.] Thomas Mallett; [b.] September 21, 1944, Worcut Cr., Massachusetts; [p.] Al and Margaret Mallett; [m.] (fiance') Eveon Okun; [ch.] Dennis and Kelly; [ed.] High school; [occ.] Disability; [memb.] Shelby /Mustang All FJR Club of Syracuse; [oth. writ.] Other poems, unpublished, done for my own pleasure; [pers.] This poem was written to my daughter who since my divorce has not talked to me, I was

trying to show her my pain and also how much I love her. [a.] Syracuse, NY 13205.

MANALAC, GLORIA CARMELA D.
[b.] March 23, 1978, Zamboanga City, Philippines; [p.] Atty. Vicente and Chona Delfin Manalac; [occ.] Student, school, Pilar College Zambo City, Philippines; [hon.] Elementary, with honors, 3rd place paragraph writing, 3rd placer math contest (school), high school-top 4, 4th placer city wide math contest, elementary, Tula or Elocution contest (2nd placer); [oth. writ.] Several poems made but kept privately. [a.] Zamboanga City, 7000 Philippines.

MANGANO, KRISTA
[b.] August 16, 1978, Syracuse, New York; [p.] Mary Anne and John Mangano; [ed.] Oswego High School (sophomore); [occ.] Student; [memb.] Student of The Institute of Children's Literature; [pers.] My writing is a mirror of the pain in the world that everyone can see themselves in. [a.] Oswego, NY 13126.

MANJARES, MELCHOR M.
[pen.] Chorman; [b.] January 6, 1945, Putiao,Pilar, Sorsogon, Philippines; [p.] Felix L. Manjares and Elizabeth R. Miraflor; [m.] Salvacion G. Garais, January 21,1980; [ch.] Christopher, Cherry, Charity, Charina, Christian, Charles, Chester and Charmaine; [ed.] B.S. Architecture, Technological Institute of the Philippines; [occ.] Utility clerk, Rack and Sack, Kempsville Road, VA; [memb.] Missionary Association of Mary Immaculate, The Highlander Club; [hon.] Golden Poet 1992, World of Poetry; [pers.] Hallelujah! The Lord is my strength. [a.] Virginia Beach, VA.

MANTOOTH, MICHAEL DAVID
[pen.] Michael David Mantooth; [b.] January 4, 1948, Oklahoma City, Oklahoma; [p.] John Wesley and Ruth Mantooth; [m.] Patricia Ann Mantooth, August 31, 1968; [ch.] John Wesley Mantooth, Jr., James Robert Mantooth; [ed.] B.S., Oklahoma State University, (Animal Science), MDIV, Texas Christian University; [occ.] Ordained Minister, Christian Church (Disciples of Christ), United States Army Chaplain; [hon.] Three awards of Meritorious Service Medal; [oth. writ.] Write monthly column published in military newspaper, distributed down Eastern Seaboard and in Europe; [pers.] All of my writings stem from personal experiences. I try to reflect our need for each other and for our Creator. [a.] Bayonne, NJ 07002.

MAPLE, ROCHELLE
[b.] July 11, 1973, Orangeburg, South Carolina; [p.] Harry C. and Mary L. Maple; [m.] Single; [ed.] Orangeburg-Wilkinson High School, Northern Virginia Community College, South Carolina State University; [occ.] Unemployed, student; [memb.] National Black Child Development Institute; [hon.] Recipient of Bronze Medallion for academic performance; [oth. writ.] "Why", "Parents" and "Reflection"; [pers.] In my poetry, I struggle to find answers to the difficult and overwhelming obstacles in my life. Hopefully through my method of expression, I can help, not only myself, but others like me to realize that out time is coming... someday. [a.] Orangeburg, SC 29115.

MARCELLUS, GREGG
[b.] December 19,1958, Syracuse, New York; [p.] Clyde and Betty Marcellus; [ed.] Bachelor of Science in Marketing, Syracuse University; [occ.] Currently T.V. Production/director effective August 20, 1993, English Instructor in Okayama, Japan; [pers.] I believer the quality of my life is equal to the quality of the questions I ask myself. [a.] Bridgeport, NY.

MARIAN, SUMMER
[b.] July 5, 1977, Philadelphia, Pennsylvania; [p.] Donna Marian and Joe Siravo; [ed.] 9th grade, Souderton Area High School, Souderton, PA; [occ.] Student; [hon.] None yet (intrack); [oth. writ.] I've never really had any interest in poetry before, until my friend Ben died. It effected me so much that I put all of my feelings down on paper; [pers.] My soul is one with poetry, now and forever. [a.] Souderton, PA.

MARKIEWICZ, NORBERT FRANCIS
[b.] January 14, 1963, New Haven, Connecticut; [p.] Jan and Gertrude Markiewicz; [m.] Angela Markiewicz, April 16, 1994; [ed.] B.A. in Journalism from Southern Connecticut State University, A.O.S. in Culinary Arts from Johnson and Wales University; [occ.] Assistant Chef at Walt Disney World; [memb.] Church drama group; [hon.] College Dean's List; [oth. writ.] Poem published in "American Collegiate Poets"-1984 anthology, " Listen to The Light" a private publication of my poetry, personal biographical novel of my family, editor and writer for college newspaper, short stories; [pers.] I strive to reflect the love and salvation of my Lord and Savior Jesus Christ, and those I love who have influenced me. I like to reflect my travels and the romantic side of life. Writers I admire-Walt Whitman, Hemingway, Steinbeck, romantic poets. [a.] Orlando, FL.

MARQUIS, ANTHONY J.
[b.] July 4, 1935, Peabody, Massachusetts; [p.] Philip and Alice (Ferrante) Marquis; [ch.] Jill-Ann Marquis; [ed.] Lowell University, Northern Essex; [occ.] Landscaper; [oth. writ.] " I Must Pass", " Dream International Quarterly # 18, 1990, " Gardening Tips", Methuen Weekly news and self-published Gardner's Crosswords; [pers.] The study of nature and how it effects us all. We should work with nature not against it, to follow a natural order in all things created. [a.] Lawrence, MA 01843.

MARRELLI, GIOVANNA
[b.] July 30, 1971, Toronto, Ontario; [p.] Mario and Carmela Marrelli; [m.] Joe Accettura; [ed.] McGraw Hill Universities, Woodbridge High School, Brother Edmund Rice and Pope Paul Elementary; [occ.] Medical Receptionist/sales representative; [memb.] Leukemia Research Fund volunteer; [hon.] Highest honors, McGraw Hill Business Award; [oth. writ.] Several poems published in local newspapers, The Toronto Sun Poet's Corner; [pers.] In the words of my parents, " The World Always Turns", my influence is my heart, for love is the strongest power. I love you mom and dad. [a.] Woodbridge, ON L4L 3E4.

MARSEE, ELLA MAE
[b.] May 18, 1934, Middlesboro, Kentucky; [p.] Fannie and Bert Goins; [m.] Ralph Marsee (deceased), February 6, 1952; [ch.] Marcia Marsee Parker and Marc Marsee; [ed.] High school graduate, correspondent dress designing, retail merchandise graduate; [occ.] Retired; [hon.] Poetry, 1989 Golden Poet, 1990 Silver Poet and Who's Who In Poetry 1990, 1992 Golden Poet and 1990 Honorable Mention Award; [oth. writ.] Biography " Beauty to Tragedy" published 1990, several manuscripts; [pers.] My writing comes from my heart and soul to be simple and easy to understand. The happening that have occurred in my life are the roots of my success. [a.] Harrogate, TN 37752.

MARSHALL, DALLAS RAY
[b.] September 13, 1955; [ed.] B.A. University of Nebraska, Classics Department-1984, Practical English Career Institute 1990; [memb.] Evangelical Free Church; [hon.] Grace I. Bridge Classics scholarships, 1980-81, 1982-83; [oth. writ.] Victorious Glory; [pers.] These compositions were written from the perspective of recording an emotional interpretation of my belief in God. [a.] Omaha, NE 68114.

MARSHALL, TARA
[b.] December 6, 1979, Takoma Park, Maryland; [p.] Raymond and Veronica Marshall; [ed.] 7th grade student; [hon.] Honor Roll.

MARTELL, DANIELLE ALEXIS
[b.] Born when I was very young, in the summer; [m.] Single; [ch.] One son named Cousteau; [ed.] I believe I was kicked out of kindergarten for some subversive activity, can't quiet remember what it was; [memb.] I am a volunteer at the Mayo Clinic in Scottsdale, Arizona, I give guided tours of the " Nature Trail" at the clinic, and do a slide show on all the plants and animals in the desert; [pers.] I have been writing poetry since I was a small child. Ever since I can remember all my friends have said "You should be a writer or a poet". After 30 years of hearing those words over and over again I finally took the first step by entering The National Library of Poetry's contest. I amy truly honored to have been selected for publication. [a.] Scottsdale, AZ 85259.

MARTIN, DEBBIE
[pen.] Duchess Dawn; [b.] April 25, 1979, Conrot, Texas; [p.] John and Debra Martin; [ed.] Tarkington Elementary, Cleveland, Texas, Palestine Middle School, Palestine, Texas; [occ.] Student; [hon.] Perfect Attendance Award, Patriotic Award by the Cleveland V.F.W.; [pers.] I believe that teenagers and adults have a talent if they could find it and develop it. [a.] Cleveland, TX 77328.

MARTIN, HAZEL BALDWIN
[b.] March 17, 1912, Owen County, Kentucky; [p.] John Crowder and Gertrude Thomason Baldwin; [m.] Roscoe Martin, February 5, 1933; [ed.] Owenton High, Georgetown College (BA); [occ.] Teacher (Elementary and Junior High); [memb.] Owen County Retired Teacher, Kentucky Retired Teachers, National Retired Teachers Association Lona Ridge Baptist Church; [hon.] Cum Laude (Georgetown College), Kentucky Colonel, Meritorious Service to 4-H; [oth. writ.] Newspaper articles, skits for 4-H Clubs; [pers.] Organist and/or Pianist for 60 years, have served in all youth activities during the years, church and school. [a.] Owenton, KY 40359.

MARTIN, LEE
[b.] July 4, 1970, Cornwall; [ed.] Observation; [occ.] Hopelessly seeking perfection;[oth. writ.] Many unpublished verses, I am also an artist of the post modern kind; [pers.] I merely display probables for the

present path and the importance of inner reflections and liberation of self from surrounds, inside space and time, outside man's mechanics which by-pass insight for avarice. [a.] Cornwall, PL242QQ England.

MARTIN, LINDA (RYAN)
[b.] 1946, in a small New York town, Marion; [p.] George and Evelyn Ryan; [m.] Donald R. Martin; [ch.] Tammy Marie and Tina Lynn Martin; [ed.] Graduated in 1964 from Marion Central High; [memb.] International Society of Poets; [oth. writ.] First 3 poems ever sent out were published by three different publishers; [pers.] A firm believer that a home should never be empty, so I have devoted my time and love to my family and home. I am just now enjoying my own talents as a writer and poet. Family life today has greatly changed, commitment and devotion is not the same. My heart goes out to all women who truly have no choice today. For a lot of these women carry a great deal of pain, as well as the heaviest burdens.

MARTIN, MARGARET
[b.] July 27, 1933, Hickory Grove, South Carolina; [p.] James and Mary Wylie; [m.] Arthur Martin, March 6, 1955; [ch.] Bonita Louann, Regina Sue and Matilda Kaye; [ed.] Blacksburg High School; [occ.] Housewife; [pers.] I have always endeavored to express my love in words and writing. [a.] Blacksburg, SC 29702.

MARTIN, MARIO A.
[b.] May 4, 1974, El Dorado, Arkansas; [p.] Sharon Martin; [ed.] El Dorado High School, South Arkansas Community College (one year); [hon.] Dean's List; [oth. writ.] Rhythm of The Delta and Mahogany Blues, a play, have had several editorials published in local paper, Forty Acres and A Mule, numerous poems and essays; [pers.] I try to show and capture the essence of black life. Many of my writings I did with the friendship, love and family. I believe that with out these we are nothing. I try to reflect life in motion, influenced by Maya Angelou. [a.] El Dorado, AR 71730.

MARTIN, MARY D.
[pen.] Bunny Martin; [b.] March 26, 1971, Killeen, Texas; [p.] Nancy Lynn Martin; [m.] Michael S. Verner (fiance), January 8, 1994; [ed.] Killeen High School, Central Texas College; [occ.] Clerk, One Day Cleaners, Killeen; [memb.] Art Club, We Can Do It Club, Central Texas College Student Government Association; [hon.] Diplomas from K.H.S., Certificates of Appreciation from different clubs; [oth. writ.] Numerous personal stories about me; [pers.] I would like the people who read this poem to understand people with disabilities and not to make fun of them. [a.] Killeen, TX 76541.

MARTINEZ, SABRINA
[pen.] Sabrina Martinez; [b.] January 20, 1979, Hollywood, Florida; [p.] Juan and Iowi Martinez, (brothers) Juan M. and Aberto M.; [ed.] Still in school in the 8th grade, age 14; [hon.] Always honor student since kindergarten; [oth. writ.] Likes writing poems. [a.] Plantation, FL 33317.

MARTINEZ, ZANDRIA K.
[pen.] Zee; [b.] Washington, District of Columbia, raised in Virginia; [p.] Mr. and Mrs. Karl P. Duckwitz and William A. Prokos; [ch.] Eric D. Wallace and Elizabeth K. Daisey; [ed.] Fairfax High School, class

of 72, Fairfax, Virginia, Fort Bend Beauty School, Rosenberg, Texas; [occ.] Cosmetologist, author.poet; [memb.] First United Methodist Church of Rosenberg; [oth.writ.] I enjoy writing romantic short stories as well as poetry; [pers.] This poem was written in honor of John "Red Bird" Moore, the gentle giant who will always be in my heart. A written word will help us to remember, for time changes images, but a written word will stay forever. [a.] Rosenberg, TX.

MASKEL, HAZEL
[b.] May 7, 1916, Georgetown, Illinois; [p.] Fredric and Mary Ruth Morrison; [m.] Boyd N. Maskel, 1937; [ch.] Arthur, Daryl, James, George, Fredrick; [ed.] Georgetown High; [occ.] Homemaker, playground and lunchroom supervisor for Georgetown school; [memb.] Georgetown Homemakers Exten., Vermilion Co. Board HEA, Georgetown Historical Society, Community Choir, United Methodist Women's Society, chairboard; [hon.] Charter member National Honor Society in high school, 1985 Silver Award and 1987, 1988, 1989, 1990, 1991 and 1992 Golden Awards from World of Poetry, in Who's Who in Poetry in 1990 and 1992 by invitation; [oth.writ.] Some anthologies by World of Poetry, " His Precious Love" by American Arts Association, local newspaper and senior citizen letter; [pers.] Friendship is a knot tied by an Angel's hand-or every evil deed, every unkind act carries a roundtrip ticket and always comes back. [a.] Georgetown, IL.

MASON, GREGORY C.
[b.] January 6, 1961, Macomb, Illinois; [p.] George K. and Barbara S. Mason; [m.] Alexandra Mason, October 5, 1990; [ch.] Georgia Eve Mason; [ed.] Hazelwood Central High School, Arizona G.E.D.; [occ.] Arizona State Prison, Inmate; [oth. writ.] Several other unpublished poems; [pers.] I will never be able to express my deep regret for having hurt the person I most love, for all the words I would use to explain everything hang just outside my reach! [a.] Florence, AZ 85232.

MASON, MARVA L.
[b.] March 31, 1968, Toledo, Ohio; [p.] Levi and Vernice Mason; [ed.] Associates with University of Maryland; [occ.] NCO in the United Stated Air Force; [memb.] Air Force Association, Black Heritage Club, American Red Cross blood donor; [hon.] Air Force Achievement Medal with an oak leaf cluster; [oth. writ.] Several unpublished personal poems; [pers.] The gift of life has been given to you so take it graciously and make your dreams come true. [a.] Toledo, OH 43607.

MASON, RONALD H.
[pen.] Ronald H. Mason; [b.] July 28, 1963, Macon, Georgia; [p.] James M. Mason and Geneva Howard; [m.] Anita R. Mason, February 26, 1987; [ch.] Melissa L. Mason; [ed.] Central Lanier High School, Fayetteville Technical Community College; [occ.] Soldier/finance clerk; [memb.] Finance Corps Association; [oth. writ.] Several poems entered in poetry contests and receiving Honorable Mention; [pers.] My poems are just an expression in writing of what state of mind that I'm in at that time. [a.] 8815 Peter Saurach, Germany.

MATE, ROBERTA
[b.] December 16, 1951, Washington, Pennsylvania; [p.] Robert Hawley and Helen Moore; [m.] Thomas

Mate, September 28, 1984; [ch.] Melissa. Laura and Jonathan; [ed.] High school graduate, Beauty School, Eastern Illinois University School of continuing Cosmetology; [occ.] Hairdresser; [memb.] Aurora Area Writer's and Artists Group; [oth. writ.] I have written over 200 poems; [pers.] For every star that falls to earth a new one glows, for every dream that fades away a new one grows. I adopt this philosophy by Rod McKuen, I have too many of my own to pick one. [a.] Aurora, IL 60506.

MATHEWS, GARLINDA TROUT
[b.] September 13, 1933, Brazil, Indiana; [p.] William D. Trout and Schellia (Trout) Aker; [m.] Lyle E. Mathews, Sr., June 27, 1953; [ed.] Brazil High School graduate; [occ.] Reelsville Elementary School Cook; [memb.] Pleasant Gardeners Homemakers' Club-Baptist Church; [hon.] Homemaker of the Year Award 1987-Putnam Co. Fair Bake-off 3rd place winner 1991 and 1992, 4th place winner 1990; [oth. writ.] This is the first poem I shared; [pers.] I live in Putnam County, one of the most beautiful countries in Indiana, especially in the Fall, writing poetry is a hobby for me. [a.] Reelsville, IN 46171-9701.

MATSON, MARIE
[pen.] Maria; [b.] July 20, 1920, California; [p.] Mr. and Mrs. A.V. Amet; [m.] Warner C. Matson, April 13, 1941; [ch.] Christine, Tom and Jim; [ed.] Some college; [occ.] Taught in Junior College for 6 years, had my own Floral Business; [memb.] Altrua Study Club, Four Seasons Garden Club, Tacoma Lawn Tennis Club; [hon.] Many awards for flower arranging; [oth. writ.] Many of my expressions are done in oil on canvas; [pers.] Wife, mother, grandmother to 7. My home and children have always has top priority. I'm a nurturer and will always help others when needed. [a.] Tacoma, WA 98407.

MAURER, JAMES E.
[pen.] Poetry Pal; [b.] January 24, 1920, Philipsburg, Pennsylvania; [p.] William and Mary Maurer; [m.] Sara J. Maurer, April 3, 1973; [ch.] 5; [ed.] High school, O.T.C. in service in Chemical Warfare, Edgewood, MD,- school for officers; [occ.] Service U.S. Army 1943-1946, A & T Co. employee 34 years-retired; [memb.] Church-Am Vets, fire department, service clubs, etc.; [hon.] Army Service Awards, (500th West Pacific) with stars and ribbons, service awards (34 years A&T Co.) honored for my christian work and teaching with children, to show them the love of God and our universe He made, I served my parents in childhood, I served my country in my youth and I've served my Lord in my entire life; [oth. writ.] I have written many poems since I was 12 years old, given many readings in churches in local areas, wrote several for local paper (The Daily Journal) under pen name "Poetry Pal", 1940-1946; [pers.] I have strived to reflect the goodness and love of God thru my poetry. I have been inspired my own struggle thru life to succeed, still writing at 73 years. [a.] Philipsburg, PA 16866-9719.

MAURICE, HEATHER
[pen.] Liz; [b.] May 13, 1979, Marquette, Michigan; [p.] Michelle Cornell; [ed.] 8th grade Springbrook Middle School; [hon.] 2 writing Scholarships, Adrian College, Meap for Math and Science. [a.] Adrian, MI 49221.

MAWUSI, DEBBIE
[pen.] Debbie Mawusi; [b.] October 12, 1970, Oliver, BC; [p.] Kathy Morgan and Ken Pettifer; [m.] Anthony Mawusi, April 22, 1989; [ch.] Amanda Lynn Mawusi and Michael Wayne Mawusi; [ed.] Killarney; [occ.] Homemaker; [pers.] I am only 23 years old, but know more about life than I would like. This poem is one of many things that I have thought of and written down. My greatest wish is to write not only poems but books as well. My life in itself is a book.

MAXWELL, DONNA LEE
[pen.] Donna Lee Maxwell; [b.] Born and raised in New England; [ed.] Bishop Keough High School, Katharine Kibbs School, East Side, Providence, B.A. Liberal Arts, Providence College, studied abroad at University College Cork, Ireland, International Summer School, Irish Studies Program, attended the W.B. Yeats International Summer School, Sligo, Ireland studying poetry, drama and literature; [occ.] Presently a M.Ed. candidate in Counseling at Providence College, Rhode Island; [pers.] Donna Lee's love of New England inspire many of her writings. [a.] Pawtucket, RI 02860.

MAXWELL, MARIAN W.
[b.] July 4, 1926, Harlan (Harlan County), Kentucky; [p.] Sallie L. and J.R. Weiler; [m.] Howard H. Maxwell, Jr. (deceased), August 24, 1950; [ch.] Beverly M. Burden, Anne H. Maxwell and Don Jonas Maxwell; [ed.] B.A. Maryville College, Tennessee, M.A. George Peabody College, Nashville, Tennessee, Special Ed., University of Kentucky; [occ.] Retired Music Teacher/special ed. teacher, now professional musician; [memb.] Sigma Alpha Iota Music Sorority, American Guild of English Handbell Ringers, Centenary United Methodist Church, Kentucky Music Educators Association; [hon.] Honorable Order of Kentucky Colonels, Golden Poet Award; [oth. writ.] Handbell music, " Bell Folly" published by National Music Publisher, California, handbell and inspirational music written for specific occasions and or choirs; [pers.] I write poetry as a means of expressing an emotion or feeling that could not be expressed thru mere conversation or that cannot be spoken aloud. [a.] Shelbyville, KY 40065.

MAY, MARIA E.
[b.] November 10, 1965, Los Angeles, California; [p.] Thomas H. May and Rose S. Caswell; [m.] Charles B. Mapes; [ch.] Kristina Rosemary, Charlene Eloise, Benjamin Charles; [ed.] Moreno Valley High School; [occ.] Homemaker; [memb.] PTA Rainbow Ridge Elementary; [oth. writ.] Many more waiting for publication; [pers.] I write what I feel in my heart and soul to share my feelings with everyone. [a.] Pernis, CA 92570.

MAYFIELD, SUE ANN
[pen.] Sue Mayfield; [b.] June 15, 1935, Connersville, Indiana; [p.] John A. Allen and Catherine M. Jones; [m.] Willard Lee Mayfield, July 16, 1955; [ch.] Alan, Debra, David, Teresa and Karen; [ed.] G.E.D.; [occ.] Housewife; [memb.] Bethany Baptist Church; [oth.writ.] Most of my writings are for relatives and friends, none have been published; [pers.] I write the way I feel about certain subjects and hope to stir the feelings of others. [a.] Somerset, KY 42501-8447.

MAYNARD, JAMES H.
[b.] May 16, 1968, Palm Springs, California; [p.] James R. Maynard and Annette Margot Bendtsen; [m.] Jacquie Y. Maynard, August 18, 1991; [ch.] James R. Maynard; [ed.] Indio High School, U.S. Army Infantry School, U.S. Army Airborne School; [hon.] 3 Army Achievement Medals, Good Conduct Medal, Kuwait Liberation Medals, South West Asia Service Medal/with 2 stars, National Defense Service Medal, Army Service Ribbon; [pers.] I like to write poems to make people feel better. This poem was to my wife Jacquie, I wanted her to be happy even though I was far away. [a.] Banning, CA 92220.

MAYR, IMOGENE
[pen.] Jene Napier; [b.] September 26, 1930, St. Albans, Long Island, New York; [p.] Margaret E. and Julius Troy Mayr (surveyor, U.S. Army-seal # 102); [ch.] 3 children; [ed.] St. Agnes Academy Lynbrook High School, New York, Junior College, G.R., M.I.; [occ.] Secretary and teacher; [memb.] Immanuel Evangelical Lutheran Church, Las Vegas, N.M.; [hon.] Senior Citizen-State of New Mexico Olympics, gold, silver, bronze-swimming, artist-2nd and 3rd place, Mi., Colorado; [oth. writ.] Short stories, poetry, cookbook, knitting brochure " Food For Thought" and " Thoughts On Food"; [pers.] " Where standards, institutions, reputations all fail-christian families, churches and friends do prevail", credit my grandmother Adeline Peele. [a.] Denver, CO 80202.

MAZZA, JOSEPH
[pen.] Pie; [b.] March 20, 1973, Bronx, New York; [p.] Mary G. and Louis R. Mazza; [ed.] Fordham Preparatory High School, Iona College; [memb.] Editor of the Cornelian Literary Magazine, Iona College; [hon.] National Honor Society, Dean's Scholarship, Dean's List; [oth. writ.] Several works published in college literary magazine, poem published in another hardbound anthology; [pers.] Some of the best things I have ever said have been written, not spoken. [a.] Bronx, NY 10469.

McADAMS, MARTHA
[pen.] Mikki; [b.] November 6, 1977, Baton Rouge, Louisiana; [p.] Michael and Susan McAdams; [ed.] Currently attending Baton Rouge High, graduated from Baton Rouge Lutheran School; [occ.] Student; [memb.] Trinity Youth, Koinonia Choir, Baton Rouge High Choir; [hon.] Valedictorian of Baton Rouge Lutheran School, Superior rating at Solo/ensemble Festival, Woodmen of the World, Presidential Academic Fitness Award; [oth. writ.] Poems published in youth newsletters; [pers.] I pray that everyone may find their joy in life as I have in singing and writing. [a.] Baton Rouge, LA 70816.

McADOO, CRYSTAL D.
[pen.] Crystal; [b.] June 24, 1959, Gatesville, Texas; [p.] Thomas Jasper and Ruth White; [m.] Single parent; [ch.] Crystal Joe, Matthew, Christopher, Angela and Micheal; [ed.] Gatesville High School, Temple Junior College and now working on ADN Degree; [occ.] Licensed Vocational Nurse, Day Surgery, King's Daughters Hospital, Temple, Texas; [memb.] Northside Church of Christ, Temple, Texas, Coordinator-Attention Deficit Hyperactive Disorder Support Group, Temple, Texas; [oth., writ.] Numerous other non-published poems; [pers.] I have been writing since I was a child. I write according to my feelings which then reflect how I feel. [a.] Troy, TX

McALEER, R.
[pen.] Finney McCloud, Frost, [b.] February 2, 1969, Moontownship, Pennsylvania; [p.] Mary and John; [ed.] Dropped out of junior college, graduated Estancia High School 1987; [occ.] Unemployed actor; [memb.] Member of Two Rocky Horror casts, (1) Lipp Service in Montclair, CA., (2) Tonights Menu in Redondo Beach, CA.; [hon.] None noteworthy; [oth. writ.] No previously publicated work; [pers.] Our lives are reflected by art, art is reflected by our lives. After our death, our art survives. Thanks cruel world for your pain, my poetry proves it's not in vain. [a.] Garden Grove, CA 92641.

McCAA, ANNIECE
[b.] April 30, 1939, Aliceville, Alabama; [ed.] Summerville Industrial High School, Bronx Community College, Pratt Institute of Technology, Pace University and Consad Research Institute; [occ.] Educational Associate, P.S. 178X Board of Education, New York City; [memb.] Union Grove Baptist Church; [hon.] Parents and Teachers Association, Para-Professional of The Year and Martin Luther King, Jr.; [oth. writ.] Several poems published, "New Voices In American Poetry", "Vantage Press", newspapers, Mercy College and The United Federation of Teachers Para-Scope, displays of poetry Mercy College and The United States Holocaust Memorial Museum Permanent Collection Archives; [pers.] My joys comes from working with young people. My writings are reflections of inner, "Bitter and Sweet Inspirations"@, I am also touched by the humility and the writing style of Dr. Maya Angelou. [a.] Bronx, NE 10472.

McCARTER, JENNIFER
[pen.] Jena; [b.] July 27, 1978, Parkersburg, West Virginia; [p.] Janice and Dr. Joseph McCarter; [ed.] Currently in Parkersburg High School; [memb.] Camden-Clark Volunteer Services; [hon.] Wood Whispers; [oth. writ.] None that have been published except Wood Whispers (Wood County school's art magazine); [pers.] Poetry, to me is my emotions being revealed in a way that everyone interprets differently;. [a.] Parkersburg, WV 26101.

McCARTHY, FRANCIS LEE
[pen.] Francis Lee; [b.] February 22, 1929, Detroit, Michigan; [p.] Richard George and Mary Lee (Quigley) McCarthy; [m.] Polly Louise (Jent) McCarthy; [ch.] Richard Lee, Robert Louis, Kevin Michael, Kathleen Marie, Brian Joseph, Allan Patrick, Susan Darlene, David Michael, Lori Colleen, Timothy Patrick McCarthy; [ed.] Roseville High School, Roseville, Michigan, Great Lakes College (Architecture), Detroit, Michigan, University of Toledo (Paralegal), Toledo, Ohio; [occ.] Furniture and cabinetmaker; [memb.] Friends of the Vietnam Veterans Memorial, Knights of Columbus, Moose; [hon.] Phi Theta Kappa; [oth. writ.] Political essays, Op Ed; [pers.] To each his own. [a.] Angola, IN.

McCARTHY, RHONDA
[b.] January 30, 1958, Cottage Grove, Oregon; [p.] Max Parsons and Norma Parsons, Sr.; [m.] Robert McCarthy, Jr., September 9, 1989; [ch.] Monique and baby girl McCarthy (not yet born); [oth. writ.] " One Special Day", published in A Break In The Clouds, published by The National Library of Poetry; [pers.] " Don't give up, try together". [a.] Oswego, NY.

McCARTY, FLOYD
[pen.] "Reach"; [b.] May 1, 1955, Monroe, Louisiana; [pers.] A dream can only be expressed by trying to live it. [a.] Kennedale, TX 76060-2616.

McCLAIN, AJANET DANGRE
[b.] April 10,1978, Cedar Falls, Iowa; [p.] Gregory Dan and Janet Elaine Williams McClain; [ed.] Northern University High School, sophomore (fall 1993); [occ.] Student; [memb.] High school track, basketball, volleyball, orchestra, chorus, TEMCA; [hon.] University of Northern Iowa Young Scholars Science, Minorities in Teaching Program, Loras College Math Camp for Girls; [oth. writ.] Several poems, essays, short stories and plays; [pers.] Write for feeling, write for emotion, write for creativeness, write for imagination, be right to write on. [a.] Cedar Falls, IA 50613.

McCLELLAND, JEAN
[b.] February 22, 1968, Pittsburgh, Pennsylvania; [ed.] B.A., Duquesne University; [occ.] Secretary - The Carnegie, Pittsburgh, PA. [a.] Pittsburgh, PA 15216.

McCLISTER, JEAN
[pen.] Jeannie; [b.] March 2, 1953, Peoria, Illinois; [p.] Frank and Rosamond McNutt; [m.] Robert Eugene McClister, December 5, 1981; [ch.] Heather Lynn (9 1/2), Bobby Kenneth (8 1/2) and Jimmy Franklin (5 1/2); [ed.] 2 years college, Beauty School, correspondence school course for teacher's aide; [occ.] Homemaker; [oth. writ.] Written and have several poems; [pers.] Take time no matter how busy you are to enjoy people, yourself and life, don't put off tomorrow what needs done now. [a.] Gautier, MS 39553.

McCLURE, MARGARET
[b.] April 23, 1916, Pendleton, Oregon; [p.] Long deceased; [m.] James McClure, November 30, 1936; [ch.] 7; [ed.] Very limited; [occ.] Grandmother, mother and wife; [oth.writ.] Poetry, unpublished. [a.] Elgin, OR 97827.

McCOLLUM, WILLIAM G.
[pen.] William G. McCollum; [b.] January 10, 1967, Pittsburgh, Pennsylvania; [p.] George R. and Janice C. McCollum; [m.] Margaret Mary McCollum, May 19, 1990; [ch.] Conor Seamus and Shane George Robert McCollum; [ed.] Shadyside Academy (grammar/high school), Boston University; [occ.] V.P. Sales/marketing Pittsburgh Homecare Products, Inc.; [memb.] South Hills Republican Club, Pittsburgh Athletic Association, Pennsylvania Association Medical Suppliers; [hon.] Dean's Citation 91986), Boston University; [oth. writ.] Numerous -unpublished "I've filled notebooks of poetry and short stories since the age of thirteen"; [pers.] " I only write about things of a personal nature-trying to link with universal experiences. Since I've become a husband and a father, my writings have become focused upon the sentiment of our family life". [a.] Pittsburgh, PA 15211.

McCONNELL, SHAWN LEA
[b.] September 10, 1980, West Union, West Virginia; [p.] Joseph and Marla McConnell; [ed.] Sixth grade, Doddridge County Middle School, West Union, West Virginia; [hon.] "A" Honor Roll Student, selected as " Student of The Week", Talent Award for poetry writing; [oth. writ.] Several poems written for school

assignments or for pleasure however this is the first one to ever to be published; [pers.] Through my poetry I try to express my concerns for the problems in the world today. [a.] West Union, WV 26456.

McCORKLE, STEPHANIE J.
[pen.] Stephanie McCorkle; [b.] November 13, 1973, Raleigh, North Carolina; [ed.] Sanderson High, Bennett College; [occ.] College student; [memb.] Ethics Club, Campus Scouts, Martin Street Baptist Church Usher Board, co-writer of Ebony Vibes, a campus television production; [hon.] Dean's List, Honor Roll, National Dean's List; [oth. writ.] The North Carolina Federation of Women's Clubs Inc. local, district and merit awards; [pers.] I can accomplish all things, through God, who strengthens me. Life experiences are my writing inspirations. [a.] Raleigh, NC 27610.

McCORMICK, REBECCA ANN
[b.] December 21, 1976, Milwaukee, Wisconsin; [p.] Ronald and Rose Marie McCormick; [ed.] Manitawoc Lincoln High School; [occ.] Student; [oth. writ.] Short stories and several other poems (non-published); [pers.] Most of my poetry reflects the emotions of a young teenage girl. I've been influenced by friends and family to put my feelings into words of poetry. [a.] Manitawoc, WI 54220.

McCORTNEY, JOE
[b.] January 28, 1976, Condell Hospital, Mondelein, Illinois; [p.] Margaret and Eugene Techmanski; [occ.] Student. [a.] Round Lake Park, IL 60073.

McCOY, CHRIS GRIMES
[pen.] Chris Grimes McCoy; [b.] June 23, 1929, Rotan, Texas; [p.] Selly and Myrtle Grimes; [m.] Lynn McCoy, September 29,1950; [ch.] One son, Randy; [ed.] High school; [occ.] Retired-housewife; [memb.] All this I just can't recall, but lots of my life has been being a Choir Director/singer; [hon.] Nothing worth mentioning, don't like to brag; [oth. writ.] " Signs of Love" published in Where Dreams Begin, "A Daily Prayer" in On The Threshold of A Dream, "Everyday Thanksgiving" in Wind In The Night Sky, all published by THE NATIONAL LIBRARY OF POETRY; [pers.] I believe in "God Is Love". I believe in doing for others without expections of getting something in return. I believe in treating others as you would like to be treated, all this adds up to "God Is Love". [a.] Goldthwaite, TX 76844.

McCREA, TREY
[b.] November 21, 1977, Houston, Texas; [p.] Llew and Diane McCrea; [ed.] 1992-3 -Freshman Belton High School, Belton, Texas; [occ.] High school student; [memb.] National Junior Honor Society; [hon.] Recipient of Presidential Academic Fitness Award - 1989 and 1992, DAR Citizenship Award - 1991, Outstanding Student -Advanced Physical Science - 1993, Outstanding Student - Advanced Geometry -1993. [a.] Belton, TX.

McCREE, MARTHA
[pen.] Dolly Dimples; [b.] January 30, 1946, Waycross, Georgia; [p.] John and Martha Bradely; [ch.] Walnita Lovettee McCree, daughter, grandkids, Lashawn McCree, Lashira, Lamira and Lakera Smith; [ed.] Tivoli High graduate, Southern Ohio graduate medical, certificates for keypunch, retail sales, diplomas high school and college; [occ.] Sears employee;

[memb.] Hopefully the future; [hon.] Academic list, atheltic awards in high school; [oth. writ.] Several poems published for National Library of Poetry; [pers.] I strive to be know greatly by mankind and the media also hope poems influence early romantic poets as so did their for me.

McCURDY, WARREN WILLIAM
[pen.] WWM; [b.] December 14, 1936, Washington, District Columbia; [p.] Walter and VonZelle McCurdy; [m.] Kathleen Mary (Brooks) McCurdy, December 3, 1965; [ch.] Collin (25) and Neil (21) McCurdy; [ed.] BS Philosophy, Kansas State, MA Spanish, Middlebury, certificate Salamanca, Spain; [occ.] Retired USIA Foreign Service Officer (magazine editor); [memb.] Diplomatic and Consular Officers retired, USIA Alumni Association; [hon.] Dean's list,USIA Meritorious Honor Award; [oth. writ.] Since the mid 60's, I have written about 100 unpublished poems to my wife, sons and good friends. most are extremely topical, for insiders only, for 5 years in the 70's I was a reporter and wrote much; [pers.] I particularly enjoy writing limericks even when they are not bawdy or funny. I do look for humorous endings, no matter what the style. [a.] San Diego, CA 92124.

McDANIEL, CHRISTINE L.
[pen.] Chrissei Teenie; [b.] January 27, 1965, Youngstown, Ohio; [p.] John Burl and Helen L. (Slaton) McDaniel; [ch.] Nathaniel Burl R. McDaniel; [ed.] Carrolton High School, Buckeye Joint Vocational School, South Eastern Academy; [occ.] Homemaker, mother; [hon.] 1982 Most Outstanding Student, B.J.V.S. Auto Mechanics class; [oth. writ.] Have no other poems published, have my own personal book, I've worked on and added to since age 12; [pers.] All my poems reflect back to special times in my life, they help me through the rough times. [a.] Carrolton, OH 44615.

McDANIEL, DORI
[b.] May 19, 1972, Macon, Georgia; [m.] Darren McDaniel, November 7, 1992; [occ.] U.S. Army, Executive Administrative Assistant (Secretary); [pers.] All I ever really want from my poetry is for people to understand what I am saying and possibly remember and learn. [a.] Copperas Cove, TX.

McDANIELS, ELAINE
[b.] April 23, 1932, Lake Norden, South Dakota; [p.] Hjalmar and Jennie Efraimson; [m.] Lyle McDaniels, April 10, 1959; [ch.] Paul, Stan, Carolyn, Susan, Terry, Teresa, Julie and Charles; [ed.] Bryant High, 1 year of college, Madison, SD, General Beadle Teachers College; [occ.] Former school teacher, housewife; [oth. writ.] Just Call Me Putter, a book on poetry about an old Model A Ford car, published by Scott Publishing Kalispell, Montana, 1992; [pers.] As a hobby I do artistic woodburning and painting and sell my work at bazaars and on consignment. [a.] Lonepine, MT.

McFARLAND, ANGEL
[b.] October 6, 1978, Waterville, Maine; [p.] Adopted at age 5 by David and Beverly McFarland; [ed.] An eighth grader of Boothbay Region Elementary School; [pers.] This poem was written shortly after the death of my grandfather, who I never got to say goodbye to. [a.] Boothbay, ME.

McGEE, ANTHONY ELLIS
[b.] September 24, 1961, Chicago, Illinois; [p.] Jessye H. and Charles W. McGee; [ed.] Mendel Catholic Prep, Western Illinois University, Control Data Institute; [occ.] Service order writer, Illinois Bell Ameritech; [mem.] Member of Trinity United Church of Christ; [oth. writ.] Several poems to be compiled for a book of poetry; [pers.] I feel God has given me a gift, I want to cultivate the talent the Lord has blessed me with. I hope to inspire people in my writing. [a.] Chicago, IL 60628.

MCGIFFEN-NEWKIRK, LESLIE
[pen.] Leslie McGiffen-Newkirk; [b.] May 2, 1979, Louisville, Kentucky; [p.] Dawn McGiffen-Newkirk; [ed.] Graduate May 27, 1993 from Junior High, Sacred Heart Model School/Louisville; [occ.] Student; [hon.] Math Counts/city/3rd place/1988, Science Fair/Sacred Heart Model School/Honorable Mention/1990 Social Studies Fair/Scared Heart Model School first place/1991; [oth. writ.] "Quest of a Dream Publication", poetry. [a.] Louisville, KY 40207.

McGINNIS, STACEY
[b.] October 27, 1979, Madison, Wisconsin; [p.] Teresa K. and Robert N. McGinnis; [ed.] I am currently graduating from middle school and next year I will be entering Poynette High School; [hon.] I won third place in the Helen Mears Art contest for my painting titled " Here Kitty, Kitty"; [oth.writ.] I have no published writings, but I am thinking of writing a collection of short stories; [pers.] A good friend of mine said " If you let something go and it comes back it's yours to keep forever". [a.] Poynette, WI 53955.

McGREGOR, SALIMA
[pen.] Pebbles; [b.] November 30, 1979, Alexandria, Louisiana; [p.] Edward and Sonia McGregor; [ed.] Honors level, 8th grade Missouri City Middle School; [mem.] Junior Engineering and Technology Society, Prosecuting Attorney in Teencourt, Sisters of Intellect, Windsor Village Usher Board; [hon.] Runner-up in speech contest, moral authority, middle school level diploma, award for participation in graduation (invocation); [oth. writ.] Starting a book "Chronicles", poetry, children's, " Lies Are Like Flies", adult, " Dad, Sweet Dreams", " I Am Proud To Be Me", "We Ain't Gonna Cry", " The Left's Point of View", " I Heard", " A Girl Once Said"; [pers.] " Correct me if I am wrong and I promise not to label you jealous, for only a villain would allow me to make a fool of myself". [a.] Missouri City, TX 77489.

McGREW, KELLY L.
[b.] October 29, 1970, Three Rivers Hospital; [p.] Carl and Norma Wittendorf; [m.] Claude A. McGrew, August 29, 1989; [ch.] Brittany Lee, Brandy Lee and Frank Willson; [occ.] Housewife and mother; [pers.] I believe that I have the two greatest parents in the world who have given me more love and support than anyone could hope for. I only wish I'll be able to do as good as they have. [a.] Constantine, MI 49042.

McGRORY, TINA MARIE
[b.] August 23, 1977, Brooklyn, New York; [p.] Joseph F. and Ann McGrory; [ed.] A sophomore at Longwood High, in the future I plan to attend college and study law; [mem.] Treasurer of the FBLA;

[hon.] I am enrolled in the Renaissance program with first honors, I have also received various awards in physical fitness, Girl Scouts and ballet; [pers.] "101 Famous Poems", a gift from my grandmother, originally sparked my interest in reading poetry, the overwhelming love and support always given to me by my family in all my endeavors was the inspiration behind writing poetry. [a.] Coram, NY.

McGUIRE, BARBARA
[b.] September 14, 1938, Salida, Colorado; [p.] Robert and Viola Jackson; [m.] 1st marriage March 1, 1957; [ch.] Ernest, Jerry, Barbara, Evan and Tiffanie; [ed.] High school, 2 years of college; [occ.] Housewife; [oth. writ.] Cowboy's Sweetheart, Fastfood Places, Those Two Squirrels, Look at That Squirrel, The Fortune Cookie; [pers.] I have been writing poetry ever since my children were small. [a.] Arapahoe, WY.

McHONE, LACY
[b.] May 24, 1978, Denver, Colorado; [p.] Linda and Steve McHone; [ed.] Freshman in high school.

McILROY, DIANE
[b.] September 23, 1956, Mason City, Iowa; [p.] Dallas Read and Winifred Morrison; [m.] Allen McIlroy, September 3, 1977; [ch.] Phillip, Mary, Sharah, Anna, Jordan, Revekah, Jeshanah; [ed.] Ozark High, Westark College and Henderson College; [occ.] Homemaker, homeschool teacher; [mem.] National Right to Life, Concerned Woman for America, AWANA Clubs International, Lighthouse Baptist Church, Christian Homeschool Association; [pers.] Any talent or success that I may have or obtain comes from the Lord Jesus, without Him I am nothing. [a.] Pottersville, NY 12860.

McINTOSH, JUANITA (MRS.)
[b.] December 20, 1932, Kentucky; [p.] Ford and Ida (Morris) Spurlock; [m.] William J. McIntosh, August 5, 1953; [ch.] Larry, Ventia Lynn, Jerry Gwyn and Darlene Marie; [ed.] 8th grade; [occ.] Homemaker; [oth. writ.] Several poems, I have always loved poetry; [pers.] My family, always comes first above everything. I love the outdoors and raising flowers, my hobbies are embordery, reading and crafts. [a.] Buckhorn, KY 41721.

McINTOSH, LILLIE BURKE
[b.] October 10, 1957, Jacksonville, Florida; [p.] Pauline Rouse and William Burke; [m.] Levi H. McIntosh, Jr., April 11, 1992; [ch.] Jeremiah Way (nephew); [ed.] William M. Raines Senior High, Florida A & M University, Nova University; [occ.] Elementary school principal, Chimney Lakes Elementary; [mem.] Delta Sigma Theta Sorority, Greater Grant Memorial A.M.E. Church, National State and Local Elementary Principals' Association; [hon.] Alpha Kappa Mu, Kappa Delta Pi, Phi Delta Kappa, Outstanding Young Women of America (1988), Who's Who Among Students in Colleges and Universities; [oth. writ.] Various articles and poems have been penned for school-related and family functions; [pers.] In all that you do, work 'til you're through. Always give your best, and your reward will be just. [a.] Jacksonville, FL 43512.

McISAAC, LORRAINE VICTORIA
[b.] April 1, 1921, Boston, Massachusetts; [p.] Marie and Harry True; [m.] Nolan McIsaac, November 8,

1975; [ed.] Elementary and high school, Gerham, Maine, attended Licenced Vocational School of Nursing, Winthrop, Mass., attended 1 year Bible College, Sweetwater of the Valley, Arizona, U.S.A., three years training, Christ Centered Missions Grandview Washington State - Evangelical Church, nursed at Cider Lebon Hospital, Los Angeles, CA; [occ.] Counseling youth; [memb.] Full Gospel Assembly, Chilliwack, B.C.; [oth. writ.] In 1990 wrote a small book of spirit lead poems, for Christmas gifts, title On The Wings of The Spirit-I Will Lead You- I Will Guide You For You Are My People; [pers.] A good friend, Robert Barnett, encouraged me and I am grateful to him. [a.] Chilliwack, BC V2P 4H9.

McKEEVER, ANN
[pen.] Ann McKeever; [b.] 1955, Belfast; [ch.] 5; [ed.] Dominican College, Fort William; [memb.] Belfast Writer's Group; [oth. writ.] " Poetry Ireland", " New Irish Writing:, " Fortnight Magazine", " The Catholic Teacher", " The Belfast Telegram" and " The News Letter". [a.] Belfast, 14 6JY N Ireland.

McKENNON, EARL W.
[b.] December 23, 1949, Nanticoke, Pennsylvania; [p.] Fred and Grace McKennon; [ch.] Earl Jr., and Kerry; [ed.] Northwest Area, Northeastern; [occ.] Engineer.

McKENZIE, MAVIS
[b.] November 29, 1914, Hope, Arkansas; [m.] William T. Mckenzie; [ed.] A.B. University of Pittsburgh, MA Wayne Stare University; [occ.] Retired school administrator, Detroit, Michigan Public Schools; [memb.] AAUW, Delta Sigma Theta Sorority, Life Member National Council of Black Women; [oth. writ.] Several poems published in anthologies, magazines and a college textbook published by Harcourt Brace Jovanich; [pers.] I am seventy-eight years old and I have been writing poetry two years. My poems hopefully inspires more truth, love and kindness in human behavior. [a.] Los Angeles, CA.

McKENZIE, UNA B.
[b.] May 1, 1931, Detroit, Michigan; [p.] Josephine and Clarence McKenzie; [ed.] Central High, Detroit, MI., Central State College, Ohio, B.S. degree and M. Ed. degree at Eastern Michigan University; [occ.] Teacher, retired; [memb.] A member of the Poetry Society of Michigan; [hon.] Good Neighbor Award from the Mayor of Detroit, Achievement Award from Children's Library, Detroit Service Award from Top Ladies of Distinction, Inc., Detroit; [oth. writ.] My first book, Poems from the Heart by Una B. McKenzie, my poems have been published in Golden Song, an anthology, Peninsula Poets, published by Poetry Society of Michigan and American Poetry Anthology 1983 by John Frost; [pers.] To all neophyte poets who love poetry, always keep trying.

McKEON, RICHARD C. (MR.)
[b.] May 20, 1916, Lockport, New York; [p.] James McKeon and Mary E. Pascoe; [occ.] Hospital worker, June 1937-June 10, 1971; [hon.] Retired June 10, 1971; [pers.] I grab the opportunity to compliment the National Library of Poetry for doing this much needed work. [a.] Gowanda, NY 14070.

McKINNON-GEE, JUANITA BIROG IOLUC CARMILLE
[pen.] Ioluc Matthews; [b.] December 8, 1969,

Otautahi/Christchurch, Aotearoal, New Zealand; [p.] John Matthew William McKinnon and Nan Clara Gee; [ed.] Hagley High School, University of Cantersbury (New Zealand), Telford College (Edinburgh); [occ.] Bookshop worker; [hon.] 1989 Scottish International Open Poetry competition, 1991 Scottish International Open Poetry competition; [pers.] My main interest include poetry, (writers-Hone Tuwhare, Ted Hughes, Plath and Basho), painting, history, religious studies (Indo-European branches especially), Celtic languages and Celtic studies in general and genealogy. [a.] Christchurch, NZ.

McKLVEEN, GILBERT D.
[b.] June 5, 1911, Greensburg, Pennsylvania; [p.] John H. and Della A. McKlveen; [m.] Lola A. McKlveen, August 29, 1976; [ch.] 2nd marriage for both, we each lost our first spouse by death, I had 2 children and wife has 4; [ed.] Greensburg High School-1929, Junlata College-1953, University of Pittsburgh, M.Ed and D. Ed; [occ.] Retired, had 40 years of teaching, elementary, high school and college; [memb.] Zion U M Church -Myerstown, American Association of Retired Persons, AARP; [hon.] Poem, The Wretch, printed by Anderie Poetry Press, Allentown, PA; [oth writ.] A complete anthology of some sixty of my poems, in printed and bound form, publication of poems in local newspaper, one one act play " The Road to View Haven: [pers.] It was once written; " The kind of a man Mark Hopkins is, is the kind of man I hope to be". If my students say that of me, my life has been a crowning achievement. I love life. If some of my humor and philosophy inspires others, I have received my reward for living. [a.] Myerstown, PA 17067.

McLEAN, DANIEL
[pen.] Daniel McLean; [b.] March 27, 1982, Fort Walton Beach, Florida; [p.] Hubert M. and Pamela K. McLean; [ed.] Edwins Elementary School; [occ.] Student; [hon.] Second place, local Young Author's contest (1993). [a.] Fort Walton Beach, FL 32548.

McLELLAND, EVA
[pen.] Koni Falcon; [b.] May 4, 1916, Laurel Hill, Florida; [p.] William and Dora Howard; [ed.] High school and correspondence courses; [occ.] Retired Civil Service Secretary; [memb.] Nature Conservancy, National Wildlife, Methodist Church; [oth. writ.] Short stories and articles soon to be published (hopefully); [pers.] Since early childhood my every inspiration has stemmed from manifestations of nature. [a.] Troy, NY 36081.

McLEOD, T. WAYNE
[pen.] TWMc; [b.] May 20, 1943, Crenshaw Co., Alabama; [p.] Opal and Herman; [m.] Mary, July 5, 1966; [ch.] Thomas Timothy and April Dawn; [ed.] Winter Haven Senior High; [occ.] Communications-Florida Department of Agriculture; [memb.] 1st Baptist Church, Eagle Lake, Winter Haven F & Am # 186; [oth. writ.] Yes; [pers.] God, moves the heart, life pens the words; [a.] Winter Haven, FL 33880.

McMILLAN, FRIAR JOHN-DOUGLAS
(OFM CONV.)[b.] February 8, 1947, New York City; [p.] The late James and Irene McMillan; [ed.] Xavier University of Louisiana Th.M, University of Pittsburgh B.A.; [occ.] Director, Office for Black Catholic Ministries; [memb.] National Association of Black Catholic Administrators, National Association

of Black Catholic Clergy. [a.] Syracuse, NY 13208.

McNALLY, MARK MENDEX
[pen.] Marquis de McNally; [b.] May 5, 1927, Republic of Hoyti, West Indies; [p.] Anthony McNally of Scottish parentage; [m.] Marie Therese McNally, July 4, 1957; [ch.] Minerva, Minosa, Jerry, Gloria, Patricia,, Valentine, Magadalena and Harold; [ed.] Lycee Petion, high school, college, University of Hoyti, certificates, diplomas have been presented to me; [occ.] Specialist in Physical Theraphy, massage, hydrotherapy, etc.; [memb.] International Traders member, American Physical Theraphy Association; [hon.] "Pot O Gold"; [oth.writ.] Poems, editor publisher; [pers.] I was born in Haiti, West Indies and was descended from a distinguished family of Scottish and Hoytian parentage. [a.] Brooklyn, NY.

McNAMARA, KAREN
[pen.] Karen McNamara; [b.] March 8, 1977, Research Medical Center, Kansas City, Missouri; [p.] John Thomas and Margaret Sue McNamara; [ed.] Wyandotte High School; [occ.] Still attending high school; [hon.] State Finalist Teen Pageant 1992 and 1993; [oth. writ.] Essay for the Youth Motivation Program. [a.] Kansas City, KS 66102.

McQUEEN, ROSA L.
[b.] October 18, 1937, Philadelphia, Pennsylvania; [p.] Lena Outtin and Clop Garey; [m.] Divorced; [ch.] Cynthia, David, Dorleen, Mary, Delphine, Joseph, Rosa, Garry, Darrell and Anthony; [ed.] High school; [occ.] Student, American School; [pers.] Keep trust within yourself and believe in you. [a.] APO, AE 09821 (Izmir, Turkey).

McQUEEN, TAWANDA
[pen.] Wanda McQueen; [b.] January 6, 1951, Jasper, Alabama; [p.] Callos and Doris Brown, (sis.) Carla Brown; [m.] Glenn John McQueen, July 13, 1989; [ch.] Cody (deceased), Stephen Jeffery, Angeloni (step daughter) Laurie J. Still; [ed.] Forest Hill High School W.P.B., Medical Assistant and Surgical Technician; [occ.] Self-employed, retirement home for the elderly; [memb.] P I Fish, National Med. Assistant, Training Div., CCST Hope Hospice; [oth.writ.] Numerous poetry writings, but have never tried to publish any previously; [pers.] I strongly believe in Equality and Unity for all of mankind, strong family ties and magic in the power of words to change the course of one's life by inspiration. [a.] St. James City, FL 33956.

McREYNOLDS, JOHN
[b.] December 15, 1920, Seattle, Washington; [p.] Lee and Helen McReynolds; [m.] Camilla McReynolds, September 26, 1942; [ch.] Anita Hammet; [ed.] West Settle High, University of Washington; [occ.] Retired; [memb.] United States Power Squadrons (past); [oth.writ.] Anita's Cat, Mary's Cat and other poems for children; [pers.] Enjoy reading literature and poetry. [a.] Vashon, WA 98070.

McSORLEY, RANDALL GENE
[b.] October 24, 1955, Portland, Oregon; [p.] Joseph and Marvelle McSorley; [m.] Janette (deceased), 1974; [ch.] Amber Marie McSorley; [ed.] 11th grade; [occ.] Roofer; [memb.] B.P.O.E.; [oth. writ.] None published; [pers.] In memory of Janette Marie Hansen, 1956-1992, we will always remember her. [a.] Portland, OR 97266.

McTHENIA, CARRIE L.
[b.] December 3, 1924; [m.] Charles D. McThenia (deceased); [pers.] This poem was written in memory of my husband, Charles McThenia who died February 11, 1993. [a.] Richmond, KY.

McWILLIAMS, DONNY
[b.] June 30, 1976, Meridian, Mississippi; [p.] Nell Fulton and Harry McWilliams. [a.] DeKalb, MS 39328.

MEADE, ETHEL M.
[b.] October 12, 1904, Toledo, Ohio; [p.] Louis and Susie Miller; [m.] Deceased, June 4, 1924; [ch.] Melvin C. and Joyce Arthur Meade; [ed.] St. Ursula High School, Toledo, Ohio; [occ.] Retired; [memb.] Toledo Artists' Club and Northwestern Ohio Water Color Society; [oth. writ.] " Toledo" in the The Scroll which is an Ursula School publication; [pers.] I enjoy art, music and poetry. [a.] Bowling Green, OH 43402-1724.

MEADOR, EDDIE
[b.] October 26, 1951, Clifton, Texas; [p.] Charlie and Bethel Meador; [m.] Charlotte Meador, June 22, 1981; [ed.] Morgan High; [occ.] Electrician, disabled; [hon.] Valedictorian; [oth. writ.] Several pieces of prose, none published, also an artist, some pieces include an ink drawing, this piece will depict the Crucifixion of Christ; [pers.] It has been said, I have the ability to place myself in the shoes of another, becoming the person, writing what one feels. [a.] Morgan, TX 76671.

MEADOWS, RICHARD L.
[b.] January 4, 1949, Chewelah, Washington; [p.] Roy and Myrtle Meadows; [m.] Linda Meadows, June 24, 1972; [ch.] Richard H.N. and Tina E.M.; [ed.] 12 years at Jenkins High School; [occ.] Sawmill worker; [memb.] I just belong; [hon.] Honored to serve my country and awarded a good life; [oth. writ.] Poetry written from the heart for my own pleasure and satisfaction; [pers.] Poetry comes easy with the love of family and friends, to my loving wife, Linda. [a.] Chewelah, WA.

MEAGHER, TONI R.
[pen.] Toni, Robin; [b.] March 6, 1981, Alamdea, California; [p.] Laurie Summers and John Meagher; [ed.] Entering 7th grade; [occ.] Student; [memb.] School paper editor, Girls Club Alameda; [oth. writ.] Short stories and poems. [a.] Redwood City, CA.

MEAIKE, TAMMIE
[b.] December 8, 1964, Yuma, Arizona; [p.] Jean and James Hand; [m.] Lance Meaike, May 22, 1991; [ch.] Christinna and Jerry Meaike; [ed.] Antelope Union High; [occ.] Housewife; [memb.] St. John's Lutheran Church; [oth. writ.] Yeah when I write my poems it seems to take my pain away cause its down on paper and its not a letter to anyone, I enjoy writing poems; [pers.] I write my poems with my feelings inside of me and how I feel or what I feel like at the time, I wrote the poem I was going thru some hard times. [a.] Audubon, IA 50025.

MEDINA, MELISSA
[pen.] Murry Full; [b.] August 14, 1979, South Bend, Indiana; [p.] Harold and Mary McNally; [ed.] In grade 8 at the moment; [hon.] Third place in Optimist International Optimist Club, Oratorical contest, on

our oxygen, animals and our rain forest; [pers.] I wish to take life one step at a time, and I hope to be the best I can be. [a.] Regina, Saskatchewan S4S 5X7.

MEDFORD, CONSTANCE
[pen.] Connie; [b.] July 17, 1970, Washington; [p.] Wilburn Yates and Linda Lou McDaniel; [m.] Brian Keith Medford, April 2, 1988; [ch.] Bradley Keith Medford; [occ.] Certified Nurse's Aid; [pers.] I wrote this poem especially for my mother, whom I love very much. [a.] Ellenboro, NC 28040.

MEDVEDEV, ALICE
[b.] September 11, 1980, Moscow, USSR; [p.] Galina Medvedev and Alex Kartashov; [ed.] Walsh Middle School; [occ.] High school student; [pers.] I am 13 and this is my first publication, I am an immigrant and have lived in this country only for two years. I feel very good. [a.] Framingham, MA 01701.

MEIER, ROBIN S.
[b.] December 26, 1960, Poughkeepsie, New York; [p.] Robert and Kathel Greenwood; [m.] Mario Meier, December 30, 1985; [ch.] Conlan Andrew, Arlo Hans and Della Nalina; [ed.] Northwestern Regional High School # 7, Northwestern CT Community College; [occ., membs.] Member of the Hutterian Brethren, which is a total life commitment, we live in complete community of goods as did the Early Christian Church; [oth. writ.] This is my first work to be published though I have written poetry and stories for my family; [pers.] The joy that a life of dedication and love to Jesus and all men brings, also brings appreciation of all aspects of childhood, life, nature and family. This is the source of my poetry. [a.] Rifton, NY 12471.

MEINECKE, GALE GOODFRIEND
[pen.] Gale Goodfriend; [b.] July 8, 1963, Chicago, Illinois; [p.] Alvin and Bernice Goodfriend; [m.] Scott Meinecke, October 10, 1992; [ed.] Mather High School, University of Illinois; [occ.] Pediatric Nursing Supervisor, M & B degree; [memb.] Society of Pediatric Nurses, Association of Pediatric Oncology Nurses, American Nurses Association; [hon.] Peers Award recipient for excellence in scholarship and service; [oth. writ.] And A Nation's Tears (unpublished manuscript), a romantic drama about three children who learn about life during the Civil War; [pers.] My love for children is what motivates my writing, nothing can be compared to a child's curiosity, inate goodness and creativity. [a.] Chicago, IL 60625.

MEJIA, EDGAR
[pen.] Eddie Write; [b.] November 16, 1971, Brownsville, Texas; [p.] Tomasa Naranjo and Eduardo Mejia; [ed.] Oak Park Junior High, Gage Park High and Lewis University; [occ.] Student, Lewis University, Romeoville, Illinois; [memb.] Alpha Gamma Chi Fr, Latin American Student Organization and Aviation Management Society Club; [oth. writ.] Few others sacred poems not yet released for publication; [pers.] It is through poetry that I allow my emotions to be seen. Love and hate are the two things that inspire me to write. [a.] Chicago, IL 60632.

MELENDREZ, JESS
[pen.] Jess Melendrez; [b.] February 13, 1965, Cerritos, California; [p.] Frank and Evelyn Melendrez; [ed.] 12 years school, 7 1/2 Cerritos College; [pers.]

This poem is dedicated to my best friend, my German Shepard Smokey.

MENA, MARIANA
[b.] September 24, East Lansing, Michigan; [p.] Lorenza and Ascencion Mena; [ed.] Sixth grade, Charles Middle School, El Paso, Texas; [occ.] Student; [memb.] Honor Student; [hon.] Honor Student; [pers.] I believe in goodness, honesty, kindness and the love of God. Shel Silverstein ia a big influence in me. his poems are funny and I enjoy them. [a.] El Paso, TX.

MENDOZA, JR., A.
[pen.] A. Mendoza, Jr.; [b.] November 7, 1963, St. Bernard Parish, Louisiana; [p.] Anthony and Linda Mendoza, the two people I thank for their love and support; [ch.] Bethiney Lynn Mendoza (Godchild); [ed.] I am a product of Chalmette High School, one of St. Bernard Parishes fine public schools; [oth. writ.] I have many other unpublished poems; [pers.] I take an abstract look at life, hopefully it shows in my writing. A friend once said " Ya'll just cross his path and he'll write a poem about ya". [a.] Arabi, LA 70032.

MENK, KIRSTEN
[b.] February 11, 1970, Haiger, Germany; [p.] Rudi and Irmtraut Menk; [ed.] Gymnasium Neunkirchen; [occ.] Toolmaker; [memb.] YMCA, Country Dance Club; [oth. writ.] Several country and country-gospel songs which have not been published yet; [pers.] I like to write positive songs and try to put my Christian belief in them. [a.] 57290 Neunkirchen, Germany.

MERAU-ROSS, YVONNE
[pen.] Yvonne Ross; [b.] March 18, 1924, Paris, France; [p.] Germaine Lesain and Roger Merau; [m.] Densil L. Ross (deceased), December 15, 1946; [ch.] Bertrand, Suzanne and Roger; [ed.] High school and business France, Nursing and Health Information Management USA-A.S.; [occ.] Health Information Manager, Nurse; [memb.] AH.IMA, Red Cross, Battle of Normandie, VFW, V.VA, Nature Conservancy, Clearwater, International Health Records; [hon.] Certificate of Appreciation, Battle of Normandie, American Red Cross; [oth. writ.] My Old Coat (poem), " The Prisoner" (true story), The Soldier-Hospitals Are Not Always Sad, (short stories), " The Adventures of Coco, The French Parrot" (poem), The Brooklyn Bridge"; [pers.] I love mankind and all its people, each so different and interesting, yet basically just like me. I am thankful for having lived, studied and worked on two continents, I have had the best of two worlds. [a.] Ferndale, NY.

MERKEL, TAMI
[b.] October 23, 1971, Lincoln, Nebraska; [p.] Ronald and Judy Merkel; [pers.] I wrote this poem as a tribute to my grandmother for her 80th birthday. This poem relates to my philosophy of the influence grandmothers have on their grandchildren. [a.] Omaha, NE.

MERRICK, THAIS V.
[pen.] Darcy; [b.] October 10,1926, Chicago, Illinois; [ed.] U.S.C. Pre-med; [occ.] Semi-retired; [memb.] Pomona Humane Society; [oth. writ.] Short stories for children published in local school magazines; [pers.] Try to tell stories that moralize situations in a pleasant but firm manner. [a.] Pomona, CA.

METKO, BETTY
[b.] May 18, 1922, Chicago, Illinois; [p.] Frank Peter and Anna Schlobohm Keller; [m.] Earl D. Metko, September 22, 1945; [ch.] Lisa M. and Dan E. Metko; [ed.] Steinmetz High School, class of '40; [occ.] Homemaker; [memb.] AARP, '25 Dance Club (Naperville, Il.), Chorales (women's singing chorus), PTA, Dever PTA Chorus; [memb.] National Honor Society, Life PTA Membership, Mother of the Year (from my kids); [oth. writ.] True to life animal poems, four poems published in two separate books, personal poems to friends; [pers.] Learn how to laugh at yourself, don't waste your time on regrets, learn to enjoy everything. [a.] Chicago, IL 60635.

METROS, ROSE
[b.] June 28, 1932, Chicago, Illinois; [p.] Katherine and Gust Metros; [ed.] Austin High, Chicago Teachers College, University of Chicago; [occ.] Former teacher, free-lance writer; [memb.] American Association for Retired Persons, St. George Green Orthodox Church; [hon.] National Honor Society; [oth. writ.] Elementary school newspaper " The McLavenite Encyclopedia Britannica", Society For Visual Education", Sears Roebuck and Company, these were technical writings; [pers.] I am writing poetry to reflect the struggle and survival of disabled persons. [a.] Chicago, IL 60657.

MEYER, HENRY J.
[b.] September 21, 1940, Cleveland, Ohio; [ed.] BBA, Ohio University, Athens, Ohio, 1963; [occ.] Computing Professional (since 1964); [memb.] Mensa (inactive); [oth. writ.] Works of 60-90 lines titled " Life", " Truth", "War", "do", "$", " Times", "Each Other", " Man and Nature", " Governing", " Progress", unpublished, except as individual copies to c., 1000 people, about 100 of whom have responded, including Nobel Laureates, ambassadors, senators, governors, mayors, also c. 10,000 lines on 30-40 other topics, not yet composed into formal works; [pers.] I regard my work as simply "thought", though most who comment on it commend my " poetry". [a.] University Heights, OH 4418.

MEYER, STEPHEN
[pen.] Zhivago in L.A.; [b.] June 14, 1945, New York City, New York; [p.] Arthur and Estelle Myer; [m.] Lisa, May 26, 1993; [ch.] Justin, age 16, 1st marriage; [ed.] B.A.-University of Miami, Coral Gables, Florida; [occ.] Writer/consultant; [hon.] L.A. Writer's Silver Crest Award-1986; [oth. writ.] Songs, including "Everytime I Hear An Elvis Presley Song I Cry"; [pers.] " The supreme happiness in life is the conviction we are loved". [a.] Studio CIty, CA 91604.

MICEK, JOHN L.
[b.] June 3, 1970, Hartford, Connecticut; [ed.] Manhattanville College, Purchase, New York; [occ.] Journalist; [pers.] Remember Hemingway, find the mot juste, and write the truest sentence that you know. [a.] Canton, CT.

MILIARESIS, CRISTINA MARIA
[b.] March 3,1975, New York, New York; [p.] Licia and George Miliaresis; [hon.] National Honor Society, Principal's Honor Roll, PTSA Scholarship; [oth.writ.] Several poems published in the Olive Branch, Dept of Defense Schools poetry anthology; [pers.] "Give me by all means the shorter and nobler

life, instead of one that is longer but of less account", Epictetus. [a.] Jackson Heights, NY.

MILLER III, HANK
[b.] November 12, 1976, Camden, New Jersey; [p.] Lois and Henry Miller; [ed.] Collingswood High School, sophomore; [occ.] Would like to be a computer programmer; [memb.] Boy Scouts of America, St. Pauls Lutheran Youth Group; [hon.] Many trophies for baseball and soccer, merits for Boy Scouts of America, holding Rank of Star; [oth. writ.] Several unpublished poems, I will soon submit into contests and newspapers; [pers.] I hope to show people that there's more to life than what is right in front of their faces. [a.] Collingswood, NJ 08108.

MILLER, HELEN ELIZABETH (DAILY)
[pen.] Helen Daily; [b.] February 21, 1918, Fairmount, Indiana; [p.] Olive E. (Johnson) and James Arthur Daly; [m.] Deceased, November 1, 1936; [ch.] James P., Julia E., Joan E., Janice E., Jean E., Robert E. and J. Richard; [ed.] Fairmount High School, 1936; [occ.] Retired glass worker; [memb.] First Christian Church, Christian Women's Fellowship, GPPAW Local # 38 ; [hon.] Girls Athletic Award, Extra Curricular Award - Sub-teaching and making signs for the school. [a.] Marion, IN.

MILLER, JACKIE
[pen.] Jackie Miller; [b.] September 25, (6), Vancouver, BC.; [p.] Barbara Mickels and Jack Worrall; [m.] Gary Miller, March 13, 1957; [ch.] Amanda JoAnn, Michelle Anne, Kathleen Luanne (P.K.U. child); [ed.] Grade 12, Salmo, B.C., Jr., Sr. Secondary, Salmo, BC; [occ.] Mom; [memb.] Director, Canadian Society for Metabolic Disease; [oth. writ.] Letters to local newspapers regarding the Canadian Society for Metabolic Disease, regarding exposure and funding for our kids; [pers.] I would like to dedicate my poem to The Biochemical Diseases Clinic at B.C. Children's Hospital and Dr. Arnie Emery, Laurie, Mary and " of course Amanda, Michelle and Katie". [a.] Ladner, BC V4K 3H4 Canada.

MILLER, JACQUELYNN RAE
[pen.] Jackie; [b.] July 14, 1978, Halifax, Nova Scotia; [p.] Connie and Brian Miller; [sib.] 1 brother, Scott; [ed.] Attends Hants North Rural High School; [occ.] Grade nine student; [hon.] High Honors Student (Principal's List); [pers.] I enjoy music, reading and sports.[a.] Nova Scotia, Canada.

MILLER, JENNIFER
[b.] April 16, 1977, Princeton, BC. [p.] Robert and Valerie Miller; [ed.] High school student, grade 10, Barriere Secondary; [occ.] Student; [memb.] Peer Counselling Club; [pers.] After high school I want to study psychology and work with emotionally disturbed children. [a.] Barriere,BC V0E 1E0.

MILLER, KIMBERLY ELAINE
[b.] January 2, 1972, Bainbridge, Georgia; [p.] Slyvester and Jessie Mae Harris, John Henry and Christine Malone; [ed.] Bainbridge High School, Bainbridge College; [pers.] Art is the agony within a silent heart that gives it a need for poetic expression.

MILLER, SHARON A. (MRS.)
[b.] April 28, 1947, Columbus, Ohio; [p.] Mr. and Mrs. Lonnie Pigg; [m.] John R. Miller, Sr., October 6, 1977; [ch.] Norene Elizabeth (age 12) and John R.

Miller, Jr., (age 14); [ed.] North High School, Columbus, Ohio 1965; [occ.] Farm wife, mother and homeschool teacher; [memb.] Family gospel group called Rush County Believers, and church affiliation; [hon.] Volunteer awards from local nursing homes and residential facilities; [pers.] My poems reflect my feelings about God, my family, and everyday life. My thoughts simply come from my heart. [a.] Rushville, IN 46173.

MILLS, JERE'
[pen.] Jere' Mills; [b.] February 28, 1978, Long Beach, California; [p.] Julie and James Mills; [ed.] High school, 9th grade; [occ.] Student; [hon.] Certificate of Merit for Scholastic Achievement 1991, participation and achievement in the C Sulb Young Writers Camp 1989; [oth. writ.] I have written a couple of stories and more poems, but none of them have been published; [pers.] I love to write, and I hope that in the near future my poems will come clear to someone and help them out. [a.] Colton, CA 92324.

MILLS, JON K. (Psy.D.)
[pen.] Jon Mills; [b.] November 3, 1964, Springfield, Illinois; [p.] Richard and Rachel Mills; [ch.] McKensi Rae Mills, age 5; [ed.] Doctor of Psychology degree, in Clinical Psychology from the Illinois School of Professional Psych.; [occ.] Assistant Professor of Psychology, Director of Training, Graduate Program Lewis University; [hon.] Outstanding Doctor Graduate of the Year Award, 1992; [oth. writ.] Numerous articles published in professional journals;[pers.] Existential and psychoanalytic principles permeate my thinking. Truth can always be found within. [a.] Romeoville, IL.

MILTON, CHRISTINE SNYDER
[b.] May 21, 1949, War, West Virginia; [p.] Forrest Dale and Hazel Marie Snyder; [m.] William Alan Milton, November 25; [ch.] Curtis Randall Aragon, (grandchildren) Jaime Lynn Aragon; [ed.] Hampton High School; [occ.] Artist/writer and homemaker; [memb.] Memorial Baptist Church, American Red Cross; [oth. writ.] At this time I have several poems under contract for possible publication; [pers.] I try to write from my heart, to be honest about the emotions and beliefs that I have. Gibran and Rod McKuen are two of my favorite poets. [a.] Hampton, VA 23661.

MINES, ROSETTE
[b.] April 1, 1929, Brooklyn, New York; [p.] Samuel and Esther Mines; [ed.] Erasmus High School, Brooklyn, night courses in advanced art, Brooklyn College, 12 years; [occ.] Own business, customer service; [memb.] Artist League of Brooklyn; [hon.] Poetry, Honorable Mention World of Poetry-1991, will be in Feelings Magazine-1993; [oth. writ.]" Lonely", " Last Rose of Summer" and " Feelings," I was published in World of Poetry -1991, I will be in 1993 in _Feelings_ magazine summer and fall; [pers.] My poems come from things as simple as a leaf twirling on the ground or a big HELLO from the cashier in the subway station. The friendly faces and things all around us seem to create a need deep in me to be expressed. Hoping you too will see and fill my inner needs. [a.] Brooklyn, NY 11218.

MINNIS, ROBERT B.
[pen.] Barry Minnis; [b.] March 26, 1970, Nashville, Tennessee; [p.] Judy Wilson and Kelly Minnis; [m.] Cynthia M. Minnis, November 20, 1989; [ch.] Barry

Matthew and Kayla Marie Minnis; [ed.] Springfield High School; [occ.] Manager of Ponderosa, Springfield, Tennessee; [hon.] President, Jobs for Tennessee graduates, Dela; [pers.] I have been greatly influenced by my friends and family to accomplish the highest goals in everything I do. [a.] Springfield, TN 37172.

MITCHELL, RAYMOND
[b.] November 3, 1920, Newcastle upon Tyne, U.K.; [p.] Charles and Margaret Ann Mitchell; [m.] Joan Mitchell (nee Jeffrey), August 29, 1953; [ch.] Jacqueline, Sandra, Carolyn and Jonathan Jeffrey; [ed.] Heaton Grammar School, Newcastle upon Tyne; [occ.] Civil Engineer (Rtd); [memb.] Institution of Civil Engineers, Royal Marines Historical Society, Normandy Veterans Association; [hon.] WWII Campaign medals, 1939-45 Star, Italy Star, France and Germany Star, Defence Medal, War Medal; [oth. writ.] Several technical articles and reports, largely on Waste Derived Fuel, I published book "Marine Commando" (Sicily and Salermo) and a follow-up (NW Europe) ready, a history of 41 Ronal Marines Commando; [pers.] My sole aim is to present the facts as I see them, whether in scientific matters, historical events or human relationships. [a.] Newcastle upon Tyne, NE7 7BB England UK.

MITCHELL, TIM
[b.] October 22, 1963, Omaha, Nebraska; [p.] Charles Thomas and Florence Marie (Lutwitze) Mitchell; [ed.] St. Cecilia's Elementary, Cathedral High, St. John's U. (MN), Creighton U., Un-Omaha (B.G.S./M.A.-English); [occ.] Cataloging assistant at Un-Omaha Library/grad. assistant-Clarion U.(P.A.) Library Science Department (Sp "93/Fall '93); [memb.] Phia Kappa Phi, Alpha Sigma Lambda, Golden Key National Honor Societies; [oth. writ.] The Shaping of Real Time, a study of chapters 24, 25, 26 in The Log from the Sea of Cortez, John Steinbeck Library, Archives Salinas, CA. [a.] Omaha, NE 68131-1437.

MIZE, ERIN MAUREEN
[pen.] Erin M. Mize; [b.] February 3, 1971, Plattsburgh, New York; [p.] Mr. and Mrs. David E. Mize; [ed.] Graduate of Wesleyan College, Macon, Georgia, high school, William Henry Shaw, Columbus, Georgia; [occ.] Worker/volunteer, Museum of Arts and Sciences; [memb.] Catholic Campus Ministry; [hon.] Sang in the Wesleyan Concert Choir and sang with the Macon Symphony Orchestra's " Side by Side" Concert Choir; [pers.] Without music, words or signs the world would be dead, so always look and listen or the world will pass-away. [a.] Macon, GA 31204.

MOAT, MARION A.
[pen.] Moh; [b.] Chester, Pennsylvania; [p.] Celestine and Chesterfield L. Moat; [ch.] Eddie Jamal and Liimab Imaui; [ed.] Sociology, U.D.C.; [hon.] Dean's List; [oth. writ.] True Blues, True Blues II and Hearts Near; [pers.] To give one's self to the development of mankind, is to be one who lives a glorious life. [a.] Washington, DC 20002.

MOBLEY, PAXTON
[b.] September 10, 1970, Shreveport, Louisiana; [p.] Tommy Mobley and Peggy Jones; [ed.] B.A., Queens College, Charlotte, North Carolina, Concentration Studio Art/Art History; [occ.] Surreal painter/sculptor; [hon.] Artist of The Year, Queens College,

Charlotte, North Carolina, National Dean's List 91; [oth. writ.] Short story published in Queens College Literary pamphlet and Athens State College Literary pamphlet; [pers.] I hope to bring to life, in those who observe my art, the imaginative world that we hold in the depth of our minds. [a.] Monterey, CA 93940.

MOECKEL, DEBI HENSLEY
[b.] October 19, 1955, Hazard, Kentucky; [p.] Paul and Ernestine Hensley; [m.] Richard Moeckel, December 13, 1986; [ed.] Hazard High, University of Kentucky. [a.] Palm Harbor, FL 34684.

MOEN, GEORGIANNA
[b.] February 22, 1911, Clearbrook, Minnesota; [p.] Herman and Minnie Rydren; [m.] James Moen, May 25, 1931; [ch.] Ernest, James, David (deceased), Richard, Judy and Mary; [ed.] 8th grade Clearbrook High School, 1 1/2 college; [occ.] Farmer's wife; [memb.] Senior Citizen's Elim Lutheran Brethren Church; [hon.] 1979 Senior Citizen Queen, Clearwater County; [oth. writ.] Farm Journals, Clearwater County Poet used in special occasions; [pers.] Early American poets inspired my thoughts and desire to write and compose poetry. [a.] Clearbrook, MN 56634.

MOKER, MARISA ANNE
[b.] September 18, 1981, Long Beach, California; [p.] Russell and Sheila Moker; [ed.] Home schooled by mother, 2nd -5th, West Sedona School; [occ.] Student; [memb.] Girl Scouts; [hon.] Scholastic Honor Roll. [a.] Sedona, AZ 86339.

MOLLER, SHARON
[pen.] C.B.S.; [b.] July 15, 1952, Stratford, Iowa; [p.] Marvin and Pauline Peterson (father deceased); [m.] Divorced; [ch.] Rhiannon Lynne and Ryan Alan; [ed.] Stratford High School, Bellevue College (B.A.) Psychology Sociology, Masters of Art in Management in progress, Bellevue College; [occ.] Asst. Director to Academic Advising, Bellevue College, Bellevuene; [hon.] Alpha Chi Honor Society, Dean's List, Who's Who American University, Magna Cum Laude; [oth. writ.] The Bellwether, Bellevue College's publishing of poems; [pers.] Please, Lord teach us to laugh again, but God, don't ever let us forget that we cried, your attitude determines your attitude. [a.] Bellevue, NE 68005.

MONCRIEF JR., CHARLES ROBERT
[pen.] Charles; [b.] September 18, 1935, Thomasville, Georgia; [p.] Essie White and Charles Robert Montcrief, Sr.; [m.] Charlotte Ann Montcrief, February 14, 1988; [ch.] Charles Greg, Joni, Cindy, Charles Robert, Nicolette Ca-Tice and Lisa; [ed.] Thomasville Senior High, Bob Jones University, University of Southern California, University of Santa Barbara; [occ.] Organizational Consultant, trainer; [memb.] American Management Association, American Society for Training and Development, Los Angeles Federal Executive Board-College Federal Council; [hon.] Education Partnership Award 1985-1986-1987; [oth. writ.] Sparrowgrass Poetry Forum, Archives of the Arts; [pers.] Keep on keeping on-anything worth doing is worth doing right. [a.] Camanillo, CA 93012.

MONTGOMERY, SARA
[b.] February 2, 1971, Kingston, Ontario Canada; [ed.] Queen's University; [occ.] Student; [oth. writ.] Just started writing my first novel; [pers.] Sometimes

it is best to live as if there is no middle ground, for only on these outer fringes can true intensity of the soul be found. [a.] Kingston, Ontario Canada K7L 4V1.

MOONEY, DIANE E.
[b.] June 11, 1963, Imperial, Sask, Canada; [p.] David Norman and Racheal Cleone Mooney; [ed.] Imperial School, Sask, S.T.I., Moose Jaw, Sask., N.A.I.T., Edmonton, A.B.; [occ.] Chef; [pers.] Positions open immediately, good, honest, hard working individuals needed to help care for Mother Earth, on the job training. [a.] Edmonton, Alberta Canada T5H 3N3.

MOONEY, FRANCES D.
[pen.] Dollie; [b.] December 27, 1934, Clintwood, Virginia; [p.] Fassie and Earnest Mullins; [m.] Crit Mooney, June 6, 1990; [ch.] Gary-deceased, Billy, Greg, Lisa and Randy; [ed.] High school-Clintwood, GED-1990, Huntsville, AL; [occ.] Retail sales, housewife and mother; [memb.] Valley Fellowship, Huntsville, AL., 700 Club; [hon.] The handmade cards and gifts of my children and their love; [oth. writ.] Several poems, not published, written for family members; [pers.] My mother died when I was three months old, my grandparents raised me. My biggest desire was and is to be a good mother and a friend. [a.] Clintwood, VA.

MOORE, HEATHER
[pen.] Heather Moore; [b.] September 19,1977, Orange, Texas; [p.] Shiela Moore; [ed.] Vidor High School; [occ.] I'm not old enough to work yet; [oth. writ.] Flowers, Rain, Ode to A Mother, The Tree, People to Love; [pers.] I believe everyone is a work of art in the things they do and say. I value life and try to get the most out of it. If I touched just one person with my poetry that's good enough for me. [a.] Vidor, TX.

MOORE, PATRICIA W.
[pen.] Trish; [b.] April 24, 1963, Walsh, Colorado; [p.] Bill and Cherie Beamer; [m.] Dave "O" Moore, March 19, 1993; [ch.] David and Valerie McCready and step-daughter, Crystal Moore; [oth. writ.] I have a lot of other poems, all written about what I've felt about the "times " in my life; [pers.] Life in general is deep down in your soul. How you choose to live it, is what will make you whole. [a.] Phoenix, AZ.

MOORE, PAUL ALLEN
[b.] October 9, 1975, Columbus, Ohio; [p.] Ernest Lee and Wilma Jean Moore; [ed.] Junior in West High School; [occ.] Mail sorter; [hon.] Honor roll at school; [oth. writ.] A lot of unpublished poetry; [pers.] I never tell people the meaning of my poetry, I always let people form their own meanings. If I told them, then I would control their minds, because they would agree with my meaning. [a.] Columbus, OH 43204.

MOORE, PEGGY L.
[b.] November 26, 1930, Parsons, West Virginia; [p.] Roy and Regina Vanscoy; [m.] Theodore Moore; [ch.] Deborah Kaye and Vicki Lynne; [ed.] Elkins (WOA) High School; [occ.] Retired, worked in Traffic and Transportation; [oth. writ.] " Before Tomorrow"; [pers.] This poem was written as a tribute to my dad, who went to be with our Lord, October 1, 1992. [a.] Niles, OH.

MORALES, C. NICHOLAS
[b.] February 8,1969, Elmhurst, New York; [p.] Nicholas and Carmen Morales; [ed.] John Bowne High School, Queens Borough Community College; [occ.] Student of Psychology, Music, Astrology and poetry; [pers.] Life is a mystery to be lived which reveals itself to those whose are willing. [a.] Flushing, NY.

MORALEZ, JESSICA
[pen.] Jessica Moralez; [b.] January 21, 1980, Long Beach, California; [p.] Cindy and Max Bertzing, Nacho and Teresa Moralez; [ed.] I am currently attending Nicolas Junior High and in 7th grade; [hon.] In elementary school I received an award for writing; [oth. writ.] In my spare time I love to express my feelings through the poems I write; [pers.] I'd like to thank my parents and best friend Kimberly Clark for their support and encouragement. [a.] Fullerton, CA.

MORAMARCO, ADAM
[b.] October 19, 1970, Long Island, New York; [p.] Cathy and Gene Moramarco; [ed.] Carle Place High, Fairleigh Dickinson University, Adelphi University; [occ.] Student/tutor; [memb.] Humane Society; [hon.] Honor's List at Fairleigh Dickinson, Academic Honor Scholarship to Adelphi University; [pers.] My interest of writing was introduced and influenced by my English teacher Mrs. Ziminiski and my inspiration is dedicated to a special freind-words alone can not only be heard they can be seen and felt, presentation is the key. [a.] Westbury, NY.

MORES, JEFF
[b.] January 19,1974, Joliet, Illinois; [p.] Robert and Carol Mores; [ed.] St. Paul The Apostle grade school, Joliet West High School, Millikin University; [hon.] Who's Who Among American High School Students 1992, 1st place award in high school Art Show, member of N.H.S. 1990-1992, Honorable Mention All Area in football 1992; [oth. writ.] I have written many other poems over the years but nothing that has been published, "The Hourglass" is the first poem I've ever entered into a contest; [pers.] Music inspires me to write poetry. Jimi Hendrix and Dave Mustaine are my biggest poetic influences, I try to put deep thought into my poetry. I also enjoy making/creating art and participating in sports. [a.] Joliet, IL.

MORGAN, RUTH BARBARA
[b.] Cincinnati, Ohio; [p.] Frank Morgan and Barbara Koehler; [ch.] Sons David and Bob, grandchildren, Christopher, Crystal and Justin; [occ.] Administrative Secretary and Certified Dental Assistant; [hon.] U.S. Patent, 1990 Keyboards for Homes, Inc., Instant Typing Computer Keyboard; [pers.] The Golden Rule, "Do Unto Others As You Would Have Them Do Unto You", Psalm 19: verse 14, prayer my grandmother taught when I was 8, " May the words of my mouth and the meditation of my heart, be acceptable in thy sight oh Lord, my strength and my Redeemer". [a.] Arlington, VA.

MORLEY, ALBERT JOHN
[pen.] John Morley; [b.] October 29, 1921, London, England; [m.] Deceased, 1950; [ch.] 2; [ed.] English; [occ.] Retired; [hon.] Battle of Britain Medal and Nurma Star; [oth. writ.] 3 unpublished children's books of poetry; [pers.] I love him who lives in order to know and seems to know in order to live. [a.] Tehachapi, CA 93561.

MORRISON, DANIEL DAVID
[pen.] Daniel David Morrison; [b.] November 20, 1931, Sarasota, Florida, (date of death March 13, 1993); [p.] Warren and Anne Morrison; [m.] Jeannee Elswick-Morrison, November 21, 1992; [ch.] Eric, Robin, Lisa and J.J.; [ed.] B.S. -Florida State University, (was working on Ph.D. when he died); [occ.] U.S.A.F. Major (retired) pilot; [hon.] Several military honors and awards; [pers.] Daniel believed music and poetry were food for the mind and soul. [a.] Quincy, FL 32351.

MORRISON, DELORES JEAN
[pen.] Delores Jean Morrison; [b.] October 20, 1939, Lake Providence, Louisiana; [p.] Fred and Essie Harris; [m.] Norman Morrison; [ch.] Carol A. Johnson and Sharon M. Irvine; [ed.] Graduate of Christian Fenger High School, June 24, 1957; [occ.] Universal teller for Northern Trust Bank; [hon.] Certificate for role in grammar school play " Hansel and Gretel"; [oth. writ.] Unpublished poems that vary in style and content; [pers.] My philosophy of life is to fill your heart with love, surround yourself with beauty, let your mind create, all the negative, alleviate, let nature warm your soul and let the good book take control. [a.] Chicago, IL 60628.

MORRISON, ELIZABETH
[b.] August 5, 1947, Trenton, Michigan; [p.] Adopted by Henry and Gladys Erat; [m.] David Morrison, August 26, 1990; [ch.] Too many to mention here; [ed.] Gaylord High, M.S.U. and U. of D.; [occ.] Teacher of History and freshman English; [memb.] Circle of Life Lutheran Church, Northern Cheyenne Tribe by Marriage; [oth. writ.] This is my first published work, I hope to be able to submit more in the future; [pers.] I write what I feel in my heart, I am proud to be an American Indian. [a.] Busby, MT 59016.

MORTON, CHARLES W.
[b.] August 6, 1916, Knoxville, Tennessee; [p.] William P. and Jennie Morton; [m.] Norma Morton, January 19, 1946; [ch.] Nancy Ann Vest; [ed.] B.A. University of Tennessee, M B A University of Indiana; [occ.] U.S. Air Force retired; [memb.] Military Order of World Wars, Veterans of Foreign Wars; [hon.] World of Poetry "Golden Poet Award" 1991, numerous military awards; [oth. writ.] Poem "Women's Rights" published by World of Poetry. A conference presentation "Managing A Value Engineering Program" in Library of Congress; [pers.] Poetry through ear appeal and emphasis on nouns and verbs is more communicative than conventional verbage or writings. Ear appeal improves attention as President Lincoln's famous words "Four Score and Seven Years ago". [a.] San Bernardino, CA.

MOSLEY, BOBBIE JO
[b.] July 25, 1978, Ridgecrest, California; [p.] Leo and Robbin Mosley, Jr.; [ed.] 10 grade. [a.] Wynona, OK 74084.

MOSQUEDA, CHRISTINA
[b.] August 23, 1978, Tulare, California; [p.] Mike and Irene Mosqueda; [sibs.] Tony Joseph, Melissa Angelica and Serena Deborah; [ed.] Freshman at Mt. Whitney High School in Visalia, California; [occ.] Volunteer at YMCA, and volunteer with the disabled; [oth. writ.] I have written other poems but never published them. [a.] Visalia, CA.

MOSS, JOY CARR
[pen.] Joy Carr Moss; [b.] April 22, 1940, Bells, Tennessee (Crockett County); [p.] Raphael Lazelle Carr and Annie Kate Shaw; [m.] Jimmy Joe Moss, January 26, 1958; [ch.] Jimmy Michael, Shirley Jean, Linda Loy, David Raphael and Natalie Diane; [ed.] Grade school, Anderson Grammar School, Brownsville, TN. and high school -Haywood County High School, Brownsville, Tennessee; [occ.] Retired ATM Operations Officer, Union Planters National Bank, Memphis and retired part-time instructor at State Technical Institute at Memphis; [memb.] American Bankers Association; [hon.] Employee of the Month for June 1982, while at Union Planters National Bank, Memphis; [oth. writ.] I am in the process of writing a book of poems and a non-fiction novel. I have never had anything published; [pers.] I strive to reflect the beauty of personal memories and dreams in my writings. I have been greatly influenced by my late paternal grandmother who was a school teacher and two aunts who helped raised me. [a.] Memphis, TN.

MOSWEUNYANE, DAMA
[pen.] Foster; [b.] July 31, 1964, Serowe, Botswana; [p.] Leabanehg and Galefmele Mosweunyane; [ch.] Thato Gobudzlwe; [ed.] Diploma in Adult Education, University of Botswana; [occ.] Community Development Officer, Nata Extension Area; [memb.] Roman Catholic Church; [pers.] I intend to write poems to emulate Professor David Rubadirz who taught me poetry during my study at the university. My poems will reflect suffering of the people. [a.] Nata Botswana, South Africa.

MOZDZYNSKI, JACEK
[b.] February 6, 1960, Warsaw, Poland; [p.] Wanda and Edmund Mozdzynski; [m.] Monika Mozdzynski, November 12, 1989; [ch.] Karolina Mozdzynski; [ed.] High school; [occ.] Driver; [oth. writ.] None in U.S.A., some in Poland not published yet; [pers.] We need a new creative christian life. Do not look too far, life is around you, just reach you hand and you will fill it. I strive to tell anyone that now is the time to think, what happened with human beings, we have to have much more respect for ourselves, if not we will become beast, thinking again is the future. [a.] Portland, ME 04102.

MPATSOS, KATHY
[b.] January 27, 1978, Toronto, Canada; [p.] Athanasios (Tom) and Chrisoula (Soula) Mpatsos; [ed.] David and Mary Thomson Collegiate; [occ.] Full time student; [hon.] Speech Arts Award and Creative Writing Award; [oth. writ.] Several other poems and stories; [pers.] Those who work hard in what they believe in will be rewarded with success and happiness. [a.] Scarborough, Ontario Canada M2J 1R6.

MUELLING, SHAYNE
[b.] December 31, 1980, Rutland, Vermont; [p.] Maureen and Ronald Muelling; [ed.] 7th grade, Barstow School; [oth. writ.] Several other poems; [pers.] This poem is a part of me, for it reflects part of my soul. I hope that you keep it close to your heart as do I. I would also like to dedicate this poem to my wonderful sister Rowan, who gave me the little push that I needed.

MUHAMMAD, ALI
[pen.] Ali; [b.] September 28, 1971, Harvey, Illinois; [p.] Hanan Muhammad; [ed.] Rust College, Holly Springs, MS 38635; [occ.] College student; [hon.] President's List, Sigma Tau Delta (English) Honor Society; [oth. writ.] Many poems about relationships and social aspects; [pers.] Expression comes from the soul, let yourself go. [a.] Chicago, IL 60617.

MULDER, ZELLA S.
[pen.] Zella; [b.] July 24, 1919, Burley, Idaho; [hon.] Poetry awards from local radio stations; [oth. writ.] Poetry has always been my first love but I have just completed my life history; [pers.] The inspiration for this poem was because of a very dear friend who had undergone years of Cancer treatments on her face, she was so depressed and felt that her looks were unpleasant to others, this poem was my way of showing her how truly beautiful she is to all that know her. [a.] Twin Falls, ID.

MULLIGAN, EUGENIA R.
[pen.] Jean Mulligan; [b.] January 17, 1932, Greenpoint, Brooklyn, New York; [p.] Effie and Bernard Meyer; [m.] Thomas Michael Mulligan, April 5, 1953; [ch.] Lynn, Thomas A., David, (grandchildren) Shannon, Darren, Jennifer and Thomas II; [ed.] Washington Irving High School, graduate of Institute of Children's Literature, Connecticut; [occ.] Housewife, firematic volunteer; [memb.] Secretary Allied Community Fire Co., Clintondale, New York, Ulster County Fire Police Association, provisional Director State N.Y. Fire Police Association, Ulster Co. Firemen's Association, Clintondale Friends Church, Education Committee; [hon.] For service on committee, Certificate Award 1983 Firefighters Burn Fund, soft ball marathon, plaque 1993 dedicated Service Award, Ulster County Fire Police Association (secretary 10 years), I am also a past secretary-treasurer of NYS Fire Police, Area 2 (7 years); [oth. writ.] Many children's stories, numerous scripts, plays, skits, songs and poems: Scouting and churches, poetry read on WKIP radio, Poughkeepsie, New York, during Burn Fund Marathon 1982 and 1983, article (firematic) in the Consumer Report Newspaper, various poems and articles in Firematic Newspapers: [pers.] I believe there is nothing more precious than a friend, for you never know when you need one. I have delighted in sharing my God given talents in life with others, especially friends. [a.] Highland, NY 12528-2246.

MURELLO, STACEY
[b.] April 24, 1979, Webster Spring, West Virginia; [p.] Frank and Donna Murello; [ed.] Finished 8th grade in June of 93, Webster Springs Junior High School, WV; [memb.] Former basketball and softball player, cheerleader, in school bands as well as a Heavy Metal Band; [hon.] First place and 2nd place in school writing contest, honor roll, many cheerleading awards, band awards; [oth. writ.] Many other poems and short stories which have won awards in the 5th and 6th grades though none have been published. [a.] Parcoal, WV 26288.

MURILLO, JANET A.
[b.] October 30, 1942, Kingston, Jamaica West Indies; [ed.] Graduated from University of the West Indies and University of Puerto Rico; [occ.] Teacher of English and Spanish; [oth. writ.] Materials for teach-

ing Spanish as a second language, one short story in English published in New York in 1989. [a.] Miami, Fl.

MURNEY, JOHN C.
[b.] August 9,1971, Regina, Saskatchewan, Canada; [p.] Kelly and Mary Murney; [m.] Single; [ed.] High school diploma 1989, Broadcast certificate, Prairie Broadcast 1991/ Training Institute, Regina Sk., Canada; [occ.] Radio Reporter/anchor at 900 CKBI/ Power 99FM Radio, Prince Albert, Sk.; [memb.] None current; [hon.] Academic Awards in high school, writing awards for Royal Canadian Legion, oratorical awards in high school, high school drama awards, two high school debating awards, one curling (sport) award; [oth. writ.] Nothing published; [pers.] Regardless a person's background, all people share three qualities that make us equal, we all have minds, we all harbour emotions and we all dream dreams. [a.] Prince Albert, Sask., Canada S6V 3S1.

MURPHY, JR., BOB
[b.] August 3, 1958, Sterling, Illinois; [p.] Bob and JoAnn Murphy, Sr.; [ch.] Jeremy Lee and Brittany Diane; [ed.] Sterling High School; [occ.] Disabled; [oth. writ.] Poems published in local newspapers; [pers.] I always write about my own feelings and experiences of life, as well as feelings of people I know. [a.] Iowa City, IA.

MURPHY, L.K.C.
[b.] January 9, 1930, San Francisco, California; [p.] Joseph and Eva; [ed.] M.A. Special Education; [occ.] Retired teacher of 30 years; [memb.] CTA, NEA, AAUW, Haynie Grange, Custer, WA, DUPI Garden Club, Aftermath (Women's Club); [oth. writ.] Innumerable " Educationist" tracts in " Educationese"; [pers.] I hope to continue my retirement actively pursing humanitarian and creative aims. [a.] Blaine, WA 98231-3076.

MURRAY, JANA
[b.] July 5, 1980, Elkins Park, Pennsylvania; [p.] Jana Ann and James Eli Murray; [ed.] Hope Lutheran Elementary School and I am still attending McConnellsburg High School; [memb.] Library, Nature Center; [hon.] Citizenship Award, school honor roll, softball; [oth. writ.] Violet Hill (short story), Fear, My Jar and other poems, I am previously writing another short story; [pers.] All of the poems I write have a meaning behind them whether it be a dream I had, a feeling for humor or the way I see the future, it's up to you to find the meaning. [a.] McConnellsburg, PA 17233.

MURRAY, RACHAEL
[b.] June 17, 1975, Galesburg, Illinois; [p.] Lois Chisholm and Greg Murray (divorced); [ed.] Knoxville High and transferred to Macomb High;[occ.] Student; [oth. writ.] Wrote for school paper "Sentinel", published poem in "Treasured Poems of America" winter 1991, fiction short story published; [pers.] My poetry comes to me in bursts of inspiration, if I don't write it down immediately, it disappears. This poem was on such burst. [a.] Macomb, IL 61455.

MURRELL, SHELDINE
[b.] December 20, 1978, Brooklyn, New York; [p.] Lucille and Lemuel Murrell; [sib.] Todd Murrell; [ed.] Student of Springfield Garden High School;

[memb.] Member of Springfield Gardens Future Business Leaders of America- Church-St. Barnabas Episcopal; [hon.] Award in academic excellence in English, merit and handwriting skills; [pers.] I have been inspired by great poets like Maya Angelou and I hope that people can someday be inspired by my work also. [a.] Queens Village, NY.

MUZIKIR, JALEES
[b.] January 30, 1974, Washington, District of Columbia; [[p.] Abdul and Sultana Muzikir; [ed.] The Islamic Saudi Academy, The American University; [occ.] College student; [memb.] Washington Arlington Catholic, Forensic League, Northern Virginia Speech League; [hon.] Qur'an recitation contest 1st Director Generals Award, Principals Award, Science Fair Regionals; [oth. writ.] Several poems, stories and artwork published in high school literary magazine; [pers.] Above all I thank the Creator for receiving such an honor. I also thank my parents, A.R and B.R. for always encouraging me to pursue my writing. They have helped me achieve my most desired personal goal. [a.] Silver Spring, MD.

MYERS, MARSHA (AGE 14)
[b.] June 3, 1978, Morgan City, Louisiana; [p.] Sandra and David Cantrell, Marshall and Ruth Myers; [ed.] Ellender High School; [oth. writ.] None published; [pers.] I write what I know and what my imagination enables me too. [a.] Houma, LA.

MYERS, MARY LOUISE
[b.] May 6, 1945, Roanoke, Virginia; [p.] James Ernest Walker (father); [m.] Dennis Ray Myers, Sr., November 4, 1961; [ch.] Cynthia, Penny, Tammy, Laura and Dennis Jr.; [ed.] Lord Batetourt High; [occ.] Homemaker; [memb.] Lighthouse Baptist Church; [oth. writ.] I have written two songs and several poems, (I strive to reflect the beauty of God in my writings). [a.] Rocky Mt., VA.

MYRA, TINA MICHELLE
[pen.] Bubber and Tinker; [b.] February 9, 1967, Lunenburg Hospital; [p.] Carmon and Ella Myra; [ed.] Grade 10; [occ.] Attending Forest Heights Community School; [pers.] I enjoy writing about nature in the way I see it and would like others to see it too. [a.] Lun, Co, Nova Scotia

NAND, VINEETA
[b.] march 24, 1975, Suva, Fiji Islands; [p.] Bechan Satyanand I.S.O. and Prabha Satyanand; [ed.] Samabula Primary School, Yat-Sen Secondary School; [occ.] School student, Yat-Sen Secondary School; [memb.] South Pacific Action Committee on Human Ecology and Environment (Spachee), Yon Jun Do International; [oth. writ.] Poems on prejudice, religion, love and life, some of which have been published in The Yat-Sen Secondary School magazines 1991 and 1992; [pers.] Appreciate the gift of life that God has given to you, prepare your gift to God, a life lived righteously, a life lived true. [a.] Samabula, Fiji Islands.

NAPPI, ROBERT ANDREW
[pen.] R.A. Nappi; [b.] September 26, 1954, Yonkers, New York; [p.] Rocco and Francis; [m.] Single; [ed.] Saunders T & T High School; [occ.] Construction Worker; [memb.] U.S. Army Signal Corps; [hon.] Good conduct medal overseas service, National Defense medals (U.S. Army); [oth. writ.]

Many poems as yet unpublished; [pers.] Man should be measured with eyes and time because the eyes see what he does and time always shows what is truly in his heart. [a.] Yonkers, NY.

NARDI, ANTHONY
[pen.] Tony Nardi; [b.] May 26, 1952, Hackensack, New Jersey; [p.] Louis F. Nardi (deceased) and Doreen Nardi; [m.] Gwyneth, September 5, 1979; [ch.] Ryan (12) and Jayme Lee (10); [ed.] Graduate Lodi High School, 1970; [occ.] Postal worker 19 years, stand-up comedy, 7 years, partime; [memb.] President APWU # 4884 Local, Youth Coaches National Association; [hon.] Creative Writer's Award, Lodi High School 1969, Youth Coach Volunteer Award 1990-1993; [oth. writ.] Many original poems (2 volumes) not published, sports editor, rampages, local high school sports page; [pers.] Treasured memories of those I love can live forever on pages written with the ink that flows through my heart. [a.] Hasbrouck Heights, NJ 07604.

NASHED, NANCY S.
[b.] November 13, 1974, Boston, Massachusetts; [p.] Samir and Madleen Nashed, (sis.) Neveen and Nagwa Nashed; [ed.] Liverpool High School, St. John Fisher College (still attending); [oth. writ.] This is the first; [pers.] I believe that inspiration is the key which unlocks the door to success, and I give my heartfelt thanks to my family, my friends (especially at St. John Fisher) and those who love me for giving me this key. [a.] Liverpool, NY 13090.

NASZ, ANNA
[b.] October 3, 1963, Budapest, Hungary; [p.] Janos Bednarik and Anna Urban; [m.] Laszlo Nasz, July 24, 1982; [ch.] Natalie, David, Anthony and Robert; [ed.] High school
Budapest Beta Bavdok Conservatory of Music, Liszt Terenc College of Music/not finished due to immigration; [occ.] Music Teacher; [hon.] Several scholarships in music while studying in Hungary; [oth. writ.] Songs, poems and some short stories, presently working on a musical; [pers.] I feel a need to reach out and share the love I have with everyone, together we can make this beautiful world a better place to live in-for all of us. [a.] Princeton, BC. V0X 1W0 Canada.

NAVRATIL, MICHELLE
[b.] June 10, 1980, U of A Hospital, Edmonton, Alberta Canada T8A 3N5; [p.] Paul and Leslie Navratil; [sibs.] Twin brothers Matthew and Michael (age 9); [ed.] Mills Haven Elementary and Clover Bar Junior High; [ins.] Interests, swimming, softball and shopping; [oth. writ.] Poem entitled, " Michael and Matthew" published in " Magpie" in 1986, as well as my "Grandfather" poem was published in "Stepping Stones" in 1992: In the summer of 1992 I wrote a poem entitled "Friends" which won 1st place in our summer festival; [pers.] I enjoy writing poems relating to personal experiences, my family members and close friends. [a.] Sherwood Park, Alberta, Canada T8A 3N5.

NAWASCA, EDISON
[b.] November 1, 1972, Luzon City, Phillipines; [p.] Pilar Labayog; [ed.] St. Boniface Diocesau High School 1986-90, University of Manitoba 1991; [occ.] Part-time student, part-time employee; [oth. writ.] " As Time Passes By", the one that made be believe, and several other poems someday to be recognized;

[pers.] The poem is a reflection of the heart, it was not written for a specific someone, but rather it is how I feel. I dedicate it to those who've believed in me, thank you God for this miracle, and to my inspiration - " The Friend In You" , I'll love you always. [a.] Winnipeg, MB Canada R1L 0Y3.

NAWELLS, CORINNE
[b.] May 5, 1925, Los Angeles, California; [p.] Frank and Emily Nawells; [ed.] Graduated from Hoover High School, 1947; [occ.] Composer and songwriter and poet; [memb.] Was in The World of Poetry, now in The National Library of Poetry; [hon.] Won two Golden Poets Awards (plaques) 1987 and 1988, and last August 28, 1992 I won first runner-up (40 inch banner) and plaque in talent competition at Disneyland Hotel, and won a second plaque and silver crown May 1993, too; [oth.writ.] Other poems in anthology books, "What Must God Think?", "God Bless The Statue of Liberty" and "That's Our U.S.A."; [pers.] I was listed in " Who's Who in Poetry, 1991, I have received two colored pictures from former President Reagan and Nancy Reagan and signed by both of them as well as two letters from " The White House", too.

NAZWORTHY, CYNTHIA KAY (FINCHAM)
[b.] May 28, 1954, Marshalltown, Iowa; [p.] Mariann Deeter and Donald F. Fincham (deceased); [m.] Leon Nazworthy, June 12, 1982; [ch.] Gregory A. Moughler and Alamanda M. Nazworthy; [ed.] Marshalltown High School; [occ.] Bookbinder (R.R. Donnelley & Sons); [memb.] Quarterhorse Association, American Paint Horse Association and Humane Society of United States; [hon.] Golden Poet Award, years 1989, 1990, 1991 and 1992; [pers.] Explore within the depths of your heart, put it down on paper; Love all Godly things, be it mankind or be it nature. Express all in love, this is what lonely hearts search of. [a.] St. Charles, IA 50240.

NCHUNGA, A.C.N.
[b.] Botswana; [m.] Metlha Nchunga, July 27, 1990; [ch.] One girl, Blessing; [ed.] L.L.B.-University of Botswana; [occ.] Senior Magistrate; [oth. writ.] Several love poems unpublished; [pers.] If you die, you will be dead, so don't worry about dying. [a.] Botswana, Africa.

NDERITU, JOHN GATU
[b.] 1983, Nyeri, Kenya; [p.] Samwel Thige (Late) and Ann Wahito Thige; [m.] P. Gathoni Nderitu, May 2, 1961; [ch.] F. Thige, B. Mugumo, L. Wanjiru, R. Kingori, D. Muchemi, G. Wangui and Dr. A. Wahito (Late); [ed.] Associates of Chartered Institute of Secretaries and Administrators (London); [occ.] Author; [memb.] Chairman of 4 Boards of Management of Catholic Schools and Vice-Chairman of 3 others; [oth. writ.] Have written extensively as Press Officer and newspaper reporter, have written a book in local language; [pers.] Consistent hard work is the route to success in writing.; [a.] Nyeri, Kenya

NEAL, ANGELA
[pen.] Angela Neal; [b.] November 16, 1978, Shreveport, Louisiana; [p.] Chuck and Jan Neal; [ed.] 8th grade graduate of Cross Roads, Texas, ISD; [occ.] Student; [hon.] Salutatorian of 92-93 8th grade graduation, Outstanding English Award, 1st place spelling in UIL; [oth.writ.] Jointly written poem with twin sister Aimee Neal, titled "Certified Farrier"; [pers.] Nobody's perfect. [a.] Malakoff, TX.

NEBINGER, NORMA HOFFMAN
[pen.] Nom Nebinger; [b.] August 12, 1929, Vintondale, Pennsylvania; [p.] Norman and Nora Hoffman (Galer); [m.] William Nebinger, September 6, 1972; [ch.] Nina Erhard Carson and Diane Erhard Landes; [ed.] Armagh High School, Yuba Junior College, California; [occ.] Franklin County Children Services, Columbus, Ohio; [memb.] Charter member National Museum of Women in The Arts, Washington, D.C.; [hon.] 1983 Jean Lamb Hall Memorial Award for sculpture, Cols. Museum of Art, 4th place, Beta Sigma Phi, National Poetry contest 1961, other awards too numerous to list; [oth. writ.] Currently working on small book of poetry; [pers.] When I reach an impasse in art, I turn to my old friend, poetry.

NEFOUSE, DAVID
[b.] June 23, 1980, Louisville, Texas; [p.] Barbara and Greg Nefouse; [ed.] Middle school; [memb.] Beta Club; [hon.] B. [a.] Louisville, KY.

NELSON, DARYL
[b.] January 20, 1957, Nashville, Tennessee; [p.] Ted and Dorothy Nelson; [m.] Divorce; [ch.] Steven and Heather Nelson; [ed.] Central High School, Bedford Co.; [occ.] Asst. Manager, K-Mart Corp, Tullahoma, Tennessee; [oth. writ.] Several poems I have not tried to publish; [pers.] I write from my heart in hopes it will touch someone. [a.] Winchester, TN 37398.

NELSON, DEBRA
[pen.] Debby Nelson; [b.] September 9, 1953, Cut Bank, Montana; [p.] Ben Creech and Bev Ross; [ch.] Grant and Alecia Nelson; [ed.] A.A. degree in Secretarial Technology; [occ.] Data Entry Operator for Roche Biomedical Lab; [memb.] Assembly of God Church; [oth.writ.] Daddy, Why, Even So Come, Lord Jesus, The Bee Attitude, To Die Is Gain, The Judgement of Alex Cox, Chosen and others; [pers.] I give the glory to my Lord and Savior Jesus Christ for His inspiration, and thanks to Patricia Berkram for her faithful prayers and love for me. [a.] Kalispell, MT.

NELSON, LOUIS
[pen.] Louis Nelson, Louis Olivares; [b.] July 5, 1968, San Antonio, Texas; [p.] Charles and Socorro Nelson; [ed.] San Antonio Junior College 1986-90, Texas A & M University 90 to present; [occ.] Student, currently a senior, major- Political Science/Literature; [memb.] DJ-KANM 99.9 FM " The Alternative" 1992-present; [pers.] I have so many thoughts I feel compelled to get them on paper, writing is a catharsis for me. Thank you Neil, Geddy and Alex of RUSH, Allen Ginsberg. [a.] Bryon, TX 77801.

NELSON, VANESSA
[b.] January 7, 1981, Denton, Texas; [p.] Allison and John Nelson; [ed.] 6th grader at McNair Elementary on the honor roll, and Expo Student; [memb.] Trinity Methodist Church; [hon.] Poetry contest McNair Elementary School; [pers.] Inspired by my parents and influenced by God. [a.] Corinth, TX.

NESBIT, KARL E.
[pen.] Earthling # 2.024.673.421 (appox); [b.] February 25, 1943, Aix-La-Chapelle, Germany; [m.] Marie Isabel Nesbit, 74; [ch.] Madeline Christine, George Alexander, Daniel Iqnacio and Daniela; [ed.] The University of Life; [occ.] International Coordinator Universal Wave, Environmental Organization, freelance writer, a poet; [oth.writ.] The Unimport

Person's book, various poems, essays; [pers.] Planetary improvement through life enrichment through planetary improvement. [a.] Tallahassee, FL.

NETTLES, T. HAROLD
[pen.] Tiger; [b.] March 25, Guilford, Colorado; [p.] Radie V. and Thomas L. Nettles; [ed.] Dudley High School, N.C., A & T State University, GTCC Jamestown, North Carolina; [occ.] Trans.; [memb.] American Red Cross, The Wu Shul Association. [a.] Greensboro, NC 27401.

NEUFELD, RONALD D.
[b.] August 27, 1925, Sundre, Alta; [p.] David and Kathleen Neufeld; [m.] Norma Cowitz-Neufeld, May 25, 1948; [ch.] Sharon, Blair, Brenda, Terry and Larry; [occ.] Auditor - U.F.A. Farmer, Didsbury, AB; [pers.] Ron died several weeks after writing this poem. His memory will live forever in his writings.

NEWBERRY, DANIEL ALLAN
[b.] November 20, 1963, Bluefield, West Virginia; [p.] John Price and Francis Cook Newberry, Sr.; [ch.] Madeline Lenore; [ed.] Bland High School, Bland, Virginia 1982, Wytheville Community College, 1988; [occ.] Musician and truck driver; [memb.] National Rife Association and Gun Owners of America; [pers.] Some of my favorite writers are Edgar Allan Poe, Emily Dickenson, Sylvia Plath and Anne Sexton. [a.] Wytheville, VA 24382.

NEWKIRK, LARRY D.
[b.] April 2, 1952, Sampson Co., North Carolina; [p.] William and Freda Newkirk; [ed.] Union High, Harris Barber College, Lenoir Community College; [occ.] Minster and barber; [hon.] Blue Ribbon Award Accomplishment of Merit; [oth. writ.] Three poems published the Mount Olive Review and one poem in the Southern Poetry Review; [pers.] A man that has common sense, honesty and humbleness can reach great heights in this world as long as he maintains the fear of God within him. [a.] Kinston, NC.

NEWMAN, HAROLD LLOYD
[b.] December 26, 1929, Jenny Lind, Arkansas; [p.] Sherman Durrett and Tressie Agnes Ferrari Newman; [m.] Grace B. Williams Newman, August 5, 1954; [ch.] Phillip Harold Newman and Laurie S. Newman Smith; [ed.] Hackett High School, Hackett, Arkansas, University of Alabama, Troy State University and George C. Wallace Community College; [occ.] Real Estate Broker; [memb.] National Exchange Club and The Exchange Club od Dothan Immediate Past-president, Alabama District; [hon.] Outstanding Alabama Exchangite Jimmy Rodgers Memorial Award, Co-Valedictorian of class; [oth.writ.] None published (except for articles in the Alabama Exchangite Magazine); [pers.] One of the most deplorable situations in America today it the false testimony and other unjust means by which convictions are obtained in the courts of America. The very worst is when an innocent defendant is convicted and sentenced to death when he is not guilty. [a.] Dothan, AL.

NEWSOME, BERNICE
[pen.] Bernice Newsome (Nici); [b.] December 6, 1938, Ahoskie, North Carolina; [p.] George and Elsie Newsome; [ed.] Robert L. Vann High, Fayetteville State University; [occ.] Elementary Teacher, Powellsville, North Carolina, (retired) clerk, FBI

(retired); [oth. writ.] Numerous poems and love songs (unpublished); [pers.] I am a loving and caring person, who love to see people love one another. I strive to reflect the sharing of love to people in all of my writings. I have been greatly influenced by the early music composers and romantic poets. [a.] Washington, DC 20020.

NEWTON, TAMBERLY LANE POE
[b.] December 29, 1961, Linton in Greene County; [p.] Phil and Patti Poe; [m.] Jim E. Newton, September 20, 1980; [ch.] Jeremy Brent and Joshua David Newton; [ed.] Linton Stockton High School, Lincoln Trail Community College, Vincennes University; [occ.] Special Events Director of Saratoga Inn; [memb.] Saron United Church of Christ. [a.] Saratoga, WY 82331.

NICHOLS, CATHERINE CHENOT
[pen.] Granny Nichols; [b.] may 23, 1920, Pittsburgh, Pennsylvania; [p.] Elizabeth Becker and John P. Chenot; [m.] Robert A. Nichols (deceased), 1939; [ch.] 4 adults college educated; [ed.] General education development; [occ.] Retired; [memb.] Senior Citizens, AARP, and Christian Mothers; [hon.] Resident Poet at Little Dickens Bookstore, 634 Allegheny River Blvd., Oakmont, PA (412-828-9005); [oth. writ.] Numerous poems, published stories and songs, edited by Richard Gregory of Oakmont, PA 15139, stories and songs are unpublished; [pers.] Love thy neighbor, no matter how much you hate him! [a.] Oakmont, PA 15139-1440.

NICKERSON, JEAN D.
[b.] January 29, 1943, Woodbridge, England; [p.] Doris and Douglas Orford; [m.] William J. Nickerson, January 11, 1986; [ch.] Kevin Mark, Gary Sean and Lee George. [a.] Great Falls, MT

NIHISER, JEREMY M.
[pen.] J. Michael Nihiser; [b.] March 8, 1972, Decatur, Illinois; [p.] Jerry and Jane Nihiser; [ed.] Graduate of Central Senior High, Victoria, Virginia; [occ.] Cook, Moneta/Campers Paradise Marina- Smith Mt. Lake, VA; [hon.] Several 1st and 2nd place ribbons for photography and color graphic art, 1 poem published for McDougall and Littel; [pers.] Life has no death, for death has life, philosophy of life, I love to do what makes others smile. [a.] Moneta, VA.

NISHIOKA, LIANE M.
[b.] December 27, 1973, Torrance, California; [p.] George and Charlene Nishioka; [ed.] Lincoln Elementary, North High School, CSU, Long Beach; [occ.] Student at California State University, Long Beach; [memb.] Koto String Society, Awaya Kai; [oth. writ.] Non-fiction story published in Torrance Area Reading Council book, poem published in high school anthology, couple of poems published in Poetic Voices of America; [pers.] It's never too late to say " I Care".]a.] Torrance, CA 90504.

NOBBEE, RANJEEV SANJAY
[b.] March 22, 1976, Trinidad and Tobago; [p.] Abzal and Kalawatee Nobbee; [ed.] Palm Beach Lakes Community High School, West Palm Beach, Florida; [hon.] Presidential Scholar; [oth.writ.] Published in high school annual; [pers.] Life is what you make it.[a.] Newark, NJ 07104.

NOBLE, HOLLIS H.
[b.] September 10, 1911; [m.] Widower; [ed.] 3rd grade; [occ.] Ingalls Shipbuilding, Pascagoula, MS; [memb.] First Baptist, Vancleave, MS; [hon.] Writers Unlimited 21st Annual International Literary competition 1991, " Certificate of Merit"; [oth. writ.] Fiction short stories, Fisherman's Daughter also Boyhood Memories, many humorous and spiritual poems. [a.] Ocean Springs, MS 39564.

NOGGLE, DALE G.
[pen.] Pep Noggle; [b.] August 4, 1950, Toledo, Ohio; [p.] Glen Leslie and Lillian Mary (Buffington) Noggle; [m.] Deborah Ann (Wilkins), July 27, 1973; [ch.] Nate (1/24/77), Anna (9/26/79), Amber (4/16/82) and Joe (11/4/84); [ed.] B.Ed., University of Toledo, 1974, M.Ed., University of Toledo, 1988; [occ.] Ohio Retired Teacher, Writer and Poet; [memb.] Ohio Education Association, National Education Association, The Noggle Family; [hon.] Silver Poet Award 1986 and 1991, Golden Poet Award 1987, from the World of Poetry; [oth. writ.] Currently writing " One Forgotten Monster", " The Life Story of Bud Snyder, N.F.L.; [pers.] " Jesus is Lord", Romans 10:9. [a.] Oak Harbor, OH 43449.

NOGLE, DONA MAE
[b.] February 19, 1937, Forest Grove, Oregon; [p.] LeRoy A. and Edith F. Field Elliott; [m.] Richard F. Nogle (deceased), 1955; [ch.] Sheila McWhofter, Carolyn Henle and Laura Tiffany; [ed.] High school, business college; [occ.] Medical retirement; [memb.] Eagle Aux # 2241 (Foe), Women of the Moose # 32 Senior Citizens, First Christian Church; [hon.] 1st prize Tm'Cheu art and many times in school for art; [pers.] I try to present humor involving mankind in various ways. [a.] West Richland, WA 99352.

NORABHANLOBH, CHARISMA
[b.] September 12, 1967, Los Angeles, California; [p.] Boone Norabhanlobh and Mija Chang; [ed.] California State University, Los Angeles; [occ.] Editorial Assistant, Reason magazine; [hon.] English Honors Program; [pers.] I enjoy writing about the beauty of the human spirit. I have been greatly influence by Robert Frost and Walt Whitman. [a.] West Los Angeles, CA.

NORLING, SHAWN B.A.
[pen.] Ceezart; [b.] December 1, Chicago, Illinois; [p.] Bruce and Linda Norling; [ed.] Andrew High School; [occ.] Student; [oth. writ.] Monster, Vampire Night; [pers.] When I write poems I try to write in a realistic deep form. [a.] Rolling Prairie, IN 46371.

NORRIS, DENISE M.
[b.] April 15, 1970, Greenville, Texas; [p.] Wanda and Adolf Vargas; [m.] Paul E. Norris, July 16, 1989; [ch.] Shenna Diane, Adam Daniel, Kayla Marie, Alesha Faith and Jacob Gerald; [ed.] Greenville High, Amherst Career Center; [occ.] Homemaker; [memb.] Laleche League, Variety Extension Homemaker's Club; [hon.] Dean's List, Salutatorian; [oth. writ.] Poems and short stories (unpublished); [pers.] My writing is my hobby and my faith in God provides my talent. [a.] Greenville, TX 75402.

NORTH, DOROTHY B.
[b.] February 17, 1928, Woodbine, Iowa; [p.] Martin W. Nelson (deceased) and Hazel E. Nelson; [m.]

James S.L. North, June 10, 1951; [ch.] Paula Squier, Julie Jesse, Ron, Joe, Tim and Bob North; [ed.] High school, Rockford, Iowa, 3 semesters, Simpson College, Indianola, Iowa, 3 quarters, UNI, Cedar Falls, Iowa; [occ.] Part-time newspaper office, part-time retired, former Home Health Aide Teacher; [memb.] Poetry group, Historical Society, Women's Club, United Methodist Women; [hon.] Notable American 1976-77, Charles City Day Cees Woman of The Year 1985, Outstanding Unit volunteer for American Cancer Society 1990, 25 year recognition for recording the family Cooper Clan history, " Harmony in Living" award from Barbershoppers 1991; [oth.writ.] 2 long time newspaper column "Of People and Things: and " Hi Neighbor" large book of unpublished poems, a number of songs, countless letters and journals, regular writings during several years of newspapering; [pers.] I like the Bible verse that says "Do good, as you have opportunity" and my former pastor's quote, "Have an attitude of gratitude", I hope I do both. [a.] Rockford, IA.

NOYES, HENRY
[b.] November 5, 1910, Canton, China; [p.] William Dean and Mary S. Noyes; [m.] Gertrude Sirnis, December 18, 1937; [ch.] Christopher and Nicolette; [ed.] BA., MA., University of Toronto, PhD. London University, England; [occ.] Teacher, author; [memb.] Sierra Club, Chinese Culture Foundation, Chinese Historical Association; [hon.] Jardine Memorial prize for poetry; [oth. writ.] English Heritage (co-ed), Hand Over Fist, Novel China Born, autobiography, Valley of the Sun, Sel poems '63-'93; [pers.] Special interests-justice, peace, ecology and long life. [a.] San Francisco, CA 94110.

NUZZO, MADDALENA
[b.] March 31, 1976, Newark, New Jersey; [p.] Lusia and Domenico Nuzzo; [m.] Engaged to Sean E. Neves; [ed.] Lafayette Street School, East Side High School; [occ.] Travel Agent trainee, Immigration Photographer and consultant; [oth. writ.] None published, but I have a personal notebook over 200 poems that I have written; [pers.] The people who have inspired me the most in writing my poetry are my parents, sister, family and my fiancee Sean E. Neves. [a.] Newark, NJ.

NYBERG, ARTHUR E.
[b.] February 13, 1919, Ward County, North Daktoa; [p.] Emma Marie Steen and John Adolph Nyberg; [m.] Eva M. Barnes Nyberg, February 27, 1943; [ch.] Arthur E., John M. and Randy E. Nyberg; [ed.] 8th grade, Radio School in US Army (5 major battles, World War 2, European Theater); [occ.] Presently retired farmer, bus driver, radio lay preacher; [oth. writ.] 2 boobs, Memories of Yesteryear, God and Five Campaigns; [pers.] I am a bible believing christian, knowing Jesus died for my sins, as well as for all who trust Him ever lasting life. [a.] Lemmon, SD.

OAKE, DWAYNE
[b.] September 10, 1981, Central Newfoundland Health Center, Grand Falls, Newfoundland; [p.] Ruby and Selby Oake; [ed.] R.W. Parsons Collegiate, Roberts Arm; [occ.] Student; [hon.] Trophies in kindergarten and grade 1 for honors in my class; [pers.] I wrote this poem for my friend for homework. I never thought it would be in a book.

OATES, VICKIE J.
[b.] November 30, 1960, Winchester, Virginia; [p.] Harry W. and Mary "Jean" Oates; [ch.] Justin Harry Oates; [ed.] Hampshire High; [occ.] Homemaker; [pers.] This is my first published poem and I am very excited that others will get to see how much I enjoy writing them. [a.] Bloomery, WV 26817.

OBAOB, SOCORRO F.
[pen.] Cora; [b.] December 21, 1911, Mambusao, Capiz Philippines; [p.] Nicolas Fernandez and Nasavia Camporaco, all deceased; [m.] Aniceto Obaob, January 1945; [ch.] Rosemary Romero Mittenthal, MSN, Myrna O Aquila, R.N/BSI, Miguel Obaob Fernandez, Medical Tech.; [ed.] Elementary Educ.-Philippine Normal College, M-A Arellano University, Philippines; [occ.] Special Education Teacher, Philippines, substitute-Archdiocese of Chicago (retired); [memb.] Fil-Am Catholic Guild, Chicago Senior Citizens Club; [hon.] Always first prize winner in academic contests of our times 1920-30, founder and first president of the Fil-Am Grandparents Association, participant-poetry reading contest-Chicago Department of Aging, 1990, article-Grandparents Plea for Fairness and Justice, published in local newspapers, silver cup awardee two times in a row 1989-1990 in the Greening of College Garden contest by Mayor Daley, certificate awardee for voluntary efforts in service to community by the Chicago Department of Human Services, currently the first Ginang Pilipinas 1993 in the popularity contest launched by FAGPAC; [pers.] My motto is: if there is sacrifice there is success, if there is a problem, let the problem take care of itself.

O'BRIEN, KATHLEEN ELIZABETH
[b.] July 18, 1912, Iowa Falls, Iowa; [p.] John and Sarah Convery Thines; [m.] William John O'Brien, January 8, 1938; [ch.] Colonel Maurice O'Brien, Mary Pat Cole and Michael O'Brien; [ed.] 2 years college, Iowa State Teachers, Cedar Falls, Iowa, 1 year Art School, Chicago, Illinois; [occ.] Now retired postmaster, taught school, U.S. Postmaster- Chapin, Iowa, twice postmaster at Geneva, Iowa 50633; [memb.] National Retired Federal Employees, National League of Postmasters; [hon.] Valedictorian of high school class at age 16, Honorary Society in college; [pers.] I enjoy reading poetry, especially Henry Wadsworth Longfellow. [a.] Geneva, IA 50633.

O'BRIEN, SALLY SHERRY
[b.] January 24, 1917, Alamogordo, New Mexico; [ch.] Bella Frye, granddaughters, Consuelo Barragan and Jessica Frye; [occ.] Activist; [memb.] California State Central Committee Peace and Freedom Party.

OCHOA, JOSEPHINE
[pen.] Josie Ochoa; [b.] August 11, 1976, Waynesboro, Pennsylvania; [p.] Feliseo M.F. and Rizalina Ochoa; [ed.] Waynesboro Area School District, Saint Andrew (1-6) Wams (7-8) Wash (9); [occ.] Full time student and sometimes when not busy I volunteer at the hospital; [memb.] Supporting member of The Dream Come True Organization, Hagerstown, Maryland, and supporting member of The National Kidney Foundation, D.C., W-Boro volunteer; [pers.] Even at my early age, I can view my life as lucky seeing how much I have gone through with kidney disease and knowing people around me care. I would like to return the loving, caring attention by being the best I can be and by helping others. [a.] Waynesboro, PA 17268.

O'CONNOR, ELIZABETH
[b.] March 24, 1942, New York City; [m.] Thomas O'Connor, March 18, 1967; [ch.] Eight; [ed.] B.A. English Literature, M.S. Education; [occ.] Teacher-English and French; [memb.] National Council of Teachers of English, NCTE, Lambda Iota Tau, National English Honor Society; [hon.] Dean's List, college years, grant recipient, field of writing; [oth. writ.] Poetry collection, novel in process; [pers.] Poetry is music and should convey the beauty of one's soul and the rhythm of life in all its aspects. [a.] Poughkeepsie, NY.

O'DONNELL, CHARLOTTE
[pen.] Charlotte Wild; [b.] July 22, 1933, Wilmington, Delaware; [p.] Grace and David Wild; [m.] John Barry O'Donnell, July 5, 1958; [ch.] Maureen born 61, Bill born 64 and died 87, Ellen Foster born 66; [ed.] Bachelor of Science, University of Delaware, Associate Arts degree, Green Mt. Junior College; [occ.] Teacher/caretaker for senior citizens; [memb.] AAUW, Niles Congregational Church, Board of Christian Education, Niles Unity Association, Earthquake prep. group; [oth. writ.] Several poems, children articles, an oral history of a ninety eight year old friend, Rosie Bellas; [pers.] Each of us is creating the image of God, each born a unique individual with the capacity to love and be loved. My creativity is a grift I am pleased to share with the world. [a.] Fremont, CA.

O'DONNELL, HUGH
[pen.] Hugh O'Donnell; [b.] April 16, 1938, Philadelphia, Pennsylvania; [p.] Hugh and Mary O'Donnell; [m.] Carol O'Donnell, March 1971; [ch.] Shawn, Brent, Hugh, Christopher, Lisa and Angela; [ed.] North Catholic, Philadelphia, Pennsylvania; [occ.] Musician, composer, songwriter, realtor, guitarist, organist and vocalist; [memb.] Musician Local 77, Philadelphia, Atlantic County Board of Realtors; [hon.] 1986 Salesman of The Year, Atlantic County Board of Realtors; [oth. writ.] Mr. Bean, children's novel, The Green and Gold, an epic novel, The life and Times of Duffy Donovan, Poems of Hugh O'Donnell, All By Myself, an autobiography; [pers.] I wish I could freeze the morning in time, those hours of sunrise, when the world is quiet and solitude is everywhere... when thoughts come from the air, ideas from nothing and the creative process surrounds you. [a.] Brigantine, NJ 08203.

OGBURN, EARL
[b.] July 7, 1981, Columbia, South Carolina; [p.] Brian and Mary Ogburn; [ed.] 6th grade; [occ.] Student; [memb.] J.V. Basketball Team; [hon.] Certificates and trophies for basketball. [a.] Winnsboro, SC 29180.

OBUNNIYI, KEMI
[pen.] Kemi O; [b.] April 3, 1973, Ibadan; [p.] Mr. and Mrs. Obunniyi; [ed.] University Undergraduate; [occ.] Student; [memb.] Student Union Journalism, Faculty Press Member; [oth.writ.] A collection of short stories (unpublished), a collection of poems (unpublished); [pers.] It is true that after the love of God, there is no great love than that of a mother. Love wins all. [a.] Ilesa Osum State, Nigeria.

OLIVER, LUCILLE
[b.] September 29, 1919, Salvisia, Kentucky; [p.] Tom and Olive McGough; [m.] Lee R. Oliver, December 1, 1939; [ch.] Robert, Carol and John; [ed.] Midway College, Midway Kentucky; [occ.] Retired; [memb.] R.L. D.S. Church; [oth. writ.] 3 books, Celebrate Your Existence, Crystal Mountain and Cry for the World; [pers.] Our greatest need is to establish a relationship with God, our creator, I believe we are put on earth to help each other and to follow God's commandments. [a.] Lady Lake, FL 32159.

OLSON, APRIL LYNN
[b.] December 21, 1976, Carroll, Iowa; [p.] Kathleen and Roger Olson; [ed.] Paton-Churdan High School; [memb.] Paton-Churdan Student Council, Speech, County Church Group; [oth. writ.] A poem published in "Feelings of the Past"; [pers.] Be your own poetry writer, don't let anyone tell you how and what to write. My poem reflects the life of a great poet James D. Morrison. [a.] Churdan, IA.

OMBAKA, CHRISTINE (MRS.)
[b.] November 23, 1954, Kisumu-Kenya; [p.] Jacob and Elizabeth Owaga Ochola; [m.] Wycliffe Oduor Ombaka, April 2, 1982; [ed.] M.A. in Linguistics (Lancaster-U.K.), B. Ed. (Hons), Nairobi University-Kenya; [occ.] Lecturer in English Maseno University College; [memb.] Association of African Women in Research and Development (AAWORD), Kenya Oral Literature Association (Kola), Friends of Lake Victoria (Osienala) The Kenya Red Cross Society, International Child Resource Centre (1CRC); [hon.] The British Council Awards; [oth. writ.] I have a collection of poems and short stories most of which have not been published. I am looking for a publisher; [pers.] I strive to recreate human experiences in a troubled world in order for the reader to become informed and educated, thus to me, the poem or the song is a powerful medium of communicating human experiences, valves and aspirations. [a.] Maseno-Kenya.

O'MEARA, SHAMUS P.
[b.] October 14, 1961, Minneapolis, Minnesota; [ed.] University of Minnesota, William Mitchell College of Law; [occ.] Attorney; [memb.] American Bar Association, Minnesota State Bar Association, Ramsey County Volunteer Attorney Program; [pers.] Determine that the thing can and should be done... and then find a way. [a.] Saint Paul, MN 55105.

O'NEAL, ADELLA DARDEN
[pen.] Della Darden; [b.] November 1, 1938, Wilson, North Carolina; [p.] William and Ethel Darden; [m.] Freddie O'Neal, June 27, 1981; [ch.] Arvis and Veronica Grace; [ed.] Key West High, Queensborough Community College, Lynn University; [occ.] Registered Nurse, Funeral Director; [memb.] Christian Temple AME Church, American Nurses' Association; [oth. writ.] Several songs-unpublished, collection of poems-unpublished, several spiritual skits used in churches, several speeches used in churches; [pers.] In my writings, I endeavor to encourage, to inspire and to instill hope in the hearts and minds of people. [a.] Royal Palm Beach, FL 33411.

O'NEILL, MILDRED
[b.] Astoria, Long Island, New York; [p.] Ethel and Leo Hughes; [m.] Donald O'Neill; [ch.] Peggy Conaghan, Donna Porzio, Maureen O'Neill and 6 grandchildren; [ed.] High school; [occ.] Retired school aide of Brentwood High School, Brentwood, New

York; [oth. writ.] Poems and I am presently working on a book, the poem submitted was written for my grandson, others were written for family and friends; [pers.] My writings reflect my feelings of oneness with each other and God, by which I hope to inspire others. [a.] Brentwood, NY 11717.

O'NEILL, REBECCA M.
[pen.] Becky; [b.] September 3, 1966, Trenton, New Jersey; [p.] Linda and Felix O'Neill; [ch.] Angelo O'Neill; [occ.] Professional cook; [hon.] Honorable Mention for a poem called "He Who Dares"; [pers.] I believe when you write a poem you are sending a message to both yourself and others, young and old. [a.] Trenton, NJ.

OOSTERHOUS, LUCILLE J.
[b.] January 28, 1911, Oshkosh, Wisconsin; [p.] Carl Schwartz and Maude Douglas; [m.] Lawrence A. Oosterhous, June 11, 1938; [ch.] James, Jerry and Nancy; [ed.] B.A. Lawrence University, additional credits from U. of Md. and G.W. University; [occ.] Retired school teacher, elementary now volunteering is my thing; [memb.] MSTA, P.G.T.A., Phi Ma, Oasis, Homemakers Charter Member, Grace U.M. Church, Tak Park; [hon.] Md. Mother of the Year 1963, poems (3) published in Mynd P.G. Community College magazine 1963; [oth. writ.] "Oops Here Goes Perry", a book of Md. Geography for el. schools " Mr. Fixit Goes to Mixit", picture book for pre-schoolers (teaches values); [pers.] In this sometimes sad and old world children need to identify with and enjoy the characters they read about. I like to put touches of humor in the things I write. [a.] Silver Spring, MD 20906.

ORANE, ALEXIS
[b.] April 6, 1979, Brooklyn, New York 11221; [p.] Charlene Orane and Jeffery Walker; [ed.] Belhim Middle School, J.H.S. 324; [hon.] Honor roll; [pers.] I try to write about what happens to me and what could happen to me. [a.] Brooklyn, NY 11221.

O'ROONEY, SEAN
[pen.] Sean O'Rooney; [b.] February 25,1908, New York City; [p.] Maby Armstrong and John Rooney; [m.] Ann Patricia Rooney, September 1946; [ed.] No former education; [occ.] Soldier, 1st Lt. U.S. Army; [memb.] Retired Officers Association,DAV Chapter 43, Masquers of Hollywood; [hon.] Military; [oth.writ.] " The Best of Friends", : My Shadows and Other Poems", " Wounded Tigers", "Nanine", " Feed The Birds Wild Rice"; [pers.] " If you don't have the words bring flowers". [a.] Sherman Oaks, CA 91403.

O'ROURKE, JR., RONALD J.
[b.] July 30, 1959, New Orleans, Louisiana; [p.] Ronald and Rose O'Rourke; [m.] Michele, June 12, 1993; [ch.] David and Brittany; [ed.] Archbishop Shaw High School, Louisiana State University, John Tyler Community College; [occ.] US Army; [pers.] I started writing to feel what was missing in my life. In time my life and my writing both developed new and exciting feelings and directions. [a.] Hopewell, BA 23860.

ORTWEIN, MICHELLE
[b.] December 11, 1980, Rochester, New York; [p.] Anne and Bill Ortwein; [ed.] Still attending 6th grade; [hon.] Daughters of The American Revolution, essay

contest 1992, 1st place 5th grade; [oth. writ.] Many, many short stories and poems; [pers.] In my work, I try to stress that even though I have a learning disability that does not conflict with my ability to express my complex thoughts. [a.] Batavia, NY.

OSBORNE, IAN S.
[b.] September 29,1971, Columbus, Ohio; [p.] Nancy S. and John E. Osborne, Captain USN; [m.] Terry L. Wilkinson, to be announced; [ch.] Zacharey; [ed.] Columbus Military Academy, Columbus College of Art and Design; [occ.] Student, photographer and poet; [memb.] Citizen of The World; [oth. writ.] Wrote an essay on Emergency Medical Service member which was published in West Virginia Emergency 911 newsletter; [pers.] The world is a terrible place, we all have to strive for peace and unity. Bob Dylan and Dylan Thomas are both strong influences in my life.[a.] Columbus, OH 43223.

O'SHAUGHNESSY, KRYSTAL
[pen.] Krystal O'Shaughnessy; [[b.] July 2,1978, Fort Saskatchewan, Alberta; [p.] David and Sandra O'Shaughnessy; [ed.] Win Ferguson Community School, Landing Trail School; [memb.] Gibbons 4-H Light Horse Club, school band; [hon.] Academic honors, drama award 1992, most potential in Intermediate Ballet 1990. [a.] Edmonton, Alberta Canada T5E 5S7.

O'SHAUGHNESSY, PATRICK S.
[pen.] P.S. O'Shaughnessy; [b.] May 19, 1969, Toronto, Ontario Canada; [p.] Jacqueline O'Shaughnessy; [m.] Colleen Elizabeth O'Shaughnessy, April 5, 1990; [ch.] Christian Walter O'Shaughnessy; [ed.] Sutherland Secondary, Westminster College; [occ.] U.S. Navy Seaman, San Diego, CA.: [memb.] Green Peace; [hon.] U.S. Navy musician, S.D.C.S.L., MVP, All-Navy Soccer, All-Navy Hockey, National Defense medal, South East Asia campaign; [oth. writ.] Short stories and poems in a personal journal; [pers.] I've been blessed with 2 loving families and with the warm and thoughtful guidance of my dear mother. [a.] Rifle, CO.

OSWALD, DEBBIE
[pen.] Little White Bird; [b.] June 7, 1952, Van Nuys, California;[p.] James R. Oswald and Dorothy J. Meahl; [ed.] Grant High, Pierce College; [occ.] Carpenter; [memb.] Women in The Trades, Southern California Tradeswomen; [hon.] Dean's List; [oth. writ.] A series of poems, reflecting respect for the earth and the American Indian Philosophy, I wish to publish these in book form someday; [pers.] We as humans are merely a string in the web of life, we are not the web itself. We are guardians, not Gods, I strive to love, nurture and strength myself and others and to celebrate our individual beauty. [a.] Sylmon, CA.

OSWALD, ERNEST J.
[b.] January 20, 1943, New York City; [p.] Ernest Oswald and Theresa Wagner; [ed.] Fordham University, BA, English Literature, Bronx Community College, AAS, Retail Business Management; [occ.] Documents Administrator/Researchist; [memb.] Poets and Writers, Literary Agents of North America, International Whose Who in Poetry (UK); [hon.] Certificate of Merit, No. California Poetry Organization of Women (1979); [oth.writ.] Poems and small press book reviews published in U.S. and Western Europe; [pers.] "Commute" first appeared in a German trans-

lation by Helma Giannone in Vienna, Austria for the publication Log Zeitschrift Fur Internationale Literatur (1984). [a.] San Francisco, CA.

OTTE, CLIFFORD N.
[b.] October 24, 1971, Paris, KY; [p.] Harry B. and Judy T. Otte; [ed.] Bourbon Co. High School; [occ.] United States Air Force; [a.] Castle AFB, CA

OTTO, FRANCIS
[b.] March 7, 1981, Valley Stream, New York; [p.] Frank and Helen Otto; [ed.] Malverne Jewish Center, Grace Lutheran, Our Lady of Lourdes grade school; [memb.] Boy Scouts, Our Lady of Lourdes Knights of the Altar; [hon.] Arrow of Light, B.S.A., Honors Society O.L.L.; [oth. writ.] Spring and What The American Flag Means to Me. [a.] Malverne, NY 11565.

OWEN, VELMA O.
[b.] Central, South Carolina; [p.] William and Josie Owen; [ch.] Dolores S. von Rosen and Betty Jo S. Scurry; [ed.] Central High, Central College, Lander University, Greenwood, South Carolina; [occ.] Retired teacher, church organist; [memb.] First Baptist Church, Greenwood, South Carolina, S.C. Federation Music Clubs, American Guild of Organists, Retired Teachers Association; [hon.] Teacher of The Year, Greenwood, Honorary Speaker, Central College; [pers.] I strive to build beautiful memories into my life each day. [a.] Ninety Six, SC 29666.

OWENS, CLARENCE M.
[b.] February 22, 1927, Liberty, New York; [p.] Archie and Alice Owens; [m.] Shirley (Steele) Owens, September 1953; [ch.] Steven, Lee, Kim, Alice and Lori; [ed.] High school; [occ.] Building contractor; [memb.] V.F.W.; [oth. writ.] I have only written about my younger life while growing up on my grandparent's farm. This was for my children to read, most of the poems are about things that happened there.. The story is called" Reminiscence"; [pers.] The Golden Rule. [a.] Albuquerque, NM 87114.

PADDOCK, MICHAEL J.
[pen.] John Michael; [p.] Sam and Judy Paddock; [occ.] Poet, free-lance writer; [memb.] The Wilderness Society; [pers.] The grace of our Lord Jesus Christ be with you all, Amen, Rev. 22:21. [a.] Randolph, VT 05060.

PAINAGA, MARY DIVINE GRACE DINSAY
[pen.] Divine; [b.] February 4,1978, Zamboanga City; [p.] Jessie Dinsay and Antonio Trazona Painaga; [ed.] Artuio Eustaguio Memorial Science High School; [occ.] 3rd year high school student. [a.] Zamboanga City, Philippines.

PALAZZOLO, JAMES
[pen.] Litchfield Purgor; [b.] October 13, 1973; [p.] Leonora and Richard; [hon.] Published once before in "Windows of The World II, 1st place senior year in high school Literary Magazine "Visions", 2nd place in 9th grade in "Visions"; [pers.] "Always go with the underdog". [a.] Babylon, NY 11702.

PANICO, ANTHONY T.
[b.] July 16, 1950, Brooklyn, New York; [p.] Salvator and Lucy; [m.] Donise M., January 8, 1983; [ch.] Thomas A., Christopher S. and John T.; [ed.] Patchogue High, various college courses, Ass. De-

gree Electronics; [occ.] Sales and marketing of Insurance and Investment Products; [memb.] National Association of Life, Father and Children for Equality; [pers.] To me poetry is the combining of structure, melody and message in a rhythmic harmony.

PANTTILA, GARY A.
[b.] July 28, 1954, Melrose Park, Illinois; [p.] Bonnie and Allan Panttila, Helmi Panttila-grandmother; [m.] Shelley J. Panttila, May 1, 1982; [ch.] Lisa, John and Gary; [ed.] Hinsaale South High School, various universities; [occ.] Service Technician; [hon.] Humanitarian-Fire Rescue of Neighbors; [oth. writ.] Various newsletters, editor; [pers.] To share my perception of the complexities of the world with few simple words that will be heard for years to come. [a.] Romeoville, IL 60441.

PARKER, MAZELL
[pen.] Zetta; [b.] Mt. Holly, Arkansas; [p.] Willie and Lillian Jones Jr.; [ch.] Garry D. Ridgie and Kenneth Parker; [ed.] Bachelor of Art, Dommga Hill University, Carson, CA.; [occ.] Social Worker, Department of Children Services, Los Angeles County, L.A., CA 90057; [memb.] Bethel A.M.E. Church; [oth. writ.] Several poems not published. [a.] Los Angeles, CA 90044.

PARKEY, CHASE
[b.] May 8, 1979, Kansas City, Missouri; [ed.] Still in school, will start 9th grade next year; [hon.] Top 10 Citizenship Award at school, out of 1,000 students, honor roll; [pers.] I believe all mankind are equal and that we should do our best to always help others, I care about people, that's what inspired me to write this poem. [a.] Lee's Summit, MO 64063.

PARKS, PHYLLIS
[b.] March 15, 1937, Marion, Illinois; [p.] Wendell and Mildred Pulley; [ed.] Marion High School, Southern Illinois University; [occ.] Retired elementary teacher and Guidance Counselor; [memb.] American Diabetes Association; [hon.] 2 Golden Poet Awards, World of Poetry, semi-finalist in National Library of Poetry contest; [oth. writ.] Two newspaper articles in Marion paper, 2 other poems in anthologies; [pers.] I enjoy writing poetry about my family and simple pleasures in my life, dogs, my students, friends and hometown. [a.] Marion, IL 62959.

PARKS, RUTH V.
[pen.] Elizabeth Hiemer; [b.] March 15, 1932, Texas; [p.] Reuben and Viola Parks; [ed.] AA Degree, Artist, Secretary, Dental Technician, beautician operator; [occ.] Retired, I am also a barber, certificate in shorthand; [hon.] My art is on exhibit during art shows, it is at (524 Hayes Street, 415-255-0415); [oth. writ.] Short stories; [pers.] I draw pictures and I draw people, my art work is at the State of The Art Studio, at Hayes and Octavia Streets in San Francisco. [a.] San Francisco, CA 94112.

PATER, EDWARD R.
[b.] November 6, 1941, St Alban's, Hertfordshire, England; [p.] Dr. John Edward Pater, CB, MA (Cantab) and Margaret Anderson Furtado, MA (Cantab); [m.] Susan Caroline Heap, BSc (Lond) PGCE, August 29, 1975; [ch.] Ruth Margaret, Hannah Rachel Meriel Liesel; [ed.] Whitgift School and Queens' College, University of Cambridge; [occ.] University Administrator at Queen Mary and Westfield College, Univer-

sity of London; [memb.] Association of University Administrators, Minack Theatre Society, Croydon Histrionic Society; [hon.] MA(Cantab); [pers.] By upbringing, education, profession and inclination, I am a Wordsmith. This Haiku was a gift to family friends on their return to Japan. I write for the fun of it. [a.] South Croydon, Surrey CR2 0BZ United Kingdom.

PATMON, JUNE ROBERTA
[b.] June 10, 1953, Barbados, West Indies; [p.] John and Margaret Lovell; [m.] Divorced; [ch.] Reba-Lee and Gabrielle Patmon; [ed.] High school, presently going to Southern Illinois University on base for BA in Vocational Education and Development; [occ.] Hospital Corpsman; [memb.] Downs Syndrome; [hon.] Citations and (3) three good conduct awards from the military, numerous letters of appreciation; [pers.] I am a British West Indian from Barbados, now in the United States Navy. I love my job, I love people, I function as a divorced/single parent with my best friends Reba and Gabrielle. [a.] Bangor, WA 98315.

PATT, LYNN
[pen.] Lynn Patt; [b.] May 3, 1949, Paterson, New Jersey; [p.] Anne and Peter Redyke; [m.] Walter E. Patt, Jr., January 10, 1970; [ch.] Robert Daniel and Edward Jonathan; [ed.] Fairlawn Senior High School; [occ.] Homemaker, singer and author; [memb.] Tampa Bay Opera Company; [hon.] Golden Poet Awards 1989 and 1990; [oth. writ.] Book of poetry published in 1988 "Reflections on Life; [pers.] Someday I hope to have one of my poems put to music. [a.] Pinellas Park, Fl 34665.

PATTERSON, JoCAROL COX
[b.] April 11, 1941, Maury Co., Columbia, Tenn. 38401; [p.] Mr. and Mrs. William H. Cox, Jr., 308 W 17th Street, Columbia, Tenn. 38401; [m.] Deceased, January 22, 1966; [ch.] Jan Kristen Patterson, Larry S. Patterson, Jr. and Zane Blake Patterson; [ed.] Columbia Central High School, St. Thomas School of Nursing 3 year diploma degree; [occ.] Unemployed/houseperson; [hon.] Invitation International Poets Society, wife of a deceased Arkansas Congressman Larry S. Patterson, 3 term state Congressman, astute and prestigious, deceased 15 years; [oth. writ.] Pacific Rone, Seattle Washington, several poems published in National Library of Poetry, one on John Campbell, California publisher; [pers.] I write poetry to find reason for my existence to make my life sublime. [a.] Columbia, TN.

PATTERSON, KATIE ANN
[b.] September 28, 1977, Westfield, Massachusetts; [p.] Patricia Ann and John Russell Patterson; [ed.] Westfield High School; [occ.] I work with my parents in their business; [oth.writ.] I have a whole notebook full of my poems just waiting to publish, just like this one; [pers.] I write poems to express my feelings and thoughts. I hope other people can relate to my poem and enjoy it. I have been influenced by my mother's poetry. [a.] Westfield, MA.

PATTERSON, RHONDA
[pen.] Rhonda Patterson; [b.] November 1, 1961, Clinton, Oklahoma; [p.] Phillip and Geneva Risher; [m.] Lawrence Patterson, Jr., May 7, 1988; [ed.] Mustang High, 1980 graduate, New Life Bible College attended 3 years; [occ.] Housewife; [memb.] 7

year church member New Life Chapel, Udall, Kansas; [oth. writ.] Written several more poems with compassion, deep feeling and emotion in them, have written short stories; [pers.] I write about how our wonderful creator, God works and moves in my life and what He can do for others as well. [a.] Wichita, KS 67207.

PATTON, LARRY G.
[b.] September 8, 1940, E. Prairie, Missouri; [p.] Thomas and Lorene Patton; [ch.] Jeffrey, Scott and Michael; [ed.] Elm Grove Elementary, Ferguson Junior and Senior High, American Business School; [occ.] Asst. Mgr./corporate services, Western Reserve Life; [memb.] Sunset Pt. Baptist Church; [hon.] Golden Poet, Silver Poet from World of Poetry; [oth. writ.] Several poems published thru World of Poetry, local paper and monthly work paper; [pers.] I try to write what I feel, positive and uplifting poetry. [a.] Clearwater, FL 34615.

PATZ, DORIS E.
[b.] Pittsburgh, Pennsylvania; [m.] Nathan Patz; [ch.] Three daughters, nine grandchildren and five great-grandchildren; [ed.] Educated at Carnegie Tech., College of Fine Arts; [occ.] Taught violin and viola, gave numerous recitals, performed my original composition for violin and piano at Carnegie Hall in Pittsburgh; [memb.] Member of Baltimore Womens' String Symphony Orchestra, Gettysburg Symphony Orchestra under Dr. William Sebastian Hart: active with P.A.C.E. (Performing Arts for Childrens' Education), an affiliate of the Baltimore Music Club, Inc., a cultural enrichment program which reaches approximately 200,000 school children in Baltimore City and the adjoining counties, Baltimore and State President of the National League of American Penwomen, Inc., a national organization of Professional Artists, Writers, and Composers, member of Board of Girl Scouts of Central Maryland, member of Board of Baltimore Music Club, Inc; [hon.] Won several first and second prizes for poetry and short stories in N.L.A.P.W.-National, State and Local competitions, served on the Advisory Board of the Arts and Humanities at the University of Maryland, College Park, Maryland, established in conjunction with my husband, Nathan Patz, the first Board of Regents Scholarship for the top student in the Arts, University of Maryland, established with Ms. Bylee Massey, a permanent collection of over 200 works in every facet of the Arts, of Distinguished Maryland Artists, on display at the University of Maryland, Adult Education Center, College Park, Maryland, I was conferred an honorary membership of the University of Maryland Alumni Association-International, appeared In Person at Maryland Public Television for a half hour interview with host Rich Breitenfeld about my musical activities in Pittsburgh, Interlochen and Baltimore, appointed by County Executive, Roger Hayden to Commission on the Arts and Sciences; [oth. writ.] Wrote and produced several musical shows throughout Baltimore; [pers.] The Arts, to me, are an exercise of joy. I have always been drawn to express my innermost feelings through my compositions, my violin and my writing. [a.] Baltimore, MD.

PAYAN, STEVEN PATRICK
[pen.] Steve Payan; [b.] December 9, 1979, Los Angeles, California; [p.] Mary Ann and Michael Hector Payan; [oth. writ.] Renee, Black Rose, Blackheart At Last, Last Wish and Black Rain. [a.] Morreno

Valley, CA 92553.

PAYNE, LISA-ANNE
[pen.] Lou/Lou Belle; [b.] December 28, 1977, Cowansville, Quebec Canada; [p.] Grant Payne and Evelyn Morson; [ed.] Presently attending at Massey-Vanier Cowansville, Quebec; [occ.] Student; [memb.] Youth Groups, Student Council; [hon.] Public speaking, school sports; [pers.] I was extremely influenced by the death of my dear father, this one's for you dad. Thanks. [a.] Knowlton, Quebec Canada.

PAYNE, JOHNNY F.
[b.] May 26,1963, Gary, Indiana; [p.] Floyd and Audrey Payne; [m.] Debra Ann Payne, September 9, 1989; [ed.] Appalachian Bible College; [occ.] Student, Pastoral-Creek; [memb.] Disabled American Veterans, Stanford Road Baptist Church, Beckerly, West Virginia; [hon.] Joint Service Commendation Medal, Air Force Commendation Medal, Good Conduct Medal (Air Force); [pers.] I strive to show and acknowledge the goodness of God and His principles by which man can live, plus man's need for the Creator himself (Jesus Christ). [a.] Bradely, West Virginia.

PAYNE, NORMA DOTSON
[b.] January 22, 1918, Forest, Illinois; [p.] Mr. and Mrs. Emery Lincoln Dotson; [m.] Jess Willard Payne, March 3, 1948; [ch.] Teri Ann Payne Nunnally; [ed.] B.S. Northwestern University, MS University of Illinois, attended Chicago University -James Millikin University; [occ.] Retired teacher and counselor, educator; [memb.] AXSL-Women's Study Club, Deer Run Golf Club, AM Legion Aux., MSTA; [hon.] 1946 American National Red Cross Overseas Service Certificate, 1971 Leader of American Secondary Ed., 1973 Certificate of Recognition by Mo Dept Ed., 1975 Who's Who in Mo. Ed, 1978 World's Who's Who of Women (4th Ed.); [oth. writ.] Contributor of Careers Education Guides K-12; [pers.] Was influenced by my English teacher while in high school, she encouraged writing thoughts in poetry form. [a.] Van Buren, MO 63965.

PAYNE, TIM R.
[pen.] Kemp Keng; [b.] November 5, 1972, Lexington, North Carolina; [p.] Gid W. and Brenda J. Payne,Jr.; (best friend, Buckley Shoaf; [ed.] West Davidson High, work experience and life experience; [memb.] (God Father) of Joshawa Keith Williams, son of Laura and Darran Williams; [hon.] Congressional honors, song writing contracts, Who's Who Honor; [oth. writ.] Poetry of a Dreamer, a Realist and The Balance between it all, by Kemp King (future work) is The Fantasy, short story, entitled The Dream Star; [pers.] The sword of life, at its heart lies the dreamer, he is the strength and force, at the sharpest edge is the realist who always sees life's physical needs. The iron of the sword is the balance, the three make the whole without them life could not be. [a.] Lexington, NC 27292.

PEALE, DEBORAH H.
[b.] September 17, 1952, Clarksburg, West Virginia; [p.] John and Delores Holt; [m.] William L. Peale, June 28, 1987; [ch.] Amy Renae, Kelly Marie and Matthew; [ed.] Moorefield High, Potomac State College, West Virginia University, James Madison University, Florida International University; [occ.] Educator; [memb.] Council for Exceptional Children,

International/Florida/Dade Reading Associations, Epilepsy Foundations, Association for Retarded Citizens; [hon.] 1994 Dade County Teacher of The Year; [oth. writ.] Newspaper articles, grant proposals, thesis, poems and stories; [pers.] "To laugh often and much; to win the respect of intelligent people and the affection of children, to earn the appreciation of honest critics and endure the betrayal of false friends, to appreciate beauty to find the best in others, to leave the world a bit better, whether by a healthy child, a garden patch or a redeemed social condition, to know even one life has breathed easier because you lived. This is to have succeeded" Walt Whitmam. [a.] Miami, FL 33143.

PEARCE, RAYMOND JOSEPH
[pen.] Ray Pearce; [b.] December 2, 1935, Northampton, England; [m.] Lucy Pearce, March 31, 1973; [ed.] Waterloo Grammar School, Liverpool 22 England; [occ.] Retired Banker (in management for 25 years); [hon.] Associate of Chartered Institute of Bankers, London, England, on their official list of speakers; [oth. writ.] Article on the end of British Empire as seen by me (a young soldier in Malaya in 1954/55); [pers.] Since retiring two years ago, I lecture all over U.K. on (1) Rogues I have known, (2) A history of Lloyds Bank and Birmingham. [a.] Birmingham B36 0EH England.

PEARCE, SHEILA
[b.] November 2, 1945, Romford, England; [p.] Miriam Laxton and John Gardner (John Gardner deceased 1984); [m.] Peter Charles Pearce, November 23, 1985; [ch.] Gillian Clare (Campbell) 21 years, Colin Robert (Campbell) 15 years; [ed.] G.C.E. England "O" level, 3 year diploma in education, Nottingham B.A. Philosophy, Laurentian University Ontario; [occ.] Teacher, private tutor, homemaker; [memb.] St. Peter's Anglican Church, Comox B.C., Vancouver Island, North Island Choir; [hon.] Queen's Guide Award, England 1960, Royal Life Saving Society Bronze 1983, received an award in 1959 for first prize in a Scripture reading contest for the SOuth East of England in London; [oth. writ.] " Source of Joy" March 1993, a poem on the unconditional love of God, submitted to Diocesan Post B.C., April 93; [pers.] My recent poetry, I sense has been inspired during prayerful attitudes towards God, concerning people, events and the spirit of goodwill. [a.] Comox, British Columbia, Canada V9N 4R8.

PEER, ELSIE
[pen.] Elsie Peer; [m.] Robert Peer; [ch.] David and Beverly Peer; [occ.] Homemaker.

PELTON, LAURETTA E.
[b.] October 24,1924, Iowa; [ed.] Masters in School Administration; [occ.] College professor, school principal, junior high teacher; [memb.] Formerly, National Principal Association, National Council for Mathematics; [hon.] Multiple awards, local and National Golden Poet of the Year 1990-1991; [oth.writ.] Professional books (2) Out To Discover (poetry), multiple newspaper articles, editorials, etc. [a.] Tucson, AZ.

PELLEGRINI, SILVANA E.
[b.] December 7, 1958, Sydney, Australia; [m.] Bartolomeo, June 29, 1979; [ch.] Stephen E., Sabrina E., Silvio E. and Samanta E.; [ed.] Pfarrer Graf High, Karlsruhe Technical Trade Academy, Kirtland Com-

munity College, Army Military Intelligence (SGT/ E5); [occ.] Presently artist; [memb.] NRA; [hon.] Too many to mention; [oth. writ.] German poems published in German magazines; [pers.] The day when mankind stops searching for the unknown, will be the day this world will end. [a.] Grayling, MI 49738.

PEMBERTON, EDITH DALE
[pen.] E. Dale Pemberton; [b.] March 28, 1949, Vancouver, British Columbia Canada; [p.] Albert William and Kathleen Eva Pemberton; [m.] Terrance Edwin Hann; [ch.] Shawna Rae Hammond and Kathleen Pemberton; [ed.] Graduate-Fairview College, Alta Canada, attended Northern Light College, British Columbia, Canada; [occ.] Equine Instructor, rancher, mother-plus; [memb.] Appaloosa Horse Club of Canada, Canadian Charolais Association; [oth.writ.] "Rebirth", American Poetry Anthology, Volume IX, number 3 1989, "Rebirth and Baltic Zephyr" Best New Poets of 1989, themes, Spring's Imagery in Alaska and on The North Slope; [pers.] When children look to us for help and guidance, they can be our inspiration, understanding that our greatest gifts are the simplest, I f we only open our eyes and see! [a.] Manning, Alberta Canada T0H 2M0.

PENASKOVIC, THOMAS J.
[pen.] Thomas J. Penaskovic; [b.] May 15,1947, Bayonne, New Jersey 07002; [p.] Frank and Jean; [ed.] 2 years of college; [occ.] Retired; [memb.] Marine Corps League and American Legion; [oth. writ.] Many, but I never attempted to publish any till recently; [pers.] God is great, God is good, God lives in our neighborhood.

PENNEBAKER, WANDA
[b.] February 15, 1925, Memphis, Tennessee; [p.] Marvin and Sudye Pennebaker; [m.] Single; [ed.] Finished several high school studies by correspondence; [occ.] Do volunteer work at dieters claim; [hon.] Received pin for volunteer work, received ribbon for being a participant in helping hand olympics; [oth. writ.] Have composed several songs, one was played over local radio station; [pers.] I truly believe that this poem of mine was God's work, and that he put it into my mind. [a.] Kerrville, TX.

PENNINGTON, AMBER LYNN
[pen.] Amber Lynn Pennington; [b.] April 11, 1983, St Louis, Missouri; [p.] Doug and Christie Pennington; [ch.] 1 Ragdoll Kitty named Flossie; [ed.] West Chester Friends School, West Chester, PA, 3rd grade; [occ.] Student; [hon.] Tops in reading and math group, # a daughter to Doug and Christie.[a.] St Louis, MO.

PEREZ, BENJAMIN de SOUZA
[b.] June 18, 1969, Sonoma, California; [p.] Cherie Perez; [ed.] Transferring to the University of California at Berkeley in the spring semester of 94; [memb.] Feminists on Campus, Santa Rosa Junior College; [hon.] Dr.Pearl Konttas Scholarship, Doyle Scholarship, Dean's Honors; [oth. writ.] Two poems published in local paper, MEMO (366 N Main, Ft. Bragg, CA 95437); [pers.] All of my poetry is ultimately inspired by my mother's personal power and struggle (a power and struggle illustrated universally in the myths of Lilith, Kali and Artemis and furthermore seen in the faces of all women I have ever met). [a.] Santa Rosa, CA.

PEREZ, PABLO
[b.] August 26, 1960, Havana, Cuba; [p.] Medel Perez and Victoria Gonzalez; [m.] Alina Calderin, July 1, 1992; [ed.] University of Havana School of Medicine, 5 years Computer Systems Institute, Havana; [occ.] Computer Programmer; [memb.] League Against Cancer, Inc.; [pers.] Poetry is a continuing battle for free expression, I write to break through the thought barriers of human society. [a.] Miami, FL.

PEREZ, TERESA
[b.] July 6, 1980; [p.] Dr. Jose and Patricia Walsh Perez; [ed.] 7th grade at Gelinas Junior High; [occ.] Full time student; [hon.] Honor student, honored in Suffolk County for Theatre Arts Founder award for Earth Club at Setauket School; [oth. writ.] This poem was inspired and is dedicated to my late grandmother Mrs. Jean Walsh, I love you grandma. [a.] East Setauket, NY.

PERKINS, RICHARD H.
[b.] August 24,1966, Lower Bucks County, Pennsylvania; [p.] Judith H. Wentworth and James H. Perkins, Jr.; [m.] Jamin Badersbach Perkins, November 22, 1992; [ed.] Harrison Central High School; [occ.] U.S. Army Servicemember; [memb.] Non-commissioned Officer of America; [hon.] Good Conduct Medal, Air Assault Badge; [oth. writ.] Several poems published in Harrison Central High School, literature magazine " The Phoenix"; [pers.] Writing helped me to get thru the turmoils of a teenagers life and also made my thoughts take on new and more important meanings to me. [a.] Saucier, MS.

PERRINE, KEVIN D.
[b.] April 3, 1955, Gurdon, Arkansas; [p.] Harlan E. and Nancy L. Perrine; [ch.] Amanda K. and Kala A. Perrine; [ed.] Jefferson High, U. S. Marines and a lot of hard knocks; [occ.] Welder for Sabine Mining Co.; [oth. writ.] One poem being coincident by Blue Mountain Arts and one done by Company Magazine; [pers.] Hope we all take the time to see the children they're too precious to overlook, I hope one day for more time to write. [a.] Jefferson, TX 75657.

PESONEN, LIISA
[b.] September 25, 1980, Grande Cache; [p.] Kaija and Seppo Pesonen;[ed.] Student; [occ.] Student; [memb.] New Member, (4-H); [oth. writ.] All I have to say is I'm glad you chose me and this my first time; [pers.] I hope other people try this (kids too). [a.] Black Creek B.C. V0R 1C0.

PETERSHEIM, MEREDITH-JOY
[pen.] M.J., Ember; [b.] July 11, 1981, Rochester, New York; [p.] Mark and Sharon Petersheim; [ed.] 6th grade-mother of Sorrows School; [memb.] Youth group at Holy Name of Jesus Church and The Mother of Sorrows Sports Program; [hon.] National Honor Roll; [pers.] I strive to be good in everything. If I put my mind to it I can do it. [a.] Rochester, NY.

PETERSON, DONNA
[b.] May 25, 1932, Calgary, Alberta Canada; [p.] Conrad and Lillian Pfeifer; [m.] Arnt Peterson, August 13,1955; [ch.] Carla and Brett Peterson; [ed.] B.Ed. University of Alberta, English major; [occ.] Teacher, elementary retired; [memb.] Canadian Schizophrenia Foundation; [hon.] Public Speaking Award (Toastmistress International) Silver Pin Award for editing university newspaper; [oth. writ.] Article

on nutrition "Journal of Home Economics Education" book and music reviews letters and poetry in local newspapers; [pers.] We must develop our potential to the fullest and use it responsibly. [a.] St. Albert Alberta T8N 0H1.

PETERSON, ELMER J. (BUTCH)
[pen.] Elmer J. Peterson; [b.] May 30, 1945, Paradise Hill, Sask; [p.] Louis and Edith Peterson; [m.] Alice, December 6, 1969; [ch.] Michael age 22 and Jimmy age 20; [ed.] Grade 10; [occ.] Trucker to 1979, then heavy equipment operator; [memb.] Nor-Sask Gun Club, Saskatchewan Wildlife Western Canada Songwriters' Association; [hon.] My first poem submitted to the National Library of Poetry, (A Parent's Prayer) was chosen for recording by Cynthia Stevens on " The Sound of Poetry"; [oth. writ.] Poem to be published in A Break In The Clouds, (A Parent's Prayer), two songs published in Canada, one to soon be recorded; [pers.] A poem is not always about the way things are, but how you'd like them to be, then you read it and can pretend that's the way it is. [a.] Saskatchewan, Canada S0M 2T0.

PETERSON, MERALYN EVANS
[pen.] Meralyn Evans Peterson; [b.] July 21, 1938, Hinton, West Virginia; [p.] Leslie and Mary Lucille Evans; [m.] Jack Peterson; [ch.] Patti P. Carroll, Mike, Lisa P. Potter, Mark, and Amy P. Dale; [ed.] Clinton High School, Delta State College, University of Southern Mississippi, Hinds Community College; [memb.] Christian Writers Group, Alta Woods Baptist Church, Prayer Coordinator for Alta Woods B.C. and Hinds-Madison Baptist Association, Jackson, Mississippi; [oth. writ.] Devotionals for a Christmas Devotional book put out by Alta Woods Baptist Church, Jackson, Mississippi; [pers.] My delight is to share with others the encouragement, hope, joy, wonder and very real help with which I have been blessed by my Lord. [a.] Clinton, MS.

PETERSON. ULRICA LYNNE MARYES
[pen.] Rica; [b.] November 17, 1972, Bunnell, Florida;[p.] Otis and Cynthia Maryes, Bunnell, Florida; [m.] Jerry Allen Peterson, December 17, 1990; [ch.] Julia Eve Peterson; [ed.] Graduated, Flagler Palm Coast Junior Senior High; [occ.] Housewife and mother; [pers.] Today's moments become tomorrow's special memories. [a.] Pierson, FL.

PETRIE, CALVIN ROY
[b.] November 5, 1962, Winnipeg, Manitoba Canada; [p.] Roy and Donna Petrie; [ed.] Grade 12 graduate, Hope Secondary, Creative Writing Community College; [occ.] Mentally Handicap Support worker, parttime model and movie extra; [oth.writ.] Published political and opinion columns and letters to district newspaper editors; [pers.] Love is expression and expression is love, as vulnerable, as it may be, it will free you. My writings are inspired by the early Calvalier artistry. [a.] Hope BC Canada V0X 1L0.

PETROSKEY, KELTIA
[b.] May 22, 1978, Hammond, Indiana; [p.] Ed and Phyllis Jones and Ken Petroskey; [ed.] Going to be a sophomore at Bethel-Tate High School, (Bethel, Ohio); [occ.] Student; [memb.] The Poets Lauriette at my school (poetry club); [hon.] Honors Art Society Award; [oth. writ.] I've written other poems as a hobby but not published; [pers.] I write poetry to express my feelings and what I feel about life, it's the

way I get feelings out in the open that bottled up inside. [a.] Bethel, OH 45106.

PHAN, LEMINH
[b.] November 1, 1977, Westminster, California; [p.] Charlie and Khanh Phan; [ed.] I am presently going to Crescenta Valley High School, I am a sophomore; [occ.] Student (high school); [pers.] F Flight (my ROTC class last year) inspired me to write this poem, we created many memories that will last forever. To me this poem will always symbolize F Flight, thank you. [a.] La Crescenta, CA 91214.

PHIFER, MIRIAM D.
[b.] January 20, 1917, Austin, Minneapolis; [p.] Ernest Foote Dunning and Elene (Mickelson) Dunning; [m.] Emmett Roberts Phifer (deceased), November 5, 1941; [ch.] Twins, Michael Craig and Malcolm Roy Phifer; [ed.] Austin High; [occ.] Retired legal secretary, Dep. Clerk Municipal Court, columnist and church organist; [memb.] Magna Charta Dames, Colonial Dames of the Seventeenth Century, Daughters of 1812, Daughters of American Colonist, Daughters of the American Revolution, Daughters of Colonial Physicians and Chirurgiens, Daughter of Union Vietnam of the Civil War, American Legion Aux.; [memb.] 1st place on poem, Raleigh Woman's Club, 2nd prize in "Christmas Memories Contest", St. Paul (MN) Dispatch, plaque and member of Board Emeritus, Foote Family Association of America; [oth. writ.] Editor: " Time to Operate in The Kitchen", cookbook for Regina Memorial Hospital Aux. (Hastings, MN), columnist for MN Fire Chiefs Association magazine, columnist for Hastings Gazette, columnist for Mississippi Valley Star, editor of "Footeprints) newsletter (7 years) for Foote Family Association of American, currently editor of newsletter for Caswell-Nash Chapter, DAR, 'Hymn of Faith", " Morning in The Garden" and other anthems. [a.] Raleigh, NC.

PHILLIPS, EMERSTA
[b.] November 17, 1934, Colby, Wisconsin; [p.] Rudolph and Olivia Schoelzel; [m.] Rayford Phillips, December 5, 1953; [ch.] Keith, Linda, Doug, Amanda and John. [a.] Blooming Prairie, MN 55917.

PHILLIPS, MARION P.
[b.] March 12, 1950, Jeff Davis Co., Hazelhurst, Georgia; [p.] Albert and Olif Partin (both deceased); [m.] Donnie L. Phillips, October 1, 1966; [ch.] One daughter, Donna, 26 years old, married; [ed.] South Georgia College since September 91, going for degree as RN; [occ.] Housewife and student; [memb.] First Assembly of God Church located in Douglas, Georgia, Joy Fellowship member; [hon.] Mother of The Year 1993 and 1988, Honoree of Month for January 1993, Ladies Joy Fellowship; [oth.writ.] Several poems published in newspaper, " Mother - We'll Remember You", " Playing in That Heavenly Choir", Christmas programs, " The Greatest Gift of All", songs " Bais of Prison" and " A Heaven to Gain"; [pers.] I love to write, I am founder and editor of our church bulletin for 4 years now, I write many poems for local people for different occasions. [a.] Douglas, GA 31533.

PHILLIPS, MIKE
[b.] July 31, 1958, Nurnberg, Germany; [p.] David D. and Edith S. Phillips; [m.] Bambie Lee Phillips, May 31, 1985; [ch.] Christina Ann and David Michael

Pierce; [ed.] Master of Divinity (in progress) B.S. in Botanical Science, Christian Theological Seminary and Butler University, Indianapolis; [occ.] Student and part time bookseller; [hon.] Editor' Choice, National Library of Poetry, 1989; [oth. writ.] Several poems in National Library of Poetry Anthologies, "Days of Future Past" and "Diamonds and Rust", articles in Christian Theological Seminary; [pers.] I am fascinated by Middle Age mysteries in the Arabic, Christian and Jewish Communities, I am studying Process Philosophy and Theology to articulate my personal faith. [a.] Waldron, IN 46182.

PHILLIPS, REGINA F.
[b.] February 26, 1951, Pittsburgh, Pennsylvania; [p.] Dr. Robert and Alma Rydze; [ch.] Janine and Chelsey Phillips; [ed.] B.S. Slippery Rock St. College, M.Ed. Duquesne University; [occ.] Elementary teacher, Seminole County Schools; [memb.] International Reading Association; [hon.] Disney Teacheriffic Award 1990, 1991 and 1993. [a.] Lake Mary, FL 32746.

PHINNY, CAROLYN
[b.] November 21, 1964, Waco, Texas; [p.] James and Nell Phinny of Baytown; [ed.] Working towards Bachelors degree in Sociology with minor in English; [occ.] Postal worker; [pers.] I love to read and write about the macabre, I feel everyone has a dark side. Favorite authors are Poe and Kippling. [a.] Baytown, TX 77520.

PICHETTO, HELEN T.
[pen.] Helen Pichetto; [b.] March 2, 1917, Carlstadt, New Jersey; [p.] Karl and Margaret Blaut; [m.] Frank A. Pichetto, August 17, 1941; [ch.] Robert Pichetto and Linda Geribo; [ed.] High school; [occ.] Retired; [memb.] " Sunrise" Chapter, Sweet Adeline, Inc. 4 Part Harmony, Rosary Alter Soc.-Sr. Citizen Organization; [hon.] Honorary emcee for " Sunrise Sweet Adeline, Inc., performances and just being myself is an honor for me; [oth. writ.] Comedy skits, many poems for all types of things, director and writer of many shows (amateur) poems published in church bulletin and local papers; [pers.] I write poetry as the mood strikes me, comedy, prayerful loving, etc., usually they trend to become spiritual, if I can see that someone receives pleasure, that's my reward. [a.] East Rutherford, NJ 07073.

PIERCE, DIXIE B.
[pen.] Dixie Pierce; [b.] December 28, 1938, Cache, Oklahoma; [p.] Cecil and Jewish Blunt; [m.] Larry D. Pierce, December 21, 1958; [ch.] William B. and Jeffrey D.; [ed.] Center High School (CO); [occ.] Freelance writer and secretary; [memb.] Senior Citizen Advisory Committee, AARP, American Contract Bridge League; [hon.] American Legion Award, English Award, Economic Development Award, Golden Poet; [oth. writ.] Poetry for all occasions written since childhood, editor, Baca Grande Newsletter, little theater scripts; [pers.] " We wouldn't worry so much about what other people think of us, if we knew how seldom they do". [a.] Montrose, CO 81401-8230.

PIERCE, HELEN CECIL
[pen.] Helen Cecil Pierce; [b.] October 22, 1908, New York City, New York; [p.] Lyllian and Alexander King; [m.] Divorced; [ch.] Jeanna Marie Pierce; [ed.] High school, Laney College, Vista College; [occ.]

Retired; [memb.] R.S.V.P., Stagebridge Theatre Company; [hon.] Featured in book called " Gifts of Age", actress with senior performing group, artist, paint animals and birds; [oth. writ.] Published in "Contemporary American Poetry", and " Across The Generations", and " World of Poetry: [pers.] I take the ordinary things in life and turn them into poetry, I like to make people laugh, that is my gift to people. [a.] Berkeley, CA.

PIPITONE, CAMMY
[pen.] Alexandra Camille; [b.] November 15, 1959, Burbank, California; [p.] Nino and Charlene Pipitone; [ed.] High school, college degree also senior at University Reno acquiring dual degrees Psy-Social Work; [occ.] Musician, dealer (cards); [memb.] Mensa; [hon.] Dean's List, Silver Pen Award from our newspaper; [oth. writ.] Other poems printed in Mensa newsletters, Reader's Digest; [pers.] Be the best person you can be for yourself, live and let live. Don't judge others.[a.] Reno, NV.

PIROZZI, THOMAS L.
[b.] November 6, 1961, Bayonne, New Jersey 07002; [p.] Elia (Eli) and Elaine B. Pirozzi; [m.] Wendy Lestarchick, August 25,1984; [ch.] Lauren Ann and Thomas L. Jr.; [ed.] Graduated Rutgers University, May 1983; [occ.] Captain, U.S. Army.

PISTILLI, DONNA
[pen.] Donna Marie; [b.] January 26, 1958, Queens, New York; [p.] Frances and Michael Ricciardi; [m.] Anthony Pistilli, September 28,1980; [ch.] Gina Marie, Michael Anthony and Anthony Joseph; [ed.] Francis Lewis High, St. John's; [occ.] Housewife; [memb.] St. Kevins Choir Group, Magical Singing Group; [pers.[I have been greatly influenced by my faith, voice and poetry writing. [a.] Bayside, NY.

PITSENBERGER JR., JOHN D.
[pen.] Satchiel; [b.] July 27, 1969, Huntington, West Virginia; [p.] L.J. and David Pitsenberger; [ed.] Point Pleasant High School, Pt. Pleasant, West Virginia. [a.] Beckley, WV.

PLAZEK SR., EDWARD L.
[b.] January 22,1960, Garfield Heights, Ohio; [p.] Edgar and Mary Plazek; [ch.] Kelly Ann and Edward Jr.; [ed.] Bedford High School; [occ.] Tool maker; [memb.] Bill W. and Dr. Bobs Assembly; [pers.] To ask God each day to grant me the serenity to accept the things I cannot change, the courage to change the things I can and the wisdom to know the difference. [a.] Twinsburg, OH.

PLOURDE, TANSI D.
[b.] October 4, 1977, Berlin, New Hampshire; [p.] Mr. and Mrs. Benton I. Monk, Sr.; [ed.] 9th grade, Berlin High School; [occ.] Student; [memb.] Field-hockey, plays, dancing school; [hon.] Vice-president of class (9th) field hockey, dancing; [pers.] To appreciate the beauty in life and enjoy it to its fullest. [a.] Berlin, NH.

POETE, SHAUNA
[pen.] Tessa V. Baden; [b.] December 19, 1979, San Bernadino, California; [p.] Grandmother, Leonor Fajardo and mother, Victoria Gonzalez; [ed.] Carol City Middle School, 6th - 8th grade and Carol City Senior High; [occ.] Student; [memb.] School Service

Club, Math Club, Youth Crime Watch, Journalism; [hon.] National Junior Honor Society, Dade County Youth Fair Exposition; [oth. writ.] Neighborhood Drug Free and Proud, Dade COunty Youth Fair Exposition; [pers.] Reach out your hand and get a tight grip on your dream and let it guide and lead you to your future. [a.] Miami, FL 33055.

POIRIER, JOYCE A.
[pen.] NYM KIM; [b.] October 9, 1938, Peabody, Massachusetts; [p.] Joseph E. and Florence E. (Langan) Poirier (both deceased); [m.] Single; [ed.] Salem, MA High class of 56, B.A. English, College of St. Elizabeth, Convent Station, NJ, M.A. English, Fairfield University, Fairfield, CT; [occ.] High school English Teacher, Beverly, MA 01915; [memb.] National Council of Teachers of English, MA Council Teachers of English, National Education Association, MA Education Association, Beverly Teachers Association, The International Society of Poetry; [hon.] The Ledger Person of the Year, 1991, nominee-Massachusetts Teacher of the Year 1991, Who's Who Among American Teachers 1992; [oth.writ.] Published "Last Respects" in National Library of Poetry, Wind In The Night Sky c. 1993, 2 copyrighted collections of poetry, Revelations One, and Christalized (80 poems) another 65 poems not yet copyrighted and several works in process; [pers.] As a young child, I collected "words", their power lured me to manipulate them, however not until 2 1/2 years ago, when Chris Bavaro inspired me, did I plumb my depths and realize the hidden treasures of my poetry there. The volume Christalized is dedicated to her, as I may never have found my gift without her. [a.] Danvers, MA.

POISSON, ANNE WARREN
[b.] July 8,1973, Berlin, Hew Hampshire; [p.] Mary Elizabeth Oleson; [ed.] Berlin High, St. Patrick's College of Sutherland, Australia St. Oalf College; [occ.] Full time student; [hon.] Graduated with high honors from Berlin High class of 1991; [oth.writ.] Several short autobiographical essays none of which are published; [pers.] Through writing, I gain a more lucid understanding of myself and human nature. My writing is derived mainly from personal experience, experience equals inspiration. [a.] Berlin, NH.

POLLEY, MARIE
[b.] January 22, 1977, Seattle, Washington; [p.] Rosemary Dontje and John Polley; [ed.] High school student; [pers.] I am one in a lost generation, trapped in a society that refuses to accept us for who we are and not who they want us to be. [a.] Issaquah, WA 98027.

POPE III, GEORGE E.
[pen.] George E. Pope, III; [b.] March 11, 1950, Columbus, Georgia; [p.] Johnsie Peterson and George E. Pope Jr.; [m.] Dorothy Alexander Pope, February 19, 1972; [ch.] Bryan Edward, Candace, Gabrielle, Kimberly Alison and Jonathan Eliott; [ed.] University of Maryland; [occ.] System Engineer; [memb.] Alpha Phi Alpha; [hon.] Chief Petty Officer, USNR; [oth. writ.] Poetry and Prose by George E. Pope; [pers.] People and life, good, bad or indifferent, you must love them both to discover who you really are. [a.] Fort Washington, MD 20744.

POPE, LLOYD
[b.] October 17, 1929, Cleveland, Mississippi; [p.] Eddie Ree and Jessie Gray Pope; [m.] Myrtle Wright

Pope, June 20, 1953; [ch.] Larry Glenn, Debra Gale and Roy G.; [ed.] Arcola, Ms., Pensacola Junior College, University of West Florida; [occ.] 28 years U.S. Army, 6 years State of Florida Employment Service; [hon.] Salutatorian high school, Citizenship high school, numerous military awards, BSM, Arcom, Meritorious Service; [oth. writ.] " Class of 83", published local paper, I quite often write event poetry, sometimes on my own, sometimes by request, I had a "ball" during election campaigns '92 most of my poems are longer than allowed for this contest; [pers.] I often try to point out the absurd (i.e. who is deader, one murdered by abortion or by genocide. [a.] Milton, FL 32583.

PORTER, BEULAH M.
[pen.] Beulah Langston Porter; [b.] Decatur, Texas, Wise County; [p.] Henry and Rachel Langston; [m.] Harold W. Porter (deceased), August 27, 1928; [ch.] William Henry Flenniken, Liberty Lake, WA., Clifford C. Porter, Spokane and Nola F. Stezaker, Los Angeles, CA.; [oth. writ.] Several other poems and words to 4 recorded songs, several poems published in Our World's Favorite Gold and Silver poems", Anthology of Poetry, World of Poetry; [pers.] Good poetry comes from the soul and the heart of the writer. [a.] Spokane, WA.

PORTER, YOLANDE
[b.] March 1927, Jamaica, West Indies; [p.] Herbert Chandos and Mildred Louise Silvera; [m.] Richard Frederick Porter (deceased), August 2, 1957; [ch.] Anne Marie; [ed.] Hampton High School, Jamaica, George Brown College, Toronto, Florence Italy, (Wilfred Laurier University) University of Toronto; [occ.] Visual Artist; [memb.] Robert MacLaughlin Gallery, volunteer committee, The Station Gallery, All Saints' Anglican Church, Whitby, Newcomers ORganization, Whitby; [hon.] Two first awards for painting, Carmel, CA; [oth. writ.] Many which sit in a file. My activities to date have been in fine art/ exhibitions, but it may be time for me to attend to my writing; [pers.] The world is full of mediocrity so one should strive to be better. [a.] Whitby, Ontario L1P 1B8.

POSEY, KRISTI
[b.] July 2, 1977, Newnan, Georgia; [p.] Jerry and Melissa Posey; [ed.] Newnan High School, I am currently a sophomore; [memb.] French Club, Environmental Club, History Club, Honors Club, Media CLub; [hon.] Who's Who Among American High School Students. [a.] Grantville, GA 30220.

POTTER, LESSA J.
[b.] February 5, 19610, Lansing, Michigan; [p.] William J. and Lillian D. Potter; [ed.] Laingsburg High School, graduated 1979, Lansing Community College, 14th year; [occ.] Vec. maintenance worker; [pers.] Thank you, Wendy for sharing my experiences and beliefs, also thanks to Pat for helping me verbalize. [a.] Lansing, MI 48915.

POTTS, WILLIAM M.
[pen.] The Kid; [b.] January 17, 1971, Fordyce, Nebraska; [p.] Marcus and Madonna Potts; [ed.] Cedar Catholic High School, Northeast Community College; [occ.] Service repairman technician; [oth. writ.] " Listen to Your Heart", " Someone Special", " Friends ", " The Most Wonderful Gift"; [pers.] My poems express feelings for special people to say things

they can not say themselves or find in a card. [a.] Crofton, NE.

POWELL, JOHN RITZ
[b.] November 16, 1951, Schenectady, NY; [p.] Gordon and Colleen Powell; [m.] Holly A. Krill Powell; [oth. writ.] "Best Friends" written in 1992, "Wishing Star" written in 1992; [pers.] This poem is for someone very special with much love.

POWELL, MARY FRANCES
[b.] January 30,19836, Talladega, Alabama; [p.] Willey Bennett Powell and Vera Johnston Spivey; [ch.] Denise, Leslie and Anita Moody; [pers.] Tragic and current events inspire my poems, it seems that out of these rhymes and lines start to form in my mind. [a.] Robert, LA.

POWERS, JEFFREY T.
[pen.] Zachery Crow; [b.] December 15, 1971, Youngstown, Ohio; [p.] Frances Powers; [ed.] Austintown Fitch High School, Youngstown State University (current); [occ.] Student; [memb.] Member and co-captain of Youngstown State University football team; [hon.] Dean's List, Scholar Athlete Awards; [pers.] In my writing, I attempt to uproot the fear, love and hatred captured in the dark side of the human psyche. The writings of Jim Morrison, poet, influence me. [a.] Youngstown, OH.

PRATT, REYNDA
[pen.] Reynda Pratt; [b.] January 13, 1975, Fort Smith, Arkansas; [p.] Jim and Helen Pratt; [ed.] High school diploma (June 1993); [memb.] National Thesbians; [oth. writ.] None published; [pers.] My writings reflect how I feel about the world around me. [a.] Fort Smith, AR.

PRESTON, GRANT
[b.] September 8,1974, Gloversville, New York; [p.] Larry and Carol Preston; [ed.] Johnstown High School, Johnstown, New York 12095; [occ.] Student at SUNY Oneonta majoring in Art and English; [oth. writ.] Fight On, Johnny (honorable mention in the Russell Sage College writing contest); [pers.] I write so that others may hear what I can not always say. [a.] Johnstown, NY.

PRETZER, MARIE JON
[pen.] Marie Jon Gallet-maiden name; [b.] February 23, 1964, Los Angeles, California; [p.] William Joseph and Helen Frances Wass Gallet; [m.] Jack R. Pretzer, AKA Randy Pretzer, May 19, 1990, Lake Tahoe; [ed.] St. Augustines Catholic School, Los Angeles,California, Mariposa Count High School; [occ.] Receptionist at Mariposa Family Medicine, caregiver for my 99 year old grandmother, homemaker; [memb.] Member of the J.C. Freemont Hospital Volunteers in Mariposa, Girl Scout for 10 years; [hon.] I won the Editor's Choice Award for outstanding achievement in poetry presented by The National Library of Poetry, 1993, received the Marion Award, the highest award a Catholic Girl Scout could ever achieve, it took 2 years to complete; [oth.writ.] In 1993 I had a poem " Randy, Randy" in the Wind In The Night Sky and have approximately 50 others not yet published. I take great pride in each poem I write, and hope to someday write a book of my poetry; [pers.] I took good care of my father thru his last days of life, before he went to be with my mother in Heaven. Safely, with his arms loving around him, he passed on. From his arms, he then entrusted his little

girl to the arms of her husband, her husbands family and her caring friends, with the many signs from above, I received during my parents death, there is a true loving God. [a.] Mariposa, CA.

PRICE, NIKKI LYNN
[b.] June 14, 1977, Farmington Hills, Michigan; [ed.] 2 years of high school; [occ.] Red Cross Lifeguard; [memb.] Member of Walled Lake Western Symphony Orchestra; [pers.] I would like to thank my school counselor Chriss Golden for her support of me and in believing in my poetry. [a.] Walled Lake, MI 48390.

PRIEST, CRYPTICION 'MANES'
[pen.] Raum; [b.] October 13, 1967, Cook County, Illinois; [p.] Henry and mary Brown; [ed.] Vast self skepticism over high school graduation; [occ.] Artist; [oth. writ.] Words baring gamery God/state in general/ imaginable aspects; [pers.] No comment bares my lifes every loss enlighten moment. [a.] Milwaukee, WI 53233.

PRINCE, ERIK A.
[b.] November 29, 1967, Silver Springs, Maryland; [p.] Leslie and Brenda Prince; [ed.] Stafford High, Virginia Commonwealth University; [occ.] Air crewmember, USAF. [a.] Plattsburgh AFB, NY.

PRINCE, JESSICA
[pen.] Jessica Prince; [b.] February 19, 1984, Ottawa, Ontario Canada; [p.] Karen Wallace and Michael John Prince; [ed.] I am in grade 3 at Glenlyon Norfolk School, Victoria, British Columbia, Canada; [occ.] Student; [oth. writ.] I like to write stories and poems, but this is my first published poem. [pers.] I'm 9 years old and haven't yet developed a philosophical statement. [a.] Victoria B.C. Canada V8R 5X7.

PRITCHETT, WADE
[b.] May 19, 1963, Marion, Illinois; [p.] Bill and Clairus Pritchett; [m.] Susan Pritchett, November 7, 1987; [ch.] Brooke (11), Brandi (9) and Ashley (4); [ed.] High school graduate, Goreville High School, Goreville, IL.; [occ.] Factory worker, Birmingham Bolt Company, Marion, IL.; [oth. writ.] This was my first attempt at getting a writing published, I am currently writing songs and children's stories; [pers.] Keep a positive outlook, never stop trying to fulfill your dreams. [a.] Goreville, IL 62939.

PROGAR, MERISSA ANN
[b.] May 28, 1978, Gettysburg, Maryland; [p.] Nancy and Joe Progar; [ed.] Catoctin High School; [occ.] Student; [memb.] Deborah A Lewis Dance Studio, Catoctin High School soccer; [hon.] Numerous dance awards; [oth. writ.] Personal, Nightmares, is first effort at publication; [pers.] If you have a dream, take hold of it and never ever let go for a dream is the key to find true happiness. [a.] Thurmont, MD.

PROTHRO, JUDY ANN
[b.] August 9, 1949, Panama City, Florida; [p.] Joseph and Modell Williams; [m.] Harris Prothro, July 18, 1986; [ch.] Tammy Neel, Tracy Foster, Russell Prothro and Sylvia Turnmeyer, Charles Prothro and grandchildren, Jessica Neel and Tiffany Foster; [pers.] My professor, Dr. Betty Jo McCarty was my inspiration for writing this poem, she instilled in me the importance of what I think, feel and say as an individual. [a.] Panama City, FL.

PRUITT, KAREN VICTORIA
[pen.] Alanna Briana and Daphne Jade; [b.] September 18,1977, Galveston, Texas; [p.] Victor and Debbie Pruitt; [ed.] Nandua High School, currently a sophomore, 1992-93; [occ.] Student; [memb.] Delmarva Morgan Horse Club, International Arabian Horse Association; [hon.] Numerous awards related to horseback riding; [oth.writ.] A poem titled "Specks On The Seashore" and a short story titled "Journey Into A Heart; [pers.] We have not inherited the earth from our ancestors, we are borrowing it from our children. [a.] Anancock, VA.

PUENNER, JOHN DAVID
[b.] December 12,1970, Chicago, Illinois; [p.] Carol Ann and Frank C. Puenner; [ed.] Lane Tech High School, Chicago, University of Arizona, Tucson, AZ; [occ.] Student, Media Arts University of Arizona; [memb.] National Academy of Television Arts and Sciences, Southern Arizona Film Commission; [oth.writ.] Several poems published in national anthologies; [pers.] The greatest beauty in nature compares only to a good woman's heart. [a.] Chicago, IL.

PURVIS, LISA
[b.] April 6, 1976, Arnprior, Ontario; [p.] Steve Purvis (father) Linda and Paul Benson (step-father); [ed.] Grade 11, Haliburton Highlands Secondary School; [pers.] In an ever changing society, I find stability in my faith. [a.] Eagle Lake, Ontario K0M 1M0.

PUTMAN, MARVIN JAMES
[b.] May 27,1958, Hanover, Pennsylvania; [p.] Fannie V. and Galen L. Putman; [ch.] Nathan J. and Chad M. Putman; [ed.] 12 years high school, South Western; [occ.] Quality Control Inspector. [a.] Hanover, PA.

QUANTZ, MONICA C.
[pen.] Monique C. Quantz; [b.] September 13, 1972, Halifax Hospital, Daytona Beach, Florida; [p.] Dennis B.P. (the first) and Chong Quantz; [ch.] Melinda Lela Quantz; [ed.] Clarmont High School, South Western College of Business (I'm still attending); [occ.] Studying to be LPN and eventually a RN; [hon.] Good Achievement Awards in English and gymnastics during grammar and high school; [oth. writ.] I have several personal poems that I have written to my loved ones. I also have had an offer from Broadway Music Production to produce song melodies from one of my poems; [pers.] I try to capture emotion and feelings in my poems, I want anyone who reads my poem to feel as if they have been there or felt the feeling of the poem. I'm planning to move back to Florida,I'm just going to college up here in Ohio. [a.] Dayton, OH 45404.

QUELCH, SHAWN
[b.] September 25, 1972, Bellows Falls, Texas; [p.] Henry and Judy Quelch; [ed.] Fall Mountain Regional High School, Franklin Pierce College; [occ.] Full time student, part time grocery clerk, Shop n Save, Claremont, New Hampshire; [hon.] Asparagus Club Scholarship winner, Dean's Honor List. [a.] Charlestown, NH 03603.

QUIGLEY, MARIE-ANNE
[b.] April 14, 1957, Cap-De-La-Madeleine, Quebec; [p.] Denis and Pauline Quigley and 12 siblings; [m.] Peter Diederichs, July 2, 1982; [ch.] Michael (23) and Sandra (20); [ed.] High school diploma and a lot of life

experience; [occ.] Bilingual Secretary; [oth. writ.] Several short stories and poems published in local publications; [pers.] My goal is to help people realize that every individual effort counts in making our world a better world to live in, through my writings. [a.] British Columbia, Canada V0K 2G0.

RACINE, KELLY JOHN (MR.)
[b.] April 5, 1967, Malone, New York; [p.] John and Joyce Racine; [ed.] Franklin Academy High School, Canton Agricultural Technical College; [occ.] Police Officer; [memb.] Fraternal Order of Police; [oth. writ.] Poems published in college newspaper; [pers.] My poems are symbolic reminders of my feelings or of different stages in my life.[a.] Fairfax, VA 22032.

RAETHER, ARNOLD L.
[pen.] Arnie,Arn; [b.] May 23,1954, Eau Claire, Wisconsin; [p.] Lawrence and Doris Raether; [ch.] Alisha Susan and Amanda Lynn Raether, (Eau Claire, Wis); [ed.] Augusta High School, Augusta, Wisconsin; [occ.] Hardware Sales Assistant, Busy Bee Hardware, 1521 Santa Monica Blvd, Santa Monica, CA 90404; [memb.] Pilgrim Lutheran Church, 1730 Wilshire Blvd, Santa Moncia, CA 90403; [hon.] Editor's Choice Award, 1993 National Library of Poetry; [oth.writ .] Red-eye He Was Quite The Guy, The National Library of Poetry, Wind In The Night Sky , (Library of Congress ISBN 1-56167-041-3); [pers.] My parents were the best 2 people to know in my life time, I honor them with this poem. I'll always love them! [a.] Santa Monica, CA 90405.

RAFFA, LUISA MARIA
[b.] October 21, 1975, Toronto, Ontario; [p.] Stefano and Rosalba Raffa; [ed.] High school, grade 12, St. Patrick's; [hon.] Italian and French Awards; [oth.writ.] Courage, A Night and Gale, War and Peace; [pers.] " Follow your dream to where-ever it leads". [a.] Toronto, Ontario Canada M4J 1R8.

RAINERI, PAUL
[pen.] Stan Maxwel; [b.] January 22, 1965, Panorama City, California; [p.] John Raineri, Jr. and Loraie Godwin; [occ.] Full time student of journalism at Palomar College, 3rd year; [hon.] Honorable Mention in On-The-Spot editorial writing from Journalism Association of Community College newspaper (The Telescope) over 30 unsubmitted poems and short stories; [pers.] The individual can only be empowered by giving his/her power to the betterment of the people who's lives are touched by the individual. [a.] Temecula, CA 92592.

RAJSKA, DANUTA
[b.] May 8, 1975, Szamotuly, Poland; [p.] Dorota and Janusz Rajski; [ed.] Royal West Academy, Marianopolis College; [occ.] Student, Marianopolis College, Montreal, Canada; [oth. writ.] Various poems in school arts publications; [pers.] In life, art is the point, science and imagination are looks and people inspiration (shining armor was inspired by Sebastian MacDougall). [a.] West Quebec, H4X 1Z4 Canada.

RALEIGH, HOWARD WENDELL
(US-52-040-699-KOREAN WAR)[pen.] Wen Surname-Poet Name; [b.] November 25, 1927, Glen Campbell, Pennsylvania; [p.] Arthur and Mildred Raleigh; [ed.] Public high school, 1948 Curwensville, PA; [occ.] Retired; [oth. writ.] Between Us, A L-O-

V-E, by my permission, two verses from that poem, quoted in Life Magazine, September 13, 1953, pages 149-160 in a pawnshop story, the two lines, They say it is Your;s Heavenly Luck, having E-Y-E-S- which are Charmed Deluxe, quoted, there are your's soft tender lips, here-a kiss, if I don't miss, other poems of mine, Journey In Feelings, my best, Them-We-Us, Out's Father, Kind, Strong, Welcome Home-Mother, High Quality,Step Mother, Brothers and Sisters, Endearments Here I Am: There You Are , Love Poems, Oneies-Twoies (this poem: I Out Did Myself-Great. [a.]Bronx, NY.

RAMOLEFHE, PATRICK
[pen.] Patrick Ramolefhe; [b.] October 22, 1957, Ramotswa; [p.] Motshabi Ramolefhe; [m.] Yobe Shonga and Russ Molosiwa, April 28, 1989; [ch.] Four, Kaone, Thobo, Shimo and Dikaelo; [ed.] Form II; [occ.] Soldier; [memb.] WABO, Botswana Writer's Association; [oth. writ.] My poems are published in a local magazine Kutlwano (Mutual Understanding); [pers.] Writing makes me communicate with those who understand what it is about, I open their ears and eyes to see, let them wonder and find the "ans" writing came naturally into me. [a.] Botswana, Southern Africa.

RAMSEY, EVELYN F.
[pen.] Evelyn F. Ramsey; [b.] April 10, 1940, Lockport, New York; [p.] Llewellyn and Rose Printup ; [ch.] Ronda, Mark, Robert, Michael, Christine and Pamula, Michael died at age 23,April 1919; [ed.] High school, Southern College, Orlando, Florida; [occ.] One Hour Photo Lab, Orlando, Florida; [oth. writ.] Other poems but not published; [pers.] I have learned that it helps to get things out, and though my poetry I feel I can do that, and maybe it will help others.

RATCLIFFE, DERITA RENEE'
[b.] October 19, 1966, Portsmouth, Virginia; [p.] Nina B. and William A. Ratcliffe; [ed.] James Madison University, Virginia Polytechnic Institute and State University, I.C. Norcom High; [occ.] Graduate student, Clinical Psychology; [memb.] Delta Sigma Theta Sorority, Virginia Psychological Association, Health Psychology Division of APA; [hon.] Dean's List, Virginia Council of Higher Education Fellow (1990-92); [oth.writ.] Several poems, none published; [pers.] Food and water allow me to survive. Loving and writing allow me to live. [a.] Portsmouth, VA.

RAY, OLA ROWENA
[pen.] Ro-Rose-Weinie; [b.] November 10, 1948, Andrews Memorial Hospital; [p.] Ruben Will and Olene Mason Guffey; [m.] Shelby (Nelson) Ray, July 6, 1982; [ch.] Brandon Nelson and CHristopher Sheldon Ray; [ed.] G.E.D., college 1 year general office; [occ.] Housewife; [oth. writ.] Poem published in local newspaper, song copy written, Library of Congress, Raleigh, North Carolina, also recorded a record in 1980 (I'd Rather Be The Other Woman); [pers.] I hope to be able to get my work published and out so the public can enjoy it. [a.] Robbinsville, NC 28771.

RAYMOND, JASON
[pen.] J.A. Raymond, November 26, 1973, Plattsburgh, New York; [p.] Zepher and Mary Raymond; [ed.] Batavia High School, Temple Uni-

versity; [occ.] Student; [pers.] Every person can create a single reality every single day of their entire life. [a.] Batavia, NY 14020.

READ, JANICE LYNN
[hon.] Navy and Unit Meritorious Commendation, Sea Service Deployment (3), Southwest Asia Service with bronze star, National Defense Service Medal, Armed Forces Expeditionary Medal, Battle "E" Ribbon, first and second Good Conduct Medals; [pers.] Giving is the better part of getting. [a.] Imperial Beach, CA 91932.

RECONNU, EVERETT E.
[pen.] "Q"; [b.] May 18, 1943, Charleroi, Pennsylvania; [p.] David A. and Helen V. Reconnu; [m.] Joan Fox Reconnu, June 15, 1963; [ch.] Rhett, Tracey, Bethany and Erynn; [ed.] B.A., Furman University '65, M.R.E., New Orleans Baptist Theological Seminary "70; [occ.] Southern Baptist Minister Providence Baptist Church; [memb.] Providence Disaster Relief Team; [oth. writ.] " Thoughts Thunk While Thinking" (collection of musing) many poems and "Selah" series; [pers.] " My desire is to reflect God's mercy, love and grace in all that I say and do, because without His strength and guidance, I am nothing..." Q. [a.] Moncks Corner, SC 29456.

REDMAN, PATRICIA ANN
[pen.] Patti; [b.] October 21, 1954, Newton, Mississippi; [p.] N.B. Alford and Julia Olive; [m.] Ronnie Daniel Redman, April 12, 1986; [ch.] Laurie, Christian and Jessica Will; [ed.] Central High, Jackson, Mississippi, College of the Redwoods, Crescent City, California; [occ.] Housewife; [memb.] Faith Baptist Church, Westfield, NC.; [hon.] Golden Poet 1991, Honorable Mention " A Star is Born," June 6, 1991; [oth. writ.] Divine Time, Living Memories, Mother's Day 1993, How Much Time, The Long and Dusty Road, He Was Thinking of Me, Jesus Will Get You By; [pers.] I love to write to glorify my Saviour and Lord Jesus Christ, He had given me back all that I lost and more. Praise His name forever. [a.] King, NC 27021.

REGAN, SHAWN PATRICK
[pen.] Schwin; [b.] December 11, 1969, Saint Cloud, Minnesota; [p.] David and Patricia Regan; [ed.] Apollo High, Saint John's University, SCSU; [occ.] Student; [hon.] Winner Upper Mississippi Harvest poetry contest; [oth. writ.] A few poems published in local magazines; [pers.] To be human is to love, to love is to taste bitterness, to taste bitterness and still love is poetry. [a.] St. Cloud, MN 56303.

REICHELT, ROBERT DUANE
[b.] March 16, 1966 5"-7", 150 lt.br. blue eyes, Canoga Park, California; [p.] Duane and Daurine Reichelt; [ed.] 10th grade, MGM Program 72-78; [occ.] Mechanic, plumber, etc., etc.; oth. writ.] None documented, writing stories, songs, poems since 10 years; [pers.] Life is but a series of up and downs, so the more peaceful we are the less we notice. Kindness and a smile will take you farther than a knife or a gun. Be good to yourself. [a.] Riverside, CA.

REILLY, TROY
[pen.] Tro; [b.] September 7, 1958, Lima, Ohio; [p.] Donald and Mary Reilly; [ch.] Amy Reilly, May 18, 1991; [ch.] Bryan, Kristen and Eric; [ed.] Macomber

Vocational Technical School; [occ.] Sign Artist, Longshoreman, I.L.A. Local 153; [memb.] Toledo Songwriters Association; [pers.] I have written lyrics for songs, put them to music and have enjoyed playing them for family and friends. [a.] Toledo, OH 43614.

REINHART, STEVEN LEE
[pen.] S.L. Reinhart; [b.] August 29, 1951, Carroll, Iowa; [p.] John S. (+) and Kathleen M. Reinhart (i.e., father deceased); [ed.] University of Nebraska, University of Georgia, foreign-studies, Sorbonne, Paris (oriental languages), Germany (Philosophy); [occ.] English and Foreign-Language Arts teacher, graduate-studies, comparative-literature(s); [hon.] Undergraduate Dean's List, Bachelor-degree cum laude; [oth. writ.] (None published. Certain 'German' criticisms and versifications contributed to semi-formal alternative publications of dubious quality, anonymously, for which I'd like to claim no authorship, ATT.); [pers.] My poetry reflects the influences od lengthy foreign travels in Europe and S. Asia. The work of Baudelaires and les symbolistes, Heine and die Romantiker; and Tagore, Kabir and the Baal and Sufic traditions, as well as T.S. Eliot, Ezra Pound and W.B. Yeats, are my essentials. [a.] Glidden, IA 51443-0413.

REINHART, VANESSA
[pen.] Lidia; [b.] April 18, 1976, Las Vegas, Nevada; [p.] Charles Reinhart, Joan and Kevin Treadway; [ed.] Seymour Senior High; [pers.] Poetry and music are the universal language in which to express your outlooks and emotions on life and nature as a whole. [a.] Seymour, IN 47274.

RESENDES, MARK
[b.] December 10, 1973, Fall River, Massachusetts; [p.] Joseph and Cleofa Resendes; [ed.] Currently at Boston University; [occ.] Student; [memb.] Amnesty International; [pers.] Greatly influenced by the music of R.E.M., to live with yourself you must be able to mock yourself. [a.] Fall River, MA 02721.

REYES, MARILY A.
[pen.] MAR; [b.] April 10, 1048, Havana, Cuba; [p.] Miguel Benitez and Nilda Domingves; [m.] Frank Reyes, September 7, 1968; [ch.] Frances and Alexis Reyes; [ed.] Immaculate-La Salle High School, Miami Dade Community College, The Institute of Children's Literature; [occ.] Free lance writer and poet;[memb.] South Florida Poetry Institute (Vicepresident), National Writers Club, Circulo Poetico Pan Americano; [hon.] Dade County Wide Florida, MDCC Hispanic Festival Poetry contest 1986 award and honors, Amherst Society Certificate of Poetic Achievement-Poetry Merit Certificates, presented at National Theater in Guatemala 1992 "7 Writers and Interpreter"; [oth.writ.] Several poems published in magazines, newspapers and books. self published poetry book and some articles; [pers.] I go through life in the rhythms of the tides, trying to fuse into one the feeling, the word, the poem and the poet. [a.] Miami, FL.

REYES, SARAH MARIE
[b.] October 4, 1980, Parkersburg, West Virginia; [p.] Dr. Charles and Linda Reyes; [sib.] One brother, Sean; [ed.] Student (7th grade), Belpre Junior High School; [occ.[Student; [memb.] 1992-1993 girl's basketball, 1993 Girl Scouts (Junior Cadet), 1993 junior high school varsity cheerleader (7th grade),

member Belpre Heights United Methodist Church; [hon.] National Institute, Library of Poetry semifinalist poetry contest, America's Modern Miss, Ohio Pre-teen, 1991 Leadership Award, America's Miss Ohio Pre-teen, 1993 Just Say No Award winner, Miss Personality winner, Girl Scout T-Shirt winner, straight A, Honor Student, Masters Certificate of Academic Achievement, Presidential Academic Fitness Award 1993, American Coed Ohio State Winner Academic Achievement Award 1993. [pers.] I've been very blessed especially with a loving and supportive family, "it's not how you handle the good days that counts, but how well you handle the bad days". [a.] Belpre, OH.

REYNOLDS, SHANNON T.
[pen.] Shannon T. Reynolds; [b.] October 3, 1967, Madison, Wisconsin; [ed.] B.S. in Mathematics Education at Florida State University, Tallahassee, Florida; [occ.] Delivery driver for major pizza chain; [pers.] My inspiration comes during a time when many people are confronted with a parallel in life. Once inspired, it only takes 5 minutes to write the poem. [a.] Cape Coral, FL 33904.

RHULE, WALT
[b.] 15 August 16, Coquille, Oregon; [p.] Deceased; [m.] M. Anne Rhule, February 25, 1950; [ch.] James, Deborah, (granddaughters, Laura, Amanda and Clarissa; [ed.] 3 years college; [occ.] Retired Army, retired Civil Service, currently working as the Docket Officer, Juvenile Court; [memb.] Catholic church, Masonic Lodge, Knights of Columbus, Military Order of World Wars; [oth. writ.] Will soon, privately publish 116/120 book of poetry that I have written off and on over past 50 years. Several articles in Army newspapers during WWII and in Comptrollers magazine while working for Civil Service. [a.] Odenton, MD 21113.

RICE, MARCIE DOMINIQUE
[b.] April 16, 1985, Richmond, VA; [p.] Denise Rice and Eric Rice; [ed.] 2nd Grade, Totaro Elementary School, Lawrenceville, VA - current student; [memb.] Talented and Gifted Program; Just Say No International; First Baptist Church Youth Choir; [hon.] First Place - Essay Contest; Most Outstanding Member - Just Say No Club; Outstanding TAG Participation; Richmond Times Dispatch and The National Spelling Bee Classroom Champion 1992 and 1993; Richmond Times Dispatch and The National Spelling Bee Grade Level Champion 1992 and 1993; National Fitness Award; Outstanding Citizenship Award; Young Author's Contest - Prose; 2nd Place 1991, 3rd Place 1992; Honorable Mention 1993; Young Author's Contest - Poetry 2nd Place 1993; [oth. writ.] "The Princess and the Magic Rabbit," "The Magic Wizard," "The Penguin Who Lived In a Doghouse"; [pers.] I believe that anyone can succeed if they try.; [a.] Lawrenceville, VA.

RICE, JR., NORMAN JOHN-CHRISTOPHER
[b.] September 19, 1973, Grosse Pointe Farms, Michigan; [p.] Norman and Clementine Rice; [ed.] Current student at United States Military Academy, West Point, New York; [occ.] Student; [memb.] Rugby, swimming, football and skiing teams; [hon.] National Honor Society, MVP Army football, fall of '92; [oth. writ.] Several unpublished poems, descriptive essays and works on the Counter Culture of the Sixties; [pers.] " There are things that are known, and

things that are unknown, in between are the doors"- William Blake. [a.] Grosse Pointe, MI.

RICHARDS, CINDY LEE
[b.] July 19, 1965, New York;[p.] Marlene and Joseph Richards; [m.] George Dombek; [pers.] If but one can find solace through the strength of my words, then I will have achieved my greatest quest. [a.] Mineola, NY 11501.

RICHARDS, KIMBERLY J.
[b.] June 18, 1979, Houston, Texas; [p.] Janice and Steven R. Richards; [ed.] Completed middle school; [occ.] Schooling; [memb.] John Wesley United Methodist Church, honors classes, speech and debate, band council; [hon.] Nomination for top English student in my grade; [oth. writ.] Un-published; [pers.] I wrote this poem thinking of my late grandfather, knowing that I needed as much courage as he had. [a.] Houston, TX.

RIDDLE, NATHAN
[b.] November 12, 1975, Simcoe on Canada; [p.] Howard and Bonnie Riddle; [ed.] Attending Waterford District High School; [occ.] Student. [a.] Wilsonville on Canada.

RIELAND, SARAH
[b.] October 7, 1980, Minnesota; [p.] Maura and Tom Rieland; [ed.] 6th grade student; [hon.] Honor Roll at Nava Elementary; [oth. writ.] The Darkness, The Best Friend; [pers.] Started writing poems in 4th grade and really enjoy it. [a.] Santa Fe, NM.

RIESCH, LOUIS
[pen.] Shaya Sabayoth;[b.] August 15, 1925, West Bend, Wisconsin; [p.] Mr. & Mrs. Louis Riesch,Sr.; [ed.] College degree and Bachelor of Divinity; [occ.] Administration (now retired); [oth. writ.] A trilogy of books, (in poetic form) Beyond Today, Beyond Tomorrow , Beyond Forever; [pers.] I believe all persons can continue to mature all the days of their lives... if provided the simple ways and means to do so. [a.] West Bend, WI 53095.

RIFE, ARNOLD D.
[pen.] Arnold from Varney; [b.] August 22, 1945, Varney, West Virginia; [p.] Jodie P. and Ethel Justice Rife; [m.] Cynthia Anderson Rife, April 26, 1981; [ch.] Teresa Ann and Jason Rife; [ed.] 2 years, Marshall University, Htgn., West Virginia (40 years, school of hard knocks and U.S. Roads Scholar); [occ.] Office Manager (Jack of all trades and master of nothing); [memb.] Of the human race; [hon.] U.S. Army Leadership 1968, Best speaker in Junior Division, Marshall University, Honorable Mention and Appreciation of Suc., to disaster victims by Department of Housing and Urban Development, letter of request for comments by U.S.A. Today News; [oth. writ.] Book, From These Mountain, (not published), poems, "Where Is God", " A Reason For An Untold Story", "Where May I Wash My Hands", "Just Before Dawn"; [pers.] Man is an unfinished product, until he is satisfied with himself. [a.] Varney, WV 25696.

RIGGS, LYNETTE A.
ed.] Utah State University, B.S.-major, English, minor-music, Utah State University, M.S.-English, Idaho State University-Doctoral student, English; [occ.] High school/college instructor; [a.] Wellsville, UT.

RILEY, KERRA
[b.] September 2, 1943, Birmingham, Alabama; [p.] James and Alice Humphreys; [ch.] Joshua Kerr Sallin; [ed.] Ramsay High School, University of South Alabama; [occ.] Secondary school teacher, (I will be soon); [memb.] National Council of Teacher's of English, National Educational Association; [hon.] (Most meaningful) Summma Cum Laude, (members Phi Kappa Phi, Omicron Delta Kappa, Kappa Delta Pi, Sigma Tau Delta -finalist, Outstanding Student of the Year, College of Education, President's List 4 years, Presidential Scholarships, Kappa Delta Pi Scholarship Award, Phi Kappa Phi High Scholarship recognition, National Dean's List 4 years; [oth. writ.] First place winner 1992 and 1993, Southern Literary Festival writing competition (6 state), informal essay (including publication in Festival Publication, essays published in " The Harbinger"; [pers.] I write, always in awe of the poems of children.[a.] Mobile, AL 36609.

RILEY-WHITE, JOHNNIE
[b.] January 14, 1935, Gantt, Alabama; [p.] Tennie Gunter and John Dupree Riley; [m.] Divorced; [ch.] Lynne Dupree Kartsakalis and David Kennedy White; [ed.] B.A., Judson College, Marion, Alabama; [occ.] Retired Legal Assistant; [memb.] Stage Crafters, Ft. Walton Beach Florida Historic Preservation Society, SC Genealogical Association. [a.] Santa Rosa Beach, Fl 32459.

RIOLA, SARA HEWITT
[pen.] Naomi Brightwater, Sara; [b.] June 28, 1916, Brooklyn, New York; [p.] Frances-May Mann and Ralston Coffin Hewitt; [m.] William Renaldo Riola, October 18, 1935; [ch.] Peter, William, Jr. and Richard; [ed.] Harrisonburg Teachers College; [occ.] Retired Trust Officer Bankers Trust Company, New York; [oth. writ.] "Anecdotes of One American Family (anthology of family-related stories) "Missy" (collection of youth oriented stories) " Moments" (poetry) and various local publications; [pers.] Indeed, have I been gifted much, though so it may not seem, that life again has let me touch my heart upon a dream. [a.] Lakewood, NJ 08701.

RIOS-PERIN, JOSE' MARC
[pen.] Jose' Marc Rios; [b.] July 26, 1958, Jean D'Arc USAF Hospital, Toule Des Martin France; [p.] Marie Joseph Rich-Perin and Leo L. Rich; [ch.] Amy E. Chastain; [ed.] Old Trooper University (high school) Ft. Riley, Kansas, Community College of The Air Force; [occ.] Emergency Medical Tech., Ft. Riley EMS, Kansas; [memb.] National Registry EMS, American Heart Association, Air & Space Smithsonian; [pers.] I endeavor to write on the emotional state of the heart in relation to man's perceptions, environment and experiences. [a.] Junction City, KS 66441.

RIPLEY, LINDA SUE
[b.] October 31, 1952, Hamilton, New York; [p.] Ames and Mary Ripley; [ch.] Keith, Kam, Katie and Kristopher; [ed.] Fairleigh Dickinson University, Drew University Theological School Master of Divinity; [oth.writ.] Not Just Another Book About God- non-fiction, "Easter Dawn", short story; [pers.] I believe that all of creation deserves to be treated with love dignity and respect. [a.] Hopetcong, NJ.

RIVEL, NEIL D.
[pen.] Gerhart Schnable III; [b.] August 1, 1971, Philadelphia, Pennsylvania; [p.] Ingrid and Thomas Rivel, Jr.; [ed.] Upper Dublin Senior High, University of Pittsburgh at Johnstown; [occ.] Student; [memb.] Quaker City Citroea Car Club; [oth.writ.] Some articles published by Ocean County Review; [pers.] Write what is close to your heart, the truth is writing is sometimes surprising. [a.] Ft Washington, PA.

RIVERA, BERNICE R.
[b.] April 3, 1980, Tucson, Arizona; [ed.] Booth Math/Science Magnet Elementary School, Pistor Middle School; [occ.] Student; [memb.] Member of National Junior Honor Society; [hon.] National Junior Honor Society; [pers.] " Why" is the universal question and "Because" is the universal answer. [a.] Tucson, AZ 85714.

ROATH, GEORGE A. H.
[b.] March 28, 1928, Little Rock, Arkansas; [p.] George Abram Roath and Sina L. M. Tweedie; [m.] Phoebe Ellen Roath; [ch.] Karen, Sharon and Annette; [ed.] Gardena California High, A.S. Prelaw Business AD., Tarleton State, Texas B.A. Behavioral Science Cal Poly, Pomona, California; [occ.] Ret. Finance, supply officer, USCG, Ret. tool and die maker, Tohr, Riverside, CA.; [oth. writ.] The Plow; [pers.] Pay attention to the center of creation. [a.] Grand Terrace, CA.

ROBBINS, JEANNY
[b.] March 4, 1960, Bakersfield, California; [p.] Gene and Rosemary Whitton; [m.] Michael Robbins, January 9, 1981; [ch.] (horses and dogs) Horses, Boone and Chad, dog, Chester, no children; [ed.] Graduate Tehachapi High School 1978, Community College, Bakersfield, CA; [occ.] Housewife (cowgirl), work on cattle ranch with father; [memb.] Tehachapi Mountain Flyers Mounted Drill Team, PRCA (Professional Rodeo Cowboys Association), members (drillmaster); [hon.] Honor Roll in high school; [oth. writ.] 20 other "Cowboy poems", newspaper articles for Flyers Drill Team; [pers.] When looking out at the landscape, I imagine, 100 years ago and 100 years from now. How empty this country must have been, how crowed it will be. [a.] Keene, CA (6,400 acres).

ROBBINS, JESSICA I.
[pen.] Seka; [b.] September 13,1980, Michigan; [p.] Darlene F. Robbins; [ed.] Attends L'Anse Creuse North; [occ.] Student; [memb.] National Honor Society, Student Council and Gold-dusters Drill team; [hon.] Citizen of the Month and Honor Society; [oth.writ.] Wrote a poetry book for a literature class; [pers.] Poems are a way of putting my feelings and thoughts on paper. [a.] Chesterfield Twp., MI 48051.

ROBERTS, AMY
[b.] December 10,1976, Rockville Centre, New York; [p.] Bonnie and Alfred J. Roberts; [ed.] South Side High School; [memb.] Honor Society, Peer Counciling, Helping Hands, Senior Citizen Services; [hon.] Honor Society; [oth.writ.] Several poems and short stories published in local papers; [pers.] Through words the mind is excited and the soul is set free. [a.] Rockville Centre, NY 11570.

ROBERTS, BLEU
[pen.] Weldon Bleu; [b.] June 7, 1979, Jacksonville, Florida; [p.] Marcia Kaplan and J.R. Roberts; [ed.] Laing Middle School, 7th grade presently; [occ.] Student; [memb.] Tae Kwon Doe, Theatre Works Spoleto; [hon.] Chosen for Gian Carlos Mennotti's Production of Parsifal (the opera) and numerous other productions; [oth. writ.] Many poems, short stories, plays and songs; [pers.] My words are from the mind, my inspirations are from daily experiences and emotions. [a.] Mt. Pleasant, SC 29464.

ROBERTS, CAROLYN J.
[b.] June 18, 1956, Wheeling, West Virginia; [ed.] University of Notre Dame, University of Kentucky (Baccalaureate), University of Kentucky, University of Louisville (Master's and Post-master's); [occ.] Teacher, Fairdale Elementary, Jefferson County Kentucky; [memb.] NSTA, NCTE, NCTM, National Writing Project; [hon.] Dean's List, bachelor's and master's degrees with honor; [oth. writ.] Up to this point, I have written mostly for my own soul searching and amusement; [pers.] The survivors of the Vietnam War (or victims if you wish) include the many widows and children whose lives were shattered and immeasurably changed by death and the prejudices of that war, their needs are ignored all to often. [a.] Louisville, KY 40214.

ROBERTS, DETRA
[pen.] Lady D; [b.] May 30, 1954, Kendall, Florida; [p.] Elvera Crittendon and Floyd Bethel; [m.] Nelson H. Roberts, October 18, 1986; [ch.] Tameka Arianne, Andrae Michael, Jameka Aisha, Bakori and Ashante; [ed.] University of North Dakota, Grand Forks, North Dakota; [occ.] Elementary teacher, Bent Tree Elementary; [memb.] Reading Council; [oth. writ.] Poems published in college newspaper, wrote poems for weddings and other occasion; [pers.] My feelings about life comes through my poem. To search is to find, to believe is to seek, to reach is to touch. [a.] Miami, FL 33157.

ROBERTS, PAUL G.
[b.] January 7, 1960, Koblenz, Germany; [m.] Elizabeth Roberts, August 4, 1989; [ch.] Brande' and Casey; [ed.] Associate degree, general studies, Central Texas College; [occ.] Sergeant First Class in the US Army Rangers; [oth. writ.] Several poems and songs, none published; [pers.] I try to echo my feelings on a subject through my writings and maybe causing the same feelings to be felt by the reader. [a.] APO, AIA 34005-5000.

ROBERTSON, SHARON RUTH
[b.] December 27, 1979, Milford Hospital; [p.] Kara M. and William Robertson; [hon.] Award on a book I wrote called "The A.B.C. Book", it is a children's book; [oth. writ.] Other poems published in my school newspaper. [a.] Uxbridge, MA 01569.

ROBERTSON, WYVONNE HUEBSCH
[b.] September 10, 1935, Westminster, Texas; [p.] Brodie Ezekiel and Olivia Elizabeth (nee) Cleveland Huebsch; [m.] Dudley Edward Robertson (deceased), June 12, 1953; [ch.] Ray, Clay, Alan and Shelly; [ed.] Westminster High, Collin County Community College, Assoc. Art Degree; [occ.] Retired banker, farmer, beekeeper, house painter/decorating, artist, sculpture; [memb.] First Methodist Church, Collin County Hobby Beekeepers Association, Dallas Mu-

seum, Heard Museum, Dallas Arboretum, Channel 13; [hon.] Beekeeper of the Year, 1993 1st place in honey taste; [oth. writ.] None published, Editor for the CCHBA; [pers.] I have a very deep devotion to the land that I grew up on and to the land that we now farm. I love children, the animals, the trees and flowers, and even the weeds in the fence rows. I see poetry in the very existence of life and even in death. I am influenced mostly by my love for my God, Michelangelo, Beethoven and my late mother. [a.] Allen, TX.

ROBINS, LYNN
[b.] May 13, 1953, Mt. Clemens, Michigan; [p.] Helen and Edward Warner; [m.] Michael Robins, July 7, 1973; [ch.] Joshua, Jesse, Caleb-Matthew, Jehonathan and Michael Robins; [ed.] Fordson High; [occ.] Housewife; [memb.] Jehovah's Witness; [hon.] Golden Poet Award; [pers.] Inspiration is the key to my success, my husband and my children. [a.] Monroe, MI.

ROBINSON, CHRISTINA
[b.] October 13, 1977, Portland, Oregon; [p.] Diana Robinson; [ed.] Mooberry Elementary, 2 years school in Mexico, Blue Ridge Elementary, Pioneer Middle, Walla Walla High; [occ.] I want to become a lawyer, I speak 5 languages; [memb.] F.H.A., Latino Club, National Junior Honor Society, (NJHS), A.J.B.; [hon.] N.J.H.S. awards in fairs and in modeling invitations; [oth. writ.] Poems, short stories and many other stories that are just for school activities; [pers.] I believe that everyone can be who they want to be if they put their mind and soul to it, go for it. [a.] Milton Freewater, OR 97862.

ROBINSON, JENNIFER R.
[pen.] Jen Robinson; [b.] November 1, 1979, Columbia, South Carolina; [p.] Carol G. and Van B. Robinson; [ed.] 7th grader at Richard Winn Academy; [pers.] Enjoys piano, horse back riding (hunt seat), tennis and swimming. [a.] Winnsboro, SC 29180.

ROBINSON, PATRICIA
[pen.] Pat; [b.] October 12, 1958, Athens, Ohio; [p.] Alva and Alice Robinson; [ch.] None, but have 18-20 nieces and nephews; [ed.] Completed G.E.D., quit school, but went back; [occ.] Unemployed at this time, have good work history; [hon.] Got an award from truck driving school and from passenger assistant training; [oth. writ.] I've wrote several songs, that maybe someday will be sung. several different poems, I love to write and try to sing; [pers.] Never been married, far as kids go I have my nieces and nephews to enjoy. I started writing when I was young. It comes from the heart. [a.] Albany, OH.

ROBINSON, ROSETTA
[b.] May 17, 1950, Brooklyn, New York; [p.] Mr. and Mrs. Alfred Robinson; [ed.] B.S. Education, New York University, M.S. Cornell University 1974; [occ.] Independent/freelance writer/producer/reporter; [memb.] Disciples of Christ Church; [hon.] AAUW Letter of Recognition Award, 1993, National Fed. of Community Broadcasters Award, 1990, Outstanding Young Woman of America 1978; [oth. writ.] Articles published in The Washington Post, Essence Magazine, Commentary in The Washington Times and The Washington Informer; [pers.] I understand

that my writing and communications abilities are a gift from God. My goal is to inform, educate, restore and to help persons attain a new vision of self worth. [a.] Washington, DC.

ROBINSON, SHARITA
[pen.] Rita Sams; [b.] March 8, 1979, Providence Rhode Island; [p.] Dr. Rita and Sam Robinson; [ed.] Copely-Fairlawn Middle School, Copley, Ohio; [occ.] Student; [memb.] Builders Club, 2 years Pres. 3, Student Council, Youth President St. John C.M.E., C.F.M.S. band; [hon.] Honor student, Kiwaina Club Honors, Community Leader; [oth. writ.] Published poem entitled "Aids" Snodgrass, unpublished children's book entitled "A Dream Too Many"; [pers.] "By the grace and goodness of God all and everything will be, will be, and by the goodness of God all that will not, will never". [a.] Akron, OH.

ROCKNOWSKI, JAMES
[b.] November 28, 1958, Kenosha, Wisconsin; [p.] John and Lois Rocknowski; [ed.] Cal State University, Long Beach; [occ.] Vice-president, Speed Racer Enterprises; [oth. writ.] Over 200 poems in my private collection, poem published in Voices od America Publication; [pers.] " Love is a dog from hell". [a.] San Pedro, CA 90732.

RODRIGUEZ, JAN
[b.] July 3, 1972, Sault St. Marie, Michigan; [p.] Raul and Susan Rodriguez; [ed.] (Class of 90') Wasilla High School; [occ.] Retail salesman at local record/ music store; [hon.] 2nd place in fighting at AAU Karate Nationals in 1990, 4th place in State Fencing Tournament in 1991; [oth. writ.] This is my first published writing; [pers.] I believe that poetry and music are the most effective of expressing one's deeper emotions. My major influences are Jim Morrison, Javan, Trent Reznor and Lao-Tzu. [a.] Wasilla, AK 99645.

ROE, JASON C.
[b.] April 27, 1976, Jacksonville, Florida; [p.] Susan and Clifford Roe; [ed.] Exeter Area High School, Exeter, New Hampshire; [occ.] Student, work at a private school, drummer/teacher; [memb.] Kentucky Colonel; [oth. writ.] Several used in a musical setting as lyrics; [pers.] I try to reflect the thought that although nothing is perfect, goodness and beauty is part of everyone and everything. [a.] Exeter, NH 03833.

ROGAHN, GREGORY C.
[pen.] El Sr. Gallo Rojo; [b.] June 5, 1947, Chicago, Illinois; [ch.] Matthew, Aaron and Andrew Peter; [ed.] BA., Concordia College, St. Paul, MN., M-Div Concordia Theological, Springfield, Illinois; [occ.] 4th grade teacher, H.D. Hilley Elementary School; [memb.] National Lutheran Association of Scouters, National Horseless Carriage Club; [hon.] Pro Deo et Patria Emblem and Lamb Award; [oth. writ.] Articles in the Outreach and the Intouch newsletters; [pers.] I attempt to be sensitive to the emotional struggles within myself and those around me. [a.] El Paso, TX 79936.

ROGERS, RANEY
[b.] April 8, 1956; [p.] Reverend and Mrs. Norman E. Gossett, Sr.; [m.] Kenneth Rogers, December 16, 1979; [ch.] Elizabeth Raney; [ed.] East Carolina University; [occ.] Artist/painter; [memb.] North Caro-

lina Nature Artists Association, World Wildlife Fund, East African Wildlife Society; [hon.] Numerous awards won in shows throughout Southeast and a one woman show March 93; [oth. writ.] Poem published in high school paper about Clouds, which later evolved into a painting; [pers.] As a nature artist my goal is to bring my viewer closer to our environment and truly appreciate the natural beauty of our world, it seemed only right that one could write about such things as well. [a.] Warrensville, NC 28693.

ROHLF, DEBORAH
[b.] August 20, 1968, Fridely, Minnesota; [p.] Ronald and Sandra Rohlf; [ed.] Wylie High School, Texas State Technical Institute Sweetwater; [occ.] Telephone Operator, Abilene, Texas; [hon.] President and Dean's List; [oth. writ.] One other published poem; [pers.] I draw on personal experiences for my poems. [a.] Abilene, TX 79606.

ROLSON, JUNE RITA
[pen.]] Andreana Seaton; [b.] April 9, 1939, Toronto, Ontario; [p.] Robert E.G. and Mary Margaret (Rutledgge) Atkins; [m.] Donald J. Rolson, August 18, 1970; [ed.] Grade 12 plus 4 college credits; [occ.] Housewife, parttime teacher and writer; [memb.] B.C. Writers Association; [oth. writ.] I have written 5 complete Juvenile Adventure stories yet to be published; [pers.] I believe in books for children. There aren't enough on the market today, children are getting away from reading and that's a shame. I'll continue to write for children until I get published. [a.] Forest Grove, B C Canada V0K 1M0.

ROMAN, NICHOLAS
[b.] May 25, 1926, Chilliwack, BC Canada; [p.] Nicholas Romanuck and Helen Duff; [ed.] Completed grade X, Philip Shefield High School, Abbotsford BC, Canada; [occ.] Real Estate Salesman, prior to that worked in tugs on the British Columbia Coast; [oth. writ.] Many letters to the West Coast Mariner and West Coast Fisherman, Vancouver BC, Canada. [a.] Orlando, FL 32808-1808.

ROMERO, MICHELLE (13 YEARS OLD)
[b.] November 11, 1979, Abbeville, Louisiana; [p.] Bonnie Romero; [ed.] J.H. Williams Middle School; [occ.] Student; [memb.] 4-H Club, band, Creative Scholars; [hon.] Band Award, Honor Roll Award, Science Project Awards, Creative Scholars Awards, 4-H Awards; [oth. writ.] Several other poems; [pers.] I try to be creative and imaginative as I most possibly can. I am greatly influenced by teachers, family and friends. [a.] Abbeville, LA.

ROMINE, DEBRA D.
[pen.] Debra D. Romine; [b.] March 17, 1954, Umatilla, Oregon; [m.] Larry J. Romine; [oth. writ.] First published work; [pers.] In a tiny little town, in a rambling house with four kittens to bring me a mouse, two young souls adorning my crown helping me fly: keeping my feet on the ground, husband number one (and only I'm sure) keeps me aware love is so pure, write me with comments and other remarks (no threats, please: my house is surrounded by sharks). [a.] LaGrande, OR.

ROSE, MARY C.
[b.] November 13, 1926, Wildwood, New Jersey; [p.] Alda and William Baldwin; [m.] Alfred G. Rose, August 18, 1946; [ch.] William George, James Allen,

Sue Ann, (Mary C.) Cathy; [ed.] Graduate-Cape May High, Cape May Co. Vocational School; [occ.] Ceramic Teacher, housewife; [memb.] Green Creek Fire Co. Auxiliary; [hon.] Community Volunteer-Baptist Church -Green Creek Fire Co.; [oth. writ.] Some have been published in newspapers type, "Poetry Journals", one poem was set to music, and is sung in church; [pers.] I write mainly about clowns and their inner-most feelings, for we all at sometime play the part of a clown. I also write in a religious vein. [a.] Green Creek, NJ.

ROSE, ROLAND
[b.] October 1, 1939, Oklahoma City, Oklahoma; [p.] Frank and Lena Rose; [m.] Josie R. Rose; [ch.] Laura Elena and Noel Christopher; [ed.] BA, Med; [occ.] Art Instructor, Freelance Illustrator, cartoonist, mural artist; [pers.] Reflection, interpretation, inspiration comes from observation and contemplation, when all five becomes one then the moment of creating was begun. [a.] Andrews, TX 79714.

ROSE, TAMARA
[b.] February 11, 1977, Iran; [p.] Joanne Shorthill and Alan Rose; [ed.] I am currently enrolled in high school as a junior; [occ.] Student; [memb.] National Honor Society, March of Dimes; [hon.] Honor Roll; [oth. writ.] One in a Santa Monica Gallery, California; [pers.] My poetry is a reflection of my feelings and nothing else. [a.] Plano, TX 75023-8111.

ROSENBERG, ESTHER
[b.] August 23,1978, Brooklyn, New York; [p.] Sheila Grinberg and Victor Rosenberg; [ed.] Shulamith Elementary School, Shulamith High School; [pers.] Exhaustion is the aftermath to success. [a.] Brooklyn, NY 11218.

ROSS, ANGELIA
[b.] November 2, 1971, Scott County, Tennessee; [p.] Billy and Judy Ross; [ed.] McCreary Central High; [hon.] Student of the Month, best Chemistry notebook and best flower collection; [oth. writ.] Two poems published by Quill Books and one poem published by Western Poetry Association.[a.] Pine Knot, KY 42635.

ROSS, KATHLEEN
[b.] 1916, England; [m.] Widow; [ch.] 6 daughters; [occ.] Registered Nurse CN; [hon.] (Hobbies) Sending appropriate poems to other artists and musicians for example, Sir Yehudi Munhin and Prof. Hanes (Prof. of English Literature at Princeton University); [oth. writ.] I've been writing poetry for 25 years. [a.] Bournemouth, BH6 5QF.

ROSS, TAMMI
[b.] May 9, 1976, Eugene, Oregon; [p.] Kathi and Larry Ross; [ed.] Preschool through 7th, then homeschool, will graduate in 1994; [hon.] Won 1st place on an essay contest three years ago, then the next year I won an Honorable Mention in the next years contest; [pers.] Never give up- if you try hard enough you will always win, at least in your heart. [a.] Cottage Grove, OR 97424.

ROSSIER, MOENSIE
[b.] January 5, 1973, Cardiff, Wales U.K.; [p.] Achmat and Gadija Rossier; [ed.] The Queen's School, Chester, U.K., King's College, Cambridge University; [occ.] Student Reading Philosophy at Cambridge

University (rising 3rd year); [hon.] Final year school prizes in maths and physics for outstanding work at advanced level, ICI Young Analyst prize-Chemistry; [oth. writ.] Poem published in Cadbury's book of children's poetry. [a.] Cambridge, CB2 1ST, England.

ROTH, CLARK
[pen.] Sigmund; [b.] September 15, 1976, Tokyo, Japan; [p.] Dale and Eileen Roth; [occ.] Student; [pers.] I have a pair of beautiful black shoes, they are quite Gothic, with a strap and buckle rather than laces. [a.] Columbus, NE 68601.

ROUBIAN, SUSAN
[b.] June 18,1977, Landstuhl, West Germany; [p.] Dr. Armen S. and Cynthia Roubian; [ed.] Currently entering junior year of high school at Rome Free Academy; [occ.] Student; [memb.] J.O.Y. Presbyterian Youth Group, Rome Free Academy Varsity Swim Team, Leatherstocking Swim Team; [hon.] Junior National Honor Society, Varsity Swim Team Most Valuable Swimmer 1992, Onandago All-Star Swim League 1992; [oth. writ.] None published; [pers.] "Eternity" was written in January 1992, on the death of my grandfather, John H. Allan. I dedicate it to his memory and to my grandmother, Olive B. Allan, who encourages me. [a.] Rome, NY.

ROULSTON, BOBBI-LEE
[b.] February 14, 1978, Windsor, Nova Scotia; [p.] Norman and Elizabeth Roulston; [ed.] Grade nine student, Harts North Rural High School, Kennetcook, Nova Scotia, Canada; [occ.] Student; [hon.] English Award grade 8, Math Award grade 7, regards to top student in subject area; [pers.] I write about material that influences my life and the issues that students my age must deal with in our society. [a.] Harts County, Nova Scotia B0N 1P0 Canada.

ROWNEY, DAVID A.
[pen.] Alan B. Schaefer; [b.] November 6, 1962, Woburn, Massachusetts; [ed.] Bachelor of Arts 1985, University of New Hampshire; [occ.] Student (Mechanical Engineering) University of Arizona. [a.] Tucson, AZ.

ROYNON, VERONICA
[b.] December 31, 1938, England; [ch.] David Edward and Bettine Helen; [occ.] R.N., Midwife I; [occ.] Director -Day Care Center; [memb.] Anglican Church; [oth. writ.] Several poems; [pers.] I am guided by the love of God and influenced by the Christian Mystics.[a.] Port Sydney, Ontario Canada P0B 1L0.

RUCKER, DRIFTWOOD H.
[b.] January 6, 1918, Calhoun County, South Carolina; [p.] Bogan H. and Pearl Blanche Rucker; [m.] Bernice Jernigan Rucker, August 25, 1944; [ch.] Hayne Jernigan and Daniel Wray Rucker; [ed.] AB from Wooford College, Spartanburg, South Carolina and M-Div. from Duke Divinity School, Durham, North Carolina; [occ.] Retired United Methodist Minister in Alabama-West Florida Conference; [memb.] A Commissioned Chaplain with the Veterans Administration; [hon.] Chairman District Missions, Chairman Rural Life Com., Chairman of Blue Lake Commission, specialized in Evangelism, (college honors: Who's Who, President of Sigma Tav Alpha Frat., Block "W" Club; [oth. writ.] Heavenly

Prayers for Earthly Settings (a book of prayers mostly for worship services) Gathered Fragments; [pers.] While geared to a spiritual frequency, I'm aware of the burdens and anxiety and frustrations people are carrying. I enjoy using humor, wit and puns as a diversion for lifting furrows from brows. [a.] Pensacola, FL 32504

RUDRICK, JULIE A.
[b.] June 28, 1958, Regina, Sask; [p.] Patrick and Louise; [m.] Ex-spouse, Dr. Brian Rudrick, October 22, 1983; [ch.] Adina (9) and Stephen (8); [ed.] B.F.A.-Advertising Art, B.E.A.D.-Arts Education (visual art major, literature minor); [occ.] Senior Education student; [hon.] Dean's List; [pers.] Interested in the connections of humans to nature and to both secular and spiritual institutions and how "action" and "meaning" are related. [a.] Regina, Sask S4N 4K9 Canada.

RUNDBERG, KAREN
[b.] April 9, 1930, Estevan-Sask, Canada; [p.] Signe and Josef Svorkfal; [m.] October 2, 1951; [ch.] Kathryn Lynn Watson, Calgary-Alberta; [ed.] Grade 10, plus technical school; [occ.] Advertising, copywriting and display manager, now retired; [memb.] Highwood Lutheran Church; [hon.] Have won a few times in local and national display contests within the company I was employed; [oth. writ.] Many poems and song, personal to family and friends, won 1st prize re: small injured bird I found, nursed back to health and released, this was in the 30's and was published in Winnipeg Free Press in Pathfinders column; [pers.] My poem, 'Tribute to Mother" was started in 1965, I couldn't seem to finish it, so I tucked it away then in 1985 I was inspired to finish it. I did and gave it to mom on December 12, 1985, she passed away suddenly 2 weeks later at age 91, I loved her. [a.] Regina-Sask, Canada S4R 4Y1.

RUNYON, THEODORE H.
[pen.] Ted; [b.] November 8, 1919, Newark, New Jersey; [p.] T. W. S. and Martha C. (Radke) Runyon; [m.] Mildred C. (Kyle) (Carol) Runyon, May 10, 1946; [ch.] Susan, Ted, Bill and Dan; [ed.] Brown Military Academy High School, University of California, Berkeley, California, Engr. Mech., George Washington U for Foreign Affairs, Dean's List, So. Western College, as Real Estate Cmd. and General Staff, Air Cmd. and General Staff, NATO Def, Coll; [occ.] 32 years Navy, Army, AF., Ret. Colonel AF, Instr. R.E. So. Western College, R.E. Broker Prudential Cal. Reality; [memb.] US Navy Lg., the Retired Officers Association, Lutheran Church Council, past, president of each, R.E. Certificate, Inst. Ca. Ed. Association, Coronado Association of Re California Education Association; [hon.] Comd. Pilot, Master Missileman Legion of Merit, DFC, Air Medal, Purple Heart, POW Medal, Campaign Medals, American and ETO Alpha Sigma Lambda; [oth. writ.] Honor thesis " Military in Space, What Should Be Done", The National War College, Washington, DC., 1963. Top secret study on Middle East, India, Pakistan, participant, Real Estate column local newspaper, numerous poems for church poet's corner; [pers.] I believe that poetry like beautiful music brings joy to the heart and peace to the mind. " Now good shepherd hear the prayer of good sheep her and everywhere" from my poem " Your Sheep Are Calling". [a.] Coronado, CA 92118.

RUSHING, CHRISTY
[b.] August 28, 1980, Pensacola, Florida; [p.] Steve and Linda Rushing; [ed.] Meigs Middle School, student (7th grade); [occ.] Student; [hon.] Athlete lettered in varsity soccer and track, football manager, Duke University Talent Identification Program recipient for 7th grade gifted students; [pers.] " Why settle for less, when I can try to do my best". [a.] Fort Walton Beach. FL 32548.

RUSS, SEAN DAVID NICHOLAS
[pen.] Sean D. Russ; [b.] February 7, 1970, Fairfax, Virginia; [p.] David and Linda Russ; [m.] Anita D. Tracy-Russ (current wife), September 29, 1992; [ch.] Lauren and Ryan Russ, (children by 1st wife); [ed.] G.E.D.; [occ.] Automotive Defamer (self-employed) and deliver driver; [memb.] Nicholasville Fire Department (volunteer firefighter), Jessamine Co. Little League Association (assistant baseball coach); [oth. writ.] 1st published and 1st submitted, currently working on a personal collection of poems and reflections; [pers.] I strive to express my heart and soul through my writing. [a.] Nicholasville, KY 40356.

RUSSELL, MILDRED E. CLEARWATER
[b.] January 23, 1915, Elmira, New York Township; [p.] Frank L. Clearwater and Lovina; [m.] S.A. Russell, 1949; [ch.] One son; [ed.] High school; [occ.] Housewife and mother; [memb.] V.F.W.A. and D.A.V.A. [hon.] Chaplain -Lake Havasu City V.F.W.A. 1981-2, lettered material for V.F.W. at one time -1979, Chaplain -Lake Havasu City, AZ; [oth. writ.] Editor, Robert Nelson 1988, " God's T.V. -The Sky" page 109, " The Milk Man of Santa Cruz, editor-John Frost page 379, reports to V.F.W. (Provo, Utah); [pers.] " Take the rose the thorn forget" that I've done all my life. [a.] Lake Havasu City, AZ, home of London Bridge.

RUSSO, TARA RAYE
[pen.] Lee Way Spindle; [b.] March 13, 1971, Glenridge, New Jersey; [ed.] Passaic Valley High School, School of Visual Arts, New York City, L'Escola Massana, Bacelona Spain 1992; [memb.] Montclair Art Museum, MACA, Montclair Arts and Cultural Alliance, City Without Walls, Alternative Gallery Space, Newark, New Jersey; [hon.] The Colors of Conflict Juried Show, The Paterson Museum, Paterson, New Jersey; [oth. writ.] Ebb and Flow, spoken work at the Right to Exist Bookstore, Paterson, NJ, Hidden Beauty 10th anniversary poetry contest, West Paterson Public Library, West Paterson, New Jersey; [pers.] Until grasped by the artist and individually realized, art is the reflection of conceptions, captured in a fleeting moment and is as delicate a process as a far away star twinkling in a mother's eye. [a.] Little Falls, NJ 07424.

RUTLEDGE, KATHY WINTON
[pen.] Kathy Rutledge; [b.] February 13, 1958, Manchester, Tennessee; [p.] Bobby and Julie Elledge; [m.] Billy Lee Rutledge, May 3, 1991; [ch.] Kevin and Marc Rutledge, Jennifer and Kelly Winton; [ed.] Grundy Co. High, Motlow State College; [occ.] Customer Service/buyer; [memb.] Lighthouse Bible Church; [pers.] If you learn but one thing in life, understand who you are and what you stand for, and let Jesus Christ be your guide. [a.] McMinnville, TN 37110.

RYAN, SHARON
[pen.] "Ryan" or "Roni"; [b.] April 29, 1958, Los Angeles, California; [p.] Roger (deceased) and Margaret Ryan; [m.] Divorced; [ch.] Edwon, April and Christopher; [ed.] Compton, California, graduated, Compton Senior High, attended Compton Community College; [occ.] Self-employed, writing service; [memb.] Theatrical Club, Paul Robeson Players, Los Angeles, California (1977); [hon.] Several high school achievements; [oth. writ.] An extensive list of various other poems that cover a span of over fifteen years, over a variety of topics from both male and female points of view; [pers.] Creativity is the vehicle of the imagination. Poetry is an endangered pastime. They both should be reborn. [a.] Baton Rouge, LA.

RZADKOWOLSKA, KATIE
[b.] November 9, 1978, Warsaw, Poland; [p.] Ewa Bolesta and Bogdan Rzadkowolska; [ed.] High school, freshman Aliso Niguel High School; [occ.] Student; [memb.] Volunteer work at community park; [oth. writ.] Written several poems and a few published in school year book; [pers.] Life is tough, but you should never give up. [a.] Laguna Niguel, CA 92677.

SAAH, DAVID JR.
[b.] November 4, 1972, Bethesda, Maryland; [p.] David and Renee Daah; [ed.] Magruder High, Montgomery College; [occ.] Auto mechanic, part-time carpenter; [memb.] Program Council, The Spur newspaper, WROC radio on college campus; [hon.] Letter in chorus, other writings, certificate of achievement in program council; [oth. writ.] Song lyrics, other poems not published yet, stories; [pers.] I always finish what I've started and never quit. [a.] Gaithersburg, MD 20877.

SAARELA, TUULI
[b.] September 15, 1979, Helsinki, Finland; [p.] Tapio and Ulla Saarela; [ed.] Starting high school september 1993 (Beverly Hills); [occ.] Student; [pers.] I have been influenced to write poems from my personal experiences and the happenings around me. [a.] Los Angeles, CA 90049.

SAAVEDRA, MANUEL
[b.] March 12, 1956, Valparaiso, Chile; [p.] Manuel Saavedra and Rosa Duran; [ed.] High school, commercial institute; [occ.] Seaman in merchant ships; [oth. writ.] Poems, short stories, songs, and novels waiting for publication in a short future; [pers.] If through a simple poem I am able to offer a positive message to the humankind about the small details hidden at every corner of this wonderful planet, then I will write on forever! [a.] Valparaiso, Chile (South America).

SACK, ATHENA
[b.] February 9, 1981, Long Beach, California; [p.] Helen and Enno Sack, sister, Athena; [ed.] Withrow Elementary School; [memb.] Koala Club, U.S.A. Olympic Penpal Club; [hon.] Honor Roll, Student of the Month, Good Citizenship award; [oth. writ.] Coordinator and editor for "The Other End" section of school newsletter; [pers.] I am 12 years old and enjoy reading and writing very much. My goal is to become an accomplished author and be able to support myself as a writer. [a.] Lake Elsinore, CA 92530.

SAENZ, CHRISTOPHER LEE
[b.] March 22, 1975, McAllen, Texas; [p.] Juan E. Jr. and Mary S. Saenz; [ed.] Zapata High School; [oth. writ.] Several poems written in my personal journal. [a.] Zapata, TX 78076.

SAGER, ANNIE LAVERLE
[b.] February 1, 1941, Leachville, Arkansas; [p.] Cecil and Imogene Cope; [m.] deceased; [ch.] Edward Douglas, Jeffrey William, Cheri Marie, Kristina Ann Sager Overhiser; [ed.] Lake City Arkansas Elementary School, Old Central Continuing Education, Parsons Business School, Kalamazoo, Michigan; [occ.] Sales representative, Sears Roebuck and Co.; [memb.] Valley View Bible Church, Poem/Church Bulletin, Eternal Springtime; [oth. writ.] Collections of poems, prayers, and songs; [pers.] I enjoy writing about God, His love, and the beauty of nature. [a.] Kalamazoo, MI 49008.

SAHLER, ABRAHAM
November 5, 1911, Bronx, New York; [p.] Moses and Minnie Sahler; [m.] Sarah Sahler, December 28, 1938; [ch.] Anne, Joseph; [ed.] High School; [occ.] Taxi driver; [memb.] Taxi Union, Society of Janina, WMCA, [hon.] Volunteered for numerous charities, WMCA, March of Dimes, Heart Association, Leukemia Society; [oth. writ.] Several poems written lovingly to wife and family members; [pers.] Mr. Sahler is deceased as of 3/18/93. My loving husband was a loving father, grandfather, and great-grandfather with a wonderful sense of humor that saw many of us through some very tough times. [a.] Bronx, NY 10473.

SAIS, JOEY O. JR.
[pen.] JOS Jr.; [b.] December 15, 1971, Pueblo, Colorado; [p.] Joe and Margaret Sais; [ed.] College sophomore. [a.] Pueblo, CO 81001.

SAMPSON, BILLIE JOE
[pen.] Billie Joe Taylor; [b.] December 24, 1953, Wellington, Kansas; [p.] Alpine and Joseph Taylor; [m.] Ronnie Sampson, December 18, 1970; [ch.] Joseph Earl, Cary Ronald, Bobbie Joe; [ed.] West High School, Butler County Community College; [occ.] Artist, restaurant owner/operator, earning Bachelor degree in psychology; [pers.] My personal experiences are reflected in my writings. I have always has a deep love for poetry. [a.] Severy, KS 67137.

SANBORN, CLYDE
[b.] April 21, 1948, Oakland, California; [p.] Clyde and Gwendolyn Sanborn; [ed.] Stagg High School, San Joaquin Delta College; [oth. writ.] Poems since the age of 14 published in various small presses; [pers.] Currently reside on a riverboat near La Conner, north of Seattle, Washington, studying ornithology, meteorology, and estuary dynamics. Pursuing a career in visual arts and philosophy. [a.] Lodi, CA 95242.

SANCHEZ, WADE
[pen.] Wade Samuels; [b.] December 31, 1969, Dayton, Texas; [p.] Alex C. and Adelina Sanchez; [ed.] Robinson High School, 1988, presently a senior at the University of Mary Hardin-Baylor in Belton, Texas; [occ.] Future spanish teacher; [pers.] A quote by Johann von Goethe that I strive to remind myself of daily, "Nothing should be prized more highly than the value of each day". [a.] Waco, TX 76706.

SANDERS, MYRON H.
[b.] November 2, 1914, Burlington, Wyoming; [p.] Frank Edmond and Eva Gribble Sanders; [m.] Elaine Richards, June 28, 1933; [ch.] Lynn M, Lyla (twins), Karon; [ed.] Completed 8th grade, graduated from Barber School, many classes in oil painting; [occ.] Barber; [memb.] Idaho Falls Writers League, Church of Latter-Day Saints; [oth. writ.] Fiction novel Gypsie Freedom, book of poems; [pers.] I have received a conviction that in many of my writings I have felt a greater power than my own dictation, some of the words I write, for which I am grateful. [a.] Basalt, ID 83218.

SANDERS, SCOTT
[b.] April 20, 1970, Atlanta, Georgia; [p.] Tom and Margaret Sanders; [m.] girlfriend, Jocelyn Altizer; [ch.] Expecting child in October 1993; [ed.] Whittier College, Virginia Tech; [occ.] Waiter, bartender; [oth. writ.] Plenty of poems and stories looking for homes; [pers.] I like to shock and surprise the reader. I like to make people think. [a.] Floyd, VA 24091.

SANDKNOP, L.A. (SILVERWING)
[pen.] Silverwing; [b.] March 17, 1946, San Diego, California; [p.] Mildred H. Sandknop-Steele; [ed.] Dr. L.A. Sandknop Silverwing P.H.D./D.D.; [occ.] Counselor, teacher, minister; [memb.] Gem and Mineral Society, Art League, UCM minister; [hon.] Newspaper articles, local, published 7 times in various poetry books, partial scholarship for my P.H.D., Columbia P. University; [oth. writ.] 4 novels, The Inbetweeners, My Rainbow Bridge (Lamar and Lania), Helen's Hallucinations, My Real Home Is a Starbase (children's book); [pers.] May there be world peace and prosperity for every living human being on the planet in our NOW, not tomorrow, or some other day! [a.] Oceanside, CA 92057.

SANDLIN, KIMBERLY D.
[b.] September 6, 1969, Indianapolis, Indiana; [p.] Earl and Rose M. Sandlin; [pers.] Enjoy living life to its fullest extent today, but let us not forget what the consequences of tomorrow may become. I want to extend a heartfelt feeling of gratitude to my 3 main sources of inspiration: Alan Hopewell, Don Stansberry, and also the famous novelist, Stephen King. Thank you especially to my two greatest supporters of my writing ability, my mother, Rose, and my best friend, Greg Dierlam. Favorite pasttimes include reading and writing (naturally), listening to music (preferably Billy Joel), and spending time with my one and only sibling, my little sister, Amber. [a.] Cynthiana, IN 47612.

SANTINI, LUCIANO
[b.] December 25, 1961, Palermo, Italy; [m.] Laura Schmidt, July 17, 1989; [ch.] Brittani Renee; [ed.] High school graduate, attending Santa Monica College; [occ.] Business; [hon.] Middle school, high school awards in writing; [oth. writ.] Too many to put on paper. Someday I would love to share them with the world; [pers.] I love writing, it's a way for a person to show their true emotions and who they really are. [a.] North Hollywood, CA 91606.

SANTMIER, REV. DEWEY
[b.] September 11, 1944, Glens Falls, New York; [p.] Rev. and Mrs. Dwight Santmier; [m.] Beverly Brewer, March 27, 1975; [ch.] Jennifer, Joshua; [ed.] Orlando Junior College, Tennessee Temple University, Temple Baptist Seminary; [occ.] Christian schoolteacher and coach; [memb.] National Rifle Association, National Forensic League, Phi Rho Pi; [hon.] Who's Who Among America's Teachers 1992, Yearbook dedications 1974, 1989; [oth writ.] A poem published in The Titan, literary publication of Tennessee Temple University, numerous letters published in The Miami Herald; [pers.] Tanks to Rick Dixon who helped me catch my first bass, Mike Hicks who sometimes outfishes me, and my favorite partner, Joshua. [a.] Pt. St. Lucie FL 34952.

SANTONGUE, CYNTHIA CHRISTINE
[b.] July 15, 1980, Las Vegas, Nevada; [p.] Michael Joseph and Dianne Santongue; [ed.] Junior high school, 7th grade; [hon.] National History and Government Award; [oth. writ.] None that were published; [pers.] I hope my writings will influence young and elderly readers to understand about the world today. [a.] Las Vegas, NV 89120.

SANTOS, THERESA ANN
[pen.] Terry, [b.] November 29, 1972, Hyannis, Massachusetts; [p.] JoAnn and Ferdinand F. Santos; [ed.] Dennis-Yarmouth Regional High School; [occ.] manager/clerk; [memb.] Dennis-Yarmouth High Chorus, Dennis-Yarmouth High School Marching and Concert Band; [hon.] Dennis-Yarmouth High Academic All Star Team College Scholarship; [pers.] Life is a special gift we get. We are all very special people who should try to give life as much as we can, and take from it without any fear. [a.] Yarmouthport, MA 02675.

SAPIGAO, DAISY
[pen.] Daisy Sapigao; [b.] April 16, 1915, Laina Lu Molokai; [p.] Charles and Luci Travis Kaahonui; [m.] Florentino Sapigao, July 22, 1953; [ch.] Henry, Edward, Flo, Theola, Lucille; [ed.] Kaluaaha High School, Kapiolani School of Nursing and Cafeteria Dieting; [occ.] Nursing, Lunalilo Home, private home for elderly; [memb.] American Heart; [hon.] Government award for helping family from burning home (child); [oth. writ.] For patients in hospital, churches; [pers.] Poems published in Kula Hospital, Maui. Loving and goodness of patients in my handwriting. [a.] Waionoe, HI 96792.

SAPPINGTON, ESTHER "COOKIE"
[pen.] Cookie Sappington; [b.] July 21, 1959, poplar Bluff, Missouri; [p.] Grady N, and Ruby M. Sappington; [m.] Divorced; [ch.] John Schultz, Jennifer Schultz, Angel De La Garza; [ed.] National Education Center, The Institute of Children's Literature; [occ.] Medical assistant, AHCCCS coordinator, PMT ambulance; [hon.] Survivor of four divorces with no visual residual damage; [oth. writ.] Several non-submitted/nonpublished poems and songs; [pers.] My writings reflect the struggle, perseverance, defeat, and victories of the single working mother. I have been greatly influenced by experience. [a.] Phoenix, AZ 85008.

SARGENT, HAROLD L.
[pen.] Kopy Kat; [b.] September 24, 1917; [ed.] High school graduate, 2 years graduate SUNY Canton,

New York, Rochester Business Institute; [occ.] Retired; [memb.] Syracuse Writers Guild, VFW Post 7290, AARP, Syracuse; [hon.] Inducted into the Prestigious Homer International Society of Poets, December 1992; [oth. writ.] Published 3 children's and 1 teenage stories; [pers.] No greater love hath a man than this, that he lay down his life for his friends. (John 15:13). [a.] N. Syracuse, NY 13212.

SCAFE, VELMA BERRY

[b.] January 11, 1907, Paragon, West Virginia; [p.] Wiley A. and Viola Catherine Berry; [m.] Elton K. Scafe, December 14, 1946; [ch.] William Kuchon; [ed.] Grade school only, country school in West Virginia; [occ.] Retired L.P.N.; [hon.] Won prize in 6th grade for essay on United States Navy; [oth. writ.] Have written several poems of life's happenings (none submitted for publishing), "Hello Kiddo" was some of my best childhood memories; [pers.] We are making memories each day of our lives. Children should be taught to make theirs good ones. They are going to live with them, but surely! [a.] Charleston, WV 25302.

SCALONE, BETH JULIA

[b.] March 30, 1974, Chicago, Illinois; [p.] Peter and Anita Scalone; [ed.] George Washington High, Calumet College of St. Joseph; [occ.] Student. [a.] Chicago, IL 60633.

SCARBEARY, ROSEMARIE MOEWS

[b.] August 10, 1950, Bloomington, Illinois; [p.] Paul and Florence Moews; [m.] Divorced; [ch.] Paul, 9 yrs old, loves Star Trek, Clare, 7 yrs old, loves tumbling; [ed.] Central Catholic High, Bloomington, Illinois, Illinois State University, Maryknoll Seminary, Maryknoll, New York, Cloud County Community College, Concordia Kansas, Baron County Community College, Great Bend, Kansas; [occ.] Certified Nurses' Aide for mentally ill, mentally retarded, developmentally disabled and geriatric residents, El Paso Health Care, El Paso, Illinois; [memb.] Kappa Omicron Phi, Peace Corps, in Phillipines, VISTA in Chicago, worked with an Irish missionary in Nigeria, Public Relations Committee for Walk for Children (formerly Walk for Mankind), past member Church Women United and Amnesty International; [oth. writ.] Letters to the editor and newspaper articles regarding current happenings, I hope to write a book one day; [pers.] I am interested in peace and justice issues and how they affect my community and global family. I have adopted two children, one Caucasian and one African-American. I am a mother without custody. Throughout most of my adult life I've worked for others to gain basic human rights, Now I find I must also work for these rights for myself and my children. [a.] El Paso, IL 61738.

SCHANZ, MARGARET

[pen.] Margaret Lea Schanz; [b.] August 21, 1923, Owensboro, Kentucky, [p.] Ervin and Daisy Lea Stone; pm.] Donald Leroy (deceased), August 23, 1947; [ch.] William F. Schanz, Patricia Lee Harhold; [ed.] Associate of Arts; [occ.] Retired bookkeeper, office manager; [memb.] American Business Women's Association, The International Society of Poets, National Audubon Society; [hon.] ABWA Woman of the Year, Dearborn Chapter 1983, Poetry Awards with "World of Poetry", honorable mention: "First Snow", 1990, honorable mention, "Days Beginning", 2992, honorable mention "Bowling", 1991, Golden Poet,

1991; [oth. writ.] Just poetry; [pers.] The spoken word is music to my ears, life would be dull without it. [a.] Novi, MI 48375.

SCHAUBEL, DANNA

[b.] March 1, 1973, Port Colborne, Ontario; [p.] Joan Schaubel of Welland; [ed.] Welland High, Eastdale Secondary School (grades in English and Math); [occ.] Teller at credit union here in Welland, 3 years; [memb.] Active participant in Canada's annual "Terry Fox Run"; [hon.] Awarded a plaque after winning an essay contest for my district and then won regionally. This was an essay about our environment. The contest was called the "Marion Drysdale Award"; [oth. writ.] Two poems published in 1992. Several printed in local newspaper; [pers.] My writing is an easy way for me to release my feelings. I am influenced by simple things we sometimes take for granted, like the sun, the trees, love and relationships. [a.] Welland, Ontario L3C 6N3.

SCHEFF, JEREMY

[b.] October 6, 1985, Turnersville, New Jersey; Steven and Cindy Scheff; [ed.] First grade, Carl T. Mitnick Elementary School, Cape May, New Jersey; [occ.] Student; [memb.] Lego Club, Youth Tee-ball, Basketball, and Soccer teams; [hon.] God Medal-World Book Partners in Excellence Reading Award, 1992. Music Award, Piano Recital, 1993; [oth. writ.] I have written many other poems and short stories, none yet published; [pers.] I like sports, writing, and music. I play baseball, soccer, basketball, and piano. When I grow up I might want to be a builder, a basketball player, or a writer. [a.] N. Cape May, NJ 08204.

SCHETTINO, ELAINE F.

[b.] December 4, 1956, White Plains, New York; [p.] Kohn and Rita DeGennaro Schettino; [ed.] M.B.A., New York University, B.F.A., New York University; [occ.] Loan officer, Globe Mortgage Company, Mortgage Bankers; [memb.] Westchester Business Executives, The Builders Institute, Women's Council of Realtors; [hon.] Who's Who in the East, Who's Who of American Women, The World Who's Who of Women, International Who's Who of Professional and Business Women, Hall of Fame, Advertising Club of Westchester, Founders' Day Award, New York University, Alpha Phi Sigma, Dean's List; [oth. writ.] Co-author, Here Comes The Sales Trainers, Royal Publishing, Glendora, Ca., columnist, Impact, The Builders Institute; [pers.] My best work is that which is emotionally charged-coming straight from the heart. I mince no words-I call situations by their right names. I make no apologies. [a.] New Rochelle, NY 10805.

SCHIBIG, SHARYNN ROSE

[b.] April 25, 1962, Seattle, Washington; [p.] Harold Joseph and Lois Marie Stephens Schibig; [ed.] Issaquah High graduate, 1980, business student graduate, 1993; [memb.] the American Rose Society, Patriotic Community; [hon.] Various small press publications, words of appreciation from world-class tenor and pianist; [oth. writ.] Over 20 poems accepted by publishers in over 10 states from January 1993 to March 1993; [pers.] The best is yet to come. [a.] Seattle, WA 98138.

SCHIPPER, AMELIA

[b.] September 29, 1924, Applington, Iowa; [p.] Reihhold and Bernadine Block Wust; [m.] Steno J. Schipper, March 12, 1946; [ch.] Dr. Darwin L. Schipper, Judy Kay Schipper Kellogg; [ed.] Rural Allison, Iowa, Jackson #7, 8th grade; [occ.] Retired, housewife; [memb.] St. James Lutheran Church, Allison Garden Club, American Legion Auxiliary, Friends of Iowa, National Wildlife; [hon.] Graduated with honors, rural Jackson #7, received the golden letter "I" for graduating with honors; [oth. writ.] "Thankful for the Little Things", in Poetic Voices of America, by Sparrowgrass Poetry Forum, Inc.; [pers.] I like to write from the heart, whatever I feel at the time. [a.] Allison IA 50602.

SCHMIDT, JODIE LYNN

[b.] March 3, 1976, Altona, Manitoba; [p.] Harry and Ellen Schmidt; [ed.] Grade 11 student at W.C. Miller Collegiate; [memb.] Vice-president of Kronsweide Youth. [a.] Rosenfeld, Manitoba, Canada R0G 1X0.

SCHMIDT, RYAN MATTHEW

[pen.] R. Matthew Schmidt; [b.] January 30, 1975, Moline Illinois; [p.] John August and Catherine Louise Cervantes Schmidt; [ed.] Wood Junior High School, Davenport North High School, St. Ambrose University; [occ.] Student, musician, actor; [memb.] Founder of the band "Davenport North"; [hon.] MVP Award for 1993 Norwica staff, Who's Who Among American Students, 1991-92; [oth. writ.] Poetry: "Wash Away", "sand", "Who?", "The Loved Wall, songs: "Nagina", "In America", "Catharsis", "Way It Is", "Undub"; [pers.] No two persons will EVER perceive ANYTHING identically. [a.] Davenport, IA 52806.

SCHMIDT, STANLEY W.

[pen.] S.W. Schmidt; [b.] September 16, 1927, Denzil, Saskatchewan, Canada; [p.] Frank and Emily Schmidt; [m.] Marie, December 4, 1952; [ch.] Wellington, Marla, Brickford; [oth. writ.] "Poets Corner" in Norco News, a weekly publication (published from 1989-1993); [pers] "Gestalts": Planting wheat or sowing thoughts farmers and poets work different plots, the one or both with passion or not on fields of dreams...or rocks. [a.] Norco, CA 91760.

SCHRADER, KARRIE

[pen.] K C Schrader; [b.] May 17, 1977, Wichita, Kansas; [p.] Valerie and Jim Schrader; [ch.] Kirk Smit, Jr.,; [ed.] Metro-Midtown High; [hon.] Best Poet award in junior high; [oth. writ.] Prayer in "Quest of a Dream"; [pers.] The wonders of life inspire me to write what I feel. [a.] Wichita, KS 67212.

SCHRADER, MARGARET A.

[b.] August 28, 1942, Wilmington, Delaware; [p.] William H. and Margaret E. Armento; [m.] Julius J. Schrader, August 20, 1983; [ed.] Albany High School, B.A. from State University of New York at Albany, M.S. from University of New York at Oneonta, Ed.S. from University of Missouri-Columbia; [occ.] Administrative assistant at University of Missouri Law School; [memb.] Campus Lutheran Church, volunteer with Missouri State Conservation Department; [hon.] EPDA Summer Institute for Group Counselors at North Texas State University, G.E. Summer Guidance Fellowship at Boston University, EPDA Institute for Junior College Counselors at the University of

Missouri-Columbia; [pers.] I believe in being a source of encouragement and support to others. Through my poetry I seek to express feelings and concerns that are common to the human experience with which others may therefore identify. [a.] Columbia, MO 65202.

SCHULTZ, JUNE H.

[b.] June 3, 1958, Milwaukee, Wisconsin; [p.] Lucille and John Roblek; [m.] Michael J. Schultz, April 7, 1990; [ch.] Russell John; [ed.] B.S. degree Art/Anthropology; [occ.] Sales secretary-Pella Windows; [memb.] Past volunteer of the Milwaukee Public Museum; [oth. writ.] I've written poems occasionally since high school; [pers.] I am a lover of life, art, and nature. I strive to be creative. Writing poetry is one form of that. My son has become my latest inspiration. [a.] Menononee Falls, WI.

SCHULTZ, LINDA J.

[pen.] L,S. Waldo; [b.] May 18, 1958, Holland, Michigan; [p.] Merlin and Eliner Schultz; [ed.] Fennville High School, 12th grade; [oth. writ.] Numerous other poems. [a.] Fennville, MI 49408.

SCHULZ, RENEE

[b.] October 8, 1981, Detroit, Michigan; [p.] Denise Schulz; [ed.] Eagle Ridge Elementary, Phoenix, Arizona; [occ.] Student; [pers.] I wrote this poem in the summer of 1992 when I was 10 years old. [a.] Phoenix, AZ 85024.

SCHWARTZ, BRADLEY

[b.] November 12, 1956, Long Beach, California; [p.] Leon Schwartz, Arthur and Virginia Heineman; [ed.] Buena Park High School, U.C. Davis, U.C. Santa Cruz; [oth. writ.] About 10 or 12 poems, and a group of political science editorials, which I hope to someday publish; [pers.] I try to write honestly, and from my heart. [a.] W. Los Angeles, CA 90025.

SCHWARTZ, MONICA D.

[b.] February 1, 1974, New Jersey; [p.] Allen and Leona Schwartz, sister Paulette Schwartz; [ed.] Trumbull High, Fairfield University; [occ.] Sales; [pers.] Without Jason, my only love, and my family behind me, I would not be the person I am today. [a.] Trumbull, CT.

SCHWEIGER, LAURAL JEANNE

[b.] March 28, 1981, Queen of the Valley Hospital; [p.] Karl A. and Patricia J.C. Schweiger, siblings Jeremy, Michelle; [ed.] 6th grade; [hon.] School writing contest, 1st place, Honor Roll; [oth. writ.] Various poems and stories. [a.] Napa, CA 94558.

SCHWIEN, TAMMY LYNN

[b.] February 9, 1977, Davenport, Iowa; [ed.] Central Clinton High School, Dewitt Iowa; [occ.] Student; [oth. writ.] Several nonpublished poems that I have enjoyed writing for my own collection; [pers.] The Poetry Unit in my Language class has inspired me to try writing poems. I now enjoy it very much. [a.] Welton, IA.

SCOTT, ROSAMOND ELLIS

[b.] December 19, 1910, New Jersey; [p.] Susan MacDonald and Halcolm Ellis; [m.] David Harlow Scott (deceased), March 29, 1941; [ed.] Educated abroad, France, Belgium, England. Schools n Pasadena, California and New York City; [occ.] Interior

designer; [memb.] English Speaking Union; [oth. writ.] Poems and articles published in various newspapers; [pers.] Poetry seems to be the very distilled essence of thought-going straight to the heart, and should provide what the heart needs in comfort, joy, inspiration, originality and feel a closeness to nature. [a.] Washington, DC 20007.

SCOTTI, JOHN R.

[b.] May 8, 1944, Mahanoy City, Pennsylvania; [p.] Dr. and Mrs. John Scotti; [m.] Pat Brown Scotti, May 9, 1992; [ch.] Devin, Todd, Scott; [ed.] Garden City High, SUNY at Stonybrook, University of Delaware; [occ.] Instructor of English, Bowie State University, Bowie, Maryland; [memb.] National Council of Teachers of English, Society for Technical Communication; [hon.] American Field Service Scholarship to Brazil, Athletic Scholarship; [oth. writ.] Publisher/writer for Imago Dei, a Roman Catholic quarterly, byline column for newspaper The Business Exchange, several articles in international newspapers; [pers.] The Lord Jesus Christ is the author of life. Pat, my wife, in reflecting his love for us, inspires my poetry. [a.] Rockville, MD.

SEARS, LOU ANN

[b.] October 12, 1961, Butler, Pennsylvania; [p.] Floyd and Joan Osborne; [m.] David Sears, May 30, 1987; [ed.] Slippery Rock University, Master of Arts degree in English, Bachelor of Science degree in Education, Butler Community College, Associate in Arts degree in General Studies; [occ.] Part-time instructor of English at Butler County Community College, Butler Pa. and Westmoreland Co. Community College, Youngwood, Pa.; [hon.] 8 poems published, accepted invitation to read one of my new poems (1993) at Broad Street Bookstore and Cafe in Grove City, Pa, Summa cum laude graduate of S.R.U. (1989), Magna cum laude graduate of S.R.U. (1983)m Sigma Tau Delta English honorary, Kappa Delta Pi Education honorary, Dean's list ar S.R.U. and Butler Community College, Cum laude graduate of Butler Co. Community College (1981), Phi Theta Kappa academic fraternity; [oth. writ.] 6 poems published in Slippery Rock University's Ginger Hill literary magazine (1989, 1993), 2 poems published in Butler Co. Community College's Facets literary magazine (1993), wrote a 60-poem collection called "Second Glances" (as a thesis project at S.R.U. (1989); [pers.] Actively seeking employment as a full-time instructor of English (in Western Pa.)! [a.] Cabot, PA 16023.

SEAY, ELIZABETH D.

[pen.] Beth Davis, Liz Seay; [b.] May 27, 1923, Grizzard, Virginia; [p.] Howard and Margaret Hayes; [m.] Claude Davis (deceased), Charles Seay, June 15, 1974; [ch.] Claude, Ted, Anne Davis; [ed.] South Hill High, Ferguson High G.E.D., Henderson Business College; [occ.] Factory work (sewing), clerk, cashier; [memb.] Zion Methodist Church Sunday School teacher and choir member, secretary and treasurer Y.A.F. Zion Church, S.T of H.D. Club; [hon.] H.D Fashion Show Grand Prize winner, modeled dress on Peggy Mann, TV, WTVD, Durham, N.C.; [oth. writ.] Several poems published in local newspapers; [pers.] Do unto others as I would have them do unto me. My favorite authors: Elizabeth Barrett Browning and Emily Dickerson. [a.] Newport News VA 23606.

SEELEY, WILLIAM P. JR

[pen.] Bill Seeley Jr.; [b.] November 25, 1975, New London, Connecticut; [ed.] Susquehannock High School, will attend California University of Pennsylvania; [memb.] Exchange student to Sweden; [hon.] National Honor Society. [a.] Shrewsbury, PA 17361.

SEELKE, RONNELLE

[b.] May 17, 1975, Belflower, California; [p.] James and Vicki Crawford; [ed.] Senior at John Glenn High School. I will be attending Cypress College in the Fall 1993; [occ.] Market Research Interviewer; [memb.] Yearbook Editor, Project Interdependence, Wrestling Stats, Track, Cross Country and Hand 'n' Hand; [hon.] Honor Roll, Team Commitment Medal (C.C.); [oth. writ.] Many other poems written for family and friends. Poem to be published in this year's annual. A poem published in "On A Threshold of A Dream. Vol. III", another poem published in local newspaper; [pers.] Anything is possible as long as you believe that it can become a reality. This poem is dedicated to my Grandfather who struggled through the last years of his life with cancer. [a.] Downey, CA 90242.

SEIWALD, GRETCHEN T.

[b.] February 11, 1980, Lawrence, Kansas; [p.] Linda and Eric Seiwald; [ed.] 7th grade completed May 1993; [pers.] Peace! [a.] Lawrence KS 66046.

SELBY, SUSAN F.

[ed.] Central Michigan University, Bachelors degree, University of Michigan, Masters degree, Toledo University; [occ.] Elementary teacher, 19 years, exchange teacher, Priestmead Infants School, Middlesex, England, teacher and principal, Wheelus Field Dependents School, Tripoli, Libya, North Africa; [memb.] Sigma Tau Delta, Kappa Delta Pi, Mt. Pleasant Teachers Club, president 1953, University of Michigan Graduate Club, Monroe, president 1959, board of directors 1963, Michigan Education Association, International Relations M.E.A. convention panel member, Ann Arbor Michigan, Board of Regents, University of Michigan 1960, Science Committee, Monroe Schools, 1960; [hon.] Freshman Speech Award for Public Speaking, Central Michigan University, graduated from Central-Summa cum Laude; [oth. writ.] Complete story of our years in Africa, 10 children's books, enough poems to make a complete book; [pers.] "Bridge of Love" You can build a bridge, Or you can build a wall: If you build a wall, Your world is small: If you build a bridge, Of love for all: It will be a way that, Conquers all. This is my philosophy of life. I am truly singing in my heart at such a great honor. [a.] Leesburg, FL 34788.

SELIM, LILA

[b.] October 28, 1983, Syracuse, New York; [p.] Mohamed and Marilyn Selim; [ed.] 4th grade student at John Kennedy School in Batavia New York; [pers.] I would like to thank my parents for their support, my brothers Alexander and Andre for not driving me crazy all the time, and Danielle Rotundo for being the best friend a person could have. [a.] Batavia, NY.

SELLERS, BELINDA

[b.] March 3, 1962, Memphis, Tennessee; [p.] Ann Herron, Minnie Ector, Martha Skinner; [ch.] William Downey III, Shara Denese, Ikeisha Lenee; [ed.] Trezevant High, Shelby State Community College, Rutledge College, Sea Isle Vo-Tech, Mid-Town Computer; [occ.] Facilitator for drug elimination, nurse technician; [memb.] American Heart Association

(CPR); [hon.] Dean's list, Computer Literacy certificate; [oth. writ.] Newsletters, poems for the sick, wedding poems, sympathy poems; [pers.] My writings reflect my innermost personal experiences and my everyday surroundings. Putting it into writing gives me strength for a positive faith in myself. [a.] Memphis, TN 38105.

SELLERS, KIMBERLY

[b.] September 16, 1969, Bronx, New York; [p.] Paul and Linda Baker; [m.] Chad Sellers, July 30, 1988 ; [ch.] Kyle Paul Sellers, Welsey Jon-Michael Sellers; [ed.] Tecumseh High School, Jackson Community College; [oth. writ.] Several poems on various topics that have never been published; [pers.] Poetry brings inner peace and softens the hard trials of everyday life. Poetry enlightens my heart and helps me to appreciate the little things in my life that I love most. [a.] Tecumseh, MI 49286.

SEMCHUK, KARLA LEIGH

[pen.] Gabrielle Leigh; [b.] October 30, 1974, Danbury, Connecticut; [p.] James c. and Terry Semchuk; [ed.[Danbury High School, class of 1992; [hon.] Golden Poet of 1991 and 1992 (World of Poetry, Sacramento, California); [oth. writ.] Have written several hundred poems over the past six years, was published in a compilation in California by age sixteen; [pers.] I have tried to capture truth in my poetry, real feelings from the heart. For what is poetry if it does not come born from within? [a.] Danbury, CT 06811.

SESHADRI, SHEILA

[b.] November 16, 1978, Boston, Massachusetts; [p.] Ramakrishnan and Lalita Seshadri; [ed.] White Station High School; [memb.] United Way Youth Board, Students Against Drunk Driving (S.A.D.D.); [hon.] Honor Roll; [pers.] Through my poetry I hope to address the problems of society and make the world a better place in which to live. [a.] Memphis, TN 38139.

SEVERINI, FELICIA C.

[b.] September 23, 1927, Red Bank, New Jersey; [p.] Mariano Binaco and Benedetta Pace; [m.] Camillo George, September 14, 1946; [ch.] George, Robert, Linda; [ed.] High school, Red Bank; [occ.] Former telephone operator; [oth. writ.] Other poems, none published; [pers.] Imagination and memories, I want so much to express it when I write. [a.] Eatontown, NJ 07724.

SEXTON, SANDRA

[b.] June 10, 1977' [p.] Joel and Carol Sexton; [ed.] Woodland elementary, Kelly Junior High, still attending East Detroit High School; [occ.] Lifeguard; [hon.] Michigan Educational Assessment Program awards; [oth. writ.] Several poems, not published. [a.] Eastpointe, MI 48021.

SHARE, DONU K.

[pen.] Donu Karuneenu-Avulon; [b.] January 7, 1931, Greenville, South Carolina; [p.] Katherine and Paul Hunt; [ch.] Karen Rae, Kyle Evans, Theron Keith, Donya Karla; [ed.] High school, workshops, and home studies; [occ.] Regression therapist, artist, potter, writer; [memb.] Shuswap Environmental Association, Unitarian Universalist Women's Association, Amnesty International; [hon.] International Canadian Wildlife Federation; [oth. writ.] "Let'c rite it like wee cae it" and "The wae tu Hevun goes thru Hel" (in progress); [pers.] I beleive we are here to transform what we get into something better.To know who we are and what we have to offer we need to remember where and how we have been. [a.] Sorrento, B.C. Canada V0E 2W0

SHARMA, ASHLESA

[pen.] Ash, Ashu; [b.] March 17, 1978, Indore (M.P.), India; [p.] Anant Deo and Vijay Laxmu Sharma; [ed.] Sophomore at Washington High School, Two Rivers, Wisconsin; [memb.] Various school clubs including Ecology club, Interact, school newspaper, Band, Math club, Forensics and Pit Orchestra; [hon.] 9th grade Geography Bee award, 8th grade Presidential Academic Fitness award, 10th grade Chemistry award; [oth. writ.] A story published in the literary magazine at Platteville High School (Wisconsin), stories in school newspaper at Platteville High School and Washington High School, (Two rivers, Wisconsin); [pers.] I always leave some room in life for miracles and surprises. [a.] Clinton, IA 52732.

SHARP, JESSICA MARIE

[pen.] Tomie Williams; [b.] July 20. 1977, Peoria, Illinois; [p.] Sandra Sue Sharp, brother Shane Michael Sharp; [ed.] Peoria High School; [occ.] Counter clerk, Zip Tone Cleaners; [memb.] Orchestra, Key Club; [hon.] Seven years orchestra; [oth. writ.] Poem published in a book call All My Tomorrows, titled "Distant Glance", record contract for lyrics I wrote, "No One Sees"; [pers.] I always say what I feel. I love to express myself in my writing. My motto to live by is: "Peace. Love, and Hope always". [a.] Peoria, IL

SHAW, JENNELL

[b.] October 18, 1978, Dunedin, Florida; [p.] Margaret and Scott Shaw; [ed.] High school, 9th grade; 1993 8th grade graduate at Most Holy Redeemer School; [occ.] Student at Tampa Catholic High School, Fall 1993; [memb.] School newspaper, soccer player for 10 years; [hon.] Honor Roll student; [oth. writ.] Various poems in the school newspaper; [pers.] Poetry brings out the beauty in the world and helps us forget the violence of today. [a.] Tampa FL 33624.

SHELLITO, CHRISTINE M.

[b.] April 2, 1950, Union City, Pennsylvania; [p.] Elmo and Enid Smiley; [m.] Divorced; [ch.] Becky Shellito; [ed.] Union City High School; [occ.] Mother; [hon.] Written other poems such as "Guide Me to Health My Lord", "Time To Go"; [pers.] I love to write poems. Whatever comes to my mind, I start writing. [a.] Union City, PA 16438.

SHEEDY, NANCY DORIS

[pen.] Nancy D.W. Sheedy; [b.] February 18, 1963, Rahway, New Jersey; [p.] David F. and Madeline R. Sheedy; [ch.] Brian M., Daniel F., [ed.] High school, nurse's aide; [occ.] None, EpsteinBarr virus; [memb.] Our Lady of Perpetual Help Catholic Church, International Society of Poets (ISP) 1992-93; [hon.] American Legion Post 211, Sayeville, New Jersey 1975 Medal of Honor, Poet of Merit award from ISP, have also had my poetry read over the air on WXPN 88.5 FM University of Pennsylvania Editor's Choice Award, National Library of Poetry, 1993; [oth. writ] "A Question of Balance", "Where Dreams Begin", Most Distinguished Poets of America, The National Library of Poetry, my poems have been published in the Holy Spirit Newsletter, in a local publication The

Bulletin, and in my own newsletter Angel's Dove, no longer in circulation; [pers.] "Peace" One man's eye to another man's hand. I do believe that the two will meet and become friends as we all learn to become a part of Peace. Be love to love. [a.] Maple Shade, NJ 08052.

SHEPARD, ANGIE LOUISE

[b.] January 14, 1976, Shelbyville, Indiana; [p.] Terry and Rebecca Sue Pike Shepard; [oth. writ.] Short stories for young authors which is part of the International Reading Association, short stories and articles for Vagabond, which is a school newspaper; [pers.] To me poetry is one of the most beautiful forms of writing, a way to express emotions and feelings from the heart that deals with all things in life. [a.] Connersville, IN 47331.

SHEPHARD, NORMA

[b.] May 6. 1952, Montreal, Quebec; [p.] Rev. Norman and Iris Thoms Hillyer; [m.] Jim Shephard, August 25, 1973; [ch.] Ardra Leah, Norma Corinne, James Adam Hillyer; [ed.] Delta High, Vanier College, McMaster University; [occ.] Registered nurse; [hon.] The Canadian Achiever's Award; [pers.] I was inspired to write this grace by my father, Henry Norman Hillyer. [a.] Burlington, Ont L7R 3B5.

SHEPPARD, BRANDY

[b.] April 27, 1973, Macon, Georgia; [p.] Sherry and Arthur Williams; [m.] G.K. Sheppard II, March 11, 1992; [ed.] Taylor County High School; [occ.] Bookkeeper, Citizen's Bank of Perry, Florida. [a.] Perry, FL 32347.

SHERMAN, GLEN C.

[pen.] G.C. Sherman;[b.] December 28, 1948, Chestertown, New York; [p.] William and Veronica Sherman; [ed.] Chestertown Central School, studied restoration at Lawrence University, Appleton Wisconsin; [occ.] Restorer of pottery and porcelain; [oth. writ.] "The Eagle's Eye", "The Arena", currently working on a novel Immortal Son; [pers.] Admirer of John Burroughs. The relativity of perfection lies in infinity and is not within reach of the human hand. [a.] Chestertown, NY 12817.

SHIFFLETT, BOBBIE

[b.] September 18, 1937, Helena, Alabama; [p.] John and Ethyl Martin; [m.] Charles Shifflett, July 1, 1959; [ch.] Franklin, Terry, William Parks, Karen Jackson, Melissa Shifflett; [ed.] Thompson High, 10th grade; [occ.] Housewife, raising two grandsons; [memb.] International Society of Poets; [hon.] Honorable mention poem "A Country Mile", by Eddie Lou Cole, "Editor's Choice" award by National Library of Poetry; [oth. writ.] Three poems published by Quill Books, two poems published by National Library of Poetry; [pers.] I enjoy writing poems about my childhood, growing up in a big family. Daddy teaching us to be honest and to "reach for the stars". [a.] Calera, AL 35040.

SHOWERS, ZAC

[pen.] Eli Shiver, P. Floyd; [b.] September 2, 1977, Lawton, Oklahoma; [p.] Edward and Debi Showers; [ed.] Geneva High School; [occ.] High school student; [memb.] Beta Club, Band, English Club, Science Olympiad, Boy Scouts, College Bowl, Honor;s Society; [hon.] Numerous College Bowl championships, Alabama State Scholar's Bowl all-star 1990,

1991, 1992; [oth. writ.] I am currently working on a fantasy novel entitled, The Diamond Rook, several of my poems have been published in local/school newspapers; [pers.] I portray the vast realm of human emotion in my poems and stories, from the delightfully frivolous to the deeply sinister. [a.] Black, AL 36314.

SIBTHORPE, RON SR.
[pen.] Bull Shooter; [b.] December, 23, 1936, London, England; [p.] George and May Sibthorpe; [m.] Sarah McAllister Sibthorpe, November 17, 1962; [ch.] Ronald G., Mark J., Barbara A., Roberta A., Michael D.; [ed.] Harben Secondary School, London, England; [occ.] Disability pension, Northern Telecom Co Ltd; [memb.] Royal Canadian :Legion, Ste. Anne De Bellevue P.O.; [hon.] President and Provincial Dart Champ Quebec (RCL) 1975, secondary school athletic champ 1948; [oth. writ.] "Origin of Darts" published in Darts World 1976, a portrayal of events leading up to present day practice done with a twisted version; [pers.] A special thanks to national health programs in England and in Canada for allowing me to progress through life's difficulties on an equal footing after suffering paralysis at an early age. [a.] P.Q. Canada H9X 1G5.

SICILIANO, CARMELA M.
[b.] April 24, 1915, Atlantic City, New Jersey; [p.] Sebastian and Grazia Rifice; [m.] Charles J. Siciliano, September 30, 1943; [ch.] None of our own, raised three nephews; [ed.] High school and graduate of Vocational School of Cosmetology; [occ.] self-employed cosmetologist; [memb.] Hospital auxiliary, past regent Catholic Daughter of America, board member Baby Keepwell, Child Fed., chairman Columbus Day Com. Scholarship; [hon.] Humanitarian award O.S.O.I. Bishop's Medal of Honor, Columbus Day Com. special award; [oth. writ.] For friends birthdays, anniversaries, most are written inspired by my love for him, about him, to him; [pers.] After 48 years of endless love, lost my love, my friend and part of my heart. Ours was Romeo and Juliet, without the tragedy. [a.] Atlantic City, NJ 08401.

SIDDIQUI, NAIM
[b.] February 18, 1940, Hyderabad, India; [p.] Mr. Burhanuddin and Mrs. Mehboob Siddiqui; [m.] Mrs. Abida Siddiqui, March 11, 1964; [ch.] Pervin Hussaini, Zaheer Siddiqui, Tasneem Sayeed; [ed.] M.A. English, Osmania University, India, M.A. English Language and Literature, Oxford University, England; [occ.] Professor of English; [memb.] The Oxford Society, The Poetry Society U.K., Modern Language Association of America, The Poetry Society of America; [hon.] Distinction (A) in B.A. and M.A. degrees; [oth. writ.] Published several poems, several general articles and short stories, several research articles (literary criticism); [pers.] Poetry has to be rehabilitated after its present decline, and its potential for a tremendous impact on the human mind has to be utilized. [a.] Corona, CA 91720.

SIDLO, JENNIFER R.
[b.] February 17, 1963, Framingham, Massachusetts; [p.] Clarence M. and E.C. Sidlo; [ed.] Framingham North High School, Keene State College; [occ.] Programmer/analyst, Seiler's, Waltham, Massachusetts. [a.] Framingham, MA 01701.

SILER, IVA
[b.] February 6, 1910, Finleyville, Pennsylvania; [p.] Mr. and Mrs. John V. Biddle; [m.] deceased, December 7, 1928; [ch.] eight; [ed.] High school, 4 years; [occ.] Dispatcher, airlines; [oth. writ.] "Shepard of the Hills", "Alone:, "America Shores of Freedom", "Pennsylvania Hills", "Our Trail". [a.] Venetia, PA 15367.

SIMMONS, BILLY R. JR.
[b.] May 22, 1976, Homestead AFB, Florida; [p.] Billy and Sandra Simmons; [ed.] Junior at Franklin County High; [memb.] Fellowship of Christian Athletes, Forensics Club, Art Club, Student Volunteers, soccer and football teams; [hon.] Numerous awards in art, including watercolor, sculpture, oils and pencil; [oth. writ.] I am the author of a wide variety of untitled poetry; [pers.] As a member of the first Baptist Church on Winchester, I am an active choir member and youth group member. When you are not within your spiritual boundaries, He is asking you where you are.. Genesis 3:9. [a.] Winchester, TN 37398.

SIMMONS, LINDA GAIL HUNTER
[pen.] Hunter Gayle; [b.] May 6, 1942, North Carolina; [p.] Robert C. and Helen Hunter; [ch.] Joey, Eric, Cindy; [occ.] Registered nurse; [pers.] As a registered nurse, I have seen beauty in the relationships of mankind and devastation when those relationships are not honored. [a.] Pilot Mountain, NC 27041.

SIMON, FLOYD A.
[b.] July 21, 1928, Youngstown, Ohio; [p.] Floyd E. (deceased) and Christine Simon (deceased); [m.] Fiona P. Simon; [ch.] five, previous marriage; [ed.] Quit 11th grade; [memb.] Teamsters, Elks; [hon.] Golden Poet Award; [oth. writ.] Two are included plus I have numerous others that have not been published; [pers.] I enjoy writing and drawing, but my arthritis is getting the best of me. Also enjoy collecting antiques. [a.] Battle Ground WA 98604.

SIMON, JEWEL WOODARD
[b.] July 28, 1911, Houston, Texas; [p.] Chester Arthur and Rachel Williams Woodard; [m.] Edward Lloyd Simon (deceased), February 19, 1939; [ch.] Edward Lloyd Simon Jr, Margaret Jewel Simon Summersour; [ed.] B.F.A. and B.A. Summa cum laude, Atlanta University, additional study in Art under Hale Woodruff and Alice Dunbar, also B.F.A. was received from Atlanta College of Art; [occ.] Homemaker after marriage, head of Mathematics Dept. at Yates High School, Houston, Texas; [memb.] AAUW, Associates of Emory University, Kappa Omega, Alpha Kappa Alpha sorority; [hon.] Atlanta University Special Recognition for distinguished contribution to the Arts, Golden Dove award, AKA sorority, James Weldon Johnson Atlanta NAACP, A.U. President's Alumni Award for Outstanding Achievement, and many other awards, included in many books, Who's Who of American Women, Who's Who in American Art, The Best Poems of the 90's and many others.

SIMONTEN, REBECCA
[b.] April 17, 1976, Flint, Michigan; [p.] Roger and Jacqueline; [ed.] Perry High; [occ.] Student; [memb.] Publications-yearbook staff; [hon.] Spelling Bee, 100 % Math Meap Score, perfect attendance; [oth.writ.] Several stories published in school newspaper and yearbook, and several other poems and stories unpublished; [pers.] I want to thank my parents and my sister for encouraging me to write. To my friends for being there through all my troubles. And especially to Mrs. Jessica Bentley for her help. [a.] Owasso, MI.

SIMPSON, SHIRLEY
[b.] September 19, 1935, Birmingham, U.K.; [p.] Ethel and Charles Abbott; [m.] Arthur Simpson, November 2, 1956; [ch.] Kim Anthony, Kelly Anne, Kandy Sue, Kate Samantha, Krayton Charles, Claire Rachael; [ed.] Torquay Girls Grammar School; [occ.] Jane of all trades!; [oth. writ.] Several published poems in newspapers, in book of Devonshire poets, read on radio, etc, short stories never published; [pers.] If everyone had more poetry in their hearts there would be less room for hate. [a.] Plymouth, S. Devon, U.K.

SINCLAIR, MATTHEW
[b.] March 17, 1968, Summit, New Jersey; [p.] W. Robert and Helen Sinclair; [ed.] Lafayette College; [occ.] YMCA Youth Program director, freelance writer; [memb.] Summit Volunteer First Aid Squad, Phi Gamma Delta fraternity; [oth. writ.] Former editor of "Mid-Week" , a weekly campus newsletter at Drew University, I have also written several newspaper articles, I am a short story writer, with one, "Sebastians Story" published at Lafayette College; [pers.] Personal interaction says more than any philosophical statement. My writing is an extension of that interaction. [a.] Summit, NJ 07901.

SINGH, ATUL
[b.] March 15, 1973, Vasco-da-gama, Goa, India; [p.] Lt. Col.(Dr.) I.P. Singh (Plastic and recons surgeon), and Mrs Sudha Singh (B.A. Hons.); [ed.] Doing graduation in Lucknow University with English, History, Political Science as my subjects; [occ.] Student; [memb.] The American Center Library, New Delhi, The British Library, Lucknow; [oth. writ.] Poems, essays, short stories and an unfinished novel; [pers.] To understand the universe to the utmost. (My brother Amit has always helped me to believe in myself). [a.] Lucknow-226 016, India.

SINGH, PROMEET
[b.] May 15, 1971, Poona; [p.] Dr Shama and Dr. Jaswant Singh; [ed.] St.Vincent's High School, Ness Wadia College, Bachelor of Commerce; [occ.] Student; [hon.] 1st prize for poem in MTV's (Asian) contest, award from German Consulate for Language; [oth. writ.] Poems published in college magazine and church bulletins; [pers.] My poems have been inspired by Gospel singer Keith Green's songs. I write in my leisure on topics which touch me deeply. [a.] Poona-411 048, India.

SIRONEN, GORDON
[b.] October 19, 1953, Grand Rapids, Michigan; [p.] Richard and Beverly Sironen; [m.] Jane Sironen; [ch.] Tanya Ann, Angela Lynn, Jason Robert; [occ.] Owner of Monarch Metal Mfg.; [pers.] As in Hebrews 11:13-16, This earth is not our real home, we're just strangers visiting down here, living for heaven, for God has made a heavenly city for us. [a.] Comstock Park, MI 49321.

SKAW, ORAN K.
[b.] September 23, 1915, Turin, Iowa; [p.] Nels C. and Grace A. Skaw; [m.] Mariam A. Skaw, Novem-

ber 19, 1941; [ch.] Loran Kent, John Kenneth, and Steven Keith; [ed.] Onawa High School and Armored force School at Ft. Knox, Kentucky; [occ.] Retired farmer and factory machine operator; [oth. writ.] Several poems in two World of Poetry books, Our World's Favorite Gold and Silver Poems and Poems That Will Live Forever; [pers.] I write spiritual, humorous, and poems that carry a message. I employ rhyme and rhythm in my writings. [a.] Magnolia, IA 51550.

SKIERSKI, ANGELA
[b.] July 12, 1975, Irving, Texas; [p.] Ramona Skierski (mother) and Naomia Morton (grandmother); [ed.] I am about to graduate high school at Denton High School; [occ.] None yet, but I am majoring in nursing; [hon.] National Council on Youth Leadership, 1st place in solo and ensemble; [oth. writ.] I've written several little poems; [pers.] Be real! And be honest! God will know anyway. [a.] Denton, TX 76201.

SLAVIN, LEON
[p.] lazar and Vera Slavin; [ed.] B.A. Ohio State University, M.A. in History, DePaul University; [occ.] Retired teacher, Cleveland Ohio school system; [memb.] Interboro Discussion Group of New York. [a.] New York, NY 10128.

SLEET, LENA IRENE HURD
[pen.] Lena Sleet; [b.] April 10, 1930, Oxford, Ohio; [p.] George and Addie Mae Mize Hurd; [m.] Bruce Emerson Sleet, March 10th 1950; [ch.] Dona Marie, vicki Juanita, Bruce Ricky; [ed.] Union City West Side High, Union City, Indiana; [occ.] Nurse's aide; [memb.] Full Gospel Trinity Church; [hon.] Plaque for poems written!; [oth. writ.] Same poem published in World of Poetry and mentioned in local paper Connersville News-Examiner; [pers.] I have written many poems, "Anectdotes of a Christian Aide" and my biography. I write mostly truth and some fiction. Influenced by mother. [a.] Connersville, IN 47331.

SLEGER, EDWARD J. JR.
[b.] November 14, 1926, Wrightstown, Wisconsin; [p.] Edward J. Sleger and Caroline Eckstine; [m.] Diane J. Sleger (Otto), August 19, 1953; [ch.] Edward III, Helen, Jonathan, Mark, Constance, Renee, David, Patricia, Robert, Mary; [ed.] St. Horbert High School, DePere Wisconsin, Carroll College, Waukesha, Wisconsin (B.S.), University of Wisconsin-Milwaukee (M.S.); [occ.] Retired teacher of Math and Physics in high school in 1987 after 36 years of teaching; [hon.] Received National Science Foundation (NSF) scholarship to pursue Masters degree at University of Wisconsin-Milwaukee, 1961-1965; [pers.] John Bunyan's Pilgrim's Progress was an inspiration to attempt a work on "Salvation Enacted" which is in progress. [a.] Kewaskum, WI 53040.

SLEPPY, DAVID A.
[b.] December 26, 1955, Heidelberg, West Germany; [p.] JoAnn and Alan sleppy; [m.] Patricia A. McGill, July 2, 1983; [ch.] Joseph Mcgill sleppy; [ed.] Bonn American High School, Gettysburg College, George Washington University Law School; [occ.] Attorney, Herman & Sleppy PC; [memb.] ATLA, GTLA; [hon.] Phi Beta Kappa, Pi Lambda Sigma; [oth. writ.] A lot of appellate briefs. [a.] Atlanta, GA.

SMALE, SEASON
[b.] October 31, 1979, Milwaukee, Wisconsin; [p.] Sam and Janet Smale; [ed.] Richland Middle School; [occ.] Student; [memb.] S.A.D.D.(Students Against Drunk Driving); [hon.] Presidential Academic Fitness award; [oth. writ.] Lots of poems, short stories, and composed a song; [pers.] I like to write in my spare time. Ideas come to me easily. I live in the country and I like it because there are lots of animals. [a.] Soldiers Grove, WI 54655.

SMITH, ALTA F.
[pen.] Alta Shill Smith; [b.] October 9, 1930, Malta, Idaho; [p.] Jesse and Lavilla Shill; [m.] Merle Smith, October 27, 1949; [ch.] Kerry, Kent (twins), Bob, Alan; [ed.] Raft River High School; [occ.] Housewife; [memb.] Institute of American West, Idaho Historical Society, Daughters of the Utah Pioneers; [hon.] Two time finalist in Idaho Poet Laureate (writer in residence); [oth. writ.] "Dusty Memories", a collection of 150 original poems, numerous essays and newspaper articles, eulogies, greeting cards; [pers.] I always write about the positive side of everything. [a.] Oakley ID 83346.

SMITH, ANNETTE
[b.] August 8, 1972, Iowa City, Iowa; [p.] Robert and Nancy Smith; [ed.] West Liberty Junior and Senior High; [occ.] Soldier in the United States Army Reserves; [pers.] Poetry is a way for me to express how I feel about anything, without really having to worry about what anyone is going to say about them. [a.] West Liberty, IA 52776.

SMITH, BERNIECE
[b.] April 3, 1908, Elkhart Indiana; [p.] Clyde L. and Catharine Marsh Mead; [m.] Stewart James Smith M.D., January 10, 1936; [ch.] Sara K. Jamieson, Jonathan c. Smith PhD.; [ed.] B.S., O.S.U., M.A. Ohio Wesleyan, additional work University of Michigan; [occ.] Retired teacher and social worker, volunteer various community organizations; [memb.] League of Women Voters, Presbyterian Church, Genealogical Society, Historical Society, Friends of Library, hospital auxiliary et al; [hon.] Woman of the Year, 1967, Bowling Green, Ohio Chamber of Commerce; [oth. writ.] "Davidson-Stewart Genealogy of Wood County, Ohio", other historical paper, poems, "Healthomania"m "attic Sale", "RorryRobin", Leaha's Revenge", "Gold Rush", "Mike","Class Reunion" et al, numerous news/feature items for newspapers; [pers.] Reading and writing are both great means of promoting understanding. Humor and human interest are valuable elements. [a.] Bowling Green, OH 43402.

SMITH, BRYAN PATRICK
[b.] December 5, 1981, Nashville, Tennessee; [p.] Michael and Paula Smith, Jared (brother), Rachel (sister); [ed.} 5th grade going on 6th; [occ.] Student; [memb.] "Classic Black" member, Band member; [hon.] "Young Authors 1991", "David Small", 1st place contest 191 winner, "Jack in the Box" story contest 1st place 1990, Honor Roll, Principal's List since preschool, honors on Michigan M.E.A.P. tests 100%; [oth. writ.] "How Jack Got in the Box", "Dream of Wings That Fly!"; [pers.] I"m only 11 years old but I write stories all the time for school. I love to read! My favorite author is John Bellairs. [a.] Kalamazoo, MI 49008.

SMITH, DARYL EUGENE
[b.] April 10, 1917, Richland County, Ohio; [p.] Eugene Preston and Abbie Jane Smith (deceased); [m.] Theresa Marie Moore Smith, July 3, 1939; [ch.] Cathy Ann, Dianne Ellen, Regg Eugene, Patti Sue, Bryan Dayne; [ed.] Graduate She;by Ohio High School, 3yrs Ohio S.U. and Wright S. U.; [occ.] Retired-USAF civilian federal employee; [memb.] AARP, DAV, NCPSSM; [hon.] God's good gifts; [oth. writ.] Many unpublished and unsubmitted poems and song lyrics; [pers.] I love, my thankfulness to God for love, life, wife, family and country. Greed and lack of caring are deteriorating mankind's chances of survivability. Change attitudes now! [a.] Dayton, OH 45426.

SMITH, FRANCES TAYLOR
[pen.] Frances Taylor Smith; [b.] February 18, 1921, Greenville, Mississippi; [p.] James W. Taylor and Bessie Mae Hollis; [m.] Clarence A. Smith Jr., October 17, 1942; [ch.] Clarence A. Smith III (Alvin), Gayle Evans Smith; [ed.] Sulphur High School, Sulphur Louisiana, King's Daughters School of Nursing, Greenville, Mississippi, (RN); [occ.] Retired; [memb.] Mississippi Art Association, Mississippi Artists Guild; [hon.] American Legion Scholarship Award, Scholastic Scholarship to LA Tech, numerous Best of Show 1st, 2nd, 3rd place and Honorable Mentions in local art shows; [oth. writ.] Poems published in R.N. Magazine in 1940's, Treasured Poems of America, Summer 1990 and Let His Light Shine; [pers.] As a Christian, I know that all of our strengths and talents stem from God. My desire is to be a good and useful steward of all that He has entrusted to me, both the tangibles and intangibles. [a.] Jackson, MS 39209.

SMITH, GEOFFREY L.
[pen.] Geoffrey L. Smith; [b.] September 9, 1967, Hutchinson, Kansas; [p.] Natrhalee and Dennis Smith; [ed.] Hutchinson High School and everyday life experiences; [occ.] Records clerk of underground vaults and storage, also a liquor store clerk; [memb.] Several local video stores and some drinking establishments; [hon.] To be part of this great country and a registered independent voter; [oth. writ.] One editorial in the Hutchinson News, and a whole notebook of my own private poems, phrases and thoughts; [pers.] Explore all you can explore...learn all you can learn...teach all you can teach, then please help me to do the same and then we'll find freedom together. [a.] Hutchinson, KS 67501.

SMITH, ISOREL
[b.] December 6, 1949, Tillicoultry, Scotland; [p.] Mary S. Todd and Gavin L. Johnson; [ch.] Jade Elizabeth Smith, 6 years old (adopted from Phillipines); [ed.] Tillicoultry Primary School, Alloa Academy Senior Sec. School; [occ.] Retired hairstylist /salon owner; [hon.] I do have my advanced City Guilds (London) which I acquired after 3 years at Regent Rd. College, Edinburgh, which qualifies to teach hairdressing; [oth. writ.] Notes and scribbles over the years thrown in a drawer, nothing of any serious note, The poem forwarded my first attempt; [pers.] Either deep pain or true joy prompts one to commit the feelings of life to remembrance, thus words written from the soul. [a.] Nassau, Bahamas.

SMITH, LEE A.
[b.] July 11, 1961. Whitehorse, Yukon Terr; [p.] Mel (deceased) and Nora Smith; [ch.] Michelle Lee Smith-Irnie; [ed.] Kwantlen college, Surrey B.C. Canada; [oth. writ.] No others published, but I have a personal collection of many poems and short stories; [pers.] My writing has always been a reflection of what is where the best of all things comes from. [a.] Langley, B.C. Canada V3A 4B7.

SMITH. LORRIE
[pers.] I want to glorify God in my writings. [a.] Cedar Falls, IA 50613.

SMITH, MARY JANE
[b.] April 28, 1950, Windsor Nova Scotia; [ch.] Deanna Lee; [ed.] Grade 7, part of grade 8; [oth. writ.] I have written just a few poems but they are not published as yet; [pers.] Loss is the renewal or beginning of something else and the completion of a circle. [a.] Beaverbanks, Nova Scotia, Canada B4G 1E7.

SMITH, MELISSA
[pen.] Melissa Jaylene Smith; [b.] October 12, 1978, Roseburg, Oregon; [p.] James and Betty Smith; [ed.] Freshman, high school; [occ.] Student; [oth. writ.] Unpublished poems and short stories; [pers.] When I write I let my true feelings show. I take pride in my writing and I hope others do too. [a.] Wrangell, AK 99929.

SMITH MELISSA ANN
[b.] May 24, 1979, Fort Collins, Colorado; [p.] Howard and Linda Smith; [ed.] 8th grade; [memb.] Summerville Presbyterian Church, Softball, Basketball, Marching Band and Band; [hon.] Excellence in Writing, excellence in Band, Presidential Physical Fitness Award; [oth. writ.] Poem published in the junior high edition of the High School Writer; [pers.] I like to capture the beauty of nature in my poems because if we don't take care of it now, it will start to disappear. [a.] Summerville, GA 30747.

SMITH, MELODY A.
[b.] August 21, 1963, Greencastle, Indiana; [p.] Patricia Slaybaugh and Tom Smith; [ch.] Kristin Carter, Ashley Carter; [ed.] Bloomington High School South; [occ.] EMT; [memb.] Bloomington Township Volunteer Fire Dept.; [pers.] Writing poems is God's gift to me. It fulfills my heart to share God's word to others. [a.] Unionville, IN 47468.

SMITH, MISSY
[b.] July 7, 1977, Wise, Virginia; [p.] Billy and Judy Smith; [ed.] J.J. Kelly High; [occ.] High school, 10th grade; [pers.] This poem is dedicated to my grandfather, Carl Yates, who passed away in October of 1992. Even though he has passed away, he will live on forever in my heart. [a.] Wise, VA 24293.

SMITH, NORMA J.
[pen.] Norma J. Smith; [b.] February 10, 1943, Philipsburg, Pennsylvania; [p.] Robert and Margaret Richards; [m.] Arthur C. Smith, March 27, 1965; [ch.] Rhonda Kay, Kathie Jean; [ed.] Graduate of West Branch Area High School, Allport Institute of Children's Literature, West Reading, Pennsylvania; [occ.] Business office manager, The Progress (newspaper), Philipsburg, Pennsylvania; [pers.] I love watching an idea shape into an article or story. Every

new idea is a new challenge. [a.] Morrisdale PA.

SMITH, TERRY
[b.] November 22, 1968, Fall River, Massachusetts; [p.] Paul and Juanita Smith; [ed.] 1986 graduate of Weatherly Area High School, Weatherly Pennsylvania; [oth. writ.] "Tammy" published 1993 by the Amherst Society, a song recorded by Five Star Music Co. "No More Time for Dreams"; [pers.] Due to my having dyslexia I didn't learn to read until I was a senior in high school. Now writing has become the greatest joy in my life. Remember nothing is impossible until you stop trying. [a.] Wilkes-Barre, PA 18702.

SMITH, ZELDA M.
[pen.] Zel Les, Lucky, Zelma M.; [b.] September 7, 1928, Riverton, Wyoming; [p.] Harvey A. Eaton, Osborne Kansas, and Goldie G. Eaton, Gardner, Missouri; [m.] Lester C. Smith Jr., Avalon, California, October 7, 1948; [ch.] Dana G. Smith, Darlene M. Purcell, 4 grandchildren; [ed.] Graduated Riverton High School 1947, excelled in writing and business; [occ.] Retired at present, have worked many jobs, working at the radio station and desk clerk; [memb.] Riverton Rebekah Lodge #25; [hon.] Noble Grand of Rebekah Lodge #25, soloist, Rebekah Assembly of Wyoming; [oth. writ.] Spent time growing up writing short stories and poetry, animal stories not published; [pers.] I try not to judge myself...I let others do that. Published "Ode to a Desk Clerk" in Super 8 magazine 1992. [a.] Riverton, Wy.

SMITHEM, DUANE B. JR.
[b.] October 28, 1949, Tacoma Washington; [ed.] Westmont High School, San Jose California, Institute of Children's Literature, Connecticut, New York Institute of Photography, New York; [occ.] Courier, Timberland Regional Library System, Olympia Washington; [memb.] TCTV Public Access TV station, volunteer time as cameraman and director for local programs; [hon.] Numerous photo awards for scenic and candid photos; [oth. writ.] Published in Poetry; An American Heritage; [pers.] It is through writing that I can express a wide range of heartfelt emotions, seeking new personal adventures in all aspects of life either real or imagined.; [a.] Olympia, WA 98512.

SNELL, COURTNEY RENE
[b.] April 29, 1976, Grass Valley; [p.] Cheryl Sullivan; [ed.] Union Hill Elementary School, Nevada Union High School; [hon.] Who's Who of American High School Students; [pers.] My personal feelings are shown through my writings. I enjoy writing about the many things in this world which we always wonder about.

SNOW, RICHARD ALVIN JR.
[b.] July 5, 1956, Savannah, Georgia; [p.] Richard Alvin Sr. and Betty Jean Snow; [ed.] Riverside City College, Sacramento City College, California State University, Sacramento; [hon.] A 1991 Golden Poet Award, as well as Award of Merit certificates, a 1981 SAA/EOPS student intern; [oth. writ.] This is the second to be published others will be forthcoming; [pers.] The exposure received from writing has greatly enriched my life and I would hope the peoples lives I have touched. [a.] San Bernardino, CA.
SNYDER, BERTHA

[b.] September 24, 1911, Yukon, Canada; [p.] William F. and Florence C. William Peck; [m.] Gilbert R. Snyder, June 20, 1935; [ch.] Vea Lynne Snyder, Sue Anne Snyder Wickens; [ed.] Hannibal LaGrange College, Hannibal, Missouri, MacMurray College, Jackson, Illinois, Rockford College, Rockford, Illinois; [occ.] Retired elementary teacher; [hon.] Lead in freshman play; [pers.] Wife, mother and teacher. My husband is deceased. My children are grown. I have time for my first love, poetry. [a.] Winston-Salem, NC.

SNYDER, JAMES M.
[pen.] Jim Snyder; [b.] February 22, 1939, Benton, Illinois; [p.] Claude and Irene Snyder; [m.] Betty Snyder, June 8, 1973; [ch.] James C., Ramona D., John V. Anthony P., F. Therese, Carole M., Christine M, Jimmie L., Glen D., Lora J., Rose A.; [ed.] Wallace High, Rend Lake College; [occ.] Maintenance custodian; [hon.] Dean's List; [oth. writ.] Various poems, essays, ghost stories, treasure stories, one published in Treasure magazine; [pers.] I have always tried to keep the insight and enthusiasm of a child, so I could see things as they do. [a.] Benton, IL 62812.

SNYDER-HAMMAN, REBA MAE
[pen.] Reb; [b.] March 6, 1929, Three Springs, Pennsylvania; [p.] Ralph Rannells and Cloma Mae Thomas Snyder, 2 sisters, Madeline and Evone; [m.] Howard Elliott Hamman, February 29, 1948; [ch.] Carol, Charlotte, Cheryl, Charlene, Christine; [ed.] Three Springs Grade School, Saltillo High School; [occ.] Housewife; [memb.] Newton Hamilton Brethren in Christ Church; [hon.] High school Honor Roll, Three Springs School Huntingdon Co. school Field Day champion, two medals, one for relay run race, one for overall activities, 1941, high jump, broad jump, ball throw, 100 yard dash, sang alto in Huntingdon Co. High School chorus; [oth. writ.] This is a first time for "Mud Dolls", school poems and stories, I want to write a book about my childhood and would like to have it made into a series of movies like Little House stories; [pers.] I try to write and tell things that life in itself is worth more than money which can buy many things. I find stories and poems about one's life and our Earth brings laughter and joy and much learning "education". [a.] McVeytown, PA.

SOCHA, DON
[pers.] I strive to demonstrate that it is to everyone's advantage to eliminate unbalanced forms of power, privilege and profit. [a.] Mount Pleasant, MI 48858.

SOLOMON, SHARRON L
[pen.] Na Na Yaa; [b.] December 8, 1955, Detroit, Michigan; [p.] Jesse Solomon and Mattie R. Tolbert; [ch.] Avery Scott McWhorter (12), Jason Lowell "McW" (11), Matthew Henry "McW" (5); [ed.] University of Michigan, 1980, B.A. degree Journalism/Communications; [occ.] Writer; [memb.] Alpha Kappa Alpha sorority, The Black Writers Guild, Fellowship Chapel Church; [oth. writ.] A compilation of poetry entitled experiences of a lifetime; [pers.] If thine pen succeeds at raising consciousness, write on! [a.] Detroit, MI 48228.

SOMMER, PAMELA
[b.] May 22, 1974, Stanford, California; [p.] Fred and Olga Sommer; [ed.] Sacred Heart Preparatory, Woodbury University; [occ.] Fulltime student as an Architecture major; [hon.] Dean's List; [oth. writ.] Several poems and short stories. [a.] Foster City, CA 94404.

SOMMERS JENNIFER J.
[b.] January 15, 1975, Harbor Beach, Michigan 48441; [p.] Richard I. and Joan K. Sommers; [ed.] Graduated June 6, 1993 plans for college in Michigan at E.M.U. fall 1993; [occ.] Will be student in college; [memb.] American Red Cross donor; [hon.] Couple of poems published, Who's Who Among American High School Students, Multiple Year award; [oth. writ.] Almost 100 poems, a few have been published, a true life short story about the worst and hardest part of my life, hopefully this and my poems will someday all be published; [pers.] My note to all is: NO matter what life hands you always go after what you want. Don't let anything stand in your way (keep it legal though). Even if you think the worst has taken it all, fight, don't give up! Succeed in life, reach your dreams! [a.] Caribou, ME 04736.

SOREY, FRANCIA B.
[pen.] Sister Nancy, Lady D.J.; [b.] November 16, 1949, Columbia, South Carolina; [p.] Mae Frances and Frank Nathaniel Bowden; [m.] Divorced, December 29, 1968; [ch.] Donald Lee, Ronald LeSean, Otto Rashad, Rodd Everson; [ed.] Miami Jackson High School, Barry University, Nova University (studying M.A.); [occ.] Teacher K-6 Esol Adults Liberty City Elementary, Miami Florida; [memb.] South Broward Organization Forum; [hon.] Chapter 1 North Central Office Recognition of Achievement; [oth. writ.] My first entry! other topics not published, "Inspiration", "Wisdom", "Romance", "Song"; [pers.] Responsibility to fulfill our purpose in life is the duty of all through whatever means afforded us, then life is worth living. [a.] Miramar, FL 33023.

SOTO, VALERIE
[b.] February 13,1980, Brooklyn, New York; [p.] Marta and Jose Alvarado; [ed.] Currently in Satellite West J.H.S. 7th grade; [occ.] Student; [oth. writ.] "We Are Free", "She", "Running", (non-published); [pers.] Think of our future generations. Don't kill our "Mother". [a.] Brooklyn, NY 11205.

SOULE, SARAH E.
[b.] July 17, 1979, Brocton, Massachusetts; [p.] George and Janet Soule; [ed.] Middleboro Junior High School; [occ.] Student; [memb.] Middleboro Softball League; [hon.] Honor Roll, Sportmanship Award; [pers.] Writing poetry is a good way of expressing my thoughts and feelings. [a.] Middleboro, MA 02346.

SOULIERE, LAURA
[b.] January 11, 1978, Pawtucket, Rhode Island; [p.] Susan Souliere; [ed.] Burrillville High School; [occ.] Student; [memb.] Varsity cheerleader; [hon.] Winner of 'Youth Authors' contest, grades 5 and 8; [pers.] To: Mom and Marc, I've come a long way thanks to you. You've helped me make my dreams come true. [a.] Glendale, RI 02826.

SOUTHERS, DONNA G.
[b.] September 19, 1952, Apple Grove, North Carolina; [p.] Ray R. Sr. (deceased) and Ilene V. Greeson; [m.] Jerry D. Southers, February 14, 1990; [ch.] Pamela Dawn, Toni Marie, Laura Jean, Paula Ilene; [ed.] Finished the 8th grade, but still study a lot; [occ.] Contract painter for Interrex Inc. I paint gnomes at home; [oth. writ.] I have written other poetry, but this is my first publication, I never have sent my poems to anyone for publication; [pers.] I love writing, I also write short stories. I took some classes from the Institute of Children's Literature. I like writing, it's a pleasure. [a.] Catawba, NC 28609.

SPALDING, MARLENE CAROL
[b.] March 11, 1941, Bradford, Pennsylvania; [p.] Victor and Olive Cornelius; [m.] Rev. Neil K. Spalding, November 30, 1963; [ch.] Grant Kenyon, Sara Lynn Wright, Derek Ashley; [ed.] Bradford High, Roberts Wesleyan College; [occ.] Minister, singer, writer, composer; [memb.] Association of Faith churches & Ministers; [hon.] Alpha Kappa Sigma Christian Writers Conference Award; [oth. writ.] Book: Power Serve, newspaper articles, gospel songs, children's songs, musical; [pers.] Words are precious, carrying life or death. We must share life-giving words to bless, challenge, or encourage others. [a.] Sodus, NY 14551.

SPEARS, ANNIE LAURA
[pen.] Kitty Spears; [b.] December 3, 1949, Potts Camp, Mississippi; [p.] Theodore and Lida Ella Hancock; [m.] Travis Spears, September 4, 1970; [ed.] Graduate of Potts Camp High School; [occ.] Housewife, Avon lady; [memb.] Evangel Full gospel Church; [oth. writ.] None so far, writing a book about my life and family called Days Gone By; [pers.] I try to express God's love and my love for him in my writing.; [a.] Holly Springs, MS 38635.

SPEARS, JENNIFER
[pen.] Jennifer Spears; [b.] October 10, 1976, San Francisco, California; [p.] Yong Ae (Spears) Cho; [ed.] Airline High School; [occ.] Student, class of 94; [hon.] Placed 2nd in statewide French literacy contest-prose, United States Achievement Academy award winner sophomore and junior years; [oth. writ.] "Une Lettre Pour Mon Amour" published in la Gazette de la Louisiane (en francais); [a.] Bossier City, LA 71111.

SPECK, KRISTINA DANNIELLE
[pen.] Kris, Kristi, Dannie; [b.] December 21, 1977, Houston, Texas; [p.] Hal and Cheri Kaelin; [ed.] South Houston Int. up to 8th grade; [occ.] Student; [oth. writ.] Personal writings; [pers.] In my writing I always bring out the way I feel. And I am inspired very greatly by my mother, father, and my best friend Olivia DeLaGarca. [a.] South Houston, TX 77587.

SPENCE, WAYNE J.
[pen.] Wayne; [b.] December 14, 1924, Willow Springs, Missouri; [p.] Lyman C. and Charlotte May Pottle Spence; [ed.] B.S. in Sc., S.W. Missouri University, Springfield, Missouri, Naval Midshipman School, Columbia University, New York, New York, Navy Postgrad School, Monterey, California; [occ.] Retired Navy pilot (30 years, flew off 13 aircraft carriers and served during three wars); [memb.] Naval Officers Retirement Association, Experimental Aircraft Association, Trinity Baptist Church, Willow Springs, Missouri, Willow Springs Country Club, Ozarks Genealogical Society, Springfield, Missouri, Rhea County Hist. and Gen. Soc., Dayton, Tennessee; [hon.] Four air-medals plus numerous other flight medals, numerous awards in music and music instruments; [oth. writ.] Wayne's World of Verse, a small book of poetry I had printed November 92 (120 copies) for friends. It was a compilation of a lifetime of short verses put in a file and finally put them all together. I have 57 of my poems in it, "A New Look At Shorts; (short stories of a Navy pilot's adventures-not yet complete. Ten chapters now done.), genealogical histories of mine and other families, several poems in local newspapers; [pers.] Once a friend of James A. Michener as he lived six weeks with my group of Navy pilots getting information for the book The Bridges of Toko-Ri. He was a bad poker player. Also I flew with Neil Armstrong and shared Ready Rooms and Quarters with him. We traveled some in Japan together, photographing Japanese families and the country of Japan. I had a stroke two years ago and all writing must be done with left hand on my computer. It is slow but very satisfying to be able to write something others might enjoy. Thirty years of flying fighter aircraft in three wars makes for many sea stories. I am writing them now.

SPENCER, CHLOE
[b.] June 5, 1980, Washington, D.C.; [p.] Daryl and Gail Spencer; [ed.] Stephan Decatur Middle School; [hon.] Straight "A" student, being able to sing in Honors Chorus 3 years; [oth. writ.] I've written other poems, but "My Get Away Path" was the first one to get published; [pers.] I wrote this poem on the destruction of the Earth by using metaphors and the sun beaming on it. [a.] Clinton, MD 20735.

SPENCER, MATTHEW
[b.] July 15, 1977, Vincennes, Indiana; [p.] Stephen and Saundra Spencer; [ed.] Center Grove High School, class of '96; [occ.] Student; [oth. writ.] "I Look Away", " The Distance"; [pers.] It's a small man's world, so you've gotta live big. [a.] Greenwood, IN 46145.

SPENCER, TIMOTHY DAVID
[b.] January 13, 1976, Louisville, Kentucky; [p.] Deana and David Spencer; [ed.] Charlestown High; [memb.] Boy Scouts of America; [pers.] Beauty is the true essence of life; a necessity. For without it, life is worthless. [a.] Charlestown, IN 47111.

SPENO, ROBERT R.
[b.] January 20, 1926, N Tarrytown, New York; [p.] Ethel and George E. Speno Jr.; [m.] Nancy J,. Speno, January 12, 1951; [ch.] Jeffrey Speno, Cynthia Meyers, Polly Crenshaw Price and Robert R. Speno (twins), Brently Speno and Priscilla Steluti (twins); [ed.] Washington Irving High School, Kent State University, B.S.; [occ.] Retired, insurance; [memb.] Delta Tau Delta; [oth. writ.] Some poems have been published in local newspapers and trade papers; [pers.] Some of my poems experiences of WWII, and some project an attitude, both political and personal. [a.] Titusville, FL 327.

SPILLMAN, KATHRYN
[b.] Akron, Ohio; [p.] Stephen and Julianna Peck Papai; [m.] Ronald Spillman; [ch.] Glenn Richard, wife Rita, grandson, Erik, wife Carolyn, granddaughters Ann Kathryn, Elisabeth Jane; [ed.] B.S. in

Education, Masters in Reading, Library Certification, Post Masters; [occ.] Elementary teacher, elementary school librarian; [memb.] Association of School Librarians, Retired Teachers Association, elder in church, Delta Kappa Gamma, International Reading Association; [hon.] Graduated Summa cum laude, received $4000 grant for writing operetta, received a number of baking and cooking awards; [oth. writ.] Children's operetta, other children's musical productions and plays, numerous Haiku, various articles in professional journals; [pers.] I believe that all children (adults as well) have innate creative abilities and I have endeavored to develop these aptitudes so the quality of lives may be enriched. [a.] New Waterford, OH 44445.

SPITZ, ROSE
[b.] September 27, 1979, Milwaukee, Wisconsin; [p.] Mary Spitz; [ed.] K-7th grade; [oth. writ.] "Eagle". [a.] Rockland, MI 49960.

SPIVEY, EDWIN P.
[b.] January 4, 1912. Manchester, England; [p.] John Edwin (deceased) and Elizabeth Bishop Spivey (deceased); [m.] Thetis Rosina Bridge Spivey, September 25, 1937, Lavanira Dell Bailey Spivey, July 31, 1974 (both deceased); [ed.] Irish National School; [occ.] Telecommunication Engineer; [memb.] World of Poetry, National Library of Poetry; [hon.] 17 award of merit, 4 fourth prizes, Golden poet Award, 1987-1992, all above awards with world of poetry; [oth. writ.] Poetry only writings; [pers.] Try to follow father's ideas to live in peace, be tolerant, and patient. Also the life styles of both my wives who both were great believers of the 2nd commandment...to love their neighbors and friends, irrespective of whatever colour, race, or creed they happened to be, which are my own beliefs entirely. [a.] New Iberia, LA 70560.

SPRINGER, SHEILA MARIE
[b.] October 5, 1970, Doylestown, Pennsylvania; [p.] Frank and Gail Springer; [m.] Joseph Stankiewitch, October 2, 1993. [a.] Ottsville, PA 18942.

SPRUNG, JOHN GEORGE
[b.] March 4, 1913, St. Louis, Missouri; [p.] John Nicholas and Magdelena Tremel Sprung; [m.] Loa Ruth Sprung, April 26, 1947; [ch.] John Leon Sprung, Lori Lee Sprung; [ed.] B.S. Degree, Northwestern University 1939, Scholarship Art Institute, Chicago; [occ.] Retired plastics engineer; [memb.] Delta Beta Phi, Society of Plastics Engineers; [oth. writ.] Poetry in stereo first syllable of each line rhymes with the last syllable of the line. [a.] San Pedro, CA 90732.

SPUHLER, FREDERICK MORGAN
[pen.] Fred Morgan; [b.] May 31, 1910, Winona, Minnesota; [p.] A. J. and Eva Morgan Spuhler; [m.] Mariom Kuethe Spuhler, July 23, 1933; [ch.] F.M. Spuhler Jr.; [ed.] Winona High; Notre Dame University 1928-29, University of Minnesota 1929-31, Winona State Teachers College 1932-33 (junior high teacher); [occ.] Marketing management, Swift Baystate Milling, TransWorld Airlines, International Milling Co; [memb.] Past member Elks, Shrine, Kiwanis, B.S.A., Junior Chamber of Commerce, Life Sigma Chi Tau Seniors Club, Desert Hills Lutheran Church of Green Valley, Green Valley Lodge #71; [hon.] High school Class President, founder and 7 year president, Green Valley A.Z. Sigma Chi Atlantic Club, 1989 Best Alumni Officer Sigma Chi alumni

chapters, past president Albuquerque Kiwanis Club, member executive comm Albuquerque Chamber of Commerce, officer and director several country clubs, past Col Aide de Camp several New Mexico governors; [oth. writ.] Humor column college newspapers, wrote one and contributed to others; [pers.] When seeking true friendship make sure you also give what you seek (this may have been said by others but it is my personal philosophy). [a.] Green Valley, AZ 85614.

SQUICCERINI, LISA MARIE
[b.] May 12, 1977, Flushing, New York; [p.] Michael and Christine Squiccerini; [ed.] High school student; [oth. writ.] Poetry written for personal pleasure; [pers.] My writing is influenced by all the people I love or have loved and lost. I try to reflect my innermost feelings in my poetry. [a.] Hicksville, NY 11801.

STA ANA, GUADALUPE S.
[pen.] Danga; [b.] December 12, 1938, Calabanga Cam Sur Phillipines; [p.] Pedro E. and Francisca Azuela Sola; [m.] Levi T. Sta Ana, June 26, 1968; [ch.] Cyril, Levi Jr., Lyn, Edward, Johan Peter, Eugene Cecil, and John Paul; BSEED, Academic requirement in Master of Arts in Education; [occ.] Elementary grades teacher; [hon.] College awards: Magna cum laude, excellence in English, division award for Module Writing (Guro Kasagip); [oth. writ.] Stories and poems published in The Elizabethan, and Kislap Graphic, module and workbooks for elementary grades in English; [pers.] I am deeply grateful for this rare opportunity to express the Filipino in English poetry. [a.] Sabang, Calabanga, Cam Sur, Phillipines.

STAEBLER, LLOYD A.
March 19, 1909, Ann Arbor , Michigan; [m.] Mary Ciminnisi-Staebler, May 3, 1991; [ed.] B.S. in Engineering; [occ.] retired engineer; [memb.] ASHRAE, Sigma Xi; [hon.] Who's Who in Engineering; [oth. writ.] All technical; [pers.] This poem was inspired by "On His Blindness", by John Milton. My first poem written at age 84! [a.] North East, PA 16428.

STAFFIERI, J. A.
[b.] August 4, 1960, Atlantic City, New Jersey; [m.] Andrea; [ed.] Mainland Reg. High, American Art Institute; [occ.] Singer/songwriter, performing artist, composer of acoustic bohemian poetry; [hon.] Many performing arts awards for charities and music associations; [oth. writ.] Many interviews on my music and world views have been published in highly established entertainment journals such as The Aquarian, Asbury Park Press, E.C. Rocker, The Whoot, and many more; [pers.] I believe in powerful poetry, full of emotion and haunting reality. I believe in stretching boundaries and creating lasting works. My writing comes from a tortured soul. I live my words, I represent the true world vision of a new age in poetry. [a.] Mays Landing, NJ 08330.

STAFFORD, ARTHUR
[b.] March 22, 1914, Elwood, Indiana; [p.] Emma Porter and Lester Stafford; [m.] Agnes, April 13, 1940; [ch.] Janis, David; [ed.] Anderson High, Anderson Indiana, DePaul University, A.B. degree; [occ.] Accountant, retired; [memb.] AHA Association; [hon.] President, Chicago Hotel Accountants' Association; [oth. writ.] Just a few random poems, a reflection of

time so precious, time so short; [pers.] Writing from day one was "prime time" for me, but only after retirement have I pursued any efforts although amateur, but obsessive. [a.] Louisville, KY 40243.

STAKER, JOE J.
[pen.] The Old Scribbler; [b.] March 29, 1916, Beaver County, Oklahoma; [p.] Oscar C. and Dora Swan Staker; [m.] Kathryn R. Long Staker, January 1, 1939; [ch.] Marlene K. Staker Mitchell, Thomas Joe Staker; [oth. writ.] Poetry, prose, many short stories, and children's stories. [a.] Liberal, KS 67905.

STANLEY, CHRISTINE
[pen.] Chris; [b.] July 30, 1925, Dyersburg, Tennessee; [p.] Ben E. and Lou Ester Walk Tyler; [m.] John E. Stanley, May 13, 1951; [ch.] Kim Renee Stanley Grossman, granddaughter Julie Tyler Grossman; [ed.] Dyersburg High, correspondence courses; [occ.] Professional volunteer; [memb.] Faith Assembly, National Travel Club, International Society of Poets; [hon.] Golden Poet Award and World of Poetry's Hall of Fame; [oth. writ.] Local newspapers in Indiana and Tennessee, church bulletins, child's book and historical story of church, plays for church; [pers.] The blessings we enjoy today are the results of prayers we prayed yesterday. C.S. [a.] Hobart, IN 46342.

STANLEY, FRED C.
[b.] November 30, 1902, Cleburne, Texas; [p.] W. H. and Nancy Elizabeth Kirkland Stanley; [m.] Beulah Mae Hollis Stanley (deceased), November 26, 1929; [ch.] Fred C. Stanley Jr. (deceased), Jan Philip Stanley; [ed.] Tarleton State University; [occ.] Construction engineer, retired; [memb.] American Society of Professional Engineers, Texas Society of Professional Engineers, First Baptist Church, Lubbock, Texas; [hon.] Baptist deacon 57 years; [oth. writ.] Several poems published and others not submitted for publication; [pers.] Aim: To search for truth and tell it with plain talk. [a.] Lubbock, TX 79405.

STANLEY, SANDRA C.
[b.] April 12, 1945, Portsmouth, Virginia; [p.] Clarence Andrew (deceased) and Doris Muriel Crawford; [m.] Royce Daile Stanley (deceased), May 22, 1962; [ch.] Anthony Dale, Bryan Clay; [ed.] Woodrow Wilson, Portsmouth, Virginia; [occ.] Owner/operator, Country Classics, Shallotte, North Carolina; [memb.] Sudan Temple A.A.O.N.M.S., New Bern, North Carolina; [pers.] I strive to share the gift that I have been given with others. [a.] Charlotte, NC 28459.

STANLEY, SARAH ELIZABETH
[pen.] Sarah Beth; [b.] April 12, 1955, Reid Memorial Hospital; [p.] Ruth Sophiah and Freeman Enyart Stanley; [ed.] Graduate of Richmond Senior High School; [memb.] First Church of God, Anderson, Bible Study Fellowship International; [hon.] Numerous awards from World of poetry, honorable mentions and golden awards; [oth. writ.] In church bulletins, the newsletters, The Palladium item and graphic in print are special occasions, religious, anniversaries, Mother's Day, Valentine's Day, and retirement on Mom's fortieth year of teaching, published in World of Poetry, a poem on Mother's Day, in anthology entitled: The Golden Treasury of Great Poems; [pers.] A profound interest I've had in Helen Steiner Rice known as the poet laureate of popular verse. Rice's impact and inspirational influence

touched my life. God spoke to me through her writings. It was also through a friend named Wes: a God-given vessel that captivated my poetic abilities. The inspiring. gracious incentive Wes who is helping make my dreams a reality. I owe gratitude to the one that's pursuing tenaciously regardless of what others may think, and standing by me, my sister. That I might hope to accomplish having a book published and entitled Promising Prayers of Praise. To God be all the glory and praise for friends like these, and the greatest friend of all is our Lord Jesus Christ. [a.] Richmond, IN 47374.

STANTOM, LUTHER D.
[pen.] The Golden Artist; [b.] July 29, 1947, Dallas, Texas; [p.] Luther and Ruth Mildred Barnes Stanton; [ch.] Steven D. Stanton, granddaughters, Amanda D. and Lauren A. Stanton; [ed.] B.S. in Technology (Industrial Arts), minor in Education, certified in several areas of Aerospace Technology; [occ. Industrial specialist with U.S. Government Dept. of Defense; [memb.] Church of Christ; [hon.] Vietnam veteran, received a number of awards in the field of industrial arts; [oth. writ.] "California Love Dust", Juneteenth", Emancipation Proclamation" and several other poems,. songs , and paintings published and marketed including a campaign song for ex-president Jimmy Carter; [pers.] If you do not plant any seeds you cannot expect anything to grow! [a.] Los Angeles, Ca 90019.

STAPP, ROBERT M.
[b.] November 12, 1933, Loma Linda, California; [m.] Roselyn Stapp, June 27, 1953; [ch.] Three sons; [ed.] Two years college; [occ.] Civil Service supervisor; [memb.] St. Paul's Episcopal Church; [hon.] Numerous awards in visual art; [pers.] For many years I have practiced the art of sculpting, and only recently have I become interested in writing. I have found considerable pleasure in both art forms, each providing me an avenue of expressing my philosophy of life. [a.] Barstow, CA 92311.

STARGEL, LOUANN RUSSELL
[b.] December 30, 1956, Columbia, Kentucky; [p.] Wayne and Ann Hankins Russell; [m.] Gary Stargel, June 7, 1989; [ch.] Glynn Parker-15, Carrie Campbell-13; [ed.] Adair Co. High graduate, Somerset Cosmetology graduate, E.M.T. and health-aide training; [occ.] Housewife, farmer, co-owner Poor Boys' Appliances; [memb.] Tabernacle Christian Church; [hon.] Honorable mention for "Fate of Death" published in Treasured Poems of America, Fall 1991; [oth. writ.] Several poems published in local newspaper; [pers.] My writings are my feelings. They come from deep within my heart. My entire family is my inspiration. I write to help others, which is truly my calling. [a.] Russell Springs, KY 42642.

STEINBAUER, EMILY KAY
[b.] July 30,1980, Clay Center, Kansas; [p.] Jeffrey Robert and Jackie Kay Steinbauer; [ed.] 6th grade graduate, Cimarron Middle School, Edmond, Oklahoma; [memb.] National Honor Society, First Presbyterian Church, Gymnastics Association, Creative Writing Association; [hon.] I have won many awards and certificates from school and from sports. Honor Roll in middle school; [oth. writ.] I have had my poems published in yearbooks and newspapers in my town and school; [pers.] I love to write and I plan to become an author or a journalist. Follow your dreams

and listen to your heart so you may become whatever you wish. [a.] Edmond, OK 73013.

STEINIGER, ELAINE ANNETTE
[b.] June 17, 1958, Detorit, Michigan; [p.] Emily and Phillip Steiniger (deceased); [ed.] Our Lady Gate of Heaven grade school, Cody High School, Wayne County Community College, Wayne State University, 3 years; [occ.] Preschool teacher, Best Child Care Academy and poet; [memb.] National Library of Poetry; [hon.] Received 6 awards for my performance as teacher for Sleepy Hollow Ed. Center 1980-1991; [oth. writ.] Had poem "Friends" published in Selected Works of Poetry; [pers.] Wrote poetry for 15 years and worked with children for 15 years now. I write and work for all humankind and animals for the grace of God. [a.] Detroit, MI 48228.

STEPHENS, JAMES O. JR.
[b.] November 17, 1951, Valdosta, Georgia; [p.] James and Margaret Stephens; [ch.] John Phillip Stephens; [ed.] Various military; [occ.] Chief Warrant Officer 4, (Avionics officer in the United States Marine Corps); [hon.] Marine Corps Aviation Association Electronic Technician of the Year 1981, various military awards; [oth. writ.] Several poems unpublished; [pers.] All my poetry is militarily inspired and I hope someday to publish my own anthology. [a.] Jacksonville, NC 28540.

STEPHENS, JEAN HAWKS
[pen.] Jean Hawks; [b.] March 20, 1939, Southwold, Suffolk, England; [p.] Henry Hurr and Kathleen Coe; [ch.] John, Dennis Kevin, Paul Brian; [ed.] English High School, U.S. G.E.D., 1 year college, cosmetology school; [occ.] Housewife, retired cosmetologist; [hon.] Two winnings of hairstyles; [oth. writ.] Poetry, children stories, nothing published except this poem; [pers.] I write in the direction of helping children, in self-esteem with the insight of nature, God, and parents. So to enjoy life, school and homework. To enjoy life, to understand and be themselves. [a.] Tigret, TN 38070.

STEPHENS, MARY
[b.] August 28, 1948, Chattanooga, Tennessee; [p.] June C. and Howard L. Stephens; [ed.] A.B. Math U.T.C, Med. West Georgia College; [occ.] Educator; [memb.] CEA/GAE/NEA, NCTM, Delta Kappa Gamma, Pilot Club; [pers.] Dedicated to the students who have allowed me to make a difference in this world. [a.] Rossville, GA 30741.

STEPHENSON, EDIE
[b.] December 10, 1949, Roundup, Montana; [p.] Katie and Mick Stephenson; [ch.] Ryan Joseph; [ed.] Broadview High School, St. Vincent's School of Nursing, Sierra School of Integrative Therapy; [occ.] Registered nurse, certified massage therapist; [memb.] American and Californian Association of Post-Anesthesia Nurses, Professional Nurse Healer Association, Nurse Massage Therapists Association; [hon.] Nurse of the Month, Roseville Hospital, Dean's List, St. Vincent's School of Nursing; [oth. writ.] "Ode to Australia" and "Forgiveness" (unpublished); [pers.] My poems reflect my journey of inner growth and opening of my heartspace. I thank all those who have touched me in this process. [a.] Carmichael, Ca 95608.

STESLOW, MICHAEL G.
[b.] October 7, 1957, Chester, Pennsylvania; [p.] Lawrence and Mary Steslow; [m.] Deborah, September 20, 1986; [ch.] Tobiao, Matthew and Alex; [ed.] Wilson High School, Berks Vocational School, Lincoln Technical Institute; [occ.] Security Supervisor; [memb.] Mt. Pleasant Fire and Rescue Scout Master of Boy Scout Troop 113; [oth. writ.] Non published; [pers.] My works are dedicated to my inspiration - my wife. [a.] Bernville, PA 19506.

STEVENS, BUDDY
[pen.] O.D.D.; [b.] June 4, 1974, Shreveport, Louisiana; [p.] David and Tresa Olsen; [ed.] Ross Sterling of Baytown, Sam Houston State University; [oth. writ.] Several anthology publications; [pers.] Influences: Mother, God, Trent Reznor, Pink Floyd. You've got to bleed a little while you sing unless the words don't mean no thing. [a.] LaPorte, TX 77571.

STEVENS, EDGAR HARRISON
[pen.] Edgar H. Stevens, Brother Harry; [b.] December 12, 1907, Faulkner County , Arkansas; [p.] Elmer Henry and Charlotte Isabell Shilcutt Stevens; [m.] Eula E. Glover Stevens,m November 27, 1941; [ch.] Edgar Larence (died at birth), Donald Harry, Charlotte Rebecca; [ed.] B.S.E. University of Central Arkansas, Masters in Public School Administration, University of Arkansas; [occ.] public schoolteacher and administrator; [memb.] Southern Baptist, Masons, Disabled American Veteran; [hon.] Good Conduct Medal, Combat Infantryman Badge, Bronze Star, Presidential Citation; [oth. writ.] "Reflections of Brother Harry": This is a collection of about 70 of my poems, published by my church to raise money for our building fund, as a fundraiser it was quite successful and I have received many compliments, including four libraries; [pers.] I only write poetry when I feel compelled to because I cannot express my thoughts and feelings in any other way. [a.] Greenbrier, AR 72058.

STEVENS, GINA M. PEABODY
[b.] November 26, 1965, Bozeman, Montana; [p.] Gene and Sandra Peabody; [m.] John alan Stevens, August 19, 1989; [ed.] Sherodan High, Montana State University; [occ.] Rancher; [memb.] American Angus Association, National Stockgrowers, National Cattlewomen, Farm Bureau; [oth. writ.] Various poems published in local newspapers and magazines, book of my poems published; [pers.] I write about everyday events in ranching life. [a.] Busby, MT 59016.

STEVENSON, JULIA A.
[pen.] Julia; [b.] March 2, 1953, Augusta, Georgia; [p.] Mr. and Mrs. Hubert G. Stevenson; [ed.] MCHS Chatsworth, Georgia; [pers.] Though the body be not perfect, the mind has great intelligence.

STEVENSON, KIRSTY L.
[pen.] Kirsty Louise Stevenson; [b.] April 8, 1974, Mansfield, Nottinghamshire; [p.] Jennifer and Trevor Stevenson; [ed.] Nth Sonercotres Primary School, Healing Comprehensive and Grimsby College of Technology and Arts; [occ.] Student aiming to become a psychotherapist and writer; [memb.] Stevie Nicks "The Connection"; [hon.] 9 GCSES and 3 'A' levels in Sociology, Politics, and English; [oth. writ.] Poem published in the local newspaper called "The Wall"; [pers.] My writing reflects my true self. Hope

to inspire in others appreciation of the emotional quality of words, which Stevie's music has inspired in me. [a.] S. Hunberside, DN37 9NW England.

STEVENSON, LAURALEE T.
[b.] October 11, 1928, Lynchburg, Virginia; [p.] Blanche Rudd and Jason Bruffy Trent; [m.] Divorced, May 25, 1946; [ch.] Jed, Treni, Martha; [ed.] Gunston Hall, Wash. D.C., Hunter College B.A. Art History, M.A. Art History; [occ.] Retired; [memb.] Metropolitan Club, St. George Society, D.A.R., G.D.C., English Speaking Union, A.F.A.; [oth. writ.] "Confederate Soldier Artists in the Civil War" to be published December 1994 by White Mane Publishers, Columbia Md.; [pers.] Poetry is God's music to the world. [a.[New York, NY 10021.

STEVER, CINDY FAYE
[pen.] Cindy Campbell Stever; [b.] July 29, 1954, Sacramento, California; [p.] Irving S. and Betty Jo Campbell; [m.] Douglas George Stever, May 28, 1977; [ch.] JoAnne Michelle, Cynthia Jenelle, Sean Douglas, Christopher Riyse, Aaron Tyler, Matthew Benjamin and Joshua Scott; [ed.] High school, taking gradual college courses; [occ.[] Mother, wife, writer; [memb.] The Church of Jesus Christ of Latter Day Saints; [hon.] Returned missionary for church; [oth. writ.] Several children's books to be submitted, also a couple of teen adventures as well as adult humor and romance; [pers.] Writing has always been a love of mine along with singing, music, sewing, cooking and my greatest loves, church and family! [a.] Placerville, CA 95667.

STEWART, IRENE ELIZABETH
[pen.] Elizabeth Stewart; [b.] July 30, 1930, Springfield, Illinois; [p.] William H. and Ruby E. Watts; [m.] Robert J. Stewart (deceased), October 17, 1947, [ch.] Judith L. Stewart, Robert G. Stewart; [ed.] Lanphier High School, McClernand Grade School, Iles Grade School; [occ.] Data entry operator, input/output clerk; [memb.] Body of Christ of Buffalo Illinois Church; [hon.] 1993 Employees Choice Awards on my own time poem, "The Potter an the Clay", 1993 Famous Poets Society, poem "Love"; [oth. writ.] Several poems published in church paper, I have written from 1950-1993, a book of poems containing over one hundred poems unpublished as yet; [pers.] Life is not always happy or perfect. In my writing, I try to bring a little hope, peace, joy, and comfort to my readers. [a.] Springfield, IL 62704.

STIGERS, MARY D.
[b.] November 11, 1909, Amarilla, Texas; [p.] William and Sardina Dudgeon; [m.] Melburne Stigers (deceased), October 11, 1931; [ch.] William, Stephanie, Nina, Charles; [ed.] Graduate of University of Arizona; [occ.] Retired; [memb.] Church Mormon; [oth. writ.] Published 2 books of poetry, 1 novel, 2 books of musical theory; [pers.] My efforts have been directed toward educating children to develop skills in all areas of the arts, visual, musical, dance, and drama. [a.] Tucson, AZ 85926.

STINSON, THERESA
[pen.] Theresa Stinson; [b.] January 8, 1981, [p.] Susan and Michael C. Stinson; [ed.] Lakeview Elementary; [occ.] Student; [memb.] Church Chorus, Girl Scouts; [hon.] Running awards, beauty pageant awards, group writing awards; [oth. writ.] Long stories; [pers.] When I write, it's like getting away to

some magical or powerful place. Like leaving behind the badness in our world. [a.] Phoenix, AZ 85029.

STITH, MARGARET A.
[pen.] Natasha Vanessa Terrence; [b.] January 24, 1939, Canton, Ohio; [ed.] Graduate of E. Canton High, Kent State, Akton U, Stark Tech, N.M.S.U.; [occ.] Clerical; [hon.] National Honor Society, high school; [pers.] I was thrilled to learn my poem would be published since it is my first writing, but I hope to have more. [a.] Canton, OH.

STIVERS, TAMMY
[b.] January 7, 1977, Louisville, Kentucky; [p.] Charlotte Hall and Danny Stivers Sr,; [ed.] Moore High Career Magnet Academy; [occ.] Sales associate at a Deb Clothing Store; [memb.] Secretary of the Junior Class, and a F.B.L.A. student; [hon.] Received the Ambassador of Goodwill Award and I am in all Honors classes with a 4.0 grade point average; [pers.] This poem was written about my teacher and best friend. She was a beautiful person who was taken from us with cancer. She is greatly missed/1 This is for her. [a.] Louisville, KY 40229.

STOCKMAN, DOROTHY
[pen.] Dottie Stockman; [b.] September 6, 1940, Knoxville, Tennessee; [p.] Lillie McCoy and Harvey E. Green; [ch.] Teresa, Charles, Douglas, Daniel, and Alecia; [ed.] Consumnes River College, Placerville, California; [occ.] Student, studying to become a writer; [memb.] Center for Creative Living, Cameno, California, a metaphysical church; [oth. writ.] Other poetry, none published; [pers.] I believe that our accomplishments in life can be anything that we believe within ourselves is possible. [a.] Cameron Park, CA 95682.

STONE, MARY J.
[b.] July 6, 1050, Claremont, New Hampshire; [p.] William Henry and Marie E. Cummings; [m.] Harold W. Stone, December 16, 1972; [ch.] Laurie J. and Lesley M. Stone; [occ.] Housewife and love to write poems; [memb.] Women of the Moose; [pers.] Would like this poem dedicated to my mother, Marie A. Cummings and late father William H. Cummings Sr. I write for the joy of others. [a.] Colorado Springs, CO 80910.

STOREY, ELVIN E. (REV)
[b.] March 3, 1925, Grattan, Michigan; [p.] Louland and Lila Storey; [m.] Ruth Storey, August 30, 1952; [ch.] Janet Storey LeFevre, Roger Duane, Ronald Leslie, Terry Allen; [ed.] Belding High School, Grand Rapids School of Bible and Music, Grand Rapids Baptist Bible College; [occ.] Clergyman, pastored 6 churches, ordained May 15, 1959; [memb.] American Poetry Society, honorary charter member of the International Society of Poets; [hon.] Golden Poet Award 1992, awarded by World Of Poetry; [oth. writ.] Author of poetical book Trailways of Poetical Thought, and Poems of Inspiration and Devotion; [pers.] In my service to God and country, I felt deeply honored to have served in the U.S. Armed Forces, and to have served 37 years in the Christian ministry. My greatest reward is helping people that I have ministered to. [a.] Tucson, AZ 85706.

STOWE, JANE TELFAIR
[b.] January 24, 1942, Springfield, Massachusetts; [p.] David and Mary Swift Telfair; [m.] Peter Stowe,

August 22, 1964; [ch.] Timothy David Stowe; [ed.] Olney Friends School, Earlham College, Southern Illinois University; [occ.] Administrative assistant, formerly elementary teacher; [memb.] Adelphi Friends Meeting, Women's Center and Referral Service, COPRED (peace research),CCRC (conflict resolution), Center for Partnership Education; [oth. writ.] Poems and articles published in newsletters, poem published in Friendly Woman; [pers.] My poetry reflects my deepest feelings which focus on my love of nature, human bonds and political justice, while striving for Quaker simplicity. [a.] Silver Spring, MD 20903.

STRAHM, EDNA L.
[b.] January 17, 1923, Clark County, Indiana; [p.] Paul and Minnie Montgomery Smith; [m.] Raymond Strahm (deceased); [ch.] Steven W. Strahm; [ed.] Swayzee High School; [occ.] Homemaker, care for elderly, part-time merchandiser; [memb.] Church of Christ, AARP; [oth. writ.] Several poems printed in local church bulletins, sold a "A Christian's Christmas" to Gibson Greeting Card Co., 1st prize, Montpelier, Indiana 1966 poetry contest; [pers.] Due to a need in m,y life I became a Bible scholar in my early twenties. I feel this has greatly helped me to be a stronger person. If there is any merit in what I write I am glad for an opportunity to have it published. [a.] Hartford City IN 47348.

STRATTOPN, CARL F.
[b.] January 27, 1931, Fulton, New York; [p.] William Harlowe and Della Anne;]   [m.] Patricia Jean, April 24, 1954; [ch.] Dennis, David, Sharon; [ed.] North Western University (corporation management); [occ.] Retired; [memb.] V.F.W.; [hon.] Golden Poet 10901, Who's Who of Poetry 1002, Golden Poet 1992, Homer Honor Society; [oth. writ.] Poems in Great oems of Our Time, poems will be in Whispers in the Wind and The Coming of Dawn in local newspaper; [pers.] If all the world's population were poets there would be no more hatred and no more wars. [a.] Wooddale Il 60191.

STEICKLAND, DEBORAH J.
[b.] March 30, 1952. Litchfield, Minnesota; [p.] Donald V. Robinson, and Cora E. Blazer; [m.] Will Strickland Jr., November 20, 1987, [ch.] Three; [ed.] High school degree, Tech school; [oth. writ.] This is the first time I have ever submitted anything in a contest.; [pers.] When I write poetry I try to use words to draw the picture I see in my head. [a.] Longville, MN 56655.

STRUBLE, JANICE
[b.] April 14, 1954, Monroe, Michigan; [p.] Robert Nagy and Virginia Talley; [m.] Douglas Struble, November 16, 1972; [ch.] Douglas J. Wesley, Olivia, Ben, and Neil; [ed.] Airport High, Monroe County Community College, Wayne County Community College; [occ.] Homemaker; [memb.] Right to Life of Michigan, Relief Society, Church of Jesus Christ of Latter Day Saints; [oth. writ.] "My Psalm" and "For What it's Worth
both written for church recital; [pers.] I truly believe there is a purpose in my writing. We need to focus more on God and less on the world. I feel very strongly about this matter. [a.] Riverview, MI 48192.

STRUCKMEYER, DOUGLAS J.
[b.] June 29, 1970, San Diego, California; [p.] Robert W. and Diana L. Struckmeyer; [ed.] First Colonial High School, Virginia Tech; [occ.] Student/engineer; [memb.] American Nuclear Society, American Society of Mechanical Engineers; [hon.] Dean's List. [a.] Virginia Beach, VA 23452.

STUMPF, EUNICE HELEN
[pen]. Eunice Helen Francisco Stumpf; [b.] March 21, 2926, Schenectady, New York; [p.] Bert and Anna Francisco; [m.] Andrew Stumpf, November 27, 1946; [ch.] Andrew L. Stumpf; [ed.] Robert G. Shaw Jr. High, West Roxbury, Massachusetts, Army Quartermaster School WWII, Fort Lee, Virginia; [memb.] U.S. Army Sgt. WWII; [hon.] Won several blue ribbons for my ceramics, won 1 Best of Show ribbon at Colorado State Fair, Senior Division; [oth. writ.] Wrote some political articles published in local papers. [a.] Colorado Springs, Co 80911.

STURGEON, HAZEN WARREN
[pen.] H.W. Shortfellow; [b.] May 30, 1921, Blackville, New Brunswick; [p.] Henry and Maria; [m.] Mary Roselyn, December 24, 1942; [ch.] Garnett Hazen, William David; [ed.] Grade 8 public school, one room country schoolhouse; [occ.] Purchasing agent nd traffic manager, retired; [memb.] Life member The Royal Canadian Legion; [hon.] Meritorious medal assisting, advising veterans and families of veterans; [oth. writ.] "The Hillside Lumberjacks", "The Miramichi" (River), "'Tis April", "The Orphan's Song", "Boyhood Days". [a.] Toronto, Ontario M4L 2Z7.

STURGEON, MARCI
[b.] March 20, 1974, New Britain, Connecticut; [p.] David and Melissa Sturgeon; [ed.] Stayton High School, Chemeketa Community College; [occ.] College student; [pers.[I strive to capture emotion in my poetry to find new perspectives of everyday life. [a.] Scio, OR 97374.

STURGEON, WILLIAM T.
[pen.] Tommy; [b.] March 1, 1926, Wawota, Saskatchewan; [p.] Fred Sturgeon and Annie Mabel Newman; [m.] Susan Hance, May 14, 1960; [ch.] Marvin, Brian, Doreena, Teresa; [ed.] Completed grade 9 in school, completed 4th class marine engineering, worked on ferry boats, housepainter for 2 years, completed apartment manager's course; [oth. writ.] I have many poems I have composed over the years. Nature poems, religious poems, some set to music, others accepted I had sent to newspapers; [pers.] I give all credit for the gift of poetry to my heavenly Father, and I love all things in nature, I behold all beauty in people, in flowers, in scenery, and all creatures great and small. [a.] Kamloops, B.C. Canada V2C 6C3.

STURGILL, DEAN
[pen.] Ole Booger; [b.] October 14, 1934, Lansing, North Carolina; [p.] Carl and Blannie Spencer Sturgill; [m.] Phyllis Walls, May 26, 1972; [ch.] Greely Dean, Johnny Allen; [ed.] Lansing High School; [occ.] Farmer; [hon.] Blue ribbon, Old Time Fiddler; [oth. writ.] An Old Fiddler's Book of Rhymes, An Old Fiddler's Book of Rhymes II; [pers.] If I can get a man to laugh I will have eased some of his pain. [a.] Lansing, MI 28643.

SUHR, LOIS W.
[b.] April 13, 1939, Sayre, Pennsylvania; [p.] Myron Paul and Thelma Root Wilson; [m.] Frederick L, Suhr, September 14, 1957; [ch.] Connie Suhr Boiano; [ed.] Wellsboro Sr. High School; [occ.] Secretary, Boyer Kantz and Associates; [memb.] Friends of Green Free Library, Tioga County Historical Society; [pers.] My writings reflect my love of home and family., It is my hope that future generations will hold these values also and treasure the memories. [a.] Wellsboro, PA 16901.

SULAK, KATHY
[pen.] Kathy Churchill-Sulak; [b.] December 13, 1957, Schotter, Germany; [p.] John and Norma Churchill; [m.] William J. Sulak, June 24, 1978; [ch.] Michael Joseph, 6 years old; [ed.] Belton High School graduate, 1976, Belton Texas; [occ.] Pathology secretary/transcriptionist; [memb.] Homer Poet's Society; [hon.] Golden Poet Award 1989-1993, Gold Medal of Honor, 1993; [oth. writ.] Poems published in Great Poems of the Western World, Treasured Poems of America, Poems That Will Live Forever, Anthology of Great Poems.

SUMMER, EDDIE
[b.] December 2, 1956, Newberry; [p.] Brad and Sara Summer; [ed.] High School, 1 year college; [hon.] Handicapped since 1976, quadriplegic, use eye control computer to write; [oth. writ.] Stories published in Quad Unlimited and Penthouse, 2 chap books published, poems in many books and newspapers; [pers.] I lost my health, I lost my life, When I write, I dream of living. [a.] Callells, SC 29037.

SUMMERS MARY
[pen.] Penny Louise; [b.] May 12, 1980, Columbus, Ohio; [p.] James and Sue Summers; [ed.] Elementary school, middle school, I'm only in 8th grade; [hon.] Honor roll, goal Achiever award; [oth. writ.] I'm currently writing a book on my aunt Penny's life; [pers.] I am greatly influenced by my mother and Aunt Penny, who's hardships of losing her sons helped me write this poem. [a.] Columbus, OH 43204.

SUNDERLAND, TERRY
[pen.] Terja; [b.] November 5, 1950, Baltimore, Maryland; [p.] Shirley and Roland Sunderland; [m.] Marc, divorced, May 25, 1969; [ch.] Lisa Elaine Kabik, Eric Neal Kabik; [ed.] Southern High, CCB College; [occ.] Finance manager, bookkeeper for Columbia Auto Sales; [memb.] New Poet; [oth. writ.] Only my personal ones; [pers.] My poems are dedicated to my children and George K. Romantic, in love with the beauty in this world and people. George K. and my children who have been my inspiration in love and life, my champions. [a.] Columbia MD 21045.

SUNS, WAYNE E.
[b.] October 24, 1941, Huntsville, Alabama; [m.] Jerri Ann Martin, May 14, 1966; [ch.] Stephanie, Jennifer, Wayne Jr.; [ed.] M.S. Southeastern Institute of Technology; [occ.] Corporate executive; [oth. writ.] Short stories, essays, literary criticism. [a.] Huntsville, AL.

SUTCLIFFE, CHRISTIE
[b.] July 20, 1975, Wilmington, Delaware; [p.] Dona Kelly and Chuck Kelly and Shirley Reed; [ch.] Jacob Lee, 2 years old; [ed.] Graduate from Delcastle Vocational Technical High School; [occ.] Unit clerk,

Alfred I. Dupont Children's Hospital; [oth. writ.] I have written several poems that have not yet been published. but I am looking forward to possibly getting them published; [pers.] My writing comes from within me and only me!

SUTHERLAND, IRENE
[pen.] Irene Sutherland; [b.] September 30, 1058, Calgary, Alta., Canada; [p.] Lois and Olie 'Deschampos, Agnes Sutherland; [m.] John Sutherland, July 6, 1985; [ch.] Teresa Christine, Jarrett, Chad, Kimberly and Jay; [occ.] Residential service provider for mentally challenged; [pers,] May we all learn from those less fortunate, the lesson of life. [a.] Granges, B.C., Canada V0S 1E0.

SUTTON, RICHARD
[b.] December, 1947; [m.] My pen; [e.] B.Sc., B.Ed., Life; [hon.] A smile, a thought; [oth. writ. Other poems; [pers.] Words strung together by spaces. Synchronicity. Balance. Connection. Allowing mystery, but finding a home in a reader's experience. My constellations for you. [a.] Regina, Saskatchewan, Canada.

SWAFFORD, JENNIFER L.
[n.] November 28, 1980, Kirksville, Missouri; [p.] Donald and Sheila Swafford; [ed.] Adair Co. R-1 School, Novinger; [memb.] Novinger Renewal, Inc, Novinger United Methodist Church. [a.] Novinger, MO 63559.

SWANN, ARNSTEAD H, JR.
[pen.] Meadaris Shanni; [b.] March 24, 1959, Danville, Virginia; [p.] Armstead Sr. and Barbara Swann (passed away); [m.] Carolyn Swann, April 25, 1992; [ch.] Cammie Swann, step Chinetta and Sheila Swann; [ed.] George Washington High, Marine Corps Institute; [occ.] Quilter, J.P. Stevens and Co., Inc, Burlington, North Carolina; [memb.] Mt. Calvary Baptist Church, American Red Cross vol. blood donor; [hon.] Marine Corps Institute, Wash., D.C., 2nd plaques U.S.M.C. football team; [oth. writ.] I do have many poems at my home that have not been read by National Library of Poetry; [pers.] I always try and do my best at whatever task or hobby before me, learning a little about any and everything helps me be well-rounded person that I may be able to give back to mankind and my Lord and Master. [a.] Yanceyville, NC 27379.

SWART, SUSAN
[b.] July 9, 1947, Jackson, Mississippi; [m.] Kenneth Swart, April 25, 1981; [ed.] Masters of Business Management, Aquinas College; [occ.] Sr. Territorial marketing rep; [memb.] State Poetry Society, International Society of Poets, lay Eucharist minister, Episcopal Diocese of Michigan; [oth. writ.] This is my eleventh poem published in a variety of anthologies and Christian magazines; [pers.] Poetry comes out of the depths of my being where I experience God's great goodness and love. [a.] Birmingham, MI 48009.

SWEARINGEN, ROBERT
[b.] January 22, 1979, Panama City, Florida; [p.] Edward and Deborah Swearingen; [ed.] Millville Elementary, Rosenwald Middle School; [memb.] Millville Melodie Airs, Lois Lawrence, instructor, Rosenwald yearbook staff, M. Davis; [hon.] Most Outstanding Business Student, from Mary Davis; [oth. writ.] "Friends", a poem, "Christmas", a short

story, "Granny", a poem about my grandmother, Sarah Swearingen; [pers.] I thank all of my teachers from Millville and Rosenwald, especially my parents, Mike and Debbie Swearingen, and grandparents Ed and Sarah Swearingen. [a.] Panama City, FL 32401.

SWEENEY, MARIE T.
[pen.] Trina; [b.] July 4, 1915, Naples, Florida; [p.] Lorenzo and Sarafina Mattia; [m.] John Joseph Sweeney, June 27, 1937; [ch.] Margaret Ami, 3 grandchildren, 3 great-grandchildren; [ed.] High school; [occ.] Retired beautician; [hon.] Three poems, honorable mention awards; [oth. writ.] "Do Not Weep For Me", "Your Wedding Day", "Robert and Ami", "Jesus Loves Me". [a.] Clinton, MD 20735.

SWEETING, TRESKA TAMARA
[b.] February 1, 1978, Nassua, Bahamas; [p.] Laura Lowe and Vincent Sweeting; [ed.] Palmdale Primary , C.I. Gibson Secondary; [occ.] Student; [hon.] Math, Spelling, speech, B.J.C's 9; [oth. writ.] Only a few poems I write in my spare time; [pers.] I enjoy writing poems., I really hope you liked my poem and I am very thankful that you accepted my poem. [a.] Nassau, Bahamas.

SWINFORD, IVA MAE
[b.] December 6, 1931, Mason, Texas; [p.] Archie Lonnie and Winnie Dianrha Eingfield Keith; [m.] Joseph Arthur Swinford (deceased), February 20, 1968; [ch.] Lonnie O'Dell Sturdivant, Shirley Ann Sturdivant Wilkins; [ed.] 10th grade high school, nursing training; [occ.] Nurse, retired, write poetry, make dolls; [memb.] Rebekah Genealogical Society; [hon.] Best New Song 1968, Best New Poem in Top Ten of 1992, 2 honorable mentions 1988, 1989; [oth. writ.] Poems published in Earthshine Vol II, Poetry press, The American Muse, Fine Arts Press, Our World's Most Treasured Poems, Great Poems of Our Times, senior citizen newsletter; [pers.] To keep my faith in my God, my country, and my fellow man. To help others whenever I can and to give to others some of the joy and happiness in life that I have had. [a.] Hobbs, New Mexico 88240.

SWIFT, LIZ
[pen.] Liz Smith; [b.] July 4, 1947, West Ridge, Arkansas; [p.] Clyde and Viola Howard; [m.] Bert Swift, May 19, 1989; [ch.] Gilbert, Andy, Dennis, Danny and Libby; [ed.] 11th grade; [occ.] Resident manager for National Church Residences; [memb.] Chamber of Commerce; [oth. writ.] Submission is first poem, but other poems have ben written; [pers.] The poems that I have written has been a gift from God. I feel like a new world has opened up to me through my poems. It is an honor that my first poem was selected. [a.] Bedford, TX 76021.

SYMPSON, BILL
[pen.] Bill Sympson; [b.] December 25, 1953, Indianapolis, Indiana; [p.] William I, Sympson, Wanda M. Davis; [m.] Tonya L. Sympson, October 15, 1991; [ch.] Brandi Star Sympson, Tim W. Sympson, Jimmy L. Schindler; [ed.] Western High School, Louisville, Kentucky, Associate degree from Louisville Tech College, Louisville Kentucky; [occ.] Machine operator, Koetler Woodworking, Borden, Indiana; [hon.] Honor Roll in high school, Dean's List in college, 5 awards and honors from World of Poetry for other poems; [oth. writ.] Many writings published in World of Poetry, also many other poems I have in my

personal collection; [pers.] Most all my writings are from my personal experiences in life, love, happiness, and sadness. I hope people can read my poems and it can touch their lives in special ways. [a.] New Albany, IN 47150.

TADOORI, HIMA
[pen.] Hima, Tadoori; [b.] February 15, 1979, Parma, Ohio; [p.] Pandu and Padma Tadoori; [ed.] Student attending Baldwin Junior High School, 8th grade; [memb.] Baldwin Junior High School Honors Society; [hon.] High honor roll, participated and place in 6 Spelling Bees, awards in cheerleading, music, art, NYSSMA, math, Social Studies, Science, Presidential Academic Fitness Award; [pers.] I owe thanks to mom, dad, Rekha, Swathis, Abhiskek and all my friends and teachers, I was truly inspired by author Shad Helmstetter, Ph.D., my saying is "c'est la vie! Be fearless of it". [a.] Baldwin, NY.

TAIT, JOHN SAMUEL
[b.] May 5, 1908, Enfield, St. Mary, Jamaica, West Indies; [p.] John Samuel and Lydia Victoria Tait; [m.] Margaret May Tait, July 27, 1937; [ch.] Sheila May and Noel Emmanuel Hewitt Tait; [ed.] Enfield Elementary School, St. John's College, Kingston Jamaica, London Matric. Corres. course-University Corresp. College London, England; [occ.] Pharmacist (Jamaica); [memb.] Pharmaceutical Society of Jamacia, Jamaica Cricket Club; [hon.] Officer of the Order of Distinction-Jamacia Government, Serving Brother-Order of St. John, medal of merit and bar-Jamaica Scouts Association; [oth. writ.] Twelve (12) poems (unpublished); [pers.] Writing poetry helps me to develop an inquiring mind, to seek lessons in ordinary things and phenomena, and to record historical facts in pleasant form. It increases my power of expression and memory and helps me to meditate even in unfavourable situations. Above all it perpetrates my thoughts. [a.] Toronto Ontario, Canada M6S 1H2.

TALLURI, SOLOMON SUVARNA RAJ
[pen.] Jaazu; [b.] August 14, 1974, Guntur; [p.] T. Joseph Suvarna Raj and T. Suguna Kumari; [ed.] Lutheran English Medium High, Andhra Christian College; [occ.] Student; [memb.] YMCA, St. Matthew's Church North Parish; [hon.] Poet of Merit 92, International Poet of Merit 93; [pers.] I try to bring peace and goodness for mankind in my poetry. [a.] Guntur 522-002 A.P. India.

TAUER, SANDY
[b.] May 26, 1946, Chicago, Illinois (Cook County); [p.] Original unknown, adopted-Walter and Irene Block; [m.] Kenneth C. Tauer, April 8, 1967; [ch.] Eugene Charles and Jason Eric; [ed.] Cathedral High, graduated; [occ.] Housewife; [pers.] For me, the beauty of nature is my mentor, my compass. It compliments and completes my sense of well-being, it enriches my life, like minerals enrich the soil. [a.] New Ulm, MN.

TAYLOR, ANNE GROVE
[pen.] Anne G. Taylor; [b.] December 8, 1944, Cullman, Alabama; [p.] Dorothy Rowland Grove and Rev. Woodfin Kirk Grove; [m.] James (Jim) W. Taylor, December 30, 1988; [ch.] Jonathan (John) Grove Stiff, born January 6, 1971; [ed.] Banks High School, Birmingham University of Alabama, Tuscaloosa Sanford University, Birmingham; [occ.] Professional photoglazer, owner/president Anne Tay-

lor Originals; [memb.] Active member of Trinity United Methodist Church, Charter member and officer of Metro Humane Shelter Guild, member of Greater Birmingham Humane Society, Patron member of The Broadway Series/Town and Gown / Summerfest, member Heart Association, Handbell Choir, Church Ambassador; [oth. writ.] Editor/publisher of Booster Beat Newsletter, several articles in local newspaper; [pers.] I write poetry for the enjoyment of my family, friends and myself. "Oh John, My Son: was written for and about my son, Corp. Johnathan (John) Grove Stiff, U.S.M.C., when he was on stand-by for Saudi Arabia. The words and the meaning were a comfort when he served in Somalia. My poetry flows from my heart almost faster than I can capture it on paper. [a.] Birmingham, AL.

TAYLOR, FRANCES MOSS
[b.] June 6, Danville, Virginia; [p.] Robert and Elizabeth Moss; [m.] Ronald Taylor, June 9; [ch.] Monte William Taylor; [oth. writ.] Published poetry; [pers.] Beleving life ia a gift of God, and gratitude is expressed in many forms. The written word has been a treasure for me conveying the wisdom of the ancients, teaching me to celebrate life today with joy and grace. My writing expresses my gratitude to God. [a.] Danville, VA.

TAYLOR, JESSIE
[pen.] Jessie Taylor; [b.] July 4, 1917, Bethel, Wise Co., Texas; [p.] John and Jannie Read;[m.] Clyde Terry Taylor, April 24, 1971; [ch.] Two daughters, one step-daughter and two stepsons; [ed.] High school, Business College and Life Underwriters; [occ.] Retired Insurance Saleslady; [memb.] Eastern Star, Lutc and Baptist Church; [hon.] National Quality Award; [pers.] Born on a farm, have three sisters and two brothers living. [a.] Aledo, TX 76008.

TAYLOR, LINDA G.
[b.] September 17, 1952, Pittsburgh, Pennsylvania; [p.] Harry P. and Helen G. Muders; [m.] Samuel J. Taylor, August 18, 1973; [ch.] Ashley Lynn Taylor; [ed.] Quaker Valley High, Robert Morris College, U.S. Naval School of Health Sciences (operating room and pharmacy); [occ.] Pharmacy Technician, U.S. Navy; [memb.] American Association of Pharmacy Technicians, Celiac Disease Foundation; [pers.] I believe that anything you want to achieve, you can and each day brings something new to learn. [a.] Honolulu, HI 96818.

TAYLOR, RACHEL MARIAH
[b.] December 14, 1984, Lansing, Michigan; [p.] Stacey L. Taylor-Milks and Max Leon Taylor, Jr.; [ch.] Wants 2 when she grows up, (she used to want 12) for real; [ed.] 3rd grader at Averill Elementary, Carol Shank is Rachel's 3rd grade teacher, Mr. Roichowiak is her principal; [occ.] School, Girl's Scouts and church; [memb.] Member of Life Christian Church of Lansing, Michigan and Girl Scouts Troop # 202; [hon.] Kindergarten: Principals Honor Roll, 1st grade: Gifted and Talented Program, Good Citizenship Award, Reading Achievement Award, Writing Award and Certificate of Recognition, Good Behavior and Student of the Month Award, 2nd grade, Gifted and Talented Program, Certificate of Proficiency in Education Awareness, Student of the Month Award and Girl Scouts, 3rd grade, Gifted and Talent Program, Girl Scouts, Certificate of Merit in the Arts; [oth. writ.] Oh Yes, Here at Home and at

School, not published yet; [pers.] Lee Bennet Hopkins told me the most about poetry, he taught me how to write them. [a.] Lansing, MI 48911.

TAYLOR, SEAN M.
[b.] February 8, 1971, Bellevue, Washington; [p.] Jim and Sandy Taylor; [ed.] Sammammish High School, Bellevue Community College, University of Idaho; [occ.] Psychology major, University of Idaho; [memb.] Order of DeMolay; [hon.] Chevalier degree, Order of DeMolay; [oth. writ.] (in) Fugue, the literary digest of The University of Idaho; [pers.] " Poetry is my emotional and spiritual center, it is the fulcrum that gives my life balance. [a.] Bellevue, WA 98008.

TAYLOR, WALTER (TOMMY) THOMAS
[pen.] Tommy Taylor; [b.] December 1, 1974, Ohio; [p.] George and Wanda Taylor; [ed.] Grimsley High School, attending Guilford College; [oth.writ.] Poetry for a new age, not published yet; [pers.] Do what thou wilt, love is the law, love under will. [a.] Greensboro, NC.

TEMPLEMAN, ANGELA
[b.] April 26, 1974, Marceline, Missouri; [p.] Mike and Linda Templeman; [m.] Michael Frakes (fiancee'); [ch.] Michael Dans; [occ.] Mother of Michael, 4 months old; [oth. writ.] Many non-published; [pers.] Reach for what you want, someday you'll have it in your hold. [a.] Liberty, MO 64068.

TERNES, ESTHER
[pen.] Esther Ternes; [b.] January 26, 1943, Dodsland, Saskatchewan; [ch.] Norman Walter and Leslie Wade; [occ.] Secretary; [oth. writ.] Several unpublished poems. [a.] Stettler, Alberta T0C 2L2.

TERRY, JUDITH E.
[pen.] Judy Terry; [b.] November 8, 1941, Kansas City, Missouri; [p.] Robert E. and Melba D. Wilson; [m.] James E. Terry, August 25, 1962; [ch.] Jama Elaine and Jason Lee; [ed.] Paoli High School, In, Indiana State University, B.S., Indiana University, M.S.; [occ.] Elementary teacher; [memb.] North Lawrence Education Association, Indiana State Teachers Association, National Education Association, Delta Kappa Gamma International Society; [hon.] Received nominations for: Who's Who in Universities, Who's Who in Education; [oth. writ.] I have approximately 80 poems in a "personal growth file". This is the first time I've ever submitted any work for publishing; [pers.] Thanks to my son who helped pick up the garbage, my daughter who encouraged me to submit a poem, my parents who taught me to be sensitive aware of my world and to continue to grow.[a.] Bedford, IN.

TERRY, ROBERT DANIEL
[b.] September 28, 1949, Concord, Massachusetts; [p.] Barbara Rose and Thomas D. Terry; [ed.] Weare High School, Weare, New Hampshire; [oth. writ.] An unpublished collection of prose and poetry entitled "The Woodpile" ; [pers.] To live without acknowledging our memories, both good and bad, is to be as a tree without bark. [a.] Wartburg, TN 37887.

TESSENSOHN, LESA
[b.] February 24, 1957, Wiltshire County, England; [p.] William and Delores McCallister; [m.] James H. Tessensohn, March 1, 1975; [ch.] Judith Amanda, Jeanna Christine and Jessica Amber; [occ.] Validation/Calibration Technician; [oth. writ.] Poems published in local papers.

THACKER, BEATRICE F.
[b.] June 13, 1910, Grundy, Virginia; [p.] John A. Fields and Mae Ratliff; [m.] Marvin Thacker (deceased), September 17, 1927; [ch.] Bill, Bruce, Geneva and Robert; [ed.] B.A. degree in Elementary Education; [occ.] Retired elementary teacher, Kentucky; [memb.] Kentucky Retired Teachers; [oth. writ.] I Am A Mountaineer, I have some stories written about the Mountaineers, never published; [pers.] I love nature. We can learn from nature, we need to listen and observe the wonders nature has for us. [a.] Gloucester, VA 23061.

THAO, BLIA
[b.] September 10,1980, Chicago, Illinois; [p.] Ngia Va and Chia Thao; [ed.] C.M. Goethe Middle School; [occ.] Student; [oth.writ.] First Love, Still Holding On, Memories and several more poems; [pers.] My older sister's social life inspired me to write love poems. "It is pride and inspiration that will ge me to the top". [a.] Sacramento, CA.

THARP, SHEILA
[pen.] Dreamer; [b.] March 25, 1967, Glendale, West Virginia; [p.] Kenneth and Betty Jean Weese; [m.] S. Robert Tharp, August 1, 1987; [ch.] Kendra Nicole Tharp; [ed.] Piedmont Virginia Community College; [occ.] Student, preparing to attend University Illinois, September 93; [memb.] Amnesty International; [hon.] Dean's List, PVCC Honors Program, Vice President, Phi Theta Kappa; [oth. writ.] Several poems published in college newspaper; [pers.] On pages I pour out my sour. Searching for a sliver of contentment, or at least some understanding of the world around me. [a.] Glendale Heights, IL 60139.

THEIS, TRICIA ANNE
[b.] August 30, 1976, Bridgeport, Connecticut; [p.] Patricia and Thomas Theis; [pets.] Ethel (dog), Toby (cat) and Darby (dog); [ed.] Meadowside Elementary, Jonathan Law High School; [occ.] Student; [memb.] Educational Center for the Arts, Ecology Club, Literary Magazine, school newspaper, Quill and Scroll; [hon.] Quill and Scroll Honors Society, 1st and 2nd honors, Young Author's Award; [oth. writ.] Poetry in 8th grade yearbook, school newspaper (articles) short stories for Young Authors; [pers.] Poetry is more than words on paper, it reaches down into your soul to soother it or tear it apart. [a.] Milford, CT.

THOMAS, DOROTHY
[b.] Scotland; [m.] Evan Andrew Thomas; [ch.] Andrew and Adelaide; [ed.] High school and college and nursing college; [occ.] Teacher/registered psychiatric nurse; [memb.] U.K.C.C; [hon.] Diploma RMN RGN; [oth.writ.] "Living Death" (poem), " No One Out There Listens", (Psychiatric Thriller) not yet published; [pers.] Judge not a man until you have walked two moons in his proverbs. [a.] England, SG17 505.

THOMAS, ELEANOR K.
[pen.] Eleanor K. Thomas; [b.] September 26, 1935, Boston, Massachusetts; [p.] Elizabeth and Walter Francis; [m.] Joseph F. Thomas, December 19, 1953; [ch.] Renee', Joseph, Paula, John and James; [ed.] High school graduate; [occ.] Librarian, reading teacher;

[hon.] 1st place in a National Americanism contest; [oth. writ.] Several poems in local newspaper; [pers.] I find I write how I feel in my heart. This poem was written to my children on my 55th birthday, September 26, 1990. [a.] Lady Lake, FL.

THOMAS, JAMILA HAMISI
[pen.] Jamila Hamisi Thomas; [b.] December 8, 1978 (at 6:12 p.m.), Dallas, Texas at St. Paul Hospital; [p.] Duane Julius Thomas and Imani Pamoja; [ed.] High Pointe Elementary, City Temple Junior Academy, Roger Q. Mills School and Sarah Zumwalt; [occ.] Student; [memb.] Vice-president of Student Council, Vice-president of Sarah Zumwalt Choral Choir; [hon.] Excellent in choral music, maintaining an average of 80 or above, best all around and Martin Luther King, Jr. Peace Award; [oth. writ.] I have entered many contest before with my poetry and I've always won 1st place. Poems printed in school newspaper; [pers.] I began writing poetry when I was in the 6th grade. I was influenced by my mother and Science teacher from Sarah Zumwalt, Mrs. Merrick, also Mrs. Kimble. [a.] Dallas, TX.

THOMAS, JOHNNY BLANTON
[b.] September 7, 1972, Carthage, Mississippi; [p.] Blanche Dianne and Johnnie W. Thomas; [ed.] Carthage High School, East Central Community College; [occ.] Student; [memb.] Phi Theta Kappa, Mu Alpha Theta; [hon.] All American Scholar, Who's Who Among College Students, College Republicans, Baptist Student Union, Student Missionary; [oth writ.] I've only been writing a few months, I have written several things, but nothing that has been published; [pers.] My writing very much depends on my mood at the time, I often try to reflect hope in my writing, but much of it is very realistic. [a.] Lena, MS 39094.

THOMAS, KATHLEEN
[pen.] Kay Tee Thomas; [b.] March 4, 1935, LeLand, Michigan; [m.] Richard F. Thomas, September 3, 1966; [ed.] Traverse City Public Schools and Nursing; [occ.] Retired Psychiatric Nurse; [memb.] Aries Eagle Lodge, Michigan Retiree Association, Michigan United Conservation Club; [oth.writ.] I have 10 other poems, never published yet; [pers.] I study the beauty of nature and all the things that surround me. My love of animals, people and friends inspire me to write. [a.] Grawn, MI 49637-9733.

THOMAS, LAURIE
[b.] December 12, 1956, Tacoma, Washington; [p.] Wayne and Cleo Ross; [m.] Lowell S. Thomas, October 24, 1975; [ch.] Justin and Jeremy Thomas; [ed.] High school, 25 credits from Arts and Sciences, degree in Chemical Dependency; [occ.] Cosmetologist, Counselor Trainee (Chemical Dependency); [oth. writ.] " Parable of The Good Shepherd", "Jim", tribute to Jim Morrison, poetry, " Dreams", " Thoughts", Haiku-" Peaceful Spirit"; [pers.] I desire to help others discover themselves through client centered therapy, this to me is the greatest human experience. [a.] Tacoma, WA.

THOMAS, SOPHIA
[pen.] Nicholas S. George; [b.] December 1, 1972, Tulsa, Oklahoma; [p.] George G. and Magdaline S. Thomas; [ed.] Junior at Arizona State University, Putnam City High School; [occ.] Student. [a.] Scottsdale, AZ 85251.

THOMAS, WILLIAM ARTHUR
[pen.] William Arthur Thomas; [b.] August 11, 1961, Tacoma, Washington; [p.] Earl A. and Betty M. Thomas; [m.] Linley E.J. Thomas, June 12,1992; [ch.] John Douglas, Erin Sue and William Arthur, Jr.; [ed.] G.E.D. at 16, Tacoma Public Schools; [occ.] Painter; [memb.] North American Fishing Club; [hon.] Certificate of Participation for Growing In Christ Seminar "1989"; [oth. writ.] Several poems to my wife and children, plus a few about my parents, as well as other subjects; [pers.] I dedicate this poem with love and total devotion to my darling wife, Linley Elspeth Jeanie Thomas, she is my influence and inspiration. [a.] Elk, WA 99009.

THOMPSON-MARKS, LOIS P.
[pen.] Lois T; [b.] May 10, 1932, Dewitt, Arkansas; [p.] Lem and Margia Phillips (deceased); [ch.] Michele Thompson Ford, 2 grandchildren, Micherai Thompson and Paul Ford Jr.; [ed.] Fargo High School, Brinkley, Arkansas, University of Arkansas at Pine Bluff, Arkansas, University of Miami Florida; [occ.] Retired Federal Employee; [memb.] FEW, NARFE, AARP, St. Paul Baptist Church, NAACP, PTA, America Cancer Society; [hon.] Outstanding Achievements Award, Meritorious Service Award; [oth. writ.] Poems published in work bulletin and newspaper, delivered a speech written as a poem for school Parents Teachers Guild; [pers.] Capturing thoughts of the mind with humorous connotations is my way of sharing the gift of life with all human beings. [a.] Sacramento, CA.

THOMPSON, PAULINE GRANT
[b.] Chester Co., South Carolina; [p.] Jimmie Graham Grant and Bessie Hudson Grant; [m.] Henry Martin Thompson, December 2, 1939; [ch.] Robert John and Jimmie Grant Thompson; [ed.] Chester High School, Chester, South Carolina; [occ.] Retired-Enro Shirt Co., Woodruff, South Carolina; [memb;] Emma Gray United Methodist Church, Woodfurr, S.C., Chester Historical Society, Chester, S.C. ; [pers.] I respect and enjoy nature the outdoors and the masters creation. [a.] Woodruff, SC.

THOMPSON, SAMUEL H.
[b.] April 1, 1983, Sanford, Maine; [p.] Don and Martha Thompson. [a.] North Berwick, ME 03906.

THOMPSON, VIRGINIA L.
[pen.] Virginia Lisenby Thompson; [b.] November 12,1936, Dale Co., Alabama; [p.] Grady Crawfor and Mary Inez (Long Lisenby; [m.] Ray Thompson; [ch.] Michael Ray and Taresa; [ed.] Midland City High School, Wallace Community College, Private Art Teachers; [occ.] Bookkeeper/accounting, artist-visual art; [memb.] Dothan Wiregrass Art League, Wiregrass Museum of Art, Sylvan Grove Methodist Church; [hon.] First entry for poetry, several awards in visual art contest, 3rd place Art For Heart, 3rd place DWAL Art Show, 2nd place WTVY Art contest; [oth. writ.] I have other poems written, this is the first I have entered in any competition and have never presented any to a publisher; I have written just for putting down thoughts as they come to me; [pers.] Most of my writings are influenced by some personal experience, sometimes what I write is from thoughts that come to me that help me through a particular experience or that might help someone else. [a.] Midland City, AL.

THORMAN, RICHARD I.
[b.] July 27, 1929, Toronto, Ontario Canada; [p.] Mary Edna and Richard Thorman; [ed.] B. Comm. University of Toronto, Chartered Accountant; [occ.] Ret. Comptroller of Finance Metropolitan Toronto School Board, Ret., VP and Comptroller Canadian Operations Prudential Insurance Company of America; [oth. writ.] Short stories and poetry in the genres of speculative fiction, humorous, philosophy, horror and adventure; [pers.] A rollicking rambler through life's realities and beyond, an almost eternal optimist who has smelt the roses, touched the brambles and loved every damned second. a[.] Toronto, Ontario Canada M4M 2Z3.

THORNTON, CATHY LEE
[b.] February 9, 1967, Trenton, New Jersey; [p.] Raymond and Louise Mulrine; [m.] Keith A. Thornton, October 3,1992; [ch.] Ashley and Matthew Thornton; [ed.] Graduate; [occ.] Clerk typist; [oth. writ.] Mary, non-published poems; [pers.] If dreams could come true, they would. [a.] Trenton, NJ.

THORNTON, CHARLES H.
[pen.] Ni Ni Ichi; [b.] October 19, 1920, Crystal Springs, Mississippi; [p.] Henry F. and Mildren Nemon (Didlake) Thornton; [m.] Gladys Marie (Malone) Thornton, April 3, 1948; [ch.] Amy Carol (Thornton) Plamer; [ed.] Crystal Springs Consolidated School, MS, Mississippi College, Clinton, MS, BS degree Chemistry; [occ.] United States Air Force (retired), University Mississippi Department Clinical Lab Sciences (retired); [memb.] American Legion, American POW, Pilgrims Rest Baptist Church, MS Baptist Disaster Team, Army Mars, America Radio Relay league, Copiah Writers Group; [hon.] World of Poetry Golden Poet 1992, 1993 Copiah-Lincoln Community College Literary Hall of Fame, Congress of Freedom Awards; [oth. writ.] Contributor: Death March Survivors of Battaan by Don Knox, American POW History book, History of The Defenders of The Philippines Guam and Wake Islands 1941-1945, songs of the Hedge Hopper by Ni Ni Ichi, other published poems and articles; [pers.] Writing began as personal therapy as a prisoner of war in the Far East. It has evolved as a medium to try to make a difference in our troubled world. [a.] Crystal Springs,MS 39059.

THORNTON, SCOTT
[b.] December 9, 1971, Jackson, Mississippi; [p.] Mike and Barbara Thornton; [ed.] High school, East Rankin Academy, college-Hinds Community College; [occ.] Emergency Medical Technician; [memb.] Antioch Baptist Church, Mississippi Firefighters Association, Walters Vol. Fire Department; [hon.] Dean's List 92-93; [pers.] I am fascinated by the brief beauty of this strange existence we call life. Not just human life but all of life in nature, I try to give a voice to the things I see around me. [a.] Brandon, MS 39042.

TIDWELL, KIMBERLY ANN
[b.] April 7, 1961, St. Louis, Missouri; [p.] Rosa Lee Keys and Roosevelt Tidwell Sr. (father deceased); [ed.] Sophomore at Warner Pacific College, Portland, Oregon, major -Religion; [occ.] Data Entry Clerk at Envoy Global, Inc.; [memb.] Immanuel Free Methodist Church; [hon.] Warner Pacific Garlington Fellow Scholarship; [oth. writ.] Many poems written for family and friends; [pers.] My goal when writing is to edify and encourage the reader. I strive to remind many and introduce to those that don't know God, a God with power. [a.] Portland, OR 97232.

TIDWELL, MICHELLE
[b.] November 3, 1977, Eugene, Oregon; [p.] Eddie and Linda Tidwell; [ed.] West Valley High School; [occ.] Junior/student; [oth. writ.] First poem sent in and published; [pers.] This poem focuses on love and the way life can often be. One day I hope to become an author. [a.] Yakima, WA.

TIMMINS, RACHEL E.
[b.] 14, 2nd September 1981, Calgary, Canada; [p.] Peter and Ann Timmins; [ed.] Grade 6; [occ.] Student; [pers.] Like to create happiness and peace. [a.] Lloydminster, Alberta Canada T9V 2N1.

TIRTADIHARDJA, SALLY
[pen.] Sally; [b] February 5, 1975, Malang, East Java-Indonesta: [p.] Tirtadihardja, Yahuda Muono and Lidia Julian; [ed.] Branksome Hall High (Canada), Marymount College (Palos Verdes, California); [occ.] Student; [hon.] Dean's List, Marymount International of the Year 1992-1993; [pers.] I believe that each human being is very special, I also believe that no one is better than anybody else in all aspects of life. [a.] San Pedro, CA 90732.

TITA, REBECCA LYNN
[pen.] Becky Tita; [b.] April 11, 1977, Rochester, Pennsylvania; [p.] David P. and Lindy L. Tita; [ed.] Student at Big Beaver Falls School District, Beaver Falls, PA 15010; [occ.] High school student; [memb.] Big Beaver Falls Marching Band, SADD, Lab Biology Club; [hon.] August 1988, Life Saving Citation from Pennsylvania House of Representatives for saving life of 11 year old cousin in a choking accident, won essay contest by Maxwell House Corp., nominated her father as a Maxwell House Real Hero in 1992, PADI certified scuba diver; [oth. writ.] Beaver County Times letters to the editor; [pers.] Carpe Diem-Sieze the day. [a.] Beaver Falls, ZPA 15010.

TKACHUK, REV. MIKE HENRY
[pen.] Mohat; [b.] February 26, 1939, Silver Creek Munc., Manitoba; [p.] Harry and Annie Tkachuk; [m.] Delores, October 31, 1970; [ed.] B.A., M. Ed.; [occ.] Teacher/principal Riverside School, Assistant Administrator Ukrainian Catholic Church-Neepawa; [memb.] Knights of Columbus; [oth. writ.] Several poems published in local newspaper. [Thesis for Master Degree in Education, " The Volenti Defense in Torts for Educators and Boards", presently compiling a book of my own poetry; [pers.] Nature is a very intriguing and fascinating subject. Many of my poems are about nature. [a.] Minnedosa, Manitoba Canada R0J 1E0.

TODD, VIRGINIA RUTH JANNEY (McMICHAEL) [pen.] Petuna Flowere; [b.] July 16, 1925, Toledo, Ohio; [p.] Charles Sumner and Thelma Linzie Janney; [m.] Forrest McMichael, June 19, 1945 (deceased) now C.D. Todd, January 15, 1982; [ch.] Donald, David and Karen McMichael; [ed.] Bachelor degree, Toledo, Ohio, Master's Degree Early Childhood; [occ.] Teacher-34 years in Toledo, Ohio, Lambertville, MI., Gainesville, Texas; [hon.] 112 ribbons and awards for paintings, oils, acrylic and watercolor, 2nd place song contest (Texas Federation of Music Clubs, song " Behold The Lord Cometh"

1969, two songs published in " From Texas With Love" a glow song book 1987, also an article about " My Guinea Pigs At School" in 1982 in Instructor Magazine: [oth. writ.] 22 Christian songs 32 poems published in " Poetry Time from My Heart A Line"; [pers.] I express the feelings of my heart as I walk the pathway of life here on earth desiring to give God the glory for the talents He's given me. [a.] Gainesville, TX 76240.

TOHILL, ALICE MAE
[pen.] Alice Tohill; [b.] October 1, 1913, West York, Illinois; [p.] William and Clara Blaker; [m.] Herman Tohill, August 19, 1934; [ch.] Keith Leon, Kenneth Wayne and Vivian Kaye; [ed.] Hutsonville High School, attended Eastern Illinois State Teachers College; [occ.] Homemaker; [memb.] Free Methodist Church; [pers.] I enjoy writing poetry for family, friends and church. [a.] Robinson, IL.

TOO-CHUNG, CINDY
[b.] March 19, 1962, Essequibo, Guyana, South America; [p.] Conrad and Agnes Too-Chung; [occ.] Private and Confidential Secretary; [oth. writ.] Several poems (unpublished); [pers.] If I had one wish, it would be for this world to live in peace and harmony. We are only here for a short time, and power matters not. What matters is goodness of heart and soul; not only for us, but more importantly for our children.; [a.] Georgetown, Guyana, South America

TOOLEY, RUTH MARY FELLNER
[pen.] Ruth; [b.] July 20, 1911, Wausau, Wisconsin; [p.] Mr. and Mrs. Fred Fellner, Antigo, WI.; [m.] George Tooley, November 23, 1931; [ch.] Eight, 4 boys and 4 girls; [occ.] Housewife; [memb.] St. Rose ALter Society for four terms, for twenty years was in charge of comfort and feeding at funerals with two groups of twenty helpers; [oth. writ.] I have many articles from talks I gave around the area on the Downs Syndrome Child. My number eight son is Downs, but he is very talented and so easy to get along with. A real joy to have, he is presently 34 years old. [a.] Clintonville, WI 54929.

TOOMEY, LIL
[b.] January 11, 1943, Owosso, Michigan; [p.] Warren and Lorena Hibbard Morgan; [m.] David Toomey, November 5, 1960; [ch.] Robin and Criner Timothy Toomey; [ed.] Bryon High, Christian Writer's Institute, Lansing Community College (graduated Summa Cum Laude); [occ.] Supervisor for the Senior Companion Program, Lansing, Michigan; [memb.] State Association of Foster Grandparent/Senior Companion Programs, Wesleyan Church, American Association of Retired Persons; [oth. writ.] I have written many poems but this is the first I've submitted for publication. I was influenced by my grandfather and great uncle on mother's side, they both wrote poetry; [pers.] Within the heart of each soul, lies a fragrance, though for some it is released only through suffering. This is how my poetry was born. There is a silver lining within each storm cloud, we must sometimes change our focus to see it. [a.] Owosso, MI 48867.

TORPILA, FRANK T.
[b.] December 21, 1951, New Jersey; [p.] Frank and Ann; [ed.] Hamilton West; [occ.] Artist; [oth. writ.] " Wolf Tales", " Like WOW", "Rose Marie", "Prayer", " Wishes", " Star Gazer", " Eyes For You", " La Fornarina", " Wonderin", " Foul Weather Blues"; [pers.] Thanks to Rose Marie Calla for inspiring me. [a.] Yardville, NJ.

TRAN, THANH
[b.] March 20, 1977, Cam Ranh, Vietnam; [p.] Loc Le and Trinh Nguyen Tran; [ed.] St. Pius X School, Bishop Lynch High School; [occ.] Student, Bishop Lynch High School; [memb.] Cross Country Team Art Club, Spanish Club, Scholar Program; [hon.] Art Division winner in State Fair of Texas, Bishop Lynch High School Scholarship recipient; [oth.writ.] Several poems published in school's annual literary Arts Journal "The Bridge"; [pers.] Live each day to the fullest because you are one day closer to your final destination. [a.] Dallas, TX.

TRELLER, TREVOR
[pen.] T. M. Treller; [b.] May 6, 1972, Long Beach, California; [p.] Gary and Margaret Treller; [ed.] Lakewood High School; [occ.] Journalist in U.S. Navy; [oth. writ.] Several dozen poems that I've never submitted for publication; [pers.] " Love is my inspiration-and my medium. It is the greatest of emotions". William Shakespeare is my mentor. [a.] FPO, AP 96649-2535.

TREZONA, BETTY
[b.] March 13, 1927, Omaha, Nebraska; [p.] Edith and Sherman Holderness; [m.] Johnny Trezona, May 22, 1949; [ch.] David, Ross and Kevin; [ed.] North High, Omaha, University of Nebraska at Omaha, Black Hills State University; [occ.] Teacher-28 years, retired 1992; [memb.] Delta Kappa Gamma, A.A.U.W., Beta Sigma Phi, United Church of Christ, Literary Council of Black Hills; [hon.] Spearfish Teacher of The Year-1977; [oth. writ.] Poems in "Prairie Winds" magazine; [pers.] Poetry is an expression of the emotional response to an event or situation;. [a.] Spearfish, SD 57783.

TREZZA, ARTHUR
[b.] Orange, New Jersey; [p.] Frank and Sarah Trezza; [occ.] Former Horse Trainer; [hon.] Won many awards showing horses; [pers.] I strive to bring love an joy in my writings to everyone. [a.] Honey Brook, PA 19344.

TRIPLITT, LOIS
[pen.] Lois Smith Triplitt; [b.] April 9, 1917, Bay City, Michigan; [p.] John and Edith Smith of Bay City, Michigan; [m.] Irvion Darrel Triplitt (expired in '73), May 27, 1950; [ed.] Masters degree, UCLA; [occ.] Nursing Education Consultant (retired); [oth. writ.] Poems, " Massai Village", " Dumb Bird # 2", " I'd Know You in The Dark", 'Premonition", "Enchanted Room"; [pers.] " I would look up and laugh and love and lift". [a.] Rocklin, CA.

TROTT, MYRTLE I.
[pen.] LMC Scott; [b.] April 8, 1930, Fond du lac, Wisconsin; [p.] Gertrude and Emmett Freiberg; [m.] Ex-spouse, Ken Trott, December 30, 1953; [ch.] David, (deceased), Bob, Journalist 37 years old; [ed.] No Fond Du Lac High School, graduated 1948; [occ.] Retired secretary and cook; [memb.] Wisconsin Fellowship of Poets (just accepted), FDL Area Writers Club; [hon.] Being called by God to give the good news of His kingdom message, actively engaged as one of Jehovah's Witnesses; [oth.writ.] Published in a number of small poetry magazines, hope to get a book out soon, two anthologies, one local "Thoughts and Feelings; [pers.] Spiritual gifts in people inspire me, honoring these expresses thanks to God for His indescribable free gifts. [a.] Fond Du Lac, WI.

TROUT, SHERRI L.
[b.] September 9,1948, Van Nuys, California; [p.] Ralph Warren White and Marie Louise Ortega; [m.] Phillip William Trout, June 21; [ch.] Jamie Michael and Jody Robert Schoolcraft; [ed.] AA Commercial Art, Moorpark College, BS in Recreation from C.S.U.N., Certified Activity Director, Techniques of teaching; [occ.] Program Coordinator; [memb.] Delta Society, Roar Foundation; [hon.] NCCAP-Activity Director Certified, Senior Concerns volunteer recognition, USO 112 hours service; [oth. writ.] A book of poetry not yet published, doing the illustration myself; [pers.] Life should be a breath of love, caring, friendships and a knowledge that its the hardest to keep, hold onto and give out.. God willing, it can be done. [a.] Simi Valley, CA.

TROVATO, JESSICA T.
[pen.] Jessie Trovato; [b.] July 5, 1977, Summitt County, Akron, Ohio; [p.] Paul and Carolyn Trovato; [ed.] 9th grade, Valley Forge High School, Parma Heights, Ohio 44130; [occ.] Student; [memb.] Drama Club, S.A.D.D., Ski Club, Yearbook Staff; [hon.] English Horse Back Riding competition, place 3rd and 5th 1991; [oth. writ.] Private collection, this is the 1st that I have entered in a contest; [pers.] I try to project my "Feelings" on paper thru poetry. My philosophy is to show your talents and stand-up for what you believe in. [a.] Parma Heights, OH 44130.

TSANTIS, STEVE
[pen.] Papa Steve, Evets; [b.] March 27, 1964, Chicago, Illinois; [p.] John and Marta Tsantis; [ed.] Rich Central High, Prairie State College; [occ.] Flight Stewart, Las Vegas, NV.; [memb.] Community Action Against Rape, United Blood Services, Green Peace, MIA's, POW's; [oth. writ.] Poems published in high school, college and church news letters; [pers.] In life you can get advise, but always do what you think is best so if you screw up, you only have yourself to blame. [a.] Las Vegas, NV 89115.

TUCKER, DARRIN DARNELL
[pen.]"D"; [b.] November 7, 1980, Kansas City, Missouri; [p.] Glen D. and Sanita R. Tucker; [ed.] Taft School, Enid, Oklahoma 6th grade; [memb.] Progressive Baptist Church Choir, Youth Group, YMCA, Boy Scouts; [hon.] Baseball, football, basketball, soccer; [pers.] I strive to reflect the goodness of my people in my writings and to reflect a positive image of the youth of today. [a.] Enid, Ok.

TUCKER, PEGGY
[b.] December 3, 1951, Seattle, Washington; [p.] Gordon and Maureen Tucker; [ed.] Holy Angels High, Shoreline Junior College, North Seattle Junior College; [occ.] Domestic Engineer; [hon.] North Seattle COmmunity College Honor Roll (1976); [oth. writ.] Working on several other poems; [pers.] I've always enjoyed writing, especially poetry. There's an endless supply of ideas to write about creatively. [a.] Seattle, WA 98125-3931.

TURBYFILL, LORI F.
[b.] October 5, 1966, Raleigh, North Carolina; [p.] David and Harriet Fuquay, Jr.; [m.] Joseph D. Turbyfill, December 28, 1985; [ed.] Garner Senior High School; [occ.] CLerk-typist III with State of North Carolina, Dorothea Dix Hospital; [memb.] North Carolina State Employees' Association; [oth. writ.] Poems published by the following: The National Library of Poetry -On The Threshold of A Dream Vol. # 2 and 3, Quill Books, All My Tomorrows,and 3, Pacific Rim Publications Quest For a Dream; [pers.] My ambition with my writing is to create an expression of my thoughts through verse which I am hopeful others may be able to visualize in their minds and personally relate to. [a.] Raleigh, NC.

TURNER, JR. II, AARON M.
[pen.] Chuy, Speedy and Crazy Legs; [b.] Walnut Creek, California; [p.] Aaron and Glorian Turner, Aaron Matthew Turner, Sr. and Gloria Jean Roberts; [m.] Single; [ed.] Now attending Middletown High School, sophomore; [occ.] Yoder Construction Company; [memb.] Friday Night Live Organization, Honor Roll Student; [hon.] Best Dressed Male at Middletown High School, MVP of the Middletown JV Football team; [oth. writ.] I have been writing poems since I was 12 years old. I have over 40 poems that I composed into a book, I call this book "For Your Eyes Only" and I hope to soon have it published; [pers.] First of all I would like to thank God for giving me the strength and knowledge to understand and write poems. Poetry is a true way to release your feelings, and for me, it is a way of life. [a.] Middletown, CA.

TURNER, HEATHER
[b.] January 14,1980, Memorial Mission Hospital, Ashville; [p.] Jim and Tami; [hon.] Terrific Kid, tennis, medals, soccer. [a.] Ashville, NC.

TURNER, MARY B.
[b.] January 3, 1932, Cleveland Co., Landale, North Carolina; [p.] Alston Blackett and Louella Morrison; [m.] Herman Turner, April 9, 1951; [ch.] 3 sons and two daughters (Rickey, Ronnie, Jimmy, Sherry and Jackie); [ed.] High school, 2 years of college; [occ.] Nurse; [hon.] Degree in Nursing and certified in intravenous therapy; [oth. writ.] None except poetry, I have other poems; [pers.] I was inspired to write the poem after having my baby daughter, I sit down and wrote about her. [a.] Hickory, NC 28602.

TURNER, REBECCA
[pen.] Becky Jean; [b.] November 10, 1978, Hamlin, Texas; [p.] Wyatt and Pirley Turner; [ed.] Hamlin Junior High; [occ.] Student; [memb.] Band, P.A.L., P.R.Y.D.E.; [hon.] A-B Honor Scholarship; [oth.writ.] Poems not published; [pers.] I appreciate my boyfriend Shannon for being there so I could write about him, thanks to my family, I love you all. [a.] Hamlin, TX 79520.

TURTLE, LITTLE
[p.] Parents of Native American Ancestry; [ed.] Tourtelotte High and numerous courses in Art, Literature and Anthropology; [occ.] Illustrator/writer; [hon.] Several awards by Native American Tribal groups and Press Organizations; [oth. writ.] Little Bird, Medicine Bag and many poem in Native Publication, frequently published in Cultural and Anthropological magazines; [pers.] A socially conscious medicine man (Nipmuck Tribe) who enjoys life, the arts, all living things and a frequent shot of hot country rock. [a.] East Douglas, MA 01516-2504.

TUSA, BOBBI
[pen.] Bobbi Tusa; [b.] June 25, 1939, Pittsburgh, Pennsylvania; [p.] Rae Holliger and Robert Sloan Woodling; [m.] Donald C. Tusa; [ch.] Daniel, Leslie, Susan and Amy; [ed.] St. Benedicts Academy, Earl Wheeler Finishing School; [occ.] Artist\model; [memb.] Artist and Craftsmans Guild; [hon.] Selected " Girl Most Likely To Succeed" by E.W. Finishing School; [oth. writ.] 1 other published poem while in high school; [pers.] Thank you to my wonderful mother, who has always inspired and supported me. [a.] Zelienople, PA 16063.

TVEDTEN, DANIELLE
[b.] December 27, 1981, Blue Earth, Minnesota; p.] David and Diane Tvedten; [ed.] Elmore Elementary School; [occ.] Student; [memb.] 4-H, Student Council and band; [hon.] Basketball and volleyball awards, Science Fair Award. [a.] Elmore, MN 56027.

TYLER, EPHRHIM DAVID
[b.] January 10, 1884, Grand Cane, Louisiana -- Deceased 6/30/69; [p.] William and Isabella Peace Tyler; [m.] Emily Barney Tyler (died December 30,1965), June 20, 1926; [ch.] Anna Mae Tyler Martin; [ed.] Coleman College, Gibsland, Louisiana; [occ.] Brief career in teaching, writing was his job; [memb.] YMCA, Alpha Omega Retirement Club, Evergreen Baptist Church, Special Representative and Booster of M.W. St. John's Grand Lodge A.F.and MM State LA; [hon.] YMCA and YWCA honored him Black History, Presidents, Eisenhower, Kennedy, Johnson has written thank you notes to him for poems he wrote about them, governors also has written him; [oth. writ.] Two books, Tyler's Poems of Today and Tyler's Poems of Everyday Life, quite a few sheet poems, thanks cards, sympathy cards, Xmas cards, cards of appreciation; [pers.] I was born in Louisiana, eighteen hundred and eighty four. I am just a Negro subject, nothing less and nothing more, I am just a lowly peasant, just an humble son of Ham, but give me a few years longer, the world will know who I am.[a.] Shreveport, LA.

UGAH, ADA
[b.] March 6, 1958, Iga Okpaya; [p.] Mr. Ugah Otondo and Mrs. Iyada Ugah; [ed.] B.A. (hons.) University of Calabar, M.A. (University Bordeaux III, France), B.SC (University Bordeaux III, France), Ph.D. University Bordeaux IV France; [occ.] Writer/ University Lecturer; [memb.] Member, Association of Mataian Authors (ANA), member Pen International Nigerian Centre, Literary Society of Nigeria; [hon.] Laureate University prize (1980), winner 1991 Association of Nigerian Author's poetry prize and runner-up (1992) Index on Censorship/Skoob Books International poetry prize; [oth.writ.] Naked Hearts (poems) 1982, song of Talakaina (poems) 1983, Reves Interdicts (poems in French) 1983, Haninis Parade (novel) 1985, Ballads of Unknown Soldier (poems) 1983, Colours of The Rainbow (poems) 1991 and The Rainmaker's Daughter and other stories (short stories) 1993 (all published); [pers.] I write in order to witness about my times. [a.] 1115 Calabar, Nigeria.

UMBDENSTOCK, LORRAINE
[b.] October 19, 1919, Geneva, Illinois; [p.] Frank and Lois Brown; [m.] Raymond (died on November 17, 1988), October 21, 1939; [ch.] Lois Mary Bushman, 312 Deerfield Way, Geneva, IL 60134; [ed.] Bachelor of Science in Education, 19 hrs. graduate hours in Art from Northern Illinois College, now a university; [occ.] Retired teacher, homemaker, widow; [memb.] Life member N.E.A., Retired Teachers, member of Yorkville Methodist Church, inactive member of Gamma Rh branch of the Delta Kappa Gamma Society International, among others; [hon.] Awarded Medal of Honor at World of Poetry Convention in San Francisco 1992, grandmother of 6, great grandmother of 1; [oth. writ.] 2 poems titled "Mouse House" and "Seasons" in book Selected Works of Our World's Best Poets, written in 1972 for Circle Center second graders, numerous others; [pers.] I have liked and written poetry throughout my life. Writing for children when I was teaching was the most satisfying.

URBAN, JOHN S.
[b.] January 31, 1945, Trenton, New Jersey 08611; [p.] John S. and Catherine A. Urban; [m.] Single; [ed.] Trenton High, University of Pennsylvania, Rider College; [occ.] Senior Business Analyst; [hon.] Summa Cum Laude, Alpha Epsilon Zeta Honor Society; [oth. writ.] First publication; [pers.] I strive to express the essence of my innermost feelings in my poetry. I have been greatly influenced by the classical poets of antiquity. [a.] Trenton, NJ 08611.

USKERT, MILLICENT WALTERS
[b.] May 17, 1976, Birmingham, Alabama; [p.] John and Pysche Uskert; [ed.] Senior, Rutherford High School; [occ.] Student; [memb.] Key Club, Young Republicans, French Club, St. John Catholic Church, Northwest Florida Ballet, Panama City Mall Fashion Board, Drama Club. [a.] Panama City, FL.

VANASSENDELFT, MARIE
[b.] September 30, 1978, San Jose, California; [p.] Fred and Jean Vanassendelft; [ed.] Attending Oakmont High School; [memb.] " S" Club, IKF membership; [hon.] Honor's list, first place in the 1990 National Kar Dance competition; [oth. writ.] None published; [pers.] Emotions, feelings and family influence my writing. [a.] Granite Bay, CA.

VAN DEN BERG, PATRICIA S.
[pen.] Patricia S. Van Den Berg; [b.] November 1, 1943, Detroit, Michigan; [p.] Michael and Anna Ruth Selepak; [m.] Anthony Van Den Berg, October 20, 1962; [ch.] Juliann C. Gardner (married name), Anette R., Michele R. and Andrew J.; [ed.] Southeastern High School, Madonna University; [occ.] Secretary/interpreter/Sign Language Instructor; [memb.] Registry of Interpreters for The Deaf,Inc., Michigan Registry of Interpreters for The Deaf, Children's Reading Round Table, National Association of The Deaf; [hon.] Dean's List; [oth.writ.] Activity book for Deaf Children, Sign "O" (game for learning Sign Language); [pers.] Continue in the things you have learned. [a.] St. Clair Shores, MI.

VAN DUSEN, TAMI
[b.] January 24, 1967, Provost, Alberta; [p.] Bud and Gloria Masson; [m.] Tony Van Dusen, August 5,1991; [ch.] Frankie (Cathryn Frances) born February 19,1992; [ed.] High school, Lethbridge Community

College, Journalism course; [occ.] Reporter for the Crowsnest Pass Promoter; [oth. writ.] Various newspaper articles; [pers.] Grandma, Frances Maull, was very influential for me as a child. I admire her very much for her zest for life. The title of the poem is "Grandma". [a.] Coleman, A.B. T0K 0M0.

VANKOPPEN, VERONICA
[b.] August 6, 1914, Manchester, New York; [p.] Sarah Veronica Fitzpatrick and Harry Greenway; [m.] Nicholas VanKoppen, February 3,1933; [ch.] Nicholas and Marilyn Ann; [ed.] Elementary and 2 years high school, Our Lady of Victory, Patterson, New Jersey; [occ.] Retired; [memb.] Lower Bucks Senior Center, YWCA-Patterson, New Jersey; [hon.] Writing lyrics, manuscripts-copywrites, collaborate with music writers; [oth. writ.] Other poetry and poems, lyrics in music; [pers.] I like to write about my own true feelings and expresses these feelings trying to give other people a note of self confidence. [a.] Bristol, PA 19007.

VARGA, JONATHAN M.
[pen.] Psyris Mach; [b.] June 17, 1971, Philadelphia, Pennsylvania; [p.] Peter Varga and Lynne Lichtman; [ed.] George Washington High, Delaware Valley High; [occ.] Truck driver, student; [pers.] I like to look beyond the realm of reality, for in the dreams of men, the greatest adventures await their birth. Fantasy is our art and our passion and our love. [a.] Philadelphia, PA 19020.

VARGA, LASZLO, M.D., Ph.D.
[pen.] Laszlo Varga; [b.] October 30, 1920, Hungary; [p.] Deceased; [m.] Divorced; [ch.] I have three adult married daughters; [ed.] Medical Doctor; [occ.] Medical Director, Odyssey Harbor a non-profit neuropsychiatric residential center for children; [memb.] APA, AM. Academy of Neurology, Am. Neuropsych Association; [hon.] Fellow: New York Academy of Science; [oth. writ.] Dr. Varga is a practicing physician, among numerous scientific papers, he published articles on literary and art problems from psychoanalytical point of view. This is his first published poem, by the way his Ph. D. degree is in physics; [pers.] Wer das Wort Kennte, hatte auch Gewalt uber die Sache. (Goethe). [a.] Keene, TX 76059.

VARIATH, P. A.
[pen.] P.A. Variath; [b.] June 11, 1950, Cheranalloor, India; [p.] Auseph and Alia Poonoly; [m.] Mable Variath; [ch.] Caroline, Jacqueline and Josephine; [ed.] B.Sc > Engineering, College of Engineering Trivandrum, India; [occ.] Engineering manager; [memb.] Institute of Engineers (India), Indian Society for Technical Education; [oth. writ.] "Your Destiny" a published treatise on the hereditary and environmental influences on man, "A Challenge to Christianity" yet to be published and several poems published in Zimbabwe; [pers.] There is no point in adulating a winner or despising a loser, success and failure are largely nature's work. We do not make what we are. [a.] Masvingo, Zimbabwe.

VARNER, JESSIE FRANK
[b.] February 4, 1949, Louisville, Kentucky; [p.] Jefferson Washington and Rosann (Roberts) Varner; [m.] Diana Marie (Walter) Varner, March 17, 1992; [ch.] Jesse J., Kiasha J., Jessica D. and Bryan L.

Varner, Rebecca A. and Michael B. Degener; [ed.] GED, 2 years of college and one year of Technical School; [occ.] Postmaster of Park City, Kentucky; [memb.] Green St. Baptist Church, NAPS and Phoenix Association; [hon.] Founder and owner of Varner's Tax Service; [oth. writ.] A collection of poems; [pers.] A special thank to my childhood inspirers Fred and Anna Bond, and to Suzanne Waldrop of Park City. Thank you to God, my mother and my wife. [a.] Smiths Grove, KY.

VASQUEZ, REBEKA
[pen.] Becky (Half Pint); [b.] October 3, 1960, East Chicago, Indiana; [p.] Robert E. and Maria C. Martinez; [m.] Martin Serrano Vasquez, October 16; [ch.] Adrian (boy 6 years old) and Jessica Vazquez, 3 years old; [ed.] High school; [occ.] Housewife (occassionally odd jobs); [oth. writ.] High school; [pers.] I may not have achieved many goals the most important one I achieved, my children, which I'm very proud of. [a.] East Chicago, IN.

VEAL, ARONDA
[p.] Mr. and Mrs. Gilbert Spland (Gilbert and Bernice); [pers.] "There are no "Dumb" people, only lazy ones who use the phrase, "I don't know how to do that" as an excuse for not achieving. [a.] Baton Rouge, LA.

VER BECKE, W. EDWIN
[b.] July 21, 1913, Sidney, Iowa; [p.] Dora Abigail Thorne and Walter Earle Verbeck; [m.] Countess Eugenia Chavessey (deceased), July 1945; [ch.] 1 son; [ed.] BA., University of Minnesota, Duluth State Teachers College, private studies; [occ.] Painter, poet, realalist and dramatist; [memb.] American Poetry Society, Composes Artists, Authors of America, New York Poetry Forum, Universal Church of the Master, Dramatist Guild; [hon.] Many painting awards and honors; [oth. writ.] "Poems of The Spirit", "Life of The Virgin Mary", "Line in Painting", stories in ElfMagazine, Berkeley Journal, Bay Quarterly, Christian Science Manilor; [pers.] I am over sixty five years, constantly active in the arts and literature. I was an early surrealist exhibiting in "Art of this century" New York City. [a.] New York, NY.

VERMA, KRISHAN KANT
[pen.] Vivek; [b.] September 30, 1958, Village Dadal (Solan) HP, India; [p.] Rishi Ram and Sevati Verma; [m.] Satya Verma, June 17, 1985; [ch.] Anupam Kant and Sukriti Verma; [ed.] B. Comm., Caiib, M.B.A., high school Bhumati, degree College Dharamsala, Osmania University; [occ.] Banking, Free Lance Author; [memb.] Founder Association for Secularism and Human Amity India; [hon.] Ashirvad Award for Creative Writing, honours from various Socio-cultural Organizations; [oth.writ.] Several poems, short stories, dramas and essays published, regular free lance contributor to various Indian newspapers and magazines and professional journals; [pers.] No war, no strife, no destruction, no challenge or no human and even supernatural effort can destroy it .. it was.. it is.. and it will.. yes..it is love.. do it.. spreadit. [a.] Solan,Himachal Pradesh, Pin 173 212 India.

VESTERBY, MISTY KARIN
[b.] August 11, 1979, Upland, California; [p.] Don and Marta Vesterby. [a.] Ardmore, OK 73402.

VIANNA, RUTH P.
[pen.] Ruth Vianna; [b.] November 27, 1935, Alegria-RJ, Brazil; [p.] Antonio and Cenyra Santos; [m.] Gether M. Vianna, December 22, 1956; [ch.] Flavia Cristina, Claudia Marcia; [ed.] Suam University in Brazil; [occ.] Geography Teacher; [memb.] West Essex Baptist Church, in Livingston, NJ; [hon.] CEPA International contest, Folha Do Brasil contest, poetry and prose; [oth. writ.] Several poems published in local magazines and newspapers, articles for many newspapers in Brazil and America, special column in Brazilian voice newspaper, Newark; [pers.] The most important thing in my life is to spread the inner peace around the world through my poems, because I see each day as a precious gift from God. [a.] Montclair. NJ.

VIELBAUM, KRISTEN NOEL
[pen.] Kristen N. Vielbaum; [b.] December 15, 1978, Hartford, Wisconsin; [p.] Michael J. and Diane R. Vielbaum; [ed.] Central Middle School; [memb.] Forensic "Playacting", Swing Choir, Solo Ensemble; [hon.] Forensics, Swing Choir, Solo Ensemble; [pers.] I dedicate this poem to my sister, Tina Vielbaum, and my Aunt Gail Wagner, who also enjoy writing poetry. [a.] Hartford, WI.

VILLARREAL, DENISE
b.] May 4, 1974, El Paso, Texas; [p.] Edna J. Salcido and Jose Amos Villarreal; [m.] Single; [ed.] Eastwood High; [oth. writ.] Several feature stories published in high school's Salute; [pers.] I don't plan on changing the world with my writings. All I really want is for people to read my feelings and say " I remember when...", because memories are the best keepsakes. [a.] El Paso, TX 79936.

VINAL, DENNIS G.
[b.] November 30, 1970, Manassas, Virginia; [p.] Henry and Ruby Vinal; [ed.] W.T. Woodson High School, George Mason University; [occ.] Intelligence Assistant, Langley, Virginia; [pers.] If that cow truly jumped over the moon, don't you think that he would of been killed upon impact? [a.] Manassas, VA.

VINE, KRISTYNE
[b.] August 20, 1977, Gloversville, New York; [p.] Floyd S. and Mary M. Vine; [ed.] High school junior; [occ.] Student; [pers.] If you see life as a gift you'll always fine happiness buried within, even the most tragic of incidences. On the other hand, if you see life as a curse, any gift which is bestowed upon you becomes a burden. Another misery upon your back. So look at life with new eyes every waking moment and discover a life fulfilled. [a.] Bolingbrook, IL.

VIOLA, A.L.A.
[pen.] For First Time, Johnny Viola; [b.] March 4, 1922, Pago Pago American Samoa; [p.] Juan L. Viola and Lily Allen, I am a blend of Filipino, American Indian, (Cherokee), Samoan and English; [m.] Tamiko Viola, August 10, 1972; [ed.] After retirement from U.S. Coast Guard, I attended an adult school and completed high school level; [occ.] Semi-retired Sail Merchant ships now and then, gave up tugboats; [memb.] Veterans of Foreign Wars, Sailors Union of the Pacific, Tn Land Boat Men's Union of the Pacific, U.S. Coast Guard Chief Petty Officers Association; [hon.] Ribbons of World War II (Pacific), had a 4.0 marking across the board as Chief Boatswain Mate in 28 years service in U.S. Coast Guard. I have always

felt that that 4.0 marking was the apex of my U.S. Coast Guard career and have tried to use it as a gauge in my new fields; [oth. writ.] I've been writing poetry since my middle teens and lost all those poems from about 1948 to this very day, I have so much writings that have never been published, I am now trying to re-write; [pers.] Most of my writings come from an instant thought coming from all the moods of man like sadness and happiness. Reading something I wrote 50 years ago floods me with young memories, I have always believe that like wine I must age to attain the ultimate flavor. [a.] Honolulu, HI 96813-2422.

VISCOUNT, LORETTA
[b.] August 11, 1959, New Hyde Park, New York; [m.] Michael J. Viscount, Jr., October 16, 1982; [ch.] Nicholas James; [ed.] B.A., Long Island University, J.D., University of Richmond; [occ.] Casino La Horney, Atlantic City, New Jersey. [a.] Linwood, NJ 08221.

VITALOS, ROBERT F.
[b.] October 31, 1947, Allentown, Pennsylvania;[p.] Joseph J. and Elizabeth M. Vitalos; [ed.] Allentown Central Catholic High School class of 1965; [occ.] Electrical Worker for A.T.& T. Micro Electronics; [memb.] Verse Writers Guild of Ohio, International Society of Poets, Academy of American Poets, Conservatory of American Letters; [hon.] American Poetry Association Poet of Merit 1989-1990, International Society of Poets, Poet of Merit 1991-1992, International Biographical Centre, 20th Century Achievement Award; [oth. writ.] Books, Arrows From A Golden Quiver, 1990, The Milk White Sea, 1993. [a.] Bethlehem, PA.

VITEK, STEVE
[b.] July 9, 1967, Southbend, Indiana; [p.] Jerry and Martha Vitek; [m.] Single; [ed.] High school graduate, 2 years college; [occ.] Artist/musician; [oth. writ.] Numerous poems, music (guitarist); [pers.] When I can go no farther, I will teach. [a.] Buchanan, MI.

VIXO, LEONA JEAN
[pen.] Leah Jean Vixo; [b.] May 5, 1931, White Earth, North Dakota; [p.] Hjalmer and Rachael Frostad; [m.] Darby P.Vixo, August 21,1949; [ch.] Lynette Denaye, Darcy Lynn and Danna La Mae; [ed.] Tioga High, South Puget Sound Community College; [occ.] Job Service Specialist II; [memb.] Faith Assembly of Lacey, W2 Prison Ministries, Sweet Adelines Choral Group; [hon.] 3 Washington State Dept. of Corrections Certificate of Appreciation awards, 2 brainstorm suggestions Certificate of Commendations awards, Certificate of Recognition award for music instruction, appreciation award for more than 24 years of public service rendered for the state of Washington, two year Bible study completion award; [oth. writ.] Several poems published in local newspapers, school papers, Tioga Historical Society, Norman Lutheran Church, copyrights in the National Library of Congress in Washington, DC.; [pers.] I was greatly influenced by my elementary literary teacher who delved into the meaning of each poetic authors writings with intent expression, as she recited poetry before the class. I give all glory to God for the gift given me to write poetry. [a.] Olympia, WA.

VODVARKA, JAMI
[b.] July 17, 1977, West Point, Nebraska; [p.] Sharlene and James Vodvarka (father deceased); [ed.] Howells High School currently attending; [memb.] Cheerleading squad, FHA, 4-H, Spirit Club, basketball team and volleyball team; [pers.] The least important is to be perfect, the most important is to set a goal and achieve it. [a.] Howells, NE.

VOGT, JASON R.
[pen.] Jason R.Vogt; [b.] June 24, 1977, Albany, New York; [p.] Robert H. and Carol M. Vogt; [m.] Single; [ed.] La Salle Institute; [occ.] Student; [hon.] Bronze Honors; [pers.] Live and let live, do unto others as you want done with you. [a.] Troy, NY 12180.

VOLL, BRANDI CHRISTINE
[b.] June 5, 1975, Tecumseh, Michigan; [p.] Fred and Peg Voll; [ed.] Clinton High School; [occ.] Graduating student, soon to be active Navy personnel; [oth. writ.] I have written many other poems but this is the first to be sent anywhere' [pers.] This poem was written for James Edward Coffelt. [a.] Clinton, MI 49236.

VOLOSY, CHRISTOPHER M.
[b.] September 24, 1976, Perth Amboy, New Jersey; [p.] Marlene Lechowitz and Joseph Volosy; [ed.] Vivian Gaither Senior High School; [occ.] Junior at Gaither High; [memb.] Mu Alpha Theta (Math Honors); [hon.] French Merit Award, High Honor Roll; [pers.] My deepest and sincere thanks to my parents for believing in me, and to Mrs. Sara Durst my English teacher for teaching and having her students write poetry, it was these things and her praise that made this publication possible. [a.] Tampa, FL 33626.

VOSS, FREDERIC W.
[b.] June 12, 1974, Wellsville, New York; [ed.] GED; [occ.] Unemployed-odd jobs, construction and roofing; [oth. writ.] Other poems; [pers.] Be flexible. [a.] Canisteo, NY 14823.

VOSS, LINDA D.
[b.] South Bend, Indiana; [ed.] M.A. English, University of Massachusetts 1985, B.A. Journalism with Science minor, Indiana University 1979; [occ.] Write about Science and Technology and romance; [memb.] Washington Independent Writers (WIW); [hon.] Dean's List, merit scholarship, National delegate for the Society of Professional Journalists, SDX, Louisville Courier Journal reporting internship; [oth. writ.] Author of book on virtual reality, published articles on space; [pers.] This poem was written in Malio West Africa when I was in the Peace Corps, 1986. [a.] Arlington, VA 22209.

WAGNER, TIMOTHY B.
[b.] July 15, 1970, Kwang-Ju Korea; [p.] Bill and Doreen Wagner; [ed.] Attended Rochester Community College, Art;[oth. writ.] I've been writing poetry since 1970's, mostly 1990's are my best poems; [pers.] Poetry is another way like painting to express one's idea and feelings to another. Most of my poetry deals with humanity and nature.[a.] Pembroke Pines, FL.

WAHLI, TERACH
[pen.] Kristine Law; [b.] February 26,1970, Fort Wayne, Indiana; [p.] Shmuel and Rut Wahli; [m.]

Mark Hoeppner, August 813, 1993; [ed.] Woodland High, Derek Modeling, IPFW (Indiana -Purdue of Fort Wayne) College, Praise in Motion dance; [occ.] Secretary; [memb.] National Arbor Association; [hon.] Invite to Beta Beta Bets, Dean's List, 3rd in State Forestry; [oth. writ.] Newspaper articles on IPFW College; [pers.] And so faith, hope, love abide, these three: but the greatest of these is love I Cor. 13:13. [a.] Fort Wayne, IN.

WALCZAK, JENNIFER JEAN ELIZABETH
[pen.] Jennifer Jean Walczak;[b.] December 10, 1973, Des Plaines, Illinois; [p.] Dawn Marie and Thomas Lee Walczak; [ed.] Mark Twain Elementary School, Rudd Junior High School, Pinson Valley High School; [hon.] High school diploma; [oth. writ.] I wrote other poems and non fiction or fiction stories, that will be publish someday; [pers.] I try to express how I feel when I do, it has a meaning to it that I try to tell. My influence is a personal influence, I write what I feel, I try to be different. I don't want to be like anyone else. [a.] Pinson, AL.

WALDON, ANN LYNN
[b.] March 31, 1959, Lawrenceburg, Indiana; [p.] Louis H. and Kathryn C. Behr; [m.] Robert (Bob) Waldon, November 20, 1979; [ch.] Michelle Renee' and Autumn Dawn [ed.] Lawrenceburg High School; [occ.] Police Communications Officer; [oth. writ.] I have a large collection of poems written from my childhood through the present. None others yet published but each holding a special place in my heart; [pers.] My poems are words spoken by my heart. Words that express what can't pass over my lips. My inspirations are many but mostly are my love, my family and friends. My goal is to grow through my poems. Explore my inner self. [a.] Lawrenceburg, IN.

WALKER, ANDREA
[b.] January 29, 1979, Royal Oak, Michigan; [p.] Martin and Ellen Walker, Tom and Connie Crites; [ed.] Freshman in high school, Rocky River High School; [occ.] Student; [pers.] Writing comes from the heart and soul. Reserve the right to express yourself. [a.] Rocky River, OH.

WALKER, BILLY L.
[pen.] Billy L. Walker; [b.] April 17, 1928, Marshall County, Kentucky; [p.] Bennie and Jennie Walker; [m.] Betty Walker, August 30, 1947; [ch.] Mike, Pat, Necia and Marty; [ed.] One room elementary school, 2 years college, Murray State and Pad. Community College, diploma at ITI 3 years; [occ.] Chemist (electronics, amateur astronomer); [memb.] National Geo. Society, Charter member of the Planetary Society, Vagun's Chapel C.P. Church; [oth.writ.] Short plays, songs and magazine, newspaper articles and poems; [pers.] I thank God for the ten talents He has given me and I am happy to share them with other people. [a.] Possum Trot, KY.

WALKER, JAMES
[pen.] Jimmy; [b.] February 24,1962, Savannah, Georgia; [p.] Charlie H. and Sandra K. Walker; [m.] Single; [ed.] 12th grade education, 2 1/2 years USAF, Richland Northeast High School; [occ.] Correctional Office, S.C. Dept. of Corrections; [hon.] 2 Honorable Mention "The Dream" "I Wonder What Went Wrong", " The Dream" was published in " Great Poets of Our Time" by the National Library of Poetry;

[oth. writ.] None published, 172 total poems; [pers.] My poems are written from the heart by the influence of a few beautiful young ladies, Jaci, Jami and Abi; [a.] Cola, SC.

WALKER, ROBERTA J.
[b.] October 5, 1963, Marion, Indiana; [p.] Maudie A. Thornton; [m.] Charles R. Walker, November 28, 1987; [ed.] Quit school in the 10th grade, due to hospital stay; [occ.] All Safe Allied Security Guard; [oth. writ.] Kids, A Minute or Two To Share Your Name, my poems; [pers.] All my writings came from experience and lots of mixed feelings. I hope they help you in some way. [a.] Phoenix, AZ.

WALKER, SHARON R.
[b.] July 22, 1940, East Jordan, Michigan; [p.] Ralph and Sophia Walker; [ed.] 12 grade, East Jordan Michigan, attended Modeling School; [occ.] Unemployed; [oth.writ.] Several articles in newspapers; [pers.] I love to write poetry for people they seem to love them. [a.] East Jordan, MI.

WALKER, VIRGINIA LEE
[pen.] Virginia Jensen, G. Jensen; [b.] March 25, 1960, Clearwater, Florida; [p.] Deceased; [m.] Larry Dale Walker, June 29, 1992; [ch.] Misty Lee and Chad Michael; [ed.] Shaker High, Latham, New York; [occ.] Salesperson, PJ's Fishy Business, Mary Esther, Florida; [memb.] Postal Commemorative Society; [hon.] Chosen for the Coming of Dawn; [oth. writ.] A Stone in My SHoe, a collection of my poetry, (c) 1992 (unpublished); [pers.] Writing has always come natural for me. I enjoy challenging others to look inward, to see life and the world through a different perspective. Poetry to me is therapy without expense. [a.] Mary Esther, FL.

WALLACE, ALFRED LEON
[pen.] Alfred Leon Wallace; [b.] April 24, 1931, Rome, Georgia; [p.] Howard Marion and Leola Corley Wallace; [ed.] Mount Berry High School for Boys, Writer's Digest School Famous Writers School; [occ.] Poet; [memb.] ACLU, Veterans of Foreign Wars of the United States; [oth. writ.] Live, If I Were A Butterfly, Love Is Pure Baloney, Have You Ever Been Thankful, I Am A Slave. [a.] Rome, GA.

WALLACE-JENKINS, SIENNA A.
[pen.] Sienna A.W.; [b.] August 17, 1979, Hawaii; [p.] Yanett and Corwin Jenkins; [ed.] 7th passing over to the 8th grade in 93-94; [occ.] Dishes (chores); [hon.] Academic Awards; [oth. writ.] Yes; [pers.] I am so happy to receive this privilege. I write cause my heart and mind can't hold half the troubles in life, so I put the burden on paper. [a.] Killeen, TX.

WALLACE, JOSHUA DAVID
[b.] October 11, 1978, Richmond, Virginia; [p.] Barbara MacKinnon and Patrick Wallace; [ed.] Currently in 9th grade at Patrick Henry High School; [occ.] Student; [memb.] International Society of Poets, Church of Our Saviour Acolytes. [a.] Montpelier, VA.

WALLER, CATALINO
[pen.] Lee Waller; [b.] March 9, 1976, New York City, New York; [ed.] High school, junior year; [occ.] Student. [a.] Claremont, NH.

WALLIS, IONE I.
[b.] November 21, 1917, Brainerd, Minnesota; [p.] Rose Turner and Cooper Holleman; [m.] Clarence Wallis (deceased July 92), May 22, 1937; [ch.] Carol Hawbaker and Marjorie Niemann; [ed.] High school; [occ.] Retired school secretary; [memb.] Usual; [hon.] Life Membership in Indiana State P.T.A.;[oth. writ.] Poems (Friends) not sure it was published, have 3 manuscripts (children's books), so far too costly to publish; [pers.] Love to read. [a.] South Bend, IN.

WALTER, TAMMY S.
[pen.] Tammy Rose Walter; [b.] February 27,1964, Spartanburg, South Carolina;[p.] Tom and Emma Lou Loftin; [m.] Tom Walter, December 28, 1991; [ch.] Lelia, Carrie-Anna, Sommer and Casey; [ed.] Technical College; [occ.] Self-employed Marketing and Computer Work; [memb.] Vice President of Boiling Springs Elementary School PTA, Ways and Means; [hon.] 1991-S.C. Speech competition, 1st place in Original Oratory; [pers.] I write primarily about and for the family that I love dearly, my husband and children are my greatest inspiration; [a.] Inman, SC.

WALTON SR., RICHARD
[b.] February 15, 1923, Columbus, Georgia; [p.] Richard and Leanna Walton; [m.] Dorothy Walton, July 10, 1931; [ch.] Richard Joseph, Carolyn, Michael, Jeffery and Bernard;[ed.] 12 grade;[occ.] Retired Army; [memb.] Mt. Zion Baptist Church; [oth. writ.] Several poems in newspaper and church newsletter. [a.] Aberdeen, MD.

WA'NDEDA, MANGENI PATRICK
[b.] Busia, South-Eastern Uganda; [p.] Charles Wafula Ndeda and Virginia Ajwangi Wafula; [ed.] Marchison Bay, Bunyide, Pece, Soroti and Nahayaka Primary Schools, Sebei College, Kitgum High School, Makerere University, Leeds University; [occ.] Lecturer in playwriting and television drama, Makerere University; [oth. writ.] Several poems, some published in magazines, many plays for radio, television and the stage and a variety of short stories, some published. [a.] Kampala, Uganda.

WARD, CHARLES CECIL
[b.] August 13,1948, Mishawaka, Indiana;[p.] Rufus Cecil and Luella Jean; [m.] Judy Rae Berwanger, April 5, 1984; [ch.] Harold Jay, Christopher Cecil, Charles Robert and Joshua Scott;[ed.] Lincoln Elementary, Mishawake High; [occ.] Construction Tradesman and struggling writer; [hon.] Honored, Houston Texas 1978 for pulling 2 policemen from crashed helicopter; [oth. writ.] Have been working 20 plus years on children's stories and a book The Lands of Dawn also, writing songs and Gothic horror tales; [pers.] My dreams are for the children, and to one day see the "Lands of Dawn" in print. [a.] Phoenix, AZ.

WARD, SAMUEL W.
[pen.] Krymson Daain; [b.] March 6,1973, Oakland, California; [p.] Charles D. and Cheryl J. Ward;[ed.] Graduated basic high school, Henderson NV, class of 1991;[occ.] Communication Center Operator United States Marine Corps; [pers.] I try to provoke feelings, emotions and/or thought within my writing. I want you to feel, I want you to think, most of all I want you to understand, not my writing but what I'm writing about. [a.] Las Vegas, NV.

WARE, JENNIFER STAR
[b.] November 10, 1977, Pompton Plains, New Jersey; [p.] Cathy and Richard Deska; [ed.] Wanaque Elementary, St. Mary's and Lakeland Regional High School; [occ.]Student; [hon.] Class of '92 Humanitarian Award. [a.] Ringwood, NJ.

WARNER, DAVID GERALD R.
[pen.] Jerry Warner; [b.] August 29, 1977, Crossville, Tennessee; [p.] David E. and Deborah Warner; [ed.] Cumberland Co. High School; [occ.] Student; [memb.] CCHS Band, soccer; [oth. writ.] All poetry (none published); [pers.] In all the world there is no one as devoted as a miner, for it will never lie. [a.] Crossville, TN.

WARNER, MARGARET
[pen.] Marge Warner; [b.] July 30, 1949, Dayton, Ohio; [p.] Jerry and Olive Welling; [m.] David J. Warner, July 11, 1981; [ch.] Eric David and Rebecca Marie;[ed.] Wright State University B.S. in Education; [occ.] Elementary Teacher, Titus Elementary, Huber Heights, Ohio; [memb.] St. Matthew's Lutheran Church; [hon.] Dean's List, Phi Eta Tau Honor Society; [oth. writ.] Poems for various school events; [pers.] Preserve and enjoy the beauty of nature. [a.] Bradford, OH.

WASNAK, FRED
[pen.] Fred; [b.] February 2, 1951, Kittanning, Pennsylvania; [p.] Mary and Harry Wasnak; [ch.] Amie and Julia; [ed.] Sayreville War Memorial High School, Middlesex County College, Indiana University of Pennsylvania; [occ.] Free Lance Computer Graphic Artist, writer; [oth. writ.] Numerous songs, articles and poems; [pers.] I am Jack of the Jack of all trades. My predicament was born of abhorrence of boredom. [a.] South Amboy, NJ.

WASSEL, STEPHAN PAUL
[b.] February 24, 1950, Worchester, Massachusetts, [p.] Paul Wassel and Eugenia Brzezinska; [m.] Diana Fenton, October 2,1982; [ed.] Quinsigamond College-ASE, University of Massachusetts-BSEE, Old Dominion University-MBA; [occ.] Engineering Supervisor; [hon.] Cum Laude, Dean's List; [pers.] The nail that stands out gets hammered down, don't ever stop standing out. [a.] Arlington, VA.

WATFORD JR., RICHARD ALTO
[pen.] Richie; [b.] May 20, 1980, Okeechobee, Florida; [p.] Richard A. and Marcia L, Watford, Sr.; [ed.] I'm in junior high school, I began 8th grade 93-94; [hon.] English outstanding work; [oth. writ.] Mothers Day, poem Dad's Birthday, poem and Gramma's Birthday, poem; [pers.] I'm a growing boy that loves fishing, baseball. I love my hometown of Okeechobee. It's the second largest lake of U.S. [a.] Okeechobee, FL.

WATKINS, BRANDON
[b.] August 8, 1976; [p.] Steven Edward Watkins and Cynthia Ann Madsen; [ed.] 10th grade, high school; [pers.] I enjoy writing and making others inspired by my work. I also like leaving people contemplating on what I've written.

WATKINS, TAYRAN
[pen.] Tay; [b.] January 29,1974, Canton, Georgia;[p.] Mickey and Rita Watkins; [ed.] High school-Sequoyah High School, Reinhartd College, freshman; [occ.]

Early Childhood Educational Therapist at Little People's Corner Day Care; [memb.] Arbor Hill Baptist Church; [hon.] Honor Roll, Canton Rotary Club Scholarship, President's Academic Letter; [oth.writ.] Other personal writings given to people as gifts; [pers.] I believe that Jesus truly is my comfort and guide. I rely on him to get me through life. I also believe that we should live our life to the best of our ability because we may be the only Bible some people ever read. [a.] Canton, GA.

WATSON, MILTON CODY
[pen.] Milton Cody Watson; [b.] December 7,1931, Big Spring, Texas; [p.] Courtney B. Watson and Anna M. Watson (mother deceased); [m.] Unmarried, therefore no children, but I wish I was married; [ed.] Odessa High School, a Vocational School, plans for college courses; [occ.] Retired; [memb.] Disabled American Veterans, American Legion; [hon.] Ninety Second (92nd) in class of 293, high school-Who's Who Wittiest, first place (blue ribbon), Canterbury North, Christmas (1992) door decoration; [oth. writ.] Another, poem's entry into the National Library of Poetry, contest, also other unpublished poems and verses; [oth. writ.] My, mentors are Seventeenth (17th) Century poets, much as a symphony does with musical notes, I strive for the imagery of poets, to reach the deepest parts of a person's being. [a.] Big Spring, TX.

WATTS, LORI A.
[pen.] Noni (9); [b.] December 13,1970, Bridgeport, Connecticut; [p.] Herman T. and Margaret D. Watts; [ed.] Central Magnet Component High School, The Institute of Children's Literature; [occ.] Cleaning Service; [oth. writ.] Many other poems that have not been published; [pers.] Writing about your life and experiences are the best pieces of poetry anyone can create.[a.] Bridgeport, CT.

WEAVER, GRACE MARGARET
[b.] September 4, 1909, Philadelphia, Pennsylvania; [p.] James Henry (Harry) and Beulah Grace (Dans) Weaver; [ed.] Glassboro Normal School, Glassboro, NJ, Morningside College, Sioux City, Iowa (BA), Iliff School of Theology, Denver, Colo., (ThM); [occ.] Former school teacher, NJ., Home Missionary, (Utah), United Methodist Minster ; [hon.] Several certificates of Merit from World of Poetry. [a.] Salem, OR.

WEAVER, RONNIE
[b.] October 22,1967, Keywest, Florida; [p.] Lee and Teresita Weaver; [ed.] McIntosh High School, Clayton State College; [occ.] Security Officer, Atlanta Renaissance Hotel; [oth. writ.] Personal, poetry, Theology and Philosophy; [pers.] Believe in yourself and your abilities. Pursue happiness and let life take its course. [a.] Peachtree City, GA 30269.

WEBB, CHRISTINE
[b.] July 29, 1936, Gary, Indiana; [p.] Chrystena Key and Harry Taylor, Sr.; [m.] Divorced; [ch.] Harold, Jr.and Robin Webb Owsley; [ed.] Roosevelt High School, 1954, Indiana University, BS. 1959, MS. 1972;[occ.] Teacher, Business and Prof. Writer, proposals, resumes, South Shore Community Academy, Chicago; [memb.] Kappa Delta Pi, Education Honorary, CAABSE; [hon.] Sigrid Stark Award, poetry and essay; [oth. writ.] Essays, songs, poems, Technical writing-proposals; [pers.] How magnifi-

cent id life's journey, duty, ecstacy, endurance, celebration. [a.] Chicago, IL.

WEBB, NIKI
[b.] June 20, 1973, Los Angeles, California; [p.] Rosalind Belcher and Donald Webb; [ed.] Immaculate Heart High School, University of San Francisco; [occ.] Full time student; [memb.] Ward African Methodist Episcopal Church, NAACP; [pers.] Be honest and tactful, pray and give praise omit pettiness from your life and live for better future days. [a.] Los Angeles, CA.

WEBSTER, JAMIE
[b.] July 26, 1977, Merrillville, IN; [p.] Robert and Judy Webster; [ed.] Willowcreek Middle School and Portage High School; [hon.] Grand Prize and First Place for Writing, "Unheard Cries in the Dark"; [oth. writ.] "Unheard Cries in the Dark," and also "Party Time, Deadly Time"; [pers.] Thank you to the people who influence me the most. Bryon and Cindy Weck. I love you!; [a.] Portage, IN

WEBSTER, MILTON R.
[b.] April 16, 1912, St. Joseph, Missouri; [p.] Ben A. and Leora Smith Webster; [m.] Emily R. Stuessi Webster, October 16, 1935; [ch.] Richard David Webster and Mary Ann Lippincott Guildner; [ed.] B.S. in Business, University of Kansas '34; [occ.] Reti5red Accountant, Bookkeeper; [memb.] OMA, Phi Mu Alpha, National Music Fraternity; [hon.] K.U. Vocal Quartett "34, K.U. Men's Glee Club '34, The "Melody Masters" Quartet (tenor), St. Joseph, MO, 1932-1945, had male lead in "Naughty Marietta" St. Joseph J.C. 1932; [oth. writ.] "Felix cum Amor", "The Dilemma of Dialogue", "A Limpid Limmerick To Lament"; [pers.] My compilation of poems exempted me from taking final exam in English Literature, high school senior 1932, Central High School, St. Joseph, MO. [a.] Gladstone, MO.

WEBSTER, TAMARA JOAN
[pen.] Tami Webster; [b.] January 8, 1982, Lowell, Massachusetts; [p.] Russell R. and Cherie A. Webster; [ed.] 5th grade; [memb.] Tyngsboro Elementary band; [hon.] High Honor Roll, Kindergarten-3rd grade. [a.] Tyngsboro, MA.

WEDAN, RODGER
[b.] August 17, 1942, Duluth, Minnesota; [p.] Ivan and Kathleen Wedan; [m.] Marsha Wedan, May 14, 1960; [ch.] Lydia Ann and Joanne Marie; [ed.] High school, Shasta Junior College, Shasta Bible College; [occ.] Custodian, student; [memb.] Lake Blvd. Baptist, North Valley Baptist Church; [oth. writ.] Several poems, newspaper articles, various occasion cards; [pers.] My writing reflects personal experiences. Having lived what I write gives me the opportunity to show the sufficiency of Jesus Christ, to the greater glory of God. [a.] Redding, CA.

WEDEMAN, D.V. (JOE)
[b.] January 27, 1919, Texas farm boy; [m.] Honey Wedeman; [ch.] Mark and Willa, four grandchildren; [occ.] WWII U.S. Marine pilot, airport crash rescue vehicle manufacturer and now estate property trustee; [oth. writ.] I have written many poems for friends as they relate to special occasions or current events. Never before have I offered an item for publication; [pers.] As I reflect upon my seventy-four years, my youth was really not so great as I once thought and

notwithstanding, life on earth can never be the way it was. The only time for all of us is now. [a.] Honolulu, HI.

WEEKS, BEULAH M.
[pen.] Bea Weeks; [b.] July 18, 1926, Battle Creek, Michigan; [p.] Clinton and Beulah Ferguson ; [m.] Widowed, (Gerold F. Weeks died March 3, 1993), November 16, 1943; [ch.] Pamela, Deborah, son Rona Keith; [ed.] High school; [occ.] Wife, mother, cashier, part-time writer, Amway Dist.; [memb.] Honorary member of Iota Chapter Alpha Beta Epsilon from Western Michigan University; [oth. writ.] Many poems published in local newspaper in Battle Creek, Michigan;[pers.] I volunteer my time at 3 schools, introducing 1st through 6th grades to poetry.[a.] Climax, MI.

WEGRZYN, JOSEPH L.
[pen.] Joseph L. Wegrzyn; [b.] September 16,1917, East St. Louis, Illinois; [p.] John and Agata Wegrzyn; [m.] Genevieve A. Wegrzyn, April 27, 1957; [ch.] Catherine Ann, Janet Marie and John Paul; [ed.] East St. Louis Senior High, Aerial Gunnery, World War II Air Corps, Marine Drill Instructor, Korean Conflict; [occ.] Railroad carman; [memb.] Retired Transport Workers Union, American Legion Post 58, Belleville, Illinois, Polish American War Veterans, Caseyville, ILlinois; [hon.] Queen of Peace Church; [oth. writ.] Retired Correspondent St. Louis, Missouri area for Mutual Magazine, a railroad publication based Philadelphia, Pennsylvania; [pers.] Try to follow St. Francis, prayer for peace. [a.] Belleville, IL.

WEINER, SAMANTHA
[b.] February 18, 1978, Plainview, New York; [p.] Alan and Madeline Weiner; [occ.] Student in high school; [memb.] Western Poetry Association, Some Music Club; [oth. writ.] " Spong of You", a poem published in Poetry an American Heritage, an article in the school newspaper; [pers.] I sing with my group, I dance, I write lyrics to songs, and all of these things help me with poetry and life. I've been influenced by my parents, friends, singers, songwriters and dancers all over the world. [a.] Plainview, Long Island, NY.

WEIR, S.J.
[b.] February 14, 1978, Syracuse, New York; [p.] Robert and Eileen Weit; [ed.] Freshman, Henninger High School; [oth. writ.] Many poems written only one published; [pers.] It's hard to see what's within, when you are blinded by what's without. [a.] Syracuse, NY.

WEISHAN, ANNABELLE
[b.] September 28, 1934, West Allis, Wisconsin; [p.] Charles and Ida Beutler of Swiss decent; [m.] John F. Weishan, August 21, 1954; [ch.] (10) Mike, Mark, Karen, Kim, Kathy, Kristi, Kelly, John, James and Kay; [ed.] High school graduate Central High, West Allis; [occ.] Homemaker, grandmother of 13; [memb.] St.John's Lutheran church, Sunday School teacher 2nd year; [hon.] Region F. Advisor on the Wisconsin State PTA Board of Directors, PTA Honorary Life and the PTA Martinson Memorial Award; [oth. writ.] Does Santa Belong to The PTA and There's Room for You, in PTA bulletins, " A Man for All Seasons" published in the Wisconsin Outdoor Journal, March 1993, Conservation Issue; [pers.] Don't worry so much about what you don't have, be grateful for the good things that you have. [a.] West Allis, WI.

WEISS, GABRIELLE
[b.] June 19, 1936, New York City; [p.] Esther and Edwin Repp; [m.] Divorced, September 29, 1956; [ch.] Christopher, Wendy and Maureen; [ed.] Bachelors of Professional study primarily life experiences State University of New York; [occ.] Health Care Administration and Director Sudden Infant Death Syndrome Center; [memb.] Association of Death Education and death Related Counseling; [oth. writ.] Approximately 60 unpublished poems relating to spirituality and relationships; [pers.] Learning how to love is the most important complicated difficult and joyful component of life. [a.] Naples, NY.

WEISSER, LAURA
[b.] September 3,1967, Reading, Pennsylvania; [p.] Thomas C. and Yvonne M. Davies; [m.] Bradley Weisser, September 19, 1987; [ch.] Drew Alan; [ed.] Gov. Mifflin High School, Penn State University, Berks Campus; [memb.] Calvary United Methodist Church; [oth. writ.] " Adventures in The Forest", "Learning About Litter", "Where do Lightning Bugs Go In The Winter", "Emily's Nightmare", 'How Do Worms Survive", all are pending publication; [pers.] Always be true to yourself and appreciate everything around you, life is too short to do otherwise. [a.] Reading, PA.

WELCH, HARRIETTE A.
[pen.] Kitty Welch; [b.] April 19, 1915, New Jersey; [p.] Harriet L. Pfleger and Victor E. Weber; [m.] William Addams Welch, June 25, 1934; [ch.] Wendy Addams Reiner and Heather Addams Tuckfield; [ed.] Cliffside Park High, Business College, New York School of Interior Design; [occ.] Sales, F. Schumacher and Co., New York; [memb.] President United Methodist Church, North Hollywood, CA., P.E.O., Sherman Oaks, California; [hon.] Chamber of Commerce, North Hollywood, California, Woman of the Year, Methodist District Special Award, North Hollywood, California; [oth. writ.] Poems for church work-P.E.O., publication-Leisure Word Paper; [pers.] My spirit is romantic, adventuresome eager to explore the unknown and to live life as a faithful friend. [a.] Mesa, AZ.

WELCH, KEVIN
[b.] August 31, 1969, Brooklyn, New York; [p.] Elwyn Welch; [ed.] High school, 2 years trade school degree, data processing and programming; [occ.] Merchandiser, Jamesway Dept. store and bouncer, bartender, Silver Bullet Saloon; [pers.] " With change, there is opportunity. To Every end, there's a new beginning! [a.] Owenota, NY.

WELLS, JAMES MITCHELL
[b.] May 28, 1956, Winchester, Virginia; [p.] John and Joyce Wells; [m.] Karen Denise Wells, June 3, 1977; [ch.] Katie, John and James; [ed.] Hampshire High, Potomac State College, Eastern Christian College, Johnson Bible College, BA, MA, Emmanuel School of Religion; [occ.] Minister; [hon.] Fig Tree Scholarship, a finalist of The Alexander Campbell Scholarship, named "An Outstanding Young Minister" in 1989 at the North American Christian Convention; [oth. writ.] Articles in The Lookout, The Christian Standard, Preaching. [a.] Norton, VA.

WELLS, LINDA
[b.] December 5, 1977, Philadelphia, Pennsylvania; [p.] Sandra and Michael Wells; [ed.] Presently a junior at the Central High School of Philadelphia; [occ.] Student; [hon.] Kiwanis Club of Olney Award; [oth. writ.] I have many other personal writings but none of them has ever been published; [pers.] In my writing I try to show the real deal of this world through my own eyes and the eyes of others. [a.] Philadelphia, PA.

WELSH, VERNA L.
[b.] December 20, 1917, Newton, Kansas; [p.] Rhoda and Ben Northcott; [m.] Leo Dan Welsh, January 15, 1941; [ch.] Jeanette, Leorena and George; [ed.] Newton High School, Bethel College in Newton, Kansas, Northland Pioneer College, Winslow, Arizona; [occ.] Retired; [memb.] First Christian Church, Scroptimist International, UTU Ladies Auxiliary, Santa Fe Woman's club; [hon.] National Honor society, Beta Sigma Phi Poetry contest;[oth. writ.] Miscellaneous poetry, many for family and friends honoring their lives and achievements, many religious poems; [pers.] God made it possible for me to have my talent and He gives me the inspiration for the poetry I write and because of this I strive to have the majority of my writings include His goodness and blessings. [a.] Winslow, AZ.

WENZEL, ANDREA
[b.] July 13, 1977, Elhart, Indiana; [p.] John and Stephanie Wenzel;[ed.] Elkhart Central High School (class of 95); [occ.] Student; [memb.] National Thespians Society, National Forensics League, school newspaper-Opinion Editor, Symphony Orchestra, founder and president of Student Coalition for Peace, various environmental and political organizations; [hon.] Science Fair, American center for Quality Control 1st place award and Sigman XI Award, Rotary Youth Leadership Award recipient, qualified to travel to China as Student Ambassador and to Israel as an Exchange Student; [oth. writ.] Editorial published in local paper, various articles in school newspaper; [pers.] I believe that social messages can be communicated through poetry in a much more intense form than can be translated into factual reports. Through poetry can provide avenues of escape, social poetry should raise the awareness and concern of its readers. [a.] Elkhart, IN.

WERNER, BETTY J.
[b.] September 15, 1924, Wells, Minnesota; [p.] Silas and Irene Passer; [m.] Ray H. Werner, September 11, 1940; [ch.] Richard Werner, Jean Osmundson, Dean and Jack Werner, Linda Blair, Laura Colbert and Susan Bigelow; [occ.] Bookkeeper, store owner, waitress; [oth.writ.] Several poems about her family and special occasions; [pers.] Betty has been diagnosed with Alzheimers Disease and has been in a nursing home since January 1991. [a.] Albert Lea, MN.

WESTBROOKS, ADRIANNA ASHEIA
[b.] October 20, 1979, Fort Payne, Alabama, Baptist Medical Center;[p.] Michael Timothy Westbrooks and Donna Lynn Freeman; [ed.] 7th grade (going into 8th) Ider High School; [memb.] Junior Bata Club, Ider High School Band, School Spirit Club; [hon.] Highest Achievement in Journalism, music award, Science awards, Honor Roll; [oth. writ.] If There Were No Tomorrow and Mother, were two other

poems written, but not published and one other dedication to my great-grandfather which was in the newspaper; [pers.] I love to write and get highest grades and honors in journalism. In my opinion writing is the perfect way to express your feelings and emotions. [a.] Ider, AL.

WESTERBACK, MICHAEL
[b.] June 20, 1968, Worchester, Massachusetts; [p.] Paul and Nancy Westerback; [ed.] St. John's High School, Worcester State College; [pers.] I see hope in the eyes of children and beauty in a quiet sunset but nothing lasts forever. [a.] Leicester, MA.

WETZLER, MARIAN ARDEN
[pen.] M. Arden Wetzler; [b.] March 2, 1929, Grand Forks, North Dakota; [p.] Erle J. and Emma E. Pope; [m.] Jack L. Wetzler (died 1/23/91), March 31, 1948; [ch.] Jacqueline, Patti Rae, Michael, Terry Lee, and Sherry Lynn (twins), eight grandchildren; [ed.] High school graduate; [occ.] Retired; [memb.] Ladies Auxiliary, Fleet Reserve Association, First Presbyterian Church, Senior Friends, AARP, Winnebago Itascha Traverlers; [oth. writ.] "A Smile" published in a local senior's paper, other poetry to date unpublished; [pers.] " The House You Call Home" was written for Patti Rae and Tim Arnold, when they were the first of my children to own their own home. [a.] Fort Walton Beach, FL.

WHALEY, RENEE DANETTE
[b.] July 4, 1975, Rockford, Illinois; [p.] Jack and Caroline Whaley; [ed.] Stillman Valley High School; [hon.] 4 year Honor Roll, 4 year wrestling cheerleader, 2 year captain, 2 year Students for Students. [a.] Stillman Valley, IL.

WHEATLEY, KEMBERLEY D. LOUANNA
[pen.] Kem; [b.] April 9, 1976, Charlotte Amalie, St. Thomas, Virgin Island; [p.] William L. and Ann L. Wheatley; [ed.] Apostolic Faith and Prophecy Elementary Schools, Bertha Boschulte Junior High, Ivanna Eudora Kean High; [occ.] Student; [memb.] Kean Strivers, Spanish Club, U.S. Naval Sea Cadets, New Creation (church choir); [hon.] National Honor Society, Spanish Honor Society. [a.] St. Thomas, VI.

WHEELER, BRIGITTE
[b.] April 21, 1943, Munich, Germany; [p.] Annia Miller (Henning) [m.] Michael Wheeler, August 18, 1972; [ch.] James, Michael, Teresa and Alan; [ed.] High school, Hanamer Schule The Gold Schmidt College of Business; [occ.] Writer; [memb.] Foothill Farms Cabana Club # 2 ; [hon.] Top Honors Gold Schmidt College, Gold medal figure skating-roller; [oth. writ.] Complete short works of poetry; [pers.] I came to America not knowing the language, I taught myself to write and read English. My goal is to touch as many people as I can with my writings, maybe it will help. [a.] Sacramento, CA.

WHEELER, REX
[pen.] Rex Wheeler; [b.] January 2, 1954, Des Moines, Iowa;[p.] James and Mildred; [ch.] Jeremiah and Elizabeth; [ed.] East High, Army Education, Des Moines Area XI Community College; [occ.] Laborer; [memb.] American Legion, VFW, Viet Nam Vets of American, A.B.A.T.E., Freedom of Road Riders, Bros Club; [oth. writ.] 1st poem printed in Leetown News at age of 13, other poems were published by World of Poetry, 5 Golden Poet Awards, 2 books of

my poetry written and gathering dust; [pers.] I write to get my feelings out, so that others may see that they are not alone in their feelings and that there is no shame in showing feelings and emotion. [a.] Des Moines, IA.

WHETSELL, JoANN
[pen.] J. P. Lawrence; [b.] October 1, 1976, Morristown, New Jersey; [p.] Harold and Yvonne Whetsell; [ed.] The Lawrenceville School (will be a senior at time of publication); [occ.] Student; [hon.] Dean's List, High Honors twice, 9th grade English prize; [oth. writ.] I write both poetry and short stories, one story was published in the school literary magazine in the fall; [pers.] I write from inspiration, as a communication of feelings about myself and my world. [a.] Florham Park, NJ.

WHITE, BRINDA E.
[pen.] Frenche; [b.] June 15, 1949, Jacksonville, Florida; [p.] Clifford H. White I and Jessie B. Pelham; [m.] Richard J. William I, engaged; [ch.] Richardo, Monica, Uriah, Derrick and Aldreka; [ed.] Florida Junior Community College, Florida Medical and Dental College, Jones Medical College; [occ.] PResently homemaker at home and do Missionary work to help others; [memb.] Member of Multiple Sclerosis Association, Cancer Society; [hon.] Received awards in Medical College for High Honors and achievement; [oth. writ.] I've written several poems of poetry to various and would like to contribute a portion of my award money to a good cause, I have Multiple Sclerosis of the spine; [pers.] I enjoy writing poems, its a hobby for me, and it gives an opinion in expressing views in reacting good awareness with others. [a.] Jacksonville, FL.

WHITE, JAN
[b.] December 27,1950, Lauderdale County; [p.] Jr. and Gearldine Thigpen; [m.] Terry A. White, Sr., May 16, 1970; [ch.] Terry Allen, Jr., Eric Lee, Jeremy Wayne, daughter-in-law Cyndi; [ed.] Lauderdale County High School, Rogersville, AL; [occ.] School bus driver, Anderson Junior High and preschool teacher-Mars Hill Bible School. [a.] Rogersville, AL.

WHITE, JEAN D. (EVANGELIST)
[b.] November 23, 1934, Washington, District Columbia; [p.] Herman R. and Dorothy E. Duley; [m.] Charles L. White, January 19, 1985; [ch.] Robert G. Smith and Annette D. Cardona; [ed.] Graduated from Gaithersburg High School; [occ.] Retired; [memb.] New Convenant Baptist Church, Reverend A. Norris Smith, pastor; [hon.] I have received The Golden Poets Award for, 1989-90, 1991-1992; [oth. writ.] I published my true story which I wrote"The Road Back", my book was written in 3 days, thru the Holy Spirit; [pers.] I have come from a "cult" to "religion" to a personal relationship with Jesus Christ. All of my poems are inspired by God thru His Holy Spirit. [a.] Beltsville, MD.

WHITE, JOHN EDWARD
[b.] March 3, 1963, Spokane, Washington; [p.] Rose and Leron White; [m.] April Lucille White, January 18,1990; [ch.] Jenifer and Jesica White; [ed.] High school graduate; [occ.] Antique Radio Rebuilder; [pers.] In writing this poem it is my intent to express the certainty of better things to come no matter how bad things seem and that the possibilities of positive

change are abundantly eminent in the coming of a new day. [a.] Spokane, WA.

WHITE, KEVIN ANTHONY
[b.] February 23, 1976, Jamestown, New York; [p.] Gerald and Beverly White; [ed.] I am currently a junior attending Jamestown High School; [memb.] National Honor Society, Jamestown High School "Red Raider" Marching Band, Jamestown High School Concert Band and Orchestra; [hon.] Several times selected for Area All County and Sectional All State Bands for trumpet; [oth.writ.] Several poems published in a section of my local newspaper which honors student writing and art; [pers.] I would like to like thank my family and my English teacher, Miss Dorman for her guidance and help. It's amazing how powerful human emotion is, and it's wonderful what a person can create with those emotions. [a.] Jamestown, NY.

WHITE, MISTY
[b.] July 31, 1977, Houston, Missouri; [p.] Mildred and Frank White; [ed.] High school; [occ.] Student; [memb.] FHA, band, choir, cheerleading, Hi-Step, track; [hon.] Who's Who Among Students, Girl Scouts; [pers.] Dedicated to Jeff, the one who can understand me by reading my poems. The poems opens a window into my innermost feelings. [a.] Houston, MO.

WHITE, NICOLE
[pen.] Shadow; [b.] November 29, 1974, Los Angeles, California; [p.] Alan and Lynda White; [pers.] Solitaire is lonely without the cards. [a.] Los Angeles, CA.

WHITE, POLLY E.
[b.] February 2, 1966, Murray, Kentucky; [p.] Rev. Billy G. White and Doris E. Moon; [ed.] Henry County High-Tenn, University of Tennessee, Martin, University of Texas, Arlington; [occ.] Computer Systems Analyst, Computer Science Corporation; [memb.] Alpaha Chi National Honor Society, Beta Gamma Sigma National Business Honor Society; [hon.] National Dean's List, Alpha Chi National Honor Society, Beta Gamma Sigma National Business Honor Society, Honorary Historian Recognition, Bachelor of Science with High Honors, National Dean's List for College Students;[pers.] I strive to reflect the natural beauty in romance, nature and simple daily life. [a.] Ft. Worth. TX.

WHITE, STEPHANIE
[b.] February 7, Macon, Missouri; [p.] Sheila (Grant) and Harold White; [ed.] Currently attending Macon High School, class of 1995; [hon.] A Honor Roll, winner of a school poetry contest in 1993; [oth. writ.] Small collection of poetry; [pers.] If everyone in the world communicated only by expressing themselves through nature, there would be on hatred, only love and concern for the things that count. [a.] Macon, MO.

WHITEHEAD, KIM
[b.] August 1, 1980, Tulsa, Oklahoma; [p.] Wayne and Laura Whitehead; [ed.] Choctaw Elementary, Nicoma Park Intermediate, Choctaw Junior High; [occ.] Junior high student; [memb.] Eastland Hills Baptist Church Awana Group; [hon.] Presidential Academic Fitness Award (6th grade) Honor Roll; [oth. writ.] I have written several poems, however this

is the first one I have submitted; [pers.] I try to show the way the world is or was in my poems. I believe if people take matters into their own hands, they can make a difference. [a.] Choctaw, OK.

WHITELEY, LISA
[pen.] Lindsey; [b.] January 26, 1959, Long Branch, New Jersey; [p.] Richard G. and Joyce Budd; [m.] Keith R. Whiteley, January 7, 1978; [ch.] Misty Noel, Lindsey Marie and Ashley Michelle; [ed.] St. Lukes Catholic School, Temple City High, McLean High and Pasadena City College, Photography and Journalism; [occ.] Hair Designer and Teachers Aide; [memb.] R.I.F. Program Reading is Fundamental, Gifted and Talented Education, G.A.T.E.; [hon.] Writing Celebration local poetry contests placed 1st, 3rd and Honorable Mention; [oth. writ.] Numerous sonnets, poems and short stories for local schools. My inspiration Linda Skaggs, my motivation and respect Miranda Zienowicz; [pers.] To attain your highest goals you must challenge perfection. Influenced solely by the exquisite and complete works of Edgar A. Poe. [a.] Rialto, CA.

WHITEMAN, MARCI
[b.] May 26, 1970, Jackson, Michigan; [p.] Raymond and E. Jean Whiteman; [ed.] BA, Wheaton College; [occ.] Full time student, MA program Wheaton College; [memb.] Modern Poetry Association; [hon.] Alpha Kappa Petta, Dean's List, Lowell-Grabill Creative Writing contest; [oth. writ.] Upcoming book review in Christianity Today, poem published in Wheaton College literary publication; [pers.] "All writing comes by the grace of God and all doing and having". [a.] Carol Stream, IL.

WHITESEL, CHARLOTTE E.
[b.] January 25, 1939, Denver, Colorado; [p.] Charles and Clara Colborg; [ch.] David Allan, Ross Lee and Alan James; [ed.] St. Francis grade and high, 1 year course in writing; [occ.] Retired US West Comm., present. Total Petroleum, Purchasing Department; [hon.] "World of Poetry" (2) merit, 1, Honorable Mention, 3 Golden Awards, 1 Silver Award; [oth. writ.] World of Poetry, "The Gift of Nature", To Mother With Love", " My Special Friend"; [pers.] A "Special Child", A " Special Friend" in his own beautiful world and all his love, has been a great inspiration to me in my writing. If everyone could see the world through the eyes of a child, what a wonderful world this would be. [a.] Broomfield, CO.

WHITNEY, KIM E.
[b.] January 6, 1961, Ann Arbor, Michigan; [p.] Harvey A.K. and Tina Whitney; [ed.] Sycamore High, University of Cinn.; [occ.] Assistant Business Manager, continuing Ed. Manager for Harvey Whitney Books, Co.; [pers.] I have always had a passion for words and expressing myself in writing. Some of my best kept secrets are those I've camouflaged in poetry. [a.] Loveland, OH.

WHITTLESEY, NINA MERLE
[b.] December 7, 1927, Beatrice, Nebraska; [p.] Richard and Bonnie Ruth Brubaker; [m.] Dr. Wellington W. Whittlesey (professor), December 28,1947; [ed.] Baton Rouge H.C., in Louisiana, B.A. Wm. Penn Col., Oskaloosa, Louisiana, M.A. State University, IA., (Science Ed.); [occ.] Retired teacher, W. Penn College, (Biology), Bear Creek Elementary 5th grade, St. Pete, Florida; [memb.] Pi Lambda

Theta, AARP; [hon.] Cum Laude Wm Penn College, Sop. soloist, WPC, member Blue Angels' Choir, Pasadena Community Church, Meth. St. Petersburg, Fl, Bd. of Trustees and Official Bd. volunteer work at St. Pete Theological Seminary; [oth. writ.] Composed other poems for friends and composed religious choruses with music; [pers.] From the time I took my first science course and began to see the vastness and depth of creation, the many references to nature in the Bible took on new meaning, I see God's creation as an indication of the depth of His love for all who respond to it. Look at a star or seed and be overwhelmed. [a.] St. Petersburg, FL.

WIGHT, JEFF
[b.] April 30, 1954, Piqua, Ohio; [p.] Martha and Bill Wight; [ch.] Chastity (20), Jeffrey (7) and Jesse (5); [occ.] Electrical sales; [memb.] Many; [hon.] Dale Carnegie Public Speaking; [oth. writ.] Not available now; [pers.] Enjoy having fun in the sun and on the water skiing or fishing. [a.] Holmes, NY.

WIJE-TILLAKE, OLIVER
[pen.] Oliver Lake; [b.] January 12, 1934, Hevadiwela, Sri Lanka; [p.] Alice Wije-Tillake and (late) Bastian Wije-Tillake; [m.] Prema Wije-Tillake, December 22, 1966; [ed.] St. Mary's College, Kegalla, Ceylon Law College, Monash University (Aust.) L.L.M. and M (Env) Sc; [occ.] Attorney at Law, Solicitor, Lecturer in law and former Judge; [memb.] Commonwealth Mag. Association, Marath Alumni; [hon.] Post-graduate Award, Monash University (Australia); [oth.writ.] Numerous of published articles on law, environmental law, sentencing, two books published, two to be published Sabina and Count Down To Extinction; [pers.] Do not do to others, what you do not like to be done to yourself. Read and follow -St. Matthew Ch.5,6 and 7. Buddha said "Your salvation is in your own hands". [a.] Black River, Qld, Australia.

WILBER, ALICE O.
[b.] August 5, 1925, West Avon, Connecticut; [p.] Bernhard and Martha Krueger; [m.] Robert G. Wilber, Sr., January 23, 1945; [ch.] Robert G. Jr., Catharine Margaret, Donald Lawrence and James Carl; [ed.] Thru 2 years college; [occ.] Ret. former pre-school teacher/owner, floral designer; [memb.] College Lutheran; [oth. writ.] Articles in Lutheran publication, pre-school curriculum, LCA, monthly church newsletter 20 years; [pers.] My first reading was from the poems of R.L. Stevenson and H.W. Longfellow. I fell in love with the rythmn of words then and have written poetry, short stories, etc. ever since. [a.] La Mesa, CA.

WILBORN, PATRICIA
[pen.] Pat Wilborn; [b.] July 14, 1955, Virginia Beach, Virginia; [p.] William H. Walker and Mollie B. Wilborn; [m.] Teddy Lee Wilborn, August 6, 1981; [ch.] Salena, William and Jerry Nabors; [occ.] Housewife; [oth. writ.] I have written many poems and songs but I have never published any of them, also I've made many cards for friends to give their loved ones; [pers.] My poetry is inspired from my heart and my thoughts. [a.] Trenton, GA.

WILHELMY, SR., ARTHUR F.
[b.] June 29, 1920, Cerro Gordo, Illinois; [p.] Lino and Naomi Wilhelmy; [m.] Winifred, June 9, 1946; [ch.] Lino, Steve, Almitta, Jack, Janet and Arthur Jr.; [ed.] Decatur High School, various schools while

serving in the U.S.A. Army; [occ.] Retired, Electronic Tech; [memb.] Life member American Legion, Life V.F.W., charter member Music Society of America; [hon.] 3 awards from the Cal. American Legion, 2nd place for historical scrap book of Cal. State American Legion; [oth. writ.] Weekly column for The Desert Reporter, many editorial columns for Hi-Desert Star Yucca Valley; [pers.] To express your feelings write to hold on to your opinion fight to sit back and let things go, this solves nothing and this is so my friends to find your nitch, get in there, give it your best pitch, write, fight, say what is true everyone will know its you. [a.] Yucca Valley, CA.

WILHITE, PAULA DIANE
[pen.] Guinn Marie Ratliff; [b.] August 5, 1956, Mena, Arkansas; [p.] Paul M. and Charlene Guinn; [m.] Dennis Dale Wilhite, March 14, 1980; [ch.] Dina Diane Wilhite; [ed.] Mena High School, DeQueen Vo-Tech, in DeQueen, Arkansas; [occ.] Machine operator, Aalfs Manufacturing, Mena, Arkansas; [pers.] I am greatly honored to be associated with The National Library of Poetry and to also be mentioned in your upcoming anthology The Coming of Dawn. I would like to dedicate this poem to my daughter, mother and in loving memory of my grandmothers. [a.] Mena, AR.

WILKINSON, REBECCA
[b.] September 1, 1980, London, England; [p.] Alan and Angelika Wilkinson; [ed.] University Elementary School and Harvard Westlake School; [occ.] Student at Harvard Westlake; [hon.] One of the highest scorers in the State (for age group) for the S.A.T. Verbal; [oth. writ.] Nothing published but I write a lot of poetry in my free time, I also like to write stories and hope to one day write a novel. [pers.] I use poetry as a release of my feelings and feel that it is a good way of relieving stress. I love to read poetry and have a great respect for all writers. [a.] Los Angeles, CA.

WILLCOX, EMILY JEAN
[pen.] Emily Jean Willcox; [b.] December 4, 1980, Framingham, Massachusetts; [p.] Arthur Raymond and Linda Alice Willcox; [hon.] The awards I got were in gymnastics; [oth. writ.] This is the first I have ever entered, the others I kept to myself; [pers.] I'm just a kid, what ever bugs me, I just write it down instead of fighting, drugs or alcohol. [a.] Clinton, MA.

WILLEMS, PATRICIA (CSJ)
[b.] Chicago, Illinois; [p.] Ferdinand and Margaret Willems; [ed.] DePaul U., Notre Dame U., Loyola U., Chicago; [occ.] Artist/spiritual director; [memb.] Sisters of St. Joseph, National Expressive Art Therapy Association, La Grange Art League; [hon.] Morton Arboretum Art Guild, local poetry award; [oth. writ.] Published articles, watercolor art printed into note cards with full color; [pers.] When we waste and pollute our natural habitat our inner life suffers. Yet nature becomes the very revelation of the Sacred when we take time to become aware of the beauty, mystery and unity of matter. Poetry and painting are ways to internalize the energy in creation and to appreciate the symphony of all that is. We then stand in awe and gratitude in its presence and share this with others. [a.] La Grange Park, IL.

WILLETT, MARIA L.
[b.] February 11, 1976, Louisville, Kentucky; [p.] Charles and Dorothy Willett; [ed.] Junior in high school, class of 94; [memb.] Red Cross and SADD; [oth. writ.] Other poems; [pers.] Writing poetry has been an enjoyable experience for me. I strive to get into the hearts of people with my poems. [a.] Louisville, KY.

WILLIAMS, ALBERTA N.
[pen.] A. Williams, Sonia Davis; [b.] April 22, 1908, Olds Alberta, Canada; [p.] Albert E. Suedekum and Leola Bell Myers Suedekum Martin; [m.] Billy D. Williams, September 4, 1928; [ch.] Neppie Rebecca Williams and Billy Williams, Jr.; [occ.] Rancher, writer, bookkeeper; [memb.] NLAPW, G.F.W.C., D.A.R., Poetry Society of Co., Territorial Daughters of Southern Co., Hvertano Co. Cowbelles; [oth. writ.] Pearls of A Lady, poetry booklet (60 poems) 1976, "Potpourri of A Poet", 80 poems, 1992, my life story "Prairie Bird" 1993; [pers.] I also write short stories, plays, Haiku, articles, book reports, compose music with words, play the piano, guitar, banjo, mandolin, hunt arrowheads and artifacts. I am president of "Verses of The Valley" poets and Sec. of The Territorial Daughters. [a.] Rye, CO.

WILLIAMS, BRANDY
[pen.] Rose; [b.] August 26, 1979, Monroe County Hospital; [p.] Debbie and Willis Green Williams, Jr.; [ed.] Azalea Middle School, Monroe Middle and Elementary School; [occ.] Student at Azalea Middle School, 7th grade Mobile, AL; [memb.] Mexia United Methodist Church; [oth. writ.] Other poems (non-published); [pers.] I write only when I'm sad of bored. It relaxes me, I'm greatly influenced by Jim Morrison and early beatniks poems. [a.] Mobile, AL.

WILLIAMS, EVIE KITTRELL
[b.] January 3, 1919, Jacksonville, North Carolina; [p.] Viola Wetherington and Tilma Willard Kittrell; [m.] Jack Oliver Williams, August 24, 1941; [ch.] Donald Lee, Oliva Ann, Mary Joyce, Jacqulyn, Nancy Jean, Jack Oliver Jr. and Clara Kay; [ed.] Morehead City High School of 12 years in 1937; [occ.] Housewife and mother of seven children; [memb.] United Methodist Church, Beaufort, North Carolina for 50 years, chairperson, 2 years of Ann Neal Circle; [hon.] For three years consecutive I was honored for Mother of Most Children present on Mother's Day; [oth. writ.] I sent off one of my many poems and had music put to it in a song, name At The Foot of The Cross, I didn't have it published. [a.] Beaufort, NC.

WILLIAMS, GAIL
[pen.] Gail Williams; [b.] September 3, 1951, Buffalo, New York; [p.] Deceased; [m.] Divorced, September 17, 1971; [ed.] St. Augustine Erie Community College, City Campus, Independent studies; [occ.] Laundry aid work with soil linen; [memb.] Under influence of the Rosicrucians since 1977; [hon.] Beliefs based on credence and credit promised N.D. degree in five years after guidance of Rosicrucians for 20 years, bona fide right now, Alpha Sigma Theta; [oth. writ.] The book Imagination from office of Mental Hygiene under married name Trait, poem So Can You; [pers.] I'm an artist first, my poetry inspires my artwork, my life's problems in love, nature, sorrow, God, etc., etc. [a.] Geneva, NY.

WILLIAMS, LAURA
[b.] Born and raised in the Pennsylvania Dutch Country; [p.] Harriette and Cloyd Eberly; [ch.] One daughter, Heather; [ed.] Hershey Junior College, PA, Elizabethtown College, PA, Northern Arizona University; [occ.] Community College Instructor, Social Sciences and Child Development; [oth. writ.] Several poems published in small poetry publications, short stories and poetry published in community college Writers' Guild publication; [pers.] I enjoy the challenge of writing poetry in different forms. I have been greatly influenced by Frost, Dickinson and of course, Shakespeare and Nash just for fun. [a.] Lake Havasu City, AZ.

WILLIAMS, MICHAEL GERALD
[pen.] Michael Gerald; [b.] may 4, 1964, Washington, District Columbia; [p.] Avie L. and Helen M. Williams; [m.] Engaged to be married to Diane M. Redd, March 19, 1994; [ed.] Bachelor of Science Degree in Computer Information Systems from Devry Institute of Technology, Cols, OH.; [occ.] Computer Programmer Analyst for the Ohio Attorney General's Office; [oth. writ.] A number of unpublished song lyrics and poems; [pers.] Without a strong faith in God, one only exists instead of truly living. [a.] Columbus, OH.

WILLIAMS, MILDRED
[pers,] Our English teacher, Mable J. Bourquin, taught the students who wanted to be poets. We stayed after school and learned what a gift she was. I have written my life in poetry. [a.] Fostoria, OH.

WILLIAMS, NORMA JEAN
[pen.] Norma Jean Williams; [b.] February 6, 1939, Omaha, Nebraska; [p.] Gerald and Inez Dueling; [m.] Richard L. Williams, September 24,1955; [ch.] Rick, Tonja, Jeff; [ed.] Tech High; [occ.] Homemaker; [memb.] Ladies Auxiliary, National Library Poetry; [hon.] Watermark Press; [oth. writ.] Local newspapers, Senator Bob Kerry has one of my poems, Richard Simmons read one of my poems on national T.V.; [pers.] If I can bring out one emotion in someone sad, happy, angry or any other, I have accomplished what I have set out to do. [a.] Omaha, NE.

WILLIAMS, PAUL D.
[b.] December 9, 1973, Indiana; [p.] David O. and Judy A. Williams; [ed.] High school and will have Bachelors of Arts Degree (AA) by next year; [occ.] Independent Contractor currently employed by Technical Dispersions; [oth. writ.] None published, but I have many song lyrics, poems and other short stories, I would love to eventually write a short novel; [pers.] I write for me, I don't write things to get them published. I believe it's only art if it comes natural and from the heart. [a.] Hoffman Estates, IL 60194.

WILLIAMS, RAYLEMISHA VANCONDRIA
[pen.] Ray; [b.] December 6, 1972, Columbus, Georgia; [p.] Vandolph and Adelaide Williams; [ed.] Kendrick High School, Columbus College; [occ.] Student Assistant/dispatcher at Public Safety Department of Columbus College; [memb.] I Fellowship at Cuessta Road Church of Christ; [hon.] The National Honor Society, Spanish Honor Society, Who's Who Among American High School, top 5% of freshman class and top 10% in senior class during my high school years; [oth. writ.] I've written several other

poems that have not been published but they are called Queen Elizabeth, The Maid In Waiting, Nature, Strawbery, The Characters, Wanting to Make A Change, The Reach of Innocence, The Depths of The SHell and a lot more; [pers.] Never will there be any success if I am self-willed, but remembering to put God first in every positive thing that I do will make a big difference. [a.] Columbus, GA.

WILLIAMS, RICK
[pen.] Rick Rhythm; [b.] May 1, 1963, Minneapolis, Minnesota; [p.] Loretta Williams; [ch.] Charity Rose Partridge and Angle May Williams; [ed.] Edison High; [occ.] Automotive Cooling Tech.; [memb.] MN Song Writer Association, MN Music Academy, Upper Mississippi Blues Society, MN Street Rod Association; [hon.] Honored for volunteer services with the UMBS and other non-profit organizations; [oth. writ.] I have other poems and songs being used both published and recorded in MN, WV, NY, MD; [pers.] The circle of life it very tight, if you think it will be easy, that's elementary sight. You must work and work and work some more, to try and find the open door. [a.] Minneapolis, MN.

WILLIS, LARRY HARDY
[b.] March 17,1945, Raeford, North Carolina; [p.] Hardy B. and Desdrie Willis; [ed.] Lawrinburg High, Pembroke State, Chesterfield Marlboro Tec., College, Jefferson Community College; [occ.] Real Estate Investment; [oth. writ.] Several poems published in anthologies, various political essays in local newspapers; [pers.] I see the reality of God in most things, I strive and often fail to please Him but strive I must. [a.] Clarksville, IN 47129.

WILLIS, TERESA
[b.] November 3, 1955, Clintwood, Virginia; [p.] Bobby Lee and Janet (Stanley) Elkins; [m.] Harold Willis, June 3, 1977; [ch.] Amy and Kristi Willis, step-son Shawn Mullins; [ed.] Graduated Clintwood High School; [occ.] Housewife; [memb.] Georges Fork Old Regular Baptist Church; [oth. writ.] I have written many poems but have never had any published; [pers.] Most of what I write seems to be from a personal moment that has touched me or my life in some way. Family and friendships are my best inspirations. [a.] Clintwood, VA.

WILLS , CHRISTA ILENE
[pen.] Christa Wills; [b.] March 9, 1970, Indianapolis, Indiana; [p.] Sandy Harden and Jim Maze; [m.] Rick Wills, April 7, 1990; [ed.] South Decatur High School; [occ.] Housewife; [memb.] Greensburg Club Golf Course; [pers.] I have found writing poems as a hobby as well as a way to release feelings. It is a talent I never knew that I had, and it's something I'm very proud of. [a.] Westport, IN.

WILSON, EMERSON
[pen.] Em Wilson; [b.] December 13,1931, New York, New York; [p.] James and Helen Wilson; [ed.] BS/MS in the Social Sciences and Education, SUNY, Oneonta, New York; [occ.] Teacher, (retired) and associated with Wal Mart,Inc.; [hon.] From Deland Chapter Florida State Poets Association, Golden Poet Award; [oth. writ.] Poems in local newspaper, published in The Other Side of The Mirror 1992 and The Golden Treasury of Great Poems 1989. [a.] Flagler Beach, FL.

WILSON, LUCIOUS
[b.] March 5, 1974, Champagne; [p.] Micheal Wilson and Marilyn Addison; [m.] Jennifer Davies; [ed.] The Buckley School, The Hotchkiss School, Pitzer College; [occ.] Student. [a.] New York, NY.

WILSON, MARY JO
[b.] August 19, 1952, Richwood, West Virginia; [p.] Wendell and Beverly Seabolt; [m.] Tony Jack Wilson, July 7, 1975; [ch.] Jennifer Kristen Seabolt; [ed.] Richwood High School; [occ.] Bookkeeper/co-owner of T.J's Auto Service and Salvage; [oth.writ.] Several poems published in RHS Woodchopper, numerous articles published in West Virginia Heritage Encyclopedia. [a.] Cowen, WV.

WILSON, MELANIE
[b.] August 12,1979, Bremerhavenm, West Germany; [p.] Roy and Elizabeth Wilson; [ed.] Junior high school, Baumholder, Germany; [occ.] Student; [memb.] National Junior Honor Society, Red Cross, Girl Scouts, Chapel of the Good Samaritan; [hon.] 2nd place in city -wide essay contest, 3rd place in class-wide speech contest, 1st place in 7th grade Spelling Bee, Pillar of Support volunteer award, 2nd place in wood-working project, 1993 Presidential Academic Award; [pers.] I enjoy reading and writing poetry because it is fun, when you write poetry you can express anything, love, hate, fear of bravery. My opinion is that other lines of work are probably also interesting. [a.] Baumholder, Germany.

WILSON, RHODA E.
[b.] February 20, 1916, Hanley Falls, Minnesota; [p.] Fred and Elizabeth Cullickson; [m.] Ralph E. Wilson (deceased), April 1, 1949; [ch.] Cynthia S. and Ralph E.; [ed.] Graduated from Hanley Falls High School, one year at Denver U., Denver, Colorado, majoring in art; [occ.] Retired; [oth. writ.] A few poems and one story, I am trying to have published-fiction. [a.] Bruna Park, CA 90620.

WINGERTER, GRECHEN LYNNE
[pen.] G. Tristan Lynne; [b.] July 13, 1970, Newport, Rhode Island; [p.] Carol Fox and Curt Wingerter; [ed.] Guilford High School, Rockford, IL, 1988, Illinois State University -BA/Theatre, 1992, University of Illinois-MS/Library and Information Science 1993; [occ.] Intern-New American Theater, Rockford, IL; [memb.] American Library Association; [hon.] Illinois State University College of Fine Arts Dean's List; [oth. writ.] Several unpublished poems, one short story in progress;[pers.] To quote Tennessee Williams: "All true work of an artist must be personal, whether directly or obliquely, it must and it does reflect the emotional climates of its creator". [a.] Rockford, IL.

WINTER, CHRISTIE ANN
[b.] November 12,1950, Riverdale, Maryland; [p.] Charles E. and Betty L. Winter; [ed.] Loma Linda University - B.S., 1973 (nursing), M.S., 1980 (nursing), Chaffey Community College -A.S., 1990 (art); [occ.] Assistant Professor, Nursing Department, San Bernardino Valley College; [memb.] Association of Seventh Day Adventist Nurses, The Nature Conservancy; [hon.] Sigma Theta Tau, National Honor Society of Nursing, Outstanding Young Women of America 1982; [pers.] My poems are a diary for me, the record of an experience, an expression of feelings, or painting word pictures of the beauty of nature. [a.]

Loma Linda, CA.

WINTERS, MAJORIE A.
[pen.] Marj Winters; [b.] April 25, 1946, Duluth, Minnesota; [p.] Dorothy and Lyle Winters; [occ.] Wedding and Corporate Event Planner; [oth. writ.] I have written and privately published six books over a number of years. This was a way to share my writings with family and friends; [pers.] Poetry is my way of capturing a feeling or a moment in time, there to share or to revisit like an old friend. [a.] Carrollton, TX.

WIRTH, ABBY
[b.] September 10, 1980, Boston, Massachusetts; [p.] Richard Gordon and Patricia Anne Wirth; [ed.] Fairview Elementary School, Burke, Virginia, Parkside Middle School, Manassas, Virginia, Hilton Head Prepatory School, Hilton Head Island, South Carolina; [hon.] Consistent member of Honor Roll, Geography Award, Math Award, conduct award; [oth. writ.] "Beautiful Bride", "On The Shore", " Feelings", " Choices of Life", " The Worst Day"; [pers.] " Just go where the day takes you"," people call this the end when its really only the end of the beginning". [a.] Hilton Head Island, SC.

WOLFHEART
[pen.] Wolfheart; [b.] September 17, 1958, Tokyo, Japan; [ed.] B.S. Cum Laude-The University of Tennessee, MA candidate in Native American History and Literature, Western Carolina University; [occ.] Poet, writer, painter, photographer; [memb.] Native American Intertribal Federation Chickamaugee Cherokee Tribe; [hon.] Honor graduate of The University of Tennessee, University Grant and Research Assistantship from Western Carolina University, American Foundations Scholarship, Reynolda House Museum of American Art, Wake Forest University; [oth. writ.] Wolfheart is completing, Songs of The Chickamugee, a collection of poems and short stories of the Chickamaugee people and Raven Fire, a book of Shamanistic poetry at this time; [pers.] "Orinda", the title of my poem refers to the Chickamaugee word for spiritual harmony as the desired center of ones life path. This "Orinda" is the goal of all Cherokee endeavor. [a.] Roswell, GA.

WOLFINGTON, BARBARA MONEY
[pen.] Barbara Money Wolfington; [b.] June 21, 1935, Houston Co, Dothan, Alabama; [p.] Marvin W. and Freddie M. Money; [m.] Robert "Bob" J. Wolfington, October 12, 1985; [ch.] Jenean Bagwell-Hendricks, Robert J. Wolfington, Jr. and Maxwell R. Bagwell (deceased); [ed.] 13 years-Rehobeth High School, Gulf Coast Community College; [occ.] Executive Secretary; [memb.] AAAA (Army Aviation Association of America), Beta Sigma Phi-Business and Professional Women, Legal Secretaries Association, American National Red Cross; [oth. writ.] Manuscript, "The Peace and Joy of Forgiveness", personal experience surrounding the murder of my son; [pers.] Upon learning of my brother's terminal illness, I was determined to be strong and courageous for him, only to have him show me what true courage is in the face of death. [a.] Enterprise, AL.

WOLFORD, DOUGLAS L.
[b.] June 27, 1961, Buffalo, New York; [p.] Donald and Dolores Wolford; [m.] Karen Wolford, June 11, 1983; [ed.] North Carolina State University, The Sorbonne, University of Maryland;[occ.] Director-

External Affairs, National Academy of Engineering; [memb.] Adjunct Faculty, Johns Hopkins University; [hon.] Tau Beta Pi, Beta Gamma Sigma; [oth. writ.] Abandon, a novel, articles published in various periodicals; [pers.] Poetry exists to reveal what one already knows, but may not know one knows. [a.] Rockville, MD.

WOLFORD, JOHN B.
[b.] April 29,1934, Fremont, Michigan; [m.] Keon Wolford, October 4, 1963; [ch.] Linda Ann, Lisa Marie, Laurie Beth and Jeffrey John; [ed.] Newaygo Public Schools, Michigan State College, Grand Rapids J.C. Occupational Training; [occ.] General woodworker; [memb.] International Society of Poets, U.S. Navy Memorial Foundation, Smithsonian Associate; [oth. writ.] Two poems published in Selected Works of Our World's Best Poets (c) 1992 by World of Poetry PRess, ISBN 0-910147-21-3; [pers.] As a pronounced realist, I write of humankind's world as I have personally experienced it, without the benefit of makeup! [a.] Kent City, MI.

WOLLIN, HOLLY MARIE
[pen.] Lil'En, Fruitcake; [b.] May 5, 1971; [p.] David Leray Wollin and Catherine Gail Simpson; [ed.] Freshman in high school; [oth. writ.] I have only written poetry; [pers.] I love to read and write poetry, to me poetry tells how you're feeling inside. Most poetry is very beautiful. [a.] Sugarloaf, CA.

WOLTERING, WAYNE
[pen.] Wayne Woltering; [b.] November 25, 1967, Breeze, Illinois; [p.] Nancy Halsted and Melvin Woltering; [ed.] Roosevelt High; [occ.] Labor, welder, painter; [oth. writ.] Several poems, none published; [pers.] My poetry is the only way to express feelings and desires that I otherwise would have trouble expressing. [a.] St. Louis, MO.

WOMACK, RAMONA KNIGHT
[pen.] Mona; [b.] June 18, 1952, Boloxi, Mississippi; [p.] Dorothy and Harvey L. Knight, Sr.; [m.] James Womack, December 17, 1971; [ch.] Mark A. (23), Brian J. (18) and Bobby L,. Womack (16); [ed.] Lincoln High, Tacoma Community College, Bates Technical College; [occ.] Sales Associates, Klopfensteins The Bon Marche' Norstrom; [memb.] Shiloh Baptist Church, N.A.A.C.P. member, Advocate for Children; [hon.] Certificate of Award, Christian Teaching-Shiloh Baptist Church School, Bon Marcle Par-excellence, top achiever in general merchandise; [oth. writ.] Several poems published in local newspapers, Shilho Baptist Church, article for Northwest Dispatch Morning News Tribune; [pers.] My divine desire is to inspire all people of every color that we are but one in Christ Jesus. I'm compelled to write what the spirit in powers me with to wake up those that sleep.[a.] Tacoma, WA 98404.

WONG, HELEN
[b.] May 16, 1973, Los Angeles; [p.] Shew Yue and Yu Har Wong; [memb.] Ephebian Society, Red Cross; [hon.] Byron Scholarship, Los Angeles Chinese Women Scholarship. [a.] Los Angeles, CA.

WOOD, DONALD A.
[b.] August 23,1953, Penn Yan, New York; [p.] C. Leonard and Evelyn Wood; [ed.] Penn Yan Academy and Monroe Community College; [occ.] Police Chief; [memb.] M.B.S.I., A.M.I.C.A., P.Y. Flying Club;

[oth.writ.] 1 other non-published poem; [pers.] My father's close brush with death and the wonderful nurses that took care of him were my inspiration for this poem. God bless them. [a.] Penn Yan, NY.

WOODCOCK, SEAN
[b.] December 21, 1968, Fort Lauderdale, Florida; [p.] Ileen Woodcock; [ed.] Graduate, Cypress Lake High; [occ.] Poet; [oth. writ.] Yes, a book of poetry; [pers.] I would like in the future to publish my book. [a.] Cape Coral, FL 33904.

WOODLEY, BARBARA J.
[b.] September 2,1951, Broward County, Florida; [p.] William and Mary Lee Shiver; [m.] Charlie C. Woodley, Jr., December 21, 1987; [ch.] Ishmael, Jacob, Esther and George Swinton, Jr. [a.] Pompano Beach, FL.

WOODRIN, LESLIE
[pen.] Les; [b.] February 15, 1981, Madisonville, Kentucky; [p.] Kathy Scott and Larry Woodring; [ed.] Thompkins Middle School; [hon.] Hopkins Co, Language Arts Festival, 1991; [oth. writ.] Butterflies (poem). [a.] Evansville, IN.

WOODS, EARL J.
[b.] February 25, 1969, Flin Flon, Manitoba; [p.] Robert and Elizabeth Woods; [ed.] Bachelor of Arts, University of Alberta; [occ.] Student; [memb.] Alberta Writer's Guild, University of Alberta, Star Trek Club; [hon.] Rutherford Scholarship; [oth. writ.] Various works in progress, including the satirical adventure epic Tomb of The Radish; [pers.] Humanity's future can be grand if we have the will and the courage to make it so. [a.] Edmonton Alberta, Canada T5H 3A6.

WOODS, EDMOND C.
[b.] May 31, 1924, Webster County, West Virginia; [p.] Ira E. and Clora L. Pugh Woods; [m.] Jennie L. Woods, September 16, 1946; [ch.] Robert C., Shirley J. and David E. Woods; [ed.] Grade 8; [occ.] Factory, stock expeditor; [memb.] Church, retirement community; [hon.] "Merit Award Certificates" from World of Poetry; [oth. writ.] Local newspaper, 2 bi-monthly publication; [pers.] Inspired by " Lillie Myres", published in the " Grit". Though I would, become famous achieving honor and acclaim, if no heart I've touched in writing, I have written all in vain. [a.] Mentor, OH.

WOODS, MARY
[b.] November 28, 1959, Columbia, South Carolina, Richland County; [p.] Raised by grandparents, Ethel M. Muller and the late Austin Muller; [ed.] Graduated from Swansea High School and Ruthledge College; [occ.] Civil Engineering, South Carolina State Highways; [memb.] International Society of Poets;[hon.] Editor's Choice Award from another contest, recognized by the mayor of Newberry for my winning poem and is displayed in the Chamber of Commerce of Newberry County; [oth. writ.] Destination Unknown, The Time Has Come, also published in a book of anthology "Destination Unknown"; [pers.] Often times you can become a stranger to yourself, a reflection from a mirror can introduce you to that stranger. [a.] Newberry, SC.

WORRELL, TRICIA LYNN
[b.] March 8, 1974, Killeen, Texas; [p.] Clara F. Sawtelle and step-father Col. Floyd J. Boyce; [ed.]

Received G.E.D., February 1993; [memb.] Y.M.C.A.; [oth. writ.] Several poems on many subjects written over the past 6 years; [pers.] My poetry is based on "hope". Hope in which we may grow to see one another as companions on a journey through life, other than enemies. [a.] Warren, OH.

WRIGHT, AUTUMN
[b.] December 22, 1975, Eureka, California; [p.] Mother Earth; [occ.] Hope to be writer or commercial artist; [hon.] Blue ribbon for watercolor painting, Golden Poet Award at age 11; [oth. writ.] Several unpublished stories and poems; [pers.] Creativity is the combination of body and soul. [a.] Rathfrum, ID.

WRIGHT, CHARLES W.
[b.] May 26, 1949, Owingsville; [p.] James R. and Lena B. Wright; [m.] Sandra Trusty Wright, APril 30, 1990; [ed.] High school, one year college; [occ.] U.S. Army retired store manager; [memb.] VFW, Shriver, Masonic Lodge; [hon.] Outstanding graduate of the U.S. Army Culinary Institute; [oth. writ.] Several poems not yet published; [pers.] My poems are based on truth and beauty. [a.] Owingsville, KY.

WRIGHT, CAROLYN
[p.] Carolyn Wright; [b.] July 9, 1947, Rockledge, Georgia; [p.] William Preston and Christine Smith; [m.] Wilbur L. Wright, July 24,1970; [ch.] Christopher and Eric; [ed.] Miller High School, Computer Tech-Macon, Georgia; [occ.] Airborne Express; [memb.] Second Baptist Church; [pers.] Before my mother passed away she wanted my sister and me to put together a country basket to place at the head of her casket and told me to write a poem about it. I told her I was no poet, she told me that God would help me and that the poem was going to travel. [a.] Macon, GA.

WRIGHT, CYNTHIA
[b.] July 8, 1958, St. Joseph, Missouri; [p.] Edwin and Elizabeth Irwin Hatten; [m.] John Wright, June 17, 1978; [ch.] Jordan Michael and Lindsay Elizabeth; [ed.] East Bakersfield High School, California Baptist College, California State University, Fullerton; [occ.] Donor Relations, California Baptist College; [memb.] City of Riverside Human Relations Commission; [hon.] Dean's List, President's List, California Baptist College. [a.] Riverside, CA.

WRIGHT, JAMES KEITH
[[pen.] Mr. Wright; [b.] August 3, 1964, Kansas City, Missouri; [ed.] Southwest High School, Central Missouri State University Career Enrichment Program; [memb.] Phi Beta Sigma Fraternity Inc., Greater Corinthian Church of The Christ; [oth.writ.] "Expression of Poetry for Black Woman" by Mr. Wright; [pers.] If it wasn't for the grace of God, give praise, live a righteous life, praise the Lord. [a.] Kansas City, MO.

WRIGHT, KATHERINE S.
[pen.] Katie; [b.] June 1, 1978, Petoskey, Michigan; [p.] James R. and Sharon Wright; [ed.] Freshman, Harbor Springs High School; [hon.] Honor student. [a.] Harbor Springs, MI.

WRIGHT, SARAH RUTH
[b.] August 4, 1981, Okinawa, Japan; [p.] Kyle James and Mary Ann Vandervort Wright; [ed.] 6th grade 92-93, Keflavik Iceland Nato Base Resident; [memb.] Girl Scouts of the USA; [hon.] D.A.R.E. - Drug

Abuse Resistance Education Award Recipient; [oth. writ.] Many other poems and short stories.; [pers.] I love writing poetry and short stories especially for children my age and younger.; [a.] Plano, TX

WRIGHT, TERRY W.
[b.] August 16, 1953, Jefferson, Iowa; [p.] Paul and Ruth Wright; [m.] Elizabeth Wright, April 28, 1978; [ch.] Melissa, Melinda and Jessica; [ed.] Jefferson High School, Des Moines Area Community College; [occ.] General Manager Sut Hill Auto and Truck Center; [memb.] Elk, Toastmasters, Rotary; [hon.] Selected to Writers Workshop University of Iowa 1971; [oth. writ.] Newspaper columns, short story; [pers.] Over the years, I have written poems and short stories as a hobby. Someday, I would like to have a book published. [a.] Brookfield, MA.

WUNDER, FAITH G.
[pen.] FGW; [b.] June 11, 1944; [ch.] Tracy E. Wunder; [ed.] Keveny Memorial Academy, SUNY Cobleskill, SUNY Regents College, Albany; [occ.] Academic Advisor; [memb.] NYS Association of Women in Higher Education, National Academic Advisor Association; [hon.] Kellog Foundation Fellowship Nomination, Outstanding Advisor at Regents College 1990; [pers.] I write to soothe my soul. [a.] Waterford, NY.

WURTZ, CHARLES E.
[b.] August 29, 1920, Detroit, Michigan; [p.] Charles E. and Martha (Waddell) Wurtz; [m.] Nadine J. (Woltmann) Wurtz, November 18, 1964; [ch.] Julia L. Learned, Brenda K. Braumbaugh and Robert A. Wurtz; [ed.] College undergraduate; [occ.] Jocky, military, laboratory tech., Cardiopulmonary Tech., with Veterans Administration, auctioneer and (now retired); [memb.] NARFE (National Association Retired Federal Employees), Boy Scouts, Air Force Sergeants Association, VFW and Lutheran Brotherhood; [hon.] NARFE Special Service Award, Boy Scout Silver Beaver and District Award of Merit VFW Life Member; [oth. writ.] Poem, " The Mighty Umpqua" (Oregon River) writings for a creative writing class, short church Christmas plays; [pers.] "Enjoy new challenges and look at defeat as a opportunity for doing it another way". [a.] Southerlin, OR.

WYATT, DAVID B.
[b.] January 18, 1959, Hamilton, Ontario; [m.] Therese Wyatt; [ch.] Katlin Marjorie and Jesse George Bradley; [pers.] The love of God inspires all. [a.] Grimsby, Ontario Canada.

WYATT, JANICE A.
[pen.] Janice A. Wyatt; [b.] June 12, 1965, Petersburg, Virginia; [p.] Norma Jean and Earnest Earl Wyatt; [ch.] Kara Jean and Jacob Green; [ed.] Prince George High School, John Tyler Community College; [oth. writ.] Several other poems and short stories; [pers.] Writing poetry is a great need that must be fulfilled. The words and feelings are of such great intensity that I am overcome and my hand can barely control my pen. [a.] Claremont, VA.

WYNESS, HERBERT CLIFF
[b.] March 17, 1936; [p.] Alexander and Nellie Wyness; [ed.] Masters of Business Administration; [occ.] Vice-president Grande Prairie Regional College; [pers.] Home-spun, earth-made and basic raw,

I am intellectual, wordy and cultured, I am not. [a.] Grand Prairie, Alberta Canada T8V 5X1.

YACCO, STEVEN D.
[b.] April 5, 1975; [ed.] West Milford High (so far); [occ.] Burger Flipper, Butler, New Jersey; [pers.] Nothing abstract is real. Emotions aren't cut and dried. A mind is a path to depressing, irrational thoughts that are outside regular.

YAGERIC, BARBARA A.
[b.] April 2, 1937, Cleveland, Ohio; [p.] Olga M. and Joseph S. Yageric; [ed.] Mt. St. Mary Academy (HS), University of VA at Alexandria, VA, SUNY Buffalo at Amherst, Amherst, NY; [occ.] Freelance Writer, Public Relations/advertising Promotion; [memb.] Amherst Museum, Mt. St. Mary Alumnae Board, Daeman College Association Board and Zonta Club of Amherst; [hon.] Honor Roll, Volunteer of Year-Amherst Museum; [oth. writ.] Many poems-some won a ribbon at Country Fair-Amherst Museum, play for State Convention, short story and articles; [pers.] Some of my poetry is a tribute to my wonderful parents, to nature and life which they taught me to appreciate. My short stories and articles are about children and senior citizens. [a.] Williamsville, NY.

YANKULOU, AMBER
[ed.] I go to Jennings Middle School in Akron, Ohio; [pers.] I am 13 years old and I live with my brother, mother and sister. I have 3 cats, my hobbies are reading and writing. I started writing poetry about 5-7 months ago.

YARBROUGH, ANGIE
[b.] Angie Yarbrough; [b.] August 2, 1977, Winston-Salem, North Carolina; [p.] Paul T. Yarbrough and Betty Accetura; [ed.] Sophomore at North Forsyth High School; [oth.writ.] This is the first poem that I've ever sent to anyone but I have plenty of writings; [pers.] I just like for everyone even if inside they feel dark and gloomy, they can look on the bright side of life and find something to cheer them up, in other words, no matter what happens try to stay on the sunny side of life. [a.] Winston-Salem, NC.

YARBROUGH, JASEN
[b.] November 23, 10978, N. Charleston, South Carolina; [p.] Robert Julius and Sarah Susan Yarbrough; [oth. writ.] I have written several other poems of a romantic nature. I was influenced greatly by Shakespeare and Edgar Allan Poe; [pers.] I would like to thank a lot of people especially, Johanna Melissa Winn, you are my inspiration and strength. [a.] Younges Island, SC.

YIP, HANG CHING
[pen.] Green Yip, Kyou Yip; [b.] November 12, 1929, Taisun City, China; [p.] Tonghor and Kam Lun Chou Yip; [m.] Ngan Ling Chan Yip, April 6, 1954; [ed.] Taisun CIty First High School, Shanghai Chemical Engineer University, Chicago National College, Malcolm X College; [occ.] Former principal Kong Tai Elementary School, former chemical engineer in China, Chinese American Service League, Chicago, Illinois; [memb.] The Chinese Artist Association of North American, Golden Mountain Poetry Association, Chicago Chinese Poetry , Arts, Literature Society (one of establisher); [hon.] The 1992 Operation Able Twelfth Annual Older Worker Awards luncheon; [oth.writ.] Essay, Horse, Rams, several po-

ems and proses published in local or in China newspapers or magazines; pers.] I am an American citizen, I like to describe the beautiful world and strive to reflect the goodness of mankind and advance peace of the world in my writing. [a.] Chicago, IL.

YOON, MI HEE
[pen.] So Wael Kim; [b.[August 10, 1962, Seoul, Korea; [p.] Joung You and Im Oh; [m.] Dae Sop Yoon (June 26, 1957), October 8, 1986; [ch.] Paul S. Yoon; [ed.] Chun-An High, Red Cross College of Nursing; [occ.] Housewife; [memb.] Korean Poets and Writers Group in Washington Area; [oth. writ.] Several poems published in local newspaper, article for The Saturday Evening Post, a collection of member's poems. [a.] Gaithersburg, MD.

YORK, JAMES V.
[pen.] J. York; [b.] September 6, 1935, Silo, Oklahoma; [p.] Jim and Robbie York; [m.] Alta V. York, November 20, 2959; [ch.] Russell W. York and Deborah R. Evans; [ed.] Silo Grade School, Cobb High School, Southeastern Oklahoma State University; [occ.] Locksmith at SOSU; [memb.] Durant Masonic Lodge #45, Scottish Rite Bodies of McAlester Oklahoma; [oth. writ.] Views and Treasures of James V. York , Library of Congress cat. # TXU535693. [a.] Durant, OK.

YOSHIDA, KAREN K.C.
[b.] September 18, 1964, Honolulu, Hawaii; [p.] William Francis and Masako Cateel; [m.] Ken Yutaka Yoshida, August 4, 1990; [ed.] University of Hawaii, Hawaii Pacific University (previously known as Hi Pacific College); [occ.] Manager of Communications and Public Relations Hi State Bar Association; [memb.] KHPR Community Advisory Board, member, Sons and Daughters of 442nd RCT, Hawaii Pacific University Alumni Association; [hon.] 1990 Who's Who in The West, 1989 Magna Cum Laude, HPC, 1989 Who's Who Among Students in American Universities and Colleges, etc, 1982 Executive Women's International contest, Western Region alternate winner, Hawaii State winner (1st place), 1982 Distributive Education Clubs of America, 2nd place in Food Marketing category, 1981 Who's Who Among American High School Students; [oth. writ.] Ghost writer for article in the Honolulu Star bulletin, short articles in the Hawaii Bar Journal, poem and short story in high school publication, articles in high school newspaper; [pers.] I enjoy focusing my writing on emotional experiences. Writing provides me with pleasure and is an excellent stress reliever. [a.] Honolulu, HI.

YOST, DAWNELLE A.
[pen.] Dawn Yost; [b.] September 16, Reading, Pennsylvania; [p.] Charles F. and (late Jacqueline F.) Yost; [m.] Divorced; [ch.] Jodi Lynn; [ed.] Reading Senior High School; [occ.] Artist; [oth. writ.] One other poem published "Be For It Is Too Late"; [pers.] So often I hear some one say " I have all those dishes to do", I instantly think, gosh, at least that means you've had food to eat, some people aren't so fortunate. That's just how I see life. No matter what the problems are, there are always blessings to be found. [a.] Blandon, FL.

YOUNG, FANNIE ANN
[b.] August 7, 1949, Orange, Texas; [p.] James, Ambers, Pearl Ambers and Henry Randall; [m.] Abron Young, Jr., April 28, 1972; [ch.] Crystal Ann

and Angela La shun;l [ed.] Lutcher Starks High, Bishop College, El Centro College, Langston University; [occ.] Administrative Assistant to the Business Manager; [memb.] The Church of The Living God, Escort of Langston University Ladies Basketball team; [hon.] Academic Scholarship, poetry awards, Sunday School Teacher Awards, Bible Speaker Awards, awards of appreciation; [oth. writ.] God Is Not Dead, Manners, Then You Can Depend Upon The Lord, Wealthy Man, Listen, Weeping Jesus, We Must Come To A Compromise, Low Self-Esteem; [pers.] I am who I am because of God's love. I try to give our youth and my fellowman an encouraging word, I am concerned about our society's well being. [a.] Langston, OK.

YOUNG, SHARI ARLENE
[b.] June 9, 1965, Burlingame, California; [p.] Richard J. and David A. McColgan; [m.] David McColgan, August 22, 1992; [ed.] B.A. English, Humboldt State University, Arcata, California; [occ.] Private Tutor; [pers.] " That love is all there is, is all we know of love, Emily Dickinson. [a.] South Lake Tahoe, CA.

YOUNKINS, GALE H.
[b.] January 10, 1947, Frederick, Maryland; [ch.] Paul L. and David H. Younkins; [ed.] Bachelor of Arts, University of Maryland, Master of Divinity, Eastern Mennonite Seminary; [pers.] I am a Christian. I believe that following Jesus Christ as Savior and Lord is the only "way" to abundant/eternal life. My high school English teacher sparked my literary interest. The poetry of Robert Frost has been very influential. [a.] Johnstown, PA.

YOUST, YVONNE
[b.] January 1, 1927, Kansas City, Missouri; [p.] Edith Bair and W. Lester Youst; [ed.] Northfield Mount Hermon School, Skidmore College, Phoenix School of Design; [occ.] Writer, co-founder of Evergreen Press, New Hampton, NH, composer, classical and popular vocal music done in concert, on radio and TV; [oth.writ.] Self-published by Evergreen Press, Snowgarden (poetry), The Journey of Life (poetic philosophy), The Peaceful Climb (poetic philosophy), co-author, All About New Hampshire (history). [a.] New Hampton, NH.

YOUTZ, ELIZABETH McFERREN
[pen.] Elizabeth McFerren Youtz; [b.] July 14, 1924, Lebanon, Pennsylvania; [p.] Esther Carroll and Claude Reed McFerren; [m.] Earl Youtz, January 20, 1950; [ch.] Michael Earl, Andrea Lynn and Laurie Susan; [ed.] Lebanon High School and studying many, many books, "self taught"; [occ.] Retired, formerly owner of Keepsake Art Gallery; [memb.] Berks Art Alliance; [hon.] 1st and 2nd prizes for oil and watercolor paintings 1970 thru 1986; [oth.writ.] More poetry, none published except for two others, "Christmas In My Valley" and " The Train" published by Ideals Magazine; [pers.] Through art, music and the written word, one becomes immortal. The world and relationships are so beautiful. I like to record them in my way. [a.] West Lawn, PA.

YU, DIANA
[b.] February 5, 1936, Choong Nam, Korea; [p.] Yu Chin San (father) and Kim Hyun Shin (mother); [m.] Thomas M. Tull, Jr., January 15, 1977; [ch.] Alisa, Karen and Judith; [ed.] Ewha Girl's School, Seoul Korea, Arizona State University, BA and MA, The

George Washington University, Ed.D; [occ.] Writer and lecturer; [memb.] The Women's Institute of Washington, DC. Advisory Board, Arizona Author's Association; [hon.] Kappa Delta Pi, Pi Lamda Theta, 4.o GPA for doctorate, former president Korean-American Citizens COuncil of Maryland, first book, Winds of Change, was 1991 National Press Club selection; [oth. writ.] Winds of Change, Korean Women in America (Silver Springs, Maryland, Women's Institute Press 1991), 392 pp, co-author "The Role of International Education in American Higher Education", Educational Horizons (March 1983) p. 144; [pers.] My very first teacher -and greatest, was my grandfather, Yu Kyung Duk. He instilled in me as appreciation for reading, writing and gender equality at a very young age. [a.] Scottsdale, AZ.

YURY, CHARLOTTE
b.] July 2, 1974, The Pas, Manitoba; [p.] Zane and Elise Yury; [ed.] Graduate of Margaret Barbour Collegiate Institute; [oth.writ.] Several other poems I have written throughout the years; [pers.] I love poetry and enjoy writing poems about romance and other life situations. [a.] The Pas, Manitoba R9A 1K4.

ZACH, KAREN
[b.] April 4, 1978, LaCrosse, Wisconsin; [p.] Paul and Roseann Zach; [ed.] 8th grade student of Seneca High School; [occ.] A farmer's daughter and a babysitter; [hon.] Band solo, choir solo, Honor Roll student; [pers.] I enjoy playing sports like softball, basketball, volleyball and cheerleading, I also enjoy riding bike and playing with the farm animals. [a.] Eastman, WI.

ZALDIVAR GLADYS
[pen.] Gladys, Zaldivar; [b.] November 5, 1936, Camaguey, Cuba; [p.] Juan Zaldivar and Virginia Alvarez; [ed.] University of Miami, doctoral studies, University of Maryland at College Park, master's degree; [occ.] English instructor, the English Center, Dade County Public Schools; [memb.] South Florida Poetry Institute, Save The Manatee club (Florida Audobon Society), etc.; [hon.] Phi Kappa Phi, Sigma Delta Pi, Distinguished Woman Author" (1988), according to Miami-Dade Community College (North Campus); [oth. writ.] Five published books of poems, 6 articles included in different books of literary criticism on Cuban authors, 2 short stories in 2 anthologies, several articles for the Miami Herald, etc.; [pers.] My poetry blends two traditions, The Hispanic and the Angelo-Saxon, and my urge to write orginiates in compassion and the need to restore harmony through beauty. [a.] Miami, FL.

ZALEWSKA, DOBI
[b.] January 19, 1980, Warsaw, Poland; [p.] Maria and Janusz Zalewska; [ed.] Junior high school student; [hon.] Participation in Duke University's 7-graders Talent Identification Program, 1993; [oth.writ.] Short stories, " The Final Challenge" "Dear Santa" and others; [pers.] I am mostly interested in studying weird sides of human nature and reflecting it in poems, stories and drawings. [a.] San Marcos, TX.

ZAVALA, JR., ARMANDO
[b.] January 19, 1979, El Paso, Texas; [p.] Armando and Elia Zavala, Jr.; [ed.] Eastern Hills Elementary, William James College Readiness Academy; [occ.]

Student; [hon.] Project A.B.L.E., Duke Talent Iden-
tification Program, Advance Summer Residential
Program at Northwestern State University; [pers.] No
matter how good things seem, they can always get
better. [a.] Fort Worth, TX.

ZHANG, JIM JUNFENG
[ed.] M.S. Chemistry, M.S. Environmental Sciences;
[occ.] Ph.D. student; [memb.] International Society
of Exposure Assessment; [hon.] The first place in the
National Hongyu (Rainbow and Rain) Cup contest of
words and poetry in China, B.S. with honors, Peking
University; [oth. writ.] Several poems published in
China, a popular science book on Environmental
Knowledge (in Chinese), Scientific Research papers
published in Scientific Journals; [pers.] I strive to
discover the beauty of nature and the goodness of
human being by means of both science and art. [a.]
Piscataway, NJ.

ZIEMANN, LOIS J.
[pen.] Sonora Sea; [b.] January 8, 1953, Newark,
New Jersey; [p.] Francis X and Adele M. Wazeter;
[m.] Divorced; [ch.] Michael R. Ziemann; [ed.]
B.S.N. (nursing), Loyola University, M.A. (Coun-
seling Psychology) from National University; [occ.]
Vice president Irad COrp., Fort Myers, FA; [hon.]
Black belt -Tae Kwon Do; [pers.] My poems reflect
the spiritual and philosophical part of myself.[a.]
Cape Coral, FL>

ZILLMER, RONNIE ALLEN
[pen.] Ron Zillmer; [b.] November 1, 1957,
Wiesbaden, W.Germany; [p.] Danny Zillmer and
Gertrude Becker; [m.] Karen Sue Zillmer, August
9,1987; [ch.] Collin Allan and Brandon Alec Zillmer;
[ed.] High school, Institute of Hard Knocks, and self
motivation university; [occ.] You name it; [oth.writ.]
Numerous poems, short stories and with novel under
construction; [pers.] One should never stop learning
until one's death, after that? [a.] Fergus Falls, MN.

ZIMMER, ARDIE
[b.] September 24,1941, Milwaukee, Wisconsin; [p.]
Jerome and Rose Zimmer; [m.] Nancy Zimmer,
September 28,1963; [ch.] Greg, Susan and Ann; [ed.]
School of Hard Knocks, BA Street Smarts; [occ.]
Small business owner, Pyro Kleen; [memb.] St.
Hubert Church, Germantown Chamber of Com-
merce; [hon.] Many awards for public service and
volunteerism; [oth.writ.] Numerous poems; [pers.]
Yesterday is gone don't worry about it, today is here
enjoy it, tomorrow is coming plan for it. [a.] Hubertus,
WI.

ZIMMERLY, STEPHEN C.
[b.] July 7, 1972, Agana, Guam; [p.] Mr. and Mrs.
Stephen J. Zimmerly; [ed.] University of Arizona, De
Paul University; [occ.] Student; [memb.] Alpha Tau
Omega; [oth.writ.] Recently published book The
Beach Is A Great Conversation; [pers.] The envelope
of our experiences is only limited by our willingness
to explore. [a.] Dallas, TX.

INDEX

Brock, R. H. 325
Brockwell, Kathleen H. 538
Broe, Lisa M. 379
Broekhuizen, Victoria J. 77
Brohl, Ted 106
Brooks, Aleisha 204
Brooks, Crystal LeeAnn 303
Brookshire, Mel 510
Brookter, Raymond Charles 479
Broome, Peter 114
Broome, Ruth 108
Brosco, Irene 51
Broughton, Nilsa 241
Broumley, Bobbie Russell 284
Broussard, Evelyn 271
Brown Sr., Robert N. 158
Brown, Barbara L. 449
Brown, Betty P. 137
Brown, Carla J. 198
Brown, Elaine 281
Brown, George F. 548
Brown, Gregory D. 148
Brown, Harley Michael 33
Brown, Hellen 586
Brown, Joan Ray 383
Brown, Judy Ann 171
Brown, Karl A.D. 290
Brown, Kay 614
Brown, Leah 173
Brown, Leslie 346
Brown, Linda 621
Brown, Sara J. 652
Brown, Sunshine L. 458
Brown, Thomas F. 327
Brown, Tiffany 241
Brown, Tom D. 205
Brown, Tom D. 94
Brown, Velma Lipe 113
Brown, Wayde Kenji 331
Brown, evelyn 367
Browne, Brian W. 175
Browning, Benton 303
Brownlee, Curt 335
Bruchmiller, Velma 102
Brummer, Isabelle 278
Brundage, Jenny 195
Brunei, Vickie 324
Bruning, Jean 59
Brunson III, Hugh 204
Bruss, Tobbin A. 3
Bruzzese, Angela 588
Bryan, L. Wayne 473
Bryan, Trisha 207
Bryant, Frances Marie Leigh 201
Bryant, Melissa Jo 407
Bryant, Ph.D., Carlyle R. 49
Bryant, Verna Wooten 414
Bryce, Doris M. 133
Buarques Sr., Raymond 227
Buchanan, Judy Ann 588
Buchanan, Kathleen 429
Buckland, Andrew C. 429
Buckland, Herb 311

Budge, Bruce 193
Buehler, Evelyn Judy 137
Buels, Valen 444
Buenrustro, Monica 655
Buffum Sr., Carroll 296
Bullard, John 162
Bullard, Trina 469
Buller, Dorothy J. 18
Bullock, Ada 251
Bullock, Ree 84
Bundschuh, June A. 152
Bunker, Jessica 258
Bunton, Sharon E. 113
Burcham, Matthew 317
Burchfield, Carolyn 480
Burger, Jo Ann 612
Burgess, Brenda I. J. 362
Burgess, Jr., J Roy 57
Burgess, Theresa M. 513
Burian, Lorraine Cordileone 614
Burk, Mona R. 86
Burke, Andrea 182
Burkett, Tina Christine 467
Burkhardt, Samantha 243
Burkhart-Navarro, Victoria A. 499
Burkholder, Anthony Otis 319
Burkitt, Marcie 206
Burleigh, Berta 319
Burleigh, Doris L. 201
Burmester, Kim 265
Burnette, Gloria J. 271
Burnham, Sheila 318
Burns, Bonnie 551
Burns, Finny J. 186
Burns, Isobella 183
Burns, John M. 607
Burns, Maggie 175
Burns, Ozella 450
Burns, Sr., Roy Lee 468
Burns, Terrie M. 96
Burnside, Rebecca 78
Burrell, Alan O. 70
Burrell, Laura Lambe 616
Burt-Hedrick, Keshet 225
Burton, Holly 620
Busby, Evelyn 172
Busch, Shawn 552
Bushacker, Evangeline 200
Buskirk, Jennifer 599
Bussiere, Natalie 345
Butler, A. Lois 507
Butler, Beth Anne 424
Butler, Catherine 28
Butler, Jennifer 519
Butler, Joy 292
Butt, Lee 309
Buzzell, Donna 546
Bye, Darcie 53
Byerly, Willie R. 82
Bynum, Barbara K. 561
Byrne, Duane 588
Byrne, Michael 429
Byrns, Kenneth A. 536

Byron, Virginia 498
Byttner, Mark E. 271
Caesar, Amanda 85
Cagg, Richard D. 643
Caggiano, Renee 436
Cahill-Epstein, Kellie-Ann 317
Cain, M.R. 491
Cain, M.R. 558
Caldwell, Christy 203
Caldwell, Fred 291
Callaghan, Gerry 336
Callahan, Susan 477
Callas, John 285
Calleja, Carmel 125
Callison, Elizabeth Trouve' 544
Camacho, Mercedes 454
Caminiti, Lauren Ann 490
Campbell, Carrie A. 596
Campbell, Gregory B. 284
Campbell, Iva 550
Campbell, Karen Jean 124
Campbell, Mickey 432
Campbell, Robert P. 255
Campbell, William S. 566
Campos, Nanette 223
Candee, Jean 159
Canfield, Bethany L. 192
Cannon, Cara 12
Cantella, Charles N. 301
Cantner, Christopher Adam 45
Cantu, Ercilia 203
Canty, Patricia 313
Capalbo, Richard 447
Carbone, Jill 177
Card, Jean 328
Cardinel, Ruth M. 160
Carey, Brian 333
Carey, Meredith 226
Carje, Petre 374
Carleton, Jessica Honor 572
Carlson, Jody 35
Carlson, Judy 641
Carman, Donald Russell 100
Carmichael, Tim 313
Carnaghi, Emma L. 54
Carnes, Timothy C. 652
Carnes, Todi S. 526
Carney, Karen 558
Carothers, Kristin 390
Carpenter, Deborah 326
Carpenter, Donald Gilbert 564
Carr, Jean Costen 546
Carr, Jill 168
Carr, Kathleen Goodin 572
Carr, Paul 416
Carson, Allan 415
Carson, James 338
Carstensen, Jens. T. 252
Carte, Cindy 133
Carter, Amber 326
Carter, Carissa 586
Carter, Frances Tunnell 70
Carter, Gary W. 40

Carter, Gayle 528
Carter, John A. 122
Carter, K.S. 320
Carter, Timothy J. 237
Cartwright, Theodachia E. 266
Casalinuovo, Sandra Stevens 470
Casarietti, John 184
Cascio, Anthony 232
Case, Mary 94
Cassar, Natalie 83
Casteel, Cindi 611
Castillo, Venessa 110
Castro, Jewell 289
Cavanaugh, Leigh 138
Cavins, Deanna L. 280
Cecchetti, Teresa 234
Cecil, Walter R. 178
Celani, Lois 164
Center, Dorothy M. 282
Century, 46
Ceriani, Sr., Joseph D. 12
Cerniglia, Josephine 326
Cervantes, Eleonora 140
Cervantes, Michelle L. 259
Chalar, Laura 369
Chalone, Ingrid 61
Chamaillard, Krystal 345
Chamberlain, Clair H. 35
Chamberlain, Deborah 151
Chance, Mark L. 595
Chancey, Angela 216
Chandler, Heather 369
Chandler, Jr., Thomas W. 513
Changamire, Waunidi 249
Chapman, Erik 203
Chapman, J. Thaddeus 405
Chapman, Louise 10
Chapman, Marie 122
Chapman, Mary Elizabeth 374
Charran, Sherry Ann 222
Chase, Elsa L. 4
Chase, Ervin H. 390
Chase, Ervin H. 51
Chase-Garagan, Jeannette 126
Chateauneuf, Ellen 46
Chau, Angie 235
Chavez, Danielle 62
Cheaqui, Helen M. 25
Cheng, Yi 381
Cherni, Tammy 524
Chesney,, Reghan M. 77
Chia, C.H. 367
Chiang, Jennifer 211
Chiaramonte, Gary 60
Chiasson, Jana 259
Childers, Brenda G. 630
Childree, Diane M. 623
Chimwaso, David K. 118
Chinchillo, Jean 415
Chism, Gloria 154
Chism, Rose 74
Choi, Moon 504
Chow, Pete 73

Rojas, Romina 283
Rolson, June 350
Roman, Matt 247
Roman, Nicholas 320
Romano, Karen L. 216
Romero, Michelle 407
Romine, Debra 25
Root, Carr O. 549
Rose, Mary C. 78
Rose, Morgen Sizer 440
Rose, Penny 380
Rose, Roland 514
Rose, Tamara J. 326
Rose, Yvonne F. 260
Roseburrough, Susan 326
Roseman, Karl 323
Rosenbach, Scotty 210
Rosenberg, Esther 567
Rosenberg, Helene 150
Rosenkrantz, Emanuel 539
Rosenman, Harriet M. 567
Rosenthal, Angela 574
Rosenthal, Courtney 630
Ross, Angelia 463
Ross, Deloris L. 657
Ross, Donna 616
Ross, Jerry D. 139
Ross, Kathleen 352
Ross, Susan 516
Ross, Tammi 312
Ross, Vernon 377
Ross, Yvonne 250
Rossario, Lisa 645
Rossier, Moensie 641
Roth, Myrtle 643
Roubian, Susan L. 32
Roulston, Bobbi 119
Roumm, Phyllis G. 633
Rowbottom, Herbie 201
Rowe, Donna Belle 562
Rowney, David A. 189
Roy, Callonie 124
Roy, Geraldean B. 291
Rubadeau, Phyllis 449
Rubadeau, Phyllis 632
Ruckdeschel, Hugh. W. 393
Rucker, Driftwood H. 195
Rucker, Susan 213
Rude, Helen 65
Rude, Linda Caray 436
Rudolph, Melissa 505
Rudrick, Julie 127
Ruffing, Sean 530
Ruhannah, Rachel 121
Ruiz, Laureen 134
Ruiz, Nike S. 497
Rundberg, Karen 350
Runyon, Theodore H. 375
Rush, A.L. 40
Rush, Edna 183
Rushing, Christina 280
Russ, Sean D. 431
Russell, Billie R. 405

Russell, Claire 116
Russell, Harold L. 585
Russell, Jana 50
Russell, Jonathan 50
Russell, Mildred 105
Russo, Barbara 35
Russo, Tara Raye 96
Russo, Wayne J. 105
Ruthledge, Kathy Ann 300
Ruzicka, Dolores A. 290
Ryan, Guy V. 305
Ryan, Mary A. 256
Ryan, Sharon 647
Ryk, Mary A. 640
Rzadkowolska, Katie 541
Saah, Jr., David 13
Saarela, Tuuli 402
Sack, Etanna 543
Saelzer, Karen 16
Saenz, Christophe Lee 54
Saey, Sarah O. 266
Sagan, Stanley D. 218
Sage, Arleta M. 458
Sager, La Verle 149
Sahler, A. 526
Sais, Jr., Joey O. 328
Salmon, Andrew 116
Salsburg, David 596
Salvo, Emilia 25
Samon, Grico 555
Sampson, Billie Joe Taylor 584
Sams, Bob 591
Sanborn, Clyde 132
Sanchez, Rebekah Anne 417
Sanchez, Rosa 511
Sanchez, Wade 228
Sanders, Margaret L. 586
Sanders, Myron H. 267
Sanders, Scott 435
Sanders, Sharon L. 523
Sanderson, Kaye 209
Sandknop, Linda A. 438
Sandlin, Kimberly D. 11
Sandridge, Clara Ingram 542
Sanfratello, T. 651
Santana, John L. 4
Santini, Luciano 613
Santmier, Dewey 12
Santogue, Cynthia 280
Santos, Theresa Ann 221
Sappington, Cookie 202
Sarauer, Jessie 493
Sargent, Doris Fontaine 180
Sargent, Harold L. 59
Sarras, Jamie 286
Sarrasin, Chantale 356
Sarrgent, Jennifer 250
Satchidanand, Antara 522
Saum, Jeffrey A. 483
Sauter, John D. 476
Savage, Michelle 122
Sawyer, Hazel 52
Saxon, Randall Lee 485

Sayarot, Alan 227
Saylor, Carla 301
Scacco, Sara 387
Scafe, Velma 379
Scalone, Beth 505
Scarbeary, Rosemarie Moews 99
Scarbrough, Lacy 302
Scaro, Patricia 638
Schade, Troy S. 468
Schanz, Margaret 388
Schaubel, Danna Marie 354
Scheff, Jeremy 319
Schell, Dennis 294
Scherley, Eugene J. 596
Schettino, Elaine F. 43
Schibig, Sharynn Rose 446
Schipper, Amelia 241
Schittone Jr., Robert V. 216
Schlank, Katey 378
Schlichenmayer, Judy 348
Schlinkman, Kay 76
Schlumpberger, Jill 380
Schmidt, Jodie 126
Schmidt, Ryan 48
Schmidt, Stanley W. 653
Schmitt, Virginia Ann 207
Schmitz, David 558
Schneider, Roberta 339
Schneller, Peter L. 239
Schnoor, Robert 425
Schooley, Mary C. 218
Schopmeyer, Rebecca 453
Schorr, Nancy 134
Schott, Megan 239
Schrader, Karrie 581
Schrader, Lillian L. 568
Schrader, Margaret A. 11
Schrotenboer, Marilyn 254
Schubert, Brenda 332
Schuller, Henrietta 198
Schultz, June H. 169
Schwartz, Bradley 170, 359
Schwartz, Wm. R. 412
Schwatz, Monica D. 389
Schweiger, Laural 546
Schwemer, Gretchen 144
Schwien, Tammy 644
Scott, Evelyn Fuller 540
Scott, Jo 255
Scott, Judy Kay 581
Scott, Margurite 562
Scott, Rosamond Ellis 475
Scotti, Jr., John R. 302
Scriven, Norman E. 275
Scrutchin, Dorothy 570
Scura, Tom 122
Seabon, Lori D. 281
Seales, Joan P. 399
Seaman, Tammy E. 527
Sears, Lou Ann 563
Seay, Elizabeth D. 154
Seehaver, Adam 444
Seeley Jr., William P. 262

Seelke, Ronnelle 236
Seese, Christine 377
Seestadt, Jean 593
Seifrid, Phyllis 71
Seipel, Margaret Ann 153
Seiser, Bonnie 61
Seiwald, Gretchen 138
Selby, Susan F. 421
Selim, Lila 337
Sellers, Alex 258
Sellers, Belinda 452
Sellers, Kim 521
Semczuk, Karla 287
Senette, Allison C. 521
Senger, Elizabeth Smith 42
Senser, Richard A. 471
Senter, Alice H. 37
Sergent, Gary Lee 201
Serpa, Albertina C. 413
Seshadri, Sheila 502
Sethi, Sonia Dass 341
Severance, Janice 137
Severini, Felicia C. 273
Sexton, Jason 145
Sexton, Jean L. 491
Sexton, Sandra 321
Seyller, Crystal M. 588
Shaaber, Caroline-Louise 64
Shabazz, Ama Folayan 114
Shabazz, Faiz 15
Shadov, M.M. 130
Shaffer, John 293
Shaffer, John Nevin 531
Shah, Darshana 174
Shaltz, Justin 288
Shanker, Elaine 632
Shannon, Harold F. 58
Shantz, David 294
Shapiro, Yael 335
Share, Donu Karuneenu 335
Shari, 425
Sharma, Ashlesha 397
Sharp, Jessica M. 476
Shauger, Aerie 392
Shaw, Addie 130
Shaw, Duane P. 528
Shaw, Jennell 96
Shaw, Letty M. 575
Shaw, Shawna Marie 387
Sheedy, Nancy D.W. 322
Sheffield, Gregory John 37
Sheldon, Helen M. 22
Shelley, Katherine 589
Shellito, Christine M. 590
Shelton, Sherry 92
Shepard, Angie L. 186
Sheppard, Brandy 272
Sheppard, Meryl 79
Sheppard, Stephanie 81
Sheridan, Keith 89
Sherlock, Karen W. 410
Sherman, Glen C. 134
Sherman, Sabrina 582